arihant

SUCCESS AND NOTHING LESS

ARIHANT PRAKASHAN (SERIES), MEERUT

Skills in Mathematics

JEE Main & Advanced

Coordinate Geometry

Dr. SK Goyal

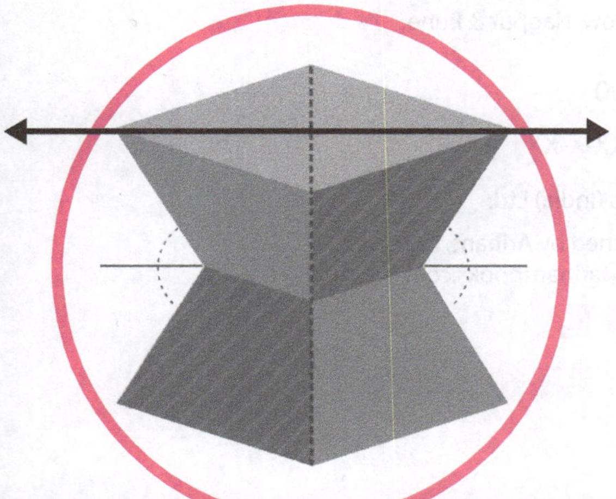

arihant
SUCCESS AND NOTHING LESS

Arihant Prakashan (Series), Meerut

卐 **Administrative & Production Offices**

Regd. Office

'Ramchhaya' 4577/15, Agarwal Road, Darya Ganj, New Delhi -110002
Tele: 011- 47630600, 43518550

卐 **Head Office**

Kalindi, TP Nagar, Meerut (UP) - 250002 Tel: 0121-7156203, 7156204

卐 **Sales & Support Offices**

Agra, Ahmedabad, Bengaluru, Bareilly, Chennai, Delhi, Guwahati, Hyderabad, Jaipur, Jhansi, Kolkata, Lucknow, Nagpur & Pune.

卐 **PRICE**: ₹ 655.00

卐 **PO No :** TXT-XX-XXXXXXX-X-XX

Published by Arihant Publications (India) Ltd.

For further information about the books published by Arihant, log on to www.arihantbooks.com or e-mail at info@arihantbooks.com

Follow us on

Preface

It is a matter of great pride and honour for me to have received such an overwhelming response to the previous editions of this book from the readers. In a way, this has inspired me to revise this book thoroughly as per the changed pattern of JEE Main & Advanced. I have tried to make the contents more relevant as per the needs of students, many topics have been re-written, a lot of new problems of new types have been added. All possible efforts are made to remove all the printing errors that had crept in previous editions. The book is now in such a shape that the students would feel at ease while going through the problems, which will in turn clear their concepts too.

A Summary of changes that have been made in Revised & Enhanced Edition

- Theory has been completely updated so as to accommodate all the changes made in JEE Syllabus & Pattern in recent years.
- The most important point about this new edition is, now the whole text matter of each chapter has been divided into small milestones with practice exercise in each milestones. This will help reader in step by step learning
- Theory of each milestone is more precise with **JEE focus Points** and **JEE Spike**.
- **JEE Scanners** are incorporated in theory for more synced learning with JEE Main and Advanced PYQs.
- Just after completion of theory, Solved Examples of all JEE types have been given, providing the students a complete understanding of all the formats of JEE questions & the level of difficulty of questions generally asked in JEE.
- Along with exercises given with each Milestone, following three exercises have been given at the end of each chapter.
- Practice Milestone 1- JEE Main Pattern Exercises.
- Practice Milestone 2- JEE Advanced Pattern Exercises.
- Practice Milestone 3- Challenging Problems Exercises.
- Previous Years questions asked in JEE Main and Advanced have been incorporated in all the exercises.

However I have made the best efforts and put my all teaching experience in revising this book. Still I am looking forward to get the valuable suggestions and criticism from my own fraternity i.e. the fraternity of JEE teachers. I strongly believe that

"YOU CAN DO ANYTHING IF YOU SET YOUR MIND FOR IT. I ALWAYS BELIEVE THE MOST IMPORTANT FORMULA IS

COURAGE + DREAMS = SUCCESS"

I would also like to motivate the students to send their suggestions or the changes that they want to be incorporated in this book. All the suggestions given by you all will be kept in prime focus at the time of next revision of the book.

Dr. SK Goyal

Enhanced Features

JEE Focus Points

- The distance of the point $P(x, y)$ f origin $O(0, 0)$ is given by
  $$|OP| = \sqrt{(x-0)^2 + (y-0)^2} = \backslash$$
- If PQ is parallel to X-axis, then $y_1 = y_2$ and so
  $$|PQ| = \sqrt{(x_2 - x_1)^2} = |x_2 - x_1|$$
- If PQ is parallel to Y-axis, then $x_1 = x_2$ and so
  $$|PQ| = \sqrt{(y_2 - y_1)^2} = |y_2 - y_1|$$
- If (x_1, y_1) and (x_2, y_2) are the ends of the hypotenuse of a right angled isosceles triangle, then the third vertex is given by
  $$\left(\frac{(x_1 + x_2) \pm (y_1 - y_2)}{2}, \frac{(y_1 + y_2) \mp (x_1 - x_2)}{2}\right)$$
- If two vertices of an equilateral triangle are (x_1, y_1) and (x_2, y_2), then coordinates of the third vertex are
  $$\left(\frac{x_1 + x_2 \mp \sqrt{3}(y_2 - y_1)}{2}, \frac{y_1 + y_2 \pm \sqrt{3}(x_2 - x_1)}{2}\right)$$

Concept Inside Video

A collection of Key Points/Results prime from JEE Preparation point of View. These are further elaborated with support videos.

Seggregated most valuable Pointers for JEE preparation

JEE SPIKE

Usually, we use the formula, $\tan 2\theta = \dfrac{2h}{a-b}$ for finding the angle of rotation θ.

However, if $a = b$, we use $\cot 2\theta = \dfrac{a-b}{2h}$ as in this case $\tan 2\theta$ is not defined.

JEE SCANNER

Example Similar to PYQ Asked in JEE Main 2024

If the locus of the point whose distances from the point (3, 1) and (1, 4) are in the ratio 4 : 3 is $ax^2 + by^2 + cxy + dx + ey + 182 = 0$, *then the value of* $a^2 + b^2 + d + e$ *is equal to*

(a) 5 (b) 10 (c) 15 (d) 2

Sol. (b) Let the point be (h, k).

According to the question, $\dfrac{\sqrt{(h-3)^2 + (k-1)^2}}{\sqrt{(h-1)^2 + (k-4)^2}} = \dfrac{4}{3}$

On squaring and simplifying, we get
$$9[(h-3)^2 + (k-1)^2] = 16[(h-1)^2 + (k-4)^2]$$
$$\Rightarrow \quad 7h^2 + 7k^2 + 22h - 110k + 182 = 0$$

Now, replace (h, k) with (x, y), so the locus is
$$7x^2 + 7y^2 + 22x - 110y + 182 = 0$$

On comparing it with
$$ax^2 + by^2 + cxy + dx + ey + 182 = 0, \text{ we have}$$
$$a = 7, b = 7, c = 0, d = 22, e = -110$$
$$\therefore \quad a^2 + b^2 + d + e = 49 + 49 + 22 - 110 = 10$$

Skill Builder

If the locus of the point whose distances from the point (2, 3) and (5, 4) are in the ratio 3 : 2 is $ax^2 + by^2 + cxy + dx + ey + 317 = 0$, then the value of $a^3 + b^3 + d + e$ is equal to

(a) 225 (b) 124

(c) 128 (d) 258

For Sol.

- **For more Practice** See Q. 6 of Milestone Practice 1.4.

Unmatched Concept elevation tool helpful in syncing recent JEE Main & Advanced PYQs with theory and provide additional practice through Skill Builders.

Contents

Syllabus

JEE Main

Cartesian system of rectangular coordinates in a plane, distance formula, section formula, locus and its equation, translation of axes, slope of a line, parallel and perpendicular lines, intercepts of a line on the coordinate axes.

Straight Lines

Various forms of equations of a line, intersection of lines, angles between two lines, conditions for concurrence of three lines, distance of a point from a line, equations of internal and external bisectors of angles between two lines, coordinates of centroid, orthocentre and circumcentre of a triangle.

Circles, Conic Sections

Standard form of equation of a circle, general form of the equation of a circle, its radius and centre, equation of a circle when the end points of a diameter are given, points of intersection of a line and a circle with the centre at the origin and condition for a line to be tangent to a circle, equation of the tangent. Sections of cones, equations of conic sections (parabola, ellipse and hyperbola) in standard forms.

JEE Advanced

Coordinate Geometry

Cartesian coordinates, distance between two points, section formulae, shift of origin.
Equation of a straight line in various forms, angle between two lines, distance of a point from a line; Lines through the point of intersection of two given lines, equation of the bisector of the angle between two lines, concurrency of lines; Centroid, orthocentre, incentre and circumcentre of a triangle.

Equation of a circle in various forms, equations of tangent, normal and chord. Parametric equations of a circle, intersection of a circle with a straight line or a circle, equation of a circle through the points of intersection of two circles and those of a circle and a straight line.
Equations of a parabola, ellipse and hyperbola in standard form, their foci, directrices and eccentricity, parametric equations, equations of tangent and normal.
Locus problems.

“

If people do not believe that Mathematics is simple, it is only because they do not realize how complicated life is.

–John Von Neumann

1

Coordinate System and Coordinates

Learning Milestones

Milestone 1 System of Coordinates

- Coordinate Axes
- Rectangular Cartesian Coordinates of a Point
- Polar Coordinates System
- Relation Between the Polar and Cartesian Coordinates

Milestone 2 Distance Formula

- Distance Between Two Points
- Choice of Axes
- Distance Between Two Points in Oblique Coordinates
- Distance Between Two Points in Polar Coordinates

Milestone 3 Section Formula

- Definition of Section Formula
- Standard Points of a Triangle
- Centroid of a Triangle
- Incentre of a Triangle
- Excentre of a Triangle
- Circumcentre of a Triangle
- Orthocentre of a Triangle
- Nine-Point Centre of a Triangle
- Area of Triangle

Milestone 4 Locus and its Equation

- Equation of a Locus
- Transformation of Axes
- Removal of the Term xy From $f(x, y) = ax^2 + 2hxy + by^2$ Without Changing the Origin
- Position of a Point which Lies Inside a Triangle

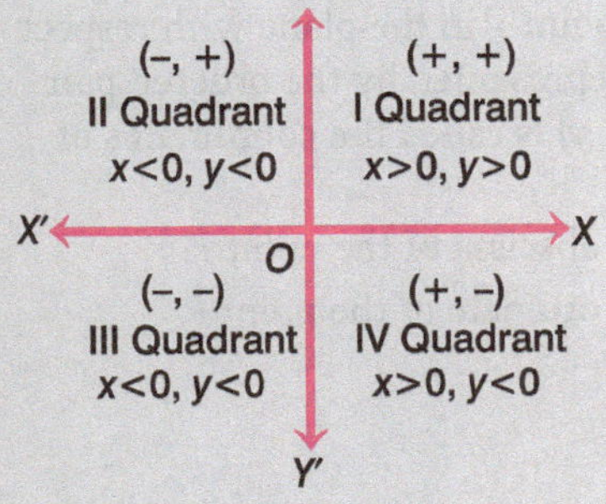

Practice Milestones

Practice Milestone 1 - JEE Main Pattern

Practice Milestone 2 - JEE Advanced Pattern

Practice Milestone 3 - Challenging Problems

Milestone 1 System of Coordinates

• Coordinate Axes • Rectangular Cartesian Coordinates of a Point • Polar Coordinates System
• Relation Between the Polar and Cartesian Coordinates

The great philospher and mathematician of France **Rane Descartes** (1596-1665) published a book 'La Geometric' in 1637.

Descartes established a relationship between the Algebra and Geometry. This relationship is called system of coordinates.

i.e. each point in a plane is expressed by an ordered pair of algebraic real numbers like $(x, y), (r, \theta)$ etc. called coordinates of the point.

The point (x, y) is called cartesian coordinates and (r, θ) is called polar coordinates of the point. Then, represents different forms of equations which are developed for all types of straight lines and curves.

Thus, the Coordinate Geometry (or Analytical Geometry) is that branch of mathematics in which geometrical problems are solved with the help of Algebra.

1.1 Coordinate Axes

The position of a point in a plane is determined with reference to two intersecting straight lines called the coordinate axes and their point of intersection is called the origin of coordinates.

If these two axes of reference (generally we call them X and Y-axes) cut each other at right angle, they are called rectangular axes. The axes divide the coordinate plane in four quadrants.

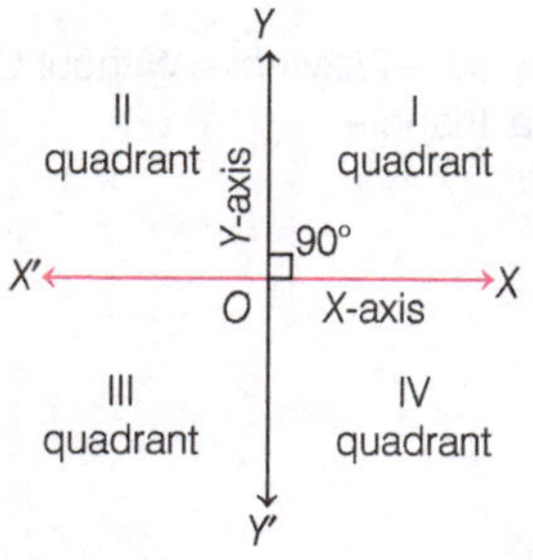

Table for conversion sign of coordinates.

Quadrants	XOY (I)	$X'OY$ (II)	$X'OY'$ (III)	XOY' (IV)
Sign of x-coordinate	+	−	−	+
Sign of y-coordinate	+	+	−	−
Sign of (x, y)	(+, +)	(−, +)	(−, −)	(+, −)

1.2 Rectangular Cartesian Coordinates of a Point

Coordinates of a point are the real variables associated with point to describe its location.

Let $X'OX$ and $Y'OY$ be two perpendicular axes in the plane of paper intersecting at O. Let P be any point in the plane of the paper. Draw PM perpendicular to OX. Then, the lengths OM and PM are called the rectangular cartesian coordinates or briefly the coordinates of P.

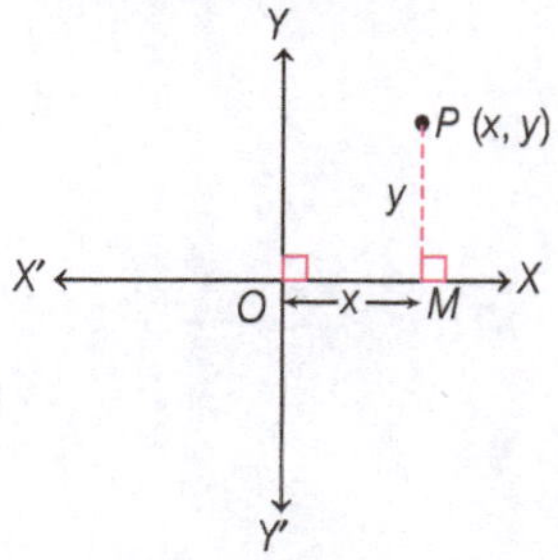

Let $OM = x$ and $MP = y$

Then, the position of the point P in the plane with respect to the coordinate axes is represented by the ordered pair (x, y). The ordered pair (x, y) is called the coordinates of point P.

i.e. $OM = x$-coordinate or abscissa of the point P

and $MP = y$-coordinate or ordinate of the point P.

JEE Focus Points

- The ordinate of every point on X-axis is 0.
- The abscissa of every point on Y-axis is 0.
- The abscissa and ordinate of the origin $O(0, 0)$ are both zero.
- The absolute value of abscissa and ordinate of a point are the perpendicular distance from Y-axis and X-axis respectively.
- Equation of X-axis is $y = 0$ and equation of Y-axis is $x = 0$.
- **Lattice point** A point whose abscissa and ordinate are integers.
  Here, the two lines XOX' and YOY' divide the plane in four quadrants. XOY, YOX', $X'OY'$, $Y'OX$ are called the first, second, third and fourth quadrant, respectively. The direction of OX, OY is positive and the direction of OX' and OY' is negative.

Example 1. Locate $(1, 2)$, $(-1, 2)$, $(-1, -2)$ and $(1, -2)$ in rectangular coordinate system and then find the area of figure obtained by joining them in the given order.

Sol. Let $A(1, 2)$, $B(-1, 2)$, $C(-1, -2)$ and $D(1, -2)$ be the points of rectangular coordinate system. Firstly, we draw the two perpendicular axes i.e. $X'OX$ and $Y'OY$, then plot the points according to sign of coordinates as shown below

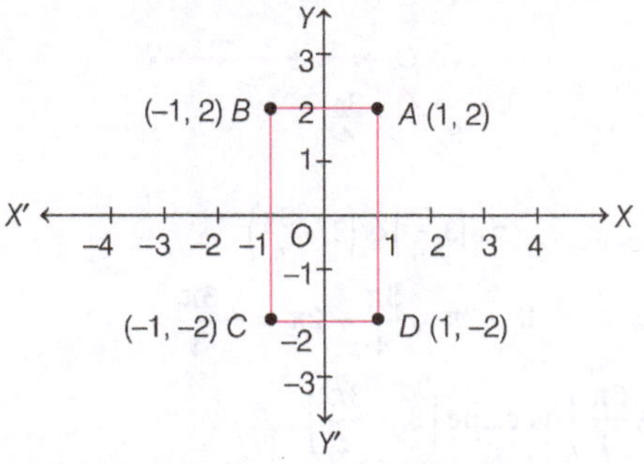

Clearly, the figure formed is rectangle $ABCD$.

Now, area of $ABCD = AB \times BC$

$= 2 \times 4 = 8$ sq units

Example 2. Locate the position of the following points in the correct quadrant.

(i) $(a\alpha^2 + b\alpha + c,\ b^2 - 4ac)$, $\forall\, \alpha \in R$, $a > 0$, $b^2 < 4ac$

(ii) $\left(\cos 10° - \cos 13°,\ \tan\dfrac{\pi}{7} - \tan\dfrac{\pi}{9}\right)$

Sol. (i) Given, $b^2 < 4ac \Rightarrow b^2 - 4ac < 0$

$\therefore\ a\alpha^2 + b\alpha + c$ has same sign as its leading coefficient.

Now, $a > 0$

$\Rightarrow\ x = a\alpha^2 + b\alpha + c > 0$

and $b^2 - 4ac < 0$

$\Rightarrow\ y = b^2 - 4ac < 0$

So, the point lies in IV quadrant.

(ii) We know that

$\cos 10° > \cos 13°$

$\Rightarrow\ \cos 10° - \cos 13° > 0$

$\therefore\ x = \cos 10° - \cos 13° > 0$

Again, $\dfrac{\pi}{7} > \dfrac{\pi}{9}$

$\Rightarrow\ \tan\dfrac{\pi}{7} > \tan\dfrac{\pi}{9}$

$\Rightarrow\ \tan\dfrac{\pi}{7} - \tan\dfrac{\pi}{9} > 0$

$\therefore\ y = \tan\dfrac{\pi}{7} - \tan\dfrac{\pi}{9} > 0$

So, the point lies in I quadrant.

Oblique Coordinate System

If the two axes are not perpendicular i.e. inclined at certain angle $\omega (\neq 90°)$, then they are known as oblique coordinate system.

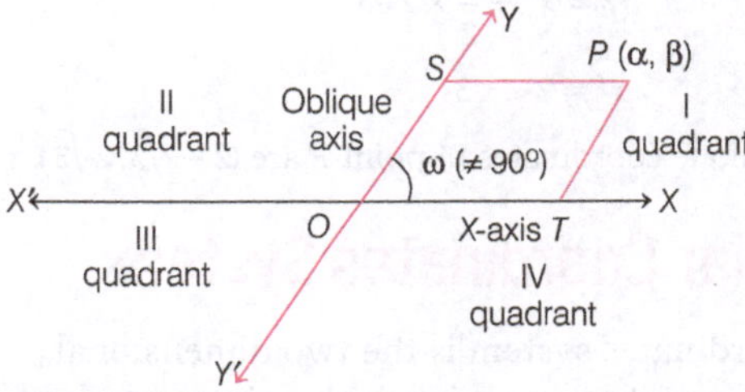

Consider the two lines $X'OX$ and $Y'OY$ intersecting at the origin. Let the angle between them be $\omega\ (\omega \neq 90°)$.

Here, a point P is given by two real numbers indicating the positions of the projections from the point to each axis.

The oblique coordinates (α, β) of point P can be determined by drawing the lines parallel to each oblique axis and measuring, where they cut at oblique axis.

Relation between Rectangular and Oblique Coordinate System

Consider a point P having its rectangular coordinates (x, y) and oblique coordinates (x', y').

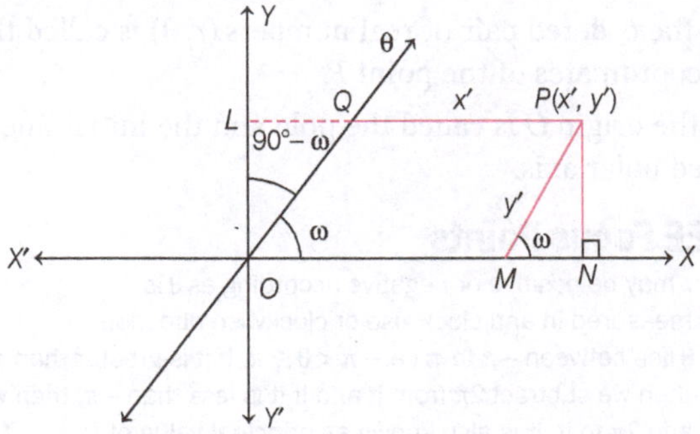

Then, $x = LP = LQ + QP = y' \cos\omega + x'$

and $y = PN = y' \sin\omega$

$\therefore$ Coordinates of (x, y) are $(x' + y'\cos\omega,\ y'\sin\omega)$.

Example 3. Let $P(2, 3)$ be a point in a rectangular coordinate system. Then, obtain this point with respect to oblique coordinate system, where angle between two axes is $60°$.

Sol. We know that

$$x = x' + y' \cos\omega$$

$$\Rightarrow \quad 2 = x' + y' \cos 60°$$

$$\Rightarrow \quad 2 = x' + \frac{1}{2}y' \quad \text{...(i)}$$

$$\text{and} \quad y = y' \sin\omega \Rightarrow 3 = y' \sin 60°$$

$$\Rightarrow \quad 3 = \frac{\sqrt{3}}{2}y'$$

$$\Rightarrow \quad y' = 2\sqrt{3} \quad \text{...(ii)}$$

From Eqs. (i) and (ii), we get

$$2 = x' + \frac{1}{2} \times 2\sqrt{3}$$

$$\Rightarrow \quad x' = 2 - \sqrt{3}$$

$\therefore$ Oblique coordinates of point P are $(2-\sqrt{3}, 2\sqrt{3})$.

1.3 Polar Coordinates System

Polar coordinates system is the two dimensional coordinates system in which each point on a plane has a unique distance and specific angle from a reference point.

Here, the point P is at distance of r from origin.

If $\quad OP = r \quad$ [radius vector]

and $\angle XOP = \theta \quad$ [vectorial angle]

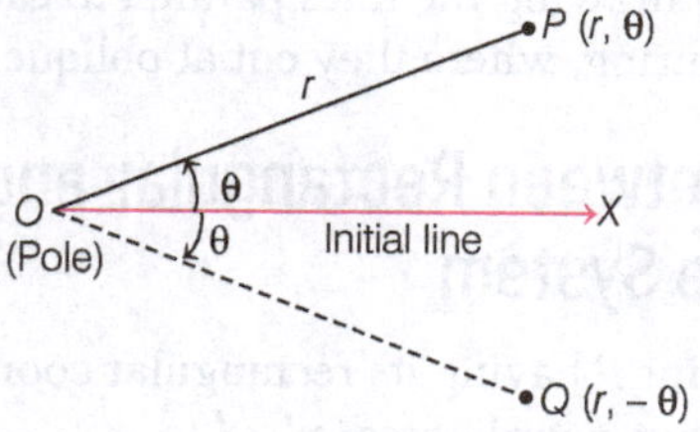

Then, the ordered pair of real numbers (r, θ) is called the polar coordinates of the point P.

Here, the origin O is called the pole and the initial line OX is called polar axis.

JEE Focus Points

- r may be positive or negative according as θ is measured in anti-clockwise or clockwise direction. θ lies between $-\pi$ to π i.e. $-\pi < \theta \le \pi$. If it is greater than π, then we subtract 2π from it and if it is less than $-\pi$, then we add 2π to it. It is also known as principal value of P.
- Always taken θ in radian.

Example 4. Draw the polar coordinates $\left(2, \frac{\pi}{3}\right), \left(-2, \frac{\pi}{3}\right), \left(-2, -\frac{\pi}{3}\right)$ and $\left(2, -\frac{\pi}{3}\right)$ on the plane.

Sol. The points $P\left(2, \frac{\pi}{3}\right), Q\left(-2, \frac{\pi}{3}\right), R\left(-2, -\frac{\pi}{3}\right)$ and $S\left(2, -\frac{\pi}{3}\right)$ are points of polar coordinates as shown below.

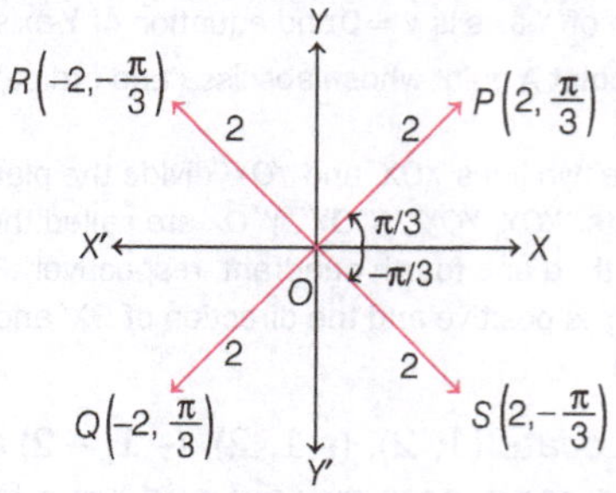

Example 5. Draw the polar coordinates $\left(3, \frac{5\pi}{4}\right)$ on the plane.

Sol. Here, $\quad \theta = \frac{5\pi}{4} > \pi$

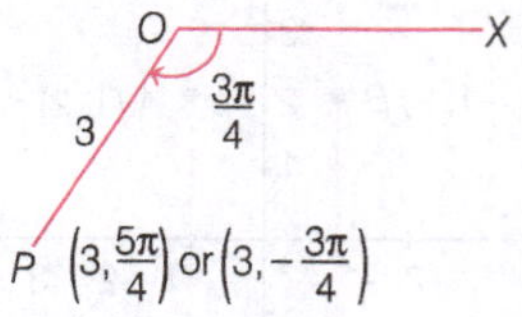

Then, $\quad \theta - 2\pi = \frac{5\pi}{4} - 2\pi = -\frac{3\pi}{4}$

$\therefore \quad \left(3, \frac{5\pi}{4}\right)$ is same $\left(3, -\frac{3\pi}{4}\right)$.

1.4 Relation between the Polar and Cartesian Coordinates

Let $P(x, y)$ be the cartesian coordinates with respect to axes OX and OY and (r, θ) be its polar coordinates with respect to pole O and initial line OX.

It is clear from figure,

$$OM = x = r\cos\theta \quad \text{...(i)}$$

$$\text{and} \quad MP = y = r\sin\theta \quad \text{...(ii)}$$

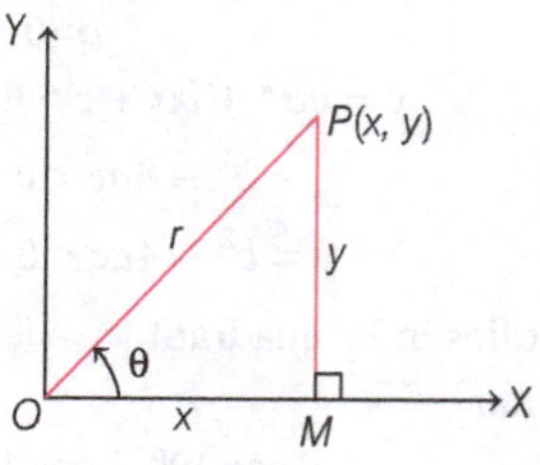

On squaring and adding Eqs. (i) and (ii), we get

$$x^2+y^2=r^2 \quad \text{or} \quad r=\sqrt{(x^2+y^2)}$$

On dividing Eq. (ii) by Eq. (i), we get

$$\tan\theta=\left(\frac{y}{x}\right) \quad \text{or} \quad \theta=\tan^{-1}\left(\frac{y}{x}\right)$$

i.e. $(r\cos\theta, r\sin\theta) \Rightarrow (x,y)$ ...(iii)

and $\left(\sqrt{(x^2+y^2)}, \tan^{-1}\left(\frac{y}{x}\right)\right) \Rightarrow (r,\theta)$ ...(iv)

If r and θ are known, then we can find (x,y) from Eq. (iii) and if x and y are known, then we can find (r,θ) from Eq. (iv).

$\because$ $\theta=\tan^{-1}\left(\frac{y}{x}\right)$

If $\alpha=\tan^{-1}\left|\frac{y}{x}\right|$

Then, values of θ in four quadrants.

Quadrants	I	II	III	IV
θ	α	$\pi-\alpha$	$-\pi+\alpha$	$-\alpha$

Example 6. Find the cartesian coordinates of the points whose polar coordinates are

(i) $\left(5, \pi-\tan^{-1}\left(\frac{4}{3}\right)\right)$ (ii) $\left(5\sqrt{2}, \frac{\pi}{4}\right)$

Sol. (i) Given, $r=5, \theta=\pi-\tan^{-1}\left(\frac{4}{3}\right)$

Now, $x=r\cos\theta=5\cos\left(\pi-\tan^{-1}\left(\frac{4}{3}\right)\right)$

$=-5\cos\left(\tan^{-1}\left(\frac{4}{3}\right)\right)$

$=-5\cos\left(\cos^{-1}\left(\frac{3}{5}\right)\right)=-5\times\frac{3}{5}=-3$

and $y=r\sin\theta=5\sin\left(\pi-\tan^{-1}\left(\frac{4}{3}\right)\right)$

$=5\sin\left(\tan^{-1}\left(\frac{4}{3}\right)\right)$

$=5\sin\left(\sin^{-1}\left(\frac{4}{5}\right)\right)$

$=5\times\frac{4}{5}=4$

Hence, cartesian coordinates of the given point will be $(-3, 4)$.

(ii) Given, $r=5\sqrt{2}, \theta=\frac{\pi}{4}$

Now, $x=r\cos\theta=5\sqrt{2}\cos\left(\frac{\pi}{4}\right)$

$=5\sqrt{2}\times\frac{1}{\sqrt{2}}=5$

and $y=r\sin\theta=5\sqrt{2}\sin\left(\frac{\pi}{4}\right)$

$=5\sqrt{2}\times\frac{1}{\sqrt{2}}=5$

Hence, cartesian coordinates of the given point will be $(5, 5)$.

Example 7. Find the polar coordinates of the points whose cartesian coordinates are

(i) $(-2,-2)$ (ii) $(-3,4)$

Sol. (i) Given, $x=-2, y=-2$

$\therefore$ $r=\sqrt{(x^2+y^2)}=\sqrt{(4+4)}=2\sqrt{2}$

and $\alpha=\tan^{-1}\left|\frac{y}{x}\right|=\tan^{-1}\left|\frac{-2}{-2}\right|$

$=\tan^{-1}1=\frac{\pi}{4}$

Since, point $(-2,-2)$ lies in III quadrant.

$\therefore$ $\theta=-\pi+\alpha=-\pi+\frac{\pi}{4}=-\frac{3\pi}{4}$

Hence, polar coordinates of the given points will be $\left(2\sqrt{2}, -\frac{3\pi}{4}\right)$.

(ii) Given, $x=-3, y=4$

$\therefore$ $r=\sqrt{(x^2+y^2)}=\sqrt{(9+16)}=5$

and $\alpha=\tan^{-1}\left|\frac{y}{x}\right|=\tan^{-1}\left|\frac{4}{-3}\right|=\tan^{-1}\left(\frac{4}{3}\right)$

Since, point $(-3, 4)$ lies in II quadrant.

$\therefore$ $\theta=\pi-\alpha=\pi-\tan^{-1}\left(\frac{4}{3}\right)$

Hence, polar coordinates of the given points will be $\left(5, \pi-\tan^{-1}\left(\frac{4}{3}\right)\right)$.

Example 8. Transform the equation $x^2+y^2=ax$ into polar form.

Sol. Since, $x=r\cos\theta$

and $y=r\sin\theta$

Given, $x^2+y^2=ax$

$\Rightarrow$ $r^2=a(r\cos\theta)$

or $r=a\cos\theta$

This is the required equation in polar form.

Example 9. Transform the equation $r^2 = a^2 \cos 2\theta$ into cartesian form.

Sol. $r^2 = a^2 \cos 2\theta$ or $r^2 = a^2 (\cos^2\theta - \sin^2\theta)$ ...(i)

$\because$ $x = r\cos\theta$

and $y = r\sin\theta$

and $r^2 = x^2 + y^2$

Then, $r^2 = a^2\left(\frac{x^2}{r^2} - \frac{y^2}{r^2}\right)$ [from Eq. (i)]

or $r^4 = a^2(x^2 - y^2)$

or $(x^2 + y^2)^2 = a^2(x^2 - y^2)$

Alternate Solution

Since, $r = \sqrt{(x^2 + y^2)}$ and $\theta = \tan^{-1}\left(\frac{y}{x}\right)$

or $r^2 = (x^2 + y^2)$ and $\tan\theta = \frac{y}{x}$

Given, $r^2 = a^2 \cos 2\theta = a^2\left(\frac{1 - \tan^2\theta}{1 + \tan^2\theta}\right)$

or $(x^2 + y^2) = a^2\left(\frac{1 - \frac{y^2}{x^2}}{1 + \frac{y^2}{x^2}}\right)$ or $(x^2 + y^2)^2 = a^2(x^2 - y^2)$

This is the required equation in cartesian form.

Milestone Practice 1.1

1. Locate the position of following points in the correct quadrant.

(i) $(\cos\theta + \sin\theta, \cos\theta - \sin\theta), \theta \in \left(\frac{\pi}{4}, \frac{3\pi}{4}\right)$

(ii) $(\sec^2 9° - \tan^2 9°, \cos 17° - 1)$.

2. Let $A(3, 2)$ in a rectangular coordinate system. Then, obtain this point with respect to oblique coordinate system, where angle between two axes is 45°.

3. The polar coordinates of the point whose cartesian coordinates are $(-1, -1)$ is

(a) $\left(\sqrt{2}, \frac{\pi}{4}\right)$ (b) $\left(\sqrt{2}, \frac{3\pi}{4}\right)$

(c) $\left(\sqrt{2}, -\frac{\pi}{4}\right)$ (d) $\left(\sqrt{2}, -\frac{3\pi}{4}\right)$

4. The cartesian coordinates of the point whose polar coordinates are $\left(13, \pi - \tan^{-1}\left(\frac{5}{12}\right)\right)$ is

(a) (12, 5) (b) (−12, 5)

(c) (−12, −5) (d) (12, −5)

5. The transform equation of $r^2\cos^2\theta = a^2\cos 2\theta$ to cartesian form is $(x^2 + y^2)\,x^2 = a^2\lambda$, then value of λ is

(a) $y^2 - x^2$ (b) $x^2 - y^2$

(c) xy (d) x^2y^2

6. The coordinates of P' in the figure are

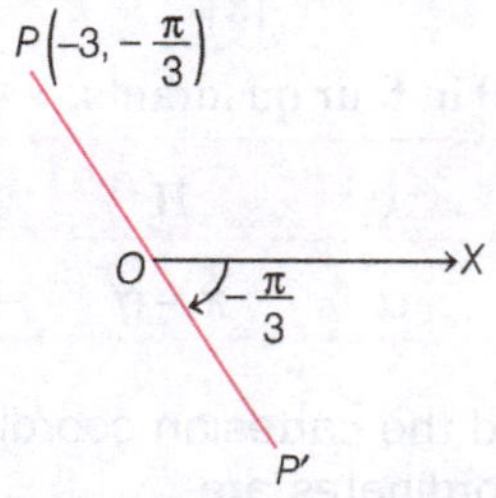

(a) $\left(3, \frac{\pi}{3}\right)$ (b) $\left(3, -\frac{\pi}{3}\right)$ (c) $\left(-3, -\frac{\pi}{3}\right)$ (d) $\left(-3, \frac{\pi}{3}\right)$

7. The cartesian coordinates of the point Q in the figure are

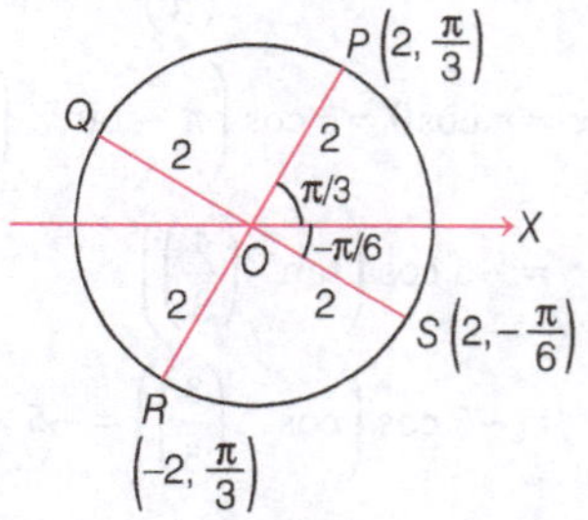

(a) $(\sqrt{3}, 1)$ (b) $(-\sqrt{3}, 1)$ (c) $(-\sqrt{3}, -1)$ (d) $(\sqrt{3}, -1)$

8. Transform the equation $y = x\tan\alpha$ to polar form.

9. Transform the equation $r = 2a\cos\theta$ to cartesian form.

Answer Key

1. (i) IV quadrant (ii) IV quadrant		**2.** $(1, 2\sqrt{2})$	**3.** (d)
4. (b)	**5.** (b)	**6.** (b)	**7.** (b)
8. $(r, \theta) = (r, \alpha)$	**9.** $x^2 + y^2 = 2ax$		

For Detailed Solution

Milestone 2 Distance Formula

• Distance Between Two Points • Choice of Axes • Distance Between Two Points in Oblique Coordinates
• Distance Between Two Points in Polar Coordinates

1.5 Distance Between Two Points

Theorem The distance between two points $P(x_1, y_1)$ and $Q(x_2, y_2)$ is given by

$$|PQ| = \sqrt{(x_2 - x_1)^2 + (y_2 - y_1)^2}$$

Proof Let $P(x_1, y_1)$ and $Q(x_2, y_2)$ be any two points in the plane. Let us assume that the points P and Q are both in I quadrant (for the sake of exactness).

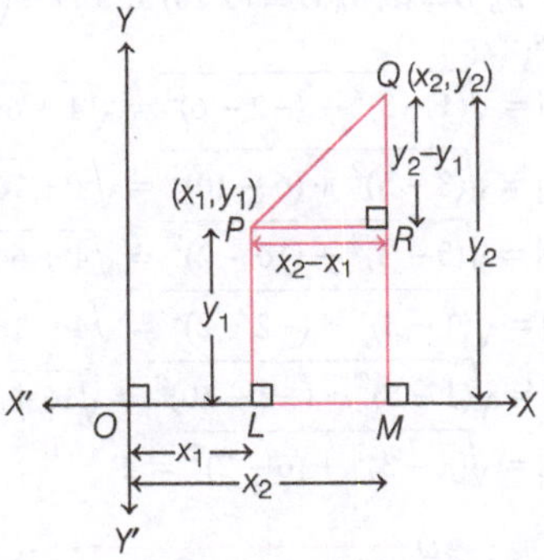

From P and Q, draw PL and QM perpendiculars to X-axis. From P, draw PR perpendicular to QM and join PQ.

Then, $OL = x_1, OM = x_2, PL = y_1, QM = y_2$

$\therefore$ $PR = LM = OM - OL = x_2 - x_1$

and $QR = QM - RM = QM - PL = y_2 - y_1$

Since, PRQ is a right angled triangle.

$\therefore$ By Pythagoras theorem,

$$(PQ)^2 = (PR)^2 + (QR)^2$$

$$\therefore \quad |PQ| = \sqrt{(PR)^2 + (QR)^2} \quad [\because PQ \text{ is always positive}]$$

$$= \sqrt{(x_2 - x_1)^2 + (y_2 - y_1)^2}$$

$\therefore$ The distance PQ between the points $P(x_1, y_1)$ and $Q(x_2, y_2)$ is given by $\sqrt{(x_2 - x_1)^2 + (y_2 - y_1)^2}$

or $\sqrt{(\text{difference in } x \text{ coordinates})^2 + (\text{difference in } y \text{ coordinates})^2}$

or $\sqrt{(\text{difference of abscissaes})^2 + (\text{difference of ordinates})^2}$

Notations We shall denote the distance between two points P and Q of the coordinate plane, either by $|PQ|$ or by $\overline{PQ}$.

Concept Inside Video

JEE Focus Points

- The distance of the point $P(x, y)$ from the origin $O(0, 0)$ is given by
  $$|OP| = \sqrt{(x-0)^2 + (y-0)^2} = \sqrt{(x^2 + y^2)}$$
- If PQ is parallel to X-axis, then $y_1 = y_2$ and so
  $$|PQ| = \sqrt{(x_2 - x_1)^2} = |x_2 - x_1|$$
- If PQ is parallel to Y-axis, then $x_1 = x_2$ and so
  $$|PQ| = \sqrt{(y_2 - y_1)^2} = |y_2 - y_1|$$
- If (x_1, y_1) and (x_2, y_2) are the ends of the hypotenuse of a right angled isosceles triangle, then the third vertex is given by
  $$\left(\frac{(x_1 + x_2) \pm (y_1 - y_2)}{2}, \frac{(y_1 + y_2) \mp (x_1 - x_2)}{2}\right)$$
- If two vertices of an equilateral triangle are (x_1, y_1) and (x_2, y_2), then coordinates of the third vertex are
  $$\left(\frac{x_1 + x_2 \mp \sqrt{3}(y_2 - y_1)}{2}, \frac{y_1 + y_2 \pm \sqrt{3}(x_2 - x_1)}{2}\right)$$

Example 10. Find the distance between the points $(a\cos\alpha, a\sin\alpha)$ and $(a\cos\beta, a\sin\beta)$, where $a > 0$.

Sol. Let $P \equiv (a\cos\alpha, a\sin\alpha)$ and $Q \equiv (a\cos\beta, a\sin\beta)$

Then, $|PQ| = \sqrt{(a\cos\alpha - a\cos\beta)^2 + (a\sin\alpha - a\sin\beta)^2}$

$$= \sqrt{a^2\{(\cos\alpha - \cos\beta)^2 + (\sin\alpha - \sin\beta)^2\}}$$

$$= \sqrt{a^2\{\cos^2\alpha + \cos^2\beta - 2\cos\alpha\cos\beta + \sin^2\alpha + \sin^2\beta - 2\sin\alpha\sin\beta\}}$$

$$= \sqrt{a^2\{1 + 1 - 2(\cos\alpha\cos\beta + \sin\alpha\sin\beta)\}}$$

$$= \sqrt{a^2(2 - 2\cos(\alpha - \beta))}$$

$$= \sqrt{2a^2(1 - \cos(\alpha - \beta))}$$

$$= \sqrt{\left(2a^2 \cdot 2\sin^2\left(\frac{\alpha-\beta}{2}\right)\right)}$$

$$= \sqrt{4a^2 \sin^2\left(\frac{\alpha-\beta}{2}\right)}$$

$$= \left|2a \sin\left(\frac{\alpha-\beta}{2}\right)\right|$$

$$= 2a\left|\sin\left(\frac{\alpha-\beta}{2}\right)\right| \qquad [\because a > 0]$$

Example 11. If the distance between the points $(3, b)$ and $(5, 7)$ is 12, then b is

(a) $2 \pm 3\sqrt{35}$ (b) $7 \pm 2\sqrt{35}$
(c) $3 \pm 3\sqrt{35}$ (d) $2 \pm 7\sqrt{35}$

Sol. (b) Let $(x_1, y_1) \equiv (3, b)$ and $(x_2, y_2) \equiv (5, 7)$ be two points.

Given distance between two points = 12

$$\sqrt{(x_2 - x_1)^2 + (y_2 - y_1)^2} = 12$$

$$\Rightarrow \quad \sqrt{(5-3)^2 + (7-b)^2} = 12$$

On squaring both sides, we get

$$4 + (7-b)^2 = 144$$

$$\Rightarrow \quad 4 + 49 - 14b + b^2 = 144$$

$$\Rightarrow \quad b^2 - 14b - 91 = 0$$

$$\Rightarrow \quad b = \frac{14 \pm \sqrt{196 + 364}}{2}$$

$$\Rightarrow \quad b = 7 \pm 2\sqrt{35}$$

Example 12. Prove that the distance of the point $(a\cos\alpha, a\sin\alpha)$ from the origin is independent of α.

Sol. Let $P \equiv (a\cos\alpha, a\sin\alpha)$ and $O \equiv (0, 0)$

Then, $|OP| = \sqrt{(a\cos\alpha - 0)^2 + (a\sin\alpha - 0)^2}$

$$= \sqrt{(a^2\cos^2\alpha + a^2\sin^2\alpha)}$$

$$= \sqrt{a^2(\cos^2\alpha + \sin^2\alpha)} = \sqrt{a^2}$$

$= |a|$, which is independent of α.

Example 13. If the point (x, y) is equidistant from the points $(6, -1)$ and $(2, 3)$, then prove that $x - y = 3$.

Sol. Let $P \equiv (x, y)$, $A \equiv (6, -1)$ and $B \equiv (2, 3)$

By the given condition, $PA = PB$

$$\Rightarrow \quad \sqrt{(x-6)^2 + (y+1)^2} = \sqrt{(x-2)^2 + (y-3)^2}$$

or $\quad (x-6)^2 + (y+1)^2 = (x-2)^2 + (y-3)^2$

or $\quad x^2 - 12x + 36 + y^2 + 2y + 1 = x^2 - 4x + 4 + y^2 - 6y + 9$

or $\quad 8x - 8y = 24$

or $\quad x - y = 3$

Example 14. Using distance formula, show that the points $(1, 5)$, $(2, 4)$ and $(3, 3)$ are collinear.

Sol. Let $A \equiv (1, 5)$, $B \equiv (2, 4)$ and $C \equiv (3, 3)$ be the given points.

Then, $|AB| = \sqrt{(1-2)^2 + (5-4)^2} = \sqrt{2}$,

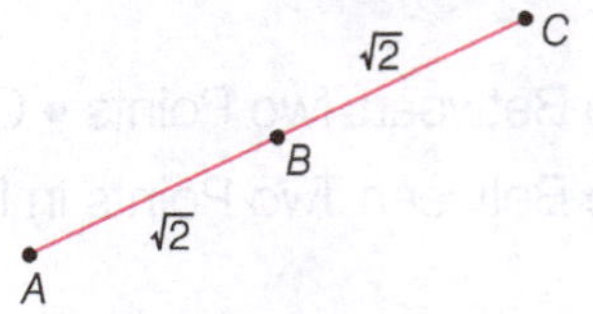

$$|BC| = \sqrt{(2-3)^2 + (4-3)^2} = \sqrt{2}$$

and $\quad |AC| = \sqrt{(1-3)^2 + (5-3)^2} = 2\sqrt{2}$

Clearly, $|AB| + |BC| = \sqrt{2} + \sqrt{2} = 2\sqrt{2} = |AC|$

Hence, A, B and C are collinear.

Example 15. Show that four points $(1, -2)$, $(3, 6)$, $(5, 10)$ and $(3, 2)$ are the vertices of a parallelogram.

Sol. Let $A \equiv (1, -2)$, $B \equiv (3, 6)$, $C \equiv (5, 10)$ and $D \equiv (3, 2)$ be the given points.

Then, $|AB| = \sqrt{(1-3)^2 + (-2-6)^2} = \sqrt{4 + 64} = 2\sqrt{17}$,

$|BC| = \sqrt{(3-5)^2 + (6-10)^2} = \sqrt{4 + 16} = 2\sqrt{5}$,

$|CD| = \sqrt{(5-3)^2 + (10-2)^2} = \sqrt{4 + 64} = 2\sqrt{17}$,

$|AD| = \sqrt{(1-3)^2 + (-2-2)^2} = \sqrt{4 + 16} = 2\sqrt{5}$,

$|AC| = \sqrt{(1-5)^2 + (-2-10)^2} = \sqrt{16 + 144} = 4\sqrt{10}$

and $\quad |BD| = \sqrt{(3-3)^2 + (6-2)^2} = 4$

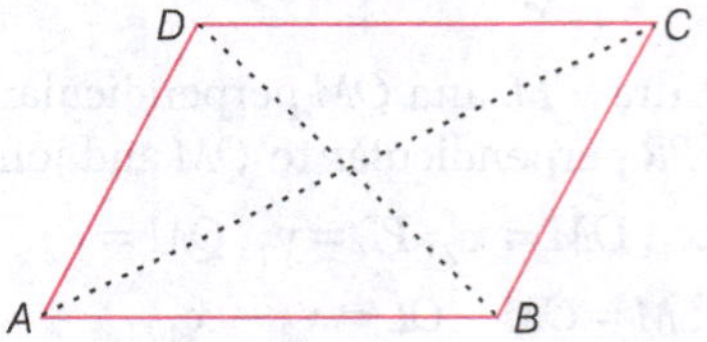

Clearly, $|AB| = |CD|$, $|BC| = |AD|$ and $|AC| \neq |BD|$

Hence, $ABCD$ is a parallelogram.

Example 16. Find the circumcentre of the triangle whose vertices are $(-2, -3)$, $(-1, 0)$ and $(7, -6)$. Also, find the radius of the circumcircle.

Sol. Let $A \equiv (-2, -3)$, $B \equiv (-1, 0)$ and $C \equiv (7, -6)$.

Let $P \equiv (x, y)$ be the circumcentre of ΔABC.

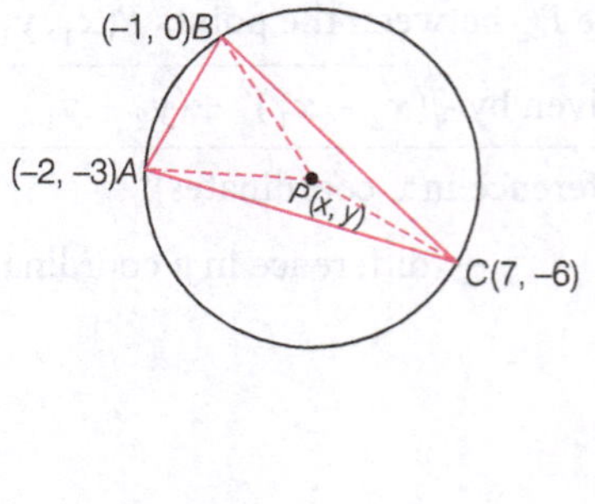

Since, P is the circumcentre.

$\therefore \quad |PA| = |PB| = |PC| \Rightarrow (PA)^2 = (PB)^2 = (PC)^2$

$$(x+2)^2 + (y+3)^2 = (x+1)^2 + (y-0)^2 = (x-7)^2 + (y+6)^2$$

$$\Rightarrow \quad x^2 + y^2 + 4x + 6y + 13 = x^2 + y^2 + 2x + 1 = x^2 + y^2 - 14x + 12y + 85$$

On taking first two members, we get

$$x + 3y + 6 = 0 \quad \text{...(i)}$$

On taking first and last member, then we get

$$3x - y - 12 = 0 \quad \text{...(ii)}$$

On solving Eqs. (i) and (ii), we get

$$x = 3 \text{ and } y = -3$$

Hence, circumcentre is $(3, -3)$.

Radius of the circumcircle $= PB = \sqrt{(3+1)^2 + (-3-0)^2} = \sqrt{16+9} = 5$ units

Example 17. Let the opposite angular points of a square be $(3, 4)$ and $(1, -1)$. Find the coordinates of the remaining angular points.

Sol. Let $A(3, 4)$ and $C(1, -1)$ be the given angular points of a square $ABCD$ and let $B(x, y)$ be the unknown vertex.

Then, $\quad AB = BC$

$$\Rightarrow \quad (AB)^2 = (BC)^2$$

$$\Rightarrow \quad (x-3)^2 + (y-4)^2 = (x-1)^2 + (y+1)^2$$

$$\Rightarrow \quad 4x + 10y - 23 = 0$$

$$\Rightarrow \quad x = \left(\frac{23 - 10y}{4}\right) \quad \text{...(i)}$$

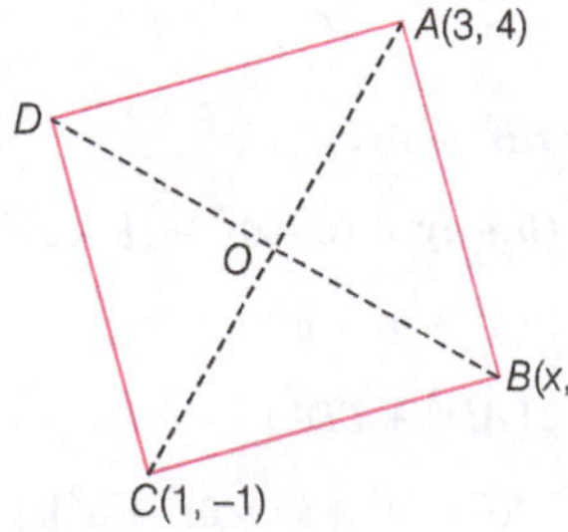

Also, in ΔABC,

$$(AB)^2 + (BC)^2 = (AC)^2$$

$$\Rightarrow \quad (x-3)^2 + (y-4)^2 + (x-1)^2 + (y+1)^2 = (3-1)^2 + (4+1)^2$$

$$\Rightarrow \quad x^2 + y^2 - 4x - 3y - 1 = 0 \quad \text{...(ii)}$$

On substituting the value of x from Eq. (i) in Eq. (ii), we get

$$\left(\frac{23-10y}{4}\right)^2 + y^2 - 4\left(\frac{23-10y}{4}\right) - 3y - 1 = 0$$

$$\Rightarrow \quad 4y^2 - 12y + 5 = 0 \text{ or } (2y-1)(2y-5) = 0$$

$$\therefore \quad y = \frac{1}{2} \text{ or } \frac{5}{2}$$

On putting $y = \frac{1}{2}$ in Eq. (i), we get $x = \frac{9}{2}$,

and on putting $y = \frac{5}{2}$ in Eq. (i), we get $x = -\frac{1}{2}$

Hence, the required vertices of the square are $\left(\frac{9}{2}, \frac{1}{2}\right)$ and $\left(-\frac{1}{2}, \frac{5}{2}\right)$.

Example 18. An equilateral triangle has one vertex at the point $(0, 0)$ and another at $(3, \sqrt{3})$. Find the coordinates of the third vertex.

Sol. Let $O \equiv (0, 0)$ and $A \equiv (3, \sqrt{3})$ be the given points and let $B \equiv (x, y)$ be the required point.

Then, $\quad OA = OB = AB$

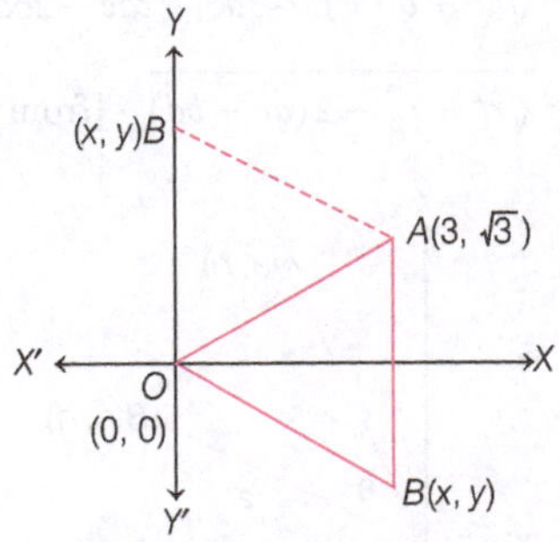

$$\Rightarrow \quad (OA)^2 = (OB)^2 = (AB)^2$$

$$\Rightarrow \quad (3-0)^2 + (\sqrt{3}-0)^2 = (x-0)^2 + (y-0)^2 = (x-3)^2 + (y-\sqrt{3})^2$$

$$\Rightarrow \quad 12 = x^2 + y^2 = x^2 + y^2 - 6x - 2\sqrt{3}y + 12$$

On taking first two members, then

$$x^2 + y^2 = 12 \quad \text{...(i)}$$

and on taking last two members, then

$$6x + 2\sqrt{3}y = 12 \text{ or } y = \sqrt{3}(2-x) \quad \text{...(ii)}$$

From Eqs. (i) and (ii), we get

$$x^2 + 3(2-x)^2 = 12$$

or $\quad 4x^2 - 12x = 0 \Rightarrow x = 0, 3$

On putting $x = 0, 3$ in Eq. (ii), we get

$$y = 2\sqrt{3}, -\sqrt{3}$$

Hence, the coordinates of the third vertex B are $(0, 2\sqrt{3})$ or $(3, -\sqrt{3})$.

Time Saving Technique

Given two vertices of an equilateral triangle are $(0, 0)$ and $(3, \sqrt{3})$, then the coordinates of third vertex are

$$\left(\frac{x_1 + x_2 \mp \sqrt{3}(y_2 - y_1)}{2}, \frac{y_1 + y_2 \pm \sqrt{3}(x_2 - x_1)}{2}\right)$$

i.e. $\quad \left(\frac{0 + 3 \mp \sqrt{3}(\sqrt{3} - 0)}{2}, \frac{0 + \sqrt{3} \pm \sqrt{3}(3 - 0)}{2}\right)$

or $\quad \left(\frac{3 \mp 3}{2}, \frac{\sqrt{3} \pm 3\sqrt{3}}{2}\right) \Rightarrow (0, 2\sqrt{3}) \text{ or } (3, -\sqrt{3})$

Example 19. If the line segment joining the points $A(a, b)$ and $B(c, d)$ subtends an angle θ at the origin O, then prove that $\cos\theta = \dfrac{ac + bd}{\sqrt{(a^2 + b^2)(c^2 + d^2)}}$

or $\quad OA \cdot OB \cos\theta = ac + bd$

Sol. Let $OA = r_1$ and $OB = r_2$

Now, $r_1 = |OA| = \sqrt{(a^2 + b^2)}$ ...(i)

and $r_2 = |OB| = \sqrt{(c^2 + d^2)}$ ...(ii)

Also, $|AB| = \sqrt{(a-c)^2 + (b-d)^2}$

$= \sqrt{a^2 + b^2 + c^2 + d^2 - 2ac - 2bd}$

$= \sqrt{r_1^2 + r_2^2 - 2(ac + bd)}$ [from Eqs. (i) and (ii)]

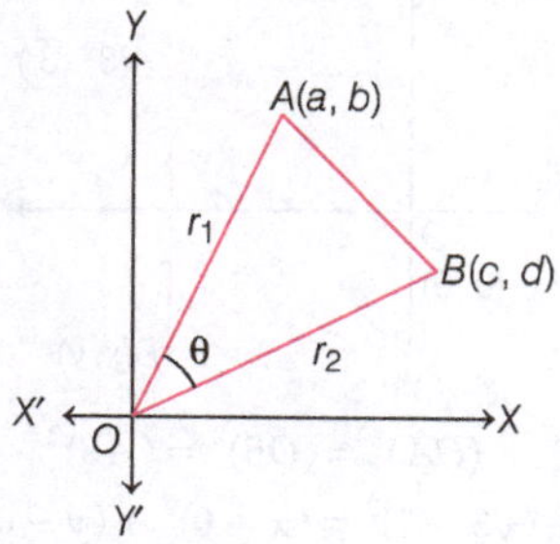

By using cosine formula, in ΔAOB,

$$\cos\theta = \frac{(OA)^2 + (OB)^2 - (AB)^2}{2 \cdot OA \cdot OB}$$

$$= \frac{r_1^2 + r_2^2 - (r_1^2 + r_2^2 - 2(ac + bd))}{2r_1 r_2}$$

$$= \frac{2(ac + bd)}{2r_1 r_2}$$

$$= \frac{(ac + bd)}{r_1 r_2} \quad \text{...(iii)}$$

$$= \frac{(ac + bd)}{\sqrt{(a^2 + b^2)}\sqrt{(c^2 + d^2)}} \quad \text{[from Eqs. (i) and (ii)]}$$

Also, from Eq. (iii), $r_1 r_2 \cos\theta = ac + bd$

or $\quad OA \cdot OB \cos\theta = ac + bd$

1.6 Choice of Axes

For simplification, we carefully choose the axes or the origin. Some situations are given below.

(i) If two lines are perpendicular, then point of intersection is taken as origin and these lines must be taken as the coordinate axes.

(ii) If two fixed points A and B are given, then we take $|AB| = 2a$ and the mid-point of AB as origin O, line AOB as X-axis and the line perpendicular to AB through O is taken as Y-axis, then the coordinates of the fixed points are $(\pm a, 0)$.
Similarly, if AOB as Y-axis and the line perpendicular to AB through O is taken as X-axis, then the coordinates of the fixed points are $(0, \pm a)$.

(iii) If there is a symmetry of any kind, then take the coordinates of the points in a general way i.e. $(x_i, y_i), i = 1, 2, 3, \ldots$ etc.

Example 20. In any ΔABC, show that $AB^2 + AC^2 = 2(AD^2 + BD^2)$, where D is the middle point of BC.

Sol. Let D as the origin and DC and DY as the X and Y-axes, respectively.

Let $BC = 2a$, then $B \equiv (-a, 0), C \equiv (a, 0)$

and let $A \equiv (b, c)$

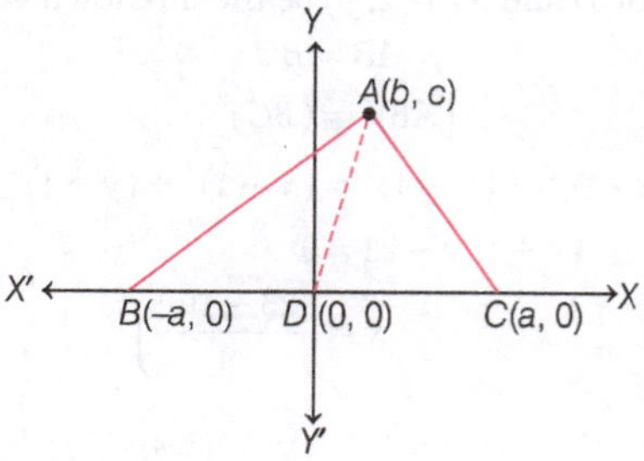

Now, $\quad \text{LHS} = AB^2 + AC^2$

$= (b + a)^2 + (c - 0)^2 + (b - a)^2 + (c - 0)^2$

$= 2(a^2 + b^2 + c^2)$ ...(i)

and $\quad \text{RHS} = 2(AD^2 + BD^2)$

$= 2\{(b - 0)^2 + (c - 0)^2 + a^2\}$

$= 2(a^2 + b^2 + c^2)$ ...(ii)

From Eqs. (i) and (ii), we get

$AB^2 + AC^2 = 2(AD^2 + BD^2)$

Example 21. Let $ABCD$ be a rectangle and P be any point in its plane. Show that $PA^2 + PC^2 = PB^2 + PD^2$.

Sol. Let A as the origin and AB and AD as the X and Y-axes, respectively.

Let $\quad AB = a$

and $\quad AD = b$

then $\quad B \equiv (a, 0), D \equiv (0, b)$ and $C \equiv (a, b)$

Let $P \equiv (\alpha, \beta)$

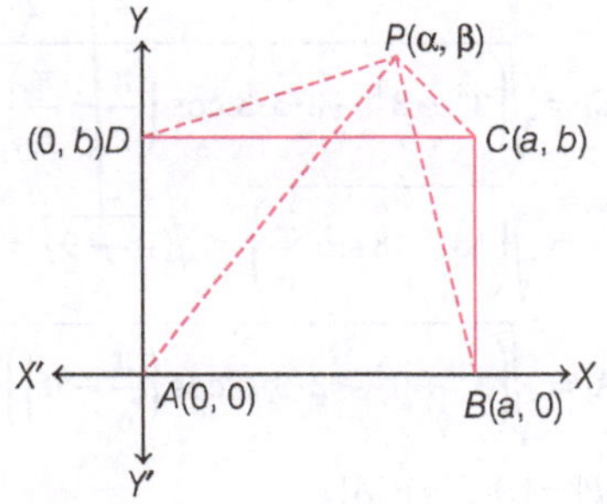

Now, LHS $= PA^2 + PC^2$

$$= (\alpha - 0)^2 + (\beta - 0)^2 + (\alpha - a)^2 + (\beta - b)^2$$

$$= 2\alpha^2 + 2\beta^2 - 2a\alpha - 2b\beta + a^2 + b^2 \quad \ldots\text{(i)}$$

and RHS $= PB^2 + PD^2$

$$= (\alpha - a)^2 + (\beta - 0)^2 + (\alpha - 0)^2 + (\beta - b)^2$$

$$= 2\alpha^2 + 2\beta^2 - 2a\alpha - 2b\beta + a^2 + b^2 \quad \ldots\text{(ii)}$$

From Eqs. (i) and (ii), we get

$$PA^2 + PC^2 = PB^2 + PD^2$$

1.7 Distance between Two Points in Oblique Coordinates

Let $P(x_1, y_1)$ and $Q(x_2, y_2)$ be two points in oblique coordinate system, where axes are inclined at an angle $\omega (\neq 90°)$.

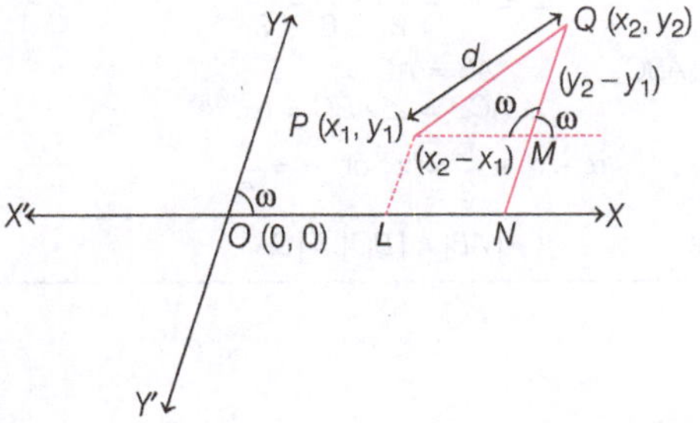

Then, the distance between the points P and Q will be given by

$$PQ = d = \sqrt{(x_2 - x_1)^2 + (y_2 - y_1)^2 + 2(x_2 - x_1)(y_2 - y_1)\cos\omega}$$

Proof In ΔPMQ, using cosine formula,

$$\cos(\angle QPM) = \frac{PM^2 + QM^2 - PQ^2}{2PM \cdot QM}$$

$$\cos(\pi - \omega) = \frac{(x_2 - x_1)^2 + (y_2 - y_1)^2 - d^2}{2(x_2 - x_1)(y_2 - y_1)}$$

$$\Rightarrow d^2 = (x_2 - x_1)^2 + (y_2 - y_1)^2 + 2(x_2 - x_1)(y_2 - y_1)\cos\omega$$

$$\Rightarrow d = \sqrt{(x_2 - x_1)^2 + (y_2 - y_1)^2 + 2(x_2 - x_1)(y_2 - y_1)\cos\omega}$$

Example 22. Let $A(4, 5)$ and $B(2, 3)$ be two points in an oblique coordinate system, in which the axes are inclined at an angle of 30°. Then, find the distance between A and B.

Sol. We have, $A(x_1, y_1) \equiv (4, 5)$, $B(x_2, y_2) \equiv (2, 3)$ and $\omega = 30°$

$$\therefore \quad AB = \sqrt{(x_2 - x_1)^2 + (y_2 - y_1)^2 + 2(x_2 - x_1)(y_2 - y_1)\cos\omega}$$

$$= \sqrt{(2-4)^2 + (3-5)^2 + 2(2-4)(3-5)\cos 30°}$$

$$= \sqrt{4 + 4 + 4\sqrt{3}}$$

$$= 2\sqrt{2 + \sqrt{3}} \text{ units}$$

Example 23. If the distance between two points $P(2, 3)$ and $Q(9, 7)$ in an oblique coordinate system is $2\sqrt{3}$, then the angle in which axes are inclined is

(a) $\pi - \cos^{-1}\left(\frac{23}{56}\right)$

(b) $\pi - \cos^{-1}\left(\frac{11}{56}\right)$

(c) $\pi - \cos^{-1}\left(\frac{53}{56}\right)$

(d) $\pi - \cos^{-1}\left(\frac{25}{56}\right)$

Sol. (c) Given, $P(x_1, y_1) \equiv (2, 3)$ and $Q(x_2, y_2) \equiv (9, 7)$ and $d = 2\sqrt{3}$.

Let the angle between the axes be ω.

According to distance formula,

$$d^2 = (x_2 - x_1)^2 + (y_2 - y_1)^2 + 2(x_2 - x_1)(y_2 - y_1)\cos\omega$$

$$(2\sqrt{3})^2 = (9-2)^2 + (7-3)^2 + 2(9-2)(7-3)\cos\omega$$

$$12 = 49 + 16 + 56\cos\omega$$

$$\Rightarrow \quad 56\cos\omega = 12 - 49 - 16 = -53$$

$$\Rightarrow \quad \cos\omega = -\frac{53}{56}$$

$$\Rightarrow \quad \omega = \cos^{-1}\left(\frac{-53}{56}\right)$$

Hence, the angle ω between the two axes is $\pi - \cos^{-1}\left(\frac{53}{56}\right)$.

1.8 Distance between Two Points in Polar Coordinates

Let O be the pole and OX be the initial line. Let P and Q be two given points whose polar coordinates are (r_1, θ_1) and (r_2, θ_2), respectively.

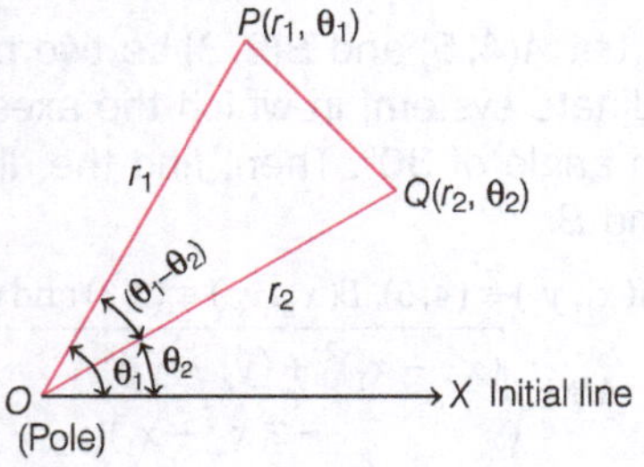

Then, $\quad OP = r_1, OQ = r_2$

and $\quad \angle POX = \theta_1, \angle QOX = \theta_2$

$\therefore \quad \angle POQ = \theta_1 - \theta_2$

Using cosine formula, in ΔPOQ,

$$\cos(\angle POQ) = \frac{(OP)^2 + (OQ)^2 - (PQ)^2}{2(OP)(OQ)}$$

or $$\cos(\theta_1 - \theta_2) = \frac{r_1^2 + r_2^2 - (PQ)^2}{2 r_1 r_2}$$

$$\therefore \quad |PQ| = \sqrt{(r_1^2 + r_2^2 - 2 r_1 r_2 \cos(\theta_1 - \theta_2))}$$

Example 24. Prove that the points (0, 0), $\left(3, \frac{\pi}{2}\right)$ and $\left(3, \frac{\pi}{6}\right)$ are the vertices of an equilateral triangle.

Sol. Let $A \equiv (0, 0)$, $B \equiv \left(3, \frac{\pi}{2}\right)$ and $C \equiv \left(3, \frac{\pi}{6}\right)$

Here, given coordinates are in polar form.

$$\therefore \quad |AB| = \sqrt{\left(0^2 + 3^2 - 2\cdot 0\cdot 3 \cos\left(\frac{\pi}{2} - 0\right)\right)} = 3 \text{ units}$$

$$|BC| = \sqrt{\left(3^2 + 3^2 - 2\cdot 3\cdot 3 \cos\left(\frac{\pi}{2} - \frac{\pi}{6}\right)\right)}$$

$$= \sqrt{\left(18 - 18 \sin\frac{\pi}{6}\right)} = \sqrt{(18 - 9)} = 3 \text{ units}$$

and $$|CA| = \sqrt{\left(3^2 + 0^2 - 2\cdot 3\cdot 0 \cos\left(\frac{\pi}{6} - 0\right)\right)} = 3 \text{ units}$$

$\therefore \quad |AB| = |BC| = |CA|$

Hence, points A, B and C are the vertices of an equilateral triangle.

Alternate Solution

Since, $\quad \angle BAX = \frac{\pi}{2}$ and $\angle CAX = \frac{\pi}{6}$

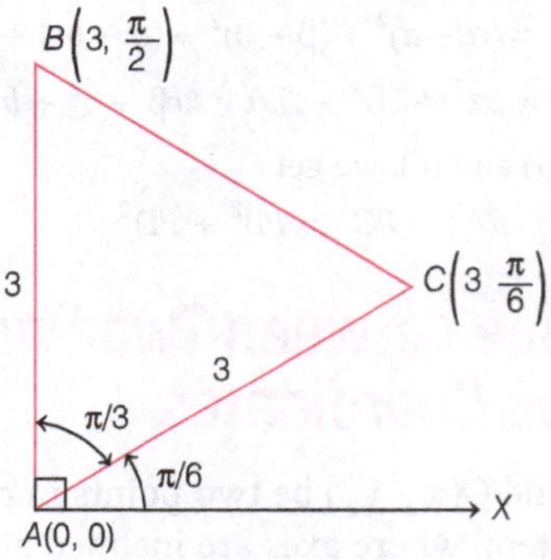

$\therefore \quad \angle BAC = \frac{\pi}{2} - \frac{\pi}{6} = \frac{\pi}{3}$

$\because$ In ΔABC, $\quad AB = AC$

$\therefore \quad \angle ACB = \angle ABC = \alpha$ [say]

$\therefore \quad \alpha + \alpha + \frac{\pi}{3} = \pi$ or $\alpha = \frac{\pi}{3}$

Hence, $\quad |AB| = |BC| = |CA|$.

Milestone Practice 1.2

1. If the distance between the points $(a, 2)$ and $(3, 4)$ be 8, then a equals to
(a) $2+3\sqrt{15}$ (b) $2-3\sqrt{15}$
(c) $2\pm 3\sqrt{15}$ (d) $3\pm 2\sqrt{15}$

2. Let $A(6,-1)$, $B(1,3)$ and $C(x,8)$ be three points such that $AB=BC$, then the value of x are
(a) 3, 5 (b) –3, 5
(c) 3, –5 (d) –3, –5

3. The points $(a+1,1)$, $(2a+1,3)$ and $(2a+2,2a)$ are collinear, if
(a) $a=-1,2$ (b) $a=\frac{1}{2},2$
(c) $a=2,1$ (d) $a=-\frac{1}{2},2$

4. If $A\equiv(3,4)$ and B is a variable point on the lines $|x|=6$. If $AB\le 4$, then the number of positions of B with integral coordinates is
(a) 5 (b) 6
(c) 10 (d) 12

5. The number of points on X-axis which are at a distance c units $(c<3)$ from $(2,3)$, is
(a) 1 (b) 2
(c) 0 (d) 3

6. The point on the axis of Y which its equidistant from $(-1,2)$ and $(3,4)$, is
(a) (0, 3)
(b) (0, 4)
(c) (0, 5)
(d) (0, –6)

7. Find the distance between the points $(at_1^2, 2at_1)$ and $(at_2^2, 2at_2)$, where t_1 and t_2 are the roots of the equation $x^2-2\sqrt{3}x+2=0$ and $a>0$.

8. If $P(at^2, 2at)$, $Q\left(\frac{a}{t^2}, -\frac{2a}{t}\right)$ and $S(a,0)$ are any three points, then show that $\frac{1}{SP}+\frac{1}{SQ}$ is independent of t.

9. Find the circumcentre and circumradius of the triangle whose vertices are $(-2,3)$, $(2,-1)$ and $(4,0)$.

10. The vertices of a triangle are $A(1,1)$, $B(4,5)$ and $C(6,13)$. Find $\cos A$.

11. Two opposite vertices of a square are $(2,6)$ and $(0,-2)$. Find the coordinates of the other vertices.

12. If the point (x,y) is equidistant from the points $(a+b, b-a)$ and $(a-b, a+b)$, then prove that $bx=ay$.

13. If a and b are real numbers between 0 and 1 such that the points $(a,1)$, $(1,b)$ and $(0,0)$ form an equilateral triangle, then find a and b.

14. An equilateral triangle has one vertex at $(3,4)$ and another at $(-2,3)$. Find the coordinates of the third vertex.

15. If P is any point in the plane of square $ABCD$, then prove that $PA^2+PC^2=PB^2+PD^2$

16. Let $P(3,1)$ and $Q(1,2)$ be two points in an oblique coordinate system, in which the axes are inclined at an angle of 60°. Then, find PQ.

17. The distance between the points $\left(3,\frac{\pi}{4}\right)$ and $\left(7,\frac{5\pi}{4}\right)$ is
(a) 8 (b) 10
(c) 12 (d) 14

Answer Key

1. (d) 2. (b) 3. (d) 4. (a) 5. (c) 6. (c)
7. $8a$ 9. $\left(\frac{3}{2},\frac{5}{2}\right), \frac{5\sqrt{2}}{2}$ units 10. $\frac{63}{65}$ 11. (5, 1) and (–3, 3)
13. $a=b=2-\sqrt{3}$ 14. $\left(\frac{1\pm\sqrt{3}}{2}, \frac{7\pm 5\sqrt{3}}{2}\right)$ 16. $\sqrt{7}$ 17. (b).

For Detailed Solution

Milestone 3 Section Formula

• Definition of Section Formula • Standard Points of a Triangle • Centroid of a Triangle • Incentre of a Triangle • Excentre of a Triangle • Circumcentre of a Triangle • Orthocentre of a Triangle • Nine-point Centre • Area of Triangle

1.9 Definition of Section Formula

If P is any point on the line AB between A and B, then we say that P divides segment AB internally in the ratio $AP : PB$.

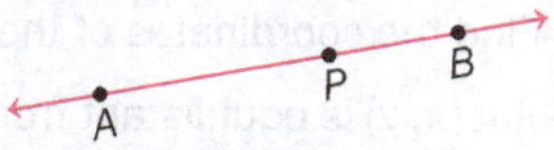

Also, if P is any point on the line AB but not between A and B (P may be to the right or the left of the points A, B), then P divides AB externally in the ratio $AP : PB$.

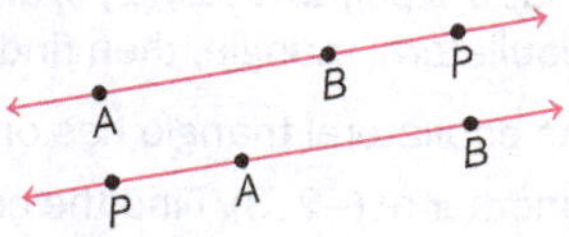

JEE SPIKE

If P be the point on the line AB, then

$$\frac{AP}{PB} = \begin{cases} \text{Positive, in internally division} \\ \text{Negative, in externally division} \end{cases}$$

Formula for Internal Division

Theorem If the point $P(x, y)$ divides the line segment joining the points $A(x_1, y_1)$ and $B(x_2, y_2)$ internally in the ratio $m : n$, then $x = \dfrac{mx_2 + nx_1}{m+n}$

and $y = \dfrac{my_2 + ny_1}{m+n}$

Proof The given points are $A(x_1, y_1)$ and $B(x_2, y_2)$. Let us assume that the points A and B are both in I quadrant (for the sake of exactness). Since, $P(x, y)$ divides AB internally in the ratio $m : n$ i.e. $AP : PB = m : n$. From A, B and P, draw AL, BM and PN perpendiculars to X-axis. From A and P, draw AH and PJ perpendiculars to PN and BM respectively, then

$OL = x_1, ON = x, OM = x_2, AL = y_1, PN = y$ and $BM = y_2$

$\therefore \quad AH = LN = ON - OL = x - x_1$

$PJ = NM = OM - ON = x_2 - x$

$PH = PN - HN = PN - AL = y - y_1$

and $\quad BJ = BM - JM = BM - PN = y_2 - y$

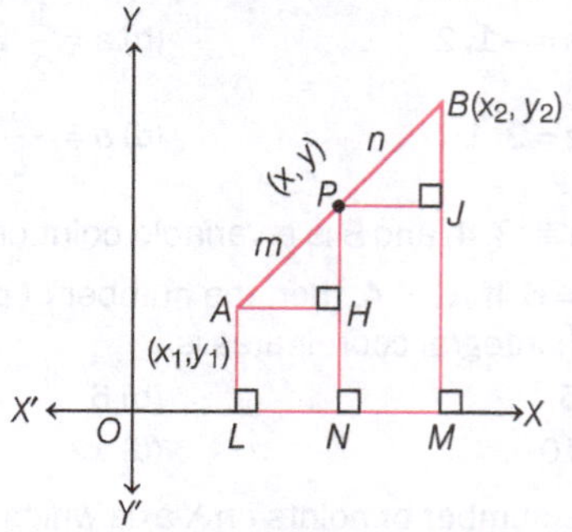

Clearly, ΔAHP and ΔPJB are similar and therefore, their sides are proportional.

$$\therefore \quad \frac{AH}{PJ} = \frac{PH}{BJ} = \frac{AP}{PB}$$

$$\text{or} \quad \underset{\text{(i)}}{\frac{x - x_1}{x_2 - x}} = \underset{\text{(ii)}}{\frac{y - y_1}{y_2 - y}} = \underset{\text{(iii)}}{\frac{m}{n}}$$

From (i) and (iii), we get

$$\frac{x - x_1}{x_2 - x} = \frac{m}{n}$$

$$\Rightarrow \quad nx - nx_1 = mx_2 - mx$$

$$\Rightarrow \quad (m + n)\, x = mx_2 + nx_1$$

$$\therefore \quad x = \frac{mx_2 + nx_1}{m + n}$$

From (ii) and (iii), we get

$$\frac{y - y_1}{y_2 - y} = \frac{m}{n}$$

$$\Rightarrow \quad ny - ny_1 = my_2 - my \Rightarrow (m + n)\, y = my_2 + ny_1$$

$$\therefore \quad y = \frac{my_2 + ny_1}{m + n}$$

Thus, the coordinates of P are

$$\left(\frac{mx_2 + nx_1}{m + n}, \frac{my_2 + ny_1}{m + n}\right).$$

JEE Focus Points

- If P is the mid-point of AB, then $m = n$.
- The coordinates of the middle point of AB are $\left(\frac{x_1 + x_2}{2}, \frac{y_1 + y_2}{2}\right)$

Concept Inside Video

- If $P(\alpha, \beta)$ is the mid-point of AB and if coordinates of A are (λ, μ), then the coordinates of B are $(2\alpha - \lambda, 2\beta - \mu)$.
- The following diagram will help to remember the section formula.

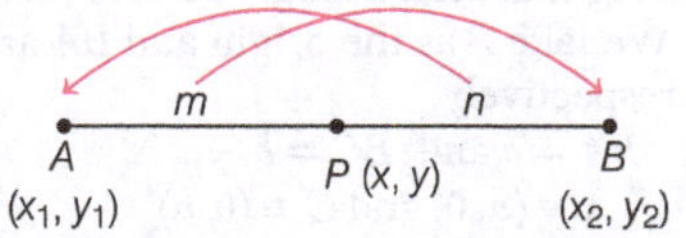

- The straight line $ax + by + c = 0$ divides the join of points $A(x_1, y_1)$ and $B(x_2, y_2)$ in the ratio

$$\frac{AP}{PB} = \frac{\lambda}{1} = -\frac{(ax_1 + by_1 + c)}{(ax_2 + by_2 + c)}$$

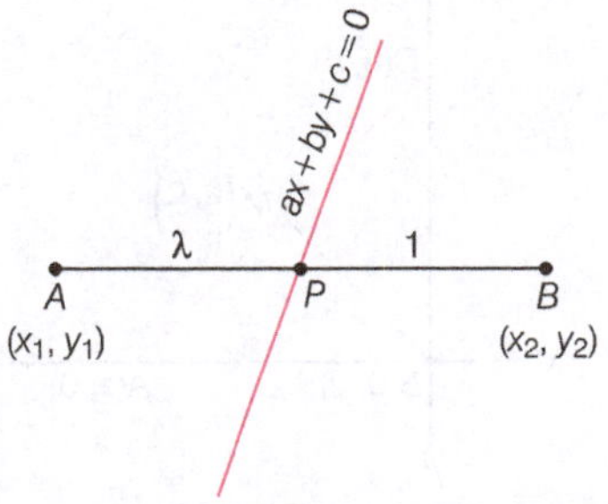

- The line joining the points (x_1, y_1) and (x_2, y_2) is divided by the X-axis in the ratio $-\frac{y_1}{y_2}$ and by Y-axis in the ratio $-\frac{x_1}{x_2}$.

Example 25. Find the coordinates of the point which divides the line segment joining the points $(5, -2)$ and $(9, 6)$ in the ratio 3 : 1 internally.

Sol. Let the required point be (x, y).

Then,
$$x = \left(\frac{3 \times 9 + 1 \times 5}{3 + 1}\right) = 8$$
and
$$y = \left(\frac{3 \times 6 + 1 \times (-2)}{3 + 1}\right) = 4$$

Thus, the coordinates of the required point are $(8, 4)$.

Example 26. Find the length of median through A of a triangle whose vertices are $A(-1, 3)$, $B(1, -1)$ and $C(5, 1)$.

Sol. Let D be the mid-point of BC.

Then, coordinates of D are $\left(\frac{1+5}{2}, \frac{-1+1}{2}\right)$ i.e. $(3, 0)$

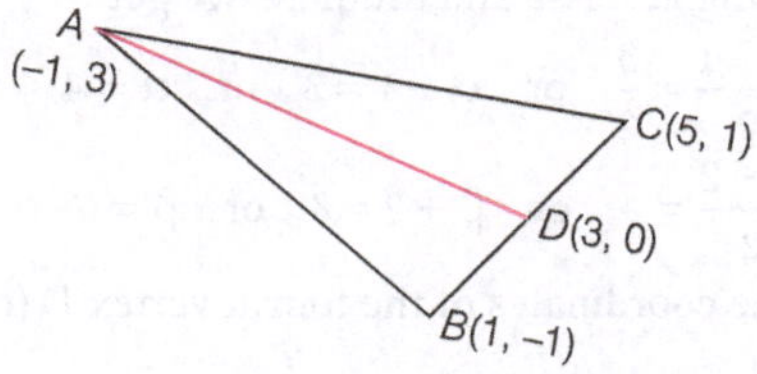

$\therefore$ Length of median, $AD = \sqrt{(3+1)^2 + (0-3)^2}$
$= \sqrt{16 + 9}$
$= \sqrt{25}$
$= 5$ units

Example 27. Determine the ratio in which $y - x + 2 = 0$ divides the line joining $(3, -1)$ and $(8, 9)$.

Sol. Suppose the line $y - x + 2 = 0$ divides the line segment joining $A(3, -1)$ and $B(8, 9)$ in the ratio $\lambda : 1$ at point P, then the coordinates of the point P are $\left(\frac{8\lambda + 3}{\lambda + 1}, \frac{9\lambda - 1}{\lambda + 1}\right)$.

But P lies on $y - x + 2 = 0$

$$\therefore \quad \left(\frac{9\lambda - 1}{\lambda + 1}\right) - \left(\frac{8\lambda + 3}{\lambda + 1}\right) + 2 = 0$$
$$\Rightarrow \quad 9\lambda - 1 - 8\lambda - 3 + 2\lambda + 2 = 0$$
$$\Rightarrow \quad 3\lambda - 2 = 0 \text{ or } \lambda = \frac{2}{3}$$

So, the required ratio is $\frac{2}{3} : 1$ i.e. 2 : 3 (internally), since here λ is positive.

Example 28. The coordinates of three consecutive vertices of a parallelogram are $(1, 3)$, $(-1, 2)$ and $(2, 5)$. Then, find the coordinates of the fourth vertex.

Sol. Let the fourth vertex be $D(\alpha, \beta)$. Since, $ABCD$ is a parallelogram, the diagonals bisect each other.
i.e. mid-point of BD = mid-point of AC

$$\therefore \quad \left(\frac{\alpha - 1}{2}, \frac{\beta + 2}{2}\right) = \left(\frac{2+1}{2}, \frac{5+3}{2}\right)$$
or
$$\left(\frac{\alpha - 1}{2}, \frac{\beta + 2}{2}\right) = \left(\frac{3}{2}, 4\right)$$

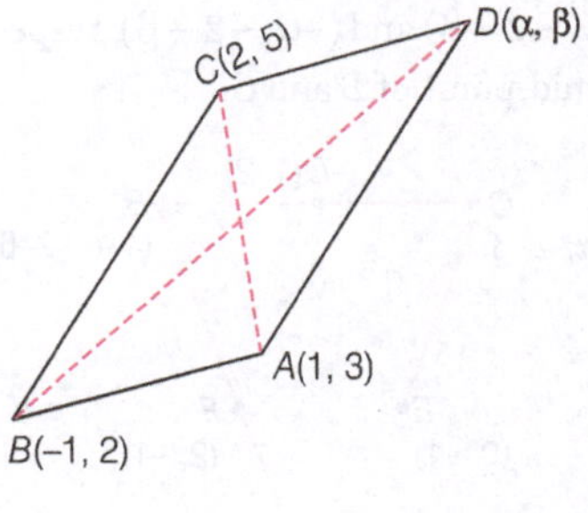

On equating abscissa and ordinate, we get

$$\frac{\alpha - 1}{2} = \frac{3}{2} \quad \text{or} \quad \alpha - 1 = 3 \quad \text{or} \quad \alpha = 4$$

and $$\frac{\beta + 2}{2} = 4 \quad \text{or} \quad \beta + 2 = 8 \quad \text{or} \quad \beta = 6$$

Hence, the coordinates of the fourth vertex $D(\alpha, \beta)$ are $(4, 6)$.

Example 29. In what ratio does X-axis divide the line segment joining $(2, -3)$ and $(5, 6)$?

Sol. Let the given points be $A(2, -3)$ and $B(5, 6)$. Let AB be divided by the X-axis at $P(x, 0)$ in the ratio $\lambda : 1$ internally. Considering the ordinate of P, then

$$0 = \frac{\lambda \times 6 + 1 \times (-3)}{\lambda + 1} \quad \text{or} \quad \lambda = \frac{1}{2}$$

$\therefore$ The ratio is $\frac{1}{2} : 1$ i.e. $1 : 2$ [internally]

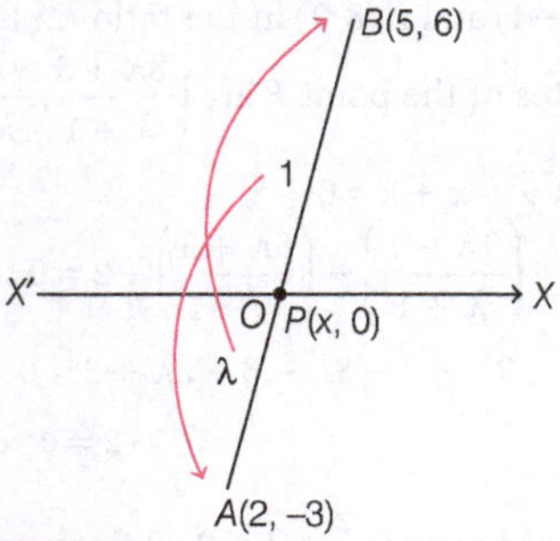

Time Saving Technique

$$\frac{\lambda}{1} = -\frac{y_1}{y_2} = \frac{-(-3)}{6} = \frac{1}{2}$$

$\therefore$ The ratio is $\frac{1}{2} : 1$ i.e. $1 : 2$ (internally)

Example 30. The mid-points of the sides of a triangle are $(1, 2), (0, -1)$ and $(2, -1)$. Find the coordinates of the vertices of a triangle with the help of two unknowns.

Sol. Let $D(1, 2)$, $E(0, -1)$ and $F(2, -1)$ be the mid-points of side BC, CA and AB, respectively.

Let the coordinates of A be (α, β), then coordinates of B and C are $(4 - \alpha, -2 - \beta)$ and $(-\alpha, -2 - \beta)$, respectively.

$\because$ D is the mid-point of B and C.

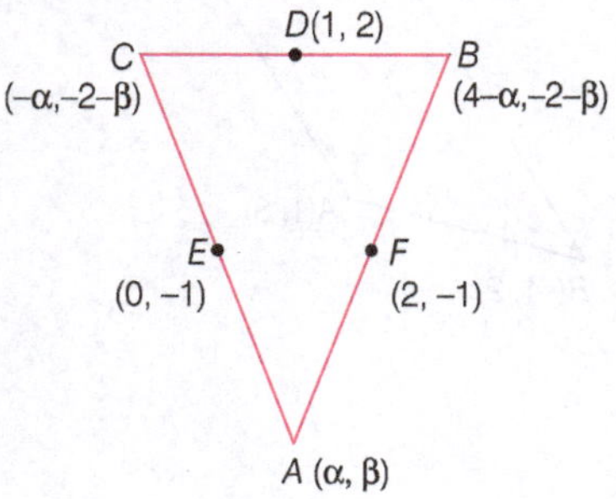

Then, $$1 = \frac{4 - \alpha - \alpha}{2} \Rightarrow 1 = 2 - \alpha \quad \text{or} \quad \alpha = 1$$

and $$2 = \frac{-2 - \beta - 2 - \beta}{2} \Rightarrow 2 = -2 - \beta \text{ or } \beta = -4$$

Hence, coordinates of A, B and C are $(1, -4), (3, 2)$ and $(-1, 2)$, respectively.

Example 31. Prove that in a right angled triangle the mid-point of the hypotenuse is equidistant from its vertices.

Sol. Let the given right angled triangle be ABC, with right angled at B. We take B as the origin and BA and BC as the X and Y-axes, respectively.

Let $BA = a$ and $BC = b$

Then, $A \equiv (a, 0)$ and $C \equiv (0, b)$

Let M to be the mid-point of the hypotenuse AC, then coordinates of M are $\left(\frac{a}{2}, \frac{b}{2}\right)$.

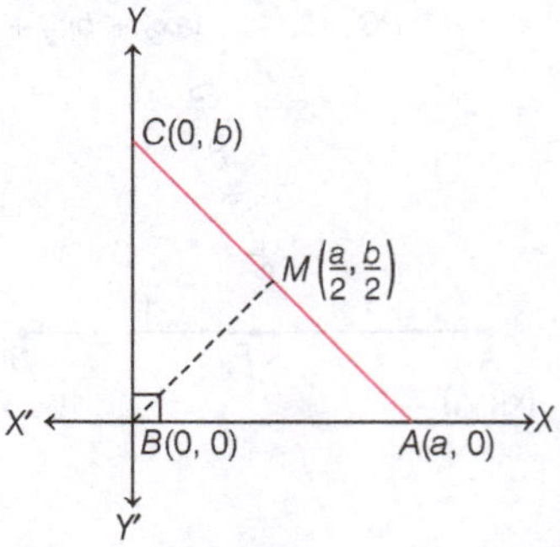

$$\therefore \quad |AM| = \sqrt{\left(a - \frac{a}{2}\right)^2 + \left(0 - \frac{b}{2}\right)^2} = \frac{\sqrt{(a^2 + b^2)}}{2} \quad \text{... (i)}$$

$$|BM| = \sqrt{\left(0 - \frac{a}{2}\right)^2 + \left(0 - \frac{b}{2}\right)^2} = \frac{\sqrt{(a^2 + b^2)}}{2} \quad \text{...(ii)}$$

and $$|CM| = \sqrt{\left(0 - \frac{a}{2}\right)^2 + \left(b - \frac{b}{2}\right)^2} = \frac{\sqrt{(a^2 + b^2)}}{2} \quad \text{...(iii)}$$

From Eqs. (i), (ii) and (iii), we get

$$|AM| = |BM| = |CM|$$

Example 32 The line joining the mid-points of any two sides of a triangle is $1/k$ times the third side. Then, find the value of k.

Sol. We take O as the origin and OC and OY as the X and Y-axes respectively.

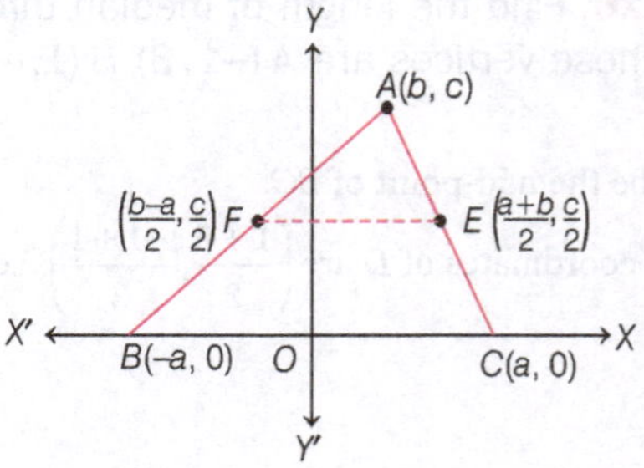

Let $BC = 2a$, then $B \equiv (-a, 0)$, $C \equiv (a, 0)$

Let $A \equiv (b, c)$, if E and F are the mid-points of sides AC and AB, respectively.

Then, $\quad E \equiv \left(\frac{a+b}{2}, \frac{c}{2}\right)$ and $F \equiv \left(\frac{b-a}{2}, \frac{c}{2}\right)$

Now, $\quad FE = \sqrt{\left(\frac{a+b}{2} - \frac{b-a}{2}\right)^2 + \left(\frac{c}{2} - \frac{c}{2}\right)^2} = a$

$$= \frac{1}{2}(2a) = \frac{1}{2}(BC)$$

So, $\quad \frac{1}{k} = \frac{1}{2}$

Hence, $\quad k = 2$

Example 33. Find the coordinates of the points which trisect the line segment joining $(1, -2)$ and $(-3, 4)$.

Sol. Let the points which trisect the line segment AB be $C(p, q)$ and $D(r, s)$.

$\therefore \quad AC = CD = DB$

$\because \quad \frac{AC}{CB} = \frac{1}{2}$ and $\frac{AD}{DB} = \frac{2}{1}$

So, $C(p, q)$ divides AB in $1:2$ ratio.

$\therefore \quad p = \frac{1(-3) + 2 \times 1}{1+2} = -\frac{1}{3}$

and $\quad q = \frac{1 \times 4 + 2(-2)}{1+2} = 0$

$\therefore \quad C\left(-\frac{1}{3}, 0\right)$

Again, $D(r, s)$ divides AB in $2:1$ ratio.

$\therefore \quad r = \frac{2(-3) + 1 \times 1}{2+1} = \frac{-5}{3}$

and $\quad s = \frac{2 \times 4 + 1 \times (-2)}{2+1} = 2$

$\therefore \quad D\left(\frac{-5}{3}, 2\right)$

(ii) Formula for External Division

Theorem If the point $P(x, y)$ divides the line joining the points $A(x_1, y_1)$ and $B(x_2, y_2)$ externally in the ratio $m:n$, then

$$x = \frac{mx_2 - nx_1}{m-n}, y = \frac{my_2 - ny_1}{m-n}$$

Proof The given points are $A(x_1, y_1)$ and $B(x_2, y_2)$. Let us assume that the points A and B are both in the I quadrant (for the sake of exactness).

Let $P(x, y)$ be the point which divides AB externally in the ratio $m:n$, so that $\frac{AP}{BP} = \frac{m}{n}$.

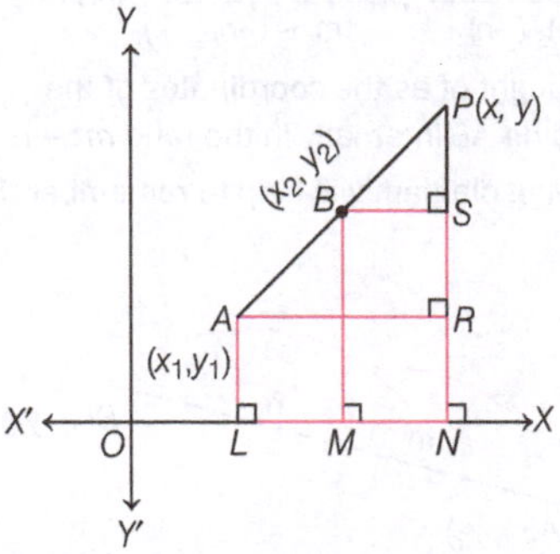

From A, B and P, draw AL, BM and PN perpendiculars on X-axis. Also, from A and B, draw AR and BS perpendiculars on PN.

Then, $\quad AR = LN = ON - OL = x - x_1$

$BS = MN = ON - OM = x - x_2$

$PR = PN - RN = PN - AL = y - y_1$

and $\quad PS = PN - SN = PN - BM = y - y_2$

Clearly, the ΔAPR and ΔBPS are similar and therefore their sides are proportional.

$\therefore \quad \frac{AP}{PB} = \frac{AR}{BS} = \frac{PR}{PS}$

or $\quad \frac{m}{n} = \frac{x - x_1}{x - x_2} = \frac{y - y_1}{y - y_2}$

(i) (ii) (iii)

From (i) and (ii), we get

$$\frac{m}{n} = \frac{x - x_1}{x - x_2}$$

$\Rightarrow \quad mx - mx_2 = nx - nx_1$

$\Rightarrow \quad (m-n)x = mx_2 - nx_1$

or $\quad x = \frac{mx_2 - nx_1}{m-n}$

Also, from (i) and (iii), we get

$$\frac{m}{n} = \frac{y - y_1}{y - y_2}$$

$\Rightarrow \quad my - my_2 = ny - ny_1$

$\Rightarrow \quad (m-n)y = my_2 - ny_1$

or $\quad y = \frac{my_2 - ny_1}{m-n}$

Thus, the coordinates of P are $\left(\frac{mx_2 - nx_1}{m-n}, \frac{my_2 - ny_1}{m-n}\right)$.

(here, $m \neq n$)

JEE Focus Points

- The above coordinates can also be expressed as $\left(\frac{mx_2 + (-n)\,x_1}{m + (-n)}, \frac{my_2 + (-n)\,y_1}{m + (-n)}\right)$ and this can be thought of as the coordinates of the point dividing AB internally in the ratio $m : -n$.

Concept Inside Video

- The following diagram will help to remember the section formula

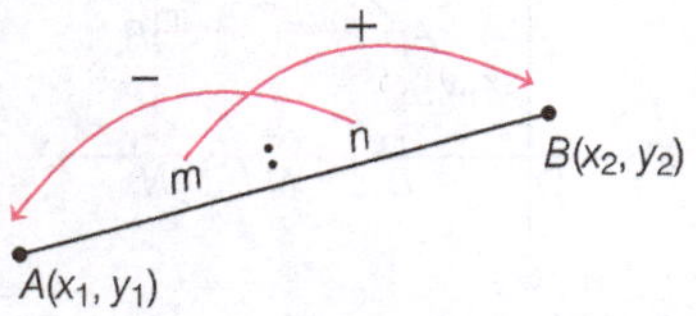

- Let $\frac{m}{n} = \lambda$, then $\left(\frac{mx_2 - nx_1}{m - n}, \frac{my_2 - ny_1}{m - n}\right)$

or $\left(\frac{\frac{m}{n}x_2 - x_1}{\frac{m}{n} - 1}, \frac{\frac{m}{n}y_2 - y_1}{\frac{m}{n} - 1}\right)$ or $\left(\frac{\lambda x_2 - x_1}{\lambda - 1}, \frac{\lambda y_2 - y_1}{\lambda - 1}\right)$

- If A, B and C are collinear, then let C divides AB in the ratio $\lambda : 1$ internally.

  If $\lambda =$ positive rational, then divide internally and if $\lambda =$ negative rational, then divide externally.

Example 34. Find the coordinates of a point which divides externally the line joining $(1, -3)$ and $(-3, 9)$ in the ratio $1 : 3$.

Sol. Let the coordinates of the required point be $P(x, y)$.

Then, $x = \left(\frac{1 \times (-3) - 3 \times 1}{1 - 3}\right)$ and $y = \left(\frac{1 \times 9 - 3 \times (-3)}{1 - 3}\right)$

i.e. $x = 3$ and $y = -9$

Hence, the required point is $(3, -9)$.

Example 35. Using section formula, show that the points $(1, -1)$, $(2, 1)$ and $(4, 5)$ are collinear.

Sol. Let $A \equiv (1, -1)$, $B \equiv (2, 1)$ and $C \equiv (4, 5)$

Suppose C divides AB in the ratio $\lambda : 1$ internally, then

$$4 = \frac{\lambda \times 2 + 1 \times 1}{\lambda + 1} \Rightarrow 4\lambda + 4 = 2\lambda + 1 \text{ or } \lambda = -\frac{3}{2}$$

$$\text{and } 5 = \frac{\lambda \times 1 + 1 \times (-1)}{\lambda + 1} \Rightarrow 5\lambda + 5 = \lambda - 1 \Rightarrow \lambda = \frac{-3}{2}$$

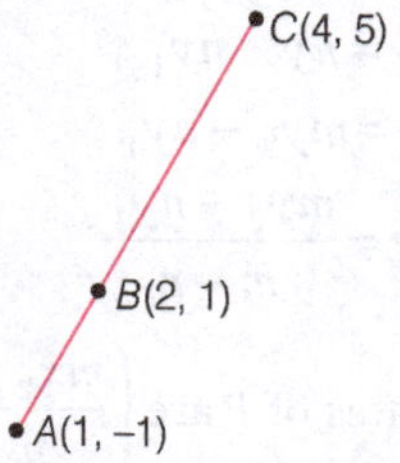

i.e. C divides AB in the ratio $3 : 2$ (externally).

Hence, A, B and C are collinear.

Example 36. Find the ratio in which the point $(2, y)$ divides the line segment joining $(4, 3)$ and $(6, 3)$ and hence find the value of y.

Sol. Let $A \equiv (4, 3)$, $B \equiv (6, 3)$ and $P \equiv (2, y)$

Let P divides AB internally in the ratio $\lambda : 1$.

Then, $2 = \frac{6\lambda + 4}{\lambda + 1} \Rightarrow 2\lambda + 2 = 6\lambda + 4$

$\Rightarrow$ $-4\lambda = 2$ or $\lambda = -\frac{1}{2}$

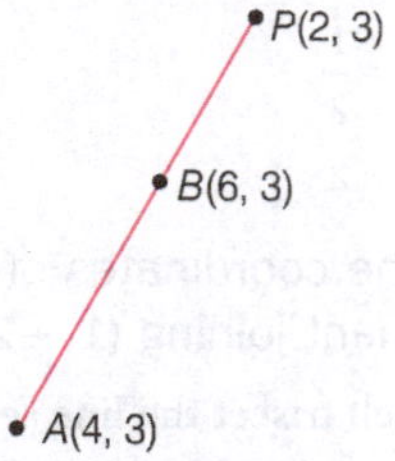

$\therefore$ P divides AB externally in the ratio $1 : 2$. ($\because \lambda$ is negative)

Now, $y = \frac{1 \times 3 - 2 \times 3}{1 - 2} = 3$

Example 37. The line segment joining $A(6, 3)$ to $B(-1, -4)$ is doubled in length by having its length added to each end. Find the coordinates of the new ends.

Sol. Let P and Q be the required new ends.

Let the coordinates of P be (x_1, y_1).

Given, $AB = 2AP \Rightarrow \frac{AB}{AP} = \frac{2}{1}$

i.e. A divides BP internally in the ratio $2 : 1$.

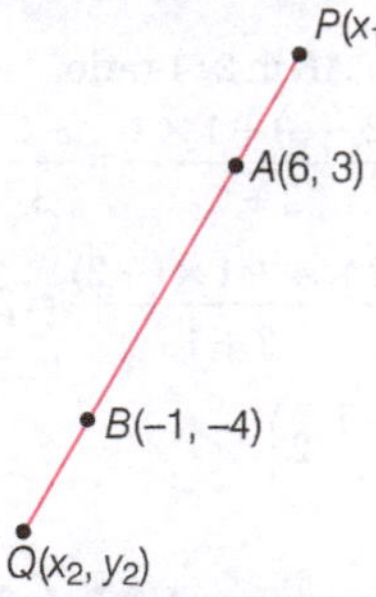

Then, $6 = \frac{2 \times x_1 + 1 \times (-1)}{2 + 1} \Rightarrow 19 = 2x_1$ or $x_1 = \frac{19}{2}$

and $3 = \frac{2 \times y_1 + 1 \times (-4)}{2 + 1} \Rightarrow 13 = 2y_1$ or $y_1 = \frac{13}{2}$

$\therefore$ Coordinates of P are $\left(\frac{19}{2}, \frac{13}{2}\right)$.

Also, let coordinates of Q be (x_2, y_2).

Given, $AB = 2BQ \Rightarrow \frac{AB}{BQ} = \frac{2}{1}$

i.e. B divides AQ internally in the ratio $2 : 1$.

Then, $-1 = \dfrac{2 \times x_2 + 1 \times 6}{2+1} \Rightarrow -9 = 2x_2$ or $x_2 = -\dfrac{9}{2}$

and $-4 = \dfrac{2 \times y_2 + 1 \times 3}{2+1}$

$\Rightarrow$ $-15 = 2y_2$ or $y_2 = -\dfrac{15}{2}$

$\therefore$ Coordinates of Q are $\left(-\dfrac{9}{2}, -\dfrac{15}{2}\right)$.

Alternate Solution

$\because$ $AB = 2AP$

$\Rightarrow \dfrac{AB}{AP} = \dfrac{2}{1} \Rightarrow \dfrac{AB}{AP} + 1 = \dfrac{2}{1} + 1$

$\Rightarrow \dfrac{AB + AP}{AP} = \dfrac{3}{1} \Rightarrow \dfrac{BP}{AP} = \dfrac{3}{1}$

$\therefore$ P divides AB externally in the ratio 1 : 3.

Then, $x_1 = \dfrac{1 \times (-1) - 3 \times 6}{1 - 3} = \dfrac{19}{2}$ and $y_1 = \dfrac{1 \times (-4) - 3 \times 3}{1 - 3} = \dfrac{13}{2}$

$\therefore$ Coordinates of P are $\left(\dfrac{19}{2}, \dfrac{13}{2}\right)$.

Also, $AB = 2BQ$

$\Rightarrow \dfrac{AB}{BQ} = \dfrac{2}{1} \Rightarrow \dfrac{AB}{BQ} + 1 = \dfrac{2}{1} + 1$

$\Rightarrow \dfrac{AB + BQ}{BQ} = \dfrac{3}{1} \Rightarrow \dfrac{AQ}{BQ} = \dfrac{3}{1}$

$\therefore$ Q divides AB externally in the ratio 3 : 1.

Then, $x_2 = \dfrac{3 \times (-1) - 1 \times 6}{3 - 1} = -\dfrac{9}{2}$

and $y_2 = \dfrac{3 \times (-4) - 1 \times 3}{3 - 1} = -\dfrac{15}{2}$

$\therefore$ Coordinates of Q are $\left(-\dfrac{9}{2}, -\dfrac{15}{2}\right)$

(iii) Harmonic Conjugates

Points Q and S are the harmonic conjugates of each other with respect to points P and R if Q divides PR in the ratio $\lambda : 1$ internally, then S divides PR in the ratio $\lambda : 1$ externally.

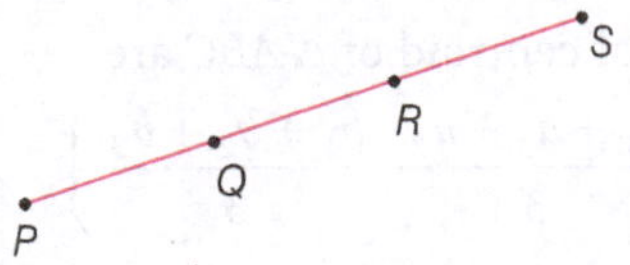

$\therefore \dfrac{PQ}{RQ} = \dfrac{\lambda}{1} \Rightarrow PQ : RQ = \lambda : 1$ (internally)

and $\dfrac{SP}{SR} = \dfrac{-\lambda}{1} \Rightarrow SP : SR = -\lambda : 1$ (externally)

Example 38. Find the harmonic conjugates of the point $R(5, 1)$ with respect to the points $P(2, 10)$ and $Q(6, -2)$.

Sol. Let $S(\alpha, \beta)$ be the harmonic conjugates of the point $R(5, 1)$.

Suppose R divides PQ in the ratio $\lambda : 1$ internally, then S divides PQ in the ratio $\lambda : 1$ externally.

Then, $5 = \dfrac{6\lambda + 2}{\lambda + 1} \Rightarrow 5\lambda + 5 = 6\lambda + 2$

$\therefore$ $\lambda = 3$

Also, $1 = \dfrac{-2\lambda + 10}{\lambda + 1}$

$\lambda + 1 = -2\lambda + 10 \Rightarrow 3\lambda = 9$

$\therefore$ $\lambda = 3$

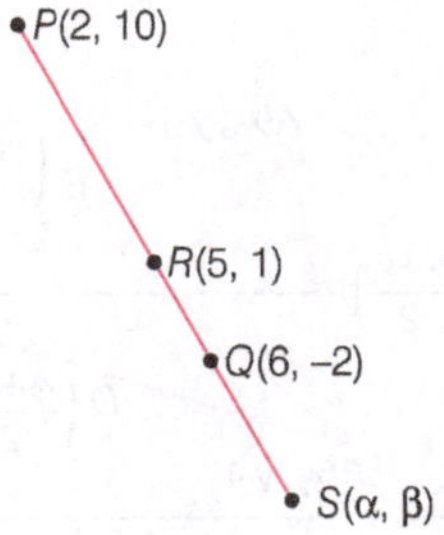

Now, $\alpha = \dfrac{3 \times 6 - 1 \times 2}{3 - 1} = 8$

and $\beta = \dfrac{3 \times (-2) - 1 \times 10}{3 - 1} = -8$

Hence, harmonic conjugate of $R(5, 1)$ is $S(8, -8)$.

1.10 Standard Points of a Triangle

The triangle is an amazing geometric figure, which has many cyclic and symmetrical properties. In a triangle, medians, altitudes, perpendicular bisectors of sides, internal angle bisector, two external and one internal angle bisectors all are concurrent and their points of concurrency are, respectively known as centroid G, orthocentre O or H, circumcentre (C), incentre (I) and excentres I_1, I_2 and I_3.

1.11 Centroid of a Triangle

The point of intersection of the medians of a triangle is called the centroid of the triangle and it divides the median internally in the ratio 2 : 1.

Theorem The coordinates of the centroid of the triangle whose vertices are $(x_1, y_1), (x_2, y_2)$ and (x_3, y_3) are $\left(\dfrac{x_1 + x_2 + x_3}{3}, \dfrac{y_1 + y_2 + y_3}{3}\right)$. Also, the medians of a triangle are concurrent.

Proof Let $A \equiv (x_1, y_1)$, $B \equiv (x_2, y_2)$ and $C \equiv (x_3, y_3)$ be the vertices of the ΔABC. Let us assume that the points A, B and C are in the I quadrant (for the sake of exactness) whose medians are AD, BE and CF respectively, so D, E and F are respectively the mid-points of BC, CA and AB, then the coordinates of D, E, F are

$$D \equiv \left(\frac{x_2+x_3}{2}, \frac{y_2+y_3}{2}\right)$$

$$E \equiv \left(\frac{x_3+x_1}{2}, \frac{y_3+y_1}{2}\right)$$

and $$F \equiv \left(\frac{x_1+x_2}{2}, \frac{y_1+y_2}{2}\right)$$

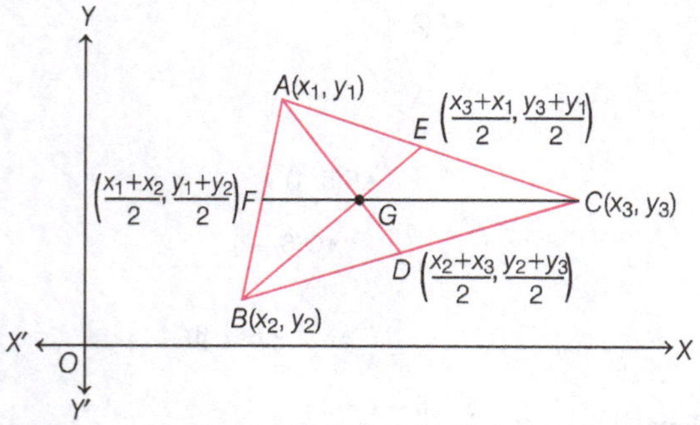

The coordinates of a point dividing AD in the ratio $2:1$ are

$$\left(\frac{2\cdot\left(\frac{x_2+x_3}{2}\right)+1\cdot x_1}{2+1}, \frac{2\cdot\left(\frac{y_2+y_3}{2}\right)+1\cdot y_1}{2+1}\right)$$

or $$\left(\frac{x_1+x_2+x_3}{3}, \frac{y_1+y_2+y_3}{3}\right)$$

and the coordinates of a point dividing BE in the ratio $2:1$ are

$$\left(\frac{2\cdot\left(\frac{x_3+x_1}{2}\right)+1\cdot x_2}{2+1}, \frac{2\cdot\left(\frac{y_3+y_1}{2}\right)+1\cdot y_2}{2+1}\right)$$

or $$\left(\frac{x_1+x_2+x_3}{3}, \frac{y_1+y_2+y_3}{3}\right)$$

Similarly, the coordinates of a point dividing CF in the ratio $2:1$ are

$$\left(\frac{x_1+x_2+x_3}{3}, \frac{y_1+y_2+y_3}{3}\right)$$

$\therefore$ The common point which divides AD, BE and CF in the ratio $2:1$ is

$$\left(\frac{x_1+x_2+x_3}{3}, \frac{y_1+y_2+y_3}{3}\right)$$

Hence, medians of a triangle are concurrent and the coordinates of the centroid are

$$\left(\frac{x_1+x_2+x_3}{3}, \frac{y_1+y_2+y_3}{3}\right)$$

Important Theorem

Centroid of the triangle obtained by joining the middle points of the sides of a triangle is the same as the centroid of the original triangle.

Or

If (a_1, b_1), (a_2, b_2) and (a_3, b_3) are the mid-points of the sides of a triangle, then its centroid is given by

$$\left(\frac{a_1+a_2+a_3}{3}, \frac{b_1+b_2+b_3}{3}\right)$$

Proof Let D, E and F be the mid-points of BC, CA and AB respectively now let coordinates of A are (α, β), then coordinates of B and C are $(2a_3-\alpha, 2b_3-\beta)$ and $(2a_2-\alpha, 2b_2-\beta)$, respectively.

$\because$ $D(a_1, b_1)$ is the mid-point of B and C, then

$$2a_1 = 2a_3 - \alpha + 2a_2 - \alpha \quad \Rightarrow \quad \alpha = a_2 + a_3 - a_1$$

and $$2b_1 = 2b_3 - \beta + 2b_2 - \beta \quad \Rightarrow \quad \beta = b_2 + b_3 - b_1$$

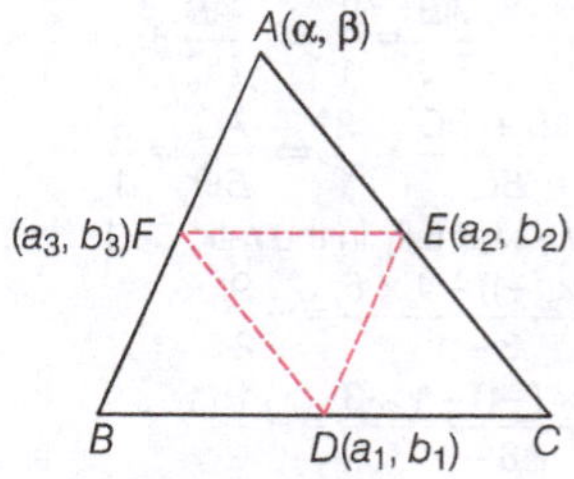

Now, coordinates of B are $(2a_3-\alpha, 2b_3-\beta)$

or $(a_3+a_1-a_2, b_3+b_1-b_2)$

and coordinates of C are $(2a_2-\alpha, 2b_2-\beta)$

or $(a_2+a_1-a_3, b_2+b_1-b_3)$

Hence, coordinates of A, B and C are

$$A \equiv (a_2+a_3-a_1, b_2+b_3-b_1),$$
$$B \equiv (a_3+a_1-a_2, b_3+b_1-b_2)$$

and $$C \equiv (a_2+a_1-a_3, b_2+b_1-b_3)$$

$\therefore$ Coordinates of centroid of ΔABC are

$$\left(\frac{a_1+a_2+a_3}{3}, \frac{b_1+b_2+b_3}{3}\right)$$

which is same as the centroid of ΔDEF.

JEE Focus Points

- **(Finger Rule)** If mid-points of the sides of a triangle are (x_1, y_1), (x_2, y_2) and (x_3, y_3), then coordinates of the original triangle are $(x_2+x_3-x_1, y_2+y_3-y_1)$, $(x_3+x_1-x_2, y_3+y_1-y_2)$ and $(x_1+x_2-x_3, y_1+y_2-y_3)$.
- If two vertices of a triangle are (x_1, y_1) and (x_2, y_2) and the coordinates of centroid are (α, β), then coordinates of the third vertex are $(3\alpha - x_1 - x_2, 3\beta - y_1 - y_2)$.

Example 39. Two vertices of a triangle are $(-1, 4)$ and $(5, 2)$. If its centroid is $(0, -3)$, find the third vertex.

Sol. Let the third vertex be (x, y), then the coordinates of the centroid of triangle are

$$\left(\frac{-1+5+x}{3}, \frac{4+2+y}{3}\right) \text{ i.e. } \left(\frac{4+x}{3}, \frac{6+y}{3}\right)$$

Now, $$\left(\frac{4+x}{3}, \frac{6+y}{3}\right) = (0, -3)$$

$$\Rightarrow \quad \frac{4+x}{3} = 0 \quad \text{and} \quad \frac{6+y}{3} = -3$$

$$\Rightarrow \quad 4+x=0 \quad \text{and} \quad y+6=-9$$

or $$x=-4 \quad \text{and} \quad y=-15$$

Hence, the third vertex is $(-4, -15)$.

Time Saving Technique

Given two vertices of a triangle are $(-1, 4)$ and $(5, 2)$, then the coordinates of third vertex are

$$(x, y) = (3\times 0-(-1)-5, 3\times(-3)-4-2) = (-4, -15)$$

Example 40. The vertices of a triangle are $(1, 2)$, $(h, -3)$ and $(-4, k)$. If the centroid of the triangle be at the point $(5, -1)$, then find the value of $\sqrt{\{(h+k)^2+(h+3k)^2\}}$.

Sol. Here, $\dfrac{1+h-4}{3} = 5$ and $\dfrac{2-3+k}{3} = -1$

Then, we get $h = 18$ and $k = -2$

$$\therefore \quad \sqrt{(h+k)^2+(h+3k)^2} = \sqrt{(18-2)^2+(18-6)^2}$$

$$= \sqrt{(16^2+12^2)} = 20$$

Example 41. If $D(-2, 3)$, $E(4, -3)$ and $F(4, 5)$ are the mid-points of the sides BC, CA and AB of ΔABC, then find $\sqrt{(|AG|^2+|BG|^2-|CG|^2)}$, where G is the centroid of ΔABC.

Sol. Let the coordinates of A be (α, β).

Then coordinates of B are $(8-\alpha, 10-\beta)$ and coordinates of C are $(8-\alpha, -6-\beta)$

$\because D$ is the mid-point of BC, then

$$\frac{8-\alpha+8-\alpha}{2} = -2 \text{ and } \frac{10-\beta-6-\beta}{2} = 3$$

i.e. $$\alpha = 10 \quad \text{and} \quad \beta = -1$$

$\therefore$ Coordinates of A, B and C are $(10, -1)$, $(-2, 11)$ and $(-2, -5)$ respectively.

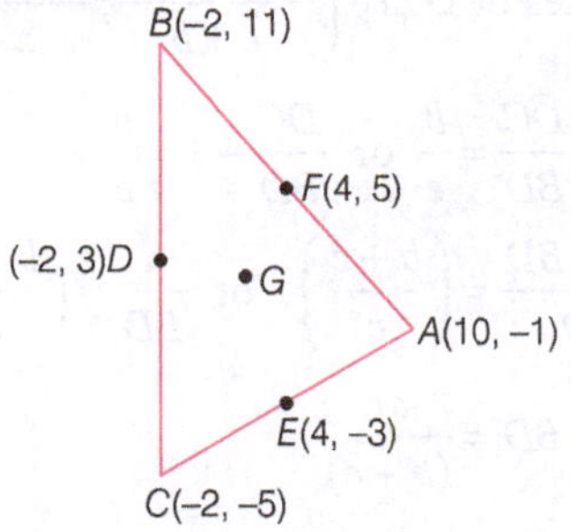

Now, coordinates of centroid

$$G \equiv \left(\frac{10-2-2}{3}, \frac{-1+11-5}{3}\right)$$

i.e. $$G \equiv \left(2, \frac{5}{3}\right)$$

$$\therefore \quad AG = \sqrt{(10-2)^2+\left(-1-\frac{5}{3}\right)^2}$$

$$= \sqrt{\left(64+\frac{64}{9}\right)} = \frac{8}{3}\sqrt{10}$$

$$BG = \sqrt{(-2-2)^2+\left(11-\frac{5}{3}\right)^2}$$

$$= \sqrt{16+\frac{(28)^2}{9}} = \frac{4}{3}\sqrt{58}$$

and $$CG = \sqrt{(-2-2)^2+\left(-5-\frac{5}{3}\right)^2}$$

$$= \sqrt{\left(16+\frac{400}{9}\right)} = \frac{4}{3}\sqrt{34}$$

Hence, $\sqrt{(|AG|^2+|BG|^2-|CG|^2)}$

$$= \sqrt{\left(\frac{64}{9}\times 10+\frac{16}{9}\times 58-\frac{16}{9}\times 34\right)}$$

$$= \sqrt{\frac{32}{9}(20+29-17)} = \sqrt{\left(\frac{32}{9}\times 32\right)} = \frac{32}{3}$$

Example 42. If G be the centroid of the ΔABC and O be any other point in the plane of the ΔABC, then show that

$$OA^2+OB^2+OC^2 = GA^2+GB^2+GC^2+3GO^2.$$

Sol. Let G be the origin and GO be X-axis.

$O \equiv (a, 0)$, $A \equiv (x_1, y_1)$, $B \equiv (x_2, y_2)$ and $C \equiv (x_3, y_3)$

Now, LHS $= OA^2+OB^2+OC^2$

$$= (x_1-a)^2+y_1^2+(x_2-a)^2+y_2^2+(x_3-a)^2+y_3^2$$

$$= (x_1^2+x_2^2+x_3^2)+(y_1^2+y_2^2+y_3^2) - 2a(x_1+x_2+x_3)+3a^2$$

$$= \sum x_1^2+\sum y_1^2-0+3a^2 \quad \left[\because \frac{x_1+x_2+x_3}{3} = 0 \text{ i.e. } x_1+x_2+x_3 = 0\right]$$

$$= \sum x_1^2+\sum y_1^2+3a^2 \quad \text{...(i)}$$

RHS $= GA^2+GB^2+GC^2+3GO^2$

$$= x_1^2+y_1^2+x_2^2+y_2^2+x_3^2+y_3^2+3\{(a-0)^2\}$$

$$= \sum x_1^2+\sum y_1^2+3a^2 \quad \text{... (ii)}$$

Hence, from Eqs. (i) and (ii), we get

$$OA^2+OB^2+OC^2 = GA^2+GB^2+GC^2+3GO^2$$

Example 43. If G be the centroid of ΔABC, show that

$$AB^2 + BC^2 + CA^2 = 3(GA^2 + GB^2 + GC^2).$$

Sol. We take B as the origin and BC and BY as the X and Y-axes, respectively.

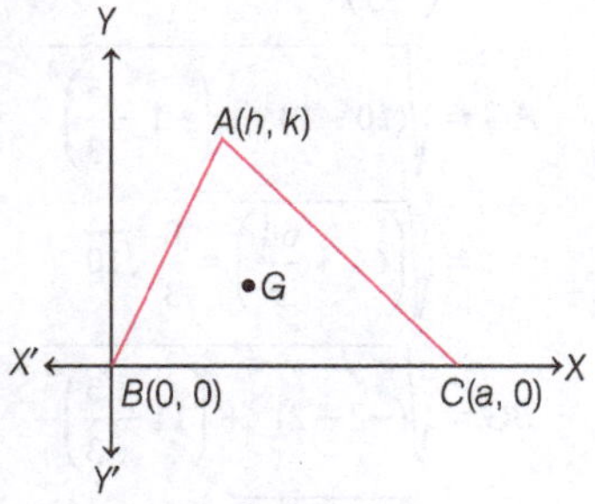

Let $BC = a$, then $B \equiv (0, 0)$ and $C \equiv (a, 0)$ and let $A \equiv (h, k)$.

Then, coordinates of G will be

$$\left(\frac{h+0+a}{3}, \frac{k+0+0}{3}\right) \text{ i.e. } \left(\frac{h+a}{3}, \frac{k}{3}\right)$$

Take ΔABC as in I quadrant (for the sake of exactness).

Now, $\text{LHS} = (AB)^2 + (BC)^2 + (CA)^2$

$$= (h-0)^2 + (k-0)^2 + a^2 + (h-a)^2 + (k-0)^2$$

$$= 2h^2 + 2k^2 - 2ah + 2a^2 \quad \text{... (i)}$$

$$\text{RHS} = 3((GA)^2 + (GB)^2 + (GC)^2)$$

$$= 3\left\{\left(\frac{a+h}{3} - h\right)^2 + \left(\frac{k}{3} - k\right)^2 + \left(\frac{a+h}{3} - 0\right)^2 + \left(\frac{k}{3} - 0\right)^2 + \left(\frac{a+h}{3} - a\right)^2 + \left(\frac{k}{3} - 0\right)^2\right\}$$

$$= \frac{3}{9}\{(a-2h)^2 + (-2k)^2 + (a+h)^2 + k^2 + (h-2a)^2 + k^2\}$$

$$= \frac{1}{3}\{6a^2 + 6h^2 + 6k^2 - 6ah\}$$

$$= 2h^2 + 2k^2 - 2ah + 2a^2 \quad \text{... (ii)}$$

Hence, from Eqs. (i) and (ii), we get

$$AB^2 + BC^2 + CA^2 = 3(GA^2 + GB^2 + GC^2)$$

Example 44. The vertices of a triangle are $(1, a)$, $(2, b)$ and $(c^2, -3)$.

(i) Prove that its centroid can not lie on the Y-axis.

(ii) Find the condition that the centroid may lie on the X-axis.

Sol. Centroid of the triangle is

$$G \equiv \left(\frac{1+2+c^2}{3}, \frac{a+b-3}{3}\right) \text{ i.e. } \left(\frac{3+c^2}{3}, \frac{a+b-3}{3}\right)$$

(i) $\because$ G will lie on Y-axis, then

$$\frac{3+c^2}{3} = 0 \Rightarrow c^2 = -3 \text{ or } c = \pm i\sqrt{3}$$

$\because$ Both values of c are imaginary.

Hence, G cannot lie on Y-axis.

(ii) $\because$ G will lie on X-axis, then

$$\frac{a+b-3}{3} = 0$$

$$\Rightarrow \quad a + b - 3 = 0 \text{ or } a + b = 3$$

1.12 Incentre of a Triangle

The point of intersection of internal angle bisectors of triangle is called the incentre of the triangle.

Theorem The coordinates of the incentre of a triangle whose vertices are $A(x_1, y_1)$, $B(x_2, y_2)$ and $C(x_3, y_3)$ are $\left(\frac{ax_1 + bx_2 + cx_3}{a+b+c}, \frac{ay_1 + by_2 + cy_3}{a+b+c}\right)$

where a, b and c are the lengths of sides BC, CA and AB respectively.

Also, the internal bisectors of the angles of a triangle are concurrent.

Proof Given, $A \equiv (x_1, y_1)$, $B \equiv (x_2, y_2)$ and $C \equiv (x_3, y_3)$ be the vertices of ΔABC and $BC = a$, $CA = b$ and $AB = c$. Let AD be the bisector of $\angle A$. We know that the bisector of an angle of a triangle divides the opposite side in the ratio of the sides containing the triangle.

$$\therefore \quad \frac{BD}{DC} = \frac{AB}{AC} = \frac{c}{b} \quad \text{... (i)}$$

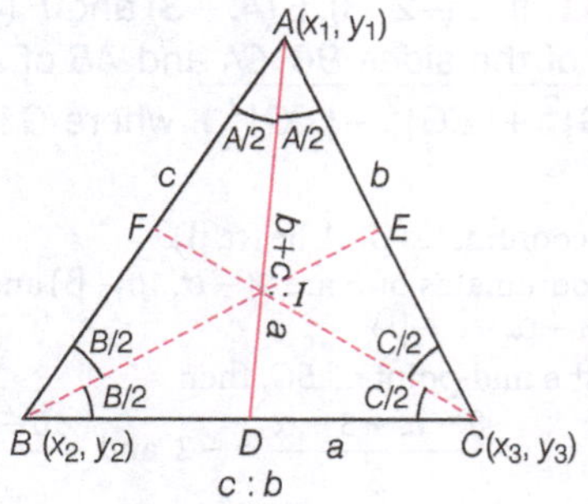

Hence, D divides BC in the ratio $c : b$.

$\therefore$ Coordinates of D are $\left(\frac{cx_3 + bx_2}{c+b}, \frac{cy_3 + by_2}{c+b}\right)$

From Eq. (i), $\frac{DC}{BD} = \frac{b}{c}$ or $\frac{DC}{BD} + 1 = \frac{b}{c} + 1$

or $\frac{DC + BD}{BD} = \left(\frac{b+c}{c}\right)$ or $\frac{a}{BD} = \left(\frac{b+c}{c}\right)$

$$\therefore \quad BD = \frac{ac}{(b+c)}$$

Also, in ΔABD, BI is the bisector of B.

Then, $$\frac{AI}{ID} = \frac{AB}{BD} = \frac{c}{\left(\frac{ac}{b+c}\right)} = \frac{b+c}{a}$$

$\therefore$ I divides AD in the ratio $b+c:a$.

$\therefore$ Coordinates of I are

$$\left(\frac{(b+c)\cdot\frac{cx_3+bx_2}{c+b}+a\cdot x_1}{b+c+a}, \frac{(b+c)\cdot\frac{cy_3+by_2}{c+b}+a\cdot y_1}{b+c+a}\right)$$

i.e. $$\left(\frac{ax_1+bx_2+cx_3}{a+b+c}, \frac{ay_1+by_2+cy_3}{a+b+c}\right)$$

Similarly, we can show that the coordinates of the point which divides BE internally in the ratio $c+a:b$ and the coordinates of the point which divides CF internally in the ratio $a+b:c$ will be each

$$\left(\frac{ax_1+bx_2+cx_3}{a+b+c}, \frac{ay_1+by_2+cy_3}{a+b+c}\right)$$

and $$CE = \frac{ab}{(c+a)}, AE = \frac{bc}{(c+a)},$$

$$AF = \frac{bc}{a+b}, BF = \frac{ac}{a+b}$$

Thus, the three internal bisectors of the angles of a triangle meet at a point I.

$$I \equiv \left(\frac{ax_1+bx_2+cx_3}{a+b+c}, \frac{ay_1+by_2+cy_3}{a+b+c}\right)$$

COROLLARY 1 If ΔABC is equilateral, then $a=b=c$, then

$$\text{incentre} = \left(\frac{x_1+x_2+x_3}{3}, \frac{y_1+y_2+y_3}{3}\right) = \text{centroid}$$

i.e. incentre and centroid coincide in equilateral triangle.

COROLLARY 2

$$AE = AF = s-a$$
$$BD = BF = s-b$$
$$CD = CE = s-c$$

where, $$s = \frac{a+b+c}{2}$$

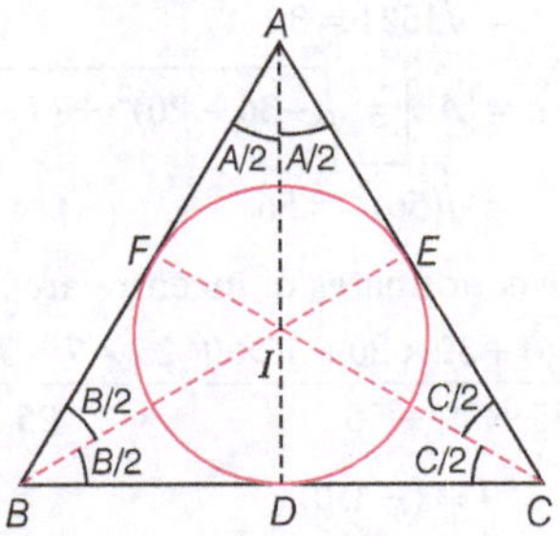

and $$|BC| = a, |CA| = b, |AB| = c$$

Proof Let $AE = AF = \alpha$

[$\because$ length of tangents are equal from a point to a circle]

$$BD = BF = \beta$$
$$CD = CE = \gamma$$

Also, $$a = BC = BD + DC = \beta + \gamma \quad \text{....(i)}$$
$$b = CA = CE + AE = \gamma + \alpha \quad \text{...(ii)}$$
and $$c = AB = AF + BF = \alpha + \beta \quad \text{...(iii)}$$

On adding Eqs. (i), (ii) and (iii), we get

$$a+b+c = 2(\alpha+\beta+\gamma)$$
or $$2s = 2(\alpha+\beta+\gamma)$$
$\therefore$ $$s = \alpha+\beta+\gamma$$

From Eqs. (i), (ii) and (iii), we get

$$\alpha = s-a, \beta = s-b, \gamma = s-c$$

Example 45. Find the coordinates of incentre of the triangle whose vertices are $(4,-2)$, $(-2,4)$ and $(5,5)$.

Sol. Let $A(4,-2)$, $B(-2,4)$ and $C(5,5)$ be the vertices of the given triangle. Then,

$$a = BC = \sqrt{(-2-5)^2+(4-5)^2} = \sqrt{50} = 5\sqrt{2},$$
$$b = CA = \sqrt{(5-4)^2+(5+2)^2} = \sqrt{50} = 5\sqrt{2}$$
and $$c = AB = \sqrt{(4+2)^2+(-2-4)^2} = \sqrt{72} = 6\sqrt{2}$$

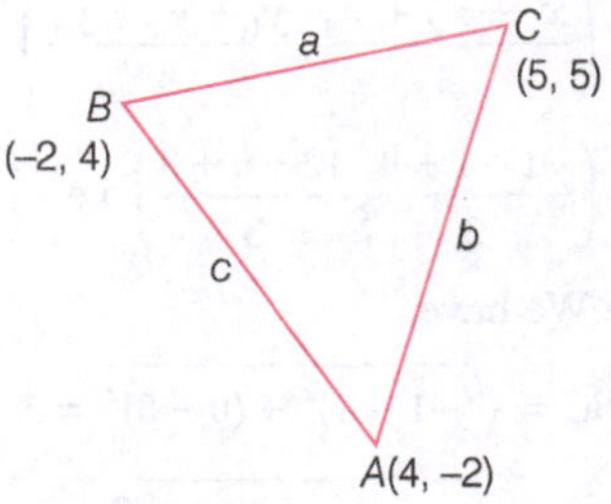

Let (x, y) be the coordinates of incentre of ΔABC. Then,

$$x = \frac{ax_1+bx_2+cx_3}{a+b+c}$$
$$= \frac{5\sqrt{2}\times 4 + 5\sqrt{2}\times(-2) + 6\sqrt{2}\times 5}{5\sqrt{2}+5\sqrt{2}+6\sqrt{2}}$$
$$= \frac{20\sqrt{2}-10\sqrt{2}+30\sqrt{2}}{16\sqrt{2}} = \frac{40}{16} = \frac{5}{2}$$

and $$y = \frac{ay_1+by_2+cy_3}{a+b+c}$$
$$= \frac{5\sqrt{2}\times(-2)+5\sqrt{2}\times 4+6\sqrt{2}\times 5}{5\sqrt{2}+5\sqrt{2}+6\sqrt{2}}$$
$$= \frac{40}{16} = \frac{5}{2}$$

$\therefore$ The coordinates of the incentre are $\left(\frac{5}{2}, \frac{5}{2}\right)$.

Example 46. If $\left(\frac{3}{2},0\right),\left(\frac{3}{2},6\right)$ and $(-1,6)$ are mid-points of the sides of a triangle, then find
(i) centroid of the triangle.
(ii) incentre of the triangle.

Sol. Let $A \equiv (\alpha, \beta)$, then coordinates of $B \equiv (-2-\alpha, 12-\beta)$ and coordinates of $C \equiv (3-\alpha, 12-\beta)$.

But mid-point of BC is $\left(\frac{3}{2},0\right)$.

Then, $3 = -2-\alpha+3-\alpha \Rightarrow \alpha = -1$

and $0 = 12-\beta+12-\beta \Rightarrow \beta = 12$

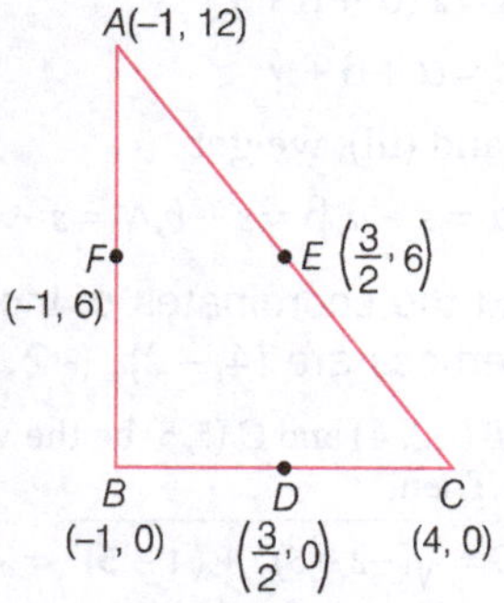

$\therefore$ Coordinates of vertices are

$A \equiv (-1, 12), B \equiv (-1, 0)$ and $C \equiv (4, 0)$.

(i) Centroid The centroid of ΔABC is

$$\left(\frac{x_1+x_2+x_3}{3}, \frac{y_1+y_2+y_3}{3}\right)$$

or $$\left(\frac{-1-1+4}{3}, \frac{12+0+0}{3}\right) \text{ i.e. } \left(\frac{2}{3}, 4\right)$$

(ii) Incentre We have,

$$a = BC = \sqrt{(-1-4)^2+(0-0)^2} = 5$$

$$b = CA = \sqrt{(4+1)^2+(0-12)^2} = 13$$

and $$c = AB = \sqrt{(-1+1)^2+(12-0)^2} = 12$$

$\therefore$ The incentre of ΔABC is

$$\left(\frac{ax_1+bx_2+cx_3}{a+b+c}, \frac{ay_1+by_2+cy_3}{a+b+c}\right)$$

or $$\left(\frac{5\times(-1)+13\times(-1)+12\times 4}{5+13+12}, \frac{5\times 12+13\times 0+12\times 0}{5+13+12}\right)$$

i.e. $(1, 2)$

Example 47. If a vertex of a triangle be $(1, 1)$ and the middle points of two sides through it be $(-2, 3)$ and $(5, 2)$, then find the centroid and the incentre of the triangle.

Sol. Let coordinates of A be $(1, 1)$ and mid-points of AB and AC are F and E.

$\therefore$ $F \equiv (-2, 3)$ and $E \equiv (5, 2)$

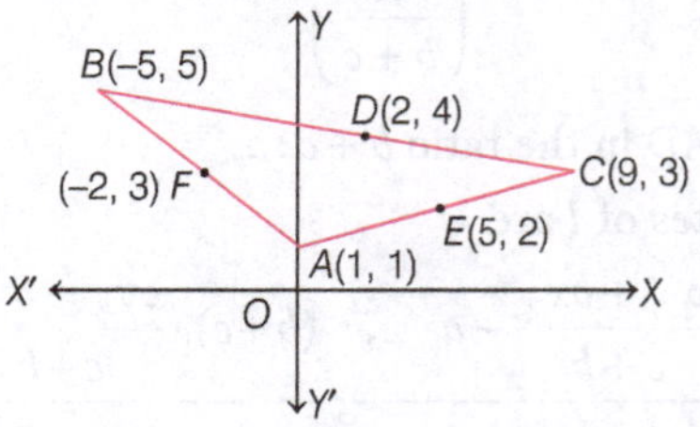

Hence, coordinates of B and C are $(2(-2)-1, 2\times 3-1)$ and $(2(5)-1, 2(2)-1)$ respectively.

i.e. $B \equiv (-5, 5)$ and $C \equiv (9, 3)$

Then, centroid is $\left(\frac{1-5+9}{3}, \frac{1+5+3}{3}\right)$ i.e. $\left(\frac{5}{3}, 3\right)$

Also, $a = |BC| = \sqrt{(-5-9)^2+(5-3)^2} = \sqrt{200} = 10\sqrt{2}$,

$$b = |CA| = \sqrt{(9-1)^2+(3-1)^2} = \sqrt{68} = 2\sqrt{17}$$

and $$c = |AB| = \sqrt{(1+5)^2+(1-5)^2} = \sqrt{52} = 2\sqrt{13}$$

Then, incentre is

$$\left(\frac{10\sqrt{2}\times 1+2\sqrt{17}\times(-5)+2\sqrt{13}\times 9}{10\sqrt{2}+2\sqrt{17}+2\sqrt{13}}, \frac{10\sqrt{2}\times 1+2\sqrt{17}\times 5+2\sqrt{13}\times 3}{10\sqrt{2}+2\sqrt{17}+2\sqrt{13}}\right)$$

i.e. $$\left(\frac{5\sqrt{2}-5\sqrt{17}+9\sqrt{13}}{5\sqrt{2}+\sqrt{17}+\sqrt{13}}, \frac{5\sqrt{2}+5\sqrt{17}+3\sqrt{13}}{5\sqrt{2}+\sqrt{17}+\sqrt{13}}\right)$$

Example 48. If G be the centroid and I be the incentre of the triangle with vertices $A(-36, 7), B(20, 7)$ and $C(0, -8)$ and $GI = \frac{25}{3}\sqrt{(205)}\,\lambda$, then find the value of λ.

Sol. Coordinates of centroid are $G \equiv \left(-\frac{16}{3}, 2\right)$

and $$a = |BC| = \sqrt{(20-0)^2+(7+8)^2}$$

$$= \sqrt{625} = 25$$

$$b = |CA| = \sqrt{(0+36)^2+(-8-7)^2}$$

$$= \sqrt{1521} = 39$$

$$c = |AB| = \sqrt{(-36-20)^2+(7-7)^2}$$

$$= \sqrt{(56)^2} = 56$$

Therefore, the coordinates of incentre are

$$I \equiv \left(\frac{25\times(-36)+39\times 20+56\times 0}{25+39+56}, \frac{25\times 7+39\times 7+56\times(-8)}{25+39+56}\right)$$

i.e. $I \equiv (-1, 0)$

$$\therefore \quad GI = \sqrt{\left(-\frac{16}{3}+1\right)^2 + (2-0)^2} = \frac{\sqrt{(205)}}{3}$$

But given that $GI = \frac{25}{3}\sqrt{(205)}\,\lambda$

$$\therefore \quad \frac{1}{3}\sqrt{(205)} = \frac{25}{3}\sqrt{(205)}\,\lambda$$

$$\Rightarrow \quad \lambda = \frac{1}{25}$$

1.13 Excentres of a Triangle

This is the point of intersection of the external bisectors of the angles of a triangle.

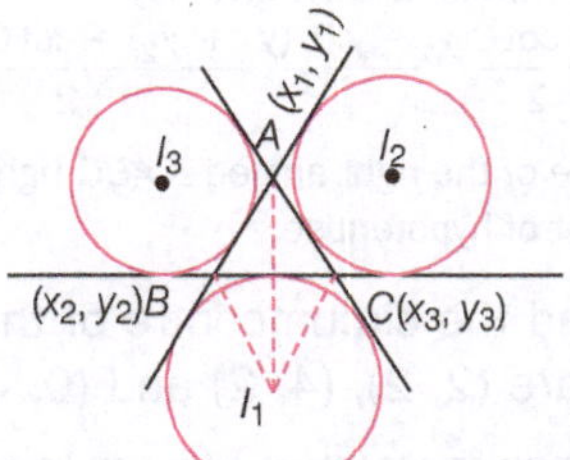

The circle opposite to the vertex A is called the escribed circle opposite A or the circle escribed to the side BC. If I_1 is the point of intersection of internal bisector of $\angle BAC$ and external bisector of $\angle ABC$ and $\angle ACB$, then

$$I_1 \equiv \left(\frac{ax_1 - bx_2 - cx_3}{a-b-c}, \frac{ay_1 - by_2 - cy_3}{a-b-c}\right)$$

or
$$I_1 \equiv \left(\frac{-ax_1 + bx_2 + cx_3}{-a+b+c}, \frac{-ay_1 + by_2 + cy_3}{-a+b+c}\right)$$

Similarly,
$$I_2 \equiv \left(\frac{ax_1 - bx_2 + cx_3}{a-b+c}, \frac{ay_1 - by_2 + cy_3}{a-b+c}\right)$$

and
$$I_3 \equiv \left(\frac{ax_1 + bx_2 - cx_3}{a+b-c}, \frac{ay_1 + by_2 - cy_3}{a+b-c}\right)$$

where, $|BC| = a, |CA| = b$ and $|AB| = c$

Example 49. If the coordinates of the mid-points of sides BC, CA and AB of ΔABC are (1, 1), (2, – 3) and (3, 4), then find the excentre opposite to the vertex A.

Sol. Let $D(1, 1)$, $E(2, -3)$ and $F(3, 4)$ are the mid-points of the sides of the triangle BC, CA and AB respectively.

Let $A \equiv (\alpha, \beta)$

Then, $B \equiv (6-\alpha, 8-\beta)$

and $C \equiv (4-\alpha, -6-\beta)$

Also, D is the mid-point of B and C, then

$$1 = \frac{6-\alpha+4-\alpha}{2}$$

$$\Rightarrow \quad \alpha = 4$$

and
$$1 = \frac{8-\beta-6-\beta}{2}$$

$$\Rightarrow \quad \beta = 0$$

$\therefore$ $A \equiv (4, 0)$, $B \equiv (2, 8)$ and $C \equiv (0, -6)$, then

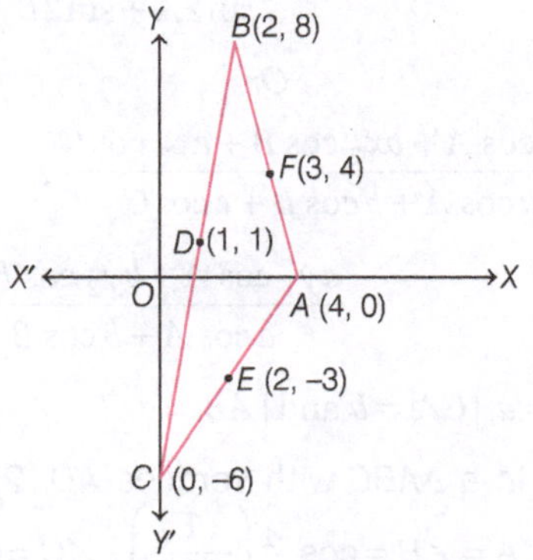

$$a = |BC| = \sqrt{(2-0)^2 + (8+6)^2} = \sqrt{200} = 10\sqrt{2},$$

$$b = |CA| = \sqrt{(0-4)^2 + (-6-0)^2} = \sqrt{52} = 2\sqrt{13}$$

and
$$c = |AB| = \sqrt{(4-2)^2 + (0-8)^2} = \sqrt{68} = 2\sqrt{17}$$

Hence, the coordinates of the excentre opposite to A are

$$\left(\frac{-ax_1 + bx_2 + cx_3}{-a+b+c}, \frac{-ay_1 + by_2 + cy_3}{-a+b+c}\right)$$

i.e.
$$\left(\frac{-10\sqrt{2}\times 4 + 2\sqrt{13}\times 2 + 2\sqrt{17}\times 0}{-10\sqrt{2} + 2\sqrt{13} + 2\sqrt{17}}, \frac{-10\sqrt{2}\times 0 + 2\sqrt{13}\times 8 + 2\sqrt{17}\times(-6)}{-10\sqrt{2} + 2\sqrt{13} + 2\sqrt{17}}\right)$$

or
$$\left(\frac{-20\sqrt{2} + 2\sqrt{13}}{-5\sqrt{2} + \sqrt{13} + \sqrt{17}}, \frac{8\sqrt{13} - 6\sqrt{17}}{-5\sqrt{2} + \sqrt{13} + \sqrt{17}}\right)$$

1.14 Circumcentre of a Triangle

The circumcentre of a triangle is the point of intersection of the perpendicular bisectors of the sides of a triangle (i.e. the lines through the mid-point of a side and perpendicular to it). Let $A(x_1, y_1)$, $B(x_2, y_2)$ and $C(x_3, y_3)$ be the vertices of ΔABC and if angles of ΔABC are given.

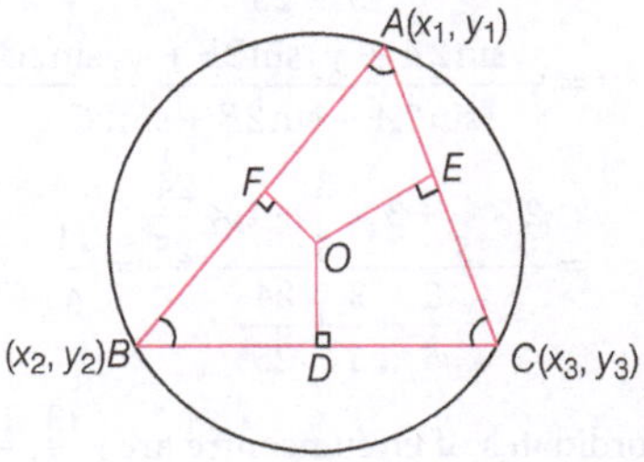

Then, coordinates of circumcentre

are $\left(\dfrac{x_1 \sin 2A + x_2 \sin 2B + x_3 \sin 2C}{\sin 2A + \sin 2B + \sin 2C}, \dfrac{y_1 \sin 2A + y_2 \sin 2B + y_3 \sin 2C}{\sin 2A + \sin 2B + \sin 2C}\right)$

Or

$$\left(\frac{ax_1 \cos A + bx_2 \cos B + cx_3 \cos C}{a\cos A + b\cos B + c\cos C}, \frac{ay_1 \cos A + by_2 \cos B + cy_3 \cos C}{a\cos A + b\cos B + c\cos C}\right)$$

where, $|BC| = a, |CA| = b$ and $|AB| = c$

Example 50. In a ΔABC with vertices $A(1,2)$, $B(2,3)$ and $C(3,1)$ and $\angle A = \angle B = \cos^{-1}\left(\dfrac{1}{\sqrt{10}}\right)$, $\angle C = \cos^{-1}\left(\dfrac{4}{5}\right)$, then find the circumcentre of ΔABC.

Sol. Since, $\angle A = \angle B = \cos^{-1}\left(\dfrac{1}{\sqrt{10}}\right)$

$\Rightarrow \quad \cos A = \cos B = \dfrac{1}{\sqrt{10}}$

Then, $\sin A = \sin B = \dfrac{3}{\sqrt{10}}$

$\therefore \quad \sin 2A = \sin 2B = 2 \times \dfrac{3}{\sqrt{10}} \times \dfrac{1}{\sqrt{10}} = \dfrac{3}{5}$

and $\quad \angle C = \cos^{-1}\left(\dfrac{4}{5}\right)$

$\Rightarrow \quad \cos C = \dfrac{4}{5}$, then $\sin C = \dfrac{3}{5}$

$\therefore \quad \sin 2C = 2 \times \dfrac{3}{5} \times \dfrac{4}{5} = \dfrac{24}{25}$

Let the circumcentre be (x, y), then

$$x = \frac{x_1 \sin 2A + x_2 \sin 2B + x_3 \sin 2C}{\sin 2A + \sin 2B + \sin 2C}$$

$$= \frac{1 \times \frac{3}{5} + 2 \times \frac{3}{5} + 3 \times \frac{24}{25}}{\frac{3}{5} + \frac{3}{5} + \frac{24}{25}} = \frac{13}{6}$$

and $$y = \frac{y_1 \sin 2A + y_2 \sin 2B + y_3 \sin 2C}{\sin 2A + \sin 2B + \sin 2C}$$

$$= \frac{2 \times \frac{3}{5} + 3 \times \frac{3}{5} + 1 \times \frac{24}{25}}{\frac{3}{5} + \frac{3}{5} + \frac{24}{25}} = \frac{11}{6}$$

Hence, coordinates of circumcentre are $\left(\dfrac{13}{6}, \dfrac{11}{6}\right)$.

JEE Focus Points

Concept Inside Video

- If angles of ΔABC are not given and the vertices $A(x_1, y_1)$, $B(x_2, y_2)$ and $C(x_3, y_3)$ are given, then the circumcentre of the ΔABC is given by

$$\left(\frac{(x_1 + x_2) + \lambda(y_1 - y_2)}{2}, \frac{(y_1 + y_2) - \lambda(x_1 - x_2)}{2}\right)$$

where, $P = \begin{bmatrix} x_1 - x_3 & y_1 - y_3 \\ x_2 - x_3 & y_2 - y_3 \end{bmatrix}$

$\therefore \quad \lambda = \dfrac{\text{Row}_1 \cdot \text{Row}_2}{|P|}$

- If the angle C is given instead of coordinates of the vertex C and the vertices $A(x_1, y_1)$, $B(x_2, y_2)$ of ΔABC are given, then the circumcentre of ΔABC is given by

$$\left(\frac{(x_1 + x_2) \pm \cot C(y_1 - y_2)}{2}, \frac{(y_1 + y_2) \mp \cot C(x_1 - x_2)}{2}\right)$$

- Circumcentre of the right angled ΔABC, right angled at A is the mid-point of hypotenuse.

Example 51. Find the circumcentre of the triangle whose vertices are (2, 2), (4, 2) and (0, 4).

Sol. Let the given points are (x_1, y_1), (x_2, y_2) and (x_3, y_3) respectively.

For the matrix

$$P = \begin{bmatrix} x_1 - x_3 & y_1 - y_3 \\ x_2 - x_3 & y_2 - y_3 \end{bmatrix} = \begin{bmatrix} 2 & -2 \\ 4 & -2 \end{bmatrix}$$

$$\therefore \quad \lambda = \frac{\text{Row}_1 \cdot \text{Row}_2}{|P|}$$

$$= \frac{2 \times 4 + (-2) \times (-2)}{|2 \times (-2) - 4 \times (-2)|} = \frac{12}{4} = 3$$

$\therefore$ Circumcentre of the triangle

$$\equiv \left(\frac{(x_1 + x_2) + \lambda(y_1 - y_2)}{2}, \frac{(y_1 + y_2) - \lambda(x_1 - x_2)}{2}\right)$$

$$\equiv \left(\frac{2 + 4 + 3(2 - 2)}{2}, \frac{2 + 2 - 3(2 - 4)}{2}\right) \equiv (3, 5)$$

Example 52. Find the circumcentre of ΔABC, if $A \equiv (7, 4)$, $B \equiv (3, -2)$ and $\angle C = \dfrac{\pi}{3}$.

Sol. Here, $x_1 = 7, y_1 = 4, x_2 = 3, y_2 = -2$ and $\angle C = \dfrac{\pi}{3}$

$\therefore$ The circumcentre of ΔABC

$$\equiv \left(\frac{(x_1 + x_2) \pm \cot C(y_1 - y_2)}{2}, \frac{(y_1 + y_2) \mp \cot C(x_1 - x_2)}{2}\right)$$

$$\equiv \left(\frac{(7 + 3) \pm \frac{1}{\sqrt{3}}(4 + 2)}{2}, \frac{(4 - 2) \mp \frac{1}{\sqrt{3}}(7 - 3)}{2}\right)$$

$$\equiv \left(5 + \sqrt{3}, 1 - \frac{2}{\sqrt{3}}\right) \text{ or } \left(5 - \sqrt{3}, 1 + \frac{2}{\sqrt{3}}\right)$$

1.15 Orthocentre of a Triangle

The orthocentre of a triangle is the point of intersection of altitudes (i.e. the lines through the vertices and perpendicular to opposite sides).

Let $A(x_1, y_1)$, $B(x_2, y_2)$ and $C(x_3, y_3)$ be the vertices of ΔABC and if angles of ΔABC are given, then coordinates of orthocentre are

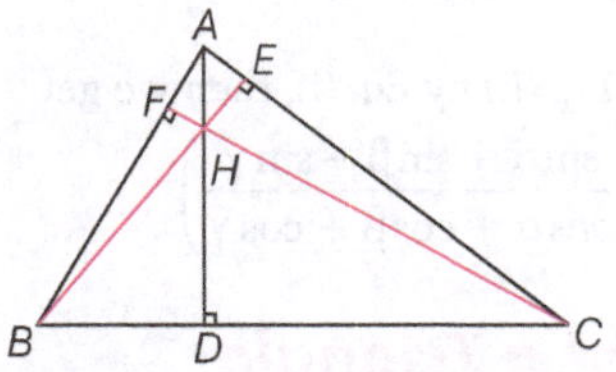

$$\left(\frac{x_1 \tan A + x_2 \tan B + x_3 \tan C}{\tan A + \tan B + \tan C}, \frac{y_1 \tan A + y_2 \tan B + y_3 \tan C}{\tan A + \tan B + \tan C}\right)$$

or $$\left(\frac{ax_1 \sec A + bx_2 \sec B + cx_3 \sec C}{a \sec A + b \sec B + c \sec C}, \frac{ay_1 \sec A + by_2 \sec B + cy_3 \sec C}{a \sec A + b \sec B + c \sec C}\right)$$

where, $|BC| = a, |CA| = b$ and $|AB| = c$

JEE Focus Points

Concept Inside Video

- Orthocentre of the triangle whose vertices are $(0, 0)$, (x_1, y_1) and (x_2, y_2) is given by $$(\lambda(y_2 - y_1), -\lambda(x_2 - x_1))$$ where, $\lambda = \dfrac{x_1x_2 + y_1y_2}{x_1y_2 - x_2y_1}$
- The orthocentre of a triangle having vertices (α, β), (β, α) and (α, α) is (α, α).
- The orthocentre of a triangle having vertices $\left(\alpha, \dfrac{1}{\alpha}\right)$, $\left(\beta, \dfrac{1}{\beta}\right)$ and $\left(\gamma, \dfrac{1}{\gamma}\right)$ is $\left(-\dfrac{1}{\alpha\beta\gamma}, -\alpha\beta\gamma\right)$
- The orthocentre of right angled ΔABC, right angled at A is vertex A.
- The distance between the orthocentre and circumcentre in an equilateral triangle is zero.
- If the circumcentre and centroid of a triangle are respectively (α, β) (γ, δ), then orthocentre will be $(3\gamma - 2\alpha, 3\delta - 2\beta)$.

Example 53. Find the orthocentre of ΔABC, if $A \equiv (0, 0)$, $B \equiv (3, 5)$ and $C \equiv (4, 7)$.

Sol. Here, $x_1 = 3, y_1 = 5, x_2 = 4, y_2 = 7$

$$\therefore \quad \lambda = \frac{3 \times 4 + 5 \times 7}{3 \times 7 - 4 \times 5} = 47$$

Hence, orthocentre of $\Delta ABC \equiv (47(7 - 5), -47(4 - 3))$
$\equiv (94, -47)$

1.16 Nine Point Centre of a Triangle

If a circle passing through the feet of perpendiculars (i.e. D, E, F), mid-points of sides BC, CA, AB respectively (i.e. H, I, J) and the mid-points of the line joining the orthocentre O to the angular points A, B, C (i.e. K, L, M), thus the nine points D, E, F, H, I, J, K, L and M all lie on a circle.

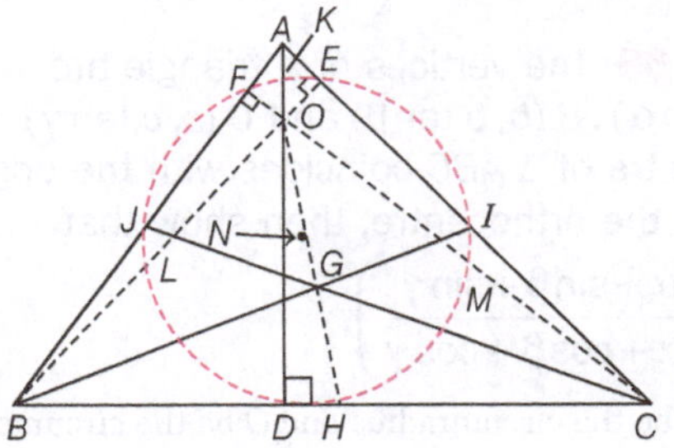

This circle is known as nine point circle and its centre is called the nine point centre. The nine point centre of a triangle is collinear with the circumcentre and the orthocentre and bisects the segments joining them and radius of nine point circle of a triangle is half the radius of the circumcircle.

COROLLARY 1 The orthocentre, the nine point centre, the centroid and the circumcentre are all lie on a straight line.

COROLLARY 2 If O is orthocentre, N is nine point centre, G is centroid and C is circumcentre, then G divides O and C in the ratio 2 : 1 (internally).

We can remember it by *ONGC* (i.e. Oil Natural Gas Corporation).

Since, the letters in left of G are 2 and in right is 1.

COROLLARY 3 N is the mid-point of O and C.

COROLLARY 4 Radius of nine point circle $= \dfrac{1}{2} \times$ Radius of circumcircle.

Example 54. If a triangle has its orthocentre at (1,1) and circumcentre at $\left(\frac{3}{2}, \frac{3}{4}\right)$, then find the centroid and nine point centre.

Sol. Since, centroid divides the orthocentre and circumcentre in the ratio 2 : 1 (internally) and if centroid $G(x, y)$, then

$$O(1,1) \overset{2}{\text{———}} G(x,y) \overset{1}{\text{———}} C\left(\frac{3}{2}, \frac{3}{4}\right)$$

$$x = \frac{2 \times \frac{3}{2} + 1 \times 1}{2+1} = \frac{4}{3} \text{ and } y = \frac{2 \times \frac{3}{4} + 1 \times 1}{2+1} = \frac{5}{6}$$

$\therefore$ Centroid is $\left(\frac{4}{3}, \frac{5}{6}\right)$ and nine point centre is the mid-point of orthocentre and circumcentre.

$$\therefore \text{ Nine point centre is } \left(\frac{1+\frac{3}{2}}{2}, \frac{1+\frac{3}{4}}{2}\right) \text{ i.e. } \left(\frac{5}{4}, \frac{7}{8}\right).$$

Example 55. The vertices of a triangle are $A(a, a\tan\alpha)$, $B(b, b\tan\beta)$ and $C(c, c\tan\gamma)$. If the circumcentre of ΔABC coincides with the origin and $H(\bar{x}, \bar{y})$ is the orthocentre, then show that

$$\frac{\bar{y}}{\bar{x}} = \left(\frac{\sin\alpha + \sin\beta + \sin\gamma}{\cos\alpha + \cos\beta + \cos\gamma}\right).$$

Sol. Let R be the circumradius and O be the circumcentre

Then, $OA = OB = OC = R$

or $\sqrt{(a^2 + a^2\tan^2\alpha)} = \sqrt{(b^2 + b^2\tan^2\beta)}$
$= \sqrt{(c^2 + c^2\tan^2\gamma)} = R$

or $a\sec\alpha = b\sec\beta = c\sec\gamma = R$

or $a = R\cos\alpha, b = R\cos\beta, c = R\cos\gamma$

Then, $a\tan\alpha = R\cos\alpha \cdot \frac{\sin\alpha}{\cos\alpha} = R\sin\alpha$

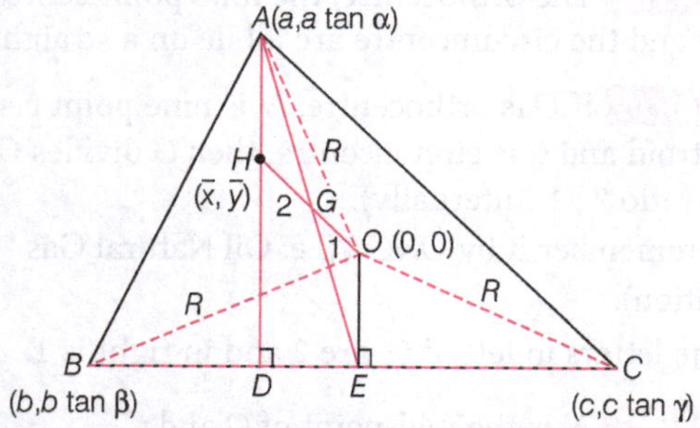

Similarly, $b\tan\beta = R\sin\beta$ and $c\tan\gamma = R\sin\gamma$

$\therefore$ Coordinates of the vertices of a triangle are

$A(R\cos\alpha, R\sin\alpha)$, $B(R\cos\beta, R\sin\beta)$ and $C(R\cos\gamma, R\sin\gamma)$.

$\therefore$ Centroid (G)

$$\equiv \left(\frac{R(\cos\alpha + \cos\beta + \cos\gamma)}{3}, \frac{R(\sin\alpha + \sin\beta + \sin\gamma)}{3}\right)$$

Since, G divides H and O in the ratio 2 : 1 (internally), then

$$\frac{R}{3}(\cos\alpha + \cos\beta + \cos\gamma) = \frac{2 \cdot 0 + 1 \cdot \bar{x}}{2+1}$$

or $$\frac{R}{3}(\cos\alpha + \cos\beta + \cos\gamma) = \frac{\bar{x}}{3} \quad \text{...(i)}$$

and $$\frac{R}{3}(\sin\alpha + \sin\beta + \sin\gamma) = \frac{2 \cdot 0 + 1 \cdot \bar{y}}{2+1}$$

or $$\frac{R}{3}(\sin\alpha + \sin\beta + \sin\gamma) = \frac{\bar{y}}{3} \quad \text{...(ii)}$$

On dividing Eq. (ii) by Eq. (i), then we get

$$\frac{\bar{y}}{\bar{x}} = \left(\frac{\sin\alpha + \sin\beta + \sin\gamma}{\cos\alpha + \cos\beta + \cos\gamma}\right)$$

Hence proved.

1.17 Area of a Triangle

Theorem The area of a triangle, the coordinates of whose vertices are $(x_1, y_1), (x_2, y_2)$ and (x_3, y_3) is

$$\frac{1}{2}|x_1(y_2 - y_3) + x_2(y_3 - y_1) + x_3(y_1 - y_2)|$$

or $$\frac{1}{2}\left|\begin{vmatrix} x_1 & y_1 & 1 \\ x_2 & y_2 & 1 \\ x_3 & y_3 & 1 \end{vmatrix}\right|$$

Proof Let ABC be a triangle with vertices $A(x_1, y_1)$, $B(x_2, y_2)$ and $C(x_3, y_3)$. Let us assume that the points A, B and C are in I quadrant (for the sake of exactness). Draw AL, BM and CN perpendicular on X-axis.

Let Δ be the required area of the triangle ABC, then

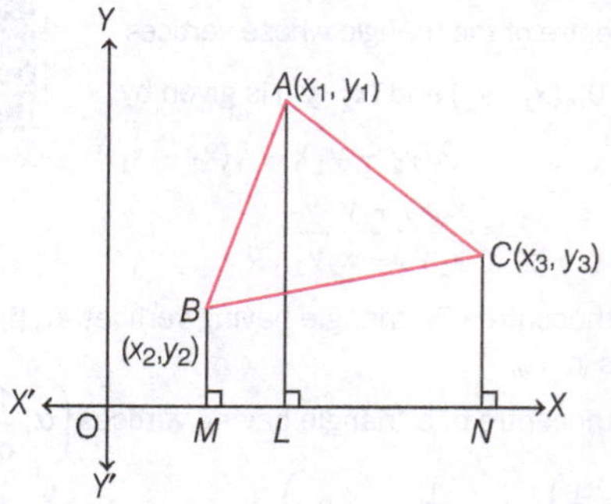

Δ = Area of triangle ABC

= [Area of trapezium $ABML$ + Area of trapezium $ALNC$ − Area of trapezium $BMNC$]

$$\therefore \Delta = \left[\frac{1}{2}(BM + AL)(ML) + \frac{1}{2}(AL + CN)(LN) - \frac{1}{2}(BM + CN)(MN)\right]$$

[$\because$ Area of trapezium $= \frac{1}{2}$ (Sum of parallel sides) × (Distance between them)]

$$=\left[\frac{1}{2}(BM+AL)(OL-OM)+\frac{1}{2}(AL+CN)(ON-OL)-\frac{1}{2}(BM+CN)(ON-OM)\right]$$

$$=\left[\frac{1}{2}(y_2+y_1)(x_1-x_2)+\frac{1}{2}(y_1+y_3)(x_3-x_1)-\frac{1}{2}(y_2+y_3)(x_3-x_2)\right]$$

$$=\frac{1}{2}[x_1(y_2+y_1-y_1-y_3)+x_2(-y_2-y_1+y_2+y_3)+x_3(y_1+y_3-y_2-y_3)]$$

$$=\frac{1}{2}[x_1(y_2-y_3)+x_2(y_3-y_1)+x_3(y_1-y_2)]$$

The area of ΔABC will come out to be a positive quantity only when the vertices A, B and C are taken in anti-clockwise direction and if points A, B and C are taken in clockwise direction, then the area will be negative and if the points A, B and C are taken arbitrary, then the area will be positive or negative, the numerical value being the same in all cases.

Thus, Area of $\Delta\, ABC=\frac{1}{2}|\,x_1(y_2-y_3)+x_2(y_3-y_1)+x_3(y_1-y_2)\,|$

This expression can be written in determinant form as follows

$$\Delta=\frac{1}{2}\left|\begin{vmatrix}x_1 & y_1 & 1\\ x_2 & y_2 & 1\\ x_3 & y_3 & 1\end{vmatrix}\right|$$

COROLLARY 1 Area of triangle can also be found by easy method

$$\Delta=\left|\frac{1}{2}\begin{vmatrix}x_1 & y_1\\ x_2 & y_2\end{vmatrix}+\frac{1}{2}\begin{vmatrix}x_2 & y_2\\ x_3 & y_3\end{vmatrix}+\frac{1}{2}\begin{vmatrix}x_3 & y_3\\ x_1 & y_1\end{vmatrix}\right|$$

Area of Quadrilateral *ABCD*

The area of a quadrilateral can be found out by dividing the quadrilateral into two triangles.

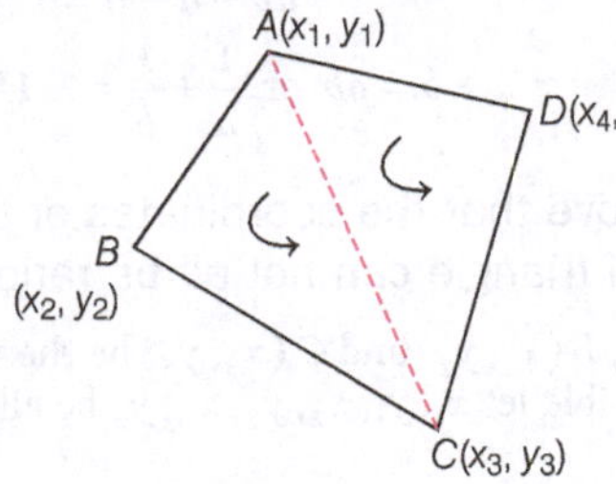

$\therefore$ Area of quadrilateral $ABCD$

$=$ Area of ΔABC + Area of ΔDAC

$$=\frac{1}{2}\begin{vmatrix}x_1 & y_1\\ x_2 & y_2\end{vmatrix}+\frac{1}{2}\begin{vmatrix}x_2 & y_2\\ x_3 & y_3\end{vmatrix}+\frac{1}{2}\begin{vmatrix}x_3 & y_3\\ x_1 & y_1\end{vmatrix}+\frac{1}{2}\begin{vmatrix}x_4 & y_4\\ x_1 & y_1\end{vmatrix}+\frac{1}{2}\begin{vmatrix}x_1 & y_1\\ x_3 & y_3\end{vmatrix}+\frac{1}{2}\begin{vmatrix}x_3 & y_3\\ x_4 & y_4\end{vmatrix}$$

$$=\left|\frac{1}{2}\begin{vmatrix}x_1 & y_1\\ x_2 & y_2\end{vmatrix}+\frac{1}{2}\begin{vmatrix}x_2 & y_2\\ x_3 & y_3\end{vmatrix}+\frac{1}{2}\begin{vmatrix}x_3 & y_3\\ x_4 & y_4\end{vmatrix}+\frac{1}{2}\begin{vmatrix}x_4 & y_4\\ x_1 & y_1\end{vmatrix}\right|$$

$$\left[\because \begin{vmatrix}x_3 & y_3\\ x_1 & y_1\end{vmatrix}=-\begin{vmatrix}x_1 & y_1\\ x_3 & y_3\end{vmatrix}\right]$$

$\therefore$ Area of polygon whose vertices are $(x_1,y_1),(x_2,y_2),(x_3,y_3),\ldots,(x_n,y_n)$ is

$$\frac{1}{2}\left|\begin{vmatrix}x_1 & y_1\\ x_2 & y_2\end{vmatrix}+\begin{vmatrix}x_2 & y_2\\ x_3 & y_3\end{vmatrix}+\begin{vmatrix}x_3 & y_3\\ x_4 & y_4\end{vmatrix}+\ldots+\begin{vmatrix}x_n & y_n\\ x_1 & y_1\end{vmatrix}\right|$$

Or

Stair Method

Repeat first coordinates one time in last for down arrow use positive sign and for up arrow use negative sign.

$\therefore$ Area of polygon $=\frac{1}{2}\left|\ \right|$

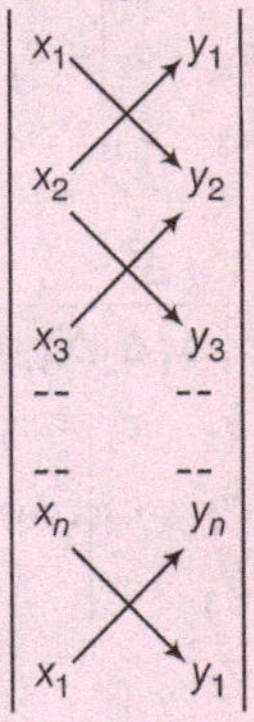

$$=\frac{1}{2}|\{(x_1y_2+x_2y_3+\ldots+x_ny_1)-(y_1x_2+y_2x_3+\ldots+y_nx_1)\}|$$

COROLLARY 2 If the coordinates of the vertices of the triangle are given in polar form i.e. $A(r_1,\theta_1)$, $B(r_2,\theta_2)$ and $C(r_3,\theta_3)$.

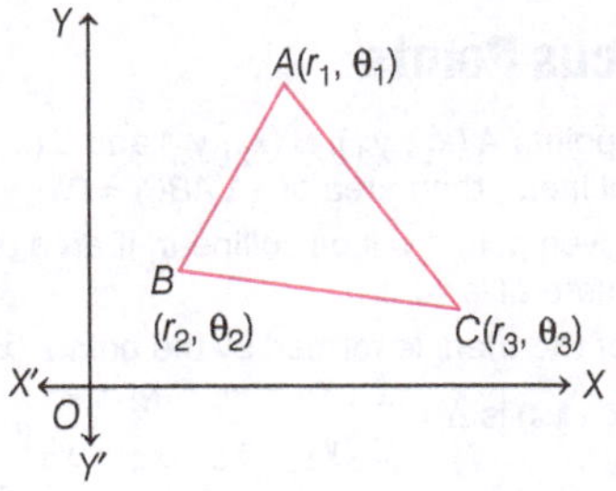

Then, area of triangle

$$= \frac{1}{2} | r_1 r_2 \sin(\theta_1 - \theta_2) + r_2 r_3 \sin(\theta_2 - \theta_3) + r_3 r_1 \sin(\theta_3 - \theta_1)|$$

$$= \frac{1}{2} \left| \sum r_1 r_2 \sin(\theta_1 - \theta_2) \right|$$

COROLLARY 3 If $a_1 x + b_1 y + c_1 = 0$, $a_2 x + b_2 y + c_2 = 0$ and $a_3 x + b_3 y + c_3 = 0$ are the sides of a triangle, then the area of the triangle is given by (without solving for vertices)

$$\Delta = \frac{1}{2|C_1 C_2 C_3|} \begin{vmatrix} a_1 & b_1 & c_1 \\ a_2 & b_2 & c_2 \\ a_3 & b_3 & c_3 \end{vmatrix}^2$$

where, C_1, C_2, C_3 are the cofactors of c_1, c_2, c_3 in the determinant.

Here, $$C_1 = \begin{vmatrix} a_2 & b_2 \\ a_3 & b_3 \end{vmatrix} = (a_2 b_3 - a_3 b_2)$$

$$C_2 = \begin{vmatrix} a_3 & b_3 \\ a_1 & b_1 \end{vmatrix} = (a_3 b_1 - a_1 b_3)$$

and $$C_3 = \begin{vmatrix} a_1 & b_1 \\ a_2 & b_2 \end{vmatrix} = (a_1 b_2 - a_2 b_1)$$

and $$\begin{vmatrix} a_1 & b_1 & c_1 \\ a_2 & b_2 & c_2 \\ a_3 & b_3 & c_3 \end{vmatrix} = c_1 C_1 + c_2 C_2 + c_3 C_3$$

Or

$$\text{Area of triangle} = \frac{\Delta^2}{2|\Delta_1 \Delta_2 \Delta_3|}$$

where, $\Delta = \begin{vmatrix} a_1 & b_1 & c_1 \\ a_2 & b_2 & c_2 \\ a_3 & b_3 & c_3 \end{vmatrix}$, $\Delta_1 = \begin{vmatrix} a_1 & b_1 \\ a_2 & b_2 \end{vmatrix}$, $\Delta_2 = \begin{vmatrix} a_2 & b_2 \\ a_3 & b_3 \end{vmatrix}$

and $\Delta_3 = \begin{vmatrix} a_3 & b_3 \\ a_1 & b_1 \end{vmatrix}$

COROLLARY 4 Area of the triangle formed by the lines of the form $y = m_1 x + c_1$, $y = m_2 x + c_2$ and $y = m_3 x + c_3$ is

$$\Delta = \frac{1}{2} \left| \frac{(c_2 - c_3)^2}{(m_2 - m_3)} + \frac{(c_3 - c_1)^2}{(m_3 - m_1)} + \frac{(c_1 - c_2)^2}{(m_1 - m_2)} \right|$$

JEE Focus Points

Concept Inside Video

1. If the points $A(x_1, y_1)$, $B(x_2, y_2)$ and $C(x_3, y_3)$ are collinear, then area of $(\Delta ABC) = 0$.
2. Four given points will be collinear, if area of the quadrilateral is zero.
3. Area of the triangle formed by the points (x_1, y_1), (x_2, y_2) and (x_3, y_3) is $\Delta = \frac{1}{2} \begin{vmatrix} x_1 - x_3 & x_2 - x_3 \\ y_1 - y_3 & y_2 - y_3 \end{vmatrix}$
4. If one vertex (x_3, y_3) is at $(0, 0)$, then $\Delta = \frac{1}{2} | x_1 y_2 - x_2 y_1 |$

Example 56. The coordinates of A, B and C are $(6, 3), (-3, 5)$ and $(4, -2)$, respectively and P is any points (x, y). Show that the ratio of the areas of the ΔPBC and ΔABC is $\frac{|x + y - 2|}{7}$.

Sol. We have,

$$\frac{\text{Area of } \Delta PBC}{\text{Area of } \Delta ABC} = \frac{\frac{1}{2}|\{x(5+2) - 3(-2-y) + 4(y-5)\}|}{\frac{1}{2}|\{6(5+2) - 3(-2-3) + 4(3-5)\}|}$$

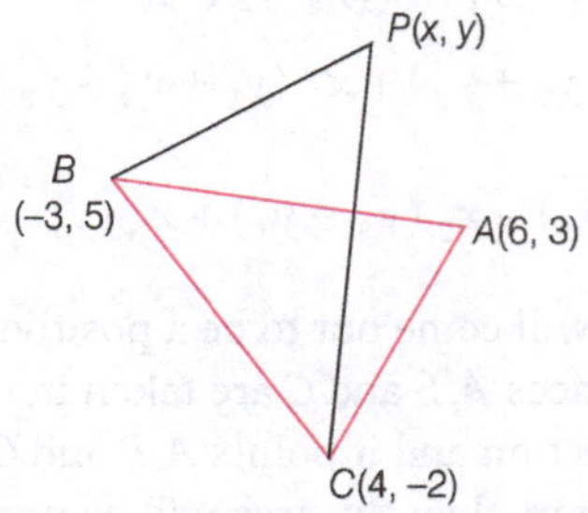

$$= \frac{|7x + 7y - 14|}{|49|} = \frac{7|x + y - 2|}{49} = \frac{|x + y - 2|}{7}$$

Example 57. Find the area of the pentagon whose vertices are $A(1, 1), B(7, 21), C(7, -3), D(12, 2)$ and $E(0, -3)$.

Sol. The required area

$$= \frac{1}{2} \left| \begin{vmatrix} 1 & 1 \\ 7 & 21 \end{vmatrix} + \begin{vmatrix} 7 & 21 \\ 7 & -3 \end{vmatrix} + \begin{vmatrix} 7 & -3 \\ 12 & 2 \end{vmatrix} + \begin{vmatrix} 12 & 2 \\ 0 & -3 \end{vmatrix} + \begin{vmatrix} 0 & -3 \\ 1 & 1 \end{vmatrix} \right|$$

$$= \frac{1}{2} |(21 - 7) + (-21 - 147) + (14 + 36) + (-36 - 0) + (0 + 3)|$$

$$= \frac{1}{2} |-137| = \frac{137}{2} \text{ sq units}$$

Example 58. Show that the points $(a, 0), (0, b)$ and $(1, 1)$ are collinear, if $\frac{1}{a} + \frac{1}{b} = 1$.

Sol. Let $A \equiv (a, 0)$, $B \equiv (0, b)$ and $C \equiv (1, 1)$

Now, points A, B and C will be collinear, if

Area of $\Delta ABC = 0$

or $$\frac{1}{2} \left| \begin{vmatrix} a & 0 \\ 0 & b \end{vmatrix} + \begin{vmatrix} 0 & b \\ 1 & 1 \end{vmatrix} + \begin{vmatrix} 1 & 1 \\ a & 0 \end{vmatrix} \right| = 0$$

$\Rightarrow$ $$|(ab - 0) + (0 - b) + (0 - a)| = 0$$

or $$ab - a - b = 0$$

or $$a + b = ab \text{ or } \frac{1}{a} + \frac{1}{b} = 1$$ **Hence proved.**

Example 59. Prove that the coordinates of the vertices of an equilateral triangle can not all be rational.

Sol. Let $A(x_1, y_1)$, $B(x_2, y_2)$ and $C(x_3, y_3)$ be the vertices of a ΔABC. If possible let $x_1, y_1, x_2, y_2, x_3, y_3$ be all rational.

Now, area of $\Delta ABC = \frac{1}{2}|x_1(y_2 - y_3) + x_2(y_3 - y_1) + x_3(y_1 - y_2)|$

$= \text{Rational}$ ...(i)

Since, ΔABC is equilateral.

$\therefore$ Area of $\Delta ABC = \frac{\sqrt{3}}{4}(\text{Side})^2$

$= \frac{\sqrt{3}}{4}(AB)^2$

$= \frac{\sqrt{3}}{4}\{(x_1 - x_2)^2 + (y_1 - y_2)^2\}$

$= \text{Irrational}$ ...(ii)

From Eqs. (i) and (ii), we get

Rational = Irrational

which is a contradiction.

Hence, all $x_1, y_1, x_2, y_2, x_3, y_3$ cannot be rational.

Example 60. The coordinates of two points A and B are (3, 4) and (5, −2) respectively. Find the coordinates of any point P if $PA = PB$ and area of ΔAPB is 10.

Sol. Let coordinates of P be (h, k).

$\because \quad PA = PB \Rightarrow (PA)^2 = (PB)^2$

$\Rightarrow (h-3)^2 + (k-4)^2 = (h-5)^2 + (k+2)^2$

$\Rightarrow (h-3)^2 - (h-5)^2 + (k-4)^2 - (k+2)^2 = 0$

$\Rightarrow (2h-8)(2) + (2k-2)(-6) = 0$

$\Rightarrow (h-4) - 3(k-1) = 0$

$\Rightarrow h - 3k - 1 = 0$ ...(i)

Now, area of $\Delta PAB = \frac{1}{2}\left|\begin{vmatrix} h & k & 1 \\ 3 & 4 & 1 \\ 5 & -2 & 1 \end{vmatrix}\right| = 10$

or $6h + 2k - 26 = \pm 20$

$\Rightarrow 6h + 2k - 46 = 0$

or $6h + 2k - 6 = 0$

$\Rightarrow 3h + k - 23 = 0$

or $3h + k - 3 = 0$

On solving $h - 3k - 1 = 0$ and $3h + k - 23 = 0$, we get

$h = 7, k = 2$

On solving $h - 3k - 1 = 0$ and $3h + k - 3 = 0$, we get

$h = 1, k = 0$

Hence, the coordinates of P are (7, 2) or (1, 0).

Example 61. Find the area of the triangle formed by the straight lines $7x - 2y + 10 = 0$, $7x + 2y - 10 = 0$ and $9x + y + 2 = 0$ (without solving the vertices of the triangle).

Sol. The given lines are

$7x - 2y + 10 = 0$

$7x + 2y - 10 = 0.$

and $9x + y + 2 = 0$

$\therefore$ Area of triangle $= \frac{1}{2|C_1C_2C_3|}\begin{vmatrix} 7 & -2 & 10 \\ 7 & 2 & -10 \\ 9 & 1 & 2 \end{vmatrix}^2$ ...(i)

where, $C_1 = \begin{vmatrix} 7 & 2 \\ 9 & 1 \end{vmatrix} = 7 - 18 = -11,$

$C_2 = \begin{vmatrix} 9 & 1 \\ 7 & -2 \end{vmatrix} = -18 - 7 = -25$

and $C_3 = \begin{vmatrix} 7 & -2 \\ 7 & 2 \end{vmatrix} = 14 + 14 = 28,$

and $\begin{vmatrix} 7 & -2 & 10 \\ 7 & 2 & -10 \\ 9 & 1 & 2 \end{vmatrix} = 10C_1 - 10C_2 + 2C_3$

$= 10 \times (-11) - 10 \times (-25) + 2 \times 28 = 196$

$\therefore$ From Eq. (i), $\Delta = \frac{1}{2|-11 \times (-25) \times 28|} \times (196)^2$

$= \frac{196 \times 196}{2 \times 11 \times 25 \times 28} = \frac{686}{275}$ sq units

Example 62. If Δ_1 is the area of the triangle with vertices $(0, 0)$, $(a\tan\alpha, b\cot\alpha)$, $(a\sin\alpha, b\cos\alpha)$; Δ_2 is the area of the triangle with vertices (a, b), $(a\sec^2\alpha, b\,\text{cosec}^2\alpha)$, $(a + a\sin^2\alpha, b + b\cos^2\alpha)$ and Δ_3 is the area of the triangle with vertices $(0, 0)$, $(a\tan\alpha, -b\cot\alpha)$, $(a\sin\alpha, b\cos\alpha)$. Show that there is no value of α for which Δ_1, Δ_2 and Δ_3 are in GP.

Sol. We have, $\Delta_1 = \frac{1}{2}|(a\tan\alpha)(b\cos\alpha) - (a\sin\alpha)(b\cot\alpha)|$

[$\because$ one vertex is (0,0)]

$= \frac{1}{2}|ab||\sin\alpha - \cos\alpha|$ ... (i)

and $\Delta_2 = \frac{1}{2}\left|\begin{vmatrix} a - (a + a\sin^2\alpha) & a\sec^2\alpha - (a + a\sin^2\alpha) \\ b - (b + b\cos^2\alpha) & b\,\text{cosec}^2\alpha - (b + b\cos^2\alpha) \end{vmatrix}\right|$

$= \frac{1}{2}\left|\begin{vmatrix} -a\sin^2\alpha & a(\tan^2\alpha - \sin^2\alpha) \\ -b\cos^2\alpha & b(\cot^2\alpha - \cos^2\alpha) \end{vmatrix}\right|$

$= \frac{1}{2}|ab| \times \left|\begin{vmatrix} -\sin^2\alpha & \sin^2\alpha(\sec^2\alpha - 1) \\ -\cos^2\alpha & \cos^2\alpha(\text{cosec}^2\alpha - 1) \end{vmatrix}\right|$

$= \frac{1}{2}|ab| \times \left|\begin{vmatrix} -\sin^2\alpha & \sin^2\alpha\tan^2\alpha \\ -\cos^2\alpha & \cos^2\alpha\cot^2\alpha \end{vmatrix}\right|$

$= \frac{1}{2}|ab| \times |-\sin^2\alpha\cos^2\alpha\cot^2\alpha + \sin^2\alpha\cos^2\alpha\tan^2\alpha|$

$= \frac{1}{2}|ab| \times |-\cos^4\alpha + \sin^4\alpha|$

$= \frac{1}{2}|ab| \times |\sin^2\alpha + \cos^2\alpha| \times |\sin^2\alpha - \cos^2\alpha|$

$= \frac{1}{2}|ab| \times |1| \times |-\cos 2\alpha| = \frac{1}{2}|ab| \times |\cos 2\alpha|$ ... (ii) and $\Delta_3 = \frac{1}{2}|(a\tan\alpha)(b\cos\alpha) - (-b\cot\alpha)(a\sin\alpha)|$

$$= \frac{1}{2}|ab||\sin\alpha + \cos\alpha| \quad \text{... (iii)}$$

Since, $\Delta_1, \Delta_2, \Delta_3$ are in GP, then $\Delta_1\Delta_3 = \Delta_2^2$

$\Rightarrow \quad \frac{1}{2}|ab||\sin\alpha - \cos\alpha| \times \frac{1}{2}|ab||\sin\alpha + \cos\alpha|$

$= \frac{1}{4}|ab|^2|\cos 2\alpha|^2$ [from Eqs. (i), (ii) and (iii)]

$\Rightarrow \quad |\sin^2\alpha - \cos^2\alpha| = |\cos 2\alpha|^2$

$\Rightarrow \quad |-\cos 2\alpha| = |\cos 2\alpha|^2$

$\Rightarrow \quad |\cos 2\alpha| = |\cos 2\alpha|^2$

$\Rightarrow \quad |\cos 2\alpha|(1 - |\cos 2\alpha|) = 0$

$\therefore \quad 1 - |\cos 2\alpha| = 0 \quad [\because |\cos 2\alpha| \neq 0]$

$\Rightarrow \quad |\cos 2\alpha| = 1$

or $\quad \cos 2\alpha = \pm 1$

or $\quad \cos 2\alpha = 1$ and $\cos 2\alpha = -1$

or $\quad 2\alpha = 2n\pi, 2\alpha = (2p+1)\pi$

or $\quad \alpha = n\pi, \alpha = p\pi + \frac{\pi}{2}, n, p \in I$

For these values of α the vertices of the given triangles are not defined. Hence, Δ_1, Δ_2 and Δ_3 cannot be in GP for any value of α.

JEE SCANNER

Example Similar to PYQ Asked in JEE Main 2023

Let $A(\alpha, -2)$, $B(\alpha, 6)$ and $C\left(\frac{\alpha}{4}, 2\right)$ be the vertices of ΔABC. If $\left(\frac{3}{2}, \beta\right)$ is the centroid of ΔABC, and area and perimeter of ΔABC is k and $8 + \sqrt{m}$ respectively, then the value of $k + m$ is ......

Sol. (79) We have, $A(\alpha, -2)$, $B(\alpha, 6)$ and $C\left(\frac{\alpha}{4}, 2\right)$ and $G\left(\frac{3}{2}, \beta\right)$

$$\therefore \quad \frac{\alpha + \alpha + \frac{\alpha}{4}}{3} = \frac{3}{2} \text{ and } \frac{-2+6+2}{3} = \beta$$

$\Rightarrow \quad \alpha = 2$ and $\beta = 2$

$\therefore \quad A(2, -2), B(2, 6)$ and $C\left(\frac{1}{2}, 2\right)$

Now, area $(\Delta ABC) = \frac{1}{2}\left\|\begin{matrix} x_1 & y_1 & 1 \\ x_2 & y_2 & 1 \\ x_3 & y_3 & 1 \end{matrix}\right\|$

$$= \frac{1}{2}\left\|\begin{matrix} 2 & -2 & 1 \\ 2 & 6 & 1 \\ \frac{1}{2} & 2 & 1 \end{matrix}\right\| = \frac{1}{2}\left|\left[2(6-2) + 2\left(2 - \frac{1}{2}\right) + 1(4-3)\right]\right|$$

$$= \frac{1}{2}|[8 + 3 + 1]| = 6 \text{ sq units}$$

$\therefore \quad k = 6$

Again, $AB = \sqrt{(2-2)^2 + (6+2)^2} = 8$,

$$BC = \sqrt{\left(\frac{1}{2} - 2\right)^2 + (2-6)^2}$$

$$= \sqrt{\frac{9}{4} + 16} = \frac{\sqrt{73}}{2}$$

and $\quad CA = \sqrt{\left(2 - \frac{1}{2}\right)^2 + (-2-2)^2}$

$$= \sqrt{\frac{9}{4} + 16} = \frac{\sqrt{73}}{2}$$

$\therefore$ Perimeter of $\Delta ABC = 8 + \sqrt{73}$

$\therefore \quad m = 73$

Hence, $\quad k + m = 79$

Skill Builder

For Sol.

Let $A(2a, b)$, $B\left(\frac{a}{3}, \frac{-b}{2}\right)$ and $C(-a, 3b)$ be the vertices of ΔABC. If $(4, 14)$ is the centroid of ΔABC, and its area and perimeter are k and $\sqrt{549} + 6\sqrt{m} + 3\sqrt{n}$ respectively, then the value of $k - (m+n)$ is ....

■ **For more Practice** See Q. 17 of Milestone Practice 1.3.

Milestone Practice 1.3

1. The coordinates of the middle points of the sides of a triangle are (4, 2), (3, 3) and (2, 2), then coordinates of centroid are
   (a) $\left(3, \frac{7}{3}\right)$ (b) (3, 3)
   (c) (4, 3) (d) (3, 4)

2. The incentre of the triangle whose vertices are (−36, 7), (20, 7) and (0, −8) is
   (a) (0, −1) (b) (−1, 0)
   (c) (1, 1) (d) $\left(\frac{1}{2}, 1\right)$

3. If the orthocentre and centroid of a triangle are (−3, 5) and (3, 3), then its circumcentre is
   (a) (6, 2) (b) (3, −1) (c) (−3, 5) (d) (−3, 1)

4. The vertices of a triangle are $A(0,0)$, $B(0,2)$ and $C(2,0)$. The distance between circumcentre and orthocentre is
   (a) $\sqrt{2}$ (b) $\frac{1}{\sqrt{2}}$ (c) 2 (d) $\frac{1}{2}$

5. $A(a, b)$, $B(x_1, y_1)$ and $C(x_2, y_2)$ are the vertices of a triangle. If a, x_1, x_2 are in GP with common ratio r and b, y_1, y_2 are in GP with common ratio s, then area of ΔABC is
   (a) $ab(r-1)(s-1)(s-r)$ (b) $\frac{1}{2}ab(r+1)(s+1)(s-r)$
   (c) $\frac{1}{2}ab(r-1)(s-1)(s-r)$ (d) $ab(r+1)(s+1)(r-s)$

6. The points $(x+1, 2)$, $(1, x+2)$, $\left(\frac{1}{x+1}, \frac{2}{x+1}\right)$ are collinear, then x is equal to
   (a) −4 (b) −8 (c) 4 (d) 8

7. The vertices of a triangle are (6, 0), (0, 6) and (6, 6). Then, distance between its circumcentre and centroid, is
   (a) $2\sqrt{2}$ (b) 2 (c) $\sqrt{2}$ (d) 1

8. The incentre of the triangle with vertices $(1, \sqrt{3})$, (0, 0) and (2, 0) is
   (a) $\left(1, \frac{\sqrt{3}}{2}\right)$ (b) $\left(\frac{2}{3}, \frac{1}{\sqrt{3}}\right)$
   (c) $\left(\frac{2}{3}, \frac{\sqrt{3}}{2}\right)$ (d) $\left(1, \frac{1}{\sqrt{3}}\right)$

9. The vertices of a triangle are (0, 0), (1, 0) and (0, 1). Then, excentre opposite to (0, 0) is
   (a) $\left(1-\frac{1}{\sqrt{2}}, 1+\frac{1}{\sqrt{2}}\right)$ (b) $\left(1+\frac{1}{\sqrt{2}}, 1+\frac{1}{\sqrt{2}}\right)$
   (c) $\left(1+\frac{1}{\sqrt{2}}, 1-\frac{1}{\sqrt{2}}\right)$ (d) $\left(1-\frac{1}{\sqrt{2}}, 1-\frac{1}{\sqrt{2}}\right)$

10. If α, β and γ are the real roots of the equation $x^3 - 3px^2 + 3qx - 1 = 0$, then find the centroid of the triangle whose vertices are $\left(\alpha, \frac{1}{\alpha}\right)$, $\left(\beta, \frac{1}{\beta}\right)$ and $\left(\gamma, \frac{1}{\gamma}\right)$.

11. Find the number of values of b for which in an acute ΔABC, the coordinates of orthocentre H are $(4, b)$, centroid G are $(b, 2b-8)$ and circumcentre S are $(-4, 8)$.

12. Show that the area of the triangle with vertices $(\lambda, \lambda-2)$, $(\lambda+3, \lambda)$ and $(\lambda+2, \lambda+2)$ is independent of λ.

13. If the points (x_1, y_1), (x_2, y_2) and (x_3, y_3) are collinear, show that $\sum\left(\frac{y_1-y_2}{x_1x_2}\right) = 0$ i.e.
$$\frac{y_1-y_2}{x_1x_2} + \frac{y_2-y_3}{x_2x_3} + \frac{y_3-y_1}{x_3x_1} = 0$$

14. Let (a, b) be the centroid of the triangle formed by the lines $x + y = 4$, $-x + y = 4$, $y = 6$. Then, find the quadratic equation whose roots are $2a + b$ and $a + 2b$.

15. The coordinates of points A, B, C and D are $(-3, 5)$, $(4, -2)$, $(x, 3x)$ and $(6, 3)$ respectively and $\frac{\text{Area of } \Delta ABC}{\text{Area of } \Delta BCD} = \frac{2}{3}$, find x.

16. Find the area of the hexagon whose vertices taken in order are (5, 0), (4, 2), (1, 3), (−2, 2), (−3, −1) and (0, −4).

17. Let $A\left(\frac{\alpha}{4}, \beta\right)$, $B\left(-\alpha, \frac{\beta}{2}\right)$ and $C(\alpha, \beta)$ be the vertices of ΔABC. If $\left(\frac{1}{4}, \frac{5}{6}\right)$ is the centroid of ΔABC, then find its area and perimeter.

Answer Key

1. (a)	2. (b)	3. (a)	4. (a)	5. (c)	6. (a)
7. (c)	8. (d)	9. (b)	10. (p, q)	11. 0	
14. $9x^2 - 144x + 512 = 0$		15. $-\frac{3}{43}$ or $\frac{45}{41}$	16. 34 sq. units	17. $\frac{9}{16}, \frac{9+\sqrt{229}+2\sqrt{145}}{4}$	

For Detailed Solution

Milestone 4 Locus and its Equation

• Equation of a Locus • Transformation of Axes • Removal of the term xy from $f(x,y)=ax^2+2hxy+by^2$ without changing the origin • Position of a Point which lies Inside a Triangle

The **locus** of a moving point is the path traced out by that point under one or more given conditions.

e.g. If a point P moves in a plane such that whose distance from a fixed point O (say) in the plane is always constant distance a. Thus, the locus of the moving point P is clearly a circle with centre O and radius a.

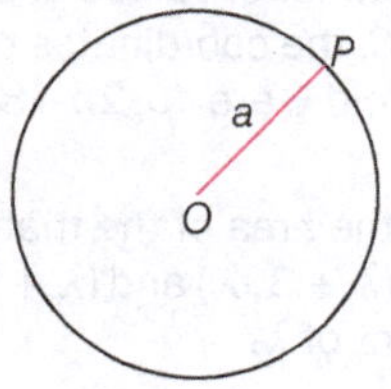

e.g. If a point P moves in a plane such that whose distance from two fixed points A and B (say) are always equal i.e. $PA = PB$

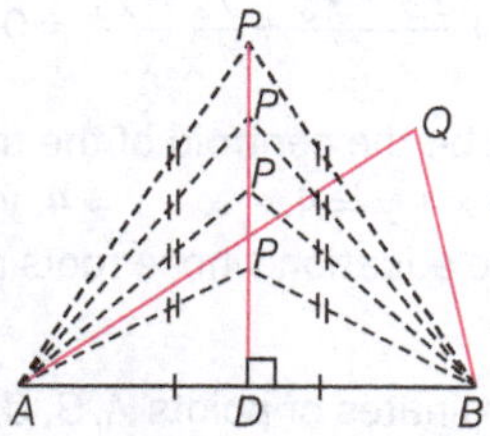

(the point P cannot be at Q because $AQ \neq BQ$)

Obviously all the positions of the moving point P lies on the right bisector of AB. Thus, the locus of the moving point P is the right bisector of AB.

1.18 Equation of a Locus

A relation $f(x, y)=0$ between x and y which is satisfied by each point on the locus and such that each point satisfying the equation is on the locus is called the equation of the locus.

How to Find the Locus of a Point

Let (x_1, y_1) be the coordinates of the moving point say P. Now, apply the geometrical conditions on x_1 and y_1. This gives a relation between x_1 and y_1. Now, replace x_1 by x and y_1 by y in the eliminant and resulting equation would be the equation of the locus.

COROLLARY 1 If x and y are not there in the question, the coordinates of P may also be taken as (x, y).

COROLLARY 2 If coordinates and equation are not given in the question, suitable choice of origin and axes may be made.

COROLLARY 3 To find the locus of the point of intersection of two straight lines, eliminate the parameter or parameters from the given lines. If more than one parameter, then additional condition or conditions will also be given.

Example 63. Find the locus of a point which moves such that its distance from the point (0, 0) is twice its distance from the Y-axis.

Sol. Let $P(x_1, y_1)$ be the moving point whose locus is required.

By hypothesis $|OP| = 2|PM|$ [$\because P$ can lie in any quadrant]

$\Rightarrow \sqrt{(x_1^2 + y_1^2)} = 2|x_1|$

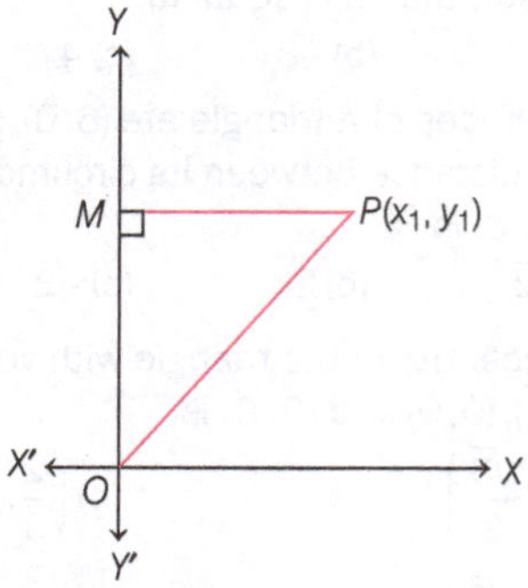

On squaring both sides, then

$$x_1^2 + y_1^2 = 4x_1^2$$

$$\Rightarrow \quad 3x_1^2 - y_1^2 = 0$$

Replacing (x_1, y_1) to (x, y), then

$$3x^2 - y^2 = 0$$

which is the required locus of P.

Example 64. Find the locus of the moving point P such that $2PA = 3PB$, where A is $(0, 0)$ and B is $(4, -3)$.

Sol. Let $P(x_1, y_1)$ be the moving point whose locus is required.

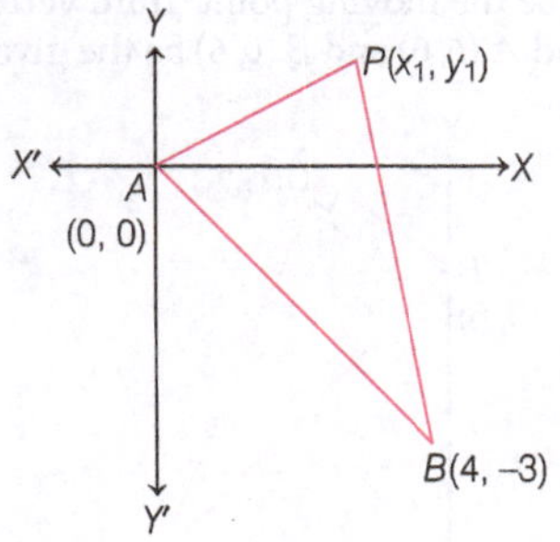

By hypothesis,

$$2PA = 3PB \text{ or } 4(PA)^2 = 9(PB)^2$$

$$\Rightarrow \quad 4\{x_1^2 + y_1^2\} = 9\{(x_1 - 4)^2 + (y_1 + 3)^2\}$$

$$\Rightarrow \quad 4(x_1^2 + y_1^2) = 9(x_1^2 + y_1^2 - 8x_1 + 6y_1 + 25)$$

$$\text{or} \quad 5x_1^2 + 5y_1^2 - 72x_1 + 54y_1 + 225 = 0$$

Replacing (x_1, y_1) to (x, y), then

$$5x^2 + 5y^2 - 72x + 54y + 225 = 0$$

which is the required locus of P.

Example 65. A point moves so that the sum of the squares of its distances from two fixed points $A(a, 0)$ and $B(-a, 0)$ is constant and equal to $2c^2$, find the locus of the point.

Sol. Let $P(x_1, y_1)$ be the moving point whose locus is required.

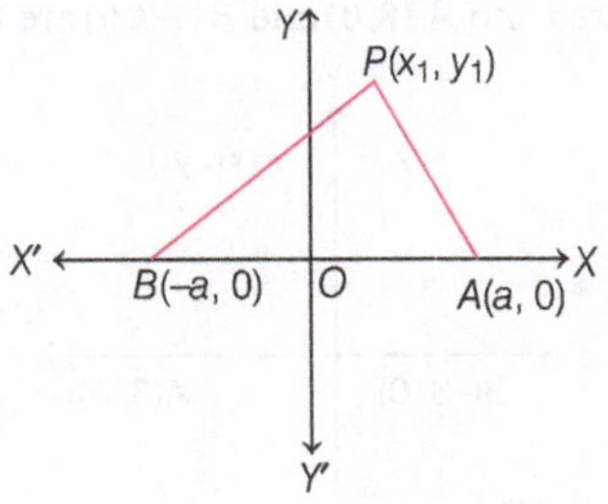

By hypothesis, $(PA)^2 + (PB)^2 = 2c^2$

$$\Rightarrow (x_1 - a)^2 + (y_1 - 0)^2 + (x_1 + a)^2 + (y_1 - 0)^2 = 2c^2$$

$$\Rightarrow \quad 2x_1^2 + 2y_1^2 + 2a^2 = 2c^2$$

$$\text{or} \quad x_1^2 + y_1^2 = c^2 - a^2$$

Replacing (x_1, y_1) to (x, y), then

$$x^2 + y^2 = c^2 - a^2$$

which is the required locus of P.

Example 66. A point moves such that the sum of its distances from two fixed points $(ae, 0)$ and $(-ae, 0)$ is always $2a$. Prove that the equation of the locus is $\frac{x^2}{a^2} + \frac{y^2}{b^2} = 1$, where $b^2 = a^2(1 - e^2)$

Sol. Let $P(x_1, y_1)$ be the moving point whose locus is required and $A(ae, 0)$ and $B(-ae, 0)$ be the given fixed points.

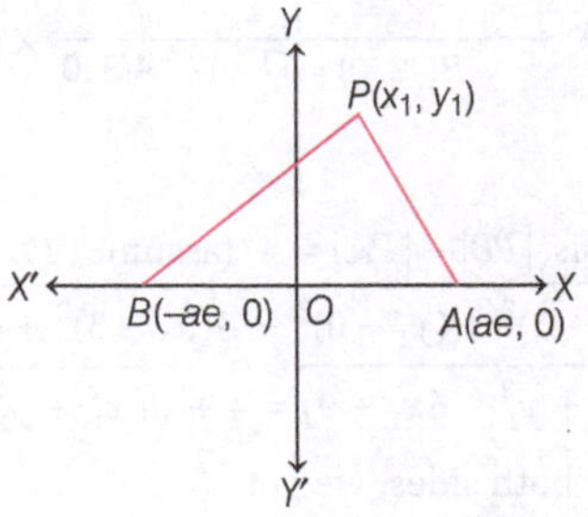

By hypothesis, $\quad |PA| + |PB| = 2a$

$$\text{or} \quad \sqrt{(x_1 - ae)^2 + (y_1 - 0)^2} + \sqrt{(x_1 + ae)^2 + (y_1 - 0)^2} = 2a$$

$$\text{or} \quad \sqrt{(x_1^2 + y_1^2 - 2aex_1 + a^2e^2)} + \sqrt{(x_1^2 + y_1^2 + 2aex_1 + a^2e^2)} = 2a \quad \text{...(i)}$$

Let $\quad l = x_1^2 + y_1^2 - 2aex_1 + a^2e^2$

and $\quad m = x_1^2 + y_1^2 + 2aex_1 + a^2e^2 \quad$ [$l - m$ method]

Then, Eq. (i) can be written as

$$\sqrt{l} + \sqrt{m} = 2a \quad \text{...(ii)}$$

$$\text{and} \quad l - m = -4aex_1$$

$$\text{or} \quad (\sqrt{l} + \sqrt{m})(\sqrt{l} - \sqrt{m}) = -4aex_1$$

$$\text{or} \quad 2a(\sqrt{l} - \sqrt{m}) = -4aex_1 \quad \text{[from Eq. (ii)]}$$

$$\text{or} \quad \sqrt{l} - \sqrt{m} = -2ex_1 \quad \text{...(iii)}$$

On adding Eqs. (ii) and (iii), we get

$$2\sqrt{l} = 2a - 2ex_1 \text{ or } \sqrt{l} = a - ex_1$$

On squaring both sides, we get

$$l = a^2 - 2aex_1 + e^2x_1^2$$

$$\Rightarrow \quad x_1^2 + y_1^2 - 2aex_1 + a^2e^2 = a^2 - 2aex_1 + e^2x_1^2$$

$$\Rightarrow \quad (1 - e^2)x_1^2 + y_1^2 = a^2(1 - e^2)$$

$$\text{or} \quad \frac{x_1^2}{a^2} + \frac{y_1^2}{a^2(1 - e^2)} = 1$$

$$\text{or} \quad \frac{x_1^2}{a^2} + \frac{y_1^2}{b^2} = 1 \quad [\because b^2 = a^2(1 - e^2)]$$

Replacing (x_1, y_1) to (x, y), then

$$\frac{x^2}{a^2} + \frac{y^2}{b^2} = 1$$

which is the required locus of P. **Hence proved.**

Example 67. Find the equation of the locus of a point which moves so that the difference of its distances from the points (3, 0) and (–3, 0) is 4 units.

Sol. Let $P(x_1, y_1)$ be the moving point whose locus is required and $A(3, 0)$ and $B(-3, 0)$ be the given fixed points.

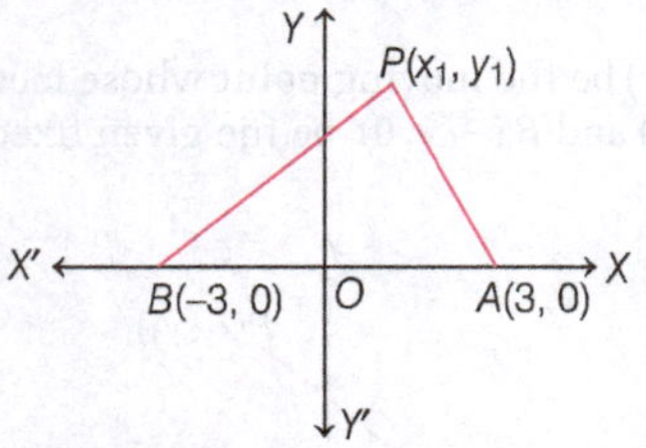

By hypothesis, $|PB| - |PA| = 4$ (assume $|PB| > |PA|$)

$$\Rightarrow \sqrt{(x_1+3)^2 + (y_1-0)^2} - \sqrt{(x_1-3)^2 + (y_1-0)^2} = 4$$

$$\Rightarrow \sqrt{(x_1^2 + y_1^2 + 6x_1 + 9)} = 4 + \sqrt{(x_1^2 + y_1^2 - 6x_1 + 9)}$$

On squaring both sides, we get

$$x_1^2 + y_1^2 + 6x_1 + 9 = 16 + x_1^2 + y_1^2 - 6x_1 + 9 + 8\sqrt{(x_1^2 + y_1^2 - 6x_1 + 9)}$$

or $$(12x_1 - 16) = 8\sqrt{(x_1^2 + y_1^2 - 6x_1 + 9)}$$

or $$(3x_1 - 4) = 2\sqrt{(x_1^2 + y_1^2 - 6x_1 + 9)}$$

Again, on squaring both sides, we get

$$9x_1^2 - 24x_1 + 16 = 4x_1^2 + 4y_1^2 - 24x_1 + 36$$

or $$5x_1^2 - 4y_1^2 = 20 \Rightarrow \frac{x_1^2}{4} - \frac{y_1^2}{5} = 1$$

Replacing (x_1, y_1) by (x, y), then $\frac{x^2}{4} - \frac{y^2}{5} = 1$

which is the required locus of P.

Alternate Solution

($l - m$ method)

Since, $|PB| - |PA| = 4$

$$\Rightarrow \sqrt{(x_1+3)^2 + (y_1-0)^2} - \sqrt{(x_1-3)^2 + (y_1-0)^2} = 4$$

$$\Rightarrow \sqrt{(x_1^2 + y_1^2 + 6x_1 + 9)} - \sqrt{(x_1^2 + y_1^2 - 6x_1 + 9)} = 4 \quad \text{...(i)}$$

Let $l = x_1^2 + y_1^2 + 6x_1 + 9$

and $m = x_1^2 + y_1^2 - 6x_1 + 9$

Then, Eq. (i) can be written as

$$\sqrt{l} - \sqrt{m} = 4 \quad \text{... (ii)}$$

and $l - m = 12x_1$

$$\Rightarrow (\sqrt{l} + \sqrt{m})(\sqrt{l} - \sqrt{m}) = 12x_1$$

$$\Rightarrow (\sqrt{l} + \sqrt{m})(4) = 12x_1 \quad \text{[from Eq. (ii)]}$$

$$\Rightarrow \sqrt{l} + \sqrt{m} = 3x_1 \quad \text{...(iii)}$$

On adding Eqs. (ii) and (iii), we get $2\sqrt{l} = (3x_1 + 4)$

On squaring both sides, we get $4l = 9x_1^2 + 24x_1 + 16$

$$\Rightarrow 4(x_1^2 + y_1^2 + 6x_1 + 9) = 9x_1^2 + 24x_1 + 16$$

$$\Rightarrow 5x_1^2 - 4y_1^2 = 20 \text{ or } \frac{x_1^2}{4} - \frac{y_1^2}{5} = 1$$

Replacing (x_1, y_1) by (x, y), then $\frac{x^2}{4} - \frac{y^2}{5} = 1$

which is the required locus of P.

Example 68. The ends of the hypotenuse of a right angled triangle are (6, 0) and (0, 6). Find the locus of the third vertex.

Sol. Let $C(x_1, y_1)$ be the moving point (third vertex) whose locus is required and $A(6, 0)$ and $B(0, 6)$ be the given vertices.

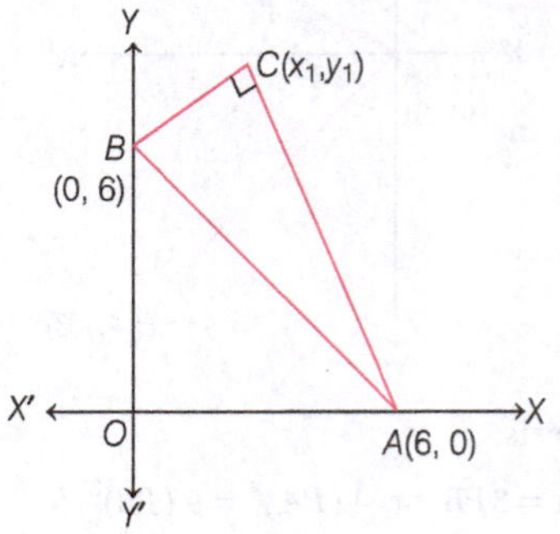

By hypothesis,

$$(AC)^2 + (BC)^2 = (AB)^2 \quad [\because \angle ACB = 90^\circ]$$

$$\Rightarrow (x_1-6)^2 + (y_1-0)^2 + (x_1-0)^2 + (y_1-6)^2 = 6^2 + 6^2$$

$$\Rightarrow 2x_1^2 + 2y_1^2 - 12x_1 - 12y_1 = 0$$

or $$x_1^2 + y_1^2 - 6x_1 - 6y_1 = 0$$

Replacing (x_1, y_1) by (x, y), then

$$x^2 + y^2 - 6x - 6y = 0$$

which is the required locus of third vertex C.

Example 69. Find the equation of the locus of a point which moves so that the sum of their distances from (3, 0) and (–3, 0) is less than 9.

Sol. Let $P(x_1, y_1)$ be the moving point whose locus is required and $A(3, 0)$ and $B(-3, 0)$ are the given points.

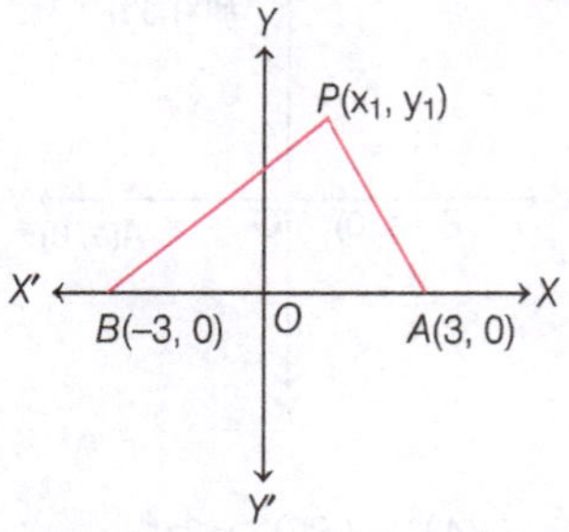

By hypothesis, $|PA| + |PB| < 9$

$$\Rightarrow \sqrt{\{(x_1-3)^2 + (y_1-0)^2\}} + \sqrt{\{(x_1+3)^2 + (y_1-0)^2\}} < 9$$

$$\Rightarrow \sqrt{(x_1^2 + y_1^2 - 6x_1 + 9)} < 9 - \sqrt{(x_1^2 + y_1^2 + 6x_1 + 9)}$$

On squaring, we get

$$(x_1^2 + y_1^2 - 6x_1 + 9) < (81 + x_1^2 + y_1^2 + 6x_1 + 9 - 18\sqrt{(x_1^2 + y_1^2 + 6x_1 + 9)})$$

$$[\because a < b \Rightarrow a^2 < b^2 \text{ provided } a > 0]$$

$$\Rightarrow -12x_1 - 81 < -18\sqrt{(x_1^2 + y_1^2 + 6x_1 + 9)}$$

$$\Rightarrow \quad (4x_1 + 27) > 6\sqrt{(x_1^2 + y_1^2 + 6x_1 + 9)}$$

$[\because$ if $a > b$, then $-a < -b]$

On squaring, we get

$$16x_1^2 + 729 + 216x_1 > 36x_1^2 + 36y_1^2 + 216x_1 + 324$$

$$\Rightarrow \quad 20x_1^2 + 36y_1^2 < 405$$

Replacing (x_1, y_1) by (x, y), then

$$20x^2 + 36y^2 < 405$$

which is the required locus of P.

Example 70. Find the locus of a point whose coordinate are given by $x = t + t^2$, $y = 2t + 1$, where t is variable.

Sol. Given, $\quad x = t + t^2 \quad$ ...(i)

and $\quad y = 2t + 1 \quad$ ...(ii)

From Eq. (ii), $\quad t = \left(\dfrac{y-1}{2}\right) \quad$ ...(iii)

On eliminating t from Eqs. (i) and (iii), we get required locus as

$$x = \left(\frac{y-1}{2}\right) + \left(\frac{y-1}{2}\right)^2$$

$$\Rightarrow \quad x = \left(\frac{y-1}{2}\right)\left(1 + \frac{y-1}{2}\right) \Rightarrow x = \left(\frac{y-1}{2}\right)\left(\frac{y+1}{2}\right)$$

or $\quad 4x = y^2 - 1 \quad$ or $\quad y^2 = 4x + 1$

Example 71. A stick of length l rests against the floor and a wall of a room. If the stick begins to slide on the floor, find the locus of its middle point.

Sol. Let the cross section of the floor and wall be taken as the coordinate axes and AB be one of the position of the stick. Let the mid-point of AB be $P(x_1, y_1)$, then coordinates of A and B are $(2x_1, 0)$ and $(0, 2y_1)$ respectively.

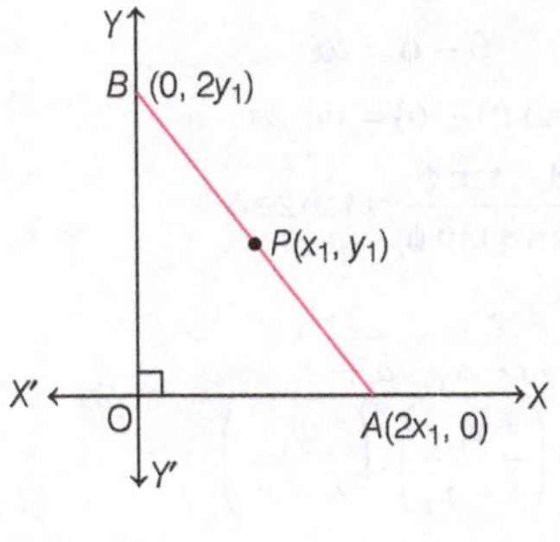

But given, $|AB| = l$

$$\Rightarrow \quad (AB)^2 = l^2$$

$$\Rightarrow \quad (2x_1 - 0)^2 + (0 - 2y_1)^2 = l^2$$

$$\Rightarrow \quad 4x_1^2 + 4y_1^2 = l^2$$

Replacing (x_1, y_1) by (x, y), then

$$4(x^2 + y^2) = l^2$$

which is the required locus of P.

Alternate Solution

Since, $\quad |AB| = l$

Let $\quad \angle OAB = \alpha$

$\therefore \quad OA = l\cos\alpha \quad$ and $\quad OB = l\sin\alpha$

Then, $\quad A \equiv (l\cos\alpha, 0)$

and $\quad B \equiv (0, l\sin\alpha)$

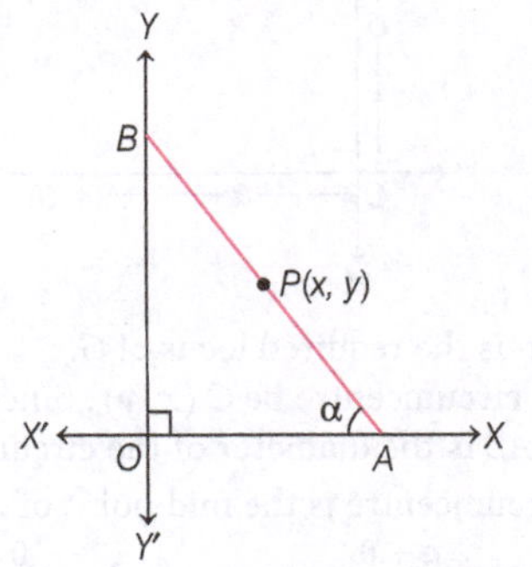

Let $P(x, y)$ be the mid-point of AB, then

$2x = l\cos\alpha \quad$ ...(i)

$2y = l\sin\alpha \quad$ ...(ii)

On squaring and then adding Eqs. (i) and (ii), we get

$$4(x^2 + y^2) = l^2$$

which is the required locus of P.

Example 72. Find the locus of the point of intersection of the lines $x\cos\alpha + y\sin\alpha = a$ and $x\sin\alpha - y\cos\alpha = b$, where α is variable.

Sol. Given equations are

$x\cos\alpha + y\sin\alpha = a \quad$ ...(i)

and $\quad x\sin\alpha - y\cos\alpha = b \quad$ ...(ii)

Here, α is a variable. On squaring and adding Eqs. (i) and (ii), we get required locus as

$$(x\cos\alpha + y\sin\alpha)^2 + (x\sin\alpha - y\cos\alpha)^2 = a^2 + b^2$$

or $\quad (x^2\cos^2\alpha + y^2\sin^2\alpha + 2xy\cos\alpha\sin\alpha)$

$$+ (x^2\sin^2\alpha + y^2\cos^2\alpha - 2xy\sin\alpha\cos\alpha) = a^2 + b^2$$

$$\Rightarrow \quad x^2(\cos^2\alpha + \sin^2\alpha) + y^2(\sin^2\alpha + \cos^2\alpha) = a^2 + b^2$$

$$\therefore \quad x^2 + y^2 = a^2 + b^2$$

Example 73. A variable line cuts X-axis at A, Y-axis at B, where $OA = a$, $OB = b$ (O as origin) such that $a^2 + b^2 = 1$.

Find the locus of

(i) centroid of ΔOAB. (ii) circumcentre of ΔOAB.

Sol. (i) Coordinates of A and B are $(a, 0)$ and $(0, b)$ respectively. If centroid of ΔOAB be $G(x, y)$.

Then, $\quad x = \dfrac{0 + a + 0}{3} \Rightarrow a = 3x$

and $\quad y = \dfrac{0 + 0 + b}{3} \Rightarrow b = 3y$

On substituting the values of a and b in $a^2 + b^2 = 1$, we get

$$(3x)^2 + (3y)^2 = 1 \text{ or } x^2 + y^2 = \frac{1}{9}$$

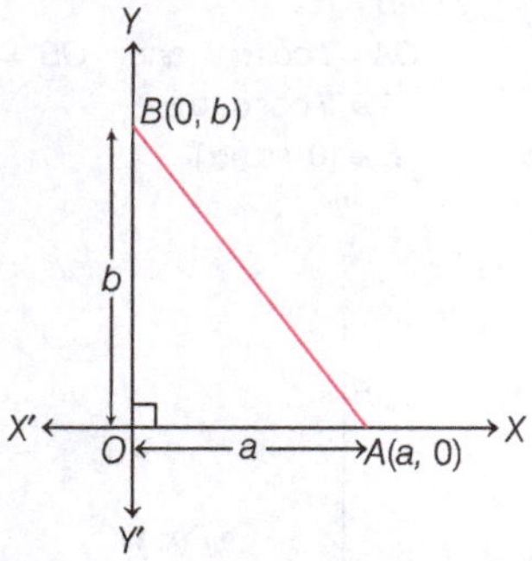

which is the required locus of G.

(ii) If the circumcentre be $C(x, y)$. Since, $\angle AOB = 90°$, then AB is the diameter of the circumcircle OAB.

∴ Circumcentre is the mid-point of AB.

Then, $x = \frac{a+0}{2} \Rightarrow a = 2x$ and $y = \frac{0+b}{2} \Rightarrow b = 2y$

On substituting the values of a and b in $a^2 + b^2 = 1$, we get

$$(2x)^2 + (2y)^2 = 1 \text{ or } x^2 + y^2 = \frac{1}{4}$$

which is the required locus of C.

JEE SCANNER

Example Similar to PYQ Asked in JEE Main 2024

If the locus of the point whose distances from the point (3, 1) and (1, 4) are in the ratio 4 : 3 is $ax^2 + by^2 + cxy + dx + ey + 182 = 0$, then the value of $a^2 + b^2 + d + e$ is equal to

(a) 5 (b) 10 (c) 15 (d) 2

Sol. (b) Let the point be (h, k).

According to the question, $\frac{\sqrt{(h-3)^2 + (k-1)^2}}{\sqrt{(h-1)^2 + (k-4)^2}} = \frac{4}{3}$

On squaring and simplifying, we get

$$9[(h-3)^2 + (k-1)^2] = 16[(h-1)^2 + (k-4)^2]$$

$$\Rightarrow 7h^2 + 7k^2 + 22h - 110k + 182 = 0$$

Now, replace (h, k) with (x, y), so the locus is

$$7x^2 + 7y^2 + 22x - 110y + 182 = 0$$

On comparing it with

$ax^2 + by^2 + cxy + dx + ey + 182 = 0$, we have

$$a = 7, b = 7, c = 0, d = 22, e = -110$$

$$\therefore a^2 + b^2 + d + e = 49 + 49 + 22 - 110 = 10$$

Skill Builder

If the locus of the point whose distances from the points (2, 3) and (5, 4) are in the ratio 3 : 2 is $ax^2 + by^2 + cxy + dx + ey + 317 = 0$, then the value of $a^3 + b^3 + d + e$ is equal to

(a) 225 (b) 124

(c) 128 (d) 258

For Sol.

■ **For more Practice** See Q. 6 of Milestone Practice 1.4.

Example 74. Two points P and Q are given, R is a variable point on one side of the line PQ such that $\angle RPQ - \angle RQP$ is a positive constant 2α. Find the locus of the point R.

Sol. Let the X-axis along QP and the middle point of PQ be origin and let coordinates of moving point R be (x_1, y_1).

Let $OP = OQ = a$

Then, coordinates of P and Q are $(a, 0)$ and $(-a, 0)$, respectively.

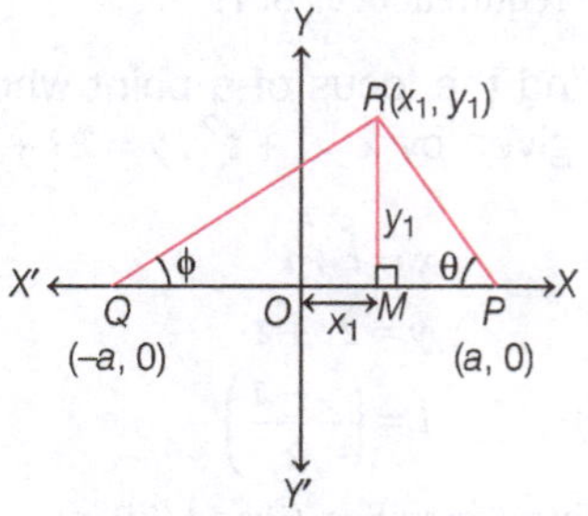

Draw RM perpendicular on QP

$\therefore \quad OM = x_1$

and $\quad MR = y_1$

and let $\quad \angle RPM = \theta$

and $\quad \angle RQM = \phi$

Now, in ΔRMP,

$$\tan\theta = \frac{RM}{MP} = \frac{RM}{OP - OM} = \frac{y_1}{a - x_1} \quad \text{...(i)}$$

and in ΔRMQ,

$$\tan\phi = \frac{RM}{QM} = \frac{RM}{OQ + OM} = \frac{y_1}{a + x_1} \quad \text{...(ii)}$$

But given

$$\angle RPQ - \angle RQP = 2\alpha \quad \text{[constant]}$$

$$\Rightarrow \theta - \phi = 2\alpha$$

$$\therefore \tan(\theta - \phi) = \tan 2\alpha$$

$$\Rightarrow \frac{\tan\theta - \tan\phi}{1 + \tan\theta \tan\phi} = \tan 2\alpha$$

$$\Rightarrow \frac{\frac{y_1}{a - x_1} - \frac{y_1}{a + x_1}}{1 + \left(\frac{y_1}{a - x_1}\right) \cdot \left(\frac{y_1}{a + x_1}\right)} = \tan 2\alpha$$

[from Eqs. (i) and (ii)]

$$\Rightarrow \frac{2x_1y_1}{a^2 - x_1^2 + y_1^2} = \tan 2\alpha$$

or $$a^2 - x_1^2 + y_1^2 = 2x_1y_1 \cot 2\alpha$$

or $$x_1^2 - y_1^2 + 2x_1y_1 \cot 2\alpha = a^2$$

Hence, locus of the point $R(x_1, y_1)$ is

$$x^2 - y^2 + 2xy \cot 2\alpha = a^2$$

1.19 Transformations of Axes

In coordinate geometry, we have discussed the coordinates of a point or the equation of a curve are always considered on taking a fixed point O as the origin and two perpendicular straight lines through O as the coordinates axes. For convenience the coordinates of the point or the equation of the curve changes when either the origin is changed or the direction of axes or both suitably. These processes in coordinate geometry are known as the transformations or change of axes.

This process of transformation of coordinates will be of great advantage to solve most of the problems very easily.

(i) Change of origin *OR* Shifting of origin (Translation of Axes)

To change the origin of coordinates to another point (h, k) whereas the directions of axes remain unaltered.

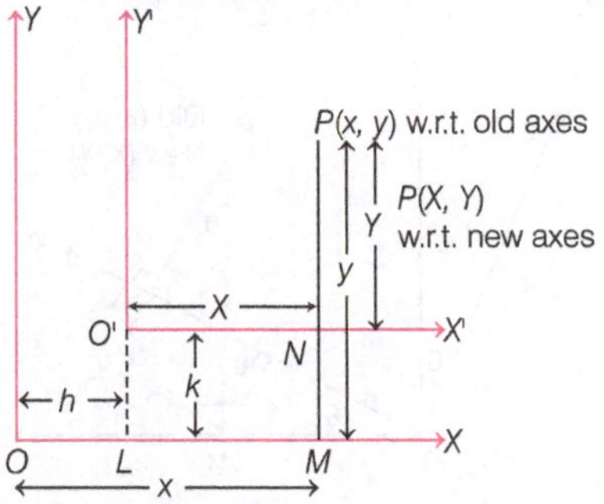

Let O be the origin of coordinates and OX, OY be the original coordinate axes. Let O' be the new origin and (h, k) its coordinates referred to the original axes. Draw two lines $O'X'$ and $O'Y'$ through O' and parallel to OX and OY, respectively.

Let $P(x, y)$ be any point referred to the original axes OX, OY. Again, suppose that the coordinates of the same point P referred to the new axes $O'X', O'Y'$ are (X, Y).

From O' draw $O'L$ perpendicular to OX, from P draw PM perpendicular to OX to meet $O'X'$ in N. Then,

$$OL = h, O'L = k, OM = x, PM = y, O'N = X$$

and $PN = Y$

We have, $x = OM = OL + LM = OL + O'N = h + X$

i.e. $\boldsymbol{x = X + h}$ ...(i)

and $y = PM = PN + NM = PN + O'L = Y + k$

i.e. $\boldsymbol{y = Y + k}$ ...(ii)

From Eqs. (i) and (ii), we get

$$X = x - h$$

and $Y = y - k$

Thus, if origin is shifted to point (h, k) without rotation of axes, then new equation of curve can be obtained by putting $x + h$ in place of x and $y + k$ in place of y.

In this case, axes are shifted parallel to themselves, then it is also called **Transformation by parallel axes.**

JEE Focus Points

1. **Inverse translation or shifting the origin back** Sometimes it is required to shift the new origin back. Then, putting $x - h$ in place of x and $y - k$ in place of y in any equation of curve referred to the new origin to get the corresponding equation referred to the old origin.
2. The above transformation is true whether the axes be rectangular or oblique.

Concept Inside Video

Example 75. Find the equation of the curve $2x^2 + y^2 - 3x + 5y - 8 = 0$ when the origin is transferred to the point $(-1, 2)$ without changing the direction of axes.

Sol. Here, we want to shift the origin to the point $(-1, 2)$ without changing the direction of axes. Then, we replace x by $x - 1$ and y by $y + 2$ in the equation of given curve, then the transformed equation is

$$2(x-1)^2 + (y+2)^2 - 3(x-1) + 5(y+2) - 8 = 0$$

$$\Rightarrow \quad 2x^2 + y^2 - 7x + 9y + 11 = 0$$

Example 76. The equation of a curve referred to the new axes, axes retaining their direction and origin is $(4, 5)$ is $x^2 + y^2 = 36$. Find the equation referred to the original axes.

Sol. Here, we want to shift $(4, 5)$ to the origin without changing the direction of axes. Then, we replace x by $x - 4$ and y by $y - 5$ in the equation of given curve, then the required equation is

$$(x-4)^2 + (y-5)^2 = 36$$

$$\Rightarrow \quad x^2 + y^2 - 8x - 10y + 5 = 0$$

Example 77. Shift the origin to a suitable point so that the equation $y^2 + 4y + 8x - 2 = 0$ will not contain term in y and the constant.

Sol. Let the origin be shifted to the point (h, k) without changing the direction of axes. Then, we replace x by $x + h$ and y by $y + k$ in the equation of the given, curve then the transformed equation is

$$(y+k)^2 + 4(y+k) + 8(x+h) - 2 = 0$$

$$\Rightarrow \quad y^2 + (2k+4)y + 8x + (k^2 + 4k + 8h - 2) = 0$$

Since, this equation is required to be free from the term containing y and the constant, we get

$$2k + 4 = 0 \quad \text{and} \quad k^2 + 4k + 8h - 2 = 0$$

$$\therefore \quad k = -2 \quad \text{and} \quad h = \frac{3}{4}$$

Hence, the point to which the origin be shifted is $\left(\frac{3}{4}, -2\right)$.

Example 78. At what point the origin be shifted, if the coordinates of a point $(-1, 8)$ become $(-7, 3)$?

Sol. Let the origin be shifted to the point (h, k) without changing the direction of axes. Then, we replace x by $x+h$ and y by $y+k$ and we get new coordinates. Here, given old coordinates and new coordinates are $(-1, 8)$ and $(-7, 3)$, respectively.

Here, $-1+h=-7$ and $8+k=3$

$\Rightarrow$ $h=-6$ and $k=-5$

Hence, the origin must be shifted to $(-6, -5)$.

(ii) Rotation of Axes (Change of Directions of Axes)

To find the change in the coordinates of a point when the directions of axes are rotated through an angle θ, the origin being fixed.

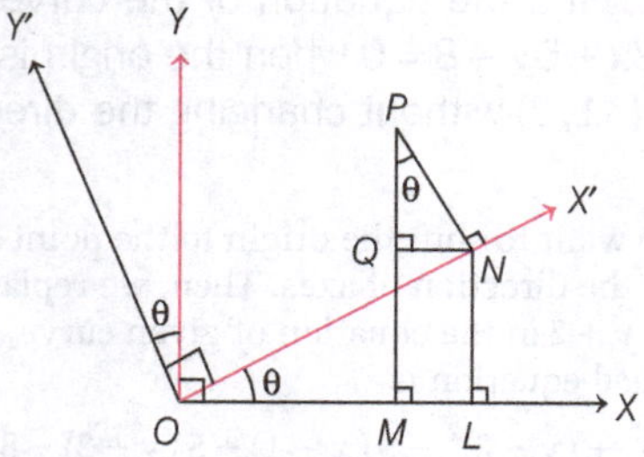

Let OX and OY be the original system of coordinate axes. Let OX' and OY' be the new axes obtained by rotating the original axes through an angle θ. Let P be a point in the plane whose coordinates be (x, y) and (X, Y) referred to old and new axes, respectively. Draw PM and PN perpendiculars to OX and OX' and also NL and NQ perpendiculars to OX and PM, we get

$$OM = x, PM = y, ON = X \text{ and } PN = Y$$

$\because$ Angle between any two lines = angle between their perpendiculars i.e. $\angle XOX' = \angle NPM = \theta$

Now, $x = OM = OL - ML$

$= OL - QN = ON\cos\theta - PN\sin\theta$

$= X\cos\theta - Y\sin\theta$

i.e. $x = X\cos\theta - Y\sin\theta$ ...(i)

and $y = PM = PQ + QM = PQ + NL$

$= PN\cos\theta + ON\sin\theta$

$= Y\cos\theta + X\sin\theta$

i.e. $y = X\sin\theta + Y\cos\theta$ ...(ii)

Now, multiplying Eq. (i) by $\cos\theta$ and Eq. (ii) by $\sin\theta$ and adding we get

$$X = x\cos\theta + y\sin\theta \quad ...(iii)$$

Also, on subtracting the product of Eq. (i) by $\sin\theta$ from the product of Eq. (ii) by $\cos\theta$, we get

$$Y = -x\sin\theta + y\cos\theta \quad ...(iv)$$

Also, $x^2 + y^2 = X^2 + Y^2 = OP^2$ are unchanged

i.e. the distance of the point P from the origin O remains unaffected by the rotation of axes.

JEE SPIKE

When the axes are rotated through θ, replace (x, y) by $(x\cos\theta - y\sin\theta, x\sin\theta + y\cos\theta)$.

Shifting the coordinate axes back Some times it is required to shift the new coordinates axes back. Then, replace (x, y) by $(x\cos\theta + y\sin\theta, -x\sin\theta + y\cos\theta)$.

Independent Proof (Alternate)

The relations $X = x\cos\theta + y\sin\theta$ and $Y = -x\sin\theta + y\cos\theta$ can be obtained independently.

Proof Draw PM and PN perpendiculars to OX and OX' and also ML and MQ perpendiculars to PN and OX', respectively.

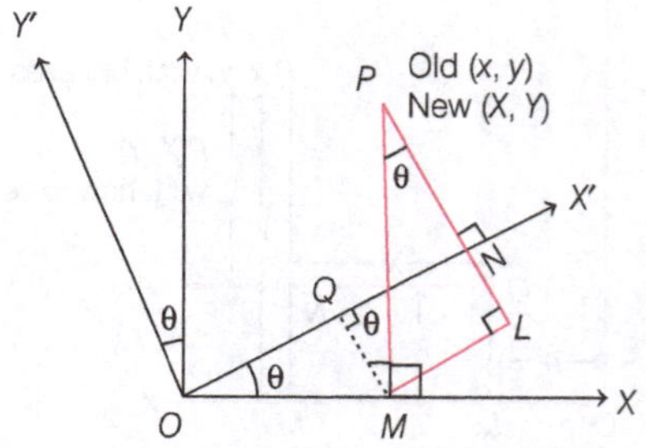

We have, $OM = x, PM = y, ON = X$ and $PN = Y$

Also, angle between any two lines

= angle between their perpendiculars lines

i.e. $\angle XOX' = \angle MPN = \angle PMQ = \theta$

$\therefore$ $X = ON = OQ + QN$

$= OQ + ML$

$= OM\cos\theta + PM\sin\theta$

$[\because OQ = OM\cos\theta \text{ and } ML = PM\sin\theta]$

$= x\cos\theta + y\sin\theta$

i.e. $X = x\cos\theta + y\sin\theta$

and $Y = PN = PL - NL = PL - QM$

$= PM\cos\theta - OM\sin\theta$

$[\because PL = PM\cos\theta \text{ and } QM = OM\sin\theta]$

$= y\cos\theta - x\sin\theta$

i.e. $Y = -x\sin\theta + y\cos\theta$

The results in Eqs. (i), (ii), (iii) and (iv) can be conveniently remembered by the following methods.

(i) **Light heavy method** Let x, y be light and X, Y be heavy, then heavy X, Y down and x, y up, then

	x	y
X	$\cos\theta$	$\sin\theta$
Y	$-\sin\theta$	$\cos\theta$

third row is obtained by differentiating second row with respect to θ.

For remembrance C S (Civil Services)

$$\begin{matrix} C & S \\ \downarrow & \downarrow \\ \cos\theta & \sin\theta \\ \downarrow & \downarrow \\ -\sin\theta & \cos\theta \end{matrix} \quad \left(\text{i.e. } \begin{matrix} C \to \cos\theta \\ S \to \sin\theta \end{matrix}\right) \quad \left(\begin{matrix} (\cos\theta)' = -\sin\theta \\ (\sin\theta)' = \cos\theta \end{matrix}\right)$$

(a) Finding x and y in terms of X and Y

x = sum of the products of the elements in the left most column with the corresponding elements of the first column

i.e. $x = X\cos\theta - Y\sin\theta$

and y = sum of the products of the elements in the left most column with the corresponding elements of the second column

i.e. $y = X\sin\theta + Y\cos\theta$

Hence, $\left.\begin{aligned} x &= X\cos\theta - Y\sin\theta \\ y &= X\sin\theta + Y\cos\theta \end{aligned}\right\}$

(b) Finding X and Y in terms of x and y

X = sum of the products of the elements of top-row with the corresponding elements of first row.

i.e. $X = x\cos\theta + y\sin\theta$

and Y = sum of the products of the elements of top-row with the corresponding elements of second row

i.e. $Y = -x\sin\theta + y\cos\theta$

Hence, $\left.\begin{aligned} X &= x\cos\theta + y\sin\theta \\ Y &= -x\sin\theta + y\cos\theta \end{aligned}\right\}$

(ii) **Matrix method**

$$\begin{bmatrix} X \\ Y \end{bmatrix} = \begin{bmatrix} \cos\theta & \sin\theta \\ -\sin\theta & \cos\theta \end{bmatrix} \begin{bmatrix} x \\ y \end{bmatrix} = A \begin{bmatrix} x \\ y \end{bmatrix} \quad \text{[say]}$$

and $$\begin{bmatrix} x \\ y \end{bmatrix} = \begin{bmatrix} \cos\theta & -\sin\theta \\ \sin\theta & \cos\theta \end{bmatrix} \begin{bmatrix} X \\ Y \end{bmatrix} = A' \begin{bmatrix} X \\ Y \end{bmatrix}$$

where A' is the transpose matrix of A.

(iii) **Complex number method**

Let $z = x + iy$

and $Z = X + iY$, where $i = \sqrt{-1}$

Then, $z = Ze^{i\theta}$ ...(i)

i.e. $(x + iy) = (X + iY)(\cos\theta + i\sin\theta)$

On comparing real and imaginary parts, we get

$$\left.\begin{aligned} x &= X\cos\theta - Y\sin\theta \\ y &= X\sin\theta + Y\cos\theta \end{aligned}\right\}$$

Again, from Eq. (i), $Z = ze^{-i\theta}$

i.e. $(X + iY) = (x + iy)(\cos\theta - i\sin\theta)$

On comparing real and imaginary parts, we get

$$\left.\begin{aligned} X &= x\cos\theta + y\sin\theta \\ Y &= -x\sin\theta + y\cos\theta \end{aligned}\right\}$$

Example 79. If the axes are turned through 45°, then find the transformed form of the equation $3x^2 + 3y^2 + 2xy = 2$.

Sol. Here, $\theta = 45°$

So, $\sin\theta = \cos\theta = \dfrac{1}{\sqrt{2}}$

Replacing (x, y) by $(x\cos\theta - y\sin\theta, x\sin\theta + y\cos\theta)$

i.e. $\left(\dfrac{x-y}{\sqrt{2}}, \dfrac{x+y}{\sqrt{2}}\right)$

Then, $3x^2 + 3y^2 + 2xy = 2$ becomes

$$3\left(\frac{x-y}{\sqrt{2}}\right)^2 + 3\left(\frac{x+y}{\sqrt{2}}\right)^2 + 2\left(\frac{x-y}{\sqrt{2}}\right)\left(\frac{x+y}{\sqrt{2}}\right) = 2$$

$\Rightarrow$ $3(2x^2 + 2y^2) + 2(x^2 - y^2) = 4$

$\Rightarrow$ $8x^2 + 4y^2 = 4$

or $2x^2 + y^2 = 1$

which is free from the term containing xy.

Example 80. Prove that if the axes be turned through $\dfrac{\pi}{4}$ the equation $x^2 - y^2 = a^2$ is transformed to the form $xy = \lambda$. Find the value of λ.

Sol. Here, $\theta = \dfrac{\pi}{4}$

So, $\sin\theta = \cos\theta = \dfrac{1}{\sqrt{2}}$

Replacing (x, y) by $(x\cos\theta - y\sin\theta, x\sin\theta + y\cos\theta)$

i.e. $\left(\dfrac{x-y}{\sqrt{2}}, \dfrac{x+y}{\sqrt{2}}\right)$,

then $x^2 - y^2 = a^2$ becomes

$$\left(\frac{x-y}{\sqrt{2}}\right)^2 - \left(\frac{x+y}{\sqrt{2}}\right)^2 = a^2$$

$$\Rightarrow \left(\frac{x-y}{\sqrt{2}}+\frac{x+y}{\sqrt{2}}\right)\left(\frac{x-y}{\sqrt{2}}-\frac{x+y}{\sqrt{2}}\right)=a^2$$

$$\Rightarrow \left(\frac{2x}{\sqrt{2}}\right)\left(\frac{-2y}{\sqrt{2}}\right)=a^2 \quad \text{or} \quad xy=-\frac{a^2}{2}$$

On comparing it with $xy=\lambda$, then we get

$$\lambda=-\frac{a^2}{2}.$$

Example 81. Through what angle should the axes be rotated so that the equation $9x^2-2\sqrt{3}\,xy+7y^2=10$ may be changed to $3x^2+5y^2=5$?

Sol. Let angle be θ. Then, replacing (x, y) by $(x\cos\theta-y\sin\theta,\ x\sin\theta+y\cos\theta)$

Then, $9x^2-2\sqrt{3}xy+7y^2=10$ becomes

$$9(x\cos\theta-y\sin\theta)^2-2\sqrt{3}(x\cos\theta-y\sin\theta)(x\sin\theta+y\cos\theta)+7(x\sin\theta+y\cos\theta)^2=10$$

$$\Rightarrow x^2(9\cos^2\theta-2\sqrt{3}\sin\theta\cos\theta+7\sin^2\theta)+2xy(-9\sin\theta\cos\theta-\sqrt{3}\cos 2\theta+7\sin\theta\cos\theta)+y^2(9\sin^2\theta+2\sqrt{3}\sin\theta\cos\theta+7\cos^2\theta)=10$$

On comparing with $3x^2+5y^2=5$, we get

coefficient of $xy=0$

$$-9\sin\theta\cos\theta-\sqrt{3}\cos 2\theta+7\sin\theta\cos\theta=0$$

or $\quad \sin 2\theta=-\sqrt{3}\cos 2\theta$

or $\quad \tan 2\theta=-\sqrt{3}=\tan(180°-60°)$

or $\quad 2\theta=120°$

$\therefore \quad \theta=60°$

Example 82. If (x, y) and (X, Y) are the coordinates of the same point referred to two sets of rectangular axes with the same origin and if $ux+vy$, when u and v are independent of X and Y become $VX+UY$, show that $u^2+v^2=U^2+V^2$

Sol. Let the axes rotate through an angle θ and (x, y) the point with respect to old axes and (X, Y) be the coordinates with respect to new axes.

Then, $x+iy=(X+iY)e^{i\theta}=(X+iY)(\cos\theta+i\sin\theta)$

On comparing real and imaginary parts, we get

$$\begin{cases} x=X\cos\theta-Y\sin\theta \\ y=X\sin\theta+Y\cos\theta \end{cases}$$

Then, $ux+vy=u(X\cos\theta-Y\sin\theta)+v(X\sin\theta+Y\cos\theta)$
$=(u\cos\theta+v\sin\theta)X+(-u\sin\theta+v\cos\theta)Y$

but given new curve $VX+UY$.

Then, $VX+UY=(u\cos\theta+v\sin\theta)X+(-u\sin\theta+v\cos\theta)Y$

On comparing the coefficients of X and Y, we get

$$V=u\cos\theta+v\sin\theta \quad \text{...(i)}$$

and $$U=-u\sin\theta+v\cos\theta \quad \text{...(ii)}$$

On squaring and adding Eqs. (i) and (ii), we get

$$V^2+U^2=(u\cos\theta+v\sin\theta)^2+(-u\sin\theta+v\cos\theta)^2=u^2+v^2$$

Hence, $\quad u^2+v^2=U^2+V^2$

Alternate Solution

$$\begin{bmatrix} x \\ y \end{bmatrix}=\begin{bmatrix} \cos\theta & -\sin\theta \\ \sin\theta & \cos\theta \end{bmatrix}\begin{bmatrix} X \\ Y \end{bmatrix}=\begin{bmatrix} X\cos\theta-Y\sin\theta \\ X\sin\theta+Y\cos\theta \end{bmatrix} \quad \text{...(i)}$$

$$\because\ ux+vy=[u\ \ v]\begin{bmatrix} x \\ y \end{bmatrix}=[u\ v]\begin{bmatrix} X\cos\theta-Y\sin\theta \\ X\sin\theta+Y\cos\theta \end{bmatrix} \quad \text{[from Eq. (i)]}$$

$$=uX\cos\theta-uY\sin\theta+vX\sin\theta+vY\cos\theta$$
$$=X(u\cos\theta+v\sin\theta)+Y(-u\sin\theta+v\cos\theta)$$

but given new curve $VX+UY$.

Then, $VX+UY=X(u\cos\theta+v\sin\theta)+Y(-u\sin\theta+v\cos\theta)$

On comparing the coefficients of X and Y, we get

$$V=u\cos\theta+v\sin\theta \quad \text{...(ii)}$$
$$U=-u\sin\theta+v\cos\theta \quad \text{...(iii)}$$

On squaring and adding Eqs. (ii) and (iii), we get

$$u^2+v^2=U^2+V^2$$

Time Saving Technique

$$ux+vy=R_e((u-iv)(x+iy))=R_e((u-iv)(X+iY)e^{i\theta}) \quad \text{...(i)}$$

and $$VX+UY=R_e((V-iU)(X+iY)) \quad \text{...(ii)}$$

From Eqs. (i) and (ii), we get

$$V-iU=(u-iv)e^{i\theta}$$

On taking modulus both sides, then

$$|V-iU|=|u-iv||e^{i\theta}|$$

$$\Rightarrow \sqrt{(V^2+U^2)}=\sqrt{u^2+v^2}\cdot 1$$

or $\quad u^2+v^2=U^2+V^2$

(iii) Double Transformation (Origin Shifted and Axes Rotated)

If origin is shifted to the point $O'(h, k)$ and at the same time the directions of axes are rotated through an angle θ in the anti-clockwise sense such that new coordinates of $P(x, y)$ become (X, Y).

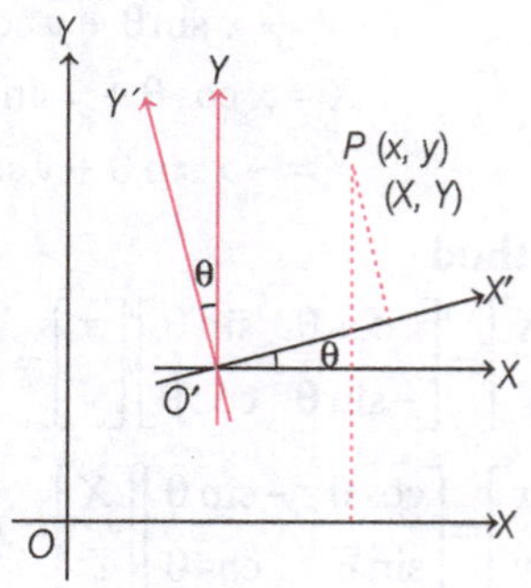

Then, $\quad x=h+X\cos\theta-Y\sin\theta \quad \text{...(i)}$

and $\quad y=k+X\sin\theta+Y\cos\theta \quad \text{...(ii)}$

Example 83. What does the equation $2x^2 + 4xy - 5y^2 + 20x - 22y - 14 = 0$ becomes when referred to rectangular axes through the point $(-2, -3)$, the new axes being inclined at an angle of $45°$ with the old ?

Sol. Let $O'(-2, -3)$ be the new origin and axes are rotated about O' through an angle 45° in anti-clockwise direction, then replacing x and y by

$$-2 + x\cos 45° - y\sin 45°$$

and $$-3 + x\sin 45° + y\cos 45°$$

i.e. $-2 + \left(\frac{x-y}{\sqrt{2}}\right)$ and $-3 + \left(\frac{x+y}{\sqrt{2}}\right)$ respectively in the given curve, then the new equation of curve will be

$$2\left\{-2 + \left(\frac{x-y}{\sqrt{2}}\right)\right\}^2 + 4\left\{-2 + \left(\frac{x-y}{\sqrt{2}}\right)\right\}\left\{-3 + \left(\frac{x+y}{\sqrt{2}}\right)\right\}$$
$$-5\left\{-3 + \left(\frac{x+y}{\sqrt{2}}\right)\right\}^2 + 20\left\{-2 + \left(\frac{x-y}{\sqrt{2}}\right)\right\}$$
$$-22\left\{-3 + \left(\frac{x+y}{\sqrt{2}}\right)\right\} - 14 = 0$$

$$\Rightarrow \quad x^2 - 14xy - 7y^2 - 2 = 0$$

1.20 Removal of the Term *xy* from $f(x, y) = ax^2 + 2hxy + by^2$ without Changing the Origin

Rotating the axes through an angle θ, we get

$$x = X\cos\theta - Y\sin\theta$$

and $$y = X\sin\theta + Y\cos\theta$$

$$\because \quad f(x, y) = ax^2 + 2hxy + by^2$$

After rotation, new equation is

$$F(X, Y) = (a\cos^2\theta + 2h\cos\theta\sin\theta + b\sin^2\theta)X^2$$
$$+ 2\{(b-a)\cos\theta\sin\theta + h(\cos^2\theta - \sin^2\theta)\}XY$$
$$+ (a\sin^2\theta - 2h\cos\theta\sin\theta + b\cos^2\theta)Y^2$$

Now, coefficient of $XY = 0$.

Then, we get $\cot 2\theta = \frac{a-b}{2h}$ [clearly, $h \neq 0$]

JEE SPIKE

Usually, we use the formula, $\tan 2\theta = \frac{2h}{a-b}$ for finding the angle of rotation θ.

However, if $a = b$, we use $\cot 2\theta = \frac{a-b}{2h}$ as in this case $\tan 2\theta$ is not defined.

Example 84. Given the equation $4x^2 + 2\sqrt{3}xy + 2y^2 = 1$, through what angle should the axes be rotated so that the term xy is removed from the transformed equation.

Sol. On comparing the given equation with $ax^2 + 2hxy + by^2$, we get $a = 4$, $h = \sqrt{3}$ and $b = 2$. If axes are to be rotated at θ, then

$$\tan 2\theta = \frac{2h}{a-b} = \frac{2\sqrt{3}}{2} = \sqrt{3} = \tan\frac{\pi}{3}$$

$$2\theta = \frac{\pi}{3}, \pi + \frac{\pi}{3} \Rightarrow 2\theta = \frac{\pi}{3}, \frac{4\pi}{3}$$

$$\therefore \quad \theta = \frac{\pi}{6}, \frac{2\pi}{3}$$

1.21 Position of a Point which Lies Inside a Triangle

If any point P lies within the ΔABC,

then $\Delta_1 + \Delta_2 + \Delta_3 = \Delta$

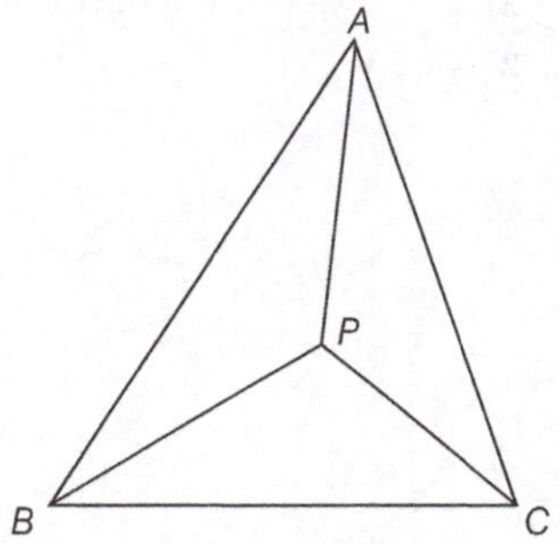

where, $\Delta =$ Area of ΔABC,

$\Delta_1 =$ Area of ΔPBC,

$\Delta_2 =$ Area of ΔPCA

and $\Delta_3 =$ Area of ΔPAB

Also, $\Delta_1 \neq 0, \Delta_2 \neq 0, \Delta_3 \neq 0$ and $\Delta \neq 0$

[each individual area must be non-zero]

Example 85. Find λ if $(\lambda, \lambda + 1)$ is an interior point of ΔABC, where $A \equiv (0, 3)$, $B \equiv (-2, 0)$ and $C \equiv (6, 1)$.

Sol. The point $P(\lambda, \lambda + 1)$ will be inside the ΔABC. Then,

Area of ΔPBC + Area of ΔPCA + Area of ΔPAB = Area of ΔABC

$$\Rightarrow \frac{1}{2}\left|\begin{vmatrix} \lambda & \lambda+1 & 1 \\ -2 & 0 & 1 \\ 6 & 1 & 1 \end{vmatrix}\right| + \frac{1}{2}\left|\begin{vmatrix} \lambda & \lambda+1 & 1 \\ 6 & 1 & 1 \\ 0 & 3 & 1 \end{vmatrix}\right| + \frac{1}{2}\left|\begin{vmatrix} \lambda & \lambda+1 & 1 \\ 0 & 3 & 1 \\ -2 & 0 & 1 \end{vmatrix}\right|$$

$$= \frac{1}{2}\left|\begin{vmatrix} 0 & 3 & 1 \\ -2 & 0 & 1 \\ 6 & 1 & 1 \end{vmatrix}\right|$$

$$\Rightarrow \quad |7\lambda + 6| + |8\lambda - 12| + |\lambda + 4| = 22$$

For $\lambda < -4$

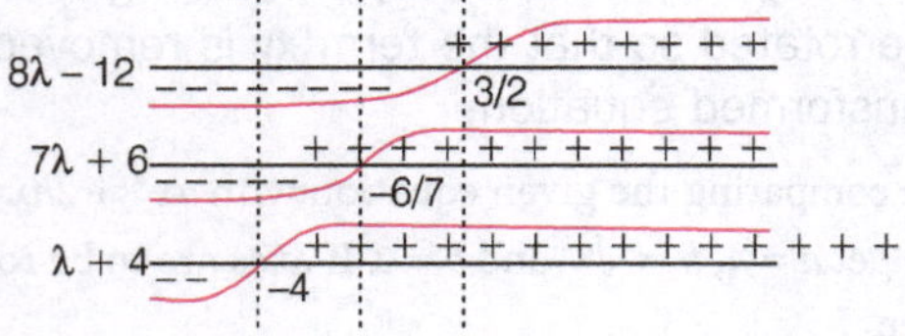

Then, $\quad -(7\lambda + 6) - (8\lambda - 12) - (\lambda + 4) = 22$

$\Rightarrow \quad -16\lambda = 20$

$\therefore \quad \lambda = -\dfrac{5}{4}$

which is impossible.

For $-4 \le \lambda < -\dfrac{6}{7}$

Then, $\quad -(7\lambda + 6) - (8\lambda - 12) + (\lambda + 4) = 22$

$\Rightarrow \quad -14\lambda = 12$

$\therefore \quad = -\dfrac{6}{7}$

which is impossible.

For $-\dfrac{6}{7} \le \lambda < \dfrac{3}{2}$

Then, $(7\lambda + 6) - (8\lambda - 12) + \lambda + 4 = 22 \Rightarrow 22 = 22$

$\because$ At $\lambda = -\dfrac{6}{7}$, area of $\Delta PBC = 0$

$\therefore \quad \lambda \ne \dfrac{-6}{7}$

$\therefore \quad \lambda \in \left(-\dfrac{6}{7}, \dfrac{3}{2}\right)$

For $\lambda \ge \dfrac{3}{2}$

Then, $7\lambda + 6 + 8\lambda - 12 + \lambda + 4 = 22$

$\Rightarrow \quad 16\lambda = 24$

$\therefore \quad \lambda = \dfrac{3}{2}$

$\because$ At $\lambda = \dfrac{3}{2}$, area of $\Delta PCA = 0$

$\therefore \quad \lambda \ne \dfrac{3}{2}$

Hence, value of $\lambda \in \left(-\dfrac{6}{7}, \dfrac{3}{2}\right)$.

Milestone Practice 1.4

1. The equation of the locus of points equidistant from $(-1, -1)$ and $(4, 2)$ is
(a) $3x-5y-7=0$ (b) $5x+3y-9=0$
(c) $4x+3y+2=0$ (d) $x-3y+5=0$

2. The equation of the locus of a point which moves so that its distance from the point $(ak, 0)$ is k times its distance from the point $\left(\frac{a}{k}, 0\right)$, $(k \neq 1)$ is
(a) $x^2 - y^2 = a^2$ (b) $2x^2 - y^2 = 2a^2$
(c) $xy = a^2$ (d) $x^2 + y^2 = a^2$

3. If the coordinates of a variable point P be $\left(t+\frac{1}{t}, t-\frac{1}{t}\right)$, where t is the variable quantity, then the locus of P is
(a) $xy = 8$ (b) $2x^2 - y^2 = 8$
(c) $x^2 - y^2 = 4$ (d) $2x^2 + 3y^2 = 5$

4. If the coordinates of a variable point P be $(\cos\theta + \sin\theta, \sin\theta - \cos\theta)$, where θ is the parameter, then the locus of P is
(a) $x^2 - y^2 = 4$ (b) $x^2 + y^2 = 2$
(c) $xy = 3$ (d) $x^2 + 2y^2 = 3$

5. If a point moves such that twice its distance from the axis of X exceeds its distance from the axis of Y by 2, then its locus is
(a) $x-2y=2$ (b) $x+2y=2$
(c) $2y-x=2$ (d) $2y-3x=5$

6. If the locus of the point whose distances from the point (5, 2) and (2, 3) are in the ratio 4 : 1 is $ax^2 + by^2 + dx + ey + 179 = 0$, then find the value of $a+b+d-e$.

7. OA and OB are two perpendicular straight lines. A straight line AB is drawn in such a manner that $OA + OB = 8$. Find the locus of the mid-point of AB.

8. The ends of a rod of length l move on two mutually perpendicular lines. Find the locus of the point on the rod which divides it in the ratio 1 : 2.

9. The coordinates of three points O, A and B are (0, 0), (0, 4) and (6, 0), respectively. A point P moves so that the area of ΔPOA is always twice the area of ΔPOB. Find the equation to both parts of the locus of P.

10. What does the equation $(a-b)(x^2+y^2) - 2abx = 0$ become, if the origin be moved to the point $\left(\frac{ab}{a-b}, 0\right)$?

11. The equation $x^2 + 2xy + 4 = 0$ is transformed to the parallel axes through the point $(6, \lambda)$. For what value of λ its new form passes through the new origin ?

12. The equation $4xy - 3x^2 = a^2$ becomes when the axes are turned through an angle $\tan^{-1} 2$ is
(a) $x^2 + 4y^2 = a^2$ (b) $x^2 - 4y^2 = a^2$
(c) $4x^2 + y^2 = a^2$ (d) $4x^2 - y^2 = a^2$

13. Transform the equation $x^2 - 3xy + 11x - 12y + 36 = 0$ to parallel axes through the point $(-4, 1)$ becomes $ax^2 + bxy + 1 = 0$. Then, $b^2 - a$ is
(a) $\frac{1}{4}$ (b) $\frac{1}{16}$ (c) $\frac{1}{64}$ (d) $\frac{1}{256}$

14. Show that if the axes be turned through $7\frac{1°}{2}$, the equation $\sqrt{3}x^2 + (\sqrt{3}-1)xy - y^2 = 0$ become free of xy in its new form.

15. Find the angle through which the axes may be turned so that the equation $Ax + By + C = 0$ may reduce to the form $x=$ constant and determine the value of this constant.

16. Transform $12x^2 + 7xy - 12y^2 - 17x - 31y - 7 = 0$ to rectangular axes through the point $(1, -1)$ inclined at an angle $\tan^{-1}\left(\frac{4}{3}\right)$ to the original axes.

Answer Key

1. (b) 2. (d) 3. (c) 4. (b) 5. (c)
6. 68 7. $x+y=4$ 8. $9x^2 + 36y^2 = 4l^2$ 9. $x-3y=0$ and $x+3y=0$
10. $(a-b)^2(x'^2 + y'^2) = a^2b^2$ 11. $-\frac{10}{3}$ 12. (b) 13. (c)
15. $\tan^{-1}\left(\frac{B}{A}\right), \frac{-C}{\sqrt{A^2+B^2}}$ 16. $xy = 0$

For Detailed Solution

JEE Pattern EXAMPLES

Single Option Correct Type Questions

Example 1 *The quadrant in which the point* $\left(\log_2\left(\frac{x}{x^2+1}\right), \log_{1/2}(x^2+x+1)\right), \forall x \in R^+$ *lies, is*

(a) I quadrant (b) II quadrant
(c) III quadrant (d) IV quadrant

Sol. (c) Let $y = \frac{x}{x^2+1}, x \in R^+$

$$\Rightarrow \quad yx^2 - x - y = 0$$

Since, $\quad x \in R^+$

$$\therefore \quad D \geq 0$$

$$\Rightarrow \quad 1 - 4y^2 \geq 0$$

$$\Rightarrow \quad -\frac{1}{2} \leq y \leq \frac{1}{2}$$

Also, $x \in R^+$ and $y = \frac{x}{1+x^2}$

$$\therefore \quad y > 0$$

$$\Rightarrow \quad y \in \left(0, \frac{1}{2}\right]$$

$$\Rightarrow \quad \log_2\left(\frac{x}{x^2+1}\right) < 0$$

Now, $\quad x^2 + x + 1 = \left(x + \frac{1}{2}\right)^2 + \frac{3}{4} \geq \frac{3}{4}$

$$\therefore \quad x^2 + x + 1 \in \left[\frac{3}{4}, \infty\right)$$

But $x \in R^+$

$$\therefore \quad x^2 + x + 1 \in [1, \infty)$$

$$\Rightarrow \quad \log_{1/2}(x^2 + x + 1) < 0$$

So, the point lies in III quadrant.

Example 2 *If O is the origin and* $P(x_1, y_1), Q(x_2, y_2)$ *are two points, then* $OP \cdot OQ \cos(\angle POQ)$ *is equal to*

(a) $x_1x_2 + y_1y_2$ (b) $x_1y_2 + x_2y_1$
(c) $|x_1y_2 - x_2y_1|$ (d) None of these

Sol. (a)

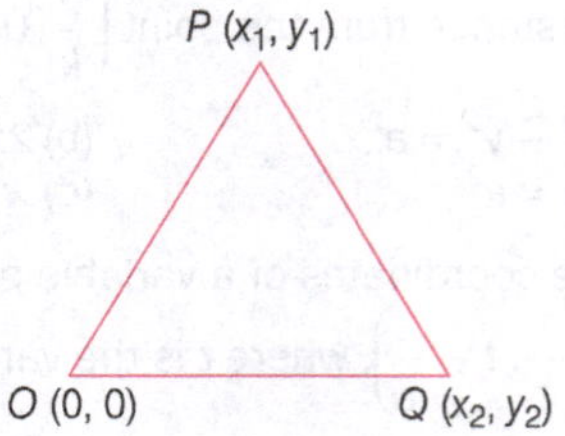

In ΔPOQ,

$$\cos(\angle POQ) = \frac{OP^2 + OQ^2 - PQ^2}{2OP \times OQ} \quad \text{[using cosine rule]}$$

$$\Rightarrow \quad PQ^2 = OP^2 + OQ^2 - 2OP \times OQ \cos(\angle POQ)$$

$$\Rightarrow \quad (x_2 - x_1)^2 + (y_2 - y_1)^2 = x_1^2 + y_1^2 + x_2^2 + y_2^2 - 2OP \times OQ \cos(\angle POQ)$$

$$\Rightarrow \quad OP \cdot OQ \cos(\angle POQ) = x_1x_2 + y_1y_2$$

Example 3 *Let* $A(a, b)$ *be a fixed point and O be the origin. If* A_1 *is the mid-point of OA,* A_2 *is the mid-point of* AA_1, A_3 *is the mid-point of* AA_2 *and so on. Then, the coordinates of* A_n *are*

(a) $(a(1-2^{-n}), b(1-2^{-n}))$
(b) $(a(2^{-n}-1), b(2^{-n}-1))$
(c) $(a(1-2^{-(n+1)}), b(1-2^{-(n+1)}))$
(d) $(a(1+2^{-(n-1)}), b(1+2^{-(n-1)}))$

Sol.

Decoding the Question

To find the sum of finite (n) terms of a GP

$S_n = a\frac{(1-r^n)}{1-r}$ if $r < 1$

(a) We have, $A_1 = \left(\frac{a}{2}, \frac{b}{2}\right)$

$$\therefore \quad A_2 = \left(\frac{a + \frac{a}{2}}{2}, \frac{b + \frac{b}{2}}{2}\right) = \left(\frac{a}{2} + \frac{a}{2^2}, \frac{b}{2} + \frac{b}{2^2}\right)$$

$$A_3 = \left(\frac{a + \frac{a}{2} + \frac{a}{2^2}}{2}, \frac{b + \frac{b}{2} + \frac{b}{2^2}}{2}\right)$$

$$= \left(\frac{a}{2} + \frac{a}{2^2} + \frac{a}{2^3}, \frac{b}{2} + \frac{b}{2^2} + \frac{b}{2^3}\right)$$

$$\therefore \quad A_n = \left(\frac{a}{2}+\frac{a}{2^2}+\frac{a}{2^3}+\ldots+\frac{a}{2^n}, \frac{b}{2}+\frac{b}{2^2}+\frac{b}{2^3}+\ldots+\frac{b}{2^n}\right)$$

$$= \left(a\left(1-\frac{1}{2^n}\right), b\left(1-\frac{1}{2^n}\right)\right)$$

$$= (a(1-2^{-n}), b(1-2^{-n}))$$

Example 4 *A rectangular billiard table has vertices at $P(0, 0)$, $Q(0, 7)$, $R(10, 7)$ and $S(10, 0)$. A small billiard ball starts at $M(3, 4)$, moves in a straight line to the top of the table, bounce to the right side of the table and then comes to rest at $N(7, 1)$. The y-coordinate of the point, where it hits the right side is*

(a) 3.7 (b) 3.8 (c) 3.9 (d) 4

Sol. (a) We have,

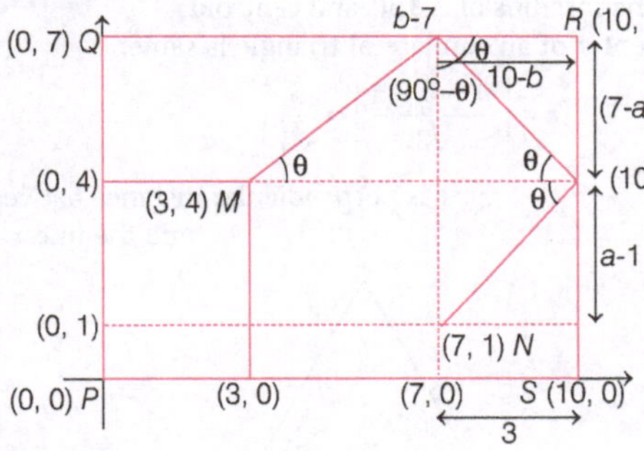

$$\tan\theta = \frac{a-1}{3} = \frac{7-a}{10-b}$$

Also, $\tan\theta = \dfrac{7-4}{b-3} = \dfrac{3}{b-3}$

$$\therefore \quad \underset{\text{I}}{\frac{3}{b-3}} = \underset{\text{II}}{\frac{a-1}{3}} = \underset{\text{III}}{\frac{7-a}{10-b}}$$

On taking I and II terms,

$\Rightarrow \quad 9 = ab - b - 3a + 3$

$\Rightarrow \quad 3a + 6 = ab - b$ ...(i)

and from II and III terms,

$10a - ab - 10 + b = 21 - 3a$

$\Rightarrow \quad 13a - ab + b = 31$ ...(ii)

From Eqs. (i) and (ii), we get

$3a + 6 = 13a - 31$

$\Rightarrow \quad a = 3.7$

Example 5 *Let $A \equiv (3, -4)$, $B \equiv (1, 2)$ and $P \equiv (2k-1, 2k+1)$ are three points such that $PA + PB$ is minimum. Then, the value of k is*

(a) $\dfrac{7}{9}$ (b) 0

(c) $\dfrac{7}{8}$ (d) None of these

Sol. **Decoding the Question**

If three points $A(x_1, y_1)$, $B(x_2, y_2)$ and $C(x_3, y_3)$ are collinear, then $AB + BC = AC$ and area of triangle formed by three points is zero.

(c) By triangle inequality, we have

$$PA + PB \geq AB$$

So, $PA + PB$ is minimum, if $PA + PB = AB$.

$\therefore A$, B and P are collinear.

Therefore,

$$\begin{vmatrix} 3 & -4 & 1 \\ 1 & 2 & 1 \\ 2k-1 & 2k+1 & 1 \end{vmatrix} = 0$$

$\Rightarrow \quad 3(2-2k-1) + 4(1-2k+1) + 1(2k+1-4k+2) = 0$

$\Rightarrow \quad 3 - 6k + 8 - 8k - 2k + 3 = 0$

$\Rightarrow \quad 16k - 14 = 0$

$\Rightarrow \quad k = \dfrac{7}{8}$

Example 6 *Three vertices of triangle are $A(4, 3)$, $B(1, -1)$ and $C(7, k)$. The value of k for which centroid, orthocentre, incentre and circumcentre of ΔABC lies on the same straight line, is*

(a) 7 (b) –1

(c) $\dfrac{5}{4}$ (d) None of these

Sol. (a) Given, centroid, orthocentre, incentre and circumcentre of ΔABC lies on the same line.

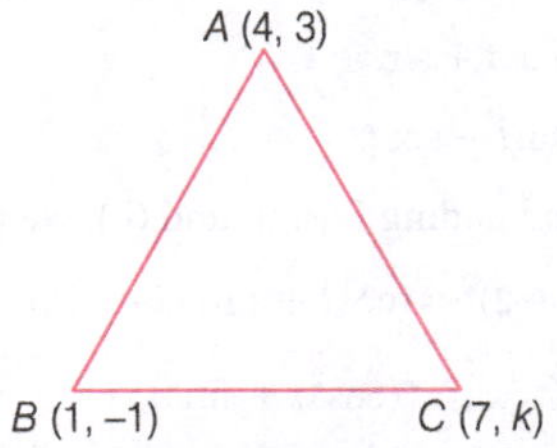

ΔABC must be isosceles. Therefore,

$AB = BC$

$\Rightarrow \quad AB^2 = BC^2$

$\Rightarrow \quad 9 + 16 = 36 + (k+1)^2$

$\Rightarrow \quad (k+1)^2 = -11$ [not possible]

Similarly, $BC = CA$

$\Rightarrow \quad BC^2 = CA^2$

$\Rightarrow \quad 36 + (k+1)^2 = 9 + (k-3)^2$

$\Rightarrow \quad 37 - 18 = -8k$

$k = \dfrac{-19}{8}$

Similarly, $AB = AC$

$\Rightarrow \quad AB^2 = AC^2$

$\Rightarrow \quad 25 = 9 + (k-3)^2$

$\Rightarrow \quad k - 3 = \pm 4$

$\Rightarrow \quad k = \pm 4 + 3$

$\Rightarrow \quad k = -1, +7$

But $k = 7$ $\quad$ [$\because$ A, B, C becomes collinear for $k = -1$]

Example 7 *ABC is a variable triangle with the fixed vertex $C(1, 2)$ and A, B having the coordinates $(\cos t, \sin t)$, $(\sin t, -\cos t)$ respectively, where t is a parameter. The locus of centroid of the ΔABC is*

(a) $3(x^2 + y^2) - 2x - 4y - 1 = 0$

(b) $3(x^2 + y^2) - 2x - 4y + 1 = 0$

(c) $3(x^2 + y^2) + 2x + 4y - 1 = 0$

(d) $3(x^2 + y^2) + 2x + 4y + 1 = 0$

Sol. (b) Let $G(\alpha, \beta)$ be the centroid in any position.

Then, $(\alpha, \beta) = \left(\dfrac{1 + \cos t + \sin t}{3}, \dfrac{2 + \sin t - \cos t}{3}\right)$

$\therefore \quad \alpha = \dfrac{1 + \cos t + \sin t}{3}$,

$\beta = \dfrac{2 + \sin t - \cos t}{3}$

or $\quad 3\alpha - 1 = \cos t + \sin t$ $\quad$ ...(i)

and $\quad 3\beta - 2 = \sin t - \cos t$ $\quad$ ...(ii)

On squaring and adding Eqs. (i) and (ii), we get

$$(3\alpha - 1)^2 + (3\beta - 2)^2 = (\cos t + \sin t)^2 + (\sin t - \cos t)^2$$

$$= 2(\cos^2 t + \sin^2 t)$$

$$= 2$$

$\therefore$ The equation of locus of the centroid is

$$(3x - 1)^2 + (3y - 2)^2 = 2$$

$\Rightarrow \quad 9(x^2 + y^2) - 6x - 12y + 3 = 0$

$\Rightarrow \quad 3(x^2 + y^2) - 2x - 4y + 1 = 0$

JEE SCANNER

Example 8 Similar to PYQ Asked in JEE Main 2021

Let the centroid of an equilateral ΔABC be at origin. Let one of the sides of equilateral triangle be along the straight line $x + y = 5$. If R and r be the radius of circumcircle and incircle of ΔABC, respectively. Then, $\dfrac{R+r}{5}$ is equal to

(a) $3\sqrt{2}$ units $\quad$ (b) $\dfrac{3}{\sqrt{2}}$ units

(c) $5\sqrt{2}$ units $\quad$ (d) $\dfrac{9}{\sqrt{2}}$ units

Sol. (b) Given r is the radius of incircle of ΔABC.

$\therefore$ r be the inradius of ΔABC and centroid and incenter of an equilateral triangle is same.

$$r = \left|\frac{0 + 0 - 5}{\sqrt{2}}\right| = \frac{5}{\sqrt{2}}. \quad \text{..(i)}$$

[$\because$ r is perpendicular distance between $(0, 0)$ and the line $x + y = 5$]

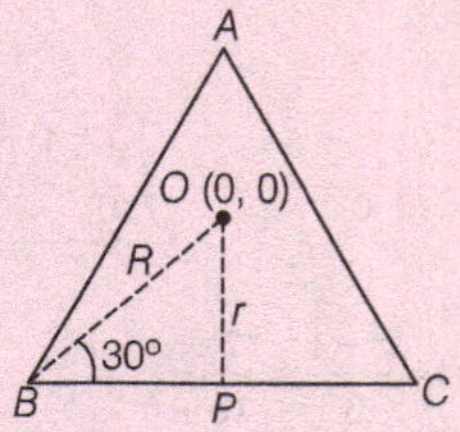

In ΔOBP, $\sin 30° = \dfrac{r}{R} \Rightarrow \dfrac{1}{2} = \dfrac{r}{R} \Rightarrow R = 2r$

$$\therefore \quad \frac{R+r}{5} = \frac{2r+r}{5} = \frac{3r}{5} = \frac{3}{5} \times \frac{5}{\sqrt{2}} \quad \text{[from Eq. (i)]}$$

$$= \frac{3}{\sqrt{2}} \text{ units}$$

Skill Builder

Let the centroid of an equilateral ΔPQR be at origin. Let one of the sides of equilateral triangle be along the straight line $5x + 6y = 7$. If R_1 and r_1 be the radius of circumcircle and incircle of ΔPQR respectively, then $R_1 + r_1$ is equal to

(a) $\dfrac{23}{\sqrt{61}}$ units $\quad$ (b) $\dfrac{13}{\sqrt{61}}$ units

(c) $\dfrac{21}{\sqrt{61}}$ units $\quad$ (d) $\dfrac{11}{\sqrt{61}}$ units

For Sol.

Example 9 *The incentre of triangle with vertices* $(1, \sqrt{3})$, $(0, 0)$ *and* $(2, 0)$ *is*

(a) $\left(1, \frac{\sqrt{3}}{2}\right)$ (b) $\left(\frac{2}{3}, \frac{1}{\sqrt{3}}\right)$ (c) $\left(\frac{2}{3}, \frac{\sqrt{3}}{2}\right)$ (d) $\left(1, \frac{1}{\sqrt{3}}\right)$

Sol. (d)

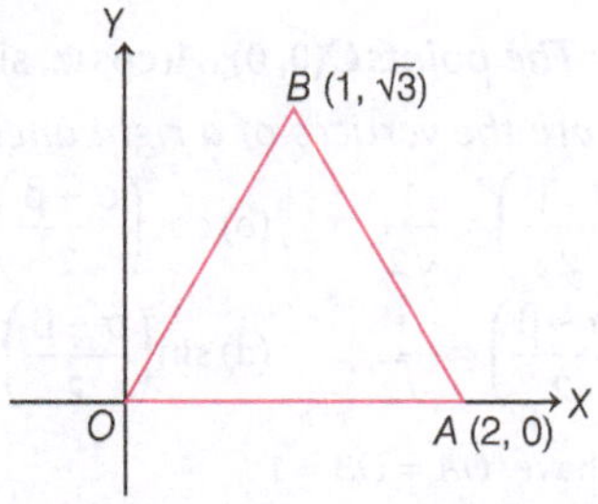

Let $O \equiv (0, 0)$, $A \equiv (2, 0)$ and $B \equiv (1, \sqrt{3})$

$\because \quad OA = 2 = OB = AB$

$\Rightarrow \Delta OAB$ is an equilateral triangle.

$\therefore$ Incentre = Centroid

$$\equiv \left(\frac{0+2+1}{3}, \frac{0+0+\sqrt{3}}{3}\right)$$

$\therefore$ Incentre $\equiv \left(1, \frac{1}{\sqrt{3}}\right)$

Example 10 *Orthocentre of triangle with vertices* $(0, 0)$, $(3, 4)$ *and* $(4, 0)$ *is*

(a) $\left(3, \frac{5}{4}\right)$ (b) $(3, 12)$ (c) $\left(3, \frac{3}{4}\right)$ (d) $(3, 9)$

Sol. (c) Denote the points as (x_1, y_1), (x_2, y_2) and (x_3, y_3), to form the matrix.

$$P = \begin{bmatrix} x_1 - x_3 & y_1 - y_3 \\ x_2 - x_3 & y_2 - y_3 \end{bmatrix} = \begin{bmatrix} -4 & 0 \\ -1 & 4 \end{bmatrix}$$

$$\therefore \quad \lambda = \frac{\vec{R_1} \cdot \vec{R_2}}{|P|} = \frac{(-4)(-1) + 0}{-16} = -\frac{1}{4}$$

$\therefore$ Circumcentre of the triangle

$$\equiv \left(\frac{x_1 + x_2 + \lambda(y_1 - y_2)}{2}, \frac{y_1 + y_2 - \lambda(x_1 - x_2)}{2}\right)$$

$$\equiv \left(\frac{3 - 4\lambda}{2}, \frac{4 + 3\lambda}{2}\right) \equiv \left(2, \frac{13}{8}\right)$$

i.e. $C \equiv \left(2, \frac{13}{8}\right)$

and centroid, $G \equiv \left(\frac{7}{3}, \frac{4}{3}\right)$

$\therefore$ Orthocentre, $H \equiv \left(3 \times \frac{7}{3} - 2 \times 2, 3 \times \frac{4}{3} - 2 \times \frac{13}{8}\right) \equiv \left(3, \frac{3}{4}\right)$

Alternate Solution

Let orthocentre be $H \equiv (\alpha, \beta)$.

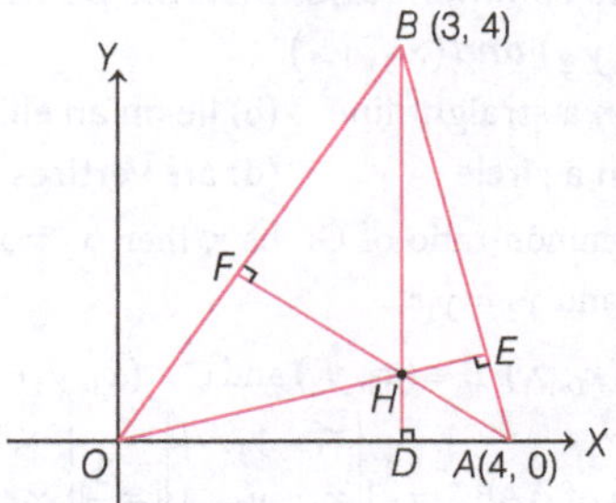

$\therefore$ Slope of $BH \times$ Slope of $OA = -1$

$\Rightarrow \quad \left(\frac{\beta - 4}{\alpha - 3}\right) \times \left(\frac{0}{4}\right) = -1$

$\therefore \quad \alpha - 3 = 0$

$\Rightarrow \quad \alpha = 3 \quad \quad$ ...(i)

and slope of $AH \times$ slope of $OB = -1$

$\Rightarrow \quad \left(\frac{\beta - 0}{\alpha - 4}\right) \times \left(\frac{4}{3}\right) = -1$

$\Rightarrow \quad \beta = \frac{3}{4} \quad \quad$ [from Eq. (i)]

Hence, orthocentre is $\left(3, \frac{3}{4}\right)$.

Example 11 *Locus of centroid of the triangle whose vertices are* $(a \cos t, a \sin t)$, $(b \sin t, -b \cos t)$ *and* $(1, 0)$, *where t is a parameter, is*

(a) $(3x - 1)^2 + (3y)^2 = a^2 - b^2$

(b) $(3x - 1)^2 + (3y)^2 = a^2 + b^2$

(c) $(3x + 1)^2 + (3y)^2 = a^2 + b^2$

(d) $(3x + 1)^2 + 3y^2 = a^2 - b^2$

Decoding the Question

The coordinates of centroid of the triangle whose vertices are (x_1, y_1), (x_2, y_2) and (x_3, y_3) are $\left(\frac{x_1 + x_2 + x_3}{3}, \frac{y_1 + y_2 + y_3}{3}\right)$.

Sol. (b) Let $A \equiv (a \cos t, a \sin t)$, $B \equiv (b \sin t, -b \cos t)$ and $C \equiv (1, 0)$

$\therefore$ Centroid $\equiv \left(\frac{a \cos t + b \sin t + 1}{3}, \frac{a \sin t - b \cos t}{3}\right)$

Let $x = \frac{a \cos t + b \sin t + 1}{3} \Rightarrow 3x - 1 = a \cos t + b \sin t \quad$ ...(i)

and $y = \frac{a \sin t - b \cos t}{3} \Rightarrow 3y = a \sin t - b \cos t \quad$ ...(ii)

On squaring and adding Eqs. (i) and (ii), we get

$$(3x - 1)^2 + (3y)^2 = a^2 + b^2$$

which is the locus of centroid.

Example 12 *If x_1, x_2, x_3 as well as y_1, y_2, y_3 are in GP, with the same common ratio, then the points $(x_1, y_1), (x_2, y_2)$ and (x_3, y_3)*

(a) lie on a straight line (b) lie on an ellipse

(c) lie on a circle (d) are vertices of a triangle

Sol. (a) Let common ratio of GP be r, then $x_2 = x_1 r$, $x_3 = x_1 r^2$, $y_2 = y_1 r$ and $y_3 = y_1 r^2$.

Let $A \equiv (x_1, y_1)$, $B \equiv (x_2, y_2)$ and $C \equiv (x_3, y_3)$

$$\therefore \quad \text{Area of } \Delta ABC = \frac{1}{2}\left|\begin{vmatrix} x_1 & y_1 & 1 \\ x_2 & y_2 & 1 \\ x_3 & y_3 & 1 \end{vmatrix}\right| = \frac{1}{2}\left|\begin{vmatrix} x_1 & y_1 & 1 \\ x_1 r & y_1 r & 1 \\ x_1 r^2 & y_1 r^2 & 1 \end{vmatrix}\right|$$

$$= \frac{1}{2}|x_1 y_1|\left|\begin{vmatrix} 1 & 1 & 1 \\ r & r & 1 \\ r^2 & r^2 & 1 \end{vmatrix}\right| = 0$$

[$\because C_1$ and C_2 are identical]

$\Rightarrow$ Points A, B and C are collinear.

Example 13 *Let A be the image of $(2, -1)$ with respect to Y-axis. Without transforming the origin, coordinate axis are turned at an angle 45° in the clockwise direction. Then, the coordiates of A in the new system are*

(a) $\left(\frac{1}{\sqrt{2}}, \frac{3}{\sqrt{2}}\right)$ (b) $\left(-\frac{3}{\sqrt{2}}, -\frac{1}{\sqrt{2}}\right)$

(c) $\left(\frac{1}{\sqrt{2}}, \frac{3}{\sqrt{2}}\right)$ (d) $\left(\frac{3}{\sqrt{2}}, \frac{1}{\sqrt{2}}\right)$

Sol. (a) Since, the image of (h, k) w.r.t. Y-axis is $(-h, k)$.

$\therefore$ Coordinate of A are $(-2, -1)$.

If (X, Y) are the coordinates of A w.r.t. the new coordinate axes obtained by turning the axes through an angle 45° in the clockwise direction, then

$$X = -2\cos(-45°) - \sin(-45°)$$
$$= -\frac{2}{\sqrt{2}} + \frac{1}{\sqrt{2}} = -\frac{1}{\sqrt{2}}$$

and
$$Y = 2\sin(-45°) - \cos(-45°)$$
$$= -\frac{2}{\sqrt{2}} - \frac{1}{\sqrt{2}} = -\frac{3}{\sqrt{2}}$$

$\therefore$ Required coordinates are $\left(-\frac{1}{\sqrt{2}}, -\frac{3}{\sqrt{2}}\right)$.

More than One Correct Option Type Questions

Example 14 *ABC is an isosceles triangle. If the coordinates of the base are B(1, 3) and C (−2, 7). The coordinates of vertex A can be*

(a) (1, 6) (b) $\left(-\frac{1}{2}, 5\right)$ (c) $\left(\frac{5}{6}, 6\right)$ (d) $\left(-7, \frac{1}{8}\right)$

Sol. (b,c,d) Let vertex of the ΔABC be $A(x, y)$

$$\therefore \quad AB = AC \Rightarrow (AB)^2 = (AC)^2$$

$$\Rightarrow \quad (x-1)^2 + (y-3)^2 = (x+2)^2 + (y-7)^2$$

$$\Rightarrow \quad 6x - 8y + 43 = 0 \quad \text{...(i)}$$

Here, we observe that the coordinates $\left(-\frac{1}{2}, 5\right), \left(\frac{5}{6}, 6\right)$ and $\left(-7, \frac{1}{8}\right)$ satisfy the Eq. (i).

Example 15 *The points O(0, 0), A(cos α, sin α) and B(cos β, sin β) are the vertices of a right angle triangle, if*

(a) $\sin\left(\frac{\alpha-\beta}{2}\right) = \frac{1}{\sqrt{2}}$ (b) $\cos\left(\frac{\alpha-\beta}{2}\right) = \frac{-1}{\sqrt{2}}$

(c) $\cos\left(\frac{\alpha-\beta}{2}\right) = \frac{1}{\sqrt{2}}$ (d) $\sin\left(\frac{\alpha-\beta}{2}\right) = \frac{-1}{\sqrt{2}}$

Sol. (a,c) We have, $OA = OB = 1$

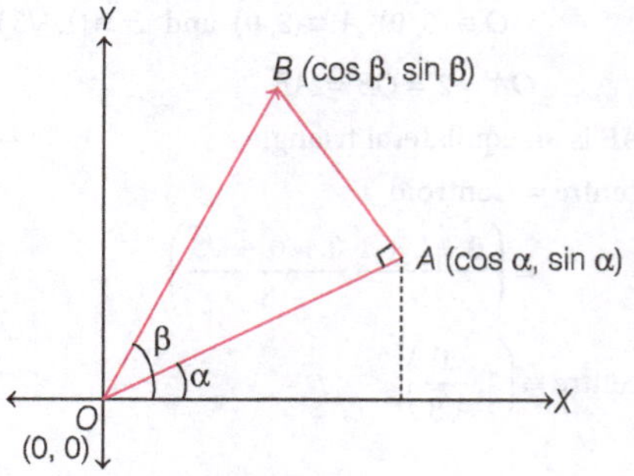

$\therefore$ $OA = OB$ and ΔOAB is right angle triangle

i.e. $\angle O = 90°$

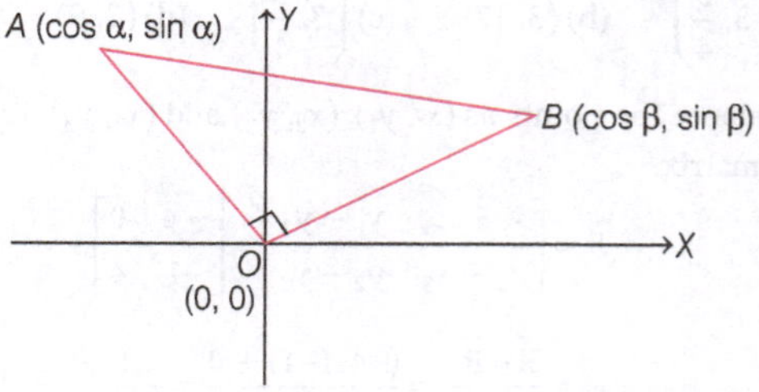

$$\therefore \quad \alpha - \beta = 90°$$

$$\cos\left(\frac{\alpha-\beta}{2}\right) = \cos 45° = \frac{1}{\sqrt{2}},$$

and
$$\sin\left(\frac{\alpha-\beta}{2}\right) = \sin 45° = \frac{1}{\sqrt{2}}$$

Example 16 *The straight line $3x + 4y - 12 = 0$ meets the coordinate axes at A and B. An equilateral ΔABC is constructed. The possible coordinates of vertex C are*

(a) $\left\{2\left(1+\frac{1}{4}\sqrt{5}\right), \frac{3}{2}+\frac{2}{3}\sqrt{5}\right\}$ (b) $\left\{-2(1+\sqrt{3}), \frac{3}{2}(1-\sqrt{3})\right\}$

(c) $\left\{2(1+\sqrt{3}), \frac{3}{2}(1+\sqrt{3})\right\}$ (d) $\left\{2\left(1-\frac{1}{4}\sqrt{5}\right), \frac{3}{2}-\frac{2}{3}\sqrt{5}\right\}$

Sol. (a, d) $3x+4y-12=0$

For *A*

Let $y=0$, then $x=4$

and **for *B***

Let $x=0$, then $y=3$

$AB=5$

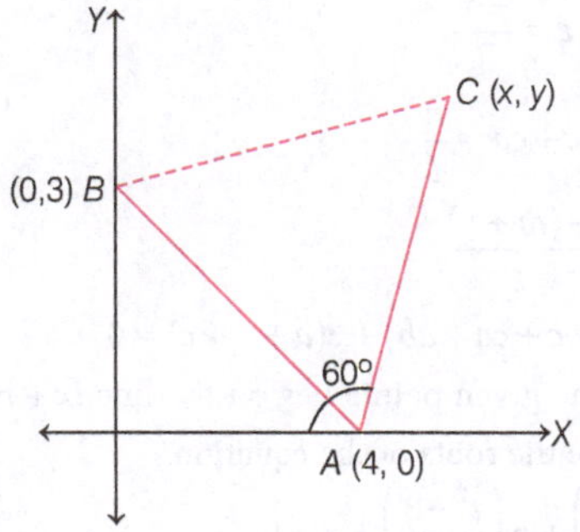

$\therefore \quad AB=BC=AC$

$AC=5=\sqrt{(x-4)^2+y^2}$

$\Rightarrow \quad (x-4)^2+y^2=25 \quad$ ...(i)

$\therefore \quad BC=\sqrt{x^2+(y-3)^2}=5$

$\Rightarrow \quad x^2+(y-3)^2=25 \quad$ ...(ii)

On subtracting Eq. (ii) from Eq. (i), we get

$x^2+16-8x-x^2+y^2-y^2+6y-9=0$

$\Rightarrow \quad -8x+6y=-7$

$\Rightarrow \quad 8x-6y=7 \Rightarrow 6y=8x-7$

$\Rightarrow \quad y=\frac{8x}{6}-\frac{7}{6}=\frac{4x}{3}-\frac{7}{6}$

From Eq. (i), $x^2+16-8x+\frac{16x^2}{9}+\frac{49}{36}-\frac{56x}{18}=25$

$\Rightarrow \quad \frac{25x^2}{9}-\frac{72x+28x}{9}+\frac{49}{36}-9=0$

$\Rightarrow \quad \frac{25x^2}{9}-\frac{100}{9}x+\frac{49-324}{36}=0$

$\Rightarrow \quad 100x^2-400x-275=0$

$\Rightarrow \quad x=2\left(1+\frac{1}{4}\sqrt{5}\right), 2\left(1-\frac{1}{4}\sqrt{5}\right)$

Then, $\quad y=\frac{3}{2}+\frac{2}{3}\sqrt{5}, \frac{3}{2}-\frac{2}{3}\sqrt{5}$

Example 17 *Two sides of a rhombus OABC (lying entirely in I quadrant or III quadrant) of area equal to 2 sq units are $y=\frac{x}{\sqrt{3}}, y=\sqrt{3}x$. Then, possible coordinate of B is/are (O being origin)*

(a) $(1+\sqrt{3}, 1+\sqrt{3})$ (b) $(-1-\sqrt{3}, -1-\sqrt{3})$

(c) $(3+\sqrt{3}, 3+\sqrt{3})$ (d) $(\sqrt{3}-1, \sqrt{3}-1)$

Sol. (a,b) $\because \angle COA=\angle COX-\angle AOX=60°-30°=30°$

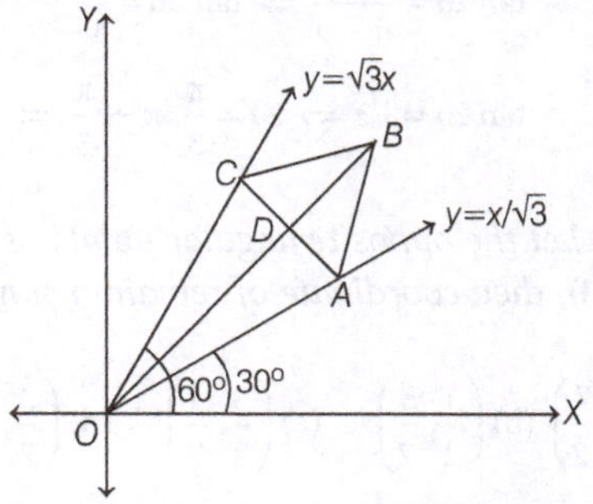

$\therefore$ Area of rhombus $=2\times\frac{1}{2}\times OA\times OC\sin 30° \Rightarrow 2=\frac{1}{2}x^2$

$OA=OC=2$

Also, $\angle OAB=180°-30°=150°$

$\cos 150°=\frac{OA^2+AB^2-OB^2}{2\times OA\times AB} \Rightarrow OB^2=8+4\sqrt{3}$

$\Rightarrow \quad OB=\sqrt{2}(\sqrt{3}+1) \quad [\because 8+4\sqrt{3}=(\sqrt{6}+\sqrt{2})^2]$

Coordinates of B are $\{\pm\sqrt{2}(\sqrt{3}+1)\cos 45°, \pm\sqrt{2}(\sqrt{3}+1)\sin 45°\}$

$\Rightarrow \quad \{\pm(\sqrt{3}+1), \pm(\sqrt{3}+1)\}$

$\Rightarrow \quad (\sqrt{3}+1, \sqrt{3}+1)$ and $(-\sqrt{3}-1, -\sqrt{3}-1)$

Example 18 *Let $S_1, S_2, \ldots$, be squares such that for each $n\geq 1$, the length of a side of S_n equals the length of a diagonal of S_{n+1}. If the length of a side S_1 is 10 cm, then for which of the following value of n is the area of S_n less than 1 sq cm?*

(a) 7 (b) 8 (c) 9 (d) 10

Sol. (b,c,d) If a be the side of the square, then diagonal $d=a\sqrt{2}$

By hypothesis

$a_n=\sqrt{2}\,a_{n+1}$

$\Rightarrow \quad a_{n+1}=\frac{a_n}{\sqrt{2}}=\frac{a_{n-1}}{(\sqrt{2})^2}=\frac{a_{n-2}}{(\sqrt{2})^3}=\ldots=\frac{a_1}{(\sqrt{2})^n}$

$\Rightarrow \quad a_n=\frac{a_1}{(\sqrt{2})^{n-1}}=\frac{10}{(2)^{(n-1)/2}}$

$\because \quad$ Area of $S_n<1 \Rightarrow a_n^2<1$

$\Rightarrow \quad \frac{100}{2^{n-1}}<1 \Rightarrow 2^{n-1}>100>2^6$

$\Rightarrow \quad n-1>6 \Rightarrow n>7$

$\therefore \quad n=8, 9, 10, \ldots$

Example 19 *If the equation $4x^2+2\sqrt{3}xy+2y^2=1$ is rotated through an angle θ such that the term xy gets removed, then the value of θ is*

(a) $\frac{\pi}{6}$ (b) $\frac{\pi}{3}$ (c) $\frac{2\pi}{3}$ (d) $\frac{5\pi}{6}$

Sol. (a, c) On comparing the given equation with $ax^2+2hxy+by^2$, we get

$a=4, b=2$ and $h=\sqrt{3}$

Now, $\tan 2\theta = \dfrac{2h}{a-b} \Rightarrow \tan 2\theta = \dfrac{2\sqrt{3}}{4-2}$

$\Rightarrow \tan 2\theta = \sqrt{3} \Rightarrow 2\theta = \dfrac{\pi}{3}, \pi + \dfrac{\pi}{3} \Rightarrow \theta = \dfrac{\pi}{6}, \dfrac{2\pi}{3}$

Example 20 *Let the opposite angular points of a square be (2, 3) and (−1, 1), then coordinate of remaining angular points is*

(a) $\left(\dfrac{-1}{2}, \dfrac{7}{2}\right)$ (b) $\left(\dfrac{1}{2}, \dfrac{5}{2}\right)$ (c) $\left(\dfrac{3}{2}, \dfrac{1}{2}\right)$ (d) $\left(\dfrac{3}{2}, \dfrac{7}{2}\right)$

Sol. (a, c) Let $A(2, 3)$ and $C(-1, 1)$ be the given angular points of a square $ABCD$ and let $B(x, y)$ be the unknown vertex.

Then, $AB = BC$

$\Rightarrow (AB)^2 = (BC)^2$

$\Rightarrow (x-2)^2 + (y-3)^2 = (x+1)^2 + (y-1)^2$

$\Rightarrow x^2 - 4x + 4 + y^2 - 6y + 9 = x^2 + 2x + 1 + y^2 - 2y + 1$

$\Rightarrow 6x + 4y - 11 = 0$

$\Rightarrow x = \dfrac{11-4y}{6}$ ...(i)

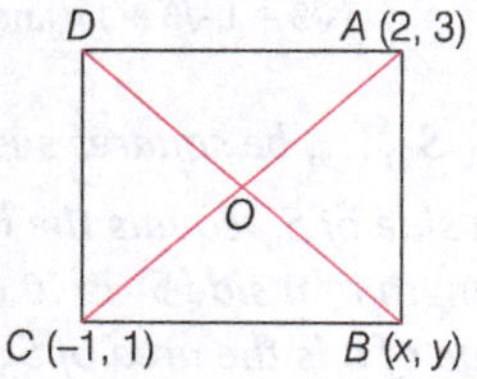

Also, in ΔABC,

$(AB)^2 + (BC)^2 = (AC)^2$

$\Rightarrow (x-2)^2 + (y-3)^2 + (x+1)^2 + (y-1)^2 = (3)^2 + (2)^2$

$\Rightarrow x^2 + y^2 - x - 4y + 1 = 0$

On putting the value of x from Eq. (i), we get

$\left(\dfrac{11-4y}{6}\right)^2 + y^2 - \left(\dfrac{11-4y}{6}\right) - 4y + 1 = 0$

$\Rightarrow 4y^2 - 16y + 7 = 0$

$\Rightarrow 4y^2 - 14y - 2y + 7 = 0$

$\Rightarrow 2y(2y-7) - 1(2y-7) = 0$

$\Rightarrow (2y-7)(2y-1) = 0 \Rightarrow y = \dfrac{7}{2}$ or $\dfrac{1}{2}$

when $y = \dfrac{7}{2}$, then $x = \dfrac{-1}{2}$

when $y = \dfrac{1}{2}$, then $x = \dfrac{3}{2}$

$\therefore$ Coordinate of remaining angular points is $\left(\dfrac{-1}{2}, \dfrac{7}{2}\right)$ and $\left(\dfrac{3}{2}, \dfrac{1}{2}\right)$.

Example 21 *If the points* $\left(\dfrac{a^3}{a-1}, \dfrac{a^2-3}{a-1}\right), \left(\dfrac{b^3}{b-1}, \dfrac{b^2-3}{b-1}\right)$ *and* $\left(\dfrac{c^3}{c-1}, \dfrac{c^2-3}{c-1}\right)$, *where* $a, b, c \neq 1$, *lie on the line* $lx + my + n = 0$, *then*

(a) $a + b + c = \dfrac{-m}{l}$

(b) $ab + bc + ca = \dfrac{n}{l}$

(c) $abc = \dfrac{-(m+n)}{l}$

(d) $abc - (bc + ca + ab) + 3(a + b + c) = 0$

Sol. (a,b,d) $\because$ The given points lies on the line $lx + my + n = 0$.

So, a, b, c are the roots of the equation.

$l\left(\dfrac{t^3}{t-1}\right) + m\left(\dfrac{t^2-3}{t-1}\right) + n = 0$

$\Rightarrow lt^3 + mt^2 + nt - (3m + n) = 0$

$\therefore a + b + c = \dfrac{-m}{l}$ ...(i)

$ab + bc + ca = \dfrac{n}{l}$ ...(ii)

$abc = \dfrac{3m+n}{l}$ ...(iii)

$\Rightarrow abc - \left(\dfrac{3m+n}{l}\right) = 0$ [from Eq. (iii)]

From Eqs. (i), (ii) and (iii),

$abc - (bc + ca + ab) + 3(a + b + c) = 0$

Passage Based Questions

Passage I

(Ex. Nos. 22 to 23)

If $A\left(\alpha, \dfrac{1}{\alpha}\right), B\left(\beta, \dfrac{1}{\beta}\right)$ and $C\left(\gamma, \dfrac{1}{\gamma}\right)$ be the vertices of a ΔABC, where α, β are the roots of $x^2 - 6ax + 2 = 0$ and β, γ are the roots of $x^2 - 6bx + 3 = 0$ and γ, α are the roots of $x^2 - 6cx + 6 = 0$, where a, b and c being positive.

Example 22 *The value of* $a + b + c$ *is*

(a) 1 (b) 2

(c) 3 (d) 5

Example 23 *The coordinates of centroid of* ΔABC *is*

(a) $\left(1, \dfrac{11}{9}\right)$ (b) $\left(\dfrac{1}{3}, \dfrac{11}{18}\right)$

(c) $\left(2, \dfrac{11}{18}\right)$ (d) $\left(\dfrac{2}{3}, \dfrac{11}{19}\right)$

Sol. (Ex. Nos. 22 and 23)

$\because \alpha, \beta$ are the roots of $x^2 - 6ax + 2 = 0$

$$\therefore \quad \alpha + \beta = 6a \quad \text{...(i)}$$

$$\text{and} \quad \alpha\beta = 2 \quad \text{...(ii)}$$

Again, β, γ are the roots of $x^2 - 6bx + 3 = 0$

$$\therefore \quad \beta + \gamma = 6b \quad \text{...(iii)}$$

$$\text{and} \quad \beta\gamma = 3 \quad \text{...(iv)}$$

Again, γ, α are the roots of $x^2 - 6cx + 6 = 0$

$$\therefore \quad \gamma + \alpha = 6c \quad \text{...(v)}$$

$$\text{and} \quad \gamma\alpha = 6 \quad \text{...(vi)}$$

From Eqs. (ii), (iv) and (vi), we get

$$\alpha\beta \cdot \beta\gamma \cdot \gamma\alpha = 2 \cdot 3 \cdot 6 \Rightarrow \alpha\beta\gamma = 6$$

$$\therefore \quad \alpha = 2, \beta = 1 \text{ and } \gamma = 3$$

22. (b) On adding Eqs. (i), (iii) and (v), we get

$$2(\alpha + \beta + \gamma) = 6(a + b + c)$$

$$\text{or} \quad a + b + c = \frac{1}{3}(2 + 1 + 3) = 2$$

23. (c) Centroid of $\Delta ABC \equiv \left(\frac{\Sigma\alpha}{3}, \frac{\Sigma\alpha\beta}{3\alpha\beta\gamma}\right)$

$$\equiv \left(\frac{2+1+3}{3}, \frac{2\cdot1 + 1\cdot3 + 3\cdot2}{3\cdot2\cdot1\cdot3}\right)$$

$$\equiv \left(2, \frac{11}{18}\right)$$

Passage II

(Ex. Nos. 23 to 24)

$A(P, 0)$, $B(4, 0)$, $C(5, 6)$ and $D(1, 4)$ are the vertices of a quadrilateral $ABCD$.

Example 24 *If $\angle ADC$ is obtuse, then the maximum integral value of P is equal to*

(a) 1 (b) 2 (c) 3 (d) 0

Example 25 *If two sides of the quadrilateral AB and AD are equal, then area of the quadrilateral is*

(a) $\frac{25}{3}$ sq units (b) 11 sq units

(c) $\frac{58}{3}$ sq units (d) $\frac{23}{3}$ sq units

Sol. (Ex. Nos. 24 and 25)

24. (b) $\because \angle ADC$ is obtuse.

Using cosine rule, we get

$$\cos \angle ADC = \frac{AD^2 + CD^2 - AC^2}{2AD \cdot CD} < 0$$

$$\Rightarrow \quad AD^2 + CD^2 < AC^2$$

$$\Rightarrow \quad (P-1)^2 + 4^2 + (5-1)^2 + (6-4)^2 < (P-5)^2 + 6^2$$

$$\Rightarrow \quad 8P < 24 \Rightarrow P < 3$$

$\therefore$ Maximum integral value of P is 2.

25. (c) $AB^2 = AD^2$

$$\Rightarrow \quad (P-4)^2 = (P-1)^2 + 4^2$$

$$P = -\frac{1}{6}$$

$\therefore$ Area of quadrilateral $ABCD$

$$= \text{Area of } \Delta ABD + \text{Area of } \Delta BDC$$

$$= \frac{1}{2}\left\| \begin{matrix} -\frac{1}{6} & 0 & 1 \\ 4 & 0 & 1 \\ 1 & 4 & 1 \end{matrix} \right\| + \frac{1}{2}\left\| \begin{matrix} 4 & 0 & 1 \\ 1 & 4 & 1 \\ 5 & 6 & 1 \end{matrix} \right\|$$

$$= \frac{25}{3} + 11$$

$$= \frac{58}{3} \text{ sq units}$$

Stem Based Questions

Stem I

(Ex. Nos. 26 to 27)

Consider three non-collinear points $A(9,3)$, $B(7,-1)$ and $C(1,-1)$. Let $P(a, b)$ be the centre and R is the radius of circle S passing through points A, B and C. Also, $H(\bar{x}, \bar{y})$ are the coordinates of the orthocentre of ΔABC whose area is denoted by Δ.

Example 26 *If D, E and F are the middle points of BC, CA and AB respectively, then the area of ΔDEF is ......*

Example 27 *The value of $a + b + R$ is ......*

Sol. (Ex. Nos. 26 and 27)

26. (3) $\therefore$ Area of $\Delta DEF = \frac{1}{4}$ Area of ΔABC

$$= \frac{1}{4} \times \left(\frac{1}{2} \times \text{base} \times \text{height}\right)$$

$$= \frac{1}{4} \times \frac{1}{2} \times BC \times AM$$

$$= \frac{1}{4} \times \frac{1}{2} \times 6 \times 4$$

$$= 3 \text{ sq units}$$

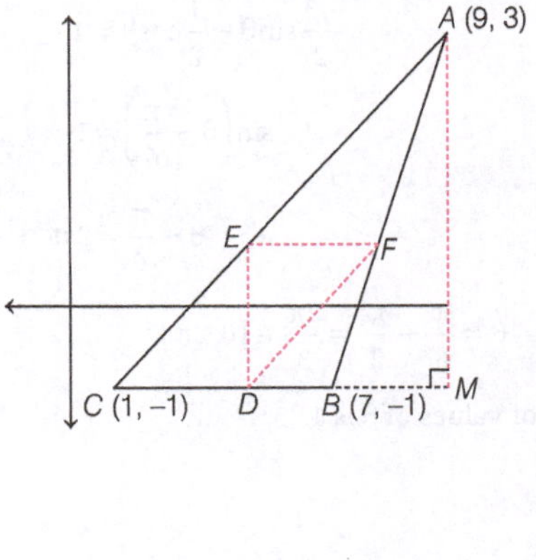

27. (12) D is mid-point BC, E is mid-point AC

For circumcentre,

$$OA = OB = OC$$

$\Rightarrow$ $OA = OB$

$\Rightarrow$ $(a-9)^2 + (b-3)^2 = (a-7)^2 + (b+1)^2$

$\Rightarrow$ $a + 2b = 10$

and $OB = OC$

$\Rightarrow$ $(a-1)^2 + (b+1)^2 = (a-7)^2 + (b+1)^2$

$\Rightarrow$ $a = 4$

$\therefore b = 3$

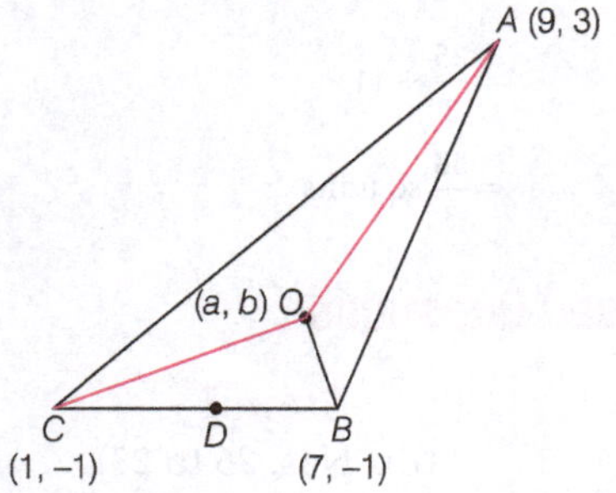

Circumcentre $= (a, b) = (4, 3)$

$\Rightarrow$ $R = OA = \sqrt{(4-1)^2 + (3+1)^2} = 5$

$a + b + R = 4 + 3 + 5 = 12$

Single Integer Answer Type Questions

Example 28 *If the points* $(-2, 0)$, $\left(-1, \frac{1}{\sqrt{3}}\right)$ *and* $(\cos\theta, \sin\theta)$ *are collinear, then the number of values of* $\theta \in [0, 2\pi]$ *is*

Sol. (1) Since, the given points are collinear, then

$$\begin{vmatrix} -2 & 0 & 1 \\ -1 & \frac{1}{\sqrt{3}} & 1 \\ \cos\theta & \sin\theta & 1 \end{vmatrix} = 0$$

$\Rightarrow$ $-2\left(\frac{1}{\sqrt{3}} - \sin\theta\right) - 0 + 1\left(-\sin\theta - \frac{\cos\theta}{\sqrt{3}}\right) = 0$

$\Rightarrow$ $\sqrt{3}\sin\theta - \cos\theta = 2$

$\Rightarrow$ $\frac{\sqrt{3}}{2}\sin\theta - \frac{1}{2}\cos\theta = 1$

or $\sin\left(\theta - \frac{\pi}{6}\right) = 1$

or $\theta - \frac{\pi}{6} = 2n\pi + \frac{\pi}{2}$

For $n = 0$, $\theta = \frac{\pi}{6} + \frac{\pi}{2} = \frac{2\pi}{3} \in [0, 2\pi]$

Number of values of θ is 1.

Example 29 *If the line segment joining the points* $(-1, 2)$ *and* $(4, -5)$ *is divided by the line* $x - 5y - 5 = 0$ *internally in the ratio* $k_1 : k_2$, *then the value of* $(k_1)^{k_2} + (k_2)^{k_1}$ *is .....*

Sol. (17) Let $A(-1, 2)$ and $B(4, -5)$. Then, CD is divided by the line

$\therefore$ $x - 5y - 5 = 0$ in the ratio

$$\frac{k_1}{k_2} = \frac{-L(-1, 2)}{L(4, -5)}$$

$$= \frac{-(-1-10-5)}{4+25-5} = \frac{16}{24} = \frac{2}{3}$$

$\therefore$ $k_1 = 2$ and $k_2 = 3$

So, $(k_1)^{k_2} + (k_2)^{k_1} = 2^3 + 3^2 = 17$

JEE SCANNER

Example 30 Similar to PYQ Asked in JEE Main 2022

Let a, b and c be the length of sides of a ΔABC such that $\frac{a+b}{7} = \frac{b+c}{8} = \frac{c+a}{9}$. *If r and R are the radius of incircle and radius of circumcircle of the ΔABC, respectively, then the value of* $\frac{2R}{r}$ *is equal to*

(a) 5 (b) 2 (c) 3 (d) 1

Sol. (a) Let $\frac{a+b}{7} = \frac{b+c}{8} = \frac{c+a}{9} = \lambda$

$a + b = 7\lambda$, $b + c = 8\lambda$, $a + c = 9\lambda$

$\Rightarrow$ $a + b + c = 12\lambda$

Now, $a = 4\lambda$, $b = 3\lambda$, $c = 5\lambda$

$\therefore$ $c^2 = b^2 + a^2$

$\angle C = 90°$

$\Delta = \frac{1}{2}ab\sin C = \frac{1}{2}ab$

$2\frac{R}{r} = 2 \times \frac{c}{2\sin C} \times \frac{S}{\Delta}$

$= 2 \times \frac{c}{2} \times \frac{6\lambda}{\frac{1}{2}ab} = \frac{c}{ab} \times 6\lambda = 5$

Skill Builder

Let a, b and c be the length of sides of a ΔABC such that $\frac{a+b}{9} = \frac{b+c}{8} = \frac{c+a}{7}$. If r and R are the radius of incircle and radius of circumcircle of the ΔABC respectively, then the value of $\frac{R}{r}$ is equal to

(a) $\frac{5}{2}$ (b) $\frac{3}{2}$

(c) $\frac{1}{2}$ (d) 1

For Sol.

Example 31 *One of the diameters of the circle circumscribing the rectangle ABCD is $4y = x + 7$. If A and B are the points $(-3, 4)$ and $(5, 4)$ respectively, then the area of rectangle ABCD, is ....*

Sol. (32) Ordinates of A and B are same.

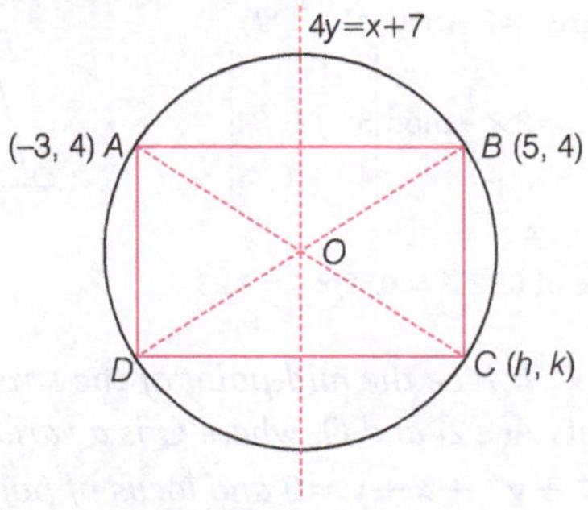

$\therefore$ This is parallel to X-axis and $AB = 8$

Now, BC is parallel to Y-axis. $[\because AB$ perpendicular on $BC]$

$\therefore$ x-coordinate will same

$$\Rightarrow \quad 5 = h$$

$$\text{Mid-point of } AC \equiv \left(\frac{-3+h}{2}, \frac{4+k}{2}\right) = \left(1, \frac{4+k}{2}\right)$$

O lies on $4y = x + 7$

$$\Rightarrow \quad 4\left(\frac{4+k}{2}\right) = 1 + 7$$

$$\Rightarrow \quad 4 + k = 4$$

$$\Rightarrow \quad k = 0$$

$$\therefore \quad C = (5, 0)$$

$$\therefore \quad BC = 4$$

$\therefore$ Area of rectangle $ABCD = AB \times BC = 8 \times 4 = 32$ sq units

Example 32 *The length of angle bisector of $\angle B$ of ΔABC having vertices $A(-1, -7)$, $B(5, 1)$ and $C(1, 4)$ is l, then the value of $\left[\frac{l}{4}\right]$, {[·] denotes greatest integer function}, is ....*

Sol. (1) $AB = \sqrt{6^2 + 8^2} = 10$ and $BC = \sqrt{4^2 + 3^2} = 5$

$\because$ We know that $\dfrac{DA}{DC} = \dfrac{BA}{BC}$

$$\therefore \quad \frac{AD}{CD} = \frac{10}{5} = \frac{2}{1}$$

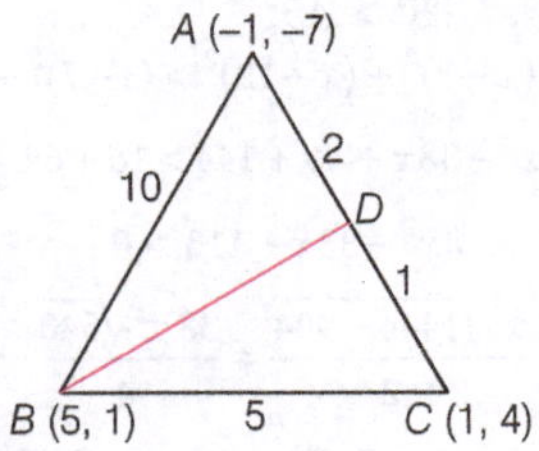

$$\therefore \quad D = \left(\frac{2(1) + 1(-1)}{2+1}, \frac{4 \times 2 + (1)(-7)}{2+1}\right) = \left(\frac{1}{3}, \frac{1}{3}\right)$$

$\therefore$ Length of angle bisector

$$BD = \sqrt{\left(5 - \frac{1}{3}\right)^2 + \left(1 - \frac{1}{3}\right)^2} = \sqrt{\frac{196}{9} + \frac{4}{9}} = \sqrt{\frac{200}{9}} = \frac{10}{3}\sqrt{2}$$

$$\Rightarrow \quad l = \frac{10\sqrt{2}}{3} \Rightarrow \left[\frac{l}{4}\right] = 1$$

Example 33 *Number of values of b for which in an acute ΔABC, if the coordinates of orthocentre H are $(4, b)$, centroid G are $(b, 2b - 8)$ and circumcentre S are $(-4, 8)$, is ......*

> **Decoding the Question**
>
> In any triangle orthocentre, circumcentre and centroid are collienar and the distance between the centroid and orthocentre is twice the distance between the centroid and circumcentre.

Sol. (0) We know that H, G and S are collinear.

$$\therefore \quad \begin{vmatrix} 4 & b & 1 \\ b & 2b-8 & 1 \\ -4 & 8 & 1 \end{vmatrix} = 0$$

Applying $R_2 \to R_2 - R_1$ and $R_3 \to R_3 - R_2$, we get

$$\begin{vmatrix} 4 & b & 1 \\ b-4 & b-8 & 0 \\ -(b+4) & 16-2b & 0 \end{vmatrix} = 0$$

$$\therefore \quad (b-4)(16-2b) + (b-8)(b+4) = 0$$

$$\Rightarrow \quad (b-8)(b-12) = 0$$

$$\therefore \quad b = 8 \text{ or } 12$$

$$\text{But} \quad \frac{-8+4}{3} = b \Rightarrow b = \frac{-4}{3}$$

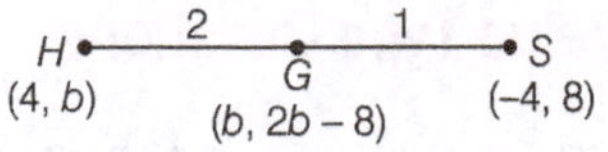

$$\text{and} \quad \frac{16+b}{3} = 2b - 8 \Rightarrow b = 8$$

But no common value of b is possible.

Hence, number of possible values of $b = 0$.

Example 34 *$P(3, 1)$, $Q(6, 5)$ and $R(x, y)$ are three points such that $\angle PRQ$ is right angle and the area of ΔPRQ is 7 sq units, then number of such points R is ......*

Sol. (0) $PQ = \sqrt{(6-3)^2 + (5-1)^2} = \sqrt{3^2 + 4^2} = 5$

Area of $\Delta PQR = 7$ sq units

$$\Rightarrow \quad \frac{1}{2} \times PQ \times h = 7 \Rightarrow h = \frac{2 \times 7}{5} = \frac{14}{5}$$

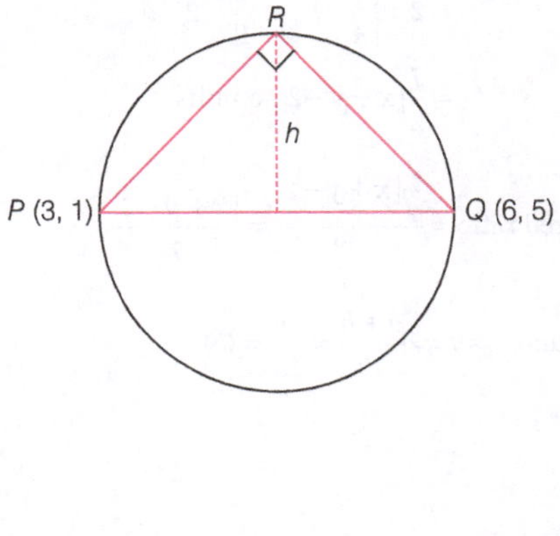

But h_{max} = Radius of circle with diameter PQ

$$= \frac{5}{2} < \frac{14}{5}$$

$\Rightarrow$ No such triangle exists.

Example 35 *In a ΔABC, the vertex A is (1,1) and orthocentre is (2,4). If the sides AB and BC are members of the family of straight lines $ax + by + c = 0$, where a, b, c are in AP, then the coordinates of vertex C are (h, k). The value of $2h + 12k$ is ......*

Sol. (14) a, b, c are in AP

$$2b = a + c$$
$$a + c - 2b = 0$$

Now, $ax + by + c = 0$ passes through a fixed point $(1, -2)$.

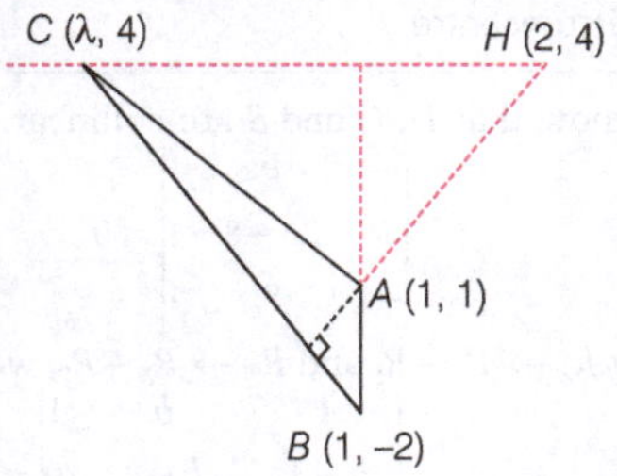

$$\text{Slope of } BC = \frac{-(2-1)}{4-1} = \frac{4+2}{\lambda - 1}$$

$\Rightarrow \quad \lambda = -17$

$\therefore \quad C \equiv (-17, 4) = (h, k)$

$\Rightarrow \; 2h + 12k = -34 + 48 = 14$

Numerical Value Type Questions

Example 36 *The coordinates of A, B, C are (6, 3), (–3, 5), (4, – 2), respectively and P is any point (x, y), if ratio of area of ΔPBC to ΔABC is $\frac{|x+y-a|}{b}$, then the value of $\frac{a+b}{10}$ is ....*

Sol. (0.9) $\therefore$ Area of $\Delta ABC = \frac{1}{2} \times \begin{vmatrix} 6 & 3 & 1 \\ -3 & 5 & 1 \\ 4 & -2 & 1 \end{vmatrix} = \frac{49}{2}$ sq units

$$\therefore \text{Area of } \Delta PBC = \frac{1}{2} \times \begin{vmatrix} x & y & 1 \\ -3 & 5 & 1 \\ 4 & -2 & 1 \end{vmatrix} = \frac{1}{2}|7x + 7y - 14|$$

$$= \frac{7}{2}|x + y - 2| \text{ sq units}$$

$$\therefore \text{Required ratio} = \frac{\frac{7}{2}|x+y-2|}{\frac{49}{2}} = \frac{|x+y-2|}{7}$$

$$\therefore a = 2 \text{ and } b = 7 \Rightarrow \frac{a+b}{10} = \frac{9}{10} = 0.9$$

Example 37 *P(2, 1), Q(3, 2) and R(4, – 1) are the vertices of a triangle and it through P and R lines parallel to opposite sides are drawn to intersect in S. If the area of PQRS is A, then the value of 0.32A is ....*

Sol. (1.28) Here, $PQRS$ is parallelogram.

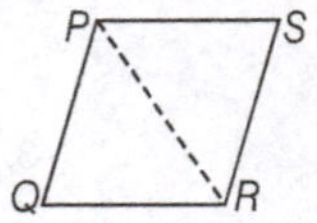

$\therefore \quad$ Area $= 2$ Area of (ΔPQR)

$$= 2 \times \frac{1}{2} \text{ mod} \begin{vmatrix} 2 & 1 & 1 \\ 3 & 2 & 1 \\ 4 & -1 & 1 \end{vmatrix}$$

$$A = 4$$

$\therefore$ Value of $0.32\,A = 0.32 \times 4 = 1.28$

Example 38 *If P be the mid-point of the straight line joining the points A(1, 2) and Q, where Q is a variable point on the curve $x^2 + y^2 + x + y = 0$ and locus of point P is $p(x^2 + y^2) + qx + ry + s$, then the value of $\frac{4p+q+r+s}{25}$ is ....*

Sol. (0.2) Let $P(h, k)$ be mid-point of AQ.

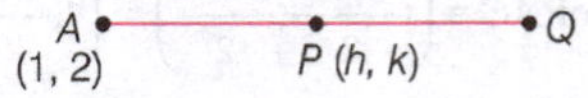

$\therefore$ Q is $(2h - 1, 2k - 2)$.

$\because$ It lies on the curve $x^2 + y^2 + x + y = 0$

$\therefore$ It will satisfy the equation

$$(2h-1)^2 + (2k-2)^2 + (2h-1) + (2k-2) = 0$$

$$\Rightarrow \quad 4h^2 - 4h + 1 + 4k^2 + 4 - 8k + 2h - 1 + 2k - 2 = 0$$

$$\Rightarrow \quad 4h^2 + 4k^2 - 2h - 6k + 2 = 0$$

$$\Rightarrow \quad 2(h^2 + k^2) - h - 3k + 1 = 0$$

$$p = 2, q = -1, r = -3 \text{ and } s = 1$$

$$\therefore \quad \frac{4p+q+r+s}{25} = \frac{8-1-3+1}{25} = \frac{5}{25} = \frac{1}{5} = 0.2$$

Example 39 *If points A(3, 4), B(7, 12) and P(x, y) are such that $PA^2 > PB^2 > AB^2$, then sum of integral value of x less than 99 and divisible by 4, is ....*

Sol. (1176) $\quad PA^2 > PB^2$

$$(x-3)^2 + (x-4)^2 > (x-7)^2 + (x-12)^2$$

$$\Rightarrow \quad 24x - 168 > 0 \Rightarrow x > 7 \quad \text{...(i)}$$

Now, $\quad PB^2 > AB^2$

$$\Rightarrow \quad (x-7)^2 + (x-12)^2 > (3-7)^2 + (4-12)^2$$

$$\Rightarrow \quad 2x^2 - 38x + 49 + 144 > 16 + 64$$

$$\Rightarrow \quad 2x^2 - 38x + 113 > 0$$

$$\Rightarrow \quad x = \frac{38 \pm \sqrt{1444 - 904}}{2 \times 2} = \frac{38 \pm \sqrt{540}}{4}$$

$$x \in \left(-\infty, \frac{38 - \sqrt{540}}{4}\right) \cup \left(\frac{38 + \sqrt{540}}{4}, \infty\right) \quad \text{...(ii)}$$

By Eqs. (i) and (ii), $x \in \left(\frac{19+\sqrt{135}}{2}, \infty\right)$

$\therefore$ Possible integral values are 16,17,18....

Now, required series

$\Rightarrow \quad 16+20+\ldots 96$

$\therefore \quad 96 = 16+(n-1)4$

$\Rightarrow \quad \frac{80}{4} = n-1 \Rightarrow n = 21$

$\therefore \quad S_n = \frac{n}{2}(a+l) = \frac{21}{2}(16+96) = 21\times 56 = 1176$

Example 40 *ΔABC with $AB = 13$, $BC = 5$ and $AC = 12$ slides on the coordinates axis with A and B on the positive X-axis and positive Y-axis, respectively. The locus of vertex C is $ax - by$, then value of $a+b$ is ......*

Sol. (17) $\angle BCA = 90°$

Points A, O, B, C are concyclic.

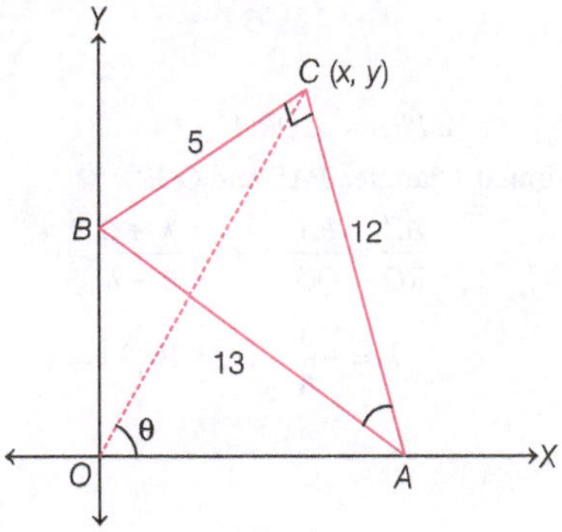

Let $\angle AOC = \theta$

$\therefore \quad \angle BOC = \angle BAC$

$\Rightarrow \quad \tan\left(\frac{\pi}{2}-\theta\right) = \frac{5}{12} \Rightarrow \frac{x}{y} = \frac{5}{12} \Rightarrow 12x - 5y = 0$

Focus of vertex C is $ax - by = 0$, comparing, we get

$a = 12$ and $b = 5$

$a + b = 12 + 5 = 17$

Matching Type Questions

Example 41 *ABCD is a rectangle in the clockwise direction. The coordinates of A are (1, 3) and of C are (5, 1). Coordinates of vertices B and D satisfy $y = 2x + c$, the coordinates of*

	Column I		Column II
A.	Middle point of BD	(p)	(2,0)
B.	Middle point of AB	(q)	(3,2)
C.	Middle point of BC	(r)	$\left(\frac{5}{2}, \frac{7}{2}\right)$
D.	The point D	(s)	$\left(\frac{9}{2}, \frac{5}{2}\right)$

Sol. (A) → q, (B) → r, (C) → s, (D) → p

(A) Let M be the point of intersection of the diagonals which bisects each of the diagonal.

$\therefore$ The coordinates of the middle point M of AC (mid-point of AC = mid-point of BD)

$= \left(\frac{5+1}{2}, \frac{3+1}{2}\right) = (3, 2)$

(B) If $x = 4$

i.e. $B = (4, 4)$

$\therefore$ Mid-point of $AB = \left(\frac{4+1}{2}, \frac{4+3}{2}\right) = \left(\frac{5}{2}, \frac{7}{2}\right)$

(C) $\therefore$ Mid-point of $BC = \left(\frac{5+4}{2}, \frac{1+4}{2}\right) = \left(\frac{9}{2}, \frac{5}{2}\right)$

(D) M satisfy $y = 2x + c$

$\Rightarrow \quad 2 = 6 + c \Rightarrow c = -4$

Let the coordinates of D which satisfies $y = 2x - 4$ be $(x, 2x-4)$.

$\Rightarrow \quad AD^2 + DC^2 = AC^2$

$\Rightarrow \quad (x-1)^2 + (2x-4-3)^2 + (x-5)^2 + (2x-4-1)^2 = (5-1)^2 + (1-3)^2$

$\Rightarrow \quad x^2 - 6x + 8 = 0 \Rightarrow x = 2$ or 4

$\therefore \quad D = (2, 0)$

Example 42 *Match the following*

	Column I		Column II
A.	The points $(\lambda+1, 1)$, $(2\lambda+1, 3)$ and $(2\lambda+2, 2\lambda)$ are collinear then number of values of λ is	(p)	3
B.	Area of ΔABC is 20 sq units, where A, B and C are (4, 6), (10, 14) and (x, y) respectively. AC is perpendicular to BC, then number of positions of C is	(q)	2
C.	In a ΔABC coordinates of orthocentre, centroid and vertex A are respectively (2, 2), (2, 1) and (0, 2). The x-coordinate of vertex B is	(r)	6
D.	A man starts from $P(-3, 4)$ and reaches the point $Q(0, 1)$ touching the X-axis at $R(\lambda, 0)$ such that $PR + RQ$ is minimum, then $10\|\lambda\|$ is	(s)	4

Sol. (A) → (q), (B) → (s), (C) → (p), (D) → (r)

(A) $\because$ Points are collinear.

$$\therefore \quad \begin{vmatrix} \lambda+1 & 1 & 1 \\ 2\lambda+1 & 3 & 1 \\ 2\lambda+2 & 2\lambda & 1 \end{vmatrix} = 0$$

$\Rightarrow \quad (\lambda+1)(3-2\lambda) - 1(2\lambda+1-2\lambda-2) + 1(4\lambda^2+2\lambda-6\lambda-6) = 0$

or $\quad 2\lambda^2 - 3\lambda - 2 = 0$

or $\quad (2\lambda+1)(\lambda-2) = 0$

$\therefore \quad \lambda = 2, -\frac{1}{2}$

Number of values of λ is 2.

(B) $\because$ Area of ΔABC is 20 sq units.

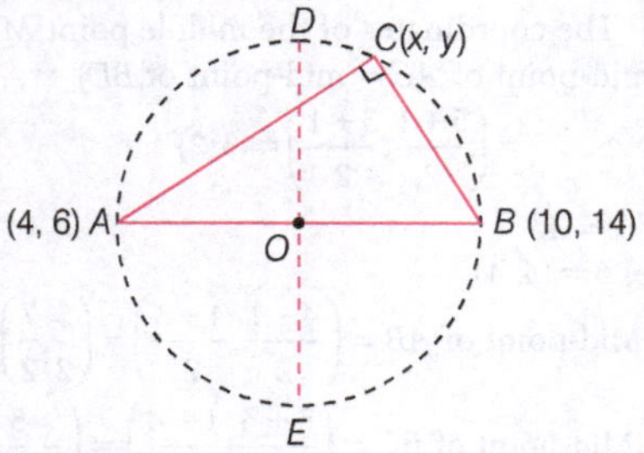

$\because$ C can not be at D and E.

$\therefore$ Four positions are possible two above AB and two below AB.

(C)

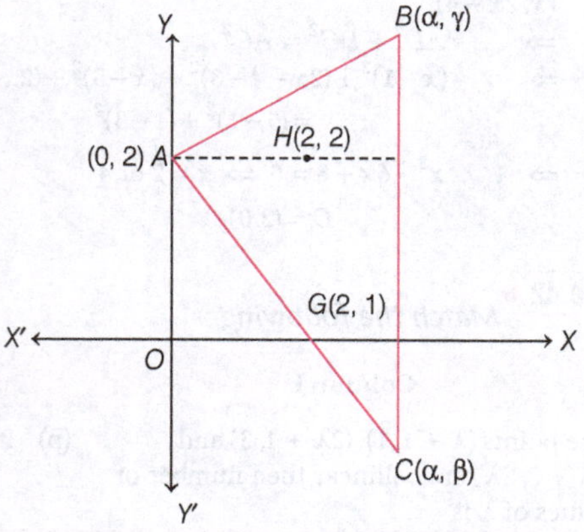

$$\because \quad \frac{\alpha + \alpha + 0}{3} = 2$$

$$\therefore \quad \alpha = 3$$

$\Rightarrow$ x-coordinates of vertex $B = 3$

(D) For $PR + RQ$ to be minimum, it should be the path of light

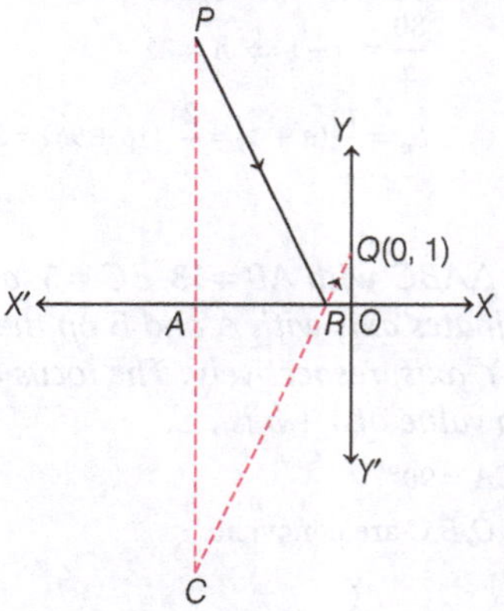

$$\because \quad \angle PRA = \angle QRO$$

From similar triangles PAR and QOR

$$\frac{AR}{RO} = \frac{PA}{QO} \quad \text{or} \quad \frac{\lambda + 3}{0 - \lambda} = \frac{4}{1}$$

or $\quad \lambda = -\frac{3}{5} \quad \therefore \; 10\,|\lambda| = 6.$

EXERCISE 1

JEE Main Pattern

Single Option Correct Type Questions

1. The distance between the points $(a \cos \alpha, a \sin \alpha)$ and $(a \cos \beta, a \sin \beta)$ is

(a) $a \cos\left(\frac{\alpha - \beta}{2}\right)$ (b) $2a \cos\left(\frac{\alpha - \beta}{2}\right)$

(c) $a \sin\left(\frac{\alpha - \beta}{2}\right)$ (d) $2a \sin\left(\frac{\alpha - \beta}{2}\right)$

2. Let A be $(3, 4)$ and B is a variable point on the lines $|x| = 6$. If $AB \leq 4$, then the number of position of point B with integral coordinates is

(a) 3 (b) 4

(c) 5 (d) 6

3. The vertices of a triangle are $A(-1, -7)$, $B(5, 1)$ and $C(1, 4)$. If the internal angle bisector of $\angle B$ meets the side AC in D, then the length of BD is

(a) $\frac{10}{3}$ (b) $\frac{10\sqrt{2}}{3}$

(c) $\frac{20}{3}$ (d) $\frac{20\sqrt{2}}{3}$

4. If (x_i, y_i), $i = 1, 2, 3$ are the vertices of an equilateral triangle such that $(x_1 + 2)^2 + (y_1 - 3)^2 = (x_2 + 2)^2 + (y_2 - 3)^2 = (x_3 + 2)^2 + (y_3 - 3)^2$, then the value of $\frac{x_1 + x_2 + x_3}{y_1 + y_2 + y_3}$ is

(a) $-\frac{2}{3}$ (b) $-\frac{1}{3}$

(c) $\frac{1}{3}$ (d) $\frac{2}{3}$

5. A variable line through point $P(2, 1)$ meets the axes at A and B. Then, the locus of the circumcentre of ΔOAB (where O is origin) is

(a) $2x + y - 2xy = 0$

(b) $x + 2y - 2xy = 0$

(c) $2x + y + 2xy = 0$

(d) $x + 2y + 2xy = 0$

6. An equivalent cartesian equation of polar equation $r = 4 \tan \theta \sec \theta$ is

(a) $x^2 = 2y$ (b) $y^2 = 2x$

(c) $x^2 = 4y$ (d) $y^2 = 4x$

7. $OPQR$ is a square and M, N are the middle points of the sides PQ and QR, respectively. Then, the ratio of the area of the square to that of ΔOMN is

(a) 4 : 1 (b) 2 : 1

(c) 8 : 3 (d) 7 : 3

8. If the point $(x_1 + t(x_2 - x_1), y_1 + t(y_2 - y_1))$ divides the join of (x_1, y_1) and (x_2, y_2) internally, then

(a) $t < 0$ (b) $0 < t < 1$

(c) $t > 1$ (d) $t = 1$

9. If by shifting the origin to the point $(1, 2)$ without rotating the coordinate axes, the equation $y^2 - 8x - 4y + 12 = 0$ changes to $y^2 = 4ax$, then a is equal to

(a) 1 (b) 2

(c) -2 (d) -1

10. If the axes are rotated through an angle of $30°$ in the clockwise direction, then the point $(4, 2\sqrt{3})$ in the new system is

(a) $(2, 3)$ (b) $(2, \sqrt{3})$

(c) $(\sqrt{3}, 2)$ (d) $(\sqrt{3}, 5)$

11. Vertices of a variable triangle are $(3, 4)$, $(5 \cos \theta, 5 \sin \theta)$ and $(5 \sin \theta, -5 \cos \theta)$, where $\theta \in R$. Locus of its orthocentre is

(a) $x^2 + y^2 + 6x + 8y - 25 = 0$

(b) $x^2 + y^2 - 6x + 8y - 25 = 0$

(c) $x^2 + y^2 + 6x - 8y - 25 = 0$

(d) $x^2 + y^2 - 6x - 8y - 25 = 0$

12. If a rod AB of length 2 units slides on coordinate axes in the first quadrant. An equilateral ΔABC is completed with C on the side away from O. Then, locus of C is

(a) $x^2 + y^2 - xy + 1 = 0$

(b) $x^2 + y^2 - xy\sqrt{3} + 1 = 0$

(c) $x^2 + y^2 + xy\sqrt{3} - 1 = 0$

(d) $x^2 + y^2 - xy\sqrt{3} - 1 = 0$

13. The sides of a triangle are $3x + 4y$, $4x + 3y$ and $5x + 5y$ units, where $x > 0$, $y > 0$. The triangle is

(a) right angled (b) acute angled

(c) obtuse angled (d) isosceles

14. Let P and Q be the points on the line joining $A(-2,5)$ and $B(3,1)$ such that $AP = PQ = QB$. Then, the mid-point of PQ is

(a) $\left(\frac{1}{2}, 3\right)$ (b) $\left(-\frac{1}{4}, 4\right)$
(c) $(2, 3)$ (d) $(-1, 4)$

15. A ΔABC right angled at A has points A and B as $(2, 3)$ and $(0, -1)$, respectively. If $BC = 5$ units, then the point C is

(a) $(4, 2)$ (b) $(-4, 2)$
(c) $(-4, 4)$ (d) $(4, -4)$

16. The x-coordinate of the incentre of the triangle that has the coordinates of mid-points of its sides as $(0, 1)$, $(1, 1)$ and $(1, 0)$ is

(a) $2+\sqrt{2}$ (b) $2-\sqrt{2}$
(c) $1+\sqrt{2}$ (d) $1-\sqrt{2}$

17. The number of points, having both coordinates are integers, that lie in the interior of the triangle with vertices $(0, 0)$, $(0, 41)$ and $(41, 0)$ is

(a) 820 (b) 780
(c) 901 (d) 861

18. Let k be an integer such that the triangle with vertices $(k, -3k)$, $(5, k)$ and $(-k, 2)$ has area 28 sq. units. Then, the orthocentre of this triangle is at the point

(a) $\left(2, \frac{1}{2}\right)$ (b) $\left(2, -\frac{1}{2}\right)$
(c) $\left(1, \frac{3}{4}\right)$ (d) $\left(1, -\frac{3}{4}\right)$

19. Harmonic conjugate of the point $C(5,1)$ with respect to the point $A(2,10)$, $B(6,-2)$ is circumcentre and $(3,-4)$ is the orthocentre of triangle, then its centroid is

(a) $\left(\frac{19}{3}, \frac{20}{3}\right)$ (b) $\left(\frac{19}{3}, -\frac{20}{3}\right)$
(c) $\left(\frac{20}{3}, \frac{-19}{3}\right)$ (d) None of these

20. If in the equation $2x^2 + 4xy - 5y^2 + 20x - 22y - 14 = 0$, when if referred to rectangular axes through the point $(-2, -3)$ and the new equation formed which inclined to an angle of 45° with the old axes, is

(a) $x^2 - 14xy - 7y^2 + 2 = 0$
(b) $x^2 - 14xy - 7y^2 - 2 = 0$
(c) $x^2 - 14xy + 7y^2 - 14 = 0$
(d) None of the above

Numerical Value Type Questions

21. A point A divides the join of $P(-5, 1)$ and $Q(3, 5)$ in the ratio $k:1$. Then, the integral value of k for which the area of ΔABC, where B is $(1, 5)$ and C is $(7, -2)$, is equal to 2 units in magnitude is ....

22. If the perpendicular bisector of the line segment joining $P(1, 4)$ and $Q(\alpha, 3)$ cut Y-axis at -4, then the positive integral value of α is ....

23. The sum of absolute values of integral values of m for which the x-coordinate of the point of intersection of the lines $3x + 4y = 9$ and $y = mx + 1$ is also an integer is ....

24. The vertices of a triangle are $(6, 0)$, $(0, 6)$ and $(6, 6)$. If the distance between its circumcentre and orthocentre is $\alpha\sqrt{\beta}$, then minimum value of $\alpha\beta$ $(\alpha, \beta \in N)$ is equal to ....

25. In a ΔABC, coordinates of A is $(1,2)$ and the equations of the medians through B and C are $x + y = 5$ and $x = 4$, respectively. Then, area of ΔABC is

26. Let $A(1, k)$, $B(1, 1)$ and $C(2, 1)$ be the vertices of a right angled triangle with AC as its hypotenuse. If the area of the triangle is 1, then the positive integral value of k is ......

27. The ratio in which the line $r = \dfrac{4}{\sin\theta - \cos\theta}$ divides the line joining the points $\left(3, \frac{\pi}{2}\right)$ and $\left(3, \frac{\pi}{6}\right)$ externally is $a + b\sqrt{3} : c$, then $a + b - c$ is ......

28. Let $A(0, 1)$, $B(1, 1)$, $C(1, -1)$, $D(-1, 0)$ be four points. If P is any point, then $PA + PB + PC + PD \ge d$, then, $[d]$ is ...., where $[\cdot]$ denotes GIF.

29. Numbers of values of b for which ΔABC is an acute angle and coordinate of orthocentre H is $(4, b)$, centroid $G(b, 2b - 8)$ and circumcentre S is $(-4, 8)$ are collinear is ......

30. Let the coordinates of the feet of perpendiculars from the vertices of a triangle on the opposite sides are $(20, 25)$, $(8, 16)$ and $(8, 9)$. If the orthocentre of the triangle lies at the point (α, β), then $\beta - \alpha$ is ....

Previous Years Questions

31. If the locus of the point whose distances from the points $(2, 1)$ and $(1, 3)$ are in the ratio $5:4$, is $ax^2 + by^2 + cxy + dx + ey + 170 = 0$, then the value of $a^2 + 2b + 3c + 4d + e$ is equal to

[Single Correct Type, 2024 Main]

(a) 5 (b) 37 (c) 437 (d) -27

32. Let $\left(5, \frac{a}{4}\right)$ be the circumcenter of a triangle with vertices $A(a, -2)$, $B(a, 6)$ and $C\left(\frac{a}{4}, -2\right)$. Let α denote the circumradius, β denote the area and γ denote the perimeter of the triangle. Then, $\alpha + \beta + \gamma$ is

[Single Correct Type, 2024 Main]

(a) 30 (b) 60 (c) 53 (d) 62

33. Let $A(\alpha, -2)$, $B(\alpha, 6)$ and $C\left(\frac{\alpha}{4}, -2\right)$ be vertices of a ΔABC. If $\left(5, \frac{\alpha}{4}\right)$ is the circumcentre of ΔABC, then which of the following is not correct about ΔABC?

[Single Correct Type, 2024 Main]

(a) area is 24 (b) perimeter is 25
(c) circumradius is 5 (d) inradius is 2

34. Let a, b and c be the length of sides of a $\Delta\ ABC$ such that $\frac{a+b}{7} = \frac{b+c}{8} = \frac{c+a}{9}$. If r and R are the radius of incircle and radius of circumcircle of the ΔABC, respectively, then the value of $\frac{R}{r}$ is equal to

[Single Correct Type, 2022 Main]

(a) $\frac{5}{2}$

(b) 2

(c) $\frac{3}{2}$

(d) 1

35. A point P moves so that the sum of squares of its distances from the points (1, 2) and (– 2, 1) is 14. Let $f(x, y) = 0$ be the locus of P, which intersects the X-axis at the points A, B and the Y-axis at the points C, D. Then, the area of the quadrilateral $ACBD$ is equal to

[Single Correct Type, 2022 Main]

(a) $\frac{9}{2}$ (b) $\frac{3\sqrt{17}}{2}$ (c) $\frac{3\sqrt{17}}{4}$ (d) 9

36. Let $A\left(\frac{3}{\sqrt{a}}, \sqrt{a}\right)$, $a > 0$, be a fixed point in the XY-plane. The image of A in Y -axis be B and the image of B in X-axis be C. If $D(3\cos\theta, a\sin\theta)$ is a point in the fourth quadrant such that the maximum area of ΔACD is 12 sq. units, then a is equal to

[Numerical Value Type, 2021 Main]

37. A ΔABC lying in the first quadrant has two vertices as $A(1, 2)$ and $B(3, 1)$. If $\angle BAC = 90°$, and area of $(\Delta ABC) = 5\sqrt{5}$ sq. units, then the abscissa of the vertex C is **[Numerical Value Type, 2020 Main]**

(a) $2 + \sqrt{5}$ (b) $1 + 2\sqrt{5}$
(c) $2\sqrt{5} - 1$ (d) $1 + \sqrt{5}$

EXERCISE 2

JEE Advanced Pattern

Single Option Correct Type Questions

1. The points with the coordinates $(2a, 3a)$, $(3b, 2b)$ and (c, c) are collinear

(a) for no value of a, b, c
(b) for all values of a, b, c
(c) if $a, \frac{c}{5}, b$ are in HP
(d) if $a, \frac{2c}{5}, b$ are in HP

2. Consider three points $P\{-\sin(\beta - \alpha), -\cos\beta\}$, $Q\{\cos(\beta - \alpha), \sin\beta\}$ and $R\{\cos(\beta - \alpha + \theta), \sin(\beta - \theta)\}$, where $0 < \alpha, \beta, \theta < \frac{\pi}{4}$. Then,

(a) P lies on the line segment RQ.
(b) Q lies on the line segment PR.
(c) R lies on the line segment QP.
(d) P, Q, R are non-collinear.

3. ABC is an equilateral triangle such that the vertices B and C lie on two parallel lines at a distance 6. If A lies between the parallel lines at a distance 4 from one of them, then the length of a side of the equilateral triangle is

(a) 8 (b) $\sqrt{\frac{88}{3}}$
(c) $\frac{4\sqrt{7}}{\sqrt{3}}$ (d) None of these

4. (i) The points $(-1, 0)$, $(4, -2)$ and $(\cos 2\theta, \sin 2\theta)$ are collinear.

(ii) The points $(-1, 0)$, $(4, -2)$ and $\left(\frac{1-\tan^2\theta}{1+\tan^2\theta}, \frac{2\tan\theta}{1+\tan^2\theta}\right)$ are collinear.

(a) Both statements are equivalent
(b) Statement (i) has more solution than statement (ii) for θ
(c) Statement (ii) has more solution than statement (i) for θ
(d) None of the above

5. If $\alpha_1, \alpha_2, \alpha_3, \beta_1, \beta_2, \beta_3$ are the values of n for which $\sum_{r=0}^{n-1} x^{2r}$ is divisible by $\sum_{r=0}^{n-1} x^r$, then the triangle having vertices $(\alpha_1, \beta_1), (\alpha_2, \beta_2)$ and (α_3, β_3) cannot be
(a) an isosceles triangle
(b) a right angled isosceles triangle
(c) a right angled triangle
(d) an equilateral triangle

6. The coordinates of three points $A(-4,0)$, $B(2,1)$ and $C(3,1)$ determine the vertices of an equilateral trapezium $ABCD$. The coordinates of vertex D is
(a) (6, 0) (b) (−3, 0)
(c) (−5, 0) (d) (9, 0)

7. Each side of a square is of length 4 units. The centre of the square is (3,7) and one of its diagonal is parallel to $y = x$, then the coordinates of its vertices are
(a) (1, 5) (1, 9) (5, 9) (5, 5) (b) (−1, 5) (−1, 9) (−2, 3) (−5, 5)
(c) Both (a) and (b) (d) None of the above

8. m and n are integer with $o < n < m$. A is the point (m, n) on the cartesian plane. B is the reflection of A in the line $y = x$. C is the reflection of B in the Y-axis. D is the reflection of C in the X-axis and E is the reflection of D in the Y-axis. The area (sq units) of pentagon $ABCDE$ is
(a) $2m(m+n)$ (b) $m(m+3n)$
(c) $m(2m+3n)$ (d) $2m(m+3n)$

9. The vertices of a triangle are (0, 3), (−3, 0) and (3, 0). The coordinates of its orthocentre are
(a) (0, −2) (b) (0, 2) (c) (0, 3) (d) (0, −3)

10. A, B, C are respectively the points (1, 2), (4, 2), (4, 5). If T_1, T_2 are the points of trisection of the line segment AC and S_1, S_2 are the points of trisection of the line segment BC, then the area of the quadrilateral $T_1S_1S_2T_2$ is
(a) 1 (b) $\frac{3}{2}$ (c) 2 (d) $\frac{5}{2}$

11. A ΔABC with vertices $A(-1, 0)$, $B\left(-2, \frac{3}{4}\right)$ and $C\left(-3, -\frac{7}{6}\right)$ has its orthocentre at H. Then, the orthocentre of ΔBCH will be
(a) (−3, −2) (b) (1, 3)
(c) (−1, 2) (d) None of these

12. If $\sum_{i=1}^{4} (x_i^2 + y_i^2) \le 2x_1x_3 + 2x_2x_4 + 2y_2y_3 + 2y_1y_4$, then the points $(x_1, y_1), (x_2, y_2), (x_3, y_3), (x_4, y_4)$ are
(a) the vertices of a rectangle
(b) collinear
(c) the vertices of a trapezium
(d) None of the above

13. The locus of a point P which divides the line joining (1, 0) and $(2\cos\theta, 2\sin\theta)$ internally in the ratio 2 : 3 for all θ, is
(a) a straight line (b) a circle
(c) a pair of straight lines (d) a parabola

14. A rod of length k slides in a vertical plane, its ends touching the coordinate axes, then the locus of the foot of perpendicular from origin to rod is
(a) $(x^2+y^2)^3 = kx^2y^2$ (b) $(x^2+y^2)^3 = k^2x^2y^2$
(c) $(x^2+y^2)^2 = k^2x^2y^2$ (d) None of these

15. Without change of axes the origin is shifted to (h, k), then from the equation $x^2 + y^2 - 4x + 6y - 7 = 0$, then term containing linear powers are missing, then point (h, k) is
(a) (3, 2) (b) (−3, 2)
(c) (2, −3) (d) (−2, −3)

More than One Correct Option Type Questions

16. Coordinates of a point P are (a, b), where a is root of the equation $x^2 + x - 42 = 0$ and b is an integral root of the equation $x^2 + ax + a^2 - 37 = 0$. The coordinates of P can be
(a) (6, 4) (b) (−7, 4) (c) (−7, 3) (d) (6, −3)

17. If (−6, −4), (3, 5), (−2, 1) are the vertices of a parallelogram, then remaining vertex can be
(a) (0, −1) (b) (−1, 0) (c) (−11, −8) (d) (7, 10)

18. If the point $P(x, y)$ be equidistant from the points $A(a+b, a-b)$ and $B(a-b, a+b)$, then
(a) $ax = by$ (b) $bx = ay$
(c) $x^2 - y^2 = 2(ax + by)$ (d) P can be (a, b)

19. If the coordinates of the vertices of a triangle are rational numbers, then which of the following points of the triangle will always have rational coordinates?
(a) centroid (b) incentre
(c) circumcentre (d) orthocentre

20. The points $A(-4, -1)$, $B(-2, -4)$, $C(4, 0)$ and $D(2, 3)$ are the vertices of a
(a) parallelogram (b) rectangle
(c) rhombus (d) square

21. The medians AD and BE of the triangle with vertices $A(0, b)$, $B(0, 0)$ and $C(a, 0)$ are mutually perpendicular if
(a) $b = a\sqrt{2}$ (b) $a = b\sqrt{2}$
(c) $b = -a\sqrt{2}$ (d) $a = -b\sqrt{2}$

22. The points $A(x, y)$, $B(y, z)$ and $C(z, x)$ represents the vertices of a right angled triangle, if
(a) $x = y$ (b) $y = z$
(c) $z = x$ (d) $x = y = z$

23. Let the base of a triangle lie along the line $x = a$ and be of length $2a$. The area of this triangles is a^2, if the vertex lies on the line

(a) $x = -a$ (b) $x = 0$ (c) $x = \frac{a}{2}$ (d) $x = 2a$

24. Two sides of a rhombus $OABC$ (lying entirely in I quadrant or III quadrant) of area equal to 2 sq units are $y = \frac{x}{\sqrt{3}}, y = \sqrt{3}x$. Then, possible coordinate of B is/are (O being origin)

(a) $(1+\sqrt{3}, 1+\sqrt{3})$ (b) $(-1-\sqrt{3}, -1-\sqrt{3})$

(c) $(3+\sqrt{3}, 3+\sqrt{3})$ (d) $(\sqrt{3}-1, \sqrt{3}-1)$

25. If G be the centroid and I be the incentre of the triangle with vertices $A(-15, 3)$, $B(6, 3)$ and $C(0, -5)$ and $GI = \lambda$, then

(a) $\lambda = \frac{13}{6}$ (b) $G \equiv \left(-3, \frac{1}{3}\right)$

(c) $G \equiv \left(-2, \frac{1}{3}\right)$ (d) $\lambda = \frac{5}{6}$

Passage Based Questions

Passage I

(Q. Nos. 26 and 27)

- ABC is a triangle right angled at A, $AB = 2AC$. $A \equiv (1, 2)$, $B \equiv (-3, 1)$. ACD is an equilateral triangle. The vertices of two triangles are in anti-clockwise sense. $BCEF$ is a square with vertices in clockwise sense.

26. If area of ΔACF is S, then the value of $8S$ is

(a) 42 (b) 51 (c) 62 (d) 102

27. Length of DE is

(a) $\sqrt{17}\sqrt{(4-\sqrt{3})}$ (b) $\frac{\sqrt{17}}{2}\sqrt{(8+\sqrt{3})}$

(c) $\frac{\sqrt{17}}{2}\sqrt{(4+\sqrt{3})}$ (d) $\sqrt{15}\sqrt{(4+\sqrt{3})}$

Passage I

(Q. Nos. 28 and 29)

- Let $O(0,0)$, $A(2,0)$ and $B\left(1, \frac{1}{\sqrt{3}}\right)$ be the vertices of a triangle. Let R be the region consisting of all those points P inside ΔOAB satisfying. $d(P, OA) \le \min \{d(P, OB), d(P, AB)\}$, where, d denotes the distance from the point P to the corresponding line. Let M be the peak of region R.

28. Length of perpendicular from M to OA is equal to

(a) $\sqrt{3}$ (b) $\frac{1}{\sqrt{3}}$ (c) 3 (d) $2-\sqrt{3}$

29. The perimeter of region R is equal to

(a) $4-\sqrt{3}$

(b) $4+\sqrt{3}$

(c) $4+3\sqrt{3}$

(d) $2+4\sqrt{(2-\sqrt{3})}$

Stem Based Questions

Stem I

(Q. Nos. 30 and 31)

- Consider three non-collinear points $A(9, 3)$, $B(7, -1)$ and $C(1, -1)$. Let $P(a, b)$ be the centre and R is the radius of circle S passing through points A, B and C. Also $h(\bar{x}, \bar{y})$ are the coordinates of the orthocentre of ΔABC whose area be denoted by Δ.

30. If D, E and F are the middle points of BC, CA and AB respectively, then the area of ΔDEF is ......

31. The value of $a + b + R$ is ......

Single Integer Type Questions

32. The distance between the points $(t_1^3, \sqrt{2}t_1)$ and $(t_2^3, -\sqrt{2}t_2)$, if t_1 and t_2 are the roots of $x^2 - 2\sqrt{2}x + 1 = 0$, is $\alpha\sqrt{53}$, then the value of α is equal to ....

33. Find the number of triangles with sides of integer length whose perimeter is 10 units, is ......

34. Suppose the bisector AD of the interior angle A of ΔABC divides the sides BC into segments $BD = 4$, $DC = 2$, then the maximum value of k is ......

35. If the area of the triangle formed by the points $(2a, b)$, $(a+b, 2b+a)$ and $(2b, 2a)$ be Δ_1 and the area of the triangle whose vertices are $(a+b, a-b)$, $(3b-a, b+3a)$ and $(3a-b, 3b-a)$ be Δ_2, then the value of Δ_2/Δ_1 is ......

36. The diameter of the nine point circle of the triangle with vertices $(3, 4)$, $(5\cos\theta, 5\sin\theta)$ and $(5\sin\theta, -5\cos\theta)$, where $\theta \in R$, is ......

37. The ends of the base of an isosceles triangle are $(2\sqrt{2}, 0)$ and $(0, \sqrt{2})$. One side is of length $2\sqrt{2}$. If Δ be the area of triangle, then the value of $[\Delta]$ is ...... (where $[\cdot]$ denotes the greatest integer function)

38. If (x, y) is the incentre of the triangle formed by the points $(3, 4)$, $(4, 3)$ and $(1, 2)$, then the value of x^2 is ......

39. Let P and Q be points on the line joining $A(-2, 5)$ and $B(3, 1)$ such that $AP = PQ = QB$. If mid-point of PQ is (a, b), then the value of $\frac{b}{a}$ is ......

Numerical Value Type Questions

40. The vertices of ΔABC are $(4, 3), (1, -1)$ and $(7, 7)$. The bisector of $\angle ABC$ meets the opposite side in the point D. If the length of angle bisector BD is $\sqrt{\frac{\alpha}{\beta}}$, then $\frac{\alpha+\beta}{100}$ is .... (where α and β are coprime numbers)

41. If $P(3, 7)$, $Q(8, 9)$ and $R(11, 23)$ are three vertices of ΔPQR. S divides PQ in the ratio $2:3$ and T divides QR in the ratio $3:2$. Then, $5(ST)^2$ is ....

42. The parallelogram is bounded by the lines $y = ax + c$, $y = ax + d$ and $y = bx + c$, $y = bx + d$ and has the area equal to 18 sq units. Also, the parallelogram bounded by the lines $y = ax + c$, $y = ax - d$ and $y = bx + c$, $y = bx - d$ has area 72 sq units. Given, a, b, c and d are positive integers, then the smallest possible value of $a + b + c + d$ is ....

43. In a ΔABC, $A \equiv (\alpha, \beta)$, $B \equiv (1, 2)$, $C \equiv (2, 3)$ and point A lies on the line $y = 2x + 3$ where $\alpha, \beta \in I$. If the area of ΔABC be such that $[\Delta] = 2$, where $[\cdot]$ denotes the greatest integer function, then number of possible coordinates of A is λ, then λ^2 is equal to ....

44. Let S be the square of unit area. Consider any quadrilateral which has one vertex on each side of S. If a, b, c and d denote the lengths of the sides of the quadrilateral and $\alpha \le a^2 + b^2 + c^2 + d^2 \le \beta$, then $\alpha^2 + \beta^2$ is .....

Matching Type Questions

45. Consider the triangle with vertices $A(0, 0)$, $B(5, 12)$ and $C(16, 12)$.

	Column I		Column II
A.	If (λ, μ) are the coordinates of centroid of ΔABC, then $(\lambda + \mu)$ is divisible by	(p)	3
B.	If (λ, μ) are the coordinates of circumcentre of ΔABC, then 2λ is divisible by	(q)	5
C.	If (λ, μ) are the coordinates of incentre of ΔABC, then μ is divisible by	(r)	7
D.	If (λ, μ) are the coordinates of excentre opposite to vertex B, then $\lambda + \mu$ is divisible by	(s)	9

46. The vertices of a triangle are $A(-10, 8)$, $B(14, 8)$ and $C(-10, 26)$. Let G, I, H, O be the centroid, incentre, orthocentre, circumcentre respectively of ΔABC.

	Column I		Column II
A.	The inradius r is	(p)	6
B.	The circumradius R is	(q)	3
C.	The area of ΔIGH is	(r)	5
D.	The area of ΔOGI is	(s)	15

EXERCISE 3
Challenging Problems

1. If x coordinates of two points B and C are the roots of equation $x^2 + 4x + 3 = 0$ and their y coordinates are the roots of equation $x^2 - x - 6 = 0$. If x coordinate of B is less than x coordinate of C and y coordinate of B is greater than the y coordinate of C and coordinates of a third point A be $(3, -5)$, find the length of the bisector of the interior angle at A.

2. The distance between two parallel lines is unity. A point P lies between the lines at a distance a units from one of them. Find the length of a side of an equilateral triangle PQR, vertex Q of which lies on one of the parallel lines and vertex R lies on the other line.

3. If $A(x_1, y_1), B(x_2, y_2)$ and $C(x_3, y_3)$ are the vertices of a ΔABC and (x, y) be a point on the internal bisector of angle A, then prove that
$$b\begin{vmatrix} x & y & 1 \\ x_1 & y_1 & 1 \\ x_2 & y_2 & 1 \end{vmatrix} + c\begin{vmatrix} x & y & 1 \\ x_1 & y_1 & 1 \\ x_3 & y_3 & 1 \end{vmatrix} = 0,$$ where, $AC = b$ and $AB = c$.

4. A line L intersects three sides BC, CA and AB of a triangle in P, Q, R respectively, show that
$$\frac{BP}{PC} \cdot \frac{CQ}{QA} \cdot \frac{AR}{RB} = -1.$$

5. Show that the area of the triangle whose sides are $a_r x + b_r y + c_r = 0, r = 1, 2, 3$ is $\dfrac{\Delta^2}{2|C_1C_2C_3|}$, where C_1, C_2 and C_3 are the cofactors of c_1, c_2 and c_3 respectively in the determinant $\Delta = \begin{vmatrix} a_1 & b_1 & c_1 \\ a_2 & b_2 & c_2 \\ a_3 & b_3 & c_3 \end{vmatrix}$.

6. If $A_1, A_2, A_3, \ldots, A_n$ are n points in a plane whose coordinates are $(x_1, y_1), (x_2, y_2), (x_3, y_3), \ldots, (x_n, y_n)$ respectively. A_1A_2 is bisected in the point G_1; G_1A_3 is divided at G_2 in the ratio $1:2$; G_2A_4 is divided at G_3 in the ratio $1:3$; G_3A_5 at G_4 in the $1:4$ and so on until all the points are exhausted. Show that the coordinates of the final point so obtained are
$$\frac{x_1 + x_2 + \ldots + x_n}{n} \text{ and } \frac{y_1 + y_2 + \ldots + y_n}{n}.$$

7. If by change of axes without change of origin, the expression $ax^2 + 2hxy + by^2$ becomes $a_1x_1^2 + 2h_1x_1y_1 + b_1y_1^2$, prove that
   (i) $a + b = a_1 + b_1$
   (ii) $ab - h^2 = a_1b_1 - h_1^2$
   (iii) $(a - b)^2 + 4h^2 = (a_1 - b_1)^2 + 4h_1^2$

Answer Key

Exercise 1

1. (d)	2. (c)	3. (b)	4. (a)	5. (b)	6. (c)	7. (c)	8. (b)	9. (b)	10. (d)
11. (d)	12. (d)	13. (c)	14. (a)	15. (a)	16. (b)	17. (b)	18. (a)	19. (b)	20. (b)
21. (7)	22. (4)	23. (3)	24. (6)	25. (9)	26. (3)	27. (6)	28. (4)	29. (0)	30. (5)
31. (b)	32. (c)	33. (b)	34. (a)	35. (b)	36. (8)	37. (b)			

Exercise 2

1. (d)	2. (d)	3. (c)	4. (b)	5. (d)	6. (b)	7. (a)	8. (b)	9. (c)	10. (b)
11. (d)	12. (a)	13. (b)	14. (b)	15. (c)	16. (b,c)	17. (b,c,d)	18. (a,b,d)	19. (a,c,d)	20. (a,b)
21. (b,d)	22. (a,b,c)	23. (b,d)	24. (a,b)	25. (a,b)	26. (b)	27. (b)	28. (d)	29. (d)	30. (3)
31. (12)	32. (2)	33. (2)	34. (4)	35. (4)	36. (5)	37. (3)	38. (9)	39. (6)	40. (307)
41. (576)	42. (16)	43. (16)	44. (20)						

45. (A) → (p,q), (B) → (p,r), (C) → (p,s), (D) → (p)   46. (A) → (p), (B) → (s), (C) → (p), (D) → (q)

Solutions

Exercise 1 - JEE Main Pattern

1. Required distance

$$= \sqrt{(a\cos\alpha - a\cos\beta)^2 + (a\sin\alpha - a\sin\beta)^2}$$

$$= a\sqrt{\cos^2\alpha + \cos^2\beta - 2\cos\alpha\cos\beta + \sin^2\alpha + \sin^2\beta - 2\sin\alpha\sin\beta}$$

$$= a\sqrt{2 - 2\cos(\alpha - \beta)}$$

$$= a\sqrt{2(1 - \cos(\alpha - \beta))}$$

$$= a\sqrt{2 \times 2\sin^2\left(\frac{\alpha - \beta}{2}\right)} = 2a\sin\left(\frac{\alpha - \beta}{2}\right)$$

2. Let B be $(\pm 6, y)$.

Now, $AB \le 4$

$\Rightarrow \quad (3 \pm 6)^2 + (y - 4)^2 \le 16$

$\Rightarrow \quad 9 + (y - 4)^2 \le 16$

$[\because 81 + (y - 4)^2 \le 16$ is not possible$]$

$\Rightarrow \quad y^2 - 8y + 9 \le 0$

$\Rightarrow \quad 4 - \sqrt{7} \le y \le 4 + \sqrt{7}$

But $\quad y \in Z$

$\therefore \quad y = 2, 3, 4, 5, 6$

3. Let BD be the bisector of $\angle ABC$. Then,

$AD : DC = AB : BC$

and $\quad AB = \sqrt{(5 + 1)^2 + (1 + 7)^2} = 10$

$BC = \sqrt{(5 - 1)^2 + (1 - 4)^2} = 5$

$\therefore \quad AD : DC = 2 : 1$

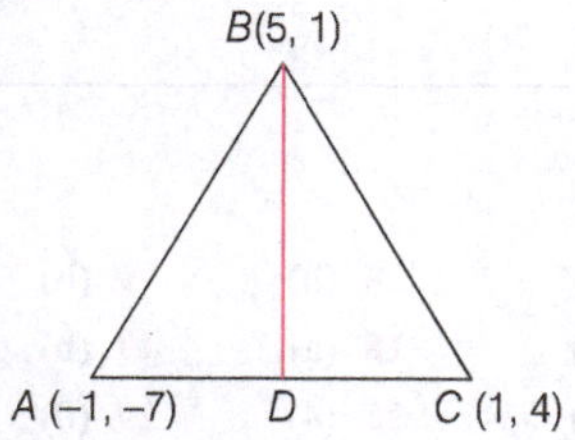

Using section formula,

$$D = \left(\frac{-1 \times 1 + 1 \times 2}{2 + 1}, \frac{-7 \times 1 + 4 \times 2}{2 + 1}\right)$$

$$= \left(\frac{1}{3}, \frac{1}{3}\right)$$

$$\therefore \quad BD = \sqrt{\left(5 - \frac{1}{3}\right)^2 + \left(1 - \frac{1}{3}\right)^2} = \sqrt{\frac{196}{9} + \frac{4}{9}} = \frac{10\sqrt{2}}{3}$$

4. We have,

$$(x_1 + 2)^2 + (y_1 - 3)^2 = (x_2 + 2)^2 + (y_2 - 3)^2 = (x_3 + 2)^2 + (y_3 - 3)^2$$

$\therefore (x_i, y_i), i = 1, 2, 3$ lies on a circle with centre $(-2, 3)$.

Since, triangle is an equilateral triangle.

So, centroid and circumcentre coincide.

$\therefore$ Centroid is $(-2, 3)$. Therefore,

$$\frac{x_1 + x_2 + x_3}{3} = -2 \text{ and } \frac{y_1 + y_2 + y_3}{3} = 3$$

$$\therefore \quad \frac{x_1 + x_2 + x_3}{y_1 + y_2 + y_3} = -\frac{2}{3}$$

5. Since, ΔOAB is right angled triangle. Its circumcentre is the mid-point of hypotenuse AB.

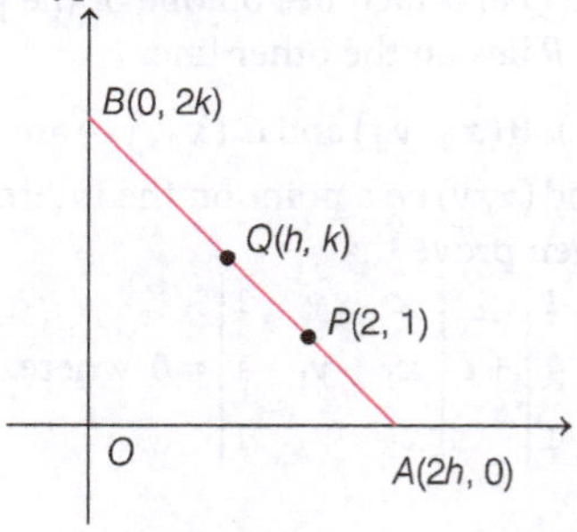

So, let the mid-point of AB be $Q(h, k)$. Then, the coordinates of A and B will be $(2h, 0)$ and $(0, 2k)$, respectively.

Now, A, P and B are collinear. Therefore,

$$\begin{vmatrix} 2h & 0 & 1 \\ 0 & 2k & 1 \\ 2 & 1 & 1 \end{vmatrix} = 0$$

$\Rightarrow \quad 2h(2k - 1) + 1(0 - 4k) = 0$

$\Rightarrow \quad 4hk - 2h - 4k = 0$

$\Rightarrow \quad h + 2k - 2hk = 0$

So, locus of circumcentre is $x + 2y - 2xy = 0$.

6. We have,

$$r = 4\tan\theta\sec\theta$$

$\Rightarrow \quad r = \dfrac{4\sin\theta}{\cos^2\theta}$

$\Rightarrow \quad r\cos^2\theta = 4\sin\theta$

$\Rightarrow \quad r^2\cos^2\theta = 4r\sin\theta$

$\Rightarrow \quad x^2 = 4y$

7. Let the coordinates of vertices O, P, Q, R be $(0, 0), (a, 0), (a, a), (0, a)$, respectively. Then, $M = \left(a, \dfrac{a}{2}\right)$ and $N = \left(\dfrac{a}{2}, a\right)$.

$$\therefore \text{Area of } (\Delta OMN) = \frac{1}{2}\begin{vmatrix} 0 & 0 & 1 \\ a & \frac{a}{2} & 1 \\ \frac{a}{2} & a & 1 \end{vmatrix} = \frac{3a^2}{8}$$

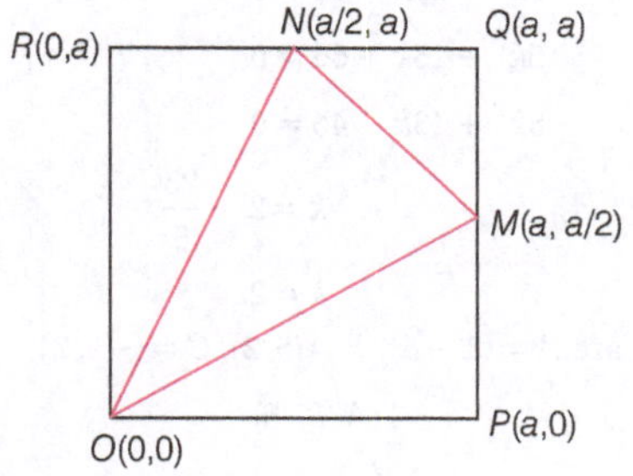

Also, area of square $= a^2$

$\therefore$ Required ratio $= 8:3$

8. We have, $(x_1 + t(x_2 - x_1), y_1 + t(y_2 - y_1))$

$$\equiv (x_1(1-t) + tx_2, y_1(1-t) + ty_2)$$

$\therefore$ The given point divides (x_1, y_1) and (x_2, y_2) in the ratio $t:(1-t)$.

Since, it divides internally.

$\therefore \quad t > 0, 1 - t > 0 \Rightarrow t > 0, t < 1$

$\therefore \quad 0 < t < 1$

9. By shifting the origin at (1, 2), we have

$$x = X + 1, y = Y + 2.$$

On substituting these values in $y^2 - 8x - 4y + 12 = 0$, we get

$$(Y+2)^2 - 8(X+1) - 4(Y+2) + 12 = 0$$

$\Rightarrow \quad Y^2 - 8X = 0 \Rightarrow Y^2 = 8X$

On comparing this with $Y^2 = 4aX$, we get

$$4a = 8 \Rightarrow a = 2$$

10. We have, $x = 4, y = 2\sqrt{3}$ and $\theta = -30°$

$\therefore \quad X = x\cos\theta + y\sin\theta$

$$= 4\cos(-30°) + 2\sqrt{3}\sin(-30°) = 2\sqrt{3} - \sqrt{3} = \sqrt{3}$$

and $\quad Y = -x\sin\theta + y\cos\theta$

$$= -4\sin(-30°) + 2\sqrt{3}\cos(-30°) = 2 + 3 = 5$$

$\therefore$ The given point in new system is $(\sqrt{3}, 5)$.

11. **Decoding the Question**

To solve this problem, use the following formula as orthocentre, centroid and circumcentre are collinear and the centroid divides the line joining the orthocentre and circumcentre in the ratio of 2 : 1.

Since, the distance of all points from $O(0, 0) = 5$

$\therefore O(0, 0)$ be the circumcentre.

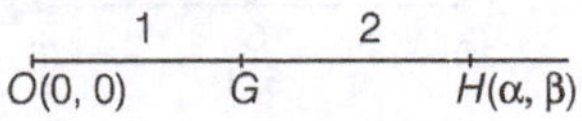

Centroid of triangle, (G)

$$\equiv \left(\frac{3 + 5\cos\theta + 5\sin\theta}{3}, \frac{4 + 5\sin\theta - 5\cos\theta}{3}\right)$$

Let $H(\alpha, \beta)$ be the orthocentre of the triangle, then

$$\alpha = 3 + 5\cos\theta + 5\sin\theta$$

$\Rightarrow \quad (\alpha - 3) = 5\cos\theta + 5\sin\theta \quad$ ...(i)

and $\quad \beta = 4 + 5\sin\theta - 5\cos\theta$

$\Rightarrow \quad (\beta - 4) = 5\sin\theta - 5\cos\theta \quad$ ...(ii)

On squaring and adding Eqs. (i) and (ii), we get

$$(\alpha - 3)^2 + (\beta - 4)^2 = 25 + 25$$

$\Rightarrow \quad \alpha^2 + \beta^2 - 6\alpha - 8\beta - 25 = 0$

Hence, the locus of $H(\alpha, \beta)$ is

$$x^2 + y^2 - 6x - 8y - 25 = 0$$

12.

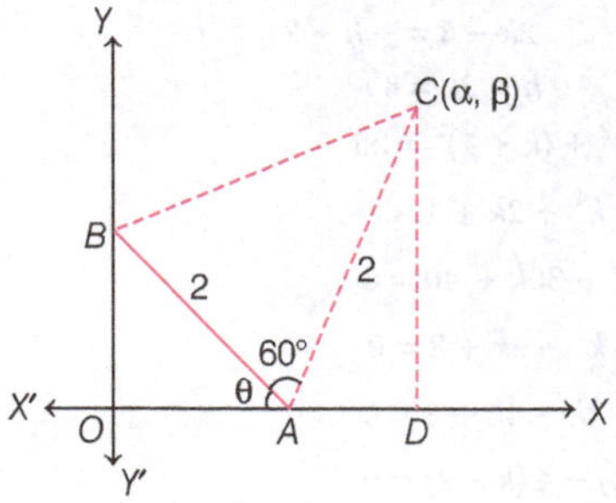

Let $\quad AB = AC = 2$

and $\quad \angle BAO = \theta$

Let $\quad C \equiv (\alpha, \beta)$

$\therefore \quad \alpha = 2\cos\theta + 2\cos(180° - (60° + \theta))$

$$= 2\cos\theta - 2\cos(60° + \theta)$$

$$= 2\cos\theta - 2\left\{\cos\theta \times \frac{1}{2} - \sin\theta \times \frac{\sqrt{3}}{2}\right\}$$

$$= \cos\theta + \sqrt{3}\sin\theta \quad \text{...(i)}$$

and $\quad \beta = 2\sin(180° - (60° + \theta)) = 2\sin(60° + \theta)$

$$= 2\left(\sin\theta \times \frac{1}{2} + \cos\theta \times \frac{\sqrt{3}}{2}\right)$$

$$= \sin\theta + \sqrt{3}\cos\theta \quad \text{...(ii)}$$

On eliminating θ from Eqs. (i) and (ii), we get

$$\alpha^2 + \beta^2 - \alpha\beta\sqrt{3} - 1 = 0$$

Hence, the locus of $H(\alpha, \beta)$ is

$$x^2 + y^2 - xy\sqrt{3} - 1 = 0$$

13. Let $a = 3x + 4y, b = 4x + 3y, c = 5x + 5y$

$$\therefore \quad \cos C = \frac{a^2 + b^2 - c^2}{2ab}$$

$$= \frac{(3x+4y)^2 + (4x+3y)^2 - (5x+5y)^2}{2(3x+4y)(4x+3y)}$$

$$= -\frac{xy}{(3x+4y)(4x+3y)} < 0$$

$\Rightarrow \quad C > 90°$

Hence, triangle is obtuse angled.

14.

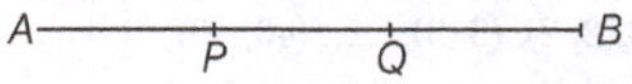

$\because \quad AP = PQ = QB$

$\therefore$ Mid-point of PQ = Mid-point of $AB = \left(\frac{1}{2}, 3\right)$

15. Let the point C be (h, k).

Given, $AC = 5$

$\Rightarrow \quad h^2 + (k+1)^2 = 25 \quad \text{...(i)}$

Now, slope of $AC \times$ slope of $AB = -1$

$$\Rightarrow \quad \frac{k-3}{h-2} \times \frac{3+1}{2-0} = -1$$

$$\Rightarrow \quad \frac{k-3}{h-2} \times 2 = -1$$

$\Rightarrow \quad 2k - 6 = -h + 2$

$\Rightarrow \quad h + 2k = 8 \quad \text{...(ii)}$

From Eq. (i), $(8-2k)^2 + (k+1)^2 = 25$

$\Rightarrow 64 + 4k^2 - 32k + k^2 + 2k + 1 = 2$

$\Rightarrow \quad 5k^2 - 30k + 40 = 0$

$\Rightarrow \quad k^2 - 6k + 8 = 0$

$\Rightarrow \quad k^2 - 2k - 4k + 8 = 0$

$\Rightarrow \quad k(k-2) - 4(k-2) = 0$

$\Rightarrow \quad (k-2)(k-4) = 0$

$\Rightarrow \quad k = 2, 4$

When $k = 2, h = 8 - 2(2) = 8 - 4 = 4$

When, $k = 4, h = 8 - 2(4) = 8 - 8 = 0$

$\therefore \quad C \equiv (4, 2)$ or $(0, 4)$

16. From the figure, we have

$a = 2, b = 2\sqrt{2}, c = 2 \quad [\because BC = a, CA = b, AB = c]$

$x_1 = 0, x_2 = 0, x_3 = 2$

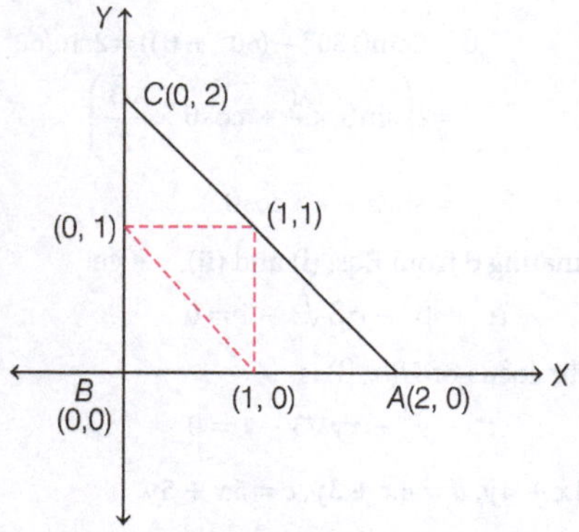

Now, x-coordinate of incentre

$$= \frac{2 \times 0 + 2\sqrt{2} \times 0 + 2 \times 2}{2 + 2 + 2\sqrt{2}}$$

$$= \frac{2}{2 + \sqrt{2}} = 2 - \sqrt{2}$$

17. Total number of integral points inside the square

$OABC = 40 \times 40 = 1600$

Number of integral points on AC = Number of integral points on OB = 40 (namely (1, 1),(2, 2), (3, 3), ... (40, 40)

Hence, number of integral points inside the ΔOAC

$$= \frac{1600 - 40}{2} = 780$$

18. Given,
$$\frac{1}{2}\begin{vmatrix} k & -3k & 1 \\ 5 & k & 1 \\ -k & 2 & 1 \end{vmatrix} = \pm 28$$

$\Rightarrow \quad 5k^2 + 13k + 10 = \pm 56$

$\Rightarrow \quad 5k^2 + 13k - 46 = 0$

or $\quad 5k^2 + 13k + 66 = 0 \quad [\because D < 0]$

$\therefore \quad 5k^2 + 13k - 46 = 0$

$$\Rightarrow \quad k = 2, -\frac{23}{5}$$

$\therefore \quad k = 2 \quad [\because k \in I]$

$\therefore$ Vertices are $A = (2, -6)$, $B = (5, 2)$, $C = (-2, 2)$

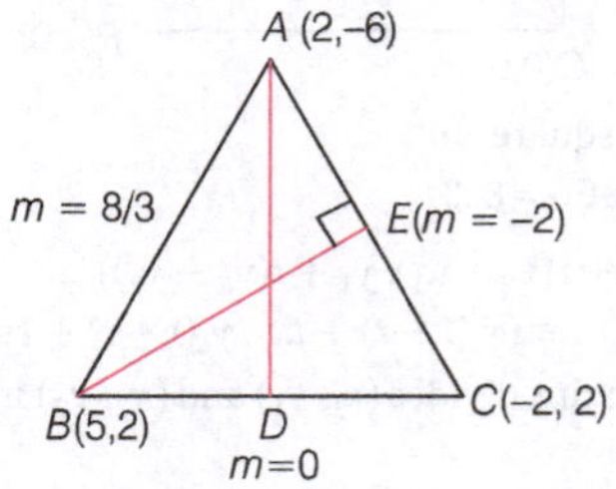

The orthocentre of a triangle is the point of intersection of lines AD and BE. Let its coordinates be (x, y).

Now, slope of line AD is infinite, hence the x-coordinate of its orthocentre will be 2 because the line AD passes through $(2, -6)$.

Line BE is perpendicular on AC, hence, its slope will be equal to

$m_{BE} \times m_{AC} = -1 \quad [\because BE \perp AC]$

$\Rightarrow \quad m_{BE} \times -2 = -1$

$$\Rightarrow \quad m_{BE} = \frac{1}{2}$$

Now, the equation of line BE will be

$y - y_1 = m_{BE}(x - x_1)$

$$\Rightarrow \quad y - 2 = \frac{1}{2}(x - 5)$$

$$\Rightarrow \quad y = \frac{1}{2}(2-5) + 2 \quad [x = 2]$$

$$\Rightarrow \quad y = \frac{-3}{2} + 2 \Rightarrow y = \frac{1}{2}$$

Therefore, the coordinates of orthocentre are $\left(2, \frac{1}{2}\right)$.

19. Harmonic conjugate of $C(5,1)$ w.r.t. $A(2, 10)$ and $B(6, -2)$.

Let C divides AB in $k : 1$.

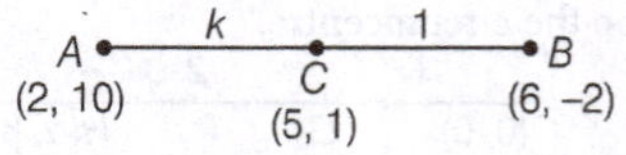

$$\Rightarrow \quad \frac{-2k + 10}{k + 1} = 1$$

$\Rightarrow \quad -2k + 10 = k + 1$

$\Rightarrow \quad 3k = 9 \Rightarrow k = 3$

Harmonic conjugate is

$$\left[\frac{3\times 6-1\times 2}{3-1},\left(\frac{3\times(-2)-1\times 10}{3-1}\right)\right]$$

$$=\left(\frac{16}{2},\frac{-16}{2}\right)=(8,-8)$$

$\therefore$ Circumcentre, $O=(8,-8)$

and orthocentre, $H=(3,-4)$

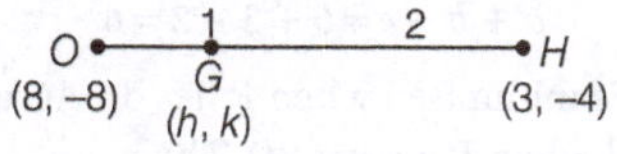

$$\therefore \quad G=\left(\frac{3+16}{2+1},\frac{-4-16}{2+1}\right)=\left(\frac{19}{3},\frac{-20}{3}\right)$$

20. Let O' be $(-2,-3)$. Since, the axes are rotated about O' by an angle of 45° in anti-clockwise direction. Let (x', y') be the new axes and (x, y) be the coordinates with respect to old axes, then

$$x=-2+x'\cos 45°-y'\sin 45°$$

$$\Rightarrow \quad x=-2+\left(\frac{x'-y'}{\sqrt{2}}\right)$$

and $y=-3+x'\sin 45°+y'\cos 45°$

$$\Rightarrow \quad y=-3+\left(\frac{x'+y'}{\sqrt{2}}\right)$$

The new equation will be

$$2\left\{-2+\left(\frac{x'-y'}{\sqrt{2}}\right)\right\}^2+4\left\{\left(-2+\frac{(x'-y')}{\sqrt{2}}\right)\left(-3+\frac{(x'+y')}{\sqrt{2}}\right)\right\}$$

$$-5\left\{-3+\left(\frac{x'+y'}{\sqrt{2}}\right)\right\}^2+20\left\{-2+\left(\frac{x'-y'}{\sqrt{2}}\right)\right\}$$

$$-22\left\{-3+\frac{(x'+y')}{\sqrt{2}}\right\}-14=0$$

$$\Rightarrow \quad (x')^2-14x'y'-7(y')^2-2=0$$

New equation of curve is

$$x^2-14xy-7y^2-2=0$$

21. Using section formula, $A\equiv\left(\frac{3k-5}{k+1},\frac{5k+1}{k+1}\right)$

Now, area of $\Delta ABC=2$

$$\Rightarrow \quad \frac{1}{2}\begin{vmatrix}1 & 5 & 1\\ 7 & -2 & 1\\ \frac{3k-5}{k+1} & \frac{5k+1}{k+1} & 1\end{vmatrix}=\pm 2$$

$$\Rightarrow \quad \begin{vmatrix}1 & 5 & 1\\ 7 & -2 & 1\\ \frac{3k-5}{k+1} & \frac{5k+1}{k+1} & 1\end{vmatrix}=\pm 4$$

$$\Rightarrow 1\left[-2-\frac{5k+1}{k+1}\right]-5\left[7-\frac{3k-5}{k+1}\right]$$

$$+1\left[\frac{7(5k+1)}{k+1}+\frac{2(3k-5)}{k+1}\right]=\pm 4$$

$$\Rightarrow \quad \left[\frac{-2k-2-5k-1}{k+1}\right]-5\left[\frac{7k+7-3k+5}{k+1}\right]$$

$$+\left[\frac{35k+7+6k-10}{k+1}\right]=\pm 4$$

$$\Rightarrow \quad -7k-3-20k-60+41k-3=\pm 4(k+1)$$

$$\Rightarrow \quad 14k-66=\pm 4(k+1)$$

$$\Rightarrow \quad k=7,\frac{31}{9}$$

22. Every point (x,y) on the perpendicular bisector of PQ is equidistant from both P and Q, we have

$$(x-1)^2+(y-4)^2=(x-\alpha)^2+(y-3)^2$$

$$\Rightarrow \quad -2x-8y+17=-2\alpha x+\alpha^2-6y+9$$

$\therefore$ It cuts X-axis at -4.

At $\quad x=0, y=-4$

$$\Rightarrow \quad -8(-4)+17=\alpha^2-6(-4)+9$$

$$\Rightarrow \quad \alpha^2=16$$

$$\Rightarrow \quad \alpha=\pm 4$$

$\therefore$ The positive integral value of α is 4.

23. We have, $3x+4y=9$ and $y=mx+1$,

On solving, we get

$$x=\frac{5}{4m+3}$$

Since, x-coordinate is an integer.

$\therefore \quad 4m+3=\pm 5$

or $\quad 4m+3=\pm 1$

$$\Rightarrow \quad m=\frac{1}{2},-2,-\frac{1}{2},-1$$

$\therefore$ Required sum $=|-2|+|-1|=2+1=3$

24. Clearly, triangle with vertices $A(6, 0)$, $B(0, 6)$ and $C(6, 6)$ is a right angled triangle, right angled at C. So, the coordinates of its orthocentre are $(6, 6)$ and the circumcentre is the mid-point of hypotenuse AB. Thus, the coordinates of the circumcentre are $(3, 3)$.

Hence, the required distance $=\sqrt{(6-3)^2+(6-3)^2}=3\sqrt{2}$

For minimum $\alpha\beta$,

$\therefore \quad \alpha=3, \beta=2 \quad [\because \alpha, \beta\in N]$

So, $\quad \alpha\beta=6$

25. Equation of median through B and C are $x+y=5$ and $x=4$.

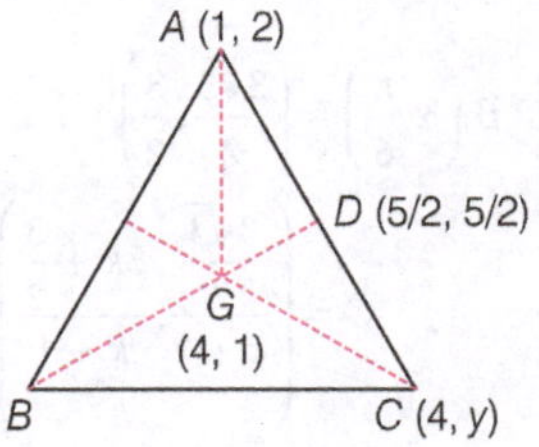

Let $C(4, y)$.

Now, mid-point of $AC=\left(\frac{1+4}{2},\frac{2+y}{2}\right)=\left(\frac{5}{2},\frac{2+y}{2}\right)$

It lies on BD.

$$\frac{5}{2}+\frac{2+y}{2}=5$$

$\Rightarrow \quad 2+y=5$

$\Rightarrow \quad y=3 \Rightarrow C=(4,3)$

and centroid G is point of intersection of median.

$\therefore \quad G=(4,1)$

$\therefore$ Area of $\Delta AGC=\frac{1}{3}\times$ Area of (ΔABC)

$$\therefore \quad \text{Area of } \Delta ABC = 3\times\frac{1}{2}\begin{vmatrix}1 & 2 & 1\\ 4 & 3 & 1\\ 4 & 1 & 1\end{vmatrix}$$

$$=\frac{3}{2}\{|2-8|\}=\frac{3}{2}\times 6=9 \text{ sq units}$$

26. Given, the vertices of a right angled triangle are $A(1, k)$, $B(1, 1)$ and $C(2, 1)$ and area of $\Delta ABC = 1$ sq. unit

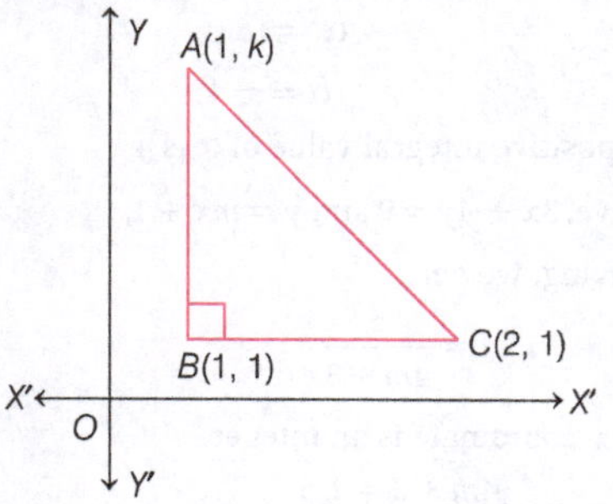

We know that area of right angled triangle

$$=\frac{1}{2}\times BC\times AB=\frac{1}{2}(1)(k-1)$$

$$=\frac{1}{2}\ |k-1| \ \Rightarrow \pm(k-1)=2$$

$\Rightarrow \quad k=-1, 3$

$\therefore$ The positive integral value of k is 3.

27. Let the line $r=\dfrac{4}{\sin\theta-\cos\theta}$ divides the line joining the points $\left(3, \dfrac{\pi}{2}\right)$ and $\left(3, \dfrac{\pi}{6}\right)$ in the ratio $k:1$ and point is C.

Now, $\quad A=\left(3, \dfrac{\pi}{2}\right)=(0, 3)$

$$r=3, \theta=\frac{\pi}{2}, x=r\cos\theta, y=r\sin\theta$$

$$B\left(3, \frac{\pi}{6}\right)=\left(\frac{3\sqrt{3}}{2}, \frac{3}{2}\right)$$

$$\therefore \quad C=\left(\frac{\frac{3\sqrt{3}}{2}}{k+1}, \frac{3k+\frac{3}{2}}{k+1}\right)=\left(\frac{3\sqrt{3}}{2(k+1)}, \frac{6k+3}{2(k+1)}\right)$$

Now, equation of line, $r=\dfrac{4}{\sin\theta-\cos\theta}$

$\Rightarrow \quad r\sin\theta-r\cos\theta=4 \Rightarrow y-x=4$

and C lies on line $\dfrac{6k+3}{2(k+1)}-\dfrac{3\sqrt{3}}{2(k+1)}=4$

$\Rightarrow \quad 6k+3-3\sqrt{3}=8k+8$

$\Rightarrow \quad 2k=-5-3\sqrt{3}\Rightarrow k=-\left(\dfrac{5+3\sqrt{3}}{2}\right)$

$\therefore$ C divides AB externally in the ratio $5+3\sqrt{3}:2=a+b\sqrt{3}:c$

$\Rightarrow \quad a=5, b=3$ and $c=2$

$\therefore \quad a+b-c=5+3-2=6$

28. $AP+PC$ is minimised when P lies on AC and $BP+PD$ is minimised when P lies on BD. Thus,

$$AP+PB+PC+PD=AC+BD$$

$$=\sqrt{(1-D)^2+(-1-1)^2}+\sqrt{(-1-1)^2+(0-1)^2}=2\sqrt{5}$$

$\therefore \quad d=2\sqrt{5}$

$\therefore \quad [d]=4$

29. As H, G and S are collinear, we have

$$\begin{vmatrix}4 & b & 1\\ b & 2b-8 & 1\\ -4 & 8 & 1\end{vmatrix}=0$$

$$\Rightarrow \quad \begin{vmatrix}14 & b & 1\\ b-4 & b-8 & 0\\ -(b+4) & 16-2b & 0\end{vmatrix}=0$$

$\Rightarrow \quad (b-4)(16-2b)+(b+4)(b-8)=0$

$\Rightarrow \quad 2(b-4)(8-b)+(b+4)(b-8)=0$

$\Rightarrow \quad (8-b)[(2b-8)-(b+4)]=0$

$\Rightarrow \quad (8-b)(b-12)=0$

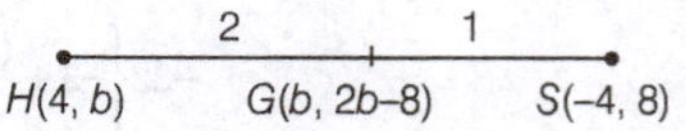

From above figure,

$$\frac{-8+4}{3}=b\Rightarrow b=-\frac{4}{3}$$

and $\quad \dfrac{16+b}{3}=2b-8\Rightarrow b=8$

But no common value of b is possible.

30. Let A, B and C be the vertices of triangle and D, E, F are feet of perpendicular.

$\because$ Orthocentre of ΔABC is incentre of its pedal ΔDEF.

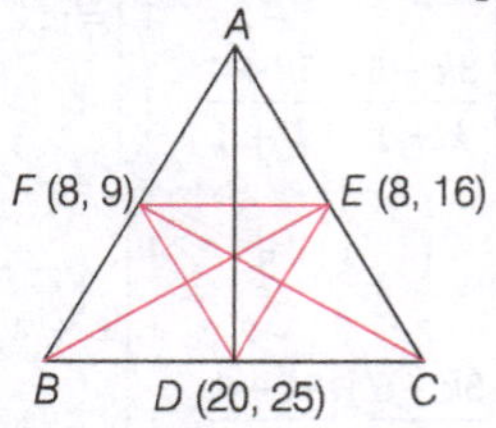

Now, $\quad DE=\sqrt{(12)^2+(9)^2}=15$

$$EF=\sqrt{0^2+(7)^2}=7$$

$$FD=\sqrt{(12)^2+(16)^2}=20$$

$\therefore$ Required point $= \left(\dfrac{ax_1 + bx_2 + cx_3}{a+b+c}, \dfrac{ay_1 + by_2 + cy_3}{a+b+c}\right)$

$= \left(\dfrac{20(7) + 8(20) + 8(15)}{7 + 20 + 15}, \dfrac{25(7) + 16(20) + 9(15)}{7 + 20 + 15}\right)$

$= (10, 15) = (\alpha, \beta)$

$\therefore \quad \beta - \alpha = 15 - 10 = 5$

31. Let the point be (h, k).

According to the question,

$$\frac{\sqrt{(h-2)^2 + (k-1)^2}}{\sqrt{(h-1)^2 + (k-3)^2}} = \frac{5}{4}$$

By squaring and simplification,

$16[(h-2)^2 + (k-1)^2] = 25[(h-1)^2 + (k-3)^2]$

$\Rightarrow 16[h^2 + 4 - 4h + k^2 + 1 - 2k]$

$= 25[h^2 + 1 - 2h + k^2 + 9 - 6k]$

$\Rightarrow 9h^2 + 9k^2 + 14h - 118k + 170 = 0$

Now, replace (h, k) with (x, y), so the locus is

$$9x^2 + 9y^2 + 14x - 118y + 170 = 0$$

Now, comparing it with $ax^2 + by^2 + cxy + dx + ey + 170 = 0$, we have

$$a = 9, b = 9, c = 0, d = 14, e = -118$$

So, the value of

$a^2 + 2b + 3c + 4d + e = 81 + 18 + 0 + 56 - 118 = 37$

32. We have,

$A(a, -2), B(a, 6)$ and $C\left(\dfrac{a}{4}, -2\right)$ and $O\left(5, \dfrac{a}{4}\right)$

$\therefore \quad AO = BO$

$\Rightarrow (a-5)^2 + \left(-2 - \dfrac{a}{4}\right)^2 = (a-5)^2 + \left(6 - \dfrac{a}{4}\right)^2$

$\Rightarrow a^2 + 25 - 10a + 4 + \dfrac{a^2}{16} + a$

$= a^2 + 25 - 10a + 36 + \dfrac{a^2}{16} - 3a$

$\Rightarrow \quad a = 8$

$AB = 8, AC = 6$ and $BC = 10$

$\therefore \quad \alpha = 5, \beta = 24$ and $\gamma = 24$

$\therefore \quad \alpha + \beta + \gamma = 5 + 24 + 24 = 53$

33. Given, $A(\alpha, -2)\ B(\alpha, 6), C\left(\dfrac{\alpha}{4}, -2\right)$

$AB = \sqrt{0^2 + 8^2} = 8$

$AC = \sqrt{\left(\alpha - \dfrac{\alpha}{4}\right)^2 + 0} = \dfrac{3\alpha}{4}$

$BC = \sqrt{\left(\alpha - \dfrac{\alpha}{4}\right)^2 + (6+2)^2} = \sqrt{\left(\dfrac{3\alpha}{4}\right)^2 + 64}$

So, $\quad (AB)^2 + (AC)^2 = (BC)^2$

Also, AC is perpendicular to AB.

Hence, ΔABC is a right angled triangle at A

Now, circumcentre is mid-point of BC.

$$\left(5, \frac{\alpha}{4}\right) = \left(\frac{\alpha + \frac{\alpha}{4}}{2}, \frac{6-2}{2}\right)$$

So, $\quad \dfrac{\alpha}{4} = 2 \Rightarrow \alpha = 8$

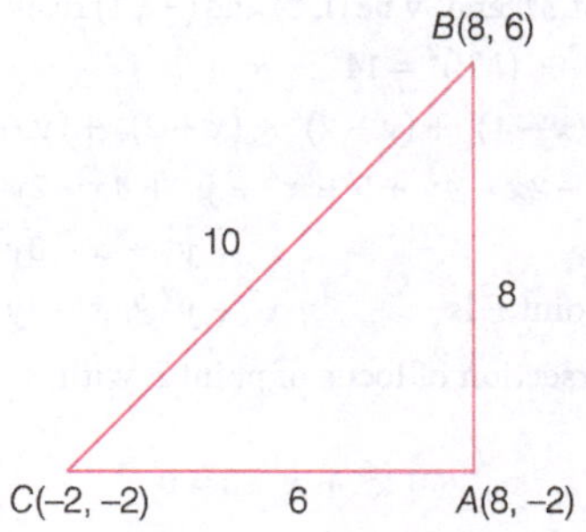

So, area of $\Delta ABC = \dfrac{1}{2} \times 6 \times 8 = 24$

Perimeter $= 6 + 8 + 10 = 24$

Circumradius $= \dfrac{BC}{2} = \dfrac{10}{2} = 5$

Inradius $= \dfrac{\Delta}{S} = \dfrac{24}{12} = 2 \qquad \left[\because x = \dfrac{a+b+c}{2}\right]$

34. Let $\dfrac{a+b}{7} = \dfrac{b+c}{8} = \dfrac{c+a}{9} = K$

$\therefore \quad a + b = 7K, b + c = 8K$ and $c + a = 9K$

Semi-perimeter of triangles,

$(s) = \dfrac{a+b+c}{2} = \dfrac{2(a+b+c)}{4}$

$= \dfrac{(a+b) + (b+c) + (c+a)}{4}$

$= \dfrac{7K + 8K + 9K}{4} = 6K$

$a = 2s - (b+c) = 12K - 8K = 4K$

Similarly, $\quad b = 3K$ and $c = 5K$

Now, $\quad \Delta = \sqrt{s(s-a)(s-b)(s-c)}$

$= \sqrt{6K(2K)(3K)(K)} = 6K^2$

Radius of incircle $(r) = \dfrac{\Delta}{S} = \dfrac{6K^2}{6K} = K$

Radius of circumcircle $(R) = \dfrac{abc}{4\Delta}$

$= \dfrac{4K \times 3K \times 5K}{4 \times 6K^2} = \dfrac{5K}{2}$

$\therefore \quad \dfrac{R}{r} = \dfrac{5K}{2} \div K$

$= \dfrac{5}{2}$

35. **Decoding the Question**

(i) The orthocentre of a triangle is the point where the perpendicular drawn from the vertices to the opposite sides of the triangle intersect each other.

(ii) For perpendicular lines, product of their slopes is equal to = − 1

Let the coordinates of point P be (x, y).

Let the point M and N be $(1, 2)$ and $(-2, 1)$ respectively.

Given, $(MP)^2 + (NP)^2 = 14$

$$(x-1)^2 + (y-2)^2 + (x+2)^2 + (y-1)^2 = 14$$

$$\Rightarrow x^2 + y^2 - 2x - 4y + 5 + x^2 + y^2 + 4x - 2y + 5 = 14$$

$$\Rightarrow \quad x^2 + y^2 + x - 3y - 2 = 0$$

$\therefore$ Locus of point P is $\quad x^2 + y^2 + x - 3y - 2 = 0$

For the intersection of locus of point P with X-axis, substitute $y = 0$

$$\Rightarrow \quad x^2 + x - 2 = 0$$

$$\Rightarrow \quad x(x+2) - 1(x+2) = 0 \Rightarrow x = -2, 1$$

Let point $A(-2, 0)$ and $B(1, 0)$.

For the intersection of locus of point P with Y-axis, substitute $x = 0$,

$$\Rightarrow \quad y^2 - 3y - 2 = 0$$

$$\Rightarrow \quad y = \frac{3 \pm \sqrt{9+8}}{2} = \frac{3 \pm \sqrt{17}}{2}$$

$\therefore$ Point $C\left(0, \frac{3+\sqrt{17}}{2}\right)$ and point $D\left(0, \frac{3-\sqrt{17}}{2}\right)$.

$$\text{Area of quadrilateral } = \frac{1}{2}\begin{vmatrix} x_1 - x_3 & x_2 - x_4 \\ y_1 - y_3 & y_2 - y_4 \end{vmatrix}$$

$$= \frac{1}{2}\begin{vmatrix} -2-1 & 0-0 \\ 0-0 & \frac{3+\sqrt{17}}{2} - \frac{3-\sqrt{17}}{2} \end{vmatrix}$$

$$= \frac{1}{2}|-3(\sqrt{17})| = \frac{3\sqrt{17}}{2} \text{ sq. units}$$

36. Given that $A\left(\frac{3}{\sqrt{a}}, \sqrt{a}\right)$, $a > 0$ be a fixed point in the XY-plane, the image of A in Y-axis is $B\left(-\frac{3}{\sqrt{a}}, \sqrt{a}\right)$ and the image of B in X-axis is $C\left(\frac{-3}{\sqrt{a}}, -\sqrt{a}\right)$ and also given $D(3\cos\theta, a\sin\theta)$ in the IV quadrant.

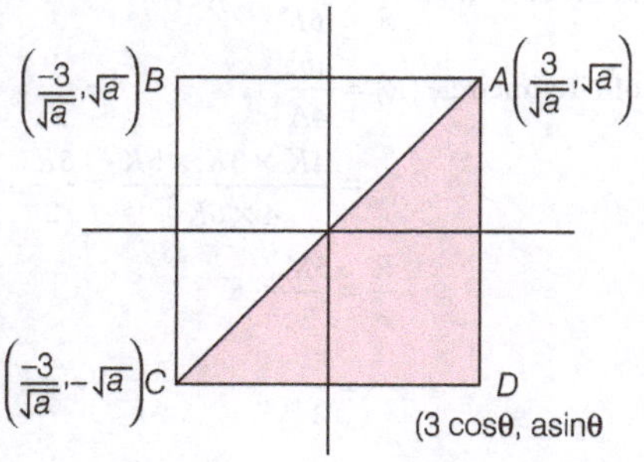

Thus, area of ΔACD

$$\Delta = \frac{1}{2}\begin{vmatrix} \frac{3}{\sqrt{a}} & \sqrt{a} & 1 \\ -\frac{3}{\sqrt{a}} & -\sqrt{a} & 1 \\ 3\cos\theta & a\sin\theta & 1 \end{vmatrix}$$

Applying $R_1 \to R_1 + R_2$,

$$\Rightarrow \quad \Delta = \frac{1}{2}\begin{vmatrix} 0 & 0 & 2 \\ -\frac{3}{\sqrt{a}} & -\sqrt{a} & 1 \\ 3\cos\theta & a\sin\theta & 1 \end{vmatrix}$$

$$\Rightarrow \quad \Delta = \left|\frac{1}{2} 2\{-3\sqrt{a}\sin\theta + 3\sqrt{a}\cos\theta\}\right|$$

$$\Rightarrow \quad \Delta = |3\sqrt{a}(-\sin\theta + \cos\theta)|$$

$$\Rightarrow \quad \Delta = 3\sqrt{a}|-\sin\theta + \cos\theta|$$

$$\therefore \quad \Delta_{\max} = 3\sqrt{a} \cdot \sqrt{2} = 12 \text{ (given)}$$

$$\Rightarrow \quad \sqrt{a} = 2\sqrt{2}$$

$$\Rightarrow \quad a = (2\sqrt{2})^2 = 8$$

37. According to given information,

Let $AC = l$

and $AB = \sqrt{(3-1)^2 + (1-2)^2} = \sqrt{5}$

$\therefore$ The area of right angled ΔABC

$$= \frac{1}{2}(AC)(AB) = 5\sqrt{5} \quad \text{[given]}$$

$$\Rightarrow \quad \frac{1}{2}l(\sqrt{5}) = 5\sqrt{5}$$

$$\Rightarrow \quad l = 10 \text{ units}$$

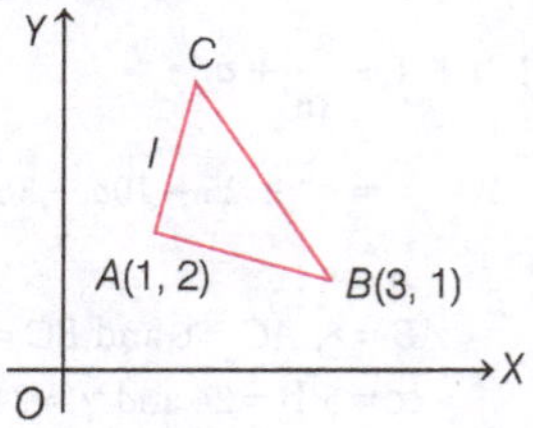

Now, according to concept of rotation abscissa of the vertex C we will get easily if we write the coordinate of the vertices in complex form, like $A(1 + 2i)$, $B(3 + i)$ and let $C(x_1 + iy_1)$.

$$\text{Then,} \quad \frac{x_1 + iy_1 - 1 - 2i}{3 + i - 1 - 2i} = \frac{AC}{AB} e^{i\frac{\pi}{2}}$$

$$\Rightarrow \quad \frac{(x_1 - 1) + i(y_1 - 2)}{2 - i} = \frac{10}{\sqrt{5}} i$$

$$\Rightarrow \quad (x_1 - 1) + i(y_1 - 2) = 2\sqrt{5}i(2 - i)$$

$$\Rightarrow \quad (x_1 - 1) + i(y_{12} - 2) = 2\sqrt{5} + 4\sqrt{5}i$$

$\therefore \quad x_1 = 1 + 2\sqrt{5}$ is abscissa of the vertex C.

Exercise 2 - JEE Advanced Pattern

1. $\frac{1}{2}\begin{vmatrix} 2a & 3a & 1 \\ 3b & 2b & 1 \\ c & c & 1 \end{vmatrix} = 0$

$\Rightarrow \quad 2a(2b - c) - 3a(3b - c) + 1(3bc - 2bc) = 0$

or $\quad -5ab + ac + bc = 0$

or $\quad c = \dfrac{5ab}{a+b}$

or $\quad \dfrac{2c}{5} = \dfrac{2ab}{a+b}$

Hence, $a, \frac{2c}{5}, b$ are in HP.

2. We have,

$$P = \{-\sin(\beta - \alpha), -\cos\beta\} \equiv (x_1, y_1)$$
$$Q = (\cos(\beta - \alpha), \sin\beta) \equiv (x_2, y_2)$$
$$R = \{\cos(\beta - \alpha + \theta), \sin(\beta - \theta)\}$$

The x-coordinate and y-coordinate of R are

$$X_R = x_2\cos\theta + x_1\sin\theta$$
$$Y_R = y_2\cos\theta + y_1\sin\theta$$

The points

$$\left(\frac{x_2\cos\theta + x_1\sin\theta}{\cos\theta + \sin\theta}, \frac{y_2\cos\theta + y_1\sin\theta}{\cos\theta + \sin\theta}\right)$$

lies on PQ. But R does not lies on PQ. For it to lie on PQ, $\cos\theta$ and $\sin\theta$ must be related by $\cos\theta + \sin\theta = 1$ which is not given.

$\therefore$ P, Q, R are non-collinear.

3. Let coordinates of A be $(0, 0)$.

Coordinates of B are $(2\cot\theta, 2)$ and coordinates of C are $(4\cot(60° - \theta), -4)$

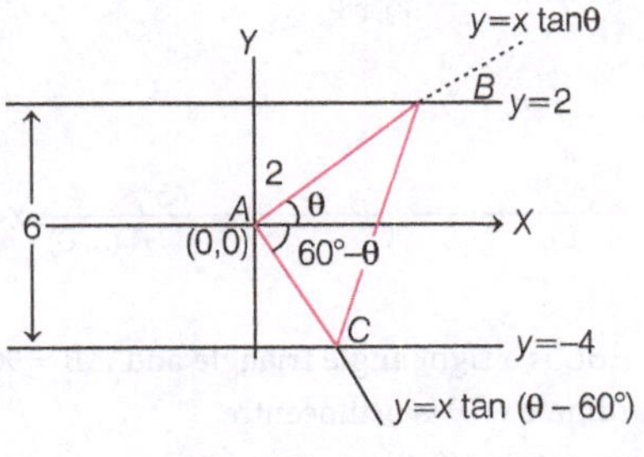

$\therefore \quad AB = AC$

$\Rightarrow \quad (AB)^2 = (AC)^2$

$\Rightarrow \quad 4\cot^2\theta + 4 = 16\cot^2(60° - \theta) + 16$

$\Rightarrow \quad 4\operatorname{cosec}^2\theta = 16\operatorname{cosec}^2(60° - \theta)$

$\Rightarrow \quad \sin(60° - \theta) = 2\sin\theta$

$\Rightarrow \quad \left(\frac{\sqrt{3}}{2}\cos\theta - \frac{1}{2}\sin\theta\right) = 2\sin\theta$

$\therefore \quad \tan\theta = \dfrac{\sqrt{3}}{5}$

$\therefore$ The required length $= AB$

$$= \sqrt{(4\cot^2\theta + 4)}$$
$$= 2\sqrt{\frac{28}{3}} = \frac{4\sqrt{7}}{\sqrt{3}}$$

4. **Statement (i)**

$\because$ Points $(-1, 0)$, $(4, -2)$ and $(\cos 2\theta, \sin 2\theta)$ are collinear.

$\therefore \quad \begin{vmatrix} -1 - \cos 2\theta & 0 - \sin 2\theta \\ 4 - \cos 2\theta & -2 - \sin 2\theta \end{vmatrix} = 0$

$\Rightarrow \quad 2 + \sin 2\theta + 2\cos 2\theta + \sin 2\theta \cos 2\theta$
$\qquad + 4\sin 2\theta - \sin 2\theta \cos 2\theta = 0$

$\Rightarrow \quad 5\sin 2\theta + 2(1 + \cos 2\theta) = 0$

$\Rightarrow \quad 10\sin\theta\cos\theta + 4\cos^2\theta = 0$

$\Rightarrow \quad 2\cos\theta(5\sin\theta + 2\cos\theta) = 0$

$\Rightarrow \quad \cos\theta = 0$ and $\tan\theta = -\dfrac{2}{5}$

$\Rightarrow \quad \theta = m\pi + \dfrac{\pi}{2}$

and $\quad \theta = n\pi + \tan^{-1}\left(\dfrac{-2}{5}\right); m, n \in I$

Statement (ii)

$\because$ Points $(-1, 0)$, $(4, -2)$ and $\left(\dfrac{1 - \tan^2\theta}{1 + \tan^2\theta}, \dfrac{2\tan\theta}{1 + \tan^2\theta}\right)$ are collinear.

$$\therefore \quad \begin{vmatrix} -1 - \dfrac{1 - \tan^2\theta}{1 + \tan^2\theta} & 0 - \dfrac{2\tan\theta}{1 + \tan^2\theta} \\ 4 - \dfrac{1 - \tan^2\theta}{1 + \tan^2\theta} & -2 - \dfrac{2\tan^2\theta}{1 + \tan^2\theta} \end{vmatrix} = 0$$

$\Rightarrow \quad 10\tan^3\theta + 4\tan^2\theta + 10\tan\theta + 4 = 0$

or $\quad (2\tan^2\theta + 2)(5\tan\theta + 2) = 0$ or $\tan^2\theta \neq -1$

$\therefore \quad \tan\theta = -\dfrac{2}{5}$

$\Rightarrow \quad \theta = p\pi + \tan^{-1}\left(\dfrac{-2}{5}\right), p \in I$

5. $\because \quad \dfrac{\sum_{r=0}^{n-1} x^{2r}}{\sum_{r=0}^{n-1} x^r} = $ Integer

$\Rightarrow \quad \dfrac{\dfrac{1\cdot(1 - x^{2n})}{(1 - x^2)}}{\dfrac{1\cdot(1 - x^n)}{(1 - x)}} = $ Integer

$\Rightarrow \quad \dfrac{1 + x^n}{1 + x} = $ Integer

n must be 1, 3, 5, 7, 9, 11, ...

$\therefore$ Vertices are (1, 7), (3, 9), (5, 11)

Here, $(AB)^2 = 8, (BC)^2 = 8$ and $(CA)^2 = 32$

$\therefore$ Triangle cannot be an equilateral triangle.

6. $ABCD$ is equilateral trapezium.

$\Rightarrow AB \parallel CD$ and $AD = BC$

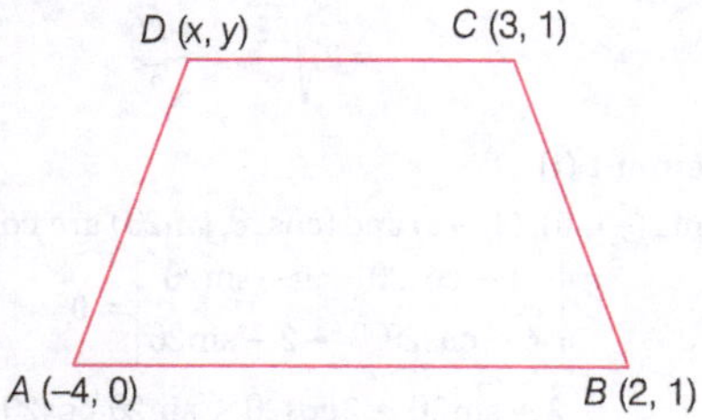

Now, $AD = BC$

$\Rightarrow \quad AD^2 = BC^2$

$\Rightarrow \quad (x+4)^2 + y^2 = 1 \quad \text{...(i)}$

$\because \quad AB \parallel CD$

Slope of AB = Slope of CD

$\Rightarrow \quad \dfrac{1-0}{2+4} = \dfrac{y-1}{x-3} \quad \left[\because \text{Slope} = \dfrac{y_2 - y_1}{x_2 - x_1}\right]$

$\Rightarrow \quad \dfrac{1}{6} = \dfrac{y-1}{x-3}$

$\Rightarrow \quad 6y - 6 = x - 3 \Rightarrow x - 6y = -3$

$x = 6y - 3$

From Eq. (i),

$(6y+1)^2 + y^2 = 1$

$\Rightarrow \quad 36y^2 + 12y + 1 + y^2 = 1$

$\Rightarrow \quad 37y^2 + 12y = 0$

$\Rightarrow \quad y(37y + 12) = 0$

$\Rightarrow \quad y = 0$ and $x = -3$

$\therefore$ Coordinate of D are $(-3, 0)$.

7. Let the line AC is parallel to $y = x$

$\therefore$ Side of square $= a = 4$

$\Rightarrow$ Diagonal $= a\sqrt{2} = 4\sqrt{2}$

$OA = OC = 2\sqrt{2}$

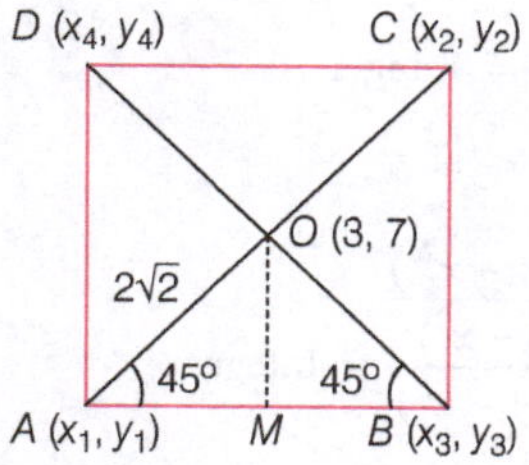

In ΔOAM, $\quad \sin 45^\circ = \dfrac{7 - y_1}{2\sqrt{2}} \Rightarrow \dfrac{7 - y_1}{2} = 1$

$\Rightarrow \quad 7 - y_1 = 2$

$\Rightarrow \quad y_1 = 5$

and $\quad \cos 45^\circ = \dfrac{AM}{2\sqrt{2}} \Rightarrow \dfrac{3 - x_1}{2\sqrt{2}} = \dfrac{1}{\sqrt{2}}$

$\Rightarrow \quad x_1 = 3 - 2 = 1$

O is mid-point of AC.

$\therefore \quad A = (1, 5), O(3, 7)$ and $C = (5, 9)$

Similarly, in ΔOBM,

$\because \quad \sin 45^\circ = \dfrac{7 - y_3}{2\sqrt{2}} \Rightarrow 7 - y_3 = 2 \Rightarrow y_3 = 5$

and $\quad \cos 45^\circ = \dfrac{x_3 - 3}{2\sqrt{2}} \Rightarrow x_3 - 3 = 2 \Rightarrow x_3 = 5$

$\therefore \quad B = (5, 5)$

O is mid-point of BD,

$B(5, 5), O(3, 7)$ and $D = (1, 9)$

$\therefore$ Vertices are $A(1,5), B(5,5), C(5,9)$ and $D(1,9)$.

8. $A = (m, n)$

B = reflection of A w.r.t. $y = x \equiv (n, m)$

C = reflection of B in Y-axis $\equiv (-n, m)$

D = reflection of C in X-axis $\equiv (-n, -m)$

E = reflection of D in Y-axis $\equiv (n, -m)$

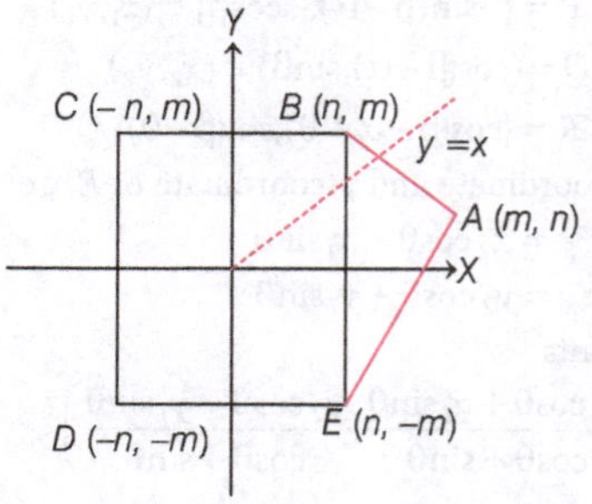

$\therefore$ Area of pentagon $ABCDE$

= Area of rectangle $BCDE$ + Area of ΔABE

$= 2m \times 2n + \dfrac{1}{2}(2m)(m - n) = m^2 + 3mn = m(m + 3n)$

9.

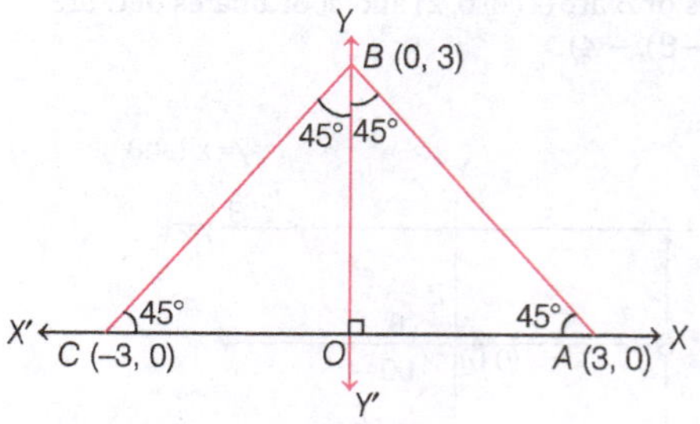

Here, ABC is a right angle triangle and $\angle B = 90^\circ$

$\therefore$ Coordinate of B is orthocentre.

$\therefore$ Orthocentre is (0, 3).

10.

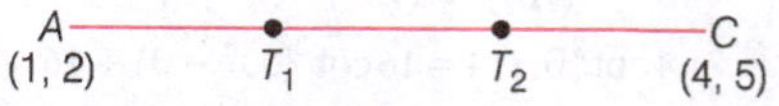

$\because \quad A \equiv (1, 2), B \equiv (4, 2)$ and $C \equiv (4, 5) \quad [\because AT_1 = T_1T_2 = T_2C]$

T_1 divides AC in the ratio 1 : 2 internally, then

$$T_1 \equiv \left(\frac{1 \times 4 + 2 \times 1}{1 + 2}, \frac{1 \times 5 + 2 \times 2}{1 + 2}\right) \text{ or } T_1 \equiv (2, 3)$$

and T_2 is the mid-point of T_1 and C, then

$$T_2 \equiv \left(\frac{2 + 4}{2}, \frac{3 + 5}{2}\right) \text{ or } T_2 \equiv (3, 4)$$

S_1 divides BC in the ratio 1 : 2 (internally), then

$$[\because BS_1 = S_1S_2 = S_2C]$$

$$S_1 \equiv \left(\frac{1\times 4 + 2\times 4}{1+2}, \frac{1\times 5 + 2\times 2}{1+2}\right)$$

or $\quad S_1 \equiv (4, 3)$

and S_2 is the mid-point of S_1 and C, then

$$S_2 \equiv \left(\frac{4+4}{2}, \frac{3+5}{2}\right) \text{ or } S_2 = (4, 4)$$

$$\text{Area of quadrilateral } T_1S_1S_2T_2 = \frac{1}{2}\begin{vmatrix} 2 & 3 \\ 4 & 3 \\ 4 & 4 \\ 3 & 4 \\ 2 & 3 \end{vmatrix}$$

$$= \frac{1}{2}|(6+16+16+9)-(12+12+12+8)|$$

$$= \frac{3}{2} \text{ sq units}$$

11. The orthocentre of ΔBCH is the intersection point of BA and CA i.e. $A(-1, 0)$

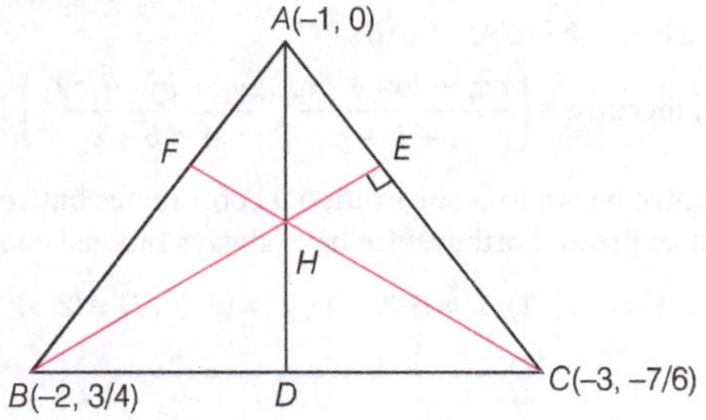

12. Given, $x_1^2 + y_1^2 + x_2^2 + y_2^2 + x_3^2 + y_3^2 + x_4^2 + y_4^2$

$$\le 2x_1x_3 + 2x_2x_4 + 2y_2y_3 + 2y_1y_4$$

$$\Rightarrow (x_1 - x_3)^2 + (x_2 - x_4)^2 + (y_2 - y_3)^2 + (y_1 - y_4)^2 \le 0$$

or $\quad (x_1 - x_3)^2 + (x_2 - x_4)^2 + (y_2 - y_3)^2 + (y_1 - y_4)^2 = 0$

or $\quad x_1 = x_3, x_2 = x_4, y_2 = y_3, y_1 = y_4$

or $\quad \dfrac{x_1 + x_2}{2} = \dfrac{x_3 + x_4}{2}$ and $\dfrac{y_1 + y_2}{2} = \dfrac{y_3 + y_4}{2}$

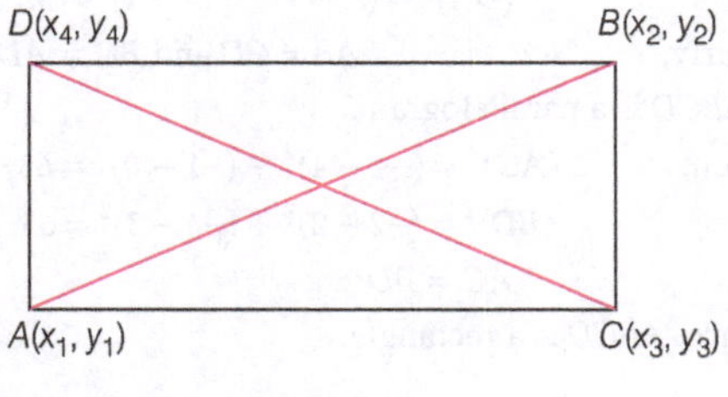

Hence, AB and CD bisect each other.

Therefore, $ACBD$ is a parallelogram. Also,

$$(AB)^2 = (x_1 - x_2)^2 + (y_1 - y_2)^2 = (x_3 - x_4)^2 + (y_3 - y_4)^2 = (CD)^2$$

Thus, $ACBD$ is a parallelogram and $AB = CD$.

Hence, it is a rectangle.

13. Let $P \equiv (h, k)$, $A \equiv (1, 0)$ and $B \equiv (2\cos\theta, 2\sin\theta)$

$\because \quad PA : PB = 2 : 3$

$$\therefore \quad h = \frac{4\cos\theta + 3}{5} \Rightarrow 5h - 3 = 4\cos\theta \quad \text{...(i)}$$

$$\text{and} \quad k = \frac{4\sin\theta + 0}{5} \Rightarrow 5k = 4\sin\theta \quad \text{...(ii)}$$

On squaring and adding Eqs. (i) and (ii), we get

$$(5h - 3)^2 + (5k)^2 = 16$$

$\therefore$ Locus of C is $(5x - 3)^2 + (5y)^2 = 16$

or $\quad 25(x^2 + y^2) - 30x - 7 = 0$

which is a circle.

14. $AB =$ Length of rod $= k$

$$AB = \sqrt{a^2 + b^2} = k$$

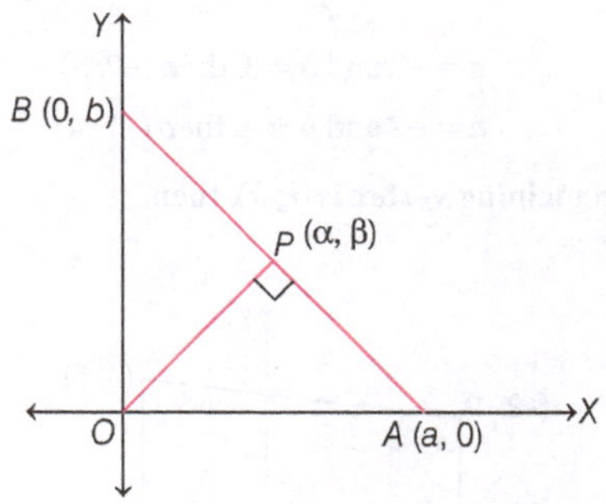

In ΔOPA, $\quad OP^2 + AP^2 = OA^2$

$$\Rightarrow \alpha^2 + \beta^2 + \alpha^2 - 2a\alpha + a^2 + \beta^2 = a^2$$

$$\Rightarrow 2\alpha^2 + 2\beta^2 - 2a\alpha = 0$$

$$\Rightarrow a = \frac{\alpha^2 + \beta^2}{\alpha}$$

In ΔOPB,

$$OP^2 + PB^2 = OB^2$$

$$\Rightarrow \alpha^2 + \beta^2 + \alpha^2 + \beta^2 - 2b\beta + b^2 = b^2$$

$$\Rightarrow 2\alpha^2 + 2\beta^2 - 2b\beta = 0$$

$$\Rightarrow b = \frac{\alpha^2 + \beta^2}{\beta}$$

Now, $\quad a^2 + b^2 = k^2$

$$\Rightarrow \frac{(\alpha^2 + \beta^2)^2}{\alpha^2} + \frac{(\alpha^2 + \beta^2)^2}{\beta^2} = k^2$$

$$\Rightarrow (\alpha^2 + \beta^2)^3 = k^2\alpha^2\beta^2$$

$\therefore$ Locus is $(x^2 + y^2)^3 = k^2x^2y^2$.

15. $(x+h)^2 + (y+k)^2 - 4(x+h) + 6(y+k) - 7 = 0$

$\Rightarrow x^2 + y^2 + 2x(h-2) + 2y(k+3) + (h^2 + k^2 - 4h + 6k - 7) = 0$

According to the question

$$h - 2 = 0,\ k + 3 = 0$$

$\therefore$ $h = 2, k = -3$

Hence, $(h, k) \equiv (2, -3)$.

16. $\because a$ is root of $x^2 + x - 42 = 0$.

$\Rightarrow$ $a^2 + a - 42 = 0$

$\Rightarrow$ $(a+7)(a-6) = 0$

$$a = -7, 6$$

$\because b$ is a root of $x^2 + ax + a^2 - 37 = 0$

For $a = -7,\ x^2 - 7x + 12 = 0$

$\Rightarrow$ $(x-4)(x-3) = 0$

$\Rightarrow$ $x = 3, 4$

$\Rightarrow$ $b = 3, 4$

and for $a = 6 \Rightarrow x^2 + 6x - 1 = 0$

$\Rightarrow$ $x = \dfrac{-6 \pm \sqrt{36+4}}{2} = \dfrac{-6 \pm \sqrt{40}}{2}$ [not integral]

$a = -7$ and $b = 3$, then $(-7, 3)$

$a = -7$ and $b = 4$, then $(-7, 4)$

17. If the remaining vertex is (h, k), then

Case I

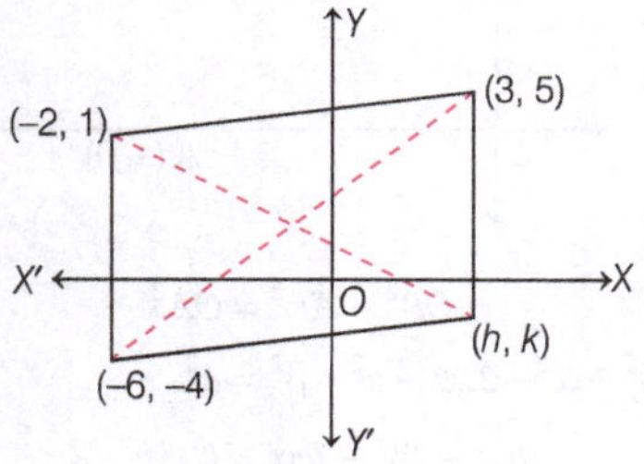

$$h - 2 = 3 - 6,\ k + 1 = 5 - 4$$

or $h = -1, k = 0$

$\therefore$ Fourth vertex is $(-1, 0)$.

Case II

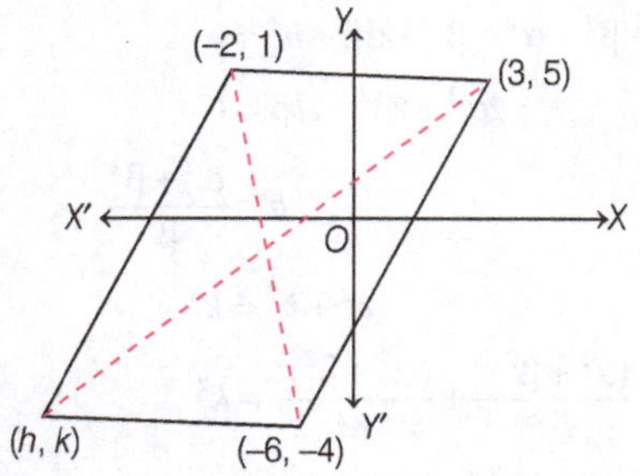

$h + 3 = -2 - 6, k + 5 = 1 - 4$ or $h = -11, k = -8$

$\therefore$ Fourth vertex is $(-11, -8)$.

Case III

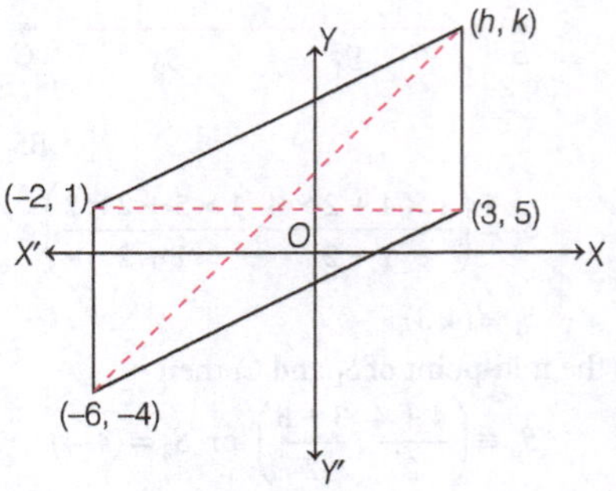

$$h - 6 = -2 + 3, k - 4 = 1 + 5$$

or $h = 7, k = 10$

$\therefore$ Fourth vertex is (7, 10).

18. $(PA)^2 = (PB)^2$

$\Rightarrow (x - a - b)^2 + (y - a + b)^2 = (x - a + b)^2 + (y - a - b)^2$

$\Rightarrow (x - a + b)^2 - (x - a - b)^2 = (y - a + b)^2 - (y - a - b)^2$

$\Rightarrow$ $(2x - 2a)(2b) = (2y - 2a)(2b)$

or $x = y$

and P is the mid-point of AB i.e. (a, a)

If P is (a, b), then $bx = ay$ $[\because a = b]$

19. Let vertices of ΔABC are

$$A \equiv (x_1, y_1), B \equiv (x_2, y_2) \text{ and } C \equiv (x_3, y_3)$$

where, $x_1, x_2, x_3, y_1, y_2, y_3 \in Q$

$\therefore$ $a = BC = \sqrt{(x_2 - x_3)^2 + (y_2 - y_3)^2}$

= rational or irrational

Similarly, $b = CA, c = AB$

Then, incentre $\equiv \left(\dfrac{ax_1 + bx_2 + cx_3}{a+b+c}, \dfrac{ay_1 + by_2 + cy_3}{a+b+c} \right)$

$\therefore$ Incentre has rational or irrational coordinates but centroid, circumcentre and orthocentre have always rational coordinates.

20. Since, $A \equiv (-4 -1), B \equiv (-2, -4), C \equiv (4, 0), D \equiv (2, 3)$

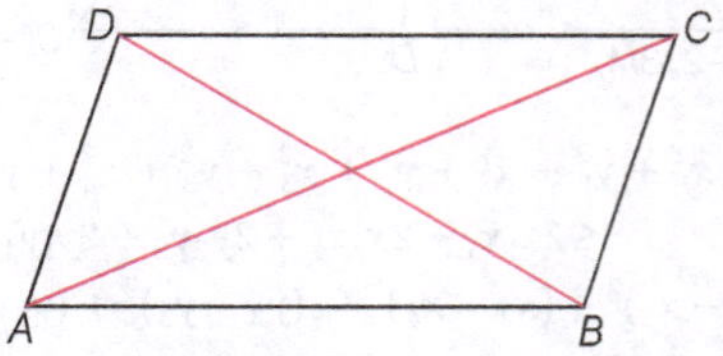

$\therefore$ $(AB)^2 = (-4+2)^2 + (-1+4)^2 = 13$

$(BC)^2 = (-2-4)^2 + (-4-0)^2 = 52$

$(CD)^2 = (4-2)^2 + (0-3)^2 = 13$

and $(DA)^2 = (2+4)^2 + (3+1)^2 = 52$

Clearly, $AB = CD$ and $BC = AD$

$\therefore$ $ABCD$ is a parallelogram.

Again, $(AC)^2 = (-4-4)^2 + (-1-0)^2 = 65$

and $(BD)^2 = (-2-2)^2 + (-4-3)^2 = 65$

$\therefore$ $AC = BD$

Hence, $ABCD$ is a rectangle.

21.

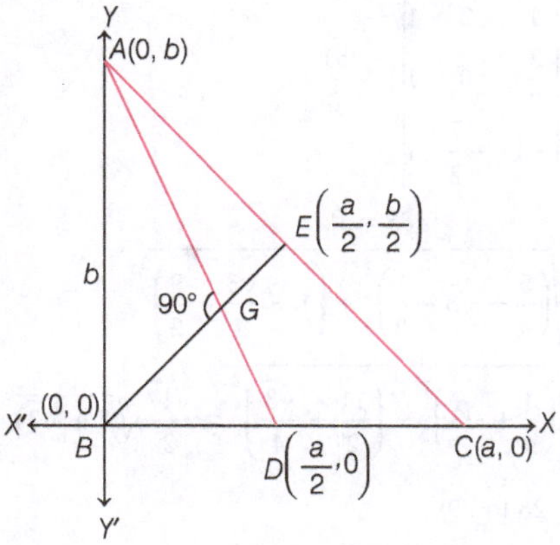

$\because \quad BG = \frac{2}{3} BE = \frac{2}{3} \times \frac{\sqrt{(a^2 + b^2)}}{2}$

$\Rightarrow \quad (BG)^2 = \frac{1}{9}(a^2 + b^2) \quad$ ...(i)

and $\quad AG = \frac{2}{3} AD = \frac{2}{3} \times \sqrt{\left(\frac{a^2}{4} + b^2\right)} \quad$ ...(ii)

$\Rightarrow \quad (AG)^2 = \frac{1}{9}(a^2 + 4b^2)$

Now, in right angled ΔABG,

$(BA)^2 = (AG)^2 + (BG)^2$

$\Rightarrow \quad b^2 = \frac{1}{9}(a^2 + 4b^2) + \frac{1}{9}(a^2 + b^2)$

[from Eqs. (i) and (ii)]

$\Rightarrow \quad a^2 = 2b^2$

$\therefore \quad a = \pm b\sqrt{2}$

22. $\because \quad (AB)^2 = (x - y)^2 + (y - z)^2$

$(BC)^2 = (y - z)^2 + (z - x)^2$

and $\quad (CA)^2 = (z - x)^2 + (x - y)^2$

Case I If $x = y$, then

$(AB)^2 + (CA)^2 = (BC)^2$

Case II If $y = z$, then

$(AB)^2 + (BC)^2 = (CA)^2$

Case III If $z = x$, then

$(BC)^2 + (CA)^2 = (AB)^2$

23.

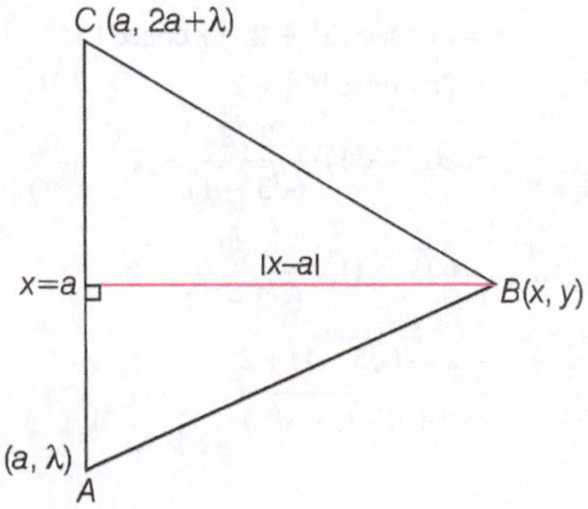

Let $\quad A \equiv (a, \lambda)$

Then, $\quad B \equiv (a, 2a + \lambda)$

and $\quad C \equiv (x, y)$

Area of $\Delta ABC = a^2 \quad$ (given)

$\Rightarrow \quad \frac{1}{2} \times 2a \times |x - a| = a^2$

$\Rightarrow \quad |x - a| = a \Rightarrow x - a = \pm a$

$\Rightarrow \quad x = 0, x = 2a$

24. $\because \angle COA = \angle COX - \angle AOX = 60° - 30° = 30°$

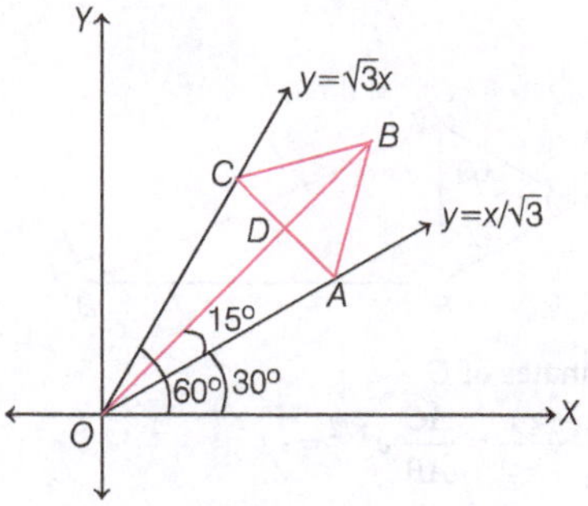

$\therefore$ Area of rhombus $= 2 \times \frac{1}{2} \times OA \times OC \sin 30°$

$\Rightarrow \quad 2 = \frac{1}{2} x^2 \quad$ [let $OA = OC = x$]

$\Rightarrow \quad OA = OC = 2$

Also, $\quad \angle OAB = 180° - 30° = 150°$

$\because \quad \cos 150° = \frac{OA^2 + AB^2 - OB^2}{2 \times OA \times AB}$

$\Rightarrow \quad OB^2 = 8 + 4\sqrt{3}$

$\Rightarrow \quad OB = \sqrt{2}(\sqrt{3} + 1) \quad [\because 8 + 4\sqrt{3} = (\sqrt{6} + \sqrt{2})^2]$

Coordinates of B are $\{\pm \sqrt{2}(\sqrt{3} + 1)\cos 45°, \pm \sqrt{2}(\sqrt{3} + 1)\sin 45°\}$

$\Rightarrow \quad \{\pm(\sqrt{3} + 1), \pm(\sqrt{3} + 1)\}$

$\Rightarrow \quad (\sqrt{3} + 1, \sqrt{3} + 1)$ and $(-\sqrt{3} - 1, -\sqrt{3} - 1)$

25. Coordinates of centroid are $G \equiv \left(-3, \frac{1}{3}\right)$

$a = |BC| = \sqrt{(6 - 0)^2 + (3 + 5)^2} = \sqrt{36 + 64} = 10,$

$b = |CA| = \sqrt{(0 + 15)^2 + (-5 - 3)^2} = \sqrt{225 + 64} = 17$

and $c = |AB| = \sqrt{(-15 - 6)^2 + (3 - 3)^2} = \sqrt{(21)^2} = 21$

$\therefore$ The coordinates of incentre are

$$I \equiv \left(\frac{10 \times (-15) + 17 \times 6 + 21 \times 0}{10 + 17 + 21}, \frac{10 \times 3 + 17 \times 3 + 21 \times (-5)}{10 + 17 + 21}\right)$$

i.e. $\quad I \equiv \left(-1, -\frac{1}{2}\right)$

$\therefore \quad GI = \sqrt{(-3 + 1)^2 + \left(\frac{1}{3} + \frac{1}{2}\right)^2} = \sqrt{\frac{169}{36}} = \frac{13}{6}$

$\because \quad GI = \lambda \quad$ [given]

$\therefore \quad \lambda = \frac{13}{6}$

Sol. (Q. Nos. 26 to 27)

$$AB = \sqrt{(1+3)^2 + (2-1)^2} = \sqrt{17}$$

$$AC = \frac{1}{2} AB = \frac{1}{2}\sqrt{17}$$

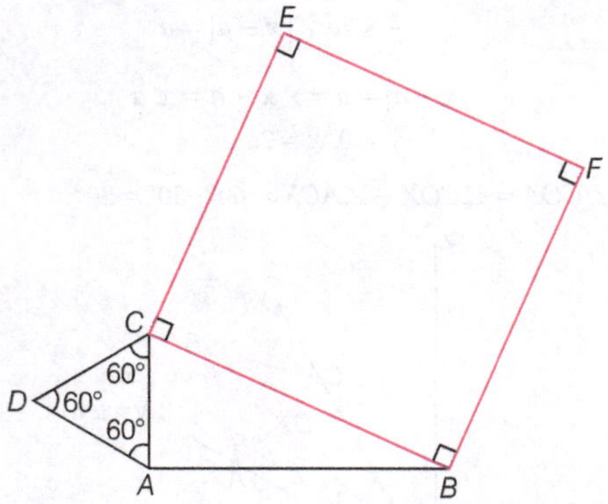

For coordinates of C,

$$\frac{z_c - z_A}{z_B - z_A} = \frac{AC}{AB} e^{i\pi/2} = \frac{i}{2}$$

$$\Rightarrow z_c - (1+2i) = \frac{i}{2}(-3+i-1-2i)$$

$$= \frac{i}{2}(-4-i) = -2i + \frac{1}{2}$$

or $$z_c = \frac{3}{2}$$

$\therefore$ $$C \equiv \left(\frac{3}{2}, 0\right)$$

For coordinates of D,

$$\frac{z_D - z_A}{z_C - z_A} = e^{i\pi/3}$$

$$\Rightarrow z_D - (1+2i) = \left(\frac{1}{2} + \frac{i\sqrt{3}}{2}\right)\left(\frac{1}{2} - 2i\right)$$

$$= \frac{1}{4} + \sqrt{3} - i + \frac{i\sqrt{3}}{4}$$

or $$z_D = \left(\frac{5}{4} + \sqrt{3}\right) + i\left(1 + \frac{\sqrt{3}}{4}\right)$$

$\therefore$ $$D \equiv \left(\frac{5}{4} + \sqrt{3}, 1 + \frac{\sqrt{3}}{4}\right)$$

For coordinates of F,

$$\frac{z_F - z_B}{z_C - z_B} = e^{-i\pi/2} = -i$$

$$\Rightarrow z_F - (-3+i) = -i\left(\frac{9}{2} - i\right)$$

$$\Rightarrow z_F = -4 - \frac{7}{2}i$$

$\therefore$ $F \equiv \left(-4, -\frac{7}{2}\right)$, then

$$E \equiv \left(\frac{1}{2}, -\frac{9}{2}\right)$$

26. $$S = \frac{1}{2}\left|\begin{vmatrix} 1 & 2 & 1 \\ \frac{3}{2} & 0 & 1 \\ -4 & -\frac{7}{2} & 1 \end{vmatrix}\right| = \frac{51}{8}$$

$\therefore$ $$8S = 51$$

27. $$DE = \sqrt{\left(\frac{5}{4} + \sqrt{3} - \frac{1}{2}\right)^2 + \left(1 + \frac{\sqrt{3}}{4} + \frac{9}{2}\right)^2}$$

$$= \sqrt{\left(\frac{3}{4} + \sqrt{3}\right)^2 + \left(\frac{11}{2} + \frac{\sqrt{3}}{4}\right)^2} = \frac{\sqrt{17}}{2}\sqrt{(8+\sqrt{3})}$$

Sol. (Q. Nos. 28 to 29)

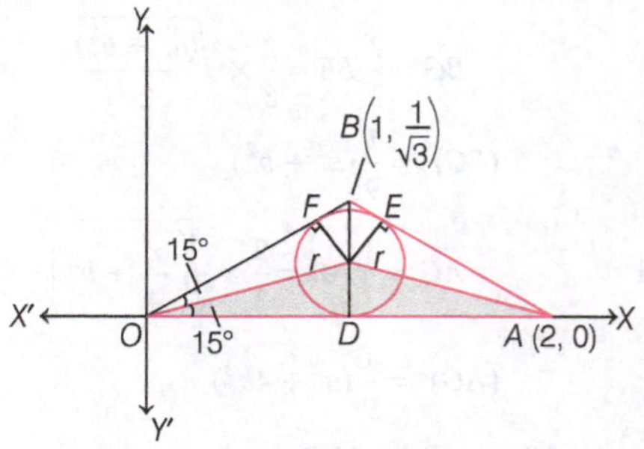

Given, $O \equiv (0, 0)$ $A \equiv (2, 0)$

and $B \equiv \left(1, \frac{1}{\sqrt{3}}\right)$

Let $P \equiv (x, y)$

I be the incentre of ΔOAB.

If in radius $= r$, then

$ID = IE = IF = r$, if P at I,

$d(P, OA) = d(P, OB) = d(P, AB) = r$,

But $d(P, OA) \le \min.\{d(P, OB), d(P, AB)\}$

which is possible only P lies in the ΔOIA.

$\therefore$ M be the peak of region R.

$\therefore$ $M = I$

28. Length of perpendicular from M to $OA = ID = r = OD \tan 15°$

$$= 1 \times (2 - \sqrt{3})$$

$$= 2 - \sqrt{3}$$

29. Perimeter of region,

$$R = IO + OA + AI$$

$$= r \operatorname{cosec} 15° + 2 + r \operatorname{cosec} 15°$$

$$= 2r \operatorname{cosec} 15° + 2$$

$$= 2(2-\sqrt{3}) \cdot \frac{2\sqrt{2}}{(\sqrt{3}-1)} + 2$$

$$= (\sqrt{3}-1)^2 \cdot \frac{2\sqrt{2}}{(\sqrt{3}-1)} + 2$$

$$= 2\sqrt{2}(\sqrt{3}-1) + 2$$

$\Rightarrow$ $$= 2 + 4\sqrt{(2-\sqrt{3})}$$

30. $\therefore$ Area of $\Delta DEF = \frac{1}{4}$ Area of ΔABC

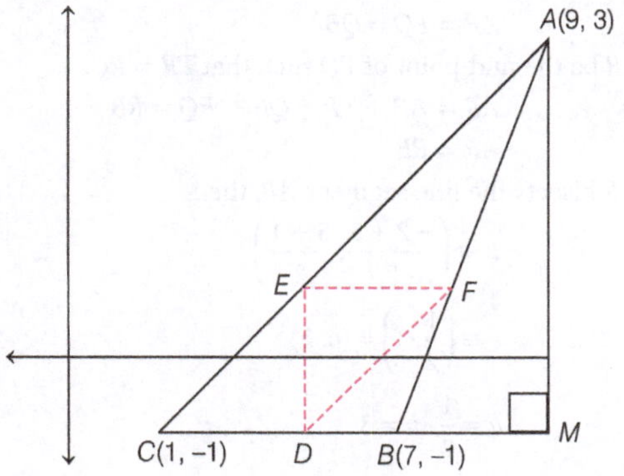

$$= \frac{1}{4} \times \left(\frac{1}{2} \times \text{base } \times \text{height}\right)$$

$$= \frac{1}{4} \times \frac{1}{2} \times BC \times AM$$

$$= \frac{1}{4} \times \frac{1}{2} \times 6 \times 4 = 3 \text{ sq. units}$$

31. D is mid-point BC, E is mid-point AC, for circumcentre

$$OA = OB = OC$$

Now, $OA = OB$

$\therefore (a-9)^2 + (b-3)^2 = (a-7)^2 + (b+1)^2$

$\Rightarrow$ $a + 2b = 10$

and $OB = OC$

$(a-1)^2 + (b+1)^2 = (a-7)^2 + (b+1)^2$

$\Rightarrow$ $a = 4$

$\therefore$ $b = 3$

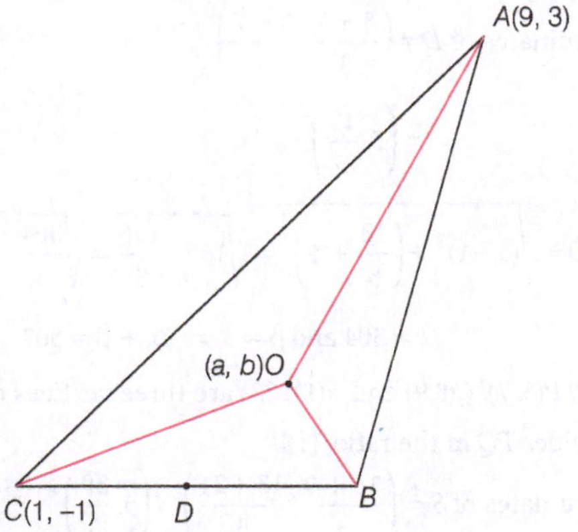

Circumcentre $= (a, b) = (4, 3)$

$\Rightarrow$ $R = OA = \sqrt{(4-1)^2 + (3+1)^2} = 5$

$$a + b + R = 4 + 3 + 5 = 12$$

32. $P(t_1^3, \sqrt{2}t_1)$ and $Q(t_2^3, -\sqrt{2}t_2)$

$\because$ t_1 and t_2 are the the roots of $x^2 - 2\sqrt{2}x + 1 = 0$.

$\therefore$ $t_1 + t_2 = 2\sqrt{2}$ and $t_1t_2 = 1$

Now, $PQ = \sqrt{(t_2^3 - t_1^3)^2 + (-\sqrt{2}t_2 - \sqrt{2}t_1)^2}$

$$= \sqrt{(t_2 - t_1)^2(t_2^2 + t_1^2 + t_1t_2)^2 + 2(t_2 + t_1)^2}$$

$\because$ $t_2 - t_1 = \sqrt{(t_1 + t_2)^2 - 4t_1t_2} = \sqrt{8-4} = \sqrt{4} = 2$

$\because$ $t_2^2 + t_1^2 = (t_1 + t_2)^2 - 2t_1t_2 = 8 - 2 = 6$

$\therefore$ $PQ = \sqrt{4(6+1)^2 + 2(2\sqrt{2})^2}$

$$= \sqrt{196 + 16} = \sqrt{212} = 2\sqrt{53} \text{ units}$$

$\therefore$ $\alpha = 2$

33. Let the sides are $x, y, 10-(x+y)$ and $x, y \in N$

Now, $x + y > 10 - (x+y)$

$\Rightarrow$ $x + y > 5$ ...(i)

$\Rightarrow$ $x + 10 - (x+y) > y$

$\Rightarrow$ $10 - y > y$

$\Rightarrow$ $y < 5$

$\Rightarrow$ $0 < y < 5$

and $y + 10 - (x+y) > x$

$\Rightarrow$ $x < 5$

$\Rightarrow$ $0 < x < 5$

Put $x = 1 \Rightarrow x + y > 5$

From Eq. (i),

$\Rightarrow$ $y > 4$

$\therefore$ $y = 5, 6...$

But $y < 5$ [not possible]

Put $x = 2 \Rightarrow y > 3 \Rightarrow y = 4 \Rightarrow z = 10 - (x+y) = 4$

Put $x = 3 \Rightarrow y > 2 \Rightarrow y = 3, 4 \Rightarrow z = 4, 3$

Put $x = 4 \Rightarrow y > 1 \Rightarrow y = 2, 3, 4 \Rightarrow z = 4, 3, 2$

Only 2 different types of triangle having sides (2,4,4) and (3,3,4).

$\therefore$ Number of triangles = 2

34. Taking B as origin and BC as X-axis. Let A be (h,k).

Since, AD is angle bisector of $\angle A$.

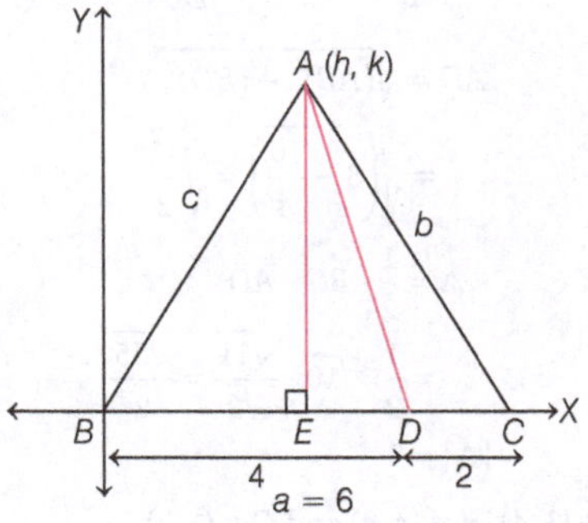

$\therefore$ $\frac{AB}{AC} = \frac{BD}{CD} \Rightarrow c = 2b$

Now, we know that in any triangle.

Sum of two sides > Third side

In ΔABC, $b + c > a \Rightarrow b + c > 6$

$\Rightarrow$ $3b > 6 \Rightarrow b > 2$

Again, $\cos A = \frac{b^2 + c^2 - 36}{2bc} < 1$

$\Rightarrow$ $5b^2 - 36 < 4b^2$ $[\because c = 2b]$

$\Rightarrow$ $b^2 - 36 < 0$

$\Rightarrow$ $(b-6)(b+6) < 0$

$\Rightarrow \quad 0 < b < 6 \quad [\because b \text{ is '+' ve}]$

$\therefore \quad 2 < b < 6$

Now, in ΔABE,

$$h^2 + k^2 = c^2$$

$$\Rightarrow \quad h^2 + k^2 = 4b^2 \quad \text{...(i)}$$

In ΔAEC, $(h-6)^2 + k^2 = b^2$ ...(ii)

From Eqs. (i) and (ii), $3b^2 = h^2 - (h-6)^2$

$$\Rightarrow \quad 3b^2 = 12h - 36 \Rightarrow b^2 = 4h - 12$$

$$\Rightarrow \quad k^2 = 16 - (h-8)^2$$

$\therefore$ Maximum value of $k = 4$

35. We know that the area of the triangle formed by joining the mid-points of any triangle is one fourth of that triangle, then

$$\Delta_2 = 4\Delta_1$$

$$\therefore \quad \frac{\Delta_2}{\Delta_1} = 4$$

36. Since, the distance of all points from $O(0, 0) = 5$

$\therefore$ Circumradius $(R) = 5$

Hence, diameter of nine point circle $= R = 5$

37. Let $B \equiv (2\sqrt{2}, 0)$, $C \equiv (0, \sqrt{2})$

$$\therefore \quad BC = \sqrt{(8+2)} = \sqrt{10}$$

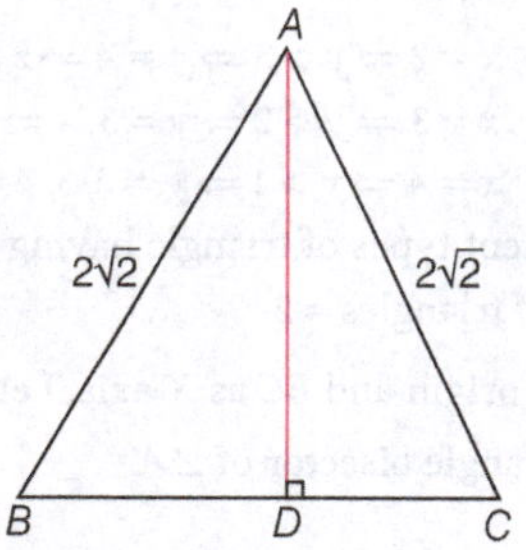

and $\quad AD = \sqrt{(AB)^2 - (BD)^2}$

$$= \sqrt{\left(8 - \frac{10}{4}\right)} = \sqrt{\frac{11}{2}}$$

$$\therefore \quad \Delta = \frac{1}{2} \cdot BC \cdot AD$$

$$= \frac{1}{2} \cdot \sqrt{10} \cdot \frac{\sqrt{11}}{\sqrt{2}} = \frac{\sqrt{55}}{2}$$

$$\Rightarrow \quad [\Delta] = 3$$

38. Let $A \equiv (3, 4)$, $B \equiv (4, 3)$ and $C \equiv (1, 2)$

$$\therefore \quad a = |BC| = \sqrt{(9+1)} = \sqrt{10}$$

$$b = |CA| = \sqrt{(4+4)} = 2\sqrt{2}$$

$$c = |AB| = \sqrt{(1+1)} = \sqrt{2}$$

$$\Rightarrow \quad x = \frac{\sqrt{10} \times 3 + 2\sqrt{2} \times 4 + \sqrt{2} \times 1}{\sqrt{10} + 2\sqrt{2} + \sqrt{2}}$$

$$= \frac{3(\sqrt{10} + 3\sqrt{2})}{(\sqrt{10} + 3\sqrt{2})} = 3$$

$$\therefore \quad x^2 = 9$$

39.

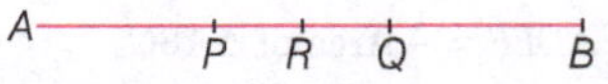

$$\because \quad AP = PQ = QB$$

Let R be the mid-point of PQ such that $PR = RQ$.

Now, $\quad AR = AP + PR = QB + RQ = RB$

$$\Rightarrow \quad AR = RB$$

$\therefore \quad R$ bisects the line segment AB, then

$$R \equiv \left(\frac{-2+3}{2}, \frac{5+1}{2}\right)$$

$$\equiv \left(\frac{1}{2}, 3\right) = (a, b) \quad \text{(given)}$$

$$\therefore \quad a = \frac{1}{2},\ b = 3$$

$$\Rightarrow \quad \frac{b}{a} = 6$$

40. Given, $A(4,3)$, $B(1,-1)$ and $C(7,7)$ are vertices of ΔABC.

$\therefore AB = 5$ and $BC = 10$

$\because$ Angle bisector divides the opposite sides on the ratio of its containing sides.

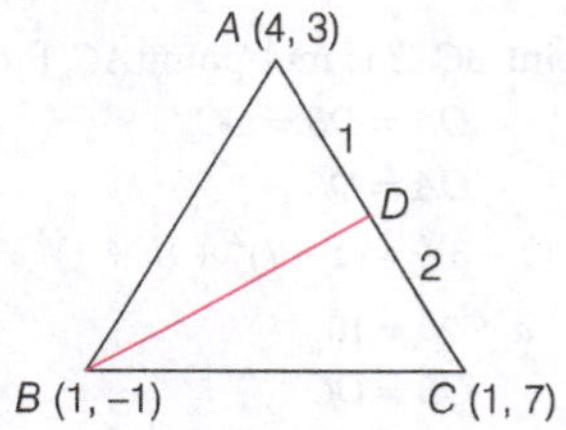

$$\therefore \quad \frac{AD}{CD} = \frac{AB}{BC} = \frac{5}{10} = \frac{1}{2}$$

$$\therefore \text{Coordinates of } D = \left(\frac{8+7}{3}, \frac{6+7}{3}\right)$$

$$= \left(5, \frac{13}{3}\right)$$

$$\therefore \quad BD = \sqrt{(5-1)^2 + \left(\frac{13}{3} + 1\right)^2} = \sqrt{16 + \frac{256}{3}} = \sqrt{\frac{304}{3}}$$

$$\therefore \quad \alpha = 304 \text{ and } \beta = 3 \Rightarrow \alpha + \beta = 307$$

41. Given, $P(3, 7)$, $Q(8, 9)$ and $R(11, 23)$ are three vertices of ΔPQR.

$\because S$ divides PQ in the ratio $2:3$.

$$\therefore \text{Coordinates of } S = \left(\frac{16+9}{5}, \frac{18+21}{5}\right) = \left(5, \frac{39}{5}\right)$$

and T divides QR in the ratio $3:2$.

$$\therefore \text{Coordinates of } T = \left(\frac{33+16}{5}, \frac{69+18}{5}\right) = \left(\frac{49}{5}, \frac{87}{5}\right)$$

$$\therefore \quad (ST)^2 = \left(5 - \frac{49}{5}\right)^2 + \left(\frac{39}{5} - \frac{87}{5}\right)^2 = \frac{576}{5}$$

$$\therefore \quad 5(ST)^2 = 5\left(\frac{576}{5}\right) = 576$$

42. $\therefore$ Area of parallelogram $= \dfrac{|c_1 - c_2||d_1 - d_2|}{|m_1 - m_2|}$

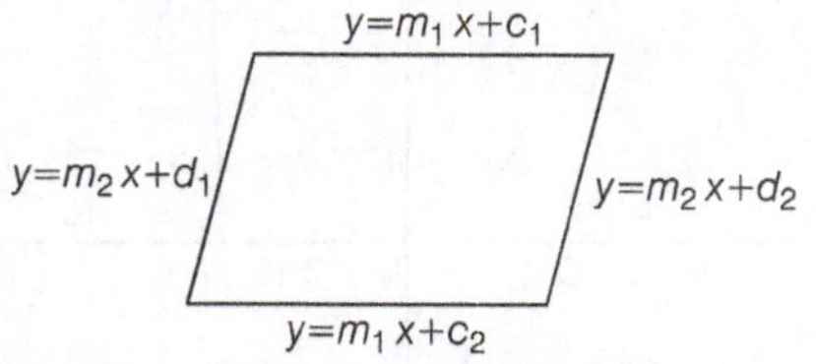

$\therefore$ Area of parallelogram formed by the first set of 4 lines

$$\frac{|c-d|^2}{|a-b|} = 18 \quad \text{...(i)}$$

and area of parallelogram formed by the second set of 4 lines

$$\frac{|c+d|^2}{|a-b|} = 72 \quad \text{...(ii)}$$

By Eqs. (i) and (ii), $\quad |c-d|^2 = |a-b|(18)$

$$|c+d|^2 = |a-b|(72)$$

$\because$ $a, b, c, d \in N$

$\therefore$ RHS must be a perfect square for some least value of $(a-b)$ which obviously can be equal to 2

$$|a-b| = 2 \Rightarrow a = 1 \text{ and } b = 3$$

$\therefore$ $\quad c - d = 6$ and $c + d = 12$

$$c = 9 \text{ and } d = 3$$

$\therefore$ $a + b + c + d = 16$

43. $\because$ $A(\alpha, \beta)$ lies on $y = 2x + 3$

Then, $\quad \beta = 2\alpha + 3$

Thus, the coordinates of A are $(\alpha, 2\alpha + 3)$.

$$\Delta = \frac{1}{2}\begin{vmatrix} \alpha & 2\alpha + 3 & 1 \\ 1 & 2 & 1 \\ 2 & 3 & 1 \end{vmatrix} = \frac{1}{2}|\alpha + 2|$$

But $[\Delta] = 2$ $\quad$ [given]

$\Rightarrow$ $\quad \left[\frac{1}{2}|\alpha + 2|\right] = 2 \Rightarrow 2 \le \frac{|\alpha + 2|}{2} < 3$

$\Rightarrow$ $\quad 4 \le \alpha + 2 < 6$ and $-6 < \alpha + 2 \le -4$

$\Rightarrow$ $\quad 2 \le \alpha < 4$ and $-8 < \alpha \le -6$

$\because$ $\quad \alpha \in I$

$\therefore$ $\quad \alpha = 2, 3, -7, -6$

Hence, total possible coordinates of A are $(2, 7), (3, 9), (-7, -11)$ and $(-6, -9)$ i.e. 4.

$\therefore$ $\quad \lambda = 4 \Rightarrow \lambda^2 = 4^2 = 16$

44. Given, S be the area of square with vertices $O(0, 0)$, $A(1, 0)$, $B(1, 1)$ and $C(0, 1)$.

Let $PQRM$ be the quadrilateral with vertices $P(p, 0)$, $Q(1, q)$, $R(r, 1)$ and $M(0, m)$ and sides $MP = a$, $PQ = b$, $QR = c$, $RM = d$

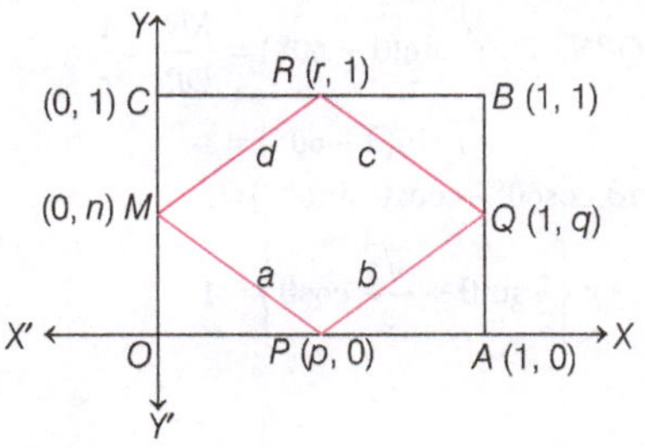

Then, $\quad a^2 = p^2 + m^2, \; b^2 = (1-p)^2 + q^2$

$$c^2 = (1-q)^2 + (1-r)^2, \; d^2 = r^2 + (1-m)^2$$

$\therefore$ $a^2 + b^2 + c^2 + d^2$

$$= p^2 + (1-p)^2 + q^2 + (1-q)^2 + r^2 + (1-r)^2 + m^2 + (1-m)^2$$

$$= 2[p^2 + q^2 + r^2 + m^2 - p - q - r - m + 2]$$

$$= 2\left[\left(p - \frac{1}{2}\right)^2 + \left(q - \frac{1}{2}\right)^2 + \left(r - \frac{1}{2}\right)^2 + \left(m - \frac{1}{2}\right)^2 + 1\right] \ge 2$$

$\Rightarrow$ $\quad a^2 + b^2 + c^2 + d^2 \ge 2 \quad$ ...(i)

Also, since $0 \le x \le 1$

$\therefore$ $\quad x^2 \le 1$

$\therefore$ $\quad a^2 \le 1, b^2 \le 1, c^2 \le 1, d^2 \le 1$

$\Rightarrow$ $\quad a^2 + b^2 + c^2 + d^2 \le 4 \quad$ ...(ii)

From Eqs. (i) and (ii), we get

$$2 \le a^2 + b^2 + c^2 + d^2 \le 4$$

$\therefore$ $\quad \alpha = 2$ and $\beta = 4$

$\Rightarrow$ $\quad \alpha^2 + \beta^2 = (2)^2 + (4)^2 = 4 + 16 = 20$

45. **(A)** Centroid of ΔABC is $\left(\dfrac{0 + 5 + 16}{3}, \dfrac{0 + 12 + 12}{3}\right) \equiv (7, 8)$

Here, $\quad \lambda = 7$ and $\mu = 8$

$\therefore$ $\quad \lambda + \mu = 15$

(B)

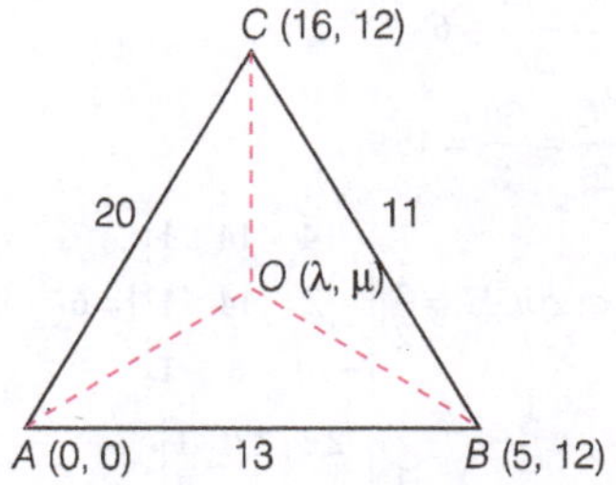

$$(OA)^2 = (OB)^2 = (OC)^2$$

$\Rightarrow$ $\quad \lambda^2 + \mu^2 = (\lambda - 5)^2 + (\mu - 12)^2$

$$= (\lambda - 16)^2 + (\mu - 12)^2$$

$\Rightarrow$ $\quad (\lambda - 5)^2 + (\mu - 12)^2 = (\lambda - 16)^2 + (\mu - 12)^2$

or $\quad (\lambda - 5) = -(\lambda - 16)$

$\therefore$ $\quad \lambda = \dfrac{21}{2} \Rightarrow 2\lambda = 21$

(C) Incentre of ΔABC is

$$\left(\frac{11 \times 0 + 13 \times 16 + 20 \times 5}{11 + 13 + 20}, \frac{11 \times 0 + 13 \times 12 + 20 \times 12}{11 + 13 + 20}\right)$$

$$\equiv (7, 9)$$

Here, $\quad \mu = 9$

(D) Excentre opposite to vertex B is

$$\left(\frac{11 \times 0 + 13 \times 16 - 20 \times 5}{11 + 13 - 20}, \frac{11 \times 0 + 13 \times 12 - 20 \times 12}{11 + 13 - 20}\right)$$

$$\equiv (27, -21)$$

Here, $\quad \lambda = 27$ and $\mu = -21$

$\therefore$ $\quad \lambda + \mu = 6$

46.

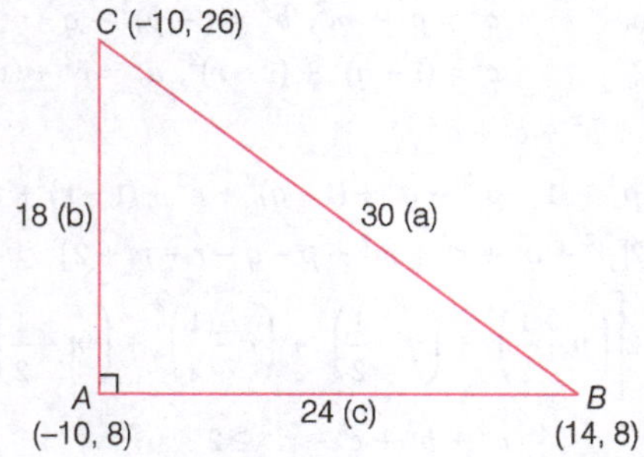

$$\Delta = \frac{1}{2}\left|\begin{vmatrix} -10 & 8 & 1 \\ 14 & 8 & 1 \\ -10 & 26 & 1 \end{vmatrix}\right| = 216$$

$$s = \frac{a+b+c}{2} = \frac{30+18+24}{2} = 36$$

$$G \equiv \left(\frac{-10+14-10}{3}, \frac{8+8+26}{3}\right)$$

$$\equiv (-2, 14)$$

$$I \equiv \left(\frac{30\times -10 + 24 \times -10 + 18 \times 14}{30+24+18}, \frac{30 \times 8 + 24 \times 26 + 18 \times 8}{30+24+18}\right)$$

$$\equiv (-4, 14)$$

$$H = A \equiv (-10, 8)$$

$O =$ mid-point of $BC \equiv (2, 17)$

(A) $r = \dfrac{\Delta}{s} = \dfrac{216}{36} = 6$

(B) $R = \dfrac{BC}{2} = \dfrac{30}{2} = 15$

(C) Area of $\Delta IGH = \dfrac{1}{2}\left|\begin{vmatrix} -4 & 14 & 1 \\ -2 & 14 & 1 \\ -10 & 8 & 1 \end{vmatrix}\right| = 6$

(D) Area of $\Delta OGI = \dfrac{1}{2}\left|\begin{vmatrix} 2 & 17 & 1 \\ -2 & 14 & 1 \\ -4 & 14 & 1 \end{vmatrix}\right| = 3$

Exercise 3 - Challenging Problems

1. $\because \quad x^2 + 4x + 3 = 0 \Rightarrow x = -1, -3$

and $\quad x^2 - x - 6 = 0 \Rightarrow x = -2, 3$

Also, given that x and y coordinates of B are respectively less than and greater than the corresponding coordinates of C.

$\therefore \quad B \equiv (-3, 3)$ and $C \equiv (-1, -2)$

Now, $\quad AB = \sqrt{(3+3)^2 + (-5-3)^2} = 10$

and $\quad AC = \sqrt{(3+1)^2 + (-5+2)^2} = 5$

$\therefore \quad \dfrac{AB}{AC} = \dfrac{2}{1}$

Let AD be the bisector of $\angle BAC$, then

$$\frac{BD}{DC} = \frac{AB}{AC} = \frac{2}{1}$$

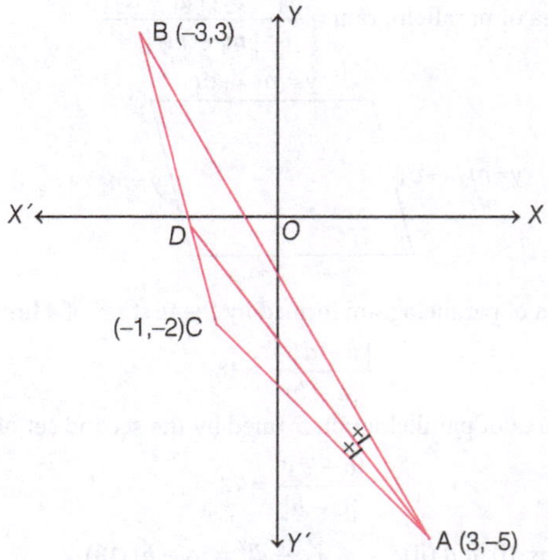

Thus, D divides BC internally in the ratio 2 : 1

$$\therefore \quad D \equiv \left(\frac{2(-1)+1(-3)}{2+1}, \frac{2(-2)+1(3)}{2+1}\right)$$

Thus, $\quad D \equiv \left(-\dfrac{5}{3}, -\dfrac{1}{3}\right)$

Now, $\quad AD = \sqrt{\left(3+\dfrac{5}{3}\right)^2 + \left(-5+\dfrac{1}{3}\right)^2}$

$$= \sqrt{\frac{196}{9} + \frac{196}{9}} = \frac{14\sqrt{2}}{3} \text{ units}$$

2. Let $PQ = QR = RP = r$

and $\quad \angle PQL = \theta$

Then, $\quad \angle XQR = \theta + 60°$

Given, $\quad PL = a$ and $RN = 1$ unit

In ΔPQL, $\quad \sin\theta = \dfrac{PL}{QP} = \dfrac{a}{r}$

$\therefore \quad a = r\sin\theta \quad$ ...(i)

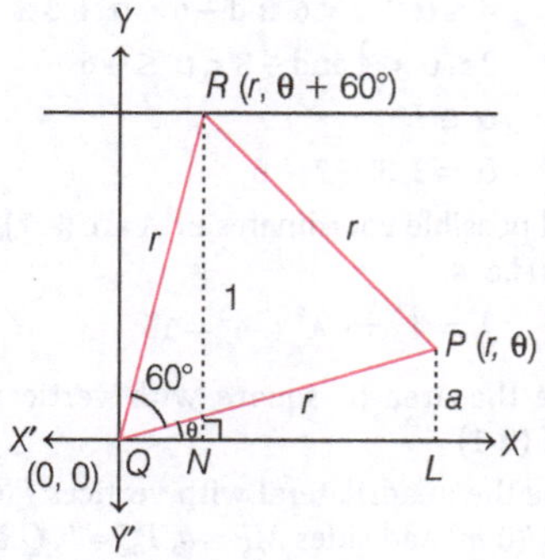

and in ΔQRN, $\quad \sin(\theta + 60°) = \dfrac{RN}{QR} = \dfrac{1}{r}$

$\therefore \quad r\sin(\theta + 60°) = 1$

$\Rightarrow \quad r\{\sin\theta\cos 60° + \cos\theta \sin 60°\} = 1$

$\Rightarrow \quad r\left\{\dfrac{1}{2}\sin\theta + \dfrac{\sqrt{3}}{2}\cos\theta\right\} = 1$

$$\Rightarrow \quad r\left\{\frac{1}{2}\times\frac{a}{r}+\frac{\sqrt{3}}{2}\times\sqrt{1-\frac{a^2}{r^2}}\right\}=1 \qquad \text{[from Eq. (i)]}$$

$$\Rightarrow \quad \frac{a}{2}+\frac{\sqrt{3}}{2}\sqrt{(r^2-a^2)}=1$$

$$\Rightarrow \quad \frac{\sqrt{3}}{2}\sqrt{(r^2-a^2)}=1-\frac{a}{2}$$

or
$$\frac{3}{4}(r^2-a^2)=1+\frac{a^2}{4}-a$$

$$\Rightarrow \quad 3r^2-3a^2=4+a^2-4a$$

$$\Rightarrow \quad 3r^2=4a^2-4a+4$$

$$=4(a^2-a+1)$$

$$\therefore \quad r=\frac{2}{\sqrt{3}}\sqrt{(a^2-a+1)}$$

Hence, length of side of an equilateral triangle

$$=\frac{2}{\sqrt{3}}\sqrt{(a^2-a+1)} \text{ units}$$

3. Let AD be the internal bisector of angle A.

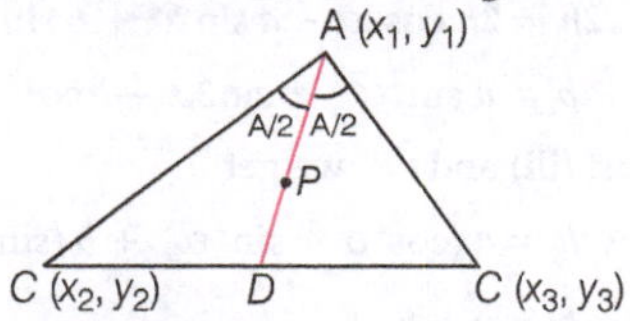

Then,
$$\frac{BD}{DC}=\frac{AB}{AC}=\frac{c}{b}$$

$$\therefore \quad D\equiv\left(\frac{cx_3+bx_2}{c+b},\frac{cy_3+by_2}{c+b}\right)$$

Let $P\equiv(x,y)$. According to question, $P(x,y)$ lies on AD, therefore P, A, D are collinear

$$\therefore \quad \begin{vmatrix} x & y & 1\\ x_1 & y_1 & 1\\ \dfrac{cx_3+bx_2}{c+b} & \dfrac{cy_3+by_2}{c+b} & 1\end{vmatrix}=0$$

or
$$\frac{1}{(c+b)}\begin{vmatrix} x & y & 1\\ x_1 & y_1 & 1\\ cx_3+bx_2 & cy_3+by_2 & c+b\end{vmatrix}=0$$

or
$$\begin{vmatrix} x & y & 1\\ x_1 & y_1 & 1\\ cx_3 & cy_3 & c\end{vmatrix}+\begin{vmatrix} x & y & 1\\ x_1 & y_1 & 1\\ bx_2 & by_2 & b\end{vmatrix}=0$$

[using the addition property of determinants]

or
$$c\begin{vmatrix} x & y & 1\\ x_1 & y_1 & 1\\ x_3 & y_3 & 1\end{vmatrix}+b\begin{vmatrix} x & y & 1\\ x_1 & y_1 & 1\\ x_2 & y_2 & 1\end{vmatrix}=0$$

Hence,
$$b\begin{vmatrix} x & y & 1\\ x_1 & y_1 & 1\\ x_2 & y_2 & 1\end{vmatrix}+c\begin{vmatrix} x & y & 1\\ x_1 & y_1 & 1\\ x_3 & y_3 & 1\end{vmatrix}=0$$

4. Suppose the equation of the line L is $ax+by+c=0$. Let the coordinates of A, B, C be respectively $(x_1, y_1); (x_2, y_2); (x_3, y_3)$. Suppose P divides BC in the ratio $\lambda:1$, then coordinates of P are $\left(\dfrac{\lambda x_3+x_2}{\lambda+1},\dfrac{\lambda y_3+y_2}{\lambda+1}\right)$ since P lies on L.

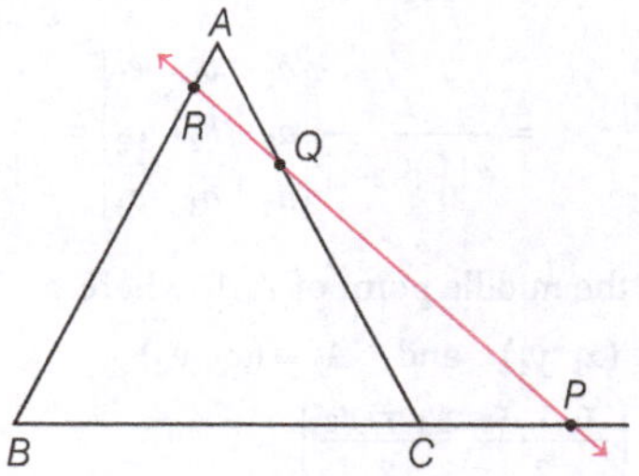

$$\Rightarrow \quad a\left(\frac{\lambda x_3+x_2}{\lambda+1}\right)+b\left(\frac{\lambda y_3+y_2}{\lambda+1}\right)+c=0$$

$$\Rightarrow \quad a(\lambda x_3+x_2)+b(\lambda y_3+y_2)+c(\lambda+1)=0$$

$$\Rightarrow \quad \lambda(ax_3+by_3+c)+(ax_2+by_2+c)=0$$

$$\therefore \quad \frac{\lambda}{1}=\frac{BP}{CP}=-\frac{(ax_2+by_2+c)}{(ax_3+by_3+c)}$$

Similarly,
$$\frac{CQ}{QA}=-\frac{(ax_3+by_3+c)}{(ax_1+by_1+c)}$$

and
$$\frac{AR}{RB}=-\frac{(ax_1+by_1+c)}{(ax_2+by_2+c)}$$

Hence,
$$\frac{BP}{PC}\cdot\frac{CQ}{QA}\cdot\frac{AR}{RB}=-1$$

5. $\because \Delta^c=\Delta^2$

where, Δ^c be the determinant of cofactors of Δ.

Let,
$$\Delta^c=\begin{vmatrix} A_1 & B_1 & C_1\\ A_2 & B_2 & C_2\\ A_3 & B_3 & C_3\end{vmatrix}$$

then,
$$A_1=b_2c_3-b_3c_2,\ B_1=a_3c_2-a_2c_3,\ C_1=a_2b_3-a_3b_2$$
$$A_2=b_3c_1-b_1c_3,\ B_2=c_3a_1-c_1a_3,\ C_2=a_3b_1-a_1b_3$$
$$A_3=b_1c_2-b_2c_1,\ B_3=a_2c_1-a_1c_2,\ C_3=a_1b_2-a_2b_1$$

Given lines are

$$a_1x+b_1y+c_1=0 \qquad \text{...(i)}$$
$$a_2x+b_2y+c_2=0 \qquad \text{...(ii)}$$
$$a_3x+b_3y+c_3=0 \qquad \text{...(iii)}$$

Let P be the point of intersection of Eqs. (ii) and (iii), then

$$\frac{x}{b_2c_3-b_3c_2}=\frac{y}{c_2a_3-c_3a_2}=\frac{1}{a_2b_3-a_3b_2}$$

i.e.
$$\frac{x}{A_1}=\frac{y}{B_1}=\frac{1}{C_1}$$

$$\therefore \quad P\equiv\left(\frac{A_1}{C_1},\frac{B_1}{C_1}\right)$$

Similarly, if Q and R be the points of intersections of Eqs. (iii) and (i) and Eqs. (i) and (ii) respectively, then

$$Q\equiv\left(\frac{A_2}{C_2},\frac{B_2}{C_2}\right),\ R\equiv\left(\frac{A_3}{C_3},\frac{B_3}{C_3}\right)$$

$$\therefore \text{ Area of } \Delta PQR = \frac{1}{2}\left|\begin{vmatrix} \frac{A_1}{C_1} & \frac{B_1}{C_1} & 1 \\ \frac{A_2}{C_2} & \frac{B_2}{C_2} & 1 \\ \frac{A_3}{C_3} & \frac{B_3}{C_3} & 1 \end{vmatrix}\right| = \frac{1}{2\,|C_1C_2C_3|}\begin{vmatrix} A_1 & B_1 & C_1 \\ A_2 & B_2 & C_2 \\ A_3 & B_3 & C_3 \end{vmatrix}$$

$$= \frac{1}{2\,|C_1C_2C_3|}\begin{vmatrix} a_1 & b_1 & c_1 \\ a_2 & b_2 & c_2 \\ a_3 & b_3 & c_3 \end{vmatrix}^2 = \frac{\Delta^2}{2\,|C_1C_2C_3|}$$

6. Since, G_1 is the middle point of A_1A_2 where

$$A_1 \equiv (x_1, y_1) \text{ and } A_2 \equiv (x_2, y_2)$$

$$\therefore \quad G_1 \equiv \left(\frac{x_1 + x_2}{2}, \frac{y_1 + y_2}{2}\right)$$

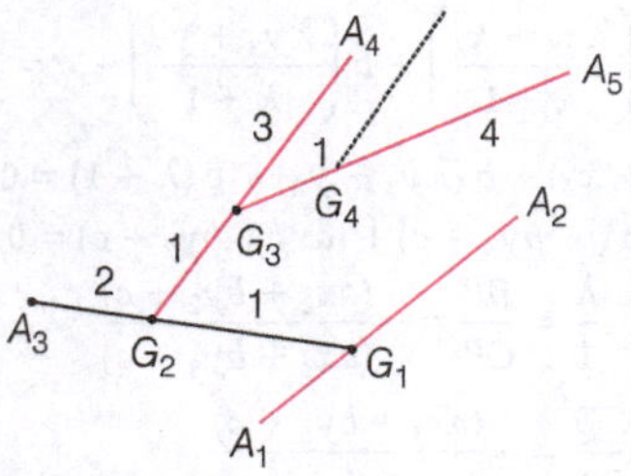

Since, G_2 divided G_1A_3 internally in the ratio 1:2

$$\therefore \quad G_2 \equiv \left(\frac{2\cdot\left(\frac{x_1 + x_2}{2}\right) + 1.\, x_3}{2+1}, \frac{2\cdot\left(\frac{y_1 + y_2}{2}\right) + 1.\, y_3}{2+1}\right)$$

$$\text{i.e.} \quad G_2 \equiv \left(\frac{x_1 + x_2 + x_3}{3}, \frac{y_1 + y_2 + y_3}{3}\right)$$

Again G_3 divides G_2A_4 internally in the ratio 1:3

$$\therefore \quad G_3 \equiv \left(\frac{3\cdot\left(\frac{x_1 + x_2 + x_3}{3}\right) + 1.\, x_4}{3+1}, \frac{3\cdot\left(\frac{y_1 + y_2 + y_3}{3}\right) + 1.\, y_4}{3+1}\right)$$

$$\text{i.e.} \quad G_3 \equiv \left(\frac{x_1 + x_2 + x_3 + x_4}{4}, \frac{y_1 + y_2 + y_3 + y_4}{4}\right)$$

Proceeding in this way, we can show that

$$G_{n-1} \equiv \left(\frac{x_1 + x_2 + \ldots + x_n}{n}, \frac{y_1 + y_2 + \ldots + y_n}{n}\right)$$

or we can say that the coordinates of the final point are

$$\frac{x_1 + x_2 + \ldots + x_n}{n} \text{ and } \frac{y_1 + y_2 + \ldots + y_n}{n}$$

7. Let the axes be rotated through an angle α, since (x, y) be the coordinates with respect to old axes and (x_1, y_1) be the coordinates with respect to new axes, then

$$x = x_1 \cos\alpha - y_1 \sin\alpha$$

and $$y = x_1 \sin\alpha + y_1 \cos\alpha$$

Now, the expression $ax^2 + 2hxy + by^2$ becomes

$$a(x_1\cos\alpha - y_1\sin\alpha)^2 + 2h(x_1\cos\alpha - y_1\sin\alpha)(x_1\sin\alpha + y_1\cos\alpha) + b(x_1\sin\alpha + y_1\cos\alpha)^2$$

$$\Rightarrow \quad x_1^2(a\cos^2\alpha + h\sin 2\alpha + b\sin^2\alpha) + x_1y_1(2h\cos 2\alpha - a\sin 2\alpha + b\sin 2\alpha) + y_1^2(a\sin^2\alpha - h\sin 2\alpha + b\cos^2\alpha) \quad \ldots\text{(i)}$$

But, from question the expression $ax^2 + 2hxy + by^2$ transforms into

$$a_1x_1^2 + 2h_1x_1y_1 + b_1y_1^2 \quad \ldots\text{(ii)}$$

Therefore, the expressions (i) and (ii) are the same. Hence, equating the coefficients, we get

$$a_1 = a\cos^2\alpha + h\sin 2\alpha + b\sin^2\alpha \quad \ldots\text{(iii)}$$

$$2h_1 = 2h\cos 2\alpha - a\sin 2\alpha + b\sin 2\alpha \quad \ldots\text{(iv)}$$

$$b_1 = a\sin^2\alpha - h\sin 2\alpha + b\cos^2\alpha \quad \ldots\text{(v)}$$

On adding Eqs. (iii) and (v), we get

$$a_1 + b_1 = a(\cos^2\alpha + \sin^2\alpha) + b(\sin^2\alpha + \cos^2\alpha)$$

or $$a_1 + b_1 = a + b \quad \ldots\text{(vi)}$$

Again, $$a_1 - b_1 = a(\cos^2\alpha - \sin^2\alpha) + 2h\sin 2\alpha + b(\sin^2\alpha - \cos^2\alpha)$$

$$\Rightarrow \quad (a_1 - b_1) = (a - b)\cos 2\alpha + 2h\sin 2\alpha$$

$$\Rightarrow \quad (a_1 - b_1)^2 = (a - b)^2\cos^2 2\alpha + 4h^2\sin^2 2\alpha + 4h(a - b)\sin 2\alpha\cos 2\alpha \quad \ldots\text{(vii)}$$

Again, from Eq. (iv)

$$2h_1 = 2h\cos 2\alpha - (a - b)\sin 2\alpha$$

$$\therefore \quad 4h_1^2 = 4h^2\cos^2 2\alpha + (a - b)^2\sin^2 2\alpha - 4h(a - b)\sin 2\alpha\cos 2\alpha \quad \ldots\text{(viii)}$$

On adding Eqs. (vii) and (viii), we get

$$(a_1 - b_1)^2 + 4h_1^2 = (a - b)^2 + 4h^2$$

Again, $$4a_1b_1 - 4h_1^2 = (a_1 + b_1)^2 - (a_1 - b_1)^2 - 4h^2$$

$$= (a + b)^2 - (a - b)^2 - 4h^2 \quad \text{[from Eq. (vi)]}$$

Hence, $$a_1b_1 - h_1^2 = ab - h^2$$

2

> *An equation means nothing to me unless it express a through of God.*
>
> **-Shri Srinivasa Ramanujan**

Straight Lines

Learning Milestones

Milestone 1 Equation of Straight Line

- Definition
- Angle of Inclination of a Line
- Lines Parallel to Coordinate Axes
- Reduction of General Equation to Standard Form
- The distance Form or Symmetric Form or Parametric Form of a Line

Milestone 2 Position of Two Points Relative to a Given Line

- Position of two Points relative to a given Line
- Position of a Point which lies inside a triangle
- Distance of a Point From a Line
- Distance between Two Parallel Lines
- Area of a Parallelogram

Milestone 3 Point of Intersection of Two lines

- Points of Intersection of two lines
- Concurrent Lines
- Family of Lines

Milestone 4 Equation of Angle Bisector of Lines

- Equations of Straight lines Passing through a given point and making angle with a given line
- A line Equally inclined with two lines
- Equation of the bisectors

Milestone 5 The foot of Perpendicular

- The foot of Perpendicular Drawn from the Point (x_1, y_1) to the line $ax+by+c=0$
- Image or Reflection of a Point (x_1, y_1) About a line Mirror
- Image or Reflection of a Point in Different Cases
- Use of Image or Reflection

Milestone 6 Reflection of a Light

- Reflection of a Light
- Refraction of Light

Practice Milestones

Practice Milestone 1- JEE Main Pattern

Practice Milestone 2 - JEE Advanced Pattern

Practice Milestone 3 - Challenging Problems

Milestone 1 Equation of Straight Line

• Definition • Angle of Inclination of a Line • Lines Parallel to Coordinate Axes • Reduction of General Equation to Standard Form • The Distance Form or Symmetric Form or Parametric Form of a Line

2.1 Definition

A straight line defined as the curve which is such that the line segment joining any two points on it lies wholly on it.

Theorem The general equation of the first degree in x, y represents a straight line.

Proof The general equation of the first degree is

$$ax + by + c = 0 \quad \text{...(i)}$$

Let $P(x_1, y_1)$ and $Q(x_2, y_2)$ be the coordinates of any two points on the curve given by Eq. (i), then

$$ax_1 + by_1 + c = 0 \quad \text{...(ii)}$$

$$ax_2 + by_2 + c = 0 \quad \text{...(iii)}$$

Multiplying Eq. (iii) by λ and adding to Eq. (ii), we have

$$a(x_1 + \lambda x_2) + b(y_1 + \lambda y_2) + c(1 + \lambda) = 0$$

or $$a\left(\frac{x_1 + \lambda x_2}{1 + \lambda}\right) + b\left(\frac{y_1 + \lambda y_2}{1 + \lambda}\right) + c = 0 \quad (\lambda \neq -1)$$

This relation shows that the point $\left(\frac{x_1 + \lambda x_2}{1 + \lambda}, \frac{y_1 + \lambda y_2}{1 + \lambda}\right)$ lies on Eq. (i).

But from previous chapter we know that this point divides the join of $P(x_1, y_1)$ and $Q(x_2, y_2)$ in the ratio $\lambda : 1$.

Since, λ can have any value, so each point on the line PQ lies on Eq. (i) i.e. the line wholly lies on Eq. (i). Hence, by the definition of the straight line as given above we conclude that Eq. (i) represents a straight line.

Hence, the general equation of first degree in x, y *viz* $ax + by + c = 0$ represents a straight line.

JEE Focus Points

- The number of arbitrary constants in the equation of a straight line is two (we observe three constants a, b and c in the equation $ax + by + c = 0$ of a straight line). The given equation of line can be rewritten as $\left(\frac{a}{c}\right)x + \left(\frac{b}{c}\right)y + 1 = 0$ or $px + qy + 1 = 0$, where $p = \frac{a}{c}$ and $q = \frac{b}{c}$.

  Thus, we have only two arbitrary constants p and q in the equation of a straight line. Hence, to completely determine the equation of a straight line, we require two conditions to determine the two unknowns in general.
- A straight line is briefly written as a 'line.'
- The equation of a straight line is the relation between x and y, which is satisfied by the coordinates of each and every point on that line.

2.2 Angle of Inclination of a Line

The angle of inclination of a line is the measure of the angle between the X-axis and the line measured in the anti-clockwise direction.

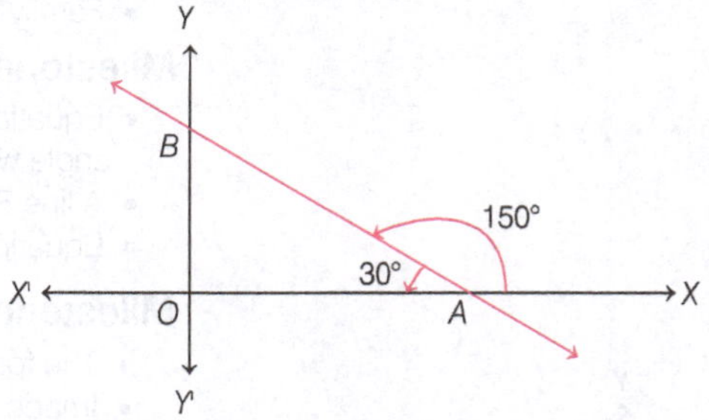

Here, angle of inclination of line $AB = 150°$.

Slope or Gradient of a Line

If inclination of a line is θ $(\theta \neq 90°)$ and $0° < \theta < 180°$, then $\tan\theta$ is called the slope or gradient of the line. It is usually denoted by m.

θ is positive or negative according as it is measured in anti-clockwise or clockwise direction.

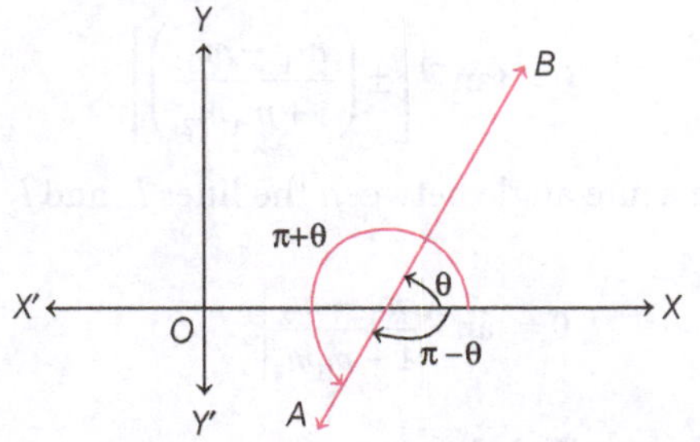

i.e. Slope of $AB = m$ of $AB = m(AB)$

$$= \tan\theta \text{ or } \tan[-(\pi-\theta)] = \tan(\pi+\theta)$$

$$= \text{slope of } BA = m \text{ of } BA = m(BA)$$

$\therefore \quad m(AB) = m(BA)$

Hence, we do not take into consideration the direction of a line segment while talking of its slope.

Concept Inside Video

JEE Focus Points

- Slope of a line is not the angle but is the tangent of the angle of inclination of the line.
- If a line is parallel to *X*-axis, then its slope = tan0° = 0.
- Slope of a line parallel to *Y*-axis or perpendicular to *X*-axis is not defined.
- If a line is equally inclined to the axes, then it will make an angle of 45° or 135° with the positive direction of *X*-axis. Slope in this case will be tan 45° or tan135° i.e. ± 1

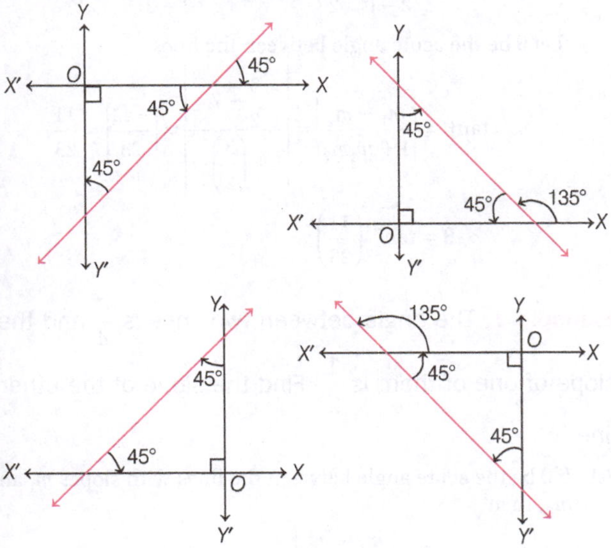

Example 1. Find the slope of line such that line substends an angle of 15° with positive direction of *X*-axis measured anti-clockwise.

Sol. Given, $\theta = 15°$

So, slope $m = \tan 15° = \tan(45° - 30°)$ $[\because m = \tan\theta]$

$$\Rightarrow m = \frac{\tan 45° - \tan 30°}{1 + \tan 45° \tan 30°} = \frac{1 - \frac{1}{\sqrt{3}}}{1 + \frac{1}{\sqrt{3}}} = \frac{\sqrt{3}-1}{\sqrt{3}+1} = 2 - \sqrt{3}$$

Example 2. Find the angle of inclination of a line whose slope is $-\frac{1}{\sqrt{3}}$.

Sol. Let angle α be the inclination of a line, then its slope = tan α

$$\therefore \quad \tan\alpha = -\frac{1}{\sqrt{3}} = -\tan 30° = \tan(180° - 30°) = \tan 150°$$

$$\Rightarrow \quad \alpha = 150°$$

Slope-in point form

If $P(x_1, y_1)$ and $Q(x_2, y_2)$ are two points on a line *l*, then the slope *m* of the line *l* is given by

$$m = \frac{y_2 - y_1}{x_2 - x_1}, x_1 \neq x_2$$

If $x_1 = x_2$, then *m* is not defined. In that case the line is perpendicular to *X*-axis.

Example 3. Determine λ, so that 2 is the slope of the line through (2, 5) and (λ, 3).

Sol. Slope of the line joining (2, 5) and (λ, 3).

$$= \frac{3-5}{\lambda-2} = \frac{-2}{\lambda-2} = 2 \quad \text{[given]}$$

$$\Rightarrow \quad -2 = 2\lambda - 4 \Rightarrow 2\lambda = 2$$

$$\therefore \quad \lambda = 1$$

Example 4. Show that the line joining the points (2, −3) and (−5, 1) is parallel to the line joining the points (7, −1) and (0, 3).

Sol. Slope of the line joining the points (2, −3) and (−5, 1) is

$$m_1 = \frac{1-(-3)}{-5-2} = -\frac{4}{7}$$

and slope of the line joining the points (7, −1) and (0, 3) is

$$m_2 = \frac{3-(-1)}{0-7} = \frac{-4}{7}$$

Here, $m_1 = m_2$

Hence, lines are parallel.

Example 5. For what value of *k*, the points $(k, 2-2k)$, $(-k+1, 2k)$ and $(-4-k, 6-2k)$ are collinear ?

Sol. Let $A \equiv (k, 2-2k)$, $B \equiv (-k+1, 2k)$ and $C \equiv (-4-k, 6-2k)$ are collinear, then

Slope of *AB* = Slope of *AC*

$$\Rightarrow \quad \frac{2k-(2-2k)}{-k+1-k} = \frac{6-2k-(2-2k)}{-4-k-k}$$

$$\Rightarrow \quad \frac{4k-2}{-2k+1}=\frac{4}{-4-2k}$$

$$\left[k \neq \frac{1}{2} (\because \text{denominator} \neq 0)\right]$$

$$\Rightarrow \quad (4k-2)(-4-2k)=4(-2k+1)$$

$$\Rightarrow \quad (2k-1)(-2-k)-(-2k+1)=0$$

$$\Rightarrow \quad (2k-1)(-2-k+1)=0$$

$$\because \quad k \neq \frac{1}{2}$$

$$\therefore \quad k=-1$$

Angle Between Two Lines

The acute angle θ between the lines having slopes m_1 and m_2 is given by

$$\theta = \tan^{-1}\left|\frac{m_1-m_2}{1+m_1m_2}\right|$$

Proof Let l_1 and l_2 be two non-perpendicular lines, neither of which is parallel to the Y-axis.

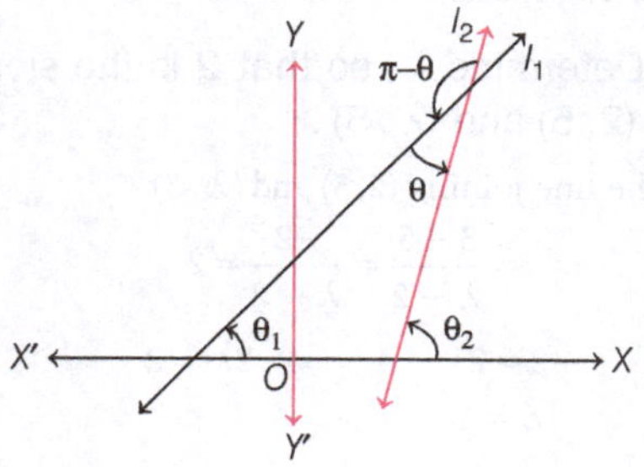

Let m_1 and m_2 be the slopes of two given lines l_1 and l_2 respectively.

Let θ_1 and θ_2 be the inclinations of these lines.

$$\therefore \quad m_1=\tan\theta_1 \text{ and } m_2=\tan\theta_2$$

Let θ and $\pi-\theta$ be the angles between the lines $\left(\theta \neq \frac{\pi}{2}\right)$.

Then, $\quad \theta_2=\theta+\theta_1$ or $\theta=\theta_2-\theta_1$

$$\Rightarrow \quad \tan\theta=\tan(\theta_2-\theta_1)$$

$$\Rightarrow \quad \tan\theta=\left(\frac{\tan\theta_2-\tan\theta_1}{1+\tan\theta_2\tan\theta_1}\right)=\left(\frac{m_2-m_1}{1+m_1m_2}\right) \quad \text{...(i)}$$

Also, $\quad \tan(\pi-\theta)=-\tan\theta=-\left(\dfrac{m_2-m_1}{1+m_2m_1}\right) \quad$ ...(ii)

From Eqs. (i) and (ii) the angle between two lines of slopes m_1 and m_2 is given by

$$\tan\theta=\pm\left(\frac{m_1-m_2}{1+m_1m_2}\right)$$

$$\Rightarrow \quad \theta=\tan^{-1}\left[\pm\left(\frac{m_1-m_2}{1+m_1m_2}\right)\right]$$

Hence, the acute angle between the lines l_1 and l_2 is given by

$$\theta=\tan^{-1}\left|\frac{m_1-m_2}{1+m_1m_2}\right|.$$

JEE Focus Points

- If two lines, whose slopes are m_1 and m_2 are parallel, then $m_1=m_2$. Thus, when two lines are parallel, their slopes are equal.
- If two lines, whose slopes are m_1 and m_2 are perpendicular, then $m_1m_2=-1$. Thus, when two lines are perpendicular, the product of their slopes is -1.
- If m is the slope of a line, then the slope of a line perpendicular to it is $-\frac{1}{m}$.

Example 6. Find the angle between the lines joining the points $(0,0),(2,3)$ and $(2,-2),(3,5)$.

Sol. Let the given points be $A\equiv(0,0)$, $B\equiv(2,3)$, $C\equiv(2,-2)$ and $D\equiv(3,5)$. Let m_1 and m_2 be the slopes of the lines AB and CD respectively.

$$\therefore \quad m_1=\frac{3-0}{2-0}=\frac{3}{2} \text{ and } m_2=\frac{5-(-2)}{3-2}=7$$

Let θ be the acute angle between the lines

$$\therefore \quad \tan\theta=\left|\frac{m_1-m_2}{1+m_1m_2}\right|=\left|\frac{\frac{3}{2}-7}{1+\left(\frac{3}{2}\right)\cdot 7}\right|=\left|\frac{-11}{23}\right|=\frac{11}{23}$$

$$\therefore \quad \theta=\tan^{-1}\left(\frac{11}{23}\right)$$

Example 7. The angle between two lines is $\frac{\pi}{4}$ and the slope of one of them is $\frac{1}{2}$. Find the slope of the other line.

Sol. If θ be the acute angle between the lines with slopes m_1 and m_2, then

$$\tan\theta=\left|\frac{m_1-m_2}{1+m_1m_2}\right|$$

Given, $\quad \theta=\dfrac{\pi}{4}$ and $m_1=\dfrac{1}{2}$

Then, $\tan\frac{\pi}{4} = \left|\frac{\frac{1}{2} - m_2}{1 + \frac{1}{2}\cdot m_2}\right| \Rightarrow 1 = \left|\frac{1 - 2m_2}{2 + m_2}\right|$

$$\Rightarrow \quad \frac{1 - 2m_2}{2 + m_2} = \pm 1$$

Taking positive sign, then

$$1 - 2m_2 = 2 + m_2$$

$$\therefore \quad m_2 = -\frac{1}{3}$$

and taking negative sign, then

$$1 - 2m_2 = -2 - m_2$$

$$\therefore \quad m_2 = 3$$

Hence, the slope of the other line is either $-\frac{1}{3}$ or 3.

Example 8. A line passes through the points $A(2, -3)$ and $B(6, 3)$. Find the slopes of the lines which are

(i) parallel to AB (ii) perpendicular to AB

Sol. Let m be the slope of AB. Then, $m = \frac{3 - (-3)}{6 - 2} = \frac{6}{4} = \frac{3}{2}$

(i) Let m_1 be the slope of a line parallel to AB, then

$$m_1 = m = \frac{3}{2}$$

(ii) The slope of a line perpendicular to AB is

$$-\frac{1}{m} = -\frac{1}{\frac{3}{2}} = -\frac{2}{3}$$

Example 9. Find the equation to the sides of an isosceles right angled triangle, the equation of whose hypotenuse is $3x + 4y = 4$ and the opposite vertex is $(2, 2)$.

Sol. We need to find out equation to the straight lines passing through the given point (2, 2) and making equal angles of 45° with the given straight line $3x + 4y = 4$.

$\therefore$ Slope of line $3x + 4y - 4 = 0$ is $m_2 = \frac{-3}{4}$

$$\Rightarrow \quad \tan 45° = \pm\left(\frac{m_1 - m_2}{1 + m_1 m_2}\right)$$

$$1 = \pm\left(\frac{m_1 + \frac{3}{4}}{1 - \frac{3}{4}m_1}\right)$$

On solving, we get $m_1 = \frac{1}{7}$ and -7.

Hence, required equation of two lines are

$$7y - x - 12 = 0 \text{ and } 7x + y = 16$$

Example 10. In an isosceles ΔABC, $AB = AC$, $B(1, 2)$ and $C(2, 1)$. If the equation of line AB is $y = 2x$, then find the equation of line AC.

Sol. Slope of $BC = \frac{2 - 1}{1 - 2} = -1$

Also, slope of $AB = 2$

Let slope of AC be m

$$\therefore \quad \tan\theta = \left|\frac{2 - (-1)}{1 + 2(-1)}\right| = \left|\frac{m - (-1)}{1 + m(-1)}\right|$$

$$= \frac{m + 1}{1 - m} = \pm 3$$

$$\Rightarrow \quad m = \frac{1}{2} \text{ or } 2$$

Since, the slope of AB is also 2, so the slope of AC must be $\frac{1}{2}$.

So, its equation is $2(y - 1) = x - 2$ or $2y = x$

Example 11. Show that the triangle which has one of the angles as 60°, can not have all vertices with integral coordinates.

Sol. Let ABC be a triangle whose vertices are $A(x_1, y_1), B(x_2, y_2)$ and $C(x_3, y_3)$. Assume $x_1, x_2, x_3, y_1, y_2, y_3$ all are integers.

Let $\angle BAC = 60°$

Slope of $AC = \frac{y_3 - y_1}{x_3 - x_1} = m_1$ [say]

and slope of $AB = \frac{y_2 - y_1}{x_2 - x_1} = m_2$ [say]

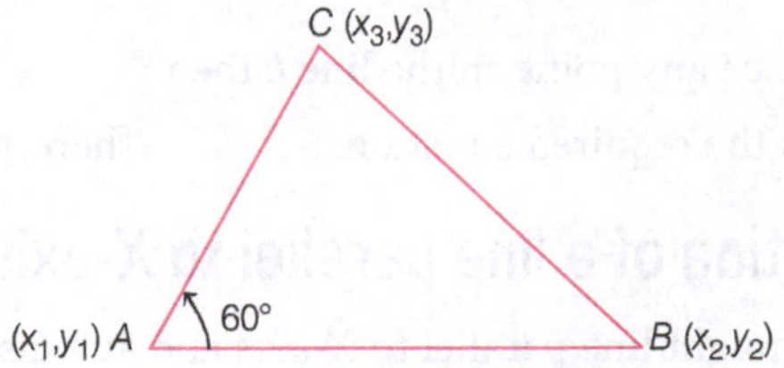

Here, m_1 and m_2 are rational numbers

[$\because x_1, x_2, x_3, y_1, y_2, y_3$ are integers]

$$\therefore \quad \tan(\angle BAC) = \frac{m_1 - m_2}{1 + m_1 m_2}$$

$= \text{Rational}$ [$\because m_1$ and m_2 are rational]

But $\tan(\angle BAC) = \tan 60° = \sqrt{3} =$ Irrational

$\because$ Rational number $\neq$ Irrational number

which is contradiction so our assumption that the vertices are integers is wrong.

Hence, the triangle having one angle of 60° can not have all vertices with integral coordinates.

2.3 Lines Parallel to Coordinate Axes

(i) Equation of a line parallel to Y-axis

Let l be a straight line parallel to Y-axis and at a distance a from it, a being the directed distance of the line from the Y-axis.

Therefore, the line lies on the right of Y-axis, if $a > 0$ and if $a < 0$, then the line would lies on the left of Y-axis.

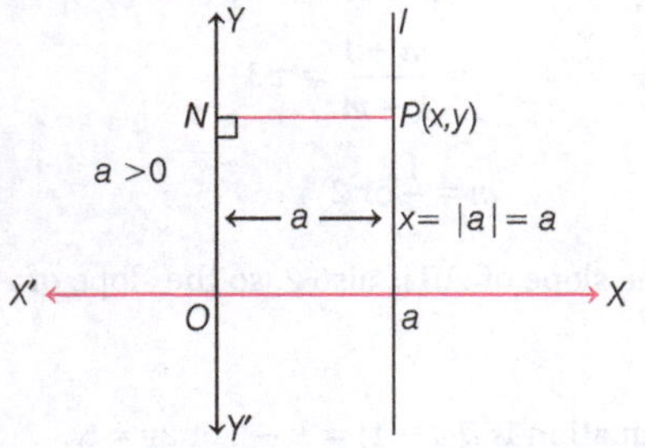

Here, $|a| = a$

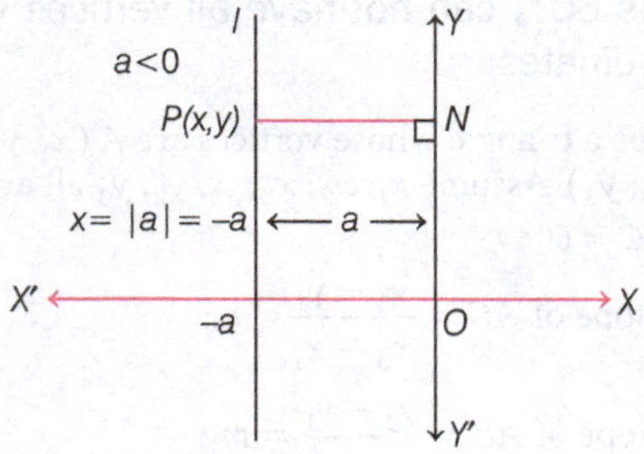

Here, $|a| = -a$

Let $P(x, y)$ be any point on the line l, then

$x = a$ is the required equation. [here, $|a| = a$]

(ii) Equation of a line parallel to X-axis

Let l be a straight line parallel to X-axis and at a distance b from it, b being the directed distance of the line from the X-axis.

Therefore, the line lies above the X-axis, if $b > 0$ and if $b < 0$, then the line would lie below the X-axis.

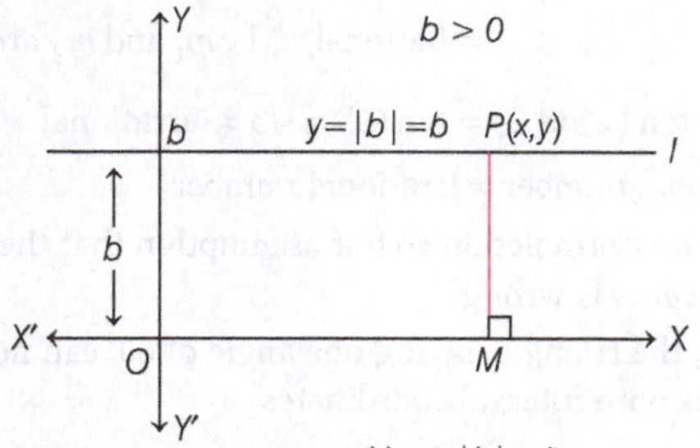

Here, $|b| = b$

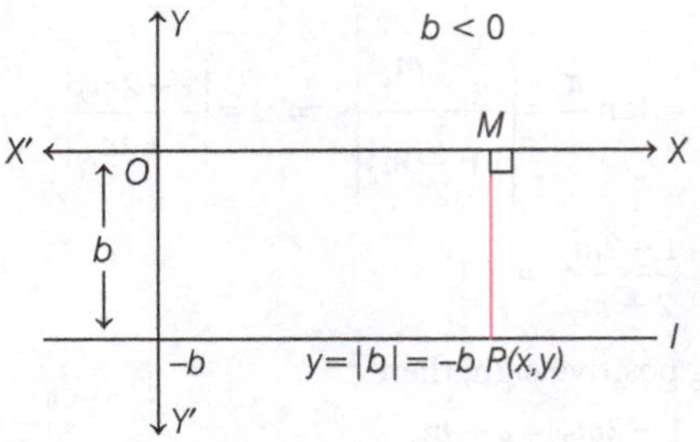

Here, $|b| = -b$

Let $P(x, y)$ be any point on the line l, then $y = b$ is the required equation. [here, $|b| = b$]

JEE Focus Points

- A line parallel to Y-axis at a distance a from it and is on the negative side of Y-axis, then its equation is $x = -a$.
- A line parallel to X-axis at a distance b from it and is on the negative side of X-axis, then its equation is $y = -b$.

Example 12. Find the equation of the straight line which passes through the point $(2, -3)$ and is

(i) parallel to the X-axis

(ii) perpendicular to the X-axis

Sol. (i) Let equation of any line parallel to X-axis is

$$y = b \quad \text{....(i)}$$

Since, it passes through the point $(2, -3)$.

Putting $y = -3$ in Eq. (i), then

$$b = -3$$

Hence, required equation of the line is $y = -3$.

(ii) Let equation of any line perpendicular to X-axis

= Equation of any line parallel to Y-axis is

$$x = a \quad \text{...(ii)}$$

Since, it passes through the point $(2, -3)$ putting $x = 2$ in Eq. (ii), we get

$$2 = a \Rightarrow a = 2$$

Hence, required equation of the line $x = 2$.

Example 13. Find the equation of line passing through the point $(2, -7)$ which is perpendicular to the line $3x + 2y - 4 = 0$

Sol. Slope of line perpendicular to line $3x + 2y - 4 = 0$ is $\frac{2}{3}$.

Thus, equation of line is $y + 7 = \frac{2}{3}(x - 2)$

$$\Rightarrow \quad 2x - 3y - 25 = 0$$

Example 14. Find the equation of a line which is equidistant from the lines $x = -\frac{7}{2}$ and $x = \frac{15}{2}$.

Sol. Since, the given (both) lines are parallel to Y-axis and the required line is equidistant from these lines, so it is also parallel to Y-axis. Let equation of any line parallel to Y-axis is

$$x = a$$

Here, $a = \dfrac{\left(-\dfrac{7}{2}+\dfrac{15}{2}\right)}{2} = \dfrac{8}{4} = 2$ units

Hence, its equation is $x = 2$.

Example 15. Find the direction in which a straight line must be drawn through the point $(-1, 2)$ so that its point of intersection with the line $x + y = 4$ may be at a distance of 3 units from this point.

Sol. Let the slope of line be m. Then, line through point $P(-1, 2)$ is

$$y - 2 = m(x+1)$$

$$y = mx + 2 + m \quad \text{...(i)}$$

The given line is $x + y = 4$. ...(ii)

From Eqs. (i) and (ii), we get

$$Q\left(\frac{2-m}{m+1}, \frac{5m+2}{m+1}\right)$$

Given, $PQ = 3$

$$\therefore \quad \sqrt{\left(\frac{2-m}{m+1}+1\right)^2 + \left(\frac{5m+2}{m+1}-2\right)^2} = 3$$

$$\Rightarrow \quad \frac{9}{(m+1)^2} + \frac{9m^2}{(m+1)^2} = 9$$

$$\Rightarrow \quad 1 + m^2 = m^2 + 1 + 2m$$

$$\Rightarrow \quad 2m = 0 \Rightarrow m = 0$$

Thus, slope of required line must be zero i.e. the line must be parallel to X-axis.

Example 16. Find the line passing through the point $\left(-1, \dfrac{\pi}{2}\right)$ and perpendicular to the straight line $\sqrt{3}\sin\theta + 2\cos\theta = \dfrac{4}{r}$.

Sol. Point $P\left(-1, \dfrac{\pi}{2}\right) = (0, -1)$

Given line, $\sqrt{3}r\sin\theta + 2r\cos\theta = 4$

Put $x = r\cos\theta$ and $y = r\sin\theta$

$$\sqrt{3}y + 2x = 4$$

$$m = \frac{-2}{\sqrt{3}}$$

$$\therefore \text{ Required line is } y + 1 = \frac{\sqrt{3}}{2}(x - 0)$$

$$2y + 2 = \sqrt{3}x$$

$$\Rightarrow \quad \sqrt{3}r\cos\theta - 2r\sin\theta = 2$$

Intercepts of a Line on Axes

If a line cuts X-axis at $A(a, 0)$ and the Y-axis at $B(0, b)$, then OA and OB are known as the intercepts of the line on X-axis and Y-axis respectively. $|a|$ is called the length of intercept of the line on X-axis. Intercept of a line on X-axis may be positive or negative and $|b|$ is called the length of intercept of the line on Y-axis. Intercept of a line on Y-axis may be positive or negative.

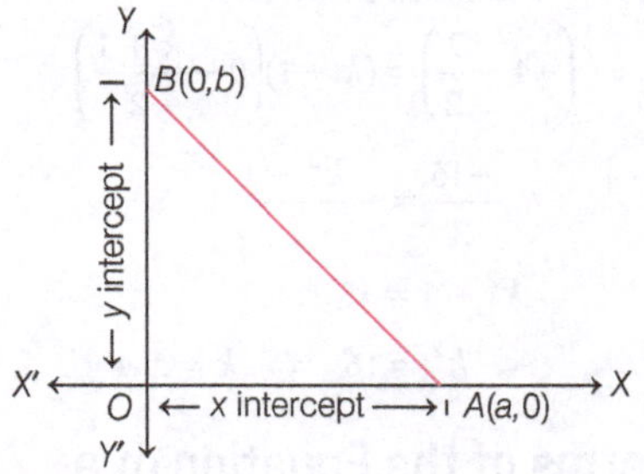

JEE SPIKE

If a line parallel to Y-axis, then its intercept on Y-axis is not defined and if a line parallel to X-axis, then its intercept on X-axis is not defined.

Example 17. If the line passing through the points $(m, -9)$ and $(7, m)$ has a slope m, then find the x-intercept of this line.

Sol. Slope of line

$$m = \frac{y_2 - y_1}{x_2 - x_1} = \frac{m+9}{7-m}$$

$$\Rightarrow \quad 7m - m^2 = m + 9$$

$$\Rightarrow \quad m^2 - 6m + 9 = 0$$

$$\Rightarrow \quad (m-3)^2 = 0 \Rightarrow m = 3$$

$\therefore$ The points are $(3, -9)$ and $(7, 3)$.

The equation of the line passing through the point $(3, -9)$ is $(y + 9) = 3(x - 3)$

$$\Rightarrow \quad 3x - y - 18 = 0$$

Put $y = 0$ in the above equation to get x-intercept

$$\therefore \quad x = 6$$

Hence, the x-intercept of line is $x = 6$.

Example 18. Perpendicular bisector of the line segment joining $P(1, 4)$ and $Q(k, 3)$ has y-intercept is -4, then find the possible values of k.

Sol. Slope of line $PQ = \dfrac{y_2 - y_1}{x_2 - x_1} = \dfrac{3-4}{k-1} = \dfrac{-1}{k-1}$

Slope of perpendicular bisector of $PQ = k - 1$

Also, mid-point of $PQ = \left(\dfrac{k+1}{2}, \dfrac{7}{2}\right)$

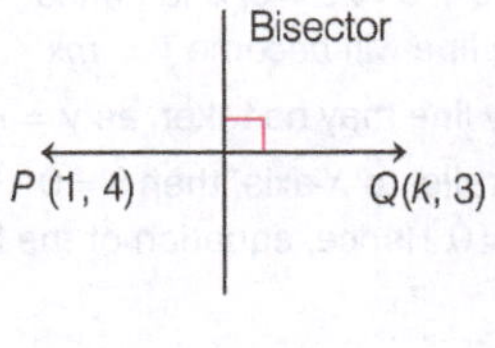

The equation of bisector of PQ is

$$y - \frac{7}{2} = (k-1)\left(x - \frac{k+1}{2}\right)$$

as $x = 0, y = -4$ satisfies it, we have

$$\left(-4 - \frac{7}{2}\right) = (k-1)\left(0 - \frac{k+1}{2}\right)$$

$$\Rightarrow \quad \frac{-15}{2} = -\frac{k^2-1}{2}$$

$$\Rightarrow \quad k^2 - 1 = 15$$

$$\Rightarrow \quad k^2 = 16 \Rightarrow k = \pm 4$$

Different Forms of the Equation of a Straight Line

(i) Slope-Intercept Form

The equation of the straight line whose slope is m and which cuts an intercept c on the Y-axis is

$$y = mx + c$$

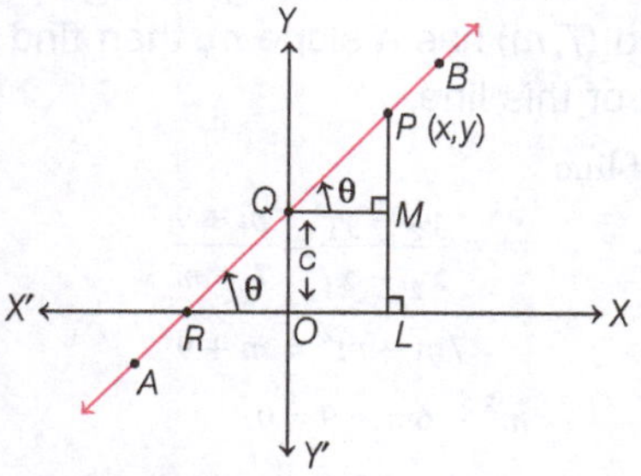

Proof Let AB be a line whose slope is m and which cuts an intercept c on Y-axis. Let $P(x, y)$ be any point on the line. Draw $PL \perp$ to X-axis and $QM \perp$ to PL.

Then, from figure,

$$\angle PRL = \angle PQM = \theta, OQ = c$$

$$\therefore \quad PM = PL - ML = PL - OQ = y - c$$

and $$QM = OL = x$$

Now, in ΔPQM, $$\tan\theta = \frac{PM}{QM}$$

$$\Rightarrow \quad m = \frac{y-c}{x} \Rightarrow y = mx + c$$

which is the required equation of the line.

JEE Focus Points

- If the line passes through the origin, then $c = 0 (\because 0 = m \cdot 0 + c \Rightarrow c = 0)$ and hence equation of the line will become $y = mx$.
- Equation of any line may be taken as $y = mx + c$.
- If the line is parallel to X-axis, then $\theta = 0°$ i.e. $m = \tan 0° = 0$. Hence, equation of the line parallel to X-axis is $y = c$.

Concept Inside Video

Example 19. If the straight line $y = mx + c$ passes through the points $(2, 4)$ and $(-3, 6)$, find the values of m and c.

Sol. Since, $(2, 4)$ lies on $y = mx + c$

$$\therefore \quad 4 = 2m + c \quad \text{...(i)}$$

Again, $(-3, 6)$ lies on $y = mx + c$

$$\therefore \quad 6 = -3m + c \quad \text{...(ii)}$$

On solving Eqs. (i) and (ii), we get

$$m = -\frac{2}{5}, c = \frac{24}{5}$$

Example 20. Find the equation of the straight line cutting off an intercept of 3 units on negative direction of Y-axis and inclined at an angle $\tan^{-1}\left(\frac{3}{5}\right)$ to the axis of X.

Sol. Here, $c = -3$ and $\theta = \tan^{-1}\left(\frac{3}{5}\right)$

or $$\tan\theta = \frac{3}{5} = m$$

Hence, the equation of the line $y = mx + c$

i.e., $$y = \frac{3}{5}x - 3$$

$$\therefore \quad 3x - 5y - 15 = 0$$

Example 21. Find the equations of the bisectors of the angle between the coordinate axes.

Sol. Let L_1 and L_2 be the straight lines bisecting the coordinate axes.

Both L_1 and L_2 pass through origin.

$\therefore$ Equation of line through origin is $y = mx$

For L_1, $m = \tan 45° = 1$

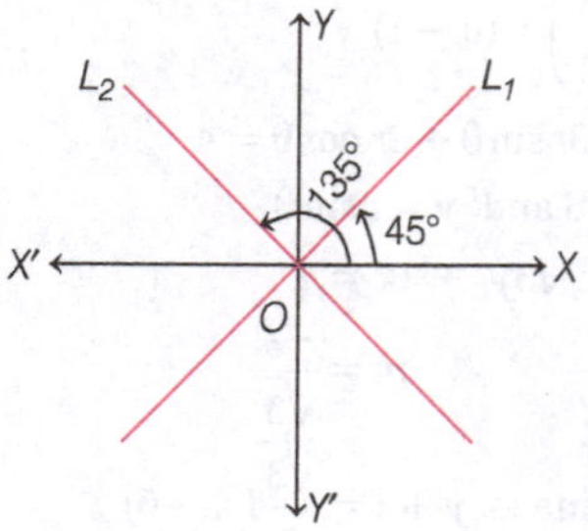

$\therefore$ Equation of line L_1 is $y = x$

i.e. $$x - y = 0$$

For L_2, $m = \tan 135° = -1$

$\therefore$ Equation of line L_2 is $y = -x$

i.e. $$x + y = 0$$

Hence, equations of the bisectors of the angle between the coordinate axes are $x \pm y = 0$.

(ii) The Point-Slope Form of a Line

The equation of the straight line which passes through the point (x_1, y_1) and has the slope m is

$$y - y_1 = m(x - x_1)$$

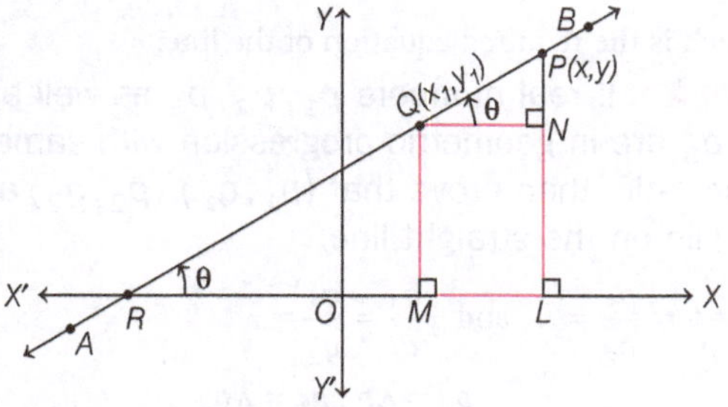

Let the equation of the required line be

$$y = mx + c \quad \text{...(i)}$$

where, m is the slope of the line.

Since, line in Eq. (i) passes through the point (x_1, y_1), therefore

$$y_1 = mx_1 + c \quad \text{...(ii)}$$

On subtracting Eq. (ii) from Eq. (i), we get

$$y - y_1 = m(x - x_1)$$

which is the required equation of the line.

JEE SPIKE

If the line passes through the origin, then putting $x_1 = 0$ and $y_1 = 0$ in $y - y_1 = m(x - x_1)$.

It becomes $y = mx$, which is the equation of the line passing through the origin and having slope m.

The equation $y - y_1 = m(x - x_1)$ is called point-slope form or one point form of the equation.

Example 22. Find the equation of the straight line bisecting the segment joining the points $(5, 3)$ and $(4, 4)$ and making an angle of 45° with the positive direction of X-axis.

Sol. Here, m = slope of the line = $\tan 45° = 1$.

Let A be the mid-point of $(5, 3)$ and $(4, 4)$. Then, the coordinates of A are

$$\left(\frac{5+4}{2}, \frac{3+4}{2}\right) \text{ i.e. } \left(\frac{9}{2}, \frac{7}{2}\right).$$

Hence, the required equation of the line is

$$y - \frac{7}{2} = 1\left(x - \frac{9}{2}\right)$$

or $\quad x - y - 1 = 0$

Example 23. Find the equation of the right bisector of the line joining $(1, 1)$ and $(3, 5)$.

Sol. Let m be the slope of the line joining $(1, 1)$ and $(3, 5)$.

Then, $\quad m = \frac{5-1}{3-1} = \frac{4}{2} = 2$

∴ Slope (M) of right bisector of the join of $(1, 1)$ and $(3, 5)$

$$= -\frac{1}{m}$$

∴ $\quad M = -\frac{1}{2}$

Mid-point of the join of $(1, 1)$ and $(3, 5)$ is $\left(\frac{1+3}{2}, \frac{1+5}{2}\right)$

i.e. $(2, 3)$.

Hence, equation of the right bisector passing through $(2, 3)$ and having slope $M = -\frac{1}{2}$ is

$$y - 3 = -\frac{1}{2}(x - 2)$$

or $\quad x + 2y - 8 = 0$

(iii) The Two-Point Form of a Line

The equation of a line passing through two given points (x_1, y_1) and (x_2, y_2) is given by

$$y - y_1 = \left(\frac{y_2 - y_1}{x_2 - x_1}\right)(x - x_1)$$

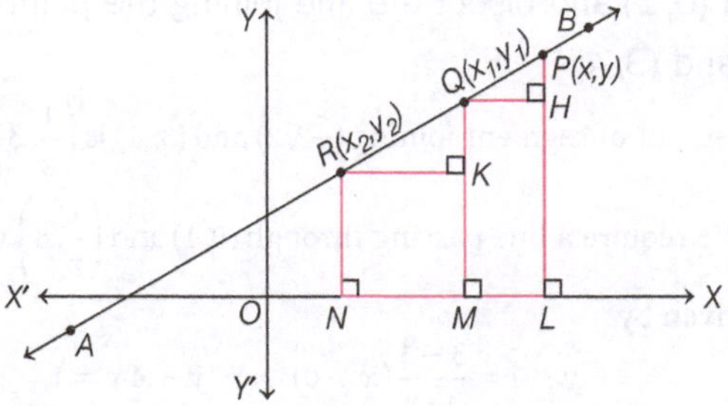

Proof Let the equation of the required line be

$$y = mx + c \quad \text{...(i)}$$

where m is the slope of the line.

Since, line in Eq. (i) passes through the points (x_1, y_1) and (x_2, y_2), therefore

$$y_1 = mx_1 + c \quad \text{...(ii)}$$

and $\quad y_2 = mx_2 + c \quad \text{...(iii)}$

On subtracting Eq. (ii) from Eq. (i), we get

$$y - y_1 = m(x - x_1) \quad \text{...(iv)}$$

and subtracting Eq. (ii) from Eq. (iii), we get

$$y_2 - y_1 = m(x_2 - x_1) \quad \text{...(v)}$$

Dividing Eq. (iv) by Eq. (v), then we get

$$\frac{y-y_1}{y_2-y_1}=\frac{x-x_1}{x_2-x_1}$$

or $$y-y_1=\left(\frac{y_2-y_1}{x_2-x_1}\right)(x-x_1)$$

which is the required equation of the line.

Example 24. Find the equation of the straight line joining the points $\left(at_1, \frac{a}{t_1}\right)$ and $\left(at_2, \frac{a}{t_2}\right)$.

Sol. The equation of the line joining the points $\left(at_1, \frac{a}{t_1}\right)$ and $\left(at_2, \frac{a}{t_2}\right)$ is

$$y-\frac{a}{t_1}=\left(\frac{\frac{a}{t_2}-\frac{a}{t_1}}{at_2-at_1}\right)(x-at_1)$$

$$\Rightarrow \quad y-\frac{a}{t_1}=-\frac{a(t_1-t_2)}{at_1t_2(t_1-t_2)}(x-at_1)$$

or $$y-\frac{a}{t_1}=-\frac{1}{t_1t_2}(x-at_1)$$

or $t_1t_2y-at_2=-x+at_1$ or $x+t_1t_2y=a(t_1+t_2)$

which is the required equation of the line.

Example 25. Find the equation of the line which passes through (0, 1) and bisect the line joining the points (−2, 2) and (3, 4).

Sol. Mid-point of segment joining (−2, 2) and (3, 4) is $\left(\frac{1}{2}, 3\right)$.

∴ We require a line passing through (0, 1) and $\left(\frac{1}{2}, 3\right)$ which is given by

$$y-1=\frac{3-1}{1/2}(x-0) \Rightarrow y-4x=1$$

Example 26. Let ABC be a triangle with $A(-1,-5)$, $B(0,0)$ and $C(2,2)$ and let D be the middle point of BC. Find the equation of the perpendicular drawn from B to AD.

Sol. ∵ D is the middle point of BC.

∴ Coordinates of D are $\left(\frac{0+2}{2}, \frac{0+2}{2}\right)$ i.e. $D(1, 1)$

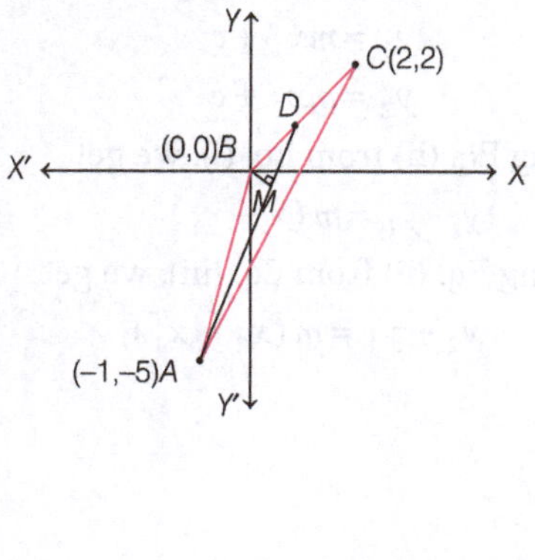

Slope of median $AD=\frac{1+5}{1+1}=3$

∴ Slope of BM which is perpendicular to $AD=-\frac{1}{3}$.

Hence, equation of the line BM is

$$y-0=-\frac{1}{3}(x-0) \Rightarrow x+3y=0$$

which is the required equation of the line.

Example 27. If real numbers p_1, p_2, p_3 as well as q_1, q_2, q_3 are in geometric progression with same common ratio, then prove that (p_1, q_1), (p_2, q_2) and (p_3, q_3) lie on the straight line.

Sol. Let $\frac{p_2}{p_1}=\frac{p_3}{p_2}=\lambda$ and $\frac{q_2}{q_1}=\frac{q_3}{q_2}=\lambda$

$$p_2=\lambda p_1, p_3=\lambda p_2$$

and $$q_2=q_1\lambda, q_3=q_2\lambda$$

It will be sufficient to prove that area subtended by three point = 0

Thus, $\Delta=\frac{1}{2}\begin{vmatrix} p_1 & q_1 & 1 \\ p_2 & q_2 & 1 \\ p_3 & q_3 & 1 \end{vmatrix} \Rightarrow \Delta=\frac{1}{2}\begin{vmatrix} p_1 & q_1 & 1 \\ \lambda p_1 & \lambda q_1 & 1 \\ \lambda^2 p_1 & \lambda^2 q_1 & 1 \end{vmatrix}$

$$=\frac{1}{2}p_1q_1\begin{vmatrix} 1 & 1 & 1 \\ \lambda & \lambda & 1 \\ \lambda^2 & \lambda^2 & 1 \end{vmatrix}=0 \quad [\because C_1 \text{ and } C_2 \text{ are identical}]$$

∴ They lie on the straight line.

Example 28. Find the ratio in which the line segment joining the points (2, 3) and (4, 5) is divided by the line joining (6, 8) and (−3, −2).

Sol. The equation of line passing through (6, 8) and (−3, −2) are

$$y-8=\frac{-2-8}{-3-6}(x-6)$$

$$\Rightarrow \quad 9y-72=10x-60$$

or $$10x-9y+12=0 \quad \text{...(i)}$$

Let the required ratio be $\lambda : 1$.

Now, the coordinates of the point P which divide the line segment joining the points (2, 3) and (4, 5) in the ratio $\lambda : 1$ are

$$P\left(\frac{2+4\lambda}{1+\lambda}, \frac{3+5\lambda}{1+\lambda}\right)$$

Clearly, P lies on Eq. (i), then

$$10\left(\frac{2+4\lambda}{1+\lambda}\right)-9\left(\frac{3+5\lambda}{1+\lambda}\right)+12=0$$

or $$20+40\lambda-27-45\lambda+12+12\lambda=0$$

or $$7\lambda+5=0 \text{ or } \lambda=-\frac{5}{7}$$

∴ The required ratio $=\lambda:1=-\frac{5}{7}:1=-5:7$

Hence, the required ratio is 5 : 7 (externally).

(iv) The Intercept Form of a Line

The equation of the straight line which cuts off intercepts a and b on X-axis and Y-axis respectively, is

$$\frac{x}{a}+\frac{y}{b}=1$$

Proof Let QR be a line which cuts off intercepts $OA=a$ and $OB=b$ on the X-axis and Y-axis respectively, where $a\neq 0$.

The line is non vertical, because b is finite. Let $P(x, y)$ be a general point on the line.

Draw PL and PM perpendiculars on X-axis and Y-axis respectively. Then, $PL=y$ and $OL=x$, also join OP.

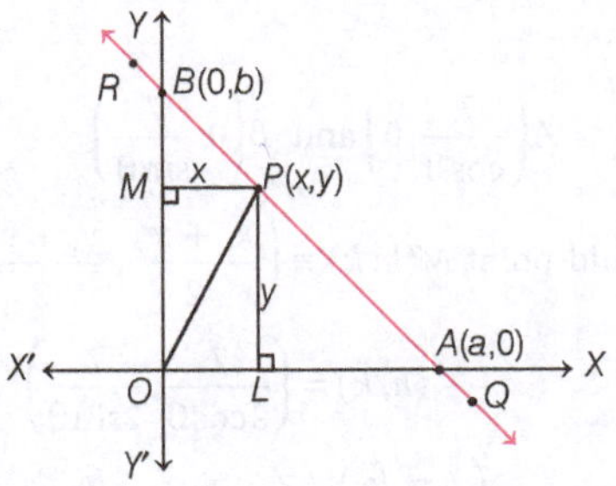

Clearly, Area of $\Delta OAB=$ Area of $\Delta OAP+$ Area of ΔOPB

$$\Rightarrow \quad \frac{1}{2}\cdot OA\cdot OB=\frac{1}{2}\cdot OA\cdot PL+\frac{1}{2}\cdot OB\cdot PM$$

$$\Rightarrow \quad \frac{1}{2}\cdot OA\cdot OB=\frac{1}{2}\cdot OA\cdot PL+\frac{1}{2}\cdot OB\cdot OL$$

or $$\frac{1}{2}ab=\frac{1}{2}ay+\frac{1}{2}bx$$

$$\Rightarrow \quad ab=ay+bx$$

or $$\frac{x}{a}+\frac{y}{b}=1$$

which is the required equation of the line.

Example 29. Find the equation of the line through $(2, 3)$ so that the segment of the line intercepted between the axes is bisected at this point.

Sol. Let the required line segment be AB.

Let O be the origin and $OA=a$ and $OB=b$.

Then, the coordinates of A and B are $(a, 0)$ and $(0, b)$, respectively.

$$\therefore \quad \frac{a+0}{2}=2$$

$$\Rightarrow \quad a=4$$

and $$\frac{0+b}{2}=3$$

$$\Rightarrow \quad b=6$$

Hence, the equation of the required line is

$$\frac{x}{4}+\frac{y}{6}=1$$

i.e. $$3x+2y=12$$

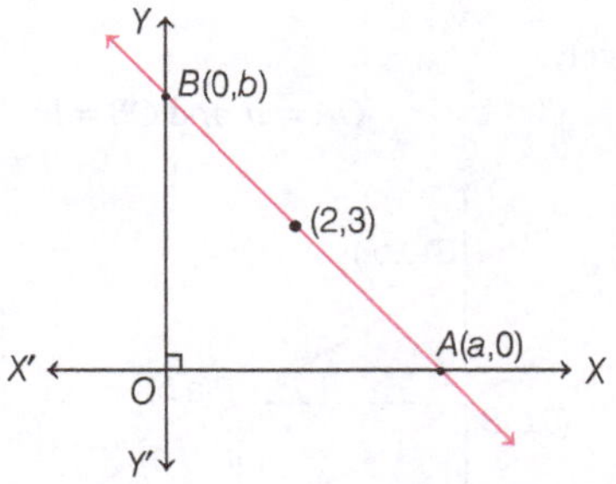

Example 30. Find the equation to the straight line which passes through the point $(3, 4)$ and have intercepts on the axes

(a) equal in magnitude but opposite in sign

(b) such that their sum is 14

Sol. (a) Let intercepts on the axes be a and $-a$ respectively.

$\therefore$ The equation of the line in intercept form is

$$\frac{x}{a}+\frac{y}{-a}=1 \quad \text{or} \quad x-y=a \qquad \text{...(i)}$$

Since, Eq. (i) passes through $(3, 4)$, then

$$3-4=a$$

$$\therefore \quad a=-1$$

From Eq. (i), $\quad x-y+1=0$

which is the required equation of the line.

(b) Let the equation of the line be $\frac{x}{a}+\frac{y}{b}=1$

This passes through $(3, 4)$.

Therefore, $$\frac{3}{a}+\frac{4}{b}=1 \qquad \text{...(ii)}$$

It is given that $a+b=14$

$$\therefore \quad b=14-a$$

Putting $b=14-a$ in Eq. (ii), we get

$$\frac{3}{a}+\frac{4}{14-a}=1$$

$$\Rightarrow \quad 42-3a+4a=14a-a^2$$

$$\Rightarrow \quad a^2-13a+42=0$$

$$\Rightarrow \quad (a-7)(a-6)=0$$

$$\therefore \quad a=6, 7$$

Then, $$b=8, 7 \qquad [\because b=14-a]$$

Hence, the required equations are

$$\frac{x}{6}+\frac{y}{8}=1 \quad \text{and} \quad \frac{x}{7}+\frac{y}{7}=1$$

i.e. $$4x+3y=24 \quad \text{and} \quad x+y=7$$

Example 31. Find the equation of the straight line through the point $P(a, b)$ parallel to the line $\frac{x}{a}+\frac{y}{b}=1$. Also, find the intercepts made by it on the axes.

Sol. Let the line $\frac{x}{a}+\frac{y}{b}=1$ meets the axes in A and B respectively.

So that $\quad OA = a$ and $OB = b$

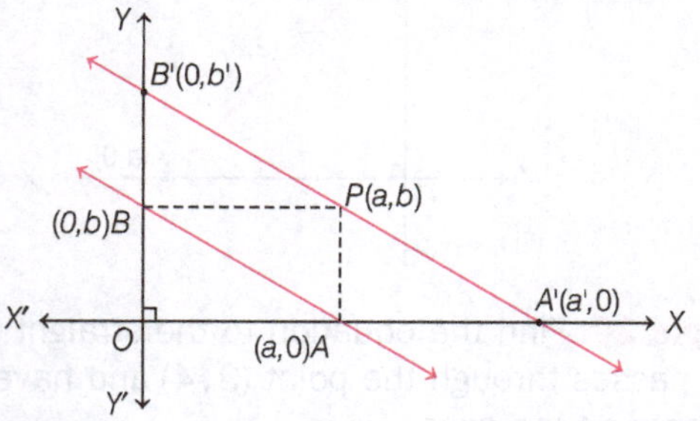

Let the required parallel line meet in A' and B' respectively, so that

$$OA' = a' \quad \text{[say]}$$

and $$OB' = b' \quad \text{[say]}$$

∴ Equation of required line is

$$\frac{x}{a'}+\frac{y}{b'}=1 \quad \text{...(i)}$$

Since, Δ's OAB and $OA'B'$ are similar, then

$$\frac{OA'}{OA}=\frac{OB'}{OB}$$

i.e. $$\frac{a'}{a}=\frac{b'}{b}=\lambda \quad \text{[say]}$$

$$\Rightarrow \quad a' = a\lambda,\ b' = b\lambda$$

Substituting these values in Eq. (i), then

$$\frac{x}{a\lambda}+\frac{y}{b\lambda}=1 \quad \text{...(ii)}$$

It passes through (a, b), then

$$\frac{a}{a\lambda}+\frac{b}{b\lambda}=1$$

$$\Rightarrow \quad \frac{2}{\lambda}=1 \text{ or } \lambda = 2$$

From Eq. (ii), required equation is

$$\frac{x}{2a}+\frac{y}{2b}=1$$

Evidently intercepts on the axes are $2a$ and $2b$.

Example 32. If the point $\left(\beta, \frac{7\sqrt{2}}{2}\right)$ lies on the curve traced by the mid-point of the line segment of the line $x\cos\theta + y\sin\theta = 7$, $\theta \in \left(0, \frac{\pi}{2}\right)$ between the coordinates axes, then find the value of β.

Sol. $x\cos\theta + y\sin\theta = 7$

So, x-intercept $= \frac{7}{\cos\theta}$

and y-intercept $= \frac{7}{\sin\theta}$

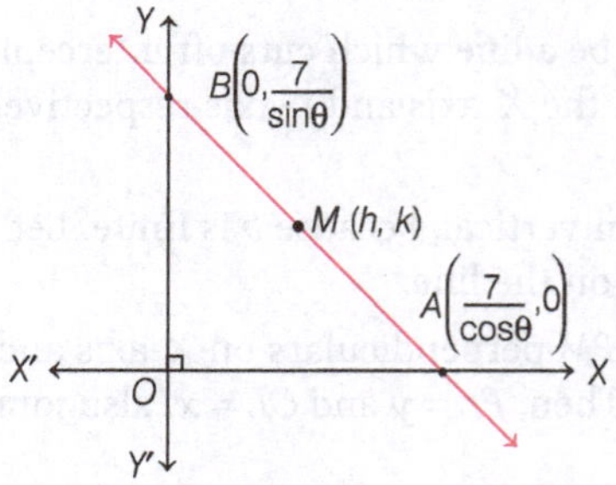

$$A\left(\frac{7}{\cos\theta}, 0\right) \text{ and } B\left(0, \frac{7}{\sin\theta}\right)$$

Locus of mid-point $M(h, k) \equiv \left(\frac{x_1+x_2}{2}, \frac{y_1+y_2}{2}\right)$

$$\Rightarrow \quad (h, k) = \left(\frac{7}{2\cos\theta}, \frac{7}{2\sin\theta}\right)$$

$$\Rightarrow \quad \left(\beta, \frac{7\sqrt{2}}{2}\right) = \left(\frac{7}{2\cos\theta}, \frac{7}{2\sin\theta}\right)$$

$$\Rightarrow \quad \beta = \frac{7}{2\cos\theta}, \frac{7\sqrt{2}}{2} = \frac{7}{2\sin\theta}$$

$$\Rightarrow \quad \sin\theta = \frac{1}{\sqrt{2}} \Rightarrow \theta = 45°$$

$$\therefore \quad \beta = \frac{7}{2\cos 45°}$$

$$\Rightarrow \quad \beta = \frac{7}{2 \times \frac{1}{\sqrt{2}}} = \frac{7}{\sqrt{2}}$$

Example 33. If x-intercept of some line L is double as that of the line $3x+4y=12$ and y-intercept of L is half as that of the same line, then find the slope of L.

Sol. Given line $3x + 4y = 12$ can be rewritten as

$$\frac{3x}{12}+\frac{4y}{12}=1 \Rightarrow \frac{x}{4}+\frac{y}{3}=1$$

∴ x-intercept = 4 and y-intercept = 3

Let the required line be

$$L : \frac{x}{a}+\frac{y}{b}=1, \text{ where}$$

a = x-intercept and b = y-intercept

According to the question,

If x-intercept is doubled $= (2a, 0)$

and y-intercept is halved $= \left(0, \frac{b}{2}\right)$

$\Rightarrow \quad a = 4 \times 2 = 8$ and $b = \dfrac{3}{2}$

$\therefore$ Required line is $\dfrac{x}{8} + \dfrac{2y}{3} = 1$

$\Rightarrow \quad 3x + 16y = 24$

$\Rightarrow \quad y = \dfrac{-3}{16}x + \dfrac{24}{16}$

Hence, required slope $= -\dfrac{3}{16}$

(v) The Normal Form or Perpendicular Form of a Line

Theorem The equation of the straight line upon which the length of perpendicular from the origin is p and this normal makes an angle α with the positive direction of X-axis is

$$x \cos\alpha + y \sin\alpha = p$$

Proof Let AB be a line such that the length of perpendicular from O to the line be p

i.e. $\quad ON = p$ and $\angle NOX = \alpha$

Let $P(x, y)$ be any point on the line. Draw PL perpendicular from P on X-axis.

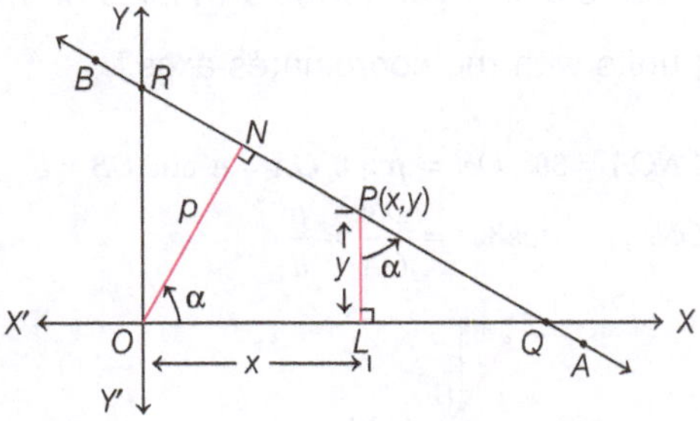

Let line AB cuts X and Y-axes at Q and R, respectively.

Now, $\quad \angle NQO = 90° - \alpha$

$\therefore \quad \angle LPQ = 90° - (90° - \alpha) = \alpha$

In ΔPLQ, $\quad \tan\alpha = \dfrac{LQ}{PL} = \dfrac{LQ}{y}$

$\therefore \quad LQ = y \tan\alpha \quad$ ...(i)

Also, in ΔONQ, $\quad \cos\alpha = \dfrac{ON}{OQ}$

$\Rightarrow \quad \cos\alpha = \dfrac{p}{OL + LQ}$

$\Rightarrow \quad OL\cos\alpha + LQ\cos\alpha = p$

$\Rightarrow \quad x\cos\alpha + y\tan\alpha\cos\alpha = p$

$[\because OL = x$ and $LQ = y\tan\alpha]$

$\therefore \quad x\cos\alpha + y\sin\alpha = p$

which is the required equation of the line AB.

COROLLARY 1 If $\alpha = 0°$, then equation $x\cos\alpha + y\sin\alpha = p$ becomes $x\cos 0° + y\sin 0° = p$

i.e. $x = p$ (equation of line parallel to Y-axis)

COROLLARY 2 If $\alpha = \dfrac{\pi}{2}$, then equation $x\cos\alpha + y\sin\alpha = p$

becomes $x\cos\left(\dfrac{\pi}{2}\right) + y\sin\left(\dfrac{\pi}{2}\right) = p$

i.e. $y = p$ (equation of line parallel to X-axis).

COROLLARY 3 If $\alpha = 0°$, $p = 0$ then equation $x\cos\alpha + y\sin\alpha = p$ becomes $x\cos 0° + y\sin 0° = 0$

i.e. $x = 0$ (equation of Y-axis)

COROLLARY 4 If $\alpha = \dfrac{\pi}{2}$, $p = 0$ then equation

$x\cos\alpha + y\sin\alpha = p$ becomes $x\cos\left(\dfrac{\pi}{2}\right) + y\sin\left(\dfrac{\pi}{2}\right) = 0$

i.e. $\quad y = 0$ (equation of X-axis)

Concept Inside Video

JEE Focus Points

- Here, p is always taken as positive and α is measured from positive direction of X-axis in anti-clockwise direction between 0 and 2π (i.e. $0 \le \alpha < 2\pi$).
- (Coefficient of x)^2 + (Coefficient of y)^2 $= \cos^2\alpha + \sin^2\alpha = 1$
- $\cos\alpha$ and $\cos(90° - \alpha)$ are the direction cosines of ON.
-

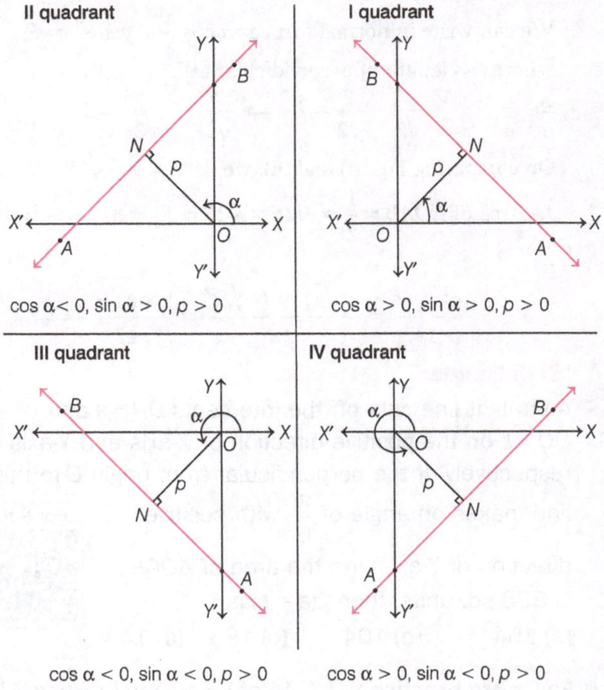

JEE SCANNER

Example Similar to PYQ Asked in JEE Main 2023

A straight line cuts off the intercepts $OA = a$ and $OB = b$ on the positive directions of X-axis and Y-axis, respectively. If the perpendicular from origin O to this line makes an angle of $\frac{\pi}{4}$ with positive direction of Y-axis and the area of ΔOAB is 81 sq. units, then $\frac{a^2+b^2}{12}$ is equal to

(a) 27 (b) 38 (c) 19 (d) 59

Sol. (a) Given, $OA = a$ and $OB = b$

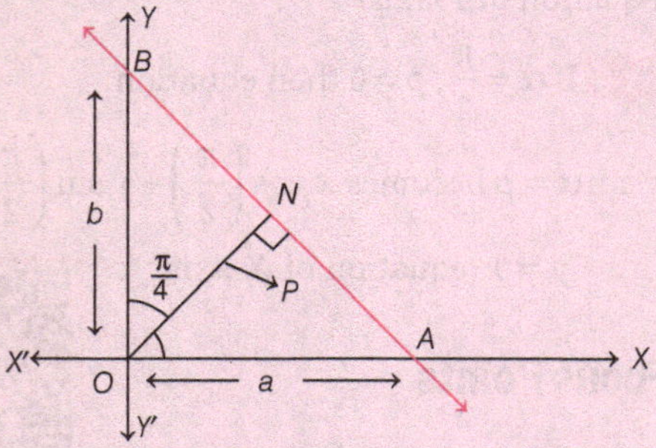

Let N be foot of perpendicular drawn from O to AB.

$\therefore \quad \angle NOA = \frac{\pi}{4}$ and $\angle NOB = \frac{\pi}{4}$ [given]

$\because$ Equation of straight line (in intercepts form) is

$$\frac{x}{a} + \frac{y}{b} = 1 \quad \text{...(i)}$$

We can write in normal form as $x\cos\frac{\pi}{4} + y\sin\frac{\pi}{4} = P$, where P = length of perpendicular ON.

$$\Rightarrow \quad \frac{x}{\sqrt{2}} + \frac{y}{\sqrt{2}} = P \Rightarrow \frac{x}{\sqrt{2}P} + \frac{y}{\sqrt{2}P} = 1 \quad \text{...(ii)}$$

On comparing Eqs. (i) and (ii), we get $a = b = \sqrt{2}P$

$\therefore$ Area of $\Delta OAB = \frac{1}{2} \times \sqrt{2}P \times \sqrt{2}P = P^2 = 81$ [given]

$\Rightarrow \quad P = 9$

$$\therefore \quad \frac{a^2+b^2}{12} = \frac{(9\sqrt{2})^2 + (9\sqrt{2})^2}{12} = \frac{2\times 81\times 2}{12} = 27$$

Skill Builder

A straight line cuts off the intercepts $OP = a$ and $OQ = b$ on the positive direction of X-axis and Y-axis respectively. If the perpendicular from origin O to this line makes on angle of $\frac{\pi}{6}$ with positive direction of Y-axis and the area of ΔOQP is 338 sq. units, then $2(a+b)$ is

For Sol.

(a) 154 (b) 104 (c) 196 (d) 144

■ **For more practice** See Q.14 of Milestone Practice 2.1.

Example 34. The length of perpendicular from the origin to a line is 9 and the line makes an angle of 120° with the positive direction of Y-axis. Find the equation of the line.

Sol. Here, $\alpha = 60°$ and $p = 9$.

$\therefore$ Equation of the required line is

$$x\cos 60° + y\sin 60° = 9$$

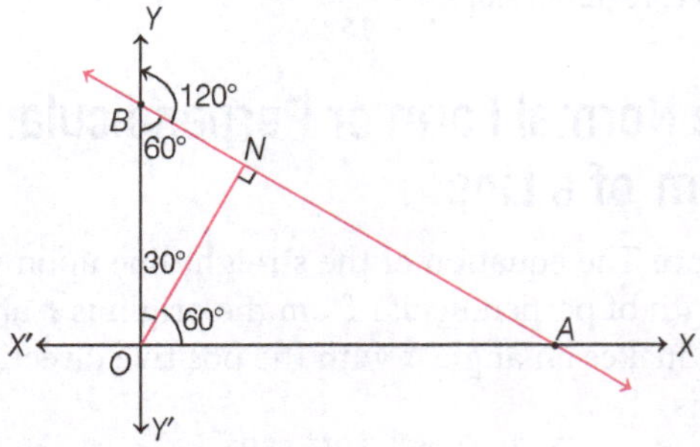

$$\Rightarrow \quad x\left(\frac{1}{2}\right) + y\left(\frac{\sqrt{3}}{2}\right) = 9$$

or $\quad x + y\sqrt{3} = 18$

Example 35. Find the equation of the straight line on which the perpendicular from origin makes an angle of 30° with X-axis and which forms a triangle of area $\left(\frac{50}{\sqrt{3}}\right)$ sq units with the coordinates axes.

Sol. Let $\angle NOA = 30°$, $ON = p > 0$, $OA = a$ and $OB = b$

In ΔONA, $\quad \cos 30° = \frac{ON}{OA} = \frac{p}{a}$

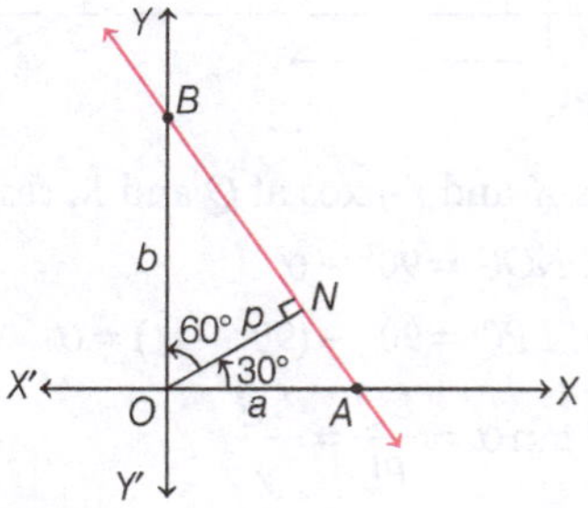

$$\Rightarrow \quad \frac{\sqrt{3}}{2} = \frac{p}{a} \text{ or } a = \frac{2p}{\sqrt{3}}$$

In ΔONB, $\cos 60° = \frac{ON}{OB} = \frac{p}{b}$

$$\Rightarrow \quad \frac{1}{2} = \frac{p}{b} \text{ or } b = 2p$$

$\therefore \quad$ Area of $\Delta OAB = \frac{1}{2}ab$

$$= \frac{1}{2}\left(\frac{2p}{\sqrt{3}}\right)(2p) = \frac{2p^2}{\sqrt{3}}$$

$$\therefore \quad \frac{2p^2}{\sqrt{3}} = \frac{50}{\sqrt{3}} \quad \text{[given]}$$

$$\Rightarrow \quad p^2 = 25$$

or $\quad p = 5 \quad [\because p > 0]$

$\therefore$ Using $x \cos\alpha + y \sin\alpha = p$, the equation of the line AB is

$$x \cos 30° + y \sin 30° = 5$$

or $\quad x\sqrt{3} + y = 10$

2.4 Reduction of General Equation to Standard Form

Let $Ax + By + C = 0$ be the general equation of a straight line where A and B are not both zero.

(i) Reduction of 'Slope-Intercept' Form

Given equation is $Ax + By + C = 0$

$$\Rightarrow \quad By = -Ax - C$$

$$\Rightarrow \quad y = \left(-\frac{A}{B}\right)x + \left(-\frac{C}{B}\right) \quad [\text{assuming } B \neq 0]$$

Comparing it with $y = mx + c$,

we get $\quad$ slope $(m) = -\dfrac{A}{B} = -\dfrac{\text{coefficient of } x}{\text{coefficient of } y}$

and $\quad$ y intercept $(c) = -\dfrac{C}{B} = -\dfrac{\text{constant term}}{\text{coefficient of } y}$

COROLLARY 1 Find angle between the lines

$$A_1x + B_1y + C_1 = 0 \text{ and } A_2x + B_2y + C_2 = 0.$$

Slope of the line

$$A_1x + B_1y + C_1 = 0 \text{ is } -\frac{A_1}{B_1} = m_1 \quad \text{(say)}$$

and slope of the line

$$A_2x + B_2y + C_2 = 0 \text{ is } -\frac{A_2}{B_2} = m_2 \quad \text{(say)}$$

If θ is the angle between the two lines, then

$$\tan\theta = \left|\frac{m_1 - m_2}{1 + m_1m_2}\right| = \left|\frac{\left(-\frac{A_1}{B_1}\right) - \left(-\frac{A_2}{B_2}\right)}{1 + \left(-\frac{A_1}{B_1}\right)\left(-\frac{A_2}{B_2}\right)}\right|$$

$$= \left|\frac{A_1B_2 - A_2B_1}{A_1A_2 + B_1B_2}\right|$$

$$\therefore \quad \theta = \tan^{-1}\left|\frac{A_1B_2 - A_2B_1}{A_1A_2 + B_1B_2}\right|$$

COROLLARY 2 Find the condition of (i) parallelism (ii) perpendicularity of the lines

$$A_1x + B_1y + C_1 = 0$$

and $\quad A_2x + B_2y + C_2 = 0$

(i) If the two lines are parallel, $\theta = 0°$

$$\therefore \quad \tan\theta = \tan 0° = 0$$

$$\Rightarrow \quad \left|\frac{A_1B_2 - A_2B_1}{A_1A_2 + B_1B_2}\right| = 0$$

$$\Rightarrow \quad A_1B_2 - A_2B_1 = 0$$

or $\quad \dfrac{A_1}{A_2} = \dfrac{B_1}{B_2} \quad$ (remember)

which is required condition of parallelism.

(ii) If the two lines are perpendicular, $\theta = 90°$

$$\therefore \quad \tan\theta = \tan 90° = \infty$$

$$\Rightarrow \quad \left|\frac{A_1B_2 - A_2B_1}{A_1A_2 + B_1B_2}\right| = \infty$$

$$\Rightarrow \quad A_1A_2 + B_1B_2 = 0 \quad \text{(remember)}$$

which is required condition of perpendicularity.

JEE SPIKE

If two lines are coincident, then

$$\frac{A_1}{A_2} = \frac{B_1}{B_2} = \frac{C_1}{C_2} \quad \text{[remember]}$$

(ii) Reduction to 'Intercept' Form

Given equation is $Ax + By + C = 0$

$$\Rightarrow \quad Ax + By = -C$$

$$\Rightarrow \quad \frac{A}{-C}x + \frac{B}{-C}y = 1 \quad (\text{assuming } C \neq 0)$$

$$\Rightarrow \quad \frac{x}{(-C/A)} + \frac{y}{(-C/B)} = 1 \quad (\text{assuming } A \neq 0, B \neq 0)$$

Comparing with $\dfrac{x}{a} + \dfrac{y}{b} = 1$, we get

x-intercept $(a) = -\dfrac{C}{A} = -\dfrac{\text{constant term}}{\text{coefficient of } x}$

and y-intercept $(b) = -\dfrac{C}{B} = -\dfrac{\text{constant term}}{\text{coefficient of } y}$

(iii) Reduction to 'Normal' Form

Given equation is $Ax + By + C = 0$. Let its **normal form** be $x\cos\alpha + y\sin\alpha = p$.

Clearly, equations $Ax + By + C = 0$ and $x\cos\alpha + y\sin\alpha = p$ represent the same line.

Therefore, $$\frac{A}{\cos\alpha} = \frac{B}{\sin\alpha} = \frac{C}{-p}$$

$$\Rightarrow \quad \cos\alpha = -\frac{Ap}{C}$$

and $$\sin\alpha = -\frac{Bp}{C} \quad \text{...(i)}$$

$$\cos^2\alpha + \sin^2\alpha = 1$$

$$\Rightarrow \quad \left(-\frac{Ap}{C}\right)^2 + \left(-\frac{Bp}{C}\right)^2 = 1$$

or $$p^2 = \frac{C^2}{A^2 + B^2}$$

$$\Rightarrow \quad p = \frac{|C|}{\sqrt{(A^2 + B^2)}}$$

From Eq. (i), $$\cos\alpha = -\frac{|C|}{C} \cdot \frac{A}{\sqrt{(A^2 + B^2)}},$$

and $$\sin\alpha = -\frac{|C|}{C} \cdot \frac{B}{\sqrt{(A^2 + B^2)}}.$$

On putting the values of $\cos\alpha, \sin\alpha$ and p in $x\cos\alpha + y\sin\alpha = p$, we get

$$x\left(\frac{-|C|}{C} \cdot \frac{A}{\sqrt{(A^2 + B^2)}}\right) + y\left(\frac{-|C|}{C} \cdot \frac{B}{\sqrt{(A^2 + B^2)}}\right) = \frac{|C|}{\sqrt{(A^2 + B^2)}}$$

$$\Rightarrow \quad \left(-\frac{A}{\sqrt{(A^2 + B^2)}}\right)x + \left(-\frac{B}{\sqrt{(A^2 + B^2)}}\right)y = \frac{C}{\sqrt{(A^2 + B^2)}}$$

This is the normal form of the line $Ax + By + C = 0$.

Example 36. Find the measure of the angle of intersection of the lines whose equations are $3x + 4y + 7 = 0$ and $4x - 3y + 5 = 0$.

Sol. Given lines are $3x + 4y + 7 = 0$, $4x - 3y + 5 = 0$.

Comparing the given lines with $A_1x + B_1y + C_1 = 0$, $A_2x + B_2y + C_2 = 0$ respectively, we get

$$A_1 = 3, B_1 = 4 \text{ and } A_2 = 4, B_2 = -3$$

$$\because \quad A_1A_2 + B_1B_2 = 3 \times 4 + 4(-3) = 0$$

Hence, the given lines are perpendicular.

Example 37. Reduce $x + \sqrt{3}y + 4 = 0$ to the

(i) Slope-intercept form and find its slope and y-intercept.

(ii) Intercept form and find its intercepts on the axes.

(iii) Normal form and find the values of p and α.

Sol. (i) Given equation is $x + \sqrt{3}\,y + 4 = 0$

$$\Rightarrow \quad \sqrt{3}y = -x - 4$$

$$\Rightarrow \quad y = \left(-\frac{1}{\sqrt{3}}\right)x + \left(-\frac{4}{\sqrt{3}}\right)$$

which is in the slope-intercept form $y = mx + c$

where slope $(m) = -\frac{1}{\sqrt{3}}$ and y-intercept $(c) = -\frac{4}{\sqrt{3}}$

(ii) Given equation is

$$x + \sqrt{3}y + 4 = 0$$

$$\Rightarrow \quad x + \sqrt{3}y = -4$$

$$\Rightarrow \quad \frac{x}{-4} + \frac{\sqrt{3}y}{-4} = 1$$

$$\Rightarrow \quad \frac{x}{-4} + \frac{y}{-4/\sqrt{3}} = 1$$

which is in the intercept form $\frac{x}{a} + \frac{y}{b} = 1$

where x-intercept $(a) = -4$ and y-intercept $(b) = -\frac{4}{\sqrt{3}}$

(iii) Given equation is $x + \sqrt{3}y + 4 = 0$

$$\Rightarrow \quad x + \sqrt{3}y = -4$$

$$\Rightarrow \quad -x - \sqrt{3}y = 4 \quad \text{[RHS made positive]}$$

Dividing both sides by $\sqrt{(-1)^2 + (-\sqrt{3})^2} = 2$, we get

$$\left(-\frac{1}{2}\right)x + \left(-\frac{\sqrt{3}}{2}\right)y = 2$$

Which is the normal form $x\cos\alpha + y\sin\alpha = p$.

where, $$\cos\alpha = -\frac{1}{2} = -\cos 60^\circ$$

$$= \cos(180^\circ - 60^\circ) \text{ or } \cos(180^\circ + 60^\circ)$$

$$\therefore \quad \alpha = 120^\circ \text{ or } 240^\circ$$

and $$\sin\alpha = -\frac{\sqrt{3}}{2} = -\sin 60^\circ$$

$$= \sin(180^\circ + 60^\circ) \text{ or } \sin(360^\circ - 60^\circ)$$

$\therefore \quad \alpha = 240^\circ$ or 300°

Hence, $\quad \alpha = 240^\circ$ and $p = 2$

$\therefore$ Required normal form is

$$x \cos 240^\circ + y \sin 240^\circ = 2$$

Example 38. Find the angle between the lines $(a^2 - ab)\,y = (ab + b^2)\,x + b^3$ and $(ab + a^2)\,y = (ab - b^2)\,x + a^3$, where $a > b > 0$.

Sol. The given equations of lines can be written as

$$(ab + b^2)\,x - (a^2 - ab)\,y + b^3 = 0 \quad \text{...(i)}$$

and $$(ab - b^2)\,x - (ab + a^2)\,y + a^3 = 0 \quad \text{...(ii)}$$

Comparing the given lines (i) and (ii) with the lines

$$A_1x + B_1y + C_1 = 0 \quad \text{and} \quad A_2x + B_2y + C_2 = 0$$

respectively, we get

$$A_1 = ab + b^2,\ B_1 = -(a^2 - ab)$$

and $$A_2 = ab - b^2,\ B_2 = -(ab + a^2)$$

Let θ be the acute angle between the lines, then

$$\tan\theta = \left|\frac{A_1B_2 - A_2B_1}{A_1A_2 + B_1B_2}\right|$$

$$\tan\theta = \left|\frac{(ab + b^2) \times (-(ab + a^2)) - (ab - b^2) \times (-(a^2 - ab))}{(ab + b^2)(ab - b^2) + (a^2 - ab)(ab + a^2)}\right|$$

$$= \left|\frac{-\{a^2b^2 + a^3b + ab^3 + a^2b^2 - a^3b + a^2b^2 + a^2b^2 - b^3a\}}{(a^2b^2 - b^4 + a^4 - a^2b^2)}\right|$$

$$= \left|\frac{-4a^2b^2}{a^4 - b^4}\right| = \frac{4a^2b^2}{a^4 - b^4}$$

$$\therefore \quad \theta = \tan^{-1}\left(\frac{4a^2b^2}{a^4 - b^4}\right)$$

Example 39. Find the distance of the line from origin and inclination of normal to the line with X-axis and reduce the line $2x - 3y + 5 = 0$ in slope intercept, intercept and normal from.

Sol. Equation of given line is $2x - 3y + 5 = 0$

$$y = \frac{2x}{3} + \frac{5}{3}$$

This is of the form of $y = mx + c$

Slope of line, $m = \tan\theta = \dfrac{2}{3}$ and y-intercept is $c = \dfrac{5}{3}$

Here, θ is the angle of line with positive X-axis

$\therefore$ Intercept form is $\dfrac{x}{\left(\dfrac{-5}{2}\right)} + \dfrac{y}{\left(\dfrac{5}{3}\right)} = 1,$

where x-intercept is $a = \dfrac{-5}{2}$ and y-intercept is $b = \dfrac{5}{3}$

To get equation in normal form, divide both sides by

$$\sqrt{2^2 + 3^2} = \sqrt{13}$$

On comparing with standard equation $x\cos\alpha + y\sin\alpha = P$

$$\cos\alpha = \frac{-2}{\sqrt{13}} \text{ and } \sin\alpha = \frac{3}{\sqrt{13}}$$

and $P = \dfrac{5}{\sqrt{13}}$ = Distance of line from origin

So, inclination of normal to the line is

$$\alpha = 180^\circ - \sin^{-1}\frac{3}{\sqrt{13}}$$

2.5 The Distance Form or Symmetric Form or Parametric Form of a Line

Theorem The equation of the straight line passing through (x_1, y_1) and making an angle θ with the positive direction of X-axis is

$$\frac{x - x_1}{\cos\theta} = \frac{y - y_1}{\sin\theta} = r$$

where, r is the directed distance between the points (x, y) and (x_1, y_1).

Proof Let AB be a line which passes through the point $Q(x_1, y_1)$ and meet X-axis at R and makes an angle θ with the positive direction of X-axis.

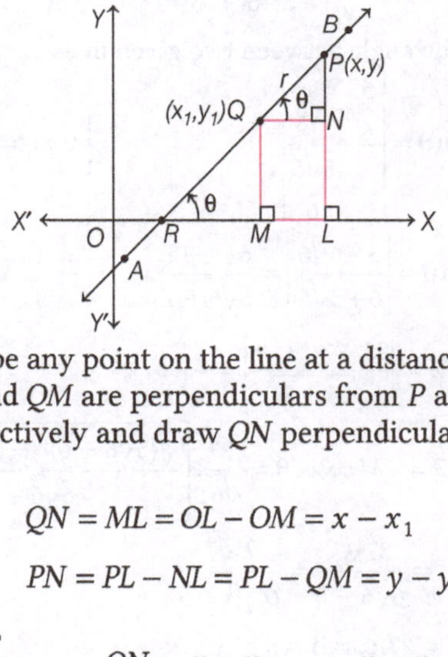

Let $P(x, y)$ be any point on the line at a distance r from Q. Draws PL and QM are perpendiculars from P and Q on X-axis respectively and draw QN perpendicular on PL. Then,

$$QN = ML = OL - OM = x - x_1$$

and $$PN = PL - NL = PL - QM = y - y_1$$

From ΔPQN,

$$\cos\theta = \frac{QN}{PQ} = \frac{x - x_1}{r} \quad \text{or} \quad \frac{x - x_1}{\cos\theta} = r \quad \text{...(i)}$$

and $$\sin\theta = \frac{PN}{PQ} = \frac{y - y_1}{r} \quad \text{or} \quad \frac{y - y_1}{\sin\theta} = r \quad \text{...(ii)}$$

From Eqs. (i) and (ii), we get

$$\frac{x - x_1}{\cos\theta} = \frac{y - y_1}{\sin\theta} = r$$

COROLLARY 1 $\because \dfrac{x-x_1}{\cos\theta}=\dfrac{y-y_1}{\sin\theta}=r$, then

$$\left.\begin{array}{l} x=x_1+r\cos\theta \\ y=y_1+r\sin\theta \end{array}\right\} \text{parametric form of straight line } AB.$$

COROLLARY 2 If point P above Q then r is positive then coordinates of P are $(x_1+r\cos\theta, y_1+r\sin\theta)$ and if P below Q then r is negative then coordinates of P are $(x_1-r\cos\theta, y_1-r\sin\theta)$.

JEE SCANNER

Example Similar to PYQ Asked in JEE Main 2023

The distance of the point (5, 6) from the line $5x-6y+38=0$, measured parallel to the line $\sqrt{6}x-y+1=0$ is equal to $\dfrac{\lambda\sqrt{7}}{\alpha\sqrt{\beta}-5}$, then $\dfrac{\lambda}{\alpha\beta}$ is

(a) $\dfrac{5}{4}$ (b) $\dfrac{7}{4}$ (c) $\dfrac{3}{4}$ (d) $\dfrac{1}{4}$

Sol. (c) The distance of $P(5, 6)$ from the line $5x-6y+38=0$ measured parallel to line $\sqrt{6}x-y+1=0$ is PQ

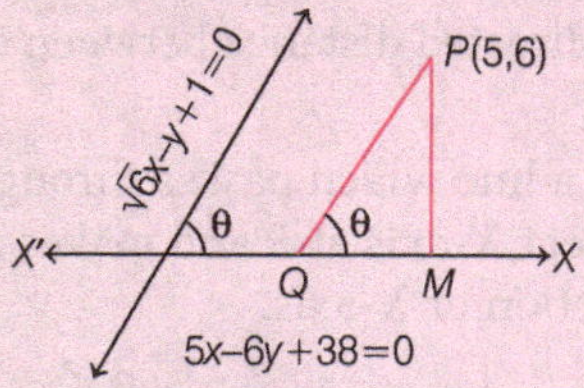

Let θ be the angle between two given lines

$$\tan\theta=\left|\frac{\frac{5}{6}-\sqrt{6}}{1+\frac{5\sqrt{6}}{6}}\right| \qquad \left[\because m_1=\frac{5}{6}, m_2=\sqrt{6}\right]$$

$$\Rightarrow \quad \tan\theta=\left|\frac{5-6\sqrt{6}}{6+5\sqrt{6}}\right|=\frac{6\sqrt{6}-5}{5\sqrt{6}+6}$$

Now, $$PM=\left|\frac{25-36+38}{\sqrt{25+36}}\right|=\frac{27}{\sqrt{61}}$$

$$\because \quad PQ=PM\operatorname{cosec}\theta=\frac{27}{\sqrt{61}}\left[\frac{\sqrt{(5\sqrt{6}+6)^2+(6\sqrt{6}-5)^2}}{6\sqrt{6}-5}\right]$$

$$=\frac{27\sqrt{7}}{6\sqrt{6}-5}=\frac{\lambda\sqrt{7}}{\alpha\sqrt{\beta}-5}$$

$$\Rightarrow \quad \lambda=27, \alpha=\beta=6$$

$$\therefore \quad \frac{\lambda}{\alpha\beta}=\frac{27}{36}=\frac{3}{4}.$$

Skill Builder

The distance of the point (2, 3) from the line $2x-3y+9=0$ measured along the line $2x-2y+5=0$, is

(a) 5/2 (b) $4\sqrt{2}$ (c) $\sqrt{2}$ (d) $2\sqrt{2}$

For Sol.

■ **For more practice** See Q.16 of Milestone Practice 2.1

Example 40. The slope of a straight line through $A(3, 2)$ is $\dfrac{3}{4}$. Find the coordinates of the points on the line that are 5 units away from A.

Sol. Let straight line makes an angle θ with positive direction of X-axis.

Then, $\tan\theta=\dfrac{3}{4}$

$\therefore \quad \sin\theta=\dfrac{3}{5}$ and $\cos\theta=\dfrac{4}{5}$

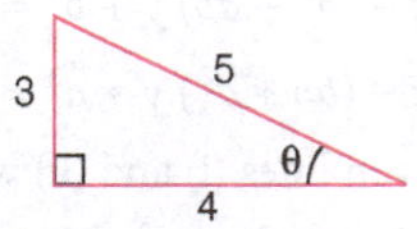

$\therefore$ Equation of the straight line through $A(3, 2)$ in parametric form is

$$\frac{x-3}{\cos\theta}=\frac{y-2}{\sin\theta}=\pm 5$$

$$\therefore \quad x=3\pm 5\cos\theta=3\pm 5\times\frac{4}{5}=3\pm 4=7 \text{ or } -1$$

and $$y=2\pm 5\sin\theta=2\pm 5\times\frac{3}{5}=2\pm 3=5 \text{ or } -1$$

Hence, the coordinates of the required points are (7, 5) and (−1, −1).

Example 41. Find the direction in which a straight line must be drawn through the point (1, 2) so that its point of intersection with the line $x+y=4$ may be at a distance $\dfrac{1}{3}\sqrt{6}$ from this point.

Sol. Let the straight line makes an angle θ with the positive direction of X-axis.

$\therefore$ Equation of the line through (1, 2) in parametric form is

$$\frac{x-1}{\cos\theta}=\frac{y-2}{\sin\theta}=\frac{1}{3}\sqrt{6}$$

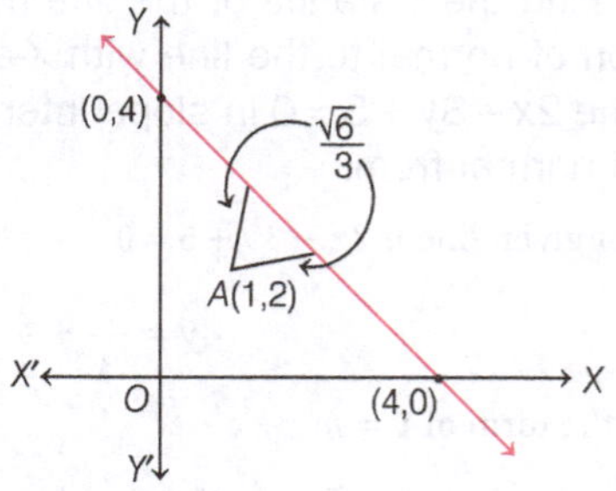

or $$x=1+\frac{\sqrt{6}}{3}\cos\theta$$

and $$y=2+\frac{\sqrt{6}}{3}\sin\theta$$

Since, the point $\left(1+\dfrac{\sqrt{6}}{3}\cos\theta, 2+\dfrac{\sqrt{6}}{3}\sin\theta\right)$ lies on the line $x+y=4$

$$\therefore \quad 1+\frac{\sqrt6}{3}\cos\theta+2+\frac{\sqrt6}{3}\sin\theta=4$$

$$\Rightarrow \quad \frac{\sqrt6}{3}(\cos\theta+\sin\theta)=1$$

$$\Rightarrow \quad \cos\theta+\sin\theta=\frac{3}{\sqrt6}=\frac{\sqrt3}{\sqrt2}$$

$$\Rightarrow \quad \frac{1}{\sqrt2}\cos\theta+\frac{1}{\sqrt2}\sin\theta=\frac{\sqrt3}{2}$$

$$\Rightarrow \quad \cos\left(\theta-\frac{\pi}{4}\right)=\cos\left(\frac{\pi}{6}\right)$$

$$\Rightarrow \quad \theta-\frac{\pi}{4}=2n\pi\pm\frac{\pi}{6};\ n\in I$$

For $n=0$, $\theta=\pm\frac{\pi}{6}+\frac{\pi}{4}$ $\quad [\because 0\le\theta<\pi]$

$=15°, 75°$

Example 42. A line through $(2, 3)$ makes an angle $\frac{3\pi}{4}$ with the negative direction of X-axis. Find the length of the line segment cut off between $(2, 3)$ and the line $x+y-7=0$.

Sol. $\because$ Line makes an angle $\frac{3\pi}{4}$ with the negative direction of X-axis.

$\therefore$ Line makes an angle $\frac{\pi}{4}$ with the positive direction of X-axis.

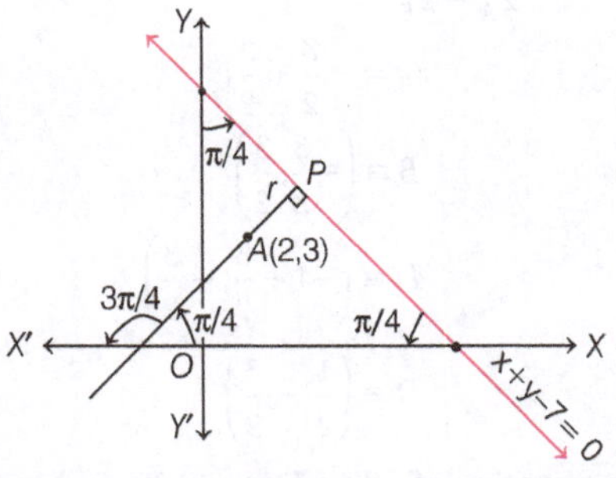

$\therefore$ The equation of the line through (2, 3) in parametric form is

$$\frac{x-2}{\cos\left(\frac{\pi}{4}\right)}=\frac{y-3}{\sin\left(\frac{\pi}{4}\right)}=r$$

i.e. $$\frac{x-2}{\frac{1}{\sqrt2}}=\frac{y-3}{\frac{1}{\sqrt2}}=r \quad ...(i)$$

$$\therefore \quad x=2+\frac{r}{\sqrt2} \text{ and } y=3+\frac{r}{\sqrt2}$$

Let the line (i) meet the line $x+y-7=0$ at point P.

$\therefore$ Coordinates of $P\left(2+\frac{r}{\sqrt2}, 3+\frac{r}{\sqrt2}\right)$ lies on $x+y-7=0$.

Then, $$2+\frac{r}{\sqrt2}+3+\frac{r}{\sqrt2}-7=0$$

or $$\frac{2r}{\sqrt2}=2 \text{ or } r=\sqrt2$$

$$\therefore \quad AP=\sqrt2$$

Special Corollaries

(i) **Angle made by AB with positive X-axis (where A and B are given points)** Let AB makes an angle θ with the positive direction of X-axis and let d be the distance between A and B. Then Let $A(x_1, y_1)$ and $B(x_2, y_2)$

$$\cos\theta=\frac{x_2-x_1}{d}, \sin\theta=\frac{y_2-y_1}{d}$$

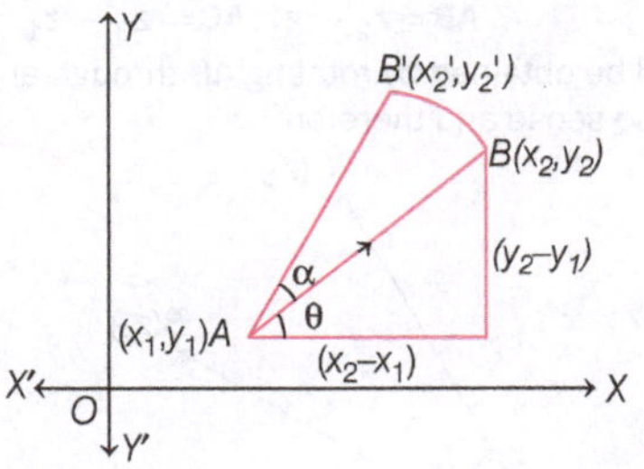

where, $d=\sqrt{(x_2-x_1)^2+(y_2-y_1)^2}=AB$

and $\quad x_2=x_1+d\cos\theta, y_2=y_1+d\sin\theta$

If AB rotates an angle α about A, then new coordinates of B are

$$x_2'=x_1+d\cos(\theta+\alpha),$$
$$y_2'=y_1+d\sin(\theta+\alpha)$$

and here, $\quad AB=AB'=d$.

(ii) **Complex number as a rotating arrow in Argand plane**

Let $\quad z=r(\cos\theta+i\sin\theta)=re^{i\theta}$, where $i=\sqrt{-1}$ ... (i)

be a complex number representing a point P in the Argand plane.

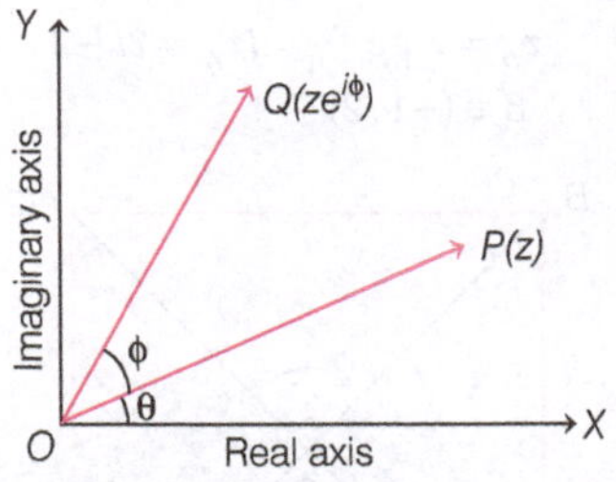

Then, $\quad OP=|z|=r$ and $\angle POX=\theta$

Now, consider complex number $z_1 = ze^{i\phi}$

or $\quad z_1 = re^{i\theta} \cdot e^{i\phi} = r \cdot e^{i(\theta+\phi)}$ [from Eq. (i)]

Clearly, the complex number z_1 represents a point Q in the Argand plane, when

$$OQ = r \quad \text{and} \quad \angle QOX = \theta + \phi$$

Clearly, multiplication of z with $e^{i\phi}$ rotates the vector **OP** through angle ϕ in anti-clockwise sense. Similarly, multiplication of z with $e^{-i\phi}$ will rotate the vector **OP** in clockwise sense.

JEE SPIKE

If z_1, z_2 and z_3 are the affixes of the three points A, B and C such that $AC = AB$ and $\angle CAB = \theta$. Therefore,

$$\mathbf{AB} = z_2 - z_1, \mathbf{AC} = z_3 - z_1$$

Then, **AC** will be obtained by rotating **AB** through an angle θ in anti-clockwise sense and therefore

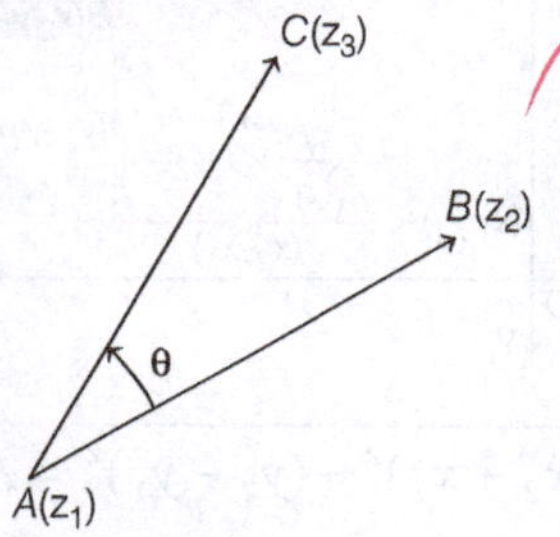

Concept Inside Video

$$\mathbf{AC} = \mathbf{AB}e^{i\theta}$$

or $\quad (z_3 - z_1) = (z_2 - z_1)\, e^{i\theta}$ or $\left(\dfrac{z_3 - z_1}{z_2 - z_1}\right) = e^{i\theta}$

Example 43. The centre of a square is at the origin and one vertex is $A(2, 1)$. Find the coordinates of other vertices of the square.

Sol. By special corollary (ii).

$\because \quad A \equiv (2, 1)$

$\therefore \quad z_A = 2 + i$, where $i = \sqrt{-1}$

Now, in ΔAOB,

$$OA = OB, \angle AOB = 90° = \frac{\pi}{2}$$

$\therefore \quad z_B = z_A\, e^{i\frac{\pi}{2}} = iz_A = 2i - 1$

$\therefore \quad B \equiv (-1, 2)$

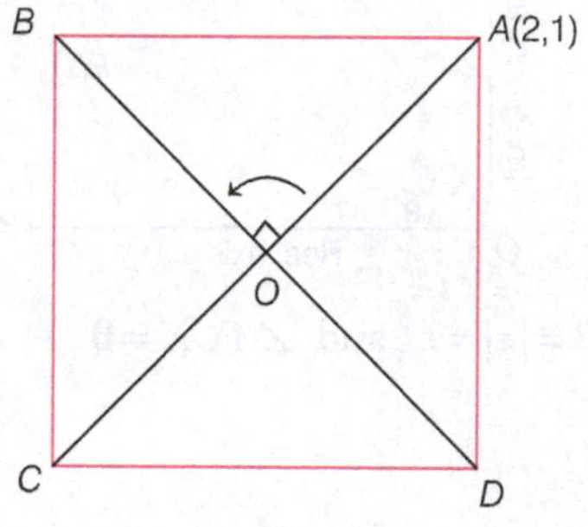

$\because O$ is the mid-point of AC and BD

$\therefore \quad C \equiv (-2, -1)$ and $D \equiv (1, -2)$.

Example 44. The extremities of the diagonal of a square are $(1, 1)$, $(-2, -1)$. Obtain the other two vertices and the equation of the other diagonal.

Sol. By special corollary (ii),

$\because \quad A \equiv (1, 1)$

$\therefore \quad z_A = 1 + i$, where $i = \sqrt{-1}$ and $C \equiv (-2, -1)$

$\therefore \quad z_C = -2 - i$

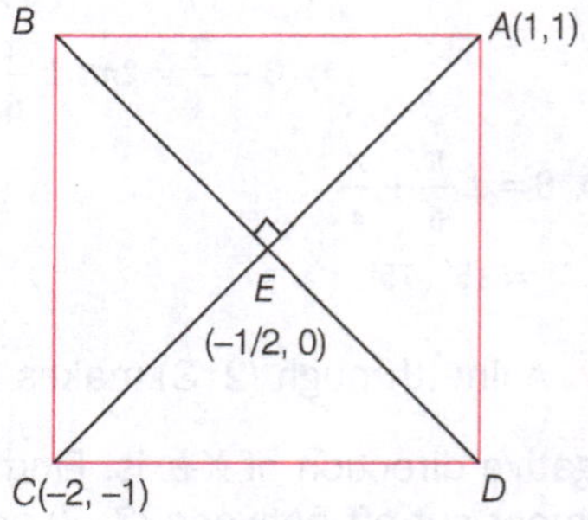

Then, centre of square $E \equiv \left(-\dfrac{1}{2}, 0\right)$

$\therefore \quad z_E = -\dfrac{1}{2}$

Now, in ΔAEB, $EA = EB$,

$$\frac{z_B - z_E}{z_A - z_E} = e^{i\frac{\pi}{2}} = i \Rightarrow z_B + \frac{1}{2} = i\left(1 + i + \frac{1}{2}\right)$$

$\therefore \quad z_B = -\dfrac{3}{2} + \dfrac{3}{2}i$

$\Rightarrow \quad B \equiv \left(-\dfrac{3}{2}, \dfrac{3}{2}\right)$

then $\quad D \equiv \left(-1 + \dfrac{3}{2}, -\dfrac{3}{2}\right)$

or $\quad D \equiv \left(\dfrac{1}{2}, -\dfrac{3}{2}\right)$

Hence, equation of other diagonal BD is

$$y - \frac{3}{2} = \frac{-\frac{3}{2} - \frac{3}{2}}{\frac{3}{2} + \frac{1}{2}}\left(x + \frac{3}{2}\right)$$

$\Rightarrow \quad 6x + 4y + 3 = 0$

Example 45. The line joining the points $A(2, 0)$ and $B(3, 1)$ is rotated about A in the anticlockwise direction through an angle of $15°$. Find the equation of the line in the new position. If B goes to C in the new position, what will be the coordinates of C?

Sol. By special corollary (i),

Here, $\quad AB = \sqrt{(2-3)^2 + (0-1)^2} = \sqrt{2}$

and slope of $AB = \dfrac{1-0}{3-2} = 1 = \tan 45°$

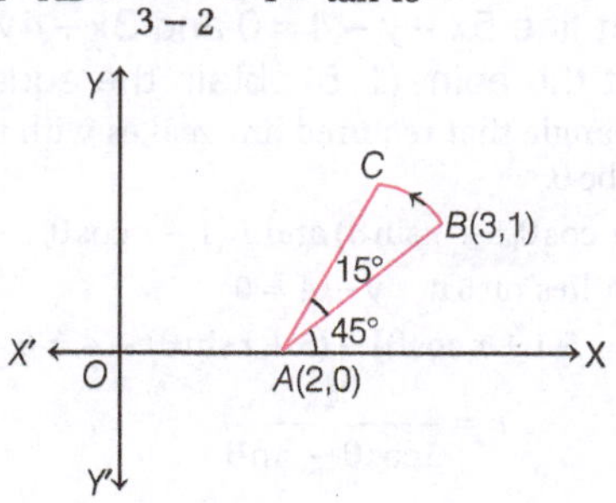

$\therefore \quad \angle BAX = 45°$

Now, line AB is rotated through an angle of 15°

$\Rightarrow \quad \angle CAX = 45° + 15° = 60°$

and $\quad AB = AC = \sqrt{2}$

Equation of line AC in parametric form is

$$\left.\begin{aligned} x &= 2 + r\cos 60° \\ y &= 0 + r\sin 60° \end{aligned}\right\} \qquad \text{...(i)}$$

Since, $\quad AC = r = \sqrt{2}$

Put $r = \sqrt{2}$ in Eq. (i), then

$$x = 2 + \sqrt{2}\cdot\frac{1}{2} = \frac{4+\sqrt{2}}{2} \text{ and } y = \sqrt{2}\,.\frac{\sqrt{3}}{2} = \frac{\sqrt{6}}{2}$$

Equation of the line AC is

$$\frac{x-2}{y} = \cot 60° = \frac{1}{\sqrt{3}}$$

or $\quad x\sqrt{3} - y - 2\sqrt{3} = 0$

and coordinates of C are $\left(\dfrac{4+\sqrt{2}}{2}, \dfrac{\sqrt{6}}{2}\right)$

Alternate Solution

(By special corollary (ii))

$\because \quad A \equiv (2, 0), B \equiv (3, 1)$, let $C \equiv (x, y)$

$\therefore \quad z_A = 2, z_B = 3 + i,$

$z_C = x + iy$, where $i = \sqrt{-1}$

$$\frac{z_C - z_A}{z_B - z_A} = e^{i\frac{\pi}{12}} \qquad \left[\because 15° = \frac{\pi}{12}\right]$$

$\Rightarrow \quad z_C - 2 = (1 + i)(\cos 15° + i\sin 15°)$

or $\quad z_C = 2 + (1+i)\left(\dfrac{\sqrt{3}+1}{2\sqrt{2}} + i\left(\dfrac{\sqrt{3}-1}{2\sqrt{2}}\right)\right)$

$$= \left(2 + \frac{\sqrt{3}+1}{2\sqrt{2}} - \frac{\sqrt{3}-1}{2\sqrt{2}}\right) + i\left(\frac{\sqrt{3}+1}{2\sqrt{2}} + \frac{\sqrt{3}-1}{2\sqrt{2}}\right)$$

$$= \left(2 + \frac{1}{\sqrt{2}}\right) + i\left(\frac{\sqrt{3}}{\sqrt{2}}\right) = \frac{4+\sqrt{2}}{2} + i\left(\frac{\sqrt{6}}{2}\right)$$

$\therefore \quad C \equiv \left(\dfrac{4+\sqrt{2}}{2}, \dfrac{\sqrt{6}}{2}\right)$

and equation of AC is

$$y - 0 = \tan 60°\,(x - 2)$$

$\Rightarrow \quad x\sqrt{3} - y - 2\sqrt{3} = 0$

Example 46. If the circumcentre of a triangle lies at the origin and the centroid is the middle point of the line joining the points (a^2+1, a^2+1) and $(2a, -2a)$ find the equation of line on which orthocentre lies ?

Sol. $\because$ Orthocentre (O), Centroid (G) and Circumcentre (C) of a triangle are collinear.

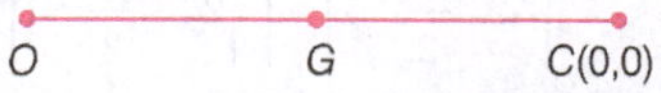

Orthocentre lies on the line joining the circumcentre (0, 0) and centroid which is the middle point of line joining the points.

$$G\left(\frac{a^2+1+2a}{2}, \frac{a^2+1-2a}{2}\right) \equiv \left(\frac{(a+1)^2}{2}, \frac{(a-1)^2}{2}\right)$$

$\therefore$ Orthocentre lies on the line.

$$(y - 0) = m(x - 0),$$

where $\quad m = \dfrac{\dfrac{(a-1)^2}{2} - 0}{\dfrac{(a+1)^2}{2} - 0}$

$$y - 0 = \frac{\dfrac{(a-1)^2}{2}}{\dfrac{(a+1)^2}{2}}(x - 0)$$

$$(a+1)^2 y = (a-1)^2 x$$

or $\quad (a-1)^2 x - (a+1)^2 y = 0$

Example 47. If the extremities of the base of an isosceles triangle are the points $(2a, 0)$ and $(0, a)$ and the equation of one of the sides is $x = 2a$, then find the area of the triangle in squares units.

Sol. Let y-coordinate of $C = b$

$\therefore \quad C = (2a, b)$

$$AB = \sqrt{4a^2 + a^2} = \sqrt{5}a$$

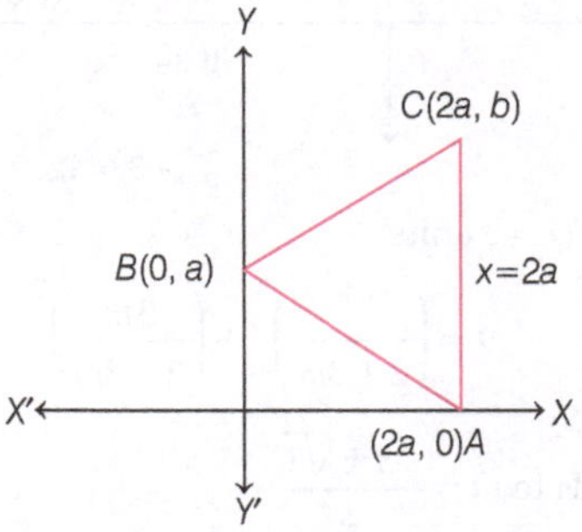

Now, $\quad AC = BC \Rightarrow b = \sqrt{4a^2 + (b-a)^2}$

$\Rightarrow \quad b^2 = 4a^2 + b^2 + a^2 - 2ab$

$\Rightarrow \quad 2ab = 5a^2$

$\Rightarrow \quad b = \dfrac{5a}{2}$

$\therefore \quad C\left(2a, \frac{5a}{2}\right)$

Hence, area of triangle

$$= \frac{1}{2}\begin{vmatrix} 2a & 0 & 1 \\ 0 & a & 1 \\ 2a & \frac{5a}{2} & 1 \end{vmatrix} = \left|\frac{1}{2}\begin{vmatrix} 2a & 0 & 1 \\ 0 & a & 1 \\ 2a & \frac{5a}{2} & 1 \end{vmatrix}\right|$$

$$= \frac{1}{2} \times 2a \times \left(\frac{-5a}{2}\right)$$

$$= \left|\frac{-5a^2}{2}\right|$$

$$= \frac{5a^2}{2} \text{ sq. units.}$$

Example 48. Find the equation of straight line through the origin whose intercept between the straight line $2x + 3y = 12$ and $2x + 3y = 15$ is 3 units.

Sol. Equation of required line, $y = mx$

The intersection of this line with $2x + 3y = 12$ is

$$P = \left(\frac{12}{2+3m}, \frac{12m}{2+3m}\right)$$

and with $2x + 3y = 15$ is

$$Q = \left(\frac{15}{2+3m}, \frac{15m}{2+3m}\right)$$

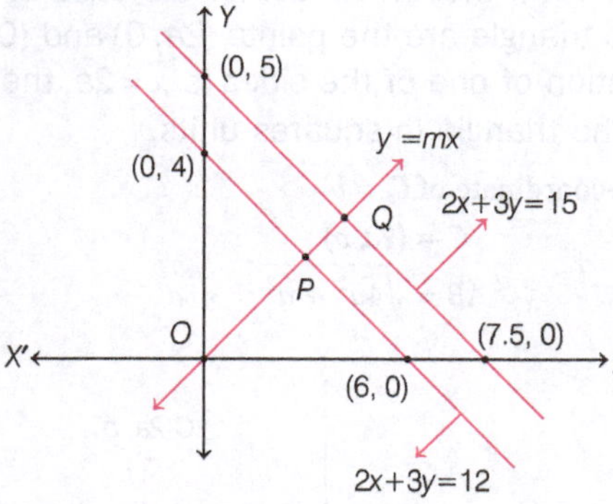

Distance, $PQ = 3$ units

So, $$9 = \left(\frac{3}{2+3m}\right)^2 + \left(\frac{3m}{2+3m}\right)^2$$

Which leads to $m = \frac{-3 \pm \sqrt{3}}{4}$

Hence, the required lines are

$$y = \frac{-3+\sqrt{3}}{4}x$$

and $$y = \frac{-3-\sqrt{3}}{4}x$$

Example 49. A line is such that its segment between the straight line $5x - y - 4 = 0$ and $3x + 4y - 4 = 0$ is bisected at the point $(1, 5)$ obtain the equation of line.

Sol. Let the angle that required line makes with the positive X-axis be θ.

$A(1 + r\cos\theta, 5 + r\sin\theta)$ and $B(1 - r\cos\theta, 5 - r\sin\theta)$

Point A lies on $5x - y - 4 = 0$

Then, $5(1 + r\cos\theta) - (5 + r\sin\theta) - 4 = 0$

$$r = \frac{4}{5\cos\theta - \sin\theta} \quad \text{...(i)}$$

Point B lies on $3x + 4y - 4 = 0$ and

$3(1 - r\cos\theta) + 4(5 - r\sin\theta) - 4 = 0$

$$r = \frac{19}{3\cos\theta + 4\sin\theta} \quad \text{...(ii)}$$

On equating Eqs. (i) and (ii),

$$\frac{4}{5\cos\theta - \sin\theta} = \frac{19}{3\cos\theta + 4\sin\theta}$$

$\Rightarrow \quad 12 + 16\tan\theta = 95 - 19\tan\theta$

$\Rightarrow \quad m = \tan\theta = \frac{83}{35}$

Equation of line AB is

$$y - 5 = \frac{83}{35}(x - 1) \Rightarrow 83x - 35y + 92 = 0$$

Example 50. Given $P(0, 0)$ and $Q(x, y)$ with $x \in (0, 1)$ and $y > 0$. Let the slope of line PQ be m_1. Point R lies on the line $x = 1$ such that the slope of QR is equal to m_2 where $0 < m_2 < m_1$. If the area of ΔPQR can be expressed as $(m_1 - m_2) f(x)$, then find the largest possible value of $f(x)$.

Sol. Let the coordinates of R be $(1, c)$. Then,

$$m_2 = \frac{c - y}{1 - x} \Rightarrow m_2 = \frac{c - m_1x}{1 - x}$$

$\Rightarrow \quad m_2 - m_2x = c - m_1x$

$\Rightarrow \quad (m_1 - m_2)x = c - m_2$

$\Rightarrow \quad c = (m_1 - m_2)x + m_2$

Now, area of ΔPQR

$$\frac{1}{2}\begin{vmatrix} 0 & 0 & 1 \\ x & m_1x & 1 \\ 1 & c & 1 \end{vmatrix} = \frac{1}{2}|[cx - m_1x]|$$

$$= \frac{1}{2}|[\{(m_1 - m_2)x + m_2\}x - m_1x]|$$

$$= \frac{1}{2}(m_1 - m_2)(x - x^2)$$

$[\because x > x^2 \text{ in } (0, 1)]$

Hence, $$f(x) = \frac{1}{2}(x - x^2)$$

$$f_{\max} = \frac{1}{8}, \text{ where } x = \frac{1}{2}$$

Example 51. A square of side a above the X-axis has one vertex at the origin. The side passing through the origin makes an angle $\alpha(0<\alpha<\pi/4)$ with the positive direction of X-axis. Find the equation of its diagonal not passing through the origin.

Sol. Coordinates of A are $(a\cos\alpha, a\sin\alpha)$ and C are

$$\left[a\cos\left(\frac{\pi}{2}+\alpha\right), a\sin\left(\frac{\pi}{2}+\alpha\right)\right]=[-a\sin\alpha, a\cos\alpha]$$

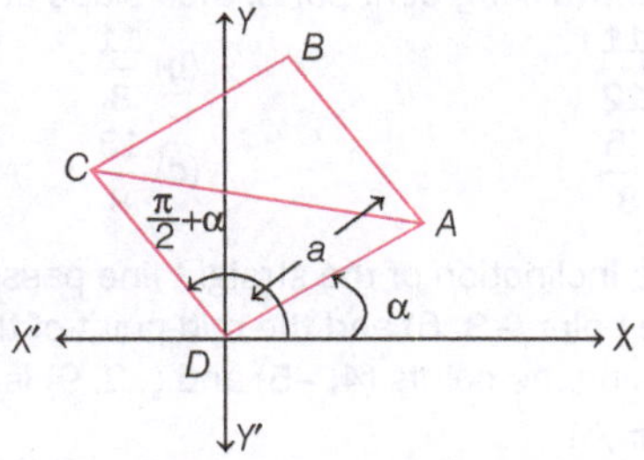

$\therefore$ By two point form equation of AC will be

$$(y-a\sin\alpha)=\frac{a\cos\alpha-a\sin\alpha}{-a\sin\alpha-a\cos\alpha}(x-a\cos\alpha)$$

$$\Rightarrow \quad y\sin\alpha-a\sin^2\alpha+y\cos\alpha-a\sin\alpha\cos\alpha$$
$$=x\sin\alpha-a\sin\alpha\cos\alpha-x\cos\alpha+a\cos^2\alpha$$
$$\Rightarrow \quad x\sin\alpha-x\cos\alpha-y\sin\alpha-y\cos\alpha+a=0$$
or
$$y(\sin\alpha+\cos\alpha)+x(\cos\alpha-\sin\alpha)=a$$

Example 52. Prove that the four straight lines $\frac{x}{a}+\frac{y}{b}=1, \frac{x}{b}+\frac{y}{a}=1, \frac{x}{a}+\frac{y}{b}=2$ and $\frac{x}{b}+\frac{y}{a}=2$ form a rhombus. Find its area.

Sol. The equations of the four sides are

$$\frac{x}{a}+\frac{y}{b}=1 \quad \text{...(i)}$$

$$\frac{x}{b}+\frac{y}{a}=1 \quad \text{...(ii)}$$

$$\frac{x}{a}+\frac{y}{b}=2 \quad \text{...(iii)}$$

and

$$\frac{x}{b}+\frac{y}{a}=2 \quad \text{...(iv)}$$

Clearly, Eqs. (i), (iii) and Eqs. (ii), (iv) form two sets of parallel lines.

So, the four lines form a parallelogram.

Let p_1 be the distance between parallel Eqs. (i) and (iii) and p_2 be the distance between parallel Eqs. (ii) and (iv).

Then,

$$p_1=\left|\frac{2-1}{\sqrt{\frac{1}{a^2}+\frac{1}{b^2}}}\right|=\frac{ab}{\sqrt{a^2+b^2}}$$

$$\left[\because d=\left|\frac{c_1-c_2}{\sqrt{a^2+b^2}}\right|\right]$$

and

$$p_2=\left|\frac{2-1}{\sqrt{\frac{1}{a^2}+\frac{1}{b^2}}}\right|=\frac{ab}{\sqrt{a^2+b^2}}$$

Clearly, $p_1=p_2$.

So, the given lines form a rhombus.

$$\text{Area of the rhombus}=\frac{(2-1)(2-1)}{\begin{vmatrix}\frac{1}{a} & \frac{1}{b}\\ \frac{1}{b} & \frac{1}{a}\end{vmatrix}}$$

$$=\frac{1}{\left(\frac{1}{a^2}-\frac{1}{b^2}\right)}$$

$$=\frac{a^2b^2}{|b^2-a^2|}$$

Example 53. Find the coordinates of P, if the line $\frac{x}{a}+\frac{y}{b}=1$ meets the X-axis at A and Y-axis at B and the line $y=x$ at P such that the area of ΔAOP is twice the area of ΔBOP.

Sol. Given ar $\Delta AOP=2$ (ar ΔBOP)

$$\frac{1}{2}(OA)(x_1)=2\times\frac{1}{2}\times OB\times x_1 \Rightarrow a=2b$$

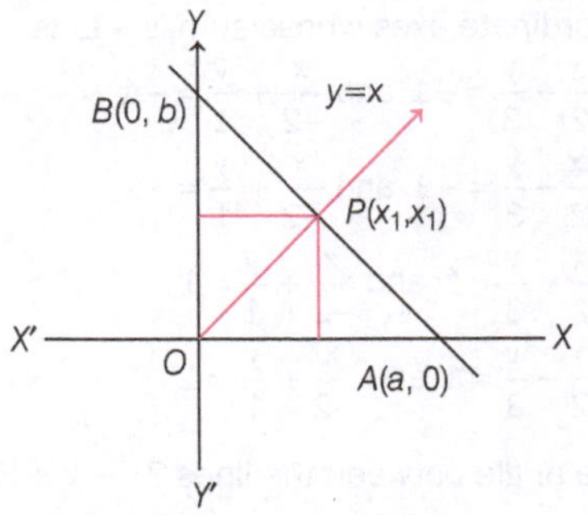

Equation of AB is

$$\frac{x}{a}+\frac{y}{b}=1 \quad \text{...(i)}$$

$$\frac{x}{2b}+\frac{y}{b}=1 \quad \text{...(ii)}$$

Since, point P lies on line (ii), we have

$$\frac{x_1}{2b}+\frac{x_1}{b}=1$$

$$\Rightarrow \quad x_1=\frac{2b}{3}=\frac{a}{3}$$

or

$$P\equiv\left(\frac{2b}{3},\frac{2b}{3}\right)$$

Milestone Practice 2.1

1. The lines $x\cos\alpha + y\sin\alpha = p_1$ and $x\cos\beta + y\sin\beta = p_2$ will be perpendicular, if

(a) $\alpha = \beta$ (b) $|\alpha - \beta| = \pi/2$

(c) $\alpha = \pi/2$ (d) $\alpha \pm \beta = \pi/2$

2. A beam of light is sent along the line $x - y = 1$ which after refraction from the X-axis enters the opposite side by turning through 30° away from the normal at the point of incidence on the X-axis, then the equation of refracted ray is

(a) $(2-\sqrt{3})x - y = 2+\sqrt{3}$

(b) $(2+\sqrt{3})x - y = 2+\sqrt{3}$

(c) $(2-\sqrt{3})x + y = 2+\sqrt{3}$

(d) $y = (2-\sqrt{3})(x-1)$

3. If each of the points $(x_1, 4), (-2, y_1)$ lies on the line joining the points $(2,-1), (5,-3)$, then the point $P(x_1, y_1)$ lies on the line

(a) $6(x+y) - 25 = 0$ (b) $2x + 6y + 1 = 0$

(c) $2x + 3y - 6 = 0$ (d) $6(x+y) + 25 = 0$

4. The equation of the straight line passing through the point (4, 3) and making intercepts on the coordinate axes whose sum is –1, is

(a) $\frac{x}{2} + \frac{y}{3} = -1$ and $\frac{x}{-2} + \frac{y}{1} = -1$

(b) $\frac{x}{2} - \frac{y}{3} = -1$ and $\frac{x}{-2} + \frac{y}{1} = -1$

(c) $\frac{x}{2} + \frac{y}{3} = 1$ and $\frac{x}{-2} + \frac{y}{1} = 1$

(d) $\frac{x}{2} - \frac{y}{3} = 1$ and $\frac{x}{-2} + \frac{y}{1} = 1$

5. The angle between the lines $2x - y + 3 = 0$ and $x + 2y + 3 = 0$ is

(a) 30° (b) 45° (c) 60° (d) 90°

6. If the straight lines $ax + by + c = 0$ and $x\cos\alpha + y\sin\alpha = c$ enclose an angle $\frac{\pi}{4}$ between them and meet the straight line $x\sin\alpha - y\cos\alpha = 0$ in the same point, then

(a) $a^2 + b^2 = c^2$ (b) $a^2 + b^2 = 2$

(c) $a^2 + b^2 = 2c^2$ (d) $a^2 + b^2 = 4$

7. $OPQR$ is a square and M, N are the middle point of the sides PQ and QR respectively, then the ratio of the area of the square and the ΔOMN is

(a) 4 : 1

(b) 2 : 1

(c) 8 : 3

(d) 7 : 3

8. Vertices of a parallelogram $ABCD$ are $A(3,1), B(13,6), C(13,12)$ and $D(3,16)$ if a line passing through origin divides the parallelogram into two congruent parts, then slope of the line is

(a) $\frac{11}{12}$ (b) $\frac{11}{8}$

(c) $\frac{25}{8}$ (d) $\frac{13}{8}$

9. The inclination of the straight line passing through the point (–3, 6) and the mid-point of the line joining the points (4, –5) and (–2, 9) is

(a) $\pi/4$

(b) $\pi/2$

(c) $3\pi/4$

(d) π

10. A square of side a lies above the X-axis and has one vertex at the origin. The side passing through the origin makes an angle $\pi/6$ with the positive direction of X-axis. The equation of its diagonal not passing through the origin is

(a) $y(\sqrt{3}-1) - x(1-\sqrt{3}) = 2a$

(b) $y(\sqrt{3}+1) + x(1-\sqrt{3}) = 2a$

(c) $y(\sqrt{3}+1) + x(1+\sqrt{3}) = 2a$

(d) $y(\sqrt{3}+1) + x(\sqrt{3}-1) = 2a$

11. $A(1,3)$ and $C(7,5)$ are two opposite vertices of a square. The equation of side through A is

(a) $x + 2y - 7 = 0$

(b) $x - 2y + 5 = 0$

(c) $2x + y - 5 = 0$

(d) $2x - y + 1 = 0$

12. One diagonal of a square is along the line $8x - 15y = 0$ and one its vertex is $(1, 2)$. Then, the equations of the sides of the square passing through this vertex are

(a) $23x + 7y = 9, 7x + 23y = 53$

(b) $23x - 7y + 9 = 0, 7x + 23y + 53 = 0$

(c) $23x - 7y - 9 = 0, 7x + 23y - 53 = 0$

(d) None of the above

13. The equation of a straight line passing through the point $(-5, 4)$ and which cuts off an intercept of $\sqrt{2}$ units between the lines $x + y + 1 = 0$ and $x + y - 1 = 0$ is

(a) $x - 2y + 13 = 0$

(b) $2x - y + 14 = 0$

(c) $x - y + 9 = 0$

(d) $x - y + 10 = 0$

14. Equation to the straight line cutting off an intercept 2 from negative direction of the axis of y and inclined at 30° to the positive direction of axis of x is

(a) $y + x - \sqrt{3} = 0$ (b) $y - x + 2 = 0$
(c) $y - x\sqrt{3} - 2 = 0$ (d) $y\sqrt{3} - x + 2\sqrt{3} = 0$

15. If the straight line through the point $P(3, 4)$ makes an angle $\frac{\pi}{6}$ with X-axis and meets the line $12x + 5y + 10 = 0$ at Q, find the length of PQ.

16. The distance of the point (3, 5) from the line $2x + 3y - 14 = 0$ measured parallel to the line $x - 2y = 1$ is

(a) $\frac{7}{\sqrt{5}}$ (b) $\frac{7}{\sqrt{13}}$ (c) $\sqrt{5}$ (d) $\sqrt{13}$

17. A line is such that its segment between the straight line $5x - y + 4 = 0$ and $3x + 4y - 4 = 0$ is bisected at the point $(1, 5)$. Obtain the equation.

18. The equations of sides AB and AC of a ΔABC are respectively $2x + 3y = 29$ and $x + 2y = 16$. If the mid-point of BC is (5, 6), then find the equation of BC.

19. Find the equation of one of the straight lines which passes through the point (1, 3) and makes an angle $\tan^{-1}(\sqrt{2})$ with the straight line $y + 1 = 3\sqrt{2}x$.

20. The circumcentre of a triangle with vertices $A(a, 3)$, $B(b, 5)$ and $C(a, b)$, $ab > 0$ be $P(1, 1)$. If the line AP intersects the line BC at point $Q(k_1, k_2)$, then find the value of $(k_1 + k_2)$.

Answer Key

1. (b)	2. (d)	3. (b)	4. (d)	5. (d)	6. (b)
7. (c)	8. (b)	9. (c)	10. (d)	11. (a)	12. (c)
13. (c)	14. (d)	15. $\frac{132}{12\sqrt{3} + 5}$	16. (c)	17. $107x - 3y - 92 = 0$	
18. $x + y = 11$	19. $7y - 2\sqrt{2}x - (21 - 2\sqrt{2}) = 0$ or $4\sqrt{2}x + 5y - (15 + 4\sqrt{2}) = 0$			20. $\frac{4}{7}$	

For Detailed Solution

Milestone 2 Position of Two Points Relative to a Given Line

- Position of two Points Relative to a Given Line • Position of a Point which Lies inside a Triangle
- Distance of a Point From a Line • Distance between Two Parallel Lines • Area of Parallelogram

2.6 Position of Two Points Relative to a Given Line

Theorem The points $P(x_1, y_1)$ and $Q(x_2, y_2)$ lie on the same or opposite sides of the line $ax + by + c = 0$ according as

$$\frac{ax_1 + by_1 + c}{ax_2 + by_2 + c} > 0 \text{ or } < 0$$

Proof Let the line PQ be divided by the line $ax + by + c = 0$ in the ratio $\lambda : 1$ (internally) at the point R.

$\therefore$ The coordinates of R are $\left(\frac{x_1 + \lambda x_2}{1+\lambda}, \frac{y_1 + \lambda y_2}{1+\lambda}\right)$.

The point of R lies on the line $ax + by + c = 0$

then $$a\left(\frac{x_1 + \lambda x_2}{1+\lambda}\right) + b\left(\frac{y_1 + \lambda y_2}{1+\lambda}\right) + c = 0$$

$$\Rightarrow \quad \lambda(ax_2 + by_2 + c) + (ax_1 + by_1 + c) = 0$$

$$\Rightarrow \quad \lambda = -\left(\frac{ax_1 + by_1 + c}{ax_2 + by_2 + c}\right) \qquad [\because ax_2 + by_2 + c \neq 0]$$

Case I Let P and Q are on same side of the line $ax + by + c = 0$.

$\therefore$ R divides PQ externally.

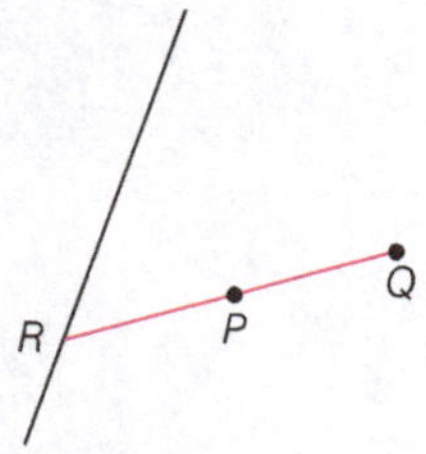

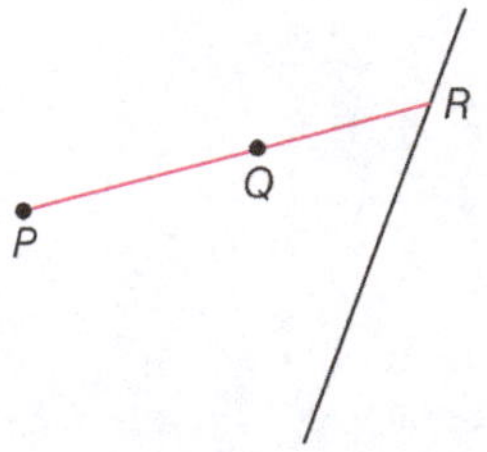

$\therefore$ λ is negative

$$\Rightarrow \quad -\left(\frac{ax_1 + by_1 + c}{ax_2 + by_2 + c}\right) < 0$$

$$\Rightarrow \quad \left(\frac{ax_1 + by_1 + c}{a x_2 + by_2 + c}\right) > 0$$

or $$\frac{f(x_1, y_1)}{f(x_2, y_2)} > 0$$

where, $f(x, y) \equiv ax + by + c$.

Case II Let P and Q are on opposite sides of the line $ax + by + c = 0$

$\therefore$ R divides PQ internally.

$\therefore$ λ is positive.

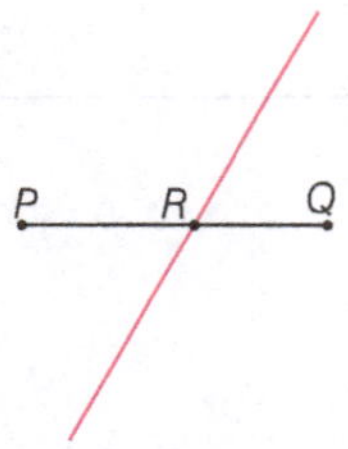

$$\Rightarrow \quad -\left(\frac{ax_1 + by_1 + c}{ax_2 + by_2 + c}\right) > 0$$

$$\Rightarrow \quad \left(\frac{ax_1 + by_1 + c}{ax_2 + by_2 + c}\right) < 0$$

or $$\frac{f(x_1, y_1)}{f(x_2, y_2)} < 0$$

where, $f(x, y) = ax + by + c$

Concept Inside Video

JEE Focus Points

1. The side of the line where origin lies is known as origin side.
2. A point (α, β) will lie on origin side of the line $ax + by + c = 0$, if $a\alpha + b\beta + c$ and c have same sign.
3. A point (α, β) will lie on non-origin side of the line $ax + by + c = 0$, if $a\alpha + b\beta + c$ and c have opposite sign.

Example 54. Are the points (2, 1) and (−3, 5) on the same or opposite side of the line $3x-2y+1=0$?

Sol. Let $f(x, y) \equiv 3x - 2y + 1$

$$\therefore \quad \frac{f(2,1)}{f(-3,5)} = \frac{3(2)-2(1)+1}{3(-3)-2(5)+1} = -\frac{5}{18} < 0$$

Therefore, the two points are on the opposite sides of the given line.

Example 55. Find the set of positive values of λ for which the origin and the point (1, 1) lies on the same side of the straight line $a^2x + a\lambda y + 1 = 0 \ \forall a \in R$.

Sol. Point (0, 0) and (1, 1) lie on the same side of the line $a^2x + a\lambda y + 1 = 0$

For (0, 0), we have

$$a^2(0) + a\lambda(0) + 1 > 0$$

For (1, 1), we must have

$$a^2 + \lambda a + 1 > 0 \ \forall a \in R$$

$$D < 0$$

$$\Rightarrow \quad \lambda^2 - 4 < 0$$

$$\Rightarrow \quad \lambda \in (-2, 2)$$

But $\quad \lambda > 0$

$$\Rightarrow \quad \lambda \in (0, 2)$$

Example 56. If point $(P^2, P+1)$ lies in the angle between the line $3x - y + 1 = 0$ and $x + 2y - 5 = 0$ containing the origin, then find the values of P.

Sol. Given lines are $L_1 = 3x - y + 1 = 0$

and $\quad L_2 = x + 2y - 5 = 0$

$P(P^2, P+1)$ lies in the angle formed by above two lines containing $O(0, 0)$, then O and P must lie on the same side with respect to both the lines.

Now, $\quad L_1(0, 0) = 1 > 0$

So, $\quad L_1(P^2, P+1) > 0$

$$3P^2 - (P+1) + 1 > 0$$

$$P(3P-1) > 0$$

$$\Rightarrow \quad P \in (-\infty, 0) \cup \left(\frac{1}{3}, \infty\right) \quad \text{...(i)}$$

$$L_2(0, 0) = -5 < 0$$

$$\therefore \quad L_2(P^2, P+1) < 0$$

$$P^2 + 2(P+1) - 5 < 0$$

$$(P-1)(P+3) < 0$$

$$P \in (-3, 1) \quad \text{...(ii)}$$

From Eqs. (i) and (ii), we get

$$P \in (-3, 0) \cup \left(\frac{1}{3}, 1\right)$$

Example 57. If $A\left(\frac{\sin\alpha}{3} - 1, \frac{\cos\alpha}{2} - 1\right)$ and $B(1, 1), \alpha \in [-\pi, \pi]$ are two points on the same side of the line $3x - 2y + 1 = 0$, then which interval does α belongs ?

Sol. $3x - 2y + 1 = 0$ and points A and B satisfy the equation of line.

$$\therefore \ 3\left(\frac{\sin\alpha}{3} - 1\right) - 2\left(\frac{\cos\alpha}{2} - 1\right) + 1 > 0$$

and $3(1) - 2(1) + 1 > 0$ have same sign

i.e. $\quad \sin\alpha - \cos\alpha > 0 \Rightarrow \sin\alpha > \cos\alpha$

$$\alpha \in \left[-\pi, \frac{3\pi}{4}\right) \cup \left(\frac{\pi}{4}, \pi\right]$$

2.7 Position of a Point Which Lies Inside a Triangle

Let $P(x_1, y_1)$ be the point and equations of the sides of a triangle are

$$BC: a_1x + b_1y + c_1 = 0$$

$$CA: a_2x + b_2y + c_2 = 0$$

and $\quad AB: a_3x + b_3y + c_3 = 0$

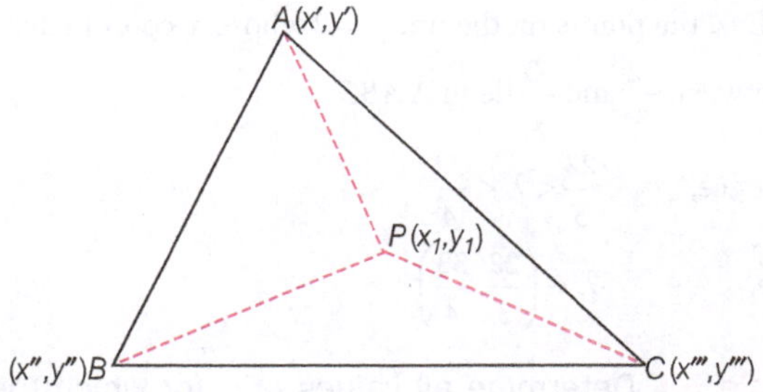

First find the coordinates of A, B and C say,

$$A \equiv (x', y');\ B \equiv (x'', y'') \text{ and } C \equiv (x''', y''')$$

and if coordinates of A, B, C are given, then find equations of BC, CA and AB.

If $P(x_1, y_1)$ lies inside the triangle, then P and A must be on the same side of BC, P and B must be on the same side of AC, P and C must be on the same side of AB, then

$$\frac{a_1x_1 + b_1y_1 + c_1}{a_1x' + b_1y' + c_1} > 0 \quad \text{...(i)}$$

$$\frac{a_2x_1 + b_2y_1 + c_2}{a_2x'' + b_2y'' + c_2} > 0 \quad \text{...(ii)}$$

and $$\frac{a_3x_1 + b_3y_1 + c_3}{a_3x''' + b_3y''' + c_3} > 0 \quad \text{...(iii)}$$

The required values of $P(x_1, y_1)$ must be intersection of these inequalities Eqs. (i), (ii) and (iii).

Example 58. Find λ if $(\lambda, 2)$ is an interior point of ΔABC formed by $x+y=4$, $3x-7y=8$ and $4x-y=31$.

Sol. Let $P \equiv (\lambda, 2)$

First draw the exact diagram of ΔABC, the point $P(\lambda, 2)$ move on the line $y = 2$ for all λ.

Now, D and E are the intersection of

$$3x - 7y = 8, \; y = 2$$

and $4x - y = 31, y = 2$ respectively.

$$\therefore \quad D \equiv \left(\frac{22}{3}, 2\right) \text{ and } E \equiv \left(\frac{33}{4}, 2\right)$$

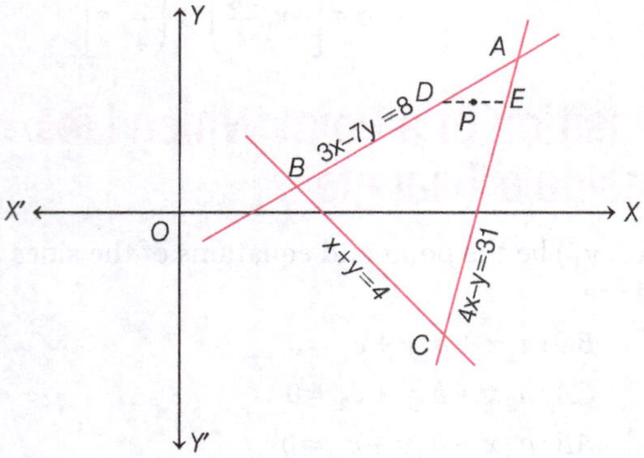

Thus, the points on the line $y = 2$ whose x-coordinates lies between $\frac{22}{3}$ and $\frac{33}{4}$ lie in ΔABC.

Hence, $\frac{22}{3} < \lambda < \frac{33}{4}$

i.e. $\lambda \in \left(\frac{22}{3}, \frac{33}{4}\right)$

Example 59. Determine all values of α for which the point (α, α^2) lies inside the triangle formed by the lines $2x+3y-1=0$, $x+2y-3=0$ and $5x-6y-1=0$.

Sol. The coordinates of the vertices are

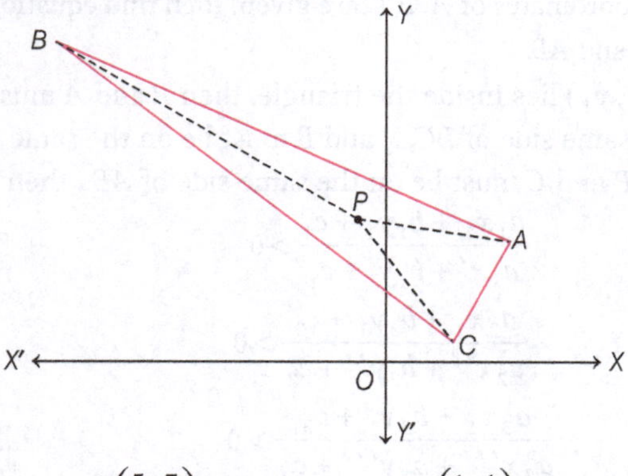

$$A\left(\frac{5}{4}, \frac{7}{8}\right), B(-7, 5) \text{ and } C\left(\frac{1}{3}, \frac{1}{9}\right)$$

$\because P(\alpha, \alpha^2)$ lies inside the ΔABC, then

(i) A and P must lie on the same side of BC.

(ii) B and P must lie on the same side of CA.

(iii) C and P must lie on the same side of AB, then

$$\frac{\frac{5}{2} + \frac{21}{8} - 1}{2\alpha + 3\alpha^2 - 1} > 0 \Rightarrow \frac{33}{2\alpha + 3\alpha^2 - 1} > 0$$

or $\quad 3\alpha^2 + 2\alpha - 1 > 0$

$$\Rightarrow \quad (\alpha + 1)\left(\alpha - \frac{1}{3}\right) > 0$$

$$\Rightarrow \quad \alpha \in (-\infty, -1) \cup \left(\frac{1}{3}, \infty\right) \quad \text{...(i)}$$

and $\quad \frac{-35 - 30 - 1}{5\alpha - 6\alpha^2 - 1} > 0 \Rightarrow 5\alpha - 6\alpha^2 - 1 < 0$

$$\Rightarrow \quad \left(\alpha - \frac{1}{3}\right)\left(\alpha - \frac{1}{2}\right) > 0$$

$$\therefore \quad \alpha \in (-\infty, 1/3) \cup (1/2, \infty) \quad \text{..(ii)}$$

and $\quad \frac{\frac{1}{3} + \frac{2}{9} - 3}{\alpha + 2\alpha^2 - 3} > 0$

$$\Rightarrow \quad \alpha + 2\alpha^2 - 3 < 0$$

$$\Rightarrow \quad (2\alpha + 3)(\alpha - 1) < 0$$

$$\therefore \quad \alpha \in (-3/2, 1) \quad \text{...(iii)}$$

From Eqs. (i), (ii) and (iii), we get

$$\alpha \in (-3/2, -1) \cup (1/2, 1)$$

Example 60. Find the value of β such that the variable point $(\beta, \tan\beta)$ lie inside the triangle whose sides are $y = x + \sqrt{3} - \frac{\pi}{3}$, $x + y + \frac{1}{\sqrt{3}} + \frac{\pi}{6} = 0$ and $x - \frac{\pi}{2} = 0$.

Sol. Given lines are $\quad y = x + \sqrt{3} - \frac{\pi}{3} \quad$ ...(i)

$$x + y + \frac{1}{\sqrt{3}} + \frac{\pi}{6} = 0 \quad \text{...(ii)}$$

and $\quad x - \frac{\pi}{2} = 0 \quad$ ...(iii)

Variable point $(\beta, \tan\beta)$ lies on the curve $y = \tan x$, so we draw the given lines and curve $y = \tan x$.

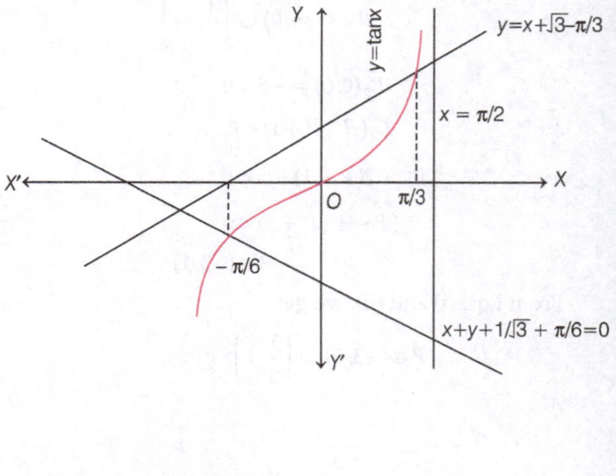

By hit and trial method, we find that line (i) cuts the curve $y = \tan x$ for $x = \frac{\pi}{3}$ and line (i) cuts the curve for $x = \frac{-\pi}{6}$

Hence, point $(\beta, \tan\beta)$ lie inside the triangle, if

$$\frac{-\pi}{6} < \beta < \frac{\pi}{3}$$

Equation of Lines Parallel and Perpendicular to a Given Line

Theorem 1 The equation of line parallel to $ax + by + c = 0$ is $ax + by + \lambda = 0$, where λ is some constant.

Proof The given line is

$$ax + by + c = 0 \quad \text{...(i)}$$

Its slope $= -\frac{a}{b}$

Thus, any line parallel to Eq. (i) is given by

$$y = \left(-\frac{a}{b}\right)x + \lambda_1$$

$\Rightarrow \quad ax + by - b\lambda_1 = 0$

$\Rightarrow \quad ax + by + \lambda = 0 \quad$ [writing λ for $-b\lambda_1$]

where, λ is some constant.

Working Rule

(i) Keep the terms containing x and y unaltered.

(ii) Change the constant.

(iii) The constant λ is determined from an additional condition given in the problem.

Theorem 2 The equation of the line perpendicular to the line $ax + by + c = 0$ is $bx - ay + \lambda = 0$, where λ is some constant.

Proof The given line is

$$ax + by + c = 0 \quad \text{...(i)}$$

Its slope $= -\frac{a}{b}$

Slope of perpendicular line of Eq. (i) is $\frac{b}{a}$.

Thus, any line perpendicular to Eq. (i) is given by

$$y = \left(\frac{b}{a}\right)x + \lambda_1$$

$\Rightarrow \quad bx - ay + a\lambda_1 = 0$

or $\quad bx - ay + \lambda = 0 \quad$ [writing λ for $a\lambda_1$]

where, λ is some constant.

Working Rule

(i) Interchange the coefficients of x and y and changing sign of one of these coefficients.

(ii) Changing the constant term.

(iii) The value of λ can be determined from an additional condition given in the problem.

JEE Focus Points

- The equation of the line parallel to $ax + by + c = 0$ and passing through (x_1, y_1) is $a(x - x_1) + b(y - y_1) = 0$
- The equation of the line through (x_1, y_1) and perpendicular to $ax + by + c = 0$ is $b(x - x_1) - a(y - y_1) = 0$
- The equation of the line perpendicular to $ax + by + c = 0$ is written as $\frac{x}{a} - \frac{y}{b} + k = 0$, where k is some constant.

Concept Inside Video

Example 61. Find the general equation of the line which is parallel to $3x - 4y + 5 = 0$. Also, find such line through the point $(-1, 2)$.

Sol. Equation of any parallel to $3x - 4y + 5 = 0$ is

$$3x - 4y + \lambda = 0 \quad \text{...(i)}$$

which is general equation of the line.

Also, Eq. (i) passes through $(-1, 2)$, then

$$3(-1) - 4(2) + \lambda = 0$$

$\therefore \quad \lambda = 11$

Then, from Eq. (i) required line is $3x - 4y + 11 = 0$

Example 62. Find the equation of line perpendicular to $2x + 3y - 2012 = 0$ and passing through $(3, 4)$.

Sol. Equation of any line perpendicular to

$2x + 3y - 2012 = 0$ is

$$3x - 2y + \lambda = 0 \quad \text{...(i)}$$

which is passing through $(3, 4)$.

Eq. (i) passes through $(3, 4)$, then

$$3(3) - 2(4) + \lambda = 0 \Rightarrow \lambda = -1$$

Then, from Eq. (i) required line is $3x - 2y - 1 = 0$

2.8 Distance of a Point From a Line

Theorem The length of perpendicular from a point (x_1, y_1) to the line $ax + by + c = 0$ is $\frac{|ax_1 + by_1 + c|}{\sqrt{(a^2 + b^2)}}$

Proof Given line is $ax + by + c = 0$

$$\Rightarrow \quad \frac{x}{\left(-\frac{c}{a}\right)} + \frac{y}{\left(-\frac{c}{b}\right)} = 1$$

Let the given line intersects the X-axis and Y-axis at A and B respectively, then coordinates of A and B are $\left(-\frac{c}{a}, 0\right)$ and $\left(0, -\frac{c}{b}\right)$, respectively.

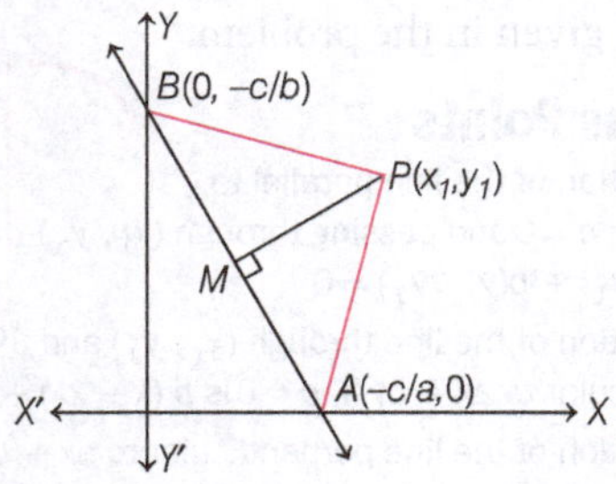

Draw PM perpendicular to AB.

Now, area of ΔPAB

$$= \frac{1}{2}\left| x_1\left(0+\frac{c}{b}\right) - \frac{c}{a}\left(-\frac{c}{b}-y_1\right) + 0(y_1 - 0)\right|$$

$$= \frac{1}{2}\left|\frac{c}{ab}\right| |ax_1 + by_1 + c| \quad \text{...(i)}$$

Let $PM = p$

Also, area of ΔPAB

$$= \frac{1}{2} \cdot AB \cdot PM$$

$$= \frac{1}{2}\sqrt{\left\{\left(-\frac{c}{a}-0\right)^2 + \left(0+\frac{c}{b}\right)^2\right\}} \cdot p$$

$$= \frac{1}{2}\left|\frac{c}{ab}\right| \sqrt{(a^2+b^2)} \cdot p \quad \text{... (ii)}$$

From Eqs. (i) and (ii), we have

$$\frac{1}{2}\left|\frac{c}{ab}\right| \sqrt{(a^2+b^2)} \cdot p = \frac{1}{2}\left|\frac{c}{ab}\right| |ax_1 + by_1 + c|$$

or
$$p = \frac{|ax_1 + by_1 + c|}{\sqrt{(a^2+b^2)}}$$

JEE Focus Points

- The length of perpendicular from the origin to the line $ax + by + c = 0$ is $\frac{|a \cdot 0 + b \cdot 0 + c|}{\sqrt{(a^2+b^2)}}$ i.e. $\frac{|c|}{\sqrt{(a^2+b^2)}}$.
- The length of perpendicular from (x_1, y_1) to the line $x\cos\alpha + y\sin\alpha = p$ is
$$\frac{|x_1\cos\alpha + y_1\sin\alpha - p|}{\sqrt{(\cos^2\alpha + \sin^2\alpha)}} = |x_1\cos\alpha + y_1\sin\alpha - p|$$

Example 63. Find the sum of the abscissas of all the points on the line $x + y = 4$ that lie at a unit distance from the line $4x + 3y - 10 = 0$.

Sol. Any point on the line $x + y = 4$ can be taken as $(x_1, 4 - x_1)$. As it is at a unit distance from the line $4x + 3y - 10 = 0$, we get

$$\frac{|4x_1 + 3(4 - x_1) - 10|}{\sqrt{(4^2 + 3^2)}} = 1$$

$$\Rightarrow \quad |x_1 + 2| = 5$$

$$\Rightarrow \quad x_1 + 2 = \pm 5$$

$$\Rightarrow \quad x_1 = 3 \text{ or } -7$$

$\therefore$ Required sum $= 3 - 7 = -4$

Example 64. A line is drawn from $P(x_1, y_1)$ in the direction with X-axis, to meet $Ax + By + C = 0$ at Q, then find the length PQ.

Sol. The equation of line passing through $P(x_1, y_1)$ and makes an angle θ with X-axis is

$$\frac{x - x_1}{\cos\theta} = \frac{y - y_1}{\sin\theta}$$

Let $PQ = r$

Then, the coordinates of Q are given by

$$x = x_1 + r\cos\theta$$
$$y = y_1 + r\sin\theta$$

Clearly Q lies on the line $ax + by + c = 0$

$$\therefore \quad a(x_1 + r\cos\theta) + b(y_1 + r\sin\theta) + c = 0$$

$$\Rightarrow \quad r = \frac{-(ax_1 + by_1 + c)}{a\cos\theta + b\sin\theta}$$

$$\therefore \quad PQ = \left|\frac{ax_1 + by_1 + c}{a\cos\theta + b\sin\theta}\right|$$

Example 65. If p and p' are the length of the perpendiculars from the origin to the straight lines whose equations are $x\sec\theta + y\,\mathrm{cosec}\,\theta = a$ and $x\cos\theta - y\sin\theta = a\cos 2\theta$, then find the value of $4p^2 + p'^2$.

Sol. We have, $p = \frac{|-a|}{\sqrt{(\sec^2\theta + \mathrm{cosec}^2\theta)}}$

$$\therefore \quad p^2 = \frac{a^2}{\sec^2\theta + \mathrm{cosec}^2\theta} = \frac{a^2\sin^2\theta\cos^2\theta}{1}$$

$$\Rightarrow \quad 4p^2 = a^2\sin^2 2\theta \quad \text{...(i)}$$

and
$$p' = \frac{|-a\cos 2\theta|}{\sqrt{(\cos^2\theta + \sin^2\theta)}} = |-a\cos 2\theta|$$

$$\therefore \quad (p')^2 = a^2\cos^2 2\theta \quad \text{...(ii)}$$

$\therefore$ Adding Eqs. (i) and (ii), we get

$$4p^2 + p'^2 = a^2$$

Example 66. Find the distance between the two points A and A' which lies on $y=2$ such that both the line segments AB and $A'B$ (where B is the point (2, 3)) substend angle $\frac{\pi}{4}$ at the origin.

Sol. Let origin O, slope $M_{OB}=\frac{3-0}{2-0}=\frac{3}{2}$

$$M_{OA}=\frac{2-0}{x-0}=\frac{2}{x}$$

Then, $$\tan\theta=\left|\frac{M_{OB}-M_{OA}}{1+M_{OB}M_{OA}}\right|$$

$$\Rightarrow \tan\frac{\pi}{4}=\left|\frac{\frac{3}{2}-\frac{2}{x}}{1+\frac{6}{2x}}\right|$$

$$\Rightarrow 1=\left|\frac{\frac{3}{2}-\frac{2}{x}}{1+\frac{6}{2x}}\right|$$

$$\Rightarrow x=10 \text{ and } x=\frac{-2}{5}$$

$$\Rightarrow A\equiv(10,2) \text{ and } A'\equiv\left(\frac{-2}{5},2\right)$$

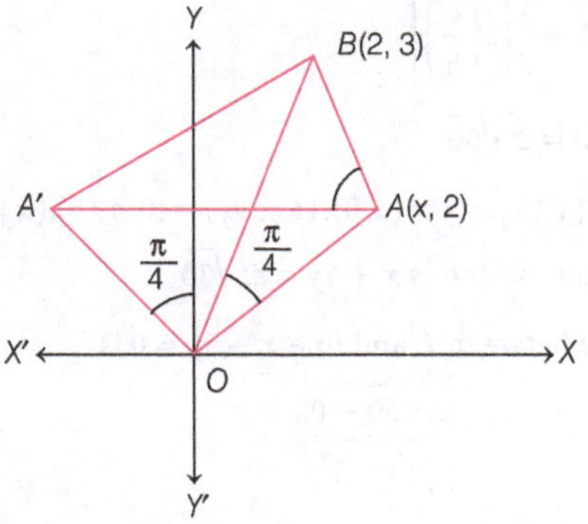

By distance formula,

$$AA'=\sqrt{\left(10+\frac{2}{5}\right)^2+(2-2)^2}$$

$$=\frac{52}{5} \text{ units}$$

2.9 Distance between Two Parallel Lines

Let the two parallel lines be

$$ax+by+c=0 \quad \text{and} \quad ax+by+c_1=0$$

The distance between the parallel lines is the perpendicular distance of any point on one line from the other line.

Let (x_1, y_1) be any point on $ax+by+c=0$

$$\therefore \quad ax_1+by_1+c=0 \qquad \text{...(i)}$$

Now, perpendicular distance of the point (x_1, y_1) from the line $ax+by+c_1=0$ is

$$\frac{|ax_1+by_1+c_1|}{\sqrt{(a^2+b^2)}}=\frac{|c_1-c|}{\sqrt{(a^2+b^2)}} \quad \text{[from Eq. (i)]}$$

This is required distance between the given parallel lines.

Alternate method

The distance between the lines is

$$d=\frac{\lambda}{\sqrt{(a^2+b^2)}}$$

(i) $\lambda=|c_1-c|$, if both the lines are on the same side of the origin.

(ii) $\lambda=|c_1|+|c|$, if the lines are on the opposite side of the origin.

Example 67. Find the distance between the lines $5x-12y+2=0$ and $5x-12y-3=0$.

Sol. The distance between the lines

$$5x-12y+2=0 \quad \text{and} \quad 5x-12y-3=0 \text{ is}$$

$$\frac{|2-(-3)|}{\sqrt{(5)^2+(-12)^2}}=\frac{5}{13}$$

Alternate Solution

Putting $y=0$ in $5x-12y-3=0$, then $x=\frac{3}{5}$

$\therefore$ $\left(\frac{3}{5},0\right)$ lie on $5x-12y-3=0$

Hence, distance between the lines

$5x-12y+2=0$ and $5x-12y-3=0$

$=$ Distance from $\left(\frac{3}{5},0\right)$ to the line $5x-12y+2=0$

$$=\frac{\left|5\times\frac{3}{5}-0+2\right|}{\sqrt{5^2+(-12)^2}}=\frac{5}{13}$$

Example 68. Find the equations of the line parallel to $5x-12y+26=0$ and at a distance of 4 units from it.

Sol. Equation of any line parallel to $5x-12y+26=0$ is

$$5x-12y+\lambda=0 \qquad \text{...(i)}$$

Since, the distance between the parallel lines is 4 units, then

$$\frac{|\lambda-26|}{\sqrt{(5)^2+(-12)^2}}=4$$

or $|\lambda-26|=52$ or $\lambda-26=\pm 52$

or $\lambda=26\pm 52$

$\therefore$ $\lambda=-26$ or 78

Substituting the values of λ in Eq. (i), we get

$5x-12y-26=0$

and $5x-12y+78=0$

JEE SCANNER

Example Similar to PYQ Asked in JEE Main 2022

If the line $3x - y + 5 = 0$ is at a distance $\frac{1}{\sqrt{10}}$ and $\frac{3}{\sqrt{10}}$ from the lines $6x - 2y + \alpha = 0$ and $9x - 3y + \beta = 0$ respectively, then the sum of all possible values of α and β is ....

Sol. (34) It is given that distance between lines $3x - y + 5 = 0$ or $6x - 2y + 10 = 0$ and $6x - 2y + \alpha = 0$ is $\frac{1}{\sqrt{10}}$.

$$\therefore \quad \frac{|10-\alpha|}{\sqrt{36+4}} = \frac{1}{\sqrt{10}}$$

$$\Rightarrow \quad |10-\alpha| = 2$$

$$\Rightarrow \quad \alpha = -8, 12$$

and it is also given that distance between lines $3x - y + 5 = 0$ or $9x - 3y + 15 = 0$ and $9x - 3y + \beta = 0$ is $\frac{3}{\sqrt{10}}$.

$$\therefore \quad \frac{|\beta - 15|}{\sqrt{81+9}} = \frac{3}{\sqrt{10}}$$

$$\Rightarrow \quad |\beta - 15| = 9$$

$$\Rightarrow \quad \beta = 24, 6$$

So, sum of all possible values of α and β

$$= -8 + 12 + 24 + 6 = 34$$

Skill Builder

If the line $5x - y + 3 = 0$ is at a distance $\frac{1}{\sqrt{26}}$ and $\frac{5}{\sqrt{26}}$ from the lines $10x - 2y + \alpha = 0$ and $15x - 3y + \beta = 0$, respectively, then sum of all possible values of α and β is ....

For Sol.

■ **For more practice** See Q.5 of Milestone Practice 2.2.

Example 69. Let the point $P(\alpha, \beta)$ be at a unit distance from each other the two lines $L_1 : 3x - 4y + 12 = 0$ and $L_2 : 8x + 6y + 11 = 0$. If P lies below L_1 and above L_2, then find the value of $100(\alpha + \beta)$.

Sol. Distance from (α, β) to the line $3x - 4y + 12 = 0$ and $8x + 6y + 11 = 0$ is 1 unit

Now, $$\left|\frac{3\alpha - 4\beta + 12}{\sqrt{3^2 + 4^2}}\right| = 1$$

$$\Rightarrow \quad 3\alpha - 4\beta + 7 = 0 \quad \text{...(i)}$$

Similarly, $$\left|\frac{8\alpha + 6\beta + 11}{\sqrt{8^2 + 6^2}}\right| = 1$$

$$8\alpha + 6\beta + 1 = 0 \quad \text{...(ii)}$$

From Eqs. (i) and (ii),

$$\alpha = \frac{-23}{25}, \beta = \frac{106}{100}$$

$$\therefore \quad 100(\alpha + \beta) = 106 - 92 = 14$$

Example 70. If a line L is perpendicular to the line $5x - y = 1$ and the area of the triangle formed by the line L and the coordinate axes is 5, then find the distance of line L from the line $x + 5y = 0$.

Sol. Let equation of line L perpendicular to $5x - y = 1$ be $x + 5y = c$.

Given that area of ΔAOB is 5.

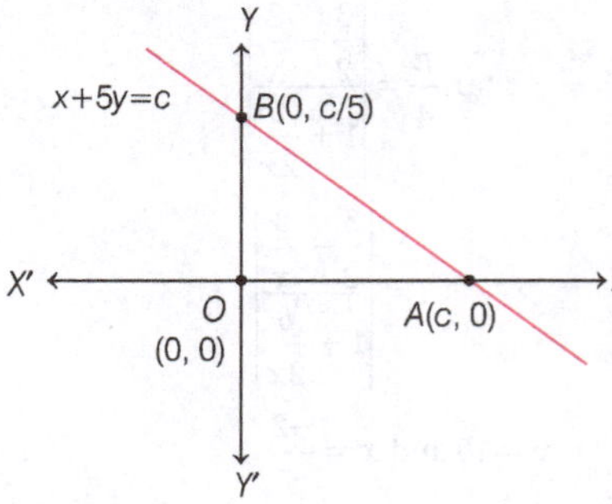

Area, $A = \frac{1}{2}[x_1(y_2 - y_3) + x_2(y_3 - y_1) + x_3(y_1 - y_2)]$

$$\Rightarrow \quad 5 = \frac{1}{2}\left[c\left(\frac{c}{5}\right)\right]$$

$$\Rightarrow \quad c = \pm\sqrt{50}$$

$[\because (x_1, y_1) = (c, 0), (x_2, y_2) = (0, c/5), (x_3, y_3) = (0, 0)]$

$\therefore$ Equation of line is $x + 5y = \pm\sqrt{50}$

Distance between L and line $x + 5y = 0$ is

$$d = \left|\frac{\pm\sqrt{50} - 0}{\sqrt{1^2 + 5^2}}\right|$$

$$= \frac{\sqrt{50}}{\sqrt{26}} = \frac{5}{\sqrt{13}}$$

2.10 Area of Parallelogram

Theorem Area of parallelogram $ABCD$ whose sides AB, BC, CD and DA are represented by $a_1x + b_1y + c_1 = 0$, $a_2x + b_2y + c_2 = 0$, $a_1x + b_1y + d_1 = 0$ and $a_2x + b_2y + d_2 = 0$ is

$$\frac{p_1p_2}{\sin\theta} \quad \text{or} \quad \frac{|c_1 - d_1||c_2 - d_2|}{\left|\begin{vmatrix} a_1 & b_1 \\ a_2 & b_2 \end{vmatrix}\right|}$$

where, p_1 and p_2 are the distances between parallel sides and θ is the angle between two adjacent sides.

Proof Since, p_1 and p_2 are the distances between the pairs of parallel sides of the parallelogram and θ is the angle between two adjacent sides, then

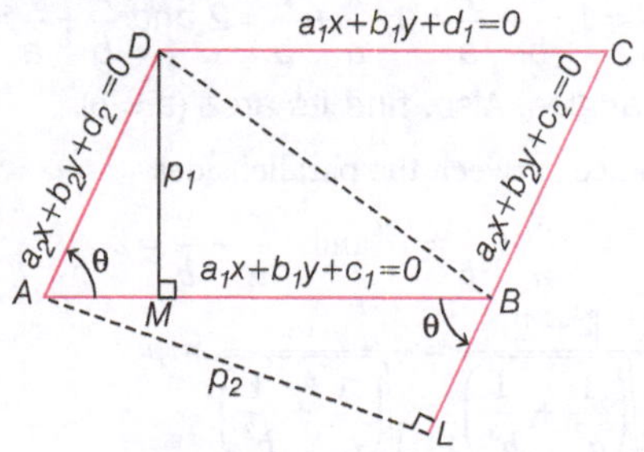

Area of parallelogram $ABCD = 2 \times$ Area of ΔABD

$$= 2 \times \frac{1}{2} \times AB \times p_1 = AB \times p_1$$

$$= \frac{p_2}{\sin\theta} \times p_1 \qquad \left[\because \text{ in } \Delta ABL, \sin\theta = \frac{p_2}{AB}\right]$$

$$= \frac{p_1 p_2}{\sin\theta} \qquad \ldots\text{(i)}$$

Now, p_1 = Distance between parallel sides AB and DC

$$= \frac{|c_1 - d_1|}{\sqrt{(a_1^2 + b_1^2)}}$$

and p_2 = Distance between parallel sides AD and BC

$$= \frac{|c_2 - d_2|}{\sqrt{(a_2^2 + b_2^2)}}$$

Also, $$\tan\theta = \left|\frac{m_1 - m_2}{1 + m_1 m_2}\right| = \left|\frac{-\frac{a_1}{b_1} - \left(-\frac{a_2}{b_2}\right)}{1 + \left(-\frac{a_1}{b_1}\right)\left(-\frac{a_2}{b_2}\right)}\right|$$

$$\left[\begin{array}{l}\because m_1 = \text{slope of } AB = -\frac{a_1}{b_1} \\ \text{and } m_2 = \text{slope of } AD = -\frac{a_2}{b_2}\end{array}\right]$$

$$= \left|\frac{a_1 b_2 - a_2 b_1}{a_1 a_2 + b_1 b_2}\right|$$

$$\therefore \quad \sin\theta = \frac{|a_1 b_2 - a_2 b_1|}{\sqrt{(a_1^2 + b_1^2)(a_2^2 + b_2^2)}}$$

Now, substitute the values of p_1, p_2 and $\sin\theta$ in Eq. (i)

$$\therefore \text{ Area of parallelogram } ABCD = \frac{|c_1 - d_1||c_2 - d_2|}{|a_1 b_2 - a_2 b_1|}$$

$$= \frac{|c_1 - d_1||c_2 - d_2|}{\left|\begin{vmatrix} a_1 & b_1 \\ a_2 & b_2 \end{vmatrix}\right|}$$

JEE Focus Points

- If $p_1 = p_2$, then $ABCD$ becomes a rhombus

  $$\therefore \text{ Area of rhombus } ABCD = \frac{p_1^2}{\sin\theta}$$

  $$= \frac{(c_1 - d_1)^2}{|a_1 b_2 - a_2 b_1| \sqrt{\left(\frac{a_1^2 + b_1^2}{a_2^2 + b_2^2}\right)}}$$

- If d_1 and d_2 are the lengths of two perpendicular diagonals of a rhombus, then

  $$\text{Area of rhombus} = \frac{1}{2} d_1 d_2$$

- Area of the parallelogram whose sides are $y = mx + a$, $y = mx + b$, $y = nx + c$ and $y = nx + d$ is $\dfrac{|a - b||c - d|}{|m - n|}$.

Example 71. Find the area of the parallelogram formed by the lines $x + 3y - a = 0$, $3x - 2y + 3a = 0$, $x + 3y + 4a = 0$ and $3x - 2y + 7a = 0$.

Sol. Required area of the parallelogram

$$= \frac{|-a - 4a||3a - 7a|}{\left|\begin{vmatrix} 1 & 3 \\ 3 & -2 \end{vmatrix}\right|}$$

$$= \frac{20}{11} a^2 \text{ sq units}$$

Example 72. Find the area of the parallelogram formed by the lines

$$x\cos\alpha + y\sin\alpha = p,\ x\cos\alpha + y\sin\alpha = q,$$
$$x\cos\beta + y\sin\beta = r,\ x\cos\beta + y\sin\beta = s.$$

Sol. The equation of sides of the parallelogram are

$$x\cos\alpha + y\sin\alpha - p = 0,$$
$$x\cos\alpha + y\sin\alpha - q = 0,$$
$$x\cos\beta + y\sin\beta - r = 0,$$
and $$x\cos\beta + y\sin\beta - s = 0$$

$\therefore$ Required area of the parallelogram

$$= \frac{|-p - (-q)||-r - (-s)|}{\left|\begin{vmatrix} \cos\alpha & \sin\alpha \\ \cos\beta & \sin\beta \end{vmatrix}\right|}$$

$$= \frac{|p - q||r - s|}{|\sin(\beta - \alpha)|}$$

$$= |(p - q)(r - s)\operatorname{cosec}(\alpha - \beta)|$$

JEE SCANNER

Example Similar to PYQ Asked in JEE Main 2021

Two sides of a parallelogram are along the lines $2x+3y=0$ and $5x+y=0$. If the equation of one of the diagonals of the parallelogram is $7x+4y=12$, then other diagonal passes through the point

(a) (6, 9) (b) (3, 1) (b) (5, 2) (d) (8, 9)

Sol. (a) Given, two sides of parallelogram are $2x+3y=0$ and $5x+y=0$, both lines are passing through origin.

Thus, point $A=(0,0)$ the equation of one diagonal is $7x+4y=12$, point D is the point of intersection of $2x+3y=0$ and $7x+4y=12$

$\therefore$ Coordinates of $D=\left(\frac{36}{13},\frac{-24}{13}\right)$

Also, point B is the point of intersection of $5x+y=0$ and $7x+4y=12$

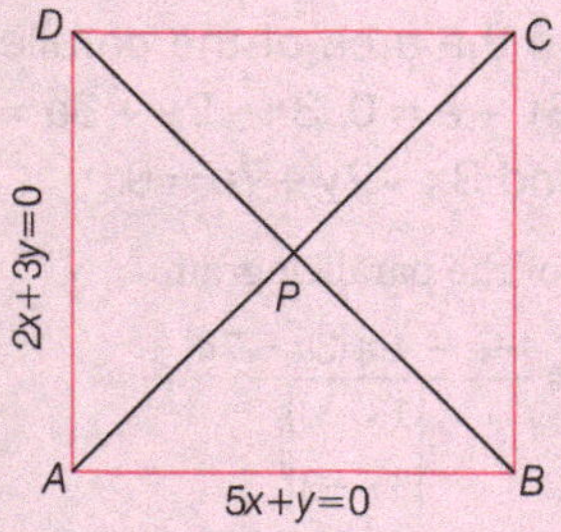

$\therefore$ Coordinates of $B=\left(\frac{-12}{13},\frac{60}{13}\right)$

$\because$ Diagonals of parallelogram bisects each other.

Let P be the middle point of BD.

So, coordinates of $P=\left(\frac{12}{13},\frac{18}{13}\right)$

Now, equation of diagonal AC is

$$y-0=\frac{\frac{18}{13}-0}{\frac{12}{13}-0}(x-0)\Rightarrow y=\frac{3}{2}x$$

$\therefore$ Diagonal AC passes through (6, 9).

Skill Builder

Two sides of a parallelogram are along the lines $8x+5y=0$ and $9x+4y=0$. If the equation of one of the diagonals of the parallelogram is $3x+5y=15$, then the equation of other diagonal is

(a) $249y+465x=0$

(b) $265y+489x=0$

(c) $265x+489y=0$

(d) $271y+47x=0$

For Sol.

■ **For more practice** See Q.8 of Milestone Practice 2.2.

Example 73. Prove that the diagonals of the parallelogram formed by the lines

$$\frac{x}{a}+\frac{y}{b}=1,\ \frac{x}{b}+\frac{y}{a}=1,\ \frac{x}{a}+\frac{y}{b}=2 \text{ and } \frac{x}{b}+\frac{y}{a}=2$$

are at right angles. Also, find its area ($a\neq b$).

Sol. The distance between the parallel sides

$$\frac{x}{a}+\frac{y}{b}=1 \text{ and } \frac{x}{a}+\frac{y}{b}=2$$

is $$\frac{|2-1|}{\sqrt{\left(\frac{1}{a^2}+\frac{1}{b^2}\right)}}=\frac{1}{\sqrt{\left(\frac{1}{a^2}+\frac{1}{b^2}\right)}}=p_1 \quad \text{[say]}$$

and the distance between the parallel sides

$$\frac{x}{b}+\frac{y}{a}=1 \text{ and } \frac{x}{b}+\frac{y}{a}=2$$

is $$\frac{|2-1|}{\sqrt{\left(\frac{1}{b^2}+\frac{1}{a^2}\right)}}=\frac{1}{\sqrt{\left(\frac{1}{a^2}+\frac{1}{b^2}\right)}}=p_2 \quad \text{[say]}$$

Here, $p_1=p_2$

$\therefore$ Parallelogram is a rhombus.

But we know that diagonals of rhombus are perpendicular to each other.

$$\therefore \quad \text{Area of the rhombus}=\frac{|(-1+2)(-1+2)|}{\left|\begin{vmatrix}\frac{1}{a} & \frac{1}{b}\\ \frac{1}{b} & \frac{1}{a}\end{vmatrix}\right|}$$

$$=\frac{a^2b^2}{|b^2-a^2|}(a\neq b)$$

Example 74. *PQR* is an equilateral triangle with *P*(0, 0) and *Q*(*a*, 0), (*a* > 0) *L*, *M* and *N* are foot of the perpendiculars drawn from a point *P* to the sides *PQ*, *QR*, *PR* respectively. If *A* lies inside the triangle and satisfies the condition $AL^2=AM\cdot AN$, then find the locus of *A*.

Sol. The equation of lines PR and QR are respectively given by

$$y-\sqrt{3}x=0$$

$$y+\sqrt{3}(x-a)=0$$

Let $A(h,k)$ be the coordinates of the point whose locus is to be found.

Now, using condition

$$AL^2=AM\cdot AN$$

$$k^2=\left|\frac{k-\sqrt{3}h}{2}\right|\cdot\left|\frac{k+\sqrt{3}(h-a)}{2}\right|$$

i.e. $$4k^2=(k-\sqrt{3}h)[k+\sqrt{3}(h-a)]$$

$\because$ A lies below both the lines.

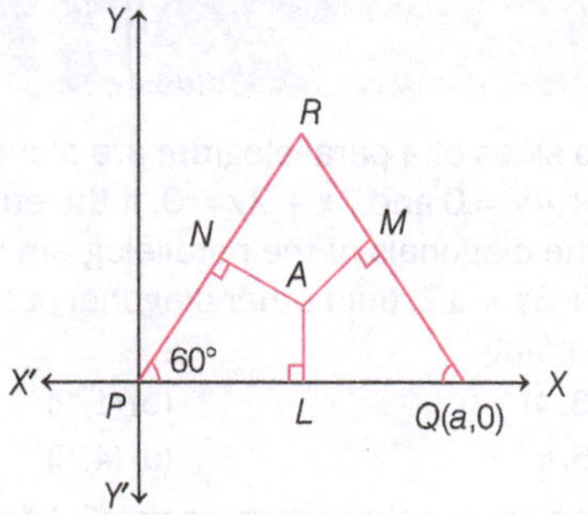

i.e. $$3(h^2 + k^2) - 3ah + \sqrt{3}ak = 0$$

$$\Rightarrow \quad h^2 + k^2 - ah + \frac{a}{\sqrt{3}}k = 0$$

Putting (x, y) in place of (h, k). Required equation of locus is

$$x^2 + y^2 - ax + \frac{a}{\sqrt{3}}y = 0$$

Example 75. If an intercept of length 3 between the straight lines $4x + 3y = 12$ and $4x + 3y = 3$ passing through $(-2, -7)$, then find the equation of straight lines.

Sol. Given lines are

$$4x + 3y = 12 \quad \text{...(i)}$$

$$4x + 3y = 3 \quad \text{...(ii)}$$

Given, $AB = 3$

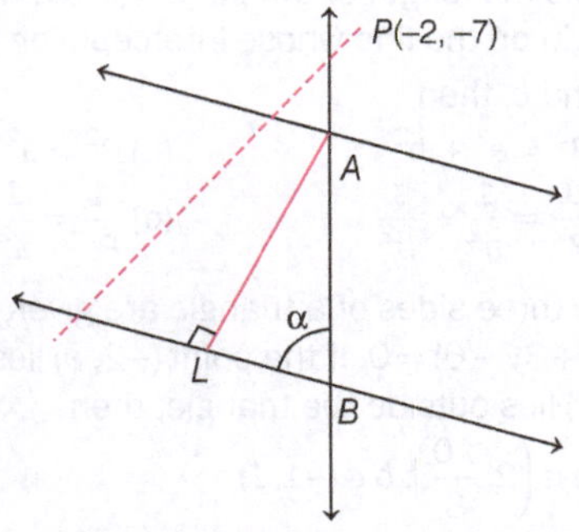

Distance between parallel lines

$$AL = \frac{|-12 + 3|}{\sqrt{4^2 + 3^2}} = \frac{9}{5}$$

From ΔALB, we get

$$LB^2 = AB^2 - AL^2$$

$$= 3^2 - \frac{81}{25} = 9 \times \frac{16}{25}$$

$$\therefore \quad LB = \frac{12}{5}$$

and $$\tan\alpha = \frac{AL}{LB} = \frac{3}{4}$$

$$\tan\theta = \text{slope of line (i)} = \frac{-4}{3}$$

Let the slope of PB be m,

$$\tan\alpha = \frac{3}{4} = \left|\frac{m - \left(\frac{-4}{3}\right)}{1 + m\left(\frac{-4}{3}\right)}\right| = \frac{|3m + 4|}{|3 - 4m|}$$

$$m = \infty \text{ or } m = \frac{-7}{24}$$

$\therefore$ Equation of the line is

$$x + 2 = 0 \text{ and } y + 7 = \frac{-7}{24}(x + 2)$$

$$x + 2 = 0 \text{ and } 7x + 24y + 182 = 0$$

Example 76. A line L is drawn from $P(4, 3)$ to meet the line L_1 and L_2 given by $3x + 4y + 5 = 0$ and $3x + 4y + 15 = 0$ at points A and B respectively. From 'A' a line perpendicular to L is drawn meeting the line L_2 at A_1. Similarly from point 'B' a line perpendicular to L is drawn meeting the line L_1 at B_1. Thus, a parallelogram AA_1BB_1 is formed then the equation of L so that find the least area of the parallelogram AA_1BB_1.

Sol. The given line (L_1 and L_2) parallel and distance between (BC or AD) is $(15 - 5)/5 = 2$ units

Let $$\angle BCA = \theta$$

$$AB = BC \operatorname{cosec}\theta = 2 \operatorname{cosec}\theta$$

$$AA_1 = AD\sec\theta = 2\sec\theta$$

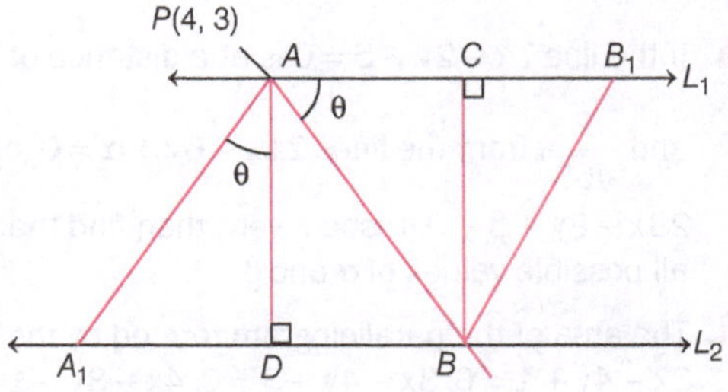

Now, area of parallelogram

$$= AB \times AA_1 = 4\sec\theta\operatorname{cosec}\theta = \frac{8}{\sin 2\theta}$$

Clearly, area is least for $\theta = \frac{\pi}{4}$. Let slope of AB be m.

Then, $$1 = \left|\frac{m + \frac{3}{4}}{1 - \frac{3m}{4}}\right|$$

$$\Rightarrow \quad 4m + 3 = \pm(4 - 3m)$$

$$\Rightarrow \quad m = \frac{1}{7} \text{ or } -7$$

Hence, the equation of L is $x - 7y + 17 = 0$

or $$7x + y - 31 = 0$$

Milestone Practice 2.2

1. The number of lines that are parallel to $2x + 6y - 7 = 0$ and have an intercept 10 between the coordinate axes is

(a) 1 (b) 2

(c) 4 (d) infinitely many

2. The shortest distance between the line $y - x = 1$ and the curve $x = y^2$ is

(a) $\frac{2\sqrt{3}}{8}$ (b) $\frac{3\sqrt{2}}{5}$

(c) $\frac{\sqrt{3}}{4}$ (d) $\frac{3\sqrt{2}}{8}$

3. If the algebraic sum of the perpendicular distances from the points (2, 0), (0, 2) and (1, 1) to a variable straight line is zero, then the line passes through the point

(a) (1, 1) (b) (−1, 1)

(c) (−1, −1) (d) (1, −1)

4. If the quadrilateral formed by the lines $ax + by + c = 0$, $a'x + b'y + c' = 0$, $ax + by + c' = 0$ and $a'x + b'y + c' = 0$ have perpendicular diagonals, then

(a) $b^2 + c^2 = b'^2 + c'^2$ (b) $c^2 + a^2 = c'^2 + a'^2$

(c) $a^2 + b^2 = a'^2 + b'^2$ (d) None of these

5. If the line $7x - 2y + 5 = 0$ is at a distance of $\frac{1}{\sqrt{53}}$ and $\frac{2}{\sqrt{53}}$, from the lines $21x - 6y + \alpha = 0$ and $28x - 8y + \beta + 0$, respectively, then find the sum of all possible values of α and β.

6. The area of the parallelogram formed by the lines $3x - 4y + 1 = 0$, $3x - 4y + 3 = 0$, $4x - 3y - 1 = 0$ and $4x - 3y - 2 = 0$, is

(a) $\frac{1}{7}$ sq units (b) $\frac{2}{7}$ sq units

(c) $\frac{3}{7}$ sq units (d) $\frac{4}{7}$ sq units

7. If $A\left(\sin\alpha, \frac{1}{\sqrt{2}}\right)$ and $B\left(\frac{1}{\sqrt{2}}, \cos\alpha\right)$, $-\pi \le \alpha \le \pi$ are two points on the same side of the line $x - y = 0$ then α belongs to the interval

(a) $\left(-\frac{\pi}{4}, \frac{\pi}{4}\right) \cup \left(\frac{\pi}{4}, \frac{3\pi}{4}\right)$ (b) $\left(-\frac{\pi}{4}, \frac{\pi}{4}\right)$

(c) $\left(\frac{\pi}{4}, \frac{3\pi}{4}\right)$ (d) None of these

8. Two sides of a parallelogram are along the line $3x + 4y = 0$ and $7x + 2y = 0$. If the equation of one of the diagonals of the parallelogram is $5x + 3y = 12$, then other diagonal passes through the point

(a) (3, 4) (b) (1, 2)

(c) (5, 6) (d) (4, 5)

9. A line passes through the point (2, 2) and is perpendicular to the line $3x + y = 3$, then its y-intercept is

(a) $-\frac{2}{3}$ (b) $\frac{2}{3}$

(c) $-\frac{4}{3}$ (d) $\frac{4}{3}$

10. If the points (1, 2) and (3, 4) are to be on the opposite side of the line $3x - 5y + a = 0$, then

(a) $7 < a < 11$ (b) $a = 7$

(c) $a = 11$ (d) $a < 7$ or $a > 11$

11. The lines $y = mx$, $y + 2x = 0$, $y = 2x + k$ and $y + mx = k$ form a rhombus if m equals

(a) −1 (b) $\frac{1}{2}$

(c) 1 (d) 2

12. If P is the length of the perpendicular from the origin on the line whose intercepts on the axes are a and b, then

(a) $P^2 = a^2 + b^2$ (b) $P^2 = a^2 - b^2$

(c) $\frac{1}{P^2} = \frac{1}{a^2} + \frac{1}{b^2}$ (d) $\frac{1}{P^2} = \frac{1}{a^2} - \frac{1}{b^2}$

13. The three sides of a triangle are given by $(x^2 - y^2)(2x + 3y - 6) = 0$. If the point $(-2, a)$ lies inside and $(b, 1)$ lies outside the triangle, then

(a) $a \in \left(2, \frac{10}{3}\right)$; $b \in (-1, 1)$

(b) $a \in \left(-2, \frac{10}{3}\right)$; $b \in \left(-1, \frac{9}{2}\right)$

(c) $a \in \left(1, \frac{10}{3}\right)$; $b \in (-3, 5)$

(d) None of the above

14. Are the points (3, 4) and (2, −6) on the same or opposite sides of the line $3x - 4y = 8$?

15. Find the equations of lines parallel to $3x - 4y - 5 = 0$ at a unit distance from it.

16. Find the range of β for which the points $(\beta, 2+\beta)$ and $\left(\frac{3\beta}{2}, \beta^2\right)$ lie on opposite sides of the line $2x+3y=6$.

17. Find the product of the length of perpendiculars from the points $(\pm\sqrt{a^2-b^2}, 0)$ to the line $\frac{x}{a}\cos\theta + \frac{y}{b}\sin\theta = 1$.

18. Find the number of points on the line $3x+4y=5$, which are at a distance of $\sec^2\theta + 2\text{cosec}^2\theta, \theta \in R$ from the point $(1, 3)$.

19. The vertices of a ΔOBC are $O(0, 0), B(-3, -1), C(-1, -3)$. Find the equation of the line parallel to BC and intersecting the sides OB and OC and whose perpendicular distance from the origin is $\frac{1}{2}$.

20. Two points A and B move on the positive direction of X-axis and Y-axis respectively such that $OA+OB=k$, then find the locus of the foot of the perpendicular from the origin O on the line AB.

Answer Key

1. (b)	**2.** (d)	**3.** (a)	**4.** (c)	**5.** (70)	**6.** (b)
7. (a)	**8.** (b)	**9.** (d)	**10.** (a)	**11.** (d)	**12.** (c)
13. (a)	**14.** opposite sides	**15.** $3x-4y=0$ and $3x-4y-10=0$		**16.** $B \in (-\infty, -2) \cup (0, 1)$	
17. (b^2)	**18.** (2)	**19.** $2x+2y+\sqrt{2}=0$			
20. $(x^2+y^2)(x+y)=kxy$					

For Detailed Solution

Milestone 3 Point of Intersection of Two Lines

• Point of Intersection of Two Lines • Concurrent Lines • Family of Lines

2.11 Points of Intersection of Two Lines

Let $a_1x + b_1y + c_1 = 0$ and $a_2x + b_2y + c_2 = 0$ be two non-parallel lines. If (x_1, y_1) be the coordinates of their point of intersection,

then $a_1x_1 + b_1y_1 + c_1 = 0$ and $a_2x_1 + b_2y_1 + c_2 = 0$

Solving these two by cross multiplication, then

$$\frac{x_1}{b_1c_2 - b_2c_1} = \frac{y_1}{c_1a_2 - c_2a_1} = \frac{1}{a_1b_2 - a_2b_1}$$

we get, $$(x_1, y_1) \equiv \left(\frac{b_1c_2 - b_2c_1}{a_1b_2 - a_2b_1}, \frac{c_1a_2 - c_2a_1}{a_1b_2 - a_2b_1}\right)$$

$$\equiv \left(\frac{\begin{vmatrix} b_1 & b_2 \\ c_1 & c_2 \end{vmatrix}}{\begin{vmatrix} a_1 & a_2 \\ b_1 & b_2 \end{vmatrix}}, \frac{\begin{vmatrix} c_1 & c_2 \\ a_1 & a_2 \end{vmatrix}}{\begin{vmatrix} a_1 & a_2 \\ b_1 & b_2 \end{vmatrix}}\right)$$

JEE Focus Points

1. Here lines are not parallel, they have unequal slopes, then $a_1b_2 - a_2b_1 \neq 0$
2. In solving numerical questions, we should not be remember the coordinates (x_1, y_1) given above, but we solve the equations directly.

Example 77. Find the number of integral values of m, for which the x-coordinate of the point of intersection of lines $3x + 4y = 9$ and $y = mx + 1$ is also an integer.

Sol. We solve the equations directly

$$3x + 4y = 9 \quad \text{...(i)}$$

$$y = mx + 1 \quad \text{...(ii)}$$

On putting Eq. (ii) in Eq. (i), we get

$$3x + 4(mx + 1) = 9$$

$$x(3 + 4m) + 4 = 9$$

$$x = \frac{5}{3 + 4m}$$

For x to be an integer,

$$3 + 4m = \pm 5 \quad \text{or} \quad \pm 1 \quad \text{...(iii)}$$

∴ Four possible values of m are possible and given by

$$m = -2, -1, \frac{-1}{2}, \frac{1}{2} \quad \text{[by solving Eq. (iii)]}$$

So, there are two integral values of m i.e. -2 and -1.

Example 78. The straight lines L_1 and L_2 pass through the origin and trisect the line segment of the line $5x + 9y = 45$ between the axes. If m_1 and m_2 are the slopes of lines L_1 and L_2, then find the point of intersection of the line $y = (m_1 + m_2)x$ with L.

Sol. Given, the straight lines L_1 and L_2 pass through the origin and trisect the line segment of the line $L \equiv 5x + 9y = 45$ between the axes. Also m_1 and m_2 are the slopes of lines L_1 and L_2.

Now, on plotting the diagram, we get

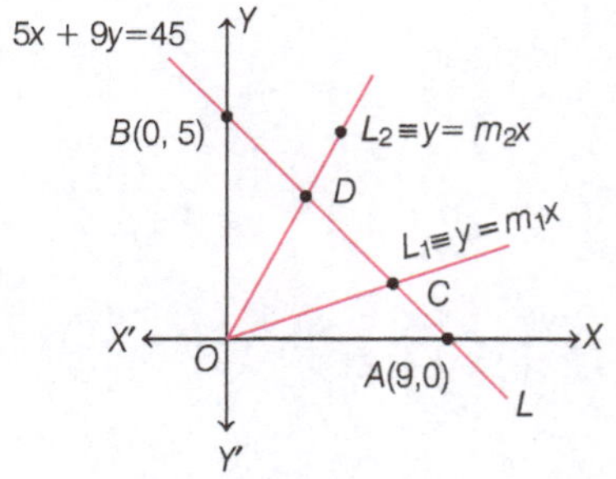

Given, equation of line $L \equiv 5x + 9y = 45$.

Now, using the section formula between points $A(9, 0)$ and $B(0, 5)$, we get the value of point C and D

$$D \equiv \left(3, \frac{10}{3}\right) \text{ and } C \equiv \left(6, \frac{5}{3}\right)$$

Now, finding the slopes m_1 and m_2, we get

$$m_2 = \frac{\frac{10}{3}}{3} = \frac{10}{9} \text{ and } m_1 = \frac{\frac{5}{3}}{6} = \frac{5}{18}$$

$$\left[\because m_1 = \text{slope of } OC = \frac{y}{x}, m_2 = \text{slope of } OD = \frac{y}{x}\right]$$

So, equation of line $y = (m_2 + m_1)x$ will be

$$y = \left(\frac{10}{9} + \frac{5}{18}\right)x = \frac{(20 + 5)x}{18} = \frac{25}{18}x$$

So, intersection of point with L will be

$$5x + 9\left(\frac{25}{18}\right)x = 45$$

$$\frac{35x}{2} = 45 \Rightarrow x = \frac{18}{7}.$$

$$y = \frac{25}{18}x$$

$$y = \frac{25}{7} \quad \text{[on putting value of } x \text{ from above]}$$

Hence, point of intersection is $\left(\frac{18}{7}, \frac{25}{7}\right)$.

2.12 Concurrent Lines

Three given lines are said to be concurrent, if they pass through a common point. Hence to prove that three given lines are concurrent, we proceed as follows :

METHOD I Find the point of intersection of any two lines by solving them simultaneously. If this point satisfies the third equation also, then the given lines are concurrent.

METHOD II The three lines $a_i x + b_i y + c_i = 0, i = 1, 2, 3$ are concurrent if

$$\begin{vmatrix} a_1 & b_1 & c_1 \\ a_2 & b_2 & c_2 \\ a_3 & b_3 & c_3 \end{vmatrix} = 0$$

METHOD III The condition for the lines $P = 0, Q = 0$ and $R = 0$ to be concurrent is that three constants l, m, n (not all zeros at the same time) can be obtained such that

$$lP + mQ + nR = 0$$

Example 79. Show that the lines

$$2x + 3y - 8 = 0,\ x - 5y + 9 = 0 \text{ and } 3x + 4y - 11 = 0$$

are concurrent.

Sol. Method I Solving the first two equations, we see that their point of intersection is (1, 2) which also satisfies the third equation,

$$3 \times 1 + 4 \times 2 - 11 = 0$$

Hence, the given lines are concurrent.

Method II We have, $\begin{vmatrix} a_1 & b_1 & c_1 \\ a_2 & b_2 & c_2 \\ a_3 & b_3 & c_3 \end{vmatrix} = \begin{vmatrix} 2 & 3 & -8 \\ 1 & -5 & 9 \\ 3 & 4 & -11 \end{vmatrix}$

Applying, $C_3 \to C_3 + C_1 + 2C_2$,

$$= \begin{vmatrix} 2 & 3 & 0 \\ 1 & -5 & 0 \\ 3 & 4 & 0 \end{vmatrix} = 0$$

Hence, the given lines are concurrent.

Method III Suppose

$$l(2x + 3y - 8) + m(x - 5y + 9) + n(3x + 4y - 11) = 0$$

$$\Rightarrow x(2l + m + 3n) + y(3l - 5m + 4n) + (-8l + 9m - 11n) = 0$$
$$= 0 \cdot x + 0 \cdot y + 0$$

On comparing, we get

$$2l + m + 3n = 0,\ 3l - 5m + 4n = 0$$

and $\quad -8l + 9m - 11n = 0$

After solving, we get $l = 19, m = 1$ and $n = -13$

So, $\quad 19(2x + 3y - 8) + (x - 5y + 9) - 13(3x + 4y - 11) = 0$

Hence, the given lines are concurrent.

Example 80. Find the value of P, if lines $3x - 4y - 13 = 0$, $8x - 11y - 33 = 0$ and $2x - 3y + P = 0$ are concurrent.

Sol. The given lines are concurrent if

$$\begin{vmatrix} 3 & -4 & -13 \\ 8 & -11 & -33 \\ 2 & -3 & P \end{vmatrix} = 0$$

or $\quad 3(-11P - 99) + 4(8P + 66) - 13(-24 + 22) = 0$

$$-P - 7 = 0 \Rightarrow P = -7$$

Example 81. If the lines $ax + y + 1 = 0$, $x + by + 1 = 0$ and $x + y + c = 0$ (a, b and c being distinct and different from 1) are concurrent, then find the value of $\frac{1}{1-a} + \frac{1}{1-b} + \frac{1}{1-c}$.

Sol. The given lines are concurrent, then

$$\begin{vmatrix} a & 1 & 1 \\ 1 & b & 1 \\ 1 & 1 & c \end{vmatrix} = 0 \Rightarrow \begin{vmatrix} a & 1-a & 1-a \\ 1 & b-1 & 0 \\ 1 & 0 & c-1 \end{vmatrix} = 0$$

[applying $C_2 \to C_2 - C_1$ and $C_3 \to C_3 - C_1$]

Expanding along first row,

$$\Rightarrow a(b-1)(c-1) - (1-a)(c-1) - (1-a)(b-1) = 0$$

$$\Rightarrow a(1-b)(1-c) + (1-a)(1-c) + (1-a)(1-b) = 0$$

On dividing by $(1-a)(1-b)(1-c)$, then

$$\frac{a}{1-a} + \frac{1}{1-b} + \frac{1}{1-c} = 0$$

$$\Rightarrow \quad -1 + \frac{1}{1-a} + \frac{1}{1-b} + \frac{1}{1-c} = 0$$

Hence, $\quad \frac{1}{1-a} + \frac{1}{1-b} + \frac{1}{1-c} = 1$

Example 82. Find the set of real values of k for which the lines $x + 3y + 1 = 0$, $kx + 2y - 2 = 0$ and $2x - y + 3 = 0$ from a triangle.

Sol. Given, lines from a triangle.

$\therefore$ $x + 3y + 1 = 0$ is not parallel to $kx + 2y - 2 = 0$

$$-\frac{k}{2} \neq \frac{-1}{3}$$

$$\Rightarrow \quad k \neq \frac{2}{3}$$

Also, line $2x - y + 3 = 0$ is not parallel to $kx + 2y - 2 = 0$

$$\frac{-k}{2} \neq 2 \Rightarrow k \neq -4$$

For non-concurrency,

$$\begin{vmatrix} 1 & 3 & 1 \\ k & 2 & -2 \\ 2 & -1 & 3 \end{vmatrix} \neq 0$$

$$\Rightarrow \quad -10k \neq 12 \Rightarrow k \neq \frac{-6}{5}$$

Hence, $$k \in R - \left\{-4, \frac{-6}{5}, \frac{2}{3}\right\}$$

Example 83. Find the possible values of m for which the lines $x + y - 1 = 0$, $(m-1)x + (m^2 - 7)y - 5 = 0$ and $(m-2)x + (2m-5)y = 0$ are concurrent.

Sol. If the lines are concurrent, then $\Delta = 0$

$$\begin{vmatrix} 1 & 1 & -1 \\ m-1 & m^2-7 & -5 \\ m-2 & 2m-5 & 0 \end{vmatrix} = 0$$

$$\Rightarrow \quad (m-2)(-5+m^2-7) - (2m-5)(-5+m-1) + 0 = 0$$

$$(m-2)(m^2-12) - (2m-5)(m-6) = 0$$

$$m^3 - 4m^2 + 5m - 6 = 0$$

$$(m-3)(m^2 - m + 2) = 0$$

Here, $m = 3$ but $m^2 - m + 2 = 0$ has no real roots if $m = 3$, then the two lines are parallel.

So, no real value of m for which lines are concurrent.

2.13 Family of Lines

Theorem Any line through the point of intersection of the lines $a_1x + b_1y + c_1 = 0$ and $a_2x + b_2y + c_2 = 0$ can be represented by the equation

$$(a_1x + b_1y + c_1) + \lambda(a_2x + b_2y + c_2) = 0$$

where λ is a parameter which depends on the other property of line.

Proof The equations of the lines are

$$a_1x + b_1y + c_1 = 0 \quad \text{...(i)}$$

and $$a_2x + b_2y + c_2 = 0 \quad \text{...(ii)}$$

Multiplying by μ and ν in Eqs. (i) and (ii) and then adding, we get

$$\mu(a_1x + b_1y + c_1) + \nu(a_2x + b_2y + c_2) = 0$$

where μ, ν are any constants not both zero.

Dividing both sides by μ, then

$$(a_1x + b_1y + c_1) + \frac{\nu}{\mu}(a_2x + b_2y + c_2) = 0$$

$$\Rightarrow (a_1x + b_1y + c_1) + \lambda(a_2x + b_2y + c_2) = 0 \left(\text{where, } \lambda = \frac{\nu}{\mu}\right)$$

It is a first degree equation in x and y. So it represents family of lines through the point of intersection of Eqs. (i) and (ii).

Thus, the family of straight lines through the intersection of lines $L_1 \equiv a_1x + b_1y + c_1 = 0$ and $L_2 \equiv a_2x + b_2y + c_2 = 0$ is

$$(a_1x + b_1y + c_1) + \lambda(a_2x + b_2y + c_2) = 0$$

i.e. $$L_1 + \lambda L_2 = 0$$

JEE Focus Points

Concept Inside Video

1. The equation $L_1 + \lambda L_2 = 0$ or $\mu L_1 + \nu L_2 = 0$ represent a line passing through the intersection of the lines $L_1 = 0$ and $L_2 = 0$ which is a fixed point, where λ, μ, ν are constants.
2. To finding fixed point, the number of constants in family of lines are one or two. If number of constants more than two, then convert in two or one constant form.

Example 84. Find the equation of the straight line passing through the point $(2, 1)$ and through the point of intersection of the lines $x + 2y = 3$ and $2x - 3y = 4$.

Sol. Equation of any straight line passing through the intersection of the lines $x + 2y = 3$ and $2x - 3y = 4$ is

$$\lambda(x + 2y - 3) + (2x - 3y - 4) = 0 \quad \text{...(i)}$$

Since, it passes through the point (2, 1)

$$\therefore \quad \lambda(2 + 2 - 3) + (4 - 3 - 4) = 0$$

$$\Rightarrow \quad \lambda - 3 = 0$$

$$\therefore \quad \lambda = 3$$

Now, substituting this value of λ in Eq. (i), we get

$$3(x + 2y - 3) + (2x - 3y - 4) = 0$$

i.e. $$5x + 3y - 13 = 0$$

which is the equation of required line.

Example 85. If $3a + 2b + 6c = 0$ the family of straight lines $ax + by + c = 0$ passes through a fixed point. Find the coordinates of fixed point.

Sol. Given, $3a + 2b + 6c = 0$

or $$\frac{a}{2} + \frac{b}{3} + c = 0 \quad \text{...(i)}$$

and family of straight lines is

$$ax + by + c = 0 \quad \text{...(ii)}$$

On subtracting Eq. (i) from Eq. (ii), then

$$a\left(x - \frac{1}{2}\right) + b\left(y - \frac{1}{3}\right) = 0$$

which is equation of a line passing through the point of intersection of the lines.

$$\Rightarrow \quad x - \frac{1}{2} = 0 \text{ and } y - \frac{1}{3} = 0$$

$\therefore$ The coordinates of fixed point are $\left(\frac{1}{2}, \frac{1}{3}\right)$.

Example 86. If $4a^2+9b^2-c^2+12ab=0$, then the family of straight line $ax+by+c=0$ is either concurrent at (m,n) or (p,q). Find the value of $m+n+p+q+10$.

Sol. We have, $4a^2+9b^2-c^2+12ab=0$

$$\Rightarrow \quad (4a^2+9b^2+12ab)-c^2=0$$
$$\Rightarrow \quad (2a+3b)^2-c^2=0$$
$$\Rightarrow \quad (2a+3b+c)(2a+3b-c)=0$$
$$\Rightarrow \quad (2a+3b+c)=0 \text{ and } (2a+3b-c)=0$$

Given family of lines are

$$ax+by+c=0 \qquad \text{...(i)}$$

and also the given conditions are

$$(2a+3b+c)=0 \qquad \text{...(ii)}$$

and $$(2a+3b-c)=0 \qquad \text{...(iii)}$$

From Eqs. (i) and (ii), we get

$$\Rightarrow \quad ax+by-2a-3b=0$$
$$\Rightarrow \quad a(x-2)+b(y-3)=0$$
$$\Rightarrow \quad (x-2)+\frac{b}{a}(y-3)=0$$
$$\Rightarrow \quad x=2 \text{ and } y=3$$
$$\Rightarrow \quad m=2 \text{ and } n=3$$

From Eqs. (i) and (iii), we get

$$ax+by+2a+3b=0$$
$$\Rightarrow \quad a(x+2)+b(y+3)=0$$
$$\Rightarrow \quad (x+2)+\frac{b}{a}(y+3)=0$$
$$\Rightarrow \quad x=-2 \text{ and } y=-3$$
$$\Rightarrow \quad p=-2 \text{ and } q=-3$$

Thus, the value of

$$m+n+p+q+10=2+3-2-3+10=10$$

Example 87. Find the equation of straight line which passes through the intersection of the straight lines

$3x-4y+1=0$ and $5x+y-1=0$

and cuts off equal intercepts from the axes.

Sol. Equation of any line passing through the intersection of the given lines is

$$(3x-4y+1)+\lambda(5x+y-1)=0$$
$$\Rightarrow \quad x(3+5\lambda)+y(-4+\lambda)+(1-\lambda)=0 \qquad \text{...(i)}$$
$$\Rightarrow \quad \frac{x}{\left(\frac{\lambda-1}{3+5\lambda}\right)}+\frac{y}{\left(\frac{\lambda-1}{\lambda-4}\right)}=1$$

Given, x-intercept $=$ y-intercept

i.e. $$\left(\frac{\lambda-1}{3+5\lambda}\right)=\left(\frac{\lambda-1}{\lambda-4}\right)$$

$$\Rightarrow \quad \frac{1}{3+5\lambda}=\frac{1}{\lambda-4}$$

[$\lambda \neq 1 \because$ if $\lambda=1$, then line (i) passes through origin]

$$\therefore \quad \lambda-4=3+5\lambda$$

or $$4\lambda=-7$$

$$\therefore \quad \lambda=-\frac{7}{4}$$

On substituting the value of λ in Eq. (i), we get required equation is

$$23x+23y=11.$$

Example 88. Find the equation of line which is equally inclined to the axes and passes through the common point of family of lines

$4acx+y(ab+bc+ca-abc)+abc=0$; where $a,b,c>0$ are in HP.

Sol. Given, $a,b,c>0$ in HP

$$\therefore \quad \frac{2}{b}=\frac{1}{a}+\frac{1}{c}$$
$$\Rightarrow \quad \frac{2}{b}=\frac{a+c}{ac}$$
$$\Rightarrow \quad 2ac=ab+bc \qquad \text{...(i)}$$

Given, $4acx+y(ab+bc+ca-abc)+abc=0$

From Eq. (i),

$$4acx+y(2ac+ca-abc)+abc=0$$
$$\Rightarrow \quad 4acx+y(3ac-abc)+abc=0$$
$$\Rightarrow \quad ac(4x+3y)+abc(-y+1)=0$$

On dividing whole equation by ac, we get

$$(4x+3y)+b(-y+1)=0$$
$$\Rightarrow \quad -y+1=0 \text{ and } 4x+3y=0$$
$$\Rightarrow \quad y=1 \text{ and } 4x+3(1)=0$$
$$\Rightarrow \quad 4x=-3$$
$$\Rightarrow \quad x=\frac{-3}{4}$$

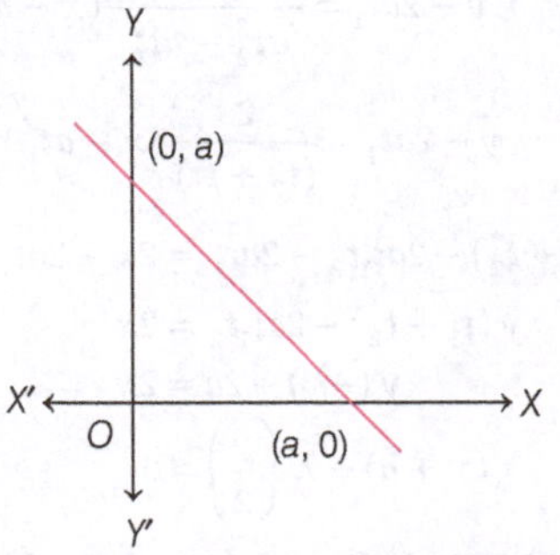

$\because$ The lines are concurrent at the point of intersection of lines at $\left(\frac{-3}{4},1\right)$.

Equation of line is $x+y=a$

$$a=\frac{-3}{4}\pm 1=\frac{-7}{4},\frac{1}{4}$$

$$\therefore \quad x\pm y=\frac{-7}{4},\frac{1}{4}$$

Hence, the required equation of lines are $y-x=\frac{7}{4}$ and $y+x=\frac{1}{4}$.

Example 89. If $\frac{a}{\sqrt{bc}} - 2 = \sqrt{\frac{b}{c}} + \sqrt{\frac{c}{b}}$ where $a, b, c > 0$, then find the fixed point which passes through the family of lines $\sqrt{a}x + \sqrt{b}y + \sqrt{c} = 0$.

Sol. $\frac{a}{\sqrt{bc}} - 2 = \sqrt{\frac{b}{c}} + \sqrt{\frac{c}{b}}$

$\Rightarrow \quad a = b + c + 2\sqrt{bc}$

$\Rightarrow \quad a = (\sqrt{b} + \sqrt{c})^2$

$\Rightarrow \quad (\sqrt{a} - \sqrt{b} - \sqrt{c})(\sqrt{a} + \sqrt{b} + \sqrt{c}) = 0$

$\Rightarrow \quad \sqrt{a} - \sqrt{b} - \sqrt{c} = 0$ ...(i)

$[\because \sqrt{a} + \sqrt{b} + \sqrt{c} \neq 0 \ (\because a, b, c > 0)]$

On comparing equation with $\sqrt{a}x + \sqrt{b}y + \sqrt{c} = 0$, we get

$$x = -1, y = 1$$

$[\because -\sqrt{a} + \sqrt{b} + \sqrt{c} = 0 \text{ or } \sqrt{a} - \sqrt{b} - \sqrt{c} = 0]$

$\therefore$ Point $(-1, 1)$ passes through the line.

Example 90. If t_1 and t_2 are roots of the equation $t^2 + \lambda t + 1 = 0$, where λ is an arbitrary constant. Then, prove that the line joining the points $(at_1^2, 2at_1)$ and $(at_2^2, 2at_2)$ always passes through a fixed point. Also, find coordinates of that point.

Sol. Given that t_1 and t_2 are the roots of the equation $t^2 + \lambda t + 1 = 0$

$\therefore \quad t_1 + t_2 = -\lambda$ and $t_1 t_2 = 1$ ...(i)

Equation of the line joining the points $(at_1^2, 2at_1)$ and $(at_2^2, 2at_2)$ is

$$y - 2at_1 = \frac{2at_2 - 2at_1}{at_2^2 - at_1^2}(x - at_1^2)$$

$\Rightarrow \quad y - 2at_1 = \frac{2}{(t_2 + t_1)}(x - at_1^2)$

$\Rightarrow \quad y(t_1 + t_2) - 2at_1t_2 - 2at_1^2 = 2x - 2at_1^2$

$\Rightarrow \quad y(t_1 + t_2) - 2at_1t_2 = 2x$

$\Rightarrow \quad y(-\lambda) - 2a = 2x$ [from Eq. (i)]

or $\quad (x + a) + \lambda\left(\frac{y}{2}\right) = 0$

which is equation of a line passing through the point of intersection of the lines $x + a = 0$ and $\frac{y}{2} = 0$ or $y = 0$.

$\therefore$ Coordinates of fixed point are $(-a, 0)$.

Example 91. Find the equation of the line passing through the point of intersection of the lines $x + 5y + 7 = 0, 3x + 2y - 5 = 0$

and (a) parallel to the line $7x + 2y - 5 = 0$

(b) perpendicular to the line $7x + 2y - 5 = 0$

Sol. Any line passing through the point of intersection of the given lines is $(x + 5y + 7) + \lambda(3x + 2y - 5) = 0$.

$\Rightarrow \quad x(1 + 3\lambda) + y(5 + 2\lambda) + (7 - 5\lambda) = 0$ ...(i)

Its slope $= -\frac{(1 + 3\lambda)}{(5 + 2\lambda)}$

(a) Line Eq. (i) is to be parallel to $7x + 2y - 5 = 0$

then $\quad -\frac{(1 + 3\lambda)}{(5 + 2\lambda)} = -\frac{7}{2}$

$\Rightarrow \quad 2 + 6\lambda = 35 + 14\lambda \Rightarrow 8\lambda = -33$

$\Rightarrow \quad \lambda = -\frac{33}{8}$

On substituting this value of λ in Eq. (i), we get the required equation as $7x + 2y - 17 = 0$

(b) Line (i) is to be perpendicular to $7x + 2y - 5 = 0$

$\therefore \quad -\frac{(1 + 3\lambda)}{(5 + 2\lambda)} \times -\left(\frac{7}{2}\right) = -1$ or $7 + 21\lambda = -10 - 4\lambda$

$\therefore \quad \lambda = -\frac{17}{25}$

On substituting this value of λ in Eq. (i), we get the required equation as

$$2x - 7y - 20 = 0.$$

Time Saving Technique

The point of intersection of the given lines

$x + 5y + 7 = 0$ and $3x + 2y - 5 = 0$ is $(3, -2)$.

$\therefore$ Equation of line through $(3, -2)$ is

$y + 2 = m(x - 3)$ ...(ii)

(a) Line (ii) is parallel to $7x + 2y - 5 = 0$,

$\therefore \quad m = -\frac{7}{2}$

Hence, the equation of the required line is

$y + 2 = -\frac{7}{2}(x - 3)$

or $\quad 7x + 2y - 17 = 0$

(b) Line (ii) is perpendicular to $7x + 2y - 5 = 0$

then $\quad m \times \left(-\frac{7}{2}\right) = -1$ or $m = \frac{2}{7}$

Hence, the equation of the required line is

$y + 2 = \frac{2}{7}(x - 3)$ or $2x - 7y - 20 = 0$

How to Find Circumcentre and Orthocentre by Slopes

(i) Circumcentre

The circumcentre of a triangle is the point of intersection of the perpendicular bisectors of the sides of a triangle. It is the centre of the circle which passes through the vertices of the triangle and so its distance from the vertices of the triangle is same as radius of circle and this distance is known as the **circumradius** of the triangle.

Let $O(x, y)$ be the circumcentre.

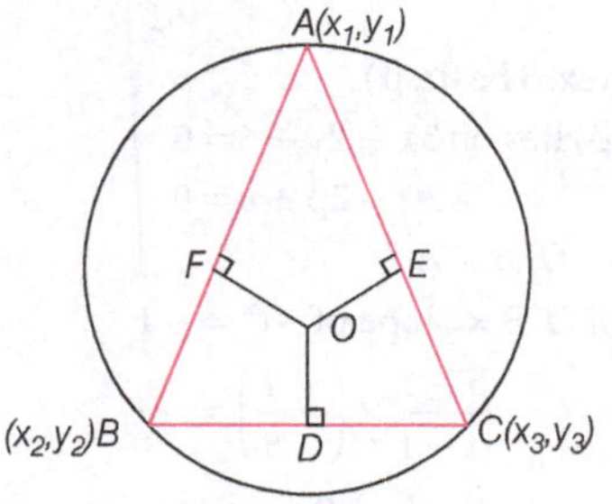

If D, E and F are the mid-points of BC, CA and AB, respectively and $OD \perp BC, OE \perp CA$ and $OF \perp AB$

$\therefore$ slope of $OD \times$ slope of $BC = -1$

and slope of $OE \times$ slope of $CA = -1$

and slope of $OF \times$ slope of $AB = -1$

On solving any two, we get (x, y).

Example 92. Find the coordinates of the circumcentre of the triangle whose vertices are $A(5, -1)$, $B(-1, 5)$ and $C(6, 6)$. Find circumradius also.

Sol. Let circumcentre be $O'(\alpha, \beta)$ and mid-points of sides BC, CA and AB are $D\left(\frac{5}{2}, \frac{11}{2}\right)$, $E\left(\frac{11}{2}, \frac{5}{2}\right)$ and $F(2, 2)$, respectively. Since, $O'D \perp BC$.

$\therefore$ Slope of $O'D \times$ Slope of $BC = -1$

$$\Rightarrow \quad \frac{\beta - \frac{11}{2}}{\alpha - \frac{5}{2}} \times \frac{6-5}{6+1} = -1$$

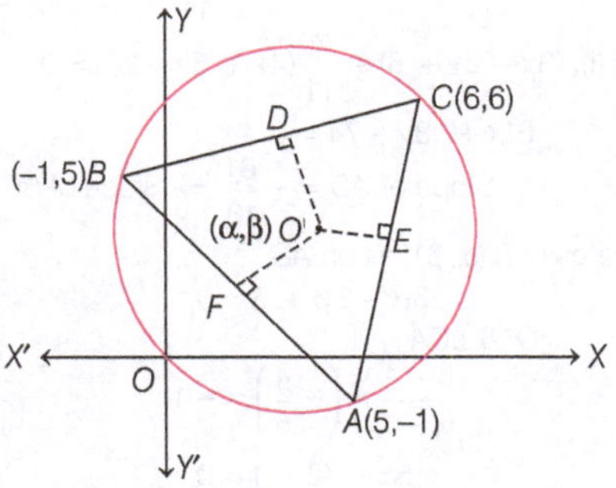

$$\Rightarrow \quad \frac{2\beta - 11}{7(2\alpha - 5)} = -1$$

$\Rightarrow \quad 2\beta - 11 = -14\alpha + 35 \Rightarrow 14\alpha + 2\beta = 46$

$\therefore \quad 7\alpha + \beta = 23$ ...(i)

and $\quad O'E \perp CA$

$\therefore$ Slope of $O'E \times$ Slope of $CA = -1$

$$\Rightarrow \quad \frac{\beta - \frac{5}{2}}{\alpha - \frac{11}{2}} \times \frac{-1-6}{5-6} = -1$$

$$\Rightarrow \quad \frac{2\beta - 5}{2\alpha - 11} \times \frac{7}{1} = -1$$

$\Rightarrow \quad 14\beta - 35 = -2\alpha + 11$

$\therefore \quad 2\alpha + 14\beta = 46$

$\therefore \quad \alpha + 7\beta = 23$ ... (ii)

On solving Eqs. (i) and (ii), we get

$$\alpha = \beta = \frac{23}{8}$$

$\therefore$ Circumcentre $= \left(\frac{23}{8}, \frac{23}{8}\right)$

$\therefore$ Circumradius $= O'A = O'B = O'C$

$$= O'C = \sqrt{(\alpha - 6)^2 + (\beta - 6)^2}$$

$$= \sqrt{\left(\frac{23}{8} - 6\right)^2 + \left(\frac{23}{8} - 6\right)^2}$$

$$= \sqrt{\left(\frac{25}{8}\right)^2 + \left(\frac{25}{8}\right)^2} = \frac{25\sqrt{2}}{8} \text{ units.}$$

JEE SCANNER

Example Similar to PYQ Asked in JEE Main 2023

Let $O\left(3, \frac{a}{2}\right)$ be the circumcentre of a triangle with vertices $A(a, -4)$, $B(a, 12)$ and $C\left(\frac{a}{2}, -4\right)$. Let α denotes the circumradius, β denotes the area and γ denotes the perimeter of the ΔABC. Then, $\beta + \gamma - 2\alpha$ is equal to ...

Sol. (52) We have, $A(a, -4)$, $B(a, 12)$, $C\left(\frac{a}{2}, -4\right)$ and $O\left(3, \frac{a}{2}\right)$.

$\therefore \quad AO = BO$

$$\Rightarrow \quad (a-3)^2 + \left(-4 - \frac{a}{2}\right)^2 = (a-3)^2 + \left(12 - \frac{a}{2}\right)^2$$

$$\Rightarrow \quad 16 + 4a + \frac{a^2}{4} = 144 - 12a + \frac{a^2}{4}$$

$\Rightarrow \quad 16a = 128 \Rightarrow a = 8$

$\therefore \quad AB = 16, AC = 4$ and $BC = 4\sqrt{17}$

$\therefore \quad \alpha = 2\sqrt{17}, \beta = 32$ and $\gamma = 20 + 4\sqrt{17}$

$\Rightarrow \quad \beta + \gamma - 2\alpha = 32 + 20 + 4\sqrt{17} - 4\sqrt{17} = 52$

Skill Builder

Let $O\left(4, \frac{a}{3}\right)$ be the circumcentre of a triangle with vertices $P(a, -5)$, $Q(a, 10)$ and $R\left(\frac{a}{3}, -5\right)$. Let α denotes the circumradius, β denotes the area and γ denotes the perimeter of ΔPQR. Then, the value of $2(\alpha + \beta) - \gamma$ is ......

For Sol.

■ **For more practice** See Q.13 of Milestone Practice 2.3.

(ii) Orthocentre

The orthocentre of a triangle is the point of intersection of altitudes.

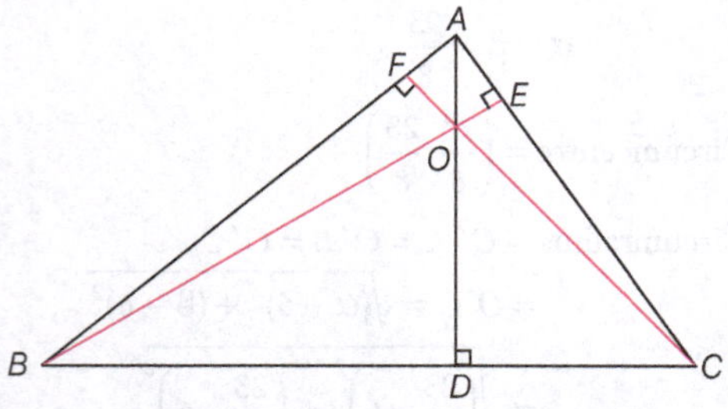

Here, O is the orthocentre since $AD \perp BC$, $BE \perp CA$ and $CF \perp AB$, then $OA \perp BC$, $OB \perp CA$ and $OC \perp AB$.

Solving any two we can get coordinates of O.

JEE SPIKE

If any two lines out of three lines i.e. AB, BC and CA are perpendicular, then orthocentre is the point of intersection of two perpendicular lines.

Example 93. The equations of two sides of a triangle are $3x - 2y + 6 = 0$ and $4x + 5y = 20$ and the orthocentre is $(1, 1)$. Find the equation of the third side.

Sol. Let $3x - 2y + 6 = 0$ and $4x + 5y = 20$ are the equations of the sides AB and AC. The point of intersection of AB and AC is $\left(\frac{10}{23}, \frac{84}{23}\right)$. Let slope of BC is m, since $O'A \perp BC$.

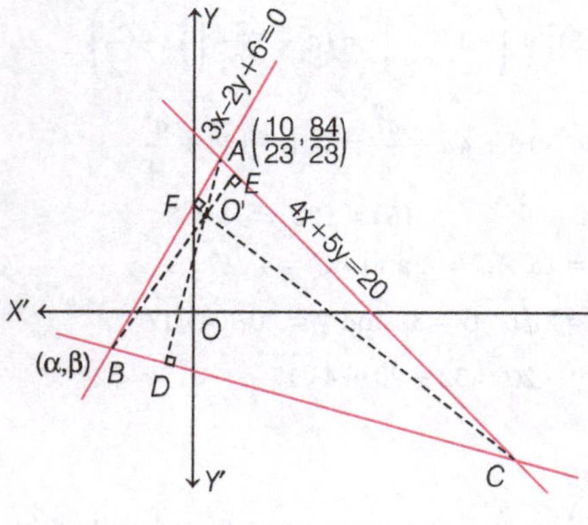

$\therefore$ Slope of $O'A \times$ Slope of $BC = -1$

$$\Rightarrow \quad \frac{\frac{84}{23} - 1}{\frac{10}{23} - 1} \times m = -1$$

$$\Rightarrow \quad \frac{61}{-13} m = -1$$

$$\therefore \quad m = \frac{13}{61}$$

Let the vertex B be (α, β).

(α, β) lies on $3x - 2y + 6 = 0$

$$\therefore \quad 3\alpha - 2\beta + 6 = 0 \quad \text{...(i)}$$

and $\quad O'B \perp AC$

$\therefore$ Slope of $O'B \times$ Slope of $AC = -1$

$$\frac{\beta - 1}{\alpha - 1} \times \left(-\frac{4}{5}\right) = -1$$

$$\Rightarrow \quad 4\beta - 4 = 5\alpha - 5$$

$$\Rightarrow \quad 5\alpha - 4\beta - 1 = 0 \quad \text{...(ii)}$$

On solving Eqs. (i) and (ii), we get

$$\alpha = -13 \text{ and } \beta = -\frac{33}{2}$$

Since, third side passes through $\left(-13, -\frac{33}{2}\right)$ with slope $\frac{13}{61}$, therefore its equation is

$$y + \frac{33}{2} = \frac{13}{61}(x + 13)$$

$$\Rightarrow \quad 122y + 33 \times 61 = 26x + 2 \times 169$$

$$\Rightarrow \quad 26x - 122y - 1675 = 0$$

Alternate Solution

The equation of line through A i.e. point of intersection of AB and AC is

$$(3x - 2y + 6) + \lambda(4x + 5y - 20) = 0 \quad \text{...(i)}$$

It passes through (1, 1), then

$$(3 - 2 + 6) + \lambda(4 + 5 - 20) = 0 \Rightarrow 7 - 11\lambda = 0$$

$$\therefore \quad \lambda = \frac{7}{11}$$

From Eq. (i), $(3x - 2y + 6) + \frac{7}{11}(4x + 5y - 20) = 0$

$$\Rightarrow \quad 61x + 13y - 74 = 0$$

$\therefore$ Slope of $AD = -\frac{61}{13} \Rightarrow$ Slope of $BC = \frac{13}{61}$

If coordinates of $B(\alpha, \beta)$ lies on AB

$$\therefore \quad 3\alpha - 2\beta + 6 = 0 \quad \text{...(ii)}$$

and $\quad O'B \perp CA$

Then, $\quad \frac{\beta - 1}{\alpha - 1} \times \left(-\frac{4}{5}\right) = -1$

$$\Rightarrow \quad 5\alpha - 4\beta - 1 = 0 \quad \text{...(iii)}$$

On solving Eqs. (ii) and (iii), we get

$$\alpha = -13 \text{ and } \beta = -\frac{33}{2}$$

$\therefore$ Equation of third side i.e. BC is $y + \frac{33}{2} = \frac{13}{61}(x + 13)$

$$\therefore \quad 26x - 122y - 1675 = 0$$

Example 94. Find the orthocentre of the ΔABC whose angular points are $A(1, 2)$, $B(2, 3)$ and $C(4, 3)$.

Sol. Now, slope of $BC = \frac{3 - 3}{4 - 2} = 0$

$$\text{Slope of } CA = \frac{2 - 3}{1 - 4} = \frac{1}{3}$$

and $\quad$ slope of $AB = \dfrac{3-2}{2-1} = 1$

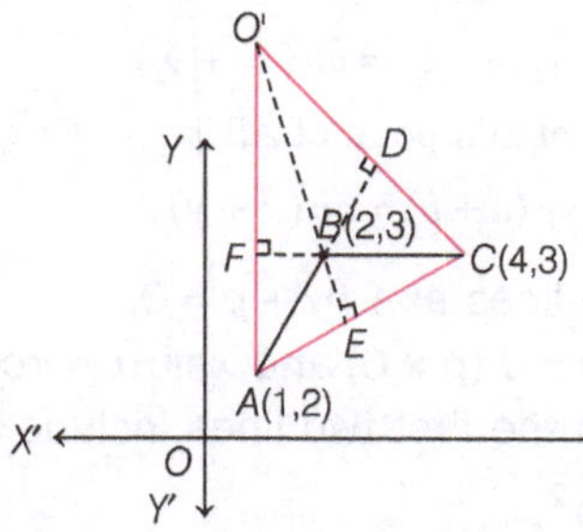

Let orthocentre be $O'(\alpha, \beta)$, then

Slope of $O'A \times$ Slope of $BC = -1$

$$\frac{2-\beta}{1-\alpha} \times 0 = -1$$

$$\Rightarrow \quad \frac{0}{1-\alpha} = -1$$

$$\Rightarrow \quad 1 - \alpha = 0$$

$$\therefore \quad \alpha = 1$$

and Slope of $O'B \times$ Slope of $CA = -1$

$$\Rightarrow \quad \frac{3-\beta}{2-\alpha} \times \frac{1}{3} = -1$$

$$\Rightarrow \quad 3 - \beta = 3\alpha - 6$$

$$\Rightarrow \quad 3\alpha + \beta = 9$$

$$\therefore \quad \beta = 6 \qquad [\because \alpha = 1]$$

Hence, orthocentre of the given triangle is $(1, 6)$.

Example 95. If the orthocentre of the triangle formed by the lines $2x + 3y - 1 = 0$, $x + 2y - 1 = 0$, $ax + by - 1 = 0$ is at origin, then find (a, b).

Sol. The equation of a line through A i.e. the point of intersection of AB and AC, is

$$(2x + 3y - 1) + \lambda\,(ax + by - 1) = 0 \qquad \text{...(i)}$$

It passes through $O\,(0, 0)$, then

$$-1 - \lambda = 0$$

$$\therefore \quad \lambda = -1$$

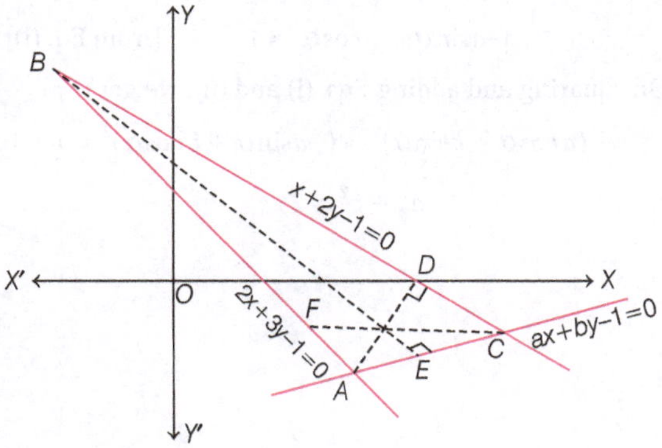

From Eq. (i), we get

$$2x + 3y - 1 - ax - by + 1 = 0$$

$$\Rightarrow \quad (2-a)\,x + (3-b)\,y = 0$$

Since, $AD \perp BC$

$$\therefore \quad -\frac{(2-a)}{(3-b)} \times \left(-\frac{1}{2}\right) = -1$$

$$\Rightarrow \quad 2 - a = -6 + 2b$$

$$\Rightarrow \quad a + 2b = 8 \qquad \text{...(ii)}$$

Similarly, $BE \perp AC$, we get

$$a + b = 0 \qquad \text{...(iii)}$$

On solving Eqs. (ii) and (iii), we get

$$b = 8 \quad \text{and} \quad a = -8$$

$\therefore$ Points (a, b) is $(-8, 8)$.

JEE SCANNER

Example Similar to PYQ Asked in JEE Main 2023

If (α, β) is the orthocentre of the ΔABC with vertices $A(2, -5)$, $B(-3, 2)$ and $C(5, 6)$, then $\beta - 3\alpha$ is equal to

(a) $\dfrac{159}{19}$ (b) $\dfrac{101}{19}$ (c) $\dfrac{105}{19}$ (d) $\dfrac{111}{19}$

Sol. (b) Let $O(\alpha, \beta)$ be the orthocentre of the ΔABC.

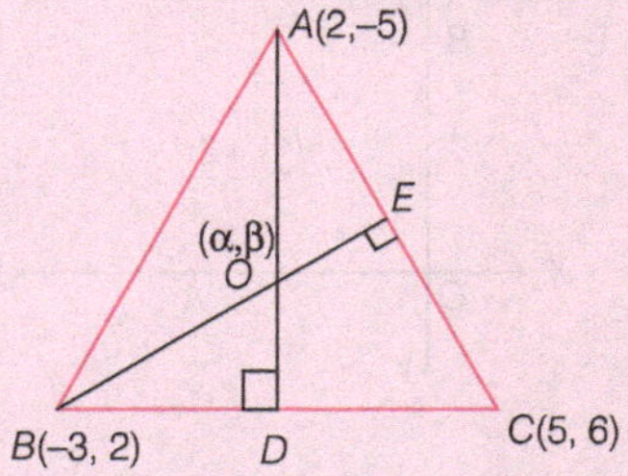

$$m_{AD} = \frac{-1}{m_{BC}} = -2 \qquad \left[\because m_{BC} = \frac{6-2}{5+3} = \frac{1}{2}\right]$$

$$m_{AC} = \frac{6+5}{5-2} = \frac{11}{3},\ m_{BE} = \frac{-3}{11}.$$

$$AD : (y+5) = -2(x-2) \Rightarrow 2x + y + 1 = 0 \qquad \text{...(i)}$$

$$BE : (y-2) = \frac{-3}{11}(x+3) \Rightarrow 3x + 11y - 13 = 0 \qquad \text{...(ii)}$$

From Eq. (ii), $\quad x = \dfrac{-11y + 13}{3}$

On putting the value of x in Eq. (i), we get $y = \dfrac{29}{19}$

$$\Rightarrow \quad x = \frac{-72}{57} \text{ and } y = \frac{29}{19}$$

$$\therefore \quad \text{Orthocentre } (\alpha, \beta) = \left(\frac{-72}{57}, \frac{29}{19}\right)$$

$$\therefore \quad \beta - 3\alpha = \frac{29}{19} - 3\left(\frac{-72}{57}\right) = \frac{29}{19} + \frac{72}{19} = \frac{101}{19}$$

Skill Builder

If (p, q) is the orthocentre of the ΔPQR with vertices $P(7, -2)$, $Q(-5, 3)$ and $R(9, 7)$, then $59(p + q)$ is

(a) 580 (b) 400

(c) 380 (d) 581

For Sol.

■ **For more practice** See Q.16 of Milestone Practice 2.3.

Example 96. A variable straight line through the point of intersection of the lines $\frac{x}{a}+\frac{y}{b}=1$ and $\frac{x}{b}+\frac{y}{a}=1$ meets the coordinate axes at A and B. Find the locus of the mid-point of AB.

Sol. Any line through the point of intersection of given lines is

$$\left(\frac{x}{a}+\frac{y}{b}-1\right)+\lambda\left(\frac{x}{b}+\frac{y}{a}-1\right)=0$$

$$\Rightarrow \quad x\left(\frac{1}{a}+\frac{\lambda}{b}\right)+y\left(\frac{1}{b}+\frac{\lambda}{a}\right)=(1+\lambda)$$

$$\Rightarrow \quad x\left(\frac{b+a\lambda}{ab}\right)+y\left(\frac{a+b\lambda}{ab}\right)=(1+\lambda)$$

$$\Rightarrow \quad \frac{x}{\left\{\frac{ab(1+\lambda)}{b+a\lambda}\right\}}+\frac{y}{\left\{\frac{ab(1+\lambda)}{a+b\lambda}\right\}}=1$$

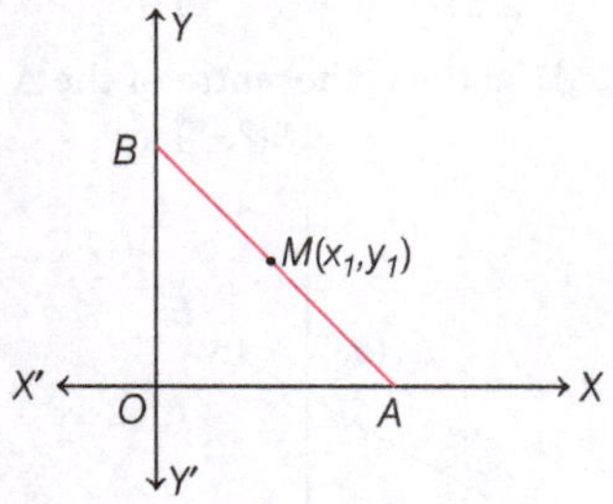

This meets the X-axis at $A\equiv\left(\frac{ab(1+\lambda)}{b+a\lambda},0\right)$

and meets the Y-axis at $B\equiv\left(0,\frac{ab(1+\lambda)}{a+b\lambda}\right)$.

Let the mid-point of AB is $M(x_1, y_1)$, then

$$x_1=\frac{ab(1+\lambda)}{2(b+a\lambda)}$$

and $$y_1=\frac{ab(1+\lambda)}{2(a+b\lambda)}$$

$$\therefore \quad \frac{1}{x_1}+\frac{1}{y_1}=\frac{2(b+a\lambda)}{ab(1+\lambda)}+\frac{2(a+b\lambda)}{ab(1+\lambda)}$$

$$=\frac{2}{ab(1+\lambda)}(b+a\lambda+a+b\lambda)$$

$$=\frac{2}{ab(1+\lambda)}(a+b)(1+\lambda)$$

$$\Rightarrow \quad \frac{(x_1+y_1)}{x_1y_1}=\frac{2(a+b)}{ab}$$

$$\Rightarrow \quad 2x_1y_1(a+b)=ab(x_1+y_1)$$

Hence, the locus of mid-point of AB is

$$2xy(a+b)=ab(x+y).$$

Example 97. If the lines $ax+by+p=0$, $x\cos\alpha+y\sin\alpha-p=0$ $(p\neq 0)$ and $x\sin\alpha-y\cos\alpha=0$ are concurrent and the first two lines include an angle $\frac{\pi}{4}$, then find a^2+b^2.

Sol. Since, the given lines are concurrent

$$\therefore \quad \begin{vmatrix} a & b & p \\ \cos\alpha & \sin\alpha & -p \\ \sin\alpha & -\cos\alpha & 0 \end{vmatrix}=0$$

$$\Rightarrow \quad a\cos\alpha+b\sin\alpha+1=0 \quad \text{...(i)}$$

As $ax+by+p=0$ and $x\cos\alpha+y\sin\alpha-p=0$ include an angle $\frac{\pi}{4}$.

$\therefore$ Slope of $ax+by+p=0$, $m_1=-\frac{a}{b}$

and slope of $x\cos\alpha+y\sin\alpha-p=0$, $m_2=\frac{-\cos\alpha}{\sin\alpha}$

$$\tan\theta=\left|\frac{m_1-m_2}{1+m_1m_2}\right|$$

$$\Rightarrow \quad \tan\frac{\pi}{4}=\left|\frac{\frac{-a}{b}+\frac{\cos\alpha}{\sin\alpha}}{1+\frac{a\cos\alpha}{b\sin\alpha}}\right|$$

$$\Rightarrow \quad 1=\left|\frac{\frac{-a}{b}+\frac{\cos\alpha}{\sin\alpha}}{1+\frac{a\cos\alpha}{b\sin\alpha}}\right|$$

$$\Rightarrow \quad |-a\sin\alpha+b\cos\alpha|=|b\sin\alpha+a\cos\alpha|$$

$$|-a\sin\alpha+b\cos\alpha|=1 \quad \text{[from Eq. (i)] ...(ii)}$$

On squaring and adding Eqs. (i) and (ii), we get

$$(a\cos\alpha+b\sin\alpha)^2+(-a\sin\alpha+b\cos\alpha)^2=1+1$$

$$\therefore \quad a^2+b^2=2$$

Milestone Practice 2.3

1. The locus of the point of intersection of lines $x\cos\alpha + y\sin\alpha = a$ and $x \sin \alpha - y \cos \alpha = b$ (α is a parameter) is

(a) $2(x^2 + y^2) = a^2 + b^2$
(b) $x^2 - y^2 = a^2 - b^2$
(c) $x^2 + y^2 = a^2 + b^2$
(d) $x^2 - y^2 = a^2 + b^2$

2. The set of lines $ax + by + c = 0$, where $3a + 2b + 4c = 0$ is concurrent at the point

(a) $\left(\frac{3}{4}, \frac{1}{2}\right)$
(b) $\left(\frac{1}{2}, \frac{3}{4}\right)$
(c) $\left(-\frac{3}{4}, -\frac{1}{2}\right)$
(d) $\left(-\frac{1}{2}, -\frac{3}{4}\right)$

3. If $u \equiv a_1x + b_1y + c_1 = 0$ and $v \equiv a_2x + b_2y + c_2 = 0$ and $\frac{a_1}{a_2} = \frac{b_1}{b_2} = \frac{c_1}{c_2}$, then $u + kv = 0$ represents

(a) $u = 0$
(b) a family of concurrent lines
(c) a family of parallel lines
(d) None of the above

4. The straight lines $x + 2y - 9 = 0, 3x + 5y - 5 = 0$ and $ax + by - 1 = 0$ are concurrent, if the straight line $35x - 22y + 1 = 0$ passes through the point

(a) (a, b)
(b) (b, a)
(c) $(a, -b)$
(d) $(-a, b)$

5. Vertices of a triangle are (3, 4), $(5\cos\theta, 5\sin\theta)$ and $(5\sin\theta, -5\cos\theta)$, where $\theta \in R$. Locus of its orthocentre is

(a) $(x+y-1)^2 + (x-y-7)^2 = 100$
(b) $(x+y-7)^2 + (x-y-1)^2 = 100$
(c) $(x+y-7)^2 + (x+y-1)^2 = 100$
(d) $(x+y-7)^2 + (x-y+1)^2 = 100$

6. ABC is a variable triangle such that A is $(1, 2)$ B and C lie on line $y = x + \lambda$ (where λ is a variable), then locus of the orthocentre of ΔABC is

(a) $(x-1)^2 + y^2 = 4$
(b) $x + y = 3$
(c) $2x - y = 0$
(d) None of these

7. If the equations of three sides of a triangle are $x + y = 1, 3x + 5y = 2$ and $x - y = 0$, then the orthocentre of the triangle lies on the line/lines

(a) $5x - 3y = 1$
(b) $5y - 3x = 1$
(c) $2x - 3y = 1$
(d) $5x - 3y = 2$

8. If the equation of any two diagonals of a regular pentagon belongs to family of lines $(1 + 2\lambda)y - (2 + \lambda)x + 1 - \lambda = 0$ and their lengths are $\sin 36°$, then locus of centre of circle circumscribing the given pentagon (the triangles formed by these diagonals with slides of pentagon have no side common is

(a) $x^2 + y^2 - 2x - 2y + 1 + \sin^2 72° = 0$
(b) $x^2 + y^2 - 2x - 2y + 1 + \cos^2 72° = 0$
(c) $x^2 + y^2 - 2x - 2y + \cos^2 72° = 0$
(d) $x^2 + y^2 - 2x - 2y + \sin^2 72° = 0$

9. Find the equation of the line through the intersection of $2x - 3y + 4 = 0$ and $3x + 4y - 5 = 0$ and perpendicular to $6x - 7y + 8 = 0$

(a) $199y + 120x = 125$
(b) $199y - 120x = 125$
(c) $119x + 102y = 125$
(d) $119x - 102y = 125$

10. If an triangle ABC, $A \equiv (1, 10)$, circumcentre $\equiv \left(-\frac{1}{3}, \frac{2}{3}\right)$ and orthocentre $\equiv \left(\frac{11}{3}, \frac{4}{3}\right)$, then the coordinates of mid-point of side opposite to A is

(a) $\left(1, -\frac{11}{3}\right)$
(b) (1, 5)
(c) (1, −3)
(d) (1, 6)

11. Find the condition on a and b, such that the portion of the line $ax + by - 1 = 0$, intercepted between the lines $ax + y = 0$ and $x + by = 0$ subtends a right angled at the origin.

12. If $\left(2, \frac{a}{5}\right)$ be the circumcentre of a triangle with vertices $A(a, -3)$, $B(a, 9)$ and $C\left(\frac{a}{5}, -3\right)$. Let α denote the circumradius, β denote the area and γ denote the perimeter of ΔABC. Then, find $\gamma + \beta - 2\alpha$.

13. Find the equation of the straight line which passes through the intersection of the lines $x - y - 1 = 0$ and $2x - 3y + 1 = 0$ and is parallel to (i) X-axis (ii) Y-axis (iii) $3x + 4y = 14$.

14. If $6a^2 - 3b^2 - c^2 + 7ab - ac + 4bc = 0$, then family of lines $ax + by + c = 0\,(|a| + |b| \neq 0)$ is concurrent at which points.

15. If the orthocentre of the Δ formed by $2x + 3y - 1 = 0$, $x + 2y - 1 = 0$ and $ax + by - 1 = 0$ is at origin, then find $\frac{b-a}{4}$.

16. A straight line passes through the point of intersection $x - 2y - 2 = 0$ and $2x - by - 6 = 0$ and the origin, then find the complete set of values of b for which the acute angle between this line and $y = 0$ is less than 45°.

Answer Key

1. (c)	**2.** (a)	**3.** (a)	**4.** (a)	**5.** (d)	6. (b)
7. (a,b)	**8.** (a)	**9.** (c)	**10.** (a)	**11.** $a + b = 0$	
12. (94)	**13.** $3x + 4y = 24$	**14.** $(3, -1)$ and $(-2, -3)$		**15.** (4)	
16. $b \in (-\infty, 4) \cup (4, 5) \cup (7, \infty)$					

For Detailed Solution

Milestone 4 Equation of Angle Bisector of Lines

- Equation of Straight line Passing Through a Given Point and Making a Angle with a Given Line
- A Line Equally Inclined with Two Lines • Equation of the Bisectors

2.14 Equations of Straight Lines Passing Through a Given Point and Making a Given Angle with a Given Line

Theorem Prove that the equations of the straight lines which pass through a given point (x_1, y_1) and make a given angle α with the given straight line $y = mx + c$ are

$$y - y_1 = \tan(\theta \pm \alpha)(x - x_1)$$

where, $m = \tan\theta$.

Proof Let AB be the given line which makes an angle θ with X-axis.

$\therefore \quad m = \tan\theta$

Let CD and EF are two required lines which make angle α with the given line.

Let these lines meet the given line AB at Q and R, respectively.

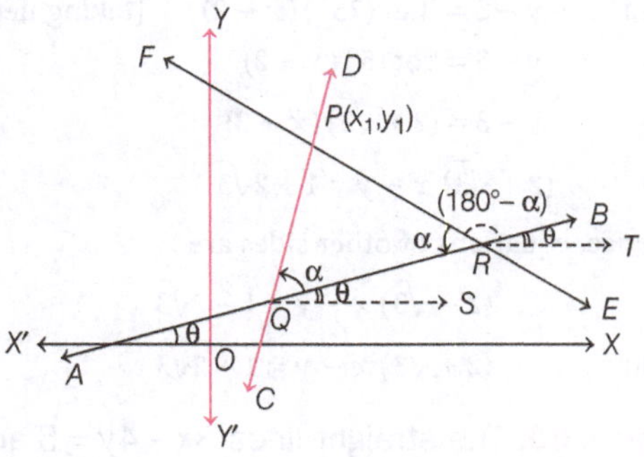

$\therefore \quad \angle DQS = \angle PQR + \angle RQS = (\alpha + \theta)$

$\therefore$ Equation of line CD is

$$y - y_1 = \tan(\theta + \alpha)(x - x_1) \qquad \text{...(i)}$$

and $\quad \angle FRT = \angle FRB + \angle BRT$

$$= 180^\circ - \alpha + \theta$$

$$= 180^\circ + (\theta - \alpha)$$

$\therefore$ Equation of line EF is

$$y - y_1 = \tan(180^\circ + \theta - \alpha)(x - x_1)$$

or $\quad y - y_1 = \tan(\theta - \alpha)(x - x_1) \qquad \text{...(ii)}$

From Eqs. (i) and (ii), we get

$$y - y_1 = \tan(\theta \pm \alpha)(x - x_1)$$

These are the equations of the two required lines.

Example 98. Find the equations of the straight lines passing through the point $(2, 3)$ and inclined at $\pi/4$ radians to the line $2x + 3y = 5$.

Sol. Let the line $2x + 3y = 5$ make an angle θ with positive X-axis.

Then, $\quad \tan\theta = -\frac{2}{3}$

Now, $\quad \tan\theta \cdot \tan\frac{\pi}{4} = -\frac{2}{3} \times 1 = -\frac{2}{3} \neq \pm 1$

Slopes of required lines are

$$\tan\left(\theta + \frac{\pi}{4}\right) \text{ and } \tan\left(\theta - \frac{\pi}{4}\right).$$

$$\therefore \quad \tan\left(\theta + \frac{\pi}{4}\right) = \frac{\tan\theta + \tan\left(\frac{\pi}{4}\right)}{1 - \tan\theta \tan\left(\frac{\pi}{4}\right)} = \frac{\left(-\frac{2}{3}\right) + 1}{1 - \left(-\frac{2}{3}\right)(1)} = \frac{1}{5}$$

and $$\tan\left(\theta - \frac{\pi}{4}\right) = \frac{\tan\theta - \tan\left(\frac{\pi}{4}\right)}{1 + \tan\theta \tan\left(\frac{\pi}{4}\right)}$$

$$= \frac{\left(-\frac{2}{3}\right) - 1}{1 + \left(-\frac{2}{3}\right)(1)} = -5$$

$\therefore$ Equations of required lines are

$$y - 3 = \frac{1}{5}(x - 2) \text{ and } y - 3 = -5(x - 2)$$

i.e. $\quad x - 5y + 13 = 0$ and $5x + y - 13 = 0$

JEE SCANNER

Example Similar to PYQ Asked in JEE Main 2023

The equation of one of the straight line which passes through the point (2, 3) and makes an angle of $\tan^{-1}(\sqrt{3})$ *with the straight line* $3x+y+1=0$ *is* $(\lambda+5\sqrt{3})x-\beta y+(27-10\sqrt{3})=0$*, then* $\lambda+\beta$ *is equal to ....*

Sol. (19) Let m = slope of the required line

$\therefore$ Equation of required line is $y-3=m(x-2)$ ...(i)

Given equation of line is $3x+y+1=0$ ...(ii)

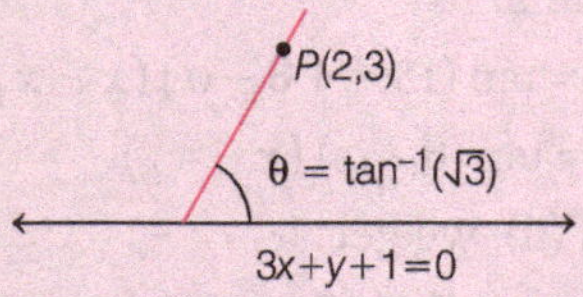

$\because$ Angle between Eqs. (i) and (ii) is $\tan^{-1}(\sqrt{3})$.

$$\Rightarrow \quad \tan\theta=\sqrt{3}$$

$$\Rightarrow \quad \left|\frac{m+3}{1-3m}\right|=\sqrt{3}$$

$$\Rightarrow \quad m+3=\pm\sqrt{3}(1-3m)$$

On squaring both sides, we get

$$m^2+6m+9=3(1+9m^2-6m)$$

$$\Rightarrow \quad 13m^2-12m-3=0$$

$$\Rightarrow \quad m=\frac{12\pm\sqrt{144+156}}{26}=\frac{6\pm5\sqrt{3}}{13}$$

For $m=\dfrac{6+5\sqrt{3}}{13}$ and point (2, 3), equation of line will be

$$y-3=\frac{6+5\sqrt{3}}{13}(x-2),$$

$$\Rightarrow \quad (6+5\sqrt{3})x-13y+(27-10\sqrt{3})=0 \quad ...(iii)$$

For $m=\dfrac{6-5\sqrt{3}}{13}$ and point (2, 3), equation of line will be

$$y-3=\frac{6-5\sqrt{3}}{13}(x-2)$$

$$\Rightarrow \quad (6-5\sqrt{3})x-13y+(27+10\sqrt{3})=0 \quad ...(iv)$$

$\therefore$ From Eq. (iii), $\lambda=6, \beta=13 \Rightarrow \lambda+\beta=19$

Skill Builder

The equation of one of the straight line which passes through the point (1, 5) and makes an angle of $\tan^{-1}(\sqrt{2})$ with the straight line $2x-y+1=0$ is $(\alpha+5\sqrt{2})x+\beta y-(\lambda+5\sqrt{2})=0$, then the value of $\alpha+\beta+\lambda$ is ......

For Sol.

■ **For more practice** See Q.13 of Milestone Practice 2.4.

Example 99. A vertex of an equilateral triangle is (2, 3) and the opposite side is $x+y=2$. Find the equations of the other sides.

Sol. Let $A(2, 3)$ be one vertex and $x+y=2$ be the opposite side of an equilateral triangle. Clearly, remaining two sides pass through the point $A(2, 3)$ and make an angle 60° with $x+y=2$.

$\because$ Slope of $x+y=2$ is -1

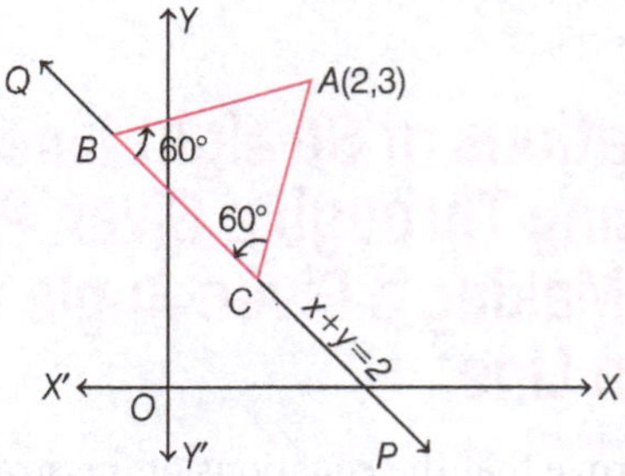

Let $\tan\theta=-1$

$\therefore \quad \theta=135°$

$\therefore$ Equations of the other two sides are

$$y-3=\tan(135°\pm60°)(x-2)$$

i.e. sides are

$$y-3=\tan(195°)(x-2) \quad \text{[taking positive sign]}$$

$$\Rightarrow \quad y-3=\tan(180°+15°)(x-2)$$

$$\Rightarrow \quad y-3=\tan15°(x-2)$$

$$\Rightarrow \quad y-3=(2-\sqrt{3})(x-2)$$

$$\Rightarrow \quad (2-\sqrt{3})x-y=1-2\sqrt{3}$$

and $$y-3=\tan(75°)(x-2) \quad \text{[taking negative sign]}$$

$$\Rightarrow \quad y-3=\cot15°(x-2)$$

$$\Rightarrow \quad y-3=(2+\sqrt{3})(x-2)$$

$$\Rightarrow \quad (2+\sqrt{3})x-y=1+2\sqrt{3}$$

Hence, equations of other sides are

$$(2-\sqrt{3})x-y=1-2\sqrt{3}$$

and $$(2+\sqrt{3})x-y=1+2\sqrt{3}$$

Example 100. The straight lines $3x+4y=5$ and $4x-3y=15$ intersect at a point A. On these lines, the points B and C are chosen, so that $AB=AC$. Find the possible equations of the line BC passing through the point (1, 2).

Sol. Clearly, $\angle BAC=90°$

$\because \quad AB=AC$

$\therefore \quad \angle ABC=\angle BCA=45° \Rightarrow \alpha=45°$

$\because$ Slope of $3x+4y=5$ is $-\dfrac{3}{4}$.

Let $\tan\theta = -\dfrac{3}{4}$

So, possible equations of BC are given by

$$y - 2 = \tan(\theta \pm \alpha)(x - 1)$$

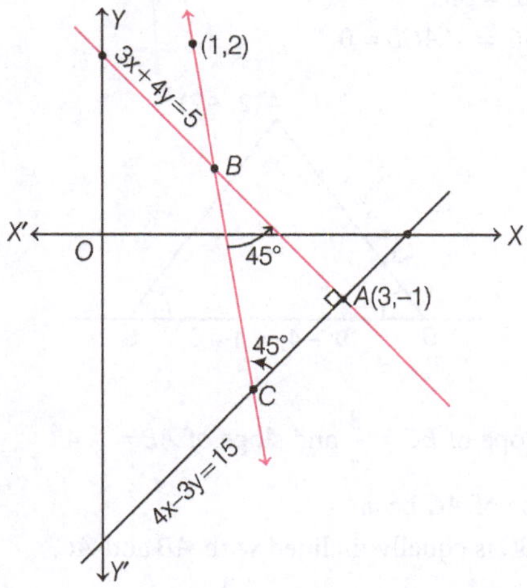

$$\Rightarrow \quad y - 2 = \left(\frac{\tan\theta \pm \tan\alpha}{1 \mp \tan\theta\tan\alpha}\right)(x - 1)$$

$$\Rightarrow \quad y - 2 = \left(\frac{-\frac{3}{4} \pm 1}{1 \mp \left(-\frac{3}{4}\right)(1)}\right)(x - 1)$$

$$\Rightarrow \quad y - 2 = \left(\frac{-3 \pm 4}{4 \mp (-3)}\right)(x - 1)$$

$$\Rightarrow \quad y - 2 = \frac{1}{4 - (-3)}(x - 1) \qquad \text{[taking upper sign]}$$

or $\quad x - 7y + 13 = 0$

and $\quad y - 2 = \dfrac{(-3 - 4)}{(4 + (-3))}(x - 1) \qquad$ [taking below sign]

or $\;7x + y - 9 = 0$

Hence, possible equation of the line BC are $x - 7y + 13 = 0$ and $7x + y - 9 = 0$

2.15 A Line Equally Inclined with Two Lines

Theorem If two lines with slopes m_1 and m_2 be equally inclined to a line with slope m, then

$$\left(\frac{m_1 - m}{1 + mm_1}\right) = -\left(\frac{m_2 - m}{1 + mm_2}\right)$$

Proof Let two lines of slopes be m_1 and m_2 intersecting at a point P.

Let $\quad \angle CPA = \angle BPC = \theta$

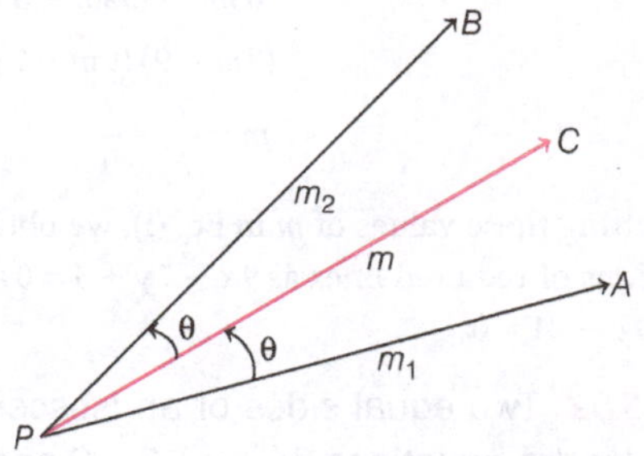

$$\therefore \quad \tan(\angle CPA) = \left(\frac{m - m_1}{1 + mm_1}\right)$$

or $\quad \tan\theta = \left(\dfrac{m - m_1}{1 + mm_1}\right) \qquad [\because m > m_1]$ ...(i)

and $\quad \tan(\angle BPC) = \left(\dfrac{m_2 - m}{1 + m_2 m}\right)$

or $\quad \tan\theta = \left(\dfrac{m_2 - m}{1 + m_2 m}\right) \qquad [\because m_2 > m]$ ... (ii)

From Eqs. (i) and (ii), we get

$$\left(\frac{m - m_1}{1 + mm_1}\right) = \left(\frac{m_2 - m}{1 + m_2 m}\right) \text{ or } \left(\frac{m_1 - m}{1 + mm_1}\right) = -\left(\frac{m_2 - m}{1 + mm_2}\right)$$

JEE Focus Points

1. The above equation gives two values of m which are the slopes of the lines parallel to the bisectors of the angles between the two given lines.
2. Sign of m in both brackets is same.

Example 101. Find the equations of the straight lines passing through the point $(2, 3)$ and equally inclined to the lines $3x - 4y - 7 = 0$ and $12x - 5y + 6 = 0$.

Sol. Let m be the slope of the required line. Then, its equation is

$$y - 3 = m(x - 2) \qquad \text{...(i)}$$

It is given that line (i) is equally inclined to the lines

$3x - 4y - 7 = 0$ and $12x - 5y + 6 = 0$, then

$$\Rightarrow \quad \left(\frac{\frac{3}{4} - m}{1 + \frac{3}{4}m}\right) = -\left(\frac{\frac{12}{5} - m}{1 + \frac{12}{5}m}\right)$$

$\left[\because \text{ slope of } 3x - 4y - 7 = 0 \text{ is } \dfrac{3}{4} \text{ and slope of } 12x - 5y + 6 = 0 \text{ is } \dfrac{12}{5}\right]$

$$\Rightarrow \quad \left(\frac{3 - 4m}{4 + 3m}\right) = -\left(\frac{12 - 5m}{5 + 12m}\right)$$

$\Rightarrow \quad (3-4m)(5+12m)+(4+3m)(12-5m)=0$

$\Rightarrow \quad 63m^2-32m-63=0$

$\Rightarrow \quad (7m-9)(9m+7)=0$

$\therefore \quad m=\frac{9}{7},-\frac{7}{9}$

On putting these values of m in Eq. (i), we obtain the equations of required lines as $9x-7y+3=0$ and $7x+9y-41=0$.

Example 102. Two equal sides of an isosceles triangle are given by the equations $7x-y+3=0$ and $x+y-3=0$ and its third side passes through the point $(1,-10)$. Determine the equation of the third side.

Sol. Let m be the slope of BC, since $AB=AC$.

Therefore, BC makes equal angles with AB and AC.

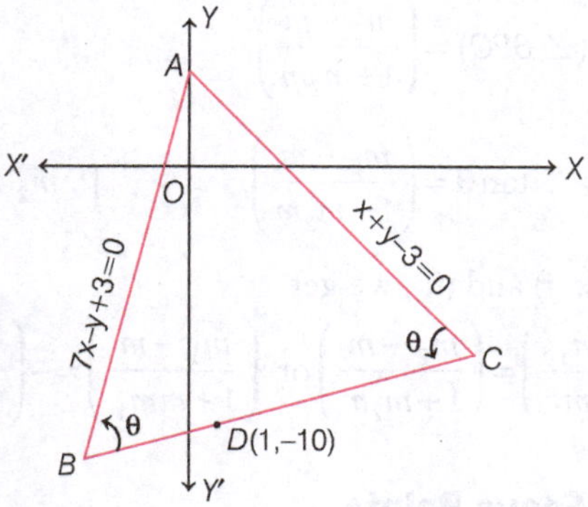

Then, $\left(\frac{7-m}{1+7m}\right)=-\left(\frac{-1-m}{1+(-1)m}\right)$

$\Rightarrow (7-m)(1-m)-(1+7m)(1+m)=0$

$\Rightarrow \quad 6m^2+16m-6=0$

$\Rightarrow \quad 3m^2+8m-3=0$

$\Rightarrow \quad (3m-1)(m+3)=0$

$\Rightarrow \quad m=\frac{1}{3},-3$

Equation of third side BC is $y+10=m(x-1)$

i.e. $\quad y+10=\frac{1}{3}(x-1)$

and $\quad y+10=-3(x-1)$

or $\quad x-3y-31=0$

and $\quad 3x+y+7=0$

Example 103. A line $4x+y=1$ through the point $A(2,-7)$ meets the line BC whose equation is $3x-4y+1=0$ at the point B. If $AB=AC$, then find the equation of the line AC.

Sol. Since, $AB=AC$

$\therefore \angle ABC=\angle ACB=\theta$ [say]

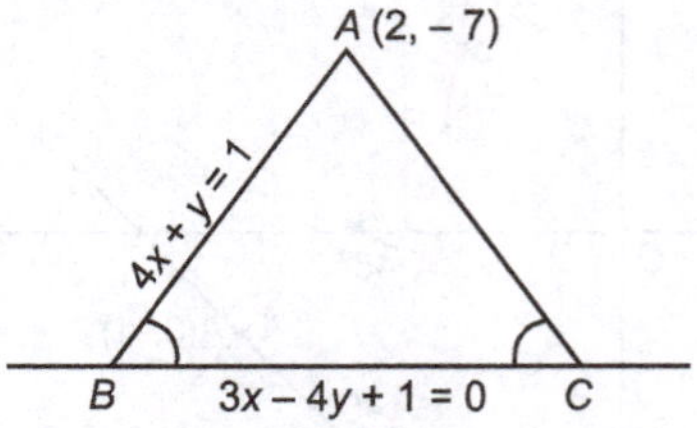

Now, slope of $BC=\frac{3}{4}$ and slope of $AB=-4$

Let slope of AC be m.

Since, BC is equally inclined with AB and AC.

$$\frac{\frac{3}{4}+4}{1-4\cdot\frac{3}{4}}=\frac{m-\frac{3}{4}}{1+\frac{3}{4}m}$$

$\Rightarrow \quad \frac{19}{8}=\frac{3-4m}{4+3m}$

$\Rightarrow \quad 76+57m=24-32m$

$\Rightarrow \quad m=-\frac{52}{89}$

$\therefore$ Equation of AC is $(y+7)=-\frac{52}{89}(x-2)$

$\Rightarrow \quad 52x+89y+519=0$

2.16 Equation of the Bisectors

Theorem Prove that the equation of the bisectors of the angles between the lines

$$a_1x+b_1y+c_1=0 \quad \text{and} \quad a_2x+b_2y+c_2=0$$

are given by $\quad \frac{(a_1x+b_1y+c_1)}{\sqrt{(a_1^2+b_1^2)}}=\pm\frac{(a_2x+b_2y+c_2)}{\sqrt{(a_2^2+b_2^2)}}$

Proof Let the given lines be AA' and BB' whose equations are

$a_1x+b_1y+c_1=0$ ...(i)

and $\quad a_2x+b_2y+c_2=0$ ...(ii)

Since, bisectors of the angles between the two lines are the locus of a point which moves in a plane such that whose distance from two lines are equal.

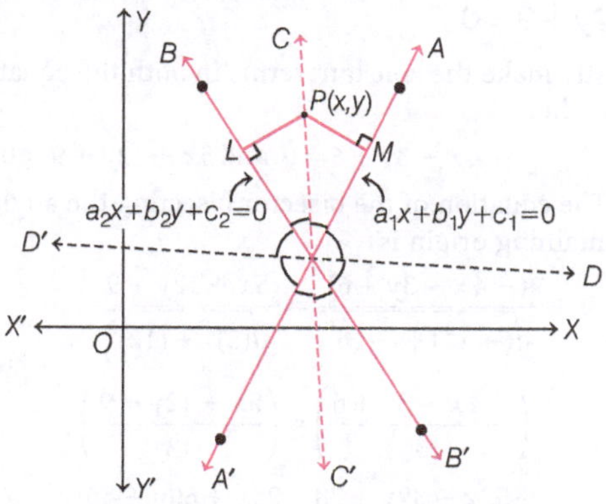

Let CC' and DD' be the two bisectors of the angle between the lines AA' and BB'. Let $P(x, y)$ be any point on CC', then length of the perpendicular from P on AA'

= length of the perpendicular from P on BB'

$$\therefore \quad \frac{|a_1x+b_1y+c_1|}{\sqrt{(a_1^2+b_1^2)}} = \frac{|a_2x+b_2y+c_2|}{\sqrt{(a_2^2+b_2^2)}}$$

or $$\frac{(a_1x+b_1y+c_1)}{\sqrt{(a_1^2+b_1^2)}} = \pm\frac{(a_2x+b_2y+c_2)}{\sqrt{(a_2^2+b_2^2)}}$$

These are the required equations of the bisectors.

JEE SPIKE

The two bisectors are perpendicular to each other.

Example 104. Find the equations of the bisectors of the angles between the straight lines $3x-4y+7=0$ and $12x+5y-2=0$.

Sol. The equations of the bisectors of the angles between $3x-4y+7=0$ and $12x+5y-2=0$ are

$$\frac{(3x-4y+7)}{\sqrt{(3)^2+(-4)^2}} = \pm\frac{(12x+5y-2)}{\sqrt{(12)^2+(5)^2}}$$

or $$\frac{(3x-4y+7)}{5} = \pm\frac{(12x+5y-2)}{13}$$

or $$(39x-52y+91) = \pm(60x+25y-10)$$

On taking the positive sign, we get

$21x+77y-101=0$ as the first bisector.

On taking the negative sign, we get $99x-77y+81=0$ as the second bisector.

Example 105. Two sides of a rhombus $ABCD$ are parallel to the lines $y=x+2$ and $y=7x+3$. If the diagonals of the rhombus intersect at the point $(1, 2)$ and the vertex A is on Y-axis. Find the equations of diagonals and hence, find the possible coordinates of A.

Sol. Let the coordinates of A be $(0, a)$.

As the sides of the rhombus are parallel to line $y=x+2$ and $y=7x+3$, the diagonal of the rhombus are parallel to the bisectors of the angle between given lines.

Equation of the bisectors of the angles between the lines $y=x+2$ and $y=7x+3$ are

$$\frac{y-x-2}{\sqrt{1+1}} = \pm\frac{y-7x-3}{\sqrt{1+49}} \quad \text{or} \quad 5(y-x-2) = \pm(y-7x-3)$$

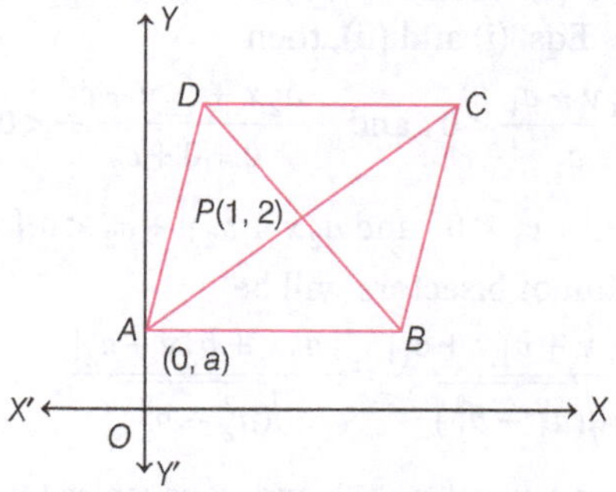

Thus, the diagonals are parallel to lines $2x+4y-7=0$ and $12x-6y+13=0$.

Let P be the point of intersection of diagonals $P \equiv (1, 2)$.

Equation of bisectors will be $(y-2) = -\frac{1}{2}(x-1)$ and $(y-2) = 2(x-1)$

i.e. $\quad x+2y-5=0$ and $2x-y=0$.

Therefore, slope of AP is either 2 or $\frac{-1}{2}$

$$\therefore \quad \frac{a-2}{0-1} = 2 \text{ or } -\frac{1}{2} \Rightarrow a = 0, \frac{5}{2}$$

Hence, the possible coordinates of A are $(0, 0)$ and $\left(0, \frac{5}{2}\right)$.

Bisector of the Angle Containing the Origin

Let equations of lines be

$$a_1x+b_1y+c_1=0 \quad \text{...(i)}$$
$$a_2x+b_2y+c_2=0 \quad \text{...(ii)}$$

where c_1 and c_2 are positive.

Let $P(x, y)$ be taken on the bisector of the angle which contains the origin.

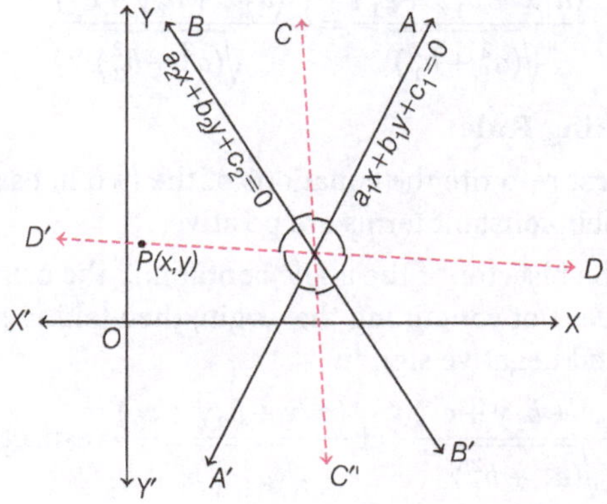

Let $P(x, y)$ lies on DD', then either $O(0,0)$ and $P(x, y)$ will lie on the same side of the two lines Eqs. (i) and (ii), then

$$\frac{a_1x+b_1y+c_1}{0+0+c_1}>0 \text{ and } \frac{a_2x+b_2y+c_2}{0+0+c_2}>0$$

or $\quad a_1x+b_1y+c_1>0$

and $\quad a_2x+b_2y+c_2>0 \qquad [\because c_1, c_2>0]$

If the origin $O(0,0)$ and $P(x, y)$ lie on the opposite side of the two lines Eqs. (i) and (ii), then

$$\frac{a_1x+b_1y+c_1}{0+0+c_1}<0 \text{ and } \frac{a_2x+b_2y+c_2}{0+0+c_2}<0$$

or $\quad a_1x+b_1y+c_1<0$ and $a_2x+b_2y+c_2<0 \; [\because c_1, c_2>0]$

Then, equation of bisectors will be

$$\frac{|a_1x+b_1y+c_1|}{\sqrt{(a_1^2+b_1^2)}}=\frac{|a_2x+b_2y+c_2|}{\sqrt{(a_2^2+b_2^2)}}$$

Case I If $a_1x+b_1y+c_1>0$ and $a_2x+b_2y+c_2>0$,

then $\quad \dfrac{(a_1x+b_1y+c_1)}{\sqrt{(a_1^2+b_1^2)}}=\dfrac{(a_2x+b_2y+c_2)}{\sqrt{(a_2^2+b_2^2)}}$

Case II If $a_1x+b_1y+c_1<0$ and $a_2x+b_2y+c_2<0$,

then $\quad -\dfrac{(a_1x+b_1y+c_1)}{\sqrt{(a_1^2+b_1^2)}}=-\dfrac{(a_2x+b_2y+c_2)}{\sqrt{(a_2^2+b_2^2)}}$

i.e. $\quad \dfrac{(a_1x+b_1y+c_1)}{\sqrt{(a_1^2+b_1^2)}}=\dfrac{(a_2x+b_2y+c_2)}{\sqrt{(a_2^2+b_2^2)}}$

Thus, the equation of the bisector containing the origin, when c_1 and c_2 are positive is

$$\frac{(a_1x+b_1y+c_1)}{\sqrt{(a_1^2+b_1^2)}}=\frac{(a_2x+b_2y+c_2)}{\sqrt{(a_2^2+b_2^2)}}$$

and equation of the bisector of the angle between the lines

$$a_1x+b_1y+c_1=0 \quad \text{and} \quad a_2x+b_2y+c_2=0$$

which does not contain the origin when c_1 and c_2 are positive is

$$\frac{(a_1x+b_1y+c_1)}{\sqrt{(a_1^2+b_1^2)}}=-\frac{(a_2x+b_2y+c_2)}{\sqrt{(a_2^2+b_2^2)}}$$

Working Rule

(i) First re-write the equations of the two lines so that their constant terms are positive.

(ii) The bisector of the angle containing the origin and does not containing the origin, then taking positive and negative sign in

$$\frac{(a_1x+b_1y+c_1)}{\sqrt{(a_1^2+b_1^2)}}=\pm\frac{(a_2x+b_2y+c_2)}{\sqrt{(a_2^2+b_2^2)}} \text{ respectively.}$$

Example 106. Find the equations of angular bisector bisecting the angle containing the origin and not containing the origin of the lines $4x+3y-6=0$ and $5x+12y+9=0$.

Sol. Firstly make the constant terms in both the equation positive, then

$$-4x-3y+6=0 \text{ and } 5x+12y+9=0$$

$\therefore$ The equation of the bisector bisecting the angle containing origin is

$$\frac{(-4x-3y+6)}{\sqrt{(-4^2)+(-3)^2}}=\frac{(5x+12y+9)}{\sqrt{(5)^2+(12)^2}}$$

$$\Rightarrow \left(\frac{-4x-3y+6}{5}\right)=\left(\frac{5x+12y+9}{13}\right)$$

$$\Rightarrow -52x-39y+78=25x+60y+45$$

$$\Rightarrow 77x+99y-33=0 \text{ or } 7x+9y-3=0$$

and the equation of the bisector bisecting the angle not containing origin is

$$\frac{(-4x-3y+6)}{\sqrt{(-4)^2+(-3)^2)}}=-\frac{(5x+12y+9)}{\sqrt{(5^2)+(12)^2}}$$

$$\Rightarrow \left(\frac{-4x-3y+6}{5}\right)=-\left(\frac{5x+12y+9}{13}\right)$$

$$\Rightarrow -52x-39y+78=-25x-60y-45$$

$$\Rightarrow 27x-21y-123=0 \text{ or } 9x-7y-41=0$$

Equation of that Bisector of the Angle between Two Lines which Contains a Given Point

Let the equations of the two lines be

$$a_1x+b_1y+c_1=0 \qquad \text{...(i)}$$

and $$a_2x+b_2y+c_2=0 \qquad \text{...(ii)}$$

The equation of the bisector of the angle between the two lines containing the points (h, k) will be

$$\frac{(a_1x+b_1y+c_1)}{\sqrt{(a_1^2+b_1^2)}}=\frac{(a_2x+b_2y+c_2)}{\sqrt{(a_2^2+b_2^2)}}$$

or $$\frac{(a_1x+b_1y+c_1)}{\sqrt{(a_1^2+b_1^2)}}=-\frac{(a_2x+b_2y+c_2)}{\sqrt{(a_2^2+b_2^2)}}$$

according as $a_1h+b_1k+c_1$ and $a_2h+b_2k+c_2$ are of the same sign or opposite sign.

Example 107. Find the bisector of the angle between the lines $2x+y-6=0$ and $2x-4y+7=0$ which contains the point (1, 2).

Sol. Value of $2x+y-6$ at (1, 2) is -2 [negative]

and value of $2x-4y+7$ at (1, 2) is 1 [positive]

i.e. opposite sign.

$\therefore$ Equation of bisector containing the point (1, 2) is

$$\frac{(2x + y - 6)}{\sqrt{(2^2 + 1^2)}} = -\frac{(2x - 4y + 7)}{\sqrt{(2)^2 + (-4)^2}}$$

$\Rightarrow \quad 2(2x + y - 6) + (2x - 4y + 7) = 0$

or $\quad 6x - 2y - 5 = 0$

How to Distinguish the Acute (Internal) and Obtuse (External) Angle Bisectors?

Let the equations of the two lines be

$$a_1 x + b_1 y + c_1 = 0 \quad \text{...(i)}$$

and $$a_2 x + b_2 y + c_2 = 0 \quad \text{...(ii)}$$

where, $c_1 > 0, c_2 > 0$.

$\because$ Equations of bisectors are

$$\frac{(a_1 x + b_1 y + c_1)}{\sqrt{(a_1^2 + b_1^2)}} = \pm \frac{(a_2 x + b_2 y + c_2)}{\sqrt{(a_2^2 + b_2^2)}} \quad \text{...(iii)}$$

when Eq. (iii) be simplified, let the bisectors be

$$p_1 x + q_1 y + r_1 = 0 \quad \text{...(iv)}$$

and $$p_2 x + q_2 y + r_2 = 0 \quad \text{...(v)}$$

Since, the two bisectors are at right angles, the angle α between the acute (internal) bisector and any one of the given lines must lie between 0 and 45° i.e. $0 < \alpha < 45°$.

$\therefore \quad 0 < \tan \alpha < 1$

If m_1 and m_2 are the slopes of Eqs. (i) and (iv) respectively.

Then, $\quad m_1 = -\frac{a_1}{b_1}$ and $m_2 = -\frac{p_1}{q_1}$

$$\therefore \quad \tan \alpha = \left| \frac{m_1 - m_2}{1 + m_1 m_2} \right|$$

$$= \left| \frac{\left(-\frac{a_1}{b_1}\right) - \left(-\frac{p_1}{q_1}\right)}{1 + \left(-\frac{a_1}{b_1}\right)\left(-\frac{p_1}{q_1}\right)} \right| = \left| \frac{a_1 q_1 - b_1 p_1}{b_1 q_1 + a_1 p_1} \right|$$

Hence, if $0 < \tan \alpha < 1$, $p_1 x + q_1 y + r_1 = 0$ is the acute (internal) bisector and if $\tan \alpha > 1$, $p_2 x + q_2 y + r_2 = 0$ is the obtuse (external) bisector.

Shortcut Method for finding Acute (Internal) and Obtuse (External) Angle Bisectors

Let the equations of the two lines be

$$a_1 x + b_1 y + c_1 = 0$$
$$a_2 x + b_2 y + c_2 = 0$$

On taking, $c_1 > 0, c_2 > 0$ and $a_1 b_2 \neq a_2 b_1$.

Then, equations of the bisectors are

$$\frac{(a_1 x + b_1 y + c_1)}{\sqrt{(a_1^2 + b_1^2)}} = \pm \frac{(a_2 x` + b_2 y + c_2)}{\sqrt{(a_2^2 + b_2^2)}}$$

Conditions	Acute angle bisector	Obtuse angle bisector
$a_1 a_2 + b_1 b_2 > 0$	$-$	$+$
$a_1 a_2 + b_1 b_2 < 0$	$+$	$-$

JEE Focus Points

1. If $a_1 a_2 + b_1 b_2 = 0$, then the Bisectors are perpendiculars to each other.
2. Positive sign gives the bisector of the angle containing origin.
3. If $a_1 a_2 + b_1 b_2 > 0$, then the origin lies in obtuse angle and if $a_1 a_2 + b_1 b_2 < 0$, then the origin lies in acute angle.

Concept Inside Video

Example 108. Find the equation of the bisector of the obtuse angle between the lines $3x - 4y + 7 = 0$ and $12x + 5y - 2 = 0$.

Sol. Firstly, make the constant terms (c_1, c_2) positive

$3x - 4y + 7 = 0$

and $-12x - 5y + 2 = 0$

$\because \quad a_1 a_2 + b_1 b_2 = (3)(-12) + (-4)(-5) = -36 + 20 = -16$

$\therefore \quad a_1 a_2 + b_1 b_2 < 0$

Hence, negative sign gives the obtuse angle bisector.

$\therefore$ Obtuse angle bisector is

$$\frac{(3x - 4y + 7)}{\sqrt{(3)^2 + (-4)^2}} = -\frac{(-12x - 5y + 2)}{\sqrt{(-12)^2 + (-5)^2}}$$

$\Rightarrow \quad 13(3x - 4y + 7) = -5(-12x - 5y + 2)$

$\therefore \quad 21x + 77y - 101 = 0$ is the obtuse angle bisector.

Example 109. Find the bisector of acute angle between the lines $x + y - 3 = 0$ and $7x - y + 5 = 0$.

Sol. Firstly, make the constant terms (c_1, c_2) positive, then

$-x - y + 3 = 0$ and $7x - y + 5 = 0$

$\because \quad a_1 a_2 + b_1 b_2 = (-1)(7) + (-1)(-1) = -7 + 1 = -6$

i.e. $\quad a_1 a_2 + b_1 b_2 < 0$

Hence, positive sign gives the acute angle bisector.

$$\therefore \text{Acute angle bisector is } \frac{(-x - y + 3)}{\sqrt{(-1)^2 + (-1)^2}} = + \frac{(7x - y + 5)}{\sqrt{(7)^2 + (-1)^2}}$$

$$\Rightarrow \quad \frac{-x - y + 3}{\sqrt{2}} = \frac{7x - y + 5}{5\sqrt{2}}$$

$\Rightarrow \quad -5x - 5y + 15 = 7x - y + 5$

$\therefore \quad 12x + 4y - 10 = 0$

or $\quad 6x + 2y - 5 = 0$

is the acute angle bisector.

Example 110. Find the coordinates of incentre of the triangle. The equation of whose sides are $AB: x+y-1=0, BC: 7x-y-15=0$ and $CA: x-y-1=0$.

Sol. Firstly, make the constant terms $(c_1, c_2$, and $c_3)$ positive

i.e.
$$AB: -x-y+1=0 \quad \text{...(i)}$$
$$BC: -7x+y+15=0 \quad \text{...(ii)}$$
$$CA: -x+y+1=0 \quad \text{...(iii)}$$

$\because$ The incentre of triangle is the point of intersection of internal or acute angle bisectors.

Internal bisector of AB and BC

$$-x-y+1=0$$
$$-7x+y+15=0$$

$\because \quad a_1a_2+b_1b_2=(-1)(-7)+(-1)(1)=6>0$

$\therefore$ Acute or internal bisector is

$$\frac{(-x-y+1)}{\sqrt{(-1)^2+(-1)^2}}=-\frac{(-7x+y+15)}{\sqrt{(-7)^2+(1)^2}}$$

$$\Rightarrow \quad \frac{(-x-y+1)}{\sqrt{2}}=-\frac{(-7x+y+15)}{5\sqrt{2}}$$

$$\Rightarrow \quad -5x-5y+5=7x-y-15$$

or $\quad 12x+4y-20=0$

or $\quad 3x+y-5=0 \quad \text{...(iv)}$

Internal bisector of BC and CA

$$-7x+y+15=0$$
$$-x+y+1=0$$

$\because \quad a_1a_2+b_1b_2=(-7)(-1)+(1)(1)=8>0$

$\therefore$ Acute or internal bisector is

$$\frac{(-7x+y+15)}{\sqrt{(-7)^2+(1)^2}}=-\frac{(-x+y+1)}{\sqrt{(-1)^2+(1)^2}}$$

$$\Rightarrow \quad \frac{-7x+y+15}{5\sqrt{2}}=\frac{(x-y-1)}{\sqrt{2}}$$

$$\Rightarrow \quad -7x+y+15=5x-5y-5$$

or $\quad 12x-6y-20=0$

or $\quad 6x-3y-10=0 \quad \text{...(v)}$

On solving Eqs. (iv) and (v), we get

$$x=\frac{5}{3} \text{ and } y=0$$

Hence, coordinates of incentre are $\left(\frac{5}{3}, 0\right)$.

Example 111. If $6x+6y+m=0$ is acute angle between the lines $x+2y+4=0$ and $4x+2y-1=0$, then find the value of m.

Sol. Given, $\quad x+2y+4=0 \quad \text{...(i)}$

$\quad 4x+2y-1=0 \quad \text{...(ii)}$

Equation of bisectors between Eqs. (i) and (ii),

$$\frac{x+2y+4}{\sqrt{5}}=\pm\frac{4x+2y-1}{\sqrt{20}}$$

$\because \quad a_1a_2+b_1b_2=1(4)+2(2)>0$

Thus, equation of angle bisector of acute angle is with opposite sign.

$$2(x+2y+4)=-(4x+2y-1)$$

$$\Rightarrow \quad 2x+4y+8=-4x-2y+1$$

$$\Rightarrow \quad 6x+6y+7=0$$

On comparing with equation $6x+6y+m=0$

$\therefore \quad m=7$

Milestone Practice 2.4

1. The straight lines $2x+11y-5=0$, $24x+7y-20=0$ and $4x-3y-2=0$

(a) form a triangle

(b) are only concurrent

(c) are concurrent with one line bisecting the angle between the other two

(d) None of the above

2. The line $x+3y-2=0$ bisects the angle between a pair of straight lines of which one has the equation $x-7y+5=0$. The equation of other line is

(a) $3x+3y-1=0$ (b) $x-3y+2=0$

(c) $5x+5y+3=0$ (d) $5x+5y-3=0$

3. In a triangle ABC, the bisectors of angles B and C lie along the lines $x=y$ and $y=0$. If A is (1, 2), then the equation of line BC is

(a) $2x+y=1$ (b) $3x-y=5$

(c) $x-2y=3$ (d) $x+3y=1$

4. If θ_1 and θ_2 are the inclination of lines L_1 and L_2 with is L_1 and L_2 passes through $P(x_1\ y_1)$, then equation of one of the angle bisector of these lines are

(a) $\dfrac{x-x_1}{\cos\left(\dfrac{\theta_1-\theta_2}{2}\right)}=\dfrac{y-y_1}{\sin\left(\dfrac{\theta_1+\theta_2}{2}\right)}$

(b) $\dfrac{x-x_1}{-\sin\left(\dfrac{\theta_1-\theta_2}{2}\right)}=\dfrac{y-y_1}{\cos\left(\dfrac{\theta_1-\theta_2}{2}\right)}$

(c) $\dfrac{x-x_1}{\sin\left(\dfrac{\theta_1-\theta_2}{2}\right)}=\dfrac{y-y_1}{\cos\left(\dfrac{\theta_1-\theta_2}{2}\right)}$

(d) $\dfrac{x-x_1}{-\sin\left(\dfrac{\theta_1+\theta_2}{2}\right)}=\dfrac{y-y_1}{\cos\left(\dfrac{\theta_1+\theta_2}{2}\right)}$

5. The vertex P of ΔPQR is $(3, -1)$. The equation of median QE and angle bisector RF are $x - 4y + 10 = 0$ and $6x + 10y - 59 = 0$ respectively, then equation of PR is

(a) $5x + 18y = 87$
(b) $15x + 8y = 37$
(c) $15x - 8y = 37$
(d) $15x + 8y + 37 = 0$

6. The equation of the bisector of that angle between the lines $x + y = 3$ and $2x - y = 2$ which contains the point (1, 1) is

(a) $(\sqrt{5} - 2\sqrt{2})x + (\sqrt{5} + \sqrt{2})y = 3\sqrt{5} - 2\sqrt{2}$
(b) $(\sqrt{5} + 2\sqrt{2})x + (\sqrt{5} - \sqrt{2})y = 3\sqrt{5} + 2\sqrt{2}$
(c) $3x = 10$
(d) $3x - 5y + 2 = 0$

7. The equation of the straight line which bisects the intercepts made by the axes on the lines $x + y = 2$ and $2x + 3y = 6$ is

(a) $2x = 3$
(b) $y = 1$
(c) $2y = 3$
(d) $x = 1$

8. The equation of the bisector of the acute angle between the lines $2x - y + 4 = 0$ and $x - 2y = 1$ is

(a) $x + y + 5 = 0$
(b) $x - y + 1 = 0$
(c) $x - y = 5$
(d) $x - y + 5 = 0$

9. Find the equations of the bisectors of the angle between the lines $y - b = \frac{2m}{1 - m^2}(x - a)$ and $y - b = \frac{2'}{1 - (m')^2}(x - a)$.

10. Equation of straight line passing through the point (4, 5) and equally inclined to the lines $3x = 4y + 7$ and $5y = 12x + 6$.

11. Let $P \equiv (-1, 0)$, $Q \equiv (0, 0)$ and $R \equiv (3, 3\sqrt{3})$ be three points. Find th equation of the angle bisector of $\angle PQR$.

12. Find the equations of the two straight lines through (7, 9) and making an angle of 60° with the line $x - \sqrt{3}y - 2\sqrt{3} = 0$.

13. Find the equation of the bisector of the angle between the lines $x + 2y - 11 = 0$ and $3x - 6y - 5 = 0$ which contains the point (1, −3).

14. The bisector of two lines L_1 and L_2 are given by $3x^2 - 8xy - 3y^2 + 10x + 20y - 25 = 0$. If the line L_1 passes through origin, find the equation of line L_2.

15. Find the equation of the bisector of the angle between the lines $2x - 3y - 5 = 0$ and $6x - 4y + 7 = 0$ which is the supplement of the angle containing the point (2, −1).

16. In a triangle ABC, if $A(2, -1)$ and $3x - 2y + 5 = 0$ and $7x - 10y + 1 = 0$ are equations of an angle bisector and an altitude respectively drawn from B, then find equation of BC.

Answer Key

1. (c) **2.** (d) **3.** (b) **4.** (d) **5.** (b) **6.** (a)

7. (b) **8.** (b) **9.** $y - b = \frac{m + m'}{1 - mm'}(x - a)$ or $y - b = \frac{mm' - 1}{m + m'}(x - a)$

10. $7x + 9y = 73$ and $9x - 7y = -1$ **11.** $\sqrt{3}x + y = 0$ **12.** $x = 7$ and $x + \sqrt{3}y = 7 + 9\sqrt{3}$

13. $3x = 19$ **14.** $x + 2y = 5$ **15.** $10x - 10y - 3 = 0$ **16.** $5x + y + 17 = 0$

For Detailed Solution

Milestone 5 The Foot of Perpendicular

- The Foot of Perpendicular Drawn from the Point (x_1, y_1) to the Line $ax+by+c=0$
- Image or Reflection of a Point (x_1, y_1) About a Line Mirror
- Image or Reflection of a Point in Different Cases
- Use of Image or Reflection

2.17 The Foot of Perpendicular Drawn from the Point (x_1, y_1) to the Line $ax+by+c=0$

Let $P \equiv (x_1, y_1)$ and let M be the foot of perpendicular drawn from P on $ax+by+c=0$.

In order to find the coordinates of M, find the equation of the line PM which is perpendicular to RS and passes through $P(x_1, y_1)$, i.e. $bx - ay = bx_1 - ay_1$

or $b(x - x_1) - a(y - y_1) = 0$ and solving it with $ax + by + c = 0$, then we get coordinates of M.

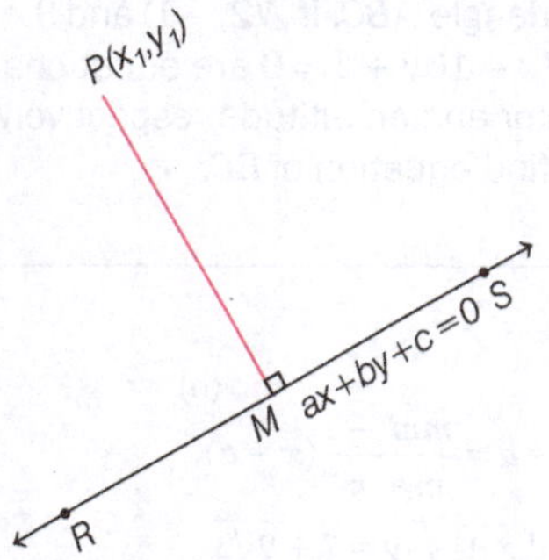

Proof Let the coordinates of M be (x_2, y_2). Then, $M(x_2, y_2)$ lies on $ax + by + c = 0$

$$\Rightarrow \quad ax_2 + by_2 + c = 0 \qquad \text{...(i)}$$

$$\because \quad PM \perp RS$$

$\therefore$ (Slope of PM) (Slope of RS) $= -1$

$$\Rightarrow \quad \left(\frac{y_2 - y_1}{x_2 - x_1}\right) \times \left(-\frac{a}{b}\right) = -1$$

$$\text{or} \quad bx_2 - ay_2 = bx_1 - ay_1 \qquad \text{...(ii)}$$

On solving Eqs. (i) and (ii), we get (x_2, y_2).

Alternate Proof Let the coordinates of M are (x_2, y_2)

Then, M lies on $\quad ax + by + c = 0$

$$\text{i.e.} \quad ax_2 + by_2 + c = 0 \qquad \text{...(iii)}$$

$$\because \quad PM \perp RS$$

$$\therefore \quad \left(\frac{y_2 - y_1}{x_2 - x_1}\right) \times \left(-\frac{a}{b}\right) = -1$$

$$\text{or} \quad \frac{x_2 - x_1}{a} = \frac{y_2 - y_1}{b}$$

$$\text{or} \quad \frac{x_2 - x_1}{a} = \frac{y_2 - y_1}{b} = \frac{a(x_2 - x_1) + b(y_2 - y_1)}{(a^2 + b^2)}$$

(by ratio proportion method)

$$= \frac{(ax_2 + by_2) - (ax_1 + by_1)}{a^2 + b^2}$$

$$= \frac{-c - (ax_1 + by_1)}{a^2 + b^2} \qquad \text{[from Eq. (iii)]}$$

$$\text{or} \quad \frac{x_2 - x_1}{a} = \frac{y_2 - y_1}{b} = -\frac{(ax_1 + by_1 + c)}{(a^2 + b^2)}$$

Example 112. Find the coordinates of the foot of the perpendicular drawn from the point (2, 3) to the line $y = 3x + 4$.

Sol. Given line is $3x - y + 4 = 0 \qquad$ ...(i)

Let M be the foot of perpendicular drawn from $P(2, 3)$ on RS.

Then, equation of PM passes through $P(2, 3)$ and perpendicular to RS is

$$x + 3y - (2 + 3 \times 3) = 0$$

$$\text{i.e.} \quad x + 3y - 11 = 0 \qquad \text{...(ii)}$$

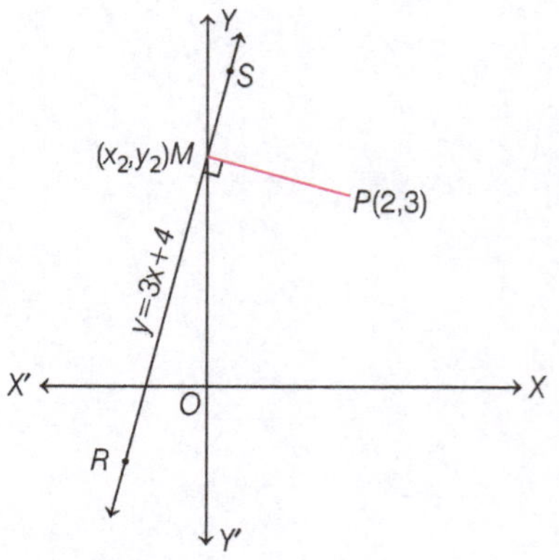

On solving Eqs. (i) and (ii), we get

$$x = \frac{1}{10}, y = \frac{37}{10}$$

$$\therefore \quad M \equiv \left(-\frac{1}{10}, \frac{37}{10}\right)$$

Alternate Solution

Let the coordinates of M be (x_2, y_2). Then, $M\ (x_2, y_2)$ lies on $3x - y + 4 = 0$

$$\Rightarrow \quad 3x_2 - y_2 + 4 = 0 \quad \ldots\text{(iii)}$$

$$\because \quad PM \perp RS$$

$$\therefore \ (\text{Slope of } PM) \times (\text{Slope of } RS) = -1$$

$$\Rightarrow \quad \left(\frac{y_2 - 3}{x_2 - 2}\right) \times (3) = -1$$

or $\quad x_2 + 3y_2 - 11 = 0 \quad \ldots$(iv)

On solving Eqs. (iii) and (iv), we get

$$x_2 = -\frac{1}{10}, y_2 = \frac{37}{10}$$

$$\therefore \quad M \equiv \left(-\frac{1}{10}, \frac{37}{10}\right)$$

Example 113. If $\frac{x}{a} + \frac{y}{b} = 1$ is a variable line, where $\frac{1}{a^2} + \frac{1}{b^2} = \frac{1}{c^2}$, then find the locus of the foot of the perpendicular drawn from the origin.

Sol. Given variable line is

$$\frac{x}{a} + \frac{y}{b} = 1$$

and $\quad \frac{1}{a^2} + \frac{1}{b^2} = \frac{1}{c^2}$

Foot of the perpendicular from origin $O(0, 0)$ to $\frac{x}{a} + \frac{y}{b} = 1$ is $P(h, k)$.

So, by Ratio proportion method,

$$\frac{h - 0}{\frac{1}{a}} = \frac{k - 0}{\frac{1}{b}} = -\frac{\left(\frac{0}{a} + \frac{0}{b} - 1\right)}{\frac{1}{a^2} + \frac{1}{b^2}} = c^2$$

$$\therefore \quad h = \frac{ab^2}{a^2 + b^2} \quad \ldots\text{(i)}$$

and $\quad k = \frac{a^2 b}{b^2 + a^2} \quad \ldots$(ii)

On squaring and adding Eqs. (i) and (ii), we get

$$h^2 + k^2 = \frac{a^2 b^2}{a^2 + b^2} = c^2$$

$\therefore$ Required locus equation is $x^2 + y^2 = c^2$.

Example 114. In a ΔPQR the vertex P is $(-4, 6)$, the base QR lies on the line $x - y + 2 = 0$. If PM is the altitude, then find the coordinates of M.

Sol. Let M be the foot of perpendicular drawn from P on QR.

By Ratio proportion method,

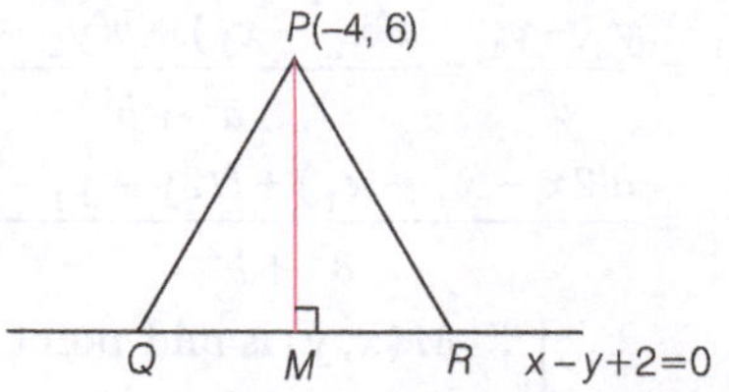

$$\frac{x - x_1}{a} = \frac{y - y_1}{b} = \frac{-(ax_1 + by_1 + c)}{(a^2 + b^2)}$$

$$\frac{x + 4}{1} = \frac{y - 6}{-1} = \frac{-(-4 - 6 + 2)}{2}$$

$$x + 4 = -y + 6 = 4$$

$$x + 4 = 4, -y + 6 = 4 \Rightarrow x = 0, y = 2$$

$\therefore$ Coordinates of M are $(0, 2)$.

Example 115. If the foot of the perpendicular from $(-4, 5)$ to the straight line is $3x - 4y - 18 = 0$ is (α, β), then find the value of $(\alpha + \beta)$.

Sol. Given, $(x_1, y_1) \equiv (-4, 5)$

Line $3x - 4y - 18 = 0$

where $\quad a = 3, b = -4, c = -18$

Since, (α, β) is foot of perpendicular

$$\frac{\alpha - x_1}{a} = \frac{\beta - y_1}{b} = \frac{-(ax_1 + by_1 + c)}{a^2 + b^2}$$

$$\Rightarrow \quad \frac{\alpha + 4}{3} = \frac{\beta - 5}{-4} = \frac{-(-12 - 20 - 18)}{25}$$

$$\Rightarrow \quad \frac{\alpha + 4}{3} = \frac{\beta - 5}{-4} = \frac{50}{25} = 2 \Rightarrow \frac{\alpha + 4}{3} = 2; \frac{\beta - 5}{-4} = 2$$

$$\alpha = 2; \beta = -3$$

$$\therefore \quad \alpha + \beta = 2 - 3 = -1$$

2.18 Image or Reflection of a Point (x_1, y_1) About a Line Mirror

Let $Q \equiv (x_2, y_2)$ be the image of $P \equiv (x_1, y_1)$ then find coordinates of the foot of perpendicular M drawn from the point $P(x_1, y_1)$ on RS and use fact that M is the mid- point P and Q.

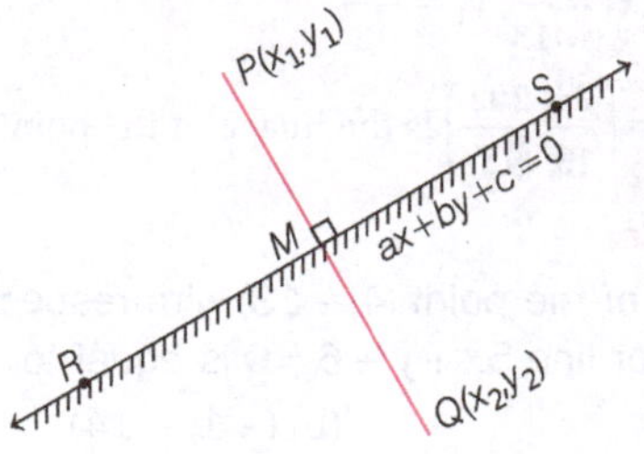

i.e. $\quad M \equiv \left(\frac{x_1 + x_2}{2}, \frac{y_1 + y_2}{2}\right).$

Aliter Ratio Proportion Method

$\because \quad PQ \perp RS$

$\therefore$ (Slope of PQ) $\times$ (Slope of RS) $= -1$

or $\left(\dfrac{y_2 - y_1}{x_2 - x_1}\right) \times \left(-\dfrac{a}{b}\right) = -1$ or $\dfrac{(x_2 - x_1)}{a} = \dfrac{(y_2 - y_1)}{b}$

or $\dfrac{x_2 - x_1}{a} = \dfrac{y_2 - y_1}{b} = \dfrac{a(x_2 - x_1) + b(y_2 - y_1)}{a^2 + b^2}$

$$= \frac{a(2x - x_1 - x_1) + b(2y - y_1 - y_1)}{a^2 + b^2}$$

$\left[\begin{array}{l}\because M(x, y) \text{ is mid-point of } P \text{ and } Q \\ \therefore x_2 = 2x - x_1 \text{ and } y_2 = 2y - y_1\end{array}\right]$

$$= \frac{-2ax_1 - 2by_1 + 2(ax + by)}{a^2 + b^2}$$

$$= \frac{-2ax_1 - 2by_1 + 2(-c)}{a^2 + b^2} \quad [\because ax + by = -c]$$

$$= \frac{-2(ax_1 + by_1 + c)}{(a^2 + b^2)}$$

i.e. $\dfrac{x_2 - x_1}{a} = \dfrac{y_2 - y_1}{b} = -\dfrac{2(ax_1 + by_1 + c)}{(a^2 + b^2)}$

JEE SCANNER

Example Similar to PYQ Asked in JEE Main 2023

Let L denote the line in XY-plane with x and y-intercepts as 5 and 1, respectively. Then, the image of the point (–1, –6) in this line is

(a) $\left(\dfrac{23}{13}, \dfrac{102}{13}\right)$ (b) $\left(\dfrac{-23}{13}, \dfrac{102}{13}\right)$

(c) $\left(\dfrac{102}{13}, \dfrac{23}{13}\right)$ (d) $\left(\dfrac{23}{13}, \dfrac{-102}{13}\right)$

Sol. (a) Given, line L made x and y-intercepts 5 and 1 respectively.

So, equation of line L is $\dfrac{x}{5} + \dfrac{y}{1} = 1 \Rightarrow x + 5y = 5$ ...(i)

Now, image of point $(-1, -6)$ with respect to line (i) is (x_1, y_1), then

$$\frac{x_1 + 1}{1} = \frac{y_1 + 6}{5} = \frac{-2(-1 - 30 - 5)}{1 + 25} = \frac{36}{13}$$

$$\Rightarrow \quad x_1 = \frac{23}{13}, y_1 = \frac{102}{13}$$

$\therefore (x_1, y_1) = \left(\dfrac{23}{13}, \dfrac{102}{13}\right)$ is the image of the point $(-1, -6)$.

Skill Builder

The image of the point $(4, -13)$ with respect to the mirror line $5x + y + 6 = 0$ is equal to

(a) (1, 14) (b) (– 1, – 14)

(c) (3, 14) (d) (14, 1)

For Sol.

■ **For more practice** See Q.7 of Milestone Practice 2.5.

Example 116. The equation of the line segment AB is $y = x$. If A and B lie on the same side of the line mirror $2x - y = 1$, then find the equation of the image of AB.

Sol. Let $Q(x_2, y_2)$ be the image of $P(0, 0)$ with respect to line mirror $2x - y = 1$, then

$$\frac{x_2 - 0}{2} = \frac{y_2 - 0}{-1} = -2\left(\frac{2 \times 0 - 0 \times 0 - 1}{4 + 1}\right)$$

$$\frac{x_2 - 0}{2} = \frac{2}{5}$$

and $\dfrac{y_2 - 0}{-1} = \dfrac{2}{5}$

$$x_2 = \frac{4}{5} \text{ and } y_2 = \frac{-2}{5}$$

Thus, required line passing through (1, 1) and $\left(\dfrac{4}{5}, \dfrac{-2}{5}\right)$.

So, its equation is $y - 1 = \dfrac{\dfrac{-2}{5} - 1}{\dfrac{4}{5} - 1}(x - 1)$

$$y - 1 = 7(x - 1)$$

$\Rightarrow \quad 7x - y - 6 = 0$

Example 117. Find the centre of the square and other vertices. If one of the vertices of a square is (3, 2) and one of the diagonals is along the line $3x + 4y + 8 = 0$.

Sol. Let coordinates of A be (3, 2). Clearly, point (3, 2) does not satisfy the line $3x + 4y + 8 = 0$.

Thus, diagonal BD is along this line.

Let $M(x_2, y_2)$ be centre of the square which is the foot of perpendicular from vertex A on the diagonal BD.

$\therefore \quad \dfrac{x_2 - 3}{3} = \dfrac{y_2 - 2}{4} = -\left(\dfrac{3(3) + 4(2) + 8}{3^2 + 4^2}\right)$

$\Rightarrow \quad \dfrac{x_2 - 3}{3} = \dfrac{y_2 - 2}{4} = -1$

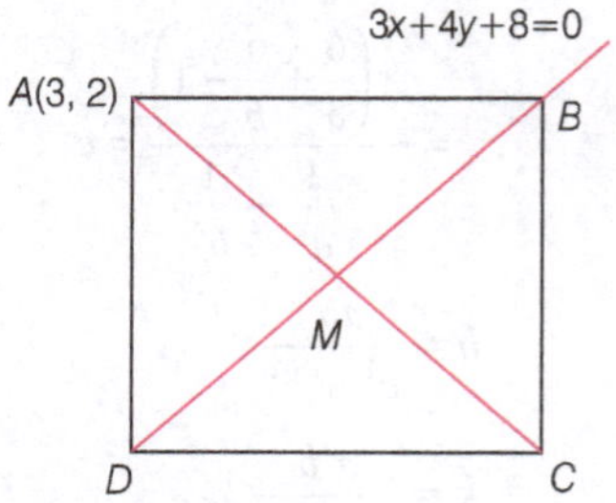

$\because \quad \dfrac{x_2 - 3}{3} = -1$ and $\dfrac{y_2 - 2}{4} = -1$

$$x_2 = 0 \text{ and } y_2 = -2$$

which is the centre of square.

$\because M$ is the mid-point of AC

$\therefore \quad C \equiv (-3, -6)$

Now, $AM = \dfrac{|3(3)+4(2)+8|}{\sqrt{3^2+4^2}} = \left|\dfrac{9+8+8}{\sqrt{25}}\right| = \dfrac{25}{5} = 5$

$\therefore \quad MB = MD = 5$

Slope of $BD = \dfrac{-3}{4} = \tan\theta$ of line $3x+4y+8=0$, where θ is inclination of BD with X-axis.

$\therefore$ Coordinates of B and D are $(0 \pm 5\cos\theta, -2 \pm 5\sin\theta)$

$$\equiv \left(0 \pm 5\left(\frac{-4}{5}\right), -2 \pm 5\left(\frac{3}{5}\right)\right)$$

$$\equiv (\mp 4, -2 \pm 3) \equiv (-4, 1), (4, -5)$$

2.19 Image or Reflection of a Point in Different Cases

(i) The image or reflection of a point with respect to X-axis

Let $P(\alpha, \beta)$ be any point and $Q(x, y)$ be its image about X-axis, then (M is the mid-point of PQ).

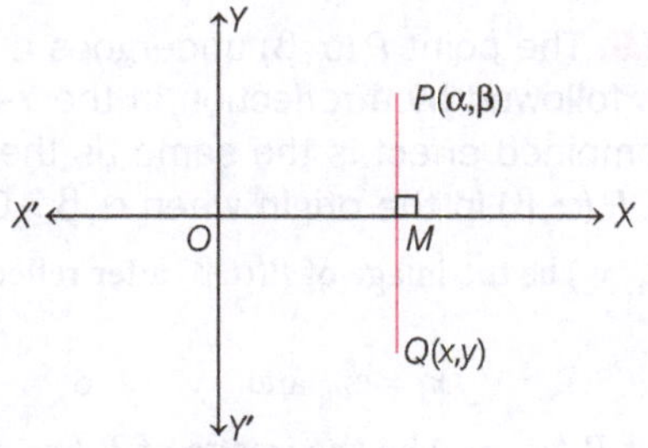

$x = \alpha$ and $y = -\beta$

$\therefore \quad Q \equiv (\alpha, -\beta)$

i.e. sign change of ordinate.

(ii) The image or reflection of a point with respect to Y-axis

Let $P(\alpha, \beta)$ be any point and $Q(x, y)$ be its image about Y-axis, then (M is the mid-point of PQ)

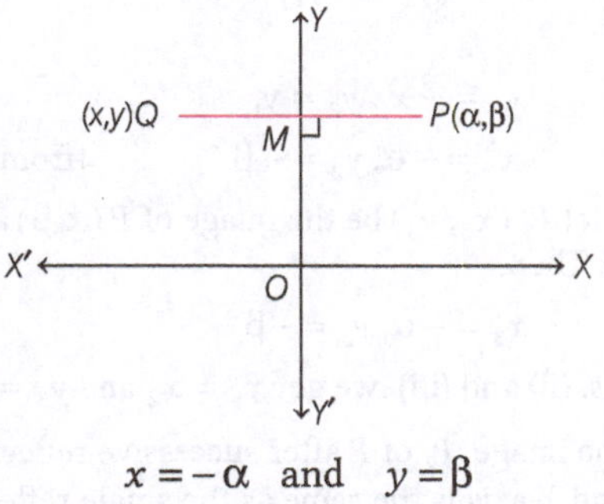

$x = -\alpha$ and $y = \beta$

$\therefore \quad Q \equiv (-\alpha, \beta)$

i.e. sign change of abscissa.

(iii) The image or reflection of a point with respect to origin

Let $P(\alpha, \beta)$ be any point and $Q(x, y)$ be its image about the origin (O is the mid-point of PQ), then

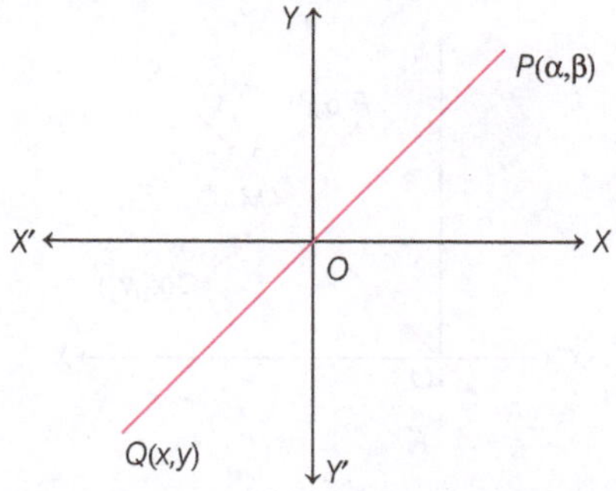

$x = -\alpha$ and $y = -\beta$

$\therefore \quad Q \equiv (-\alpha, -\beta)$

i.e. sign change of abscissa and ordinate.

(iv) The image or reflection of a point with respect to the line $x = a$

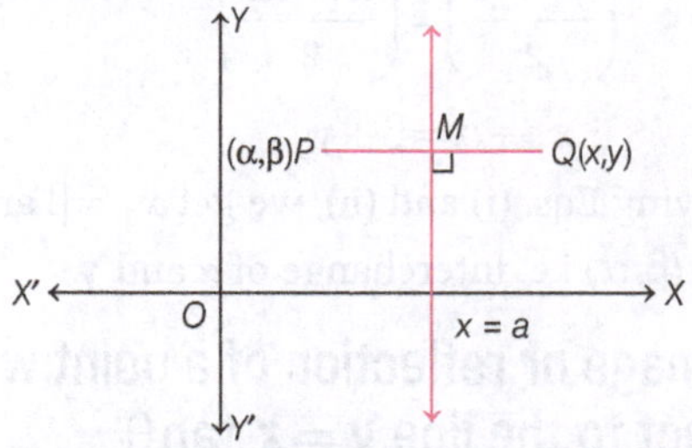

Let $P(\alpha, \beta)$ be any point and $Q(x, y)$ be its image about the line $x = a$, then $y = \beta$

$\therefore$ Coordinates of M are (a, β)

$\because$ M is the mid-point of PQ

$\therefore \quad Q \equiv (2a - \alpha, \beta)$

(v) The image or reflection of a point with respect to the line $y = b$

Let $P(\alpha, \beta)$ be any point and $Q(x, y)$ be its image about the line $y = b$, then $x = \alpha$

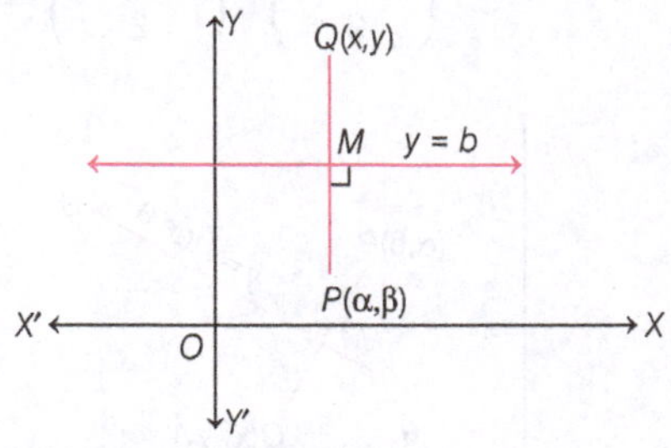

$\therefore$ Coordinates of M are (α, b)

$\because$ M is the mid-point of PQ.

$\therefore \quad Q \equiv (\alpha, 2b - \beta)$

(vi) The image or reflection of a point with respect to the line $y = x$

Let $P(\alpha, \beta)$ be any point and $Q(x_1, y_1)$ be its image about the line $y = x$ (RS), then $PQ \perp RS$.

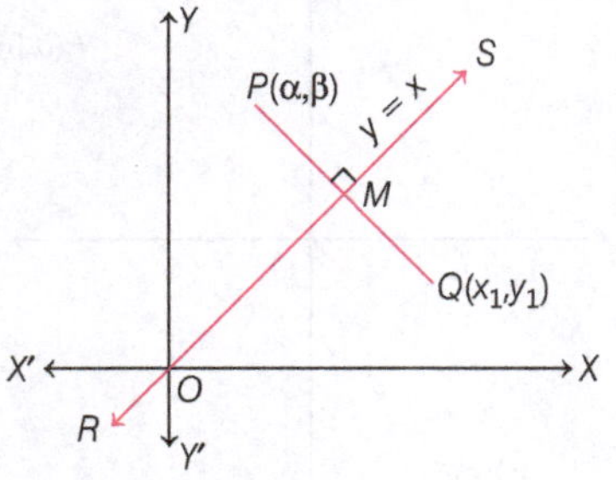

$\therefore$ (Slope of PQ) $\times$ (Slope of RS) $= -1$

or $$\frac{y_1 - \beta}{x_1 - \alpha} \times 1 = -1$$

or $$x_1 - \alpha = \beta - y_1 \quad \text{...(i)}$$

and mid-point of PQ lies on $y = x$

i.e. $$\left(\frac{y_1 + \beta}{2}\right) = \left(\frac{x_1 + \alpha}{2}\right)$$

or $$x_1 + \alpha = \beta + y_1 \quad \text{...(ii)}$$

On solving Eqs. (i) and (ii), we get $x_1 = \beta$ and $y_1 = \alpha$

$\therefore$ $Q \equiv (\beta, \alpha)$ i.e. interchange of x and y.

(vii) The image or reflection of a point with respect to the line $y = x \tan\theta$

Let $P(\alpha, \beta)$ be any point and $Q(x_1, y_1)$ be its image about the line $y = x \tan\theta$ (RS), then $PQ \perp RS$

$\therefore$ (Slope of PQ) $\times$ (Slope of RS) $= -1$

$$\Rightarrow \quad \frac{y_1 - \beta}{x_1 - \alpha} \times \tan\theta = -1$$

$$\Rightarrow \quad y_1 - \beta = (\alpha - x_1)\cot\theta \quad \text{...(i)}$$

and mid-point of PQ lie on $y = x \tan\theta$

i.e. $$\left(\frac{y_1 + \beta}{2}\right) = \left(\frac{x_1 + \alpha}{2}\right)\tan\theta$$

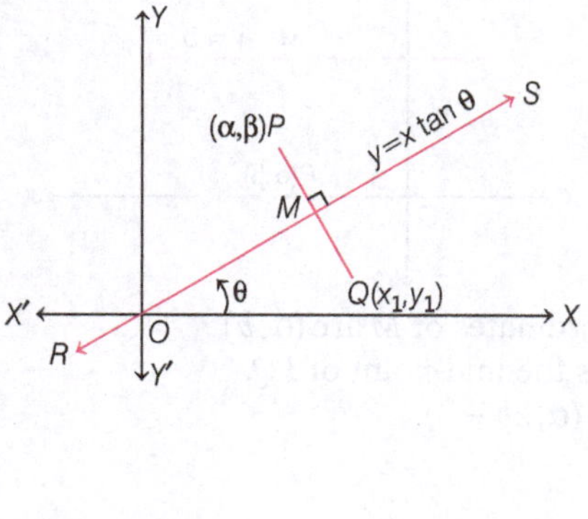

$$\Rightarrow \quad y_1 + \beta = (x_1 + \alpha)\tan\theta \quad \text{...(ii)}$$

On solving Eqs. (i) and (ii), we get

$$x_1 = \alpha\cos 2\theta + \beta\sin 2\theta$$

and $$y_1 = \alpha\sin 2\theta - \beta\cos 2\theta$$

$$\therefore \quad Q \equiv (\alpha\cos 2\theta + \beta\sin 2\theta, \alpha\sin 2\theta - \beta\cos 2\theta)$$

JEE Focus Points

- The image of the line $ax + by + c = 0$ about X-axis is $$ax - by + c = 0$$
- The image of the line $ax + by + c = 0$ about Y-axis is $$-ax + by + c = 0$$
- The image of the line $ax + by + c = 0$ about origin is $$-ax - by + c = 0.$$
- The image of the line $ax + by + c = 0$ about the line $x = \lambda$ is $$a(2\lambda - x) + by + c = 0$$
- The image of the line $ax + by + c = 0$ about the line $y = \mu$ is $$ax + b(2\mu - y) + c = 0.$$
- The image of the line $ax + by + c = 0$ about the line $y = x$ is $$ay + bx + c = 0.$$

Example 118. The point $P(\alpha, \beta)$ undergoes a reflection in the X-axis followed by a reflection in the Y-axis. Show that their combined effect is the same as the single reflection of $P(\alpha, \beta)$ in the origin when $\alpha, \beta > 0$.

Sol. Let $P_1(x_1, y_1)$ be the image of $P(\alpha, \beta)$ after reflection in the X-axis.

Then, $$x_1 = \alpha \quad \text{and} \quad y_1 = -\beta \quad \text{...(i)}$$

Now, let $P_2(x_2, y_2)$ be the image of $P_1(x_1, y_1)$ in the Y-axis.

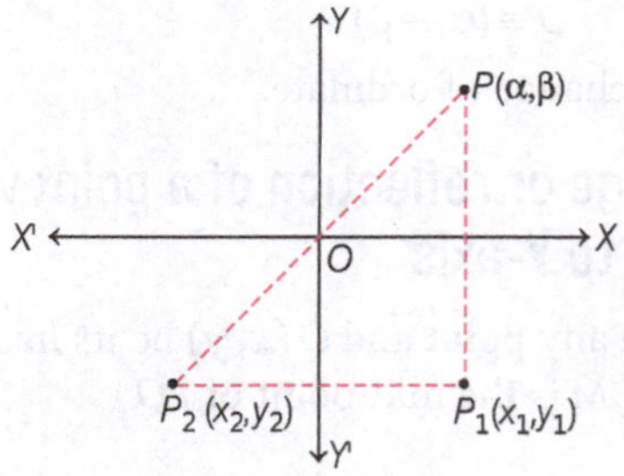

Then, $$x_2 = -x_1, y_2 = y_1$$

$$\Rightarrow \quad x_2 = -\alpha, y_2 = -\beta \quad \text{[from Eq. (i)] ...(ii)}$$

Further, let $P_3(x_3, y_3)$ be the image of $P(\alpha, \beta)$ about the origin O. Then,

$$x_3 = -\alpha, y_3 = -\beta \quad \text{...(iii)}$$

From Eqs. (ii) and (iii), we get $x_3 = x_2$ and $y_3 = y_2$.

Hence the image P_2 of P after successive reflection in their X-axis and Y-axis is the same as the single reflection of P about the origin.

Example 119. Find the image of the point $(-2,-7)$ under the transformations $(x, y) \to (x-2y, -3x+y)$.

Sol. Let (x_1, y_1) be the image of the point (x, y) under the given transformation. Then,

$$x_1 = x - 2y = (-2) - 2(-7) = 12$$

$$\therefore \quad x_1 = 12 \text{ and } y_1 = -3x + y = -3(-2) - 7 = -1$$

$$\therefore \quad y_1 = -1$$

Hence, the image is $(12, -1)$.

Example 120. The image of the point $A(1,2)$ by the line mirror $y = x$ is the point B and the image of B by the line mirror $y = 0$ is the point (α, β). Find α and β.

Sol. Let (x_1, y_1) be the image of the point $(1, 2)$ about the line $y = x$.

Then, $\quad x_1 = 2, y_1 = 1 \quad$ ...(i)

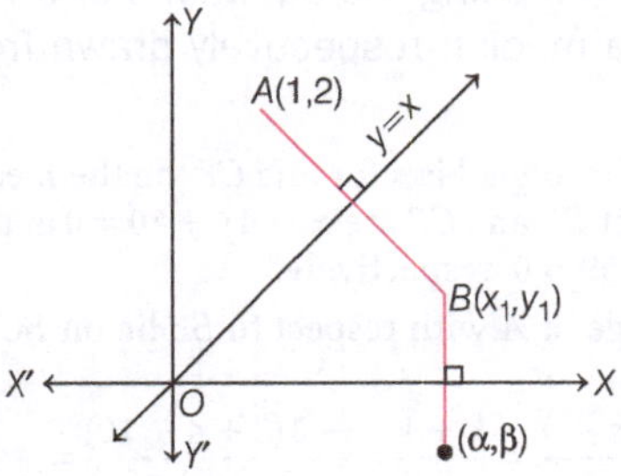

Also given, image of $B(x_1, y_1)$ by the line mirror $y = 0$ is (α, β). Then, $\alpha = x_1 = 2$

and $\quad \beta = -y_1 = -1 \quad$ [from Eq. (i)]

Hence, $\quad \alpha = 2 \text{ and } \beta = -1$

Example 121. The point $(4, 1)$ undergoes the following three transformations successively

(i) Reflection about the line $y = x$.

(ii) Translation through a distance 2 units along the positive direction of X-axis.

(iii) Rotation through an angle $\pi/4$ about the origin in the anti-clockwise direction.

Then, find the coordinates of the final position.

Sol. Let $Q(x_1, y_1)$ be the reflection of P about the line $y = x$.

Then,

$$\left.\begin{aligned} x_1 &= 1 \\ y_1 &= 4 \end{aligned}\right\}$$

$\therefore$ Coordinates of Q are $(1, 4)$.

Given that Q moves 2 units along the positive direction of X-axis.

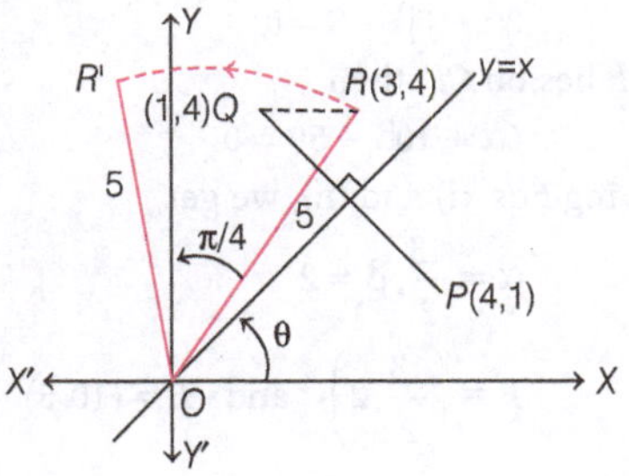

$\therefore$ Coordinates of R are $(x_1 + 2, y_1)$

or $\quad R(3, 4)$

If OR makes an angle θ, then

$$\tan\theta = \frac{4}{3}$$

$$\therefore \quad \sin\theta = \frac{4}{5}$$

$$\text{and} \quad \cos\theta = \frac{3}{5}$$

After rotation of $\frac{\pi}{4}$, let new position of R be R' and

$$OR = OR' = \sqrt{3^2 + 4^2} = 5$$

$\therefore$ OR' makes an angle $(\pi/4 + \theta)$ with X-axis.

Coordinates of $R'\left(OR' \cos\left(\frac{\pi}{4} + \theta\right), OR' \sin\left(\frac{\pi}{4} + \theta\right)\right)$

i.e.
$$\left[R'\left(OR'\left(\frac{1}{\sqrt{2}}\cos\theta - \frac{1}{\sqrt{2}}\sin\theta\right), OR'\left(\frac{1}{\sqrt{2}}\cos\theta + \frac{1}{\sqrt{2}}\sin\theta\right)\right)\right]$$

$$\Rightarrow \quad R'\left(5\left(\frac{3}{5\sqrt{2}} - \frac{4}{5\sqrt{2}}\right), 5\left(\frac{3}{5\sqrt{2}} + \frac{4}{5\sqrt{2}}\right)\right)$$

$$\Rightarrow \quad R'\left(-\frac{1}{\sqrt{2}}, \frac{7}{\sqrt{2}}\right)$$

> **Alternate Solution**
>
> Let Q be the reflection of $P(4, 1)$ about the line $y = x$, then $Q(1, 4)$
>
> $\because Q$ move 2 units alongs the + ve direction of X-axis, if new point is
>
> R, then $\quad R = (3, 4)$
>
> If $\quad R(3, 4) = R(z_1)$
>
> when $\quad z_1 = (3 + 4i)$
>
> Then, $\quad R'(x, y) = R'(z_2)$
>
> $\therefore \quad z_2 = ze^{i\pi/4} \quad \left[\because \angle ROR' = \frac{\pi}{4}\right]$
>
> $$= (3 + 4i)\left(\cos\frac{\pi}{4} + i\sin\frac{\pi}{4}\right)$$
>
> $$= (3 + 4i)\left(\frac{1}{\sqrt{2}} + \frac{i}{\sqrt{2}}\right) = \left(-\frac{1}{\sqrt{2}} + \frac{7i}{\sqrt{2}}\right)$$
>
> Hence, new coordinates are $\left(-\frac{1}{\sqrt{2}}, \frac{7}{\sqrt{2}}\right)$.

2.20 Use of Image or Reflection

To make problems simpler and easier use Image or reflection.

Types of problems

(i) If vertex of a ΔABC and equations of perpendicular bisectors of AB and AC are given, then B and C are the images or reflections of A about the perpendicular bisectors of AB and AC.

(where M and N are the mid-points of AB and AC).

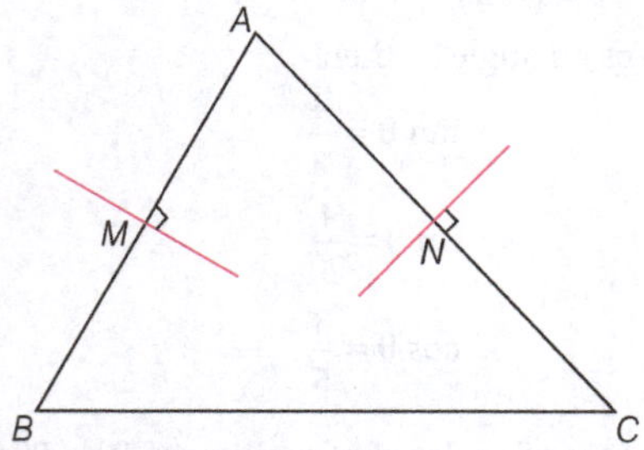

Example 122. The base of a triangle passes through a fixed point (f, g) and its sides are respectively bisected at right angles by the lines $y + x = 0$ and $y - 9x = 0$. Determine the locus of its vertex.

Sol. Let $A \equiv (\alpha, \beta)$, the image of $A\ (\alpha, \beta)$ about $y + x = 0$ is B, then $B \equiv (-\beta, -\alpha)$ and if image of $A\ (\alpha, \beta)$ about $y - 9x = 0$ is $C\ (x_2, y_2)$, then $\dfrac{x_2 - \alpha}{-9} = \dfrac{y_2 - \beta}{1} = \dfrac{-2(\beta - 9\alpha)}{1 + 81}$

$$\therefore \quad x_2 = \frac{9\beta - 40\alpha}{41} \text{ and } y_2 = \frac{40\beta + 9\alpha}{41}$$

$$\therefore \quad C \equiv \left(\frac{9\beta - 40\alpha}{41}, \frac{40\beta + 9\alpha}{41}\right)$$

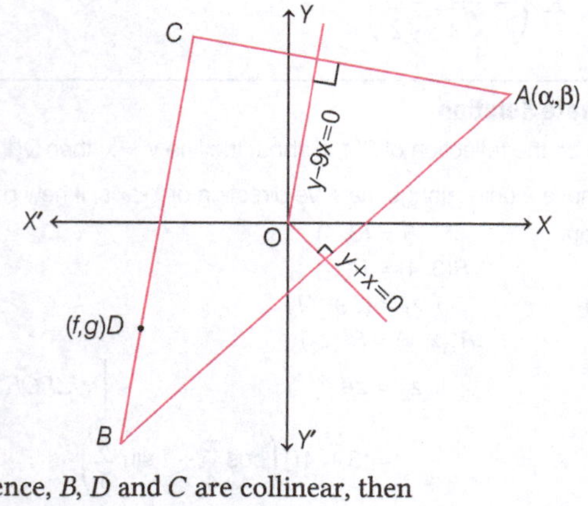

Hence, B, D and C are collinear, then

$$\frac{1}{2}\begin{vmatrix} -\beta & -\alpha & 1 \\ f & g & 1 \\ \dfrac{9\beta - 40\alpha}{41} & \dfrac{40\beta + 9\alpha}{41} & 1 \end{vmatrix} = 0$$

$$\Rightarrow \quad 4(\alpha^2 + \beta^2) + (4g + 5f)\alpha + (4f - 5g)\beta = 0$$

Hence, locus of vertex is

$$4(x^2 + y^2) + (4g + 5f)x + (4f - 5g)y = 0$$

(ii) The images or reflections of vertex A of a ΔABC about the angular bisectors of angles B and C lie on the side BC. (By congruence) A_1 and A_2 are the images of A about the angle bisectors BE and CF respectively, where M and N are the mid-points of AA_1 and AA_2.

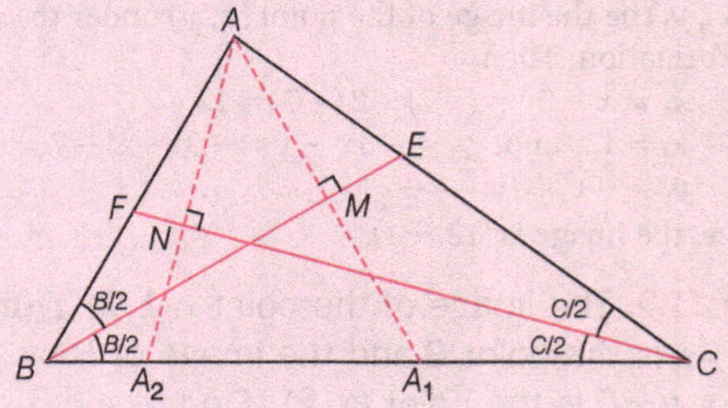

Example 123. Find the equations of the sides of the triangle having $(3, -1)$ as a vertex, $x - 4y + 10 = 0$ and $6x + 10y - 59 = 0$ being the equations of an angle bisector and a median respectively drawn from different vertices.

Sol. Let BE be the angle bisector and CF be the median. Given equations of BE and CF are $x - 4y + 10 = 0$ and $6x + 10y - 59 = 0$ respectively.

Since, image of A with respect to BE lie on BC. If image of A is $L(h, k)$.

$$\text{Then,} \quad \frac{h - 3}{1} = \frac{k + 1}{-4} = \frac{-2(3 + 4 + 10)}{1^2 + (-4)^2} = -2$$

i.e. $\quad h = 1, k = 7$

$\therefore \quad L \equiv (1, 7)$

$\because$ F is the mid-point of AB.

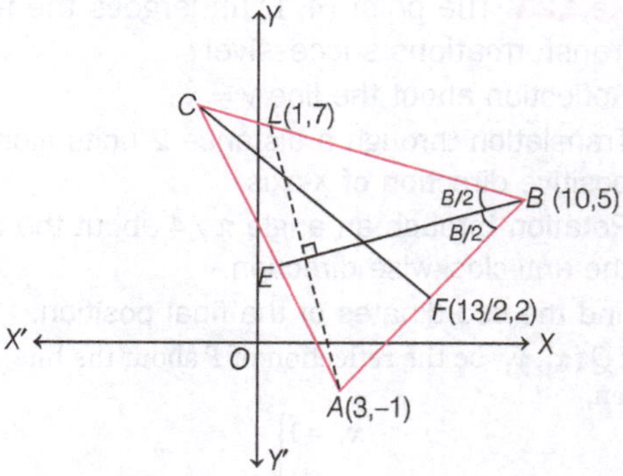

Let $\quad F \equiv (\alpha, \beta)$

Then, $\quad B \equiv (2\alpha - 3, 2\beta + 1)$

$\because$ B lies on BE, then $(2\alpha - 3) - 4(2\beta + 1) + 10 = 0$

i.e. $\quad 2\alpha - 8\beta + 3 = 0 \quad$ ...(i)

and $\quad F$ lies on CF, then

$$6\alpha + 10\beta - 59 = 0 \quad \text{...(ii)}$$

On solving Eqs. (i) and (ii), we get

$$\alpha = \frac{13}{2}, \beta = 2$$

Then, $\quad F \equiv \left(\dfrac{13}{2}, 2\right)$ and $B = (10, 5)$

$\therefore$ Equation of AB is $y + 1 = \dfrac{2+1}{\dfrac{13}{2} - 3}(x - 3)$

$\Rightarrow \quad y + 1 = \dfrac{6}{7}(x - 3)$

$\Rightarrow \quad 6x - 7y - 25 = 0$

Equation of BC is $y - 5 = \dfrac{7-5}{1-10}(x - 10)$

$\Rightarrow \quad y - 5 = -\dfrac{2}{9}(x - 10)$

$\Rightarrow \quad 2x + 9y - 65 = 0$

$\because$ CA is the family of lines of CB and CF.

Then, $(2x + 9y - 65) + \lambda(6x + 10y - 59) = 0$ ...(iii)

It passes through $A(3, -1)$.

Then, $(6 - 9 - 65) + \lambda(18 - 10 - 59) = 0$

$\therefore \quad \lambda = -\dfrac{4}{3}$

From Eq. (iii), we get equation of AC is

$$18x + 13y - 41 = 0$$

(iii) Minimisation Let A and B are two given points on the same side of line $ax + by + c = 0$.

Suppose we want to determine a point P on $ax + by + c = 0$ such that $PA + PB$ is minimum.

For that find the image of A or B about the line $ax + by + c = 0$ (say A' or B'), then join B' with A or A' with B wherever it intersects $ax + by + c = 0$ is the required point.

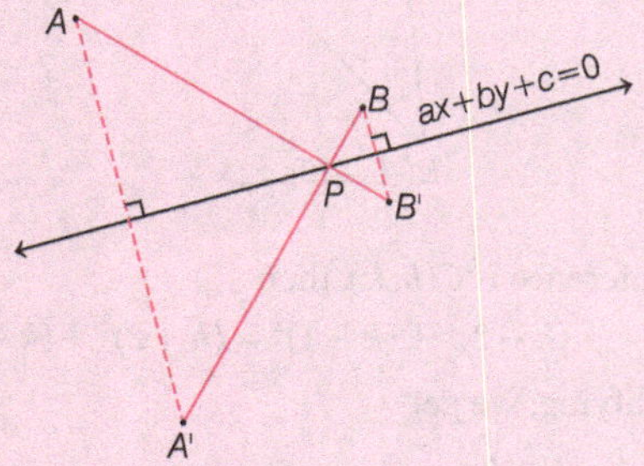

$\therefore \quad PA + PB = PA + PB'$

$\Rightarrow \quad PA + PB = PA' + PB$

Example 124. Find a point R on the X-axis such that $PR + RQ$ is the minimum, when $P \equiv (1, 1)$ and $Q \equiv (3, 2)$.

Sol. Since, P and Q lie on the same side of X-axis.

The image of $Q(3, 2)$ about X-axis is $Q'(3, -2)$, then the equation of line PQ' is

$$y - 1 = \frac{-2-1}{3-1}(x - 1)$$

$\Rightarrow \quad 3x + 2y - 5 = 0$

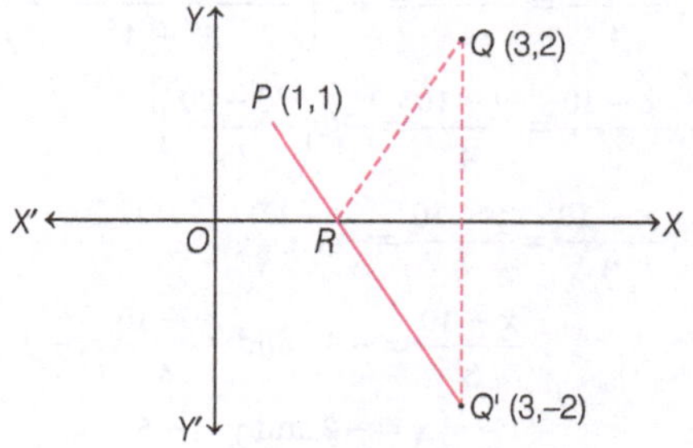

This line meets X-axis at $R\left(\dfrac{5}{3}, 0\right)$, which is the required point.

Example 125. A person starts from the point $P(-3, 4)$ and reaches point $Q(0, 1)$ touching X-axis at R such that $PR + RQ$ is minimum, then find point R.

Sol. Since, P and Q lie on the same side of X-axis,

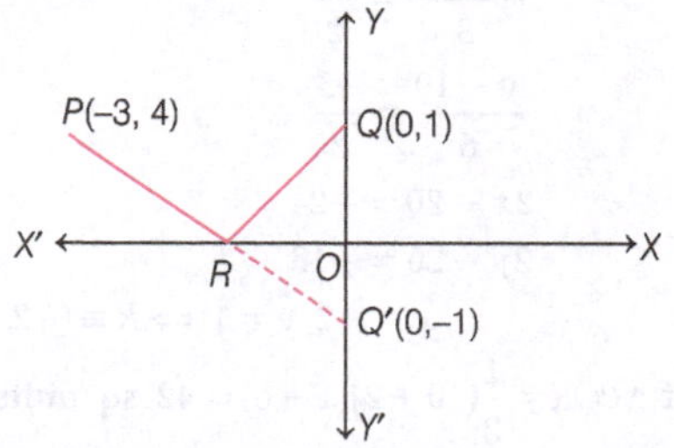

Therefore, the image of $Q(0, 1)$ about X-axis is $Q'(0, -1)$, then equation of line PQ' is

$$y - 4 = \frac{-1-4}{0+3}(x + 3) \Rightarrow y - 4 = -\frac{5}{3}(x + 3)$$

$\Rightarrow \quad 3y - 12 = -5x - 15$

$\Rightarrow \quad 5x + 3y + 3 = 0$

This line meets X-axis at $R\left(\dfrac{-3}{5}, 0\right)$, which is the required point.

Example 126. In a triangle PQR, the equations of perpendicular bisectors of sides PQ and PR are $3x + 4y = 20$ and $8x + 6y = 65$, respectively. If the vertex P is $(10, 10)$, then find the area of ΔPQR.

Sol. Given, the perpendicular bisector of PQ is $3x + 4y - 20 = 0$ and perpendicular bisector of PR is $8x + 6y - 65 = 0$. Image of P with respect to $3x + 4y - 20 = 0$ is Q and image of P with respect to $8x + 6y - 65 = 0$ is R.

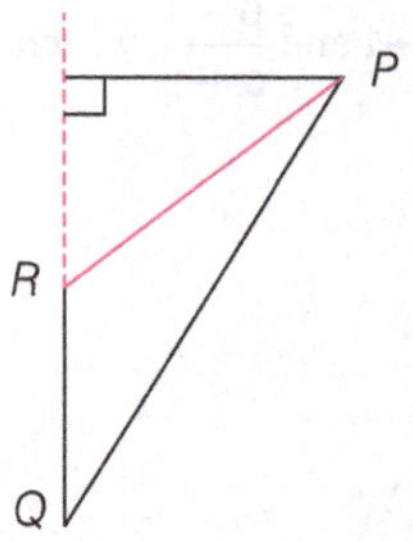

For Q, $\frac{x-10}{3}=\frac{y-10}{4}=-2\left(\frac{3(10)+4(10)-20}{3^2+4^2}\right)$

$\Rightarrow \quad \frac{x-10}{3}=\frac{y-10}{4}=-2\left(\frac{70-20}{25}\right)$

$\Rightarrow \quad \frac{x-10}{3}=\frac{y-10}{4}=-4$

$\Rightarrow \quad \frac{x-10}{3}=-4$ and $\frac{y-10}{4}=-4$

$\Rightarrow \quad x=-2$ and $y=-6$

$\Rightarrow \quad Q\equiv(-2,-6)$

For R, $\frac{x-10}{8}=\frac{y-10}{6}=-2\left(\frac{8(10)+6(10)-65}{8^2+6^2}\right)$

$\Rightarrow \quad \frac{x-10}{8}=\frac{y-10}{6}=-2\left(\frac{140-65}{100}\right)=\frac{-3}{2}$

$\Rightarrow \quad \frac{x-10}{8}=\frac{-3}{2}$

and $\quad \frac{y-10}{6}=\frac{-3}{2}$

$\Rightarrow \quad 2x-20=-24$

and $\quad 2y-20=-18$

$x=-2,\ y=1 \Rightarrow R\equiv(-2,1)$

$\therefore$ Area of $\Delta PQR=\frac{1}{2}(10+2)(1+6)=42$ sq. units

Example 127. Let image of point $A(3,1)$ about the line $x+y+7=0$ be $B(\alpha,\beta)$ and image of $B(\alpha,\beta)$ about line $x-2y+4=0$ be $C(\gamma,8)$, then find the circumcentre of ΔABC.

Sol. We know that any point and its image point are at same distance from the mirror line.

The mid-point of them will be on the line.

The mid-point of $A(3,1)$ and $B(\alpha,\beta)$ is

$$M\equiv\left(\frac{3+\alpha}{2},\frac{1+\beta}{2}\right)$$

$\because M$ lies on the line $x+y+7=0$, which means the coordinates satisfy the equation.

$\therefore \quad \frac{3+\alpha}{2}+\frac{1+\beta}{2}+7=0$

$\Rightarrow \quad 18+\alpha+\beta=0 \quad$ ...(i)

These lines are also perpendicular to each other. $A(3,1)$ is on the perpendicular of $x+y+7=0$.

$\therefore \quad$ Slopes are -1 and $\frac{\beta-1}{\alpha-3}$, which gives

$$\frac{\beta-1}{\alpha-3}\times(-1)=-1$$

$\Rightarrow \quad \beta-1=\alpha-3$

$\Rightarrow \quad \alpha-\beta-2=0 \quad$ ...(ii)

On solving Eqs. (i) and (ii), we get

$$\alpha=-8,\beta=-10$$

$\therefore$ Coordinates of B are $(-8,-10)$.

Now, similarly the mid-point of B and C is N.

$\therefore \quad N\equiv\left(\frac{-8+\gamma}{2},\frac{-10+8}{2}\right)\equiv\left(\frac{-8+\gamma}{2},-1\right)$

N lies on line $x-2y+4=0$, which means coordinates satisfy equation

$\therefore \quad \frac{-8+\gamma}{2}+2+4=0$

$\Rightarrow \quad \gamma=-4$

Point C is $(-4,8)$.

Now, the points are $A(3,1)$, $B(-8,-10)$ and $C(-4,8)$.

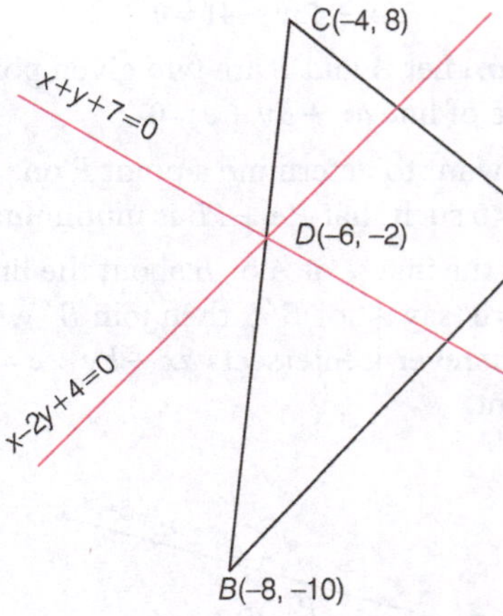

$\therefore$ Circumference is $C(h,k)$, then

$$(h-3)^2+(k-1)^2=(h+8)^2+(k+10)^2$$

On simplifying, we get

$h+k=-7 \quad$ ...(iii)

Also, $(h+4)^2+(k-8)^2=(h+8)^2+(k+10)^2$

Again, on simplifying, we get $2h+9k=-21 \quad$ ...(iv)

From Eqs. (iii) and (iv), we get

$$h=-6 \text{ and } k=-1$$

Milestone Practice 2.5

1. The coordinates of the foot of the perpendicular from (2, 3) to the line $3x+4y-6=0$ are

(a) $\left(-\frac{14}{25}, -\frac{27}{25}\right)$

(b) $\left(\frac{14}{25}, -\frac{17}{25}\right)$

(c) $\left(-\frac{14}{25}, \frac{17}{25}\right)$

(d) $\left(\frac{14}{25}, \frac{27}{25}\right)$

2. If the foot of the perpendicular from the origin to a straight line is at the point $P(3, -4)$. Then, the equation of the line is

(a) $3x-4y=25$ (b) $3x-4y+25=0$

(c) $4x+3y-25=0$ (d) $4x-3y+25=0$

3. A is a point on either of two $y+\sqrt{3}|x|=2$ at a distance of $3\sqrt{3}$ units from their point of intersection. The coordinates of the foot of the perpendicular from A on the bisector of angle between them are

(a) $(2/\sqrt{3}, 2)$ (b) (0, 0)

(c) $(2\sqrt{3}, 2)$ (d) (0, 4)

4. If $A(2, -1)$ and $B(6, 5)$ are two points, then the ratio in which the foot of the perpendicular from (4, 1) to the line AB divides it, is

(a) 8 : 15 (b) 5 : 8

(c) −5 : 8 (d) 8 : 5

5. The coordinates of the foot of the perpendicular from (a, 0) on the line $y=mx+\frac{a}{m}$ are

(a) $\left(0, -\frac{1}{a}\right)$

(b) $\left(0, \frac{a}{m}\right)$

(c) $\left(0, -\frac{a}{m}\right)$

(d) $\left(0, \frac{1}{a}\right)$

6. If the equation of the locus of a point equidistant from the points (a_1, b_1) and (a_2, b_2) is $(a_1-a_2)x+(b_1-b_2)y+c=0$, then the value of c is

(a) $a_1^2-a_2^2+b_1^2-b_2^2$

(b) $\sqrt{(a_1^2+b_1^2-a_2^2-b_2^2}$

(c) $\frac{1}{2}(a_1^2+a_2^2+b_1^2+b_2^2)$

(d) $\frac{1}{2}(a_2^2+b_2^2-a_1^2-b_1^2)$

7. Let L denote the line in the XY-plane with x and y intercepts as 7 and $\frac{7}{3}$, respectively. Then, the image of the point (3, 8) is

(a) (1, 4) (b) (4, 1)

(c) (−1, −4) (d) (−4, −1)

8. The image of the point (4, −3) with respect to the line $y=x$ is

(a) (−4, −3) (b) (3, 4)

(c) (−4, 3) (d) (−3, 4)

9. The coordinates of the image of the origin O with respect to the straight line $x+y+1=0$ are

(a) $\left(-\frac{1}{2}, -\frac{1}{2}\right)$ (b) (−2, −2)

(c) (1, 1) (d) (−1, −1)

10. If (−2, 6) is the image of the point (4, 2) with respect to the line $L=0$, then $L\equiv$

(a) $6x-4y-7=0$ (b) $2x-3y-5=0$

(c) $3x-2y+5=0$ (d) $3x-2y+10=0$

11. Locus of the image of the point (2, 3) in the line $(x-2y+3)+\lambda(2x-3y+4)=0$ is, $(\lambda \in R)$

(a) $x^2+y^2-3x-4y-4=0$

(b) $x^2+y^2-2x-4y+4=0$

(c) $2x^2+2y^2-9x+4y=0$

(d) None of the above

12. The image of $P(a, b)$ on the line $y=-x$ is Q and the image of Q on the line $y=x$ is R. Then, the mid-point of PR is

(a) $(a+b, a+b)$ (b) $\left(\frac{a+b}{2}, \frac{b+2}{2}\right)$

(c) $(a-b, b-a)$ (d) (0, 0)

13. Consider the points $A(0, 1)$ and $B(2, 0)$ and P be a point on the line $4x+3y+9=0$. The coordinates of P such that $|PA-PB|$ is maximum are

(a) $\left(-\frac{12}{5}, \frac{17}{5}\right)$ (b) $\left(-\frac{24}{5}, \frac{17}{5}\right)$

(c) $\left(-\frac{6}{5}, \frac{17}{5}\right)$ (d) (0, −3)

14. Consider the points $A(3, 4)$ and $B(7, 13)$. If P is a point on the line $y=x$ such that $PA+PB$ is minimum, then lies coordinates of P are

(a) $\left(\frac{12}{7}, \frac{12}{7}\right)$

(b) $\left(\frac{13}{6}, \frac{13}{5}\right)$

(c) $\left(\frac{31}{7}, \frac{31}{7}\right)$

(d) (0, 0)

15. In a ΔABC, the equation of the perpendicular bisector of AC is $3x - 2y + 8 = 0$. If the coordinates of the point A and B are $(1, -1)$ and $(3, 1)$ respectively, find the equation of the line BC and the centre of the circumcircle of ΔABC.

16. Is there a real value of λ for which the image of the point $(\lambda, \lambda - 1)$ by the line mirror $3x + y = 6\lambda$ is the point $(\lambda^2 + 1, \lambda)$? If so find λ.

17. If the image of the $M(\lambda, \lambda^2)$ in the line $x + y = \lambda^2$ is $(0, 2)$, then find λ.

18. A ray of light is sent along the line $x - 6y = 8$. After refracting across the line $x + y = 1$, it enters the opposite side after turning by $15°$ away from the line $x + y = 1$. Find the equation of the line along with the reflected ray travels.

19. Find the equation of sides of a triangle having $(4, -1)$ as a vertex, if the lines $x - 1 = 0$ and $x - y - 1 = 0$ are equations of two internal bisectors of its angles.

Answer Key

1. (d) **2.** (a) **3.** (b) **4.** (b) **5.** (b) **6.** (d)

7. (c) **8.** (d) **9.** (d) **10.** (c) **11.** (d) **12.** (d)

13. (b) **14.** (c) **15.** $x + 4y - 7 = 0, \left(-\frac{4}{5}, \frac{14}{5}\right)$ **16.** $\lambda = \frac{1}{3}, 2$

17. $\lambda = -1, 2$ **18.** $y + 1 = \frac{13 - 6\sqrt{3}}{4 + \sqrt{3}}(x - 2)$ **19.** $2x + y = 3$, $2x + 3y = 5$ and $x + 2y = 2$

For Detailed Solution

Milestone 6 Reflection of Light

- Reflection of Light • Refraction of Light

2.21 Reflection of Light

When a ray of light falls on a smooth polished surface (Mirror) separating two media, a part of it is reflected back into the first medium.

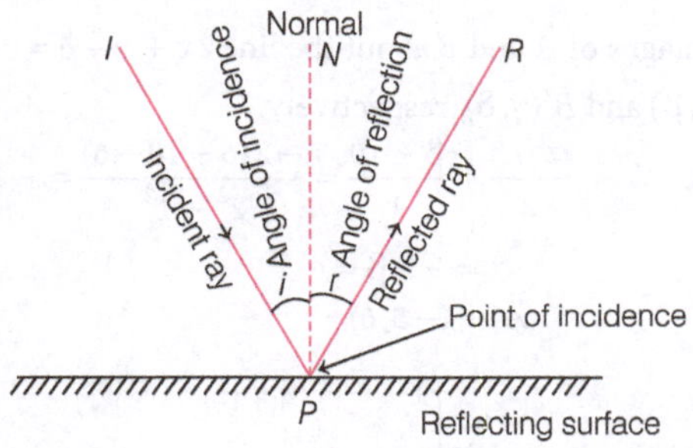

IP is the incident ray and *PR* is the reflected ray. A perpendicular drawn to the surface, at the point of incidence *P* is called the normal. Hence, *PN* is the normal. The angle between the incident ray and the normal ($\angle IPN$) is called the **angle of incidence** which is represented by $\angle i$

i.e. $\angle IPN = \angle i =$ angle of incidence and the angle between the reflected ray and the normal ($\angle IPR$) is called the **angle of reflection**, which is represented by $\angle r$.

i.e. $\angle RPN = \angle r =$ Angle of reflection.

Laws of Reflection

(i) The incident ray, normal and the reflected ray to a surface at the point of incidence all lie in the same plane.

(ii) The angle of incidence = angle of reflection

i.e. $\angle i = \angle r$

Example 128. A ray of light is sent along the line $x - 2y - 3 = 0$. Upon reaching the line $3x - 2y - 5 = 0$, the ray is reflected from it. Find the equation of the line containing the reflected ray.

Sol. To get coordinates of point *P*, we solve the given equation of lines together as

$$x - 2y - 3 = 0$$
$$3x - 2y - 5 = 0$$
$$\therefore \quad x = 1, y = -1$$

$\therefore$ Coordinates of *P* are $(1, -1)$.

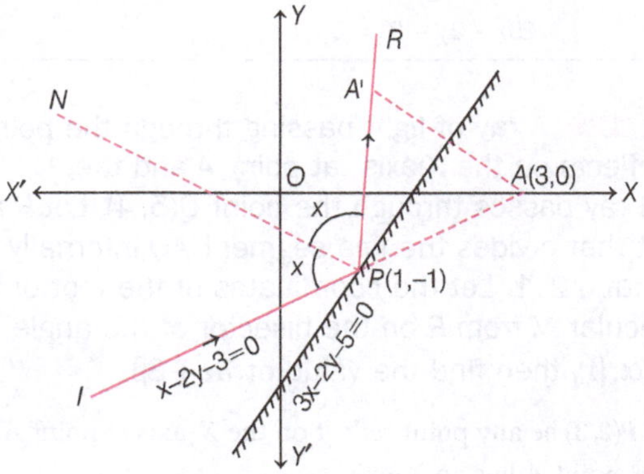

Let slope of reflected ray be *m*.

Since, slope of line mirror is 3/2.

$\therefore$ Slope of $PN = -2/3$ and slope of $IP = 1/2$, line *PN* is equally inclined to *IP* and *PR*, then

$$\left(\frac{m - \left(-\frac{2}{3}\right)}{1 + m\left(-\frac{2}{3}\right)}\right) = -\left(\frac{\frac{1}{2} - \left(-\frac{2}{3}\right)}{1 + \frac{1}{2}\left(-\frac{2}{3}\right)}\right)$$

$$\Rightarrow \quad \frac{3m + 2}{3 - 2m} = -\frac{7}{4}$$

$$\Rightarrow \quad 12m + 8 = -21 + 14m$$

$$\therefore \quad 2m = 29$$

$$\Rightarrow \quad m = \frac{29}{2}$$

$\therefore$ Equation of reflected ray $y + 1 = \frac{29}{2}(x - 1)$

$$\Rightarrow \quad 2y + 2 = 29x - 29$$

$$\Rightarrow \quad 29x - 2y - 31 = 0.$$

Alternate Solution

Image method Take A (3, 0) be any point on IP and if $A'(\alpha, \beta)$ be the image of A about the mirror line $3x - 2y - 5 = 0$, then

$$\frac{\alpha - 3}{3} = \frac{\beta - 0}{-2} = \frac{-2(9 - 0 - 5)}{9 + 4}$$

$$\therefore \quad \alpha = \frac{15}{13}$$

and $$\beta = \frac{16}{13}$$

$$\therefore \quad A' \equiv \left(\frac{15}{13}, \frac{16}{13}\right)$$

$\therefore$ Equation of $A'P$ is the equation of the reflected ray, then its equation is,

$$y + 1 = \frac{\left(\frac{16}{13} + 1\right)}{\left(\frac{15}{13} - 1\right)}(x - 1)$$

$$\Rightarrow \quad y + 1 = \frac{29}{2}(x - 1)$$

or $$29x - 2y - 31 = 0$$

Example 129. A ray of light passing through the points $P(2, 3)$ reflects on the X-axis at point A and the reflected ray passes through the point $Q(5, 4)$. Let R be the point that divides the line segment AQ internally into the ratio 2 : 1. Let the coordinates of the foot of the perpendicular M from R on the bisector of the angle PAQ be (α, β), then find the value of $7\alpha + 3\beta$.

Sol. Take $P(2, 3)$ be any point reflect on the X-axis at point A.

Since, point A lies on X-axis.

$\therefore$ Coordinates of A would be $(\alpha, 0)$.

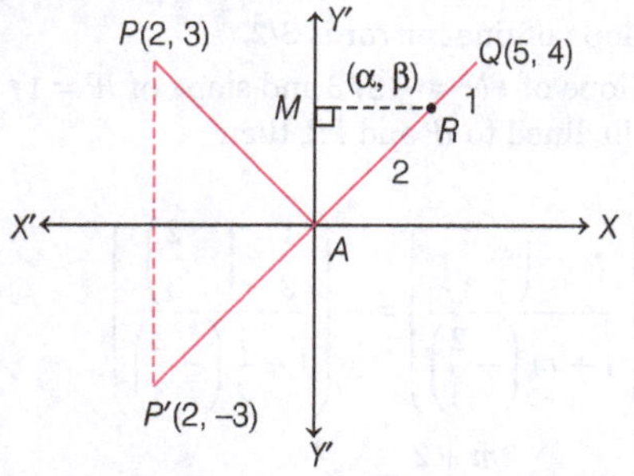

Now, again reflected ray passes through point $Q(5, 4)$.

Draw a line R perpendicular to QP' where R divides QP' in 2 : 1.

$$P' = \text{Image of } P \text{ w.r.t. } y = 0$$

$$P' \equiv (2, -3)$$

$\therefore$ Equation of $P'Q$,

$$y + 3 = \frac{4 + 3}{5 - 2}(x - 2)$$

$$\Rightarrow \quad 3y + 9 = 7x - 14$$

$$\Rightarrow \quad 3y = 7x - 23 \qquad \text{...(i)}$$

On putting $y = 0$ in above Eq. (i)

$$\Rightarrow \quad 3(0) = 7\alpha - 23$$

$$\Rightarrow \quad \alpha = \frac{23}{7}$$

Coordinates of A will be $\left(\frac{23}{7}, 0\right)$

$\because$ β will be y coordinate of R

$$\Rightarrow \quad \beta = \frac{2 \times 4 + 1 \times 0}{2 + 1} = \frac{8}{3}$$

$$\therefore \quad 7\alpha + 3\beta = 23 + 8 = 31$$

Example 130. A light beam, emanating from the point (3, 10) reflects from the straight line $2x + y - 6 = 0$ and then passes through the point (7, 2). Find the equations of the incident and reflected beams.

Sol. Let images of A and B about the line $2x + y - 6 = 0$ be $A'(\alpha, \beta)$ and $B'(\gamma, \delta)$, respectively.

Then, $$\frac{\alpha - 3}{2} = \frac{\beta - 10}{1} = \frac{-2(6 + 10 - 6)}{2^2 + 1^2} = -4$$

$$\therefore \quad \alpha = -5, \beta = 6$$

i.e. $$A' \equiv (-5, 6)$$

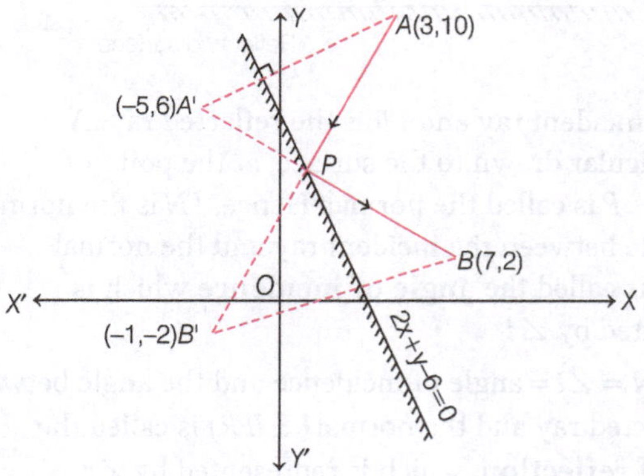

and $$\frac{\gamma - 7}{2} = \frac{\delta - 2}{1} = \frac{-2(14 + 2 - 6)}{2^2 + 1^2} = -4$$

$$\therefore \quad \gamma = -1, \delta = -2$$

i.e. $$B' \equiv (-1, -2).$$

$\therefore$ Equation of incident ray AB' is

$$y + 2 = \frac{10 + 2}{3 + 1}(x + 1)$$

or $3x - y + 1 = 0$

and equation of reflected ray $A'B$ is

$$y - 6 = \frac{2 - 6}{7 + 5}(x + 5)$$

$$\Rightarrow \quad y - 6 = -\frac{1}{3}(x + 5)$$

or $x + 3y - 13 = 0$

JEE SCANNER

Example Similar to PYQ Asked in JEE Main 2023

Let a ray of light passing through the point $(5, 11)$ reflects on the line $3x + y = 9$ and the reflected ray passes through the point $(9, 4)$. If the equation of the incident ray is $ax - by + c = 0$, then the value of $c - a - b$ is ......

Sol. (118) Let $A \equiv (5, 11)$ and $B \equiv (9, 4)$

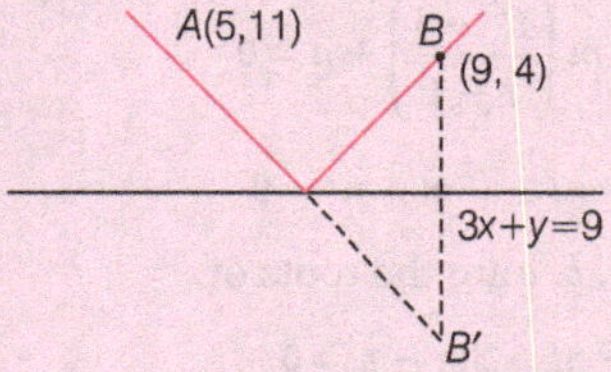

For B', $\dfrac{x-9}{3} = \dfrac{y-4}{1} = -2\left(\dfrac{27+4-9}{9+1}\right)$

$\Rightarrow \quad \dfrac{x-9}{3} = y - 4 = \dfrac{-22}{5} \Rightarrow x = \dfrac{-21}{5}, y = \dfrac{-2}{5}$

$\therefore \quad B' \equiv \left(\dfrac{-21}{5}, \dfrac{-2}{5}\right) \Rightarrow$ Slope of $AB' = \dfrac{57}{46}$

$\therefore \quad$ Equation of $AB' = \left(y + \dfrac{2}{5}\right) = \dfrac{57}{46}\left(x + \dfrac{21}{5}\right)$

$\Rightarrow \quad 57x - 46y + 221 = 0$

$\therefore \quad a = 57, b = 46$ and $c = 221$

$\Rightarrow \quad c - a - b = 221 - 57 - 46 = 118$

Skill Builder

A ray of light passing through the point $(3, 5)$ reflects on the line $2x + 3y = 6$ and the reflected ray passes through the point $(6, 5)$. If the equation of the incident ray is $ax - by - 221 = 0$, then the value of $a - b$ is ......

For Sol.

■ **For more practice** See Q.6 of Milestone Practice 2.6.

2.22 Refraction of Light

When a ray of light falls on the boundary separating the two transparent media, there is a change in direction of ray. This phenomenon is called refraction.

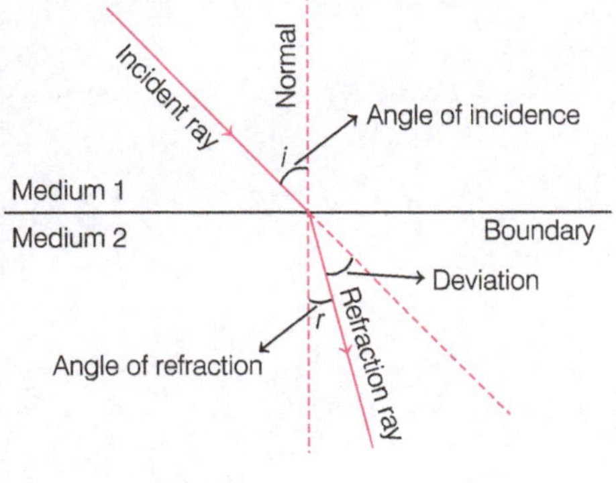

Laws of Refraction

(i) The incident ray, normal and the refracted ray to the surface separating the two transparent media all lie in the same plane.

(ii) The ratio of sine of angle of incidence to the sine of the angle of refraction is constant for the two given media. The constant is called the refractive index of medium 2 with respect to medium 1.

i.e. $\quad {}_1\mu_2 = \dfrac{\sin i}{\sin r}$

Example 131. A ray of light is sent along the line $x - 6y = 8$. After refracting across the line $x + y = 1$ it enters the opposite side after turning by $15°$ away from the line $x + y = 1$. Find the equation of the line along which the refracted ray travels.

Sol. The point of intersection of $x - 6y = 8$ and $x + y = 1$ is $A \equiv (2, -1)$. Let the required ray have the slope $= m$.

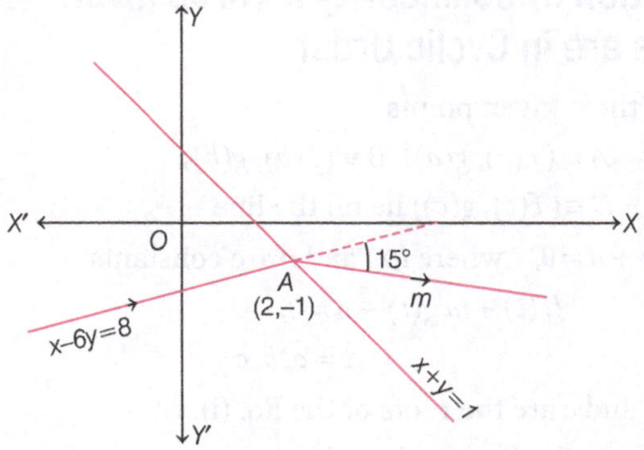

Then, $\quad \tan 15° = \left|\dfrac{m - \frac{1}{6}}{1 + \frac{m}{6}}\right|$

$\Rightarrow \quad 2 - \sqrt{3} = \pm\left(\dfrac{6m - 1}{m + 6}\right)$

Then, $\quad \dfrac{6m-1}{m+6} = 2 - \sqrt{3}$ or $\sqrt{3} - 2$

$\Rightarrow \quad m = \dfrac{70 - 37\sqrt{3}}{13}$ or $m = \dfrac{37\sqrt{3} - 70}{61}$

Let the angle between $x + y = 1$ and the line through $A(2, -1)$ with the slope $\dfrac{70 - 37\sqrt{3}}{13}$ be α.

Then, $\tan \alpha = \left|\dfrac{\dfrac{70-37\sqrt{3}}{13} - (-1)}{1 - \left(\dfrac{70-37\sqrt{3}}{13}\right)}\right| = \left|\dfrac{83 - 37\sqrt{3}}{37\sqrt{3} - 57}\right|$

$= \dfrac{83 - 37\sqrt{3}}{37\sqrt{3} - 57}$

and if angle between $x+y=1$ and the line through $A(2,-1)$ with the slope $\frac{37\sqrt{3}-70}{61}$ be β, then

$$\tan\beta=\left|\frac{\frac{37\sqrt{3}-70}{61}-(-1)}{1-\left(\frac{37\sqrt{3}-70}{61}\right)}\right|=\left|\frac{37\sqrt{3}-9}{131-37\sqrt{3}}\right|=\frac{37\sqrt{3}-9}{131-37\sqrt{3}}$$

Here, $\tan\alpha>\tan\beta, \therefore \alpha>\beta$

Therefore, the slope of the refracted ray $=\frac{70-37\sqrt{3}}{13}$

$\therefore$ The equation of the refracted ray is

$$y+1=\frac{(70-37\sqrt{3})}{13}(x-2)$$

$$\Rightarrow \quad 13y+13=(70-37\sqrt{3})\,x-140+74\sqrt{3}$$

or $\quad (70-37\sqrt{3})\,x-13y-153+74\sqrt{3}=0$

Condition of Collinearity if Three given points are in Cyclic Order

Let the three given points

$$A\equiv(f(a),g(a)),\ B\equiv(f(b),g(b))$$

and $\quad C\equiv(f(c),g(c))$ lie on the line

$lx+my+n=0$, where l,m and n are constants.

Then, $\quad lf(t)+m\,g(t)+n=0, \quad$ ...(i)

where $\quad t=a,b,c$

i.e. a, b and c are the roots of the Eq. (i).

In this case, Eq. (i) must be cubic in t.

$\Rightarrow \quad At^3+Bt^2+Ct+D=0 \quad$ (say)

Then, $\quad a+b+c=-\frac{B}{A},\ ab+bc+ca=\frac{C}{A}$

and $\quad abc=-\frac{D}{A}$

which are the required conditions.

Example 132. If the points $\left(\frac{a^3}{a-1},\frac{a^2-3}{a-1}\right),\left(\frac{b^3}{b-1},\frac{b^2-3}{b-1}\right)$ and $\left(\frac{c^3}{c-1},\frac{c^2-3}{c-1}\right)$ are collinear for three distinct values a,b,c and different from 1, then show that $abc-(bc+ca+ab)+3(a+b+c)=0$.

Sol. Let the three given points lie on the line

$lx+my+n=0$, where l, m and n are constants.

Then, $\quad l\left(\frac{t^3}{t-1}\right)+m\left(\frac{t^2-3}{t-1}\right)+n=0$

$\Rightarrow \quad lt^3+mt^2+nt-(3m+n)=0$

For $t=a,b,c$ i.e. a,b,c are the roots of

$$lt^3+mt^2+nt-3m-n=0$$

Then, $\quad a+b+c=-\frac{m}{l},\ ab+bc+ca=\frac{n}{l}$

and $\quad abc=\left(\frac{3m+n}{l}\right)$

Now, $abc-(bc+ca+ab)+3(a+b+c)$

$$=\left(\frac{3m+n}{l}\right)-\frac{n}{l}-\frac{3m}{l}=0$$

Hence, $abc-(bc+ca+ab)+3(a+b+c)=0$

Example 133. If t_1, t_2 and t_3 are distinct, the points $(t_1, 2at_1+at_1^3), (t_2, 2at_2+at_2^3)$ and $(t_3, 2at_3+at_3^3)$ are collinear, then prove that $t_1+t_2+t_3=0$.

Sol. Let the three given points lie on the line $lx+my+n=0$, where l, m and n are constants. Then,

$$l(t)+m(2at+at^3)+n=0$$

$\Rightarrow \quad (am)t^3+(2am+l)t+n=0 \quad$ ...(i)

For $t=t_1,t_2,t_3$

i.e. $\quad t_1,t_2,t_3$ are the roots of Eq. (i), then

$$t_1+t_2+t_3=0$$

Milestone Practice 2.6

1. A ray of light passing through the point (1, 2) is reflected on the X-axis at a point P and passes through the point (5, 3). The abscissa of the point P is

(a) 3 (b) $\frac{13}{3}$ (c) $\frac{13}{5}$ (d) $\frac{13}{4}$

2. The equation of the line segment AB is $y = x$. If A and B lie on the same side of the line mirror $2x - y = 1$, then the image of AB has the equation

(a) $x + y = 2$ (b) $8x + y = 9$
(c) $7x - y = 6$ (d) None of these

3. A ray of light travelling along the line $x + y = 1$ is incident on the X-axis and after refraction it enters the other side of the X-axis by turning $\pi/6$ away from the X-axis. The equation of the line along which the refracted ray travels is

(a) $x + (2 - \sqrt{3})\, y = 1$ (b) $x(2 + \sqrt{3}) + y = 2 - \sqrt{3}$
(c) $(2 - \sqrt{3})x + y = 1$ (d) $x + (2 + \sqrt{3})y = (2 + \sqrt{3})$

4. All the points lying inside the triangle formed by the points (0, 4), (2, 5) and (6, 2) satisfy

(a) $3x + 2y + 8 \ge 0$ (b) $2x + y - 10 \ge 0$
(c) $2x - 3y - 11 \ge 0$ (d) $-2x + y - 3 \ge 0$

5. Let O be the origin and let $A(1, 0)$, $B(0, 1)$ be two points. If $P(x, y)$ is a point such that $xy > 0$ and $x + y < 1$, then

(a) P lies either inside in ΔOAB or in third quadrant
(b) P cannot be inside in ΔOAB
(c) P lies inside the ΔOAB
(d) None of the above

6. A ray of light coming along the line $3x + 4y - 5 = 0$ gets reflected from the line $ax + by - 1 = 0$ and goes along the line $5x - 12y - 10 = 0$ then

(a) $a = \frac{64}{115}, b = \frac{112}{15}$ (b) $a = -\frac{64}{115}, b = \frac{8}{115}$
(c) $a = \frac{64}{115}, b = \frac{-8}{115}$ (d) $a = -\frac{64}{115}, b = \frac{-8}{115}$

7. Two sides of a triangle have the joint equation $x^2 - 2xy - 3y^2 + 8y - 4 = 0$. The third side, which is variable, always passes through the point $(-5, -1)$. Find the range of values of the slope of the third side, so that the origin is an interior point of the triangle.

8. Let $P(\sin\theta, \cos\theta)$, where $0 \le \theta \le 2\pi$ be a point and let OAB be a triangle with vertices (0, 0), $\left(\frac{\sqrt{3}}{2}, 0\right)$ and $\left(0, \frac{\sqrt{3}}{2}\right)$. Find θ if P lies inside the ΔOAB.

9. Determine whether the point $(-3, 2)$ lies inside or outside the triangle whose sides are given by the equations $x + y - 4 = 0$, $3x - 7y + 8 = 0$ and $4x - y - 31 = 0$.

10. A ray of light is sent along the line $x - 2y + 5 = 0$, upon reaching the line $3x - 2y + 7 = 0$, the ray is reflected from it. Find the equation of the line containing the reflected ray.

11. If a ray initiated from $P(6, 4)$ is reflected about X-axis and passes through $Q(12, 16)$, then find the equation of reflected ray.

Answer Key

1. (c) **2.** (c) **3.** (a) **4.** (a) **5.** (a) **6.** (c)
7. $m \in \left(-1, \frac{1}{5}\right)$ **8.** $\theta \in \left(0, \frac{\pi}{12}\right) \cup \left(\frac{5\pi}{12}, \frac{\pi}{12}\right)$ **9.** Outside **10.** $29x - 2y + 33 = 0$
11. $10x - 3y = 72$

For Detailed Solution

JEE Pattern EXAMPLES

Single Option Correct Type Questions

Example 1 *A rectangle ABCD has its side AB parallel to $y = x$ and vertices A, B and D lie on $y = 1$, $x = 2$ and $x = -2$ respectively, then locus of vertex C is*

(a) $x = 5$

(b) $x - y = 5$

(c) $y = 5$

(d) $x + y = 5$

Sol. (c) Given, AB is parallel to $y = x$.

$\therefore$ Equation of AB is $y = x + a$ [say]

$\because$ A lies on $y = 1$

$\therefore$ $A \equiv (1 - a, 1)$

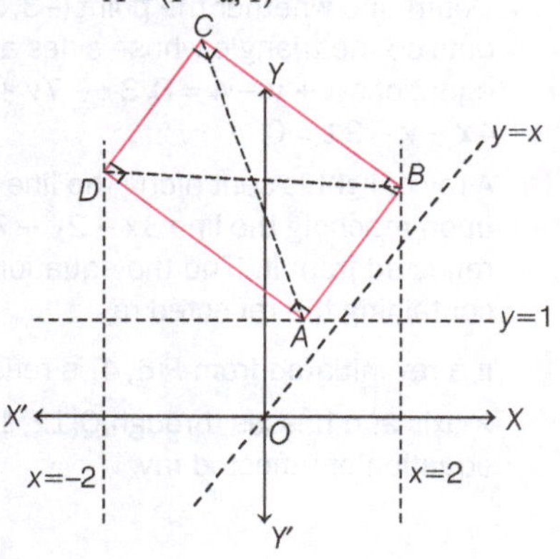

Again, B lies on $x = 2$

$\therefore$ $B = (2, 2 + a)$

$\Rightarrow$ Equation of AD is

$$y - 1 = -[x - (1 - a)] \text{ or } y = 2 - x - a$$

$\because$ D lies on $x = -2$

$\therefore$ $D \equiv (-2, 4 - a)$

Let $C \equiv (h, k)$

$\because$ Diagonals of rectangle bisects to each other

$\therefore$ $h + 1 - a = 2 - 2$

$\Rightarrow$ $a = 1 + h$

and $k + 1 = 2 + a + 4 - a$

$\Rightarrow$ $k = 5$

$\therefore$ Locus of C is $y = 5$

Example 2 *The line $(\lambda + 1)^2 x + \lambda y - 2\lambda^2 - 2 = 0$ passes through a point regardless of the value λ. Which of the following is the line with slope 2 passing through the point?*

(a) $y = 2x - 8$ (b) $y = 2x - 5$

(c) $y = 2x - 4$ (d) $y = 2x + 8$

Sol. (a) Given, $(\lambda + 1)^2 x + \lambda y - 2\lambda^2 - 2 = 0$

or $(\lambda^2 + 2\lambda + 1)x + \lambda y - 2\lambda^2 - 2 = 0$

or $(\lambda^2 + 1)(x - 2) + \lambda(2x + y) = 0$

Now, for fixed point, $x - 2 = 0$ and $2x + y = 0$

$\therefore$ Fixed point is $(2, -4)$.

$\therefore$ Equation of required line is $y + 4 = 2(x - 2)$

or $y = 2x - 8$

Example 3 *If the point $P(a, a^2)$ lies inside the triangle formed by the lines $x = 0$, $y = 0$ and $x + y = 2$, then exhaustive range of a is*

(a) $(0, 1)$ (b) $(1, \sqrt{2})$

(c) $(\sqrt{2} - 1, 1)$ (d) $(\sqrt{2} - 1, 2)$

Sol. (a) Since, the point $P(a, a^2)$ lies on $y = x^2$

On solving, $y = x^2$

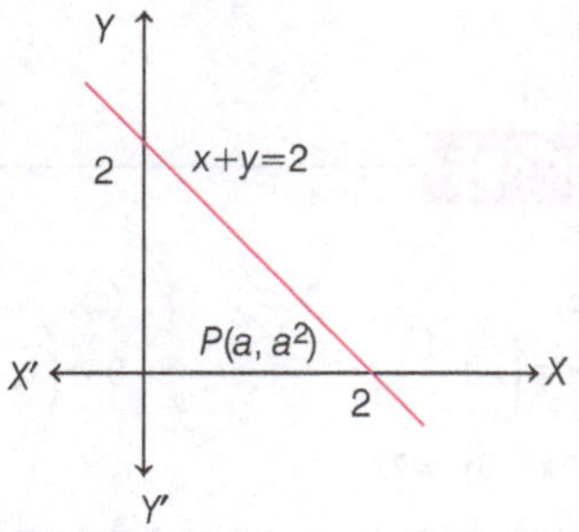

and $x + y = 2$, we get

$$a^2 + a - 2 < 0$$

$\Rightarrow$ $(a + 2)(a - 1) < 0 \Rightarrow a \in (-2, 1)$

It is clear from figure, $P(a, a^2)$ lies in 1st quadrant.

Also, $a > 0$ for Ist quadrant.

$\therefore$ $a \in (0, 1)$

Example 4 *If $5a + 4b + 20c = t$, then the value of t for which the line $ax + by + c - 1 = 0$ always passes through a fixed point is*

(a) 0 (b) 20 (c) 30 (d) None of these

Sol. (b) Equation of line $\frac{ax}{c-1} + \frac{by}{c-1} + 1 = 0$ has two independent parameters. It can pass through a fixed point if it contains only one independent parameter. Now, there must be one relation between $\frac{a}{c-1}$ and $\frac{b}{c-1}$ independent of a, b and c so that $\frac{a}{c-1}$ can be expressed in terms of $\frac{b}{c-1}$ and straight line contains only one independent parameter. Now that given relation can be expressed as $\frac{5a}{c-1} + \frac{4b}{c-1} = \frac{t-20c}{c-1}$.

RHS is independent of c if $t = 20$.

Example 5 *If the straight lines, $ax + amy + 1 = 0$, $bx + (m+1)by + 1 = 0$ and $cx + (m+2)cy + 1 = 0$, $(m \neq 0)$ are concurrent, then a, b and c are in*

(a) AP only for $m = 1$ (b) AP for all m

(c) GP for all m (d) HP for all m

Sol. (d) The three lines are concurrent if $\begin{vmatrix} a & am & 1 \\ b & m+1 & 1 \\ c & (m+2)c & 1 \end{vmatrix} = 0$

On applying $C_2 \to C_2 - mC_1$, then $\begin{vmatrix} a & 0 & 1 \\ b & b & 1 \\ c & 2c & 1 \end{vmatrix} = 0$

or $a(b - 2c) - 0 + 1(2bc - bc) = 0$

or $b = \frac{2ac}{a+c}$, which is independent of m.

$\therefore$ a, b and c are in HP for all m.

Example 6 *Two sides of a rhombus are along the lines, $x - y + 1 = 0$ and $7x - y - 5 = 0$. If its diagonals intersect at $(-1, -2)$, then which one of the following is a vertex of this rhombus?*

(a) $(-3, -9)$ (b) $(-3, -8)$

(c) $\left(\frac{1}{3}, -\frac{8}{3}\right)$ (d) $\left(-\frac{10}{3}, -\frac{7}{3}\right)$

Sol. (c) As the given lines $x - y + 1 = 0$ and $7x - y - 5 = 0$ are not parallel, therefore they represent the adjacent sides of the rhombus.

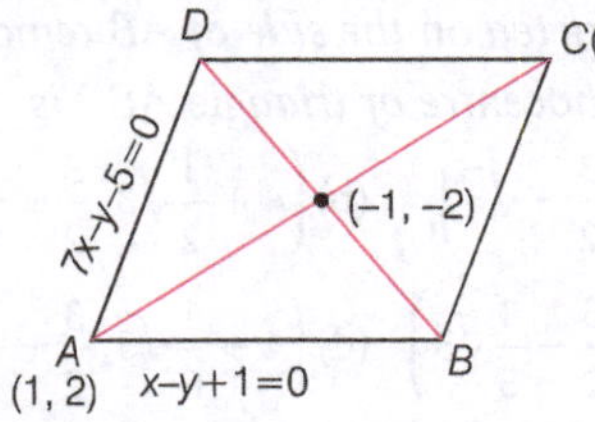

On solving $x - y + 1 = 0$ and $7x - y - 5 = 0$, we get $x = 1$ and $y = 2$. Thus, one of the vertex is $A(1, 2)$.

Let the coordinate of point C be (x, y).

Then, $-1 = \frac{x+1}{2}$ and $-2 = \frac{y+2}{2}$

$\Rightarrow$ $x + 1 = -2$ and $y = -4 - 2$

$\Rightarrow$ $x = -3$ and $y = -6$

Hence, coordinate of point C be $(-3, -6)$.

Note that vertices B and D will satisfy $x - y + 1 = 0$ and $7x - y - 5 = 0$, respectively.

Since, option (c) satisfies $7x - y - 5 = 0$, therefore coordinate of vertex D is $\left(\frac{1}{3}, \frac{-8}{3}\right)$.

Example 7 *Through the point $P(\alpha, \beta)$, when $\alpha\beta > 0$, the straight line $\frac{x}{a} + \frac{y}{b} = 1$ is drawn so as to form with coordinate axes a triangle of area Δ. If $ab > 0$, then the least value of Δ is*

(a) $\alpha\beta$ (b) $2\alpha\beta$ (c) $4\alpha\beta$ (d) $8\alpha\beta$

Sol. (b) Given line is $\frac{x}{a} + \frac{y}{b} = 1$ ...(i)

$\therefore$ $A \equiv (a, 0)$ and $B \equiv (0, b)$

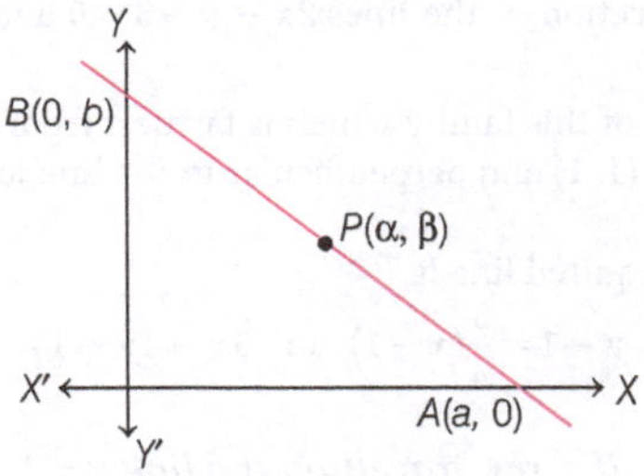

$\because$ Area of $(\Delta AOB) = \Delta$

$\therefore$ $\frac{1}{2}|ab| = \Delta \Rightarrow ab = 2\Delta$ $[\because ab > 0]$

Since, the line Eq. (i) passes through the point $P(\alpha, \beta)$.

$\therefore$ $\frac{\alpha}{a} + \frac{\beta}{b} = 1 \Rightarrow \frac{\alpha}{a} + \frac{a\beta}{2\Delta} = 1$ $\left[\because b = \frac{2\Delta}{a}\right]$

$\Rightarrow a^2\beta - 2a\Delta + 2\Delta\alpha = 0$

$\therefore$ $D \geq 0$ $[\because a$ is real$]$

$\Rightarrow$ $4\Delta^2 - 4\beta(2\Delta\alpha) \geq 0$ or $\Delta \geq 2\alpha\beta$

$\therefore$ Least value of Δ is $2\alpha\beta$.

Example 8 *The coordinates of the point P on the line $2x + 3y + 1 = 0$, such that $|PA - PB|$ is maximum, where A is $(2, 0)$ and B is $(0, 2)$, is*

(a) $(5, -3)$ (b) $(7, -5)$ (c) $(9, -7)$ (d) $(11, -9)$

Sol. (b) $|PA - PB| \leq |AB|$

Maximum value of $|PA - PB|$ is $|AB|$, which is possible only when P, A, B are collinear.

If $P(x, y)$, then equation AB is

$$\frac{x}{2} + \frac{y}{2} = 1$$

$\Rightarrow \quad x + y = 2 \quad$ ...(i)

Now, solving Eq. (i)

and $\quad 2x + 3y + 1 = 0 \quad$ ...(ii)

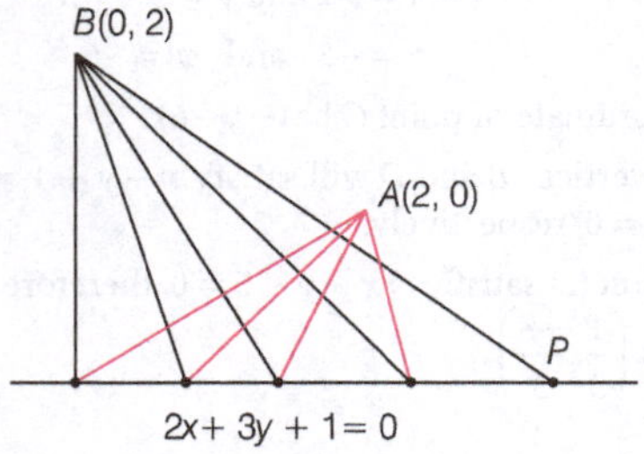

Then, $\quad x = 7, y = -5$

$\therefore \quad P \equiv (7, -5)$

Example 9 *Equation of the straight line which belongs to the system of straight lines $a(2x + y - 3) + b(3x + 2y - 5) = 0$ and is farthest from the point $(4, -3)$ is*

(a) $4x + 11y - 15 = 0$ (b) $3x - 4y + 1 = 0$

(c) $7x + y - 8 = 0$ (d) None of these

Sol. (b) The system of straight lines $a(2x + y - 3) + b(3x + 2y - 5) = 0)$ passes through the point of intersection of the lines $2x + y - 3 = 0$ and $3x + 2y - 5 = 0$ i.e. $(1, 1)$.

The line of this family which is farthest from $(4, -3)$ is the line through $(1, 1)$ and perpendicular to the line joining $(1, 1)$ and $(4, -3)$.

$\therefore$ The required line is

$$y - 1 = \frac{3}{4}(x - 1) \quad \text{or} \quad 3x - 4y + 1 = 0$$

Example 10 *If a ray travelling the line $x = 1$ gets reflected the line $x + y = 1$, then the equation of the line along which the reflected ray travels is*

(a) $y = 0$ (b) $x - y = 1$ (c) $x = 0$ (d) None of these

Sol.

Decoding the Question

The angle of the reflected ray is equal to the angle of the incident ray, with respect to the normal to the surface that is to a line perpendicular to the surface at the point of contact.

(a) Reflected ray is X-axis.

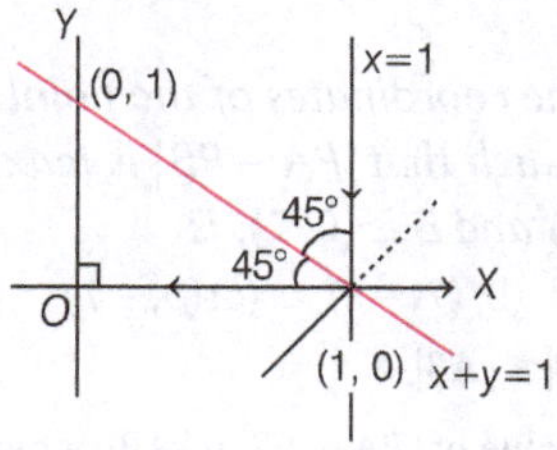

$\therefore$ Equation is $y = 0$.

JEE SCANNER

Example 11 Similar to PYQ Asked in JEE Main 2023

Let two straight line drawn from the origin O intersect the line $2x+3y=6$ at the points P and Q such that ΔOPQ is an isosceles triangle and $\angle POQ = 90°$. If $l = OP^2 + PQ^2 + QO^2$, then the greatest integer less than or equal to l is

(a) 24 (b) 22 (c) 21 (d) 23

Sol. (b) Given, ΔOPQ is an isosceles triangle and $\angle POQ = 90°$ and $OP = OQ$.

Equation of PQ is $2x + 3y - 6 = 0$

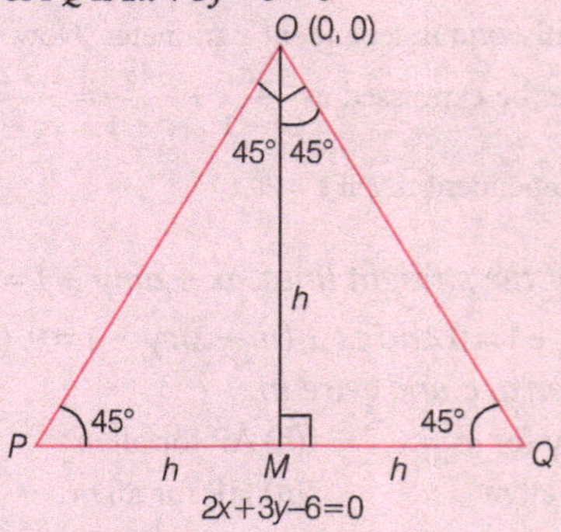

and length of OM be h.

$$\therefore \quad h = \left|\frac{-6}{\sqrt{4+9}}\right| = \frac{6}{\sqrt{13}}$$

$$\therefore \quad OP = OQ = h\sqrt{2} = \frac{6\sqrt{2}}{\sqrt{13}} \text{ and } PQ = 2h = \frac{12}{\sqrt{13}}$$

$$l = OP^2 + OQ^2 + PQ^2 = \left(\frac{6\sqrt{2}}{\sqrt{13}}\right)^2 + \left(\frac{6\sqrt{2}}{\sqrt{13}}\right)^2 + \left(\frac{12}{\sqrt{13}}\right)^2$$

$$= \frac{72 + 72 + 144}{13} = \frac{288}{13}$$

$$\therefore \quad [l] = \left[\frac{288}{13}\right] = 22$$

Skill Builder

Let two straight lines drawn from the origin O intersect the line $3x+4y=15$ at the points P and Q such that ΔOPQ is an isosceles triangle and $\angle POQ = 90°$. If $l = OP^2 + PQ^2 + QO^2$, then l is

For Sol.

(a) 76 (b) 75 (c) 72 (d) 108

Example 12 *Let $A \equiv (3, 2)$ and $B \equiv (5, 1)$. ABP is an equilateral triangle constructed on the side of AB remote from origin, then the orthocentre of triangle ABP is*

(a) $\left(4 - \frac{1}{2}\sqrt{3}, \frac{3}{2} - \sqrt{3}\right)$ (b) $\left(4 + \frac{1}{2}\sqrt{3}, \frac{3}{2} + \sqrt{3}\right)$

(c) $\left(4 - \frac{1}{6}\sqrt{3}, \frac{3}{2} - \frac{1}{3}\sqrt{3}\right)$ (d) $\left(4 + \frac{1}{6}\sqrt{3}, \frac{3}{2} + \frac{1}{3}\sqrt{3}\right)$

Sol. $AB = \sqrt{(5-3)^2 + (1-2)^2} = \sqrt{5}$

$\therefore PA = PB$

$\Rightarrow \quad \sqrt{(x-3)^2 + (y-2)^2} = \sqrt{(x-5)^2 + (y-1)^2}$

$\Rightarrow x^2 + 9 - 6x + y^2 - 4y + 4 = x^2 + 25 - 10x + y^2 - 2y + 1$

$\Rightarrow \quad 4x - 2y = 13 \quad \text{...(i)}$

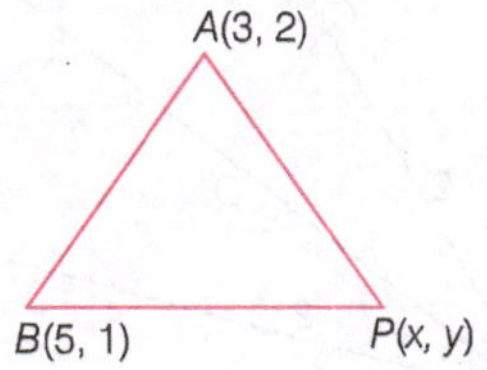

$\therefore$ Area of $\Delta ABC = \frac{1}{2}\begin{vmatrix} 3 & 2 & 1 \\ 5 & 1 & 1 \\ x & y & 1 \end{vmatrix} = \frac{5\sqrt{3}}{4}$

$\Rightarrow 3 + 5y + 2x - x - 3y - 10 = \frac{5\sqrt{3}}{2}$

$\Rightarrow \quad x + 2y = 7 + \frac{5\sqrt{3}}{2}$

$\Rightarrow \quad x + 2y = \frac{14 + 5\sqrt{3}}{2}$

$\Rightarrow \quad 2x + 4y = 14 + 5\sqrt{3} \quad \text{...(ii)}$

On solving Eqs. (i) and (ii), we get

$$\left(x = 4 + \frac{\sqrt{3}}{2}, y = \frac{3}{2} + \sqrt{3}\right)$$

More than One Correct Type Questions

Example 13 *The vertices of a square inscribed in the triangle with vertices A(0, 0), B(2, 1) and C(3, 0), given that two of its vertices are on the side AC, are*

(a) $\left(\frac{3}{2}, 0\right)$ (b) $\left(\frac{3}{2}, \frac{3}{4}\right)$

(c) $\left(\frac{9}{4}, \frac{3}{4}\right)$ (d) $\left(\frac{9}{4}, 0\right)$

Sol. (a, b, c, d)

Let $PQRS$ be a square inscribed in ΔABC and

$PQ = QR = RS = SP = \lambda$ (say)

Let $P \equiv (a, 0)$,

$\therefore \quad Q \equiv (a + \lambda, \lambda), R \equiv (a + \lambda, \lambda)$ and $S \equiv (a, \lambda)$

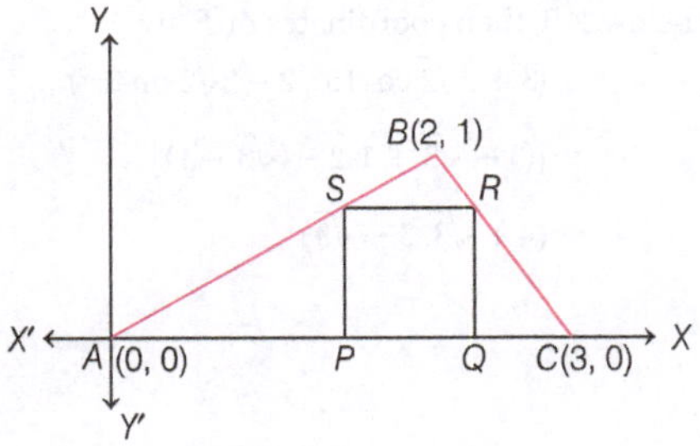

Now, equation of AB is

$$x - 2y = 0 \quad \text{...(i)}$$

and equation of BC is

$$x + y - 3 = 0 \quad \text{...(ii)}$$

$\because$ S lies on AB, then

$$a - 2\lambda = 0 \quad \text{...(iii)}$$

and R lies on BC, then

$$a + \lambda + \lambda - 3 = 0 \text{ or } a + 2\lambda - 3 = 0 \quad \text{...(iv)}$$

From Eqs. (iii) and (iv), we get

$$a = \frac{3}{2}, \lambda = \frac{3}{4}$$

Hence, $P \equiv \left(\frac{3}{2}, 0\right)$, $Q \equiv \left(\frac{9}{4}, 0\right)$,

$R \equiv \left(\frac{9}{4}, \frac{3}{2}\right)$ and $S \equiv \left(\frac{3}{2}, \frac{3}{4}\right)$

Example 14 *Line $\frac{x}{a} + \frac{y}{b} = 1$ cuts the coordinate axes at $A(a, 0)$ and $B(0, b)$ and the line $\frac{x}{a'} + \frac{y}{b'} = -1$ at $A'(-a', 0)$ and $B'(0, -b')$. If the points A, B, A' and B' are concyclic, then the orthocentre of the triangle ABA' is*

(a) $(0, 0)$ (b) $(0, b')$

(c) $\left(0, \frac{-aa'}{b}\right)$ (d) $\left(0, \frac{bb'}{a}\right)$

Sol. (b, c) $\because$ A, B, A', B' are concyclic then,

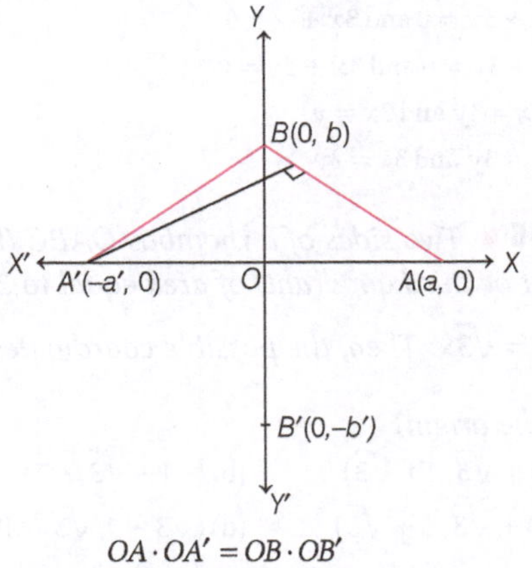

$$OA \cdot OA' = OB \cdot OB'$$

or $\quad (a) \cdot (-a') = (b) \cdot (-b')$

or $\quad aa' = bb' \quad \text{...(i)}$

The equation of altitude through A' is

$$y - 0 = \frac{a}{b}(x + a')$$

It intersects the altitude

$$x = 0 \text{ at } y = \frac{aa'}{b}$$

$\therefore$ Orthocentre is $\left(0, \frac{aa'}{b}\right)$ or $(0, b')$ [from Eq. (i)]

Example 15 *Two straight lines $u=0$ and $v=0$ pass through the origin and angle between them is $\tan^{-1}\left(\frac{7}{9}\right)$. If the ratio of the slope of $v=0$ and $u=0$ is $\frac{9}{2}$, then their equations are*

(a) $y = 3x$ and $3y = 2x$
(b) $2y = 3x$ and $3y = x$
(c) $y + 3x = 0$ and $3y + 2x = 0$
(d) $2y + 3x = 0$ and $3y + x = 0$

Sol. (a, b, c, d)

Let the slope of $u=0$ be m, then the slope of $v=0$ is $\frac{9m}{2}$.

Therefore, $$\left|\frac{m-\frac{9m}{2}}{1+m\times\frac{9m}{2}}\right|=\frac{7}{9}$$

or $$\left|\frac{-7m}{2+9m^2}\right|=\frac{7}{9}$$

$\Rightarrow$ $$9m^2+9m+2=0$$

or $$9m^2-9m+2=0$$

$\Rightarrow$ $$m=-\frac{2}{3},-\frac{1}{3}$$

or $$m=\frac{2}{3},\frac{1}{3}$$

Therefore, the equation of lines are

(i) $2x+3y=0$ and $3x+y=0$
(ii) $x+3y=0$ and $3x+2y=0$
(iii) $2x=3y$ and $3x=y$
(iv) $x=3y$ and $3x=2y$

Example 16 *Two sides of a rhombus OABC (lying entirely in the first or third quadrant) of area equal to 2 sq units are $y=\frac{x}{\sqrt{3}}$, $y=\sqrt{3}x$. Then, the possible coordinates of B is/are (O being the origin)*

(a) $(1+\sqrt{3}, 1+\sqrt{3})$
(b) $(-1-\sqrt{3}, -1-\sqrt{3})$
(c) $(3+\sqrt{3}, 3+\sqrt{3})$
(d) $(\sqrt{3}-1, \sqrt{3}-1)$

Sol. (a, b) Here, $\angle COA = 30°$

Let $OA = AB = BC = CO = x$

$\because$ Area of rhombus $OABC$

$$=2\times\frac{1}{2}\times x\times x\sin 30°$$

$$=\frac{x^2}{2}=2 \quad \text{[given]}$$

$\therefore$ $x=2$

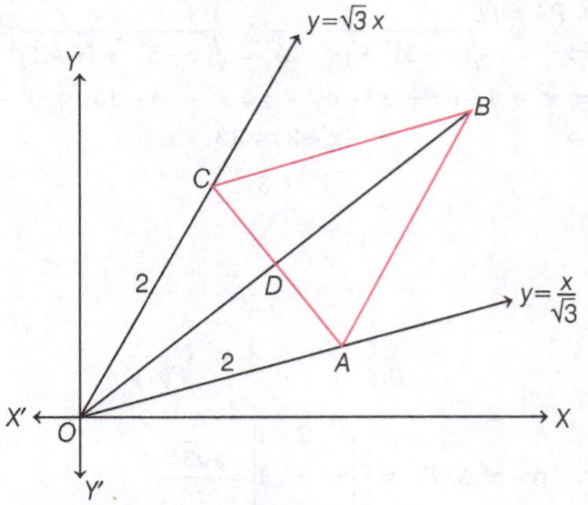

Coordinates of A and C are $(\sqrt{3}, 1)$ and $(1, \sqrt{3})$ in I quadrant and in III quadrant are $(-\sqrt{3}, -1)$ and $(-1, -\sqrt{3})$

Hence, coordinates of B are $(\sqrt{3}+1, \sqrt{3}+1)$ and $(-\sqrt{3}-1, -\sqrt{3}-1)$.

Example 17 *A and B are two fixed points whose coordinates are (3, 2) and (5, 4), respectively. The coordinates of a point P, if ABP is an equilateral triangle are*

(a) $(4-\sqrt{3}, 3+\sqrt{3})$
(b) $(4+\sqrt{3}, 3-\sqrt{3})$
(c) $(3-\sqrt{3}, 4+\sqrt{3})$
(d) $(3+\sqrt{3}, 4-\sqrt{3})$

Sol. (a, b)

$\because$ $AB = AP = BP = 2\sqrt{2}$

$\therefore$ Coordinates of P are $(3+2\sqrt{2}\cos 105°,\ 2+2\sqrt{2}\sin 105°)$

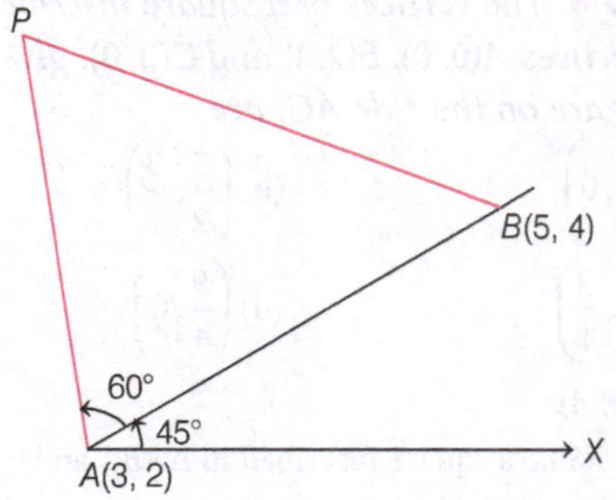

or $(3-(\sqrt{3}-1), 2+\sqrt{3}+1)$

or $(4-\sqrt{3}, 3+\sqrt{3})$

If P below AB, then coordinates of P are

$(3+2\sqrt{2}\cos 15°, 2-2\sqrt{2}\sin 15°)$

or $[(3+\sqrt{3}+1, 2-(\sqrt{3}-1)]$

or $(4+\sqrt{3}, 3-\sqrt{3})$

Example 18 *If the points* $\left(\frac{a^3}{a-1}, \frac{a^2-3}{a-1}\right), \left(\frac{b^3}{a-1}, \frac{b^2-3}{b-1}\right)$ *and* $\left(\frac{c^3}{c-1}, \frac{c^2-3}{c-1}\right)$ *when a, b and c are different from 1, lie on the line* $lx + my + n$*, then*

(a) $ab + bc + ca = \frac{h}{l}$

(b) $abc = \left(\frac{m+n}{l}\right)$

(c) $a + b + c = \frac{-m}{l}$

(d) $abc - (bc + ca + ab) + 3(a + b + c) = 0$

Sol. (a, c, d)

Since, the given points lie on the line $lx + my + n = 0$,

a, b and c are the roots of the equation

$$l\left(\frac{t^3}{t-1}\right) + m\left(\frac{t^2-3}{t-1}\right) + n = 0$$

$$\Rightarrow \quad lt^3 + mt^2 + nt - (3m + n) = 0 \quad \text{...(i)}$$

Hence, $$a + b + c = \frac{-m}{l}$$

$$ab + bc + ca = \frac{n}{l} \quad \text{...(ii)}$$

$$abc = \frac{3m + n}{l} \quad \text{...(iii)}$$

So, from Eqs. (i), (ii) and (iii), we get

$$abc - (bc + ca + ab) + 3(a + b + c) = 0$$

Passage Based Questions

Passage I

(Q. Nos. 19 and 20)

Let $d(P, OA) \le \min \cdot \{d(P, AB), d(P, BC), d(P, OC)\}$, where d denotes the distance from the point to the corresponding the line and R be the region consisting of all those points P inside the rectangle $OABC$ such that $O \equiv (0, 0)$, $A \equiv (3, 0)$, $B \equiv (3, 2)$ and $C \equiv (0, 2)$. Let M be the peak of region R.

Example 19 *Length of the perpendicular from M to OA is*

(a) 4 (b) 3

(c) 2 (d) 1

Example 20 *If λ be the perimeter of region R, then λ is*

(a) $4 - \sqrt{2}$

(b) $4 + \sqrt{2}$

(c) $4 + 2\sqrt{2}$

(d) 10

Sol. Let $P \equiv (x, y)$

$\because \quad d(P, OA) \le \min \cdot \{d(P, AB), d(P, BC), d(P, OC)\}$

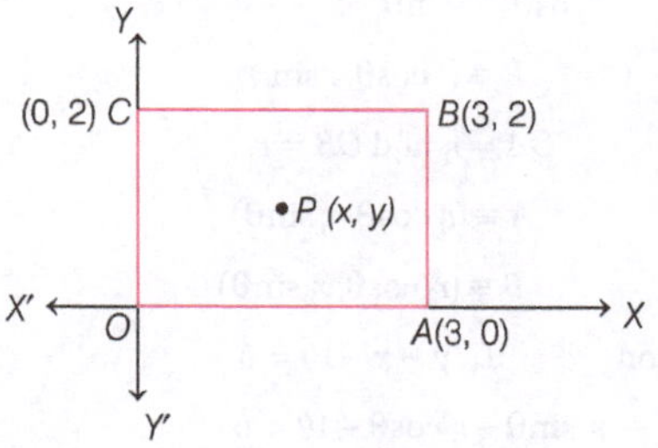

$\Rightarrow \quad |y| \le \min \{|3 - x|, |2 - y|, |x|\}$

As the rectangle $OABC$ lies in I quadrant,

$\therefore \quad y \le \min \cdot [3 - x, 2 - y, x]$

We draw the graph of

$\Rightarrow \quad y = 3 - x, y = 2 - y, y = x$

or $\quad x + y = 3, y = 1, y = x$

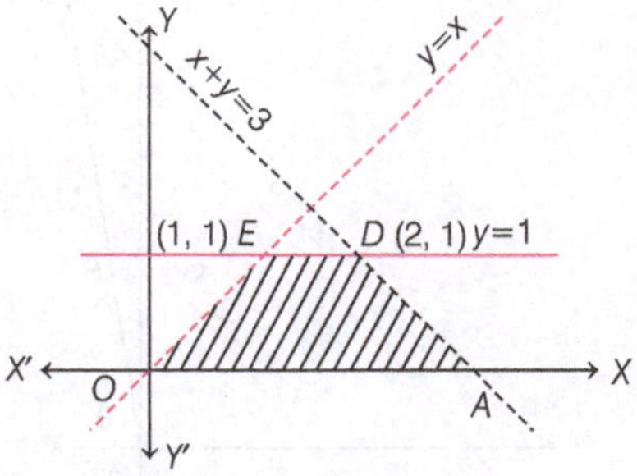

$\therefore \quad E \equiv (1, 1)$ and $D \equiv (2, 1)$

19. (d) $\because$ M lie on $y = 1$

$\therefore$ Length of perpendicular from M to OA is 1.

20. (c) λ = Perimeter of region R

$= OA + AD + DE + EO$

$= 3 + \sqrt{2} + 1 + \sqrt{2} = 4 + 2\sqrt{2}$

Passage II

(Q. Nos. 21 and 22)

A variable straight line L is drawn through $O(0, 0)$ to meet this lines $L_1 : y - x - 10 = 0$ and $L_2 : y - x - 20 = 0$ at the points A and B respectively.

Example 21 *A point P is taken on L such that* $\frac{2}{OP} = \frac{1}{OA} + \frac{1}{OB}$*, then the locus of P is*

(a) $3x + 3y - 40 = 0$ (b) $3x + 3y + 40 = 0$

(c) $3x - 3y - 40 = 0$ (d) $3x - 3y + 40 = 0$

Example 22 *A point P is taken on L such that* $(OP)^2 = OA \cdot OB$*, then the locus of P is*

(a) $(y - x)^2 = 25$ (b) $(y - x)^2 = 50$

(c) $(y - x)^2 = 100$ (d) $(y - x)^2 = 200$

Sol. Let the equation of line L through origin is

$$\frac{x-0}{\cos\theta}=\frac{y-0}{\sin\theta}=r$$

$\therefore \quad P\equiv(r\cos\theta, r\sin\theta)$

Let $\quad OA=r_1$ and $OB=r_2$

$\therefore \quad A\equiv(r_1\cos\theta, r_1\sin\theta)$

and $\quad B\equiv(r_2\cos\theta, r_2\sin\theta)$

A lies on $\quad L_1: y-x-10=0$

$\therefore \quad r_1\sin\theta-r_1\cos\theta-10=0$

$$\Rightarrow \quad r_1=\frac{10}{\sin\theta-\cos\theta} \quad \text{...(i)}$$

$\Rightarrow \quad B$ lies on $L_1: y-x-20=0$

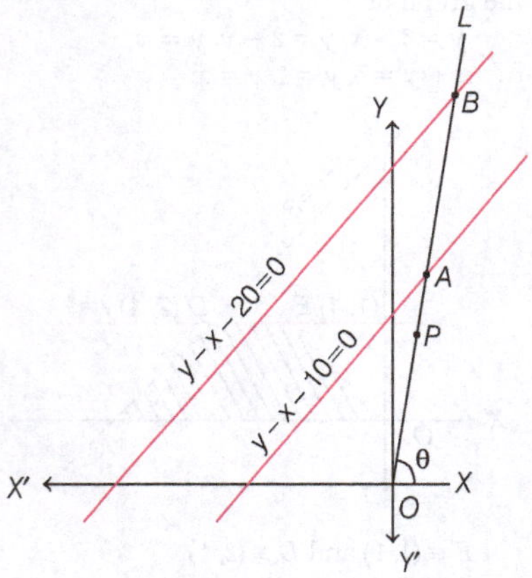

$\therefore \quad r_2\sin\theta-r_2\cos\theta-20=0$

$$\Rightarrow \quad r_2=\frac{20}{\sin\theta-\cos\theta} \quad \text{...(ii)}$$

21. (d) $\because \dfrac{2}{OP}=\dfrac{1}{OA}+\dfrac{1}{OB} \Rightarrow \dfrac{2}{r}=\dfrac{1}{r_1}+\dfrac{1}{r_2}$

$$\Rightarrow \quad \frac{2}{r}=\frac{\sin\theta-\cos\theta}{10}+\frac{\sin\theta-\cos\theta}{20} \quad \text{[from Eqs. (i) and (ii)]}$$

or $\quad 2=\dfrac{r\sin\theta-r\cos\theta}{10}+\dfrac{r\sin\theta-r\cos\theta}{20}$

or $\quad 2=\dfrac{y-x}{10}+\dfrac{y-x}{20} \quad [\because P\equiv(r\cos, r\sin\theta)]$

$\therefore$ Locus of P is $3x-3y+40=0$

22. (d) $\because (OP)^2=OA\cdot OB$

$\Rightarrow \quad r^2=r_1\cdot r_2$

$$\Rightarrow r^2=\frac{10}{(\sin\theta-\cos\theta)}\cdot\frac{20}{(\sin\theta-\cos\theta)} \quad \text{[from Eqs. (i) and (ii)]}$$

or $\quad (r\sin\theta-r\cos\theta)^2=200$

$\therefore$ Locus of P is $(y-x)^2=200$

Stem Based Questions

Stem I

(Q. Nos. 23 and 24)

Consider 3 non-collinear points $A(9,3)$, $B(7,-1)$ and $C(1,-1)$. Let $P(a,b)$ be the centre and R is the radius of circle S passing through A, B, C. Also $H(\bar{x},\bar{y})$ are the coordinates of the orthocentre of triangle ABC whose area is denoted by Δ.

Example 23 *The value of $a+b+R$ is ....*

Example 24 *If D, E and F are the middle points of BC, CA and AB respectively, then the area of triangle DEF is ....*

23. (12) Equation of perpendicular bisector of AC is

$$y-1=-2(x-5)$$

$$y+2x=11 \quad \text{...(i)}$$

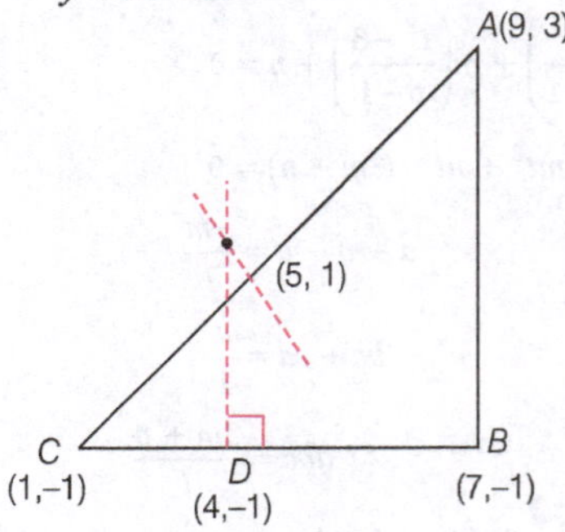

Equation of perpendicular bisector of BC is

$$x=4$$

$\therefore$ Circumcentre $\equiv(4,3) \quad [\because$ put $x=4$ in Eq. (i), we get $y=3]$

$$\Rightarrow \quad R=\sqrt{(4-1)^2+(3+1)^2}=5$$

$$\therefore \quad a+b+R=4+3+5=12$$

24. (3) Area of $\Delta DEF=\dfrac{1}{4}\times$ area of ABC

$$=\frac{1}{4}\times\frac{1}{2}\times6\times4=3 \text{ sq. units}$$

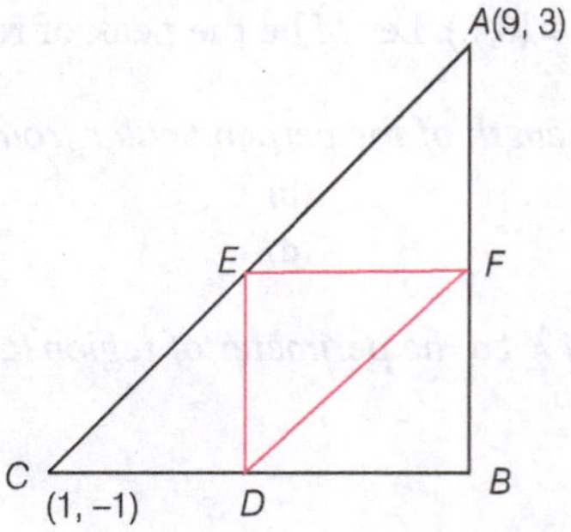

Single Integer Answer Type Questions

Example 25 *$P(x, y)$ is called a natural point if $x, y \in N$. The total number of points lying inside the quadrilateral formed by the lines $2x + y = 2$, $x = 0$, $y = 0$ and $x + y = 5$ is ....*

Sol. (6) First, we construct the graph of the given quadrilateral.

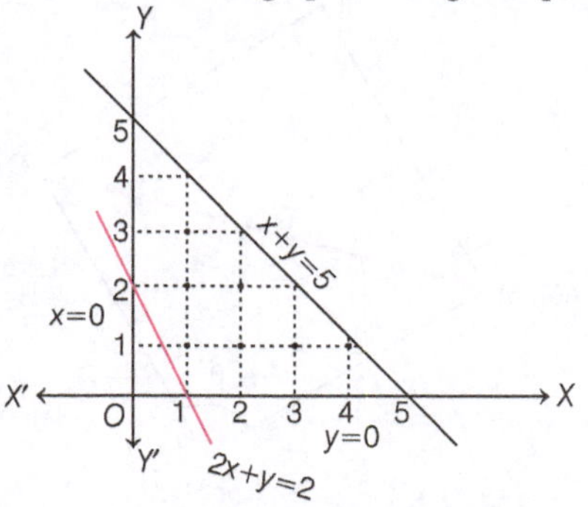

It is clear from the graph that there are six points lying inside the quadrilateral.

Example 26 *The distance of the point (x, y) from the origin is defined as $d = \max\{|x|, |y|\}$. Then the distance of the common point for the family of lines $x(1+\lambda) + \lambda y + 2 + \lambda = 0$ (λ being parameter) from the origin is ....*

Sol. (2) Given family of lines is

$$x(1+\lambda) + \lambda y + 2 + \lambda = 0$$

$$\Rightarrow \quad (x+2) + \lambda(x + y + 1) = 0$$

for common point or fixed point

$$x + 2 = 0$$

and $\quad x + y + 1 = 0$ or $x = -2, y = 1$

$\therefore$ Common point is $(-2, 1)$

or $\quad d = \max\{|-2|, |1|\} = \max\{2, 1\} = 2$

Example 27 *Let A, B and C lie on lines $y = x$, $y = 2x$ and $y = 3x$ respectively. Also, AB passes through fixed point $(1, 0)$, BC passes through fixed point $(0, -1)$, then AC also passes through fixed point (h, k). The value of $h + k$ is ....*

Sol. (0) Slope of $AB = \dfrac{\alpha}{\alpha - 1} = \dfrac{2\beta}{\beta - 1} \Rightarrow \alpha = \dfrac{2\beta}{\beta + 1}$

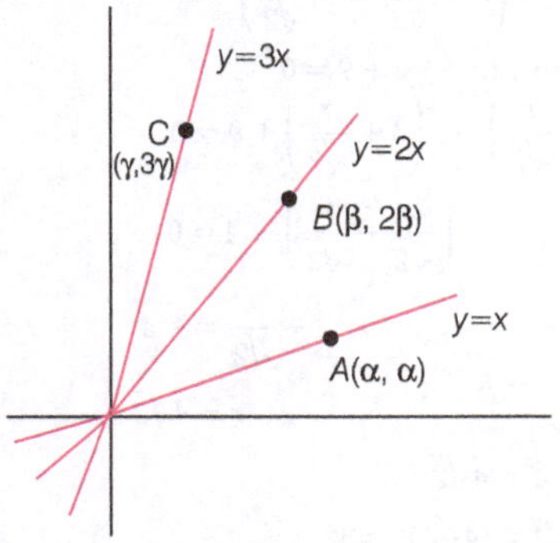

Slope of $BC = \dfrac{2\beta + 1}{\beta} = \dfrac{3\gamma + 1}{\gamma}$

$$\Rightarrow \quad \gamma = \frac{\beta}{1 - \beta}$$

Equation of AC is $y - \dfrac{2\beta}{\beta + 1} = \left(\dfrac{\dfrac{3\beta}{1-\beta} - \dfrac{2\beta}{\beta+1}}{\dfrac{\beta}{1-\beta} - \dfrac{2\beta}{\beta+1}}\right)\left(x - \dfrac{2\beta}{\beta+1}\right)$

$$\Rightarrow (x + y) - \beta(3y - 5x + 4) = 0$$

which passes through fixed point $\left(\dfrac{1}{2}, -\dfrac{1}{2}\right)$

$\therefore \quad h + k = 0$

JEE SCANNER

Example 28 Similar to PYQ Asked in JEE Main 2024

Let $A(-2, 1)$ and $B(3, 4)$ be two points and P be a variable point above the line AB such that the area of ΔPAB is 10. If the locus of P is $ax + by - 9 = 0$, then $a - b$ is equal to ....

Sol. (8)

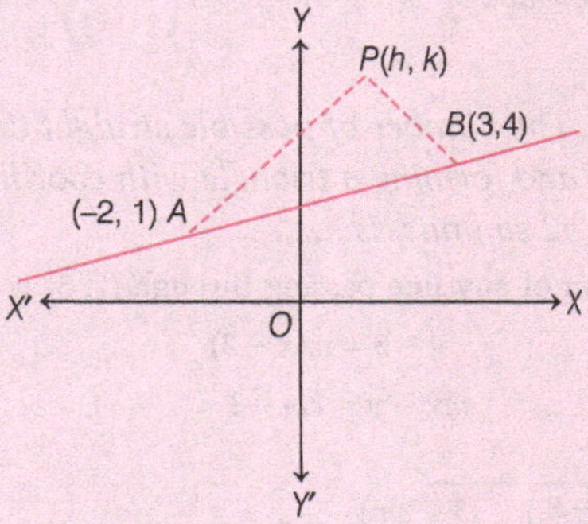

Area of $\Delta PAB = 10$

$$\frac{1}{2}\begin{vmatrix} h & k & 1 \\ -2 & 1 & 1 \\ 3 & 4 & 1 \end{vmatrix} = 10 \Rightarrow |h(-3) - k(-5) - 11| = 20$$

$\Rightarrow -3h + 5k - 11 = \pm 20 \Rightarrow 3h - 5k + 31 = 0$ or $3h - 5k - 9 = 0$

$\because$ Given locus is $ax + by - 9 = 0$

$3h - 5k - 9 = 0 \Rightarrow a = 3, b = -5 \Rightarrow a - b = 8$

Skill Builder

Let $A(-1, 2)$ and $B(2, 5)$ be two points and P be a variable point above the line AB such that the area of ΔPAB is 5. If the locus of P is $ax + by - 1 = 0$, then $a - b$ is equal to ....

For Sol.

Example 29 *Let the algebraic sum of the perpendicular distances from the points (3, 0), (0, 3) and (2, 2) to a variable straight line be zero, the line passing through a fixed point whose co-ordinates are (p, q), where $3(p+q) - 2$ is ....*

Sol. (8) Let the line be $ax + by + c = 0$ ...(i)

Let p_1, p_2 and p_3 are the perpendicular distances from the line Eq. (i).

Clearly, $p_1 + p_2 + p_3 = 0$

$$\Rightarrow \frac{3a+c}{\sqrt{a^2+b^2}} + \frac{3bc+c}{\sqrt{a^2+b^2}} + \frac{2a+2b+c}{\sqrt{a^2+b^2}} = 0$$

$$\Rightarrow \frac{3a+c+3b+c+2a+2b+c}{\sqrt{a^2+b^2}} = 0$$

$$\Rightarrow \frac{5a+5b+3c}{\sqrt{a^2+b^2}} = 0$$

$$\Rightarrow 5a+5b+3c = 0$$

$$\Rightarrow \frac{5}{3}a + \frac{5}{3}b + c = 0$$

which passes through a fixed point $\left(\frac{5}{3}, \frac{5}{3}\right)$.

Thus, $p = \frac{5}{3}, q = \frac{5}{3}$

Hence, the value of $3(p+q) - 2 = 3\left(\frac{5}{3} + \frac{5}{3}\right) - 2 = 10 - 2 = 8$

Example 30 *The number of possible straight lines passing through (2, 3) and forming a triangle with coordinate axes, whose area is 12 sq units, is ....*

Sol. (3) Equation of any line passing through (2, 3) is

$$y - 3 = m(x-2)$$

$$\Rightarrow mx - y = 2m - 3$$

$$\Rightarrow \frac{x}{\left(\frac{2m-3}{m}\right)} + \frac{y}{(3-2m)} = 1$$

It is given that

$$\frac{1}{2} \times \left(\frac{2m-3}{m}\right) \times (3-3m) = \pm 12$$

$$\Rightarrow (3-2m)^2 = \mp 24m$$

$$\Rightarrow 9 - 12m + 4m^2 = \mp 24m$$

$$4m^2 + 12m + 9 = 0, 4m^2 - 36m + 9 = 0$$

$$\Rightarrow (2m+3)^2 = 0, 4m^2 - 36m + 9 = 0$$

$$\Rightarrow (2m+3) = 0, 4m^2 - 36m + 9 = 0$$

$$\Rightarrow m = -\frac{3}{2}, D > 0$$

So, the number of lines is 3.

Numerical Value Type Questions

Example 31 *If one side of a rhombus has end points (4, 5) and (1, 1) such that the maximum area of the rhombus is .... (in sq. units).*

Sol. (25) We have, $AB = \sqrt{(4-1)^2 + (5-1)^2}$

$$= \sqrt{9+16}$$

$$= \sqrt{25}$$

$$= 5$$

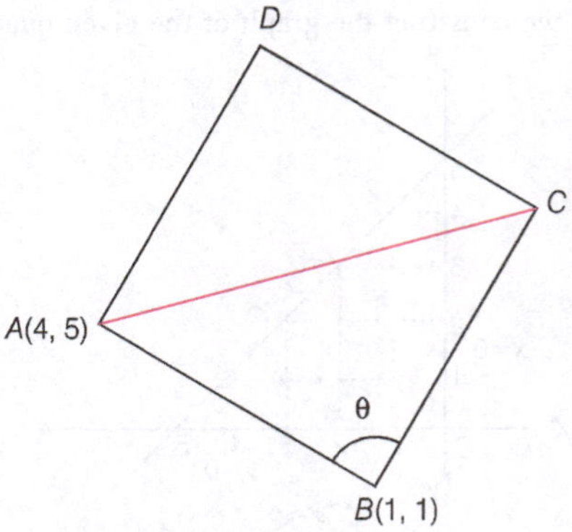

Area of the rhombus $= 2ar(\Delta ABC)$

$$= 2\left(\frac{1}{2} \times 5 \times 5 \sin\theta\right)$$

$$= 25 \sin\theta$$

Maximum area of a rhombus is 25 sq. units

Example 32 *If the distance of the point (2, 3) from the line $2x - 3y + 9 = 0$ measured along the line $2x - 2y + 5 = 0$ is d, then d^2 is equal to ....*

Sol. (32) Clearly, slope of the line $2x - 2y + 5 = 0$ is 1,

i.e. $\theta = \frac{\pi}{4}$.

Equation of any line passing through (2, 3) and making an angle $\frac{\pi}{4}$ is $\frac{x-2}{\cos\left(\frac{\pi}{4}\right)} = \frac{y-3}{\sin\left(\frac{\pi}{4}\right)} = r$

$$\Rightarrow \frac{x-2}{\frac{1}{\sqrt{2}}} = \frac{y-3}{\frac{1}{\sqrt{2}}} = r$$

$$\Rightarrow (x-2) = (y-3) = \frac{r}{\sqrt{2}} \quad \text{...(i)}$$

Thus, any point on the line Eq. (i) is

$$\left(2 + \frac{r}{\sqrt{2}}, 3 + \frac{r}{\sqrt{2}}\right)$$

which lies on $2x - 3y + 9 = 0$

So, $2\left(2 + \frac{r}{\sqrt{2}}\right) - 3\left(3 + \frac{r}{\sqrt{2}}\right) + 9 = 0$

$$\Rightarrow \left(\frac{2r}{\sqrt{2}} - \frac{3r}{\sqrt{2}}\right) + 4 = 0$$

$$\Rightarrow -\frac{r}{\sqrt{2}} = -4$$

$$\Rightarrow r = 4\sqrt{2}$$

Here, $d = 4\sqrt{2}$

$\therefore$ $d^2 = (4\sqrt{2})^2 = 32$

Example 33 *Let $P(\sin\theta, \cos\theta)(0 \le \theta \le 2\pi)$ be a point and let OAB be a triangle with vertices $(0, 0)$, $\left(\sqrt{\frac{3}{2}}, 0\right)$ and $\left(0, \sqrt{\frac{\sqrt{3}}{2}}\right)$. θ if P lies inside the ΔOAB and $\pi K / 24 < \theta < \pi/2$, then the value of k is ....*

Sol. (10) Equation of lines along OA, OB and AB are $y = 0$, $x = 0$, and $x + y = \sqrt{\frac{3}{2}}$ respectively. Now, P and B will lie on the same side of $y = 0$ if $\cos\theta > 0$. Similarly, P and A will lie on the same side of $x = 0$ if $\sin\theta > 0$ and P and O will lie on the same side of $x + y = \sqrt{\frac{3}{2}}$ if $\sin\theta + \cos\theta < \sqrt{\frac{3}{2}}$. Hence, P will lie inside the ΔABC, if $\sin\theta > 0$, $\cos\theta > 0$ and $\sin\theta + \cos\theta < \sqrt{\frac{3}{2}}$.

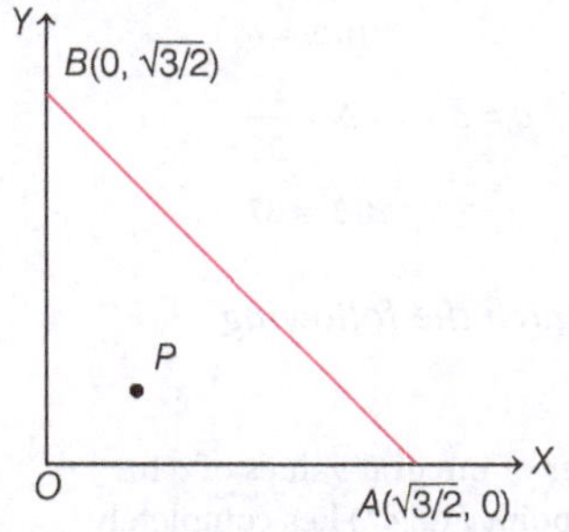

Now, $\sin\theta + \cos\theta < \sqrt{\frac{3}{2}} \Rightarrow \sin(\theta + \pi/4) < \frac{\sqrt{3}}{2}$

i.e. $0 < \theta + \pi/4 < \pi/3$ or $\frac{2\pi}{3} < \theta + \pi/4 < \pi$

Since, $\sin\theta > 0$ and $\cos\theta > 0$, so $0 < \theta < \frac{\pi}{12}$ or $\frac{5\pi}{12} < \theta < \pi/2$.

$\therefore k = 10$

Example 34 *A ray of light generated from the source kept at $(-3, 4)$ strikes the line $2x + y = 7$ at R and then terminated at $(0, 1)$. The sum of coordinates of point R so that ray travels through the shortest distance is λ, then $100\{\lambda\}$ is .... (where $\{\cdot\}$ denotes fractional part function).*

Sol. (32) Slope of the line $2x + y = 7$ is -2.

Let R be $(a, 7 - 2a)$, $P(-3, 4)$ and $Q(0, 1)$.

$\therefore$ Slope of $PR = \frac{3 - 2a}{a + 3}$, Slope of $RQ = \frac{6 - 2a}{a}$

Now, ray travels through the shortest distance so, PR must be incident ray and RQ must be reflected ray.

$$\frac{\frac{3 - 2a}{a + 3} + 2}{1 - 2\left(\frac{3 - 2a}{a + 3}\right)} = \frac{-2 - \frac{6 - 2a}{a}}{1 - 2\left(\frac{6 - 2a}{a}\right)} \Rightarrow a = \frac{42}{25}$$

Hence, R is $\left(\frac{42}{25}, \frac{91}{25}\right)$. Required sum is 5.32 $\Rightarrow \lambda = 5.32$

$\therefore 100\{\lambda\} = 100\{5.32\} = 100 \times 0.32 = 32$

Example 35 *If the line $y = \sqrt{3}x$ cuts the curve $x^4 + ax^2y + bxy + cx + dy + 6 = 0$ at A, B, C and D, then $OA \cdot OB \cdot OC \cdot OD$ (where O is the origin) is ....*

Sol. (96) The line $y = \sqrt{3}x$ can be written as $x = \frac{r}{2}$, $y = \frac{r\sqrt{3}}{2}$.

If this line cuts the given curve, then

$$\frac{r^4}{16} + \frac{ar^3\sqrt{3}}{8} + \frac{br^2\sqrt{3}}{4} + \frac{cr}{2} + \frac{dr\sqrt{3}}{2} + 6 = 0.$$

Therefore, $OA \cdot OB \cdot OC \cdot OD = |r_1||r_2||r_3||r_4| = |r_1r_2r_3r_4| = 96$

Example 36 *If the straight lines $ax + by + p = 0$ and $x\cos\alpha + y\sin\alpha = p$ are inclined at an angle $\frac{\pi}{4}$ and concurrent with the straight line $x\sin\alpha - y\cos\alpha = 0$, then the value of $10(a^2 + b^2)$ is ....*

Sol. (29). $ON = p$

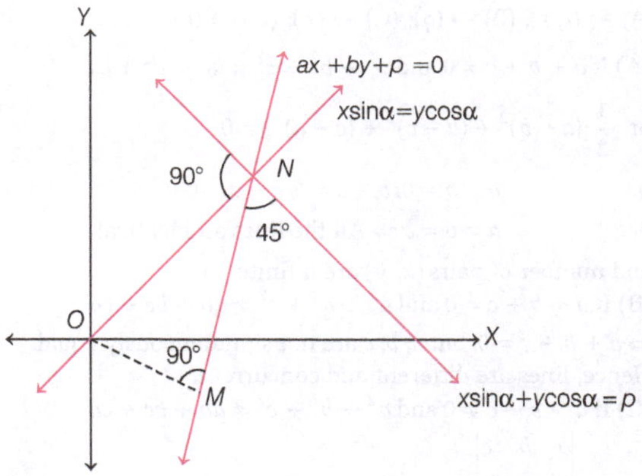

OM = Perpendicular distance of O from $ax + by + p = 0$

$$= \frac{p}{\sqrt{a^2 + b^2}} = ON\sin\frac{\pi}{4} = \frac{p}{\sqrt{2}}$$

Hence, $a^2 + b^2 = 2 \Rightarrow 10(a^2 + b^2) = 20$

Example 37 *Let ABC be a triangle. Let A be the point $(1, 2)$, $y = x$ is the perpendicular bisector of AB and $x - 2y + 1 = 0$ is the angle bisector of $\angle C$. If equation of BC is given by $ax + by - 5 = 0$, then the value of $10(a + b)$ is*

Sol. (20) The point B is $(2, 1)$.

Image of $A(1, 2)$ in the line $x - 2y + 1 = 0$ is given by

$$\frac{x - 1}{1} = \frac{y - 2}{2} = \frac{4}{5}$$

$\therefore$ Coordinates of the point are $\left(\frac{9}{5}, \frac{2}{5}\right)$.

Since, this point lies on BC.

$\therefore$ Equation of BC is $3x - y - 5 = 0$

$\therefore \quad a + b = 2 \Rightarrow 10(a + b) = 20$

Matching Type Questions

Example 38 *Consider the following linear equations in x and y* $ax + by + c = 0, bx + cy + a = 0, cx + ay + b = 0$.

Column I	Column II
(A) $a + b + c \neq 0$ and $a^2 + b^2 + c^2 = ab + bc + ca$	(p) Lines are sides of a triangle
(B) $a + b + c = 0$ and $a^2 + b^2 + c^2 \neq ab + bc + ca$	(q) Lines are different and concurrent
(C) $a + b + c \neq 0$ and $a^2 + b^2 + c^2 \neq ab + bc + ca$	(r) Number of pair (x, y) satisfying the equations are infinite
(D) $a + b + c = 0$ and $a^2 + b^2 + c^2 = ab + bc + ca$	(s) Lines are identical

Sol. (A) → (r, s); (B) → (q); (C) → (p); (D) → (r)

(A) if $a + b + c \neq 0$ and $a^2 + b^2 + c^2 = ab + bc + ca$

or $\frac{1}{2}\{(a-b)^2 + (b-c)^2 + (c-a)^2\} = 0$

or $a - b = 0, b - c = 0, c - a = 0$

or $a = b = c \Rightarrow$ All the lines an identical

and number of pairs (x, y) are infinite.

(B) If $a + b + c = 0$ and $a^2 + b^2 + c^2 \neq ab + bc + ca$

$\Rightarrow a + b + c = 0$, but a, b, c are not simultaneously equal.

Hence, lines are different and concurrent.

(C) If $a + b + c \neq 0$ and $a^2 + b^2 + c^2 \neq ab + bc + ca$

$$\Rightarrow \Delta = \begin{vmatrix} a & b & c \\ b & c & a \\ c & a & b \end{vmatrix} \neq 0 \text{ and } a, b, c \text{ are not all simultaneously equal.}$$

∴ Lines are sides of a triangle.

(D) If $a + b + c = 0$ and $a^2 + b^2 + c^2 = ab + bc + ca$

$\Rightarrow \Delta = 0$ and $a = b = c$

∴ Equations are satisfied for any (x, y).

Example 39 *The equation of the sides of a triangle are* $x + 2y + 1 = 0, 2x + y + 2 = 0$ *and* $px + qy + 1 = 0$ *and area of triangle is* Δ.

Column I		Column II
(A) $p = 2, q = 3$, then 8Δ is divisible by	(p)	3
(B) $p = 3, q = 2$, then 8Δ is divisible by	(q)	4
(C) $p = 3, q = 4$, then 10Δ is divisible by	(r)	6
(D) $p = 4, q = 3$, then 20Δ is divisible by	(s)	9

Sol. (A) → (p); (B) → (p, q, r); (C) → (p, r); (D) → (p, s)

$$\because \quad \Delta = \frac{D^2}{2|C_1 C_2 C_3|}, \text{ where } D = \begin{vmatrix} 1 & 2 & 1 \\ 2 & 1 & 2 \\ p & q & 1 \end{vmatrix} = 3(p-1)$$

and C_1, C_2, C_3 are co-factors of third column, then

$$C_1 = 2q - p, C_2 = 2p - q, C_3 = -3$$

$$\therefore \quad \Delta = \frac{3(p-1)^2}{2|2q-p||2p-q|}$$

(A) For $p = 2, q = 3 \Rightarrow \Delta = \frac{3}{8}$

∴ $8\Delta = 3$

(B) For $p = 3, q = 2 \Rightarrow \Delta = \frac{3}{2}$

∴ $8\Delta = 12$

(C) For $p = 3, q = 4 \Rightarrow \Delta = \frac{6}{10}$

∴ $10\Delta = 6$

(D) For $p = 4, q = 3 \Rightarrow \Delta = \frac{27}{20}$

∴ $20\Delta = 27$

Example 40 *Match the following*

Column I	Column II
(A) The number of integral values of a for which the point $P(a, a^2)$ lies completely inside the triangle by the lines $x = 0, y = 0$, and $x + 2y = 3$.	(p) 1
(B) ΔABC with $AB = 13, BC = 5$ and $AC = 12$ sides on the coordinates axis with A and B on the positive X-axis and positive Y-axis respectively,. the locus of vertex C is a line $12x - ky = 0$, then the value of k is	(q) 4
(C) The reflection of the point $(t-1, 2t+2)$ in a line is $(2t+1, t)$, then the line has slope equals to	(r) 3
(D) In the ΔABC the bisector of angles B and C lie along the lines $x = y$ and $y = 0$. If A is $(1, 2)$, then $\sqrt{10}d(A, B, C)$, where $d(A, BC)$ represents distance of point A form side BC.	(s) 5

Sol. (A) → (t), (B) → (s), (C) → (p), (D) → (q)

(A) For point (a, a^2) to lie inside the triangle formed by line $x = 0, y = 0$ and $x + 2y - 3 = 0$.

$$a > 0 \quad \text{...(i)}$$

$$a^2 > 0 \quad \text{...(ii)}$$

and $$a + 2a^2 - 3 < 0 \quad \text{...(iii)}$$

$$(2a+3)(a-1) < 0$$

$\Rightarrow$ $$a < 1 \Rightarrow a \in (0, 1)$$

(B) Since, $\angle BCA = 90°$

Points A, O, B, C are concyclic.

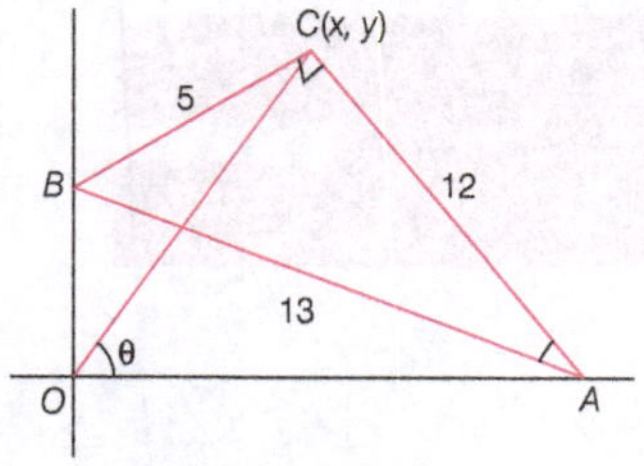

Let $\angle AOC = \theta$, $\angle BOC = \angle BAC$

$$\tan\left(\frac{\pi}{2} - \theta\right) = \frac{5}{12} \Rightarrow \frac{x}{y} = \frac{5}{12} \Rightarrow 12x - 5y = 0$$

(C) Slope of line joining the point $(t-1, 2t+2)$ and its image $(2t+1, t)$ is $\dfrac{(2t+2)-t}{t-1-2t-1} = \dfrac{t+2}{-(t+2)} = -1.$

So, slope of line is 1.

(D) Image of point $A(1, 2)$ in bisector of angles B and C lie on the line BC. Image of A in $x = y$ is $(2, 1)$ and image of A in $y = 0$ is $(1, -2)$. So, equation of line BC is $y = 3x - 5$

So, $d(A, BC) = \dfrac{4}{\sqrt{10}}$. So, $\sqrt{10}d(A, BC) = 4$

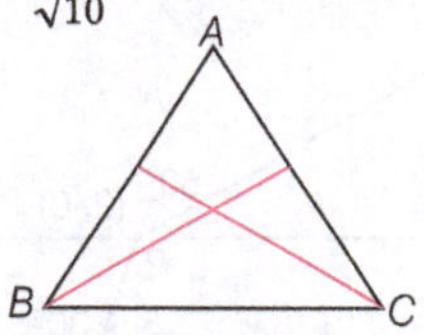

Example 41 *Match the following table.*

	Column I	Column II
(A)	Area of the region enclosed by $2\|x\| + 3\|y\| \le 6$ is	(p) 12
(B)	The extremities of the base of an isosceles ΔABC are the points $A(2, 0)$ and $B(0, 1)$. If the equation of the side AC is $x = 2$ and m be the slope of side BC, then $4m$ equals to	(q) 4
(C)	Area of ΔABC is 20 sq. units, where points A, B and C are $(4, 6), (10, 14)$ and (x, y) respectively. If AC is perpendicular to BC, then number of positions of C is	(r) 5
(D)	In a ΔABC coordinates of orthocentre, centroid and vertex A are respectively $(2, 2)$, $(2, 1)$ and $(0, 2)$. Then, x-coordinate of vertex B is	(s) 3 (t) 2

Sol. (A) → (p), (B) → (s), (C) → (q), (D) → (s)

$\therefore$ (A) $2|x| + 3|y| \le 6$ will represent the shaded region as shown in figure.

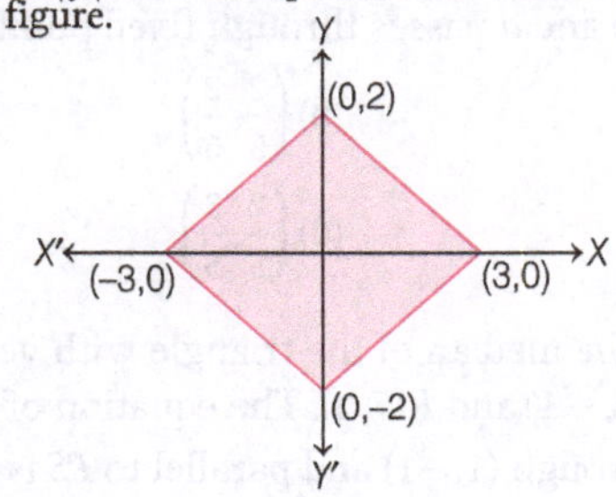

$\therefore$ Required area $= 4 \times \dfrac{1}{2} \times 3 \times 2 = 12$ sq. units.

(B) $\therefore D\left(1, \dfrac{1}{2}\right)$

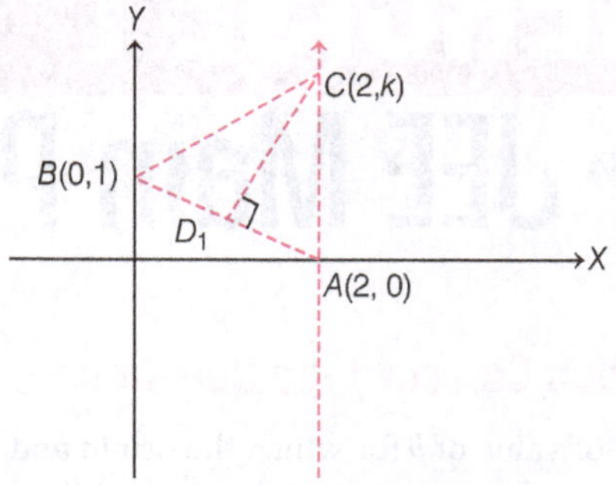

$\therefore CD$ is perpendicular AB.

$$\Rightarrow \quad \frac{k - \frac{1}{2}}{2 - 1} = 2$$

$$\Rightarrow \quad k = \frac{5}{2}$$

$\therefore$ Slope of $BC = \dfrac{3}{4}$

$\therefore 4m = 3$

(C) $\therefore$ Area of $\Delta ABC = 20$ sq units

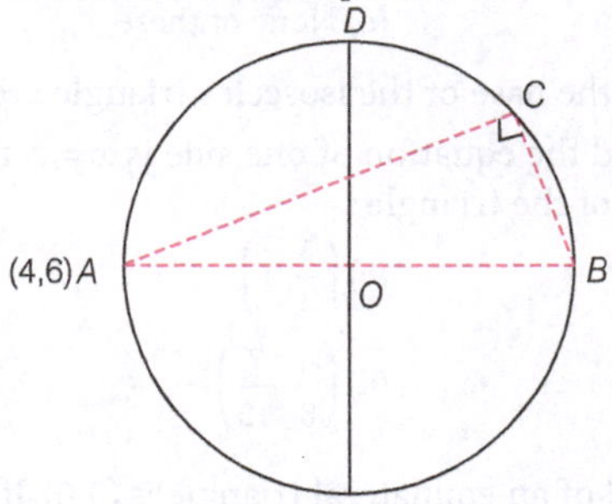

$\therefore C$ cannot be at D and E.

$\therefore$ Four positions are possible two above AB and two below AB.

(D) $\therefore \dfrac{\alpha + \alpha + 0}{3} = 2$

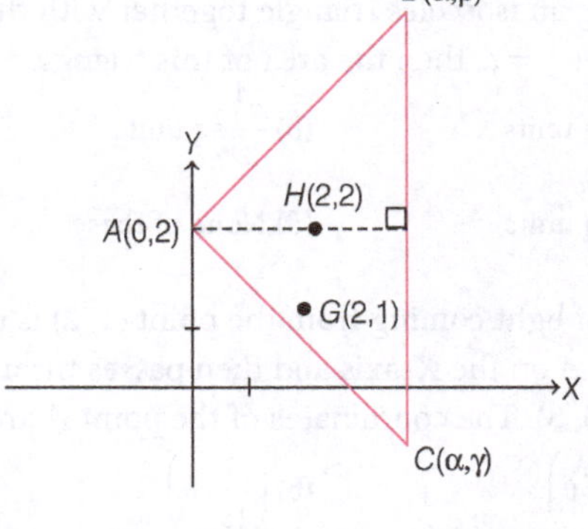

$$\Rightarrow \quad \alpha = 3$$

$\therefore$ x-coordinate of $B = 3$

EXERCISE 1

JEE Main Pattern

Single Option Correct Type Questions

1. The set of value of b for which the origin and the point (1, 1) lie on the same side of the straight line $a^2x + aby + 1 = 0 \forall a \in R, b > 0$ are
(a) $b \in (2, 4)$ (b) $b \in (0, 2)$
(c) $b \in [0, 2]$ (d) None of these

2. If $A\left(\frac{\sin\alpha}{3} - 1, \frac{\cos\alpha}{2} - 1\right)$ and $B(1, 1), \alpha \in [-\pi, \pi]$ are two points on the same side of the line $3x - 2y + 1 = 0$, then α belongs to the interval
(a) $\left(-\pi, -\frac{3\pi}{4}\right] \cup \left(\frac{\pi}{4}, \pi\right)$ (b) $[-\pi, \pi]$
(c) ϕ (d) None of these

3. The ends of the base of the isosceles triangle are at (2, 0) and (0, 1) and the equation of one side is $x = 2$, then the orthocentre of the triangle is
(a) $\left(\frac{3}{4}, \frac{3}{2}\right)$ (b) $\left(\frac{5}{4}, 1\right)$
(c) $\left(\frac{3}{4}, 1\right)$ (d) $\left(\frac{4}{3}, \frac{7}{12}\right)$

4. The centroid of an equilateral triangle is (0, 0). If two vertices of triangle lie on $x + y = 2\sqrt{2}$, then one of them will have its coordinates.
(a) $(\sqrt{2} + \sqrt{6}, \sqrt{2} - \sqrt{6})$ (b) $(\sqrt{2} + \sqrt{3}, \sqrt{2} - \sqrt{3})$
(c) $(\sqrt{2} + \sqrt{5}, \sqrt{2} - \sqrt{5})$ (d) None of these

5. Drawn from origin are two mutually perpendicular lines forming an isosceles triangle together with the straight line $2x + y = a$, then the area of this triangle is
(a) $\frac{a^2}{2}$ sq units (b) $\frac{a^2}{3}$ sq units
(c) $\frac{a^2}{5}$ sq units (d) None of these

6. A ray of light coming from the point (1, 2) is reflected at a point A on the X-axis and then passes through the point (5, 3). The coordinates of the point A are
(a) $\left(\frac{13}{5}, 0\right)$ (b) $\left(\frac{5}{13}, 0\right)$
(c) $(-7, 0)$ (d) None of these

7. In ΔABC equation of the right bisectors of the sides AB and AC are $x + y = 0$ and $x - y = 0$ respectively. If $A \equiv (5, 7)$, then equation of side BC is
(a) $7y = 5x$ (b) $5x = y$ (c) $5y = 7x$ (d) $5y = x$

8. In the adjacent figure, combined equation of the incident and refracted ray is

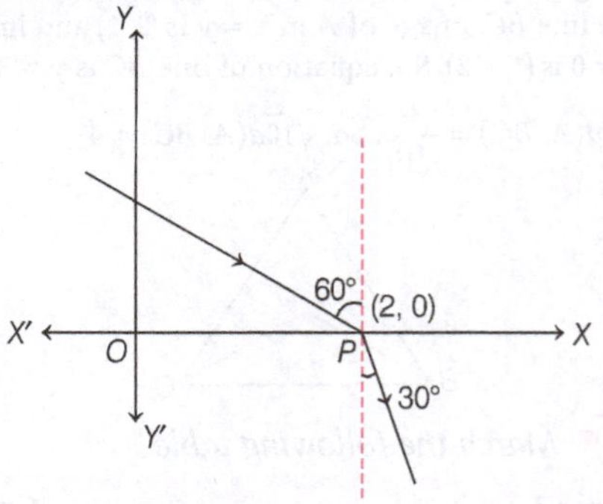

(a) $(x-2)^2 + y^2 + \frac{4}{\sqrt{3}}(x-2)y = 0$
(b) $(x-2)^2 + y^2 - \frac{4}{\sqrt{3}}(x-2)y = 0$
(c) $(x-2)^2 + y^2 + \frac{y}{\sqrt{3}}(x-2) = 0$
(d) $(x-2)^2 + y^2 - \frac{y}{\sqrt{3}}(x-2) = 0$

9. The equation of the lines through the point (2, 3) and making an intercept of length 2 units between the lines $2x + y = 3$ and $2x + y = 5$ are
(a) $x + 3 = 0, 3x + 4y = 12$ (b) $y - 2 = 0, 4x - 3y = 6$
(c) $x - 2 = 0, 3x + 4y = 18$ (d) None of these

10. The lines $(p + 2q)x + (p - 3q)y = p - q$ for different values of p and q passes through fixed point
(a) $\left(\frac{3}{2}, \frac{5}{2}\right)$ (b) $\left(\frac{2}{5}, \frac{2}{5}\right)$
(c) $\left(\frac{3}{5}, \frac{2}{5}\right)$ (d) $\left(\frac{2}{5}, \frac{3}{5}\right)$

11. Let PS be the median of the triangle with vertices $P(2, 2), Q(6, -1)$ and $R(7, 3)$. The equation of the line passing through $(1, -1)$ and parallel to PS is
(a) $2x - 9y - 7 = 0$ (b) $2x - 9y - 11 = 0$
(c) $2x + 9y - 11 = 0$ (d) $2x + 9y + 7 = 0$

12. The equation of the base of an equilateral triangle is $x+y=2$ and vertex is $(2,-1)$. The length of its side is

(a) $\sqrt{\frac{1}{2}}$ (b) $\sqrt{\frac{3}{2}}$ (c) $\sqrt{\frac{2}{3}}$ (d) $\sqrt{2}$

13. The distance between the lines $4x+3y=11$ and $8x+6y=15$ is

(a) $\frac{7}{2}$ (b) $\frac{7}{3}$

(c) $\frac{7}{5}$ (d) $\frac{7}{10}$

14. For $a>b>c>0$, the distance between $(1, 1)$ and the point of intersection of the lines $ax+by+c=0$ and $bx+ay+c=0$ is less than $2\sqrt{2}$. Then,

(a) $a+b-c>0$ (b) $a-b+c<0$

(c) $a-2b+c>0$ (d) $a+b-c<0$

15. The straight line $2x+3y+1=0$ bisects the angle between two straight lines of which one line is $3x+2y+4=0$. Then, the equation of the other line is

(a) $9x+26y=48$ (b) $9x+46y=28$

(c) $9x+26y=28$ (d) $3x+26y=48$

16. The graph of the function $\cos x\cos(x+2)-\cos^2(x+1)$ is

(a) a straight line passing through $(0, \sin^2 1)$ with slope 2

(b) a straight line passing through $(0, 0)$

(c) a parabola with vertex $(1, -\sin^2 1)$

(d) a straight line passing through the point $\left(\frac{\pi}{2}, -\sin^2 1\right)$ and parallel to the X-axis.

17. The orthocentre of the triangle formed by the lines $xy=0$ and $x+y=1$ is

(a) $\left(\frac{1}{2}, \frac{1}{2}\right)$ (b) $\left(\frac{1}{3}, \frac{1}{3}\right)$

(c) $(0, 0)$ (d) $\left(\frac{1}{4}, \frac{1}{4}\right)$

18. If $P=(1, 0)$, $Q=(-1, 0)$ and $R=(2, 0)$ are three given points, then locus of the points satisfying the relation $SQ^2+SR^2=2SP^2$, is

(a) a straight line parallel to X-axis

(b) a circle passing through the origin

(c) a circle with the centre at the origin

(d) a straight line parallel to Y-axis.

19. The point $(4, 1)$ undergoes the following three transformation successively

I. Reflection about the line $y=x$.

II. Transformation through a distance 2 units along the positive direction of X-axis.

III. Rotation through an angle $\frac{\pi}{4}$ about the origin in the counter clockwise direction. Then, the final position of the point is given by the coordinates

(a) $\left(\frac{1}{\sqrt{2}}, \frac{7}{\sqrt{2}}\right)$ (b) $(-\sqrt{2}, 7\sqrt{2})$

(c) $\left(-\frac{1}{\sqrt{2}}, \frac{7}{\sqrt{2}}\right)$ (d) $(\sqrt{2}, 7\sqrt{2})$

20. The incentre of the triangle with vertices $(1, \sqrt{3})$, $(0, 0)$ and $(2, 0)$ is

(a) $\left(1, \frac{\sqrt{3}}{2}\right)$ (b) $\left(\frac{2}{3}, \frac{1}{\sqrt{3}}\right)$ (c) $\left(\frac{2}{3}, \frac{\sqrt{3}}{2}\right)$ (d) $\left(1, \frac{1}{\sqrt{3}}\right)$

21. Let $a, \lambda, \mu \in R$. Consider the system of linear equations $ax+2y=\lambda$ and $3x-2y=\mu$.

Which of the following statement(s) is/are correct ?

(a) If $a=-3$, then the system has infinitely many solutions for all values of, λ and μ

(b) If $a\neq 3$, then the system has infinitely many solutions for all values of λ and μ

(c) If $a\neq -3$, then the system has a unique solution for all values of λ and μ

(d) If $\lambda+\mu\neq 0$, then the system has no solution for $a=-3$

Numerical Value Type Questions

22. A variable line passes through $P(2, 3)$ and cuts the coordinates axes at A and B. If the parallelogram $OACB$ (where O is the origin) is completed, then number of order pair (x, y) of integers which lie on the locus of point C is ....

23. The portion of the line $ax+3y-1=0$, intercepted between the lines $ax+y+1=0$ and $x+3y=0$ subtend a right angle at origin, then the value of $2|a|$ is ......

24. The equation of adjacent sides AB and AD of a parallelogram $ABCD$ are $3x-4y+21=0$ and $4x-3y-14=0$, respectively. The perpendicular distances between the parallel sides AB, DC and AD, BC are $\frac{14}{5}$ and $\frac{7}{5}$, respectively. If area of parallelogram is $2k$ sq units, then the value of k is ....

25. In a plane there are two families of lines : $y=x+n$, $y=-x+n$, where $n\in\{0, 1, 2, 3, 4\}$. The number of squares of the diagonal of length 2 formed by these lines is ...

26. The vertices B and C of a ΔABC lie on the lines $3y=4x$ and $y=0$ respectively and the sides BC passes through the point $\left(\frac{2}{3}, \frac{2}{3}\right)$. If $ABOC$ is a rhombus, O being the origin. If coordinates of vertex A is (α, β), then the value of $5(\alpha+\beta)$ is ....

27. If $(\lambda, \lambda+1)$ is an interior point of ΔABC, where $A \equiv (0,3)$, $B \equiv (-2,0)$ and $C \equiv (6,1)$, then the number of integral values of λ is ......

28. For all real values of a and b, lines $(2a+b)x+(a+3b)y+(b-3a)=0$, $\lambda x+2y+6=0$ and $\lambda x+2y+6=0$ are concurrent, then the value of $|\lambda|$ is ......

29. If from point (4, 4) perpendiculars to the straight lines $3x+4y+5=0$ and $y=mx+7$ meet at Q and R and area of triangle PQR is maximum, then the value of $9m$ is ......

30. If the vertices of a ΔABC are $(\lambda, 2-2\lambda)$, $(-\lambda+1, 2\lambda)$ and $(-4-\lambda, 6-2\lambda)$. If its area be 70 sq. units, the number of integral values of λ is ......

31. The sum of the abcissae of all the points on the line $x+y=4$ that lie at a unit distance from the line $4x+3y-10=0$ is λ, then $(100-\lambda)$ is equal to ....

32. If the straight line, $2x-3y+17=0$ is perpendicular to the line passing through the points (7, 17) and $(15, \beta)$, then (5β) equals ......

33. A rectangle is inscribed in a circle with a diameter lying along the line $3y=x+7$. If the two adjacent vertices of the rectangle are (−8, 5) and (6, 5), then the area of the rectangle (in sq. units) is ......

34. If $4a^2+9b^2-c^2+12ab=0$, the family of the straight lines $ax+by+c=0$ is either concurrent at (m, n) or (p, q) then, the value jkof $m+n+p+q+10$ is equal to ......

35. If the distance of the point (2, 3) from the line $2x-3y+9=0$ measured along the line $2x-2y+5=0$ is $d\sqrt{2}$, then the value of $d+2$ is ....

36. If the point (a^2, a) lies in the region corresponding to the acute angle between the lines $2y=x$ and $4y=x$ such that the value of a lies in (p, q), when $p, q \in N$, then the value of $(p+q+1)^2$ is equal to ......

Previous Years Questions

37. Let $\left(5, \frac{a}{4}\right)$ be the circumcenter of a triangle with vertices $A(a, -2)$, $B(a, 6)$ and $C\left(\frac{a}{4}, -2\right)$. Let α denote the circumradius, β denote the area and γ denote the perimeter of the triangle. Then, $\alpha+\beta+\gamma$ is **[Single Correct Type, 2024 Main]**

(a) 30 (b) 60
(c) 53 (d) 62

38. Let two straight lines drawn from the origin O intersect the line $3x+4y=12$ at the points P and Q such that ΔOPQ is an isosceles triangle and $\angle POQ=90°$. If $l=OP^2+PQ^2+QO^2$, then the greatest integer less than or equal to l is **[Single Correct Type, 2024 Main]**

(a) 44 (b) 42
(c) 46 (d) 48

39. The distance of the point (2, 3) from the line $2x-3y+28=0$, measured parallel to the line $\sqrt{3}x-y+1=0$ is equal to **[Single Correct Type, 2024 Main]**

(a) $6\sqrt{3}$ (b) $3+4\sqrt{2}$
(c) $4\sqrt{2}$ (d) $4+6\sqrt{3}$

40. In a ΔABC, suppose $y=x$ is the equation of the bisector of the $\angle B$ and the equation of the side AC is $2x-y=2$. If $2AB=BC$ and the points A and B are respectively (4, 6) and (α, β), then $\alpha+2\beta$ is equal to **[Single Correct Type, 2024 Main]**

(a) 42 (b) 45
(c) 48 (d) 39

41. Let R be the interior region between the lines $3x-y+1=0$ and $x+2y-5=0$ containing the origin. The set of all values of a, for which the points $(a^2, a+1)$ lie in R, is **[Single Correct Type, 2024 Main]**

(a) $(-3, -1) \cup \left(\frac{1}{3}, 1\right)$

(b) $(-3, 0) \cup \left(\frac{2}{3}, 1\right)$

(c) $(-3, -1) \cup \left(-\frac{1}{3}, 1\right)$

(d) $(-3, 0) \cup \left(\frac{1}{3}, 1\right)$

42. The portion of the line $4x+5y=20$ in the first quadrant is trisected by the lines L_1 and L_2 passing through the origin. The tangent of an angle between the lines L_1 and L_2 is **[Single Correct Type, 2024 Main]**

(a) $\frac{25}{41}$ (b) $\frac{30}{41}$ (c) $\frac{2}{5}$ (d) $\frac{8}{5}$

43. Let a ray of light passing through the point (3, 10) reflects on the line $2x+y=6$ and the reflected ray passes through the point (7, 2). If the equation of the incident ray is $ax+by+1=0$, then a^2+b^2+3ab is equal to .... **[Numerical Value Type, 2024 Main]**

44. Let ABC be an isosceles triangle in which A is at (−1, 0), $\angle A = \frac{2\pi}{3}$, $AB=AC$ and B is on the positive X-axis. If $BC=4\sqrt{3}$ and the line BC intersects the line $y=x+3$ at (α, β), then $\frac{\beta^4}{\alpha^2}$ is .... **[Numerical Value Type, 2024 Main]**

45. If (α, β) is the orthocenter of the ΔABC with vertices $A(3, -7)$, $B(-1, 2)$ and $C(4, 5)$, then $9\alpha - 6\beta + 60$ is equal to **[Single Correct Type, 2023 Main]**

(a) 30 (b) 35 (c) 40 (d) 25

46. If the point $\left(\alpha, \frac{7\sqrt{3}}{3}\right)$ lies on the curve traced by the mid-points of the line segments of the lines $x\cos\theta + y\sin\theta = 7, \theta \in \left(0, \frac{\pi}{2}\right)$ between the coordinate axes, then α is equal to **[Single Correct Type, 2023 Main]**

(a) $7\sqrt{3}$ (b) 7

(c) $-7\sqrt{3}$ (d) -7

47. Let $C(\alpha, \beta)$ be the circumcenter of the triangle formed by the lines $4x + 3y = 69$, $4y - 3x = 17$ and $x + 7y = 61$ Then, $(\alpha - \beta)^2 + \alpha + \beta$ is equal to **[Single Correct Type, 2023 Main]**

(a) 16 (b) 17

(c) 18 (d) 15

48. If the orthocentre of the triangle, whose vertices are (1, 2), (2, 3) and (3, 1) is (α, β), then the quadratic equation whose roots are $\alpha + 4\beta$ and $4\alpha + \beta$, is **[Single Correct Type, 2023 Main]**

(a) $x^2 - 20x + 99 = 0$ (b) $x^2 - 19x + 90 = 0$

(c) $x^2 - 18x + 80 = 0$ (d) $x^2 - 22x + 120 = 0$

49. A straight line cuts off the intercepts $OA = a$ and $OB = b$ on the positive directions of X-axis and Y-axis, respectively. If the perpendicular from origin O to this line makes an angle of $\frac{\pi}{6}$ with positive direction of Y-axis and the area of ΔOAB is $\frac{98}{3}\sqrt{3}$, then $a^2 - b^2$ is equal to **[Single Correct Type, 2023 Main]**

(a) $\frac{392}{3}$ (b) $\frac{196}{3}$

(c) 196 (d) 98

50. Let the equations of two adjacent sides of a parallelogram $ABCD$ be $2x - 3y = -23$ and $5x + 4y = 23$. If the equation of its one diagonal AC is $3x + 7y = 23$ and the distance of A from the other diagonal is d, then $50d^2$ is equal to .... **[Numerical Value Type, 2023 Main]**

51. Let α_1, α_2 $(\alpha_1 < \alpha_2)$ be the values of α for the points $(\alpha, -3)$, $(2, 0)$ and $(1, \alpha)$ to be collinear. Then the equation of the line, passing through (α_1, α_2) and making an angle of $\frac{\pi}{3}$ with the positive direction of the X-axis, is **[Single Correct Type, 2022 Main]**

(a) $x - \sqrt{3}y - 3\sqrt{3} - 1 = 0$ (b) $\sqrt{3}x - y + \sqrt{3} + 3 = 0$

(c) $x - \sqrt{3}y + 3\sqrt{3} + 1 = 0$ (d) $\sqrt{3}x - y + \sqrt{3} - 3 = 0$

52. Let m_1, m_2 be the slopes of two adjacent sides of a square of side a such that $a^2 + 11a + 3(m_1^2 + m_2^2) = 220$. If one vertex of the square is $10(\cos\alpha - \sin\alpha)$, $10(\sin\alpha + \cos\alpha)$, where $\alpha \in \left(0, \frac{\pi}{2}\right)$ and the equation of one diagonal is $(\cos\alpha - \sin\alpha)x + (\sin\alpha + \cos\alpha)y = 10$, then $72(\sin^4\alpha + \cos^4 x) + a^2 - 3a + 13$ is equal to **[Single Correct Type, 2022 Main]**

(a) 119 (b) 128

(c) 145 (d) 155

53. Let $A(\alpha, -2)$, $B(\alpha, 6)$ and $C\left(\frac{\alpha}{4}, -2\right)$ be vertices of a ΔABC. If $\left(5, \frac{\alpha}{4}\right)$ is the circumcentre of ΔABC, then which of the following is not correct about ΔABC **[Single Correct Type, 2022 Main]**

(a) area is 24 units (b) perimeter is 25 units

(c) circumradius is 5 units (d) inradius is 2 units

54. The equations of the sides AB, BC and CA of a ΔABC are $2x + y = 0$, $x + py = 39$ and $x - y = 3$ respectively and $P(2, 3)$ is its circumcentre. Then, which of the following is not true? **[Single Correct Type, 2022 Main]**

(a) $(AC)^2 = 9p$ (b) $(AC)^2 + p^2 = 136$

(c) $32 <$ area $(\Delta ABC) < 36$ (d) $34 <$ area $(\Delta ABC) < 38$

55. Let $A(1, 1)$, $B(-4, 3)$, $C(-2, -5)$ be vertices of a ΔABC, P be a point on side BC, and Δ_1 and Δ_2 be the areas of ΔAPB and ΔABC, respectively. If $\Delta_1 : \Delta_2 = 4:7$, then the area enclosed by the lines AP, AC and the X-axis is **[Single Correct Type, 2022 Main]**

(a) $\frac{1}{4}$ (b) $\frac{3}{4}$

(c) $\frac{1}{2}$ (d) 1

56. A point P moves so that the sum of squares of its distances from the points (1, 2) and (–2, 1) is 14. Let $f(x, y) = 0$ be the locus of P, which intersects the X-axis at the points A and B and the Y-axis at the points C and D. Then, the area of the quadrilateral $ABCD$ is equal to **[Single Correct Type, 2022 Main]**

(a) $\frac{9}{2}$ (b) $\frac{3\sqrt{17}}{2}$ (c) $\frac{3\sqrt{17}}{4}$ (d) 9

57. The distance between two points A and A' which lie on $y = 2$ such that both the line segments AB and $A'B$ (where B is the point (2, 3)) subtend angle $\frac{\pi}{4}$ at the origin, is equal to **[Single Correct Type, 2022 Main]**

(a) 10 (b) $\frac{48}{5}$

(c) $\frac{52}{5}$ (d) 3

58. Let a triangle be bounded by the lines $L_1 : 2x + 5y = 10$; $L_2 : -4x + 3y = 12$ and the line L_3, which passes through the point $P(2, 3)$, intersects L_2 at A and L_1 at B. If the point P divides the line segment AB, internally in the ratio 1 : 3, then the area of the triangle is equal to **[Single Correct Type, 2022 Main]**

(a) $\frac{110}{13}$ (b) $\frac{132}{13}$ (c) $\frac{142}{13}$ (d) $\frac{151}{13}$

59. Let a, b and c be the length of sides of a ΔABC such that $\frac{a+b}{7} = \frac{b+c}{8} = \frac{c+a}{9}$. If r and R are the radius of incircle and radius of circumcircle of the ΔABC, respectively, then the value of R/r is equal to **[Single Correct Type, 2022 Main]**

(a) $\frac{5}{2}$ (b) 2 (c) $\frac{3}{2}$ (d) 1

60. The equation of the sides AB, BC and CA of a ΔABC are $2x + y = 0$, $x + py = 15a$ and $x - y = 3$, respectively. If its orthocentre is $(2, a)$, $-\frac{1}{2} < a < 2$, then p is equal to .... **[Numerical Value Type, 2022 Main]**

61. Let $A\left(\frac{3}{\sqrt{a}}, \sqrt{a}\right)$, $a > 0$, be a fixed point in the XY-plane. The image of A in Y-axis be B and the image of B in X-axis be C. If $D(3\cos\theta, a\sin\theta)$ is a point in the fourth quadrant such that the maximum area of ΔACD is 12 sq units, then a is equal to ...... **[Numerical Value Type, 2022 Main]**

62. If p and q are the lengths of the perpendiculars from the origin on the lines, $x \operatorname{cosec}\alpha - y\sec\alpha = k\cot 2\alpha$ and $x\sin\alpha + y\cos\alpha = k\sin 2\alpha$ respectively, then k^2 is equal to **[Single Correct Type, 2021 Main]**

(a) $4p^2 + q^2$ (b) $2p^2 + q^2$

(c) $p^2 + 2q^2$ (d) $p^2 + 4q^2$

63. Let A be a fixed point $(0, 6)$ and B be a moving point $(2t, 0)$. Let M be the mid-point of AB and the perpendicular bisector of AB meets the Y-axis at C. The locus of the mid-point P of MC is **[Single Correct Type, 2021 Main]**

(a) $3x^2 - 2y - 6 = 0$ (b) $3x^2 + 2y - 6 = 0$

(c) $2x^2 + 3y - 9 = 0$ (d) $2x^2 - 3y + 9 = 0$

64. Let ABC be a triangle with $A(-3, 1)$ and $\angle ACB = \theta$, $0 < \theta < \frac{\pi}{2}$. If the equation of the median through B is $2x + y - 3 = 0$ and the equation of angle bisector of C is $7x - 4y - 1 = 0$, then $\tan\theta$ is equal to **[Single Correct Type, 2021 Main]**

(a) $\frac{1}{2}$ (b) $\frac{3}{4}$ (c) $\frac{4}{3}$ (d) 2

65. Two sides of a parallelogram are along the lines $4x + 5y = 0$ and $7x + 2y = 0$. If the equation of one of the diagonals of the parallelogram is $11x + 7y = 9$, then other diagonal passes through the point **[Single Correct Type, 2021 Main]**

(a) (1, 2) (b) (2, 2) (c) (2, 1) (d) (1, 3)

66. The equation of one of the straight lines which passes through the point (1,3) and makes an angle $\tan^{-1}(\sqrt{2})$ with the straight line, $y + 1 = 3\sqrt{2}x$ is **[Single Correct Type, 2021 Main]**

(a) $4\sqrt{2}x + 5y - (15 + 4\sqrt{2}) = 0$

(b) $5\sqrt{2}x + 4y - (15 + 4\sqrt{2}) = 0$

(c) $4\sqrt{2}x + 5y - 4\sqrt{2} = 0$

(d) $4\sqrt{2}x - 5y - (5 + 4\sqrt{2}) = 0$

67. In a ΔPQR, the coordinates of the points P and Q are $(-2, 4)$ and $(4, -2)$, respectively. If the equation of the perpendicular bisector of PR is $2x - y + 2 = 0$, then the centre of the circumcircle of the ΔPQR is **[Single Correct Type, 2021 Main]**

(a) (−1, 0) (b) (−2, −2) (c) (0, 2) (d) (1, 4)

68. Let $A(-1, 1)$, $B(3, 4)$ and $C(2, 0)$ be given three points. A line $y = mx$, $m > 0$ intersects lines AC and BC at point P and Q, respectively. Let A_1 and A_2 be the areas of ΔABC and ΔPQC, respectively, such that $A_1 = 3A_2$, then the value of m is equal to **[Single Correct Type, 2021 Main]**

(a) 4/15 (b) 1 (c) 2 (d) 3

69. The intersection of three lines $x - y = 0$, $x + 2y = 3$ and $2x + y = 6$ is a **[Single Correct Type, 2021 Main]**

(a) right angled triangle (b) equilateral triangle

(c) isosceles triangle (d) None of these

70. If the curve $x^2 + 2y^2 = 2$ intersects the line $x + y = 1$ at two points P and Q, then the angle subtended by the line segment PQ at the origin is **[Single Correct Type, 2021 Main]**

(a) $\frac{\pi}{2} + \tan^{-1}\left(\frac{1}{4}\right)$ (b) $\frac{\pi}{2} - \tan^{-1}\left(\frac{1}{4}\right)$

(c) $\frac{\pi}{2} + \tan^{-1}\left(\frac{1}{3}\right)$ (d) $\frac{\pi}{2} - \tan^{-1}\left(\frac{1}{3}\right)$

71. The image of the point (3, 5) on the line $x - y + 1 = 0$, lies on **[Single Correct Type, 2021 Main]**

(a) $(x-2)^2 + (y-2)^2 = 12$ (b) $(x-4)^2 + (y+2)^2 = 16$

(c) $(x-4)^2 + (y-4)^2 = 8$ (d) $(x-2)^2 + (y-4)^2 = 4$

72. A man is walking on a straight line. The arithmetic mean of the reciprocals of the intercepts of this line on the coordinate axes is 1/4. Three stones A, B and C are placed at the points (1,1), (2, 2) and (4, 4), respectively. Then, which of these stones is / are on the path of the man ? **[Single Correct Type, 2021 Main]**

(a) A only (b) B only

(c) C only (d) All the three

73. A man starts walking from the point $P(-3, 4)$, touches the X-axis at R, and then turns to reach at the point $Q(0, 2)$. The man is walking at a constant speed. If the man reaches the point Q in the minimum time, then $50((PR)^2 + (RQ)^2)$ is equal to ....

[Numerical Value Type, 2021 Main]

74. Let the points of intersections of the lines $x - y + 1 = 0$, $x - 2y + 3 = 0$ and $2x - 5y + 11 = 0$ are the mid points of the sides of a ΔABC. Then, the area of the ΔABC is ....

[Numerical Value Type, 2021 Main]

75. Let L denote the line in the XY-plane with x and y-intercepts as 3 and 1 respectively. Then, the image of the point $(-1, -4)$ in this line is

[Single Correct Type, 2020 Main]

(a) $\left(\frac{11}{5}, \frac{28}{5}\right)$ (b) $\left(\frac{29}{5}, \frac{8}{5}\right)$ (c) $\left(\frac{8}{5}, \frac{29}{5}\right)$ (d) $\left(\frac{29}{5}, \frac{11}{5}\right)$

76. If the perpendicular bisector of the line segment joining the points $P(1, 4)$ and $Q(k, 3)$ has y-intercept equal to -4, then a value of k is **[Single Correct Type, 2020 Main]**

(a) $\sqrt{15}$ (b) -4 (c) $\sqrt{14}$ (d) -2

77. A ΔABC lying in the first quadrant has two vertices as $A(1, 2)$ and $B(3, 1)$. If $\angle BAC = 90°$, and ar $(\Delta ABC) = 5\sqrt{5}$ sq units, then the abscissa of the vertex C is **[Single Correct Type, 2020 Main]**

(a) $2 + \sqrt{5}$ (b) $1 + 2\sqrt{5}$ (c) $2\sqrt{5} - 1$ (d) $1 + \sqrt{5}$

78. If a ΔABC has vertices $A(-1, 7)$, $B(-7, 1)$ and $C(5, -5)$, then its orthocentre has coordinates

[Single Correct Type, 2020 Main]

(a) $(3, -3)$ (b) $(-3, 3)$ (c) $\left(-\frac{3}{5}, \frac{3}{5}\right)$ (d) $\left(\frac{3}{5}, -\frac{3}{5}\right)$

79. The locus of the mid-points of the perpendiculars drawn from points on the line, $x = 2y$ to the line $x = y$ is

[Single Correct Type, 2020 Main]

(a) $5x - 7y = 0$ (b) $2x - 3y = 0$
(c) $3x - 2y = 0$ (d) $7x - 5y = 0$

80. If the line, $2x - y + 3 = 0$ is at a distance $\frac{1}{\sqrt{5}}$ and $\frac{2}{\sqrt{5}}$ from the lines $4x - 2y + \alpha = 0$ and $6x - 3y + \beta = 0$, respectively, then the sum of all possible values of α and β is ....

[Numerical Value Type, 2020 Main]

EXERCISE 2

JEE Advanced Pattern

Single Option Correct Type Questions

1. The straight line $y = x - 2$ rotates about a point where it cuts X-axis and becomes perpendicular on the straight line $ax + by + c = 0$, then its equation is

(a) $ax + by + 2a = 0$ (b) $ay - bx + 2b = 0$
(c) $ax + by + 2b = 0$ (d) None of these

2. If $\frac{2}{1!9!} + \frac{2}{3!7!} + \frac{1}{5!5!} = \frac{2^m}{n!}$, then orthocentre of the triangle having sides $x - y + 1 = 0$, $x + y + 3 = 0$ and $2x + 5y - 2 = 0$ is

(a) $(2m - 2n, m - n)$ (b) $(2m - 2n, n - m)$
(c) $(2m - n, m + n)$ (d) $(2m - n, m - n)$

3. If $f(x + y) = f(x)f(y)\ \forall\ x, y \in R$ and $f(1) = 2$, then area enclosed by $3|x| + 2|y| \le 8$ is

(a) $f(4)$ sq units (b) $\frac{1}{2}f(6)$ sq units
(c) $\frac{1}{3}f(6)$ sq units (d) $\frac{1}{3}f(5)$ sq units

4. A line passing through the point (2, 2) and the axes enclose an area λ. The intercepts on the axes made by the line are given by the two roots of

(a) $x^2 - 2|\lambda|x + |\lambda| = 0$ (b) $x^2 + |\lambda|x + 2|\lambda| = 0$
(c) $x^2 - |\lambda|x + 2|\lambda| = 0$ (d) None of these

5. If p_1, p_2 and p_3 be the perpendiculars from the points $(m^2, 2m)$, $(mm', m + m')$ and $(m'^2, 2m')$ respectively on the line $x\cos\alpha + y\sin\alpha + \frac{\sin^2\alpha}{\cos\alpha} = 0$, then p_1, p_2, p_3 are in

(a) AP (b) GP
(c) HP (d) None of these

6. The line $x + y = a$ meets the axes of X and Y at A and B respectively. A triangle AMN is inscribed in the triangle OAB, O being the origin, with right angle at N, M and N lie respectively on OB and AB. If the area of the triangle AMN is $\frac{3}{8}$ of the area of the triangle OAB, then $\frac{AN}{BN}$ is equal to

(a) 1 (b) 2 (c) 3 (d) 4

7. The line $x + y = 1$ meets X-axis at A and Y-axis at B, P is the mid-point of AB. P_1 is the foot of the perpendicular from P to OA; M_1 is that of P_1 from OP; P_2 is that of M_1 from OA; M_2 is that of P_2 from OP; P_3 is that of M_2 from OA and so on. If P_n denotes the nth foot of the perpendicular on OA form M_{n-1}, then OP_n is equal to

(a) $\frac{1}{2n}$ (b) $\frac{1}{2^n}$
(c) $2^n - 1$ (d) $2^n + 3$

8. The line $x = c$ cuts the triangle with corners (0, 0), (1, 1) and (9, 1) into two regions. For the area of the two regions to be the same, then c must be equal to

(a) $\frac{5}{2}$ (b) 3
(c) $\frac{7}{2}$ (d) 3 or 15

9. A straight line L with negative slope passes through the point (8, 2) and cuts the positive coordinates axes at points P and Q. As L varies, the absolute minimum value of $OP + OQ$ is (O is origin)

(a) 10 (b) 18 (c) 16 (d) 12

10. Consider the family of lines
$5x + 3y - 2 + \lambda(3x - y - 4) = 0$ and
$x - y + 1 + \mu(2x - y - 2) = 0$. Equation of straight line that belongs to both families is $ax + by - 7 = 0$, then $a + b$ is

(a) 1 (b) 3 (c) 5 (d) 7

11. The opposite angular points of a square are (3, 4) and (1, − 1), the other two vertices are

(a) $\left(-\frac{1}{2}, \frac{5}{2}\right), \left(\frac{9}{2}, \frac{1}{2}\right)$ (b) $\left(\frac{9}{2}, \frac{1}{2}\right), \left(\frac{7}{2}, \frac{1}{2}\right)$
(c) $\left(\frac{7}{2}, \frac{1}{2}\right), \left(-\frac{7}{2}, -\frac{1}{2}\right)$ (d) $\left(-\frac{7}{2}, -\frac{1}{2}\right), \left(-\frac{7}{2}, -\frac{9}{2}\right)$

12. A line through $A(-5, -4)$ meets the lines $x + 3y + 2 = 0$, $2x + y + 4 = 0$ and $x - y - 5 = 0$ at B, C and D respectively. If $\left(\frac{15}{AB}\right)^2 + \left(\frac{10}{AC}\right)^2 = \left(\frac{6}{AD}\right)^2$, the equation of the line is

(a) $2x + 3y + 22 = 0$ (b) $5x - 4y + 7 = 0$
(c) $3x - 2y + 3 = 0$ (d) None of these

13. The sides AB, BC, CD and DA of a quadrilateral are $x + 2y = 3$, $x = 1$, $x - 3y = 4$ and $5x + y + 12 = 0$ respectively. The angle between diagonals AC and BD is

(a) 45° (b) 60° (c) 90° (d) 30°

14. In a ΔABC, the vertex is $A(1, 1)$ and orthocentre is (2, 4). If sides AB and BC are members of the family of straight line $ax + by + c = 0$ where a, b and c are in AP then the coordinates of vertex C are (h, k). Then, the value of $2h + 12k$ is

(a) 14 (b) 12 (c) 3 (d) 9

15. Let A_0, A_1, A_2, A_3, A_4 and A_5 be a regular hexagon inscribed in a circle of unit radius. Then, the product of the length of the line segments A_0A_1, A_0A_2 and A_0A_4 is

(a) $\frac{3}{4}$ (b) $3\sqrt{3}$ (c) 3 (d) $\frac{3\sqrt{3}}{2}$

More than One Correct Option Type Questions

16. The equations $(b - c)x + (c - a)y + a - b = 0$ and $(b^3 - c^3)x + (c^3 - a^3)y + a^3 - b^3 = 0$ will represent the same line, if

(a) $b = c$ (b) $c = a$
(c) $a = b$ (d) $a + b + c = 0$

17. If the lines $x - 2y - 6 = 0$, $3x + y - 4 = 0$ and $\lambda x + 4y + \lambda^2 = 0$ are concurrent, then

(a) $\lambda = 2$ (b) $\lambda = -3$
(c) $\lambda = 4$ (d) $\lambda = -4$

18. If the line $ax + by + c = 0$, $bx + cy + a = 0$ and $cx + ay + b = 0$ are concurrent $(a + b + c \neq 0)$, then

(a) $a^3 + b^3 + c^3 - 3abc = 0$
(b) $a = b$
(c) $a = b = c$
(d) $a^2 + b^2 + c^2 - bc - ca - ab = 0$

19. $A(1, 3)$ and $C(7, 5)$ are two opposite vertices of a square. The equation of a side through A is

(a) $x + 2y - 7 = 0$ (b) $x - 2y + 5 = 0$
(c) $2x + y - 5 = 0$ (d) $2x - y + 1 = 0$

20. If $6a^2 - 3b^2 - c^2 + 7ab - ac + 4bc = 0$, then the family of lines $ax + by + c = 0$ is concurrent at

(a) (−2, −3) (b) (3, −1)
(c) (2, 3) (d) (−3, 1)

21. Two roads are represented by the equations $y - x = 6$ and $x + y = 8$. An inspection bungalow has to be so constructed that it is at a distance of 100 from each of the roads. Possible location of the bungalow is given by

(a) $(100\sqrt{2} + 1, 7)$ (b) $(1 - 100\sqrt{2}, 7)$
(c) $(1, 7 + 100\sqrt{2})$ (d) $(1, 7 - 100\sqrt{2})$

22. If (a, b) be an end of a diagonal of a square and the other diagonal has the equation $x - y = a$, then another vertex of the square can be

(a) $(a - b, a)$ (b) $(a, 0)$
(c) $(0, -a)$ (d) $(a + b, b)$

23. Consider the equation $y - y_1 = m(x - x_1)$. If m and x_1 are fixed and different lines are drawn for different values of y_1, then

(a) the lines will pass through a fixed point
(b) there will be a set of parallel lines
(c) all the lines intersect the line $x = x_1$
(d) all the lines will be parallel to the line $y = x_1$

24. Let $L_1 \equiv ax + by + a\sqrt[3]{b} = 0$ and $L_2 \equiv bx - ay + b\sqrt[3]{a} = 0$ be two straight lines. The equations of the bisectors of the angle formed by the foci whose equations are $\lambda_1 L_1 - \lambda_2 L_2 = 0$ and $\lambda_1 L_1 + \lambda_2 L_2 = 0$, λ_1 and λ_2 being non-zero real numbers, are given by

(a) $L_1 = 0$ (b) $L_2 = 0$

(c) $\lambda_1 L_1 + \lambda_2 L_2 = 0$ (d) $\lambda_2 L_1 - \lambda_1 L_2 = 0$

25. The equation of the bisectors of the angles between the two intersecting lines $\frac{x-3}{\cos\theta} = \frac{y+5}{\sin\theta}$ and $\frac{x-3}{\cos\phi} = \frac{y+5}{\sin\phi}$ are $\frac{x-3}{\cos\alpha} = \frac{y+5}{\sin\alpha}$ and $\frac{x-3}{\beta} = \frac{y+5}{\gamma}$, then

(a) $\alpha = \frac{\theta+\phi}{2}$ (b) $\beta = -\sin\alpha$

(c) $\gamma = \cos\alpha$ (d) $\beta = \sin\alpha$

Passage Based Questions

Passage I

(Q. Nos. 26 and 27)

- For points $P \equiv (x_1, y_1)$ and $Q = (x_2, y_2)$ of the coordinate plane, a new distance $d(P, Q)$ is defined by
$$d(P, Q) = |x_1 - x_2| + |y_1 - y_2|$$
Let $O \equiv (0, 0)$, $A \equiv (1, 2)$, $B \equiv (2, 3)$ and $C \equiv (4, 3)$ are four fixed points on XY-plane.

26. Let $R(x, y)$, such that R is equidistant from the point O and A with respect to new distance and if $0 \le x < 1$ and $0 \le y < 2$, then R lie on a line segment whose equation is

(a) $x + y = 3$ (b) $x + 2y = 3$

(c) $2x + y = 3$ (d) $2x + 2y = 3$

27. Let $S(x, y)$ such that S is equidistant from points O and B with respect to new distance and if $x \ge 2$ and $0 \le y < 3$, then locus of S is

(a) a line segment of finite length

(b) a line of infinite length

(c) a ray of finite length

(d) a ray of infinite length

Passage II

(Q. Nos. 28 and 29)

- In a triangle ABC, if the equation of sides AB, BC and CA are $2x - y + 4 = 0$, $x - 2y - 1 = 0$ and $x + 3y - 3 = 0$ respectively.

28. The equation of external bisector of angle B is

(a) $x - y - 1 = 0$ (b) $x - y + 1 = 0$

(c) $x + y - 5 = 0$ (d) $x + y + 5 = 0$

29. The image of point B w.r.t. the side CA is

(a) $\left(-\frac{3}{5}, \frac{26}{5}\right)$ (b) $\left(-\frac{3}{5}, -\frac{26}{5}\right)$

(c) $\left(\frac{3}{5}, -\frac{26}{5}\right)$ (d) $\left(\frac{3}{5}, \frac{26}{5}\right)$

Passage III

(Q. Nos. 30 and 31)

- $A(1, 3)$ and $C\left(-\frac{2}{5}, \frac{-2}{5}\right)$ are the vertices of a triangle ABC and the equation of the angle bisector of $\angle ABC$ is $x + y = 2$.

30. Equation of BC is

(a) $7x + 3y - 4 = 0$ (b) $7x + 3y + 4 = 0$

(c) $7x - 3y + 4 = 0$ (d) $7x - 3y - 4 = 0$

31. Equation of AB is

(a) $3x + 7y = 24$ (b) $3x + 7y + 24 = 0$

(c) $13x + 7y + 8 = 0$ (d) $13x - 7y + 8 = 0$

Passage IV

(Q. Nos. 32 and 33)

- Let $S' = 0$ be the image or reflection of the curve $S = 0$ about line mirror $L = 0$. Suppose P be any point on the curve $S = 0$ and Q be the image or reflection about the line mirror $L = 0$, then Q will lie on $S' = 0$.
How to find the image or reflection of a curve?

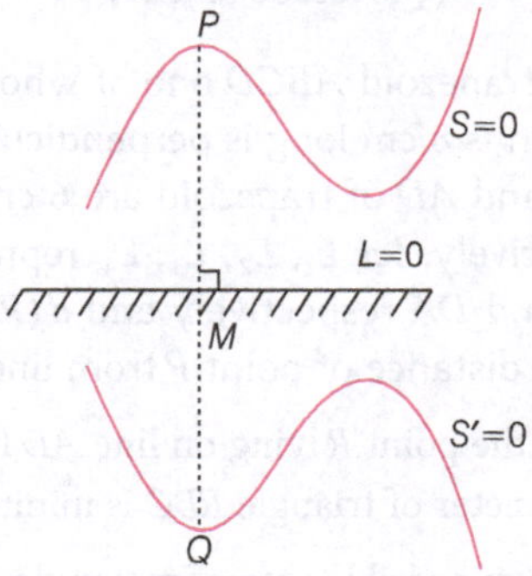

Let the given curve be $S: f(x, y) = 0$ and line mirror $L: ax + by + c = 0$. We take a point P on the given curve in parametric form. Suppose Q be the image or reflection of point P about line mirror $L = 0$, which again contains the same parameter. Let $Q \equiv (\phi(t), \psi(t))$, where t is parameter. Now, let $x = \phi(t)$ and $y = \psi(t)$. Eliminating t, we get the equation of the reflected curve S'.

32. The image of the line $3x - y = 2$ in the line $y = x - 1$ is

(a) $x + 3y = 2$ (b) $3x + y = 2$

(c) $x - 3y = 2$ (d) $x + y = 2$

33. The image of the circle $x^2 + y^2 = 4$ in the line $x + y = 2$ is

(a) $x^2 + y^2 - 2x - 2y = 0$ (b) $x^2 + y^2 - 4x - 4y + 6 = 0$

(c) $x^2 + y^2 - 2x - 2y + 2 = 0$ (d) $x^2 + y^2 - 4x - 4y + 4 = 0$

Passage V

(Q. Nos. 34 and 35)

- In a ΔABC, the equation of the side BC is $2x - y = 3$ and its circumcentre and orhtocentre are $(2, 4)$ and $(1, 2)$ respectively.

34. Circumradius of ΔABC is

(a) $\sqrt{\frac{61}{5}}$ (b) $\sqrt{\frac{51}{5}}$

(c) $\sqrt{\frac{41}{5}}$ (d) $\sqrt{\frac{43}{5}}$

35. The distance of orthocentre from vertex A is

(a) $\frac{1}{\sqrt{5}}$ (b) $\frac{6}{\sqrt{5}}$ (c) $\frac{3}{\sqrt{5}}$ (d) $\frac{2}{\sqrt{5}}$

Stem Based Questions

Stem I

(Q. Nos. 36 and 37)

- Let $ABCD$ be a square with sides of unit length. Point E and F are taken on sides AB and AD respectively so that $AE = AF$. Let P be any point inside the square.

36. The maximum area of quadrilateral $CDFE$ is ....

37. The value of $(PA)^2 - (PB)^2 + (PC)^2 - (PD)^2$ is equal to ....

Stem II

(Q. Nos. 38 and 39)

- Consider the trapezoid $ABCD$ one of whose non-parallel sides AB which is 8 cm long is perpendicular to the base. The base BC and AD of trapezoid are 6 cm and 10 cm in length respectively, let L_1, L_2, L_3, L_4 represent the lines AB, BC, CD and DA respectively and $d(P, L)$ denote the perpendicular distance of point P from line L.

38. Distance of the point R lying on line AD from vertex A so that perimeter of triangle RBC is minimum is ....

39. The maximum possible area of rectangle inscribed in the trapezoid so that one of its sides lies on the larger base of trapezoid is ....

Single Integer Type Questions

40. The equation of a line through the mid-point of the sides AB and AD of rhombus $ABCD$, whose one diagonal is $3x - 4y + 5 = 0$ and one vertex is $A(3, 1)$, is $ax + by + c = 0$. The absolute value of $(a + b + c)$, where a, b and c are integers expressed in lowest form is ....

41. Consider a ΔABC whose sides AB, BC and CA are represent by the straight lines $2x + y = 0$, $x + py = q$ and $x - y = 3$, respectively. If the point $P(2, 3)$ is orthocenter, then the value of $(p + q)/10$ is ....

42. If the area of the triangular region in the first quadrant bounded on the left by the Y-axis, bounded above by the line $7x + 4y = 168$ and bounded below by the line $5x + 3y = 121$ is A, then the value of $\frac{3A}{10}$ is ......

43. Number of value of b for which it is acute ΔABC, if the coordinates of orthocentre 'H' are $(4, b)$, centroid G are $(b, 2b - 8)$ and circumcentre S are $(-4, 8)$, is ....

44. A man starts from the point $P(-3, 4)$ and reaches point $Q(0, 1)$ touching X-axis at $R(\alpha, 0)$ such that $|PR + RQ|$ is minimum when $5|\alpha|$ is ....

Numerical Value Type Questions

45. A diagonal of rhombus $ABCD$ is member of both the families of lines $(x + y - 1) + \lambda_1 (2x + 3y - 2) = 0$ and $(x - y + 2) + \lambda_2 (2x - 3y + 5) = 0$, where $\lambda_1, \lambda_2 \in R$ and one of the vertex of the rhombus is $(3, 2)$. If area of rhombus is $12\sqrt{5}$ sq units, then the length of longer diagonal of the rhombus is ....

46. Let the point $M(2, 1)$ be shifted through a distance $3\sqrt{2}$ units measured parallel to the line $L: x + y - 1 = 0$ in the direction of decreasing ordinates, to reach at N. If the image of N in the line L is R and Q. If the distance of R from the line $3x - 4y + 25 = 0$ is d, then the value of d^2 is ......

47. The equation of adjacent sides AB and AD of a parallelogram $ABCD$ are $3x - 4y + 21 = 0$ and $4x - 3y - 14 = 0$, respectively. The perpendicular distance between the parallel sides AB, DC and AD, BC are $\frac{14}{5}$ and $\frac{7}{5}$, respectively. Then, area of parallelogram is ....

48. In acute angle ΔABC, equation of side BC is $4x - 3y + 3 = 0$, orthocentre is $(1, 2)$ and the circumcentre 0 is $(2, 3)$. The circum radius of ΔABC is $\frac{\sqrt{m}}{n}$ $gcd(m, n) = 1$, then the value of $m + n$ is ......

49. The parallelogram is bounded by the lines $y = ax = c$, $y = ax + d$ and $y = bx + c$, $y = bx + d$ and has the area equal to 18 sq. units. Also, the parallelogram bounded by the lines $y = ax + c$, $y = ax - d$ and $y = bx + c$, $y = bx - d$ has area 72 sq units. Given, a, b, c and d are positive integers, then the smallest possible value of $a + b + c + d$ is ....

50. Consider two lines L_1 and L_2 given by $x - y = 0$ and $x + y = 0$, respectively and a moving point $P(x, y)$. Let $d(P, L_i)i = 1, 2$ represents the distance of point 'P' from the line L_i. If point P moves in certain region 'R' in such a way that $2 \le d(P, L_1) + d(P, L_2) \le 4$, then the area of region R is ....

51. A line through $A(-5, -4)$ meets the lines $x + 3y + 2 = 0$, $2x + y + 4 = 0$ and $x - y - 5 = 0$ at points B, C and D, then the value of $25a - c$ is ....

Matching Type Questions

52. Match the Columns

Column I	Column II
(A) Lines $x-2y-6=0, 3x+y-4=0$ and $\lambda x+4y+\lambda^2=0$ are concurrent, then the value of $\|\lambda\|$ is	(p) 2
(B) The variable straight line $3x(a+1)+4y(a-1)-3(a-1)=0$ for different value of 'a' passes through a fixed point (p, q) if $\lambda = p-q$, then the value of $4\|\lambda\|$ is	(q) 3
(C) If the line $x+y-1-\left\|\frac{\lambda}{2}\right\|=0$ passing through the intersection of $x-y+1=0$ and $3x+y-5=0$, is perpendicular to one of them, then the value of $\|\lambda+1\|$ is	(r) 4
(D) If the line $y-x-1+\lambda=0$ is equidistant from the points $(1,-2)$ and $(3, 4)$, then the value of $\|\lambda\|$ is	(s) 5

53. Consider the triangle formed by the lines $y+3x+2=0$, $3y-2x-5=0$ and $4y+x-14=0$

Column I	Column II
(A) If $(0, \lambda)$ lies inside the triangle, then integral values are less than $\|3\lambda\|$	(p) 4
(B) If $(1, \lambda)$ lies inside the triangle, then integral values are less than $\|3\lambda\|$	(q) 5
(C) If $(\lambda, 2)$ lies inside the triangle, then integral values of $\|6\lambda\|$ are	(r) 6
(D) If $(\lambda, 7/2)$ lies inside the triangle, then integral value of $\|6\lambda\|$ are	(s) 7

54. Match the Column

Column I	Column II
(A) A straight line with negative slope passing through (1, 4) meets the coordinate axes at A and B. The minimum length of $OA+OB$, O being origin is	(p) $5\sqrt{2}$
(B) If the point $P(4,-1)$ is symmetric to the point Q with respect to the bisector of the first quadrant, then the length of PQ is	(q) $3\sqrt{2}$
(C) On the portion of the straight line $xd+y=2$ between the axis a square is constructed away from the origin, with this portion as one of its sides. If 'd' denotes the perpendicular distance of a side of this square from the origin, then maximum value of d is	(r) 9/2
(D) If the parametric equation of a line is given by $x=4+\lambda/\sqrt{2}$ and $y=4+\sqrt{2}\lambda$, where λ is a parameter, then the intercept made by the line on the X-axis is	(s) 9

55. Match the Column

Column I	Column II
(A) If lines $3x+y-4=0$, $x-2y-6=0$ and $\lambda x+4y+\lambda^2=0$ are concurrent, then the values of λ is	(p) −4
(B) If the points $(\lambda+1, 1), (2\lambda+1, 3)$ and $(2\lambda+2, 2\lambda)$ are collinear, then the value of λ is	(q) −1 / 2
(C) If line $x+y-1-\|\lambda/2\|=0$ passing through the intersection of $x-y+1=0$ and $3x+y-5=0$ is perpendicular to one of them, then the value of λ is	(r) 4
(D) If line $y-x-1+\lambda=0$ is equidistant from the point $(1,-2)$ and $(3, 4)$, then λ is	(s) 2

Previous Year Questions

56. Let $a = 3\sqrt{2}$ and $b = \dfrac{1}{5^{1/6}\sqrt{6}}$. If $x, y \in R$ are such that $3x + 2y = \log_a (18)^{5/4}$ and $2x - y = \log_b(\sqrt{1080})$, then $4x + 5y$ is equal to .... **[Numerical Value Type, 2024 Adv.]**

Stem

- Consider the lines L_1 and L_2 defined by $L_1 : x\sqrt{2} + y - 1 = 0$ and $L_2 : x\sqrt{2} - y + 1 = 0$ For a fixed constant λ, let C be the locus of a point P such that the product of the distance of P from L_1 and the distance of P from L_2 is λ_2. The line $y = 2x + 1$ meets C at two points R and S, where the distance between R and $S\sqrt{270}$. Let the3 perpendicular bisector of RS meet C at two distinct points R' and S'. Let D be the square of the distance between R' and S'. **[Stem Type, 2021 Adv.]**

57. The value of λ^2 is ....

58. The value of D is ....

EXERCISE 3

Challenging Problems

1. If $A(x_1, y_1), B(x_2, y_2)$ and $C(x_3, y_3)$ are the vertices of a triangle, then show that the equation of the line joining A and the circumcentre is given by $(\sin 2B)\begin{vmatrix} x & y & 1 \\ x_1 & y_1 & 1 \\ x_2 & y_2 & 1 \end{vmatrix} + (\sin 2C)\begin{vmatrix} x & y & 1 \\ x_1 & y_1 & 1 \\ x_3 & y_3 & 1 \end{vmatrix} = 0.$

2. Find the coordinates of the point at unit distance from the lines $3x - 4y + 1 = 0, 8x + 6y + 1 = 0$.

3. A variable line makes intercepts on the coordinate axes, the sum of whose squares is constant and equal to k^2. Show that the locus of the foot of the perpendicular from the origin to this line is $(x^2 + y^2)^2 (x^{-2} + y^{-2}) = k^2$.

4. A variable line intersects n lines $y = mx, (m = 1, 2, 3, \ldots, n)$ in the points $A_1, A_2, A_3, \ldots, A_n$ respectively. If $\sum_{p=1}^{n} \dfrac{1}{OA_p} = c$ (constant). Show that line passes through a fixed point. Find the coordinates of this fixed point (O being origin).

5. Given n straight lines and a fixed point O. A straight line is drawn through O meeting these lines in the points $R_1, R_2, R_3, \ldots, R_n$ and a point R is taken on it such that $\dfrac{n}{OR} = \sum_{r=1}^{n} \dfrac{1}{OR_r}$. Prove that the locus of R is a straight line.

6. P is any point on the line $x - a = 0$. If A is the point $(a, 0)$ and PQ, the bisector of the angle OPA, meets the X-axis in Q. Prove that the locus of the foot of the perpendicular from Q on OP is $(x - a)^2 (x^2 + y^2) = a^2 y^2$.

7. A variable line is drawn through O to cut two fixed straight lines L_1 and L_2 in R and S. A point P is chosen on the variable line such that $\dfrac{m+n}{OP} = \dfrac{m}{OR} + \dfrac{n}{OS}$. Show that the locus of P is a straight line passing through the point of intersection of L_1 and L_2.

Answer Key

Exercise 1

1. (b)	2. (d)	3. (b)	4. (a)	5. (c)	6. (a)	7. (a)	8. (a)	9. (c)	10. (d)
11. (d)	12. (c)	13. (d)	14. (a)	15. (b)	16. (d)	17. (c)	18. (d)	19. (c)	20. (d)
21. (c)	22. (8)	23. (12)	24. (7)	25. (9)	26. (12)	27. (2)	28. (2)	29. (12)	30. (0)
31. (104)	32. (25)	33. (84)	34. (10)	35. (6)	36. (49)	37. (c)	38. (c)	39. (d)	40. (a)
41. (d)	42. (b)	43. (1)	44. (36)	45. (d)	46. (b)	47. (b)	48. (a)	49. (a)	50. (529)
51. (b)	52. (b)	53. (b)	54. (d)	55. (c)	56. (b)	57. (c)	58. (b)	59. (a)	60. (3)
61. (8)	62. (a)	63. (c)	64. (c)	65. (b)	66. (a)	67. (b)	68. (b)	69. (c)	70. (a)
71. (d)	72. (b)	73. (1250)	74. (6)	75. (a)	76. (b)	77. (b)	78. (b)	79. (a)	80. (30)

Exercise 2

1. (b)	2. (a)	3. (c)	4. (c)	5. (b)	6. (c)	7. (b)	8. (b)	9. (b)	10. (b)
11. (a)	12. (a)	13. (c)	14. (a)	15. (c)	16. (c,d)	17. (a,d)	18. (a,b,c,d)	19. (a,d)	20. (a,b)
21. (a,b,c,d)	22. (b,d)	23. (a,b,c)	24. (a,b)	25. (a,b,c)	26. (d)	27. (d)	28. (d)	29. (a)	30. (b)
31. (a)	32. (c)	33. (d)	34. (a)	35. (b)	36. (0.625)	37. (0)	38. (3)	39. (48)	40. (1)
41. (5)	42. (5)	43. (0)	44. (3)	45. (10)	46. (100)	47. (14)	48. (63)	49. (16)	50. (24)
51. (28)									

52. (A) → (p,r), (B) → (q), (C) → (q,s), (D) → (p)

53. (A) → (p,q), (B) → (p,q,r,s), (C) → (p,q,r,s), (D) → (p,q,r,s)

54. (A) → (s), (B) → (p), (C) → (q), (D) → (r)

55. (A) → (p,s), (B) → (q,s), (C) → (p,r), (D) → (s)

56. (8) 57. (9) 58. (77.14)

Solutions

Exercise 1 - JEE Main Pattern

1. $\dfrac{\text{Value of } (a^2x + aby + 1) \text{ at } (1, 1)}{\text{Value of } (a^2x + aby + 1) \text{ at } (0, 0)} > 0$

or $\qquad \dfrac{a^2 + ab + 1}{1} > 0, \forall a \in R$

or $\qquad a^2 + ab + 1 > 0, \forall a \in R$

$\therefore \qquad D < 0$

$\Rightarrow \qquad b^2 - 4 < 0$

$\Rightarrow \qquad -2 < b < 2 \text{ but } b > 0$

$\therefore \qquad 0 < b < 2 \text{ i.e. } b \in (0, 2)$

2. $\dfrac{\text{Value of } (3x - 2y + 1) \text{ at } A}{\text{Value of } (3x - 2y + 1) \text{ at } B} > 0$

$\Rightarrow \dfrac{(\sin\alpha - 3) - (\cos\alpha - 2) + 1}{(3 - 2 + 1)} > 0$

$\Rightarrow \sin\alpha - \cos\alpha > 0 \Rightarrow \sin\alpha > \cos\alpha$

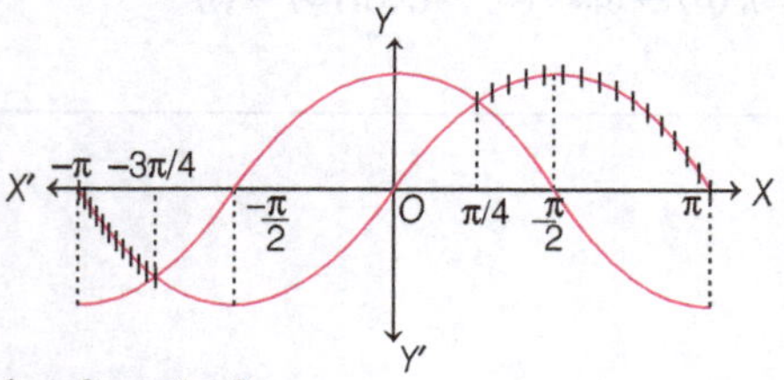

It is clear from the figure,

$$\alpha \in \left[-\pi, \frac{-3\pi}{4}\right) \cup \left(\frac{\pi}{4}, \pi\right]$$

3. $\because BC = AC$

$\Rightarrow \qquad 2^2 + (\lambda - 1)^2 = \lambda^2$

$\Rightarrow \qquad 4 = \lambda^2 - (\lambda - 1)^2 = (2\lambda - 1)(1)$

$\therefore \qquad \lambda = \dfrac{5}{2}$

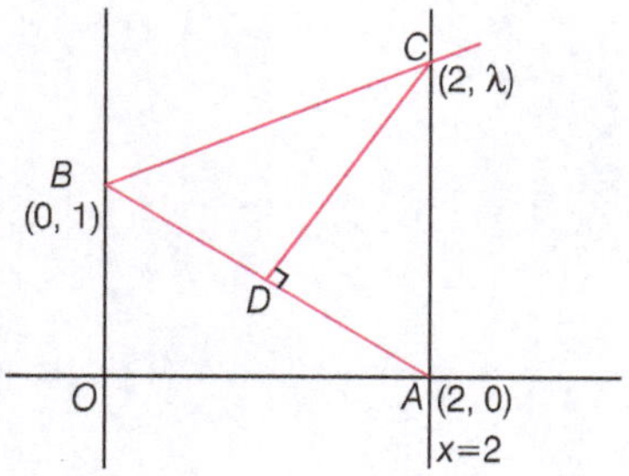

$\because$ Equation of AB is $\dfrac{x}{2} + \dfrac{y}{1} = 1, D \equiv \left(1, \dfrac{1}{2}\right)$ [mid-point of AB]

$\therefore$ Equation of CD is $2x - y = \mu$

$\because$ CD pass through D, thus $2 - \dfrac{1}{2} = \mu$ or $\mu = \dfrac{3}{2}$

$\therefore$ Equation of CD is $2x - y = \dfrac{3}{2}$ ...(i)

and Eq. (i) of line perpendicular to AC and pass through B is $y = 1$ ...(ii)

From Eqs. (i) and (ii), we get

Orthocentre $\equiv \left(\dfrac{5}{4}, 1\right)$

4. Let the vertices B and C lie on the given line.

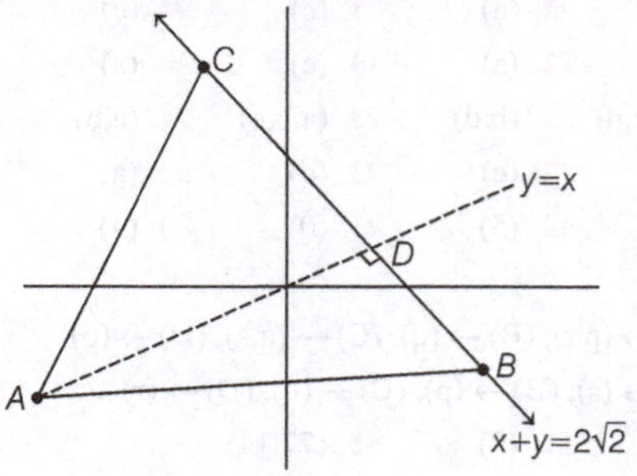

Then, $OD = \dfrac{2\sqrt{2}}{\sqrt{2}} = 2$

$\therefore$ Equation of OD is $y = x \Rightarrow x = y = \sqrt{2}$ for point D.

Also, $BD = OD \times \tan 60°$

$= 2\sqrt{3}$ for the coordinates of B and C.

Using parametric equation of line, we get

$$\frac{x - \sqrt{2}}{-\frac{1}{\sqrt{2}}} = \frac{y - \sqrt{2}}{\frac{1}{\sqrt{2}}} = \pm 2\sqrt{3}$$

$$C = (\sqrt{2} + \sqrt{6}, \sqrt{2} - \sqrt{6}) \text{ and } B = (\sqrt{2} - \sqrt{6}, \sqrt{2} + \sqrt{6})$$

5. Let the two perpendiculars through the origin intersect $2x + y = a$ at A and B so that the triangle OAB is isosceles.

OM = length of perpendicular from O to AB, $OM = \dfrac{a}{\sqrt{5}}$.

Also, $AM = MB = OM \Rightarrow AB = \dfrac{2a}{\sqrt{5}}$

Area of $\Delta OAB = \dfrac{1}{2} \cdot AB \cdot OM = \dfrac{1}{2} \cdot \dfrac{2a}{\sqrt{5}} \cdot \dfrac{a}{\sqrt{5}} = \dfrac{a^2}{5}$

6. Let the coordinates of A be $(a, 0)$. Then, the slope of the reflected ray is

$$\frac{3 - 0}{5 - a} = \tan\theta \qquad \text{(say) ...(i)}$$

Then, the slope of the incident ray $= \dfrac{2 - 0}{1 - a} = \tan(\pi - \theta)$ ...(ii)

From Eqs. (i) and (ii), we get

$$\tan\theta + \tan(\pi - \theta) = 0 \Rightarrow \frac{3}{5 - a} + \frac{2}{1 - a} = 0$$

$$\Rightarrow \quad 3 - 3a + 10 - 2a = 0$$

$$a = \frac{13}{5}$$

Thus, the coordinates of A are $\left(\frac{13}{5}, 0\right)$.

7. $\because$ B is the reflection of $A(5, 7)$ w.r.t the line $x + y = 0$

$\therefore \quad B \equiv (-7, -5)$

and C is the reflection of $A(5, 7)$ w.r.t the line $x - y = 0$

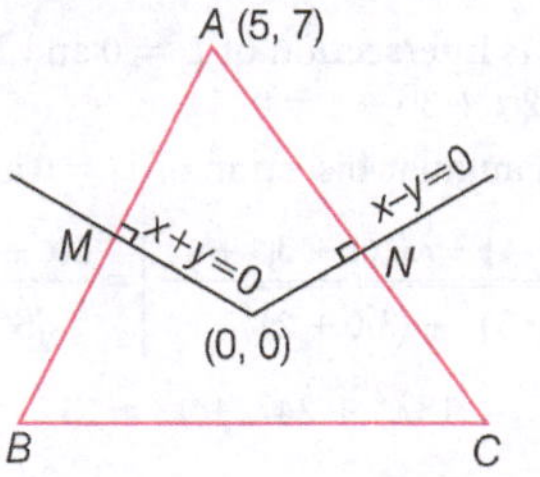

$\therefore \quad C \equiv (7, 5)$

$\therefore$ Equation of BC is $y + 5 = \frac{5+5}{7+7}(x+7)$ or $7y = 5x$

8. Equation of incident ray is

$$y - 0 = \tan(90° + 60°)(x - 2)$$

or $$y = -\frac{1}{\sqrt{3}}(x - 2)$$

or $$(x - 2) + y\sqrt{3} = 0$$

and equation of refracted ray is

$$y - 0 = -\tan 60°(x - 2)$$

or $$y = -\sqrt{3}(x - 2)$$

or $$(x - 2) + \frac{y}{\sqrt{3}} = 0$$

$\therefore$ Combined equation is

$$[(x - 2) + y\sqrt{3}]\left[(x - 2) + \frac{y}{\sqrt{3}}\right] = 0$$

i.e. $$(x - 2)^2 + y^2 + \frac{4}{\sqrt{3}}(x - 2)y = 0$$

9. **Decoding the Question**

Distances between parallel lines $a_1x + b_1y + c_1 = 0$ and $a_2x + b_2y + c_2 = 0$ is $d = \frac{|c_1 - c_2|}{\sqrt{a^2 + b^2}}$ to this formula make sure coefficient of x and y should be same for both the lines.

As the lines are parallel, distance between them

$$= \frac{|5 - 3|}{\sqrt{4 + 1}} = \frac{2}{\sqrt{5}} = BC$$

$\therefore$ $$AB = \sqrt{4 - \frac{4}{5}} = \frac{4}{\sqrt{5}}$$

From ΔABC, $\tan\theta = \frac{\left(\frac{2}{\sqrt{5}}\right)}{\left(\frac{4}{\sqrt{5}}\right)} = \frac{1}{2}$

Slope of the given line is 2.

Let m_1 be the slope of the required line.

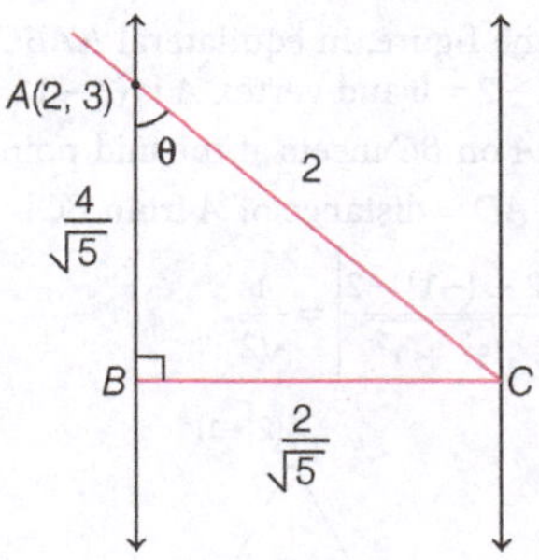

Now, $\tan\theta = \frac{1}{2} = \left|\frac{m_1 + 2}{1 - 2m_1}\right| \Rightarrow \frac{m_1 + 2}{1 - 2m_1} = \pm\frac{1}{2}$

Consider $\frac{1}{2} = \frac{m_1 + 2}{1 - 2m_1} \Rightarrow 1 - 2m_1 = 2m_1 + 4$

$$\Rightarrow \quad 4m_1 = -3 \Rightarrow m_1 = -\frac{3}{4}$$

Similarly, by taking $-\frac{1}{2}$, other value of m_1 undefined.

The equation of the line having slope m and passing through the point (x_1, y_1) is $y - y_1 = m(x - x_1)$

$$\Rightarrow \quad y - 3 = -\frac{3}{4}(x - 2) \text{ and } y - 3 = \frac{1}{0}(x - 2)$$

$\therefore$ Equations to the required lines are $3x + 4y - 18 = 0$ and $x = 2$.

10. $p(x + y - 1) + q(2x - 3y + 1) = 0$

$$(x + y - 1) + \frac{q}{p}(2x - 3y + 1) = 0$$

Always passes through intersection of $x + y - 1 = 0$ and $2x - 3y + 1 = 0$ which is $\left(\frac{2}{5}, \frac{3}{5}\right)$.

11. PS being the median of ΔPQR, S is the mid-point of QR

i.e. coordinates of $S \equiv \left(\frac{6+7}{2}, \frac{-1+3}{2}\right) = \left(\frac{13}{2}, 1\right)$

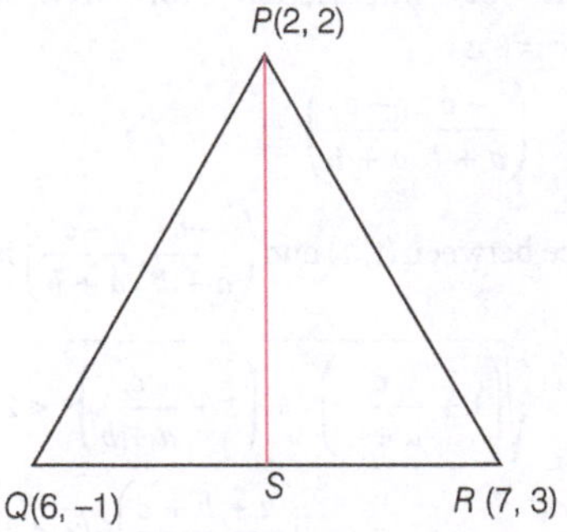

Slope of line parallel to PS = Slope of PS

$$= \frac{1 - 2}{\frac{13}{2} - 2} = \frac{-1}{\frac{9}{2}} = \frac{-2}{9}.$$

$\therefore$ Equation of a line parallel to PS passing through the point $(1, 1)$ is

$$(y + 1) = \frac{-2}{9}(x - 1) \text{ i.e. } 9y + 9 = -2x + 2$$

$$\Rightarrow \quad 2x + 9y + 7 = 0$$

12. As shown in the figure, in equilateral ΔABC, BC is base along the line $x + y - 2 = 0$ and vertex A is $(2 - 1)$.

Altitude from A on BC meets at the mid-point of BC.

Now, distance AD = distance of A from BC

$$\Rightarrow \quad \left|\frac{2 + (-1) - 2}{\sqrt{1^2 + 1^2}}\right| = \frac{1}{\sqrt{2}}$$

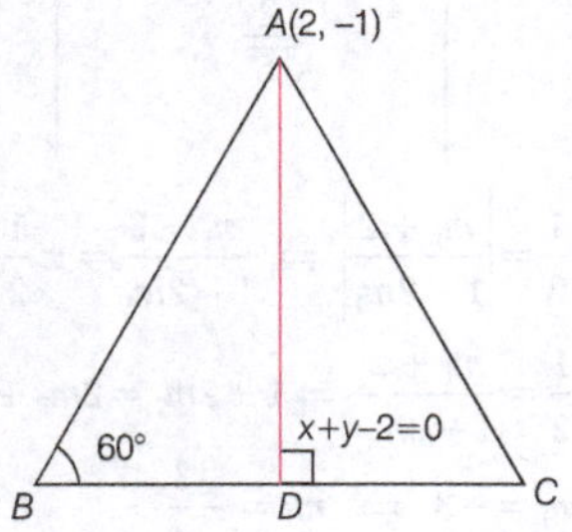

Also, in ΔABD, $\sin 60° = \dfrac{AD}{AB} \Rightarrow AB = \dfrac{AD}{\sin 60°} = \dfrac{\frac{1}{\sqrt{2}}}{\frac{\sqrt{3}}{2}}$

$$AB = \left(\sqrt{\frac{2}{3}}\right)$$

13. The given lines can be written as

$$4x + 3y - 11 = 0 \quad \text{...(i)}$$

$$8x + 6y - 15 = 0$$

$$\Rightarrow \quad 4x + 3y - \frac{15}{2} = 0 \quad \text{...(ii)}$$

Let d be the distance between the lines (i) and (ii), then

$$d = \left|\frac{-11 - \left(\frac{15}{2}\right)}{\sqrt{4^2 + 3^2}}\right| = \frac{7}{10} \text{ units}$$

14. The point of intersection for $ax + by + c = 0$ and $bx + ay + c = 0$ is

i.e. $\left(\dfrac{-c}{a+b}, \dfrac{-c}{a+b}\right)$

The distance between (1, 1) and $\left(\dfrac{-c}{a+b}, \dfrac{-c}{a+b}\right)$ is less than $2\sqrt{2}$

$$\Rightarrow \quad \sqrt{\left(1 + \frac{c}{a+b}\right)^2 + \left(1 + \frac{c}{a+b}\right)^2} < 2\sqrt{2}$$

$$\Rightarrow \quad \left(\frac{a+b+c}{a+b}\right)\sqrt{2} < 2\sqrt{2}$$

$$\Rightarrow \quad a + b + c < 2a + 2b$$

$$\Rightarrow \quad a + b - c > 0$$

15. Let $L_1 = 3x + 2y + 4 = 0$, $L = 2x + 3y + 1 = 0$ and $L_2 = 0$ be the required line

$\because$ The line $L_2 = 0$ passes through point of intersection of the lines $L_1 = 0$ and $L = 0$

$\therefore$ By family of lines $L_2 = (3x + 2y + 4) + \lambda(2x + 3y + 1) = 0$

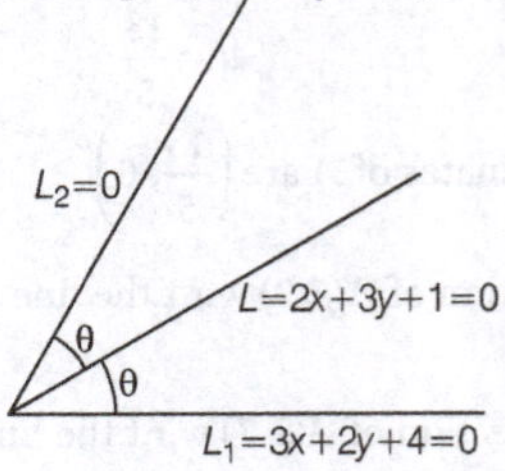

Suppose, (α, β) is intersection of $L_1 = 0$ and $L = 0$ is a point on $L = 0$ so that $2\alpha + 3\beta + 1 = 0$ ...(i)

But $L = 0$ is an angular bisection of $L_1 = 0$ and $L_2 = 0$

$$\Rightarrow \quad \left|\frac{(3\alpha + 2\beta + 4) + \lambda(2\alpha + 3\beta + 1)}{\sqrt{(2\lambda + 3)^2 + (3\lambda + 2)^2}}\right| = \frac{3\alpha + 2\beta + 4}{\sqrt{3^2 + 2^2}}$$

$$\Rightarrow \quad 13\lambda^2 + 24\lambda + 13 = 13 \quad \text{[from Eq. (i)]}$$

$$\Rightarrow \quad \lambda = 0 \text{ or } \lambda = -\frac{24}{13}$$

$$\lambda = 0 \text{ gives } L_1 = 0$$

and $\lambda = -\dfrac{24}{13}$ gives the lines

$$L_2 = 3x + 2y + 4$$

$$-\frac{24}{13}(2x + 3y + 1) = 0$$

$$\Rightarrow \quad -9x - 46y + 28 = 0 \Rightarrow 9x + 46y = 28$$

16. Let $y = \cos x \cos(x + 2) - \cos^2(x + 1)$

$$= \cos(x + 1 - 1)\cos(x + 1 + 1) - \cos^2(x + 1)$$

$$= \cos^2(x + 1) - \sin^2 1 - \cos^2(x + 1)$$

$$\Rightarrow \quad y = -\sin^2 1$$

This is a staright line which is parallel to X-axis.

It passes through $\left(\dfrac{\pi}{2}, -\sin^2 1\right)$.

17. Orthocentre of right angled triangle is at the vertex of right angle. Therefore, orthocentre of the triangle is at (0, 0).

18. Let the coordinate of S be (x, y).

$\therefore \quad SQ^2 + SR^2 = 2SP^2$

$$\Rightarrow \quad (x + 1)^2 + y^2 + (x - 2)^2 + y^2 = 2[(x - 1)^2 + y^2]$$

$$\Rightarrow \quad x^2 + x + 1 + y^2 + x^2 - 4x + 4 + y^2$$

$$= 2(x^2 - 2x + 1 + y^2)$$

$$\Rightarrow \quad 2x + 3 = 0 \Rightarrow x = -\frac{3}{2}$$

Hence, it is a straight line parallel to Y-axis.

19. Let B, C and D be the position of the point $A(4, 1)$ after the three operations I, II and III, respectively.

Then, B is (1, 4), $C(1 + 2, 4)$ i.e. (3, 4). The point D is obtained from C by rotating the coordinate axes through an angle $\dfrac{\pi}{4}$ in anti-clockwise direction.

Therefore, the coordinates of D are given by

$$X = 3\cos\frac{\pi}{4} - 4\sin\frac{\pi}{4} = -\frac{1}{\sqrt{2}}$$

and $$Y = 3\sin\frac{\pi}{4} + 4\cos\frac{\pi}{4} = \frac{7}{\sqrt{2}}$$

$\therefore$ Coordinates of D are $\left(-\frac{1}{\sqrt{2}}, \frac{7}{\sqrt{2}}\right)$.

20. **Decoding the Question**

To solve this problem, use formula for centroid of Δ

i.e. $\left(\frac{x_1+x_2+x_3}{3}, \frac{y_1+y_2+y_3}{3}\right)$.

Let the vertices of triangle be $A(1, \sqrt{3})$, $B(0, 0)$ and $C(2, 0)$. Here, $AB = BC = CA = 2$

Therefore, it is an equilateral triangle.

So, the incentre coincides with centroid.

$$\therefore \quad I \equiv \left(\frac{1+0+2}{3}, \frac{\sqrt{3}+0+0}{3}\right) \Rightarrow I \equiv \left(1, \frac{1}{\sqrt{3}}\right)$$

21. Here, $ax + 2y = \lambda$ and $3x - 2y = \mu$

For $a = -3$ above equations will be parallel or coincident, i.e. for parallel $\lambda + \mu \neq 0$ and coincident, if $\lambda \neq \mu = 0$ and if $a \neq -3$, equations are intersecting i.e. unique solution.

22. Line AB is $\frac{x}{a} + \frac{y}{b} = 1$

Point (2, 3) lies on it.

$$\therefore \quad \frac{2}{a} + \frac{3}{b} = 1$$

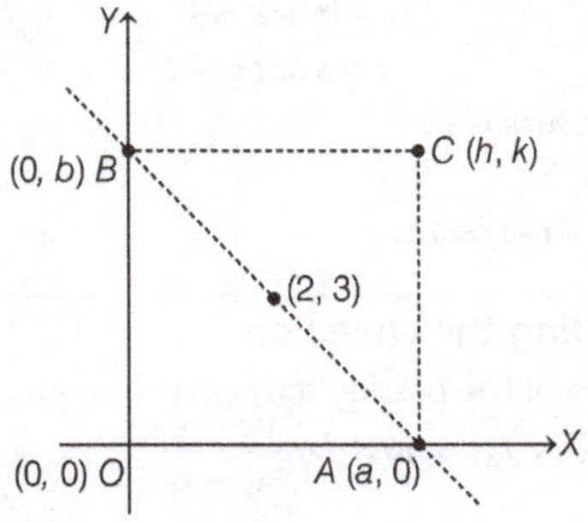

Point $C(h,k)$

$$h = a \text{ and } k = b$$

$$\therefore \quad \frac{2}{h} + \frac{3}{k} = 1 \Rightarrow \frac{2}{x} + \frac{3}{y} = 1 \text{ which is locus of } C$$

$$\frac{2}{x} = 1 - \frac{3}{y} \Rightarrow \frac{2}{x} = \frac{y-3}{y} \Rightarrow x = \frac{2y}{y-3}$$

$\therefore x = \frac{6}{y-3} + 2$ for x is to be integer.

$y - 3 = \pm 1, \pm 2, \pm 3, \pm 6$

$\therefore$ Total 8 points.

23. $\because$ Point of intersection of $ax + 3y - 1 = 0$ and $ax + y + 1 = 0$ is $A\left(\frac{-2}{a}, 1\right)$ and point of intersection of $ax + 3y - 1 = 0$ and $x + 3y = 0$ is $B\left(\frac{1}{a-1}, \frac{-1}{3(a-1)}\right)$

Slope of OA is $m_{OA} = \frac{-a}{2}$

Slope of OB is $m_{OB} = -\frac{1}{3}$

$$\therefore \quad m_{OA} \times m_{OB} = -1 \Rightarrow \frac{-a}{2} \times \frac{-1}{3} = -1 \Rightarrow a = -6$$

$$\therefore \quad |a| = 6$$

Hence, $2|a| = 12$

24.

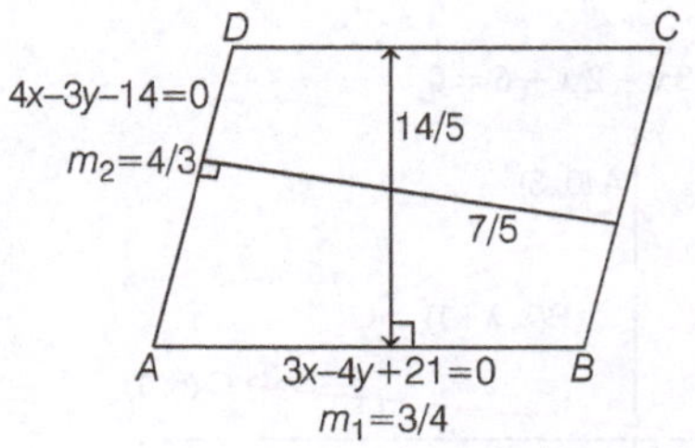

$$\tan\theta = \left|\frac{m_2 - m_1}{1 + m_1 m_2}\right| = \left|\frac{\frac{4}{3} - \frac{3}{4}}{1+1}\right| = \left|\frac{16-9}{12} \times \frac{1}{2}\right| = \frac{7}{24}$$

$$\therefore \sin\theta = \frac{7}{25}$$

$$\therefore \text{ Area of parallelogram} = \frac{1}{\sin\theta} p_1 p_2 = \frac{\frac{14}{5} \times \frac{7}{5}}{\frac{7}{25}} = 14$$

$$\Rightarrow \quad 2k = 14 \Rightarrow k = 7$$

25. Let a be the length of side of square

$$\therefore \quad a^2 + a^2 = 2^2 \Rightarrow a = \sqrt{2}$$

i.e. distance between parallel lines is $\sqrt{2}$.

Now, let two lines of family $y = x + n$ are $y = x + n_1$ and $y = x + n_2$, where

$$n_1, n_2 \in \{0, 1, 2, 3, 4\}$$

$$\therefore \quad \frac{|n_1 - n_2|}{\sqrt{2}} = \sqrt{2} \text{ or } |n_1 - n_2| = 2$$

$\Rightarrow \{n_1, n_2\}$ are $\{0, 2\}$, $\{1, 3\}$ and $\{2, 4\}$.

Hence, both the family have three such pairs. So, the number of possible squares is $3 \times 3 = 9$.

26. Let $OC = a$

$\therefore OC = CA = AB = BO = a$

Let $\left(x_1, \frac{4x_1}{3}\right) \Rightarrow A\left(a + x_1, \frac{4x_1}{3}\right)$

So, $x_1^2 + \frac{16x_1^2}{9} = a^2$ [$\because$ ODB is a right angle triangle]

$$\therefore \quad a = \frac{5x_1}{3}$$

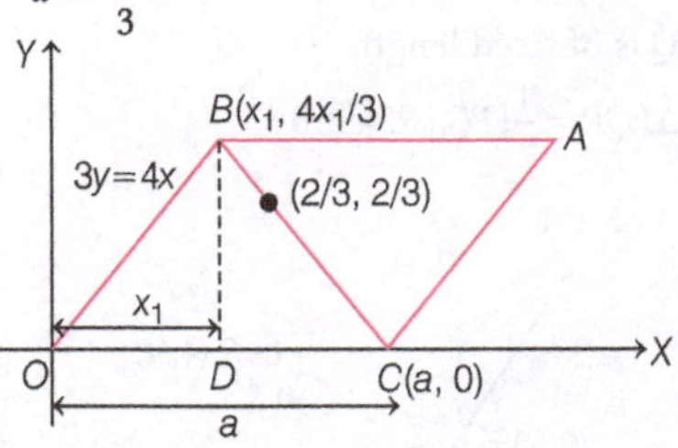

Now, equation of BC is $y - 0 = \frac{\frac{4x_1}{3} - 0}{x_1 - a}(x - a)$.

$\therefore \quad a = \frac{5x_1}{3} \Rightarrow y = -2x + \frac{10x_1}{3}$

Now, BC passes through $\left(\frac{2}{3}, \frac{2}{3}\right)$

$\therefore \quad x_1 = \frac{3}{5}$ and $a = 1$

$\Rightarrow \quad A\left(1 + \frac{3}{5}, \frac{4}{3} \times \frac{3}{5}\right) \Rightarrow A\left(\frac{8}{5}, \frac{4}{5}\right)$

$\therefore \quad 5(\alpha + \beta) = 12$

27. Equation of AB is $3x - 2y + 6 = 0$

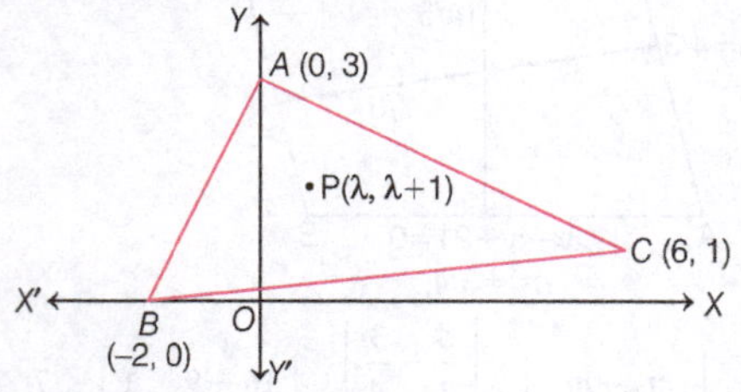

Equation of BC is $x - 8y + 2 = 0$ and

Equation of CA is $x + 3y - 9 = 0$.

Let $\quad P \equiv (\lambda, \lambda + 1)$

$\because$ B and P lie on one side of AC, then

$$\frac{\lambda + 3(\lambda + 1) - 9}{-2 + 0 - 9} > 0 \text{ or } 4\lambda - 6 < 0 \text{ or } \lambda < \frac{3}{2} \quad \text{...(i)}$$

and C and P lie on one side of AB, then

$$\frac{3\lambda - 2(\lambda + 1) + 6}{18 - 2 + 6} > 0$$

or $\quad \lambda + 4 > 0$ or $\lambda > -4$ ...(ii)

Finally, A and P lie on one side of BC, then

$$\frac{\lambda - 8(\lambda + 1) + 2}{0 - 24 + 2} > 0 \text{ or } -7\lambda - 6 < 0$$

or $\quad \lambda > -\frac{6}{7}$ ...(iii)

From Eqs. (i), (ii) and (iii), we get

$$-\frac{6}{7} < \lambda < \frac{3}{2}$$

Integral values of λ are 0 and 1.

Hence, number of integral values of λ is 2.

28. Lines $\quad (2a + b)x + (a + 3b)y + b - 3a = 0$

or $\quad a(2x + y - 3) + b(x + 3y + 1) = 0$

are concurrent at the point of intersection of lines $2x + y - 3 = 0$ and $x + 3y + 1 = 0$, which is $(2, -1)$.

Now, line $\lambda x + 2y + 6 = 0$ must pass through $(2, -1)$, therefore,

$$2\lambda - 2 + 6 \text{ or } \lambda = -2$$

$\therefore \quad |\lambda| = 2$

29. Since, PQ is of fixed length.

Area of $\Delta PQR = \frac{1}{2}|PQ||RP|\sin\theta$

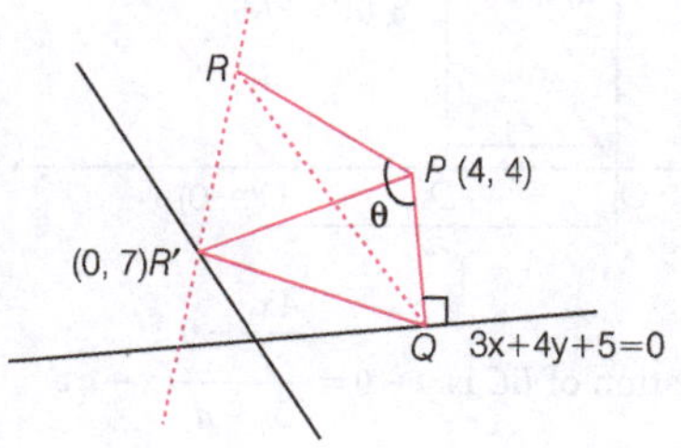

This will be maximum if $\sin\theta = 1$ and RP is maximum,

Since, line $y = mx + 7$ rotates about $(0, 7)$ and PR' is perpendicular to the line than PR' is maximum value of PR

$$m = -\left(\frac{4 - 0}{4 - 7}\right) = \frac{4}{3}$$

Hence, $\quad 9m = 12$

30. Given, the vertices of ΔABC.

$A(\lambda, 2 - \lambda)$, $B(-\lambda + 1, 2\lambda)$ and $C(-4 - \lambda, 6 - 2\lambda)$.

Total area = 70 sq. units [given]

Area of triangle $= \frac{1}{2}[x_1(y_2 - y_3) + x_2(y_3 - y_1) + x_3(y_1 - y_2)]$

$\Rightarrow \quad \frac{1}{2}[[2\lambda - 6 + 2\lambda] + (1 - \lambda)[6 - 2\lambda - 2 + \lambda]$
$\qquad - (4 + \lambda)[2 - \lambda - 2\lambda]] = 70$

$\Rightarrow \quad \lambda(4\lambda - 6) + (1 - \lambda)(4 - \lambda) - (4 + \lambda)(2 - 3\lambda) = 2 \times 70$

$\Rightarrow \quad 4\lambda^2 - 6\lambda + 4 - 5\lambda + \lambda^2 - [8 - 12\lambda + 2\lambda - 3\lambda^2] = 140$

$\Rightarrow \quad 5\lambda^2 - 11\lambda + 4 - 8 + 10\lambda + 3\lambda^2 = 140$

$\Rightarrow \quad 8\lambda^2 - \lambda = 144$

$\lambda = 4.305, -4.180$

$\therefore$ Number of integral value of λ is 0.

31. Any point on the line $x + y = 4$ is $(t, 4 - t)$ where, $t \in R$.

Now, distance of this point from the line

$4x + 3y - 10 = 0$ is 1.

$\Rightarrow \quad \frac{|4t + 3(4 - t) - 10|}{5} = 1$

or $\quad |t + 2| = 5$

$t = 3$ or $t = -7$

$\therefore$ Sum of values is -4.

So, $\lambda = -4$

Hence, $100 - (-4) = 104$

32.

> **Decoding the Question**
>
> (i) Slope of line passing through two given points (x_1, y_1) and (x_2, y_2) is given by $\frac{y_2 - y_1}{x_2 - x_1}$.
>
> (ii) If two lines are perpendicular, then product of their slope is equal to –1.

Slope of the line $2x - 3y + 17 = 0$ is

$$\frac{2}{3} = m_1 \quad \text{[let]}$$

and the slope of line joining the points $(7, 17)$ and $(15, \beta)$ is

$$\frac{\beta - 17}{15 - 7} = \frac{\beta - 17}{8} = m_2 \quad \text{[let]}$$

According to the question, $m_1 m_2 = -1$

$\Rightarrow \quad \frac{2}{3} \times \frac{\beta - 17}{8} = -1$

$\Rightarrow \quad \beta - 17 = -12$

$\Rightarrow \quad \beta = 5$

Hence, $5\beta = 25$

33. Given, perpendicular bisector of AB will pass from centre.

$\therefore$ Equation of perpendicular bisector is $x = -1$.

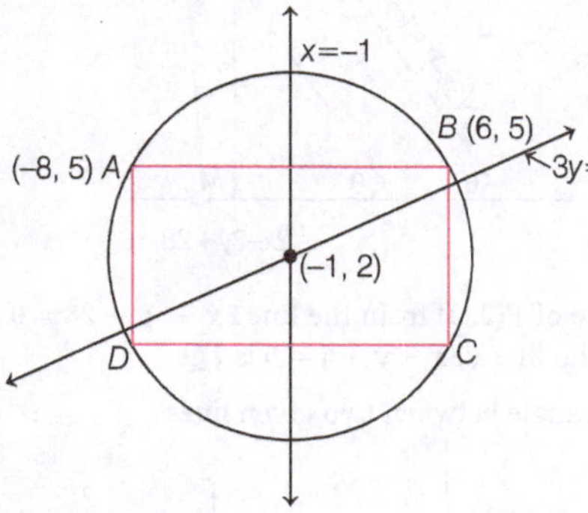

Hence, centre of the circle is $(-1, 2)$.

Let coordinate of D be (x, y).

$\Rightarrow \quad \dfrac{x+6}{2} = -1$ and $\dfrac{y+5}{2} = 2$

$\Rightarrow \quad x = -8$ and $y = -1$

$\therefore \quad D \equiv (-8, -1)$

$|AD| = 6$ and $|AB| = 14$

Area of the rectangle $= 6 \times 14 = 84$

34. We have, $\quad 4a^2 + 9b^2 - c^2 + 12ab = 0$

$\Rightarrow \quad (4a^2 + 9b^2 + 12ab) - c^2 = 0$

$\Rightarrow \quad (2a + 3b)^2 - c^2 = 0$

$\Rightarrow \quad (2a + 3b + c)(2a + 3b - c) = 0$

$\Rightarrow \quad (2a + 3b + c) = 0$ or $(2a + 3b - c) = 0$

Given family of lines are

$$ax + by + c = 0 \quad \text{...(i)}$$

and also the given conditions are

$$2a + 3b + c = 0 \quad \text{...(ii)}$$

$$2a + 3b - c = 0 \quad \text{...(iii)}$$

From Eqs. (i) and (ii), we get

$ax + by - 2a - 3b = 0$

$\Rightarrow \quad a(x-2) + b(y-3) = 0$

$\Rightarrow \quad (x-2) + \dfrac{b}{a}(y-3) = 0$

$\Rightarrow \quad x = 2$ and $y = 3$

$\Rightarrow \quad m = 2$ and $n = 3$

From Eqs. (i) and (iii), we get

$ax + by + 2a + 3b = 0$

$\Rightarrow \quad a(x+2) + b(y+3) = 0$

$\Rightarrow \quad (x+2) + \dfrac{b}{a}(y+3) = 0$

$\Rightarrow \quad x = -2$ and $y = -3$

$\Rightarrow \quad p = -2$ and $2 = -3$

Hence, $m + n + p + q + 10$

$= 2 + 3 - 2 - 3 + 10 = 10$

35. Clearly, slope of line $2x - 2y + 5 = 0$ is 1

$\Rightarrow \quad \theta = \dfrac{\pi}{4}$

Equation of any line passing through $(2, 3)$ and making an angle $\dfrac{\pi}{4}$ is

$$\frac{x-2}{\cos\frac{\pi}{4}} = \frac{y-3}{\sin\frac{\pi}{4}} = r \Rightarrow x - 2 = y - 3 = \frac{r}{\sqrt{2}}$$

$\Rightarrow \quad x = 2 + \dfrac{r}{\sqrt{2}}$ and $y = 3 + \dfrac{r}{\sqrt{2}}$

which lies on $2x - 3y + 9 = 0$

$\Rightarrow 2\left(2 + \dfrac{r}{\sqrt{2}}\right) - 3\left(3 + \dfrac{r}{\sqrt{2}}\right) + 9 = 0$

$\Rightarrow \quad \dfrac{2r}{\sqrt{2}} - \dfrac{3r}{\sqrt{2}} + 4 = 0$

$\Rightarrow \quad -\dfrac{r}{\sqrt{2}} = -4 \Rightarrow r = 4\sqrt{2}$

$\therefore \quad d\sqrt{2} = 4\sqrt{2}$

$d = 4$

$d + 2 = 6$

36. Given lines are $2y = x$ and $4y = x$

$\Rightarrow \quad y = \dfrac{x}{2}$ and $y = \dfrac{x}{4}$

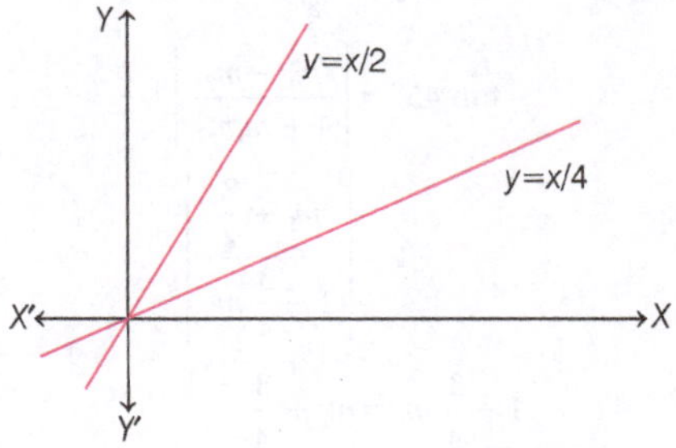

We have, $\quad a - \dfrac{a^2}{4} > 0$ and $a - \dfrac{a^2}{2} < 0$

$\Rightarrow \quad (4a - a^2) > 0$ and $(2a - a^2) < 0$

$\Rightarrow \quad (a^2 - 4a) < 0$ and $(a^2 - 2a) > 0$

$\Rightarrow \quad a(a-4) < 0$ and $a(a-2) > 0$

$\Rightarrow \quad 0 < a < 4$ and $a < 0, a > 2$

$\Rightarrow \quad 2 < a < 4$

$\Rightarrow \quad a \in (2, 4) \equiv (p, q)$

Hence, the value of $(p + q + 1)^2 = (2 + 4 + 1)^2 = (7)^2 = 49$

37. We have, $A(a, -2)$, $B(a, 6)$ and $C\left(\dfrac{a}{4}, -2\right)$ and $O\left(5, \dfrac{a}{4}\right)$

$\therefore \quad AO = BO$

$\Rightarrow \quad (a-5)^2 + \left(-2 - \dfrac{a}{4}\right)^2 = (a-5)^2 + \left(6 - \dfrac{a}{4}\right)^2$

$\Rightarrow \quad a^2 + 25 - 10a + 4 + \dfrac{a^2}{16} + a = a^2 + 25 - 10a + 36 + \dfrac{a^2}{16} - 3a$

$\Rightarrow \quad a = 8$

$AB = 8$, $AC = 6$ and $BC = 10$

$\therefore \quad \alpha = 5, \beta = 24$ and $\gamma = 24$

$\therefore \quad \alpha + \beta + \gamma = 5 + 24 + 24 = 53$

38. Given, ΔOPQ be isosceles triangle and $\angle POQ = 90°$.

Here, $OP = OQ = a$

$\therefore \quad PQ = \sqrt{2}a$

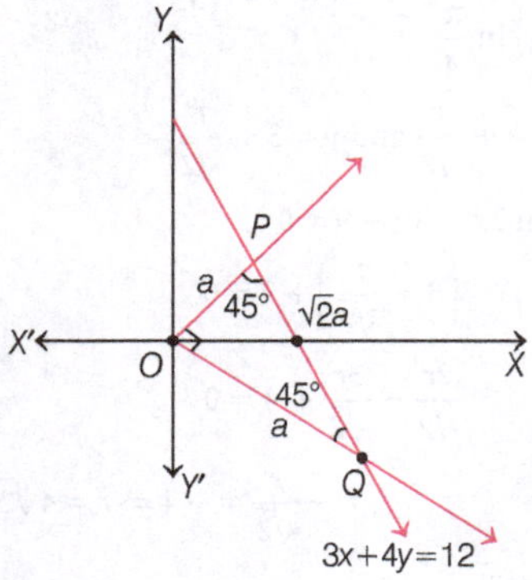

Let slope of OP be m_1.

$\therefore$ Equation of line OP is $y = m_1 x$

and slope of $3x + 4y = 12$ is $-\dfrac{3}{4}$

i.e. $\quad m_2 = -\dfrac{3}{4}$

Now, $\quad \tan 45° = \left|\dfrac{m_1 - m_2}{1 + m_1 m_2}\right|$

$\Rightarrow \quad 1 = \left|\dfrac{m_1 + \frac{3}{4}}{1 - \frac{3}{4} m_1}\right|$

$\Rightarrow \quad 1 - \dfrac{3}{4} m_1 = m_1 + \dfrac{3}{4}$

$\Rightarrow \quad \dfrac{7}{4} m_1 = \dfrac{1}{4}$

$\Rightarrow \quad m_1 = \dfrac{1}{7}$

$\therefore$ Equation of line OP is $y = \dfrac{1}{7} x$

Intersecting point of lines $y = \dfrac{1}{7} x$ and $3x + 4y = 12$ is $P\left(\dfrac{84}{25}, \dfrac{12}{25}\right)$.

and $\quad OP^2 = a^2 = \left(\dfrac{84}{25} - 0\right)^2 + \left(\dfrac{12}{25} - 0\right)^2$

$\Rightarrow \quad a^2 = \dfrac{7056}{625} + \dfrac{144}{625} = \dfrac{7200}{625} = \dfrac{288}{25}$

$\therefore \quad l = OP^2 + PQ^2 + OQ^2$

$= a^2 + 2a^2 + a^2 = 4a^2$

$= 4 \times \dfrac{288}{25} = 46.08$

$\therefore \quad [l] = 46$

39.

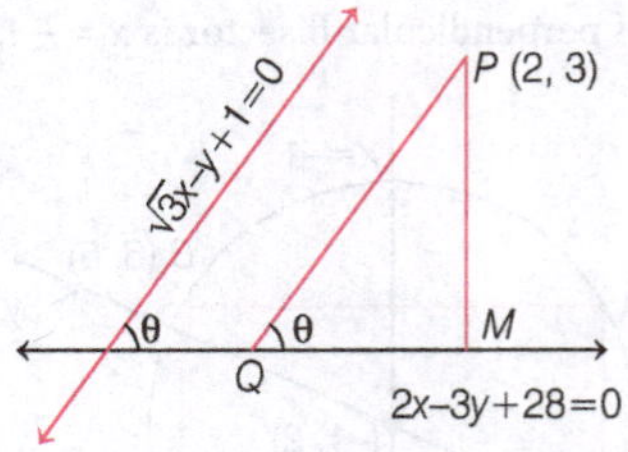

The distance of $P(2, 3)$ from the line $2x - 3y + 28 = 0$ measured parallel to the line $\sqrt{3}x - y + 1 = 0$ is PQ.

Let θ be the angle between two given lines

$$\tan\theta = \left|\frac{\frac{2}{3} - \sqrt{3}}{1 + \frac{2}{3}\sqrt{3}}\right| \quad \left[\because m_1 = \frac{2}{3} \text{ and } n_2 = -\sqrt{3}\right]$$

$$= \tan\theta = \left|\frac{2 - 3\sqrt{3}}{3 + 2\sqrt{3}}\right|$$

$$\tan\theta = \frac{3\sqrt{3} - 2}{2\sqrt{3} + 3}$$

Now, $\quad PM = \left|\dfrac{2(2) - 3(3) + 28}{\sqrt{4 + 9}}\right| = \dfrac{23}{\sqrt{13}}$

$\because \quad PQ = \dfrac{PM}{\sin\theta} = PM \operatorname{cosec}\theta$

$$= \frac{23}{\sqrt{13}}\left[\frac{\sqrt{(2\sqrt{3} + 3)^2 + (3\sqrt{3} - 2)^2}}{3\sqrt{3} - 2}\right]$$

$$= \frac{23}{\sqrt{13}}\left(\frac{\sqrt{12 + 9 + 12\sqrt{3} + 27 + 4 - 12\sqrt{3}}}{3\sqrt{3} - 2}\right)$$

$$= \frac{23}{\sqrt{13}} \times \frac{\sqrt{52}}{(3\sqrt{3} - 2)} = \frac{46}{3\sqrt{3} - 2} \times \frac{3\sqrt{3} + 2}{3\sqrt{3} + 2}$$

$$= \frac{46(3\sqrt{3} + 2)}{23} = 4 + 6\sqrt{3}$$

40. Given, $\quad 2AB = BC$

$\Rightarrow \quad \dfrac{AB}{BC} = \dfrac{1}{2}$

$\Rightarrow \quad AP = PC = 1 = 2$

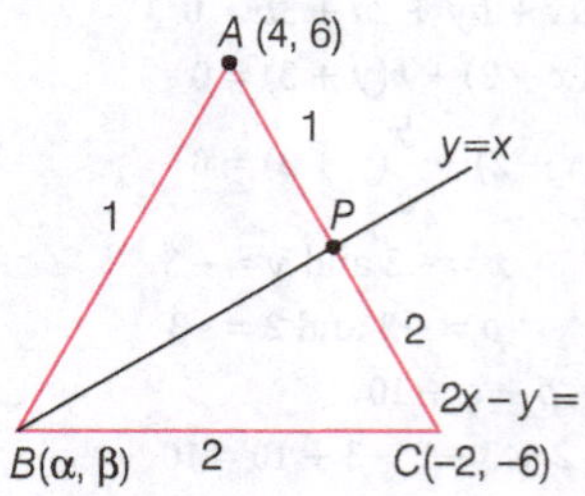

We have, $\quad y = x \quad$ ...(i)

$2x - y = 2 \quad$ ...(ii)

On solving Eqs. (i) and (ii), we get point $P(2, 2)$

Let coordinates of C be (x, y).

$\therefore$ By section formula, we have

$$2 = \frac{1 \times x + 2 \times 4}{1+2} \Rightarrow x = -2$$

and $$2 = \frac{1 \times y + 2 \times 6}{1+2} \Rightarrow y = -6$$

$\therefore$ $C \equiv (-2, -6)$

$\because$ Point B lies on $y = x$

$\therefore$ $(\alpha = \beta)$

$\because$ $$\frac{AB}{BC} = \frac{1}{2} \Rightarrow |BC| = 2|AB|$$

$$\Rightarrow \sqrt{(\alpha+2)^2 + (\alpha+6)^2} = 2\sqrt{(\alpha-4)^2 + (\alpha-6)^2}$$

$$\Rightarrow (\alpha+2)^2 + (\alpha+6)^2 = 4[(\alpha-4)^2 + (\alpha-6)^2]$$

$$\Rightarrow \alpha^2 - 16\alpha + 28 = 0 \Rightarrow \alpha = 2, 14$$

$\alpha = 2$ given point P, $\Rightarrow \alpha = 14$

$\therefore \alpha + 2\beta = \alpha + 2\alpha = 3\alpha = 3 \times 14 = 42$

41.

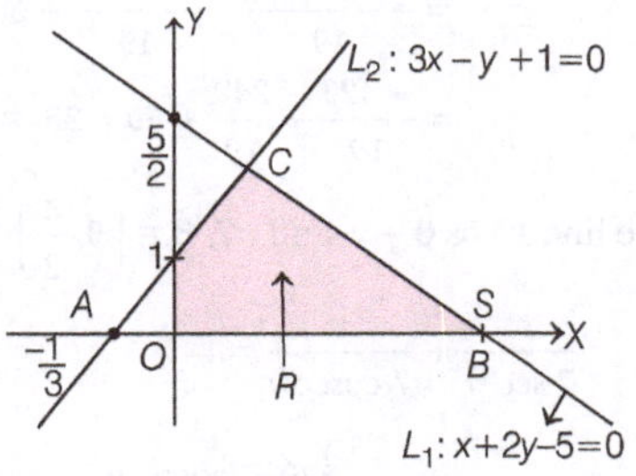

Let $L_1 : x + 2y - 5 = 0$

$L_2 : 3x - y + 1 = 0$

R = Shaded region, where $P(a^2, a+1)$ should lie.

For line L_1 Origin and P lies same side w.r.t. L_1

$$L_1(O) \cdot L_1(P) < 0$$

$$\Rightarrow a^2 + 2(a+1) - 5 < 0$$

$$\Rightarrow a^2 + 2a - 3 < 0$$

$$\Rightarrow (a-1)(a+3) < 0$$

$$\Rightarrow -3 < a < 1 \quad \text{...(i)}$$

For line L_2

$$L_2(O) \cdot L_2(P) > 0$$

$$\Rightarrow 3a^2 - a - 1 + 1 > 0$$

$$\Rightarrow 3a^2 - a > 0$$

$$\Rightarrow a(3a-1) > 0$$

$$\Rightarrow a < 0 \text{ or } a > \frac{1}{3} \quad \text{...(ii)}$$

From Eqs. (i) and (ii), we have

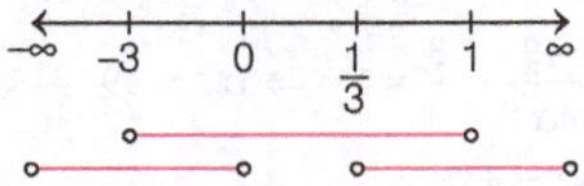

$$\Rightarrow a \in (-3, 0) \cup \left(\frac{1}{3}, 1\right)$$

42. Let θ = Angle between L_1 and L_2

According to the question,

$PA = AB = BQ$

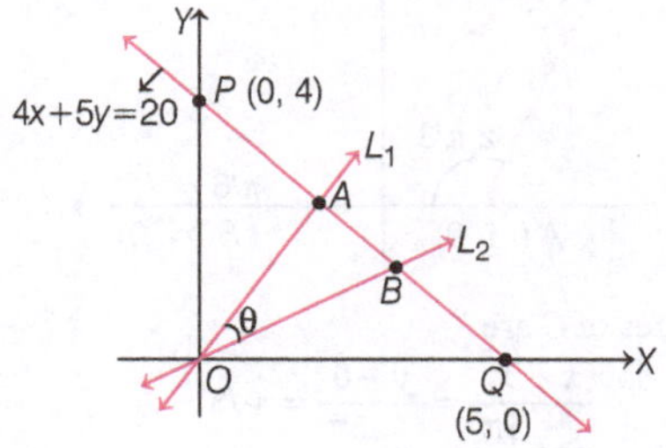

So, coordinates of $A \equiv \left(\frac{5}{3}, \frac{8}{3}\right)$

and coordinates of $B \equiv \left(\frac{10}{3}, \frac{4}{3}\right)$

$$\therefore m_{OA} = \text{Slope of } OA = \frac{\frac{8}{3} - 0}{\frac{5}{3} - 0} = \frac{8}{5}$$

$$m_{OB} = \text{Slope of } OB = \frac{\frac{4}{3} - 0}{\frac{10}{3} - 0} = \frac{2}{5}$$

$$\text{Now, } \tan\theta = \left|\frac{m_{OA} - m_{OB}}{1 + m_{OA} \times m_{OB}}\right|$$

$$= \left|\frac{\frac{8}{5} - \frac{2}{5}}{1 + \frac{8}{5} \times \frac{2}{5}}\right| = \left|\frac{\frac{6}{5}}{\frac{25+16}{25}}\right|$$

$$= \frac{30}{41}$$

43.

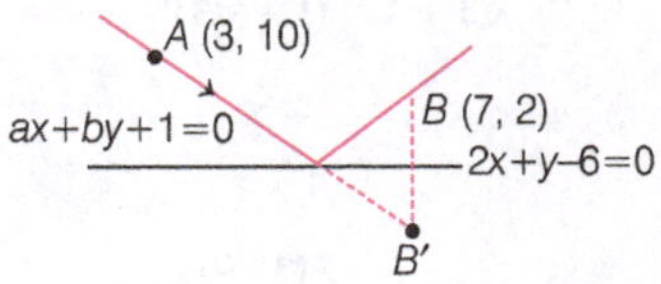

For B',

$$\frac{x-7}{2} = \frac{y-2}{1} = -2\left(\frac{14+2-6}{5}\right)$$

$$\Rightarrow \frac{x-7}{2} = y - 2 = -4$$

$$\Rightarrow x = -1, y = -2$$

So, $B'(-1, -2)$

Slope $(AB') = 3$

Equation of AB'

$$y + 2 = 3(x+1)$$

$$\Rightarrow 3x - y + 1 = 0$$

$$\Rightarrow a = 3, b = -1$$

Therefore, $a^2 + b^2 + 3ab = 9 + 1 - 9 = 1$

44. We have,

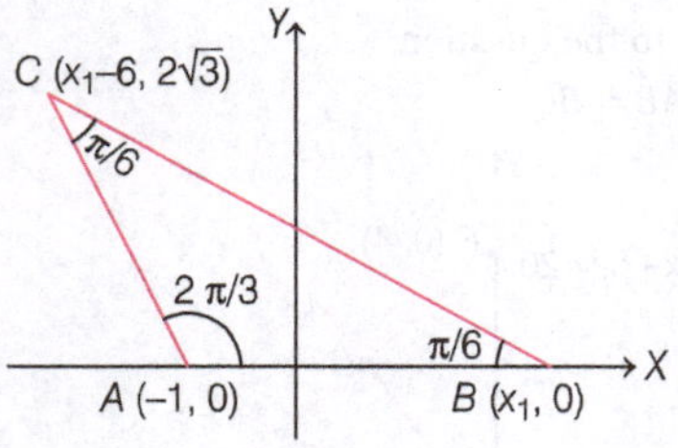

Coordinates of C are

$$\frac{x - x_1}{\cos\frac{5\pi}{6}} = \frac{y - 0}{\sin\frac{5\pi}{6}} = 4\sqrt{3}$$

$\therefore \quad x = 4\sqrt{3}\cos\frac{5\pi}{6} + x_1 = 4\sqrt{3}\left(\frac{-\sqrt{3}}{2}\right) + x_1$

$\Rightarrow \quad x = x_1 - 6$

and $\quad y = 4\sqrt{3}\sin\frac{5\pi}{6}$

$\Rightarrow \quad y = 4\sqrt{3} \times \frac{1}{2} = 2\sqrt{3}$

$C(x_1 - 6, 2\sqrt{3})$

$$M_{AC} = -\sqrt{3}$$

$\therefore \quad \frac{0 - 2\sqrt{3}}{-1 - x_1 + 6} = -\sqrt{3} \Rightarrow x_1 = 3$

Equation of BC: $x + \sqrt{3}y = 3$

Point of intersection of BC and $y = x + 3$ is

$y - 3 + \sqrt{3}y = 3$

$\Rightarrow \quad y = \frac{6}{\sqrt{3}+1},$

and $\quad x = \frac{6}{\sqrt{3}+1} - 3 = \frac{6 - 3\sqrt{3} - 3}{\sqrt{3}+1}$

$\Rightarrow \quad x = \frac{3 - 3\sqrt{3}}{\sqrt{3}+1} = \frac{-6}{(1+\sqrt{3})^2}$

So, $\frac{\beta^4}{\alpha^2} = 36$

45.

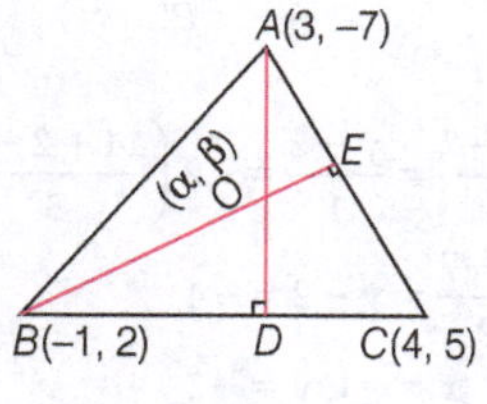

$m_{AD} = \frac{-1}{m_{BC}} = \frac{-5}{3} \qquad \left[\because m_{BC} = \frac{5-2}{4+1} = \frac{3}{5}\right]$

$m_{AC} = \frac{5+7}{4-3} = \frac{12}{1}, m_{BE} = -\frac{1}{12}$

Equation of AD: $(y + 7) = \frac{-5}{3}(x - 3)$

$\Rightarrow \quad 3y + 21 = -5x + 15$

$\Rightarrow \quad 5x + 3y + 21 - 15 = 0$

$\Rightarrow \quad 5x + 3y + 6 = 0 \qquad$ ...(i)

Equation of BE: $(y - 2) = \frac{-1}{12}(x + 1)$

$\Rightarrow \quad 12y - 24 = -x - 1$

$\Rightarrow \quad x + 12y - 24 + 1 = 0$

$\Rightarrow \quad x + 12y - 23 = 0$

$\Rightarrow \quad x = 23 - 12y \qquad$ ...(ii)

On putting the value of x in Eq. (i), we get

$5(23 - 12y) + 3y + 6 = 0$

$\Rightarrow \quad 115 - 60y + 3y + 6 = 0$

$\Rightarrow \quad y = \frac{121}{57}$

and $\quad x = 23 - \frac{12 \times 121}{57} = \frac{141}{57}$

Orthocentre $O(\alpha, \beta) = \left(\frac{-141}{57}, \frac{121}{57}\right)$

$= 9\alpha - 6\beta + 60$

$= 9 \times \left(\frac{-141}{57}\right) - 6\left(\frac{121}{57}\right) + 60$

$= \frac{3 \times (-141)}{19} - \frac{2 \times 121}{19} + 60$

$= \frac{-423}{19} - \frac{242}{19} + 60 = 25$

46. We have the line $x\cos\theta + y\sin\theta = 7$, $\theta \in \left(0, \frac{\pi}{2}\right)$

$\Rightarrow \quad \frac{x}{7\sec\theta} + \frac{y}{7\,\text{cosec}\,\theta} = 1$

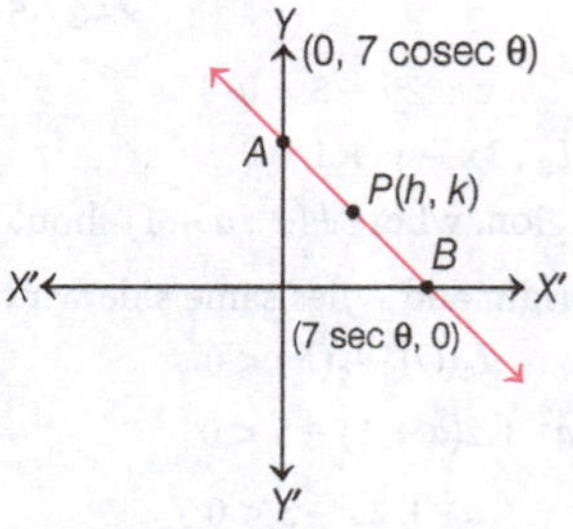

Let $P(h, k)$ be mid-point of the line segment AB.

$\therefore \quad h = \frac{7\sec\theta}{2}, k = \frac{7\,\text{cosec}\,\theta}{2}$

Since, $\theta \in \left(0, \frac{\pi}{2}\right) \Rightarrow h$ and k are positive. Now, $\cos\theta = \frac{7}{2h},$

and $\quad \sin\theta = \frac{7}{2k} \Rightarrow \left(\frac{7}{2h}\right)^2 + \left(\frac{7}{2k}\right)^2 = 1$

Also, $\left(\alpha, \frac{7\sqrt{3}}{3}\right)$ lies on this curve

$\Rightarrow \quad \left(\frac{7}{2\alpha}\right)^2 + \left(\frac{7 \cdot 3}{2 \cdot 7\sqrt{3}}\right)^2 = 1$

$\Rightarrow \quad \frac{49}{4\alpha^2} + \frac{3}{4} = 1 \quad \Rightarrow \alpha^2 = 49$

$\Rightarrow \quad \alpha = \pm 7$

Since, $h > 0$ i.e. x-coordinate of points on curve are positive.

$\therefore \quad \alpha = 7$

47. Given, sides of triangle

$$4x + 3y = 69 \quad \text{...(i)}$$
$$4y - 3x = 17$$
$$\Rightarrow \quad 3x - 4y = -17 \quad \text{...(ii)}$$
$$x + 7y = 61 \quad \text{...(iii)}$$

Lines (i) and (ii) are perpendicular.

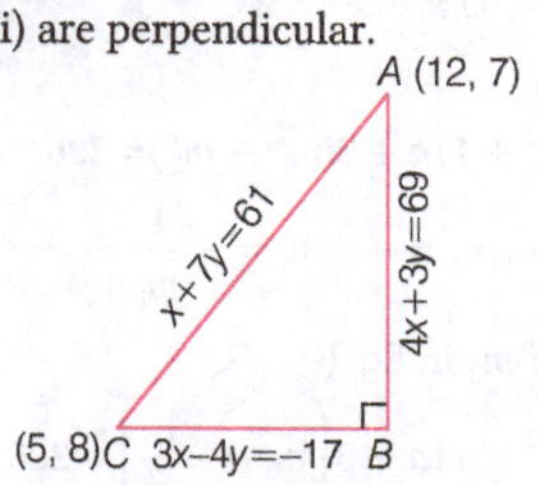

$\therefore$ Circumcentre of a right angled triangle is the mid-point of the hypotenuse.

Solving Eqs. (i) and (iii) after multiply by 4 in Eq (iii),

$$4x + 3y = 69$$
$$\underline{\underset{-}{}4x \underset{-}{+} 28y \underset{-}{=} 244}$$
$$-25y = -175$$

$$\Rightarrow \quad y = 7 \text{ and } x = 12$$

$A(12, 7)$

Solving Eqs. (ii) and (iii) for C

$$3x - 4y = -17$$
$$\underline{3x + 21y = 183}$$
$$-25y = -200$$

$\Rightarrow$ $y = 8$ and $x = 5$

$C(5, 8)$

Coordinate of circumcentre = mid-point of AC

$$= \left(\frac{5+12}{2}, \frac{7+8}{2}\right)$$

$$\therefore \quad \alpha = \frac{17}{2}, \beta = \frac{15}{2}$$

$$\therefore \quad (\alpha - \beta)^2 + \alpha + \beta = 1 + 16 = 17$$

48.

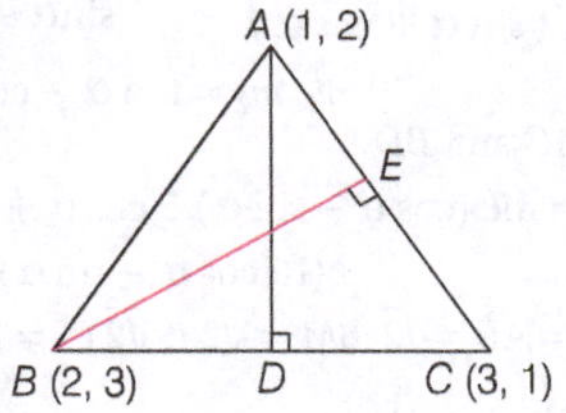

Slope of BC, $m_{BC} = \dfrac{1-3}{3-2} = \dfrac{-2}{1} = -2$

$\therefore$ Slope of AD, $m_{AD} = \dfrac{-1}{m_{BC}} = \dfrac{-1}{-2} = \dfrac{1}{2}$

So, equation of line AD is

$$y - 2 = \frac{1}{2}(x - 1)$$

$$\Rightarrow \quad x - 2y + 3 = 0 \quad \text{...(i)}$$

Slope of AC, $m_{AC} = \dfrac{2-1}{1-3} = \dfrac{1}{-2} = \dfrac{-1}{2}$

$\therefore$ Slope of BE, $m_{BE} = \dfrac{-1}{m_{AC}} = \dfrac{-1}{\left(-\frac{1}{2}\right)} = 2$

So, equation of line BE is

$$y - 3 = 2(x - 2)$$

$$\Rightarrow \quad 2x - y - 1 = 0 \quad \text{...(ii)}$$

On solving Eqs. (i) and (ii), we get

$$x = \frac{5}{3}, y = \frac{7}{3}$$

$\therefore$ Orthocentre of ΔABC is $\left(\dfrac{5}{3}, \dfrac{7}{3}\right)$.

$$\therefore \quad \alpha = \frac{5}{3} \text{ and } \beta = \frac{7}{3}$$

Now, Let $\alpha_1 = \alpha + 4\beta$

and $\beta_1 = 4\alpha + \beta$.

Then, $\alpha_1 = \alpha + 4\beta = \dfrac{5}{3} + 4 \times \dfrac{7}{3} = \dfrac{33}{3} = 11$

and $\beta_1 = 4\alpha + \beta = 4 \times \dfrac{5}{3} + \dfrac{7}{3} = \dfrac{27}{3} = 9$

Again, $\alpha_1 + \beta_1 = 11 + 9 = 20$

and $\alpha_1\beta_1 = 11 \times 9 = 99$

So, quadratic equation, whose roots are α_1 and β_1 is

$$x^2 - (\alpha_1 + \beta_1)x + \alpha_1\beta_1 = 0$$

$$\Rightarrow \quad x^2 - 20x + 99 = 0$$

49. Given, $OA = a$, $OB = b$

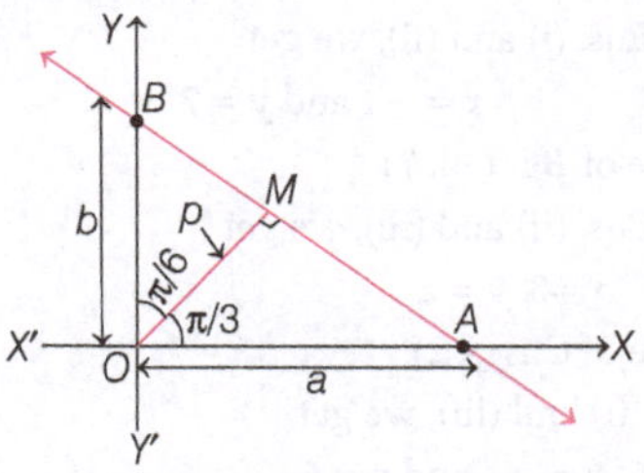

Let M = foot of perpendicular drawn from O to AB.

$$\angle MOA = \frac{\pi}{3} \text{ and } \angle MOB = \frac{\pi}{6} \quad \text{(given)}$$

Since, we know that equation of straight line (in intercept form) is given by

$$\frac{x}{a} + \frac{y}{b} = 1 \quad \text{...(i)}$$

Also, we can write equation of straight line in normal form as

$$x\cos\frac{\pi}{3} + y\sin\frac{\pi}{3} = p$$

where p = length of perpendicular drawn from origin to the given line AB.

$$\Rightarrow \quad \frac{x}{2} + \frac{y\sqrt{3}}{2} = p \Rightarrow \frac{x}{2p} + \frac{\sqrt{3}y}{2p} = 1$$

$$\Rightarrow \quad \frac{x}{2p} + \frac{y}{\left(\frac{2p}{\sqrt{3}}\right)} = 1 \quad \text{...(ii)}$$

On comparing Eqs. (i) and (ii), we get

$$a = 2p \text{ and } b = \frac{2p}{\sqrt{3}}$$

Now, area of $\Delta OAB = \frac{1}{2} \times a \times b = \frac{1}{2} \times (2p) \times \left(\frac{2p}{\sqrt{3}}\right)$

$$\Rightarrow \quad \frac{98}{3} \times \sqrt{3} = \frac{1}{2} \times 2 \times 2 \times \frac{p^2}{\sqrt{3}}$$

$$\Rightarrow \quad 2p^2 = 98 \Rightarrow p^2 = 49$$

Hence, $a^2 - b^2 = (2p)^2 - \left(\frac{2p}{\sqrt{3}}\right)^2$

$$= 4p^2 - \frac{4p^2}{3} = \frac{8}{3}p^2$$

$$\Rightarrow \quad a^2 - b^2 = \frac{8}{3} \times 49 = \frac{392}{3}$$

50.

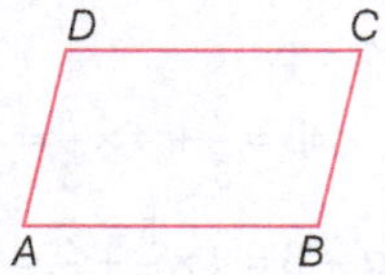

We have, $ABCD$ is a parallelogram.

Let equation of AB be

$$2x - 3y = -23 \quad \text{...(i)}$$

and equation of BC be

$$5x + 4y = 23 \quad \text{...(ii)}$$

Equation of AC is

$$3x + 7y = 23 \quad \text{...(iii)}$$

On solving Eqs. (i) and (ii), we get

$$x = -1 \text{ and } y = 7$$

$\therefore$ Coordinate of B is $(-1, 7)$

On solving Eqs. (ii) and (iii), we get

$$x = 3, y = 2$$

$\therefore$ Coordinate of C is $(3, 2)$.

Solving Eqs. (i) and (iii), we get

$$x = -4 \text{ and } y = 5$$

$\therefore$ Coordinate of A is $(-4, 5)$.

Let M be the intersection point of diagonal.

Coordinate of M is $\left(\frac{-4+3}{2}, \frac{5+2}{2}\right)$ or $\left(-\frac{1}{2}, \frac{7}{2}\right)$.

Equation of BD is $y - 7 = \left(\frac{7 - \frac{7}{2}}{-1 + \frac{1}{2}}\right)(x + 1)$

$$\Rightarrow \quad 7x + y = 0$$

Distance of A from diagonal BD

$$d = \frac{|7 \times (-4) + 5|}{\sqrt{7^2 + 1^2}}$$

$$\therefore \quad d = \frac{23}{\sqrt{50}}$$

Hence, $\quad 50d^2 = (23)^2 = 529$

51. Given point $(\alpha, -3)$, $(2, 0)$ and $(1, \alpha)$.

For collinear, $\left(\frac{\alpha - 0}{-1}\right) = \frac{\alpha + 3}{1 - \alpha} \Rightarrow \alpha = -1, 3$

$$\Rightarrow \quad \alpha_1 = -1, \alpha_2 = 3$$

Equation is $(y - y_1) = m(x - x_1) \Rightarrow y - 3 = \sqrt{3}(x + 1)$

52. Given equation,

$$a^2 + 11a + 3(m_1^2 + m_2^2) = 220 \quad \text{...(i)}$$

$$m_1 m_2 = -1, m_2 = -\frac{1}{m_1}$$

Put the value of m_2 in Eq. (i)

$$a^2 + 11a + 3\left(m_1^2 + \frac{1}{m_1^2}\right) = 220$$

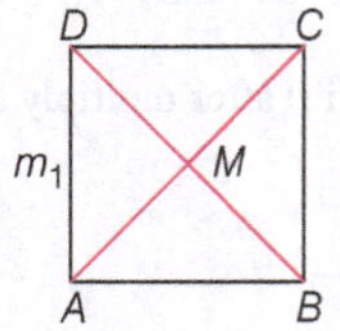

Equation of diagonal AC,

$$(\cos\alpha - \sin\alpha)x + (\sin\alpha + \cos\alpha)y = 10$$

Equation of diagonal BD,

$$(\sin\alpha - \cos\alpha)x + (\sin\alpha - \cos\alpha)y = 0$$

One vertex of square $= [10(\cos\alpha - \sin\alpha), 10(\sin\alpha - \cos\alpha)]$

Slope of $AC = \left(\frac{\sin\alpha - \cos\alpha}{\sin\alpha + \cos\alpha}\right)$

Equation of line making an angle $\frac{\pi}{4}$ with AC

$$(m_1, m_2) = \frac{m \pm \tan\frac{\pi}{4}}{1 \pm m\tan\frac{\pi}{4}} = \frac{m+1}{1-m} \text{ or } \frac{m-1}{1+m}$$

$$\frac{\frac{\sin\alpha - \cos\alpha}{\sin\alpha + \cos\alpha} + 1}{1 - \left(\frac{\sin\alpha - \cos\alpha}{\sin\alpha + \cos\alpha}\right)} = \frac{\frac{\sin\alpha - \cos\alpha}{\sin\alpha + \cos\alpha} - 1}{1 + \frac{\sin\alpha - \cos\alpha}{\sin\alpha + \cos\alpha}}$$

$$m_1, m_2 = \tan\alpha, -\cot\alpha$$

Mid-point of AC and BD

$$= M(5(\cos\alpha - \sin\alpha), 5(\cos\alpha + \sin\alpha))$$

$$B(10(\cos\alpha - \sin\alpha), 10(\cos\alpha + \sin\alpha))$$

$$\therefore \quad a = AB = \sqrt{2}\, BM = \sqrt{2}\,(5\sqrt{2}) \quad = 10a = 10$$

$$\because \; a^2 + 11a + 3\left(m_1^2 + \frac{1}{m_1^2}\right) = 220$$

Hence $\tan^2\alpha = 3, \tan^2\alpha = \frac{1}{3}$,

$$\alpha = \frac{\pi}{3} \text{ or } \frac{\pi}{6}.$$

Now, $72(\sin^4\alpha + \cos^4\alpha) + a^2 - 3a + 13$

$$= 72\left(\frac{9}{16} + \frac{1}{16}\right) + 100 - 30 + 13$$

$$= 72\left(\frac{5}{8}\right) + 83 = 45 + 83 = 128$$

53. Given, $A(\alpha, -2)$, $B(\alpha, 6)$, $C\left(\frac{\alpha}{4}, -2\right)$.

$$AB = \sqrt{0^2 + 8^2} = 8$$

$$AC = \sqrt{\left(\alpha - \frac{\alpha}{4}\right)^2 + 0} = \frac{3\alpha}{4}$$

$$BC = \sqrt{\left(\alpha - \frac{\alpha}{4}\right)^2 + (6+2)^2} = \sqrt{\left(\frac{3\alpha}{4}\right)^2 + 64}$$

So, $(AB)^2 + (AC)^2 = (BC)^2$

Also, AC is perpendicular to AB.

Hence, ΔABC is a right angled triangle at A.

Now circumcentre is mid-point of BC.

$$\left(5, \frac{\alpha}{4}\right) \equiv \left(\frac{\alpha + \frac{\alpha}{4}}{2}, \frac{6-2}{2}\right)$$

So, $\alpha/4 = 2 \Rightarrow \alpha = 8$

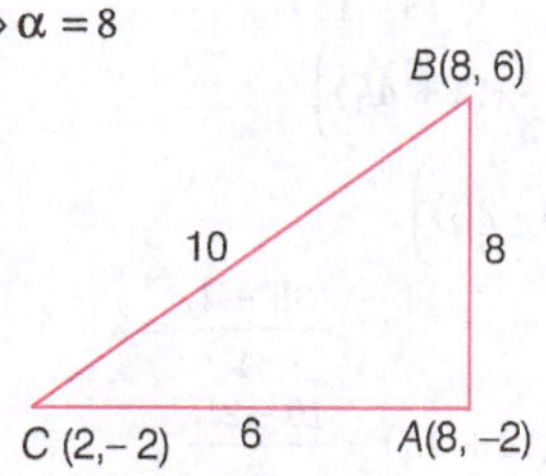

So, area of $\Delta ABC = \frac{1}{2} \times 6 \times 8 = 24$

Perimeter $= 6 + 8 + 10 = 24$

Circumradius $= \frac{BC}{2} = \frac{10}{2} = 5$

Inradius $= \frac{\Delta}{S} = \frac{24}{12} = 2$ $\left[\because s = \frac{a+b+c}{2}\right]$

54. $AB \rightarrow 2x + y = 0$

$AC \rightarrow x - y = 3$

$BC \rightarrow x + py = 39$

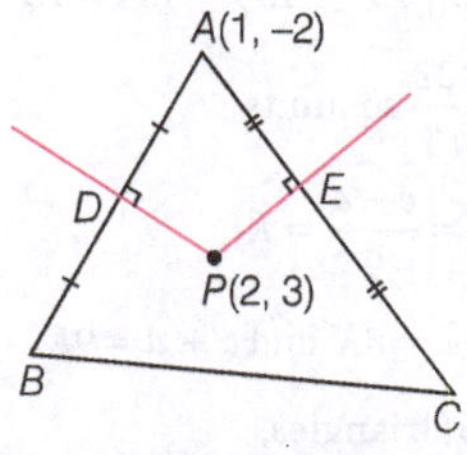

Point of intersection of AB, AC is vertex $A = (1, -2)$

Let PD be perpendicular bisector of AB.

Slope of $AB = -2$

$\therefore$ Slope of $PD = \frac{1}{2}$

$\therefore$ Equation of PD is $x - 2y = -4$

$\therefore$ Point D is $\left(\frac{-4}{5}, \frac{8}{5}\right)$.

$\therefore$ Point B is $\left(\frac{-13}{5}, \frac{26}{5}\right)$.

Similarly, equation of PE is $x + y = 5$.

Point E is (4, 1).

$\therefore$ Point C is (7, 4).

$$\therefore \quad AC = \sqrt{(1-7)^2 + (-2-4)^2} = 6\sqrt{2}$$

Also, C satisfies BC.

$$\therefore \quad 7 + 4p = 39 \Rightarrow p = 8$$

$$\Rightarrow \quad (AC)^2 = 72 = 8 \times 9 = 9p$$

$$\Rightarrow \quad (AC)^2 + p^2 = 72 + 64 = 136$$

Area of ΔABC

$$= \frac{1}{2}\begin{vmatrix} 1 & -2 & 1 \\ \frac{-13}{5} & \frac{26}{5} & 1 \\ 7 & 4 & 1 \end{vmatrix}$$

$$= \left|\frac{1}{2}\left[1\left(\frac{26}{5} - 4\right) + 2\left(\frac{-13}{5} - 7\right) + 1\left(\frac{-52}{5} - \frac{182}{5}\right)\right]\right|$$

$$= \left|\frac{1}{2}\left[\frac{6}{5} - \frac{96}{5} - \frac{234}{5}\right]\right| = 32.4$$

55.

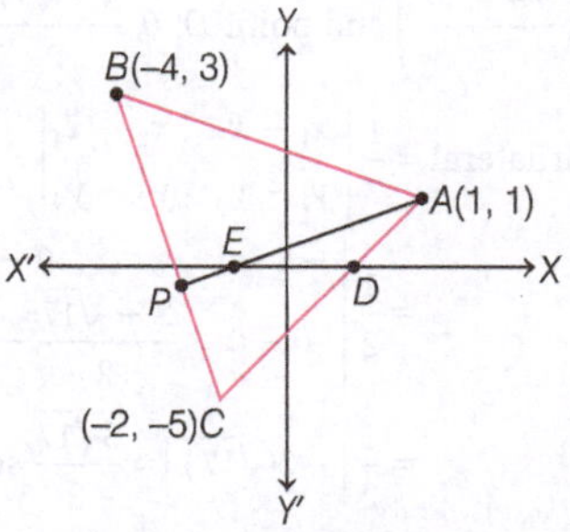

$$\Delta_1 = \text{ar}(\Delta APB),\ \Delta_2 = \text{ar}(\Delta ABC)$$

Now, $\frac{\Delta_1}{\Delta_2} = \frac{4}{7} \Rightarrow \frac{\text{ar}(\Delta PAB)}{\text{ar}(\Delta APC)} = \frac{4}{3}$

$$\therefore \quad \frac{BP}{PC} = \frac{4}{3}$$

$$\therefore \quad P = \left(\frac{(-4)\times 3 + (-2)\times 4}{3+4}, \frac{3\times 3 + (-5)\times 4}{3+4}\right)$$

$$\Rightarrow \quad P = \left(\frac{-20}{7}, \frac{-11}{7}\right)$$

Let D be $(h, 0) \Rightarrow \frac{1-0}{1-h} = \frac{-5-0}{-2-h}$

$$\Rightarrow \quad D = \left(\frac{1}{2}, 0\right).$$

Let E be $(k, 0) \Rightarrow \frac{1-0}{1-k} = \frac{\frac{-11}{7} - 0}{\frac{-20}{7} - k}$

$$\Rightarrow \quad E = \left(\frac{-1}{2}, 0\right).$$

$\therefore$ ar$(\Delta AED) = \frac{1}{2} \times 1 \times 1 = \frac{1}{2}$

56. Let the coordinates of point P be (x, y).

Let the point M and N be $(1, 2)$ and $(-2, 1)$ respectively.

Given, $(MP)^2 + (NP)^2 = 14$

$$(x-1)^2 + (y-2)^2 + (x+2)^2 + (y-1)^2 = 14$$

$$\Rightarrow x^2 + y^2 - 2x - 4y + 5 + x^2 + y^2 + 4x - 2y + 5 = 14$$

$$\Rightarrow \quad x^2 + y^2 + x - 3y - 2 = 0$$

$\therefore$ Locus of point P is $x^2 + y^2 + x - 3y - 2 = 0$

For the intersection of locus of point P with X-axis, substitute $y = 0$

$$\Rightarrow \quad x^2 + x - 2 = 0$$

$$\Rightarrow \quad x(x+2) - 1(x+2) = 0$$

$$\Rightarrow \quad x = -2, 1$$

Let point $A(-2, 0)$ and $B(1, 0)$.

For the intersection of locus of point P with Y-axis, substitute $x = 0$.

$$y^2 - 3y - 2 = 0$$

$$\Rightarrow \quad y = \frac{3 \pm \sqrt{9+8}}{2} = \frac{3 \pm \sqrt{17}}{2}$$

$\therefore$ Point $C\left(0, \frac{3+\sqrt{17}}{2}\right)$ and point $D\left(0, \frac{3-\sqrt{17}}{2}\right)$.

$$\text{Area of quadrilateral} = \frac{1}{2}\begin{vmatrix} x_1 - x_3 & x_2 - x_4 \\ y_1 - y_3 & y_2 - y_4 \end{vmatrix}$$

$$= \frac{1}{2}\begin{vmatrix} -2-1 & 0-0 \\ 0-0 & \frac{3+\sqrt{17}}{2} - \frac{3-\sqrt{17}}{2} \end{vmatrix}$$

$$= \frac{1}{2}\left|-3(\sqrt{17})\right| = \frac{3\sqrt{17}}{2} \text{ sq. units}$$

57. A and A' lie on the line $y = 2$

And point B is $(2, 3)$.

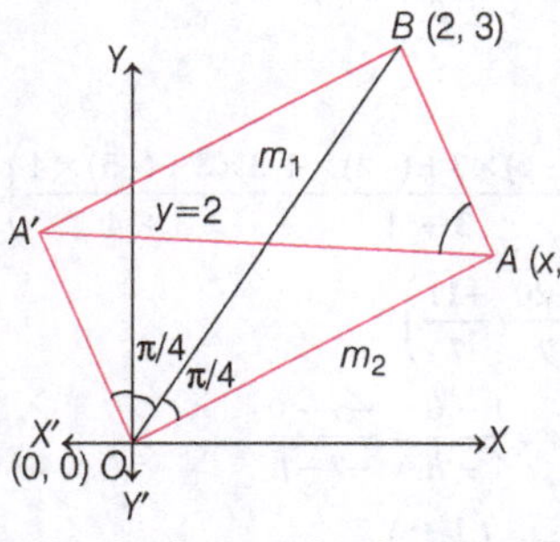

$$m_1 = \frac{3-0}{2-0} = \frac{3}{2}, \; m_2 = \frac{2-0}{x-0} = \frac{2}{x}$$

$$\tan\theta = \left|\frac{m_1 - m_2}{1 + m_1 m_2}\right|$$

$$\Rightarrow \quad \tan\frac{\pi}{4} = \left|\frac{\frac{3}{2} - \frac{2}{x}}{1 + \frac{3}{2}\cdot\frac{2}{x}}\right| \Rightarrow 1 = \left|\frac{3x-4}{2x+6}\right|$$

$$\Rightarrow \pm(2x+6) = 3x - 4$$

It gives $\quad x = -\frac{2}{5}, 10; \; x_1 = -\frac{2}{5}$

and $\quad x_2 = 10$

$$\therefore \quad AA' = \sqrt{\left(10 + \frac{2}{5}\right)^2 + (2-2)^2} = 10 + \frac{2}{5} = \frac{52}{5}$$

58. Given, $\quad L_1 : 2x + 5y = 10$

$$L_2 : -4x + 3y = 12$$

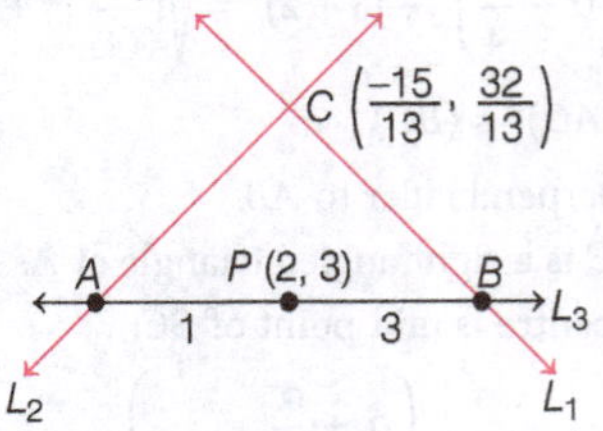

On solving L_1 and L_2, we get

$$C \equiv \left(\frac{-15}{13}, \frac{32}{13}\right)$$

Now, let $A\left(l_1, \frac{1}{3}(12 + 4l_1)\right)$

and $B\left(l_2, \frac{1}{5}(10 - 2l_2)\right)$

$$\therefore \quad \frac{3l_1 + l_2}{4} = 2$$

and $$\frac{(12 + 4l_1) + \frac{10 - 2l_2}{5}}{4} = 3$$

So, $\quad 3l_1 + l_2 = 8 \quad$ ...(i)

and $\quad 10l_1 - l_2 = -5 \quad$ ...(ii)

Solving Eqs. (i) and (ii), we get

$$(l_1, l_2) = \left(\frac{3}{13}, \frac{95}{13}\right)$$

$$\therefore \quad A = \left(\frac{3}{13}, \frac{56}{13}\right) \text{ and } B = \left(\frac{95}{13}, -\frac{12}{13}\right)$$

$$\text{Area of } \Delta ABC = \left|\frac{1}{2}\left[\frac{3}{13}\left(-\frac{44}{13}\right) - \frac{56}{13}\left(\frac{110}{13}\right) + 1\left(\frac{2860}{169}\right)\right]\right|$$

$$= \frac{132}{13} \text{ sq. units}$$

59. Let $\frac{a+b}{7} = \frac{b+c}{8} = \frac{c+a}{9} = K$

$\therefore a + b = 7K$, $b + c = 8K$ and $c + a = 9K$

Semi-perimeter of triangles,

$$(s) = \frac{a+b+c}{2} = \frac{2(a+b+c)}{4}$$

$$= \frac{(a+b) + (b+c) + (c+a)}{4}$$

$$= \frac{7K + 8K + 9K}{4} = 6K$$

$$a = 2s - (b + c) = 12K - 8K$$

$$= 4K$$

Similarly, $b = 3K$ and $c = 5K$

Now, $\Delta = \sqrt{s(s-a)(s-b)(s-c)}$

$= \sqrt{6K(2K)(3K)(K)} = 6K^2$

Radius of incircle $(r) = \dfrac{\Delta}{S} = \dfrac{6K^2}{6K} = K$

Radius of circumcircle $(R) = \dfrac{abc}{4\Delta}$

$= \dfrac{4K \times 3K \times 5K}{4 \times 6K^2} = \dfrac{5K}{2}$

$\therefore \quad \dfrac{R}{r} = \dfrac{5K}{2} \div K = \dfrac{5}{2}$

60.

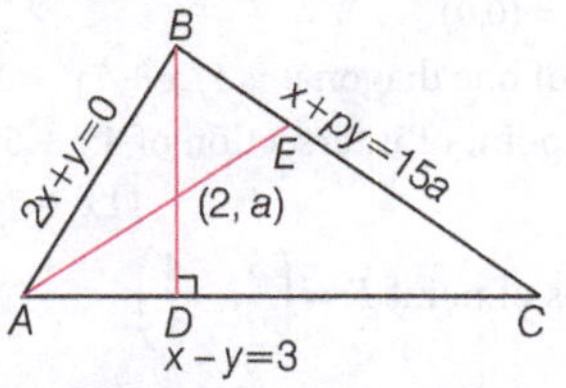

For determining coordinate of point *A*,

$2x + y = 0 \Rightarrow y = -2x$

and $\quad x - y = 3$

$\Rightarrow \quad x - (-2x) = 3$

$\Rightarrow \quad x = 1$

Coordinates of *A* is (1, − 2).

For determining coordinate of point *B*.

On putting $y = -2x$ in equation $x + py = 15a$, we get

$x - 2px = 15a$

$\Rightarrow \quad x = \dfrac{15a}{1-2p}$

$\therefore$ Coordinates of *B* is $\left(\dfrac{15a}{1-2p}, \dfrac{-30a}{1-2p}\right)$.

Slope of $AE = \dfrac{a+2}{2-1} = a + 2$

Slope of $BD = \dfrac{a + \dfrac{30a}{1-2p}}{2 - \dfrac{15a}{1-2p}} = \dfrac{31a - 2ap}{2 - 4p - 15a}$

Slope of $BC = -\dfrac{1}{p}$

Slope of $AC = 1$

As *AE* is perpendicular to *BC*,

Slope of *AE* × Slope of *BC* = − 1

$\Rightarrow \quad (a+2)\left(-\dfrac{1}{p}\right) = -1$

$\Rightarrow \quad a + 2 = p$

$\Rightarrow \quad a = p - 2 \qquad$ ...(i)

As *BD* is perpendicular to *AC*,

Slope of *BD* × Slope of *AC* = − 1

$\Rightarrow \quad \dfrac{31a - 2ap}{2 - 4p - 15a} \times 1 = (-1)$

$\Rightarrow \quad 16a - 2ap - 4p + 2 = 0$

$\Rightarrow \quad 16(p-2) - 2p(p-2) - 4p + 2 = 0$

$\Rightarrow \quad p^2 - 8p + 15 = 0$

$\Rightarrow \quad p = 3 \text{ or } 5$

If $p = 3$, then $a = 1$ and if $p = 5$, then $a = 3$

As, $\quad -\dfrac{1}{2} < a < 2, a \neq 3 \Rightarrow p \neq 5$

Hence, $p = 3$

61. Given that $A\left(\dfrac{3}{\sqrt{a}}, \sqrt{a}\right)$, $a > 0$ be a fixed point in the *xy*-plane, the image of *A* in *Y*-axis is $B\left(-\dfrac{3}{\sqrt{a}}, \sqrt{a}\right)$ and the image of *B* in *X*-axis is $C\left(\dfrac{-3}{\sqrt{a}}, -\sqrt{a}\right)$ and also given $D(3\cos\theta, a\sin\theta)$ in the fourth quadrant.

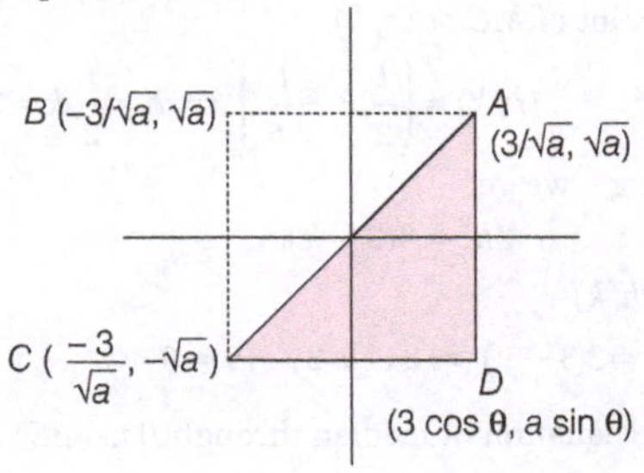

Thus, area of $\Delta ACD = \dfrac{1}{2}\begin{vmatrix} \dfrac{3}{\sqrt{a}} & \sqrt{a} & 1 \\ -\dfrac{3}{\sqrt{a}} & -\sqrt{a} & 1 \\ 3\cos\theta & a\sin\theta & 1 \end{vmatrix}$

Applying $R_1 \to R_1 + R_2$,

$\Delta = \dfrac{1}{2}\begin{vmatrix} 0 & 0 & 2 \\ -\dfrac{3}{\sqrt{a}} & -\sqrt{a} & 1 \\ 3\cos\theta & a\sin\theta & 1 \end{vmatrix}$

$\Rightarrow \quad \Delta = \left|\dfrac{1}{2} 2\{-3\sqrt{a}\sin\theta + 3\sqrt{a}\cos\theta\}\right|$

$\Rightarrow \quad \Delta = |3\sqrt{a}(-\sin\theta + \cos\theta)|$

$\Rightarrow \quad \Delta = 3\sqrt{a}\,|-\sin\theta + \cos\theta|$

$\therefore \quad \Delta_{max} = 3\sqrt{a} \cdot \sqrt{2} = 12$ (given)

$\Rightarrow \quad \sqrt{a} = 2\sqrt{2} \Rightarrow a = (2\sqrt{2})^2 = 8$

62. $\quad p = \dfrac{k\cot 2\alpha}{\sqrt{\operatorname{cosec}^2\alpha + \sec^2\alpha}}$

and $\quad q = \dfrac{k\sin 2\alpha}{\sqrt{\sin^2\alpha + \cos^2\alpha}}$

$\Rightarrow \quad p = \dfrac{k\left(\dfrac{\cos 2\alpha}{\sin 2\alpha}\right)}{\sqrt{\dfrac{\sin^2\alpha + \cos^2\alpha}{\sin^2\alpha\cos^2\alpha}}} = \dfrac{k\cos 2\alpha}{\sin 2\alpha} \times \sin\alpha\cos\alpha$

$$\Rightarrow \quad p = \left(\frac{k}{2}\right)\cos 2\alpha \text{ and } q = k\sin 2\alpha$$

$$\Rightarrow \cos 2\alpha = (2p/k) \text{ and } \sin 2\alpha = (q/k)$$

$$\Rightarrow \quad \sin^2 2\alpha + \cos^2 2\alpha = 1$$

$$\Rightarrow \quad \frac{4p^2}{k^2} + \frac{q^2}{k^2} = 1 \Rightarrow 4p^2 + q^2 = k^2$$

63. Given, $A(0, 6)$ and $B(2t, 0)$.

Mid-point of $AB = M(t, 3)$

Equation of perpendicular bisector of AB passes through M.

$$\therefore \quad y - 3 = \frac{t}{3}(x - t) \quad \text{...(i)}$$

Intersection of Eq. (i) on Y-axis

$$C\left(0, 3 - \frac{t^2}{3}\right)$$

Let mid-point of MC be (h, k).

$$\text{Then,} \quad (h, k) = \left(\frac{t}{2}, 3 - \frac{t^2}{6}\right) \Rightarrow h = \frac{t}{2}, k = 3 - \frac{t^2}{6}$$

Eliminating t, we get

$$2h^2 = 3(3 - k)$$

Locus of (h, k)

$$2x^2 = 3(3 - y) \Rightarrow 2x^2 + 3y - 9 = 0$$

64. Given, the equation of median through B i.e. $BE : 2x + y - 3 = 0$

Equation of angle bisector of $\angle C$ i.e. $CD : 7x - 4y = 1$

Since, E satisfies the equation of BE.

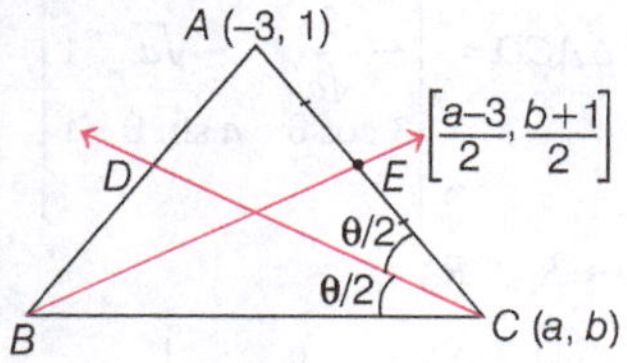

$$\therefore \quad 2\left(\frac{a-3}{2}\right) + \left(\frac{b+1}{2}\right) - 3 = 0$$

$$\Rightarrow \quad 2a - 6 + b + 1 - 6 = 0$$

$$\Rightarrow \quad 2a + b = 11 \quad \text{...(i)}$$

Since, C satisfies CD.

$$\therefore \quad 7a - 4b = 1 \quad \text{...(ii)}$$

On solving Eqs. (i) and (ii), we get

$$a = 3, b = 5$$

$$\text{Slope of } AC = \frac{2}{3},$$

$$\text{Slope of } CD = \frac{7}{4}$$

$$\therefore \quad \tan\left(\frac{\theta}{2}\right) = \left|\frac{\frac{2}{3} - \frac{7}{4}}{1 + \frac{14}{12}}\right| = \frac{1}{2}$$

$$\text{Now,} \quad \tan\theta = \frac{2\tan\left(\frac{\theta}{2}\right)}{1 - \tan^2\left(\frac{\theta}{2}\right)} = \frac{2\left(\frac{1}{2}\right)}{1 - \frac{1}{4}} = \frac{4}{3}$$

65. Given, two sides of parallelogram are

$$4x + 5y = 0 \text{ and } 7x + 2y = 0$$

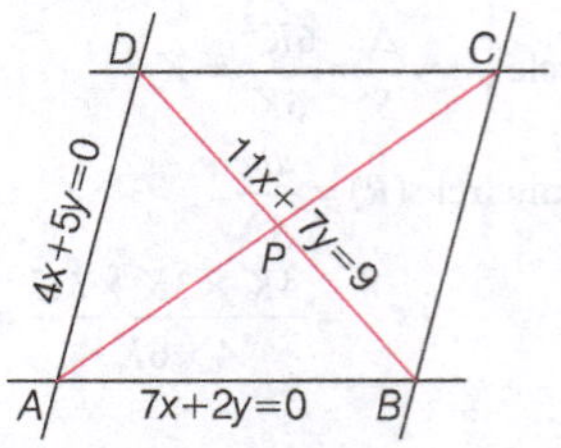

Both lines are passing through origin.

Thus, point $A = (0,0)$

The equation of one diagonal is $11x + 7y = 9$

Point D is the point of intersection of $4x + 5y = 0$

and $\quad 11x + 7y = 9$

So, coordinates of point $D = \left(\frac{5}{3}, -\frac{4}{3}\right)$

Also, point B is the point of intersection of $7x + 2y = 0$ and $11x + 7y = 9$

So, coordinates of point $B = \left(-\frac{2}{3}, \frac{7}{3}\right)$

We know that, diagonals of parallelogram bisects each other.

Let P is the middle point of BD.

$$\text{So, coordinates of } P = \left(\frac{\frac{5}{3} + \left(-\frac{2}{3}\right)}{2}, \frac{-\frac{4}{3} + \frac{7}{3}}{2}\right) = \left(\frac{1}{2}, \frac{1}{2}\right)$$

Now, equation of diagonal AC

$$y - 0 = \frac{\frac{1}{2} - 0}{\frac{1}{2} - 0}(x - 0) \Rightarrow y = \frac{\frac{1}{2}}{\frac{1}{2}}x$$

$$\Rightarrow \quad y = x$$

$\therefore$ Diagonal AC passes through $(2, 2)$.

66. Let $m =$ Slope of required line

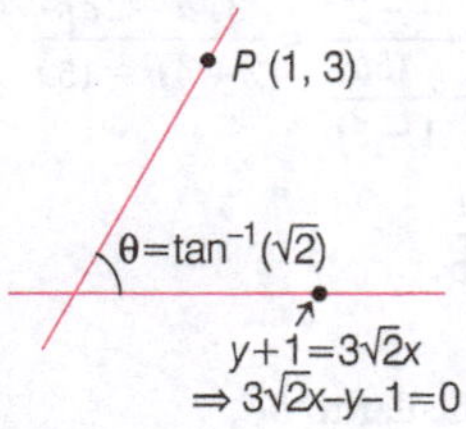

$\therefore$ Equation of required line

$$y - 3 = m(x - 1) \quad \text{...(i)}$$

Given, equation of line is

$$3\sqrt{2}x - y - 1 = 0 \quad \text{...(ii)}$$

Since, angle θ between Eqs. (i) and (ii) is $\tan^{-1}(\sqrt{2})$

i.e. $\quad \tan\theta = \sqrt{2}$

$$\Rightarrow \quad \left|\frac{m - 3\sqrt{2}}{1 + 3\sqrt{2}m}\right| = \sqrt{2} \quad (m = 3\sqrt{2})$$

[$\because$ slope of Eq. (i) $= m$ and slope of Eq. (ii) $= 3\sqrt{2}$]

Squaring on both sides,

$$m^2 - 6\sqrt{2}m + 18 = 2(1 + 18m^2 + 6\sqrt{2}m)$$

$$\Rightarrow \quad 35m^2 + 18\sqrt{2}m - 16 = 0$$

$$\therefore \quad m = \frac{-18\sqrt{2} \pm \sqrt{648 + 2240}}{70}$$

$$= \frac{-18\sqrt{2} \pm 38\sqrt{2}}{70}$$

$$\Rightarrow \quad m = \frac{2\sqrt{2}}{7}, -\frac{4}{5}\sqrt{2}$$

For $m = \frac{2\sqrt{2}}{7}$ and point (1, 3) equation of required line will be

$$y - 3 = \frac{2\sqrt{2}}{7}(x - 1)$$

$$\Rightarrow 2\sqrt{2}x - 7y + 21 - 2\sqrt{2} = 0$$

(options are not matching so, neglect this)

For $m = \frac{-4\sqrt{2}}{5}$, equation of required line will be

$$y - 3 = \frac{-4\sqrt{2}}{5}(x - 1)$$

$$\Rightarrow \quad 5y - 15 = -4\sqrt{2}x + 4\sqrt{2}$$

$$\Rightarrow \quad 4\sqrt{2}x + 5y - 15 - 4\sqrt{2} = 0$$

$$\Rightarrow \quad 4\sqrt{2}x + 5y - (15 + 4\sqrt{2}) = 0$$

Alternate Solution

Let equation of required line is $y = mx + c$ ...(i)

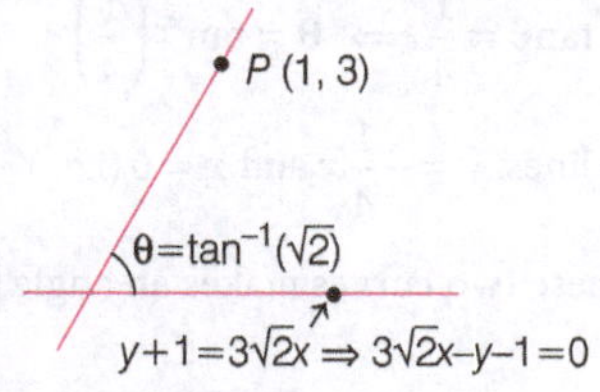

$\because$ Eq (i) passes through (1, 3).

$$\therefore \quad 3 = m + c$$

$$\Rightarrow \quad c = 3 - m \qquad \text{...(ii)}$$

Let θ = angle between Eq. (i) and the given line

$$y + 1 = 3\sqrt{2}x = \tan^{-1}(\sqrt{2})$$

$$\therefore \quad \tan\theta = \sqrt{2}$$

$$\Rightarrow \quad \left|\frac{m - 3\sqrt{2}}{1 + 3\sqrt{2}m}\right| = \sqrt{2}$$

$$\Rightarrow \quad \frac{m - 3\sqrt{2}}{1 + 3\sqrt{2}m} = \pm\sqrt{2}$$ [using $|x| = a, a > 0; \therefore x = \pm a$]

$$\Rightarrow \quad \frac{m - 3\sqrt{2}}{1 + 3\sqrt{2}m} = \sqrt{2} \text{ or } \frac{m - 3\sqrt{2}}{1 + 3\sqrt{2}m} = \sqrt{2}$$

$$\Rightarrow \quad \sqrt{2} + 6m = m - 3\sqrt{2}$$

or

$$-\sqrt{2} - 6m = m - 3\sqrt{2}$$

$$\Rightarrow \quad 5m = -4\sqrt{2} \text{ or } -7m = -2\sqrt{2}$$

$$\Rightarrow \quad m = \frac{-4\sqrt{2}}{5} \text{ or } m = \frac{2\sqrt{2}}{7}$$

For the value of $m = \frac{2\sqrt{2}}{7}$ equation of required line will not match to the given options.

So, neglect this value of m.

From Eq. (ii),

$$c = 3 - m$$

$$= 3 + \frac{4\sqrt{2}}{5} \qquad \left[\because m = \frac{-4\sqrt{2}}{5}\right]$$

$$= \frac{15 + 4\sqrt{2}}{5}$$

From Eq. (i), $y = \frac{-4\sqrt{2}}{5}x + \frac{15 + 4\sqrt{2}}{5}$

$$\Rightarrow \quad 4\sqrt{2}x + 5y - (15 + 4\sqrt{2}) = 0$$

67. Let O be the centre of the circumcircle.

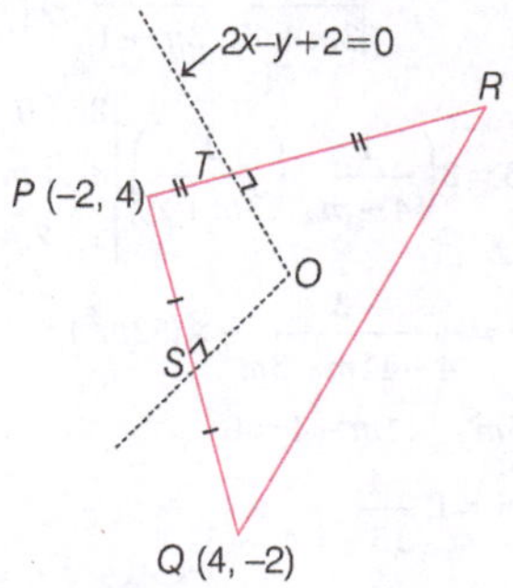

And T be the mid-point of PR.

So, equation of OT is given as

$$2x - y + 2 = 0$$

Let S be the mid-point of PQ.

Now, S will be $\left(\frac{-2 + 4}{2}, \frac{4 - 2}{2}\right) = (1, 1)$

Slope of the line $PQ = \frac{-2 - 4}{4 + 2} = -1$

Equation of OS : $y - 1 = 1(x - 1) \Rightarrow y = x$

Now, coordinates of O will be the intersection of lines OS and OT.

$$\begin{cases} y = x \\ 2x - y + 2 = 0 \end{cases}$$

$$\Rightarrow \quad 2x - x + 2 = 0 \Rightarrow x = -2$$

$$\Rightarrow \quad y = -2 \Rightarrow O = (-2, -2)$$

68. Given, points $A(-1, 1)$, $B(3, 4)$, $C(2, 0)$.

Equation of AC is $\frac{y - 1}{x + 1} = \frac{0 - 1}{2 + 1}$

$$\Rightarrow \quad 3y - 3 = -x - 1$$

$$\Rightarrow \quad x + 3y = 2 \qquad \text{...(i)}$$

On solving Eq. (i) and $y = mx$, we get $P\left(\frac{2}{3m+1}, \frac{2m}{3m+1}\right)$

Equation of BC, $\frac{y - 0}{x - 2} = \frac{4 - 0}{3 - 2}$

$$\Rightarrow \quad y = 4x - 8 \qquad \text{...(ii)}$$

Similarly, on solving Eq. (ii) and $y = mx$, we get

$$Q\left(\frac{8}{4 - m}, \frac{8m}{4 - m}\right)$$

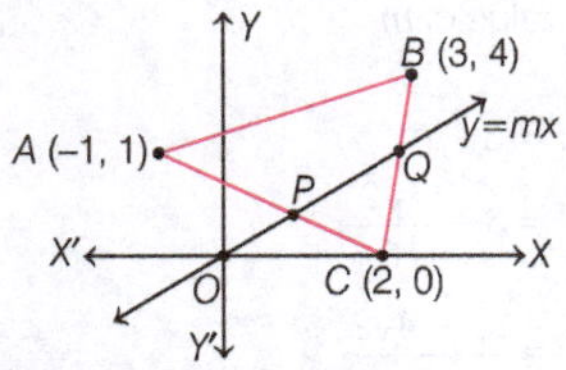

Area of $\Delta ABC = 3$ Area of ΔPQC (given)

$$\frac{1}{2}\begin{vmatrix} -1 & 1 & 1 \\ 2 & 0 & 1 \\ 3 & 4 & 1 \end{vmatrix} = 3 \times \frac{1}{2}\begin{vmatrix} 2 & 0 & 1 \\ \frac{8}{4-m} & \frac{8m}{4-m} & 1 \\ \frac{2}{3m+1} & \frac{2m}{3m+1} & 1 \end{vmatrix}$$

$$\Rightarrow \quad 13 = 3\left(\frac{1}{4-m}\right)\left(\frac{1}{3m+1}\right)\begin{vmatrix} 2 & 0 & 1 \\ 8 & 8m & 4-m \\ 2 & 2m & 3m+1 \end{vmatrix}$$

$$\Rightarrow \quad 13 = \frac{3}{4+11m-3m^2} \times (52m^2)$$

$$\Rightarrow \quad 15m^2 - 11m - 4 = 0$$

$$\Rightarrow \quad m = 1, \frac{-4}{15} \qquad [\text{but } m > 0]$$

$$\Rightarrow \quad m = 1$$

69. Given lines, $x - y = 0$, $x + 2y = 3$, $2x + y = 6$

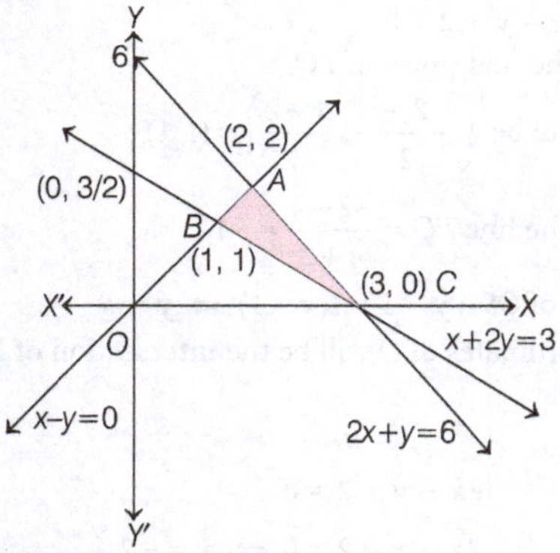

The only triangle which include all three lines is ΔABC.

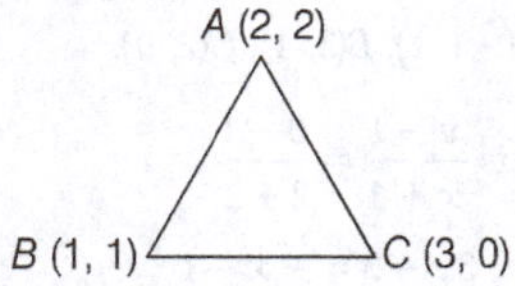

Now, $AB = \sqrt{(2-1)^2 + (2-1)^2} = \sqrt{2}$

$AC = \sqrt{(2-3)^2 + (2-0)^2} = \sqrt{5}$

$BC = \sqrt{(3-1)^2 + (0-1)^2} = \sqrt{5}$

$\Rightarrow$ $AC = BC$ (two sides are equal)

$\Rightarrow \Delta ABC$ is isosceles triangle.

70. Curve $x^2 + 2y^2 = 2$ intersect the line $x + y = 1$ at points P and Q. First we have to find any common relation between these two curves. Use substitution for the same as follows,

$$x^2 + 2y^2 = 2 \qquad \text{...(i)}$$

and $\quad x + y = 1$

then $\quad (x+y)^2 = 1^2$

$$\Rightarrow \quad x^2 + y^2 + 2xy = 1 \qquad \text{...(ii)}$$

We can write Eq. (i) as,

$$x^2 + 2y^2 - 2(1)^2 = 0$$

$$\Rightarrow \quad x^2 + 2y^2 - 2(x+y)^2 = 0 \qquad [\text{using Eq. (ii) in Eq. (i)}]$$

$$\Rightarrow \quad x^2 + 2y^2 - 2x^2 - 2y^2 - 4xy = 0$$

$$\Rightarrow \quad -x^2 - 4xy = 0 \Rightarrow -x(x + 4y) = 0$$

Given, $x = 0$ and $x + 4y = 0$ or $y = \dfrac{-1}{4}x$

Draw the line $y = \dfrac{-1}{4}x$ on graph and take arbitrary point (any one) as follows,

From given graph,

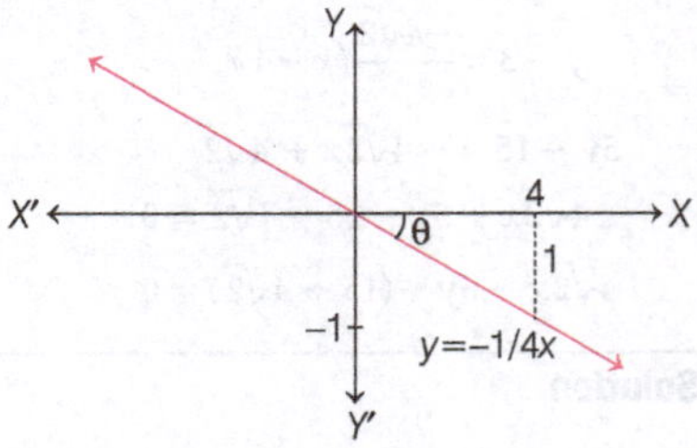

$$\tan\theta = \frac{1}{4} \Rightarrow \theta = \tan^{-1}\left(\frac{1}{4}\right)$$

We have two lines, $y = -\dfrac{1}{4}x$ and $x = 0$ (i.e. Y - axis). Thus, any line joining these two curves makes an angle $\left(\dfrac{\pi}{2} + \theta\right)$ at origin.

$\therefore$ Required answer is $\dfrac{\pi}{2} + \tan^{-1}\left(\dfrac{1}{4}\right)$.

71. Image of $P(3, 5)$ on the line $x - y + 1 = 0$ is

$$\frac{x-3}{1} = \frac{y-5}{-1} = \frac{-2(3-5+1)}{2}$$

$$\Rightarrow \quad \frac{x-3}{1} = \frac{y-5}{-1} = 1$$

$$\Rightarrow \quad \frac{x-3}{1} = 1 \text{ and } \frac{y-5}{-1} = 1$$

$$x = 4, y = 4$$

$\therefore$ Required image is at (4, 4).

Clearly, this point lies on $(x-2)^2 + (y-4)^2 = 4$ as (4, 4) satisfies this equation.

72. Given, position of $A = (1, 1)$

Position of $B = (2, 2)$

Position of $C = (4, 4)$

Let x-intercept be a and y-intercept be b.

Equation of line traced is $\dfrac{x}{a} + \dfrac{y}{b} = 1$

This is the equation of path, let a point (h, k) lie on this path, then

$$\frac{h}{a} + \frac{k}{b} = 1 \qquad \text{...(i)}$$

Also, arithmetic mean of reciprocal of a and $b = \frac{1}{4}$

$$\therefore \quad \frac{\frac{1}{a} + \frac{1}{b}}{2} = \frac{1}{4} \Rightarrow \frac{1}{a} + \frac{1}{b} = \frac{1}{2} \qquad \text{...(ii)}$$

On comparing Eqs. (i) and (ii), we get

$$(h, k) = (2, 2).$$

73. Let P' be the mirror image of P about X-axis.

$\therefore \quad PR = P'R$

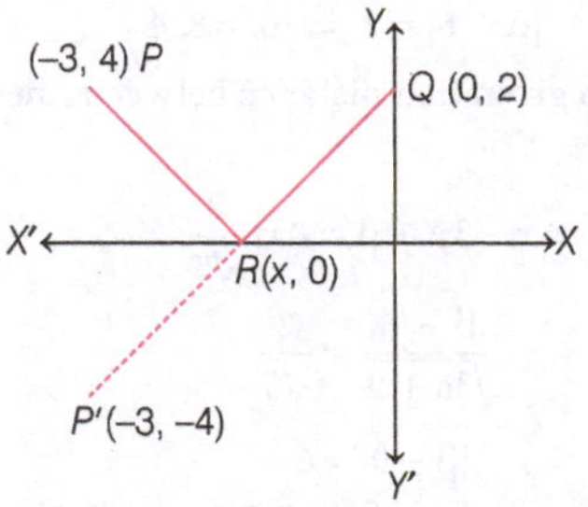

For minimum distance, $PR + RQ = P'R + RQ$

P', R, Q are collinear.

$\Rightarrow$ Slope of $P'R$ = Slope of RQ

$$\Rightarrow \quad \frac{-4-0}{-3-x} = \frac{2-0}{0-x} \Rightarrow 4x = -6 - 2x$$

$$\Rightarrow \quad x = -1 \Rightarrow R = (-1, 0)$$

$$\therefore PR^2 + RQ^2 = P'R^2 + RQ^2 = (-3+1)^2 + (-4)^2 + 1^2 + 2^2 = 25$$

So, $50 \times (PR^2 + RQ^2) = 50 \times 25 = 1250$

74. Let point of intersection of lines are A, B, C.

Solving system of equations, we get point of intersections $(1, 2), (7, 5), (2, 3)$

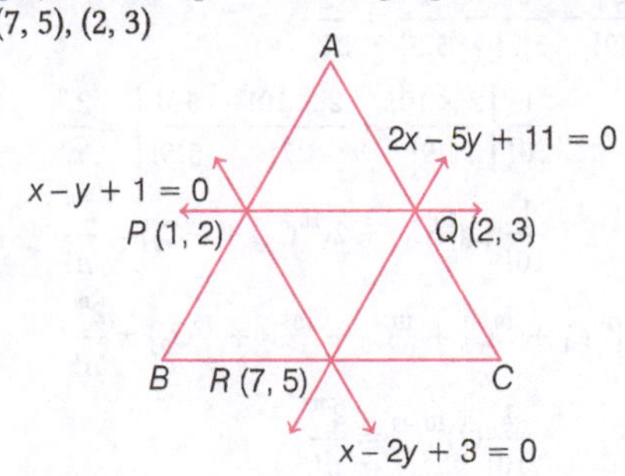

$$\text{Area of } \Delta PQR = \frac{1}{2}\begin{vmatrix} 1 & 2 & 1 \\ 7 & 5 & 1 \\ 2 & 3 & 1 \end{vmatrix} = \frac{1}{2}(3) = \frac{3}{2}$$

$$\text{Area of } \Delta ABC = 4 \times \Delta PQR = 4\left(\frac{3}{2}\right) = 6 \text{ sq units}$$

75. It is given that the line 'L' made x and y intercepts 3 and 1 respectively, so equation of line L is

$$\frac{x}{3} + \frac{y}{1} = 1 \Rightarrow x + 3y = 3 \qquad \text{...(i)}$$

Now, image of point $(-1, -4)$ with respect to line (i) is (x_1, y_1), then

$$\frac{x_1 + 1}{1} = \frac{y_1 + 4}{3} = -2\left(\frac{-1-12-3}{1+9}\right) = \frac{16}{5}$$

Since, image (h, k) or (x_1, y_1) w.r.t. the line mirror $ax + by + c = 0$ is given by

$$\left[\frac{h - x_1}{a} = \frac{k - y_1}{b} = \frac{-2(ax_1 + by_1 + c)}{a^2 + b^2}\right]$$

$$\Rightarrow \quad x_1 = \frac{16}{5} - 1 = \frac{11}{5} \text{ and } y_1 = \left(\frac{16}{5} \times 3\right) - 4 = \frac{28}{5}$$

$$\therefore \quad (x_1, y_1) = \left(\frac{11}{5}, \frac{28}{5}\right)$$

76. The mid-point of line joining points $P(1, 4)$ and $Q(k, 3)$ is $M\left(\frac{1+k}{2}, \frac{4+3}{2}\right)$ and slope of line perpendicular to line PQ is $-\frac{1-k}{4-3} = k - 1$.

$\therefore$ Equation of perpendicular bisector of the line segment joining the points P and Q is

$$y - \frac{7}{2} = (k-1)\left(x - \frac{1+k}{2}\right) \qquad \text{...(i)}$$

and line (i) passes through $(0, -4)$, so

$$-4 - \frac{7}{2} = (k-1)\left(-\frac{1+k}{2}\right)$$

$$\Rightarrow \quad 15 = k^2 - 1 \Rightarrow k = \pm 4$$

77. According to given information,

Let $AC = l$ and $AB = \sqrt{(3-1)^2 + (1-2)^2} = \sqrt{5}$

$\therefore$ The area of right angled ΔABC

$$= \frac{1}{2}(AC)(AB) = 5\sqrt{5} \qquad \text{[given]}$$

$$\Rightarrow \quad \frac{1}{2}l(\sqrt{5}) = 5\sqrt{5} \Rightarrow l = 10 \text{ units}$$

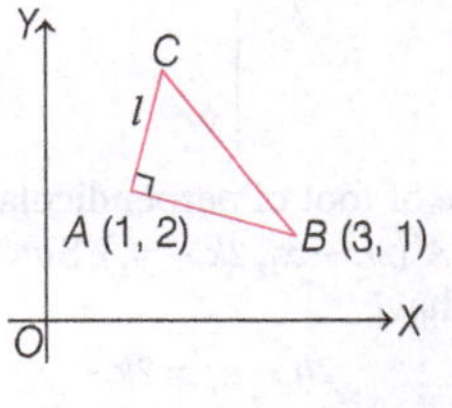

Now according to concept of rotation abscissa of the vertex C we will get easily if we write the coordinate of the vertices in complex form, like $A(1 + 2i)$, $B(3 + i)$ and let $C(x_1 + iy_1)$.

$$\text{Then, } \frac{x_1 + iy_1 - 1 - 2i}{3 + i - 1 - 2i} = \frac{AC}{AB} e^{i\frac{\pi}{2}}$$

$$\Rightarrow \quad \frac{(x_1 - 1) + i(y_1 - 2)}{2 - i} = \frac{10}{\sqrt{5}} i$$

$$\Rightarrow \quad (x_1 - 1) + i(y_1 - 2) = 2\sqrt{5}i(2 - i)$$

$$\Rightarrow \quad (x_1 - 1) + i(y_1 - 2) = 2\sqrt{5} + 4\sqrt{5}i$$

$$\therefore \quad x_1 = 1 + 2\sqrt{5} \text{ is abscissa of the vertex } C.$$

78. The vertices of given ΔABC are $A(-1, 7)$, $B(-7, 1)$ and $C(5, -5)$.

Since, slope of line BC is $m_1 = \frac{-5-1}{5+7} = \frac{-6}{12} = -\frac{1}{2}$

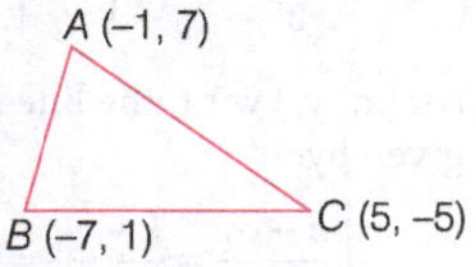

So, slope of altitude through vertex A is

$$m_1' = -\frac{1}{m} = 2$$

$\therefore$ Equation of altitude through vertex A is $y - 7 = 2(x + 1)$

$$\Rightarrow \quad 2x - y + 9 = 0 \quad \text{...(i)}$$

Similarly, the slope of line CA is

$$m_2 = \frac{7-(-5)}{-1-5} = \frac{12}{-6} = -2$$

So, slope of altitude through vertex B is $m_2' = \frac{1}{2}$

$\therefore$ Equation of altitude through vertex B is

$$y - 1 = \frac{1}{2}(x + 7)$$

$$\Rightarrow \quad x - 2y + 9 = 0 \quad \text{...(ii)}$$

As, the point of intersection of altitudes (i) and (ii) is the orthocentre. Then, the orthocentre is $(-3, 3)$.

79. Let a point $A(x_1, y_1)$ on the line $x = 2y$ and the middle point of the perpendicular drawn from point $A(x_1, y_1)$ to the line $x = y$ is $P(h, k)$.

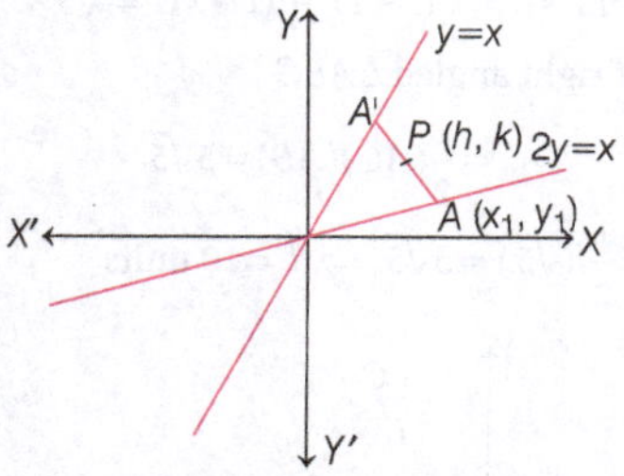

So, the coordinate of foot of perpendicular to line $y = x$ from point $A(x_1, y_1)$ is $A'(2h - x_1, 2k - y_1)$. Since, the point A' lies on line $y = x$, so we have

$$2h - x_1 = 2k - y_1 \quad \text{...(i)}$$

and as point A lies on line $2y = x$, so we have

$$x_1 = 2y_1 \quad \text{...(ii)}$$

and as PA is perpendicular to line $y = x$, so

$$\frac{y_1 - k}{x_1 - h} = -1$$

$$\Rightarrow \quad y_1 - k = -x_1 + h \quad \text{...(iii)}$$

From Eqs. (i) and (ii), we get

$$2h = 2k + y_1 \quad \text{...(iv)}$$

From Eqs. (ii) and (iii), we get

$$h = -k + 3y_1 \quad \text{...(v)}$$

On the elimination of y_1, from Eqs. (iv) and (v), we get

$$h + k = 3(2h - 2k)$$

$$\Rightarrow \quad 5h = 7k$$

On taking the locus of point $P(h, k)$, we get

$$5x - 7y = 0$$

80. It is given that distance between lines $2x - y + 3 = 0$ and $4x - 2y + \alpha = 0$ is $\frac{1}{\sqrt{5}}$

$$\therefore \quad \frac{|6-\alpha|}{\sqrt{16+4}} = \frac{1}{\sqrt{5}}$$

$$\Rightarrow \quad |\alpha - 6| = 2 \Rightarrow \alpha = 8, 4$$

And it is also given that distance between lines $2x - y + 3 = 0$ and

$$6x - 3y + \beta = 0 \text{ is } \frac{2}{\sqrt{5}}.$$

$$\therefore \quad \frac{|\beta - 9|}{\sqrt{36+9}} = \frac{2}{\sqrt{5}}$$

$$\Rightarrow \quad |\beta - 9| = 6$$

$$\Rightarrow \quad \beta = 15, 3$$

So, sum of all possible values of α and $\beta = 4 + 8 + 3 + 15 = 30$.

Exercise 2 - JEE Advanced Pattern

1. Equation of line passing through (2, 0) and perpendicular to $ax + by + c = 0$

Then, required equation is

$$y - 0 = \frac{b}{a}(x - 2)$$

$$ay = bx - 2b$$

$$\therefore \quad ay - bx + 2b = 0$$

2. Given, $\frac{2}{1!9!} + \frac{2}{3!7!} + \frac{1}{5!5!} = \frac{2^m}{n!}$

$$\Rightarrow \quad \frac{1}{10!}\left\{\frac{2 \times 10!}{1!9!} + \frac{2 \times 10!}{3!7!} + \frac{10!}{5!5!}\right\} = \frac{2^m}{n!}$$

$$\Rightarrow \quad \frac{1}{10!}\{2({}^{10}C_1) + 2({}^{10}C_3) + {}^{10}C_5\} = \frac{2^m}{n!}$$

$$\Rightarrow \quad \frac{1}{10!}\{{}^{10}C_1 + {}^{10}C_3 + {}^{10}C_5 + {}^{10}C_7 + {}^{10}C_9\} = \frac{2^m}{n!}$$

$$\Rightarrow \quad \frac{1}{10!}(2)^{10-1} = \frac{2^m}{n!}$$

$$\therefore \quad m = 9 \text{ and } n = 10$$

Hence, $x - y + 1 = 0$ and $x + y + 3 = 0$ are perpendicular to each other, then orthocentre is the point of intersection which is $(-2, -1)$,

$$\therefore \quad -2 = 2m - 2n \text{ and } -1 = m - n$$

$\therefore$ Point is $(2m - 2n, m - n)$.

3. $\therefore$ Required area $= 4 \times \frac{1}{2}\left(\frac{8}{3} \times 4\right) = \frac{64}{3} = \frac{2^6}{3}$ ...(i)

$\because \quad f(x+y) = f(x)f(y) \Rightarrow f(2) = [f(1)]^2 = 2^2$

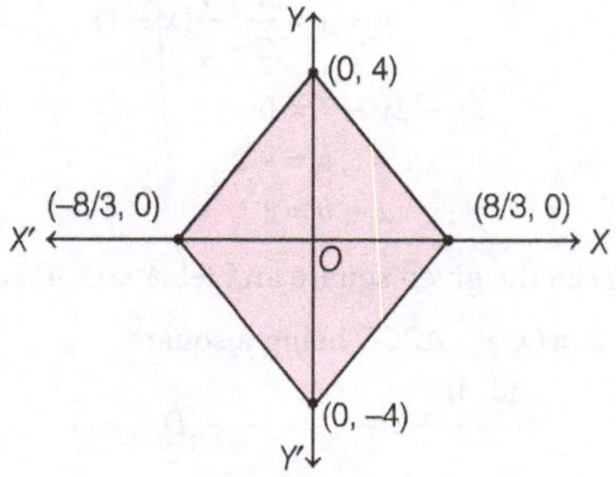

and $\quad f(3) = f(1+2) = f(1)f(2) = 2^3$

....

....

$\therefore \quad f(n) = 2^n$

$\therefore \quad \text{Area} = \frac{2^6}{3} = \frac{f(6)}{3}$ sq units

4. Let line $\frac{x}{a} + \frac{y}{b} = 1$ ...(i)

It passes through (2, 2), then

$\frac{2}{a} + \frac{2}{b} = 1 \Rightarrow 2(a+b) = ab$ ...(ii)

$\because$ Area of $\Delta AOB = \frac{1}{2}ab = |\lambda|$ [given]

$\therefore \quad ab = 2|\lambda|$

from Eq. (ii), $\quad a + b = |\lambda|$

Hence, required equation is

$x^2 - (a+b)x + ab = 0$

or $\quad x^2 - |\lambda|x + 2|\lambda| = 0$

5. $P_1 = |m^2\cos\alpha + 2m\sin\alpha + \frac{\sin^2\alpha}{\cos\alpha}|$

$= \frac{(m\cos\alpha + \sin\alpha)^2}{|\cos\alpha|}$

and $\quad p_2 = \left|mm'\cos\alpha + (m+m')\sin\alpha + \frac{\sin^2\alpha}{\cos\alpha}\right|$

$= \frac{|(m\cos\alpha + \sin\alpha)|\,|m'\cos\alpha + \sin\alpha|}{|\cos\alpha|}$

and $\quad p_3 = |m'^2\cos\alpha + 2m'\sin\alpha + \frac{\sin^2\alpha}{\cos\alpha}|$

$= \frac{(m'\cos\alpha + \sin\alpha)^2}{|\cos\alpha|}$

$\because \quad p_2^2 = p_1 p_3$

Hence, p_1, p_2 and p_3 are in GP.

6. Let $\frac{AN}{BN} = \lambda$

Then, coordinate of N are $\left(\frac{a}{1+\lambda}, \frac{a\lambda}{1+\lambda}\right)$

$\because \quad$ Slope of $AB = -1$

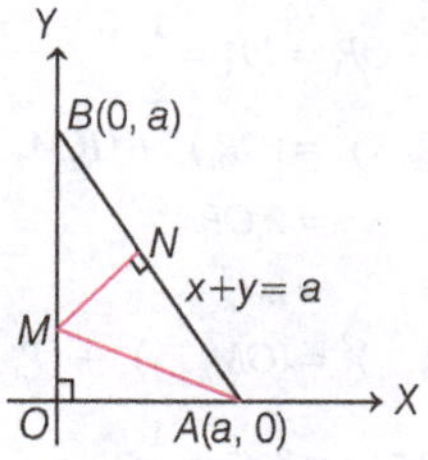

$\therefore \quad$ Slope of $MN = 1$

$\therefore \quad$ Equation on MN is

$y - \frac{a\lambda}{1+\lambda} = x - \frac{a}{1+\lambda} \Rightarrow x - y = a\left(\frac{1-\lambda}{\lambda+1}\right)$

So, the coordinates of M are $\left(0, a\left(\frac{\lambda-1}{\lambda+1}\right)\right)$

Therefore, area of $\Delta AMN = \frac{3}{8}$ area of ΔOAB

$\Rightarrow \quad \frac{1}{2} \cdot AN \cdot MN = \frac{3}{8} \cdot \frac{1}{2} a \cdot a$

$\Rightarrow \quad \frac{1}{2}\left|\frac{a\lambda\sqrt{2}}{1+\lambda} \cdot \frac{a\sqrt{2}}{1+\lambda}\right| = \frac{3}{8} \cdot \frac{1}{2} a \cdot a \Rightarrow \frac{a^2\lambda}{(1+\lambda)^2} = \frac{3}{8} \cdot \frac{1}{2} a^2$

$\therefore \quad \lambda = 3 \text{ or } \lambda = \frac{1}{3}$

For $\lambda = \frac{1}{3}$, then M lies outside the segment OB and hence the required value of $\lambda = 3$.

7. $\because$ Equation of AB is $x + y = 1$, then coordinates of A and B are (1, 0) and (0, 1), respectively.

$\therefore \quad$ Coordinates of P are $\left(\frac{1}{2}, \frac{1}{2}\right)$

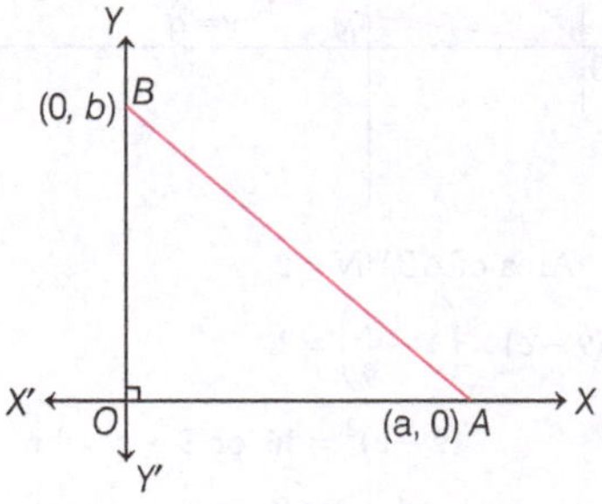

$\because \quad PP_1$ is perpendicular to OA,

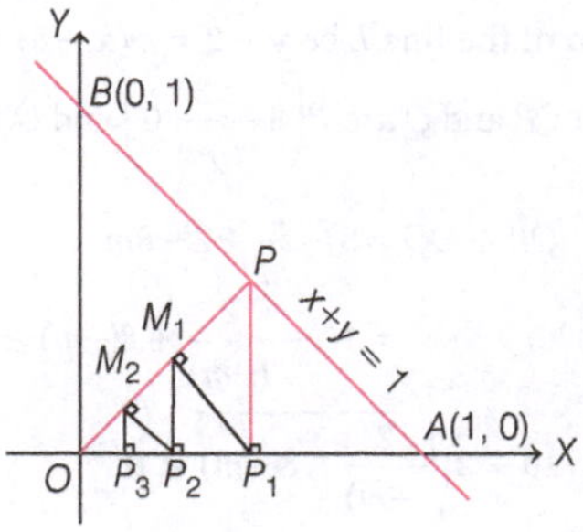

Equation of OP is $y = x$

Then, $OP_1 = PP_1 = \frac{1}{2}$

We have, $(OM_{n-1})^2 = (OP_n)^2 + (P_nM_{n-1})^2$

$= 2(OP_n)^2$ $[\because y = x]$

$= 2\alpha_n^2$ (say)

Also, $(OP_{n-1})^2 = (OM_{n-1})^2 + (P_{n-1}M_{n-1})^2$

$\Rightarrow \quad \alpha_{n-1}^2 = 2\alpha_n^2 + \frac{1}{2}\alpha_{n-1}^2$

$\Rightarrow \quad \frac{1}{2}\alpha_{n-1}^2 = 2\alpha_n^2 \Rightarrow \alpha_n = \frac{1}{2}\alpha_{n-1}$

$\therefore \quad OP_n = \alpha_n = \frac{1}{2}\alpha_{n-1}$

$= \frac{1}{2^2}\alpha_{n-2} = \frac{1}{2^3}\alpha_{n-3}$

....

....

....

$= \frac{1}{2^{n-1}}\alpha_1 = \frac{1}{2^{n-1}}\left(\frac{1}{2}\right) = \frac{1}{2^n}.$

8. Let $O \equiv (0, 0)$, $A \equiv (1, 1)$ and $B \equiv (9, 1)$

Area of $\Delta OAB = \frac{1}{2} \times 8 \times 1 = 4$

It is clear that $1 < c < 9$

and $M \equiv (c, 1)$ and $N \equiv \left(c, \frac{c}{9}\right)$

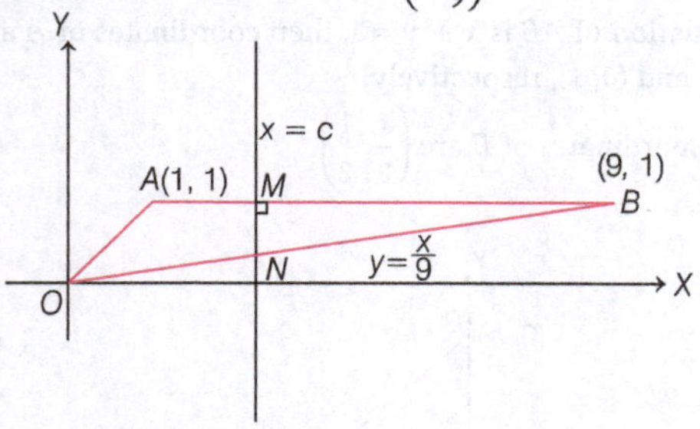

$\therefore$ Area of $\Delta BMN = 2$ [given]

$\Rightarrow \frac{1}{2} \times (9 - c) \times \left(1 - \frac{c}{9}\right) = 2$

or $(9 - c)^2 = 36$ or $9 - c = \pm 6 \Rightarrow c = 3$ or 15

but $1 < c < 9$

$\therefore \quad c = 3$

9. The equation of the line L be $y - 2 = m(x - 8)$, $m < 0$ coordinates of P and Q are $P\left(8 - \frac{2}{m}, 0\right)$ and $Q(0, 2 - 8m)$.

So, $OP + OQ = 8 - \frac{2}{m} + 2 - 8m$

$= 10 + \frac{2}{(-m)} + 8(-m) \geq$

$10 + 2\sqrt{\frac{2}{(-m)} \times 8(-m)} \geq 18$

So, absolute minimum value of $OP + OQ = 18$

10. Lines $5x + 3y - 2 + \lambda(3x - y - 4) = 0$ are concurrent at $(1, -1)$ and lines $x - y + 1 + \mu(2x - y - 2) = 0$ are concurrent at $(3, 4)$. Thus, equation of line common to both family is

$$y + 1 = \frac{4 + 1}{3 - 1}(x - 1)$$

or $5x - 2y - 7 = 0$

$\Rightarrow \quad a = 5, b = -2$

$\therefore \quad a + b = 3$

11. Let $ABCD$ be the given square and let $A \equiv (3, 4)$ and $C \equiv (1, -1)$. Also, let $B \equiv (x, y)$, $ABCD$ being a square.

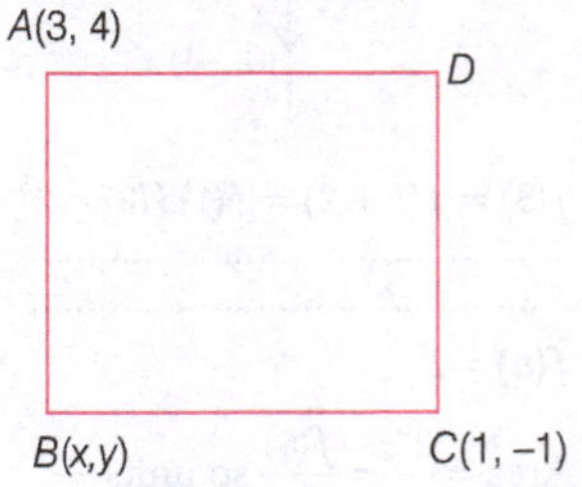

$AB = BC \Rightarrow AB^2 = BC^2, \angle ABC = 90°$

$(\sqrt{(x-3)^2 + (y-4)^2})^2 = (\sqrt{(x-1)^2 + (y+1)^2})^2$

$\Rightarrow \quad x^2 - 6x + 9 + y^2 - 8y + 16$

$= x^2 - 2x + 1 + y^2 + 2y + 1$

$\Rightarrow \quad 4x + 10y + 23 = 0$

$\Rightarrow \quad x = \frac{23 - 10y}{4}$ ...(i)

Also, in ΔABC, $\angle B = 90°$

$\Rightarrow \quad AB^2 + BC^2 = AC^2$

$\Rightarrow (x-3)^2 + (y-4)^2 + (x-1)^2 + (y+1)^2 = (3-1)^2 + (4+1)^2$

$\Rightarrow x^2 - 6x + 9 + y^2 - 8y + 16 + x^2 - 2x + 1 + y^2 + 2y + 1$

$= 4 + 25$

$\Rightarrow \quad 2x^2 + 2y^2 - 8x - 6y + 27 = 29$

$\Rightarrow \quad 2x^2 + 2y^2 - 8x - 6y - 2 = 0$

$\Rightarrow \quad x^2 + y^2 - 4x - 3y - 1 = 0$ ...(ii)

Now, substitute the value of x from Eq. (i), we get

$$\left(\frac{23 - 10y}{4}\right)^2 + y^2 - (23 - 10y) - 3y - 1 = 0$$

$\Rightarrow \quad (23 - 10y)^2 + 16y^2 - 16(23 - 10y) - 48y - 16 = 0$

$\Rightarrow \quad 529 - 460y + 100y^2 + 16y^2 - 368 + 160y - 48y - 16 = 0$

$\Rightarrow \quad 116y^2 - 348y + 145 = 0$

$\Rightarrow \quad 4y^2 - 12y + 5 = 0$

$\Rightarrow \quad (2y - 1)(2y - 5) = 0$

$\Rightarrow \quad y = \frac{1}{2}$ or $\frac{5}{2}$

On putting $y = \frac{1}{2}$ and $\frac{5}{2}$ respectively in Eq. (i), we get $x = \frac{9}{2}$ and $x = -\frac{1}{2}$

$\therefore$ The required vertices of the square are $\left(\frac{9}{2}, \frac{1}{2}\right)$ and $\left(-\frac{1}{2}, \frac{5}{2}\right)$.

12. Let the line through $A(-5,-4)$ be $\frac{x+5}{\cos\theta}=\frac{y+4}{\sin\theta}=\gamma$

Therefore, every point on the line is of the form

$$x=-5+\gamma\cos\theta,\ y=-4+\gamma\sin\theta.$$

Let $AB=\gamma_1$, $AC=\gamma_2$ and $AD=\gamma_3$.

Since, $B=(-5+\gamma_1\cos\theta, -4+\gamma_1\sin\theta)$

we have, $(-5+\gamma_1\cos\theta)+3(-4+\gamma_1\sin\theta)+2=0$

[$\because$ B lies on $x+3y+2=0$]

Therefore,

$$\gamma_1=\frac{15}{\cos\theta+3\sin\theta}$$

Hence, $\frac{15}{AB}=\cos\theta+3\sin\theta$ [$\because \gamma_1=AB$] ...(i)

Similarly, points C and D lie on $2x+y+4=0$ and $x-y-5=0$, respectively. We have,

$$\frac{10}{AC}=2\cos\theta+\sin\theta \quad \text{...(ii)}$$

and $\frac{6}{AD}=\cos\theta-\sin\theta$ ...(iii)

Now, by hypothesis,

$$\left(\frac{15}{AB}\right)^2+\left(\frac{10}{AC}\right)^2=\left(\frac{6}{AD}\right)^2$$

Hence, from Eqs. (i), (ii) and (iii), we get

$$(\cos\theta+3\sin\theta)^2+(2\cos\theta+\sin\theta)^2=(\cos\theta-\sin\theta)^2$$

$$\Rightarrow 5\cos^2\theta+10\sin^2\theta+10\sin\theta\cos\theta$$

$$=\cos^2\theta+\sin^2\theta-2\sin\theta\cos\theta$$

$$\Rightarrow 4\cos^2\theta+9\sin^2\theta+12\sin\theta\cos\theta=0$$

$$\Rightarrow (2\cos\theta+3\sin\theta)^2=0$$

Therefore, $2\cos\theta+3\sin\theta=0$ or $\tan\theta=\frac{-2}{3}$

Hence, the equation of the line is

$$y+4=-\frac{2}{3}(x+5) \text{ or } 2x+3y+22=0$$

13. Slope of AC, $m_1=\frac{-1-3}{1-(-3)}=-1$

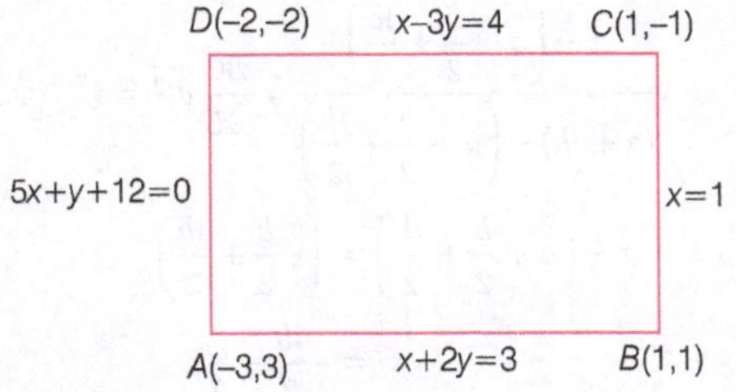

$\therefore$ Slope of BD, $m_2=\frac{-2-1}{-2-1}=1$

$\because$ $m_1\times m_2=-1$

$\therefore$ Angle between diagonal is 90°.

14. Given, a, b and c are in AP.

So, $a+c-2b=0$

$\Rightarrow$ $ax+by+c=0$ passes through fixed point $(1,-2)$.

$\therefore$ $B\equiv(1,-2)$

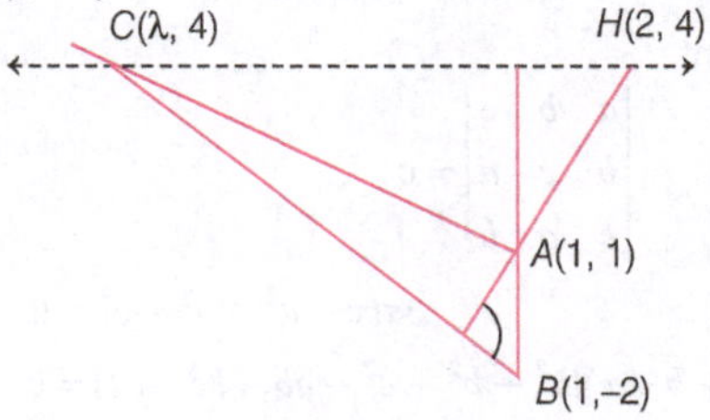

Slope of $BC=\frac{2-1}{4-1}=\frac{4+2}{\lambda-1}$

$$\Rightarrow \lambda-1=-18$$

$$\Rightarrow \lambda=-17$$

$$\Rightarrow c\equiv(-17,4)\equiv(h,k)$$

$$\therefore 2h+12k=-34+48=14$$

15. Now, $(A_0A_1)^2=\left(1-\frac{1}{2}\right)^2+\left(0-\frac{\sqrt{3}}{2}\right)^2$

$$=\left(\frac{1}{2}\right)^2+\left(\frac{\sqrt{3}}{2}\right)^2=\frac{1}{4}+\frac{3}{4}=1$$

$$\Rightarrow A_0A_1=1$$

$$(A_1A_2)^2=\left(1+\frac{1}{2}\right)^2+\left(0-\frac{\sqrt{3}}{2}\right)^2$$

$$=\left(\frac{3}{2}\right)^2+\left(-\frac{\sqrt{3}}{2}\right)^2=\frac{9}{4}+\frac{3}{4}=\frac{12}{4}=3$$

$$\Rightarrow A_0A_2=\sqrt{3}$$

and $(A_0A_4)^2=\left(1+\frac{1}{2}\right)^2+\left(0+\frac{\sqrt{3}}{2}\right)^2$

$$=\left(\frac{3}{2}\right)^2+\left(\frac{3}{4}\right)=\frac{9}{4}+\frac{3}{4}=\frac{12}{4}=3$$

$$\Rightarrow A_0A_4=\sqrt{3}$$

$$\Rightarrow (A_0A_1)(A_0A_2)(A_0A_4)=3$$

16. The two lines will be identical if their exists some real number k such that

$$b^3-c^3=k(b-c),\ c^3-a^3=k(c-a) \text{ and } a^3-b^3=k(a-b)$$

$$\Rightarrow b-c=0 \text{ or } b^2+c^2+bc=k$$

$$c-a=0 \text{ or } c^2+a^2+ca=k$$

and $a-b=0$ or $a^2+b^2+ab=k$

$$\Rightarrow a=b \text{ or } b=c \text{ or } c=a$$

or $b^2+c^2+bc=c^2+a^2+ca$

$$\Rightarrow b=c \text{ or } c=a$$

or $a=b$ or $a+b+c=0$

17. $\begin{vmatrix}1 & -2 & -6\\ 3 & 1 & -4\\ \lambda & 4 & \lambda^2\end{vmatrix}=0$

$$\Rightarrow \lambda^2+2\lambda-8=0$$

$$\therefore (\lambda+4)(\lambda-2)=0 \Rightarrow \lambda=-4,2$$

18. Since, $ax + by + c = 0$, $bx + cy + a = 0$ and $cx + ay + b = 0$ are concurrent.

$$\therefore \quad \begin{vmatrix} a & b & c \\ b & c & a \\ c & a & b \end{vmatrix} = 0$$

$$\Rightarrow \quad 3abc - a^3 - b^3 - c^3 = 0$$

$$\Rightarrow - (a + b + c)(a^2 + b^2 + c^2 - ab - bc - ca) = 0$$

$$a + b + c \neq 0$$

$$\therefore \quad a^2 + b^2 + c^2 - ab - bc - ca = 0$$

$$\frac{1}{2}\{(a - b)^2 + (b - c)^2 + (c - a)^2\} = 0$$

As a, b and c are real numbers

$$\therefore \quad b - c = 0, c - a = 0, a - b = 0$$

$$\Rightarrow \quad a = b = c$$

19. Since, $E \equiv (4, 4)$

$\therefore z_C = 7 + 5i$, $z_E = 4 + 4i$

Now, in ΔBEC,

$$\frac{z_B - z_E}{z_C - z_E} = e^{i\frac{\pi}{2}} = i$$

$$\Rightarrow \quad z_B - 4 - 4i = i(7 + 5i - 4 - 4i)$$

or $\quad z_B = 3 + 7i$

$\therefore \quad B \equiv (3, 7)$, then $D \equiv (5, 1)$

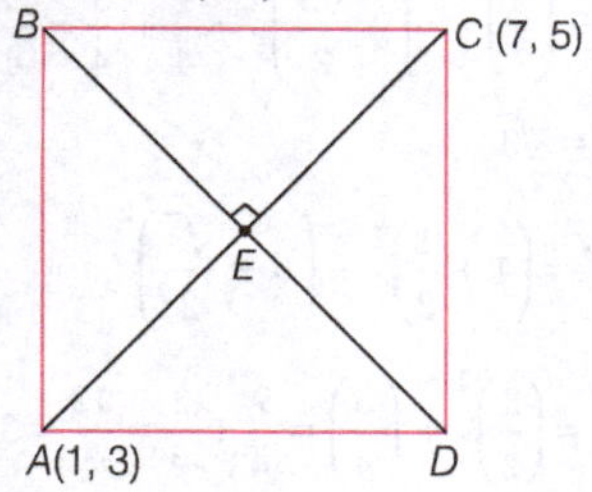

Equation of AB is

$$y - 3 = \frac{7 - 3}{3 - 1}(x - 1) \text{ or } 2x - y + 1 = 0$$

and equation of AD is

$$y - 3 = \frac{1 - 3}{5 - 1}(x - 1) \text{ or } x + 2y - 7 = 0$$

20. Given, $6a^2 - 3b^2 - c^2 + 7ab - ac + 4bc = 0$

$$\Rightarrow \quad 6a^2 + (7b - c)a - (3b^2 - 4bc + c^2) = 0$$

$$\Rightarrow a = \frac{-(7b - c) \pm \sqrt{(7b - c)^2 + 24(3b^2 - 4bc + c^2)}}{12}$$

$$\Rightarrow \quad 12a + 7b - c = \pm(11b - 5c)$$

$$\Rightarrow \quad 12a - 4b + 4c = 0$$

or $\quad 12a + 18b - 6c = 0 \Rightarrow 3a - b + c = 0$

or $\quad -2a - 3b + c = 0$

Hence $(3, -1)$ or $(-2, -3)$ lies on the line $ax + by + c = 0$.

21. Let position of bunglow be $P(x_1, y_1)$. Then, $PM = 100$ and $PN = 100$

$$\therefore \quad \frac{x_1 + y_1 - 8}{\sqrt{2}} = \pm 100$$

and $\quad \dfrac{x_1 - y_1 + 6}{\sqrt{2}} = \pm 100$

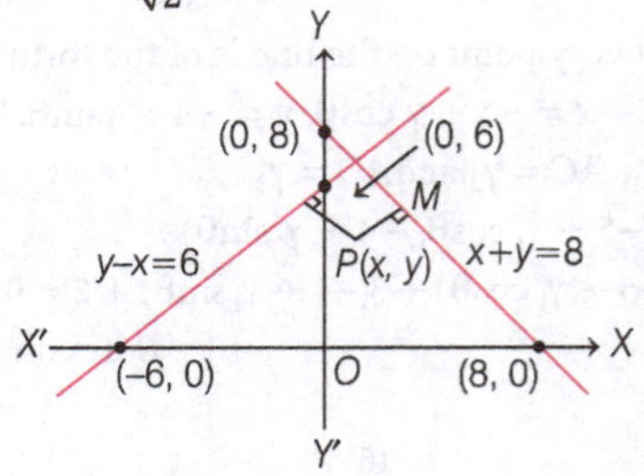

After solving, we get

$$x_1 = 1 \pm 100\sqrt{2}, 1$$

and $\quad y_1 = 7, 7 \pm 100\sqrt{2}$

Hence, $\quad (1 + 100\sqrt{2}, 7), (1 - 100\sqrt{2}, 7),$
$(1, 7 + 100\sqrt{2}), (1, 7 - 100\sqrt{2})$

22. Equation of the other diagonal is $x + y = \lambda$ which pass through (a, b), then $a + b = \lambda$

$\therefore$ Equation of other diagonal is $x + y = a + b$

i.e. centre of the square is the point of intersection of $x - y = a$ and $x + y = a + b$ is $\left(a + \frac{b}{2}, \frac{b}{2}\right)$. Then, vertex

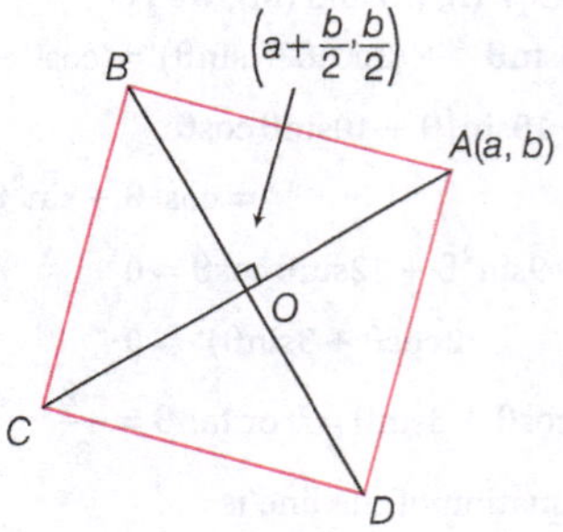

$$C \equiv (2a + b - a, b - b)$$

$$\therefore \quad C \equiv (a + b, 0)$$

If $\quad B \equiv z$,

then
$$\frac{z - \left(a + \frac{b}{2} + \frac{ib}{2}\right)}{(a + ib) - \left(a + \frac{b}{2} + \frac{ib}{2}\right)} = \frac{BO}{AO} e^{i\frac{\pi}{2}} = i \quad [\because BO = AO]$$

$$\Rightarrow \quad z - \left(a + \frac{b}{2} + \frac{ib}{2}\right) = i\left(-\frac{b}{2} + \frac{ib}{2}\right)$$

$$= -\frac{ib}{2} - \frac{b}{2}$$

$$\therefore \quad z = a$$

$$\therefore \quad B \equiv (a, 0)$$

Then, $\quad D \equiv (a + b, b)$

Hence, other vertices are $(a + b, 0)$, $(a, 0)$ and $(a + b, b)$.

23. $(y - y_1) - m(x - x_1) = 0$ is family of lines

$$\therefore \quad y - y_1 = 0, x - x_1 = 0$$

Then, $\quad y = y_1$ and $x = x_1$

24. Given lines $L_1 = 0$ and $L_2 = 0$ are perpendicular and given bisectors are $\lambda_1 L_1 - \lambda_2 L_2 = 0$ and $\lambda_1 L_1 + \lambda_2 L_2 = 0$

$\therefore$ Bisectors are perpendicular to each other.

Hence, bisectors of $\lambda_1 L_1 - \lambda_2 L_2 = 0$ and $\lambda_1 L_1 + \lambda_2 L_2 = 0$ are $L_1 = 0$ and $L_2 = 0$.

25. Given, one bisector makes an angle $\left(\frac{\theta+\phi}{2}\right)$ with X-axis, then other bisector makes an angle $90° + \left(\frac{\theta+\phi}{2}\right)$ with X-axis.

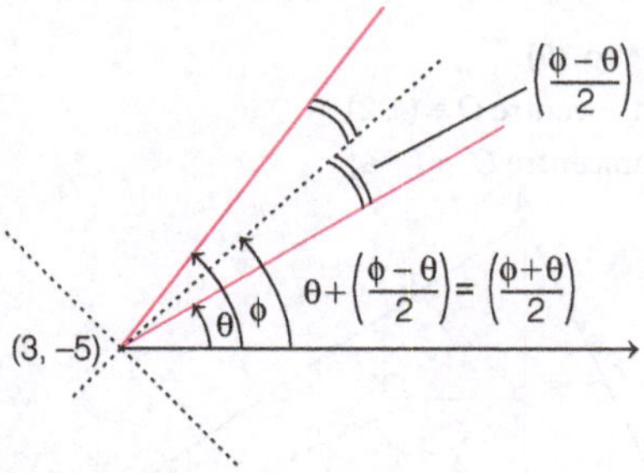

$\therefore$ Equations of bisectors are

$$\frac{x-3}{\cos\left(\frac{\theta+\phi}{2}\right)} = \frac{y+5}{\sin\left(\frac{\theta+\phi}{2}\right)} \quad \text{...(i)}$$

and
$$\frac{x-3}{\cos\left(\frac{\pi}{2}+\frac{\theta+\phi}{2}\right)} = \frac{y+5}{\sin\left(\frac{\pi}{2}+\frac{\theta+\phi}{2}\right)}$$

$$\Rightarrow \quad \frac{x-3}{-\sin\left(\frac{\theta+\phi}{2}\right)} = \frac{y+5}{\cos\left(\frac{\theta+\phi}{2}\right)} \quad \text{...(ii)}$$

But given bisector are $\frac{x-3}{\cos\alpha} = \frac{y+5}{\sin\alpha}$

$$\therefore \quad \alpha = \frac{\theta+\phi}{2} \text{ and } \frac{x-3}{\beta} = \frac{y+5}{\gamma} \quad \text{[from Eq. (i)]...(iii)}$$

$$\therefore \quad \beta = -\sin\left(\frac{\theta+\phi}{2}\right) = -\sin\alpha \quad \text{[from Eq. (ii)]}$$

and
$$\gamma = \cos\left(\frac{\theta+\phi}{2}\right) = \cos\alpha$$

26. Since, $OR = AR$

$\Rightarrow \quad |x-0| + |y-0| = |x-1| + |y-2|$

$\Rightarrow \quad |x| + |y| = |x-1| + |y-2|$

$\because \quad 0 \le x < 1$ and $0 \le y < 2$

$\therefore \quad x + y = -(x-1) - (y-2)$

$\Rightarrow \quad 2x + 2y = 3$

27. $OS = BS$

$\Rightarrow |x-0| + |y-0| = |x-2| + |y-3|$

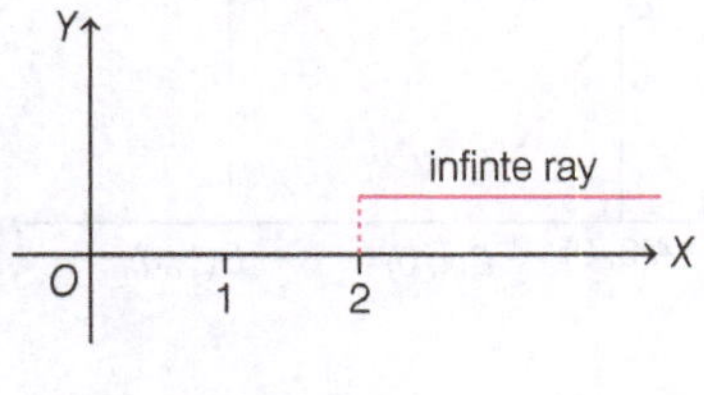

$\Rightarrow \quad |x| + |y| = |x-2| + |y-3|$

$\because \quad x \ge 2$ and $0 \le y < 3$

$\therefore \quad x + y = x - 2 + 3 - y$

$\Rightarrow \quad 2y = 1$

$\therefore \quad y = \frac{1}{2}$

Sol. (Q. Nos. 28 to 29)

$AB : 2x - y + 4 = 0,$

$BC : x - 2y - 1 = 0$

and $\quad CA : x + 3y - 3 = 0$

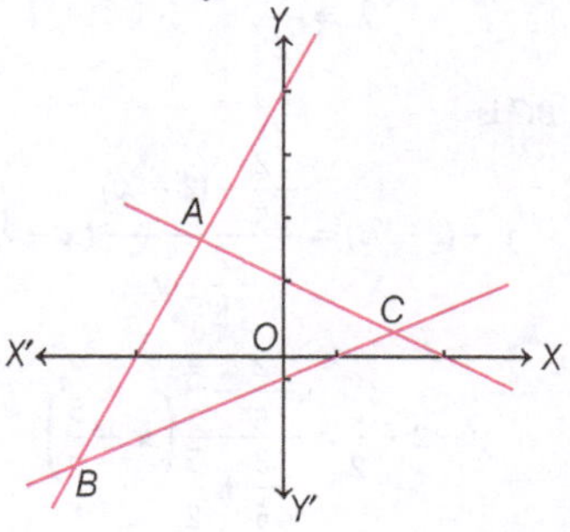

$\therefore \quad m_{AB} = m_1 = 2$

$m_{BC} = m_2 = \frac{1}{2}$

and $\quad m_{CA} = m_3 = -\frac{1}{3}$

$\because \quad m_1 > m_2 > m_3$

28. For external bisector of B

$AB : 2x - y + 4 = 0$

$BC : -x + 2y + 1 = 0$

$\because \quad (2)(-1) + (-1)(2) = -4 < 0$

$\therefore$ External bisector of B is

$$\left(\frac{2x-y+4}{\sqrt{5}}\right) = -\frac{(-x+2y+1)}{\sqrt{5}}$$

or $\quad x + y + 5 = 0$

29. Let (α, β) be the image of $B(-3, -2)$ w.r.t. the line $x + 3y - 3 = 0$, then

$$\frac{\alpha+3}{1} = \frac{\beta+2}{3} = \frac{-2(-3-6-3)}{1+9}$$

or
$$\frac{\alpha+3}{1} = \frac{\beta+2}{3} = \frac{12}{5}$$

or
$$\alpha = -\frac{3}{5} \text{ and } \beta = \frac{26}{5}$$

$\therefore$ Required image is $\left(-\frac{3}{5}, \frac{26}{5}\right)$.

Sol. (Q. Nos. 30 to 31)

Let $\quad B \equiv (\lambda, 2-\lambda) \quad [\because B$ lies on $x + y = 2]$

Slope of line $AB = m_1 = \frac{1+\lambda}{1-\lambda}$

and slope of line $BC = m_2 = \frac{5\lambda - 12}{-5\lambda - 2} = \frac{12-5\lambda}{2+5\lambda}$

Let slope of bisector $(x + y = 2) = m_3 = -1$

Now, $$\frac{m_3 - m_1}{1 + m_3 m_1} = \frac{m_2 - m_3}{1 + m_2 m_3}$$

$$\Rightarrow \quad \frac{-1 - \dfrac{1+\lambda}{1-\lambda}}{1 - \dfrac{1+\lambda}{1-\lambda}} = \frac{\dfrac{12-5\lambda}{2+5\lambda} + 1}{1 - \dfrac{12-5\lambda}{2+5\lambda}}$$

or $$\frac{-2}{-2\lambda} = \frac{14}{-10+10\lambda}$$

or $$14\lambda = -10 + 10\lambda$$

$$\therefore \quad \lambda = \frac{-5}{2}$$

30. Equation of BC is

$$y - (2 - \lambda) = \frac{-\dfrac{2}{5} - (2 - \lambda)}{-\dfrac{2}{5} - \lambda}(x - \lambda)$$

or $$y - 2 - \frac{5}{2} = \frac{-\dfrac{2}{5} - \dfrac{9}{2}}{-\dfrac{2}{5} + \dfrac{5}{2}}\left(x + \frac{5}{2}\right)$$

or $$7x + 3y + 4 = 0$$

31. Coordinates of vertex B are $(\lambda, 2 - \lambda)$

i.e. $$\left(-\frac{5}{2}, \frac{9}{2}\right)$$ [from Eq. (i)]

$A \equiv (1, 3)$ and $B \equiv \left(-\dfrac{5}{2}, \dfrac{9}{2}\right)$

$\therefore$ Equation of AB is

$$y - 3 = \frac{\dfrac{9}{2} - 3}{-\dfrac{5}{2} - 1}(x - 1) \text{ or } 3x + 7y = 24$$

Sol. (Q. Nos. 32 to 33)

32. Any point on the line $3x - y = 2$ is $(t, 3t - 2)$, t being parameter. If (x, y) be image of the point $(t, 3t - 2)$ in the line $y = x - 1$ or $x - y - 1 = 0$, then

$$\frac{x - t}{1} = \frac{y - (3t - 2)}{-1} = -\frac{2(t - 3t + 2 - 1)}{1 + 1}$$

$$\Rightarrow \quad \frac{x - t}{1} = \frac{y - 3t + 2}{-1} = 2t - 1$$

or $x - t = 2t - 1 \Rightarrow x + 1 = 3t$ ...(i)

and $y - 3t + 2 = -2t + 1 \Rightarrow y + 1 = t$ ...(ii)

From Eqs. (i) and (ii), we get

$$x + 1 = 3(y + 1)$$

$$\Rightarrow \quad x - 3y = 2$$

33. Any point on the circle $x^2 + y^2 = 4$ is $(2\cos\theta, 2\sin\theta)$, θ being parameter.

If (x, y) be image of the point $(2\cos\theta, 2\sin\theta)$, in the line $x + y = 2$, then

$$\frac{x - 2\cos\theta}{1} = \frac{y - 2\sin\theta}{1} = \frac{-2(2\cos\theta + 2\sin\theta - 2)}{1 + 1}$$

or $$x - 2\cos\theta = y - 2\sin\theta = -2\cos\theta - 2\sin\theta + 2 \quad \text{...(i)}$$

or $$x - 2\cos\theta = -2\cos\theta - 2\sin\theta + 2$$

$$\Rightarrow \quad x - 2 = -2\sin\theta$$

and $$y - 2\sin\theta = -2\cos\theta - 2\sin\theta + 2$$

$$\Rightarrow \quad y - 2 = -2\cos\theta \quad \text{...(ii)}$$

From Eqs. (i) and (ii), we get

$$(x - 2)^2 + (y - 2)^2 = 4$$

$$\Rightarrow \quad x^2 + y^2 - 4x - 4y + 4 = 0$$

Sol. (Q. Nos. 34 to 35)

Given orthocentre $O \equiv (1, 2)$

and circumcentre $O' = (2, 4)$

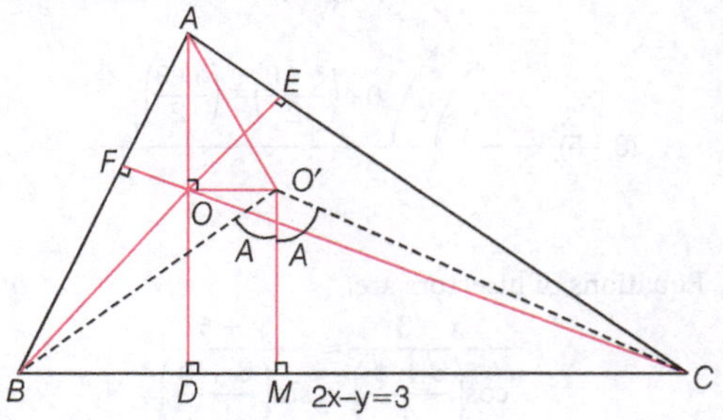

$\because$ Slope of OO' = Slope of $(2x - y = 3)$

and $$OD = O'M = \frac{3}{\sqrt{5}}$$

Let R be the circumradius

$$\therefore \quad O'M = R\cos A$$

$$\Rightarrow \quad R\cos A = \frac{3}{\sqrt{5}} \quad \text{...(i)}$$

34. $$R = AO' = \sqrt{(AO)^2 + (OO')^2} = \sqrt{(2R\cos A)^2 + 5}$$

$$= \sqrt{\left(\frac{6}{\sqrt{5}}\right)^2 + 5} \quad \text{[from Eq. (i)]}$$

$$= \sqrt{\frac{61}{5}}$$

35. $\because$ $$AO = 2R\cos A$$

$$= 2 \times \frac{3}{\sqrt{5}} \quad \text{[from Eq. (i)]}$$

$$= \frac{6}{\sqrt{5}}$$

36. Area of $CDFE$, $A(x) = 1 - \dfrac{1}{2}x^2 - \dfrac{1}{2}(1 - x) = \dfrac{1 + x - x^2}{2}$

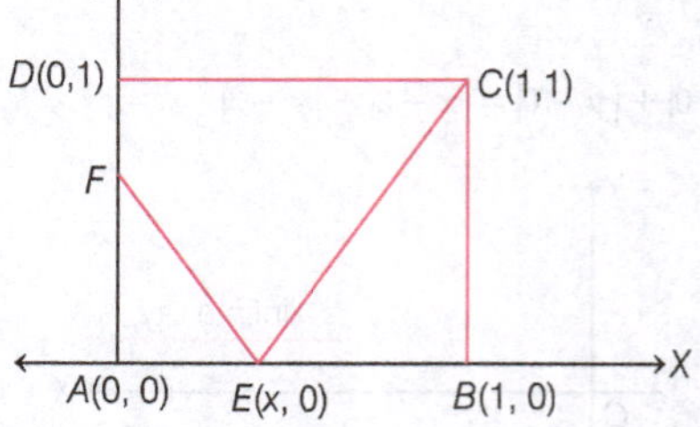

$$A_{max} = A\left(\frac{1}{2}\right) = \frac{1 + \frac{1}{2} - \frac{1}{4}}{2} = \frac{5}{8}$$

At $x = \frac{1}{2}$, $\quad A_{(max)} = 0.625$

37. $PA^2 - PB^2 + PC^2 - PD^2 = (\alpha^2 + \gamma^2) - (\alpha^2 + \delta^2) + (\beta^2 + \delta^2) - (\gamma^2 + \beta^2) = 0$

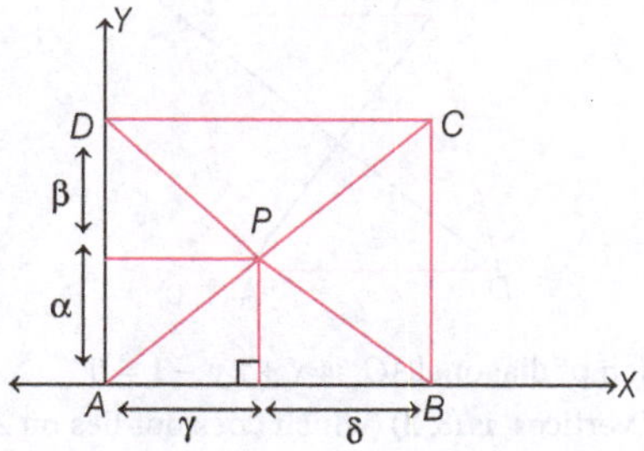

38. $(\text{Perimeter of } \Delta RBC)_{min} = (RB + RC)_{min} + BC$

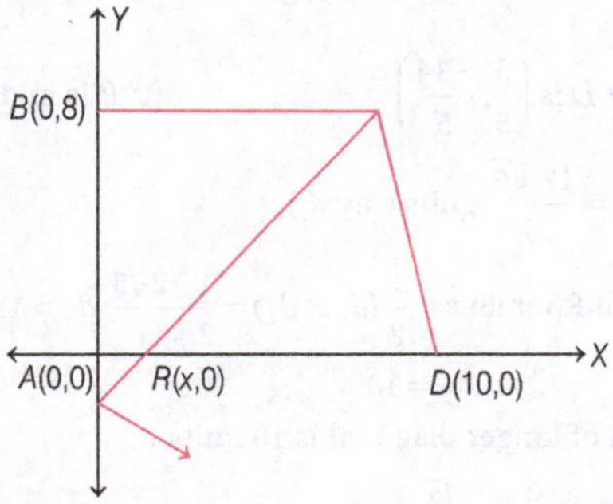

$$= (RB' + RC)_{min} + BC$$
$$= B'C + BC$$
$$= \frac{8}{6 - x} = \frac{16}{6}$$
$$\Rightarrow \quad x = 3$$

39. $\frac{y}{8} = \frac{10 - x}{10 - 6}$

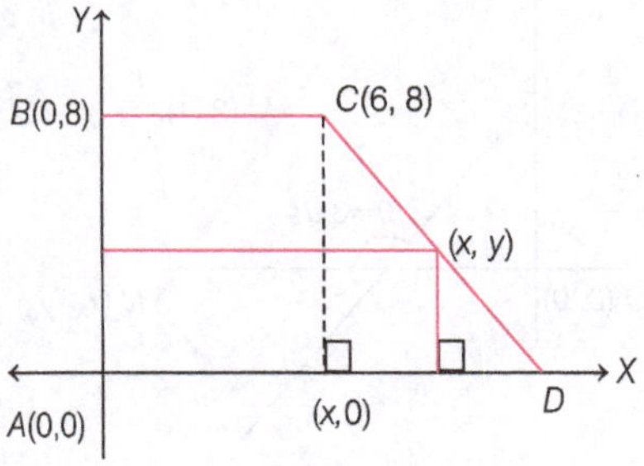

$$y = 2(10 - x)$$

Area of rectangle, $A(x) = 2x(10 - x)$

$$x \in [6, 10]$$
$$A_{max} = A(6) = 2 \times 6(10 - 6) = 48$$

40. Equation of line AC, which is perpendicular to BD is $4x + 3y = \lambda$.

Since, line AC is passing through (3, 1).

$\therefore$ Equation of AC is $4x + 3y - 15 = 0$.

Point E is the intersection of AC and BD.

Solving $4x + 3y - 15 = 0$ and $3x - 4y + 5 = 0$, we get

Line L passing through mid-point of sides AB and AD passes through F.

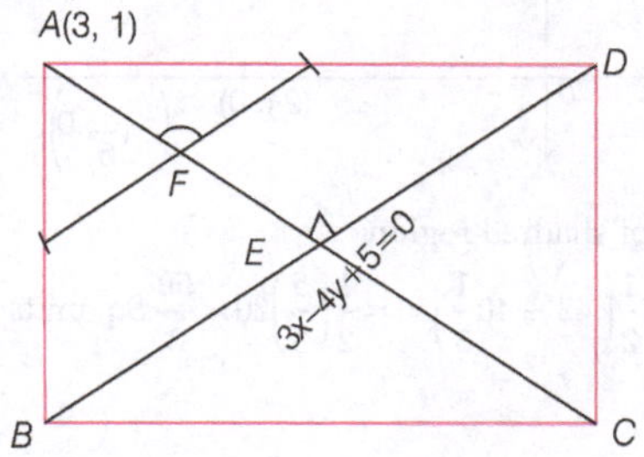

$$F \equiv \left(\frac{3 + \frac{9}{5}}{2}, \frac{\frac{13}{5} + 1}{2}\right) \equiv \left(\frac{12}{5}, \frac{9}{5}\right)$$

Equation of line L is $3x - 4y = \frac{36}{5} - \frac{36}{5} = 0$

$$\Rightarrow \quad 3x - 4y = 0$$
$$\Rightarrow \quad |a + b + c| = |3 - 4| = 1$$

41. P is orthocenter

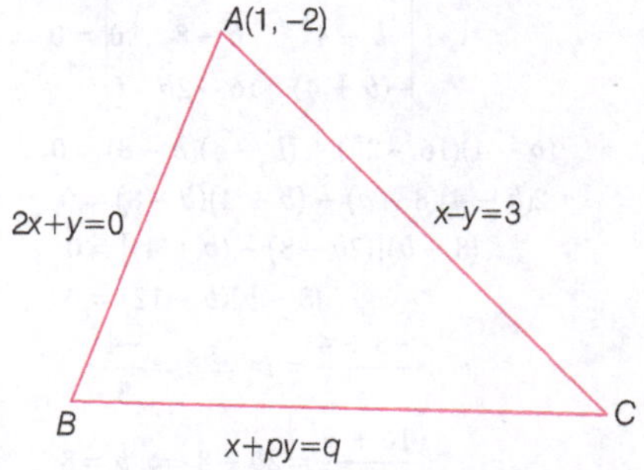

$$\therefore \quad AP \perp BC$$
$$\Rightarrow \quad \left(\frac{-1}{p}\right)\left(\frac{3 + 2}{2 - 1}\right) = -1$$
$$\Rightarrow \quad \frac{5}{p} \Rightarrow p = 5$$
$$\because \quad BC \perp AC$$
$$\Rightarrow \quad \frac{27 - 2q}{18 + q} = -1$$
$$\Rightarrow \quad q = 27 + 18$$
$$\Rightarrow \quad q = 45$$
$$\therefore \quad p + q = 5 + 45 = 50$$
$$\frac{p + q}{10} = \frac{50}{10} = 5$$

42. The given lines $7x + 4y = 168$ and $5x + 3y = 121$ intersect at $P(20, 7)$

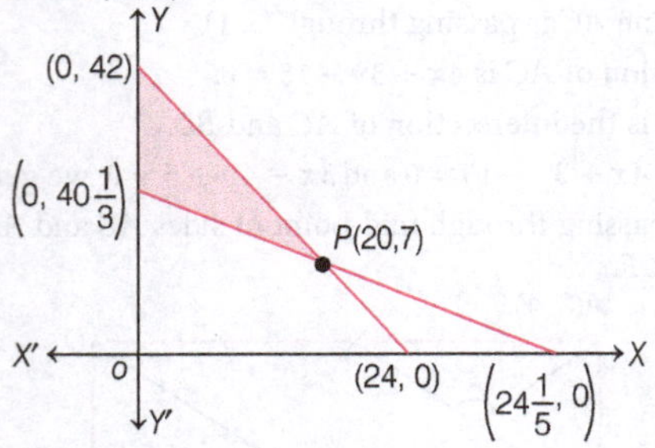

$\therefore$ Area of shadred region,

$$A = \frac{1}{2}\left(42 - 40\frac{1}{3}\right)20 = \frac{1}{2}\left(\frac{5}{3}\right)20 = \frac{50}{3} \text{ Sq. units}$$

$$\frac{3A}{10} = 5$$

43. As H, G and S are collinear

$$\therefore \begin{vmatrix} 4 & b & 1 \\ b & 2b-8 & 1 \\ -4 & 8 & 1 \end{vmatrix} = 0 \text{ and } HG : GS = 2 : 1$$

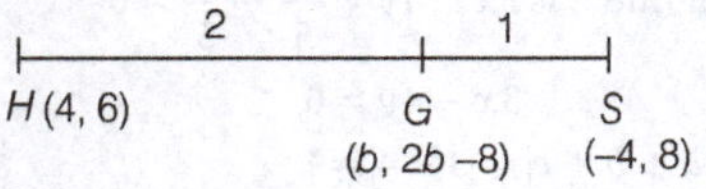

$$\Rightarrow \begin{vmatrix} 4 & b & 1 \\ b-4 & b-8 & 0 \\ -(b+4) & 16-2b & 0 \end{vmatrix} = 0$$

$$\Rightarrow (b-4)(16-2b) + (b+4)(b-8) = 0$$

$$\Rightarrow 2(b-4)(8-b) + (b+4)(b-8) = 0$$

$$\Rightarrow (8-b)[(2b-8) - (b+4)] = 0$$

$$(8-b)(b-12) = 0$$

Also, $\dfrac{-8+4}{3} = b \Rightarrow b = \dfrac{-4}{3}$

and $\dfrac{16+b}{3} = 2b - 8 \Rightarrow b = 8$

$\therefore$ No common value of b is possible.

Hence, the number of value of b is 0.

44. For $|PR + RQ|$ to be minimum, it should be the path of light

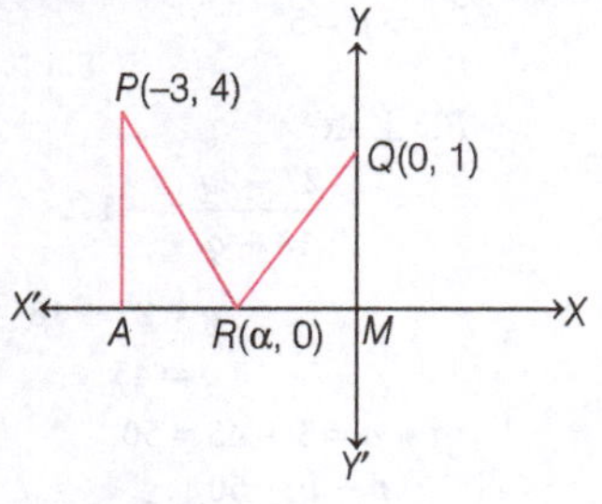

$$\therefore \angle PRA = \angle QRM$$

From similar ΔPAR and ΔQMR,

$$\frac{AR}{RM} = \frac{PA}{QM}$$

$$\Rightarrow \frac{\alpha+3}{0-\alpha} = \frac{4}{1} \Rightarrow \alpha = \frac{-3}{5}$$

$$\Rightarrow 5|\alpha| = 5\left|\frac{-3}{5}\right| = 3$$

45. $\because$ Diagonal is member of both the given families of line, so it will pass through the points $(1, 0)$ and $(-1, 1)$

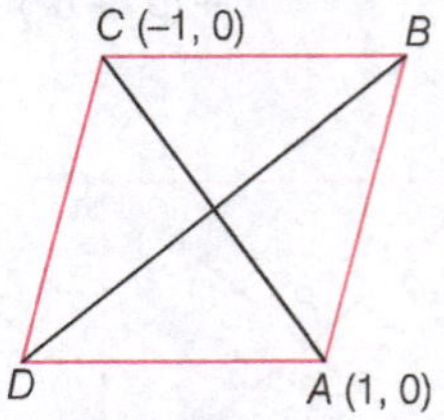

$\Rightarrow$ Equation of diagonal AC is $x + 2y - 1 = 0$

$\therefore$ One of vertices is $(3, 2)$ (which does not lies on AC)

So, equation of diagonal BD is $2x - y = 4$

$\Rightarrow$ Point of intersection of diagonals AC and BD is $P\left(\frac{9}{5}, -\frac{2}{5}\right)$

$\Rightarrow$ Vertex D is $\left(\frac{3}{5}, \frac{-14}{5}\right)$ [$\because P$ is mid-point of BD]

Also, $BD = \dfrac{12\sqrt{5}}{5}$ units (say d_1)

$\therefore$ Area of Rhombus $= \dfrac{1}{2}(d_1 \times d_2) = \dfrac{1}{2}\dfrac{12\sqrt{5}}{5} d_2 = 12\sqrt{5}$

$$d_2 = 10$$

$\therefore$ Length of longer diagonal is 10 units.

46. We have, $MN = 3\sqrt{2}$

$$X_N = 2 - 3\sqrt{2}\left(-\frac{1}{\sqrt{2}}\right) = 5$$

$$Y_N = 1 - 3\sqrt{2}\left(\frac{1}{\sqrt{2}}\right) = -2$$

So, $N = (5, -2)$

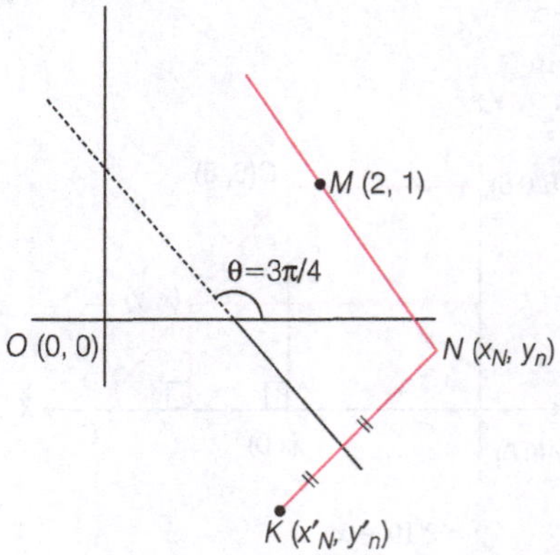

Image of N with respect to $x + y - 1 = 0$

$$\Rightarrow \frac{h-5}{1} = \frac{k+2}{1} = \frac{-2(5-2-1)}{(1^2+1^2)}$$

$$\Rightarrow h - 5 = -2 \Rightarrow h = 3$$

$$kl = -4$$

$\therefore \quad R = (3, -4)$

$$\therefore \quad d = \left|\frac{3(3) - 4(-4) + 25}{\sqrt{3^2 + (-4)^2}}\right| = \left|\frac{50}{5}\right| = 10 \text{ units}$$

$\therefore \quad d^2 = 100$ units

47. $$\tan\theta = \left|\frac{m_2 - m_1}{1 + m_1 m_2}\right| = \left|\frac{\frac{4}{3} - \frac{3}{4}}{1+1}\right| = \left|\frac{16 \quad 9}{12} \times \frac{1}{2}\right| = \frac{7}{24}$$

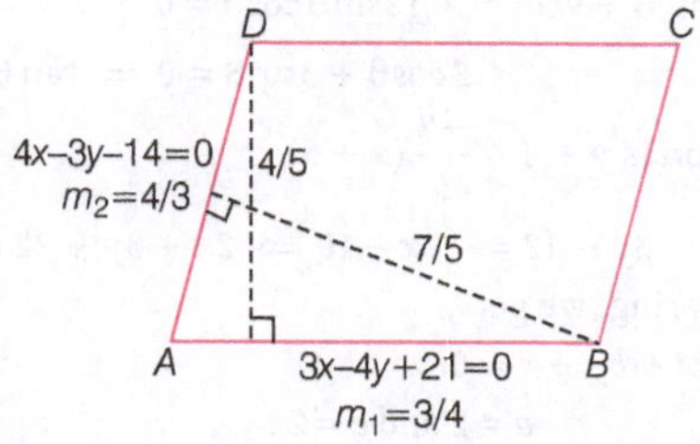

$\therefore \quad \sin\theta = \dfrac{7}{25}$

$$\therefore \quad \text{Area of parallelogram} = \frac{1}{\sin\theta}\, p_1 p_2 = \frac{\frac{14}{5} \times \frac{7}{5}}{\frac{7}{25}} = 14$$

48. Let the image of the orthocentre $H(1, 2)$ to the side BC is $H'(h, k)$.

$H'(h, k)$ is images of line $4x - 3y + 3 = 0$ of $H(1, 2)$

$$\therefore \quad \frac{h-1}{4} = \frac{k-2}{-3} = \frac{-2(4-6+3)}{4^2+3^2}$$

$$\frac{h-1}{4} = \frac{k-2}{-3} = \frac{-2}{25}$$

$$h = 1 - \frac{8}{25} = \frac{17}{25}$$

$$k = 2 + \frac{6}{25} = \frac{56}{25}$$

$$\therefore \quad H' \equiv \left(\frac{17}{25}, \frac{56}{25}\right)$$

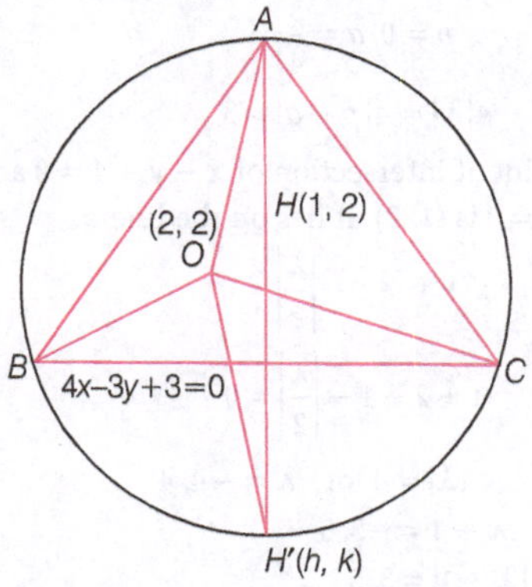

$$\therefore \text{Circumradius of } \Delta ABC = OH' = \sqrt{\left(2 - \frac{17}{25}\right)^2 + \left(3 - \frac{56}{25}\right)^2}$$

$$OH' = \frac{\sqrt{58}}{5}$$

$\therefore \quad m = 58$ and $n = 5$

$\Rightarrow m + n = 65 + 5 = 63$

49. $$\therefore \text{ Area of parallelogram} = \frac{|c_1 - c_2||d_1 - d_2|}{|m_1 - m_2|}$$

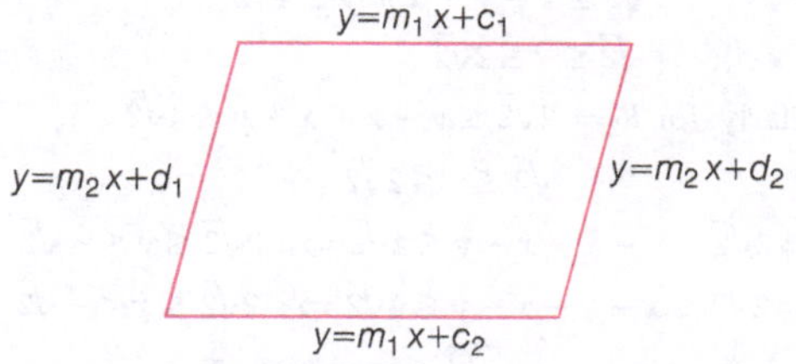

$\therefore$ Area of parallelogram formed by the first set of 4 lines

$$\frac{|c-d|^2}{|a-b|} = 18 \qquad \text{...(i)}$$

and area of parallelogram formed by the second set of 4 lines

$$\frac{|c+d|^2}{|a-b|} = 72 \qquad \text{...(ii)}$$

By Eqs. (i) and (ii),

$$|c-d|^2 = |a-b|(18)$$
$$|c+d|^2 = |a-b|(72)$$

$\because a, b, c, d \in N$

$\therefore$ RHS must be a perfect square for some least value of $(a - b)$ which obviously can be equal to 2.

$$|a - b| = 2$$

$\therefore$ For smallest values of a and b

$\Rightarrow \quad a = 1$ and $b = 3$

$\therefore \quad c - d = 6$ and $c + d = 12$

$c = 9$ and $d = 3$

$\therefore \quad a + b + c + d = 16$

50.

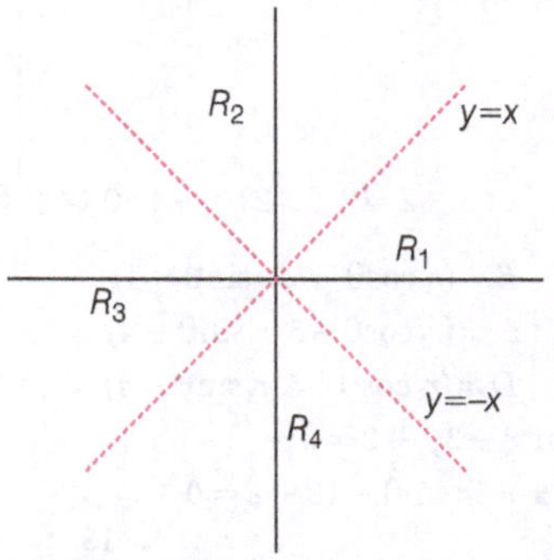

$$\therefore \quad d(P, L_1) = \left|\frac{x-y}{\sqrt{2}}\right|$$

$$\therefore \quad d(P, L_2) = \left|\frac{x+y}{\sqrt{2}}\right|$$

Now, we have $2 \le d(P, L_1) + d(P, L_2) \le 4$

$$2\sqrt{2} \le |x - y| + |x + y| \le 4\sqrt{2} \qquad \text{...(i)}$$

Now, let us consider the four region namely R_1, R_2, R_3 and R_4 in the lines L_1 and L_2 dividing the coordinate plane.

In R_1, we have $y < x, y > -x$

In R_2, we have $y > x, y > -x$

In R_3, we have $y > x, y < -x$

In R_4, we have $y < x, y < -x$

Thus, in R_1 Eq. (i) becomes

$$2\sqrt{2} \le x - y + x + y \le 4\sqrt{2}$$

$$\Rightarrow \quad \sqrt{2} \le x \le 2\sqrt{2}$$

Similarly, for $R_2 \Rightarrow 2\sqrt{2} \le y - x + x + y \le 4\sqrt{2}$

$$\Rightarrow \quad \sqrt{2} \le y \le 2\sqrt{2}$$

$R_3 \Rightarrow 2\sqrt{2} \le y - x - x - y \le 4\sqrt{2} \Rightarrow -2\sqrt{2} \le y \le -\sqrt{2}$

$R_4 \Rightarrow 2\sqrt{2} \le x - y - x - y \le 4\sqrt{2} \Rightarrow -2\sqrt{2} \le x < -\sqrt{2}$

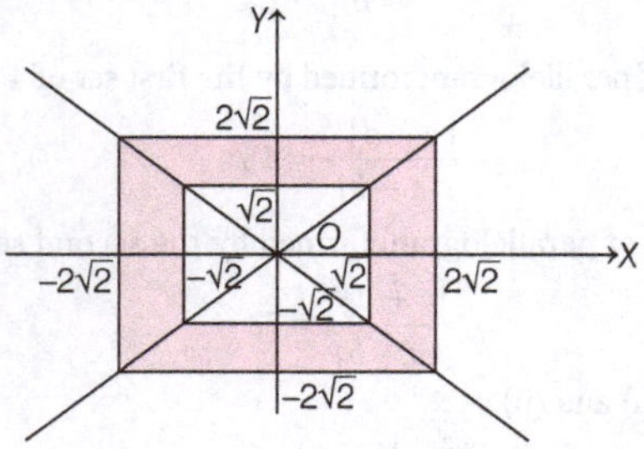

$\therefore$ R will be the region between concentric squares formed by lines

$x = \pm\sqrt{2}, y = \pm\sqrt{2}$ and $x = \pm 2\sqrt{2}, y = \pm 2\sqrt{2}$

Thus, the required area $\Rightarrow (4\sqrt{2})^2 - (2\sqrt{2})^2 = 24$ sq units

51. Let θ be the inclination of the line through $A(-5, -4)$.

Then, equation of the line is $\dfrac{x+5}{\cos\theta} = \dfrac{y+4}{\sin\theta} = r$

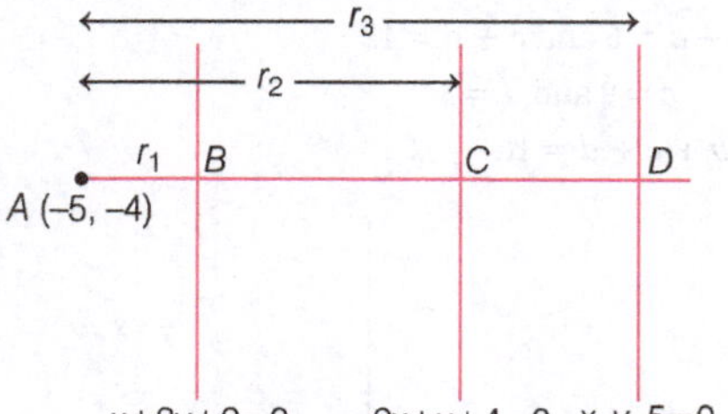

$$B = (r_1\cos\theta - 5, r_1\sin\theta - 4)$$

$$C = (r_2\cos\theta - 5, r_2\sin\theta - 4)$$

$$D = (r_3\cos\theta - 5, r_3\sin\theta - 4)$$

But B lies on $x + 3y + 2 = 0$

$\therefore$ $r_1\cos\theta - 5 + 3r_1\sin\theta - 12 + 2 = 0$

$$\Rightarrow \quad r_1 = \frac{15}{\cos\theta + 3\sin\theta} = AB$$

$$\Rightarrow \quad \frac{15}{AB} = \cos\theta + 3\sin\theta \quad \text{...(i)}$$

As C lies on $2x + y + 4 = 0$

$\because$ $2(r_2\cos\theta - 5) + (r_2\sin\theta - 4) + 4 = 0$

$$\frac{10}{r_2} = 2\cos\theta + \sin\theta \Rightarrow \frac{10}{AC} = 2\cos\theta + \sin\theta$$

Similarly, D lies on $x - y - 5 = 0$

$\therefore$ $r_3\cos\theta - 5 - r_3\sin\theta + 4 - 5 = 0$

$$\Rightarrow \quad r_3 = \frac{6}{\cos\theta - \sin\theta} = AD$$

$$\Rightarrow \quad \frac{6}{AD} = \cos\theta - \sin\theta \quad \text{...(iii)}$$

Now, given that $\left(\dfrac{15}{AB}\right)^2 + \left(\dfrac{10}{AC}\right)^2 = \left(\dfrac{6}{AD}\right)^2$

$\Rightarrow (\cos\theta + 3\sin\theta)^2 + (2\cos\theta + \sin\theta)^2 = (\cos\theta - \sin\theta)^2$

[by Eqs. (i), (ii) and (iii)]

$$\Rightarrow \quad 4\cos^2\theta + 9\sin^2\theta + 12\sin\theta\cos\theta = 0$$

$$\Rightarrow \quad 2\cos\theta + 3\sin\theta = 0 \Rightarrow \tan\theta = -2/3$$

$\therefore$ Equation is $y + 4 = \dfrac{-2}{3}(x+5)$

$$\Rightarrow \quad 3y + 12 = -2x - 10 \Rightarrow 2x + 3y + 22 = 0$$

On comparing, we get

$$ax + by + c = 0$$

$$\Rightarrow \quad a = 2 \text{ and } c = 22$$

$$\therefore \quad 25a - c \Rightarrow 50 - 22 = 28$$

52. **(A)** The given lines an concurrent.

So, $\begin{vmatrix} 1 & -2 & -6 \\ 3 & 1 & -4 \\ \lambda & 4 & \lambda^2 \end{vmatrix} = 0$

or $\quad \lambda^2 + 2\lambda - 8 = 0$

or $\quad \lambda = 2, -4$

$\therefore$ $\quad |\lambda| = 2, 4$

(B) Given family is

$$3x(a+1) + 4y(a-1) - 3(a-1) = 0$$

or $\quad a(3x + 4y - 3) + (3x - 4y + 3) = 0$

for fixed point=

$$3x + 4y - 3 = 0$$

and $\quad 3x - 4y + 3 = 0$

$\therefore$ $\quad x = 0, y = \dfrac{3}{4}$

Fixed point is $\left(0, \dfrac{3}{4}\right)$,

Here, $\quad p = 0, q = \dfrac{3}{4}$

$\therefore$ $\quad 4|\lambda| = 4|p - q| = 3$

(C) The point of intersection of $x - y + 1 = 0$ and $3x + y - 5 = 0$ is (1, 2). It lies on the line

$$x + y - 1 - \left|\frac{\lambda}{2}\right| = 0$$

$$\Rightarrow \quad 1 + 2 - 1 - \left|\frac{\lambda}{2}\right| = 0$$

or $\quad |\lambda| = 4$ or $\lambda = -4, 4$

$\therefore$ $\quad \lambda + 1 = -3, 5$

or $\quad |\lambda + 1| = 3, 5$

(D) The mid-point of (1, −2) and (3, 4) will satisfy

$$y - x - 1 + \lambda = 0$$

or $\quad 1 - 2 - 1 + \lambda = 0$

$\therefore$ $\quad \lambda = 2$ or $|\lambda| = 2$

53.

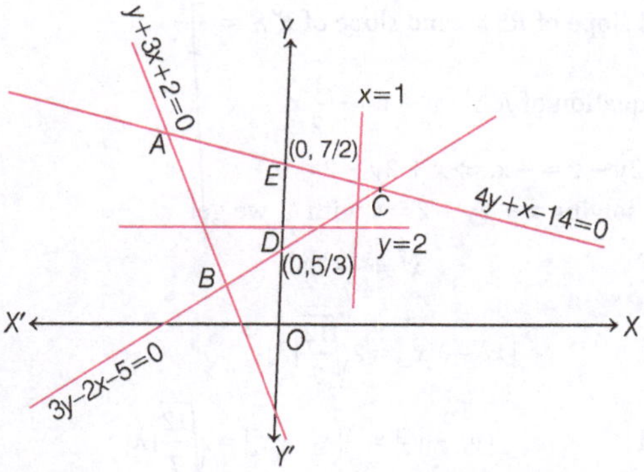

(A) The points on the line $x = 0$, whose y-coordinate lies between $\frac{5}{3}$ and $\frac{7}{2}$ inside the ΔABC.

$\therefore \quad \frac{5}{3} < \lambda < \frac{7}{2}$ or $5 < 3\lambda < 10.5$

$\therefore \quad |3\lambda| = 6, 7, 8, 9, 10$

(B) $\because C \equiv (2, 3)$

The points on the line $x = 1$, whose y-coordinate lies between

$\frac{8}{3}$ [put $x = 1$ in $3y - 2x - 5 = 0$]

and $\frac{13}{4}$ [put $x = 1$ in $4y + x - 14 = 0$]

$\therefore \quad \frac{8}{3} < \lambda < \frac{13}{4}$ or $8 < 3\lambda < 9.75$

$\therefore \quad |3\lambda| = 9$

(C) $\because B \equiv (-1, 1)$

The point on the line $y = 2$, whose x-coordinate lies between

$\frac{-4}{3}$ (put $y = 2$ in $y + 3x + 2 = 0$)

and $\frac{1}{2}$ (put $y = 2$ in $3y - 2x - 5 = 0$)

$\therefore \quad \frac{-4}{3} < \lambda < \frac{1}{2}$ or $-8 < 6\lambda < 3$

Integral values of 6λ are

$-7, -6, -5, -4, -3, -2, -1, 0, 1, 2$

$\therefore \quad |6\lambda| = 7, 6, 5, 4, 3, 2, 1, 0$

(D) $\because A \equiv (-2, 4)$

The points on the line $y = \frac{7}{2}$, whose x-coordinates lies between

0 (put $y = \frac{7}{2}$ in $4y + x - 14 = 0$)

and $\frac{-11}{6}$ (put $y = \frac{7}{2}$ in $y + 3x + 2 = 0$)

$\therefore \quad \frac{-11}{6} < \lambda < 0$

or $\quad -11 < 6\lambda < 0$

Integral values of 6λ are

$-10, -9, -8, -7, -6, -3, -2, -1$

$\therefore \quad |6\lambda| = 10, 9, 8, 7, 6, 5, 4, 3, 2, 1$

54. (A) $OA = 1 + 4\cot\theta$

$OB = 4 + \tan\theta$

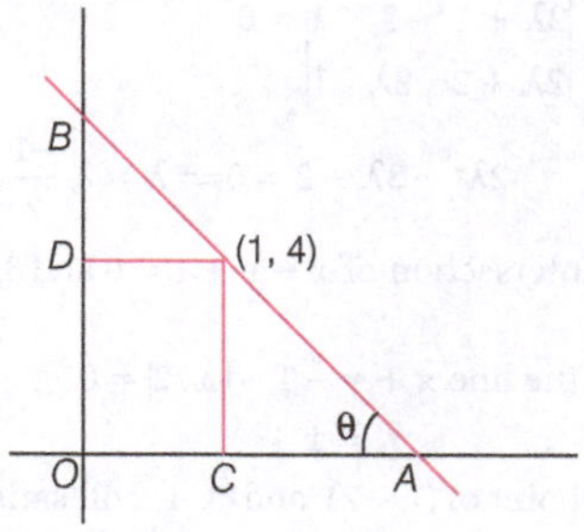

$$\therefore \quad OA + OB = 5 + 4\cot\theta + \tan\theta$$
$$\geq 5 + 2\sqrt{4\cot\theta \tan\theta}$$
$$= 5 + 2 \times 2 = 9$$

(B) Reflection of $P(4, -1)$ in $y = x$ is $Q(-1, 4)$.

$$\therefore \quad PQ = \sqrt{(4+1)^2 + (-1-4)^2}$$
$$= \sqrt{50} = 5\sqrt{2}$$

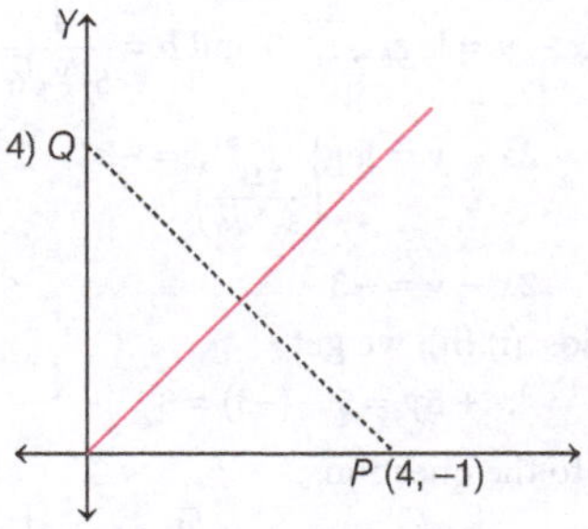

(C) $AB = 2\sqrt{2}$ and $OC = \sqrt{2}$

Maximum value of d is

$\Rightarrow OF = \sqrt{2} + 2\sqrt{2} = 3\sqrt{2}$

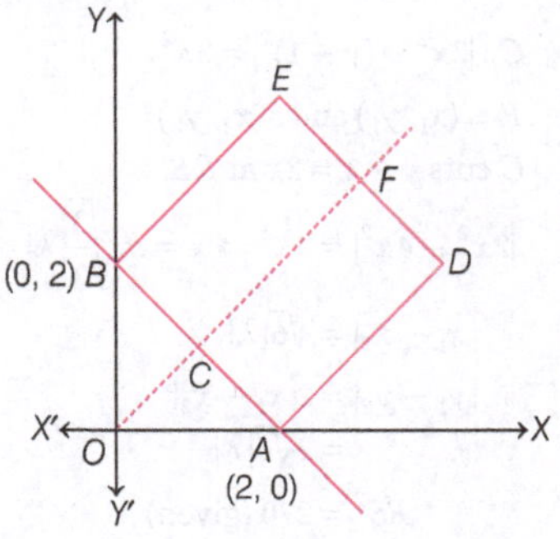

(D) The given line $x = 4 + \frac{1}{\sqrt{2}}\left(\frac{y+1}{\sqrt{2}}\right)$

$$y = 2x - 9$$

$\therefore$ Intercept made by X-axis is 9/2.

55. (A) Given, lines are concurrent so

$$\begin{vmatrix} 3 & 1 & -4 \\ 1 & -2 & -6 \\ \lambda & 4 & \lambda^2 \end{vmatrix}$$

$\Rightarrow \quad \lambda^2 + 2\lambda - 8 = 0 \Rightarrow \lambda = 2, -4$

(B) Points are collinear

i.e. $\begin{vmatrix} \lambda+1 & 1 & 1 \\ 2\lambda+1 & 3 & 1 \\ 2\lambda+2 & 2\lambda & 1 \end{vmatrix} = 0$

$\Rightarrow \quad 2\lambda^2 - 3\lambda - 2 = 0 \Rightarrow \lambda = 2, \dfrac{-1}{2}$

(C) Point of intersection of $x - y + 1 = 0$ and $3x + y - 5 + 0$ is $(1, 2)$

It lies on the line $x + y - 1 - |\lambda/2| = 0$

$\Rightarrow \quad \lambda = \pm 4$

(D) The mid-point of $(1, -2)$ and $(3, 4)$ will satisfy.

$y - x - 1 + \lambda = 0 \Rightarrow \lambda = 2$

56. Given, $3x + 2y = \log_a (18)^{5/4}$ and $a = 3\sqrt{2}$

$a = 3\sqrt{2}$

$\Rightarrow 3x + 2y = \log_{3\sqrt{2}} (3\sqrt{2})^{5/2} = 5/2$

$[\because \log_b a^m = m \log_b a]$ ...(i)

$\Rightarrow 6x + 4y = 5$

Also, $2x - y = \log_b \sqrt{1080}$ and $b = \dfrac{1}{5^{1/6}\sqrt{6}}$

$\Rightarrow \quad 2x - y = \log_{\left(\frac{1}{5^{1/6}\sqrt{6}}\right)} (5^{1/6}\sqrt{6})^3 = -3$

$\Rightarrow \quad 2x - y = -3$

From Eqs. (i) (ii), we get

$4x + 5y = 5 - (-3) = 8$

57. According to the question,

$C: \left|\dfrac{x\sqrt{2} - y - 1}{\sqrt{3}}\right| \left|\dfrac{x\sqrt{2} - y + 1}{\sqrt{3}}\right| = \lambda^2$

$\Rightarrow \quad C: \dfrac{|(x\sqrt{2})^2 - (y-1)^2|}{\sqrt{3} \times \sqrt{3}} = \lambda^2$

$\Rightarrow \quad C: |2x^2 - (y-1)^2| = 3\lambda^2$

Let $\quad R \equiv (x_1, y_1)$ and $S(x_2, y_2)$

$\because \quad C$ cuts $y - 1 = 2x$ at RS.

So, $\quad |2x^2 - 4x^2| = 3\lambda^2 \Rightarrow x = \pm\sqrt{\dfrac{3}{2}}|\lambda|$

$\therefore \quad |x_1 - x_2| = \sqrt{6}|\lambda|$

and $\quad |y_1 - y_2| = 2|x_1 - x_2|$

$= 2\sqrt{6}|\lambda|$

$\because \quad RS^2 = 270$ (given)

$\Rightarrow (x_1 - x_2)^2 + (y_1 - y_2)^2 = 270$

$\Rightarrow \quad (\sqrt{6}\lambda)^2 + (2\sqrt{6}|\lambda|)^2 = 270$

$\Rightarrow \quad 30\lambda^2 = 270$

$\Rightarrow \quad \lambda^2 = 9$

58. Now, l mid-point of RS is

$\left(\dfrac{x_1 + x_2}{2}, \dfrac{y_1 + y_2}{2}\right) \equiv (0, 1)$

and slope of $RS = 2$and slope of $R'S' = \dfrac{-1}{2}$

$\therefore$Equation of $R'S' : y - 1 = -\dfrac{1}{2}x$

i.e. $2y - 2 = -x. \Rightarrow x + 2y - 2 = 0$

On solving $x + 2y - 2 = 0$ with C, we get

$x^2 = \dfrac{12}{7}\lambda^2$

$\Rightarrow \quad |x_1 - 0\, x_2| = 2\sqrt{\dfrac{12}{7}}|\lambda|$

and $\quad |y_1 - y_2| = \dfrac{1}{2}|x_1 - x_2| = \sqrt{\dfrac{12}{7}}|\lambda|$

Hence, $\quad D = (R'S')^2 = (x_1 - x_2)^2 + (y_1 - y_2)^2$

$= \dfrac{12}{7} \times 9 \times 5 = \dfrac{12 \times 45}{7} \approx 77.14$

Exercise 3 - Challenging Problems

1. In ΔOBD, $\quad \dfrac{BD}{\sin(\pi - 2C)} = \dfrac{R}{\sin\theta}$ ...(i)

In ΔODC, $\quad \dfrac{DC}{\sin(\pi - 2B)} = \dfrac{R}{\sin(\pi - \theta)}$ ...(ii)

From Eqs. (i) and (ii), $\dfrac{BD}{DC} = \dfrac{\sin 2C}{\sin 2B}$

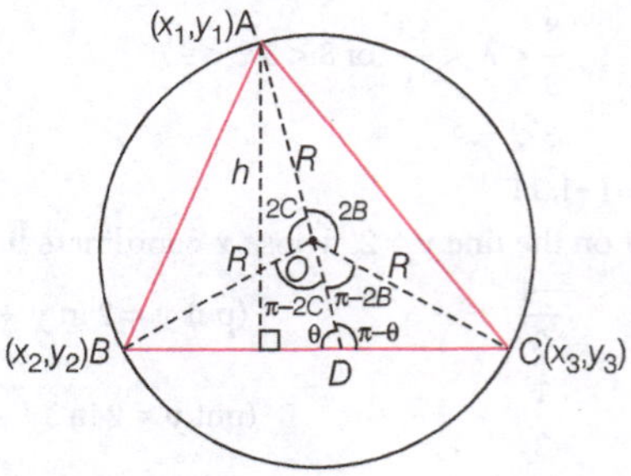

$\therefore$ Coordinates of D are

$\left(\dfrac{x_2 \sin 2B + x_3 \sin 2C}{\sin 2B + \sin 2C}, \dfrac{y_2 \sin 2B + y_3 \sin 2C}{\sin 2B + \sin 2C}\right)$

Let (x, y) be any point on AD, then equation of AD is

$\begin{vmatrix} x & y & 1 \\ x_1 & y_1 & 1 \\ \dfrac{x_2 \sin 2B + x_3 \sin 2C}{\sin 2B + \sin 2C} & \dfrac{y_2 \sin 2B + y_3 \sin 2C}{\sin 2B + \sin 2C} & 1 \end{vmatrix} = 0$

or $\begin{vmatrix} x & y & 1 \\ x_1 & y_1 & 1 \\ x_2 \sin 2B + x_3 \sin 2C & y_2 \sin 2B + y_3 \sin 2C & \sin 2B + \sin 2C \end{vmatrix} = 0$

$$\text{or} \quad \begin{vmatrix} x & y & 1 \\ x_1 & y_1 & 1 \\ x_2 \sin 2B & y_2 \sin 2B & \sin 2B \end{vmatrix} + \begin{vmatrix} x & y & 1 \\ x_1 & y_1 & 1 \\ x_3 \sin 2C & y_3 \sin 2C & \sin 2C \end{vmatrix} = 0$$

$$\text{or} \quad (\sin 2B) \begin{vmatrix} x & y & 1 \\ x_1 & y_1 & 1 \\ x_2 & y_2 & 1 \end{vmatrix} + (\sin 2C) \begin{vmatrix} x & y & 1 \\ x_1 & y_1 & 1 \\ x_3 & y_3 & 1 \end{vmatrix} = 0$$

2. Let (x_1, y_1) be the coordinates of a point at unit distance from each of the given lines.

$$\Rightarrow \quad \frac{|3x_1 - 4y_1 + 1|}{\sqrt{3^2 + 4^2}} = 1 \text{ and } \frac{|8x_1 + 6y_1 + 1|}{\sqrt{8^2 + 6^2}} = 1$$

$$\Rightarrow \quad 3x_1 - 4y_1 + 1 = \pm 5 \text{ and } 8x_1 + 6y_1 + 1 = \pm 10$$

$$\Rightarrow \quad 3x_1 - 4y_1 - 4 = 0 \quad \text{...(i)}$$

$$\text{or} \quad 3x_1 - 4y_1 + 6 = 0 \quad \text{...(ii)}$$

$$8x_1 + 6y_1 - 9 = 0 \quad \text{...(iii)}$$

$$\text{or} \quad 8x_1 + 6y_1 + 11 = 0 \quad \text{...(iv)}$$

By intersection Eq. (i) and (iii), we get

$$\Rightarrow \quad x_1 / 60 = y_1 / -5 = 1/50,$$

$$\therefore \quad (x_1, y_1) = \left(\frac{6}{5}, -\frac{1}{10}\right)$$

By intersection Eq. (i) and (iv), we get

$$\Rightarrow \quad x_1 / -20 = y_1 / -65 = 1/50,$$

$$\therefore \quad (x_1, y_1) = \left(-\frac{2}{5}, -\frac{13}{10}\right)$$

By intersection Eq. (ii) and (iii), we get

$$\Rightarrow \quad x_1 / 0 = y_1 / 75 = 1/50, \therefore (x_1, y_1) = (0, 3/2)$$

By intersection Eq. (ii) and (iv), we get

$$\Rightarrow \quad x_1 / -80 = y_1 / 15 = 1/50, \therefore (x_1, y_1) = \left(-\frac{8}{5}, \frac{3}{10}\right)$$

Hence, the required four points have the coordinates are

$$\left(\frac{6}{5}, -\frac{1}{10}\right), \left(-\frac{2}{5}, -\frac{13}{10}\right), \left(0, \frac{3}{2}\right) \text{ and } \left(-\frac{8}{5}, \frac{3}{10}\right).$$

3. Let $\angle OAB = \alpha$

$$\therefore \quad OA = AB \cos \alpha \text{ and } OB = AB \sin \alpha$$

$$\because \quad (OA)^2 + (OB)^2 = k^2$$

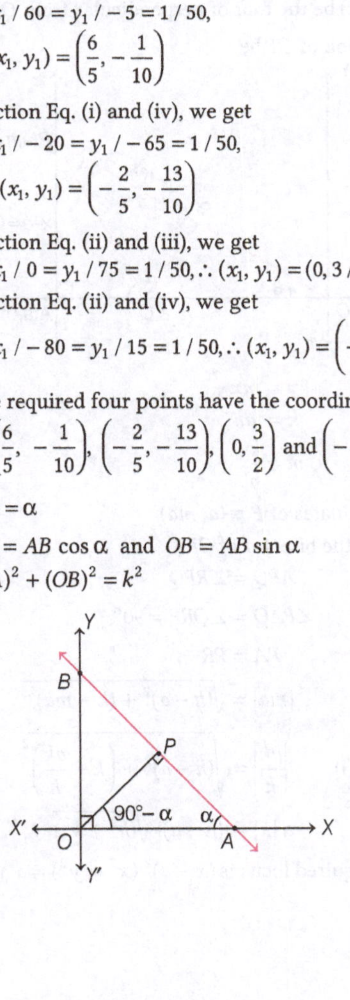

$$\text{i.e.} \quad (AB)^2 (\cos^2\alpha + \sin^2\alpha) = k^2$$

$$\text{or} \quad AB = k$$

Then, $OA = k \cos \alpha$ and $OB = k \sin \alpha$

$$\therefore \text{ Equation of } AB \text{ is } \frac{x}{k \cos \alpha} + \frac{y}{k \sin \alpha} = 1$$

$$\text{or} \quad \frac{x}{\cos \alpha} + \frac{y}{\sin \alpha} = k \quad \text{...(i)}$$

Let P be the foot of perpendicular from O on AB.

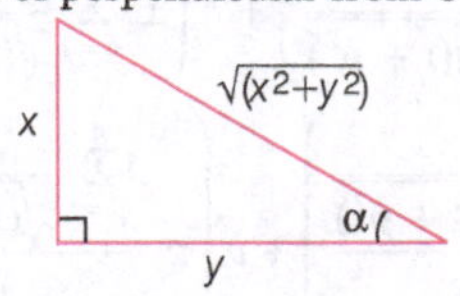

$$\therefore \text{ Equation of } OP \text{ is } y = x \tan (90° - \alpha)$$

$$\text{or} \quad \cot \alpha = \frac{y}{x}$$

$$\therefore \quad \sin \alpha = \frac{x}{\sqrt{(x^2 + y^2)}}$$

$$\text{and} \quad \cos \alpha = \frac{y}{\sqrt{(x^2 + y^2)}} \quad \text{...(ii)}$$

Substituting the values of $\sin \alpha$ and $\cos \alpha$ from Eq. (i) in (i) then we get the required locus of P

$$\therefore \quad \frac{x}{y / \sqrt{(x^2 + y^2)}} + \frac{y}{x / \sqrt{(x^2 + y^2)}} = k$$

$$\Rightarrow \quad (x^2 + y^2) \sqrt{(x^2 + y^2)} = kxy$$

Squaring both sides, we get

$$(x^2 + y^2)^2 (x^2 + y^2) = k^2 x^2 y^2$$

$$\text{or} \quad (x^2 + y^2)^2 \left(\frac{x^2}{x^2 y^2} + \frac{y^2}{x^2 y^2}\right) = k^2$$

$$\text{or} \quad (x^2 + y^2)^2 (x^{-2} + y^{-2}) = k^2$$

4. Let the equation of variable line be $ax + by = 1$. Then, the coordinates of A_p will be

$$A_p \equiv \left(\frac{1}{a + bp}, \frac{p}{a + bp}\right)$$

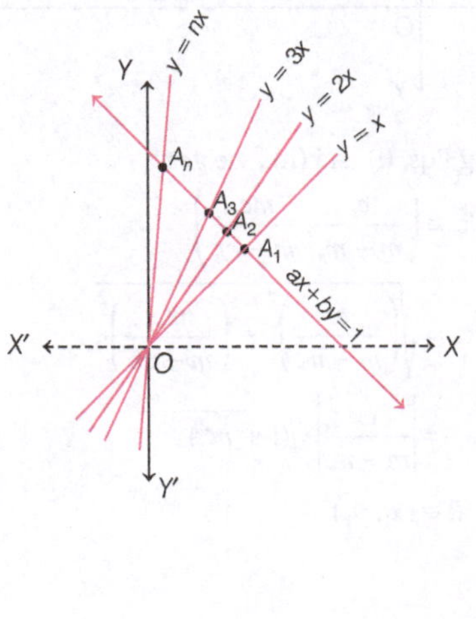

$\therefore \quad OA_p = \dfrac{\sqrt{(1+p^2)}}{|a+bp|}$ ...(i)

Given, $\displaystyle\sum_{p=1}^{n} \frac{1}{OA_p} = c$

$\Rightarrow \displaystyle\sum_{p=1}^{n} \frac{|a+bp|}{\sqrt{(1+p^2)}} = c$ [from Eq. (1)]

$\Rightarrow \quad a\left(\pm \displaystyle\sum_{p=1}^{n} \frac{1}{\sqrt{(1+p^2)}}\right) + b\left(\pm \displaystyle\sum_{p=1}^{n} \frac{p}{\sqrt{(1+p^2)}}\right) = c$

or $\quad a\left(\pm \dfrac{\displaystyle\sum_{p=1}^{n} \frac{1}{\sqrt{(1+p^2)}}}{c}\right) + b\left(\pm \dfrac{\displaystyle\sum_{p=1}^{n} \frac{p}{\sqrt{(1+p^2)}}}{c}\right) = 1$

So, line always passes through a fixed point whose coordinates are

$$\left(\pm \frac{\displaystyle\sum_{p=1}^{n} \frac{1}{\sqrt{(1+p^2)}}}{c}, \pm \frac{\displaystyle\sum_{p=1}^{n} \frac{p}{\sqrt{(1+p^2)}}}{c}\right)$$

5. Let the equation of given n lines be $y = m_r x + c_r$,

where $\quad r = 1, 2, 3, \ldots, n$ ...(i)

Let equation of line through origin O be

$y = mx$ ...(ii)

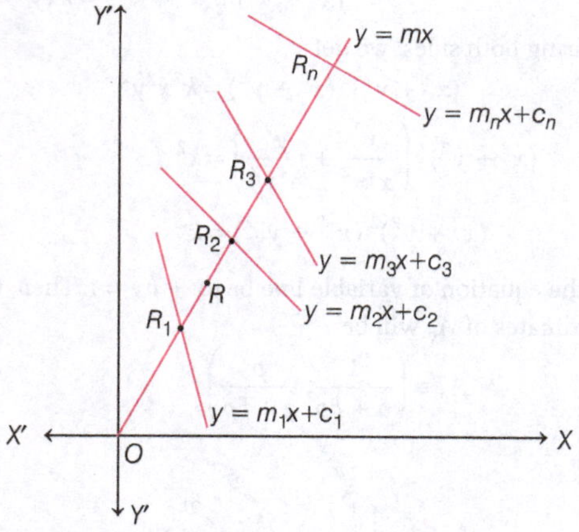

On solving Eqs. (i) and (ii) , we get

$R_r \equiv \left(\dfrac{c_r}{m-m_r}, \dfrac{mc_r}{m-m_r}\right)$

$\therefore \quad OR_r = \sqrt{\left(\dfrac{c_r}{m-m_r}\right)^2 + \left(\dfrac{m\,c_r}{m-m_r}\right)^2}$

$= \left|\dfrac{c_r}{m-m_r}\right| \sqrt{(1+m^2)}$ ...(iii)

Let $\quad R \equiv (x_1, y_1)$

$\therefore \quad y_1 = mx_1 \Rightarrow m = \dfrac{y_1}{x_1}$ ...(iv)

Given, $\dfrac{n}{OR} = \displaystyle\sum_{r=1}^{n} \frac{1}{OR_r}$

$\Rightarrow \dfrac{n}{\sqrt{(x_1^2+y_1^2)}} = \displaystyle\sum_{r=1}^{n} \left|\frac{m-m_r}{c_r}\right| \frac{1}{\sqrt{(1+m^2)}}$ [from Eq . (iii)]

$= \dfrac{1}{\sqrt{(1+m^2)}} \left\{m\left(\displaystyle\sum_{r=1}^{n}\left(\pm\frac{1}{c_r}\right)\right) + \displaystyle\sum_{r=1}^{n}\left(\mp\frac{m_r}{c_r}\right)\right\}$

$= \dfrac{1}{\sqrt{(1+m^2)}}(ma+b)$

where $a = \displaystyle\sum_{r=1}^{n}\left(\pm\frac{1}{c_r}\right)$ and $b = \displaystyle\sum_{r=1}^{n}\left(\mp\frac{m_r}{c_r}\right)$

then $\dfrac{n}{\sqrt{(x_1^2+y_1^2)}} = \dfrac{\dfrac{y_1}{x_1}a+b}{\sqrt{1+\left(\dfrac{y_1}{x_1}\right)^2}}$ [from Eq. (iv)]

$\Rightarrow \quad n = ay_1 + bx_1$

Hence, locus of point R is $bx + ay = n$.

6. Let $R\,(h, k)$ be the foot of perpendicular from Q on OP.

Let equation of OP be

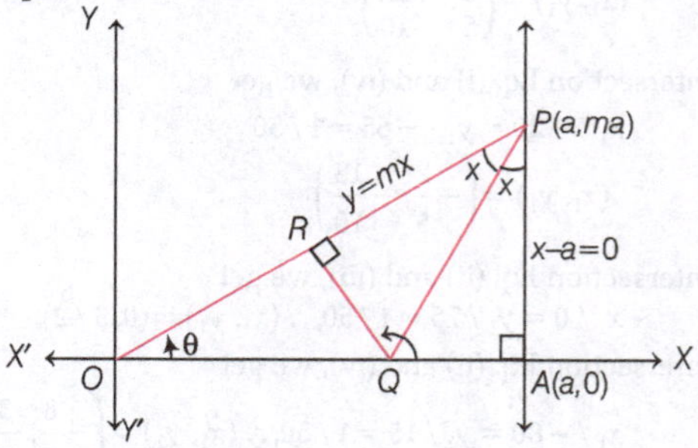

$y = mx$

then $\quad k = mh$

or $\quad m = \dfrac{k}{h}$ ...(i)

and coordinates of $P \equiv (a, ma)$

$\because \quad PQ$ is the bisector of OPA

$\therefore \quad \angle APQ = \angle RPQ$

and $\quad \angle PAQ = \angle QRP = 90°$

$\therefore \quad PA = PR$

then $\quad |ma| = \sqrt{(h-a)^2 + (k-ma)^2}$

From Eq. (i), $\quad \left|\dfrac{ak}{h}\right| = \sqrt{(h-a)^2 + \left(k - \dfrac{ak}{h}\right)^2}$

$\Rightarrow \quad a\,|k| = |(h-a)|\,\sqrt{(h^2+k^2)}$

Hence, required locus is $(x-a)^2\,(x^2+y^2) = a^2y^2$

7. Let the equation of the variable line through be

$$\frac{x}{\cos\theta}=\frac{y}{\sin\theta}$$

and let $OR = r_1$, $OS = r_2$ and $OP = r_3$

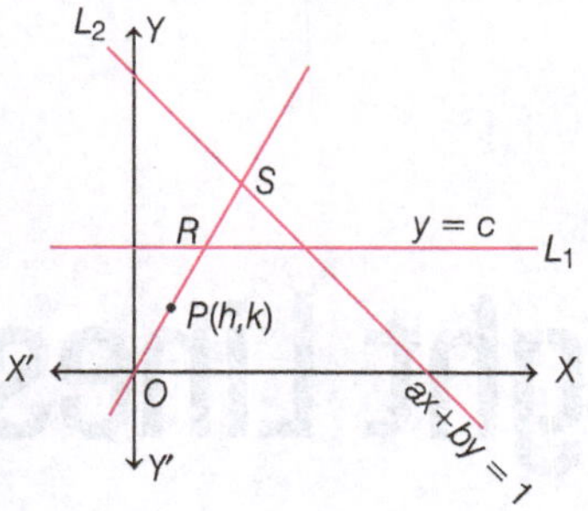

Then, coordinates of R, S and P are

$R(r_1\cos\theta, r_1\sin\theta)$, $S(r_2\cos\theta, r_2\sin\theta)$, $P(r_3\cos\theta, r_3\sin\theta)$

R lies on L_1 and S lies on L_2.

Let $L_1 \equiv y - c = 0$

and $L_2 \equiv ax + by - 1 = 0$

$\therefore$ $r_1\sin\theta = c$ and $ar_2\cos\theta + br_2\sin\theta = 1$

$\therefore$ $r_1 = \dfrac{c}{\sin\theta}$ and $r_2 = \dfrac{1}{a\cos\theta + b\sin\theta}$

From the given condition, $\dfrac{m+n}{r_3} = \dfrac{m}{r_1} + \dfrac{n}{r_2}$

$$\Rightarrow \frac{m+n}{r_3} = \frac{m\sin\theta}{c} + n(a\cos\theta + b\sin\theta) \quad \text{...(i)}$$

Let the coordinates of P be (h, k).

Then, $h = r_3\cos\theta$, $k = r_3\sin\theta$

From Eq. (i), $m + n = \dfrac{mr_3\sin\theta}{c} + n(ar_3\cos\theta + br_3\sin\theta)$

$$\Rightarrow m + n = \frac{mk}{c} + n(ah + bk)$$

Locus of P is $n(ax + by) + \dfrac{my}{c} = (m + n)$

$$\Rightarrow n(ax + by - 1) + \frac{m}{c}(y - c) = 0$$

$$\Rightarrow (ax + by - 1) + \frac{m}{nc}(y - c) = 0$$

$$\Rightarrow L_2 + \lambda L_1 = 0 \quad \left(\text{where } \lambda = \frac{m}{nc}\right)$$

Hence, locus of P is a point of intersection of L_1 and L_2.

3

> "*I have always enjoyed mathematics. It is the most precise and concise way of expressing an idea.*"
>
> **-N.R. Narayana Murthy**

Pair of Straight Lines

Learning Milestones

Milestone 1 Homogeneous Equation in Two Variables

- Definition
- Homogeneous Equation in Two Variables
- Pair of Straight Lines Through the Origin

Milestone 2 Angle Between the pairs of lines

- Angle Between the Pair of Lines $ax^2+2hxy+by^2 = 0$
- Bisectors of the Angle Between the Lines Given by a Homogeneous Equation

Milestone 3 General Equation of Second Degree

- General Equation of Second Degree
- Angle Between Lines Represented by $ax^2+2hxy+by^2 + 2gx+2fy+c=0$
- Point of Intersection of the Lines Represented by $ax^2+2hxy+by^2 + 2gx + 2fy+c=0$
- To Find the Point of Intersection of Lines Represented by $ax^2+2hxy+by^2+2gx +2fy +c=0$ Using Partial Differentiation
- Equation of the Angle Bisectors of Pair of Straight lines $ax^2+2hxy+by^2 + 2gx + 2fy+c=0$
- Equation of the Lines Joining the Origin to the Points of Intersection of a Given Line and a Given Curve

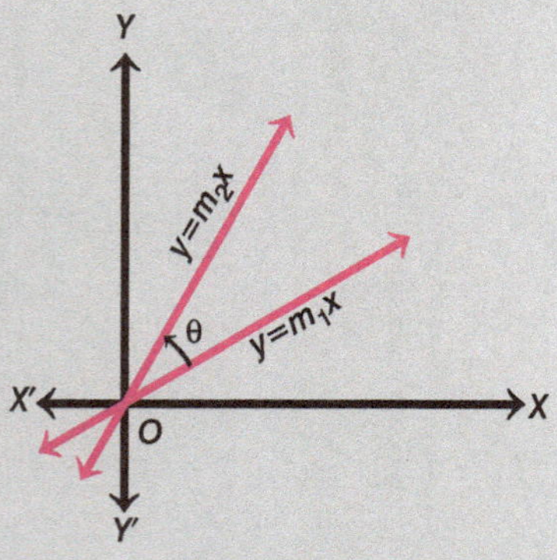

Practice Milestones

Practice Milestone 1- JEE Main Pattern

Practice Milestone 2 - JEE Advanced Pattern

Practice Milestone 3 - Challenging Problems

Milestone 1 Homogeneous Equation in Two Variables

• Definition • Homogeneous Equation in Two Variables • Pair of Straight Lines Through the Origin

3.1 Definition

Let the equation of two lines be

$$ax + by + c = 0 \quad \text{...(i)}$$

and $$a_1 x + b_1 y + c_1 = 0 \quad \text{...(ii)}$$

Hence, $(ax + by + c)(a_1 x + b_1 y + c_1) = 0$ is called the joint equation of lines Eqs. (i) and (ii) and conversely, if joint equation of two lines be

$$(ax + by + c)(a_1 x + b_1 y + c_1) = 0,$$

then their separate equations will be

$$ax + by + c = 0 \quad \text{and} \quad a_1 x + b_1 y + c_1 = 0$$

Example 1. Find the joint equation of lines $y = x$ and $y = -x$.

Sol. The given lines can be rewritten as

$$x - y = 0 \quad \text{and} \quad x + y = 0$$

$\therefore$ Joint equation of lines is $(x - y)(x + y) = 0$

or $$x^2 - y^2 = 0$$

Wrong process Since, the lines are

$$y = x \quad \text{and} \quad y = -x$$

Then, joint equation is $y^2 = -x^2$

$$\Rightarrow \quad x^2 + y^2 = 0$$

This process is wrong, since RHS of two equations are not equal to zero.

Example 2. Find the separate equation of lines represented by the equation $x^2 - 6xy + 8y^2 = 0$.

Sol. Separate equation of lines represented by the equation

$$x^2 - 6xy + 8y^2 = 0$$

i.e. $$(x - 4y)(x - 2y) = 0$$

$$\Rightarrow \quad x - 4y = 0 \quad \text{and} \quad x - 2y = 0$$

Alternate Solution

We have, $x^2 - 6xy + 8y^2 = 0$

By Shri Dharacharya method,

$$x = \frac{6y \pm \sqrt{(-6y)^2 - 4 \cdot 8y^2}}{2}$$

$$\Rightarrow \quad x = 3y \pm y\sqrt{(9-8)}$$

$$x = 3y \pm y$$

$$\therefore \quad x = 4y \quad \text{and} \quad x = 2y$$

Hence, the lines are $x - 4y = 0$ and $x - 2y = 0$.

Example 3. Does equation $x^2 + 2y^2 - 2\sqrt{3}x - 4y + 5 = 0$ represent pair of straight lines ?

Sol. We have,

$$x^2 + 2y^2 - 2\sqrt{3}x - 4y + 5 = 0$$

$$\Rightarrow \quad (x^2 - 2\sqrt{3}x) + 2(y^2 - 2y) + 5 = 0$$

$$\Rightarrow \quad (x - \sqrt{3})^2 - 3 + 2(y - 1)^2 - 2 + 5 = 0$$

$$\Rightarrow \quad (x - \sqrt{3})^2 + 2(y - 1)^2 = 0$$

Hence, it denotes only a point $(\sqrt{3}, 1)$ but not a pair of straight lines.

3.2 Homogeneous Equation in Two Variables

An equation of the form

$$a_0 y^n + a_1 y^{n-1} x + a_2 y^{n-2} x^2 + \dots + a_n x^n = 0 \quad \text{...(i)}$$

in which the sum of the powers of x and y in every term is the same (here n), is called a **homogeneous** equation (of degree n).

We will prove that Eq. (i) represents n straight lines passing through the origin.

$$a_0 y^n + a_1 y^{n-1} x + a_2 y^{n-2} x^2 + \dots + a_n x^n = 0$$

On dividing each term by x^n, we get

$$a_0 \left(\frac{y}{x}\right)^n + a_1 \left(\frac{y}{x}\right)^{n-1} + a_2 \left(\frac{y}{x}\right)^{n-2} + \dots + a_n = 0$$

Above is an equation of nth degree in $\frac{y}{x}$.

Let the roots of this equation be $m_1, m_2, m_3, \dots, m_n$.

Then, the above equation will be identical with

$$a_0 \left(\frac{y}{x} - m_1\right)\left(\frac{y}{x} - m_2\right)\left(\frac{y}{x} - m_3\right) \dots \left(\frac{y}{x} - m_n\right) = 0$$

$$\Rightarrow a_0 (y - m_1 x)(y - m_2 x)(y - m_3 x) \dots (y - m_n x) = 0$$

Hence, Eq. (i) represents n straight lines

$$y - m_1 x = 0, y - m_2 x = 0,$$
$$y - m_3 x = 0, \dots, y - m_n x = 0$$

all of which clearly pass through the origin.

3.3 Pair of Straight Lines Through the Origin.

Since, $ax^2 + 2hxy + by^2 = 0$ is a homogeneous equation of second degree, it represents two straight lines through origin.

The given equation is

$$ax^2 + 2hxy + by^2 = 0 \quad \text{...(i)}$$

Dividing by x^2, we get

$$a + 2h\left(\frac{y}{x}\right) + b\left(\frac{y}{x}\right)^2 = 0$$

$$\Rightarrow \quad b\left(\frac{y}{x}\right)^2 + 2h\left(\frac{y}{x}\right) + a = 0 \quad \text{...(ii)}$$

On putting $\frac{y}{x} = m$,

then $$bm^2 + 2hm + a = 0 \quad \text{...(iii)}$$

If m_1 and m_2 be two roots, then

$$m_1 + m_2 = -\frac{2h}{b} = -\frac{\text{coefficient of } xy}{\text{coefficient of } y^2}$$

and $$m_1 m_2 = \frac{a}{b} = \frac{\text{coefficient of } x^2}{\text{coefficient of } y^2}$$

$$\therefore \quad |m_1 - m_2| = \sqrt{\{(m_1 + m_2)^2 - 4m_1 m_2\}}$$

$$= \frac{2}{|b|}\sqrt{(h^2 - ab)}$$

Thus, $y = m_1 x$ and $y = m_2 x$ are two straight lines which are given by Eq. (i). Also, from Eq. (iii),

$$m = \frac{-2h \pm 2\sqrt{(h^2 - ab)}}{2b}$$

$$= \frac{-h \pm \sqrt{(h^2 - ab)}}{b} = \frac{y}{x} \qquad \left[\because m = \frac{y}{x}\right]$$

$$\therefore \quad by = \{-h + \sqrt{(h^2 - ab)}\}x$$

and $$by = \{-h - \sqrt{(h^2 - ab)}\}x$$

$\therefore$ These are two separate lines represented by the equation $ax^2 + 2hxy + by^2 = 0$.

JEE Focus Points

Concept Inside Video

- The lines are real and distinct, if $h^2 - ab > 0$.
- The lines are coincident, if $h^2 - ab = 0$.
- The lines are imaginary, if $h^2 - ab < 0$.
- When lines represented by

$$ax^2 + 2hxy + by^2 = 0$$

pass through the origin, let their equations be

$$y = m_1 x \text{ and } y = m_2 x$$

Then, $(y - m_1 x)$ and $(y - m_2 x)$ must be factors of $ax^2 + 2hxy + by^2 = 0$

then $ax^2 + 2hxy + by^2 = b(y - m_1 x)(y - m_2 x)$

[making coefficient of y^2 equal on both sides]

Now, comparing both sides, we get

$$2h = -b(m_1 + m_2) \text{ and } a = bm_1 m_2$$

$$\therefore \quad m_1 + m_2 = -\frac{2h}{b} \text{ and } m_1 m_2 = \frac{a}{b}$$

Example 4. Find the values of λ, if the equation $2x^2 + \lambda xy + 2y^2 = 0$ represents a pair of real and distinct lines.

Sol. We have, $2x^2 + \lambda xy + 2y^2 = 0$

$$\therefore \quad a = 2, b = 2 \text{ and } h = \frac{\lambda}{2}$$

The given equation represents real and distinct pair of straight lines.

$$\therefore \quad h^2 > ab$$

$$\Rightarrow \quad \frac{\lambda^2}{4} > 4$$

$$\Rightarrow \quad \lambda^2 - 16 > 0$$

$$\Rightarrow \quad \lambda \in (-\infty, -4) \cup (4, \infty)$$

Example 5. Find the condition that the slope of one of the lines represented by $ax^2 + 2hxy + by^2 = 0$ should be n times the slope of the other.

Sol. Let the lines represented by $ax^2 + 2hxy + by^2 = 0$ are

$$y = m_1 x \quad \text{and} \quad y = m_2 x.$$

Therefore, $$m_1 + m_2 = -\frac{2h}{b} \quad \text{...(i)}$$

and $$m_1 m_2 = \frac{a}{b} \quad \text{...(ii)}$$

Given, $$m_2 = nm_1$$

From Eq. (i), $$m_1 + nm_1 = -\frac{2h}{b}$$

$$\therefore \quad m_1 = -\frac{2h}{b(1+n)} \quad \text{...(iii)}$$

From Eq. (ii), $m_1(nm_1) = \frac{a}{b}$

$\therefore \quad nm_1^2 = \frac{a}{b}$

$\Rightarrow \quad n\left\{\frac{-2h}{b(1+n)}\right\}^2 = \frac{a}{b}$ [from Eq. (iii)]

$\Rightarrow \quad \frac{4nh^2}{b^2(1+n)^2} = \frac{a}{b}$

$\Rightarrow \quad 4nh^2 = ab(1+n)^2$ ...(iv)

This is the required condition.

Example 6. If the slope of one of the lines represented by $ax^2 + 2hxy + by^2 = 0$ be the nth power of the other, prove that $(ab^n)^{\frac{1}{n+1}} + (a^n b)^{\frac{1}{n+1}} + 2h = 0$.

Sol. Let m and m^n be the slopes of the lines represented by

$$ax^2 + 2hxy + by^2 = 0$$

Then, $m + m^n = -\frac{2h}{b}$ ...(i)

and $m \cdot m^n = \frac{a}{b}$

$\Rightarrow \quad m^{n+1} = \frac{a}{b}$

$\Rightarrow \quad m = \left(\frac{a}{b}\right)^{\frac{1}{(n+1)}}$ ...(ii)

On substituting the value of m from Eq. (ii) in Eq. (i), we get

$$\left(\frac{a}{b}\right)^{\frac{1}{(n+1)}} + \left(\frac{a}{b}\right)^{\left(\frac{n}{n+1}\right)} = -\frac{2h}{b}$$

$\Rightarrow \quad a^{\frac{1}{n+1}} \cdot b^{\frac{n}{n+1}} + a^{\frac{n}{n+1}} \cdot b^{\frac{1}{n+1}} + 2h = 0$

Hence, $(ab^n)^{\frac{1}{n+1}} + (a^n b)^{\frac{1}{n+1}} + 2h = 0$

Example 7. If the sum of the slopes of the lines given by $x^2 - 2cxy - 7y^2 = 0$ is four times their product, then find the value of c.

Sol. We have, $x^2 - 2cxy - 7y^2 = 0$ ...(i)

Let the slopes of lines represented by Eq. (i) be m_1 and m_2, then

$$m_1 + m_2 = \frac{-2h}{b} = -\frac{2c}{7}$$

and $m_1 m_2 = \frac{a}{b} = \frac{-1}{7}$

Now, we have $m_1 + m_2 = 4m_1m_2$

$\Rightarrow \quad \frac{-2c}{7} = \frac{-4}{7} \Rightarrow c = 2$

Example 8. Find the product of the perpendiculars drawn from the point (x_1, y_1) on the lines $ax^2 + 2hxy + by^2 = 0$.

Sol. Let the lines represented by $ax^2 + 2hxy + by^2 = 0$ be $y = m_1 x$ and $y = m_2 x$.

Therefore, $m_1 + m_2 = -\frac{2h}{b}$

and $m_1 m_2 = \frac{a}{b}$

The lengths of the perpendiculars from (x_1, y_1) on these lines are

$$\frac{|y_1 - m_1x_1|}{\sqrt{1+m_1^2}} \text{ and } \frac{|y_1 - m_2x_1|}{\sqrt{1+m_2^2}}$$

Their product $= \frac{|y_1 - m_1x_1|}{\sqrt{1+m_1^2}} \times \frac{|y_1 - m_2x_1|}{\sqrt{1+m_2^2}}$

$$= \frac{|(y_1 - m_1x_1)(y_1 - m_2x_1)|}{\sqrt{(1+m_1^2)(1+m_2^2)}}$$

$$= \frac{|y_1^2 - (m_1+m_2)x_1y_1 + m_1m_2x_1^2|}{\sqrt{1+m_1^2+m_2^2+m_1^2m_2^2}}$$

$$= \frac{|y_1^2 - (m_1+m_2)x_1y_1 + m_1m_2x_1^2|}{\sqrt{1+(m_1+m_2)^2 - 2m_1m_2 + (m_1m_2)^2}}$$

$$= \frac{\left|y_1^2 + \frac{2h}{b}x_1y_1 + \frac{a}{b}x_1^2\right|}{\sqrt{\left(1 + \frac{4h^2}{b^2} - \frac{2a}{b} + \frac{a^2}{b^2}\right)}}$$

$$= \frac{|ax_1^2 + 2hx_1y_1 + by_1^2|}{\sqrt{[(a-b)^2 + 4h^2]}}$$

Example 9 Find the condition that one of the lines given by $ax^2 + 2hxy + by^2 = 0$ may be perpendicular to one of the lines given by $a'x^2 + 2h'xy + b'y^2 = 0$.

Sol. Since, both pair are passing through origin, let $y = mx$ be one of the lines represented by

$$ax^2 + 2hxy + by^2 = 0$$

Then, $ax^2 + 2hx(mx) + b(mx)^2 = 0$

$\Rightarrow \quad bm^2 + 2hm + a = 0$ ...(i)

Let $y = -\frac{1}{m}x$ be one of the line represented by

$$a'x^2 + 2h'xy + b'y^2 = 0$$

$\left[\because y = -\frac{1}{m}x \text{ is perpendicular to } y = mx \text{ and passing through origin}\right]$

Then, $a'x^2 + 2h'x\left(-\frac{1}{m}x\right) + b'\left(-\frac{1}{m}x\right)^2 = 0$

$$\Rightarrow \quad a'm^2 - 2h'm + b' = 0 \quad \text{...(ii)}$$

On solving Eqs. (i) and (ii), by cross-multiplication rule

i.e.
$$\begin{array}{ccc} m^2 & m & 1 \\ b & 2h & a \\ a' & -2h' & b' \end{array}$$

$$\Rightarrow \quad \frac{m^2}{2hb' + 2h'a} = \frac{m}{aa' - bb'} = \frac{1}{-2h'b - 2a'h}$$

$$\therefore \quad m^2 = -\frac{(hb' + h'a)}{(h'b + a'h)}, m = \frac{(bb' - aa')}{2(a'h + h'b)}$$

On eliminating m, we obtain

$$4(ha' + h'b)(h'a + hb') + (bb' - aa')^2 = 0.$$

Example 10. Show that the centroid (x', y') of the triangle with sides $ax^2 + 2hxy + by^2 = 0$ and $lx + my = 1$, is given by

$$\frac{x'}{bl - hm} = \frac{y'}{am - hl} = \frac{2}{3(am^2 - 2hlm + bl^2)}.$$

Sol. Let the lines represented by $ax^2 + 2hxy + by^2 = 0$ be $y = m_1x$ and $y = m_2x$.

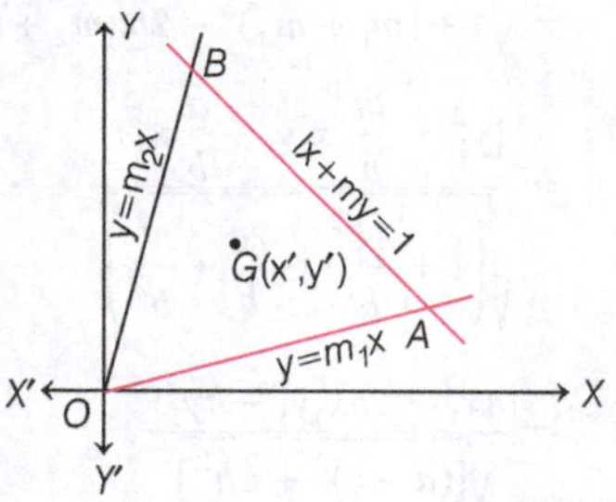

Therefore, $m_1 + m_2 = -\frac{2h}{b}$

and $\quad m_1m_2 = \frac{a}{b}$

Coordinates of A and B are

$$\left(\frac{1}{l + mm_1}, \frac{m_1}{l + mm_1}\right) \text{ and } \left(\frac{1}{l + mm_2}, \frac{m_2}{l + mm_2}\right)$$

Since, centroid $= (x', y')$

$$\text{Therefore, } x' = \left(\frac{\frac{1}{l + mm_1} + \frac{1}{l + mm_2} + 0}{3}\right)$$

$$= \left(\frac{2l + m(m_1 + m_2)}{3\{l^2 + ml(m_1 + m_2) + m^2m_1m_2\}}\right)$$

$$= \left(\frac{2l - \frac{2hm}{b}}{3\left(l^2 - \frac{2hml}{b} + \frac{m^2a}{b}\right)}\right)$$

$$= \frac{2}{3} \cdot \frac{(bl - hm)}{(am^2 - 2hlm + bl^2)} \quad \text{...(i)}$$

and
$$y' = \left(\frac{\frac{m_1}{l + mm_1} + \frac{m_2}{l + mm_2} + 0}{3}\right)$$

$$= \left(\frac{l(m_1 + m_2) + 2mm_1m_2}{3\{l^2 + lm(m_1 + m_2) + m^2m_1m_2\}}\right)$$

$$= \left(\frac{-\frac{2hl}{b} + \frac{2ma}{b}}{3\left(l^2 - \frac{2hlm}{b} + \frac{m^2a}{b}\right)}\right)$$

$$= \frac{2}{3} \cdot \frac{(am - hl)}{(am^2 - 2hlm + bl^2)} \quad \text{...(ii)}$$

From Eqs. (i) and (ii), we get

$$\frac{x'}{bl - hm} = \frac{y'}{am - hl} = \frac{2}{3(am^2 - 2hlm + bl^2)}$$

Example 11. Show that the area of the triangle formed by the lines $ax^2 + 2hxy + by^2 = 0$ and $lx + my + n = 0$ is $\frac{n^2\sqrt{(h^2 - ab)}}{|(am^2 - 2hlm + bl^2)|}$.

Sol. Let equation of lines represented by $ax^2 + 2hxy + by^2 = 0$ be $y = m_1x$ and $y = m_2x$.

Therefore, $m_1 + m_2 = -\frac{2h}{b}$ and $m_1m_2 = \frac{a}{b}$.

Coordinates of A and B are

$$\left(\frac{-n}{l + mm_1}, \frac{-nm_1}{l + mm_1}\right) \text{ and } \left(\frac{-n}{l + mm_2}, \frac{-nm_2}{l + mm_2}\right),$$

respectively.

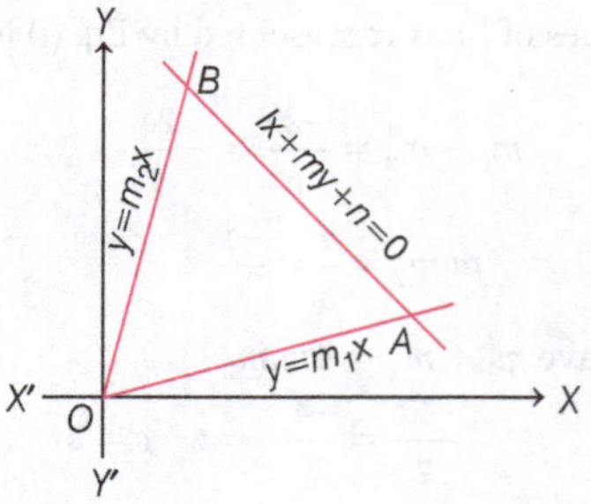

Then, required area

$$=\frac{1}{2}\left|\left(\frac{-n}{l+mm_1}\right)\left(\frac{-nm_2}{l+mm_2}\right)-\left(\frac{-n}{l+mm_2}\right)\left(\frac{-nm_1}{l+mm_1}\right)\right|$$

[$\because$ if coordinates are $(0, 0), (x_1, y_1)$ and (x_2, y_2), then area $=\frac{1}{2}|x_1y_2 - x_2y_1|$]

$$=\frac{1}{2}\left|\frac{n^2(m_2-m_1)}{l^2+lm(m_1+m_2)+m^2m_1m_2}\right|$$

$$=\frac{1}{2}\left|\frac{n^2\sqrt{(m_1+m_2)^2-4m_1m_2}}{l^2+lm(m_1+m_2)+m^2m_1m_2}\right|$$

$$=\frac{1}{2}\left|\frac{n^2\sqrt{\left(\frac{4h^2}{b^2}-\frac{4a}{b}\right)}}{l^2-\frac{2hlm}{b}+\frac{m^2a}{b}}\right|$$

$$=\frac{n^2\sqrt{(h^2-ab)}}{|(am^2-2hlm+bl^2)|}$$

Example 12. Show that the two straight lines $x^2(\tan^2\theta+\cos^2\theta)-2xy\tan\theta+y^2\sin^2\theta=0$ move with the axis of x angles such that the difference of their tangents is 2.

Sol. Given equation is

$$x^2(\tan^2\theta+\cos^2\theta)-2xy\tan\theta+y^2\sin^2\theta=0 \quad \text{...(i)}$$

and homogeneous equation of second degree is

$$ax^2+2hxy+by^2=0 \quad \text{...(ii)}$$

On comparing Eqs. (i) and (ii), we get

$$a=\tan^2\theta+\cos^2\theta,$$
$$h=-\tan\theta$$
and $$b=\sin^2\theta$$

Let separate lines of Eq. (ii) be

$$y=m_1x$$
and $$y=m_2x$$
where, $$m_1=\tan\theta_1$$
and $$m_2=\tan\theta_2$$

Therefore, $$m_1+m_2=-\frac{2h}{b}=\frac{2\tan\theta}{\sin^2\theta}$$

and $$m_1\cdot m_2=\frac{a}{b}=\frac{\tan^2\theta+\cos^2\theta}{\sin^2\theta}$$

$\because$ $$m_1-m_2=\sqrt{(m_1+m_2)^2-4m_1m_2}$$

$$\Rightarrow \tan\theta_1-\tan\theta_2=\sqrt{\frac{4\tan^2\theta}{\sin^4\theta}-\frac{4(\tan^2\theta+\cos^2\theta)}{\sin^2\theta}}$$

$$=\frac{2}{\sin^2\theta}\sqrt{\tan^2\theta-\sin^2\theta(\tan^2\theta+\cos^2\theta)}$$

$$=\frac{2\sin\theta}{\sin^2\theta}\sqrt{(\sec^2\theta-\tan^2\theta-\cos^2\theta)}$$

$$=\frac{2\sin\theta}{\sin^2\theta}\sqrt{(1-\cos^2\theta)}$$

$$=\frac{2}{\sin\theta}\sin\theta=2$$

Milestone Practice 3.1

1. The lines given by the equation $(2y^2+3xy-2x^2)(x+y-1)=0$ form a triangle which is
   (a) equilateral
   (b) isosceles
   (c) right angled
   (d) obtuse angled

2. Area of the triangle formed by the lines $y^2-9xy+18x^2=0$ and $y=9$ is
   (a) 27/4
   (b) 0
   (c) 9/4
   (d) 27

3. The equation $3x^2+2hxy+3y^2=0$ represents a pair of straight lines passing through the origin. The two lines are
   (a) real and distinct, if $h^2>3$
   (b) real and distinct, if $h^2>9$
   (c) real and coincident, if $h^2=3$
   (d) real and coincident, if $h^2>3$

4. If one of the line of the pair $ax^2+2hxy+by^2=0$ bisects the angle between positive directions of the axes, then a, b and h satisfy the relation
   (a) $a+b=2|h|$
   (b) $a+b=-2h$
   (c) $a-b=2|h|$
   (d) $(a-b)^2=4h^2$

5. If the slope of one of the lines given by $a^2x^2+2hxy+b^2y^2=0$ be three times of the other, then h is equal to
   (a) $2\sqrt{3}\,ab$ (b) $-2\sqrt{3}\,ab$
   (c) $\frac{2}{\sqrt{3}}ab$ (d) $-\frac{2}{\sqrt{3}}ab$

6. Find the separate equations of two straight lines whose joint equation is $ab(x^2-y^2)+(a^2-b^2)xy=0$.

7. Find the coordinates of the centroid of the triangle whose sides are $12x^2-20xy+7y^2=0$ and $2x-3y+4=0$.

8. If the lines $ax^2+2hxy+by^2=0$ be two sides of a parallelogram and the line $lx+my=1$ be one of its diagonal. Then, the equation of the other diagonal is ....

9. Find the condition that one of the lines given by $ax^2+2hxy+by^2=0$ may coincide with one of the lines given by $a'x^2+2h'xy+b'y^2=0$.

10. If the sum of the slopes of the lines given by $4x^2+2kxy-7y^2=0$ is equal to the product of its slopes, then the value of k is ....

11. If the lines $px^2-qxy-y^2=0$ make angles α and β with the X-axis, then the value of $\tan(\alpha+\beta)$ is ......

12. If the pair of straight lines $ax^2+2hxy+by^2=0$ is rotated about the origin through 90°, then the equation in the new position is ....

Answer Key

1. (c) 2. (a) 3. (b) 4. (b) 5. (c, d)
6. $bx+ay=0$ and $ax-by=0$ 7. $\left(\frac{8}{3},\frac{8}{3}\right)$ 8. $y(bl-hm)=x(am-hl)$
9. $(ab'-a'b)^2=4(ha'-h'a)(bh'-b'h)$ 10. (-2) 11. $\left(\frac{-q}{1+p}\right)$
12. $bx^2-2hxy+ay^2=0$

For Detailed Solution

Milestone 2 Angle Between the Pair of Lines

- Angle Between the Pair of Lines $ax^2 + 2hxy + by^2 = 0$
- Bisectors of the Angle Between the Lines Given by a Homogeneous Equation

3.4 Angle Between the Pair of Lines $ax^2 + 2hxy + by^2 = 0$

Theorem The angle θ between the pair of lines represented by $ax^2 + 2hxy + by^2 = 0$

is given by $\theta = \tan^{-1}\left\{\frac{2\sqrt{(h^2 - ab)}}{|a+b|}\right\}$.

Proof Let $y = m_1 x$ and $y = m_2 x$ be the lines represented by

$$ax^2 + 2hxy + by^2 = 0.$$

Then, $m_1 + m_2 = -\frac{2h}{b}$ and $m_1 m_2 = \frac{a}{b}$

Since, θ be the angle between the lines

$$y = m_1 x \quad \text{and} \quad y = m_2 x.$$

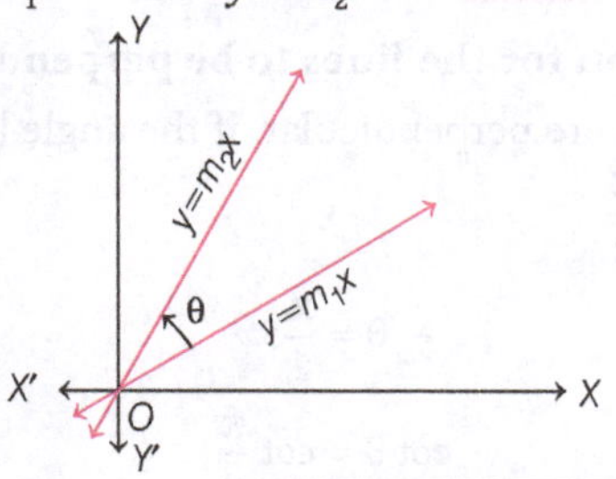

Then, $\tan\theta = \left|\frac{m_1 - m_2}{1 + m_1 m_2}\right| = \frac{\sqrt{(m_1 + m_2)^2 - 4m_1 m_2}}{|1 + m_1 m_2|}$

$$= \frac{\sqrt{\left(\frac{-2h}{b}\right)^2 - 4\left(\frac{a}{b}\right)}}{\left|1 + \frac{a}{b}\right|} = \frac{2\sqrt{(h^2 - ab)}}{|a+b|}$$

$\therefore \quad \theta = \tan^{-1}\left\{\frac{2\sqrt{(h^2 - ab)}}{|a+b|}\right\}$

JEE SPIKE

The angle θ between the pair of lines in terms of sine is

$$\theta = \sin^{-1}\left\{\frac{2\sqrt{h^2 - ab}}{\sqrt{(a-b)^2 + 4h^2}}\right\}$$

Example 13. Find the angle between the pair of lines represented by $2x^2 - 7xy + 3y^2 = 0$.

Sol. We have, $2x^2 - 7xy + 3y^2 = 0$

$\therefore \quad a = 2, b = 3$ and $h = \frac{-7}{2}$

Let θ be the angle between the lines.

Then, $\tan\theta = \frac{2\sqrt{h^2 - ab}}{|a+b|} = \frac{2\sqrt{\frac{49}{4} - 6}}{5} = 1$

$\therefore \quad \theta = 45°$ or $\frac{\pi}{4}$

Example 14. Find the angle between the lines $(x^2 + y^2)\sin^2\alpha = (x\cos\beta - y\sin\beta)^2$.

Sol. Given equation is

$$(x^2 + y^2)\sin^2\alpha = (x\cos\beta - y\sin\beta)^2$$

$$\Rightarrow \quad x^2(\sin^2\alpha - \cos^2\beta) + 2xy\sin\beta\cos\beta + y^2(\sin^2\alpha - \sin^2\beta) = 0 \quad \text{...(i)}$$

The homogeneous equation of second degree is

$$ax^2 + 2hxy + by^2 = 0 \quad \text{...(ii)}$$

On comparing Eqs. (i) and (ii), we get

$$a = \sin^2\alpha - \cos^2\beta, h = \sin\beta\cos\beta,$$

and $\quad b = \sin^2\alpha - \sin^2\beta$

Let the angle between the lines representing by Eq. (i) be θ.

$\therefore \tan\theta = 2\frac{\sqrt{h^2 - ab}}{|a+b|}$

$$= 2\frac{\sqrt{\sin^2\beta\cos^2\beta - (\sin^2\alpha - \cos^2\beta)(\sin^2\alpha - \sin^2\beta)}}{|\sin^2\alpha - \cos^2\beta + \sin^2\alpha - \sin^2\beta|}$$

$$= 2\frac{\sqrt{\{\sin^2\beta\cos^2\beta - \sin^4\alpha + \sin^2\alpha\sin^2\beta + \sin^2\alpha\cos^2\beta - \sin^2\beta\cos^2\beta\}}}{|(2\sin^2\alpha - 1)|}$$

$$= 2\frac{\sqrt{\sin^2\alpha(1 - \sin^2\alpha)}}{|-\cos 2\alpha|} = \frac{2\sin\alpha\cos\alpha}{|-\cos 2\alpha|} = \tan 2\alpha$$

$\therefore \quad \theta = 2\alpha$

Example 15. Show that the angle between the lines given by $(a+2hm+bm^2)x^2+2\{(b-a)m-(m^2-1)h\}xy+(am^2-2hm+b)y^2=0$ is the same whatever be the value of m.

Sol. Given equation is

$$(a+2hm+bm^2)x^2+2\{(b-a)m-(m^2-1)h\}xy+(am^2-2hm+b)y^2=0 \quad ...(i)$$

The homogeneous equation of second degree is

$$Ax^2+2Hxy+By^2=0 \quad ...(ii)$$

On comparing Eqs. (i) and (ii), we get

$$A=a+2hm+bm^2,\ H=(b-a)m-(m^2-1)h,$$

and $B=am^2-2hm+b$

Let the angle between the lines representing by Eq. (i) is θ.

$$\therefore \tan\theta=\frac{2\sqrt{(H^2-AB)}}{|A+B|}$$

$$=\frac{2\sqrt{\{(b-a)m-(m^2-1)h\}^2-(a+2hm+bm^2)(am^2-2hm+b)}}{|a+2hm+bm^2+am^2-2hm+b|}$$

$$=\frac{2\sqrt{(m^2+1)^2(h^2-ab)}}{|a+b|(m^2+1)}=\frac{2\sqrt{(h^2-ab)}}{|a+b|}$$

$$\Rightarrow \theta=\tan^{-1}\left\{\frac{2\sqrt{(h^2-ab)}}{|a+b|}\right\}$$

which is independent of m. Hence, the angle between the lines representing by Eq. (i) is same for all values of m.

Example 16. Show that the straight lines $x^2+4xy+y^2=0$ and the line $x-y=4$ form an equilateral triangle.

Sol. Equation $x^2+4xy+y^2=0$ ...(i)

is a homogeneous equation of second degree in x and y. Therefore, it represents two lines OP and OQ through the origin.

Equation $x-y=4$ ...(ii)

represents the line PQ.

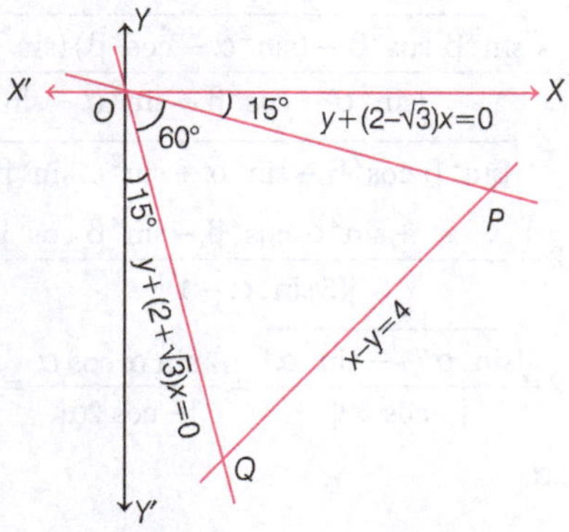

Let $\angle POQ=\theta$.

Then, $\tan\theta=\frac{2\sqrt{[(2)^2-1\cdot 1]}}{|1+1|}=\sqrt{3}$

$\therefore \theta=60°$

From Eq. (i), we get

$$x^2+4xy+y^2=0$$

$$\Rightarrow \left(\frac{y}{x}\right)^2+4\left(\frac{y}{x}\right)+1=0$$

$$\Rightarrow \frac{y}{x}=\frac{-4\pm\sqrt{(4^2-4)}}{2}=-2\pm\sqrt{3}$$

$$\Rightarrow y=(-2\pm\sqrt{3})x$$

i.e. $OP: y+(2-\sqrt{3})x=0$

and $OQ: y+(2+\sqrt{3})x=0$

$\because$ Slope of $PQ=1$ and slope of $OP=-(2-\sqrt{3})$.

If $\angle OPQ=\alpha$, then

$$\tan\alpha=\left|\frac{1-(-2+\sqrt{3})}{1-2+\sqrt{3}}\right|=\left|\frac{3-\sqrt{3}}{-1+\sqrt{3}}\right|=\sqrt{3}$$

$\therefore \alpha=60°$

Hence, $\angle OQP=180°-(60°+60°)=60°$

Hence, ΔOPQ is an equilateral triangle.

IMPORTANT POINTS

1. **Condition for the lines to be perpendicular.**

The lines are perpendicular, if the angle between them is $\frac{\pi}{2}$.

i.e. $\theta=\frac{\pi}{2}$

$$\Rightarrow \cot\theta=\cot\frac{\pi}{2}$$

$$\Rightarrow \cot\theta=0$$

$$\Rightarrow \frac{|a+b|}{2\sqrt{(h^2-ab)}}=0$$

$$\Rightarrow a+b=0$$

i.e. Coefficient of x^2 + Coefficient of $y^2=0$

Hence, the lines represented by $ax^2+2hxy+by^2=0$ are perpendicular iff $a+b=0$

i.e. coefficient of x^2 + coefficient of $y^2=0$.

2. **Pair of any two perpendicular lines through the origin.**

$\because$ Lines represented by $ax^2+2hxy+by^2=0$ be perpendicular, then $a+b=0$ or $b=-a$

Hence, the equation becomes

$$ax^2 + 2hxy - ay^2 = 0$$

$$\Rightarrow \quad x^2 + \left(\frac{2h}{a}\right)xy - y^2 = 0$$

$$\Rightarrow \quad x^2 + pxy - y^2 = 0$$, where p is any constant.

3. **Pair of lines perpendicular to the lines represented by $ax^2 + 2hxy + by^2 = 0$ and through origin.**

Let lines represented by

$ax^2 + 2hxy + by^2 = 0$ be $y = m_1 x$ and $y = m_2 x$.

Then, $$m_1 + m_2 = -\frac{2h}{b}$$

and $$m_1 m_2 = \frac{a}{b}$$

Lines perpendiculars to $y = m_1 x$ and $y = m_2 x$ and passing through origin are $y = -\frac{1}{m_1} x$ and $y = -\frac{1}{m_2} x$ respectively.

Then, pair is $\left(y + \frac{x}{m_1}\right)\left(y + \frac{x}{m_2}\right) = 0$

$$\Rightarrow x^2 + xy\,(m_1 + m_2) + m_1 m_2 y^2 = 0$$

$$\Rightarrow \quad x^2 - \frac{2hxy}{b} + \frac{a}{b} y^2 = 0$$

$$\therefore \quad bx^2 - 2hxy + ay^2 = 0$$

Aid to memory For perpendicular pairs interchange the coefficients of x^2 and y^2 and change the sign of xy.

4. **Condition for the lines to be coincident**

The lines are coincident, if the angle between them is $0°$ (or π).

i.e. $$\theta = 0 \text{ (or } \pi)$$

$$\therefore \quad \tan\theta = 0°$$

$$\Rightarrow \quad \frac{2\sqrt{(h^2 - ab)}}{|a + b|} = 0$$

$$\Rightarrow \quad h^2 - ab = 0$$

$$\Rightarrow \quad h^2 = ab$$

Hence, the lines represented by $ax^2 + 2hxy + by^2 = 0$ are coincident, iff $h^2 = ab$, then $ax^2 + 2hxy + by^2$ is a perfect square.

The parallel lines will be coincident only as both pass through a point.

Example 17. Find the value of a for which the lines represented by $ax^2 + 5xy + 2y^2 = 0$ are mutually perpendicular.

Sol. We have, $ax^2 + 5xy + 2y^2 = 0.$

Since, the lines are mutually perpendicular.

$$\therefore \quad a + 2 = 0$$

$$\Rightarrow \quad a = -2$$

Example 18. How many values of a are possible for which the pair of lines represented by $3ax^2 + 5xy + (a^2 - 2)y^2 = 0$ are perpendicular to each other.

Sol. The pair of lines is given as

$$3ax^2 + 5xy + (a^2 - 2)y^2 = 0$$

Since, lines are perpendicular.

$\therefore$ Coefficient of x^2 + Coefficient of $y^2 = 0$

$$\Rightarrow \quad 3a + (a^2 - 2) = 0$$

$$\Rightarrow \quad a^2 + 3a - 2 = 0$$

$$\Rightarrow \quad a = \frac{-3 \pm \sqrt{17}}{2}$$

$\therefore$ There are two possible values of a.

Example 19. Show that the condition that two of the three lines represented by $ax^3 + bx^2y + cxy^2 + dy^3 = 0$ may be at right angles is $a^2 + ac + bd + d^2 = 0$.

Sol. The given equation being homogeneous of third degree represents three straight lines through the origin. Since, two of these lines are to be at right angles.

Let pair of these lines be $(x^2 + pxy - y^2)$, p is constant and the other factor is $(ax - dy)$.

Hence, $ax^3 + bx^2y + cxy^2 + dy^3 = (x^2 + pxy - y^2)(ax - dy)$

On comparing the coefficients of similar terms, we get

$$b = ap - d \quad \text{...(i)}$$

$$c = -pd - a \quad \text{...(ii)}$$

On multiplying Eq. (i) by d and Eq. (ii) by a and then adding, we get

$$bd + ac = -d^2 - a^2$$

$$\Rightarrow \quad a^2 + ac + bd + d^2 = 0$$

Alternate Solution

Let $y = m_1x$, $y = m_2x$ and $y = m_3x$ be the lines represented by the equation

$$ax^3 + bx^2y + cxy^2 + dy^3 = 0.$$

Then, $ax^3 + bx^2y + cxy^2 + dy^3$

$$= d\,(y - m_1x)\,(y - m_2x)\,(y - m_3x) \quad \text{...(i)}$$

On equating the coefficients of x^3, x^2y and xy^2 on both sides, we get

$$m_1 + m_2 + m_3 = -\frac{c}{d}$$

$$m_1m_2 + m_2m_3 + m_3m_1 = \frac{b}{d}$$

and $$m_1m_2m_3 = -\frac{a}{d} \quad \text{...(ii)}$$

Let the perpendicular lines be $y = m_1x$ and $y = m_2x$, then

$$m_1m_2 = -1$$

From Eq. (ii), $$m_3 = \frac{a}{d} \quad \text{...(iii)}$$

On putting $y = m_3x$ in Eq. (i), we get

$$ax^3 + bm_3x^3 + cm_3^2x^3 + dm_3^3x^3 = 0$$

$$\Rightarrow \quad dm_3^3 + cm_3^2 + bm_3 + a = 0$$

$$\Rightarrow \quad d\left(\frac{a}{d}\right)^3 + c\left(\frac{a}{d}\right)^2 + b\left(\frac{a}{d}\right) + a = 0 \quad \text{[from Eq. (iii)]}$$

Hence, $$a^2 + ac + bd + d^2 = 0$$

3.5 Bisectors of the Angle between the Lines Given by a Homogeneous Equation

Theorem The joint equation of the bisectors of the angles between the lines represented by the equation

$$ax^2 + 2hxy + by^2 = 0 \quad \text{is} \quad \frac{x^2 - y^2}{a - b} = \frac{xy}{h}.$$

Proof Let the lines represented by $ax^2 + 2hxy + by^2 = 0$ be $y - m_1x = 0$ and $y - m_2x = 0$, then

$$m_1 + m_2 = -\frac{2h}{b} \text{ and } m_1m_2 = \frac{a}{b}$$

Since, the bisectors of the angles between the lines are the locus of a point which is equidistant from the two given lines.

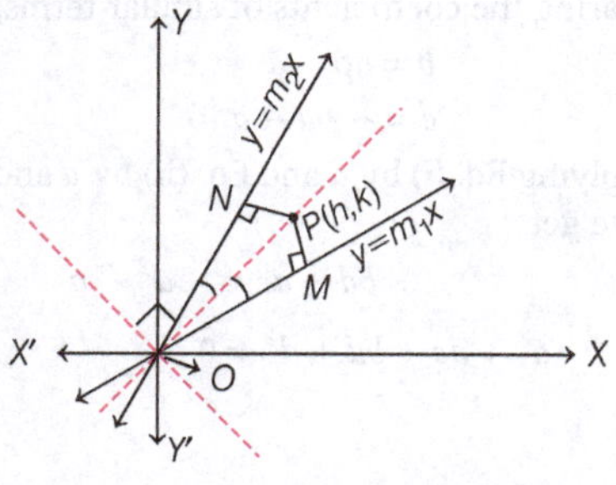

Let $P(h, k)$ be a point on a bisector of the angle between the given lines.

Then, $$PM = PN$$

$$\Rightarrow \quad \frac{|k - m_1h|}{\sqrt{(1 + m_1^2)}} = \frac{|k - m_2h|}{\sqrt{(1 + m_2^2)}}$$

$$\Rightarrow \quad \frac{(k - m_1h)}{\sqrt{(1 + m_1^2)}} = \pm\frac{(k - m_2h)}{\sqrt{(1 + m_2^2)}}$$

Hence, the locus of a $P(h, k)$ is

$$\frac{(y - m_1x)}{\sqrt{(1 + m_1^2)}} = \pm\frac{(y - m_2x)}{\sqrt{(1 + m_2^2)}}$$

$\therefore$ The pair of bisectors is

$$\left(\frac{(y - m_1x)}{\sqrt{(1 + m_1^2)}} + \frac{(y - m_2x)}{\sqrt{(1 + m_2^2)}}\right)\left(\frac{(y - m_1x)}{\sqrt{(1 + m_1^2)}} - \frac{(y - m_2x)}{\sqrt{(1 + m_2^2)}}\right) = 0$$

$$\Rightarrow \quad \frac{(y - m_1x)^2}{(1 + m_1^2)} - \frac{(y - m_2x)^2}{(1 + m_2^2)} = 0$$

$$\Rightarrow \quad (1 + m_2^2)(y^2 + m_1^2x^2 - 2m_1xy) - (1 + m_1^2)(y^2 + m_2^2x^2 - 2m_2xy) = 0$$

$$\Rightarrow \quad (m_2^2 - m_1^2)y^2 - (m_2^2 - m_1^2)x^2 + 2xy(m_2 - m_1) - 2m_1m_2(m_2 - m_1)xy = 0$$

$$\Rightarrow \quad (m_2 + m_1)(y^2 - x^2) + 2xy - 2m_1m_2xy = 0 \quad [\because m_1 - m_2 \neq 0]$$

$$\Rightarrow \quad (x^2 - y^2)\left(-\frac{2h}{b}\right) = 2xy\left(1 - \frac{a}{b}\right) \quad \left[\because m_1 + m_2 = -\frac{2h}{b},\ m_1m_2 = \frac{a}{b}\right]$$

$$\therefore \quad \frac{x^2 - y^2}{a - b} = \frac{xy}{h} \quad [\because b \neq 0]$$

Example 20. Find the equation of the bisectors of the angle between the lines represented by $3x^2 - 5xy + 4y^2 = 0$.

Sol. Given equation is $3x^2 - 5xy + 4y^2 = 0$ ...(i)

Comparing it with the equation

$ax^2 + 2hxy + by^2 = 0$, we get

$$a = 3,\ h = -\frac{5}{2} \text{ and } b = 4$$

Hence, the equation of bisectors of the angle between the pair of the lines (i) is

$$\frac{x^2 - y^2}{3 - 4} = \frac{xy}{-5/2} \Rightarrow \frac{x^2 - y^2}{-1} = \frac{2xy}{-5}$$

$$\therefore \quad 5x^2 - 2xy - 5y^2 = 0$$

JEE SCANNER

Example Similar to PYQ Asked in JEE Main 2023

Let the equation of the pair of lines, $y = px$ and $y = qx$ can be written as $(y - px)(y - qx) = 0$. Then, the equation of the pair of the angle bisectors of the line $2x^2 - 3xy - y^2 = 0$ is

(a) $x^2 - 3xy + y^2 = 0$ (b) $x^2 + 4xy - y^2 = 0$
(c) $x^2 + 2xy - y^2 = 0$ (d) $x^2 - 3xy - y^2 = 0$

Sol. (c) Equation of angle bisectors of homogeneous equation of pair of straight line $ax^2 + 2hxy + by^2 = 0$ is

$$\frac{x^2 - y^2}{a - b} = \frac{xy}{h}$$

For $2x^2 - 3xy - y^2 = 0$,

$$a = 2, h = \frac{-3}{2} \text{ and } b = -1$$

So, equation of angle bisectors is

$$\frac{x^2 - y^2}{2 + 1} = \frac{xy}{-3/2}$$

$$\Rightarrow \frac{x^2 - y^2}{3} = \frac{-2xy}{3}$$

$$\Rightarrow x^2 + 2xy - y^2 = 0$$

$\therefore$ The equation of the pair of angle bisectors of the lines $2x^2 - 3xy - y^2 = 0$ is $x^2 + 2xy - y^2 = 0$.

Skill Builder

Let the equation of the pair of lines, $y = px$ and $y = qx$ can be written as $(y - px)(y - qx) = 0$. Then, the combined equation of the pair of the angle bisectors of the line $5x^2 - 2xy + y^2 = 0$ is

(a) $x^2 - 3xy + y^2 = 0$
(b) $x^2 + 4xy - y^2 = 0$
(c) $x^2 + 2xy - y^2 = 0$
(d) $x^2 - 3xy - y^2 = 0$

For Sol.

- **For more practice** See Q.8 of Milestone Practice 3.2.

Example 21. Show that the line $y = mx$ bisects the angle between the lines $ax^2 - 2hxy + by^2 = 0$, if $h(1 - m^2) + m(a - b) = 0$.

Sol. Equation of pair of bisectors of angles between lines $ax^2 - 2hxy + by^2 = 0$ is

$$\frac{x^2 - y^2}{a - b} = \frac{xy}{-h} \Rightarrow -h(x^2 - y^2) = (a - b)xy \quad \text{...(i)}$$

But $y = mx$ is one of these lines, then it will satisfy it. Substituting $y = mx$ in Eq. (i),

$$-h(x^2 - m^2x^2) = (a - b)x \cdot mx$$

Dividing by x^2, $h(1 - m^2) + m(a - b) = 0$

Example 22. If pairs of straight lines $x^2 - 2pxy - y^2 = 0$ and $x^2 - 2qxy - y^2 = 0$ be such that each pair bisects the angle between the other pair, then prove that $pq = -1$.

Sol. According to the question, the equation of the bisectors of the angle between the lines

$$x^2 - 2pxy - y^2 = 0 \quad \text{...(i)}$$

and

$$x^2 - 2qxy - y^2 = 0 \quad \text{...(ii)}$$

$\therefore$ The equation of bisectors of the angle between the lines (i) is

$$\frac{x^2 - y^2}{1 - (-1)} = \frac{xy}{-p}$$

$$\Rightarrow -px^2 - 2xy + py^2 = 0 \quad \text{...(iii)}$$

Since, Eqs. (ii) and (iii) are identical, comparing Eqs. (ii) and (iii), we get

$$\frac{1}{-p} = \frac{-2q}{-2} = \frac{-1}{p}$$

Hence, $pq = -1$

Example 23. Prove that the angle between one of the lines given by $ax^2 + 2hxy + by^2 = 0$ and one of the lines $ax^2 + 2hxy + by^2 + \lambda(x^2 + y^2) = 0$ is equal to angle between other two lines of the system.

Sol. The equation of the bisectors of the angle between the lines

$$ax^2 + 2hxy + by^2 = 0 \quad \text{...(i)}$$

is

$$\frac{x^2 - y^2}{a - b} = \frac{xy}{h}$$

and the equation of bisectors of the angle between the lines

$$ax^2 + 2hxy + by^2 + \lambda(x^2 + y^2) = 0 \quad \text{...(ii)}$$

$$\Rightarrow (a + \lambda)x^2 + 2hxy + (b + \lambda)y^2 = 0$$

$$\Rightarrow \frac{x^2 - y^2}{(a + \lambda) - (b + \lambda)} = \frac{xy}{h}$$

$$\Rightarrow \frac{x^2 - y^2}{a - b} = \frac{xy}{h}$$

$\therefore$ Bisectors of angles between lines given by Eqs. (i) and (ii) are the same.

Example 24. Show that the pair of lines given by $a^2x^2 + 2h(a + b)xy + b^2y^2 = 0$ is equally inclined to the pair given by $ax^2 + 2hxy + by^2 = 0$.

Sol. Given pair of lines are

$$a^2x^2 + 2h(a + b)xy + b^2y^2 = 0 \quad \text{...(i)}$$

and

$$ax^2 + 2hxy + by^2 = 0 \quad \text{...(ii)}$$

Equation of bisectors of first pair is

$$\frac{x^2 - y^2}{a^2 - b^2} = \frac{xy}{h(a+b)}$$

$$\Rightarrow \quad \frac{x^2 - y^2}{a - b} = \frac{xy}{h}$$

which are also the bisectors of the second pair.

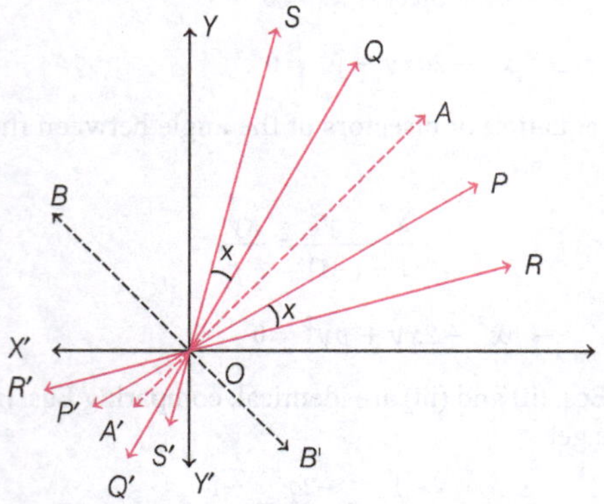

Let $P'OP$, $Q'OQ$, $R'OR$, $S'OS$ be the lines of the Eqs. (i) and (ii) pairs respectively and $A'OA$ and $B'OB$ be their bisectors. We have,

$$\angle ROA = \angle SOA$$

and $\quad \angle POA = \angle QOA$

$$\Rightarrow \quad \angle ROA - \angle POA = \angle SOA - \angle QOA$$

$$\Rightarrow \quad \angle ROP = \angle SOQ$$

Example 25. If the lines represented by $x^2 - 2pxy - y^2 = 0$ are rotated about the origin through an angle θ, one in clockwise direction and the other in anti-clockwise direction, then find the equation of the bisectors of the angle between the lines in the new position.

Sol. Since, lines represented by $x^2 - 2pxy - y^2 = 0$ are perpendicular to each other. The bisectors of the angles between the lines in new position are same as the bisectors of the angles between their old positions. i.e. OC, OD and OA, OB be the old and new pairs respectively and OE and OF be their bisectors, we have

$$\angle COE = \angle DOE$$

and $\quad \angle COA = \angle DOB = \theta$ [given]

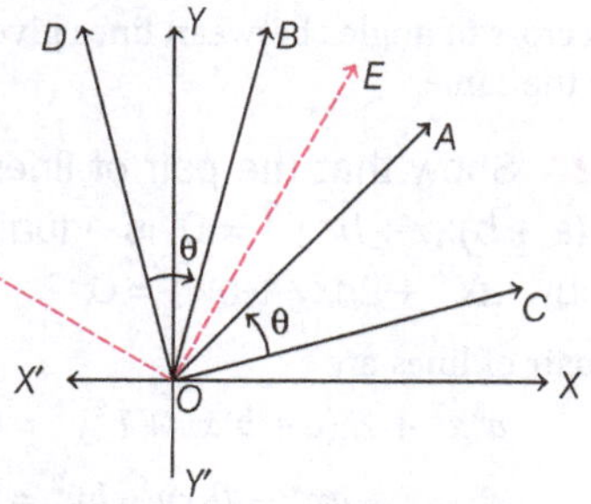

$$\Rightarrow \quad \angle COE - \angle COA = \angle DOE - \angle DOB$$

$$\Rightarrow \quad \angle AOE = \angle BOE$$

Therefore, the required equation is $\dfrac{x^2 - y^2}{1-(-1)} = \dfrac{xy}{-p}$

i.e. $\quad px^2 + 2xy - py^2 = 0.$

JEE SCANNER

Example Similar to PYQ Asked in JEE Main 2023

If the line $l_1 : 2y - 3x = -2$ is the angular bisector of the lines $l_2 : x + y - 1 = -2$ and $l_3 : \alpha x + \beta y + 17 = 0$, then $\beta^2 - \alpha^2$ is equal to ....

Sol. (240) Given, l_1 is angular bisector of l_2 and l_3.

Let angle between l_1 and l_2 be θ.

Then, $\quad \tan\theta = \left|\dfrac{m_1 - m_2}{1 + m_1 m_2}\right|$

Here, $\quad m_1 = \dfrac{3}{2}, m_2 = -1$

$$\therefore \quad \tan\theta = \left|\frac{\frac{3}{2} + 1}{1 + \frac{3}{2}(-1)}\right| = \left|\frac{\frac{5}{2}}{\frac{-1}{2}}\right| = 5$$

$$\therefore \quad \tan\theta = 5 = \left|\frac{m_1 - m_3}{1 + m_1 m_3}\right| \Rightarrow \left|\frac{m - \frac{3}{2}}{1 + \frac{3m}{2}}\right| = 5$$

$$\Rightarrow \quad 5 + \frac{15m}{2} = \pm\left(m - \frac{3}{2}\right)$$

$$\Rightarrow \quad 5 + \frac{15}{2}m = m - \frac{3}{2} \Rightarrow \frac{13}{2}m = -\frac{13}{2}$$

[taking + ve sign]

$\Rightarrow \quad m = -1$ [same as slope of L_2]

and $\quad 5 + \dfrac{15}{2}m = -m + \dfrac{3}{2} \Rightarrow \dfrac{17}{2}m = \dfrac{-7}{2}$

[taking − ve sign]

$$\Rightarrow \quad m = \frac{-7}{17}$$

$\therefore$ Point of intersection l_1 and l_2 is $(0, -1)$

$\Rightarrow \quad l_3$ passes through $(0, -1)$

$$\Rightarrow \quad y + 1 = \frac{-7}{17}x$$

$$\Rightarrow \quad 17y + 17 = -7x$$

$$\therefore \quad \alpha = 7, \beta = 17$$

Hence, $\beta^2 - \alpha^2 = 289 - 49 = 240$

Skill Builder

If the line $l_1 : y - 3x = -1$ is the angular bisector of the lines $l_2 : x + y + 1 = 0$ and $l_3 : \alpha x + \beta y - 7 = 0$, then $\alpha - \beta$ is equal to ......

For Sol.

■ **For more practice** See Q.14 of Milestone Practice 3.2.

Milestone Practice 3.2

1. The angle between the pair of straight lines $y^2\sin^2\theta - xy\sin^2\theta + x^2(\cos^2\theta - 1) = 0$ is

   (a) $\frac{\pi}{4}$ (b) $\frac{\pi}{2}$

   (c) $\frac{\pi}{3}$ (d) $\frac{2\pi}{3}$

2. The angle between the lines given by the equation $ay^2 - (1+\lambda^2)\,xy - ax^2 = 0$ is same as the angle between the lines

   (a) $5x^2 + 2xy - 3y^2 = 0$

   (b) $x^2 - 2xy - 3y^2 = 0$

   (c) $x^2 + y^2 = 100$

   (d) $xy = 0$

3. Which of the following pair of straight lines intersect at right angles ?

   (a) $2x^2 = y(x + 2y)$

   (b) $(x + y)^2 = x(y + 3x)$

   (c) $2y(x + y) = xy$

   (d) $y = \mp 2x$

4. Equation $ax^3 - 9x^2y - xy^2 + 4y^3 = 0$ represents three straight lines. If the two of the lines are perpendicular, then a is/are equal to

   (a) -5 (b) 5

   (c) -4 (d) 4

5. If coordinate axes are the angle bisectors of the pair of lines $ax^2 + 2hxy + by^2 = 0$, then

   (a) $a = b$ (b) $h = 0$

   (c) $a^2 + b = 0$ (d) $a + b^2 = 0$

6. If the line $y = mx$ is one of the angle bisector of the angle between the lines represented by $x^2 + 4xy - y^2 = 0$, then the value of m is/are

   (a) $\frac{\sqrt{5}-1}{2}$ (b) $\frac{\sqrt{5}+1}{2}$

   (c) $-\left(\frac{\sqrt{5}+1}{2}\right)$ (d) $-\left(\frac{\sqrt{5}-1}{2}\right)$

7. If one of the lines of $my^2 + (1 - m^2)\,xy - mx^2 = 0$ is a bisector of the angle between the lines $xy = 0$, then $\cos^{-1}(m)$ is/are

   (a) 0 (b) $\pi/2$

   (c) π (d) $3\pi/2$

8. Let the equation of the pair of lines, $y = \alpha x$ and $y = \beta x$ can be written as $(y - \alpha x)(y - \beta x) = 0$. Then, the equation of the pair of the angle bisectors of the line represented by $3x^2 - 7xy - 5y^2 = 0$ is

   (a) $5x^2 + 16xy - 5y^2 = 0$ (b) $7x^2 + 16xy - 7y^2 = 0$

   (c) $3x^2 + 16xy - 7y^2 = 0$ (d) $7x^2 + 19xy - 7y^2 = 0$

9. Find the angle between the lines whose joint equation is $2x^2 - 3xy + y^2 = 0$.

10. Find the angle between the lines represented by the equation $x^2 - 2pxy + y^2 = 0$.

11. Show that the lines $x^2 - 4xy + y^2 = 0$ and $x + y = 1$ form an equilateral triangle and find its area.

12. Prove that the triangle formed by the lines $ax^2 + 2hxy + by^2 = 0$ and $lx + my = 1$ is isosceles, if $h(l^2 - m^2) = (a - b)\,lm$.

13. If the pairs of straight lines $ax^2 + 2hxy - ay^2 = 0$ and $bx^2 + 2gxy - by^2 = 0$ be such that each bisects the angles between the other, then prove that $hg + ab = 0$.

14. If the line $l_1 : 3y - 5x = -3$ is the angular bisector of the lines $l_2 : x + y + 1 = 0$ and $l_3 : \alpha x + \beta y + 23 = 0$, then find the value of $\beta - \alpha$.

15. Prove that the bisectors of the angle between the lines $ax^2 + acxy + cy^2 = 0$ and $\left(3 + \frac{1}{c}\right)x^2 + xy + \left(3 + \frac{1}{a}\right)y^2 = 0$ are always the same.

16. The lines represented by $x^2 + 2\lambda xy + 2y^2 = 0$ and the lines represented by $(1 + \lambda)x^2 - 8xy + y^2 = 0$ are equally inclined, find the values of λ.

Answer Key

1. (b)
2. (d)
3. (a)
4. (b)
5. (b,c)
6. (a,c)
7. (a, c)
8. (b)
9. $\tan^{-1}\left(\frac{1}{3}\right)$
10. $\tan^{-1}(\sqrt{p^2 - 1})$
11. $\frac{1}{2\sqrt{3}}$ sq units
14. 16
16. (± 2)

For Detailed Solution

Milestone 3 General Equation of Second Degree

- General Equation of Second Degree • Angle Between Lines Represented by $ax^2+2hxy+by^2+2gx+2fy+c=0$
- Point of Intersection of the Lines Represented by $ax^2+2hxy+by^2+2gx+2fy+c=0$
- To Find the Point of Intersection of Lines Represented by $ax^2+2hxy+by^2+2gx+2fy+c=0$ Using Partial Differentiation
- Equation of the Angle Bisector of Pair of Straight Lines $ax^2+2hxy+by^2+2gx+2fy+c=0$
- Equation of the Lines Joining the Origin to the Points of Intersection of a Given Line and a Given Curve

3.6 General Equation of Second Degree

The equation $ax^2+2hxy+by^2+2gx+2fy+c=0$ is the general equation of second degree and represents a conics (pair of straight lines, circle, parabola, ellipse, hyperbola). It contains six constants a, b, c, f, g, h.

i.e. $a=$ coefficient of x^2

$b=$ coefficient of y^2

$c=$ constant term

$g=$ half the coefficient of x

$f=$ half the coefficient of y

and $h=$ half the coefficient of xy.

Condition for the General Equation to Represent a Pair of Straight lines

Theorem The necessary and sufficient condition for $ax^2+2hxy+by^2+2gx+2fy+c=0$ to represent a pair of straight lines is that

$$abc+2fgh-af^2-bg^2-ch^2=0 \text{ or } \begin{vmatrix} a & h & g \\ h & b & f \\ g & f & c \end{vmatrix}=0.$$

Proof Let the equation be

$$ax^2+2hxy+by^2+2gx+2fy+c=0 \qquad \text{...(i)}$$

represent a pair of lines.

Assuming that these lines are not parallel, we suppose that their point of intersection is (x_1, y_1).

Shifting the origin at (x_1, y_1) without rotating the coordinate axes, we have the Eq. (i) transforms to

$$a(X+x_1)^2+2h(X+x_1)(Y+y_1)+b(Y+y_1)^2$$
$$+2g(X+x_1)+2f(Y+y_1)+c=0 \qquad \text{...(ii)}$$

Now, this Eq. (ii) represents a pair of lines through the new origin and consequently, it is homogeneous in X and Y.

Hence, the coefficients of X and Y and the constant term in Eq. (ii) must vanish separately.

i.e. coefficient of $X=$ coefficient of $Y=$ constant term $=0$

$$\Rightarrow \quad ax_1+hy_1+g=0 \qquad \text{...(iii)}$$
$$hx_1+by_1+f=0 \qquad \text{...(iv)}$$
$$\text{and} \quad ax_1^2+2hx_1y_1+by_1^2+2gx_1+2fy_1+c=0 \qquad \text{...(v)}$$

Now, $ax_1^2+2hx_1y_1+by_1^2+2gx_1+2fy_1+c=0$

$$\Rightarrow \quad x_1(ax_1+hy_1+g)+y_1(hx_1+by_1+f)+(gx_1+fy_1+c)=0$$
$$\Rightarrow \quad x_1\cdot 0+y_1\cdot 0+gx_1+fy_1+c=0$$

[from Eqs. (iii) and (iv)]

$$\Rightarrow \quad gx_1+fy_1+c=0 \qquad \text{...(vi)}$$

On eliminating x_1, y_1 from Eqs. (iii), (iv) and (vi), we get the determinant

$$\begin{vmatrix} a & h & g \\ h & b & f \\ g & f & c \end{vmatrix}=0$$

$\therefore$ $abc+2fgh-af^2-bg^2-ch^2=0$ as the required condition.

Alternate proof

Let the lines represented by

$$ax^2 + 2hxy + by^2 + 2gx + 2fy + c = 0 \quad \text{...(i)}$$

be $\quad lx + my + n = 0 \quad$ and $\quad l'x + m'y + n' = 0$

then $\quad ax^2 + 2hxy + by^2 + 2gx + 2fy + c$

$$\equiv (lx + my + n)(l'x + m'y + n') \quad \text{...(ii)}$$

Comparing the coefficients of similar terms in both sides of Eq. (ii), we get

$$\left.\begin{array}{l} ll' = a, mm' = b, nn' = c \\ lm' + l'm = 2h, ln' + l'n = 2g, \\ mn' + m'n = 2f \end{array}\right\} \quad \text{...(iii)}$$

We now eliminate l, m, n, l', m' and n' from these equations,

we have $\quad \begin{vmatrix} l & l' & 0 \\ m & m' & 0 \\ n & n' & 0 \end{vmatrix} \times \begin{vmatrix} l' & l & 0 \\ m' & m & 0 \\ n' & n & 0 \end{vmatrix} = 0$

[$\because$ each determinant $= 0$]

$$\Rightarrow \begin{vmatrix} 2ll' & lm' + l'm & ln' + l'n \\ ml' + m'l & 2mm' & mn' + m'n \\ nl' + n'l & nm' + n'm & 2nn' \end{vmatrix} = 0$$

$$\Rightarrow \begin{vmatrix} 2a & 2h & 2g \\ 2h & 2b & 2f \\ 2g & 2f & 2c \end{vmatrix} = 0$$

$$\Rightarrow \quad \Delta = \begin{vmatrix} a & h & g \\ h & b & f \\ g & f & c \end{vmatrix} = 0$$

$\therefore \quad \Delta = abc + 2fgh - af^2 - bg^2 - ch^2 = 0,$

which is the required necessary condition.

Sufficient condition (Conversely)

Here, we have to show that the equation $ax^2 + 2hxy + by^2 + 2gx + 2fy + c = 0$ represents a pair of straight lines.

$$\begin{vmatrix} a & h & g \\ h & b & f \\ g & f & c \end{vmatrix} = 0$$

i.e. lines $ax + hy + g = 0$, $hx + by + f = 0$, $gx + fy + c = 0$ are concurrent.

Let the point of concurrency be (x_1, y_1).

Then, $\quad ax_1 + hy_1 + g = 0 \quad$ ...(iii)

$\quad hx_1 + by_1 + f = 0 \quad$ ...(iv)

and $\quad gx_1 + fy_1 + c = 0 \quad$ ...(v)

Now, shifting the origin at (x_1, y_1) without rotating the coordinate axes the equation $ax^2 + 2hxy + by^2 + 2gx + 2fy + c = 0$ reduces to

$$a(X + x_1)^2 + 2h(X + x_1)(Y + y_1) + b(Y + y_1)^2 + 2g(X + x_1) + 2f(Y + y_1) + c = 0$$

$$\Rightarrow aX^2 + 2hXY + bY^2 + 2X(ax_1 + hy_1 + g) + 2Y(hx_1 + by_1 + f) + x_1(ax_1 + hy_1 + g) + y_1(hx_1 + by_1 + f) + (gx_1 + fy_1 + c) = 0$$

$$\Rightarrow \quad aX^2 + 2hXY + bY^2 + 0 + 0 + 0 + 0 + 0 = 0$$

[from Eqs. (iii), (iv) and (v)]

i.e. $\quad aX^2 + 2hXY + bY^2 = 0$

It is homogeneous equation of second degree. So, it represents a pair of straight lines through the new origin. Hence, the equation $ax^2 + 2hxy + by^2 + 2gx + 2fy + c = 0$ represents a pair of straight lines, if

$$abc + 2fgh - af^2 - bg^2 - ch^2 = 0.$$

JEE Focus Points

- If the lines given by $ax^2 + 2hxy + by^2 + 2gx + 2fy + c = 0$ are parallel, then in this case necessary condition that represents two straight lines is $abc + 2fgh - af^2 - bg^2 - ch^2 = 0$ can be obtained by without using determinant.

  Concept Inside Video

  Now, $(lm' + l'm)(ln' + l'n)(mn' + m'n) = 2h \cdot 2g \cdot 2f$

  $\Rightarrow \quad 2ll'mm'nn' + ll'(m^2n'^2 + m'^2n^2) + mm'(n^2l'^2 + n'^2l^2) + nn'(l^2m'^2 + l'^2m^2) = 8fgh$

  $\Rightarrow \quad 2ll'mm'nn' + ll'\{(mn' + m'n)^2 - 2mm'nn'\} + mm'\{(nl' + n'l)^2 - 2nn'll'\} + nn'\{(lm' + l'm)^2 - 2ll'mm'\} = 8fgh$ [from Eq. (iii)]

  $\Rightarrow \quad 2abc + a(4f^2 - 2bc) + b(4g^2 - 2ca) + c(4h^2 - 2ab) = 8fgh$

  $\therefore \quad abc + 2fgh - af^2 - bg^2 - ch^2 = 0,$

  which is the required necessary condition.

- If equation $ax^2 + 2hxy + by^2 + 2gx + 2fy + c = 0$ represents two lines $y = m_1x + c_1$ and $y = m_2x + c_2$, then

  $$b(y - m_1x - c_1)(y - m_2x - c_2) = 0$$

  i.e. $b(m_1m_2x^2 - (m_1 + m_2)xy + y^2 + (m_1c_2 + m_2c_1)x - (c_1 + c_2)y + c_1c_2) = 0$

  On equating coefficients, we get

  $$m_1 + m_2 = -\frac{2h}{b}, m_1m_2 = \frac{a}{b}, m_1c_2 + m_2c_1 = \frac{2g}{b},$$

  $$c_1 + c_2 = -\frac{2f}{b} \text{ and } c_1c_2 = \frac{c}{b}$$

- The product of perpendiculars drawn from (x_1, y_1) to the pair of lines given by $ax^2 + 2hxy + by^2 + 2gx + 2fy + c = 0$ is

  $$\left|\frac{ax_1^2 + 2hx_1y_1 + by_1^2 + 2gx_1 + 2fy_1 + c}{\sqrt{(a - b)^2 + 4b^2}}\right|$$

Example 26. Show that the equation $3x^2+7xy+2y^2+5x+5y+2=0$ represents a pair of straight lines.

Sol. We have, $3x^2+7xy+2y^2+5x+5y+2=0$

On comparing with general equation, we get

$$a=3, h=\frac{7}{2}, b=2, g=\frac{5}{2}, f=\frac{5}{2} \text{ and } c=2$$

Now, $abc+2fgh-af^2-bg^2-ch^2$

$$=12+2\times\frac{5}{2}\times\frac{5}{2}\times\frac{7}{2}-3\left(\frac{5}{2}\right)^2-2\left(\frac{5}{2}\right)^2-2\left(\frac{7}{2}\right)^2=0$$

Hence, the given equation represents a pair of straight lines.

Example 27. Find the value of λ, if $2x^2+7xy+3y^2+8x+14y+\lambda=0$

Sol. We have, $2x^2+7xy+3y^2+8x+14y+\lambda=0$

On comparing with general equation, we get

$$a=2, h=\frac{7}{2}, b=3, g=4, f=7 \text{ and } c=\lambda$$

Now, $\quad abc+2fgh-af^2-bg^2-ch^2=0$

$$\Rightarrow 6\lambda+2(7)(4)\left(\frac{7}{2}\right)-2(7)^2-3(4)^2-\lambda\left(\frac{7}{2}\right)^2=0$$

$$\Rightarrow 6\lambda+196-98-48-\frac{49\lambda}{4}=0$$

$$\Rightarrow \frac{25\lambda}{4}=50 \Rightarrow \lambda=8$$

3.7 Angle Between Lines Represented by $ax^2+2hxy+by^2+2gx+2fy+c=0$

The angle between the lines represented by

$$ax^2+2hxy+by^2+2gx+2fy+c=0$$

is given by $\theta=\tan^{-1}\left\{\dfrac{2\sqrt{(h^2-ab)}}{|a+b|}\right\}$.

Proof Let $y=m_1x+c_1$ and $y=m_2x+c_2$ be the lines represented by

$$ax^2+2hxy+by^2+2gx+2fy+c=0,$$

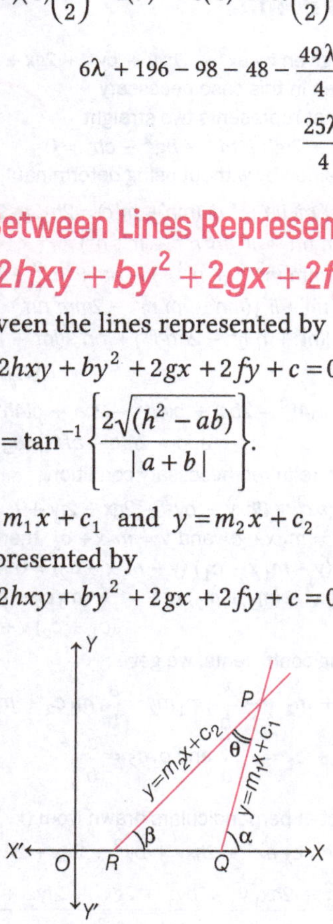

where $m_1=\tan\alpha$ and $m_2=\tan\beta$

Then, $ax^2+2hxy+by^2+2gx+2fy+c$

$$\equiv(y-m_1x-c_1)(y-m_2x-c_2)$$

On comparing coefficients of like powers, we obtain

$$m_1+m_2=-\frac{2h}{b} \text{ and } m_1m_2=\frac{a}{b}$$

Now, if θ be the acute angle between the lines $y=m_1x+c_1$ and $y=m_2x+c_2$, then

$$\tan\theta=\left|\frac{m_1-m_2}{1+m_1m_2}\right|=\frac{\sqrt{(m_1+m_2)^2-4m_1m_2}}{|1+m_1m_2|}$$

$$=\frac{\sqrt{\left(-\frac{2h}{b}\right)^2-4\left(\frac{a}{b}\right)}}{\left|1+\frac{a}{b}\right|}=\frac{2\sqrt{(h^2-ab)}}{|a+b|}$$

$$\therefore \quad \theta=\tan^{-1}\left\{\frac{2\sqrt{(h^2-ab)}}{|a+b|}\right\}$$

Theorem The lines represented by $ax^2+2hxy+by^2+2gx+2fy+c=0$ will be coincident, if $h^2-ab=0$, $g^2-ac=0$ and $f^2-bc=0$.

Proof Let the lines represented by

$$ax^2+2hxy+by^2+2gx+2fy+c=0$$

be $\quad lx+my+n=0$ and $l'x+m'y+n'=0$

then $\quad ax^2+2hxy+by^2+2gx+2fy+c$

$$\equiv(lx+my+n)(l'x+m'y+n')$$

On comparing the coefficients of similar terms in both sides, we get

$$\left.\begin{array}{l} ll'=a, mm'=b, nn'=c \\ lm'+l'm=2h, ln'+l'n=2g \\ mn'+m'n=2f \end{array}\right]$$

$\because$ Lines $lx+my+n=0$ and $l'x+m'y+n'=0$ are coincident.

Then, $\quad \dfrac{l}{l'}=\dfrac{m}{m'}=\dfrac{n}{n'}$.

On taking the ratios in pairs, then

$$lm'-l'm=0, mn'-m'n=0 \text{ and } ln'-l'n=0$$

$$\Rightarrow \sqrt{(lm'+l'm)^2-4ll'mm'}=0,$$

$$\sqrt{(mn'+m'n)^2-4mm'nn'}=0$$

and $\quad \sqrt{(ln'+l'n)^2-4ll'nn'}=0$

$$\Rightarrow \sqrt{(4h^2-4ab)}=0, \sqrt{(4f^2-4bc)}=0$$

and $\quad \sqrt{(4g^2-4ac)}=0$

i.e. $\quad h^2-ab=0, f^2-bc=0, g^2-ac=0$

JEE Focus Points

Concept Inside Video

- The angle between the lines represented by $ax^2 + 2hxy + by^2 + 2gx + 2fy + c = 0$ is same as the angle between the lines represented by $ax^2 + 2hxy + by^2 = 0$.
- The lines represented by $$ax^2 + 2hxy + by^2 + 2gx + 2fy + c = 0$$ are perpendicular iff $a + b = 0$ and parallel iff $h^2 = ab$.
- If the equation $ax^2 + 2hxy + by^2 + 2gx + 2fy + c = 0$ represents a pair of parallel lines, then the distance between them is $2\sqrt{\dfrac{(g^2 - ac)}{a(a+b)}}$.
- If $ax^2 + 2hxy + by^2 + 2gx + 2fy + c = 0$ represents two straight lines, then the equation of lines through the origin and parallel to them is $ax^2 + 2hxy + by^2 = 0$.

Example 28. For what value of λ does the equation $12x^2 - 10xy + 2y^2 + 11x - 5y + \lambda = 0$ represent a pair of straight lines? Find their equations and the angle between them.

Sol. On comparing the given equation with the equation $ax^2 + 2hxy + by^2 + 2gx + 2fy + c = 0$, we get

$$a = 12, h = -5, b = 2, g = \frac{11}{2}, f = -\frac{5}{2} \text{ and } c = \lambda$$

If the given equation represents a pair of straight lines, then

$$abc + 2fgh - af^2 - bg^2 - ch^2 = 0$$

$$\Rightarrow \quad 12 \times 2 \times \lambda + 2 \times \left(-\frac{5}{2}\right) \times \frac{11}{2} \times (-5) - 12 \times \frac{25}{4} - 2 \times \frac{121}{4} - \lambda \times 25 = 0$$

$$\therefore \quad \lambda = 2 \text{ and } h^2 - ab = 25 - 24 = 1 > 0$$

$\therefore$ The given equation will represent a pair of straight lines, if $\lambda = 2$.

To find the two lines

On substituting $\lambda = 2$ in the given equation, we get

$$12x^2 - 10xy + 2y^2 + 11x - 5y + 2 = 0 \quad \text{...(i)}$$

Since, $\quad 12x^2 - 10xy + 2y^2 = 2(3x - y)(2x - y)$

Factors of Eq. (i) can be taken as

$$2(3x - y + l)(2x - y + m)$$
$$= 12x^2 - 10xy + 2y^2 + 2(2l + 3m)x + 2(-l - m)y + 2lm$$

On comparing, $2l + 3m = \dfrac{11}{2}, l + m = \dfrac{5}{2}, lm = 1$

On solving, we get $l = 2, m = \dfrac{1}{2}$.

Thus, the factors of Eq. (i) are

$$2(3x - y + 2)\left(2x - y + \frac{1}{2}\right) = 0$$

or $\quad (3x - y + 2)(4x - 2y + 1) = 0.$

$\therefore$ The two straight lines represented by the given equation are $3x - y + 2 = 0$ and $4x - 2y + 1 = 0$.

To find the angle between the lines

If θ is the angle between the lines, then

$$\tan\theta = \frac{2\sqrt{h^2 - ab}}{|a + b|} = \frac{2\sqrt{25 - 24}}{|12 + 2|} = \frac{1}{7} \Rightarrow \theta = \tan^{-1}\left(\frac{1}{7}\right)$$

Example 29. Prove that the equation $8x^2 + 8xy + 2y^2 + 26x + 13y + 15 = 0$ represents a pair of parallel straight lines. Also, find the perpendicular distance between them.

Sol. Given equation is

$$8x^2 + 8xy + 2y^2 + 26x + 13y + 15 = 0 \quad \text{...(i)}$$

Writing Eq. (i) as quadratic equation in x, we get

$$8x^2 + 2x(4y + 13) + 2y^2 + 13y + 15 = 0$$

$$\therefore \quad x = \frac{-2(4y + 13) \pm \sqrt{4(4y + 13)^2 - 32(2y^2 + 13y + 15)}}{16}$$

$$\Rightarrow \quad x = \frac{-(4y + 13) \pm \sqrt{(4y + 13)^2 - 8(2y^2 + 13y + 15)}}{8}$$

$$\Rightarrow \quad x = \frac{-(4y + 13) \pm 7}{8}$$

$\Rightarrow \quad 8x = -4y - 13 + 7$, i.e. $4x + 2y + 3 = 0$

and $\quad 8x = -4y - 13 - 7$, i.e. $2x + y + 5 = 0$

i.e. the given Eq. (i) represents two straight lines

$$2x + y + 5 = 0 \text{ and } 4x + 2y + 3 = 0$$

i.e. $\quad 2x + y + \dfrac{3}{2} = 0$

Hence, both lines are parallel.

Also, comparing Eq. (i) with general equation, we get

$$a = 8, h = 4, b = 2, g = 13, f = \frac{13}{2} \text{ and } c = 15$$

$\therefore$ Distance between them

$$= 2\sqrt{\frac{g^2 - ac}{a(a+b)}} = 2\sqrt{\frac{169 - 120}{8 \times 10}} = \frac{7}{2\sqrt{5}}$$

Alternate Solution

Here, $\Delta = 8 \times 2 \times 15 + 2 \times \dfrac{13}{2} \times 13 \times 4 - 8 \times \left(\dfrac{13}{2}\right)^2 - 2 \times (13)^2 - 15 \times (4)^2 = 0$

and $\quad h^2 = (4)^2 = 16 = 8 \times 2 = ab$

$\therefore$ Given equation $8x^2 + 8xy + 2y^2 + 26x + 13y + 15 = 0 \quad \text{...(i)}$

represents two parallel straight lines.

Since, $\quad 8x^2 + 8xy + 2y^2 = 2(2x + y)^2$

Factors of Eq. (i) can be taken as

$$2(2x + y + l)(2x + y + m)$$
$$= 8x^2 + 8xy + 2y^2 + 2(2m + 2l)x + 2(m + l)y + 2lm$$

On comparing, we get $l + m = \dfrac{13}{2}$ and $lm = \dfrac{15}{2}$

$\therefore$ Distance between them

$$= \frac{|l - m|}{\sqrt{(2^2 + 1^2)}} = \frac{\sqrt{(l + m)^2 - 4lm}}{\sqrt{5}} = \frac{\sqrt{\dfrac{169}{4} - \dfrac{60}{2}}}{\sqrt{5}} = \frac{7}{2\sqrt{5}}$$

Example 30. Find the combined equation of the straight lines passing through the point (1, 1) and parallel to the lines represented by the equation $x^2 - 5xy + 4y^2 + x + 2y - 2 = 0$.

Sol. Given equation of lines is

$$x^2 - 5xy + 4y^2 + x + 2y - 2 = 0. \quad \text{...(i)}$$

Since, $x^2 - 5xy + 4y^2 = (x - 4y)(x - y)$

Factors of Eq. (i) can be taken as $(x - 4y + l)(x - y + m)$.

Now, equation of line through (1, 1) and parallel to $x - 4y + l = 0$ is

$$x - 4y + \lambda = 0 \text{ i.e. } 1 - 4 + \lambda = 0$$

$$\therefore \quad \lambda = 3$$

Then, line is $x - 4y + 3 = 0$ ...(ii)

and equation of line through (1, 1) and parallel to $x - y + m = 0$ is

$$x - y + \mu = 0 \text{ i.e. } 1 - 1 + \mu = 0$$

$$\therefore \quad \mu = 0$$

Then, line is $\quad x - y = 0$ ...(iii)

Hence, from Eqs. (ii) and (iii), the combined equation of lines is

$$(x - 4y + 3)(x - y) = 0$$

i.e. $$x^2 - 5xy + 4y^2 + 3x - 3y = 0$$

3.8 Point of Intersection of the lines Represented by $ax^2 + 2hxy + by^2 + 2gx + 2fy + c = 0$

The point of intersection of the lines represented by $ax^2 + 2hxy + by^2 + 2gx + 2fy + c = 0$ is

$$\left(\sqrt{\left(\frac{f^2 - bc}{h^2 - ab}\right)}, \sqrt{\left(\frac{g^2 - ca}{h^2 - ab}\right)}\right) \text{ or } \left(\frac{bg - hf}{h^2 - ab}, \frac{af - gh}{h^2 - ab}\right).$$

Proof Let the lines represented by

$$ax^2 + 2hxy + by^2 + 2gx + 2fy + c = 0$$

be $\quad lx + my + n = 0 \quad$ and $\quad l'x + m'y + n' = 0$

Then, $ax^2 + 2hxy + by^2 + 2gx + 2fy + c$

$$\equiv (lx + my + n)(l'x + m'y + n')$$

Comparing the coefficients of similar terms in both sides, then

$$ll' = a, mm' = b, nn' = c$$

$$lm' + l'm = 2h, ln' + l'n = 2g \text{ and } mn' + m'n = 2f$$

$$\Rightarrow \quad (lm' - l'm) = \sqrt{(lm' + l'm)^2 - 4ll'mm'} = 2\sqrt{(h^2 - ab)}$$

$$\Rightarrow \quad (nl' - n'l) = \sqrt{(ln' + l'n)^2 - 4ll'nn'} = 2\sqrt{(g^2 - ac)}$$

and $$(mn' - m'n) = \sqrt{(mn' + m'n)^2 - 4mm'nn'} = 2\sqrt{(f^2 - bc)}$$

Now, solving $lx + my + n = 0$ and $l'x + m'y + n' = 0$,

then $$\frac{x}{(mn' - m'n)} = \frac{y}{(nl' - n'l)} = \frac{1}{(lm' - l'm)}$$

$$\Rightarrow \quad \frac{x}{2\sqrt{(f^2 - bc)}} = \frac{y}{2\sqrt{(g^2 - ac)}} = \frac{1}{2\sqrt{(h^2 - ab)}}$$

$$\therefore \quad (x, y) = \left(\sqrt{\left(\frac{f^2 - bc}{h^2 - ab}\right)}, \sqrt{\left(\frac{g^2 - ac}{h^2 - ab}\right)}\right)$$

Also, $$x = \sqrt{\left(\frac{f^2 - bc}{h^2 - ab}\right)} = \frac{\sqrt{(f^2 - bc)(h^2 - ab)}}{(h^2 - ab)}$$

$$= \frac{\sqrt{f^2h^2 - abf^2 - bch^2 + b(abc)}}{(h^2 - ab)}$$

$$= \frac{\sqrt{f^2h^2 - abf^2 - bch^2 + b(af^2 + bg^2 + ch^2 - 2fgh)}}{(h^2 - ab)}$$

$$[\because abc + 2fgh - af^2 - bg^2 - ch^2 = 0]$$

$$= \frac{\sqrt{(f^2h^2 + b^2g^2 - 2bfgh)}}{(h^2 - ab)} = \frac{\sqrt{(bg - hf)^2}}{(h^2 - ab)}$$

$$= \left(\frac{bg - hf}{h^2 - ab}\right)$$

Similarly, $$y = \left(\frac{af - gh}{h^2 - ab}\right)$$

Hence, $$(x, y) = \left(\frac{bg - hf}{h^2 - ab}, \frac{af - gh}{h^2 - ab}\right).$$

Alternate Method (for first point)

$$\Delta = \begin{vmatrix} a & h & g \\ h & b & f \\ g & f & c \end{vmatrix}$$

Cofactors of leading diagonal are C_{11}, C_{22}, C_{33}

$$\because \quad C_{11} = \begin{vmatrix} b & f \\ f & c \end{vmatrix} = bc - f^2, \; C_{22} = \begin{vmatrix} a & g \\ g & c \end{vmatrix} = ac - g^2$$

and $$C_{33} = \begin{vmatrix} a & h \\ h & b \end{vmatrix} = ab - h^2$$

$\therefore$ Point of intersection are $\left(\sqrt{\dfrac{C_{11}}{C_{33}}}, \sqrt{\dfrac{C_{22}}{C_{33}}}\right)$

i.e. $$\left(\sqrt{\left(\frac{bc - f^2}{ab - h^2}\right)}, \sqrt{\left(\frac{ac - g^2}{ab - h^2}\right)}\right)$$

or $$\left(\sqrt{\left(\frac{f^2 - bc}{h^2 - ab}\right)}, \sqrt{\left(\frac{g^2 - ac}{h^2 - ab}\right)}\right)$$

Alternate Method (For second point)

Since, $\Delta = \begin{vmatrix} a & h & g \\ h & b & f \\ g & f & c \end{vmatrix}$

Taking first two rows (repeat first column)

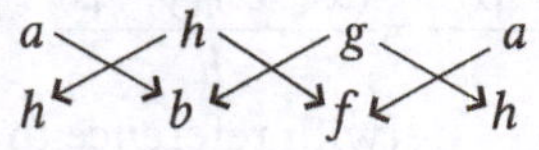

$\Rightarrow \quad ab - h^2, hf - bg, gh - af$

$\Rightarrow \quad h^2 - ab, bg - hf, af - gh$

$\Rightarrow \quad 1, \dfrac{bg - hf}{h^2 - ab}, \dfrac{af - gh}{h^2 - ab}$

Hence, point of intersection is $\left(\dfrac{bg - hf}{h^2 - ab}, \dfrac{af - gh}{h^2 - ab}\right)$.

Or

Cofactors of third column are C_{13}, C_{23}, C_{33}

$\because \quad C_{13} = \begin{vmatrix} h & b \\ g & f \end{vmatrix} = hf - bg,$

$C_{23} = -\begin{vmatrix} a & h \\ g & f \end{vmatrix} = hg - af$

and $\quad C_{33} = \begin{vmatrix} a & h \\ h & b \end{vmatrix} = ab - h^2$

$\therefore$ Point of intersection is $\left(\dfrac{C_{13}}{C_{33}}, \dfrac{C_{23}}{C_{33}}\right)$

i.e. $\quad \left(\dfrac{hf - bg}{ab - h^2}, \dfrac{hg - af}{ab - h^2}\right)$ or $\left(\dfrac{bg - hf}{h^2 - ab}, \dfrac{af - hg}{h^2 - ab}\right)$.

Example 31. Find the point of intersection of pair of straight lines $x^2 - xy + 2y^2 - y - 5x - 6 = 0$.

Sol. We have, $x^2 - xy + 2y^2 - y - 5x - 6 = 0$

On comparing with general equation, we get

$$a = 1, h = -\frac{1}{2}, b = 2, g = -\frac{5}{2}, f = -\frac{1}{2} \text{ and } c = -6$$

$\therefore$ Point of intersection is given by

$$x = \frac{bg - hf}{h^2 - ab} = \frac{2 \times \left(-\frac{5}{2}\right) - \left(-\frac{1}{2}\right)\left(-\frac{1}{2}\right)}{\left(-\frac{1}{2}\right)^2 - 1 \times 2}$$

$$= \frac{-5 - \frac{1}{4}}{\frac{1}{4} - 2} = \frac{-21}{-7} = 3$$

and $$y = \frac{af - gh}{h^2 - ab} = \frac{1 \times \left(\frac{-1}{2}\right) - \left(\frac{-5}{2}\right)\left(\frac{-1}{2}\right)}{\left(\frac{-1}{2}\right)^2 - 1 \times 2}$$

$$= \frac{-\frac{1}{2} - \frac{5}{4}}{\frac{1}{4} - 2} = \frac{-7}{-7} = 1$$

$\therefore$ Point of intersection is (3, 1).

3.9 To Find the Point of Intersection of Lines Represented by $ax^2 + 2hxy + by^2 + 2gx + 2fy + c = 0$ Using Partial Differentiation

Let $\phi(x, y) \equiv ax^2 + 2hxy + by^2 + 2gx + 2fy + c = 0$

$\therefore \quad \dfrac{\partial \phi}{\partial x} = 2ax + 2hy + 2g \qquad$ [treating y as constant]

and $\quad \dfrac{\partial \phi}{\partial y} = 2hx + 2by + 2f \qquad$ [treating x as constant]

For point of intersection $\dfrac{\partial \phi}{\partial x} = 0$ and $\dfrac{\partial \phi}{\partial y} = 0$, we obtain

$$ax + hy + g = 0$$

and $$hx + by + f = 0$$

On solving them,

$$\frac{x}{fh - bg} = \frac{y}{gh - af} = \frac{1}{ab - h^2}$$

$$(x, y) = \left(\frac{bg - fh}{h^2 - ab}, \frac{af - gh}{h^2 - ab}\right)$$

Alternate Method (without use of partial derivatives)

Since, $\Delta = \begin{vmatrix} a & h & g \\ h & b & f \\ g & f & c \end{vmatrix}$

from first two rows

$a \quad h \quad g \quad \Rightarrow \quad ax + hy + g = 0$

and $\quad h \quad b \quad f \quad \Rightarrow \quad hx + by + f = 0$

and then solve.

Example 32. Find the point of intersection of lines represented by $2x^2 - 7xy - 4y^2 - x + 22y - 10 = 0$.

Sol. Let $\quad \phi \equiv 2x^2 - 7xy - 4y^2 - x + 22y - 10 = 0$

$\therefore \quad \dfrac{\partial \phi}{\partial x} \equiv 4x - 7y - 1 = 0 \qquad$ ...(i)

and $\quad \dfrac{\partial \phi}{\partial y} \equiv -7x - 8y + 22 = 0 \qquad$ ...(ii)

On solving Eqs. (i) and (ii), we get $x = 2$ and $y = 1$
Then, the point of intersection is $(x, y) = (2, 1)$.

Alternate Solution

Given, $2x^2 - 7xy - 4y^2 - x + 22y - 10 = 0$

On comparing with general equation, we get

$$a = 2, h = -\frac{7}{2}, b = -4, g = -\frac{1}{2}, f = 11 \text{ and } c = -10$$

$\therefore$ Point of intersection is given by

$$x = \frac{bg - hf}{h^2 - ab} = \frac{(-4)\left(\frac{-1}{2}\right) - \left(\frac{-7}{2}\right)(11)}{\left(\frac{-7}{2}\right)^2 - (2)(-4)} = \frac{\frac{81}{2}}{\frac{81}{4}} = 2$$

and $$y = \frac{af - gh}{h^2 - ab} = \frac{2 \times 11 - \left(\frac{-1}{2}\right)\left(\frac{-7}{2}\right)}{\left(\frac{-7}{2}\right)^2 - (2)(-4)} = \frac{\frac{81}{4}}{\frac{81}{4}} = 1$$

$\therefore$ Point of intersection is (2, 1).

3.10 Equation of the Angle Bisectors of Pair of Straight lines $ax^2 + 2hxy + by^2 + 2gx + 2fy + c = 0$

The pair of bisectors of the lines represented by

$$ax^2 + 2hxy + by^2 + 2gx + 2fy + c = 0,$$

is $$\frac{(x - \alpha)^2 - (y - \beta)^2}{(a - b)} = \frac{(x - \alpha)(y - \beta)}{h}$$

where (α, β) be the point of intersection of the pair of straight lines represented by Eq. (i).

Proof Since, (α, β) be the point of intersection of the lines represented by $ax^2 + 2hxy + by^2 + 2gx + 2fy + c = 0$ ...(i)

Shifting the origin at (α, β) without rotating the coordinate axes, then Eq. (i) reduces to

$$a(X + \alpha)^2 + 2h(X + \alpha)(Y + \beta) + b(Y + \beta)^2 + 2g(X + \alpha) + 2f(Y + \beta) + c = 0$$

$[\because x = X + \alpha \text{ and } y = Y + \beta]$

$$\Rightarrow (aX^2 + 2hXY + bY^2) + 2X(a\alpha + h\beta + g) + 2Y(h\alpha + b\beta + f) + a\alpha^2 + 2h\alpha\beta + b\beta^2 + 2g\alpha + 2f\beta + c = 0 \quad \text{...(ii)}$$

This equation represents a pair of straight lines passing through the new origin. So, it must be homogeneous equation of second degree in X and Y.

$$\therefore \quad a\alpha + h\beta + g = 0, \quad \text{...(iii)}$$

$$h\alpha + b\beta + f = 0 \quad \text{....(iv)}$$

and $$a\alpha^2 + 2h\alpha\beta + b\beta^2 + 2g\alpha + 2f\beta + c = 0 \quad \text{...(v)}$$

Now, from Eq. (ii), $$aX^2 + 2hXY + bY^2 = 0 \quad \text{...(vi)}$$

The equation of the bisectors of the angles between the lines given by Eq. (vi) is $$\frac{X^2 - Y^2}{a - b} = \frac{XY}{h} \quad \text{...(vii)}$$

[with reference to new origin]

Replacing X by $x - \alpha$ and Y by $y - \beta$ in Eq. (vii), then

$$\frac{(x - \alpha)^2 - (y - \beta)^2}{(a - b)} = \frac{(x - \alpha)(y - \beta)}{h}$$

[with reference to old origin]

which is the required equation of the bisectors of the angles between the lines given by Eq. (i).

Example 33. If $ax^2 + 2hxy + by^2 + 2gx + 2fy + c = 0$ represents a pair of lines, prove that the area of the triangle formed by their bisectors and axis of X is $\frac{\sqrt{(a - b)^2 + 4h^2}}{|2h|} \left| \frac{ca - g^2}{ab - h^2} \right|$.

Sol. Given, $ax^2 + 2hxy + by^2 + 2gx + 2fy + c = 0$ ...(i)

The points of intersections of the lines given by Eq. (i) are

$$\alpha = \sqrt{\left(\frac{f^2 - bc}{h^2 - ab}\right)}, \beta = \sqrt{\left(\frac{g^2 - ca}{h^2 - ab}\right)}$$

Hence, equation of the bisectors of the lines given by Eq. (i) is

$$\frac{(x - \alpha)^2 - (y - \beta)^2}{a - b} = \frac{(x - \alpha)(y - \beta)}{h}$$

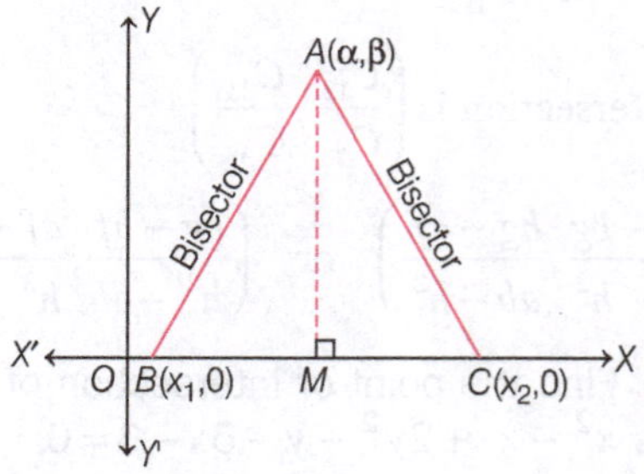

For X-axis, $y = 0$,

$$\therefore \quad \frac{(x - \alpha)^2 - \beta^2}{a - b} = \frac{-\beta(x - \alpha)}{h}$$

or $$h(x - \alpha)^2 + \beta(x - \alpha)(a - b) - h\beta^2 = 0 \quad \text{...(ii)}$$

Eq. (ii) is a quadratic in $(x - \alpha)$ and let two values of x be x_1 and x_2, so that its roots are $x_1 - \alpha$ and $x_2 - \alpha$.

$$\therefore \quad (x_1 - \alpha) + (x_2 - \alpha) = \text{Sum of roots} = \frac{-\beta(a - b)}{h}$$

$$(x_1 - \alpha)(x_2 - \alpha) = \text{Products of roots} = -\beta^2$$

$$\therefore \quad |x_2 - x_1| = |(x_2 - \alpha) - (x_1 - \alpha)|$$

$$= \sqrt{[(x_2 - \alpha) + (x_1 - \alpha)]^2 - 4(x_2 - \alpha)(x_1 - \alpha)}$$

$$\therefore\ |x_2 - x_1| = \sqrt{\left\{\frac{\beta^2 (a-b)^2}{h^2} + 4\beta^2\right\}}$$

$$= \left|\frac{\beta}{h}\right| \sqrt{(a-b)^2 + 4h^2}$$

$$\therefore \text{ Area of } \Delta ABC = \frac{1}{2}|BC||AM|$$

$$= \frac{1}{2}|x_2 - x_1||\beta|$$

$$= \frac{1}{2}\left|\frac{\beta}{h}\right|\sqrt{(a-b)^2 + 4h^2} \times |\beta|$$

$$= \frac{\sqrt{(a-b)^2 + 4h^2}}{|2h|} . \beta^2$$

$$= \frac{\sqrt{(a-b)^2 + 4h^2}}{|2h|} . \left|\frac{ca - g^2}{ab - h^2}\right|$$

3.11 Equation of the Lines Joining the Origin to the Points of Intersection of a Given Line and a Given Curve

Theorem The combined equation of the straight lines joining the origin to the points of intersection of a second degree curve $ax^2 + 2hxy + by^2 + 2gx + 2fy + c = 0$ and a straight line $lx + my + n = 0$ is

$$ax^2 + 2hxy + by^2 + 2gx\left(\frac{lx + my}{-n}\right) + 2fy\left(\frac{lx + my}{-n}\right) + c\left(\frac{lx + my}{-n}\right)^2 = 0$$

Proof The equation of the curve (PAQ) is

$$ax^2 + 2hxy + by^2 + 2gx + 2fy + c = 0 \quad \text{...(i)}$$

and the equation of the line PQ be

$$lx + my + n = 0 \quad \text{...(ii)}$$

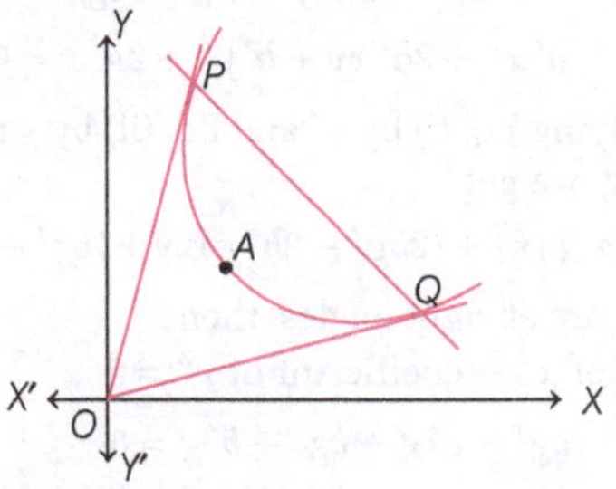

From the equation of the line Eq. (ii), the value of 1 in terms of x and y,

i.e. $$\frac{lx + my}{-n} = 1 \quad \text{...(iii)}$$

Now, the Eq. (i) can be written as

or $$ax^2 + 2hxy + by^2 + (2gx + 2fy)(1) + c(1)^2 = 0$$

or $$ax^2 + 2hxy + by^2 + (2gx + 2fy)\left(\frac{lx + my}{-n}\right) + c\left(\frac{lx + my}{-n}\right)^2 = 0 \quad \text{...(iv)}$$

[replacing 1 by $\frac{lx + my}{-n}$ from Eq. (iii)]

Hence, the Eq. (iv) is homogeneous equation of second degree.

Above Eq. (iv) on simplification will be of the form $Ax^2 + 2Hxy + By^2 = 0$ and will represent the required straight lines.

If θ be the angle between them, then

$$\theta = \tan^{-1}\left(\frac{2\sqrt{(H^2 - AB)}}{|A + B|}\right)$$

Hence, the equation of pairs of straight lines passing through the origin and the points of intersection of a curve and a line is obtained by making the curve homogeneous with the help of the line.

Example 34. Prove that the angle between the lines joining the origin to the points of intersection of the straight line $y = 3x + 2$ with the curve $x^2 + 2xy + 3y^2 + 4x + 8y - 11 = 0$ is $\tan^{-1}\left(\frac{2\sqrt{2}}{3}\right)$.

Sol. Equation of curve is $x^2 + 2xy + 3y^2 + 4x + 8y - 11 = 0$ ...(i)

and line $\quad y = 3x + 2 \Rightarrow \frac{y - 3x}{2} = 1$ ...(ii)

Making Eq. (i) homogeneous with the help of Eq. (ii), then

$$x^2 + 2xy + 3y^2 + 4x\left(\frac{y - 3x}{2}\right) + 8y\left(\frac{y - 3x}{2}\right) - 11\left(\frac{y - 3x}{2}\right)^2 = 0$$

$$\Rightarrow x^2 + 2xy + 3y^2 + 2xy - 6x^2 + 4y^2 - 12xy - \frac{11}{4}(y - 3x)^2 = 0$$

$$\Rightarrow \quad -5x^2 - 8xy + 7y^2 - \frac{11}{4}(y^2 - 6xy + 9x^2) = 0$$

$$\Rightarrow -20x^2 - 32xy + 28y^2 - 11y^2 + 66xy - 99x^2 = 0$$

$$\Rightarrow \quad 119x^2 - 34xy - 17y^2 = 0$$

$$\Rightarrow \quad 7x^2 - 2xy - y^2 = 0 \quad \text{...(iii)}$$

This is the equation of lines joining the origin to the points of intersection of Eqs. (i) and (ii).

On comparing Eq. (iii) with $ax^2 + 2hxy + by^2 = 0$, we get

$$a = 7, h = -1 \text{ and } b = -1$$

If θ is the acute angle between pair of lines of Eq. (iii), then

$$\tan\theta = \frac{2\sqrt{h^2 - ab}}{|a+b|} = \frac{2\sqrt{(1+7)}}{|7-1|}$$

$$= \frac{2\sqrt{8}}{6} = \frac{4\sqrt{2}}{6} = \frac{2\sqrt{2}}{3}$$

$$\therefore \quad \theta = \tan^{-1}\left(\frac{2\sqrt{2}}{3}\right)$$

Example 35. Find the condition that the pair of straight lines joining the origin to the intersections of the line $y = mx + c$ and the circle $x^2 + y^2 = a^2$ may be at right angles.

Sol. The equations of the line and the circle are

$$y = mx + c \quad \text{...(i)}$$

and

$$x^2 + y^2 = a^2 \quad \text{...(ii)}$$

The pair of straight lines joining the origin to the intersections of Eqs. (i) and (ii), is obtained by making homogeneous Eq. (ii) with the help of Eq. (i).

$$\because \quad y = mx + c \Rightarrow \frac{y - mx}{c} = 1$$

$$\therefore \quad x^2 + y^2 = a^2(1)^2 \Rightarrow x^2 + y^2 = a^2\left(\frac{y - mx}{c}\right)^2$$

$$\Rightarrow x^2(c^2 - a^2m^2) + 2ma^2xy + y^2(c^2 - a^2) = 0 \quad \text{...(iii)}$$

The lines given by Eq. (iii), are at right angles, then coefficient of x^2 + coefficient of $y^2 = 0$

$$\Rightarrow c^2 - a^2m^2 + c^2 - a^2 = 0$$

$$\therefore \quad 2c^2 = a^2(1 + m^2)$$

which is the required condition.

Example 36. Prove that the pair of lines joining the origin to the intersection of the curve $\frac{x^2}{a^2} + \frac{y^2}{b^2} = 1$ by the line $lx + my + n = 0$ are coincident, if $a^2l^2 + b^2m^2 = n^2$.

Sol. The given curve is

$$\frac{x^2}{a^2} + \frac{y^2}{b^2} = 1 \quad \text{...(i)}$$

and line

$$lx + my + n = 0$$

$$\Rightarrow \quad lx + my = -n$$

$$\Rightarrow \quad \frac{lx + my}{-n} = 1 \quad \text{...(ii)}$$

Making Eq. (i) homogeneous with the help of Eq. (ii), then

$$\frac{x^2}{a^2} + \frac{y^2}{b^2} = \left(\frac{lx + my}{-n}\right)^2$$

$$\Rightarrow \quad \frac{n^2x^2}{a^2} + \frac{n^2y^2}{b^2} = l^2x^2 + m^2y^2 + 2lmxy$$

$$\Rightarrow \quad \left(\frac{n^2}{a^2} - l^2\right)x^2 - 2lmxy + \left(\frac{n^2}{b^2} - m^2\right)y^2 = 0 \quad \text{...(iii)}$$

This is of the form $Ax^2 + 2Hxy + By^2 = 0$,

then $A = \frac{n^2}{a^2} - l^2, H = -lm$ and $B = \frac{n^2}{b^2} - m^2$

The lines given by Eq. (iii) will be coincident, if

$$H^2 - AB = 0 \Rightarrow H^2 = AB$$

$$\Rightarrow \quad l^2m^2 = \left(\frac{n^2}{a^2} - l^2\right)\left(\frac{n^2}{b^2} - m^2\right)$$

$$\Rightarrow \quad l^2m^2 = \frac{n^4}{a^2b^2} - \frac{n^2m^2}{a^2} - \frac{l^2n^2}{b^2} + l^2m^2$$

$$\Rightarrow \quad \frac{n^4}{a^2b^2} = \frac{n^2m^2}{a^2} + \frac{n^2l^2}{b^2}$$

$$\Rightarrow \quad n^2 = b^2m^2 + a^2l^2$$

$$\Rightarrow \quad a^2l^2 + b^2m^2 = n^2$$

Example 37. Show that the straight lines joining the origin to the points of intersection of curves

$$ax^2 + 2hxy + by^2 + 2gx = 0$$

and

$$a'x^2 + 2h'xy + b'y^2 + 2g'x = 0$$

are at right angles, if $g'(a + b) = g(a' + b')$.

Sol. The two curves meet in two points and the required lines joining the origin to these points will be obtained by making one equation homogeneous with the help of the other.

$$ax^2 + 2hxy + by^2 + 2gx = 0 \quad \text{...(i)}$$

$$a'x^2 + 2h'xy + b'y^2 + 2g'x = 0 \quad \text{...(ii)}$$

On multiplying Eq. (i) by g' and Eq. (ii) by g and subtracting, we get

$$(ag' - a'g)x^2 + (2hg' - 2h'g)xy + (bg' - b'g)y^2 = 0$$

If the lines are at right angles, then coefficient of x^2 + coefficient of $y^2 = 0$

$$\Rightarrow \quad ag' - a'g + bg' - b'g = 0$$

$$\therefore \quad (a + b)g' = (a' + b')g$$

Milestone Practice 3.3

1. If $\lambda x^2 + 10xy + 3y^2 - 15x - 21y + 18 = 0$ represents a pair of straight lines. Then, the value of λ is

   (a) – 3 (b) 3 (c) 4 (d) – 4

2. The equation of second degree $x^2 + 2\sqrt{2}xy + 2y^2 + 4x + 4\sqrt{2}\,y + 1 = 0$ represents a pair of straight lines, the distance between them is

   (a) 2 (b) $2\sqrt{3}$ (c) 4 (d) $4\sqrt{3}$

3. If the angle between the two lines represented by $2x^2 + 5xy + 3y^2 + 6x + 7y + 4 = 0$ is $\tan^{-1}(m)$, then m is/are equal to

   (a) $-\frac{1}{5}$ (b) $\frac{1}{5}$ (c) $-\frac{3}{5}$ (d) $\frac{3}{5}$

4. If the equation $12x^2 + 7xy - py^2 - 18x + qy + 6 = 0$ represents two perpendicular lines, then the value of p and q are

   (a) 12, 1 (b) 12, – 1 (c) 12, $\frac{23}{2}$ (d) 12, $-\frac{23}{2}$

5. The point of intersection of the straight lines given by the equation $3y^2 - 8xy - 3x^2 - 29x + 3y - 18 = 0$ is

   (a) $\left(1, \frac{1}{2}\right)$ (b) $\left(1, -\frac{1}{2}\right)$

   (c) $\left(-\frac{3}{2}, \frac{5}{2}\right)$ (d) $\left(-\frac{3}{2}, -\frac{5}{2}\right)$

6. If the straight lines joining origin to the points of intersection of the line $x + y = 1$ with the curve $x^2 + y^2 + x - 2y - m = 0$ are perpendicular to each other, then the value of m should be

   (a) $-\frac{1}{2}$ (b) 0 (c) $\frac{1}{2}$ (d) 1

7. The pair of straight lines joining the origin to the common points of $x^2 + y^2 = 4$ and $y = 3x + c$ are perpendicular, if c^2 is equal to

   (a) –1 (b) 6 (c) 13 (d) 20

8. The lines joining the origin to the points of intersection of $2x^2 + 3xy - 4x + 1 = 0$ and $3x + y = 1$ are given by

   (a) $x^2 - y^2 - 5xy = 0$ (b) $x^2 - y^2 + 5xy = 0$
   (c) $x^2 + y^2 - 5xy = 0$ (d) $x^2 + y^2 + 5xy = 0$

9. The equation of the line joining the origin to the point of intersection of the lines $2x^2 + xy - y^2 + 5x - y + 2 = 0$ is

   (a) $x + y = 0$ (b) $x - y = 0$
   (c) $x - 2y = 0$ (d) $2x + y = 0$

10. The area of the parallelogram formed by the lines $2x^2 + 5xy + 3y^2 = 0$ and $2x^2 + 5xy + 3y^2 + 3x + 4y + 1 = 0$ is ....

11. Find the locus of the incentre of the triangle formed by $xy - 4x - 4y + 16 = 0$ and $x + y = a$ ($a > 4, a \neq 4\sqrt{2}$ and a is the parameter).

12. If the equation $2hxy + 2gx + 2fy + c = 0$ represents two straight lines, then show that they form a rectangle of area $\frac{|fg|}{h^2}$ with the coordinate axes.

13. The area of the triangle formed by the lines represented by $ax^2 + 2hxy + by^2 + 2gx + 2fy + c = 0$ and axis of X is ....

14. The equations of the straight lines passing through the point (1, 1) and parallel to the lines represented by the equation $x^2 - 5xy + 4y^2 + x + 2y - 2 = 0$ is ....

15. Find the equation of the lines joining the origin to the points of intersection of $3x - 2y = 1$ with $3x^2 + 5xy - 3y^2 + 2x + 3y = 0$ and show that they are at right angles.

16. If the straight line joining the origin and the points of intersection of $y = mx + 1$ and $x^2 + y^2 = 1$ be perpendicular to each other, then the value of m is ....

17. Prove that the straight lines joining the origin to the points of intersection of the straight line $kx + hy = 2hk$ with the curve $(x - h)^2 + (y - k)^2 = c^2$ are at right angles, if $h^2 + k^2 = c^2$.

18. Show that for all values of λ, the lines joining the origin to the points common to $x^2 + hxy - y^2 + gx + fy = 0$ and $fx - gy = \lambda$ are at right angles.

19. The combined equation of the straight lines joining the origin to the points of intersection of the curves given by $x^2 + y^2 - 4x - 2y = 0$ and $x^2 + y^2 - 2x - 4y = 4$ is ....

Answer Key

1. (b)	2. (a)	3. (a, b)	4. (a, d)	5. (d)	6. (c)	7. (d)
8. (a)	9. (b)	10. (1)	11. $x - y = 0$	13. $\frac{gh - af}{h^2 - ab}\frac{\sqrt{g^2 - ac}}{a}$		
14. $x^2 + 4y^2 - 5xy + 3x - 3y = 0$			15. $9x^2 + 10xy - 9y^2 = 0$	16. ±1	19. $x^2 - 2xy + y^2 = 0$	

For Detailed Solution

JEE Pattern EXAMPLES

Single Option Correct Type Questions

Example 1 *If the pairs of lines $x^2 + 2xy + \lambda y^2 = 0$ and $\lambda x^2 + 2xy + y^2 = 0$ have exactly one line in common, then the joint equation of the other two lines is given by*

(a) $3x^2 + 8xy - 3y^2 = 0$ (b) $3x^2 + 10xy + 3y^2 = 0$

(c) $x^2 + 2xy - 3y^2 = 0$ (d) $3x^2 + 2xy - y^2 = 0$

Sol. (b) Let $y = mx$ be a line common to the given pairs of lines.

Then, $\lambda m^2 + 2m + 1 = 0$ and $m^2 + 2m + \lambda = 0$

$$\Rightarrow \frac{m^2}{2(\lambda - 1)} = \frac{m}{(1 - \lambda^2)} = \frac{1}{2(\lambda - 1)}$$

$$\Rightarrow m^2 = 1 \text{ and } m = -\frac{1}{2}(\lambda + 1)$$

$$\Rightarrow (\lambda + 1)^2 = 4 \Rightarrow \lambda + 1 = 2, -2$$

$$\therefore \lambda = 1 \text{ or } -3$$

But for $\lambda = 1$, the two pairs have both the lines common.

So, $\lambda = -3$ and the slope m of the line common to both the pairs is 1.

Now, $x^2 + 2xy + \lambda y^2 = x^2 + 2xy - 3y^2 = (x - y)(x + 3y)$

and $\lambda x^2 + 2xy + y^2 = -3x^2 + 2xy + y^2$

$$= -(x - y)(3x + y)$$

Hence, the joint equation of other two lines is

$$(x + 3y)(3x + y) = 0 \text{ or } 3x^2 + 10xy + 3y^2 = 0.$$

Example 2 *The combined equation of the lines l_1 and l_2 is $2x^2 + 6xy + y^2 = 0$ and that of the lines m_1 and m_2 is $4x^2 + 18xy + y^2 = 0$. If the angle between l_1 and m_2 is α, then the angle between l_2 and m_1 will be*

(a) $\frac{\pi}{2} - \alpha$ (b) $\frac{\pi}{4} + \alpha$

(c) α (d) 2α

Sol. (c) The combined equation of the bisectors of the angles between the lines of the first pair is

$$\frac{x^2 - y^2}{2 - 1} = \frac{xy}{3} \Rightarrow x^2 - y^2 = \frac{1}{3}xy$$

and the combined equation of the bisectors of the angles between the lines of the second pair is

$$\frac{x^2 - y^2}{4 - 1} = \frac{xy}{9} \Rightarrow x^2 - y^2 = \frac{1}{3}xy$$

It is clear that the two pairs are equally inclined to each other.

Hence, the angle between l_2 and m_1 is α.

Example 3 *The pair of lines $\sqrt{3}x^2 - 4xy + \sqrt{3}y^2 = 0$ are rotated about the origin by $\frac{\pi}{6}$ in the anti-clockwise sense. The equation of the pair in the new position is*

(a) $x^2 - \sqrt{3}xy = 0$ (b) $y^2 - \sqrt{3}xy = 0$

(c) $\sqrt{3}x^2 - xy = 0$ (d) $\sqrt{3}y^2 - xy = 0$

Sol. (c) The given equation of pair of straight lines can be written as

$$(\sqrt{3}x - y)(x - \sqrt{3}y) = 0$$

$$\Rightarrow y = \sqrt{3}x \text{ and } y = \frac{1}{\sqrt{3}}x$$

$$\Rightarrow y = x \tan 60° \text{ and } y = x \tan 30°$$

After rotation, the separate equations are

$$y = x \tan 90° \text{ and } y = x \tan 60°$$

$$\Rightarrow x = 0 \text{ and } y = x\sqrt{3}$$

Hence, the combined equation in the new position is

$$x(\sqrt{3}x - y) = 0 \text{ or } \sqrt{3}x^2 - xy = 0.$$

Example 4 *If the pair of lines $ax^2 - 2xy + by^2 = 0$ and $bx^2 - 2xy + ay^2 = 0$ be such that each pair bisects the angle between the other pair, then $|a - b|$ equals to*

(a) 1 (b) 2

(c) 3 (d) 4

Sol.

Decoding the Question

The equation of pair of lines bisecting the angle between the lines given by $ax^2 + 2hxy + by^2 = 0$ is $\frac{x^2 - y^2}{a - b} = \frac{xy}{h}$

(b) The equation of the bisectors of the angle between the lines

$$ax^2 - 2xy + by^2 = 0 \quad \text{...(i)}$$

is $$bx^2 - 2xy + ay^2 = 0 \quad \text{...(ii)}$$

$\therefore$ The equation of bisectors of the angle between the lines Eq. (i) is

$$\frac{x^2 - y^2}{a-b} = \frac{xy}{-1}$$

$$\Rightarrow \quad x^2 + (a-b)xy - y^2 = 0 \quad \text{...(iii)}$$

Since, Eqs. (ii) and (iii) are identical, comparing Eqs. (ii) and (iii), we get

$$\frac{b}{1} = \frac{-2}{a-b} = \frac{a}{-1}$$

$$\Rightarrow \quad (a-b)b = -2 \text{ and } (a-b)a = 2$$

$$\therefore \quad (a-b)^2 = 4$$

or $$|a-b| = 2$$

Example 5 *The equation of line which is parallel to the line common to the pair of lines given by $3x^2 + xy - 4y^2 = 0$ and $6x^2 + 11xy + 4y^2 = 0$ and at a distance of 2 units from it is*

(a) $3x - 4y = -10$ (b) $x - y = 2$
(c) $3x + 4y = 10$ (d) $2x + y = -2$

Sol. (c) We have, $3x^2 + xy - 4y^2 = 0$

or $$(x-y)(3x+4y) = 0 \quad \text{...(i)}$$

and $$6x^2 + 11xy + 4y^2 = 0$$

or $$(2x+y)(3x+4y) = 0 \quad \text{...(ii)}$$

Equation of line common to Eqs. (i) and (ii) is

$$3x + 4y = 0 \quad \text{...(iii)}$$

Equation of any line parallel to Eq. (iii) is

$$3x + 4y = \lambda$$

Since, its distance from Eq. (iii) is 2, we get

$$\frac{|\lambda - 0|}{\sqrt{(3^2 + 4^2)}} = 2 \text{ or } \lambda = \pm 10$$

Hence, required lines are $3x + 4y = \pm 10$.

Example 6 *The lines joining the origin to the points of intersection of $x^2 + y^2 + 2gx + c = 0$ and $x^2 + y^2 + 2fy - c = 0$ are at right angles, if*

(a) $g^2 + f^2 = c$ (b) $g^2 - f^2 = c$
(c) $g^2 - f^2 = 2c$ (d) $g^2 + f^2 = c^2$

Sol. (c) Given, $x^2 + y^2 + 2gx + c = 0 \quad \text{...(i)}$

and $$x^2 + y^2 + 2fy - c = 0 \quad \text{...(ii)}$$

On subtracting Eq. (ii) from Eq. (i), we get

$$2gx - 2fy + 2c = 0$$

or $$\frac{fy - gx}{c} = 1 \quad \text{...(iii)}$$

On adding Eqs. (i) and (ii), we get

$$2(x^2 + y^2 + gx + fy) = 0$$

or $$x^2 + y^2 + gx + fy = 0 \quad \text{...(iv)}$$

Homogenising Eq. (iv) with the help of Eq. (iii), then

$$x^2 + y^2 + (gx + fy)\left(\frac{fy - gx}{c}\right) = 0$$

$\therefore$ The lines will be at right angles, when

$$\left(1 - \frac{g^2}{c}\right) + \left(1 + \frac{f^2}{c}\right) = 0 \Rightarrow g^2 - f^2 = 2c$$

Example 7 *The square of the distance between the point of intersection of the lines represented by the equation $ax^2 + 2hxy + by^2 + 2gx + 2fy + c = 0$ and origin is*

(a) $\dfrac{c(a+b) - f^2 - g^2}{ab - h^2}$ (b) $\dfrac{c(a-b) + f^2 + g^2}{\sqrt{ab - h^2}}$

(c) $\dfrac{c(a+b) - f^2 - g^2}{ab + h^2}$ (d) None of these

Sol. (d) Let the lines represented by given equation be

$$y = m_1x + c_1 \text{ and } y = m_2x + c_2$$

Then, $ax^2 + 2hxy + by^2 + 2gx + 2fy + c = 0$

$$\Rightarrow \quad b(y - m_1x - c_1)(y - m_2x - c_2) = 0$$

Comparing the coefficients of x^2, xy, x, y and constant term, we get

$$m_1m_2 = \frac{a}{b} \text{ and } m_1m_2 = -\frac{2h}{b}$$

$$m_1c_2 + m_2c_1 = \frac{2g}{b}$$

$$c_1 + c_2 = \frac{2f}{b} \text{ and } c_1c_2 = \frac{c}{b}$$

Also point of intersection of $y = m_1x + c_1$ and $y = m_2x + c_2$ is $\left(\dfrac{c_2 - c_1}{m_1 - m_2}, \dfrac{m_1c_2 - m_2c_1}{m_1 - m_2}\right)$.

The square of distance of this point from origin is

$$\frac{(c_2 - c_1)^2}{(m_1 - m_2)^2} + \frac{(m_1c_2 - c_1m_2)^2}{(m_1 - m_2)^2}$$

$$= \frac{[(c_1 + c_2)^2 - 4c_1c_2][(m_1c_2 + m_2c_1)^2 - 4m_1m_2 - c_1c_2]}{(m_1 + m_2)^2 - 4m_1m_2}$$

On putting the values, we get

$$\frac{-c(a+b) + f^2 + g^2}{h^2 - ab}$$

Example 8 *The distance between the two lines represented by the equation $9x^2 - 24xy + 16y^2 - 12x + 16y - 12$ is d, then find the pair of straight line passing through origin and $(d, 1)$ and $(1, d)$ is*

(a) $40(x^2 + y^2) + 89xy = 0$ (b) $40(x^2 + y^2) - 89xy = 0$
(c) $40x^2 + 40y^2 - 59xy = 0$ (d) None of these

Sol. (b) Given, $9x^2-24xy+16y^2-12x+16y-12=0$

$\Rightarrow \quad (3x-4y+2)(3x-4y-6)=0$

$\Rightarrow 3x-4y+2=0$ and $3x-4y-6=0$

$\because$ Lines are parallel.

$$\therefore \quad d=\left|\frac{(c_1-c_2)}{\sqrt{a^2+b^2}}\right|=\left|\frac{2+6}{\sqrt{3^2+4^2}}\right|=\frac{8}{5}$$

$\therefore$ The required points are $\left(\frac{8}{5},1\right)$ and $\left(1,\frac{8}{5}\right)$.

Now, equation of pair of lines passing through origin

$$(y-m_1x)(y-m_2x)=0$$

$$\Rightarrow \left(y-\frac{5}{8}x\right)\left(y-\frac{8}{5}x\right)=0$$

$$\Rightarrow (8y-5x)(5y-8x)=0$$

$$\Rightarrow 40y^2+40x^2-89xy=0 \quad \left[\because m_1=\frac{1}{8/5} \text{ and } m_2=\frac{8}{5}\right]$$

Example 9 *If the equation*
$12x^2+7xy-py^2-18x+qy+6=0$ *represents two perpendicular lines, then the value of* $p+q+7$ *is*

(a) 15 (b) 20

(c) 25 (d) 30

Decoding the Question

An equation of the form $ax^2+2hxy+by^2+2gx+2fy+c=0$ represents two perpendicular lines if $a+b=0$.

Sol. (b) Given equation, $12x^2+7xy-py^2-18x+qy+6=0$ represents a pair of straight line

where, $a=12, b=-p, c=6, h=\frac{7}{2}, g=-9$ and $f=\frac{q}{2}$

$$\therefore \quad \Delta=\begin{vmatrix} a & h & g \\ h & b & f \\ g & f & c \end{vmatrix}=0$$

$$=\begin{vmatrix} 12 & \frac{7}{2} & -9 \\ \frac{7}{2} & -p & \frac{q}{2} \\ -9 & \frac{q}{2} & 6 \end{vmatrix}=0$$

$$\Rightarrow 12\left(-6p-\frac{q^2}{4}\right)-\frac{7}{2}\left(21+\frac{9q}{2}\right)-9\left(\frac{7q}{4}-9p\right)=0$$

$$\Rightarrow -72p-3q^2-\frac{147}{2}-\frac{63q}{4}-\frac{63q}{4}+81p=0$$

$$\Rightarrow 9p-3q^2-\frac{63}{2}q-\frac{147}{2}=0$$

$$\Rightarrow 18p-6q^2-63q-147=0 \quad \text{...(i)}$$

Lines are perpendicular.

$$\therefore \quad a+b=0$$

$$\Rightarrow \quad 12-p=0 \Rightarrow p=12$$

Put $p=12$ in Eq. (i), we get

$$12\times18-6q^2-63q-147=0$$

$$\Rightarrow 216-147-6q^2-63q=0$$

$$\Rightarrow 6q^2+63q-69=0$$

$$\Rightarrow 2q^2+21q-23=0$$

$$\Rightarrow 2q^2+23q-2q-23=0$$

$$\Rightarrow q(2q+23)-1(2q+23)=0$$

$$\Rightarrow (q-1)(2q+23)=0$$

$$\Rightarrow q=1, q=-\frac{23}{2}$$

Hence, at $q=1$,

$$p+q+7=12+1+7=20$$

At $q=-\frac{23}{2}$,

$$p+q+7=12-\frac{23}{2}+7$$

$$=\frac{38-23}{2}=\frac{15}{2}$$

$$\therefore \quad p+q+7=20$$

Example 10 *The pair of straight lines joining the origin to the points of intersection of the line* $y=2\sqrt{2}x+c$ *and the circle* $x^2+y^2=2$ *are at right angles, if*

(a) $c^2-4=0$ (b) $c^2-8=0$

(c) $c^2-9=0$ (d) $c^2-10=0$

Sol. (c) Given line $y=2\sqrt{2}x+c$

$$\Rightarrow \frac{y-2\sqrt{2}x}{c}=1$$

Circle $x^2+y^2=2$

By homogenisation,

$$x^2+y^2=2\left(\frac{y-2\sqrt{2}x}{c}\right)^2$$

$$\Rightarrow c^2(x^2+y^2)=2(y^2+8x^2-4\sqrt{2}xy)$$

$$\Rightarrow x^2(c^2-16)+y^2(c^2-2)+8\sqrt{2}xy=0 \quad \text{...(i)}$$

$\because$ Eq. (i) represents a pair of straight line and lines are perpendicular to each other

$$\Rightarrow a+b=0$$

$$\Rightarrow c^2-16+c^2-2=0$$

$$\Rightarrow 2c^2-18=0$$

$$\Rightarrow c^2-9=0$$

$$\Rightarrow c=\pm3$$

More than One Correct Option Type Questions

Example 11 *The lines joining the origin to the point of intersection of $3x^2 + mxy - 4x + 1 = 0$ and $2x + y - 1 = 0$ are at right angles. Which of the following is/are possible value of m?*

(a) -4 (b) 3

(c) 4 (d) 7

Sol. (a,b,c,d) Given line is $2x + y = 1$ ...(i)

and curve is $3x^2 + mxy - 4x + 1 = 0$ ...(ii)

Homogenising Eq. (ii) with the help of Eq. (i), then

$$3x^2 + mxy - 4x(2x + y) + (2x + y)^2 = 0$$

or $$-x^2 + mxy + y^2 = 0$$

The lines are at right angles as $a + b = 0$

Then, $$h^2 \geq ab$$

i.e. $$\frac{m^2}{4} + 1 \geq 0$$

which is true for all $m \in R$.

Example 12 *The lines $(lx + my)^2 - 3(mx - ly)^2 = 0$ and $lx + my + n = 0$ form*

(a) an isosceles triangle

(b) a right angled triangle

(c) an equilateral triangle

(d) None of the above

Sol. (a,c) $(lx + my)^2 - 3(mx - ly)^2 = 0$

$\Rightarrow (l^2 - 3m^2)x^2 + 8mlxy + (m^2 - 3l^2)y^2 = 0$

$\Rightarrow \{(l + m\sqrt{3})x + (m - l\sqrt{3})y\}\{(l - \sqrt{3}m)x + (m + \sqrt{3}l)y\} = 0$

Let slope of $(l + m\sqrt{3})x + (m - l\sqrt{3})y = 0$ be m_1 and slope of $(l - m\sqrt{3})x + (m + l\sqrt{3})y = 0$ be m_2 and slope of $lx + my + n = 0$ be m_3.

Then, $$\tan\theta_1 = \left|\frac{m_3 - m_1}{1 + m_3 m_1}\right| = \left|\frac{-\frac{l}{m} + \frac{l + m\sqrt{3}}{m - l\sqrt{3}}}{1 + \frac{l}{m}\cdot\left(\frac{l + m\sqrt{3}}{m - l\sqrt{3}}\right)}\right|$$

$$= \left|\frac{\sqrt{3}(l^2 + m^2)}{(l^2 + m^2)}\right| = \sqrt{3}$$

$\Rightarrow$ $$\theta_1 = 60°$$

Similarly, $$\tan\theta_2 = \left|\frac{m_2 - m_1}{1 + m_2 m_1}\right| = \sqrt{3}$$

$\Rightarrow$ $$\theta_2 = 60°$$

Hence, an equilateral triangle is formed which is also an isosceles one.

Example 13 *If the equation $ax^2 - 6xy + y^2 + bx + cy + d = 0$ represents a pair of lines whose slopes are m and m^2, then the value(s) of a is/are*

(a) -27 (b) -8

(c) 8 (d) 27

Sol. (a,c) Since, m and m^2 are the roots of the equation

$$\left(\frac{y}{x}\right)^2 - 6\left(\frac{y}{x}\right) + a = 0$$

$\therefore$ $$m + m^2 = 6 \text{ and } m \cdot m^2 = a \quad ...(i)$$

Now, $$(m + m^2)^3 = (6)^3$$

$\Rightarrow$ $$m^3 + m^6 + 3m \cdot m^2(m + m^2) = 216$$

$\Rightarrow$ $$a + a^2 + 3a(6) = 216 \quad \text{[from Eq. (i)]}$$

$\Rightarrow$ $$a^2 + 19a - 216 = 0$$

$\Rightarrow$ $$(a + 27)(a - 8) = 0$$

$\therefore$ $$a = -27, 8$$

Example 14 *If $x^2 + 2hxy + y^2 = 0$ represents the equation of the straight lines through the origin which make an angle α with the straight line $y + x = 0$, then*

(a) $\sec 2\alpha = h$ (b) $\cos\alpha = \sqrt{\frac{1+h}{2h}}$

(c) $2\sin\alpha = \sqrt{\frac{1+h}{n}}$ (d) $\cot\alpha = \sqrt{\frac{h+1}{h-1}}$

Sol. (a,b,d) Equation of the lines given by $x^2 + 2hxy + y^2 = 0$ be $y = m_1 x$ and $y = m_2 x$.

$\therefore$ These make an angle α with $y + x = 0$ whose slope is -1.

So, $$\frac{m_1 + 1}{1 - m_1} = \tan\alpha = \frac{-1 - m_2}{1 - m_2}$$

$\therefore$ $$m_1 + m_2 = \frac{(\tan\alpha - 1)^2 + (\tan\alpha + 1)^2}{\tan^2\alpha - 1}$$

$\Rightarrow$ $$\frac{-2h}{1} = -\frac{2\sec^2\alpha \times \cos^2\alpha}{\cos 2\alpha}$$

$\Rightarrow$ $$-2\sec 2\alpha = -2h \Rightarrow \sec 2\alpha = h$$

$\Rightarrow$ $$\cos 2\alpha = \frac{1}{h} \Rightarrow 2\cos^2\alpha - 1 = \frac{1}{h}$$

$\Rightarrow$ $$\cos\alpha = \sqrt{\frac{1+h}{2h}} \Rightarrow \cot\alpha = \sqrt{\frac{h+1}{h-1}}$$

Example 15 *If one of the lines given by the equation $2x^2 + pxy + 3y^2 = 0$ coincide with one of those given by $2x^2 + qxy - 3y^2 = 0$ and the other lines represented by them be perpendicular, then*

(a) $p = 5$ (b) $p = -5$

(c) $q = -1$ (d) $q = 1$

Sol. (a, b, c, d) Let $\frac{2}{3}x^2 + \frac{p}{3}xy + y^2 = (y - mx)(y - m'x)$

and $-\frac{2}{3}x^2 + \frac{q}{-3}xy + y^2 = \left(y + \frac{1}{m}x\right)(y - m'x)$

Then, $m + m' = -\frac{p}{3}, mm' = \frac{2}{3}$ ...(i)

$\frac{1}{m} - m' = -\frac{q}{3}, -\frac{m'}{m} = -\frac{2}{3}$ ...(ii)

From Eqs. (i) and (ii), we get

$m^2 = 1 \Rightarrow m = \pm 1$

If $m = 1$ and $m' = \frac{2}{3}$

So, $p = -5, q = -1$

and if $m = -1$ and $m' = -\frac{2}{3}$

So, $p = 5, q = 1$

Passage Based Question

Passage

(Ex. Nos. 16 and 17)

Consider the equation of a pair of straight lines as $\lambda xy - 8x + 9y - 12 = 0$.

Example 16 *The value of λ is*

(a) 0 (b) 2

(c) 4 (d) 6

Example 17 *The point of intersection of lines is (α, β), then the equation whose roots are α and β, is*

(a) $4x^2 + x - 8 = 0$ (b) $6x^2 + x - 12 = 0$

(c) $4x^2 - x - 8 = 0$ (d) $6x^2 - x - 12 = 0$

Sol. (Ex. Nos. 16 and 17)

Given equation is, $\lambda xy - 8x + 9y - 12 = 0$

Here, $a = 0, b = 0, c = -12, f = \frac{9}{2}, g = -4$ and $h = \frac{\lambda}{2}$

16. (d) For $\Delta = 0$,

$$0 + 2 \times \frac{9}{2} \times -4 \times \frac{\lambda}{2} - 0 - 0 + 12 \times \frac{\lambda^2}{4} = 0 \Rightarrow 3\lambda^2 - 18\lambda = 0$$

$\therefore \lambda = 0, 6$

Hence, $\lambda = 6$

[$\because$ for $\lambda = 0$, it will give an equation of first degree]

17. (b) Let $f(x, y) = 6xy - 8x + 9y - 12$ [$\because \lambda = 6$]

$\therefore \frac{\partial f}{\partial x} = 6y - 8$ and $\frac{\partial f}{\partial y} = 6x + 9$

For point of intersection $\frac{\partial f}{\partial x} = 0$ and $\frac{\partial f}{\partial y} = 0$, we get

$x = -\frac{3}{2}$ and $y = \frac{4}{3}$

$\therefore \alpha = -\frac{3}{2}$ and $\beta = \frac{4}{3}$

Hence, required equation is

$$x^2 - \left(-\frac{3}{2} + \frac{4}{3}\right)x - 2 = 0$$

$\Rightarrow 6x^2 + x - 12 = 0$

Stem Based Questions

Stem

(Ex. Nos. 18 to 19)

Consider the equation of a pair of straight lines as $x^2 - 3xy + \lambda y^2 + 3x - 5y + 2 = 0$.

Example 18 *The value of λ is ....*

Example 19 *The point of intersection of lines is (α, β), then the value of $\alpha^2 + \beta^2$ is ....*

Sol. (Ex. Nos. 18 to 19)

Given equation is $x^2 - 3xy + \lambda y^2 + 3x - 5y + 2 = 0$.

Here, $a = 1, b = \lambda, c = 2, f = -\frac{5}{2}, g = \frac{3}{2}$ and $h = -\frac{3}{2}$.

18. (2) $\Delta = 0$

$$\Rightarrow 1 \times \lambda \times 2 + 2 \times -\frac{5}{2} \times \frac{3}{2} \times -\frac{3}{2} - 1 \times \frac{25}{4} - \lambda \times \frac{9}{4} - 2 \times \frac{9}{4} = 0$$

$$\Rightarrow 2\lambda + \frac{45}{4} - \frac{25}{4} - \frac{9\lambda}{4} - \frac{9}{2} = 0 \Rightarrow -\frac{\lambda}{4} + \frac{1}{2} = 0$$

$\therefore \lambda = 2$

19. (10) Let $f(x, y) = x^2 - 3xy + 2y^2 + 3x - 5y + 2$ [$\because \lambda = 2$]

$\therefore \frac{\partial f}{\partial x} = 2x - 3y + 3, \frac{\partial f}{\partial y} = -3x + 4y - 5$

For point of intersection $\frac{\partial f}{\partial x} = 0$ and $\frac{\partial f}{\partial y} = 0$, we get

$x = -3$ and $y = -1$

$\therefore \alpha = -3$ and $\beta = -1$

$\therefore$ The value of $\alpha^2 + \beta^2$ is 10.

Single Integer Type Question

Example 20 *If the sum of the slopes of the lines given by $x^2 - 2cxy - 7y^2 = 0$ is four times their product, then the value of c is ....*

Sol. (2) Given, $m_1 + m_2 = 4m_1m_2$

$\Rightarrow -\frac{2h}{b} = 4 \cdot \frac{a}{b}$

$\Rightarrow h = -2a$

$\therefore -c = -2 \times 1 \Rightarrow c = 2$

Example 21 *If one of the lines given by* $6x^2 - xy + 4cy^2 = 0$ *is* $3x + 4y = 0$*, then the value of* $|c|$ *is ...*

Sol. (3) Since, $3x + 4y = 0$ is one of the lines given by $6x^2 - xy + 4cy^2 = 0$, then

$$6x^2 - x\left(-\frac{3x}{4}\right) + 4c\left(-\frac{3x}{4}\right)^2 = 0 \qquad \left[\because y = -\frac{3x}{4}\right]$$

$$\Rightarrow \quad 6 + \frac{3}{4} + \frac{9c}{4} = 0$$

$$\therefore \quad c = -3$$

Hence, $|c| = 3$

Example 22 *If the lines* $x^2 + 2xy - 35y^2 - 4x + 44y - 12 = 0$ *and* $5x + \lambda y - 8 = 0$ *are concurrent, then the value of* λ *is ....*

Sol. (2) Given equation is

$$f = x^2 + 2xy - 35y^2 - 4x + 44y - 12 = 0 \qquad \text{...(i)}$$

For point of intersection $\frac{\partial f}{\partial x} = 0$ and $\frac{\partial f}{\partial y} = 0$

$$2x + 2y - 4 = 0 \quad \text{and} \quad 2x - 70y + 44 = 0$$

Solving $72y = 48$

$$\Rightarrow \quad y = \frac{48}{72}$$

$$\Rightarrow \quad y = \frac{2}{3}$$

$$\therefore \quad x = \frac{4}{3}$$

$\therefore$ Point of intersection $\left(\frac{4}{3}, \frac{2}{3}\right)$.

$\because$ Line $5x + \lambda y - 8 = 0$ is concurrent with line (i)

$$\therefore \quad 5\left(\frac{4}{3}\right) + \lambda\left(\frac{2}{3}\right) - 8 = 0$$

$$\Rightarrow \quad 20 + 2\lambda - 24 = 0$$

$$\Rightarrow \quad \lambda = 2$$

Example 23 *The sides of a triangle have the combined equation* $x^2 - 3y^2 - 2xy + 8y - 4 = 0$*. The third side, which is variable always passes through the point* $(-5, -1)$*. If the range of values of the slope of third line is such that the origin is an interior point of the triangle is* (a, b)*, then the value of* $\left(a + \frac{1}{b}\right)$ *is ....*

Sol. (4) Given pair of straight lines $x^2 - 3y^2 - 2xy + 8y - 4 = 0$

$$\Rightarrow \quad (x - 3y + 2)(x + y - 2) = 0$$

Now, $(-5, -1)$ lies on $x - 3y + 2 = 0$.

In limiting case, line passing through $(-5, -1)$ and can be parallel to $x + y - 2 = 0$ i.e. $m > -1$

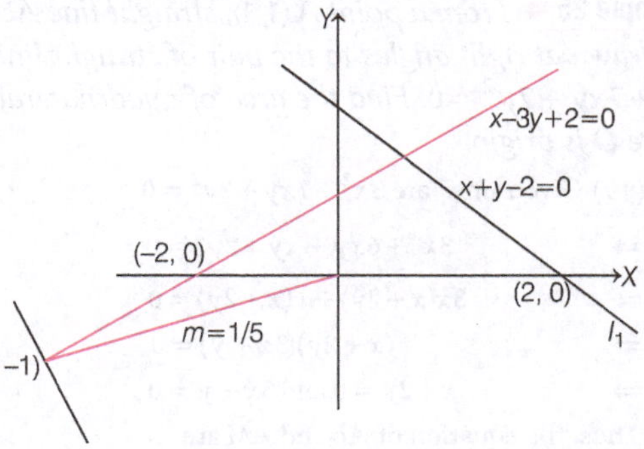

and maximum slope can occur if it passes through (0, 0),

i.e. $m < \frac{1}{5} \Rightarrow m \in \left(-1, \frac{1}{5}\right)$

$$\Rightarrow \quad a = -1 \text{ and } b = \frac{1}{5}$$

$$\therefore \quad a + \frac{1}{b} = -1 + 5 = 4$$

Example 24 *If area of the triangle formed by the lines* $x + y = 3$ *and the angle bisectors of the pair of lines* $x^2 - y^2 + 4y - 4 = 0$ *is A. Then, the value of* $16A$ *is ....*

Sol. (8) Given pair of lines $x^2 - (y^2 - 4y + 4) = 0$

$$\Rightarrow \quad x^2 - (y - 2)^2 = 0$$

$$\Rightarrow \quad (x - y + 2)(x + y - 2) = 0$$

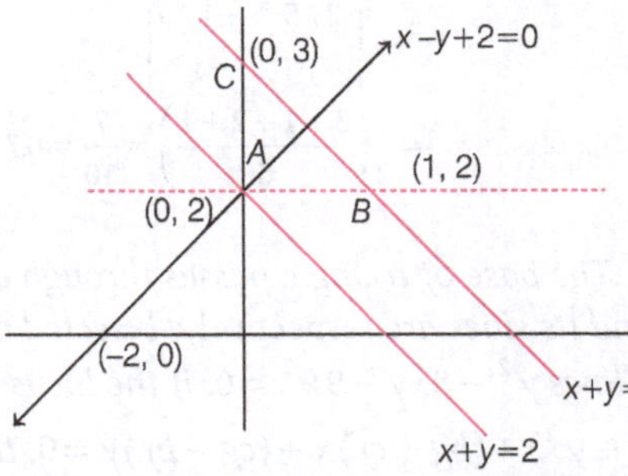

$\therefore$ Equation lines which bisect the angle between the lines $x - y + 2 = 0$ and $x + y - 2 = 0$ is $y = 2$ and $x = 0$.

Now, the vertices of triangle with $y = 2$, $x = 0$ and $x + y = 3$

$$A = (0, 2), B = (1, 2), C = (0, 3)$$

$\because$ ABC is right angled triangle.

$$\therefore \quad A = \frac{1}{2} \times AB \times AC$$

$$= \frac{1}{2} \times 1 \times 1 = \frac{1}{2}$$

$$\therefore \quad 16A = 16 \times \frac{1}{2} = 8 \text{ sq units}$$

Numerical Value Type Questions

Example 25 *From a point $A(1, 1)$, straight line AL and AM are drawn at right angles to the pair of straight lines $3x^2+7xy+2y^2=0$. Find the area of quadrilateral ALOM where O is origin.*

Sol. (0.7) Given lines are $3x^2+7xy+2y^2=0$

$$\Rightarrow \quad 3x^2+6xy+xy+2y^2=0$$

$$\Rightarrow \quad 3x(x+2y)+y(x+2y)=0$$

$$\Rightarrow \quad (x+2y)(3x+y)=0$$

$$\Rightarrow \quad x+2y=0 \text{ and } 3x+y=0$$

Thus, the equation of AL and AM are

$$2x-y+\lambda=0$$

$$3y-x+\mu=0$$

which passes through $A(1, 1)$

$$\lambda=-1 \text{ and } \mu=-2$$

$\therefore$ Equation are $2x-y-1=0, 3y-x-2=0$

Solving $x+2y=0$ and $3y-x-2=0$, we get

$$M\left(\frac{2}{5}, \frac{-1}{5}\right)$$

Solving $3x+y=0$ and $2x-y-1=0$, we get

$$L\left(\frac{-1}{5}, \frac{3}{5}\right)$$

$\therefore$ Area of the quadrilateral $ALMO$

$$=\frac{1}{2}\begin{vmatrix} 1 & 1 \\ -1/5 & 3/5 \\ 0 & 0 \\ 2/5 & -1/5 \\ 1 & 1 \end{vmatrix}$$

$$=\frac{1}{2}\left(\frac{3+1+2+1}{5}\right)=\frac{7}{10}=0.7 \text{ sq unit}$$

Example 26 *The base of triangle passes through a fixed point (f, g) and its sides are respectively, bisected at right angles by the lines $y^2-8xy-9x^2=0$, if the locus of its vertex is $a(x^2+y^2)+(bg+cf)x+(cg-bf)y=0$, then find $\frac{a+b+c}{5}$.*

Sol. (2.6) Given lines are $y^2-8xy-9x^2=0$

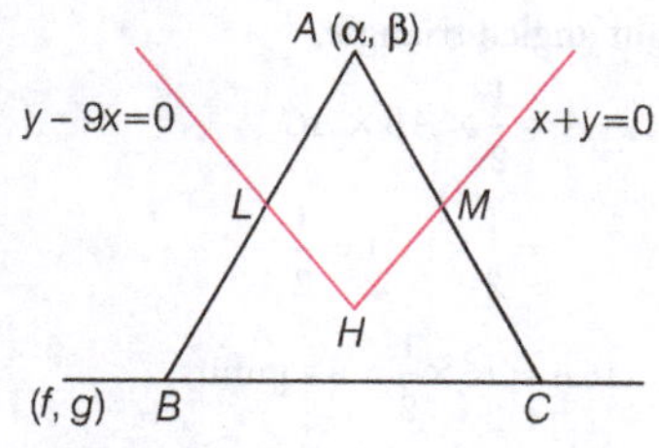

$$\Rightarrow \quad y^2-9xy+xy-9x^2=0$$

$$\Rightarrow \quad y(y-9x)+x(y-9x)=0$$

$$\Rightarrow \quad (y-9x)(y+x)=0$$

$$\Rightarrow \quad y+x=0, y-9x=0$$

Equations of AB and AC are

$$x+9y=\alpha+9\beta \text{ and } x-y=\alpha+\beta$$

Here, B and C are the images of A w.r.t. the lines $y=9x$ and $y=-x$.

So, $\quad C=(-\beta, -\alpha)$

and $\quad B=\left(\frac{9\beta-40\alpha}{41}, \frac{40\beta+9\alpha}{41}\right)$

Now, P, B and C are collinear, so

$$\begin{vmatrix} f & g & 1 \\ \frac{9\beta-40\alpha}{41} & \frac{40\beta+9\alpha}{41} & 1 \\ -\beta & -\alpha & 1 \end{vmatrix}=0$$

$$\Rightarrow \quad \begin{vmatrix} f & g & 1 \\ 9\beta-40\alpha & 40\beta+9\alpha & 41 \\ \beta & \alpha & -1 \end{vmatrix}=0$$

$$\Rightarrow \quad \begin{vmatrix} f & g & 1 \\ 9\beta-40\alpha & 40\beta+9\alpha & 41 \\ f+\beta & g+\alpha & 0 \end{vmatrix}=0$$

$$\Rightarrow \quad \begin{vmatrix} 9\beta-40\alpha & 40\beta+9\alpha \\ f+\beta & g+\alpha \end{vmatrix}-41\begin{vmatrix} f & g \\ f+\beta & g+\alpha \end{vmatrix}=0$$

$$\Rightarrow (g+\alpha)(9\beta-40\alpha)-(f+\beta)(40\beta+9\alpha)-41(f\alpha-g\beta)=0$$

$$\Rightarrow 40(\alpha^2+\beta^2)+10(4g+5f)\alpha+10(4f-5g)\beta=0$$

$$\Rightarrow \quad 4(\alpha^2+\beta^2)+(4g+5f)\alpha+(4f-5g)\beta=0$$

Hence, the locus $A(\alpha, \beta)$ is

$$4(x^2+y^2)+(4g+5f)x+(4f-5g)y=0$$

Given, $\quad a(x^2+y^2)+(bg+cf)x+(cf-bg)y=0$

$\therefore \quad a=4, b=4$ and $c=5$

Now, $\quad \frac{a+b+c}{5}=\frac{4+4+5}{5}=\frac{13}{5}=2.6$

Example 27 *The equation $9x^3+9x^2y-45x^2=4y^3+4xy^2-20y^3$ represents 3 straight lines, two of which pass through the origin. Find the area of the triangle formed by these lines (in sq units).*

Sol. (30) Given, $9x^3+9x^2y-45x^2=4y^3+4xy^2-20y^3$

$$\Rightarrow \quad 9x^2(x+y-5)=4y^2(y+x-5)$$

$$\Rightarrow \quad (9x^2-4y^2)(x+y-5)=0$$

$$\Rightarrow (x+y-5)(3x-2y)(3x+2y)=0$$

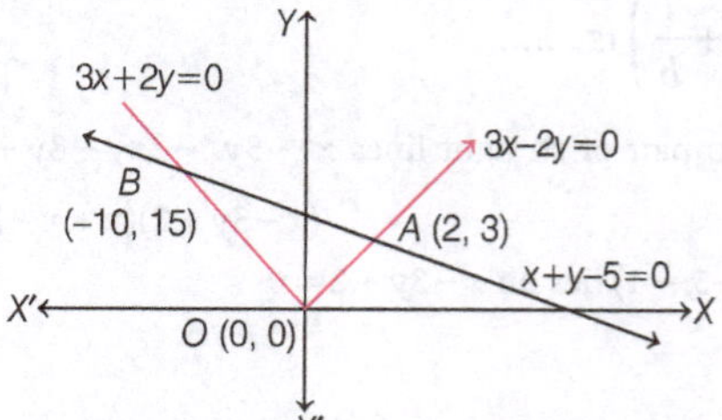

$\therefore$ Lines are $\quad x + y - 5 = 0 \quad$ ...(i)

$3x - 2y = 0 \quad$ ...(ii)

$3x + 2y = 0 \quad$ ...(iii)

Points of intersections of Eqs. (i), (ii) and (iii) are A, B, O.

By solving $A(2, 3), O(0, 0), B(-10, 15)$

$$\therefore \text{ Area of } \Delta ABO = \frac{1}{2}\begin{vmatrix} 0 & 0 & 1 \\ 2 & 3 & 1 \\ -10 & 15 & 1 \end{vmatrix}$$

$$= \frac{1}{2}\{(30 + 30)\}$$

$$= 30 \text{ sq units}$$

JEE SCANNER

Example 28 Similar to PYQ Asked in JEE Main 2023

If the locus of the point whose distance from the points (5, 1) and (1, 4) are in the ratio 4 : 3 is, $ax^2 + by^2 + cxy + dx + ey + 38 = 0$, then the value of $a^2 + b + 2c + 5d + e$ is equal to ....

Sol. (16) Given points are (5, 1) and (1, 4) in the ratio 4 : 3.

Let the point Y be (h, k).

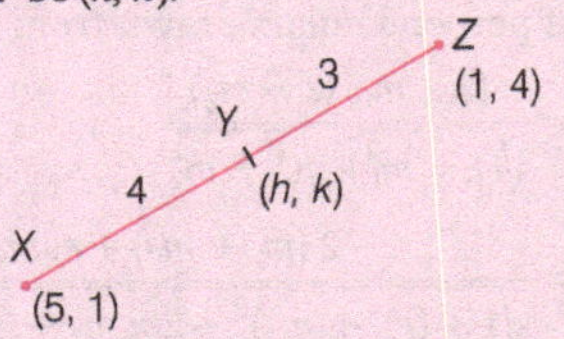

$$\therefore \quad \frac{(h-5)^2 + (k-1)^2}{(h-1)^2 + (k-4)^2} = \frac{16}{9}$$

$$\Rightarrow \quad \frac{h^2 + k^2 - 10h - 2k + 26}{h^2 + k^2 - 2h - 8k + 17} = \frac{16}{9}$$

Replacing $h \to x$ and $k \to y$, we get

$$\frac{x^2 + y^2 - 10x - 2y + 26}{x^2 + y^2 - 2x - 8y + 17} = \frac{16}{9}$$

$$\Rightarrow \quad 7x^2 + 7y^2 + 58x - 110y + 38 = 0$$

$$\Rightarrow \quad a = 7, b = 7, c = 0, d = 58$$

and $\quad e = -110$

$$\therefore \quad a^2 + b + 2c + 5d + e = 49 + 7 + 0 + 290 - 330$$

$$= 16$$

Skill Builder

If the locus of the point whose distance from the points (3, 2) and (2, 5) are in the ratio 3 : 2, is $ax^2 + by^2 + cxy + dx + ey + 209 = 0$, then the value of $|a^2 + b^2 + c + 2(d + e)|$ is ....

For Sol.

Example 29 *A triangle has the lines $ax^2 + 2hxy + by^2 = 0$ for two of its sides and the point (l, m) for its orthocentre, then if the third side has the equation. $(a + b)(lx + my) = \lambda am^2 - \mu hlm + bl^2$, then find the value of $\sqrt{\lambda^2 + \mu^2}$ upto two decimal.*

Sol. (2.23) Let the lines be $y = m_1 x$ and $y = m_2 x$,

where $\quad m_1 + m_2 = -\dfrac{2h}{b}$ and $m_1 m_2 = \dfrac{a}{b}$

Equation of OA is $y = m_1 x$

BE is perpendicular to OA.

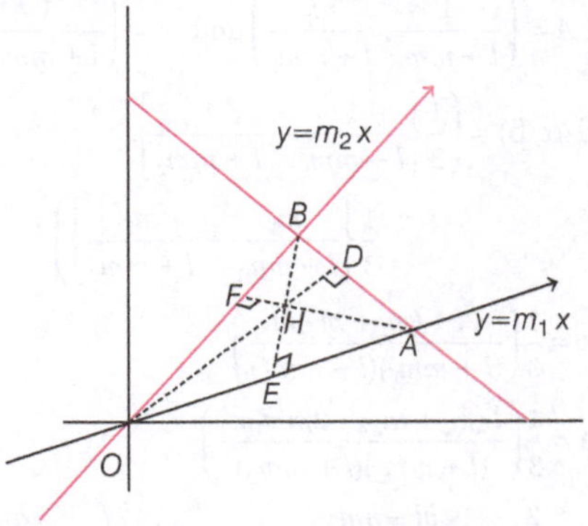

So, $BE : x + m_1 y + \lambda_1 = 0$ which is passing through $H(l, m)$, we get $l + mm_1 + \lambda_1 = 0$

$$\Rightarrow \quad \lambda_1 = -(l + mm)$$

Thus, $BE : x + m_1 y - (l + mm_1) = 0$

Similarly, $AF : x + m_2 y - (l + mm_2) = 0$

On solving OA and AF, we get $A = \left(\dfrac{l + mm_2}{1 + m_1 m_2}, \dfrac{m_1(l + mm_2)}{1 + m_1 m_2}\right)$

On solving OB and BE, we get $B = \left(\dfrac{l + mm_1}{1 + m_1 m_2}, \dfrac{m_2(l + mm_2)}{1 + m_1 m_2}\right)$

Equation of AB is $lx + my + \lambda_3 = 0$

which is passing through A.

$$\text{So, } l\left(\frac{l + mm_2}{1 + m_1 m_2}\right) + m\left(\frac{m_1(l + mm_2)}{1 + m_1 m_2}\right) + \lambda_3 = 0$$

$$\lambda_3 = -\left(\frac{l^2 + lm(m_2 + m_1) + m^2(m_1 m_2)}{1 + m_1 m_2}\right)$$

$$= -\frac{\left[l^2 - \left(\frac{2h}{b}\right)lm + \frac{a}{b}m^2\right]}{1 + \frac{a}{b}} = -\left(\frac{bl^2 - 2hlm + am^2}{a + b}\right)$$

Hence, equation of third side is

$$lx + my = \left(\frac{bl^2 - 2hlm + am^2}{a + b}\right)$$

$$\Rightarrow \quad (lx + my)(a + b) = (bl^2 - 2hlm + am^2)$$

$$\lambda = 1 \text{ and } \mu = 2$$

$$\Rightarrow \quad \sqrt{\lambda^2 + \mu^2} = \sqrt{1 + 4} = \sqrt{5} = 2.23$$

Example 30 *If (α, β) is the centroid of the triangle whose sides are the lines $ax^2 + 2hxy + by^2 = 0$ and $lx + my = 1$ and a relation $\frac{\alpha}{bl - hm} = \frac{\beta}{am - hl} = \frac{p}{q} \frac{1}{bl^2 - 2hlm + ah^2}$ follow, then find $\frac{p+q}{10}$, where p, q are coprime*

Sol. (0.5) Let the lines be $y = m_1x$ and $y = m_2x$,

where $$m_1 + m_2 = -\frac{2h}{b} \text{ and } m_1m_2 = \frac{a}{b}$$

Thus, the point O, A and B are

$$O(0, 0),\ A = \left(\frac{1}{l + mm_1}, \frac{m_1}{l + mm_1}\right) \text{ and } B = \left(\frac{1}{l + mm_2}, \frac{m_2}{l + mm_2}\right)$$

$$\text{Centroid } (\alpha, \beta) = \left(\frac{1}{3}\left\{\frac{1}{l + mm_1} + \frac{1}{l + mm_2}\right\}, \frac{1}{3}\left\{\frac{m_1}{l + mm_1} + \frac{m_2}{l + mm_2}\right\}\right)$$

$$\therefore \quad \alpha = \frac{1}{3}\left(\frac{2l + (m_1 + m_2)m}{(l + mm_1)(l + mm_2)}\right)$$

$$\text{and} \quad \beta = \frac{1}{3}\left(\frac{l(m_1 + m_2) + 2mm_1m_2}{(l + mm_1)(l + mm_2)}\right)$$

$$\Rightarrow \quad \alpha = \frac{2}{3}\left(\frac{bl - hm}{bl^2 - 2hlm + am^2}\right) \text{ and } \beta = \frac{2}{3}\left(\frac{am - hl}{bl^2 - 2hlm + am^2}\right)$$

$$\text{Thus, } \frac{\alpha}{bl - hm} = \frac{\beta}{am - hl} = \frac{2}{3}\left(\frac{1}{bl^2 - 2hlm + am^2}\right)$$

$$\frac{\alpha}{bl - hm} = \frac{\beta}{am - hl} = \frac{p}{q}\left(\frac{l}{bl^2 - 2hlm + am^2}\right) \quad \text{[given]}$$

$$\therefore \quad \frac{p+q}{10} = \frac{2+3}{10} = \frac{5}{10} = 0.5$$

Matching Type Questions

Example 31 *Match the following*

Column I		Column II
(A) If the slope of one of the lines represented by $ax^2 + 2hxy + by^2 = 0$ is the square of the other, then $\frac{a+b}{h} + \frac{8h^2}{ab}$ is a	(p)	2
(B) The product of perpendiculars drawn from the point (1, 2) to the pair of lines $x^2 + 4xy + y^2 = 0$ is λ units, then $[\lambda]$ is a (where $[\cdot]$ denotes the greatest integer function).	(q)	6
(C) Distance between two lines represented by the line pair $x^2 - 4xy + 4y^2 + x - 2y - 6 = 0$ is λ unit, then $[\lambda]$ is a (where $[\cdot]$ denotes the greatest integer function).	(r)	4
(D) If the pairs $a_1x^2 + 2h_1xy + b_1y^2 = 0$ and $a_2x^2 + 2h_2xy + b_2y^2 = 0$ have one line common, then $\frac{(a_1b_2 - a_2b_1)^2}{(b_1h_2 - b_2h_1)(a_2h_1 - a_1h_2)}$ is a	(s)	3

Sol. (A) → (q); (B) → (s); (C) → (p); (D) → (r)

(A) Let m and m^2 be the slopes of the lines represented by $ax^2 + 2hxy + by^2 = 0$.

Then,
$$m + m^2 = -\frac{2h}{b} \quad \text{...(i)}$$

and
$$m \cdot m^2 = \frac{a}{b} \quad \text{...(ii)}$$

From Eq. (i),
$$(m + m^2)^3 = \left(-\frac{2h}{b}\right)^3$$

$$\Rightarrow m^3 + m^6 + 3m \cdot m^2(m + m^2) = -\frac{8h^3}{b^3}$$

$$\Rightarrow \frac{a}{b} + \frac{a^2}{b^2} + \frac{3a}{b}\left(-\frac{2h}{b}\right) = -\frac{8h^3}{b^3}$$

[from Eqs. (i) and (ii)]

$$\Rightarrow ab + a^2 - 6ah = -\frac{8h^3}{b}$$

$$\therefore \quad \frac{a+b}{h} + \frac{8h^2}{ab} = 6$$

(B) Let $y = m_1x$ and $y = m_2x$ lines represented by $x^2 + 4xy + y^2 = 0$, then $m_1 + m_2 = -4$, $m_1m_2 = 1$. Then, product of perpendiculars drawn from the point (1, 2)

$$= \frac{|(2 - m_1)(2 - m_2)|}{\sqrt{(1 + m_1^2)}\sqrt{(1 + m_2^2)}}$$

$$= \frac{|4 - 2(m_1 + m_2) + m_1m_2|}{\sqrt{1 + (m_1 + m_2)^2 - 2m_1m_2 + (m_1m_2)^2}}$$

$$= \frac{|4 + 8 + 1|}{\sqrt{(1 + 16 - 2 + 1)}} = \frac{13}{4} \text{ units}$$

$$\because \quad \lambda = \frac{13}{4}$$

$$\therefore \quad [\lambda] = 3$$

(C) Given, line pair is $x^2 - 4xy + 4y^2 + x - 2y - 6 = 0$

$$\Rightarrow (x - 2y)^2 + (x - 2y) - 6 = 0$$

$$\Rightarrow (x - 2y + 3)(x - 2y - 2) = 0$$

∴ Lines are $x - 2y + 3 = 0$ and $x - 2y - 2 = 0$.

Hence, distance between lines $= \frac{|3 - (-2)|}{\sqrt{1 + 4}} = \sqrt{5}$ unit

$$\therefore \quad \lambda = \sqrt{5}$$

Hence, $[\lambda] = [\sqrt{5}] = 2$

(D) Let $y = mx$ be the common line, then $b_1m^2 + 2h_1m + a_1 = 0$ and $b_2m^2 + 2h_2m + a_2 = 0$.

$$\Rightarrow \begin{vmatrix} b_1 & 2h_1 \\ b_2 & 2h_2 \end{vmatrix} \times \begin{vmatrix} 2h_1 & a_1 \\ 2h_2 & a_2 \end{vmatrix} = \begin{vmatrix} a_1 & b_1 \\ a_2 & b_2 \end{vmatrix}^2$$

$$\Rightarrow 4(b_1h_2 - b_2h_1)(a_2h_1 - a_1h_2) = (a_1b_2 - a_2b_1)^2$$

$$\therefore \quad \frac{(a_1b_2 - a_2b_1)^2}{(b_1h_2 - b_2h_1)(a_2h_1 - a_1h_2)} = 4$$

EXERCISE 1

JEE Main Pattern

Single Option Correct Type Questions

1. Number of points lying on the line $7x + 4y + 2 = 0$ which is equidistant from the lines $15x^2 + 56xy + 48y^2 = 0$ is

(a) 0 (b) 1
(c) 2 (d) 4

2. Orthocentre of the triangle formed by the lines $xy - 3x - 5y + 15 = 0$ and $3x + 5y = 15$ is

(a) $(-5, -3)$ (b) $(5, 3)$
(c) $(-3, -5)$ (d) $(3, 5)$

3. Two of the straight lines given by $3x^3 + 3x^2y - 3xy^2 + dy^3 = 0$ are at right angles, if d equal to

(a) -4 (b) -3
(c) -2 (d) -1

4. Two lines are given by $(x - 2y)^2 + \lambda(x - 2y) = 0$. The value of $|\lambda|$ so that the distance between them is 3, is

(a) $\sqrt{5}$ (b) $2\sqrt{5}$
(c) $3\sqrt{5}$ (d) $4\sqrt{5}$

5. The four straight lines given by the equations $12x^2 + 7xy - 12y^2 = 0$ and $12x^2 + 7xy - 12y^2 - x + 7y - 1 = 0$ lie along the sides of a

(a) square (b) rhombus
(c) rectangle (d) parallelogram

6. Distance between the parallel lines $4x^2 + 20xy + 25y^2 + 2x + 5y - 12 = 0$ is

(a) $\frac{3}{\sqrt{29}}$ (b) $\frac{5}{\sqrt{29}}$
(c) $\frac{7}{\sqrt{29}}$ (d) $\frac{9}{\sqrt{29}}$

7. The point of intersection of the two lines given by $2x^2 - 5xy + 2y^2 + 3x + 3y + 1 = 0$ is

(a) $(-2, 2)$ (b) $(-3, 3)$
(c) $(3, 3)$ (d) $(2, 2)$

8. If $\alpha, \beta > 0$ and $\alpha < \beta$ and $\alpha x^2 + 4\gamma xy + \beta y^2 + 4p(x + y + 1) = 0$ represents a pair of straight lines, then

(a) $\alpha \le p \le \beta$ (b) $p \le \alpha$
(c) $p \ge \alpha$ (d) $p \le \alpha$ or $p \ge \beta$

9. If the equation of the pair of straight lines passing through the point (1, 1), one making an angle θ with the positive direction of the X-axis and the other making the same angle with the positive direction of the Y-axis, is $x^2 - (a+2)xy + y^2 + a(x + y - 1) = 0, a \ne -2$, then the value of $\sin 2\theta$ is

(a) $a - 2$ (b) $a + 2$
(c) $\frac{2}{(a+2)}$ (d) $\frac{2}{a}$

10. If the pair of lines $ax^2 + 2(a+b)xy + by^2 = 0$ lie along the diameters of a circle and divide the circle into four sectors such that the area of one of the sector is thrice the area of the another sector, then

(a) $3a^2 + 2ab + 3b^2 = 0$
(b) $3a^2 + 10ab + 3b^2 = 0$
(c) $3a^2 - 2ab + 3b^2 = 0$
(d) $3a^2 - 10ab + 3b^2 = 0$

11. If one of the lines of $my^2 + (1 - m^2)xy - mx^2 = 0$ is a bisector of the angle between the lines $xy = 0$, then m^2 is

(a) $-\frac{1}{2}$ (b) -2
(c) 1 (d) 2

12. The line $x - 2y = 0$ will be a bisector of the angle between the lines represented by the equation $x^2 - 2hxy - 2y^2 = 0$, then h is equal to

(a) $\frac{1}{2}$ (b) 2
(c) -2 (d) $\left(-\frac{1}{2}\right)$

13. If the lines represented by the equation $3y^2 - x^2 + 2\sqrt{3}x - 3 = 0$ are rotated about the point $(\sqrt{3}, 0)$ through an angle 15° in clockwise direction and other in anti-clockwise direction so that they become perpendicular, then the equation of the pair of lines in the new position is

(a) $y^2 - x^2 + 2\sqrt{3}x + 3 = 0$
(b) $y^2 - x^2 + 2\sqrt{3}x - 3 = 0$
(c) $y^2 - x^2 - 2\sqrt{3}x + 3 = 0$
(d) $y^2 - x^2 + 3 = 0$

14. If two of the lines represented by $x^4+x^3y+cx^2y^2-xy^3+y^4=0$ bisects the angle between the other two, then the value of c is

(a) 0 (b) −1 (c) 1 (d) −6

15. The angle between the pair of lines whose equation is $4x^2+10xy+my^2+5x+10y=0$ is

(a) $\tan^{-1}\left(\frac{3}{8}\right)$

(b) $\tan^{-1}\left(\frac{3}{4}\right)$

(c) $\tan^{-1}\left(\frac{2\sqrt{25-4m}}{m+1}\right), m \geq n$

(d) None of the above

Numerical Value Type Questions

16. Equation $\lambda x^3-10x^2y-xy^2+4y^3=0$ represents three straight lines, out of these three, two lines makes equal angle with $y=x$ and $\lambda>0$, then the value of λ is ......

17. Area enclosed by curves $y^2-5xy+6x^2+3x-y=0$ and $y^2-5xy+6x^2+2x-y=0$ is λ sq units, then the value of λ is ......

18. The lines represented by $x^2+2\lambda xy+2y^2=0$ and $(\lambda+1)x^2-8xy+y^2=0$ are equally inclined, then the value of $|\lambda|$ is ......

19. If the lines joining the origin to the intersection of the line $y=nx+2$ and the curve $x^2+y^2=1$ are at right angles, then the value of n^2 is ......

20. If area of the triangle formed by the line $x+y=3$ and the angle bisectors of the pair of straight lines $x^2-y^2+2y=1$ is λ sq units, then the value of λ is ......

21. If $ax^3-9x^2y-xy^2+4y^3=0$ represents three straight lines such that two of them are perpendicular, then the sum of the values of a is ....

22. If the angle between the lines joining the points of intersection of line $y=3x+2$ and the curve $x^2+2xy+3y^2+4x+8y-11=0$ to the origin is $\tan^{-1}\left(\frac{m\sqrt{m}}{n}\right)$, then mn is equal to ......

23. If the distance between the pair of straight lines represented by $x^2+2\sqrt{2}xy+2y^2+4x+4\sqrt{2}y+1=0$ is λ units, then λ is ......

Previous Years Questions

24. If the line $l_1: 3y-2x=3$ is the angular bisector of the lines $l_2: x-y+1=0$ and $l_3: \alpha x+\beta y+17=0$, then $\alpha^2+\beta^2-\alpha-\beta$ is equal to......

[Numerical Value Type, 2023 Main]

25. Let the equation of the pair of lines, $y=px$ and $y=qx$ can be written as $(y-px)(y-qx)=0$. Then, the equation of the pair of the angle bisectors of the line $x^2-4xy-5y^2=0$ is

[Single Option Correct Type, 2021 Main]

(a) $x^2-3xy+y^2=0$ (b) $x^2+4xy-y^2=0$

(c) $x^2+3xy-y^2=0$ (d) $x^2-3xy-y^2=0$

EXERCISE 2

JEE Advanced Pattern

Single Correct Type Questions

1. A is a point on the X-axis through the point A, a line is drawn parallel to Y-axis so as to meet the lines $ax^2+2hxy+by^2=0$ at B and C. If $AB=BC$, then

(a) $9h^2=8ab$ (b) $8h^2=9ab$

(c) $4b^2=3ab$ (d) $3h^2=8ab$

2. A variable line L passing through the point $B(2,5)$ intersects the lines $2x^2-5xy+2y^2=0$ at P and Q, then the locus of point R on L such that distances BP, BR and BQ are in harmonic progression, is

(a) $17x-10y=0$ (b) $17x+10y=0$

(c) $10x-17y=0$ (d) None of these

3. Let a and b be non-zero and real number. Then, the equation $(ax^2+by^2+c)(x^2-5xy+6y^2)=0$ represents

(a) four straight line when $c=0$ and a, b are of the same sign

(b) two straight lines and a circle when $a=b$ and c is of sign opposite to that of a

(c) two straight lines and a circle when a and b are of the same sign and c is of opposite to that of a

(d) a circle and pair of straight lines when a and b are at the same sign and c is at sign opposite to that of a

4. If the pair of straight lines $ax^2 + 2hxy + by^2 = 0$ represents the adjacent sides of a parallelogram, then the equation of second diagonal if one is $lx + my = 1$ will be
(a) $(am + hl)x = (bl + hm)y$
(b) $(am - hl)x = (bl - hm)y$
(c) $(am - hl)x = (bl + hm)y$
(d) None of the above

5. The angle between the lines $(x^2 + y^2)\sin^2\alpha = (x\cos\beta - y\sin\beta)^2$ is
(a) 2β (b) 2α
(c) α (d) None of these

6. A straight line is drawn through (1, 0) to the curve $x^2 + y^2 + 6x - 10y + 1 = 0$ such that the intercept made on it by the curve subtends a right angle at the origin. Then , the slope of the line is
(a) 1 or $\frac{1}{9}$ (b) -1 or $-\frac{1}{9}$
(c) -1 or $\frac{1}{9}$ (d) 1 or $-\frac{1}{9}$

7. Let PQR be a right angled isosceles triangle, right angled at $P(2, 1)$. If the equation of line QR is $2x + y = 3$ then combined equation representing the pair of lines PQ and PR is
(a) $3x^2 - 3y^2 + 8xy + 20x + 10y + 25 = 0$
(b) $3x^2 - 3y^2 - 8xy - 4x + 22y - 7 = 0$
(c) $3x^2 - 3y^2 + 8xy + 10x + 15y + 20 = 0$
(d) $3x^2 - 3y^2 - 8xy - 10x - 15y - 20 = 0$

8. The square of distance of the point of intersection of the lines represented by the equation $ax^2 + 2hxy + by^2 + 2gx + 2fy + c = 0$ and origin is
(a) $\frac{c(a+b) - f^2 - g^2}{ab - h^2}$ (b) $\frac{c(a-b) + f^2 + g^2}{\sqrt{ab - h^2}}$
(c) $\frac{c(a+b) - f^2 - g^2}{ab + h^2}$ (d) None of these

9. Let the lines represented by $2x^2 - 5xy + 2y^2 = 0$ be the two sides of a parallelogram and the line $5x + 2y = 1$ be one of its diagonal. Then, the area of the parallelogram is
(a) $\frac{1}{36}$ sq unit (b) $\frac{1}{54}$ sq unit
(c) $\frac{1}{72}$ sq unit (d) $\frac{1}{96}$ sq unit

10. The lines L_1 and L_2 denoted by $3x^2 + 10xy + 8y^2 + 14x + 22y + 15 = 0$ intersect at the point P and have gradients m_1 and m_2, respectively. If acute angle between them is θ, then $\cos\theta$ is equal to
(a) $\frac{2}{5\sqrt{5}}$ (b) $\frac{11}{5\sqrt{5}}$ (c) $\frac{2}{11}$ (d) $\frac{5\sqrt{5}}{11}$

11. The equation of image of pair of lines $y = |x - 1|$ in Y-axis is
(a) $y = |x + 1|$
(b) $y = |x - 1| + 3$
(c) $x^2 - y^2 + 2x + 1 = 0$
(d) $x^2 - y^2 + 2x - 1 = 0$

12. The equation $ax^2 + by^2 + cx + cy = 0$ represents a pair of straight lines, if
(a) $a + b = 0$ (b) $c = 0$
(c) $a + c = 0$ (d) $c(a + b) = 0$

More than One Option Correct Type Questions

13. If $x^2 + \alpha y^2 + 2\beta y = a^2$ represents a pair of perpendicular straight lines, then
(a) $\alpha = 1, \beta = a$
(b) $\alpha = 1, \beta = -a$
(c) $\alpha = -1, \beta = -a$
(d) $\alpha = -1, \beta = a$

14. If the pair of lines $ax^2 + 2hxy + by^2 + 2gx + 2fy + c = 0$ intersect on Y-axis, then
(a) $f^2 = bc$
(b) $abc = 2fgh$
(c) $bg^2 \neq ch^2$
(d) $2fgh = bg^2 + ch^2$

15. The combined equation of three sides of a triangle is $(x^2 - y^2)(2x + 3y - 6) = 0$. If $(-2, a)$ is an interior and $(b, 1)$ is an exterior point of the triangle, then
(a) $2 < a < \frac{10}{3}$ (b) $-2 < a < \frac{10}{3}$
(c) $-1 < b < \frac{9}{2}$ (d) $-1 < b < 1$

Passage Based Questions

Passage I

(Q. Nos. 16 to 17)

- Consider a pair of perpendicular straight lines $2x^2 + 3xy + by^2 - 11x + 13y + c = 0$

16. The value of c is
(a) -2 (b) 2
(c) -3 (d) 3

17. If point of intersection of lines is C and points of intersection of the lines with the X-axis are A and B, if distance between the orthocentre and the circumcentre of ΔABC is λ, then $[\lambda]$ is (where [.] denotes the greatest integer function)
(a) 2 (b) 3
(c) 4 (d) 5

Passage II

(Q. Nos. 18 to 19)

- Let $f_1(x, y) \equiv ax^2 + 2hxy + by^2 = 0$ and let $f_{i+1}(x, y) = 0$ denote the equation of the bisectors of $f_i(x, y) = 0$ for all $i = 1, 2, 3, \ldots$

18. $f_3(x, y) = 0$ is

(a) $hx^2 - (a-b)xy - hy^2 = 0$

(b) $(a-b)x^2 + 4hxy - (a-b)y^2 = 0$

(c) $ax^2 + 2hxy + by^2 = 0$

(d) None of the above

19. The value of $\sum_{n=2}^{5} \frac{f_{n+2}(x, y)}{f_n(x, y)}$ is

(a) 14 (b) 4

(c) 54 (d) 6

Stem Based Questions

Stem I

(Q. Nos. 20 to 21)

- Consider a line pair $ax^2 + 3xy - 2y^2 - 5x + 5y + c = 0$ representing perpendicular lines intersecting each other at C and forming a ΔABC with the X-axis.

20. If x_1 and x_2 are intercepts on the X-axis and y_1 and y_2 are the intercepts on the Y-axis, then the sum $(x_1 + x_2 + y_1 + y_2)$ is equal to ....

21. Distance between orthocentre and circumcentre of the ΔABC is ....

Stem II

(Q. Nos. 22 to 23)

- Suppose a line $lx + my = 1$ meets a second degree curve $ax^2 + 2hxy + by^2 + 2gx + 2fy + c = 0$ at two points A and B. Then, the combined equation of the pair of lines OA and OB is $ax^2 + 2hxy + by^2 + (2gx + 2fy)(lx + my) + c(lx + my)^2 = 0$ which is a second degree homogeneous equation.

22. If all chords of the curve $3x^2 - y^2 - 2x + 4y = 0$ which subtend right angle at the origin will pass through a fixed point whose coordinates are (m, n), then $m - n$ is ....

23. If the intercept of the line $lx + my = 1$ made by the curve $x^2 + y^2 - a^2 = 0$ subtend right angle at the origin and $l^2 + m^2 = \frac{\lambda}{a^2}$, then 2λ is ....

Single Integer Type Questions

24. If the area of quadrilateral formed by given lines $3x^2 + 8xy - 3y^2 = 0$ and $3x^2 + 8xy - 3y^2 + 2x - 4y - 1 = 0$ is $\frac{1}{m}$, then $\frac{m}{2}$ is equal to ....

25. The combined equation of three sides of a triangle is $(x^2 - y^2)(2x + 3y - 6) = 0$. If $(-2, a)$ is the interior point of the triangle, then the integral value of a is ....

26. Two conics $a_1x^2 + 2h_1xy + b_1y^2 = c_1$ and $a_2x^2 + 2h_2xy + b_2y^2 = c_2$ intersect at 4 concylic points, where $(a_1 - b_1)h_2 = \lambda(a_2 - b_2)h_1$, then λ is equal to ......

27. There exists two ordered triplets (a_1, b_1, c_1) and (a_2, b_2, c_2) for (a, b, c) for which the equation $4x^2 - 4xy + ay^2 + bx + cy + 1 = 0$ represents a pair of identical straight lines in XY-plane. Then, the value of $a_1 + b_1 + c_1 + a_2 + b_2 + c_2$ is ......

28. If the pair of lines $9x^2 + 14xy + 16y^2 = 0$ are equally inclined to the lines $3x^2 + 2xy + \lambda y^2 = 0$, then the value of λ is ....

Numerical Value Type Questions

29. If the angle between the pair of straight lines represented by the equation $x^2 - 3xy + \lambda y^2 + 3x - 5y + 2 = 0$ is $\tan^{-1}\left(\frac{1}{3}\right)$, where λ is non-negative real number, then $5[\lambda]$ is (where [.] denotes the greatest integer function) ....

30. Area of the triangle formed by the lines $y^2 - 9xy + 18x^2 = 0$ and $y = 9$, is ....

31. If the equation $ax^2 + 2hxy + by^2 + 2gx + 2fy + c = 0$ represents two straight lines and the product of the perpendiculars drawn from the origin to the lines is $\frac{mc}{\sqrt{(a-b)^2 + nh^2}}$, then $4(m+n)$ is ....

32. If the equation $12x^2 + 7xy - py^2 - 18x + 9y + 6 = 0$ represents two perpendicular lines, then the value of $p + q$ is, ... (where p and q are positive integers)

33. A point moves so that the distance between the feet of perpendiculars drawn from it to the lines $ax^2 + 2hxy + by^2 = 0$ is a constant $2n$ and the locus of the point is $(x^2 + y^2)(h^2 - ab) = n^2((a-b)^2 + \lambda h^2)$, then $\frac{\lambda}{10}$ is equal to ....

Matching Type Questions

34. Match the following

Column I		Column II
(A) The pair of lines joining the origin to the points of intersection of the curve $9x^2 + 16y^2 = 144$ by the line $2x + 2y + \lambda = 0$ are coincident, then $\lvert \lambda \rvert$ is divisible by	(p)	2
(B) If the straight lines joining the origin to the points of intersection of the straight line $4x + 3y = 24$ and the curve $(x-3)^2 + (y-4)^2 = \lambda^2$, are at right angles, then $\lvert\lambda\rvert$ is divisible by	(q)	3
(C) The two line pairs $y^2 - 4y + 3 = 0$ and $x^2 + 4xy + 4y^2 - 5x - 10y + 4 = 0$ enclose a 4 sided convex polygon, if area of polygon is λ sq units, then λ is divisible by	(r)	5
(D) If the pairs of lines $3x^2 - 2pxy - 3y^2 = 0$ and $5x^2 - 2qxy - 5y^2 = 0$ are such that each pair bisects the angle between the other pair. If $\lambda = \lvert pq \rvert$, then λ is divisible by	(s)	6

35. Match the items of column I with those of column II.

Column I		Column II
(A) If $6x^2 + 5xy - 6y^2 + 9x + 20y + c = 0$ represents a pair of lines, then c is equal to	(p)	$\frac{\pi}{2}$
(B) The angle between the lines joining the origin to the points of intersection of the curve $2x^2 + 6xy + 3y^2 + 4x + 2y - 36 = 0$ and line $x - 2y - 6 = 0$ is	(q)	8
(C) If the lines joining the origin to the points of intersection of the curve $2x^2 - 2xy + 3y^2 + 2x - y - 1 = 0$ and the line $x + 2y = k$ are at right angles, then the value of k is	(r)	1
(D) If d is the distance between the parallel lines represented by the equation $9x^2 - 24xy + 16y^2 - 12x + 16y - 12 = 0$, then the value of $5d$ is	(s)	-6
	(t)	-1

EXERCISE 3

Challenging Problems

1. Show that the straight lines $(A^2 - 3B^2)x^2 + 8ABxy + (B^2 - 3A^2)y^2 = 0$ form with the line $Ax + By + C = 0$ are equilateral triangle whose area is $\frac{C^2}{\sqrt{3}(A^2 + B^2)}$.

2. Prove that the equation $(a + 2h + b)x^2 - 2(a - b)xy + (a - 2h + b)y^2 = 0$ represents a pair of lines each inclined at an angle of 45° to one or other of the lines given by, $ax^2 + 2hxy + by^2 = 0$.

3. If $u \equiv ax^2 + 2hxy + by^2 + 2gx + 2fy + c = 0$ represents a pair of straight lines, prove that the equation of the third pair of straight lines passing through the points where these meet the axes is $cu + 4(fg - ch)xy = 0$.

4. If the equation $ax^2 + 2hxy + by^2 + 2gx + 2fy + c = 0$ represents a pair of parallel lines, prove that

(i) $h = \sqrt{ab}$ and $g\sqrt{b} = f\sqrt{a}$ or $(h = -\sqrt{ab}$ and $g\sqrt{b} = -f\sqrt{a})$.

(ii) the distance between them is $2\sqrt{\left(\frac{g^2 - ac}{a(a + b)}\right)}$.

5. A parallelogram is formed by the lines $ax^2 + 2hxy + by^2 = 0$ and the lines through (p, q) parallel to them. Show that the equation of the diagonal of the parallelogram which does not pass through origin is $(2x - p)(ap + hq) + (2y - q)(hp + bq) = 0$.
Show also that the area of the parallelogram is $|(ap^2 + 2hpq + bq^2)| / 2\sqrt{(h^2 - ab)}$.

6. A triangle has the line $y = m_1 x$ and $y = m_2 x$ for two of its sides with m_1 and m_2 being roots of the equation $bx^2 + 2hx + a = 0$. If $H(a, b)$ is the orthocentre of the triangle, then find the equation of the third side.

7. Show that if two of the lines $ax^3 + bx^2 y + cxy^2 + dy^3 = 0 (a \neq 0)$ make complementary angles with X-axis in anti-clockwise sense, then $a(a - c) + d(b - d) = 0$.

8. Show that the equation $a(x^4 + y^4) - 4bxy(x^2 - y^2) + 6cx^2 y^2 = 0$ represents two pairs of lines at right angles and that if $2b^2 = a^2 + 3ac$, the two pairs will coincide.

9. Show that the locus of a point such that the product of the perpendiculars drawn from it on three lines represented by $ay^3 + by^2 x + cyx^2 + dx^3 = 0$ is constant $= k^3$, is $ay^3 + by^2 x + cyx^2 + dx^3 = k^3 \sqrt{(a-c)^2 + (b-d)^2}$.

10. If one of the lines given by the equation $ax^2 + 2hxy + by^2 = 0$ coincides with one of the lines given by $a'x^2 + 2h'xy + b'y^2 = 0$ and the other lines represented by them be perpendicular, then $\frac{ha'b'}{b' - a'} = \frac{h'ab}{b - a} = \frac{1}{2}\sqrt{(-aa'bb')}$.

Answer Key

Exercise 1

1. (c)	2. (b)	3. (b)	4. (c)	5. (a)	6. (c)	7. (c)	8. (d)	9. (c)	10. (a)
11. (c)	12. (c)	13. (b)	14. (d)	15. (b)	16. (7)	17. (1)	18. (2)	19. (7)	20. (2)
21. (1)	22. (6)	23. (2)	24. (348)	25. (c)					

Exercise 2

1. (b)	2. (a)	3. (b)	4. (b)	5. (b)	6. (b)	7. (b)	8. (a)	9. (a)	10. (b)
11. (c)	12. (d)	13. (c,d)	14. (a,d)	15. (a,d)	16. (a)	17. (c)	18. (b)	19. (b)	20. (5)
21. (1.75)	22. (3)	23. (4)	24. (5)	25. (3)	26. (1)	27. (2)	28. (4)	29. (10)	30. (6.75)
31. (20)	32. (13)	33. (0.4)							

34. (A) → (p,r); (B) → (r); (C) → (p,q,s); (D) → (q,r)

35. (A) → (s); (B) → (p); (C) → (r,t); (D) → (q)

Solutions

Exercise 1 - JEE Main Pattern

1. Given, $15x^2 + 56xy + 48y^2 = 0$ ...(i)

$\Rightarrow \quad (3x + 4y)(5x + 12y) = 0$

Equation of lines represented by Eq. (i) are

$$3x + 4y = 0 \text{ and } 5x + 12y = 0$$

Let any point on $7x + 4y + 2 = 0$ be $\left(\lambda, \dfrac{-7\lambda - 2}{4}\right)$.

According to the question,

$$\left| \frac{3\lambda + 4\left(\dfrac{-7\lambda - 2}{4}\right)}{5} \right| = \left| \frac{5\lambda + 12\left(\dfrac{-7\lambda - 2}{4}\right)}{13} \right|$$

$\Rightarrow \quad \dfrac{1}{5}|-4\lambda - 2| = \dfrac{1}{13}|-16\lambda - 6|$

$\Rightarrow \quad \dfrac{|2\lambda + 1|}{5} = \dfrac{|8\lambda + 3|}{13}$

$\Rightarrow \quad 13(2\lambda + 1) = \pm 5(8\lambda + 3)$

$\therefore \quad \lambda = -\dfrac{1}{7}, -\dfrac{14}{33}$

Hence, the number of points lying on the line $7x + 4y + 2 = 0$, which is equidistant from lines $15x^2 + 56xy + 48y^2 = 0$ is 2.

2. Given lines are $xy - 3x - 5y + 15 = 0$

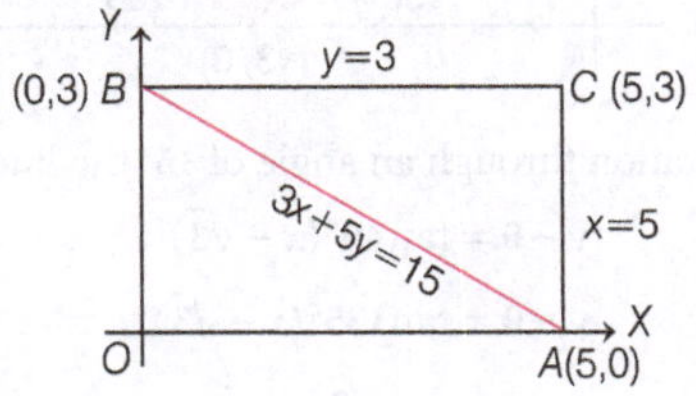

$\Rightarrow \quad (x - 5)(y - 3) = 0$

$\therefore \quad x = 5 \text{ and } y = 3$

Hence, orthocentre is (5, 3).

3. $3x^3 + 3x^2y - 3xy^2 + dy^3 = (x^2 + pxy - y^2)(3x - dy)$

On comparing coefficients of x^2y and xy^2, we get

$$3p - d = 3 \quad \text{and} \quad -3 - pd = -3$$

$\therefore \quad p = 0 \text{ and } d = -3$

4. Given, $(x - 2y)^2 + \lambda(x - 2y) = 0$

$\Rightarrow \quad (x - 2y)(x - 2y + \lambda) = 0$

$\therefore$ Lines are $x - 2y = 0$ and $x - 2y + \lambda = 0$.

Distance between the lines = 3 (given)

$\Rightarrow \quad \dfrac{|\lambda - 0|}{\sqrt{(1 + 4)}} = 3$

$\therefore \quad |\lambda| = 3\sqrt{5}$

5. Given, $12x^2 + 7xy - 12y^2 = 0$ ...(i)

$\Rightarrow \quad (3x + 4y)(4x - 3y) = 0$

$\therefore$ Lines represented by Eq. (i) are

$$3x + 4y = 0 \text{ and } 4x - 3y = 0$$

and $\quad 12x^2 + 7xy - 12y^2 - x + 7y - 1 = 0$ ...(ii)

$\Rightarrow \quad (3x + 4y - 1)(4x - 3y + 1) = 0$

$\therefore$ Lines represented by Eq. (ii) are

$$3x + 4y - 1 = 0 \text{ and } 4x - 3y + 1 = 0$$

Distance between parallel lines $3x + 4y = 0$ and $3x + 4y - 1 = 0$ is $\dfrac{1}{5}$.

And distance between parallel lines $4x - 3y = 0$ and $4x - 3y + 1 = 0$ is $\dfrac{1}{5}$.

Hence, all lines lie along the sides of a square.

6. Given, $4x^2 + 20xy + 25y^2 + 2x + 5y - 12 = 0$ ...(i)

$\Rightarrow \quad (2x + 5y)^2 + (2x + 5y) - 12 = 0$

$\Rightarrow \quad (2x + 5y + 4)(2x + 5y - 3) = 0$

$\therefore$ Lines represented by Eq. (i) are

$$2x + 5y + 4 = 0 \text{ and } 2x + 5y - 3 = 0$$

Hence, distance between parallel lines $= \dfrac{|4 - (-3)|}{\sqrt{4 + 25}} = \dfrac{7}{\sqrt{29}}$.

7. Let $f(x, y) \equiv 2x^2 - 5xy + 2y^2 + 3x + 3y + 1 = 0$

$\therefore \quad \dfrac{\partial f}{\partial x} = 4x - 5y + 3 \text{ and } \dfrac{\partial f}{\partial y} = -5x + 4y + 3$

For point of intersection, $\dfrac{\partial f}{\partial x} = 0$ and $\dfrac{\partial f}{\partial y} = 0$

$\Rightarrow \quad 4x - 5y + 3 = 0$ and $-5x + 4y + 3 = 0$, we get $x = 3$ and $y = 3$.

$\therefore$ Point of intersection is (3, 3).

8. Given equation $\alpha x^2 + 4\gamma xy + \beta y^2 + 4p(x + y + 1) = 0$ represents a pair of straight lines.

$\therefore \Delta = 0$

$\Rightarrow \quad 4\alpha\beta p + 16p^2\gamma - 4p^2\alpha - 4p^2\beta - 16\gamma^2 p = 0$

$\Rightarrow \quad (16p)\gamma^2 - 16p^2\gamma + 4p(p\alpha + p\beta - \alpha\beta) = 0$

$\therefore \quad B^2 - 4AC \geq 0$

$\Rightarrow \quad (16p^2)^2 - 4 \cdot (16p) \cdot 4p(p\alpha + p\beta - \alpha\beta) \geq 0$

$\Rightarrow \quad p^2(p^2 - p\alpha - p\beta + \alpha\beta) \geq 0$

$\Rightarrow \quad (p - \alpha)(p - \beta) \geq 0$

$\therefore \quad p \leq \alpha \text{ or } p \geq \beta \qquad [\because \alpha < \beta]$

9. Equation of first line is $y-1=\tan\theta(x-1)$

Equation of second line is $y-1=\cot\theta(x-1)$

So, their joint equation is

$$[(y-1)-\tan\theta\,(x-1)][(y-1)-\cot\theta\,(x-1)]=0$$

$$\Rightarrow (y-1)^2-(x-1)(y-1)(\tan\theta+\cot\theta)+(x-1)^2=0$$

$$\Rightarrow x^2-(\tan\theta+\cot\theta)xy+y^2$$
$$+(\tan\theta+\cot\theta-2)(x+y-1)=0$$

On comparing with the given equation, we get

$$\tan\theta+\cot\theta=a+2$$

or $$\frac{1}{\sin\theta\cos\theta}=a+2$$

or $$\sin 2\theta=\frac{2}{(a+2)}$$

10. Let A be the area of small sector, then area of major sector is $3A$.

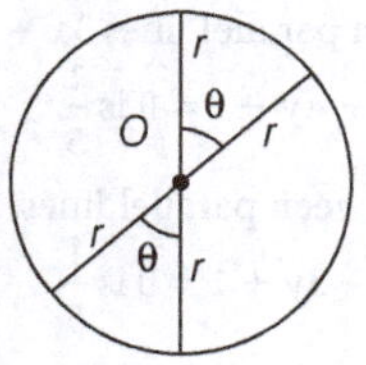

$$\therefore \quad A+3A+A+3A=\pi r^2$$

$$\Rightarrow \quad A=\frac{\pi}{8}r^2$$

$$\Rightarrow \quad \frac{1}{2}r^2\theta=\frac{\pi}{8}r^2 \quad \left[\because \text{area of sector}=\frac{1}{2}r^2\theta\right]$$

$$\therefore \quad \theta=\frac{\pi}{4}$$

$\therefore$ Angle between lines represented by

$$ax^2+2(a+b)xy+by^2=0 \text{ is } \frac{\pi}{4}.$$

$$\Rightarrow \quad \tan\frac{\pi}{4}=\frac{2\sqrt{(a+b)^2-ab}}{|a+b|}$$

$$\Rightarrow \quad 1=\frac{2\sqrt{(a+b)^2-ab}}{|a+b|}$$

$$\Rightarrow \quad (a+b)^2=4(a+b)^2-4ab$$

$$\therefore \quad 3a^2+2ab+3b^2=0$$

11. The equation of the bisectors of the lines $xy=0$ are $y=\pm x$.

On putting $y=\pm x$ in $my^2+(1-m^2)xy-mx^2=0$, we get

$$\pm(1-m^2)x^2=0$$

$$\therefore \quad m^2=1$$

12. Given, $x^2-2hxy-2y^2=0$ be a pair of straight lines whose one bisector is line $x=2y$.

Now, equation of bisectors of given equation

$$\frac{x^2-y^2}{a-b}=\frac{xy}{h'}$$

Here, $a=1, b=-2$ and $h'=-h$

$$\therefore \quad \frac{x^2-y^2}{1-(-2)}=\frac{xy}{-h}$$

$$\Rightarrow \quad \frac{x^2-y^2}{3}=\frac{xy}{-h} \quad \text{...(i)}$$

and $x=2y$ is a bisector.

It will satisfy Eq. (i).

So, $$\frac{4y^2-y^2}{3}=\frac{2y^2}{-h}$$

$$\Rightarrow \quad \frac{3y^2}{3}=\frac{2y^2}{-h}$$

$$\Rightarrow \quad -h=2$$

$$\therefore \quad h=-2$$

13. The given equation is

$$3y^2-x^2+2\sqrt{3}x-3=0$$

$$\Rightarrow \quad (\sqrt{3}y-x+\sqrt{3})(\sqrt{3}y+x-\sqrt{3})=0$$

$$\Rightarrow \quad \sqrt{3}y-x+\sqrt{3}=0 \text{ and } \sqrt{3}y+x-\sqrt{3}=0$$

$$\Rightarrow \quad y=\frac{1}{\sqrt{3}}x-1 \text{ and } y=-\frac{1}{\sqrt{3}}x+1$$

$$\Rightarrow \quad y=(\tan 30^\circ)x-1 \text{ and } y=(\tan 150^\circ)x+1$$

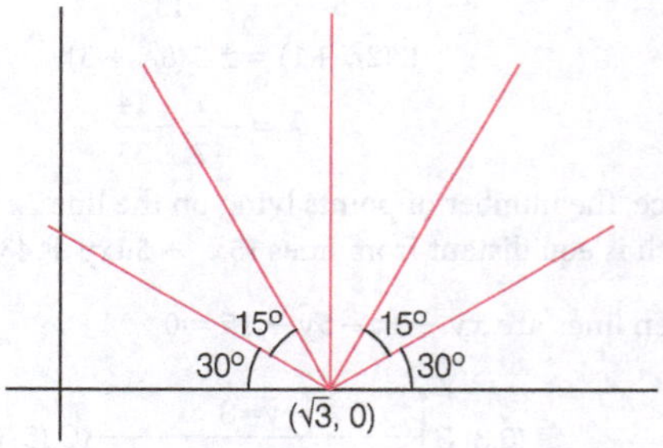

After rotation through an angle of 15° the lines are

$$y-0=\tan 45^\circ(x-\sqrt{3})$$

and $$y-0=\tan 135^\circ(x-\sqrt{3})$$

$$\Rightarrow \quad y=x-\sqrt{3}$$

and $$y=-x+\sqrt{3}$$

Combined equation is

$$(y-x+\sqrt{3})(y+x-\sqrt{3})=0$$

$$\therefore \quad y^2-x^2+2\sqrt{3}x-3=0$$

14. Given equation is

$$x^4+x^3y+cx^2y^2-xy^3+y^4=0 \quad \text{...(i)}$$

Let m_1, m_2, m_3 and m_4 be slopes of 4 lines represented by Eq. (i), then

$$m_1m_2m_3m_4=1$$

The product of the slopes of the 4 lines represented by Eq. (i) and a pair of lines represented by the bisectors of the angles between the other two, is -1.

So, let the equation of one pair be

$$ax^2 + 2hxy - ay^2 = 0,$$

then equation of its bisector is

$$\frac{x^2 - y^2}{2a} = \frac{xy}{h}$$

$$\Rightarrow \quad hx^2 - hy^2 - 2axy = 0$$

By hypothesis,

$$x^4 + x^3y + cx^2y^2 - xy^3 + y^4$$
$$= (ax^2 + 2hxy - ay^2)(hx^2 - 2axy - hy^2)$$
$$= ah(x^4 + y^4) + 2(h^2 - a^2)(x^3y - xy^3) - 6ahx^2y^2$$

By comparing, we get

$$ah = 1, 2(h^2 - a^2) = 1 \text{ and } -6ah = c$$

$$\therefore \quad c = -6 \quad [\text{put } ah = 1]$$

15. **Decoding the Question**

If $ax^2 + 2hxy + by^2 + 2gx + 2fy + c = 0$ represents pair of straight lines. Then, angle between the pair of lines is given by $\tan\theta = \frac{2\sqrt{h^2 - ab}}{|a + b|}$.

Given equation is

$$4x^2 + 10xy + my^2 + 5x + 10y = 0$$

$$\therefore \quad a = 4, b = m, h = 5, g = \frac{5}{2}, f = 5 \text{ and } c = 0$$

For pair of straight lines

$$abc + 2fgh - af^2 - bg^2 - ch^2 = 0$$

$$\Rightarrow 4(m)(0) + 2(5)\left(\frac{5}{2}\right)(5) - 4(5)^2 - m\left(\frac{5}{2}\right)^2 - 0(5)^2 = 0$$

$$\Rightarrow \quad 125 - 100 - \frac{25}{4}m = 0$$

$$\Rightarrow \quad \frac{25}{4}m = 25 \Rightarrow m = 4$$

and angle between the lines

$$\theta = \tan^{-1}\left\{\frac{2\sqrt{h^2 - ab}}{a + b}\right\}$$
$$= \tan^{-1}\left(\frac{2\sqrt{5^2 - 4m}}{4 + m}\right)$$
$$= \tan^{-1}\left(\frac{2\sqrt{25 - 4m}}{m + 4}\right)$$
$$= \tan^{-1}\left(\frac{2\sqrt{25 - 16}}{4 + 4}\right)$$
$$= \tan^{-1}\left(\frac{6}{8}\right) = \tan^{-1}\left(\frac{3}{4}\right)$$

16. Given, $4y^3 - xy^2 - 10x^2y + \lambda x^3 = 0$

$$\Rightarrow \quad 4\left(\frac{y}{x}\right)^3 - \left(\frac{y}{x}\right)^2 - 10\left(\frac{y}{x}\right) + \lambda = 0$$

Let $y = mx$, then

$$4m^3 - m^2 - 10m + \lambda = 0$$

and let m_1, m_2, m_3 be the slopes of three lines, then

$$m_1 + m_2 + m_3 = \frac{1}{4} \quad \text{...(i)}$$

$$m_1m_2 + m_2m_3 + m_3m_1 = -\frac{10}{4} \quad \text{...(ii)}$$

$$m_1m_2m_3 = -\frac{\lambda}{4} \quad \text{...(iii)}$$

Since, two lines are equally inclined with $y = x$, so let $m_2m_3 = 1$

From Eq. (iii), $\quad m_1 = -\frac{\lambda}{4}$

From Eq. (i), $\quad m_2 + m_3 = \frac{\lambda + 1}{4} \quad \text{...(iv)}$

and from Eq. (ii), $\quad 1 + \left(-\frac{\lambda}{4}\right)\left(\frac{\lambda + 1}{4}\right) = -\frac{10}{4}$

$$\Rightarrow \quad 16 - \lambda^2 - \lambda = -40$$

$$\Rightarrow \quad \lambda^2 + \lambda - 56 = 0$$

$$\Rightarrow \quad (\lambda + 8)(\lambda - 7) = 0$$

$$\lambda = -8, 7$$

Hence, $\quad \lambda = 7 \quad [\because \lambda > 0]$

17. Given, $y^2 - 5xy + 6x^2 + 3x - y = 0$

$$\Rightarrow \quad (3x - y)(2x - y + 1) = 0$$

and $\quad y^2 - 5xy + 6x^2 + 2x - y = 0$

$$\Rightarrow \quad (3x - y + 1)(2x - y) = 0$$

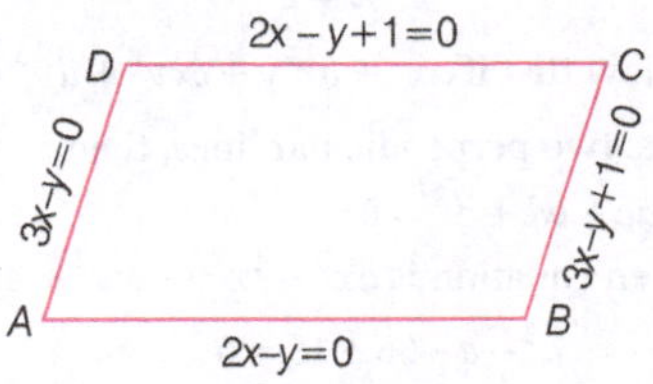

$$\therefore \text{Required area} = \frac{(1 - 0)(1 - 0)}{\begin{vmatrix} 3 & -1 \\ 2 & -1 \end{vmatrix}} = 1 \text{ sq unit}$$

[$\because$ *ABCD* is parallelogram]

$$\therefore \quad \lambda = 1$$

18. Given pairs are $x^2 + 2\lambda xy + 2y^2 = 0 \quad \text{...(i)}$

and $\quad (\lambda + 1)x^2 - 8xy + y^2 = 0 \quad \text{...(ii)}$

$\because$ Equations of angle bisectors of Eqs. (i) and (ii) are equal

$$\Rightarrow \frac{x^2 - y^2}{1 - 2} = \frac{xy}{\lambda} \text{ and } \frac{x^2 - y^2}{(\lambda + 1) - 1} = \frac{xy}{-4} \text{ must be same.}$$

$$\Rightarrow \quad \frac{\lambda}{-1} = -\frac{4}{\lambda}$$

$$\Rightarrow \quad \lambda^2 = 4 \Rightarrow \lambda = \pm 2$$

$$\therefore \quad |\lambda| = 2$$

19. Given, $\quad \frac{y - nx}{2} = 1 \quad \text{...(i)}$

and $\quad x^2 + y^2 = 1 \quad \text{...(ii)}$

Homogenising Eq. (ii) with Eq. (i), we get

$$x^2 + y^2 = \left(\frac{y - nx}{2}\right)^2$$

$$\Rightarrow \left(\frac{n^2}{4}-1\right)x^2 - nxy + \left(\frac{1}{4}-1\right)y^2 = 0$$

or $(n^2-4)x^2 - 4nxy - 3y^2 = 0$

The lines will be at right angles, when

$$(n^2-4)+(-3)=0$$

$\therefore$ $n^2 = 7$

20. Given, $x^2 - y^2 + 2y = 1$

$\Rightarrow$ $x^2 = (y^2 - 2y + 1) = (y-1)^2$

$\Rightarrow$ $x = \pm (y-1)$

i.e. $x - y + 1 = 0$ and $x + y - 1 = 0$

$\therefore$ Bisectors are $y = 1$ and $x = 0$

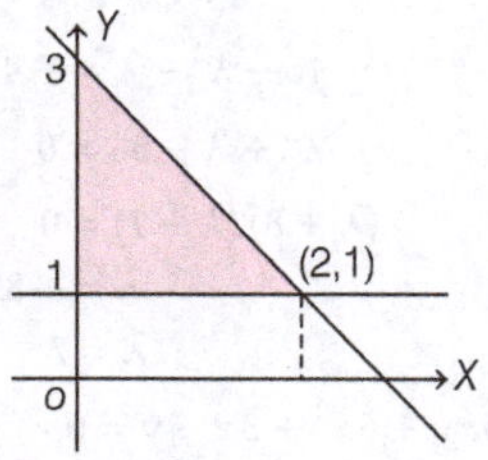

So, area between $x = 0$, $y = 1$ and $x + y = 3$ is given by

$$\frac{1}{2}\times 2\times 2 = 2 \text{ sq units}$$

$\therefore$ $\lambda = 2$

21. As we know that if $ax^3 + bx^2y + cxy^2 + dy^3 = 0$ represents two perpendicular lines, then

$$a^2 + ac + bd + d^2 = 0$$

Now, given equation is $ax^3 - 9x^2y - xy^2 + 4y^3 = 0$

$\therefore$ $a^2 - a - 36 + 16 = 0$

$\Rightarrow$ $a^2 - a - 20 = 0$

$\Rightarrow$ $(a-5)(a+4) = 0$

$\Rightarrow$ $a = 5, -4$

$\therefore$ Sum of the values of a is 1.

22. Given line, $y = 3x + 2$

Given, equation of pair of straight lines

$$x^2 + 2xy + 3y^2 + 4x + 8y - 11 = 0$$

Now, by homogenising, we get

$$x^2 + 2xy + 3y^2 + 4x\left(\frac{y-3x}{2}\right) + 8y\left(\frac{y-3x}{2}\right) - 11\left(\frac{y-3x}{2}\right)^2 = 0$$

$$\Rightarrow x^2 + 2xy + 3y^2 + 2xy - 6x^2 + 4y^2 - 12xy - \frac{11}{4}(y^2 + 9x^2 - 6xy) = 0$$

$$\Rightarrow x^2\left(1 - 6 - \frac{99}{4}\right) + y^2\left(3 + 4 - \frac{11}{4}\right) + xy\left(-8 + \frac{66}{4}\right) = 0$$

$$\Rightarrow -\frac{119}{4}x^2 + \frac{17}{4}y^2 + \frac{34}{4}xy = 0$$

$$\Rightarrow -7x^2 + 2xy + y^2 = 0$$

$$\therefore \tan\theta = \left|\frac{2\sqrt{h^2 - ab}}{a+b}\right| = \left|\frac{2\sqrt{1^2 - (-7)}}{-7+1}\right| = \frac{2\sqrt{2}}{3}$$

$$\Rightarrow \theta = \tan^{-1}\left(\frac{2\sqrt{2}}{3}\right)$$

Here, $m = 2$ and $n = 3$

$\therefore$ $mn = 2\times 3 = 6$

23. **Decoding the Question**

If $ax + by + c_1 = 0$ and $ax + by + c_2 = 0$ are two parallel lines, then distance between them is given by

$$d = \left|\frac{c_2 - c_1}{\sqrt{a^2+b^2}}\right|$$

Given combined equation is

$$x^2 + 2\sqrt{2}xy + 2y^2 + 4x + 4\sqrt{2}y + 1 = 0$$

$$\Rightarrow x^2 + x(2\sqrt{2}y + 4) + 2y^2 + 4\sqrt{2}y + 1 = 0$$

On taking above equation as a quadratic in x,

$$a = 1, b = 2\sqrt{2}y + 4 \text{ and } c = 2y^2 + 4\sqrt{2}y + 1$$

$$x = \frac{-(2\sqrt{2}y+4) \pm \sqrt{(2\sqrt{2}y+4)^2 - 4(1)(2y^2 + 4\sqrt{2}y + 1)}}{2(1)}$$

$$\Rightarrow x = \frac{-(2\sqrt{2}y+4) \pm \sqrt{8y^2 + 16 - 16\sqrt{2}y - 8y^2 - 16\sqrt{2}y - 4}}{2}$$

$$\Rightarrow x = \frac{-2(\sqrt{2})y - 4 \pm \sqrt{12}}{2}$$

$$\Rightarrow 2x = -2\sqrt{2}y - 4 \pm 2\sqrt{3}$$

$$\Rightarrow x = -\sqrt{2}y - 2 \pm \sqrt{3}$$

$\therefore$ Equation are

$$\sqrt{2}y + x + 2 - \sqrt{3} = 0$$

and $$\sqrt{2}y + x + 2 + \sqrt{3} = 0$$

$\Rightarrow$ $$x + \sqrt{2}y + 2 - \sqrt{3} = 0$$

and $$x + \sqrt{2}y + 2 + \sqrt{3} = 0$$

$$\because \frac{b_1}{b_2} = \frac{\sqrt{2}}{\sqrt{2}} = 1 \text{ and } \frac{a_1}{a_2} = \frac{1}{1} = 1$$

$$\Rightarrow \frac{a_1}{a_2} = \frac{b_1}{b_2} = 1$$

Lines are parallel.

$\therefore$ Distance between them

$$= \left|\frac{c_1 - c_2}{\sqrt{a^2+b^2}}\right| = \left|\frac{2-\sqrt{3}-2-\sqrt{3}}{\sqrt{2+1}}\right|$$

$$= \left|\frac{2\sqrt{3}}{\sqrt{3}}\right|$$

$$= 2 \text{ units}$$

$\therefore$ $\lambda = 2$

24. Given, l_1 is angular bisector of l_2 and l_3.

Let angle between l_1 and l_2 be θ.

Then, $\tan\theta = \left|\dfrac{m_1 - m_2}{1 + m_1 m_2}\right|$

$$\tan\theta = \left|\frac{\frac{2}{3} - 1}{1 + \frac{2}{3}}\right| = \frac{1}{5} \qquad \left[\because m_1 = \frac{2}{3}, m_2 = 1\right]$$

Then, $\tan\theta = \dfrac{1}{5} = \left|\dfrac{m_1 - m_3}{1 + m_1 m_3}\right|$

$$\Rightarrow \left|\frac{m - \frac{2}{3}}{1 + \frac{2m}{3}}\right| = \frac{1}{5} \Rightarrow 5m - \frac{10}{3} = \left(1 + \frac{2m}{3}\right)$$

and $5m - \dfrac{10}{3} = -\left(1 + \dfrac{2m}{3}\right)$

$$m = 1, m = \frac{7}{17}$$

$\therefore$ Point of intersection l_1 and l_2 passes through is (0, 1) and also satisfy l_3.

$\Rightarrow \quad y - 1 = \dfrac{7x}{17}$

$\Rightarrow \quad 7x - 17y + 17 = 0$

$\alpha = 7$

and $\beta = -17$

Hence, $\alpha^2 + \beta^2 - \alpha - \beta$

$= 49 + 289 - 7 + 17$

$= 49 + 289 + 10$

$= 338 + 10 = 348$

25. **Decoding the Question**

The joint equation of bisectors of the angles between the lines represented by the equation $ax^2 + 2hxy + by^2 = 0$ is

$$\frac{x^2 - y^2}{a - b} = \frac{xy}{h}$$

$\Rightarrow \quad hx^2 - (a - b)xy - hy^2 = 0$

Equation of angle bisectors of homogeneous equation of pair of straight lines $ax^2 + 2hxy + by^2 = 0$ is

$$\frac{x^2 - y^2}{a - b} = \frac{xy}{h}$$

For $\quad x^2 - 4xy - 5y^2 = 0$

$\therefore \quad a = 1, h = 2$ and $b = -5$

So, combined equation of angle bisectors is

$$\frac{x^2 - y^2}{1 - (-5)} = \frac{xy}{-2}$$

$\Rightarrow \quad x^2 - y^2 = -3xy$

$\Rightarrow \quad x^2 + 3xy - y^2 = 0$

So, combined equation of angle bisectors is

$$x^2 + 3xy - y^2 = 0$$

Exercise 2 - JEE Advanced Pattern

1. Let $y = m_1 x$ and $y = m_2 x$ be the lines represented by

$$ax^2 + 2hxy + by^2 = 0$$

$\therefore \quad m_1 + m_2 = -\dfrac{2h}{b} \quad$ ...(i)

$m_1 m_2 = \dfrac{a}{b} \quad$ ...(ii)

Suppose $A(\alpha, 0)$ and the line $x = \alpha$ meets

$y = m_1 x$ at point B and $y = m_2 x$ at point C

Thus, $B = (\alpha, m_1\alpha)$ and $C(\alpha, m_2\alpha)$

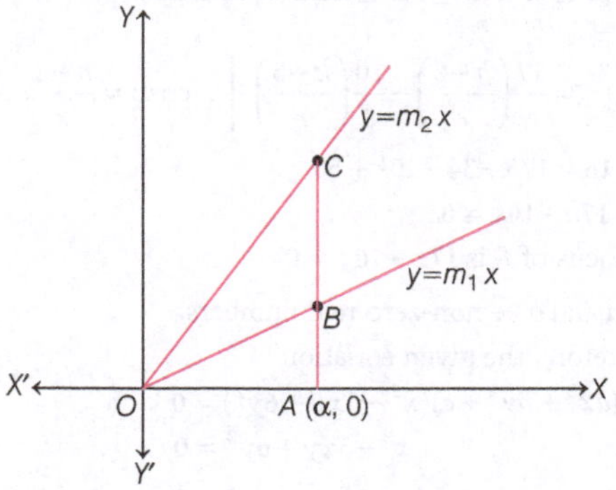

So, $\quad AB = BC$

$\Rightarrow \quad \dfrac{m_2\alpha + 0}{2} = m_1\alpha \Rightarrow m_2 = 2m_1$

By Eq. (i), $\quad 3m_1 = -\dfrac{2h}{b} \Rightarrow m_1 = -\dfrac{2h}{3b}$

and by Eq. (ii), $\quad 2m_1^2 = \dfrac{a}{b}$

$\Rightarrow \quad 2\left(\dfrac{-2h}{3b}\right)^2 = \dfrac{a}{b}$

$\therefore \quad 8h^2 = 9ab$

2. We have, $2x^2 - 5xy + 2y^2 = 0$

$\Rightarrow \quad 2x^2 - 4xy - xy + 2y^2 = 0$

$\Rightarrow \quad 2x(x - 2y) - y(x - 2y) = 0$

$\Rightarrow \quad (x - 2y)(2x - y) = 0$

$\Rightarrow \quad x - 2y = 0$ and $2x - y = 0$

Let $\quad P = (a, b), Q = (c, d)$ and $R = (h, k)$

and $RB = r$, $PB = r_1$ and $QB = r_2$

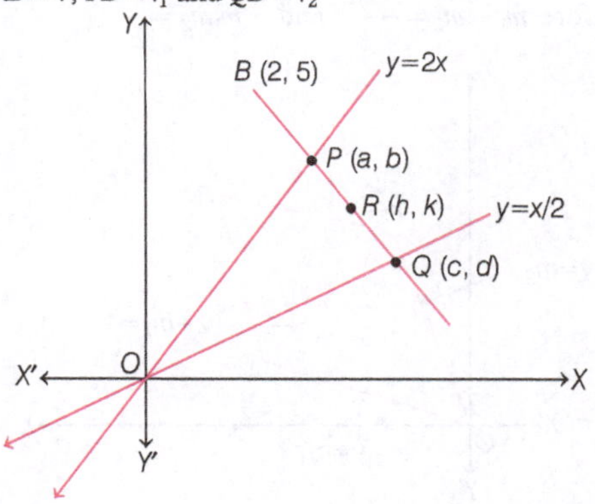

So, $P = (2 + r_1\cos\theta, 5 + r_1\sin\theta)$,

$Q = (2 + r_2\cos\theta, 5 + r_2\sin\theta)$

and $R = (2 + r\cos\theta, 5 + r\sin\theta)$

$\because$ P lies on $y = 2x$.

$\therefore \quad \frac{1}{r_1} = 2\cos\theta - \sin\theta$

Also, Q lies on $x = 2y$

$\Rightarrow \quad \frac{1}{r_2} = \frac{\cos\theta - 2\sin\theta}{8}$

Given, r_1, r and r_2 are in HP.

$$\therefore \quad \frac{2}{r} = \frac{1}{r_1} + \frac{1}{r_2} \Rightarrow \frac{2}{r} = \frac{17\cos\theta - 10\sin\theta}{8}$$

$$= \frac{17}{8}\left(\frac{h-2}{r}\right) - \frac{10}{8}\left(\frac{k-5}{r}\right) \quad \left[\because \cos\theta = \frac{h-2}{r}, \sin\theta = \frac{k-5}{r}\right]$$

$\Rightarrow \quad 16 = 17h - 34 - 10k + 50$

$\Rightarrow \quad 17h - 10k = 0$

$\therefore$ Locus of R is $17x - 10y = 0$

3. Let a and b be non-zero real numbers.

Therefore, the given equation

$$(ax^2 + by^2 + c)(x^2 - 5xy + 6y^2) = 0$$

$$\Rightarrow \quad x^2 - 5xy + 6y^2 = 0$$

$$\Rightarrow \quad (x - 2y)(x - 3y) = 0$$

$$\Rightarrow \quad x = 2y \text{ and } x = 3y$$

represents two straight lines passing through origin or

$$ax^2 + by^2 + c = 0$$

When $c = 0$ and a and b are of same sign.

Then, $ax^2 + by^2 + c = 0, x = 0, y = 0$

which is a point specified as the origin.

When $a = b$ and c is sign opposite to that of a

$$ax^2 + by^2 + c = 0 \Rightarrow a(x^2 + y^2) = c$$

$$\Rightarrow \quad x^2 + y^2 = \frac{c}{a} \text{ represents a circle.}$$

$\therefore$ The given equation $(ax^2 + by^2 + c)(x^2 - 5xy + 6y^2) = 0$ may represent two straight lines and a circle.

4. Let the equation of lines represented by $ax^2 + 2hxy + by^2 = 0$ be $y - m_1x = 0$ and $y - m_2x = 0$ and one diagonal AC be $lx + my = 1$

Therefore, $m_1 + m_2 = -\frac{2h}{b}$ and $m_1m_2 = \frac{a}{b}$

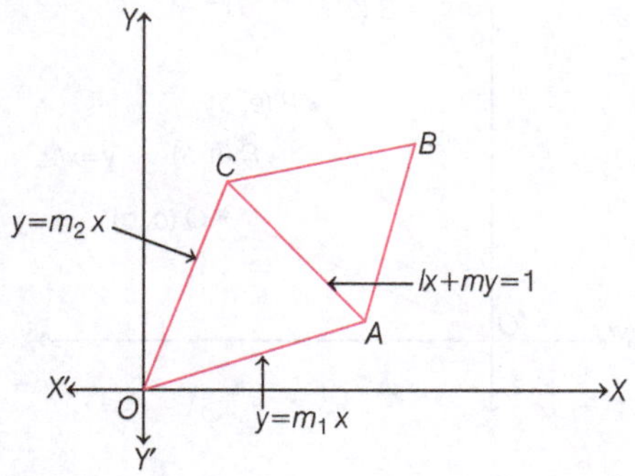

Now, solving the equation of OA and OC with the line AC, we get the coordinates of

$$A\left(\frac{1}{l + mm_1}, \frac{m_1}{l + mm_1}\right) \text{ and } C\left(\frac{1}{l + mm_2}, \frac{m_2}{l + mm_2}\right).$$

Now, find the coordinates of mid-point of AC and the equation of diagonal through this mid-point and origin.

The required equation is $x(am - hl) = (lb - mh)y$.

5. (b) Given equation is $(x^2 + y^2)\sin^2\alpha = (x\cos\beta - y\sin\beta)^2$

$$x^2(\sin^2\alpha - \cos^2\beta) + 2xy\sin\beta\cos\beta + y^2(\sin^2\alpha - \sin^2\beta) = 0 \quad \text{...(i)}$$

The homogeneous equation of second degree is

$$ax^2 + 2hxy + by^2 = 0 \quad \text{...(ii)}$$

On comparing Eqs. (i) and (ii), we get

$$a = \sin^2\alpha - \cos^2\beta,$$

$$h = \sin\beta\cos\beta$$

and $$b = \sin^2\alpha - \sin^2\beta$$

Let the angle between the lines representing by Eq. (i) is θ.

$$\therefore \quad \tan\theta = 2\frac{\sqrt{h^2 - ab}}{|a + b|}$$

$$= 2\frac{\sqrt{\sin^2\beta\cos^2\beta - (\sin^2\alpha - \cos^2\beta)(\sin^2\alpha - \sin^2\beta)}}{|\sin^2\alpha - \cos^2\beta + \sin^2\alpha - \sin^2\beta|}$$

$$= \frac{2\sqrt{\sin^2\beta\cos^2\beta - \sin^4\alpha + \sin^2\alpha\sin^2\beta + \sin^2\alpha\cos^2\beta - \sin^2\beta\cos^2\beta}}{|2\sin^2\alpha - 1|}$$

$$= \frac{2\sqrt{\sin^2\alpha(-\sin^2\alpha + \sin^2\beta + \cos^2\beta)}}{|2\sin^2\alpha - 1|}$$

$$= \frac{2\sqrt{\sin^2\alpha(1 - \sin^2\alpha)}}{|-\cos 2\alpha|}$$

$$= \frac{2\sin\alpha\cos\alpha}{\cos 2\alpha} = \tan 2\alpha$$

$$\therefore \quad \theta = 2\alpha$$

6. Let $y = m(x - 1)$ be the line meeting the curve at the points A and B.

The combined equation of the pair of lines OA and OB is

$$x^2 + y^2 + (6x - 10y)\frac{(mx - y)}{m} + 1 \cdot \frac{(mx - y)^2}{m^2} = 0$$

$\because$ $\angle AOB = 90°$, from the above equation, we get

coefficient of x^2 + coefficient of $y^2 = 0$

$$\Rightarrow \quad (1 + 6 + 1) + \left(1 + \frac{10}{m} + \frac{1}{m^2}\right) = 0$$

$$\Rightarrow \quad 9m^2 + 10m + 1 = 0$$

$$\Rightarrow \quad (9m + 1)(m + 1) = 0$$

$$\therefore \quad m = -\frac{1}{9} \text{ or } -1$$

7. Clearly, the slope of PM is $-\frac{1}{2}$.

Here, PM is equally inclined with PQ and PR.

Let the slope of PQ be m, then the slope of PR will be $-\frac{1}{m}$.

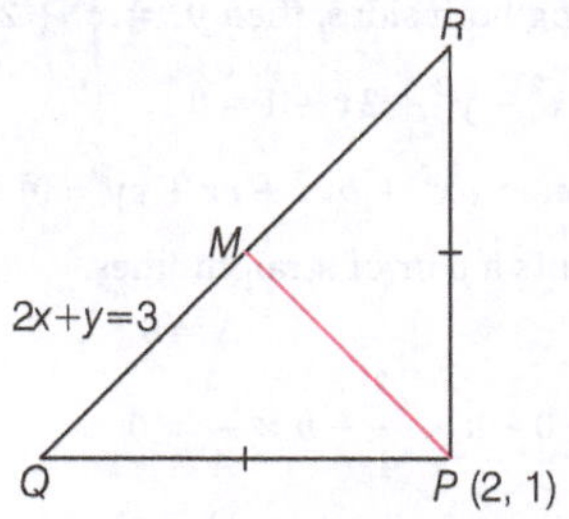

Thus, $$\frac{m-\left(-\frac{1}{2}\right)}{1+m\left(-\frac{1}{2}\right)}=\frac{-\frac{1}{2}-\left(-\frac{1}{m}\right)}{1+\left(-\frac{1}{2}\right)\left(-\frac{1}{m}\right)}$$

$$\Rightarrow \quad \frac{2m+1}{2-m}=\frac{2-m}{2m+1}$$

$$\Rightarrow \quad (2m+1)^2=(2-m)^2$$

$$\Rightarrow \quad 4m^2+4m+1=4-4m+m^2$$

$$\Rightarrow \quad 3m^2+8m-3=0$$

$$\Rightarrow \quad 3m^2+9m-m-3=0$$

$$\Rightarrow \quad 3m(m+3)-1(m+3)=0$$

$$\Rightarrow \quad (m+3)(3m-1)=0$$

$$\Rightarrow \quad m=-3, \frac{1}{3}$$

Thus, the equations of PQ and PR are

$$(y-1)=-3(x-2)$$

and $$y-1=\frac{1}{3}(x-2)$$

$$\Rightarrow \quad y-1=-3(x-2),$$

$$3(y-1)=(x-2)$$

Then, joint equation is

$$\{(y-1)+3(x-2)\}\{3(y-1)-(x-2)\}=0$$

$$\Rightarrow \quad \{y-1+3x-6\}\{3y-3-x+2\}=0$$

$$\Rightarrow \quad (y+3x-7)(3y-x-1)=0$$

$$\Rightarrow 3y^2-xy-y+9xy-3x^2-3x-21y+7x+7=0$$

$$\Rightarrow \quad 3y^2-3x^2+8xy+4x-22y+7=0$$

$$\Rightarrow \quad 3x^2-3y^2-8xy-4x+22y-7=0$$

8. **Decoding the Question**

If the equation of pair of straight lines is $ax^2+2hxy+by^2+2gx+2fy+c=0$, then the point of intersection is $\left(\frac{hf-bg}{ab-h^2}, \frac{gh-af}{ab-h^2}\right)$

Let $f(x, y)=ax^2+2hxy+by^2+2gx+2fy+c$

This point of intersection of the lines given by

$$ax^2+2hxy+by^2+2gx+2fy+c=0$$

is obtained by solving $\frac{\partial f}{\partial x}=0$ and $\frac{\partial f}{\partial y}=0$

i.e. $$ax+hy+g=0$$

and $$hx+by+f=0$$

The coordinates of point of intersection are

$$P\left(\frac{hf-bg}{ab-h^2}, \frac{hg-af}{ab-h^2}\right)$$

$\therefore$ Distance between the origin and point P is given by

$$OP=\sqrt{\frac{(hf-bg)^2+(hg-af)^2}{(ab-h^2)^2}}$$

$$=\sqrt{\frac{f^2(h^2+a^2)+g^2(h^2+b^2)-2fgh(a+b)}{(ab-h^2)^2}}$$

$$=\sqrt{\frac{f^2(h^2+a^2)+g^2(h^2+b^2)-(a+b)(af^2+bg^2+ch^2-abc)}{(ab-h^2)^2}}$$

$$[\because abc+2fgh-af^2-bg^2-ch^2=0]$$

$$=\sqrt{\frac{ac(ab-h^2)+bc(ab-h^2)-f^2(ab-h^2)-g^2(ab-h^2)}{(ab-h^2)^2}}$$

$$=\sqrt{\frac{c(a+b)-f^2-g^2}{(ab-h^2)}}$$

$$\therefore OP^2=\frac{c(a+b)-f^2-g^2}{(ab-h^2)}$$

9. Given line $2x^2-5xy+2y^2=0$ is the two sides of a parallelogram.

$$\therefore \quad 2x^2-5xy+2y^2=0$$

$$2x^2-4xy-xy+2y^2=0$$

$$2x(x-2y)-y(x-2y)=0$$

$$(x-2y)(2x-y)=0$$

$$x-2y=0, \; 2x-y=0$$

$$y=\frac{x}{2} \text{ and } y=2x$$

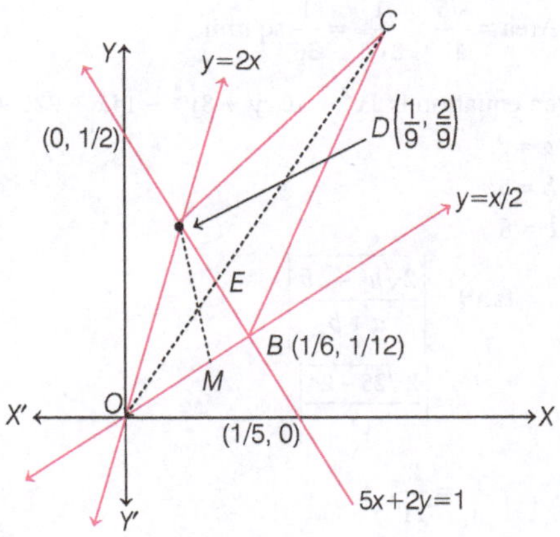

On solving $y=\frac{x}{2}$ and $5x+2y=1$, we get

$$5x+x=1$$

$\Rightarrow \quad 6x = 1$

$\Rightarrow \quad x = \frac{1}{6}$

$\Rightarrow \quad y = \frac{1}{12}$

$\therefore$ Points B is $\left(\frac{1}{6}, \frac{1}{12}\right)$,

and for point D solving $y = 2x$ and $5x + 2y = 1$,

$$9x = 1$$

$$x = \frac{1}{9} \text{ and } y = \frac{2}{9}$$

$\therefore$ Point $D\left(\frac{1}{9}, \frac{2}{9}\right)$

$$\text{Mid-point of } BD = \left(\frac{\frac{1}{6}+\frac{1}{9}}{2}, \frac{\frac{1}{12}+\frac{2}{9}}{2}\right)$$

$$= \left(\frac{5}{36}, \frac{11}{72}\right)$$

Area of parallelogram = Base × Height = $OB \times DM$

$$OB = \sqrt{\left(\frac{1}{6}\right)^2 + \left(\frac{1}{12}\right)^2}$$

$$= \frac{1}{6}\sqrt{1 + \frac{1}{4}}$$

$$= \frac{\sqrt{5}}{12}$$

$$DM = \left|\frac{\frac{1}{9} - \frac{4}{9}}{\sqrt{1+4}}\right|$$

$\left[\because \text{ line } x - 2y = 0, \text{ point } \left(\frac{1}{9}, \frac{2}{9}\right)\right]$

$$= \frac{1}{3\sqrt{5}}$$

$\therefore \quad \text{Area} = \frac{\sqrt{5}}{12} \times \frac{1}{3\sqrt{5}} = \frac{1}{36}$ sq unit

10. Given equation is $3x^2 + 10xy + 8y^2 + 14x + 22y + 15 = 0$

$\because \quad a = 3,$

$h = 5$

and $b = 8$

$$\therefore \quad \tan\theta = \left|\frac{2\sqrt{h^2 - ab}}{a+b}\right|$$

$$= \left|\frac{2\sqrt{25-24}}{11}\right|$$

$$= \frac{2}{11}$$

$$\therefore \quad \cos\theta = \frac{11}{5\sqrt{5}}$$

11. For image w.r.t. Y-axis, then replace x by $-x$, then required image of lines is

$$y = |-x - 1|$$

or $\quad y = |x + 1|$

and on squaring both sides, then $y^2 = x^2 + 2x + 1$

$\therefore \quad x^2 - y^2 + 2x + 1 = 0$

12. Given equation is $ax^2 + by^2 + cx + cy = 0$ ...(i)

Eq. (i) represents a pair of straight lines.

$\therefore \quad \Delta = 0$

$\Rightarrow \quad 0 + 2 \cdot 0 - a \times \frac{c^2}{4} - b \times \frac{c^2}{4} = 0$

or $\quad c^2(a + b) = 0$

$\therefore \quad c = 0 \text{ or } a + b = 0$

13. Given equation is $x^2 + \alpha y^2 + 2\beta y - a^2 = 0$ ...(i)

Eq. (i) represents a pair of perpendicular straight lines.

$\therefore \Delta = 0$ and coefficient of x^2 + coefficient of $y^2 = 0$

$\Rightarrow \quad -a^2\alpha - \beta^2 = 0 \text{ and } 1 + \alpha = 0$

$\therefore \quad \alpha = -1 \text{ and } \beta = \pm a$

14. Given pair of lines is

$$ax^2 + 2hxy + by^2 + 2gx + 2fy + c = 0 \quad \text{...(i)}$$

$\because$ Point of intersection of lines represented by Eq. (i) is

$$\left(\frac{hf - bg}{ab - h^2}, \frac{gh - af}{ab - h^2}\right)$$

or $\quad \left(\sqrt{\left(\frac{f^2 - bc}{h^2 - ab}\right)}, \sqrt{\left(\frac{g^2 - ac}{h^2 - ab}\right)}\right)$

For Y-axis, put $x = 0$

$\therefore \quad hf = bg, f^2 = bc \text{ and } h^2 \neq ab$

Also, $\quad \Delta = 0$

$\therefore \quad abc + 2fgh - af^2 - bg^2 - ch^2 = 0$

For $f^2 = bc$, $2fgh = bg^2 + ch^2$

15. The separate equations of the sides are $x + y = 0$, $x - y = 0$ and $\frac{x}{3} + \frac{y}{2} = 1$.

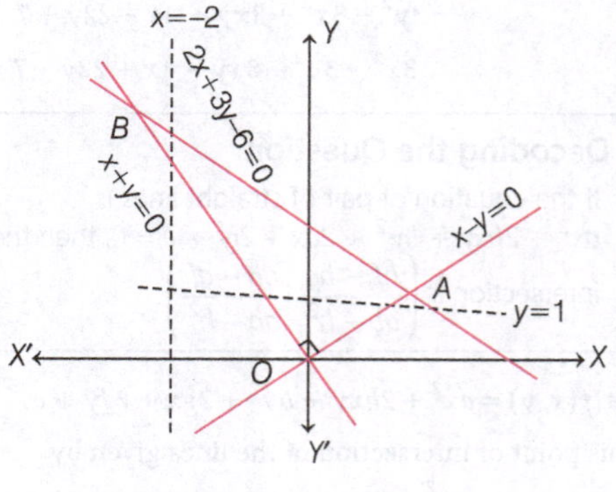

Intersection of $x = -2$ with $y = -x$ and $2x + 3y - 6 = 0$ gives the range of values of a

$$\therefore \quad 2 < a < \frac{10}{3}$$

and intersection of $y = 1$ with $y = x$ and $2x + 3y - 6 = 0$ gives the range of values of b, $-1 < b < 1$. [$\because$ $(b, 1)$ is exterior point]

Sol. (Q. Nos. 16 to 17)

For perpendicular straight lines, then coefficient of x^2 + coefficient of $y^2 = 0$

$$\Rightarrow \quad 2 + b = 0$$

$$\therefore \quad b = -2$$

16. $2x^2 + 3xy - 2y^2 - 11x + 13y + c = 0$ represents a pair of straight lines, then we get

$$2 \times -2 \times c + 2 \times \frac{13}{2} \times -\frac{11}{2} \times \frac{3}{2} - 2 \times \frac{169}{4} + 2 \times \frac{121}{4} - c \times \frac{9}{4} = 0$$

$$\Rightarrow \quad -4c - \frac{429}{4} - \frac{169}{2} + \frac{121}{2} - \frac{9c}{4} = 0$$

$$\therefore \quad c = -2$$

17. Now, pair of lines is $2x^2 + 3xy - 2y^2 - 11x + 13y - 2 = 0$

Let $f(x, y) \equiv 2x^2 + 3xy - 2y^2 - 11x + 13y - 2 = 0$

$$\therefore \quad \frac{\partial f}{\partial x} = 4x + 3y - 11 \text{ and } \frac{\partial f}{\partial y} = 3x - 4y + 13$$

For point of intersection, $\frac{\partial f}{dx} = 0$ and $\frac{\partial f}{\partial y} = 0$

$$\Rightarrow \quad 4x + 3y - 11 = 0 \text{ and } 3x - 4y + 13 = 0$$

$$\therefore \quad C \equiv \left(\frac{1}{5}, \frac{19}{5}\right)$$

Also, intersection on X-axis put $y = 0$.

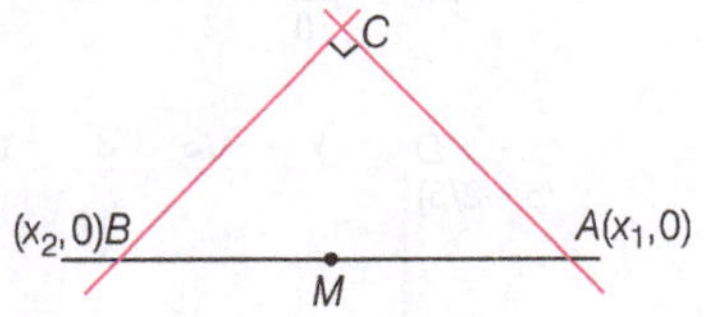

$$\because \quad 2x^2 - 11x + 2 = 0 \Rightarrow x_1 + x_2 = \frac{11}{2}$$

$\therefore$ Circumcentre of ΔABC, $M\left(\frac{x_1 + x_2}{2}, 0\right)$

[$\because$ for right angled triangle circumcentre is mid-point of hypotenuse]

$$\therefore \quad M \equiv \left(\frac{11}{4}, 0\right)$$

and orthocentre is $\quad C \equiv \left(\frac{1}{5}, \frac{19}{5}\right)$

$$\therefore \text{ Required distance} = \sqrt{\left(\frac{11}{4} - \frac{1}{5}\right)^2 + \left(0 - \frac{19}{5}\right)^2}$$

$$\therefore \quad \lambda = \sqrt{\frac{8377}{400}} = \sqrt{20.94} = 4.57$$

$$[\lambda] = [4.57] = 4$$

Sol. (Q. Nos. 18 to 19)

18. Let $f_1(x, y) \equiv ax^2 + 2hxy + by^2 = 0$ ...(i)

bisectors of $f_1(x, y)$ is $f_2(x, y)$.

$\therefore$ Equation of bisectors of Eq. (i) is $\frac{x^2 - y^2}{a - b} = \frac{xy}{h}$

$$\Rightarrow \quad hx^2 - (a - b)xy - hy^2 = 0$$

$$\therefore \quad f_2(x, y) \equiv hx^2 - (a - b)xy - hy^2 = 0 \quad \text{...(ii)}$$

Now, equation of bisectors of Eq. (ii) is

$$\frac{x^2 - y^2}{h - (-h)} = \frac{xy}{-\frac{(a - b)}{2}}$$

$$\Rightarrow \quad \frac{x^2 - y^2}{2h} = -\frac{2xy}{(a - b)}$$

$$\Rightarrow \quad (a - b)x^2 + 4hxy - (a - b)y^2 = 0$$

$$\therefore \quad f_3(x, y) \equiv (a - b)x^2 + 4hxy - (a - b)y^2 = 0$$

19. For all $n \geq 2$, $f_{n+2}(x, y) = f_n(x, y)$

$$\therefore \quad \frac{f_{n+2}(x, y)}{f_n(x, y)} = 1$$

$$\text{Now,} \quad \sum_{n=2}^{5} \frac{f_{n+2}(x, y)}{f_n(x, y)} = \sum_{n=2}^{5} 1$$

$$= 1 + 1 + 1 + 1 = 4$$

Sol. (Q. Nos. 20 to 21)

$$ax^2 + 3xy - 2y^2 - 5x + 5y + c = 0$$

$$a = a, b = -2, h = \frac{3}{2}, g = -\frac{5}{2}, f = \frac{5}{2}$$

and $c = c$

20. As lines are perpendicular.

$$\therefore \quad a - 2 = 0$$

$$\Rightarrow \quad a = 2$$

[$\because$ coefficient of x^2 + coefficient of $y^2 = 0$]

Using $\Delta = 0$,

$$abc + 2fgh - af^2 - bg^2 - ch^2 = 0$$

$$2(-2)c + 2\left(\frac{5}{2}\right)\left(-\frac{5}{2}\right)\left(\frac{3}{2}\right) - 2\left(\frac{5}{2}\right)^2 - (-2)\left(-\frac{5}{2}\right)^2 - c\left(\frac{3}{2}\right)^2 = 0$$

$$\Rightarrow \quad c + 3 = 0$$

$$\Rightarrow \quad c = -3$$

The two lines of $2x^2 + 3xy - 3y^2 - 5x + 5y - 3 = 0$

are $\quad x + 2y - 3 = 0$ and $2x - y + 1 = 0$

So, x-intercepts, $x_1 = 3$ and $x_2 = -\frac{1}{2}$

y-intercepts, $y_1 = \frac{3}{2}$ and $y_2 = 1$

$$\therefore \quad x_1 + x_2 + y_1 + y_2 = 5$$

21. $CM^2 = \left(\frac{5}{4} - \frac{1}{5}\right)^2 + \frac{49}{25}$

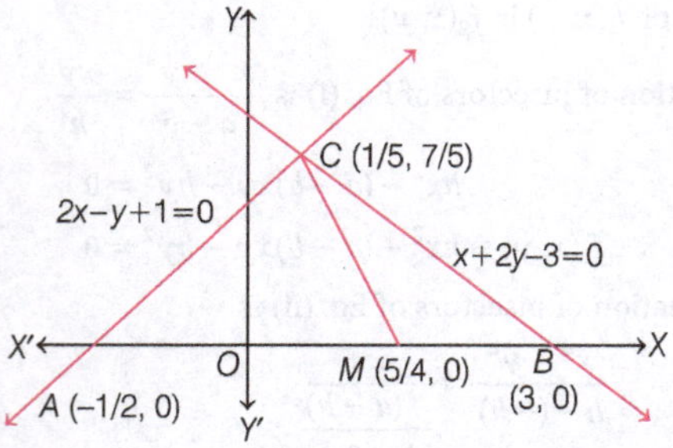

$$= \frac{441}{400} + \frac{49}{25}$$

$$= \frac{441 + 784}{400} = \frac{1225}{400} = \frac{49}{16} = \frac{7}{4} = 1.75$$

Sol. (Q. Nos. 22 to 23)

22. Suppose $lx + my = 1$ be a line meeting the curve $3x^2 - y^2 - 2x + 4y = 0$ at points A and B.

Therefore, the combined equation of the pair of lines OA and OB is $3x^2 - y^2 - (2x - 4y)(lx + my) = 0$

$\because \quad \angle AOB = 90°$

$\therefore$ Coefficient of x^2 + Coefficient of $y^2 = 0$

$$3 - 2l + (-1 + 4m) = 0$$

$\Rightarrow \quad l - 2m - 1 = 0$

$\therefore$ Line $lx + my - 1 = 0$ passes through the point $(1, -2)$.

$\therefore \quad (m, n) = (1, -2)$

$\Rightarrow \quad m = 1$ and $n = -2$

$\therefore \quad m - n = 1 - (-2) = 3$

23. Suppose the line $lx + my = 1$ intersects $x^2 + y^2 = a^2$ at points A and B.

$\therefore$ The combined equation of pair of lines OA and OB is

$$x^2 + y^2 - a^2(lx + my)^2 = 0$$

$$\angle AOB = 90°$$

$\therefore$ Coefficient of x^2 + Coefficient of $y^2 = 0$

$$(1 - a^2l^2) + (1 - a^2m^2) = 0$$

$\Rightarrow \quad a^2(l^2 + m^2) = 2 \Rightarrow l^2 + m^2 = \frac{2}{a^2}$

$\Rightarrow \quad \frac{\lambda}{a^2} = \frac{2}{a^2}$

$\Rightarrow \quad \lambda = 2$

$\therefore \quad 2\lambda = 4$

24. Given, $3x^2 + 8xy - 3y^2 = 0$

$$3x^2 + 9xy - xy - 3y^2 = 0$$

$$3x(x + 3y) - y(x + 3y) = 0$$

$$(x + 3y)(3x - y) = 0$$

$\therefore \quad y = -\frac{1}{3}x$ and $y = 3x$ are two lines

$$m_1 = -\frac{1}{3} \text{ and } m_2 = 3$$

$\therefore \quad m_1 m_2 = -1$

$\therefore$ Both are perpendicular.

Now, $\quad 3x^2 + 8xy - 3y^2 + 2x - 4y - 1 = 0$

$\Rightarrow \quad (x + 3y)(3x - y) + 2x - 4y - 1 = 0 \quad$ ...(i)

Let us assume Eq. (i) is

$$(x + 3y + c_1)(3x - y + c_2) = 0$$

$\Rightarrow (x + 3y)(3x - y) + (3c_1 + c_2)x - (c_1 - 3c_2)y + c_1c_2 = 0 \quad$ ...(ii)

By comparing Eqs. (i) and (ii),

$$3c_1 + c_2 = 2, c_1 - 3c_2 = 4 \text{ and } c_1c_2 = -1$$

On solving, we get $c_1 = 1, c_2 = -1$

$\therefore$ Separate equations are

$$(x + 3y + 1) = 0$$

$$y = -\frac{1}{3}x - \frac{1}{3}$$

$$m_3 = -\frac{1}{3}$$

and $\quad 3x - y - 1 = 0$

$$y = 3x - 1$$

$$m_4 = 3$$

$\Rightarrow \quad m_3 \cdot m_4 = -1$

$\Rightarrow$ Both are perpendicular.

and $m_1 = m_3$ and $m_4 = m_2$

$\therefore \quad y = -\frac{x}{3}$ and $y = -\frac{x}{3} - \frac{1}{3}$

and $y = 3x$ and $y = 3x - 1$ are parallel and

$$AB = AD = \frac{1}{\sqrt{10}}$$

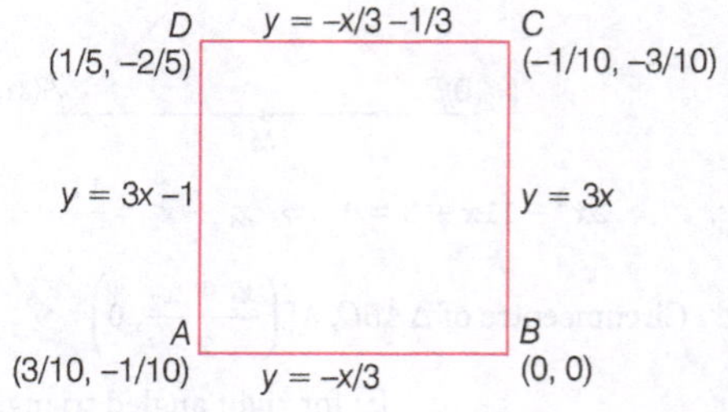

Quadrilateral formed by these four lines is square.

$\therefore \quad$ Area = $(\text{side})^2 = \left(\frac{1}{\sqrt{10}}\right)^2 = \frac{1}{10}$ sq units

$\Rightarrow \quad \frac{1}{m} = \frac{1}{10}$

$\Rightarrow \quad m = 10$

$\therefore \quad \frac{m}{2} = \frac{10}{2} = 5$

25. The sides of the triangle are given

$$(x^2 - y^2)(2x + 3y - 6) = 0$$

$\Rightarrow$ $x - y = 0$

or $x + y = 0$

$2x + 3y - 6 = 0$

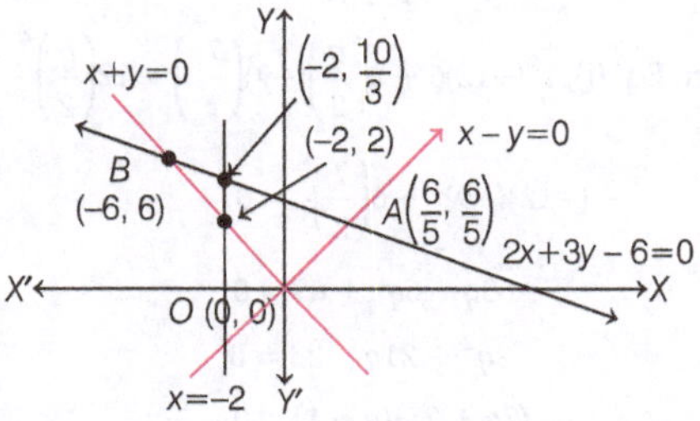

We observe that the point $(-2, a)$ moves on $x = -2$.

Thus, $2 < a < \frac{10}{3}$

$\therefore$ $a = 3$

26. Given, $a_1x^2 + 2h_1xy + b_1y^2 = c_1$ ...(i)

and $a_2x^2 + 2h_2xy + b_2y^2 = c_2$ ...(ii)

The equation of a conic passing through the intersection of the given conic is

$$(a_1x^2 + 2h_1xy + b_1y^2 - c_1) + \lambda(a_2^2 + 2h_2xy + b_2y^2 - c_2) = 0$$

This equation will represent a circle, if

coefficient of x^2 = coefficient of y^2 and coefficient of $xy = 0$

$\Rightarrow$ $(a_1 + \lambda a_2) = (b_1 + \lambda b_2)$

and $2h_1 + 2\lambda h_2 = 0$

Eliminating λ from these two equations, we get

$$a_1 - b_1 = \frac{h_1}{h_2}(a_2 - b_2)$$

$\Rightarrow$ $(a_1 - b_2)\, h_2 = (a_2 - b_2)h_1$

But it is given that

$$(a_1 - b_1)h_2 = \lambda(a_2 - b_2)h_1$$

$\therefore$ $\lambda = 1$

27. The given equation is $4x^2 - 4xy + ay^2 + bx + cy + 1 = 0$

$\therefore$It represents a pair of identical lines.

It will be perfect square

$$(\alpha + \beta + \gamma)^2 = \alpha^2 + \beta^2 + \gamma^2 + 2\alpha\beta + 2\beta\gamma + 2\gamma\alpha$$

$\therefore$ $4x^2 - 4xy + y^2 - y^2 + ay^2 + bx + cy + 1 = 0$

$\Rightarrow$ $(2x - y)^2 + (a - 1)y^2 + bx + cy + 1 = 0$

$\Rightarrow$ $(2x - y)^2 + 2(2x - y) - 2(2x - y) + (a - 1)y^2 + bx + cy + 1 = 0$

So, there are two situations.

Case I $(2x - y)^2 + 2(2x - y) + 1 + (a - 1)y^2 + x(b - 4) + y(c + 2) = 0$

$$(2x - y + 1)^2 + (a - 1)y^2 + x(b - 4) + y(c + 2) = 0$$

It represents identical pair of straight lines.

$\therefore$ $a = 1, b = 4$ and $c = -2$

or $a_1 = 1, b_1 = 4$ and $c_1 = -2$

Case II

$$(2x - y)^2 - 2(2x - y) + 1 + (a - 1)y^2 + x(b + 4) + y(c - 2) = 0$$

$\Rightarrow$ $(2x - y + 1)^2 + (a - 1)y^2 + x(b + 4) + y(c - 2) = 0$

$\therefore$If represents identical pair of straight lines.

$\therefore$ $a - 1 = 0, b + 4 = 0, c - 2 = 0$

$a = 1, b = -4$ and $c = 2$

$\therefore$ $a_2 = 1, b_2 = -4$ and $c_2 = 2$

Now, the value $a_1 + b_1 + c_1 + a_2 + b_2 + c_2$

$= 1 + 4 - 2 + 1 - 4 + 2 = 2$

28. **Decoding the Question**

The two pair of lines are equally inclined, if two pair of straight lines have same angle bisector.

The given pairs of lines are

$9x^2 + 14xy + 16y^2 = 0$ and $3x^2 + 2xy + \lambda y^2 = 0$.

$\therefore$The equation of bisector of angle between the lines represented by $9x^2 + 14xy + 16y^2 = 0$.

$a = 9, b = 16$ and $h = 7$

$\Rightarrow$ $\frac{x^2 - y^2}{9 - 16} = \frac{xy}{7}$

$\Rightarrow$ $x^2 + xy - y^2 = 0$ ...(i)

and the equation of bisector of angle between the lines represented by $3x^2 + 2xy + \lambda y^2 = 0$

$\Rightarrow$ $\frac{x^2 - y^2}{3 - \lambda} = \frac{xy}{1}$ [$\because a = 3, b = \lambda, h = 1$]

$\Rightarrow$ $x^2 - y^2 + (\lambda - 3)xy = 0$ ...(ii)

On comparing Eqs. (i) and (ii), we get

$\lambda - 3 = 1$

$\therefore$ $\lambda = 4$

29. We have, $x^2 - 3xy + \lambda y^2 + 3x - 5y + 2 = 0$ ...(i)

Let θ be the angle between the line represented by Eq. (i).

$\therefore$ $\theta = \tan^{-1}\left(\frac{1}{3}\right) \Rightarrow \tan\theta = \frac{1}{3}$

Now, $\tan\theta = \left|\frac{2\sqrt{h^2 - ab}}{a + b}\right| = \left|\frac{2\sqrt{\frac{9}{4} - \lambda}}{1 + \lambda}\right|$

$\Rightarrow$ $\frac{1}{3} = \left|\frac{\sqrt{9 - 4\lambda}}{1 + \lambda}\right| \Rightarrow \frac{\sqrt{9 - 4\lambda}}{1 + \lambda} = \pm\frac{1}{3}$

On squaring both sides, we get

$81 - 36\lambda = 1 + \lambda^2 + 2\lambda$

$\Rightarrow$ $\lambda^2 + 38\lambda - 80 = 0$

$\Rightarrow$ $(\lambda + 40)(\lambda - 2) = 0$

$\Rightarrow$ $\lambda = 2$ and -40

$\Rightarrow$ $\lambda = 2$ [$\because \lambda$ is non-negative]

$\therefore$ $[\lambda] = [2] = 2$

$\Rightarrow$ $5[\lambda] = 10$

30. We have, $y^2 - 9xy + 18x^2 = 0$ ...(i)

and $y = 9$ ...(ii)

Eq. (i) is homogeneous equation of second degree, it represents pair of straight lines passing through the origin.

Let one of the lines be $y = mx$.

$$\therefore \quad m^2x^2 - 9mx^2 + 18x^2 = 0$$

$$\Rightarrow \quad m^2 - 9m + 18 = 0$$

$$\Rightarrow \quad m = \frac{9 \pm \sqrt{81 - 72}}{2} = \frac{9 \pm 3}{2}$$

$$\Rightarrow \quad m = 6, 3$$

$\therefore$ Lines are $y = 6x$ ...(iii)

and $y = 3x$ ...(iv)

On taking mutual intersection of sides of triangle, we get vertices of triangle as $(0, 0), \left(\frac{3}{2}, 9\right)$ and $(3, 9)$.

$$\therefore \quad \text{Area} = \frac{1}{2}\begin{vmatrix} 0 & 0 & 1 \\ 3/2 & 9 & 1 \\ 3 & 9 & 1 \end{vmatrix}$$

$$= \frac{1}{2}\left|\frac{27}{2} - 27\right| = \frac{1}{2} \times \frac{27}{2} = \frac{27}{4}$$

Hence, area of triangle = 6.75 sq units.

31. Let $x^2 + 2hxy + by^2 + 2gx + 2fy + c = 0$

$$\Rightarrow \quad (lx + my + n)(l_1x + m_1y + n_1) = 0$$

$$\Rightarrow \quad ll_1x^2 + mm_1y^2 + (lm_1 + l_1m)xy + (ln_1 + l_1n)x + (mn_1 + nm_1)y + nn_1 = 0$$

On comparing the coefficients, we get

$ll_1 = a$, $mm_1 = b$, $nn_1 = c$ and $lm_1 + ml_1 = 2h$,

$ln_1 + nl_1 = 2g$ and $mn_1 + nm_1 = 2f$

Let P_1 and P_2 be the length of perpendicular from the origin.

$$\text{Thus, } P_1 \cdot P_2 = \frac{n}{\sqrt{l^2 + m^2}} \times \frac{n_1}{\sqrt{l_1^2 + m_1^2}}$$

$$= \frac{nn_1}{\sqrt{(l^2 + m^2)(l_1^2 + m_1^2)}} = \frac{nn_1}{\sqrt{l^2l_1^2 + m^2m_1^2 + l^2m_1^2 + l_1^2m^2}}$$

$$\Rightarrow \frac{nn_1}{\sqrt{l^2l_1^2 + m^2m_1^2 + (lm_1 + l_1m)^2 - 2ll_1mm_1}}$$

$$= \frac{c}{\sqrt{a^2 + b^2 + 4h^2 - 2ab}}$$

$$= \frac{c}{\sqrt{(a - b)^2 + 4h^2}}$$

$$\Rightarrow \quad m = 1 \text{ and } n = 4$$

$$\therefore \quad 4(m + n) = 4(1 + 4) = 20.$$

32. The equation represents pair of straight lines

$$\Delta \equiv abc + 2fgh - af^2 - bg^2 - ch^2 = 0 \quad \text{...(i)}$$

and also both are perpendicular.

$$\therefore \quad a + b = 0 \quad \text{...(ii)}$$

Now, given equation is

$$12x^2 + 7xy - py^2 - 18x + qy + 6 = 0$$

$$\Rightarrow \quad a = 12, h = \frac{7}{2}, b = -p, g = -9 \text{ and } f = \frac{q}{2}, c = 6$$

From Eq. (ii), $12 + (-p) = 0$

$$\Rightarrow \quad p = 12$$

From Eq. (i), $12(-12)6 + 2\left(\frac{q}{2}\right)(-9)\left(\frac{7}{2}\right) - 12\left(\frac{q}{2}\right)^2$

$$\Rightarrow \quad -(-12)(-9)^2 - 6\left(\frac{7}{2}\right)^2 = 0$$

$$\Rightarrow \quad -63q - 6q^2 + 69 = 0$$

$$\Rightarrow \quad 2q^2 + 21q - 23 = 0$$

$$\Rightarrow \quad (2q + 23)(q - 1) = 0$$

$$\Rightarrow \quad q = 1, \frac{-23}{2}$$

$$\Rightarrow \quad q = 1 \quad [\because q \text{ is positive integral}]$$

$$\therefore \quad p + q = 12 + 1 = 13$$

33. $\angle ONP = \angle OMP = \frac{\pi}{2}$

$\therefore O, M, P$ and N are concyclic with diameter OP.

Let $P(H, K)$ be the point.

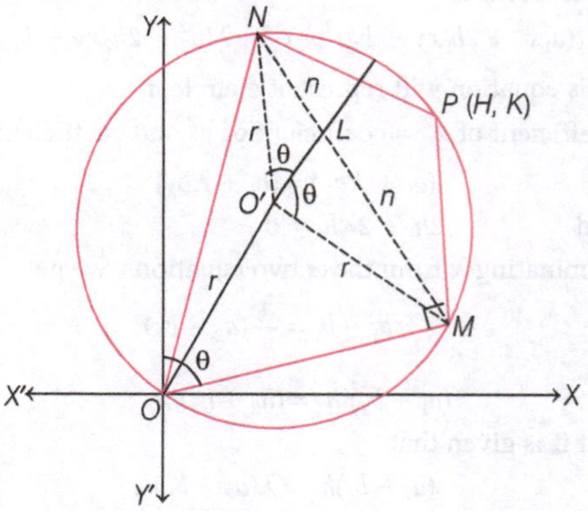

$$\therefore \text{Coordinates of } O' = \left(\frac{H}{2}, \frac{K}{2}\right)$$

$$\therefore \text{Radius,} \quad r = O'N = OM = OO'$$

$$\Rightarrow \quad \sqrt{\left(\frac{H}{2}\right)^2 + \left(\frac{K}{2}\right)^2} = \sqrt{\frac{H^2 + K^2}{4}} = \frac{\sqrt{H^2 + K^2}}{2}$$

Let $\angle MON = \theta$

$$\therefore \quad \angle MO'N = 2\theta$$

$$\Rightarrow \quad \angle NO'L = \angle MO'L = \theta$$

and given $MN = 2n$, then $NL = LM = n$

Now, in $\Delta NO'L$,

$$\sin\theta = \frac{NL}{O'N} = \frac{n}{r} = \frac{n}{\frac{\sqrt{H^2 + K^2}}{2}}$$

$$= \frac{2n}{\sqrt{H^2 + K^2}} \quad \text{...(i)}$$

But angle between the lines represented by $ax^2 + 2hxy + by^2 = 0$ is

$$\tan\theta = \frac{2\sqrt{h^2 - ab}}{|a+b|}$$

So, $$\sin\theta = \frac{2\sqrt{h^2 - ab}}{\sqrt{(a-b)^2 + 4h^2}} \quad \text{...(ii)}$$

By Eqs. (i) and (ii), we get

$$\frac{2\sqrt{h^2 - ab}}{\sqrt{(a-b)^2 + 4h^2}} = \frac{2n}{\sqrt{H^2 + K^2}}$$

On squaring both the sides, we get

$$(h^2 - ab)(H^2 + K^2) = n^2((a-b)^2 + 4h^2)$$

Locus is $$(h^2 - ab)(x^2 + y^2) = n^2((a-b)^2 + 4h^2)$$

$\therefore$ $$\lambda = 4 \text{ and } \frac{\lambda}{10} = 0.4$$

34. (A) Given, $2x + 2y + \lambda = 0$ ...(i)

and $9x^2 + 16y^2 = 144$ ...(ii)

Homogenising Eq. (ii) with Eq. (i), we get

$$9x^2 + 16y^2 = 144\left(\frac{2x + 2y}{-\lambda}\right)^2$$

$$\Rightarrow (9\lambda^2 - 576)x^2 - 1152xy + (16\lambda^2 - 576)y^2 = 0$$

The lines are coincident, then

$$(-576)^2 = (9\lambda^2 - 576)(16\lambda^2 - 576)$$

$$\Rightarrow \quad 144\lambda^4 - 576\lambda^2(25) = 0 \text{ or } \lambda^2 = 100$$

$$\therefore \quad |\lambda| = 10$$

(B) Given, $$\frac{4x + 3y}{24} = 1 \quad \text{...(i)}$$

and $(x-3)^2 + (y-4)^2 = \lambda^2$

or $x^2 + y^2 - (6x + 8y) + 25 - \lambda^2 = 0$ ...(ii)

Homogenising Eq. (ii) with Eq. (i), we get

$$x^2 + y^2 - (6x + 8y)\frac{(4x + 3y)}{24} + (25 - \lambda^2)\left(\frac{4x + 3y}{24}\right)^2 = 0$$

$$\Rightarrow \quad 16(25 - \lambda^2)x^2 + 9(25 - \lambda^2)y^2 + (-600 - 24\lambda^2)xy = 0$$

The lines will be at right angles, when

$$16(25 - \lambda^2) + 9(25 - \lambda^2) = 0$$

$$\Rightarrow \quad 625 - 25\lambda^2 = 0 \Rightarrow \lambda^2 = 25$$

$$\therefore \quad |\lambda| = 5$$

(C) The lines pairs are $(y-1)(y-3) = 0$ i.e. $y = 1$ and $y = 3$.

The other line pair is $x^2 + 4xy + 4y^2 - 5x - 10y + 4 = 0$

i.e. $(x + 2y - 4)(x + 2y - 1) = 0$

or $x + 2y - 4 = 0$ and $x + 2y - 1 = 0$

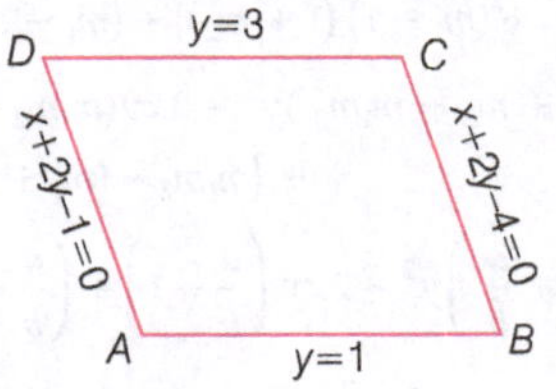

Required area $= \dfrac{(3-1)(4-1)}{\begin{vmatrix} 1 & 2 \\ 0 & 1 \end{vmatrix}} = 6$ sq units

$$\therefore \quad \lambda = 6$$

(D) Equation of the bisectors of $3x^2 - 2pxy - 3y^2 = 0$ is

$$\frac{x^2 - y^2}{3 - (-3)} = \frac{xy}{-p}$$

$$\Rightarrow px^2 + 6xy - py^2 = 0$$

which is same as $5x^2 - 2qxy - 5y^2 = 0$

i.e. $$\frac{p}{5} = \frac{6}{-2q} = \frac{-p}{-5}$$

$$\Rightarrow \quad pq = -15$$

$$\therefore \quad \lambda = |pq| = |-15| = 15$$

35. (A) $6x^2 + 5xy - 6y^2 + 9x + 20y + c = 0$

$$a = 6, b = -6, h = \frac{5}{2}, g = \frac{9}{2} \text{ and } f = 10 \quad \text{...(i)}$$

The given equation represents a pair of straight lines.

$$\therefore \quad \begin{vmatrix} 6 & 5/2 & 9/2 \\ 5/2 & -6 & 10 \\ 9/2 & 10 & c \end{vmatrix} = 0$$

$$\Rightarrow \quad 6(-6c - 100) - \frac{5}{2}\left(\frac{5c}{2} - 45\right) + \frac{9}{2}(25 + 27) = 0$$

$$\Rightarrow \quad 24(-6c - 100) - 5(5c - 90) + 18 \times 52 = 0$$

$$\Rightarrow \quad -169c - 2400 + 450 + 936 = 0$$

$$\Rightarrow \quad -169c = 1014$$

$$\therefore \quad c = -\frac{1014}{169} = -6$$

(B) Suppose the line $x - 2y - 6 = 0$ meets the given curve at points A and B.

$\therefore$ Combined equation of the pair of lines OA and OB is

$$2x^2 + 6xy + 3y^2 + (4x + 2y)\left(\frac{x - 2y}{6}\right) - 36\left(\frac{x - 2y}{6}\right)^2 = 0$$

In this equation, the coefficient of x^2 + coefficient of y^2 is 0.

$$\left(2 + \frac{2}{3} - 1\right) + \left(3 - \frac{2}{3} - 4\right) = \left(1 + \frac{2}{3}\right) + \left(-\frac{2}{3} - 1\right) = 0$$

$$\therefore \quad \angle AOB = \frac{\pi}{2}$$

(C) The combined equation of the pair of lines is

$$2x^2 - 2xy + 3y^2 + \frac{(2x - y)(x + 2y)}{k} - \left(\frac{x + 2y}{k}\right)^2 = 0$$

$\therefore$ Given two lines are at right angled.

coefficient of x^2 + coefficient of $y^2 = 0$

$$\Rightarrow \quad \left(2 + \frac{2}{k} - \frac{1}{k^2}\right) + \left(3 - \frac{2}{k} - \frac{4}{k^2}\right) = 0$$

$$\Rightarrow \quad 5k^2 - 5 = 0$$

$$\therefore \quad k = \pm 1$$

(D) If $ax^2+2hxy+by^2+2gx+2fy+c=0$ represents a pair of parallel lines, then the distance between them is

$$2\sqrt{\frac{g^2-ac}{a(a+b)}}.$$

We have, $a=9$, $b=16$, $g=-6$ and $c=-12$

$$\therefore \quad d=2\sqrt{\frac{g^2-ac}{a(a+b)}}=2\sqrt{\frac{36+108}{9\times25}}=\frac{2\times12}{3\times5}=\frac{8}{5}$$

$$\therefore \quad 5d=8$$

Exercise 3 - Challenging Problems

1. Given pair of lines is

$$(A^2-3B^2)x^2+8ABxy+(B^2-3A^2)y^2=0 \quad \text{...(i)}$$

Given line is $\quad Ax+By+C=0 \quad$ ...(ii)

On comparing Eq. (i) with $ax^2+2hxy+by^2=0$

$$a=A^2-3B^2,\ h=4AB \text{ and } b=B^2-3A^2$$

If θ is the acute angle between the lines represented by Eq. (i), then

$$\tan\theta=\frac{2\sqrt{(h^2-ab)}}{|a+b|}=\frac{2\sqrt{16A^2B^2-(A^2-3B^2)(B^2-3A^2)}}{|(A^2-3B^2+B^2-3A^2)|}$$

$$=\frac{2\sqrt{(3A^4+3B^4+6A^2B^2)}}{|-2(A^2+B^2)|}=\frac{\sqrt{3}(A^2+B^2)}{(A^2+B^2)}=\sqrt{3}$$

$$\therefore \quad \theta=60^\circ$$

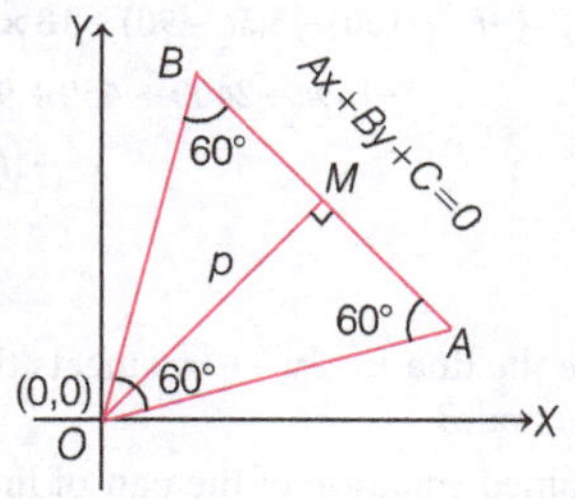

Eq. (i) can be written as

$$(B^2-3A^2)\left(\frac{y}{x}\right)^2+8AB\left(\frac{y}{x}\right)+(A^2-3B^2)=0$$

On solving for y/x, we get

$$\frac{y}{x}=\frac{-8AB\pm\sqrt{64A^2B^2-4(B^2-3A^2)(A^2-3B^2)}}{2(B^2-3A^2)}$$

$$=\frac{-4AB\pm\sqrt{16A^2B^2-(A^2B^2-3B^4-3A^4+9A^2B^2)}}{(B^2-3A^2)}$$

$$\Rightarrow \quad \frac{y}{x}=\frac{-4AB\pm\sqrt{3}(A^2+B^2)}{(B^2-3A^2)}$$

$$\Rightarrow \quad y=\left\{\frac{-4AB\pm\sqrt{3}(A^2+B^2)}{B^2-3A^2}\right\}x$$

On taking the positive sign, slope of one of the lines

$$=\frac{\sqrt{3}(A^2+B^2)-4AB}{B^2-3A^2}$$

and slope of the line $Ax+By+C=0$ is $-A/B$.

Acute angle between these lines

$$=\tan^{-1}\left|\frac{\dfrac{\sqrt{3}(A^2+B^2)-4AB}{B^2-3A^2}+\dfrac{A}{B}}{1-\left(\dfrac{A}{B}\right)\left[\dfrac{\sqrt{3}(A^2+B^2)-4AB}{B^2-3A^2}\right]}\right|$$

$$=\tan^{-1}\left|\frac{-3A^2+\sqrt{3}A^2B-3AB^2+\sqrt{3}B^3}{-\sqrt{3}A^3+A^2B-\sqrt{3}AB^2+B^3}\right|$$

$$=\tan^{-1}(\sqrt{3})=60^\circ$$

Then, remaining third angle is $180^\circ-(60^\circ+60^\circ)=60^\circ$.

$\therefore$ ΔAOB is equilateral.

In ΔOAB,

length of perpendicular from O on AB

$$=p=OM=\frac{|0+0+C|}{\sqrt{(A^2+B^2)}}$$

$$p=\frac{|C|}{\sqrt{(A^2+B^2)}}$$

and in ΔOAM, $\sin 60^\circ=\dfrac{p}{OA} \Rightarrow OA=\dfrac{2p}{\sqrt{3}}$

$$\therefore \quad OA=\frac{2|C|}{\sqrt{3}\sqrt{(A^2+B^2)}}$$

$\therefore$ Area of the equilateral triangle $=\dfrac{\sqrt{3}}{4}(\text{side})^2=\dfrac{\sqrt{3}}{4}(OA)^2$

$$=\frac{\sqrt{3}}{4}\times\frac{4|C|^2}{3\times(A^2+B^2)}=\frac{C^2}{\sqrt{3}(A^2+B^2)}$$

2. Given equation is $ax^2+2hxy+by^2=0 \quad$ ...(i)

Let the lines represented by Eq. (i) be

$$y-m_1x=0 \quad \text{...(ii)}$$

and $$y-m_2x=0 \quad \text{...(iii)}$$

Therefore, $m_1+m_2=-\dfrac{2h}{b}$ and $m_1m_2=\dfrac{a}{b}$

If $m_1=\tan\theta_1$ and $m_2=\tan\theta_2$, then equation of lines through the origin making 45° with the lines Eqs. (ii) and (iii) will be

$$y-x\tan(\theta_1-45^\circ)=0$$

and $$y-x\tan(\theta_2-45^\circ)=0$$

Their combined equation is

$$\{y-x\tan(\theta_1-45^\circ)\}\{y-x\tan(\theta_2-45^\circ)\}=0$$

$$\Rightarrow \left(y-\frac{m_1-1}{1+m_1}x\right)\left(y-\frac{m_2-1}{1+m_2}x\right)=0$$

$$\Rightarrow \{(1+m_1)y-(m_1-1)x\}\{(1+m_2)y-(m_2-1)x\}=0$$

$$\Rightarrow (1+m_1)(1+m_2)y^2-xy\{(1+m_1)(m_2-1)+(m_1-1)(1+m_2)\}+(m_1-1)(m_2-1)x^2=0$$

$$\Rightarrow (1+m_1+m_2+m_1m_2)y^2-2xy(m_1m_2-1)+\{m_1m_2-(m_1+m_2)+1\}x^2=0$$

$$\Rightarrow \left(1-\frac{2h}{b}+\frac{a}{b}\right)y^2-2xy\left(\frac{a}{b}-1\right)+\left(\frac{a}{b}+\frac{2h}{b}+1\right)x^2=0$$

$$\therefore \quad (a+2h+b)x^2-2(a-b)xy+(a-2h+b)y^2=0$$

3. $u \equiv ax^2 + 2hxy + by^2 + 2gx + 2fy + c = 0$

$\because u$ represents a pair of straight line.

Then, $\Delta = 0$

$$\therefore \quad abc + 2fgh - af^2 - bg^2 - ch^2 = 0 \quad \text{...(i)}$$

Combined equation of axes is $xy = 0$

Now, the curve through the intersection of $u = 0$ and $xy = 0$ is

$$u + \lambda xy = 0 \quad \text{...(ii)}$$

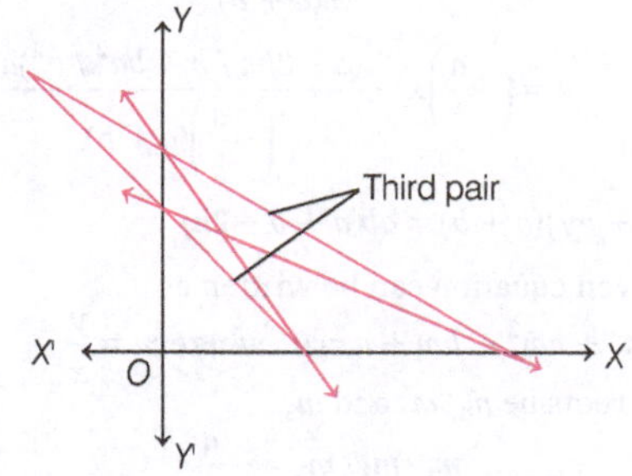

i.e. $\quad ax^2 + 2hxy + by^2 + 2gx + 2fy + c + \lambda xy = 0$

$\Rightarrow \quad ax^2 + xy(2h + \lambda) + by^2 + 2gx + 2fy + c = 0$

If it represents a pair of lines, then

$$abc + 2fg\left(h + \frac{\lambda}{2}\right) - af^2 - bg^2 - c\left(h + \frac{\lambda}{2}\right)^2 = 0$$

$$\Rightarrow (abc + 2fgh - af^2 - bg^2 - ch^2) + \lambda(fg - ch) - \frac{c\lambda^2}{4} = 0$$

$$\Rightarrow \quad 0 + \lambda(fg - ch) - \frac{c\lambda^2}{4} = 0 \quad \text{[from Eq. (i)]}$$

$$\therefore \quad \lambda = \frac{4(fg - ch)}{c} \quad \text{...(iii)}$$

Hence, the equation of third pair from Eqs. (ii) and (iii) is

$$u + \frac{4(fg - ch)}{c} xy = 0$$

$$\therefore \quad cu + 4(fg - ch)xy = 0$$

4. Given equation is, $ax^2 + 2hxy + by^2 + 2gx + 2fy + c = 0$ ...(i)

Let the equation of the parallel lines represented by Eq. (i) be $lx + my + n = 0$ and $lx + my + n_1 = 0$.

Then, $(lx + my + n)(lx + my + n_1)$

$$\equiv ax^2 + 2hxy + by^2 + 2gx + 2fy + c$$

Equating the coefficients, we get

$$l^2 = a \quad \text{...(ii)}$$

$$m^2 = b \quad \text{...(iii)}$$

$$nn_1 = c \quad \text{...(iv)}$$

$$2lm = 2h \quad \text{...(v)}$$

$$(n + n_1)l = 2g \quad \text{...(vi)}$$

$$m(n + n_1) = 2f \quad \text{...(vii)}$$

Eq. (i) From Eq. (v)

$$\Rightarrow \quad h = lm = \pm\sqrt{ab}$$

Now, $\quad h = \sqrt{ab} \quad$ or $\quad h = -\sqrt{ab}$

$\because \quad abc + 2fgh - af^2 - bg^2 - ch^2 = 0$

$\Rightarrow \quad abc + 2fg\sqrt{ab} - af^2 - bg^2 - c \cdot ab = 0$

[substituting the value of $h = \sqrt{ab}$]

$$\Rightarrow \quad -(f\sqrt{a} - g\sqrt{b})^2 = 0$$

$$\Rightarrow \quad f\sqrt{a} = g\sqrt{b}$$

Thus, the given equation represents a pair of lines.

Also, if $h = -\sqrt{ab}$,

then $-g\sqrt{b} = -f\sqrt{a}$

(ii) The distance between parallel lines

$$= \frac{|n - n_1|}{\sqrt{(l^2 + m^2)}} = \frac{\sqrt{(n + n_1)^2 - 4nn_1}}{\sqrt{l^2 + m^2}}$$

$$= \frac{\sqrt{\left(\frac{4g^2}{l^2} - 4c\right)}}{\sqrt{(a + b)}} \quad \text{[from Eqs. (vi), (ii) and (iii)]}$$

$$= 2\sqrt{\left(\frac{g^2 - ac}{a(a + b)}\right)} \quad [\because l^2 = a]$$

we show that by an example that these conditions are not sufficient because

$$h^2 = ab \quad \Rightarrow \quad h = \pm\sqrt{ab}$$

and $\quad bg^2 = af^2 \Rightarrow g\sqrt{b} = \pm f\sqrt{a}$

$\Rightarrow \quad h = \sqrt{ab},\ g\sqrt{b} = f\sqrt{a}$

or $\quad (h = -\sqrt{ab},\ g\sqrt{b} = -f\sqrt{a})$

Consider, for example, $4x^2 + 4xy + y^2 + 4x - 2y + 5 = 0$

Here, $\quad a = 4, h = 2, b = 1, g = 2, f = -1, c = 5$

and $\quad h = \sqrt{ab},\ g\sqrt{b} = -f\sqrt{a}$

But $abc + 2fgh - af^2 - bg^2 - ch^2$

$= 4 \times 1 \times 5 + 2 \times (-1) \times 2 \times 2 - 4 \times (-1)^2 - 1 \times (2)^2 - 5 \times (2)^2$

$= 20 - 8 - 4 - 4 - 20 = -16 \neq 0$

Hence, the Eq. (i) does not represent a pair of lines at all.

5. The combined equation of AB and AD is

$$S_1 \equiv ax^2 + 2hxy + by^2 = 0$$

Now, equation of lines through (p, q) and parallel to $S_1 \equiv 0$ is

$S_2 \equiv a(x - p)^2 + 2h(x - p)(y - q) + b(y - q)^2 = 0$ ...(i)

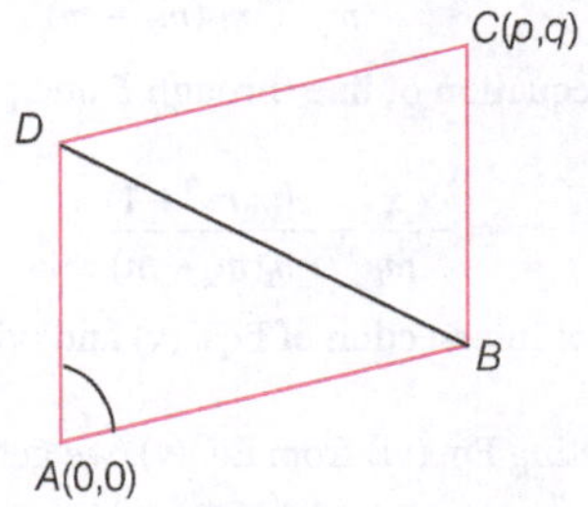

Hence, the equation of diagonal BD is

$$S_1 - S_2 = 0$$

$$a(-2xp + p^2) + 2h(-py - qx + pq) + b(-2qy + q^2) = 0$$

$$-ap(2x - p) - hq(2x - p) - hp(2y - q) - bq(2y - q) = 0$$

[$\because 2hpq$ is written as $hpq + hpq$]

Hence, diagonal of BD is

$$(2x - p)(ap + hq) + (2y - q)(bq + hp) = 0$$

Area of parallelogram $= \dfrac{p_1 p_2}{\sin\theta}$

$\Rightarrow p_1 p_2 =$ product of perpendiculars from (p, q) on AB and AD whose combined equation is

$$ax^2 + 2hxy + by^2 = 0$$

$$\therefore \quad p_1 p_2 = \frac{|ap^2 + 2hpq + bq^2|}{\sqrt{\{(a-b)^2 + 4h^2\}}}$$

$$\therefore \quad \tan\theta = \frac{2\sqrt{(h^2 - ab)}}{|(a+b)|}$$

$$\therefore \quad \sin\theta = \frac{2\sqrt{(h^2 - ab)}}{\sqrt{(a-b)^2 + 4h^2}}$$

$$\therefore \quad \text{Required area} = \frac{|ap^2 + 2hpq + bq^2|}{2\sqrt{(h^2 - ab)}}$$

6. The given lines $y = m_1 x$ and $y = m_2 x$ intersect at the origin O (0, 0). Thus, one vertex of the triangle is at the origin O. Therefore, let OAB be the triangle and OA, OB be the lines respectively

$$y = m_1 x \quad \text{...(i)}$$

and

$$y = m_2 x \quad \text{...(ii)}$$

Let the equation of the third side AB be

$$y = mx + c \quad \text{...(iii)}$$

Given that, $H(a, b)$ is the orthocentre of the ΔOAB.

$\therefore$ OH is perpendicular to AB.

$$\Rightarrow \left(\frac{b}{a}\right) \times m = -1 \Rightarrow m = -\frac{a}{b} \quad \text{...(iv)}$$

On solving Eq. (iii) with Eqs. (i) and (ii), the coordinates of A are $\left(\dfrac{c}{m_1 - m}, \dfrac{cm_1}{m_1 - m}\right)$ and those of B are $\left(\dfrac{c}{m_2 - m}, \dfrac{cm_2}{m_2 - m}\right)$.

Now, equation of the line through A and perpendicular to OB is

$$y - \frac{cm_1}{m_1 - m} = -\frac{1}{m_2}\left(x - \frac{c}{m_1 - m}\right)$$

$$\Rightarrow \quad y = -\frac{x}{m_2} + \frac{c(m_1 m_2 + 1)}{m_2(m_2 - m)} \quad \text{...(v)}$$

Similarly, equation of line through B and perpendicular to OA is

$$y = -\frac{x}{m_1} + \frac{c(m_1 m_2 + 1)}{m_1(m_2 - m)} \quad \text{...(vi)}$$

The point of intersection of Eqs. (v) and (vi) is the orthocentre $H(a, b)$.

On subtracting Eq. (vi) from Eq. (v), we get

$$x = a = \frac{-cm(m_1 m_2 + 1)}{(m_1 - m)(m_2 - m)}$$

$$\Rightarrow \quad c = \frac{-[m_1 m_2 - m(m_1 + m_2) + m^2]a}{m(m_1 m_2 + 1)} \quad \text{...(vii)}$$

Since, m_1 and m_2 are the roots of the equation $bx^2 + 2hx + a = 0$.

$$\therefore \quad m_1 + m_2 = -\frac{2h}{b} \text{ and } m_1 m_2 = \frac{a}{b}$$

$$c = \frac{-\left[\dfrac{a}{b} + \dfrac{2hm}{b} + m^2\right]a}{m\left(\dfrac{a}{b} + 1\right)} = \frac{-[a + 2hm + bm^2]a}{m(a+b)}$$

From Eq. (iii), the equation of third side AB is

$$y = mx - \frac{(a + 2hm + bm^2)a}{m(a+b)}$$

$$\Rightarrow \quad y = \left(-\frac{a}{b}\right)x - \frac{(a - 2ha/b + ba^2/b^2)a}{\left(-\dfrac{a}{b}\right)(a+b)}$$

$$\Rightarrow (ax + by)(a + b) = ab(a + b - 2h)$$

7. The given equation can be written as

$$dm^3 + cm^2 + bm + a = 0, \text{ where } m = \frac{y}{x}$$

Let its roots be m_1, m_2 and m_3.

$$\therefore \quad m_1 \cdot m_2 \cdot m_3 = -\frac{a}{d} \quad \text{...(i)}$$

If $m_1 = \tan\alpha$, then $m_2 = \tan(90° - \alpha)$

[$\because$ two lines makes complementary angles with X-axis]

$$\therefore \quad m_2 = \cot\alpha$$

Then, $m_1 m_2 = 1$

From Eq. (i), $m_3 = -\dfrac{a}{d}$

Since, m_3 is root of the above cubic, we have

$$d\left(-\frac{a^3}{d^3}\right) + c\left(\frac{a^2}{d^2}\right) + b\left(-\frac{a}{d}\right) + a = 0$$

$$\Rightarrow \quad \left(-\frac{a^3}{d^2}\right) + \left(\frac{ca^2}{d^2}\right) - \left(\frac{ab}{d}\right) + a = 0$$

$$\Rightarrow \quad -a^3 + ca^2 - abd + ad^2 = 0$$

On dividing each by a, we get

$$-a^2 + ca - bd + d^2 = 0$$

$$\therefore \quad a(a - c) + d(b - d) = 0$$

8. Given equation is

$$a(x^4 + y^4) - 4bxy(x^2 - y^2) + 6cx^2y^2 = 0 \quad \text{...(i)}$$

Eq. (i) is a homogeneous equation of fourth degree and since it represents two pairs at right angles i.e. sum of the coefficients of x^2 and y^2 should be zero.

Let $a(x^4 + y^4) - 4bxy(x^2 - y^2) + 6cx^2y^2$

$$= (ax^2 + pxy - ay^2)(x^2 + qxy - y^2),$$

where p and q are constants.

On comparing similar powers, we get

$$p + aq = -4b \quad \text{...(ii)}$$

$$-2a + pq = 6c \quad \text{...(iii)}$$

Again, given two pairs coincide, then

$$\frac{p}{a} = q \Rightarrow p = aq \quad \text{...(iv)}$$

From Eqs. (ii) and (iv), we get

$$q = -\frac{2b}{a} \text{ and } p = -2b$$

On substituting the values of p and q in Eq. (iii), we get

$$-2a + \frac{4b^2}{a} = 6c$$

$$\Rightarrow \quad -a^2 + 2b^2 = 3ac$$

$$\therefore \quad 2b^2 = a^2 + 3ac$$

9. Let the three represented lines be

$y = m_1 x$, $y = m_2 x$ and $y = m_3 x$

$$ay^3 + by^2x + cyx^2 + dx^3 = a(y - m_1x)(y - m_2x)(y - m_3x)$$

On comparing similar powers on both sides

$$\Rightarrow \quad m_1 + m_2 + m_3 = -\frac{b}{a} \quad \text{...(i)}$$

$$m_1m_2 + m_2m_3 + m_3m_1 = \frac{c}{a} \quad \text{...(ii)}$$

$$m_1m_2m_3 = -\frac{d}{a} \quad \text{...(iii)}$$

Let the point $P(x_1, y_1)$, from given condition

$$\frac{(y_1 - m_1x_1)}{\sqrt{(1+m_1^2)}} \cdot \frac{(y_1 - m_2x_1)}{\sqrt{(1+m_2^2)}} \cdot \frac{(y_1 - m_3x_1)}{\sqrt{(1+m_3^2)}} = k^3$$

$$\Rightarrow \quad \frac{1}{a}(ay_1^3 + by_1^2x_1 + cy_1x_1^2 + dx_1^3)$$

$$= k^3\sqrt{(1+m_1^2)(1+m_2^2)(1+m_3^2)}$$

$$[\because ay^3 + by^2x + cyx^2 + dx^3 = a(y - m_1x)(y - m_2x)(y - m_3x)]$$

$$\Rightarrow (ay_1^3 + by_1^2x_1 + cy_1x_1^2 + dx_1^3)$$

$$= ak^3\sqrt{(1 + \Sigma m_1^2 + \Sigma m_1^2m_2^2 + m_1^2m_2^2m_3^2)}$$

$$= ak^3\sqrt{\{1 + (\Sigma m_1)^2 - 2\Sigma m_1m_2 + (\Sigma m_1m_2)^2 - 2m_1m_2m_3\Sigma m_1 + (m_1m_2m_3)^2\}}$$

$$= ak^3\sqrt{1 + \frac{b^2}{a^2} - \frac{2c}{a} + \frac{c^2}{a^2} + \frac{2d}{a}\cdot\left(-\frac{b}{a}\right) + \left(-\frac{d}{a}\right)^2}$$

$$= k^3\sqrt{(a^2 + b^2 - 2ac + c^2 - 2bd + d^2)}$$

$$= k^3\sqrt{\{(a-c)^2 + (b-d)^2\}}$$

Hence, locus of P is

$$(ay^3 + by^2x + cyx^2 + dx^3) = k^3\sqrt{\{(a-c)^2 + (b-d)^2\}}$$

10. Let the two lines represented by

$$ax^2 + 2hxy + by^2 = 0 \quad \text{...(i)}$$

be $\quad y = m_1x$

and $\quad y = m_2x$

$$\therefore \quad m_1 + m_2 = -\frac{2h}{b} \quad \text{...(ii)}$$

$$\text{and} \quad m_1m_2 = \frac{a}{b} \quad \text{...(iii)}$$

and the lines represented by

$$a'x^2 + 2h'xy + b'y^2 = 0 \quad \text{...(iv)}$$

be $\quad y = -\frac{1}{m_1}x$ and $y = m_2x$

$$\therefore \quad -\frac{1}{m_1} + m_2 = -\frac{2h'}{b'} \quad \text{...(v)}$$

$$\text{and} \quad -\left(\frac{1}{m_1}\right)m_2 = \frac{a'}{b'} \quad \text{...(vi)}$$

From Eqs. (iii) and (vi), we get

$$-m_2^2 = \frac{aa'}{bb'}$$

$$\Rightarrow \quad m_2 = \frac{\sqrt{(-aba'b')}}{bb'}$$

From Eqs. (iii), we get $\quad m_1 = -\dfrac{\sqrt{(-aba'b')}}{a'b}$

On substituting these values of m_1 and m_2 in Eqs. (ii) and (v), we get

$$-\frac{\sqrt{-aba'b'}}{a'b} + \frac{\sqrt{-aba'b'}}{bb'} = -\frac{2h}{b}$$

$$\Rightarrow \quad \frac{ha'b'}{b'-a'} = \frac{1}{2}\sqrt{-aa'bb'} \quad \text{...(vii)}$$

$$\text{and} \quad \frac{a'b}{\sqrt{-aba'b'}} + \frac{\sqrt{-aba'b'}}{bb'} = -\frac{2h'}{b'}$$

$$\frac{h'ab}{b-a} = \frac{1}{2}\sqrt{-aba'b'} \quad \text{...(viii)}$$

From Eqs. (vii) and (viii), we get

$$\frac{ha'b'}{b'-a'} = \frac{h'ab}{b-a} = \frac{1}{2}\sqrt{-aba'b'}$$

"

Let the relation of knowledge to real life be very visible to your pupils and let them understand how by knowledge the world could be transformed.

–Bertrand Russell

4

Circle

Learning Milestones

Milestone 1 Equation of a Circle
- Definition
- Diametric Form of a Circle
- Equation of Circle Passing Through Three Non-collinear Points
- Parametric Form of a Circle

Milestone 2 Equation of Circle in Some Special Cases
- Intercepts Made on the Axes by a Circle
- Position of a Point with respect to Circle
- Maximum and Minimum Distance of a Point from the Circle

Milestone 3 Line and Circle
- Intersection of a Line and a Circle
- Length of Intercept Cut-off from a Line by a Circle
- Tangent to a Circle at a Given Point
- Normal to a Circle at a Given Point

Milestone 4 Length and Pair of Tangent
- Length of the Tangent from a Point to a Circle
- Power of a Point with respect to a Circle
- Chord of Contact
- Chord Bisected at a Given Point
- Pair of Tangents
- Director Circle

Milestone 5 Family of Circles
- Diameter of a Circle
- Common Tangents of Two Circles
- Family of Circles
- Two Circles Touch Each Other
- Common Chord of Two Circles

Milestone 6 System of Circles
- Angle of Intersection of Two Circles
- Radical Centre
- Limiting Point
- Radical Axis
- Co-axial System of Circles
- Image of the Circle by the Line Mirror

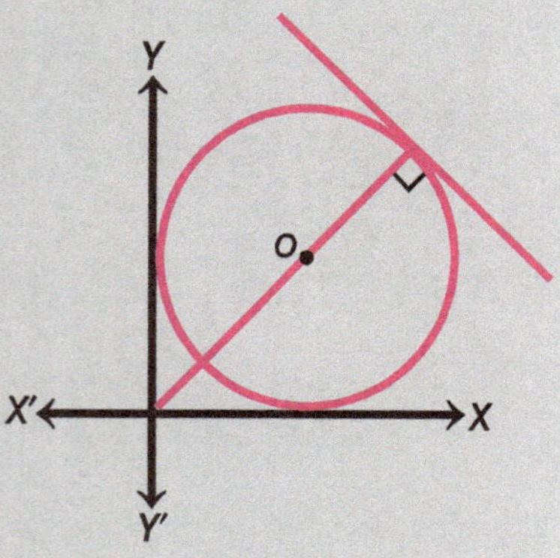

Practice Milestones

Practice Milestone 1- JEE Main Pattern

Practice Milestone 2 - JEE Advanced Pattern

Practice Milestone 3 - Challenging Problems

Milestone 1 Equation of a Circle

• Definition • Diametric Form of a Circle • Equation of Circle Passing Through Three Non-collinear Points • Parametric Form of a Circle

4.1 Definition

A circle is the locus of a point which moves in a plane, so that its distance from a fixed point in the plane is always constant. The fixed point is called the centre of the circle and the constant distance is called its radius.

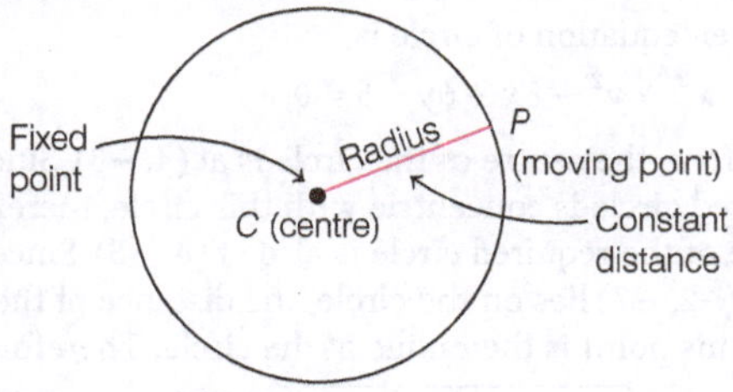

i.e. CP = constant distance = Radius

Equation of a Circle

The curve traced by the moving point is called its circumference i.e. the equation of any circle is satisfied by coordinates of all points on its circumference.

Or

The equation of the circle means the equation of the circumference.

Or

It is the set of all points lying on the circumference of the circle.

Chord and Diameter The line joining any two points on the circumference is called a chord. If any chord passing through centre of the circle, it is called its diameter.

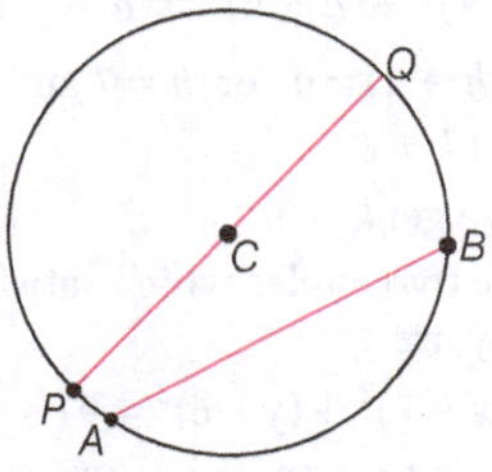

AB = Chord, PQ = Diameter

where, C is centre of the circle.

Equation of Circle in Centre-Radius Form

Let a be the radius and $C(h, k)$ be the centre of any circle.

Let $P(x, y)$ be any point on the circumference.

Then, $$CP = a$$

$$\Rightarrow \quad (CP)^2 = a^2$$

$$\Rightarrow \quad (x-h)^2 + (y-k)^2 = a^2$$

This equation is known as the central form of the equation of a circle.

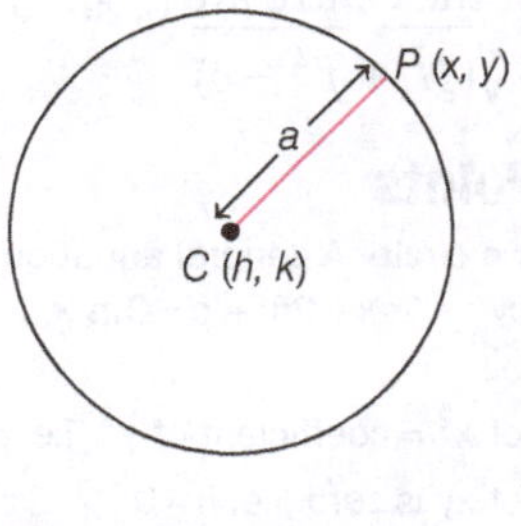

JEE SPIKE

When $C(h, k) \equiv C(0, 0)$, then equation of circle becomes $x^2 + y^2 = a^2$, which is known as standard form of the circle.

Example 1. Find the equation of a circle whose centre is at (– 2, 3) and radius is equal to 4.

Sol. We have, centre $(h, k) = (-2, 3)$ and radius, $a = 4$

So, equation of circle is $(x+2)^2 + (y-3)^2 = 16$

Example 2. Find the equation of the circle whose centre is the point of intersection of the lines $2x - 3y + 4 = 0$ and $3x + 4y - 5 = 0$ and passes through the origin.

Sol. The point of intersection of the lines

$$2x - 3y + 4 = 0 \text{ and } 3x + 4y - 5 = 0 \text{ is } \left(-\frac{1}{17}, \frac{22}{17}\right).$$

Therefore, the centre of the circle is at $\left(-\frac{1}{17}, \frac{22}{17}\right)$.

Since, the origin lies on the circle, its distance from the centre of the circle is radius of the circle, therefore

$$r = \sqrt{\left(-\frac{1}{17} - 0\right)^2 + \left(\frac{22}{17} - 0\right)^2} = \sqrt{\frac{485}{289}}$$

∴ The equation of the circle becomes

$$\left(x + \frac{1}{17}\right)^2 + \left(y - \frac{22}{17}\right)^2 = \frac{485}{289}$$

or $$17(x^2 + y^2) + 2x - 44y = 0$$

Equation of a Circle in General Form

The equation of the circle with centre (h, k) and radius a is

$$(x - h)^2 + (y - k)^2 = a^2$$

or $$x^2 + y^2 - 2hx - 2ky + h^2 + k^2 - a^2 = 0 \quad \text{...(i)}$$

which is of the form $x^2 + y^2 + 2gx + 2fy + c = 0$ ...(ii)

This is known as the **general equation** of a circle comparing Eqs. (i) and (ii), we get

$$h = -g, k = -f \quad \text{and} \quad a = \sqrt{(g^2 + f^2 - c)}$$

∴ Coordinates of the centre are $(-g, -f)$ and

$$\text{radius} = \sqrt{(g^2 + f^2 - c)} \quad [\because g^2 + f^2 \geq c]$$

JEE Focus Points

- **Conditions for a circle** A general equation of second degree $ax^2 + 2hxy + by^2 + 2gx + 2fy + c = 0$ in x, y represents a circle, if
  - coefficient of x^2 = coefficient of y^2 i.e. $a = b$
  - coefficient of xy is zero i.e. $h = 0$
- **Nature of the circle** Radius of the circle $x^2 + y^2 + 2gx + 2fy + c = 0$ is $\sqrt{(g^2 + f^2 - c)}$

  Now, the following cases are possible
  - If $g^2 + f^2 - c > 0$, then the radius of circle will be real. Hence, in this case, real circle is possible.
  - If $g^2 + f^2 - c = 0$, then the radius of circle will be real. Hence, in this case, circle is called a point circle.
  - If $g^2 + f^2 - c < 0$, then the radius of circle will be imaginary number. Hence, in this case, circle is called a virtual circle or imaginary circle.
- **Concentric circle** Two circles having the same centre $C(h, k)$ but different radii r_1 and r_2 respectively are called concentric circles. Thus, the circles $(x - h)^2 + (y - k)^2 = r_1^2$ and $(x - h)^2 + (y - k)^2 = r_2^2, r_1 \neq r_2$ are concentric circles. Therefore, the equations of concentric circles differ only in constant terms.

Concept Inside Video

Example 3. Find the centre and radius of the circle

$$2x^2 + 2y^2 = 3x - 5y + 7$$

Sol. The given equation of circle is $2x^2 + 2y^2 = 3x - 5y + 7$

or $$x^2 + y^2 - \frac{3}{2}x + \frac{5}{2}y - \frac{7}{2} = 0$$

If centre is (α, β), then

$$\alpha = -\frac{1}{2}\left(-\frac{3}{2}\right) = \frac{3}{4}$$

and $$\beta = -\frac{1}{2}\left(\frac{5}{2}\right) = -\frac{5}{4}$$

∴ Centre of circle is (α, β) i.e. $\left(\frac{3}{4}, -\frac{5}{4}\right)$

and radius of the circle

$$= \sqrt{\alpha^2 + \beta^2 - (\text{constant term})}$$

$$= \sqrt{\frac{9}{16} + \frac{25}{16} + \frac{7}{2}} = \sqrt{\frac{9 + 25 + 56}{16}} = \frac{3\sqrt{10}}{4}$$

Example 4. Find the equation of the circle concentric with the circle $x^2 + y^2 - 8x + 6y - 5 = 0$ and passing through the point $(-2, -7)$.

Sol. The given equation of circle is

$$x^2 + y^2 - 8x + 6y - 5 = 0$$

Therefore, the centre of the circle is at $(4, -3)$. Since, the required circle is concentric with this circle, therefore the centre of the required circle is also at $(4, -3)$. Since, the point $(-2, -7)$ lies on the circle, the distance of the centre from this point is the radius of the circle. Therefore, we get

$$r = \sqrt{(4 + 2)^2 + (-3 + 7)^2} = \sqrt{52}$$

Hence, the equation of the circle becomes

$$(x - 4)^2 + (y + 3)^2 = 52$$

or $$x^2 + y^2 - 8x + 6y - 27 = 0$$

Example 5. A circle has radius 3 units and its centre lies on the line $y = x - 1$. Find the equation of the circle if it passes through (7, 3).

Sol. Let the centre of the circle be (h, k). Since, the centre lies on $y = x - 1$, we get $k = h - 1$ ...(i)

Since, the circle passes through the point (7, 3), therefore the distance of the centre from this point is the radius r of the circle, we get

$$r = \sqrt{(h - 7)^2 + (k - 3)^2}$$

or $$3 = \sqrt{(h - 7)^2 + (h - 1 - 3)^2} \quad \text{[from Eq. (i)]}$$

$$\Rightarrow 9 = (h - 7)^2 + (h - 4)^2 \Rightarrow h^2 - 11h + 28 = 0$$

or $$(h - 7)(h - 4) = 0 \text{ or } h = 7 \text{ and } h = 4$$

For $h = 7$, we get $k = 6$ [from Eq. (i)]

and for $h = 4$, we get $k = 3$, [from Eq. (i)]

Hence, there are two circles which satisfy the given conditions. They are

$$(x - 7)^2 + (y - 6)^2 = 9$$

or $$x^2 + y^2 - 14x - 12y + 76 = 0$$

and $$(x - 4)^2 + (y - 3)^2 = 9$$

or $$x^2 + y^2 - 8x - 6y + 16 = 0$$

Example 6. Find the area of an equilateral triangle inscribed in the circle $x^2+y^2+2gx+2fy+c=0$.

> **Decoding the Question**
> Draw an equilateral triangle inscribed in circle. Use the concept 'a chord makes constant angle at circumference and will make twice of this angle at centre'.

Sol. Given circle is $x^2+y^2+2gx+2fy+c=0$ ...(i)

Let O be the centre and ABC be an equilateral triangle inscribed in the circle (i).

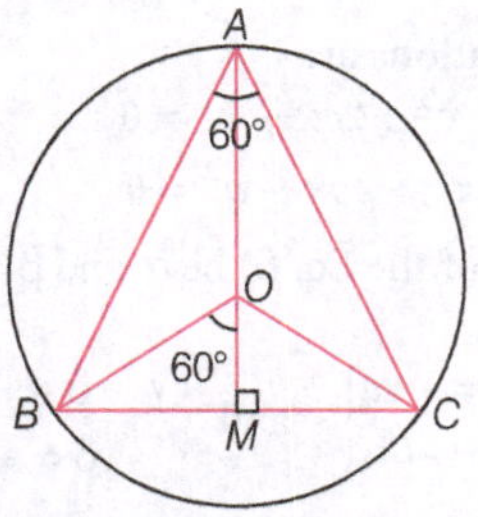

$$O \equiv (-g, -f)$$

and $$OA = OB = OC = \sqrt{g^2+f^2-c} \quad \text{...(ii)}$$

In ΔBOM, $\sin 60° = \dfrac{BM}{OB}$

$$\Rightarrow \quad BM = OB \sin 60° = (OB)\frac{\sqrt{3}}{2}$$

$$\therefore \quad BC = 2BM = \sqrt{3}\,(OB) \quad \text{...(iii)}$$

$$\therefore \text{ Area of } \Delta ABC = \frac{\sqrt{3}}{4}(BC)^2$$

$$= \frac{\sqrt{3}}{4}\,3\,(OB)^2 \quad \text{[from Eq. (iii)]}$$

$$= \frac{3\sqrt{3}}{4}(g^2+f^2-c) \text{ sq units.}$$

Example 7. If $2(x^2+y^2)+4\lambda x+\lambda^2=0$ represents a circle of meaningful radius, then the range of real values of λ is

(a) $(-\infty,\infty)$ (b) $(0,+\infty)$ (c) $(-\infty,0)$ (d) $R-\{0\}$

Sol. (d) We have, $2(x^2+y^2)+4\lambda x+\lambda^2=0$

$$x^2+y^2+2\lambda x+\frac{\lambda^2}{2}=0 \Rightarrow (x+\lambda)^2+y^2=\frac{\lambda^2}{2}$$

On comparing with $(x-h)^2+(y-k)^2=r^2$, we get

centre $(-\lambda, 0)$ and $r = \dfrac{|\lambda|}{\sqrt{2}}$

For a circle of meaningful radius,

$$r > 0$$

$$\frac{|\lambda|}{\sqrt{2}} > 0 \Rightarrow |\lambda| > 0$$

$$\therefore \quad \lambda \in R - \{0\}$$

Example 8. An isosceles triangle is inscribed in the circle $x^2+y^2=a^2$. If the vertex of the triangle is at $A(a, 0)$ and the base angle B and C be each 75°, then the coordinates of B and C are (respectively)

(a) $\left(-\dfrac{\sqrt{3}a}{2}, \dfrac{a}{2}\right)$ and $\left(-\dfrac{\sqrt{3}a}{2}, \dfrac{-a}{2}\right)$

(b) $\left(-\dfrac{\sqrt{3}a}{2}, a\right)$ and $\left(-\dfrac{\sqrt{3}a}{2}, -a\right)$

(c) $\left(\dfrac{\sqrt{3}a}{2}, \sqrt{2}a\right)$ and $\left(-\dfrac{\sqrt{3}a}{2}, -\sqrt{2}a\right)$

(d) None of the above

Sol. (a) Given circle is $x^2+y^2=a^2$

$$\angle B = \angle C = 75° \quad \text{[given]}$$

So, $\angle A$ will be 30°

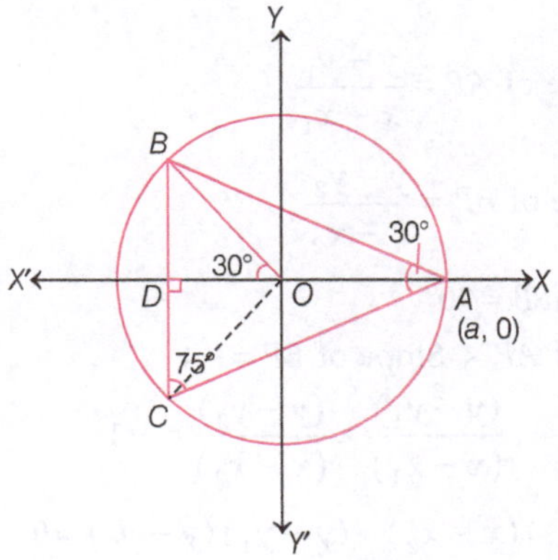

$$\Rightarrow \quad AD \perp BC$$

As in ΔADB,

$$\angle B = 75°,$$
$$\angle BDA = 90°$$

So, $$\angle BAD = 15°$$

Now, in ΔBOD, $\angle D = 90°$, $\angle BOD = 30°$, $OB = a$ (radius)

$$\sin 30° = \frac{BD}{OB}$$

$$\Rightarrow \quad BD = \frac{a}{2}$$

$$\cos 30° = \frac{OD}{OB}$$

$$\Rightarrow \quad OD = \frac{\sqrt{3}}{2}a$$

Hence, coordinates of B are $\left(-\dfrac{\sqrt{3}}{2}a, \dfrac{a}{2}\right)$ and coordinates of C are $\left(-\dfrac{\sqrt{3}}{2}a, -\dfrac{a}{2}\right)$.

4.2 Diametric Form of a Circle

Theorem The equation of the circle on the line segment joining (x_1, y_1) and (x_2, y_2) as diameter is

$$(x - x_1)(x - x_2) + (y - y_1)(y - y_2) = 0.$$

Proof Let $A(x_1, y_1)$ and $B(x_2, y_2)$ be the end points of a diameter and let $P(x, y)$ be any point on the circle.

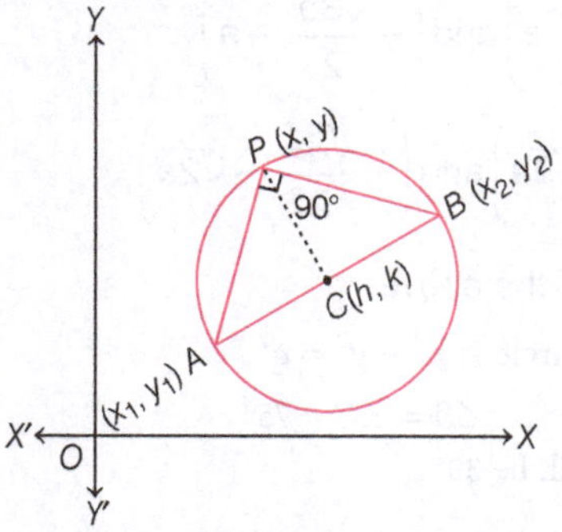

Now, slope of $AP = \dfrac{y - y_1}{x - x_1}$

and slope of $BP = \dfrac{y - y_2}{x - x_2}$

Since, $\angle APB = 90°$

$\therefore$ Slope of $AP \times$ Slope of $BP = -1$

$$\Rightarrow \quad \frac{(y - y_1)}{(x - x_1)} \times \frac{(y - y_2)}{(x - x_2)} = -1$$

$$\Rightarrow (x - x_1)(x - x_2) + (y - y_1)(y - y_2) = 0$$

Example 9. The sides of a square are $x = 2, x = 3, y = 1$ and $y = 2$. Find the equation of the circle drawn on the diagonals of the square as its diameter.

Sol. Let $ABCD$ be a square and equation of its sides AB, BC, CD and DA are $y = 1, x = 3, y = 2,$ and $x = 2$, respectively.

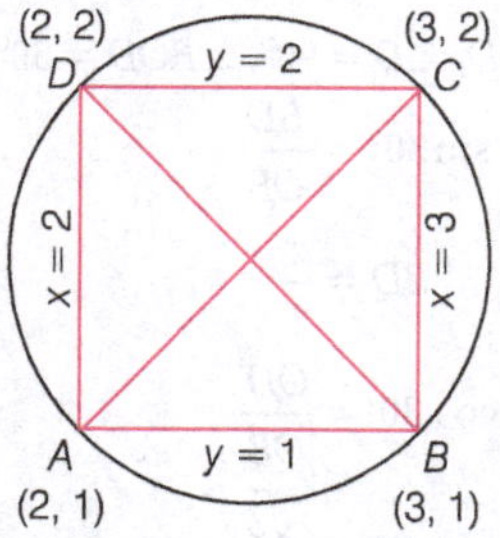

Then, $A \equiv (2, 1), B \equiv (3, 1), C \equiv (3, 2)$ and $D \equiv (2, 2)$

Since, diagonals of square are the diameters of the circle, then equation of circle is

$$(x - 2)(x - 3) + (y - 1)(y - 2) = 0$$

$$\Rightarrow \quad x^2 + y^2 - 5x - 3y + 8 = 0 \text{ [if } AC \text{ as diameter]}$$

JEE SCANNER

Example Similar to PYQ Asked in JEE Main 2022

The abscissae of two points A and B are the roots of the equation $x^2 + 2ax - b^2 = 0$ and their ordinates are the roots of the equation $x^2 + 2px - q^2 = 0$. The radius of the circle with AB as diameter is

(a) $\sqrt{(a-p)^2 + (b-q)^2}$ (b) $\sqrt{(a+p)^2 + (b+q)^2}$

(c) $\sqrt{a^2 + p^2 + b^2 + q^2}$ (d) None of these

Sol. (c) Given equations are

$$x^2 + 2ax - b^2 = 0 \quad \text{...(i)}$$

and $$x^2 + 2px - q^2 = 0 \quad \text{...(ii)}$$

Let the roots of the Eq. (i) be α and β and those of Eq. (ii) be γ and δ. Then,

$$\left.\begin{aligned}\alpha + \beta &= -2a\\ \alpha\beta &= -b^2\end{aligned}\right\} \text{ and } \left.\begin{aligned}\gamma + \delta &= -2p\\ \gamma\delta &= -q^2\end{aligned}\right\}$$

Let $A \equiv (\alpha, \gamma)$ and $B \equiv (\beta, \delta)$.

Now, equation of circle whose diameter is AB will be

$$(x - \alpha)(x - \beta) + (y - \gamma)(y - \delta) = 0$$

$$\Rightarrow x^2 + y^2 - (\alpha + \beta)x - (\gamma + \delta)y + \alpha\beta + \gamma\delta = 0$$

$$\Rightarrow \quad x^2 + y^2 + 2ax + 2py - b^2 - q^2 = 0$$

and radius $= \sqrt{(a^2 + p^2 + b^2 + q^2)}$

Skill Builder

Let the abscissae of the two points P and Q be the roots of $2x^2 - rx + p = 0$ and the ordinates of P and Q be the roots of $x^2 - sx - q = 0$. If the equation of the circle described on PQ as diameter is $2(x^2 + y^2) - 11x + 4y - 22 = 0$, then the value of $2r + s - 2q + p$ is

For Sol.

(a) -1 (b) 2

(c) 1 (d) -2

■ **For more practice** See Q.20 of Milestone Practice 4.1.

Example 10. Find the equation of the circle the end points of whose diameter are the centres of the circles $x^2 + y^2 + 6x - 14y = 1$ and $x^2 + y^2 - 4x + 10y = 2$.

Sol. The centres of the given circles

$$x^2 + y^2 + 6x - 14y - 1 = 0$$

and $x^2 + y^2 - 4x + 10y - 2 = 0$ are $(-3, 7)$ and $(2, -5)$, respectively.

According to the question, the points $(-3, 7)$ and $(2, -5)$ are the extremities of the diameter of required circle.

Hence, equation of circle is

$$(x + 3)(x - 2) + (y - 7)(y + 5) = 0$$

$$\Rightarrow \quad x^2 + y^2 + x - 2y - 41 = 0$$

4.3 Equation of Circle Passing Through Three Non-Collinear Points

Let the equation of circle be $x^2+y^2+2gx+2fy+c=0$ ...(i)

If three points $(x_1,y_1),(x_2,y_2),(x_3,y_3)$ lie on the circle (i), their coordinates must satisfy its equation. Hence, solving equations

$$x_1^2+y_1^2+2gx_1+2fy_1+c=0, \quad ...(ii)$$

$$x_2^2+y_2^2+2gx_2+2fy_2+c=0 \quad ...(iii)$$

and $$x_3^2+y_3^2+2gx_3+2fy_3+c=0, \quad ...(iv)$$

g, f, c are obtained from Eqs. (ii), (iii) and (iv). Then, we can find the circle (i).

JEE Focus Points

- **Cyclic quadrilateral** If all four vertices of a quadrilateral lie on a circle, then the quadrilateral is called a cyclic quadrilateral. The four vertices are said to be concyclic.
- **Concyclic points** If A, B, C and D are concyclic, then
  $OA \cdot OD = OB \cdot OC$
  where, O' be the centre of the circle.

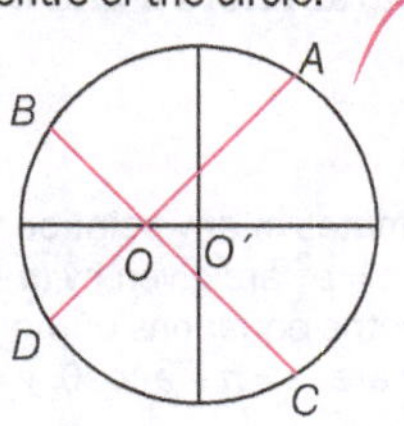

Concept Inside Video

Example 11. Find the equation of the circle which passes through the points (4, 1), (6, 5) and has its centre on the line $4x+y=16$.

Sol. Let the equation of circle be $x^2+y^2+2gx+2fy+c=0$ ...(i)

Since, the centre of Eq. (i) i.e. $(-g,-f)$ lies on $4x+y=16$

then, $-4g-f=16$

or $4g+f+16=0$ ...(ii)

Since, the points (4, 1) and (6, 5) lie on circle $x^2+y^2+2gx+2fy+c=0$, we get the equations

$$16+1+8g+2f+c=0$$

or $$17+8g+2f+c=0 \quad ...(iii)$$

and $$36+25+12g+10f+c=0$$

or $$61+12g+10f+c=0 \quad ...(iv)$$

On subtracting Eq. (iii) from Eq. (iv), we get

$$44+4g+8f=0 \quad ...(v)$$

On solving Eqs. (ii) and (v), we get

$$f=-4 \text{ and } g=-3$$

Now, from Eq. (iii), $17-24-8+c=0 \Rightarrow c=15$

Hence, the equation of circle become

$$x^2+y^2-6x-8y+15=0$$

Example 12. Find the equation of the circle passing through the three non-collinear points (1, 1), (2, −1) and (3, 2).

Sol. Let the equation of circle be

$$x^2+y^2+2gx+2fy+c=0 \quad ...(i)$$

Since, the three given points lie on circle (i), we get

$$1+1+2g+2f+c=0$$

or $$2g+2f+c+2=0 \quad ...(ii)$$

$\Rightarrow$ $$4+1+4g-2f+c=0$$

or $$4g-2f+c+5=0 \quad ...(iii)$$

$\Rightarrow$ $$9+4+6g+4f+c=0$$

or $$6g+4f+c+13=0 \quad ...(iv)$$

On subtracting Eq. (ii) from Eq. (iii) and on subtracting Eq. (iii) from Eq. (iv), we get

$$2g-4f+3=0 \quad ...(v)$$

and $$2g+6f+8=0 \quad ...(vi)$$

On solving Eqs. (v) and (vi), we get

$$f=-\frac{1}{2} \text{ and } g=-\frac{5}{2}$$

Now, from Eq. (ii), $-5-1+c+2=0$

$\therefore$ $c=4$

Hence, from Eq. (i), equation of circle is

$$x^2+y^2-5x-y+4=0$$

Alternate Solution

The centre of the circumcircle is the point of intersection of the right bisectors of the sides of the triangle and the radius is the distance of the circumcentre from any of the vertices of the triangle.

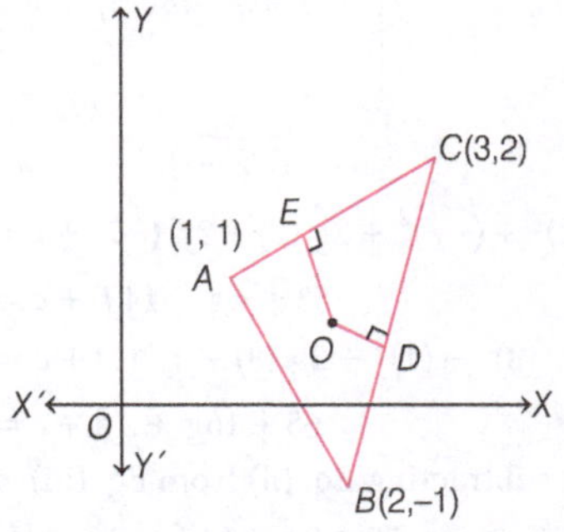

Let D and E are the mid-points of BC and CA, then

$$D \equiv \left(\frac{5}{2},\frac{1}{2}\right) \text{ and } E \equiv \left(2,\frac{3}{2}\right)$$

Slope of $BC = \dfrac{2-(-1)}{3-2}=3$

$\therefore$ Slope of $OD = -\dfrac{1}{3}$

$\therefore$ Equation of OD, $y-\dfrac{1}{2}=-\dfrac{1}{3}\left(x-\dfrac{5}{2}\right) \Rightarrow 6y-3=-2x+5$

$\therefore$ $2x+6y-8=0$ or $x+3y-4=0$ ...(i)

and Slope of $CA=\dfrac{1-2}{1-3}=\dfrac{1}{2}$

$\therefore$ Slope of $OE=-2$

$\therefore$ Equation of OE, $y-\frac{3}{2}=-2(x-2) \Rightarrow 2y-3=-4x+8$

$\Rightarrow \quad 4x+2y-11=0 \quad \text{...(ii)}$

Solving Eq. (i) and Eq. (ii), we get $x=\frac{5}{2}$ and $y=\frac{1}{2}$

$\therefore$ Circumcentre is $\left(\frac{5}{2},\frac{1}{2}\right)$

and radius, $OC=\sqrt{\left(3-\frac{5}{2}\right)^2+\left(2-\frac{1}{2}\right)^2}=\sqrt{\frac{5}{2}}$

$\therefore$ Equation of circle is

$$(x-5/2)^2+(y-1/2)^2=5/2$$

$$\Rightarrow \quad x^2+y^2-5x-y+4=0$$

Example 13. Show that the four points $(1,0),(2,-7),(8,1)$ and $(9,-6)$ are concyclic.

Sol. To show the given four points are concyclic, we have to show that they lie on a circle. Let the general equation of circle is

$$x^2+y^2+2gx+2fy+c=0 \quad \text{...(i)}$$

has three parameters, it is sufficient to obtain the equation of the circle passing through any three of these points. For concyclic, the fourth point should lie on this circle.

Let three points $A(1,0)$, $B(2,-7)$ and $D(8,1)$ lie on Eq. (i), then $1+0+2g+0+c=0$ or $1+2g+c=0 \quad \text{...(ii)}$

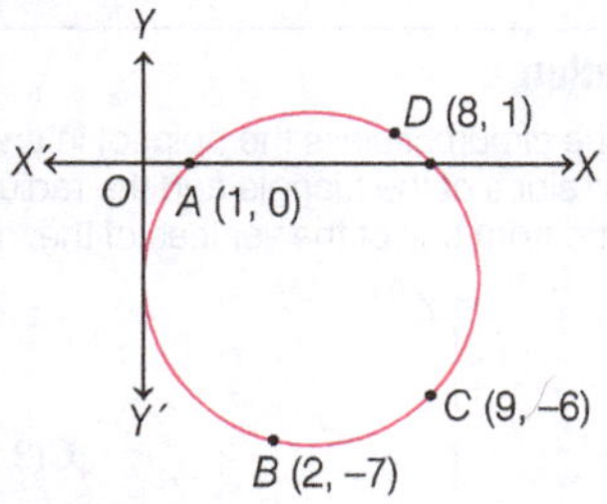

$$(2)^2+(-7)^2+2g(2)+2f(-7)+c=0$$

or $\quad 53+4g-14f+c=0 \quad \text{...(iii)}$

and $\quad (8)^2+(1)^2+2g(8)+2f(1)+c=0$

$\Rightarrow \quad 65+16g+2f+c=0 \quad \text{...(iv)}$

Now, on subtracting Eq. (ii) from Eq. (iii), we get

$$52+2g-14f=0$$

or $\quad 26+g-7f=0 \quad \text{...(v)}$

and on subtracting Eq. (iii) from Eq. (iv), we get

$$12+12g+16f=0$$

$\Rightarrow \quad 3+3g+4f=0 \quad \text{...(vi)}$

On solving Eqs. (v) and (vi), we get

$$g=-5 \text{ and } f=3$$

From Eq. (ii), $1-10+c=0$

$\therefore \quad c=9$

Therefore, equation of circle passing through these points is

$$x^2+y^2-10x+6y+9=0$$

On substituting the fourth point in the equation of this circle, we get

$$(9)^2+(-6)^2-10(9)+6(-6)+9=0$$

Hence, the point $C(9,-6)$ lies on the circle i.e. the four points are concyclic.

4.4 Parametric Form of Circle

If the radius of a circle whose centre is at $C(0,0)$ makes an angle θ with the positive direction of X-axis, then θ is called the parameter.

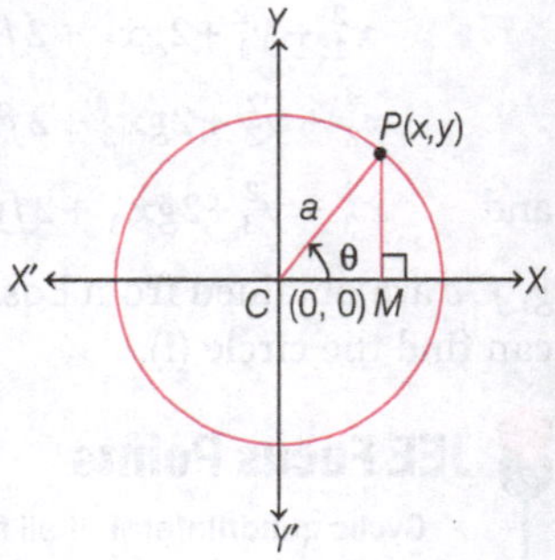

Let $\quad CP=a$

$\therefore \quad CM=x,\ PM=y$

$\Rightarrow \quad x=a\cos\theta,\ y=a\sin\theta$

Hence, $(a\cos\theta, a\sin\theta)$ or 'θ' are the parametric coordinates of the circle $x^2+y^2=a^2$ and $x=a\cos\theta$ and $y=a\sin\theta$ are called parametric equations of the circle $x^2+y^2=a^2$ with parameters a and $\theta\,(0\le\theta<2\pi)$.

JEE SPIKE

The parametric coordinates of any point on the circle $(x-h)^2+(y-k)^2=a^2$ are given by $(h+a\cos\theta, k+a\sin\theta)$ $(0\le\theta<2\pi)$ and parametric equations of the circle $(x-h)^2+(y-k)^2=a^2$ are $x=h+a\cos\theta,\ y=k+a\sin\theta$.

Example 14. Find the parametric form of the equation of the circle $x^2+y^2+px+py=0$.

Sol. Equation of the circle can be re-written in the form

$$\left(x+\frac{p}{2}\right)^2+\left(y+\frac{p}{2}\right)^2=\frac{p^2}{2}$$

Therefore, the parametric form of the equation of the given circle is $x=-\frac{p}{2}+\frac{p}{\sqrt{2}}\cos\theta=\frac{p}{2}(-1+\sqrt{2}\cos\theta)$

and $y=-\frac{p}{2}+\frac{p}{\sqrt{2}}\sin\theta=\frac{p}{2}(-1+\sqrt{2}\sin\theta)$, where $0\le\theta<2\pi$.

Example 15. If the parametric form of a circle is given by

(a) $x=-4+5\cos\theta$ and $y=-3+5\sin\theta$

(b) $x=a\cos\alpha+b\sin\alpha$ and $y=a\sin\alpha-b\cos\alpha$

find its cartesian form.

Sol. (a) The given equations are

$$x=-4+5\cos\theta \text{ and } y=-3+5\sin\theta$$

or $\quad (x+4)=5\cos\theta \quad \text{...(i)}$

and $\quad (y+3)=5\sin\theta \quad \text{...(ii)}$

On squaring and adding Eqs. (i) and (ii), we get

$$(x+4)^2+(y+3)^2=5^2$$

or $$(x+4)^2+(y+3)^2=25$$

(b) The given equations are

$$x = a\cos\alpha + b\sin\alpha \quad \text{...(iii)}$$

$$y = a\sin\alpha - b\cos\alpha \quad \text{...(iv)}$$

On squaring and adding Eqs. (iii) and (iv), we get

$$x^2+y^2=(a\cos\alpha+b\sin\alpha)^2+(a\sin\alpha-b\cos\alpha)^2$$

or $$x^2+y^2=a^2+b^2$$

Example 16. If a straight line through $C(-\sqrt{8},\sqrt{8})$, making an angle of 135° with the X-axis, cuts the circle at $x=5\cos\theta$ and $y=5\sin\theta$ at points A and B, find the length of the segment AB.

Sol. The given circle is $x^2+y^2=25$ ...(i)

Equation of line through C is

$$\frac{x+\sqrt{8}}{\cos 135^\circ}=\frac{y-\sqrt{8}}{\sin 135^\circ}=r$$

$$\Rightarrow \quad \frac{x+\sqrt{8}}{\frac{-1}{\sqrt{2}}}=\frac{y-\sqrt{8}}{\frac{1}{\sqrt{2}}}=r$$

Any point on this line is $\left(-\sqrt{8}-\frac{r}{\sqrt{2}}, \sqrt{8}+\frac{r}{\sqrt{2}}\right)$

If the point lies on the circle $x^2+y^2=25$, then

$$\left(-\sqrt{8}-\frac{r}{\sqrt{2}}\right)^2+\left(\sqrt{8}+\frac{r}{\sqrt{2}}\right)^2=25$$

$$\Rightarrow \quad 2\left(8+\frac{r^2}{2}+2\cdot\sqrt{8}\cdot\frac{r}{\sqrt{2}}\right)=25$$

$$\Rightarrow \quad 2\left(8+\frac{r^2}{2}+4r\right)=25$$

$$\Rightarrow \quad r^2+8r+16-25=0$$

$$\Rightarrow \quad r^2+9r-r-9=0$$

$$\Rightarrow \quad r=1,-9$$

$$\therefore \quad AB=|-9-1|=10$$

Locus of the Mid-point of the Chord of the Circle that Subtends an Angle of 2θ at its Centre

Let mid-point $M(x_1,y_1)$ and centre, radius of circle are (h,k), r respectively, then

$$\cos\theta=\frac{CM}{r}=\frac{\sqrt{(x_1-h)^2+(y_1-k)^2}}{r}$$

$\therefore$ Required locus is $\dfrac{(x-h)^2+(y-k)^2-r^2}{r^2}=-\sin^2\theta$

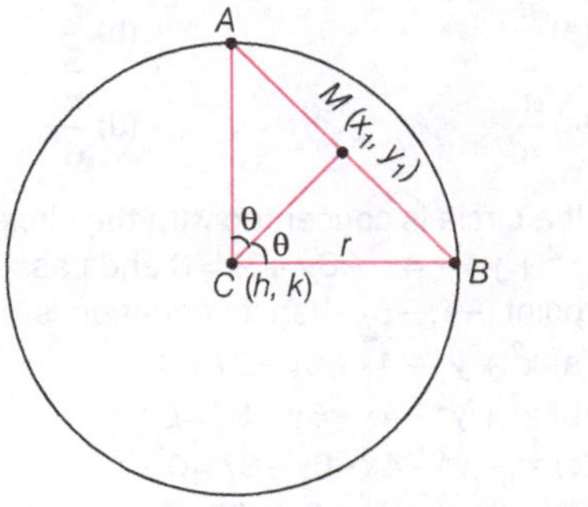

Example 17. Find the locus of mid-points of the chords of the circle $4x^2+4y^2-12x+4y+1=0$ that subtend an angle of $\frac{2\pi}{3}$ at its centre.

Sol. Here, $2\theta=\frac{2\pi}{3} \Rightarrow \theta=\frac{\pi}{3}$

Equation of circle can be written as

$$x^2+y^2-3x+y+\frac{1}{4}=0$$

$$\therefore \text{ Required locus is } \frac{x^2+y^2-3x+y+\frac{1}{4}}{\left(\sqrt{\frac{9}{4}+\frac{1}{4}-\frac{1}{4}}\right)^2}=-\sin^2\left(\frac{\pi}{3}\right)=-\frac{3}{4}$$

$$\Rightarrow \quad x^2+y^2-3x+y+\frac{1}{4}=-\frac{27}{16}$$

or $$16(x^2+y^2)-48x+16y+31=0$$

Milestone Practice 4.1

1. If $x^2+y^2-2x+2ay+a+3=0$ represents a real circle with non-zero radius, then most appropriate is

(a) $a\in(-\infty,-1)$ (b) $a\in(-1,2)$
(c) $a\in(2,\infty)$ (d) $a\in(-\infty,-1)\cup(2,\infty)$

2. If the lines $3x-4y+4=0$ and $6x-8y-7=0$ are tangents to a circle, then the diameter of the circle is

(a) $\frac{3}{2}$ (b) 3 (c) $\frac{5}{2}$ (d) 5

3. Area of a circle in which a chord of length $\sqrt{2}$ makes an angle $\frac{\pi}{2}$ at the centre is

(a) $\frac{\pi}{4}$ (b) $\frac{\pi}{2}$ (c) π (d) 2π

4. The lines $2x-3y-5=0$ and $3x-4y=7$ are diameters of a circle of area 154 sq units, then the equation of the circle is

(a) $x^2+y^2+2x-2y-62=0$
(b) $x^2+y^2+2x-2y-47=0$
(c) $x^2+y^2-2x+2y-62=0$
(d) $x^2+y^2-2x+2y-47=0$

5. The ΔPQR is inscribed in the circle $x^2+y^2=25$. If Q and R have coordinates (3, 4) and (−4,3) respectively, then $\angle QPR$ is equal to

(a) $\frac{\pi}{2}$ (b) $\frac{\pi}{3}$
(c) $\frac{\pi}{4}$ (d) $\frac{\pi}{6}$

6. If a circle is concentric with the circle $x^2+y^2-4x-6y+9=0$ and passes through the point $(-4,-5)$, then its equation is

(a) $x^2+y^2+4x+6y-87=0$
(b) $x^2+y^2-4x+6y+87=0$
(c) $x^2+y^2-4x-6y-87=0$
(d) $x^2+y^2+4x+6y+87=0$

7. Let AB be a chord of the circle $x^2+y^2=r^2$ subtending a right angle at the centre. Then, the locus of the centroid of the ΔPAB as P moves on the circle is

(a) a parabola (b) a circle
(c) an ellipse (d) a pair of straight lines

8. Prove that the centres of the circles $x^2+y^2=1, x^2+y^2+6x-2y-1=0$ and $x^2+y^2-12x+4y=1$ are collinear.

9. Prove that the locus of the centre of the circle $\frac{1}{2}(x^2+y^2)+x\cos\theta+y\sin\theta-4=0$ is $x^2+y^2=1$.

10. Find the equation of the following curves in cartesian form. If the curve is a circle, then find its centre and radius
$x=-1+2\cos\alpha, y=3+2\sin\alpha\ (0\le\alpha<2\pi)$

11. The radius of the circle, having centre at (2, 1) whose one of the chord is a diameter of the circle $x^2+y^2-2x-6y+6=0$ is

(a) 3 (b) 2 (c) 1 (d) $\sqrt{3}$

12. The centre of the circle inscribed in the square formed by the lines $x^2-8x+12=0$ and $y^2-14y+45=0$ is

(a) (4,7) (b) (7,4) (c) (9,4) (d) (4,9)

13. $ABCD$ is a square whose side is a. The equation of the circle circumscribing the square, taking AB and AD as the axes of reference is

(a) $x^2+y^2+ax+ay=0$ (b) $x^2+y^2-ax+ay=0$
(c) $x^2+y^2-ax-ay=0$ (d) $x^2+y^2+ax-ay=0$

14. The locus of the centre of the circle for which one end of the diameter is (3, 3) while the other end lies on the line $x+y=4$ is

(a) $x+y=3$ (b) $x+y=5$
(c) $x+y=7$ (d) $x+y=9$

15. The equation of the circle which passes through (1, 0) and (0, 1) and has its radius as small as possible is

(a) $x^2+y^2+x+y=0$ (b) $x^2+y^2-x+y=0$
(c) $x^2+y^2+x-y=0$ (d) $x^2+y^2-x-y=0$

16. If the points (2, 0), (0, 1), (4,5) and (0, c) are concyclic, then the value of c is

(a) 1 (b) −1 (c) $\frac{14}{3}$ (d) $-\frac{14}{3}$

17. The point on a circle nearest to the point $P(2,1)$ is at a distance of 4 units and farthest point is (6, 5), then the centre of the circle is

(a) $(3+\sqrt{2},2+\sqrt{2})$ (b) $(2+\sqrt{2},3+\sqrt{2})$
(c) $(4+\sqrt{2},3+\sqrt{2})$ (d) $(3+\sqrt{2},4+\sqrt{2})$

18. The intercept on the line $y=x$ by the circle $x^2+y^2-2x=0$ is AB. Equation of the circle on AB as a diameter is

(a) $x^2+y^2-x-y=0$ (b) $x^2+y^2-x+y=0$
(c) $x^2+y^2+x+y=0$ (d) $x^2+y^2+x-y=0$

19. Find the equation of the circle which passes through the points (3, 4), (3, −6) and (1, 2).

20. Let the abscissae of the two points P and Q be the roots of $5x^2-rx+p=0$ and the ordinates of P and Q be the roots of $2y^2-sy-q=0$. If the equation of the circle described on PQ as diameter is $10(x^2+y^2)-14x-20y-16=0$, then find the value of $r+2s+5q-2p$.

Answer Key

1. (d) **2.** (a) **3.** (c) **4.** (d) **5.** (c) **6.** (c) **7.** (b)
10. $(x+1)^2+(y-3)^2=4$, Centre $=(-1, 3)$, Radius $=2$ **11.** (a) **12.** (a)
13. (c) **14.** (b) **15.** (d) **16.** (c) **17.** (c) **18.** (a)
19. $(x-6)^2+(y+1)^2=34$ **20.** (15)

For Detailed Solution

Milestone 2 Equation of Circle in Some Special Cases

- Intercepts Made on the Axes by a Circle • Position of a Point with respect to Circle
- Maximum and Minimum Distance of a Point from the Circle

4.5 Intercepts Made on the Axes by a Circle

Let the circle $x^2+y^2+2gx+2fy+c=0$ ...(i)

Length of intercepts on X-axis and Y-axis are

$|AB|=|x_2-x_1|$ and $|CD|=|y_2-y_1|$, respectively.

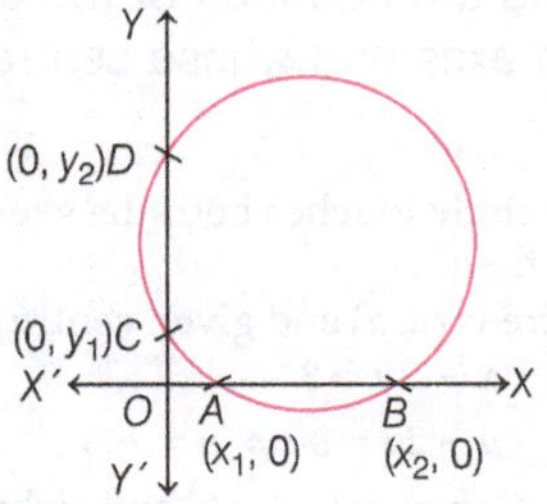

The circle intersects the X-axis, when $y=0$

Then, $x^2+2gx+c=0$

Since, the circle intersects the X-axis at $A(x_1,0)$ and $B(x_2,0)$.

Then, $x_1+x_2=-2g,\ x_1x_2=c$

$\therefore\quad |AB|=|x_2-x_1|=\sqrt{(x_2+x_1)^2-4x_1x_2}=2\sqrt{(g^2-c)}$

and the circle intersects the Y-axis, when $x=0$, then

$y^2+2fy+c=0$

Since, the circle intersects the Y-axis at $C(0,y_1)$ and $D(0,y_2)$.

Then, $y_1+y_2=-2f,\ y_1y_2=c$

$\therefore\quad |CD|=|y_2-y_1|=\sqrt{(y_2+y_1)^2-4y_2y_1}=2\sqrt{(f^2-c)}$

JEE Focus Points

- Intercepts are always positive.
- If circle touches X-axis, then $|AB|=0$

  $\therefore\quad c=g^2$

  and if circle touches Y-axis, then $|CD|=0$

  $\therefore\quad c=f^2$
- If circle touches both axes, then $|AB|=0=|CD|$

  $\therefore\quad c=g^2=f^2$

Example 18. Find the equation of the circle whose diameter is the line joining the points $(-4,3)$ and $(12,-1)$. Also, find the intercept made by it on Y-axis.

Sol. Equation of circle having $(-4,3)$ and $(12,-1)$ as the ends of a diameter is

$$(x+4)(x-12)+(y-3)(y+1)=0$$

$$\Rightarrow\quad x^2+y^2-8x-2y-51=0 \quad ...(i)$$

On comparing Eq. (i) with standard equation of circle, we get

$$x^2+y^2+2gx+2fy+c=0$$

Then, $g=-4,\ f=-1,\ c=-51$

$\therefore$ Intercept on Y-axis $=2\sqrt{(f^2-c)}=2\sqrt{(1+51)}=4\sqrt{13}$.

Example 19. If the intercepts of the variable circle on the X and Y-axes are 2 and 4 respectively, then find the locus of the centre of the circle.

Sol. We have, $2\sqrt{g^2-c}=2$ and $2\sqrt{f^2-c}=4$

$$\Rightarrow\quad g^2-c=1 \text{ and } f^2-c=4 \Rightarrow f^2-g^2=3$$

So, locus of centre is $y^2-x^2=3$

Different Forms of the Equations of a Circle

(i) When the circle passes through the origin (0, 0) and has intercepts 2α and 2β on the X-axis and Y-axis, respectively

Here, $OA=2\alpha,\ OB=2\beta$, then $OM=\alpha$ and $ON=\beta$

Centre of the circle is $C(\alpha,\beta)$ and radius

$$OC=\sqrt{(\alpha^2+\beta^2)}$$

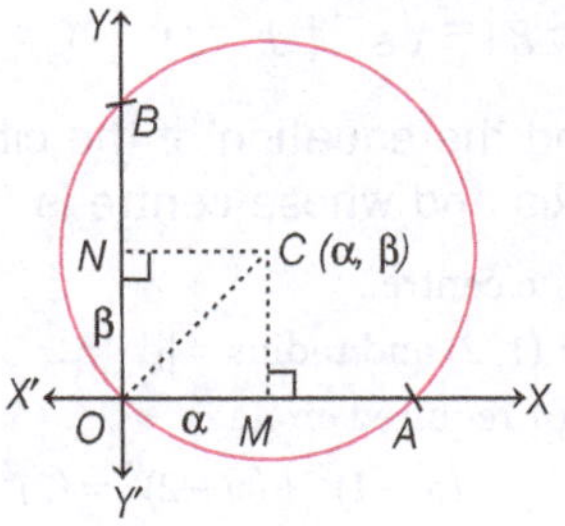

Then, equation of circle is

$$(x-\alpha)^2+(y-\beta)^2=\alpha^2+\beta^2$$

or $$x^2+y^2-2\alpha x-2\beta y=0$$

If a circle is passing through origin, then constant term is absent

i.e. $$x^2+y^2+2gx+2fy=0$$

(ii) When the circle touches *X*-axis

Let (α, β) be the centre of the circle, then radius $=|\beta|$

$\therefore$ Equation of circle is

$$(x-\alpha)^2+(y-\beta)^2=\beta^2$$

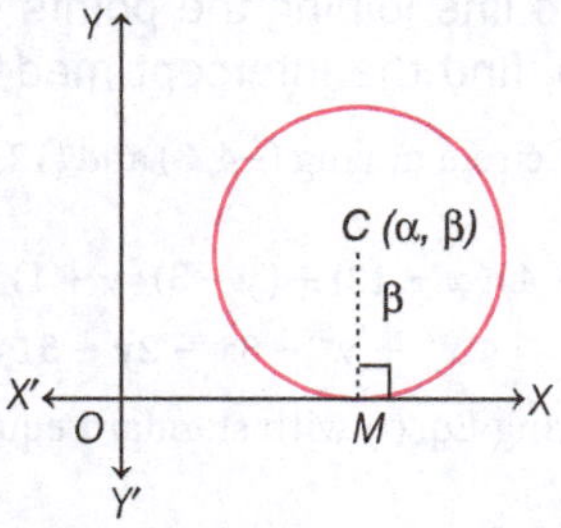

$\Rightarrow$ $$x^2+y^2-2\alpha x-2\beta y+\alpha^2=0$$

If the circle $x^2+y^2+2gx+2fy+c=0$ touches the *X*-axis, then

$$|-f|=\sqrt{g^2+f^2-c} \quad \text{or} \quad c=g^2$$

(iii) When the circle touches *Y*-axis

Let (α, β) be the centre of the circle, then radius $=|\alpha|$

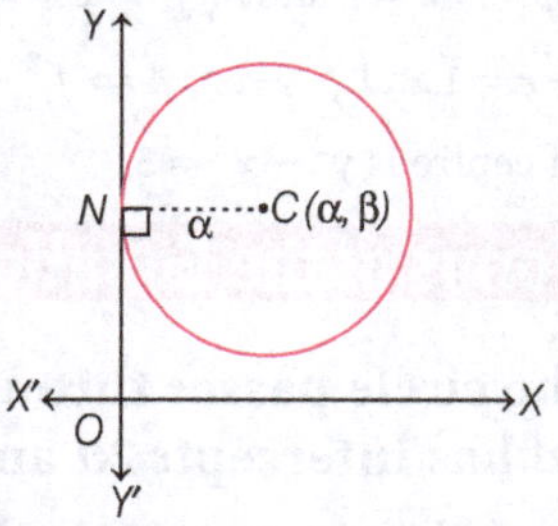

$\therefore$ Equation of circle is $(x-\alpha)^2+(y-\beta)^2=\alpha^2$

$\Rightarrow$ $$x^2+y^2-2\alpha x-2\beta y+\beta^2=0$$

If the circle $x^2+y^2+2gx+2fy+c=0$ touches the *Y*-axis, then

$$|-g|=\sqrt{g^2+f^2-c} \quad \text{or} \quad c=f^2$$

Example 20. Find the equation of the circle which touches the *X*-axis and whose centre is (1, 2).

Sol. Let (α, β) be the centre.

Then, $(\alpha, \beta)=(1, 2)$ and radius $=|\beta|=2$

$\therefore$ Equation of required circle is

$$(x-1)^2+(y-2)^2=(2)^2$$

$\Rightarrow$ $$x^2+y^2-2x-4y+1=0$$

(iv) When the circle touches both axes

Here, $|OM|=|ON|$

Since, length of tangents are equal from any point on circle.

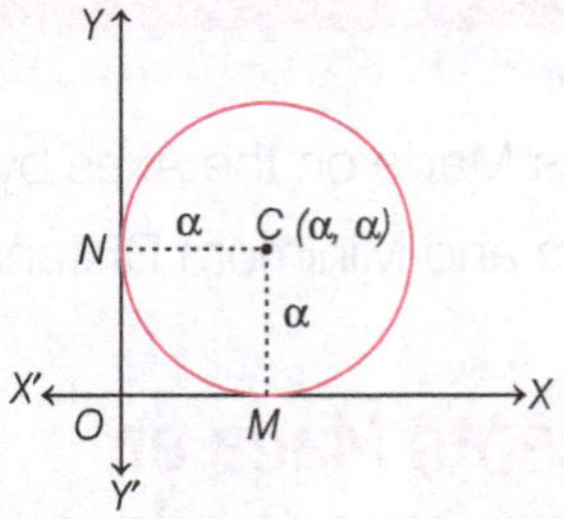

Let centre of the circle be (α, α), then radius $=\alpha$

$\therefore$ Equation of circle is $(x-\alpha)^2+(y-\alpha)^2=\alpha^2$

$\Rightarrow$ $$x^2+y^2-2\alpha x-2\alpha y+\alpha^2=0$$

Example 21. Find the equation of the circle which touches the both axes and whose centre lies on the line $x-2y=3$.

Sol. Given that the circle touches both the axes, let the radius of the circle be *a*, then

Case I If centre is (a, a) and given centre lies on

$$x-2y=3$$

$\therefore$ $$a-2a=3 \Rightarrow a=-3$$

$\therefore$ Centre $=(-3,-3)$ and radius $=|-3|=3$

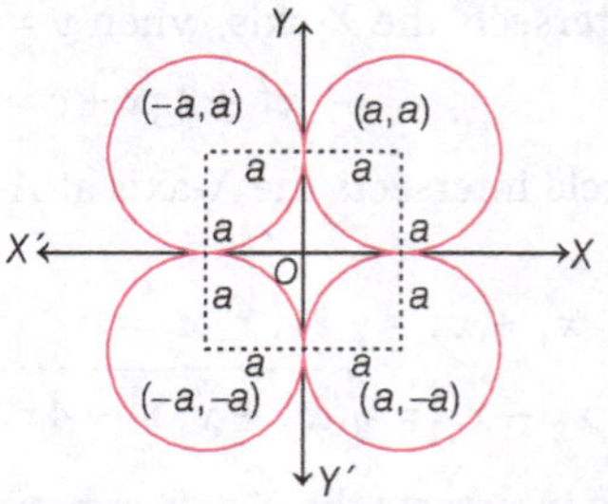

$\therefore$ Equation of circle is $(x+3)^2+(y+3)^2=3^2$

and $$x^2+y^2+6x+6y+9=0$$

Case II If centre is $(-a, a)$ and centre lies on $x-2y=3$

$\therefore$ $$-a-2a=3 \Rightarrow a=-1$$

Then, centre $=(1,-1)$ and radius $=|-1|=1$

$\therefore$ Equation of circle is $(x-1)^2+(y+1)^2=1$

or $x^2+y^2-2x+2y+1=0$

Case III If the centre $=(-a,-a)$ and centre lies on $x-2y=3$

$\therefore$ $$-a+2a=3 \Rightarrow a=3$$

Then, centre $(-3,-3)$ and radius $=|3|=3$

$\therefore$ Equation of circle is

$$(x+3)^2+(y+3)^2=3^2$$

or $$x^2+y^2+6x+6y+9=0$$

Case IV If centre = $(a, -a)$ and centre lies on $x - 2y = 3$

or $a + 2a = 3$

$\therefore$ $a = 1$

Then, centre = $(1, -1)$ and radius = 1

$\therefore$ Equation of circle is

$$(x-1)^2 + (y+1)^2 = 1 \text{ or } x^2 + y^2 - 2x + 2y + 1 = 0$$

(v) When the circle touches X-axis and cut-off intercepts on Y-axis of length $2l$

Let centre be (α, β)

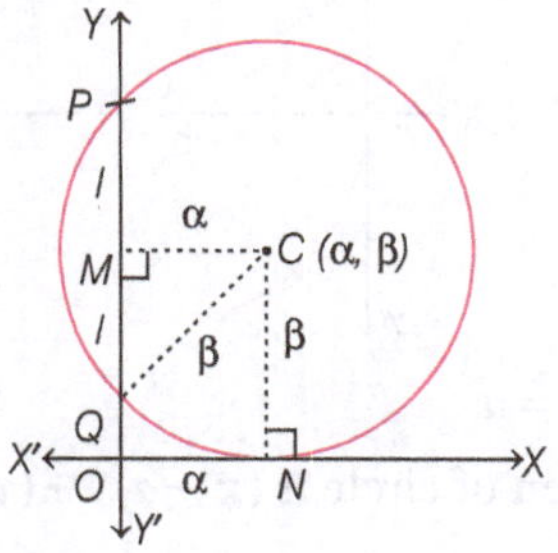

$\therefore$ Radius $= \beta \Rightarrow CQ = CN = \beta$

In ΔCMQ, $\beta^2 = \alpha^2 + l^2, \alpha = \sqrt{(\beta^2 - l^2)}$ [for I quadrant]

$\therefore$ Equation of circle is $[x - \sqrt{(\beta^2 - l^2)}]^2 + (y-\beta)^2 = \beta^2$

Example 22. A circle touching the X-axis at (3, 0) and makes a intercept of length 8 units on the Y-axis passes through the point

(a) (3, 10) (b) (3, 5)

(c) (2, 3) (d) (1, 5)

Decoding the Question

Foot of perpendicular from the centre to any chord of a circle bisects the chord.

Sol. (a) Given that circle touching the X-axis at (3, 0) and making an intercept of 8 unit on the Y-axis.

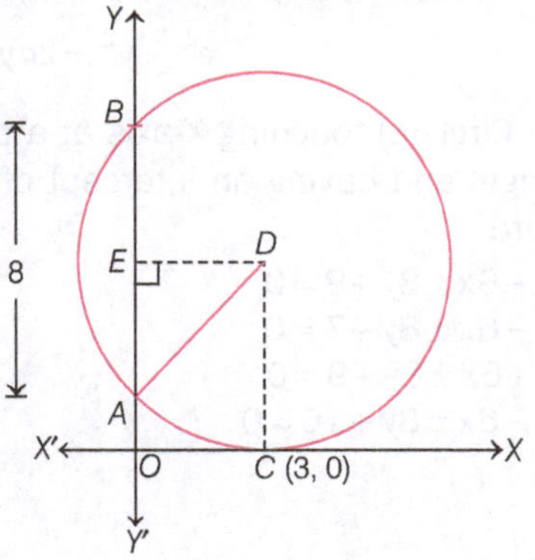

Let radius of circle be r, then the coordinates of circle will be $(3, r)$.

Now, $AE = 4, DE = 3 = OC$

In ΔAED, $AD^2 = ED^2 + AE^2$

$$r^2 = 3^2 + 4^2 \Rightarrow r = \pm 5 \Rightarrow r = 5$$

Equation of the circle with centre at (3, 5) and radius 5 units is $(x-3)^2 + (y-5)^2 = 5^2$

Now, from option (3, 10) satisfy the equation of circle.

(vi) When the circle touches Y-axis and cut-off intercept on X-axis of length $2k$

Let centre be (α, β)

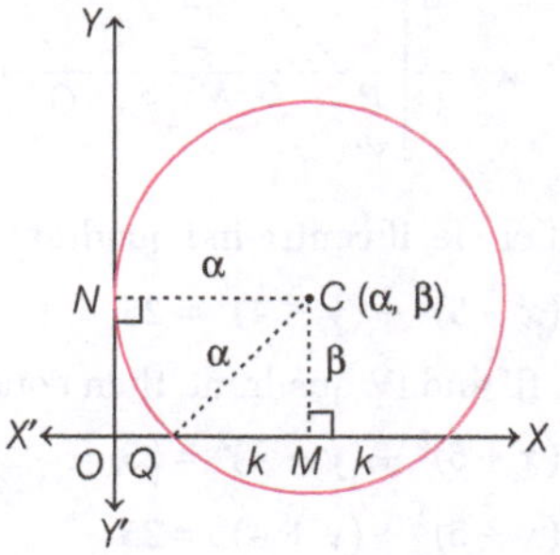

$\therefore$ Radius $= \alpha$

$$CN = CQ = \alpha$$

In ΔCMQ, $\alpha^2 = \beta^2 + k^2$

$$\beta = \sqrt{(\alpha^2 - k^2)} \quad \text{[for I quadrant]}$$

$\therefore$ Equation of circle is

$$(x-\alpha)^2 + (y - \sqrt{\alpha^2 - k^2})^2 = \alpha^2$$

JEE Focus Points

- Length of intercepts on Y-axis of the circle $x^2 + y^2 + 2gx + 2fy + c = 0$ is
  $$2l = 2\sqrt{(f^2 - c)} \text{ i.e. } l^2 = f^2 - c$$
  and also circle touches X-axis,
  then $c = g^2$
  $\therefore$ $l^2 = f^2 - g^2$
  or $l^2 = (-f)^2 - (-g)^2$
  $\therefore$ Locus of centre is $y^2 - x^2 = l^2$ (rectangular hyperbola)
- Length of intercept on X-axis of the circle $x^2 + y^2 + 2gx + 2fy + c = 0$ is
  $$2k = 2\sqrt{(g^2 - c)} \text{ i.e. } k^2 = g^2 - c$$
  and also circle touches Y-axis,
  then $c = f^2$
  $\therefore$ $k^2 = g^2 - f^2 = (-g)^2 - (-f)^2$
  $\therefore$ Locus of centre is $x^2 - y^2 = k^2$ (rectangular hyperbola)

Concept Inside Video

Example 23. Find the equation of the circle which touches the Y-axis at a distance of 4 units from the origin and cuts the intercept of 6 units from the X-axis.

Sol. Given, $CM = NO = 4$

In ΔPCM, $(PC)^2 = (3)^2 + (4)^2$

$$PC = 5$$

$\therefore$ Radius of circle = 5

$\therefore$ $NC = 5$

Centre of circle is (5, 4).

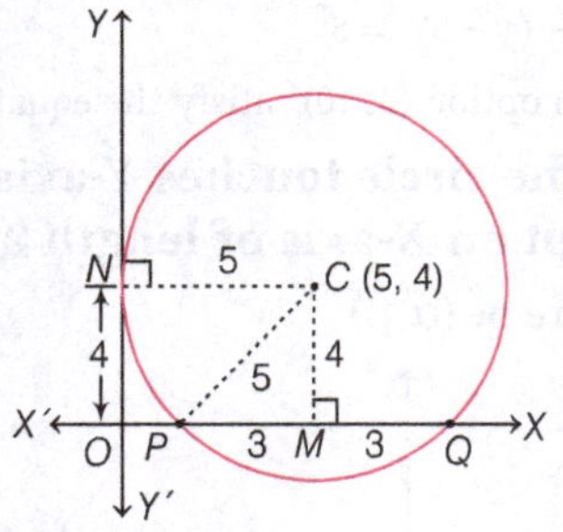

$\therefore$ Equation of circle, if centre in I quadrant

$$(x-5)^2+(y-4)^2=25$$

If centre in II, III and IV quadrant, then equations are

$$(x+5)^2+(y-4)^2=25,$$

$$(x+5)^2+(y+4)^2=25$$

and $$(x-5)^2+(y+4)^2=25$$

Hence, there are 4 circles which satisfy the given conditions. They are

$$(x\pm 5)^2+(y\pm 4)^2=25$$

or $$x^2+y^2\pm 10x\pm 8y+16=0$$

(vii) When the circle cut-off intercepts on X-axis and Y-axis of lengths 2*l* and 2*k* and not passing through origin

Let centre be (α, β)

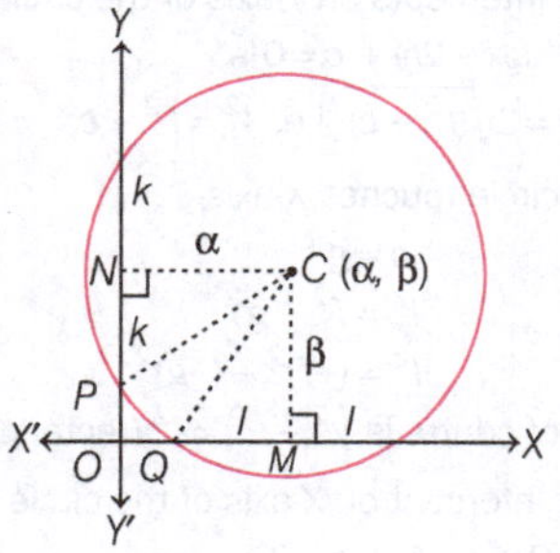

$\therefore$ Radius $= CP = CQ = \lambda$ (say)

$$(CP)^2=(CQ)^2=\lambda^2$$

$$\alpha^2+k^2=\beta^2+l^2=\lambda^2$$

$\therefore$ $\alpha=\sqrt{\lambda^2-k^2}$ and $\beta=\sqrt{\lambda^2-l^2}$ [for I quadrant]

$\therefore$ Equation of circle is

$$(x-\sqrt{\lambda^2-k^2})^2+(y-\sqrt{\lambda^2-l^2})^2=\lambda^2$$

(viii) When the circle passes through the origin and centre lies on X-axis

Let centre of circle be $C(a, 0)$

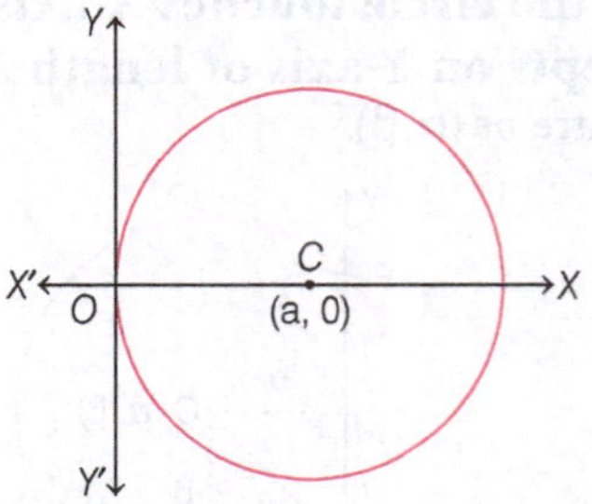

$\therefore$ Radius $= a$

$\therefore$ Equation of circle is $(x-a)^2+(y-0)^2=a^2$

or $$x^2+y^2-2ax=0$$

(ix) When the circle passes through origin and centre lies on Y-axis

Let centre of circle be $C(0, a)$

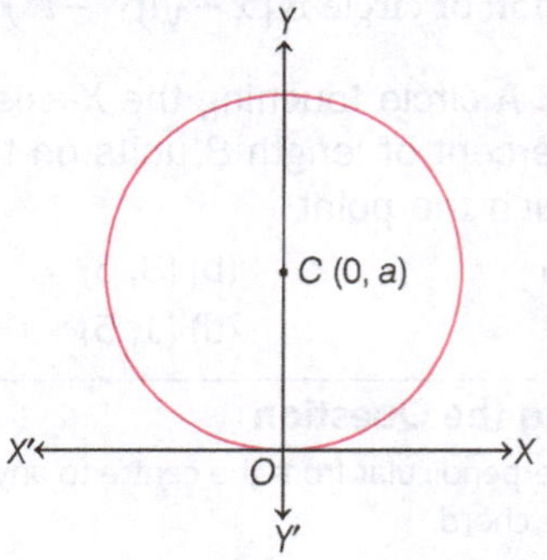

$\because$ Radius $= a$

$\therefore$ Equation of circle is $(x-0)^2+(y-a)^2=a^2$

or $$x^2+y^2-2ay=0$$

Example 24. Circle(s) touching X-axis at a distance of 3 from the origin and having an intercept of length $2\sqrt{7}$ on Y-axis is/are

(a) $x^2+y^2-6x\pm 8y+9=0$
(b) $x^2+y^2-6x\pm 8y+7=0$
(c) $x^2+y^2+6x\pm 8y+9=0$
(d) $x^2+y^2-6x\pm 8y+16=0$

Sol. (a) Given that circle touching X-axis at a distance of 3 units from origin.

So, $A \equiv (3, 0)$

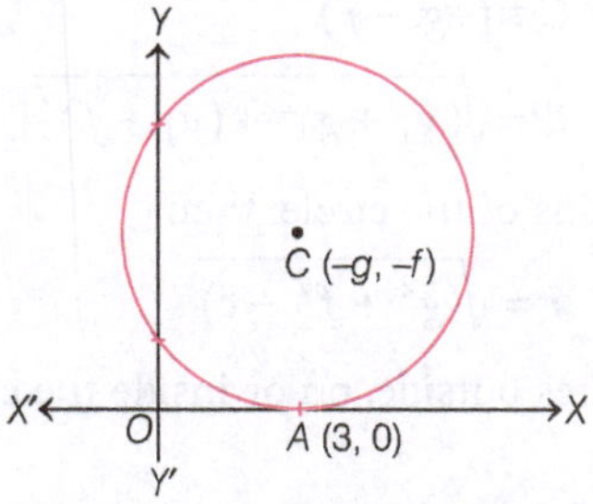

Length of intercept on Y-axis $= 2\sqrt{f^2 - c}$ for circle

$$x^2 + y^2 + 2gx + 2fy + c = 0$$

$$\Rightarrow \quad 2\sqrt{7} = 2\sqrt{f^2 - c} \Rightarrow f^2 - c = 7 \quad \text{...(i)}$$

and if circle touches X-axis, then

$$g^2 = c \quad \text{...(ii)}$$

$$AB = CD = 2\sqrt{7}$$

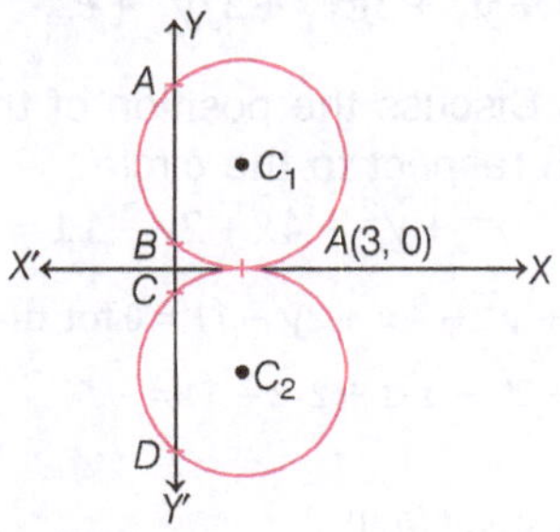

Circle passes through (3, 0)

Hence, $9 + 6g + c = 0 \quad \text{...(iii)}$

From Eqs. (i), (ii) and (iii), we get

$$g = -3, \; c = 9 \text{ and } f = \pm 4$$

$\therefore$ Required equation of circle will be

$$x^2 + y^2 - 6x \pm 8y + 9 = 0$$

Example 25. Find the equation of the circle which touches both the axes and the line $x = c$.

Sol.

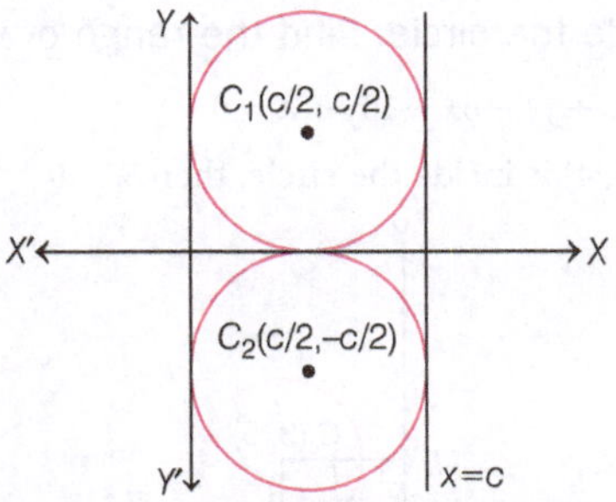

Given that the circle touches both the coordinate axes and the line $x = c$, these two circles with centers C_1 and C_2 will be in the I and IV quadrants.

$\therefore$ Diameter of the circle is c.

So, radius $= \dfrac{c}{2}$

and the coordinates of the centers are $\left(\dfrac{c}{2}, \pm \dfrac{c}{2}\right)$.

So, equation of required circle are

$$\left(x - \frac{c}{2}\right)^2 + \left(y \pm \frac{c}{2}\right)^2 = \left(\frac{c}{2}\right)^2$$

$$\therefore \quad x^2 + y^2 - cx \pm cy + \frac{c^2}{4} = 0$$

Example 26. A circle of radius 2 units lies in the first quadrant and touches both the axes of coordinates. Find the equation of the circle with centre at (6, 5) and touching the above circle externally. If two circles touch externals, then distance between centre is equal to sum of their radii.

Sol. Given, $AC = 2$ units

and $\quad A \equiv (2, 2), B \equiv (6, 5)$

Then, $\quad AB = \sqrt{(2-6)^2 + (2-5)^2} = \sqrt{16 + 9} = 5$

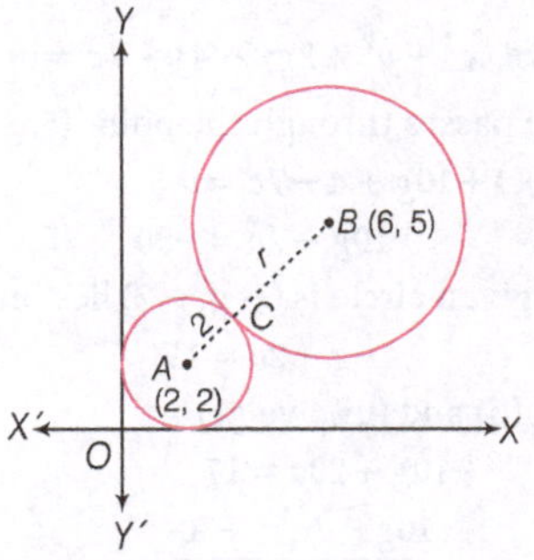

Since, $\quad AC + CB = AB$

$\therefore \quad 2 + CB = 5 \quad [\because AC = 2 \text{ units}]$

$\Rightarrow \quad CB = 3$

Hence, equation of required circle with centre at (6, 5) and radius 3 is

$$(x - 6)^2 + (y - 5)^2 = 3^2 \text{ or } x^2 + y^2 - 12x - 10y + 52 = 0$$

Example 27. A circle of radius 5 units touches the coordinate axes in first quadrant. If the circle makes one complete roll on X-axis along the positive direction of X-axis, find its equation in the new position.

Sol. Let C be the centre of the circle in its initial position and D be its centre in the new position.

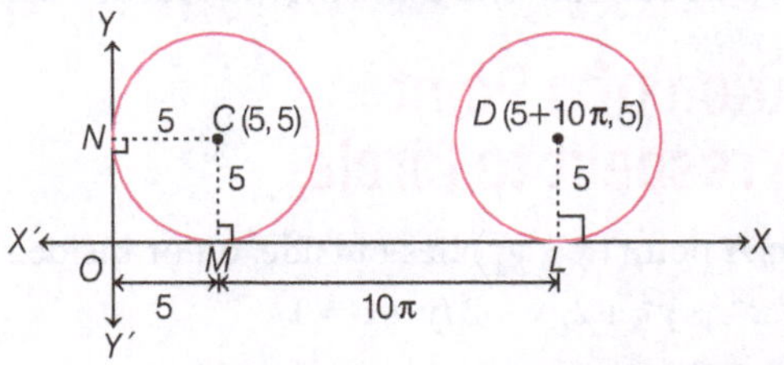

Since, the circle touches the coordinate axes in first quadrant and the radius of circle is 5 units.

$\therefore$ Centre of circle is (5, 5).

Moving length of circle = circumference of the circle

$= 2\pi r = 2\pi(5) = 10\pi$

Now, centre of circle in new position is $(5 + 10\pi, 5)$ and radius is 5 units, therefore, its equation will be

$$(x - 5 - 10\pi)^2 + (y - 5)^2 = 5^2$$

or $x^2 + y^2 - 10(1 + 2\pi)x - 10y + 100\pi^2 + 100\pi + 25 = 0$

JEE SCANNER

Example Similar to PYQ Asked in JEE Main 2022

If the circle $x^2 + y^2 + 2gx + 4y - 7c = 0$, $c \in R$ passes through the point (5, 1) and its centre lies on the line $x - cy = 1.7$, then the length of intercept made by the circle on the Y-axis is

(a) $4\sqrt{5}$ (b) $3\sqrt{5}$

(c) $\sqrt{5}$ (d) $2\sqrt{5}$

Sol. (d) We have, $x^2 + y^2 + 2gx + 4y - 7c = 0$ ...(i)

This circle passes through the point (5, 1)

$$25 + 1 + 10g + 4 - 7c = 0$$

$$10g - 7c = -30 \quad \text{...(ii)}$$

Centre of given circle is $(-g, -2)$ lies on $x - cy = 1.7$

$$-g + 2c = 1.7 \quad \text{...(iii)}$$

From Eqs. (ii) and (iii), we get

$$-10g + 20c = 17$$

$$10g - 7c = -30$$

$$13c = -13 \Rightarrow c = -1$$

From Eq. (iii), $-g - 2 = 1.7 \Rightarrow g = -3.7$

Equation of circle is $x^2 + y^2 - 7.4x + 4y + 7 = 0$.

$\therefore$ Length of y-intercept $= 2\sqrt{f^2 - c} = 2\sqrt{4 + 1} = 2\sqrt{5}$

Skill Builder

If the circle $x^2 + y^2 - 2gx + 4y - 15c = 0$, $c \in R$ passes through the point (4, 1) and its centre lies on the line $x - 4cy = -19.5$, then the length of intercept made by the circle on X-axis is

(a) $\sqrt{90.09}$ (b) $2\sqrt{90.09}$

(c) $2\sqrt{100.75}$ (d) $2\sqrt{210.09}$

For Sol.

▪ **For more practice** See Q.12 of Milestone Practice 4.2.

4.6 Position of a Point with respect to Circle

Theorem A point (x_1, y_1) lies outside, on or inside a circle $S \equiv x^2 + y^2 + 2gx + 2fy + c = 0$ according as $S_1 >, =, \text{or} < 0$

where, $S_1 = x_1^2 + y_1^2 + 2gx_1 + 2fy_1 + c$.

Proof Let $P(x_1, y_1)$ be the given point and let C be the centre of the circle.

Then, $C \equiv (-g, -f)$

$\therefore$ $CP = \sqrt{(x_1 + g)^2 + (y_1 + f)^2}$

If r is the radius of the circle, then

$$r = \sqrt{(g^2 + f^2 - c)}$$

The point P lies outside, on or inside the circle according as

$$CP >, =, \text{or} < r$$

$\Rightarrow$ $(CP)^2 >, =, \text{or} < r^2$

$\Rightarrow$ $(x_1 + g)^2 + (y_1 + f)^2 >, =, \text{or} < g^2 + f^2 - c$

$\Rightarrow$ $x_1^2 + y_1^2 + 2gx_1 + 2fy_1 + c >, =, \text{or} < 0$

$\Rightarrow$ $S_1 >, =, \text{or} < 0,$

where $S_1 = x_1^2 + y_1^2 + 2gx_1 + 2fy_1 + c$.

Example 28. Discuss the position of the points (1, 2) and (6, 0) with respect to the circle

$$x^2 + y^2 - 4x + 2y - 11 = 0.$$

Sol. Let $S \equiv x^2 + y^2 - 4x + 2y - 11 = 0$ for the point (1, 2)

$$S_1 = 1^2 + 2^2 - 4 \cdot 1 + 2 \cdot 2 - 11 = -6$$

$\therefore S_1 < 0$

and for the point (6, 0)

$$S_2 = 6^2 + 0 - 4 \cdot 6 + 2 \cdot 0 - 11$$

$$= 36 - 24 - 11$$

$$= 36 - 35 = 1$$

$\therefore$ $S_2 > 0$

Hence, the point (1, 2) lies inside the circle and the point (6, 0) lies outside the circle.

Example 29. The circle $x^2 + y^2 - 6x - 10y + \lambda = 0$ does not touch or intersect the coordinate axes and the point (1, 4) is inside the circle. Find the range of values of λ.

Sol. Let $S \equiv x^2 + y^2 - 6x - 10y + \lambda = 0$

$\because$ Point (1, 4) is inside the circle, then $S_1 < 0$

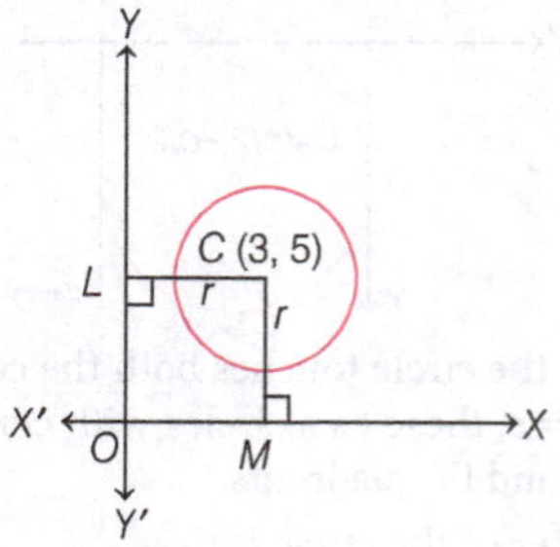

$$1 + 16 - 6 - 40 + \lambda < 0$$

$\Rightarrow$ $\lambda < 29$ ...(i)

Centre and radius of the circle are (3, 5) and $\sqrt{(34-\lambda)}$, respectively.

$\because$ Circle does not touch or intersect the coordinate axes.

$\therefore \quad 5 > r$ and $3 > r$

or $\quad 5 > \sqrt{(34-\lambda)}$ and $3 > \sqrt{(34-\lambda)}$

$\Rightarrow \quad 25 > 34 - \lambda$ and $9 > 34 - \lambda$

$\Rightarrow \quad \lambda > 9$ and $\lambda > 25$

$\therefore \quad \lambda > 25 \quad$ ...(ii)

Also, $\quad 34 - \lambda > 0$

$\therefore \quad \lambda < 34 \quad$ ...(iii)

From Eqs. (i), (ii) and (iii), we get

$$25 < \lambda < 29$$

Example 30. The values of α for which the point $(\alpha - 1, \alpha + 1)$ lies in the larger segment of the circle $x^2 + y^2 - x - y - 6 = 0$ made by the chord whose equation is $x + y - 2 = 0$, is

(a) $-1 < \alpha < 1$ (b) $0 < \alpha < 1$

(c) $-1 < \alpha < 0$ (d) $-1 \le \alpha < 1$

Sol. (a) We have,

$$S \equiv x^2 + y^2 - x - y - 6 = 0 \quad \text{...(i)}$$

Centre of circle is $C\left(\frac{1}{2}, \frac{1}{2}\right)$

It is given that the point $(\alpha - 1, \alpha + 1)$ lies in the larger segment of the circle.

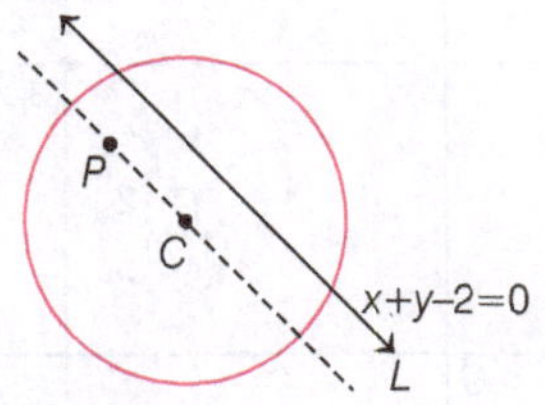

So, this point lies inside the circle

$$S(\alpha - 1, \alpha + 1) < 0$$

$$(\alpha - 1)^2 + (\alpha + 1)^2 - (\alpha - 1) - (\alpha + 1) - 6 < 0$$

$\Rightarrow \quad \alpha^2 - \alpha - 2 < 0$

$\Rightarrow \quad (\alpha - 2)(\alpha + 1) < 0$

$\Rightarrow \quad -1 < \alpha < 2 \quad$ ...(ii)

Also, points P and C must lie on the same side of the line

$$L \equiv x + y - 2 = 0$$

$L\left(\frac{1}{2}, \frac{1}{2}\right)$ and $L(\alpha - 1, \alpha + 1)$ must have the same sign.

$$L\left(\frac{1}{2}, \frac{1}{2}\right) = \frac{1}{2} + \frac{1}{2} - 2 < 0$$

$$L(\alpha - 1, \alpha + 1) = \alpha - 1 + \alpha + 1 - 2 < 0$$

$$\alpha < 1 \quad \text{...(iii)}$$

From Eqs. (ii) and (iii), we get

$$\alpha \in (-1, 1) \text{ i.e. } -1 < \alpha < 1$$

4.7 Maximum and Minimum Distance of a Point from the Circle

Let any point $P(x_1, y_1)$ and circle

$$S \equiv x^2 + y^2 + 2gx + 2fy + c = 0 \quad \text{...(i)}$$

The centre and radius of the circle are

$C(-g, -f)$ and $\sqrt{(g^2 + f^2 - c)}$ respectively.

CASE I If P inside the circle

In this case $S_1 < 0$,

$$r = \sqrt{(g^2 + f^2 - c)} = CA = CB \text{ (say)}$$

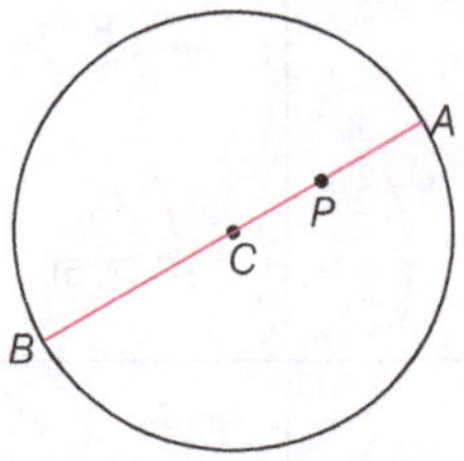

The **minimum distance** of P from circle $= PA = CA - CP$
$= r - CP$

and the **maximum distance** of P from circle $= PB$
$= CB + CP = r + CP$

CASE II If P outside the circle

In this case $S_1 > 0$, the **minimum distance** of P from circle
$= PA = CP - CA = CP - r$

and the **maximum distance** of P from the circle
$= PB = CP + CB = r + CP$

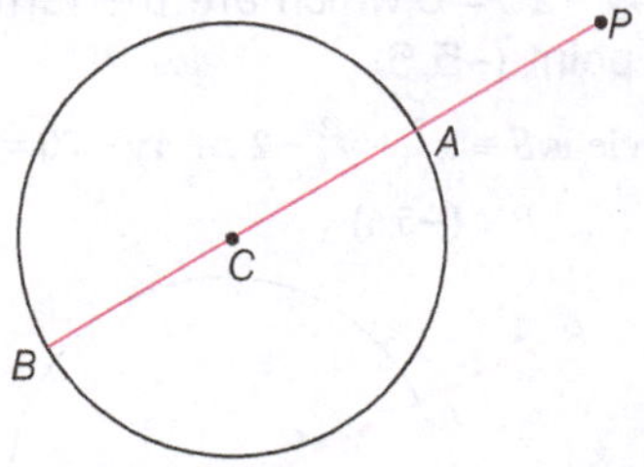

CASE III If P on the circle

In this case $S_1 = 0$,

the **minimum distance** of P from the circle $= 0$ and

the **maximum distance** of P from the circle $= PA = 2r$

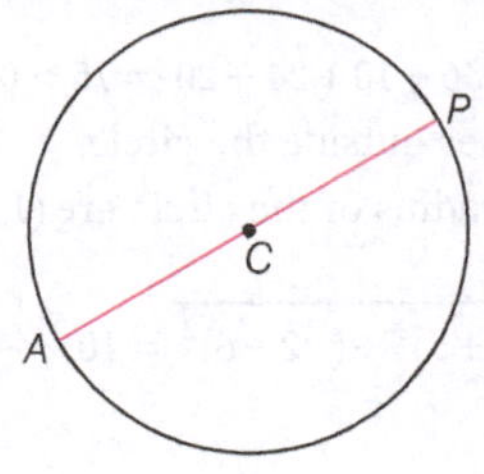

JEE SPIKE

If point P inside or outside or on the circle and centre of circle at C and radius r, then minimum distance of P from the circle $= |CP - r|$ and maximum distance of P from the circle $= CP + r$

Example 31. Find the shortest and largest distance from the point $(2, -7)$ to the circle

$$x^2 + y^2 - 14x - 10y - 151 = 0$$

Sol. Let $S \equiv x^2 + y^2 - 14x - 10y - 151 = 0$

$\therefore \quad S_1 = (2)^2 + (-7)^2 - 14(2) - 10(-7) - 151 = -56 < 0$

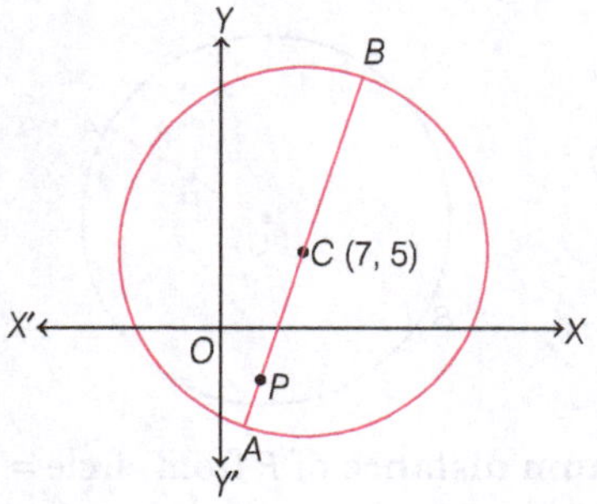

$\therefore$ $P(2, -7)$ inside the circle

radius of the circle, $r = \sqrt{(-7)^2 + (-5)^2 + 151} = 15$

$\because$ Centre of circle $C \equiv (7, 5)$

$\therefore \quad CP = \sqrt{(7-2)^2 + (5+7)^2} = 13$

$\therefore$ **Shortest distance** $= PA = r - CP = 15 - 13 = 2$

and **Largest distance** $= PB = r + CP = 15 + 13 = 28$

Example 32. Find the points on the circle $x^2 + y^2 - 2x + 4y - 20 = 0$ which are the farthest and nearest to the point $(-5, 6)$.

Sol. The given circle is $S \equiv x^2 + y^2 - 2x + 4y - 20 = 0$

Let $\quad P \equiv (-5, 6)$

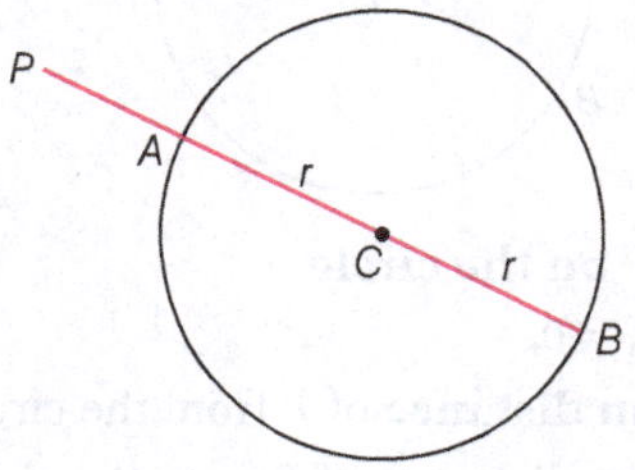

For the point P

$$S_1 = 25 + 36 + 10 + 24 - 20 = 75 > 0$$

$\therefore$ Point $P(-5, 6)$ lies outside the circle.

The centre and radius of the circle are $(1, -2)$ and 5, respectively.

$\because \quad CP = \sqrt{(1+5)^2 + (-2-6)^2} = 10$

Now, point A divides CP in the ratio

$$\frac{AP}{AC} = \frac{CP - r}{r}$$

$$= \frac{10-5}{5} = 1$$

$\therefore$ A is mid-point of CP.

$\therefore \quad A \equiv \left(\frac{1-5}{2}, \frac{-2+6}{2}\right)$ or $A \equiv (-2, 2)$

and C is the mid-point of AB.

$\therefore \quad B \equiv \{2 \times 1 - (-2), 2 \times (-2) - 2\}$

or $\quad B \equiv (4, -6)$

Hence, point $A(-2, 2)$ is nearest to P and $B(4, -6)$ is farthest from P.

JEE SCANNER

Example Similar to PYQ Asked in JEE Main 2024

Given a circle C of radius of 2 units such that it touches the lines parallel to the coordiante axes passing through (3, 4), then the minimum distance of circle from the point (6, 6) is

(a) $\sqrt{41} + 2$ (b) $\sqrt{41} + 1$ (c) $\sqrt{41} - 1$ (d) $\sqrt{41} - 2$

Sol. (d) Given that a circle C with radius 2 units and line passing through the points (3, 4) parallel to the coordinate axes.

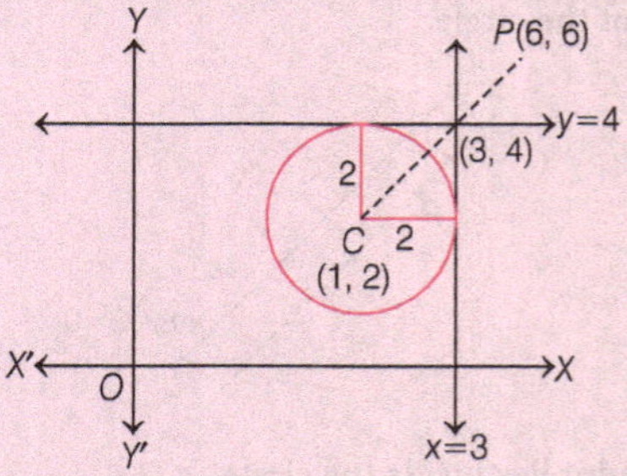

So, coordinates of circle will be $C(1, 2)$.

$\therefore$ Shortest distance of the circle C from the point (6,6)

$$= \sqrt{(6-1)^2 + (6-2)^2} - \text{radius of circle}$$

$$= \sqrt{25+16} - 2 = \sqrt{41} - 2$$

Skill Builder

Let a circle C of radius 1 unit and closer to origin be such that the line passing through the point (4, 3) and parallel to coordinate axes touch it. Then, the shortest distance of the circle C from the point (7, 7) is

For Sol.

(a) $\sqrt{41} - 1$ (b) $\sqrt{41} + 1$

(c) $\sqrt{41}$ (d) $\sqrt{31} - 1$

■ **For more practice** See Q.13 of Milestone Practice 4.2.

Milestone Practice 4.2

1. The length of intercept, the circle $x^2+y^2+10x-6y+9=0$ makes on the X-axis is
(a) 2 (b) 4 (c) 6 (d) 8

2. The locus of the centre of a circle which passes through the origin and cuts-off length $2b$ from the line $x=c$ is
(a) $y^2+2cx=b^2+c^2$ (b) $x^2+cx=b^2+c^2$
(c) $y^2+2cy=b^2+c^2$ (d) $x^2+cy=b^2+c^2$

3. If a straight line through $C(-\sqrt{8},\sqrt{8})$ making an angle of 135° with the X-axis cuts the circle $x=5\cos\theta$, $y=5\sin\theta$ at points A and B, then the length of AB is
(a) 3 (b) 5
(c) 8 (d) 10

4. If a circle of constant radius $3k$ passes through the origin and meets the axes at A and B, the locus of the centroid of ΔOAB is
(a) $x^2+y^2=k^2$ (b) $x^2+y^2=2k^2$
(c) $x^2+y^2=3k^2$ (d) $x^2+y^2=4k^2$

5. The centre of the circle touching Y-axis at $(0,3)$ and making an intercept of 2 units on positive X-axis is
(a) $(10,\sqrt{3})$ (b) $(\sqrt{3},10)$
(c) $(\sqrt{10},3)$ (d) $(3,\sqrt{10})$

6. A circle passes through the points $A(1,0)$ and $B(5,0)$ and touches the Y-axis at $C(0,\lambda)$. If $\angle ACB$ is maximum, then
(a) $|\lambda|=\sqrt{5}$ (b) $|\lambda|=2\sqrt{5}$
(c) $|\lambda|=3\sqrt{5}$ (d) $|\lambda|=4\sqrt{5}$

7. The equation of a circle whose centre is $(3,-1)$ and whose intercept chord of 6 units length on straight line $2x-5y+18=0$ is
(a) $x^2+y^2-6x+2y-28=0$
(b) $x^2+y^2+6x-2y-28=0$
(c) $x^2+y^2+4x-2y+24=0$
(d) $x^2+y^2+2x-2y-12=0$

8. The locus of the centre of a circle which touches externally the circle $x^2+y^2-6x-6y+14=0$ and also touches the Y-axis, is given by the equation
(a) $x^2-6x-10y+14=0$
(b) $x^2-10x-6y+14=0$
(c) $y^2-6x-10y+14=0$
(d) $y^2-10x-6y+14=0$

9. The locus of the centre of a circle of radius 2 which rolls on the outside of circle $x^2+y^2+3x-6y-9=0$ is
(a) $x^2+y^2+3x-6y+5=0$
(b) $x^2+y^2+3x-6y-31=0$
(c) $x^2+y^2+3x-6y+11=0$
(d) $x^2+y^2+3x-6y-36=0$

10. The point $([P+1],[P])$ is lying inside the circle $x^2+y^2-2x-15=0$. Then, the set of all values of P is (where [.] represents the greatest integer function)
(a) $[-2,3)$ (b) $(-2,3)$
(c) $[-2,0)\cup(0,3)$ (d) $[0,3)$

11. The greatest distance of the point $(10,7)$ from the circle $x^2+y^2-4x-2y-20=0$ is
(a) 5 (b) 10 (c) 15 (d) 20

12. If the circle $x^2+y^2-2gx+4y-10c=0$, $c\in R$ passes through the point $(2,1)$ and its centre lies on the line $x-cy=\frac{3}{4}$, then the length of intercept made by the circle on X-axis is
(a) $\frac{1}{2}\sqrt{393}$ (b) $\frac{1}{2}\sqrt{123}$
(c) $\sqrt{395}$ (d) $\sqrt{123}$

13. Let a circle of radius 3 units and closer to origin be such that the lines passing through the point $(5,4)$ and parallel to the coordinate axes touch it. Then, find the shortest distance of the circle from the point $(7,7)$.

Answer Key

1. (d)	2. (a)	3. (d)	4. (d)	5. (c)	6. (a)	7. (a)
8. (d)	9. (b)	10. (a)	11. (c)	12. (a)	13. $(\sqrt{61}-3)$	

For Detailed Solution

Milestone 3 Line and Circle

- Intersection of a Line and a Circle • Length of Intercept Cut-off from a Line by a Circle
- Tangent to a Circle at a Given Point • Normal to a Circle at a Given Point

4.8 Intersection of a Line and a Circle

Let the equation of the circle be

$$x^2 + y^2 = a^2 \quad \text{...(i)}$$

and the equation of the line be

$$y = mx + c \quad \text{...(ii)}$$

From Eqs. (i) and (ii),

$$x^2 + (mx + c)^2 = a^2$$

or $(1 + m^2)x^2 + 2mcx + c^2 - a^2 = 0$ ...(iii)

Case I When points of intersection are real and distinct, then Eq. (iii) has two distinct roots.

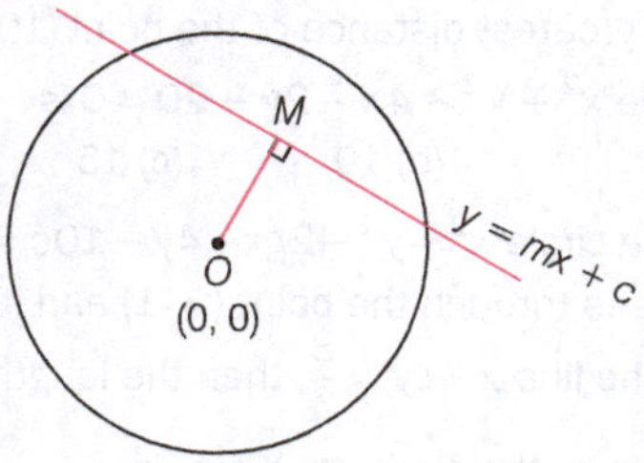

$\therefore \quad B^2 - 4AC > 0$

or $\quad 4m^2c^2 - 4(1 + m^2)(c^2 - a^2) > 0$

or $\quad a^2 > \dfrac{c^2}{1 + m^2}$

or $\quad a > \dfrac{|c|}{\sqrt{(1 + m^2)}}$ = length of perpendicular from (0, 0) to $y = mx + c$

$\Rightarrow \quad a >$ length of perpendicular from (0, 0) to $y = mx + c$.

Thus, a line intersects a given circle at two distinct points if radius of circle is greater than the length of perpendicular from centre of the circle to the line.

Case II When the points of intersection are coincident, then Eq. (iii) has two equal roots

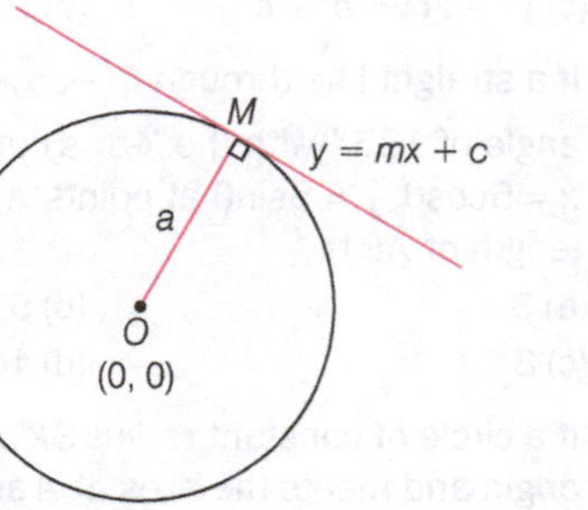

$\therefore \quad B^2 - 4AC = 0$

$\Rightarrow \quad 4m^2c^2 - 4(1 + m^2)(c^2 - a^2) = 0$

$\therefore \quad a^2 = \dfrac{c^2}{(1 + m^2)}$

or $\quad a = \dfrac{|c|}{\sqrt{(1 + m^2)}}$

a = length of the perpendicular from the point (0, 0) to $y = mx + c$

Thus, a line touches the circle if radius of circle is equal to the length of perpendicular from centre of the circle to the line.

Case III When the points of intersection are imaginary. In this case, Eq. (iii) has imaginary roots

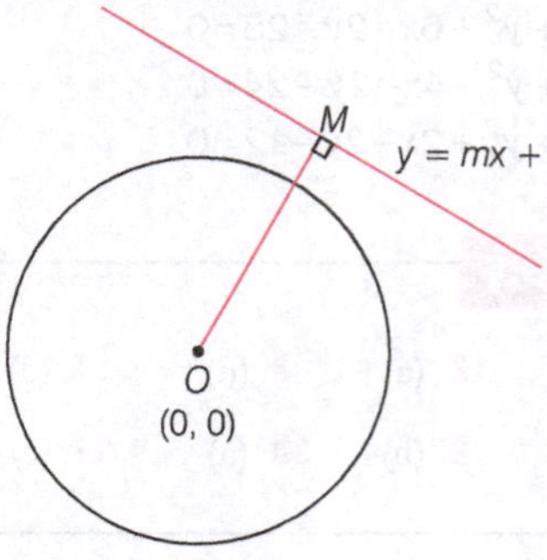

$\therefore \quad B^2 - 4AC < 0$

$$4m^2c^2 - 4(1+m^2)(c^2 - a^2) < 0$$

$$\therefore \quad a^2 < \frac{c^2}{1+m^2}$$

or $a < \dfrac{|c|}{\sqrt{1+m^2}}$ = length of perpendicular from (0, 0) to $y = mx + c$

or $a <$ length of perpendicular from (0, 0) to $y = mx + c$

Thus, a line does not intersect a circle if the radius of circle is less than the length of perpendicular from centre of the circle to the line.

Example 33. Find the points of intersection of the line $2x + 3y = 18$ and the circle $x^2 + y^2 = 25$.

Sol. We have, $2x + 3y = 18$ ....(i)

and $x^2 + y^2 = 25$ ...(ii)

From Eq. (i), $y = \dfrac{18 - 2x}{3}$

On substituting the value of y in Eq. (ii), we get

$$x^2 + \left(\frac{18 - 2x}{3}\right)^2 = 25$$

$$\Rightarrow \quad 9x^2 + 4(9 - x)^2 = 225$$

$$\Rightarrow \quad 9x^2 + 4(81 - 18x + x^2) = 225$$

$$\Rightarrow \quad 13x^2 - 72x + 324 - 225 = 0$$

$$\Rightarrow \quad 13x^2 - 72x + 99 = 0$$

$$\Rightarrow \quad (x - 3)(13x - 33) = 0$$

$$\Rightarrow \quad x = 3 \text{ or } x = \frac{33}{13}$$

From Eq. (i), $y = 4$ or $y = \dfrac{56}{13}$

Hence, the points of intersection of the given line and the given circle are (3, 4) and $\left(\dfrac{33}{13}, \dfrac{56}{13}\right)$.

Example 34. Find the value of m for which the line $y = mx + 2$ cuts the circle $x^2 + y^2 = 1$ at distinct or coincident points.

Sol. We have, $x^2 + y^2 = 1$

So, centre is (0, 0) and radius = 1.

Now, distance of the centre (0, 0) from line $y = mx + 2$ is $\dfrac{2}{\sqrt{1+m^2}}$.

For the line to cut the circle at distinct or coincident points, we have $\dfrac{2}{\sqrt{1+m^2}} \le 1$

$$\Rightarrow \quad 1 + m^2 \ge 4 \Rightarrow m^2 \ge 3$$

$$\therefore \quad m \in (-\infty, -\sqrt{3}] \cup [\sqrt{3}, \infty)$$

Product of the Algebraical Distances *PA* and *PB* is Constant when from *P*, a Secant be Drawn to Cut the Circle in the Points *A* and *B*

If a straight line through $P(\alpha, \beta)$ makes an angle θ with the positive direction of X-axis, then its equation is

$$\frac{x - \alpha}{\cos\theta} = \frac{y - \beta}{\sin\theta} = r$$

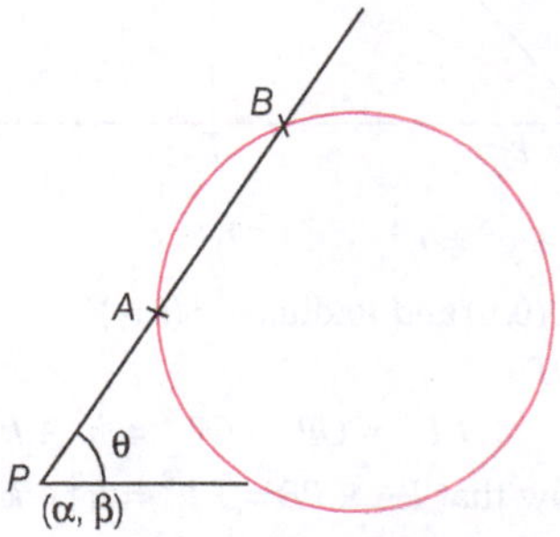

where, r is the algebraical distance of the point (x, y) from the point $P(\alpha, \beta)$.

$$\therefore \quad (x, y) = (\alpha + r\cos\theta, \beta + r\sin\theta)$$

If this point lies on the circle $x^2 + y^2 + 2gx + 2fy + c = 0$

or $(\alpha + r\cos\theta)^2 + (\beta + r\sin\theta)^2 + 2g(\alpha + r\cos\theta) + 2f(\beta + r\sin\theta) + c = 0$

$$\Rightarrow r^2 + 2r(\alpha\cos\theta + \beta\sin\theta + g\cos\theta + f\sin\theta) + (\alpha^2 + \beta^2 + 2g\alpha + 2f\beta + c) = 0$$

This is quadratic equation in r, then PA and PB are the roots of this equation.

$$\therefore \quad PA \cdot PB = \alpha^2 + \beta^2 + 2g\alpha + 2f\beta + c = \text{constant}$$

Since, RHS is independent of θ.

JEE SPIKE

If PB is secant which intersect the circle at A and B and P is tangent, then $PA \times PB = PT^2$

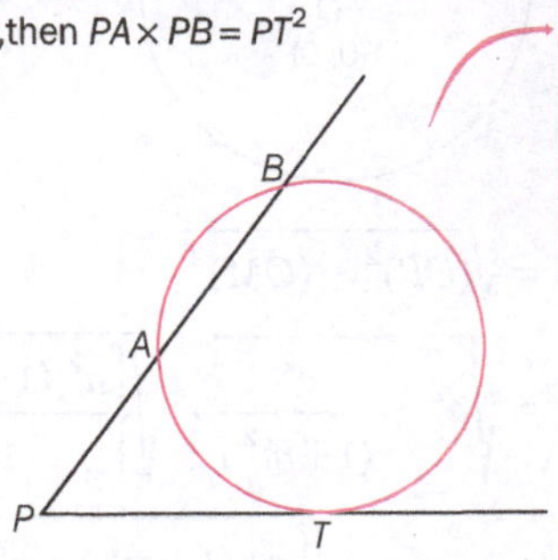

Concept Inside Video

Example 35. If a line is drawn through a fixed point $P(h, k)$ to cut the circle $x^2 + y^2 = r^2$ at A and B, then find the value of $PA \times PB$.

Sol.

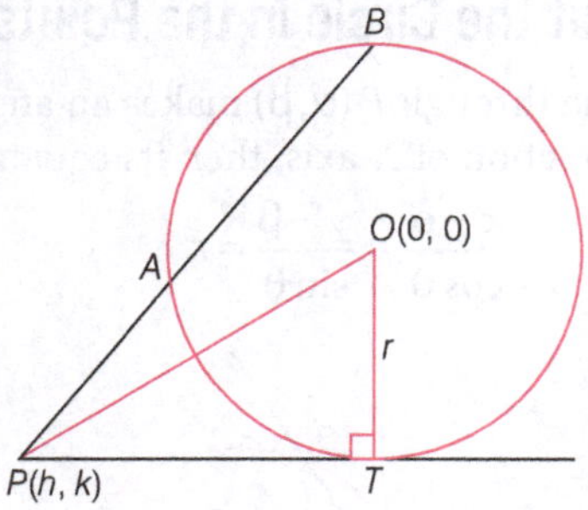

We have, $x^2 + y^2 = r^2$

$\therefore$ Centre $= O(0, 0)$ and Radius $= r$ (say)

Now, in ΔPOT

$$PT^2 = OP^2 - OT^2 = h^2 + k^2 - r^2$$

Now, we know that $PA \times PB = PT^2 = h^2 + k^2 - r^2$

4.9 Length of Intercept Cut-off from a Line by a Circle

Theorem The length of the intercept cut-off from the line $y = mx + c$ by the circle $x^2 + y^2 = a^2$ is

$$2\sqrt{\left\{\frac{a^2(1+m^2) - c^2}{(1+m^2)}\right\}}$$

Proof Draw OM perpendicular to PQ

Now, $OM =$ length of perpendicular from $O(0, 0)$ to

$$(y = mx + c) = \frac{|c|}{\sqrt{(1+m^2)}}$$

and $\quad OP =$ radius of the circle $= a$

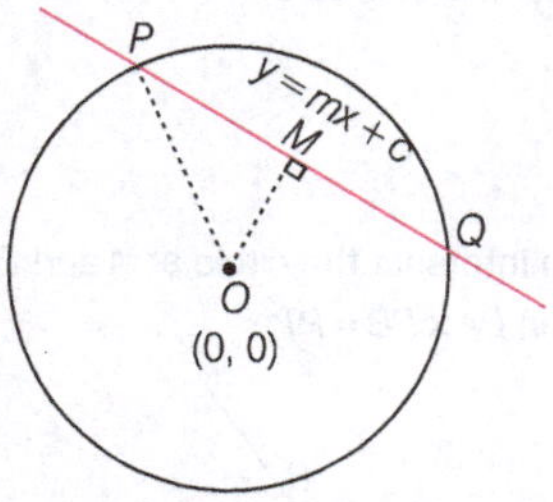

In ΔOPM, $\quad PM = \sqrt{(OP)^2 - (OM)^2}$

$$= \sqrt{a^2 - \frac{c^2}{(1+m^2)}} = \sqrt{\left\{\frac{a^2(1+m^2) - c^2}{1+m^2}\right\}}$$

$$\therefore \quad PQ = 2PM = 2\sqrt{\left\{\frac{a^2(1+m^2) - c^2}{1+m^2}\right\}}$$

JEE Focus Points

- If the line $y = mx + c$ touches the circle $x^2 + y^2 = a^2$, then intercepted length is zero

  i.e. $\quad PQ = 0 \Rightarrow 2\sqrt{\left\{\frac{a^2(1+m^2) - c^2}{1+m^2}\right\}} = 0$

  $\therefore \quad c^2 = a^2(1 + m^2)$

  which is the required condition for tangency.
- If a line touches the circle, then length of perpendicular from the centre upon the line is equal to the radius of the circle.

Concept Inside Video

Example 36. Find the length of the intercept on the straight line $4x - 3y - 10 = 0$ by the circle $x^2 + y^2 - 2x + 4y - 20 = 0$.

Sol. Centre and radius of the circle $x^2 + y^2 - 2x + 4y - 20 = 0$ are $(1, -2)$ and $\sqrt{1 + 4 + 20} = 5$, respectively.

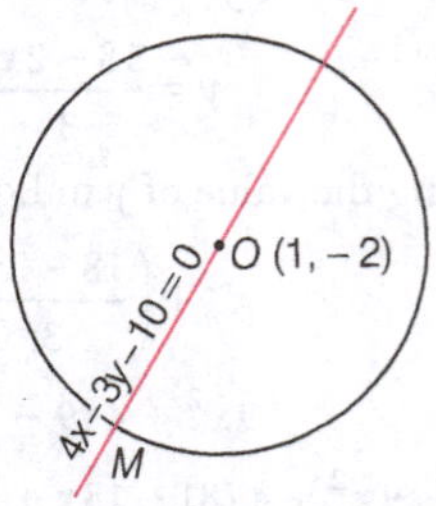

Let OM be the perpendicular from O on the line $4x - 3y - 10 = 0$

Then, $\quad OM = \frac{|4 \times 1 - 3 \times (-2) - 10|}{\sqrt{4^2 + (-3)^2}} = 0$

Hence, line $4x - 3y - 10 = 0$ passes through the centre of the circle.

Hence, intercepted length = diameter of the circle

$$= 2 \times 5 = 10$$

Example 37. Find the coordinates of the middle point of the chord which the circle $x^2 + y^2 + 4x - 2y - 3 = 0$ cuts-off the line $x - y + 2 = 0$.

Sol. Centre and radius of the circle $x^2 + y^2 + 4x - 2y - 3 = 0$ are $(-2, 1)$ and $\sqrt{4 + 1 + 3} = 2\sqrt{2}$, respectively.

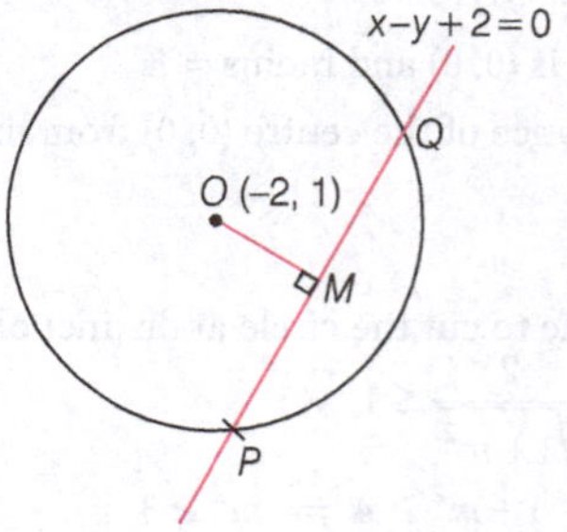

Draw perpendicular OM from O upon $x - y + 2 = 0$.

Equation of OM which is perpendicular to $x-y+2=0$ is $x+y=\lambda$, it passes through $(-2, 1)$

Then, $-2+1=\lambda \Rightarrow \lambda=-1$

$\therefore$ Equation of OM is $x+y+1=0$

Since, M is the mid-point of PQ which is point of intersection of $x-y+2=0$ and $x+y+1=0$, coordinates of M are $\left(-\frac{3}{2}, \frac{1}{2}\right)$.

Example 38. For what value of λ will the line $y=2x+\lambda$ be a tangent to the circle $x^2+y^2=5$?

Sol. On comparing the given line with $y=mx+c$, we get $m=2, c=\lambda$ and given circle with $x^2+y^2=a^2$

Then, $a^2=5$

$\because$ Condition for tangency is

$$c^2=a^2(1+m^2)$$

$$\Rightarrow \quad \lambda^2=5(1+4) \Rightarrow \lambda^2=25$$

$$\therefore \quad \lambda=\pm 5$$

Alternate Solution

Given that line $y=2x+\lambda$ or $2x-y+\lambda=0$ is the tangent to the circle $x^2+y^2=5$, then length of perpendicular from centre upon the line is equal to the radius of the circle

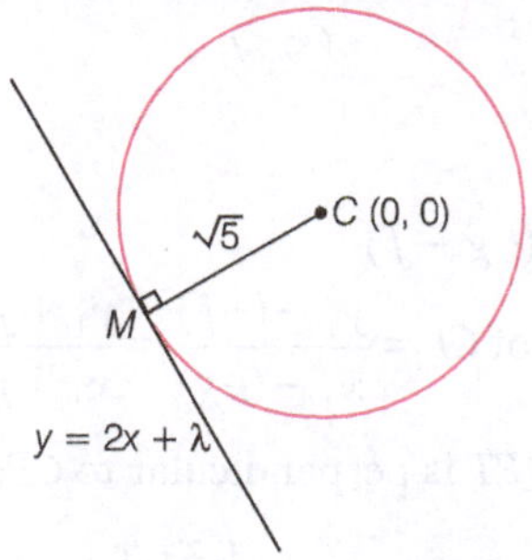

$$\therefore \quad |CM|=\sqrt{5} \text{ or } \frac{|0-0+\lambda|}{\sqrt{4+1}}=\sqrt{5}$$

$$\Rightarrow \quad \frac{|\lambda|}{\sqrt{5}}=\sqrt{5} \Rightarrow |\lambda|=5 \text{ or } \lambda=\pm 5$$

Example 39. The lines $5x+12y-10=0$ and $5x-12y-40=0$ touch a circle C_1 of diameter 6. If the centre of C_1 lies in the first quadrant, then the equation of the circle C_2 which is concentric with C_1 and cuts intercepts of length 8 units on these lines is

(a) $(x-5)^2+(y-2)^2=25$

(b) $(x-5)^2+(y+2)^2=25$

(c) $(x-5)^2+(y+2)^2=25$

(d) $(x+5)^2+(y+2)^2=25$

Sol. (a) Let the equation of tangent PAB be $5x+12y-10=0$ and that of PXY be $5x-12y-40=0$.

Let centre of circle C_1 and C_2 be $C(h, k)$, $CM \perp AB$.

Then, $CM=3$ (radius of circle C_1). It is also given that circle C_2 makes an intercept of length 8 units on PAB. So, $AM=4$.

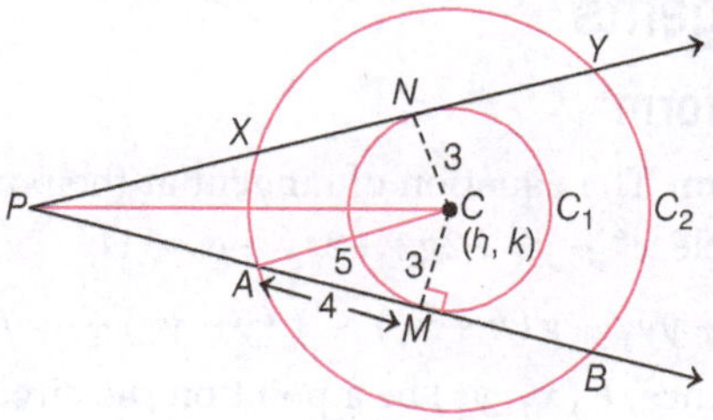

Now, in ΔAMC, $AC=\sqrt{4^2+3^2} \Rightarrow AC=5$ (radius of C_2)

$5x+12y-10$ and $15x-12y-40=0$ are tangents to C_1, the length of perpendicular from C to AB is 3 units.

$$\therefore \quad \frac{5h+12k-10}{13}=\pm 3$$

$$\Rightarrow \quad 5h+12k-49=0 \quad \text{...(i)}$$

$$5h+12k+29=0 \quad \text{...(ii)}$$

Similarly, $\frac{5h-12k-40}{13}=\pm 3$

$$\Rightarrow \quad 5h-12k-79=0 \quad \text{...(iii)}$$

$$\text{or} \quad 5h-12k-1=0 \quad \text{...(iv)}$$

As C lies in first quadrant, so h and k are positive. Therefore, $5h+12k+29=0$ is not possible as for positive values of h and k this is not satisfied.

From Eqs. (i) and (iii), we get

$$h=\frac{64}{5} \text{ and } k=-\frac{5}{4}$$

which is also not possible as $(k<0)$.

Now, from Eqs. (i) and (iv), we get

$$h=5 \text{ and } k=2$$

Thus, centre for C_2 is $(5, 2)$ and radius $r=5$.

Hence, the equation of C_2 is $(x-5)^2+(y-2)^2=25$

4.10 Tangent to a Circle at a Given Point

Let PQ be a chord and AB be a secant passing through P. Let P be the fixed point and move along the circle towards P, then the secant PQ turns about P. In the limit, when Q coincides with P, then the secant AB becomes a tangent to the circle at the point P.

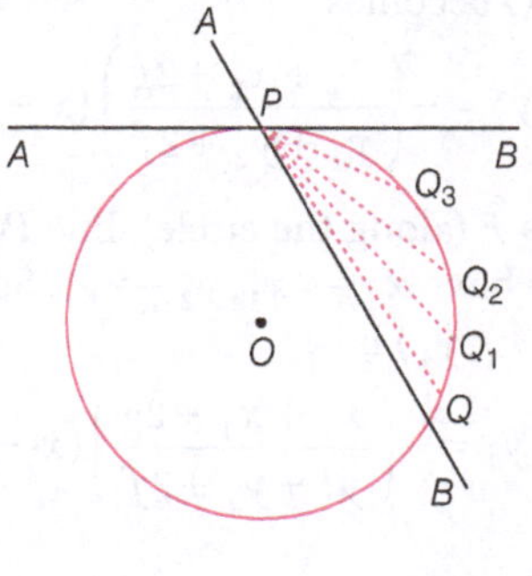

Different Forms of the Equations of Tangents

1. Point form

Theorem The equation of tangent at the point $P(x_1, y_1)$ to a circle $x^2 + y^2 + 2gx + 2fy + c = 0$ is

$$xx_1 + yy_1 + g(x + x_1) + f(y + y_1) + c = 0$$

Proof Since, $P(x_1, y_1)$ be a point on the circle

$$x^2 + y^2 + 2gx + 2fy + c = 0 \quad \text{...(i)}$$

Let $Q(x_2, y_2)$ be any other point on the circle Eq. (i).

Since, points $P(x_1, y_1)$ and $Q(x_2, y_2)$ lie on the circle, therefore

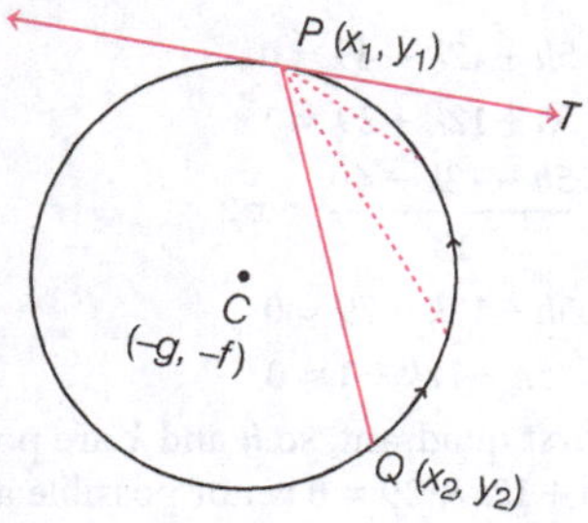

$$x_1^2 + y_1^2 + 2gx_1 + 2fy_1 + c = 0 \quad \text{...(ii)}$$

and $$x_2^2 + y_2^2 + 2gx_2 + 2fy_2 + c = 0 \quad \text{...(iii)}$$

On subtracting Eq. (ii) from Eq. (iii), we get

$$(x_2^2 - x_1^2) + (y_2^2 - y_1^2) + 2g(x_2 - x_1) + 2f(y_2 - y_1) = 0$$

$$\Rightarrow (x_2 - x_1)(x_2 + x_1 + 2g) + (y_2 - y_1)(y_2 + y_1 + 2f) = 0$$

$$\Rightarrow \left(\frac{y_2 - y_1}{x_2 - x_1}\right) = -\left(\frac{x_1 + x_2 + 2g}{y_1 + y_2 + 2f}\right) \quad \text{...(iv)}$$

Now, the equation of the chord PQ is

$$y - y_1 = \left(\frac{y_2 - y_1}{x_2 - x_1}\right)(x - x_1) \quad \text{...(v)}$$

On putting the value of $\left(\frac{y_2 - y_1}{x_2 - x_1}\right)$ from Eq. (iv) in Eq. (v), then equation PQ becomes

$$y - y_1 = -\left(\frac{x_1 + x_2 + 2g}{y_1 + y_2 + 2f}\right)(x - x_1) \quad \text{...(vi)}$$

Now, when $Q \to P$ (along the circle), line PQ becomes tangent at P, we have $x_2 \to x_1, y_2 \to y_1$. So, the equation of tangent at $P(x_1, y_1)$ is

$$y - y_1 = -\left(\frac{x_1 + x_1 + 2g}{y_1 + y_1 + 2f}\right)(x - x_1)$$

$$\Rightarrow \quad y - y_1 = -\left(\frac{x_1 + g}{y_1 + f}\right)(x - x_1)$$

$$\Rightarrow \quad (y - y_1)(y_1 + f) + (x - x_1)(x_1 + g) = 0$$

$$\Rightarrow \quad xx_1 + yy_1 + gx + fy = x_1^2 + y_1^2 + gx_1 + fy_1$$

On adding $gx_1 + fy_1 + c$ to both sides, we get

$$xx_1 + yy_1 + g(x + x_1) + f(y + y_1) + c$$
$$= x_1^2 + y_1^2 + 2gx_1 + 2fy_1 + c = 0 \quad \text{[from Eq. (ii)]}$$

$$\Rightarrow \quad xx_1 + yy_1 + g(x + x_1) + f(y + y_1) + c = 0$$

This is the required equation of the tangent PT to the circle at the point (x_1, y_1).

Alternate method

Since, circle is $\quad x^2 + y^2 + 2gx + 2fy + c = 0$

$P(x_1, y_1)$ lie on the circle

$$\therefore \quad x_1^2 + y_1^2 + 2gx_1 + 2fy_1 + c = 0 \quad \text{...(i)}$$

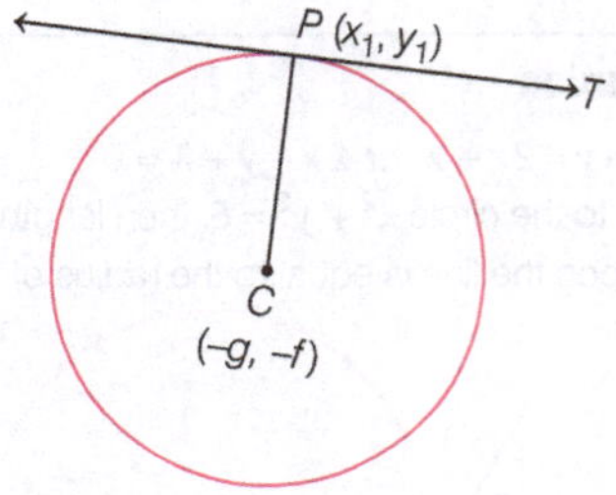

Its centre is $C(-g, -f)$

$$\therefore \quad \text{Slope of } CP = \frac{y_1 - (-f)}{x_1 - (-g)} = \frac{y_1 + f}{x_1 + g}$$

Since, tangent PT is perpendicular to CP.

$$\therefore \quad \text{Slope of tangent} = -\left(\frac{x_1 + g}{y_1 + f}\right)$$

$\therefore$ Equation of tangent at $P(x_1, y_1)$ is

$$y - y_1 = -\left(\frac{x_1 + g}{y_1 + f}\right)(x - x_1)$$

$$\Rightarrow \quad (y - y_1)(y_1 + f) + (x_1 + g)(x - x_1) = 0$$

$$\Rightarrow \quad xx_1 + yy_1 + gx + fy = x_1^2 + y_1^2 + gx_1 + fy_1$$

On adding $gx_1 + fy_1 + c$ to both sides, we get

$$xx_1 + yy_1 + g(x + x_1) + f(y + y_1) + c$$
$$= x_1^2 + y_1^2 + 2gx_1 + 2fy_1 + c = 0 \quad \text{[from Eq. (ii)]}$$

or $\quad xx_1 + yy_1 + g(x + x_1) + f(y + y_1) + c = 0$

This is the required equation of the tangent PT to the circle at the point $P(x_1, y_1)$.

Example 40. Prove that the tangents to the circle $x^2 + y^2 = 25$ at (3, 4) and (4, − 3) are perpendicular to each other.

Sol. The equations of tangents to $x^2 + y^2 = 25$ at (3, 4) and (4, − 3) are

$$3x + 4y = 25 \quad ...(i)$$

and

$$4x - 3y = 25 \quad ...(ii)$$

respectively.

Now, slope of Eq. (i) $= -\frac{3}{4} = m_1$ (say)

and slope of Eq. (ii) $= \frac{4}{3} = m_2$ (say)

Clearly, $m_1 m_2 = -1$

Hence, Eq. (i) and Eq. (ii) are perpendicular to each other.

Example 41. Find the equation of tangent to the circle $x^2 + y^2 - 2ax = 0$ at the point $[a(1 + \cos\alpha), a\sin\alpha]$.

Sol. The equation of tangent of $x^2 + y^2 - 2ax = 0$ at $[a(1 + \cos\alpha), a\sin\alpha]$ is

$$x \cdot a(1 + \cos\alpha) + y \,.\, a\sin\alpha - a[x + a(1 + \cos\alpha)] = 0$$

$$\Rightarrow \quad ax\cos\alpha + ay\sin\alpha - a^2(1 + \cos\alpha) = 0$$

or

$$x\cos\alpha + y\sin\alpha = a(1 + \cos\alpha)$$

Example 42. Show that the circles $x^2 + y^2 - 4x + 6y + 8 = 0$ and $x^2 + y^2 - 10x - 6y + 14 = 0$ touch at $(3, -1)$.

Sol. Equation of tangent at (3, − 1) of the circle $x^2 + y^2 - 4x + 6y + 8 = 0$ is

$$3x + (-1)y - 2(x + 3) + 3(y - 1) + 8 = 0$$

or

$$x + 2y - 1 = 0 \quad ...(i)$$

and equation of tangent at (3, − 1) of the circle $x^2 + y^2 - 10x - 6y + 14 = 0$ is

$$3 \cdot x + (-1) \cdot y - 5(x + 3) - 3(y - 1) + 14 = 0$$

or

$$-2x - 4y + 2 = 0$$

or

$$x + 2y - 1 = 0 \quad ...(ii)$$

which is the same as Eq (i).

Hence, the given circles touch at (3, − 1).

2. Parametric form

Theorem The equation of tangent to the circle $x^2 + y^2 = a^2$ at the point $(a\cos\theta, a\sin\theta)$ is
$x\cos\theta + y\sin\theta = a$

Proof The equation of tangent of $x^2 + y^2 = a^2$ at (x_1, y_1) is $xx_1 + yy_1 = a^2$ (using point form of the tangent)

Put $x_1 = a\cos\theta$, $y_1 = a\sin\theta$,
then, we get $x\cos\theta + y\sin\theta = a$

COROLLARY 1 Equation of chord joining $(a\cos\theta, a\sin\theta)$ and $(a\cos\phi, a\sin\phi)$ is

$$x\cos\left(\frac{\theta + \phi}{2}\right) + y\sin\left(\frac{\theta + \phi}{2}\right) = a\cos\left(\frac{\theta - \phi}{2}\right)$$

COROLLARY 2 Point of intersection of tangents at $(a\cos\theta, a\sin\theta)$ and $(a\cos\phi, a\sin\phi)$ is

$$\left(\frac{a\cos\left(\frac{\theta + \phi}{2}\right)}{\cos\left(\frac{\theta - \phi}{2}\right)}, \frac{a\sin\left(\frac{\theta + \phi}{2}\right)}{\cos\left(\frac{\theta - \phi}{2}\right)}\right)$$

COROLLARY 3 The angle between a pair of tangents from a point P to the circle $x^2 + y^2 = a^2$ is α. Then, the locus of the point P is $x^2 + y^2 = \dfrac{a^2}{\sin^2\left(\frac{\alpha}{2}\right)}$

JEE Focus Points

Concept Inside Video

- For equation of tangent of circle at (x_1, y_1), substitute xx_1 for x^2, yy_1 for y^2, $\frac{x + x_1}{2}$ for x, $\frac{y + y_1}{2}$ for y and $\frac{xy_1 + x_1 y}{2}$ for xy and keep the constant as such.
- This method of tangent at (x_1, y_1) is applied only for any conics of second degree. i.e. equation of tangent of $ax^2 + 2hxy + by^2 + 2gx + 2fy + c = 0$ at (x_1, y_1) is $axx_1 + h(xy_1 + x_1y) + byy_1 + g(x + x_1) + f(y + y_1) + c = 0$
- The angle between a pair of tangents from a point P to the circle $x^2 + y^2 + 2gx + 2fy + c = 0$ is 2θ, then the locus of P is
$$x^2 + y^2 + 2gx + 2fy + c = (g^2 + f^2 - c)\cot^2\theta$$
- If angle between a pair of tangents from a point P to the circle $x^2 + y^2 = a^2$ is $\frac{\pi}{2}$, then the locus of P is
$$x^2 + y^2 = 2a^2 \quad \left(\text{here, } \alpha = \frac{\pi}{2}\right)$$
which is director circle of $x^2 + y^2 = a^2$.
[∵ locus of point of intersection of perpendicular tangents is director circle] is
- The equation of the tangent to the circle $(x - a)^2 + (y - b)^2 = r^2$ at the point $(a + r\cos\theta, b + r\sin\theta)$ is $(x - a)\cos\theta + (y - b)\sin\theta = r$.

Example 43. The angle between a pair of tangents from a point P to the circle $x^2 + y^2 = 25$ is $\frac{\pi}{3}$. Find the equation of the locus of the point P.

Sol. Here, $\alpha = \frac{\pi}{3}$

$$\therefore \text{ Required locus is } x^2 + y^2 = \frac{25}{\sin^2\left(\frac{\pi}{6}\right)} = 100$$

i.e.

$$x^2 + y^2 = 100$$

Example 44. The angle between a pair of tangents from a point P to the circle $x^2+y^2-6x-8y+9=0$ is $\frac{\pi}{3}$. Find the equation of the locus of the point P.

Sol. Here, $2\theta = \frac{\pi}{3}$ or $\theta = \frac{\pi}{6}$

$\therefore$ Required locus is

$$x^2+y^2-6x-8y+9=(9+16-9)\cot^2\frac{\pi}{6}$$

or $$x^2+y^2-6x-8y+9=16\times 3$$

or $$x^2+y^2-6x-8y-39=0$$

3. Slope form

Theorem The equation of a tangent of slope m to the circle $x^2+y^2=a^2$ is $y=mx\pm a\sqrt{(1+m^2)}$ and the coordinates of the point of contact are

$$\left(\pm\frac{am}{\sqrt{(1+m^2)}}, \mp\frac{a}{\sqrt{(1+m^2)}}\right)$$

Proof Let $y=mx+c$ is the tangent of the circle $x^2+y^2=a^2$.

$\therefore$ Length of perpendicular from centre of circle $(0,0)$ on $(y=mx+c)$ = radius of circle

$$\therefore \quad \frac{|c|}{\sqrt{(1+m^2)}}=a$$

$$\Rightarrow \quad c=\pm a\sqrt{(1+m^2)}$$

On substituting this value of c in $y=mx+c$, we get

$$\boldsymbol{y=mx\pm a\sqrt{(1+m^2)}} \quad \text{...(i)}$$

which are the required equations of tangents.

Also, let (x_1, y_1) be the point of contact, then equation of tangent at (x_1, y_1) to the circle $x^2+y^2=a^2$ is

$$xx_1+yy_1=a^2 \quad \text{...(ii)}$$

On comparing Eq. (i) and Eq. (ii), we get

$$\frac{x_1}{m}=\frac{y_1}{-1}=\frac{a^2}{\pm a\sqrt{(1+m^2)}}$$

$$\Rightarrow \quad \frac{x_1}{m}=-\frac{y_1}{1}=\pm\frac{a}{\sqrt{(1+m^2)}}$$

$$\Rightarrow \quad x_1=\pm\frac{am}{\sqrt{1+m^2}} \text{ and } y_1=\mp\frac{a}{\sqrt{(1+m^2)}}$$

Hence, $$(x_1, y_1)=\left(\pm\frac{am}{\sqrt{(1+m^2)}}, \mp\frac{a}{\sqrt{(1+m^2)}}\right)$$

JEE Focus Points

Concept Inside Video

- There are two equations $y=mx\pm a\sqrt{1+m^2}$ i.e. two tangents, both are parallel and at the ends of diameter.
- The line $ax+by+c=0$ is tangent to the circle $x^2+y^2=r^2$ if and only if $c^2=r^2(a^2+b^2)$.
- If the line $y=mx+c$ is the tangent to the circle $x^2+y^2=r^2$, then point of contact is given by $\left(-\frac{mr^2}{c}, \frac{r^2}{c}\right)$
- If the line $ax+by+c=0$ is the tangent to the circle $x^2+y^2=r^2$, then point of contact is given by $\left(-\frac{ar^2}{c}, -\frac{br^2}{c}\right)$.
- The condition that the line $lx+my+n=0$ touches the circle $x^2+y^2+2gx+2fy+c=0$ is $(lg+mf-n)^2=(l^2+m^2)(g^2+f^2-c)$.
- Equation of tangent of the circle $x^2+y^2+2gx+2fy+c=0$ in terms of slope is $y+f=m(x+g)\pm\sqrt{(g^2+f^2-c)(1+m^2)}$
- The equation of tangents of slope m to the circle $(x-a)^2+(y-b)^2=r^2$ are given by $(y-b)=m(x-a)\pm r\sqrt{(1+m^2)}$ and the coordinates of the points of contact are $\left(a\pm\frac{mr}{\sqrt{(1+m^2)}}, b\mp\frac{r}{\sqrt{(1+m^2)}}\right)$

Example 45. Find the equations of the tangents to the circle $x^2+y^2=9$, which

(i) are parallel to the line $3x+4y-5=0$

(ii) are perpendicular to the line $2x+3y+7=0$

(iii) make an angle of 60° with the X-axis

Sol. (i) Slope of $3x+4y-5=0$ is $-\frac{3}{4}$

Let $m=-\frac{3}{4}$

and equation of circle is $x^2+y^2=9$

$\therefore$ Equations of tangents

$$y=-\frac{3}{4}x\pm 3\sqrt{\left(1+\left(-\frac{3}{4}\right)^2\right)}$$

$$\Rightarrow \quad 4y=-3x\pm 15 \text{ or } 3x+4y\pm 15=0$$

(ii) Slope of $2x+3y+7=0$ is $-\frac{2}{3}$

$\therefore$ Slope of line perpendicular to $2x+3y+7=0$ is $\frac{3}{2}=m$ (say)

and given circle is $x^2+y^2=9$.

$\therefore$ Equations of tangents perpendicular to $2x+3y+7=0$ is

$$y=\frac{3}{2}x\pm 3\sqrt{1+\left(\frac{3}{2}\right)^2} \Rightarrow 2y=3x\pm 3\sqrt{13}$$

or $$3x-2y\pm 3\sqrt{13}=0$$

(iii) Since, tangent make an angle 60° with the X-axis

$\therefore \quad m = \tan 60° = \sqrt{3}$

and given circle is $x^2 + y^2 = 9$

$\therefore$ Equation of tangents $y = \sqrt{3}x \pm 3\sqrt{1 + (\sqrt{3})^2}$

or $\quad \sqrt{3}\,x - y \pm 6 = 0$

Example 46. Prove that the line $lx + my + n = 0$ touches the circle $(x - a)^2 + (y - b)^2 = r^2$ if $(al + bm + n)^2 = r^2(l^2 + m^2)$.

Sol. If the line $lx + my + n = 0$ touches the circle $(x - a)^2 + (y - b)^2 = r^2$, then length of the perpendicular from the centre = radius

$$\frac{|la + mb + n|}{\sqrt{(l^2 + m^2)}} = r$$

$$\Rightarrow \quad (la + mb + n)^2 = r^2(l^2 + m^2)$$

Alternate Solution

Here, line is $lx + my + n = 0$ and circle is $(x - a)^2 + (y - b)^2 = r^2$.
Here, centre of circle (a, b) shift at $(0, 0)$, then replacing x by $x + a$ and y by $y + b$ in the equation of straight line $lx + my + n = 0$ and circle $(x - a)^2 + (y - b)^2 = r^2$, the new form of straight line and circle are

$$l(x + a) + m(y + b) + n = 0$$

or $\quad lx + my + (al + mb + n) = 0 \quad$ ...(i)

and $\quad x^2 + y^2 = r^2 \quad$ ...(ii)

respectively.

On comparing Eq. (i) with $y = Mx + C$,

then, $\quad M = -\dfrac{l}{m}$

and $\quad C = -\dfrac{(al + bm + n)}{m}$

Since, Eq. (i) is the tangent of Eq. (ii), then

$$C^2 = r^2(1 + M^2)$$

or $\quad \dfrac{(al + bm + n)^2}{m^2} = r^2\left(1 + \dfrac{l^2}{m^2}\right)$

or $\quad (al + bm + n)^2 = r^2(l^2 + m^2)$

Example 47. Show that the line $3x - 4y = 1$ touches the circle $x^2 + y^2 - 2x + 4y + 1 = 0$. Find the coordinates of the point of contact.

Sol. The centre and radius of the circle

$$x^2 + y^2 - 2x + 4y + 1 = 0 \text{ are } (1, -2)$$

and $\sqrt{(-1)^2 + (2)^2 - 1} = 2$ respectively.

Since, length of perpendicular from centre $(1, -2)$ on $3x - 4y = 1$ is

$$\frac{|3 \times 1 - 4 \times (-2) - 1|}{\sqrt{(3)^2 + (-4)^2}} = \frac{10}{5}$$

$= 2 =$ radius of the circle

Hence, $3x - 4y = 1$ touches the circle

$$x^2 + y^2 - 2x + 4y + 1 = 0$$

To find the coordinates of the point of contact

Let point of contact is (x_1, y_1), then tangent at (x_1, y_1) on $x^2 + y^2 - 2x + 4y + 1 = 0$ is

$$xx_1 + yy_1 - (x + x_1) + 2(y + y_1) + 1 = 0$$

$\Rightarrow \quad x(x_1 - 1) + y(y_1 + 2) - x_1 + 2y_1 + 1 = 0 \quad$ ...(i)

and given line $\quad 3x - 4y - 1 = 0 \quad$ ...(ii)

Since, Eq. (i) and Eq. (ii) are identical, then comparing Eq. (i) and Eq. (ii), we get

$$\frac{x_1 - 1}{3} = \frac{y_1 + 2}{-4} = \frac{-x_1 + 2y_1 + 1}{-1}$$

or $\quad x_1 = -\dfrac{1}{5}$ and $y_1 = -\dfrac{2}{5}$

$\therefore$ Point of contact is $\left(-\dfrac{1}{5}, -\dfrac{2}{5}\right)$

Example 48. Show that the line $(x - 2)\cos\theta + (y - 2)\sin\theta = 1$ touches a circle for all values of θ. Find the circle.

Sol. Given line is $(x - 2)\cos\theta + (y - 2)\sin\theta = 1$

$$\Rightarrow \quad (x - 2)\cos\theta + (y - 2)\sin\theta = \cos^2\theta + \sin^2\theta$$

On comparing both sides, we get

$x - 2 = \cos\theta \quad$ ...(i)

and $\quad y - 2 = \sin\theta \quad$ ...(ii)

On squaring and adding Eq. (i) and Eq. (ii), we get

$$(x - 2)^2 + (y - 2)^2 = \cos^2\theta + \sin^2\theta$$

$$\Rightarrow \quad (x - 2)^2 + (y - 2)^2 = 1$$

or $\quad x^2 + y^2 - 4x - 4y + 7 = 0$

Example 49. A tangent PT is drawn to circle $x^2 + y^2 = 4$ at the point $P(\sqrt{3}, 1)$. A straight line L, perpendicular to PT, is a tangent to the circle $(x - 3)^2 + y^2 = 1$, then a possible equation of line L is

(a) $x - \sqrt{3}y = 1$ (b) $x + \sqrt{3}y = 1$

(c) $x - \sqrt{3}y = -1$ (d) $x + 2\sqrt{2}y = 6$

Sol. (a) We have, $x^2 + y^2 = 4$

So, equation of tangent at $(\sqrt{3}, 1)$ to $x^2 + y^2 = 4$ is

$\sqrt{3}x + y = 4 \quad$ ...(i)

The slope of line perpendicular to the above tangent is $\dfrac{1}{\sqrt{3}}$.

So, the equation of tangent with slope $\dfrac{1}{\sqrt{3}}$ to $(x - 3)^2 + y^2 = 1$ will be

$$y = \frac{1}{\sqrt{3}}(x - 3) \pm 1\sqrt{1 + \frac{1}{3}}$$

or $\quad \sqrt{3}y = x - 3 \pm 2$

i.e. $\quad \sqrt{3}y = x - 1$ or $\sqrt{3}y = x - 5$

JEE SCANNER

Example Similar to PYQ Asked in JEE Main 2023

Let P and Q be points of tangency where tangents are drawn from points A(3, – 7) and B(6, – 4) respectively to the circle $x^2+y^2-3x+8y-17=0$. The tangent intersect at point R. The radius of the circle whose centre is R and the line joining A and B is its tangent, is

(a) $\frac{121}{17\sqrt{2}}$ (b) $\frac{119}{18\sqrt{2}}$ (c) $\frac{67}{6\sqrt{2}}$ (d) $\frac{117}{16\sqrt{2}}$

Sol. (c) We have $x^2+y^2-3x+8y-17=0$

Tangent at $A(3,-7)$ is $3x-7y-\frac{3}{2}(x+3)+4(y-7)-17=0$

$$6x-14y-3x-9+8y-56-34=0$$
$$3x-6y-99=0 \quad \text{...(i)}$$

Now, equation of tangent at $B(6,-4)$ is

$$6x-4y-\frac{3}{2}(x+6)+4(y-4)-17=0$$
$$12x-8y-3x-18+8y-32-34=0$$
$$9x-84=0 \Rightarrow x=\frac{84}{9} \quad \text{...(ii)}$$

Since, these tangents intersect at R, on solving Eqs. (i) and (ii), we get

$$\frac{84}{3}-6y-99=0 \Rightarrow 6y=\frac{84-297}{3}$$
$$\Rightarrow \quad y=-\frac{213}{3\times 6}=-\frac{71}{6}$$
$$R=\left(\frac{84}{9},\frac{-71}{6}\right)$$

Now, equation of line passing through A and B is

$$y+7=\frac{3}{3}(x-3) \Rightarrow x-y-10=0 \quad \text{...(iii)}$$

Now, radius of this circle = perpendicular distance from R to $x-y-10=0$

$$=\left|\frac{\frac{84}{9}+\frac{71}{6}-10}{\sqrt{2}}\right|$$
$$\Rightarrow \quad r=\frac{201}{18\sqrt{2}}=\frac{67}{6\sqrt{2}}$$

Skill Builder

Let the tangent at the points $P(-3,5)$ and $Q(6,-3)$ on the circle $x^2+y^2-4x+6y-12=0$, intersect at the point C. Then, the radius of the circle, whose centre is C and the line joining P and Q is its tangent, is equal to

(a) $\frac{2160}{32\sqrt{145}}$ (b) $\frac{2601}{32\sqrt{145}}$

(c) $\frac{2109}{32\sqrt{145}}$ (d) $\frac{2121}{32\sqrt{145}}$

For Sol.

■ **For more practice** See Q.14 of Milestone Practice 4.3.

4.11 Normal to a Circle at a Given Point

The normal of a circle at any point is a straight line which is perpendicular to the tangent at the point and always passes through the centre of the circle.

Different form of the Equation of Normals

1. Point form

Theorem The equation of normal at the point $P(x_1, y_1)$ to the circle $x^2+y^2+2gx+2fy+c=0$ is

$$\frac{x-x_1}{x_1+g}=\frac{y-y_1}{y_1+f}$$

Proof Equation of the given circle is

$$x^2+y^2+2gx+2fy+c=0 \quad \text{...(i)}$$

Its centre C is $(-g,-f)$

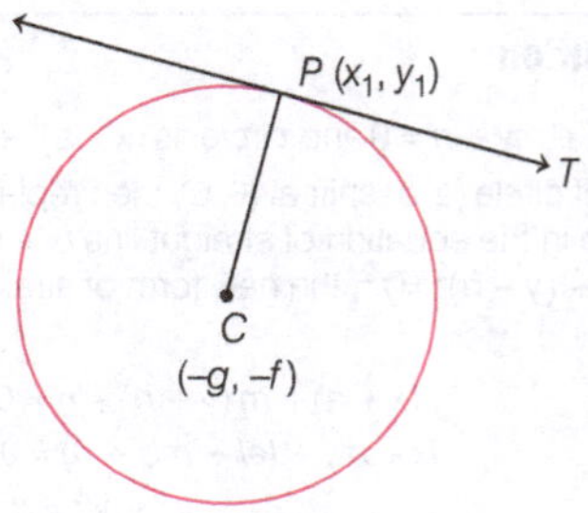

Let $P(x_1, y_1)$ be the given point.

$\because$ Normal of the circle at $P(x_1, y_1)$ passes through centre $C(-g,-f)$ of the circle.

Then, equation of normal CP passes through the points $C(-g,-f)$ and $P(x_1, y_1)$ is

$$y-y_1=\frac{(y_1+f)}{(x_1+g)}(x-x_1)$$

or
$$\frac{x-x_1}{x_1+g}=\frac{y-y_1}{y_1+f}$$

This is the required equation of normal at $P(x_1, y_1)$ of the given circle.

COROLLARY 1 Equation of normal of $x^2+y^2=a^2$ at (x_1, y_1) is

$$\frac{x-x_1}{1\cdot x_1+0+0}=\frac{y-y_1}{0+1\cdot y_1+0}$$

[here, $g, f=0$ and $a=b=1$]

$$\Rightarrow \quad \frac{x-x_1}{x_1}=\frac{y-y_1}{y_1}$$

or
$$\frac{x}{x_1}=\frac{y}{y_1}$$

COROLLARY 2 Equation of normal of $x^2+y^2+2gx+2fy+c=0$ at (x_1, y_1) is

$$\frac{x-x_1}{x_1+g}=\frac{y-y_1}{y_1+f} \quad [\text{here, } a=b=1 \text{ and } h=0]$$

Example 50. Find the equation of the normal to the circle $x^2+y^2-5x+2y-48=0$ at the point $(5, 6)$.

Sol. Equation of the normal at $(5, 6)$ is

$$\frac{x-5}{5-\frac{5}{2}}=\frac{y-6}{6+1} \Rightarrow \frac{x-5}{\frac{5}{2}}=\frac{y-6}{7} \Rightarrow \frac{2x-10}{5}=\frac{y-6}{7}$$

$$\Rightarrow \quad 14x-70=5y-30$$

$$\therefore \quad 14x-5y-40=0$$

Example 51. Find the equation of the normal to the circle $x^2+y^2=2x$, which is parallel to the line $x+2y=3$.

Sol. Given circle is $x^2+y^2-2x=0$.

$$\Rightarrow \quad (x-1)^2+y^2=1$$

Centre of given circle is $(1, 0)$.

Since, normal is parallel to $x+2y=3$,

Let the equation of normal be $x+2y=\lambda$

Since, normal passes through the centre of the circle i.e. $(1, 0)$.

$$\therefore \quad 1+0=\lambda \Rightarrow \lambda=1$$

Then, equation of normal is $x+2y=1$

or $\quad x+2y-1=0$

Alternate Solution

Equation of normal at (x_1, y_1) of $x^2+y^2-2x=0$ is

$$\frac{x-x_1}{x_1-1}=\frac{y-y_1}{y_1-0} \text{ or Slope}=\frac{y_1}{x_1-1}=m_1 \quad \text{(say)}$$

Since, normal is parallel to

$x+2y=3$

$$\therefore \quad \text{Slope}=-\frac{1}{2}=m_2 \quad \text{(say)}$$

but given $m_1=m_2$

$$\frac{y_1}{x_1-1}=-\frac{1}{2} \text{ or } x_1+2y_1-1=0$$

$\Rightarrow$ Locus of (x_1, y_1) is $x+2y-1=0$

$\therefore$ The equation of normal is $x+2y-1=0$.

2. Equation of Normal in Parametric form

Since, parametric coordinates of circle $x^2+y^2=a^2$ are $(a\cos\theta, a\sin\theta)$.

$\therefore$ Equation of normal at $(a\cos\theta, a\sin\theta)$ is

$$\frac{x}{a\cos\theta}=\frac{y}{a\sin\theta}$$

or $\quad \dfrac{x}{\cos\theta}=\dfrac{y}{\sin\theta}$ or $y=x\tan\theta$

or $\quad y=mx$, where $m=\tan\theta$

which is slope form of normal.

Example 52. The range of value of α for which the line $2y=gx+\alpha$ is a normal to the circle $x^2+y^2+2gx+2fy-2=0$, (where $f=g$) for all values of g is

(a) $[1, \infty)$ (b) $[-1, \infty)$
(c) $(0, 1)$ (d) $(-\infty, 1]$

Sol. (b) We have, $x^2+y^2+2gx+2fy-2=0$ ...(i)

Centre of given circle is $(-g, -f)$.

It is given that $2y=gx+\alpha$ is a normal to the circle Eq. (i).

We know that normal to a circle always passes through the centre of the circle.

Hence, $-2g=-g^2+\alpha$

$$\alpha=g^2-2g$$

or $\quad \alpha=g^2-2g+1-1=(g-1)^2-1\geq -1$

$$\therefore \quad \alpha\geq -1$$

$$\alpha\in[-1, \infty)$$

Example 53. If the line $ax+by=2$ is a normal to the circle $x^2+y^2-4x-4y=0$ and tangent to the circle $x^2+y^2=1$, then

(a) $a=\frac{1}{2}, b=\frac{1}{2}$ (b) $a=\frac{1\pm\sqrt{7}}{2}, b=\frac{1\mp\sqrt{7}}{2}$
(c) $a=-\frac{1}{2}, 3=\frac{1}{2}$ (d) $a=-\frac{1}{2}, b=-\frac{1}{2}$

Sol. (b) We have, $x^2+y^2-4x-4y=0$ ...(i)

The centre of circle is $(2, 2)$.

It is given that $ax+by=2$ is a normal to the circle Eq. (i), we know that normal always passes through the centre of circle.

Hence, $2a+2b=2$ or $a+b=1$ ...(ii)

Now, $ax+by=2$ touches $x^2+y^2=1$

$$1=\left|\frac{-2}{\sqrt{a^2+b^2}}\right| \text{ or } a^2+b^2=4 \quad \text{...(iii)}$$

From Eqs. (ii) and (iii), we get

$$a^2+(1-a)^2=4 \text{ or } 2a^2-2a-3=0$$

$$\therefore \quad a=\frac{2\pm\sqrt{4+24}}{4}=\frac{1\pm\sqrt{7}}{2}$$

$$b=1-a=1-\left(\frac{1\pm\sqrt{7}}{2}\right)$$

$$\Rightarrow \quad b=\frac{1\mp\sqrt{7}}{2}$$

Milestone Practice 4.3

1. The length of the chord cut-off by $y = 2x + 1$ from the circle $x^2 + y^2 = 2$ is

(a) $\frac{5}{6}$ (b) $\frac{6}{5}$ (c) $\frac{6}{\sqrt{5}}$ (d) $\frac{\sqrt{5}}{6}$

2. Circle $x^2 + y^2 - 4x - 8y - 5 = 0$ will intersect the line $3x - 4y = \lambda$ in two distinct points, if

(a) $-10 < \lambda < 5$ (b) $9 < \lambda < 20$
(c) $-35 < \lambda < 15$ (d) $-16 < \lambda < 30$

3. If the line $3x - 4y + \lambda = 0$, $(\lambda > 0)$ touches the circle $x^2 + y^2 - 4x - 8y - 5 = 0$ at (a, b), then $\lambda + a + b$ is equal to

(a) -22 (b) -20 (c) 20 (d) 22

4. Tangent which is parallel to the line $x - 3y - 2 = 0$ of the circle $x^2 + y^2 - 4x + 2y - 5 = 0$, has point/points of contact

(a) $(1, -2)$ (b) $(-1, 2)$ (c) $(3, 4)$ (d) $(3, -4)$

5. The area of the triangle formed by the tangent at the point (a, b) to the circle $x^2 + y^2 = r^2$ and the coordinate axes, is

(a) $\frac{r^4}{2ab}$ (b) $\frac{r^4}{2|ab|}$ (c) $\frac{r^4}{ab}$ (d) $\frac{r^4}{|ab|}$

6. The equation of the tangent to the circle $x^2 + y^2 + 4x - 4y + 4 = 0$ which makes equal intercepts on the positive coordinate axes is

(a) $x + y = 2$ (b) $x + y = 2\sqrt{2}$
(c) $x + y = 4$ (d) $x + y = 8$

7. If $a > 2b > 0$, then the positive value of m for which $y = mx - b\sqrt{(1 + m^2)}$ is a common tangent to $x^2 + y^2 = b^2$ and $(x - a)^2 + y^2 = b^2$ is

(a) $\frac{2b}{\sqrt{(a^2 - 4b^2)}}$ (b) $\frac{\sqrt{(a^2 - 4b^2)}}{2b}$
(c) $\frac{2b}{a - 2b}$ (d) $\frac{b}{a - 2b}$

8. The normal at the point $(3, 4)$ on a circle cuts the circle at the point $(-1, -2)$. Then, the equation of the circle is

(a) $x^2 + y^2 + 2x - 2y - 13 = 0$
(b) $x^2 + y^2 - 2x - 2y - 11 = 0$
(c) $x^2 + y^2 - 2x + 2y + 12 = 0$
(d) $x^2 + y^2 - 2x - 2y + 14 = 0$

9. The line $ax + by + c = 0$ is a normal to the circle $x^2 + y^2 = r^2$. The portion of the line $ax + by + c = 0$ intercepted by this circle is of length

(a) $\sqrt{r}$ (b) r
(c) r^2 (d) $2r$

10. If the line $ax + by + c = 0$ touches the circle $x^2 + y^2 - 2x = \frac{3}{5}$ and is normal to the circle $x^2 + y^2 + 2x - 4y + 1 = 0$, then (a, b) are

(a) $(1, 3)$ (b) $(3, 1)$
(c) $(1, 2)$ (d) $(2, 1)$

11. Show that for all values of θ, $x \sin\theta - y \cos\theta = a$ touches the circle $x^2 + y^2 = a^2$.

12. Find the equation of the family of circle which touch the pair of straight lines $x^2 - y^2 + 2y - 1 = 0$.

13. Show that the area of the triangle formed by the positive X-axis, the normal and tangent to the circle $x^2 + y^2 = 4$ at $(1, \sqrt{3})$ is $2\sqrt{3}$.

14. Let tangent at the point $P(-4, 3)$ and $(10, -3)$ on the circle $x^2 + y^2 - 4x + 6y - 12 = 0$ intersect at the point R. Then, the radius of the circle, whose centre is R and the line joining P and Q is its tangent, is equal to

(a) $\frac{10}{117\sqrt{3}}$ (b) $\frac{19}{117\sqrt{3}}$
(c) $\frac{213}{119\sqrt{5}}$ (d) None of these

Answer Key

1. (c) **2.** (c) **3.** (c) **4.** (d) **5.** (b) **6.** (b) **7.** (a) **8.** (b) **9.** (d) **10.** (b)

12. $x^2 + y^2 - 2hx - 2y - \frac{h^2}{2} + 1 = 0$ or $x^2 + y^2 - 2ky + \frac{k^2}{2} + k - \frac{1}{2} = 0$ **14.** (d)

For Detailed Solution

Milestone 4 Length and Pair of Tangent

- Length of the Tangent from a Point to a Circle • Power of a Point with respect to a Circle
- Chord of Contact • Chord Bisected at a Given Point • Pair of Tangents • Director Circle

4.12 Length of the Tangent from a Point to a Circle

Theorem The length of tangent from the point $P(x_1, y_1)$ to the circle $x^2 + y^2 + 2gx + 2fy + c = 0$ is

$$\sqrt{(x_1^2 + y_1^2 + 2gx_1 + 2fy_1 + c)} = \sqrt{S_1}$$

Proof Let PT and PT' be two tangents from the given point $P(x_1, y_1)$ to the circle $x^2 + y^2 + 2gx + 2fy + c = 0$.

Then, the centre and radius are $C(-g, -f)$ and $\sqrt{(g^2 + f^2 - c)}$ $(CT = CT')$ respectively.

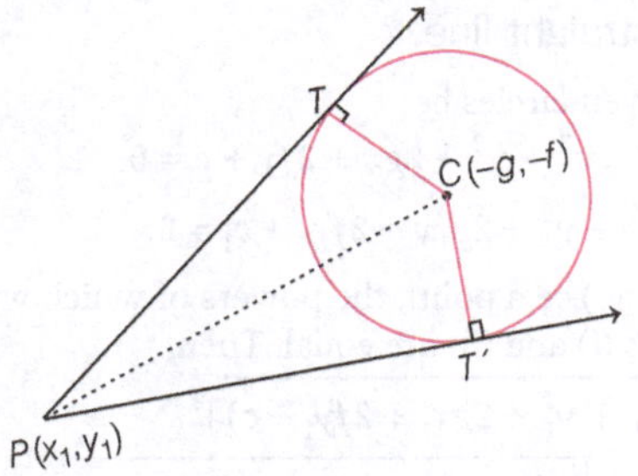

In ΔPCT, $PT = \sqrt{(PC)^2 - (CT)^2}$

$$= \sqrt{(x_1 + g)^2 + (y_1 + f)^2 - g^2 - f^2 + c}$$

$$= \sqrt{(x_1^2 + y_1^2 + 2gx_1 + 2fy_1 + c)} = \sqrt{S_1} = PT',$$

where $S_1 = x_1^2 + y_1^2 + 2gx_1 + 2fy_1 + c$

Example 54. Find the length of tangents drawn from the point $(3, -4)$ to the circle $2x^2 + 2y^2 - 7x - 9y - 13 = 0$.

Sol. The equation of the given circle is

$$2x^2 + 2y^2 - 7x - 9y - 13 = 0$$

Re-writing the given equation of the circle

i.e. $x^2 + y^2 - \frac{7}{2}x - \frac{9}{2}y - \frac{13}{2} = 0$

Let $S = x^2 + y^2 - \frac{7}{2}x - \frac{9}{2}y - \frac{13}{2}$

$\therefore$ $S_1 = (3)^2 + (-4)^2 - \frac{7}{2} \times 3 - \frac{9}{2} \times (-4) - \frac{13}{2}$

$= 25 - \frac{21}{2} + 18 - \frac{13}{2} = 43 - 17 = 26$

$\therefore$ Length of tangent $= \sqrt{S_1} = \sqrt{26}$

Example 55. If the length of tangent from (f, g) to the circle $x^2 + y^2 = 6$ be twice the length of the tangent from (f, g) to circle $x^2 + y^2 + 3x + 3y = 0$, then find the value of $f^2 + g^2 + 4f + 4g$.

Sol. According to the question,

$$\sqrt{(g^2 + f^2 - 6)} = 2\sqrt{(f^2 + g^2 + 3f + 3g)}$$

On squaring, $g^2 + f^2 - 6 = 4f^2 + 4g^2 + 12f + 12g$

or $3f^2 + 3g^2 + 12f + 12g + 6 = 0$

or $f^2 + g^2 + 4f + 4g + 2 = 0$

or $f^2 + g^2 + 4f + 4g = -2$

Example 56. Show that the length of the tangent from any point on the circle $x^2 + y^2 + 2gx + 2fy + c = 0$ to the circle $x^2 + y^2 + 2gx + 2fy + c_1 = 0$ is $\sqrt{(c_1 - c)}$.

Sol. Let (x_1, y_1) be any point on

$$x^2 + y^2 + 2gx + 2fy + c = 0$$

Then, $x_1^2 + y_1^2 + 2gx_1 + 2fy_1 + c = 0$ ...(i)

$\therefore$ Length of tangent from (x_1, y_1) to the circle $x^2 + y^2 + 2gx + 2fy + c_1 = 0$ is

$$\sqrt{x_1^2 + y_1^2 + 2gx_1 + 2fy_1 + c_1} = \sqrt{(-c + c_1)}$$

$$= \sqrt{(c_1 - c)} \quad \text{[From Eq. (i)]}$$

Example 57. Show that the area of the triangle formed by tangents from the point $(4, 3)$ to the circle $x^2 + y^2 = 9$ and the line segment joining their points of contact is $7\frac{17}{25}$ square units in length.

Sol. Since, $PQ = PR = \sqrt{4^2 + 3^2 - 9} = 4$ units

Let $\angle CPQ = \angle CPR = \alpha$

$\therefore$ $PC = \sqrt{(4 - 0)^2 + (3 - 0)^2} = 5$ units

$\therefore$ In ΔPQC, $\tan\alpha = \frac{3}{4}$,

$\therefore$ $\sin\alpha = \frac{3}{5}$ and $\cos\alpha = \frac{4}{5}$

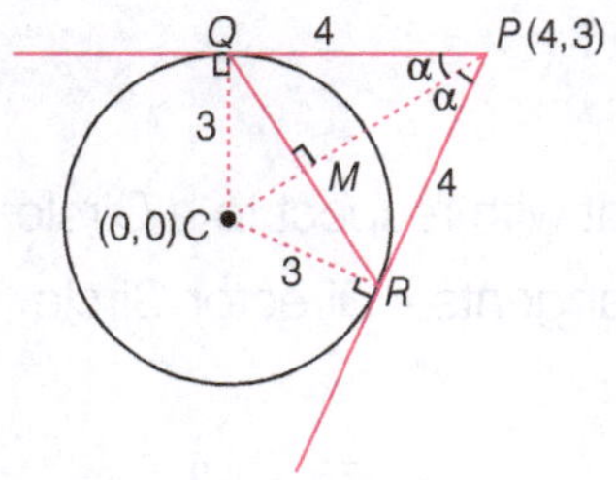

In ΔPMQ, $\cos\alpha = \frac{PM}{4} = \frac{4}{5}$

$\therefore$ $PM = \frac{16}{5}$ and $\sin\alpha = \frac{QM}{4} = \frac{3}{5}$

$\therefore$ $QM = \frac{12}{5}$

$\therefore$ Area of $\Delta PQR = \frac{1}{2} \cdot QR \cdot PM$

$= \frac{1}{2}(2QM) \cdot PM = (QM)(PM)$

$= \left(\frac{12}{5}\right)\left(\frac{16}{5}\right) = \frac{192}{25}$

$= 7\frac{17}{25}$ sq units

4.13 Power of a Point With Respect to a Circle

Theorem The power of a point $P(x_1, y_1)$ with respect to the circle

$x^2 + y^2 + 2gx + 2fy + c = 0$ is S_1

where, $S_1 = x_1^2 + y_1^2 + 2gx_1 + 2fy_1 + c$

Proof Let $P(x_1, y_1)$ be a point outside the circle and PAB and PCD are two secants. The power of $P(x_1, y_1)$ with respect to circle

$$S \equiv x^2 + y^2 + 2gx + 2fy + c = 0$$

is equal to $PA \cdot PB$ which is

$$x_1^2 + y_1^2 + 2gx_1 + 2fy_1 + c = S_1$$

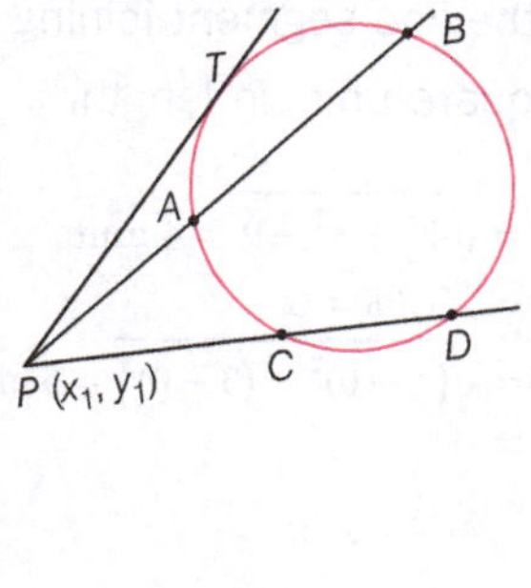

$\therefore$ Power remains constant for the circle i.e. independent of A and B.

$\therefore$ $PA \cdot PB = PC \cdot PD = (PT)^2 = S_1 = (\sqrt{S_1})^2$

$\therefore$ $PA \cdot PB = (\sqrt{S_1})^2 =$ Square of the length of tangent.

JEE SPIKE

If P is outside, inside or on the circle, then $PA \cdot PB$ is positive, negative or zero, respectively.

Example 58. Find the power of point (2, 4) with respect to the circle $x^2 + y^2 - 6x + 4y - 8 = 0$

Sol. The power of the point (2, 4) with respect to the circle $x^2 + y^2 - 6x + 4y - 8 = 0$ is $(\sqrt{S_1})^2$ or S_1

where, $S = x^2 + y^2 - 6x + 4y - 8$

$\therefore$ $S_1 = (2)^2 + (4)^2 - 6 \times 2 + 4 \times 4 - 8$

$= 4 + 16 - 12 + 16 - 8$

$= 16$

[$\because$ (2, 4) is outside the circle $x^2 + y^2 - 6x + 4y - 8 = 0$]

Example 59. Show that the locus of the point, the powers of which with respect to two given circles are equal, is a straight line.

Sol. Let the given circles be

$$x^2 + y^2 + 2gx + 2fy + c = 0 \quad \text{...(i)}$$

and $$x^2 + y^2 + 2g_1x + 2f_1y + c_1 = 0 \quad \text{...(ii)}$$

Let $P(x_1, y_1)$ be a point, the powers of which with respect to the circles (i) and (ii) are equal. Then,

$\therefore$ $[\sqrt{(x_1^2 + y_1^2 + 2gx_1 + 2fy_1 + c)}]^2$

$= [\sqrt{(x_1^2 + y_1^2 + 2g_1x_1 + 2f_1y_1 + c_1)}]^2$

or $x_1^2 + y_1^2 + 2gx_1 + 2fy_1 + c$

$= x_1^2 + y_1^2 + 2g_1x_1 + 2f_1y_1 + c_1$

$\Rightarrow$ $2(g - g_1)x_1 + 2(f - f_1)y_1 + c - c_1 = 0$

then, locus of $P(x_1, y_1)$ is

$$2(g - g_1)x + 2(f - f_1)y + c - c_1 = 0$$

which is a straight line.

4.14 Chord of Contact

From any external point, two tangents can be drawn to a given circle. The chord joining the points of contact of the two tangents is called the chord of contact of tangents.

Theorem The equation of the chord of contact of tangents drawn from a point (x_1, y_1) to the circle $x^2 + y^2 = a^2$ is $xx_1 + yy_1 = a^2$.

Sol. Let $T(x', y')$ and $T'(x'', y'')$ be the points of contact of tangents drawn from $P(x_1, y_1)$ to $x^2 + y^2 = a^2$.

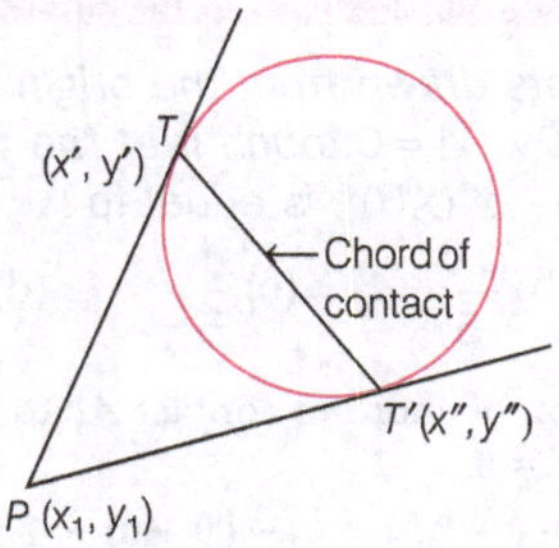

Then, equations of tangents PT and PT' are

$$xx' + yy' = a^2 \text{ and } xx'' + yy'' = a^2 \text{ respectively.}$$

Since, both tangents pass through $P(x_1, y_1)$, then

$$x_1x' + y_1y' = a^2 \text{ and } x_1x'' + y_1y'' = a^2$$

$\because$ Points $T(x', y')$ and $T'(x'', y'')$ lie on

$$xx_1 + yy_1 = a^2$$

$\therefore$ Equation of **chord of contact** TT' is $xx_1 + yy_1 = a^2$

COROLLARY 1 If R is the radius of the circle and L is the length of the tangent from $P(x_1, y_1)$ on $S = 0$.

Here, $L = \sqrt{S_1}$, then

(a) Length of chord of contact $TT' = \dfrac{2LR}{\sqrt{(R^2 + L^2)}}$

(b) Area of triangle formed by the pair of tangents and its chord of contact $= \dfrac{RL^3}{R^2 + L^2}$

(c) Angle between the pair of tangents from $P(x_1, y_1)$ $= \tan^{-1}\left(\dfrac{2RL}{L^2 - R^2}\right)$

COROLLARY 2 Equation of the circle circumscribing the triangle PTT' is

$$(x - x_1)(x + g) + (y - y_1)(y + f) = 0,$$

where $O(-g, -f)$ is the centre of the circle

$$x^2 + y^2 + 2gx + 2fy + c = 0$$

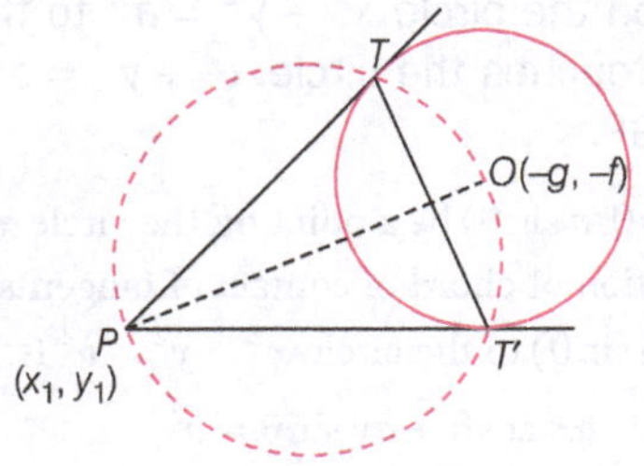

i.e. Required circle always passes through the centre of the given circle (Here, OP is the diameter of the required circle).

JEE SCANNER

Example Similar to PYQ Asked in JEE Main 2023

If the tangents at the point P and Q on the circle $x^2 + y^2 - 4x + 6y - 12 = 0$ meet at the point $R(10, 0)$, then the area of the ΔPQR is equal to

(a) $\dfrac{192\sqrt{3}}{73}$ (b) $\dfrac{960\sqrt{3}}{73}$ (c) $\dfrac{73\sqrt{3}}{960}$ (d) $\dfrac{73\sqrt{3}}{192}$

Sol. (b) We have, $x^2 + y^2 - 4x + 6y - 12 = 0$

$\therefore$ Centre, $O = (2, -3)$ and radius, $r = \sqrt{4 + 9 + 12} = 5$

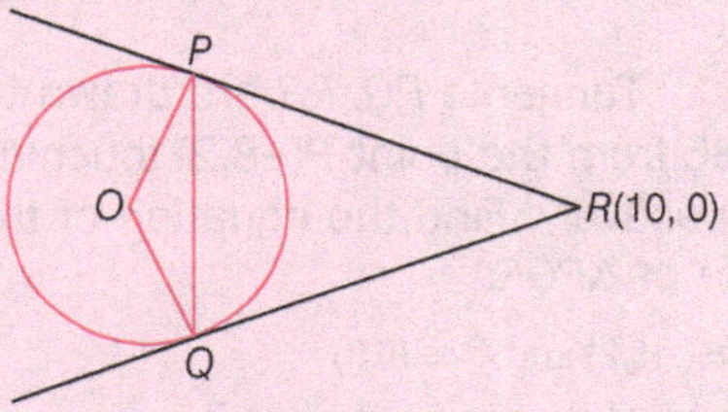

Length of tangent $PR = \sqrt{S_1}$

$\Rightarrow \quad l = \sqrt{100 + 0 - 40 + 0 - 12} = 4\sqrt{3}$

$\therefore$ Area of $\Delta PQR = \dfrac{rl^3}{r^2 + l^2}$

$= \dfrac{5 \times (4\sqrt{3})^3}{(5)^2 + (4\sqrt{3})^2} = \dfrac{5 \times 192\sqrt{3}}{25 + 48}$

$= \dfrac{960\sqrt{3}}{73}$ sq. units

Skill Builder

If the tangent at the points P and Q on the circle $x^2 + y^2 + x - 2y = 5$ meet at the point $R\left(2, \dfrac{9}{4}\right)$, then the area of ΔPQR is

(a) $\dfrac{5}{8}$ sq units (b) $\dfrac{3}{8}$ sq units

(c) $\dfrac{4}{5}$ sq units (d) $\dfrac{7}{8}$ sq units

For Sol.

■ **For more practice** See Q.14 of Milestone Practice 4.4.

Example 60. If the pair of tangents are drawn from the point (4,5) to the circle $x^2 + y^2 - 4x - 2y - 11 = 0$, then

(i) find the length of chord of contact.

(ii) find the area of the triangle formed by a pair of tangents and their chord of contact.

(iii) find the angle between the pair of tangents.

Sol. Here, $P \equiv (4,5)$, $R = \sqrt{((2)^2 + (1)^2 + 11)} = 4$

and $L = \sqrt{S_1} = \sqrt{((4)^2 + (5)^2 - 4 \times 4 - 2 \times 5 - 11)} = 2$

(i) Length of chord of contact

$$= \frac{2LR}{\sqrt{(R^2 + L^2)}} = \frac{2 \times 2 \times 4}{\sqrt{(4)^2 + (2)^2}}$$

$$= \frac{8}{\sqrt{5}} \text{ unit}$$

(ii) Area of triangle $= \frac{RL^3}{R^2 + L^2} = \frac{4 \times 8}{16 + 4} = \frac{8}{5}$ sq units

(iii) Angle between the pair of tangents

$$= \pi + \tan^{-1}\left(\frac{2 \times 4 \times 2}{2^2 - 4^2}\right)$$

$$= \pi - \tan^{-1}\left(\frac{4}{3}\right) \qquad [\because L < R]$$

Example 61. Tangents PQ, PR are drawn to the circle $x^2 + y^2 = 36$ from the point $P(-8,2)$ touching the circle at Q, R respectively. Find the equation of the circumcircle of ΔPQR.

Sol. Here, $P \equiv (-8,2)$ and $O \equiv (0,0)$

$\therefore$ Equation of the required circle is

$$(x - (-8))(x - 0) + (y - 2)(y - 0) = 0$$

or $$x^2 + y^2 + 8x - 2y = 0 \quad [\because OP \text{ is the diameter}]$$

Example 62. Find the condition that chord of contact of any external point (h, k) to the circle $x^2 + y^2 = a^2$ should subtend right angle at the centre of the circle .

Sol. Equation of chord of contact AB is $hx + ky = a^2$

For equation of pair of tangents of OA and OB, make homogeneous $x^2 + y^2 = a^2$ with the help of $hx + ky = a^2$ or $\frac{hx + ky}{a^2} = 1$

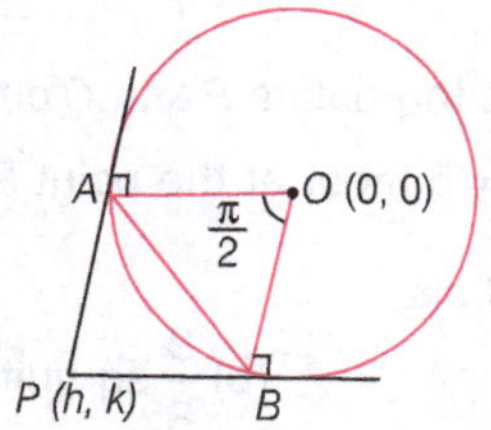

Then, $$x^2 + y^2 = a^2\left(\frac{hx + ky}{a^2}\right)^2$$

or $$a^2(x^2 + y^2) = (hx + ky)^2$$

or $$x^2(a^2 - h^2) - 2hkxy + y^2(a^2 - k^2) = 0$$

but $$\angle AOB = \frac{\pi}{2}$$

$\therefore$ Coefficient of x^2 + Coefficient of $y^2 = 0$

$\Rightarrow$ $$a^2 - h^2 + a^2 - k^2 = 0$$

or $$h^2 + k^2 = 2a^2$$

JEE SCANNER

Example Similar to PYQ Asked in JEE Main 2020

Let the tangents drawn from the origin to the circle $x^2 + y^2 - 4x - 2y + 4 = 0$ touch it at the points A and B. Then, the value of $(AB)^2$ is equal to

(a) $\frac{8}{5}$ (b) $\frac{16}{5}$ (c) $\frac{4}{5}$ (d) $\frac{32}{5}$

Sol. (b) The equation of chord of contact AB to the given circle w.r.t. (0, 0) is $T = 0$

$\Rightarrow$ $$0 \cdot x + 0 \cdot y - 2(x + 0) - (y + 0) + 4 = 0$$

$\Rightarrow$ $$2x + y - 4 = 0$$

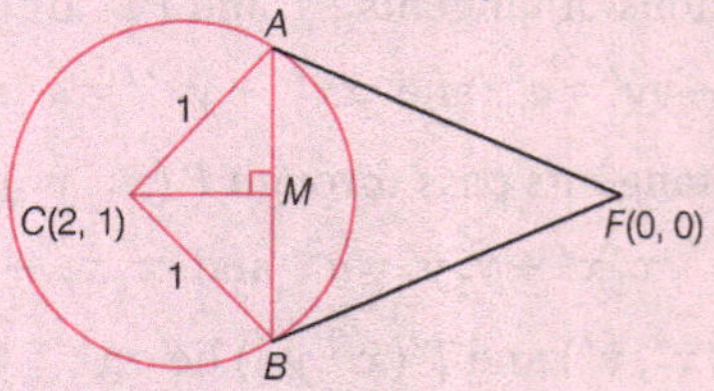

In ΔAMC, $CM = \left|\frac{2(2) + (1) - 4}{\sqrt{4 + 1}}\right| = \frac{1}{\sqrt{5}}$

$\therefore$ $$AM^2 = CA^2 - CM^2$$

$$= 1 - \left(\frac{1}{\sqrt{5}}\right)^2$$

$$= 1 - \frac{1}{5} = \frac{4}{5}$$

$\therefore$ $$AM = \frac{2}{\sqrt{5}}$$

So, $$AB^2 = (2AM)^2 = \left(2 \times \frac{2}{\sqrt{5}}\right)^2 = \frac{16}{5}$$

Skill Builder

Let the tangents drawn from the origin to the circle $x^2 + y^2 - 6x - 6y + 14 = 0$ touch it at the points A and B. Then, the value of $(AB)^2$ is equal to

(a) $\frac{131}{9}$ (b) $\frac{133}{9}$

(c) $\frac{112}{9}$ (d) $\frac{119}{9}$

For Sol.

■ **For more practice** See Q.15 of Milestone Practice 4.4.

Example 63. The chord of contact of tangents drawn from a point on the circle $x^2 + y^2 = a^2$ to the circle $x^2 + y^2 = b^2$ touches the circle $x^2 + y^2 = c^2$. Show that a, b, c are in GP.

Sol. Let $P(a\cos\theta, a\sin\theta)$ be a point on the circle $x^2 + y^2 = a^2$. Then, equation of chord of contact of tangents drawn from $P(a\cos\theta, a\sin\theta)$ to the circle $x^2 + y^2 = b^2$ is

$$ax\cos\theta + ay\sin\theta = b^2 \qquad ...(i)$$

This touches the circle $x^2 + y^2 = c^2$ ...(ii)

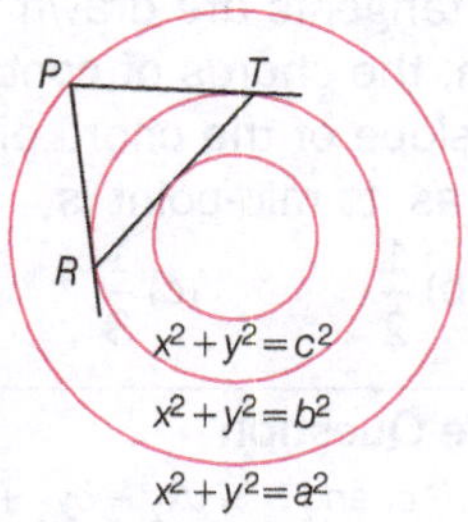

$\therefore$ Length of perpendicular from (0, 0) to Eq. (i)

= Radius of Eq. (ii)

$$\therefore \quad \frac{|0+0-b^2|}{\sqrt{(a^2\cos^2\theta + a^2\sin^2\theta)}} = c \text{ or } b^2 = ac$$

$\Rightarrow$ a, b, c are in GP.

4.15 Chord Bisected at a Given Point

Theorem The equation of the chord of the circle $x^2 + y^2 = a^2$ bisected at the point (x_1, y_1) is given by

$$xx_1 + yy_1 - a^2 = x_1^2 + y_1^2 - a^2 \text{ or } T = S_1$$

Proof Let any chord AB of the circle $x^2 + y^2 = a^2$ be bisected at $D(x_1, y_1)$. If centre of circle is represented by C

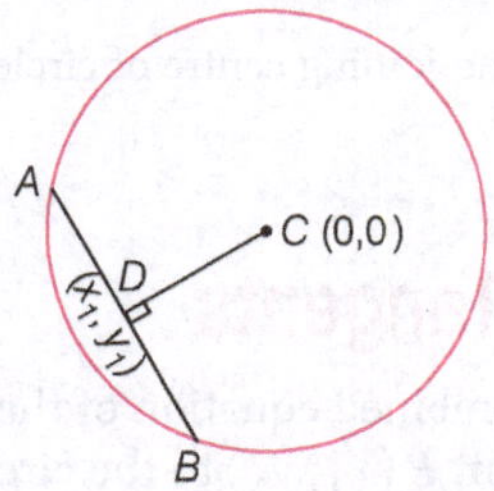

then, slope of $DC = \dfrac{0 - y_1}{0 - x_1} = \dfrac{y_1}{x_1}$

$\therefore$ Slope of the chord AB is $-\dfrac{x_1}{y_1}$ then, equation of AB is

$$y - y_1 = -\frac{x_1}{y_1}(x - x_1)$$

or $$yy_1 - y_1^2 = -xx_1 + x_1^2$$

or $$xx_1 + yy_1 = x_1^2 + y_1^2$$

or $$xx_1 + yy_1 - a^2 = x_1^2 + y_1^2 - a^2$$

or $$T = S_1$$

Example 64. Find the equation of the chord of $x^2 + y^2 - 6x + 10y - 9 = 0$ which is bisected at $(-2, 4)$.

Sol. The equation of the required chord is

$$-2x + 4y - 3(x-2) + 5(y+4) - 9$$
$$= 4 + 16 + 12 + 40 - 9$$

$\Rightarrow$ $$-5x + 9y - 46 = 0$$

or $$5x - 9y + 46 = 0$$

Example 65. Find the middle point of the chord intercepted on line $lx + my + n = 0$ by the circle $x^2 + y^2 = a^2$.

Sol. Let (x_1, y_1) be the middle point of the chord intercepted by the circle $x^2 + y^2 = a^2$ on the line $lx + my + n = 0$. Then, equation of the chord of the circle $x^2 + y^2 = a^2$, whose middle points is (x_1, y_1), is

$$xx_1 + yy_1 - a^2 = x_1^2 + y_1^2 - a^2$$

or $$xx_1 + yy_1 = x_1^2 + y_1^2 \quad \text{...(i)}$$

Clearly, $lx + my + n = 0$ and Eq. (i) represented the same line,

$$\frac{x_1}{l} = \frac{y_1}{m} = \frac{x_1^2 + y_1^2}{-n} = \lambda \quad \text{(say)}$$

$$\therefore \quad \left.\begin{array}{l} x_1 = l\lambda \\ y_1 = m\lambda \end{array}\right\} \quad \text{...(ii)}$$

and $$x_1^2 + y_1^2 = -n\lambda$$

or $$l^2\lambda^2 + m^2\lambda^2 = -n\lambda \quad \text{[from Eq. (ii)]}$$

$$\therefore \quad \lambda = -\frac{n}{l^2 + m^2}$$

So, from Eq. (ii), $x_1 = -\dfrac{nl}{l^2 + m^2}, y_1 = -\dfrac{mn}{l^2 + m^2}$

Hence, the required point is $\left(-\dfrac{nl}{l^2 + m^2}, -\dfrac{nm}{l^2 + m^2}\right)$.

Example 66. Through a fixed point (h, k), secants are drawn to the circle $x^2 + y^2 = r^2$. Show that the locus of mid-point of the portions of secants intercepted by the circle is $x^2 + y^2 = hx + ky$.

Sol. Let $P(x_1, y_1)$ be the middle point of any chord AB, which passes through the point $C(h, k)$.

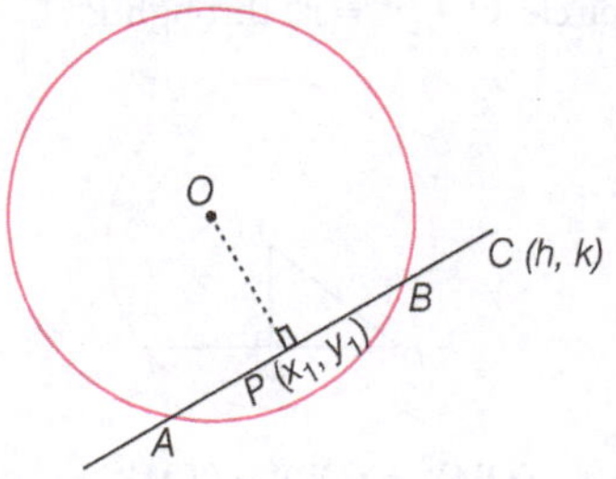

Equation of chord AB is

$$T = S_1$$

$$\therefore \quad xx_1 + yy_1 - r^2 = x_1^2 + y_1^2 - r^2$$

or $$x_1^2 + y_1^2 = xx_1 + yy_1$$

Since, AB passes through $C(h, k)$, then

$$x_1^2 + y_1^2 = hx_1 + ky_1$$

$\therefore$ Locus of $P(x_1, y_1)$ is $x^2 + y^2 = hx + ky$

Example 67. Find the locus of middle points of chords of the circle $x^2+y^2=a^2$, which subtend right angle at the point $(c, 0)$.

Sol. Let $N(h, k)$ be the middle point of any chord AB, which subtend a right angle at $P(c, 0)$.

Since, $\angle APB = 90^\circ$

$\therefore \quad NA = NB = NP$

[$\because$ distance of the vertices from middle point of the hypotenuse are equal]

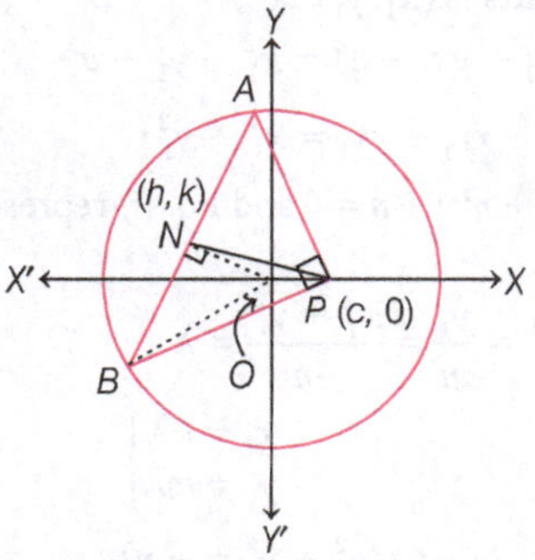

or $\quad (NA)^2 = (NB)^2 = (h-c)^2 + (k-0)^2 \quad$ ...(i)

But also $\quad \angle BNO = 90^\circ$

$\therefore \quad (OB)^2 = (ON)^2 + (NB)^2$

$\Rightarrow \quad -(NB)^2 = (ON)^2 - (OB)^2$

$\Rightarrow \quad -[(h-c)^2 + (k-0)^2] = (h^2+k^2) - a^2$

or $\quad 2(h^2+k^2) - 2ch + c^2 - a^2 = 0$

$\therefore$ Locus of $N(h, k)$ is

$$2(x^2+y^2) - 2cx + c^2 - a^2 = 0$$

Example 68. Find the equation of the chord of the circle $x^2+y^2=r^2$ passing through the point $(2, 3)$ farthest from the centre.

Sol. Let $P \equiv (2, 3)$ be the given point and M be the middle point of chord of circle $x^2+y^2=r^2$ through P.

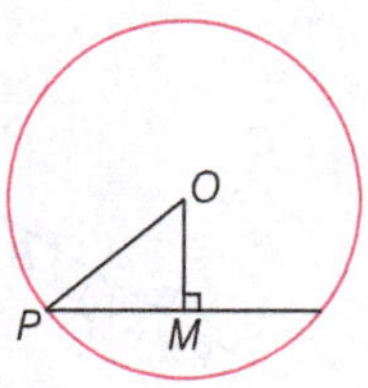

Then, $\quad (OM)^2 = (OP)^2 - (PM)^2$

If OM maximum, then PM is minimum. i.e. P coincides with M, which is middle point of the chord.

Hence, the equation of the chord is

$$T = S_1$$

i.e. $\quad 2x + 3y - r^2 = 2^2 + 3^2 - r^2$

or $\quad 2x + 3y = 13$

Example 69. From points on the straight line $3x-4y+12=0$, tangents are drawn to the circle $x^2+y^2=4$. Then, the chords of contact pass through a fixed point. The slope of the chord of the circle having this fixed points as its mid-point is

(a) $-\frac{4}{3}$ (b) $\frac{1}{2}$ (c) $\frac{1}{3}$ (d) $\frac{5}{3}$

Decoding the Question

If $L_1 = ax_1 + by_1 + c_1$ and $L_2 \equiv ax_2 + by_2 + c_2$ are two lines, then family of line is $L_1 + \lambda L_2$. This passes through a fixed point. That point will be point of intersection of $a_1x + b_1y + c_1 = 0$ and $a_2x + b_2y + c_2 = 0$.

Sol. (a) We have, $3x - 4y + 12 = 0$

Now, let any point on line be $\left(\alpha, \frac{3\alpha+12}{4}\right)$.

Then, equation of chord of contact of tangents from this point to $x^2+y^2=4$ is $\alpha x + \left(\frac{3\alpha+12}{4}\right)y - 4 = 0$

or $\quad \alpha(4x+3y) + (12y-16) = 0$

For different values of α, the above chord passes through $P\left(-1, \frac{4}{3}\right)$ which is the point of intersection of $4x+3y=0$ and $12y-16=0$.

Now, slope of line-joining centre of circle $O(0, 0)$ and point $P\left(-1, \frac{4}{3}\right)$ is $-\frac{4}{3}$.

4.16 Pair of Tangents

Theorem The combined equation of the pair of tangents drawn from a point $P(x_1, y_1)$ to the circle $x^2+y^2=a^2$ is

$$(x^2+y^2-a^2)(x_1^2+y_1^2-a^2) = (xx_1+yy_1-a^2)^2$$

or $\quad SS_1 = T^2$

where, $\quad S = x^2+y^2-a^2, S_1 = x_1^2+y_1^2-a^2$

and $\quad T = xx_1 + yy_1 - a^2$

Proof The given circle is $x^2+y^2=a^2$.

Its centre and radius are $C(0, 0)$ and a, respectively. Given external point is $P(x_1, y_1)$.

From point $P(x_1, y_1)$ two tangents PT and PR be drawn to the circle, touching circle at T and R, respectively.

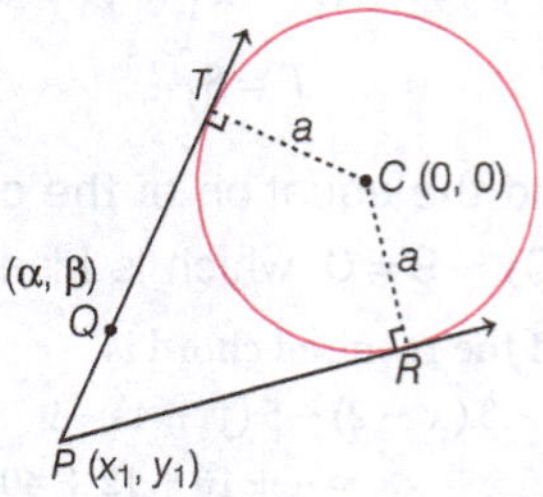

Let $Q(\alpha, \beta)$ on PT, then equation of PQ is

$$y - y_1 = \frac{\beta - y_1}{\alpha - x_1}(x - x_1)$$

or $\quad y(\alpha - x_1) - x(\beta - y_1) - \alpha y_1 + \beta x_1 = 0$

Length of perpendicular from $C(0,0)$ on $PT = a$ (radius)

$$\Rightarrow \quad \frac{|\beta x_1 - \alpha y_1|}{\sqrt{(\alpha - x_1)^2 + (\beta - y_1)^2}} = a$$

or $\quad (\beta x_1 - \alpha y_1)^2 = a^2\{(\alpha - x_1)^2 + (\beta - y_1)^2\}$

$\therefore$ Locus of $Q(\alpha, \beta)$ is

$$(yx_1 - xy_1)^2 = a^2\{(x - x_1)^2 + (y - y_1)^2\}$$

$$\Rightarrow \quad y^2x_1^2 + x^2y_1^2 - 2xyx_1y_1 = a^2\{x^2 + x_1^2 - 2xx_1 + y^2 + y_1^2 - 2yy_1\}$$

$$\Rightarrow \quad y^2(x_1^2 - a^2) + x^2(y_1^2 - a^2) - a^2(x_1^2 + y_1^2) = 2xyx_1y_1 - 2a^2xx_1 - 2a^2yy_1$$

On adding both sides $(x^2x_1^2 + y^2y_1^2 + a^4)$, we get

$$y^2(x_1^2 + y_1^2 - a^2) + x^2(x_1^2 + y_1^2 - a^2) - a^2(x_1^2 + y_1^2 - a^2) = (xx_1 + yy_1 - a^2)^2$$

$$\Rightarrow (x^2 + y^2 - a^2)(x_1^2 + y_1^2 - a^2) = (xx_1 + yy_1 - a^2)^2$$

This is the required equation of pair of tangents drawn from (x_1, y_1) to circle $x^2 + y^2 = a^2$.

Alternate method

Let circle be $x^2 + y^2 = a^2$ with centre $C(0,0)$ and radius a.
Length of tangents from $P(x_1, y_1)$ and $Q(\alpha, \beta)$ are

$$PT = \sqrt{x_1^2 + y_1^2 - a^2} \text{ and } QT = \sqrt{\alpha^2 + \beta^2 - a^2}$$

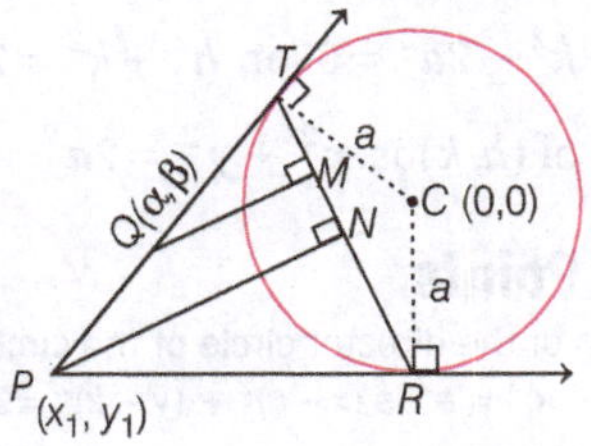

Now, equation of TR (chord of contact) is

$$xx_1 + yy_1 - a^2 = 0$$

$$\therefore \quad PN = \frac{|x_1^2 + y_1^2 - a^2|}{\sqrt{(x_1^2 + y_1^2)}} \text{ and } QM = \frac{|\alpha x_1 + \beta y_1 - a^2|}{\sqrt{(x_1^2 + y_1^2)}}$$

But from similar Δ^s PNT and QMT,

$$\frac{PN}{QM} = \frac{PT}{QT} \Rightarrow \frac{(PN)^2}{(QM)^2} = \frac{(PT)^2}{(QT)^2}$$

$$\Rightarrow \frac{\dfrac{(x_1^2 + y_1^2 - a^2)^2}{(x_1^2 + y_1^2)}}{\dfrac{(\alpha x_1 + \beta y_1 - a^2)^2}{(x_1^2 + y_1^2)}} = \frac{x_1^2 + y_1^2 - a^2}{\alpha^2 + \beta^2 - a^2}$$

$$\Rightarrow (x_1^2 + y_1^2 - a^2)(\alpha^2 + \beta^2 - a^2) = (\alpha x_1 + \beta y_1 - a^2)^2$$

$\therefore$ Locus of $Q(\alpha, \beta)$ is

$$\mathbf{(x^2 + y^2 - a^2)(x_1^2 + y_1^2 - a^2) = (xx_1 + yy_1 - a^2)^2}$$

This is the required equation of pair of tangents drawn from (x_1, y_1) to circle $x^2 + y^2 = a^2$.

JEE SPIKE

The angle between the two tangents from (x_1, y_1) to the circle $x^2 + y^2 = a^2$ is $2\tan^{-1}\left(\frac{a}{\sqrt{S_1}}\right)$, where $S_1 = x_1^2 + y_1^2 - a^2$.

Example 70. Find the equations of the tangents from the point $A(3,2)$ to the circle $x^2 + y^2 + 4x + 6y + 8 = 0$. Also, find the angle between tangents.

Sol. Combined equation of the pair of tangents drawn from $A(3,2)$ to the given circle $x^2 + y^2 + 4x + 6y + 8 = 0$ can be written in the usual notation.

$$T^2 = SS_1$$

$$\Rightarrow [3x + 2y + 2(x+3) + 3(y+2) + 8]^2 = [x^2 + y^2 + 4x + 6y + 8][9 + 4 + 12 + 12 + 8]$$

$$\Rightarrow (5x + 5y + 20)^2 = 45(x^2 + y^2 + 4x + 6y + 8)$$

$$\Rightarrow 5(x + y + 4)^2 = 9(x^2 + y^2 + 4x + 6y + 8)$$

$$\Rightarrow 5(x^2 + y^2 + 2xy + 8x + 8y + 16) = 9(x^2 + y^2 + 4x + 6y + 8)$$

$$\Rightarrow 4x^2 + 4y^2 - 10xy - 4x + 14y - 8 = 0$$

or $\quad 2x^2 + 2y^2 - 5xy - 2x + 7y - 4 = 0$

or $\quad (2x - y - 4)(x - 2y + 1) = 0$

Hence, the required tangents to the circle from $A(3,2)$ are

$$2x - y - 4 = 0 \quad \text{and} \quad x - 2y + 1 = 0$$

Now, $m_1 = \frac{1}{2}, m_2 = 2$

$\therefore$ If angle between tangent is θ, then

$$\tan\theta = \left|\frac{m_1 - m_2}{1 + m_1m_2}\right| = \left|\frac{\frac{1}{2} - 2}{1 + \frac{1}{2} \times 2}\right| = \frac{3}{4}$$

$$\therefore \quad \theta = \tan^{-1}\left(\frac{3}{4}\right)$$

Example 71. Let $2x^2 + y^2 - 3xy = 0$ be the equation of a pair of tangents drawn from the origin O to a circle of radius 3 with centre in first quadrant. If A is one of the points of contact, then the length of OA is

(a) $3(2+\sqrt{10})$ (b) $3(3-\sqrt{10})$
(c) $3(3+\sqrt{10})$ (d) $3(3+2\sqrt{10})$

Sol. (c) We have, $2x^2 + y^2 - 3xy = 0$

which represents a pair of tangents OA and OA'.
Let angle between these two tangents be 2θ.

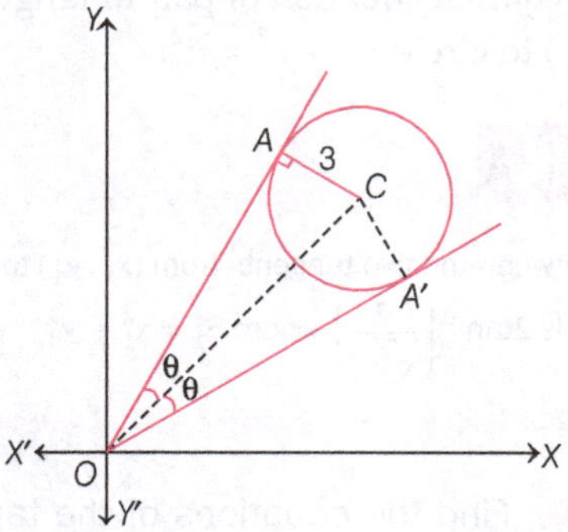

Then, $\tan 2\theta = \dfrac{2\sqrt{\left(-\frac{3}{2}\right)^2 - 2\times 1}}{2+1}$ $\left[\because \tan 2\theta = \dfrac{2\sqrt{h^2 - ab}}{a+b}\right]$

$$\frac{2\tan\theta}{1-\tan^2\theta} = \frac{1}{3} \quad \text{or} \quad \tan^2\theta + 6\tan\theta - 1 = 0$$

or $$\tan\theta = \frac{-6 \pm \sqrt{36+4}}{2} = -3 \pm \sqrt{10}$$

As θ is acute, so $\tan\theta = \sqrt{10} - 3$

From the figure, $\angle COA' = \angle COA = \theta$

In ΔCOA, $\tan\theta = \dfrac{3}{OA}$ or $OA = \dfrac{3}{(\sqrt{10}-3)}\dfrac{(\sqrt{10}+3)}{(\sqrt{10}+3)}$

$$OA = 3(3+\sqrt{10})$$

4.17 Director Circle

Director circle The locus of the point of intersection of two perpendicular tangents to a given circle is known as its director circle.

Theorem The equation of the director circle of the circle $x^2 + y^2 = a^2$ is $x^2 + y^2 = 2a^2$.

Proof The equation of any tangent to the circle

$x^2 + y^2 = a^2$ is $y = mx + a\sqrt{(1+m^2)}$ ...(i)

Let $P(h, k)$ be the point of intersection of tangents. Then $P(h, k)$ lies on Eq. (i).

$\therefore$ $$k = mh + a\sqrt{(1+m^2)}$$

or $$(k - mh)^2 = a^2(1+m^2)$$

or $$m^2(h^2 - a^2) - 2mkh + k^2 - a^2 = 0$$

This is quadratic equation in m, let two roots are m_1 and m_2. But tangents are perpendiculars, then

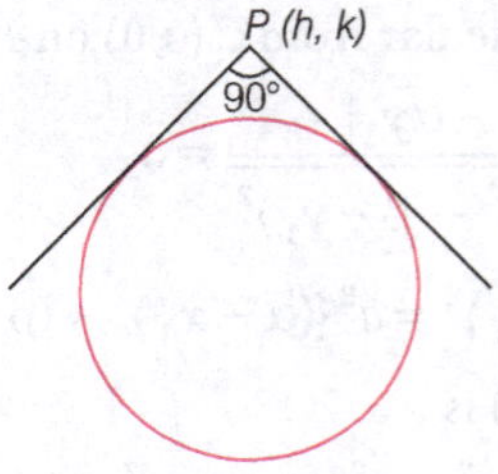

$$m_1 m_2 = -1$$

$\Rightarrow$ $$\frac{k^2 - a^2}{h^2 - a^2} = -1 \text{ or } k^2 - a^2 = -h^2 + a^2$$

or $$h^2 + k^2 = 2a^2$$

Hence, locus of $P(h, k)$ is $\boldsymbol{x^2 + y^2 = 2a^2}$

Alternate method The combined equation of the pair of tangents drawn from (h, k) to $x^2 + y^2 = a^2$ is

$$SS_1 = T^2$$

where, $$S = x^2 + y^2 - a^2$$
$$S_1 = h^2 + k^2 - a^2$$

and $$T = hx + ky - a^2$$

$\therefore$ $(x^2 + y^2 - a^2)(h^2 + k^2 - a^2) = (hx + ky - a^2)^2$

This equation will represent a pair of perpendicular lines if Coefficient of x^2 + Coefficient of $y^2 = 0$

$\Rightarrow$ $h^2 + k^2 - a^2 - h^2 + h^2 + k^2 - a^2 - k^2 = 0$

$\Rightarrow$ $h^2 + k^2 - 2a^2 = 0$ or $h^2 + k^2 = 2a^2$

Hence, the locus of (h, k) is $\boldsymbol{x^2 + y^2 = 2a^2}$

Concept Inside Video

JEE Focus Points

- The equation of the director circle of the circle $(x-h)^2 + (y-k)^2 = a^2$ is $(x-h)^2 + (y-k)^2 = 2a^2$
- The equation of the director circle of the circle $x^2 + y^2 + 2gx + 2fy + c = 0$ is $x^2 + y^2 + 2gx + 2fy + c = g^2 + f^2 - c$
- If two tangents are drawn from a point on the director circle to the circle, then angle between tangents is 90°.

Example 72. If two tangents are drawn from a point on the circle $x^2 + y^2 = 50$ to the circle $x^2 + y^2 = 25$, then find the angle between the tangents.

Sol. Given, $x^2 + y^2 = 50$ is the director circle of $x^2 + y^2 = 25$

Hence, angle between tangents $= 90°$

Milestone Practice 4.4

1. If the tangent at the point P on the circle $x^2+y^2+6x+6y=2$ meets the straight line $5x-2y+6=0$ at a point Q on the Y-axis, then the length PQ is
(a) 4 (b) $2\sqrt{5}$ (c) 5 (d) $3\sqrt{5}$

2. If the circle $x^2+y^2+2gx+2fy+c=0$ is touched by $y=x$ at P such that $OP=6\sqrt{2}$, where O is origin, then the value of c is
(a) 36 (b) 72 (c) 144 (d) 288

3. If the chord of contact of tangents from a point (x_1, y_1) to the circle $x^2+y^2=a^2$ touches the circle $(x-a)^2+y^2=a^2$, then the locus of (x_1, y_1) is
(a) a circle (b) a parabola
(c) an ellipse (d) a hyperbola

4. The locus of the mid-points of a chord of the circle $x^2+y^2=4$, which subtends a right angle at the origin is
(a) $x+y=1$ (b) $x^2+y^2=1$
(c) $x+y=2$ (d) $x^2+y^2=2$

5. The length of tangents from $P(1,-1)$ and $Q(3,3)$ to a circle are $\sqrt{2}$ and $\sqrt{6}$ respectively, then the length of tangent from $R(-2,-7)$ to the same circle is
(a) $\sqrt{41}$ (b) $\sqrt{51}$ (c) $\sqrt{61}$ (d) $\sqrt{71}$

6. If the angle between the tangents drawn to $x^2+y^2+2gx+2fy+c=0$ from (0,0) is $\frac{\pi}{2}$, then
(a) $g^2+f^2=3c$ (b) $g^2+f^2=2c$
(c) $g^2+f^2=5c$ (d) $g^2+f^2=4c$

7. The chords of contact of the pair of tangents drawn from each point on the line $2x+y=4$ to the circle $x^2+y^2=1$ pass through a fixed point
(a) (2, 4) (b) $\left(-\frac{1}{2},-\frac{1}{4}\right)$
(c) $\left(\frac{1}{2},\frac{1}{4}\right)$ (d) $(-2,-4)$

8. The length of tangent from (0, 0) to the circle $2(x^2+y^2)+x-y+5=0$ is
(a) $\sqrt{5}$ (b) $\sqrt{\left(\frac{5}{2}\right)}$ (c) $\frac{\sqrt{5}}{2}$ (d) $\sqrt{2}$

9. The perpendicular tangents to the circle $x^2+y^2=a^2$ meet at P. Then, the locus of P has the equation
(a) $x^2+y^2=2a^2$ (b) $x^2+y^2=3a^2$
(c) $x^2+y^2=4a^2$ (d) $x^2+y^2=5a^2$

10. The tangents to $x^2+y^2=a^2$ having inclinations α and β intersect at P. If $\cot\alpha+\cot\beta=0$, then the locus of P is
(a) $x+y=0$ (b) $x-y=0$ (c) $xy=0$ (d) $xy=1$

11. The exhaustive range of values of a such that the angle between the pair of tangents drawn from (a,a) to the circle $x^2+y^2-2x-2y-6=0$ lies in the range $\left(\frac{\pi}{3},\pi\right)$ is
(a) $(-1, 3)$
(b) $(-5,-3)\cup(3, 5)$
(c) $(-3, 5)$
(d) $(-3,-1)\cup(3, 5)$

12. Find the equation of that chord of the circle $x^2+y^2=15$ which is bisected at (3, 2).

13. The chords of contact of the pair of tangents to the circle $x^2+y^2=1$ drawn from any point on the line $2x+y=4$ pass through the point (α, β), then find $\alpha^2+\beta^2$.

14. If the tangents of the point P and Q on the circle $x^2+y^2-6x+4y-12=0$ meet at the point $R(0, 0)$, then find the area of the ΔPQR.

15. Let the tangents drawn from the origin to the circle $x^2+y^2-2x-4y+4=0$ must it at the point A and B. Find $(AB)^2$.

Answer Key

1. (c) 2. (b) 3. (b) 4. (d) 5. (d) 6. (b) 7. (c) 8. (b) 9. (a) 10. (c)
11. (d) 12. $3x+2y=13$ 13. $\frac{5}{16}$ 14. $\frac{280\sqrt{7}}{53}$ 15. $\frac{16}{5}$

For Detailed Solution

Milestone 5 Family of Circles

- Diameter of a Circle • Two Circles Touch Each Other • Common Tangents of Two Circles
- Common Chord of Two Circles • Family of Circles

4.18 Diameter of a Circle

The locus of the middle points of a system of parallel chords of a circle is called a diameter of the circle.

Let the circle be $x^2 + y^2 = a^2$ and equation of parallel chord is $y = mx + c$.

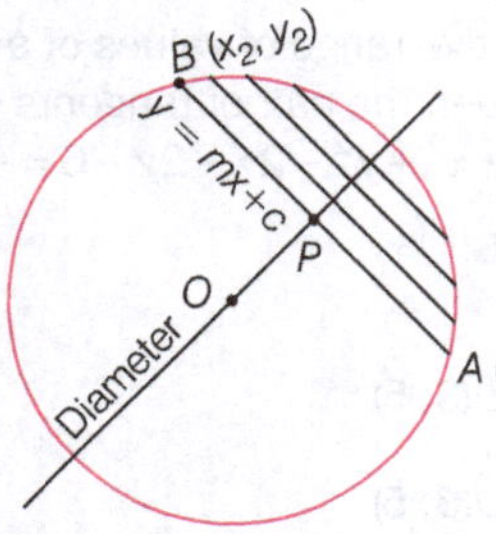

Let $P(h, k)$ be the middle point of the chord $y = mx + c$.
Since, P is the mid-point of $A(x_1\ y_1)$ and $B(x_2, y_2)$, then

$$\frac{x_1 + x_2}{2} = h \quad \text{and} \quad \frac{y_1 + y_2}{2} = k$$

or $\quad x_1 + x_2 = 2h \quad$ and $\quad y_1 + y_2 = 2k \quad$ ...(i)

$\because \quad P(h, k)$ lie on $y = mx + c$

Then, $\quad k = mh + c$

or $\quad k - mh = c \quad$ ...(ii)

Substituting $y = mx + c$ in $x^2 + y^2 = a^2$

then, $\quad x^2 + (mx + c)^2 = a^2$

or $\quad (1 + m^2)x^2 + 2mcx + c^2 - a^2 = 0 \quad$ ...(iii)

Let x_1, x_2 are roots of Eq. (iii), then

$$x_1 + x_2 = -\frac{2mc}{1 + m^2}$$

$$\Rightarrow \quad 2h = -\frac{2m}{(1 + m^2)}(k - mh)$$

[from Eq. (i) and Eq. (ii)]

$$\Rightarrow \quad h + m^2h = -mk + m^2h$$

$$\Rightarrow \quad h + mk = 0$$

Hence, locus of (h, k) is $x + my = 0$

Alternate method

Let (h, k) be the middle point of the chord $y = mx + c$ of the circle $x^2 + y^2 = a^2$

Then, $\quad T = S_1$

$$\Rightarrow \quad xh + ky = h^2 + k^2$$

$$\text{Slope} = -\frac{h}{k} = m$$

$$\Rightarrow \quad h + mk = 0$$

Hence, locus of mid-point is $x + my = 0$.

Example 73. Find the equation of the diameter of the circle $x^2 + y^2 + 2gx + 2fy + c = 0$ which corresponds to the chord $ax + by + d = 0$.

Sol. The diameter of circle passes through the centre of the circle and perpendicular to the chord $ax + by + d = 0$ is

$$bx - ay + \lambda = 0 \quad \text{...(i)}$$

which passes through centre of circle i.e. $(-g, -f)$

Then, $\quad -bg + af + \lambda = 0$

$\therefore \quad \lambda = bg - af$

From Eq. (i), the equation of the diameter is

$$bx - ay + bg - af = 0$$

4.19 Two Circles Touch Each Other

Let the two circles be $(x - x_1)^2 + (y - y_1)^2 = r_1^2$ and $(x - x_2)^2 + (y - y_2)^2 = r_2^2$ with centres $C_1(x_1, y_1)$ and $C_2(x_2, y_2)$ and radii r_1 and r_2, respectively. Then, the following cases may arises.

1. When two circles touch each other externally

Then, distance between their centres = sum of their radii

i.e. $|C_1C_2| = r_1 + r_2$

In such cases, the point of contact P divides the line joining C_1 and C_2 internally in the ratio $r_1 : r_2$

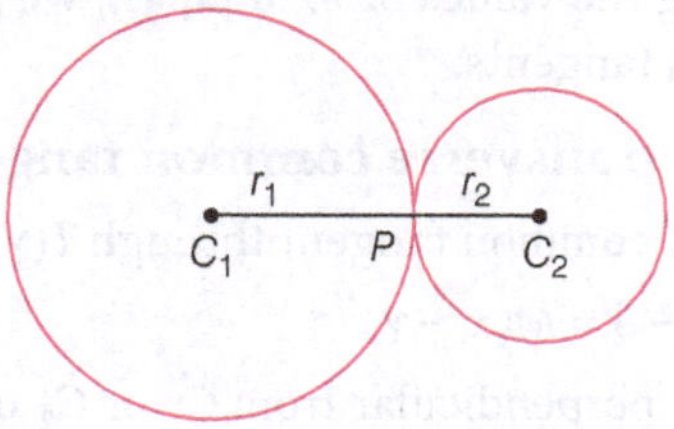

$$\Rightarrow \quad \frac{C_1P}{C_2P} = \frac{r_1}{r_2}$$

If $\quad C_1 \equiv (x_1, y_1)$ and $C_2 \equiv (x_2, y_2)$,

then coordinates of P is $\left(\dfrac{r_1x_2 + r_2x_1}{r_1 + r_2}, \dfrac{r_1y_2 + r_2y_1}{r_1 + r_2} \right)$.

2. When two circles touch each other internally

Then, distance between their centres

=difference of their radii

i.e. $|C_1C_2| = |r_1 - r_2|$

In such cases, the point of contact P divides the line joining C_1 and C_2 externally in the ratio $r_1 : r_2$.

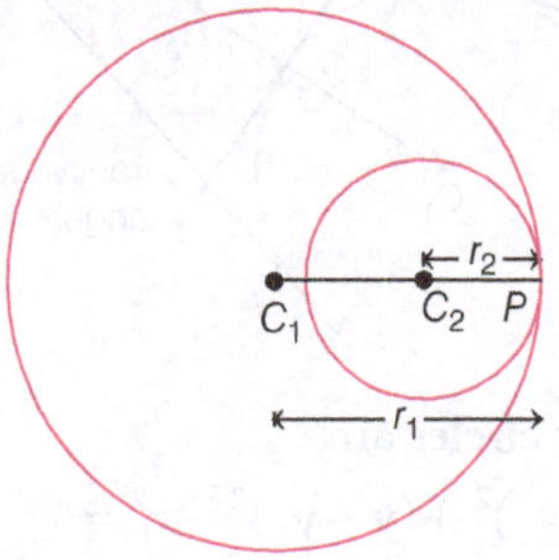

$$\Rightarrow \quad \frac{C_1P}{C_2P} = \frac{r_1}{r_2}$$

If $\quad C_1 \equiv (x_1, y_1)$ and $C_2 \equiv (x_2, y_2)$,

then coordinates of P is $\left(\dfrac{r_1x_2 - r_2x_1}{r_1 - r_2}, \dfrac{r_1y_2 - r_2y_1}{r_1 - r_2} \right)$.

Example 74. Prove that the circles $x^2 + y^2 + 2ax + c^2 = 0$ and $x^2 + y^2 + 2by + c^2 = 0$ touch each other, if $\dfrac{1}{a^2} + \dfrac{1}{b^2} = \dfrac{1}{c^2}$.

Sol. Given circles are

$$x^2 + y^2 + 2ax + c^2 = 0 \quad \text{...(i)}$$

and $$x^2 + y^2 + 2by + c^2 = 0 \quad \text{...(ii)}$$

Let C_1 and C_2 be the centres of circles of Eqs. (i) and (ii), respectively and r_1 and r_2 be their radii, then

$$C_1 = (-a, 0), C_2 = (0, -b),$$

$$r_1 = \sqrt{(a^2 - c^2)}, r_2 = \sqrt{(b^2 - c^2)}$$

For circles to touch each other,

$$|C_1C_2| = |r_1 \pm r_2|$$

or $$\sqrt{(a^2 + b^2)} = |\sqrt{(a^2 - c^2)} \pm \sqrt{(b^2 - c^2)}|$$

On squaring, we get

$$a^2 + b^2 = a^2 - c^2 + b^2 - c^2 \pm 2\sqrt{(a^2 - c^2)}\sqrt{(b^2 - c^2)}$$

or $$c^2 = \pm \sqrt{a^2b^2 - c^2(a^2 + b^2) + c^4}$$

Again, on squaring, we get $c^4 = a^2b^2 - c^2(a^2 + b^2) + c^4$

or $$c^2(a^2 + b^2) = a^2b^2 \text{ or } \frac{1}{a^2} + \frac{1}{b^2} = \frac{1}{c^2}$$

Example 75. C, C_1 and C_2 are circles of radii 5, 3 and 2, respectively. C_1 and C_2 touch each other externally and C internally. The radius of circle C_3 which touches C internally and C_1 and C_2 externally is

(a) $\dfrac{3}{2}$ (b) $\dfrac{20}{9}$ (c) $\dfrac{35}{19}$ (d) $\dfrac{30}{19}$

Decoding the Question

Using cosine rule, $\cos A = \dfrac{b^2 + c^2 - a^2}{2bc}$

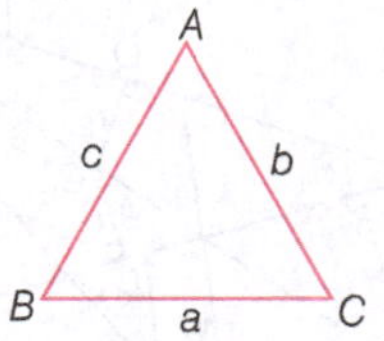

Sol. (d) Let O, O_1, O_2 and O_3 be the centre of circles C, C_1, C_2 and C_3 respectively and r the required radius of circles C_3.

$$O_1O = 2, \quad OO_2 = 3, \quad O_1O_3 = r + 3,$$

$$OO_3 = 5 - r, \quad O_2O_3 = r + 2$$

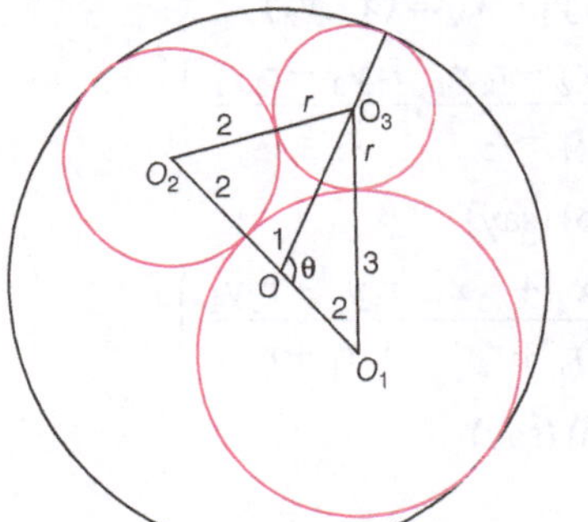

On applying cosine rule in ΔO_3OO_1, we get

$$\cos\theta = \frac{(5-r)^2 + 2^2 - (r+3)^2}{2(5-r)(2)} \quad \text{...(i)}$$

Again, on applying cosine rule in ΔO_2OO_3, we get

$$\cos(\pi - \theta) = \frac{(5-r)^2 + 3^2 - (r+2)^2}{2(5-r)3} \quad \text{...(ii)}$$

From Eqs. (i) and (ii), we get

$$r = \frac{30}{19}$$

4.20 Common Tangents of Two Circles

Different Cases of Intersection of Two Circles

Let the two circles be

$$(x - x_1)^2 + (y - y_1)^2 = r_1^2 \quad \text{...(i)}$$

and $$(x - x_2)^2 + (y - y_2)^2 = r_2^2 \quad \text{...(ii)}$$

with centres $C_1(x_1, y_1)$ and $C_2(x_2, y_2)$ and radii r_1 and r_2, respectively. Then, following cases may arise :

Case I When $|C_1C_2| > r_1 + r_2$ i.e. the distance between the centres is greater than the sum of their radii.

The two circles neither intersect nor touch each other. So, four common tangents can be drawn two are direct common and other two transverse common tangents.

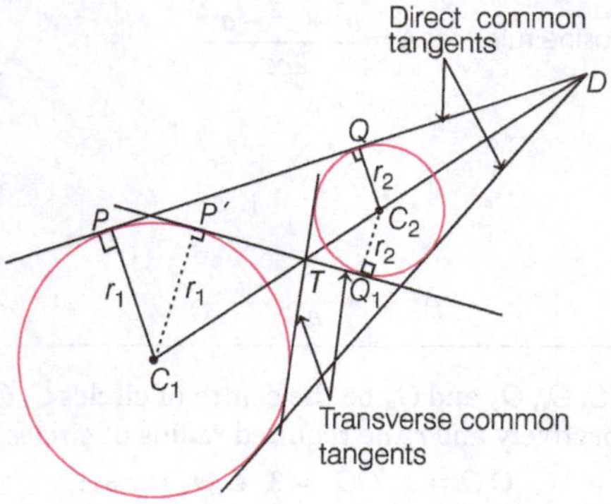

$\because \quad C_1 \equiv (x_1, y_1), C_2 \equiv (x_2, y_2)$

$$\therefore \quad D \equiv \left(\frac{r_1x_2 - r_2x_1}{r_1 - r_2}, \frac{r_1y_2 - r_2y_1}{r_1 - r_2}\right)$$

$\equiv (\alpha, \beta)$ (say)

$$\text{and } T \equiv \left(\frac{r_1x_2 + r_2x_1}{r_1 + r_2}, \frac{r_1y_2 + r_2y_1}{r_1 + r_2}\right)$$

$\equiv (\gamma, \delta)$ (say)

How to find direct common tangents

Let equation of common tangent through $D(\alpha, \beta)$ is

$$y - \beta = m(x - \alpha) \quad \text{...(i)}$$

Now, length of perpendicular from C_1 or C_2 on Eq. (i) is r_1 or r_2.

Then, we get two values of m.

On substituting the values of m in Eq. (i), we get two direct common tangents.

How to find transverse common tangents

Let equation of common tangent through $T(\gamma, \delta)$ is

$$y - \delta = M(x - \gamma) \quad \text{...(ii)}$$

Now, length of perpendicular from C_1 or C_2 on Eq. (ii) is r_1 or r_2.

Then, we get two values of M.

Substituting the values of M in Eq. (ii), we get two transverse common tangents.

Case II When $|C_1C_2| = r_1 + r_2$

i.e. the distance between the centres is equal to the sum of their radii, then the two circles touch externally.

In this case two direct common tangents are real and distinct while the transverse tangents are coincident.

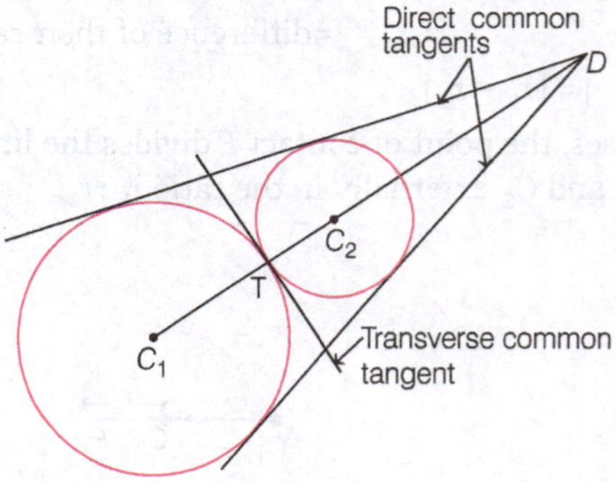

$\because$ Equation of circles are

$$S_1 \equiv (x - x_1)^2 + (y - y_1)^2 - r_1^2 = 0$$

and $$S_2 \equiv (x - x_2)^2 + (y - y_2)^2 - r_2^2 = 0$$

Then, equation of common tangent is

$$S_1 - S_2 = 0$$

which is same as equation of common chord.

Case III When $|r_1 - r_2| < |C_1C_2| < r_1 + r_2$

i.e. the distance between the centres is less than sum of their radii and greater than difference of their radii, then the two circles intersect each other at two distinct points.

In this case two direct common tangents are real and distinct while the transverse tangents are imaginary.

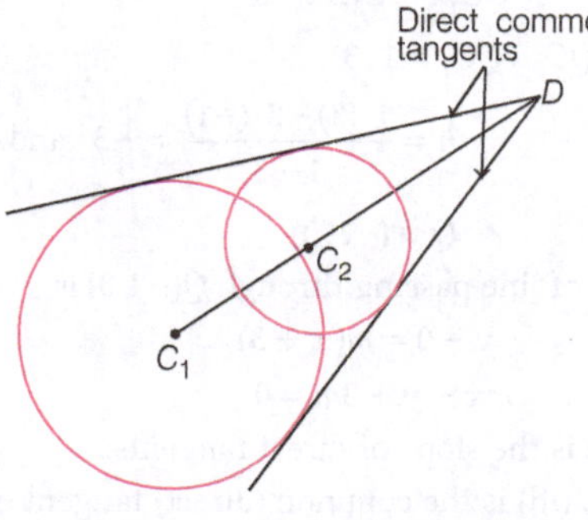

Here, D divides C_1C_2 externally in the ratio

$$\frac{C_1D}{C_2D} = \frac{r_1}{r_2}$$

Case IV When $|C_1C_2| = |r_1 - r_2|$, i.e. the distance between the centres is equal to the difference of their radii.

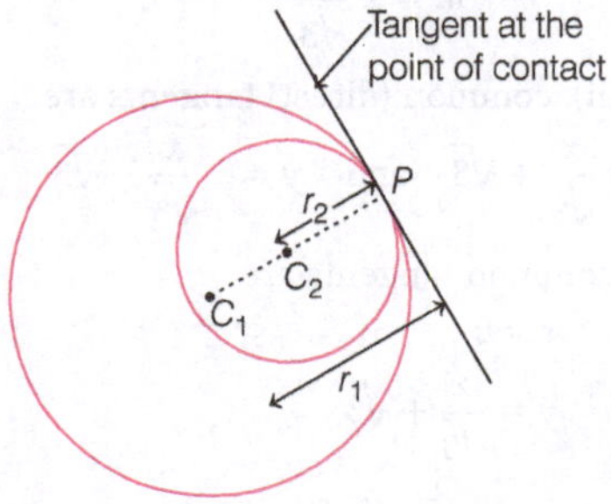

In this case two transverse common tangents are real and coincident while the other two direct tangents are imaginary.

If circles are represented by $S_1 = 0$ and $S_2 = 0$, then equation of common tangent is $S_1 - S_2 = 0$.

The point P divides C_1C_2 externally in the ratio $r_1 : r_2$

$\therefore$ Coordinates of P are $\left(\dfrac{r_1x_2 - r_2x_1}{r_1 - r_2}, \dfrac{r_1y_2 - r_2y_1}{r_1 - r_2}\right)$.

Case V When $|C_1C_2| < |r_1 - r_2|$, i.e. the distance between the centres is less than the difference of their radii.

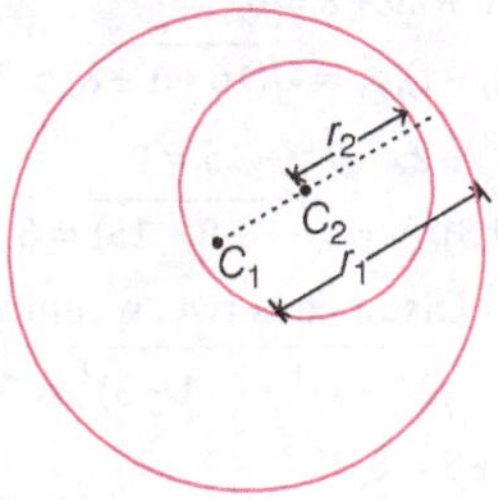

In this case, all the four common tangents are imaginary.

Common Tangents to Two Circles

If two circles with centres C_1 and C_2 and their radii are r_1 and r_2, then

Condition	Figure	Number of common tangents
(i) $\lvert C_1C_2\rvert > r_1 + r_2$	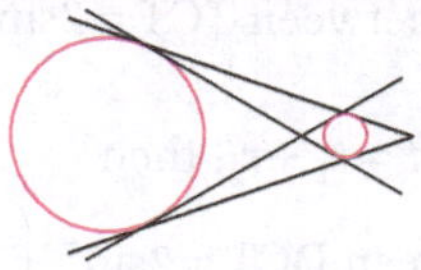	4
(ii) $\lvert C_1C_2\rvert = r_1 + r_2$	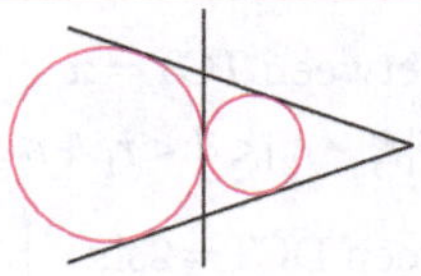	3
(iii) $\lvert r_1 - r_2\rvert < \lvert C_1C_2\rvert < r_1 + r_2$	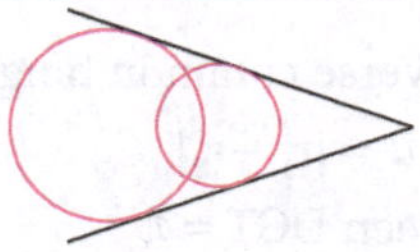	2
(iv) $\lvert C_1C_2\rvert = \lvert r_1 - r_2\rvert$	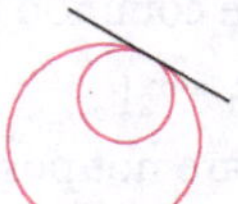	1
(v) $\lvert C_1C_2\rvert < \lvert r_1 - r_2\rvert$		0

Length of External Common Tangent and Internal Common Tangent to Two Circles

Length of external common tangent $L_{ex} = \sqrt{d^2 - (r_1 - r_2)^2}$

and length of internal common tangent

$$L_{in} = \sqrt{d^2 - (r_1 + r_2)^2}$$

[applicable only when $d > r_1 + r_2$]

where, d is the distance between the centres of two circles $|C_1C_2| = d$ and r_1, r_2 are the radii of two circles.

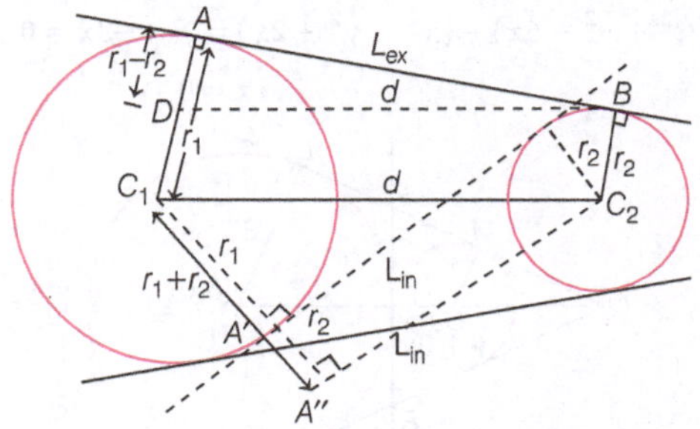

Angle between Direct Common Tangents (DCT) and Transverse Common Tangents (TCT)

Case I If $d > r_1 + r_2$, then

Angle between DCT $= 2\sin^{-1}\left(\frac{|r_1 - r_2|}{d}\right)$

And angle between TCT $= 2\sin^{-1}\left(\frac{r_1 + r_2}{d}\right)$

Case II If $d = r_1 + r_2$, then

Angle between DCT $= 2\sin^{-1}\left(\frac{|r_1 - r_2|}{d}\right)$

and angle between TCT $= \pi$

Case III If $|r_1 - r_2| < d < r_1 + r_2$, then

Angle between DCT $= 2\sin^{-1}\left(\frac{|r_1 - r_2|}{d}\right)$

Here, transverse common tangents are not possible .

Case IV If $d = |r_1 - r_2|$

Angle between DCT $= \pi$

Here, transverse common tangents are not possible.

Case V If $d < |r_1 - r_2|$

Here, tangents are not possible.

Example 76. Show that the common tangents to the circles $x^2 + y^2 - 6x = 0$ and $x^2 + y^2 + 2x = 0$ form an equilateral triangle.

Sol. The given circles are $x^2 + y^2 - 6x = 0$

or $\quad (x-3)^2 + (y-0)^2 = 9 \quad$ ...(i)

and $\quad x^2 + y^2 + 2x = 0$

or $\quad (x+1)^2 + (y-0)^2 = 1 \quad$ ...(ii)

Centres and radii of circles Eqs. (i) and (ii) are $C_1(3, 0)$, $r_1 = 3$ and $C_2(-1, 0)$, $r_2 = 1$, respectively.

$\because \quad C_1C_2 = \sqrt{[3-(-1)]^2 + 0} = 4$

$\therefore \quad C_1C_2 = r_1 + r_2$

Hence, the two circles touch each other externally, therefore there will be three common tangents. Equation of the common tangent at the point of contact is $S_1 - S_2 = 0$

$\Rightarrow \quad (x^2 + y^2 - 6x) - (x^2 + y^2 + 2x) = 0 \Rightarrow -8x = 0$

$\therefore \quad x = 0$

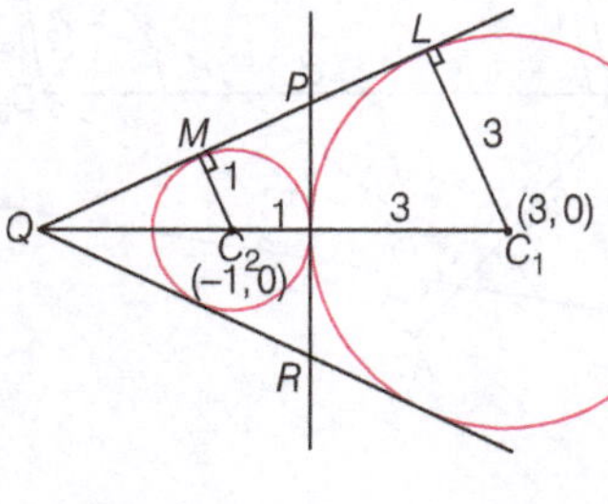

Let the coordinates of Q be (h, k), then

$$\frac{QC_2}{QC_1} = \frac{C_2M}{C_1L} = \frac{1}{3}$$

$\therefore \quad QC_2 : QC_1 = 1 : 3$

$\Rightarrow \quad h = \frac{1\cdot(3) - 3\cdot(-1)}{1-3} = -3$ and $k = 0$

$\therefore \quad Q \equiv (-3, 0)$

Equation of line passing through $Q(-3, 0)$ is

$$y - 0 = m(x + 3)$$

or $\quad mx - y + 3m = 0 \quad$ ...(iii)

where, m is the slope of direct tangents.

Since, Eq. (iii) is the common (direct) tangent of the circles Eqs. (i) and (ii), then

Length of perpendicular from centre of Eq. (ii) i.e. (–1, 0) to the Eq. (iii) = Radius of circle Eq. (ii)

$\Rightarrow \quad \frac{|-m - 0 + 3m|}{\sqrt{m^2+1}} = 1$ or $4m^2 = m^2 + 1 \Rightarrow 3m^2 = 1$

$\therefore \quad m = \pm\frac{1}{\sqrt{3}}$

From Eq. (iii), common (direct) tangents are

$$y = \frac{x}{\sqrt{3}} + \sqrt{3} \quad \text{and} \quad y = -\frac{x}{\sqrt{3}} - \sqrt{3}$$

Hence, all common tangents are

$x = 0 \quad$ ...(iv)

$y = \frac{x}{\sqrt{3}} + \sqrt{3} \quad$ ...(v)

and $\quad y = -\frac{x}{\sqrt{3}} - \sqrt{3} \quad$ ...(vi)

Let P, Q, R be the point of intersection of lines of Eqs.(iv), (v); (v), (vi) and (iv), (vi) respectively, then

$$P \equiv (0, \sqrt{3}),\ Q \equiv (-3, 0) \quad \text{and} \quad R \equiv (0, -\sqrt{3})$$

Now, $\quad PQ = QR = RP = 2\sqrt{3}$

Hence, ΔPQR is an equilateral triangle, thus common tangents form an equilateral triangle.

Example 77. Find the number of common tangents to the circles $x^2 + y^2 - 8x + 2y + 8 = 0$ and $x^2 + y^2 - 2x - 6y - 15 = 0$.

Sol. For $x^2 + y^2 - 8x + 2y + 8 = 0$

$$C_1 \equiv (4, -1),\ r_1 = \sqrt{(16 + 1 - 8)} = 3$$

and for $x^2 + y^2 - 2x - 6y - 15 = 0$

$$C_2 \equiv (1, 3),\ r_2 = \sqrt{(1 + 9 + 15)} = 5$$

Now, $\quad |C_1C_2|$ = Distance between centres

$$= \sqrt{(4-1)^2 + (-1-3)^2} = 5$$

and $r_1 + r_2 = 3 + 5 = 8$

$$|r_1 - r_2| = |3 - 5| = 2 \text{ or } |r_1 - r_2| < |C_1C_2| < r_1 + r_2$$

Hence, the two circles intersect at two distinct points.

Therefore, two common tangents can be drawn to circles.

JEE SCANNER

Example Similar to PYQ Asked in JEE Main 2023

The number of common tangents to the circles $x^2+y^2-2x-6y+9=0$ *and* $x^2+y^2+6x-2y+1=0$ *is*

(a) 1 (b) 2 (c) 3 (d) 4

Sol. (d) We have,

$$S_1 = x^2+y^2-2x-6y+9=0$$

and $S_2 = x^2+y^2+6x-2y+1=0$

Centre of circle S_1 is $C_1 \equiv (1,3)$

and centre of circle S_2 is $C_2 \equiv (-3,1)$

Radius of circle S_1 is $r_1 = \sqrt{1+9-9} = 1$

and radius of circle S_2 is $r_2 = \sqrt{9+1-1} = 3$

Distance between their centre

i.e. $|C_1C_2| = \sqrt{(-1-3)^2+(3-1)^2}$

$= \sqrt{16+4} = \sqrt{20} = 2\sqrt{5}$

$\therefore \quad r_1 + r_2 = 4$

$\Rightarrow \quad |C_1C_2| > r_1 + r_2$

$\therefore$ Circles not intersect each other.

So, the number of common tangent is 4.

Skill Builder

The number of common tangents to the circles $x^2+y^2-2x-4y-4=0$ and $x^2+y^2-4x-8y-5=0$ are

(a) 4 (b) 3

(c) 2 (d) 1

For Sol.

■ **For more practice** See Q.2 of Milestone Practice 4.5.

Example 78. Find the lengths of external and internal common tangents and also find the angle between external common tangents and internal common tangents of the circles $x^2+y^2+2x-8y+13=0$ and $x^2+y^2-8x-2y+8=0$.

Sol. The given circles are

$$x^2+y^2+2x-8y+13=0$$

$$\Rightarrow \quad (x+1)^2+(y-4)^2 = 2^2 \quad \text{...(i)}$$

and $x^2+y^2-8x-2y+8=0$

$$\Rightarrow \quad (x-4)^2+(y-1)^2 = 3^2 \quad \text{...(ii)}$$

Centres and radii of circles of Eqs. (i) and (ii) are $C_1(-1,4)$, $r_1 = 2$ and $C_2(4,1)$, $r_2 = 3$ respectively.

$$\therefore \quad |C_1C_2| = d = \sqrt{(25+9)} = \sqrt{34}$$

$$\Rightarrow \quad d > r_1 + r_2$$

Hence, the circles do not intersect each other.

$$\therefore \quad L_{ex} = \sqrt{d^2-(r_1-r_2)^2} = \sqrt{34-1} = \sqrt{33}$$

and $L_{in} = \sqrt{d^2-(r_1+r_2)^2} = \sqrt{(34-25)} = 3$

Angle between external common tangents

$$= 2\sin^{-1}\left(\frac{|r_1-r_2|}{d}\right) = 2\sin^{-1}\left(\frac{1}{\sqrt{34}}\right)$$

and angle between internal common tangent

$$= 2\sin^{-1}\left(\frac{r_1+r_2}{d}\right) = 2\sin^{-1}\left(\frac{5}{\sqrt{34}}\right)$$

4.21 Common Chord of Two Circles

The chord joining the points of intersection of two given circles is called their common chord.

Theorem The equation of common chord of two circles

$$S \equiv x^2+y^2+2gx+2fy+c=0$$

and $S' \equiv x^2+y^2+2g'x+2f'y+c'=0$

is $2x(g-g')+2y(f-f')+c-c'=0$

i.e. $S - S' = 0$

Proof $\because$ $S=0$ and $S'=0$ are two intersecting circles.

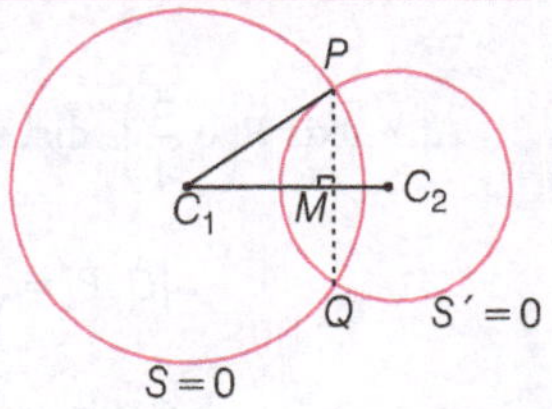

Then, $S - S' = 0$ or $2x(g-g')+2y(f-f')+c-c'=0$ is a first degree equation in x and y.

So, it represent a straight line. Also, this equation satisfied by the intersecting points of two given circles $S=0$ and $S'=0$.

Hence, $S - S' = 0$ represents the common chord of circles $S=0$ and $S'=0$.

Length of common chord

We have, $PQ = 2(PM)$ [$\because M$ is mid-point of PQ]

$$= 2\sqrt{\{(C_1P)^2-(C_1M)^2\}},$$

where C_1P = radius of the circle ($S=0$)

and C_1M = length of perpendicular from C_1 on common chord PQ.

JEE Focus Points

- The common chord PQ of two circles becomes of the maximum length when it is the diameter of the smaller one between them.
- The common chord passing through P and Q as diameter of circle, then centre of the circle lie on the common chord of two circles i.e. $S - S' = 0$.
- If the length of common chord is zero, then the two circles touch each other and the common chord becomes the common tangent to the two circles at the common point of contact.

JEE SCANNER

Example Similar to PYQ Asked in JEE Main 2023

Let the circle $C_1 : x^2 + y^2 - 4x - 4y + 5 = 0$ and C_2 be a circle having centre at $(-3, 0)$ and radius 3. If the line of common chord of C_1 and C_2 intersect the Y-axis at the point P, then the square of the distance of P from the centre of C_2 is

(a) $\frac{\sqrt{72}}{4}$ (b) $\frac{73}{16}$

(c) $\frac{\sqrt{73}}{5}$ (d) $\frac{\sqrt{73}}{5}$

Sol. (b) We have $C_1 : x^2 + y^2 - 4x - 4y + 5 = 0$ ...(i)

$C_2 : (x+3)^2 + y^2 = 9$ ...(ii)

Centre of circle C_2 is $(-3, 0)$.

Equation of common chord, $C_1 - C_2 = 0$

$\Rightarrow (x^2 + y^2 - 4x - 4y + 5) - (x^2 + y^2 + 6x) = 0$

$\Rightarrow -4x - 4y + 5 - 6x = 0$

$\Rightarrow -10x - 4y + 5 = 0$

$\Rightarrow 10x + 4y - 5 = 0$ ...(iii)

At Y-axis $P\left(0, \frac{5}{4}\right)$, distance between centre C_2 and P is

$$|C_2P| = \sqrt{3 + \frac{25}{16}} = \frac{\sqrt{73}}{4}$$

$$|C_2P|^2 = \frac{73}{16}$$

Skill Builder

Let the circle $C_1 : (x-2)^2 + (y-1)^2 = 0$ and C_2 be a circle having centre at $(-2, 0)$ and radius 6. If the line of the common chord of C_1 and C_2 intersect the Y-axis at the point P, then the cube of the distance of P from the centre C_1 is

(a) $\frac{(1240)^{3/2}}{8}$ (b) $\frac{(1244)^{3/2}}{8}$

(c) $\frac{(1241)^{3/2}}{4}$ (d) $\frac{(1241)^{3/2}}{8}$

For Sol.

■ **For more practice** See Q.10 of Milestone Practice 4.5.

Example 79. If the tangents are drawn to the circle $x^2 + y^2 = 12$ at the point where it meets the circle $x^2 + y^2 - 5x + 3y - 2 = 0$, then the point of intersection of these tangents is/are

(a) $\left(6, -\frac{18}{5}\right)$ (b) $\left(6, \frac{18}{5}\right)$

(c) $\left(\frac{18}{5}, 6\right)$ (d) $\left(-6, -\frac{18}{5}\right)$

Sol. (b) We have, $S_1 \equiv x^2 + y^2 = 12$

and $S_2 \equiv x^2 + y^2 - 5x + 3y - 2 = 0$

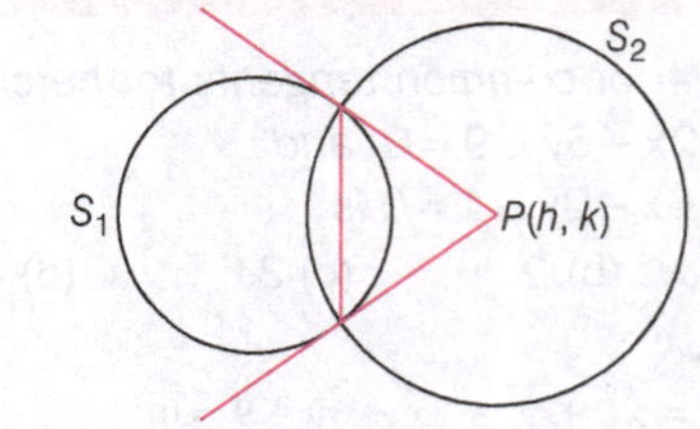

Let (h, k) be the point of intersection of the tangents.

Then, the chord of contact of the tangents is the common chord of the circle $x^2 + y^2 = 12$ and $x^2 + y^2 - 5x + 3y - 2 = 0$

It is given as $5x + 3y - 10 = 0$ ...(i)

Also, the equation of the chord of contact w.r.t. P is

$hx + ky - 12 = 0$ ...(ii)

Eqs. (i) and (ii) represent the same line

Therefore, $\frac{h}{5} = \frac{k}{3} = \frac{-12}{-10}$ or $h = 6, k = \frac{18}{5}$

Example 80. Prove that the length of the common chord of the two circles

$(x-a)^2 + (y-b)^2 = c^2$

and $(x-b)^2 + (y-a)^2 = c^2$ is $\sqrt{4c^2 - 2(a-b)^2}$.

Find also the condition when the given circles touch.

Sol. The equation of circles are

$S_1 \equiv (x-a)^2 + (y-b)^2 - c^2 = 0$ ...(i)

and $S_2 \equiv (x-b)^2 + (y-a)^2 - c^2 = 0$ ...(ii)

Then, equation of common chord is

$S_1 - S_2 = 0$

$\Rightarrow (x-a)^2 - (x-b)^2 + (y-b)^2 - (y-a)^2 = 0$

or $(2x - a - b)(-a + b) + (2y - b - a)(-b + a) = 0$

$\Rightarrow 2x - a - b - 2y + b + a = 0$

$\Rightarrow x - y = 0$

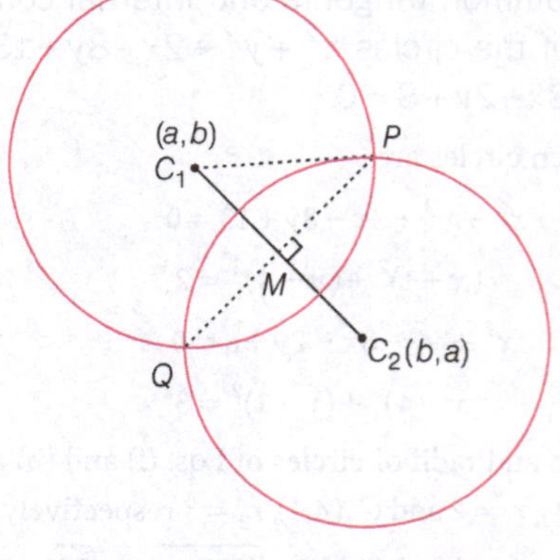

Now, C_1M = Length of perpendicular from $C_1(a, b)$ on

$PQ = \frac{|a-b|}{\sqrt{2}}$

and C_1P = radius of the circle of Eq. (i) = c

$\therefore$ In ΔPC_1M, $PM = \sqrt{(PC_1)^2 - (C_1M)^2} = \sqrt{c^2 - \frac{(a-b)^2}{2}}$

$\therefore \quad PQ = 2PM = 2\sqrt{c^2 - \frac{(a-b)^2}{2}} = \sqrt{4c^2 - 2(a-b)^2}$

Also, when the circles touch, then chord PQ becomes the tangent and $PQ = 0$.

$\therefore$ The condition of tangency is $4c^2 - 2(a-b)^2 = 0$.

i.e. $2c^2 = (a-b)^2$

4.22 Family of Circles

1. The equation of the family of circles passing through the point of intersection of two given circles $S = 0$ and $S' = 0$ is given as

$$S + \lambda S' = 0 \quad [\text{where } \lambda \text{ is a parameter, } \lambda \neq -1]$$

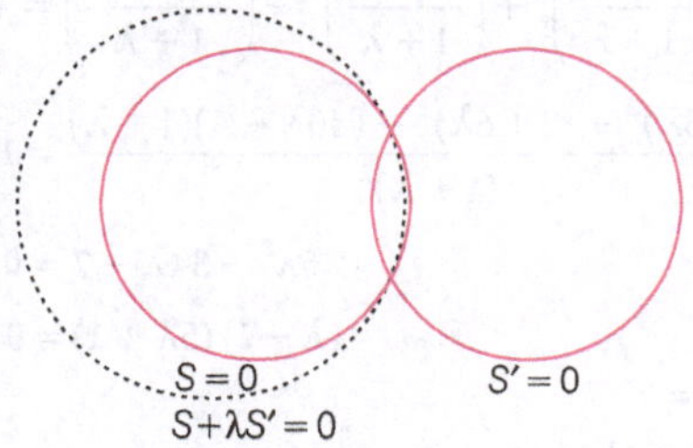

2. The equation of the family of circles passing through the point of intersection of circle $S = 0$ and a line $L = 0$ is given as

$$S + \lambda L = 0 \quad [\text{where } \lambda \text{ is a parameter}]$$

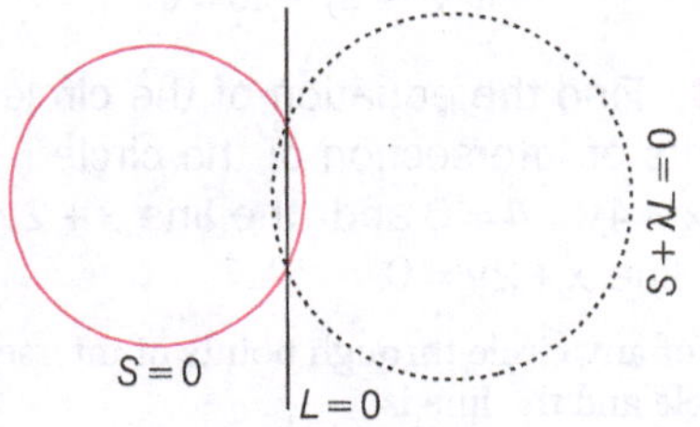

3. The equation of the family of circles touching the circle $S = 0$ and the line $L = 0$ at their point of contact P is

$$S + \lambda L = 0 \quad [\text{where } \lambda \text{ is a parameter}]$$

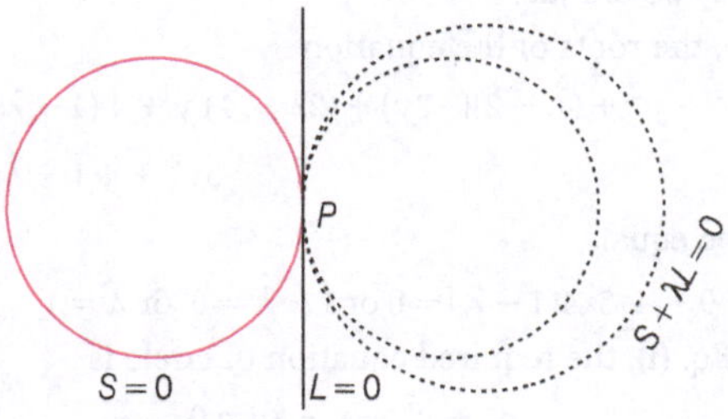

4. The equation of a family of circles passing through two given points $P(x_1, y_1)$ and $Q(x_2, y_2)$ can be written in the form

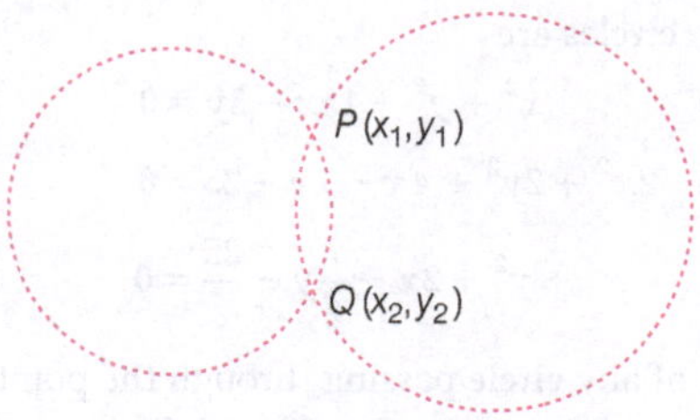

$$(x - x_1)(x - x_2) + (y - y_1)(y - y_2) + \lambda \begin{vmatrix} x & y & 1 \\ x_1 & y_1 & 1 \\ x_2 & y_2 & 1 \end{vmatrix} = 0,$$

where λ is a parameter

5. The equation of family of circles which touch $y - y_1 = m(x - x_1)$ at (x_1, y_1) for any finite m is

$$(x - x_1)^2 + (y - y_1)^2 + \lambda \{(y - y_1) - m(x - x_1)\} = 0$$

and if m is infinite, the family of circles is

$$(x - x_1)^2 + (y - y_1)^2 + \lambda(x - x_1) = 0,$$

where λ is a parameter

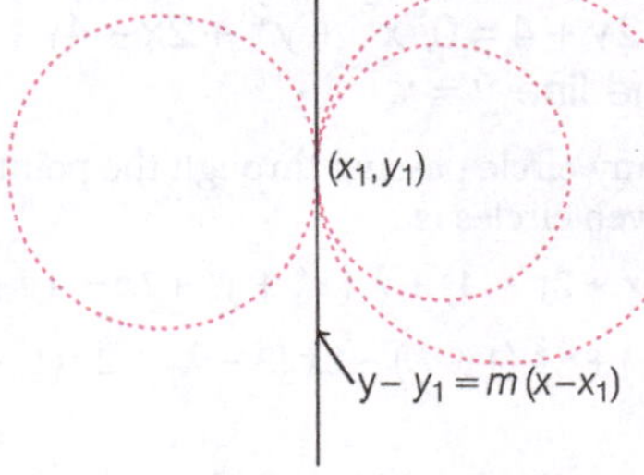

6. Equation of the circles given in diagram are

$$(x - x_1)(x - x_2) + (y - y_1)(y - y_2) \pm \cot\theta \{(x - x_1)(y - y_2) - (x - x_2)(y - y_1)\} = 0$$

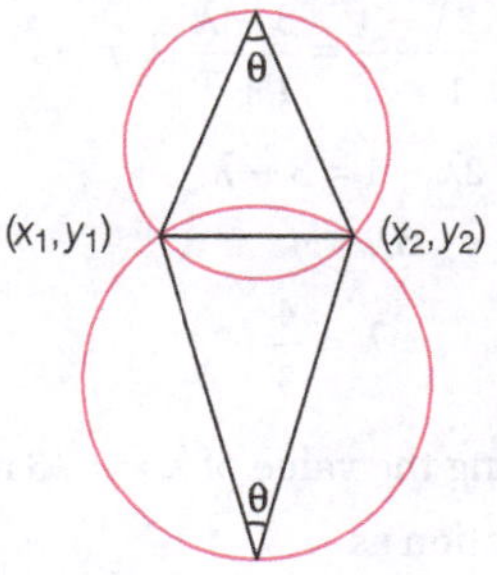

Example 81. Find the equation of the circle passing through (1, 1) and the point of intersection of the circles $x^2+y^2+13x-3y=0$ and $2x^2+2y^2+4x-7y-25=0$.

Sol. The given circles are

$$x^2+y^2+13x-3y=0 \quad \text{...(i)}$$

and $$2x^2+2y^2+4x-7y-25=0$$

or $$x^2+y^2+2x-\frac{7}{2}y-\frac{25}{2}=0 \quad \text{...(ii)}$$

Equation of any circle passing through the point of intersection of the circles Eqs. (i) and (ii) is

$$(x^2+y^2+13x-3y)+\lambda\left(x^2+y^2+2x-\frac{7}{2}y-\frac{25}{2}\right)=0 \quad \text{...(iii)}$$

Its passes through (1, 1), then

$$(1+1+13-3)+\lambda\left(1+1+2-\frac{7}{2}-\frac{25}{2}\right)=0$$

$$\Rightarrow \quad 12+\lambda(-12)=0$$

$$\therefore \quad \lambda=1$$

On substituting the value of λ in Eq. (iii), the required equation is

$$x^2+y^2+13x-3y+x^2+y^2+2x-\frac{7}{2}y-\frac{25}{2}=0$$

$$\Rightarrow \quad 2x^2+2y^2+15x-\frac{13}{2}y-\frac{25}{2}=0$$

$$\Rightarrow \quad 4x^2+4y^2+30x-13y-25=0$$

Example 82. Find the equation of the circle passing through the point of intersection of the circles $x^2+y^2-6x+2y+4=0$, $x^2+y^2+2x-4y-6=0$ and its centre on the line $y=x$.

Sol. Equation of any circle passing through the points of intersection of given circles is

$$(x^2+y^2-6x+2y+4)+\lambda(x^2+y^2+2x-4y-6)=0$$

$$\Rightarrow \quad x^2(1+\lambda)+y^2(1+\lambda)-2x(3-\lambda)+2y(1-2\lambda)+(4-6\lambda)=0$$

or $$x^2+y^2-\frac{2x(3-\lambda)}{(1+\lambda)}+\frac{2y(1-2\lambda)}{(1+\lambda)}+\frac{(4-6\lambda)}{(1+\lambda)}=0 \quad \text{...(i)}$$

Its centre $\left\{\frac{3-\lambda}{1+\lambda}, \frac{2\lambda-1}{1+\lambda}\right\}$ lies on the line $y=x$.

Then, $$\frac{2\lambda-1}{1+\lambda}=\frac{3-\lambda}{1+\lambda}, \lambda \neq -1$$

$$\therefore \quad 2\lambda-1=3-\lambda$$

or $$3\lambda=4$$

$$\therefore \quad \lambda=\frac{4}{3}$$

On substituting the value of $\lambda=4/3$ in Eq. (i), we get the required equation as

$$7x^2+7y^2-10x-10y-12=0$$

Example 83. Find the equation of the circle passing through the point of intersection of the circles $x^2+y^2-2x-4y-4=0$ and $x^2+y^2-10x-12y+40=0$ and whose radius is 4.

Sol. Equation of any circle passing through the points of intersection of given circles is

$$(x^2+y^2-2x-4y-4)+\lambda(x^2+y^2-10x-12y+40)=0$$

$$\Rightarrow \quad x^2(1+\lambda)+y^2(1+\lambda)-2x(1+5\lambda)-2y(2+6\lambda)-4+40\lambda=0$$

or $$x^2+y^2-2x\frac{(1+5\lambda)}{(1+\lambda)}-2y\frac{(2+6\lambda)}{(1+\lambda)}+\frac{(40\lambda-4)}{(1+\lambda)}=0 \quad \text{...(i)}$$

Its radius,

$$\sqrt{\left(\frac{1+5\lambda}{1+\lambda}\right)^2+\left(\frac{2+6\lambda}{1+\lambda}\right)^2-\left(\frac{40\lambda-4}{1+\lambda}\right)}=4 \quad \text{[given]}$$

$$\Rightarrow \quad \frac{(1+5\lambda)^2+(2+6\lambda)^2-(40\lambda-4)(1+\lambda)}{(1+\lambda)^2}=16$$

$$\Rightarrow \quad 5\lambda^2-34\lambda-7=0$$

or $$(\lambda-7)(5\lambda+1)=0$$

$$\therefore \quad \lambda=7$$

or $$\lambda=-\frac{1}{5}$$

On substituting the values of λ in Eq. (i), the required circles are

$$2x^2+2y^2-18x-22y+69=0$$

and $$x^2+y^2-2y-15=0$$

Example 84. Find the equation of the circle passing through points of intersection of the circle $x^2+y^2-2x-4y+4=0$ and the line $x+2y=4$ which touches the line $x+2y=0$.

Sol. Equation of any circle through points of intersection of the given circle and the line is

$$(x^2+y^2-2x-4y+4)+\lambda(x+2y-4)=0$$

or $$x^2+y^2+(\lambda-2)x+(2\lambda-4)y+4(1-\lambda)=0 \quad \text{...(i)}$$

It will touch the line $x+2y=0$, then solution of Eq. (i) and $x=-2y$ be unique.

Hence, the roots of the equation

$$(-2y)^2+y^2+(\lambda-2)(-2y)+(2\lambda-4)y+4(1-\lambda)=0$$

or $$5y^2+4(1-\lambda)=0$$

must be equal.

Then, $0-4\cdot5\cdot4(1-\lambda)=0$ or $1-\lambda=0$ or $\lambda=1$

From Eq. (i), the required equation of circle is

$$x^2+y^2-x-2y=0$$

Example 85. Find the circle whose diameter is the common chord of the circles

$$x^2 + y^2 + 2x + 3y + 1 = 0$$

and $$x^2 + y^2 + 4x + 3y + 2 = 0.$$

Sol. Given circles are

$$S \equiv x^2 + y^2 + 2x + 3y + 1 = 0$$

and $$S' \equiv x^2 + y^2 + 4x + 3y + 2 = 0$$

Hence, their common chord is

$$S - S' = 0$$

$$\Rightarrow \quad -2x - 1 = 0 \quad \text{or} \quad 2x + 1 = 0 \qquad \text{...(i)}$$

Now, the required circle must pass through the point of intersection of S and S'.

Hence, its equation is $S + \lambda S' = 0$

$$\Rightarrow (x^2 + y^2 + 2x + 3y + 1) + \lambda (x^2 + y^2 + 4x + 3y + 2) = 0$$

$$\Rightarrow x^2 (1 + \lambda) + y^2 (1 + \lambda) + 2x (1 + 2\lambda) + 3y (1 + \lambda) + (1 + 2\lambda) = 0$$

or $$x^2 + y^2 + 2x \frac{(1 + 2\lambda)}{(1 + \lambda)} + 3y + \frac{(1 + 2\lambda)}{(1 + \lambda)} = 0 \qquad \text{...(ii)}$$

Its centre is $\left(-\frac{1 + 2\lambda}{1 + \lambda}, -\frac{3}{2}\right)$

But from Eq. (i), $2x + 1 = 0$ is a diameter of this circle. Hence, its centre must lie on this line

$$\therefore \quad -2\left(\frac{1 + 2\lambda}{1 + \lambda}\right) + 1 = 0$$

$$\Rightarrow \quad -2 - 4\lambda + 1 + \lambda = 0$$

$$\Rightarrow \quad -1 - 3\lambda = 0$$

$$\therefore \quad \lambda = -\frac{1}{3}$$

Hence, from Eq. (ii), the required circle is

$$2x^2 + 2y^2 + 2x + 6y + 1 = 0$$

Example 86. If two curves, whose equations are $ax^2 + 2hxy + by^2 + 2gx + 2fy + c = 0$ and $a'x^2 + 2h'xy + b'y^2 + 2g'x + 2f'y + c' = 0$ intersect in four concyclic points, prove that $\frac{a - b}{h} = \frac{a' - b'}{h'}$

Sol. The equation of family of curves passing through the points of intersection of two curves is

$$(ax^2 + 2hxy + by^2 + 2gx + 2fy + c) + \lambda (a'x^2 + 2h'xy + b'y^2 + 2g'x + 2f'y + c') = 0$$

or $$(a + \lambda a')x^2 + 2xy(h + h'\lambda) + (b + \lambda b')y^2 + 2x(g + \lambda g') + 2y(f + \lambda f') + (c + \lambda c') = 0 \qquad \text{...(i)}$$

Four concyclic points lie on a circle, then Eq. (i) represents a circle.

Then, coefficient of x^2 = coefficient of y^2

and coefficient of $xy = 0$

$$\Rightarrow \quad a + \lambda a' = b + \lambda b'$$

or $$(a - b) = -\lambda(a' - b') \qquad \text{...(ii)}$$

and $$2(h + h'\lambda) = 0$$

or $$\lambda = -\frac{h}{h'} \qquad \text{...(iii)}$$

On substituting the value of λ from Eq. (iii) in Eq. (ii), we get

$$\frac{a - b}{h} = \frac{a' - b'}{h'}$$

Milestone Practice 4.5

1. Circles $x^2+y^2-2x-4y=0$ and $x^2+y^2-8y-4=0$

(a) touch each other internally

(b) touch each other externally

(c) cuts each other at two points

(d) None of the above

2. The number of common tangents that can be drawn to the circles $x^2+y^2-4x-6y-3=0$ and $x^2+y^2+2x+2y+1=0$ is

(a) 1 (b) 2

(c) 3 (d) 4

3. The condition that the circle $(x-3)^2+(y-4)^2=r^2$ lies entirely within the circle $x^2+y^2=R^2$ is

(a) $R+r\le 7$

(b) $R^2+r^2<49$

(c) $R^2-r^2<25$

(d) $R-r>5$

4. The circles $x^2+y^2-10x+16=0$ and $x^2+y^2=r^2$ intersect each other at two distinct points if

(a) $r<2$ (b) $r>8$

(c) $2<r<8$ (d) $2\le r\le 8$

5. If the circle $x^2+y^2+4x+22y+c=0$ bisects the circumference of the circle $x^2+y^2-2x+8y-d=0$, then $c+d$ is equal to

(a) 40 (b) 50

(c) 60 (d) 70

6. Two circles $x^2+y^2=6$ and $x^2+y^2-6x+8=0$ are given. Then, the equation of the circle through their points of intersection and the point (1, 1) is

(a) $x^2+y^2-6x+4=0$

(b) $x^2+y^2-3x+1=0$

(c) $x^2+y^2-4x+2=0$

(d) $x^2+y^2-2x+1=0$

7. The equation of the circle described on the common chord of the circles $x^2+y^2+2x=0$ and $x^2+y^2+2y=0$ as diameter is

(a) $x^2+y^2+x-y=0$ (b) $x^2+y^2-x+y=0$

(c) $x^2+y^2-x-y=0$ (d) $x^2+y^2+x+y=0$

8. The equation of the diameter of the circle $3(x^2+y^2)-2x+6y-9=0$ which is perpendicular to the line $2x+3y=12$ is

(a) $3x-2y+3=0$ (b) $3x-2y-3=0$

(c) $3x-2y+1=0$ (d) $3x-2y-1=0$

9. If the curves $ax^2+4xy+2y^2+x+y+5=0$ and $ax^2+6xy+5y^2+2x+3y+8=0$ intersect at four concyclic points, then the value of a is

(a) −6 (b) −4

(c) 4 (d) 6

10. Show that the common chord of the circles $x^2+y^2-6x-4y+9=0$ and $x^2+y^2-8x-6y+23=0$ pass through the centre of the second circle and find its length.

Answer Key

1. (a)	2. (c)	3. (d)	4. (c)	5. (b)
6. (b)	7. (d)	8. (b)	9. (b)	10. $2\sqrt{2}$

For Detailed Solution

Milestone 6 System of Circles

- Angle of Intersection of Two Circles • Radical Axis • Radical Centre
- Co-axial System of Circles • Limiting Point • Image of the Circle by the Line Mirror

4.23 Angle of Intersection of Two Circles

Let two circles

$$S \equiv x^2 + y^2 + 2gx + 2fy + c = 0$$

and $$S' \equiv x^2 + y^2 + 2g_1x + 2f_1y + c_1 = 0$$

intersect each other at points P and Q. The angle θ between two circles $S = 0$ and $S' = 0$ is defined as the angle between the tangents to the two circles at the point of intersection.

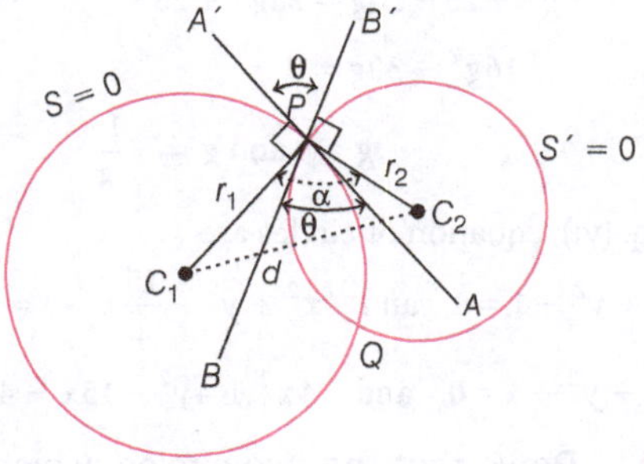

C_1 and C_2 are the centres of circles $S = 0$ and $S' = 0$, then $C_1 \equiv (-g, -f)$ and $C_2 \equiv (-g_1, -f_1)$ and radii of circles $S = 0$ and $S' = 0$ are

$$r_1 = \sqrt{(g^2 + f^2 - c)}$$

and $$r_2 = \sqrt{(g_1^2 + f_1^2 - c_1)}$$

Let $d = |C_1C_2| =$ Distance between their centres

$$= \sqrt{(-g + g_1)^2 + (-f + f_1)^2}$$

$$= \sqrt{(g^2 + f^2 + g_1^2 + f_1^2 - 2gg_1 - 2ff_1)}$$

Now, in ΔC_1PC_2, $\cos\alpha = \left(\dfrac{r_1^2 + r_2^2 - d^2}{2r_1r_2}\right)$

$$[\because \alpha + \theta + 90^\circ + 90^\circ = 360^\circ]$$

or $\cos(180^\circ - \theta) = \left(\dfrac{r_1^2 + r_2^2 - d^2}{2r_1r_2}\right)$ $[\because \alpha = 180^\circ - \theta]$

$\therefore$ $$\cos\theta = \left|\frac{r_1^2 + r_2^2 - d^2}{2r_1r_2}\right| \quad \text{...(i)}$$

Orthogonal Intersection of Circles

If the angle between the circles is 90° i.e. $\theta = 90^\circ$, then the circles are said to be **orthogonal circles** or we say that the circles cut each other **orthogonally**.

Then, from Eq. (i), $0 = \dfrac{r_1^2 + r_2^2 - d^2}{2r_1r_2}$

or $r_1^2 + r_2^2 - d^2 = 0$ or $r_1^2 + r_2^2 = d^2$

$\Rightarrow$ $g^2 + f^2 - c + g_1^2 + f_1^2 - c_1 = g^2 + f^2 + g_1^2 + f_1^2 - 2gg_1 - 2ff_1$

or $$2gg_1 + 2ff_1 = c + c_1$$

Example 87. Find the angle between the circles

$S: x^2 + y^2 - 4x + 6y + 11 = 0$

and $S': x^2 + y^2 - 2x + 8y + 13 = 0$

Sol. Centres and radii of circles S and S' are

$$C_1(2, -3),\ r_1 = \sqrt{2},\ C_2(1, -4),\ r_2 = 2.$$

Distance between centres,

$$d = |C_1C_2| = \sqrt{(2-1)^2 + (-3+4)^2} = \sqrt{2}$$

If angle between the circles is θ, then

$$\cos\theta = \left|\frac{r_1^2 + r_2^2 - d^2}{2r_1r_2}\right|$$

$$\cos\theta = \left|\frac{2 + 4 - 2}{2 \cdot \sqrt{2} \cdot 2}\right|$$

$$= \frac{1}{\sqrt{2}}$$

$\therefore$ $\theta = 45^\circ$

Example 88. Find the value of k, if the circles $2x^2+2y^2-3x+6y+k=0$ and $x^2+y^2-4x+10y+16=0$ cut each other orthogonally.

> **Decoding the Question**
> If two circles $x^2+y^2+2g_1x+2f_1y+c_1=0$ and $x^2+y^2+2g_2x+2f_2y+c_2=0$ cut orthogonally, then $2g_1g_2+2f_1f_2=c_1+c_2$.

Sol. Given circles are $C_1: 2x^2+2y^2-3x+6y+k=0$

$$\Rightarrow \quad x^2+y^2-\frac{3}{2}x+3y+\frac{k}{2}=0$$

and $\quad C_2: x^2+y^2-4x+10y+16=0$

Since, circles cut orthogonally

$$\therefore \quad 2g_1g_2+2f_1f_2=c_1+c_2$$

$$\Rightarrow \quad 2\left(-\frac{3}{4}\right)(-2)+2\left(\frac{3}{2}\right)(5)=\frac{k}{2}+16$$

$$\therefore \quad k=4$$

Example 89. Find the equation of the circle which cuts the circle $x^2+y^2+5x+7y-4=0$ orthogonally, has its centre on the line $x=2$ and passes through the point $(4,-1)$.

Sol. Let the required circle be

$$x^2+y^2+2gx+2fy+c=0 \quad \text{...(i)}$$

Since, $(4,-1)$ lie on Eq. (i), then

$$17+8g-2f+c=0 \quad \text{...(ii)}$$

Centre of Eq. (i) is $(-g,-f)$.

Since, centre lie on $x=2$ then $-g=2$

$$\therefore \quad g=-2 \quad \text{...(iii)}$$

From Eq. (ii), $1-2f+c=0$ ...(iv)

and given circle is

$$x^2+y^2+5x+7y-4=0 \quad \text{...(v)}$$

Given, the circles (i) and (v) cut each other orthogonally,

$$\therefore \quad 2g\times\frac{5}{2}+2f\times\frac{7}{2}=c-4 \text{ or } 5g+7f=c-4$$

$$-10+7f=c-4 \quad \text{[from Eq. (iii)]}$$

or $\quad -6+7f-c=0$ ...(vi)

On solving Eqs. (iv) and (vi), we get

$$f=1 \text{ and } c=1$$

On substituting the values of g, f, c in Eq. (i), we get

$$x^2+y^2-4x+2y+1=0$$

Example 90. Find the equations of the two circles which intersect the circles $x^2+y^2-6y+1=0$ and $x^2+y^2-4y+1=0$ orthogonally and touch the line $3x+4y+5=0$.

Sol. Let the required circle be

$$x^2+y^2+2gx+2fy+c=0 \quad \text{...(i)}$$

and given circles are $x^2+y^2-6y+1=0$ ...(ii)

and $\quad x^2+y^2-4y+1=0$ ...(iii)

Since, Eq. (i) cuts Eq. (ii) and Eq. (iii) orthogonally

$$\therefore \quad 2g\times 0+2f\times(-3)=c+1$$

or $\quad -6f=c+1$ ...(iv)

and $\quad 2g\times 0+2f\times(-2)=c+1$

or $\quad -4f=c+1$ ...(v)

On solving Eqs. (iv) and (v), we get

$$f=0 \quad \text{and} \quad c=-1$$

From Eq. (i), $x^2+y^2+2gx-1=0$ ...(vi)

Centre and radius of Eq. (vi) are $(-g,0)$ and $\sqrt{(g^2+1)}$, respectively.

Since, $3x+4y+5=0$ is tangent of Eq. (vi), then length of perpendicular from $(-g,0)$ to this line = radius of circle

$$\Rightarrow \quad \frac{|-3g+0+5|}{\sqrt{(9+16)}}=\sqrt{(g^2+1)}$$

$$\Rightarrow \quad |-3g+5|=5\sqrt{(g^2+1)}$$

$$\Rightarrow \quad (-3g+5)^2=25(g^2+1)$$

$$\Rightarrow \quad 9g^2+25-30g=25g^2+25$$

$$\Rightarrow \quad 16g^2+30g=0$$

$$\therefore \quad g=0 \text{ and } g=-\frac{15}{8}$$

From Eq. (vi), equation of circles are

$$x^2+y^2-1=0 \quad \text{and} \quad x^2+y^2-\frac{15}{4}x-1=0$$

$$\Rightarrow \quad x^2+y^2-1=0 \quad \text{and} \quad 4x^2+4y^2-15x-4=0.$$

Example 91. Prove that the two circles, which pass through $(0, a)$ and $(0,-a)$ and touch the line $y=mx+c$, will cut orthogonally, if $c^2=a^2(2+m^2)$

Sol. Let the equation of the circles be

$$x^2+y^2+2gx+2fy+d=0 \quad \text{...(i)}$$

Since, these circles pass through $(0, a)$ and $(0,-a)$, then

$$a^2+2fa+d=0 \quad \text{...(ii)}$$

and $\quad a^2-2fa+d=0$ ...(iii)

On solving Eq. (ii) and Eq. (iii), we get $f=0$ and $d=-a^2$.

On substituting these values of f and d in Eq. (i), we obtain

$$x^2+y^2+2gx-a^2=0 \quad \text{...(iv)}$$

Now, $y=mx+c$ touch this circle.

Therefore,

Length of the perpendicular from the centre = Radius

$$\Rightarrow \quad \frac{|-mg-0+c|}{\sqrt{1+m^2}}=\sqrt{(g^2+a^2)}$$

$$\Rightarrow \quad (c-mg)^2=(1+m^2)(g^2+a^2)$$

$$\Rightarrow g^2+2mcg+a^2(1+m^2)-c^2=0$$

Let g_1 and g_2 be the roots of this equation.

$$\therefore \quad g_1 g_2 = a^2(1+m^2) - c^2 \quad \text{...(v)}$$

Now, equation of the two circles represented by Eq. (iv) are

$$x^2 + y^2 + 2g_1 x - a^2 = 0$$

and $$x^2 + y^2 + 2g_2 x - a^2 = 0.$$

These two circles will be cut orthogonal, if

$$2g_1 g_2 + 0 = -a^2 - a^2$$

or $$g_1 g_2 = -a^2 \quad \text{...(vi)}$$

From Eqs. (v) and (vi), we get

$$-a^2 = a^2(1+m^2) - c^2$$

or $$c^2 = a^2(2+m^2)$$

which is the required condition.

Example 92. Find the equation of the circle which cuts orthogonally each of the three circles given below $x^2 + y^2 - 2x + 3y - 7 = 0$, $x^2 + y^2 + 5x - 5y + 9 = 0$ and $x^2 + y^2 + 7x - 9y + 29 = 0$.

Sol. Let the required circle be

$$x^2 + y^2 + 2gx + 2fy + c = 0 \quad \text{...(i)}$$

Since, it is orthogonal to three given circles respectively. Therefore,

$$2g \times (-1) + 2f \times \frac{3}{2} = c - 7$$

$$\Rightarrow \quad -2g + 3f = c - 7 \quad \text{...(ii)}$$

$$2g \times \frac{5}{2} + 2f \times \left(-\frac{5}{2}\right) = c + 9$$

$$\Rightarrow \quad 5g - 5f = c + 9 \quad \text{...(iii)}$$

and $$2g \times \frac{7}{2} + 2f \times \left(-\frac{9}{2}\right) = c + 29$$

or $$7g - 9f = c + 29 \quad \text{...(iv)}$$

On subtracting, Eq. (ii) from Eq. (iii), we get

$$7g - 8f = 16 \quad \text{...(v)}$$

and on subtracting Eq. (iii) from Eq. (iv), we get

$$2g - 4f = 20 \quad \text{...(vi)}$$

On solving Eq. (v) and Eq. (vi), we get

$$g = -8$$

and $$f = -9$$

On putting the values of g and f in Eq. (iii), we get

$$-40 + 45 = c + 9$$

$$\Rightarrow \quad 5 = c + 9$$

or $$c = -4$$

On substituting the values of g, f, c in Eq. (i), then required circle is

$$x^2 + y^2 - 16x - 18y - 4 = 0$$

Example 93. The equation of circle which touches the line $2x + 3y + 1 = 0$ at $(1, -1)$ and cuts orthogonally the circle having line segment having points (0, 3) and $(-2, -1)$ as diameter is

(a) $2x^2 + 2y^2 - 10x + 5y - 1 = 0$
(b) $2x^2 + 2y^2 - 10x - 5y - 1 = 0$
(c) $2x^2 + 2y^2 + 10x - 5y + 1 = 0$
(d) $2x^2 + 2y^2 - 10x - 5y + 1 = 0$

Decoding the Question

Equation of a circle touching a given line $L = 0$ at a given point $A(x_1, y_1)$ can be given as $(x - x_1)^2 + (y - y_1)^2 + \lambda L = 0$

In this case, $(x - x_1)^2 + (y - y_1)^2 = 0$ be a point circle i.e. radius is equal to zero.

Sol. (d) It is given that the line $2x + 3y + 1 = 0$, touches the circle $S = 0$ at $(1, -1)$.

So, the equation of this circle can be written as

$$(x-1)^2 + (y+1)^2 + \lambda(2x + 3y + 1) = 0, \lambda \in R$$

or $$x^2 + y^2 + 2x(\lambda - 1) + y(3\lambda + 2) + \lambda + 2 = 0 \quad \text{...(i)}$$

But this circle is orthogonal to the circle having the extremities of diameter are (0, 3) and (− 2, − 1).

i.e. $$x(x+2) + (y-3)(y+1) = 0$$

or $$x^2 + y^2 + 2x - 2y - 3 = 0 \quad \text{...(ii)}$$

On applying the condition for orthogonal of Eqs. (i) and (ii), we get

$$2(\lambda - 1) \times 1 + 2\left(\frac{3\lambda + 2}{2}\right) \times (-1) = \lambda + 2 + (-3)$$

$$[2g_1 g_2 + 2f_1 f_2 = c_1 + c_2]$$

or $$\lambda = -\frac{3}{2}$$

Put $\lambda = -\frac{3}{2}$ in Eq. (i), we get

$$2x^2 + 2y^2 - 10x - 5y + 1 = 0$$

4.24 Radical Axis

The radical axis of two circles is the locus of a point which moves such that the lengths of the tangents drawn from it to the two circles are equal.

Consider, $$S \equiv x^2 + y^2 + 2gx + 2fy + c = 0 \quad \text{...(i)}$$

and $$S' \equiv x^2 + y^2 + 2g_1 x + 2f_1 y + c_1 = 0 \quad \text{...(ii)}$$

Let $P(x_1, y_1)$ be a point such that

$$|PA| = |PB|$$

$$\Rightarrow \quad \sqrt{(x_1^2 + y_1^2 + 2gx_1 + 2fy_1 + c)} = \sqrt{(x_1^2 + y_1^2 + 2g_1 x_1 + 2f_1 y_1 + c_1)}$$

On squaring, $$x_1^2 + y_1^2 + 2gx_1 + 2fy_1 + c = x_1^2 + y_1^2 + 2g_1 x_1 + 2f_1 y_1 + c_1$$

$$\Rightarrow \quad 2(g - g_1)x_1 + 2(f - f_1)y_1 + c - c_1 = 0$$

$\therefore$ Locus of $P(x_1, y_1)$ is

$$2(g - g_1)x + 2(f - f_1)y + c - c_1 = 0$$

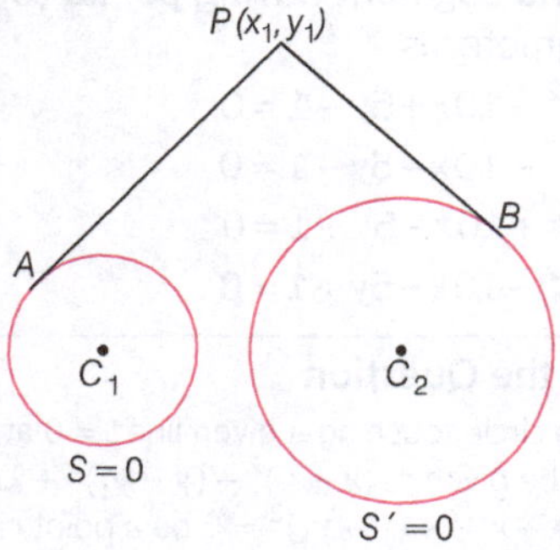

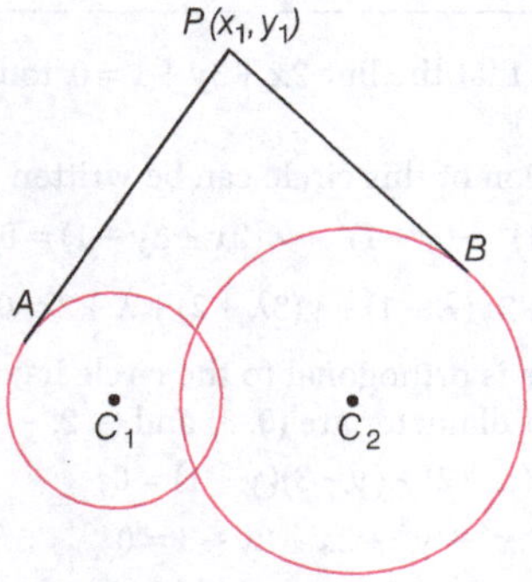

which is the required equation of radical axis of the given circles. Clearly, this is a straight line.

Some Properties of the Radical Axis

(i) **The radical axis and common chord are identical**
Since, the radical axis and common chord of two circles $S = 0$ and $S' = 0$ are the same straight line $S - S' = 0$, they are identical. The only difference is that the common chord exists only if the circles intersect in two real points, while the radical axis exists for all pair of circles irrespective of their position.

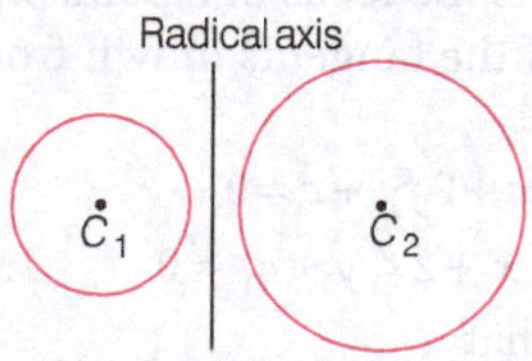

Non-intersecting circles

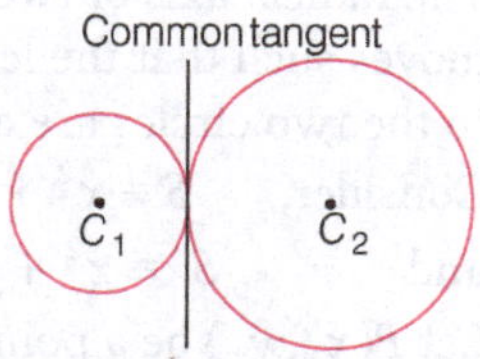

Touching circles

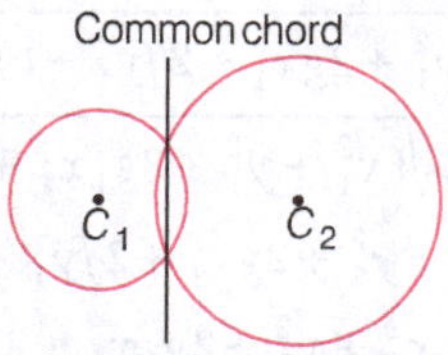

Intersecting circles

The position of the radical axis of the two circles geometrically is shown below:

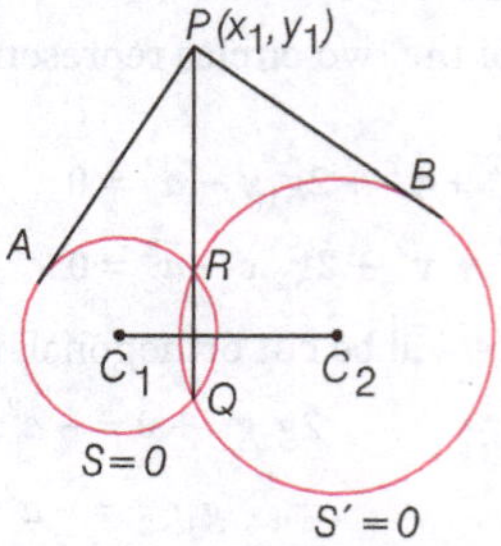

From Euclidian geometry, $(PA)^2 = PR \cdot PQ = (PB)^2$.

(ii) **The radical axis is perpendicular to the straight line which joins the centres of the circles**

Consider, $S \equiv x^2 + y^2 + 2gx + 2fy + c = 0$ ...(i)

and $S_1 \equiv x^2 + y^2 + 2g_1x + 2f_1y + c_1 = 0$ ...(ii)

Since, $C_1 \equiv (-g, -f)$ and $C_2 \equiv (-g_1, -f_1)$ are the centres of the circles of Eqs. (i) and (ii), then

$$\text{slope of } C_1C_2 = \frac{-f_1 + f}{-g_1 + g} = \frac{f - f_1}{g - g_1} = m_1 \quad \text{(say)}$$

Equation of the radical axis is

$$2(g - g_1)x + 2(f - f_1)y + c - c_1 = 0$$

$$\text{Slope of radical axis} = -\frac{(g - g_1)}{f - f_1} = m_2 \quad \text{(say)}$$

$\therefore \quad m_1 m_2 = -1$

Hence, C_1C_2 and radical axis are perpendicular to each other.

(iii) **The radical axis bisects common tangents of two circles** Let AB be the common tangent. If it meets the radical axis LM at M, then MA and MB are two tangents to the circles. Hence, $MA = MB$ since lengths of tangents are equal from any point on radical axis. Hence, radical axis bisects the common tangent AB.

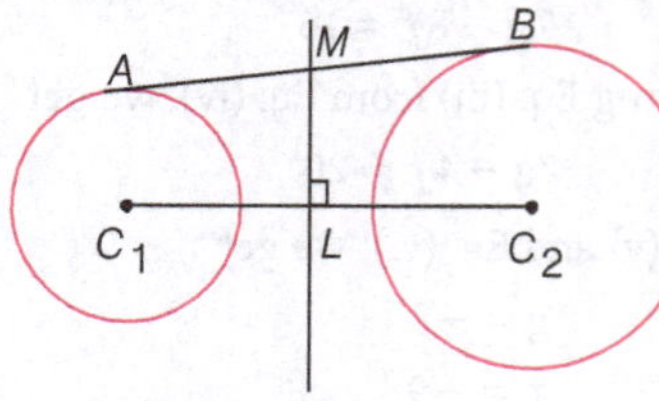

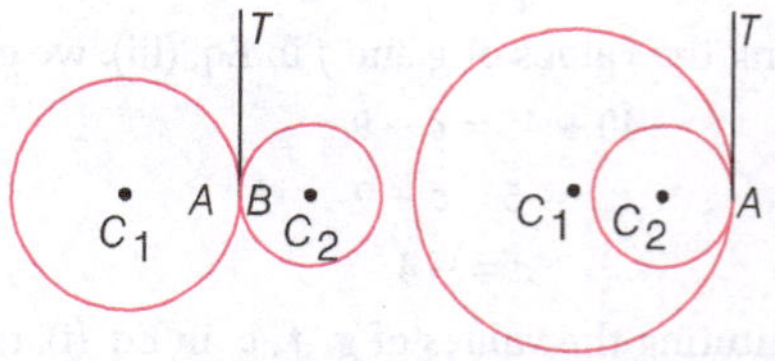

If the two circles touch each other externally or internally, then A and B coincide. In this case the common tangent itself becomes the radical axis.

(iv) **The radical axis of three circles taken in pairs are concurrent** Let the equations of three circles be

$$S_1 \equiv x^2 + y^2 + 2g_1x + 2f_1y + c_1 = 0 \quad \text{...(i)}$$

$$S_2 \equiv x^2 + y^2 + 2g_2x + 2f_2y + c_2 = 0 \quad \text{...(ii)}$$

$$S_3 \equiv x^2 + y^2 + 2g_3x + 2f_3y + c_3 = 0 \quad \text{...(iii)}$$

The radical axis of the above three circles taken in pairs are given by

$$S_1 - S_2 \equiv 2x(g_1 - g_2) + 2y(f_1 - f_2) + c_1 - c_2 = 0 \quad \text{...(iv)}$$

$$S_2 - S_3 \equiv 2x(g_2 - g_3) + 2y(f_2 - f_3) + c_2 - c_3 = 0 \quad \text{...(v)}$$

$$S_3 - S_1 \equiv 2x(g_3 - g_1) + 2y(f_3 - f_1) + c_3 - c_1 = 0 \quad \text{...(vi)}$$

Adding Eqs. (iv), (v) and (vi), we find LHS vanished. Thus, the three lines are concurrent.

Radical axis of three circles will be concurrent at a point called radical centre.

(v) **If two circles cut a third circle orthogonally, then the radical axis of the two circles will pass through the centre of the third circle.**

Or

The locus of the centre of a circle cutting two given circles orthogonally is the radical axis of the two circles.

Let $\quad S_1 \equiv x^2 + y^2 + 2g_1x + 2f_1y + c_1 = 0 \quad \text{...(i)}$

$$S_2 \equiv x^2 + y^2 + 2g_2x + 2f_2y + c_2 = 0 \quad \text{...(ii)}$$

$$S_3 \equiv x^2 + y^2 + 2g_3x + 2f_3y + c_3 = 0 \quad \text{...(iii)}$$

Since, Eqs. (i) and (ii) both cut Eq. (iii) orthogonally

$\therefore \quad 2g_1g_3 + 2f_1f_3 = c_1 + c_3$

and $\quad 2g_2g_3 + 2f_2f_3 = c_2 + c_3$

On subtracting, we get

$$2g_3(g_1 - g_2) + 2f_3(f_1 - f_2) = c_1 - c_2 \quad \text{...(iv)}$$

Now, radical axis of Eqs. (i) and (ii) is

$$S_1 - S_2 = 0$$

or $\quad 2x(g_1 - g_2) + 2y(f_1 - f_2) + c_1 - c_2 = 0$

Since, it will pass through the centre of Eq. (iii) circle

$\therefore \quad -2g_3(g_1 - g_2) - 2f_3(f_1 - f_2) + c_1 - c_2 = 0$

or $\quad 2g_3(g_1 - g_2) + 2f_3(f_1 - f_2) = c_1 - c_2 \quad \text{...(v)}$

which is true by Eq. (iv).

Example 94. If two circles $x^2 + y^2 + 2gx + 2fy = 0$ and $x^2 + y^2 + 2g'x + 2f'y = 0$ touch each other, then $f'g = fg'$.

Sol. If two circles touch each other, then their radical axis is their common tangent.

$\therefore$ Radical axis of two circles is

$$(x^2 + y^2 + 2gx + 2fy) - (x^2 + y^2 + 2g'x + 2f'y) = 0$$

or $\quad 2x(g - g') + 2y(f - f') = 0$

or $\quad x(g - g') + y(f - f') = 0 \quad \text{...(i)}$

If this touches the circle $x^2 + y^2 + 2gx + 2fy = 0$, then length of perpendicular from its centre $(-g, -f)$ to Eq. (i) $=$ radius

i.e. $$\frac{|-g(g - g') - f(f - f')|}{\sqrt{(g - g')^2 + (f - f')^2}} = \sqrt{g^2 + f^2}$$

$$\Rightarrow \{(-(g^2 + f^2) + gg' + ff')\}^2 = (g^2 + f^2)\{(g - g')^2 + (f + f')^2\}$$

$$\Rightarrow (g^2 + f^2)^2 + (gg' + ff')^2 - 2(g^2 + f^2)(gg' + ff') = (g^2 + f^2)\{(g^2 + f^2) + (g'^2 + f'^2) - 2(gg' + ff')\}$$

$$\Rightarrow (gg' + ff')^2 = (g^2 + f^2)(g'^2 + f'^2)$$

On simplifying,

$$2gg'ff' = g^2f'^2 + f^2g'^2$$

or $\quad (gf' - g'f)^2 = 0$

or $\quad gf' = g'f$

Alternate Solution

If two circles touch each other, then distance between their centres = sum or difference of their radii

$$\sqrt{(g - g')^2 + (f - f')^2} = \sqrt{(g^2 + f^2)} \pm \sqrt{(g'^2 + f'^2)}$$

$$\Rightarrow \sqrt{(g^2 + f^2 + g'^2 + f'^2 - 2gg' - 2ff')} = \sqrt{(g^2 + f^2)} \pm \sqrt{(g'^2 + f'^2)}$$

On squaring, we get

$$g^2 + f^2 + g'^2 + f'^2 - 2gg' - 2ff' = g^2 + f^2 + g'^2 + f'^2 \pm 2\sqrt{(g^2 + f^2)}\sqrt{(g'^2 + f'^2)}$$

$$\Rightarrow \quad (gg' + ff') = \pm\sqrt{(g^2 + f^2)(g'^2 + f'^2)}$$

Again, on squaring both sides, we get

$$g^2g'^2 + f^2f'^2 + 2gg'ff' = g^2g'^2 + g^2f'^2 + f^2g'^2 + f^2f'^2$$

$$\Rightarrow \quad g^2f'^2 + f^2g'^2 - 2gg'ff' = 0$$

$$\Rightarrow \quad (gf' - g'f)^2 = 0$$

$$\Rightarrow \quad gf' - g'f = 0$$

$$gf' = g'f$$

Example 95. A and B are two fixed points and P moves so that $PA = nPB$. Show that locus of P is a circle and for different values of n all the circles have a common radical axis.

Sol. Let $A \equiv (a, 0)$, $B \equiv (-a, 0)$ and $P \equiv (h, k)$

$\therefore \quad PA = \sqrt{(h-a)^2 + k^2}$

$PB = \sqrt{(h+a)^2 + k^2}$

Since, $\quad PA = nPB$

or $\quad (PA)^2 = n^2 (PB)^2$

$\Rightarrow \quad \{(h-a)^2 + k^2\} = n^2 \{(h+a)^2 + k^2\}$

$\Rightarrow \quad (h^2 + k^2 - 2ah + a^2) = n^2 (h^2 + k^2 + 2ah + a^2)$

$\Rightarrow \quad (1-n^2)h^2 + (1-n^2)k^2 - 2ah(1+n^2) + (1-n^2)a^2 = 0$

or $\quad h^2 + k^2 - 2ah \dfrac{(1+n^2)}{(1-n^2)} + a^2 = 0$

$\therefore$ Locus of P is $x^2 + y^2 - \left(\dfrac{1+n^2}{1-n^2}\right) 2ax + a^2 = 0$

which is a circle for different values of n.

If two different values of n are n_1 and n_2, then circles are

$$x^2 + y^2 - \left(\frac{1+n_1^2}{1-n_1^2}\right) 2ax + a^2 = 0 \quad \text{...(i)}$$

and $$x^2 + y^2 - \left(\frac{1+n_2^2}{1-n_2^2}\right) 2ax + a^2 = 0 \quad \text{...(ii)}$$

$\therefore$ Radical axis of Eqs. (i) and (ii) is

$$2ax\left\{\frac{1+n_2^2}{1-n_2^2} - \frac{1+n_1^2}{1-n_1^2}\right\} = 0$$

or $\quad x = 0$ or Y-axis.

Hence, for different values of n, the circles have a common radical axis.

4.25 Radical Centre

The radical axes of three circles, taken in pairs, meet at a point, which is called their radical centre. Let the three circles be

$$S_1 = 0 \quad \text{...(i)}$$
$$S_2 = 0 \quad \text{...(ii)}$$
$$S_3 = 0 \quad \text{...(iii)}$$

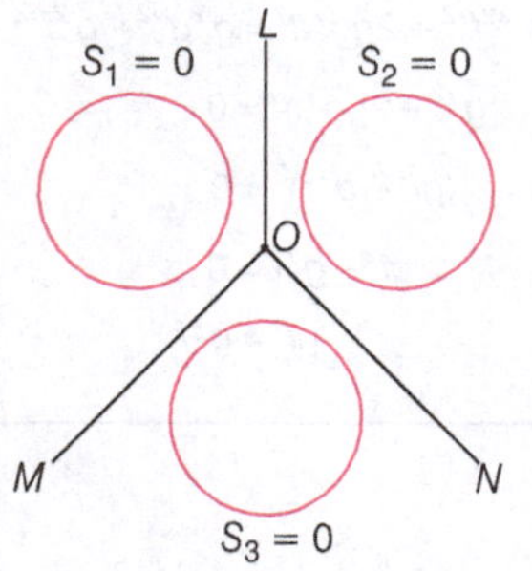

Let OL, OM and ON be radical axes of the pair of circles $\{S_1 = 0, S_2 = 0\}$, $\{S_3 = 0, S_1 = 0\}$ and $\{S_2 = 0, S_3 = 0\}$ respectively.

Equations of OL, OM and ON are respectively

$$S_1 - S_2 = 0 \quad \text{...(iv)}$$
$$S_3 - S_1 = 0 \quad \text{...(v)}$$
$$S_2 - S_3 = 0 \quad \text{...(vi)}$$

Let the straight lines of Eqs. (iv) and (v) i.e. OL and OM meet at O. The equation of any straight line passing through O is

$$(S_1 - S_2) + \lambda(S_3 - S_1) = 0$$

where λ is any constant.

For $\lambda = 1$, this equation becomes

$$S_2 - S_3 = 0$$

which is Eq. (vi) or equation of ON.

Thus, the third radical axis also passes through the point where the Eqs. (iv) and (v) meet. In the above figure, O is the **radical centre.**

Properties of Radical Centre

1. Coordinates of radical centre can be found by solving the equations
$$S_1 = S_2 = S_3 = 0$$
2. **The radical centre of three circles described on the sides of a triangle as diameters is the orthocentre of the triangle**

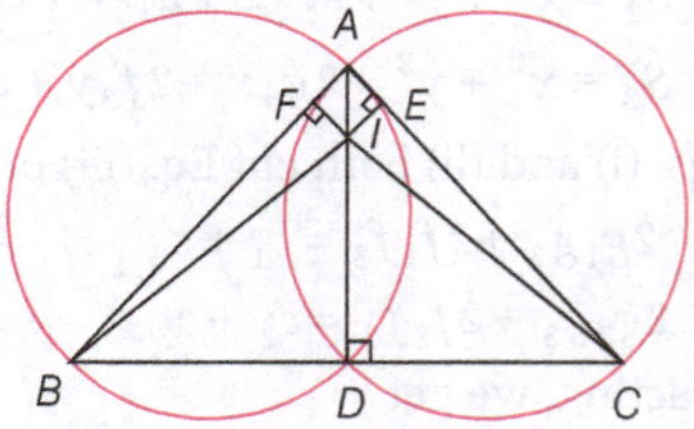

Draw perpendicular from A on BC.

$\therefore \quad \angle ADB = \angle ADC = \pi/2$

Therefore, the circles whose diameters are AB and AC passes through D and A. Hence, AD is their radical axis. Similarly, the radical axis of the circles on AB and BC as diameters is the perpendicular line from B on CA and radical axis of the circles on BC and CA as diameters is the perpendicular line from C on AB. Hence, the radial axis of three circles meet at a point. This point I is radical centre but here radical centre is the point of intersection of altitudes i.e. AD, BE and CF.

Hence, radical centre = orthocentre.

3. The radical centre of three given circles will be the centre of a fourth circle which cuts all the three circles orthogonally and the radius of the fourth circle is the length of tangent drawn from radical centre of the three given circles to any of these circles.

   Let the fourth circle be $(x-h)^2+(y-k)^2=r^2$, where (h, k) is centre of this circle and r be the radius. The centre of circle is the radical centre of the given circles and r is the length of tangent from (h, k) to any of the given three circles.

Example 96. Find the radical centre of circles $x^2+y^2+3x+2y+1=0$, $x^2+y^2-x+6y+5=0$ and $x^2+y^2+5x-8y+15=0$. Also, find the equation of the circle cutting them orthogonally.

Sol. Given circles are $S_1 \equiv x^2+y^2+3x+2y+1=0$

$$S_2 \equiv x^2+y^2-x+6y+5=0$$

$$S_3 \equiv x^2+y^2+5x-8y+15=0$$

Equations of two radical axes are

$$S_1 - S_2 \equiv 4x-4y-4=0 \quad \text{or} \quad x-y-1=0$$

and $S_2 - S_3 \equiv -6x+14y-10=0$ or $3x-7y+5=0$

Solving them, we get the radical centre i.e. (3, 2). Also, if r is the length of the tangent drawn from the radical centre (3, 2) to any one of the given circles, say S_1, we have

$$r=\sqrt{S_1}=\sqrt{3^2+2^2+3\cdot 3+2\cdot 2+1}=\sqrt{27}$$

Hence, (3, 2) is the centre and $\sqrt{27}$ is the radius of the circle intersecting them orthogonally.

$\therefore$ Its equation is

$$(x-3)^2+(y-2)^2=r^2=27 \text{ or } x^2+y^2-6x-4y-14=0$$

Alternate Solution

Let $x^2+y^2+2gx+2fy+c=0$ be the equation of the circle cutting the given circles orthogonally.

$$\therefore \quad 2g\left(\frac{3}{2}\right)+2f(1)=c+1$$

or $3g+2f=c+1$ ...(i)

and $2g\left(-\frac{1}{2}\right)+2(3)f=c+5$

or $-g+6f=c+5$ ...(ii)

and $2g\left(\frac{5}{2}\right)+2f(-4)=c+15$

or $5g-8f=c+15$ ...(iii)

On solving, Eqs. (i), (ii) and (iii), we get

$$g=-3, f=-2 \text{ and } c=-14$$

$\therefore$ Equation of required circle is

$$x^2+y^2-6x-4y-14=0$$

Example 97. Find the radical centre of three circles described on the three sides $4x-7y+10=0$, $x+y-5=0$ and $7x+4y-15=0$ of a triangle as diameters.

Sol. Since, the radical centre of three circles described on the sides of a triangle as diameters is the orthocentre of the triangle.

$\therefore$ Radical centre = orthocentre

Given sides are $4x-7y+10=0$ ...(i)

$$x+y-5=0 \quad \text{...(ii)}$$

$$7x+4y-15=0 \quad \text{...(iii)}$$

Since, lines of Eqs. (i) and (iii) are perpendiculars. The point of intersection of Eqs. (i) and (iii) is (1, 2), the orthocentre of the triangle. Hence, radical centre is (1, 2).

Example 98. Prove that if the four points of intersection of the circles $x^2+y^2+ax+by+c=0$ and $x^2+y^2+a'x+b'y+c'=0$ by the lines $Ax+By+C=0$ and $A'x+B'y+C'=0$ respectively are concyclic, then

$$\begin{vmatrix} a-a' & b-b' & c-c' \\ A & B & C \\ A' & B' & C' \end{vmatrix}=0$$

Sol. The given circles and given lines are

$$S_1 \equiv x^2+y^2+ax+by+c=0$$

$$S_2 \equiv x^2+y^2+a'x+b'y+c'=0$$

$$L_1 \equiv Ax+By+C=0$$

$$L_2 \equiv A'x+B'y+C'=0$$

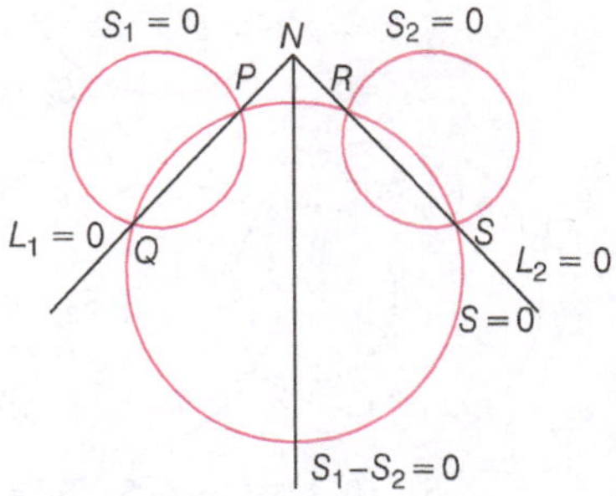

Let $S_1=0$ meet $L_1=0$ at two points P and Q and $S_2=0$ meet $L_2=0$ at two points R and S.

Further P, Q, R and S are given to be concyclic. Let the circle through them is

$$x^2+y^2+2gx+2fy+\lambda=0 \quad \text{...(i)}$$

Radical axis of $S_1=0$ and $S_2=0$ is

$$S_1-S_2=0$$

$$\Rightarrow \quad (a-a')x+(b-b')y+c-c'=0 \quad \text{...(ii)}$$

The radical axis of $S_1=0$ and $S=0$ is

$$L_1=0 \text{ or } Ax+By+C=0 \quad \text{...(iii)}$$

and radical axis of $S_2=0$ and $S=0$ is

$$L_2=0 \text{ or } A'x+B'y+C'=0 \quad \text{...(iv)}$$

Since, the radical axes of any three circles taken in pairs are concurrent. [i.e. lines of Eqs. (ii), (iii) and (iv) are concurrent].

we have $\begin{vmatrix} a-a' & b-b' & c-c' \\ A & B & C \\ A' & B' & C' \end{vmatrix}=0$

4.26 Co-axial System of Circles

A system (or a family) of circles, every pair of which have the same radical axis, are called co-axial circles.

(i) The equation of system of co-axial circles, when the equation of the radical axis and of one circle of the system are

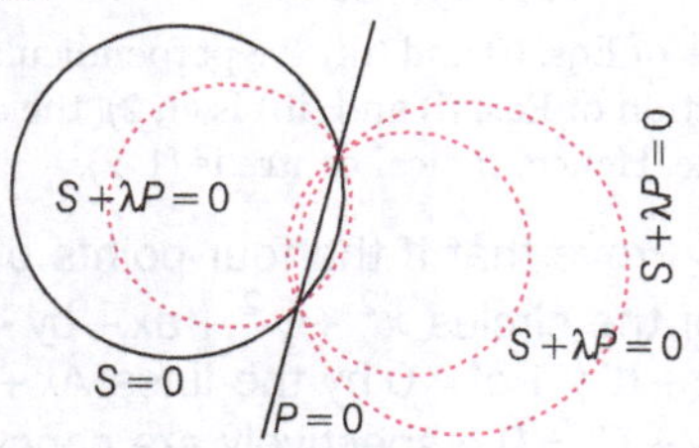

$$P \equiv lx + my + n = 0$$

and $\quad S \equiv x^2 + y^2 + 2gx + 2fy + c = 0$

respectively, is $S + \lambda P = 0$ [λ is an arbitrary constant]

(ii) The equation of co-axial system of circles, where the equation of any two circles of the system are

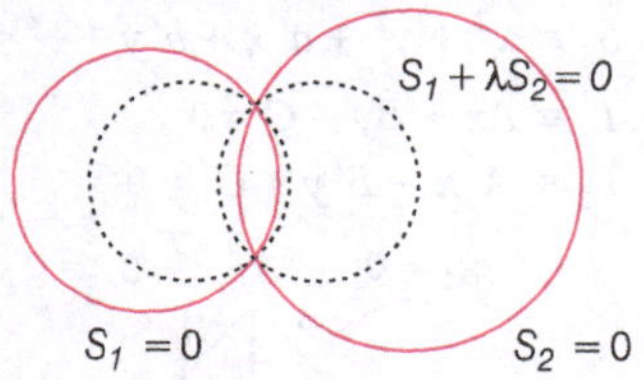

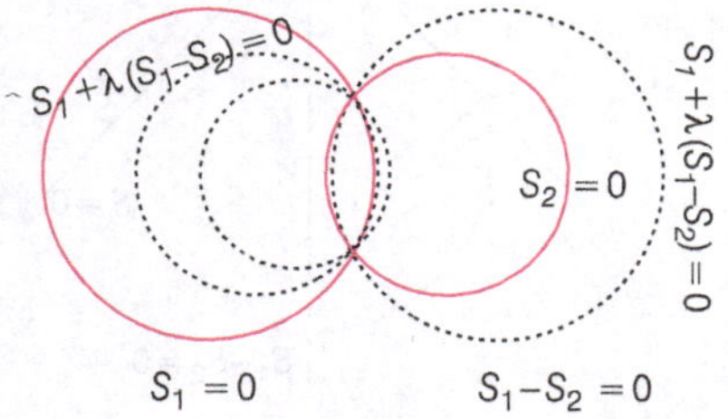

$$S_1 \equiv x^2 + y^2 + 2g_1x + 2f_1y + c_1 = 0$$

and $\quad S_2 \equiv x^2 + y^2 + 2g_2x + 2f_2y + c_2 = 0$

respectively, is $S_1 + \lambda(S_1 - S_2) = 0 \qquad (\lambda \neq -1)$

or $\quad S_2 + \lambda_1(S_1 - S_2) = 0 \qquad (\lambda_1 \neq -1)$

Other form $\quad S_1 + \lambda S_2 = 0 \qquad (\lambda \neq -1)$

(iii) The equation of system of co-axial circles in the simplest form is $x^2 + y^2 + 2gx + c = 0$

where, g is variable and c is a constant.

The common radical axis is the Y-axis

[$\because$ centre on X-axis]

and the equation of system of other co-axial circles in the simplest form is $x^2 + y^2 + 2fy + c = 0$

where, f is variable and c is a constant

The common radical axis is the X-axis.

[$\because$ centre on Y-axis]

Example 99. Find the equation of the system of circles co-axial with the circles $x^2 + y^2 + 4x + 2y + 1 = 0$ and $x^2 + y^2 - 2x + 6y - 6 = 0$. Also, find the equation of that particular circle whose centre lies on the radical axis.

Sol. Given circles are

$$S_1 \equiv x^2 + y^2 + 4x + 2y + 1 = 0$$

and $\quad S_2 \equiv x^2 + y^2 - 2x + 6y - 6 = 0$

$\therefore$ Radical axis is $\quad S_1 - S_2 = 0$

i.e. $\quad 6x - 4y + 7 = 0 \qquad$ ...(i)

Now, system of co-axial circle is $S_1 + \lambda(S_1 - S_2) = 0$

$\Rightarrow \quad (x^2 + y^2 + 4x + 2y + 1) + \lambda(6x - 4y + 7) = 0$

$\Rightarrow \quad x^2 + y^2 + 2x(2 + 3\lambda) + 2y(1 - 2\lambda) + 1 + 7\lambda = 0 \qquad$ ...(ii)

Its centre $[-(2 + 3\lambda), -(1 - 2\lambda)]$ lies on Eq. (i).

$\therefore \quad 6 \times (-(2 + 3\lambda)) - 4 \times (-(1 - 2\lambda)) + 7 = 0$

or $\quad -12 - 18\lambda + 4 - 8\lambda + 7 = 0$

or $\quad -26\lambda - 1 = 0$

$\therefore \quad \lambda = -\dfrac{1}{26}$

On substituting the value of λ in Eq. (ii), the equation of circle is

$$x^2 + y^2 + 2x\left(2 - \frac{3}{26}\right) + 2y\left(1 + \frac{2}{26}\right) + 1 - \frac{7}{26} = 0$$

$\Rightarrow \quad 26(x^2 + y^2) + 98x + 56y + 19 = 0$

Example 100. Prove that the tangents from any point of a fixed circle of co-axial system to two other fixed circles of the system are in a constant ratio.

Sol. Let the equations of the circles be

$$x^2 + y^2 + 2g_ix + c = 0, i = 1, 2, 3.$$

Since, all the three circles are fixed

$\Rightarrow g_1, g_2$ and g_3 are constants.

Let $P(h, k)$ be any point on the first circle, so that

$$h^2 + k^2 + 2g_1h + c = 0 \qquad \text{...(i)}$$

Let PQ and PR be the tangents from P on the other two circles

$\therefore \quad PQ = \sqrt{(h^2 + k^2 + 2g_2h + c)}$

and $\quad PR = \sqrt{(h^2 + k^2 + 2g_3h + c)}$

$$\therefore \quad \frac{(PQ)^2}{(PR)^2} = \frac{h^2 + k^2 + 2g_2h + c}{h^2 + k^2 + 2g_3h + c}$$

$$= \frac{-2g_1h + 2g_2h}{-2g_1h + 2g_3h} \qquad \text{[from Eq. (i)]}$$

$$= \frac{g_2 - g_1}{g_3 - g_1}$$

$= \text{constant}$

because g_1, g_2 and g_3 are constants.

Example 101. Let A, B and C be the centres of three co-axial circles and t_1, t_2, t_3 be the length of tangents to them from any point, prove that

$$\overline{BC} \cdot t_1^2 + \overline{CA} \cdot t_2^2 + \overline{AB}\ t_3^2 = 0$$

Sol. Let the equation of three circles be

$$x^2 + y^2 + 2g_i x + c = 0, i = 1, 2, 3, .$$

According to the question,

$$A \equiv (-g_1, 0), B \equiv (-g_2, 0), C \equiv (-g_3, 0)$$

Let any point be $P(h, k)$

$$\therefore \quad t_1 = \sqrt{h^2 + k^2 + 2g_1 h + c}$$

$$t_2 = \sqrt{h^2 + k^2 + 2g_2 h + c}$$

$$t_3 = \sqrt{h^2 + k^2 + 2g_3 h + c}$$

and $\overline{AB} = (g_1 - g_2)$

$$\overline{BC} = (g_2 - g_3)$$

and $\overline{CA} = (g_3 - g_1)$

Now, $\overline{BC} \cdot t_1^2 + \overline{CA} \cdot t_2^2 + \overline{AB} \cdot t_3^2$

$$= (g_2 - g_3)(h^2 + k^2 + 2g_1 h + c) + (g_3 - g_1)(h^2 + k^2 + 2g_2 h + c) + (g_1 - g_2)(h^2 + k^2 + 2g_3 h + c)$$

$$= (h^2 + k^2 + c)(g_2 - g_3 + g_3 - g_1 + g_1 - g_2) + 2h\{g_1(g_2 - g_3) + g_2(g_3 - g_1) + g_3(g_1 - g_2)\}$$

$$= (h^2 + k^2 + c)(0) + 2h(0) = 0$$

4.27 Limiting Point

Limiting points of system of co-axial circles are the centres of the point circles belonging to the family (circles whose radii are zero are called **point circles**).

1. Limiting points of the co-axial system

Let the circle be

$$x^2 + y^2 + 2gx + c = 0 \quad \text{...(i)}$$

where, g is variable and c is constant.

$\therefore$ Centre and the radius of Eq. (i) are $(-g, 0)$ and $\sqrt{(g^2 - c)}$, respectively.

Let $\sqrt{g^2 - c} = 0$

$$\therefore \quad g = \pm\sqrt{c}$$

Thus, we get the two limiting points of the given co-axial system as $(\sqrt{c}, 0)$ and $(-\sqrt{c}, 0)$.

Clearly, the above limiting points are real and distinct, real and coincident and imaginary accordingly as $c > 0, c = 0$ and $c < 0$ respectively.

2. System of co-axial circles whose two limiting points are given

Let (α, β) and (γ, δ) be the two given limiting points. Then, the corresponding point circles with zero radii are

$$(x - \alpha)^2 + (y - \beta)^2 = 0$$

and $$(x - \gamma)^2 + (y - \delta)^2 = 0$$

or $$x^2 + y^2 - 2\alpha x - 2\beta y + \alpha^2 + \beta^2 = 0$$

and $$x^2 + y^2 - 2\gamma x - 2\delta y + \gamma^2 + \delta^2 = 0$$

The equation of co-axial system is

$$(x^2 + y^2 - 2\alpha x - 2\beta y + \alpha^2 + \beta^2) + \lambda(x^2 + y^2 - 2\gamma x - 2\delta y + \gamma^2 + \delta^2) = 0,$$

where $\lambda \neq -1$ is a variable parameter.

$$\Rightarrow x^2(1 + \lambda) + y^2(1 + \lambda) - 2x(\alpha + \gamma\lambda) - 2y(\beta + \delta\lambda) + (\alpha^2 + \beta^2) + \lambda(\gamma^2 + \delta^2) = 0$$

$$\Rightarrow x^2 + y^2 - \frac{2(\alpha + \gamma\lambda)}{(1 + \lambda)}x - 2\frac{(\beta + \delta\lambda)}{(1 + \lambda)}y + \frac{(\alpha^2 + \beta^2) + \lambda(\gamma^2 + \delta^2)}{(1 + \lambda)} = 0$$

Centre of this circle is $\left(\frac{(\alpha + \gamma\lambda)}{(1 + \lambda)}, \frac{(\beta + \delta\lambda)}{(1 + \lambda)}\right)$ ...(i)

For limiting point,

Radius

$$= \sqrt{\frac{(\alpha + \gamma\lambda)^2}{(1 + \lambda)^2} + \frac{(\beta + \delta\lambda)^2}{(1 + \lambda)^2} - \frac{(\alpha^2 + \beta^2) + \lambda(\gamma^2 + \delta^2)}{(1 + \lambda)}} = 0$$

After solving, find λ. Substitute value of λ in Eq. (i), we get the limiting point of co-axial system.

Example 102. Find the coordinates of the limiting points of the system of circles determined by the two circles $x^2 + y^2 + 5x + y + 4 = 0$ and $x^2 + y^2 + 10x - 4y - 1 = 0$.

Sol. The given circles are

$$S_1 \equiv x^2 + y^2 + 5x + y + 4 = 0$$

and $$S_2 \equiv x^2 + y^2 + 10x - 4y - 1 = 0$$

$\therefore$ Equation of the co-axial system of circles is

$$S_1 + \lambda S_2 = 0$$

$$\Rightarrow (x^2 + y^2 + 5x + y + 4) + \lambda(x^2 + y^2 + 10x - 4y - 1) = 0$$

$$\Rightarrow x^2(1 + \lambda) + y^2(1 + \lambda) + 5x(1 + 2\lambda) + y(1 - 4\lambda) + (4 - \lambda) = 0$$

or $$x^2 + y^2 + \frac{5(1 + 2\lambda)}{(1 + \lambda)}x + \frac{(1 - 4\lambda)}{(1 + \lambda)}y + \frac{(4 - \lambda)}{(1 + \lambda)} = 0$$

The centre of this circles is

$$\left(\frac{-5(1+2\lambda)}{2(1+\lambda)}, \frac{(1-4\lambda)}{2(1+\lambda)}\right) \quad \text{...(i)}$$

$$\text{Radius} = \sqrt{\frac{25(1+2\lambda)^2}{4(1+\lambda)^2} + \frac{(1-4\lambda)^2}{4(1+\lambda)^2} - \frac{(4-\lambda)}{(1+\lambda)}} = 0$$

$$\Rightarrow \quad 25(1+2\lambda)^2 + (1-4\lambda)^2 - 4(4-\lambda)(1+\lambda) = 0$$

$$\Rightarrow \quad 25(4\lambda^2 + 4\lambda + 1) + (16\lambda^2 - 8\lambda + 1) - 4(-\lambda^2 + 3\lambda + 4) = 0$$

$$\Rightarrow \quad 120\lambda^2 + 80\lambda + 10 = 0 \text{ or } 12\lambda^2 + 8\lambda + 1 = 0$$

$$\Rightarrow \quad (6\lambda + 1)(2\lambda + 1) = 0$$

i.e. $\lambda = -\frac{1}{6}$ and $-\frac{1}{2}$

On substituting these values of λ in Eq. (i), we get the points $(-2, -1)$ and $(0, -3)$, which are the required limiting points.

Example 103. Let the origin be one limiting point of a system of co-axial circles of which $x^2 + y^2 + 3x + 4y + 25 = 0$ is a member, find the other limiting point.

Sol. Equation of circle with origin as limiting point is

$$(x-0)^2 + (y-0)^2 = 0 \text{ or } x^2 + y^2 = 0$$

belongs to the system of co-axial circles of which one member is $x^2 + y^2 + 3x + 4y + 25 = 0$.

Hence, the equation of the whole system is

$$(x^2 + y^2 + 3x + 4y + 25) + \lambda(x^2 + y^2) = 0$$

$$\Rightarrow \quad x^2(1+\lambda) + y^2(1+\lambda) + 3x + 4y + 25 = 0$$

$$\Rightarrow \quad x^2 + y^2 + \frac{3}{(1+\lambda)}x + \frac{4}{(1+\lambda)}y + \frac{25}{(1+\lambda)} = 0 \quad \text{...(i)}$$

$$\therefore \quad \text{Its centre} = \left(-\frac{3}{2(1+\lambda)}, -\frac{2}{(1+\lambda)}\right) \quad \text{...(ii)}$$

Radius of Eq. (i) can be zero for limiting point, then

$$\frac{9}{4(1+\lambda)^2} + \frac{4}{(1+\lambda)^2} - \frac{25}{(1+\lambda)} = 0$$

$$9 + 16 - 100(1+\lambda) = 0$$

$$\Rightarrow \quad 1 + \lambda = \frac{1}{4} \text{ or } \lambda = -\frac{3}{4}$$

From Eq. (ii), $\left(\frac{-3}{2(1-3/4)}, \frac{-2}{(1-3/4)}\right)$ or $(-6, -8)$ is the other limiting point of the system.

Example 104. Prove that the limiting points of the system $x^2 + y^2 + 2gx + c + \lambda(x^2 + y^2 + 2fx + k) = 0$ subtend a right angle at the origin, if $\frac{c}{g^2} + \frac{k}{f^2} = 2$.

Sol. The given circle is

$$x^2 + y^2 + 2gx + c + \lambda(x^2 + y^2 + 2fy + k) = 0$$

$$\Rightarrow \quad (1+\lambda)x^2 + (1+\lambda)y^2 + 2gx + 2fy\lambda + c + k\lambda = 0$$

$$\text{or} \quad x^2 + y^2 + \frac{2g}{(1+\lambda)}x + \frac{2f\lambda}{(1+\lambda)}y + \frac{c+k\lambda}{(1+\lambda)} = 0 \quad \text{...(i)}$$

$$\text{Its centre is} \left(\frac{-g}{1+\lambda}, \frac{-f\lambda}{1+\lambda}\right) \quad \text{...(ii)}$$

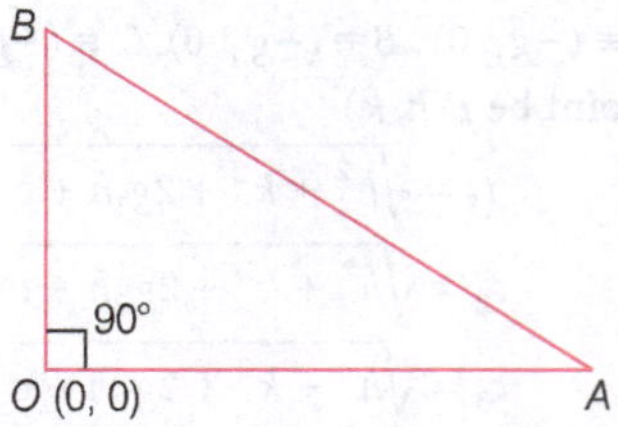

Radius of circle Eq. (i) is 0

$$\Rightarrow \quad \sqrt{\frac{g^2}{(1+\lambda)^2} + \frac{f^2\lambda^2}{(1+\lambda)^2} - \frac{(c+k\lambda)}{(1+\lambda)}} = 0$$

$$\Rightarrow \quad \lambda^2(f^2 - k) - \lambda(k + c) + g^2 - c = 0$$

which is a quadratic in λ. Let roots be λ_1 and λ_2.

$$\therefore \quad \lambda_1 + \lambda_2 = \frac{k+c}{f^2-k} \text{ and } \lambda_1\lambda_2 = \frac{g^2-c}{f^2-k} \quad \text{...(iii)}$$

Then, limiting points are

$$A\left(\frac{-g}{1+\lambda_1}, \frac{-f\lambda_1}{1+\lambda_1}\right) \text{ and } B\left(\frac{-g}{1+\lambda_2}, \frac{-f\lambda_2}{1+\lambda_2}\right) \quad \text{[from Eq. (ii)]}$$

But given that AB subtend a right angle at the origin.

$\therefore$ Slope of OA × Slope of $OB = -1$

$$\Rightarrow \quad \left(\frac{\frac{-f\lambda_1}{1+\lambda_1}}{\frac{-g}{1+\lambda_1}}\right) \times \left(\frac{\frac{-f\lambda_2}{1+\lambda_2}}{\frac{-g}{1+\lambda_2}}\right) = -1 \text{ or } \frac{f\lambda_1}{g} \times \frac{f\lambda_2}{g} = -1$$

$$\Rightarrow \quad f^2\lambda_1\lambda_2 + g^2 = 0$$

$$\Rightarrow \quad 2g^2f^2 - cf^2 - kg^2 = 0 \text{ or } 2 = \frac{c}{g^2} + \frac{k}{f^2} \quad \text{[from Eq. (iii)]}$$

Example 105. Find the radical axis of co-axial system of circles whose limiting points are (–1,2) and (2, 3).

Sol. Equations of circles with limiting points $(-1, 2)$ and $(2,3)$ are

$$(x+1)^2 + (y-2)^2 = 0$$

$$\text{or} \quad x^2 + y^2 + 2x - 4y + 5 = 0 \quad \text{...(i)}$$

$$\text{and} \quad (x-2)^2 + (y-3)^2 = 0$$

$$\text{or} \quad x^2 + y^2 - 4x - 6y + 13 = 0 \quad \text{...(ii)}$$

$\therefore$ Radical axis of circles of Eqs. (i) and (ii) is

$$(x^2 + y^2 + 2x - 4y + 5) - (x^2 + y^2 - 4x - 6y + 13) = 0$$

$$\Rightarrow \quad 6x + 2y - 8 = 0$$

$$\Rightarrow \quad 3x + y - 4 = 0$$

Example 106. Find the equation of the circle which passes through the origin and belongs to the co-axial of circles whose limiting points are (1,2) and (4,3).

Sol. Equations of circles whose limiting points are (1,2) and (4,3) are

$$(x-1)^2+(y-2)^2=0$$

$$\Rightarrow \quad x^2+y^2-2x-4y+5=0 \quad \ldots(i)$$

and

$$(x-4)^2+(y-3)^2=0$$

$$\Rightarrow \quad x^2+y^2-8x-6y+25=0 \quad \ldots(ii)$$

Therefore, the corresponding system of co-axial circles is

$$(x^2+y^2-2x-4y+5)+\lambda(x^2+y^2-8x-6y+25)=0 \quad \ldots(iii)$$

It passes through origin, then

$$5+25\lambda=0$$

$$\therefore \quad \lambda=-\frac{1}{5}$$

On substituting the value of λ in Eq. (iii), we get the required circle as

$$5(x^2+y^2-2x-4y+5)-(x^2+y^2-8x-6y+25)=0$$

$$\Rightarrow \quad 4x^2+4y^2-2x-14y=0$$

$$\Rightarrow \quad 2x^2+2y^2-x-7y=0$$

4.28 Image of the Circle by the Line Mirror

Let the circle be $x^2+y^2+2gx+2fy+c=0$ and line mirror is $lx+my+n=0$. In this condition, radius of circle remains unchanged but centres changes. Let the centre of imaged circle be (x_1, y_1).

Then, $$\frac{x_1-(-g)}{l}=\frac{y_1-(-f)}{m}=\frac{-2(-lg-mf+n)}{(l^2+m^2)}$$

we get, $$x_1=\frac{(l^2g-m^2g+2mlf-2nl)}{(l^2+m^2)}$$

and $$y_1=\frac{(m^2f-l^2f+2mlg-2mn)}{(l^2+m^2)}$$

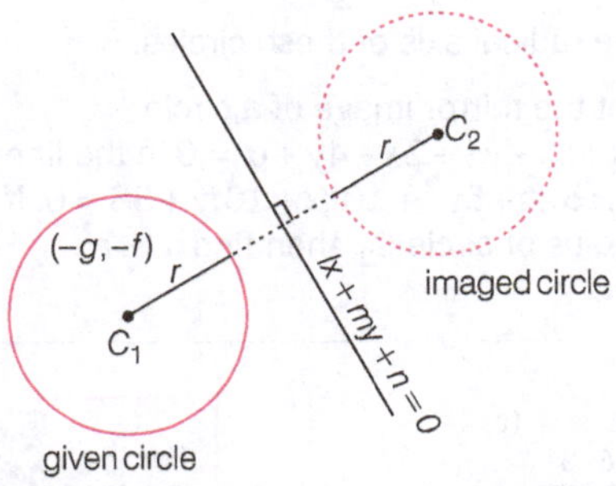

$\therefore$ Required equation of the imaged circle is

$$(x-x_1)^2+(y-y_1)^2=r^2, \text{ where } r=\sqrt{(g^2+f^2-c)}$$

JEE SCANNER

Example Similar to PYQ Asked in JEE Main 2023

Let the mirror image of a circle $C_1: x^2+y^2-2x-6y+\alpha=0$ in the line $y=x+1$ be $C_2: 5x^2+5y^2+10gx+10fy+38=0$. If r is the radius of the circle C_2, then $\alpha+6r^2$ is equal to ....

Sol. (12) We have, $C_1: x^2+y^2-2x-6y+\alpha=0$

$$C_2: x^2+y^2+2gx+2fy+\frac{38}{5}=0$$

$$L: x-y+1=0$$

Centre of circle C_1 is (1, 3) and C_2 is $(-g, -f)$.

So, $(-g, -f)$ is the image of the point (1, 3) w.r.t. the line L.

Then, $$\frac{-g-1}{1}=\frac{-f-3}{-1}=\frac{-2(1-3+1)}{1^2+(-1)^2} \Rightarrow g=f=-2$$

$\therefore$ Centre of C_2 is (2, 2)

and radius, $r=\sqrt{4+4-\frac{38}{5}}=\sqrt{\frac{2}{5}}$

Now, radius of C_1 and C_2 will be same

$$\therefore \quad \sqrt{1+9-\alpha}=\sqrt{\frac{2}{5}} \Rightarrow 10-\alpha=\frac{2}{5} \Rightarrow \alpha=\frac{48}{5}$$

$$\therefore \quad \alpha+6r^2=\frac{48}{5}+6\times\frac{2}{5}=12$$

Skill Builder

Let the mirror image of a circle. $C_1: x^2+y^2-4x-8y+\beta=0$ in the line $y=x+1$ be $C_2: 5x^2+5y^2+10gx+10fy+38=0$. If r is the radius of circle C_2, then the value of $\beta+r^2$ is ....

For Sol.

■ **For more practice** See Q.15 of Milestone Practice 4.6.

Example 107. Find the equation of the image of the circle $x^2+y^2+16x-24y+183=0$ by the line mirror $4x+7y+13=0$.

Sol. The given circle and line are

$$x^2+y^2+16x-24y+183=0 \quad \ldots(i)$$

and

$$4x+7y+13=0 \quad \ldots(ii)$$

Centre and radius of circle of Eq. (i) are (−8,12) and 5, respectively. Let the centre of the imaged circle be (x_1, y_1). Hence, (x_1, y_1) is the image of the point (−8, 12) with respect to the line $4x+7y+13=0$, then

$$\frac{x_1-(-8)}{4}=\frac{y_1-12}{7}=\frac{-2(4(-8)+7(12)+13)}{(4^2+7^2)}$$

$$\Rightarrow \quad \frac{x_1+8}{4}=\frac{y_1-12}{7}=-2$$

$\therefore$ $x_1=-16, y_1=-2$

$\therefore$ Equation of the imaged circle is $(x+16)^2+(y+2)^2=5^2$

or $$x^2+y^2+32x+4y+235=0$$

Milestone Practice 4.6

1. The circles $x^2+y^2+x+y=0$ and $x^2+y^2+x-y=0$ intersect at an angle of
   (a) $\pi/6$ (b) $\pi/4$ (c) $\pi/3$ (d) $\pi/2$

2. If the circles of same radius r and centres at (2, 3) and (5, 6) cut orthogonally, then r equals to
   (a) 1 (b) 2 (c) 3 (d) 4

3. If the circles $x^2+y^2+2x+2ky+6=0$ and $x^2+y^2+2ky+k=0$ intersect orthogonally, k is
   (a) 2 or $-\dfrac{3}{2}$ (b) -2 or $-\dfrac{3}{2}$
   (c) 2 or $\dfrac{3}{2}$ (d) -2 or $\dfrac{3}{2}$

4. If a circle passes through the point (a, b) and cuts the circle $x^2+y^2=4$ orthogonally, then the locus of its centre is
   (a) $2ax+2by+(a^2+b^2+4)=0$
   (b) $2ax+2by-(a^2+b^2+4)=0$
   (c) $2ax-2by+(a^2+b^2+4)=0$
   (d) $2ax-2by-(a^2+b^2+4)=0$

5. The locus of the centre of the circle which cuts the circle $x^2+y^2-20x+4=0$ orthogonally and which touches $x=2$ is
   (a) $x^2=16y$ (b) $x^2=16y+4$
   (c) $y^2=16x$ (d) $y^2=16x+4$

6. The equation of a circle which cuts the three circles $x^2+y^2-3x-6y+14=0$, $x^2+y^2-x-4y+8=0$ and $x^2+y^2+2x-6y+9=0$ orthogonally is
   (a) $x^2+y^2-2x-4y+1=0$
   (b) $x^2+y^2+2x+4y+1=0$
   (c) $x^2+y^2-2x+4y+1=0$
   (d) $x^2+y^2-2x-4y-1=0$

7. The equation of radical axis of the circles $x^2+y^2+x-y+2=0$ and $3x^2+3y^2-4x-12=0$ is
   (a) $2x^2+2y^2-5x+y-14=0$
   (b) $7x-3y+18=0$
   (c) $5x-y+14=0$
   (d) None of the above

8. The radical centre of the circles $x^2+y^2=1$, $x^2+y^2+10y+24=0$ and $x^2+y^2-8x+15=0$ is
   (a) $(2, 5/2)$ (b) $(-2, 5/2)$
   (c) $(-2, -5/2)$ (d) $(2, -5/2)$

9. If (1,2) is a limiting point of the co-axial system of circles containing the circle $x^2+y^2+x-5y+9=0$, then the equation of the radical axis is
   (a) $x-9y+4=0$ (b) $3x-y+4=0$
   (c) $x+3y-4=0$ (d) $9x+y-4=0$

10. The limiting points of the system of circles represented by the equation $2(x^2+y^2)+\lambda x+\dfrac{9}{2}=0$ are
    (a) $\left(\pm\dfrac{3}{2}, 0\right)$ (b) (0,0) and $\left(\dfrac{9}{2}, 0\right)$
    (c) $\left(\pm\dfrac{9}{2}, 0\right)$ (d) $(\pm 3, 0)$

11. One of the limiting points of the co-axial system of circles containing the circles $x^2+y^2-4=0$ and $x^2+y^2-x-y=0$ is
    (a) $(\sqrt{2}, \sqrt{2})$ (b) $(-\sqrt{2}, \sqrt{2})$
    (c) $(-\sqrt{2}, -\sqrt{2})$ (d) None of these

12. Find the equation of the circle which cuts orthogonally the circle $x^2+y^2-6x+4y-3=0$, passes through (3,0) and touches the axis of Y.

13. Find the coordinates of the point from which the lengths of the tangents to the following three circles be equal
    $3x^2+3y^2+4x-6y-1=0$,
    $2x^2+2y^2-3x-2y-4=0$ and
    $2x^2+2y^2-x+y-1=0$

14. Find the equation of a circle which is co-axial with the circles $x^2+y^2+4x+2y+1=0$ and $x^2+y^2-x+3y-\dfrac{3}{2}=0$ and having its centre on the radical axis of these circles.

15. Let the mirror image of a circle $C_1: x^2+y^2-2x-4y+\alpha=0$ in the line $y=x+1$ be $C_2: 5x^2+5y^2+10gx+10fy+38=0$. If r is the radius of circle C_2, then find $\alpha+r^2$.

Answer Key

1. (d) 2. (c) 3. (a) 4. (b) 5. (c) 6. (a) 7. (b) 8. (c)
9. (b) 10. (a) 11. (d) 12. $x^2+y^2-6x-6y+9=0$ 13. $\left(-\dfrac{16}{21}, \dfrac{31}{63}\right)$
14. $4x^2+4y^2+6x+5y-1=0$ 15. (5)

For Detailed Solution

JEE Pattern EXAMPLES

Single Option Correct Type Questions

Example 1 ■ *One of the diameters of the circle circumscribing the rectangle ABCD is $4y = x + 7$. If A and B are the points $(-3, 4)$ and $(5, 4)$ respectively, then the area of the rectangle is*

(a) 6 (b) 12 (c) 16 (d) 32

Sol. (d) First we note that none of the points $A(-3, 4)$ and $B(5, 4)$ lie on the diameter $4y = x + 7$.

Let $E(\alpha, \beta)$ be the centre of the circle.

Then, $4\beta = \alpha + 7$ ...(i)

Since, $ABCD$ is a rectangle.

$\therefore \quad |EA| = |EB|$

$\Rightarrow \quad EA^2 = EB^2$

$\Rightarrow \quad (\alpha + 3)^2 + (\beta - 4)^2 = (\alpha - 5)^2 + (\beta - 4)^2$

$\Rightarrow \quad 6\alpha + 9 = -10\alpha + 25$

$\Rightarrow \quad \alpha = 1$

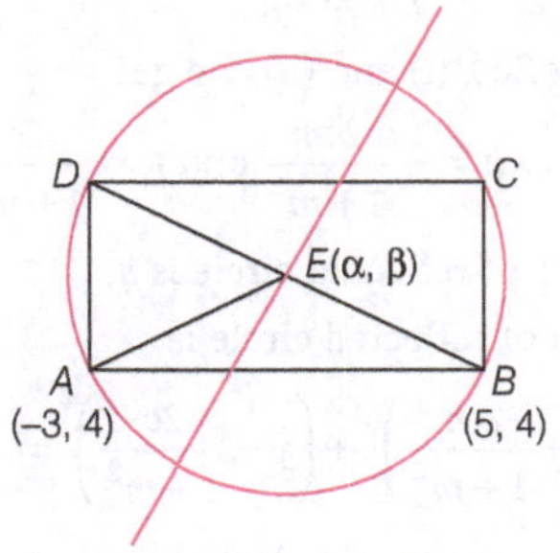

From Eq. (i), $\beta = 2$

Now, $\quad |AB| = \sqrt{(5+3)^2 + (4-4)^2} = 8$

and $\quad |BD| = 2|EB|$

$$= 2\sqrt{(5-1)^2 + (4-2)^2} = 4\sqrt{5}$$

From right angled ΔADB,

$$AD^2 = BD^2 - AB^2 = 80 - 64 = 16 \Rightarrow |AD| = 4$$

$\therefore$ Area of the rectangle $ABCD$

$$= |AB| \cdot |AD| = 8 \cdot 4 = 32 \text{ sq units}$$

JEE SCANNER

Example 2 Similar to PYQ Asked in JEE Main 2024

If $P(8, 3)$ be the orthocentre of the triangle whose vertices are $A(7, -4)$, $B(10, 5)$ and $C(h, k)$, then the point C lies on the circle

(a) $x^2 + y^2 - 52 = 0$ (b) $x^2 + y^2 - 61 = 0$

(c) $x^2 + y^2 - 65 = 0$ (d) $x^2 + y^2 - 74 = 0$

Sol. (c) Orthocentre is the intersection of altitutes.

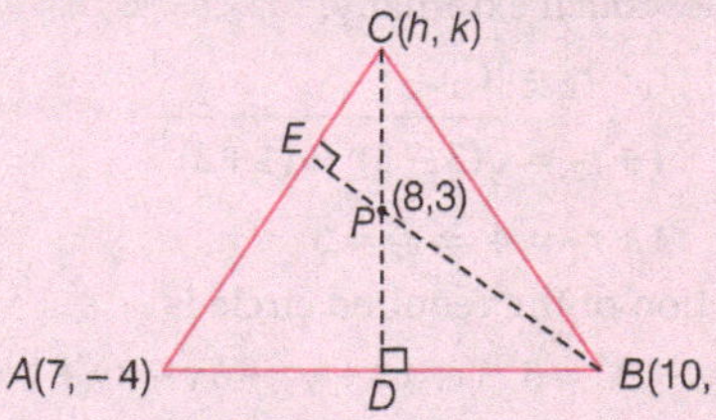

So, slope of $BP \times$ slope of $AC = -1$

$\Rightarrow \quad \left(\frac{5-3}{10-8}\right) \times \left(\frac{k+4}{h-7}\right) = -1$

$\Rightarrow \quad k + 4 = -h + 7 \Rightarrow h + k = 3$ ...(i)

and slope of $CP \times$ slope of $AB = -1$

$\left(\frac{k-3}{h-8}\right) \times \left(\frac{5+4}{10-7}\right) = -1$

$\Rightarrow \quad 3k - 9 = -h + 8 \Rightarrow h + 3k = 17$ ...(ii)

On solving Eqs. (i) and (ii), we get

$$h = -4, k = 7$$

On checking option (c) is correct.

$\therefore \quad x^2 + y^2 - 65 = 0$

Skill Builider

If $P(7, 2)$ be the orthocentre of the triangle whose vertices are $A(6, -1)$, $B(9, 4)$ and $C(h, k)$, then the point C lies on the circle

(a) $x^2 + y^2 - 52 = 0$

(b) $x^2 + y^2 - 61 = 0$

(c) $x^2 + y^2 - 65 = 0$

(d) $x^2 + y^2 - 73 = 0$

For Sol.

Example 3 *Find the equation of the circle which touches the circle $x^2+y^2-6x+6y+17=0$ externally and to which the line $x^2-3xy-3x+9y=0$ are normals.*

(a) $x^2+y^2+6x-2y+1=0$

(b) $x^2+y^2-6x-2y+1=0$

(c) $x^2+y^2-6x-2y-1=0$

(d) None of the above

> **Decoding the Question**
> Normal to a circle always passes through the centre of the circle.

Sol. (b) The centre of the given circle is $C_1(3,-3)$

and its radius $=\sqrt{9+9-17}=1$

The given lines are $x^2-3xy-3x+9y=0$

i.e. $(x-3y)(x-3)=0$

i.e. $x-3y=0$ and $x-3=0$

These lines intersect at the point C_2 (3, 1).

Since, the given lines are normals to the required circle, therefore the point C_2 (3, 1) is the centre of the required circle.

Let r_1 and r_2 be the radii of the two circles.

As the circles touch externally,

$$r_1+r_2=|C_1C_2|$$

$$\Rightarrow \quad 1+r_2=\sqrt{(3-3)^2+(1+3)^2}$$

$$\Rightarrow \quad 1+r_2=4 \Rightarrow r_2=3$$

$\therefore$ The equation of the required circle is

$(x-3)^2+(y-1)^2=3^2$ i.e. $x^2+y^2-6x-2y+1=0$.

Example 4 *The angle between a pair of tangents drawn from a point P to the circle $x^2+y^2+4x-6y+9\sin^2\alpha+13\cos^2\alpha=0$ is 2α. The equation of the locus of point P is*

(a) $x^2+y^2+4x-6y+4=0$

(b) $x^2+y^2+4x-6y-9=0$

(c) $x^2+y^2+4x-6y-4=0$

(d) $x^2+y^2+4x-6y+9=0$

Sol. (d) Let PA and PB be the tangents from the point $P(x_1,y_1)$ to the circle

$$x^2+y^2+4x-6y+9\sin^2 a+13\cos^2 a=0$$

Given, $\angle APB=2\alpha$

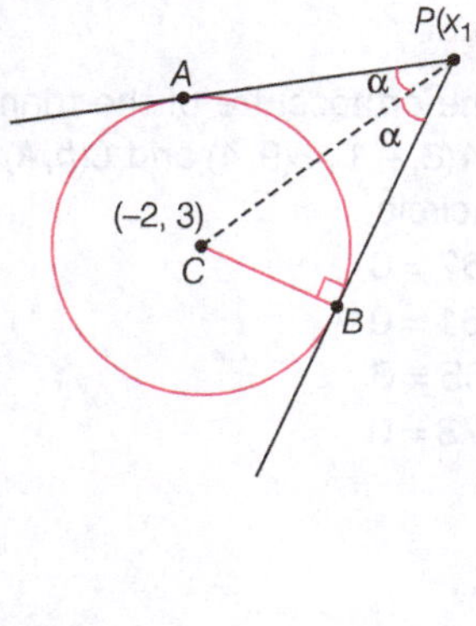

$\therefore$ $\angle CPA=\angle CPB=\alpha$, where C is the centre of the given circle.

Coordinates of centre C of the circle are $(-2,3)$.

$$\therefore \quad \sin\alpha=\frac{CB}{CP}=\frac{\sqrt{4+9-[(9\sin^2\alpha+13\cos^2\alpha)]}}{\sqrt{(x_1+2)^2+(y_1-3)^2}}$$

$$\sin\alpha=\frac{2\sin\alpha}{\sqrt{[(x_1+2)^2+(y_1-3)^2]}}$$

$$\text{or} \quad (x_1+2)^2+(y_1-3)^2=4$$

$$\text{or} \quad x_1^2+y_1^2+4x_1-6y_1+9=0$$

$\therefore$ Locus of the point $P(x_1,y_1)$ is $x^2+y^2+4x-6y+9=0$.

Example 5 *If the equation of circle obtained by reflecting the circle $x^2+y^2-a^2=0$ in the line $y=mx+c$ is $x^2+y^2+2gx+2fy+c=0$, then*

(a) $g=\frac{2cm}{1+m^2}, a^2+c=\frac{4c^2}{1+m^2}$

(b) $g=-\frac{2cm}{1+m^2}, a^2+c=\frac{4c}{1+m^2}$

(c) $f=\frac{4c}{1+m^2}, a^2+c=\frac{4c^2}{1+m^2}$

(d) None of the above

Sol. (a) Centre of the circle $x^2+y^2=a^2$ is (0, 0).

Let its reflection about the line $y=mx+c$ be (h,k).

$$\text{Then, } \left(\frac{h}{2},\frac{k}{2}\right) \text{ lies on this line } m\frac{h}{2}+c=\frac{k}{2} \quad \text{...(i)}$$

$$\text{and} \quad \frac{k}{h}\times m=-1$$

$$\Rightarrow \quad mk=-h \quad \text{...(ii)}$$

On solving Eqs. (i) and (ii), we get

$$h=-\frac{2cm}{1+m^2} \text{ and } k=\frac{2c}{1+m^2}$$

Also, radius of reflected circle is a.

$\therefore$ Equation of reflected circle is

$$\left(x+\frac{2cm}{1+m^2}\right)^2+\left(y-\frac{2c}{1+m^2}\right)^2=a^2$$

But given equation of reflected circle is

$$x^2+y^2+2gx+2fy+c=0$$

On comparing, we get

$$\frac{g}{\frac{2cm}{1+m^2}}=\frac{f}{\frac{-2c}{1+m^2}}=\frac{c}{\left(\frac{4c^2}{1+m^2}-a^2\right)}=1$$

$$\therefore \quad g=\frac{2cm}{1+m^2}, f=-\frac{2c}{1+m^2}, \frac{4c^2}{1+m^2}-a^2=c$$

Example 6 *Two distinct chords drawn from the point (p, q) on the circle $x^2 + y^2 = px + qy$, where $pq \neq 0$, are bisected by the X-axis. Then,*

(a) $|p| = |q|$ (b) $p^2 = 8q^2$ (c) $p^2 < 8q^2$ (d) $p^2 > 8q^2$

Sol. (d)

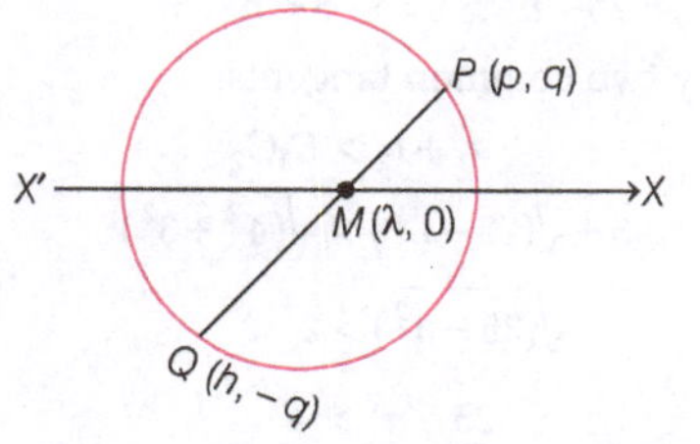

Suppose chord bisect at $M(\lambda, 0)$, then other end point of chord is $Q(h, -q)$

$\therefore \quad \lambda = \dfrac{p+h}{2}$

Point Q lies on $x^2 + y^2 = px + qy$

$\Rightarrow \quad h^2 + q^2 = ph - q^2$

$\Rightarrow \quad h^2 - ph + 2q^2 = 0$

For two distinct chords, $B^2 - 4AC > 0$

or $\quad p^2 - 4 \cdot 1 \cdot 2q^2 > 0$

or $\quad p^2 > 8q^2$

Example 7 *The values of λ for which the circle $x^2 + y^2 + 6x + 5 + \lambda(x^2 + y^2 - 8x + 7) = 0$ dwindles into a point are*

(a) $1 \pm \dfrac{\sqrt{2}}{3}$ (b) $2 \pm \dfrac{2\sqrt{2}}{3}$ (c) $2 \pm \dfrac{4\sqrt{2}}{3}$ (d) $1 \pm \dfrac{4\sqrt{2}}{3}$

Sol. (c) The given circle is

$$x^2 + y^2 + 6x + 5 + \lambda(x^2 + y^2 - 8x + 7) = 0$$

or $\quad x^2(1+\lambda) + y^2(1+\lambda) + (6 - 8\lambda)x + (5 + 7\lambda) = 0$

$\Rightarrow \quad x^2 + y^2 + \left(\dfrac{6-8\lambda}{1+\lambda}\right)x + \left(\dfrac{5+7\lambda}{1+\lambda}\right) = 0$

This will dwindle into a point circle, then radius of the circle = 0

$$\sqrt{\left(\frac{3-4\lambda}{1+\lambda}\right)^2 + 0 - \left(\frac{5+7\lambda}{1+\lambda}\right)} = 0$$

$\Rightarrow \quad (3 - 4\lambda)^2 - (5 + 7\lambda)(1 + \lambda) = 0$

$\Rightarrow \quad 9 + 16\lambda^2 - 24\lambda - 5 - 5\lambda - 7\lambda - 7\lambda^2 = 0$

$\Rightarrow \quad 9\lambda^2 - 36\lambda + 4 = 0$

$$\lambda = \frac{36 \pm \sqrt{(36)^2 - 4 \cdot 9 \cdot 4}}{2 \cdot 9}$$

$\therefore \quad \lambda = 2 \pm \dfrac{4\sqrt{2}}{3}$

Example 8 *If $f(x+y) = f(x) \cdot f(y)$ for all x and y, $f(1) = 2$ and $\alpha_n = f(n), n \in N$, then the equation of the circle having (α_1, α_2) and (α_3, α_4) as the ends of its one diameter is*

(a) $(x-2)(x-8) + (y-4)(y-16) = 0$

(b) $(x-4)(x-8) + (y-2)(y-16) = 0$

(c) $(x-2)(x-16) + (y-4)(y-8) = 0$

(d) $(x-6)(x-8) + (y-5)(y-6) = 0$

Sol. (a) Given, $\quad f(x+y) = f(x) \cdot f(y) \quad$ ...(i)

and $\quad f(1) = 2$

In Eq. (i), put $x = y = 1$,

then $\quad f(2) = f(1) \cdot f(1) = 2^2$

Now, in Eq. (i), put $x = 1, y = 2$, then

$$f(3) = f(1) f(2) = 2 \cdot 2^2 = 2^3$$

Hence, $\quad f(n) = 2^n$

$\therefore \quad \alpha_n = f(n) = 2^n \forall n \in N$

$(\alpha_1, \alpha_2) \equiv (2, 4)$

and $\quad (\alpha_3, \alpha_4) \equiv (8, 16)$

Equation of circle in diametric form is

$$(x-2)(x-8) + (y-4)(y-16) = 0$$

Example 9 *Two circles of radii a and b touching each other externally, are inscribed in the area bounded by $y = \sqrt{(1 - x^2)}$ and the X-axis. If $b = \dfrac{1}{2}$, then a is equal to*

(a) $\dfrac{1}{4}$ (b) $\dfrac{1}{8}$ (c) $\dfrac{1}{2}$ (d) $\dfrac{1}{\sqrt{2}}$

Sol. (a) Let the centres of circles be C_1 and C_2, then

$$C_1 \equiv (\sqrt{(1-2a)}, a) \text{ and } C_2 \equiv (\sqrt{(1-2b)}, b)$$

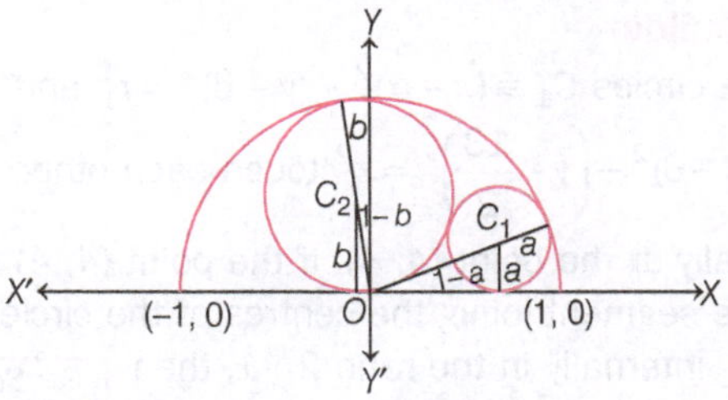

Now, $C_1C_2 = a + b$

$\Rightarrow \quad \left((\sqrt{(1-2a)})^2 + \left(a - \dfrac{1}{2}\right)^2\right) = \left(a + \dfrac{1}{2}\right)^2 \quad \left[\because b = \dfrac{1}{2}\right]$

or $\quad 1 - 2a + \left(a - \dfrac{1}{2}\right)^2 = \left(a + \dfrac{1}{2}\right)^2$

or $\quad 1 - 2a + a^2 + \dfrac{1}{4} - a = a^2 + \dfrac{1}{4} + a$

or $\quad a = \dfrac{1}{4}$

JEE SCANNER

Example 10 Similar to PYQ Asked in JEE Main 2024

Let the circles $C_1 \equiv (x-\alpha)^2 + (y-\beta)^2 = r_1^2$ and $C_2 \equiv (x-10)^2 + \left(y - \frac{17}{2}\right)^2 = r_2^2$ touch each other externally at the point (8, 8). If the point (8, 8) divides the line segment joining the centres of the circles C_1 and C_2 internally in the ratio 2 : 1, then $(\alpha+\beta) + 4(r_1^2 + r_2^2)$ equals

(a) 96 (b) 72 (c) 84 (d) 90

Sol. (a) $C_1 \equiv (x-\alpha)^2 + (y-\beta)^2 = r_1^2$

$$C_2 \equiv (x-10)^2 + \left(y - \frac{17}{2}\right)^2 = r_2^2$$

$$r_1 : r_2 = 2 : 1$$

So, $\frac{2 \times 10 + \alpha}{2+1} = 8 \Rightarrow \alpha = 4$

and $\frac{2 \times \frac{17}{2} + \beta}{2+1} = 8 \Rightarrow \beta = 7$

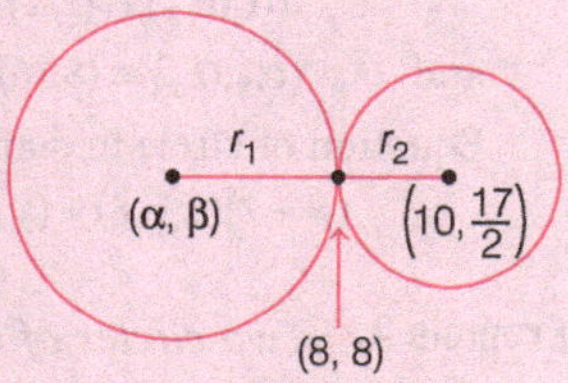

So, $(\alpha, \beta) = (4, 7)$

Now, $r_1^2 = (8-\alpha)^2 + (8-\beta)^2$

$= 4^2 + 1^2 = 16 + 1 = 17$

and $r_2^2 = (10-8)^2 + \left(\frac{17}{2} - 8\right)^2 = 4 + \frac{1}{4} = \frac{17}{4}$

$\therefore \quad (\alpha+\beta) + 4(r_1^2 + r_2^2)$

$$= (4+7) + 4\left(17 + \frac{17}{4}\right)$$

$$= 11 + 85 = 96$$

Skill Builder

Let the circles $C_1 \equiv (x-\alpha)^2 + (y-\beta)^2 = r_1^2$ and $C_2 \equiv (x-6)^2 + \left(y - \frac{13}{2}\right)^2 = r_2^2$ touch each other externally at the point (4, 4). If the point (4, 4) divides the line segment joinig the centres of the circles C_1 and C_2 internally in the ratio 2 : 1, then $(\alpha+\beta) + 4(r_1^2 + r_2^2)$ equals

(a) 296 (b) 272

(c) 284 (d) 204

For Sol.

Example 11 *There are two circles whose equations are $x^2 + y^2 = 9$ and $x^2 + y^2 - 8x - 6y + n^2 = 0, n \in I$. If the two circles have exactly two common tangents, then the number of possible values of n is*

(a) 2 (b) 7 (c) 8 (d) 9

Sol. (d) Given circles are $S_1 : x^2 + y^2 - 9 = 0$

Its centre $C_1 : (0,0)$ and radius, $r_1 = 3$

and $S_2 : x^2 + y^2 - 8x - 6y + n^2 = 0$

Its centre $C_2 : (4,3)$ and radius, $r_2 = \sqrt{(25 - n^2)}$

Here, $25 - n^2 > 0 \Rightarrow -5 < n < 5$ ...(i)

For exactly two common tangents,

$$r_1 + r_2 > C_1C_2$$

$\Rightarrow \quad 3 + \sqrt{(25-n^2)} > \sqrt{(4^2 + 3^2)}$

$\Rightarrow \quad \sqrt{(25-n^2)} > 2$

$\Rightarrow \quad 25 - n^2 > 4$

or $\quad n^2 < 21$

or $\quad -\sqrt{21} < n < \sqrt{21}$ ...(ii)

From Eqs. (i) and (ii), we get

$$-\sqrt{21} < n < \sqrt{21}$$

But $n \in I$. So, $n = -4, -3, -2, -1, 0, 1, 2, 3, 4$

Hence, number of possible values of n is 9.

Example 12 *Suppose $f(x, y) = 0$ is the equation of a circle such that $f(x, 1) = 0$ has equal roots (each equal to 2) and $f(1, x) = 0$ also has equal roots (each equal to zero). The equation of circle is*

(a) $x^2 + y^2 + 4x + 3 = 0$

(b) $x^2 + y^2 + 4y + 3 = 0$

(c) $x^2 + y^2 + 4x - 3 = 0$

(d) $x^2 + y^2 - 4x + 3 = 0$

Sol. (d) Let $f(x,y) = x^2 + y^2 + 2gx + 2fy + c$

$\Rightarrow \quad f(x,1) = x^2 + 1 + 2gx + 2f + c \equiv (x-2)^2$ [given]

then, $\quad g = -2, 2f + c = 3$ ...(i)

Also, $\quad f(1,x) = 1 + x^2 + 2g + 2fx + c \equiv (x-0)^2$ [given]

then, $\quad f = 0, 2g + c = -1$ ...(ii)

From Eqs. (i) and (ii), we get

$$g = -2, f = 0, c = 3$$

Thus, equation of circle is

$$x^2 + y^2 - 4x + 3 = 0$$

Example 13 *A variable circle C has the equation $x^2 + y^2 - 2(t^2 - 3t + 1)x - 2(t^2 + 2t)y + t = 0$, where t is a parameter. If the power of point (a, b) w.r.t. the circle C is constant, then the ordered pair (a, b) is*

(a) $\left(\frac{1}{10}, -\frac{1}{10}\right)$ (b) $\left(\frac{1}{10}, \frac{1}{10}\right)$

(c) $\left(-\frac{1}{10}, \frac{1}{10}\right)$ (d) $\left(-\frac{1}{10}, -\frac{1}{10}\right)$

Sol. (c) Given, $C: x^2 + y^2 - 2(t^2 - 3t + 1)x - 2(t^2 + 2t)y + t = 0$

Given power of circle = constant

$\therefore \quad a^2 + b^2 - 2(t^2 - 3t + 1)a - 2(t^2 + 2t)b + t = \text{constant}$

$\Rightarrow \quad -2(a + b)t^2 + (6a - 4b + 1)t + (a^2 + b^2 - 2a) = \text{constant}$

$\because$ Power of circle is constant, then

$a + b = 0$ and $6a - 4b + 1 = 0$

or $\quad b = -a$ and $6a - 4a + 1 = 0$

$\therefore \quad a = -\frac{1}{10}, b = \frac{1}{10}$

Hence, required ordered pair is $\left(-\frac{1}{10}, \frac{1}{10}\right)$

Example 14 *If the radii of the circles $(x - 1)^2 + (y - 2)^2 = 1$ and $(x - 7)^2 + (y - 10)^2 = 4$ are increasing uniformly w.r.t. time as 0.3 unit/s and 0.4 unit/s respectively, then they will touch each other at t equals to*

(a) 45 s (b) 90 s (c) 11 s (d) 135 s

Sol. (b) Given circles are $S_1: (x - 1)^2 + (y - 2)^2 = 1$

Its centre $C_1: (1, 2)$ and radius, $r_1 = 1$

and $\quad S_2: (x - 7)^2 + (y - 10)^2 = 4$

Its centre $C_2: (7, 10)$ and radius, $r_2 = 2$

$\because \quad C_1C_2 = 10 > r_1 + r_2$

Hence, the two circles are separated.

The radii of the two circles at time t are $(1 + 0.3t)$ and $(2 + 0.4t)$

For the two circles to touch each other,

$C_1C_2 = |(1 + 0.3t) \pm (2 + 0.4t)|$

$\Rightarrow \quad 10 = |3 + 0.7t| \text{ or } 10 = |-1 - 0.1t|$

$\Rightarrow \quad 0.7t + 3 = \pm 10 \text{ or } -1 - 0.1t = \pm 10$

$\Rightarrow \quad t = 10 \text{ or } t = 90 \quad [\because t > 0]$

Example 15 *A light ray gets reflected from $x = -2$. If the reflected ray touches the circle $x^2 + y^2 = 4$ and the point of incident is $(-2, -4)$, then the equation of the incident ray is*

(a) $4y + 3x + 22 = 0$ (b) $3y + 4x + 20 = 0$

(c) $4y + 2x + 20 = 0$ (d) $y + x + 6 = 0$

> **Decoding the Question**
> Use the rule of ray theory. The slope of reflected ray and incident ray is equal in opposite sign.

Sol. (a) Any tangent of $x^2 + y^2 = 4$ is $y = mx \pm 2\sqrt{(1 + m^2)}$.

If it passes through $(-2, -4)$, then $-4 = -2m \pm 2\sqrt{(1 + m^2)}$

or $\quad (m - 2)^2 = 1 + m^2 \Rightarrow m = 3/4$

Hence, the slope of the reflected ray is 3/4.

Thus, the equation of the incident ray is

$$y + 4 = -\frac{3}{4}(x + 2)$$

i.e. $\quad 4y + 3x + 22 = 0$

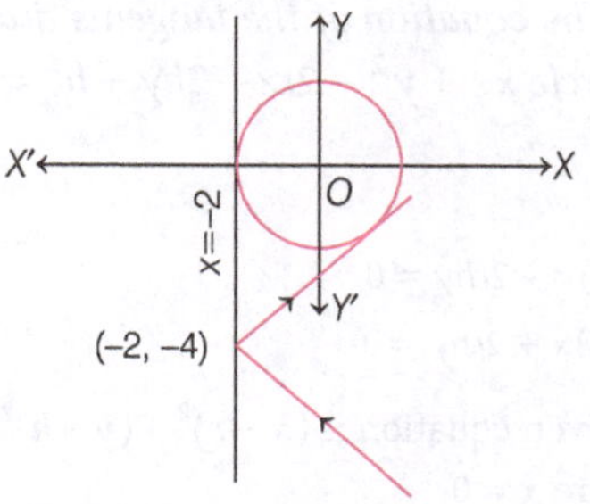

Example 16 *If a circle having centre at (α, β) radius r completely lies within two lines $x + y = 2$ and $x + y = -2$, then, $\min.(|\alpha + \beta + 2|, |\alpha + \beta - 2|)$ is*

(a) greater than $\sqrt{2}r$ (b) less than $\sqrt{2}r$

(c) greater than $2r$ (d) less than $2r$

Sol. (a) Minimum distance of the centre from line > radius of circle i.e. $\min.\left\{\frac{|\alpha + \beta + 2|}{\sqrt{2}}, \frac{|\alpha + \beta - 2|}{\sqrt{2}}\right\} > r$

or $\min.\{|\alpha + \beta + 2|, |\alpha + \beta - 2|\} > \sqrt{2}r$

More than One Correct Option Type Questions

Example 17 *If point $P(x, y)$ is called a lattice point, if $x, y \in I$. Then, the total number of lattice points in the interior of the circle $x^2 + y^2 = a^2, a \neq 0$ cannot be*

(a) 202 (b) 203 (c) 204 (d) 205

Sol. (a, b, c) Given circle is $x^2 + y^2 = a^2$ ...(i)

Clearly (0, 0) will belong the interior of circle Eq. (i). Also, other points interior to circle Eq. (i) will have the coordinates of the form

$(\pm\lambda, 0), (0, \pm\lambda)$, where $\lambda^2 < a^2$

and $(\pm\lambda, \pm\mu)$ and $(\pm\mu, \pm\lambda)$, where $\lambda^2 + \mu^2 < a^2$ and $\lambda, \mu \in I$

$\therefore$ Number of lattice points in the interior of the circle will be of the form $1 + 4r + 8t$, where $r, t = 0, 1, 2, \ldots$

$\therefore$ Number of such points must be of the form $4n + 1$, where $n = 0, 1, 2, \ldots$

Example 18 *Let x, y be real variable satisfying $x^2 + y^2 + 8x - 10y - 40 = 0$. Let $a = \max\{\sqrt{(x+2)^2 + (y-3)^2}\}$ and $b = \min\{\sqrt{(x + 2)^2 + (y - 3)^2}\}$, then*

(a) $a + b = 18$ (b) $a - b = 4\sqrt{2}$

(c) $a + b = 4\sqrt{2}$ (d) $a \cdot b = 73$

Sol. (a, b, d) Given circle is $x^2 + y^2 + 8x - 10y - 40 = 0$

The centre and radius of the circle are $(-4, 5)$ and 9, respectively.

Distance of the centre $(-4, 5)$ from $(-2, 3)$ is $\sqrt{(4 + 4)} = 2\sqrt{2}$.

Therefore, $a = 2\sqrt{2} + 9$ and $b = -2\sqrt{2} + 9$

$\therefore \quad a + b = 18, a - b = 4\sqrt{2}, ab = 73$

Example 19 ■ *The equation of the tangents drawn from the origin to the circle $x^2 + y^2 - 2rx - 2hy + h^2 = 0$, are*

(a) $x = 0$

(b) $y = 0$

(c) $(h^2 - r^2)x - 2rhy = 0$

(d) $(h^2 - r^2)x + 2rhy = 0$

Sol. (a, c) The given equation is $(x - r)^2 + (y - h)^2 = r^2$

Tangents are $x = 0$

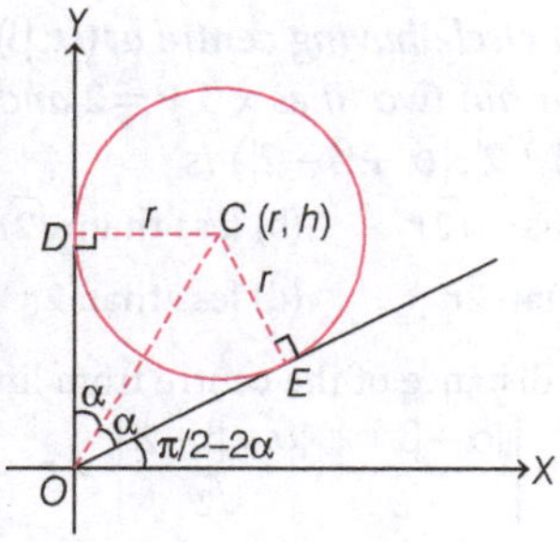

and $\quad y = x\tan\left(\dfrac{\pi}{2} - 2\alpha\right) = x\cot 2\alpha$

$$= \frac{x(1-\tan^2\alpha)}{2\tan\alpha}$$

$$y = \frac{x\left(1 - \dfrac{r^2}{h^2}\right)}{2\left(\dfrac{r}{h}\right)} \qquad \left[\because \text{ in } \Delta ODC, \tan\alpha = \frac{r}{h}\right]$$

or $\quad (h^2 - r^2)x - 2rhy = 0$

Example 20 ■ *Point M moved on the circle $(x-4)^2 + (y-8)^2 = 20$. Then it broke away from it and move along a tangent to the circle, cut the X-axis at point $(-2, 0)$. The coordinates of the point on the circle at which the moving point broke away is*

(a) $\left(\dfrac{42}{5}, \dfrac{36}{5}\right)$ (b) $\left(-\dfrac{2}{5}, \dfrac{44}{5}\right)$

(c) $(6, 4)$ (d) $(2, 4)$

Sol. (b, c) Given circle is

$$(x-4)^2 + (y-8)^2 = 20$$

or $\quad x^2 + y^2 - 8x - 16y + 60 = 0 \quad$ ...(i)

Equation of chord of contact from $(-2, 0)$ is

$$-2\cdot x + 0\cdot y - 4(x-2) - 8(y+0) + 60 = 0$$

or $\quad 3x + 4y - 34 = 0 \quad$ ...(ii)

Solving Eqs. (i) and (ii), we get

$$x^2 + \left(\frac{34-3x}{4}\right)^2 - 8x - 16\left(\frac{34-3x}{4}\right) + 60 = 0$$

or $\quad 5x^2 - 28x - 12 = 0$

or $\quad (x-6)(5x+2) = 0$

or $\quad x = 6, -\dfrac{2}{5}$

Therefore, the points are $(6, 4)$ and $\left(-\dfrac{2}{5}, \dfrac{44}{5}\right)$.

Example 21 ■ *The equations of four circles are $(x \pm a)^2 + (y \pm a)^2 = a^2$. The radius of a circle touching all the four circles is*

(a) $(\sqrt{2} - 1)a$ (b) $2\sqrt{2}a$

(c) $(\sqrt{2} + 1)a$ (d) $(2 + \sqrt{2})a$

Sol. (a, c) Radius of inner circle $= OR - a$

$$= \sqrt{(a^2 + a^2)} - a = a(\sqrt{2} - 1)$$

Radius of outer circle $= OR + RQ$

$$= a\sqrt{2} + a = a(\sqrt{2} + 1)$$

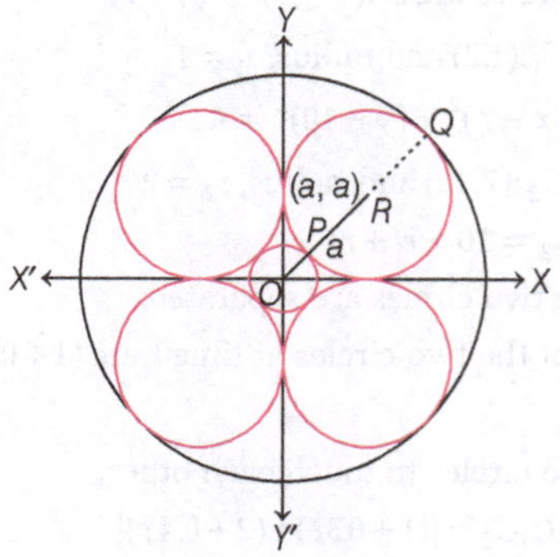

Example 22 ■ *A region in the XY-plane is bounded by the curve $y = \sqrt{(25 - x^2)}$ and the line $y = 0$. If the point $(a, a+1)$ lies in the interior of the region, then*

(a) $a \in (-4, 3)$

(b) $a \in (-\infty, -1) \cup (3, \infty)$

(c) $a \in (-1, 3)$

(d) None of the above

Sol. (c) $y = \sqrt{(25 - x^2)}$

$\Rightarrow x^2 + y^2 = 25, y \geq 0,$

$P(a, a+1)$ is inside the region

$\therefore \quad a^2 + (a+1)^2 - 25 < 0$ and $a + 1 > 0$

$\Rightarrow \quad 2a^2 + 2a - 24 < 0$ and $a > -1$

$\Rightarrow \quad a^2 + a - 12 < 0$ and $a > -1$

$\Rightarrow \quad -4 < a < 3$ and $a > -1$

$\Rightarrow \quad -1 < a < 3$

$\Rightarrow \quad a \in (-1, 3)$

Example 23 *The circles $x^2 + y^2 - 2x - 4y + 1 = 0$ and $x^2 + y^2 + 4x + 4y - 1 = 0$*

(a) touch internally

(b) touch externally

(c) have $3x + 4y - 1 = 0$ as the common tangent at the point of contact

(d) have $3x + 4y + 1 = 0$ the common tangent at the point of contact

Sol. (b,c) For the given circles

$$S_1 : x^2 + y^2 - 2x - 4y + 1 = 0$$

$$S_2 : x^2 + y^2 + 4x + 4y - 1 = 0$$

$$C_1 \equiv (1, 2), r_1 = 2, C_2 \equiv (-2, -2), r_2 = 3$$

Now, $r_1 + r_2 = 5$ and $C_1C_2 = 5$

So, $r_1 + r_2 = C_1C_2$

Hence, the circles touch externally.

Also, the common tangent at the point of contact is

$$S_1 - S_2 = 0 \Rightarrow 3x + 4y - 1 = 0$$

Example 24 *If P is a point on the circle $x^2 + y^2 = 9$, Q is a point on the line $7x + y + 3 = 0$ and the line $x - y + 1 = 0$ is the perpendicular bisector of PQ, then the coordinates of P are*

(a) (3, 0)

(b) $\left(-\frac{72}{25}, \frac{21}{25}\right)$

(c) (–3, 0)

(d) $\left(\frac{72}{125}, -\frac{21}{25}\right)$

Sol. (a, b) Let $P(x_1, y_1)$ and $Q(x_2, y_2)$ be the points on the circle $x^2 + y^2 = 9$ and the line $7x + y + 3 = 0$, respectively.

$$\therefore \quad y_2 = -(7x_2 + 3) \text{ and } x_1^2 + y_1^2 = 9$$

Since, $x - y + 1 = 0$ is perpendicular bisector of PQ.

$$\therefore \quad \frac{1}{2}(x_1 + x_2) - \frac{1}{2}[y_1 - (7x_2 + 3)] + 1 = 0$$

or $$x_1 - y_1 = (8x_2 - 5) \quad \text{...(i)}$$

Further $m_1 \times m_2 = -1$

$$\Rightarrow \quad 1\frac{(y_1 - y_2)}{(x_1 - y_2)} = -1 \Rightarrow 1\left(\frac{y_1 + 7x_2 + 3}{x_1 - x_2}\right) = -1$$

i.e. $$x_1 + y_1 = -(6x_2 + 3) \quad \text{...(iii)}$$

On squaring Eqs. (i) and (ii) and then adding, we get

$$2(x_1^2 + y_1^2) = 100x_2^2 + 116x_2 + 34$$

or $100x_2^2 + 116x_2 + 16 = 0$

$$\Rightarrow \quad x_2 = -1 \text{ or } -\frac{4}{25} \quad \text{...(iii)}$$

Hence, from Eqs. (i) and (ii), we get coordinates of P as (3, 0) and $\left(-\frac{72}{25}, \frac{21}{25}\right)$.

Passage Based Questions

Passage I

(Q. Nos. 25 and 26)

Consider the relation $4l^2 - 5m^2 + 6l + 1 = 0$, where $l, m \in R$.

Example 25 *The line $lx + my + 1 = 0$ touches a fixed circle whose equation is*

(a) $x^2 + y^2 - 4x - 5 = 0$

(b) $x^2 + y^2 + 6x + 6 = 0$

(c) $x^2 + y^2 - 6x + 4 = 0$

(d) $x^2 + y^2 + 4x - 4 = 0$

Example 26 *Tangents PA and PB are drawn to the above fixed circle from the point P on the line $x + y - 1 = 0$. Then, the chord of contact AB passes through the fixed point*

(a) $\left(\frac{1}{2}, -\frac{5}{2}\right)$

(b) $\left(\frac{1}{3}, \frac{4}{3}\right)$

(c) $\left(-\frac{1}{2}, \frac{3}{2}\right)$

(d) $\left(\frac{1}{2}, \frac{5}{2}\right)$

Sol. (Q. Nos. 25-26)

25. (c) Let the equation of the circle be

$$x^2 + y^2 + 2gx + 2fy + c = 0 \quad \text{...(i)}$$

The line $lx + my + 1 = 0$ touch circle Eq. (i), then

$$\frac{|-lg - mf + 1|}{\sqrt{(l^2 + m^2)}} = \sqrt{(g^2 + f^2 - c)}$$

$$\Rightarrow \quad (lg + mf - 1)^2 = (l^2 + m^2)(g^2 + f^2 - c)$$

or $$(f^2 - c)l^2 + (g^2 - c)m^2 - 2gflm + 2gl + 2fm - 1 = 0 \quad \text{...(ii)}$$

But the given condition is

$$4l^2 - 5m^2 + 6l + 1 = 0 \quad \text{...(iii)}$$

On comparing Eqs. (ii) and (iii), we get

$$\frac{f^2 - c}{4} = \frac{g^2 - c}{-5} = \frac{-2gf}{0} = \frac{g}{3} = \frac{2f}{0} = \frac{-1}{1}$$

Then, we get

$$g = -3, f = 0, c = 4$$

Substituting these values in Eq. (i), the equation of the circle is

$$x^2 + y^2 - 6x + 4 = 0$$

26. (a) Let any point on the line $x + y - 1 = 0$ is

$$P(\lambda, 1 - \lambda), \lambda \in R.$$

Then, equation of AB is

$$\lambda x + (1 - \lambda)y - 3(x + \lambda) + 4 = 0$$

$$\Rightarrow \quad (-3x + y + 4) + \lambda(x - y - 3) = 0$$

For fixed point $-3x + y + 4 = 0, x - y - 3 = 0$

$$\therefore \quad x = \frac{1}{2}, y = -\frac{5}{2}$$

$\therefore$ Fixed point is $\left(\frac{1}{2}, \frac{-5}{2}\right)$

Passage II

(Q. Nos. 27 and 28)

If α-chord of a circle be that chord which subtends an angle α at the centre of the circle.

Example 27 *If $x + y = 1$ is α-chord of $x^2 + y^2 = 1$, then α is equal to*

(a) $\frac{\pi}{6}$ (b) $\frac{\pi}{4}$ (c) $\frac{\pi}{2}$ (d) $\frac{3\pi}{4}$

Example 28 *If slope of a $\frac{\pi}{3}$-chord of $x^2 + y^2 = 4$ is 1, then its equation is*

(a) $x - y + \sqrt{6} = 0$ (b) $x - y + \sqrt{3} = 0$

(c) $x - y - \sqrt{3} = 0$ (d) $x - y - 2\sqrt{3} = 0$

Sol. (Q. Nos. 27-28)

27. (c) From figure,

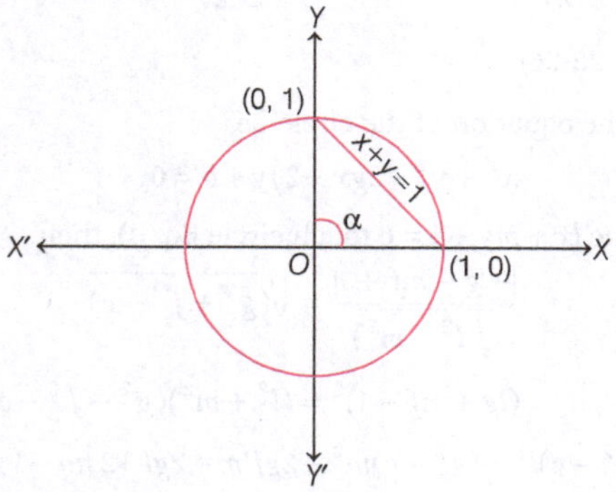

$$\alpha = \frac{\pi}{2}$$

28. (a) Given, slope of chord is 1.

Let the equation of chord be $x - y + \lambda = 0$.

$$\because \quad OM = 2\cos\left(\frac{\pi}{6}\right) = \sqrt{3}$$

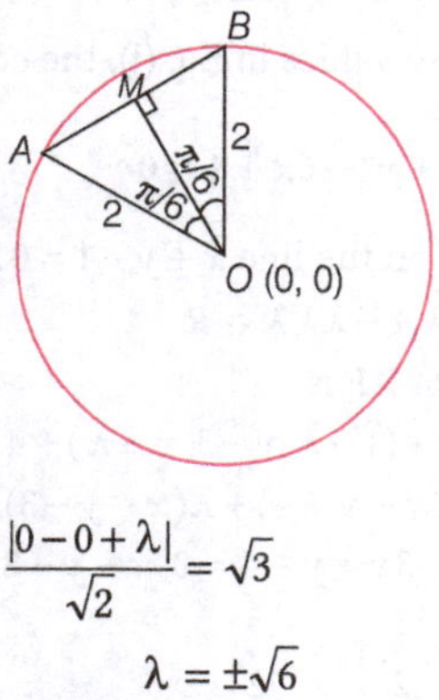

$$\therefore \quad \frac{|0 - 0 + \lambda|}{\sqrt{2}} = \sqrt{3}$$

$$\Rightarrow \quad \lambda = \pm\sqrt{6}$$

Hence, equation of chords are

$$x - y \pm \sqrt{6} = 0.$$

Stem Based Questions

Stem I

(Q. Nos. 29 and 30)

Let two circles $S_1 = 0$ and $S_2 = 0$ intersect at point A and B. $L_1 = 0$ is the line joining A and B where $S_1 \equiv x^2 + y^2 + 2ax + 2by - 5 = 0$ and $S_2 \equiv x^2 + y^2 + 2x + 4y - 4 = 0$. Let AB subtend angle θ at $(0, 0)$ and angle subtended by $S_1 = 0$ and $S_2 = 0$ at $P(3, 4)$ is α and β respectively.

Example 29 *If equation of $L_1 \equiv 3x + 4y = 7$, then the value of $7(4a + b)$ is equal to ....*

Example 30 *If $\alpha = 60°$, then (a, b) lies on a circle whose radius is r, then $9r^2$ is ....*

Sol. (Q. Nos. 29 and 30)

29. (7.14) Equation of AB as radical axis

$$2ax + 2by - 5 - 2x - 4y + 4 = 0$$

$$2x(a - 1) + 2y(b - 2) - 1 = 0 \quad \text{...(i)}$$

Also, equation of AB is $3x + 4y = 7$ ...(ii)

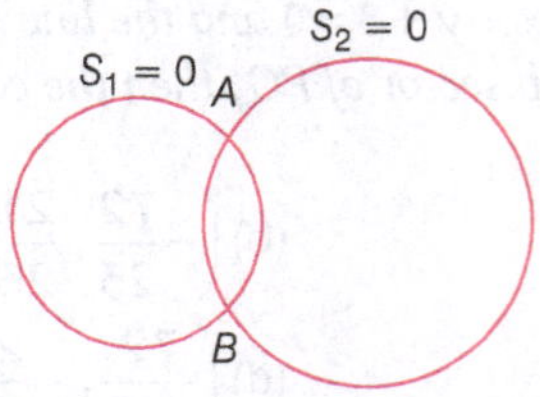

$$\Rightarrow \quad \frac{2(a-1)}{3} = \frac{2(b-2)}{4} = \frac{-1}{-7} \Rightarrow a - 1 = \frac{3}{14} \Rightarrow a = \frac{17}{14}$$

$$b = 2 + \frac{2}{7} = \frac{16}{7}$$

$$\therefore \quad 7(4a + b) = 7\left(\frac{68}{14} + \frac{32}{14}\right) = \frac{700}{14} = 50$$

30. (40) $\sin 30° = \dfrac{\sqrt{a^2 + b^2 + 5}}{\sqrt{(3 + a)^2 + (4 + b)^2}}$

$$9 + a^2 + 6a + b^2 + 8b + 16 = 4a^2 + 4b^2 + 20$$

$$3a^2 + 3b^2 - 6a - 8b - 5 = 0$$

$$a^2 + b^2 - 2a - \frac{8}{3}b - \frac{5}{3} = 0$$

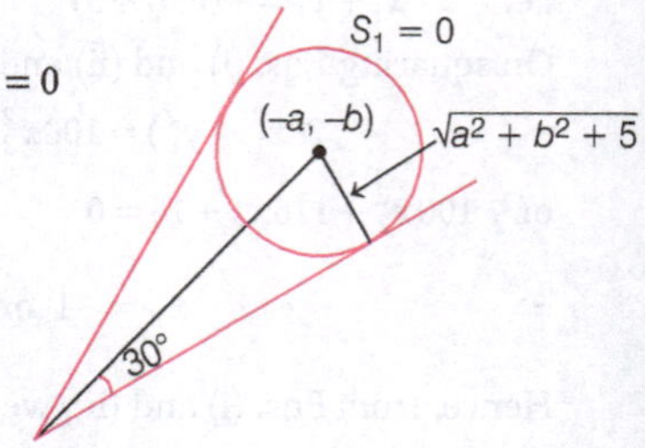

$$\text{Radius} = \sqrt{1 + \frac{16}{9} + \frac{5}{3}}$$

$$= \sqrt{\frac{40}{9}} = \frac{2\sqrt{10}}{3}$$

$$\text{Here, } 9r^2 = \frac{9 \times 4 \times 10}{9} = 40$$

Single Integer Answer Type Questions

Example 31 *A circle with centre in the first quadrant is tangent to $y = x + 10$, $y = x - 6$ and the Y-axis. Let (p, q) be the centre of the circle. If the value of $(p+q) = a + b\sqrt{a}$, when $a, b \in Q$, then the value of $|a-b|$ is*

Sol. (6) $\because$ $$CP = CR \Rightarrow \frac{|p-q+10|}{\sqrt{2}} = p$$

or $$p - q + 10 = p\sqrt{2} \quad \text{...(i)}$$

and $$CP = CQ$$

$$\frac{p-q+10}{\sqrt{2}} = -\left(\frac{p-q-6}{\sqrt{2}}\right) \text{ or } p - q = -2 \quad \text{...(ii)}$$

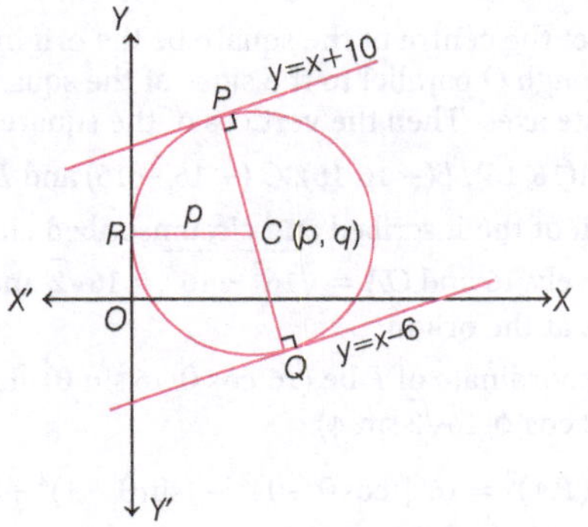

From Eqs. (i) and (ii), we get $p = 4\sqrt{2}$ and $q = 4\sqrt{2} + 2$

Now, $p + q = 2 + 8\sqrt{2} = a + b\sqrt{2}$ [given]

$\therefore$ $a = 2, b = 8$

Hence, $|a-b| = |2-8| = 6$

Example 32 *If the circles*

$x^2 + y^2 + (3 + \sin\theta)x + 2\cos\phi y = 0$ and $x^2 + y^2 + (2\cos\phi)x + 2\lambda y = 0$ touch each other, then the maximum value of λ is ....

Sol. (1) Since, both the circles are passing through the origin (0, 0), the equation of tangent at (0,0) of first circle will be same as that of the tangent at (0, 0) of second circle.

Equation of tangent at (0, 0) of first circle is

$$(3 + \sin\theta)x + (2\cos\phi)y = 0 \quad \text{...(i)}$$

Equaton of tangent at (0, 0) of second circle is

$$(2\cos\phi)x + 2\lambda y = 0 \quad \text{...(ii)}$$

Therefore, Eqs. (i) and (ii) must be identical, then

$$\frac{3+\sin\theta}{2\cos\phi} = \frac{2\cos\phi}{2\lambda}$$

or $$\lambda = \frac{2\cos^2\phi}{(3+\sin\theta)}$$

or $$\lambda_{\max} = 1 \quad [\text{when } \sin\theta = -1 \text{ and } \cos\phi = 1]$$

JEE SCANNER

Example 33 Similar to PYQ Asked in JEE Main 2023

Let the centre of a circle, passing through the points (0, 0) and (1, 0) and touching the circle $x^2 + y^2 = 4$, be (h, k). Then, for all possible values of the coordinates of the centre (h, k), then $4(h^2 + k^2)$ is equal to ....

Sol. (4) Let $C_1 \equiv x^2 + y^2 = 4$

and $C_2 \equiv (x-h)^2 + (y-k)^2 = h^2 + k^2$

$\Rightarrow$ $$x^2 + y^2 - 2hx - 2ky = 0 \quad \text{...(i)}$$

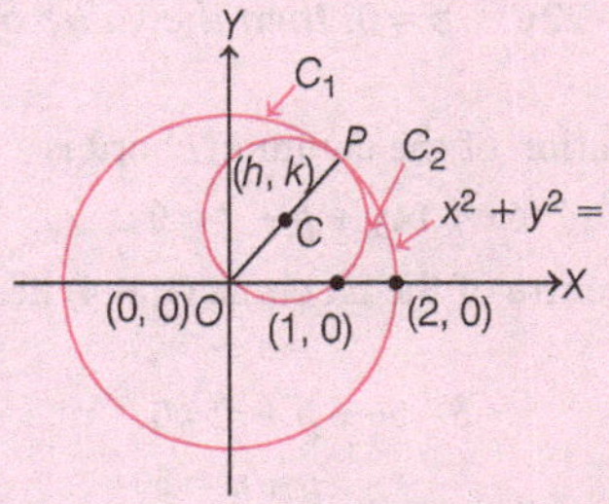

$\because$ Eq. (i) passes through (1, 0), then $1 + 0 - 2h = 0$

$\Rightarrow$ $$h = \frac{1}{2}$$

$\because$ $$OC = \frac{OP}{2}$$

$\Rightarrow$ $$\sqrt{\left(\frac{1}{2}\right)^2 + k^2} = \frac{2}{2} = 1$$

$\Rightarrow$ $$\frac{1}{4} + k^2 = 1 \Rightarrow k^2 = \frac{3}{4} \Rightarrow k = \pm\frac{\sqrt{3}}{2}$$

$\therefore$ Possible values of (h, k) are $\left(\frac{1}{2}, \frac{\sqrt{3}}{2}\right), \left(\frac{1}{2}, -\frac{\sqrt{3}}{2}\right)$

Thus, $4(h^2 + k^2) = 4\left(\frac{1}{4} + \frac{3}{4}\right) = 4$

Skill Builder

Let the centre of a circle, passing through the points (0, 0) and (1, 0) and touching the circle $x^2 + y^2 = 16$, be (h, k). Then, for all possible values of the coordiantes of the centre (h, k), then $h^2 + k^2$ is equal to ....

For Sol.

Example 34 *If $\left(m_i, \frac{1}{m_i}\right)$, $i = 1, 2, 3,$ are four distinct points on a circle, then the value of $(m_1 \cdot m_2 \cdot m_3 \cdot m_4) + 5$ is ...*

Sol. (6) Let the equation of the circle be

$$x^2 + y^2 + 2gx + 2fy + c = 0$$

and $\left(m, \frac{1}{m}\right)$ be a variable point lies on the circle.

Thus, $m^2 + \frac{1}{m^2} + 2gm + \frac{2f}{m} + c = 0$

$\Rightarrow m^4 + 1 + 2gm^3 + 2fm + cm^2 = 0$

$\Rightarrow m^4 + 2gm^3 + cm^2 + 2fm + 1 = 0$

It has four roots, say m_1, m_2, m_3 and m_4.

Thus, $m_1 \cdot m_2 \cdot m_3 \cdot m_4 = 1$

$\therefore m_1 \cdot m_2 \cdot m_3 \cdot m_4 + 5 = 6$

Example 35 *If the circumference of the circle $x^2 + y^2 - 2x + 8y - q = 0$ is bisected by the circle $x^2 + y^2 + 4x + 22y + p = 0$, then the value of $\left(\frac{p+q}{10} + 3\right)$ is*

Sol. (8) The equation of the common chord is

$$6x + 14y + p + q = 0$$

Here, the centre of the Ist circle (1, – 4) lies on the common chord.

So, $6 - 56 + p + q = 0$

$\Rightarrow \quad p + q = 50$

Hence, the value of $\left(\frac{p+q}{10} + 3\right) = 8$

Numerical Based Type Questions

Example 36 *Let $A \equiv (-4, 0)$ and $B \equiv (4, 0)$. If the number of points on the circle $x^2 + y^2 = 16$ such that the area of the triangle whose vertices are A, B and C, is a positive integer N, then the value of N is*

Sol. (62) Required area, $A = \frac{1}{2} \times 8 \times 4 \sin\theta = |16 \sin\theta|$

Now, A is an integer.

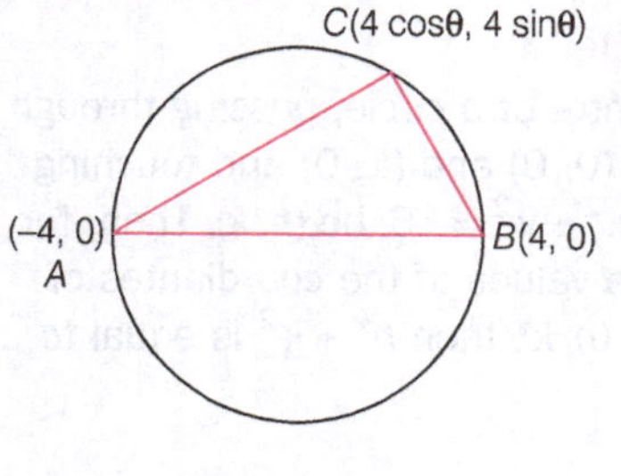

Then, the possible values of $\sin\theta$ are $\frac{1}{16}, \frac{2}{16}, \frac{3}{16}, \ldots, \frac{15}{16}$

i.e. 15 points in each quadrant or $60 + 2$ more with $\sin\theta = 1$.

$\therefore \quad N = 62$

Example 37 *If the two circles $(x-1)^2 + (y-3)^2 = r^2$ and $x^2 + y^2 - 8x + 2y + 8 = 0$ intersect in two distinct points such that $n < r < m$ where $m, n \in N$, find the value of $(m + n)$.*

Sol. (10) We have, $|r_1 - r_2| < C_1C_2 < r_1 + r_2$

$\Rightarrow \quad |r - 3| < C_1C_2 < r + 3$

$\Rightarrow \quad |r - 3| < 5 < r + 3$

$\Rightarrow \quad -5 < (r - 3) < 5, \; r + 3 > 5$

$\Rightarrow \quad -2 < r < 8, \; r > 2$

$\Rightarrow \quad 2 < r < 8$

Clearly, $n = 2, m = 8$

Hence, the value of $(m + n)$ is 10.

Example 38 *Two circles are inscribed and circumscribed about a square ABCD, length of each side of the square is 32. P and Q are two points respectively on these circles, then $[\Sigma(QA)^2 - \Sigma(PA)^2]$ is equal to*

Sol. (1024) Let the centre of the square be the origin O and the lines through O parallel to the sides of the square be the coordinate axes. Then,the vertices of the square are

$$A(16, 16), B(-16, 16), C(-16, -16) \text{ and } D(16, -16)$$

The radii of the inscribed and circumscribed circles are respectively 16 and $OA = \sqrt{16^2 + 16^2} = 16\sqrt{2}$ and their centre is at the origin.

Let the coordinate of P be $(16 \cos\theta, 16 \sin\theta)$ and that of Q be $(16\sqrt{2} \cos\phi, 16\sqrt{2} \sin\phi)$.

Then, $\Sigma(PA)^2 = 16^2[(\cos\theta - 1)^2 + (\sin\theta - 1)^2 + (\cos\theta + 1)^2 + (\sin\theta - 1)^2 + (\cos\theta + 1)^2 + (\sin\theta + 1)^2 + (\cos\theta - 1)^2 + (\sin\theta + 1)^2]$

$= 2 \times 16^2[2\cos^2\theta + 2 + 2\sin^2\theta + 2] = 12 \times (16)^2$

Similarly, $\Sigma(QA)^2 = 16 \times (16)^2$

$\therefore \quad [\Sigma(QA)^2 - \Sigma(PA)^2] = 1024$

Example 39 *Let A be the centre of the circle $x^2 + y^2 - 2x - 4y - 20 = 0$. The tangents at the points $B(1, 7)$ and $C(4, -2)$ on the circle meet at the point D. If Δ denotes the area of the quadrilateral ABCD, then $\frac{\Delta}{5}$ is equal to*

Sol. (15) Tangents at B and C are respectively

$$x + 7y - (x + 1) - 2(y + 7) - 20 = 0$$

and $\quad 4x - 2y - (x + 4) - 2(y - 2) - 20 = 0$

$\Rightarrow \quad y = 7$ and $3x - 4y - 20 = 0$

They intersect at $D(16, 7)$.

Coordinates of A are (1, 2).

Area of the quadrilateral $ABCD = 2 \times$ Area of the ΔABD

$$\Rightarrow \quad \Delta = \begin{vmatrix} 1 & 2 & 1 \\ 1 & 7 & 1 \\ 16 & 7 & 1 \end{vmatrix} = 75$$

$\therefore \quad \frac{\Delta}{5} = 15$

Matching Type Questions

Example 40 *Consider the circles C_1 of radius a and C_2 of radius b, b > a both lying the first quadrant and touching the coordinate axes.*

Column I	Column II
(A) C_1 and C_2 touch each other and $\frac{b}{a}=\lambda+\sqrt{\mu}$, $\lambda \in$ prime number and $\mu \in$ whole number, then	(p) $\lambda+\mu$ is a prime number
(B) C_1 and C_2 cut orthogonally and $\frac{b}{a}=\lambda+\sqrt{\mu}$, $\lambda \in$ prime number and $\mu \in$ whole number, then	(q) $\lambda+\mu$ is a composite number
(C) C_1 and C_2 intersect so that the common chord is longest and $\frac{b}{a}=\lambda+\sqrt{\mu}$, $\lambda \in$ prime number and $\mu \in$ whole number, then	(r) $2\lambda+\mu$ is a perfect number
(D) C_2 passes through the centre of C_1 and $\frac{b}{a}=\lambda+\sqrt{\mu}$, $\lambda \in$ prime number and $\mu \in$ whole number, then	(s) $\lvert\lambda-\mu\rvert$ is a prime number

Sol. (A)→ (p, s); (B) → (p); (C) → (p, r, s); (D) → (q, r)

$\because \quad C_1 : x^2+y^2-2ax-2ay+a^2=0$

Centre : (a,a) and radius : a

and $\quad C_2 : x^2+y^2-2bx-2by+b^2=0$

Centre : (b,b) and radius : b

(A) $\because C_1$ and C_2 touch each other, then

$$\sqrt{2}(b-a)=b+a \Rightarrow \frac{b}{a}=(\sqrt{2}+1)^2=3+\sqrt{8}$$

$\Rightarrow \quad \lambda=3, \mu=8$

(B) $\because C_1$ and C_2 intersect orthogonally, then

$$2(b-a)^2=b^2+a^2 \Rightarrow a^2+b^2-4ab=0$$

or $\quad \left(\frac{b}{a}\right)^2-4\left(\frac{b}{a}\right)+1=0$

$\therefore \quad \frac{b}{a}=\frac{4\pm\sqrt{(16-4)}}{2}=2+\sqrt{3}$

$\Rightarrow \quad \lambda=2, \mu=3$

(C) $\because C_1$ and C_2 intersect, the common chord is

$$2(b-a)(x+y)=b^2-a^2$$

given common chord is longest, then passes through (a,a)

$\Rightarrow \quad 2(b-a)(2a)=b^2-a^2$

or $\quad (b-3a)(b-a)=0$

$\because \quad b-a\neq 0 \qquad [b>a]$

$\therefore \quad b-3a=0$

or $\quad \frac{b}{a}=3 \Rightarrow \lambda=3, \mu=0$

(D) $\because C_2$ passes through (a,a), then

$$a^2+a^2-2ab-2ab+b^2=0$$

or $\quad b^2-4ab+2a^2=0$

or $\quad \left(\frac{b}{a}\right)^2-4\left(\frac{b}{a}\right)+2=0$ or $\frac{b}{a}=\frac{4\pm\sqrt{(16-8)}}{2}=2+\sqrt{2}$

$\Rightarrow \quad \lambda=2, \mu=2$

Example 41 *Match the following*

Column I	Column II
(A) The circles $x^2+y^2+2x+c=0$ $(c>0)$ and $x^2+y^2+2y+c=0$ touch each other, then the value of $2c$ is	(p) 1
(B) The circles $x^2+y^2+2x+3y+c=0$ $(c>0)$ and $x^2+y^2-x+2y+c=0$ intersect orthogonally, then the value of $2c$ is	(q) 2
(C) The circle $x^2+y^2=9$ is contains the circle $x^2+y^2-2x+1-c^2=0$ $(c>0)$, then $2c$ can be	(r) 3
(D) The circle $x^2+y^2=9$ is contains in the circle $x^2+y^2-2x+1-\frac{c^2}{4}=0$ $(c>0)$, then $(c-6)$ can be	(s) 4

Sol. (A) → (p); (B) → (q); (C) → (p, q, r); (D) → (r, s)

(A) The circles

$$S_1 : (x+1)^2+y^2=(\sqrt{(1-c)})^2$$

Centre $C_1 : (-1,0)$, radius $r_1 : \sqrt{(1-c)}$

and $\quad S_2 : x^2+(y+1)^2=(\sqrt{(1-c)})^2$

Centre $C_2 : (0,-1)$, radius : $r_2=\sqrt{(1-c)}$

Now, $C_1C_2 = \sqrt{2}$ and $r_1 = r_2$

$\therefore$ The circles will touch externally only and

$$C_1C_2 = r_1 + r_2$$

$$\Rightarrow \quad \sqrt{2} = 2\sqrt{(1-c)} \text{ or } 2c = 1$$

(B) The circles $S_1 : (x+1)^2 + \left(y + \dfrac{3}{2}\right)^2 = \left(\sqrt{\left(\dfrac{13}{4} - c\right)}\right)^2$

Centre $C_1 : \left(-1, -\dfrac{3}{2}\right)$, radius $r_1 : \sqrt{\left(\dfrac{13}{4} - c\right)}$

and $S_2 : \left(x - \dfrac{1}{2}\right)^2 + (y+1)^2 = \left(\sqrt{\left(\dfrac{5}{4} - c\right)}\right)^2$

Centre $C_2 : \left(\dfrac{1}{2}, -1\right)$, radius $r_2 : \sqrt{\left(\dfrac{5}{4} - c\right)}$

For intersect orthogonally

$$(C_1C_2)^2 = r_1^2 + r_2^2$$

$$\Rightarrow \quad \left(\frac{3}{2}\right)^2 + \left(\frac{1}{2}\right)^2 = \frac{13}{4} - c + \frac{5}{4} - c$$

or $\quad 2c = 2$

(C) The circles

$$S_1 : x^2 + y^2 = 3^2$$

Centre $C_1 : (0,0)$, radius $r_1 : 3$

and $S_2 : (x-1)^2 + y^2 = c^2$

Centre $C_2 : (1,0)$, radius $r_2 : c$

Now, S_2 will be contained in S_1, then

$$C_1C_2 < r_1 - r_2$$

or $\quad 1 < 3 - c$ or $c < 2 \Rightarrow 2c < 4$

(D) The circles

$S_1 : x^2 + y^2 = 9$

Centre $C_1 : (0,0)$, radius $r_1 : 3$ and $S_2 : (x-1)^2 + y^2 = \left(\dfrac{c}{2}\right)^2$

Centre $C_2 : (1,0)$, radius $r_2 : \dfrac{c}{2}$

Now, S_1 will be contained in S_2,

then, $\quad r_2 - r_1 > C_1C_2$

$$\Rightarrow \quad \frac{c}{2} - 3 > 1 \text{ or } c > 8$$

$$\therefore \quad (c-6) > 2$$

EXERCISE 1

JEE Main Pattern

Single Option Correct Type Questions

1. The equation of the chord of the circle $x^2+y^2-3x-4y-4=0$, which passes through the origin such that the origin divides it in the ratio 4 : 1, is
(a) $x=0$ (b) $24x+7y=0$
(c) $7x+24y=0$ (d) $7x-24y=0$

2. Two congruent circles with centered at (2, 3) and (5, 6), which intersect at right angles, have radius equal to
(a) $2\sqrt{2}$ (b) 3
(c) 4 (d) 10

3. The line $2x-y+1=0$ is tangent to the circle at the point (2, 5) and the centre of the circle lies on $x-2y=4$. The radius of the circle is
(a) $3\sqrt{5}$ (b) $5\sqrt{3}$
(c) $2\sqrt{5}$ (d) $5\sqrt{2}$

4. A pair of tangents is drawn to a unit circle with centre at the origin and these tangents intersect at A enclosing an angle of 60°. The area enclosed by these tangents and the arc of the circle is
(a) $\frac{2}{\sqrt{3}}-\frac{\pi}{6}$ (b) $\sqrt{3}-\frac{\pi}{3}$
(c) $\frac{\pi}{3}-\frac{\sqrt{3}}{6}$ (d) $\sqrt{3}\left(1-\frac{\pi}{6}\right)$

5. The point of which the line $9x+y-28=0$ is the chord of contact of the circle $2x^2+2y^2-3x+5y-7=0$ is
(a) (3, – 1) (b) (3, 1)
(c) (–3, 1) (d) None of these

6. If the distance from the origin of the centres of the three circles $x^2+y^2-2\lambda_i x=c^2, (i=1, 2, 3)$ are in GP, then the lengths of the tangents drawn to them from any point on the circle $x^2+y^2=c^2$ are in
(a) AP (b) GP
(c) HP (d) None of these

7. If the length of the common chord of two circles $x^2+y^2+8x+1=0$ and $x^2+y^2+2\mu y-1=0$ is $2\sqrt{6}$, then the value of μ are
(a) ± 2 (b) ± 3
(c) ± 4 (d) ± 5

8. The equation of the circle which has normals $(x-1)\times(y-2)=0$ and a tangent $3x+4y=6$ is
(a) $x^2+y^2-2x-4y+4=0$
(b) $x^2+y^2-2x-4y+5=0$
(c) $x^2+y^2=5$
(d) $(x-3)^2+(y-4)^2=5$

9. The locus of the mid-point of a chord of the circle $x^2+y^2=4$, which subtended a right angle at the origin is
(a) $x+y=2$ (b) $x^2+y^2=1$
(c) $x^2+y^2=2$ (d) $x+y=1$

10. If $C_1: x^2+y^2-20x+64=0$ and $C_2: x^2+y^2+30x+14y=0$, then the length of the shortest line segment PQ which touches C_1 at P and C_2 at Q is
(a) 20 (b) 15
(c) 22 (d) 27

11. The sum of the square of the length of the chord intercepted by the line $x+y=n, n\in N$ on the circle $x^2+y^2=4$ is
(a) 11 (b) 22
(c) 33 (d) None of these

12. Tangents are drawn to the circle $x^2+y^2=50$ from a point P lying on the X-axis. These tangents meet the Y-axis at points P_1 and P_2. Possible coordinates of P so that area of triangle PP_1P_2 is minimum, is
(a) (10, 0) (b) $(10\sqrt{2}, 0)$ (c) $(-10\sqrt{2}, 0)$ (d) $(10\sqrt{3}, 0)$

13. Equation of chord AB of circle $x^2+y^2=2$ passing through $P(2,2)$ such that $\frac{PB}{PA}=3$, is given by
(a) $x=3y$ (b) $x=y$
(c) $y-2=\sqrt{3}(x-2)$ (d) $y-3=\sqrt{3}(x-1)$

14. If r_1 and r_2 are the radii of smallest and largest circles which passes through (5, 6) and touches the circle $(x-2)^2+y^2=4$, then r_1r_2 is
(a) $\frac{4}{41}$ (b) $\frac{41}{4}$ (c) $\frac{5}{41}$ (d) $\frac{41}{5}$

15. Equation of circle $S(x,y)=0$, $(S(2,3)=16)$ which touches the line $3x+4y-7=0$ at $(1,1)$ is given by
(a) $x^2+y^2+x+2y-5=0$
(b) $x^2+y^2+2x+2y-7=0$
(c) $x^2+y^2+4x-6y+13=0$
(d) $x^2+y^2-4x+6y-7=0$

16. If $P(2,8)$ is an interior point of a circle $x^2+y^2-2x+4y-\lambda=0$ which neither touches nor intersects the axes, then set for λ is
(a) $(-\infty,-1)$ (b) $(-\infty,-4)$
(c) $(96,\infty)$ (d) ϕ

17. The difference between the radii of the largest and smallest circles which have their centre on the circumference of the circle $x^2+y^2+2x+4y-4=0$ and pass through the point (a,b) lying outside the given circle is
(a) 6 (b) $\sqrt{(a+1)^2+(b+2)^2}$
(c) 3 (d) $\sqrt{(a+1)^2+(b+2)^2}-3$

18. The number of rational point(s) (a point (a,b) is rational, if a and b both are rational numbers) on the circumference of a circle having centre (π, e) is
(a) atmost one (b) atleast two
(c) exactly two (d) infinite

19. Three sides of a triangle have the equations $L_r \equiv y-m_rx-c_r=0$; $r=1,2,3$. Then $\lambda L_2L_3+\mu L_3L_1+\nu L_1L_2=0$, where $\lambda\neq 0, \mu\neq 0, \nu\neq 0$ is the equation of circumcircle of triangle, if
(a) $\lambda(m_2+m_3)+\mu(m_3+m_1)+\nu(m_1+m_2)=0$
(b) $\lambda(m_2m_3-1)+\mu(m_3m_1-1)+\nu(m_1m_2-1)=0$
(c) Both (a) and (b)
(d) None of the above

20. $f(x,y)\equiv x^2+y^2+2ax+2by+c=0$ represent a circle. If $f(x,0)=0$ has equal roots, each being 2 and $f(0,y)=0$ has 2 and 3 as its roots, then the centre of the circle is
(a) $\left(2,\frac{5}{2}\right)$ (b) Data are not consistent.
(c) $\left(-2,-\frac{5}{2}\right)$ (d) Data are inconsistent.

21. If $(1+\alpha x)^n=1+8x+24x^2+\ldots$ and a line through $P(\alpha,n)$ cuts the circle $x^2+y^2=4$ in A and B, then $PA.PB$ is equal to
(a) 4 (b) 8 (c) 16 (d) 32

22. A region in the xy-plane is bounded by the curve $y=\sqrt{(25-x^2)}$ and the line $y=0$. If the point $(a,a+1)$ lies in the interior of the region, then
(a) $a\in(-4,3)$ (b) $a\in(-\infty,-1)\cup(3,\infty)$
(c) $a\in(-1,3)$ (d) None of these

23. $S(x,y)=0$ represents a circle. The equation $S(x,2)=0$ gives two identical solutions $x=1$ and the equation $S(1,y)=0$ gives two distinct solutions $y=0,2$, then the equation of the circle is
(a) $x^2+y^2+2x-2y+1=0$
(b) $x^2+y^2-2x+2y+1=0$
(c) $x^2+y^2-2x-2y-1=0$
(d) $x^2+y^2-2x-2y+1=0$

24. Let $0<\alpha<\frac{\pi}{2}$ be a fixed angle. If $P=(\cos\theta,\sin\theta)$ and $Q=(\cos(\alpha-\theta),\sin(\alpha-\theta))$, then Q is obtained from P by
(a) clockwise rotation around origin through an angle α
(b) anti-clockwise rotation around origin through an angle α
(c) reflection in the line through origin with slope $\tan\alpha$
(d) reflection in the line through origin with slope $\tan\left(\frac{\alpha}{2}\right)$

25. The number of points (x,y) having integral coordinates satisfying the condition $x^2+y^2<25$ is
(a) 69 (b) 80 (c) 81 (d) 77

26. The centre of a circle passing through the points (0, 0), (1, 0) and touching the circle $x^2+y^2=9$ is
(a) $\left(\frac{3}{2},\frac{1}{2}\right)$ (b) $\left(\frac{1}{2},\frac{3}{2}\right)$
(c) $\left(\frac{1}{2},\sqrt{2}\right)$ (d) $\left(\sqrt{2},\frac{1}{2}\right)$

27. Let L_1 be straight line passing through the origin and L_2 be the straight line $x+y=1$. If the intercepts made by the circle $x^2+y^2-x+3y=0$ on L_1 and L_2 are equal, then which of the following equation can represent L_1?
(a) $x+y=0$, $x=7y$ (b) $x-y=0$, $x+7y=0$
(c) $x+7y=0$, $x+y=0$ (d) None of these

28. Tangents TP and TQ are drawn from a point T to the circle $x^2+y^2=a^2$. If the point T lies on the line $px+qy=r$, then locus of the centre of circumcicle of ΔTPQ is
(a) $2px+2qy-r=0$ (b) $2px+2qy+r=0$
(c) $px+2qy-r=0$ (d) None of these

29. Any circle through the point of intersection of the lines $x+\sqrt{3}y=1$ and $\sqrt{3}x-y=2$ intersect these lines at points P and Q. Then, the angle subtended by the arc PQ at its centre is
(a) 180° (b) 90° (c) 120° (d) 135°

30. The locus of the centres of the circles which cut the circles $x^2+y^2+4x-6y+9=0$ and $x^2+y^2-5x+4y-2=0$ orthogonally, is
(a) $9x+10y-7=0$ (b) $x-y+2=0$
(c) $9x-10y+11=0$ (d) $9x+10y+7=0$

Numerical Value Type Questions

31. $P(a, b)$ is a point in the first quadrant. Circles are drawn through P touching the coordiante axes such that the length of common chord of these circles is maximum, if possible value of a/b is k_1 and k_2, then $k_1 + k_2$ is equal to ......

32. Let $A(-2, 2)$ and $B(2, -2)$ be two points and AB subtends an angle of 45° at any points P in the plane in such a way that area of ΔAPB is 8 sq units, then number of possible position(s) of P is ......

33. The sum of the square of the length of the chord intercepted by the line $x + y = n, n \in N$ on the circle $x^2 + y^2 = 4$ is p, then $\frac{p}{11}$ is equal to ......

34. If (α, β) is a point on the circle whose centre is on the X-axis and which touches the line $x + y = 0$ at $(2, -2)$, then $[\alpha]$ is equal to ...... (where $[\cdot]$ is GIF)

35. The number of such points $(a+1, \sqrt{3}a)$, where a is any integer, lying inside the region bounded by the circles $x^2 + y^2 - 2x - 3 = 0$ and $x^2 + y^2 - 2x - 15 = 0$, is ......

36. If the line $3x - 4y - k = 0$ touches the circle $x^2 + y^2 - 4x - 8y - 5 = 0$ at (a, b), then the positive integral value of $\frac{k+a+b}{5}$ is equal to ......

37. If two perpendicular tangents can be drawn from the origin to the circle $x^2 - 6x + y^2 - 2py + 17 = 0$, then the value of $|p|$ is ......

38. The acute angle between the line $3x - 4y = 5$ and the circle $x^2 + y^2 - 4x + 2y - 4 = 0$ is θ. Then, $9\cos\theta$ is equal to ......

39. A circle $x^2 + y^2 + 4x - 2\sqrt{2}y + c = 0$ is the director circle of the circle S_1 and S_1 is the director circle of circle S_2 and so on. If the sum of radii of all these circles is 2, then the value of $\frac{c}{\sqrt{2}}$ is ......

40. The point (1, 4) lies inside the circle $x^2 + y^2 - 6x - 10y + \lambda = 0$. If the circle neither touches nor cuts the axes, then the difference between the maximum and the minimum possible values of λ is ......

41. Consider the family of circles $x^2 + y^2 - 2x - 2\lambda y - 8 = 0$ passing through two fixed points A and B. Then the distance between the points A and B is ......

42. If $C_1 : x^2 + y^2 = (3 + 2\sqrt{2})^2$ be a circle and PA and PB are pair of tangents on C_1, where P is any point on the director circle of C_1, then the radius of the smallest circle which touches C_1 externally and also the two tangents PA and PB, is ......

43. If a circle $S(x, y) = 0$ touches the point (2,3) of the line $x + y = 5$ and $S(1, 2) = 0$, then radius of such circle is $\frac{1}{\sqrt{\lambda}}$ units, then the value of λ^2 is ......

44. If real numbers x and y satisfy $(x+5)^2 + (y-12)^2 = 196$, then the maximum value of $(x^2 + y^2)^{\frac{1}{3}}$ is ......

45. If r_1 and r_2 are the radii of smallest and largest circles which passes through (5, 6) and touches the circle $(x-2)^2 + y^2 = 4$, then $r_1 r_2$ is ......

46. Minimum radius of circle which is orthogonal with both the circles $x^2 + y^2 - 12x + 35 = 0$ and $x^2 + y^2 + 4x + 3 = 0$ is ......

47. If the circle $x^2 + y^2 + 4x + 22y + 1 = 0$ bisects the circumference of the circle $x^2 + y^2 - 2x + 8y - m = 0$, then $l + m$ is equal to ......

48. The centres of a set of circles, each of radius 3, lie on the circle $x^2 + y^2 = 25$. The locus of any point with such circle is $4 \le x^2 + y^2 \le k$, then the value of k is ......

49. Consider a family of circles passing through two fixed points A (3, 7) and B(6, 5). Show that the chords in which the circle $x^2 + y^2 - 4x - 6y - 3 = 0$ cuts the members of the family are concurrent at a point. Then, the sum of coordinates of this point is ......

Previous Year Questions

50. Let a circle passing through (2, 0) have its centre at the point (h, k). Let (x_c, y_c) be the point of intersection of the lines $3x + 5y = 1$ and $(2 + c)x + 5c^2 y = 1$. If $h = \lim_{c \to 1} x_c$ and $k = \lim_{c \to 1} y_c$, then the equation of the circle is **[Single Correct Type, 2024 Main]**

(a) $5x^2 + 5y^2 - 4x - 2y - 12 = 0$
(b) $25x^2 + 25y^2 - 2x + 2y - 60 = 0$
(c) $25x^2 + 25y^2 - 20x + 2y - 60 = 0$
(d) $5x^2 + 5y^2 - 4x + 2y - 12 = 0$

51. Let the circles $C_1 : (x - \alpha)^2 + (y - \beta)^2 = r_1^2$ and $C_2 : (x - 8)^2 + \left(y - \frac{15}{2}\right)^2 = r_2^2$ touch each other externally at the point (6, 6). If the point (6, 6) divides the line segment joining the centres of the circles C_1 and C_2 internally in the ratio 2 : 1, then $(\alpha + \beta) + 4(r_1^2 + r_2^2)$ equals **[Single Correct Type, 2024 Main]**

(a) 125
(b) 145
(c) 110
(d) 130

52. If $P(6,1)$ be the orthocentre of the triangle whose vertices are $A(5,-2)$, $B(8,3)$ and $C(h,k)$, then the point C lies on the circle **[Single Correct Type, 2024 Main]**

(a) $x^2+y^2-52=0$ (b) $x^2+y^2-61=0$

(c) $x^2+y^2-65=0$ (d) $x^2+y^2-74=0$

53. Let the circle $C_1 : x^2+y^2-2(x+y)+1=0$ and C_2 be a circle having centre at $(-1, 0)$ and radius 2. If the line of the common chord of C_1 and C_2 intersects the Y-axis at the point P, then the square of the distance of P from the centre of C_1 is **[Single Correct Type, 2024 Main]**

(a) 2 (b) 4

(c) 6 (d) 1

54. Let C be a circle with radius $\sqrt{10}$ units and centre at the origin. Let the line $x+y=2$ intersects the circle C at the points P and Q. Let MN be a chord of C of length 2 units and slope -1. Then, a distance (in units) between the chord PQ and the chord MN is **[Single Correct Type, 2024 Main]**

(a) $3-\sqrt{2}$ (b) $\sqrt{2}-1$

(c) $2-\sqrt{3}$ (d) $\sqrt{2}+1$

55. Let a circle C of radius 1 and closer to the origin be such that the lines passing through the point (3, 2) and parallel to the coordinate axes touch it. Then, the shortest distance of the circle C from the point (5,5) is **[Single Correct Type, 2024 Main]**

(a) $4\sqrt{2}$ (b) 4

(c) $2\sqrt{2}$ (d) 5

56. A square is inscribed in the circle $x^2+y^2-10x-6y+30=0$. One side of this square is parallel to $y=x+3$. If (x_i, y_i) are the vertices of the square, then $\Sigma(x_i^2+y_i^2)$ is equal to **[Single Correct Type, 2024 Main]**

(a) 156 (b) 152

(c) 148 (d) 160

57. Let a variable line passing through the centre of the circle $x^2+y^2-16x-4y=0$, meet the positive coordinate axes at the points A and B. Then, the minimum value of $OA+OB$, where O is the origin is equal to **[Single Correct Type, 2024 Main]**

(a) 18 (b) 24

(c) 20 (d) 12

58. Equations of two diameters of a circle are $2x-3y=5$ and $3x-4y=7$. The line joining the points $\left(-\frac{22}{7}, -4\right)$ and $\left(-\frac{1}{7}, 3\right)$ intersects the circle at only one point $P(\alpha, \beta)$. Then, $17\beta-\alpha$ is equal to .... . **[Numerical Value Type, 2024 Main]**

59. Let the mirror image of a circle $C_1 : x^2+y^2-2x-6y+\alpha=0$ in line $y=x+1$ be $C_2 : 5x^2+5y^2+10gx+10fy+38=0$. If r is the radius of circle C_1, then $\alpha+6r^2$ is equal to .... **[Numerical Value Type, 2024 Main]**

60. Let the centre of a circle, passing through the points (0, 0), (1, 0) and touching the circle $x^2+y^2=9$, be (h, k). Then, for all possible values of the coordinates of the centre (h, k), $4(h^2+k^2)$ is equal to .... **[Numerical Value Type, 2024 Main]**

61. The number of common tangents, to the circles $x^2+y^2-18x-15y+131=0$ and $x^2+y^2-6x-6y-7=0$, are **[Single Correct Type, 2023 Main]**

(a) 2 (b) 3

(c) 1 (d) 4

62. Let the centre of a circle C be (α, β) and its radius $r<8$. Let $3x+4y=24$ and $3x-4y=32$ be two tangents and $4x+3y=1$ be a normal to C. Then, $(\alpha-\beta+r)$ is equal to **[Single Correct Type, 2023 Main]**

(a) 6 (b) 9

(c) 7 (d) 5

63. Let A be the point (1, 2) and B be any point on the curve $x^2+y^2=16$. If the centre of the locus of the point P, which divides the line segment AB in the ratio 3 : 2 is the point $C(\alpha, \beta)$, then the length of the line segment AC is **[Single Correct Type, 2023 Main]**

(a) $\frac{3\sqrt{5}}{5}$ (b) $\frac{6\sqrt{5}}{5}$

(c) $\frac{2\sqrt{5}}{5}$ (d) $\frac{4\sqrt{5}}{5}$

64. A line segment AB of length λ moves such that the points A and B remain on the periphery of a circle of radius λ. Then, the locus of the point, that divides the line segment AB in the ratio 2 : 3, is a circle of radius **[Single Correct Type, 2023 Main]**

(a) $\frac{\sqrt{19}}{7}\lambda$ (b) $\frac{\sqrt{19}}{5}\lambda$

(c) $\frac{3}{5}\lambda$ (d) $\frac{2}{3}\lambda$

65. Let O be the origin and OP and OQ be the tangents to the circle $x^2+y^2-6x+4y+8=0$ at the points P and Q on it. If the circumcircle of the ΔOPQ passes through the point $\left(\alpha, \frac{1}{2}\right)$, then a value of α is **[Single Correct Type, 2023 Main]**

(a) 5/2 (b) 1

(c) $-1/2$ (d) 3/2

66. If the tangents at the points P and Q on the circle $x^2 + y^2 - 2x + y = 5$ meet at the point $R\left(\frac{9}{4}, 2\right)$, then the area of the ΔPQR is **[Single Correct Type, 2023 Main]**

(a) 5/4 (b) 13/4
(c) 13/8 (d) 5/8

67. The set of all values of a^2 for which the line $x + y = 0$ bisects two distinct chords drawn from a point $P\left(\frac{1+a}{2}, \frac{1-a}{2}\right)$ on the circle $2x^2 + 2y^2 - (1+a)x - (1-a)y = 0$, is equal to **[Single Correct Type, 2023 Main]**

(a) $(0, 4]$ (b) $(4, \infty)$
(c) $(8, \infty)$ (d) $(2, 12]$

68. Let a circle C_1 be obtained on rolling the circle $x^2 + y^2 - 4x - 6y + 11 = 0$ upwards 4 units on the tangent T to it at the point $(3, 2)$. Let C_2 be the image of C_1 in T. Let A and B be the centres of circles C_1 and C_2 respectively, M and N be respectively the feet of perpendiculars drawn from A and B on the X-axis. Then, the area of the trapezium $AMNB$ is **[Single Correct Type, 2023 Main]**

(a) $3 + 2\sqrt{2}$ (b) $2(2 + \sqrt{2})$
(c) $4(1 + \sqrt{2})$ (d) $2(1 + \sqrt{2})$

69. Let $y = x + 2$, $4y = 3x + 6$ and $3y = 4x + 1$ be three tangent lines to the circle $(x - h)^2 + (y - k)^2 = r^2$. Then, $h + k$ is equal to **[Single Correct Type, 2023 Main]**

(a) $5(1 + \sqrt{2})$ (b) $5\sqrt{2}$
(c) 5 (d) 6

70. Let the tangents at the points $A(4, -11)$ and $B(8, -5)$ on the circle $x^2 + y^2 - 3x + 10y - 15 = 0$, intersect at the point C. Then, the radius of the circle, whose centre is C and the line joining A and B is its tangent, is equal to **[Single Correct Type, 2023 Main]**

(a) $2\sqrt{13}$ (b) $\frac{2\sqrt{13}}{3}$
(c) $\frac{3\sqrt{3}}{4}$ (d) $\sqrt{13}$

71. The points of intersection of the line $ax + by = 0$, $(a \neq b)$ and the circle $x^2 + y^2 - 2x = 0$ are $A(\alpha, 0)$ and $B(1, \beta)$. The image of the circle with AB as a diameter in the line $x + y + 2 = 0$ is **[Single Correct Type, 2023 Main]**

(a) $x^2 + y^2 - 5x - 5y + 12 = 0$
(b) $x^2 + y^2 + 3x + 5y + 8 = 0$
(c) $x^2 + y^2 + 5x + 5y + 12 = 0$
(d) $x^2 + y^2 + 3x + 3y + 4 = 0$

72. The locus of the mid-points of the chords of the circle $C_1 : (x - 4)^2 + (y - 5)^2 = 4$ which subtend an angle θ_i at the centre of the circle C_1 is a circle of radius r_i. If $\theta_1 = \frac{\pi}{3}, \theta_3 = \frac{2\pi}{3}$ and $r_1^2 = r_2^2 + r_3^2$, then θ_2 is equal to **[Single Correct Type, 2023 Main]**

(a) $\frac{3\pi}{4}$ (b) $\frac{\pi}{4}$
(c) $\frac{\pi}{6}$ (d) $\frac{\pi}{2}$

73. Two circles in the first quadrant of radii r_1 and r_2 touch the coordinate axes. Each of them cuts off an intercept of 2 units with the line $x + y = 2$. Then, $r_1^2 + r_2^2 - r_1 r_2$ is equal to .... **[Numerical Value Type, 2023 Main]**

74. Consider a circle $C_1 : x^2 + y^2 - 4x - 2y = \alpha - 5$. Let its mirror image in the line $y = 2x + 1$ be another circle $C_2 : 5x^2 + 5y^2 - 10fx - 10gy + 36 = 0$. Let r be the radius of C_2. Then, $\alpha + r$ is equal to ..... **[Numerical Value Type, 2023 Main]**

75. A circle passing through the point $P(\alpha, \beta)$ in the first quadrant touches the two coordinate axes at the points A and B. The point P is above the line AB. The point Q on the line segment AB is the foot of perpendicular from P on AB. If PQ is equal to 11 units, then the value of $\alpha\beta$ is .... **[Numerical Value Type, 2023 Main]**

76. Let $P(a_1, b_1)$ and $Q(a_2, b_2)$ be two distinct points on a circle with center $C(\sqrt{2}, \sqrt{3})$. Let O be the origin and OC be perpendicular to both CP and CQ. If the area of ΔOCP is $\frac{\sqrt{35}}{2}$, then $a_1^2 + a_2^2 + b_1^2 + b_2^2$ is equal to .... **[Numerical Value Type, 2023 Main]**

77. A circle with centre $(2, 3)$ and radius 4 intersects the line $x + y = 3$ at the points P and Q. If the tangents at P and Q intersect at the point $S(\alpha, \beta)$, then $4\alpha - 7\beta$ is equal to .... **[Numerical Value Type, 2023 Main]**

78. Points $P(-3, 2)$, $Q(9, 10)$ and $R(\alpha, 4)$ lie on a circle C with PR as its diameter. The tangents to C at the points Q and R intersect at the point S. If S lies on the line $2x - ky = 1$, then k is equal to .... **[Numerical Value Type, 2023 Main]**

79. Let the tangents at two points A and B on the circle $x^2 + y^2 - 4x + 3 = 0$ meet at origin $O(0, 0)$. Then, the area of the ΔOAB is **[Single Correct Type, 2022 Main]**

(a) $\frac{3\sqrt{3}}{2}$ (b) $\frac{3\sqrt{3}}{4}$
(c) $\frac{3}{2\sqrt{3}}$ (d) $\frac{3}{4\sqrt{3}}$

80. Let C be the centre of the circle $x^2 + y^2 - x + 2y = \frac{11}{4}$ and P be a point on the circle. A line passes through the point C, makes an angle of $\frac{\pi}{4}$ with the line CP and intersects the circle at Q and R. Then, area of the ΔPQR (in unit^2) is **[Single Correct Type, 2022 Main]**

(a) 2 (b) $2\sqrt{2}$

(c) $8\sin\left(\frac{\pi}{8}\right)$ (d) $8\cos\left(\frac{\pi}{8}\right)$

81. For $t \in (0, 2\pi)$, if ABC is an equilateral triangle with vertices $A(\sin t, -\cos t)$, $B(\cos t, \sin t)$ and $C(a, b)$ such that its orthocentre lies on a circle with centre $\left(1, \frac{1}{3}\right)$, then $(a^2 - b^2)$ is equal to **[Single Correct Type, 2022 Main]**

(a) $\frac{8}{3}$ (b) 8

(c) $\frac{77}{9}$ (d) $\frac{80}{9}$

82. A circle C_1 passes through the origin O and has diameter 4 on the positive X-axis. The line $y = 2x$ gives a chord OA of circle C_1. Let C_2 be the circle with OA as a diameter. If the tangent to C_2 at the point A meets the X-axis at P and Y-axis at Q, then $QA : AP$ is equal to **[Single Correct Type, 2022 Main]**

(a) 1 : 4 (b) 1 : 5

(c) 2 : 5 (d) 1 : 3

83. If the circle $x^2 + y^2 - 2gx + 6y - 19c = 0$, $c \in R$ passes through the point (6, 1) and its centre lies on the line $x - 2cy = 8$, then the length of intercept made by the circle on X-axis is **[Single Correct Type, 2022 Main]**

(a) $\sqrt{11}$ (b) 4 (c) 3 (d) $2\sqrt{3}$

84. Let the abscissae of the two points P and Q on a circle be the roots $x^2 - 4x - 6 = 0$ and the ordinates of P and Q be the roots of $y^2 + 2y - 7 = 0$. If PQ is a diameter of the circle $x^2 + y^2 + 2ax + 2by + c = 0$, then the value of $(a + b - c)$ is **[Single Correct Type, 2022 Main]**

(a) 12 (b) 13 (c) 14 (d) 16

85. Consider three circles

$C_1 : x^2 + y^2 = r^2$

$C_2 : (x-1)^2 + (y-1)^2 = r^2$

$C_3 : (x-2)^2 + (y-1)^2 = r^2$

If a line $L : y = mx + c$ be a common tangent to C_1, C_2 and C_3 such that C_1 and C_3 lie on one side of line L with C_2 lies on other side, then the value of $20(r^2 + c)$ is equal to **[Single Correct Type, 2022 Main]**

(a) 23 (b) 15 (c) 12 (d) 6

86. Let a ΔABC be inscribed in the circle $x^2 - \sqrt{2}(x + y) + y^2 = 0$ such that $\angle BAC = \frac{\pi}{2}$. If the length of side AB is $\sqrt{2}$, then the area of the ΔABC is equal to **[Single Correct Type, 2022 Main]**

(a) 1 (b) $\frac{(\sqrt{6} + \sqrt{3})}{2}$

(c) $\frac{(3 + \sqrt{3})}{4}$ (d) $\frac{(\sqrt{6} + 2\sqrt{3})}{4}$

87. Let the tangent to the circle $C_1 : x^2 + y^2 = 2$ at the point $M(-1, 1)$ intersect the circle $C_2 : (x-3)^2 + (y-2)^2 = 5$, at two distinct points A and B. If the tangents to C_2 at the points A and B intersect at N, then the area of the ΔANB is equal to **[Single Correct Type, 2022 Main]**

(a) 1/2 (b) 2/3

(c) 1/6 (d) 5/3

88. If the tangents drawn at the points $O(0, 0)$ and $P(1 + \sqrt{5}, 2)$ on the circle $x^2 + y^2 - 2x - 4y = 0$ intersect at the point Q, then the area of the ΔOPQ is equal to **[Single Correct Type, 2022 Main]**

(a) $\frac{3 + \sqrt{5}}{2}$ (b) $\frac{4 + 2\sqrt{5}}{2}$

(c) $\frac{5 + 3\sqrt{5}}{2}$ (d) $\frac{7 + 3\sqrt{5}}{2}$

89. The set of values of k for which the circle $C : 4x^2 + 4y^2 - 12x + 8y + k = 0$ lies inside the fourth quadrant and the point $\left(1, -\frac{1}{3}\right)$ lies on or inside the circle C is **[Single Correct Type, 2022 Main]**

(a) an empty set (b) $\left(6, \frac{65}{9}\right]$

(c) $\left[\frac{80}{9}, 10\right)$ (d) $\left(9, \frac{92}{9}\right]$

90. Let C be a circle passing through the points $A(2, -1)$ and $B(3, 4)$. The line segment AB is not a diameter of C. If r is the radius of C and its centre lies on the circle $(x-5)^2 + (y-1)^2 = \frac{13}{2}$, then r^2 is equal to **[Single Correct Type, 2022 Main]**

(a) 32 (b) $\frac{65}{2}$ (c) $\frac{61}{2}$ (d) 30

91. Let a circle C touch the lines $L_1 : 4x - 3y + k_1 = 0$ and $L_2 : 4x - 3y + k_2 = 0$, $k_1, k_2 \in R$. If a line passing through the centre of the circle C intersects L_1 at $(-1, 2)$ and L_2 at $(3, -6)$, then the equation of the circle C is **[Single Correct Type, 2022 Main]**

(a) $(x-1)^2 + (y-2)^2 = 4$ (b) $(x+1)^2 + (y-2)^2 = 4$

(c) $(x-1)^2 + (y+2)^2 = 16$ (d) $(x-1)^2 + (y-2)^2 = 16$

92. Let AB be a chord of length 12 of the circle $(x-2)^2+(y+1)^2=169/4$. If tangents drawn to the circle at points A and B intersect at the point P, then five times the distance of point P from chord AB is equal to .... **[Numerical Value Type, 2022 Main]**

93. If the circles $x^2+y^2+6x+8y+16=0$ and $x^2+y^2+2(3-\sqrt{3})x+x+2(4-\sqrt{6})y=k+6\sqrt{3}+8\sqrt{6}$, $k>0$, touch internally at the point $P(\alpha,\beta)$, then $(\alpha+\sqrt{3})^2+(\beta+\sqrt{6})^2$ is equal to .... **[Numerical Value Type, 2022 Main]**

94. If one of the diameters of the circle $x^2+y^2-2\sqrt{2}\,x-6\sqrt{2}y+14=0$ is a chord of the circle $(x-2\sqrt{2})^2+(y-2\sqrt{2})^2=r^2$, then the value of r^2 is equal to......... . **[Numerical Value Type, 2022 Main]**

95. Let the lines $y+2x=\sqrt{11}+7\sqrt{7}$ and $2y+x=2\sqrt{11}+6\sqrt{7}$ be normal to a circle $C:(x-h)^2+(y-k)^2=r^2$. If the line $\sqrt{11}y-3x=\dfrac{5\sqrt{77}}{3}+11$ is tangent to the circle C, then the value of $(5h-8k)^2+5r^2$ is equal to .... **[Numerical Value Type, 2022 Main]**

96. Let a circle C of radius 5 lie below the X-axis. The line $L_1:4x+3y+2=0$ passes through the centre P of the circle C and intersects the line $L_2:3x-4y-11=0$ at Q. The line L_2 touches C at the point Q. Then, the distance of P from the line $5x-12y+51=0$ is .... **[Numerical Value Type, 2022 Main]**

97. A rectangle R with end points of the one of its sides as (1, 2) and (3, 6) is inscribed in a circle. If the equation of a diameter of the circle is $2x-y+4=0$, then the area of R is .... **[Numerical Value Type, 2022 Main]**

98. Let the abscissae of the two points P and Q be the roots of $2x^2-rx+p=0$ and the ordinates of P and Q be the roots of $x^2-sx-q=0$. If the equation of the circle described on PQ as diameter is $2(x^2+y^2)-11x-14y-22=0$, then $2r+s-2q+p$ is equal to .... **[Numerical Value Type, 2022 Main]**

99. Let a circle $C:(x-h)^2+(y-k)^2=r^2$, $k>0$, touch the X-axis at (1, 0). If the line $x+y=0$ intersects the circle C at P and Q such that the length of the chord PQ is 2, then the value of $h+k+r$ is equal to .... **[Numerical Value Type, 2022 Main]**

100. A circle C touches the line $x=2y$ at the point (2,1) and intersects the circle $C_1:x^2+y^2+2y-5=0$ at two points P and Q such that PQ is a diameter of C_1. Then, the diameter of C is **[Single Correct Type, 2021 Main]**

(a) $7\sqrt{5}$ (b) 15 (c) 285 (d) $4\sqrt{15}$

101. Consider a circle C which touches the Y-axis at (0, 6) and cuts off an intercept $6\sqrt{5}$ on the X-axis. Then, the radius of the circle C is equal to **[Single Correct Type, 2021 Main]**

(a) $\sqrt{53}$ (b) 9 (c) 8 (d) $\sqrt{82}$

102. Two tangents are drawn from the point $P(-1,1)$ to the circle $x^2+y^2-2x-6y+6=0$. If these tangents touch the circle at points A and B, and if D is a point on the circle such that length of the segments AB and AD are equal, then the area of the ΔABD is equal to **[Single Correct Type, 2021 Main]**

(a) 2 (b) $(3\sqrt{2}+2)$ (c) 4 (d) $3(\sqrt{2}-1)$

103. Let P and Q be two distinct points on a circle which has center at $C(2,3)$ and which passes through origin O. If OC is perpendicular to both the line segments CP and CQ, then the set $\{P,Q\}$ is equal to **[Single Correct Type, 2021 Main]**

(a) $\{(4,0),(0,6)\}$
(b) $\{(2+2\sqrt{2},3-\sqrt{3}),(2-2\sqrt{2},3+\sqrt{5})\}$
(c) $\{(2+2\sqrt{2},3+\sqrt{5}),(2-2\sqrt{2},3-\sqrt{5})\}$
(d) $\{(-1,5),(5,1)\}$

104. Let $A=\{(x,y)\in R\times R\mid 2x^2+2y^2-2x-2y=1\}$, $B=\{(x,y)\in R\times R\mid 4x^2+4y^2-16y+7=0\}$, $C=\{(x,y)\in R\times R\mid x^2+y^2-4x-2y+5\le r^2\}$.

Then, the minimum value of $|r|$ such that $A\cup B\subseteq C$ is equal to **[Single Correct Type, 2021 Main]**

(a) $\dfrac{3+\sqrt{10}}{2}$ (b) $\dfrac{2+\sqrt{10}}{2}$ (c) $\dfrac{3+2\sqrt{5}}{2}$ (d) $1+\sqrt{5}$

105. Let the circle $S:36x^2+36y^2-108x+120y+C=0$ be such that it neither intersects nor touches the coordinate axes. If the point of intersection of the lines $x-2y=4$ and $2x-y=5$ lies inside the circle S, then **[Single Correct Type, 2021 Main]**

(a) $\dfrac{25}{9}<C<\dfrac{13}{3}$ (b) $100<C<165$
(c) $81<C<156$ (d) $100<C<156$

106. Let r_1 and r_2 be the radii of the largest and smallest circles respectively, which pass through the point $(-4,1)$ and having their centres on the circumference of the circle $x^2+y^2+2x+4y-4=0$.

If $\dfrac{r_1}{r_2}=a+b\sqrt{2}$, then $a+b$ is equal to **[Single Correct Type, 2021 Main]**

(a) 3 (b) 11 (c) 5 (d) 7

107. Let $S_1\Rightarrow x^2+y^2=9$ and $S_2\Rightarrow(x-2)^2+y^2=1$. Then, the locus of center of a variable circle S which touches S_1 internally and S_2 externally always passes through the points **[Single Correct Type, 2021 Main]**

(a) $(0,\pm\sqrt{3})$ (b) $\left(\dfrac{1}{2},\pm\dfrac{\sqrt{5}}{2}\right)$
(c) $\left(2,\pm\dfrac{3}{2}\right)$ (d) $(1,\pm 2)$

108. Choose the correct statement about two circles whose equations are given below.

$x^2 + y^2 - 10x - 10y + 41 = 0$

$x^2 + y^2 - 22x - 10y + 137 = 0$

[Single Correct Type, 2021 Main]

(a) circles have same centre.
(b) circles have no meeting point.
(c) circles have only one meeting point.
(d) circles have two meeting points.

109. For the four circles M, N, O and P following four equations are given

Circle $M : x^2 + y^2 = 1$

Circle $N : x^2 + y^2 - 2x = 0$

Circle $O : x^2 + y^2 - 2x - 2y + 1 = 0$

Circle $P : x^2 + y^2 - 2y = 0$

If the centre of circle M is joined with centre of the circle N, further centre of circle N is joined with centre of the circle O, centre of circle O is joined the centre of circle P and lastly, centre of circle P is joined with centre of circle M, then these lines form the sides of a

[Single Correct Type, 2021 Main]

(a) rhombus (b) square
(c) rectangle (d) parallelogram

110. Let the tangent to the circle $x^2 + y^2 = 25$ at the point $R(3, 4)$ meet X-axis and Y-axis at points P and Q, respectively. If r is the radius of the circle passing through the origin O and having centre at the incentre of the ΔOPQ, then r^2 is equal to

[Single Correct Type, 2021 Main]

(a) $\frac{529}{64}$ (b) $\frac{625}{72}$ (c) $\frac{585}{66}$ (d) $\frac{125}{72}$

111. The line $2x - y + 1 = 0$ is a tangent to the circle at the point (2, 5) and the centre of the circle lies on $x - 2y = 4$. Then, the radius of the circle is

[Single Correct Type, 2021 Main]

(a) $3\sqrt{5}$ (b) $5\sqrt{3}$ (c) $5\sqrt{4}$ (d) $4\sqrt{5}$

112. Choose the incorrect statement about the two circles whose equations are given below

$x^2 + y^2 - 10x - 10y + 41 = 0$

and $x^2 + y^2 - 16x - 10y + 80 = 0$

[Single Correct Type, 2021 Main]

(a) Distance between two centres is the average of radii of both the circles.
(b) Both circle's centres lie inside region of one another.
(c) Both circles pass through the centre of each other.
(d) Circles have two intersection points.

113. Let the lengths of intercepts on X-axis and Y-axis made by the circle $x^2 + y^2 + ax + 2ay + c = 0, (a < 0)$ be $2\sqrt{2}$ and $2\sqrt{5}$, respectively. Then, the shortest distance from origin to a tangent to this circle which is perpendicular to the line $x + 2y = 0$, is equal to

[Single Correct Type, 2021 Main]

(a) $\sqrt{11}$ (b) $\sqrt{7}$ (c) $\sqrt{6}$ (d) $\sqrt{10}$

114. If the locus of the mid-point of the line segment from the point (3, 2) to a point on the circle, $x^2 + y^2 = 1$ is a circle of radius r, then r is equal to

[Single Correct Type, 2021 Main]

(a) 1 (b) 1/2 (c) 1/3 (d) 1/4

115. Let $A(1, 4)$ and $B(1, -5)$ be two points. Let P be a point on the circle $(x - 1)^2 + (y - 1)^2 = 1$, such that $(PA)^2 + (PB)^2$ have maximum value, then the points P, A and B lie on

[Single Correct Type, 2021 Main]

(a) a straight line (b) a hyperbola
(c) an ellipse (d) a parabola

116. In the circle given below, let $OA = 1$ unit, $OB = 13$ units and $PQ \perp OB$. Then, the area of the ΔPQB (in square units) is **[Single Correct Type, 2021 Main]**

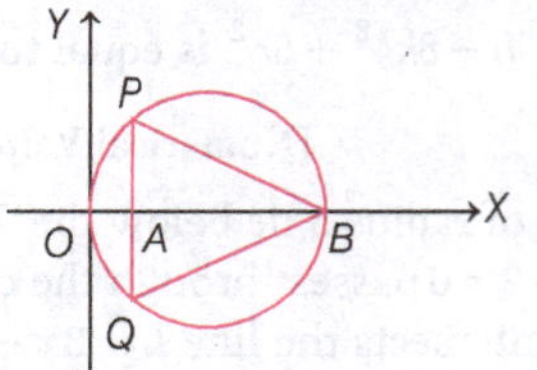

(a) $24\sqrt{2}$ (b) $24\sqrt{3}$ (c) $26\sqrt{3}$ (d) $26\sqrt{2}$

117. For which of the following curves, the line $x + \sqrt{3}y = 2\sqrt{3}$ is the tangent at the point $\left(\frac{3\sqrt{3}}{2}, \frac{1}{2}\right)$?

[Single Correct Type, 2021 Main]

(a) $x^2 + y^2 = 7$ (b) $y^2 = \frac{1}{6\sqrt{3}}x$
(c) $2x^2 - 18y^2 = 9$ (d) $x^2 + 9y^2 = 9$

118. Let B be the centre of the circle $x^2 + y^2 - 2x + 4y + 1 = 0$. Let the tangents at two points P and Q on the circle intersect at the point A (3, 1). Then $8\left(\frac{\text{area } \Delta APQ}{\text{area } \Delta BPQ}\right)$ is equal to ....

[Numerical Value Type, 2021 Main]

119. If the variable line $3x + 4y = \alpha$ lies between the two circles $(x - 1)^2 + (y - 1)^2 = 1$ and $(x - 9)^2 + (y - 1)^2 = 4$, without intercepting a chord on either circle, then the sum of all the integral values of α is ....

[Numerical Value Type, 2021 Main]

120. Two circles each of radius 5 units touch each other at the point (1, 2). If the equation of their common tangent is $4x + 3y = 10$ and $C_1(\alpha, \beta)$ and $C_2(\gamma, \delta)$, $C_1 \neq C_2$ are their centres, then $|(\alpha + \beta)(\gamma + \delta)|$ is equal to ....
[Numerical Value Type, 2021 Main]

121. Let the equation $x^2 + y^2 + px + (1 - p)y + 5 = 0$ represent circles of varying radius $r \in (0, 5]$. Then, the number of elements in the set $S = \{q : q = p^2$ and q is an integer$\}$ is ....
[Numerical Value Type, 2021 Main]

122. The locus of a point, which moves such that the sum of squares of its distances from the points (0, 0), (1, 0), (0, 1) (1, 1) is 18 units, is a circle of diameter (d). Then, d^2 is equal to ....
[Numerical Value Type, 2021 Main]

123. Let $ABCD$ be a square of side of unit length. Let a circle C_1 centred at A with unit radius is drawn. Another circle C_2, which touches C_1 and the lines AD and AB are tangent to it, is also drawn. Let a tangent line from the point C to the circle C_2 meet the side AB at E. If the length of EB is $\alpha + \sqrt{3}\beta$, where α, β are integers, then $\alpha + \beta$ is equal to .... **[Numerical Value Type, 2021 Main]**

124. Let the normals at all the points on a given curve pass through a fixed point (a, b). If the curve passes through $(3, -3)$ and $(4, -2\sqrt{2})$, and given that $a - 2\sqrt{2}b = 3$, then $(a^2 + b^2 + ab)$ is equal to ....
[Numerical Value Type, 2021 Main]

125. Let a point P be such that its distance from the point (5, 0) is thrice the distance of P from the point (– 5, 0). If the locus of the point P is a circle of radius r, then $4r^2$ is equal to ....
[Numerical Value Type, 2021 Main]

126. If the area of the triangle formed by the positive X-axis, the normal and the tangent to the circle $(x - 2)^2 + (y - 3)^2 = 25$ at the point $(5, 7)$ is A, then $24A$ is equal to .... **[Numerical Value Type, 2021 Main]**

127. If one of the diameters of the circle $x^2 + y^2 - 2x - 6y + 6 = 0$ is a chord of another circle C, whose centre is at (2, 1), then its radius is ....
[Numerical Value Type, 2021 Main]

128. If the length of the chord of the circle, $x^2 + y^2 = r^2 (r > 0)$ along the line, $y - 2x = 3$ is r, then r^2 is equal to **[Single Correct Type, 2020 Main]**

(a) 9/5 (b) 12
(c) 24/5 (d) 12/5

129. If a line, $y = mx + c$ is a tangent to the circle, $(x - 3)^2 + y^2 = 1$ and it is perpendicular to a line L_1, where L_1 is the tangent to the circle, $x^2 + y^2 = 1$ at the point $\left(\frac{1}{\sqrt{2}}, \frac{1}{\sqrt{2}}\right)$, then **[Single Correct Type, 2020 Main]**

(a) $c^2 + 7c + 6 = 0$
(b) $c^2 - 6c + 7 = 0$
(c) $c^2 - 7c + 6 = 0$
(d) $c^2 + 6c + 7 = 0$

130. Let the tangents drawn from the origin to the circle, $x^2 + y^2 - 8x - 4y + 16 = 0$ touch it at the points A and B. Then, $(AB)^2$ is equal to **[Single Correct Type, 2020 Main]**

(a) $\frac{56}{5}$ (b) $\frac{52}{5}$
(c) $\frac{64}{5}$ (d) $\frac{32}{5}$

131. The diameter of the circle, whose centre lies on the line $x + y = 2$ in the first quadrant and which touches both the lines $x = 3$ and $y = 2$, is ....
[Numerical Value Type, 2020 Main]

132. The number of integral values of k for which the line, $3x + 4y = k$ intersects the circle, $x^2 + y^2 - 2x - 4y + 4 = 0$ at two distinct points is ....
[Numerical Value Type, 2020 Main]

EXERCISE 2
JEE Advanced Pattern

Single Option Correct Type Questions

1. Lines $5x+12y-10=0$ and $5x-12y-40=0$ touch circle C_1 of diameter 6. If the centre of C_1 lies in the first quadrant, find the equation of the circle C_2 which is concentric with C_1 and cuts intercepts of lengths 8 on these lines
(a) $x^2+y^2+10x-4y+4=0$
(b) $x^2-y^2-10x-4y+4=0$
(c) $x^2+y^2-10x+4y+4=0$
(d) None of the above

2. The equation of the circle which passes through the point $(1,-1)$ and which touches the line $6x-y-18=0$ at the point $P(3,0)$.
(a) $13(x^2+y^2)-48x+5y+27=0$
(b) $13(x^2+y^2)-48x-5y-27=0$
(c) $11(x^2+y^2)-48x+5y+27=0$
(d) None of the above

3. $P(\alpha)$ and $Q(\beta)$ are the two points on the circle having origin as its centre and radius a and AB is the diameter along the axis of x. If $\alpha-\beta=2\gamma$, then the locus of intersection of AP and BQ is
(a) $x^2+y^2-2ay\cot\gamma-a=0$
(b) $x^2+y^2+2ay\tan\gamma-a=0$
(c) $x^2+y^2-2ay\tan\gamma-a^2=0$
(d) None of the above

4. P is a variable point on the line $y=4$. Tangents are drawn to the circle $x^2+y^2=4$ from P to touch it at A and B. The parallelogram $PAQB$ is completed. Then, the equation of the locus of Q is
(a) $(x^2+y^2)(y+4)=2x^2$ (b) $(x^2+y^2)(x+4)=2y^2$
(c) $(x^2+y^2)(x+4)=2x^2$ (d) $(x^2+y^2)(y+4)=2y^2$

5. The point $([P+1],[P])$, (where $[.]$ denotes the greatest integer function) lying inside the region bounded by the circle $x^2+y^2-2x-15=0$ and $x^2+y^2-2x-7=0$, then
(a) $P\in[-1,0)\cup[0,1)\cup[1,2)$
(b) $P\in[-1,2)-\{0,1\}$
(c) $P\in(-1,2)$
(d) None of the above

6. A point P lies inside the circles $x^2+y^2-4=0$ and $x^2+y^2-8x+7=0$. The point P starts moving under the conditions that its path encloses greatest possible area and it is at a fixed distance from any arbitrarily chosen fixed point in its region. Then, the locus of P is
(a) $4x^2+4y^2-12x+1=0$ (b) $4x^2+4y^2+12x-1=0$
(c) $x^2+y^2-3x-2=0$ (d) $x^2+y^2-3x+2=0$

7. The set of values of c so that the equations $y=|x|+c$ and $x^2+y^2-8|x|-9=0$ have no solution is
(a) $(-\infty,-3)\cup(3,\infty)$ (b) $(-3,3)$
(c) $(-\infty,-5\sqrt{2})\cup(5\sqrt{2},\infty)$ (d) $(5\sqrt{2}-4,\infty)$

8. If a line segment $AM=a$ moves in the plane XOY remaining parallel to OX so that the left end point A slides along the circle $x^2+y^2=a^2$, the locus of M is
(a) $x^2+y^2=4a^2$ (b) $x^2+y^2=2ax$
(c) $x^2+y^2=2ay$ (d) $x^2+y^2-2ax-2ay=0$

9. The four points of intersection of the lines $(2x-y+1)(x-2y+3)=0$ with the axes lie on a circle whose centre is at the point
(a) $\left(-\frac{7}{4},\frac{5}{4}\right)$ (b) $\left(\frac{3}{4},\frac{5}{4}\right)$ (c) $\left(\frac{9}{4},\frac{5}{4}\right)$ (d) $\left(0,\frac{5}{4}\right)$

10. The number of integral values of λ for, which $x^2+y^2+\lambda x+(1-\lambda)y+5=0$ is the equation of a circle whose radius cannot exceed 5, is
(a) 14 (b) 18 (c) 16 (d) None of these

11. Let $\phi(x,y)=0$ be the equation of a circle. If $\phi(0,\lambda)=0$ has equal roots $\lambda=2,2$ and $\phi(\lambda,0)=0$ has roots $\lambda=\frac{4}{5},5$, then the centre of the circle is
(a) $\left(2,\frac{29}{10}\right)$ (b) $\left(\frac{29}{10},2\right)$ (c) $\left(-2,\frac{29}{10}\right)$ (d) None of these

12. The locus of the point of intersection of the tangents to the circle $x=r\cos\theta, y=r\sin\theta$ at points whose parametric angles differ by $\frac{\pi}{3}$ is
(a) $x^2+y^2=4(2-\sqrt{3})r^2$ (b) $3(x^2+y^2)=1$
(c) $x^2+y^2=(2-\sqrt{3})r^2$ (d) $3(x^2+y^2)=4r^2$

13. One of the diameter of the circle circumscribing the rectangle $ABCD$ is $4y = x + 7$. If A and B are the points $(-3, 4)$ and $(5, 4)$ respectively, then the area of the rectangle is

(a) 16 sq units (b) 24 sq units
(c) 32 sq units (d) None of these

14. A, B, C and D are the points of intersection with the coordinate axes of the lines $ax + by = ab$ and $bx + ay = ab$, then

(a) A, B, C, D are concyclic
(b) A, B, C, D form a parallelogram
(c) A, B, C, D form a rhombus
(d) None of the above

15. α, β and γ are parametric angles of three points P, Q and R respectively, on the circle $x^2 + y^2 = 1$ and A is the point $(-1, 0)$. If the lengths of the chords AP, AQ and AR are in GP, then $\cos\left(\frac{\alpha}{2}\right), \cos\left(\frac{\beta}{2}\right)$ and $\cos\left(\frac{\gamma}{2}\right)$ are in

(a) AP (b) GP
(c) HP (d) None of these

16. The equation of the circle passing through (2, 0) and (0, 4) and having the minimum radius is

(a) $x^2 + y^2 = 20$
(b) $x^2 + y^2 - 2x - 4y = 0$
(c) $(x^2 + y^2 - 4) + \lambda(x^2 + y^2 - 16) = 0$
(d) None of the above

17. A circle of radius unity is centred at the origin. Two particles start moving at the same time from the point (1, 0) and move around the circle in opposite direction. One of the particle moves anti-clockwise with constant speed v and the other moves clockwise with constant speed $3v$. After leaving (1, 0), the two particles meet first at a point P and continue until they meet next at point Q. The coordinates of the point Q are

(a) (1, 0) (b) (0, 1) (c) (−1, 0) (d) (0, −1)

18. The circle $x^2 + y^2 = 4$ cuts the line joining the points $A(1, 0)$ and $B(3, 4)$ in two points P and Q. Let $\frac{BP}{PA} = \alpha$ and $\frac{BQ}{QA} = \beta$, then α and β are roots of the quadratic equation

(a) $x^2 + 2x + 7 = 0$ (b) $3x^2 + 2x - 21 = 0$
(c) $2x^2 + 3x - 27 = 0$ (d) None of these

19. The locus of the mid-points of the chords of the circle $x^2 + y^2 + 4x - 6y - 12 = 0$ which subtend an angle of $\frac{\pi}{3}$ radians at its circumference is

(a) $(x + 2)^2 + (y - 3)^2 = 6.25$ (b) $(x - 2)^2 + (y + 3)^2 = 6.25$
(c) $(x + 2)^2 + (y - 3)^2 = 18.75$ (d) $(x + 2)^2 + (y + 3)^2 = 18.75$

More than One Correct Option Type Questions

20. If OA and OB are two perpendicular chords of the circle $r = a\cos\theta + b\sin\theta$ passing through origin, then the locus of the mid-point of AB is

(a) $x^2 + y^2 = a + b$ (b) $x = \frac{a}{2}$
(c) $x^2 - y^2 = a^2 - b^2$ (d) $y = \frac{b}{2}$

21. If A and B are two points on the circle $x^2 + y^2 - 4x + 6y - 3 = 0$ which are farthest and nearest respectively, from the point (7, 2), then

(a) $A \equiv (2 - 2\sqrt{2}, -3 - 2\sqrt{2})$ (b) $A \equiv (2 + 2\sqrt{2}, -3 + 2\sqrt{2})$
(c) $B \equiv (2 + 2\sqrt{2}, -3 - 2\sqrt{2})$ (d) $B \equiv (2 - 2\sqrt{2}, -3 + 2\sqrt{2})$

22. If the circle $x^2 + y^2 + 2gx + 2fy + c = 0$ cuts each of the circles $x^2 + y^2 - 4 = 0$, $x^2 + y^2 - 6x - 8y + 10 = 0$ and $x^2 + y^2 + 2x - 4y - 2 = 0$ at the extremities of a diameter, then

(a) $c = -4$ (b) $g + f = c - 1$
(c) $g^2 + f^2 - c = 17$ (d) $gf = 6$

23. The possible value of $\lambda (\lambda > 0)$ such that the angle between the pair of tangents from point $(\lambda, 0)$ to the circle $x^2 + y^2 = 4$ lies in interval $\left(\frac{\pi}{2}, \frac{2\pi}{3}\right)$ is

(a) $\left(\frac{4}{\sqrt{3}}, 2\sqrt{2}\right)$ (b) $(0, \sqrt{2})$
(c) (1,2) (d) $\left(\frac{4}{\sqrt{3}}, \frac{5}{\sqrt{3}}\right)$

24. If a chord of the circle $x^2 + y^2 - 4x - 2y - c = 0$ is trisected at the points $\left(\frac{1}{3}, \frac{1}{3}\right)$ and $\left(\frac{8}{3}, \frac{8}{3}\right)$, then

(a) $c = 10$ (b) $c = 20$
(c) $c = 15$ (d) $c^2 - 40c + 400 = 0$

25. From the point $A(0, 3)$ on $x^2 + 4x + (y - 3)^2 = 0$, a chord AB is drawn and extended to a point M, such that $AM = 2AB$. An equation of the locus of M is

(a) $x^2 + 6x + (y - 2)^2 = 0$ (b) $x^2 + 8x + (y - 3)^2 = 0$
(c) $x^2 + y^2 + 8x - 6y + 9 = 0$ (d) $x^2 + y^2 + 6x - 4y + 4 = 0$

26. An equation of a circle touching the axes of coordinates and the line $x\cos\alpha + y\sin\alpha = 2$ can be

(a) $x^2 + y^2 - 2gx - 2gy + g^2 = 0$, where $g = \frac{2}{(\cos\alpha + \sin\alpha + 1)}$

(b) $x^2 + y^2 - 2gx - 2gy + g^2 = 0$, where $g = \frac{2}{(\cos\alpha + \sin\alpha - 1)}$

(c) $x^2 + y^2 - 2gx + 2gy + g^2 = 0$, where $g = \frac{2}{(\cos\alpha - \sin\alpha + 1)}$

(d) $x^2 + y^2 - 2gx + 2gy + g^2 = 0$, where $g = \frac{2}{(\cos\alpha - \sin\alpha - 1)}$

27. If α is the angle subtended at $P(x_1, y_1)$ by the circle $S \equiv x^2 + y^2 + 2gx + 2fy + c = 0$, then

(a) $\cot\alpha = \frac{\sqrt{S_1}}{\sqrt{(g^2+f^2-c)}}$ (b) $\cot\frac{\alpha}{2} = \frac{\sqrt{S_1}}{\sqrt{(g^2+f^2-c)}}$

(c) $\tan\alpha = \frac{2\sqrt{(g^2+f^2-c)}}{\sqrt{S_1}}$ (d) $\alpha = 2\tan^{-1}\left(\frac{\sqrt{(g^2+f^2-c)}}{\sqrt{S_1}}\right)$

28. The equation of the circle which touches the axis of coordinates and the line $\frac{x}{3} + \frac{y}{4} = 1$ and whose centre lies in the first quadrant is $x^2 + y^2 - 2\lambda x - 2\lambda y + \lambda^2 = 0$, then λ is equal to

(a) 1 (b) 2

(c) 3 (d) 6

29. If P is a point on the circle $x^2 + y^2 = 9$, Q is a point on the line $7x + y + 3 = 0$, and the line $x - y + 1 = 0$, is the perpendicular bisector of PQ, then the coordinates of P are

(a) (3, 0) (b) $\left(\frac{72}{25}, -\frac{21}{25}\right)$

(c) (0, 3) (d) $\left(-\frac{72}{25}, \frac{21}{25}\right)$

30. If a circle passes through the point $\left(3, \sqrt{\frac{7}{2}}\right)$ and touches $x + y = 1$ and $x - y = 1$, then the centre of the circle is

(a) (4,0) (b) (4, 2) (c) (6, 0) (d) (7, 9)

31. The equation of a circle C_1 is $x^2 + y^2 = 4$. The locus of the intersection of orthogonal tangents to the circle is the curve C_2 and the locus of the intersection of perpendicular tangents to the curve C_2 is the curve C_3. Then,

(a) C_3 is a circle

(b) the area enclosed by the curve C_3 is 8π

(c) C_2 and C_3 are circles with the same centre

(d) None of the above

32. Consider the circles

$C_1 \equiv x^2 + y^2 - 2x - 4y - 4 = 0$ and

$C_2 \equiv x^2 + y^2 + 2x + 4y + 4 = 0$

and the line $L \equiv x + 2y + 2 = 0$, then

(a) L is the radical axis of C_1 and C_2

(b) L is the common tangent of C_1 and C_2

(c) L is the common chord of C_1 and C_2

(d) L is perpendicular to the line joining centres of C_1 and C_2

33. A square is inscribed in the circle $x^2 + y^2 - 10x - 6y + 30 = 0$. One side of the square is parallel to $y = x + 3$, then one vertex of the square is

(a) (3, 3) (b) (7,3)

(c) $(6, 3 - \sqrt{3})$ (d) $(6, 3 + \sqrt{3})$

Passage Based Questions

Passage I

(Q. Nos. 34 and 35)

■ Consider the circle $S: x^2 + y^2 - 4x - 1 = 0$ and the line $L: y = 3x - 1$. If the line L cuts the circle at A and B.

34. Length of the chord AB is

(a) $\sqrt{5}$ (b) $\sqrt{10}$ (c) $2\sqrt{5}$ (d) $5\sqrt{2}$

35. The angle subtended by the chord AB is the minor arc of S is

(a) $\frac{\pi}{4}$ (b) $\frac{2\pi}{3}$ (c) $\frac{3\pi}{4}$ (d) $\frac{5\pi}{6}$

Passage II

(Q. Nos. 36 and 37)

■ Equation of the circumcircle of a triangle formed by the lines $L_1 = 0$, $L_2 = 0$ and $L_3 = 0$ can be written as $L_1L_2 + \lambda L_2L_3 + \mu L_3L_1 = 0$, where λ and μ are such that coefficient of x^2 = coefficient of y^2 and coefficient of $xy = 0$.

36. $L_1L_2^2 + \lambda L_2L_3^2 + \mu L_3L_1^2 = 0$ represents

(a) a curve passing through point of intersection of $L_1 = 0$, $L_2 = 0$ and $L_3 = 0$

(b) a circle is coefficient of x^2 = coefficient of y^2 and coefficient of $xy = 0$

(c) a parabola

(d) pair of straight lines

37. $L_1 = 0$, $L_2 = 0$ be the distinct parallel lines, $L_3 = 0$, $L_4 = 0$ be two other distinct parallel lines which are not parallel to $L_1 = 0$. The equation of a circle passing through the vertices of the parallelogram formed must be of the form

(a) $\lambda L_1L_4 + \mu L_2L_3 = 0$ (b) $\lambda L_1L_3 + \mu L_2L_4 = 0$

(c) $\lambda L_1L_2 + \mu L_3L_4 = 0$ (d) $\lambda L_1^2L_3 + \mu L_2^2L_4 = 0$

Passage III

(Q. Nos. 38 and 39)

■ Consider the two circles $C_1: x^2 + y^2 = a^2$ and $C_2: x^2 + y^2 = b^2$ $(a > b)$. Let A be a fixed point on the circle C_1, say $A(a, 0)$ and B be a variable point on the circle C_2. The line BA meets the circle C_2 again at C. 'O' being the origin.

38. If $(OA)^2 + (OB)^2 + (BC)^2 = \lambda$, then $\lambda \in$

(a) $[5b^2 - 3a^2, 5b^2 + a^2]$ (b) $[4b^2, 4b^2 + a^2]$

(c) $[4a^2, 4b^2]$ (d) $[5b^2 - 3a^2, 5b^2 + 3a^2]$

39. The locus of the mid-point of AB is

(a) $\left(x - \frac{a}{2}\right)^2 + y^2 = \frac{b^2}{4}$ (b) $\left(x - \frac{a}{2}\right)^2 + y^2 = \frac{a^2}{4}$

(c) $\left(x - \frac{b}{2}\right)^2 + y^2 = \frac{a^2}{4}$ (d) $\left(x - \frac{b}{2}\right)^2 + y^2 = \frac{b^2}{4}$

Passage IV

(Q. Nos. 40 and 41)

- t_1, t_2 and t_3 are lengths of tangents drawn from a point (h, k) to the circles $x^2 + y^2 = 4$, $x^2 + y^2 - 4x = 0$ and $x^2 + y^2 - 4y = 0$ respectively further, $t_1^4 = t_2^2 t_3^2 + 16$. Locus of the point (h, k) consist of a straight line L_1 and a circle C_1 passing through origin. A circle C_2, which is equal to circle C_1 is drawn touching the line L_1 and the circle C_1 externally.

40. Equation of L_1 is

(a) $x + y = 0$ (b) $x - y = 0$
(c) $2x + y = 0$ (d) $x + 2y = 0$

41. Equation of C_1 is

(a) $x^2 + y^2 - x - y = 0$ (b) $x^2 + y^2 - 2x + y = 0$
(c) $x^2 + y^2 - x + 2y = 0$ (d) $x^2 + y^2 - 2x - 2y = 0$

Stem Based Questions

Stem I

(Q. Nos. 42 and 43)

- P is a variable point on the line $L = 0$. Tangents are drawn to the circle $x^2 + y^2 = 4$ from P to touch it at Q and R. The parallelogram $PQSR$ is completed.

42. If $P \equiv (6, 8)$, then area of ΔQRS is $\frac{192}{25}\sqrt{\lambda}$ sq units. The value of λ is ....

43. If $P \equiv (3, 4)$, then the coordinates of S are (a, b), then $25|a + b|$ is ....

Stem II

(Q. Nos. 44 and 45)

- Given two circles intersecting orthogonally having the length of common chord $\frac{24}{5}$ unit. The radius of one of the circles is 3 units.

44. If radius of other circle is λ units, then λ is ....

45. If length of direct common tangent is λ units, then λ^2 is ....

Stem III

(Q. Nos. 46 and 47)

- Two variable chords AB and BC of a circle $x^2 + y^2 = a^2$ are such that $AB = BC = a$, M and N are the mid-points of AB and BC respectively such that line joining MN intersect the circle at P and Q, where P is closer to AB and O is the centre of the circle.

46. $\angle OAB$ in degree is ....

47. Angle between tangents at A and C is ...... (in degree)

Single Integer Type Questions

48. If the equation of circle circumscribing the quadrilateral formed by the lines in order are $2x + 3y = 2$, $3x - 2y = 3$, $x + 2y = 3$ and $2x - y = 1$ is given by $x^2 + y^2 + \lambda x + \mu y + \nu = 0$. Then the value of $|\lambda + 2\mu + \nu|$ is ....

49. A circle $x^2 + y^2 + 4x - 2\sqrt{2}y + c = 0$ is the director circle of the circle C_1 and C_1 is the director circle of circle C_2 and so on. If the sum of radii of all these circles is 2 and if $c = \lambda\sqrt{2}$, then the value of λ is ....

50. If the area bounded by the circles $x^2 + y^2 = r^2, r = 1, 2$ and the rays given by $2x^2 - 3xy - 2y^2 = 0, y > 0$ is $\frac{\lambda\pi}{4}$ sq units, then the value of λ is ....

51. The length of a common internal tangent of two circles is 5 and that of a common external tangent is 13. If the product of the radii of two circles is λ, then the value of $\frac{\lambda}{4}$ is ....

52. Consider a circles S with centre at the origin and radius 4. Four circles A, B, C and D each with radius unity and centres $(-3, 0), (-1, 0), (1, 0)$ and $(3, 0)$ respectively are drawn. A chord PQ of the circle S touches the circle B and passes through the centre of the circle C. If the length of this chord can be expressed as $\sqrt{\lambda}$, then the value of $\frac{\lambda}{9}$ is ......

Numerical Value Type Questions

53. The length of a common internal tangent to two circles is 7 and that of a common external tangent is 11. If the product of the radii of two circles is p, then the value of p is ......

54. Consider the family of circles $x^2 + y^2 - 2x - 2\lambda y - 8 = 0$ passing through two fixed points A and B. Then, the value of $6AB$ is ......

55. If the shortest and largest distance from the point $(3, -6)$ to the circle $x^2 + y^2 - 16x - 12y - 125 = 0$ are L and M respectively, then the value of $L + M$ is ....

56. Consider series of n concentric circle $C_1, C_2, C_3 \ldots, C_n$ with radii $r_1, r_2, r_3 \ldots, r_n$ respectively, satisfying $r_1 > r_2 > r_3 \ldots > r_n$ and $r_1 = 10$. The circles are such that the chord of contact of tangents from any point on C_i to C_{i+1} is a tangent $C_{i+2} (i = 1, 2, 3, \ldots)$. The value of $\lim_{n \to \infty} \sum_{i=1}^{n} r_i$ if the angle between the tangents from any point of C_1 to C_2 is $\frac{\pi}{3}$, is ....

Matching Type Questions

57. Consider the circles $S_1 : x^2 + y^2 - 4x - 6y + 12 = 0$ and $S_2 : (x-5)^2 + (y-6)^2 = r^2 > 1$

Column I	Column II
(A) S_1 and S_2 touch internally, then $(r-1)^2$ is divisible by	(p) 3
(B) S_1 and S_2 touch externally, then $r^2 + 2r + 3$ is divisible by	(q) 4
(C) S_1 and S_2 intersect orthogonally, then $r^2 - 1$ is divisible by	(r) 5
(D) S_1 and S_2 intersect so that the common chord is longest, then $r^2 + 5$ is divisible by	(s) 6

58. Match the following

Column I	Column II
(A) If $ax + by - 5 = 0$ is the equation of the chord of the circle $(x-3)^2 + (y-4)^2 = 4$, which passes through (2,3) and at the greatest distance from the centre of the circle, then	(p) $a + b = 1$
(B) Let O be the origin and P be a variable point on the circle $x^2 + y^2 + 2x + 2y = 0$. If the locus of mid-point of OP is $x^2 + y^2 + 2ax + 2by = 0$, then	(q) $a + b = 2$
(C) If (a, b) be coordinates of the centre of the smallest circle which cuts the circle $x^2 + y^2 - 2x - 4y - 4 = 0$ and $x^2 + y^2 - 10x + 12y + 52 = 0$ orthogonally, then	(r) $a^2 + b^2 = 2$
(D) If a and b are the slope of tangents which are drawn to the circle $x^2 + y^2 - 6\sqrt{3}x - 6y + 27 = 0$ from the origin, then	(s) $a^2 + b^2 = 3$

Previous Years Questions

59. Let the straight line $y = 2x$ touch a circle with center $(0, \alpha), \alpha > 0$ and radius r at a point A_1. Let B_1 be the point on the circle such that the line segment A_1B_1 is a diameter of the circle. Let $\alpha + r = 5 + \sqrt{5}$.

Match each entry in List I to the correct entry in List II.

[Single Correct Type, 2024 Adv.]

List I	List II
(P) α equals	(1) $(-2, 4)$
(Q) r equals	(2) $\sqrt{5}$
(R) A_1 equals	(3) $(-2, 6)$
(S) B_1 equals	(4) 5
	(5) $(2, 4)$

The correct option is

(a) (P) → (4), (Q) → (2), (R) → (1), (S) → (3)
(b) (P) → (2), (Q) → (4), (R) → (1), (S) → (3)
(c) (P) → (4), (Q) → (2), (R) → (5), (S) → (3)
(d) (P) → (2), (Q) → (4), (R) → (3), (S) → (5)

60. Let C_1 be the circle of radius 1 with centre at the origin. Let C_2 be the circle of radius r with centre at the point $A = (4, 1)$, where $1 < r < 3$. Two distinct common tangents PQ and ST of C_1 and C_2 are drawn. The tangent PQ touches C_1 at P and C_2 at Q. The tangent ST touches C_1 at S and C_2 at T. Mid-points of the line segments PQ and ST are joined to form a line which meets the X-axis at a point B. If $AB = \sqrt{5}$, then the value of r^2 is ......

[Numerical Value Type, 2023 Adv.]

61. Let G be a circle of radius $R > 0$. Let $G_1, G_2, ..., G_n$ be n circles of equal radius $r > 0$. Suppose each of the n circles $G_1, G_2, ..., G_n$ touches the circle G externally. Also, for $i = 1, 2, ... n-1$, the circle G_i touches G_{i+1} externally, and G_n touches G_1 externally. Then, which of the following statements is/are true?

[More than Correct Type, 2022 Adv.]

(a) If $n = 4$, then $(\sqrt{2} - 1) r < R$
(b) If $n = 5$, then $r < R$
(c) If $n = 8$, then $(\sqrt{2} - 1) r < R$
(d) If $n = 12$, then $\sqrt{2} (\sqrt{3} + 1) r > R$

62. Let ABC be the triangle with $AB = 1$, $AC = 3$ and $\angle BAC = \frac{\pi}{2}$. If a circle of radius $r > 0$ touches the sides AB, AC and also touches internally the circumcircle of the ΔABC, then the value of r is ....

[Numerical Value Type, 2022 Adv.]

63. Consider a triangle (Δ) whose two sides lie on the X-axis and the line $x + y + 1 = 0$. If the orthocenter of triangle is (1, 1), then the equation of the circle passing through the vertices of the triangle (Δ) is

[Single Correct Type, 2021 Adv.]

(a) $x^2 + y^2 - 3x + y = 0$ (b) $x^2 + y^2 + x + 3y = 0$
(c) $x^2 + y^2 + 2y - 1 = 0$ (d) $x^2 + y^2 + x + y = 0$

64. For any complex number $w = c + id$, let $\arg(w) \in (-\pi, \pi]$, where $i = \sqrt{-1}$. Let α and β be real numbers such that for all complex numbers $z = x + iy$ satisfying $\arg\left(\frac{z+\alpha}{z+\beta}\right) = \frac{\pi}{4}$, the ordered pair (x, y) lies on the circle $x^2 + y^2 + 5x - 3y + 4 = 0$.

Then, which of the following statements is (are) true?

[More than Correct Type, 2021 Adv.]

(a) $\alpha = -1$ (b) $\alpha\beta = 4$
(c) $\alpha\beta = -4$ (d) $\beta = 4$

Passage
(Q. Nos. 65 and 66)

- Let $M = \{(x, y) \in R \times R : x^2 + y^2 \le r^2\}$, where $r > 0$. Consider the geometric progression $a_n = \frac{1}{2^{n-1}}, n = 1, 2, 3, \ldots$. Let $S_0 = 0$ and, for $n \ge 1$, let S_n denote the sum of the first n terms of this progression. For $n \ge 1$, let C_n denote the circle with center $(S_{n-1}, 0)$ and radius a_n, and D_n denote the circle with center (S_{n-1}, S_{n-1}) and radius a_n.

[Passage Type, 2021 Adv.]

65. Consider M with $r = \frac{1025}{513}$. Let k be the number of all those circles C_n that are inside M. Let l be the maximum possible number of circles among these k circles such that no two circles intersect. Then,

(a) $k + 2l = 22$
(b) $2k + l = 26$
(c) $2k + 3l = 34$
(d) $3k + 2l = 40$

66. Consider M with $r = \frac{(2^{199} - 1)\sqrt{2}}{2^{198}}$. The number of all those circles D_n that are inside M is

(a) 198 (b) 199
(c) 200 (d) 201

67. Let O be the centre of the circle $x^2 + y^2 = r^2$, where $r > \frac{\sqrt{5}}{2}$. Suppose PQ is a chord of this circle and the equation of the line passing through P and Q is $2x + 4y = 5$. If the centre of the circumcircle of the ΔOPQ lies on the line $x + 2y = 4$, then the value of r is ……… .

[Numerical Value Type, 2020 Adv.]

EXERCISE 3
Challenging Problems

1. S is a circle having centre at $(0, a)$ and radius $b\,(b < a)$. A variable circle centred at $(\alpha, 0)$ and touching circle S, meets the X-axis at M and N. Find a point on the Y-axis. Such that $\angle MPN$ is a constant for any choice of α.

2. Prove that the equation $x^2 + y^2 - 2x - 2ay - 8 = 0$ represents a family of circles passing through two fixed points, say P and Q. Find the member of the family tangents to which at P and Q intersect on the line $x + 2y + 5 = 0$.

3. Consider a family of circles passing through the intersection point of the line $\sqrt{3}\,(y-1) = x - 1$ and $y - 1 = \sqrt{3}(x-1)$ and having its centre on the acute angle bisector of the given lines. Show that the common chords of each member of the family and the circle $x^2 + y^2 + 4x - 6y + 5 = 0$ are concurrent. Find the point of concurrency.

4. Find the range of values of λ for which the variable line $3x + 4y - \lambda = 0$ lies between the circles $x^2 + y^2 - 2x - 2y + 1 = 0$ and $x^2 + y^2 - 18x - 2y + 78 = 0$ without intercepting a chord on either circle.

5. A is one of the points of intersection of two given circles. A variable line through A meets the two circles again at point P and Q. Show that the locus of the mid-point of P and Q is also a circle passing through A.

6. Prove that there does not exist more than one rational point on circumference of the circle with center $(\sqrt{7}, \sqrt{11})$ (A point $P(x, y)$ is said to be rational, it both x and y are rational numbers)

7. A variable circle with center on X-axis and touching the fixed circle $x^2 + (y-a)^2 = b^2\,(a > b > 0)$ externally intersect X-axis at the points B and D. Find point P on positive Y-axis for which angle BPD in constant.

8. The equation of radical axis of two circles is $x + y = 1$. One of the circles has the ends of its diameter at the points $(1, -3)$ and $(4, 1)$ and the other passes through the point $(1, 2)$. Find the equations of these circles.

Answer Key

Exercise 1

1. (b)	2. (b)	3. (a)	4. (b)	5. (d)	6. (b)	7. (b)	8. (a)	9. (c)	10. (a)
11. (b)	12. (a)	13. (b)	14. (b)	15. (a)	16. (d)	17. (a)	18. (a)	19. (c)	20. (b)
21. (c)	22. (c)	23. (d)	24. (d)	25. (a)	26. (c)	27. (b)	28. (a)	29. (a)	30. (c)
31. (6)	32. (4)	33. (2)	34. (6)	35. (0)	36. (4)	37. (5)	38. (3)	39. (4)	40. (4)
41. (6)	42. (1)	43. (4)	44. (9)	45. (10.25)	46. (3.87)	47. (50)	48. (64)	49. (9.66)	50. (c)
51. (d)	52. (c)	53. (a)	54. (a)	55. (b)	56. (b)	57. (a)	58. (2)	59. (12)	60. (9)
61. (b)	62. (c)	63. (a)	64. (b)	65. (a)	66. (d)	67. (c)	68. (c)	69. (c)	70. (b)
71. (c)	72. (d)	73. (7)	74. (2)	75. (121)	76. (24)	77. (11)	78. (3)	79. (b)	80. (b)
81. (b)	82. (a)	83. (d)	84. (a)	85. (d)	86. (a)	87. (c)	88. (c)	89. (d)	90. (b)
91. (c)	92. (72)	93. (25)	94. (10)	95. (816)	96. (11)	97. (16)	98. (7)	99. (7)	100. (a)
101. (b)	102. (c)	103. (d)	104. (c)	105. (d)	106. (c)	107. (c)	108. (c)	109. (b)	110. (b)
111. (a)	112. (b)	113. (c)	114. (b)	115. (a)	116. (b)	117. (d)	118. (18)	119. (165)	120. (40)
121. (61)	122. (16)	123. (1)	124. (9)	125. (56.25)	126. (1225)	127. (3)	128. (d)	129. (d)	130. (c)
131. (3)	132. (9)								

Exercise 2

1. (b)	2. (a)	3. (c)	4. (d)	5. (d)	6. (d)	7. (d)	8. (b)	9. (a)	10. (c)
11. (b)	12. (d)	13. (c)	14. (a)	15. (b)	16. (b)	17. (c)	18. (d)	19. (a)	20. (b,d)
21. (a,b)	22. (a,b,c,d)	23. (a)	24. (b,d)	25. (b,c)	26. (a,b,c,d)	27. (b,d)	28. (a,d)	29. (a,d)	30. (a,c)
31. (a,c)	32. (a,c,d)	33. (a,b)	34. (b)	35. (c)	36. (a)	37. (c)	38. (a)	39. (a)	40. (a)
41. (d)	42. (6)	43. (119)	44. (4)	45. (24)	46. (60)	47. (60)	48. (3)	49. (4)	50. (3)
51. (9)	52. (7)	53. (18)	54. (36)	55. (30)	56. (20)	57. (A) → (p,s); (B) → (q,r); (C) → (q); (D) → (p,q,s)			
58. (A) → (q,r); (B) → (p); (C) → (p); (D) → (s)				59. (c)	60. (2)	61. (c,d)	62. (0.84)	63. (b)	64. (b,d)
65. (d)	66. (b)	67. (2)							

Solutions

Exercise 1 - JEE Main Pattern

1. Let $y = mx$ be the chord.

Then, the points of intersections are given by

$$x^2(1+m^2) - x(3+4m) - 4 = 0$$

$$\therefore \quad x_1 + x_2 = \frac{3+4m}{1+m^2} \text{ and } x_1x_2 = \frac{-4}{1+m^2}$$

Since, (0, 0) divides chord in the ratio 1 : 4 we have

$$x_2 = -4x_1$$

$$\therefore \quad -3x_1 = \frac{3+4m}{1+m^2} \text{ and } 4x_1^2 = \frac{-4}{1+m^2}$$

$$\Rightarrow \quad 9 + 9m^2 = 9 + 16m^2 + 24m$$

$$\Rightarrow \quad m = 0 \text{ or } \frac{-24}{7}$$

So, chord is $y = 0$ or $7y + 24x = 0$

2.

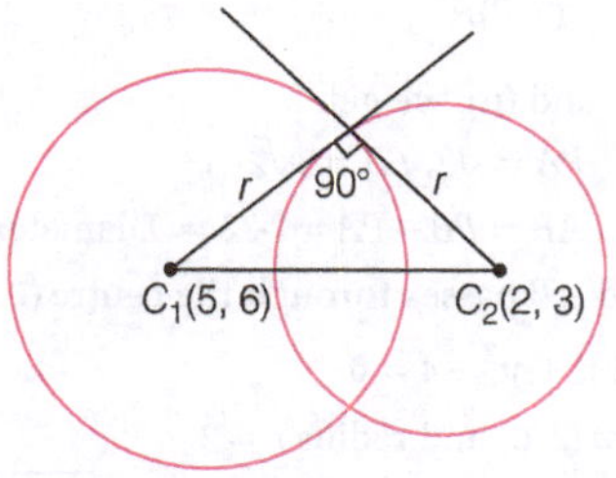

$$\therefore \quad 2r^2 = 3^2 + 3^2$$

$$\Rightarrow \quad r^2 = 9$$

$$\Rightarrow \quad r = 3 \text{ units}$$

3. $2x - y + 1 = 0$ is the tangent.

$\therefore$ Slope of line $OA = -\frac{1}{2}$

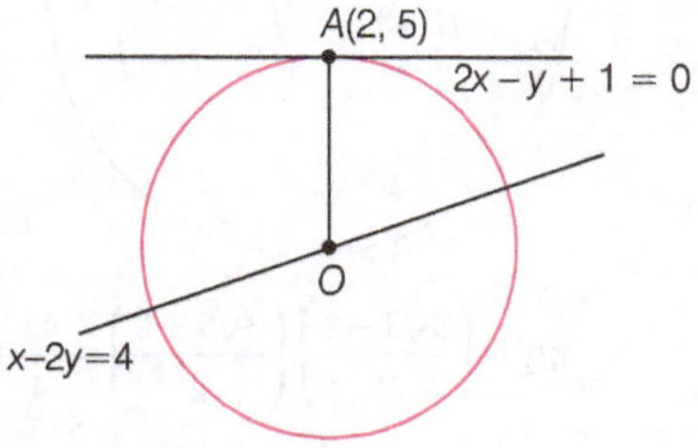

The equation of OA is $y - 5 = -\frac{1}{2}(x-2)$

$$\Rightarrow \quad x + 2y = 12$$

Centre of circle is intersection of the lines

$$x + 2y = 12 \text{ and } x - 2y = 4$$

$\therefore$ Centre = (8, 2)

Now, radius $= OA = \sqrt{(8-2)^2 + (2-5)^2} = 3\sqrt{5}$ units

4. We have,

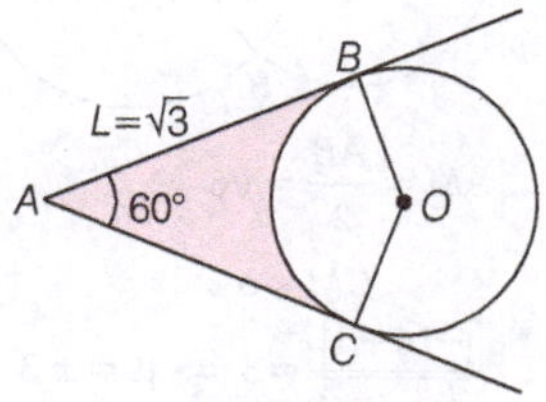

$$r = 1, L = \sqrt{3}$$

$\therefore$ Area of quadrilateral $= \sqrt{3}$

Area of sector $= \frac{1}{2} \times 1 \times \frac{2\pi}{3} = \frac{\pi}{3}$

$\therefore$ Area of shaded region $= \sqrt{3} - \frac{\pi}{3}$ sq units

5. Let the required point be (h, k). Then, its chord of contact w.r.t. the circle $S \equiv x^2 + y^2 - \left(\frac{3}{2}\right)x + \left(\frac{5}{2}\right)y - \left(\frac{7}{2}\right) = 0$ is

$$hx + ky - \left(\frac{3}{4}\right)(x+h) + \left(\frac{5}{4}\right)(y+k) - \left(\frac{7}{2}\right) = 0$$

or $\quad (4h-3)x + (4k+5)y - (3h - 5k + 14) = 0 \quad$ ...(i)

But given chord of contact is

$$9x + y - 28 = 0 \quad \text{...(ii)}$$

On comparing coefficients in Eqs. (i) and (ii), we get

$$\frac{4h-3}{9} = \frac{4k+5}{1} = \frac{3h-5k+14}{28}$$

i.e. $h - 9k = 12$ and $3h - 117k = 126 \quad$ ...(iii)

Solving, we get $h = 3$, $k = -1$

Thus, required point is (3, – 1). But this point must be outside the circle as any point inside or on the circle does not have chord of contact.

Now, $S(3, -1) = -1 < 0$

i.e. (3, – 1)

is inside the circle, so there is no point of which Eq. (ii) is the chord of contact.

6. Given circles are $x^2 + y^2 - 2\lambda_i x - c^2 = 0, i = 1, 2, 3$

Centres are $(\lambda_1, 0), (\lambda_2, 0), (\lambda_3, 0)$

Distances of the centres from origin are in GP, $\lambda_2^2 = \lambda_1 \lambda_3$

Let (x_1, y_1) be any point on the circle $x^2 + y^2 = c^2$

$$\therefore \quad x_1^2 + y_1^2 - c^2 = 0$$

Lengths of tangent from (x_1, y_1) to the three given circles are

$$l_i = \sqrt{x_1^2 + y_1^2 - 2\lambda_i x_1 - c^2} = \sqrt{-2\lambda_i, x_1}$$

$$\therefore \quad l_1^2 l_3^2 = (-2\lambda_1 x_1)(-2\lambda_3 x_1) = 4\lambda_1\lambda_3 x_1^2$$

$$= 4\lambda_2^2 x_1^2 = l_2^4 \Rightarrow l_1 l_3 = l_2^2$$

$\therefore l_1, l_2$ and l_3 are in GP.

7. The common chord is $S_1 - S_2 = 0$

$$4x - \mu y + 1 = 0$$

$\therefore$ $AC =$ Radius of first circle $= \sqrt{15}$ units

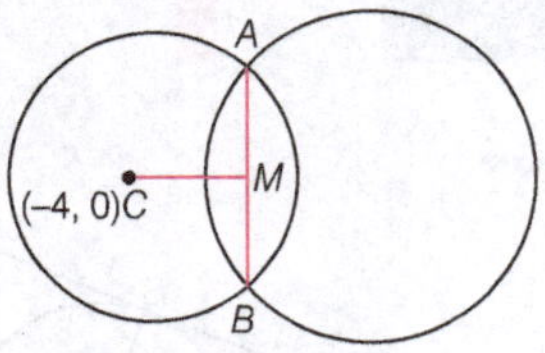

$$AM = \frac{AB}{2} = \sqrt{6}$$

$$\therefore \quad CM = 3$$

$$\therefore \quad \frac{|-16+1|}{\sqrt{16+\mu^2}} = 3 \Rightarrow \mu = \pm 3$$

8. The two normals are $x = 1$ and $y = 2$.

$\therefore$ Their point of intersection (1, 2) is the centre of the required circle.

Now, radius $= \left| \dfrac{3(1)+4(2)-6}{\sqrt{3^2+4^2}} \right| = 1$

$\therefore$ Equation of required circle is $(x-1)^2 + (y-2)^2 = 1^2$

$$\Rightarrow \quad x^2 + y^2 - 2x - 4y + 4 = 0$$

9. Let the mid-point of the chord be $P(h, k)$.

Then, $CP = \sqrt{h^2 + k^2}$, where C is the centre of the circle.

Since, the chord subtends right angle at the centre.

Radius $= \sqrt{2}\sqrt{h^2+k^2}$

$$\Rightarrow \quad 2 = \sqrt{2}\sqrt{h^2+k^2} \Rightarrow h^2 + k^2 = 2$$

So, locus of P is $x^2 + y^2 = 2$.

10. The centres are (10, 0) and (– 15, 0) and the radii are $r_1 = 6$ and $r_2 = 9$.

Also, $d = 25, r_1 + r_2 < d$

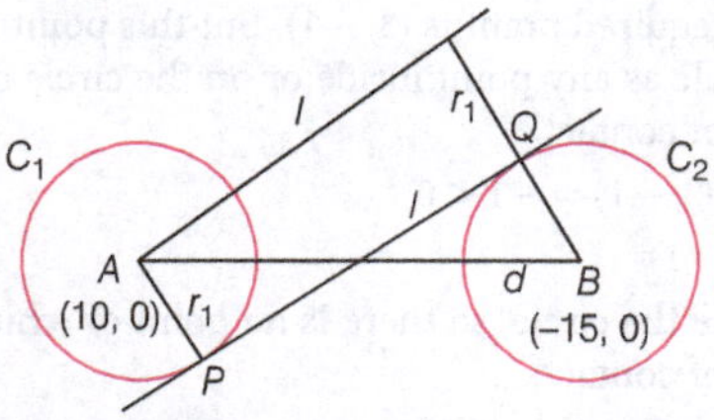

So, the circles are neither intersecting nor touching.

Therefore, $PQ = \sqrt{d^2 - (r_1 + r_2)^2} = \sqrt{625 - 225} = 20$ units

11. $AB^2 = 4AM^2 = 4\left(4 - \dfrac{n^2}{2}\right) = 2(8 - n^2)$

Hence, required sum $= 2(8 - 1^2 + 8 - 2^2) = 22$

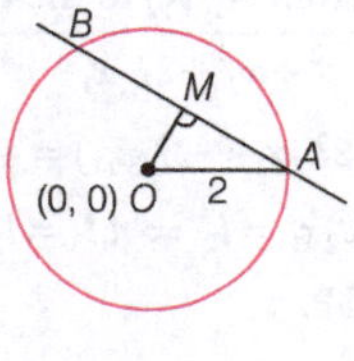

12. Tangent at $(5\sqrt{2}\cos\theta, 5\sqrt{2}\sin\theta)$ is

$$x\cos\theta + y\sin\theta = 5\sqrt{2}$$

$$\therefore \quad OP = 5\sqrt{2}\sec\theta, OP_1 = 5\sqrt{2}\operatorname{cosec}\theta$$

$\therefore$ Area $(\Delta PP_1P_2) = 2 \times$ Area of ΔOPP_1

$$= 2 \times \frac{1}{2} \times 5\sqrt{2}\sec\theta \times 5\sqrt{2}\operatorname{cosec}\theta = \frac{100}{\sin 2\theta}$$

Area $(\Delta PP_1P_2)_{\min} = 100$

$$\Rightarrow \quad \theta = \frac{\pi}{4} \Rightarrow OP = 10 \Rightarrow P \equiv (10, 0), (-10, 0)$$

13. Let $S \equiv x^2 + y^2 - 2 = 0$, $P \equiv (2, 2)$

$$\therefore \quad S_1 = 2^2 + 2^2 - 2 = 6 > 0$$

$\Rightarrow P$ lies outside the circle

$$PA.PB = (PT)^2 = S_1 = 6 \qquad \text{...(i)}$$

Given, $$\frac{PB}{PA} = 3 \qquad \text{...(ii)}$$

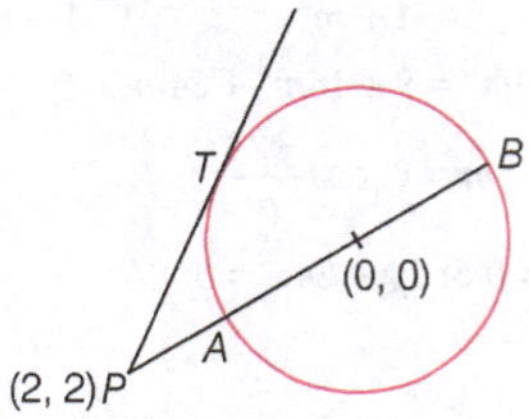

From Eqs. (i) and (ii), we get

$$PA = \sqrt{2}, PB = 3\sqrt{2}$$

$$\Rightarrow \quad AB = PB - PA = 2\sqrt{2} = \text{Diameter of circle}$$

Hence, chord AB passes through the centre $(0, 0)$, $y = x$

14. Let $S \equiv (x-2)^2 + y^2 - 4 = 0$

Its centre $C \equiv (2, 0)$ and radius $r = 2$

Distance between $C \equiv (2, 0)$ and (5, 6) is $\sqrt{(2-5)^2 + (0-6)^2}$

i.e. $3\sqrt{5}$

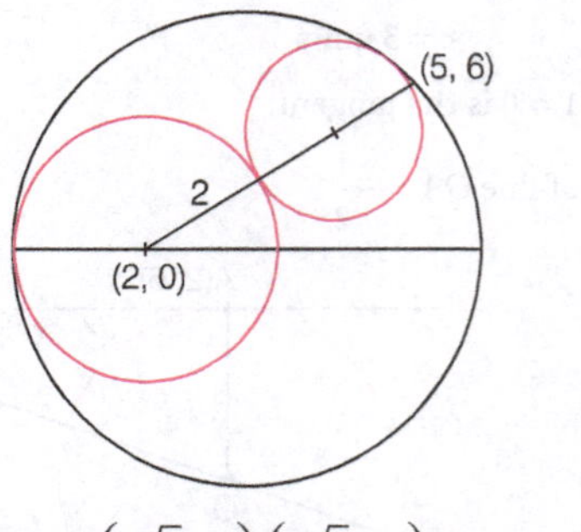

$$\therefore \quad r_1 r_2 = \left(\frac{3\sqrt{5}-2}{2}\right)\left(\frac{3\sqrt{5}+2}{2}\right) = \frac{41}{4} \text{ units}$$

15. Any circle which touches $3x + 4y - 7 = 0$ at (1, 1) will be of the form

$$S(x, y) \equiv (x-1)^2 + (y-1)^2 + \lambda(3x + 4y - 7) = 0$$

Since, $$S(2, 3) = 16 \Rightarrow 1 + 4 + \lambda(11) = 16$$

$$\therefore \quad \lambda = 1$$

So, required circle will be $x^2 + y^2 + x + 2y - 5 = 0$.

16. Let $S \equiv x^2 + y^2 - 2x + 4y - \lambda = 0$

For interval point $P(2,8)$,

$$4 + 64 - 4 + 32 - \lambda < 0 \Rightarrow \lambda > 96 \quad \text{...(i)}$$

and x-intercept $= 2\sqrt{(1+\lambda)}$ and y-intercept $= 2\sqrt{(4+\lambda)}$

given $\quad 2\sqrt{(1+\lambda)} < 0 \Rightarrow \lambda < -1 \quad$ ...(ii)

and $\quad 2\sqrt{(4+\lambda)} < 0 \Rightarrow \lambda < -4 \quad$ ...(iii)

From Eqs. (i), (ii) and (iii), we get

$$\lambda \in \phi$$

17. Let $S \equiv x^2 + y^2 + 2x + 4y - 4 = 0$

Its centre $C \equiv (-1, -2)$ and radius $r = 3$. The points on the circle which are nearest and farthest to the point $P(a, b)$ are Q and R respectively.

Thus, the circle centred at Q having radius PQ will be the smallest circle while the circle centred at R having radius PR will be the largest required circle.

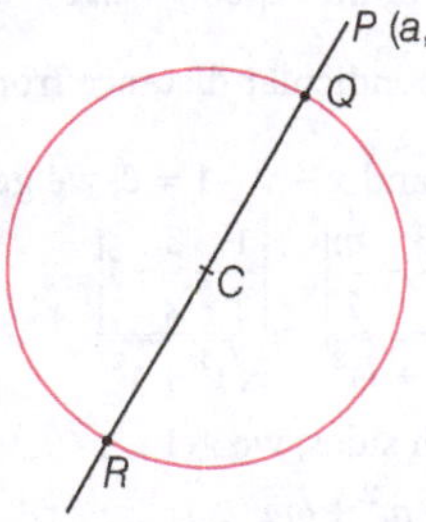

Hence, the difference between their radii is

$$PR - PQ = QR = 2 \times 3 = 6$$

18. Radius $= \sqrt{(a-\pi)^2 + (b-e)^2} = \text{irrational} = k$

$\therefore \quad$ Circle $(x-\pi)^2 + (y-e)^2 = k^2$

$$r = \sqrt{(\text{irrational})^2 + (\text{irrational})^2}$$

$\Rightarrow$ x and y are any rational number $x - \pi$ and $x - e$ are irrational.

So, atmost one point is possible.

19. Given, $\lambda L_2 L_3 + \mu L_3 L_1 + \nu L_1 L_2 = 0$

$$\Rightarrow \lambda(y - m_2 x - c_2)(y - m_3 x - c_3) + \mu(y - m_3 x - c_3)(y - m_1 x - c_1) + \nu(y - m_1 x - c_1)(y - m_2 x - c_2) = 0$$

For circle, coefficient of x^2 = coefficient of y^2 and coefficient of $xy = 0$,

then $\lambda(m_2 m_3 - 1) + \mu(m_3 m_1 - 1) + \nu(m_1 m_2 - 1) = 0$

and $\quad (m_2 + m_3)\lambda + (m_3 + m_1)\mu + (m_1 + m_2)\nu = 0$

20. $\because f(x, y) \equiv x^2 + y^2 + 2ax + 2by + c = 0$

$\Rightarrow \quad f(x, 0) = 0$

$\Rightarrow \quad x^2 + 2ax + c = (x-2)^2$

$\therefore \quad a = -2, c = 4$

and $\quad f(0, y) = 0$

$\Rightarrow \quad y^2 + 2by + c = (y-2)(y-3)$

$\therefore \quad 2b = -5, c = 6$

or $\quad b = -\dfrac{5}{2}, c = 6$

Clearly, data are not consistent.

21. Given, $(1 + \alpha x)^n = 1 + 8x + 24x^2 + \ldots$

$$\Rightarrow 1 + n(\alpha x) + \frac{n(n-1)}{1.2}(\alpha x)^2 + \ldots = 1 + 8x + 24x^2 + \ldots$$

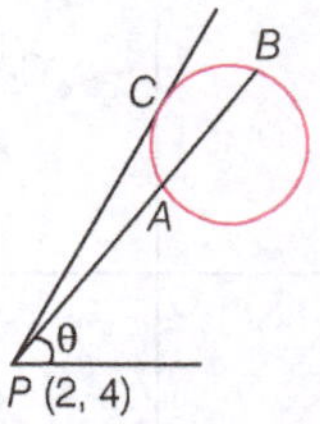

On equating the coefficients of x and x^2, we get

$$n\alpha = 8, \frac{n\alpha(n\alpha - \alpha)}{1.2} = 24$$

or $\quad \dfrac{8(8-\alpha)}{2} = 24 \Rightarrow 8 - \alpha = 6$

$\therefore \quad \alpha = 2$ and $n = 4$

Equation of line is $\dfrac{x-2}{\cos\theta} = \dfrac{y-4}{\sin\theta} = r$, then point $(2 + r\cos\theta, 4 + r\sin\theta)$ lies on the circle $x^2 + y^2 = 4$,

then, $\quad (2 + r\cos\theta)^2 + (4 + r\sin\theta)^2 = 4$

or $\quad r^2 + 4r(\cos\theta + 2\sin\theta) + 16 = 0$

$\therefore \quad PA \cdot PB = r_1 r_2 = \dfrac{16}{1} = 16$

22. For interior point $OP < 5$

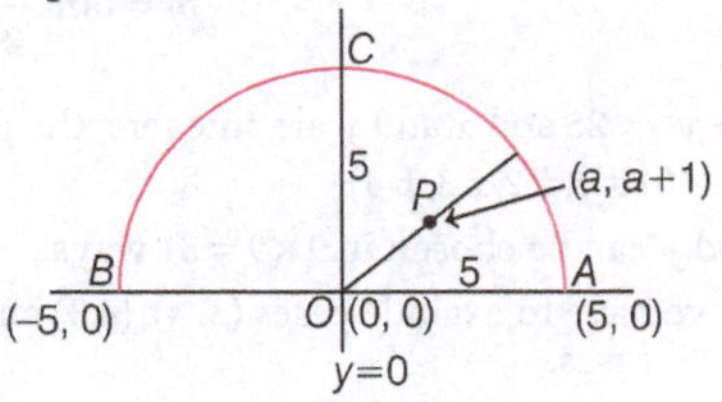

$\Rightarrow \quad \sqrt{a^2 + (a+1)^2} < 5$

$\Rightarrow \quad 2a^2 + 2a - 24 < 0$

$\therefore \quad a^2 + a - 12 < 0$

$\Rightarrow \quad (a+4)(a-3) < 0 \Rightarrow -4 < a < 3$

and for I and II quadrant

$$a + 1 > 0$$

$\therefore \quad a > -1$

Hence, $-1 < a < 3$

23. Let $S(x, y) \equiv x^2 + y^2 + 2gx + 2fy + c = 0$

$\Rightarrow \quad S(x, 2) = 0$

$\Rightarrow \quad x^2 + 4 + 2gx + 4f + c = (x-1)^2$

$\therefore \quad g = -1, 3 + 4f + c = 0 \quad$ ...(i)

and $\quad S(1, y) = 0 \Rightarrow 1 + y^2 + 2g + 2fy + c = (y-0)(y-2)$

$\therefore \quad f = -1, 1 + 2g + c = 0 \quad$ ...(ii)

From Eqs. (i) and (ii), we get

$$g = -1, f = -1, c = 1$$

$\therefore$ Equation of required circle is

$$x^2 + y^2 - 2x - 2y + 1 = 0$$

24. See the diagram. Since, there is no condition on θ, Q can be placed either at Q_1 or Q_2 for a particular position of P. So option (a) and (b) cannot be definitely true.

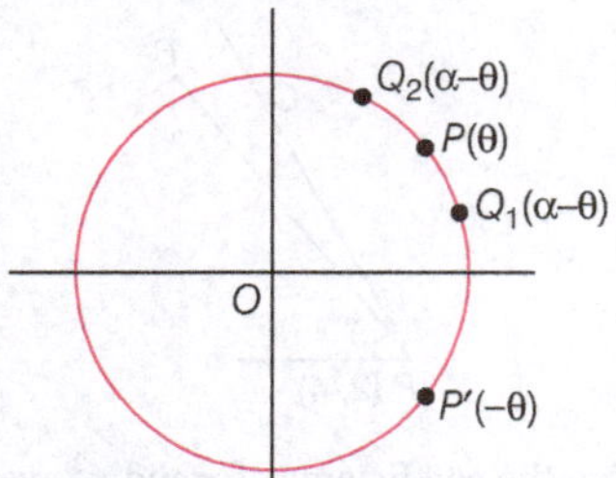

Consider a line through origin $y = mx$. If Q and P are reflection of each other with line mirror $y = mx$

(Slope of PQ) $\times m = -1$

or $$m\left(\frac{\sin\theta - \sin(\alpha-\theta)}{\cos\theta - \cos(\alpha-\theta)}\right) = -1$$

$$m\left(\frac{2\cos\left(\frac{\alpha}{2}\right).\sin\left(\frac{2\theta-\alpha}{2}\right)}{2\sin\left(\frac{\alpha}{2}\right).\sin\left(\frac{\alpha-2\theta}{2}\right)}\right) = -1$$

or $$m\left(-\cot\frac{\alpha}{2}\right) = -1$$

or $$m = \tan\left(\frac{\alpha}{2}\right)$$

25. Since, $x^2 + y^2 < 25$ and x and y are integers, the possible values of x and $y \in (0, \pm 1, \pm 2, \pm 3, \pm 4)$.

Thus, x and y can be chosen in $9 \times 9 = 81$ ways.

However, we have to exclude cases (3, 4), (4,3) and (4,4) i.e. $3 \times 4 = 12$ cases.

Hence, the number of permissible values $= 81 - 12 = 69$

26. Let the equation of the circle be

$$x^2 + y^2 + 2gx + 2fy + c = 0 \qquad \text{...(i)}$$

It passes through the points (0, 0) and (1, 0).

$\therefore$ $$c = 0 \text{ and } 1 + 2g + c = 0;\ g = -\frac{1}{2}$$

Radius of circle (i) is

$$r_1 = \sqrt{(g^2 + f^2 - c)} = \sqrt{(1/4 + f^2)}$$

The centre of the circle $x^2 + y^2 = 9$ ...(ii)

is (0, 0) and radius $r_2 = 3$

Since, the circle (i) passes through the centre (0, 0) of circle (ii) and it also touches the circle (ii), so it will touch the circle (ii) internally

$\therefore$ $$C_1C_2 = \sqrt{(g^2 + f^2)} = |r_1 - r_2|$$

$\Rightarrow$ $$\sqrt{\left(\frac{1}{4} + f^2\right)} = |3 - \sqrt{(1/4 + f^2)}|$$

$\Rightarrow$ $$f^2 = 2 \Rightarrow f = \pm\sqrt{2}$$

$\therefore$ Centres of such circles are $\left(\frac{1}{2}, \pm\sqrt{2}\right)$.

27. If the lines L_1 and L_2 make equal intercepts on the circle $x^2 + y^2 - x + 3y = 0$, then the perpendicular distance from the centre $\left(\frac{1}{2}, \frac{-3}{2}\right)$ on the two lines must be equal

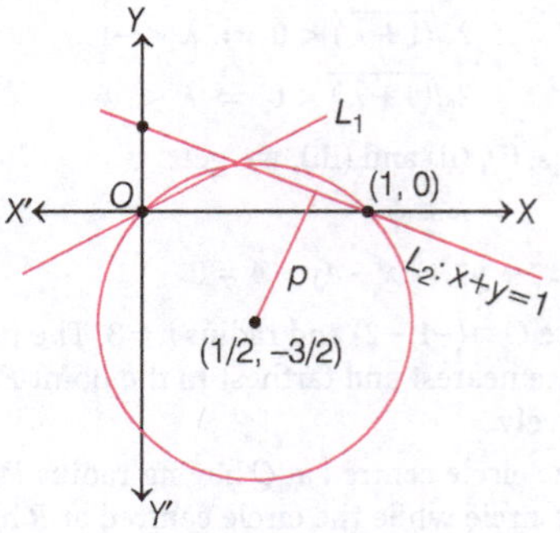

Let the equation of line L_1 be $y - mx = 0$.

By equating perpendicular distance from centre $\left(\frac{1}{2}, \frac{-3}{2}\right)$ on the lines $y - mx = 0$ and $x + y - 1 = 0$, we get

$$\frac{\left|\frac{-3}{2} - \frac{m}{2}\right|}{\sqrt{1+m^2}} = \frac{\left|\frac{1}{2} - \frac{3}{2} - 1\right|}{\sqrt{1^2+1^2}}$$

On squaring both sides, we get

$$\frac{9 + m^2 + 6m}{4(1+m^2)} = 2$$

$\Rightarrow$ $$9 + m^2 + 6m = 8 + 8m^2$$

$\Rightarrow$ $$7m^2 - 6m - 1 = 0$$

$\Rightarrow$ $$m = \frac{-1}{7}, 1$$

$\therefore$ Equations of required lines are $x - y = 0$ or $x + 7y = 0$.

28. $T(x_1, y_1)$ lies on $px + qy = r$

$\therefore$ $$px_1 + qy_1 - r = 0 \qquad \text{...(i)}$$

Equation of chord of contact of T is

$$xx_1 + yy_1 - a^2 = 0$$

Equation of circle through PQ is

$$x^2 + y^2 - a^2 + \lambda(xx_1 + yy_1 - a^2) = 0$$

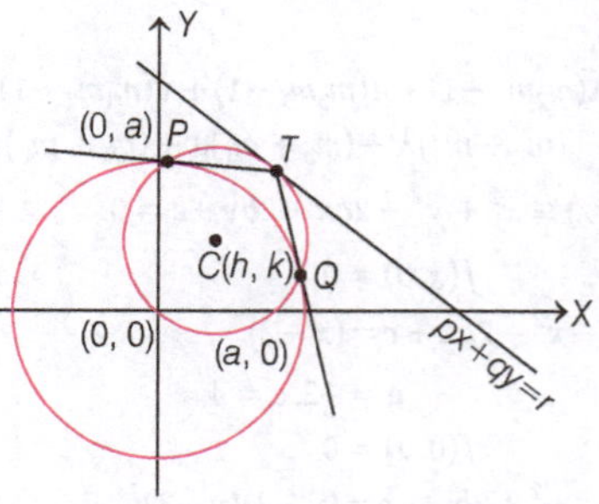

It passes through $T(x_1, y_1)$.

$\therefore$ $$x_1^2 + y_1^2 - a^2 + \lambda(x_1^2 + y_1^2 - a^2) = 0$$

$\Rightarrow$ $$\lambda = -1$$

$\therefore$ Circumcircle of ΔTPQ is $x^2 + y^2 - xx_1 - yy_1 = 0$

Its centre $C(h, k)$,

$\therefore \quad h = \frac{x_1}{2}, k = \frac{y_1}{2}$

From Eq. (i), we get

$$2ph + 2qk - r = 0$$

Hence, locus of $C(h, k)$ is $2px + 2qy - r = 0$

29.

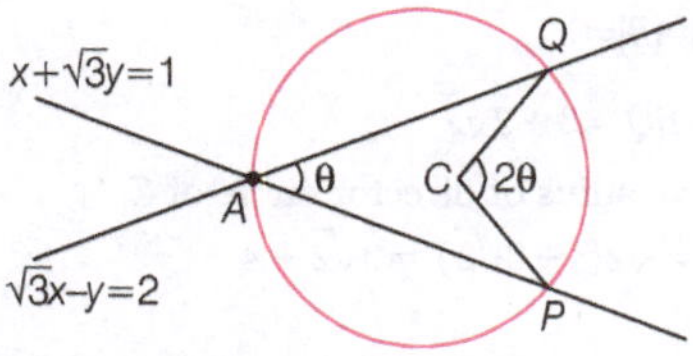

Let the point of intersection of two lines be A.

Angle subtended by PQ on centre C

$= 2 \times$ Angle subtended by PQ on A

For $x + \sqrt{3}y = 1$, $m_1 = -\frac{1}{\sqrt{3}}$

and for $\sqrt{3}x - y = 2$, $m_2 = \sqrt{3}$

Now, $m_1 \times m_2 = -\frac{1}{\sqrt{3}} \times \sqrt{3} = -1$

$\therefore \quad \angle A = 90°$

Therefore, required angle $= 2 \times 90° = 180°$

30. The locus of the centre of the circle cutting $S_1 = 0$ and $S_2 = 0$ orthogonally is the radical axis between $S_1 = 0$ and $S_2 = 0$

i.e. $\quad S_1 - S_2 = 0$

$\Rightarrow \quad 9x - 10y + 11 = 0$

31. Let r be the radius of the circle $x^2 + y^2 - 2r(x + y) + r^2 = 0$.

Since, it passes through $P(a, b)$.

$\therefore \quad a^2 + b^2 - 2r(a + b) + r^2 = 0$

Solving $r_1 = a + b + \sqrt{2ab}$ ...(i)

$r_2 = a + b - \sqrt{2ab}$ ...(ii)

The common chord is

$$S - S' = 0 = 2(x + y) = r_1 + r_2$$

For maximum length of the common chord, it must pass through the centre (r_1, r_2) of the small circle $\frac{a}{b} = 3 \pm 2\sqrt{2}$.

$\Rightarrow \quad k_1 + k_2 = 6$

32. $\therefore AB = 4$ and area of $\Delta APB = 8$

$$\frac{1}{2} \times 4 \times h = 8$$

$\Rightarrow \quad h = 4$

It is clear that P lies on circle of radius $2\sqrt{2}$ units with AB as its chord, so there are four possible positions of P.

33. $AB^2 = 4AM^2$

$$4\left(4 - \frac{n^2}{2}\right) = 2(8 - n^2), n \in N$$

$\Rightarrow \quad n = 1$ or 2

Hence, $p = 2\,(8 - 1^2 + 8 - 2^2) = 22$

$\therefore \quad \frac{p}{11} = 2$

34. If $(a, 0)$ is the centre C and P is $(2, -2)$, then

$$\angle COP = 45°$$

Since, the equation of OP is $x + y = 0$.

$\therefore \quad OP = 2\sqrt{2} = CP$

Hence, $OC = 4$

$\therefore \alpha = OB = OC + CB = 4 + 2\sqrt{2}$

$\Rightarrow \quad [\alpha] = 6$

35. The given circles are $(x - 1)^2 + y^2 = 4$ and $(x - 1)^2 + y^2 = 16$.

Then, points $(a + 1, \sqrt{3}a)$ lie on the line $y = \sqrt{3}(x - 1)$, whose slope $= \sqrt{3}$ and makes angles 60° with X-axis.

$$A = (1 + 2\cos 60°, 2\sin 60°) = (2, \sqrt{3})$$

$$B = (1 + 4\cos 60°, 4\sin 60°) = (3, 2\sqrt{3})$$

Hence, there is no point on the line segment AB.

36. $r = 5, \pm 5 = \frac{(3 \times 2) + (-4 \times 4) - k}{\sqrt{9 + 16}}$

$\Rightarrow \quad k = 15$ or -35

Take $k = 15$

Now, equation of tangent at (a, b) is

$$xa + yb - 2(x + a) - 4(y + b) - 5 = 0$$

If it represents the given line $3x - 4y - k = 0$, then

$$\frac{a - 2}{3} = \frac{b - 4}{-4} = \frac{2a + 4b + 5}{k} = \lambda$$

On simplification, $\lambda = 1$

$\Rightarrow \quad a = 5, b = 0$ and $k + a + b = 20$

$\Rightarrow \quad \frac{k + a + b}{5} = \frac{20}{5} = 4$

37. The equation of the given circle is

$$x^2 + y^2 - 6x - 2py + 17 = 0$$

$\Rightarrow \quad (x - 3)^2 + (y - p)^2 = (p^2 - 8)$ ...(i)

Also, (0, 0) lies outside the circle.

The equation of director circle of $S = 0$ will be

$(x - 3)^2 + (y - p)^2 = 2(p^2 - 8)$ ...(ii)

Tangents drawn from (0, 0) to circle (i) are perpendicular to each other.

Therefore, (0, 0) must lie on director circle.

Hence, $(0 - 3)^2 + (0 - p)^2 = 2(p^2 - 8)$

$\Rightarrow \quad p^2 = 25$

$\Rightarrow \quad p = \pm 5$

$\Rightarrow \quad |p| = 5$

38. θ is the angle between the tangent and the line.

The circle has centre (2, − 1) and radius 3.

The length of perpendicular from the centre on $3x - 4y = 5$ is

$$p = \left|\frac{6+4-5}{5}\right| = 1$$

or $$\sin(90° - \theta) = \frac{1}{3} \text{ or } \cos\theta = \frac{1}{3}$$

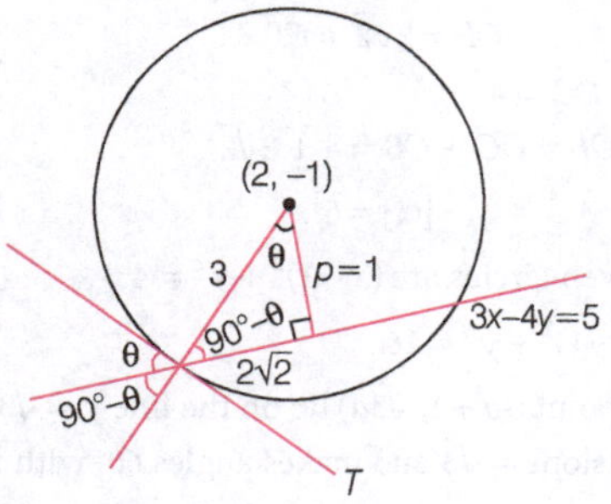

39. The radius of the given circle

$$x^2 + y^2 + 4x - 2\sqrt{2}y + c = 0$$

is $\sqrt{4+2-c} = \sqrt{6-c} = a$ [let]

Now, radius of circle, $S_1 = \frac{a}{\sqrt{2}}$

Radius of circle, $S_2 = \frac{a}{2}$ and so on.

Now, $a + \frac{a}{\sqrt{2}} + \frac{a}{2} + \dots \infty = 2$

$$\Rightarrow \quad \frac{a}{1 - \frac{1}{\sqrt{2}}} = 2$$

$$\Rightarrow \quad \frac{\sqrt{2}a}{\sqrt{2}-1} = 2$$

$$\Rightarrow \quad a = 2 - \sqrt{2} \Rightarrow \sqrt{6-c} = 2 - \sqrt{2}$$

$$\Rightarrow \quad 6 - c = 4 + 2 - 4\sqrt{2}$$

$$\Rightarrow \quad c = 4\sqrt{2} \Rightarrow \frac{c}{\sqrt{2}} = 4$$

40. The given circle is

$$S: (x-3)^2 + (y-5)^2 = (\sqrt{(34-\lambda)})^2$$

Since, point $P(1, 4)$ lies inside the circle

$$\therefore \quad S_1 < 0$$

$$\Rightarrow 1 + 16 - 6 - 40 + \lambda < 0$$

or $$\lambda < 29 \quad \text{...(i)}$$

Also, circle neither touches nor cuts the axes, then

$$3 > \sqrt{(34-\lambda)} \text{ or } \lambda > 25 \quad \text{...(ii)}$$

and $$5 > \sqrt{(34-\lambda)} \text{ or } \lambda > 9 \quad \text{...(iii)}$$

From Eqs. (i), (ii) and (iii), we get

$$25 < \lambda < 29$$

Hence, difference = 29 − 25 = 4

41. $x^2 + y^2 - 2x - 2\lambda y - 8 = 0$

or $(x^2 + y^2 - 2x - 8) - 2\lambda y = 0$

which is the form of $S + \lambda L = 0$

All the circles pass through the point of intersection of the circle $x^2 + y^2 - 2x - 8 = 0$ and $y = 0$

Solving, we get

$$x^2 - 2x - 8 = 0$$

or $$(x-4)(x+2) = 0$$

$$\therefore \quad A \equiv (-2, 0)$$

and $$B \equiv (4, 0)$$

Hence, $|AB| = 6$

42. $\because AQ = BQ = 3 + 2\sqrt{2}$

and PQ = radius of director circle of C_1

$$= \sqrt{2}(3 + 2\sqrt{2}) = 3\sqrt{2} + 4$$

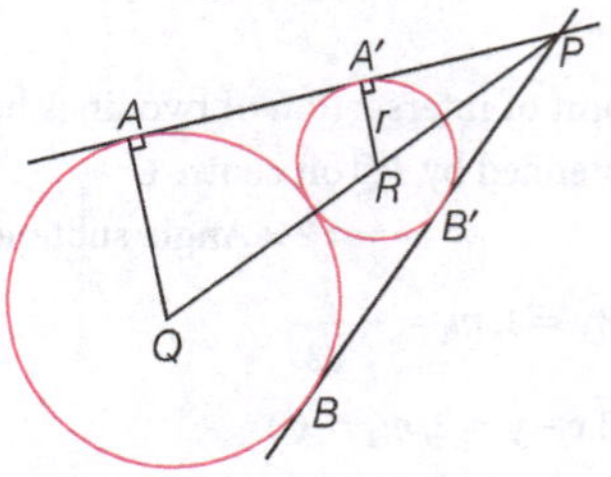

Let r be required radius.

$$\therefore \quad 3\sqrt{2} + 4 = 3 + 2\sqrt{2} + r + r\sqrt{2} \quad \left[\because \frac{PR}{PQ} = \frac{A'R}{AQ}\right]$$

$$\Rightarrow \quad r = \frac{(\sqrt{2}+1)}{(\sqrt{2}+1)} = 1$$

43. Since, $x + y - 5 = 0$ is a tangent to the circle at $P(2,3)$, so the centre of the circle lies on $x - y + 1 = 0$.

Now, $Q(1,2)$ lies on the circle.

Equation of right bisector of PQ is $x + y - 4 = 0$

∴ Centre of circle is point of intersection of $x - y + 1 = 0$ and $x + y - 4 = 0$ which is $\left(\frac{3}{2}, \frac{5}{2}\right)$

$$\therefore \quad \text{Radius, } \frac{1}{\sqrt{\lambda}} = \frac{\left|\frac{3}{2} + \frac{5}{2} - 5\right|}{\sqrt{2}} = \frac{1}{\sqrt{2}}$$

$$\therefore \quad \lambda = 2$$

Hence, $$\lambda^2 = 4$$

44. Since, given circle is $(x+5)^2 + (y-12)^2 = (14)^2$

or $$\left(\frac{x+5}{14}\right)^2 + \left(\frac{y-12}{14}\right)^2 = 1$$

Let $$\frac{x+5}{14} = \cos\theta \text{ and } \frac{y-12}{14} = \sin\theta$$

or $$x = 14\cos\theta - 5 \text{ and } y = 14\sin\theta + 12$$

$$\therefore \quad x^2 + y^2 = (14\cos\theta - 5)^2 + (14\sin\theta + 12)^2$$

$$= 196 + 25 + 144 + 28(12\sin\theta - 5\cos\theta)$$

$$= 365 + 28(12\sin\theta - 5\cos\theta)$$

Maximum value of $(x^2 + y^2) = 365 + 28 \times 13 = 729$

$[\because -13 \le 12\sin\theta - 5\cos\theta \le 13]$

or maximum value of $(x^2 + y^2)^{\frac{1}{3}} = 9$

45. $(x-2)^2+y^2=4$

Centre is (2, 0) and radius 2

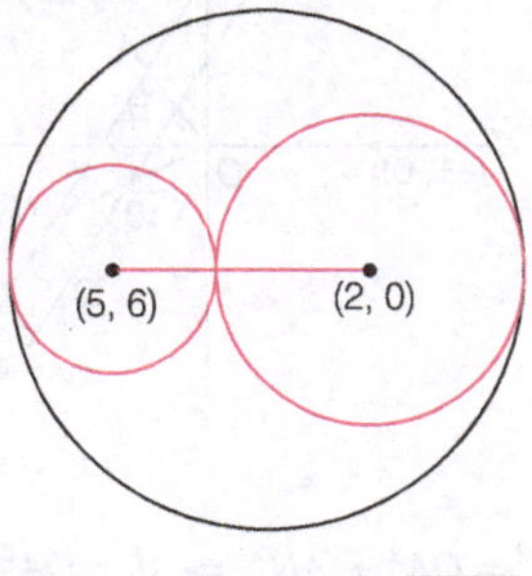

Distance between (2, 0) and (5, 6) is $\sqrt{9+36}=3\sqrt{5}$

$\therefore \quad r_1r_2=\frac{3\sqrt{5}-2}{2}\cdot\frac{3\sqrt{5}+2}{2}=\frac{41}{4}=10.25$

46. $x^2+y^2-12x+35=0 \quad \text{...(i)}$

$x^2+y^2+4x+3=0 \quad \text{...(ii)}$

Equation of radical axis of Eqs. (i) and (ii) is

$$-16x+32=0 \Rightarrow x=2$$

It intersect the line joining the centres i.e. $y=0$, at the point (2, 0).

$\therefore$ Required radius $=\sqrt{4-24+35}=\sqrt{15}=3.87$

47. The common chord of the given circles is

$$6x+14y+l+m=0 \quad \text{...(i)}$$

Since, $x^2+y^2+4x+22y+l=0$ bisects the circumference of the circle $x^2+y^2-2x+8y-m=0$.

$\therefore$ (i) passes through the centre of the second circle i.e. (1, –4)

Therefore, $6-56+l+m=0 \Rightarrow l+m=50$

48. The centre are $(5\cos\theta, 5\sin\theta)$. So equation of such circle is $(x-5\cos\theta)^2+(y-5\sin\theta)^2=9$

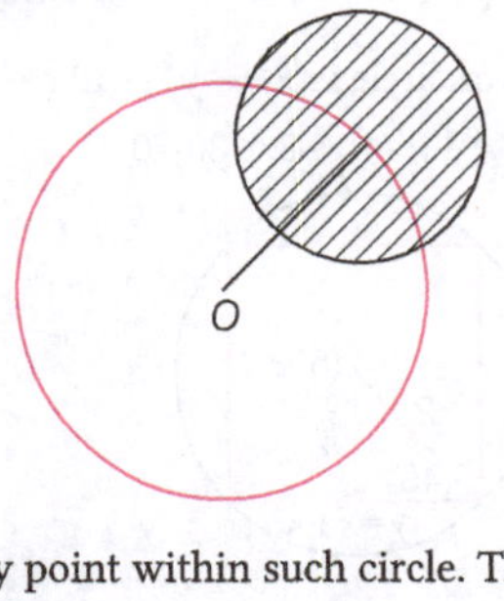

Let (h, k) be any point within such circle. Then (h, k) lie in shaded area.

$\therefore \quad 2\le$ distance of (h, k) from $0\le 8$

$\therefore \quad 4\le x^2+y^2\le 64.$

So, $\quad k=64$

49. The equation of the family of circles passing through A (3, 7) and $B(6, 5)$ is

$(x-3)(x-6)+(y-7)(y-5)+\lambda(2x+3y-27)=0$

i.e. $x^2+y^2+(2\lambda-9)x+(3\lambda-12)y+(53-27\lambda)=0 \quad \text{...(i)}$

The equation of the given circle is $x^2+y^2-4x-6y-3=0$...(ii)

Therefore, the equation of the line joining the points of intersection (i) and (ii) is

$$(2\lambda-9+4)x+(3\lambda-12+6)y+(53-27\lambda+3)=0$$

$$\Rightarrow \quad (2\lambda-5)x+(3\lambda-6)y+56-27\lambda)=0$$

$$\Rightarrow \quad \lambda(2x+3y-27)-(5x+6y-56)=0$$

which passes through the point of intersection of $2x+3y-27=0$ and $5x+6y-56=0$ for all values of λ.

$\Rightarrow$ The fixed point is $\left(2, \frac{23}{3}\right)$.

So, required sum is 9.66.

50. Since, (x_c, y_c) be the point of intersection of the lines.

$$3x+5y=1 \quad \text{...(i)}$$

and $\quad (2+c)x+5c^2y=1 \quad \text{...(ii)}$

On solving Eqs. (i) and (ii), we get

$$(2+c)x+5c^2\left(\frac{1-3x}{5}\right)=1$$

$$\Rightarrow \quad x=\frac{1-c^2}{2+c-3c^2}=\frac{(1-c)(1+c)}{(1-c)(2+3c)}$$

$$\Rightarrow \quad x=\frac{1+c}{2+3c} \quad \left[\because x_c=\frac{1+c}{2+3c}\right]$$

and $\quad y=\frac{1-3x}{5}=\frac{-1}{5(3c+2)}=y_c$

Now, $\quad h=\lim_{c\to 1}x_c=\lim_{c\to 1}\frac{(1+c)}{2+3c}=\frac{2}{5}$

$$k=\lim_{c\to 1}y_c=\lim_{c\to 1}\left[\frac{-1}{5(3c+2)}\right]=\frac{-1}{25}$$

$\therefore$ Centre $=\left(\frac{2}{5}, \frac{-1}{25}\right)$,

$$\text{Radius}=\sqrt{\left(2-\frac{2}{5}\right)^2+\left(0-\frac{1}{25}\right)^2}=\sqrt{\frac{64}{25}+\frac{1}{625}}=\frac{\sqrt{1601}}{25}$$

So, equation of the circle is

$$\left(x-\frac{2}{5}\right)^2+\left(y+\frac{1}{25}\right)^2=\frac{1601}{(25)^2}$$

$$\Rightarrow \quad 25x^2+25y^2-20x+2y-60=0$$

51. $C_1: (x-\alpha)^2+(y-\beta)^2=r_1^2$

$C_2: (x-8)^2+\left(y-\frac{15}{2}\right)^2=r_2^2$

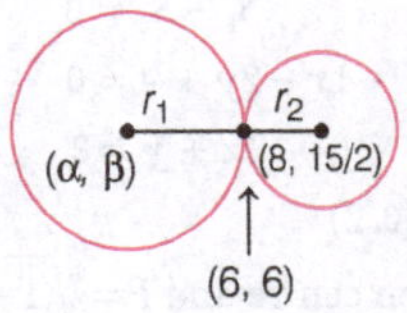

$$r_1:r_2=2:1$$

So, $\quad \frac{2\times 8+\alpha}{2+1}=6 \Rightarrow \alpha=2$

and $\quad \frac{2\times\frac{15}{2}+\beta}{2+1}=6 \Rightarrow \beta=3$

So, $(\alpha, \beta)=(2, 3)$

Now, $\quad r_1 = \sqrt{(6-\alpha)^2 + (6-\beta)^2} = \sqrt{(4)^2 + (3)^2} = 5$

$\Rightarrow \quad r_1^2 = 25$

and $\quad r_2^2 = \left(\sqrt{(8-6)^2 + \left(\dfrac{15}{2} - 6\right)^2}\right)^2 = 4 + \dfrac{9}{4} = \dfrac{25}{4}$

Therefore, $(\alpha + \beta) + 4(r_1^2 + r_2^2) = (2+3) + 4\left(25 + \dfrac{25}{4}\right)$

$$= 5 + 4 \times \frac{125}{4} = 130$$

52. Orthocentre is the intersection of altitudes.

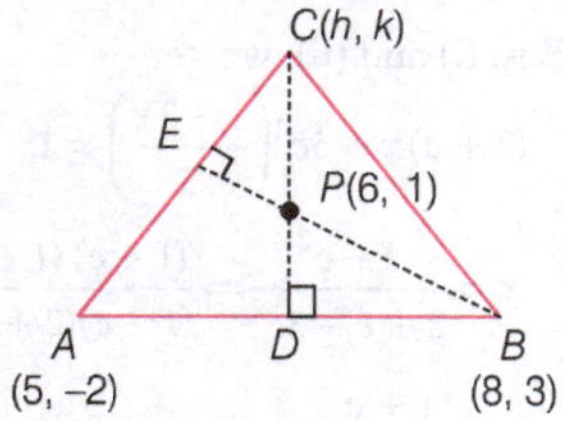

So, $\quad$ slope of $BP \times$ slope of $AC = -1$

$\Rightarrow \quad \left(\dfrac{3-1}{8-6}\right) \times \left(\dfrac{k+2}{h-5}\right) = -1$

$\Rightarrow \quad k + 2 = -h + 5$

$\Rightarrow \quad h + k = 3 \quad$ ...(i)

and $\quad$ slope of $CP \times$ slope of $AB = -1$

$\Rightarrow \quad \left(\dfrac{k-1}{h-6}\right) \times \left(\dfrac{3+2}{8-5}\right) = -1$

$\Rightarrow \quad 5k - 5 = -3h + 18$

$\Rightarrow \quad 3h + 5k = 23 \quad$ ...(ii)

On solving Eqs. (i) and (ii), we get

$$h = -4, k = 7$$

On checking, option (c) is correct.

$$x^2 + y^2 - 65 = 0$$

53. $S_1 : x^2 + y^2 - 2x - 2y + 1 = 0$

$S_2 : x^2 + y^2 + 2x - 3 = 0$

$\Rightarrow C_2(-1, 0)$ and $r = 2$

Equation of common chord

$\Rightarrow \quad S_1 - S_2 = 0$

$\Rightarrow \quad -4x - 2y + 4 = 0$

$\Rightarrow \quad 2x + y = 2$

At Y-axis $\Rightarrow P(0, 2)$

Distance between centre and $P = \sqrt{(1-0)^2 + (1-2)^2}$

$$= \sqrt{2}$$

54. $C : x^2 + y^2 = 10$

$$AN = \frac{MN}{2} = 1$$

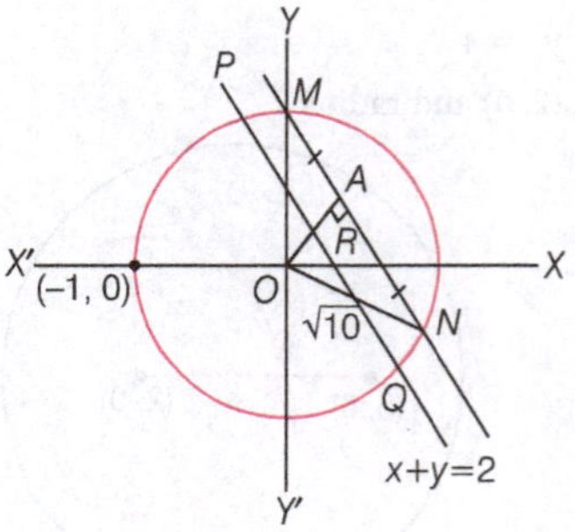

$\because$ In ΔOAN,

$$ON^2 = OA^2 + AN^2 \Rightarrow 10 = OA^2 + 1 \Rightarrow OA = 3$$

Perpendicular distance of centre from PQ

$$= \left|\frac{0+0-2}{\sqrt{2}}\right| = \sqrt{2} = OR$$

Perpendicular distance between MN and $PQ = AR = OA - OR$

$$= 3 - \sqrt{2}$$

55. We have, circle with radius 1 cm and lines passing through the point (3, 2) and parallel to the coordinate axes.

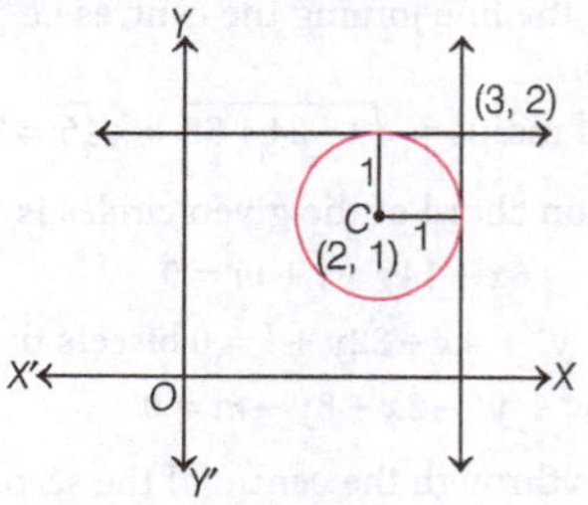

$\therefore$ Shortest distance of the circle C from the point (5, 5)

$$= \sqrt{(5-2)^2 + (5-1)^2} - \text{(radius of circle)}$$

$$= \sqrt{9 + 16} - 1 = 5 - 1 = 4 \text{ units}$$

56. Given equation of circle is $x^2 + y^2 - 10x - 6y + 30 = 0$

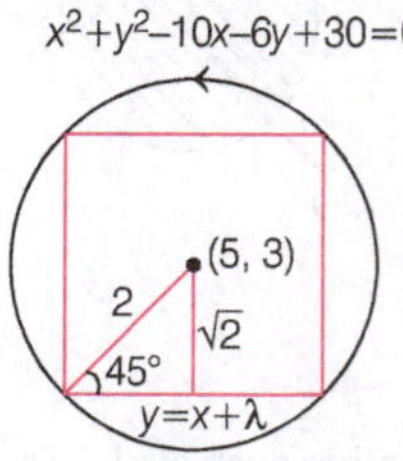

$\therefore$ Centre of the circle $= \left(-\dfrac{1}{2} \times (-10), -\dfrac{1}{2} \times (-6)\right) = (5, 3)$

Also, one side of square is parallel to the line $y = x + 3$.

So, equation of that side of square is given by, $y = x + \lambda$.

Now, distance of (5, 3) to the line $y = x + \lambda$ is $\sqrt{2}$.

$\Rightarrow \quad \left|\dfrac{3 - 5 - \lambda}{\sqrt{2}}\right| = \sqrt{2} \Rightarrow |\lambda + 2| = 2$

$\Rightarrow \quad \lambda + 2 = \pm 2 \Rightarrow \lambda = 0, -4$

So, the lines are $y = x$ and $y = x - 4$

Now, solving $y = x$ and $x^2 + y^2 - 10x - 6y + 30 = 0$, we get

$$x = 3, y = 3 \text{ and } x = 5, y = 5$$

[by putting $y = x$ in the equation of circle]

and $y = x - 4$ and $x^2 + y^2 - 10x - 6y + 30 = 0$, we get

$$x = 7, y = 3 \text{ and } x = 5, y = 1$$

So, vertices are (5, 5), (3, 3), (7, 3) and (5, 1).

Hence, $\Sigma x_i^2 + y_i^2 = 9 + 9 + 25 + 25 + 25 + 1 + 49 + 9 = 152$

57. Circle : $x^2 + y^2 - 16x - 4y = 0$

Let line passing through centre of circle C (8, 2) with slope m is $y - 2 = m(x - 8)$

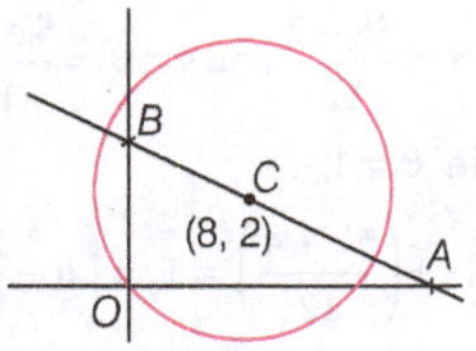

$$A = \left(8 - \frac{2}{m}, 0\right),\ B = (0, 2 - 8m)$$

$$OA + OB = 8 - \frac{2}{m} + 2 - 8m = 10 - \left(\frac{2}{m} + 8m\right)$$

Since, AM $\geq$ GM

$$\Rightarrow \quad \frac{\frac{2}{m} + 8m}{2} \geq \sqrt{\frac{2}{m} \cdot 8m}$$

$$\Rightarrow \quad \frac{2}{m} + 8m \geq 8$$

Since, $m < 0$, $\left(\frac{2}{m} + 8m\right)_{\max} = -8$

Minimum value of $OA + OB = 10 - (-8) = 18$

58. Equation of two diameters of a circle are

$$2x - 3y = 5 \quad \text{...(i)}$$

and

$$3x - 4y = 7 \quad \text{...(ii)}$$

On solving Eqs. (i) and (ii), we get

Centre of circle $C(1, -1)$

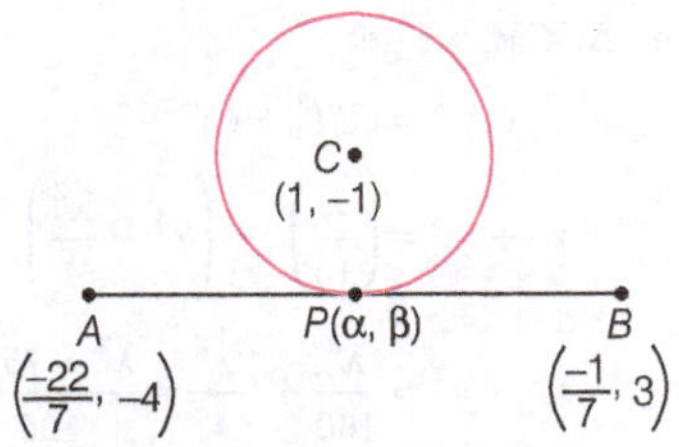

Equation of AB is $7x - 3y + 10 = 0$ ...(i)

and equation of CP is $3x + 7y + 4 = 0$ ...(ii)

On solving Eqs. (i) and (ii), we get

$$\alpha = \frac{-41}{29}, \beta = \frac{1}{29}$$

$$\therefore \quad 17\beta - \alpha = 2$$

59. Given, the equation $C_1 = x^2 + y^2 - 2x - 6y + \alpha = 0$

Image of centre $C_1 \equiv (1, 3)$ in $x - y + 1 = 0$ is given by

$$\frac{x_1 - 1}{1} = \frac{y_1 - 3}{-1} = \frac{-2(1 - 3 + 1)}{1^2 + 1^2}$$

$$\Rightarrow \quad x_1 = 2, y_1 = 2$$

Centre of circle $C_1 = (2, 2)$

$\therefore$ Equation of C_2 is $x^2 + y^2 - 4x - 4y + \frac{38}{5} = 0$

On comparing the equation $x^2 + y^2 + 2gx + 2fy + c = 0$.

Now, radius of C_2 is $\sqrt{4 + 4 - \frac{38}{5}}$

$$\Rightarrow \quad r_2 = \sqrt{2/5}$$

Now, (radius of $C_1)^2$ = (radius of $C_2)^2$

$$\Rightarrow \quad 10 - \alpha = \frac{2}{5} \Rightarrow \alpha = \frac{48}{5}$$

$$\therefore \quad \alpha + 6r^2 = \frac{48}{5} + \frac{12}{5} = 12$$

60. Let $C_1 : x^2 + y^2 = 9$

and $\quad C_2 : (x - h)^2 + (y - k)^2 = h^2 + k^2$

$$\Rightarrow \quad x^2 + y^2 - 2hx - 2ky = 0 \quad \text{...(i)}$$

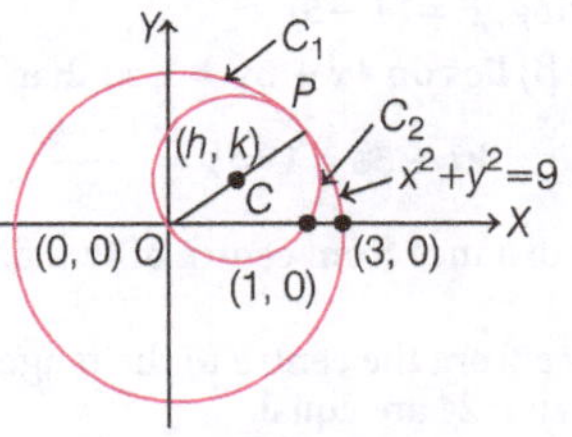

$\because$ Eq. (i) passes through (1, 0), then

$$1 + 0 - 2h = 0 \Rightarrow h = \frac{1}{2}$$

$$\because \quad OC = \frac{OP}{2}$$

$$\Rightarrow \quad \sqrt{\left(\frac{1}{2}\right)^2 + k^2} = \frac{3}{2} \Rightarrow \frac{1}{4} + k^2 = \frac{9}{4}$$

$$\Rightarrow \quad k^2 = 2 \ \Rightarrow \ k = \pm\sqrt{2}$$

$\therefore$ Possible values of (h, k) are $\left(\frac{1}{2}, \sqrt{2}\right), \left(\frac{1}{2}, -\sqrt{2}\right)$

Thus, $4(h^2 + k^2) = 4\left(\frac{1}{4} + 2\right) = 4\left(\frac{9}{4}\right) = 9$

61. $S_1 \equiv x^2 + y^2 - 18x - 15y + 131 = 0$

$$C_1 = (-g_1, -f_1) = \left(9, \frac{15}{2}\right)$$

$$S_2 \equiv x^2 + y^2 - 6x - 6y - 7 = 0$$

$$C_2 = (-g_2, -f_2) = (3, 3)$$

$$r_1 = \sqrt{g_1^2 + f_1^2 - c_1} = \sqrt{(9)^2 + \left(\frac{15}{2}\right)^2 - 131}$$

$$= \sqrt{81 + \frac{225}{4} - 131} = \frac{5}{2}$$

$$r_2 = \sqrt{(3)^2 + (3)^2 + 7} = \sqrt{9 + 9 + 7} = \sqrt{25} = 5$$

$$C_1C_2 = \sqrt{(9-3)^2 + \left(\frac{15}{2} - 3\right)^2} = \sqrt{(6)^2 + \left(\frac{9}{2}\right)^2}$$

$$= \sqrt{36 + \frac{81}{4}} = \sqrt{\frac{144 + 81}{4}} = \sqrt{\frac{225}{4}} = \frac{15}{2}$$

$$|C_1C_2| = \left|\frac{15}{2}\right| = \frac{5}{2} + \frac{5}{1} = |C_1C_2| = r_1 + r_2$$

$\Rightarrow$ Number of common tangents are 3.

62.

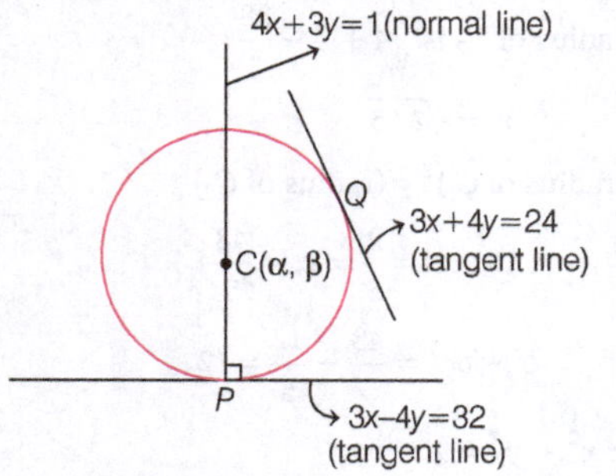

First solving equations $4x + 3y = 1$ and $3x - 4y = 32$ to get intersecting point P.

After solving, $P = (4, -5)$

Centre (α, β) lies on $4x + 3y = 1$, so that

$$4\alpha + 3\beta = 1 \Rightarrow \beta = \frac{1 - 4\alpha}{3}$$

We know distance from centre of two different tangents are equal.

So, distance from the centre to the tangent line $3x - 4y = 32$ and $3x + 4y = 24$ are equal.

Thus, $$\left|\frac{3\alpha - 4\left(\frac{1-4\alpha}{3}\right) - 32}{5}\right| = \left|\frac{3\alpha + 4\left(\frac{1-4\alpha}{3}\right) - 24}{5}\right|$$

$$\Rightarrow \left|\frac{\frac{9\alpha - 4 + 16\alpha - 96}{3}}{5}\right| \Rightarrow \left|\frac{25\alpha - 100}{15}\right| = \left|\frac{-7\alpha - 68}{15}\right|$$

$\Rightarrow \quad |25\alpha - 100| = |-7\alpha - 68|$

Either $\quad 25\alpha - 100 = -7\alpha - 68$

$\Rightarrow \quad 32\alpha = 32 \Rightarrow \alpha = 1$

or $\quad 25\alpha - 100 = -(-7\alpha - 68) = 7\alpha + 68$

$\Rightarrow \quad 18\alpha = 168 \Rightarrow \alpha = \frac{28}{3}$

For $\alpha = 1$, then $\beta = \frac{1 - 4 \times 1}{3} = \frac{-3}{3} = -1$

So, centre $(1, -1)$ and radius $= \left|\frac{3(1) - 4(-1) - 32}{\sqrt{3^2 + 4^2}}\right| = 5$

For, $\alpha = \frac{28}{3}$, then $\beta = \frac{1 - 4 \times \frac{28}{3}}{3} = \frac{-109}{9}$

So, centre $\left(\frac{28}{3}, \frac{-109}{9}\right)$

and radius $= \left|\frac{3\left(\frac{28}{3}\right) - 4\left(\frac{-109}{9}\right) - 32}{5}\right| = \frac{656}{45}$

Radius = 14.58 (neglected)

Hence, $\alpha = 1, \beta = -1, n = 5$

$\therefore \quad \alpha - \beta + r = 1 + 1 + 5 = 7$

63. We have, equation of circle is $x^2 + y^2 = 16$

Let any point on the circle be $B(4\cos\theta, 4\sin\theta)$

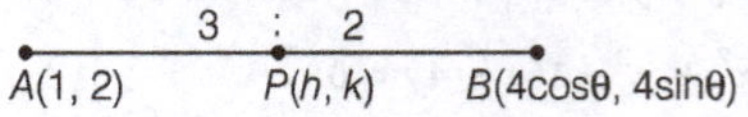

$$h = \frac{12\cos\theta + 2}{5} \text{ and } k = \frac{12\sin\theta + 4}{5}$$

$$\Rightarrow \quad \cos\theta = \frac{5h - 2}{12} \text{ and } \sin\theta = \frac{5k - 4}{12}$$

As $\cos^2\theta + \sin^2\theta = 1$,

$$\left(\frac{5h-2}{12}\right)^2 + \left(\frac{5k-4}{12}\right)^2 = 1 \Rightarrow \left(h - \frac{2}{5}\right)^2 + \left(k - \frac{4}{5}\right)^2 = 12^2$$

$\therefore$ Locus of point P is $\left(x - \frac{2}{5}\right)^2 + \left(y - \frac{4}{5}\right)^2 = 12^2$

Which is equation of circle with center $\left(\frac{2}{5}, \frac{4}{5}\right)$.

Hence, $AC = \sqrt{\left(1 - \frac{2}{5}\right)^2 + \left(2 - \frac{4}{5}\right)^2} = \frac{\sqrt{45}}{5} = \frac{3\sqrt{5}}{5}$

64. Given, length of $AB = \lambda$

So, $AC = \frac{\lambda}{2}$ and $AM = \frac{2\lambda}{5}$

$$CM = AC - AM = \frac{\lambda}{2} - \frac{2\lambda}{5} = \frac{\lambda}{10}$$

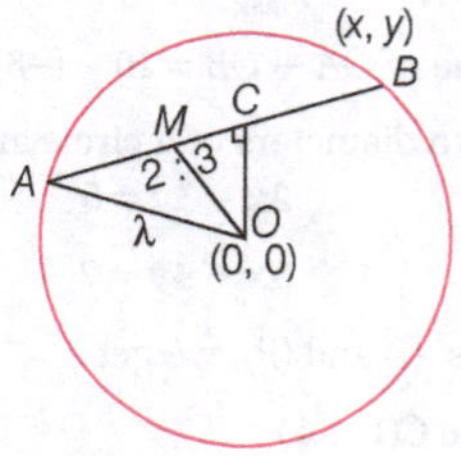

Now, from ΔOCM, we get

$$OM^2 = CM^2 + OC^2$$

$$\Rightarrow \quad x^2 + y^2 = \left(\frac{\lambda}{10}\right)^2 + \left(\lambda^2 - \frac{\lambda^2}{4}\right)$$

$$\Rightarrow \quad x^2 + y^2 = \frac{\lambda^2}{100} + \frac{3\lambda^2}{4} = \frac{\lambda^2 + 75\lambda^2}{100}$$

$$\Rightarrow \quad x^2 + y^2 = \frac{76\lambda^2}{100} = \frac{19\lambda^2}{25}$$

$$\therefore \quad x^2 + y^2 = \left(\frac{\sqrt{19}\lambda}{5}\right)^2$$

So, radius is $\frac{\sqrt{19}\lambda}{5}$.

65. Equation of circle $x^2 + y^2 - 6x + 4y + 8 = 0$

Centre = (3, – 2), Radius = $\sqrt{5}$

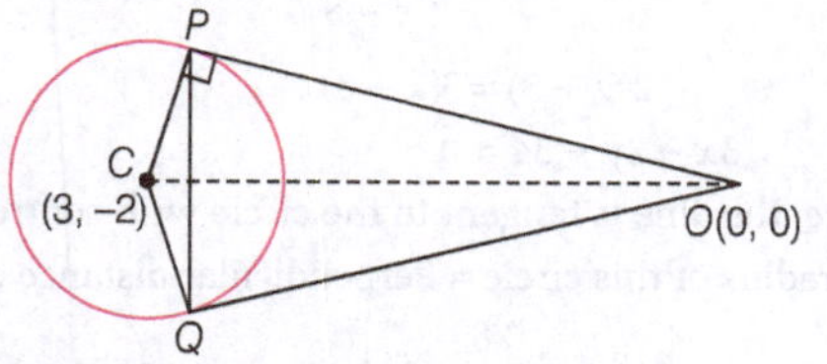

Equation of circumcircle of ΔOPQ

$$(x - 0)(x - 3) + (y - 0)(y + 2) = 0$$

$$[\because \angle OPC = 90^\circ, \therefore OC \text{ is diameter}]$$

$$\Rightarrow \quad x^2 + y^2 - 3x + 2y = 0$$

$\because$ It passes through the point (α, 1 / 2),

$$\therefore \quad \alpha^2 + \frac{1}{4} - 3\alpha + 2 \times \frac{1}{2} = 0$$

$$\Rightarrow \quad \alpha^2 - 3\alpha + \frac{5}{4} = 0$$

$$\Rightarrow \quad 4\alpha^2 - 12\alpha + 5 = 0$$

$$\Rightarrow \quad \alpha = \frac{1}{2}, \frac{5}{2}$$

66. Equation of circle $\quad x^2 + y^2 - 2x + y - 5 = 0 \quad$ ...(i)

On comparing with $x^2 + y^2 + 2gx + 2fy + c = 0$

$$\therefore \quad 2g = -2, 2f = 1, c = -5$$

$$\Rightarrow \quad g = -1, f = \frac{1}{2}, c = -5$$

$\therefore$ Radius of the circle

$$r = \sqrt{(-1)^2 + \left(\frac{1}{2}\right)^2 + 5} = \frac{5}{2}$$

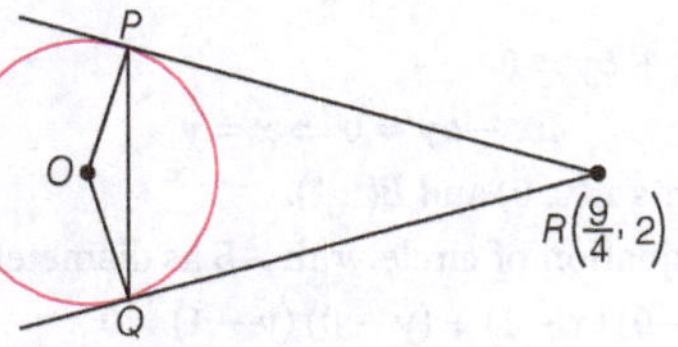

Length of tangent $PR = \sqrt{S_1}$

$$l = \sqrt{\left(\frac{9}{4}\right)^2 + (2)^2 - 2\left(\frac{9}{4}\right) + 2 - 5} = \frac{5}{4}$$

$$\therefore \text{Area of } \Delta PQR = \frac{rl^3}{r^2 + l^2} = \frac{\left(\frac{5}{2}\right)\left(\frac{5}{4}\right)^3}{\left(\frac{5}{2}\right)^2 + \left(\frac{5}{4}\right)^2} = \frac{\frac{5}{2} \times \frac{125}{64} \times 16}{125} = \frac{5}{8}$$

67. $P\left(\frac{1+a}{2}, \frac{1-a}{2}\right)$

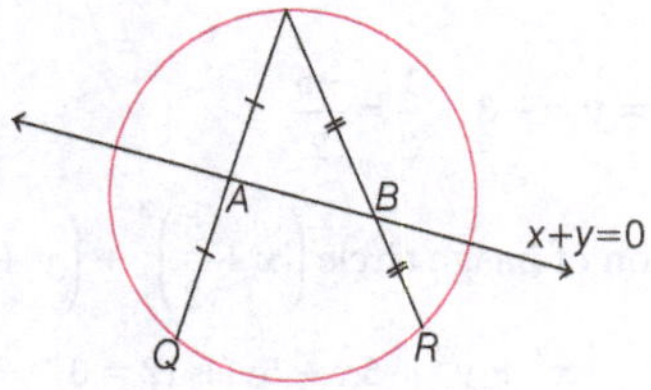

Since, point A lies on the line $x + y = 0$. So, the co-ordinates of point A are $(k, -k)$. Let the co-ordinates of Q are (α, β).

Since, A is mid-point of PQ, then

$$\left(\frac{\frac{1+a}{2} + \alpha}{2}, \frac{\frac{1-a}{2} + \beta}{2}\right) = (k, -k)$$

$$\Rightarrow \quad \alpha = 2k - \frac{(1+a)}{2} \text{ and } \beta = -2k - \frac{(1-a)}{2}$$

Now, Q lies on circle

$$2x^2 + 2y^2 - (1+a)x - (1-a)y = 0,$$

then $\quad 2\alpha^2 + 2\beta^2 - (1+a)\alpha - (1-a)\beta = 0$

$$\Rightarrow 2\left[2k - \frac{(1+a)}{2}\right]^2 + 2\left[-2k - \frac{(1-a)}{2}\right]^2$$

$$-(1+a)\left[2k - \frac{(1+a)}{2}\right] - (1-a)\left[-2k - \frac{(1-a)}{2}\right] = 0$$

$$\Rightarrow 2\left[4k^2 + \frac{(1+a)^2}{4} - 2k(1+a)\right] + 2\left[4k^2 + \frac{(1-a)^2}{4} + 2k(1-a)\right]$$

$$-2k(1+a) + \frac{(1+a)^2}{2} + 2k(1-a) + \frac{(1-a)^2}{2} = 0$$

$$\Rightarrow 16k^2 - 6k(1 + a - 1 + a) + (1+a)^2 + (1-a)^2 = 0$$

$$\Rightarrow \quad 16k^2 - 12ka + 2(1 + a^2) = 0$$

$$\Rightarrow \quad 8k^2 - 6ka + (1 + a^2) = 0$$

Since, $x + y = 0$ bisects two distinct chords, so

$$D > 0$$

$$\Rightarrow 36a^2 - 32(1 + a^2) > 0 \Rightarrow 36a^2 - 32 - 32a^2 > 0$$

$$\Rightarrow \quad 4a^2 > 32 \Rightarrow a^2 > 8$$

$$\therefore \quad a^2 \in (8, \infty)$$

68. Given, equation of circle is

$$x^2 + y^2 - 4x - 6y + 11 = 0$$

Equation of tangent to above circle at (3, 2) is

$$3x + 2y - 2(x + 3) - 3(y + 2) + 11 = 0$$

$$\Rightarrow \quad x - y - 1 = 0$$

When the circle $x^2 + y^2 - 4x - 6y + 11 = 0$ is rolled 4 units upward at the tangent $x - y - 1 = 0$, the centre of new circle C_1 becomes $(2 + 2\sqrt{2}, 3 + 2\sqrt{2})$ and radius remains same $\sqrt{21}$.

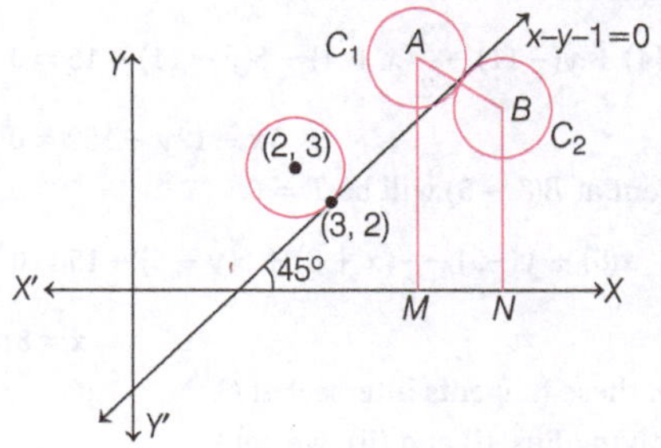

Since, C_2 is image of C_1 in tangent $x - y - 1 = 0$.

So, centre of C_2 becomes $(4 + 2\sqrt{2}, 1 + 2\sqrt{2})$.

$\therefore$ A and B are $(2 + 2\sqrt{2}, 3 + 2\sqrt{2})$ and $(4 + 2\sqrt{2}, 1 + 2\sqrt{2})$, respectively.

Again, foot of perpendicular from A and B on X-axis are $M(2 + 2\sqrt{2}, 0)$ and $N(4 + 2\sqrt{2}, 0)$.

$\therefore$ Area of trapezium $AMNB = \frac{1}{2} \times$ (Sum of parallel sides) $\times$ (Perpendicular distance between them)

$$= \frac{1}{2} \times (AM + BN) \times MN$$

$$= \frac{1}{2} \times (3 + 2\sqrt{2} + 1 + 2\sqrt{2}) \times 2$$

$$= 4 + 4\sqrt{2} = 4(1 + \sqrt{2})$$

69. Given equation of circle is

$$(x - h)^2 + (y - k)^2 = r^2 \quad \text{... (i)}$$

Let $L_1 : y = x + 2 \Rightarrow x - y + 2 = 0$

$L_2 : 4y = 3x + 6 \Rightarrow 3x - 4y + 6 = 0$

$L_3 : 3y = 4x + 1 \Rightarrow 4x - 3y + 1 = 0$

Now, equation of angle bisectors of lines L_2 and L_3 is given by

$$\frac{4x - 3y + 1}{\sqrt{4^2 + (-3)^2}} = \pm\left(\frac{3x - 4y + 6}{\sqrt{3^2 + (-4)^2}}\right)$$

$$\Rightarrow \frac{4x - 3y + 1}{5} = \pm\left(\frac{3x - 4y + 6}{5}\right)$$

$$\Rightarrow 4x - 3y + 1 = 3x - 4y + 6 \quad \text{(taking + ve sign)}$$

$$\Rightarrow x + y = 5 \quad \text{... (ii)}$$

Since, centre (h, k) lies on bisector of L_2 and L_3. So, (h, k) satisfies the Eq. (ii).

Hence, $h + k = 5$ [from Eq. (ii)]

70.

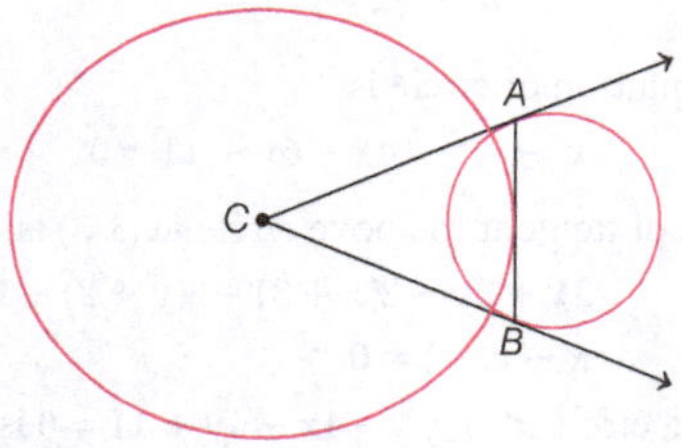

We have, circle $x^2 + y^2 - 3x + 10y - 15 = 0$

Tangent at $A(4, -11)$ will be $T = 0$

i.e. $x(4) + y(-11) - \frac{3}{2}(x + 4) + 5(y - 11) - 15 = 0$

i.e. $5x - 12y - 152 = 0$ ... (i)

Tangent at $B(8, -5)$ will be $T = 0$

i.e. $x(8) + y(-5) - \frac{3}{2}(x + 8) + 5(y - 5) - 15 = 0$

i.e. $x = 8$ ...(ii)

Since, these tangents intersect at C.

On solving Eqs. (i) and (ii), we get

$$x = 8, y = \frac{-28}{3}$$

i.e. $C\left(8, -\frac{28}{3}\right)$

Using two points of the line, equation of AB is

$$(y + 5) = \frac{(-11) + 5}{4 - 8} \times (x - 8)$$

i.e. $2(y + 5) = 3(x - 8)$

i.e. $3x - 2y - 34 = 0$ ...(iii)

Since, this line is tangent to the circle with centre C.

So, radius of this circle = Perpendicular distance of C from AB

$$\Rightarrow \text{Radius} = \frac{\left|3 \cdot 8 + 2 \cdot \frac{28}{3} - 34\right|}{\sqrt{3^2 + (-2)^2}} \text{ units}$$

$\because$ Distance of (x_1, y_1) from $ax + by + c = 0$ is $\frac{|ax_1 + by_1 + c|}{\sqrt{a^2 + b^2}}$ units. [$\because$ distance of (x_1, y_1) from $ax + by + c = 0$ is units]

$$\Rightarrow \text{Radius} = \frac{26}{3\sqrt{13}} \text{ units} = \frac{2\sqrt{13}}{3} \text{ units}$$

71. Given line, $ax + by = 0 \, (a \neq b)$ ...(i)

and circle $x^2 + y^2 - 2x = 0$ ...(ii)

From Eq. (i), $y = -\frac{ax}{b}$ puting in Eq. (ii), we get

$$x^2 + \frac{a^2}{b^2}x^2 - 2x = 0 \Rightarrow x\left(\frac{a^2 + b^2}{b^2}x - 2\right) = 0$$

$$x = 0 \text{ or } x = \frac{2b^2}{a^2 + b^2}$$

Now, circle and line cuts at $A(\alpha, 0)$ and $B(1, \beta)$.

So, only possible value is $\alpha = 0$ and $\frac{2b^2}{a^2 + b^2} = 1$

$$a^2 = b^2 \Rightarrow a = -b \quad [\because a \neq b]$$

Line $ax + by = 0$

$$ax - ay = 0 \Rightarrow x = y$$

So, points $A(0, 0)$ and $B(1, 1)$.

Now, equation of circle with AB as diameter

$$(x - 0)(x - 1) + (y - 0)(y - 1) = 0$$

$$x^2 + y^2 - x - y = 0$$

Centre $\left(\frac{1}{2}, \frac{1}{2}\right)$; $r = \sqrt{\frac{1}{4} + \frac{1}{4}} = \frac{1}{\sqrt{2}}$

Let image of $\left(\frac{1}{2}, \frac{1}{2}\right)$ in the line $x + y + 2 = 0$ is (x, y).

$$\frac{x - \frac{1}{2}}{1} = \frac{y - \frac{1}{2}}{1} = \frac{-2\left(\frac{1}{2} + \frac{1}{2} + 2\right)}{1^2 + 1^2}$$

$$x - \frac{1}{2} = y - \frac{1}{2} = -3$$

$$x = y = -3 + \frac{1}{2} = \frac{-5}{2}$$

So, equation of image circle $\left(x + \frac{5}{2}\right)^2 + \left(y + \frac{5}{2}\right)^2 = \left(\frac{1}{\sqrt{2}}\right)^2$

$$\Rightarrow x^2 + y^2 + 5x + 5y + 12 = 0$$

72. Given equation is $(x-4)^2+(y-5)^2=2^2$

$\therefore \quad r = 2$

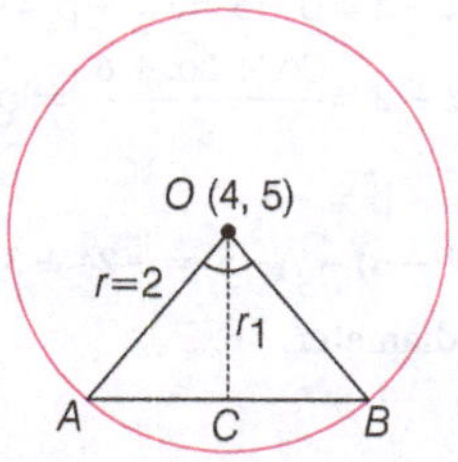

and $O(4, 5)$

$\because \quad \theta_1 = \dfrac{\pi}{3}$

$\therefore \quad \dfrac{\theta_1}{2} = \dfrac{\pi}{6}$

$\therefore$ From ΔOAC,

$$2\cos\left(\frac{\theta_1}{2}\right) = r_1$$

$$2\cos\frac{\pi}{6} = 2\times\frac{\sqrt{3}}{2} = \sqrt{3}$$

$\therefore \quad r_1 = \sqrt{3}$

If $\theta_3 = \dfrac{2\pi}{3}$

$\therefore 2\cos\left(\dfrac{\theta_3}{2}\right) = 2\cos\dfrac{\pi}{3} = 2\times\dfrac{1}{2} = 1 = r_3$

$\because \quad r_1^2 = r_2^2 + r_3^2$

$$3 = r_2^2 + 1^2 \Rightarrow r_2^2 = 2 \Rightarrow r_2 = \sqrt{2}$$

$\therefore$ From ΔOAC,

$$2\cos\left(\frac{\theta_2}{2}\right) = \sqrt{2} \Rightarrow \cos\left(\frac{\theta_2}{2}\right) = \frac{1}{\sqrt{2}}$$

$\therefore \quad \dfrac{\theta_2}{2} = \dfrac{\pi}{4}$

$\therefore \quad \theta_2 = \dfrac{\pi}{2}$

73. Let r be radius of circle touching both axes in first quadrant.

$\therefore$ Its equation is $(x-r)^2+(y-r)^2=r^2$

i.e. $x^2+y^2-2rx-2ry+r^2=0$ ...(i)

Let $A(x_1, y_1)$ and $B(x_2, y_2)$ be its points of intersection with $x+y=2$

Given, $AB = 2$ units

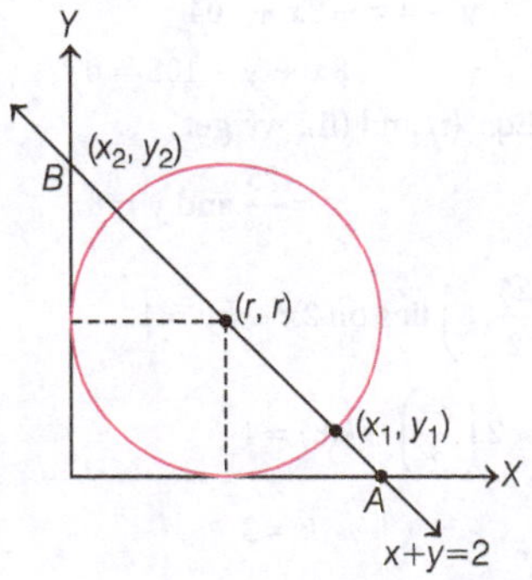

$\Rightarrow \quad AB^2 = 4$

$\Rightarrow \quad (x_1-x_2)^2+(y_1-y_2)^2 = 4$

$\Rightarrow \quad (x_1+x_2)^2 - 4(x_1x_2) + (y_1+y_2)^2 - 4(y_1y_2) = 4$ ...(ii)

Here, equation of line $x+y=2$

$\Rightarrow \quad x = 2-y$

On putting the value of $x = 2-y$ in Eq. (i), we get

$$(2-y)^2+y^2-2r(2-y)-2ry+r^2=0$$

$2y^2-4y+r^2-4r+4=0$, whose roots are y_1, y_2

$\Rightarrow \quad y_1+y_2 = -\dfrac{(-4)}{2} = 2,$

$$y_1y_2 = \frac{r^2-4r+4}{2} \quad \text{...(iii)}$$

Now, $x_1+x_2 = (2-y_1)+(2-y_2) = 4-(y_1+y_2) = 2,$

$x_1x_2 = (2-y_1)(2-y_2) = 4-2(y_1+y_2)+y_1y_2$

$$= \frac{r^2-4r+4}{2} \quad \text{...(iv)}$$

Putting in Eq. (ii),

$$2^2 - 4\left(\frac{r^2-4r+4}{2}\right) + 2^2 - 4\left(\frac{r^2-4r+4}{2}\right) = 4$$

$\Rightarrow \quad (r-2)^2 = 1, \Rightarrow r-2 = \pm 1 \Rightarrow r = 2\pm 1 \Rightarrow r = 1, 3$

Let $r_1 = 1, r_2 = 3$

$\therefore \quad r_1^2 + r_2^2 - r_1r_2 = 1^2+3^2-1\times 3 = 7$

74. Given circles, $C_1 : x^2+y^2-4x-2y = \alpha - 5$

Centre $(2, 1)$

$$C_2 : 5x^2+5y^2-10fx-10gy+36=0$$

Centre (f, g)

Line $L : y = 2x+1$

Image of $(2, 1)$ in line L in (f, g)

$$\frac{x-2}{2} = \frac{y-1}{-1} = \frac{-2(4-1+1)}{5} = -\frac{8}{5}$$

$\Rightarrow \quad x = -\dfrac{6}{5} = f \Rightarrow y = \dfrac{13}{5} = g$

Radius of both the circles is same

$\therefore \quad 4+1-(5-\alpha) = f^2+g^2-\dfrac{36}{5} \Rightarrow \alpha = 1$

$\therefore$ Radius of C_2, $r = \sqrt{\dfrac{36}{25}+\dfrac{169}{25}-\dfrac{36}{5}} = 1$

$$\alpha + r = 1+1 = 2$$

75. Let equation of circle is $(x-a)^2+(y-a)^2=a^2$ ...(i)

Since, Eq. (i) passes through $P(\alpha, \beta)$.

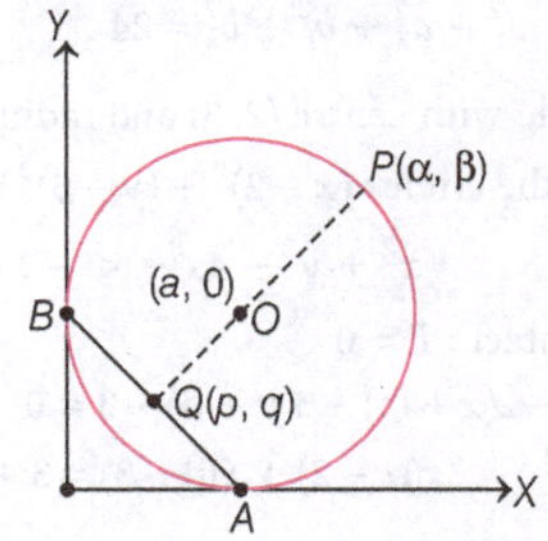

$\therefore \quad (\alpha - a)^2 + (\beta - a)^2 = a^2$

$\Rightarrow \quad \alpha^2 + \beta^2 - 2\alpha a - 2\beta a + a^2 = 0$ ...(ii)

Equation of $AB = \frac{x}{a} + \frac{y}{a} = 1 \Rightarrow x + y = a$ ...(iii)

Let $Q(p, q)$ be the foot of the perpendicular from P to line Eq. (iii)

$\therefore \quad \frac{p-\alpha}{1} = \frac{q-\beta}{1} = \frac{-(\alpha+\beta-a)}{(1)^2+(1)^2}$

$\Rightarrow \quad \frac{p-\alpha}{1} = \frac{q-\beta}{1} = \frac{-(\alpha+\beta-a)}{2}$

$\Rightarrow \quad p - \alpha = \frac{-(\alpha+\beta-a)}{2}$ and $q - \beta = \frac{-(\alpha+\beta-a)}{2}$

Now, $\quad PQ^2 = (p-\alpha)^2 + (q-\beta)^2$

$= \frac{1}{4}(\alpha+\beta-a)^2 + \frac{1}{4}(\alpha+\beta-a)^2$

$\Rightarrow \quad (11)^2 = \frac{1}{2}(\alpha+\beta-a)^2$

$\Rightarrow \quad \alpha^2 + \beta^2 + a^2 + 2\alpha\beta - 2\beta a - 2\alpha a = 242$

$\Rightarrow \quad 2\alpha\beta = 242$ [using Eq. (ii)]

$\Rightarrow \quad \alpha\beta = 121$

76. We have,

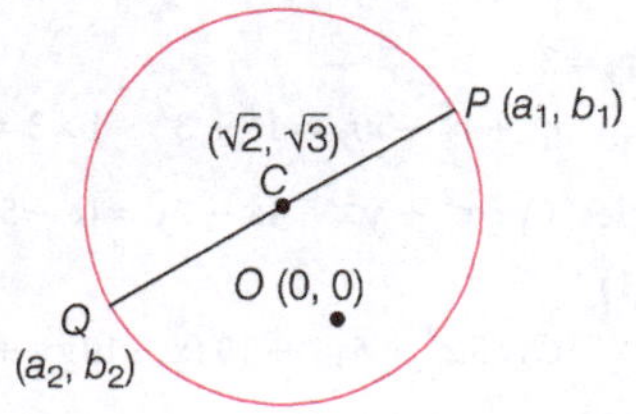

$\because OC \perp CP$ and CQ

and $OC = \sqrt{(\sqrt{2}-0)^2 + (\sqrt{3}-0)^2} = \sqrt{2+3} = \sqrt{5}$

and $PQ =$ Diameter

and Area of $\Delta OCP = \frac{1}{2}(OC) \times (CP) = \frac{\sqrt{35}}{2}$

$\Rightarrow \quad \sqrt{5} \times CP = \sqrt{35}$

$\Rightarrow \quad CP = \sqrt{7} =$ Radius of circle

Now, $\quad CP^2 + OC^2 = OP^2$

$\Rightarrow \quad a_1^2 + b_1^2 = 7 + 5 = 12$ ...(i)

and $\quad OQ^2 = CQ^2 + OC^2$ $[\because CQ = CP]$

$\Rightarrow \quad a_2^2 + b_2^2 = 12$ ...(ii)

On adding Eqs. (i) and (ii), we get

$$a_1^2 + a_2^2 + b_1^2 + b_2^2 = 24$$

77. Given, a circle with centre (2, 3) and radius 4.

Equation of the circle : $(x-2)^2 + (y-3)^2 = 16$

$\Rightarrow \quad x^2 + y^2 - 4x - 6y - 3 = 0$ ...(i)

Chord of contact : $T = 0$

$\Rightarrow \quad x\alpha + y\beta - 2(x+\alpha) - 3(y+\beta) - 3 = 0$

$\Rightarrow \quad x(\alpha - 2) + y(\beta - 3) = 3 + 2\alpha + 3\beta$

$\therefore \quad \frac{\alpha-2}{1} = \frac{\beta-3}{1} = \frac{2\alpha+3\beta+3}{3}$

$\therefore \quad \alpha - 2 = \beta - 3 \Rightarrow \alpha - \beta = -1$

$\therefore \quad \alpha - 2 = \frac{2\alpha + 3\alpha + 6}{3} \Rightarrow \alpha = -6$

$\therefore \quad \beta = -5$

So, $4\alpha - 7\beta = 4(-6) - 7(-5) = -24 + 35 = 11$

78. Given, PR is a diameter.

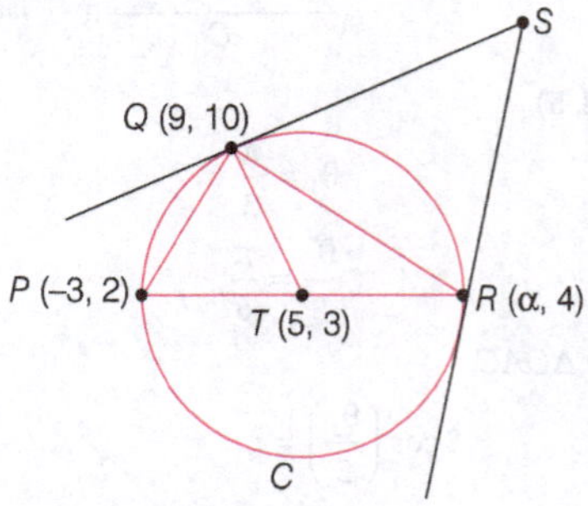

$\angle PQR = 90°$

$\Rightarrow$ Slope of $PQ \times$ Slope of $RQ = -1$

$\Rightarrow \quad \left(\frac{10-2}{9+3}\right) \times \left(\frac{10-4}{9-\alpha}\right) = -1 \Rightarrow \frac{8}{12} \times \frac{6}{9-\alpha} = -1$

$\Rightarrow \quad \alpha = 13$

Now, centre of circle, $T = T\left(\frac{13-3}{2}, \frac{4+2}{2}\right) = T(5,3)$

Since, tangents to C at the points Q and R intersect at the point $S(x, y)$

$\therefore$ Slope of $QT = \frac{10-3}{9-5} = \frac{7}{4}$

Slope of tangent, $QS = -\frac{4}{7}$

Slope of $RT = \frac{4-3}{13-5} = \frac{1}{8}$

Slope of tangent, $RS = -8$

Now, equation of QS, $y - 10 = -\frac{4}{7}(x - 9)$

$\Rightarrow \quad 4x + 7y = 106$ ...(i)

And equation of RS is

$y - 4 = (-8)(x - 13)$

$\Rightarrow \quad y - 4 = -8x + 104$

$\Rightarrow \quad 8x + y - 108 = 0$ ...(ii)

On solving Eqs. (i) and (ii), we get

$$x = \frac{25}{2} \text{ and } y = 8$$

$\therefore$ Since, $S\left(\frac{25}{2}, 8\right)$ lies on $2x - ky = 1$

$\Rightarrow \quad 2\left(\frac{25}{2}\right) - k(8) = 1$

$\therefore \quad k = 3$

79. Given, equation of circle is

$$x^2 + y^2 - 4x + 3 = 0$$

$$\Rightarrow \quad x^2 - 4x + 4 + y^2 = 4 - 3$$

$$\Rightarrow \quad (x-2)^2 + (y-0)^2 = (1)^2$$

Centre of circle is $P(2, 0)$ and radius = 1 unit

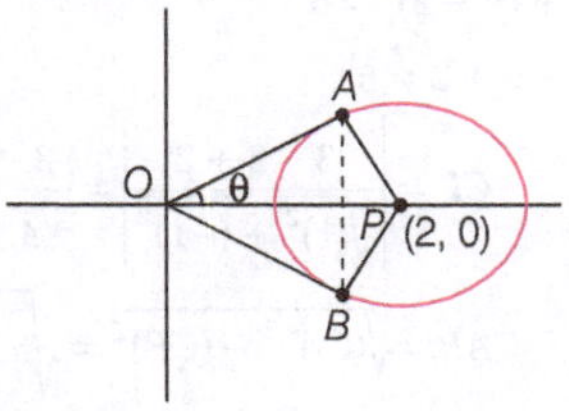

$OP = 2$ units and $AP = 1$ unit

In ΔOAP, $(OP)^2 = (OA)^2 + (AP)^2 \Rightarrow (OA)^2 = 3 \Rightarrow OA = \sqrt{3}$ units

Let $\angle AOP = \theta$

In ΔAOP, $\sin\theta = \dfrac{AP}{OP} = \dfrac{1}{2} \Rightarrow \theta = 30°$

$$\angle AOB = 60°$$

In ΔOAB, $OA = OB$

$$\therefore \quad \angle ABO = \angle BAO = \frac{180° - 60°}{2} = 60°$$

$\therefore \Delta OAB$ is an equilateral triangle.

Area of $\Delta OAB = \dfrac{\sqrt{3}}{4} \times S^2 = \dfrac{\sqrt{3}}{4} \times (OA)^2 = \dfrac{3\sqrt{3}}{4}$ sq units

80. Given, equation of circle is

$$x^2 + y^2 - x + 2y - \frac{11}{4} = 0$$

$\because$ Centre $= \left(\dfrac{1}{2}, -1\right)$ and radius $= \sqrt{\left(\dfrac{1}{2}\right)^2 + (-1)^2 - \left(\dfrac{-11}{4}\right)} = 2$

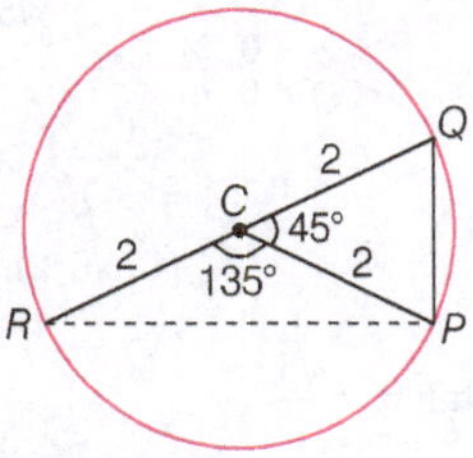

QR = Diameter = 2 × Radius = 4

$\therefore$ Area of $\Delta PQR = \dfrac{1}{2}(2)(2\sin 45°) + \dfrac{1}{2}(2)(2\sin 135°)$

$$= \frac{2}{\sqrt{2}} + \frac{2}{\sqrt{2}} = 2\sqrt{2}$$

81. Let $p \equiv \sin t$, $q \equiv \cos t$

Let orthocentre be (h, k).

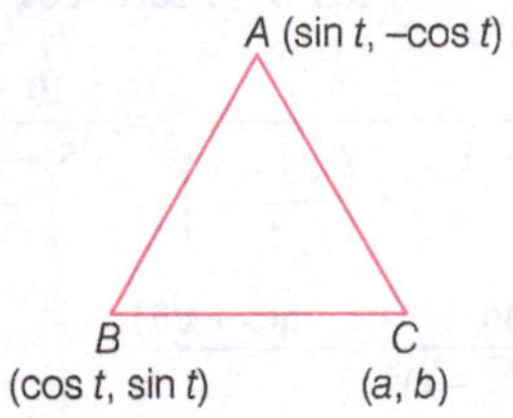

Since, if it an equilateral triangle, hence orthocentre coincides with centroid.

$$\Rightarrow \quad a + p + q = 3h,\ b + p - q = 3k$$

$$\Rightarrow \quad (3h - a)^2 + (3k - b)^2 = (p+q)^2 + (p-q)^2$$

$$= 2(p^2 + q^2) = 2$$

$$\therefore \quad \left(h - \frac{a}{3}\right)^2 + \left(k - \frac{b}{3}\right)^2 = \frac{2}{9}$$

Now, circle centre at $\left(\dfrac{a}{3}, \dfrac{b}{3}\right)$.

We are given that $\dfrac{a}{3} = 1, \dfrac{b}{3} = \dfrac{1}{3}$

$$\Rightarrow \quad a = 3, b = 1$$

$$\therefore \quad a^2 - b^2 = 8$$

82. Centre of C_1 is (2, 0).

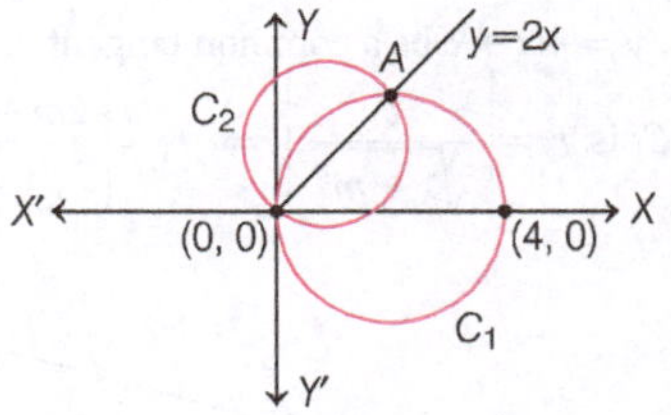

Equation of C_1 is $(x-2)^2 + y^2 = 4$

$$x^2 + y^2 - 4x = 0 \qquad \text{...(i)}$$

To find A, on putting $y = 2x$

$$x^2 + 4x^2 - 4x = 0 \Rightarrow 5x^2 - 4x = 0$$

$$\Rightarrow \quad x = 0 \text{ or } x = \frac{4}{5} \Rightarrow A = \left(\frac{4}{5}, \frac{8}{5}\right)$$

Equation of C_2 is $(x)\left(x - \dfrac{4}{5}\right) + (y)\left(y - \dfrac{8}{5}\right) = 0$

$$\Rightarrow \quad x^2 + y^2 - \frac{4x}{5} - \frac{8y}{5} = 0$$

Equation of tangent at $A\left(\dfrac{4}{5}, \dfrac{8}{5}\right)$ is $T = 0$

$$\Rightarrow \quad \frac{4}{5}x + \frac{8}{5}y - \frac{2}{5}\left(x + \frac{4}{5}\right) - \frac{4}{5}\left(y + \frac{8}{5}\right) = 0$$

$$\Rightarrow \quad \frac{2x}{5} + \frac{4y}{5} - \frac{8}{5} = 0 \Rightarrow x + 2y - 4 = 0$$

$$P \equiv (4, 0), Q \equiv (0, 2)$$

$$\therefore \quad \frac{QA}{AP} = \frac{\sqrt{\dfrac{16}{25} + \dfrac{4}{25}}}{\sqrt{\dfrac{256}{25} + \dfrac{64}{25}}} = \frac{\sqrt{20}}{\sqrt{320}} = \frac{1}{4}$$

83. Given, equation of circle is

$$x^2 + y^2 - 2gx + 6y - 19c = 0$$

passes through the point (6, 1)

$$12g + 19c = 43 \qquad \text{...(i)}$$

Centre $(g, -3)$ lies on given line.

So, $\quad g + 6c = 8 \qquad$ ...(ii)

On solving Eqs. (i) and (ii), we get

$$c = 1 \text{ and } g = 2$$

Equation of circle is $x^2 + y^2 - 4x + 6y - 19 = 0$

x-intercept $= 2\sqrt{g^2 - c} = 2\sqrt{3}$

84. Given, abscissae and ordinates of points P and Q are the roots of $x^2 - 4x - 6 = 0$ and $y^2 + 2y - 7 = 0$, respectively.

Diametric form of circle is $(x - x_1)(x - x_2) + (y - y_1)(y - y_2) = 0$

$\Rightarrow$ Equation of circle, $x^2 - 4x - 6 + y^2 + 2y - 7 = 0$

$\Rightarrow \quad x^2 + y^2 - 4x + 2y - 13 = 0$

Compare it with the given equation of circle, we get

$$a = -2, b = 1, c = -13$$

$\therefore \quad a + b - c = -2 + 1 - (-13) = -1 + 13 = 12$

85. Given, equation C_1, C_2 and C_3.

If a line $L: y = mx + c$ be a common tangent.

Let r_1 for C_1 is, $r_1 = \left|\dfrac{c}{\sqrt{1 + m^2}}\right| \Rightarrow r_3 = \left|\dfrac{2m - 1 + c}{\sqrt{1 + m^2}}\right|$

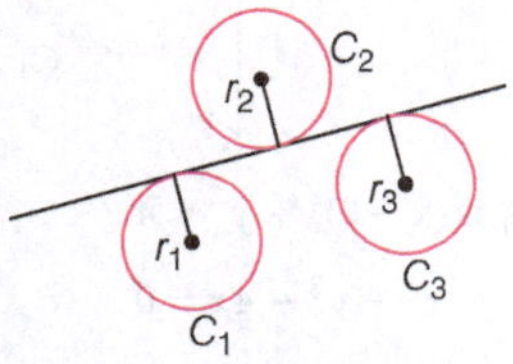

$\because \qquad m = 1/2 \qquad$ [as $r_1 = r_3 = r_2$]

For $r_2 = \left|\dfrac{m - 1 + c}{\sqrt{1 + m^2}}\right| \Rightarrow 2c = 1 - m \Rightarrow c = 1/4$

Now, $20(r^2 + c) = 20\left(\dfrac{1}{20} + \dfrac{1}{4}\right) = 6$

86. $x^2 - \sqrt{2}(x + y) + y^2 = 0$, $\angle BAC = \dfrac{\pi}{2}$ and $AB = \sqrt{2}$

$\Rightarrow \quad x^2 - \sqrt{2}x + y^2 - \sqrt{2}y = 0$

$$\Rightarrow \quad x^2 - 2\cdot(x)\cdot\left(\frac{1}{\sqrt{2}}\right) + \left(\frac{1}{\sqrt{2}}\right)^2 + y^2 - 2\cdot(y)\cdot\left(\frac{1}{\sqrt{2}}\right) + \left(\frac{1}{\sqrt{2}}\right)^2 - \left(\left(\frac{1}{\sqrt{2}}\right)^2 + \left(\frac{1}{\sqrt{2}}\right)^2\right) = 0$$

$$\Rightarrow \qquad \left(x - \frac{1}{\sqrt{2}}\right)^2 + \left(y - \frac{1}{\sqrt{2}}\right)^2 = 1^2$$

$\therefore$ Radius $= 1$ unit

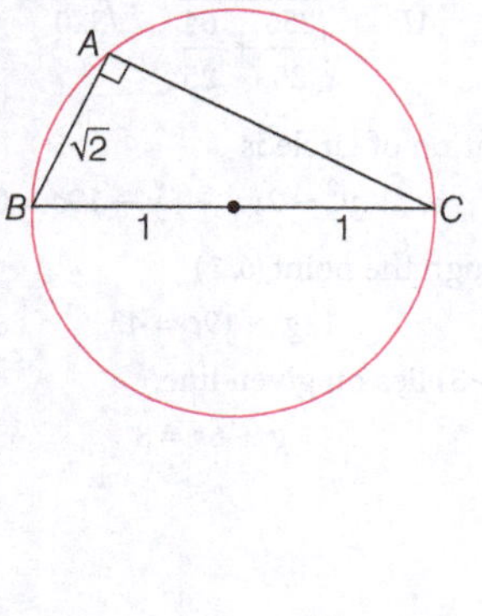

Diameter $= BC = 2$ units

$$AC = \sqrt{BC^2 - AB^2} = \sqrt{4 - 2} = \sqrt{2}$$

$$\text{ar}(\Delta ABC) = \frac{1}{2} \times AB \times AC = \frac{1}{2} \times \sqrt{2} \times \sqrt{2} = \frac{2}{2} = 1$$

87. $C_1 : x^2 + y^2 = 2$

$C_2 : (x - 3)^2 + (y - 2)^2 = 5$

Line $AB : x - y + 2 = 0$

$$CP = \left|\frac{3 - 2 + 2}{\sqrt{(1)^2 + (-1)^2}}\right| = \frac{3}{\sqrt{2}}$$

$$AP = \sqrt{(CA)^2 - (CP)^2} = \sqrt{5 - \frac{9}{2}} = \frac{1}{\sqrt{2}}$$

$$\tan\theta = \frac{CP}{AP} = \frac{\frac{3}{\sqrt{2}}}{\frac{1}{\sqrt{2}}} = 3$$

$\therefore \qquad \sin\theta = \dfrac{3}{\sqrt{1 + 9}} = \dfrac{3}{\sqrt{10}} = \dfrac{AP}{AN}$

$\therefore \qquad AN = \dfrac{\sqrt{10}}{3} \times \dfrac{1}{\sqrt{2}} = \dfrac{\sqrt{5}}{3} = BN$

Area of $\Delta ANB = \dfrac{1}{2} \times AB \times PN$

$$= \frac{1}{2} \times 2AP \times PN = \frac{1}{\sqrt{2}} \times [AN(\cos\theta)]$$

$$= \frac{1}{\sqrt{2}} \times \frac{\sqrt{5}}{3} \times \sqrt{1 - \frac{9}{10}} = \frac{1}{\sqrt{2}} \times \frac{\sqrt{5}}{3} \times \frac{1}{\sqrt{10}} = \frac{1}{6}$$

88.

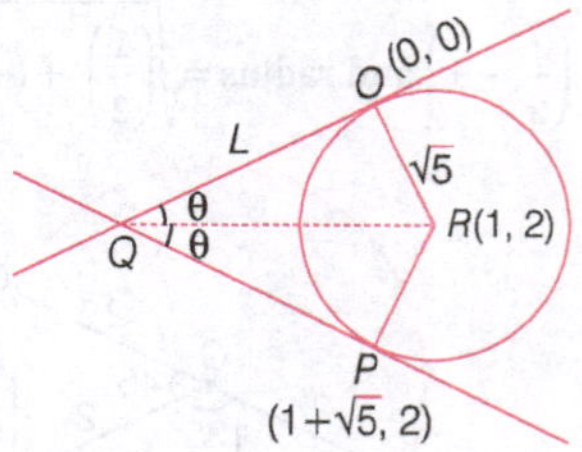

$$\tan\theta = \frac{\sqrt{5}}{L}$$

$$\tan 2\theta = 2 \Rightarrow \frac{2\tan\theta}{1 - \tan^2\theta} = 2$$

$\Rightarrow \quad \tan\theta = \dfrac{\sqrt{5} - 1}{2}$ (as θ is acute)

$$\text{Area} = \frac{1}{2}L^2 \sin 2\theta = \frac{1}{2} \cdot \frac{5}{\tan^2\theta} \cdot 2\sin\theta\cos\theta$$

$$= \frac{5\sin\theta\cos\theta}{\sin^2\theta} \cdot \cos^2\theta = 5\cot\theta \cdot \cos^2\theta$$

$$= 5 \cdot \frac{2}{\sqrt{5} - 1} \cdot \frac{1}{1 + \left(\frac{\sqrt{5} - 1}{2}\right)^2} = \frac{10}{\sqrt{5} - 1} \cdot \frac{4}{4 + 6 - 2\sqrt{5}}$$

$$= \frac{40}{2\sqrt{5}(\sqrt{5} - 1)^2} = \frac{\sqrt{5}(3 + \sqrt{5})}{2}$$

89. Given, $C: 4x^2+4y^2-12x+8y+k=0$

$$C: x^2+y^2-3x+2y+\frac{k}{4}=0 \quad \text{[divide by 4]}$$

Centre $=\left(\frac{3}{2},-1\right)$, radius $=\sqrt{\frac{9}{4}+1-\frac{k}{4}}$

According to question, radius <1

$$\Rightarrow \quad \sqrt{\frac{9}{4}+1-\frac{k}{4}}<1$$

$$\Rightarrow \quad \sqrt{\frac{13-k}{4}}<1 \Rightarrow k>9 \quad \text{...(i)}$$

Since, $\left(1,-\frac{1}{3}\right)$ lies on or inside the circle.

$$\therefore \quad 4(1)^2+4\left(\frac{-1}{3}\right)^2-12(1)+8\left(-\frac{1}{3}\right)+k\le 0$$

$$\Rightarrow \quad k\le\frac{92}{9} \quad \text{...(ii)}$$

From Eqs. (i) and (ii), we get

$$9<k\le\frac{92}{9} \text{ i.e. } k\in\left(9,\frac{92}{9}\right]$$

90. Let $C=(a,b)$

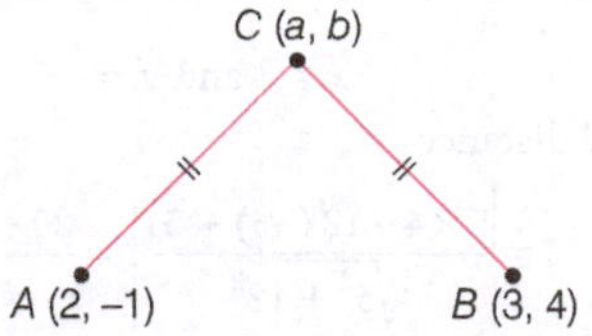

$$r^2=(CA)^2=(CB)^2$$

$$\Rightarrow \quad (CA)^2=(CB)^2$$

$$\Rightarrow (a-2)^2+(b+1)^2=(a-3)^2+(b-4)^2$$

$$\Rightarrow \quad a=10-5b \quad \text{...(i)}$$

Now, $C(a,b)$ lies on the circle

$$(x-5)^2+(y-1)^2=\frac{13}{2}$$

Then, $\quad (a-5)^2+(b-1)^2=\frac{13}{2}$

$$\Rightarrow \quad (10-5b-5)^2+(b-1)^2=\frac{13}{2}$$

$$\Rightarrow \quad (5-5b)^2+(b-1)^2=\frac{13}{2}$$

$$\Rightarrow \quad 25+25b^2-50b+b^2+1-2b=\frac{13}{2}$$

$$\Rightarrow \quad 2+2b^2-4b=\frac{1}{2}$$

$$\Rightarrow \quad 4b^2-8b+3=0$$

$$\Rightarrow \quad (2b-3)(2b-1)=0$$

$$\Rightarrow \quad b=\frac{3}{2},\frac{1}{2} \text{ and } a=\frac{5}{2},\frac{15}{2}$$

Here, $C=\left(\frac{5}{2},\frac{3}{2}\right)$ or $\left(\frac{15}{2},\frac{1}{2}\right)$

Now, $r^2=\left(\frac{15}{2}-2\right)^2+\left(\frac{1}{2}+1\right)^2=\frac{121}{4}+\frac{9}{4}=\frac{130}{4}=\frac{65}{2}$

91. The two lines L_1 and L_2 which touches the circle are parallel.

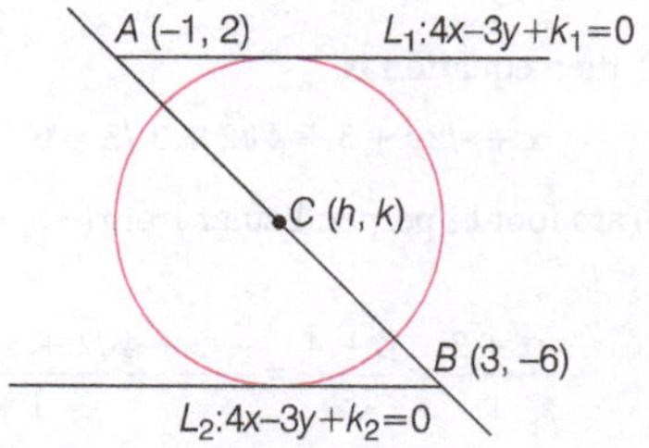

Let the centre of the circle be (h,k).

$(-1,2)$ lies on line L_1, $4(-1)-3\times 2+k_1=0$

$$\Rightarrow \quad -4-6+k_1=0$$

$$\Rightarrow \quad k_1=10$$

$(3,-6)$ lies on line L_2,

$$4(3)-3(-6)+k_2=0$$

$$\Rightarrow \quad 12+18+k_2=0\Rightarrow k_2=-30$$

Diameter of circle = Shortest distance between two given parallel lines

$$=\frac{|k_1-k_2|}{\sqrt{4^2+(-3)^2}}=\frac{|10-(-30)|}{\sqrt{16+9}}$$

$\therefore$ Radius of circle = 4 units

C is mid-point of AB.

$\Rightarrow$ Coordinates of C are $\left(\frac{-1+3}{2},\frac{2+(-6)}{2}\right)=(1,-2)$

$\therefore$ Equation of circle is $(x-1)^2+(y+2)^2=16$

92. Circle : $(x-2)^2+(y+1)^2=\frac{169}{4}$ and length of $AB=12$

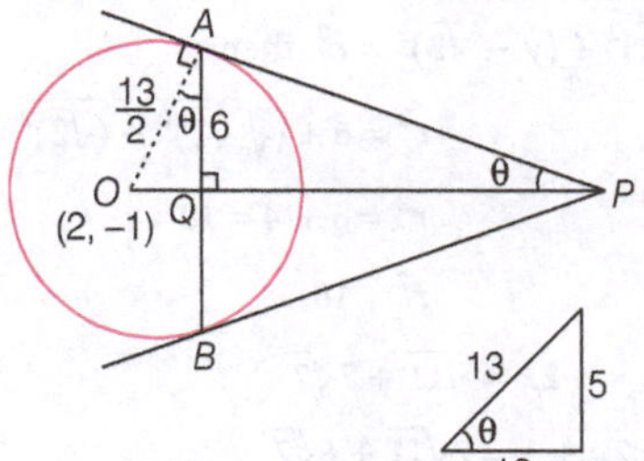

So, $\cos\theta=\frac{6}{\left(\frac{13}{2}\right)}=\frac{12}{13}\Rightarrow\tan\theta=\frac{5}{12}$

In ΔAQP, $\tan\theta=\frac{6}{QP}=\frac{5}{12}$, $QP=\frac{72}{5}$

$$\Rightarrow \quad 5QP=72$$

93. Given circle is $x^2+y^2+6x+8y+16=0$ with centre $(-3,-4)$ and radius 3 units.

The circle $x^2+y^2+2(3-\sqrt{3})x+2(4-\sqrt{6})y=k+6\sqrt{3}+8\sqrt{6}$, $k>0$ has centre $(\sqrt{3}-3,\sqrt{6}-4)$ and radius $\sqrt{k+34}$

So, these two circles touch internally hence

$\sqrt{3+6}=|\sqrt{k+34}-3|$.

Here, $k=2$ is only possible. $\quad [\because k>0]$

Equation of common tangent to two circles is

$$2\sqrt{3}x + 2\sqrt{6}y + 16 + 6\sqrt{3} + 8\sqrt{6} + k = 0$$

So, $k = 2$, then equation is

$$x + \sqrt{2}y + 3 + 4\sqrt{2} + 3\sqrt{3} = 0 \quad \text{...(i)}$$

So, (α, β) are foot of perpendicular from $(-3, -4)$ to line (i), then

$$\frac{\alpha + 3}{1} = \frac{\beta + 4}{\sqrt{2}} = \frac{-(3 - 4\sqrt{2} + 3 + 4\sqrt{2} + 3\sqrt{3})}{1 + 2}$$

$$\therefore \quad \alpha + 3 = \frac{\beta + 4}{\sqrt{2}} = -\sqrt{3}$$

$$\Rightarrow \quad (\alpha + \sqrt{3})^2 = 9 \text{ and } (\beta + \sqrt{6})^2 = 16$$

Therefore, $(\alpha + \sqrt{3})^2 + (\beta + \sqrt{6})^2 = 25$

94. Given, equation of circle $x^2 + y^2 - 2\sqrt{2}x - 6\sqrt{2}y + 14 = 0$

Centre $\equiv (\sqrt{2}, 3\sqrt{2})$

Radius $= \sqrt{(\sqrt{2})^2 + (3\sqrt{2})^2 - 14} = \sqrt{6}$

$\Rightarrow$ Diameter $= 2\sqrt{6}$

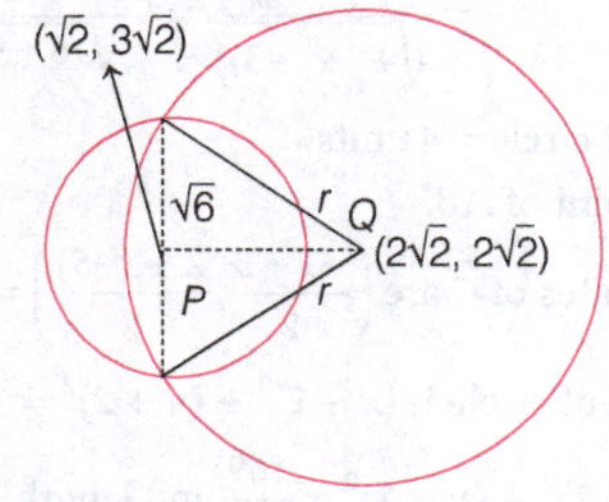

If this diameter is chord to $(x - 2\sqrt{2})^2 + (y - 2\sqrt{2})^2 = r^2$, then

$$r^2 = 6 + \left(\sqrt{(\sqrt{2})^2 + (\sqrt{2})^2}\right)^2$$

$$\Rightarrow \quad r^2 = 6 + 4 = 10$$

$$\therefore \quad r^2 = 10$$

95. Let $L_1 : y + 2x = \sqrt{11} + 7\sqrt{7}$

and $L_2 : 2y + x = 2\sqrt{11} + 6\sqrt{7}$

Point of intersection of these two lines is centre of circle

i.e. $\left(\frac{8}{3}\sqrt{7}, \sqrt{11} + \frac{5}{3}\sqrt{7}\right)$

Perpendicular from centre to line

$$3x - \sqrt{11}y + \left(\frac{5\sqrt{77}}{3} + 11\right) = 0$$

is radius of circle

$$\Rightarrow \quad r = \left|\frac{8\sqrt{7} - 11 - \frac{5}{3}\sqrt{77} + \frac{5\sqrt{77}}{3} + 11}{\sqrt{20}}\right|$$

$$= \left|4\sqrt{\frac{7}{5}}\right| = 4\sqrt{\frac{7}{5}} \text{ units}$$

So, $(5h - 8k)^2 + 5r^2$

$$= \left(\frac{40}{3}\sqrt{7} - 8\sqrt{11} - \frac{40}{3}\sqrt{7}\right)^2 + 5 \cdot 16 \cdot \frac{7}{5}$$

$$= 64 \times 11 + 112 = 816$$

96. $L_1 : 4x + 3y + 2 = 0$ ...(i)

$L_2 : 3x - 4y - 11 = 0$ ...(ii)

From Eqs. (i) and (ii), we get

$$x = 1 \text{ and } y = -2$$

$\therefore \quad Q(1, -2)$

Slope of $PQ = -\frac{4}{3} = \tan\theta$

Now, co-ordinate of P is given by, $\frac{x - 1}{\cos\theta} = \frac{y + 2}{\sin\theta} = \pm 5$

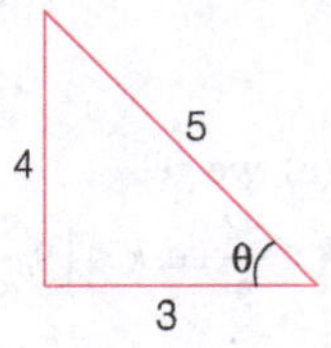

$$\Rightarrow \quad x = 1 + 5 \times \frac{3}{5} \text{ and } y = -2 - 5 \times \frac{4}{5}$$

$$x = 4 \text{ and } y = -6$$

$\therefore$ Required distance

$$= \left|\frac{5 \times 4 - 12(-6) + 51}{\sqrt{5^2 + 12^2}}\right| = \frac{20 + 72 + 51}{13} = \frac{143}{13} = 11$$

97.

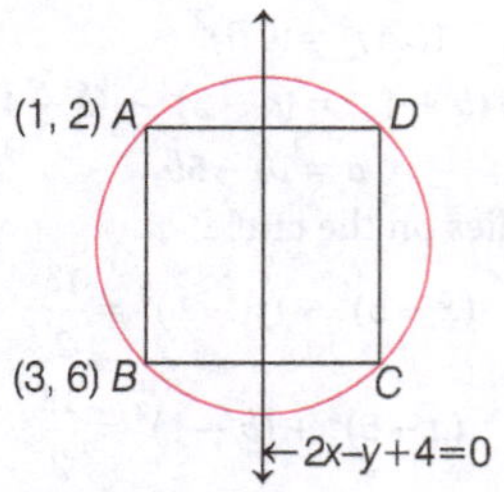

Equation of line AB, $y = 2x$

Slope of $AB = 2$

Slope of given diameter $= 2$

So, the diameter is parallel to AB.

Distance between diameter and line $AB = \frac{4}{\sqrt{4 + 1}} = \frac{4}{\sqrt{5}}$

Thus, $BC = 2 \times \frac{4}{\sqrt{5}} = \frac{8}{\sqrt{5}}$

$$AB = \sqrt{(1 - 3)^2 + (2 - 6)^2} = \sqrt{20} = 2\sqrt{5}$$

$$\text{Area} = AB \times BC = \frac{8}{\sqrt{5}} \times 2\sqrt{5} = 16$$

98. Let the coordinates of the points P and Q are (x_1, y_1) and (x_2, y_2), respectively.

According to the question,

$$x_1 + x_2 = \frac{r}{2}, \; x_1 x_2 = \frac{p}{2}$$

Also, $y_1 + y_2 = s,\ y_1 y_2 = -q$

Equation of circle with diameter PQ is

$$(x - x_1)(x - x_2) + (y - y_1)(y - y_2) = 0$$

$$\Rightarrow x^2 - (x_1 + x_2)x + y^2 - (y_1 + y_2)y + x_1 x_2 + y_1 y_2 = 0$$

Compare it with given equation of circle

$$x^2 + y^2 - \frac{11}{2}x - 7y - 11 = 0$$

$$\Rightarrow \quad x_1 + x_2 = \frac{11}{2},\ y_1 + y_2 = 7,$$

$$x_1 x_2 + y_1 y_2 = -11$$

$$\Rightarrow \quad \frac{r}{2} = \frac{11}{2},\ s = 7,\ \frac{p}{2} - q = -11$$

$$\Rightarrow \quad r = 11,\ s = 7,\ p - 2q = -22$$

$$\therefore \quad 2r + s - 2q + p = 2 \times 11 + 7 - 22 = 7$$

99. From the shown figure, the length of chord PQ is 2 units.

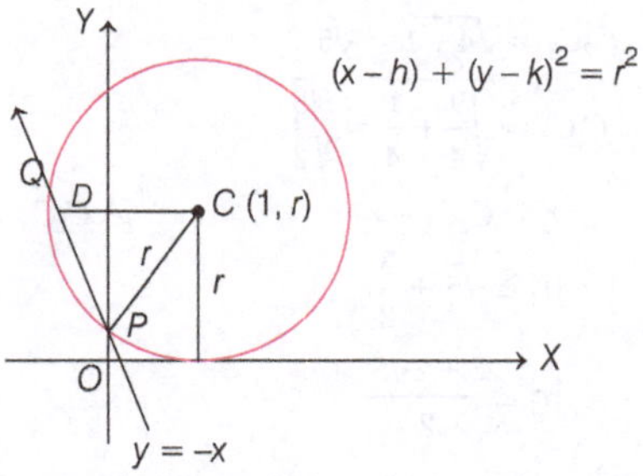

$$CD = \frac{1+r}{\sqrt{2}}$$

$$\therefore \quad PQ = 2\sqrt{r^2 - \left(\frac{1+r}{\sqrt{2}}\right)^2}$$

$$\Rightarrow \quad 2 = 2\sqrt{r^2 - \left(\frac{1+r}{\sqrt{2}}\right)^2} \Rightarrow 1 = \sqrt{r^2 - \left(\frac{1+r}{\sqrt{2}}\right)^2}$$

$$\Rightarrow \quad 2 = 2r^2 - 1 - r^2 - 2r$$

$$\Rightarrow \quad r^2 - 2r - 3 = 0 \Rightarrow (r-3)\cdot(r+1) = 0$$

$$\Rightarrow \quad r = -1 \text{ or } r = 3$$

So, $k = r = 3$ and $h = 1$ [given]

Hence, $h + k + r = 1 + 3 + 3 = 7$

100. Circle C touches $x = 2y$ at (2, 1), then equation of circle C is given by $(x-2)^2 + (y-1)^2 + \lambda(x - 2y) = 0$

$$\Rightarrow x^2 - 4x + 4 + y^2 - 2y + 1 + \lambda x - 2\lambda y = 0$$

$$\Rightarrow \quad x^2 + y^2 + x(\lambda - 4) + y(-2 - 2\lambda) + 5 = 0 \quad \text{...(i)}$$

Since, circles C and C_1 intersect each other at PQ, so PQ is common chord.

$\therefore$ Equation of PQ will be $C - C_1 = 0$

$$\Rightarrow \quad x(\lambda - 4) + y(-4 - 2\lambda) + 10 = 0$$

Again, PQ is diameter of circle C_1.

So, PQ passes through centre of C_1.

Now, equation of C_1 is $x^2 + y^2 + 2y - 5 = 0$

$\therefore$ Centre of C_1 is $(0, -1)$.

So, PQ passes through $(0, -1)$

$$\therefore \quad 0(\lambda - 4) - 1(-4 - 2\lambda) + 10 = 0$$

$$\Rightarrow \quad \lambda = -7$$

On putting $\lambda = -7$ in Eq. (i), we get equation of circle C as

$$x^2 + y^2 - 11x + 12y + 5 = 0$$

$$\therefore \quad \text{Radius of } C = \sqrt{\left(\frac{11}{2}\right)^2 + (-6)^2 - 5} = \sqrt{\frac{121}{4} + 36 - 5}$$

$$= \sqrt{\frac{245}{4}} = \frac{\sqrt{245}}{2}$$

$\therefore$ Diameter of $C = 2 \times \text{Radius} = \sqrt{245} = 7\sqrt{5}$

101. Let a circle C which touches the Y-axis at (0, 6) and cuts off an intercept $6\sqrt{5}$ on the X-axis.

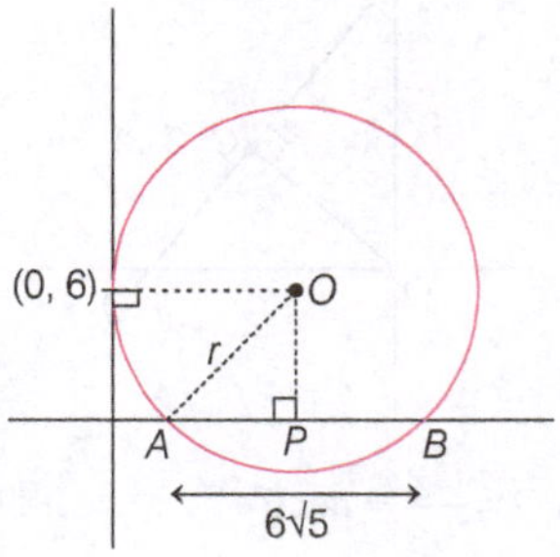

Chord $AB = 6\sqrt{5}$

So, $AP = 3\sqrt{5}$ (perpendicular from centre bisects the chord)

and $OP = 6$

In ΔAPO, $r^2 = (6)^2 + (3\sqrt{5})^2$

$$\Rightarrow \quad r = 9$$

102. $C : x^2 + y^2 - 2x - 6y + 6 = 0$

$$(x-1)^2 + (y-3)^2 = 2^2$$

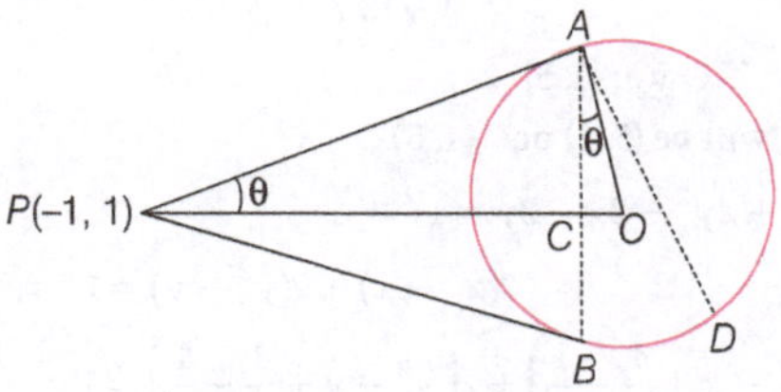

AP = Length of tangent $= \sqrt{S_1}$

$$\Rightarrow \quad AP^2 = (-1-1)^2 + (1-3)^2 - 4$$

$$\therefore \quad AP = 2$$

$$\tan\theta = \frac{AO}{AP} = \frac{2}{2} = 1 \quad (\therefore \theta = 45^\circ)$$

In ΔACO,

$$\frac{AC}{AO} = \cos\theta$$

$$\therefore \quad AC = 2 \times \frac{1}{\sqrt{2}} = \sqrt{2}$$

$$\therefore \quad \Delta OAC \cong \Delta OAM$$

$$\Delta OAC \cong \Delta OBC$$

$$\Delta OBC \cong \Delta ODM$$

$\therefore$ Area of $\Delta ABD = 4$ Area of ΔACO

$$= 4 \times \frac{1}{2}(AO \times AC \times \sin\theta)$$

$$= 2 \times 2 \times \sqrt{2} \times \frac{1}{\sqrt{2}} = 4 \text{ sq units}$$

103. Equation of circle is

$$(x-2)^2 + (y-3)^2 = (2-0)^2 + (3-0)^2$$

$$\Rightarrow \quad (x-2)^2 + (y-3)^2 = 13$$

Slope of $OC = \frac{3-0}{2-0} = \frac{3}{2}$

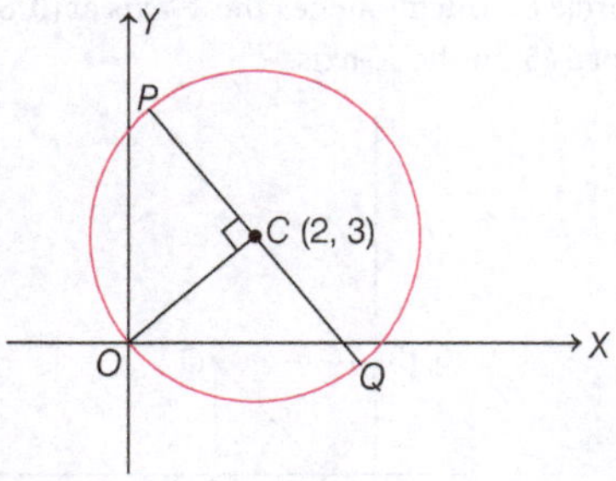

$\therefore$ Slope of $PQ = -\frac{2}{3} = \tan\theta$

Points at a distance of $\sqrt{13}$ units from O with slope $= -\frac{2}{3}$

Using, $\begin{cases} x_2 = x_1 \pm r\cos\theta \\ y_2 = y_1 \pm r\sin\theta \end{cases}$

So, $\quad x_2 = 2 \pm \sqrt{13}\left(\frac{3}{\sqrt{13}}\right) = 2 \pm 3$

$\therefore \quad x_2 : \{5, -1\}$

$$y_2 : 3 \pm \sqrt{13}\left(\frac{-2}{\sqrt{13}}\right) = 3 \pm (-2)$$

$\therefore \quad y_2 : \{1, 5\}$

$\therefore$ Point will be $(5, 1)$ or $(-1, 5)$.

104. $A : 2x^2 + 2y^2 - 2x - 2y = 1$

$$\Rightarrow \quad 2(x^2 - x) + 2(y^2 - y) = 1$$

$$\Rightarrow 2\left(x^2 - x + \frac{1}{4} - \frac{1}{4}\right) + 2\left(y^2 - y + \frac{1}{4} - \frac{1}{4}\right) = 1$$

$$\Rightarrow \quad \left(x - \frac{1}{2}\right)^2 + \left(y - \frac{1}{2}\right)^2 = 1$$

Here, $C_1 = \left(\frac{1}{2}, \frac{1}{2}\right)$ and $r_1 = 1$

$$B : 4x^2 + 4y^2 - 16y + 7 = 0$$

$$\Rightarrow \quad 4(y^2 - 4y + 4 - 4) + 4x^2 + 7 = 0$$

$$\Rightarrow \quad 4(y-2)^2 + 4x^2 + 7 - 16 = 0$$

$$\Rightarrow \quad x^2 + (y-2)^2 = \frac{9}{4}$$

Here, $C_2 = (0, 2)$ and $r_2 = \frac{3}{2}$

$$C \Rightarrow x^2 + y^2 - 4x - 2y + 5 \le r^2$$

$$(x-2)^2 + (y-1)^2 \le r^2$$

Here, $C_3 = (2, 1)$

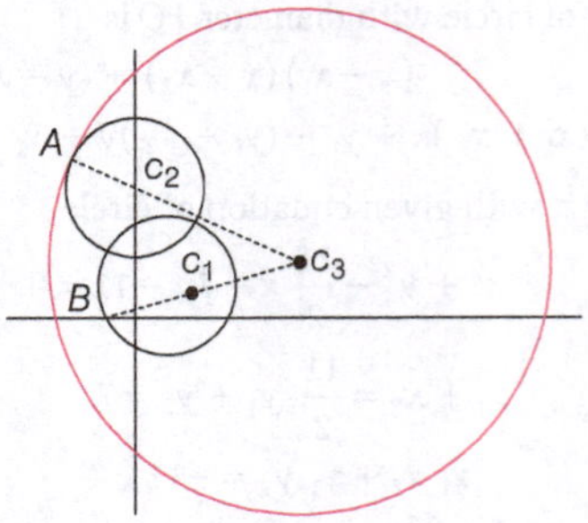

At $(2, 1)$ circle of B,

$$S_B = 2^2 + (1-2)^2 - \frac{9}{4} = 4 + 1 - \frac{9}{4} = \frac{11}{4} > 0$$

$$C_1C_2 = \sqrt{\frac{1}{4} + \frac{9}{4}} = \sqrt{\frac{5}{2}}$$

$$C_2C_3 = \sqrt{4 + 1} = \sqrt{5}$$

$$C_1C_3 = \sqrt{\frac{9}{4} + \frac{1}{4}} = \sqrt{\frac{5}{2}}$$

$r_3 \ge C_2C_3 + r_2 \qquad [\because C_2C_3 > C_1C_2 \text{ and } C_1C_3]$

$$|r| \ge \sqrt{5} + \frac{3}{2}$$

$$\Rightarrow \quad |r| \ge \frac{3 + 2\sqrt{5}}{2}$$

105. $S \Rightarrow 36x^2 + 36y^2 - 108x + 120y + C = 0$

$$x^2 + y^2 - 3x + \left(\frac{10}{3}\right)y + \frac{C}{36} = 0$$

$$\left(x - \frac{3}{2}\right)^2 + \left(y + \frac{5}{3}\right)^3 + \frac{C}{36} - \frac{9}{4} - \frac{25}{9} = 0$$

When $x = 0$, $36y^2 + 120y + C = 0$

Since, it neither touch the coordinate axis nor intersects. So, the roots of this equation must be imaginary.

$$D < 0$$

$$\Rightarrow \quad 120^2 - 4 \times 36C < 0$$

$$\Rightarrow \quad C > \frac{120 \times 120}{4 \times 36} \Rightarrow C > 100 \qquad \text{...(i)}$$

Similarly, when $y = 0$,

$$36x^2 - 108x + C = 0$$

$$108^2 - 4 \times 36\, C < 0 \Rightarrow C > 81 \qquad \text{...(ii)}$$

From Eqs. (i) and (ii), we get

$$\Rightarrow \quad C > 100$$

and point of intersection of $\begin{cases} x - 2y = 4 \\ 2x - y = 5 \end{cases}$ is $(2, -1)$.

So, $\quad S_{(2,1)} < 0$

$$\left(\frac{1}{2}\right)^2 + \left(\frac{2}{3}\right)^2 + \frac{C}{36} - \frac{9}{4} - \frac{25}{9} < 0$$

$$C < 156$$

$$C \in (100, 156)$$

106. Given, circle $x^2 + y^2 + 2x + 4y - 4 = 0$

$\Rightarrow (x^2 + 2x + 1) + (y^2 + 4y + 4) - 1 - 4 - 4 = 0$

$\Rightarrow (x + 1)^2 + (y + 2)^2 = 9$

Any point on the given circle be

$[(3\cos\theta - 1), (3\sin\theta - 2)]$

[to find the point coordinates, take $x + 1 = 3\cos\theta$ and $y + 2 = 3\sin\theta$]

Now, circle passes through $(-4, 1)$ and their centres lie on the given circle.

So, the centre coordinate of that circle be $(3\cos\theta - 1, 3\sin\theta - 2)$. Since, it passes through $(-4, 1)$, then radius of this circle be

$$r = \sqrt{(3\cos\theta - 1 + 4)^2 + (3\sin\theta - 2 - 1)^2}$$

$$= \sqrt{9\cos^2\theta + 9 + 18\cos\theta + 9\sin^2\theta + 9 - 18\sin\theta}$$

$$= \sqrt{27 + 18(\cos\theta - \sin\theta)} = 3\sqrt{3 + 2(\cos\theta - \sin\theta)}$$

Maximum radius will be when $(\cos\theta - \sin\theta)$ is maximum

i.e. $\cos\theta - \sin\theta = \frac{1}{\sqrt{2}} - \left(-\frac{1}{\sqrt{2}}\right) = \frac{2}{\sqrt{2}} = \sqrt{2}$

$\therefore \quad r_1 = r_{max} = 3\sqrt{3 + 2\sqrt{2}}$

Minimum radius will be when $(\cos\theta - \sin\theta)$ is minimum i.e. $-\sqrt{2}$.

$\therefore \quad r_2 = r_{min} = 3\sqrt{3 - 2\sqrt{2}}$

Given, $\frac{r_1}{r_2} = a + b\sqrt{2}$, then $\frac{r_1^2}{r_2^2} = (a + b\sqrt{2})^2$

$$\Rightarrow \frac{9(3 + 2\sqrt{2})}{9(3 - 2\sqrt{2})} = (a + b\sqrt{2})^2 \Rightarrow \frac{(3 + 2\sqrt{2})^2}{1} = (a + b\sqrt{2})^2$$

On comparing coefficients, we get $a = 3$ and $b = 2$

$\therefore \quad a + b = 5$

107. Given, $S_1 \Rightarrow x^2 + y^2 = 9$

$S_2 \Rightarrow (x - 2)^2 + y^2 = 1$

$\therefore \quad C_1 \equiv (0, 0)$ and $r_1 = 3$

$C_2 \equiv (2, 0)$, $r_2 = 1$

Let centre of variable circle be $P(h, k)$ and radius be r.

From the given data, it is clear that given circles touch each other internally. Hence, variable circle touches S_1 internally and S_2 externally as shown in figure below.

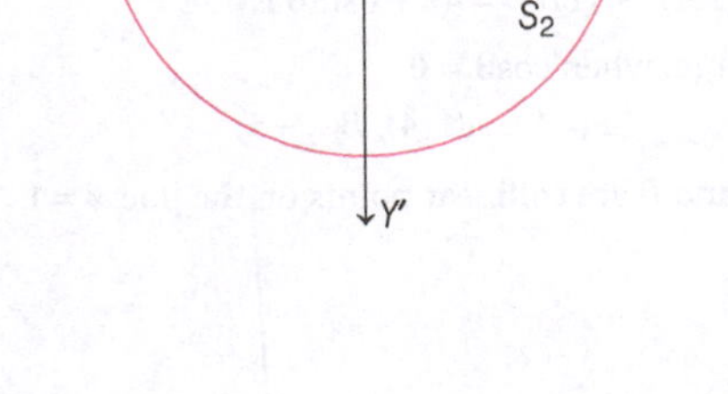

Clearly, $PC_1 = 3 - r$

and $PC_2 = 1 + r$

and $C_1C_2 = 2$

$\therefore \quad PC_1 + PC_2 = 4$

which is greater than C_1C_2.

Hence, locus of P is an ellipse whose foci are C_1 and C_2 and major axis is $2a = 4$.

and $2ae = C_1C_2 = 2 \Rightarrow e = 1/2$

$\Rightarrow \quad b^2 = 4\left(1 - \frac{1}{4}\right) = 3$

Centre is mid-point of $C_1(0, 0)$ and $C_2(2, 0)$.

$\therefore$ Centre of ellipse is $(1, 0)$.

$\frac{(x-1)^2}{4} + \frac{y^2}{3} = 1$ is the equation of locus of centre of variable circle which is satisfied by $\left(2, \pm\frac{3}{2}\right)$.

108. Given, equation of circles

$$x^2 + y^2 - 10x - 10y + 41 = 0 \quad \text{...(i)}$$

$$x^2 + y^2 - 22x - 10y + 137 = 0 \quad \text{...(ii)}$$

Centre (C_1) and radius (r_1) of Eq. (i) are $C_1 = (5, 5)$ and $r_1 = 3$ and centre (C_2) and radius (r_2) of Eq. (ii) are

$C_2 = (11, 5)$ and $r_2 = 3$

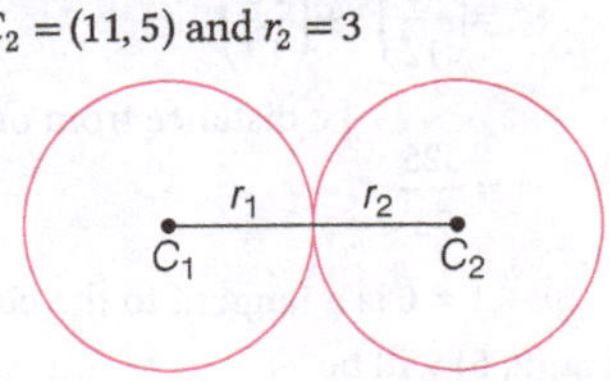

We observe that

C_1C_2 = Distance between centres

$= (11 - 5)^2 + (5 - 5)^2 = 6 = r_1 + r_2$

$\therefore$ Circles Eqs. (i) and (ii) touch each other externally. Hence, circles have only one meeting point.

109. Given,

$M \Rightarrow x^2 + y^2 = 1$, its centre $O_1 \equiv (0, 0)$

$N \Rightarrow x^2 + y^2 - 2x = 0$, its centre $O_2 \equiv (1, 0)$

$O \Rightarrow x^2 + y^2 - 2x - 2y + 1 = 0$, its centre $O_3 \equiv (1, 1)$

$P \Rightarrow x^2 + y^2 - 2y = 0$, its centre $O_4 \equiv (0, 1)$

We see that

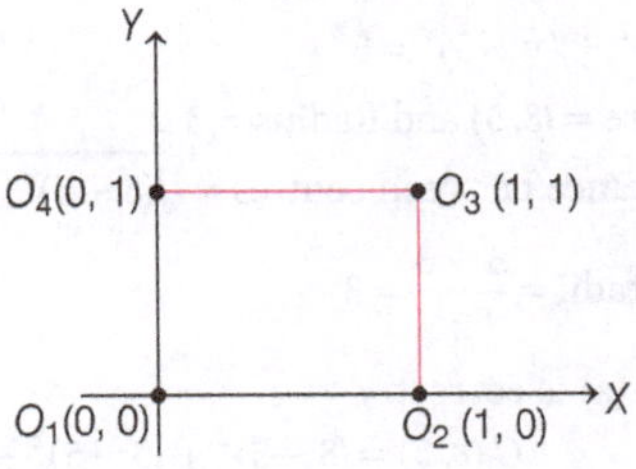

$O_1O_2 = O_2O_3 = O_3O_4 = O_4O_1$ and $O_1O_3 = O_2O_4$

Hence, O_1, O_2, O_3 and O_4 form a square.

110. Given equation of tangent to the circle $x^2 + y^2 = 25$ at the point $R(3, 4)$. Now, equation $3x + 4y = 25$.

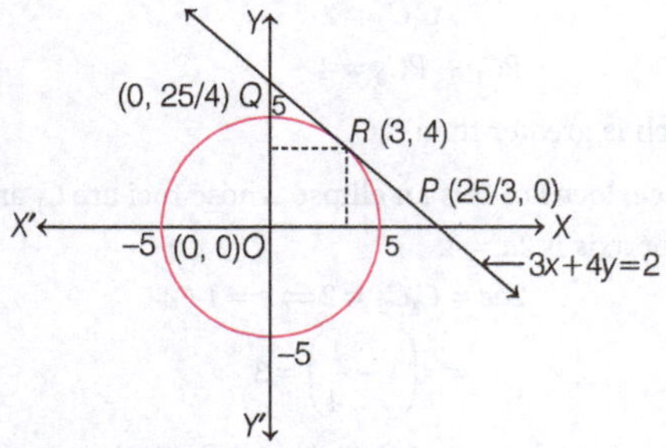

Now, point $P\left(\frac{25}{3}, 0\right)$ and $Q\left(0, \frac{25}{4}\right)$.

Now, $OP + OQ + PQ = \frac{25}{3} + \frac{25}{4} + \frac{125}{12} = 25$

Incentre of ΔOPQ

$$= \left(\frac{\frac{25}{3} \times 0 + \frac{125}{12} \times 0 + \frac{25}{4} \times \frac{25}{3}}{25}, \frac{\frac{25}{3} \times \frac{25}{4} + \frac{125}{12} \times 0 + \frac{25}{4} \times 0}{25}\right)$$

$$= \left(\frac{25}{12}, \frac{25}{12}\right)$$

$$\therefore \quad r^2 = \left(\frac{25}{12}\right)^2 + \left(\frac{25}{12}\right)^2$$

[$\because$ distance from origin to incentre is r]

$$= \frac{625}{72}$$

111. Given, $2x - y + 1 = 0$ is a tangent to the circle at $(2, 5)$.

So, normal at $(2, 5)$ will be

$$\frac{(y-5)}{(x-2)} = \frac{-1}{2} \Rightarrow x + 2y = 12 \quad \text{...(i)}$$

Now, it is also given that centre lies on $x - 2y = 4$.

On solving Eqs. (i) and (ii), we get

$$\Rightarrow \quad x = 8, y = 2$$

Radius will be the distance between $(8, 2)$ and $(2, 5)$.

$$r^2 = (8-2)^2 + (2-5)^2$$

$$\Rightarrow \quad r^2 = 36 + 9 \Rightarrow r = \sqrt{45} = 3\sqrt{5}$$

112. $C_1 \equiv x^2 + y^2 - 10x - 10y + 41 = 0$

$$\Rightarrow \quad (x-5)^2 + (y-5)^2 = 3^2$$

$\Rightarrow$ Centre $= (5, 5)$ and Radius $= 3$

$$C_2 \equiv x^2 + y^2 - 16x - 10y + 80 = 0$$

$$\Rightarrow (x-8)^2 + (y-5)^2 = 3^2$$

$\Rightarrow$ Centre $= (8, 5)$ and Radius $= 3$

Now, distance between centres $= \sqrt{(8-5)^2 + (5-5)^2} = 3$

Average radii $= \frac{3+3}{2} = 3$

$\therefore$ Option (a) is correct.

$$C_1(8, 5) = (8-5)^2 + (5-5)^2 - 9 = 0$$

$$C_2(5, 5) = (5-8)^2 + (5-5)^2 - 9 = 0$$

Centres of each other lies on circumference of each other.

113. $x^2 + y^2 + ax + 2ay + c = 0 \, (a < 0)$

For a circle in standard form $x^2 + y^2 + 2gx + 2fy + c = 0$

x-intercept $= 2\sqrt{g^2 - c}$

y-intercept $= 2\sqrt{f^2 - c}$

Here, $2g = a \Rightarrow g = \frac{a}{2}, 2f = 2a \Rightarrow f = a$

$$x\text{-intercept} \Rightarrow 2\sqrt{\frac{a^2}{4} - c} = 2\sqrt{2} \Rightarrow \frac{a^2}{4} - c = 2 \quad \text{...(i)}$$

$$y\text{-intercept} \Rightarrow 2\sqrt{a^2 - c} = 2\sqrt{5} \Rightarrow a^2 - c = 5 \quad \text{...(ii)}$$

On subtracting Eq. (ii) from Eq. (i), we get

$$\Rightarrow \quad a = \pm 2$$

As, $a < 0$, so, $a = -2, c = -1$

So, $x^2 + y^2 - 2x - 4y - 1 = 0 \Rightarrow (x-1)^2 + (y-2)^2 = 6$

Centre $(1, 2)$, Radius $= \sqrt{6}$

Equation of tangent is perpendicular to $x + 2y = 0$.

So, equation of tangent will be $2x - y + \lambda = 0$.

Now, perpendicular distance of this line from $(1, 2)$ will be $\sqrt{6}$ units.

$$\frac{|2 \cdot 1 - 2 + \lambda|}{\sqrt{5}} = \sqrt{6} \Rightarrow \lambda = \pm\sqrt{30}$$

So, $T \Rightarrow 2x - y \pm \sqrt{30} = 0$

Now, shortest distance from origin $(0, 0)$ to tangent T will be $\frac{|2 \cdot 0 - 0 \pm \sqrt{30}|}{\sqrt{2^2 + 1^2}} = \frac{\sqrt{30}}{\sqrt{5}} = \sqrt{6}$

114. Given, circle $x^2 + y^2 = 1$

Let (h, k) be the mid-point of line segment from point $(3, 2)$ to a point on circle. Let point on circle be (a, b).

Then, $h = \frac{a+3}{2} \Rightarrow a = 2h - 3$

$$k = \frac{b+2}{2} \Rightarrow b = 2k - 2$$

$\because$ (a, b) is point on circle, then

$$\Rightarrow (2h-3)^2 + (2k-2)^2 = 1$$

$$\Rightarrow \left(h - \frac{3}{2}\right)^2 + (k-1)^2 = \frac{1}{4} = \left(\frac{1}{2}\right)^2$$

which is an equation of circle with radius $1/2$.

115. Given, P be a point on circle

$$(x-1)^2 + (y-1)^2 = 1$$

So, coordinate of P will be of form $P(1 + \cos\theta, 1 + \sin\theta)$.

Given, $A(1, 4)$ and $B(1, -5)$

Then, $(PA)^2 + (PB)^2$

$$= \cos^2\theta + (\sin\theta - 3)^2 + \cos^2\theta + (\sin\theta + 6)^2$$

$$= 47 + 6\sin\theta$$

Now, $(PA)^2 + (PB)^2 = 47 + 6\sin\theta$ is

Maximum, when $\cos\theta = 0$

$$P(1, 2), A(1, 4), B(1, -5)$$

$\therefore P$, A and B are collinear points on the line $x = 1$.

116. Given, $OA = 1$ unit, $OB = 13$ units

Since, OB is diameter of circle.

Then, radius $(r) = 13/2 = 6.5$ unit

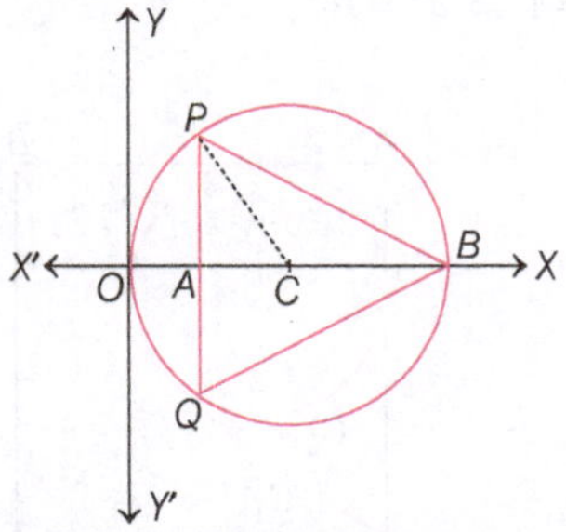

Draw a line joining points P and C, where C is the centre of the given circle.

Then, PC = radius of circle = 6.5 units

OC = radius of circle = 6.5 units

Now, $AC = OC - OA = 6.5 - 1 = 5.5$ units

Then, using Pythagoras theorem,

$$(PA)^2 = (PC)^2 - (AC)^2 = (6.5)^2 - (5.5)^2 = (1)\,(12) = 12$$

$\therefore \quad PA = \sqrt{12}$

Then, $PQ = 2PA = 2\sqrt{12}$

Hence, area of $\Delta PQB = \frac{1}{2} \times (\text{Base}) \times (\text{Height})$

$$= \frac{1}{2} \times (PQ) \times (AB) = \frac{1}{2} \times (PQ) \times (OB - OA)$$

$$= \frac{1}{2} \times (2\sqrt{12}) \times (13 - 1) = 24\sqrt{3} \text{ sq units}$$

117. Given, line $x + \sqrt{3}y = 2\sqrt{3}$ and point $\left(\frac{3\sqrt{3}}{2}, \frac{1}{2}\right)$.

From options, we take the conic $x^2 + 9y^2 = 9$

Equation of any tangent at (x_1, y_1) is $xx_1 + 9 \cdot yy_1 = 9$

$$\Rightarrow \quad \frac{3\sqrt{3}}{2}x + 9 \times \frac{1}{2} \times y = 9 \qquad \left[\because (x_1, y_1) = \left(\frac{3\sqrt{3}}{2}, \frac{1}{2}\right)\right]$$

$$\Rightarrow \quad \frac{3\sqrt{3}}{2}(x + \sqrt{3}y) = 9$$

$$\Rightarrow \quad x + \sqrt{3}y = 2\sqrt{3}$$

Clearly, $x + \sqrt{3}y = 2\sqrt{3}$ is a tangent to the curve $x^2 + 9y^2 = 9$.

118.

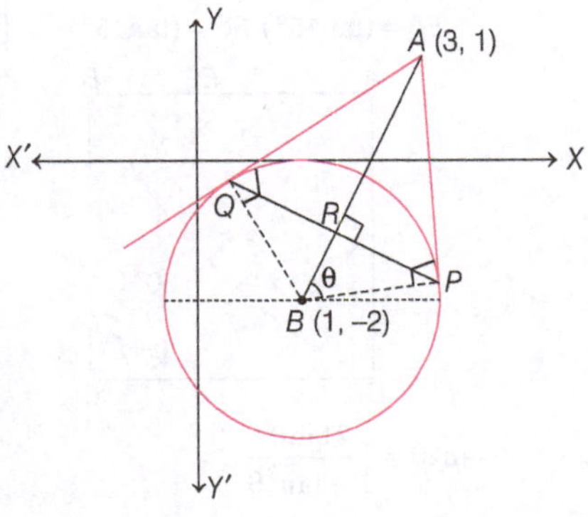

Radius $= \sqrt{1 + 4 - 1} = 2$

$$AB = \sqrt{3^2 + 2^2} = \sqrt{13}$$

In ΔABP, $\quad AP^2 = AB^2 - BP^2 = 13 - 4 = 9$

$$AP = 3$$

$\Rightarrow \quad AQ = AP = 3$

Let $\angle ABP = \theta$, $\angle BAP = 90 - \theta$

In ΔABP, $\tan\theta = 3/2$

$$\sin\theta = \frac{3}{\sqrt{13}}, \cos\theta = \frac{2}{\sqrt{13}}$$

In ΔARP, $\cos(90 - \theta) = \frac{AR}{AP}$

$\Rightarrow \quad AR = 3\sin\theta$

In ΔBRP, $\cos\theta = \frac{BR}{BP} \Rightarrow BR = 2\cos\theta$

$$= \frac{\text{ar}(\Delta APQ)}{\text{ar}(\Delta BPQ)} = \frac{\frac{1}{2} \times PQ \times AR}{\frac{1}{2} \times PQ \times BR} = \frac{AR}{RB} = \frac{3\sin\theta}{2\cos\theta} = \frac{9}{4}$$

$$\Rightarrow \quad 8\left(\frac{\text{ar}(\Delta APQ)}{\text{ar}(\Delta BPQ)}\right) = 18$$

119.

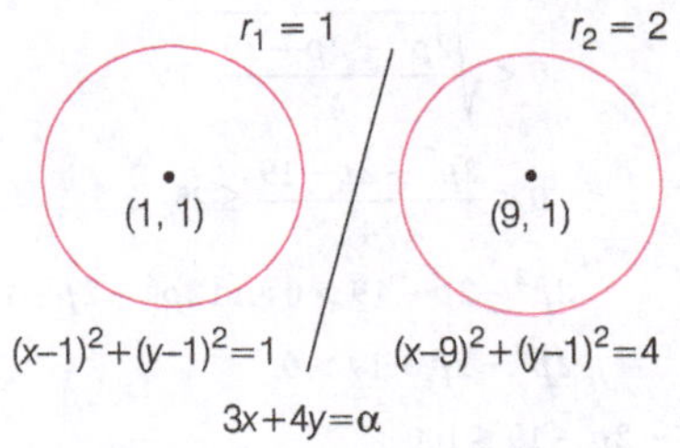

There are 2 possible cases.

1. Both centres should lie on different sides of line.
2. Line can be tangent also

Centre of both the circles are (1, 1) and (9, 1), respectively.

$$(3 + 4 - \alpha)(27 + 4 - \alpha) < 0$$

$$(7 - \alpha)(31 - \alpha) < 0$$

$$\alpha \in (7, 31) \quad \ldots (A)$$

P_1 = Distance of line from centre (1, 1)

$$P_1 \ge r_1$$

$$\frac{|3 + 4 - \alpha|}{5} \ge 1 \quad |7 - \alpha| \ge 5$$

$$\alpha \in (-\infty, 2] \cup [12, \infty) \quad \ldots (B)$$

Similarly, P_2 = Distance of line from (9, 1)

$$\frac{|27 + 4 - \alpha|}{5} \ge 2$$

$$\alpha \in (-\infty, 21] \cup [41, \infty) \quad \ldots (C)$$

Now, $(A) \cap (B) \cap (C)$

$\Rightarrow \quad \alpha \in [12, 21]$

$$\text{Sum} = (12 + 13 + 14 + \ldots + 21) = \left(\frac{21 \times 22}{2}\right) - \left(\frac{11 \times 12}{2}\right)$$

$$= 231 - 66 = 165$$

120. Equation of circles

$$(x-1)^2+(y-2)^2+\lambda(4x+3y-10)=0$$

$$x^2+y^2+(2\lambda-1)\,2x+\left(\frac{3}{2}\lambda-2\right)$$

$$2y+5-10\lambda=0$$

$$r=\sqrt{(2\lambda-1)^2+\left(\frac{3}{2}\lambda-2\right)^2-5+10\lambda}=5$$

$$\Rightarrow \quad 4\lambda^2+1-4\lambda+\frac{9}{4}\lambda^2+4-6\lambda-5+10\lambda=25$$

$$\Rightarrow \quad \frac{25}{4}\lambda^2-25=0 \Rightarrow \lambda=\pm 2$$

For $\lambda=2$,

$$x^2+y^2+6x+2y-15=0,\ C_1(-3,-1)$$

For $\lambda=-2$,

$$x^2+y^2-10x-10y+25=0,\ C_2(5,5)$$

$$|(\alpha+\beta)(\gamma+\delta)|=|-4\times 10|=40$$

121. Given equation,

$$x^2+y^2+px+(1-p)y+5=0$$

Radius, $r=\sqrt{\left(\frac{p}{2}\right)^2+\left(\frac{1-p}{2}\right)^2-5}=\sqrt{\frac{2p^2-2p-19}{4}}$

Now, $r\in(0,5] \Rightarrow 0<r\le 5$

$$\Rightarrow \quad 0<\sqrt{\frac{2p^2-2p-19}{4}}\le 5$$

$$\Rightarrow \quad 0<\frac{2p^2-2p-19}{4}\le 25$$

$$\Rightarrow \quad 2p^2-2p-19>0 \text{ and } 2p^2-2p-19\le 100$$

$$\Rightarrow \quad 2p^2-2p-19>0$$

and $2p^2-2p-19\le 100$

$$\Rightarrow \quad p\in\left(-\infty,\frac{1-\sqrt{39}}{2}\right)\cup\left(\frac{1+\sqrt{39}}{2},\infty\right)$$

and $\quad p\in\left[\frac{1-\sqrt{239}}{2},\frac{1+\sqrt{239}}{2}\right]$

$$p\in\left[\frac{1-\sqrt{239}}{2},\frac{1-\sqrt{39}}{2}\right]\cup\left[\frac{1+\sqrt{39}}{2},\frac{1+\sqrt{239}}{2}\right]$$

$$\Rightarrow \quad p^2\in\left[\left(\frac{1-\sqrt{39}}{2}\right)^2,\left(\frac{1+\sqrt{239}}{2}\right)^2\right]$$

$$\because \quad q=p^2,\ q\in Z$$

$$\Rightarrow \quad q=7,8,9,10,\ldots,67$$

$\Rightarrow$ 61 integers in S.

$$\therefore \quad n(S)=61$$

122. Let $P(x,y)$ be the required point.

Then, $(x^2+y^2)+[x^2+(y-1)^2]+[(x-1)^2+y^2]$

$$+[(x-1)^2+(y-1)^2]=18$$

$$\Rightarrow \quad 4(x^2+y^2)-4y-4x=14$$

$$\Rightarrow \quad x^2+y^2-x-y-\frac{7}{2}=0$$

$$\text{Radius}=\sqrt{\left(\frac{1}{2}\right)^2+\left(\frac{1}{2}\right)^2+\frac{7}{2}}=2$$

Diameter $=4 \Rightarrow d^2=16$

123.

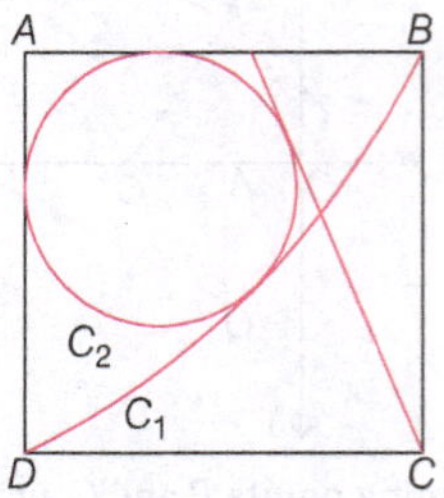

Given, $EB=\alpha+\sqrt{3}\,\beta$

Let O be the centre of circle C_2.

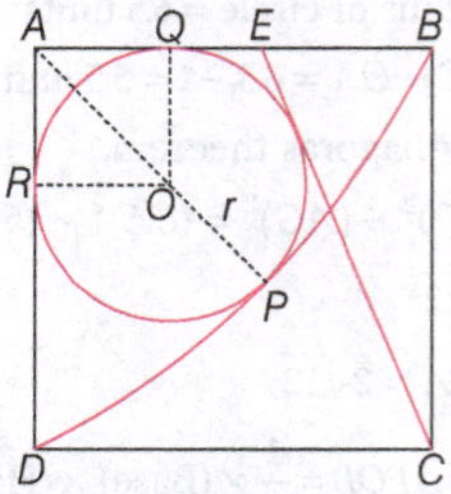

$$OQ^2+OR^2=AO^2$$

$$\Rightarrow \quad AO+OP=AP=1 \Rightarrow AO+r=1$$

$$\Rightarrow \quad r^2+r^2=(1-r)^2 \Rightarrow 2r^2=r^2+1-2r$$

$$\Rightarrow \quad r^2+2r+1=1+1 \Rightarrow (r+1)^2=2$$

$$\Rightarrow \quad r+1=\sqrt{2} \Rightarrow r=\sqrt{2}-1$$

As, $AO=1-r \Rightarrow AC=\sqrt{2}$

So, $OC=AC-AO=\sqrt{2}-(1-\sqrt{2}+1)=2(\sqrt{2}-1)$

In ΔOCN, we have

$$\frac{ON}{OC}=\sin\theta$$

$$\Rightarrow \quad \frac{\sqrt{2}-1}{2(\sqrt{2}-1)}=\frac{1}{2}=\sin\theta$$

$$\Rightarrow \quad \theta=\pi/6$$

In ΔEBC, we have

$$\frac{EB}{BC}=\tan 15^\circ$$

$$EB=(\tan 15^\circ)\,BC=(\tan 15^\circ) \qquad [\because BC=1 \text{ unit}]$$

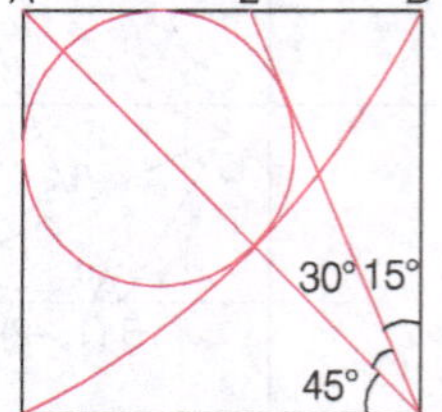

Now, $\quad \tan 2\theta=\dfrac{2\tan\theta}{1-\tan^2\theta}$

$\therefore \quad \tan 30° = \dfrac{2\tan 15°}{1-\tan^2 15°}$

$\Rightarrow \quad 1-\tan^2 15° = 2\sqrt{3}\tan 15°$

$\Rightarrow \tan^2 15° + 2\sqrt{3}\tan 15° - 1 = 0$

$$\tan 15° = \frac{-2\sqrt{3} \pm \sqrt{12+4}}{2} = -\sqrt{3}+2$$

$\therefore \quad EB = 2-\sqrt{3} = \alpha + \sqrt{3}\beta$

$\alpha = 2, \beta = -1$

$\therefore \quad \alpha + \beta = 2 + (-1) = 1$

124. All normals of circle pass through a fixed point (a, b) that is the centre

$\therefore$ Radius $= MO = NO$

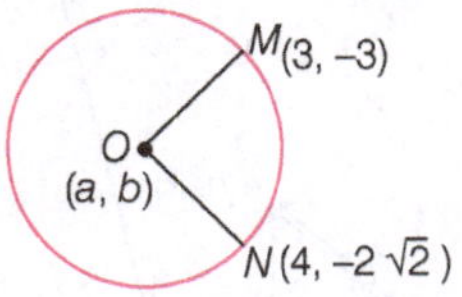

$\Rightarrow \quad (MO)^2 = (NO)^2$

$\Rightarrow \quad (a-3)^2 + (b+3)^2 = (a-4)^2 + (b+2\sqrt{2})^2$

$\Rightarrow -6a + 8a + 6b - 4\sqrt{2}b = 6$

$\Rightarrow \quad a - 2\sqrt{2}b + 3b = 3$ ...(i)

Also, given that $a - 2\sqrt{2b} = 3$ ...(ii)

On solving Eqs. (i) and (ii), we get $a = 3$ and $b = 0$

$\therefore \quad a^2 + b^2 + ab = 9$

125. Let P be (h, k), A be $(5, 0)$ and B be $(-5, 0)$.

Given $\quad PA = 3PB$

$\Rightarrow \quad PA^2 = 9PB^2$

$\Rightarrow \quad (h-5)^2 + k^2 = 9[(h+5)^2 + k^2]$

$\Rightarrow 8h^2 + 8k^2 + 100h + 200 = 0$

$\therefore$ Locus of P is $x^2 + y^2 + \dfrac{25}{2}x + 25 = 0$

Centre $= \left(\dfrac{-25}{4}, 0\right)$ and $r^2 = \left(\dfrac{-25}{4}\right)^2 + 0^2 - 25$

$= \dfrac{625}{16} - 25 = \dfrac{225}{16}$

$\therefore \quad 4r^2 = 4 \times \dfrac{225}{16} = \dfrac{225}{4} = 56.25$

126.

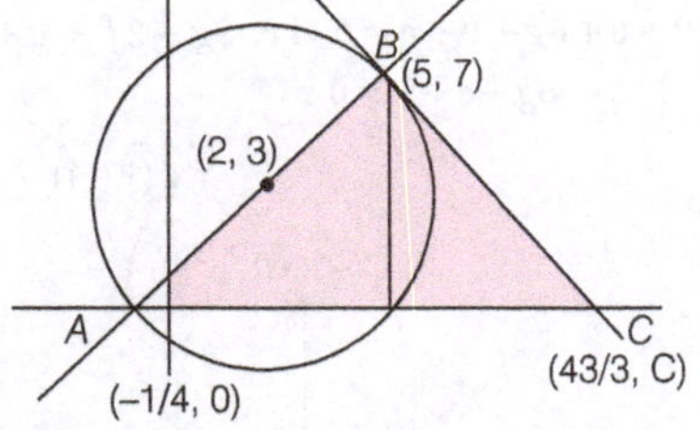

Given, equation of circle $x^2 + y^2 - 4x - 6y - 12 = 0$

Equation of normal : $\dfrac{y-y_1}{y_1+f} = \dfrac{x-x_1}{x_1+g}$

$\Rightarrow \quad 4x - 3y + 1 = 0$

Equation of tangents

$xx_1 + yy_1 + g(x+x_1) + f(y+y_1) + c = 0$

$3x + 4y - 43 = 0$

Area of triangle $= \dfrac{1}{2}\left(\dfrac{43}{3} + \dfrac{1}{4}\right) \times (7) = \dfrac{1}{2}\left(\dfrac{172+3}{12}\right) \times 7$

$\therefore \quad A = \dfrac{1225}{24} \Rightarrow 24A = 1225$

127. Given, circle $\Rightarrow x^2 + y^2 - 2x - 6y + 6 = 0$

Coordinate of $C = (1, 3)$

Radius $= r = \sqrt{1^2 + 3^2 - 6} = \sqrt{4} = 2$ units

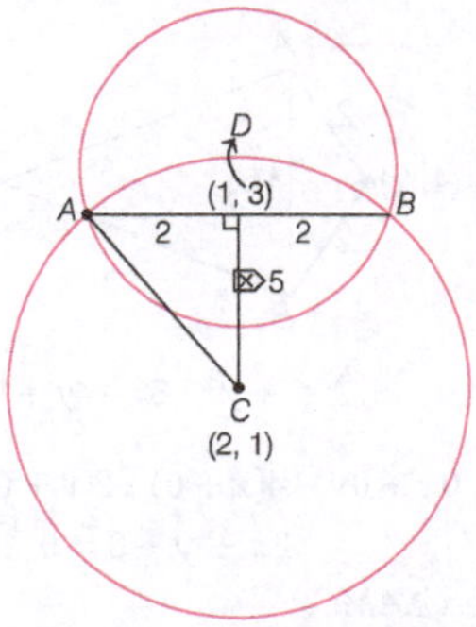

$$CD = \sqrt{(2-1)^2 + (1-3)^2} = \sqrt{1+4} = \sqrt{5}$$

Now, by using Pythagoras theorem in ΔADC,

$AC^2 = AD^2 + CD^2 = (2)^2 + (\sqrt{5})^2 = 4 + 5$

$AC = \sqrt{9} = 3$

$\therefore$ Required radius $= 3$

128. Equation of given circle

$x^2 + y^2 = r^2$ ...(i)

and the chord $y = 2x + 3$ ...(ii)

From the figure,

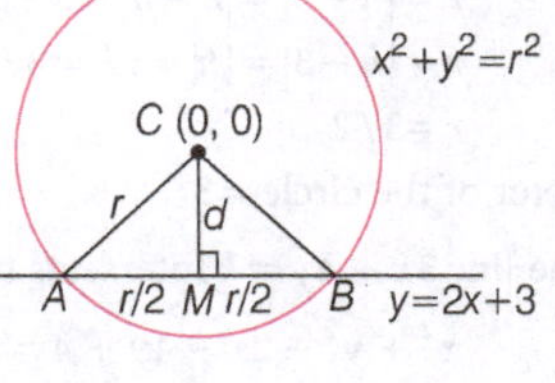

$AB = r$

$$d = \sqrt{r^2 - \frac{r^2}{4}} = \frac{\sqrt{3}}{2}r$$

and $\quad d = \dfrac{3}{\sqrt{1+4}}$

$\therefore \quad \dfrac{3}{\sqrt{5}} = \dfrac{\sqrt{3}}{2}r \Rightarrow r^2 = \dfrac{12}{5}$

129. Since, equation of tangent to the

circle $x^2 + y^2 = 1$ at point $\left(\frac{1}{\sqrt{2}}, \frac{1}{\sqrt{2}}\right)$ is $T = 0$.

$\Rightarrow \quad \frac{x}{\sqrt{2}} + \frac{y}{\sqrt{2}} = 1 \Rightarrow x + y = \sqrt{2}$ ...(i)

$\because$ Line $L_1 : x + y = \sqrt{2}$ is perpendicular to line

$y = mx + c$, so $m = 1$, since line $y = mx + c$ is tangent to the circle $(x-3)^2 + y^2 = 1$, where $m = 1$, then $y = x + c$ is

equivalent to $y = 1(x-3) \pm 1\sqrt{1 + 1^2}$.

So, $\quad c = -3 \pm \sqrt{2} \Rightarrow c + 3 = \pm\sqrt{2}$

$\Rightarrow \quad (c+3)^2 = 2 \Rightarrow c^2 + 6c + 7 = 0$

130. The equation of chord of contact AB to circle. $x^2 + y^2 - 8x - 4y + 16 = 0$ w.r.t. point origin $(0, 0)$ is $T = 0$

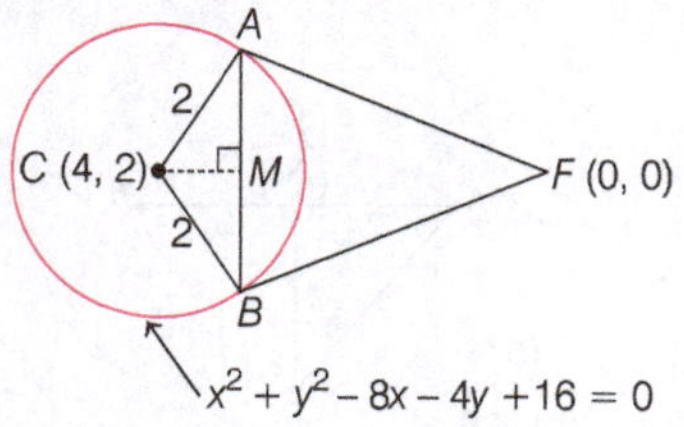

$\Rightarrow \quad 0x + 0y - 4(x+0) - 2(y+0) + 16 = 0$

$\Rightarrow \quad 2x + y - 8 = 0$ ...(i)

In right angled ΔAMC,

$$CM = \frac{|2(4) + 2 - 8|}{\sqrt{2^2 + 1^2}} = \frac{2}{\sqrt{5}}$$

$\because \quad AM^2 = CA^2 - CM^2 = 2^2 - \left(\frac{2}{\sqrt{5}}\right)^2 \Rightarrow AM = \frac{4}{\sqrt{5}}$

$\because \quad AB^2 = (2AM)^2 = \left(\frac{2 \times 4}{\sqrt{5}}\right)^2 = \frac{64}{5}$

131. Since, it is given that centre of the circle lies on the line $x + y = 2$, so let the centre is $(h, 2-h)$ lies in the first quadrant, so $h > 0$ and $2 - h > 0$

$\Rightarrow \quad 0 < h < 2$

And the circle touches the lines $x = 3$ and $y = 2$, so radius

$r = |h - 3| = |2 - h - 2|$

$\Rightarrow \quad r = |h-3| = |h| \Rightarrow h = 3/2$

$\therefore \quad r = 3/2$

$\Rightarrow$ Diameter of the circle = 3

132. Since, the line $3x + 4y = k$ intersects the circle

$x^2 + y^2 - 2x - 4y + 4 = 0$

$\Rightarrow (x-1)^2 + (y-2)^2 = 1$ at two distinct points, so perpendicular distance from centre $(1, 2)$ to the line $3x + 4y - k = 0$ must be less than the radius 1.

$\therefore \quad \left|\frac{3 + 8 - k}{\sqrt{9 + 16}}\right| < 1$

$\Rightarrow \quad |11 - k| < 5 \Rightarrow (k - 11) \in (-5, 5)$

$\Rightarrow \quad k \in (6, 16)$

$\Rightarrow \quad k = 7, 8, 9, 10, 11, 12, 13, 14, 15$

$\therefore$ Number of integral values of k is 9.

Exercise 2 - JEE Advanced Pattern

1. **Decoding the Question**

Radius of circle r whose centre (h, k) to the tangents of circle $ax + by + c = 0$ is $r = \left|\frac{ah + by + c}{\sqrt{a^2 + b^2}}\right|$.

Let $A(h, k)$ be the centre of circle C_1, where $h > 0$ and $k > 0$, as A lies in the first quadrant. As diameter of C_1 is of length 6 units, its radius = 3. Since, the circle C_1 touches the lines $5x + 12y - 10 = 0$ and $5x - 12y - 40 = 0$, we get

$$\frac{|5h + 12k - 10|}{\sqrt{5^2 + 12^2}} = 3 \text{ and } \frac{|5h - 12k - 40|}{\sqrt{5^2 + 12^2}} = 3$$

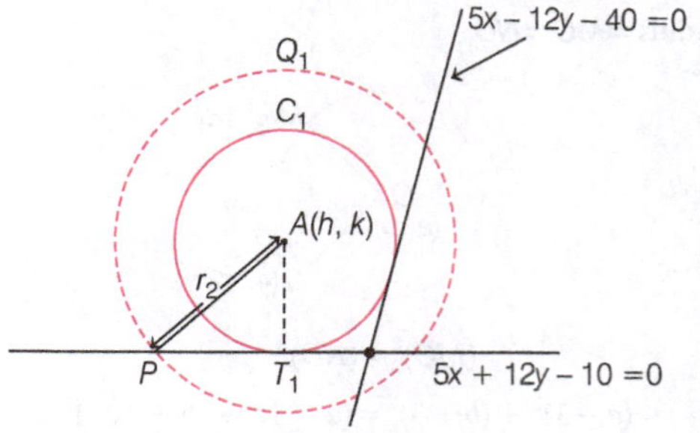

$\Rightarrow \quad |5h + 12k - 10| = |5h - 12k - 40| = 39$

$\Rightarrow \quad 5h + 12k - 10 = 5h - 12k - 40$

or $\quad 5h + 12k - 10 = -5h + 12k + 40$

$\Rightarrow \quad 24k = -30$ or $10h = 50$

$\Rightarrow \quad k = -\frac{5}{4}$ or $h = 5$ but $h > 0, k > 0 \Rightarrow h = 5$

Also, $\quad |5h + 12k - 10| = 39 \Rightarrow |25 + 12k - 10| = 39$

$\Rightarrow \quad |12k + 15| = 39 \Rightarrow (12k + 15) = \pm 39$

$\Rightarrow \quad 12k + 15 = 39$ or $12k + 15 = -39$

$\Rightarrow \quad k = 2$ or $k = -\frac{9}{2}$ but $k > 0 \Rightarrow k = 2$

Hence, centre of C_1 is $(5, 2)$.

Since, the circle C_2 cuts intercepts of length 8 on given lines.

$\therefore$ Radius of $C_2 = \sqrt{AT_1^2 + T_1P^2} = \sqrt{3^2 + 4^2} = 5$

$\therefore$ The equation of the circle C_2 is

$(x-5)^2 + (y-2)^2 = 5^2$ i.e. $x^2 + y^2 - 10x - 4y + 4 = 0$

2. Let the circle be $x^2 + y^2 + 2gx + 2fy + c = 0$ ...(i)

Its centre is $C(-g, -f)$ and radius $= \sqrt{g^2 + f^2 - c}$

Since, points $(1, -1)$, $(3, 0)$ lie on Eq. (i), we get

$1 + 1 + 2g - 2f + c = 0$

and $\quad 9 + 0 + 6g + 0 + c = 0$ i.e. $2g - 2f + c + 2 = 0$ ...(ii)

and $\quad 6g - c + 9 = 0$ ...(iii)

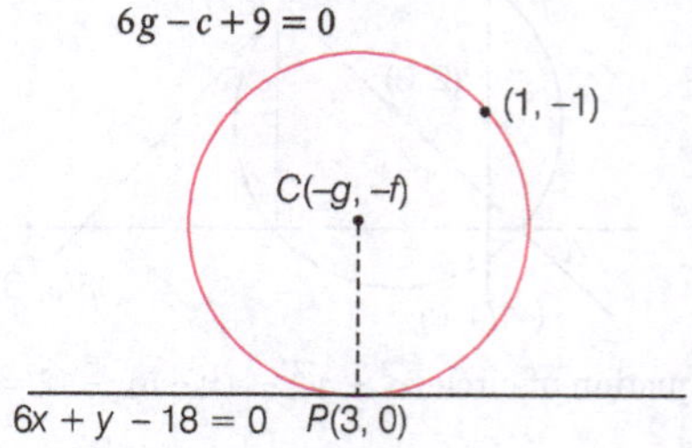

Given line is $\quad 6x + y - 18 = 0 \quad$ ...(iv)

Its slope $= -6$; Slope of $CP = \dfrac{-f-0}{-g-3} = \dfrac{f}{g+3}$

Since, the line (iv) touches circle (i) at P.

$\therefore$ CP is perpendicular to (iv).

$$\therefore \quad \frac{f}{g+3}(-6) = -1 \Rightarrow g+3 = 6f \quad \text{...(v)}$$

On solving Eqs. (ii), (iii) and (v), we get

$$g = -\frac{24}{13};\ f = \frac{5}{26} \text{ and } c = \frac{27}{13}$$

Hence, the equation of the circle is

$$x^2 + y^2 - \frac{48}{13}x + \frac{10}{26}y + \frac{27}{13} = 0$$

i.e. $\quad 13(x^2 + y^2) - 48x + 5y + 27 = 0$

3. Equation of circle with centre (0, 0) and radius a is $x^2 + y^2 = a^2$

$\therefore \quad P \equiv (a\cos\alpha, a\sin\alpha)$

and $\quad Q \equiv (a\cos\beta, a\sin\beta)$

Coordinates of A and B are $A \equiv (-a, 0)$ and $B \equiv (a, 0)$

$\therefore$ Equation AP is $y - 0 = \dfrac{a\sin\alpha - 0}{a\cos\alpha + a}(x+a)$

or $\quad y(1+\cos\alpha) = \sin\alpha\,(x+a)$

or $\quad y\left(2\cos^2\dfrac{\alpha}{2}\right) = 2\sin\left(\dfrac{\alpha}{2}\right)\cos\left(\dfrac{\alpha}{2}\right)(x+a)$

or $\quad y\cos\left(\dfrac{\alpha}{2}\right) - x\sin\left(\dfrac{\alpha}{2}\right) = a\sin\left(\dfrac{\alpha}{2}\right)$ or $\tan\left(\dfrac{\alpha}{2}\right) = \dfrac{y}{x+a}$

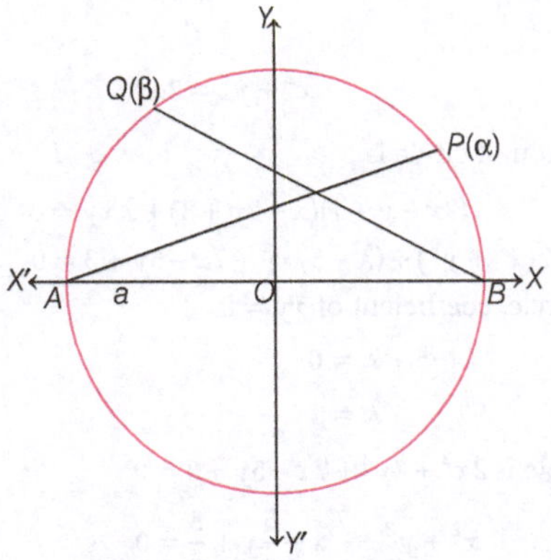

and equation of BQ is $y - 0 = \dfrac{a\sin\beta - 0}{a\cos\beta - a}(x-a)$

or $\quad y(\cos\beta - 1) = \sin\beta(x-a)$

$$\Rightarrow \quad y\left(-2\sin^2\left(\frac{\beta}{2}\right)\right) = 2\sin\left(\frac{\beta}{2}\right)\cos\left(\frac{\beta}{2}\right)(x-a)$$

$$\Rightarrow \quad y\sin\left(\frac{\beta}{2}\right) + x\cos\left(\frac{\beta}{2}\right) = a\cos\left(\frac{\beta}{2}\right)$$

$$\Rightarrow \quad \tan\left(\frac{\beta}{2}\right) = \frac{a-x}{y}$$

$$\because \quad \gamma = \frac{\alpha - \beta}{2} \quad \text{[given]}$$

$$\Rightarrow \quad \tan\gamma = \frac{\tan(\alpha/2) - \tan(\beta/2)}{1 + \tan(\alpha/2)\tan(\beta/2)} = \frac{\dfrac{y}{x+a} - \dfrac{a-x}{y}}{1 + \dfrac{a-x}{a+x}}$$

or $\quad x^2 + y^2 - 2ay\tan\gamma = a^2$

which is the locus of point of intersection of AP and BQ.

4. **Decoding the Question**

Equation of chord of contact of circle $x^2 + y^2 = r^2$ from (h, k) is $hx + ky = r^2$.

Let $P(h, 4)$ be a variable point.

Given circle is $\quad x^2 + y^2 = 4 \quad$ ...(i)

Draw tangents from $P(h, 4)$ and complete parallelogram $PAQB$.

Equation of the diagonal AB which is chord of contact of

$$x^2 + y^2 = 4 \text{ is } hx + 4y = 4 \quad \text{...(ii)}$$

Let coordinates of A and B be (x_a, y_a) and (x_b, y_b), respectively.

Since, $A(x_a, y_a)$ and $B(x_b, y_b)$ lie on Eq. (ii),

$\therefore \quad hx_a + 4y_a = 4$

and $\quad hx_b + 4y_b = 4$

$\therefore \quad h(x_a + x_b) + 4(y_a + y_b) = 8 \quad$ ...(iii)

Since, $PAQB$ is parallelogram.

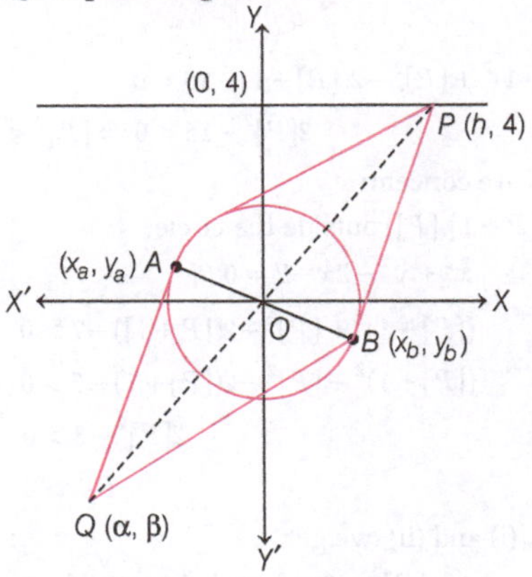

$\therefore$ Mid-point of AB = Mid-point of PQ

$$\Rightarrow \quad \frac{x_a + x_b}{2} = \frac{\alpha + h}{2} \text{ and } \frac{y_a + y_b}{2} = \frac{\beta + 4}{2} \quad \text{...(iv)}$$

On eliminating x from Eqs. (i) and (ii), we get

$$\left(\frac{4-4y}{h}\right)^2 + y^2 = 4$$

$$\Rightarrow \quad 16 + 16y^2 - 32y + h^2y^2 - 4h^2 = 0$$

$$(16 + h^2)y^2 - 32y + 16 - 4h^2 = 0$$

$$\therefore \quad y_a + y_b = \frac{32}{16+h^2} \quad \text{...(v)}$$

From Eqs. (iii) and (v), we get

$$x_a + x_b = \frac{8h}{16+h^2} \quad \text{...(vi)}$$

From Eqs. (iv) and (vi), we get

$$\beta + 4 = \frac{32}{16+h^2} \text{ or } (16+h^2)(\beta+4) = 32 \quad \text{...(vii)}$$

Also, from Eqs. (iv) and (vi), we get

$$\alpha + h = \frac{8h}{16+h^2}$$

$\Rightarrow \quad (16+h^2)(\alpha+h) = 8h \qquad$ ...(viii)

On dividing Eq. (viii) by Eq. (vii), we get

$$\frac{\alpha+h}{\beta+4} = \frac{h}{4} \text{ or } h = \frac{4\alpha}{\beta}$$

On substituting the value h in Eq. (vii), we get

$$\left(16+\frac{16\alpha^2}{\beta^2}\right)(\beta+4) = 32$$

$\Rightarrow \quad (\alpha^2+\beta^2)(\beta+4) = 2\beta^2$

Hence, locus of $Q(\alpha, \beta)$ is $(x^2+y^2)(y+4) = 2y^2$.

5. $\because$ The point $([P+1],[P])$ lies inside the circle $x^2+y^2-2x-15=0$, then $[P+1]^2+[P]^2-2[P+1]-15<0$

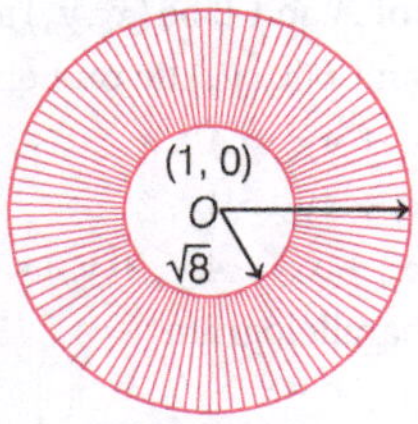

$\Rightarrow \quad ([P]+1)^2+[P]^2-2([P]+1)-15<0$

$\Rightarrow \quad 2[P]^2-16<0 \Rightarrow [P]^2<8 \qquad$ ...(i)

$\because$ Circles are concentric.

$\therefore$ Point $([P+1],[P])$ outside the circle.

$$x^2+y^2-2x-7=0$$

$\therefore \quad ([P]+1)^2+[P]^2-2([P+1])-7>0$

$\Rightarrow \quad ([P]+1)^2+[P]^2-2([P]+1)-7>0$

$\Rightarrow \quad 2[P]^2-8>0$

$\therefore \quad [P]^2>4 \qquad$ ...(ii)

From Eqs. (i) and (ii), we get

$4<[P]^2<8$, which is impossible.

$\therefore$ For no value of P the point will be within the region.

6. The circles are $x^2+y^2=2^2$ and $(x-4)^2+(y-0)^2=3^2$

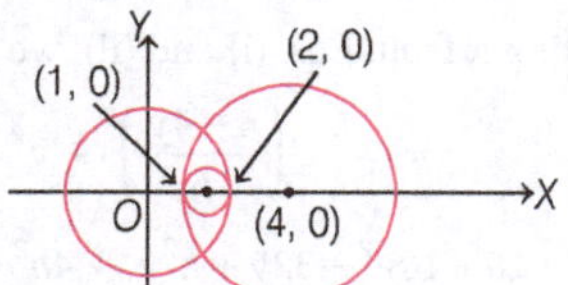

For the point P to enclose greatest area, the arbitrarily chosen point should be $\left(\frac{3}{2},0\right)$ and P should move in a circle of radius $\frac{1}{2}$.

The locus of P is $\left(x-\frac{3}{2}\right)^2+(y-0)^2=\left(\frac{1}{2}\right)^2$

$\Rightarrow \quad x^2+y^2-3x+2=0$

7. Since, $y=|x|+c$ and $x^2+y^2-8|x|-9=0$ both are symmetrical about Y-axis for $x>0$, $y=x+c$.

Equation of tangent to circle $x^2+y^2-8x-9=0$

Parallel to $y=x+c$ is $y=(x-4)+5\sqrt{(1+1)}$

$\Rightarrow \quad y=x+(5\sqrt{2}-4)$

For no solution $c>5\sqrt{2}-4$,

$\therefore \quad c\in(5\sqrt{2}-4,\infty)$

8. Let $\angle AOL=\theta$

$\therefore \quad A\equiv(a\cos\theta, a\sin\theta)$

$\therefore \quad M\equiv(a+a\cos\theta, a\sin\theta)$

$$x=a+a\cos\theta$$

$\Rightarrow \quad (x-a)=a\cos\theta \qquad$ ...(i)

and $\quad y=a\sin\theta$

From Eqs. (i) and (ii), we get

$$(x-a)^2+y^2=a^2$$

$\Rightarrow \quad x^2+y^2-2ax=0$

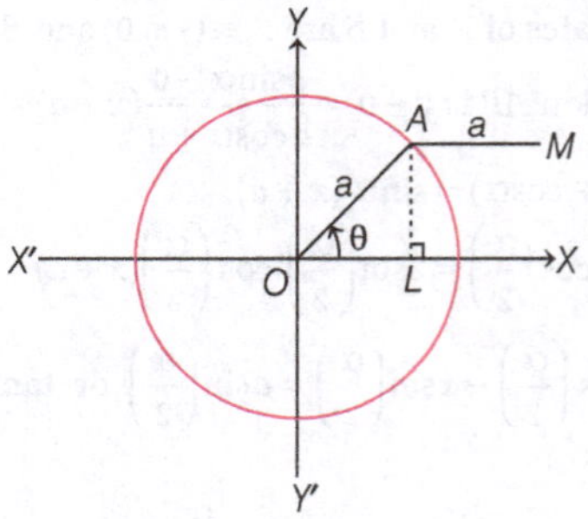

$\Rightarrow \quad x^2+y^2=2ax$

9. Equation of circle is

$$(2x-y+1)(x-2y+3)+\lambda xy=0$$

$$2(x^2+y^2)+(\lambda-5)xy+7x-5y+3=0$$

For circle, coefficient of $xy=0$

i.e. $\quad -5+\lambda=0,$

$\therefore \quad \lambda=5$

$\therefore$ Circle is $2x^2+2y^2+7x-5y+3=0$

$\Rightarrow \quad x^2+y^2+\frac{7}{2}x-\frac{5}{2}y+\frac{3}{2}=0$

$\therefore$ Centre is $\left(-\frac{7}{4},\frac{5}{4}\right)$.

10. $\sqrt{\left\{\frac{\lambda^2}{4}+\frac{(1-\lambda)^2}{4}-5\right\}}\le 5$

$\Rightarrow \quad \lambda^2+(1-\lambda)^2-20\le 100$

$\Rightarrow \quad 2\lambda^2-2\lambda-119\le 0$

$\therefore \quad \frac{1-\sqrt{239}}{2}\le\lambda\le\frac{1+\sqrt{239}}{2}$

$\Rightarrow \quad -7.2\le\lambda\le 8.2 \qquad$ [approx.]

$\therefore \quad \lambda=-7,-6,-5,\ldots,7,8$

11. Let $\phi(x,y) \equiv x^2 + y^2 + 2gx + 2fy + c = 0$

$\therefore \quad \phi(0,\lambda) = 0 + \lambda^2 + 0 + 2f\lambda + c = 0$ have equal roots.

Then, $2 + 2 = -\dfrac{2f}{1}$ and $2.2 = \dfrac{c}{1}$

$\therefore \quad f = -2$ and $c = 4$

and $\phi(\lambda, 0) \equiv \lambda^2 + 0 + 2g\lambda + 0 + c = 0$

$\therefore \quad \lambda^2 + 2g\lambda + c = 0$

Here, $c = 4$

$\therefore \quad \lambda^2 + 2g\lambda + 4 = 0$ have roots $\dfrac{4}{5}$, 5

$\therefore \quad \dfrac{4}{5} + 5 = -2g$

$\Rightarrow \quad g = -\dfrac{29}{10}$

$\therefore \quad$ Centre $\equiv (-g, -f) = \left(\dfrac{29}{10}, 2\right)$

12. Circle is $x^2 + y^2 = r^2\cos^2\theta + r^2\sin^2\theta$

$$x^2 + y^2 = r^2$$

Equation of tangent at θ is

$$x\cos\theta + y\sin\theta = r \quad \text{...(i)}$$

and at $\left(\theta + \dfrac{\pi}{3}\right)$ is $x\cos\left(\theta + \dfrac{\pi}{3}\right) + y\sin\left(\theta + \dfrac{\pi}{3}\right) = r$

$\Rightarrow \quad x\left(\dfrac{1}{2}\cos\theta - \dfrac{\sqrt{3}}{2}\sin\theta\right) + y\left(\dfrac{1}{2}\sin\theta + \dfrac{\sqrt{3}}{2}\cos\theta\right) = r$

$\Rightarrow \quad x\cos\theta + y\sin\theta - x\sqrt{3}\sin\theta + y\sqrt{3}\cos\theta = 2r$

$\Rightarrow \quad r - \sqrt{3}(x\sin\theta - y\cos\theta) = 2r$

or $\quad x\sin\theta - y\cos\theta = -\dfrac{r}{\sqrt{3}} \quad$ ...(ii)

On squaring and adding Eqs. (i) and (ii), then we get

$$x^2 + y^2 = \frac{4r^2}{3}$$

$\Rightarrow \quad 3(x^2 + y^2) = 4r^2$

13. Let MN be the diameter of the circle whose equation is

$$4y = x + 7 \quad \text{...(i)}$$

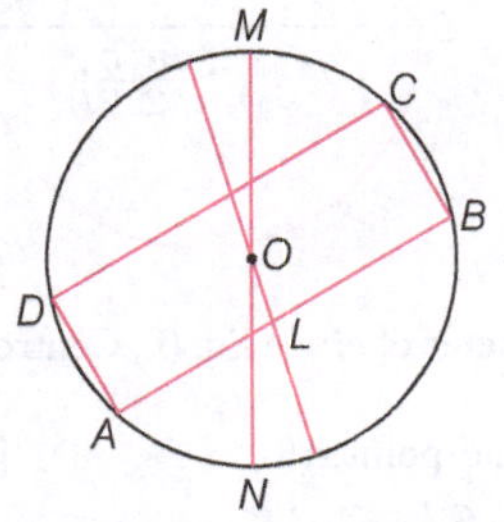

and coordinates of A and B are $(-3, 4)$ and $(5, 4)$, respectively. Equation of perpendicular bisector of AB is $[L \equiv (1, 4)]$

$$y - 4 = -\frac{1}{0}(x - 1) \quad [\because \text{slope of } AB = 0]$$

$\therefore \quad x = 1 \quad$ ...(ii)

On solving Eqs. (i) and (ii), we get the coordinates of the centre of the circle as (1, 2)

$\therefore \quad OL = \sqrt{(1-1)^2 + (4-2)^2} = 2$

$\therefore \quad BC = 2OL = 4$ units

$AB = 8$ units

$\therefore$ Area of rectangle $ABCD = 4 \times 8$

$= 32$ sq units

14. $\because \; OC \cdot OA = ab = OB \cdot OD$

$\therefore \; A, B, C, D$ are concyclic.

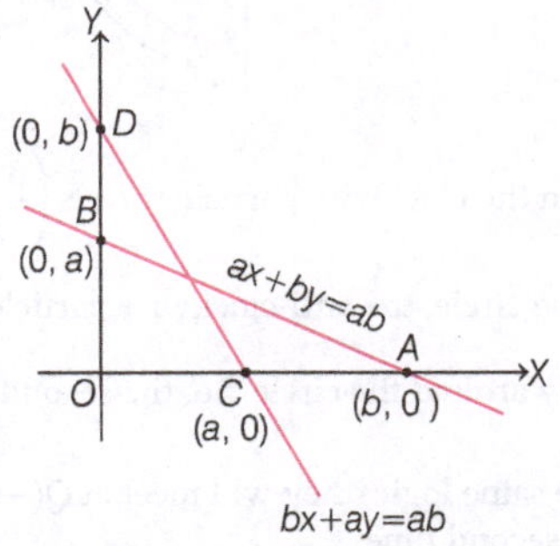

15. Coordinates of P, Q and R are $(\cos\alpha, \sin\alpha)$, $(\cos\beta, \sin\beta)$ and $(\cos\gamma, \sin\gamma)$ respectively and $A \equiv (-1, 0)$

$\therefore \quad AP = \sqrt{((1+\cos\alpha)^2 + \sin^2\alpha)} = 2\cos\left(\dfrac{\alpha}{2}\right)$

$AQ = \sqrt{((1+\cos\beta)^2 + \sin^2\beta)} = 2\cos\left(\dfrac{\beta}{2}\right)$

$AR = \sqrt{((1+\cos\gamma)^2 + \sin^2\gamma)} = 2\cos\left(\dfrac{\gamma}{2}\right)$

$\because \; AP, AQ$ and AR are in GP, then

$\cos\left(\dfrac{\alpha}{2}\right), \cos\left(\dfrac{\beta}{2}\right)$ and $\cos\left(\dfrac{\gamma}{2}\right)$ are also in GP.

16. Let equation of circle be $x^2 + y^2 + 2gx + 2fy + c = 0$

It pass through (2, 0) and (0, 4), then

$$4 + 0 + 4g + 0 + c = 0$$

$\Rightarrow \quad g = -\dfrac{(c+4)}{4}$ and $0 + 16 + 0 + 8f + c = 0$

$\Rightarrow \quad f = -\dfrac{(c+16)}{8}$

$\because \quad$ Radius, $r = \sqrt{(g^2 + f^2 - c)}$

$$= \sqrt{\left\{\frac{(c+4)^2}{16} + \frac{(c+16)^2}{64} - c\right\}}$$

$$= \sqrt{\left[\frac{4\{c^2 + 8c + 16\} + \{c^2 + 32c + 256\} - 64c}{64}\right]}$$

$$= \sqrt{\left(\frac{5c^2 + 320}{64}\right)}$$

For minimum radius, $c = 0$

$\therefore \quad g = -1$ and $f = -2$

Required circle is $x^2 + y^2 - 2x - 4y = 0$

17. The particle which moves clockwise is moving three times as fast as the particle moving anti-clockwise

($\because$ speed in clockwise $3v$ and in anti-clockwise v).

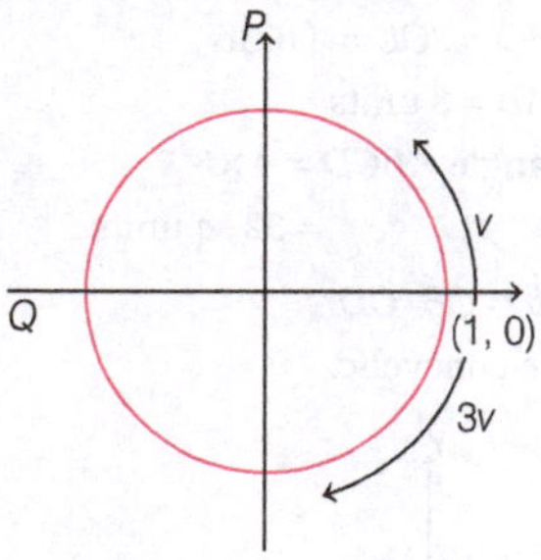

This mean the clockwise particle travels $\left(\frac{3}{4}\right)$ th of the way around the circle, the anti-clockwise particle will travel $\left(\frac{1}{4}\right)$ th of the way around the circle. So, the second particle will meet at $P(0,1)$.

Using the same logic, they will meet at $Q(-1,0)$, when they meet the second time.

18. $\because \quad \frac{BP}{PA} = \alpha$

$BP : PA = \alpha : 1$

$\therefore$ Coordinates of P is $\left(\frac{3+\alpha}{1+\alpha}, \frac{4}{\alpha+1}\right)$, P lie on $x^2 + y^2 = 4$

$\Rightarrow \quad (\alpha+3)^2 + 16 = 4(\alpha+1)^2$

$\Rightarrow \quad 3\alpha^2 + 2\alpha - 21 = 0 \quad \text{...(i)}$

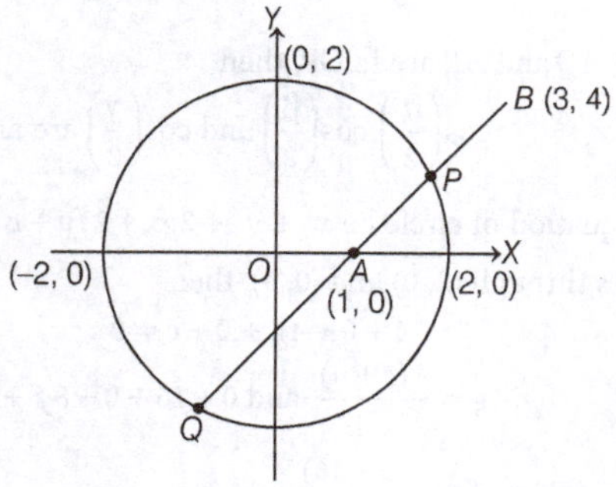

and $\quad \frac{BQ}{QA} = \frac{\beta}{1}$

$BQ : QA = \beta : 1$ or $\frac{BQ}{QA} - 1 = \beta - 1$

$\frac{AB}{QA} = \frac{(\beta - 1)}{1} \Rightarrow AB : QA = (\beta - 1) : 1$

$\therefore$ Coordinates of Q are $\left(\frac{\beta-3}{\beta-1}, \frac{-4}{\beta-1}\right)$

Q lie on $x^2 + y^2 = 4$

$\therefore \quad (\beta-3)^2 + 16 = 4(\beta-1)^2$

$\Rightarrow \quad 3\beta^2 - 21\beta - 21 = 0$

Hence, α is a root of $3x^2 + 2x - 21 = 0$

and β is a root of $3x^2 - 2x - 21 = 0$.

19. $\because \angle ACB = \frac{\pi}{3}$ [given]

$\therefore \angle AOB = \frac{2\pi}{3}$

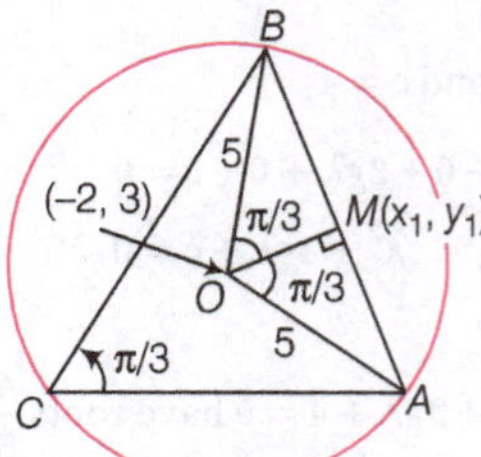

$\Rightarrow \quad \angle AOM = \angle BOM = \frac{\pi}{3}$

Let mid-point of chord AB be (x_1, y_1).

$\therefore$ In ΔAOM,

$$\cos\frac{\pi}{3} = \frac{OM}{OA} = \frac{\sqrt{(x_1+2)^2 + (y_1-3)^2}}{5}$$

or $\quad \left(\frac{5}{2}\right)^2 = (x_1+2)^2 + (y_1-3)^2$

$\Rightarrow \quad \frac{25}{4} = x_1^2 + y_1^2 + 4x_1 - 6y_1 + 13$

$$4x_1^2 + 4y_1^2 + 16x_1 - 24y_1 + 27 = 0$$

$\therefore$ Locus of mid-point is $x^2 + y^2 + 4x - 6y + \frac{27}{4} = 0$

$\Rightarrow \quad (x+2)^2 + (y-3)^2 = 6.25$

20. $\because r = a\cos\theta + b\sin\theta$

$\Rightarrow \quad r^2 = a(r\cos\theta) + b(r\sin\theta)$

or $\quad x^2 + y^2 = ax + by \quad [\because x = r\cos\theta, y = r\sin\theta]$

or $\quad x^2 + y^2 - ax - by = 0 \quad \text{...(i)}$

Circle pass through O (origin)

given $\quad \angle AOB = 90°$

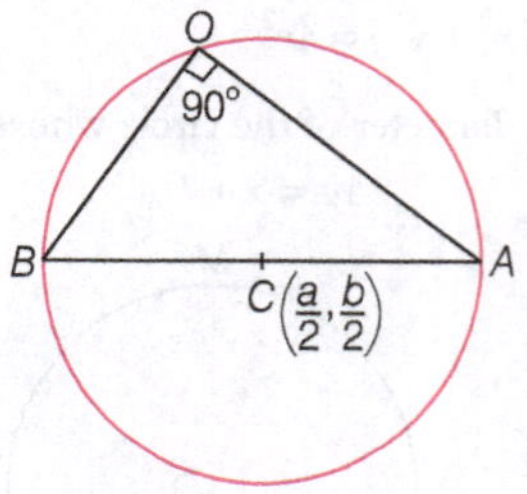

$\therefore$ AB is diameter of circle Eq. (i), Centre is $\left(\frac{a}{2}, \frac{b}{2}\right)$

$\therefore$ Locus of mid-point AB [$\because$ mid-point of AB is C]

$$x = \frac{a}{2} \text{ and } y = \frac{b}{2}$$

21. Slope of $PC = \frac{-3-2}{2-7} = 1$

If $\quad \tan\theta = 1$

$\therefore \quad \theta = 45°$

Equation of PA is $\dfrac{x-7}{\frac{1}{\sqrt{2}}}=\dfrac{y-2}{\frac{1}{\sqrt{2}}}=r$

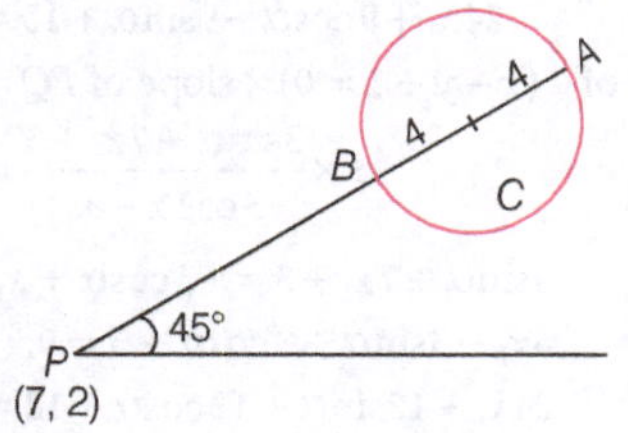

$\therefore \quad \left(7+\dfrac{r}{\sqrt{2}}, 2+\dfrac{r}{\sqrt{2}}\right)$ lie on circle,

then $\left(7+\dfrac{r}{\sqrt{2}}\right)^2+\left(2+\dfrac{r}{\sqrt{2}}\right)^2-4\left(7+\dfrac{r}{\sqrt{2}}\right)+6\left(2+\dfrac{r}{\sqrt{2}}\right)-3=0$

$\therefore \quad r^2=-5\sqrt{2}\pm 4$

$\therefore \quad r=-5\sqrt{2}\pm 4$

$\therefore$ Points $\left(7+\dfrac{-5\sqrt{2}\pm 4}{\sqrt{2}}, 2+\dfrac{-5\sqrt{2}\pm 4}{\sqrt{2}}\right)$

$\Rightarrow (2\pm 2\sqrt{2}, -3\pm 2\sqrt{2})$

Taking + ve sign for A, –ve sign for B.

22. Let $S\equiv x^2+y^2+2gx+2fy+c=0$

$$S_1\equiv x^2+y^2-4=0$$
$$S_2\equiv x^2+y^2-6x-8y+10=0$$
$$S_3\equiv x^2+y^2+2x-4y-2=0$$

$\therefore$ Common chords are

$$S-S_1\equiv 2gx+2fy+c+4=0 \quad \text{...(i)}$$
$$S-S_2\equiv (2g+6)x+(2f+8)y+c-10=0 \quad \text{...(ii)}$$
$$S-S_3\equiv (2g-2)x+(2f+4)y+c+2=0 \quad \text{...(iii)}$$

For cutting the extremities of diameter, chords Eqs. (i), (ii) and (iii) pass through the centres of S_1, S_2 and S_3 respectively, then

$\therefore \quad c+4=0, (2g+6)3+(2f+8)4+c-10=0$

and $(2g-2)(-1)+(2f+4)(2)+c+2=0$

after solving $c=-4$, $g=-2$, $f=-3$

23.

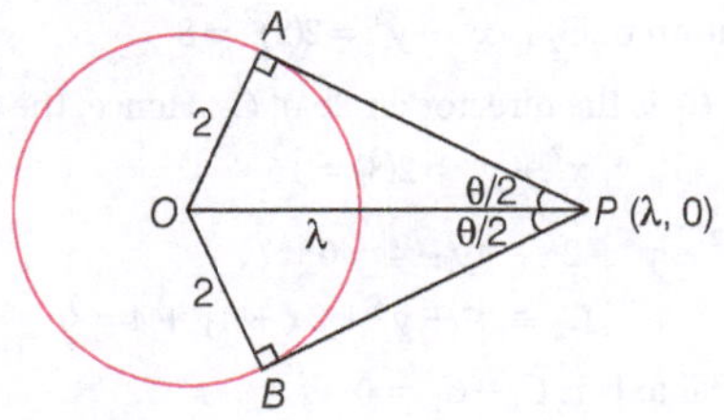

$\because \quad \dfrac{\pi}{2}<\theta<\dfrac{2\pi}{3} \Rightarrow \dfrac{\pi}{4}<\dfrac{\theta}{2}<\dfrac{\pi}{3}$

$\Rightarrow \quad \dfrac{1}{\sqrt{2}}<\sin\left(\dfrac{\theta}{2}\right)<\dfrac{\sqrt{3}}{2}$

$\Rightarrow \quad \dfrac{1}{\sqrt{2}}<\dfrac{2}{\lambda}<\dfrac{\sqrt{3}}{2}$

or $\quad \sqrt{2}>\dfrac{\lambda}{2}>\dfrac{2}{\sqrt{3}}$

or $\quad 2\sqrt{2}>\lambda>\dfrac{4}{\sqrt{3}}$ or $\dfrac{4}{\sqrt{3}}<\lambda<2\sqrt{2}$

24. It is clear that N is the mid-point of M and P.

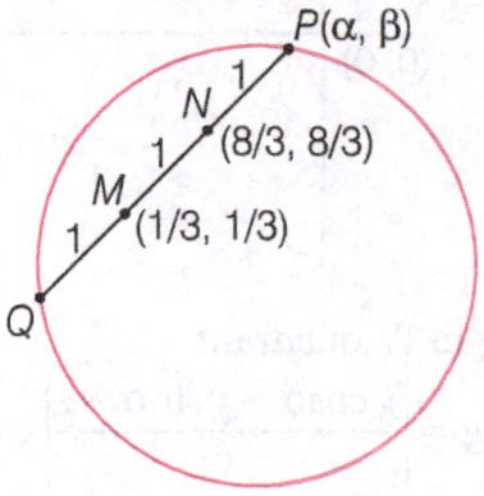

$\therefore \quad \alpha=\dfrac{16}{3}-\dfrac{1}{3}=5$

and $\quad \beta=\dfrac{16}{3}-\dfrac{1}{3}=5$

$(\alpha,\beta)\equiv(5,5)$ lie on the circle

$\therefore \quad 5^2+5^2-4\times 5-2\times 5-c=0$

$$c=20$$

or $\quad c^2-40c+400=0$

25. Let $M(\alpha,\beta)$

$\because \quad AM=2AB \Rightarrow AB+BM=2AB$

$\therefore \quad AB=BM$

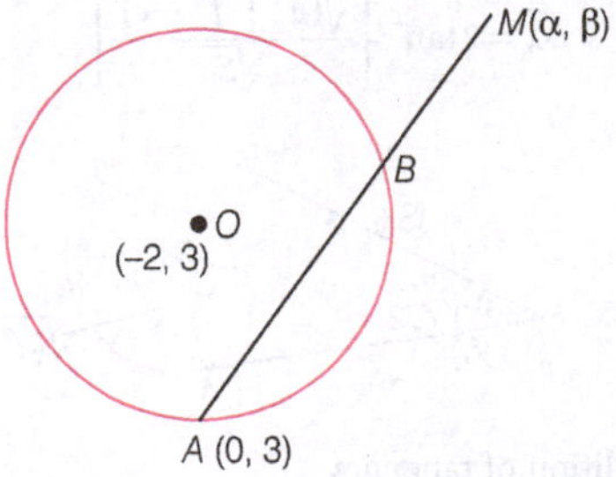

$\therefore B$ is the mid point of AM.

$\therefore$ Coordinates of B are $\left(\dfrac{\alpha}{2}, \dfrac{3+\beta}{2}\right)$ which lies on

$$x^2+4x+(y-3)^2=0$$

$$\frac{\alpha^2}{4}+4\times\frac{\alpha}{2}+\left(\frac{3+\beta}{2}-3\right)^2=0$$

$$\alpha^2+8\alpha+(\beta-3)^2=0$$

$\therefore$ Requires locus is

$$x^2+8x+(y-3)^2=0$$

or $\quad x^2+y^2+8x-6y+9=0$

26. $x\cos\alpha+y\sin\alpha=2$ or $\dfrac{x}{2\sec\alpha}+\dfrac{y}{2\ \text{cosec}\ \alpha}=1$

$2\sec\alpha = +$ ve in IV

and $\quad 2\ \text{cosec}\ \alpha = -$ ve in IV

value of g in I quadrant

$$g=\left(\frac{g\cos\alpha+g\sin\alpha-2}{\sqrt{1}}\right)$$

$\therefore \quad g = \dfrac{2}{\cos\alpha + \sin\alpha \pm 1}$

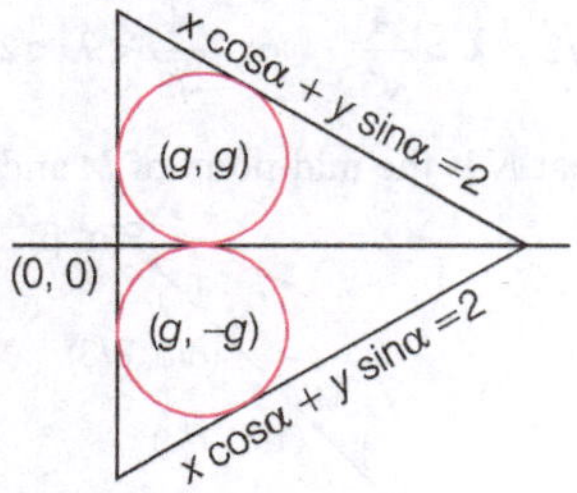

and value of g in IV quadrant

$$g = \left|\frac{g\cos\alpha - g\sin\alpha - 2}{1}\right|$$

$$\Rightarrow \quad \pm g = g(\cos\alpha - \sin\alpha) - 2$$

$$g = \frac{2}{\cos\alpha - \sin\alpha \pm 1}$$

Equation of circles in I quadrant

$$(x-g)^2 + (y-g)^2 = g^2$$

and in IV quadrant is $(x-g)^2 + (y-g)^2 = g^2$

27. Since, $\cot\left(\dfrac{\alpha}{2}\right) = \dfrac{\sqrt{S_1}}{\sqrt{(g^2+f^2-c)}}$

$$\therefore \quad \tan\left(\frac{\alpha}{2}\right) = \frac{\sqrt{(g^2+f^2-c)}}{\sqrt{S_1}}$$

$$\therefore \quad \alpha = 2\tan^{-1}\left(\frac{\sqrt{(g^2+f^2-c)}}{\sqrt{S_1}}\right)$$

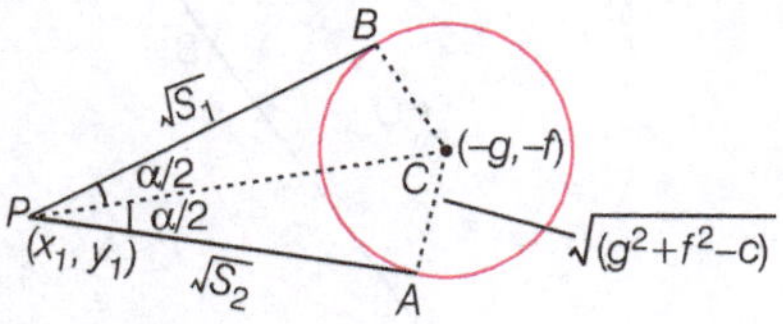

28. For condition of tangency

$$\frac{|4\lambda + 3\lambda - 12|}{5} = \lambda \Rightarrow 7\lambda - 12 = \pm 5\lambda$$

$$\therefore \quad \lambda = 1, 6$$

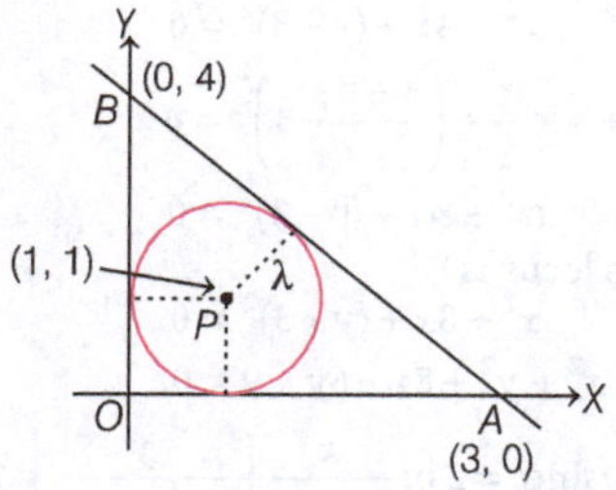

29. Let coordinates of $P \equiv (3\cos\alpha, 3\sin\alpha)$

Let x-coordinate of Q is x_1, then

y-coordinate of Q is $-7x_1 - 3$

$$\therefore \quad Q \equiv (x_1, -7x_1 - 3)$$

$\because x - y + 1 = 0$ is the perpendicular bisector of PQ, then mid-point of PQ lies on $x - y + 1 = 0$

$$\Rightarrow \quad \frac{3\cos\alpha + x_1}{2} - \frac{3\sin\alpha - 7x_1 - 3}{2} + 1 = 0$$

$$\Rightarrow \quad 8x_1 + 3\cos\alpha - 3\sin\alpha + 5 = 0$$

$$\Rightarrow \quad 24x_1 + 9\cos\alpha - 9\sin\alpha + 15 = 0 \quad \text{...(i)}$$

and slope of $(x - y + 1 = 0) \times$ slope of $PQ = -1$

$$\Rightarrow \quad 1 \times \frac{3\sin\alpha + 7x_1 + 3}{3\cos\alpha - x_1} = -1$$

$$\Rightarrow \quad 3\sin\alpha + 7x_1 + 3 = -3\cos\alpha + x_1$$

$$\Rightarrow \quad 6x_1 + 3\sin\alpha + 3\cos\alpha + 3 = 0$$

$$\Rightarrow \quad 24x_1 + 12\sin\alpha + 12\cos\alpha + 12 = 0 \quad \text{...(ii)}$$

On subtracting Eq. (i) from Eq. (ii), we obtain

$$-3\cos\alpha - 21\sin\alpha + 3 = 0$$

$$\Rightarrow \quad (1 - \cos\alpha) = 7\sin\alpha$$

$$\Rightarrow \quad (1-\cos\alpha)^2 = 49(1 - \cos^2\alpha)$$

$$\Rightarrow \quad (1-\cos\alpha)^2 = 49(1+\cos\alpha)(1-\cos\alpha)$$

$$\Rightarrow \quad (1-\cos\alpha)(1 - \cos\alpha - 49 - 49\cos\alpha) = 0$$

$$\therefore \quad \cos\alpha = 1 \text{ and } \cos\alpha = -\frac{24}{25}$$

$\therefore$ Coordinates of P are $(3, 0)$ and $\left(-\dfrac{72}{25}, \dfrac{21}{25}\right)$.

30. Circle possible in I region and centre of circle on X-axis.

If centre is $(h, 0)$, then

$$\frac{|h - 0 - 1|}{\sqrt{2}} = \sqrt{(h-3)^3 + \frac{7}{2}}$$

$$\therefore \quad h = 6, 4$$

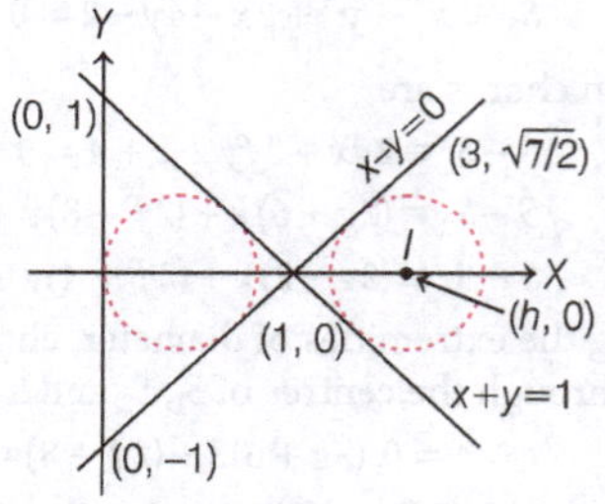

Then, centres are $(6, 0)$ and $(4, 0)$

31. $\because C_2$ is the director circle of C_1

$\therefore$ Equation of C_2 is $x^2 + y^2 = 2(2)^2 = 8$

Again, C_3 is the director circle of C_2. Hence, the equation of C_3 is

$$x^2 + y^2 = 2(8) = 16$$

32. $C_1 \equiv x^2 + y^2 - 2x - 4y - 4 = 0 \quad \text{...(i)}$

and $\quad C_2 \equiv x^2 + y^2 + 2x + 4y + 4 = 0 \quad \text{...(ii)}$

$\therefore$ Radical axis is $C_1 - C_2 = 0$

$$\Rightarrow \quad -4x - 8y - 8 = 0$$

or $x + 2y + 2 = 0$ which is $L = 0$

(a) Option is correct.

Centre and radius of $C_1 = 0$ are $(1, 2)$ and 3.

$\because$ Length of $\perp$ from $(1, 2)$ on $L = 0$

is $\dfrac{|1 + 4 + 2|}{\sqrt{1+4}} = \dfrac{7}{\sqrt{5}} \neq$ radius

$\therefore$ **(b) Option is wrong.**

L is also the common chord of C_1 and C_2.

$\therefore$ **(c) Option is correct.**

$\because$ Centres of $C_1 = 0$ and $C_2 = 0$ are (1, 2) and $(-1,-2)$

$\therefore$ Slope of Line joining centres of circles $C_1 = 0$ and $C_2 = 0$ is

$$\frac{-2-2}{-1-1} = \frac{4}{2} = 2 = m_1 \quad \text{(say)}$$

and $\quad$ slope of $L = 0$ is $-\frac{1}{2} = m_2 \quad$ (say)

$\therefore \quad m_1 m_2 = -1$

Hence, L is perpendicular to the line joining centres of C_1 and C_2.

$\therefore$ **(d) Option is correct.**

33. Let slope of OA be m.

Then, $\quad \left|\frac{m-1}{1+m}\right| = \tan 45°$

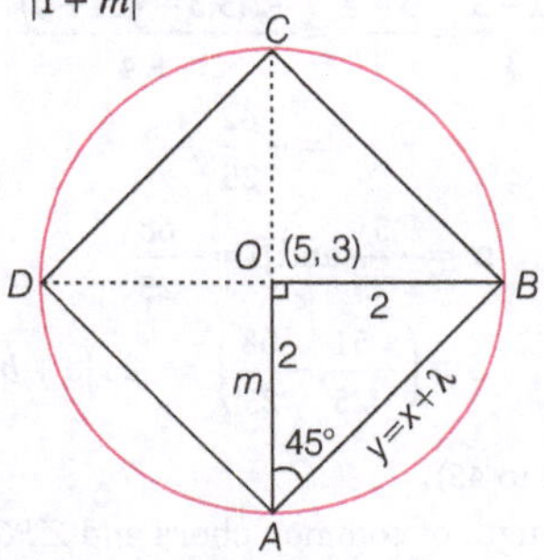

$\Rightarrow \quad \frac{m-1}{1+m} = \pm 1$ or $\frac{m-1}{m+1} = -1 \Rightarrow m-1 = -m-1$

$\therefore \quad m = 0$

$\therefore$ Equation of OA is $y = 3$

Solving $y = 3$ and $x^2 + y^2 - 10x - 6y + 30 = 0$

$\Rightarrow \quad x^2 + 9 - 10x - 18 + 30 = 0$

$\Rightarrow \quad x^2 - 10x + 21 = 0$

$\Rightarrow \quad (x-7)(x-3) = 0$ or $x = 3, 7$

$\therefore$ Two vertices are (3, 3) and (7, 3) and other diagonal is $\perp$ to $y = 3$ and through centre (5, 3) is $x = 5$.

Now, solving $x = 5$ and $x^2 + y^2 - 10x - 6y + 30 = 0$

$\Rightarrow \quad 25 + y^2 - 50 - 6y + 30 = 0$

$\Rightarrow \quad y^2 - 6y + 5 = 0$

$\Rightarrow \quad (y-1)(y-5) = 0$ or $y = 1, 5$

$\therefore$ Other two vertices are (5, 1) and (5, 5).

Sol. (Q. Nos. 34 to 35)

$S : x^2 + y^2 - 4x - 1 = 0 \quad$ ...(i)

$L : y = 3x - 1 \quad$ ...(ii)

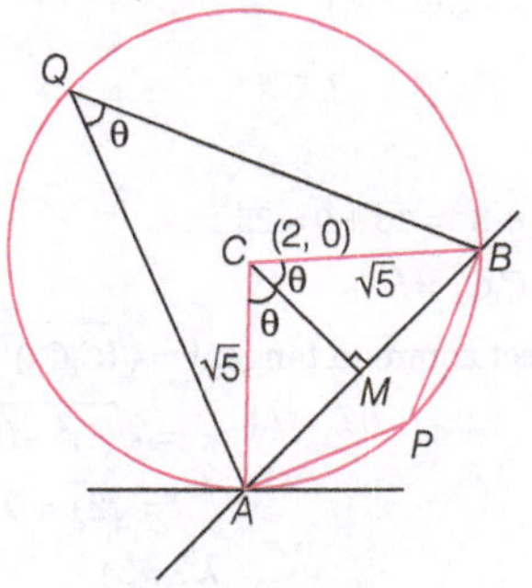

From Eqs. (i) and (ii), we get

$$x^2 + (3x-1)^2 - 4x - 1 = 0 \text{ or } 10x^2 - 10x = 0$$

$\therefore \quad x = 0$ and $x = 1$

From Eq. (ii), $y = -1$ and $y = 2$

$\therefore \quad A \equiv (0, -1)$ and $B \equiv (1, 2)$

34. $AB = \sqrt{(0-1)^2 + (-1-2)^2} = \sqrt{10}$

35. Let $\angle ACB = 2\theta$

$\therefore \quad CM = \frac{5}{\sqrt{10}} = \sqrt{\frac{5}{2}}$

$\Rightarrow \quad \cos\theta = \frac{CM}{\sqrt{5}} = \frac{1}{\sqrt{2}}$

$\therefore \quad \theta = \frac{\pi}{4}$

Required angle $= \angle APB = \pi - \theta = \pi - \frac{\pi}{4} = \frac{3\pi}{4}$

Sol. (Q. Nos. 36 to 37)

36. This is third degree equation which satisfy the point of intersection of $L_1 = 0$, $L_2 = 0$ and $L_3 = 0$.

37. $\lambda L_1 L_2 + \mu L_3 L_4 = 0$ will always pass through the vertices of the parallelogram for all $\lambda, \mu \in R \sim \{0\}$

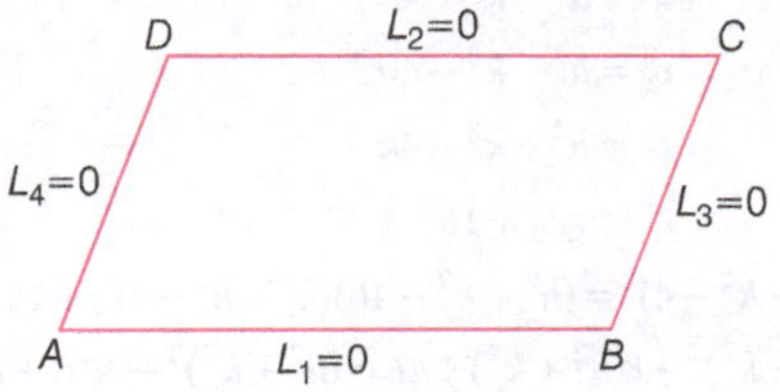

Sol. (Q. Nos. 38 to 39)

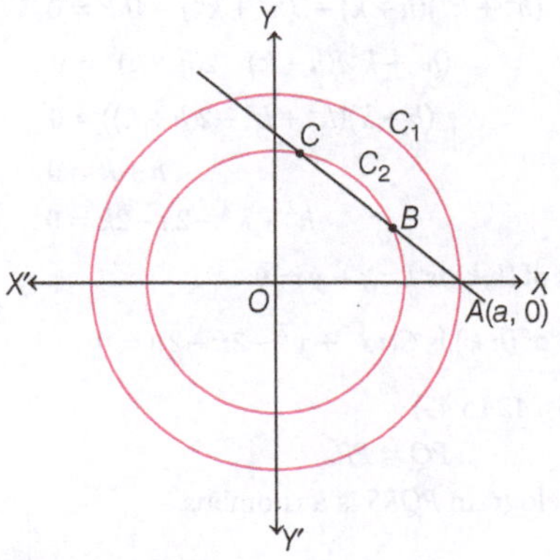

Let equation of line AB be

$$\frac{x-a}{\cos\theta} = \frac{y-0}{\sin\theta} = r$$

Coordinates of any point on the line AB is $(a + r\cos\theta, r\sin\theta)$, then

$$B \equiv (a + r_1\cos\theta, r_1\sin\theta) \text{ and } C \equiv (a + r_2\cos\theta, r_2\sin\theta)$$

38. $\lambda = (OA)^2 + (OB)^2 + (BC)^2$

$= a^2 + b^2 + (r_1 - r_2)^2\cos^2\theta + (r_1 - r_2)^2\sin^2\theta$

$= (a^2 + b^2) + (r_1 - r_2)^2$

$= (a^2 + b^2) + 4a^2\cos^2\theta - 4(a^2 - b^2)$

$\because$ B and C lie on $x^2 + y^2 = b^2$

$\therefore \quad (a + r\cos\theta)^2 + (r\sin\theta)^2 = b^2$

or $\quad r^2 + 2ar\cos\theta + a^2 - b^2 = 0$

$\therefore \quad r_1 - r_2 = \sqrt{4a^2\cos^2\theta - 4(a^2 - b^2)}$

$\Rightarrow \quad \lambda = 5b^2 - 3a^2 + 4a^2\cos^2\theta$

$\because \quad 0 \le \cos^2\theta \le 1$

$\therefore \quad \lambda \in [5b^2 - 3a^2, 5b^2 + a^2]$

39. Let (h,k) be the mid-point of AB and let (α,β) be the coordinates of B, then

$$\frac{a+\alpha}{2} = h \text{ and } \frac{0+\beta}{2} = k$$

$\Rightarrow \quad \alpha = 2h - a$ and $\beta = 2k$

Since, (α,β) lies on $x^2 + y^2 = b^2$

$$\Rightarrow \quad (2h-a)^2 + (2k)^2 = b^2 \text{ or } \left(h - \frac{a}{2}\right)^2 + k^2 = \frac{b^2}{4}$$

Hence, locus of (h,k) is $\left(x - \frac{a}{2}\right)^2 + y^2 = \frac{b^2}{4}$

Sol. (Q. Nos. 40 to 41)

Here, $\quad t_1^2 = h^2 + k^2 - 4,$

$t_2^2 = h^2 + k^2 - 4h,$

$t_3^2 = h^2 + k^2 - 4k$

given $\quad t_1^4 = t_2^2 t_3^2 + 16$

or $\quad (h^2 + k^2 - 4)^2 = (h^2 + k^2 - 4h)(h^2 + k^2 - 4k) + 16$

or $\quad (h^2 + k^2)^2 - 8(h^2 + k^2) + 16 = (h^2 + k^2)^2 - 4(h^2 + k^2)(h + k) + 16hk + 16$

or $\quad (h^2 + k^2)(h + k) - 2(h^2 + k^2) - 4hk = 0$

or $\quad (h^2 + k^2)(h + k) - 2(h + k)^2 = 0$

or $\quad (h + k)(h^2 + k^2 - 2(h + k)) = 0$

or $\quad h + k = 0 \quad$ ...(i)

and $\quad h^2 + k^2 - 2h - 2k = 0 \quad$ ...(ii)

40. Locus of (h,k) is $L_1 : x + y = 0$ [from Eq. (i)]

41. Locus of (h,k) is $C_1 : x^2 + y^2 - 2x - 2y = 0$ [from Eq. (ii)]

Sol. (Q. Nos. 42 to 43)

$\because \quad PQ = PR,$

parallelogram $PQRS$ is a rhombus.

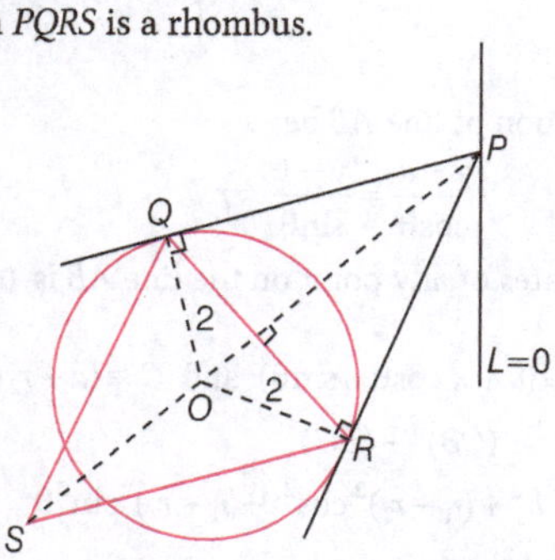

$\therefore$ Mid-point of QR = mid point of PS and $QR \perp PS$

Therefore, S in the mirror image of P w.r.t. QR.

42. Area of ΔQRS = Area of $\Delta PQR = \dfrac{RL^3}{R^2 + L^2}$ ...(i)

Here, $\quad R = 2, L = \sqrt{S_1} = \sqrt{(6^2 + 8^2 - 4)} = \sqrt{96}$

From Eq. (i),

Area of $\Delta QRS = \dfrac{2 \times 96 \times \sqrt{96}}{4 + 96} = \dfrac{192\sqrt{6}}{25}$

$= \dfrac{192\sqrt{\lambda}}{25}$ [given]

$\therefore \quad \lambda = 6$

43. Let $S \equiv (\alpha,\beta)$

$\because S$ is the mirror image of P w.r.t. QR.

Eq. (i) of QR is $3x + 4y = 4$, then

$$\frac{\alpha - 3}{3} = \frac{\beta - 4}{4} = \frac{-2(3.3 + 4.4 - 4)}{3^2 + 4^2} = -\frac{42}{25}$$

$\therefore \quad \alpha = -\dfrac{51}{25}$ and $\beta = -\dfrac{68}{25}$

Hence, $\quad S \equiv \left(-\dfrac{51}{25}, -\dfrac{68}{25}\right) \Rightarrow 25|a + b| = 119$

Sol. (Q. Nos. 44 to 45)

Let $2d$ = length of common chord and $\angle PC_1C_2 = \phi$, then

$\sin\phi = \dfrac{d}{3}$

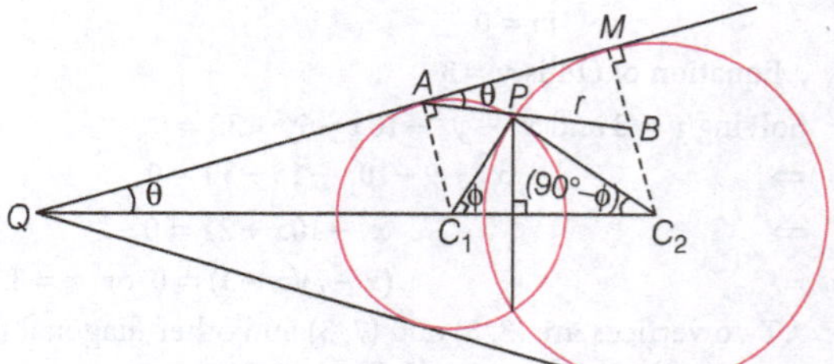

and $\sin(90° - \phi) = \dfrac{d}{r}$ or $\cos\phi = \dfrac{d}{r}$

$$1 = \frac{d^2}{9} + \frac{d^2}{r^2}$$

$\Rightarrow \quad d = \dfrac{3r}{\sqrt{9 + r^2}} = \dfrac{1}{2}\left(\dfrac{24}{5}\right)$ [given]

$\Rightarrow \quad \dfrac{r}{\sqrt{(9 - r^2)}} = \dfrac{4}{5}$

$\therefore \quad r = 4$

44. $\lambda = r = 4$

45. $\because (C_1C_2)^2 = r^2 + 3^2 = 16 + 9 = 25$

$\therefore \quad C_1C_2 = 5$

Length of direct common tangent $= \sqrt{(C_1C_2)^2 - (r-3)^2}$

$= \sqrt{(5)^2 - (1)^2}$

$= \sqrt{24} = \lambda$ [given]

$\therefore \quad \lambda^2 = 24$

Sol. (Q. Nos. 46 to 47)

46. From the figure $OA = OB = AB = a$

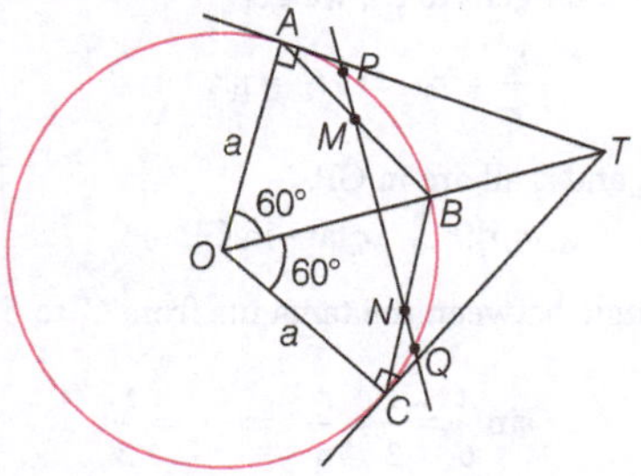

$\therefore \quad \angle OAB = 60°$

47. Let T be the point of intersection of tangents.

$\because \quad \angle AOC = 120°$

$\therefore \quad \angle ATC = 180° - 120° = 60°$

48. Let the given lines are represented by L_1, L_2, L_3 and L_4, then

$$L_1 \equiv 2x + 3y - 2 = 0 \qquad L_2 \equiv 3x - 2y - 3 = 0$$
$$L_3 \equiv x + 2y - 3 = 0 \qquad L_4 \equiv 2x - y - 1 = 0$$

Equation of second degree conic circumscribing a quadrilateral whose sides are $L_1 = 0, L_2 = 0, L_3 = 0$ and $L_4 = 0$ is

$$L_1L_3 + kL_2L_4 = 0$$

or $(2x + 3y - 2)(x + 2y - 3) + k(3x - 2y - 3)(2x - y - 1) = 0$ ...(i)

For circle, coefficient of x^2 = coefficient of y^2

or $\quad 2 + 6k = 6 + 2k$

$\therefore \quad k = 1$

From Eq. (i), required circle is

$$8x^2 + 8y^2 - 17x - 8y + 9 = 0$$

or $\quad x^2 + y^2 - \left(\frac{17}{8}\right)x - y + \left(\frac{9}{8}\right) = 0$

Here, $\quad \lambda = -\frac{17}{8}, \mu = -1, \nu = \frac{9}{8}$

Then, $\quad |\lambda + 2\mu + \nu| = 3$

49. Let radius of given circle is a.

$\therefore \quad a = \sqrt{(4 + 2 - c)} = \sqrt{(6 - c)}$ ...(i)

Now, radius of circle $C_1 = \frac{a}{\sqrt{2}}$ and radius of circle $C_2 = \frac{a}{(\sqrt{2})^2}$ and so on.

Also, $\quad a + \frac{a}{\sqrt{2}} + \frac{a}{(\sqrt{2})^2} + \ldots \infty = 2$ [given]

Then, $\quad \frac{a}{1 - \frac{1}{\sqrt{2}}} = 2$

or $\quad a = 2 - \sqrt{2} = \sqrt{6 - c}$ [from Eq. (i)]

or $\quad 4 + 2 - 4\sqrt{2} = 6 - c$

$\therefore \quad c = 4\sqrt{2}$

Hence, $\lambda = 4$

50. The rays are given as $2x^2 - 3xy - 2y^2 = 0$ i.e.

$(2x + y)(x - 2y) = 0$

$\Rightarrow y = \frac{x}{2}$ or $y = -2x$ which are perpendicular.

$\therefore$ Required area

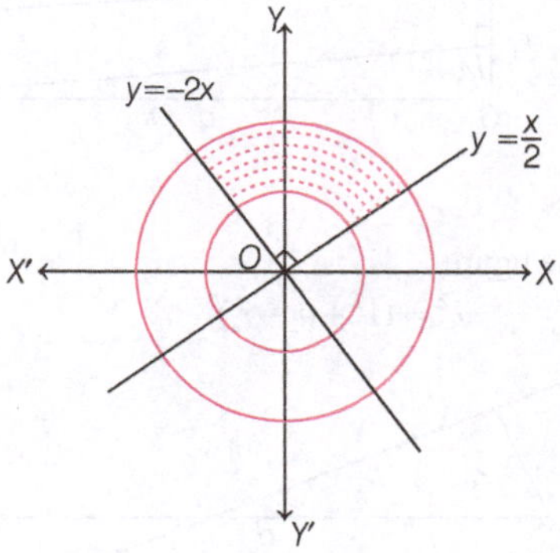

$$= \frac{1}{4}(\pi(2)^2 - \pi(1)^2) = \frac{3\pi}{4} = \frac{\lambda\pi}{4} \quad \text{[given]}$$

$\therefore \quad \lambda = 3$

51. Let radii of circles be r_1 and r_2 and distance between centres be d. Then,

$$\sqrt{d^2 - (r_1 + r_2)^2} = 5 \quad \text{...(i)}$$

and $\quad \sqrt{d^2 - (r_1 - r_2)^2} = 13$ ...(ii)

From Eqs. (i) and (ii), we get

$$(r_1 + r_2)^2 - (r_1 - r_2)^2 = (13)^2 - (5)^2$$

$\Rightarrow \quad 4r_1r_2 = 144$ or $\lambda = 36$ $\quad [\because r_1r_2 = \lambda]$

$\therefore \quad \frac{\lambda}{4} = 9$

52. Let $ax + by = 1$ be a chord PQ. ...(i)

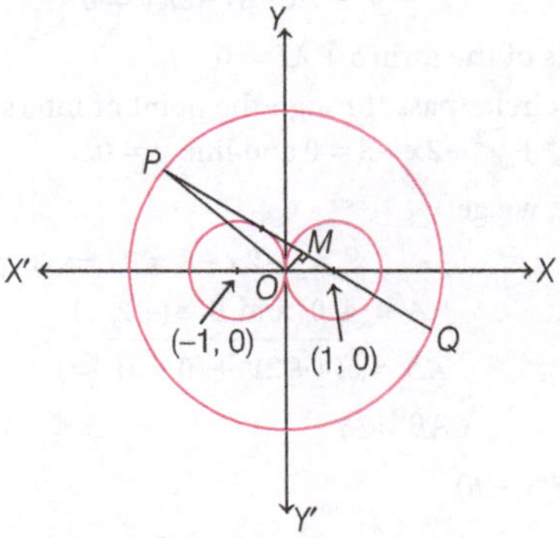

which pass through (1, 0), then $a + 0 = 1$

$\therefore \quad a = 1$

and touch circle B with centre $(-1, 0)$ and radius 1, then

$$\frac{|-a + 0 - 1|}{\sqrt{a^2 + b^2}} = 1 \text{ or } a^2 + b^2 = (a + 1)^2 \text{ or } b^2 = 2a + 1 = 3$$

$\therefore \quad b = \sqrt{3}$

From Eq. (i), equation of chord is $x + \sqrt{3}\,y = 4$

$\therefore \quad OM = \frac{1}{2}$ and $OP = 4$

$$\therefore PQ = 2PM = 2\sqrt{(OP)^2 - (OM)^2} = 2\sqrt{\left(16 - \frac{1}{4}\right)} = \sqrt{63} = \sqrt{\lambda}$$

$\therefore \quad \lambda = 63$

Hence, $\quad \frac{\lambda}{9} = 7$

53.

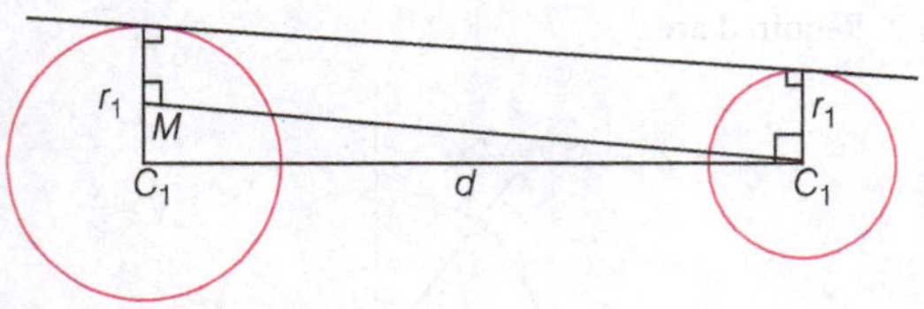

From the figure,

$$d^2 = 11^2 + (r_1 - r_2)^3 \quad \text{...(i)}$$

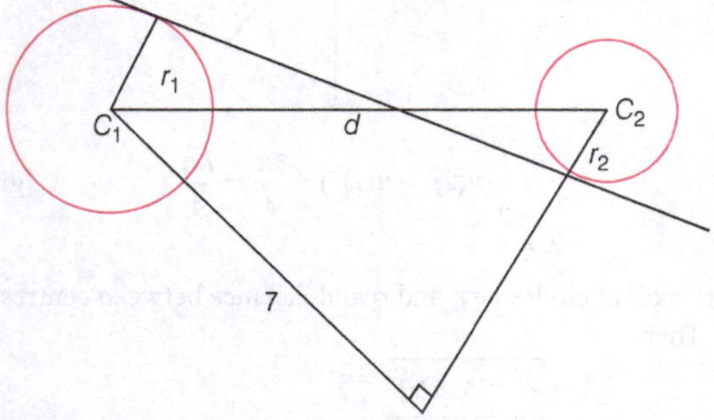

From the figure,

$$d^2 = 7^2 + (r_1 + r_2)^2 \quad \text{...(ii)}$$

From Eqs. (i) and (ii), we get

$$4r_1r_2 = 72 \Rightarrow r_1r_2 = 18$$

54. We have,

$$x^2 + y^2 - 2x - 2\lambda y - 8 = 0$$

$$\Rightarrow \quad (x^2 + y^2 - 2x - 8) - 2\lambda y = 0$$

which is of the form $S + \lambda L = 0$

All the circles pass through the point of intersection of the circle $x^2 + y^2 - 2x - 8 = 0$ and line $y = 0$.

Solving, we get

$$x^2 - 2x - 8 = 0 \Rightarrow x = 4, 2$$

$$\therefore \quad A \equiv (4, 0) \text{ and } B \equiv (-2, 0)$$

So, $\quad AB = \sqrt{(4+2)^2 + (0-0)^2} = 6$

$$\therefore \quad 6AB = 36$$

55. Given $P(3, -6)$

and $\quad S = x^2 + y^2 - 16x - 12y - 125 = 0$

$$S_1 = 9 + 36 - 48 + 72 - 125 < 0$$

$\because$ P inside the circle radius $r = \sqrt{64 + 36 + 125} = 15$

Centre $C \equiv (8, 6)$

$\because$ Shortest distance $L = r - \text{CP}$

$$= 15 - \sqrt{(8-3)^2 + (6+6)^2} = 15 - 13 = 2$$

and largest distance $M = r + \text{CP}$

$$= 15 + 13 = 28$$

$\therefore \quad \text{L} + \text{M} = 2 + 28 = 30$

56. Consider three concentric circles C_1, C_2, C_3 with radii r_1, r_2, r_3.

Let $C_1 \equiv x^2 + y^2 = r_1^2$

$$C_2 \equiv x^2 + y^2 = r_2^2$$

$$C_3 \equiv x^2 + y^2 = r_3^2$$

Equation of chord of contact of tangent from $P(x_1, y_1)$ to C_2 is $xx_1 + yy_1 - r_2^2 = 0$.

If this is a tangent to C_3, we get

$$\frac{r_2^2}{r_1} = r_3 \Rightarrow r_2^2 = r_1r_3$$

$\Rightarrow$ r_1, r_2 and r_3 all are in GP.

$\Rightarrow \quad r_1, r_2, r_3, \ldots r_n$ are in GP.

Also, angle between the tangents from C_1 to C_2 is $\frac{\pi}{3}$.

$$\Rightarrow \quad \sin\frac{\pi}{6} = \frac{1}{2} = \frac{r_2}{r_1} \Rightarrow r_2 = \frac{r_1}{2}$$

$$\Rightarrow \quad \lim_{n \to \infty} \sum_{i=1}^{n} r_i = r_1 + r_2 + \ldots \infty$$

$$= 10 + \frac{10}{2} + \frac{10}{2^2} + \ldots \infty = 10\left(1 + \frac{1}{2} + \frac{1}{2^2} + \ldots \infty\right)$$

$$= 10\left(\frac{1}{1 - \frac{1}{2}}\right) = 20$$

57. $\because \quad S_1 : (x-2)^2 + (y-3)^2 = 1$

Centre $C_1 : (2,3)$ and radius $r_1 : 1$ and $S_2 : (x-5)^2 + (y-6)^2 = r^2$

Centre $C_2 : (5,6)$ and radius $r_2 : r$

$$\Rightarrow \quad C_1C_2 = 3\sqrt{2}$$

(A) $\because$ S_1 and S_2 touch internally, then

$$C_1C_2 = r_2 - r_1$$

or $\quad 3\sqrt{2} = r - 1$

or $\quad (r-1)^2 = 18$

(B) $\because$ S_1 and S_2 touch externally, then

$$C_1C_2 = r_2 + r_1$$

or $\quad 3\sqrt{2} = r + 1$

or $\quad r^2 + 2r + 3 = (r+1)^2 + 2 = 18 + 2 = 20$

(C) $\because$ S_1 and S_2 intersect orthogonally, then

$$(C_1C_2)^2 = r_1^2 + r_2^2$$

$$\Rightarrow \quad 18 = r^2 + 1$$

or $\quad r^2 - 1 = 16$

(D) $\because$ S_1 and S_2 intersect, the common chord is $S_1 - S_2 = 0$

i.e. $\quad 6x + 6y + r^2 - 49 = 0$

Given, common chord is longest, then passes through (2, 3)

$$\Rightarrow \quad 12 + 18 + r^2 - 49 = 0$$

or $\quad r^2 = 19$

$$\therefore \quad r^2 + 5 = 24$$

58. **(A)** Since, (2, 3) lies on $ax + by - 5 = 0$

$$\therefore \quad 2a + 3b - 5 = 0 \quad \text{...(i)}$$

Since, line is at greatest distance from centre

$$\Rightarrow \quad \left(\frac{4-3}{3-2}\right)\left(-\frac{a}{b}\right) = -1 \text{ i.e. } a = b$$

From Eq. (i), $a = b = 1$

$$\therefore \quad a + b = 2 \text{ and } a^2 + b^2 = 2$$

(B) Let P be the point (h, k), then $h^2 + k^2 + 2h + 2k = 0$ ...(i)

mid-point of OP is $\left(\frac{h}{2}, \frac{k}{2}\right)$

Let $x = \frac{h}{2}, y = \frac{k}{2}$

or $h = 2x, k = 2y$

From Eq. (i), $4x^2 + 4y^2 + 4x + 4y = 0$

or $x^2 + y^2 + x + y = 0$

On comparing, we get

$2a = 1, 2b = 1$

or $a = b = \frac{1}{2}$

$\therefore$ $a + b = 1$

(C) Centre of circles are $C_1:(1, 2)$ and $C_2:(5, -6)$

Equation of C_1C_2 is $y - 2 = \frac{-6-2}{5-1}(x - 1)$

or $2x + y - 4 = 0$ ...(i)

Equation of radical axis is $8x - 16y - 56 = 0$

or $x - 2y - 7 = 0$ ...(ii)

Point of intersection of Eqs. (i) and (ii) are (3, –2)

$\therefore$ $a = 3, b = -2$

or $a + b = 1$

(D) Let $S \equiv x^2 + y^2 - 6\sqrt{3}x - 6y + 27 = 0$

$S_1 = 0^2 + 0^2 - 0 - 0 + 27 = 27$

$T = 0.x + 0.y - 3\sqrt{3}(x + 0) - 3(y + 0) + 27$

$= -3\sqrt{3}x - 3y + 27$

Equation of the pair of tangents is given by

$SS_1 = T^2$

$\Rightarrow$ $27(x^2 + y^2 - 6\sqrt{3}x - 6y + 27) = (-3\sqrt{3}x - 3y + 27)^2$

or $3(x^2 + y^2 - 6\sqrt{3}x - 6y + 27) = (\sqrt{3}x + y - 9)^2$

or $18y^2 - 18\sqrt{3}xy = 0$ or $18y(y - \sqrt{3}x) = 0$

the tangents are $y = 0, y = \sqrt{3}x$

$\therefore$ $a = 0, b = \sqrt{3}$

then, $a^2 + b^2 = 3$

59. According to the question,

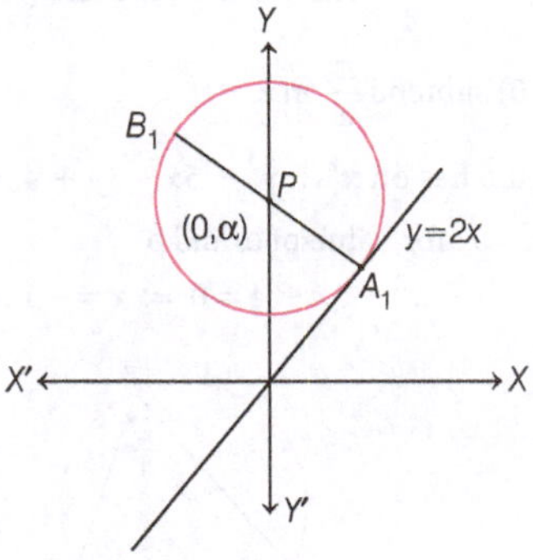

Consider centre as $P(0, \alpha), \alpha > 0$

$\Rightarrow$ $\left|\frac{2(0) - \alpha}{\sqrt{5}}\right| = r \Rightarrow |-\alpha| = \sqrt{5}\,r$

$\Rightarrow$ $\alpha = \sqrt{5}\,r$ ...(i)

Also, given $\alpha + r = 5 + \sqrt{5}$ ...(ii)

From Eq. (i), we get $\sqrt{5}r + r = 5 + \sqrt{5}$

$\Rightarrow$ $r(\sqrt{5} + 1) = \sqrt{5}(\sqrt{5} + 1)$

$\Rightarrow$ $r = \sqrt{5}$

$\Rightarrow$ $\alpha = 5$ [from Eq. (ii)]

$\therefore P(0, 5)$

Foot of perpendicular from P to line $2x - y = 0$

$\frac{x - 0}{2} = \frac{y - 5}{-1} = \frac{-(2(0) - 5)}{5} = 1$

$x = 2, y = 4$

$\Rightarrow$ $A_1 \equiv (2, 4)$

Let $B(p, q)$

$\therefore$ $\frac{p + 2}{2} = 0, \frac{q + 4}{2} = 5$

$\therefore$ $p = -2, q = 6 \Rightarrow B_1 \equiv (-2, 6)$

60. Let D and E be the mid-points of PQ and ST respectively.

$\therefore DE$ is radical axis of two circles.

$C_1 : x^2 + y^2 = 1$ ...(i)

$C_2 : (x - 4)^2 + (y - 1)^2 = r^2$

$\Rightarrow$ $x^2 + y^2 - 8x - 2y + 17 - r^2 = 0$ ...(ii)

From Eqs. (i) and (ii), we get

$8x + 2y - 18 + r^2 = 0 \rightarrow$ equation of DE

$B \equiv \left(\frac{18 - r^2}{8}, 0\right)$ [putting $y = 0$ to find x-coordinate]

and $AB = \sqrt{5}$

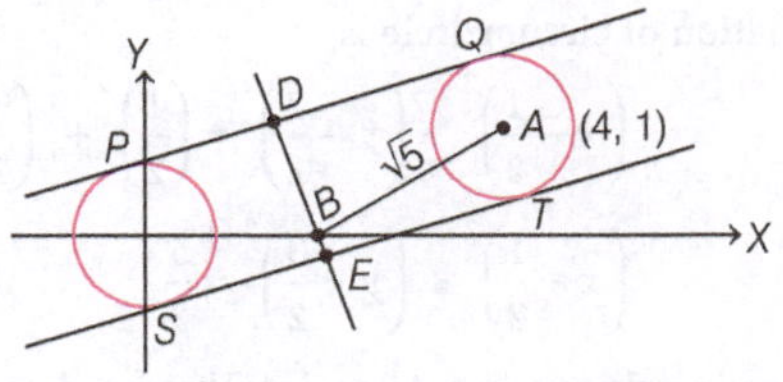

$\Rightarrow$ $\sqrt{\left(\frac{18 - r^2}{8} - 4\right)^2 + 1} = \sqrt{5} \Rightarrow \left(\frac{18 - r^2}{8} - 4\right)^2 + 1 = 5$

$\Rightarrow$ $\left(\frac{18 - r^2 - 32}{8}\right)^2 = 4 \Rightarrow r^2 = 2$

61. Refer to diagram,

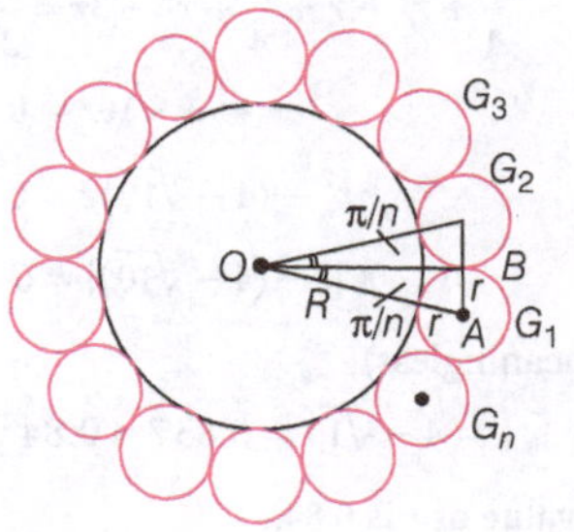

In ΔAOB, $\sin\left(\frac{\pi}{n}\right) = \frac{r}{R+r} \Rightarrow \text{cosec}\left(\frac{\pi}{n}\right) = \frac{R}{r} + 1$

$$\Rightarrow \quad R = r\left[\text{cosec}\left(\frac{\pi}{n}\right) - 1\right]$$

If $n = 4$, then $R = r(\sqrt{2} - 1)$

If $n = 5$, then $R = r\left(\text{cosec}\frac{\pi}{5} - 1\right)$

$$\because \quad \text{cosec}\frac{\pi}{5} < \text{cosec}\frac{\pi}{6}$$

$$\left(\text{cosec}\frac{\pi}{5} - 1\right) < 2 - 1 = 1; \qquad [\therefore R < r]$$

If $n = 8$, then $R = r\left(\text{cosec}\frac{\pi}{8} - 1\right)$

$$\therefore \quad \text{cosec}\frac{\pi}{8} > \text{cosec}\frac{\pi}{4}; \left(\text{cosec}\frac{\pi}{8} - 1\right) > \sqrt{2} - 1 \Rightarrow R > r(\sqrt{2} - 1)$$

If $n = 12$, then $R = r\left(\text{cosec}\frac{\pi}{12} - 1\right)$

$$R = r(\sqrt{2}(\sqrt{3}+1) - 1) \Rightarrow R < \sqrt{2}(\sqrt{3}+1)r$$

62. Let A be the origin B on X-axis, C on Y-axis are shown below the figure.

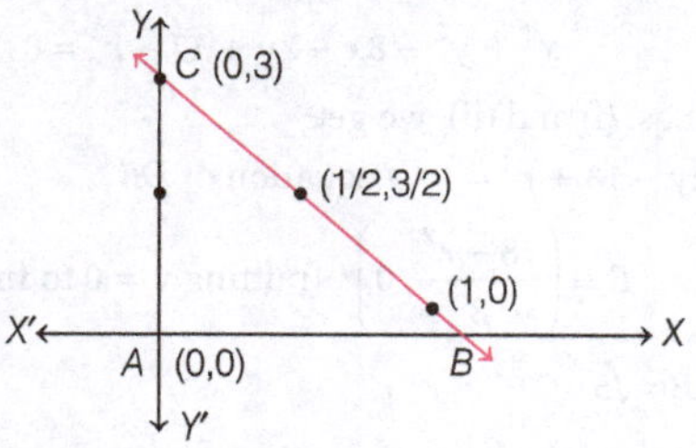

$\therefore$ Equation of circumcircle is

$$\left(x - \frac{1}{2}\right)^2 + \left(y - \frac{3}{2}\right)^2 = \left(\frac{1}{2}\right)^2 + \left(\frac{3}{2}\right)^2 = \frac{1}{4} + \frac{9}{4} = \frac{5}{2}$$

$$\therefore \quad \left(x - \frac{1}{2}\right)^2 + \left(y - \frac{3}{2}\right)^2 = \frac{5}{2} \qquad \text{...(i)}$$

Required circle touches AB and AC have radius r. Thus, equation be $(x - r)^2 + (y - r)^2 = r^2$ ...(ii)

If circle in Eq. (ii) touches circumcircle internally, we have $d_{C_1C_2} = |r_1 - r_2|$

$$\Rightarrow \quad \left(\frac{1}{2} - r\right)^2 + \left(\frac{3}{2} - r\right)^2 = \left(\left|\sqrt{\frac{5}{2}} - r\right|\right)^2$$

$$\Rightarrow \quad \frac{1}{4} + r^2 - r + \frac{9}{4} + r^2 - 3r = \frac{5}{2} + r^2 - \sqrt{10}r$$

$$\Rightarrow \quad r^2 - 4r + \sqrt{10}r = 0$$

$$\Rightarrow \quad r^2 - (4 - \sqrt{10})r = 0$$

$$\Rightarrow \quad r\{r - (4 - \sqrt{10})\} = 0$$

$\therefore$ $r = 0$ (meaningless)

or $\quad r = 4 - \sqrt{10} = 0.837 \approx 0.84$

Thus, the value of r is 0.84.

63. Method I

As we know that mirror image of orthocenter lie, on circumcircle.

Image of (1, 1), in X-axis is (1, −1).

and image of (1, 1) in $x + y + 1 = 0$ is (−2, −2).

$\therefore$ The required circle will be passing through both (1, −1) and (−2, −2).

$\therefore$ Only $x^2 + y^2 + x + 3y = 0$ satisfy both.

Method II

Equation of circle passing through $C(0, 0)$ is

$$x^2 + y^2 + 2gx + 2fy = 0 \qquad \text{... (i)}$$

Since Eq. (i), also passes through (−1, 0) and (1, −2).

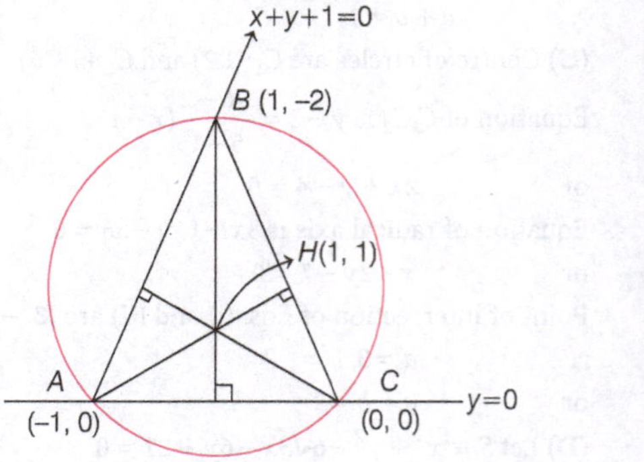

Then, $\quad 1 - 2g = 0$

$$\Rightarrow \quad g = \frac{1}{2}$$

and $\quad 5 + 1 - 4f = 0 \Rightarrow f = \frac{3}{2}$

$\therefore$ Equation of circumcircle is

$$x^2 + y^2 + 2 \times \frac{1}{2}x + 2 \times \frac{3}{2}y = 0$$

i.e. $x^2 + y^2 + x + 3y = 0$

64. Given that $\arg\left(\frac{z+\alpha}{z+\beta}\right)$

$$= \arg(z + \alpha) - \arg(z + \beta)$$

$= \frac{\pi}{4}$ implies z is on arc and $(-\alpha, 0)$

and $(-\beta, 0)$ subtend $\frac{\pi}{4}$ on z.

Given that z lies on $x^2 + y^2 + 5x - 3y + 4 = 0$

So, put $y = 0$; for value of α and β

$$x^2 + 5x + 4 = 0 \Rightarrow x = -1; x = -4$$

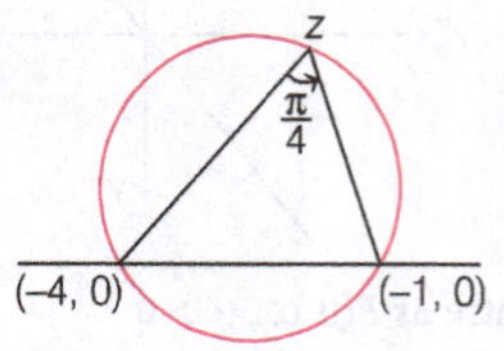

Hence, $\alpha = 1$ and $\beta = 4$

65. ∵ $a_n = \frac{1}{2^{n-1}}$ and $S_n = 2\left(1-\frac{1}{2^n}\right)$

For circle C_n to be inside M.

$$S_n < \frac{1025}{513}$$

$$\Rightarrow \quad 2\left(1-\frac{1}{2^n}\right) < \frac{1025}{513} \Rightarrow 1-\frac{1}{2^n} < \frac{1025}{1026}$$

$$\Rightarrow \quad 1-\frac{1}{2^n} < 1-\frac{1}{1026}$$

$$\Rightarrow \quad \frac{-1}{2^n} < \frac{-1}{1026} \Rightarrow \frac{1}{2^n} > \frac{1}{1026}$$

$$\Rightarrow \quad 2^n < 1026 \Rightarrow n \le 10$$

∴ Number of circles inside be $10 = k$.

Clearly, alternate circle do not intersect each other i.e. C_1, C_3, C_5, C_7, C_9 do not intersect each other as well as C_2, C_4, C_6, C_8 and C_{10} do not intersect each other.

Hence, maximum 5 set of circles do not intersect each other.

$$\therefore \quad l = 5$$

So, $3k + 2l = 40$

66. ∵ $r = \frac{(2^{199}-1)\sqrt{2}}{2^{198}}$

Now, $\sqrt{2}\, S_{n-1} + a_n < \left(\frac{2^{199}-1}{2^{198}}\right)\sqrt{2}$

$$2\sqrt{2}\left(1-\frac{1}{2^{n-1}}\right) + \frac{1}{2^{n-1}} < \left(\frac{2^{199}-1}{2^{198}}\right)\sqrt{2}$$

$$\therefore \quad 2\sqrt{2} - \frac{\sqrt{2}}{2^{n-2}} + \frac{1}{2^{n-1}} < 2\sqrt{2} - \frac{\sqrt{2}}{2^{198}}$$

$$\frac{1}{2^{n-2}}\left(\frac{1}{2}-\sqrt{2}\right) < -\frac{\sqrt{2}}{2^{198}}$$

$$\Rightarrow \quad \frac{2\sqrt{2}-1}{2\cdot 2^{n-2}} > \frac{\sqrt{2}}{2^{198}}$$

$$\Rightarrow \quad 2^{n-2} < (2 - 1/\sqrt{2})\cdot 2^{197}$$

$$\therefore \quad n \le 199$$

So, number of circles = 199

67. As we know that the equation of family of circles passes through the points of intersection of given circle $x^2 + y^2 = r^2$ and line $PQ: 2x + 4y = 5$

is, $(x^2 + y^2 - r^2) + \lambda(2x + 4y - 5) = 0$ ...(i)

Since, the circle (i) passes through the centre of circle $x^2 + y^2 = r^2$,

So, $-r^2 - 5\lambda = 0$

$\Rightarrow \quad 5\lambda + r^2 = 0$ ...(ii)

and the centre of circle (i) lies on the line $x + 2y = 4$, so centre $(-\lambda, -2\lambda)$ satisfy the line $x + 2y = 4$.

Therefore, $-\lambda - 4\lambda = 4$

$\Rightarrow \quad -5\lambda = 4$

$\Rightarrow \quad r^2 = 4$ [from Eq. (ii)]

$\Rightarrow \quad r = 2$

Exercise 3 - Challenging Problems

1. Let radius $= r$

∴ From figure, $\sqrt{\alpha^2 + a^2} = b + r$ ...(i)

Consider a point $P(0, k)$ on the Y-axis

$$M(\alpha - r, 0) \text{ and } N(\alpha + r, 0)$$

Now, slope of $MP = \frac{-k}{\alpha - r}$, slope $NP = \frac{-k}{\alpha + r}$

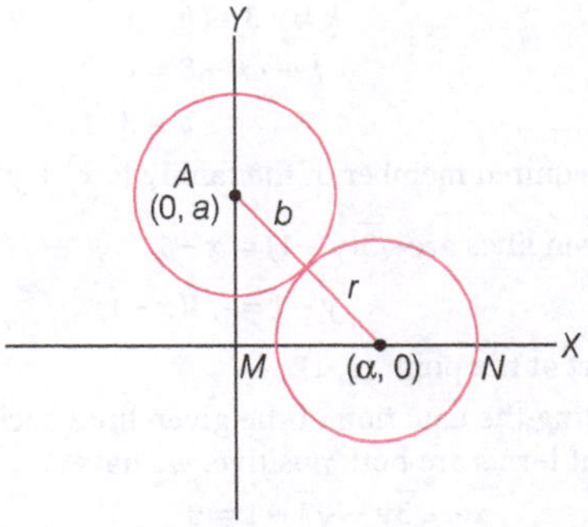

If $\angle MPN = \theta$,

then $\tan\theta = \left|\frac{\frac{k}{\alpha - r} - \frac{k}{\alpha + r}}{1 + \frac{k^2}{\alpha^2 - r^2}}\right| = \left|\frac{2kr}{\alpha^2 - r^2 + k^2}\right|$

According to the given condition, θ is a constant for any choice,

$$\alpha = \frac{2kr}{\alpha^2 - r^2 + k^2} \text{ constant}$$

i.e. $\frac{r}{\alpha^2 - r^2 + k^2} = \text{constant}$

i.e. $\frac{\sqrt{\alpha^2 + a^2} - b}{\alpha^2 - (\sqrt{\alpha^2 + a^2} - b^2)^2 + k^2} = \text{constant (from equation (i))}$

i.e. $\frac{\sqrt{\alpha^2 + a^2} - b}{2b\sqrt{\alpha^2 + a^2} - a^2 - b^2 + k^2}$

$$\frac{\sqrt{\alpha^2 + a^2} - b}{\sqrt{\alpha^2 + a^2} - \lambda} = \text{constant} \left\{\text{putting } \frac{a^2 + b^2 - k^2}{2b} = \lambda\right\}$$

which is possible only if $\lambda = b$

$$\frac{a^2 + b^2 - k^2}{2b} = b$$

$$\Rightarrow \quad k = \pm\sqrt{a^2 - b^2}$$

$$P = (0, \pm\sqrt{a^2 - b^2})$$

2. $x^2 + y^2 - 2x - 8 - 2a(y) = 0$ ...(i)

∴ It is of the $S + \lambda L = 0$

∴ It will pass through the points of intersection of

$$S: x^2 + y^2 - 2x - 8 = 0$$

$$L: y = 0$$

∴ $P(-2, 0)$ and $Q(4, 0)$

Equation of PQ is $= 0$ ...(ii)

It tangents at P and Q intersect at (h, k), then PQ is chord of contact of (h, k) whose equation is

$$x(h)+y(k)-(x+h)-a(y+k)-8=0$$

$$\therefore \quad x(h-1)+y(k-a)-(h+ak+8)=0 \quad \text{...(iii)}$$

$\therefore$ Equations (ii) and (iii) represent the same line PQ.

$\Rightarrow$ $h=1$, $k-a=$ any constant and $h+ak+8=0$

$\therefore$ (h, k) lies on $x+2y+5=0$

$$\Rightarrow \quad h+2k+5=0$$

$$\Rightarrow \quad k=-3 \text{ as } h=1$$

$$\therefore \quad h+ak+8=0$$

$$\therefore \quad a=3$$

$\therefore$ The required member of the family is $x^2+y^2-2x-6y-8=0$

3. The given lines are $\sqrt{3}(y-1)=x-1$ ...(i)

and $y-1=\sqrt{3}(x-1)$ ...(ii)

intersect at the point (1, 1).

Re-writing the equation of the given lines such that their constant terms are both positive, we have

$$x-\sqrt{3}y+\sqrt{3}-1=0 \quad \text{...(iii)}$$

and

$$-\sqrt{3}x+y+\sqrt{3}-1=0 \quad \text{...(iv)}$$

Here, we have (product of coefficients of x) + (product of coefficients of y) $=-\sqrt{3}-\sqrt{3}=-$ve quantity which implies that the acute angle between the given lines contains the origin.

Therefore, equation of the acute angle bisector of the given lines is

$$\frac{x-\sqrt{3}y+\sqrt{3}-1}{2}=+\frac{-\sqrt{3}x+y+\sqrt{3}-1}{2}$$

i.e. $y=x$

Any point on the above bisector can be chosen as (α, α) and equation of any circle passing through (1, 1) and having centre at (α, α) is $(x-\alpha)^2+(y-\alpha)^2=(1-\alpha)^2+(1-\alpha)^2$

i.e. $x^2+y^2-2\alpha x-2\alpha y+4\alpha-2=0$ ...(vi)

The common chord of the given circle

$$x^2+y^2+4x-6y+5=0 \quad \text{...(vii)}$$

and the circle represented by Eq. (vi) is

$$(4+2\alpha)x+(2\alpha-6)y+(7-4\alpha)=0$$

i.e. $(4x-6y+7)+2\alpha(x+y-2)=0$ ...(viii)

which represents a family of straight lines passing through the intersection point of the lines

$$4x-6y+7=0 \quad \text{...(ix)}$$

and

$$x+y-2=0 \quad \text{...(x)}$$

On solving Eqs. (ix) and (x) gives the coordinates of the fixed point as $\left(\frac{1}{2}, \frac{3}{2}\right)$.

4. The given circle $S_1: x^2+y^2-2x-2y+1=0$ has centre $C_1=(1, 1)$ and radius $r_1=1$

The other given circle $S_2: x^2+y^2-18x-2y+78=0$ ...(i)

has centre $C_2=(9, 1)$ and radius $r_2=2$ ...(ii)

According to the required condition, we have

$$C_1M_1 \geq r_1$$

i.e. $$\frac{|3+4-\lambda|}{\sqrt{3^2+4^2}} \geq 1$$

i.e. $(\lambda-7) \geq 5$ [$\because$ C_1 lies below the line]
[$\therefore$ $(7-\lambda)$ is a $-$ve quantity]

i.e. $\lambda \geq 12$

Also, $C_2M_2 \geq 2 \Rightarrow \frac{|27+4-\lambda|}{\sqrt{3^2+4^2}} \geq 2$

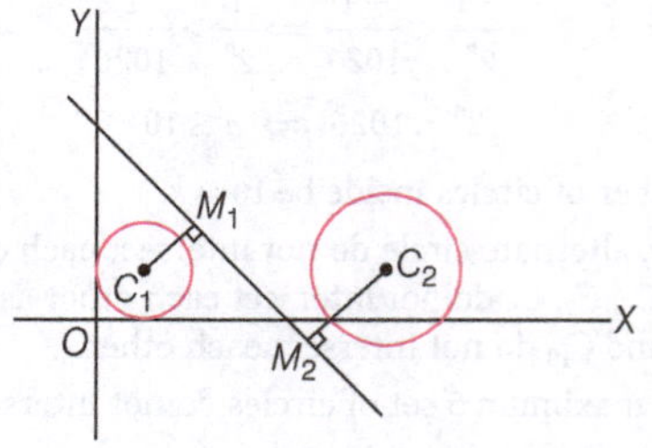

i.e. $(31-\lambda) \geq 10$ [$\because$ C_2 lies below the line]
[$\therefore$ $(31-\lambda)$ is a +ve quantity]

i.e. $\lambda \leq 21$

Hence, the range of λ is [12, 21].

5. Let us choose the intersection point A as the origin and the radical axis of the circles, as the Y-axis (fig.). Then, the equation of the circles can be chosen as

$$S_1 = x^2+y^2-2g_1x-2fy=0 \quad \text{...(i)}$$

and

$$S_2 = x^2+y^2-2g_2x-2fy=0 \quad \text{...(ii)}$$

Equation of a variable line through A can be written as $y=mx$

On putting in Eq. (i), we get

$$x^2(1+m^2)-2(g_1+mf)x=0$$

gives $x=0, \dfrac{2(g_1+mf)}{1+m^2}$

On putting in Eq. (ii), we get

$$x^2(1+m^2)-2(g_2+mf)x=0$$

gives $x=0, \dfrac{2(g_2+mf)}{1+m^2}$

Thus, we have $P=(x_1, mx_1)$ where $x_1=\dfrac{2(g_1+mf)}{1+m^2}$

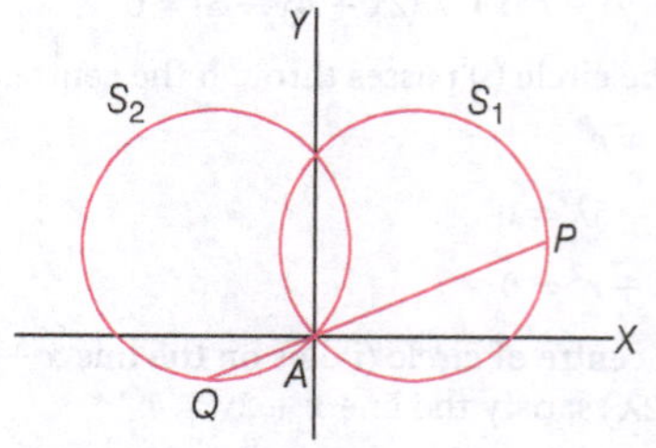

and $Q=(x_2, mx_2)$ where $x_2=\dfrac{2(g_2+mf)}{1+m^2}$

If $M(h, k)$ be the mid-point of PQ, then $2h = x_1 + x_2$

i.e. $$h(1+m^2) = g_1 + g_2 + 2mf \quad \text{...(iii)}$$

and $$2k = m(x_1 + x_2)$$

i.e. $$k(1+m^2) = m(g_1 + g_2 + 2mf) \quad \text{...(iv)}$$

On dividing Eq. (iv) by Eq. (iii), we get

$$m = \frac{k}{h}$$

On putting the above avlue of m in Eq. (iii), we get

$$h\left(1+\frac{k^2}{h^2}\right) = g_1 + g_2 + \frac{2kf}{h}$$

i.e. $h^2 + k^2 = (g_1 + g_2)h + 2fk$

On putting (x, y) in place of (h, k) gives the equation of the required locus, as $x^2 + y^2 - (g_1 + g_2)x - 2fy = 0$

which is a circle through A (0, 0).

6. Let circle be $(x-\sqrt{7})^2 + (y-\sqrt{11})^2 = r^2$

$$x^2 + y^2 - 2\sqrt{7}x - 2\sqrt{11}y + 18 - r^2 = 0.$$

If possible let circle passes through more than one rational points (x_1, y_1) and (x_2, y_2).

So, $$x_1^2 + y_1^2 - 2\sqrt{7}x_1 - 2\sqrt{11}\,y_1 + 18 - r^2 = 0 \quad \text{...(i)}$$

$$x_2^2 + y_2^2 - 2\sqrt{7}x_2 - 2\sqrt{11}y_2 + 18 - r^2 = 0 \quad \text{...(ii)}$$

From Eqs. (i) and (ii)

$\Rightarrow$ $x_1^2 + y_1^2 - 2\sqrt{7}x_1 - 2\sqrt{11}y_1 = x_2^2 + y_2^2 - 2\sqrt{7}x_2 - 2\sqrt{11}y_2$

Since, x_1, y_1, x_2 and y_2 are rational numbers,

So, comparing irrational parts, we get

$$\sqrt{7}x_1 + \sqrt{11}y_1 = \sqrt{7}x_2 + \sqrt{11}y_2$$

$\Rightarrow$ $$\sqrt{7}(x_1 - x_2) = \sqrt{11}(y_2 - y_1)$$

if $x_1 \neq x_2$, then $\dfrac{\sqrt{7}}{\sqrt{11}} = \dfrac{y_2 - y_1}{x_1 - x_2}$

$\Rightarrow$ Irrational = rational, which is a contradiction, so $x_1 = x_2$, similarly $y_1 = y_2$.

Hence, more than one rational point can not exist on the circumference of the circle with centre $(\sqrt{7}, \sqrt{11})$.

7.

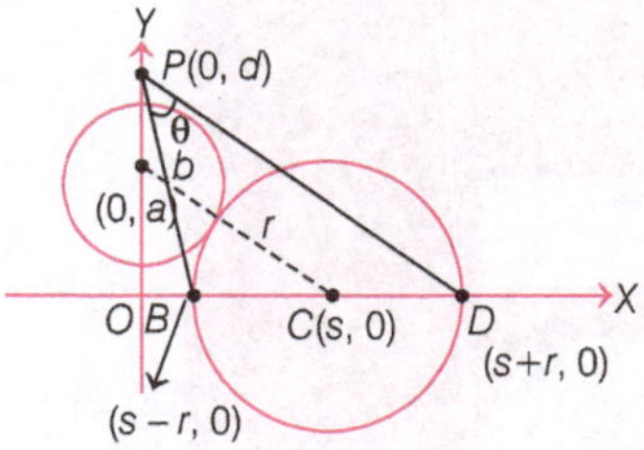

Let P be $(0, d)$.

Then, slope of $PD = \dfrac{-d}{s+r}$

and slope of $PB = \dfrac{-d}{s-r}$

Circles touch externally, so $(r+b)^2 = a^2 + s^2$

Let $\angle BPD = \theta$, then

$$\tan\theta = \frac{\dfrac{-d}{s+r} + \dfrac{d}{s-r}}{1 + \dfrac{d^2}{(s^2-r^2)}} = \frac{2dr}{s^2 - r^2 + d^2}$$

$$= \frac{2rd}{b^2 + 2rb - a^2 + d^2} = \frac{2rd}{d^2 - (a^2 - b^2) + 2rb}$$

for θ to be constant, $\tan\theta$ must be independent of r.

For it take $d^2 - (a^2 - b^2) = 0$ so, $\tan\theta = \dfrac{d}{b} = \dfrac{\sqrt{a^2 - b^2}}{b}$ and point $P = (0, \sqrt{a^2 - b^2})$.

8. Equation of the circle having the ends of diameter at (1, − 3) and (4, 1) is $(x-1)(x-4) + (y+3)(y-1) = 0$

$\Rightarrow$ $$x^2 + y^2 - 5x + 2y + 1 = 0$$

Other circle will be $x^2 + y^2 - 5x + 2y + 1 + \lambda(x + y - 1) = 0$

It passes through (1, 2).

$\Rightarrow$ $$\lambda = -\frac{5}{2}$$

$\Rightarrow$ Circle is $x^2 + y^2 - \dfrac{15}{2}x - \dfrac{y}{2} + \dfrac{7}{2} = 0.$

> To aquire knowledge, one must study; but to aquire wisdom, one must observe.
>
> **–Marilyn vos Savant**

5 Parabola

Learning Milestones

Milestone 1 Equation of Parabola

- Conic Section
- Equation of Conic Section
- How to Find the Centre of Conics
- Parabola : Definition
- Other Forms of Parabola with Latusrectum $4a$
- General Equation of a Parabola
- The Generalised Form $(y-k)^2 = 4a(x-h)$
- Parabolic Curve

Milestone 2 Line and Parabola

- Position of Points with respect to a Parabola
- Chords of Parabola
- Intersection of a Line and a Parabola
- Equation of Tangent in Different Forms
- Point of Intersection of Tangent at any Two Points on the Parabola
- Equation of Normals in Different forms
- Point of Intersection of Normals at any Two Points on the Parabola
- Co-normal Points

Milestone 3 Pair of Tangents and Chord of Contact

- Equation of Pair of Tangents
- Chord of Contact
- Equation of the Chord Bisected at a Given Point
- Diameter of a Parabola
- Length of Tangent, Subtangent, Normal and Subnormal
- Some Standard Properties of the Parabola
- Reflection Property of a Parabola

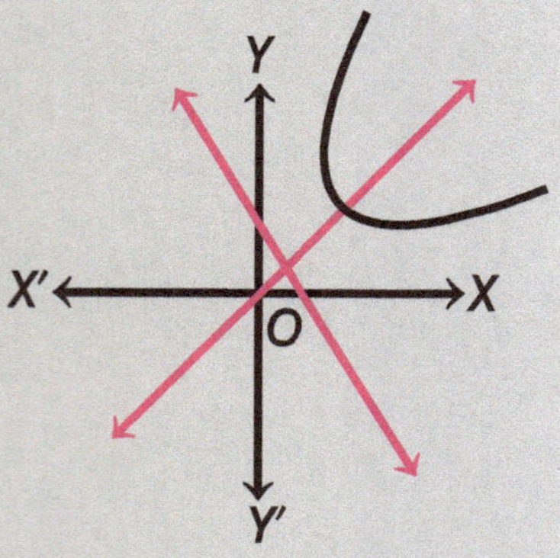

Practice Milestones

Practice Milestone 1- JEE Main Pattern
Practice Milestone 2 - JEE Advanced Pattern
Practice Milestone 3 - Challenging Problems

Milestone 1 Equation of Parabola

- Conic Section • Equation of Conic Section • How to Find the Centre of Conics
- Parabola : Definition • Other Forms of Parabola with Latusrectum $4a$ • General Equation of a Parabola
- The Generalised Form $(y-k)^2 = 4a(x-h)$ • Parabolic Curve

The famous Greek mathematician Euclid, the father of creative Geometry, near about 300 BC considering various plane sections of a right circular cone found many curves, which are called conics or conic sections.

5.1 Conic Section

Let l_1 be a fixed vertical line and l_2 be another line intersecting it at a fixed point V and inclined to it at an angle α.

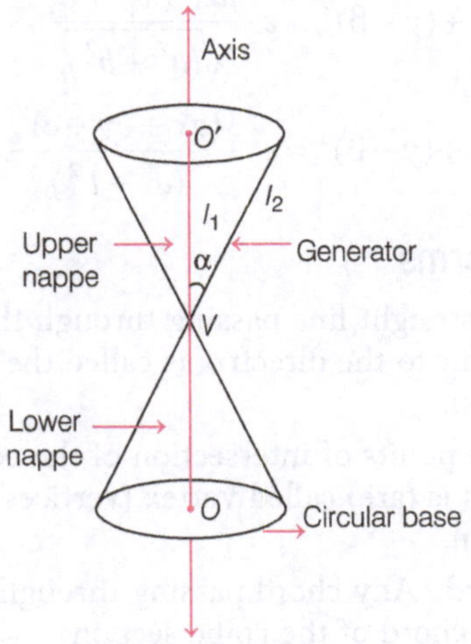

Suppose we rotate the line l_2 around the line l_1 in such a way the angle remains constant then, the surface generated is a double-napped right circular hollow cone. The point V is called the vertex, the line l_1 is the axis of the cone. The rotating line l_2 is called a generator of the cone.

The vertex separates the cone into two parts called nappes. The constant angle α is called the semi-vertical angle of the cone.

Section of a Right Circular Cone by Different Planes

1. Section of a right circular cone by a plane which is passing through its vertex is a pair of straight lines, lines always pass through the vertex of the cone.

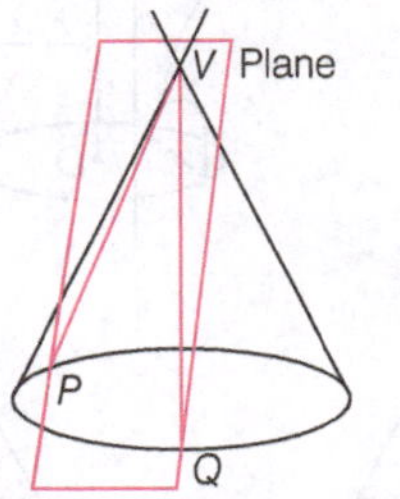

2. Section of a right circular cone by a plane which parallel to its base is a circle.

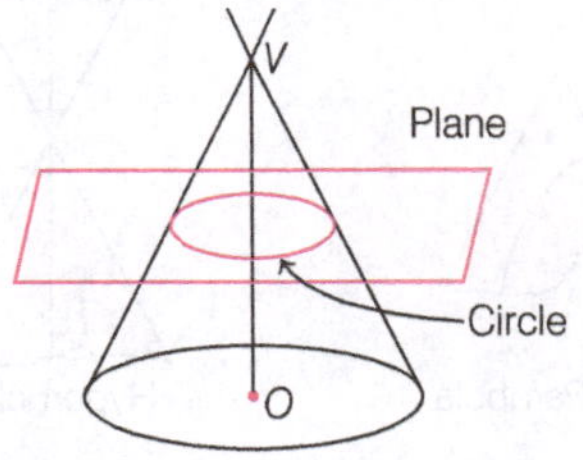

3. Section of a right circular cone by a plane which is parallel to a generator of the cone is a parabola.

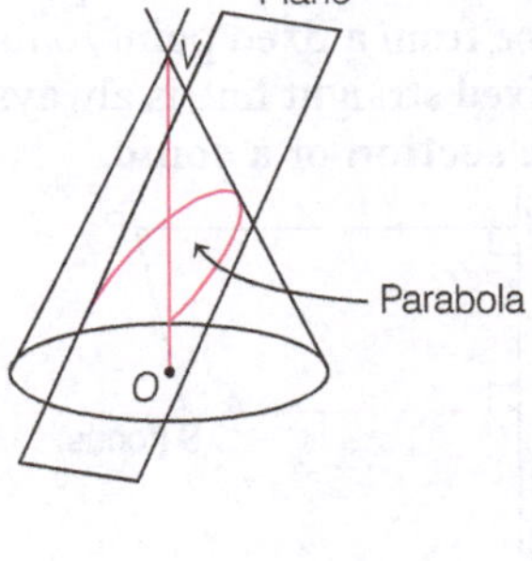

4. Section of a right circular cone by a plane which is not parallel to any generator and not parallel or perpendicular to the axis of the cone is an ellipse.

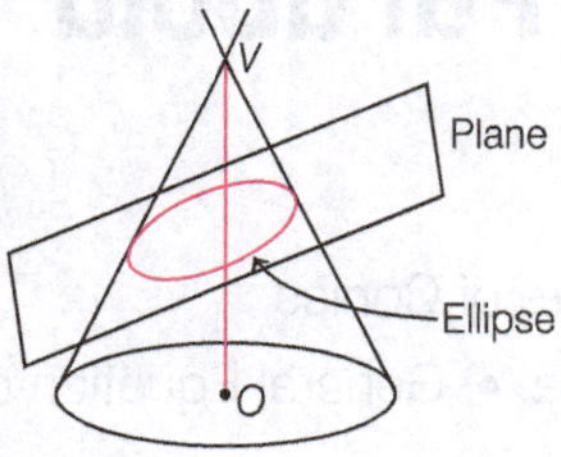

5. Section of a right circular cone by a plane which is parallel to the axis of the cone is a hyperbola.

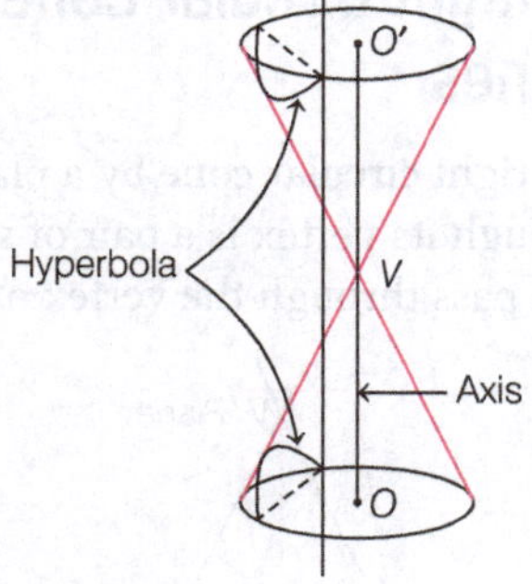

3D View

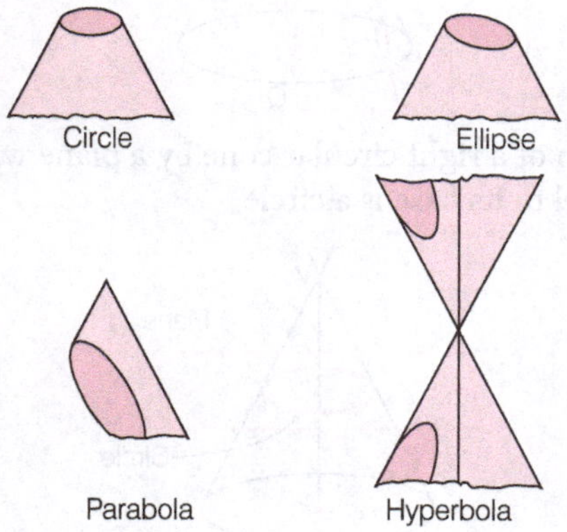

Conic Section : Definition

The locus of a point which moves in a plane such that the ratio of its distance from a fixed point to its perpendicular distance from a fixed straight line is always constant, is known as a **conic section** or a **conic.**

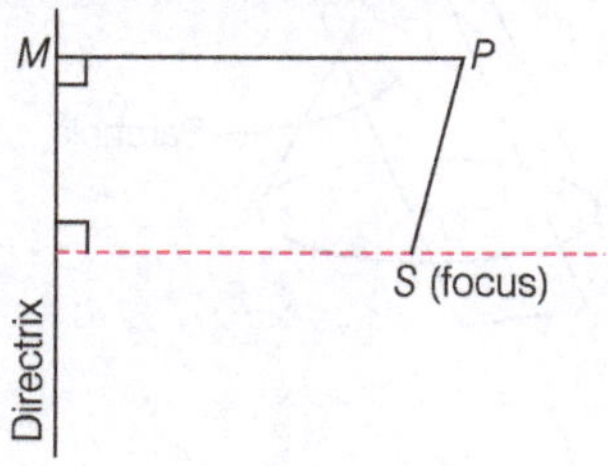

The fixed point is called the **focus** of the conic and this fixed line is called the **directrix** of the conic. Also, this constant ratio is called the **eccentricity** of the conic and is denoted by *e*.

In the figure, $\frac{SP}{PM} = \text{constant} = e$

$\Rightarrow \quad SP = e\,PM$

5.2 Equation of Conic Section

If the focus is (α, β) and the directrix is $ax + by + c = 0$, then the equation of the conic section whose eccentricity is

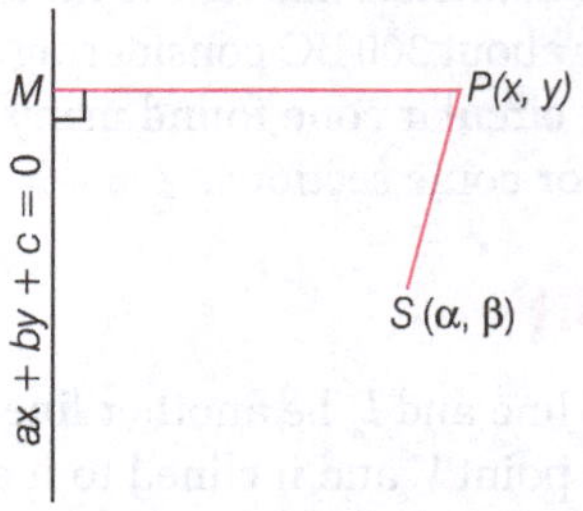

$\Rightarrow \quad SP = ePM$

$$\Rightarrow \quad \sqrt{(x-\alpha)^2 + (y-\beta)^2} = e \cdot \frac{|ax + by + c|}{\sqrt{(a^2 + b^2)}}$$

$$\Rightarrow \quad (x-\alpha)^2 + (y-\beta)^2 = e^2 \cdot \frac{(ax + by + c)^2}{(a^2 + b^2)}.$$

Important Terms

- **Axis** The straight line passing through the focus and perpendicular to the directrix is called the axis of the conic section.
- **Vertex** The points of intersection of the conic section and the axis is (are) called vertex (vertices) of the conic section.
- **Focal Chord** Any chord passing through the focus is called focal chord of the conic section.
- **Double Ordinate** A straight line drawn perpendicular to the axis and terminated at both end of the curve is a double ordinate of the conic section.
- **Latusrectum** The double ordinate passing through the focus is called the latusrectum of the conic section.
- **Centre** The point which bisects every chord of the conic passing through it, is called the centre of the conic section.

JEE SPIKE

Parabola has no centre but circle, ellipse and hyperbola have centre.

Example 1. Find the locus of a point, which moves such that its distance from the point (0, −1) is twice its distance from the line $3x+4y+1=0$.

Sol. Let $P(x_1, y_1)$ be the point, whose locus is required.

Its distance from $(0,-1) = 2\times$ its distance from the line $3x+4y+1=0$.

$$\Rightarrow \quad \sqrt{(x_1-0)^2+(y_1+1)^2} = 2\times\frac{|3x_1+4y_1+1|}{\sqrt{(3^2+4^2)}}$$

$$\Rightarrow \quad 5\sqrt{x_1^2+(y_1+1)^2} = 2|3x_1+4y_1+1|$$

On squaring and simplifying, we get

$$25(x_1^2+y_1^2+2y_1+1) = 4(9x_1^2+16y_1^2+24x_1y_1+6x_1+8y_1+1)$$

or $11x_1^2+39y_1^2+96x_1y_1+24x_1-18y_1-21=0$

Hence, the locus of (x_1, y_1) is

$$11x^2+39y^2+96xy+24x-18y-21=0$$

Recognisation of Conics

The equation of conics represented by the general equation of second degree

$$ax^2+2hxy+by^2+2gx+2fy+c=0 \quad \text{...(i)}$$

can be recognised easily by the condition given in the tabular form. For this, first we have to find discriminant of the equation. We know that the discriminant of above equation is represented by Δ, where

$$\Delta = abc+2fgh-af^2-bg^2-ch^2$$

The nature of the conic section depends upon the position of the focus *S* with respect to the directrix and also upon the value of the eccentricity *e*. Two different cases arise.

***Case* I (When the focus lies on the directrix)**

In this case, Eq. (i) represents the **Degenerate conic** whose nature is given in the following table :

Condition	Nature of Conic
$e>1, \Delta=0, h^2>ab$	The lines will be real and distinct intersecting at *S*.
$e=1, \Delta=0, h^2=ab$	The lines will coincident and will be perpendicular to directrix.
$e<1, \Delta=0, h^2<ab$	The lines will be imaginary.

***Case* II (When the focus does not lie on the directrix)**

In this case, Eq. (i) represents the **non-degenerate conic** whose nature is given in the following table :

Condition	Nature of Conic
$e=1, \Delta\neq 0, h^2=ab$	a parabola
$0<e<1, \Delta\neq 0, h^2<ab$	an ellipse
$e>1, \Delta\neq 0, h^2>ab$	a hyperbola
$e>1, \Delta\neq 0, h^2>ab, a+b=0$	rectangular hyperbola

JEE Focus Points

- If conic represents an empty set, then $\Delta\neq 0, h^2<ab$.
- If conic represents a single point, then $\Delta=0, h^2<ab$.

Concept Inside Video

Example 2. Find the value of λ if the equation $9x^2+4y^2+2\lambda xy+4x-2y+3=0$ represents a parabola.

Sol. Given equation is $9x^2+4y^2+2\lambda xy+4x-2y+3=0$

On comparing with $ax^2+by^2+2hxy+2gx+2fy+c=0$,

we get $a=9, b=4, h=\lambda, g=2, f=-1, c=3$

For representing a parabola,

$$\Delta\neq 0 \text{ and } h^2=ab$$

$$\Delta = abc+2fgh-af^2-bg^2-ch^2 \quad \text{...(i)}$$

$$\because \quad h^2=ab$$

$$\lambda^2 = 4\times 9 \Rightarrow \lambda=\pm 6$$

From Eqs. (i) for $\lambda=\pm 6$,

$$\Delta\neq 0$$

Example 3. Find the value of λ if $2x^2+7xy+3y^2+8x+14y+\lambda=0$ represents a pair of straight lines.

Sol. Given equation is $2x^2+7xy+3y^2+8x+14y+\lambda=0$

On comparing with

$ax^2+2hxy+by^2+2gx+2fy+c=0$, we get

$$a=2, h=\frac{7}{2}, b=3, g=4, f=7, c=\lambda$$

For representing a pair of straight lines,

$$abc+2fgh-af^2-bg^2-ch^2=0$$

$$6\lambda+196-98-48-\frac{49\lambda}{4}=0$$

$$\frac{24\lambda-49\lambda}{4}=-50 \Rightarrow \frac{-25\lambda}{4}=-50 \Rightarrow \lambda=8$$

Example 4. Which conic is represented by the equation $25(x^2+y^2-2x+1)=(4x-3y+1)^2$?

Sol. Given equation is

$$25(x^2+y^2-2x+1)=(4x-3y+1)^2 \quad \text{...(i)}$$

Write the right hand side of this equation, so that it appears in perpendicular distance form, then

$$(4x-3y+1)^2 = 25\left(\frac{4x-3y+1}{\sqrt{(4^2+3^2)}}\right)^2$$

Then, Eq. (i) can be re-written a

$$25[(x-1)^2+(y-0)^2] = 25\left[\frac{4x-3y+1}{\sqrt{(4^2+3^2)}}\right]^2$$

or $$\sqrt{(x-1)^2+(y-0)^2} = \frac{|4x-3y+1|}{\sqrt{(4^2+3^2)}}$$

Here, $e=1$

Thus, the given equation represents a parabola. It may noted that $(1, 0)$ is the focus and $4x-3y+1=0$ is the directrix of the parabola.

Example 5. Which conic is represented by the equation $13x^2-18xy+37y^2+2x+14y-2=0$?

Sol. Compare the given equation with

$ax^2+2hxy+by^2+2gx+2fy+c=0$, we get

$$a=13, h=-9, b=37, g=1, f=7, c=-2$$

Then, $\Delta = abc+2fgh-af^2-bg^2-ch^2$

$$= (13)(37)(-2)+2(7)(1)(-9) - 13(7)^2-37(1)^2+2(-9)^2$$

$$= -962-126-637-37+162 = -1600 \neq 0$$

and also $h^2=(-9)^2=81$ and $ab=13\times 37=481$

Here, $h^2 < ab$

So, we get $h^2<ab$ and $\Delta \neq 0$.

Hence, the given equation represents an ellipse.

Example 6. Which conic is represented by the equation $\sqrt{ax}+\sqrt{by}=1$?

Sol. Given conic is $\sqrt{ax}+\sqrt{by}=1$

On squaring both sides, we get

$$ax+by+2\sqrt{abxy}=1$$

$$\Rightarrow \quad ax+by-1=-2\sqrt{abxy}$$

Again, on squaring both sides, we get

$$(ax+by-1)^2 = 4abxy$$

$$\Rightarrow \quad a^2x^2+b^2y^2+1+2abxy-2by-2ax=4abxy$$

$$\Rightarrow \quad a^2x^2+b^2y^2-2abxy-2ax-2by+1=0$$

$$\Rightarrow \quad a^2x^2-2abxy+b^2y^2-2ax-2by+1=0 \quad \text{...(i)}$$

Comparing the Eq. (i) with the equation

$Ax^2+2Hxy+By^2+2Gx+2Fy+C=0$, we get

$$A=a^2, H=-ab, B=b^2, G=-a, F=-b, C=1$$

Then, $\Delta = ABC+2FGH-AF^2-BG^2-CH^2$

$$= a^2b^2-2a^2b^2-a^2b^2-a^2b^2-a^2b^2$$

$$= -4a^2b^2 \neq 0 \text{ and } H^2=a^2b^2=AB$$

So, we get $\Delta \neq 0$ and $H^2=AB$.

Hence, the given equation represents a parabola.

Example 7. If the equation $x^2-y^2-2x+2y+\lambda=0$ represents a degenerate conic, find the value of λ.

Sol. For degenerate conic $\Delta = 0$

Comparing the given equation of conic with

$ax^2+2hxy+by^2+2gx+2fy+c=0$, we get

$$a=1, b=-1, h=0, g=-1, f=1, c=\lambda$$

$$\therefore \quad \Delta = abc+2fgh-af^2-bg^2-ch^2=0$$

$$\Rightarrow (1)(-1)(\lambda)+0-1\times(1)^2+1\times(-1)^2-\lambda(0)^2=0$$

$$\Rightarrow \quad -\lambda-1+1=0 \Rightarrow \lambda=0$$

Example 8. If the equation $x^2+y^2-2x-2y+c=0$ represents an empty set, then find the value of c.

Sol. For empty set, $\Delta \neq 0$ and $h^2<ab$.

Now, comparing the given equation of conic with

$ax^2+2hxy+by^2+2gx+2fy+c'=0$, we get

$$a=1, h=0, b=1, g=-1, f=-1, c'=c$$

$\because \quad h^2<ab$

$\therefore \quad 0<1$, which is true.

and $\quad \Delta = abc'+2fgh-af^2-bg^2-c'h^2 \neq 0$

$\Rightarrow \quad (1)(1)(c)+0-1\times(-1)^2-1\times(-1)^2-0 \neq 0$

$\Rightarrow \quad c-2\neq 0$

$\therefore \quad c \neq 2$

Hence, $\quad c \in R\sim(2)$

Example 9. If the equation of conic

$$2x^2+xy+3y^2-3x+5y+\lambda=0$$

represents a single point, then find the value of λ.

Sol. For single point,

$$h^2<ab \text{ and } \Delta=0$$

On comparing the given equation with

$ax^2+2hxy+by^2+2gx+2fy+c=0$, we get

$$a=2, h=\frac{1}{2}, b=3, g=-\frac{3}{2}, f=\frac{5}{2}, c=\lambda.$$

$\because \quad h^2=\frac{1}{4}, ab=6$

$\therefore \quad h^2<ab$

and $\quad \Delta = abc+2fgh-af^2-bg^2-ch^2$

$$= (2)(3)(\lambda)+2\times\frac{5}{2}\times-\frac{3}{2}\times\frac{1}{2} - 2\times\frac{25}{4}-3\times\frac{9}{4}-\lambda\times\frac{1}{4}$$

$$= 6\lambda - \frac{15}{4} - \frac{25}{2} - \frac{27}{4} - \frac{\lambda}{4}$$

$$= \frac{23\lambda}{4} - 23 = 0$$

$\therefore \quad \lambda = 4$

Example 10. For what value of λ the equation of conic $2xy + 4x - 6y + \lambda = 0$ represents two intersecting straight lines, if $\lambda = 17$, then which conic is represented this equation?

Sol. On comparing the given equation of conic with $ax^2 + 2hxy + by^2 + 2gx + 2fy + c = 0$, we get

$$a = 0, b = 0, h = 1, g = 2, f = -3, c = \lambda$$

For two intersecting lines,

$$h^2 > ab, \Delta = 0$$

$\because \quad ab = 0, h = 1$

$\therefore \quad h^2 > ab$

and $\quad \Delta = abc + 2fgh - af^2 - bg^2 - ch^2$

$$= 0 + 2 \times -3 \times 2 \times 1 - 0 - 0 - \lambda\,(1)^2 = -12 - \lambda = 0$$

$\therefore \quad \lambda = -12$

For $\lambda = 17$, then the given equation of conic become $2xy + 4x - 6y + 17 = 0$ according to the first system but here $c = 17$.

$$a = 0, b = 0, h = 1, g = 2, f = -3, c = 17,$$

$\therefore \quad \Delta = abc + 2fgh - af^2 - bg^2 - ch^2$

$$= 0 + 2 \times -3 \times 2 \times 1 - 0 - 0 - 17 \times (1)^2$$

$$= -12 - 17 = -29 \neq 0$$

$\therefore \quad \Delta \neq 0$ and $h^2 > ab$

So, we have $\Delta \neq 0$ and $h^2 > ab$.

Hence, the given equation represents a hyperbola.

5.3 How to Find the Centre of Conics

If $S \equiv ax^2 + 2hxy + by^2 + 2gx + 2fy + c = 0$.

Partially differentiating w. r. t. x and y, we get

$$\frac{\partial S}{\partial x} = 2ax + 2hy + 2g \quad \text{[treating } y \text{ as constant]}$$

$$\frac{\partial S}{\partial y} = 2hx + 2by + 2f \quad \text{[treating } x \text{ as constant]}$$

For centre, $\dfrac{\partial S}{\partial x} = 0$ and $\dfrac{\partial S}{\partial y} = 0$

$\therefore \quad 2ax + 2hy + 2g = 0$

and $\quad 2hx + 2by + 2f = 0$

$\Rightarrow \quad ax + hy + g = 0$

and $\quad hx + by + f = 0$

On solving these equations, we get the centre

$$(x, y) = \left(\frac{hf - bg}{ab - h^2}, \frac{gh - af}{ab - h^2}\right).$$

Alternate Method

Since, $\quad \Delta = \begin{vmatrix} a & h & g \\ h & b & f \\ g & f & c \end{vmatrix}$

Write first two rows,

i.e. $\quad \begin{matrix} a & & h & & g & & a \\ & \times & & \times & & \times & \\ h & & b & & f & & h \end{matrix}$ [repeat Ist member]

$\therefore \quad ab - h^2, hf - bg, gh - af$

or points $\left(\dfrac{hf - bg}{ab - h^2}, \dfrac{gh - af}{ab - h^2}\right)$

Example 11. Find the centre of the conic $14x^2 - 4xy + 11y^2 - 44x - 58y + 71 = 0$.

Sol. Let $f(x, y) \equiv 14x^2 - 4xy + 11y^2 - 44x - 58y + 71 = 0$

On differentiating partially w.r.t. x and y, we get

$$\frac{\partial f}{\partial x} = 28x - 4y - 44$$

and $\quad \dfrac{\partial f}{\partial y} = -4x + 22y - 58$

For centre, $\quad \dfrac{\partial f}{\partial x} = 0$ and $\dfrac{\partial f}{\partial y} = 0,$

$\therefore \quad 28x - 4y - 44 = 0$

or $\quad 7x - y - 11 = 0 \quad$ ...(i)

and $\quad -4x + 22y - 58 = 0$

or $\quad -2x + 11y = 29 \quad$ ...(ii)

On solving Eqs. (i) and (ii), we get

$$x = 2 \text{ and } y = 3$$

$\therefore$ Centre is (2, 3).

Alternate Solution

On comparing the given conic with

$$ax^2 + 2hxy + by^2 + 2gx + 2fy + c = 0$$

$\therefore \quad a = 14, h = -2, b = 11, g = -22, f = -29, c = 71$

$\therefore \quad$ Centre $\left(\dfrac{hf - bg}{ab - h^2}, \dfrac{gh - af}{ab - h^2}\right)$

or $\quad = \left(\dfrac{(-2)(-29) - (11)(-22)}{(14)(11) - (-2)^2}, \dfrac{(-22)(-2) - (14)(-29)}{(14)(11) - (-2)^2}\right)$

or $\quad = (2, 3)$

5.4 Parabola : Definition

A parabola is the locus of a point which moves in a plane such that its distance from a fixed point (i.e. focus) is always equal to its distance from a fixed straight line (i.e. directrix).

Standard Equation of Parabola

Let S be the focus and ZM be the directrix of the parabola. Draw SZ perpendicular to ZM, let A be the mid-point of SZ, then $AS = AZ$

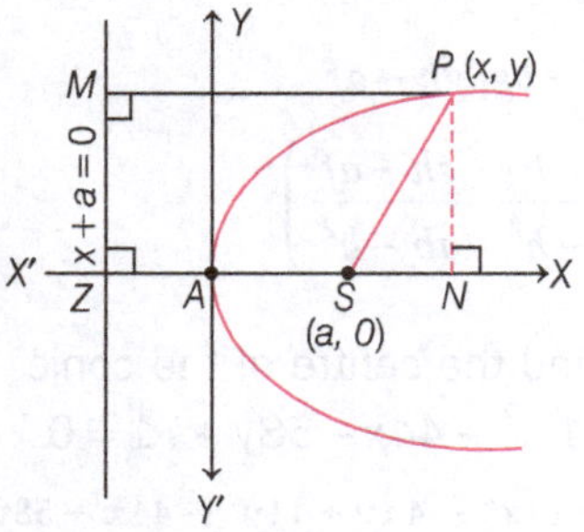

So, A lies on the parabola. Take A as the origin and a line AY through A perpendicular to AX as Y-axis.

Let $AS = AZ = a > 0$

Then, coordinate of S is $(a, 0)$ and the equation of ZM is

$$x = -a \text{ or } x + a = 0$$

Now, take $P(x, y)$ be any point on the parabola. Join SP and from P draw PM perpendicular to the directrix ZM.

Then, $SP = \sqrt{(x-a)^2 + (y-0)^2}$

$= \sqrt{(x-a)^2 + y^2}$

and $PM = ZN = AZ + AN = a + x$

Now, for the parabola $SP = PM$

$\Rightarrow$ $(SP)^2 = (PM)^2 \Rightarrow (x-a)^2 + y^2 = (a+x)^2$

$\Rightarrow$ $y^2 = (a+x)^2 - (x-a)^2 = 4ax$

$\therefore$ $y^2 = 4ax$,

which is required equation of the parabola.

JEE SPIKE

A parabola has two real foci situated on its axis one of which is the focus S and the other lies at infinity, the corresponding directrix is also at infinity.

Concept Inside Video

Some Terms Related to Parabola

1. **Axis** The axis of the parabola is the straight line which is passes through focus and perpendicular to the directrix of the parabola.

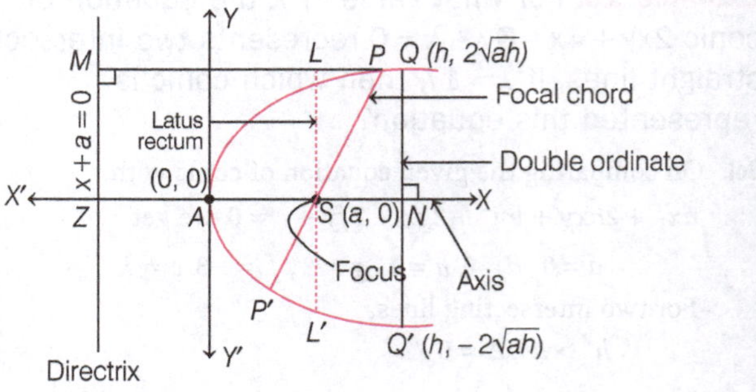

For the parabola $y^2 = 4ax$, X-axis is the **axis**.

Here, all powers of y are even in $y^2 = 4ax$, then parabola $y^2 = 4ax$ is symmetrical about its axis (i.e. X-axis).

Or

If the point (x, y) lie on the parabola $y^2 = 4ax$, then the point $(x, -y)$ also lies on it. Hence, the parabola is symmetrical about X-axis (i.e. axis of parabola).

2. **Vertex** The point of intersection of the parabola and its axis is called the vertex of the parabola. For the parabola $y^2 = 4ax$, the coordinate of vertex are $A(0, 0)$ i.e. the origin is the vertex.

3. **Double ordinate** If Q be the point on the parabola, draw QN perpendicular to the axis of parabola and produced to meet the curve again at Q', then QQ' is called a double ordinate.

   If abscissa of Q is h, then ordinate of Q,

   $y^2 = 4ah$ or $y = 2\sqrt{ah}$ (for first quadrant)

   and ordinate of Q' is $y = -2\sqrt{ah}$ (for fourth quadrant)

   Hence, coordinates of Q and Q' are $(h, 2\sqrt{ah})$ and $(h, -2\sqrt{ah})$, respectively.

4. **Latusrectum** The double ordinate LL' passes through the focus is called the latusrectum of the parabola.

   Since, focus $S(a, 0)$ the equation of the latusrectum of the parabola is $x = a$, then solving $x = a$ and $y^2 = 4ax$, we get

   $$y = \pm 2a$$

Hence, the coordinates of the extremities of the latusrectum are $L(a, 2a)$ and $L'(a, -2a)$, respectively.

Since, $LS = L'S = 2a$

$\therefore$ Length of latusrectum $LL' = 2(LS) = 2(L'S) = 4a$.

5. **Focal chord** A chord of a parabola which is passing through the focus is called a focal chord of the parabola. In the given figure, PP' and LL' are the focal chords.

6. **Focal distance** The focal distance of any point P on the parabola is its distance from the focus S i.e. SP

   Also, $SP = PM =$ Distance of P from the directrix.

   If $P \equiv (x, y)$,

   then $SP = PM = x + a$

7. **Parametric equations** From the equation of the parabola $y^2 = 4ax$, we can write $\dfrac{y}{2a} = \dfrac{2x}{y} = t$,

   where t is a parameter.

   Then, $y = 2at$ and $x = at^2$

   The equations $x = at^2$ and $y = 2at$ are called parametric equations. The point $(at^2, 2at)$ is also referred to as the point t.

5.5 Other forms of Parabola with Latusrectum 4a

(1) Parabola opening to left (i.e. $y^2 = -4ax$) : $(a > 0)$

(i) Vertex is $A(0, 0)$.

(ii) Focus is $S(-a, 0)$.

(iii) Equation of the directrix MZ is $x - a = 0$.

(iv) Equation of the axis is $y = 0$ i.e. X-axis.

(v) Equation of the tangent at the vertex is $x = 0$ i.e. Y-axis.

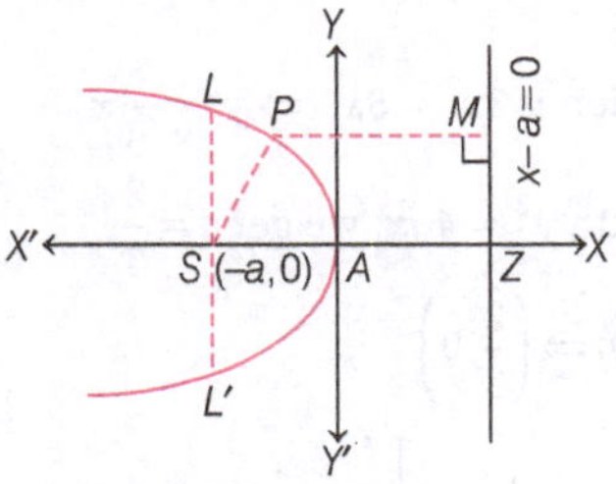

(vi) Length of latusrectum $= LL' = 4a$.

(vii) Ends of latusrectum are $L(-a, 2a)$ and $L'(-a, -2a)$.

(viii) Equation of latusrectum is $x = -a$ i.e. $x + a = 0$.

(ix) Parametric coordinates is $(-at^2, 2at)$.

(2) Parabola opening upwards (i.e. $x^2 = 4ay$) : $(a > 0)$

(i) Vertex is $A(0, 0)$.

(ii) Focus is $S(0, a)$.

(iii) Equation of the directrix MZ is $y + a = 0$.

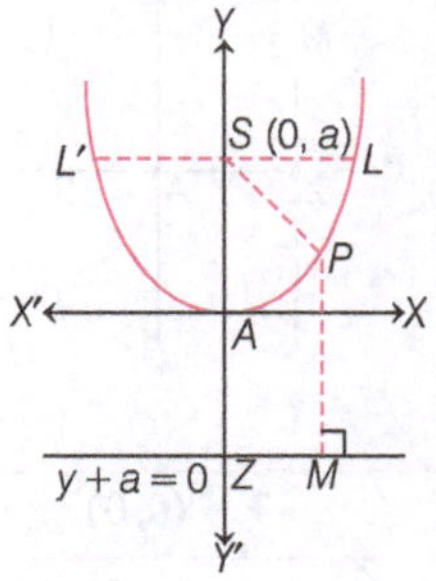

(iv) Equations of the axis is $x = 0$ i.e. Y-axis.

(v) Equation of the tangent at the vertex is $y = 0$ i.e. X-axis.

(vi) Ends of latusrectum are $L(2a, a)$ and $L'(-2a, a)$.

(vii) Length of latusrectum $= LL' = 4a$.

(viii) Equation of latusrectum is $y = a$ i.e. $y - a = 0$.

(ix) Parametric coordinates is $(2at, at^2)$.

(3) Parabola opening downwards (i.e. $x^2 = -4ay$) : $(a > 0)$

(i) Vertex is $A(0, 0)$.

(ii) Focus is $S(0, -a)$.

(iii) Equation of the directrix MZ is $y - a = 0$.

(iv) Equation of the axis is $x = 0$ i.e. Y-axis.

(v) Equation of the tangent at the vertex is $y = 0$ i.e. X-axis.

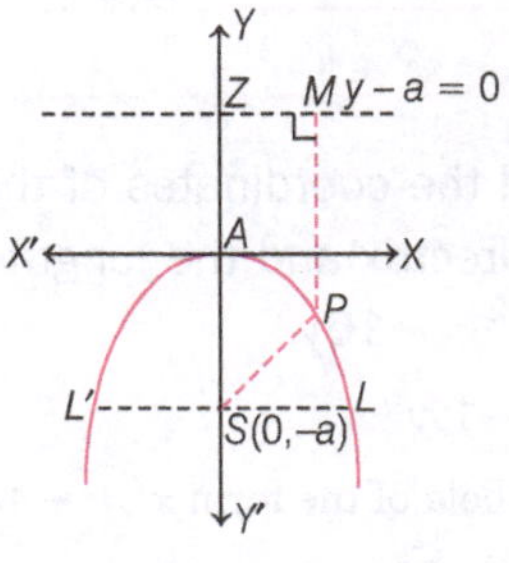

(vi) Length of latusrectum $= LL' = 4a$

(vii) Ends of latusrectum are $L(2a, -a)$ and $L'(-2a, -a)$.

(viii) Equation of latusrectum is $y = -a$ i.e. $y + a = 0$.

(ix) Parametric coordinates are $(2at, -at^2)$.

Smart Table : The Study of Standard Parabolas

Equation and Graph of the parabola	$y^2 = 4ax, a > 0$	$y^2 = -4ax, a > 0$	$x^2 = 4ay, a > 0$	$x^2 = -4ay, a > 0$
	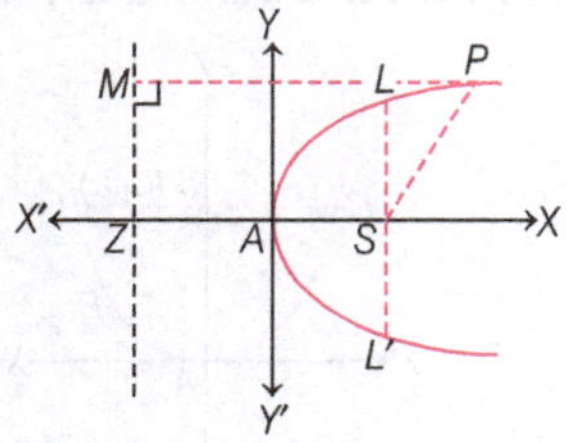	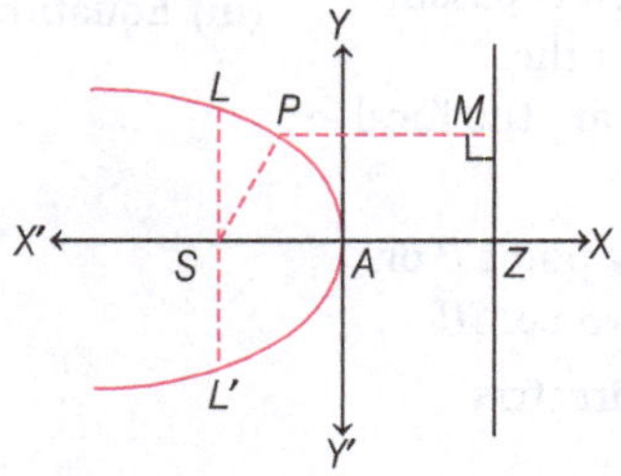	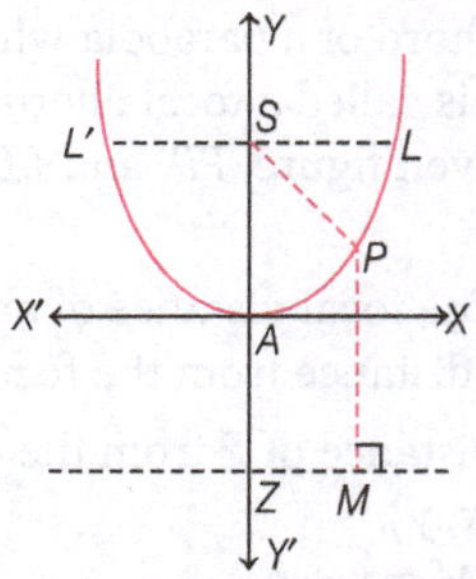	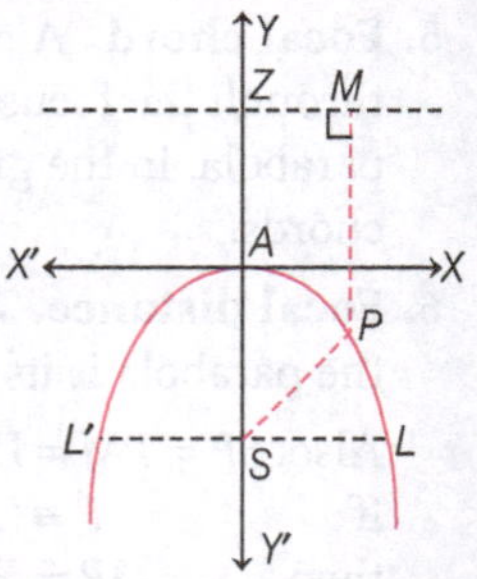
Vertex	$(0, 0)$	$(0, 0)$	$(0, 0)$	$(0, 0)$
Focus	$(a, 0)$	$(-a, 0)$	$(0, a)$	$(0, -a)$
Equation of the axis	$y = 0$	$y = 0$	$x = 0$	$x = 0$
Equation of tangent at vertex	$x = 0$	$x = 0$	$y = 0$	$y = 0$
Equation of directrix	$x + a = 0$	$x - a = 0$	$y + a = 0$	$y - a = 0$
Length of latusrectum	$4a$	$4a$	$4a$	$4a$
Ends points of latusrectum	$(a, \pm 2a)$	$(-a, \pm 2a)$	$(\pm 2a, a)$	$(\pm 2a, -a)$
Equation of latusrectum	$x - a = 0$	$x + a = 0$	$y - a = 0$	$y + a = 0$
Focal distance of a point $P(x, y)$	$x + a$	$a - x$	$y + a$	$a - y$
Parametric coordinates	$(at^2, 2at)$	$(-at^2, 2at)$	$(2at, at^2)$	$(2at, -at^2)$
Eccentricity (e)	1	1	1	1

Example 12. Find the coordinates of the focus, the equation of the directrix and the length of latusrectum of the parabola $x^2 = -16y$.

Sol. We have, $x^2 = -16y$

which is a parabola of the form $x^2 = -4ay$, where

$$4a = 16 \Rightarrow a = 4$$

Therefore,

(i) Focus $\equiv (0, -a) = (0, -4)$

(ii) Equation of directrix is $y = a \Rightarrow y = 4$

(iii) Length of the latusrectum $= 4a = 4 \times 4 = 16$

Example 13. Find the coordinates of focus, the equation of axis, the equation of the directrix and the length of latus rectum of the parabola represented by $3y^2 = 8x$.

Sol. Given equation is $3y^2 = 8x \Rightarrow y^2 = \frac{8}{3}x$

Compare with $y^2 = 4ax$, we get $a = \frac{2}{3}$

Focus $\equiv (a, 0) \Rightarrow \left(\frac{2}{3}, 0\right)$

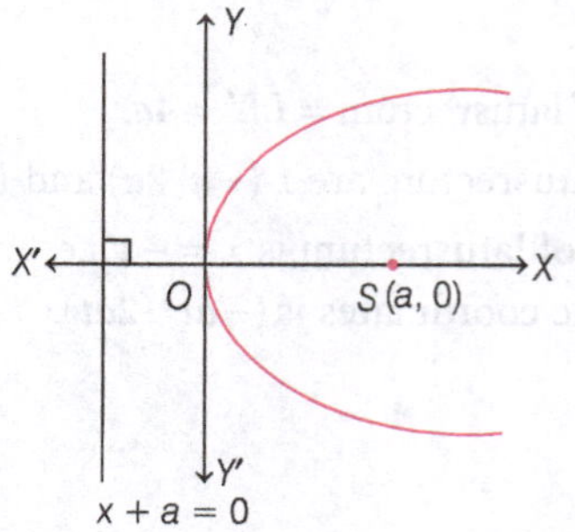

The equation of axis is $y = 0$ [i.e. equation of X-axis]
Equation of directrix $= x + a = 0$

$$\Rightarrow \quad x + \frac{2}{3} = 0$$

Length of latusrectum $= 4a = 4\left(\frac{2}{3}\right) = \frac{8}{3}$

Example 14. If a parabolic reflector is 20 cm in diameter and 5 cm deep, find the focus.

Sol. Let the origin be the vertex of the parabolic reflector in such a way that the axis of the reflector is along the positive X-axis.

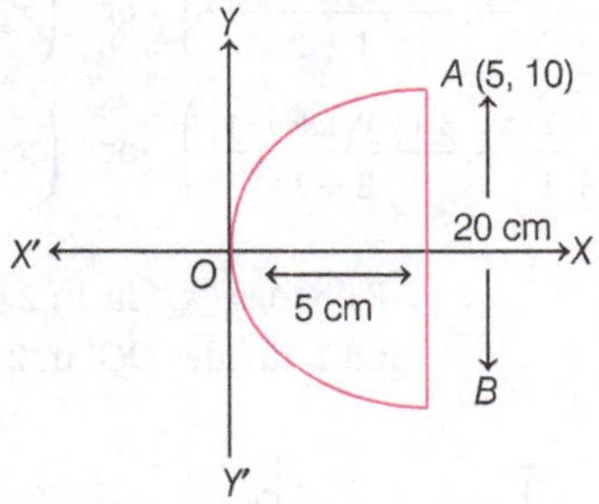

Equation of the parabola is $y^2 = 4ax$

Since, parabola passes through $A(5, 10)$

$$\therefore \quad 10^2 = 4a(5) \Rightarrow a = 5$$

So, focus is $(a, 0)$ i.e. $(5, 0)$, which is mid-point of the diameter.

Hence, focus of the reflector is the mid-point of the diameter.

5.6 General Equation of a Parabola

Let $S(a, b)$ be the focus and $lx + my + n = 0$ is the equation of the directrix. Let $P(x, y)$ be any point on the parabola. Then, by definition $SP = PM$

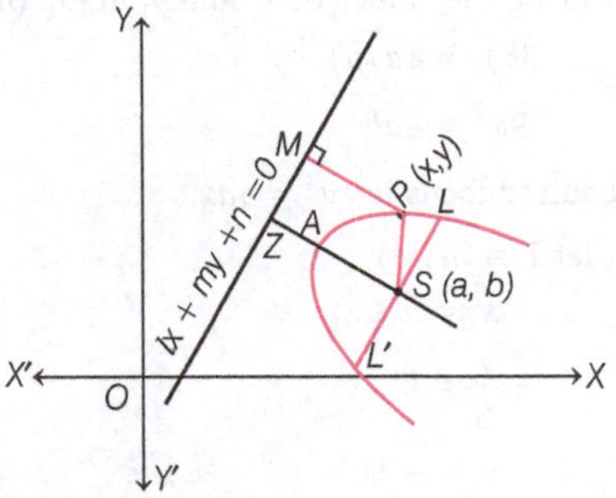

$$\Rightarrow \quad \sqrt{(x-a)^2 + (y-b)^2} = \frac{|lx + my + n|}{\sqrt{(l^2 + m^2)}}$$

$$\Rightarrow \quad (x-a)^2 + (y-b)^2 = \frac{(lx + my + n)^2}{(l^2 + m^2)}$$

$$\Rightarrow \quad m^2x^2 + l^2y^2 - 2lmxy + x \text{ term} + y \text{ term} + \text{constant} = 0$$

This is of the form $(mx - ly)^2 + 2gx + 2fy + c = 0$.

This equation is the general equation of parabola.

Example 15. Find the equation of the parabola whose focus is at $(-1, -2)$ and the directrix is the straight line $x - 2y + 3 = 0$.

Sol. Let $P(x, y)$ be any point on the parabola whose focus is $S(-1, -2)$ and the directrix $x - 2y + 3 = 0$. Draw PM perpendicular from $P(x, y)$ on the directrix $x - 2y + 3 = 0$.

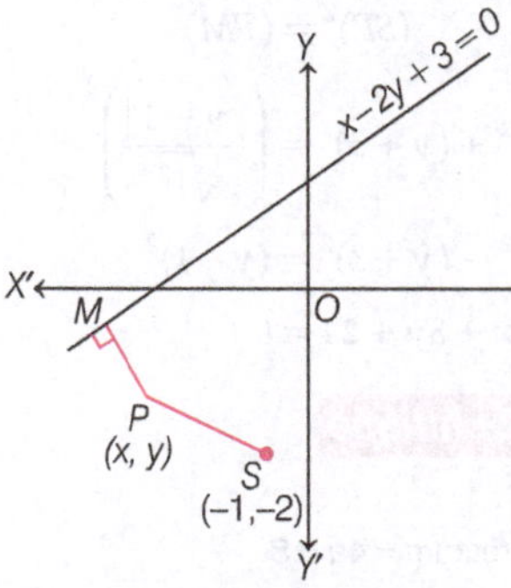

Then, by definition,

$$SP = PM$$

$$\Rightarrow \quad (SP)^2 = (PM)^2$$

$$\Rightarrow (x+1)^2 + (y+2)^2 = \left(\frac{|x - 2y + 3|}{\sqrt{(1)^2 + (-2)^2}}\right)^2$$

$$\Rightarrow 5(x^2 + y^2 + 2x + 4y + 5) = (x^2 + 4y^2 - 4xy + 6x - 12y + 9)$$

$$\therefore \quad 4x^2 + y^2 + 4xy + 4x + 32y + 16 = 0$$

Example 16. Find the equation of the parabola whose focus is $(4, -3)$ and vertex is $(4, -1)$.

Sol. Let $A(4, -1)$ be the vertex and $S(4, -3)$ be the focus.

$$\therefore \quad \text{Slope of } AS = \frac{-3 + 1}{4 - 4} = \infty$$

which is parallel to Y-axis.

$\therefore$ Directrix parallel to X-axis.

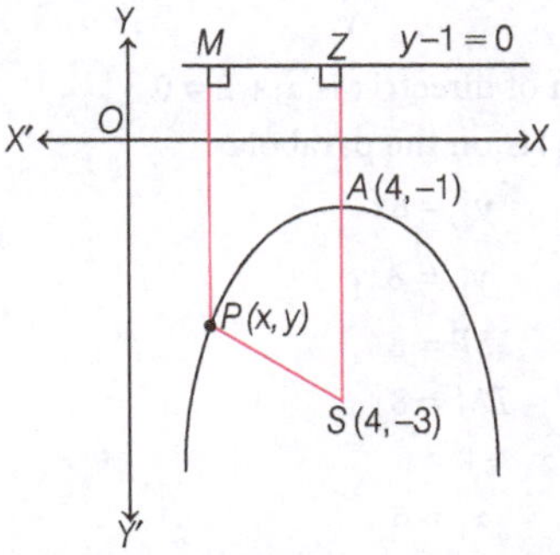

Let $Z(x_1, y_1)$ be any point on the directrix, then A is the mid-point of SZ.

$$\therefore \quad 4 = \frac{x_1 + 4}{2} \Rightarrow x_1 = 4$$

$$\text{and} \quad -1 = \frac{y_1 - 3}{2} \Rightarrow y_1 = 1$$

$$\therefore \quad Z = (4, 1)$$

Also, directrix is parallel to X-axis and passes through $Z(4,1)$, so equation of directrix is

$$y=1 \quad \text{or} \quad y-1=0$$

Now, let $P(x,y)$ be any point on the parabola. Join SP and draw PM perpendicular to the directrix. Then, by definition

$$SP = PM$$

$$\Rightarrow \quad (SP)^2 = (PM)^2$$

$$\Rightarrow \quad (x-4)^2 + (y+3)^2 = \left(\frac{|y-1|}{\sqrt{1^2}}\right)^2$$

$$\Rightarrow \quad (x-4)^2 + (y+3)^2 = (y-1)^2$$

$$\therefore \quad x^2 - 8x + 8y + 24 = 0$$

Time Saving Technique

Here, $a = AS = 2$

$\therefore$ Length of latusrectum $= 4a = 8$

Equation of parabola with vertex (0, 0) and open downward is

$$x^2 = -8y.$$

Shifting $(4, -1)$ on $(0, 0)$, we get required parabola

$$(x-4)^2 = -8(y+1)$$

$$\therefore \quad x^2 - 8x + 8y + 24 = 0$$

Example 17. The focal distance of a point on a parabola $y^2 = 8x$ is 8. Find the point.

Sol. Comparing $y^2 = 8x$ with $y^2 = 4ax$, we get

$$\therefore \quad 4a = 8 \Rightarrow a = 2$$

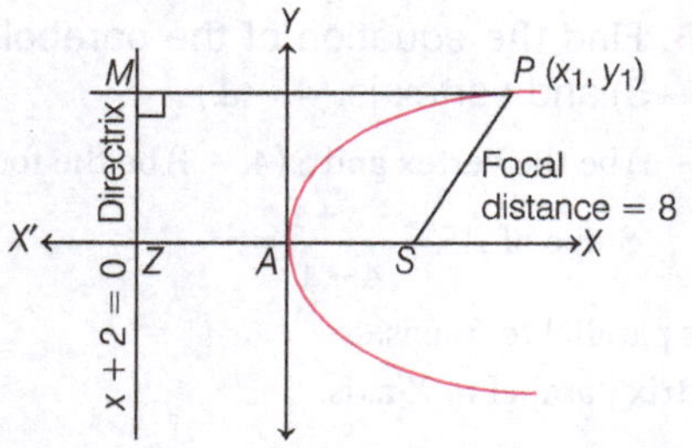

$\therefore$ Equation of directrix is $x + 2 = 0$.

Let $P(x_1, y_1)$ is on the parabola

$$y^2 = 8x$$

$$\therefore \quad y_1^2 = 8x_1 \quad \text{...(i)}$$

$$\because \quad SP = 8$$

$$\Rightarrow \quad PM = 8 \quad [\because SP = PM]$$

$$\Rightarrow \quad x_1 + 2 = 8$$

$$\text{or} \quad x_1 = 6$$

From Eq. (i),

$$y_1^2 = 8 \times 6$$

$$\therefore \quad y_1 = \pm 4\sqrt{3}$$

Hence, the required points are $(6, 4\sqrt{3})$ and $(6, -4\sqrt{3})$.

Example 18. QQ' is a double ordinate of a parabola $y^2 = 4ax$. Find the locus of its point of trisection.

Sol. Let the double ordinate QQ' meet the axis of the parabola

$$y^2 = 4ax \quad \text{...(i)}$$

Let coordinates of Q be (x_1, y_1), then coordinates of Q' be $(x_1, -y_1)$.

Since, Q and Q' lies on Eq. (i), then

$$y_1^2 = 4ax_1 \quad \text{...(ii)}$$

Let R and T be the points of trisection of QQ'. Then, the coordinates of R and T are

$$\left(\frac{1\cdot x_1 + 2\cdot x_1}{1+2}, \frac{1\cdot(-y_1) + 2\cdot y_1}{1+2}\right) \quad \text{or} \quad \left(x_1, \frac{y_1}{3}\right)$$

$$\text{and} \quad \left(\frac{2\cdot x_1 + 1\cdot x_1}{2+1}, \frac{2\cdot(-y_1) + 1\cdot y_1}{2+1}\right) \quad \text{or} \quad \left(x_1, -\frac{y_1}{3}\right),$$

respectively.

[$\because$ R divides QQ' in 1 : 2 (internally) and T divides QQ' in 2 : 1 (internally)]

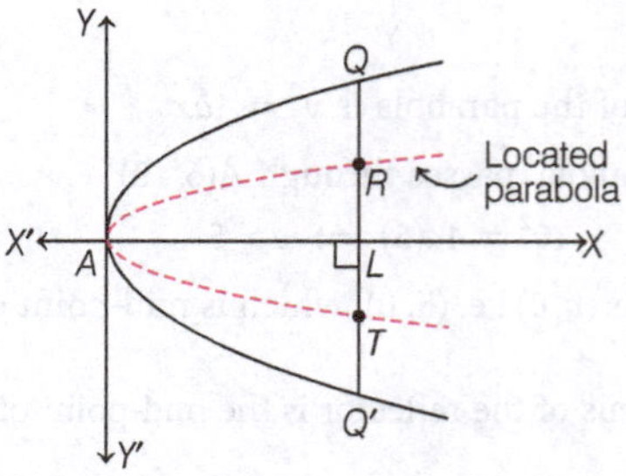

For locus, let $R(h,k)$, then

$$x_1 = h \quad \text{and} \quad \frac{y_1}{3} = k$$

$$\text{or} \quad y_1 = 3k$$

On substituting the values of x_1 and y_1 in Eq. (ii), then

$$(3k)^2 = 4a(h)$$

$$\text{or} \quad 9k^2 = 4ah$$

$\therefore$ The required locus is $9y^2 = 4ax$.

Similarly, let $T \equiv (h', k')$

$$\text{Then,} \quad x_1 = h'$$

$$\text{and} \quad -\frac{y_1}{3} = k'$$

$$\text{or} \quad y_1 = -3k'$$

On substituting the values of x_1 and y_1 in Eq. (ii), then

$$(-3k')^2 = 4a(h')$$

$$\text{or} \quad 9k'^2 = 4ah'$$

$\therefore$ The required locus is $9y^2 = 4ax$.

Hence, the locus of point of trisection is

$$9y^2 = 4ax$$

Time Saving Technique

Let R and T be the points of trisection of double ordinates QQ'. Let (h,k) be the coordinates of R.

Then, $AL = h$ and $RL = k$

$RT = RL + LT = k + k = 2k.$

$\because$ $RQ = TR = Q'T = 2k$

$\therefore$ $LQ = LR + RQ = k + 2k = 3k$

Thus, the coordinates of Q are $(h, 3k)$.

Since, $(h, 3k)$ lies on $y^2 = 4ax$

$\Rightarrow$ $9k^2 = 4ah$

Hence, the locus of point of trisection is $9y^2 = 4ax$.

Example 19. Prove that the area of the triangle inscribed in the parabola $y^2 = 4ax$ is $\frac{1}{8a}(y_1 - y_2)(y_2 - y_3)(y_3 - y_1)$, where y_1, y_2 and y_3 are the ordinates of the vertices.

Sol. Let the vertices of the triangle be $(x_1, y_1), (x_2, y_2)$ and (x_3, y_3).

$\because$ (x_1, y_1) is a point on the parabola $y^2 = 4ax$.

$$\therefore \quad y_1^2 = 4ax_1$$

$$\therefore \quad x_1 = \frac{y_1^2}{4a}$$

Similarly, $x_2 = \frac{y_2^2}{4a}$ and $x_3 = \frac{y_3^2}{4a}$

Now, vertices of triangle are

$$\left(\frac{y_1^2}{4a}, y_1\right), \left(\frac{y_2^2}{4a}, y_2\right) \text{ and } \left(\frac{y_3^2}{4a}, y_3\right).$$

$$\therefore \text{ Required area of the triangle} = \frac{1}{2}\left\|\begin{matrix} \frac{y_1^2}{4a} & y_1 & 1 \\ \frac{y_2^2}{4a} & y_2 & 1 \\ \frac{y_3^2}{4a} & y_3 & 1 \end{matrix}\right\|$$

$$= \frac{1}{8a}\left\|\begin{matrix} y_1^2 & y_1 & 1 \\ y_2^2 & y_2 & 1 \\ y_3^2 & y_3 & 1 \end{matrix}\right\| = \frac{1}{8a}(y_1 - y_2)(y_2 - y_3)(y_3 - y_1)$$

Example 20. Find the length of the side of an equilateral triangle inscribed in the parabola $y^2 = 4ax$, so that one angular point is at the vertex.

Sol. Let ABC be the inscribed equilateral triangle, with one angular point is at the vertex A of the parabola

$$y^2 = 4ax \quad \text{...(i)}$$

Let the length of the side of equilateral triangle $= l$

$\therefore$ $AB = BC = CA = l$

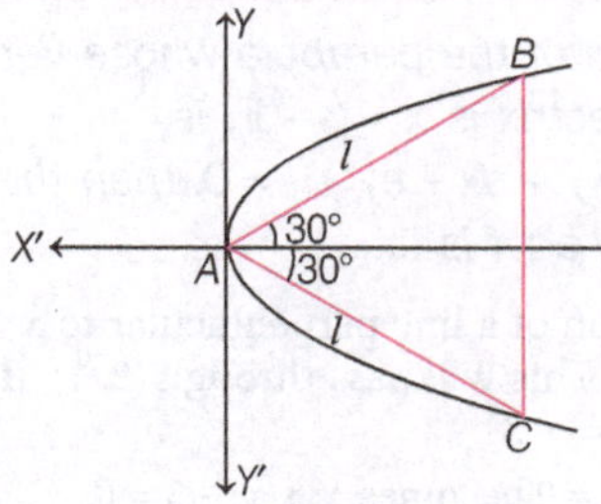

$\therefore$ The coordinates of B is $(l \cos 30°, l \sin 30°)$

i.e. $\left(\frac{l\sqrt{3}}{2}, \frac{l}{2}\right)$.

Since, B lies on Eq. (i), then $\left(\frac{l}{2}\right)^2 = 4a\left(\frac{l\sqrt{3}}{2}\right)$

or $l = 8a\sqrt{3}$

Example 21. The chord AB of the parabola $y^2 = 4ax$ cuts the axis of the parabola at C. If $A = (at_1^2, 2at_1)$, $B = (at_2^2, 2at_2)$ and $AC : AB = 1 : 3$, then find the value of $\frac{t_2}{t_1}$.

Sol. We have,

$$\frac{AC}{AB} = \frac{1}{3}$$

$$\Rightarrow \quad \frac{AC}{BC} = \frac{1}{2}$$

$$\therefore \quad C \equiv \left(\frac{2at_1^2 + at_2^2}{3}, \frac{4at_1 + 2at_2}{3}\right)$$

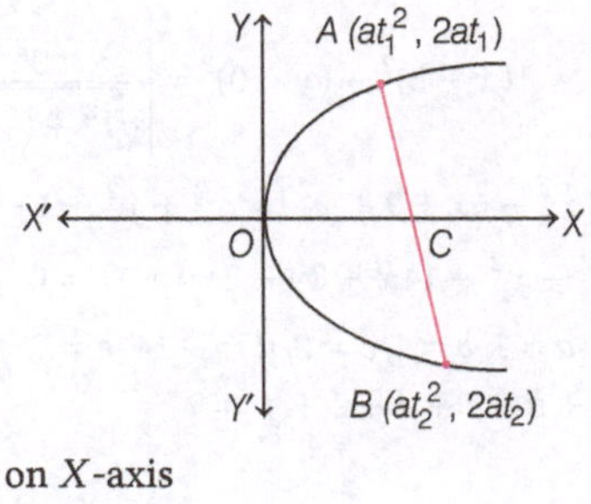

Since, C lies on X-axis

$$\therefore \quad \frac{4at_1 + 2at_2}{3} = 0$$

$$\Rightarrow \quad t_2 + 2t_1 = 0$$

$$\Rightarrow \quad \frac{t_2}{t_1} = -2$$

JEE SCANNER

Example Similar to PYQ Asked in JEE Main 2022

If the equation of the parabola whose vertex is at (2, 1) and directrix is $x = y - 1$, is $ax^2 + by^2 + cxy + dx + ey + f = 0$, then the value of $a + b + c + d + e + f$ is ....

Sol. (9) The equation of a line perpendicular to $x - y + 1 = 0$ is $x + y + \lambda = 0$. This will pass through (2, 1), if $2 + 1 + \lambda = 0$

$\Rightarrow \quad \lambda = -3$

So, $x + y + \lambda = 0$ becomes $x + y - 3 = 0$, ...(i)

which is equation of axis of parabola.

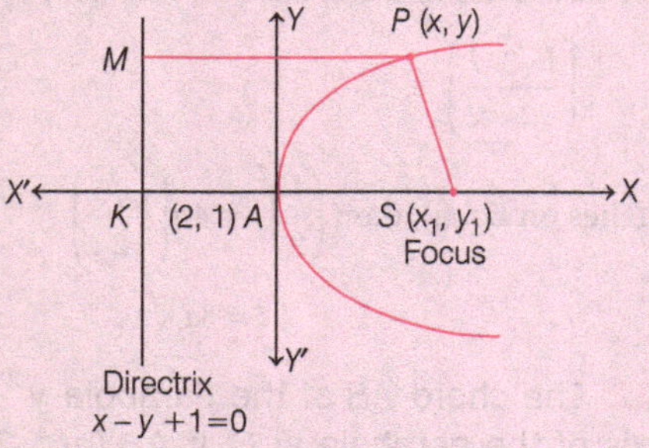

The equation of directrix is $x - y + 1 = 0$ ...(ii)

On solving Eqs. (i) and (ii), we get $x = 1$ and $y = 2$

$\therefore$ The coordinates of K are (1, 2).

Let the focus be $S(x_1, y_1)$.

Then, A is mid-point of KS

$$\therefore \quad \frac{x_1 + 1}{2} = 2 \quad \text{and} \quad \frac{y_1 + 2}{2} = 1$$

$$\Rightarrow \quad x_1 = 3 \quad \text{and} \quad y_1 = 0$$

So, focus is $S(3, 0)$.

Now, let $P(x, y)$ be any point on parabola.

Then, $\quad PS = PM \Rightarrow PS^2 = PM^2$

$$\Rightarrow \quad (x-3)^2 + (y-0)^2 = \left|\frac{x - y + 1}{\sqrt{1^2 + (-1)^2}}\right|^2$$

$$\Rightarrow \quad 2[x^2 - 6x + 9 + y^2] = x^2 + y^2 + 1 - 2xy - 2y + 2x$$

$$\Rightarrow \quad x^2 + y^2 - 14x + 2y + 2xy + 17 = 0$$

$$\therefore \quad a = 1, b = 1, c = 2, d = -14, e = 2, f = 17$$

So, $\quad a + b + c + d + e + f = 9$

Skill Builder

If the equation of the parabola whose vertex is at $(-2, -3)$ and directrix is $y + 2 = 0$ is $ax^2 + by^2 + cxy + dx + ey + f = 0$, then the value of $a + b + c + d + e + f$ is ......

For Sol.

■ **For more practice** See Q.14 of Milestone Practice 5.1.

Example 22. Prove that the equation of the parabola whose focus is (0,0) and tangent at the vertex is $x - y + 1 = 0$ is $x^2 + y^2 + 2xy - 4x + 4y - 4 = 0$.

Sol. Let focus be $S(0, 0)$ and A be the vertex of the parabola. Take any point Z such that $AS = AZ$, given tangent at vertex is $x - y + 1 = 0$, since directrix is parallel to the tangent at the vertex.

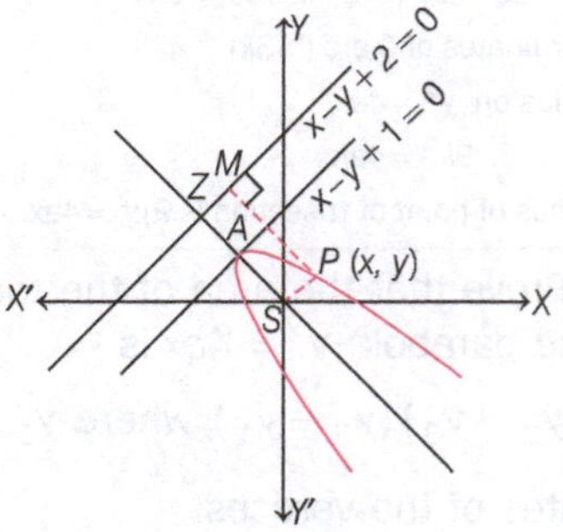

$\therefore$ Equation of directrix is $x - y + \lambda = 0$,

where λ is constant.

$\because A$ is the mid-point of SZ.

$$\therefore \quad SZ = 2SA$$

$$\Rightarrow \quad \frac{|0 - 0 + \lambda|}{\sqrt{(1^2 + (-1)^2)}} = 2 \times \frac{|0 - 0 + 1|}{\sqrt{(1^2 + (-1)^2)}}$$

$$\Rightarrow \quad \frac{|\lambda|}{\sqrt{2}} = \frac{2}{\sqrt{2}}$$

$$\therefore \quad \lambda = \pm 2 \Rightarrow \lambda = 2$$

[λ is positive, since directrix in this case always lies in II quadrant]

$\therefore$ Equation of directrix is $x - y + 2 = 0$.

Now, let $P(x, y)$ be any point on the parabola, draw $PM \perp ZM$, then from definition,

$$SP = PM \Rightarrow (SP)^2 = (PM)^2$$

$$\Rightarrow \quad (x-0)^2 + (y-0)^2 = \left(\frac{|x - y + 2|}{\sqrt{2}}\right)^2$$

$$\Rightarrow \quad 2(x^2 + y^2) = (x - y + 2)^2$$

$$\Rightarrow \quad 2x^2 + 2y^2 = x^2 + y^2 - 2xy + 4x - 4y + 4$$

$$\therefore \quad x^2 + y^2 + 2xy - 4x + 4y - 4 = 0$$

Equation of Parabola if Equation of Axis, Tangent at Vertex and Latusrectum are given

Let equation of axis is $ax + by + c = 0$ and equation of tangent at vertex is $bx - ay + d = 0$.

Equation of parabola is

$$(PM)^2 = (\text{latusrectum})\,(PN)$$

$$\Rightarrow \left(\frac{ax+by+c}{\sqrt{(a^2+b^2)}}\right)^2 = (\text{latusrectum})\left(\frac{bx-ay+d}{\sqrt{(b^2+a^2)}}\right)$$

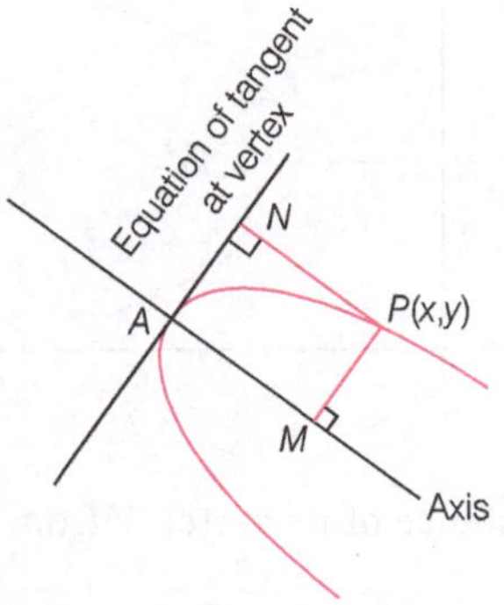

Example 23. Find the equation of the parabola whose latusrectum is 4 units, axis is the line $3x+4y-4=0$ and the tangent at the vertex is the line $4x-3y+7=0$.

Sol. Let $P(x, y)$ be any point on the parabola and let PM and PN are perpendiculars from P on the axis and tangent at the vertex respectively, then

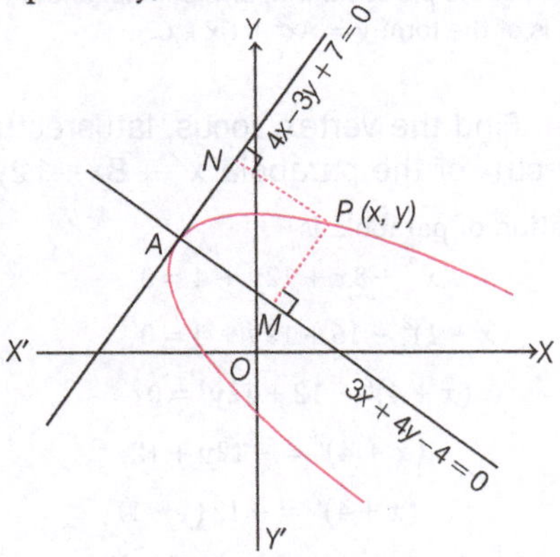

$$(PM)^2 = (\text{latusrectum})\,(PN)$$

$$\Rightarrow \left(\frac{3x+4y-4}{\sqrt{3^2+4^2}}\right)^2 = 4\left(\frac{4x-3y+7}{\sqrt{4^2+(-3)^2}}\right)$$

$$\therefore \quad (3x+4y-4)^2 = 20(4x-3y+7)$$

which is required parabola.

5.7 The Generalised form $(y-k)^2 = 4a(x-h)$

The parabola $\quad y^2 = 4ax \quad$ ...(i)

can be written as $(y-0)^2 = 4a(x-0)$.

The vertex of this parabola is $A(0,0)$.

Now, when origin is shifted at $A'(h, k)$ without changing the direction of axes, its equation becomes

$$(y-k)^2 = 4a(x-h) \quad \text{...(ii)}$$

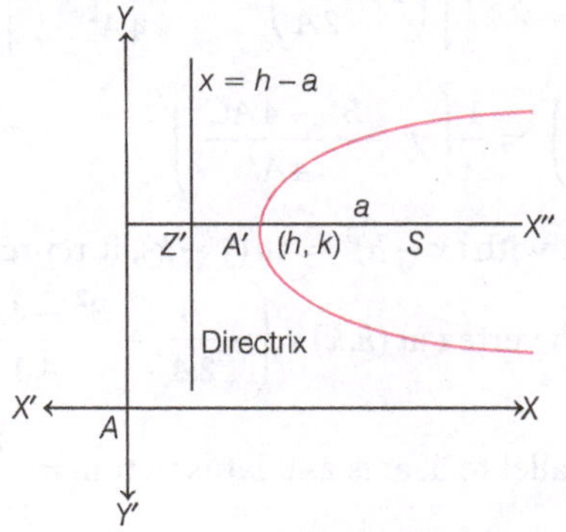

This is called generalised form of the parabola Eq. (i) and axis $A'X''\,||\,AX$ with its vertex at $A'(h, k)$. Its focus is at $(a+h, k)$ and length of latusrectum $= 4a$, the equation of the directrix is

$$x = h-a \Rightarrow x+a-h=0$$

Another form is $(x-h)^2 = 4a(y-k)$ axis parallel to

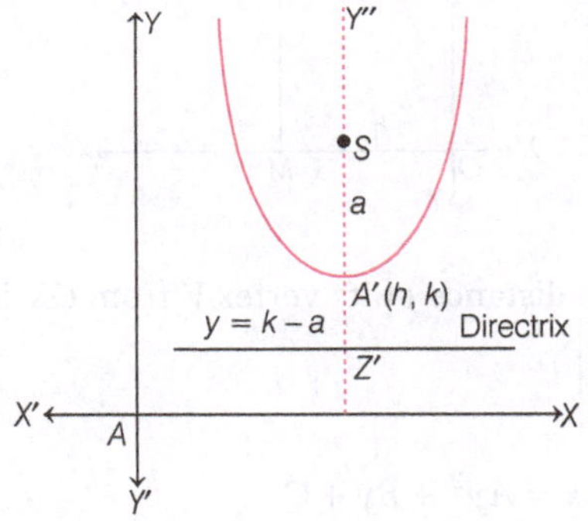

Y-axis with its vertex (h, k) its focus is at $(h, a+k)$ and length of latusrectum $= 4a$, the equation of the directrix is

$$y = k-a \Rightarrow y+a-k=0.$$

JEE SPIKE

The parametric equation of $(y-k)^2 = 4a(x-h)$ are $x = h+at^2$ and $y = k+2at$.

5.8 Parabolic Curve

The equations $y = Ax^2+Bx+C$ and $x = Ay^2+By+C$ are always represent parabolas generally called parabolic curve.

Now, $\quad y = Ax^2+Bx+C$

$$= A\left\{x^2 + \frac{B}{A}x + \frac{C}{A}\right\}$$

$$= A\left\{\left(x+\frac{B}{2A}\right)^2 - \frac{B^2}{4A^2} + \frac{C}{A}\right\}$$

$$= A\left\{\left(x + \frac{B}{2A}\right)^2 - \frac{(B^2 - 4AC)}{4A^2}\right\}$$

or $$\left(x + \frac{B}{2A}\right)^2 = \frac{1}{A}\left(y + \frac{B^2 - 4AC}{4A}\right)$$

Comparing it with $(x - h)^2 = 4a(y - k)$, it represents a parabola with vertex at $(h, k) = \left(-\frac{B}{2A}, -\frac{B^2 - 4AC}{4A}\right)$

and axis parallel to Y-axis and latusrectum $= \frac{1}{|A|}$

and the curve opening upwards and downwards depending upon the sign of A and B.

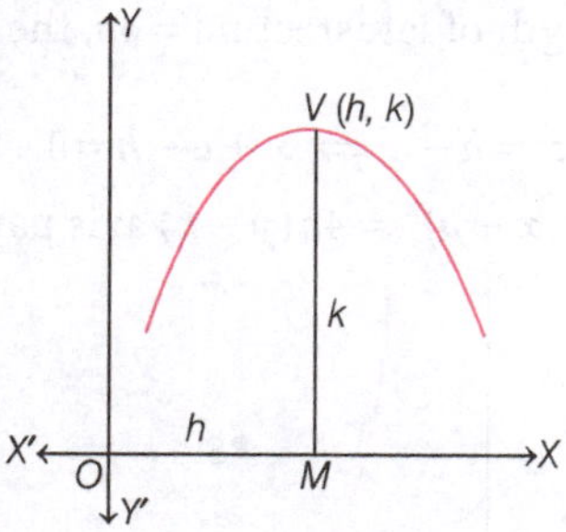

The optimum distance of its vertex V from OX is $\left|-\frac{B^2 - 4AC}{4A}\right|$

and $$x = Ay^2 + By + C$$

$$= A\left\{y^2 + \frac{B}{A}y + \frac{C}{A}\right\}$$

$$= A\left\{\left(y + \frac{B}{2A}\right)^2 - \frac{B^2}{4A^2} + \frac{C}{A}\right\}$$

$$= A\left\{\left(y + \frac{B}{2A}\right)^2 - \frac{B^2 - 4AC}{4A^2}\right\}$$

$$\Rightarrow \left(y + \frac{B}{2A}\right)^2 = \frac{1}{A}\left(x + \frac{B^2 - 4AC}{4A}\right)$$

Comparing it with $(y - k)^2 = 4a(x - h)$, it represents a parabola with vertex at

$$(h, k) = \left(-\frac{B^2 - 4AC}{4A}, -\frac{B}{2A}\right)$$

and axis parallel to X-axis and latusrectum $= \frac{1}{|A|}$

and the curve opening left and right depending upon the sign of A and B.

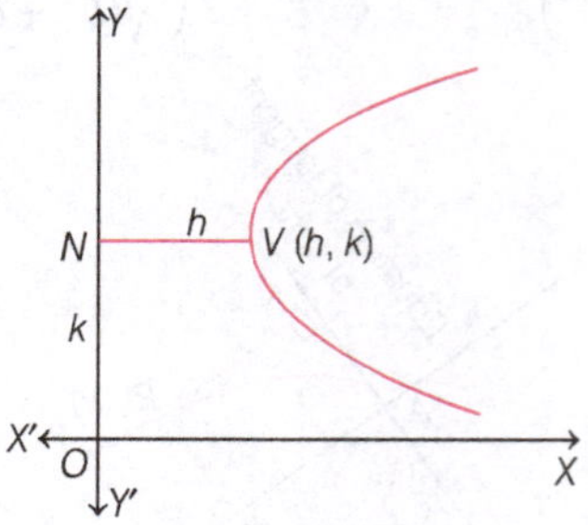

The optimum distance of its vertex V from OY is $\left|-\frac{B^2 - 4AC}{4A}\right|$.

JEE Focus Points

Concept Inside Video

- Equation of the parabola with axis parallel to the X-axis is of the form $x = Ay^2 + By + C$.
- Equation of the parabola with axis parallel to the Y-axis is of the form $y = Ax^2 + Bx + C$.

Example 24. Find the vertex, focus, latusrectum, axis and the directrix of the parabola $x^2 + 8x + 12y + 4 = 0$.

Sol. The equation of parabola is

$$x^2 + 8x + 12y + 4 = 0 \quad \text{...(i)}$$

$$\Rightarrow (x + 4)^2 - 16 + 12y + 4 = 0$$

$$\Rightarrow (x + 4)^2 - 12 + 12y = 0$$

$$\Rightarrow (x + 4)^2 = -12y + 12$$

$$\Rightarrow (x + 4)^2 = -12(y - 1)$$

Let $x + 4 = X, y - 1 = Y$ ...(ii)

$\therefore$ $X^2 = -12Y$ ...(iii)

On comparing it with $X^2 = -4aY$,

$\therefore$ $a = 3$

$\therefore$ Vertex of Eq. (iii) is (0, 0).

i.e. $X = 0, Y = 0$

From Eq. (ii),

$$x + 4 = 0, y - 1 = 0$$

$\therefore$ $x = -4, y = 1$

$\therefore$ Vertex of Eq. (i) is $(-4, 1)$.

Foucs of Eq. (iii) is $(0, -3)$

i.e. $X = 0, Y = -3$

From Eq. (ii),

$$x + 4 = 0, y - 1 = -3$$

$\therefore$ $x = -4, y = -2$

$\therefore$ Focus of Eq. (i) is $(-4, -2)$.

and latusrectum $= 4a = 12$.

Equation of axis of Eq. (iii) is $X = 0$

$\therefore$ Equation of axis of Eq. (i) is $x + 4 = 0$

Equation of directrix of Eq. (iii) is

$$Y = 3 \text{ or } y - 1 = 3$$

$$\therefore \quad y - 4 = 0$$

$\therefore$ Equation of directrix of Eq. (i) is

$$y - 4 = 0.$$

Example 25. Prove that the equation $y^2 + 2ax + 2by + c = 0$ represents a parabola whose axis is parallel to the axis of x. Find its vertex.

Sol. The equation of parabola is

$$y^2 + 2ax + 2by + c = 0$$

$$(y + b)^2 - b^2 + 2ax + c = 0$$

$$\Rightarrow \quad (y + b)^2 = -2ax + b^2 - c$$

$$\Rightarrow \quad (y + b)^2 = -2a\left(x - \frac{b^2 - c}{2a}\right) \quad \text{...(i)}$$

Let $\quad y + b = Y,\ x - \dfrac{b^2 - c}{2a} = X$

From Eq. (i),

$$Y^2 = -2aX \quad \text{...(ii)}$$

Axis of its parabola is $Y = 0$ or $y + b = 0$,

which is parallel to X-axis

and vertex of Eq. (ii) is $X = 0, Y = 0$

$$\Rightarrow \quad x - \frac{b^2 - c}{2a} = 0, \quad y + b = 0$$

$$\Rightarrow \quad x = \frac{b^2 - c}{2a}, \quad y = -b$$

$\therefore$ Vertex of given parabola is $\left(\dfrac{b^2 - c}{2a}, -b\right)$.

Example 26. Find the equation of the parabola with its vertex at (3, 2) and its focus at (5, 2).

Sol. Let vertex be $A(3, 2)$ and focus be $S(5, 2)$.

Slope of $AS = \dfrac{2 - 2}{5 - 3} = 0$, which is parallel to X-axis.

Hence, axis of parabola is parallel to X-axis.

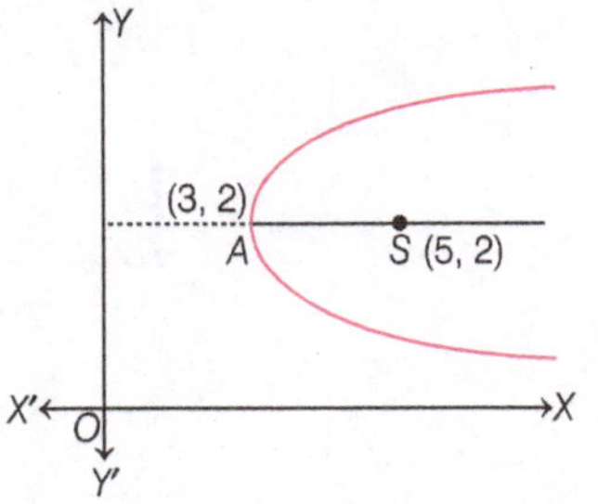

The equation is of the form

$$(y - k)^2 = 4a(x - h)$$

or $\quad (y - 2)^2 = 4a(x - 3) \quad [\because \text{veretx } (h, k) = (3, 2)]$

$a =$ distance between the focus and the vertex

$$= \sqrt{(5 - 3)^2 + (2 - 2)^2} = 2$$

Hence, the required equation is

$$(y - 2)^2 = 8(x - 3)$$

or $\quad y^2 - 8x - 4y + 28 = 0$

Example 27. Find the equation of the parabola with latusrectum joining the points (3, 6) and (3, −2).

Sol. Slope of (3,6) and (3, −2) is $\dfrac{-2 - 6}{3 - 3} = \infty$, since latusrectum is perpendicular to axis.

Hence, axis parallel to X-axis. The equation of the two possible parabolas will be of the form

$$(y - k)^2 = \pm 4a(x - h) \quad \text{...(i)}$$

Since, $\quad$ latusrectum $= \sqrt{(3 - 3)^2 + (6 + 2)^2} = 8$

$$\therefore \quad 4a = 8$$

$$\Rightarrow \quad a = 2$$

$\therefore$ From Eq. (i),

$$(y - k)^2 = \pm 8(x - h)$$

Since, (3,6) and (3, −2) lie on the parabola, then

$$(6 - k)^2 = \pm 8(3 - h) \quad \text{...(ii)}$$

and $\quad (-2 - k)^2 = \pm 8(3 - h) \quad \text{...(iii)}$

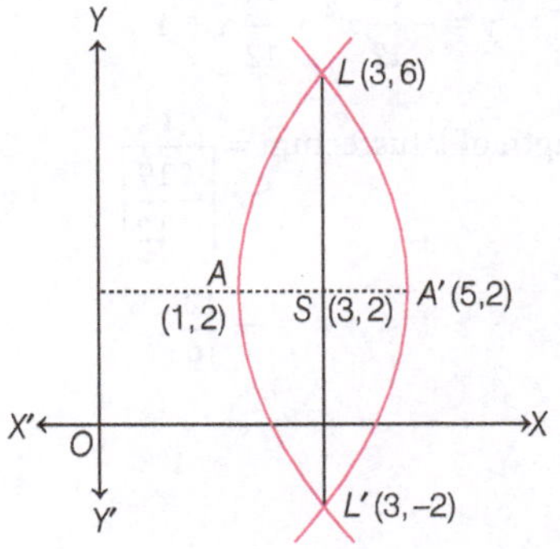

On solving Eqs. (ii) and (iii), we get

$$k = 2$$

From Eq. (ii),

$$16 = \pm 8(3 - h),$$

$$\therefore \quad h = 3 \pm 2$$

$$\therefore \quad h = 5, 1$$

Hence, values of (h, k) are (5,2) and (1, 2).

$\therefore$ The required parabola are

$$(y-2)^2 = 8(x-5)$$

and $$(y-2)^2 = -8(x-1).$$

Example 28. Find the equation of the parabola whose axis is parallel to the Y-axis and which passes through the points (0, 4) (1, 9) and (4, 5) and determine its latusrectum .

Sol. The equation of parabola parallel to Y-axis is

$$y = Ax^2 + Bx + C \quad \text{...(i)}$$

The points (0,4) , (1,9) and (4,5) lie on Eq. (i), then

$$4 = 0 + 0 + C \Rightarrow C = 4 \quad \text{...(ii)}$$

$$\Rightarrow \quad 9 = A + B + C$$

$$\Rightarrow \quad 9 = A + B + 4 \quad [\because C = 4]$$

$$\therefore \quad A + B = 5 \quad \text{...(iii)}$$

and $$5 = 16A + 4B + C \quad [\because C = 4]$$

$$\Rightarrow \quad 5 = 16A + 4B + 4$$

$$\therefore \quad 16A + 4B = 1$$

$$\Rightarrow \quad 4A + B = \frac{1}{4} \quad \text{...(iv)}$$

On solving Eqs. (iii) and (iv), we get

$$A = -\frac{19}{12}, B = \frac{79}{12} \quad \text{...(v)}$$

On substituting the values of A, B and C from Eqs. (ii) and Eq. (v) in Eq. (i), then equation of parabola is

$$y = -\frac{19}{12}x^2 + \frac{79}{12}x + 4$$

Hence, length of latusrectum $= \dfrac{1}{\left|-\dfrac{19}{12}\right|}$

$$= \frac{12}{19}$$

JEE SCANNER

Example Similar to PYQ Asked in JEE Main 2023

If area of the triangle whose one vertex is at the vertex of the parabola $y^2 + 4(x - a^2) = 0$ and the other two vertices are the points of intersections of the parabola and Y-axis, is 250 sq. units, then the value of a is

(a) $5\sqrt{5}$ (b) $(10)^{2/3}$ (c) $5(2)^{1/3}$ (d) 5

Sol. (d) Given equation of parabola is $y^2 + 4(x - a^2) = 0$ ...(i)

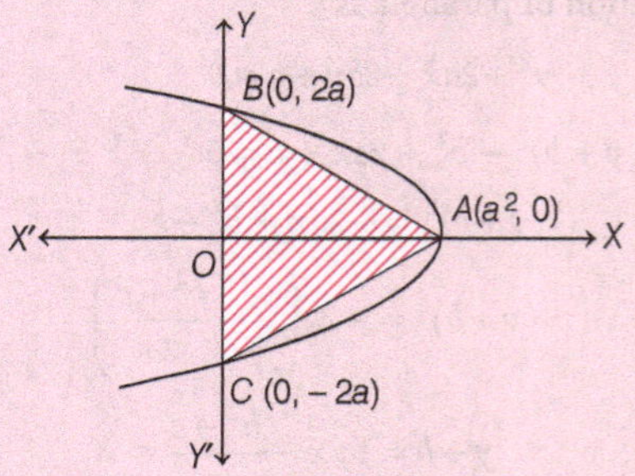

Vertex $\equiv (a^2, 0)$

For points B and C, put $x = 0$ in Eq. (i), we get

$$y^2 + 4(-a^2) = 0 \Rightarrow y = \pm 2a$$

$\therefore$ Area of $\Delta ABC = 2(\text{Area of } \Delta AOB)$

$$250 = 2\left(\frac{1}{2} \times OB \times OA\right) \Rightarrow 250 = 2a \times a^2$$

$$\Rightarrow \quad a^3 = 125 \Rightarrow a = 5$$

Skill Builder

If area of the triangle whose one vertex is at the vertex of the parabola $y^2 + 4(x - a^2) = 0$ and the other two vertices are the point of intersections of the parabola and Y-axis, is 128 sq. units, then the value of a is

(a) $4\sqrt{5}$ (b) $(8)^{2/3}$ (c) $(2)^{1/3}$ (d) 4

For Sol.

■ **For more practice** See Q.16 of Milestone Practice 5.1.

Milestone Practice 5.1

1. The vertex of the parabola $y^2 + 6x - 2y + 13 = 0$ is
(a) $(-2,1)$ (b) $(2,-1)$
(c) $(1,1)$ (d) $(1,-1)$

2. The value of p such that the vertex of $y = x^2 + 2px + 13$ is 4 units above the X-axis is
(a) ± 2 (b) 4
(c) ± 3 (d) 5

3. The length of the latusrectum of the parabola whose focus is (3,3) and directrix is $3x - 4y - 2 = 0$, is
(a) 1 (b) 2
(c) 4 (d) 8

4. If the vertex and focus of a parabola are (3,3) and (−3, 3) respectively, then its equation is
(a) $x^2 - 6x + 24y - 63 = 0$
(b) $x^2 - 6x + 24y + 81 = 0$
(c) $y^2 - 6y + 24x - 63 = 0$
(d) $y^2 - 6y - 24x + 81 = 0$

5. The directrix of the parabola $x^2 - 4x - 8y + 12 = 0$ is
(a) $y = 0$ (b) $x = 1$ (c) $y = -1$ (d) $x = -1$

6. The equation of the latusrectum of the parabola $x^2 + 4x + 2y = 0$ is
(a) $3y - 2 = 0$ (b) $3y + 2 = 0$
(c) $2y - 3 = 0$ (d) $2y + 3 = 0$

7. The focus of the parabola $x^2 - 8x + 2y + 7 = 0$ is
(a) $\left(0, -\frac{1}{2}\right)$ (b) (4,4)
(c) $\left(4, \frac{9}{2}\right)$ (d) $\left(-4, -\frac{9}{2}\right)$

8. Equation of the parabola whose axis is parallel to Y-axis and which passes through the points (1,0), (0,0) and (−2,4), is
(a) $2x^2 + 2x = 3y$ (b) $2x^2 - 2x = 3y$
(c) $2x^2 + 2x = y$ (d) $2x^2 - 2x = y$

9. The equation $ax^2 + 4xy + y^2 + ax + 3y + 2 = 0$ represents a parabola, then find the value of a.

10. Find the equation of the parabola whose axis is parallel to X-axis and which passes through the points (0, 4), (1, 9) and (−2, 6). Also, find its latusrectum.

11. Determine the name of the curve described parametrically by the equations $x = t^2 + t + 1$, $y = t^2 - t + 1$.

12. Find the name of the conic represented by $\sqrt{\left(\frac{x}{a}\right)} + \sqrt{\left(\frac{y}{b}\right)} = 1$.

13. Find the vertex, focus, axis, directrix and latusrectum of the parabola $4y^2 + 12x - 20y + 67 = 0$.

14. If the equation of the parabola whose vertex is at (5, 2) and directrix is $x - y + 1 = 0$ is $ax^2 + by^2 + cxy + dx + ey + f = 0$ then find the value of $a + b + c + d + e + f$.

15. Let $P(4, -4)$ and $Q(9, 6)$ be points on the parabola, $y^2 = 4x$. Let R be chosen on the arc POQ of the parabola, where O is the origin such that area of ΔPQR is minimum. Then, find the area of ΔPQR.

16. Find the area of an equilateral triangle inscribed in the parabola $y^2 = 16x$, with one of its vertices on the vertex of the parabola.

Answer Key

1. (a) 2. (c) 3. (b) 4. (c) 5. (c)
6. (c) 7. (b) 8. (b) 9. (4) 10. $5x = 2y^2 - 25y + 68$
11. Parabola 12. Parabola
13. Vertex $\equiv \left(-\frac{7}{2}, \frac{5}{2}\right)$, focus $\equiv \left(-\frac{17}{4}, \frac{5}{2}\right)$, axis $\equiv y = \frac{5}{2}$, directrix $\equiv x = -\frac{1}{4}$, Length of $LR = 3$
14. 73 15. $\frac{125}{4}$ sq. units 16. $768\sqrt{3}$ sq units

For Detailed Solution

Milestone 2 Line and Parabola

- Position of Points with respect to Parabola • Chords of Parabola • Intersection of a Line and a Parabola
- Equation of Tangent in Different Forms • Point of Intersection of Tangents at any Two points on the Parabola
- Equation of Normals in Different Forms • Point of Intersection of Normals at any Two Points on the Parabola
- Co-normal Points

5.9 Position of Points with respect to Parabola

Theorem The point (x_1, y_1) lies outside, on or inside the parabola $y^2 = 4ax$ according as

$$y_1^2 - 4ax_1 >, =, \text{or} < 0.$$

Proof Let $P(x_1, y_1)$ be a point. From P draw $PM \perp AX$ (on the axis of parabola) meeting the parabola $y^2 = 4ax$ at Q, let the coordinate of Q be (x_1, y_2).

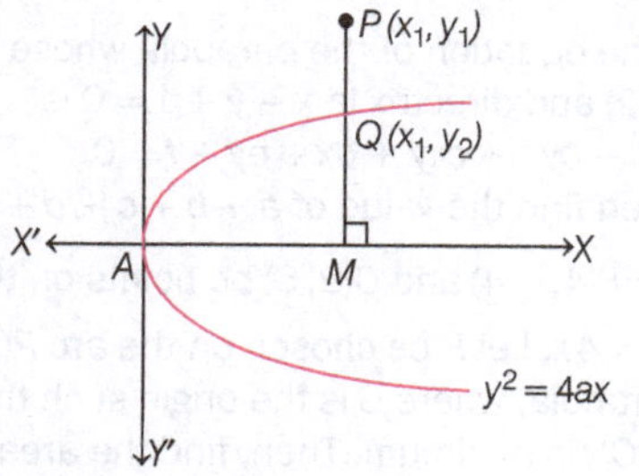

Since, $Q(x_1, y_2)$ lies on the parabola

$$y_1^2 = 4ax$$

Then, $$y_2^2 = 4ax_1 \quad \text{...(i)}$$

Now, P will be outside, on or inside the parabola $y^2 = 4ax$ according as

$$PM >, =, \text{or} < QM$$

$\Rightarrow$ $$(PM)^2 >, =, \text{or} < (QM)^2$$

$\Rightarrow$ $$y_1^2 >, =, \text{or} < y_2^2$$

$\Rightarrow$ $$y_1^2 >, =, \text{or} < 4ax_1 \quad \text{[from Eq. (i)]}$$

Hence, $$y_1^2 - 4ax_1 >, =, \text{or} < 0$$

JEE Focus Points

- The point (x_1, y_1) lies inside, on or outside $y^2 = -4ax$ according as $y_1^2 + 4ax_1 <, =, \text{or} > 0$
- The point (x_1, y_1) lies inside, on or outside $x^2 = 4ay$ according as $x_1^2 - 4ay_1 <, =, \text{or} > 0$
- The point (x_1, y_1) lies inside, on or outside $x^2 = -4ay$ according as $x_1^2 + 4ay_1 <, =, \text{or} > 0$

Concept Inside Video

Example 29. Show that the point (2, 3) lies outside the parabola $y^2 = 3x$.

Sol. Let the point $(h, k) = (2, 3)$

We have, $$k^2 - 3h = 3^2 - 3.2$$
$$= 9 - 6 = 3 > 0$$

$\therefore$ $$k^2 - 3h > 0$$

This shows that (2,3) lies outside the parabola $y^2 = 3x$.

Example 30. Find the position of the point (−2,2) with respect to the parabola $y^2 - 4y + 9x + 13 = 0$.

Sol. Let the point $(h,k) = (-2,2)$

We have, $$k^2 - 4k + 9h + 13 = (2)^2 - 4(2) + 9(-2) + 13$$
$$= 4 - 8 - 18 + 13 = -9 < 0$$

Hence, $$k^2 - 4k + 9h + 13 < 0$$

Therefore, the point (−2,2) lies inside the parabola

$$y^2 - 4y + 9x + 13 = 0.$$

Example 31. Find the values of α in the interval $\left[\frac{\pi}{2}, \frac{3\pi}{2}\right]$ for which the point $(\sin\alpha, \cos\alpha)$ does not lie outside the parabola $2y^2 + x - 2 = 0$.

Sol. If the point $(\sin\alpha, \cos\alpha)$ lies inside or on the parabola $2y^2 + x - 2 = 0$, then

$$2\cos^2\alpha + \sin\alpha - 2 \le 0$$

$\Rightarrow$ $$2 - 2\sin^2\alpha + \sin\alpha - 2 \le 0$$

$$\Rightarrow \quad -\sin\alpha\,(2\sin\alpha - 1) \geq 0$$

$$\Rightarrow \quad \sin\alpha \leq 0 \text{ or } \sin\alpha \geq \frac{1}{2}$$

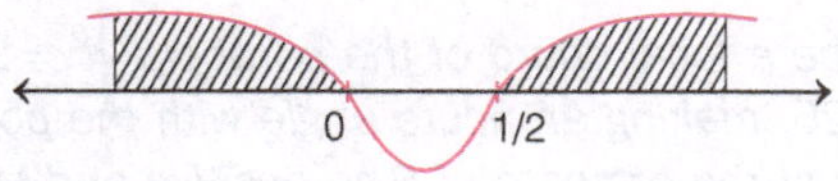

$$\Rightarrow \quad \alpha \in \left[\pi, \frac{3\pi}{2}\right] \text{ or } \alpha \in \left[\frac{\pi}{2}, \frac{5\pi}{6}\right]$$

$$\Rightarrow \quad \alpha \in \left[\frac{\pi}{2}, \frac{5\pi}{6}\right] \cup \left[\pi, \frac{3\pi}{2}\right]$$

5.10 Chords of Parabola

Given a parabola $y^2 = 4ax$, let AB be the chord joining $A(x_1, y_1)$ and $B(x_2, y_2)$

$$\Rightarrow \quad y_1^2 = 4ax_1 \text{ and } y_2^2 = 4ax_2$$

$$\Rightarrow \quad y_2^2 - y_1^2 = 4a(x_2 - x_1)$$

$$\Rightarrow \quad \frac{y_2 - y_1}{x_2 - x_1} = \frac{4a}{y_1 + y_2}$$

$$\therefore \quad \text{Slope of } AB = \frac{4a}{y_1 + y_2}$$

$$= \frac{2a}{\dfrac{y_1 + y_2}{2}}$$

and equation of $AB \Rightarrow y - y_1 = \dfrac{4a}{y_1 + y_2}(x - x_1)$

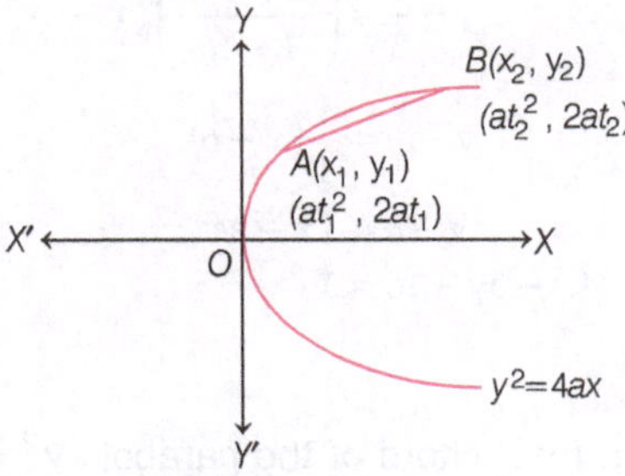

If parameteric coordinates of A and B are $(at_1^2, 2at_1)$ and $(at_2^2, 2at_2)$.

Then, slope of $AB = \dfrac{4a}{2at_2 + 2at_1} = \dfrac{2}{t_1 + t_2}$

and equation of chord AB is $y - 2at_1 = \dfrac{2}{t_1 + t_2}(x - at_1^2)$

$$\Rightarrow y(t_1 + t_2) = 2(x + at_1t_2)$$

Parametric Relation between the Coordinates of the Ends of a Focal Chord of a Parabola

Let $y^2 = 4ax$ be a parabola. If PQ is a focal chord, then $P \equiv (at_1^2, 2at_1)$ and $Q \equiv (at_2^2, 2at_2)$

Since, PQ passes through the focus $S(a, 0)$.

$\therefore \quad Q, S, P$ are collinear.

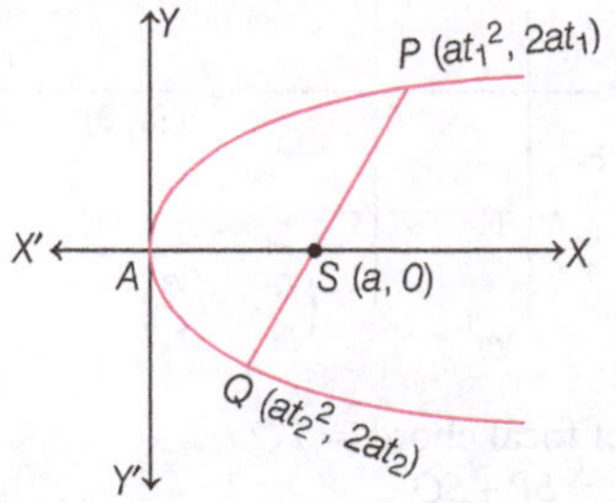

$\therefore$ Slope of PS = Slope of QS

$$\Rightarrow \quad \frac{2at_1 - 0}{at_1^2 - a} = \frac{0 - 2at_2}{a - at_2^2} \Rightarrow \frac{2t_1}{t_1^2 - 1} = \frac{2t_2}{t_2^2 - 1}$$

$$\Rightarrow \quad t_1(t_2^2 - 1) = t_2(t_1^2 - 1)$$

$$\Rightarrow \quad t_1t_2(t_2 - t_1) + (t_2 - t_1) = 0$$

$$\Rightarrow \quad t_2 - t_1 \neq 0 \quad \text{or} \quad t_1t_2 + 1 = 0$$

$$\Rightarrow \quad t_1t_2 = -1 \quad \text{or} \quad t_2 = -\frac{1}{t_1}, \quad \text{...(i)}$$

which is required relation.

JEE Focus Points

1. The length of focal chord having parameters t_1 and t_2 for its end points is $a(t_2 - t_1)^2$.
2. If l_1 and l_2 are the length of segments of a focal chord of a parabola, then its latusrectum is $\dfrac{4l_1l_2}{l_1 + l_2}$.
3. If one extremity of a focal chord is $(at_1^2, 2at_1)$, then the other extremity $(at_2^2, 2at_2)$ becomes $\left(\dfrac{a}{t_1^2}, -\dfrac{2a}{t_1}\right)$ by virtue of relation $t_2 = -\dfrac{1}{t_1}$.
4. $\left|t + \dfrac{1}{t}\right| \geq 2$, for all $t \neq 0$ $\quad$ [$\because$ AM $\geq$ GM]

   $\therefore \quad a\left(t + \dfrac{1}{t}\right)^2 \geq 4a$

   $\Rightarrow$ length of focal chord $\geq$ latusrectum i.e. the length of smallest focal chord of the parabola is $4a$. Hence, the latusrectum of a parabola is the smallest focal chord.
5. Circle described on the focal length as diameter touches the tangent at vertex.
6. Circle discribed on the focal chord as diameter touches the directrix.

Example 32. If the point $(at^2, 2at)$ be the extremity of a focal chord of parabola $y^2 = 4ax$, then show that the length of the focal chord is $a\left(t + \dfrac{1}{t}\right)^2$.

Sol. Since, one extremity of focal chord is $P(at^2, 2at)$.

Then, the other extremity is $Q\left(\frac{a}{t^2}, -\frac{2a}{t}\right)$.

[replacing t by $-1/t$]

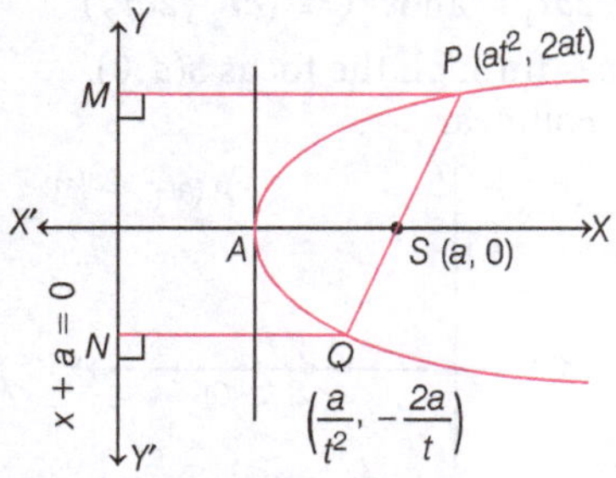

$\therefore$ Length of focal chord $= PQ$

$$= SP + SQ$$
$$= PM + QN \quad [\because SP = PM \text{ and } SQ = QN]$$
$$= at^2 + a + \frac{a}{t^2} + a$$
$$= a\left(t^2 + \frac{1}{t^2} + 2\right) = a\left(t + \frac{1}{t}\right)^2$$

Example 33. Prove that the semi-latusrectum of the parabola $y^2 = 4ax$ is the harmonic mean between the segments of any focal chord of the parabola.

Sol. Let parabola be $y^2 = 4ax$

If PQ be the focal chord, then

$$P \equiv (at^2, 2at) \text{ and } Q \equiv \left(\frac{a}{t^2}, \frac{-2a}{t}\right)$$

$\therefore$ Length of latusrectum $LL' = 4a$.

$\therefore$ Semi-latusrectum $= \frac{1}{2}(4a) = 2a$.

If sections of focal chord are k_1 and k_2,

then $k_1 = SP = PM = a + at^2 = a(1 + t^2)$

and $k_2 = SQ = QN = a + \frac{a}{t^2} = \frac{a(1+t^2)}{t^2}$

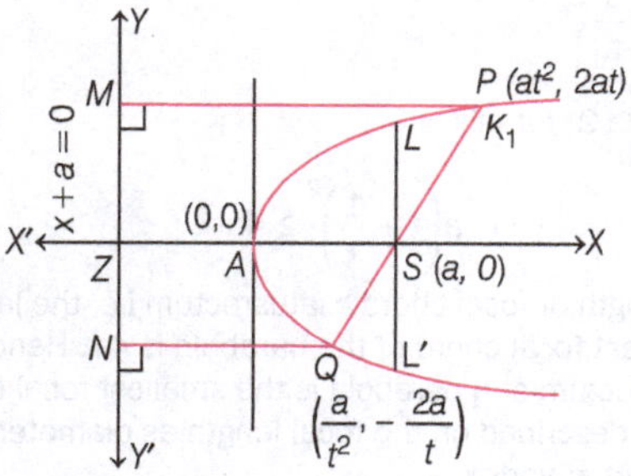

$\therefore$ Harmonic mean of k_1

and $k_2 = \frac{2k_1k_2}{k_1 + k_2} = \frac{2}{\frac{1}{k_2} + \frac{1}{k_1}} = \frac{2}{\frac{t^2}{a(1+t^2)} + \frac{1}{a(1+t^2)}}$

$$= \frac{2}{\frac{1}{a}} = 2a = \text{Semi-latusrectum.}$$

JEE SCANNER

Example Similar to PYQ Asked in JEE Main 2023

Let PQ be a focal chord of the parabola $y^2 = 16x$ of length 25, making an acute angle with the positive X-axis. Let the ordinate of P be positive and M be the point on the line segment PQ such that $PM : MQ = 2 : 1$. Then, the equation of the line passing through M and perpendicular to PQ is

(a) $9x + 12y - 86 = 0$
(b) $12x + 9y - 86 = 0$
(c) $4x - 3y - 16 = 0$
(d) $3x - 4y - 16 = 0$

Sol. (c) Given that PQ is a focal chord of the parabola $y^2 = 16x$ of length 25.

Thus, length $= 25$

$$\Rightarrow \quad 4\left(t + \frac{1}{t}\right)^2 = 25$$
$$\Rightarrow \quad \left(t + \frac{1}{t}\right)^2 = \frac{25}{4}$$
$$\Rightarrow \quad t + \frac{1}{t} = \pm\frac{5}{2}$$
$$\therefore \quad t = 2 \text{ or } \frac{1}{2}$$

Thus, $P = (16, 16)$ and $Q = (1, -4)$.

$$\therefore \quad M = \left(6, \frac{8}{3}\right)$$

Thus, required equation of line is

$$y - \frac{8}{3} = \left(\frac{-4-16}{1-16}\right)(x - 6)$$
$$\Rightarrow \quad y - \frac{8}{3} = \frac{4}{3}(x - 6)$$
$$\Rightarrow \quad 3y - 8 = 4x - 24$$
$$\therefore \quad 4x - 3y - 16 = 0$$

Skill Builder

Let PQ be a focal chord of the parabola $y^2 = 64x$ of length 289, making an acute angle with the positive X-axis. Let the ordinate of P be positive and M be the mid-point of PQ. Then, the equation of line passing through M and perpendicular to PQ is

(a) $8x - 15y - 128 = 0$
(b) $8x + 15y + 128 = 0$
(c) $8x - 15y + 128 = 0$
(d) $8x + 15y - 128 = 0$

For Sol.

■ **For more practice** See Q.4 of Milestone Practice 5.2.

Example 34. Show that the focal chord of parabola $y^2 = 4ax$ makes an angle α with the X-axis is of length $4a\,\text{cosec}^2\alpha$.

Sol. Let $P(at_1^2, 2at_1)$ and $Q(at_2^2, 2at_2)$ be the end points of a focal chord PQ which makes an angle α with the axis of the parabola. Then,

$$PQ = a(t_2 - t_1)^2$$
$$= a[(t_2 + t_1)^2 - 4t_1t_2]$$
$$= a[(t_2 + t_1)^2 + 4] \quad [\because t_1t_2 = -1] \quad \text{...(i)}$$

$\therefore \quad \tan\alpha = \text{slope of } PQ$
$$= \frac{2at_2 - 2at_1}{at_2^2 - at_1^2}$$
$$\Rightarrow \quad \tan\alpha = \frac{2}{t_2 + t_1}$$
$$\Rightarrow \quad t_2 + t_1 = 2\cot\alpha \quad \text{...(ii)}$$

On substituting the value of $t_2 + t_1$ from Eq. (ii) in Eq. (i), then

$$PQ = a(4\cot^2\alpha + 4)$$
$$= 4a\,\text{cosec}^2\alpha$$

Example 35. Prove that the length of a focal chord of a parabola varies inversely as the square of its distance from the vertex.

Sol. Let $P(at^2, 2at)$ be one end of a focal chord of the parabola $y^2 = 4ax$. The focus of its parabola is $S(a, 0)$.

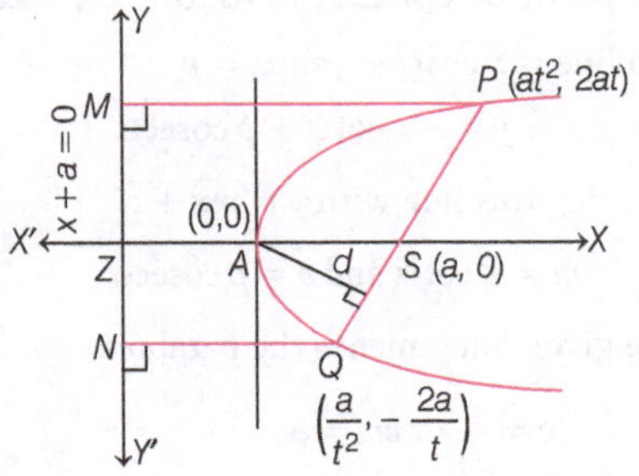

$\therefore$ Equation of focal chord (i.e. equation of PS) is

$$y - 0 = \frac{2at - 0}{at^2 - a}(x - a)$$
$$\Rightarrow \quad y = \frac{2t}{(t^2 - 1)}(x - a)$$
$$\Rightarrow \quad (t^2 - 1)y = 2tx - 2at$$
$$\Rightarrow \quad 2tx - (t^2 - 1)y - 2at = 0$$

If d be the distance of this focal chord from the vertex (0,0) of the parabola $y^2 = 4ax$, then

$$d = \frac{|0 - 0 - 2at|}{\sqrt{(2t)^2 + (t^2 - 1)^2}}$$
$$= \frac{|2at|}{(t^2 + 1)} = \frac{2a}{\left|t + \frac{1}{t}\right|}$$
$$\Rightarrow \quad d^2 = \frac{4a^2}{\left(t + \frac{1}{t}\right)^2} \quad \text{...(i)}$$

The other end of the focal chord is $Q\left(\frac{a}{t^2}, -\frac{2a}{t}\right)$.

If length of focal chord $= PQ = l$ (say)

$\therefore \quad l = PQ = PS + SQ = PM + QN$

$$\therefore \quad l = at^2 + a + \frac{a}{t^2} + a$$
$$\Rightarrow \quad l = a\left(t^2 + \frac{1}{t^2} + 2\right)$$
$$\Rightarrow \quad l = a\left(t + \frac{1}{t}\right)^2$$
$$\Rightarrow \quad \frac{l}{a} = \left(t + \frac{1}{t}\right)^2 \quad \text{...(ii)}$$

From Eqs. (i) and (ii), $d^2 = \frac{4a^2}{(l/a)} = \frac{4a^3}{l}$

$$\therefore \quad l = \frac{4a^3}{d^2} \Rightarrow l \propto \frac{1}{d^2}$$

i.e. the length of the focal chord varies inversely as the square of its distance from vertex.

5.11 Intersection of a Line and a Parabola

Let the parabola be $y^2 = 4ax$ ...(i)

and the given line be $y = mx + c$ ...(ii)

On eliminating x from Eqs. (i) and (ii), then

$$y^2 = 4a\left(\frac{y - c}{m}\right)$$
$$\Rightarrow \quad my^2 - 4ay + 4ac = 0 \quad \text{...(iii)}$$

This equation being quadratic in y, gives two values of y, shows that every straight line will cut the parabola in two points may be real, coincident or imaginary according as discriminant of Eq. (iii) $>, =, < 0$

i.e. $(-4a)^2 - 4 \cdot m \cdot 4ac >, =, < 0$

or $\quad a - mc >, =, < 0$

or $\quad a >, =, < mc$ ...(iv)

Condition of Tangency

If the line Eq. (ii) touches the parabola Eq. (i), then Eq. (iii) has equal roots.

$\therefore$ Discriminant of Eq. (iii) $=0$

$$\Rightarrow \quad (-4a)^2 - 4m \cdot 4ac = 0$$

$$\Rightarrow \quad c = \frac{a}{m}, m \neq 0 \quad \text{...(v)}$$

So, the line $y = mx + c$ touches the parabola $y^2 = 4ax$ if $c = \frac{a}{m}$ (which is condition of tangency).

On substituting the value of c from Eq. (v) in Eq. (ii), then

$$y = mx + \frac{a}{m}, m \neq 0$$

Hence, the line $y = mx + \frac{a}{m}$ will always be a tangent to the parabola $y^2 = 4ax$.

The point of contact On substituting $c = \frac{a}{m}$ in Eq. (iii), then

$$my^2 - 4ay + 4a\left(\frac{a}{m}\right) = 0$$

$$\Rightarrow \quad m^2y^2 - 4amy + 4a^2 = 0$$

$$\Rightarrow \quad (my - 2a)^2 = 0$$

$$\Rightarrow \quad my - 2a = 0 \text{ or } y = \frac{2a}{m}$$

On substituting this value of y in $y = mx + \frac{a}{m}$

$$\therefore \quad \frac{2a}{m} = mx + \frac{a}{m}$$

$$\Rightarrow \quad mx = \frac{a}{m} \text{ or } x = \frac{a}{m^2}$$

Hence, the point of contact is $\left(\frac{a}{m^2}, \frac{2a}{m}\right), (m \neq 0)$

this known as ***m*-point** on the parabola.

Example 36. Prove that the straight line $lx + my + n = 0$ touches the parabola $y^2 = 4ax$, if $ln = am^2$.

Sol. The given line is $lx + my + n = 0$.

$$\text{or} \quad y = -\frac{l}{m}x - \frac{n}{m} \quad \text{...(i)}$$

On comparing this line with $y = Mx + c$.

$$\therefore \quad M = -\frac{l}{m} \text{ and } c = -\frac{n}{m}$$

The line Eq. (i) will touch the parabola $y^2 = 4ax$, if

$$c = \frac{a}{M} \Rightarrow cM = a$$

$$\Rightarrow \quad \left(-\frac{n}{m}\right)\left(-\frac{l}{m}\right) = a$$

$$\therefore \quad ln = am^2$$

Alternate Solution

Given line $lx + my + n = 0$ ...(i)

and the parabola $y^2 = 4ax$ ...(ii)

On substituting the value of x from Eq. (i) i.e. $x = -\frac{n + my}{l}$ in Eq. (ii), then

(we should not substituting the value of y from Eq. (i), in Eq. (ii), since y is quadratic, substituting the value of x since x is linear).

$$y^2 = 4a\left(-\frac{n + my}{l}\right)$$

$$\Rightarrow \quad ly^2 + 4amy + 4an = 0 \quad \text{...(iii)}$$

Since, Eq. (i) touches the parabola Eq. (ii), then roots of Eq. (iii) must be coincident and condition for the same roots is $B^2 = 4AC$.

i.e. $$(4am)^2 = 4 \cdot l4an$$

$$\Rightarrow \quad am^2 = ln$$

$$\therefore \quad ln = am^2$$

Example 37. Show that the line $x\cos\alpha + y\sin\alpha = p$ touches the parabola $y^2 = 4ax$, if $p\cos\alpha + a\sin^2\alpha = 0$ and that the point of contact is $(a\tan^2\alpha, -2a\tan\alpha)$.

Sol. The given line is $x\cos\alpha + y\sin\alpha = p$

$$\Rightarrow \quad y = -x\cot\alpha + p\,\mathrm{cosec}\,\alpha$$

On comparing this line with $y = mx + c$,

$$\therefore \quad m = -\cot\alpha \text{ and } c = p\,\mathrm{cosec}\,\alpha$$

Since, the given line touches the parabola.

$$\therefore \quad c = \frac{a}{m} \text{ or } cm = a$$

$$\Rightarrow \quad (p\,\mathrm{cosec}\,\alpha)(-\cot\alpha) = a$$

$$\Rightarrow \quad a\sin^2\alpha + p\cos\alpha = 0$$

and point of contact is $\left(\frac{a}{m^2}, \frac{2a}{m}\right)$

$$\text{i.e.} \quad \left(\frac{a}{\cot^2\alpha}, -\frac{2a}{\cot\alpha}\right)$$

$$\text{or} \quad (a\tan^2\alpha, -2a\tan\alpha)$$

JEE SCANNER

Example Similar to PYQ Asked in JEE Main 2022

If the line $x+y-1=0$ is the tangent to the parabola $y^2=kx$ at the point P and V is the vertex of the parabola, the slope of the line through P and V is equal to $-\lambda$, then λ is ....

Sol. (2) Line $x+y-1=0$ touches the parabola $y^2=kx$ at P.

$\therefore \quad (1-x)^2 = kx$ has only one root.

$\Rightarrow \quad x^2-(k+2)x+1=0$ has only one root.

$\therefore \quad (k+2)^2-4=0$

$\Rightarrow \quad k+2=\pm 2$

$\Rightarrow \quad k=0,-4$

$\Rightarrow \quad k=-4 \qquad [\because k \neq 0]$

So, equation of parabola is $y^2=-4x$

On solving equation of line and parabola, we get

$$x=-1,\ y=2$$

So, coordinates of P are $(-1,2)$.

Now, vertex of parabola is $V(0,0)$.

$\therefore$ Slope of line $PV = \dfrac{2-0}{-1-0} = -2 = -\lambda \Rightarrow \lambda = 2$

Skill Builder

If the line $y=mx+1$ is a tangent to the parabola $y^2=4x$ at the point P and F is the focus of the parabola the slope of the line through P and F is $\tan^{-1}(\tan\theta)=\dfrac{\pi}{k}$ (where $\tan\theta$ is slope of PF), then k is equal to ....

For Sol.

■ **For more practice** See Q.5 of Milestone Practice 5.2.

Example 38. Prove that the line $\dfrac{x}{l}+\dfrac{y}{m}=1$ touches the parabola $y^2=4a(x+b)$, if $m^2(l+b)+al^2=0$.

Sol. The given parabola is $y^2=4a(x+b)$ ...(i)

Vertex of this parabola is $(-b,0)$.

Now, shifting $(0,0)$ at $(-b,0)$,

then $\quad x = X+(-b)$ and $y=Y+0$

or $\quad x+b=X \quad$ and $\quad y=Y$ ...(ii)

From Eq. (i), $Y^2=4aX$ ...(iii)

and the line $\dfrac{x}{l}+\dfrac{y}{m}=1$

reduces to $\dfrac{X-b}{l}+\dfrac{Y}{m}=1$

$$Y = m\left(1-\frac{X-b}{l}\right)$$

$\Rightarrow \quad Y=\left(-\dfrac{m}{l}\right)X + m\left(1+\dfrac{b}{l}\right)$ ...(iv)

The line Eq. (iv) will touch the parabola Eq. (iii), if

$$m\left(1+\frac{b}{l}\right)=\frac{a}{\left(-\frac{m}{l}\right)}$$

$\Rightarrow \quad \dfrac{m^2}{l}\left(1+\dfrac{b}{l}\right)=-a$

$\therefore \quad m^2(l+b)+al^2=0$

Alternate Solution

The given line and parabola are

$\dfrac{x}{l}+\dfrac{y}{m}=1$ ...(i)

and $\quad y^2=4a(x+b)$ ...(ii)

On substituting the value of x from Eq. (i)

$$x = l\left(1-\frac{y}{m}\right)$$

In Eq. (ii), $\quad y^2 = 4a\left\{l\left(1-\dfrac{y}{m}\right)+b\right\}$

or $\quad y^2+\dfrac{4al}{m}y-4a(l+b)=0$ ...(iii)

Since, the line Eq. (i) touches the parabola Eq. (ii), then the roots of Eq. (iii) are equal.

$\therefore \quad \left(\dfrac{4al}{m}\right)^2 - 4\cdot 1\{-4a(l+b)\}=0$

$\Rightarrow \quad \dfrac{al^2}{m^2}+(l+b)=0$

$\Rightarrow \quad al^2+m^2(l+b)=0$

$\Rightarrow \quad m^2(l+b)+al^2=0$

Example 39. Find the equations of the straight lines touching both $x^2+y^2=2a^2$ and $y^2=8ax$.

Sol. The given curves are

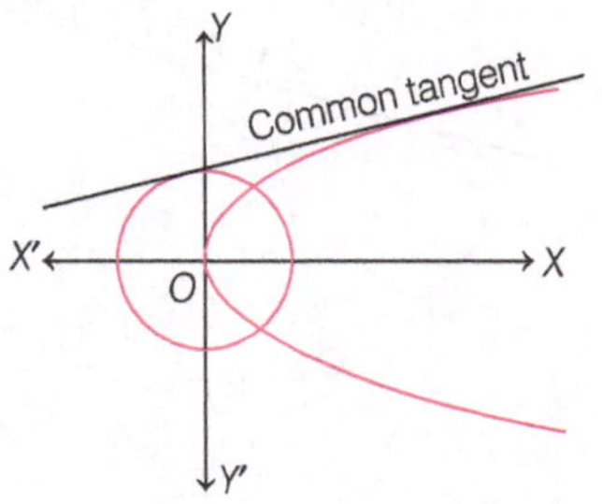

$x^2+y^2=2a^2$ ...(i)

and $\quad y^2=8ax$ ...(ii)

The parabola Eq. (ii) is $y^2=8ax$

or $\quad y^2=4(2a)x$

$\therefore$ Equation of tangent of Eq. (ii) is

$$y=mx+\frac{2a}{m}$$

or $\quad m^2x-my+2a=0$ ...(iii)

It is also tangent of Eq. (i), then the length of perpendicular from centre of Eq. (i) i.e. (0, 0) to Eq. (iii) must be equal to the radius of Eq. (i) i.e. $a\sqrt{2}$.

$$\therefore \quad \frac{|0-0+2a|}{\sqrt{(m^2)^2+(-m)^2}} = a\sqrt{2}$$

$$\Rightarrow \quad \frac{4a^2}{m^4+m^2} = 2a^2$$

$$\Rightarrow \quad m^4+m^2-2=0$$

$$\Rightarrow \quad (m^2+2)(m^2-1)=0$$

$$\Rightarrow \quad m^2+2 \neq 0$$

[$\because$ it gives the imaginary values]

$$\therefore \quad m^2-1=0$$

$$\Rightarrow \quad m=\pm 1$$

Hence, from Eq. (iii) the required tangents are

$$x \pm y + 2a = 0.$$

5.12 Equation of Tangent in Different Forms

1. Point Form

To find the equation of the tangent to the parabola $y^2 = 4ax$ at the point (x_1, y_1).

(First Principal Method) Equation of parabola is

$$y^2 = 4ax \qquad \text{...(i)}$$

Let $P \equiv (x_1, y_1)$ and $Q \equiv (x_2, y_2)$ be any two points on parabola (i), then

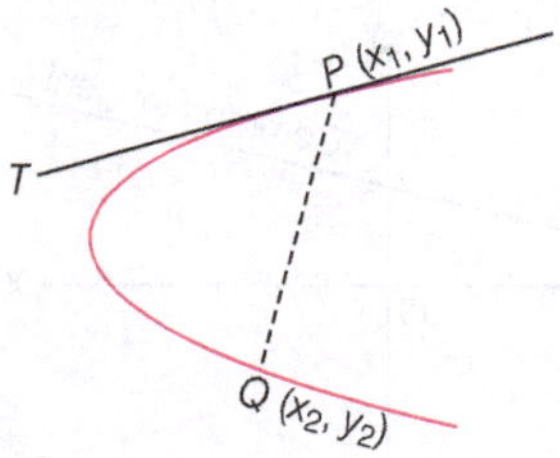

$$y_1^2 = 4ax_1 \qquad \text{...(ii)}$$

and

$$y_2^2 = 4ax_2 \qquad \text{...(iii)}$$

On subtracting Eq. (ii) from Eq. (iii), then

$$y_2^2 - y_1^2 = 4a(x_2 - x_1)$$

$$\Rightarrow \quad \frac{y_2-y_1}{x_2-x_1} = \frac{4a}{y_2+y_1} \qquad \text{...(iv)}$$

Equation of PQ is

$$y - y_1 = \frac{y_2-y_1}{x_2-x_1}(x-x_1) \qquad \text{...(v)}$$

From Eqs. (iv) and (v), then

$$y - y_1 = \frac{4a}{y_2+y_1}(x-x_1) \qquad \text{...(vi)}$$

Now, for tangent at $P, Q \to P$ i.e. $x_2 \to x_1$ and $y_2 \to y_1$, then Eq. (vi) becomes

$$y - y_1 = \frac{4a}{2y_1}(x-x_1)$$

$$\Rightarrow \quad yy_1 - y_1^2 = 2ax - 2ax_1$$

$$\Rightarrow \quad yy_1 = 2ax + y_1^2 - 2ax_1$$

$$\Rightarrow \quad yy_1 = 2ax + 4ax_1 - 2ax_1 \qquad \text{[from Eq. (ii)]}$$

$$\Rightarrow \quad yy_1 = 2ax + 2ax_1$$

$$\therefore \quad yy_1 = 2a(x+x_1),$$

which is the required equation of tangent at (x_1, y_1).

JEE Focus Points

- The equation of tangent at (x_1, y_1) can also be obtained by replacing x^2 by xx_1, y^2 by yy_1, x by $\frac{x+x_1}{2}$, y by $\frac{y+y_1}{2}$ and xy by $\frac{xy_1+x_1y}{2}$ and without changing the constant (if any) in the equation of curve of second degree in x and y.

Concept Inside Video

- Equation of tangents of all standard parabolas at (x_1, y_1).

Equations of Parabolas	Tangent at(x_1, y_1)
$y^2 = 4ax$	$yy_1 = 2a(x+x_1)$
$y^2 = -4ax$	$yy_1 = -2a(x+x_1)$
$x^2 = 4ay$	$xx_1 = 2a(y+y_1)$
$x^2 = -4ay$	$xx_1 = -2a(y+y_1)$

2. Parametric Form

To find the equation of tangent to the parabola $y^2 = 4ax$ at the point $(at^2, 2at)$ or t.

Since, the equation of tangent of the parabola $y^2 = 4ax$ at (x_1, y_1) is $yy_1 = 2a(x+x_1)$ ...(i)

On replacing x_1 by at^2 and y_1 by $2at$, then Eq. (i) becomes

$$y(2at) = 2a(x+at^2)$$

$$\Rightarrow \quad ty = x + at^2$$

The equations of tangent of all standard parabolas at 't'.

Equations of Parabolas	Parametric coordinates t	Tangent at t
$y^2 = 4ax$	$(at^2, 2at)$	$ty = x + at^2$
$y^2 = -4ax$	$(-at^2, 2at)$	$ty = -x + at^2$
$x^2 = 4ay$	$(2at, at^2)$	$tx = y + at^2$
$x^2 = -4ay$	$(2at, -at^2)$	$tx = -y + at^2$

3. Slope Form

To find the equation of tangent and point of contact in terms of m(slope) to the parabola $y^2 = 4ax$.

The equation of tangent to the parabola $y^2 = 4ax$ at (x_1, y_1) is $yy_1 = 2a(x + x_1)$. ...(i)

Since, m is the slope of the tangent, then

$$m = \frac{2a}{y_1} \Rightarrow y_1 = \frac{2a}{m}$$

Since, (x_1, y_1) lies on $y^2 = 4ax$, therefore

$$y_1^2 = 4ax_1 \Rightarrow \frac{4a^2}{m^2} = 4ax_1$$

$$\therefore \quad x_1 = \frac{a}{m^2}$$

On substituting the values of x_1 and y_1 in Eq. (i), we get

$$y = mx + \frac{a}{m} \quad \text{...(ii)}$$

Thus, $y = mx + \dfrac{a}{m}$ is a tangent to the parabola $y^2 = 4ax$, where, m is the slope of the tangent.

The coordinates of the point of contact are $\left(\dfrac{a}{m^2}, \dfrac{2a}{m}\right)$.

On comparing Eq. (ii) with $y = mx + c$,

$$c = \frac{a}{m}$$

which is condition of tangency,

when $y = mx + c$ is the tangent of $y^2 = 4ax$.

The equation of tangent, condition of tangency and point of contact in terms of slope (m) of all standard parabolas.

Equation of parabolas	Point of contact in terms of slope (m)	Equation of tangent in terms of slope (m)	Condition of tangency
$y^2 = 4ax$	$\left(\dfrac{a}{m^2}, \dfrac{2a}{m}\right)$	$y = mx + \dfrac{a}{m}$	$c = \dfrac{a}{m}$
$y^2 = -4ax$	$\left(-\dfrac{a}{m^2}, \dfrac{2a}{m}\right)$	$y = mx - \dfrac{a}{m}$	$c = -\dfrac{a}{m}$
$x^2 = 4ay$	$(2am, am^2)$	$y = mx - am^2$	$c = -am^2$
$x^2 = -4ay$	$(2am, -am^2)$	$y = mx + am^2$	$c = am^2$
$(y-k)^2 = 4a(x-h)$	$\left(h + \dfrac{a}{m^2}, k + \dfrac{2a}{m}\right)$	$y = mx - mh + k + \dfrac{a}{m}$	$c = -mh + k + \dfrac{a}{m}$
$(y-k)^2 = -4a(x-h)$	$\left(h - \dfrac{a}{m^2}, k + \dfrac{2a}{m}\right)$	$y = mx - mh + k - \dfrac{a}{m}$	$c = -mh + k - \dfrac{a}{m}$
$(x-h)^2 = 4a(y-k)$	$(h + 2am, k + am^2)$	$y = mx - mh + k - am^2$	$c = -mh + k - am^2$
$(x-h)^2 = -4a(y-k)$	$(h + 2am, k - am^2)$	$y = mx - mh + k + am^2$	$c = -mh + k + am^2$

5.14 Point of Intersection of Tangents at any Two Points on the Parabola

Let the parabola be $y^2 = 4ax$

Let two points on the parabola are

$$P \equiv (at_1^2, 2at_1) \text{ and } Q \equiv (at_2^2, 2at_2).$$

Equations of tangents at $P(at_1^2, 2at_1)$ and $Q(at_2^2, 2at_2)$

are $\quad t_1 y = x + at_1^2 \quad$ ...(i)

and $\quad t_2 y = x + at_2^2 \quad$ ...(ii)

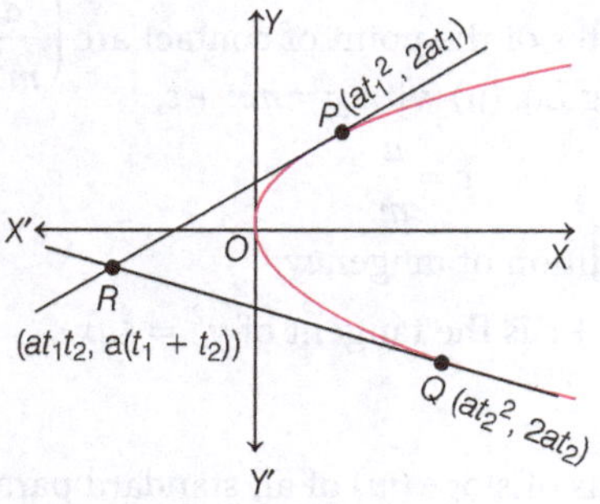

On solving these equations, we get $x = at_1 t_2, y = a(t_1 + t_2)$

Thus, the coordinates of the point of intersection of tangents at

$$(at_1^2, 2at_1) \text{ and } (at_2^2, 2at_2) \text{ are } (at_1 t_2, a(t_1 + t_2)).$$

JEE Focus Points

Concept Inside Video

- The geometric mean of the x coordinates of P and Q (i.e. $\sqrt{at_1^2 \times at_2^2} = at_1 t_2$) is the x-coordinate of the point of intersection of tangents at P and Q on the parabola. If P and Q are the ends points of focal chord, then x-coordinate of point of intersection of tangents at P and Q is $(-at_1 t_2)$.
- The arithmetic mean of the y-coordinates of P and Q $\left(\text{i.e. } \frac{2at_1 + 2at_2}{2} = a(t_1 + t_2)\right)$ is the y-coordinate of the point of intersection of tangents at P and Q on the parabola.
- Locus of foot of perpendicular from focus upon any tangent is tangent at vertex.
- Image of focus in any tangent lies on directrix.
- Locus of the point of intersection of the perpendicular tangents to the parabola $y^2 = 4ax$ is called the director circle. Its equation is $x + a = 0$, which is parabola's own directrix.

Example 40. Find the equation of the common tangents to the parabola $y^2 = 4ax$ and $x^2 = 4by$.

Sol. The equation of any tangent in terms of slope (m) to the parabola $y^2 = 4ax$ is

$$y = mx + \frac{a}{m} \quad \text{...(i)}$$

If this line is also tangent to the parabola $x^2 = 4ay$, then Eq. (i) meets $x^2 = 4by$ in two coincident points.

On substituting the value of y from Eq. (i) in $x^2 = 4by$, we

get $\quad x^2 = 4b\left(mx + \frac{a}{m}\right) \Rightarrow x^2 - 4bmx - \frac{4ab}{m} = 0$

The roots of this quadratic are equal, if

$$B^2 = 4AC$$

i.e. $\quad (-4bm)^2 = 4 \cdot 1 \left(\frac{-4ab}{m}\right)$

$\Rightarrow \quad 16b^2m^3 + 16ab = 0, m \neq 0$

or $\quad m^3 = -a/b$

$\therefore \quad m = -a^{1/3}/b^{1/3}$

On substituting the value of m in Eq. (i), then the required equation is

$$y = -\frac{a^{1/3}}{b^{1/3}}x - \frac{ab^{1/3}}{a^{1/3}}$$

$\Rightarrow \quad y = -\frac{a^{1/3}}{b^{1/3}}x - a^{2/3}b^{1/3}$

$\therefore \quad a^{1/3}x + b^{1/3}y + a^{2/3}b^{2/3} = 0$

Example 41. The tangents to the parabola $y^2 = 4ax$ make angle θ_1 and θ_2 with X-axis. Find the locus of their point of intersection, if $\cot\theta_1 + \cot\theta_2 = c$.

Sol. Let the equation of any tangent to the parabola $y^2 = 4ax$ be

$$y = mx + (a/m) \quad \text{...(i)}$$

Let (x_1, y_1) be the point of intersection of the tangents to $y^2 = 4ax$, then Eq. (i) passes through (x_1, y_1).

$\therefore \quad y_1 = mx_1 + (a/m)$

or $\quad m^2x_1 - my_1 + a = 0$

Let m_1 and m_2 be the roots of this quadratic equation, then

$$m_1 + m_2 = y_1/x_1 \text{ and } m_1m_2 = a/x_1$$

or $\quad \tan\theta_1 + \tan\theta_2 = y_1/x_1$

and $\quad \tan\theta_1 \tan\theta_2 = a/x_1 \quad$ ...(ii)

Now, $\quad \cot\theta_1 + \cot\theta_2 = c \quad$ [given]

$\Rightarrow \quad \frac{1}{\tan\theta_1} + \frac{1}{\tan\theta_2} = c$

$\Rightarrow \quad \frac{\tan\theta_1 + \tan\theta_2}{\tan\theta_1 \tan\theta_2} = c$

$$\Rightarrow \quad \frac{y_1 / x_1}{a / x_1} = c$$

$$\Rightarrow \quad y_1 = ac \quad \text{[from Eq. (ii)]}$$

The required locus is $y = ac$,

which is a line parallel to X-axis.

Example 42. Show that the locus of the points of intersection of the mutually perpendicular tangents to a parabola is the directrix of the parabola.

Sol. Let the points $P(at_1^2, 2at_1)$ and $Q(at_2^2, 2at_2)$ are on the parabola $y^2 = 4ax$. Tangents at P and Q are

$$t_1 y = x + at_1^2 \quad \text{...(i)}$$

and $$t_2 y = x + at_2^2 \quad \text{...(ii)}$$

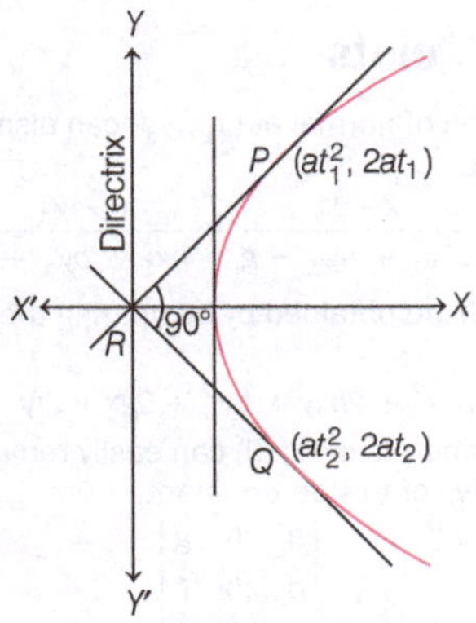

$\because$ Point of intersection of these tangents is $(at_1t_2, a(t_1 + t_2))$

Let this point be (h, k).

Then, $$h = at_1t_2 \quad \text{...(iii)}$$

and $$k = a(t_1 + t_2) \quad \text{...(iv)}$$

Slope of tangents of Eqs. (i) and (ii) are $\frac{1}{t_1}$ and $\frac{1}{t_2}$, respectively.

Since, tangents are perpendicular, then

$$\frac{1}{t_1} \times \frac{1}{t_2} = -1$$

or $$t_1 t_2 = -1 \quad \text{...(v)}$$

From Eqs. (iii) and (v), we get

$$h = -a$$

or $$h + a = 0$$

$\therefore$ Locus of the point of intersection of tangents is

$$x + a = 0.$$

which is directrix of $y^2 = 4ax$.

JEE SCANNER

Example Similar to PYQ Asked in JEE Main 2023

The distance of the point (3, 2) from the common tangent $y = mx + c$ of the curves $y^2 = 4x$ and $x^2 = 4y$ is $k\sqrt{\lambda}$, then $k \cdot \lambda$ is equal to ....

Sol. (6) Equation of tangent for parabola $y^2 = 4x$ is

$$y = mx + \frac{1}{m} \quad \text{...(i)}$$

and for parabola, $x^2 = 4y$ is

$$y = mx - m^2 \quad \text{...(ii)}$$

Since, Eqs. (i) and (ii) represent same tangent.

So, $$\frac{1}{1} = \frac{m}{m} = \frac{\frac{1}{m}}{-m^2}$$

$$\Rightarrow \quad \frac{-1}{m^3} = 1$$

$$\Rightarrow \quad m = -1$$

$\therefore$ Equation of common tangent is

$$y = -x - 1$$

$$\Rightarrow \quad x + y + 1 = 0$$

$\therefore$ Distance of point (3, 2) from common tangent

$$= \left| \frac{3 + 2 + 1}{\sqrt{1^2 + 1^2}} \right| = \frac{6}{\sqrt{2}} = 3\sqrt{2}$$

Hence, $$k\lambda = 6$$

Skill Builder

The distance of the point (0, 0) from the common tangent $y = mx + c$ of the curves $y^2 = -4x$ and $x^2 = -4y$ is $\frac{1}{\sqrt{n}}$, then n is equal to ....

For Sol.

■ **For more practice** See Q.6 of Milestone Practice 5.2.

Example 43. The tangents to the parabola $y^2 = 4ax$ at $P(at_1^2, 2at_1)$ and $Q(at_2^2, 2at_2)$ intersect at R. Prove that the area of the ΔPQR is $\frac{1}{2}a^2 |(t_1 - t_2)|^3$.

Sol. Equations of tangents at $P(at_1^2, 2at_1)$ and $Q(at_2^2, 2at_2)$ are

$$t_1 y = x + at_1^2 \quad \text{...(i)}$$

and $$t_2 y = x + at_2^2 \quad \text{...(ii)}$$

Since, point of intersection of Eqs. (i) and (ii) is $R(at_1t_2, a(t_1+t_2))$.

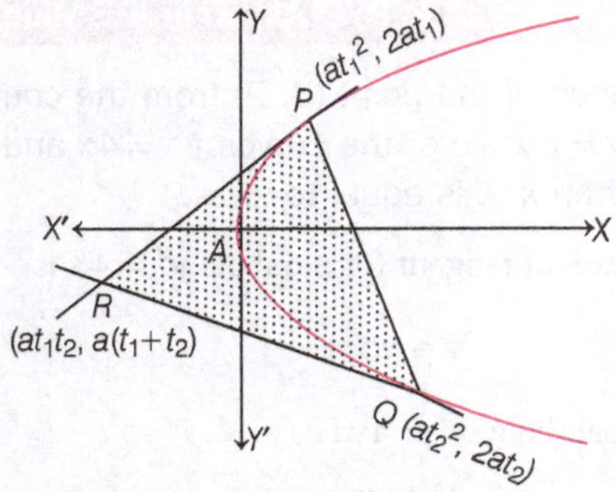

$$\therefore \text{ Area of } \Delta PQR = \frac{1}{2}\begin{vmatrix} at_1^2 & 2at_1 & 1 \\ at_2^2 & 2at_2 & 1 \\ at_1t_2 & a(t_1+t_2) & 1 \end{vmatrix}$$

Applying $R_2 \to R_2 - R_1$ and $R_3 \to R_3 - R_1$

$$= \frac{1}{2}\begin{vmatrix} at_1^2 & 2at_1 & 1 \\ a(t_2^2 - t_1^2) & 2a(t_2 - t_1) & 0 \\ at_1(t_2 - t_1) & a(t_2 - t_1) & 0 \end{vmatrix}$$

Expanding with respect to third column

$$= \frac{1}{2}\begin{vmatrix} a(t_2^2 - t_1^2) & 2a(t_2 - t_1) \\ at_1(t_2 - t_1) & a(t_2 - t_1) \end{vmatrix}$$

$$= \frac{1}{2}a^2(t_2 - t_1)^2\begin{vmatrix} t_2 + t_1 & 2 \\ t_1 & 1 \end{vmatrix}$$

$$= \frac{1}{2}a^2(t_1 - t_2)^2|(t_2 - t_1)|$$

$$= \frac{1}{2}a^2(t_1 - t_2)^2|(t_1 - t_2)|$$

$$= \frac{1}{2}a^2|(t_1 - t_2)^3|$$

5.14 Equations of Normals in Different Forms

1. Point Form

To find the equation of the normal to the parabola $y^2 = 4ax$ at the point (x_1, y_1).

Since, the equation of the tangent to the parabola $y^2 = 4ax$ at (x_1, y_1) is

$$yy_1 = 2a(x + x_1)$$

The slope of the tangent at $(x_1, y_1) = 2a / y_1$

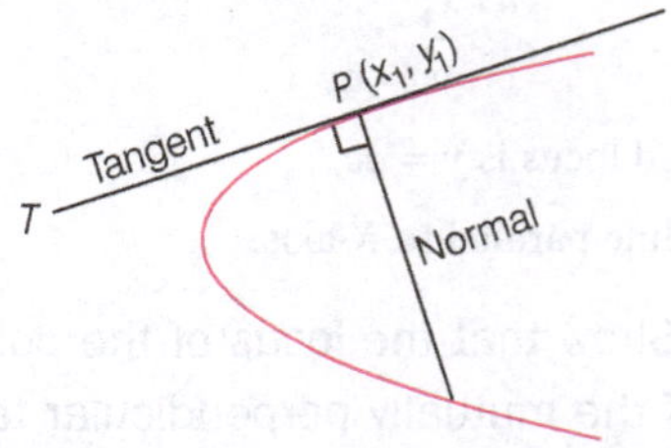

Since, the normal at (x_1, y_1) is perpendicular to the tangent at (x_1, y_1).

$\therefore$ Slope of normal at $(x_1, y_1) = -y_1 / 2a$

Hence, the equation of normal at (x_1, y_1) is

$$y - y_1 = -\frac{y_1}{2a}(x - x_1).$$

JEE Focus Points

1. The equation of normal at (x_1, y_1) can also be obtained by this method

$$\frac{x - x_1}{a'x_1 + hy_1 + g} = \frac{y - y_1}{hx_1 + by_1 + f} \quad \text{...(i)}$$

a', b, g, f, h are obtained by comparing the given parabola with

$$a'x^2 + 2hxy + by^2 + 2gx + 2fy + c = 0 \quad \text{...(ii)}$$

and denominators of Eq. (i) can easily remembered by the first two rows of this determinant

i.e. $$\begin{vmatrix} a' & h & g \\ h & b & f \\ g & f & c \end{vmatrix}$$

Concept Inside Video

Since, first row $a'(x_1) + h(y_1) + g(1)$

and second row $h(x_1) + b(y_1) + f(1)$

Here, parabola $y^2 = 4ax$

or $y^2 - 4ax = 0$ ...(iii)

On comparing Eqs. (ii) and (iii), we get

$a' = 0, b = 1, g = -2a, h = 0, f = 0$

From Eq. (i), equation of normal of Eq. (iii) is

$$\frac{x - x_1}{0 + 0 - 2a} = \frac{y - y_1}{0 + y_1 + 0} \text{ or } y - y_1 = -\frac{y_1}{2a}(x - x_1)$$

2. Equations of normals of all standard parabolas at (x_1, y_1).

Equations of Parabola	Normal at (x_1, y_1)
$y^2 = 4ax$	$y - y_1 = -\frac{y_1}{2a}(x - x_1)$
$y^2 = -4ax$	$y - y_1 = \frac{y_1}{2a}(x - x_1)$
$x^2 = 4ay$	$y - y_1 = -\frac{2a}{x_1}(x - x_1)$
$x^2 = -4ay$	$y - y_1 = \frac{2a}{x_1}(x - x_1)$

2. Parametric form

To find the equation of normal to the parabola $y^2 = 4ax$ at the point $(at^2, 2at)$ or t.

Since, the equation of normal of the parabola $y^2 = 4ax$ at (x_1, y_1) is

$$y - y_1 = -\frac{y_1}{2a}(x - x_1) \quad \text{...(i)}$$

On replacing x_1 by at^2 and y_1 by $2at$, then Eq. (i) becomes

$$y - 2at = -t(x - at^2)$$

or

$$y + tx = 2at + at^3$$

The equations of normals of all standard parabolas at t

Equation of Parabolas	Parametric coordinates t	Normals at t
$y^2 = 4ax$	$(at^2, 2at)$	$y + tx = 2at + at^3$
$y^2 = -4ax$	$(-at^2, 2at)$	$y - tx = 2at + at^3$
$x^2 = 4ay$	$(2at, at^2)$	$x + ty = 2at + at^3$
$x^2 = -4ay$	$(2at, -at^2)$	$x - ty = 2at + at^3$

3. Slope form

To find the equation of normal, condition for normality and point of contact in terms of **m (slope) to the parabola $y^2 = 4ax$**

The equation of normal to the parabola $y^2 = 4ax$ at (x_1, y_1) is

$$y - y_1 = -\frac{y_1}{2a}(x - x_1) \quad \text{...(i)}$$

Since, m is the slope of the normal.

Then, $$m = -\frac{y_1}{2a}$$

$\Rightarrow$ $$y_1 = -2am$$

Since, (x_1, y_1) lies on $y^2 = 4ax$, therefore

$$y_1^2 = 4ax_1$$

$\Rightarrow$ $$4a^2m^2 = 4ax_1$$

$\therefore$ $$x_1 = am^2$$

On substituting the values of x_1 and y_1 in Eq. (i), we get

$$y + 2am = m(x - am^2)$$

$\therefore$ $$y = mx - 2am - am^3 \quad \text{...(ii)}$$

Thus, $y = mx - 2am - am^3$ is a normal to the parabola $y^2 = 4ax$, where m is the slope of the normal. The coordinates of the point of contact are $(am^2, -2am)$

On comparing Eq. (ii) with $y = mx + c$,

$\therefore$ $$c = -2am - am^3$$

which is condition of normality when $y = mx + c$ is the normal of $y^2 = 4ax$.

- The equations of normals, point of contact and condition of normality in terms of slope (m) of all standard parabolas.

Equation of parabolas	Point of contact in terms of slope (m)	Equation of normals in terms of slope (m)	Condition of normality
$y^2 = 4ax$	$(am^2, -2am)$	$y = mx - 2am - am^3$	$c = -2am - am^3$
$y^2 = -4ax$	$(-am^2, 2am)$	$y = mx + 2am + am^3$	$c = 2am + am^3$
$x^2 = 4ay$	$\left(-\frac{2a}{m}, \frac{a}{m^2}\right)$	$y = mx + 2a + \frac{a}{m^2}$	$c = 2a + \frac{a}{m^2}$
$x^2 = -4ay$	$\left(\frac{2a}{m}, -\frac{a}{m^2}\right)$	$y = mx - 2a - \frac{a}{m^2}$	$c = -2a - \frac{a}{m^2}$
$(y-k)^2 = 4a(x-h)$	$(h + am^2, k - 2am)$	$y - k = m(x-h) - 2am - am^3$	$c = k - mh - 2am - am^3$
$(y-k)^2 = -4a(x-h)$	$(h - am^2, k + 2am)$	$y - k = m(x-h) + 2am + am^3$	$c = k - mh + 2am + am^3$
$(x-h)^2 = 4a(y-k)$	$\left(h - \frac{2a}{m}, k + \frac{a}{m^2}\right)$	$y - k = m(x-h) + 2a + \frac{a}{m^2}$	$c = k - mh + 2a + \frac{a}{m^2}$
$(x-h)^2 = -4a(y-k)$	$\left(h + \frac{2a}{m}, k - \frac{a}{m^2}\right)$	$y - k = (x-h) - 2a - \frac{a}{m^2}$	$c = k - mh - 2a - \frac{a}{m^2}$

5.15 Point of Intersection of Normals at any Two Points on the Parabola

Let the parabola be $y^2 = 4ax$.

Let the points on the parabola be

$$P \equiv (at_1^2, 2at_1) \text{ and } Q = (at_2^2, 2at_2).$$

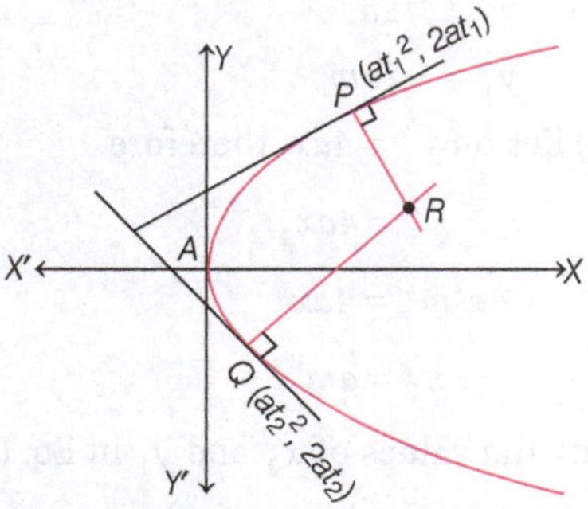

Equations of normals at $P(at_1^2, 2at_1)$ and $Q(at_2^2, 2at_2)$ are

$$y = -t_1x + 2at_1 + at_1^3 \quad \text{...(i)}$$

and $$y = -t_2x + 2at_2 + at_2^3 \quad \text{...(ii)}$$

On solving Eqs. (i) and (ii), we get

$$x = 2a + a(t_1^2 + t_2^2 + t_1t_2)$$

and $$y = -at_1t_2(t_1 + t_2)$$

If R is the point of intersection, then

$$R \equiv [2a + a(t_1^2 + t_2^2 + t_1t_2), -at_1t_2(t_1 + t_2)]$$

Point of intersection of normals at t_1 and t_2

Parabola	Equation of normal at any point t	Point of intersection of normals at t_1 and t_2
$y^2 = 4ax$	$y + tx = 2at + at^3$	$(2a + a(t_1^2 + t_1t_2 + t_2^2), -at_1t_2(t_1 + t_2))$
$y^2 = -4ax$	$y - tx = 2at + at^3$	$(-2a - a(t_1^2 + t_1t_2 + t_2^2), at_1t_2(t_1 + t_2))$
$x^2 = 4ay$	$x + ty = 2at + at^3$	$(-at_1t_2(t_1 + t_2), 2a + a(t_1^2 + t_1t_2 + t_2^2))$
$x^2 = -4ay$	$x - ty = 2at + at^3$	$(at_1t_2(t_1 + t_2), -2a - a(t_1^2 + t_1t_2 + t_2^2))$

Relation between t_1 and t_2 if Normal at t_1 Meets the Parabola Again at t_2

Let the parabola be $y^2 = 4ax$, equation of normal at $P(at_1^2, 2at_1)$ is $y = -t_1x + 2at_1 + at_1^3$ ...(i)

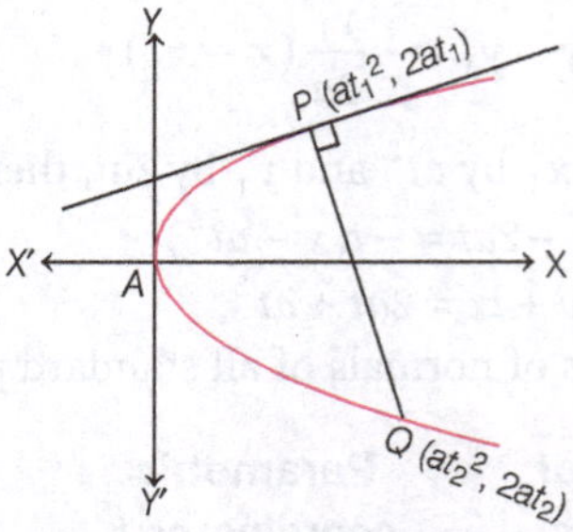

Since, it meets the parabola again at $Q(at_2^2, 2at_2)$, then Eq. (i) passes through $Q(at_2^2, 2at_2)$.

$$\therefore \quad 2at_2 = -at_1t_2^2 + 2at_1 + at_1^3$$

$$\Rightarrow \quad 2a(t_2 - t_1) + at_1(t_2^2 - t_1^2) = 0$$

$$\Rightarrow \quad a(t_2 - t_1)[2 + t_1(t_2 + t_1)] = 0$$

$$\because \quad a(t_2 - t_1) \neq 0 \quad [\because t_1 \text{ and } t_2 \text{ are different}]$$

$$\therefore \quad 2 + t_1(t_2 + t_1) = 0$$

$$\therefore \quad t_2 = -t_1 - \frac{2}{t_1}$$

Concept Inside Video

JEE Focus Points

- If normals at t_1 and t_2 meets the parabola $y^2 = 4ax$ at same point, then $t_1t_2 = 2$.
- If the normals to the parabola $y^2 = 4ax$ at the points t_1 and t_2 intersect again on the parabola at the point t_3, then $t_3 = -(t_1 + t_2)$ and the line joining t_1 and t_2 passes through a fixed point $(-2a, 0)$.
- Normal other than the axis of parabola never passes through the focus.

Example 44. Find the equation of normal to $y^2 = 16x$ with slope 3.

Sol. On comparing the given parabola with $y^2 = 4ax$, we get $a = 4$

Equation of normal in slope form is

$$y = mx - 2am - am^3$$

$$y = 3x - 2(4)(3) - 4(3)^3 \quad [\because m = 3]$$

$$y = 3x - 132$$

Example 45. If $y = x + 3$ is normal to the parabola $y^2 = 4ax$, then find value of a.

Sol. Normal to the parabola having slope m is

$$y = mx - 2am - am^3 \quad \text{...(i)}$$

Given normal is $y = x + 3$ ...(ii)

From Eqs. (i) and (ii), we get

$$m = 1 \text{ and } -2am - am^3 = 3$$

$$\Rightarrow -2a(1) - a(1)^3 = 3 \Rightarrow -2a - a = 3 \Rightarrow a = -1$$

Example 46. Show that normal to the parabola $y^2 = 8x$ at the point (2, 4) meets it again at (18, −12). Find also the length of the normal chord.

Sol. Comparing the given parabola (i.e. $y^2 = 8x$) with $y^2 = 4ax$,

$\therefore \quad 4a = 8 \Rightarrow a = 2$

Since, normal at (x_1, y_1) to the parabola $y^2 = 4ax$ is

$$y - y_1 = -\frac{y_1}{2a}(x - x_1)$$

Here, $x_1 = 2$ and $y_1 = 4$.

$\therefore$ Equation of normal is $y - 4 = -\frac{4}{4}(x - 2)$

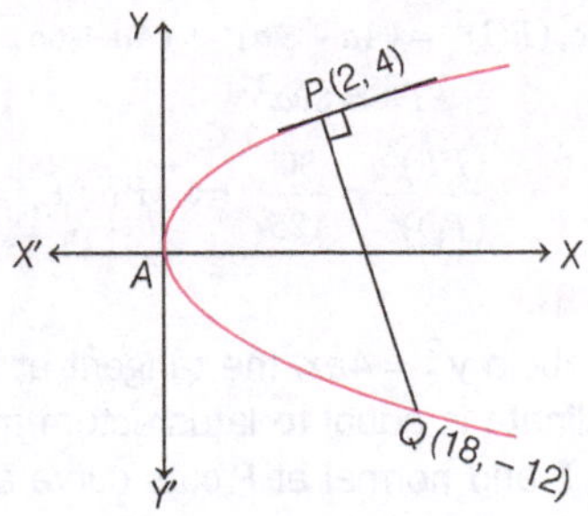

$$\Rightarrow \quad y - 4 = -x + 2$$

$$\Rightarrow \quad x + y - 6 = 0 \quad \text{...(i)}$$

On solving Eq. (i) and $y^2 = 8x$, then $y^2 = 8(6 - y)$

$$\Rightarrow \quad y^2 + 8y - 48 = 0$$

$$\Rightarrow \quad (y + 12)(y - 4) = 0$$

$\therefore \quad y = -12$ and $y = 4$

Then, $\quad x = 18$ and $x = 2$.

Hence, the point of intersection of normal and parabola are (18, −12) and (2, 4), therefore normal meets the parabola at (18, −12) and length of normal chord is distance between their points

$$= PQ = \sqrt{(18-2)^2 + (-12-4)^2} = 16\sqrt{2}$$

Example 47. Prove that the chord $y - x\sqrt{2} + 4a\sqrt{2} = 0$ is a normal chord of the parabola $y^2 = 4ax$. Also, find the point on the parabola when the given chord is normal to the parabola.

Sol. We have, $\quad y - x\sqrt{2} + 4a\sqrt{2} = 0$

i.e. $\quad y = x\sqrt{2} - 4a\sqrt{2}$ ...(i)

On comparing the Eq. (i) with the equation $y = mx + c$, then

$$m = \sqrt{2}, c = -4a\sqrt{2}$$

Since, $\quad -2am - am^3 = -2a\sqrt{2} - a(\sqrt{2})^3$

$$= -2a\sqrt{2} - 2a\sqrt{2}$$

$$= -4a\sqrt{2} = c$$

Hence, the given chord is normal to the parabola $y^2 = 4ax$.

The coordinates of the points are $(am^2, -2am)$ i.e. $(2a, -2\sqrt{2}a)$.

Example 48. If the normal to a parabola $y^2 = 4ax$, makes an angle ϕ with the axis. Show that it will cut the curve again at an angle $\tan^{-1}\left(\frac{1}{2}\tan\phi\right)$.

Sol. Let the normal at $P(at_1^2, 2at_1)$ be

$$y = -t_1x + 2at_1 + at_1^3.$$

$\therefore \quad \tan\phi = -t_1$ = slope of the normal, ...(i)

it meets the curve again at $Q(at_2^2, 2at_2)$. (say)

$$\therefore \quad t_2 = -t_1 - \frac{2}{t_1} \quad \text{...(ii)}$$

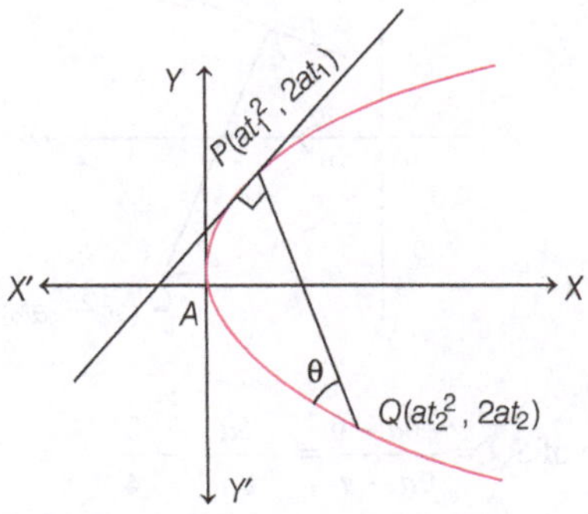

Now, angle between the normal and parabola

= angle between the normal and tangent at Q

(i.e. $t_2y = x + at_2^2$)

If θ be the angle, then

$$\tan\theta = \frac{m_1 - m_2}{1 + m_1m_2} = \frac{-t_1 - \frac{1}{t_2}}{1 + (-t_1)\left(\frac{1}{t_2}\right)} = -\frac{t_1t_2 + 1}{t_2 - t_1}$$

$$= -\frac{t_1\left(-t_1 - \frac{2}{t_1}\right) + 1}{-t_1 - \frac{2}{t_1} - t_1} \quad \text{[from Eq. (ii)]}$$

$$= -\frac{-t_1^2 - 1}{-2\left(\frac{1+t_1^2}{t_1}\right)} = -\frac{t_1}{2}$$

$$= \frac{\tan\phi}{2} \quad \text{[from Eq. (i)]}$$

$$\therefore \quad \theta = \tan^{-1}\left(\frac{1}{2}\tan\phi\right)$$

Example 49. Prove that the normal chord to a parabola $y^2 = 4ax$ at the point whose ordinate is equal to abscissa subtends a right angle at the focus.

Sol. Let the normal at $P(at_1^2, 2at_1)$ meet the curve at $Q(at_2^2, 2at_2)$.

$\therefore$ PQ is a normal chord

and $$t_2 = -t_1 - \frac{2}{t_1}. \quad \text{...(i)}$$

By given condition, $2at_1 = at_1^2$

$\therefore$ $t_1 = 2$, from Eq. (i), $t_2 = -3$

Then, $P(4a, 4a)$ and $Q(9a, -6a)$

but focus $S(a, 0)$.

$$\therefore \quad \text{Slope of } SP = \frac{4a-0}{4a-a} = \frac{4a}{3a} = \frac{4}{3}$$

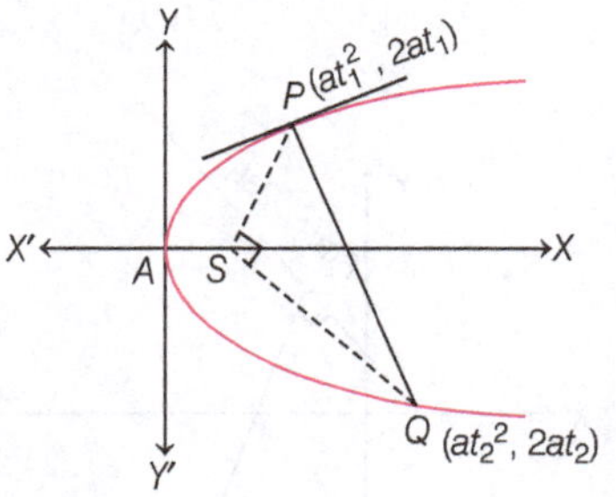

and slope of $SQ = \frac{-6a-0}{9a-a} = -\frac{6a}{8a} = -\frac{3}{4}$

$\because$ Slope of $SP \times$ Slope of $SQ = \frac{4}{3} \times -\frac{3}{4} = -1$

$$\therefore \quad \angle PSQ = \frac{\pi}{2}$$

i.e. PQ subtends a right angle at the focus S.

Example 50. If the normal to the parabola $y^2 = 4ax$ at point t_1 cuts the parabola again at point t_2, prove that $t_2^2 \geq 8$.

Sol. A normal at point t_1 cuts the parabola again at t_2. Then,

$$t_2 = -t_1 - \frac{2}{t_1}$$

$$\Rightarrow \quad t_1^2 + t_1 t_2 + 2 = 0$$

Since, t_1 is real, so $(t_2)^2 - 4 \cdot 1 \cdot 2 \geq 0$

$$\Rightarrow \quad t_2^2 \geq 8$$

JEE SCANNER

Example Similar to PYQ Asked in JEE Main 2021

In the parabola $y^2 = 4ax$, the tangent at P whose abscissa is equal to the latusrectum meets its axis at T and normal at P cuts curve again at Q, then $PT : PQ$ is equal to

(a) 3 : 5 (b) 4 : 5 (c) 5 : 4 (d) 5 : 3

Sol. (b) Given equation of parabola is $y^2 = 4ax$.

Let $P(at^2, 2at)$ be the coordinates of tangent.

Since, $at^2 = 4a$ [$\because$ abscissa = latusrectum]

$\Rightarrow$ $t = \pm 2$

Consider $t = 2$, $P \equiv (4a, 4a)$

Tangent at P is $2y = x + 4a$ which meets the X-axis at $T(-4a, 0)$.

Normal at P cuts at $Q(at_1^2, 2at_1)$.

Then, $t_1 = -t - \frac{2}{t} \Rightarrow t_1 = -3$

$\therefore$ Q is $(9a, -6a)$.

Therefore, $(PQ)^2 = (4a - 9a)^2 + (4a + 6a)^2 \Rightarrow PQ^2 = 125a^2$

Similarly, $PT^2 = 80a^2$

$$\frac{(PT)^2}{(PQ)^2} = \frac{80}{125} \Rightarrow PT : PQ = 4 : 5$$

Skill Builder

In the parabola $y^2 = 4ax$, the tangent at P whose ordinate is equal to latusrectum meets its axis at T and normal at P cuts curve again at Q, then $PT : PQ$ is equal to

(a) 5 : 3 (b) 3 : 5

(c) 5 : 4 (d) 4 : 5

For Sol.

■ **For more practice** See Q. 20 of Milestone Practice 5.2.

5.16 Co-normal Points

In general three normals can be drawn from a point to a parabola and their feet, points where they meet the parabola are called conormal points.

Let $P(h, k)$ be any given point and $y^2 = 4ax$ be a parabola. The equation of any normal to $y^2 = 4ax$ is

$$y = mx - 2am - am^3$$

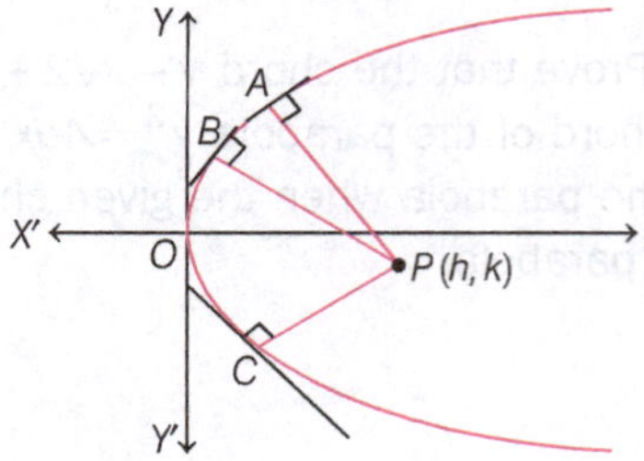

If it passes through (h, k), then

$$k = mh - 2am - am^3$$

$$\Rightarrow \quad am^3 + m(2a - h) + k = 0 \qquad \text{...(i)}$$

This is a cubic equation in m, so it has three roots, say m_1, m_2 and m_3.

$$\therefore \quad m_1 + m_2 + m_3 = 0,$$

$$m_1 m_2 + m_2 m_3 + m_3 m_1 = \frac{(2a - h)}{a},$$

$$m_1 m_2 m_3 = -\frac{k}{a} \qquad \text{...(ii)}$$

Hence, for any given point $P(h, k)$, Eq. (i) has three real or imaginary roots. Corresponding to each of these three roots, we have one normal passing through $P(h, k)$. Hence, in total, we have three normals PA, PB and PC drawn through P to the parabola.

Points A, B, C in which the three normals from $P(h, k)$ meet the parabola are **called co-normal points.**

Concept Inside Video

JEE Focus Points

- The algebraic sum of the slopes of three concurrent normals is zero.
- The algebraic sum of ordinates of the feets of three normals drawn to a parabola from a given point is zero.
- If three normals drawn to any parabola $y^2 = 4ax$ from a given point (h, k) be real, then $h > 2a$.
- If three normals drawn to any parabola $y^2 = 4ax$ from a given point (h, k) be real and distinct, then $27ak^2 < 4(h - 2a)^3$
- The centroid of the triangle formed by the feet of the three normals lies on the axis of the parabola.
- Circle passing through any three co-normal points on parabola always passes through it vertex.
- If normal at $P(t_1)$ and $Q(t_2)$ intersect at parabola it self, then $t_1 t_2 = 2$

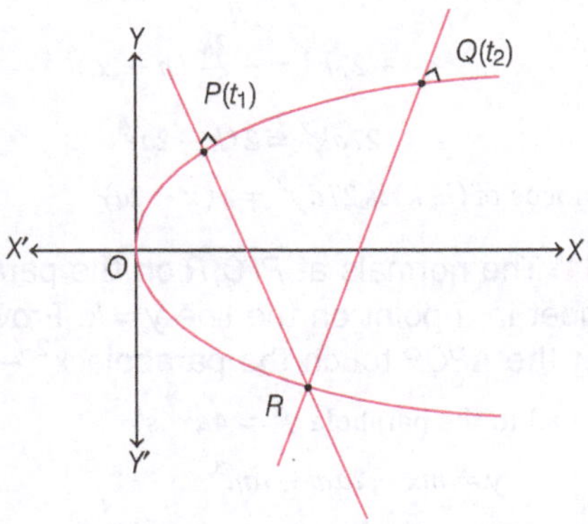

Example 51. Show that the locus of points such that two of the three normals drawn from them to the parabola $y^2 = 4ax$ coincide is $27ay^2 = 4(x - 2a)^3$.

Sol. Let (h, k) be the point of intersection of three normals to the parabola $y^2 = 4ax$. The equation of any normal to $y^2 = 4ax$ is

$$y = mx - 2am - am^3$$

If it passes through (h, k), then

$$k = mh - 2am - am^3$$

$$\Rightarrow \quad am^3 + m(2a - h) + k = 0 \qquad \text{...(i)}$$

Let the roots of Eq. (i) be m_1, m_2 and m_3.

Then, from Eq. (i), $\quad m_1 + m_2 + m_3 = 0 \qquad \text{...(ii)}$

$$m_1 m_2 + m_2 m_3 + m_3 m_1 = \frac{(2a - h)}{a} \qquad \text{...(iii)}$$

$$\text{and} \quad m_1 m_2 m_3 = -\frac{k}{a} \qquad \text{...(iv)}$$

But here, two of the three normals are given to be coincident i.e. $m_1 = m_2$.

On putting $m_1 = m_2$ in Eqs. (ii) and (iv), we get

$$2m_1 + m_3 = 0 \qquad \text{...(v)}$$

$$\text{and} \quad m_1^2 m_3 = -\frac{k}{a} \qquad \text{...(vi)}$$

On putting $m_3 = -2m_1$ from Eq. (v) in Eq. (vi), we get

$$-2m_1^3 = -\frac{k}{a} \Rightarrow m_1^3 = \frac{k}{2a}$$

Since, m_1 is a root of Eq. (i).

$$\therefore \quad am_1^3 + m_1(2a - h) + k = 0$$

$$\Rightarrow \quad a\left(\frac{k}{2a}\right) + \left(\frac{k}{2a}\right)^{1/3}(2a - h) + k = 0 \quad \left[\text{put } m_1 = \left(\frac{k}{2a}\right)^{1/3}\right]$$

$$\Rightarrow \quad \left(\frac{k}{2a}\right)^{1/3}(2a - h) = -\frac{3k}{2}$$

$$\Rightarrow \quad \frac{k}{2a}(2a - h)^3 = -\frac{27k^3}{8}$$

$$\Rightarrow \quad 27ak^2 = 4(h - 2a)^3$$

Hence, the locus of (h, k) is $27ay^2 = 4(x - 2a)^3$.

Example 52. Find the locus of the point through which three normals pass to the parabola $y^2 = 4ax$ such that two of them make angles α and β respectively with the axis such that $\tan\alpha \tan\beta = 2$.

Sol. Let (h, k) be the point of intersection of three normals to the parabola $y^2 = 4ax$.

The equation of any normal to $y^2 = 4ax$ is

$$y = mx - 2am - am^3$$

If it passes through (h,k), then

$$k = mh - 2am - am^3$$

$$\Rightarrow \quad am^3 + m(2a - h) + k = 0 \quad \text{...(i)}$$

Let roots of Eq. (i) be m_1, m_2, m_3, then from Eq. (i),

$$m_1 m_2 m_3 = -\frac{k}{a} \quad \text{...(ii)}$$

Also, $m_1 = \tan\alpha$, $m_2 = \tan\beta$ and $\tan\alpha \tan\beta = 2$

$$\therefore \quad m_1 m_2 = 2 \quad \text{...(iii)}$$

From Eqs. (ii) and (iii), $2m_3 = -\frac{k}{a}$

or $$m_3 = -\frac{k}{2a}$$

which being a root of Eq. (i) must satisfy it

i.e. $$am_3^3 + m_3(2a - h) + k = 0$$

$$\Rightarrow \quad a\left(-\frac{k}{2a}\right)^3 - \frac{k}{2a}(2a - h) + k = 0$$

$$\Rightarrow \quad -\frac{k^3}{8a^2} - k + \frac{kh}{2a} + k = 0$$

$$\Rightarrow \quad k^2 - 4ah = 0$$

$\therefore$ Required locus of (h, k) is $y^2 - 4ax = 0$.

Example 53. If the three normals from a point to the parabola $y^2 = 4ax$ cut the axis in points whose distance from the vertex are in AP, show that the point lies on the curve $27ay^2 = 2(x - 2a)^3$.

Decoding the Question

Use equation of normal in slope form and then apply concept of sum and product of zeroes of cubic polynomial.

Sol. Let (h, k) be the point of intersection of three normals to the parabola $y^2 = 4ax$. The equation of any normal to $y^2 = 4ax$ is $y = mx - 2am - am^3$ ...(i)

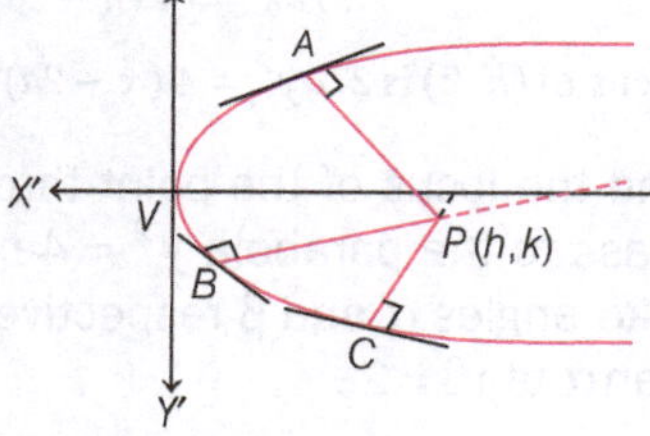

If it passes through (h, k), then

$$k = mh - 2am - am^3$$

$$\Rightarrow \quad am^3 + m(2a - h) + k = 0 \quad \text{...(ii)}$$

Let roots of Eq. (ii) be m_1, m_2 and m_3, then from Eq. (ii)

$$m_1 + m_2 + m_3 = 0 \quad \text{...(iii)}$$

$$m_1 m_2 + m_2 m_3 + m_3 m_1 = \frac{(2a - h)}{a} \quad \text{...(iv)}$$

and $$m_1 m_2 m_3 = -\frac{k}{a} \quad \text{...(v)}$$

Since, Eq. (i) cuts the axis of parabola *viz.* $y = 0$ at $(2a + am^2, 0)$.

$\therefore$ The normal through (h, k) cut the axis at $A(2a + am_1^2, 0)$, $B(2a + am_2^2, 0)$ and $C(2a + am_3^2, 0)$ and let $V(0, 0)$ be the vertex of the parabola $y^2 = 4ax$.

Then, $VA = 2a + am_1^2$, $VB = 2a + am_2^2$ and $VC = 2a + am_3^2$.

Given, VA, VB and VC are in AP.

$$\therefore \quad 2VB = VA + VC$$

$$\Rightarrow \quad 4a + 2am_2^2 = 2a + am_1^2 + 2a + am_3^2$$

$$\Rightarrow \quad 2m_2^2 = m_1^2 + m_3^2$$

$$\Rightarrow \quad 2m_2^2 = (m_1 + m_3)^2 - 2m_1 m_3$$

$$\Rightarrow \quad 2m_2^2 = (m_1 + m_2 + m_3 - m_2)^2 - \frac{2m_1 m_2 m_3}{m_2}$$

$$\Rightarrow \quad 2m_2^2 = (0 - m_2)^2 - \frac{2}{m_2}\left(-\frac{k}{a}\right)$$

[from Eqs. (iii) and (v)]

$$\Rightarrow \quad m_2^3 = \frac{2k}{a} \quad \text{...(vi)}$$

Now, from Eq. (iv), $m_2(m_1 + m_3) + m_3 m_1 = \frac{(2a - h)}{a}$

$$\Rightarrow m_2(m_1 + m_2 + m_3 - m_2) + \frac{m_1 m_2 m_3}{m_2} = \frac{(2a - h)}{a}$$

$$\Rightarrow \quad m_2(0 - m_2) - \frac{k}{am_2} = \frac{(2a - h)}{a}$$

$$\Rightarrow \quad -am_2^3 - k = m_2(2a - h)$$

$$\Rightarrow \quad (-am_2^3 - k)^3 = m_2^3(2a - h)^3$$

$$\Rightarrow \quad (-2k - k)^3 = \frac{2k}{a}(2a - h)^3 \quad \text{[from Eq. (vi)]}$$

$$\Rightarrow \quad -27k^3 = -\frac{2k}{a}(h - 2a)^3$$

$$\Rightarrow \quad 27ak^2 = 2(h - 2a)^3$$

Hence, locus of (h, k) is $27ay^2 = 2(x - 2a)^3$.

Example 54. The normals at P, Q, R on the parabola $y^2 = 4ax$ meet in a point on the line $y = k$. Prove that the sides of the ΔPQR touch the parabola $x^2 - 2ky = 0$.

Sol. Any normal to the parabola $y^2 = 4ax$ is

$$y = mx - 2am - am^3 \quad \text{...(i)}$$

Also, any point on the line $y = k$ is (x_1, k).

If Eq. (i) passes through (x_1, k) then $k = mx_1 - 2am - am^3$

or $\quad am^3 + m(2a - x_1) + k = 0$

If the roots of this equation are m_1, m_2, m_3 then we get

$$m_1 + m_2 + m_3 = 0 \quad \text{...(ii)}$$

$$m_1m_2 + m_2m_3 + m_3m_1 = \frac{(2a - x_1)}{a} \quad \text{...(iii)}$$

and $\quad m_1m_2m_3 = -\frac{k}{a} \quad$ ...(iv)

Also, coordinates of three points P, Q and R are $(am_1^2, -2am_1)(am_2^2, -2am_2)$ and $(am_3^2, -2am_3)$, respectively.

$\therefore$ The equation of the line PQ is

$$y - (-2am_1) = \frac{(-2am_2) - (-2am_1)}{am_2^2 - am_1^2}(x - am_1^2)$$

$$\Rightarrow \quad y + 2am_1 = -\frac{2}{(m_2 + m_1)}(x - am_1^2)$$

$$\Rightarrow \quad y(m_1 + m_2) + 2am_1(m_1 + m_2) = -2x + 2am_1^2$$

$$\Rightarrow \quad y(m_1 + m_2) + 2am_1m_2 = -2x$$

$$\Rightarrow \quad y(m_1 + m_2 + m_3 - m_3) + \frac{2am_1m_2m_3}{m_3} = -2x$$

$$\Rightarrow \quad y(0 - m_3) - \frac{2k}{m_3} = -2x \quad \text{[from Eqs. (ii) and (iv)]}$$

$$\Rightarrow \quad -ym_3^2 - 2k = -2m_3x$$

$$\Rightarrow \quad ym_3^2 - 2m_3x + 2k = 0,$$

which is a quadratic in m_3.

Since, PQ will touch it, then

$$B^2 - 4AC = 0$$

$$\Rightarrow \quad (-2x)^2 - 4 \cdot y \cdot 2k = 0$$

$$\therefore \quad x^2 - 2ky = 0$$

Example 55. Find the point on the axis of the parabola $3y^2 + 4y - 6x + 8 = 0$ from when three distinct normals can be drawn.

Sol. Given parabola is $3y^2 + 4y - 6x + 8 = 0$

$$\Rightarrow \quad 3\left(y^2 + \frac{4}{3}y\right) = 6x - 8$$

$$\Rightarrow \quad 3\left\{\left(y + \frac{2}{3}\right)^2 - \frac{4}{9}\right\} = 6x - 8$$

$$\Rightarrow \quad 3\left(y + \frac{2}{3}\right)^2 = \left(6x - 8 + \frac{4}{3}\right)$$

$$\therefore \quad \left(y + \frac{2}{3}\right)^2 = 2\left(x - \frac{10}{9}\right)$$

Let $\quad y + \frac{2}{3} = Y, \; x - \frac{10}{9} = X$

Then, $\quad Y^2 = 2X$

On comparing with $\quad Y^2 = 4aX$,

$$\therefore \quad a = \frac{1}{2}$$

Any point on the axis of parabola is $\left(x, -\frac{2}{3}\right)$

and $\quad X > 2a \;\Rightarrow\; x - \frac{10}{9} > 1$

$$\Rightarrow \quad x > \frac{19}{9}$$

Circle Through Co-normal Points

To find the equation of the circle passing through the three (co-normal) points on the parabola, normals at which pass through a given point (α, β).

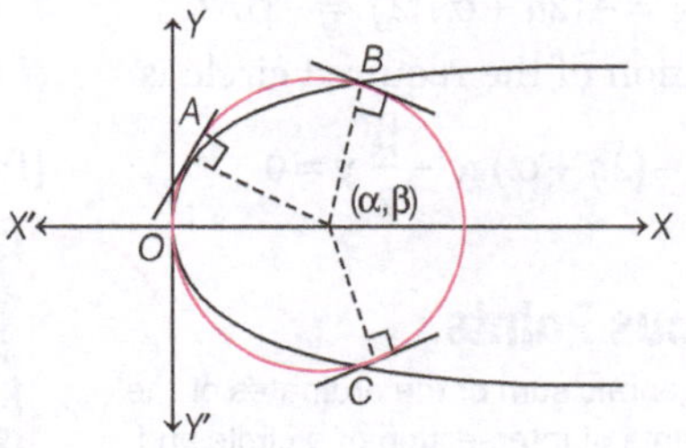

Let $A(am_1^2, -2am_1)$, $B(am_2^2, -2am_2)$ and $C(am_3^2, -2am_3)$ be the three points on the parabola

$$y^2 = 4ax$$

Since, point of intersection of normals is (α, β), then

$$am^3 + (2a - \alpha)m + \beta = 0 \quad \text{...(i)}$$

$$\therefore \quad m_1 + m_2 + m_3 = 0 \quad \text{...(ii)}$$

$$m_1m_2 + m_2m_3 + m_3m_1 = \frac{(2a - \alpha)}{a} \quad \text{... (iii)}$$

and $\quad m_1m_2m_3 = -\frac{\beta}{a} \quad$ ...(iv)

Let the equation of the circle through A, B, C be

$$x^2 + y^2 + 2gx + 2fy + c = 0 \quad \text{...(v)}$$

If the point $(am^2, -2am)$ lies on it, then

$$(am^2)^2 + (-2am)^2 + 2g(am^2) + 2f(-2am) + c = 0$$

$$\Rightarrow \quad a^2m^4 + (4a^2 + 2ag)m^2 - 4afm + c = 0 \quad \text{...(vi)}$$

This is a biquadratic equation in m. Hence, there are four values of m, say m_1, m_2, m_3 and m_4 such that the circle passes through the points.

$A(am_1^2, -2am_1)$, $B(am_2^2, -2am_2)$, $C(am_3^2, -2am_3)$ and $D(am_4^2, -2am_4)$.

$\therefore \quad m_1 + m_2 + m_3 + m_4 = 0$

$\Rightarrow \quad 0 + m_4 = 0$ [from Eq. (ii)]

$\Rightarrow \quad m_4 = 0$

$\therefore \quad (am_4^2, -2am_4) = (0, 0)$

Thus, the circle passes through the vertex of the parabola $y^2 = 4ax$ from Eq. (v),

$$0 + 0 + 0 + 0 + c = 0$$

$\therefore \quad c = 0$

From Eq. (vi), $a^2m^4 + (4a^2 + 2ag)m^2 - 4afm = 0$

$\Rightarrow \quad am^3 + (4a + 2g)m - 4f = 0$ ...(vii)

Now, Eqs. (i) and (vii) are identical.

$\therefore \quad 1 = \dfrac{4a + 2g}{2a - \alpha} = -\dfrac{4f}{\beta}$

$\therefore \quad 2g = -(2a + \alpha), 2f = -\beta/2$

$\therefore$ The equation of the required circle is

$$x^2 + y^2 - (2a + \alpha)x - \frac{\beta}{2}y = 0 \quad \text{[from Eq. (v)]}$$

Concept Inside Video

JEE Focus Points

- The algebraic sum of the ordinates of the four points of intersection of a circle and a parabola is zero.
- The common chords of a circle and a parabola are in pairs equally inclined to the axis of the parabola.

Example 56. A circle cuts the parabola $y^2 = 4ax$ at right angles and passes through the focus, show that its centre lies on the curve $y^2(a + 2x) = a(a + 3x)^2$.

Sol. Let the circle $x^2 + y^2 + 2gx + 2fy + c = 0$ ...(i)

meets the parabola $y^2 = 4ax$ at any point $P(at^2, 2at)$ cutting it at right angles.

We have to find locus of centre of circle Eq. (i),

i.e. $\quad (-g, -f)$

But given circle Eq. (i) passes through the focus $(a, 0)$, then

$$a^2 + 0 + 2ga + 0 + c = 0$$

$\Rightarrow \quad c = -a^2 - 2ag$ ...(ii)

Now, the circle and parabola intersect at $P(at^2, 2at)$ at right angles.

Since, tangent at $P(at^2, 2at)$ to the parabola $y^2 = 4ax$ is

$$ty = x + at^2$$

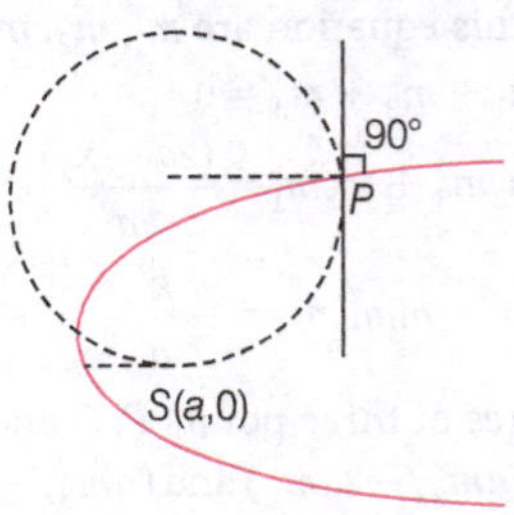

Hence, this tangent must pass through the centre $(-g, -f)$ of the circle

$\therefore \quad -ft = -g + at^2$

$\Rightarrow \quad ft = g - at^2$ ...(iii)

Also, the point $P(at^2, 2at)$ lies on the circle (i), then

$$a^2t^4 + 4a^2t^2 + 2agt^2 + 4aft + c = 0$$

Hence, from Eqs. (ii) and (iii) when we put values for c and ft.

$\therefore \quad a^2t^4 + 4a^2t^2 + 2agt^2 + 4ag - 4a^2t^2 - a^2 - 2ag = 0$

$\Rightarrow \quad a^2t^4 + 2agt^2 + 2ag - a^2 = 0$

$\Rightarrow \quad at^4 + 2gt^2 + 2g - a = 0$

$\Rightarrow \quad a(t^4 - 1) + 2g(t^2 + 1) = 0$

$\Rightarrow \quad (t^2 + 1)[a(t^2 - 1) + 2g] = 0$

But $t^2 + 1 \neq 0$

$\Rightarrow a(t^2 - 1) + 2g = 0 \Rightarrow t^2 = \dfrac{a - 2g}{a}$

Hence, from Eq. (iii),

$$f\sqrt{\left(\frac{a - 2g}{a}\right)} = g - a\left(\frac{a - 2g}{a}\right) \Rightarrow f\sqrt{\left(\frac{a - 2g}{a}\right)} = (3g - a)$$

$\Rightarrow \quad f^2(a - 2g) = a(3g - a)^2$

$\Rightarrow \quad (-f)^2[a + 2(-g)] = a(a - 3g)^2$

$\Rightarrow \quad (-f)^2[a + 2(-g)] = a[a + 3(-g)]^2$

Hence, locus of the centre $(-g, -f)$ is the curve

$$y^2(a + 2x) = a(a + 3x)^2.$$

Milestone Practice 5.2

1. The position of the point (1, 1) with respect to the parabola $y^2 - 2y + 7x + 8 = 0$ is
(a) on (b) inside (c) outside (d) none

2. If the point $(a, 2a)$ is an interior point of the region bounded by the parabola $y^2 = 16x$ and the double ordinate through the focus, then $a \in$
(a) $(-\infty, 4)$ (b) $(0, 4)$ (c) $(0, 2)$ (d) $(4, \infty)$

3. Length of the focal chord of the parabola $y^2 = 4ax$ at a distance of p from the vertex is
(a) $\frac{2a^2}{p}$ (b) $\frac{a^3}{p^2}$ (c) $\frac{4a^3}{p^2}$ (d) $\frac{p^2}{a}$

4. Let PQ be a focal chord of the parabola $y^2 = -16x$ of length 25, making an acute angle with the positive X-axis. Let the ordinates of P be positive and M be the point on the line segment PQ such that $PM : MQ = 1 : 2$. Then, find the equation of the line passing through M and perpendicular to PQ.

5. For what value of k does the line $x + y + 1 = 0$ touch the parabola $y^2 = kx$? Also, find the distance of vertex of the parabola from the point of contact.

6. Find the distance of the point $(-3, -4)$ from the common tangent of the parabolas $x^2 = 108y$ and $y^2 = 32x$.

7. If the tangent at (1, 7) to the curve $x^2 = y - 6$ touches the circle $x^2 + y^2 + 16x + 12y + c = 0$, then find the value of c.

8. If the line $ax + y = c$, touches both the curves $x^2 + y^2 = 1$ and $y^2 = 4\sqrt{2}x$, then find the value of $|c|$.

9. The ordinates of the points P and Q on the parabola $y^2 = 12x$ are in the ratio 1 : 2. Find the locus of the point of intersection of the normals to the parabola at P and Q.

10. Prove that any three tangents to a parabola whose slopes are in HP encloses a triangle of constant area.

11. A chord of parabola $y^2 = 4ax$ subtends a right angle at the vertex. Find the locus of the point of intersection of tangents at its extremities.

12. Find the point of the parabola $y^2 = 4ax$ at which the normal is inclined at 30° to the axis.

13. Find the equation of the normal to the parabola $y^2 = 8x$ which is parallel to the line $y - 2x + 3 = 0$.

14. A circle drawn on any focal chord of the parabola $y^2 = 4ax$ as diameter cuts the parabola at two points t and t' (other than the extremity of focal chord), then the value of tt' is
(a) 3 (b) 5 (c) 2 (d) 6

15. Let S be the set of all possible values of parameter a for which the points of intersection of the parabolas $y^2 = 3ax$ and $y = \frac{1}{2}(x^2 + ax + 5)$ are concyclic. Then, S contains the interval(s)
(a) $(-\infty, -3)$ (b) $(-2, 0)$ (c) $(0, 2)$ (d) $(2, \infty)$

16. The equation of the straight line(s) that touches both $x^2 + y^2 = 2a^2$ and $y^2 = 8ax$ is/are
(a) $y = x + 2a$ (b) $y = -x - a$
(c) $y = -x + 2a$ (d) $y = x - 2a$

17. If the normals at the end points of a variable chord PQ of the parabola $y^2 - 4y - 2x = 0$ are perpendicular, then the tangents at P and Q will intersect at
(a) $x + y = 3$ (b) $3x - 7 = 0$
(c) $y + 3 = 0$ (d) $2x + 5 = 0$

18. The coordinates of the point on the parabola $y^2 = 8x$, which is at minimum distance from the circle $x^2 + (y + 6)^2 = 1$ are
(a) $(2, -4)$ (b) $(18, -12)$
(c) $(2, 4)$ (d) None of these

19. Through the vertex O of a parabola $y^2 = 4x$ chords OP and OQ are drawn at right angle to one another. Show that for all position of P, PQ cuts the axis of the parabola at a fixed point. Also, find the locus of the middle point of PQ.

20. In the parabola $y^2 = 16x$, the tangent at P whose abscissa is equal to the length of latusrectum meets its axis at T and normal at P cuts curve again at Q, then $PT : PQ$ is equal to
(a) 4 : 5 (b) 5 : 4 (c) 3 : 4 (d) 4 : 3

Answer Key

1. (c)	2. (b)	3. (c)	4. $3x + 12y + 50 = 0$	5. $k = 4$ and $\frac{\sqrt{5}}{4}k$
6. $\frac{18}{13}\sqrt{13}$ units	7. (95)	8. $(\sqrt{2})$	9. $343y^2 = 12(x-6)^3$	
11. $x + 4a = 0$	12. $\left(\frac{a}{3}, \frac{-2a}{\sqrt{3}}\right)$	13. $y = 2x - 24$	14. (a)	15. (d)
16. (a)	17. (d)	18. (a)	19. $y^2 = 2x - 8$	20. (a)

For Detailed Solution

Milestone 3 Pair of Tangents and Chord of Contact

- Equation of pair of Tangents • Chord of Contact • Equation of the Chord Bisected at a Given Point
- Diameter of a Parabola • Length of Tangent, Subtangent, Normal and Subnormal
- Some Standard Properties of the Parabola • Reflection Property of a Parabola

5.17 Equation of Pair of Tangents

If $y_1^2 - 4ax_1 > 0$, then any point $P(x_1, y_1)$ lies outside the parabola and a pair of tangents PQ, PR can be drawn to it from P. We find their equation as follows.

Let $T(h, k)$ be any point on the pair of tangents PQ or PR drawn from any external point $P(x_1, y_1)$ to the parabola $y^2 = 4ax$.

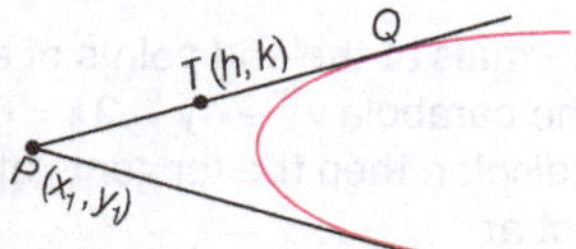

Equation of PT is

$$y - y_1 = \frac{k - y_1}{h - x_1}(x - x_1)$$

$$\Rightarrow \quad y = \left(\frac{k - y_1}{h - x_1}\right)x + \left(\frac{hy_1 - kx_1}{h - x_1}\right)$$

which is tangent to the parabola

$$y^2 = 4ax$$

$$\therefore \quad c = \frac{a}{m}$$

$$\Rightarrow \quad cm = a \Rightarrow \left(\frac{hy_1 - kx_1}{h - x_1}\right)\left(\frac{k - y_1}{h - x_1}\right) = a$$

$$\Rightarrow \quad (k - y_1)(hy_1 - kx_1) = a(h - x_1)^2$$

$\therefore$ Locus of (h, k), equation of pair of tangents is

$$(y - y_1)(xy_1 - x_1y) = a(x - x_1)^2$$

$$\Rightarrow (y^2 - 4ax)(y_1^2 - 4ax_1) = \{yy_1 - 2a(x + x_1)\}^2$$

$$\therefore \quad SS_1 = T^2$$

where, $S = y^2 - 4ax, S_1 = y_1^2 - 4ax_1$

and $T = yy_1 - 2a(x + x_1)$.

Alternate method

Let the parabola be $y^2 = 4ax$. ...(i)

Let $P(x_1, y_1)$ be any point outside the parabola. Let a chord of the parabola through the point $P(x_1, y_1)$ cut the parabola at Q and let $R(h, k)$ be any arbitrary point on the line PQ (R inside or outside).

Let Q divide PR in the ratio $\lambda : 1$, then coordinates of Q are

$$\left(\frac{\lambda h + x_1}{\lambda + 1}, \frac{\lambda k + y_1}{\lambda + 1}\right) \quad [\because PQ : QR = \lambda : 1]$$

Since, Q lies on parabola Eq. (i), then

$$\left(\frac{\lambda k + y_1}{\lambda + 1}\right)^2 = 4a\left(\frac{\lambda h + x_1}{\lambda + 1}\right)$$

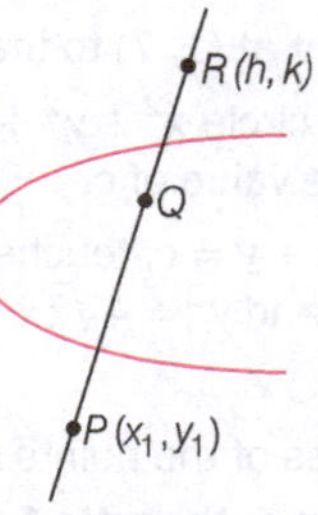

$$\Rightarrow \quad (\lambda k + y_1)^2 - 4a(\lambda h + x_1)(\lambda + 1) = 0$$

$$\Rightarrow \quad (k^2 - 4ah)\lambda^2 + 2[ky_1 - 2a(h + x_1)]\lambda + (y_1^2 - 4ax_1) = 0 \quad ...(ii)$$

Line PR will become tangent to parabola Eq. (i), then roots of Eq. (ii) are equal

$$\therefore \quad 4[ky_1 - 2a(h + x_1)]^2 - 4(k^2 - 4ah)(y_1^2 - 4ax_1) = 0$$

or $\{ky_1 - 2a(h + x_1)\}^2 = (k^2 - 4ah)(y_1^2 - 4ax_1)$

Hence, locus of $R(h, k)$ i.e. equation of pair of tangents from $P(x_1, y_1)$ is

$$\{yy_1 - 2a(x + x_1)\}^2 = (y^2 - 4ax)(y_1^2 - 4ax_1)$$

i.e. $T^2 = SS_1$ or $SS_1 = T^2$

Example 57. Find the slopes of tangents drawn from a point (4, 10) to the parabola $y^2 = 9x$.

Sol. The equation of a tangent of a slope m to the parabola $y^2 = 9x$ is

$$y = mx + \frac{9}{4m}$$

It passes through (4, 10),

$$\therefore \quad 10 = 4m + \frac{9}{4m}$$

$$\Rightarrow \quad 16m^2 - 40m + 9 = 0$$

$$\therefore \quad m = \frac{1}{4}, \frac{9}{4}$$

Example 58. Two tangents are drawn from the point (–2, –1) to the parabola $y^2 = 4x$. If α is the angle between these tangents, then find the value of $\tan\alpha$.

Sol. The equation of a tangent to the parabola $y^2 = 4x$ is

$$y = mx + \frac{1}{m}$$

It is passes through (–2, –1), then

$$-1 = -2m + \frac{1}{m} \Rightarrow 2m^2 - m - 1 = 0$$

Let m_1 and m_2 be the roots of this equation. Then,

$$m_1 + m_2 = \frac{1}{2} \quad \text{and} \quad m_1 m_2 = \frac{-1}{2}$$

Now,
$$\tan\alpha = \pm \frac{m_1 - m_2}{1 + m_1 m_2}$$

$$= \pm \left[\frac{\sqrt{(m_1 + m_2)^2 - 4m_1 m_2}}{1 + m_1 m_2}\right]$$

$$= \pm \left[\frac{\sqrt{\frac{1}{4} + \frac{4}{2}}}{1 - \frac{1}{2}}\right] = \pm 3$$

Example 59. Tangents are drawn from the point (–1, 2) on the parabola $y^2 = 4x$. Find the length such that these tangents will intercept on the line $x = 2$.

Sol.

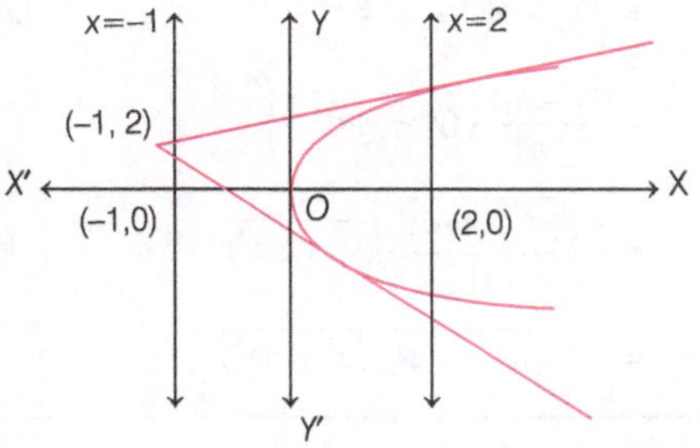

The equation of the pair of tangents from point (x_1, y_1) is

$$SS_1 = T^2$$

$$\Rightarrow \quad (y^2 - 4x)(y_1^2 - 4x_1) = [yy_1 - 2(x + x_1)]^2$$

$\therefore$ Equation of the pair of tangents from (–1, 2) is

$$(y^2 - 4x)(4 + 4) = [2y - 2(x - 1)]^2$$

$$\Rightarrow \quad 2(y^2 - 4x) = (y - x + 1)^2$$

On putting $x = 2$, we get

$$y^2 + 2y - 17 = 0$$

$$\therefore \quad y_1 + y_2 = -2 \text{ and } y_1 y_2 = -17$$

Now, $|y_1 - y_2|^2 = (y_1 + y_2)^2 - 4y_1 y_2 = 4 - 4(-17) = 72$

$$\therefore \quad |y_1 - y_2| = \sqrt{72} = 6\sqrt{2}.$$

5.18 Chord of Contact

The chord joining the points of contact of two tangents drawn from an external point to a parabola is known as the chord of contact of tangents drawn from external point.

> **Theorem** The chord of contact of tangents drawn from a point (x_1, y_1) to the parabola $y^2 = 4ax$ is
> $$yy_1 = 2a(x + x_1).$$

Proof Let PQ and PR be tangents to the parabola $y^2 = 4ax$ drawn from any external point $P(x_1, y_1)$, then QR is called **chord of contact** of the parabola $y^2 = 4ax$.

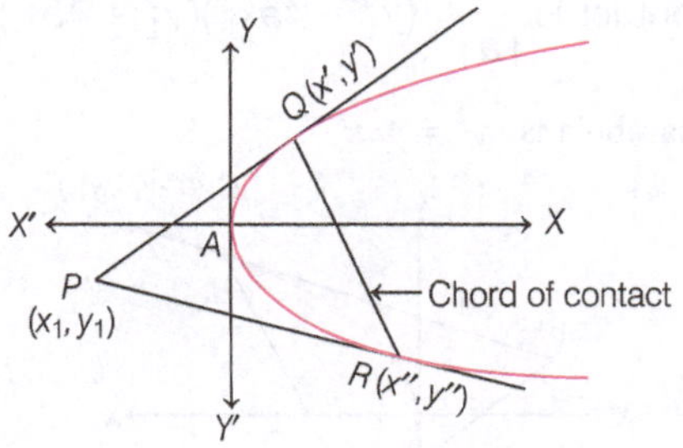

Let $\qquad Q \equiv (x', y')$ and $R \equiv (x'', y'')$

Equation of tangent PQ is

$$yy' = 2a(x + x') \qquad \text{...(i)}$$

and equation of tangent PR is

$$yy'' = 2a(x + x'') \qquad \text{...(ii)}$$

Since, lines Eqs. (i) and (ii) pass through (x_1, y_1), then

$$y_1 y' = 2a(x_1 + x') \text{ and } y_1 y'' = 2a(x_1 + x'')$$

Hence, it is clear $Q(x', y')$ and $R(x'', y'')$ lie on

$$yy_1 = 2a(x + x_1)$$

which is **chord of contact** QR.

Example 60. Find the equation of the chord of contact of tangents from (2, 5) to the parabola $y^2 = 8x$.

Sol. The equation of chord of contact is $yy_1 = 2a(x + x_i)$.

$\therefore$ Equation of chord of contact from the point (2, 5) to the parabola $y^2 = 8x$, is $5y = 4(x + 2)$.

$$\therefore \quad 4x - 5y + 8 = 0$$

Example 61. Tangents are drawn from any point on the line $x+4a=0$ to the parabola $y^2=4ax$. Then, find the angle subtended by the chord of contact at the vertex.

Sol. Let $P(at_1^2, 2at_1)$ and $Q(at_2^2, 2at_2)$ be the points of contact of tangents drawn from any point on the line $x+4a=0$.

Their point of intersection will be on this line.

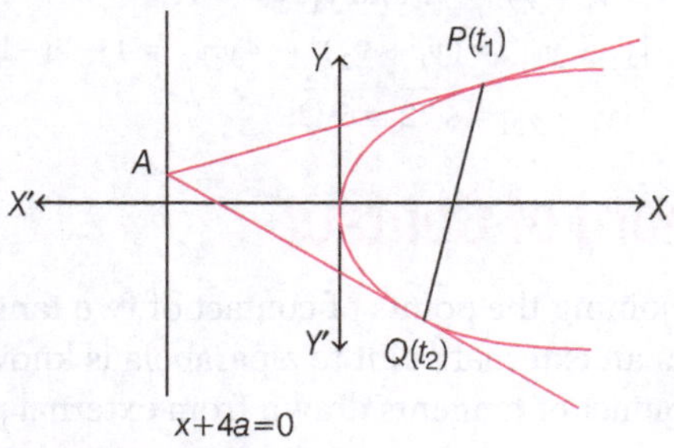

$$at_1t_2 + 4a = 0$$

$$\Rightarrow \quad t_1t_2 = -4$$

This is also the condition for chord PQ to subtend right angle at the vertex.

Example 62. Tangents are drawn from the point (x_1, y_1) to the parabola $y^2=4ax$, show that the length of their chord of contact is $\dfrac{1}{|a|}\sqrt{(y_1^2-4ax_1)(y_1^2+4a^2)}$.

Sol. Given parabola is $y^2 = 4ax$ ...(i)

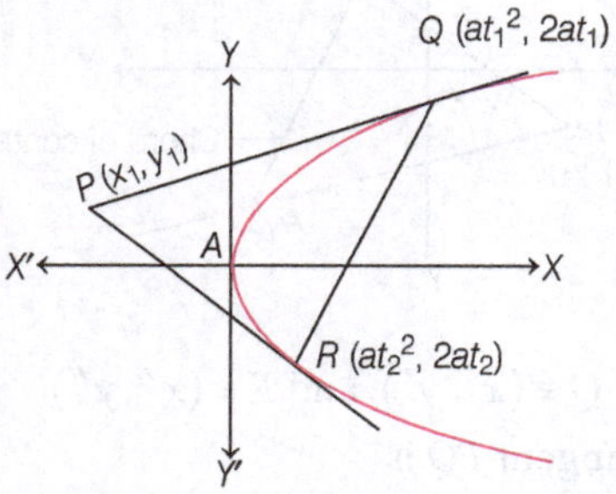

Let $P \equiv (x_1, y_1)$

and the tangents from P touch the parabola at $Q(at_1^2, 2at_1)$ and $R(at_2^2, 2at_2)$, then P is the point of intersection of tangents.

$$\therefore \quad x_1 = at_1t_2 \text{ and } y_1 = a(t_1+t_2)$$

$$\Rightarrow \quad t_1t_2 = \frac{x_1}{a} \text{ and } t_1+t_2 = \frac{y_1}{a} \quad \text{...(ii)}$$

Now, $QR = \sqrt{(at_1^2 - at_2^2)^2 + (2at_1 - 2at_2)^2}$

$$= \sqrt{a^2(t_1-t_2)^2\,[(t_1+t_2)^2+4]}$$

$$= |a|\,|t_1-t_2|\sqrt{\{(t_1+t_2)^2+4\}}$$

$$= |a|\sqrt{\{(t_1+t_2)^2-4t_1t_2\}}\sqrt{\{(t_1+t_2)^2+4\}}$$

$$= |a|\sqrt{\left(\frac{y_1^2}{a^2}-\frac{4x_1}{a}\right)}\cdot\sqrt{\left(\frac{y_1^2}{a^2}+4\right)} \quad \text{[from Eq. (ii)]}$$

$$= |a|\frac{\sqrt{(y_1^2-4ax_1)}}{|a|}\cdot\frac{\sqrt{(y_1^2+4a^2)}}{|a|}$$

$$= \frac{1}{|a|}\sqrt{(y_1^2-4ax_1)(y_1^2+4a^2)}$$

Alternate Solution

Equation of QR is $yy_1 = 2a(x+x_1)$

$$\Rightarrow \quad x = \frac{yy_1 - 2ax_1}{2a}$$

The ordinates of Q and R are the roots of the equation

$$y^2 = 4a\left(\frac{yy_1-2ax_1}{2a}\right)$$

$$\Rightarrow \quad y^2 = 2(yy_1 - 2ax_1) \quad \text{...(i)}$$

$$\Rightarrow \quad y^2 - 2yy_1 + 4ax_1 = 0$$

$$\therefore \quad k_1 + k_2 = 2y_1 \text{ and } k_1k = 4ax_1$$

$$\therefore \quad (k_2-k_1) = \sqrt{(k_1+k_2)^2 - 4k_1k_2}$$

$$= \sqrt{(4y_1^2 - 16ax_1)}$$

$$= 2\sqrt{(y_1^2-4ax_1)} \quad \text{...(ii)}$$

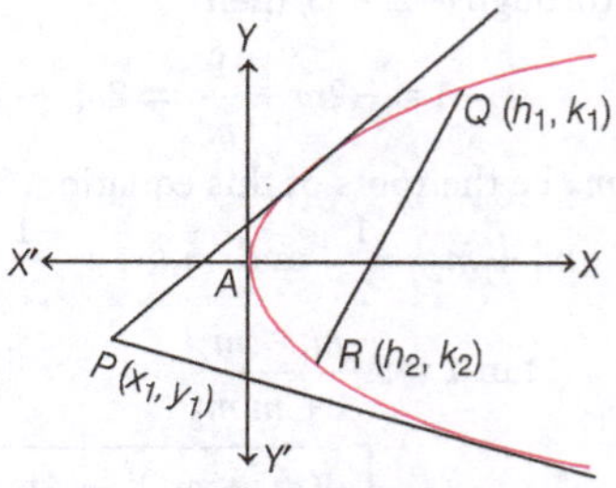

Since, $Q(h_1, k_1)$ and $R(h_2, k_2)$ lie on the parabola $y^2 = 4ax$, therefore $k_1^2 = 4ah_1$ and $k_2^2 = 4ah_2$

$$\Rightarrow \quad k_2^2 - k_1^2 = 4a(h_2 - h_1)$$

$$(k_2+k_1)(k_2-k_1) = 4a(h_2-h_1)$$

$$\Rightarrow \quad 2y_1(k_2-k_1) = 4a(h_2-h_1)$$

$$\Rightarrow \quad (h_2-h_1) = \frac{y_1(k_2-k_1)}{2a} \quad \text{...(iii)}$$

Now, $QR = \sqrt{(k_2-k_1)^2 + (h_2-h_1)^2}$

$$= \sqrt{(k_2-k_1)^2 + \frac{y_1^2(k_2-k_1)^2}{4a^2}} \quad \text{[from Eq. (iii)]}$$

$$= \frac{(k_2-k_1)}{2|a|}\sqrt{(y_1^2+4a^2)}$$

$$= \frac{2\sqrt{(y_1^2-4ax_1)}}{2|a|}\sqrt{(y_1^2+4a^2)} \quad \text{[from Eq. (ii)]}$$

$$= \frac{1}{|a|}\sqrt{(y_1^2-4ax_1)(y_1^2+4a^2)}$$

Example 63. Prove that the area of the triangle formed by the tangents drawn from (x_1, y_1) to $y^2=4ax$ and their chord of contact is $(y_1^2-4ax_1)^{3/2}/2a$.

Sol. Equation of QR (chord of contact) is

$$yy_1 = 2a(x + x_1)$$

$$\Rightarrow \quad yy_1 - 2a(x + x_1) = 0$$

$\because$ PM = Length of perpendicular from $P(x_1, y_1)$ on QR

$$= \frac{|y_1y_1 - 2a(x_1 + x_1)|}{\sqrt{(y_1^2 + 4a^2)}} = \frac{|(y_1^2 - 4ax_1)|}{\sqrt{(y_1^2 + 4a^2)}}$$

[$\because P(x_1, y_1)$ lies outside the parabola, so $y_1^2 - 4ax_1 > 0$]

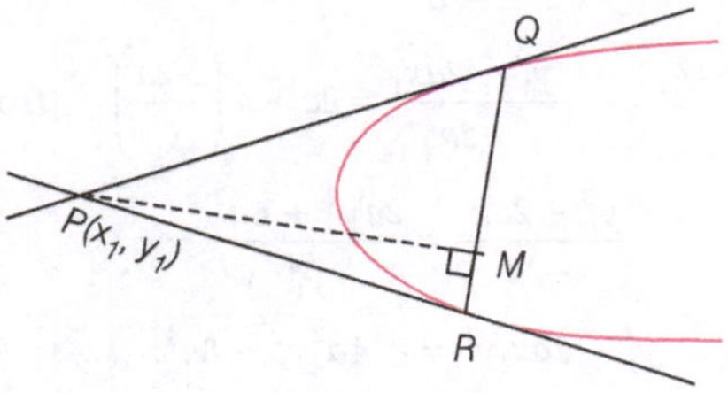

Now, area of $\Delta PQR = \frac{1}{2} QR \cdot PM$

$$= \frac{1}{2}\frac{1}{|a|}\sqrt{(y_1^2 - 4ax_1)(y_1^2 + 4a^2)}\,\frac{(y_1^2 - 4ax_1)}{\sqrt{(y_1^2 + 4a^2)}}$$

$$= (y_1^2 - 4ax_1)^{3/2} / 2a, \text{ if } a > 0$$

5.19 Equation of the Chord Bisected at a Given Point

Theorem The equation of the chord of the parabola $y^2 = 4ax$, which is bisected at (x_1, y_1) is

$$yy_1 - 2a(x + x_1) = y_1^2 - 4ax_1$$

or $\quad T = S_1,$

where, $T = yy_1 - 2a(x + x_1)$ and $S_1 = y_1^2 - 4ax_1$.

Proof Since, equation of the parabola is

$$y^2 = 4ax \quad \text{...(i)}$$

Let QR be the chord of the parabola whose mid-point is $P(x_1, y_1)$.

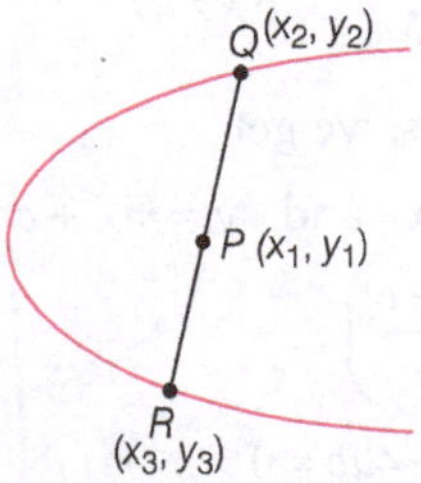

Since, Q and R lie on parabola (i), then

$$y_2^2 = 4ax_2 \text{ and } y_3^2 = 4ax_3$$

$$\therefore \quad y_3^2 - y_2^2 = 4a(x_3 - x_2)$$

$$\Rightarrow \quad \frac{y_3 - y_2}{x_3 - x_2} = \frac{4a}{y_3 + y_2}$$

$$= \frac{4a}{2y_1} \quad [\because P(x_1, y_1) \text{ is mid-point of } QR]$$

$$\therefore \quad \frac{y_3 - y_2}{x_3 - x_2} = \frac{2a}{y_1} = \text{Slope of } QR$$

Equation of QR is $\quad y - y_1 = \frac{2a}{y_1}(x - x_1)$

$$\Rightarrow \quad yy_1 - y_1^2 = 2ax - 2ax_1$$

$$\Rightarrow \quad yy_1 - 2a(x + x_1) = y_1^2 - 4ax_1$$

[subtracting $2ax_1$ from both sides]

$$\therefore \quad T = S_1,$$

where $\quad T = yy_1 - 2a(x + x_1)$ and $S_1 = y_1^2 - 4ax_1$.

Example 64. Find the equation of the chord of $y^2 = 8x$ which is bisected at $(2, -3)$.

Sol. The equation of the required chord is given by

$$T = S_1$$

$$\Rightarrow \quad -3y - 4(x + 2) = 9 - 8 \times 2$$

$$\Rightarrow \quad 4x + 3y + 1 = 0$$

Example 65. Find the mid-point of the chord intercepted on the line $4x - 3y + 4 = 0$ by the parabola $y^2 = 8x$.

Sol. Let (x_1, y_1) be the mid-point of the chord intercepted on the line $4x - 3y + 4 = 0$ by the parabola $y^2 = 8x$.

Then, the equation of the chord whose mid-point is (x_1, y_1), is

$$yy_1 - 4(x + x_1) = y_1^2 - 8x_1$$

$$\Rightarrow \quad 4x - yy_1 + y_1^2 - 4x_1 = 0 \quad \text{...(i)}$$

Now, Eq. (i) and $4x - 3y + 4 = 0$ are same, so

$$\therefore \quad \frac{4}{4} = \frac{y_1}{3} = \frac{y_1^2 - 4x_1}{4}$$

$$\Rightarrow \quad 1 = \frac{y_1}{3} = \frac{y_1^2 - 4x_1}{4}$$

$$\Rightarrow \quad y_1 = 3 \text{ and } y_1^2 - 4x_1 = 4$$

$$\Rightarrow \quad y_1 = 3 \text{ and } x_1 = \frac{5}{4}$$

So, coordinates of mid-point is $\left(\frac{5}{4}, 3\right)$.

Example 66. Find the locus of the mid-points of the chords of the parabola $y^2 = 4ax$ which subtend a right angle at the vertex of the parabola.

Sol. Let $P(h, k)$ be the mid-point of a chord QR of the parabola $y^2 = 4ax$, then equation of chord QR is

$$T = S_1$$

or $\quad yk - 2a(x + h) = k^2 - 4ah$

$\Rightarrow \quad yk - 2ax = k^2 - 2ah \quad$ ...(i)

If A is the vertex of the parabola. For combined equation of AQ and AR making homogeneous of $y^2 = 4ax$ with the help of Eq. (i).

$\therefore \quad y^2 = 4ax$

$\Rightarrow \quad y^2 = 4ax\left(\dfrac{yk - 2ax}{k^2 - 2ah}\right)$

$\Rightarrow \quad y^2(k^2 - 2ah) - 4akxy + 8a^2x^2 = 0$

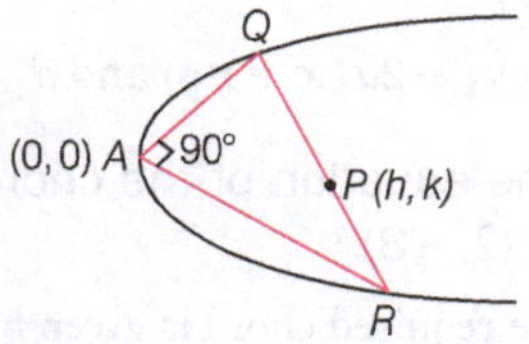

Since, $\angle QAR = 90°$

$\therefore$ Coefficient of x^2 + Coefficient of $y^2 = 0$

$$k^2 - 2ah + 8a^2 = 0$$

Hence, the locus of $P(h, k)$ is $y^2 - 2ax + 8a^2 = 0$.

Example 67. Show that the locus of the middle points of normal chords of the parabola $y^2 = 4ax$ is

$$y^4 - 2a(x - 2a)y^2 + 8a^4 = 0.$$

Decoding the Question

Find the equation of tangent at parametric point and compare with equation of chord of contact whose mid-point is given.

Sol. Equation of the normal chord at any point $(at^2, 2at)$ of the parabola $y^2 = 4ax$ is

$$y + tx = 2at + at^3 \quad \text{...(i)}$$

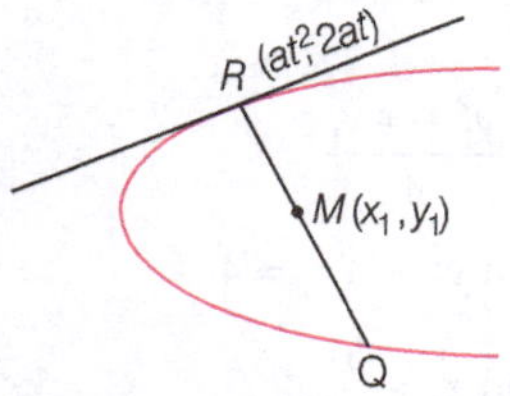

But if $M(x_1, y_1)$ be its middle point it, equation must be

$$T = S_1$$

$\Rightarrow \quad yy_1 - 2a(x + x_1) = y_1^2 - 4ax_1$

$\Rightarrow \quad yy_1 - 2ax = y_1^2 - 2ax_1 \quad$ ...(ii)

$\because$ Eqs. (i) and (ii) are identical, on comparing them

$$\frac{1}{y_1} = \frac{t}{-2a} = \frac{2at + at^3}{y_1^2 - 2ax_1}$$

From first two relations, $t = -\dfrac{2a}{y_1} \quad$ ...(iii)

From last two relations, $\dfrac{t}{-2a} = \dfrac{2at + at^3}{y_1^2 - 2ax_1}$

$\Rightarrow \quad \dfrac{y_1^2 - 2ax_1}{-2a} = 2a + at^2$

$\Rightarrow \quad \dfrac{y_1^2 - 2ax_1}{-2a} = 2a + a\left(\dfrac{-2a}{y_1}\right)^2 \quad$ [from Eq. (iii)]

$\Rightarrow \quad \dfrac{y_1^2 - 2ax_1}{-2a} = \dfrac{2ay_1^2 + 4a^3}{y_1^2}$

$\Rightarrow \quad y_1^4 - 2ax_1y_1^2 = -4a^2y_1^2 - 8a^4$

$\Rightarrow \quad y_1^4 - 2a(x_1 - 2a)y_1^2 + 8a^4 = 0$

Hence, the locus of middle point (x_1, y_1) is

$$y^4 - 2a(x - 2a)y^2 + 8a^4 = 0.$$

5.20 Diameter of a Parabola

The locus of the middle points of a system of parallel chords is called a diameter and in case of a parabola this diameter is shown to be a straight line which is parallel to the axis of the parabola.

Theorem The equation of the diameter bisecting chords of slope m of the parabola $y^2 = 4ax$ is $y = \dfrac{2a}{m}$.

Proof Let $y = mx + c$ be system of parallel chords to $y^2 = 4ax$ for different chords c varies, m remains constant. Let the extremities of any chord PQ of the set be $P(x_1, y_1)$ and $Q(x_2, y_2)$ and let its middle point be $M(h, k)$.

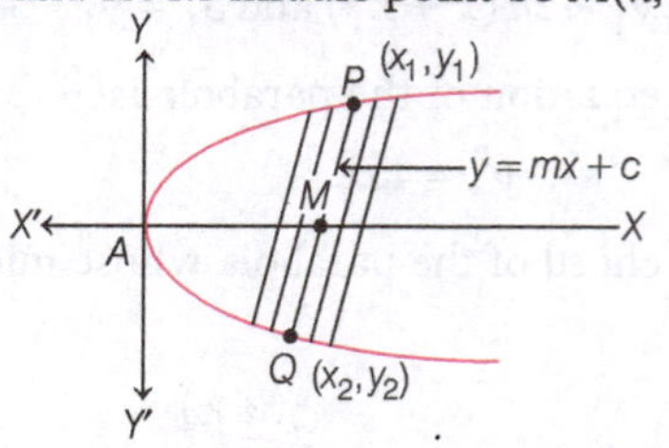

On solving equations, we get

$$y^2 = 4ax \quad \text{and} \quad y = mx + c.$$

$\therefore \quad y^2 = 4a\left(\dfrac{y - c}{m}\right)$

$\Rightarrow \quad my^2 - 4ay + 4ac = 0$

$\therefore \quad y_1 + y_2 = \dfrac{4a}{m}$ or $\dfrac{y_1 + y_2}{2} = \dfrac{2a}{m}$

[$\because$ (h, k) is the mid-point of PQ]

Hence, locus of $M(h, k)$ is $y = \dfrac{2a}{m}$.

Alternate method

Let (h, k) be the middle point of the chord $y = mx + c$ of the parabola $y^2 = 4ax$, then

$$T = S_1$$

$$\Rightarrow \quad ky - 2a(x + h) = k^2 - 4ah$$

$$\text{slope} = \frac{2a}{k} = m$$

$$\Rightarrow \quad k = \frac{2a}{m}$$

Hence, locus of the mid-point is $y = \dfrac{2a}{m}$.

JEE Focus Points

- The tangent at the extremity of a diameter of a parabola is parallel to the system of chords it bisects.
- Tangents at the end of any chord meet on the diameter which bisects the chords.

Concept Inside Video

Example 68. If the diameter through any point P of a parabola meets any chord in A and the tangent at the end of the chord meets the diameter in B and C, then prove that $PA^2 = PB \cdot PC$.

Sol. The equation of the parabola referred to the diameter through P and tangent at P as axes is

$$y^2 = 4\lambda x \qquad \text{...(i)}$$

Let QR be any chord of the parabola Eq. (i). Let the extremities Q and R be $(\lambda t_1^2, 2\lambda t_1)$ and $(\lambda t_2^2, 2\lambda t_2)$.

Then, the equation of QR is

$$y(t_1 + t_2) - 2x - 2\lambda t_1 t_2 = 0 \qquad \text{...(ii)}$$

It meets the diameter through P i.e. X-axis or $y = 0$, then Eq. (ii) reduces

$$0 - 2x - 2\lambda\, t_1 t_2 = 0$$

$$\Rightarrow \quad x = -\lambda t_1 t_2 = PA$$

Now, tangent at Q is $\quad t_1 y = x + \lambda t_1^2 \qquad \text{...(iii)}$

It meets the diameter through P i.e. X-axis or $y = 0$, then Eq. (iii) reduces

$$0 = x + \lambda t_1^2$$

$$\Rightarrow \quad x = -\lambda t_1^2 = PB \qquad \text{...(iv)}$$

Similarly, $-\lambda t_2^2 = PC \qquad \text{...(v)}$

$$\therefore \quad (PA)^2 = (-\lambda t_1 t_2)^2 = \lambda^2 t_1^2 t_2^2$$

$$= (-\lambda t_1^2)(-\lambda t_2^2) \qquad \text{[from Eqs. (iv) and (v)]}$$

$$= PB \cdot PC$$

5.21 Lengths of Tangent, Subtangent, Normal and Subnormal

Let the parabola $y^2 = 4ax$. Let the tangent and normal at $P(x, y)$ meet the axis of parabola at T and G respectively and let tangent at $P(x, y)$ makes angle ψ with the positive direction of X-axis.

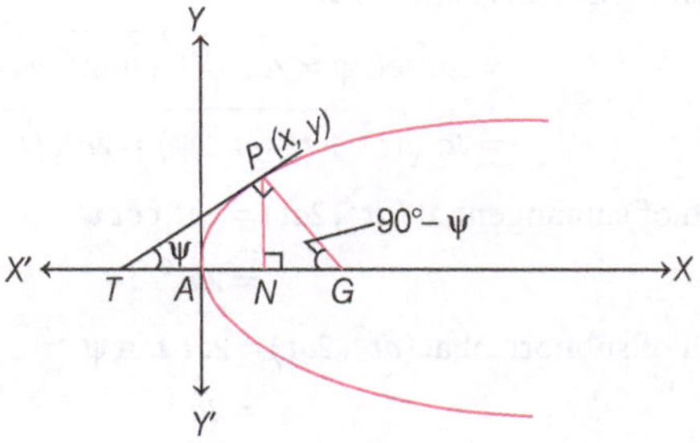

Then, $\quad PT =$ Length of Tangent

$PG =$ Length of Normal

$TN =$ Length of Subtangent

and $\quad NG =$ Length of Subnormal

If $A(0, 0)$ is the vertex of the parabola.

$\because \quad PN = y$

$\therefore \quad PT = PN \operatorname{cosec} \psi = y \operatorname{cosec} \psi$

$PG = PN \operatorname{cosec}(90° - \psi) = y \sec \psi$

$TN = PN \cot \psi = y \cot \psi$

and $\quad NG = PN \cot(90° - \psi) = y \tan \psi$

where, $\tan \psi = \dfrac{2a}{y} = m \qquad$ [slope of tangent at $P(x, y)$]

- Length of tangent $= |y\sqrt{1 + m^2}\,|$
- Length of normal $= \left| y\sqrt{1 + \dfrac{1}{m^2}} \right|$
- Length of subtengent $= \left| \dfrac{y}{m} \right|$
- Length of subnormal $= |ym|$

Example 69. Find the length of tangent, subtangent, normal and subnormal at $y^2 = 4ax$ at $(at^2, 2at)$.

Sol. $\because$ Equation of tangent at $(at^2, 2at)$ of parabola $y^2 = 4ax$ is

$$ty = x + at^2$$

Slope of this tangent $m = \dfrac{1}{t}$

Let tangent makes angle ψ with positive direction of X-axis

$$\tan\psi = \frac{1}{t}$$

Then, $t = \cot\psi$

$\therefore$ Length of tangent at $(at^2, 2at)$

$$= 2at \operatorname{cosec}\psi$$
$$= 2at\sqrt{(1+\cot^2\psi)} = 2at\sqrt{(1+t^2)}$$

Length of normals at $(at^2, 2at)$

$$= 2at\sec\psi = 2at\sqrt{(1+\tan^2\psi)}$$
$$= 2a\sqrt{(t^2+t^2\tan^2\psi)} = 2a\sqrt{(t^2+1)}$$

Length of subtangent at $(at^2, 2at) = 2at\cot\psi$

$$= 2at^2$$

Length of subnormal at $(at^2, 2at) = 2at\tan\psi$

$$= 2a$$

Example 70. Find the length of tangent, subtangent, normal and subnormal to $y^2 = 8x$ at (2, 4).

Sol. We know that parametric coordinates of $y^2 = 4ax$ is $(at^2, 2at)$.

Given parabola is $y^2 = 8x$ $[\because a = 2]$

$$\therefore \quad at^2 = 2 \text{ and } 2at = 4$$
$$t = \pm 1 \text{ and } t = 1$$

Therefore, $t = 1$

Equation of tangent to $y^2 = 4ax$ at $(at^2, 2at)$ is $ty = x + at^2$

$$\text{slope } m = \frac{1}{t} \Rightarrow m = \frac{1}{1} \Rightarrow m = 1$$

$$\text{Length of tangent} = 2at\sqrt{1+t^2}$$
$$= 4\sqrt{1+1} = 4\sqrt{2}$$

$$\text{Length of normal} = 2a\sqrt{1+t^2}$$
$$= 4\sqrt{1+1} = 4\sqrt{2}$$

$$\text{Length of subtangent} = 2at^2$$
$$= 2\times 2\times 1 = 4$$

$$\text{Length of subnormal} = 2a = 2\times 2 = 4$$

Example 71. The value of P such that the length of the subtangent and subnormal is equal for the curve $y = x^2 + 2Px + 3$ at the point (0, 3) is (are)

(a) ±1 (b) ±2 (c) $\pm\frac{1}{2}$ (d) 2

Sol. (a) We have, $y = x^2 + 2Px + 3$

On differentiating w.r.t. x, we get

$$\frac{dy}{dx} = 2x + 2P$$

$$\Rightarrow \quad \left.\frac{dy}{dx}\right|_{(0,\,3)} = 2P = m$$

$$\text{length of subtangent} = \left|\frac{y}{m}\right|$$

$$\text{length of subnormal} = |ym|$$

Given, subtangent = subnormal

$$\left|\frac{y}{m}\right| = |ym|$$
$$m = \pm 1$$
$$2P = \pm 1$$
$$\Rightarrow \quad P = \pm\frac{1}{2}$$

5.22 Some Standard Properties of the Parabola

(1) The tangents at the extremities of a focal chord intersect at right angles on the directrix.

The extremities of a focal chord PQ are

$$P \equiv (at^2, 2at) \text{ and } Q \equiv \left(\frac{a}{t^2}, -\frac{2a}{t}\right)$$

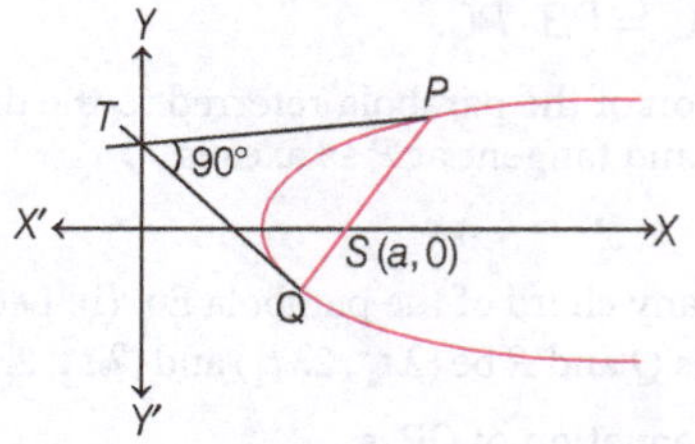

Let parabola be $y^2 = 4ax$

$\therefore$ Tangent at $P(at^2, 2at)$ is

$$ty = x + at^2 \quad \text{...(i)}$$

Its slope $\frac{1}{t} = m_1$ (say)

and tangent at $Q\left(\frac{a}{t^2}, -\frac{2a}{t}\right)$ is

$$-\frac{y}{t} = x + \frac{a}{t^2} \quad \text{...(ii)}$$

$$\Rightarrow \quad -ty = xt^2 + a$$

Its slope $-t = m_2$ (say)

$$\because \quad m_1 m_2 = -1$$
$$\therefore \quad \angle PTQ = 90°$$

and adding Eqs. (i) and (ii), we get

$$(x+a)(1+t^2) = 0 \quad \Rightarrow 1 + t^2 \neq 0$$

$\therefore$ $x + a = 0$, which is directrix.

JEE SCANNER

Example Similar to PYQ Asked in JEE Main 2023

Let $y = 3x - 8$ be the equation of the tangent at the point (7, 13) lying on a parabola whose focus is at (−1, −1). The length of the latusrectum of the parabola is

(a) $\frac{20}{\sqrt{65}}$ (b) $\frac{40}{\sqrt{65}}$ (c) $\frac{10}{\sqrt{65}}$ (d) $\frac{27}{\sqrt{65}}$

Sol. (a) The image of focus $(-1, -1)$ upon the tangent $y = 3x - 8$ is the point $(5, -3)$. It will lie on the directrix.

Slope of directrix $= -\frac{7-5}{13+3} = -\frac{1}{8}$

Its equation is $y + 3 = -\frac{1}{8}(x - 5)$

$$x + 8y + 19 = 0$$

$\therefore$ Latusrectum $= 2 \times$ (distance of focus from directrix)

$$= 2 \times \frac{|-1-8+19|}{\sqrt{65}} = \frac{20}{\sqrt{65}}$$

Skill Builder

Let $y = 3x - 8$ be the equation of the tangent at the point (6, 10) lying on the parabola whose focus is at (−1, −1), the length of latusrectum of the parabola is

(a) $\frac{60}{\sqrt{257}}$ (b) $\frac{52}{\sqrt{257}}$

(c) $\frac{28}{\sqrt{257}}$ (d) $\frac{27}{\sqrt{257}}$

For Sol.

■ **For more practice** See Q.11 of Milestone Practice 5.3.

(2) The portion of a tangent to a parabola intercepted between the directrix and the curve subtends a right angle at the focus.

The equation of the tangent to the parabola $y^2 = 4ax$ at $P(at^2, 2at)$ is

$$ty = x + at^2 \quad \text{...(i)}$$

Let Eq. (i) meets the directrix $x + a = 0$ at Q,

then coordinates of Q are $\left(-a, \frac{at^2 - a}{t}\right)$, also focus S is $(a, 0)$.

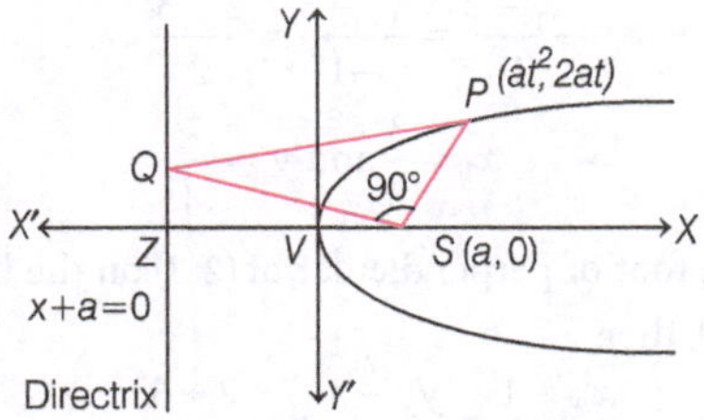

$\therefore$ Slope of $SP = \frac{2at - 0}{at^2 - a} = \frac{2t}{t^2 - 1} = m_1$ (say)

and slope of $SQ = \frac{\frac{at^2 - a}{t} - 0}{-a - a} = \frac{t^2 - 1}{-2t} = m_2$ (say)

$\therefore \quad m_1 m_2 = -1$

Therefore, SP is perpendicular to SQ i.e. $\angle PSQ = 90°$

(3) The tangent at any point P of a parabola bisects the angle between the focal chord through P and the perpendicular from P to the directrix.

Let the tangent at $P(at^2, 2at)$ to the parabola $y^2 = 4ax$ meets the axis of the parabola i.e. X-axis or $y = 0$ at T. The equation of tangent to the parabola $y^2 = 4ax$ at $P(at^2, 2at)$ is

$$ty = x + at^2$$

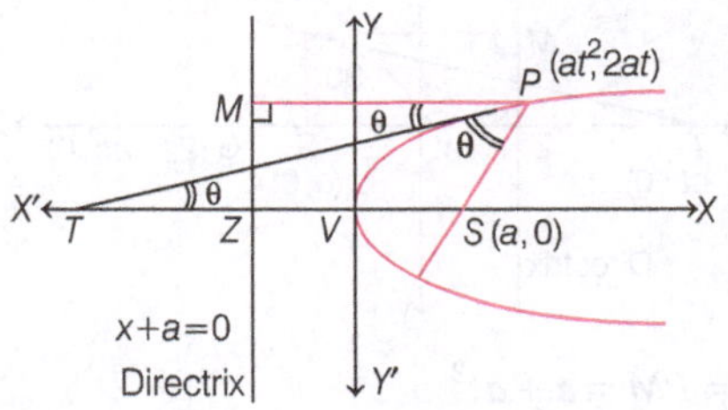

For coordinates of T solve it with $y = 0$.

$\therefore \quad T(-at^2, 0)$

$\therefore \quad ST = SV + VT = a + at^2 = a(1 + t^2)$

Also, $SP = PM = a + at^2 = a(1 + t^2)$

$\therefore \quad SP = ST$, i.e. $\angle STP = \angle SPT$

But $\angle STP = \angle MPT$ [alternate angles]

$\angle SPT = \angle MPT$

(4) The foot of the perpendicular from the focus on any tangent to a parabola lies on the tangent at the vertex.

Equation of tangent at $P(at^2, 2at)$ on the parabola $y^2 = 4ax$ is

$$ty = x + at^2$$

$\Rightarrow \quad x - ty + at^2 = 0 \quad$ ...(i)

Now, the equation of line through $S(a, 0)$ and perpendicular to Eq. (i) is

$$tx + y = \lambda$$

Since, it passes through $(a, 0)$.

$\therefore \quad ta + 0 = \lambda$

$\therefore$ Equation $tx + y = ta$ or $t^2x + ty - at^2 = 0 \quad$ ...(ii)

By adding Eqs. (i) and (ii), we get

$$x(1 + t^2) = 0$$

$\Rightarrow \quad x = 0 \quad [\because 1 + t^2 \neq 0]$

Hence, the point of intersection of Eqs. (i) and (ii) lies on $x = 0$ i.e. on Y-axis (which is tangent at the vertex of a parabola).

(5) If S be the focus of the parabola and tangent and normal at any point P meet its axis in T and G respectively, then $ST = SG = SP$.

Let $P(at^2, 2at)$ be any point on the parabola $y^2 = 4ax$, then equation of tangent and normal at $P(at^2, 2at)$ are

$$ty = x + at^2 \quad \text{and} \quad y = -tx + 2at + at^2, \text{ respectively.}$$

Since, tangent and normal meet its axis in T and G.

$\therefore$ Coordinates of T and G are $(-at^2, 0)$ and $(2a + at^2, 0)$ respectively.

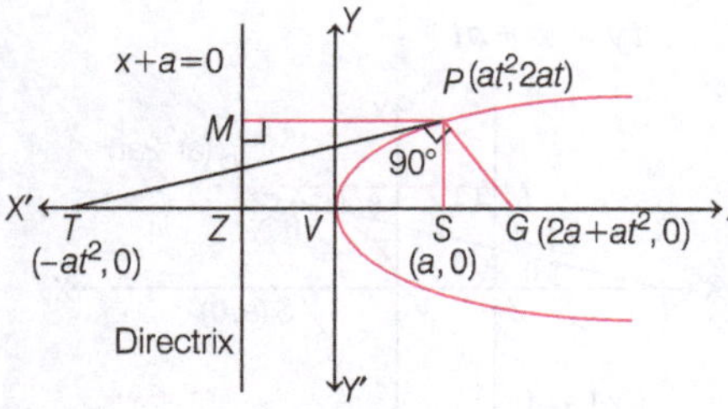

$$\therefore \quad SP = PM = a + at^2$$

$$SG = VG - VS = 2a + at^2 - a = a + at^2$$

and $\quad ST = VS + VT = a + at^2$

Hence, $SP = SG = ST$

(6) If S be the focus and SH be perpendicular to the tangent at P, then H lies on the tangent at the vertex and $SH^2 = OS \cdot SP$, where O is the vertex of the parabola.

Let $P(at^2, 2at)$ be any point on the parabola

$$y^2 = 4ax \quad \text{... (i)}$$

Then, tangent at $P(at^2, 2at)$ to the parabola Eq. (i) is

$$ty = x + at^2$$

It meets the tangent at the vertex i.e. $x = 0$.

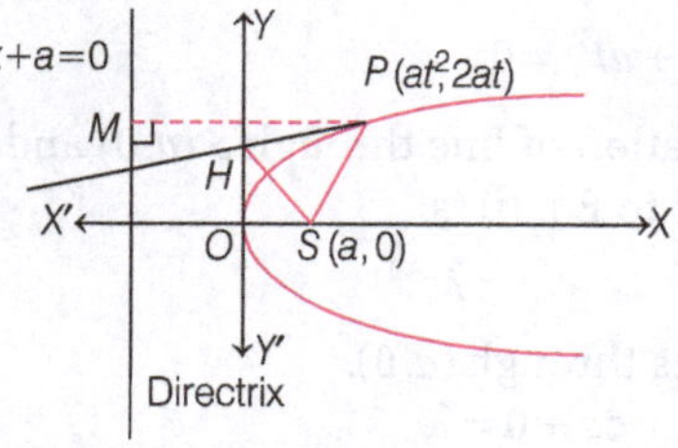

$\therefore$ Coordinates of H is $(0, at)$.

$\Rightarrow \quad SP = PM = a + at^2, \quad OS = a$

and $\quad SH = \sqrt{(a-0)^2 + (0-at)^2} = \sqrt{a^2 + a^2t^2}$

or $\quad (SH)^2 = a\{a(1+t^2)\} = OS \cdot SP$.

Example 72. The locus of the focus of the family of parabola having directrix of slope m and toching the line $x = a$ and $y = b$ is

(a) $y + mx = am + b$ (b) $y - mx = am + b$
(c) $y + mx = am - b$ (d) $y - mx = am - b$

Sol. (a) Let (h, k) be the focus of parabola.

The foot of perpendicular from (h, k) to $x = a$ is (a, k).

Similarly, for $y = b$ it is (h, b).

We know that perpendicular from the focus on any tangent meets it on the length at vertex.

Hence, the slope of tangent at vertex is $\dfrac{k-b}{a-h}$ as tangent at vertex is parallel to directrix

$$\Rightarrow \quad \frac{k-b}{a-h} = m$$

The required locus will be $y + mx = am + b$

Example 73. Two tangents on a parabola are $x - y = 0$ and $x + y = 0$. Point $(2, 3)$ is the focus of parabola, then the equation of tangent at vertex is

(a) $4x - 6y + 5 = 0$ (b) $4x - 6y + 3 = 0$
(c) $4x - 6y + 1 = 0$ (d) $4x - 6y + \frac{3}{2} = 0$

Sol. (a) We know that the foot of perpendicular from the focus upon a tangent lies on the tangent at vertex of the parabola.

Now, if the foot of perpendicular of $(2, 3)$ on the line $x - y = 0$ is (x_1, y_1), then

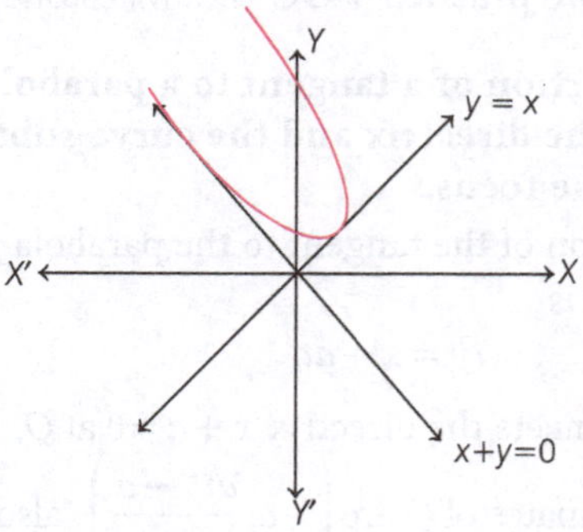

$$\frac{x_1 - 2}{1} = \frac{y_1 - 3}{-1} = \frac{2-3}{2}$$

$$\Rightarrow \quad x_1 = \frac{3}{2} \text{ and } y_1 = \frac{7}{2}$$

Similarly, foot of perpendicular of $(2, 3)$ on the line $x + y = 0$ is (x_2, y_2), then

$$\frac{x_2 - 1}{1} = \frac{y_2 - 3}{1} = -\frac{2+3}{2}$$

$$\Rightarrow \quad x_2 = -\frac{3}{2} \text{ and } y_2 = \frac{1}{2}$$

Now, tangent at vertex passes through the points $\left(\frac{3}{2}, \frac{7}{2}\right)$ and $\left(-\frac{3}{2}, \frac{1}{2}\right)$. Then, its equation is

$$y - \frac{1}{2} = \frac{3}{2}\left(x + \frac{3}{2}\right)$$

$$\therefore \quad 6x - 4y + 11 = 0$$

5.23 Reflection Property of a Parabola

The tangent (PT) and normal (PN) of the parabola

$$y^2 = 4ax$$

at P are the internal and external bisectors of $\angle SPM$ and BP is parallel to the axis of the parabola and $\angle BPN = \angle SPN$.

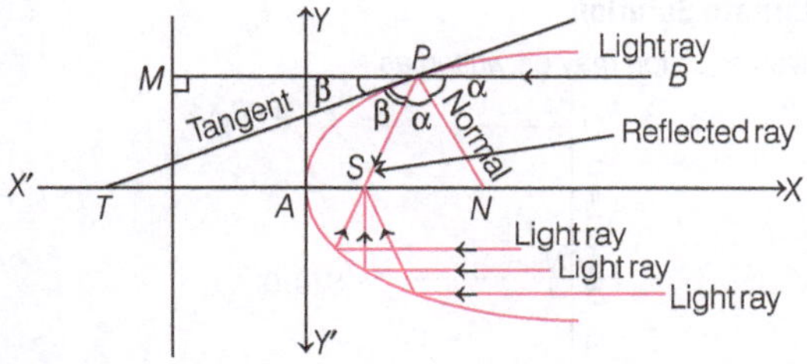

All rays of light coming from the positive direction of X-axis and parallel to the axis of the parabola after reflection pass through the focus of the parabola.

Example 74. A ray of light is coming along the line $y = b$ from the positive direction of X-axis and strikes a concave mirror whose intersection with the XY-plane is a parabola $y^2 = 4ax$. Find the equation of the reflected ray and show that it passes through the focus of the parabola. Both a and b are positive.

Sol. Given parabola is $y^2 = 4ax$

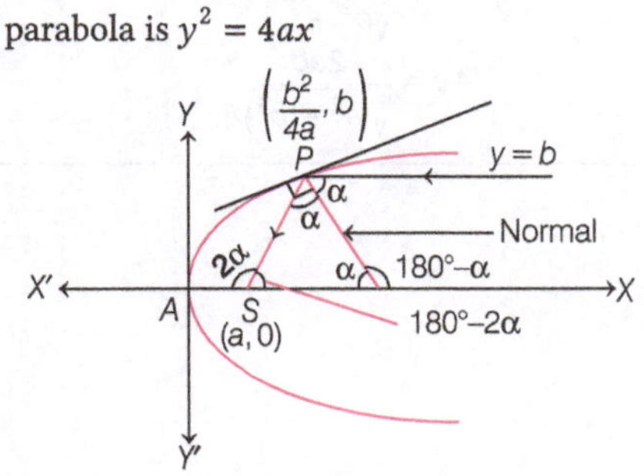

Equation of tangent at $P\left(\frac{b^2}{4a}, b\right)$ is $yb = 2a\left(x + \frac{b^2}{4a}\right)$,

Slope of tangent is $\frac{2a}{b}$.

Hence, slope of normal $= -\frac{b}{2a} = \tan(180° - \alpha)$.

$$\therefore \quad \tan\alpha = \frac{b}{2a}$$

$\therefore$ Slope of reflected ray $= \tan(180° - 2\alpha)$

$$= -\tan 2\alpha$$

$$= -\left\{\frac{2\tan\alpha}{1 - \tan^2\alpha}\right\}$$

$$= -\left\{\frac{2 \cdot \frac{b}{2a}}{1 - \frac{b^2}{4a^2}}\right\}$$

$$= -\frac{4ab}{(4a^2 - b^2)}$$

Hence, equation of reflected ray is

$$y - b = -\frac{4ab}{(4a^2 - b^2)}\left(x - \frac{b^2}{4a}\right)$$

$$\Rightarrow \quad (y - b)(4a^2 - b^2) = -b(4ax - b^2)$$

which passes through the focus $S(a, 0)$.

Study of Parabola of the Form $(\alpha x + \beta y)^2 + 2gx + 2fy + c = 0$

Given equation can be written as

$$(\alpha x + \beta y)^2 = -2gx - 2fy - c$$

Now, add an arbitrary constant λ in the square root of the second degree terms. Then, the equation will be of the form

i.e. $\quad (\alpha x + \beta y + \lambda)^2 = xf_1(\lambda) + yf_2(\lambda) + f_3(\lambda) \quad$ ...(i)

Now, choose λ such that the lines

$\alpha x + \beta y + \lambda = 0$ and $xf_1(\lambda) + yf_2(\lambda) + f_3(\lambda) = 0$

are perpendicular

i.e. (slope of $\alpha x + \beta y + \lambda = 0$) $\times$ (slope of $xf_1(\lambda) + yf_2(\lambda) + f_3(\lambda) = 0$) $= -1$

$$\Rightarrow \quad -\frac{\alpha}{\beta} \times -\frac{f_1(\lambda)}{f_2(\lambda)} = -1$$

$$\Rightarrow \quad \alpha f_1(\lambda) + \beta f_2(\lambda) = 0 \quad \text{...(ii)}$$

Now, substitute the value of λ in Eq. (i) from Eq. (ii).

On multiplying and dividing by $(\alpha^2 + \beta^2)$ in LHS of Eq. (i)

i.e. $\quad (\alpha x + \beta y + \lambda)^2 = (\alpha^2 + \beta^2)\left(\frac{\alpha x + \beta y + \lambda}{\sqrt{\alpha^2 + \beta^2}}\right)^2$

and RHS of Eq. (i) by $\sqrt{(\alpha^2 + \beta^2)}$

i.e. $\quad xf_1(\lambda) + yf_2(\lambda) + f_3(\lambda)$

$$= \sqrt{(\alpha^2 + \beta^2)}\left(\frac{xf_1(\lambda) + yf_2(\lambda) + f_3(\lambda)}{\sqrt{(\alpha^2 + \beta^2)}}\right)$$

Then, Eq. (i) reduce in the form

$$\left(\frac{\alpha x+\beta y+\lambda}{\sqrt{\alpha^2+\beta^2}}\right)^2=4\rho\left(\frac{\beta x-\alpha y+\mu}{\sqrt{(\alpha^2+\beta^2)}}\right)$$

which is of the form $Y^2=4\rho X$, where

$$Y=\frac{\alpha x+\beta y+\lambda}{\sqrt{(\alpha^2+\beta^2)}}, X=\frac{\beta x-\alpha y+\mu}{\sqrt{(\alpha^2+\beta^2)}} \text{ and } 4\rho=\frac{1}{\sqrt{(\alpha^2+\beta^2)}}.$$

Latusrectum is $4\rho=\dfrac{1}{\sqrt{(\alpha^2+\beta^2)}}$.

Axis is $Y=0$ or $\alpha x+\beta y+\lambda=0$.

Equation of tangent at vertex is

$$X=0$$

or $\beta x-\alpha y+\mu=0$.

Vertex is the point of intersection of

$$X=0 \text{ and } Y=0$$

i.e. $\beta x-\alpha y+\mu=0$ and $\alpha x+\beta y+\lambda=0$.

Equation of directrix is $X+\rho=0$.

Equation of latusrectum is $X-\rho=0$.

Focus Since, axis and latusrectum intersect at the focus S its coordinates are detained by solving

$$X-\rho=0 \text{ and } Y=0.$$

Example 75. Find the length of latusrectum of the parabola $(a^2+b^2)(x^2+y^2)=(bx+ay-ab)^2$.

Sol. Given equation may be written as

$$a^2x^2+a^2y^2+b^2x^2+b^2y^2=b^2x^2+a^2y^2+a^2b^2 + 2abxy-2a^2by-2ab^2x$$

$$\Rightarrow \quad a^2x^2-2abxy+b^2y^2=-2ab^2x-2a^2by+a^2b^2$$

$$\Rightarrow \quad (ax-by)^2=-2ab\left(bx+ay-\frac{ab}{2}\right)$$

Since, $ax-by=0$ and $bx+ay-\dfrac{ab}{2}=0$ are perpendicular.

$$\therefore\ (a^2+b^2)\left(\frac{ax-by}{\sqrt{a^2+b^2}}\right)^2=-2ab\sqrt{(a^2+b^2)}\left(\frac{bx+ay-\frac{ab}{2}}{\sqrt{(a^2+b^2)}}\right)$$

$$\Rightarrow \left(\frac{ax-by}{\sqrt{a^2+b^2}}\right)^2=\frac{-2ab}{\sqrt{(a^2+b^2)}}\left(\frac{bx+ay-\frac{ab}{2}}{\sqrt{(a^2+b^2)}}\right)$$

which is of the form $Y^2=-4\rho X$.

Therefore, the latusrectum $=4\rho$

$$=\frac{2ab}{\sqrt{(a^2+b^2)}}$$

Alternate Solution

Given equation may be written as

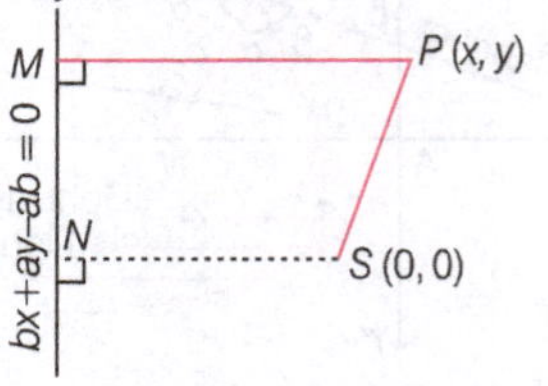

$$x^2+y^2=\frac{(bx+ay-ab)^2}{(a^2+b^2)}$$

$$\Rightarrow \quad \sqrt{(x^2+y^2)}=\frac{|bx+ay-ab|}{\sqrt{(a^2+b^2)}}$$

$$\Rightarrow \quad \sqrt{(x-0)^2+(y-0)^2}=\frac{|bx+ay-ab|}{\sqrt{(a^2+b^2)}}$$

which is of the form $SP=PM$.

Since, distance from focus S to $(bx+ay-ab=0)=\frac{1}{2}(4\rho)$

$$\Rightarrow \quad \frac{1}{2}(4\rho)=\frac{ab}{\sqrt{a^2+b^2}}$$

$$\therefore \quad 4\rho=\frac{2ab}{\sqrt{(a^2+b^2)}}$$

Milestone Practice 5.3

1. If m_1, m_2 are slopes of the two tangents that are drawn from (2, 3) to the parabola $y^2 = 4x$, then the value of $\frac{1}{m_1} + \frac{1}{m_2}$ is
   (a) -3 (b) 3
   (c) 2/3 (d) 3/2
2. The angle between the tangents drawn from the origin to the parabola $y^2 = 4a(x - a)$ is
   (a) 90° (b) 30°
   (c) $\tan^{-1}\left(\frac{1}{2}\right)$ (d) 45°
3. If (a, b) is the mid-point of chord passing through the vertex of the parabola $y^2 = 4x$, then
   (a) $a = 2b$
   (b) $2a = b$
   (c) $a^2 = 2b$
   (d) $2a = b^2$
4. The diameter of the parabola $y^2 = 6x$ corresponding to the system of parallel chords $3x - y + c = 0$ is
   (a) $y - 1 = 0$
   (b) $y - 2 = 0$
   (c) $y + 1 = 0$
   (d) $y + 2 = 0$
5. From the point (–1, 2) tangent lines are drawn to the parabola $y^2 = 4x$, the area of triangle formed by chord of contact and the tangents is given by
   (a) 8 (b) $8\sqrt{3}$
   (c) $8\sqrt{2}$ (d) None of these
6. Find the locus of the mid-point of that chord of parabola which subtends right angle on the vertex.
7. Find the locus of the point of intersection of perpendicular tangents to the parabola $y^2 = 4ax$.
8. If the distance of the point $(a, 2)$ from its chord of contact with respect to the parabola $y = 4x$ is 4, then find the value of a.
9. Prove that the locus of the point of intersection of tangents to the parabola $y^2 = 4ax$ which meet at an angle α is $(x + a)^2 \tan^2\alpha = y^2 - 4ax$.
10. Find the locus of the middle points of the chords of the parabola $y^2 = 4ax$ which passes through the focus.
11. Let $2y + 16 = 6x$ be the equation of the tangent at the point (3, 1) lying on a parabola whose focus is at (– 1, – 1). The length of the latusrectum of the parabola is
    (a) $2\sqrt{3}$ (b) $4\sqrt{5}$
    (c) $7\sqrt{5}$ (d) $2\sqrt{5}$

Answer Key

1. (b) 2. (a) 3. (d) 4. (a) 5. (c)
6. $y^2 - 2ax + 8a^2 = 0$ 7. $x = -a$ 8. $a = 1 \pm 2\sqrt{2}$ 10. $y^2 = 2ax - 2a^2$ 11. (b)

For Detailed Solution

JEE Pattern EXAMPLES

Single Option Correct Type Questions

Example 1 *AP is perpendicular to PB, where A is the vertex of the parabola $y^2 = 4x$ and P is on the parabola. B is on the axis of the parabola. Then, the locus of the centroid of ΔPAB is*

(a) point (b) circle

(c) parabola (d) None of these

Sol. (c) Let P be $(t^2, 2t)$.

$\therefore$ Slope of $AP = \frac{2}{t}$

$\therefore$ Slope of $BP = \frac{-t}{2}$

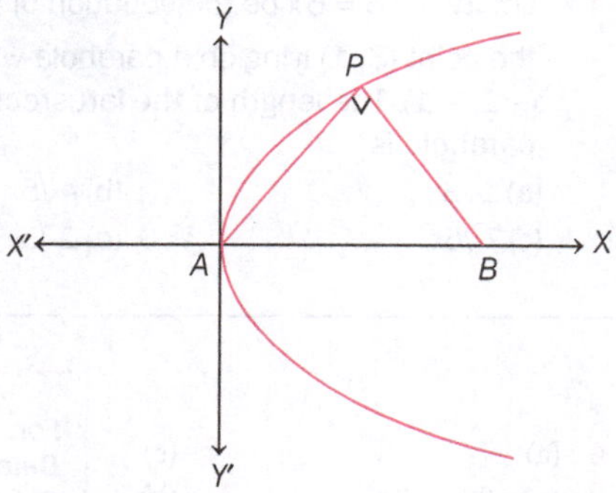

The equation of line BP is

$$y - 2t = \frac{-t}{2}(x - t^2)$$

$\therefore$ $B \equiv (t^2 + 4, 0)$

Now, let the centroid of ΔPAB be (h, k).

Then, $h = \frac{t^2 + t^2 + 4}{3}$ and $k = \frac{2t}{3}$

$\Rightarrow$ $3h - 4 = 2\left(\frac{3k}{2}\right)^2$

$\Rightarrow$ $3h - 4 = \frac{9k^2}{4}$

So, locus is $3x - 4 = \frac{9y^2}{4}$

which is a parabola.

Example 2 *If $(2, -8)$ is at an end of a focal chord of the parabola $y^2 = 32x$, then the other end of the chord is*

(a) $(32, -32)$ (b) $(2, 8)$

(c) $(32, 32)$ (d) None of these

Sol. (c) We have, $y^2 = 32x$

$\therefore$ $a = 8$

Then, any point on the parabola is $(8t^2, 16t)$.

On comparing this with the point $P(2, -8)$, we get

$$t = \frac{-1}{2}$$

Now, if PQ is the focal chord and point Q is $(8t_1^2, 16t_1)$, then

$$t_1 = \frac{-1}{t} = 2$$

$\therefore$ Point Q is $(32, 32)$.

Example 3 *The shortest distance between the line $y = x - 2$ and the parabola $y = x^2 + 3x + 2$, is*

(a) 3 (b) $\frac{3}{\sqrt{2}}$

(c) $\frac{3}{2}$ (d) $\frac{3}{2\sqrt{2}}$

Sol.

Decoding the Question

Shortest distance between the curves always lies along the common normal, so find $\frac{dy}{dx}$ of given curve and then put $\frac{dy}{dx}$ equal to slope of given line.

(b) Let $P(x_1, y_1)$ be the point closest to the line $y = x - 2$.

Then,

$$\left.\frac{dy}{dx}\right|_{(x_1, y_1)} = \text{Slope of given line}$$

$\Rightarrow$ $2x_1 + 3 = 1$

$\Rightarrow$ $x_1 = -1$

$\therefore$ $y_1 = 0$

Hence, point $(-1, 0)$ is the closest and its perpendicular distance from the line $y = x - 2$ will be the shortest distance.

$\therefore$ Shortest distance $= \left|\dfrac{-1-2}{\sqrt{(1)^2+(-1)^2}}\right|$

$= \dfrac{3}{\sqrt{2}}$

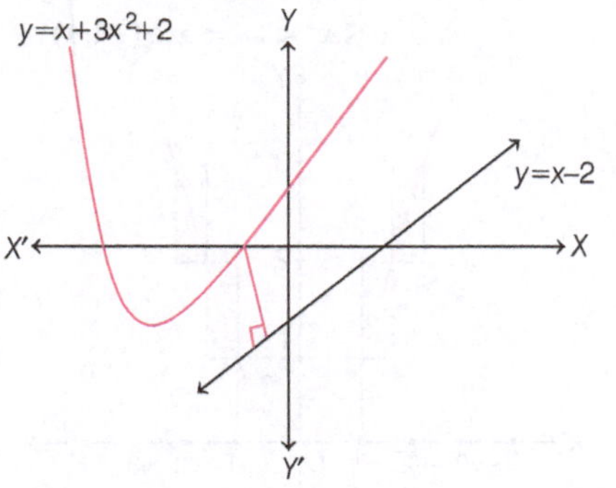

Example 4 ■ *The length of normal chord which subtends an angle of 90° at the vertex of the parabola $y^2 = 4x$*

(a) $6\sqrt{3}$ (b) $6\sqrt{2}$
(c) $7\sqrt{2}$ (d) $7\sqrt{3}$

Sol. (a) We know that the other end of normal is $t_2 = -t_1 - \dfrac{2}{t_1}$

$$t_1 = -t - \frac{2}{t}$$

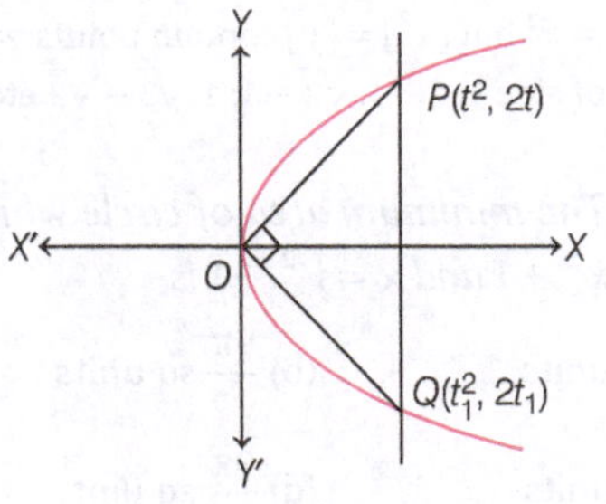

Also, $tt_1 = -4$

$\Rightarrow$ $t_1 = \dfrac{-4}{t}$

$\therefore$ $\dfrac{-4}{t} = -t - \dfrac{2}{t}$

$\Rightarrow$ $t = \dfrac{2}{t} \Rightarrow t = \sqrt{2} \Rightarrow t_1 = -2\sqrt{2}$

$\therefore$ $Q = (8, -4\sqrt{2})$ and $P \equiv (2, 2\sqrt{2})$

$\therefore$ $PQ = \sqrt{(8-2)^2 + (-4\sqrt{2} - 2\sqrt{2})^2}$

$= \sqrt{108}$

$= 6\sqrt{3}$

Example 5 ■ *If the normals from any point to the parabola $y^2 = 4x$ cut the line $x = 2$ at points whose ordinates are in AP, then the slopes of tangents at the co-normal points are in*

(a) AP (b) GP
(c) HP (d) None of these

Sol. (b) The equation of the normal to the parabola $y^2 = 4x$ is

$$y = -tx + 2t + t^3$$

Since, it intersects $x = 2$, we get $y = t^3$.

Let the three ordinates t_1^3, t_2^3 and t_3^3 are in AP.

Then, $2t_2^3 = t_1^3 + t_3^3$

$= (t_1 + t_3)^3 - 3t_1t_3(t_1 + t_3)$

Now, $t_1 + t_2 + t_3 = 0$

$\Rightarrow$ $t_1 + t_3 = -t_2$

$\therefore$ $2t_2^3 = -t_2^3 + 3t_1t_2t_3$

$\Rightarrow$ $3t_2^3 = 3t_1t_2t_3$

$\Rightarrow$ $t_2^2 = t_1t_3$

$\therefore$ t_1, t_2 and t_3 are in GP.

Hence, the slopes of tangents $\dfrac{1}{t_1}$, $\dfrac{1}{t_2}$ and $\dfrac{1}{t_3}$ are in GP.

Example 6 ■ *A ray of light travels along a line $y = 4$ and strikes the surface of curves $y^2 = 4(x + y)$, then the equation of the line along which the reflected ray travels is*

(a) $x = 0$ (b) $x = 2$
(c) $x + y = 4$ (d) $2x + y = 4$

Sol. (a) The given curve is $(y-2)^2 = 4(x+1)$

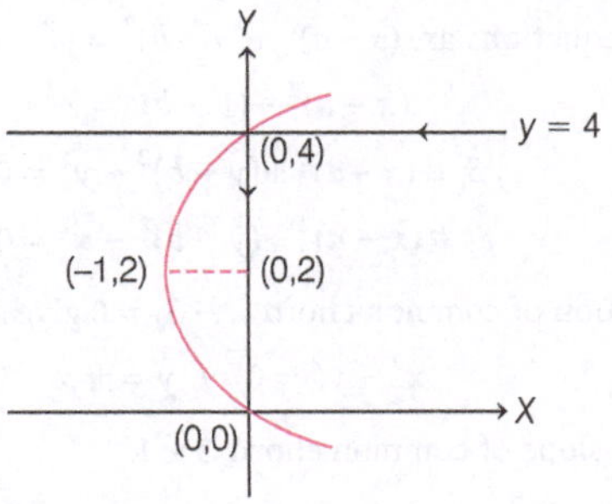

The focus is (0, 2).

The point of intersection of the curve and $y = 4$ is (0, 4).

From the reflection property of parabola the reflected ray passes through the focus.

Therefore, $x = 0$ is the reflected ray.

Example 7 *A parabola is drawn with focus at (3, 4) and vertex at the focus of the parabola $y^2 - 12x - 4y + 4 = 0$. The equation of the parabola is*

(a) $x^2 - 6x - 8y + 25 = 0$ (b) $y^2 - 8x - 6y + 25 = 0$

(c) $x^2 - 6x + 8y - 25 = 0$ (d) $x^2 + 6x - 8y - 25 = 0$

Sol. (a) $y^2 - 12x - 4y + 4 = 0 \Rightarrow (y-2)^2 = 12x$

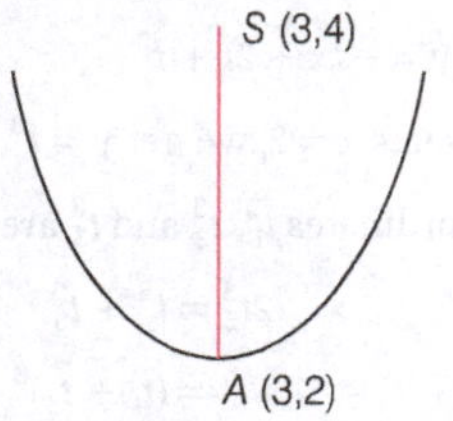

Its vertex is (0, 2) and $a = 3$,

Its focus = (3, 2).

Hence, for the required parabola, focus is (3, 4), vertex = (3, 2) and $a = 2$,

Hence, the equation of the parabola is

$$(x-3)^2 = 4(2)(y-2)$$

or $\quad x^2 - 6x - 8y + 25 = 0$

Example 8 *Two parabolas have the same focus. If their directrices are the X-axis and the Y-axis, respectively, then the slope of their common chord is*

(a) ± 1 (b) $\frac{4}{3}$

(c) $\frac{3}{4}$ (d) None of these

Sol. (a) Let the focus be (a, b).

Then, equations are $(x-a)^2 + (y-b)^2 = y^2$

and $\quad (x-a)^2 + (y-b)^2 = x^2$

If $\quad S_1 \equiv (x-a)^2 + (y-b)^2 - y^2 = 0$

and $\quad S_2 \equiv (x-a)^2 + (y-b)^2 - x^2 = 0$

∴ Equation of common chord $S_1 - S_2 = 0$ gives

$$x^2 - y^2 = 0 \text{ or } y = \pm x$$

Hence, slope of common chord is ± 1.

Example 9 *Let us define a region R in XY-plane as a set of points (x, y) satisfying $[x^2] = [y]$ (where $[x]$ denotes greatest integer $\le x$), then the region R defines*

(a) a parabola whose axis is horizontal

(b) a parabola whose axis is vertical

(c) integer point of the parabola $y = x^2$

(d) None of the above

Sol. (d) $\because [x^2] = [y]$

If $\quad 0 \le y < 1$,

Then, $\quad [y] = 0$

∴ $\quad [x^2] = 0$

$$0 \le x^2 < 1 \Rightarrow x \in (-1, 1)$$

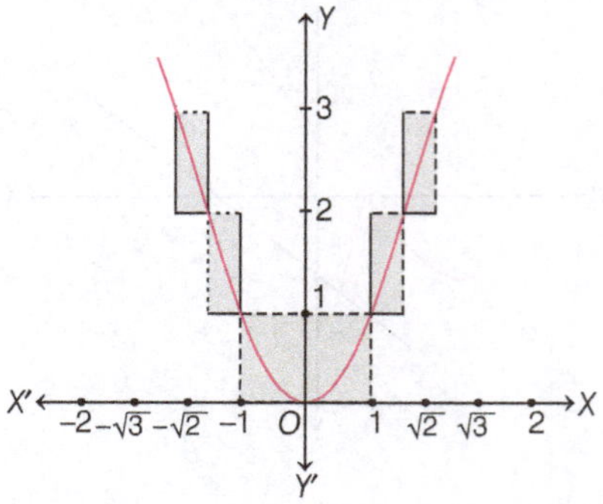

For $\quad 1 \le y < 2$,

Then, $\quad [y] = 1$

∴ $\quad [x^2] = 1 \Rightarrow 1 \le x^2 < 2$

⇒ $\quad x \in (-\sqrt{2}, -1] \cup [1, \sqrt{2})$

For $\quad 2 \le y < 3$, then $[y] = 2$

Then, $\quad [x^2] = 2 \Rightarrow 2 \le x^2 < 3$

∴ $\quad x \in (-\sqrt{3}, -\sqrt{2}] \cup [\sqrt{2}, \sqrt{3})$

The graph of the region will not only contain points of the parabola $y = x^2$ but $[x^2] = [y]$ contain points within the rectangles of side 1, 2, ; 1, $\sqrt{2} - 1$; 1, $\sqrt{3} - \sqrt{2}$ etc.

Example 10 *The minimum area of circle which touches the parabolas $y = x^2 + 1$ and $x = y^2 + 1$ is*

(a) $\frac{9\pi}{16}$ sq units (b) $\frac{9\pi}{32}$ sq units

(c) $\frac{9\pi}{8}$ sq units (d) $\frac{9\pi}{4}$ sq units

Sol. **(b)** The parabolas $y = x^2 + 1$ and $x = y^2 + 1$ are symmetrical about $y = x$.

Therefore, the tangent at point A is parallel to $y = x$,

then $\quad \frac{dy}{dx} = 2x = 1$

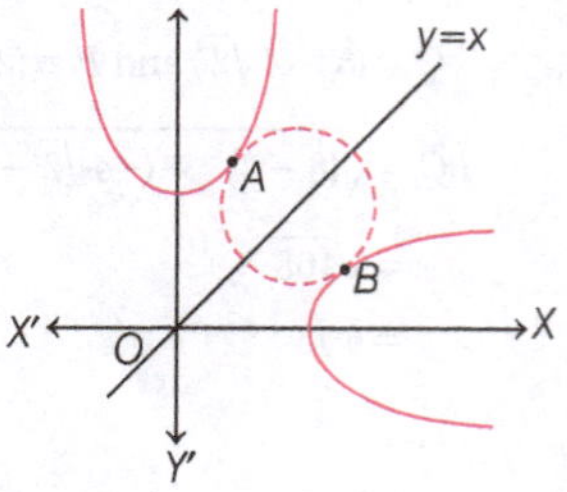

or $$x = \frac{1}{2}, y = \frac{5}{4}$$

$\therefore$ $$A \equiv \left(\frac{1}{2}, \frac{5}{4}\right) \text{ and } B \equiv \left(\frac{5}{4}, \frac{1}{2}\right)$$

Hence, radius $(r) = \frac{1}{2} AB = \frac{1}{2}\sqrt{\left(\frac{1}{2} - \frac{5}{4}\right)^2 + \left(\frac{5}{4} - \frac{1}{2}\right)^2} = \frac{3\sqrt{2}}{8}$

$\therefore$ $$\text{Area} = \pi r^2 = \frac{9\pi}{32} \text{ sq units}$$

Example 11 *Let the line $lx + my = 1$ cut the parabola $y^2 = 4ax$ in the points A and B. Normals at A and B meet at point C. Normal from C other than these two points meet the parabola at D, then the coordinate of D are*

(a) $(a, 2a)$ (b) $\left(\frac{4am}{l^2}, \frac{4a}{l}\right)$

(c) $\left(\frac{2am^2}{l^2}, \frac{2a}{l}\right)$ (d) $\left(\frac{4am^2}{l^2}, \frac{4am}{l}\right)$

Sol. (d) Let $A \equiv (am_1^2, -2am_1)$ and $B \equiv (am_2^2, -2am_2)$

Now, A and B lie on $lx + my = 1$

$\Rightarrow$ $$l(am_1^2) + m(-2am_1) = 1 \quad \text{...(i)}$$

and $$l(am_2^2) + m(-2am_2) = 1 \quad \text{...(ii)}$$

On subtracting Eq. (ii) from Eq. (i), then

$$la(m_1^2 - m_2^2) - 2am(m_1 - m_2) = 0$$

Since, $$a(m_1 - m_2) \neq 0$$

$\therefore$ $$l(m_1 + m_2) - 2m = 0$$

$\Rightarrow$ $$m_1 + m_2 = \frac{2m}{l} \quad \text{...(iii)}$$

Let $D \equiv (am_3^2, -2am_3)$ and $C \equiv (h, k)$

$\therefore$ Equation of normal in terms of slope

$$y = Mx - 2aM - aM^3$$

Then, $aM^3 - (h - 2a)M + k = 0$

$\because$ $$m_1 + m_2 + m_3 = 0 \Rightarrow \frac{2m}{l} + m_3 = 0$$

$\therefore$ $$m_3 = -\frac{2m}{l}$$

Now, $$D \equiv \left(a\left(\frac{-2m}{l}\right)^2, -2a\left(\frac{-2m}{l}\right)\right)$$

$\therefore$ $$D \equiv \left(\frac{4am^2}{l^2}, \frac{4am}{l}\right)$$

Example 12 *If d is the distance between the parallel tangents with positive slope to $y^2 = 4x$ and $x^2 + y^2 - 2x + 4y - 11 = 0$, then*

(a) $10 < d < 20$ (b) $4 < d < 6$

(c) $d < 4$ (d) None of these

Sol. (c) Tangent to the parabola $y^2 = 4x$ having slope m is

$$y = mx + \frac{1}{m}$$

and tangent to the circle $(x-1)^2 + (y+2)^2 = 4^2$ having slope m is

$$y + 2 = m(x - 1) + 4\sqrt{(1 + m^2)}$$

$\therefore$ Distance between tangents $(d) = \left|\frac{4\sqrt{(1+m^2)} - m - 2 - \frac{1}{m}}{\sqrt{(1+m^2)}}\right|$

$$= \left|4 - \frac{2}{\sqrt{(1+m^2)}} - \frac{\sqrt{(1+m^2)}}{m}\right|$$

As $m > 0$, (given)

we get $d < 4$

Example 13 *Two parabolas C and D intersect at two different points, where C is $y = x^2 - 3$ and D is $y = kx^2$. The intersection at which the value of x is positive is designated point A, and $x = a$ at this intersection the tangent line l at A to the curve D intersects curve C at point B, other than A. If x-value of point B is 1, then a is equal to*

(a) 1 (b) 2 (c) 3 (d) 4

Sol. (c) $C: y = x^2 - 3$ and $D: y = kx^2$

On solving C and D, then

$$kx^2 = x^2 - 3 \quad \text{...(i)}$$

or $$x^2 = \frac{3}{1-k},$$

$$y = \frac{3k}{1-k}$$

$\therefore$ $$A \equiv \left(\sqrt{\frac{3}{1-k}}, \frac{3k}{1-k}\right)$$

and $$a = \sqrt{\left(\frac{3}{1-k}\right)}$$

Then, $A \equiv (a, ka^2) \equiv (a, a^2 - 3)$ [from Eq. (i)]

Tangent l at A to the curve D is

$$\frac{y + a^2 - 3}{2} = kx \cdot a$$

$\Rightarrow$ $$y + a^2 - 3 = 2ax\left(1 - \frac{3}{a^2}\right) \quad \text{[from Eq. (i)] ...(ii)}$$

$\therefore$ $$B \equiv (1, -2) \quad [\because a \neq 1]$$

From Eq. (ii), $-2 + a^2 - 3 = 2a\left(1 - \frac{3}{a^2}\right)$

$\Rightarrow$ $$a^3 - 5a = 2a^2 - 6$$

$\Rightarrow$ $$a^3 - 2a^2 - 5a + 6 = 0$$

$\Rightarrow$ $$(a-1)(a+2)(a-3) = 0$$

$\therefore$ $$a = 3 \quad [\because a \neq 1, a \neq -2]$$

Example 14 *The minimum value of*

$[(x_1 - x_2)^2 + (3 + \sqrt{(1 - x_1^2)} - \sqrt{4x_2})^2], \forall\ x_1, x_2 \in R$ *is*

(a) $4\sqrt{5} + 1$ (b) $3 - 2\sqrt{2}$
(c) $\sqrt{5} + 1$ (d) $\sqrt{5} - 1$

Sol. (b) Let $y_1 = 3 + \sqrt{(1 - x_1^2)}$ and $y_2 = \sqrt{4x_2}$

or $x_1^2 + (y_1 - 3)^2 = 1$ and $y_2^2 = 4x_2$

Thus, (x_1, y_1) lies on the circle $x^2 + (y - 3)^2 = 1$ and (x_2, y_2) lies on the parabola $y^2 = 4x$.

Thus, the given expression is the shortest distance between the curve $x^2 + (y - 3)^2 = 1$ and $y^2 = 4x$.

Now, the shortest distance always occurs along the common normal to the curves and normal to the circle passes through the centre of the circle.

Normal to parabola $y^2 = 4x$ is $y = mx - 2m - m^3$. It passes through the centre of circle (0, 3).

Therefore, $3 = -2m - m^3 \Rightarrow m^3 + 2m + 3 = 0$ which has only one real value $m = -1$.

Hence, the corresponding point on the parabola is (1, 2)

$$\therefore \sqrt{(x_1 - x_2)^2 + (3 + \sqrt{(1 - x_1^2)} - \sqrt{4x_2})^2}$$
$$= \sqrt{(x_1 - x_2)^2 + (y_1 - y_2)^2}$$
$$= \text{Distance between } (1, 2) \text{ and } (0, 3) - \text{radius}$$
$$= \sqrt{(1 + 1)} - 1 = (\sqrt{2} - 1)$$

or $$(x_1 - x_2)^2 + (3 + \sqrt{(1 - x_1^2)} - \sqrt{4x_2})^2 = (\sqrt{2} - 1)^2$$

$$\therefore \quad \min \cdot [(x_1 - x_2)^2 + (3 + \sqrt{(1 - x_1^2)} - \sqrt{4x_2})^2] = 3 - 2\sqrt{2}$$

Example 15 *The condition that the parabolas $y^2 = 4c(x - d)$ and $y^2 = 4ax$ have a common normal other than X-axis $(a > 0, c > 0)$ is*

(a) $2a < 2c + d$ (b) $2c < 2a + d$
(c) $2d < 2a + c$ (d) $2d < 2c + a$

Sol. (a) Normals of parabolas $y^2 = 4ax$ and $y^2 = 4c(x - d)$ in terms of slope are

$$y = mx - 2am - am^3 \quad \text{...(i)}$$

and $$y = m(x - d) - 2cm - cm^3 \quad \text{...(ii)}$$

Subtracting Eqs. (ii) from (i), then

$$md - 2am - am^3 + 2cm + cm^3 = 0$$
$$m \neq 0$$
$$\therefore \quad d - 2a - am^2 + 2c + cm^2 = 0$$
$$\Rightarrow \quad (a - c)m^2 = d - 2a + 2c$$
$$\Rightarrow \quad m^2 = \frac{d - 2a + 2c}{(a - c)}$$
$$\Rightarrow \quad \frac{d}{a - c} - 2 > 0 \Rightarrow d > 2a - 2c$$
$$\therefore \quad 2a < 2c + d$$

JEE SCANNER

Example 16 Similar to PYQ Asked in JEE Main 2023

Let PQ be a chord of the parabola $y^2 = 16x$ and the mid-point of PQ be at (4, 3). Then, which of the following point lies on the line passing through the points P and Q?

(a) (2, 3) (b) $\left(\frac{1}{2}, \frac{1}{3}\right)$
(c) (4, –3) (d) (1, –5)

Sol. (d) On comparing with $y^2 = 4ax$, we get $a = 4$.

We know that equation of chord whose mid-point is (x_1, y_1) is given by $T = S_1$

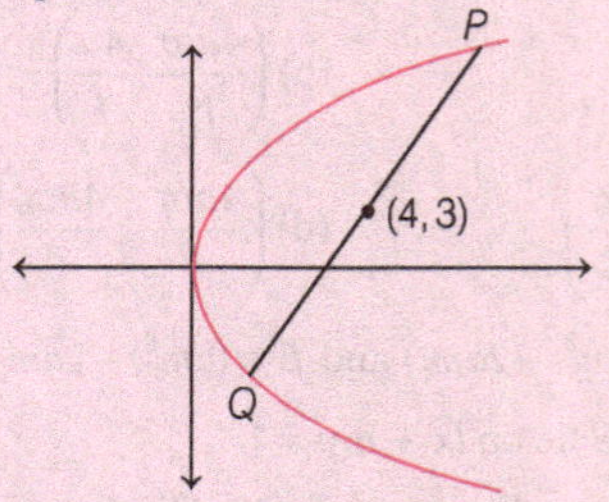

$$\Rightarrow \quad yy_1 - 2a(x + x_1) = y_1^2 - 4ax_1$$
$$\Rightarrow \quad 3y - 8(x + 4) = 9 - 64$$
$$\Rightarrow \quad 8x - 3y - 23 = 0 \quad \text{...(i)}$$

$\therefore$ Therefore, point (1, –5) will satisfy the above Eq. (i).

Hence, point (1, –5) lies on the line passing through the points P and Q.

Skill Builder

Let PQ be a chord of the parabola $y^2 = 8x$ and the mid-point of PQ be at (3, 1). Then, which of the following point lies on the line passing through the points P and Q?

(a) (2, –3) (b) $\left(\frac{1}{2}, 3\right)$
(c) (0, 4) (d) (3, –2)

For Sol.

More than one Correct Option Type Questions

Example 17 *The locus of the mid-point of the focal radii of a variable point moving on the parabola $y^2 = 4ax$ is a parabola whose*

(a) latusrectum is half the latusrectum of the original parabola
(b) vertex is $\left(\frac{a}{2}, 0\right)$
(c) directrix is Y-axis
(d) focus has the coordinates $(a, 0)$

Sol. (a, b, c, d) Let $P(at^2, 2at)$ be a point on the parabola $y^2 = 4ax$ with focus $S(a, 0)$

Now, mid-point of focal radii SP is $M\left(\frac{a}{2}(t^2 + 1), at\right)$.

Let $\quad x = \frac{a}{2}(t^2 + 1)$ and $y = at$

or $\quad x = \frac{a}{2}\left(\frac{y^2}{a^2} + 1\right)$

$\Rightarrow \quad y^2 = 2ax - a^2$ or $y^2 = 2a\left(x - \frac{a}{2}\right)$

which is a parabola with vertex $\left(\frac{a}{2}, 0\right)$ and latusrectum is $2a$,

directrix is $x - \frac{a}{2} = -\frac{a}{2}$ i.e. $x = 0$ (Y-axis) and focus $\left(\frac{a}{2} + \frac{a}{2}, 0\right)$

i.e. $(a, 0)$.

Example 18 *If P_1P_2 and Q_1Q_2, two focal chords of a parabola $y^2 = 4ax$ at right angles, then*

(a) area of the quadrilateral $P_1Q_1P_2Q_2$ is minimum when the chords are inclined at an angle $\pi / 4$ to the axis of the parabola.

(b) minimum area is twice the area of the square on the latusrectum of the parabola.

(c) minimum area of quadrilateral $P_1Q_1P_2Q_2$ cannot be found.

(d) minimum area is thrice the area of the square on the latusrectum of the parabola.

Sol. (a, b) Let coordinates of P_1 are $(at^2, 2at)$, then coordinates of P_2 are $\left(\frac{a}{t^2}, -\frac{2a}{t}\right)$.

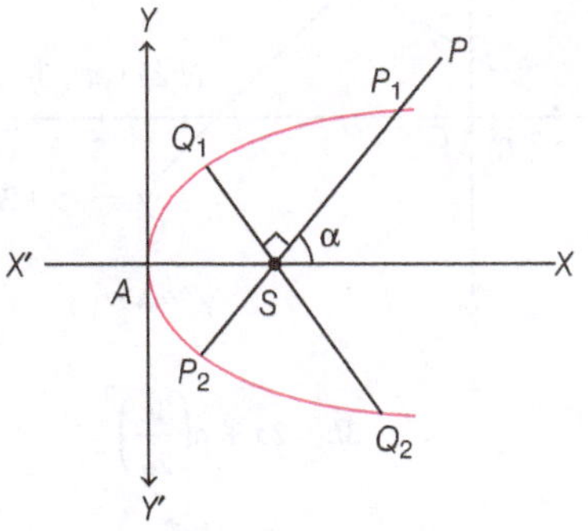

Let focal chord P_1P_2 makes an angle α with X-axis, then

$$\tan\alpha = \frac{2at - \left(-\frac{2a}{t}\right)}{at^2 - \frac{a}{t^2}} = \frac{2}{t - \frac{1}{t}}$$

$$\Rightarrow \quad t - \frac{1}{t} = 2\cot\alpha \quad \text{... (i)}$$

Now, $\quad P_1P_2 = a\left(t + \frac{1}{t}\right)^2 = a\left\{\left(t - \frac{1}{t}\right)^2 + 4\right\}$

$= a\{4\cot^2\alpha + 4\} = 4a\operatorname{cosec}^2\alpha \quad$ [from Eq. (i)]

Similarly, $\quad Q_1Q_2 = 4a\operatorname{cosec}^2(90 - \alpha) = 4a\sec^2\alpha$

$\therefore$ Area of quadrilateral $P_1Q_1P_2Q_2 = \frac{1}{2}(P_1P_2)(Q_1Q_2)$

$= 8a^2\sec^2\alpha\operatorname{cosec}^2\alpha = 32a^2\operatorname{cosec}^2 2\alpha$

$\therefore$ Minimum area $= 32a^2 = 2$ (latusrectum)^2 and is inclined at

$\alpha = \pi / 4 \quad [\because \operatorname{cosec} 2\alpha = 1]$

Example 19 *The equation of the line that touches the curves $y = x|x|$ and $x^2 + (y - 2)^2 = 4$, where $x \neq 0$, is*

(a) $y = 4\sqrt{5}x + 20$ (b) $y = 4\sqrt{3}x - 12$

(c) $y = 0$ (d) $y = -4\sqrt{5}x - 20$

Sol. (a, b, c) $\because y = x|x| = \begin{cases} x^2, & x \geq 0 \\ -x^2, & x < 0 \end{cases}$

$\because$ Equation of tangent in terms of slope (m) of $x^2 = 4ay$ is

$$y = mx - am^2 \quad \text{... (i)}$$

Also, line (i) touches the circle $x^2 + (y - 2)^2 = 4$, then

$$\frac{|2 + am^2|}{\sqrt{(1 + m^2)}} = 2 \Rightarrow 4 + a^2m^4 + 4am^2 = 4 + 4m^2$$

$\therefore \quad m^2 = \frac{4 - 4a}{a^2}$ and $m^2 = 0$

Put $4a = 1$ for $y = x^2, x \geq 0$, then $m^2 = 48$

and put $4a = -1$ for $y = -x^2, x < 0$, then $m^2 = 80$

$\therefore$ Common tangents are

$y = 0, y = 4\sqrt{3}x - 12$ and $y = 4\sqrt{5}x + 20$

Example 20 *Let V be the vertex and L be the latusrectum of the parabola $x^2 = 2y + 4x - 4$. Then, the equation of the parabola whose vertex is at V, latusrectum $L / 2$ and axis is perpendicular to the axis of the given parabola.*

(a) $y^2 = x - 2$ (b) $y^2 = x - 4$

(c) $y^2 = 2 - x$ (d) $y^2 = 4 - x$

Sol. (a, c) Given parabola is $x^2 = 2y + 4x - 4$.

$\Rightarrow \quad (x - 2)^2 = 2y$

Vertex of the parabola is (2, 0) and length of latusrectum = 2

$\therefore \quad V(2, 0)$ and $L = 2$

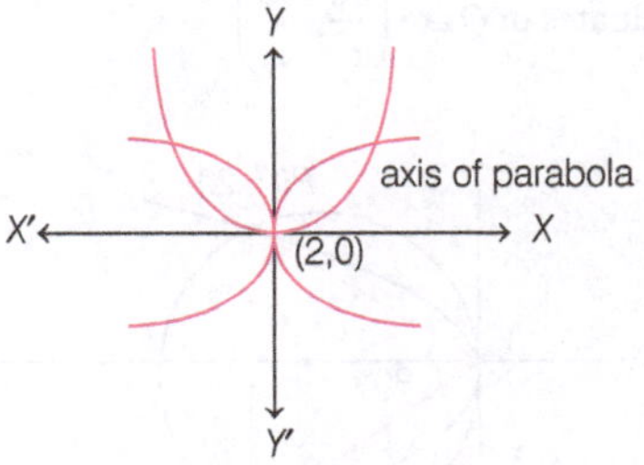

Length of latusrectum of required parabola $= L / 2 = 1$

$\therefore$ Equation of the required parabola is $(y - 0)^2 = \pm 1(x - 2)$

$\Rightarrow \quad y^2 = x - 2$ or $y^2 = -x + 2$

Example 21 *Consider a circle with its centre lying on the focus of the parabola $y^2 = 2ax$ such that it touches the directrix of the parabola. Then, a point of intersection of the circle and the parabola is*

(a) $\left(\frac{a}{2}, a\right)$ (b) $\left(\frac{a}{2}, -a\right)$ (c) $\left(-\frac{a}{2}, a\right)$ (d) $\left(-\frac{a}{2}, -a\right)$

Sol. (a, b) Given parabola is $y^2 = 2ax$. ...(i)

$\therefore$ Focus and equation of directrix are $S\left(\frac{a}{2}, 0\right)$ and $x = -\frac{a}{2}$ respectively.

$\therefore$ Equation of circle is $\left(x - \frac{a}{2}\right)^2 + (y - 0)^2 = a^2$ ... (ii)

[$\because$ radius = distance between focus and directrix]

From Eqs. (i) and (ii), we get

$$\left(x - \frac{a}{2}\right)^2 + 2ax = a^2 \Rightarrow x^2 + ax - \frac{3a^2}{4} = 0$$

or $x = \frac{a}{2}, x \neq -\frac{3a}{2}$ [$\because$ for $x = -\frac{3a}{2}$, y = imaginary]

From Eq. (i),

$$y^2 = a^2$$

$$\therefore \quad y = \pm a$$

Hence, required point of intersection are $\left(\frac{a}{2}, \pm a\right)$.

Example 22 *Let PQ be a chord of the parabola $y^2 = 4x$. A circle drawn with PQ as a diameter passes through the vertex V of the parabola. If area of $\Delta PVQ = 20$ sq units, then coordinates of P are*

(a) $(4, -4)$ (b) $(4, 4)$ (c) $(16, -8)$ (d) $(16, 8)$

Sol. (c, d) Slope of $VP = \frac{2t - 0}{t^2 - 0} = \frac{2}{t}$

$\therefore$ Slope of $VQ = \frac{-t}{2}$

Equation of VQ is $y = \frac{-t}{2}x$, solving it with $y^2 = 4x$, we get

$$\frac{t^2x^2}{4} - 4x = 0 \Rightarrow x = 0 \text{ or } \frac{16}{t^2}$$

So, coordinates of Q are $\left(\frac{16}{t^2}, \frac{-8}{t}\right)$

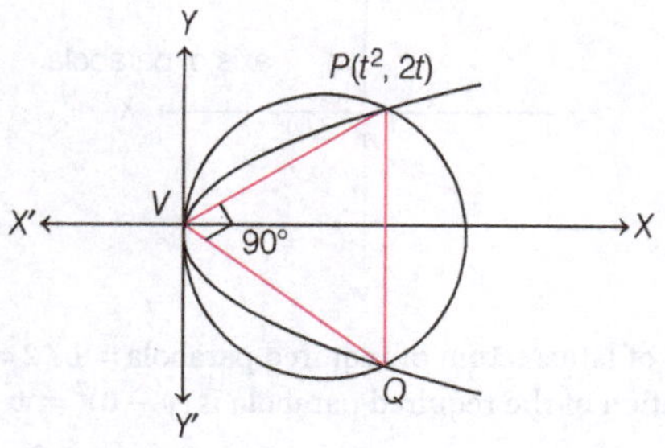

$\because$ Area of $\Delta PVQ = \frac{1}{2} \times PV \times VQ = 20$

$$\Rightarrow \quad (PV)^2(VQ)^2 = 1600$$

$$\Rightarrow \quad (t^4 + 4t^2)\left(\frac{256}{t^4} + \frac{64}{t^2}\right) = 1600$$

$$\Rightarrow \quad t^2(t^2 + 4) \cdot \frac{64}{t^4}(t^2 + 4) = 1600$$

$$\Rightarrow \quad (t^2 + 4)^2 = \frac{1600}{64}t^2$$

$$\Rightarrow \quad t^2 + 4 = \pm 5t$$

$$\Rightarrow \quad t = \pm 4, \pm 1.$$

Hence, coordinates of P are $(16, \pm 8)$ and $(1, \pm 2)$.

Example 23 *The tangent PT and the normal PN to the parabola $y^2 = 4ax$ at a point P on it meet its axis at points T and N, respectively. The locus of the centroid of the ΔPTN is a parabola whose*

(a) vertex is $\left(\frac{2a}{3}, 0\right)$ (b) directrix is $x = 0$

(c) latusrectum is $\frac{2a}{3}$ (d) focus is $(a, 0)$

Sol. (a, d) Equation of tangent and normal at point $P(at^2, 2at)$ is $ty = x + at^2$ and $y = -tx + 2at + at^3$, respectively. Let the centroid of ΔPTN is $R(h, k)$.

$$\therefore \quad h = \frac{at^2 + (-at^2) + 2a + at^2}{3} \text{ and } k = \frac{2at}{3}$$

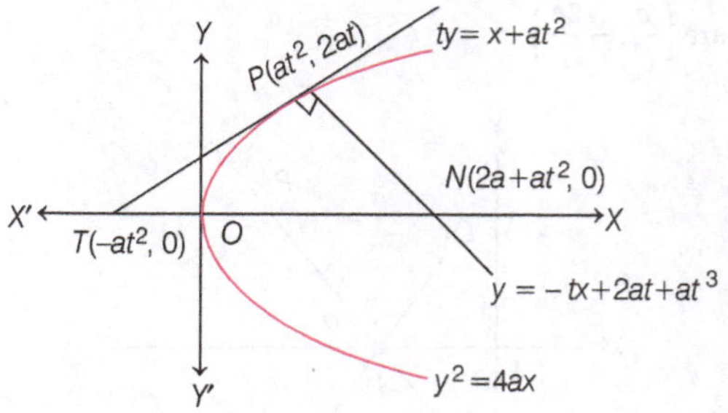

$$\Rightarrow \quad 3h = 2a + a\left(\frac{3k}{2a}\right)^2$$

$$\Rightarrow \quad 3h = 2a + \frac{9k^2}{4a} \Rightarrow 9k^2 = 4a(3h - 2a)$$

$\therefore$ Locus of centroid is $y^2 = \frac{4a}{3}\left(x - \frac{2a}{3}\right)$

which is a parabola with its vertex at $\left(\frac{2a}{3}, 0\right)$,

directrix $x - \frac{2a}{3} = \frac{-a}{3} \Rightarrow x = \frac{a}{3}$,

$\therefore$ Latusrectum $= \frac{4a}{3}$ and focus $(a, 0)$.

Passage Based Questions

Passage I

(Ex. Nos. 24 and 25)

Tangents are drawn to the parabola $y^2 = 4x$ at the point P which is the upper end of latusrectum.

Example 24 *Image of the parabola $y^2 = 4x$ in the tangent line at the point P is*

(a) $(x+4)^2 = 16y$ (b) $(x+2)^2 = 8(y-2)$

(c) $(x+1)^2 = 4(y-1)$ (d) $(x-2)^2 = 2(y-2)$

Sol. (c) The upper end of parabola is $P(1, 2)$.

The equation of tangent at P is $2y = 2(x+1) \Rightarrow x - y + 1 = 0$

Any point on the given parabola is $(t^2, 2t)$. The image of (h, k) of the point $(t^2, 2t)$ on $x - y + 1 = 0$ is given by

$$\frac{h - t^2}{1} = \frac{k - 2t}{-1} = \frac{-2(t^2 - 2t + 1)}{1 + 1}$$

$\Rightarrow$ $h = 2t - 1$ and $k = t^2 + 1$

or $k = \left(\frac{h+1}{2}\right)^2 + 1 \Rightarrow (h+1)^2 = 4(k-1)$

$\therefore$ The required equation of image is $(x+1)^2 = 4(y-1)$.

Example 25 *Radius of the circle touching the parabola $y^2 = 4x$ at the point P and passing through its focus is*

(a) 1 (b) $\sqrt{2}$ (c) $\sqrt{3}$ (d) 2

Sol. (b) $\because$ Focus is $S(1, 0)$ and P is $(1, 2)$.

Equation of circle touching the parabola at $(1, 2)$ is $(x-1)^2 + (y-2)^2 + \lambda(x - y + 1) = 0$.

It passes through $(1, 0)$.

Therefore, $4 + 2\lambda = 0$ or $\lambda = -2$

Thus, the required circle is

$$(x-1)^2 + (y-2)^2 - 2(x - y + 1) = 0$$

or $$x^2 + y^2 - 4x - 2y + 3 = 0$$

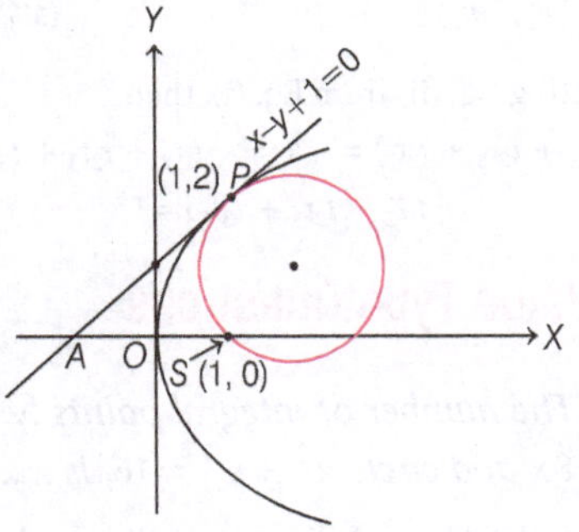

Its radius is $\sqrt{(4 + 1 - 3)} = \sqrt{2}$.

Passage II

(Ex. Nos. 26 and 27)

Let C_1 and C_2 be the parabolas $x^2 = y - 1$ and $y^2 = x - 1$ respectivley. Let P be any point on C_1 and Q be any point on C_2. Let P_1 and Q_1 be the reflections of P and Q, respectively with respect to the line $y = x$.

Example 26 *P_1 and Q_1 lie on*

(a) C_1 and C_2 respectively

(b) C_2 and C_1 respectively

(c) Cannot be determined

(d) None of the above

Example 27 *If the point $P(\lambda, \lambda^2 + 1)$ and $Q(\mu^2 + 1, \mu)$, then P_1 and Q_1 are*

(a) $(\lambda^2 + 1, \lambda)$ and $(\mu^2 + 1, \mu)$

(b) $(\lambda^2 + 1, \lambda)$ and $(\mu, \mu^2 + 1)$

(c) $(\lambda, \lambda^2 + 1)$ and $(\mu, \mu^2 + 1)$

(d) $(\lambda, \lambda^2 + 1)$ and $(\mu^2 + 1, \mu)$

Sol. Since, the reflection of a point (P, Q) with respect to line $y = x$ is (P_1, Q_1).

Let $P(\lambda, \lambda^2 + 1)$ and $Q(\mu^2 + 1, \mu)$ be points on C_1 and C_2, respectively.

$\therefore$ Reflection of $P(\lambda, \lambda^2 + 1)$ with respect to line $y = x$ is $P_1(\lambda^2 + 1, \lambda)$ and reflection of $Q(\mu^2 + 1, \mu)$ with respect to line $y = x$ is $Q_1(\mu, \mu^2 + 1)$.

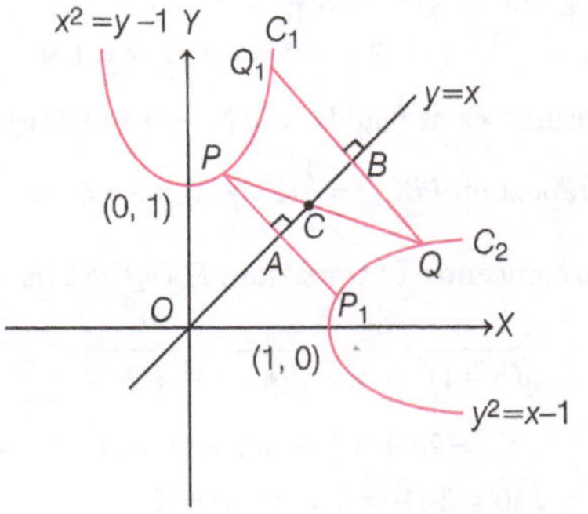

$\therefore$ P_1 and Q_1 are $(\lambda^2 + 1, \lambda)$ and $(\mu, \mu^2 + 1)$

Also, P_1 and Q_1 lie on $y^2 = x - 1$

and $x^2 = y - 1$.

Hence, P_1 and Q_1 lie on C_2 and C_1, respectively.

26. (b) **27.** (b)

Stem Based Questions

Stem I

(Ex. Nos. 28 and 29)

PQ is the double ordinate of the parabola $y^2 = 4x$ which passes through the focus. ΔPQA is an isosceles right angled triangle, where *A* is on the axis of the parabola. Line *PA* meets the parabola at *C* and *QA* meets the parabola at *B*.

Example 28 *The area of trapezium PBCQ is ....*

Example 29 *The circum radius of trapezium PBCQ is ......*

Sol. We have, $y^2 = 4x$ ...(i)

End of co-ordinates of latusrectum are $P(1, 2)$ and $Q(1, -2)$

ΔPAQ is an isosceles right angled triangle.

$\therefore$ The slope of *PA* is -1 and its equation is

$$y - 2 = -(x - 1)$$

i.e. $x + y - 3 = 0$ ...(ii)

Similarly, the equation of *QB* is $x - y - 3 = 0$ ...(iii)

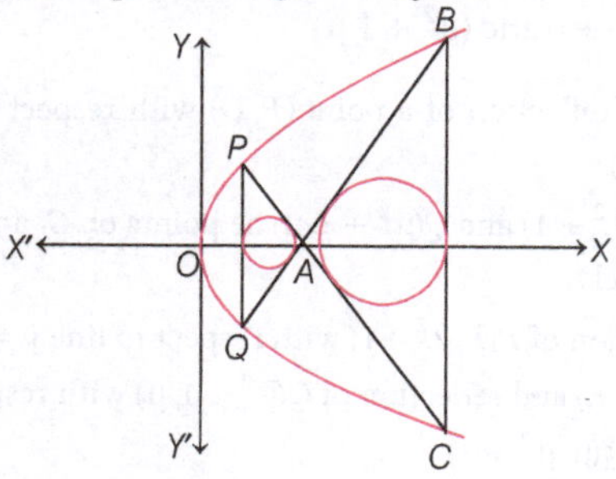

On solving Eqs. (i) and (iii), we get

$$(3 - x)^2 = 4x \Rightarrow x = 1, 9$$

$\therefore$ The coordinates of *B* and *C* are $(9, -6)$ and $(9, 6)$ respectively.

Area of trapezium $PBCQ = \frac{1}{2}(12 + 4) \times 8 = 64$ sq units

Let the circumcentre of trapezium *PBCQ* be $T(h, 0)$, then $PT = PB$

$$\sqrt{(h-1)^2 + 4} = \sqrt{(h-9)^2 + 36}$$

$\Rightarrow$ $-2h + 5 = -18h + 81 + 36 \Rightarrow h = 7$

$\therefore$ Radius $= \sqrt{40} = 2\sqrt{10} = 2 \times 3.16 = 6.32$

28. 64 sq units **29.** 6.32

Single Integer Answer Type Questions

Example 30 *Points A, B and C lie on the parabola $y^2 = 4ax$. The tangents to the parabola at A, B and C taken in pairs intersect at points P, Q and R, then the ratio of the areas of the ΔABC and ΔPQR is ....*

Sol. (2) Let $(at_1^2, 2at_1)$, $(at_2^2, 2at_2)$ and $(at_3^2, 2at_3)$ be the points *A*, *B* and *C* respectively.

$$\therefore \text{ Area of } \Delta ABC = \frac{1}{2}\left\|\begin{matrix} at_1^2 & 2at_1 & 1 \\ at_2^2 & 2at_2 & 1 \\ at_3^2 & 2at_3 & 1 \end{matrix}\right\| = a^2 \left\|\begin{matrix} 1 & t_1 & t_1^2 \\ 1 & t_2 & t_2^2 \\ 1 & t_3 & t_3^2 \end{matrix}\right\|$$

$$= a^2 \,|(t_1 - t_2)(t_2 - t_3)(t_3 - t_1)|$$

Coordinates of *P*, *Q* and *R* are $(at_2t_3, a(t_2 + t_3))$, $(at_3t_1, a(t_3 + t_1))$, $(at_1t_2, a(t_1 + t_2))$ respectively, then

$$\text{Area of } \Delta PQR = \frac{1}{2}\left\|\begin{matrix} at_2t_3 & a(t_2+t_3) & 1 \\ at_3t_1 & a(t_3+t_1) & 1 \\ at_1t_2 & a(t_1+t_2) & 1 \end{matrix}\right\| = \frac{a^2}{2}\left\|\begin{matrix} t_2t_3 & t_2+t_3 & 1 \\ t_3t_1 & t_3+t_1 & 1 \\ t_1t_2 & t_1+t_2 & 1 \end{matrix}\right\|$$

$$= \frac{a^2}{2}\,|\Sigma t_2t_3(t_3 - t_2)| = \frac{a^2}{2}\,|(t_1 - t_2)(t_2 - t_3)(t_3 - t_1)|$$

$$= \frac{1}{2} \times \text{Area of } \Delta ABC$$

$$\therefore \quad \frac{\text{Area of } \Delta ABC}{\text{Area of } \Delta PQR} = 2$$

Example 31 *If the orthocentre of the triangle formed by the points t_1, t_2 and t_3 on the parabola $y^2 = 4ax$ is the focus, then the value of $|t_1t_2 + t_2t_3 + t_3t_1|$ is ....*

Sol. (5) $\because$ *SA* is perpendicular to *BC* [*S* is focus $(a, 0)$]

$$\Rightarrow \left(\frac{2at_1 - 0}{at_1^2 - a}\right)\left(\frac{2at_3 - 2at_2}{at_3^2 - at_2^2}\right) = -1$$

$$\Rightarrow \left(\frac{2t_1}{t_1^2 - 1}\right)\left(\frac{2}{t_3 + t_2}\right) = -1$$

$$\Rightarrow \quad 4t_1 + t_1^2(t_2 + t_3) = t_2 + t_3 \quad \text{...(i)}$$

Similarly, $4t_2 + t_2^2(t_3 + t_1) = t_3 + t_1$ ...(ii)

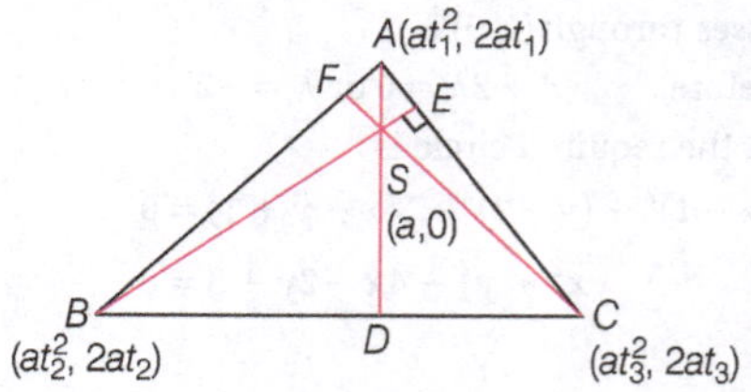

On subtracting Eq. (ii) from Eq. (i), then

$$4 + (t_1t_2 + t_2t_3 + t_3t_1) = -1 \Rightarrow t_1t_2 + t_2t_3 + t_3t_1 = -5$$

$$\therefore \quad |t_1t_2 + t_2t_3 + t_3t_1| = 5$$

Numerical Value Type Questions

Example 32 *The number of integral points lying inside the parabola $y^2 = 8x$ and circle $x^2 + y^2 = 16$, is ....*

Sol. (17) We have, let $P(x_1, y_1)$ lies inside the parabola and circle.

$$y_1^2 - 8x_1 < 0 \text{ and } x_1^2 + y_1^2 = 16, x_1 > 0$$

$\therefore$ When $x_1 = 1, y_1^2 < 8$ and $y_1^2 < 15$

$$\Rightarrow \quad y_1 = 0, \pm 1, \pm 2$$

When $x_1 = 2, y_1^2 < 16, y_1^2 < 12 \Rightarrow y_1 = 0, \pm 1, \pm 2, \pm 3$

When $x_1 = 3, y_1^2 < 27, y_1^2 < 7 \Rightarrow y_1 = 0, \pm 1, \pm 2$

$\therefore$ There are total 17 such points.

Example 33 *If the coordinates of the point on the parabola $y = x^2 + 7x + 2$, which is nearest to the straight line $y = 3x - 3$ is (k_1, k_2), then the value of $|k_1 + k_2|$ is ....*

Sol. (10) We have, $y = x^2 + 7x + 2 \Rightarrow \left(x + \frac{7}{2}\right)^2 = \left(y + \frac{41}{4}\right)$

Now, a tangent parallel to $y = 3x - 3$ will have slope $m = 3$ and its point of contact will be

$$x + \frac{7}{2} = 2am \Rightarrow x + \frac{7}{2} = 2 \times \frac{1}{4} \times 3 \Rightarrow x = -2$$

and $$y + \frac{41}{4} = am^2 \Rightarrow y + \frac{41}{4} = \frac{1}{4} \times 9 \Rightarrow y = -8.$$

Hence, the nearest point on the parabola from the line

$$y = 3x - 3 \text{ is } (-2, -8)$$

$\therefore$ $$k_1 = -2, k_2 = -8$$

So, $$|k_1 + k_2| = |-2 - 8| = 10$$

JEE SCANNER

Example 34 Similar to PYQ Asked in JEE Main 2024

Suppose AB be a focal chord of the parabola $y^2 = 16x$ of length l and slope $m < 2$. If the distance of the chord AB from the origin is d, then ld^2 is equal to ....

Sol. (256) Given equation of parabola is $y^2 = 16x$

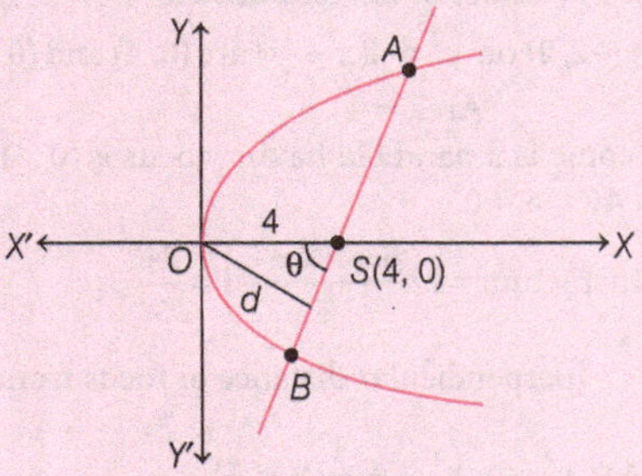

Length of focal chord AB, $l = 4a\text{cosec}^2\theta$

$$= 4 \times 4 \times \left(\frac{4}{d}\right)^2 = 16 \times \frac{16}{d^2}$$

$\therefore ld^2 = 16 \times 16 = 256$

Skill Builder

For Sol.

Suppose AB be a focal chord of the parabola $y^2 = 8x$ of length l and slope $m < \sqrt{2}$. If the distance of the chord AB from the origin is d, then ld^2 is equal to ......

Example 35 *If the normal at the end points of a variable chord PQ of the parabola $y^2 - 4y - 2x = 0$ are perpendicular and the length at P and Q will intersect at $ax + \frac{b}{2} = 0$, then the value of $a + b$ is ....*

Sol. (12) Given that normal at P and Q are perpendicular, the tangents at P and Q will also be perpendicular. But any two perpendicular tangents of a parabola always intersect on its directrix.

Given parabola is $(y - 2)^2 = 2(x + 2)$.

So, its directrix is $2x + 5 = 0$.

Compare with $ax + \frac{b}{2}$, we get $a = 2$ and $b = 10$

$\therefore$ $$a + b = 12$$

Example 36 *The equation of the directrix of the parabola with vertex at the origin and having the axis along the X-axis and a common tangent of slope 2 with the circle $x^2 + y^2 = 5$ is $x = \pm k$, then the value of k is ....*

Sol. (10) Let the line $y = 2x + c$ is a tangent to $x^2 + y^2 = 5$.

If $$c^2 = 25 \Rightarrow c \pm 5$$

Let the equation of parabola be $y^2 = 4ax$.

Then, $$\frac{a}{2} = \pm 5 \Rightarrow a = \pm 10$$

$\Rightarrow$ Equation of parabola is $y^2 = \pm 40x$

$\therefore$ Equation of the directrix are $x = \pm 10$

Hence, the value of k is ± 10.

Matching Type Questions

Example 37 *Match the following.*

	Column I	Column II	
(A)	If PQ is any focal chord of the parabola $y^2 = 32x$ and length of PQ can never be less than λ units, then λ is divisible by	(p)	2
(B)	A tangent is drawn to the parabola $y^2 = 4x$ at the point P whose abscissa lies in the interval $[1, 4]$. If maximum possible area of the triangle formed by the tangent at P, ordinate of the point P and the X-axis is λ sq units, then λ is divisible by	(q)	3
(C)	The normal at the ends of the latusrectum of the parabola $y^2 = 4x$ meet the parabola again at A and A'. If length $AA' = \lambda$ unit, then λ is divisible by	(r)	4
(D)	If two circles $(x - 1)^2 + (y - 3)^2 = r^2$ and $x^2 + y^2 - 8x + 2y + 8 = 0$ intersect in two distinct points and $2a < r < b$, then the value of b is	(s)	6
		(t)	8

Sol. (A) $\rightarrow$ (p, r, t); (B) $\rightarrow$ (p, r, t); (C) $\rightarrow$ (p, q, r, s); $D \rightarrow$ (t)

(A) Let $P(at^2, 2at)$ be any point on the parabola $y^2 = 4ax$ and $S(a, 0)$ be the focus, then the other end of focal chord through P will be $Q\left(\frac{a}{t^2}, -\frac{2a}{t}\right)$.

Then, length of focal chord $PQ = a\left(t + \frac{1}{t}\right)^2$

$\because \quad t + \frac{1}{t} \geq 2 \Rightarrow a\left(t + \frac{1}{t}\right)^2 \geq 4a$

or $\quad PQ \geq 32 \quad [\because 4a = 32]$

$\therefore \quad \lambda = 32$

(B) Equation of tangent to parabola $y^2 = 4x$ at $P(t^2, 2t)$ is

$$ty = x + t^2$$

Given, $\quad t^2 \in [1, 4]$

$\therefore$ Area of $\Delta APN = \frac{1}{2}(AN)(PN) = \frac{1}{2}(2t^2)(2t)$

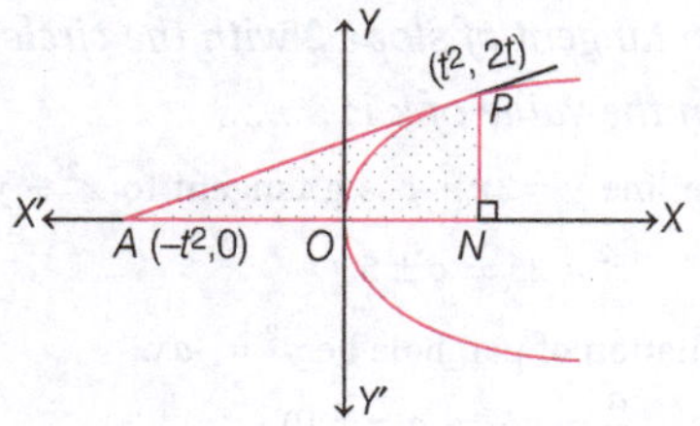

$\Rightarrow \quad \Delta = 2t^3 = 2(t^2)^{\frac{3}{2}}$

$\because \quad t^2 \in [1, 4]$

$\Rightarrow \Delta_{max}$ occurs when $t^2 = 4$

$\Rightarrow \quad \Delta_{max} = 2(4)^{\frac{3}{2}} = 16$ sq units

$\therefore \quad \lambda = 16$

(C) Given parabola is $y^2 = 4x$. Now, the ends of latusrectum are $P(1, 2)$ and $Q(1, -2)$ or $P(t^2, 2t)$ and $Q(t_1^2, 2t_1)$, where $t = 1$, $t_1 = -1$.

We know that the other end of normal is given by $t_2 = -t - \frac{2}{t}$

$\Rightarrow \quad A(t_2^2, 2t_2)$ and $A'(t_3^2, 2t_3)$,

where $t_2 = -3, t_3 = 3$

or $\quad A(9, -6)$ and $A'(9, 6)$

$\because \quad AA' = 12$ units

$\therefore \quad \lambda = 12$

(D) Given, $(x-1)^2 + (y-3)^2 = r^2 \quad$ ...(i)

and $x^2 + y^2 - 8x + 2y + 8 = 0$ or $(x-4)^2 + (y+1)^2 = 9 \quad$ ...(ii)

The centre and radius of circle (i) is (1, 3) and r.

The centre and radius of circle (ii) is (4, –1) and 3.

The distance between the centre,

$$d = \sqrt{(4-1)^2 + (-1-3)^2} = \sqrt{9+16} = 5$$

We know that condition for two distinct intersection points.

$$|r_1 - r_2| < d < r_1 + r_2 \Rightarrow |r-3| < 5 < r+3$$

If $r - 3 < 5 \Rightarrow r < 8$

and $5 < r + 3 \Rightarrow r > 2$

Thus, $2 < r < 8$

But it is given that $2a < r < b$

So, $b = 8$

Example 38 ■ *Match the following.*

	Column I	Column II
(A)	Area of a triangle formed by the tangents drawn from a point $(-2, 2)$ to the parabola $y^2 = 4(x + y)$ and their corresponding chord of contact is	(p) 8
(B)	Length of the latusrectum of the conic $25\{(x-2)^2 + (y-3)^2\} = (3x + 4y - 6)^2$ is	(q) $4\sqrt{3}$
(C)	If focal distance of a point o nthe parabola $y = x^2 - 4$ is 25/4 s and points are of the form $(\pm\sqrt{a}, b)$, then value of $a + b$ is	(r) 4
(D)	Length of side of an equilateral triangle inscribed in a parabola $y^2 - 2x - 2y - 3 = 0$ whose one angular point is vertex of the parabola, is	(s) $\frac{12}{5}$
		(t) $\frac{24}{5}$

Sol. (A) $\rightarrow$ (r), (B) $\rightarrow$ (t), (C) $\rightarrow$ (p), (D) $\rightarrow$ (q)

(A) Point of contact of tangent drawn from $(-2, 2)$ on $y^2 = 4(x + y)$ are $(0, 4)$ and $(0, 0)$

$\therefore \quad$ Area = 4

(B) The conic is a parabola having focus is $(0, 4)$ and $(0, 0)$ $3x + 4y - 6 = 0$

$\therefore$ Latusrectum $= 2\left(\frac{6 + 12 - 6}{5}\right) = \frac{24}{5}$

[perpendicular distance of focus from the directrix]

(C) $y + 4 = x^2 \Rightarrow x^2 = 4 \cdot \frac{1}{4}(y + 4)$

Focal distance $= \frac{25}{4}$

$\therefore$ Distance from directrix $\left(y = \frac{-17}{4}\right)$

$\Rightarrow$ Ordinate of points on the parabola whose focal distance is $\frac{25}{4} = \frac{-17}{4} + \frac{25}{4} = 2$

$\Rightarrow$ Points are $(\pm\sqrt{6}, 2)$.

$\therefore \quad a + b = 8$

(D) Length of side $= 8\sqrt{3}a = 8\sqrt{3}\frac{1}{2} = 4\sqrt{3}$

EXERCISE 1

JEE Main Pattern

Single Option Correct Type Questions

1. The equation of the parabola whose focus is at the point (0, 0) and the tangent at the vertex is $x - y + 1 = 0$ is

(a) $x^2 + y^2 - 2xy - 4x - 4y - 4 = 0$

(b) $x^2 + y^2 - 2xy + 4x - 4y - 4 = 0$

(c) $x^2 + y^2 + 2xy - 4x + 4y - 4 = 0$

(d) $x^2 + y^2 + 2xy - 4x - 4y + 4 = 0$

2. A water jet from a fountain reaches its maximum height of 4 m at a distance 0.5 m from the vertical passing through the point O of water outlet. The height of the jet above the horizontal OX at a distance of 0.75 m from the point O is

(a) 5 m (b) 6 m
(c) 3 m (d) 7 m

3. If the line $y - \sqrt{3}x + 3 = 0$ cuts the parabola $y^2 = x + 2$ at P and Q, then $AP \cdot AQ$ is equal to [where $A \equiv (\sqrt{3}, 0)$]

(a) $\frac{2(\sqrt{3}+2)}{3}$ (b) $\frac{4\sqrt{3}}{2}$

(c) $\frac{4(2-\sqrt{2})}{3}$ (d) $\frac{4(\sqrt{3}+2)}{3}$

4. If a line $y = 3x + 1$ cuts the parabola $x^2 - 4x - 4y + 20 = 0$ at A and B, then the tangent of the angle subtended by line segment AB at the origin is

(a) $\frac{8\sqrt{3}}{205}$ (b) $\frac{8\sqrt{3}}{209}$

(c) $\frac{8\sqrt{3}}{215}$ (d) None of these

5. The angle between the tangents to the curve $y = x^2 - 5x + 6$ at the points (2, 0) and (3, 0) is

(a) $\frac{\pi}{2}$ (b) $\frac{\pi}{3}$

(c) $\frac{\pi}{6}$ (d) $\frac{\pi}{4}$

6. Normals AO, AA_1 and AA_2 are drawn to the parabola $y^2 = 8x$ from the point $A(h, 0)$. If triangle OA_1A_2 is equilateral, then the possible value of h is

(a) 26 (b) 24
(c) 28 (d) None of these

7. If $2x + y + \lambda = 0$ is a normal to the parabola $y^2 = -8x$, then λ is

(a) 12 (b) -12
(c) 24 (d) -24

8. The largest value of a for which the circle $x^2 + y^2 = a^2$ falls totally in the interior of the parabola $y^2 = 4(x+4)$ is

(a) $4\sqrt{3}$ (b) 4

(c) $4\frac{\sqrt{6}}{7}$ (d) $2\sqrt{3}$

9. If two chords drawn from the point $A(4, 4)$ to the parabola $x^2 = 4y$ are bisected by the line $y = mx$, then the interval in which m lies is

(a) $(-2\sqrt{2}, 2\sqrt{2})$

(b) $(-\infty, -\sqrt{2}) \cup (\sqrt{2}, \infty)$

(c) $(-\infty, -2\sqrt{2} - 2) \cup (2\sqrt{2} - 2, \infty)$

(d) None of the above

10. The point of intersection of the tangents of the parabola $y^2 = 4x$ drawn at the endpoints of the chord $x + y = 2$ lies on

(a) $x - 2y = 0$ (b) $x + 2y = 0$
(c) $y - x = 0$ (d) $x + y = 0$

11. A common tangent is drawn to the circle $x^2 + y^2 = a^2$ and the parabola $y^2 = 4bx$. If the angle which this tangent makes with the axis of X is $\frac{\pi}{4}$, then the relationship between a and b is $(a, b > 0)$

(a) $b = \sqrt{2}a$ (b) $a = b\sqrt{2}$
(c) $c = 2a$ (d) $a = 2c$

12. The equation of parabola whose vertex and focus lie on the axis of X at distances a and a_1 from the origin respectively, is

(a) $y^2 = 4(a_1 - a)x$ (b) $y^2 = 4(a_1 - a)(x - a)$
(c) $y^2 = 4(a_1 - a)(x - a_1)$ (d) $y^2 = 4aa_1 x$

13. If parabolas $y^2 = ax$ and $25[(x-3)^2 + (y+2)^2] = (3x - 4y - 2)^2$ are equal, then the value of a is

(a) 3 (b) 6 (c) 7 (d) 9

14. $ABCD$ and $EFGC$ are squares and the curve $y = \lambda\sqrt{x}$ passes through the origin D and the points B and F. The ratio $\frac{FG}{BC}$ is

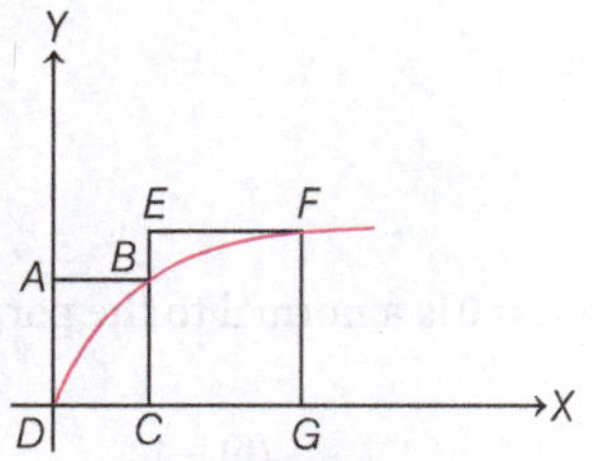

(a) $\frac{\sqrt{3}+1}{4}$ (b) $\frac{\sqrt{3}+1}{2}$
(c) $\frac{\sqrt{5}+1}{4}$ (d) $\frac{\sqrt{5}+1}{2}$

15. Let A and B be two points on a parabola $y^2 = x$ with vertex V such that VA is perpendicular to VB and θ is the angle between the chord VA and the axis of the parabola. Then, the value of $\frac{|VA|}{|VB|}$ is

(a) $\tan\theta$ (b) $\cot^2\theta$
(c) $\tan^3\theta$ (d) $\cot^3\theta$

16. The vertex of the parabola whose parametric equation is $x = t^2 - t + 1, y = t^2 + t + 1, t \in R$, is

(a) (1, 1) (b) (2, 2)
(c) (3, 3) (d) $\left(\frac{1}{2}, \frac{1}{2}\right)$

17. The circle $x^2 + y^2 + 2px = 0, p \in R$, touches the parabola $y^2 = 4x$ externally, then

(a) $p > 0$ (b) $p < 0$
(c) $p > 1$ (d) $p > 2$

18. If $a \neq 0$ and the line $2bx + 3cy + 4d = 0$ passes through the points of intersection of the parabolas $y^2 = 4ax$ and $x^2 = 4ay$, then

(a) $d^2 + (2b + 3c)^2 = 0$
(b) $d^2 + (3b + 2c)^2 = a^2$
(c) $d^2 + (2b - 3c)^2 = 0$
(d) $d^2 + (2b + 3c)^2 = a^2$

19. A parabola $y = ax^2 + bx + c$ crosses the X-axis at $(\alpha, 0)$ and $(\beta, 0)$ both to the right of the origin. A circle also passes through these two points. The length of a tangent from the origin to the circle is

(a) $\sqrt{\frac{bc}{a}}$ (b) ac^2
(c) $\frac{b}{a}$ (d) $\sqrt{\frac{c}{a}}$

20. Two mutually perpendicular tangent of the parabola $y^2 = 4ax$ meet the axis at P_1 and P_2. If S is the focus of the parabola, then $\frac{1}{SP_1} + \frac{1}{SP_2}$ is equal to

(a) $\frac{1}{4a}$ (b) $\frac{1}{a}$ (c) $\frac{2}{a}$ (d) $\frac{4}{a}$

21. If the normal to the parabola $y^2 = 4ax$ at P meets the curve again at Q and if PQ and the normal at Q make angles α and β respectively with the X-axis, then $\tan\alpha(\tan\alpha + \tan\beta)$ has the value equals to

(a) -2 (b) -1
(c) $-\frac{1}{2}$ (d) 0

22. If the normals to the parabola $y^2 = 4ax$ at three points P, Q and R meet at A and S is the focus, then $SP \cdot SQ \cdot SR$ is equal to

(a) $(SA)^2$ (b) $(SA)^3$
(c) $a\,(SA)^2$ (d) $a\,(SA)^3$

23. The length of the shortest normal chord of the parabola $y^2 = 4ax$ is

(a) $2a\sqrt{27}$ (b) $9a$
(c) $a\sqrt{54}$ (d) $18a$

24. The largest value of a for which the circle $x^2 + y^2 = a^2$ falls totally in the interior of the parabola $y^2 = 4(x + 4)$ is

(a) $4\sqrt{3}$ (b) 4
(c) $\frac{4\sqrt{6}}{7}$ (d) $2\sqrt{3}$

25. From a point $(\sin\theta, \cos\theta)$, if three normals can be drawn to the parabola $y^2 = 4ax$, then the value of a is

(a) $\left(\frac{1}{2}, 1\right)$ (b) $\left[-\frac{1}{2}, 0\right)$
(c) $\left[\frac{1}{2}, 1\right]$ (d) $\left(\frac{-1}{2}, 0\right) \cup \left(0, \frac{1}{2}\right)$

Numerical Value Type Questions

26. If the length of the latus rectum of the parabola $169\{(x-1)^2 + (y-3)^2\} = (5x - 12y + 17)^2$ is L, then the value of $\frac{13L}{4}$ is ....

27. The focal chord of $y^2 = 16x$ is tangent to $(x - 6)^2 + y^2 = 2$. Then, the possible value of the square of slope of this chord is ....

28. Two tangents are drawn from the point$(-2, -1)$ to the parabola $y^2 = 4x$. If θ is the angle between these tangents, then $\tan\theta$ is equal to ....

29. The equation of the line touching both the parabolas $y^2 = 4x$ and $x^2 = -32y$ is $ax + by + c = 0$. Then, the value of $a + b + c$ is ...

30. If the line $x + y = 6$ is a normal to the parabola $y^2 = 8x$ at the point (a, b), then the value of $a + b$ is ......

31. The locus of the mid-points of the portion of the normal to the parabola $y^2 = 16x$ intercepted between the curve and the axis is another parabola whose latusrectum is...

32. If on a given base $BC[B(0, 0)$ and $C(2, 0)]$, a triangle is described such that the sum of the tangents of the base angles is 4, then equation of the locus of the opposite vertex A is a parabola whose directrx is $y = k$. The value of $8k - 9$ is ......

33. If the length of focal chord to the parabola $y^2 = 12x$ drawn from the point (3, 6) on it is L, then the value of $L/3$ is ......

34. From the point $(-1, 2)$, tangent lines are drawn to the parabola$y^2 = 4x$. If the area of the triangle formed by the chord of contact and the tangents is A, then the value of $\frac{A}{\sqrt{2}}$ is ......

35. If the circle $(x - 6)^2 + y^2 = r^2$ and the parabola $y^2 = 4x$ have maximum number of common chords, then the least integral value of r is ....

36. The slope of the line which belong to the family of lines $(1+\lambda)x+(\lambda-1)y+2(1-\lambda)=0$ and makes shortest intercept on $x^2 = 4y - 4$, is ....

Previous Year Questions

37. Let PQ be a chord of the parabola $y^2 = 12x$ and the mid-point of PQ be at (4, 1).

Then, which of the following point lies on the line passing through the points P and Q?

[Single Correct Type, 2024 Main]

(a) $\left(\frac{3}{2}, -16\right)$ (b) $\left(\frac{1}{2}, -20\right)$

(c) $(3, -3)$ (d) $(2, -9)$

38. Let P be a parabola with vertex (2, 3) and directrix $2x + y = 6$. Let an ellipse $E: \frac{x^2}{a^2} + \frac{y^2}{b^2} = 1, a > b$, of eccentricity, $\frac{1}{\sqrt{2}}$ pass through the focus of the parabola P. Then, the square of the length of the latusrectum of E, is **[Single Correct Type, 2024 Main]**

(a) $\frac{385}{8}$ (b) $\frac{512}{25}$

(c) $\frac{656}{25}$ (d) $\frac{347}{8}$

39. If the shortest distance of the parabola $y^2 = 4x$ from the centre of the circle $x^2 + y^2 - 4x - 16y + 64 = 0$ is d, then d^2 is equal to **[Single Correct Type, 2024 Main]**

(a) 24 (b) 16

(c) 20 (d) 36

40. Consider the circle $C: x^2 + y^2 = 4$ and the parabola $P: y^2 = 8x$. If the set of all value of α, for which three chords of the circle C on three distinct lines passing through the point $(\alpha, 0)$ are bisected by the parabola P is the interval (p, q), then $(2q - p)^2$ is equal to ....

[Numerical Value Type, 2024 Main]

41. Let a line perpendicular to the line $2x - y = 10$ touch the parabola $y^2 = 4(x - 9)$ at the point P. The distance of the point P from the centre of the circle $x^2 + y^2 - 14x - 8y + 56 = 0$ is ......

[Numerical Value Type, 2024 Main]

42. Suppose AB be a focal chord of the parabola $y^2 = 12x$ of length l and slople $m < \sqrt{3}$. If the distance of the chord AB from the origin is d, then ld^2 is equal to ....

[Numerical Value Type, 2024 Main]

43. Let the length of the focal chord PQ of the parabola $y^2 = 12x$ be 15 units. If the distance of PQ from the origin is p, then $10p^2$ is equal to ......

[Numerical Value Type, 2024 Main]

44. Let $P(\alpha, \beta)$ be a point on the parabola $y^2 = 4x$. If P also lies on the chord of the parabola $x^2 = 8y$, whose mid-point is $\left(1, \frac{5}{4}\right)$, then $(\alpha - 28)(\beta - 8)$ is equal to

[Numerical Value Type, 2024 Main]

45. Let PQ be a focal chord of the parabola $y^2 = 36x$ of length 100, making an acute angle with the positive X-axis. Let the ordinate of P be positive and M be the point on the line segment PQ such that $PM : MQ = 3:1$. Then, which of the following points does not lie on the line passing through M and perpendicular to the line PQ? **[Single Correct Type, 2023 Main]**

(a) (3, 33) (b) (6, 29)

(c) (− 3, 43) (d) (− 6, 45)

46. Let R be the focus of the parabola $y^2 = 20x$ and the line $y = mx + c$ intersect the parabola at two points P and Q. Let the point $G(10, 10)$ be the centroid of the ΔPQR. If $c - m = 6$, then (PQ) is **[Single Correct Type, 2023 Main]**

(a) 325 (b) 317 (c) 296 (d) 346

47. The parabolas : $ax^2 + 2bx + cy = 0$ and $dx^2 + 2ex + fy = 0$ intersect on the line $y = 1$. If a, b, c, d, e, f are positive real numbers and a, b, c are in GP, then **[Single Correct Type, 2023 Main]**

(a) d, e and f are in AP (b) d, e and f are in GP

(c) $\frac{d}{a}, \frac{e}{b}$ and $\frac{f}{c}$ are in GP (d) $\frac{d}{a}, \frac{e}{b}$ and $\frac{f}{c}$ are in AP

48. If $P(h, k)$ be a point on the parabola $x = 4y^2$, which is nearest to the point $Q(0, 33)$, then the distance of P from the directrix of the parabola $y^2 = 4(x + y)$ is equal to **[Single Correct Type, 2023 Main]**

(a) 2 (b) 8

(c) 4 (d) 6

49. The equations of two sides of a variable triangle are $x = 0$ and $y = 3$ and its third side is a tangent to the parabola $y^2 = 6x$. The locus of its circumcentre is **[Single Correct Type, 2023 Main]**

(a) $4y^2 - 18y - 3x + 18 = 0$ (b) $4y^2 - 18y + 3x + 18 = 0$

(c) $4y^2 - 18y - 3x - 18 = 0$ (d) $4y^2 + 18y + 3x + 18 = 0$

50. The distance of the point $(6, -2\sqrt{2})$ from the common tangent $y = mx + c, m > 0$, of the curves $x = 2y^2$ and $x = 1 + y^2$ is **[Single Correct Type, 2023 Main]**

(a) 5 (b) $\frac{1}{3}$

(c) $\frac{14}{3}$ (d) $5\sqrt{3}$

51. The equations of the sides AB and AC of a triangle ABC are $(\lambda + 1)x + \lambda y = 4$ and $\lambda x + (1 - \lambda)y + \lambda = 0$, respectively. Its vertex A is on the Y-axis and its orthocentre is $(1, 2)$. The length of the tangent from the point C to the part of the parabola $y^2 = 6x$ in the first quadrant is **[Single Correct Type, 2023 Main]**

(a) $2\sqrt{2}$ (b) 2

(c) $\sqrt{6}$ (d) 4

52. Let a tangent to the curve $y^2 = 24x$ meet the curve $xy = 2$ at the points A and B. Then, the mid-points of such line segment AB lies on a parabola with the **[Single Correct Type, 2023 Main]**

(a) length of latusrectum $= 2$

(b) directrix $4x = -3$

(c) length of latusrectum $= \frac{3}{2}$

(d) directrix $4x = 3$

53. Let the tangent to the parabola $y^2 = 12x$ at the point $(3, \alpha)$ be perpendicular to the line $2x + 2y = 3$. Then, the square of distance of the point $(6, -4)$ from the normal to the hyperbola $\alpha^2 x^2 - 9y^2 = 9\alpha^2$ at its point $(\alpha - 1, \alpha + 2)$ is equal to .... **[Numerical Value Type, 2023 Main]**

54. Let a common tangent to the curves $y^2 = 4x$ and $(x - 4)^2 + y^2 = 16$ touch the curves at the points P and Q. Then, $(PQ)^2$ is equal to .... . **[Numerical Value Type, 2023 Main]**

55. The ordinates of the points P and Q on the parabola with focus $(3, 0)$ and directrix $x = -3$ are in the ratio $3 : 1$. If $R(\alpha, \beta)$ is the point of intersection of the tangents to the parabola at P and Q, then $\left(\frac{\beta}{\alpha}\right)^2$ is equal to .... **[Numerical Value Type, 2023 Main]**

56. Let the tangent to the curve $x^2 + 2x - 4y + 9 = 0$ at the point $P(1, 3)$ on it meet the Y-axis at A. Let the line passing through P and parallel to the line $x - 3y = 6$ meet the parabola $y^2 = 4x$ at B. If B lies on the line $2x - 3y = 8$, then $(AB)^2$ is equal to .... **[Numerical Value Type, 2023 Main]**

57. If the x-intercept of a focal chord of the parabola, $y^2 = 8x + 4y + 4$ is 3, then the length of this chord is equal to .... **[Numerical Value Type, 2023 Main]**

58. Let S be the set of all $a \in N$ such that the area of the triangle formed by the tangent at the point $P(b, c)$, $b, c \in N$, on the parabola $y^2 = 2ax$ and the lines $x = b$, $y = 0$ is 16 unit^2, then $\sum_{a \in S} a$ is equal to .... **[Numerical Value Type, 2023 Main]**

59. A triangle is formed by the tangents at the point $(2, 2)$ on the curves $y^2 = 2x$ and $x^2 + y^2 = 4x$ and the line $x + y + 2 = 0$. If r is the radius of its circumcircle, then r^2 is equal to .... **[Numerical Value Type, 2023 Main]**

60. If the tangents drawn at the points P and Q on the parabola $y^2 = 2x - 3$ intersect at the point $R(0, 1)$, then the orthocentre of the ΔPQR is **[Single Correct Type, 2022 Main]**

(a) $(0, 1)$ (b) $(2, -1)$

(c) $(6, 3)$ (d) $(2, 1)$

61. If the length of the latusrectum of a parabola, whose focus is (a, a) and the tangent at its vertex is $x + y = a$, is 16, then $|a|$ is equal to **[Single Correct Type, 2022 Main]**

(a) $2\sqrt{2}$ (b) $2\sqrt{3}$ (c) $4\sqrt{2}$ (d) 4

62. Let $P(a, b)$ be a point on the parabola $y^2 = 8x$ such that the tangent at P passes through the centre of the circle $x^2 + y^2 - 10x - 14y + 65 = 0$. Let A be the product of all possible values of a and B be the product of all possible values of b. Then, the value of $A + B$ is equal to **[Single Correct Type, 2022 Main]**

(a) 0 (b) 25 (c) 40 (d) 65

63. The equation of a common tangent to the parabolas $y = x^2$ and $y = -(x-2)^2$ is

[Single Correct Type, 2022 Main Main]

(a) $y = 4(x-2)$ (b) $y = 4(x-1)$
(c) $y = 4(x+1)$ (d) $y = 4(x+2)$

64. The tangents at the points $A(1, 3)$ and $B(1, -1)$ on the parabola $y^2 - 2x - 2y = 1$ meet at the point P. Then, the area (in sq. units) of the ΔPAB is

[Single Correct Type, 2022 Main]

(a) 4 (b) 6
(c) 7 (d) 8

65. Let $P : y^2 = 4ax, a > 0$ be a parabola with focus S. Let the tangents to the parabola P make an angle of $\pi/4$ with the line $y = 3x + 5$ touch the parabola P at A and B. Then, the value of a for which A, B and S are collinear is

[Single Correct Type, 2022 Main]

(a) 8 only (b) 2 only
(c) 1/4 only (d) any $a > 0$

66. If the equation of the parabola, whose vertex is at (5, 4) and the directrix is $3x + y - 29 = 0$, is $x^2 + ay^2 + bxy + cx + dy + e = 0$, then $a + b + c + d + e$ is equal to **[Single Correct Type, 2022 Main]**

(a) 575 (b) −575
(c) 576 (d) −576

67. Let the normal at the point P on the parabola $y^2 = 6x$ pass through the point (5, −8). If the tangent at P to the parabola intersects its directrix at the point Q, then the ordinate of the point Q is **[Single Correct Type, 2022 Main]**

(a) −3 (b) $-\frac{9}{4}$
(c) $-\frac{5}{2}$ (d) −2

68. If the line $y = 4 + kx, k > 0$, is the tangent to the parabola $y = x - x^2$ at the point P and V is the vertex of the parabola, then the slope of the line through P and V is

[Single Correct Type, 2022 Main]

(a) $\frac{3}{2}$ (b) $\frac{26}{9}$
(c) $\frac{5}{2}$ (d) $\frac{23}{6}$

69. Let $x = 2t, y = \frac{t^2}{3}$ be a conic. Let S be the focus and B be the point on the axis of the conic such that $SA \perp BA$, where A is any point on the conic. If k is the ordinate of the centroid of ΔSAB, then $\lim_{t \to 1} k$ is equal to

[Single Correct Type, 2022 Main]

(a) $\frac{17}{18}$ (b) $\frac{19}{18}$
(c) $\frac{11}{18}$ (d) $\frac{13}{18}$

70. If $y = m_1 x + c_1$ and $y = m_2 x + c_2, m_1 \neq m_2$ are two common tangents of circle $x^2 + y^2 = 2$ and parabola $y^2 = x$, then the value of $8|m_1 m_2|$ is equal to

[Single Correct Type, 2022 Main]

(a) $3 + 4\sqrt{2}$ (b) $-5 + 6\sqrt{2}$
(c) $-4 + 3\sqrt{2}$ (d) $7 + 6\sqrt{2}$

71. A particle is moving in the xy-plane along a curve C passing through the point (3, 3). The tangent to the curve C at the point P meets the X-axis at Q. If the Y-axis bisects the segment PQ, then C is a parabola with

[Single Correct Type, 2022 Main]

(a) length of latusrectum 3
(b) length of latusrectum 6
(c) focus $\left(\frac{4}{3}, 0\right)$
(d) focus $\left(0, \frac{3}{4}\right)$

72. Let $x^2 + y^2 + Ax + By + C = 0$ be a circle passing through (0, 6) and touching the parabola $y = x^2$ at (2, 4). Then, $A + C$ is equal to **[Single Correct Type, 2022 Main]**

(a) 16 (b) 88/5 (c) 72 (d) −8

73. Let the function $f(x) = 2x^2 - \log_e x, x > 0$, be decreasing in $(0, a)$ and increasing in $(a, 4)$. A tangent to the parabola $y^2 = 4ax$ at a point p on it passes through the point $(8a, 8a - 1)$ but does not pass through the point $\left(-\frac{1}{a}, 0\right)$. If the equation of the normal at P is $\frac{x}{\alpha} + \frac{y}{\beta} = 1$, then $\alpha + \beta$ is equal to ....

[Numerical Value Type, 2022 Main]

74. A circle of radius 2 units passes through the vertex and the focus of the parabola $y^2 = 2x$ and touches the parabola $y = \left(x - \frac{1}{4}\right)^2 + \alpha$, where $\alpha > 0$. Then, $(4\alpha - 8)^2$ is equal to .... **[Numerical Value Type, 2022 Main]**

75. Let P_1 be a parabola with vertex (3, 2) and focus (4, 4) and P_2 be its mirror image with respect to the line $x + 2y = 6$. Then, the directrix of P_2 is $x + 2y =$ ....

[Numerical Value Type, 2022 Main]

76. Consider the parabola with vertex $\left(\frac{1}{2}, \frac{3}{4}\right)$ and the directrix $y = 1/2$. Let P be the point where the parabola meets the line $x = -\frac{1}{2}$. If the normal to the parabola at P intersects the parabola again at the point Q, then $(PQ)^2$ is equal to **[Single Correct Type, 2021 Main]**

(a) 75/8 (b) 125/16
(c) 25/2 (d) 15/2

77. The length of the latusrectum of a parabola, whose vertex and focus are on the positive X-axis at a distance R and $(S > R)$ respectively from the origin, is **[Single Correct Type, 2021 Main]**

(a) $4(S + R)$ (b) $2(S - R)$
(c) $4(S - R)$ (d) $2(S + R)$

78. A tangent and a normal are drawn at the point $P(2, -4)$ on the parabola $y^2 = 8x$, which meet the directrix of the parabola at the points A and B respectively. If $Q(a, b)$ is a point such that $AQBP$ is a square, then $2a + b$ is equal to **[Single Correct Type, 2021 Main]**

(a) -16 (b) -18
(c) -12 (d) -20

79. If a line along a chord of the circle $4x^2 + 4y^2 + 120x + 675 = 0$, passes through the point $(-30, 0)$ and is tangent to the parabola $y^2 = 30x$, then the length of this chord is **[Single Correct Type, 2021 Main]**

(a) 5 (b) 7
(c) $5\sqrt{3}$ (d) $3\sqrt{5}$

80. Let a parabola P be such that its vertex and focus lie on the positive X-axis at a distance 2 and 4 units from the origin, respectively. If tangents are drawn from $O(0, 0)$ to the parabola P which meet P at S and R, then the area (in sq. units) of ΔSOR is equal to **[Single Correct Type, 2021 Main]**

(a) $16\sqrt{2}$ (b) 16
(c) 32 (d) $8\sqrt{2}$

81. Let P be a variable point on the parabola $y = 4x^2 + 1$. Then, the locus of the mid-point of the point P and the foot of the perpendicular drawn from the point P to the line $y = x$ is **[Single Correct Type, 2021 Main]**

(a) $(3x - y)^2 + (x - 3y) + 2 = 0$
(b) $2(3x - y)^2 + (x - 3y) + 2 = 0$
(c) $(3x - y)^2 + 2(x - 3y) + 2 = 0$
(d) $2(x - 3y)^2 + (3x - y) + 2 = 0$

82. Let the tangent to the parabola $S : y^2 = 2x$ at the point $P(2, 2)$ meet the X-axis at Q and normal at it meet the parabola S at the point R. Then, the area (in sq units) of ΔPQR is equal to **[Single Correct Type, 2021 Main]**

(a) 25/2 (b) 35/2
(c) 15/2 (d) 25

83. Let C be the locus of the mirror image of a point on the parabola $y^2 = 4x$ with respect to the line $y = x$. Then, the equation of tangent to C at $P(2, 1)$ is **[Single Correct Type, 2021 Main]**

(a) $x - y = 1$
(b) $2x + y = 5$
(c) $x + 3y = 5$
(d) $x + 2y = 5$

84. If the three normals drawn to the parabola, $y^2 = 2x$ pass through the point $(a, 0)$, $a \neq 0$, then a must be greater than **[Single Correct Type, 2021 Main]**

(a) $\frac{1}{2}$ (b) $-\frac{1}{2}$
(c) -1 (d) 1

85. A tangent is drawn to the parabola $y^2 = 6x$, which is perpendicular to the line $2x + y = 1$. Which of the following points does not lie on it? **[Single Correct Type, 2021 Main]**

(a) $(-6, 0)$ (b) $(4, 5)$
(c) $(5, 4)$ (d) $(0, 3)$

86. If the curve $y = ax^2 + bx + c$, $x \in R$, passes through the point (1,2) and the tangent line to this curve at origin is $y = x$, then the possible values of a, b, c are **[Single Correct Type, 2021 Main]**

(a) $a = \frac{1}{2}, b = \frac{1}{2}, c = 1$ (b) $a = 1, b = 0, c = 1$
(c) $a = 1, b = 1, c = 0$ (d) $a = -1, b = 1, c = 1$

87. If P is a point on the parabola $y = x^2 + 4$ which is closest to the straight line $y = 4x - 1$, then the coordinates of P are **[Single Correct Type, 2021 Main]**

(a) $(3, 13)$ (b) $(1, 5)$
(c) $(-2, 8)$ (d) $(2, 8)$

88. The locus of the mid-point of the line segment joining the focus of the parabola $y^2 = 4ax$ to a moving point of the parabola, is another parabola whose directrix is **[Single Correct Type, 2021 Main]**

(a) $x = a$ (b) $x = -\frac{a}{2}$
(c) $x = 0$ (d) $x = \frac{a}{2}$

89. The equation of a circle is $\text{Re}(z^2) + 2[\text{Im}(z)]^2 + 2\,\text{Re}(z) = 0$, where $z = x + iy$. A line which passes through the center of the given circle and the vertex of the parabola, $x^2 - 6x - y + 13 = 0$, has y-intercept equal to .... **[Numerical Value Type, 2021 Main]**

90. If the point on the curve $y^2 = 6x$, nearest to the point $(3, 3/2)$ is (α, β), then $2(\alpha + \beta)$ is equal to ...... **[Numerical Value Type, 2021 Main]**

91. Let $y = mx + c, m > 0$ be the focal chord of $y^2 = -64x$, which is tangent to $(x+10)^2 + y^2 = 4$. Then, the value of $4\sqrt{2}(m+c)$ is equal to ....

[Numerical Value Type, 2021 Main]

92. A line is a common tangent to the circle $(x-3)^2 + y^2 = 9$ and the parabola $y^2 = 4x$. If the two points of contact (a, b) and (c, d) are distinct and lie in the first quadrant, then $2(a+c)$ is equal to ....

[Numerical Value Type, 2021 Main]

93. The centre of the circle passing through the point (0, 1) and touching the parabola $y = x^2$ at the point (2, 4) is

[Single Correct Type, 2020 Main]

(a) $\left(\frac{-53}{10}, \frac{16}{5}\right)$

(b) $\left(\frac{6}{5}, \frac{53}{10}\right)$

(c) $\left(\frac{3}{10}, \frac{16}{5}\right)$

(d) $\left(-\frac{16}{5}, \frac{53}{10}\right)$

94. If the common tangent of the parabolas, $y^2 = 4x$ and $x^2 = 4y$ also touches the circle, $x^2 + y^2 = c^2$, then c is equal to

[Single Correct Type, 2020 Main]

(a) $\frac{1}{\sqrt{2}}$ (b) $\frac{1}{4}$

(c) $\frac{1}{2}$ (d) $\frac{1}{2\sqrt{2}}$

95. Let the latus rectum of the parabola $y^2 = 4x$ be the common chord to the circles C_1 and C_2 each of them having radius $2\sqrt{5}$. Then, the distance between the centres of the circles C_1 and C_2 is

[Single Correct Type, 2020 Main]

(a) 8 (b) $4\sqrt{5}$

(c) $8\sqrt{5}$ (d) 12

96. Let P be a point on the parabola, $y^2 = 12x$ and N be the foot of the perpendicular drawn from P on the axis of the parabola. A line is now drawn through the mid-point M and PN, parallel to its axis which meets the parabola at Q. If the y-intercept of the line NQ is 4./3, then

[Single Correct Type, 2020 Main]

(a) $PN = 4$

(b) $MQ = \frac{1}{3}$

(c) $MQ = \frac{1}{4}$

(d) $PN = 3$

97. The area (in sq. units) of an equilateral triangle inscribed in the parabola $y^2 = 8x$, with one of its vertices on the vertex of this parabola, is

[Single Correct Type, 2020 Main]

(a) $64\sqrt{3}$ (b) $256\sqrt{3}$

(c) $192\sqrt{3}$ (d) $128\sqrt{3}$

98. The locus of a point which divides the line segment joining the point (0, – 1) and a point on the parabola, $x^2 = 4y$, internally in the ratio 1 : 2, is

[Single Correct Type, 2020 Main]

(a) $4x^2 - 3y = 2$ (b) $x^2 - 3y = 2$

(c) $9x^2 - 12y = 8$ (d) $9x^2 - 3y = 2$

99. If $y = mx + 4$ is a tangent to both the parabolas, $y^2 = 4x$ and $x^2 = 2by$, then b is equal to

[Single Correct Type, 2020 Main]

(a) –32 (b) –128

(c) –64 (d) 128

EXERCISE 2

JEE Advanced Pattern

Single Option Correct Type Questions

1. If two different tangents of $y^2 = 4x$ are the normals to $x^2 = 4$ by, then

(a) $|b| < \frac{1}{2\sqrt{2}}$ (b) $|b| < \frac{1}{\sqrt{2}}$

(c) $|b| > \frac{1}{2\sqrt{2}}$ (d) $|b| > \frac{1}{\sqrt{2}}$

2. The shortest distance between the parabolas $2y^2 = 2x - 1$ and $2x^2 = 2y - 1$ is

(a) $\frac{1}{2\sqrt{2}}$ (b) $\frac{1}{2}$

(c) $2\sqrt{2}$ (d) 4

3. Normals at two points (x_1, y_1) and (x_2, y_2) of the parabola $y^2 = 4x$ meet again on the parabola, where $x_1 + x_2 = 4$, then $|y_1 + y_2|$ is equal to

(a) $\sqrt{2}$ (b) $2\sqrt{2}$

(c) $4\sqrt{2}$ (d) $8\sqrt{2}$

4. A line is drawn from $A(-2, 0)$ to intersect the curve $y^2 = 4x$ at P and Q in the first quadrant such that $\frac{1}{AP} + \frac{1}{AQ} < \frac{1}{4}$. Then, the slope of the line is always

(a) $< \frac{1}{\sqrt{3}}$ (b) $> \frac{1}{\sqrt{3}}$

(c) $> \sqrt{2}$ (d) $> \sqrt{3}$

5. An equilateral triangle SAB is inscribed in the parabola $y^2 = 4ax$ having its focus at S. If chord AB lies towards the left of S, then the length of side this triangle is

(a) $a(2 - \sqrt{3})$ (b) $2a(2 - \sqrt{3})$

(c) $4a(2 - \sqrt{3})$ (d) $8a(2 - \sqrt{3})$

6. Let C be a circle with centre $(0, 1)$ and radius unity. P is the parabola $y = ax^2$. The set of values of a for which they meet at a point other than origin is

(a) $(0, \infty)$ (b) $\left(0, \frac{1}{2}\right)$

(c) $\left(\frac{1}{4}, \frac{1}{2}\right)$ (d) $\left(\frac{1}{2}, \infty\right)$

7. Let S be the focus of $y^2 = 4x$ and a point P be moving on the curve such that its abscissa is increasing at the rate of 4 units/s. Then the rate of increase of the projection of SP on $x + y = 1$ when p is at $(4, 4)$ is

(a) $-\sqrt{2}$ (b) $-\frac{3}{\sqrt{2}}$

(c) -1 (d) $\sqrt{2}$

8. If P is a point on the parabola $y^2 = 3(2x - 3)$ and M is the foot of perpendicular drawn from P on the directrix of the parabola, then the length of each side of the equilateral triangle SMP, where S is the focus of the parabola, is

(a) 2 (b) 4

(c) 6 (d) 8

9. Consider the parabola $y^2 = 4x$. Let $A \equiv (4, -4)$ and $B \equiv (9, 6)$ be two fixed points on the parabola. Let C be a moving point on the parabola between A and B such that the area of the triangle ABC is maximum. Then the coordinates of C are

(a) $\left(\frac{1}{4}, 1\right)$ (b) $(3, -2\sqrt{3})$

(c) $(3, 2\sqrt{3})$ (d) $(4, 4)$

10. Through the vertex O of the parabola $y^2 = 4ax$, two chords OP and OQ are drawn and the circles on OP and OQ as diameters intersect at R. If θ_1, θ_2 and ϕ are the angles made with the axis by the tangents at P and Q on the parabola and by OR, then the value of $\cot\theta_1 + \cot\theta_2$ is

(a) $-2\tan\phi$ (b) $2\tan\phi$

(c) 0 (d) $2\cot\phi$

11. AB is a double ordinate of the parabola $y^2 = 4ax$. Tangents drawn to the parabola at A and B meet the Y-axis at A_1 and B_1 respectively. If the area of trapezium AA_1B_1B is equal to $24a^2$, then the angle subtended by A_1B_1 at the focus of the parabola is equal to

(a) $\tan^{-1}2$ (b) $\tan^{-1}3$

(c) $2\tan^{-1}2$ (d) $2\tan^{-1}3$

12. If the 4th term in the expansion of $\left(px + \frac{1}{x}\right)^n$, $n \in N$ is $\frac{5}{2}$ and three normals to the parabola $y^2 = x$ are drawn through a point $(q, 0)$, then
(a) $q = p$ (b) $q > p$
(c) $q < p$ (d) $pq = 1$

13. The set of points on the axis of the parabola $y^2 - 4x - 2y + 5 = 0$ from which all the three normals to the parabola are real is
(a) $(k, 0)$; $k > 1$ (b) $(k, 1)$; $k > 3$
(c) $(k, 2)$; $k > 6$ (d) $(k, 3)$; $k > 8$

14. The triangle formed by the tangent to the parabola $y = x^2$ at the point whose abscissa is x_0 ($x_0 \in [1, 2]$), the Y-axis and the straight line $y = x_0^2$ has the greatest area if x_0 is equal to
(a) 0 (b) 1
(c) 2 (d) 3

15. The set of points (x, y) whose distance from the line $y = 2x + 2$ is the same as the distance from (2, 0) is a parabola. This parabola is congruent to the parabola in standard from $y = kx^2$ for some k which is equal to
(a) $\frac{4}{\sqrt{5}}$ (b) $\frac{12}{\sqrt{5}}$
(c) $\frac{\sqrt{5}}{4}$ (d) $\frac{\sqrt{5}}{12}$

16. A circle is described whose centre is the vertex and whose diameter is three-quarters of the latusrectum of the parabola $y^2 = 4ax$. If PQ is the common chord of the circle and the parabola and L_1L_2 is the latus reactum, then the area of trapezium PL_1L_2Q
(a) $3\sqrt{2}a^2$ (b) $2\sqrt{2}a^2$
(c) $4a^2$ (d) $\left(\frac{2+\sqrt{2}}{2}\right)a^2$

17. From the point (15, 12), three normals are drawn to the parabola $y^2 = 4ax$, then centroid of triangle formed by three co-normal points is
(a) $\left(\frac{16}{3}, 0\right)$ (b) (4, 0)
(c) $\left(\frac{26}{3}, 0\right)$ (d) (6, 0)

18. If r_1 and r_2 be the lengths of the chords of the parabola $y^2 = 4ax$, which are drawn at right angles to one another from the vertex and if $r_1^{4/3} \cdot r_2^{4/3} = ka^2(r_1^{2/3} + r_2^{2/3})$, then k is equal to
(a) 16 (b) 17
(c) 18 (d) 19

19. A ray of light travels along a line $y = 4$ and strikes the surface of a curve $y^2 = 4(x + y)$, then equation of the line along reflected ray travels is
(a) $x = 0$ (b) $x = 2$
(c) $x + y = 4$ (d) $2x + y = 4$

20. If P be a point on the parabola $y^2 = 3(2x - 3)$ and M is the foot of perpendicular drawn from P on the directix of the parabola, then length of each side of an equilateral ΔSMP, where S is focus of the parabola, is
(a) 2 (b) 4 (c) 6 (d) 8

More than One Correct Option Type Questions

21. Equation of the common tangent to the circle $x^2 + y^2 = 50$ and the parabola $y^2 = 40x$ can be
(a) $x + y - 10 = 0$ (b) $x - y + 10 = 0$
(c) $x + y + 10 = 0$ (d) $x - y - 10 = 0$

22. Let PQ be a chord of the parabola $y^2 = 4x$. A circle drawn with PQ as a diameter passes through the vertex V of the parabola. If area of $\Delta PVQ = 20$ unit^2, then the coordinates of P are
(a) (16,8) (b) (16, – 8)
(c) (– 16, 8) (d) (– 16, – 8)

23. Let $y^2 = 4ax$ be a parabola and $x^2 + y^2 + 2bx = 0$ be a circle. If parabola and circle touch each other externally, then
(a) $a > 0, b < 0$ (b) $a > 0, b > 0$
(c) $a < 0, b > 0$ (d) $a < 0, b < 0$

24. Tangent is drawn at any point (x_1, y_1) other than the vertex on the parabola $y^2 = 4ax$. If tangents are drawn from any point on this tangent to the circle $x^2 + y^2 = a^2$ such that all the chords of chords of contact pass through a fixed point (x_2, y_2), then
(a) x_1, a, x_2 are in GP (b) $\frac{y_1}{2}, a, y_2$ are in GP
(c) $-4, \frac{y_1}{y_2}, \frac{x_1}{x_2}$ are in GP (d) $x_1x_2 + y_1y_2 = a^2$

25. The locus of the foot of the perpendicular from the focus on a tangent to the parabola $y^2 = 4ax$ is
(a) the directrix (b) the tangent at the vertex
(c) $x = a$ (d) $x = 0$

26. If from the vertex of a parabola $y^2 = 4ax$ a pair of chords be drawn at right angles to one another and with these chords as adjacent sides a rectangle be made, then the locus of the further angle of the rectangle is
(a) an equal parabola
(b) a parabola with focus at $(9a, 0)$
(c) a parabola with directrix as $x - 7a = 0$
(d) not a parabola

27. If two chords drawn from the point (4, 4) to the parabola $x^2 = 4y$ are divided by the line $y = mx$ in the ratio 1 : 2, then

(a) $m \in (-\infty, -\sqrt{3})$ (b) $m \in (-\infty, -\sqrt{3} - 1)$
(c) $m \in (\sqrt{3}, \infty)$ (d) $m \in (\sqrt{3} - 1, \infty)$

28. Through a point $P(-2, 0)$, tangents PQ and PR are drawn to the parabola $y^2 = 8x$. Two circles each passing through the focus of the parabola and one touching at Q and the other at R are drawn. Which of the following point (s) with respect to the triangle PQR lie (s) on the common chord of the two circles?

(a) centroid (b) orthocentre
(c) incentre (d) circumcentre

29. The set of points on the axis of the parabola $(y-2)^2 = 4\left(x - \frac{1}{2}\right)$ from which three distinct normals can be drawn to the parabola are

(a) (3, 2) (b) (1, 2) (c) (4, 2) (d) (5, 2)

30. Three normals are drawn from the point (14, 7) to the curve $y^2 - 16x - 8y = 0$. Then, the coordinates of the feet of the normals are

(a) (3, – 4) (b) (8, 16) (c) (0, 0) (d) (2, 2)

31. The equation $2y^2 + 3y - 4x - 3 = 0$ represents a parabola for which

(a) length of latus rectum is 4.
(b) equation of the axis is $4y + 3 = 0$.
(c) equation of directrix is $2x + 1 = 0$.
(d) equation of tangent at vertex is $x = -\frac{33}{32}$.

32. Let S be the set of all possible values of parameter a for which the points of intersection of the parabolas $y^2 = 3ax$ and $y = \frac{1}{2}(x^2 + ax + 5)$ are concyclic. Then, S contains the interval(s)

(a) $(-\infty, -2)$ (b) $(-2, 0)$ (c) $(0, 2)$ (d) $(2, \infty)$

33. The equation of the straight line(s) that touches both $x^2 + y^2 = 2a^2$ and $y^2 = 8ax$ is/are

(a) $y = x + 2a$ (b) $y = -x - 2a$
(c) $y = -x + 2a$ (d) $y = x - 2a$

Passage Based Questions

Passage I

(Q. Nos. 34 and 35)

- Consider a parabola P touches coordinate axes at (4, 0) and (0, 3).

34. If focus of parabola is $P(a, b)$, then the value of $b - a$ is

(a) $\frac{1}{25}$ (b) $\frac{3}{25}$ (c) $\frac{4}{25}$ (d) $\frac{12}{25}$

35. Length of latusrectum of parabola P is

(a) $\frac{72}{125}$ (b) $\frac{144}{125}$ (c) $\frac{288}{125}$ (d) $\frac{576}{125}$

Passage II

(Q. Nos. 36 and 37)

- Let C be the locus of the circumcentre of a variable triangle having sides Y-axis, $y = 2$ and $ax + by = 1$, where (a, b) lies on the parabola $y^2 = 4\lambda x$.

36. For $\lambda = 2$, the product of coordinates of the vertex of the curve C is

(a) – 8 (b) – 6
(c) 6 (d) 8

37. For $\lambda = \frac{1}{32}$, the length of smallest focal chord of the curve C is

(a) $\frac{8}{3}$ (b) 2
(c) 4 (d) 8

Passage III

(Q. Nos. 38 and 39)

- Consider a parabola (P) $x^2 - 4xy + 4y^2 - 32x + 4y + 16 = 0$.

38. The focus of the parabola (P) is

(a) (2, 1) (b) (– 2, 1)
(c) (– 2, – 1) (d) (2, – 1)

39. Length of latusrectum of the parabola (P) is

(a) $\frac{3}{\sqrt{5}}$ (b) $\frac{6}{\sqrt{5}}$
(c) $\frac{12}{\sqrt{5}}$ (d) $\frac{24}{\sqrt{5}}$

Passage IV

(Q. Nos. 40 and 41)

- If l and m are variable real numbers such that $5l^2 - 4lm + 6m^2 + 3l = 0$, then the variable line $lx + my = 1$ always touches a fixed parabola, whose axis is parallel to the X-axis.

40. If (a, b) is the vertex of the parabola, then the value of $|a - b|$ is

(a) 2 (b) 3
(c) 4 (d) 5

41. If (c, d) is the focus of the parabola, then the value of $2^{|d-c|}$ is

(a) 1 (b) 2
(c) 4 (d) 8

Passage V

(Q. Nos. 42 and 43)

- C_1 is a curve $y^2 = 4x$, C_2 is curve obtained by rotating C_1, 120° in anti-clockwise direction C_3 is reflection of C_2 with respect to $y = x$ and S_1, S_2 and S_3 are focii of C_1, C_2 and C_3 respectively, where O is origin.

42. If $(t^2, 2t)$ are parametric form of curve C_1, then the parametric form of curve C_2 is

(a) $\left(\frac{1}{2}(t^2 + 2\sqrt{3}t), \frac{1}{2}(\sqrt{3}t^2 + 2t)\right)$

(b) $\left(\frac{1}{2}(-t^2 + 2\sqrt{3}t), \frac{1}{2}(\sqrt{3}t^2 + 2t)\right)$

(c) $\left(\frac{1}{2}(-t^2 + 2\sqrt{3}t), \frac{1}{2}(-\sqrt{3}t^2 + 2t)\right)$

(d) $\left(\frac{1}{2}(-t^2 + 2\sqrt{3}t), \frac{1}{2}(-\sqrt{3}t^2 - 2t)\right)$

43. Area of ΔOS_2S_3 is

(a) $\frac{1}{8}$ (b) $\frac{1}{4}$ (c) $\frac{1}{2}$ (d) 1

Stem Based Questions

Stem I

(Q. Nos. 44 and 45)

- Tangent to the parabola $y = x^2 + ax + 1$ at the point of intersection of the Y-axis also touches the circle $x^2 + y^2 = c^2$. It is known that no point of the parabola is below X-axis.

44. The value of $5c^2$ when a attains its maximum value is ......

45. The slope of the tangent when C is maximum, is ......

Stem II

(Q. Nos. 46 and 47)

- A parabola (P) touches the conic $x^2 + xy + y^2 - 2x - 2y + 1 = 0$ at the points when it is cut by the line $x + y + 1 = 0$.

46. If equation of parabola (P) is $ax^2 + 2hxy + by^2 + 2gx + 2fy + c = 0$, then the value of $|a + b + c + f + g + h|$ is ......

47. If (a, b) is the vertex of the parabola (P), then the value of $|a - b|$ is ......

Stem III

(Q. Nos. 48 and 49)

- $y = 3x$ is tangent to the parabola $2y = ax^2 + b$.

48. The minimum value of $a + b$ is ......

49. If $(2, 6)$ is the point of contact, then the value of $2a$ is ......

Single Integer Type Questions

50. Two tangents are drawn from the point $(-2, -1)$ to the parabola $y^2 = 4x$. If θ is the angle between these tangents, then the value of $\tan\theta$ is ......

51. If the distances of two points P and Q from the focus of a parabola $y^2 = 4x$ are 4 and 9 respectively, the distance of the point of intersection of tangents at P and Q from the focus is ......

52. The tangents and normals are drawn at the extremities of the latusrectum of the parabola $y^2 = 4x$. The area of quadrilateral so formed is λ sq units, the value of λ is ......

53. Three normals are drawn from the point $(a, 0)$ to the parabola $y^2 = x$. One normal is the X-axis. If other two normals are perpendicular to each other, then the value of $4a$ is......

54. AB is the chord of the parabola $y^2 = 6x$ with the vertex at A. BC is drawn perpendicular to AB meeting the axis at C. The projection of BC on the axis is λ units, then the value of λ is ......

55. The parabolas $y = x^2 - 9$ and $y = \lambda x^2$ intersect at points A and B. If length of AB is equal to $2a$ and if $\lambda a^2 + \mu = a^2$, then the value of μ is ......

56. Radius of the largest circle which passes through the focus of the parabola $y^2 = 4x$ and contained in it, is ......

57. The slope of the line which belongs to the family of lines $(1 + a)x + (a - 1)y + 2(1 - a) = 0$ and makes shortest intercept on $x^2 - 4y + 4 = 0$ is ......

Numerical Value Type Questions

58. Let n be the number of integral points lying inside the parabola $y^2 = 8x$ and circle $x^2 + y^2 = 16$, then the value of n is ......

59. If the circle $(x - 6)^2 + y^2 = r^2$ and the parabola $y^2 = 4x$ have maximum number of common chords, then the least integral value of r is ......

60. From the point $(-1, 2)$, tangent lines are drawn to the parabola $y^2 = 4x$. If area of triangle formed by th chord of contact and the tangents is $n\sqrt{m}$, then mn is equal to ......

61. The radius of circle which passes through the focus of parabola $x^2 = 4y$ and touches it at point $(6, 9)$ is $k\sqrt{10}$, then $\frac{k}{2}$ is equal to ....

62. A parabola of latus rectum l touches a fixed equal parabola, the axes of two curves being parallel. The locus of the vertex of moving curve is a parabola of latus rectum kl, then $5k$ is ....

63. If the focus of parabola $y^2 + 8 = 4x$ coincides with one of the foci of ellipse $3x^2 + by^2 - 12x = 0$ and eccentricity of ellipse is e, then $24e$ is ....

Matching Type Questions

64. Match the following.

Column I	Column II
(A) The number of common chords of the parabola $x = y^2 - 6y + 11$ and $y = x^2 - 6x + 11$ is	(p) Prime number
(B) AB is a chord of the parabola $y^2 = 4x$ with vertex A, BC is drawn perpendicular to AB meeting the axis at C. The projection of BC on the axis of the parabola is	(q) Composite number
(C) The maximum number of common normals of $y^2 = 4ax$ and $x^2 = 4by$ is	(r) Perfect number
(D) If the locus of the middle of point of contact of tangents drawn to the parabola $y^2 = 8x$ and the foot of perpendicular drawn from its focus to the tangents is a conic, then the length of latusrectum of this conic is	(s) Even number

65. Match the following.

Column I	Column II
(A) If the parabola $x^2 = ay$ makes an intercept of length $\sqrt{40}$ on the line $y - 2x = 1$, then the values of a are	(p) -2
(B) If the tangents drawn from the point $(0, 2)$ to the parabola $y^2 = 4ax$ are inclined at an angle $\frac{3\pi}{4}$, then the values of a are	(q) 1
(C) If two distinct chords of a parabola $y^2 = 4ax$ passing through $(a, 2a)$ are bisected on the line $x + y = 1$, then the length of latusrectum can be	(r) 2
(D) If the focus of the parabola $x^2 - ay + 3 = 0$ is $(0, 2)$ and if two values of a are a_1, a_2 such that $a_1 > a_2$, then the value of $\frac{a_1}{a_2}$ is	(s) 3

66. Match the following.

Column I	Column II
(A) The common chord of the circle $x^2 + y^2 = 5$ and the parabola $6y = 5x^2 + 7x$ will passes through the point (s)	(p) $(1, 2)$
(B) Tangents are drawn from point $(2, 3)$ to the parabola $y^2 = 4x$. Then, the points of contact are	(q) $(4, 4)$
(C) From a point P on the circle $x^2 + y^2 = 5$, the equation of chord of contact to the parabola $y^2 = 4x$ is $y = 2(x - 2)$. Then, the coordinates of point P will be	(r) $(-2, 1)$
(D) $P(4, -4)$ and Q are points on the parabola $y^2 = 4x$ such that the area of ΔPOQ is 6 sq units, where O is the vertex. Then, the coordinates of Q may be	(s) $(9, -6)$

Previous Year Questions

67. Let A_1, B_1 and C_1 be three points in the XY-plane. Suppose that the lines A_1C_1 and B_1C_1 are tangents to the curve $y^2 = 8x$ at A_1 and B_1, respectively. If $O = (0, 0)$ and $C_1 = (-4, 0)$, then which of the following statements is (are) true? **[More than One Correct Type, 2024 Adv.]**

(a) The length of the line segment OA_1 is $4\sqrt{3}$.

(b) The length of the line segment A_1B_1 is 16.

(c) The orthocenter of the $\Delta A_1B_1C_1$ is $(0,0)$.

(d) The orthocenter of the $\Delta A_1B_1C_1$ is $(1, 0)$.

68. A normal with slope $\frac{1}{\sqrt{6}}$ is drawn from the point $(0, -\alpha)$ to the parabola $x^2 = -4ay$, where $a > 0$. Let L be the line passing through $(0, \alpha)$ and parallel to the directrix of the parabola. Suppose that L intersects the parabola at two points A and B. Let r denote the length of the latus rectum and s denote the square of the length of the line segment AB. If $r : s = 1 : 16$, then the value of $24a$ is ……. **[Numerical Value Type, 2024 Adv.]**

69. Let P be a point on the parabola $y^2 = 4ax$, where $a > 0$. The normal to the parabola at P meets the X-axis at a point Q. The area of the ΔPFQ, where F is the focus of the parabola is 120. If the slope m of the normal and a are both positive integers, then the pair (a, m) is **[Single Correct Type, 2023 Adv.]**

(a) $(2, 3)$ (b) $(1, 3)$ (c) $(2, 4)$ (d) $(3, 4)$

70. Consider the parabola $y^2 = 4x$. Let S be the focus of the parabola. A pair of tangents drawn to the parabola from the point $P = (-2, 1)$ meet the parabola at P_1 and P_2. Let Q_1 and Q_2 be points on the lines SP_1 and SP_2 respectively such that PQ_1 is perpendicular to SP_1 and PQ_2 is perpendicular to SP_2. Then, which of the following is/are true? **[More than One Correct Type, 2022 Adv.]**

(a) $SQ_1 = 2$ (b) $Q_1Q_2 = \frac{3\sqrt{10}}{5}$ (c) $PQ_1 = 3$ (d) $SQ_2 = 1$

71. Let E denote the parabola $y^2 = 8x$. Let $P = (-2, 4)$, and let Q and Q' be two distinct points on E such that the lines PQ and PQ' are tangents to E. Let F be the focus of E. Then, which of the following statements is (are) true? **[More than one Correct Type, 2021 Adv.]**

(a) The ΔPFQ is a right-angled triangle.

(b) The $\Delta QPQ'$ is a right-angled triangle.

(c) The distance between P and F is $5\sqrt{2}$.

(d) F lies on the line joining Q and Q'

Stem

(Q. Nos. 72 and 73)

- Consider the region $R = \{(x, y) \in R \times R : x \geq 0$ and $y^2 \leq 4 - x\}$. Let F be the family of all circles that are contained in R and have centres on the X-axis. Let C be the circle that has largest radius among the circles in F. Let (α, β) be a point, where the circle C meets the curve $y^2 = 4 - x$. **[Stem Based, 2021 Adv.]**

72. The radius of the circle C is ………

73. The value of α is ………

EXERCISE 3

Challenging Problems

1. Find the locus of the point of intersection of the tangents to the parabola $y^2 = 4ax$, the angle between them being always a given angle α.
2. Three normals from a point to the parabola $y^2 = 4ax$ meet the axis of the parabola in points whose abscissa are in AP. Find the locus of the point.
3. Find the locus of the foot of the perpendicular drawn from the vertex on a tangent to the parabola $y^2 = 4ax$.
4. From an external point P, tangents are drawn to the parabola. Find the equation of the locus of P when these tangents make angles θ_1 and θ_2 with the axis of the parabola such that $\cos\theta_1 \cos\theta_2 = \mu$, where μ is a constant.
5. Prove that all circles described on focal chords of a parabola as diameters touch the directrix of the curve and that all circle on focal radii as diameters touch the tangent at the vertex.
6. A variable chord PQ of the parabola $y^2 = 4ax$ is drawn parallel to the line $y = x$. If the parameter of the points P and Q on the parabola be t_1 and t_2 respectively, then prove that $t_1 + t_2 = 2$. Also, show that the locus of the point of intersection of the normals at P and Q is $2x - y = 12a$.
7. Find the condition that the parabolas $y^2 = 4b(x - c)$ and $y^2 = 4ax$ have a common normal other than the X-axis $(a > b > 0)$.
8. Two chords are drawn through a fixed point t of the parabola $y^2 = 4ax$ and are at right angles. Prove that the joint of their other extremities passes through a fixed point.
9. From a variable point $P(t^2, 2t)(1 \le t \le 3)$ on the parabolas $y^2 = 4x$ perpendicular PM is drawn to the tangent at the vertex of the parabola. Now, from the mid point Q of PM, perpendicular QL is drawn to the focal chord of the parabola through P. Find the maximum length of QL.
10. If a chord is normal to the parabola $y^2 = 4ax$ and is inclined at an angle θ to the positive X-axis, then find the value of θ for which the area of the triangle, formed by the chord and the tangents at its extremities, is minimum.

Answer Key

Exercise 1

1. (c)	2. (c)	3. (d)	4. (b)	5. (a)	6. (c)	7. (c)	8. (d)	9. (c)	10. (c)
11. (a)	12. (b)	13. (b)	14. (d)	15. (d)	16. (a)	17. (a)	18. (a)	19. (d)	20. (b)
21. (a)	22. (c)	23. (a)	24. (d)	25. (d)	26. (7)	27. (1)	28. (3)	29. (3)	30. (6)
31. (4)	32. (8)	33. (4)	34. (8)	35. (5)	36. (0)	37. (b)	38. (c)	39. (c)	40. (80)
41. (10)	42. (108)	43. (72)	44. (–192)	45. (c)	46. (a)	47. (d)	48. (d)	49. (b)	50. (a)
51. (a)	52. (d)	53. (116)	54. (32)	55. (16)	56. (292)	57. (16)	58. (146)	59. (10)	60. (b)
61. (c)	62. (d)	63. (b)	64. (d)	65. (d)	66. (d)	67. (b)	68. (c)	69. (d)	70. (c)
71. (a)	72. (a)	73. (45)	74. (63)	75. (10)	76. (b)	77. (c)	78. (a)	79. (d)	80. (b)
81. (b)	82. (a)	83. (a)	84. (d)	85. (c)	86. (c)	87. (d)	88. (c)	89. (1)	90. (9)
91. (34)	92. (9)	93. (d)	94. (a)	95. (a)	96. (c)	97. (c)	98. (c)	99. (b)	

Exercise 2

1. (a)	2. (a)	3. (c)	4. (d)	5. (c)	6. (d)	7. (a)	8. (c)	9. (a)	10. (a)
11. (c)	12. (b)	13. (b)	14. (c)	15. (d)	16. (d)	17. (c)	18. (a)	19. (a)	20. (c)
21. (b,c)	22. (a,b)	23. (b,d)	24. (b,c)	25. (b,d)	26. (a,b,c)	27. (b,d)	28. (a,b,c,d)	29. (a,c,d)	30. (a,b,c)
31. (b,d)	32. (a,d)	33. (a,b)	34. (d)	35. (d)	36. (b)	37. (c)	38. (d)	39. (c)	40. (b)
41. (b)	42. (d)	43. (b)	44. (1)	45. (0)	46. (12)	47. (0)	48. (6)	49. (3)	50. (3)
51. (6)	52. (8)	53. (3)	54. (6)	55. (9)	56. (4)	57. (0)	58. (16)	59. (20)	60. (16)

61. (2.5) 62. (10) 63. (12) 64. (A) $\to$ (q,r,s); (B) $\to$ (q,s); (C) $\to$ (p); (D) $\to$ (q)

65. (A) $\to$ (p,q); (B) $\to$ (p,r); (C) $\to$ (q,r,s); (D) $\to$ (s) 66. (A) $\to$ (p,r); (B) $\to$ (p,q); (C) $\to$ (r); (D) $\to$ (p,s)

67. (a,c) 68. (12) 69. (a) 70. (b,c,d) 71. (a,b,d) 72. (1.5) 73. (2)

Solutions

Exercise 1 - JEE Main Pattern

1. Tangent at the vertex is

$$x - y + 1 = 0 \quad \text{...(i)}$$

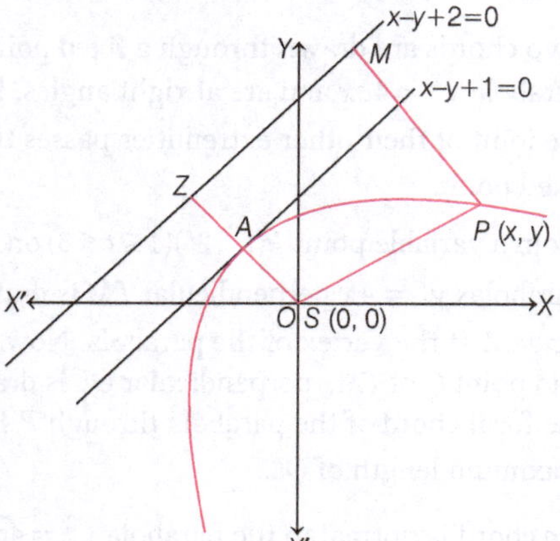

Therefore, the equation of the axis of the parabola is

$$x + y = 0 \quad \text{...(ii)}$$

Now, on solving (i) and (ii), we get $A \equiv \left(-\frac{1}{2}, \frac{1}{2}\right)$

Therefore, Z is $(-1, 1)$

Now, the directrix is $x - y + k = 0$

But this passes through $Z(-1, 1)$. Therefore, $k = 2$

So, the directrix is $x - y + 2 = 0$.

Therefore, by definition, the equation of the parabola is given by $OP = PM$

or $OP^2 = PM^2$

$$\left(\frac{x - y + 2}{\sqrt{2}}\right)^2 = x^2 + y^2$$

or $\quad (x - y + 2)^2 = 2x^2 + 2y^2$

or $\quad x^2 + y^2 + 4 - 2xy + 4x - 4y = 2x^2 + 2y^2$

or $\quad x^2 + y^2 + 2xy - 4x + 4y - 4 = 0$

2. The path of the water jet is parabola.

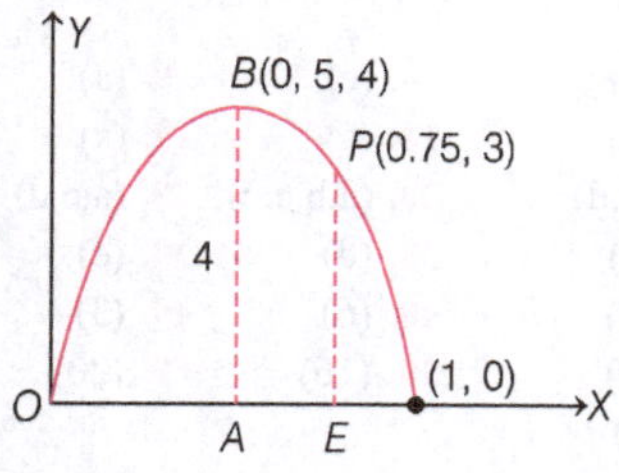

Let its equation be $y = ax^2 + bx + c$.

It should pass through (0, 0), (0.5, 4) and (1, 0).

Therefore, $c = 0$, $a = -16$, $b = 16$

$\therefore \quad y = -16x^2 + 16x$

If $\quad x = 0.75$, then $y = 3$

3. $y - \sqrt{3}\,x + 3 = 0$ can be rewritten as

$$\frac{y - 0}{\sqrt{3}/2} = \frac{x - \sqrt{3}}{1/2} = r \quad \text{...(i)}$$

On solving Eq. (i) with the parabola $y^2 = x + 2$, we get

$$\frac{3r^2}{4} = \frac{r}{2} + \sqrt{3} + 2 \text{ or } 3r^2 - 2r - (4\sqrt{3} + 8) = 0$$

Let the roots be r_1 and r_2.

$$\Rightarrow r_1 \times r_2 = \left|\frac{-(4\sqrt{3} + 8)}{3}\right| = \frac{4(\sqrt{3} + 2)}{3}$$

4. The joint equation of OA and OB is

$$x^2 - 4x(y - 3x) - 4y(y - 3x) + 20(y - 3x)^2 = 0$$

Making the equation of the parabola homogeneous using straight line, we get

$$x^2(1 + 12 + 180) - y^2(4 - 20) - xy\,(4 - 12 + 120) = 0$$

or $\quad 193x^2 + 16y^2 - 112xy = 0$

$\therefore \quad \tan\theta = \dfrac{2\sqrt{h^2 - ab}}{a + b}$

$\Rightarrow \quad \tan\theta = \dfrac{2\sqrt{56^2 - 193 \times 16}}{193 + 16} = \dfrac{8\sqrt{3}}{209}$

5. $\dfrac{dy}{dx} = 2x - 5$

$\therefore \quad m_1 = \left(\dfrac{dy}{dx}\right)_{(2,0)} = 4 - 5 = -1$

and $\quad m_2 = \left(\dfrac{dy}{dx}\right)_{(3,0)} = 6 - 5 = 1$

$\therefore \quad m_1 m_2 = -1$

Therefore, the angle between the tangent is $\dfrac{\pi}{2}$.

6. Let $A_1 \equiv (2t_1^2, 4t_1)$ and $A_2 \equiv (2t_1^2 - 4t_1)$

Clearly, $\angle A_1OA = \dfrac{\pi}{6}$

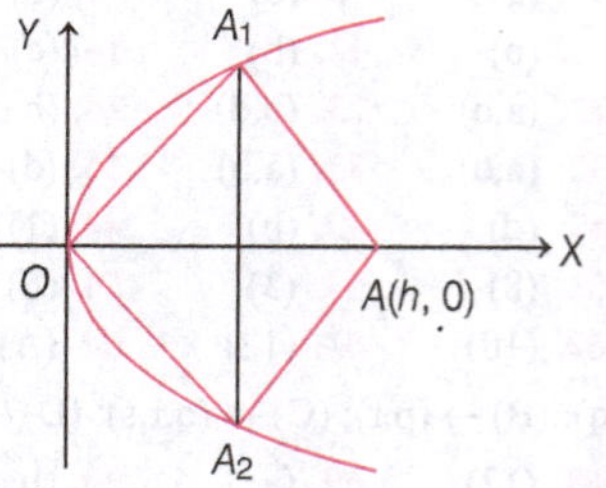

Therefore, $\frac{2}{t_1} = \frac{1}{\sqrt{3}}$

or $t_1 = 2\sqrt{3}$

The equation of normal at A_1 is $y = -t_1 x + 4t_1 + 2t_1^3$

or $h = 4 + 2t_1^2 = 4 + 2(12) = 28$

7. $y = mx + c$ is a normal to $y^2 = 4ax$ if

$$c = -2am - am^3, y = -2x - \lambda$$

or $m = -2, a = -2$

$\Rightarrow$ $c = -8 - 16 = -24$

$\therefore$ $\lambda = -c = 24$

8. On solving the equations, we get $x^2 + 4(x+4) = a^2$

If the circle and the parabola touch each other, then

$$D = 0$$

or $16 - 4(16 - a^2) = 0$

or $a = 2\sqrt{3}$

9. Point (4, 4) lies on the parabola.

Let the point of intersection of the line $y = mx$ with the chords be $(\alpha, m\alpha)$. Then,

$$\alpha = \frac{4 + x_1}{2}$$

or $x_1 = 2\alpha - 4$

and $m\alpha = \frac{4 + y_1}{2}$

$\therefore$ $y_1 = 2m\alpha - 4$

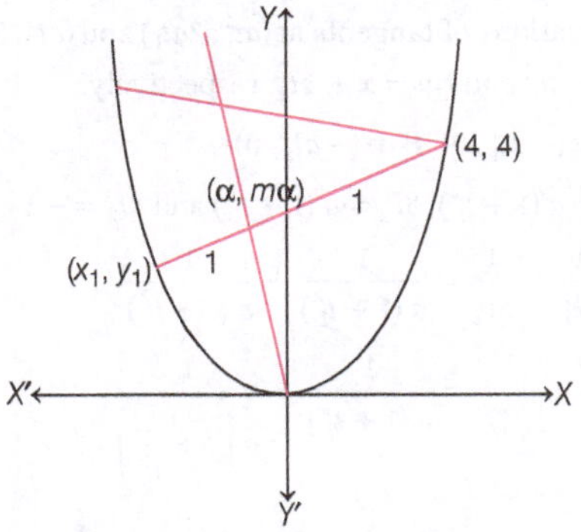

As (x_1, y_1) lies on the curve, we get

$$(2\alpha - 4)^2 = 4(2m\alpha - 4)$$

or $4\alpha^2 + 16 - 16\alpha = 8(m\alpha - 2)$

or $4\alpha^2 - 8\alpha(2 + m) + 32 = 0$

For two distinct chords, $D > 0$

$\Rightarrow$ $\{8(2 + m)\}^2 - 4(4)(32) > 0$

$\Rightarrow$ $(2 + m)^2 - 8 > 0$

$\Rightarrow$ $2 + m > 2\sqrt{2}$ or $2 + m < -2\sqrt{2}$

$\Rightarrow$ $m > 2\sqrt{2} - 2$ or $m < -2\sqrt{2} - 2$

$\Rightarrow$ $m \in (-\infty, -2 - 2\sqrt{2}) \cup (2\sqrt{2} - 2, \infty)$

10. Let the point of intersection be (α, β).

Therefore, the chord of contact w.r.t. this point is $\beta y = 2x + 2\alpha$, which is the same as $x + y = 2$.

Therefore, $\alpha = \beta = -2$

These values satisfy $y - x = 0$

11. Equation of tangent to $y^2 = 4bx$ is

$$y = mx + \frac{b}{m} \quad \text{...(i)}$$

Here, $m = \tan\frac{\pi}{4} = 1$

From Eq. (i), we get $y = x + b$

For common tangent $y = x + b$ is also tangent of circle $x^2 + y^2 = a^2$, then

$$\frac{|0 - 0 + b|}{\sqrt{1+1}} = a$$

$\Rightarrow$ $b = a\sqrt{2}$ $[\because a > 0, b > 0]$

12. The coordinates of vertex and focus of required parabola are $(a, 0)$ and $(a_1, 0)$, respectively. Therefore, the distance between the vertex and the focus is $AS = a_1 - a$. So, the length of latusrectum is $4(a_1 - a)$. Thus, the equation of the required parabola is

$$(y - 0)^2 = 4(a_1 - a)(x - a)$$

or $y^2 = 4(a_1 - a)(x - a)$.

13. The parabolas are equal if the lengths of their latusrectum are equal.

The length of latusrectum of $y^2 = ax$ is a.

The equation of second parabola can be written as

$$\sqrt{(x-3)^2 + (y+2)^2} = \left(\frac{3x - 4y - 2}{5}\right)$$

Here, focus is $(3, -2)$ and the equation of directrix is $3x - 4y - 2 = 0$.

$\therefore$Length of latusrectum$= 2 \times$ Distance between focus and directrix

$$= 2\left|\frac{9 - 4 \times -2 - 2}{\sqrt{(9 + 16)}}\right| = 6$$

Thus, the two parabolas are equal if $a = 6$.

14. Let $DC = CB = BA = AD = k$

$\therefore$ Coordinates of B are (k, k),

which lie on $y = \lambda\sqrt{x}$

$\therefore$ $k = \lambda\sqrt{k}$

$\Rightarrow$ $k = \lambda^2$

$\therefore$ $BC = k = \lambda^2$ ...(i)

Also, let $CG = GF = FE = EC = k_1$

$\therefore$Coordinates of F are $(\lambda^2 + k_1, k_1)$,

which lie on $y = \lambda\sqrt{x}$

Then, $k_1 = \lambda\sqrt{(\lambda^2 + k_1)}$

$\Rightarrow$ $k_1^2 = \lambda^4 + \lambda^2 k_1$

or $k_1^2 - \lambda^2 k_1 - \lambda^4 = 0$

$$\therefore \quad k_1 = \frac{\lambda^2 \pm \sqrt{(\lambda^4 + 4\lambda^4)}}{2}$$

or $\dfrac{k_1}{\lambda^2} = \dfrac{1 + \sqrt{5}}{2}$ $\quad [\because k_1 > 0]$

or $\dfrac{FG}{BC} = \dfrac{\sqrt{5} + 1}{2}$

15. Coordinates of A and B are

($VA \cos\theta$, $VA \sin\theta$) and ($VB \sin\theta$, $- VB \cos\theta$), respectively.

$\because$ A and B lie on $y^2 = x$, then $(VA \sin\theta)^2 = VA \cos\theta$

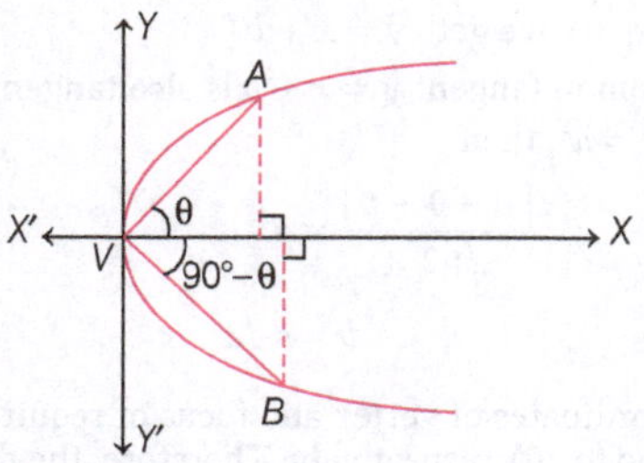

$$\Rightarrow \quad VA = \frac{\cos\theta}{\sin^2\theta}$$

Similarly, $\quad VB = \dfrac{\sin\theta}{\cos^2\theta}$

$$\therefore \quad \frac{|VA|}{|VB|} = \cot^3\theta$$

16. Since, $x = t^2 - t + 1$, $y = t^2 + t + 1$

$\therefore \quad x + y = 2t^2 + 2$ and $y - x = 2t$

or $\quad 2(x + y - 2) = 4t^2 = (2t)^2 = (y - x)^2$

or $\quad (x - y)^2 = 2(x + y - 2)$

or $\quad \left(\dfrac{x - y}{\sqrt{2}}\right)^2 = \sqrt{2}\left(\dfrac{x + y - 2}{\sqrt{2}}\right)$

For vertex, $\quad \dfrac{x - y}{\sqrt{2}} = 0$ and $\dfrac{x + y - 2}{\sqrt{2}} = 0$

or $\quad x = y$ and $x + y = 2$

$\therefore \quad x = y = 1$

Hence, vertex is (1, 1).

17. It is clear from figure,

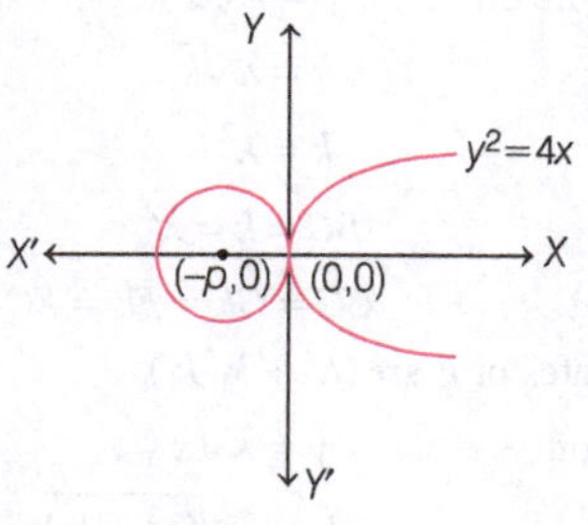

$$-p < 0 \quad \text{or} \quad p > 0$$

18. The point of intersection of the parabolas $y^2 = 4ax$ and $x^2 = 4ay$ are (0, 0) and $(4a, 4a)$ but $a \neq 0$.

Now, $2bx + 3cy + 4d = 0$ passes through (0, 0) and $(4a, 4a)$.

Therefore, $d = 0$ and $2b(4a) + 3c(4a) = 0$

i.e. $\quad 2b + 3c = 0 \quad [\because a \neq 0]$

or $\quad d^2 + (2b + 3c)^2 = 0$

19. Since, $(OT)^2 = OA \cdot OB = \alpha \cdot \beta$

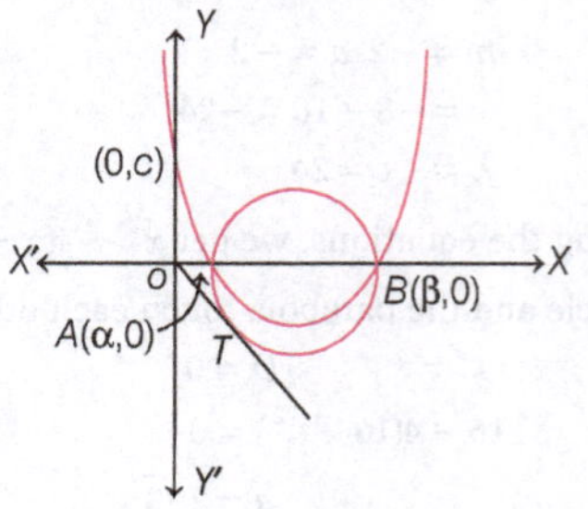

or $\quad OT = \sqrt{\alpha\beta}$ $\quad$ ...(i)

Parabola cuts X-axis at α and β.

$\therefore \alpha, \beta$ are the roots of $ax^2 + bx + c = 0$

$\Rightarrow \quad \alpha\beta = \dfrac{c}{a}$ $\quad$ ...(ii)

From Eqs. (i) and (ii), we get

$$OT = \sqrt{\frac{c}{a}}$$

20. Since, two perpendicular tangents meet a point on directrix.

Now, equations of tangents at $(at_1^2, 2at_1)$ and $(at_2^2, 2at_2)$ are $t_1 y = x + at_1^2$ and $t_2 y = x + at_2^2$, respectively.

$\therefore \quad P_1 \equiv (-at_1^2, 0)$, $P_2 \equiv (-at_2^2, 0)$

$\Rightarrow \quad SP_1 = a(1 + t_1^2)$, $SP_2 = a(1 + t_2^2)$ and $t_1 t_2 = -1$

$$\therefore \quad \frac{1}{SP_1} + \frac{1}{SP_2} = \frac{1}{a(1 + t_1^2)} + \frac{1}{a(1 + t_2^2)}$$

$$= \frac{1}{a(1 + t_1^2)} + \frac{1}{a\left(1 + \dfrac{1}{t_1^2}\right)} \quad \left[\because t_2 = -\frac{1}{t_1}\right]$$

$$= \frac{1}{a(1 + t_1^2)} + \frac{t_1^2}{a(1 + t_1^2)} = \frac{1}{a}$$

21. Let $P \equiv (at_1^2, 2at_1)$ and $Q \equiv (at_2^2, 2at_2)$

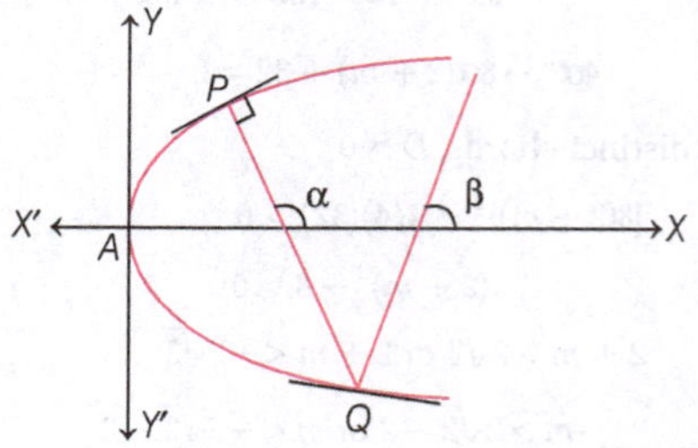

Equation of normal at P is $y + t_1 x = 2at_1 + at_1^3$

meets the curve again at Q, then

$$t_2 = -t_1 - \frac{2}{t_1} \quad \text{...(i)}$$

Here, $\tan\alpha = -t_1$ and $\tan\beta = -t_2$

From Eq. (i),

$$\therefore \quad -\tan\beta = \tan\alpha + \frac{2}{\tan\alpha}$$

$\Rightarrow \tan\alpha(\tan\alpha + \tan\beta) = -2$

22. Let $A \equiv (\alpha, \beta)$

The equation of normal at $(at^2, 2at)$ is

$$y + tx = 2at + at^3 \quad \text{...(i)}$$

Since, (α, β) lies on Eq. (i), then

$$at^3 + (2a - \alpha)t - \beta = 0 \quad \text{...(ii)}$$

Let t_1, t_2 and t_3 be the roots of Eq. (ii), then

$$at^3 + (2a - \alpha)t - \beta = a(t - t_1)(t - t_2)(t - t_3) \quad \text{...(iii)}$$

Let $P \equiv (at_1^2, 2at_1)$, $Q \equiv (at_2^2, 2at_2)$ and $R \equiv (at_3^2, 2at_3)$

Since, the focus is $S(a, 0)$.

$$\therefore \quad SP = a(1 + t_1^2),\ SQ = a(1 + t_2^2)$$

and $\quad SR = a(1 + t_3^2)$

On putting $\quad t = i = \sqrt{-1}$ in Eq. (iii), we get

$$-ai + (2a - \alpha)i - \beta = a(i - t_1)(i - t_2)(i - t_3)$$

$$\Rightarrow \quad |(a - \alpha)i - \beta| = a|i - t_1||i - t_2|i - t_3|$$

$$\Rightarrow \quad \sqrt{(a - \alpha)^2 + \beta^2} = a\sqrt{(1 + t_1^2)}\sqrt{(1 + t_2^2)}\sqrt{(1 + t_3^2)}$$

or $\quad a((a - \alpha)^2 + \beta^2) = a(1 + t_1^2) \cdot a(1 + t_2^2) \cdot a(1 + t_3^2)$

$$a(SA)^2 = SP \cdot SQ \cdot SR$$

or $\quad SP \cdot SQ \cdot SR = a(SA)^2$

23. Let AB be a normal chord, where $A \equiv (at_1^2, 2at_1)$ and $B \equiv (at_2^2, 2at_2)$, and $t_2 = -t_1 - \frac{2}{t_1}$

Now, $\quad AB = \sqrt{(at_1^2 - at_2^2)^2 + (2at_1 - 2at_2)^2}$

$$= a|t_1 - t_2|\sqrt{(t_1 + t_2)^2 + 4}$$

$$= a\left|2\left(t_1 + \frac{1}{t_1}\right)\right|\sqrt{\left(\frac{4}{t_1^2} + 4\right)}$$

$$= 4a\sqrt{\frac{(t_1^2 + 1)^3}{t_1^4}}$$

$$(AB)^2 = 16a^2\frac{(t_1^2 + 1)^3}{t_1^4}$$

$$\frac{d(AB)^2}{dt_1} = 16a^2\left\{\frac{(1 + t_1^2)^2}{t_1^5}(t_1^2 - 2)\right\}$$

For $\quad \frac{d(AB)^2}{dt_1} = 0 \Rightarrow t_1 = \sqrt{2}$,

$(AB)^2$ is minimum.

Thus, $\quad AB_{\min} = \sqrt{\frac{16a^2(2 + 1)^3}{4}} = 2a\sqrt{27}$

24. On solving $x^2 + y^2 = a^2$ and $y^2 = 4(x + 4)$

$$\Rightarrow \quad x^2 + 4(x + 4) = a^2$$

or $\quad x^2 + 4x + 16 - a^2 = 0$

If the circle and parabola touch each other, then

$$D = 0$$

$$\Rightarrow \quad 16 - 4 \cdot 1 \cdot (16 - a^2) = 0$$

$$\Rightarrow \quad a^2 = 12 \text{ or } a = 2\sqrt{3}$$

25. $\sin\theta > |2a| \quad [\because h > 2a]$

$$\Rightarrow \quad 0 < |2a| < 1 \text{ or } 0 < |a| < \frac{1}{2}$$

$$\therefore \quad a \in \left(-\frac{1}{2}, 0\right) \cup \left(0, \frac{1}{2}\right)$$

26. Here, $(x - 1)^2 + (y - 3)^2 = \left\{\frac{5x - 12y + 17}{\sqrt{5^2 + (-12)^2}}\right\}^2$

Therefore, the focus is (1, 3) and the directrix is $5x - 12y + 17 = 0$.

The distance of the focus from the directrix is

$$\left|\frac{5 \times 1 - 12 \times 3 + 17}{\sqrt{5^2 + (-12)^2}}\right| = \frac{14}{13}$$

$$\therefore \text{ Length of latusrectum, } L = 2 \times \frac{14}{13} = \frac{28}{13}$$

$$\frac{13L}{4} = \frac{13}{4} \times \frac{28}{13} = 7$$

27. The focus of $y^2 = 16x$ is (4, 0)

Any focal chord is $y - 0 = m(x - 4)$

or $\quad mx - y - 4m = 0$

This focal chord touches the circle $(x - 6)^2 + y^2 = 2$.

Then, the distance from the center of the circle to this chord is equal to the radius of the circle

i.e. $\quad \frac{|6m - 4m|}{\sqrt{m^2 + 1}} = \sqrt{2}$

or $\quad 2m = \sqrt{2} \cdot \sqrt{m^2 + 1}$

or $\quad 2m^2 = m^2 + 1 \text{ or } m^2 = 1$

28. Any tangent to the parabola $y^2 = 4x(a = 1)$, is $y = mx + \frac{1}{m}$

It passes through $(-2, -1)$. Therefore,

$$-1 = -2m + \frac{1}{m}$$

$$\Rightarrow \quad 2m^2 - m - 1 = 0$$

$$\Rightarrow \quad (2m + 1)(m - 1) = 0$$

$$\Rightarrow \quad m = \frac{1}{2} \text{ and } m = 1$$

Then, the angle between the lines is

$$\tan\theta = \left|\frac{m_1 + m_2}{1 - m_1m_2}\right| = 3$$

29. The equation of tangent in terms of the slope of the parabola $y^2 = 4x$ is

$$y = mx + \frac{1}{m} \quad ...(i)$$

Since, Eq. (i) is also the tangent of $x^2 = -32y$, we get

$$x^2 = -32\left(mx + \frac{1}{m}\right) \Rightarrow x^2 + 32mx + \frac{32}{m} = 0$$

The above equation must have equal roots.
Hence, its discriminant must be zero. Therefore,

$$(32m)^2 = 4 \times 1 \times \frac{32}{m}$$

i.e. $$m^3 = \frac{1}{8} \text{ or } m = \frac{1}{2}$$

From Eq. (i), $y = \frac{x}{2} + 2$ or $x - 2y + 4 = 0$

30. Slope of the line $= -1$

From the curve, $\frac{dy}{dx} = \frac{4}{y}$

Hence, slope of normal $= -\frac{y}{4} = -1$ or $y = 4$

On putting $y = 4$ in the equation of curve, we get $x = 2$

∴ The point is (4, 2).

Hence, $a + b = 4 + 2 = 6$

31.

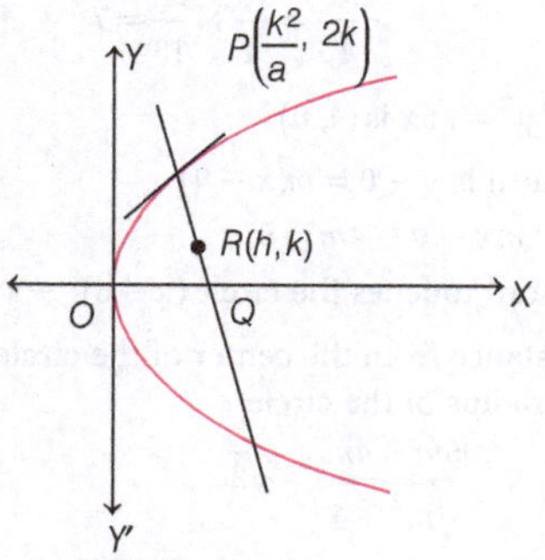

Consider the parabola $y^2 = 4ax$.

We have to find the locus of $R(h, k)$. Since, Q has ordinate 0, the ordinate of P is $2k$.

Also, P is on the curve. Then, the abscissa of P is k^2 / a.

Now, PQ is normal to the curve.

Slope of tangent to the curve at any point is

$$\frac{dy}{dx} = \frac{2a}{y}$$

Hence, the slope of normal at point P is $-k / a$.

Also, the slope of normal joining P and $R(h, k)$ is

$$\frac{2k - k}{(k^2 / a) - h}$$

Hence, comparing slopes, we get

$$\frac{2k - k}{(k^2 / a) - h} = -\frac{k}{a} \text{ or } y^2 = a(x - a)$$

For $y^2 = 16x, a = 4$. Hence, the locus is $y^2 = 4(x - 4)$.

32. Given $\tan\alpha . \tan\beta = 4$

or $$y \cdot \frac{y}{x} + \frac{y}{2 - x} = 4$$

or $$-\frac{y}{2} = x^2 - 2x = (x - 1)^2 - 1$$

or $$(x - 1)^2 = -\frac{1}{2}(y - 2)$$

Directrix $$y - 2 = \frac{1}{8} \text{ or } y = \frac{17}{8}$$

∴ $$k = \frac{17}{8}$$

⇒ $$8k - 9 = 8 \times \frac{17}{8} - 9 = 17 - 9 = 8$$

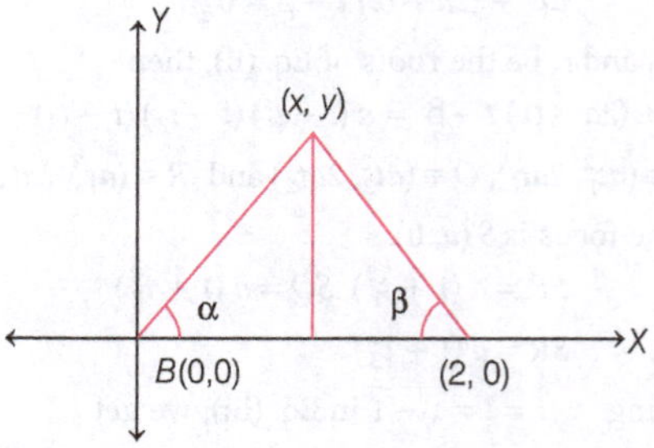

33. Here, $a = 3$

On comparing point (3, 6) with $(3t^2, 6t)$, we get $t = 1$.

Then, length of chord $= a\left(t + \frac{1}{t}\right)^2 = 3(1 + 1)^2 = 12$

Hence, the value of $\frac{L}{3} = \frac{12}{3} = 4$

34. The chord of contact w.r.t. point $O(-1, 2)$ is $y = (x - 1)$

[using $yy_1 = 2a(x + 1)$]

Solving $y = x - 1$ with the parabola, we get the points of intersection as

$$P(3 + 2\sqrt{2}, 2 + 2\sqrt{2}) \text{ and } Q(3 - 2\sqrt{2}, 2 - 2\sqrt{2})$$

∴ $$PQ^2 = 32 + 32 = 64$$

⇒ $$PQ = 8$$

Also, the length of perpendicular from $O(-1, 2)$ on PQ is $\frac{4}{\sqrt{2}}$.

Then, the required area of triangle is

$$A = \frac{1}{2} \times 8 \times \left(\frac{4}{\sqrt{2}}\right) = 8\sqrt{2} \text{ sq. units.}$$

Hence, $$\frac{A}{\sqrt{2}} = \frac{8\sqrt{2}}{\sqrt{2}} = 8$$

35. For maximum number of common chords, the circle and the parabola must intersect at four distinct points.

Let us first find the value of r when the circle and the parabola touch each other.

For that, solving the given curves, we have

$$(x - 6)^2 + 4x = r^2$$

or $$x^2 - 8x + 36 - r^2 = 0$$

The curves touch if discriminant

$$D = 64 - 4(36 - r^2) = 0$$

or $\quad r^2 = 20$

Hence, the least integral value of r for which the curves intersect is 5.

36. The family of lines $(1+\lambda)x + (\lambda - 1)y + 2(1-\lambda) = 0$ are concurrent. The focus of the parabola $x^2 = 4(y-1)$ is $(0, 2)$.

Now, the shortest intercept of the line on the parabola which passes through the focus is latus rectum,

The axis of the given parabola is the Y-axis.

Therefore, the latus rectum is parallel to the X-axis.

37. **Decoding the Question**

> Equation of chord of parabola $y^2 = 4ax$ whose mid-point is (x_1, y_1), is $yy_1 - \frac{4a(x+x_1)}{2} = y_1^2 - 4ax_1$. $\quad [T = S_1]$

Given parabola is $y^2 = 12x$

Equation of chord PQ, whose mid-point $(4, 1)$ is $T = S_1$

$$\Rightarrow \quad yy_1 - 12\left(\frac{x_1 + x}{2}\right) = y_1^2 - 12x_1$$

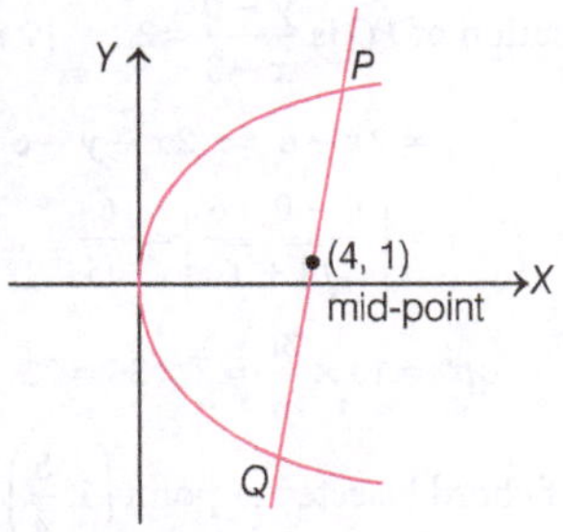

$$y(1) - \frac{12(x+4)}{2} = (1)^2 - 12(4)$$

$$\Rightarrow \quad y - 6(x+4) = 1 - 48$$

$$\Rightarrow \quad y - 6x - 24 = -47$$

$$\Rightarrow \quad 6x - y = 23$$

Since, $\left(\frac{1}{2}, -20\right)$ satisfy above equation.

$\therefore$ Line passes through $\left(\frac{1}{2}, -20\right)$.

38. First use $e = \sqrt{1 - \frac{b^2}{a^2}}$, then length of latus rectum $= \frac{2b^2}{a}$

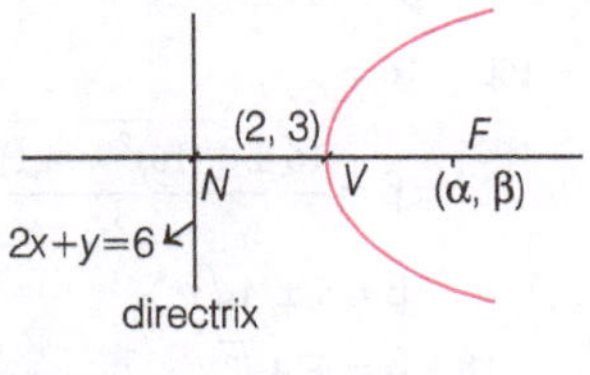

So, equation of axis is

$$y - 3 = \frac{1}{2}(x - 2)$$

$$\Rightarrow \quad x - 2y + 4 = 0$$

On solving $2x + y = 6$ and $x - 2y + 4 = 0$, we get

$$N\left(\frac{8}{5}, \frac{14}{5}\right)$$

Since, V is the mid-point of N and F

$$\therefore \quad \frac{\frac{8}{5} + \alpha}{2} = 2 \Rightarrow \alpha = 4 - \frac{8}{5} = \frac{12}{5}$$

and $$\frac{\frac{14}{5} + \beta}{2} = 3$$

$$\Rightarrow \quad \beta = 6 - \frac{14}{5} = \frac{16}{5}$$

Given that ellipse passes through (α, β).

$$\therefore \quad \frac{\alpha^2}{a^2} + \frac{\beta^2}{b^2} = 1$$

$$\Rightarrow \quad \frac{(12/5)^2}{a^2} + \frac{(16/5)^2}{b^2} = 1 \qquad \text{...(i)}$$

Also, eccentricity of ellipse is $\frac{1}{\sqrt{2}}$

$$\sqrt{1 - \frac{b^2}{a^2}} = \frac{1}{\sqrt{2}} \Rightarrow 1 - \frac{b^2}{a^2} = \frac{1}{2}$$

$$\Rightarrow \quad a^2 = 2b^2$$

Put in Eq. (i),

$$\frac{144/25}{2b^2} + \frac{256/25}{b^2} = 1$$

$$\Rightarrow \quad b^2 = \frac{72}{25} + \frac{256}{25} = \frac{328}{25}$$

Square of length of latus rectum

$$= \left(\frac{2b^2}{a}\right)^2 = \frac{4 \times b^4}{a^2}$$

$$= \frac{4b^4}{2b^2} = 2b^2 = \frac{656}{25}$$

39. Given equation of parabola is $y^2 = 4x$

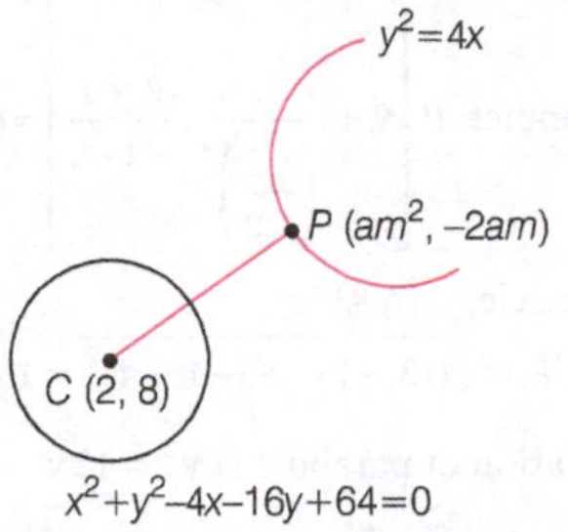

and equation of circle is

$$x^2 + y^2 - 4x - 16y + 64 = 0$$

Now, equation of normal to parabola is given by

$y = mx - 2m - m^3$, where $m =$ slope

This normal passing through centre of the circle which is $(2, 8)$.

So, $$8 = 2m - 2m - m^3$$

$$\Rightarrow \quad m^3 = -8 = (-2)^3$$

$$\Rightarrow \quad m = -2$$

Coordinates of any point P taken on given parabola is of the form $(am^2, -2am)$ i.e $(4, 4)$

Now, $CP = \sqrt{(4-2)^2 + (4-8)^2}$

$= \sqrt{4+16} = \sqrt{20} = d$ [given]

$\therefore \quad d^2 = 20$

40. $C: x^2 + y^2 = 4$

$P: y^2 = 8x$

Equation of chord bisected at $(\alpha, 0)$

$T = S_1$

$\Rightarrow x(2t^2) + y(4t) - 4 = (2t^2)^2 + (4t)^2 - 4$

$\because$ It passes through $(\alpha, 0)$

$\alpha(2t^2) = 4t^4 + 16t^2$

$\Rightarrow \quad \alpha = 2t^2 + 8$

$\Rightarrow \quad \dfrac{\alpha - 8}{2} = t^2$

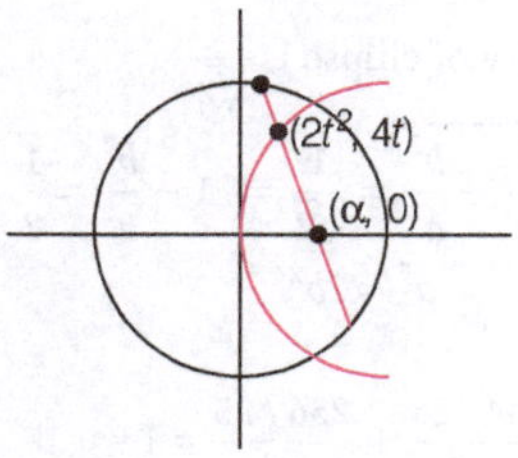

Also, $4t^4 + 16t^2 - 4 < 0$

$\therefore \quad t^2 = -2 + \sqrt{5}$

$\alpha = 4 + 2\sqrt{5}$

$\therefore \quad \alpha \in (8, 4 + 2\sqrt{5})$

$\Rightarrow \quad (2q - p)^2 = 80$

41. Given parabola $y^2 = 4(x - 9)$

Slope of tangent $= -\dfrac{1}{2}$

Point of contact, $P\left[9 + \dfrac{1}{\left(-\dfrac{1}{2}\right)^2}, \dfrac{2 \times 1}{-1/2}\right] = (13, -4)$

Centre of circle, $C\,(7, 4)$

Distance $CP = \sqrt{(13-7)^2 + (-4-4)^2} = 10$

42. Given, equation of parabola is $y^2 = 12x$

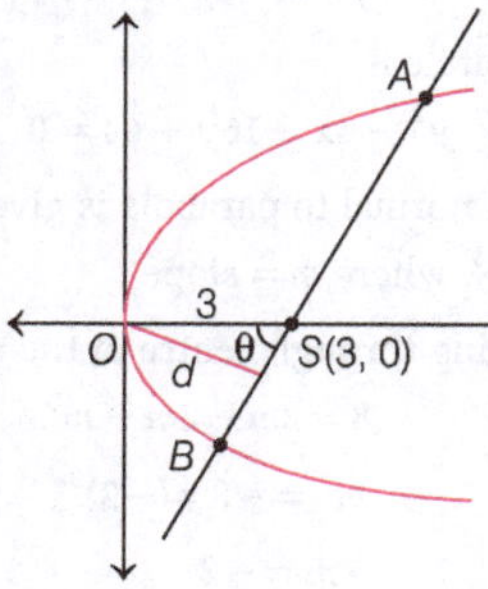

Length of focal chord AB, $l = 4a \operatorname{cosec}^2\theta$

$= 4 \times 3 \times \left(\dfrac{3}{d}\right)^2 = 12 \times \dfrac{9}{d^2}$

$\therefore \quad ld^2 = 12 \times 9 = 108$

43. Given equation of parabola is $y^2 = 12x$ and length of focal chord $= 15$

As we know that

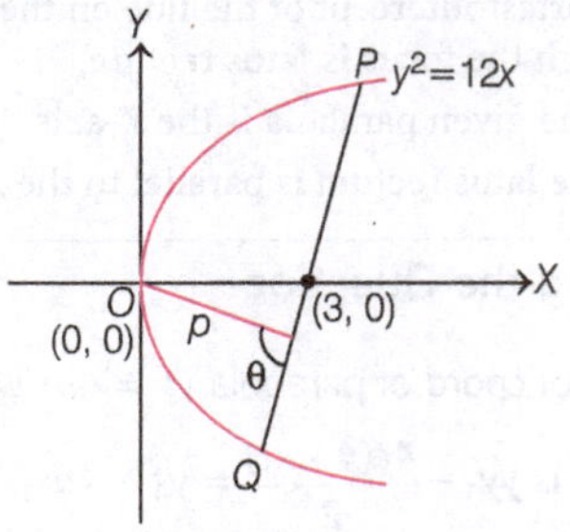

Length of focal chord $4a \operatorname{cosec}^2\theta = 15$

$\Rightarrow \quad 12 \operatorname{cosec}^2\theta = 15 \Rightarrow \sin^2\theta = \dfrac{4}{5}$

$\Rightarrow \quad \tan^2\theta = 4 \Rightarrow \tan\theta = 2$

Hence, equation of PQ is $\dfrac{y-0}{x-3} = 2 \quad [\because m = \tan\theta = 2 = \text{slope}]$

$\Rightarrow \quad y = 2x - 6 \Rightarrow 2x - y - 6 = 0$

$\therefore \quad p = \left|\dfrac{0 - 0 - 6}{\sqrt{4+1}}\right| = \dfrac{6}{\sqrt{5}}$

Hence, $\quad 10p^2 = 10 \times \dfrac{36}{5} = 2 \times 36 = 72$

44. Equation of chord bisected at point $\left(1, \dfrac{5}{4}\right)$ to parabola $x^2 = 8y$ is

$T = S_1$

$\Rightarrow \quad xx_1 - 4(y + y_1) = x_1^2 - 8y_1$

$\because \quad (x_1, y_1) = \left(1, \dfrac{5}{4}\right)$

$\Rightarrow \quad x - 4y - 5 = -9$

$\Rightarrow \quad x - 4y + 4 = 0$

$\because (\alpha, \beta)$ lies on $x - 4y + 4 = 0$ and $y^2 = 4x$

$\Rightarrow \alpha - 4\beta + 4 = 0$ and $\beta^2 = 4\alpha$

$\Rightarrow \quad \beta^2 = 4(4\beta - 4)$

$\Rightarrow \quad \beta^2 - 16\beta + 16 = 0$

$\Rightarrow \quad \beta = \dfrac{16 \pm \sqrt{(16)^2 - 4(1)(16)}}{2}$

$\Rightarrow \quad \beta = 8 \pm 4\sqrt{3}$

$\Rightarrow \quad 8 - \beta = \mp 4\sqrt{3}$

Now, $\quad \alpha = 4\beta - 4 = 28 \pm 16\sqrt{3}$

$\therefore \quad (\alpha - 28)(\beta - 8) = (\pm 16\sqrt{3})(\mp 4\sqrt{3}) = -192$

45. Given that PQ is a focal chord of the parabola $y^2 = 36x$ of length 100.

Thus, length $= 100 \Rightarrow 9\left(t+\frac{1}{t}\right)^2 = 100$

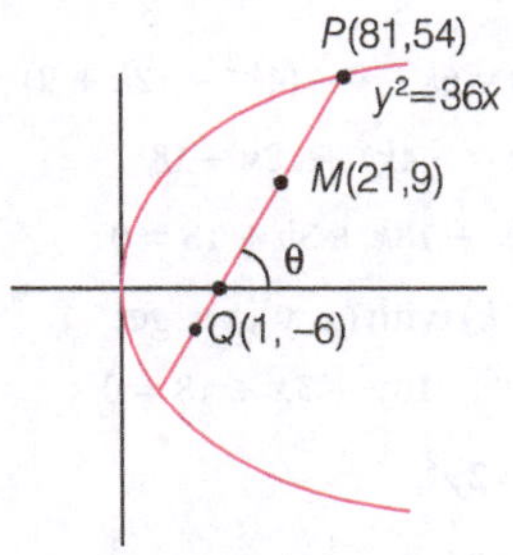

$\Rightarrow \quad \left(t+\frac{1}{t}\right)^2 = \frac{100}{9} \Rightarrow t+\frac{1}{t} = \pm\frac{10}{3}$

$\therefore \quad t = 3 \text{ or } \frac{1}{3}$

Thus, $P = (81, 54)$ and $Q = (1, -6)$ and $M = (21, 9)$

Thus, required line $y - 9 = -\frac{4}{3}(x - 21)$

$\Rightarrow \quad 3y - 27 = -4x + 84 \Rightarrow 4x + 3y = 111$

Clearly, (3, 33), (6, 29), and (–6, 45) all the points satisfies the given line which passes through $M(21, 9)$ and perpendicular to PQ.

So, only (–3, 43) not hold $4x + 3y = 111$.

46. Focus of $y^2 = 20x$ is R (5, 0)

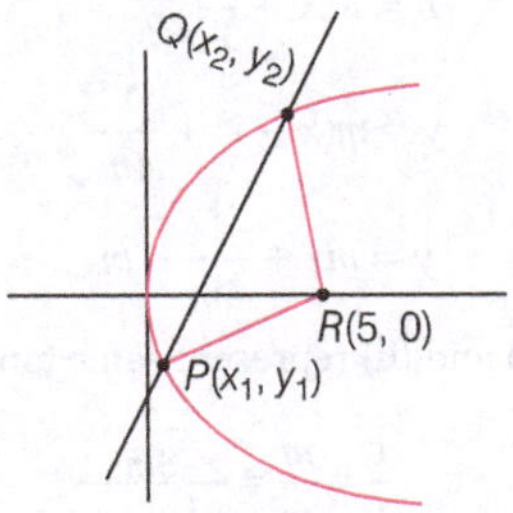

Centroid of ΔPQR is

$G(10, 10) \equiv G\left(\frac{x_1+x_2+5}{3}, \frac{y_1+y_2+0}{3}\right)$

$\Rightarrow \quad x_1 + x_2 = 25, y_1 + y_2 = 30$

and $\quad c - m = 6$

$\Rightarrow \quad c = m + 6$

line $y = mx + m + 6 \Rightarrow x = \frac{y-(m+6)}{m}$

On eliminating x in parabola $y^2 = 20x$, we get

$$y^2 = 20\left(\frac{y-(m+6)}{m}\right)$$

$\Rightarrow \quad my^2 - 20y + 20(m+6) = 0$

whose roots are y_1 and y_2, then

sum of roots are

$$y_1 + y_2 = 20/m = 30 \Rightarrow m = 2/3$$

$\therefore \quad c = \frac{2}{3} + 6 = \frac{20}{3}$

For $\quad m = 2/3$

$\Rightarrow \quad \frac{2}{3}y^2 - 20y + 20\left(\frac{2}{3}+6\right) = 0$

$\Rightarrow \quad y^2 - 30y + 200 = 0 \Rightarrow y = 20, 10$

For $y = 20$, $\quad x = 20$;

For $y = 10$, $\quad x = 5$

$$PQ^2 = (x_2 - x_1)^2 + (y_2 - y_1)^2$$
$$= (20-5)^2 + (20-10)^2 = 325$$

47. $\quad ax^2 + 2bx + c = 0 \quad$ ...(i)

and $\quad dx^2 + 2ex + f = 0 \quad$ ...(ii)

$\because a, b$ and c are in GP.

So, $\quad b^2 = ac \Rightarrow b = \sqrt{a}\sqrt{c}$

Put $b = \sqrt{ac}$ in Eq. (i), we get

$$ax^2 + 2\sqrt{a}\sqrt{c}\,x + c = 0$$

$\Rightarrow \quad (\sqrt{a}x + \sqrt{c})^2 = 0$

$\therefore \quad x = -\frac{\sqrt{c}}{\sqrt{a}}$

Put this value in Eq. (ii), we get

$$d\frac{c}{a} - 2e\cdot\frac{\sqrt{c}}{\sqrt{a}} + f = 0$$

$\Rightarrow \quad \frac{cd}{a} + f = 2e\sqrt{\frac{c}{a}}$

$\Rightarrow \quad cd + af = 2e\sqrt{ac}$

$\Rightarrow \quad cd + af = 2e\cdot b \quad [\because b = \sqrt{ac}]$

Divide by ac, $\frac{cd}{ac} + \frac{af}{ac} = \frac{2eb}{ac}$

$\frac{d}{a} + \frac{f}{c} = \frac{2eb}{b^2} \quad [\because b^2 = ac]$

$\frac{d}{a} + \frac{f}{c} = \frac{2e}{b}$

$\Rightarrow \quad \frac{d}{a}, \frac{e}{b}$ and $\frac{f}{c}$ are in AP.

48. Given equation of parabola is $x = 4y^2$.

Now, comparing it with $y^2 = 4ax$, we get $a = 1/16$

Equation of normal is

$$y = -tx + 2at + at^3$$

$\Rightarrow \quad y = -tx + \frac{2}{16}t + \frac{1}{16}t^3 \quad$ ...(i)

Since, Eq. (i) passes through (0, 33).

$\Rightarrow \quad 33 = \frac{t}{8} + \frac{t^3}{16} \Rightarrow t^3 + 2t - 528 = 0$

$\Rightarrow \quad (t-8)(t^2 + 8t + 66) = 0$

$\Rightarrow \quad t = 8 \quad [\because D < 0 \text{ for } t^2 + 8t + 66]$

$\therefore \quad P \equiv (at^2, 2at)$

$$= \left(\frac{1}{16} \times 64, 2 \times \frac{1}{16} \times 8\right) = (4, 1)$$

Given another parabola :

$$y^2 = 4(x + y)$$

$$\Rightarrow \quad y^2 - 4y = 4x$$

$$\Rightarrow \quad (y - 2)^2 = 4(x + 1)$$

$\therefore$ Equation of its directrix is by

$$x + 1 = -1 \quad \Rightarrow x = -2$$

Hence, distance of point from directrix = 6

49. Two sides of a triangle are $x = 0$ and $y = 3$

Third side is tangent to $y^2 = 6x$

Parametric coordinates of $y^2 = 6x$ are $(6t^2, 6t)$

Let point of tangency be $P(6t^2, 6t)$

$\because$ Tangent at any point (x_1, y_1) on $y^2 = 4ax$ is

$$yy_1 = 49\left(\frac{x + x_1}{2}\right)$$

So, equation of tangent at point $P(6t^2, 6t)$ on parabola is

$$y(6t) = 6\left(\frac{x + 6t^2}{2}\right)$$

$$\Rightarrow \quad 2yt = x + 6t^2$$

or $\quad x - 2yt + 6t^2 = 0$

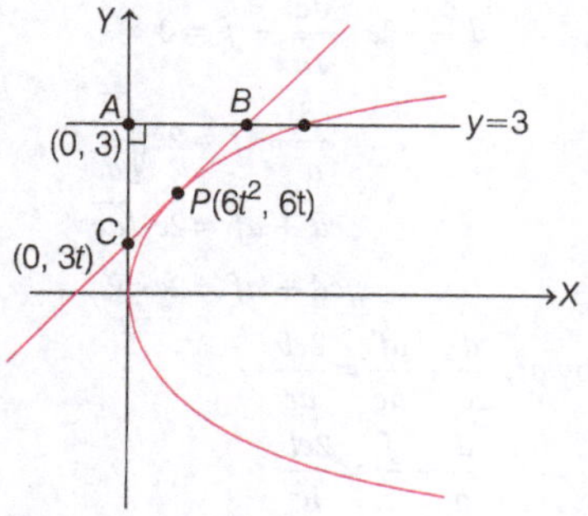

Intersection of tangent and $y = 3 \equiv$ vertex B, so put $y = 3$ in the equation of tangent

$$x - 2(3)t + 6t^2 = 0 \Rightarrow x = 6t - 6t^2 \text{ and } y = 3$$

$\therefore \quad B(6t - 6t^2, 3)$

Vertex $C \equiv$ Intersection of $x = 0$ and tangent

So, put $x = 0$ in the equation of tangent

$$0 - 2yt + 6t^2 = 0$$

$$\Rightarrow \quad y = 3t$$

Vertex $C(0, 3t)$

Now, ΔABC is right angled triangle, right angled at vertex A as $x = 0$ and $y = 3$ are perpendicular to each other.

So, Let its circumcentre is (h, k)

So, $\quad h = \dfrac{0 + 6t - 6t^2}{2} = 3t - 3t^2 \quad$ ...(i)

and $\quad k = \dfrac{3 + 3t}{2}$

or $\quad 2k - 3 = 3t$ or $t = \dfrac{(2k - 3)}{3}$

Put the value of t in Eq. (i), we get

$$h = 3\left(\frac{2k - 3}{3}\right) - 3\left(\frac{2k - 3}{3}\right)^2$$

$$\Rightarrow \quad h = \frac{6k - 9}{3} - \frac{(4k^2 - 12k + 9)}{3}$$

$$\Rightarrow \quad 3h = 6k - 9 - (4k^2 - 12k + 9)$$

$$\Rightarrow \quad 3h = -4k^2 + 18k - 18$$

$$\Rightarrow \quad 4k^2 - 18k + 3h + 18 = 0$$

Now, replace (h, k) with (x, y), we get

$$4y^2 - 18y + 3x + 18 = 0$$

50. For parabola $x = 2y^2$,

$$y^2 = 4 \times \frac{1}{8}x \Rightarrow a = \frac{1}{8}$$

Equation of tangent for parabola, $x = 2y^2$ is

$$y = mx + \frac{a}{m}$$

$$\Rightarrow \quad y = mx + \frac{1}{8m} \quad \text{... (i)}$$

and for parabola, $x = 1 + y^2$,

$$y^2 = 4 \times \frac{1}{4}(x - 1)$$

$$\Rightarrow \quad a = \frac{1}{4}$$

Equation of tangent for parabola, $x = 1 + y^2$ is

$$Y = MX + \frac{a}{m}$$

$$\Rightarrow \quad y = m(x - 1) + \frac{1}{4m}$$

$$y = mx + \frac{1}{4m} - m \quad \text{... (ii)}$$

Since, Eqs. (i) and (ii) represent same tangent.

So, $\quad \dfrac{1}{1} = \dfrac{m}{m} = \dfrac{\frac{1}{8m}}{\frac{1}{4m} - m}$

$$\frac{1}{4m} - m = \frac{1}{8m} \Rightarrow \frac{1}{8m} = m$$

$$m^2 = \frac{1}{8}$$

$$\Rightarrow \quad m = \frac{1}{2\sqrt{2}} \quad \text{[given, } m > 0]$$

Put in Eq. (i). So, common tangent is,

$$y = \frac{x}{2\sqrt{2}} + \frac{1}{2\sqrt{2}}$$

$$\Rightarrow \quad x - 2\sqrt{2}y + 1 = 0$$

Distance of the point $(6, -2\sqrt{2})$ from the common tangent $x - 2\sqrt{2}y + 1 = 0$

$$= \left|\frac{6 - 2\sqrt{2}(-2\sqrt{2}) + 1}{\sqrt{1^2 + (2\sqrt{2})^2}}\right| = \left|\frac{6 + 8 + 1}{3}\right| = 5$$

51. Given, equation of AB is

$$(\lambda + 1)x + \lambda y = 4 \quad \text{...(i)}$$

and equation of AC is

$$\lambda x + (1 - \lambda)y + \lambda = 0 \quad \text{...(ii)}$$

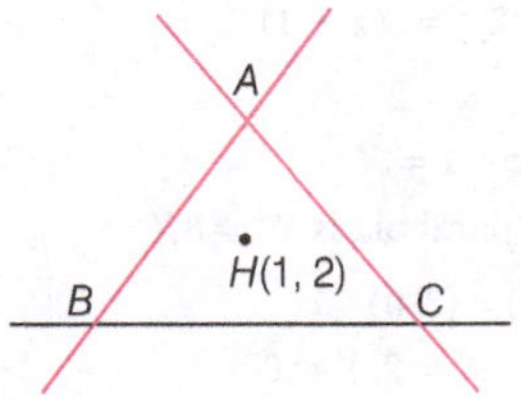

When, $x = 0$, then $\lambda = 2$

Equation of AB is $3x + 2y = 4$

and equation of AC is $2x - y + 2 = 0$

$\therefore$ Coordinates of A are $(0, 2)$.

Since, $CH \perp AB$ and let coordinates of C are (a, b).

$$\therefore \quad \left(\frac{b-2}{a-1}\right) \times \left(\frac{-3}{2}\right) = -1 \Rightarrow 3b - 6 = 2a - 2$$

$$\Rightarrow \quad 3b - 2a = 4 \quad \text{...(iii)}$$

Since, C lies on AC.

$$\therefore \quad 2a - b + 2 = 0 \quad \text{...(iv)}$$

On solving Eqs. (iii) and (iv), we get

$$a = -\frac{1}{2} \text{ and } b = 1$$

So, $\quad C\left(-\frac{1}{2}, 1\right)$

Let the equation of tangent be $y = mx + \dfrac{3}{2m}$

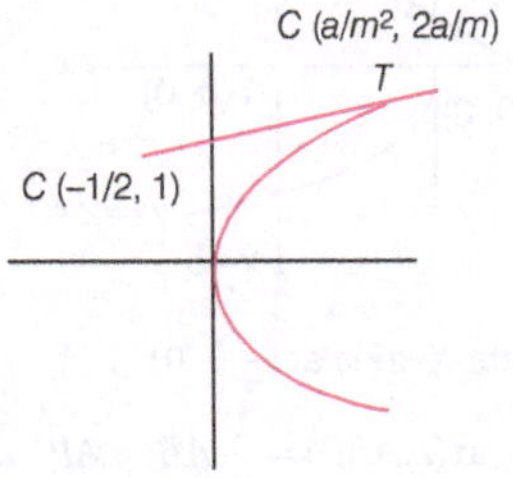

$$m^2 + 2m - 3 = 0 \Rightarrow m = 1, -3$$

So, tangent which touches in first quadrant at T is

$$T = \left(\frac{a}{m^2}, \frac{2a}{m}\right) = \left(\frac{3}{2}, 3\right)$$

$$\Rightarrow \quad CT = \sqrt{4 + 4} = 2\sqrt{2}$$

52. Given, equation of parabola is

$$y^2 = 24x \quad \text{...(i)}$$

and equation of curve (hyperbola) is

$$xy = 2 \quad \text{...(ii)}$$

On comparing Eq. (i) with $y^2 = 4ax$, we get

$$4a = 24 \Rightarrow a = 6$$

Any point taken on the parabola (i) is of the form $(at^2, 2at)$

i.e. $(6t^2, 12t)$.

$\therefore$ Equation of tangent AB at $(6t^2, 12t)$ is given by $T = 0$.

i.e. $\quad y \times (12t) = 24 \times \frac{1}{2} \times (x + 6t^2)$

$\therefore$ Equation of tangent to the parabola $y^2 = 4ax$ at (x_1, y_1) is $T = 0$

i.e. $\quad yy_1 = 4a \times \frac{1}{2} \times (x + x_1)$

$$\Rightarrow \quad ty = x + 6t^2$$

$$\Rightarrow \quad x - ty + 6t^2 = 0 \quad \text{...(iii)}$$

Also, equation of chord AB using $M(h, k)$ as mid-point is given by $T = S_1$

i.e. $\quad \dfrac{xk + yh}{2} - 2 = hk - 2$

$$\Rightarrow \quad xk + yh - 2hk = 0 \quad \text{...(iv)}$$

Now, Eqs. (iii) and (iv) represents the equation of same line.

So, $\quad \dfrac{k}{1} = \dfrac{h}{-t} = \dfrac{-2hk}{6t^2} \Rightarrow k^2 = -3h$

$\Rightarrow$ Locus of M is $y^2 = -3x$.

Hence, directrix is $4x = 3$

[$\because$ equation of directrix for the parabola $y^2 = -4ax$ is $x = a$]

53. Given, equation of parabola is $y^2 = 12x$

Since, point $(3, \alpha)$ lies on $y^2 = 12x$

$$\Rightarrow \quad \alpha^2 = 12 \times 3 = 36 \Rightarrow \alpha = \pm 6$$

Since, tangent to the parabola $y^2 = 12x$ at the point $(3, \alpha)$ be $\perp^r$ to the line $2x + 2y = 3$

So, $\quad m = -1$

$$\Rightarrow \quad \frac{6}{\alpha} = 1 7 \alpha = 6 \quad (\alpha = -6 \text{ rejected})$$

Now, the hyperbola is $\alpha^2 x^2 - 9y^2 = 9\alpha^2$

$$\Rightarrow \quad \frac{x^2}{9} - \frac{y^2}{\alpha^2} = 1 \Rightarrow \frac{x^2}{9} - \frac{y^2}{30} = 1$$

Normal to the hyperbola $\dfrac{x^2}{9} - \dfrac{y^2}{36} = 1$ at the point $(5, 8)$ is

$$\frac{9x}{5} + \frac{36y}{8} = 45$$

$$\Rightarrow \quad 72x + 180y = 1800 \Rightarrow 2x + 5y = 50$$

Now, distance of $(6, -4)$ from the normal to the given hyperbola is equal to $\left|\dfrac{2(6) + 5(-4) + 50}{\sqrt{2^2 + 5^2}}\right|$

$$= \left|\frac{12 - 20 - 50}{\sqrt{29}}\right| = \left|\frac{-56}{\sqrt{29}}\right| = \frac{58}{\sqrt{29}}$$

Distance $= 2\sqrt{29}$

$\therefore$ (Distance)$^2 = (2\sqrt{29})^2 = 4 \times 29 = 116$

54. Tangent of slope in to the parabola $y^2 = 4x$ is given by $y = mx + (1/m)$ and tangent of slope 'm' to the line $(x - 4)^2 + y^2 = 16$ is given by $y = m(x - 4) \pm 4\sqrt{1 + m^2}$

For common tangent,

$$1/m = -4m \pm 4\sqrt{1 + m^2}$$

$$\Rightarrow \quad \left(\left(\frac{1}{m}+4m\right)^2 = \left(\pm 4\sqrt{1+m^2}\right)^2\right)$$

[squaring both sides]

$$\Rightarrow \quad \frac{1}{m^2}+16m^2+8 = 16+16m^2$$

$$\Rightarrow \quad \frac{1}{m^2} = 8 \Rightarrow m = \pm\frac{1}{2\sqrt{2}}$$

Then, the point of contact on parabola is $(8, 4\sqrt{2})$.

Length of tangent PQ from $(8, 4\sqrt{2})$ on the circle is

$$\Rightarrow \quad PQ = \sqrt{(8-4)^2+(4\sqrt{2})^2-16}$$

$$\Rightarrow \quad PQ = \sqrt{16+32-16}$$

$$\Rightarrow \quad PQ = \sqrt{32} \Rightarrow (PQ)^2 = 32$$

55. Focus $= (3, 0)$

Directrix, $x = -3 \Rightarrow 2a = 6 \Rightarrow a - 3$

$\Rightarrow$ Equation of parabola $y^2 = 4 \times 3 \times x$

i.e. $$y^2 = 12x$$

We know that

$$\alpha = at_1t_2 \text{ and } \beta = a(t_1+t_2)$$

or $$\alpha = 3t\cdot 3t,\ \beta = 3(t+3t)$$

$$\alpha = 9t^2,\ \beta = 12t$$

$$\therefore \quad \left(\frac{\beta}{\alpha}\right)^2 = \frac{144t^2}{9t^2} = 16$$

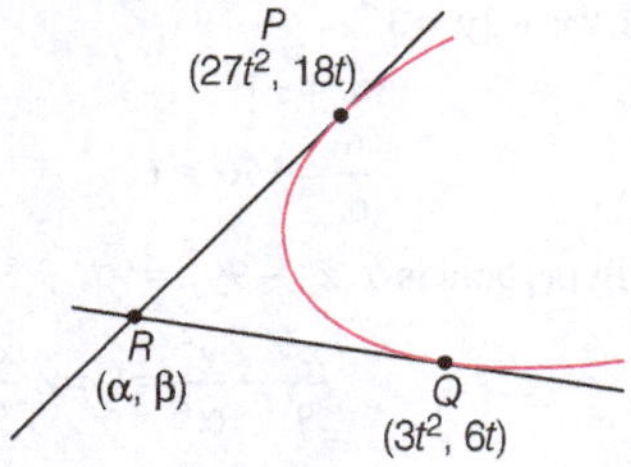

56. Given, equation of curve is

$$x^2+2x-4y+9=0 \quad \text{...(i)}$$

Equation of tangent at $P(1, 3)$ to the given curve Eq. (i),

$$x(1)+2\left(\frac{x+1}{2}\right)-4\left(\frac{y+3}{2}\right)+9=0$$

$$\Rightarrow \quad 2x+2x+2-4y-12+18=0$$

$$\Rightarrow \quad 4x-4y+8=0$$

$$\Rightarrow \quad x-y+2=0$$

which meets the Y-axis at A.

$$\therefore \quad A \equiv (0, 2)$$

Equation of line passing through P and parallel to $x-3y=6$ is

$$x-3y+8=0 \quad \text{...(ii)}$$

Since, line (ii) its meets the parabola $y^2 = 4x$ at B.

$$\therefore \quad y^2 = 4(3y-8) \Rightarrow y^2-12y+32=0$$

$$\Rightarrow \quad (y-4)(y-8)=0$$

$\therefore$ Possible coordinates of B are $(4, 4)$ and $(16, 8)$.

Since, $(4, 4)$ does not satisfies line $2x-3y=8$.

Thus, B is $(16, 8)$

$$\therefore \quad AB^2 = (16-0)^2+(8-2)^2$$

$$= 256+36 = 292$$

57. We have, $$y^2 = 8x+4y+4$$

$$\Rightarrow \quad (y-2)^2 = 8(x+1)$$

$$\therefore \quad a = 2$$

Let $y-2 = Y,\ x+1 = X$

So, equation of parabola is $Y^2 = 8X$

$\therefore$ Focus $= (a, 0) = (2, 0)$

$$\therefore \quad X = 2,\ Y = 0$$

$$\Rightarrow \quad x+1 = 2,\ y-2 = 0 \Rightarrow x = 1,\ y = 2$$

So, focus of given parabola is $(1, 2)$.

$\therefore$ Equation of focal chord of slope m is $y-2 = m(x-1)$.

But x-intercept is 3

$$\therefore \quad 0-2 = m(3-1) \Rightarrow m = -1$$

$\therefore$ Equation of focal chord is $y-2 = -1(x-1)$

$$\Rightarrow \quad x+y-3=0$$

Now, $$m = -1$$

$$\Rightarrow \quad \tan\theta = -1 \Rightarrow \theta = 135°$$

Again, length of focal chord $= 4a\operatorname{cosec}^2\theta$

$$= 4\times 2\operatorname{cosec}^2(135°) = 8(\sqrt{2})^2 = 16$$

58. Equation of tangent at $P(b, c)$ on the parabola $y^2 = 2ax$ is $cy = a(x+b)$

$$\Rightarrow \quad ax-cy+ab=0$$

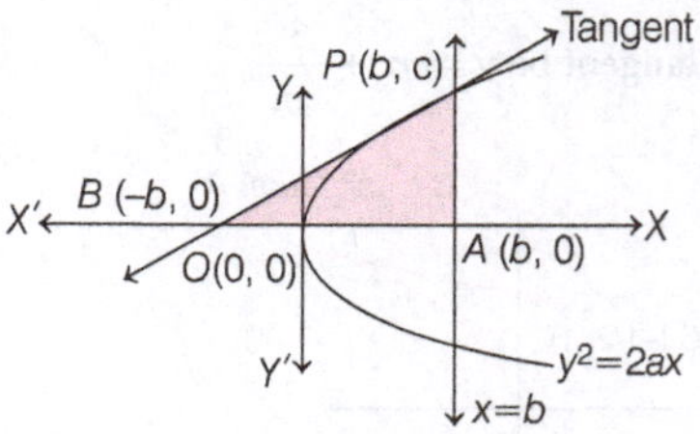

Tangent meets X-axis at $(-b, 0)$.

Now, $$\text{ar}(\Delta ABP) = \frac{1}{2}AB \times AP$$

$$= \frac{1}{2}\times(2b)\times(c) = bc$$

But $\text{ar}(\Delta ABP) = 16$

$$\therefore \quad bc = 16$$

Since, $b, c \in N$, so possible values of (b, c) are $(1, 16), (2, 8), (4, 4), (8, 2), (16, 1)$.

Now, (b, c) lies on parabola, so $c^2 = 2ab \Rightarrow a = \frac{c^2}{2b}$

On putting values of b and c, we get

$$a = 128, 16, 2, \frac{1}{4}, \frac{1}{32}$$

But $a \in N$

$$\therefore \quad a = 128, 16, 2$$

$$\therefore \quad \sum_{a\in S} a = 128+16+2 = 146$$

59. Tangent at (2, 2) on $y^2 = 2x$ is

$$x - 2y + 2 = 0$$

Tangent at (2, 2) on $x^2 + y^2 = 4x$ is

$$y = 2 \rightarrow L_1$$

Equation of line is $x + y + 2 = 0 \rightarrow L_2$

We have to find intersection point of the line and tangent on the circle at (2,2).

The intersection point of L_1 and L_2 is $A(-6, 2)$.

$$\tan(\angle A) = \left|\frac{m_1 - m_2}{1 + m_1 m_2}\right| \text{ where,}$$

$$m_1 = \text{slope of line } L_1 = 0$$

$$\Rightarrow \quad \tan A = \frac{1}{1} = 1$$

$$m_2 = \text{slope of } L_2 = -1$$

$$\Rightarrow \quad \angle A = 45°$$

Now, circumradius (radius of circumcircle) of ΔABC is

$$r = \frac{a}{2\sin A} \quad [\text{where, } a = BC = \sqrt{20}]$$

$$= \frac{\sqrt{20}}{2\sin 45°} = \frac{\sqrt{20}}{2 \cdot \frac{1}{\sqrt{2}}} = \sqrt{10}$$

Hence, $\quad r^2 = (\sqrt{10})^2 = 10$

60.

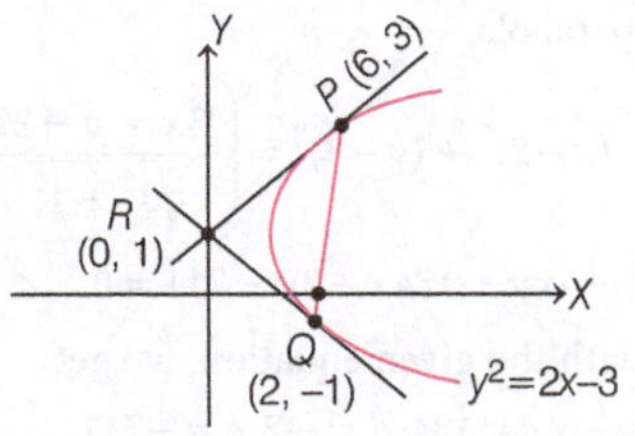

Now, equation of chord joining the points P and Q is given by

$$y + 1 = x - 2 \Rightarrow x - y = 3 \quad \text{... (i)}$$

and equation of parabola is $y^2 = 2x - 3$ ...(ii)

For finding the coordinates of P and Q, we solve the Eqs. (i) and (ii), we get $P \equiv (6, 3)$ and $Q \equiv (2, -1)$.

Now, slope of $PQ = M_{PQ} = \frac{3-(-1)}{6-2} = \frac{4}{4} = 1$

$$M_{RQ} = \frac{1-(-1)}{0-2} = \frac{2}{-2} = -1$$

$$\because \quad M_{PQ} \times M_{RQ} = -1$$

$$\therefore \quad PQ \perp RQ.$$

Hence, $\quad \angle PQR = 90°$

As we know that orthocentre of a right angled triangle is the vertex where right angle is formed.

$\therefore$ Orthocentre $= Q \equiv (2, -1)$.

61. Given, equation of tangent at vertex is $x + y - a = 0$

Focus is (a, a).

$$\therefore \quad \text{Latus rectum} = 4\left|\frac{a + a - a}{\sqrt{2}}\right| = 16$$

$$\Rightarrow \quad \left|\frac{a}{\sqrt{2}}\right| = 4 \quad \Rightarrow \frac{a^2}{2} = 16$$

$$\Rightarrow \quad a^2 = 32 \quad \Rightarrow \quad |a| = 4\sqrt{2}$$

62. $y^2 = 8x$

Let $\quad P(t) = (a, b) \Rightarrow a = 2t^2, b = 4t$

Tangent at P is $x - ty + 2t^2 = 0$

This passes through (5, 7).

$$\therefore \quad 5 - 7t + 2t^2 = 0$$

$\Rightarrow$ Two possible points are $P(t_1)$ and $P(t_2)$

where $\quad t_1 + t_2 = \frac{7}{2}, t_1 \cdot t_2 = \frac{5}{2}$

Now, $\quad A = (2t_1)^2 \times (2t_2)^2 = 4(t_1 t_2)^2$

$$= 4 \times \frac{25}{4} = 25$$

and $\quad B = (4t_1) \times (4t_2) = 16 \times \frac{5}{2} = 40$

$$\therefore \quad A + B = 65$$

63. Let the equation of the tangent of the parabola $y = x^2$ be

$$y = mx - \frac{m^2}{4}$$

Now, the tangent also touches the parabola $y = -(x-2)^2$,

so $\quad mx - \frac{m^2}{4} = -(x-2)^2$

$$\Rightarrow \quad 4mx - m^2 = -4(x^2 - 4x + 4)$$

$$\Rightarrow \quad 4mx - m^2 + 4x^2 - 16x + 16 = 0$$

$$\Rightarrow \quad 4x^2 + 4(m-4)x + 16 - m^2 = 0$$

As the tangent touches parabola at only one point, $D = 0$

$$[4(m-4)]^2 - 4 \times 4(16 - m^2) = 0$$

$$\Rightarrow \quad 16[m^2 - 8m + 16 - 16 + m^2] = 0$$

$$\Rightarrow \quad 2m^2 - 8m = 0$$

$$\Rightarrow \quad m = 0, 4$$

Equation of tangent is $y = 0$

or $\quad y = 4x - 4 = 4(x - 1)$

64. The given parabola is $y^2 - 2x - 2y = 1$

This can be written as $(y-1)^2 = 2(x+1)$

Now, from the above given information the tangent at the point $A(1, 3)$ on the parabola $y^2 - 2x - 2y = 1$ is

$$y(3) - (x + 1) - (y + 3) = 1$$

$$\Rightarrow \quad 3y - x - 1 - y - 3 = 1$$

$$\Rightarrow \quad 2y - x = 5 \quad \text{...(i)}$$

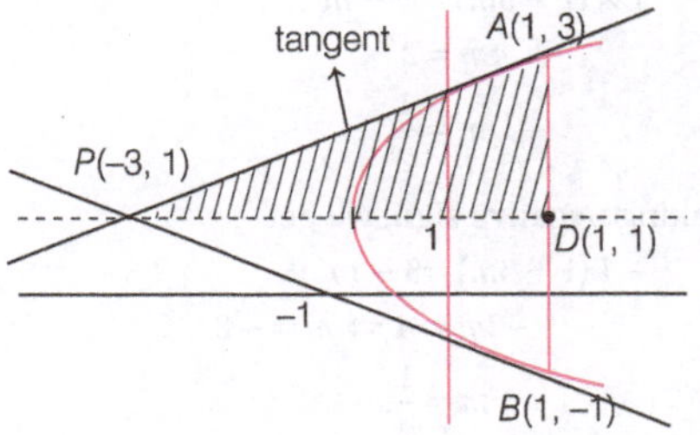

and tangent at $(1, -1)$ is

$$y(-1)-(x+1)-(y-1)=1$$

$$\Rightarrow \quad -y-x-1-y+1=1$$

$$\Rightarrow \quad x+2y=-1 \quad \text{...(ii)}$$

Now, on solving Eqs. (i) and (ii), we get

$$x=-3 \text{ and } y=1$$

Hence, the point $P(-3, 1)$

Thus, area of ΔPAB is

$$2\times\frac{1}{2}\times(1-(-3))\times(3-1)=8 \text{ sq units}$$

65. **Decoding the Question**

(i) The angle between two lines with slopes m_1 and m_2 is $\tan\theta=\left|\frac{m_1-m_2}{1+m_1m_2}\right|$

(ii) The equation of tangent to parabola $y^2=4ax$ is $y=mx+\frac{a}{m}$ and the point of contact is $\left(\frac{a}{m^2}, \frac{2a}{m}\right)$

(iii) If (x_1, y_1), (x_2, y_2) and (x_3, y_3) are collinear, then $\begin{vmatrix} x_1 & y_2 & 1\\ x_2 & y_2 & 1\\ x_3 & y_3 & 1\end{vmatrix}=0$

Given, $y^2=4ax$, $a>0$ and $y=3x+5$

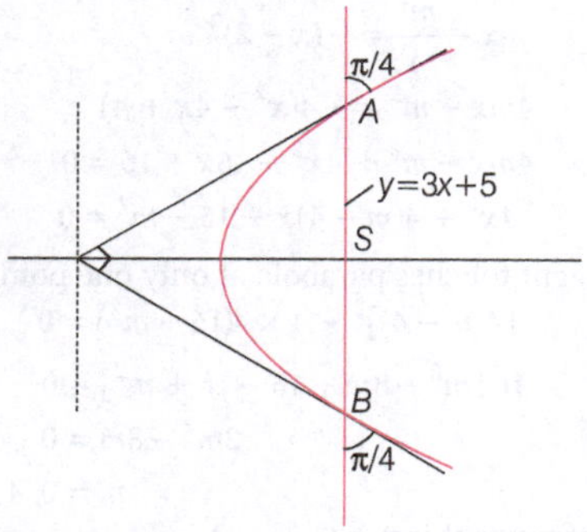

Let slope of tangent be m.

Then, $\tan\theta=\left|\frac{3-m}{1+3m}\right|$

$$\Rightarrow \quad \tan\frac{\pi}{4}=\left|\frac{3-m}{1+3m}\right|$$

$$\Rightarrow \quad \pm 1=\frac{3-m}{1+3m}$$

On taking positive sign, we get

$$1\times(1+3m)=3-m$$

$$\Rightarrow \quad 4m=2$$

$$\Rightarrow \quad m=\frac{1}{2}$$

On taking negative sign, we get

$$-1(1+3m)=3-m$$

$$\Rightarrow \quad -2m=4 \Rightarrow m=-2$$

$$\therefore \quad m=\frac{1}{2}, -2$$

It means tangents are perpendicular to each other. As we know that the tangent at extremities of a focal chord of a parabola intersect at right angle on directrix.

Therefore, A, S and B are collinear for all $a>0$.

66.

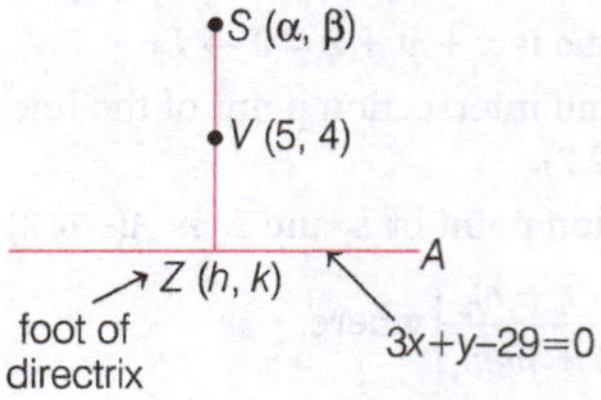

$$\frac{h-5}{3}=\frac{k-4}{1}=\frac{-(3\times5+4-29)}{10}$$

$$\Rightarrow \quad \frac{h-5}{3}=\frac{k-4}{1}=1$$

$$\Rightarrow \quad h=8, k=5$$

$$\therefore \quad Z=(8,5)$$

Now, $\frac{\alpha+8}{2}=5$

and $\frac{\beta+5}{2}=4$

$$\alpha=2, \beta=3$$

$\therefore$ Focus $\equiv S=(2,3)$

Equation of parabola,

$$(x-2)^2+(y-3)^2=\left(\frac{|3x+y-29|}{\sqrt{3^2+1^2}}\right)^2$$

$$\Rightarrow x^2+9y^2-6xy+134x-2y-711=0$$

Compare it with the given equation, we get

$$a=9, b=-6, c=134, d=-2, e=-711$$

Hence, $a+b+c+d+e=9-6+134-2-711$

$$=-576$$

67. $y^2=6x \Rightarrow 4a=6 \Rightarrow a=\frac{3}{2}$

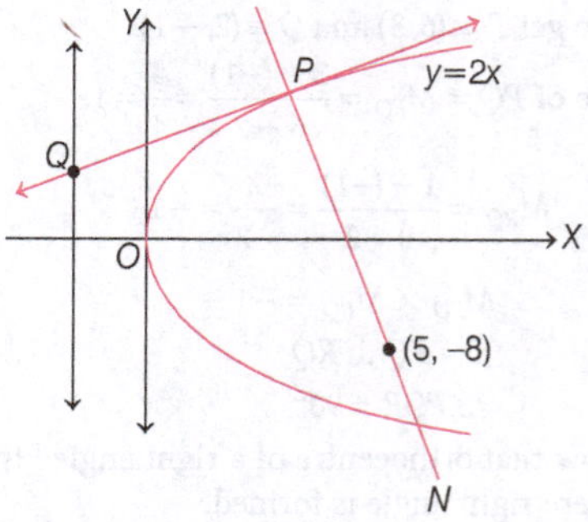

Equation of normal $y=mx-3m-\frac{3}{2}m^3$

Point (5, –8) ssatisfy this equation

$$\therefore \quad -8=5m-3m-\frac{3}{2}m^3$$

$$\Rightarrow \quad 2m - \frac{3}{2}m^3 = -8 \Rightarrow m = 2 = m_N$$

$\Rightarrow$ Slope of tangent at P, $m_T = -\frac{1}{2}$

So, equation of tangent, $y = m_T x + \frac{3}{2m_T}$

$$\Rightarrow \quad y = -\frac{x}{2} - 3$$

Equation of directrix is, $x = -\frac{3}{2}$

$$\therefore \quad y = \left(-\frac{1}{2}\right)\left(-\frac{3}{2}\right) - 3 = \frac{3}{4} - 3 = -\frac{9}{4}$$

$\therefore$ Ordinate $= -\frac{9}{4}$

68. Line $y = 4 + kx$ touches the parabola $y = x - x^2$ at point P.

$\Rightarrow \quad 4 + kx = x - x^2$ has only one root

$\Rightarrow \quad x^2 + (k-1)x + 4 = 0$ has only one root

$$\Rightarrow \quad (k-1)^2 - 4 \times 4 = 0$$

$$\Rightarrow \quad (k-1-4)(k-1+4) = 0$$

$\Rightarrow \quad k = 5, k \neq -3$, as $k > 0$

$$\therefore \quad x^2 + 4x + 4 = 0 \Rightarrow x = -2$$

If $x = -2$, then $y = -6$

$\therefore$ Coordinates of point P are $(-2, -6)$.

The given parabola is $y = x - x^2$

$$y - \frac{1}{4} = -\left(x^2 - x + \frac{1}{4}\right)$$

$$\Rightarrow \quad y - \frac{1}{4} = -\left(x - \frac{1}{2}\right)^2$$

Vertex of the parabola is $V = \left(\frac{1}{2}, \frac{1}{4}\right)$.

$$\text{Slope of } PV = \frac{\frac{1}{4} + 6}{\frac{1}{2} + 2} = \frac{\frac{25}{4}}{\frac{5}{2}} = \frac{5}{2}$$

69. Given, conic $x = 2t$, $y = \frac{t^2}{3}$

$$\Rightarrow \quad x/2 = t$$

$$\Rightarrow \quad y = \left(\frac{x}{2}\right)^2 \times \frac{1}{3}$$

$$x^2 = 12y$$

$\therefore$ The given conic is a parabola with axis on Y-axis and focus S as $(0, 3)$.

Let coordinates of B be $(0, y)$.

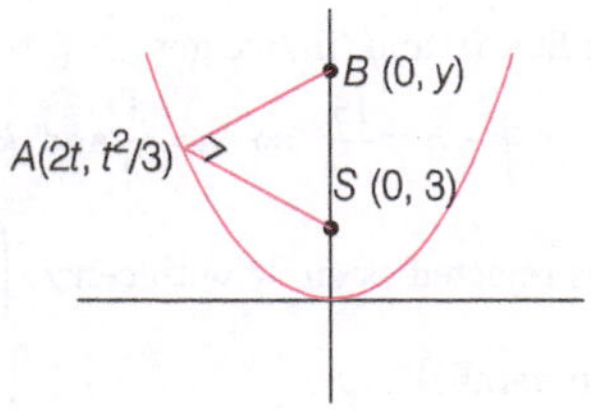

As $AB \perp AS$, $M_{AB} \times M_{AS} = -1$

$$\left(\frac{y - \frac{t^2}{3}}{0 - 2t}\right) \times \left(\frac{3 - \frac{t^2}{3}}{0 - 2t}\right) = -1$$

$$\Rightarrow \quad (3y - t^2)(9 - t^2) = -36t^2$$

$$\Rightarrow \quad 27y - 9t^2 - 3yt^2 + t^4 + 36t^2 = 0$$

$$\Rightarrow \quad y = \frac{t^4 + 27t^2}{3t^2 - 27} = \frac{t^4 + 27t^2}{3(t^2 - 9)}$$

k is ordinate of centroid of ΔSAB.

$$\therefore \quad k = \frac{3 + y + \frac{t^2}{3}}{3}$$

$$\Rightarrow \quad 9k = 9 + 3y + t^2$$

$$\Rightarrow \quad 9k = 9 + \frac{t^4 + 27t^2}{t^2 - 9} + t^2$$

$$\Rightarrow \quad 9k = \frac{9(t^2 - 9) + t^4 + 27t^2 + t^2(t^2 - 9)}{t^2 - 9}$$

$$\Rightarrow \quad k = \frac{9t^2 - 81 + t^4 + 27t^2 + t^4 - 9t^2}{9(t^2 - 9)}$$

$$\Rightarrow \quad k = \frac{2t^4 + 27t^2 - 81}{9(t^2 - 9)}$$

$$\therefore \quad \lim_{t \to 1} k = \lim_{t \to 1} \frac{2t^4 + 27t^2 - 81}{9(t^2 - 9)} = \frac{2 + 27 - 81}{9(1 - 9)} = \frac{52}{72} = \frac{13}{18}$$

70. Let the equation of tangent of parabola $y^2 = x$ is

$$y = mx + \frac{1}{4m}$$

$y = mx + \frac{1}{4m}$ is also the equation of tangent of circle

$$x^2 + y^2 = 2$$

$$\Rightarrow \quad \left(\frac{1}{4m}\right)^2 = 2(1 + m^2)$$

$$\Rightarrow \quad \frac{1}{16m^2} = 2 + 2m^2 \Rightarrow 32m^4 + 32m^2 - 1 = 0$$

$$\Rightarrow \quad m^2 = \frac{-32 \pm \sqrt{(32)^2 - 4(32)(-1)}}{2 \times 32}$$

$$\Rightarrow \quad m^2 = \frac{-32 \pm \sqrt{32 \times 36}}{2 \times 32}$$

$$\Rightarrow \quad m^2 = \frac{-32 + 24\sqrt{2}}{64} = \frac{-4 + 3\sqrt{2}}{8}$$

$$\therefore \quad m_1 \text{ and } m_2 \text{ are } \sqrt{\frac{-4 + 3\sqrt{2}}{8}} \text{ and } -\sqrt{\frac{-4 + 3\sqrt{2}}{8}}$$

$$m_1 m_2 = \sqrt{\frac{(-4 + 3\sqrt{2})^2}{(8)^2}}$$

$$\therefore \quad 8|m_1 m_2| = 8\left[\frac{-4 + 3\sqrt{2}}{8}\right] = -4 + 3\sqrt{2}$$

71. Let $P(h, k)$ be a point on the curve.

Equation of line passing (h, k) is $y - k = m(x - h)$ where $m = \frac{dy}{dx}$

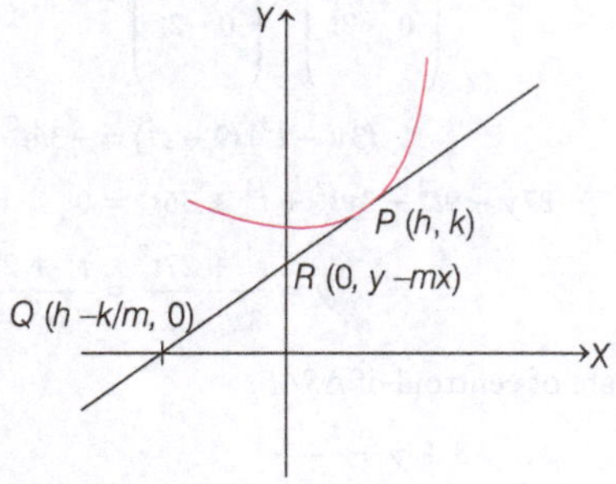

At Q, $y = 0 \Rightarrow x = h - \frac{k}{m}$

As Y-axis bisects PQ,

$$\frac{h + h - \frac{k}{m}}{2} = 0 \Rightarrow h + h - \frac{k}{m} = 0$$

$$\Rightarrow \quad \frac{dy}{y} = \frac{dx}{2x} \quad \text{[replacing } h \text{ by } x \text{ and } k \text{ by } y]$$

$\Rightarrow$ $\ln y = \frac{1}{2}\ln x + \ln C$, where C is a constant

$$\Rightarrow \quad y^2 = Cx$$

It passes through the point (3,3)

$$\Rightarrow \quad C = 3$$

Hence, $\quad y^2 = 3x$

Then, length of latus rectum is 3.

72. Given that circle is

$$x^2 + y^2 + Ax + By + C = 0 \quad \text{... (i)}$$

Parabola is $\quad y = x^2 \quad$ ... (ii)

Since, Eqs. (i) and (ii) intersect at (2, 4).

$\therefore$ (2, 4) lies on Eq. (i),

$$\Rightarrow \quad 2A + 4B + C + 20 = 0$$

$$\Rightarrow \quad 2A + 4B + C = -20 \quad \text{... (iii)}$$

Now, on differentiating Eq. (i) w.r.t. x, we get

$$2x + 2y\frac{dy}{dx} + A + B\frac{dy}{dx} = 0 \quad \text{... (iv)}$$

Also, on differentiating Eq. (ii) w.r.t. x, we get

$$\frac{dy}{dx} = 2x \Rightarrow \left.\frac{dy}{dx}\right|_{(2,4)} = 4$$

Now, from Eq. (iv), we get

$$4 + 32 + A + 4B = 0 \quad \left[\text{put } \left.\frac{dy}{dx}\right|_{(2,4)} = 4\right]$$

$$\Rightarrow \quad A + 4B = -36 \quad \text{... (v)}$$

Now, on subtracting Eq. (v) from Eq. (iii), we get

$$(2A + 4B + C) - (A + 4B) = (-20) - (-36)$$

$$\Rightarrow \quad A + C = 16$$

Thus, $A + C$ is equal to 16.

73. Given, $f(x) = 2x^2 - \log_e x$

$$f'(x) = 4x - \frac{1}{x}$$

$$f'(x) = 0 \Rightarrow 4x^2 - 1 = 0$$

$$\Rightarrow \quad x = \frac{1}{2}\left[x \neq -\frac{1}{2}\right]$$

$\therefore f(x)$ is decreasing in $\left(0, \frac{1}{2}\right)$ and increasing in $\left(\frac{1}{2}, \infty\right)$.

$\therefore$ Equation of parabola is $y^2 = 2x$

Equation of tangent of parabola $y^2 = 2x$ is

$$y = mx + \frac{1}{2m}$$

The tangent passes through $(8a, 8a - 1)$, i.e. (4, 3)

$$3 = 4m + \frac{1}{2m}$$

$$\Rightarrow \quad 8m^2 - 6m + 1 = 1 \Rightarrow m = \frac{1}{2} \text{ or } \frac{1}{4}$$

Equation of tangent can be $y = \frac{1}{2}x + 1$ or $y = \frac{1}{4}x + 2$

But the tangent $y = \frac{1}{2}x + 1$ does pass through $\left(-\frac{1}{a}, 0\right)$ i.e. $(-2, 0)$, so rejected.

$\therefore$ The required tangent of parabola is $y = \frac{1}{4}x + 2$

$\therefore$ Slope of normal is -4.

Equation of normal of parabola is

$$y = mx - 2am - am^3$$

$$\Rightarrow \quad y = -4x - 2\left(\frac{1}{2}\right)(-4) - \frac{1}{2}(-4)^3$$

$$\Rightarrow \quad 4x + y = 36 \Rightarrow \frac{x}{9} + \frac{y}{36} = 1$$

Here, $\quad \alpha = 9, \beta = 36$

$$\Rightarrow \quad \alpha + \beta = 9 + 36 = 45$$

74. Vertex and focus of parabola $y^2 = 2x$ are $V(0, 0)$ and $S\left(\frac{1}{2}, 0\right)$ respectively.

Let equation of circle be

$$(x - h)^2 + (y - k)^2 = 4$$

$\because$ Circle passes through (0, 0).

$$\Rightarrow \quad h^2 + k^2 = 4 \quad \text{...(i)}$$

$\because$ Circle passes through $\left(\frac{1}{2}, 0\right)$

$$\left(\frac{1}{2} - h\right)^2 + k^2 = 4 \Rightarrow h^2 + k^2 - h = \frac{15}{4} \quad \text{...(ii)}$$

On solving Eqs. (i) and (ii), we get

$$4 - h = \frac{15}{4} \Rightarrow h = \frac{1}{4} \text{ and } k = \frac{\sqrt{63}}{4}$$

$k = \frac{-\sqrt{63}}{4}$ is rejected as circle with centre $\left(\frac{1}{4}, \frac{-\sqrt{63}}{4}\right)$ can not touch given parabola.

Equation of circle is

$$\left(x-\frac{1}{4}\right)^2+\left(y-\frac{\sqrt{63}}{4}\right)^2=4$$

$$\Rightarrow \qquad \alpha=2+\frac{\sqrt{63}}{4}=\frac{8+\sqrt{63}}{4}$$

$$\Rightarrow \qquad 4\alpha-8=\sqrt{63}$$

$$\Rightarrow \qquad (4\alpha-8)^2=63$$

75. Given that P_1 be a parabola with vertex (3, 2) and focus (4, 4).

The point of intersection of directrix with axis of parabola $= A = (2, 0)$

Image of $A(2, 0)$ w.r.t. line $x+2y=6$ is $B(x_2, y_2)$.

$$\therefore \qquad \frac{x_2-2}{1}=\frac{y_2-0}{2}=\frac{-2(2+0-6)}{5}$$

$$\therefore \qquad B(x_2, y_2)=\left(\frac{18}{5},\frac{16}{5}\right).$$

The point B is the point of intersection of directrix with axis of parabola P_2.

Thus, $x+2y=k$ must have point $\left(\frac{18}{5},\frac{16}{5}\right)$

$$\Rightarrow \qquad \frac{18}{5}+\frac{32}{5}=k \Rightarrow k=10$$

$$\Rightarrow \qquad x+2y=10$$

76. Vertex $\left(\frac{1}{2},\frac{3}{4}\right)$

Equation of directrix is $y=\frac{1}{2}$

Equation of parabola is $\left(x-\frac{1}{2}\right)^2=y-\frac{3}{4}$

Point on parabola is $P\left(\frac{-1}{2},\frac{7}{4}\right)$

Equation of normal at $P\left(\frac{-1}{2},\frac{7}{4}\right)$ is $x=2y-4$

This normal cuts the parabola at $Q(2, 3)$

$$(PQ)^2=\left(2+\frac{1}{2}\right)^2+\left(3-\frac{7}{4}\right)^2=\frac{125}{16}$$

77.

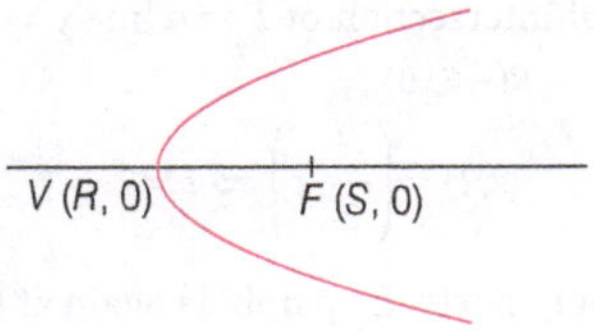

Length of LR of $y^2=4ax$ is $4a$.

Or Length of $LR = 4 \times$ [Distance between focus and vertex]

Similarly, here length of $LR = 4(S-R)$

78. Given, parabola $y^2=8x$ ...(i)

Equation of tangent at $P(2, -4)$ is

$$-4y=4(x+2)$$

Or $\qquad x+y+2=0$ ...(ii)

and Equation of normal to the parabola is

$$x-y+C=0$$

$\therefore$ Normal passes through $(2, -4)$

$$\therefore \qquad C=-6$$

Normal: $\qquad x-y=6$ ...(iii)

Equation of directrix of parabola

$$x=-2 \qquad \text{...(iv)}$$

Point of intersection of tangent and normal with directrix are $x=-2$ at $A(-2, 0)$ and $B(-2, -8)$, respectively.

$Q(a, b)$ and $P(2, -4)$ are given and $AQBP$ is a square.

Mid-point of AB = Mid-point of PQ

$$\Rightarrow \qquad (-2,-4)=\left(\frac{a+2}{2},\frac{b-4}{2}\right)$$

$$\Rightarrow \qquad a=-6, b=-4$$

$$\Rightarrow \qquad 2a+b=-16$$

79. Equation of tangent to $y^2=30x$ is

$$y=mx+\frac{30}{4m}$$

Now, this tangent passes through $(-30, 0)$.

$$\therefore \qquad 0=-30m+\frac{30}{4m}$$

$$\Rightarrow \qquad \frac{30}{4m}=30m \Rightarrow m^2=\frac{1}{4}$$

$$\Rightarrow \qquad m=\pm\frac{1}{2}$$

$\therefore$ Equation of tangent is

$$y=\frac{x}{2}+15$$

or $\qquad y=-\frac{x}{2}-15$

Now equation of circle is $x^2+y^2+30x+\frac{675}{4}=0$

Let perpendicular distance of the tangent from the centre $(-15, 0)$ of the circle $=p$

$$\therefore \qquad p=\frac{\left|\frac{-15}{2}+15\right|}{\sqrt{1+\frac{1}{4}}}=3\sqrt{5}$$

$\therefore$ Length of chord $=2\sqrt{r^2-p^2}$

$$=2\sqrt{\left(15^2+0-\frac{675}{4}\right)-45}=3\sqrt{5},$$

where r is radius of the given circle.

80.

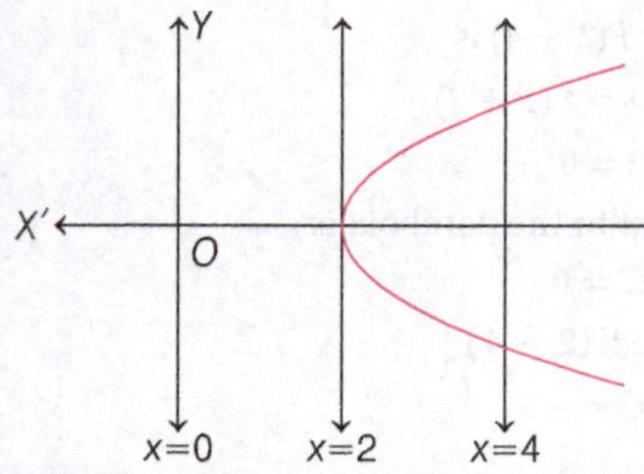

Equation of parabola is $y^2 = 4a(x-2)$

$$a = 2$$

So, $y^2 = 8(x-2)$

Equation of tangent is

$$y = m(x-2) + \frac{2}{m}$$

It passes through (0, 0),

$$0 = -2m + \frac{2}{m} \Rightarrow m^2 = 1$$

$\Rightarrow \quad m = \pm 1$

$\therefore$ Equation is $y = \pm(x-2) \pm 2$

$$y = x \text{ or } y = -x$$

If $y = x$, then $x^2 = 8(x-2)$

$\Rightarrow \quad x^2 - 8x + 16 = 0$

$\Rightarrow \quad (x-4)^2 = 0 \Rightarrow x = 4$

$\Rightarrow \quad y = \pm 4$

So, points are (4, 4), (4, –4) and (0, 0).

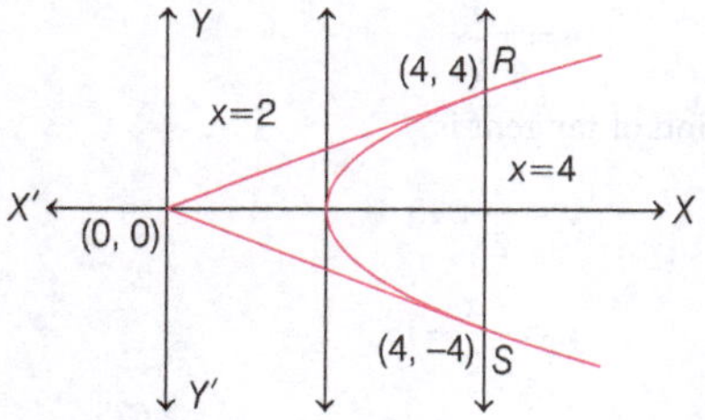

$\therefore$ Area $= \left(\frac{1}{2} \times 4 \times 4\right) \times 2 = 16$ sq units

81. Given, parabola $y = 4x^2 + 1$

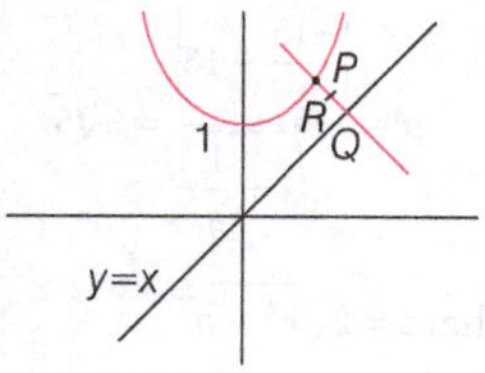

Let $R(a, b)$ be mid-point of line joining point P and Q, where PQ is perpendicular to line $y = x$.

Let coordinates of P be $P(x, y)$, $Q(q, q)$ and $R(a, b)$, then

$$a = \frac{x+q}{2}.$$

and $b = \frac{y+q}{2}$

Now, slope of line $y = x$ is $m_1 = 1$

Slope of line PQ be $\frac{b-q}{a-q} = m_2$. (say)

$\because$ Line $y = x$ and PQ are perpendicular to each other.

$\therefore \quad m_1 \cdot m_2 = -1$

$\Rightarrow \quad \frac{b-q}{a-q} = -1$

$\Rightarrow \quad b - q = q - a \Rightarrow q = \frac{b+a}{2}$

$\therefore \quad a = \frac{x+q}{2} = \frac{x + \left(\frac{b+a}{2}\right)}{2} = \frac{2x+b+a}{4}$

$\Rightarrow \quad x = \frac{4a-b-a}{2} = \frac{3a-b}{2}$

and $b = \frac{y+q}{2} = \frac{y + \left(\frac{b+a}{2}\right)}{2} = \frac{2y+b+a}{4} \Rightarrow y = \frac{3b-a}{2}$

Put (x, y) in equation of parabola as $P(x, y)$ is variable point on parabola

$$\frac{3b-a}{2} = 4\left(\frac{3a-b}{2}\right)^2 + 1$$

$\Rightarrow \quad (3b-a) = 2(3a-b)^2 + 2$

Replace (a, b) as (x, y)

$$(3y - x) = 2(3x-y)^2 + 2$$

or $\quad 2(3x-y)^2 + (x-3y) + 2 = 0$

82. $S: y^2 = 2x$

At (2, 2), equation of tangent

$\Rightarrow \quad y(2) = (x+2)$

$$T_i : 2y = x + 2$$

Normal at (2, 2)

$\Rightarrow \quad y - 2 = -2(x-2)$

$$N_i : y = -2x + 6$$

R is point of intersection of T and line $y = 0$

$\therefore \quad R(-2, 0)$

$\Rightarrow \quad (2,2) = \left(\frac{t^2}{2}, t\right) \Leftrightarrow t = 2$

If normal at t_1 meets the parabola again at t_2,

$$t_2 = -t_1 - \frac{2}{t_1}$$

$$-t_2 = -2 - \frac{2}{2} = -3$$

$\therefore \quad t_2 = 3$

$R:(at_2^2, 2at_2) \Rightarrow \left(\frac{1}{2}\cdot 9, 2\cdot\frac{1}{2}\cdot 3\right) \equiv \left(\frac{9}{2}, 3\right)$

$\therefore P(2, 2), Q(-2, 1), R\left(\frac{9}{2}, 3\right)$

$$\text{Area} = \frac{1}{2}\begin{vmatrix} 1 & 1 & 1 \\ 2 & -2 & \frac{9}{2} \\ 2 & 1 & 3 \end{vmatrix} = \frac{25}{2} \text{ sq units}$$

83. The mirror image of any point (α, β) with respect to line $y = x$ is simply (β, α).

Let (h, k) be the mirror image of a point on parabola $y^2 = 4ax$

Then, (k, h) will be the mirror image of (h, k) and it will lie on parabola.

So, $y^2 = 4x$

$h^2 = 4k$

$\Rightarrow x^2 = 4y$

Hence, locus is $x^2 = 4y$ ...(i)

For finding equation of tangent differentiate Eq. (i) w.r.t. x

$$2x = 4\frac{dy}{dx}$$

$$\Rightarrow \left(\frac{dy}{dx}\right)_{(2,1)} = \left(\frac{2}{2}\right) = 1 \Rightarrow \frac{y-1}{x-2} = 1 \qquad y = x - 1$$

$\therefore$ Equation of tangent is $y = x - 1$

$\Rightarrow x - y = 1$

84. Given, equation of parabola $y^2 = 2x$

Equation of normal of parabola, $y^2 = 4ax$ is $tx + y = 2at + at^3$

Here, $4a = 2$

So, equation of normal is

$$tx + y = t + t^3/2$$

$$\Rightarrow t^3 + (2 - 2x)t - 2y = 0$$

As, there are three normals which are passing through $(a, 0)$, so there must be three roots of this equation.

$\therefore t^3 + (2 - 2a)t - 2.0 = 0$

$\Rightarrow t^3 + (2 - 2a)t = 0$

$\therefore t_1 + t_2 + t_3 = -(2 - 2a) = 2a - 2$

and $t_1t_2 + t_2t_3 + t_3t_1 = 0, t_1, t_2, t_3 \in R$

So, $t_1^2 + t_2^2 + t_3^2 > 0$

$(t_1 + t_2 + t_3)^2 - 2(t_1t_2 + t_2t_3 + t_3t_1) > 0$

$\Rightarrow (2a - 2)^2 - 2\cdot 0 > 0$

$\Rightarrow a > 1$

Time Saving Technique

For standard parabola $y^2 = 4ax$, for more than 3 normals (on axis) $x > \frac{1}{2}$; L = length of latus rectum Now, for $y^2 = 2x$; $\left(a = \frac{1}{2}\right)$

$L.R = 2$

For point $(a, 0)$

$$a > \frac{L}{2} \Rightarrow a > 1$$

85. Given parabola is $y^2 = 6x$

$\Rightarrow y^2 = 4\left(\frac{3}{2}\right)x$ $\quad [\therefore y^2 = 4ax]$

and given line is $2x + y = 1$.

$\because$ Equation of any tangent to the parabola having slope m is

$y = mx + 3/2m$ $\quad [\because a = 3/2]$

Slope of line $2x + y = 1$ is $m_1 = -2$

$\because$ Tangent is perpendicular to this line.

$\therefore$ Slope of tangent $= m_2 = -\frac{1}{m_1} = \frac{1}{2}$

$\therefore$ Equation of tangent will be $y = \frac{1}{2}x + \frac{3}{2}\times 2$

$\Rightarrow y = \frac{x}{2} + 3$ or $2y = x + 6$

Clearly, on putting the coordinates of point (5, 4), the equation of tangent is not satisfied.

$\therefore$ Point (5, 4) does not lie on this tangent.

86. Given curve, $y = ax^2 + bx + c, x \in R$ and point (1, 2)

$\because$ The given curve passes through (1, 2).

$\therefore 2 = a + b + c$

Also, slope of tangent of $y = ax^2 + bx + c$ is $\frac{dy}{dx} = 2ax + b$

$\because$ Tangent passes through origin (0, 0).

$\therefore \left.\frac{dy}{dx}\right|_{(0,0)} = 2a \times 0 + b = b$ ... (i)

According to the question, tangent at origin is $y = x$

$\therefore$Its slope is 1. ... (ii)

From Eqs. (i) and (ii),

$b = 1$

Also, $a + b + c = 2$

$\Rightarrow a + c = 1$

From the option look for $b = 1$ and $a + c = 1$

The only correct order triplet is $a = 1, b = 1, c = 0$.

87. Given curve $y = x^2 + 4$

and line $y = 4x - 1$

Here, $y = x^2 + 4$

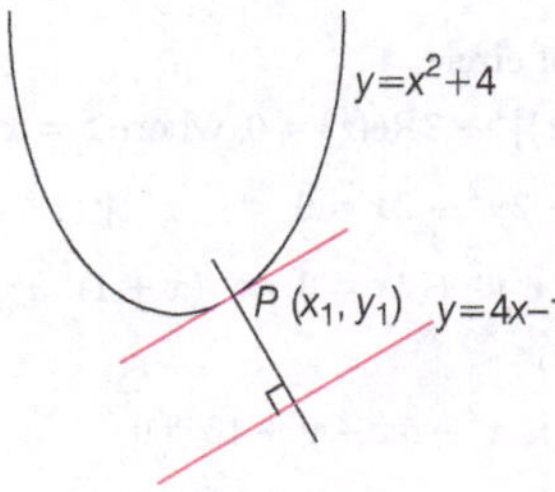

$\therefore \frac{dy}{dx} = 2x$ ... (i)

and $y = 4x - 1$

$\frac{dy}{dx} = 4$ ... (ii)

Let the required point be $P(x_1, y_1)$.

$\therefore \quad \left.\dfrac{dy}{dx}\right|_P = 2x_1$ ... (iii)

$\because$ Slopes will be equal.

$\therefore \quad 2x_1 = 4$ [from Eqs. (ii) and (iii)]

$\Rightarrow \quad x_1 = 4/2 = 2$

Now, the given point $P(x_1, y_1)$ lies on curve $y = x^2 + 4$,

$\therefore \quad y_1 = x_1^2 + 4 \Rightarrow y_1 = 2^2 + 4 = 8$

Hence, required coordinates of P are (2, 8).

88. Given, equation of parabola, $y^2 = 4ax$

Focus $= S(a, 0)$

Let any point on the parabola be $P(at^2, 2at)$.

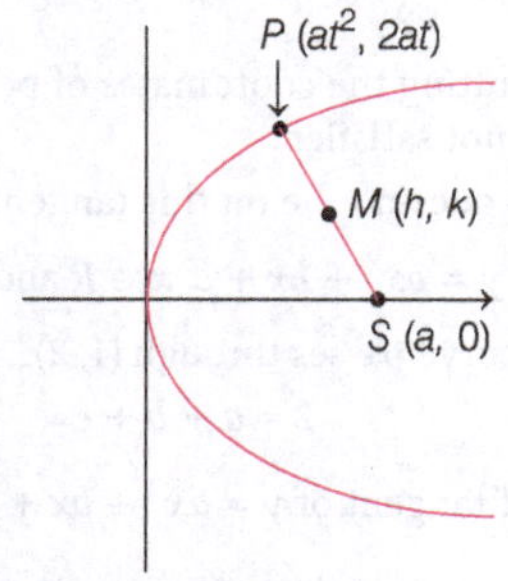

and let the mid-point of PS be $M(h, k)$.

$\therefore \quad h = \dfrac{at^2 + a}{2}, k = \dfrac{2at + 0}{2}$

$\Rightarrow \quad t^2 = \dfrac{2h - a}{a}; t = \dfrac{k}{a} \Rightarrow t^2 = \dfrac{k^2}{a^2}$

Now, $\quad \dfrac{2h - a}{a} = \dfrac{k^2}{a^2}$

$\Rightarrow \quad 2h - a = \dfrac{k^2}{a} \Rightarrow k^2 = a(2h - a)$

$\therefore$ Locus of (h, k) is $y^2 = a(2x - a)$

$$y^2 = 2a\left(x - \frac{a}{2}\right)$$

$\therefore$ The directrix of this parabola is $x - \dfrac{a}{2} = -\dfrac{a}{2} \Rightarrow x = 0.$

89. The equation of circle,

$\text{Re}(z^2) + 2[\text{Im}(z)]^2 + 2\,\text{Re}(z) = 0$, where $z = x + iy$

$\Rightarrow \quad (x^2 - y^2) + 2y^2 + 2x = 0 \quad [\because z^2 = (x^2 - y^2) + 2xyi]$

$\Rightarrow \quad x^2 + y^2 + 2x = 0 \Rightarrow (x + 1)^2 + y^2 = 1$

Centre $= (-1, 0)$

Now, parabola is $x^2 - 6x - y + 13 = 0$

$\Rightarrow \quad x^2 - 6x + 9 = y - 4 \Rightarrow (x - 3)^2 = y - 4$

Vertex = Equation of line passing through centre $(-1, 0)$ and vertex $(3, 4)$ is

$$y - 0 = \frac{4 - 0}{3 + 1}(x + 1) \Rightarrow y = x + 1$$

On comparing, $y = mx + c$

$\Rightarrow \quad y$-intercept $= 1$

90. Shortest distance is along the normal.

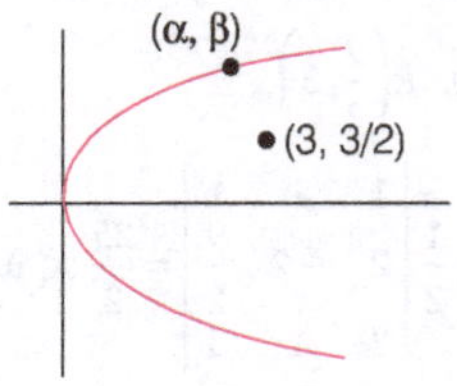

Equation of normal at (α, β)

$y - \beta = -\dfrac{\beta}{2a}(x - \alpha) \quad [\because y^2 = 4ax \Rightarrow 4a = 6 \Rightarrow 2a = 3]$

$\Rightarrow \quad 3y - 3\beta = -\beta(x - \alpha)$

This normal will pass through $\left(3, \dfrac{3}{2}\right)$.

$$\frac{9}{2} - 3\beta = -3\beta + \alpha\beta$$

$\Rightarrow \quad \alpha\beta = \dfrac{9}{2}$ ...(i)

Now, $\quad y^2 = 6\beta^2 = 6\alpha$ ...(ii)

From Eqs. (i) and (ii), we get

$$\alpha = 3/2, \beta = 3$$

$\therefore \quad 2(\alpha + \beta) = 2\left(\dfrac{3}{2} + 3\right) = 9$

91. Equation of circle, $(x + 10)^2 + y^2 = 4$

Equation of tangent to circle,

$x^2 + y^2 = a^2$ is $y = mx \pm a\sqrt{1 + m^2}$

Here, equation of tangent

$$y = m(x + 10) \pm 2\sqrt{1 + m^2}$$

$\Rightarrow \quad y = mx + 10m \pm 2\sqrt{1 + m^2}$

On comparing this equation with $y = mx + c$, we get

$c = 10m \pm 2\sqrt{1 + m^2}$ ...(i)

This equation is also a focal chord of $y^2 = -64x$ whose focus is at $(-16, 0)$.

So, it must pass through $(-16, 0)$.

$\therefore y = mx + c \Rightarrow 0 = -16m + c$

$\therefore \quad c = 16\text{ m}$ ...(ii)

From Eqs. (i) and (ii), we get

$$16m = 10m \pm 2\sqrt{1 + m^2}$$

$\Rightarrow \quad 9m^2 = 1 + m^2$

$\Rightarrow \quad m = \dfrac{1}{2\sqrt{2}}$ (as $m > 0$)

$\therefore \quad c = 16\,m = 16 \cdot \left(\dfrac{1}{2\sqrt{2}}\right) = 4\sqrt{2}$

So, $\quad 4\sqrt{2}\,(m + c) = 4\sqrt{2}\left(\dfrac{1}{2\sqrt{2}} + 4\sqrt{2}\right)$

$$= 2 + 32 = 34$$

92. Given, circle is $(x-3)^2+y^2=9$

Parabola is $y^2=4x$

Let equation of common tangent be $y=mx+\dfrac{a}{m}$

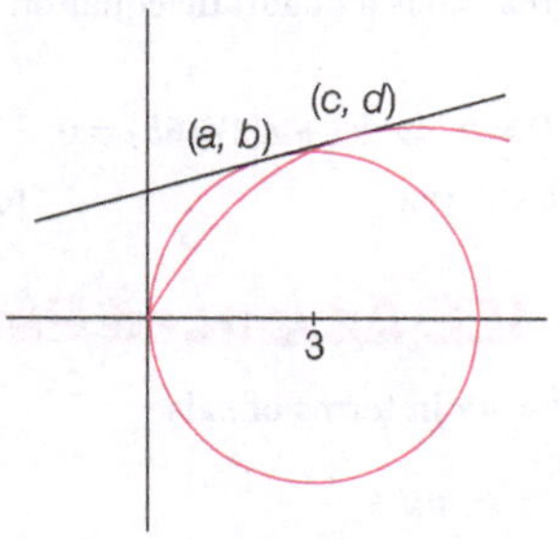

$$\Rightarrow \quad y=mx+\frac{1}{m} \qquad [\because y^2=4x]$$

$$\Rightarrow \quad m^2x-my+1=0$$

The above line is tangent to circle.

$\therefore$ Perpendicular distance from (3, 0) to line = 3

$$\Rightarrow \quad \left|\frac{(3m^2-0+1)}{\sqrt{m^2+m^4}}\right|=3$$

$$\Rightarrow \quad (3m^2+1)^2=9(m^2+m^4)$$

$$\Rightarrow \quad m=\pm\frac{1}{\sqrt{3}}$$

Tangent is $\quad y=\dfrac{1}{\sqrt{3}}x+\sqrt{3}$

$$\Rightarrow \quad m=\frac{1}{\sqrt{3}}$$

or $\quad y=\dfrac{(-1)}{\sqrt{3}}\times(-\sqrt{3})$ (rejected)

For parabola, point of contact is

$$(c,d)=\left(\frac{a}{m^2},\frac{2a}{m}\right)$$

$$\therefore \quad (c,d)=(3,2\sqrt{3})$$

Again, solve circle and line equation, we get

$$(x-3)^2+\left[\left(\frac{1}{\sqrt{3}}x+\sqrt{3}\right)\right]^2=9$$

$$\Rightarrow \quad x^2+9-6x+\frac{1}{3}x^2+3+2x=9$$

$$\Rightarrow \quad \frac{4}{3}x^2-4x+3=0$$

$$\Rightarrow \quad x=\frac{3}{2}=a$$

$$\therefore \quad 2(a+c)=2\left(\frac{3}{2}+3\right)=9$$

93. It is given that circle passes through the points $A(0,1)$ and $B(2,4)$, so the centre of the circle is point of intersection of perpendicular bisector of AB and the normal to the parabola $y=x^2$ at point $B(2,4)$, as circle touches the parabola at point $B(2,4)$ itself.

Now, equation of normal to the parabola $y=x^2$ at point $B(2,4)$ is

$$y-4=-1/4\,(x-2)$$

$$\Rightarrow \quad x+4y=18 \qquad \text{...(i)}$$

and equation of perpendicular bisector of points $A(0,1)$ and $B(2,4)$ is

$$y-5/2=-2/3\,(x-1)$$

$$\Rightarrow \quad 4x+6y=19 \qquad \text{...(ii)}$$

From Eqs. (i) and (ii), we get

$$\Rightarrow \quad y=53/10$$

$\therefore$ Coordinates of centre are $\left(-\dfrac{16}{5},\dfrac{53}{10}\right)$.

94. Equation of tangent to the parabola $y^2=4x$ having slope 'm' is

$$y=mx+\frac{1}{m} \qquad \text{...(i)}$$

$\because$ Line (i) is also tangent to the parabola $x^2=4y$

So, the discriminant of $x^2-4mx-\dfrac{4}{m}=0$ must be zero, so

$$16m^2+\frac{16}{m}=0 \Rightarrow m=-1$$

Therefore, the equation of common tangent to given parabolas is

$$x+y+1=0 \qquad \text{...(ii)}$$

It is given that line (ii) is tangent to the circle $x^2+y^2=c^2$

$$\therefore \quad c=1/\sqrt{2}$$

95. Let AB be the latus rectum of parabola $y^2=4x$ having length 4.

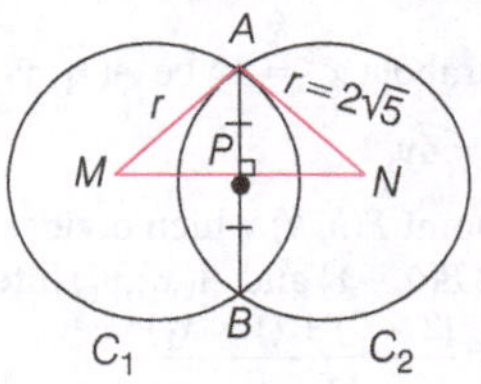

From the figure as AB divides MN equally.

So, $MN=2MP=2\sqrt{AM^2-PA^2}$ as $AB=2PA$

$$=2\sqrt{(2\sqrt{5})^2-2^2}=8$$

96. Equation of given parabola is $y^2=12x$ ...(i)

Now, let a point $P(3t^2,6t)$ on the parabola, since point N is the foot of perpendicular drawn from P on the axis of the parabola (i.e. X-axis) so coordinate of N is $(3t^2,0)$ and M is mid-point of PN, so coordinates of M are $(3t^2,3t)$. Now, equation of the parallel to the axis of parabola through point M is

$$y=3t \qquad \text{... (ii)}$$

So, point of intersection of parabola (i) and line (ii) is $Q\left(\dfrac{3t^2}{4},3t\right)$, so equation of line NQ is

$$y-0=\frac{3t}{\frac{3t^2}{4}-3t^2}(x-3t^2) \qquad \text{...(iii)}$$

For y-intercept made by line (iii) put, $x = 0$, then

$$y = \frac{1}{(1/4) - 1}(-3t) = \frac{12t}{3} = \frac{4}{3} \quad \text{[given]}$$

$$\Rightarrow \quad t = 1/3$$

$$\therefore \quad P\left(\frac{1}{3}, 2\right), N\left(\frac{1}{3}, 0\right), M\left(\frac{1}{3}, 1\right), Q\left(\frac{1}{12}, 1\right)$$

$$\therefore \quad PN = 2,$$

and $$MQ = \frac{1}{3} - \frac{1}{12} = \frac{1}{4}$$

97. Equation of given parabola is $y^2 = 8x$ and the equilateral triangle inscribed in the given parabola having one of its vertices on the vertex of the parabola, so according to symmetry other two vertices of the equilateral triangle, we can take as, $A\,(2t^2, 4t)$ and $B\,(2t^2, -4t)$

$$\therefore \quad \text{Area of } \Delta\, OAB \text{ is } \Delta = \frac{1}{2}(2t^2)\,(8t) = \frac{\sqrt{3}}{4}(8t)^2$$

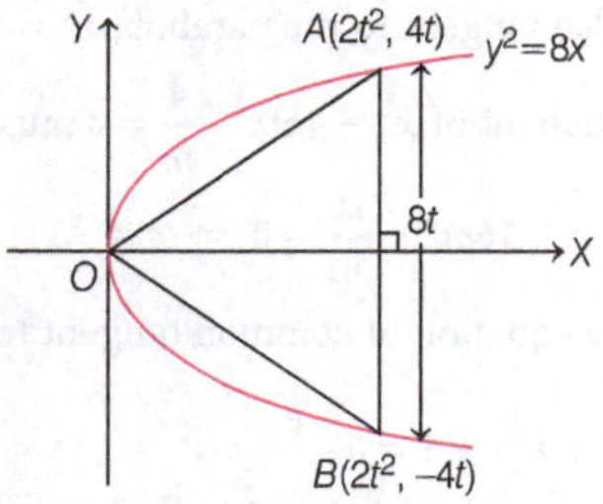

$$\Rightarrow \quad t = 2\sqrt{3}$$

$\therefore$ Area of equilateral $\Delta OAB = \dfrac{\sqrt{3}}{4}(8 \times 2\sqrt{3})^2 = 192\sqrt{3}$ sq units

98. Let a point on parabola $x^2 = 4y$ be $A(x_1, y_1)$.

So, $$x_1^2 = 4y_1 \quad \text{...(i)}$$

and an another point $P(h, k)$ which divides the line segment joining the point $B(0, -1)$ and $A(x_1, y_1)$ internally in the ratio $1 : 2$, so

$$h = \frac{(2 \times 0) + (1 \times x_1)}{2 + 1}$$

and $$k = \frac{2 \times (-1) + (1 \times y_1)}{2 + 1}$$

$$\Rightarrow \quad x_1 = 3h \text{ and } y_1 = 3k + 2 \quad \text{...(ii)}$$

Now, on the elimination of (x_1, y_1) with the help of Eq. (i) and relation (ii), we get $9h^2 = 4(3k + 2)$

On taking locus of point $P(h, k)$, we get

$$9x^2 = 12y + 8 \Rightarrow 9x^2 - 12y = 8$$

99. As we know, equation of tangent to the parabola $y^2 = 4x$, having slope m is

$$y = mx + \frac{1}{m} \quad \text{...(i)}$$

On comparing the Eq. (i) with the equation of given tangent $y = mx + 4$, we get

$$\frac{1}{m} = 4 \Rightarrow m = \frac{1}{4}$$

$\therefore$ Equation of the tangent is $y = \dfrac{1}{4}x + 4$, now it is tangent to the parabola $x^2 = 2by$, so on solving the equation of parabola $x^2 = 2by$ and tangent $y = \dfrac{1}{4}x + 4$, we must get only a common point, so $x^2 = 2b\left(\dfrac{1}{4}x + 4\right)$

$\Rightarrow 2x^2 - bx - 16b = 0$ is a quadratic equation having one solution.

So, $$D = 0 \Rightarrow b^2 + 4(2)(16b) = 0$$

$$\Rightarrow \quad b = -128 \quad [\because b \text{ cannot be zero}]$$

Exercise 2 - JEE Advanced Pattern

1. Tangent to $y^2 = 4x$ in terms of m is

$$y = mx + \frac{1}{m} \quad \text{...(i)}$$

and normal to $x^2 = 4by$ in terms of m is

$$y = mx + 2b + \frac{b}{m^2} \quad \text{...(ii)}$$

$\because$ Eqs. (i) and (ii) are same, then

$$\frac{1}{m} = 2b + \frac{b}{m^2} \Rightarrow 2bm^2 - m + b = 0$$

For two different tangents,

$$D > 0 \quad \Rightarrow 1 - 8b^3 > 0 \text{ or } |b| < \frac{1}{2\sqrt{2}}$$

2. The given parabolas $2y^2 = 2x - 1$ and $2x^2 = 2y - 1$ are symmetrical about the line $y = x$. The shortest distance occurs along the common normal which is perpendicular to the line $y = x$.

Therefore, the tangent at point A on $2y^2 = 2x - 1$ is parallel to $y = x$.

$$\therefore \quad 4y\frac{dy}{dx} = 2 \Rightarrow \frac{dy}{dx} = \frac{1}{2y} = 1$$

or $$y = \frac{1}{2} \text{ and } x = \frac{3}{4}$$

$\because$ $A \equiv \left(\dfrac{3}{4}, \dfrac{1}{2}\right)$, then coordinates of B on $2x^2 = 2y - 1$ are

$$B \equiv \left(\frac{1}{2}, \frac{3}{4}\right)$$

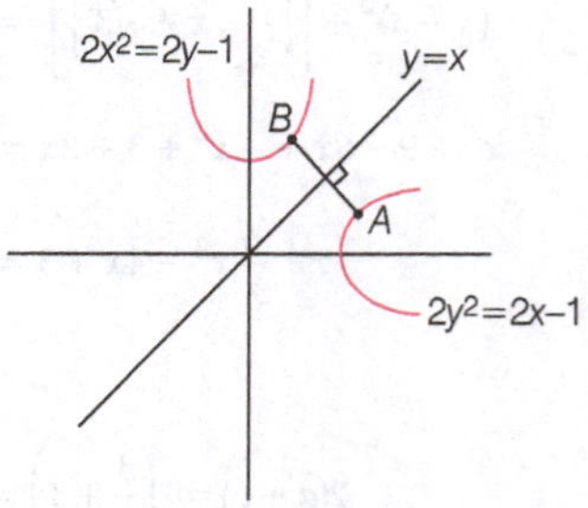

$\therefore$ Shortest distance $= AB$

$$= \sqrt{\left(\frac{3}{4} - \frac{1}{2}\right)^2 + \left(\frac{1}{2} - \frac{3}{4}\right)^2}$$

$$= \sqrt{\left(\frac{1}{16} + \frac{1}{16}\right)} = \frac{1}{\sqrt{8}} = \frac{1}{2\sqrt{2}}$$

3. We know that normals at $(at_1^2, 2at_1)$ and $(at_2^2, 2at_2)$ meet again on the parabola. Then $t_1t_2 = 2$

Here, $a = 1$

and $x_1 = at_1^2 = t_1^2$ and $y_1 = 2at_1 = 2t_1$

$x_2 = at_2^2 = t_2^2$ and $y_2 = 2at_2 = 2t_2$

Given, $x_1 + x_2 = 4 \Rightarrow t_1^2 + t_2^2 = 4$

or $(t_1 + t_2)^2 - 2t_1t_2 = 4$

$\Rightarrow (t_1 + t_2)^2 = 8$ $[\because t_1t_2 = 2]$

$\Rightarrow |t_1 + t_2| = \sqrt{8} \Rightarrow |2t_1 + 2t_2| = 2\sqrt{8}$

$\Rightarrow |y_1 + y_2| = 2\sqrt{8} = 4\sqrt{2}$

4. Let any point at distance r from A on the parabola is

$(-2 + r\cos\theta, r\sin\theta)$,

then $r^2\sin^2\theta = 4(-2 + r\cos\theta)$

or $r^2\sin^2\theta - 4r\cos\theta + 8 = 0$

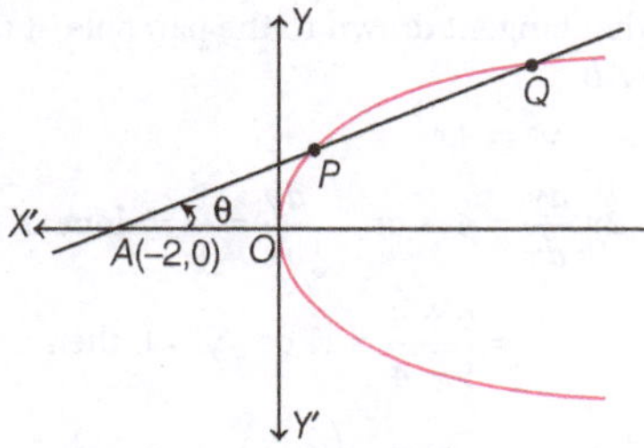

Let P and Q be distances r_1 and r_2 from A, then

$$r_1 + r_2 = \frac{4\cos\theta}{\sin^2\theta}$$

and $$r_1r_2 = \frac{8}{\sin^2\theta}$$

Now, $$\frac{1}{AP} + \frac{1}{AQ} = \frac{1}{r_1} + \frac{1}{r_2} = \frac{r_1 + r_2}{r_1r_2} = \frac{\cos\theta}{2}$$

Given that $$\frac{1}{AP} + \frac{1}{AQ} < \frac{1}{4}$$

$$\Rightarrow \frac{\cos\theta}{2} < \frac{1}{4}$$

or $$\cos\theta < \frac{1}{2} \text{ or } \tan\theta > \sqrt{3}$$

$[\because \cos\theta$ is decreasing and $\tan\theta$ is increasing in $\left(0, \frac{\pi}{2}\right)]$

$\therefore$ Slope $(m) > \sqrt{3}$

5. Coordinates of A are $(a - l\cos 30°, l\sin 30°)$

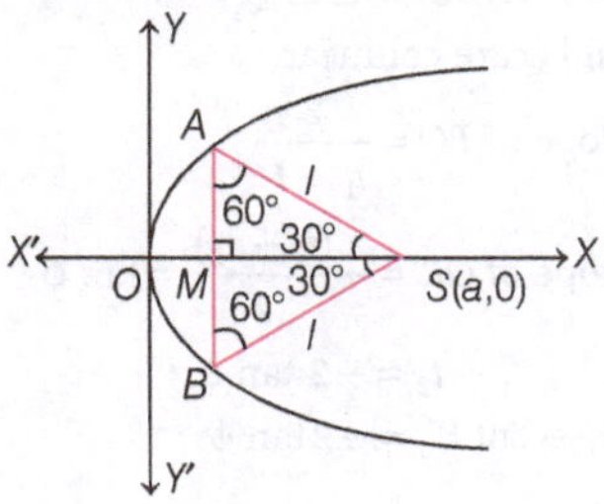

or $$A \equiv \left(a - \frac{l\sqrt{3}}{2}, \frac{l}{2}\right)$$

which lies on $y^2 = 4ax$, then

$$\frac{l^2}{4} = 4a\left(a - \frac{l\sqrt{3}}{2}\right) \Rightarrow l^2 + 8a\sqrt{3}l - 16a^2 = 0$$

$$\therefore l = \frac{-8a\sqrt{3} \pm \sqrt{(192a^2 + 64a^2)}}{2}$$

$$= \frac{-8a\sqrt{3} \pm 16a}{2}$$

$= 4a(2 - \sqrt{3})$ [taking +ve sign]

Alternate Solution

Let $A \equiv (at_1^2, 2at_1)$ and $B \equiv (at_1^2 - 2at_1)$.

Slope of $SA = \tan(180° - 30°)$

$$\frac{2at_1}{at_1^2 - a} = -\tan 30°$$

$$\frac{2t_1}{t_1^2 - 1} = -\frac{1}{\sqrt{3}}$$

or $t_1^2 + 2\sqrt{3}t_1 - 1 = 0$ or $t_1 = -\sqrt{3} \pm 2$

Thus, $t_1 = 2 - \sqrt{3}$ $[\because t_1 = -2 - \sqrt{3}$ (rejected)$]$

Here, $AB = 4at_1 = 4a(2 - \sqrt{3})$

6. $C : x^2 + (y - 1)^2 = 1$ and $P : y = ax^2$

On putting $x^2 = \frac{y}{a}$ in $x^2 + (y - 1)^2 = 1$

$$\Rightarrow \frac{y}{a} + (y - 1)^2 = 1$$

$$\Rightarrow y^2 - 2y + \frac{y}{a} = 0$$

$$\therefore y = 0$$

or $$y = 2 - \frac{1}{a}$$

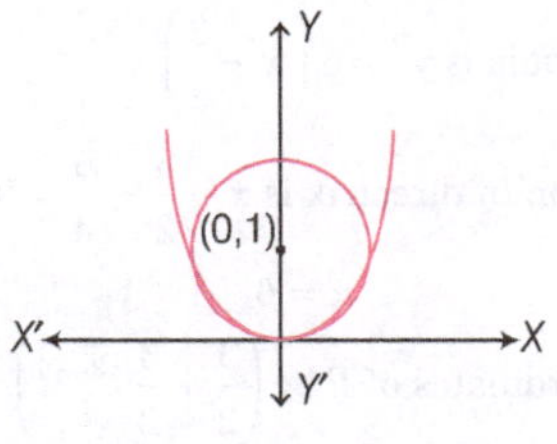

On substituting $y = 2 - \frac{1}{a}$ in $y = ax^2$, then

$$ax^2 = 2 - \frac{1}{a}$$

$$\Rightarrow x^2 = \frac{2a - 1}{a^2} > 0$$

$$\Rightarrow 2a - 1 > 0$$

$$\therefore a > \frac{1}{2}$$

or $$a \in \left(\frac{1}{2}, \infty\right)$$

7. Let SP be $\mathbf{V} = (\lambda^2 - 1)\,\hat{\mathbf{i}} + (2\lambda - 0)\,\hat{\mathbf{j}}$

$\Rightarrow \quad \mathbf{V} = (\lambda^2 - 1)\,\hat{\mathbf{i}} + (2\lambda)\,\hat{\mathbf{j}}$ ...(i)

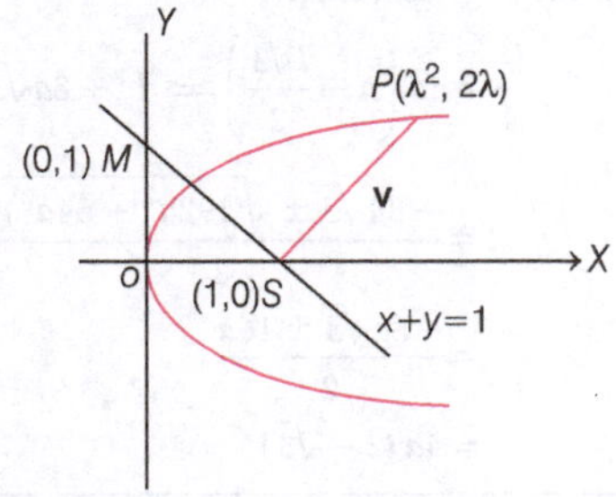

and $\quad \mathbf{SM} = \mathbf{n} = (0-1)\,\hat{\mathbf{i}} + (1-0)\,\hat{\mathbf{j}} = -\hat{\mathbf{i}} + \hat{\mathbf{j}}$

The projection of $\mathbf{V}$ on $\mathbf{n} = y$ [given]

$\therefore \quad y = \dfrac{\mathbf{V}\cdot\mathbf{n}}{|\mathbf{n}|} = \dfrac{-(\lambda^2-1)+2\lambda}{\sqrt{2}}$ ...(ii)

Given, $\quad \dfrac{dx}{dt} = 4$

$\Rightarrow \quad \dfrac{d}{dt}(\lambda^2 - 1) = 4 \Rightarrow 2\lambda\dfrac{d\lambda}{dt} = 4$

When $P \equiv (4, 4)$,

We have, $\lambda = 2$, therefore

$$\frac{d\lambda}{dt} = 1 \quad \text{...(iii)}$$

From Eq. (ii),

$$\frac{dy}{dt} = \frac{(2-2\lambda)\dfrac{d\lambda}{dt}}{\sqrt{2}} \quad \text{[from Eq. (ii)]}$$

$$= \frac{(2-4)\times 1}{\sqrt{2}} = -\sqrt{2}$$

8. Given parabola is $y^2 = 6\left(x - \dfrac{3}{2}\right)$

The equation of directrix is $x - \dfrac{3}{2} + \dfrac{6}{4} = 0$

i.e. $\quad x = 0$

Let the coordinates of P be $\left(\dfrac{3}{2} + \dfrac{3}{2}t^2, 3t\right)$.

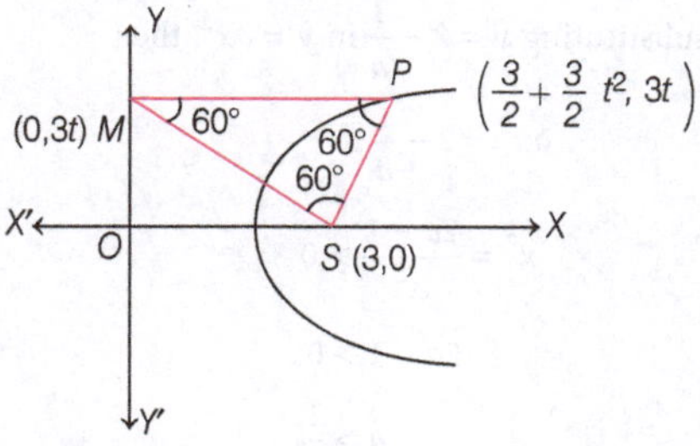

Therefore, $\quad MS = MP$

$$\sqrt{(9+9t^2)} = \frac{3}{2} + \frac{3}{2}t^2$$

or $\quad 9 + 9t^2 = \dfrac{9}{4}(1+t^2)^2$

or $\quad 1 + t^2 = 4$

$\therefore$ Length of each side $= MS$

$$= \sqrt{9(1+t^2)}$$

$$= \sqrt{36} = 6$$

9. The area of ΔABC is maximum if CD is maximum, because AB is fixed.

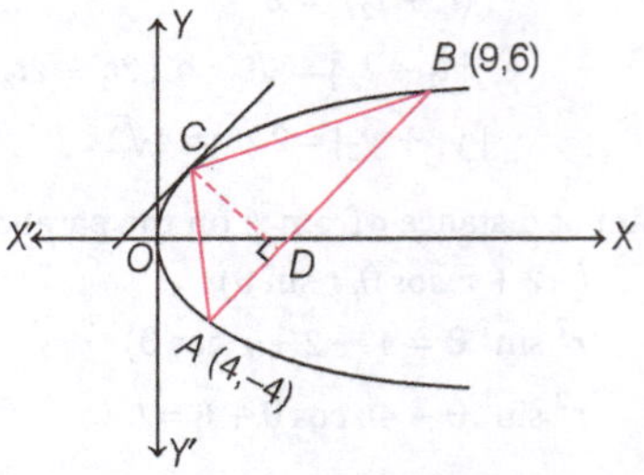

It is clear that tangent drawn to the parabola at C should be parallel to AB.

For $\quad y^2 = 4x$

$\therefore \quad 2y\dfrac{dy}{dx} = 4 \quad$ or $\quad \dfrac{dy}{dx} = \dfrac{2}{y} =$ slope of AB

$\Rightarrow \quad \dfrac{2}{y} = \dfrac{6+4}{9-4} = 2 \quad$ or $\quad y = 1$, then $x = \dfrac{1}{4}$

Hence, coordinates of C are $\left(\dfrac{1}{4}, 1\right)$.

10. $\because$ Tangent at $P(at_1^2, 2at_1)$ is $t_1 y = x + at_1^2$.

$\therefore \quad \tan\theta_1 = \dfrac{1}{t_1}$

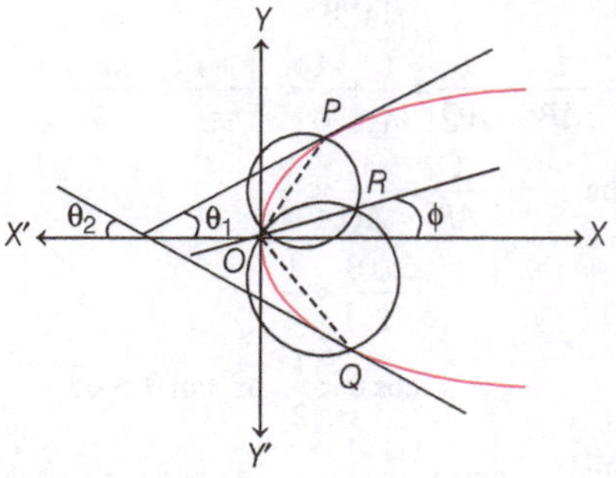

Similarly, $\quad \tan\theta_2 = \dfrac{1}{t_2}$

$\because$ Angle in a semi-circle is 90°.

$\therefore \quad \angle ORP = \angle ORQ = 90°$

$\Rightarrow$ P, R and Q are collinear.

Slope of $PQ = \dfrac{2}{t_1 + t_2}$ $\quad$ [$\because$ $OR \perp PQ$]

$\therefore \quad$ Slope of $OR = -\dfrac{(t_1+t_2)}{2} = \tan\phi$

or $\quad t_1 + t_2 = -2\tan\phi$

$\Rightarrow \quad \cot\theta_1 + \cot\theta_2 = -2\tan\phi$

11. Let $A \equiv (at^2, 2at)$ and $B \equiv (at^2, -2at)$

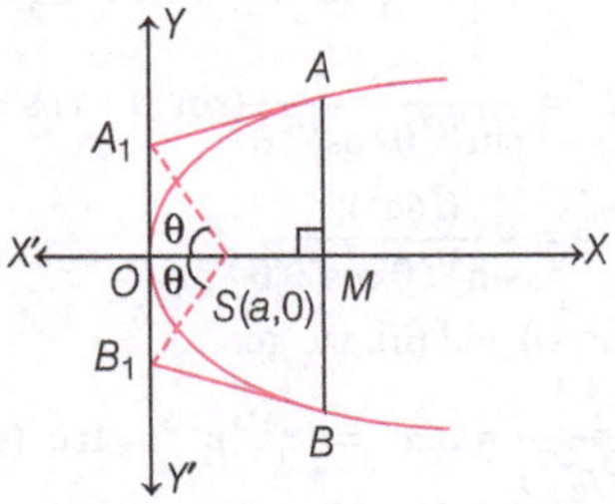

The equations of tangents at A and B are

$$ty = x + at^2 \text{ and } -ty = x + at^2.$$

These tangents meet the Y-axis at $A_1\ (0, at)$ and $B_1(0, -at)$, respectively.

Area of trapezium, $AA_1\,B_1B = \frac{1}{2}(AB + A_1B_1) \times OM$

$$24a^2 = \frac{1}{2}(4at + 2at) \times at^2$$

$$24a^2 = 3a^2t^3 \Rightarrow t^3 = 8$$

$\therefore$ $t = 2$

$\therefore$ Coordinates of A_1 and B_1 are $(0, 2a)$ and $(0, -2a)$, respectively.

If $\angle OSA_1 = \angle OSB_1 = \theta$, then

$$\tan\theta = \frac{2a}{a} = 2 \Rightarrow \theta = \tan^{-1} 2$$

Hence, subtended angle $= 2\theta = 2\tan^{-1} 2$.

12. **Decoding the Question**

To solve this problem, use the formula given as $(r+1)$ th term in $(a+b)^n$ will be ${}^nC_r\, a^{n-r} b^r$ $\left[\because {}^nC_r = \frac{n!}{r!(n-r)!}\right]$

Given, $\frac{5}{2} = {}^nC_3 (px)^{n-3}\left(\frac{1}{x}\right)^3 = {}^nC_3 \cdot p^{n-3} x^{n-6}$ ...(i)

Since, LHS of Eq. (i) is independent of x

$\therefore$ $n - 6 = 0 \Rightarrow n = 6$

From Eq. (i),

$$\frac{5}{2} = {}^6C_3 p^3 = 20p^3$$

$\Rightarrow$ $p^3 = \left(\frac{1}{2}\right)^3 \Rightarrow p = \frac{1}{2}$

Given, parabola is $y^2 = x$

Here, $4a = 1 \Rightarrow a = \frac{1}{4}$

Since, three normals are drawn from point $(q, 0)$.

$\therefore$ $q > 2a$ or $q > \frac{1}{2}$ or $q > p$ $\left[\because p = \frac{1}{2}\right]$

13. $y^2 - 4x - 2y + 5 = 0$

$\Rightarrow$ $(y-1)^2 - 4x + 4 = 0$

$\Rightarrow$ $(y-1)^2 = 4(x-1)$

Let $y - 1 = Y$ and $x - 1 = X$

Then, $y^2 = 4X$ comparing with $Y^2 = 4ax$

$\therefore$ $a = 1$

$\because$ All three normals to the parabola are real and meet on the axis of parabola, then

$$X > 2a \text{ and } Y = 0$$

i.e., $x - 1 > 2$ and $y - 1 = 0$

$\therefore$ $x > 3$ and $y = 1$

or $(k, 1),\ k > 3$

14. Let $P\,(x_0, x_0^2)$ be any point on the parabola $y = x^2$

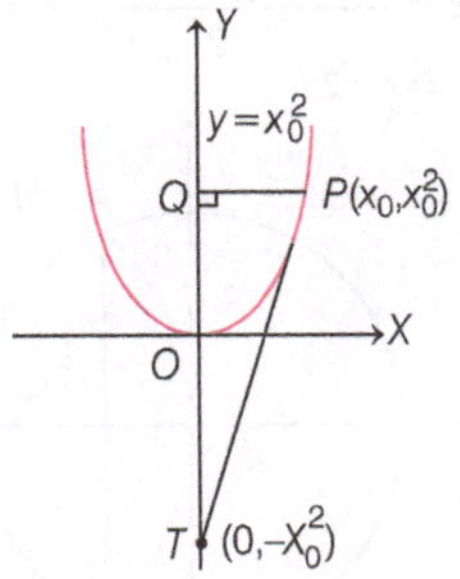

Equation of tangent at $P\,(x_0, x_0^2)$ is $xx_0 = \frac{1}{2}(y + x_0^2)$

$\Rightarrow$ $2xx_0 - y - x_0^2 = 0$

Tangent meets the Y-axis at $T\,(0, -x_0^2)$.

Hence, the area of the triangle $\Delta PTQ = \frac{1}{2} \times PQ \times QT$

$$= \frac{1}{2} \times x_0 \times 2x_0^2 = x_0^3$$

which increases in the interval $[1, 2]$ and hence is greatest when $x_0 = 2$.

15. $\left(\frac{2x - y + 2}{\sqrt{5}}\right) = \sqrt{(x-2)^2 + (y-0)^2}$ [given]

$\Rightarrow$ $(2x - y + 2)^2 = 5(x^2 + y^2 - 4x + 4)$

or $x^2 + 4y^2 + 4xy = 28x - 4y - 16$

$\Rightarrow$ $(x + 2y)^2 = 4(7x - y - 4)$

$\because$ $x + 2y = 0$ and $7x - y - 4 = 0$ and are not perpendicular.

$\therefore$ $(x + 2y + \lambda)^2 = (2\lambda + 28)\,x + (4\lambda - 4)\,y + \lambda^2 - 16$ ...(i)

Now, (slope of $x + 2y + \lambda = 0$) $\times$ (slope of $(2\lambda + 28)\,x + (4\lambda - 4)\,y + \lambda^2 - 16 = 0$) $= -1$

$\therefore$ $-\frac{1}{2} \times -\frac{(2\lambda + 28)}{(4\lambda - 4)} = -1$

$\Rightarrow$ $2\lambda + 28 = -8\lambda + 8$ or $10\lambda = -20$

$\therefore$ $\lambda = -2$

From Eq. (i),

$$(x + 2y - 2)^2 = (24x - 12y - 12)$$

$\Rightarrow$ $\left(\frac{x + 2y - 2}{\sqrt{5}}\right)^2 = \frac{12}{\sqrt{5}}\left(\frac{2x - y - 1}{\sqrt{5}}\right)$

Let $\frac{x + 2y - 2}{\sqrt{5}} = X,\ \frac{2x - y - 1}{\sqrt{5}} = Y$

or $X^2 = \frac{12}{\sqrt{5}}\,Y$ or $Y = \frac{\sqrt{5}}{12}X^2$

$\therefore$ $k = \frac{\sqrt{5}}{12}$

16. Centre (0, 0), radius $r = \frac{1}{2} \cdot \frac{3}{4} \cdot 4a = \frac{3a}{2}$

Equation of the circle is $4(x^2 + y^2) = 9a^2$ ...(i)

Equation of the parabolas is $y^2 = 4ax$ ...(ii)

On solving (i) and (ii), $x^2 + 4ax - \frac{9a^2}{4} = 0$

$$x = \frac{-4a \pm \sqrt{16a^2 + 9a^2}}{2} = \frac{-4a \pm 5a}{2}$$

$\therefore$ $x = a/2$

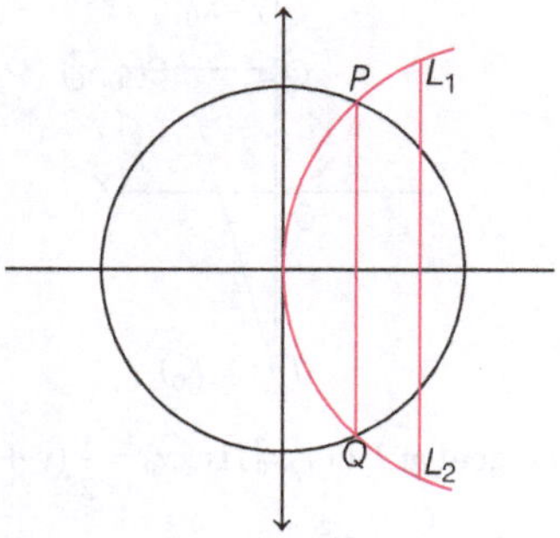

For $x = a/2, y^2 = 4ax = 4a\frac{a}{2} = 2a^2 \Rightarrow y = \pm\sqrt{2}a$

$\therefore$ The double ordinate $PQ = 2\sqrt{2}a$

and area of the trapezium and $L_1L_2 = 4a = PL_1L_2Q$

$$= \frac{1}{2}(PQ + L_1L_2) \times MN = \frac{1}{2}(2\sqrt{2} + 4)a \times \frac{a}{2} = \left(\frac{2+\sqrt{2}}{2}\right)a^2$$

17. Let the equation of any normal be $y = -tx + 2t + t^3$

Since, it passes through the point (15, 12).

Then, $12 = -15t + 2t + t^3$ *i.e.* $t^3 - 3t - 12 = 0$

$\therefore$ $t = -1, -3, 4$

So, the points are (1, −2), (9, −6), (16, 8).

$\therefore$ Centroid is $\left(\frac{26}{3}, 0\right)$.

18. Let P and Q be any two points on the parabola $y^2 = 4ax$ such that $P \equiv (r_1\cos\theta, r_1\sin\theta)$ and $Q \equiv (r_2\cos\theta, r_2\sin\theta)$.

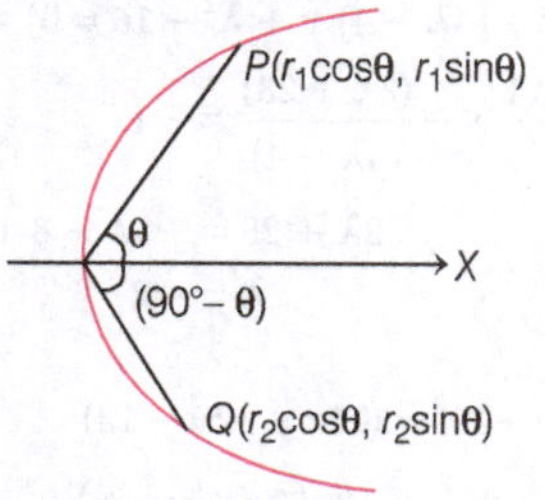

Since, P and Q lie on parabola, $r_1^2\sin^2\theta = 4ar_1\cos\theta$

$$\Rightarrow r_1 = \frac{4a\cos\theta}{\sin^2\theta} \text{ and } r_2^2\cos^2\theta = 4ar_2\sin\theta \Rightarrow r_2 = \frac{4a\sin\theta}{\cos^2\theta}$$

Now, $r_1r_2 = \frac{16a^2\cos\theta\sin\theta}{\sin^2\theta\cos^2\theta} = \frac{16a^2}{\sin\theta\cos\theta}$

$$\Rightarrow r_1^{4/3}r_2^{4/3} = \frac{(16a^2)^{4/3}}{\sin^{4/3}\theta\cos^{4/3}\theta} \quad ...(i)$$

and $r_1^{2/3} + r_2^{2/3} = (4a)^{2/3}\left\{\frac{\cos^{2/3}\theta}{\sin^{4/3}\theta} + \frac{\sin^{2/3}\theta}{\cos^{4/3}\theta}\right\}$

$$\Rightarrow r_1^{2/3} + r_2^{2/3} = \frac{(4a)^{2/3}}{\sin^{4/3}\theta\cos^{4/3}\theta}(\sin^2\theta + \cos^2\theta)$$

$$= \frac{(16a^2)^{1/3}}{\sin^{4/3}\theta\cos^{4/3}\theta} \quad ...(ii)$$

Now, from Eqs. (i) and (ii), we get

$$\frac{r_1^{4/3}r_2^{4/3}}{(r_1^{2/3} + r_2^{2/3})} = 16a^2 \Rightarrow r_1^{4/3}r_2^{4/3} = 16a^2(r_1^{2/3} + r_2^{2/3})$$

Hence, k is 16.

19. Given curves is $(y-2)^2 = 4(x+1)$

Focus $\equiv (0, 2)$

Point of intersection of the curve and $y = 4$ is (0, 4) from the reflection property of parabola reflected ray passes through the focus.

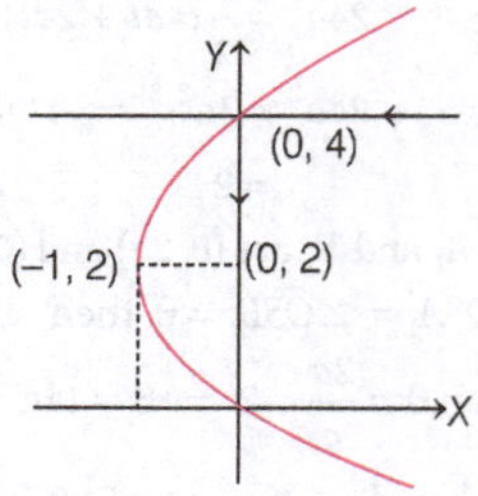

$\therefore$ $x = 0$ is required line.

20. $y^2 = 6\left(x - \frac{3}{2}\right)$

Equation of directrix $x - \frac{3}{2} = -\frac{3}{2}$ i.e. $x = 0$

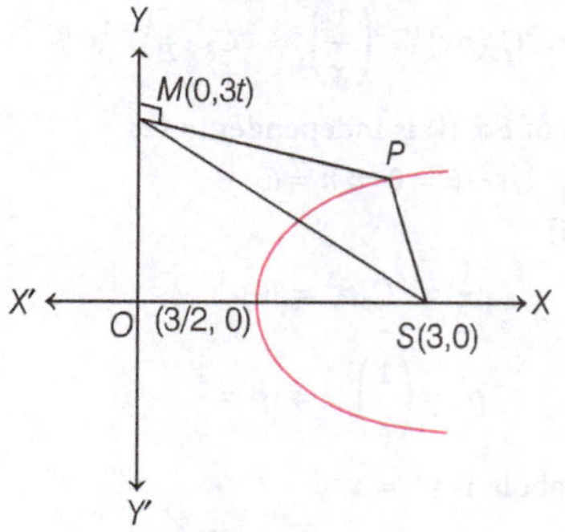

Let coordinate P be $\left(\frac{3}{2} + \frac{3}{2}t^2, 3t\right)$.

Then, coordinates of M are $(0, 3t)$

$\therefore$ $MS = \sqrt{9 + 9t^2}$

$MP = \frac{3}{2} + \frac{3}{2}t^2$.

$\therefore$ $9 + 9t^2 = \left(\frac{3}{2} + \frac{3}{2}t^2\right)^2 + \frac{9}{4}(1 + t^2)^2$

$\therefore$ Length of side = 6

21. Equation of tangent of parabola

$$y^2 = 40x \text{ is } y = mx + \frac{10}{m} \quad \text{... (i)}$$

which is also tangent of circle $x^2 + y^2 = 50$, then

$$\frac{\left|\frac{10}{m}\right|}{\sqrt{(m^2+1)}} = 5\sqrt{2}$$

$$\Rightarrow \quad m^4 + m^2 - 2 = 0 \Rightarrow (m^2+2)(m^2-1) = 0$$

$$\therefore \quad m^2 = 1, m^2 + 2 \neq 0 \text{ or } m = \pm 1$$

From Eq. (i), common tangents are

$$y = x + 10 \text{ and } y = -x - 10$$

or $\quad x - y + 10 = 0$ and $x + y + 10 = 0$

22. Let coordinates of P be $(t^2, 2t)$.

Then, slope of $PV = \dfrac{2t-0}{t^2-0} = \dfrac{2}{t}$

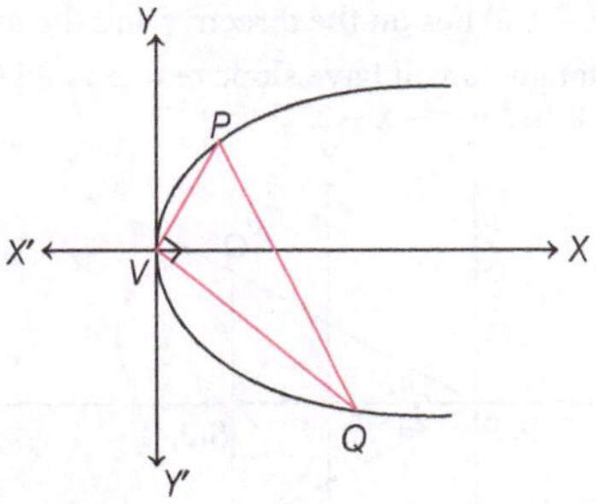

$\Rightarrow$ Slope of QV is $-\dfrac{t}{2}$.

$\therefore$ Equation of QV is $y = \dfrac{-t}{2}x$

Solving it with $y^2 = 4x$, we get $Q\left(\dfrac{16}{t^2}, \dfrac{-8}{t}\right)$

Area of $\Delta PVQ = 20$ [given]

$$\Rightarrow \quad \frac{1}{2}\left|\begin{matrix} t^2 & 2t \\ \frac{16}{t^2} & \frac{-8}{t} \end{matrix}\right| = 20 \Rightarrow t + \frac{4}{t} = \pm 5$$

$$\Rightarrow \quad t^2 - 5t + 4 = 0 \text{ or } t^2 + 5t + 4 = 0$$

$$\therefore \quad t = 1, 4 \text{ or } t = -1, -4$$

Hence, coordinates of P are (1, 2), (16, 8), (1 – 2), (16, – 8).

23. Parabola is $y^2 = 4ax$ and circle is $(x+b)^2 + (y-0)^2 = b^2$

If parabola and circle touch each other externally, then

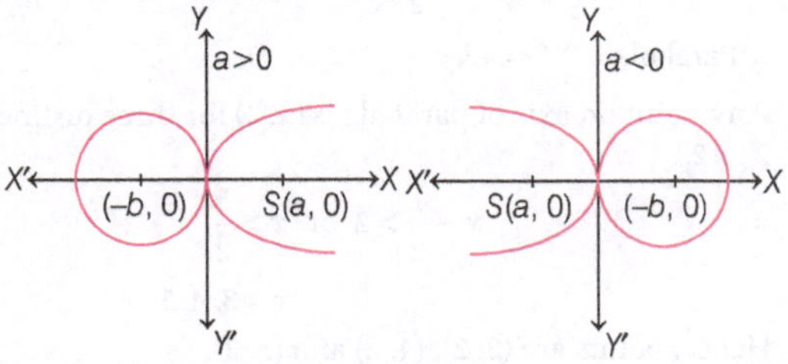

If $\quad a > 0, -b < 0$ and if $a < 0, -b > 0$

or $\quad a > 0, b > 0$ and $a < 0, b < 0$

24. Let $(x_1, y_1) \equiv (at^2, 2at)$

Equation of tangent at $(at^2, 2at)$ is $ty = x + at^2$.

Let any point on this tangent is $\left(\lambda, \dfrac{\lambda + at^2}{t}\right)$

The chord of contact of this point w.r.t the circle $x^2 + y^2 = a^2$ is

$$x \cdot \lambda + y \cdot \left(\frac{\lambda + at^2}{t}\right) = a^2$$

$$\Rightarrow \quad (aty - a^2) + \lambda \cdot \left(x + \frac{y}{t}\right) = 0$$

which is family of straight lines passing through the point of intersection of $aty - a^2 = 0$ and $x + \dfrac{y}{t} = 0$

So, the fixed point is $\left(\dfrac{-a}{t^2}, \dfrac{a}{t}\right)$.

Therefore, $x_2 = -\dfrac{a}{t^2}, \quad y_2 = \dfrac{a}{t}$

Clearly, $\quad x_1 x_2 = -a^2, \quad y_1 y_2 = 2a^2$

$$\Rightarrow \quad x_1 x_2 + y_1 y_2 = a^2$$

Also, $\quad \dfrac{x_1}{x_2} = -t^4, \quad \dfrac{y_1}{y_2} = 2t^2$

or $\quad \left(\dfrac{y_1}{y_2}\right)^2 + 4\left(\dfrac{x_1}{x_2}\right) = 0$

$\Rightarrow \; -4, \dfrac{y_1}{y_2}$ and $\dfrac{x_1}{x_2}$ are in GP.

Also, $y_1 y_2 = 2a^2 \Rightarrow \dfrac{y_1}{2}, a, y_2$ are in GP.

25. Let $M(\alpha, \beta)$ be the foot of the perpendicular from the focus $S(a, 0)$ on any tangent to the parabola at $P(at^2, 2at)$

i.e. $\quad ty + x + at^2$

$$\Rightarrow \quad \alpha - t\beta + at^2 = 0 \quad \text{...(i)}$$

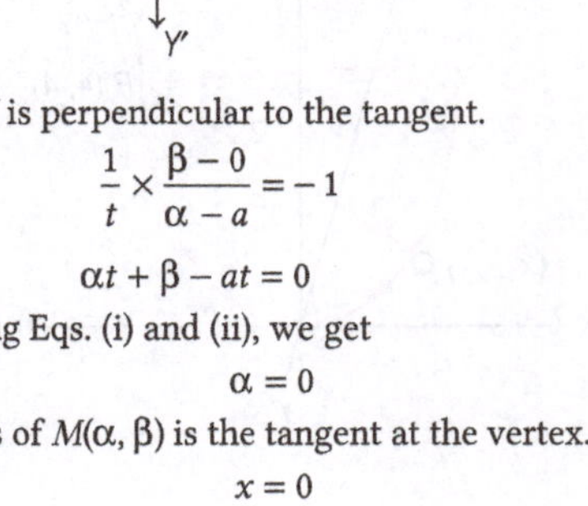

Since, SM is perpendicular to the tangent.

$$\therefore \quad \frac{1}{t} \times \frac{\beta - 0}{\alpha - a} = -1$$

$$\Rightarrow \quad \alpha t + \beta - at = 0 \quad \text{...(ii)}$$

On solving Eqs. (i) and (ii), we get

$$\alpha = 0$$

The locus of $M(\alpha, \beta)$ is the tangent at the vertex.

i.e. $\quad x = 0$

26. Let $P \equiv (at^2, 2at)$ and $R \equiv (at_1^2, 2at_1)$

$\because$ $OP \perp OR$

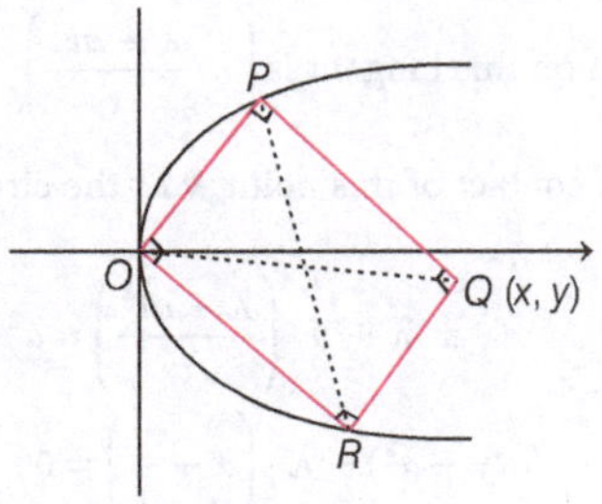

$\therefore$ Slope of $OP \times$ Slope of $OR = -1$

$$\Rightarrow \quad \frac{2}{t} \times \frac{2}{t_1} = -1$$

$$\therefore \quad t_1 = -\frac{4}{t}$$

Now, coordinates of R are $\left(\frac{16a}{t^2}, \frac{-8a}{t}\right)$.

$\because$ $OPQR$ is a rectangle.

$\therefore$ Mid-point of OQ = Mid-point of PR

$$\Rightarrow \quad x = at^2 + \frac{16a}{t^2} \quad \Rightarrow \quad \frac{x}{a} = t^2 + \frac{16}{t^2} \quad \text{... (i)}$$

and

$$y = 2at - \frac{8a}{t} \quad \Rightarrow \quad \frac{y}{2a} = t - \frac{4}{t} \quad \text{... (ii)}$$

From Eqs. (i) and (ii), we get

$$\left(\frac{y}{2a}\right)^2 = t^2 + \frac{16}{t^2} - 8 = \frac{x}{a} - 8$$

$$\Rightarrow \quad y^2 = 4ax - 32a^2$$

$$\Rightarrow \quad y^2 = 4a(x - 8a)$$

which is equal parabola and focus $(9a, 0)$ and directrix

$$x - 8a = -a$$

or

$$x - 7a = 0.$$

27. Let point of intersection of the line $y = mx$ with the chord be $(\lambda, m\lambda)$, then

$$\lambda = \frac{1.4 + 2.x_1}{1 + 2} \quad \Rightarrow \quad x_1 = \frac{3\lambda - 4}{2}$$

and

$$m\lambda = \frac{1.4 + 2.y_1}{1 + 2} \quad \Rightarrow \quad y_1 = \frac{3m\lambda - 4}{2}$$

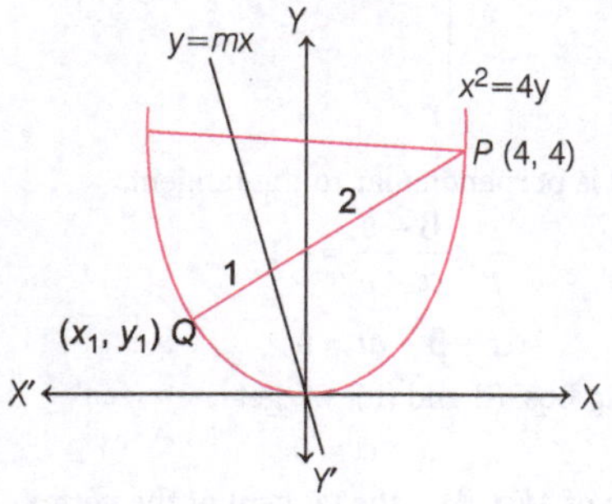

$\because$ $Q(x_1, y_1)$ lies on the parabola $x^2 = 4y$, then

$$\left(\frac{3\lambda - 4}{2}\right)^2 = 4\left(\frac{3m\lambda - 4}{2}\right)$$

$$\Rightarrow \quad 9\lambda^2 - 24\lambda(1 + m) + 48 = 0$$

For two distinct chords, $D > 0$

$$\Rightarrow \quad (24)^2 (1 + m)^2 - 4 \cdot 9 \cdot 48 > 0$$

or $\quad (1 + m)^2 > 3$

$\Rightarrow \quad 1 + m < -\sqrt{3}$

or $\quad 1 + m > \sqrt{3}$

$\Rightarrow \quad m < -\sqrt{3} - 1$

or $\quad m > \sqrt{3} - 1$

Hence , $m \in (-\infty, -\sqrt{3} - 1) \cup (\sqrt{3} - 1, \infty)$

28. The given parabola is $y^2 = 4(2)x$

$$\Rightarrow \quad a = 2$$

Since, $P(-2, 0)$ lies on the directrix and the axis.

$\Rightarrow$ The tangents will have slope $m = \pm 1$ and the equations are $y = x + 2$ and $y = -x - 2$.

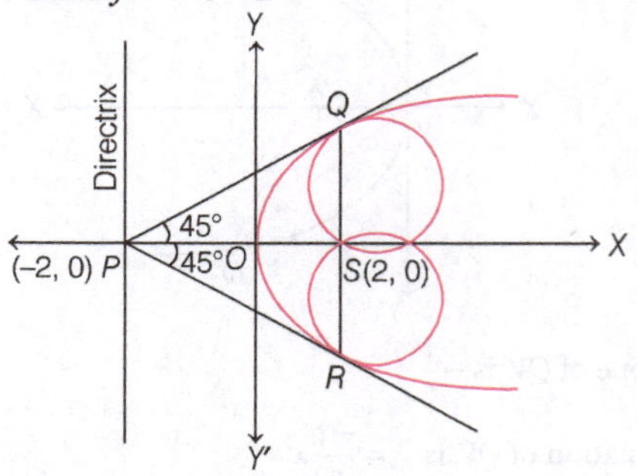

The chord of contact of tangents is QR as $x = 2$

$\because$ Common chord of two circles is X-axis.

Then, $\quad \angle QPR = 90°$

$\therefore$ Circumcentre is $S(2, 0)$ on X-axis and orthocentre is $P(-2, 0)$ on X-axis.

Centroid and incentre also lies on X-axis.

[$\because$ orthocentre, centroid, circumcentre and incentre are collinear]

29. Given parabola is $(y - 2)^2 = 4\left(x - \frac{1}{2}\right)$.

Let $\quad x - \frac{1}{2} = X, y - 2 = Y$

$\therefore$ Parabola is $Y^2 = 4X$

Any point on axis of parabola is $(x, 2)$ for three distinct normals $X > 2.1$

$$\Rightarrow \quad x - \frac{1}{2} > 2 \text{ or } x > \frac{5}{2}$$

$$\therefore \quad x = 3, 4, 5$$

Hence, points are (3, 2), (4, 2) and (5, 2).

30. The given parabola is $y^2 - 16x - 8y = 0$

$$\Rightarrow \quad (y-4)^2 = 16(x+1)$$

Shifting the origin to the point $(-1, 4)$ the equation of parabola become $y^2 = 16x$, then the coordinates of the point $(14, 7)$ becomes $(15, 3)$.

$\therefore$ Equation of any normal to the parabola is $Y + tX = 8t + 4t^3$.

Since, it passes through $(15, 3)$

$$\therefore \quad 3 + 15t = 8t + 4t^3 \Rightarrow 4t^3 - 7t - 3 = 0$$

or $\quad (t+1)(2t-3)(2t+1) = 0 \Rightarrow t = -1, \frac{3}{2}, -\frac{1}{2}$

$\therefore$ Corresponding points are $(4, -8)$, $(9, 12)$ and $(1, -4)$.
Hence, the coordinates of the feet of the normals w.r.t. the original system of coordinates are $(3, -4)$, $(8, 16)$ and $(0, 0)$.

31. The given equation can be re-written as $\left(y + \frac{3}{4}\right)^2 = 2\left(x + \frac{33}{32}\right)$

which is of the form $y^2 = 4ax$.

Hence, the vertex is $\left(-\frac{33}{32}, -\frac{3}{4}\right)$.

The, axis is $\quad y + \frac{3}{4} = 0 \Rightarrow y = -\frac{3}{4}$

The, directrix is $\quad x + a = 0$.

$$\Rightarrow \quad x + \frac{33}{32} + \frac{1}{2} = 0 \Rightarrow x = -\frac{49}{32}$$

The tangent at the vertex is

$$x + \frac{33}{32} = 0 \Rightarrow x = -\frac{33}{32}$$

Length of the latus rectum $= 4a = 2$.

32.

> **Decoding the Question**
> To solve this problem, write the equation of family of circle as $c_1 + \lambda c_2 = 0$, then apply the condition for given curve to be a circle, if coefficient of x^2 is equal to coefficient of y^2.

Family of curves passing the points of intersection of two parabolas is $y^2 - 3ax + \lambda(x^2 + ax + 5 - 2y) = 0$.

It will represents a circle if $\lambda = 1$,

$$x + y^2 - 2ax - 2y + 5 = 0$$

It represents a real circle if $a^2 + 1 - 5 > 0 \Rightarrow a^2 > 4$

$$\Rightarrow \quad a \in (-\infty, -2) \cup (2, \infty)$$

Hence, option (a) and(d) are the correct answers.

33. The equation of any tangent to the circle $x^2 + y^2 = 2a^2$ is

$$x\cos\theta + y\sin\theta = \sqrt{2}a \quad \text{...(i)}$$

The equation of any tangent to the parabola $y^2 = 8ax$ is

$$y = mx + \frac{2a}{m} \quad \text{...(ii)}$$

Since, Eqs. (i) and (ii) are identical.

$$\frac{\cos\theta}{-m} = \frac{\sin\theta}{1} = \frac{m}{\sqrt{2}}$$

$$\Rightarrow \quad \cos\theta = \frac{-m^2}{\sqrt{2}} \text{ and } \sin\theta = \frac{m}{\sqrt{2}}$$

On squaring and adding, we get

$$m^4 + m^2 - 2 = 0$$

$$\Rightarrow \quad m^2 = 1$$

$$\Rightarrow \quad m = \pm 1$$

On substituting in Eq. (ii), the equation of the required tangent is $y = \pm(x + 2a)$.

Sol. (Q. Nos. 34 to 35)

Let $A \equiv (4, 0)$ and $B \equiv (0, 3)$.

$\because$ OA and OB are mutually perpendicular tangents to the parabola. Therefore, O will lie on the directrix of the parabola.

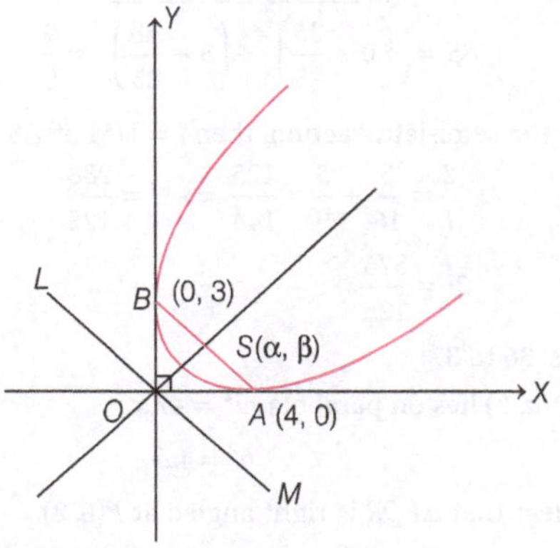

Let $S(\alpha, \beta)$ be the focus of the parabola.

$\because$ Portion of a tangent to a parabola intercepted between the directrix and point of contact subtends a right angle at the focus.

$$\therefore \quad \angle OSA = \angle OSB = \frac{\pi}{2}$$

Now, $OS \perp SA \Rightarrow$ Slope of $OS \times$ Slope of $SA = -1$

$$\Rightarrow \quad \left(\frac{\beta - 0}{\alpha - 0}\right) \times \left(\frac{\beta - 0}{\alpha - 4}\right) = -1$$

$$\Rightarrow \quad \alpha^2 + \beta^2 - 4\alpha = 0 \quad \text{...(i)}$$

Again, $OS \perp SB$

$\Rightarrow$ Slope of $OS \times$ Slope of $SB = -1$

$$\Rightarrow \quad \left(\frac{\beta - 0}{\alpha - 0}\right) \times \left(\frac{\beta - 3}{\alpha - 0}\right) = -1$$

$$\Rightarrow \quad \alpha^2 + \beta^2 - 3\beta = 0 \quad \text{...(ii)}$$

From Eqs. (i) and (ii), we get

$$4\alpha = 3\beta \quad \text{...(iii)}$$

Since, tangents AO and BO at A and B to parabola are at right angles, therefore AB will be a focal chord of the parabola.

Equation of AB is

$$\frac{x}{4} + \frac{y}{3} = 1$$

$$\Rightarrow \quad \frac{\alpha}{4} + \frac{\beta}{3} = 1$$

$$\Rightarrow \quad 3\alpha + 4\beta = 12 \quad \text{...(iv)}$$

From Eqs. (iii) and (iv), we get

$$\alpha = \frac{36}{25} \text{ and } \beta = \frac{48}{25}$$

$\therefore$ Focus of parabola is $\left(\frac{36}{25}, \frac{48}{25}\right)$.

34. $\because$ Focus is (a, b).

$$\therefore \quad b - a = \beta - \alpha = \frac{12}{25}$$

35. $\because$ $$AS = \sqrt{\left(4 - \frac{36}{25}\right)^2 + \left(0 - \frac{48}{25}\right)^2} = \frac{16}{5}$$

and $$BS = \sqrt{\left(0 - \frac{36}{25}\right)^2 + \left(3 - \frac{48}{25}\right)^2} = \frac{9}{5}$$

If l be the semi-latusrectum, then l = HM of AS and BS

$$\therefore \quad \frac{2}{l} = \frac{5}{16} + \frac{5}{9} = \frac{125}{144} \Rightarrow l = \frac{288}{125}$$

$$\therefore \quad 2l = \frac{576}{125}$$

Sol. (Q. Nos. 36 to 37)

Since, (a, b) lies on parabola, $y^2 = 4\lambda x$

$$\therefore \quad b^2 = 4a\lambda \quad \text{...(i)}$$

It is clear that ΔPQR is right angled at $P(0, 2)$.

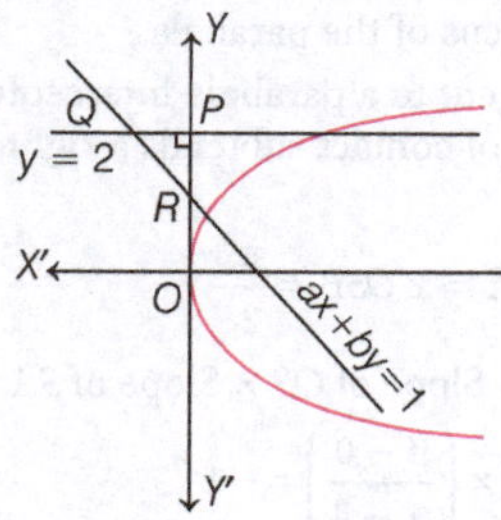

So, its circumcentre is the mid-point of Q and R, where

$$Q \equiv \left(\frac{1 - 2b}{a}, 2\right) \text{ and } R \equiv \left(0, \frac{1}{b}\right)$$

$$\therefore \quad \text{Circumcentre} \equiv \left(\frac{1 - 2b}{2a}, 1 + \frac{1}{2b}\right)$$

$$\therefore \quad x = \frac{1 - 2b}{2ab}, y = 1 + \frac{1}{2b}$$

$$\Rightarrow \quad 2b = \frac{1}{y - 1} \text{ and } 2a = \frac{(y - 2)}{x(y - 1)} \quad \text{...(ii)}$$

From Eqs. (i) and (ii), we get

$$(y - 1)(y - 2) = \frac{x}{8\lambda}$$

$$\Rightarrow \quad \left(y - \frac{3}{2}\right)^2 = \frac{1}{8\lambda}(x + 2\lambda)$$

$\therefore$ Vertex is $\left(-2\lambda, \frac{3}{2}\right)$ and length of latusrectum is $\frac{1}{8\lambda}$.

36. Product of coordinates of vertex $= -2\lambda \times \frac{3}{2} = -3\lambda$

$$= -3 \times 2 \quad [\because \lambda = 2]$$

$$= -6$$

37. Length of smallest focal chord = Length of latusrectum

$$= \frac{1}{8\lambda}$$

$$= \frac{1}{8 \times \left(\frac{1}{32}\right)} \quad \left[\because \lambda = \frac{1}{32}\right]$$

$$= 4$$

Sol. (Q. Nos. 38 to 39)

Given parabola (P) can be written as

$$(x - 2y)^2 = 32x - 4y - 16$$

On adding $2(x - 2y)\lambda + \lambda^2$ both sides, it becomes

$$(x - 2y + \lambda)^2 = 32x - 4y - 16 + 2(x - 2y)\lambda + \lambda^2$$
$$= 2(\lambda + 16)x - 4(\lambda + 1)y + \lambda^2 - 16 \quad \text{...(i)}$$

We choose λ such that lines

$$x - 2y + \lambda = 0 \text{ and } 2(\lambda + 16)x - 4(\lambda + 1)y + \lambda^2 - 16 = 0$$

are perpendicular to each other. It requires

$$\frac{1}{2} \times \frac{2(\lambda + 16)}{4(\lambda + 1)} = -1$$

$$\Rightarrow \quad \lambda + 16 = -4\lambda - 4$$

$$\Rightarrow \quad \lambda = -4$$

Hence, Eq. (i) becomes

$$(x - 2y - 4)^2 = 24x + 12y = 12(2x + y)$$

$$\Rightarrow \quad \left(\frac{x - 2y - 4}{\sqrt{5}}\right)^2 = \frac{12}{\sqrt{5}}\left(\frac{2x + y}{\sqrt{5}}\right) \Rightarrow Y^2 = 4\rho X$$

where, $$X = \frac{2x + y}{\sqrt{5}}, Y = \frac{x - 2y - 4}{\sqrt{5}}$$

and $$4\rho = \frac{12}{\sqrt{5}} \Rightarrow \rho = \frac{3}{\sqrt{5}}.$$

38. $\because$ Equation of axis is $Y = 0$.

$$\Rightarrow \quad x - 2y - 4 = 0 \quad \text{...(i)}$$

and equation of latusrectum is $X = \rho$

$$\Rightarrow \quad \frac{2x + y}{\sqrt{5}} = \frac{3}{\sqrt{5}}$$

$$\Rightarrow \quad 2x + y - 3 = 0 \quad \text{...(ii)}$$

On solving Eqs. (i) and (ii),

Focus is $(x, y) = (2, -1)$.

39. Length of latusrectum $= 4\rho = \frac{12}{\sqrt{5}}$

Sol. (Q. Nos. 40 to 41)

Any parabola whose axis is parallel to the X-axis will be of the form

$$(y - q)^2 = 4\lambda(x - p) \quad \text{...(i)}$$

Now, $lx + my = 1$ can be written as

$$(y - q) = -\frac{l}{m}(x - p) + \left(\frac{1 - mq - lp}{m}\right) \quad \text{...(ii)}$$

Eq. (ii) will touch Eq. (i), then

$$\frac{1 - mq - lp}{m} = \frac{\lambda}{-\frac{l}{m}}$$

$\Rightarrow \quad -l + mlq + l^2p = m^2\lambda$

$\Rightarrow \quad pl^2 + qlm - \lambda m^2 - l = 0$ ...(iii)

But given that

$5l^2 - 4lm + 6m^2 + 3l = 0$ ...(iv)

On comparing Eqs. (iii) and (iv), we get

$$\frac{p}{5} = \frac{q}{-4} = \frac{-\lambda}{6} = \frac{-1}{3}$$

$\Rightarrow \quad p = -\frac{5}{3}, q = \frac{4}{3}, \lambda = 2$

So, the parabola is $\left(y - \frac{4}{3}\right)^2 = 8\left(x + \frac{5}{3}\right)$.

40. $\because$ Vertex is $\left(-\frac{5}{3}, \frac{4}{3}\right)$.

Here, $a = -\frac{5}{3}$ and $b = \frac{4}{3}$

$\therefore \quad a - b = -3$

$\Rightarrow \quad |a - b| = 3$

41. For focus,

$$x + \frac{5}{3} = 2 \text{ and } y - \frac{4}{3} = 0$$

$\therefore$ Coordinates of focus are $\left(\frac{1}{3}, \frac{4}{3}\right)$.

Here, $c = \frac{1}{3}$ and $d = \frac{4}{3}$

$\therefore \quad d - c = 1$

$\Rightarrow \quad 2^{|d-c|} = 2$

Sol. (Q. Nos. 42 to 43)

$\because \quad C_1 : y^2 = 4x$

$\therefore \quad S_1 : (1, 0)$

Let $z = x + iy$ and $z_1 = x_1 + iy_1$

If z_1 is obtained by rotating z, 120° in anti-clockwise direction, then

$$z_1 = ze^{2\pi i/3} = (x + iy)\left(-\frac{1}{2} + \frac{i\sqrt{3}}{2}\right)$$

$$= \left(-\frac{x}{2} - \frac{\sqrt{3}y}{2}\right) + i\left(\frac{\sqrt{3}}{2}x - \frac{y}{2}\right)$$

$\therefore$ Equation of curve C_2 is

$$\left(\frac{\sqrt{3}}{2}x - \frac{y}{2}\right)^2 = 4\left(-\frac{x}{2} - \frac{\sqrt{3}}{2}y\right) \quad \text{...(i)}$$

For focus $-\frac{x}{2} - \frac{\sqrt{3}}{2}y = 1$ and $\frac{\sqrt{3}}{2}x - \frac{y}{2} = 0$.

$\therefore \quad x = -\frac{1}{2}, y = -\frac{\sqrt{3}}{2}$

$\Rightarrow \quad S_2 : \left(-\frac{1}{2}, -\frac{\sqrt{3}}{2}\right)$

$\because$ C_3 is reflection of C_2 with respect to $y = x$.

$\therefore \quad S_3 : \left(-\frac{\sqrt{3}}{2}, -\frac{1}{2}\right)$

42. $\because (t^2, 2t)$ are parametric form of curve C_1.

$\therefore$ From Eq. (i),

$\frac{\sqrt{3}}{2}x - \frac{y}{2} = 2t$ and $-\frac{x}{2} - \frac{\sqrt{3}}{2}y = t^2$, we get

$$x = \frac{1}{2}(-t^2 + 2\sqrt{3}t), y = \frac{1}{2}(-\sqrt{3}t^2 - 2t)$$

$\therefore$ Parametric coordinates of C_2 are

$$\left(\frac{1}{2}(-t^2 + 2\sqrt{3}t), \frac{1}{2}(-\sqrt{3}t^2 - 2t)\right).$$

43. Area of ΔOS_2S_3

$$= \frac{1}{2}\left\| \begin{matrix} -\frac{1}{2} & -\frac{\sqrt{3}}{2} \\ -\frac{\sqrt{3}}{2} & -\frac{1}{2} \end{matrix} \right\|$$

$$= \frac{1}{2}\left|\frac{1}{4} - \frac{3}{4}\right| = \frac{1}{4} \text{ sq unit}$$

Sol. (Q. Nos. 44 to 45)

Since, no point of the parabola $y = x^2 + ax + 1$ is below the X-axis.

$\therefore \quad D \le 0$

$\Rightarrow \quad a^2 - 4 \le 0$

$\Rightarrow \quad -2 \le a \le 2$

44. The maximum value of a is 2.

The equation of the parabola is $y = x^2 + 2x + 1$.

It intersect the Y-axis at (0, 1).

$\therefore$Equation of tangent at (0, 1) is

$$\frac{y + 1}{2} = 0 \cdot x + (x + 0) + 1$$

$\Rightarrow \quad y = 2x + 1$

$\Rightarrow \quad 2x - y + 1 = 0$

Since, $2x - y + 1 = 0$ touches the circle $x^2 + y^2 = c^2$, then

$$\frac{0 - 0 + 1}{\sqrt{4 + 1}} = c \quad [\because c > 0]$$

$\Rightarrow \quad c = \frac{1}{\sqrt{5}}$

$\therefore \quad 5c^2 = 1$

45. Equation of the tangent at (0, 1) to the parabola

$y = x^2 + ax + 1$ is

$\Rightarrow \quad \frac{y + 1}{2} = 0 \cdot x + \frac{a}{2}(x + 0) + 1$

$\Rightarrow \quad y = ax + 1$

$\Rightarrow \quad ax - y + 1 = 0$

As it touches the circle $x^2 + y^2 = c^2$, then

$$\frac{1}{\sqrt{(a^2 + 1)}} = c$$

i.e. c is maximum, when $a = 0$.

Therefore, the equation of the tangent is $y = 1$.

$\therefore$Slope of the tangent is 0.

Sol. (Q. Nos. 46 to 47)

The conic is $S \equiv x^2 + xy + y^2 - 2x - 2y + 1 = 0$

and the line is $L \equiv x + y + 1 = 0$

It is required to find equation of the parabola (P) which touches the conic $S = 0$ at those (two) points, where the line $L = 0$ intersect the conic.

Obviously at these points the parabola is in double contact with the conic.

$\therefore$ The equation of any such conic is $\phi \equiv S + \lambda L^2 = 0$

$\Rightarrow (x^2 + xy + y^2 - 2x - 2y + 1) + \lambda(x + y + 1)^2 = 0$ ...(i)

$\Rightarrow (1 + \lambda)x^2 + (1 + 2\lambda)xy + (1 + \lambda)y^2 + 2(\lambda - 1)x + 2(\lambda - 1)y + \lambda + 1 = 0$

It will be a parabola, if $h^2 = ab$

$\Rightarrow \frac{1}{4}(1 + 2\lambda)^2 = (1 + \lambda)^2$

$\Rightarrow 1 + 4\lambda + 4\lambda^2 = 4 + 8\lambda + 4\lambda^2$

$\therefore \lambda = -\frac{3}{4}$

Hence, from Eq. (i), the required parabola is

$(x^2 + xy + y^2 - 2x - 2y + 1) - \frac{3}{4}(x + y + 1)^2 = 0$

$\Rightarrow x^2 - 2xy + y^2 - 14x - 14y + 1 = 0$ ...(ii)

46. On comparing parabola (ii) with

$ax^2 + 2hxy + by^2 + 2gx + 2fy + c = 0,$

$\therefore a = 1, h = -1, b = 1, g = -7, f = -7, c = 1$

Now, $|a + b + c + f + g + h| = |1 + 1 + 1 - 7 - 7 - 1| = 12$

47. For vertex,

$\frac{x - y}{\sqrt{2}} = 0, \frac{14x + 14y - 1}{\sqrt{(14)^2 + (14)^2}} = 0$ [from Eq. (iii)]

$\Rightarrow x = y, 14x + 14y = 1$

$\therefore x = y = \frac{1}{28}$

Vertex is $\left(\frac{1}{28}, \frac{1}{28}\right) = (a, b)$ [given]

$\therefore |a - b| = 0$

Sol. (Q. Nos. 48 to 49)

$\because$ $y = 3x$ is tangent to the parabola

$2y = ax^2 + b$ ...(i)

$\therefore 2(3x) = ax^2 + b$

[substitute the value of $y = 3x$ in $2y = ax^2 + b$]

$\Rightarrow ax^2 - 6x + b = 0$

$D = 0$

[$\because y = 3x$ is tangent to $2y = ax^2 + b$]

$\therefore 36 - 4ab = 0$

$\Rightarrow ab = 9$ ...(ii)

From Eqs. (i) and (ii), we get

$2y = ax^2 + \frac{9}{a}$ ...(iii)

48. Since, $\frac{a + b}{2} \geq \sqrt{ab} = 3$ [from Eq. (ii)]

$\Rightarrow a + b \geq 6$

$\therefore$ Minimum value of $a + b$ is 6.

49. $\because$ (2, 6) is the point of contact.

From Eq. (iii), we get

$12 = 4a + \frac{9}{a}$

$\Rightarrow 4a^2 - 12a + 9 = 0$

$\Rightarrow (2a - 3)^2 = 0$

$\therefore 2a = 3$

50. Equation of tangent in terms of slope (m) of the parabola $y^2 = 4x$ is $y = mx + \frac{1}{m}$.

$\because$ Point of intersection of tangents is $(-2, -1)$, then

$-1 = -2m + \frac{1}{m} \Rightarrow 2m^2 - m - 1 = 0$

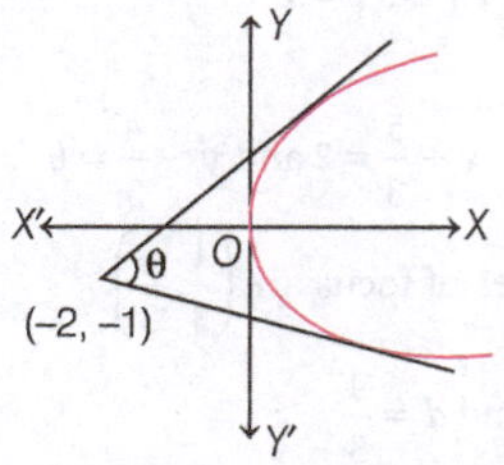

Let m_1 and m_2 be slopes of the tangents, then

$m_1 - m_2 = \frac{\sqrt{D}}{a} = \frac{\sqrt{(1 + 8)}}{2} = \frac{3}{2}$ and $m_1 m_2 = -\frac{1}{2}$

$\therefore \tan\theta = \left|\frac{m_1 - m_2}{1 + m_1 m_2}\right| = \left|\frac{3/2}{1 - 1/2}\right| = 3$

51. Let S be the focus and point of intersection of tangents at P and Q is R.

$\because (SR)^2 = SP \cdot SQ = 4 \times 9 = 36$

$\therefore SR = 6$

52. The four lines form a square. The tangents at $L(1, 2)$ and $L'(1, -2)$ are $x - y + 1 = 0$ and $x + y + 1 = 0$. They intersect at $M(-1, 0)$.

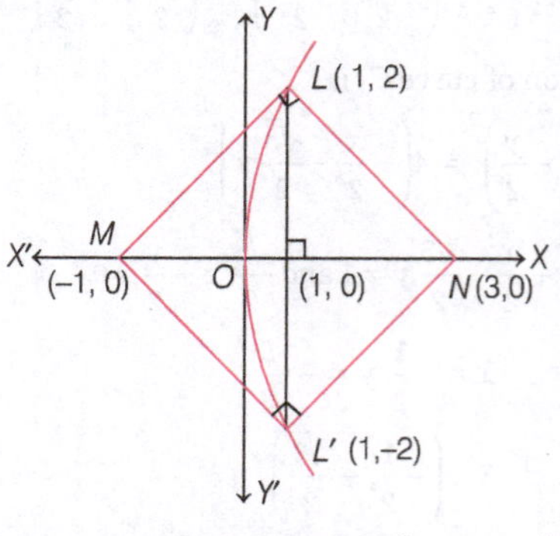

The area of the square $MLNL'$ is $(ML)^2 = (1 + 1)^2 + (2 - 0)^2 = 8$ sq units

$\therefore \lambda = 8$

53. Parabola is $y^2 = x$

$\therefore \quad a = \frac{1}{4}$

The normal at t is $tx + y = \frac{t^3}{4} + \frac{t}{2}$

It passes through $(a, 0)$.

$\therefore \quad ta = \frac{t^3}{4} + \frac{t}{2}$

$\Rightarrow \quad t^2 = 4\left(a - \frac{1}{2}\right) \Rightarrow a > \frac{1}{2}$

$\therefore \quad t_1 = 2\sqrt{\left(a - \frac{1}{2}\right)}, t_2 = -2\sqrt{\left(a - \frac{1}{2}\right)}$

The normals are perpendicular.

$\therefore \quad t_1 t_2 = -1$

$\Rightarrow \quad -4\left(a - \frac{1}{2}\right) = -1$

$\therefore \quad 4a = 3$

54. Let B as $\left(\frac{3}{2}t^2, 3t\right)$ $\left[\text{here } a = \frac{3}{2}\right]$

and let $BD \perp AC$ and $\angle DAB = \theta$

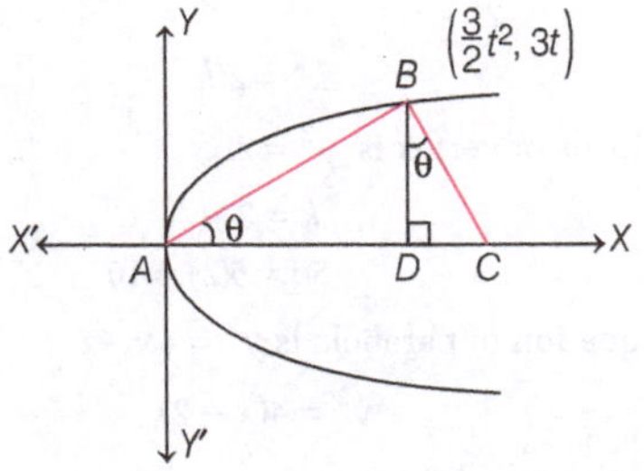

$\Rightarrow \quad \tan\theta = \frac{BD}{AD} = \frac{3t}{\frac{3}{2}t^2} = \frac{2}{t}$

$\therefore$ Projection of BC on the axis $= DC$

$= BD\tan\theta = 3t\left(\frac{2}{t}\right) = 6$ units

$\therefore \quad \lambda = 6$

55. The parabolas are $y = x^2 - 9$ and $y = \lambda x^2$.

$\Rightarrow \quad x^2 - 9 = \lambda x^2 \Rightarrow x^2(1-\lambda) = 9$

$\Rightarrow \quad x^2 = \frac{9}{1-\lambda}$

$\therefore \quad x = \pm\frac{3}{\sqrt{(1-\lambda)}}$

Now, from the symmetry about Y-axis,

$AB = 2a = \frac{6}{\sqrt{(1-\lambda)}} \Rightarrow a = \frac{3}{\sqrt{(1-\lambda)}}$

$\Rightarrow \quad a^2(1-\lambda) = 9 \Rightarrow \lambda a^2 + 9 = a^2$

$\Rightarrow \quad a^2 + \mu = a^2$ [given]

$\therefore \quad \mu = 9$

56. Focus of the parabola $y^2 = 4x$ is $S(1, 0)$.

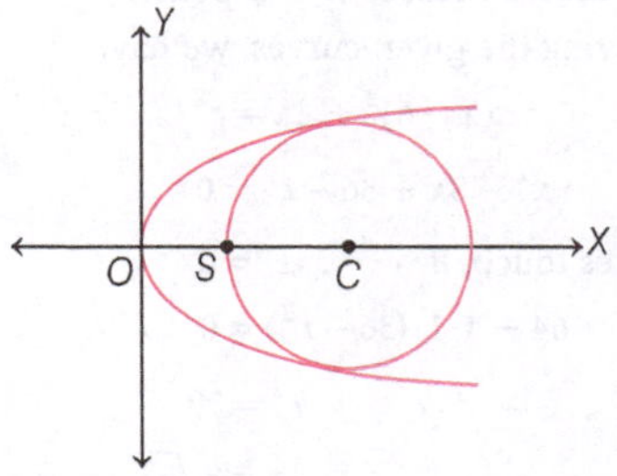

Let radius of circle be r.

$\therefore$ Centre of circle is $(1 + r, 0)$.

$\Rightarrow$ Equation of circle is $(x - 1 - r)^2 + y^2 = r^2$

$\Rightarrow \quad (x - 1 - r)^2 + 4x = r^2 \quad [\because y^2 = 4x]$

$\Rightarrow \quad x^2 + 2(2 - 1 - r)x + 2r + 1 = 0$

$\Rightarrow \quad x^2 + 2(1 - r)x + 2r + 1 = 0$

It would have same roots due to symmetry.

$\therefore \quad D = 0$

$\Rightarrow \quad 4(1-r)^2 - 4\cdot 1\cdot(2r+1) = 0$

$\therefore \quad r = 0, 4$

Hence, $\quad r = 4 \quad [\because r \neq 0]$

57. Given parabola is $x^2 = 4(y - 1)$

$\therefore$ Focus is $(0, 2)$.

Now, the shortest intercept of the line on the parabola which passes through the focus is latusrectum. The axis of the given parabola is the Y-axis.

Therefore, the latusrectum is parallel to the X-axis.

$\therefore$ Slope $= 0$

58. Given, $y^2 - 8x < 0$, $x^2 + y^2 < 16$ and $x > 0$.

For $x = 1$,

$y^2 < 8$ and $y^2 < 15$

$\Rightarrow \quad y^2 < 8$

$\therefore \quad y = 0, \pm 1, \pm 2$

$\therefore$ 5 points.

For $x = 2$,

$y^2 < 16, y^2 < 12$

$\Rightarrow \quad y^2 < 12$

$\therefore \quad y = 0, \pm 1, \pm 2, \pm 3$

$\therefore$ 7 points

For $x = 3$,

$y^2 < 24, y^2 < 7$

$\Rightarrow \quad y^2 < 7$

$\therefore \quad y = 0, \pm 1, \pm 2$

$\therefore$ 5 points

Hence, total points is 17.

$\therefore \quad n = 17$

Sum of digits of n is 8.

59. For maximum number of common chords, the circle and the parabola must intersect at four points.
Now, solving the given curves, we have

$$(x-6)^2 + 4x = r^2$$

$\Rightarrow \quad x^2 - 8x + 36 - r^2 = 0$

The curves touch, if $\quad D = 0$

$\Rightarrow \quad 64 - 4 \cdot 1 \cdot (36 - r^2) = 0$

$\Rightarrow \quad r^2 = 20$

$\therefore \quad r = 2\sqrt{5}$

60. The chord of contact with respect to point

$O(-1, 2)$ is $y = (x-1)$ $\quad$ [using $yy_1 = 2a(x + x_1)$]

On solving $y = x - 1$ with the parabola, we get the point of intersection as $P(3 + 2\sqrt{2}, 2 + 2\sqrt{2})$ and $Q(3 - 2\sqrt{2}, 2 - 2\sqrt{2})$

$\therefore \quad PQ^2 = (-4\sqrt{2})^2 + (-4\sqrt{2})^2 = 32 + 32 = 64$

$\Rightarrow \quad PQ = 8$

Also, the length of perpendicular from $O(-1, 2)$ on PQ is

$$\frac{|2+1+1|}{\sqrt{2}} = \frac{4}{\sqrt{2}}$$

Required area of triangle $= \frac{1}{2} \times 8 \times \frac{4}{\sqrt{2}} = \frac{16}{\sqrt{2}} = 8\sqrt{2}$ sq. units

$\therefore \quad 8\sqrt{2} = n\sqrt{m}$

$\Rightarrow \quad n = 8$ and $m = 2$

$\therefore \quad mn = 2 \times 8 = 16$

61. Given the equation of parabola is $x^2 = 4y$.
Its focus is $S(0, 1)$.

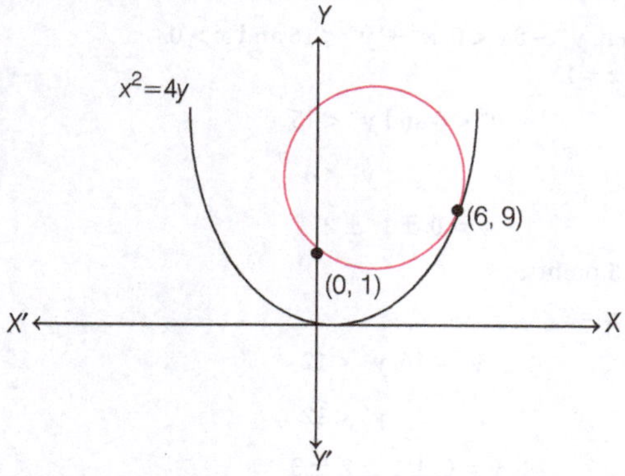

The tangent at (6, 9) is $\;6x = 2(y + 9)$

$\Rightarrow \quad 3x = y + 9$

$\Rightarrow \quad 3x - y - 9 = 0 \quad$ ...(i)

Now, equation of circle which touches at (6, 9) is
$(x-6)^2 + (y-9)^2 + \lambda(y - 3x + 9) = 0 \quad$ ...(ii)

$\because$ Circle passes through focus of parabola.
So, Eq. (ii) becomes

$$(0-6)^2 + (1-9)^2 + \lambda(1 - 3(0) + 9) = 0$$

$\Rightarrow \quad 36 + 64 + 10\lambda = 0$

$\Rightarrow \quad \lambda = -10$

On putting the value of λ in eq. (ii), we get

$$(x-6)^2 + (y-9)^2 - 10(y - 3x + 9) = 0$$

$\Rightarrow \quad x^2 + y^2 + 18x - 28y + 27 = 0$

Now, $\quad$ radius $= \sqrt{f^2 + g^2 - c^2} = \sqrt{9^2 + 14^2 - 27}$

$= \sqrt{250}$

$= 5\sqrt{10} = k\sqrt{10}$

$\Rightarrow \quad k = 5$

$\therefore \quad \frac{k}{2} = \frac{5}{2} = 2.5$

62. Let (h, k) be the coordinates of the vertex of moving parabolas and its equation be $(y-k)^2 + t(x-h) = 0$ the equation of fixed curve be $y^2 - lx = 0$, then the tangents at the point (h^3, h) to the two curves are $-2yt = x + lt^2 = 0$ and

$$y(lt - k) + \frac{x}{2} + \frac{l^2t^2}{2} + k^2 - lh - klt = 0.$$

As they are coincident $\quad \frac{k - lt}{2t} = \frac{1}{2} = \frac{l^2t^2 + 2k^2 - 2lh - 2tklt}{2lt^2}$

from which $t = \frac{k}{2l}$ and $k^2 - lh = klt$

$\Rightarrow \quad k^2 = 2lh$

Hence, locus of vertex is $y^2 = 2lx$

$\Rightarrow \quad k = 2$

$\therefore \quad 5k = 5(2) = 10$

63. Given equation of parabola is $y^2 = 4x - 8$

$\Rightarrow \quad y^2 = 4(x-2)$

and equation of ellipse is

$$3x^2 + by^2 - 12x = 0 \Rightarrow 3(x^2 - 4x) + by^2 = 0$$

$\Rightarrow \quad 3((x-2)^2 - 4) + by^2 = 0$

$\Rightarrow \quad 3(x-2)^2 + by^2 = 12$

$\Rightarrow \quad \frac{(x-2)^2}{4} + \frac{y^2}{\left(\frac{12}{b}\right)} = 1$

$\Rightarrow \quad a = 2$

$$e = \sqrt{1 - \frac{\frac{12}{b}}{4}} = \sqrt{1 - \frac{3}{b}} = \sqrt{\frac{b-3}{b}}$$

$$x = 2 + 2\sqrt{\frac{b-3}{b}} = 3$$

$\Rightarrow \quad 2\sqrt{\frac{b-3}{b}} = 1 \Rightarrow b = 4$

$\therefore \quad e = \sqrt{1 - \frac{3}{b}} = \sqrt{1 - \frac{3}{4}} = \frac{1}{2}$

$\Rightarrow \quad 24e = \frac{24}{2} = 12$

64. (A) The given parabolas are symmetrical about the line $y = x$ as shown in the figure

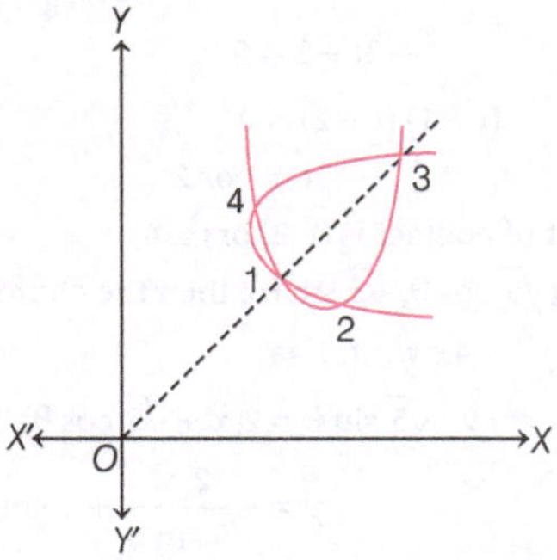

They intersect each other at four distinct points.
Hence, the number of common chords is

$$^4C_2 = \frac{4 \cdot 3}{1 \cdot 2} = 6$$

which is perfect number $[\because 1 \times 2 \times 3 = 1 + 2 + 3 = 6]$

(B) $\because$ $\tan\theta = \frac{y}{x}$ ...(i)

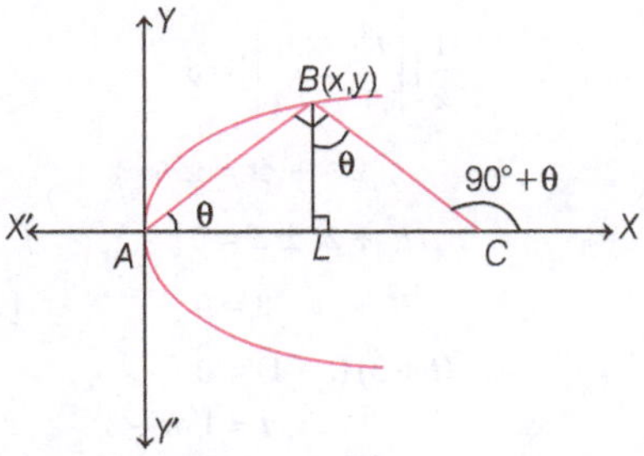

$LC =$ Projection of BC on X-axis

$$= BL \tan\theta = y \tan\theta$$

$$= y \times \frac{y}{x} \quad \text{[from Eq. (i)]}$$

$$= \frac{y^2}{x} = 4 \quad [\because y^2 = 4x]$$

(C) Normals to $y^2 = 4ax$ and $x^2 = 4by$ in terms of m are

$y = mx - 2am - am^3$ and $y = mx + 2b + \frac{b}{m^2}$.

For common normal,

$$2b + \frac{b}{m^2} = -2am - am^3$$

or $$am^5 + 2am^3 + 2bm^2 + b = 0$$

It is clear, that at most five common normals.

(D) Let middle point of P and B be (h,k), then $2h = at^2$

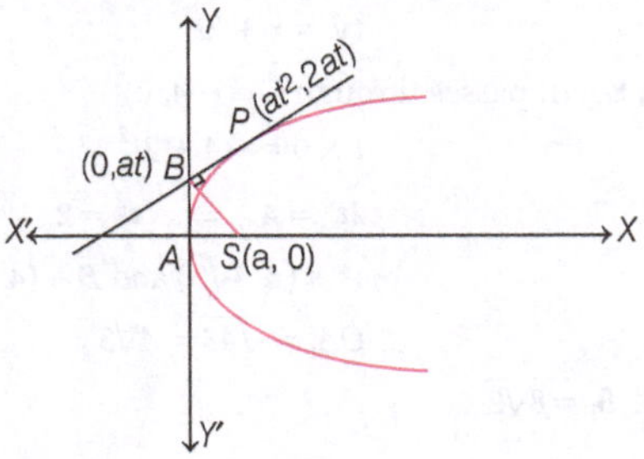

and $2k = 3at$

or $2h = a\left(\frac{2k}{3a}\right)^2$

or $2k^2 = 9ah$

$\therefore$ Locus of mid-point is $2y^2 = 9ax$.

$\therefore$ Length of latusrectum $= \frac{9a}{2}$

$$= \frac{9}{2} \times 2 \quad [\because a = 2]$$

$$= 9$$

65. (A) Given parabola is $x^2 = ay$ ...(i)

and the given line is $y - 2x = 1$ ...(ii)

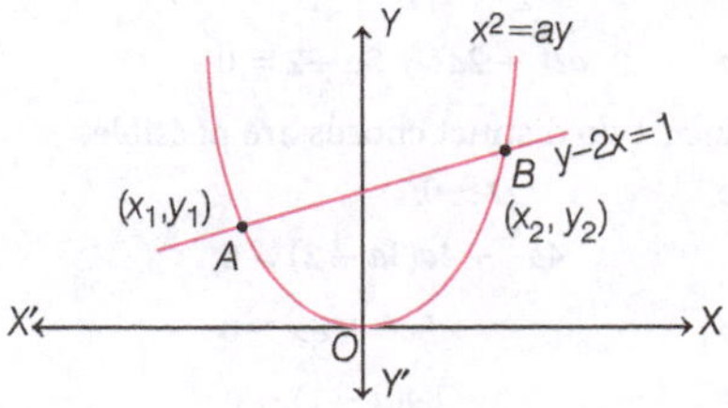

On solving Eqs. (i) and (ii), we get

$$x^2 = a(2x + 1) \Rightarrow x^2 - 2ax - a = 0$$

Let coordinates of A and B are (x_1, y_1) and (x_2, y_2), respectively, then

$$|x_1 - x_2| = \frac{\sqrt{D}}{a} = \frac{\sqrt{(4a^2 + 4a)}}{1} = 2\sqrt{(a^2 + a)} \quad \text{...(iii)}$$

Also, A, B lie on $y - 2x = 1$.

$\therefore$ $y_1 - 2x_1 = 1$ and $y_2 - 2x_2 = 1$

or $y_2 - y_1 = 2(x_2 - x_1)$ ...(iv)

$\therefore$ Length of $AB = \sqrt{(x_2 - x_1)^2 + (y_2 - y_1)^2}$

$$= \sqrt{5}\,|x_1 - x_2| \quad \text{[from Eq. (iv)]}$$

$$= 2\sqrt{5}\sqrt{(a^2 + a)} \quad \text{[from Eq. (iii)]}$$

Given, $2\sqrt{5}\sqrt{(a^2 + a)} = \sqrt{40}$

$\Rightarrow$ $a^2 + a = 2$

$\Rightarrow$ $a^2 + a - 2 = 0$

$\Rightarrow$ $(a + 2)(a - 1) = 0$

$\Rightarrow$ $a = -2, 1$

(B) If tangents are drawn from (x_1, y_1) to the parabola $y^2 = 4ax$ and angle between tangents is θ, then

$$|\tan\theta| = \frac{\sqrt{(y_1^2 - 4ax_1)}}{|x_1 + a|}$$

Here, $x_1 = 0, y_1 = 2, \theta = \frac{3\pi}{4}$, then

$$|-1| = \frac{2}{|0 + a|}$$

$\Rightarrow$ $|a| = 2$

$\therefore$ $a = \pm 2$

Alternate Solution

Observe that one tangent is the Y-axis, the other tangent is at $\theta = \frac{\pi}{4}$ and its equation is $ty = x + at^2$

for $t = 1$, we get $y = x + a$

$\Rightarrow a = 2$ from the symmetry $a = -2$ is also possible.

(C) Let the other end be at $(at^2, 2at)$

So, mid-point is $\left(\frac{at^2 + a}{2}, \frac{2at + 2a}{2}\right)$

which satisfy $x + y = 1$.

or $\frac{at^2 + a}{2} + at + a = 1$

$\Rightarrow at^2 + 2at + 3a - 2 = 0$

Since, two distinct chords are possible.

So, $D > 0$.

$\therefore 4a^2 - 4a(3a - 2) > 0$

$\Rightarrow -8a^2 + 8a > 0$

$\Rightarrow 8a(a - 1) < 0$

$\therefore 0 < a < 1$

or $0 < 4a < 4$

or $0 <$ Length of latusrectum < 4

$\therefore$ Length of latusrectum can be 1 or 2 or 3 from the given values.

(D) The given parabola is

$x^2 - ay + 3 = 0$

or $x^2 = a\left(y - \frac{3}{a}\right)$

Let $x = X, y - \frac{3}{a} = Y$

Then, the parabola is

$X^2 = aY$

For focus $X = 0, Y = \frac{a}{4}$

$\Rightarrow x = 0, y - \frac{3}{a} = \frac{a}{4}$

$\therefore$ Focus is $\left(0, \frac{3}{a} + \frac{a}{4}\right)$ given focus is $(0, 2)$.

$\therefore \frac{3}{a} + \frac{a}{4} = 2$

$\Rightarrow a^2 - 8a + 12 = 0 \Rightarrow (a - 6)(a - 2) = 0$

$\therefore a = 2, 6$

Here, $a_1 = 6, a_2 = 2$

$\therefore \frac{a_1}{a_2} = 3$

66. (A) Points $(1, 2)$ and $(-2, 1)$ satisfy both the curves.

(B) Equation of tangent at $(t^2, 2t)$ on $y^2 = 4x$ is

$ty = x + t^2$

It passes through the point $(2, 3)$, then

$3t = 2 + t^2$

$\Rightarrow t^2 - 3t + 2 = 0$

or $(t - 1)(t - 2) = 0$

or $t = 1$ or 2

The point of contact is $(1, 2)$ or $(4, 4)$.

(C) Let $P(\sqrt{5}\cos\theta, \sqrt{5}\sin\theta)$, then the chord of contact of the parabola $y^2 = 4x$ w.r.t. P is

$y \cdot \sqrt{5}\sin\theta = 2(x + \sqrt{5}\cos\theta)$

or $y = \frac{2x}{\sqrt{5}\sin\theta} + 2\cot\theta$

On comparing with $y = 2(x - 2)$, then

$\sqrt{5}\sin\theta = 1$ and $\cot\theta = -2$

or $\sqrt{5}\sin\theta = 1$ and $\sqrt{5}\cos\theta = -2$

Hence, coordinates of P are $(-2, 1)$.

(D) Let coordinates of Q be $(t^2, 2t)$.

Now, the area of ΔOPQ is

$\frac{1}{2}\left|\begin{vmatrix} t^2 & 2t \\ 4 & -4 \end{vmatrix}\right| = 6$ [given]

$\Rightarrow 2t^2 + 4t = \pm 6$

or $t^2 + 2t \pm 3 = 0$

$\therefore t^2 + 2t - 3 = 0$ $[\because t^2 + 2t + 3 \neq 0]$

$\Rightarrow (t + 3)(t - 1) = 0$

Then, $t = 1$ or -3

Hence, the point Q are $(1, 2)$ or $(9, -6)$.

67. Given, $C \equiv (-4, 0)$

and let $A_1 \equiv (2t_1^2, 4t_1)$ and $B_1 \equiv (2t_2^2, 4t_2)$

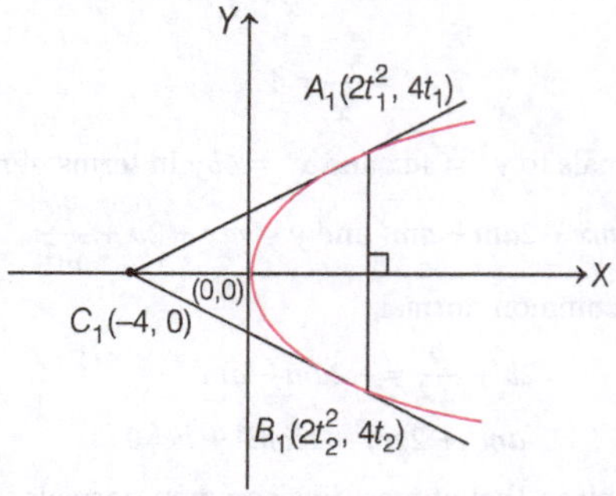

Now, equation of tangent at $(2t^2, 4t)$ is given by

$ty = x + 2t^2$ ...(i)

Since, Eq. (i) passes through $C \equiv (-4, 0)$

So, $t \times 0 = -4 + 2t^2$

$\Rightarrow 2t^2 = 4 \Rightarrow t^2 = 2 \Rightarrow t = \pm\sqrt{2}$

$\therefore A \equiv (4, 4\sqrt{2})$ and $B \equiv (4, -4\sqrt{2})$

Now, $OA_1 = \sqrt{48} = 4\sqrt{3}$

and $A_1B_1 = 8\sqrt{2}$

(Method (2) to find Coordinates of A and B) (By Short Trick)

As we know that the points of intersection of the tangents at the point t_1 and t_2 is $(at_1t_2, a(t_1 + t_2))$.

So, $\quad C \equiv (2t_1t_2, 2(t_1 + t_2)) = (-4, 0) \quad$ [here, $a = 2$]

Now, $\quad 2t_1t_2 = -4$ and $2(t_1 + t_2) = 0$

$\Rightarrow \quad t_1 = -t_2 \Rightarrow 2t_1 \times (-t_1) = -4$

$\Rightarrow \quad t_1^2 = 2 \quad \Rightarrow t_1 = \pm\sqrt{2}$

$\therefore \quad A \equiv (2t_1^2, 4t_1) \equiv (4, 4\sqrt{2})$

and $\quad B \equiv (2t_2^2, 4t_2) = (4, -4\sqrt{2})$

Now, equation of altitude of $\Delta A_1B_1C_1$ drawn from A_1 is given by

$$y - 4\sqrt{2} = \sqrt{2}(x - 4)$$

$\Rightarrow \quad \sqrt{2}x - y = 0 \quad$ ...(i)

Equation of altitude of $\Delta A_1B_1C_1$ drawn from C_1 is given by

$$x = 0 \quad \text{...(ii)}$$

On solving Eqs. (i) and (ii), we get

$$x = 0 \text{ and } y = 0$$

Hence, orthocentre $\equiv (0, 0)$

68. Given equation parabola is

$$x^2 = -4ay, a > 0 \quad \text{...(i)}$$

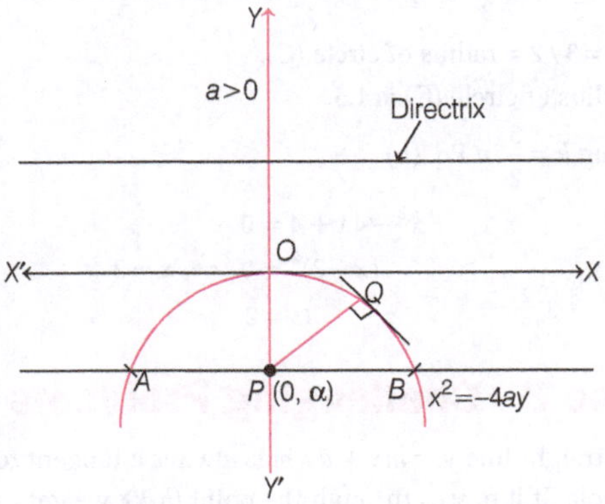

Let $P \equiv (0, -\alpha)$ and normal is PQ.

So, equation of normal PQ is

$y = mx - 2a - \dfrac{a}{m^2}$, $m =$ Slope of normal

$\because \quad PQ$ passes through P, then

$$-\alpha = 0 - 2a + \frac{a}{m^2}$$

$\Rightarrow \quad \alpha = 2a + \dfrac{a}{\left(\dfrac{1}{6}\right)} \quad \left[\text{given, } m = \dfrac{1}{\sqrt{6}}\right]$

$\Rightarrow \quad \alpha = 8a \quad$ ...(ii)

Equation of line AB is $y = -\alpha = -8a \quad$ ...(iii) [from Eq. (ii)]

On solving Eqs. (i) and (iii), to get point of intersections A and B, we get

$$x^2 = 32a^2$$

$\Rightarrow \quad x = \pm 4\sqrt{2}a = \pm 4\sqrt{2} \times \dfrac{\alpha}{8} \quad$ [from Eq. (ii)]

$\Rightarrow \quad x = \pm \dfrac{\alpha}{\sqrt{2}}$

Hence, $\quad A \equiv \left(\dfrac{\alpha}{\sqrt{2}}, -\alpha\right)$ and $B \equiv \left(\dfrac{-\alpha}{\sqrt{2}}, \alpha\right)$

$\quad AB = \sqrt{2}\alpha \quad$ ...(iv)

According to the question,

$r =$ length of latus rectum $= 4a$

and $\quad S = (AB)^2 = 2\alpha^2$

given, $\quad \dfrac{r}{S} = \dfrac{1}{16} \Rightarrow \dfrac{4a}{2\alpha^2} = \dfrac{1}{16}$

$\Rightarrow \quad \dfrac{4a}{2(64a^2)} = \dfrac{1}{16} \quad$ [from Eq. (ii)]

$\Rightarrow \quad a = \dfrac{1}{12}$

Hence, $\quad 24a = 12$

69. As we know that equation of normal at point P having slope m is given by

$$y = mx - 2am - am^3$$

Given, a rea of $\Delta PFQ = 120$

$\Rightarrow \quad \left|\dfrac{1}{2} \times (a + am^2)(-2am)\right| = 120 \quad [\because FQ = OQ - OF]$

$\Rightarrow \dfrac{1}{2} \times |a + am^2| \times |-2am| = 120$

$\Rightarrow \quad a^2(1 + m^2)m = 120 \quad$ ...(i)

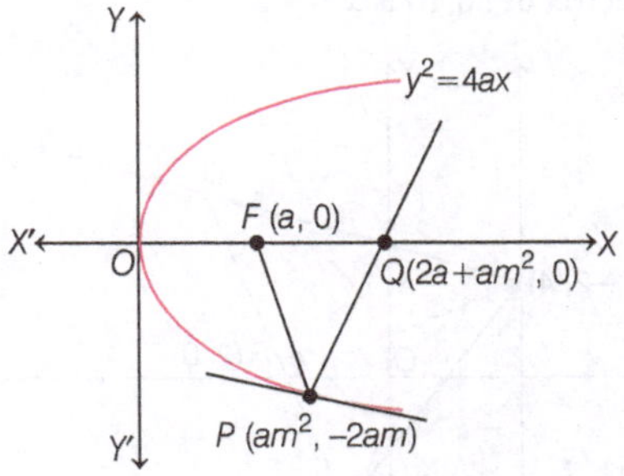

From given options, (2, 3) will satisfy Eq. (i).

$\therefore \quad (a, m) \equiv (2, 3)$

70. Given, equation of parabola is

$y^2 = 4x$ and S be the focus of the parabola.

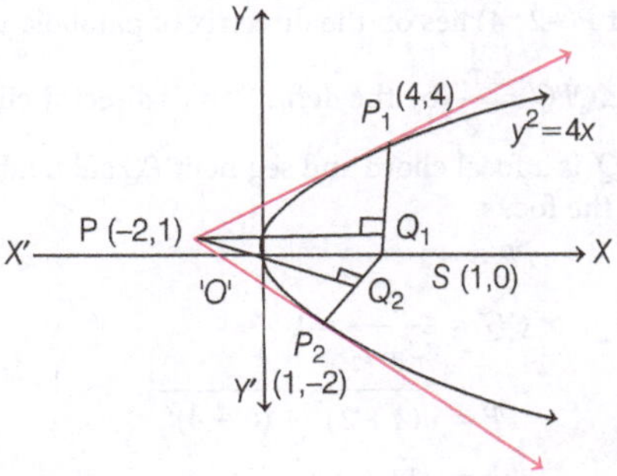

Let $P_1(t^2, 2t)$, then tangent at P_1 is $ty = x + t^2$.

Since, it passes through the point $(-2, 1)$.

Thus, $t^2 - t - 2 = 0 \Rightarrow t = 2, -1$

$\therefore$ $P_1 = (4, 4)$, $P_2 = (1, -2)$ and $S \equiv (1, 0)$

Thus, $SP_1 : 4x - 3y - 4 = 0$

and $SP_2 : x - 1 = 0$

and for $Q_1 : \dfrac{x_1 + 2}{4} = \dfrac{y_1 - 1}{-3}$

$= \dfrac{-(-8 - 3 - 4)}{25} = \dfrac{3}{5}$

$\Rightarrow$ $x_1 = \dfrac{2}{5}$ and $y_1 = -\dfrac{4}{5}$.

$\therefore$ $Q_1 = \left(\dfrac{2}{5}, \dfrac{-4}{5}\right)$

and similarly, $Q_2 = (1, 1)$

So, $SQ_1 = \sqrt{\left(1 - \dfrac{2}{5}\right)^2 + \left(\dfrac{4}{5}\right)^2} = 1$

and $Q_1Q_2 = \sqrt{\dfrac{9}{25} + \dfrac{81}{25}} = \sqrt{\dfrac{90}{25}} = \dfrac{3\sqrt{10}}{5}$

and $PQ_1 = \sqrt{\dfrac{144}{25} + \dfrac{81}{25}} = \sqrt{\dfrac{225}{25}} = \sqrt{9} = 3$

$\therefore$ $SQ_2 = \sqrt{(1-1)^2 + (0-1)^2} = 1$

71. Given, $E : y^2 = 8x$ ...(i)

and $P \equiv (-2, 4)$

Now, directrix of Eq. (i) is $x = -2$

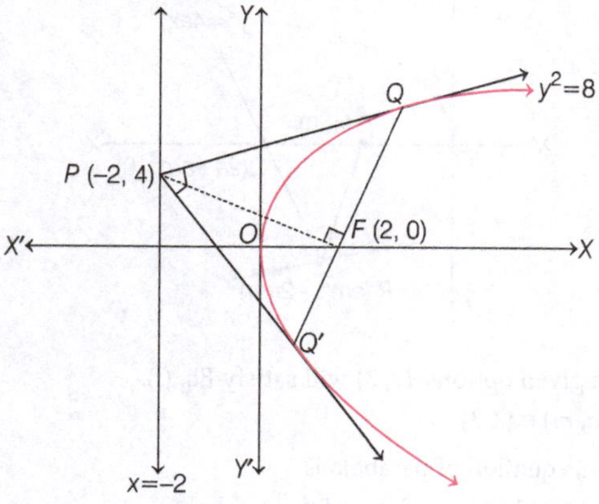

So, point $P(-2, 4)$ lies on the directrix of parabola $y^2 = 8x$.

Hence, $\angle QPQ' = \dfrac{\pi}{2}$ (by the definition of director circle) and chord QQ' is a focal chord and segment PQ subtends a right angle at the focus.

Slope of $PF = -1$ $(\because PF \perp QQ')$

Now, slope of $QQ' = \dfrac{2}{t_1 + t_2} = 1$

$\therefore$ $PF = \sqrt{(2+2)^2 + (0-4)^2}$

$= \sqrt{32} = 4\sqrt{2}$

72. Given, $x \geq 0, y^2 \leq 4 - x$

Let equation of circle be

$$(x - h)^2 + y^2 = h^2 \quad \text{...(i)}$$

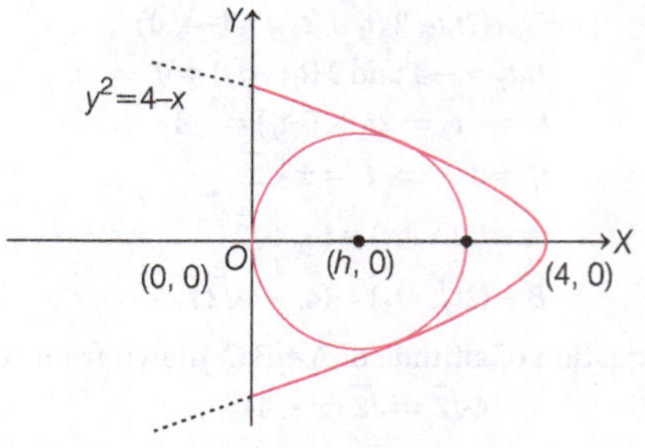

Solving Eq. (i) with $y^2 = 4 - x$, we get

$$x^2 - 2hx + 4 - x = 0$$

$\Rightarrow$ $x^2 - x(2h + 1) + 4 = 0$ ...(ii)

For touching/tangency, Discriminant $(D) = 0$

i.e. $(2h + 1)^2 = 16$

$\Rightarrow$ $2h + 1 = \pm 4 \Rightarrow 2h = \pm 4 - 1$

$\Rightarrow h = \dfrac{3}{2}, h = \dfrac{-5}{2}$ (Rejected) because part of circle lies outside R.

So, $h = 3/2$ = radius of circle (C).

$\therefore$ Radius of circle (C) is 1.5.

73. Putting $h = \dfrac{3}{2}$ in Eq. (ii),

$$x^2 - 4x + 4 = 0$$

$\Rightarrow$ $(x-2)^2 = 0 \Rightarrow x = 2$

So, $\alpha = 2$

Exercise 3 - Challenging Problems

1. The straight line $y = mx + a/m$ is always a tangent to the parabola. If it passes through the point (h, k), we get

$$m^2h - mk + a = 0 \quad \text{...(i)}$$

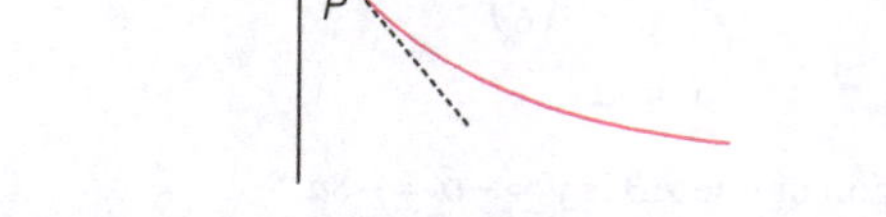

If m_1 and m_2 are the roots of this equation, then

$$m_1 + m_2 = \frac{k}{h} \quad \text{...(ii)}$$

and $$m_1m_2 = \frac{a}{h} \quad \text{...(iii)}$$

Equations of TP and TQ are $y = m_1 x + a / m_1$ and $y = m_2 x + a / m_2$, respectivley.

$$\therefore \quad \tan\alpha = \left|\frac{m_1 - m_2}{1 + m_1 m_2}\right| = \left|\frac{\sqrt{\frac{k^2}{h^2} - \frac{4a}{h}}}{1 + a/h}\right| = \left|\frac{\sqrt{k^2 - 4ah}}{a + h}\right|$$

or $$(a + h)^2 \tan^2\alpha = (k^2 - 4ah).$$

Therefore, the required locus is

$$(a + x)^2 \tan^2\alpha = (y^2 - 4ax).$$

2. The equation of any normal to the parabola is

$$y = mx - 2am - am^3$$

It passes through the point (h, k) if

$$am^3 + m(2a - h) + k = 0 \quad \text{...(i)}$$

The normal cuts the axis of the parabola viz. $y = 0$ at point where $x = 2a + am^2$

Hence, the abscissa of the points in which the normals through (h, k) meet the axis of the parabola are $x_1 = 2a + am_1^2$, $x_2 = 2a + am_2^2$ and $x_3 = 2a + am_3^2$.

Since, x_1, x_2 and x_3 are in AP.

$$(2a + am_1^2) + (2a + am_3^2) = 2(2a + am_2^2)$$

$$\Rightarrow \quad m_1^2 + m_3^2 = 2m_2^2 \quad \text{...(ii)}$$

Also, from Eq. (i),

$$m_1 + m_2 + m_3 = 0, \quad \text{...(iii)}$$

$$m_2 m_3 + m_3 m_1 + m_1 m_2 = \frac{2a - h}{a} \quad \text{...(iv)}$$

and $$m_1 m_2 m_3 = -\frac{k}{a} \quad \text{...(v)}$$

From Eq. (iii), $$(m_1 + m_3)^2 = m_2^2$$

$$\Rightarrow \quad m_1^2 + m_3^2 + 2m_1 m_3 = m_2^2$$

$$\Rightarrow \quad 2m_2^2 - 2 \cdot \frac{k}{am_2} = m_2^2 \Rightarrow m_2^2 = \frac{2k}{am_2}$$

$$\Rightarrow \quad am_2^3 = 2k \quad \text{...(vi)}$$

Since, m_2 is a root of Eq. (i).

$$\therefore \quad -\frac{k}{a}$$

$$\Rightarrow \quad 2k + m_2(2a - h) + k = 0$$

$$\Rightarrow \quad \{m_2(h - 2a)\}^3 = 27k^3$$

$$\Rightarrow \quad \frac{2k}{a}(h - 2a)^3 = 27k^3$$

$$\Rightarrow \quad 27ak^2 = 2(h - 2a)^3.$$

Hence, the locus of (h, k) is $27ay^2 = 2(x - 2a)^3$.

3. Any tangent of slope m to the parabola $y^2 = 4ax$ is

$$y = mx + a / m \quad \text{...(i)}$$

The perpendicular from the vertex on Eq. (i) is

$$x + my = 0 \quad \text{...(ii)}$$

By eliminating m between Eqs. (i) and (ii), we obtain the required locus as $xy^2 + x^3 + ay^2 = 0$

4. Let $P(h, k)$ be the point on parabola $y^2 = 4ax$.

The equation of tangents are $y = mx + \frac{a}{m}$

They pass through $P(h, k)$, so $k = mh + \frac{a}{m}$

$$m_1 + m_2 = \frac{k}{h} \text{ and } m_1 m_2 = \frac{a}{h}$$

$$\Rightarrow \quad \tan\theta_1 + \tan\theta_2 = \frac{k}{h} \text{ and } \tan\theta_1 \tan\theta_2 = \frac{a}{h}$$

$$\Rightarrow \quad \tan(\theta_1 + \theta_2) = \frac{\sin(\theta_1 + \theta_2)}{\sqrt{1 - \sin^2(\theta_1 + \theta_2)}}$$

$$\Rightarrow \quad \frac{k}{h - a} = \frac{\frac{k\mu}{h}}{\sqrt{1 - \frac{k^2\mu^2}{h^2}}} \Rightarrow \mu(h - a) = \sqrt{h^2 - k^2\mu^2}$$

$\therefore$ Locus of (h, k) is $\mu(x - a) = \sqrt{x^2 - \mu^2 y^2}$.

5. Let the equation of the parabola be $y^2 = 4ax$.

The coordinates of P and Q are $(at_1^2, 2at_1)$ and $(at_2^2, 2at_2)$, respectively. Let $S(a, 0)$ be the focus. Equation of PQ is $y(t_1 + t_2) = 2x + 2at_1 t_2$.

As it passes through $(a, 0)$ the coordinates will satisfy it, hence $0 = 2a + 2at_1 t_2$ or $t_1 t_2 = -1$

$$\therefore \quad t_2 = -1 / t_1$$

So, the coordinates of Q become $\left(\frac{a}{t_1^2}, -\frac{2a}{t_1}\right)$.

Equation of circle drawn with PQ as diameter is

$$(x - at_1^2)\left(x - \frac{a}{t_1^2}\right) + (y - 2at_1)\left(y + \frac{2a}{t_1}\right) = 0 \quad \text{...(i)}$$

The directrix $x + a = 0$ ...(ii)

intersects it at points given by

$$y^2 - 2ay\left(t_1 - \frac{1}{t_1}\right) + a^2\left(t_1 - \frac{1}{t_1}\right)^2 = 0$$

or $$\left(y - a\left(t_1 - \frac{1}{t_1}\right)\right)^2 = 0.$$

As this is a perfect square, it will give us only one value of y. So, Eq. (ii) cuts Eq. (i) at two coincident points.

Hence, Eq. (ii) is tangent to Eq. (i).

Equation of circle drawn with line PS as diameter is

$(x - at_1^2)(x - a) + (y - 2at_1)(y - 0) = 0$

[as P is $(at_1^2, 2at_1)$ and S is $(a, 0)$]

or $$x^2 + y^2 - ax(1 + t_1^2) - 2at_1 y + a^2 t_1^2 = 0 \quad \text{...(iii)}$$

Equation to the tangent at vertex is $x = 0$ ...(iv)

On solving Eqs. (iii) and (iv), we get

$$y^2 - 2ayt_1 + a^2 t_1^2 = 0$$

or $$(y - at_1)^2 = 0$$

which is again a perfect square, hence the two roots of y are coincident, therefore the Y-axis touches the circles i.e. the tangent at the vertex touches Eq. (iii).

6. Line parallel to line $y = x$ is

$$x - y + k = 0 \quad \text{...(i)}$$

Equation of variable chord PQ.

$$y - 2at_1 = \frac{2a(t_2 - t_1)}{a(t_2^2 - t_1^2)}(x - at_1^2)$$

$$(t_1 + t_2)y - 2at_1(t_1 + t_2) = 2(x - at_1^2)$$

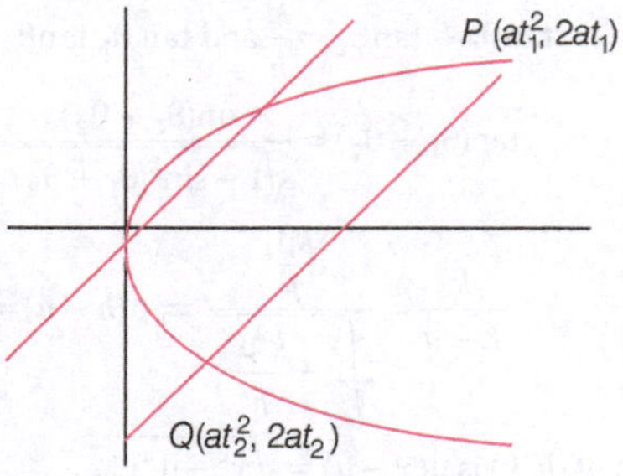

$$2x - y(t_1 + t_2)\ 2at_1t_2 = 0 \quad \text{...(ii)}$$

Eqs. (i) and (ii) denote the same line.

$$\frac{2}{1} = \frac{-(t_1 + t_2)}{-1} = \frac{2at_1t_2}{k}$$

So, $\quad t_1 + t_2 = 2 \quad$ ...(iii)

at $\quad at_1t_2 = k$

Equation of normal from points P and Q,

$$y = t_1x + 2at_1\ \ at_1^3 \quad \text{...(iv)}$$

and $\quad y = -t_2x + 2at_2 + at_2^3 \quad$ ...(v)

Intersection of Eqs. (iv) and (v) is (h, k).

So, $\quad h = 2a + a(t_1^2 + t_2^2 + t_1t_2)$

$\Rightarrow \quad k = -at_1t_2(t_1 + t_2)$

Using Eq. (iii), $\quad 2h - k = 12a$

So, locus is $\quad 2x - y = 12a.$

7. Equations of the given parabolas are

$$y^2 = 4ax \quad \text{...(i)}$$

and $\quad y^2 = 4b(x - c) \quad$ ...(ii)

Normal to Eq. (i) is given by

$$y - mx + 2am + am^3 = 0 \quad \text{...(iii)}$$

Normal to Eq. (ii) is given by

$$y - m(x - c) + 2bm + bm^3 = 0 \quad \text{...(iv)}$$

If there is a common normal, it will cut the X-axis at point $(h, 0)$ (say).

Since, Eqs. (iii) and (iv) are common normals, $(h, 0)$ lies on (3) and (4).

$\Rightarrow \quad m(am^2 + 2a - h) = 0$

and $\quad m[bm^2 + (2b + c - h)] = 0$

$\Rightarrow \quad am^2 + 2a - h = 0$ i.e. $m = \pm\sqrt{\dfrac{h - 2a}{a}} \quad [\because m \neq 0]$

Similarly, $\quad bm^2 + 2b + c - h = 0$

$\Rightarrow \quad m = \pm\sqrt{\dfrac{h - (2b + c)}{b}}$

For m to exists,

$$h > 2a \text{ and } h > 2b + c$$

and $\quad \dfrac{h - 2a}{a} = \dfrac{h - (2b + c)}{b} \quad [\because m \text{ is same}]$

$\Rightarrow \quad h = \dfrac{ac}{a - b}$ i.e. $\dfrac{ac}{a - b} > 2a$ and $\dfrac{ac}{a - b} > 2b + c$

$\Rightarrow \quad 2a < 2b + c$ from both the cases.

8. The equation of the straight line joining t_1 and t_2 is

$$y = \frac{2}{t_1 + t_2}(x + at_1t_2) \Rightarrow y(t_1 + t_2) = 2(x + at_1t_2) \quad \text{...(i)}$$

Now, the slope of the line joining t and t_1 is $\dfrac{2}{t_1 + 1}$

and that of the line joining t and t_2 is $\dfrac{2}{t + t_2}$.

Since, the two lines are at right angles, $\dfrac{2}{t + t_1} \times \dfrac{2}{t + t_2} = -1$

$\Rightarrow \quad (t + t_1)(t + t_2) = -4$

$\Rightarrow \quad t^2 + t(t_1 + t_2) + t_1t_2 = -4$

On substituting the value of t_1t_2 in the Eq. (i), we get

$$y(t_1 + t_2) = 2[x + a\{-4 - t^2 - t(t_1 + t_2)\}]$$
$$= 2\{x + a(-4 - t^2) - at(t_1 + t_2)\}$$
$$= 2(x - 4a - at^2) - 2at(t_1 + t_2)$$

$\Rightarrow \quad (t_1 + t_2)(y + 2at) = 2(x - 4a - at^2)$

$\Rightarrow \quad y + 2at = \dfrac{2}{t_1 + t_2}(x - 4a - at^2)$

which is of the form $y + 2at = \lambda(x - 4a - at^2)$, where λ is a variable. Hence, the straight line joining the points t_1 and t_2 passes through the point $(4a + at^2, -2at)$, which is a fixed point.

9. $M = (0, 2t),\ Q = \left(\dfrac{t^2}{2}, 2t\right)$

Equation of PS is $y = \dfrac{2t}{t^2 - 1}(x - 1)$

$\Rightarrow \quad y(t^2 - 1) - 2tx + 2t = 0$

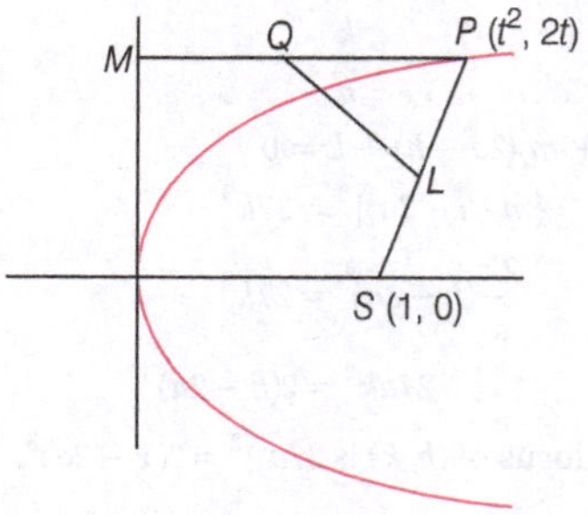

Length of perpendicular QL is

$$\frac{\left|2t(t^2 - 1) - 2t \cdot \dfrac{t^2}{2} + 2t\right|}{\sqrt{(t^2 - 1)^2 + 4t^2}} = \frac{t^3}{t^2 + 1}$$

Let $f(t) = \dfrac{t^3}{t^2+1} \Rightarrow f'(t) = \dfrac{(t^2-1)3t^2 - t^3 \cdot 2t}{(t^2+1)^2}$

$\Rightarrow \quad f'(t) = \dfrac{t^4+3t^2}{(t^2+1)^2} > 0, \ \forall \, 1 \le t \le 3.$

So, maximum value will be at $t = 3$ which is $\dfrac{27}{10}$ units.

10. Let the extremities of the normal chord be P and Q and the tangents at P and Q to the parabola $y^2 = 4ax$ meet in T.

Let the coordinates of T be (x_1, y_1).

PQ will be the chord of contact of T with respect to the parabola.

The equation of chord of contact of T will be

$$yy_1 = 2a(x + x_1) \quad \text{...(i)}$$

and equation of any normal to $y^2 = 4ax$ is

$$y = mx - 2am - am^3 \quad \text{...(ii)}$$

So, Eqs. (i) and (ii) must be identical

$\Rightarrow \quad m = \dfrac{2a}{y_1}$ and $-2am - am^3 = \dfrac{2ax_1}{y_1}$

$\Rightarrow \quad x_1 = (-2a - am^2), y_1 = \dfrac{2a}{m}$

Now, by solving $y^2 = 4ax$ and $y = mx - 2am - am^3$,

we get coordinates of P and Q as $(am^2, -2am)$ and

$\left(a\left(\dfrac{m^2+2}{m}\right)^2, 2a\left(\dfrac{m^2+2}{m}\right)\right)$, respectively.

Now, area of $\Delta TPQ = \dfrac{1}{2}\begin{vmatrix} -2a - am^2 & \dfrac{2a}{m} & 1 \\ am^2 & -2am & 1 \\ a\left(\dfrac{m^2+2}{m}\right)^2 & 2a\left(\dfrac{m^2+2}{m}\right) & 1 \end{vmatrix}$

$= \dfrac{1}{2}\begin{vmatrix} -2a - 2am^2 & \dfrac{2a}{m} + 2am & 0 \\ am^2 & -2am & 1 \\ a\left(\dfrac{m^2+2}{m}\right)^2 - am^2 & 2a\left(\dfrac{m^2+2}{m}\right) + 2am & 0 \end{vmatrix}$

$[R_1 \to R_1 - R_2, R_3 \to R_3 - R_2]$

$= \dfrac{1}{2}\begin{vmatrix} -2a(m^2+1) & 2a\dfrac{(1+m^2)}{m} & 0 \\ am^2 & -2am & 1 \\ 4a\dfrac{(m^2+1)}{m^2} & 4a\left(\dfrac{m^2+1}{m}\right) & 0 \end{vmatrix}$

$= \dfrac{1}{2}\left[-8a^2\dfrac{(m^2+1)^2}{m} - 8a^2\dfrac{(m^2+1)^2}{m^3}\right]$

$= 4a^2\dfrac{(m^2+1)^2}{m^3}[m^2+1]$

$= 4a^2\dfrac{\sec^4\theta}{\tan^3\theta}\cdot\sec^2\theta \qquad (\because m = \tan\theta)$

$= 4a^2 \cdot \dfrac{1}{\sin^3\theta\cos^3\theta} = \dfrac{32a^2}{\sin^3 2\theta}$

$\Rightarrow$ area is minimum when $\sin^3 2\theta = 1 \Rightarrow \theta = \pi/4$.

6

> *The essence of maths is not to make simple things complicated, but to make complicated things simple.*
>
> **– Stan Gudder**

Ellipse

Learning Milestones

Milestone 1 Equation of Ellipse

- Ellipse : Definition 1
- Ellipse : Definition 2
- Tracing of the Ellipse
- Parametric Equation of Ellipse
- Focal Distances of a Point

Milestone 2 Line and Ellipse

- Position of a Point with respect to an Ellipse
- Intersection of a Line and an Ellipse
- Equation of Tangents in Different Forms
- Equation of Normals in Different Forms
- Co-normal Points Lie on a Fixed Curve

Milestone 3 Pair of Tangents

- Combined Equation of Pair of Tangents
- Chord of Contact
- Diameter
- Conjugate Diameters
- Director Circle
- Concyclic Points
- Reflection Property of an Ellipse

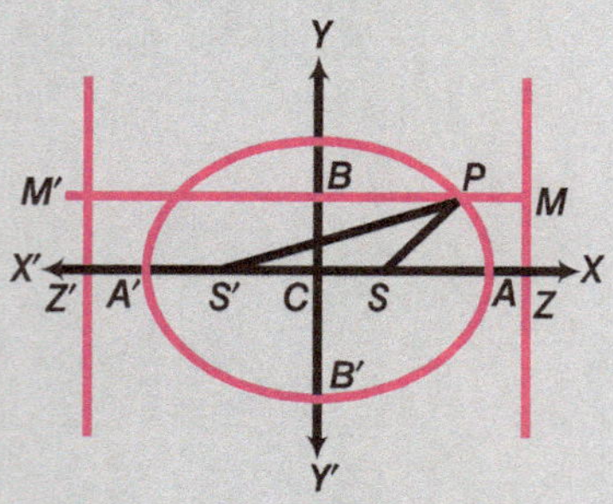

Practice Milestones

Practice Milestone 1- JEE Main Pattern
Practice Milestone 2 - JEE Advanced Pattern
Practice Milestone 3 - Challenging Problems

Milestone 1 Equation of Ellipse

• Ellipse : Definition 1 • Ellipse : Definition 2 • Tracing of the Ellipse

• Parametric Equation of Ellipse • Focal Distances of a Point

6.1 Ellipse : Definition 1

An ellipse is the locus of a point which moves in a plane such that its distance from a fixed point (i.e. focus) is a constant ratio from a fixed line (i.e. directrix).
This ratio is called eccentricity and is denoted by e.
For an ellipse $0 < e < 1$.

Standard Equation of Ellipse

Let S be the focus and ZM be the directrix of the ellipse. Draw $SZ \perp ZM$. Divide SZ internally and externally in the ratio $e:1 (0 < e < 1)$ and let A and A' be these internal and external point of division.

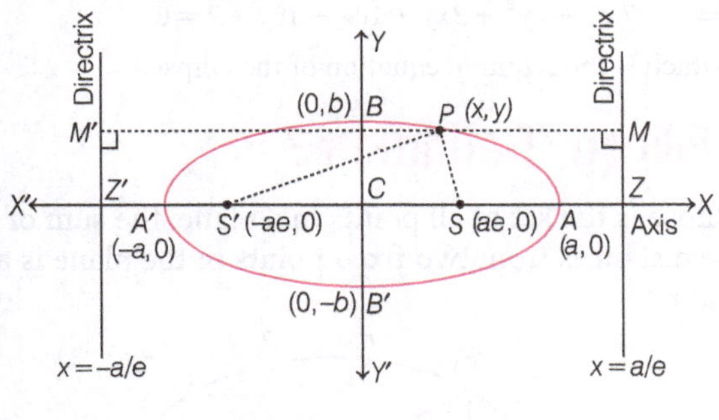

Then, $\quad SA = eAZ \quad$ ...(i)

and $\quad SA' = eA'Z \quad$ ...(ii)

Clearly, A and A' will lie on the ellipse.

Let $AA' = 2a$ and take C the mid-point of AA' as origin

$\therefore \quad CA = CA' = a \quad$ ...(iii)

Let $P(x, y)$ be any point on the ellipse referred to CA and CB as coordinate axes.

Then, adding Eqs. (i) and (ii),

$$SA + SA' = e(AZ + A'Z)$$

$\Rightarrow \quad AA' = e(CZ - CA + CA' + CZ) \quad$ [from figure]

$\Rightarrow \quad AA' = e(2CZ) \quad [\because CA = CA']$

$\Rightarrow \quad 2a = 2eCZ$

$\because \quad CZ = a/e$

$\therefore$ The directrix MZ is $\quad x = CZ = a/e$

or $\quad \frac{a}{e} - x = 0 \quad \left[\because e < 1, \therefore \frac{a}{e} > 1\right]$

and subtracting Eq. (i) from Eq. (ii), then

$$SA' - SA = e(A'Z - AZ)$$

$\Rightarrow \quad (CA' + CS) - (CA - CS) = e(AA')$

$\Rightarrow \quad 2CS = e(AA') \quad [\because CA = CA']$

$\Rightarrow \quad 2CS = e(2a)$

$\therefore \quad CS = ae$

$\therefore$ The focus S is $(CS, 0)$ i.e. $(ae, 0)$.

Now, draw $PM \perp MZ$

$\therefore \quad \frac{SP}{PM} = e$ or $(SP)^2 = e^2 (PM)^2$

$$(x - ae)^2 + (y - 0)^2 = e^2 \left(\frac{a}{e} - x\right)^2$$

$\Rightarrow \quad (x - ae)^2 + y^2 = (a - ex)^2$

$\Rightarrow \quad x^2 + a^2e^2 - 2aex + y^2 = a^2 - 2aex + e^2x^2$

$\Rightarrow \quad x^2(1 - e^2) + y^2 = a^2(1 - e^2)$

$\Rightarrow \quad \frac{x^2}{a^2} + \frac{y^2}{a^2(1 - e^2)} = 1$ or $\frac{x^2}{a^2} + \frac{y^2}{b^2} = 1$

where, $\quad b^2 = a^2(1 - e^2)$

This is the standard equation of an ellipse, AA' and BB' are called the major and minor axes of the ellipse. (here, $b < a$) and A and A' are the vertices of the ellipse.

The Foci and Two Directrices of an Ellipse

On the negative side of origin take a point S' which is such that

$$CS = CS' = ae$$

and another point Z', then $CZ = CZ' = \frac{a}{e}$

$\therefore$ Coordinates of S' are $(-ae, 0)$ and equation of second directrix (i.e. $Z'M'$) is $\quad x = -\frac{a}{e}$

Let $P(x, y)$ be any point on the ellipse, then

$$S'P = ePM'$$

or $$(S'P)^2 = e^2 (PM')^2$$

or $$(x + ae)^2 + (y - 0)^2 = e^2 \left(x + \frac{a}{e}\right)^2$$

or $$(x + ae)^2 + y^2 = (ex + a)^2$$

or $$x^2 (1 - e^2) + y^2 = a^2 (1 - e^2)$$

or $$\frac{x^2}{a^2} + \frac{y^2}{a^2 (1 - e^2)} = 1$$

or $$\frac{x^2}{a^2} + \frac{y^2}{b^2} = 1,$$

where, $$b^2 = a^2 (1 - e^2)$$

The equation being the same as that of the ellipse when $S(ae, 0)$ is focus and MZ i.e. $x = a/e$ is directrix.

Hence, coordinates of foci are $(\pm ae, 0)$ and equations of directrices are $x = \pm a / e$.

Concept Inside Video

JEE Focus Points

- Two ellipse are said to be similar if they have the same value of eccentricity.
- The equation of the ellipse, whose focus is the point (h, k) and directrix is $lx + my + n = 0$ and whose eccentricity is e, is
$$(x - h)^2 + (y - k)^2 = e^2 \cdot \frac{(lx + my + n)^2}{(l^2 + m^2)}$$
- Distance between foci $SS' = 2ae$ and distance between directrices $ZZ' = 2a / e$
- If $e = 0$, then $b^2 = a^2 (1 - 0)$
$\therefore$ $b^2 = a^2$
then equation of ellipse $\frac{x^2}{a^2} + \frac{y^2}{b^2} = 1$ changes in circle
i.e. $x^2 + y^2 = a^2$
- If ellipse $\frac{x^2}{a^2} + \frac{y^2}{b^2} = 1$, then $(PN)^2 : AN \cdot A'N = (BC)^2 : (AC)^2$

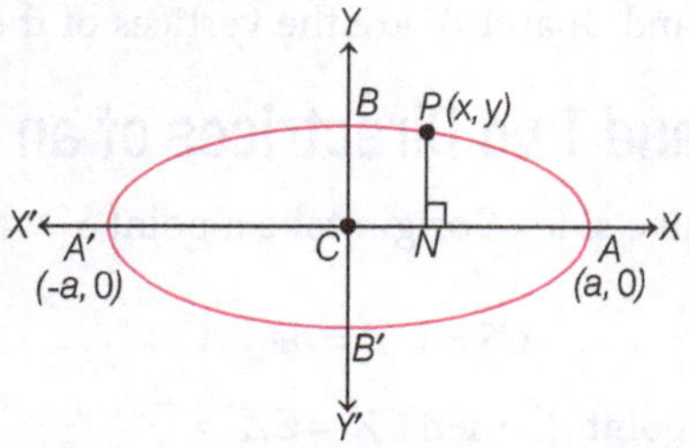

- The distance of every focus from the extremity of minor axis is equal to a.
i.e. $\sqrt{(a^2e^2 + b^2)} = \sqrt{(a^2 - b^2 + b^2)} = a$
- Area of the ellipse $\frac{x^2}{a^2} + \frac{y^2}{b^2} = 1$ is πab

Example 1. Find the equation of an ellipse whose focus is $(-1, 1)$, eccentricity is $\frac{1}{2}$ and the directrix is $x - y + 3 = 0$.

Sol. Let $P(x, y)$ be any point on the ellipse whose focus is $S(-1, 1)$ and the directrix is $x - y + 3 = 0$. Draw PM perpendicular from $P(x, y)$ on the directrix $x - y + 3 = 0$. Then, by definition

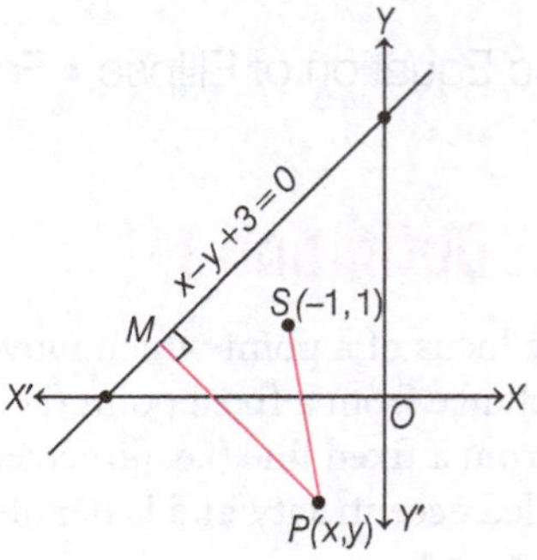

$$SP = ePM \Rightarrow (SP)^2 = e^2 (PM)^2$$

$$\Rightarrow \quad (x + 1)^2 + (y - 1)^2 = \frac{1}{4} \left\{\frac{x - y + 3}{\sqrt{2}}\right\}^2$$

$$\Rightarrow \quad 8(x^2 + y^2 + 2x - 2y + 2)$$
$$= x^2 + y^2 + 9 - 2xy + 6x - 6y$$

$$\Rightarrow \quad 7x^2 + 7y^2 + 2xy + 10x - 10y + 7 = 0$$

which is the required equation of the ellipse.

6.2 Ellipse : Definition 2

An ellipse is the set of all points in a plane, the sum of whose distances from two fixed points in the plane is a constant.

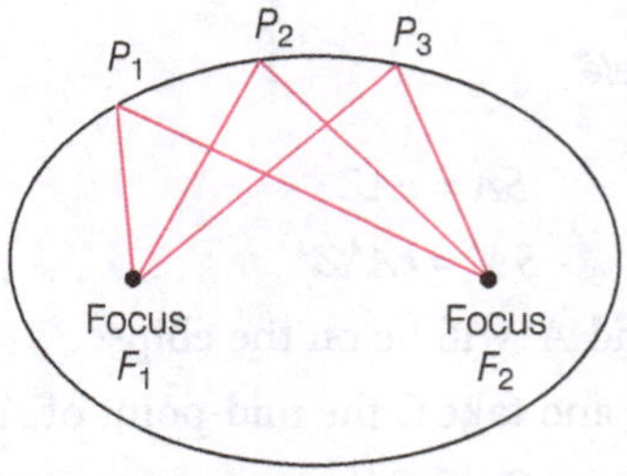

$$P_1F_1 + P_1F_2 = P_2F_1 + P_2F_2 = P_3F_1 + P_3F_2.$$

Standard Equation of an ellipse

Let the foci of an ellipse be $(\pm c, 0)$. Then, its center is $(0, 0)$.

According to the definition of an ellipse,

$$PF_1 + PF_2 = 2a \text{ (constant)}$$

$$\Rightarrow \quad \sqrt{(x - c)^2 + y^2} + \sqrt{(x + c)^2 + y^2} = 2a \quad [\because 2a > 2c] \quad \text{...(i)}$$

$$\Rightarrow \quad [(x - c)^2 + y^2] - [(x + c)^2 + y^2] = -4cx \quad \text{...(ii)}$$

On dividing Eq. (ii) by Eq. (i), we get

$$\sqrt{(x-c)^2+y^2}-\sqrt{(x+c)^2+y^2}=\frac{-2cx}{a} \quad \text{...(iii)}$$

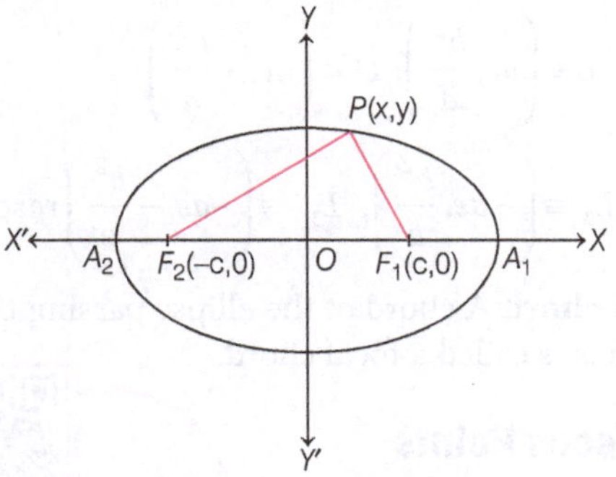

On adding Eqs. (i) and (iii), we get

$$2\sqrt{(x-c)^2+y^2}=2a-\frac{2cx}{a}$$

$$\Rightarrow \quad \sqrt{(x-c)^2+y^2}=a-\frac{cx}{a}$$

On squaring both the sides, we get

$$x^2+c^2-2cx+y^2=a^2+\frac{c^2x^2}{a^2}-2cx$$

$$\Rightarrow \quad x^2\left(1-\frac{c^2}{a^2}\right)+y^2=a^2-c^2$$

$$\Rightarrow \quad \frac{x^2}{a^2}+\frac{y^2}{a^2-c^2}=1$$

Let $a^2-c^2=b^2$, then $\frac{x^2}{a^2}+\frac{y^2}{b^2}=1$, where $a>b$

6.3 Tracing of the Ellipse

Equation of the ellipse is

$$\frac{x^2}{a^2}+\frac{y^2}{b^2}=1 \quad \text{...(i)}$$

1. The ellipse (i) cuts X-axis at $A(a,0)$ and $A'(-a,0)$ and cuts Y-axis at $B(0,b)$ and $B'(0,-b)$.
2. The Eq. (i) does not change when y is replaced by $-y$ and x is replaced by $-x$, Hence, ellipse (i) is symmetrical about both axes.
3. The Eq. (i), may be written in either of the form

$$y=\pm b\sqrt{\left(1-\frac{x^2}{a^2}\right)} \quad \text{...(ii)}$$

or

$$x=\pm a\sqrt{\left(1-\frac{y^2}{b^2}\right)} \quad \text{...(iii)}$$

From Eq. (ii), it follows that (y is real)

if $\quad 1-\frac{x^2}{a^2}\geq 0$ or $a^2-x^2\geq 0$

or $\quad x^2\leq a^2$ or $-a\leq x\leq a$

Also, from Eq. (iii), it follows that (x is real)

if $\quad 1-\frac{y^2}{b^2}\geq 0$ or $b^2-y^2\geq 0$ or $y^2\leq b^2$

$\therefore \quad -b\leq y\leq b$

Ellipse (i) is a closed curve lies entirely between the lines $x=a$ and $x=-a$ and the lines $y=b$ and $y=-b$.

Since, when x increases, then y decreases from Eq. (ii) and when y decreases, then x increases from Eq. (iii).

Some Terms Related to an Ellipse

Let the equation of the ellipse $\frac{x^2}{a^2}+\frac{y^2}{b^2}=1 \quad [a>b]$

1. **Centre** All chords passing through C is bisected at C

   Here $C\equiv(0,0)$

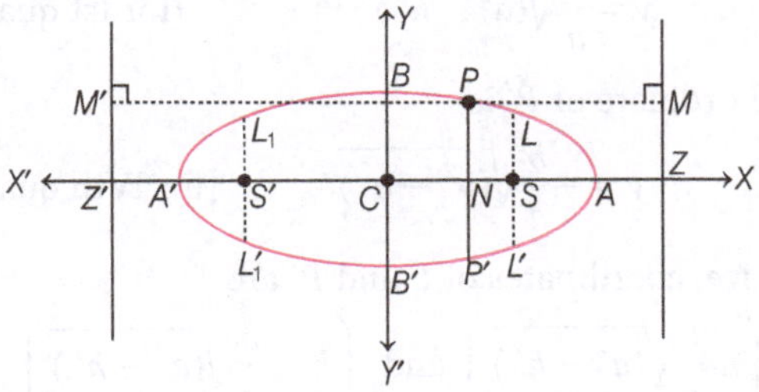

2. **Vertices** The points A and A' in above figure where the curve meets the line joining the foci S and S' are called vertices of the ellipse. The coordinates of A and A' are $(a,0)$ and $(-a,0)$, respectively.
3. **Foci** S and S' are two foci of the ellipse and their coordinates are $(ae,0)$ and $(-ae,0)$, respectively.
4. **Directrices** ZM and $Z'M'$ are two directrices of the ellipse and their equation are $x=\frac{a}{e}$ and $x=-\frac{a}{e}$, respectively.
5. **Axes** The lines AA' and BB' are called the **major** ($AA'=2a$) and **minor** axes ($BB'=2b$) of the ellipse

$\because \quad 0<e<1$

or $\quad 0<e^2<1 \quad [\therefore 0>-e^2>-1]$

or $\quad 0<1-e^2<1 \quad [\text{or } 1>1-e^2>1-1]$

or $\quad a^2(1-e^2)<a^2 \quad [\text{or } 0<1-e^2<1]$

or $\quad b^2<a^2$

i.e. $\quad b<a$

$\Rightarrow \quad 2b<2a \Rightarrow BB'<AA'$

The major and minor axis together are called **principal axes** of the ellipse.

6. Eccentricity For the ellipse $\frac{x^2}{a^2}+\frac{y^2}{b^2}=1$, we have

$$b^2 = a^2(1-e^2)$$

$$\Rightarrow \quad e^2 = 1-\frac{b^2}{a^2}$$

$$\Rightarrow \quad e = \sqrt{1-\left(\frac{\text{minor axis}}{\text{major axis}}\right)^2}$$

7. Ordinate and double ordinates If P be a point on the ellipse draw PN perpendicular to the major axis AA' of the ellipse. Then, PN is called the ordinate of P and produced to meet the curve again at P'. Then, PNP' is called a double ordinate.

If abscissa of P is h, then ordinate of P,

$$\frac{y^2}{b^2} = 1-\frac{h^2}{a^2}$$

$$y = \frac{b}{a}\sqrt{(a^2-h^2)} \qquad \text{[for Ist quadrant]}$$

and ordinate of P' is

$$y = -\frac{b}{a}\sqrt{(a^2-h^2)} \qquad \text{[for IVth quadrant]}$$

Hence, coordinates of P and P' are

$$\left(h, \frac{b}{a}\sqrt{(a^2-h^2)}\right) \text{ and } \left(h, -\frac{b}{a}\sqrt{(a^2-h^2)}\right)$$

respectively.

8. Latusrectum The double ordinates LL' and L_1L_1' are latusrectums of the ellipse. These line are perpendicular to major axis $A'A$ and through the foci S and S', respectively.

Length of the latusrectum

Now, let $LL' = 2k$,

then $LS = L'S = k$

Coordinates of L and L' are (ae, k) and $(ae, -k)$ lies on the ellipse

$$\frac{x^2}{a^2}+\frac{y^2}{b^2}=1$$

$$\therefore \quad \frac{a^2e^2}{a^2}+\frac{k^2}{b^2}=1 \text{ or } k^2 = b^2(1-e^2)$$

$$= b^2\left(\frac{b^2}{a^2}\right) \qquad [\because b^2 = a^2(1-e^2)]$$

$$\therefore \quad k = \frac{b^2}{a} \qquad [\because k>0]$$

$$\therefore \quad 2k = \frac{2b^2}{a} = LL'$$

$\therefore$ Length of latusrectum $LL' = L_1L_1' = \frac{2b^2}{a}$ and end of points of latusrectum are

$$L \equiv \left(ae, \frac{b^2}{a}\right);\ L' \equiv \left(ae, -\frac{b^2}{a}\right)$$

$$L_1 \equiv \left(-ae, \frac{b^2}{a}\right);\ L_1' \equiv \left(-ae, -\frac{b^2}{a}\right) \text{ respectively.}$$

9. Focal chord A chord of the ellipse passing through its focus is called a focal chord.

JEE Focus Points

- Latusrectum

$$= LL' = \frac{2b^2}{a} = \frac{(2b)^2}{(2a)} = \frac{(\text{Minor axis})^2}{(\text{Major axis})}$$

$$= 2a(1-e^2) = 2e\left(\frac{a}{e}-ae\right)$$

$$= 2e\,(\text{distance from focus to the corresponding directrix})$$

- Semi-latusrectum is the harmonic mean of the segments of focal chord or $\frac{1}{SP}+\frac{1}{SQ}=\frac{2a}{b^2}$, $(a>b)$, where PQ is the focal chord and S is the focus.

Concept Inside Video

Example 2. If PSQ is a focal chord of the ellipse $16x^2+25y^2=400$, such that $SP=8$, then find the length of SQ.

Sol. The given ellipse is $16x^2+25y^2=400$ or $\frac{x^2}{25}+\frac{y^2}{16}=1$

$$\because \quad \frac{1}{SP}+\frac{1}{SQ}=\frac{2a}{b^2}$$

$$\Rightarrow \quad \frac{1}{8}+\frac{1}{SQ}=\frac{2(5)}{16}=\frac{5}{8} \text{ or } \frac{1}{SQ}=\frac{1}{2}$$

$$\therefore \quad SQ = 2$$

Example 3. If the latusrectum of an ellipse is equal to half of its minor axis, then find its eccentricity.

Sol. $\because$ Latusrectum $= \frac{1}{2}$(minor axis)

$$\Rightarrow \quad \frac{2b^2}{a} = \frac{1}{2}(2b) \text{ or } 2b = a \text{ or } 4b^2 = a^2$$

$$\Rightarrow \quad 4a^2(1-e^2) = a^2 \text{ or } 4e^2 = 3$$

$$\therefore \quad e = \frac{\sqrt{3}}{2}$$

Example 4. If the distance between the directrices is thrice the distance between the foci, then find eccentricity of the ellipse.

Sol. Given, $\frac{2a}{e} = 3(2ae) \Rightarrow e^2 = \frac{1}{3}$

$$\therefore \quad e = \frac{1}{\sqrt{3}}$$

Example 5. If $P(x, y)$ be any point on the ellipse $16x^2 + 25y^2 = 400$ and $F_1 \equiv (3, 0)$, $F_2 \equiv (-3, 0)$, then find the value of $PF_1 + PF_2$.

Sol. We have, $16x^2 + 25y^2 = 400$

$$\Rightarrow \quad \frac{x^2}{5^2} + \frac{y^2}{4^2} = 1$$

$\because$ Coordinates of foci are $(\pm ae, 0)$.

or $\left(\pm \sqrt{(a^2 - b^2)}, 0\right)$

i.e. $(\pm \sqrt{(25 - 16)}, 0)$ or $(\pm 3, 0)$

Thus, F_1 and F_2 are foci of the ellipse.

$\therefore \quad PF_1 + PF_2 =$ Length of major axis $= 2a = 2 \times 5 = 10$

JEE SCANNER

Example Similar to PYQ Asked in JEE Main 2022

Let the eccentricity of an ellipse $\frac{x^2}{a^2} + \frac{y^2}{b^2} = 1$, $a > b$, be $\frac{\sqrt{7}}{4}$. If the ellipse passes through the point $\left(3, \frac{3\sqrt{7}}{4}\right)$, then the value of $a^2 + b^2$ is ......

Sol. (25) Given, $\frac{x^2}{a^2} + \frac{y^2}{b^2} = 1$, $[\because a > b]$

Now, $e^2 = 1 - \frac{b^2}{a^2}$

$$\Rightarrow \quad \frac{b^2}{a^2} = 1 - \frac{7}{16} = \frac{9}{16} \Rightarrow b^2 = \frac{9}{16}a^2$$

Again, ellipse passes through $\left(3, \frac{3\sqrt{7}}{4}\right)$

$$\therefore \quad \frac{9}{a^2} + \frac{63}{16b^2} = 1$$

$$\Rightarrow \quad \frac{9}{a^2} + \frac{63 \times 16}{16 \times 9a^2} = 1 \Rightarrow \frac{9}{a^2} + \frac{7}{a^2} = 1 \Rightarrow a^2 = 16$$

$$\therefore \quad b^2 = \frac{9}{16} \times 16 = 9$$

So, $a^2 + b^2 = 16 + 9 = 25$

Skill Builder

Let the eccentricity of an ellipse $\frac{x^2}{a^2} + \frac{y^2}{b^2} = 1$, $a > b$ be $\frac{2\sqrt{2}}{3}$. If the ellipse passes through the point $(-3\sqrt{3}, 1)$, then the value of $a^2 + b^2$ is ....

For Sol.

■ **For more practice** See Q.7 of Milestone Practice 6.1.

Example 6. Find the lengths of major and minor axes, the coordinates of foci, vertices and the eccentricity of the ellipse $3x^2 + 2y^2 = 6$. Also, find the equation of the directrices.

Sol. The equation of ellipse is

$$3x^2 + 2y^2 = 6$$

$$\Rightarrow \quad \frac{x^2}{2} + \frac{y^2}{3} = 1 \Rightarrow \frac{x^2}{(\sqrt{2})^2} + \frac{y^2}{(\sqrt{3})^2} = 1$$

On comparing this equation with,

$$\frac{x^2}{a^2} + \frac{y^2}{b^2} = 1$$

$\therefore \quad a = \sqrt{2}$ and $b = \sqrt{3}$ [here, $b > a$]

Length of major axis $= 2b = 2\sqrt{3}$

and length of minor axis $= 2a = 2\sqrt{2}$

If e be the eccentricity, then $a^2 = b^2(1 - e^2)$

$$\Rightarrow \quad 2 = 3(1 - e^2) \Rightarrow e^2 = \frac{1}{3}$$

$$\therefore \quad e = \frac{1}{\sqrt{3}}$$

Vertices $= (0, \pm b) = (0, \pm \sqrt{3})$

and foci are $(0, \pm be) = (0, \pm 1)$

and equation of the directrices are $y = \pm b/e$

$$y = \pm \frac{\sqrt{3}}{(1/\sqrt{3})}$$

$$\therefore \quad y = \pm 3$$

Example 7. Find the centre, vertices, co-vertices, length of major and minor axis, eccentricity, length of latusrectum, equation of directrices and the end-points of a latusrectum of the ellipse $2x^2 + 3y^2 - 4x - 12y + 8 = 0$

Sol. The given equation of the ellipse is

$$2x^2 + 3y^2 - 4x - 12y + 8 = 0.$$

$$\Rightarrow \quad 2(x^2 - 2x + 1) + 3(y^2 - 4y + 4) = 6$$

$$\Rightarrow \quad 2(x - 1)^2 + 3(y - 2)^2 = 6$$

$$\frac{(x-1)^2}{3} + \frac{(y-2)^2}{2} = 1$$

$\frac{X^2}{3} + \frac{Y^2}{2} = 1$, where $X = x - 1$ and $Y = y - 2$

Centre : (0, 0)

$\Rightarrow \quad X = 0, Y = 0$

$\Rightarrow \quad x - 1 = 0$

and $\quad y - 2 = 0$

$\Rightarrow \quad x = 1$

and $\quad y = 2$

Hence, the centre is (1, 2).

Vertices : $(\pm a, 0)$

$\Rightarrow$ $X = \pm a$ and $Y = 0$

$\Rightarrow$ $x - 1 = \pm\sqrt{3}$ and $y - 2 = 0$

$\Rightarrow$ $x = 1 \pm \sqrt{3}$ and $y = 2$

Hence, the vertices are $(1 + \sqrt{3}, 2)$ and $(1 - \sqrt{3}, 2)$.

Co-vertices : $(0, \pm b)$

$\Rightarrow$ $X = 0$ and $Y = \pm\sqrt{2}$

$\Rightarrow$ $x - 1 = 0$ and $y - 2 = \pm\sqrt{2}$

$\Rightarrow$ $x = 1$ and $y = 2 \pm \sqrt{2}$

Hence, the co-vertices are $(1, 2 + \sqrt{2})$ and $(1, 2 - \sqrt{2})$.

The length of the major axis $= 2a = 2\sqrt{3}$

The length of the minor axis $= 2b = 2\sqrt{2}$

The length of the latusrectum $= \dfrac{2b^2}{a} = \dfrac{2 \times 2}{\sqrt{3}} = \dfrac{4}{\sqrt{3}}$

Eccentricity, $e = \sqrt{1 - \dfrac{b^2}{a^2}} = \sqrt{1 - \dfrac{2}{3}} = \dfrac{1}{\sqrt{3}}$

Equations of the directrices

$$X = \pm \frac{a}{e} = \pm \frac{\sqrt{3}}{1/\sqrt{3}} = \pm 3$$

$$x - 1 = \pm 3$$

$\Rightarrow$ $x = 1 \pm 3 \Rightarrow x = 4, -2$

End-points of the latusrectum : $L\left(ae, \dfrac{b^2}{a}\right), L'\left(ae, -\dfrac{b^2}{a}\right)$

$$= L\left(1, \frac{2}{\sqrt{3}}\right), L'\left(1, -\frac{2}{\sqrt{3}}\right)$$

Example 8. If the angle between the straight lines joining foci and the ends of the minor axis of the ellipse $\dfrac{x^2}{a^2} + \dfrac{y^2}{b^2} = 1$, is $90°$. Find its eccentricity.

Sol. The equation of the ellipse is $\dfrac{x^2}{a^2} + \dfrac{y^2}{b^2} = 1$

Let $a > b$

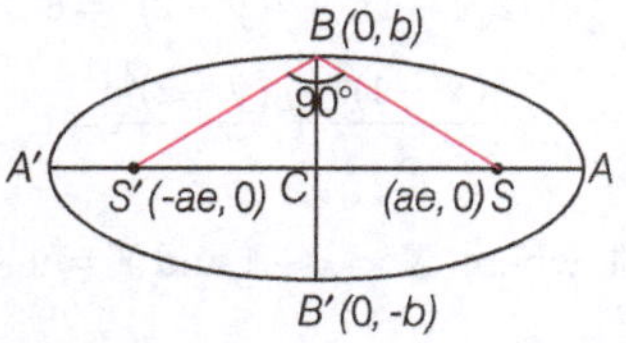

$\therefore$ The ends of minor axis are $B(0, b)$ and $B'(0, -b)$. If the eccentricity of the ellipse is e, then the foci are $S(ae, 0)$ and $S'(-ae, 0)$.

$\therefore$ Slope of BS is $m_1 = \dfrac{b - 0}{0 - ae} = -\dfrac{b}{ae}$

and slope of BS' is $m_2 = \dfrac{b - 0}{0 + ae} = \dfrac{b}{ae}$

$\because$ The angle between BS and BS' is 90°.

$\therefore$ $m_1 m_2 = -1$

$\Rightarrow$ $-\dfrac{b}{ae} \times \dfrac{b}{ae} = -1 \Rightarrow b^2 = a^2e^2$

$$a^2(1 - e^2) = a^2e^2$$

$\Rightarrow$ $1 - e^2 = e^2 \Rightarrow 2e^2 = 1$

$\therefore$ $e = \dfrac{1}{\sqrt{2}}$

Example 9. The extremities of a line segment of length l move in two fixed perpendicular straight lines. Find the locus of that point which divides this line segment in ratio 1 : 2.

Sol. Let $PA : PB = 1 : 2$

$$PA = \frac{l}{3} \quad \text{and} \quad PB = \frac{2l}{3}$$

$$k = \frac{l}{3}\sin\theta$$

or $3k = l\sin\theta$ ...(i)

and $h = \dfrac{2l}{3}\cos\theta$

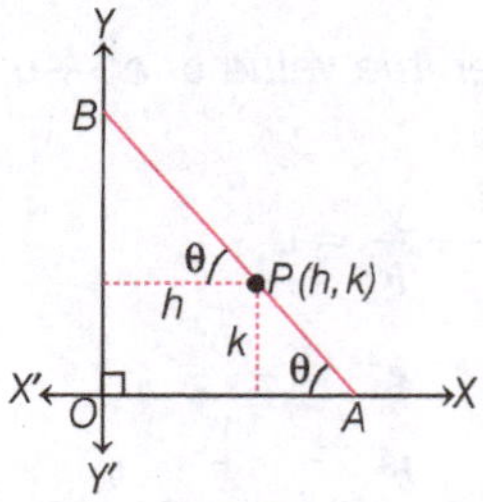

or $\dfrac{3h}{2} = l\cos\theta$ ...(ii)

On squaring and adding Eqs. (i) and (ii), we get

$$9k^2 + \frac{9h^2}{4} = l^2$$

or $9h^2 + 36k^2 = 4l^2$

$\therefore$ Locus of $P(h, k)$ is $9x^2 + 36y^2 = 4l^2$

Alternate Solution

Let $A \equiv (a, 0)$ and $B \equiv (0, b)$

$\because P(h, k)$ divide AB in the ratio 1 : 2 (internally), then

$$h = \frac{1.0 + 2.a}{1 + 2} \Rightarrow a = \frac{3h}{2}$$

and $k = \dfrac{1.b + 2.0}{1 + 2} \Rightarrow b = 3k$

$\because$ $a^2 + b^2 = l^2$

$\Rightarrow$ $\dfrac{9h^2}{4} + 9k^2 = l^2$ or $9h^2 + 36k^2 = 4l^2$

$\therefore$ Locus of $P(h, k)$ is

$$9x^2 + 36y^2 = 4l^2$$

Example 10. Find the equation of the ellipse referred to its centre whose minor axis is equal to the distance between the foci and whose latusrectum is 10.

Sol. Let the equation of the ellipse is

$$\frac{x^2}{a^2}+\frac{y^2}{b^2}=1 \quad [\text{let } a>b]$$

Then, the foci are $S(ae, 0)$ and $S'(-ae, 0)$.

Length of minor axis $BB'=2b$

and length of latusrectum $=\dfrac{2b^2}{a}$

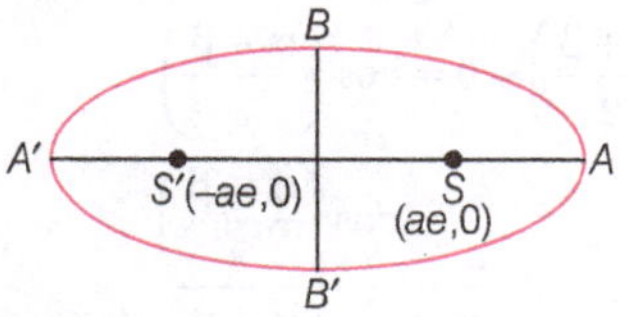

$\therefore$ According to the question,

$$BB' = SS' \Rightarrow 2b = 2ae$$

$\Rightarrow \quad b = ae \quad$ ...(i)

and $\quad \dfrac{2b^2}{a} = 10$

$\Rightarrow \quad b^2 = 5a \quad$ ...(ii)

Also, we have $\quad b^2 = a^2(1-e^2) \quad$ ...(iii)

On putting the value of b from Eq. (i) in Eq. (iii), we have

$$a^2e^2 = a^2(1-e^2)$$

$\Rightarrow \quad e^2 = 1-e^2 \Rightarrow 2e^2 = 1$

$\therefore \quad e = \dfrac{1}{\sqrt{2}}$

From Eq. (i), we have $b = \dfrac{a}{\sqrt{2}}$

$\therefore \quad b^2 = \dfrac{a^2}{2}$

$\Rightarrow \quad 5a = \dfrac{a^2}{2} \quad$ [from Eq. (ii)]

$\Rightarrow \quad a = 10$

From Eq. (ii), $b^2 = 5\times 10 = 50$

On putting the values of a and b in $\dfrac{x^2}{a^2}+\dfrac{y^2}{b^2}=1$, the equation of required ellipse is

$$\frac{x^2}{100}+\frac{y^2}{50}=1$$

$\Rightarrow \quad x^2+2y^2 = 100$

6.4 Parametric Equation of Ellipse

The circle described on the major axis of an ellipse as diameter is called the **auxiliary circle** of the ellipse.

Let the equation of ellipse be

$$\frac{x^2}{a^2}+\frac{y^2}{b^2}=1$$

$\therefore$ Equation of its auxiliary circle is

$$x^2+y^2=a^2 \quad [\because AA' \text{ is diameter of the circle}]$$

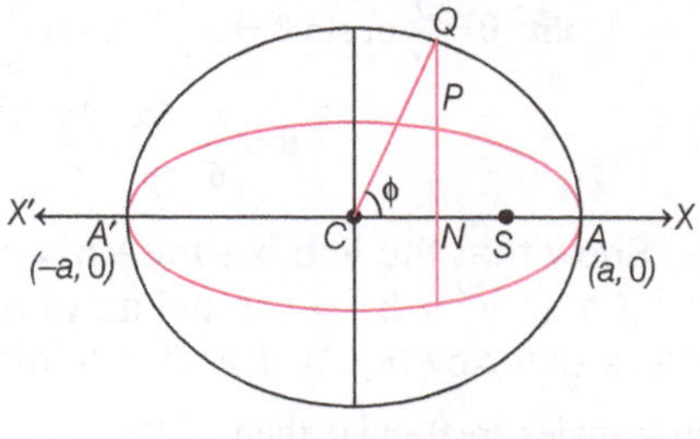

Let Q be a point on the auxiliary circle $x^2+y^2=a^2$ such that QP produced is perpendicular to the X-axis.

Then, P and Q are the **corresponding points** on the ellipse and the auxiliary circle respectively.

Let $\quad \angle QCA = \phi \quad [0 \le \phi < 2\pi]$

i.e. the eccentric angle of P on an ellipse is the angle which the radius (or **radius vector)** through the corresponding point on the auxiliary circle makes with the major axis.

$\therefore \quad Q \equiv (a\cos\phi, a\sin\phi)$

$\therefore$ Now, x-coordinate of P is $a\cos\phi$.

Let y-coordinate of P is y, then $(a\cos\phi, y)$ lies on the ellipse

$$\frac{x^2}{a^2}+\frac{y^2}{b^2}=1 \Rightarrow \frac{a^2\cos^2\phi}{a^2}+\frac{y^2}{b^2}=1 \Rightarrow y^2=b^2\sin^2\phi$$

$\therefore \quad y = \pm b\sin\phi$

$\because P$ is in Ist quadrant

$\therefore \quad y = b\sin\phi$

Coordinates of P are $(a\cos\phi, b\sin\phi)$. We have $x = a\cos\phi, y = b\sin\phi$ are called parametric equations of the ellipse.

This point $(a\cos\phi, b\sin\phi)$ is also called the point ϕ.

JEE SPIKE

If α and β are the eccentric angles of extremities of a focal chord of the ellipse $\dfrac{x^2}{a^2}+\dfrac{y^2}{b^2}=1$, then $\tan\left(\dfrac{\alpha}{2}\right)\tan\left(\dfrac{\beta}{2}\right)=\dfrac{e-1}{e+1}$ or $\dfrac{e+1}{e-1}$ according as focus $(ae, 0)$ or $(-ae, 0)$.

Example 11. Find the eccentric angle of a point on the ellipse $\dfrac{x^2}{6}+\dfrac{y^2}{2}=1$ whose distance from the center of the ellipse is $\sqrt{5}$.

Sol. Any point on the ellipse is $P(\sqrt{6}\cos\theta, \sqrt{2}\sin\theta)$.

where, $0 \le \theta < 2\pi$ and $C(0, 0)$ is center, given $CP=\sqrt{5}$

$\Rightarrow \quad (CP)^2 = 5 \Rightarrow 6\cos^2\theta + 2\sin^2\theta = 5$

$\Rightarrow \quad 6(1-\sin^2\theta) + 2\sin^2\theta = 5$

or $\quad \sin^2\theta = \frac{1}{4}$ or $\sin\theta = \pm\frac{1}{2} = \pm\sin\frac{\pi}{6}$

$\therefore \quad \theta = \frac{\pi}{6}, \frac{5\pi}{6}, \frac{7\pi}{6}, \frac{11\pi}{6}$

Example 12. Show that the line $lx + my + n = 0$ will cut the ellipse $x^2/a^2 + y^2/b^2 = 1$ in points whose eccentric angles differ by $(\pi/2)$, if $a^2l^2 + b^2m^2 = 2n^2$.

Sol. Let eccentric angles are θ and ϕ, then

$$\theta - \phi = \frac{\pi}{2} \quad \text{[given]}$$

$$\therefore \quad \theta = \frac{\pi}{2} + \phi$$

The line joining the point θ and ϕ is

$$\frac{x}{a}\cos\left(\frac{\theta+\phi}{2}\right) + \frac{y}{b}\sin\left(\frac{\theta+\phi}{2}\right) = \cos\left(\frac{\theta-\phi}{2}\right)$$

or $$\frac{x}{a}\cos\left(\frac{\pi}{4}+\phi\right) + \frac{y}{b}\sin\left(\frac{\pi}{4}+\phi\right) = \cos\frac{\pi}{4} \quad \left[\because \theta = \frac{\pi}{2}+\phi\right]$$

or $$\frac{x}{a}\cos\left(\frac{\pi}{4}+\phi\right) + \frac{y}{b}\sin\left(\frac{\pi}{4}+\phi\right) = \frac{1}{\sqrt{2}} \quad \text{...(i)}$$

and the given line is $lx + my + n = 0$

or $$lx + my = -n \quad \text{...(ii)}$$

Now, Eqs. (i) and (ii) represent the same line, so comparing them, we get

$$\frac{\cos\left(\frac{\pi}{4}+\phi\right)}{la} = \frac{\sin\left(\frac{\pi}{4}+\phi\right)}{mb} = -\frac{1}{n\sqrt{2}}$$

$$\therefore \quad \cos\left(\frac{\pi}{4}+\phi\right) = -\frac{la}{n\sqrt{2}} \quad \text{...(iii)}$$

and $$\sin\left(\frac{\pi}{4}+\phi\right) = -\frac{mb}{n\sqrt{2}} \quad \text{...(iv)}$$

On squaring and adding Eqs. (iii) and (iv), we get

$$\frac{l^2a^2}{2n^2} + \frac{m^2b^2}{2n^2} = 1$$

$$\Rightarrow \quad l^2a^2 + m^2b^2 = 2n^2$$

Example 13. If a chord joining two points whose eccentric angles are α and β, cut the major axis of an ellipse at a distance d from the centre. Show that $\tan(\alpha/2)\tan(\beta/2) = (d-a)/(d+a)$, where $2a$ is the length of major axis.

Sol. Let the equation of the ellipse be

$$\frac{x^2}{a^2} + \frac{y^2}{b^2} = 1 \quad \text{...(i)}$$

The equation of the line joining α and β on the ellipse Eq. (i) is

$$\frac{x}{a}\cos\left(\frac{\alpha+\beta}{2}\right) + \frac{y}{b}\sin\left(\frac{\alpha+\beta}{2}\right) = \cos\left(\frac{\alpha-\beta}{2}\right) \quad \text{...(ii)}$$

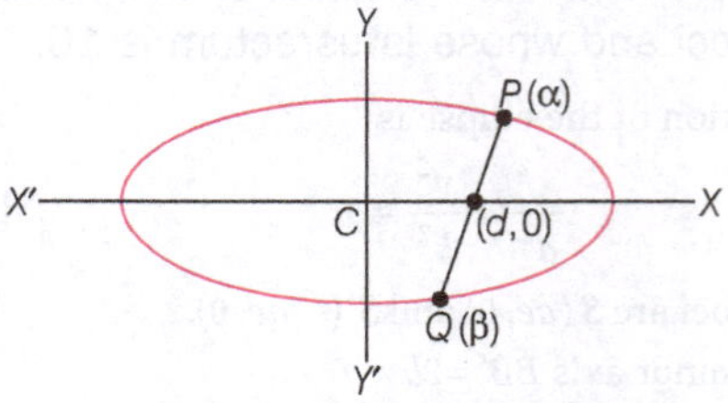

Since, it cuts the major axis of the ellipse at a distance d from the centre i.e. passes through the point $(d, 0)$, then

$$\frac{d}{a}\cos\left(\frac{\alpha+\beta}{2}\right) + 0 = \cos\left(\frac{\alpha-\beta}{2}\right)$$

or $$\frac{d}{a} = \frac{\cos\left(\frac{\alpha-\beta}{2}\right)}{\cos\left(\frac{\alpha+\beta}{2}\right)}$$

or $$\frac{d-a}{d+a} = \frac{\cos\left(\frac{\alpha-\beta}{2}\right) - \cos\left(\frac{\alpha+\beta}{2}\right)}{\cos\left(\frac{\alpha-\beta}{2}\right) + \cos\left(\frac{\alpha+\beta}{2}\right)}$$

[by componendo and dividendo]

$$= \frac{2\sin(\alpha/2)\sin(\beta/2)}{2\cos(\alpha/2)\cos(\beta/2)} = \tan(\alpha/2)\tan(\beta/2)$$

$$\therefore \quad \tan(\alpha/2)\tan(\beta/2) = \frac{d-a}{d+a}$$

Example 14. Prove that the ratio of area of any triangle PQR inscribed in the ellipse $\frac{x^2}{a^2} + \frac{y^2}{b^2} = 1$ and that of triangle formed by the corresponding points on the auxiliary circle is $\frac{b}{a}$.

Sol. Let the three points on the ellipse be $P(a\cos\alpha, b\sin\alpha)$, $Q(a\cos\beta, b\sin\beta)$ and $R(a\cos\gamma, b\sin\gamma)$.

Then, the corresponding points on the auxiliary circle are $A(a\cos\alpha, a\sin\alpha)$, $B(a\cos\beta, a\sin\beta)$ and $C(a\cos\gamma, a\sin\gamma)$, then

$$\frac{\text{Area of } \Delta PQR}{\text{Area of } \Delta ABC} = \frac{\frac{1}{2}\begin{vmatrix} a\cos\alpha & b\sin\alpha & 1 \\ a\cos\beta & b\sin\beta & 1 \\ a\cos\gamma & b\sin\gamma & 1 \end{vmatrix}}{\frac{1}{2}\begin{vmatrix} a\cos\alpha & a\sin\alpha & 1 \\ a\cos\beta & a\sin\beta & 1 \\ a\cos\gamma & a\sin\gamma & 1 \end{vmatrix}}$$

$$= \frac{ab\begin{vmatrix} \cos\alpha & \sin\alpha & 1 \\ \cos\beta & \sin\beta & 1 \\ \cos\gamma & \sin\gamma & 1 \end{vmatrix}}{a^2\begin{vmatrix} \cos\alpha & \sin\alpha & 1 \\ \cos\beta & \sin\beta & 1 \\ \cos\gamma & \sin\gamma & 1 \end{vmatrix}} = \frac{b}{a}$$

JEE SCANNER

Example Similar to PYQ Asked in JEE Main 2023

Let the ellipse $E: x^2 + 4y^2 = 4$ intersect the positive X and Y-axes at the points A and B, respectively. Let the major axis of E be a diameter of the circle C. Let the line passing through A and B meet the circle C at the point P. If the area of the triangle which vertices are A, P and the origin O, is m / n, where m and n are coprime, then m + n is equal to

(a) 8 (b) 5 (c) 13 (d) 3

Sol. (c) For line AB, $x + 2y = 2$ and circle is $x^2 + y^2 = 4$

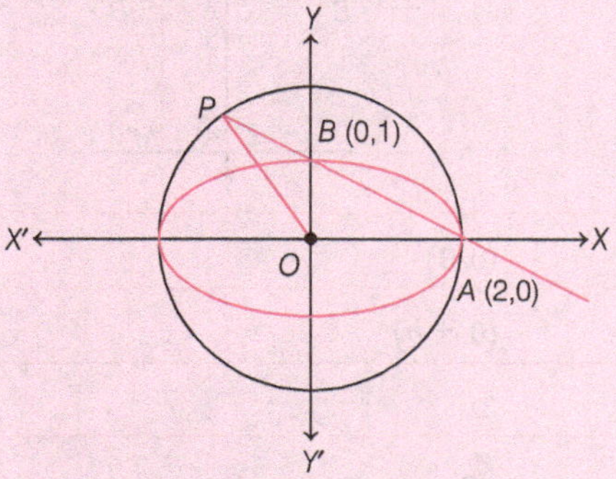

$$(2 - 2y)^2 + y^2 = 4$$

$$\Rightarrow \quad 4 + 4y^2 - 8y + y^2 = 4 \Rightarrow 5y^2 - 8y = 0$$

$$\Rightarrow \quad y = 0, \frac{8}{5}$$

$$\therefore \text{ Area} = \frac{1}{2} \times 2 \times \frac{8}{5} = \frac{8}{5} = \frac{m}{n} \Rightarrow m + n = 8 + 5 = 13$$

Skill Builder

For Sol.

Let the ellipse $E: x^2 + 16y^2 = 16$ intersect the positive X and Y-axes at the points A and B respectively. Let the major axis of E be a diameter of the circle C. Let the line passing through A and B meet the circle C at the point P. If the area of the triangle which vertices are A, P and the origin O, is m / n, where m and n are coprime, then $m + n$ is equal to

(a) 64 (b) 47 (c) 85 (d) 81

- **For More Practice** See Q.9 of Milestone Practice 6.1.

6.5 Focal Distances of a Point

The sum of focal distances of any point on the ellipse is equal to the major axis. The ellipse is

$$\frac{x^2}{a^2} + \frac{y^2}{b^2} = 1 \qquad ...(i)$$

The foci S and S' are $(ae, 0)$ and $(-ae, 0)$.

The equations of its directrices MZ and $M'Z'$ are $x = a / e$ and $x = -a / e$

Let $P(x_1, y_1)$ be any point on Eq. (i).

Now, $\quad SP = ePM = e\left(\frac{a}{e} - x_1\right) = a - ex_1$

and $\quad S'P = ePM' = e\left(\frac{a}{e} + x_1\right) = a + ex_1$

$SP + S'P = (a - ex_1) + (a + ex_1) = 2a = AA' = \text{major axis}$

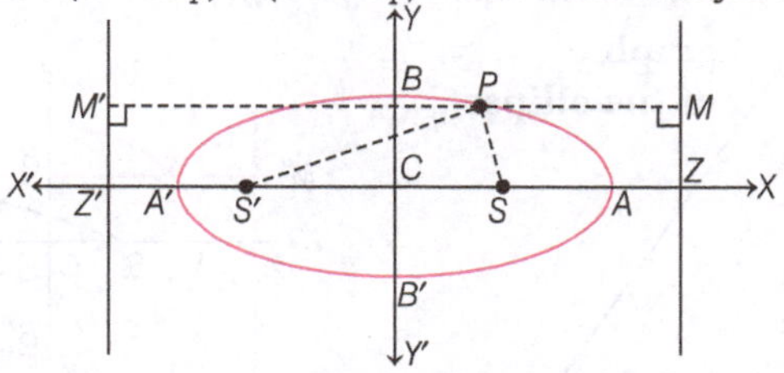

Hence, the sum of the focal distances of a point on the ellipse is constant and is equal to the length of the major axis of the ellipse.

Example 15 An ellipse having foci at (3, 3) and (–4, 4) and passing through the origin, then find eccentricity of the ellipse.

Sol. The ellipse is passing through $O(0, 0)$ and has foci $P(3, 3)$ and $Q(-4, 4)$, then $OP + OQ = 2a$ and $PQ = 2ae$

$$\therefore \quad e = \frac{PQ}{OP + OQ} = \frac{\sqrt{50}}{3\sqrt{2} + 4\sqrt{2}} = \frac{5}{7}$$

The Shape of the Ellipse $\frac{x^2}{a^2} + \frac{y^2}{b^2} = 1$, when $b > a$

In this case, major and minor-axis of the ellipse along Y-axis and X-axis respectively.

Then, $\quad AA' = 2b$ and $BB' = 2a$

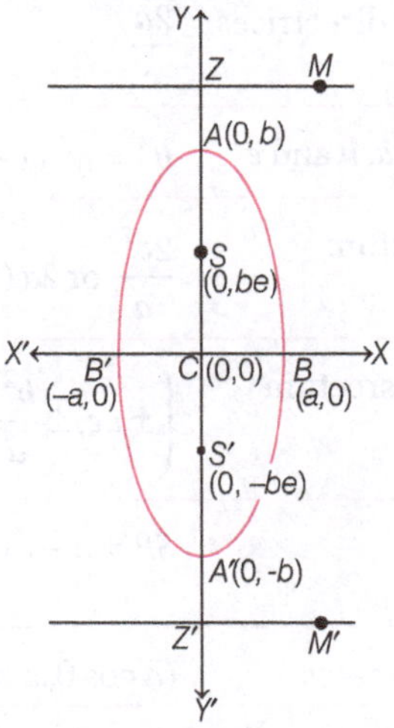

The foci S and S' are $(0, be)$ and $(0, -be)$ respectively.

The directrices are MZ and $M'Z'$ are

$$y = \frac{b}{e} \text{ and } y = -\frac{b}{e} \text{ are respectively.}$$

Smart Table

Basic Fundamental / Equation and graph of the ellipse	Horizontal ellipse	Vertical ellipse
Equation and graph of the ellipse	$\frac{x^2}{a^2}+\frac{y^2}{b^2}=1, a>b$ 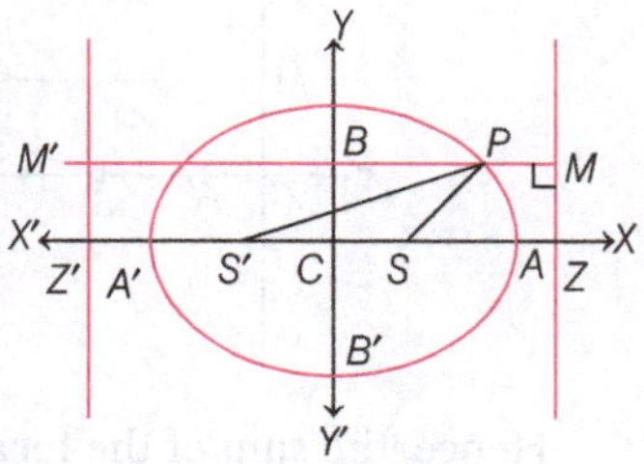	$\frac{x^2}{a^2}+\frac{y^2}{b^2}=1, a<b$ 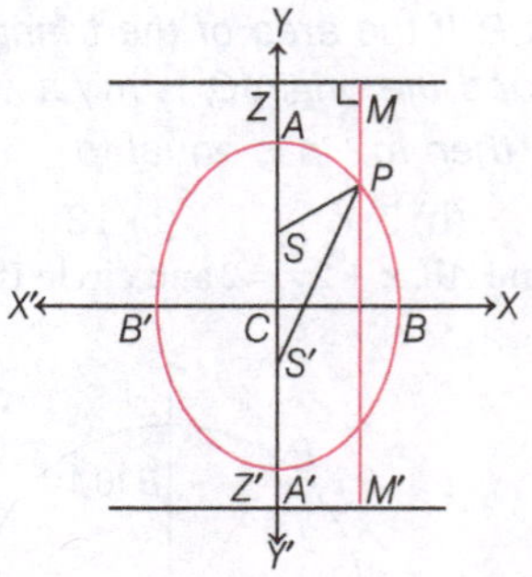
Centre	$(0,0)$	$(0,0)$
Vertices	$(\pm a,0)$	$(0,\pm b)$
Length of major axis	$2a$	$2b$
Length of minor axis	$2b$	$2a$
Foci	$(\pm ae,0)$ or $(\pm\sqrt{(a^2-b^2)},0)$	$(0,\pm be)$ or $(0,\pm\sqrt{(b^2-a^2)})$
Distance between foci	$2\,ae$ or $2\sqrt{(a^2-b^2)}$	$2\,be$ or $2\sqrt{(b^2-a^2)}$
Equation of directrices	$x=\pm\frac{a}{e}$	$y=\pm\frac{b}{e}$
Distance between directrices	$\frac{2a}{e}$	$\frac{2b}{e}$
Relation between a, b and e	$b^2=a^2(1-e^2)$	$a^2=b^2(1-e^2)$
Length of latusrectum	$\frac{2b^2}{a}$ or $2a(1-e^2)$	$\frac{2a^2}{b}$ or $2b(1-e^2)$
End points of latusrectum	$\left(\pm ae,\pm\frac{b^2}{a}\right)$	$\left(\pm\frac{a^2}{b},\pm be\right)$
Focal radii	$SP=a-ex_1, S'P=a+ex_1$ and $SP+S'P=2a$	$SP=b-ey_1, S'P=b+ey_1$ and $SP+S'P=2b$
Parametric Coordinates	$(a\cos\theta, b\sin\theta), 0\le\theta<2\pi$	$(a\cos\theta, b\sin\theta), 0\le\theta<2\pi$
Tangents at the vertices	$x=\pm a$	$y=\pm b$

Example 16 Find the lengths and equations of the focal radii drawn from the point $(4\sqrt{3}, 5)$ on the ellipse $25x^2 + 16y^2 = 1600$.

Sol. The equation of the ellipse is

$$25x^2 + 16y^2 = 1600$$

or $$\frac{x^2}{64} + \frac{y^2}{100} = 1$$

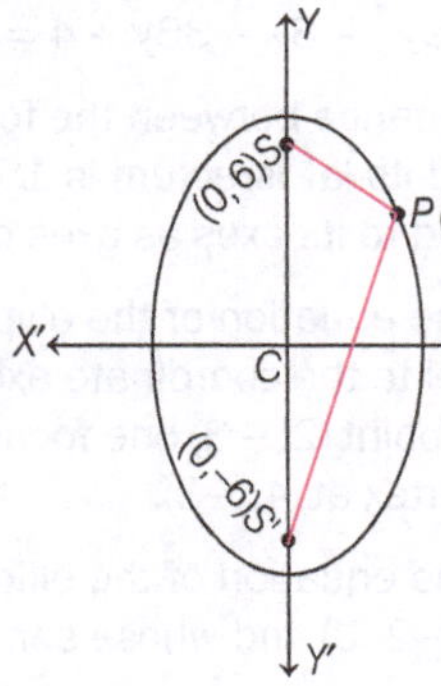

Here, $b > a$

$$a^2 = 64,\ b^2 = 100$$

$$a^2 = b^2(1 - e^2)$$

$\therefore$ $$64 = 100(1 - e^2)$$

$\Rightarrow$ $$e = 3/5$$

Let $P(x_1, y_1) \equiv (4\sqrt{3}, 5)$ be a point on the ellipse, then SP and $S'P$ are the focal radii.

$\therefore$ $$SP = b - ey_1 \text{ and } S'P = b + ey_1$$

$\therefore$ $$SP = 10 - \frac{3}{5} \times 5 \text{ and } S'P = 10 + \frac{3}{5} \times 5$$

$\Rightarrow$ $$SP = 7 \text{ and } S'P = 13$$

Also, S is $(0, be)$

i.e. $\left(0, 10 \times \frac{3}{5}\right)$ i.e. $(0, 6)$ and S' is $(0, -be)$

i.e. $\left(0, -10 \times \frac{3}{5}\right)$ i.e. $(0, -6)$

$\therefore$ Equation of SP is

$$y - 5 = \frac{6 - 5}{0 - 4\sqrt{3}}(x - 4\sqrt{3})$$

$$-4\sqrt{3}y + 20\sqrt{3} = x - 4\sqrt{3}$$

or $$x + 4\sqrt{3}y - 24\sqrt{3} = 0$$

and equation of $S'P$ is

$\therefore$ $$y - 5 = \frac{-6 - 5}{0 - 4\sqrt{3}}(x - 4\sqrt{3})$$

$\Rightarrow$ $$-4\sqrt{3}y + 20\sqrt{3} = -11x + 44\sqrt{3}$$

or $$11x - 4\sqrt{3}y - 24\sqrt{3} = 0$$

Milestone Practice 6.1

1. The length of the major axis of the ellipse $\frac{x^2}{a^2} + \frac{y^2}{b^2} = 1$, is three times the length of minor axis, its eccentricity is

(a) $\frac{1}{\sqrt{2}}$ (b) $\frac{1}{\sqrt{3}}$ (c) $\frac{2\sqrt{2}}{3}$ (d) $\frac{2\sqrt{2}}{5}$

2. The equation $\frac{x^2}{10 - a} + \frac{y^2}{4 - a} = 1$, represents an ellipse, if

(a) $a < 4$ (b) $a > 4$
(c) $4 < a < 10$ (d) $a > 10$

3. The eccentricity of an ellipse $\frac{x^2}{a^2} + \frac{y^2}{b^2} = 1$, whose latusrectum is half of its major axis, is

(a) $\frac{1}{\sqrt{3}}$ (b) $\frac{1}{\sqrt{2}}$ (c) $\frac{\sqrt{3}}{2}$ (d) $\sqrt{\left(\frac{2}{3}\right)}$

4. If the eccentricity of an ellipse is $\frac{1}{\sqrt{2}}$, then length of latusrectum is equal to its

(a) minor axis (b) semi-minor axis
(c) major axis (d) semi-major axis

5. If the distance between the foci of an ellipse is equal to its minor axis, then its eccentricity is

(a) $\frac{1}{2}$ (b) $\frac{1}{\sqrt{2}}$ (c) $\frac{1}{3}$ (d) $\frac{1}{\sqrt{3}}$

6. The eccentric angle of a point on the ellipse $\frac{x^2}{6} + \frac{y^2}{2} = 1$, whose distance from the centre of ellipse is 2, is

(a) $-\frac{\pi}{4}$ (b) $\frac{\pi}{4}$
(c) $\frac{3\pi}{2}$ (d) $\frac{5\pi}{3}$

7. If the eccentricity of the two ellipses $\frac{x^2}{169}+\frac{y^2}{25}=1$ and $\frac{x^2}{a^2}+\frac{y^2}{b^2}=1$ are equal, then the value of $\frac{a}{b}$ is

(a) $\frac{5}{13}$ (b) $\frac{6}{13}$ (c) $\frac{13}{5}$ (d) $\frac{13}{6}$

8. The ratio of the areas of triangle inscribed in ellipse $\frac{x^2}{a^2}+\frac{y^2}{b^2}=1$, to that of triangle formed by the corresponding points on the auxiliary circle is $\frac{1}{2}$, then the eccentricity of the ellipse is

(a) $\frac{1}{2}$ (b) $\frac{\sqrt{3}}{2}$ (c) $\frac{1}{\sqrt{2}}$ (d) $\frac{1}{\sqrt{3}}$

9. Let the ellipse $E: x^2+25y^2=25$ intersect the positive *X* and *Y*-axes at the points *A* and *B*, respectively. Let the major axis of *E* be a diameter of the circle *C*. Let the line passing through *A* and *B* meet the circle *C* at the point *P*. If the area of the triangle which vertices *A*, *P* and the origin *O* is $\frac{m}{n}$, where *m* and *n* are coprime, then find the value of $(m-n)$.

10. If *PSQ* is a focal chord of the ellipse $16x^2+25y^2=400$ such that $SP=8$, then find the length *SQ*.

11. Let *P* be a variable point on the ellipse $\frac{x^2}{25}+\frac{y^2}{16}=1$ with foci at *S* and *S′*. If *A* be the area of $\Delta PSS'$, then find the maximum value of *A*.

12. If *S* and *S′* are the foci of an ellipse of major axis of length 10 units and *P* is any point on the ellipse such that the perimeter of triangle *PSS′* is 15 units, then find the eccentricity of the ellipse.

13. Find the latusrectum, eccentricity, coordinates of the foci, coordinates of the vertices, the length of the axes and the centre of the ellipse $4x^2+9y^2-8x-36y+4=0$.

14. The distance between the foci of an ellipse is 10 and its latusrectum is 15, find its equation referred to its axes as axes of coordinates.

15. Find the equation of the ellipse whose axes are parallel to the coordinate axes having its centre at the point $(2,-3)$ one focus at $(3,-3)$ and one vertex at $(4,-3)$.

16. Find the equation of the ellipse whose foci are $(2,3)$, $(-2,3)$ and whose semi-minor axes is $\sqrt{5}$.

17. Find the locus of the extremities of the latusrectum of the family of ellipses $b^2x^2+y^2=a^2b^2$ having a given major axes.

18. Find the eccentricity, foci directrix and length of the latusrectum of the ellipse

$$(3x-12)^2+(3y+15)^2=\frac{(3x-4y+5)^2}{25}.$$

19. Prove that the curve represented by $x=3(\cos t+\sin t)$, $y=4(\cos t-\sin t)$, $t\in R$ is an ellipse.

Answer Key

1. (a) **2.** (b) **3.** (c) **4.** (d) **5.** (b) **6.** (b)

7. (c) **8.** (b) **9.** 99. **10.** (2) **11.** (12) **12.** $\frac{1}{2}$

13. $\frac{8}{3}, \frac{\sqrt{5}}{3}, (1\pm\sqrt{5}, 2), (-2, 2)$ and $(4, 2)$, 6, 4 and $(1, 2)$ **14.** $\frac{x^2}{100}+\frac{y^2}{75}=1$

15. $\frac{(x-2)^2}{4}+\frac{(y+3)^2}{3}=1$ **16.** $\frac{x^2}{9}+\frac{(y-3)^2}{5}=1$ **17.** $x^2\pm ay=a^2$

18. $\frac{1}{3}$, $(4,-5)$, $3x-4y+5=0$ and $\frac{2}{5}$

For Detailed Solution

Milestone 2 Line and Ellipse

• Position of a Point with respect to an Ellipse • Intersection of a Line and an Ellipse • Equations of Tangents in Different Forms • Equations of Normals in Different Forms • Co-normal points Lie on a Fixed Curve

6.6 Position of a Point with respect to an Ellipse

Theorem Prove that the point $P(x_1, y_1)$ lies outside, on or inside the ellipse $\frac{x^2}{a^2}+\frac{y^2}{b^2}=1$ according as

$$\frac{x_1^2}{a^2}+\frac{y_1^2}{b^2}-1 >, =\text{or}, < 0$$

Proof From point $P(x_1, y_1)$ draw perpendicular PM on AA' to meet the ellipse at $Q(x_1, y_2)$.

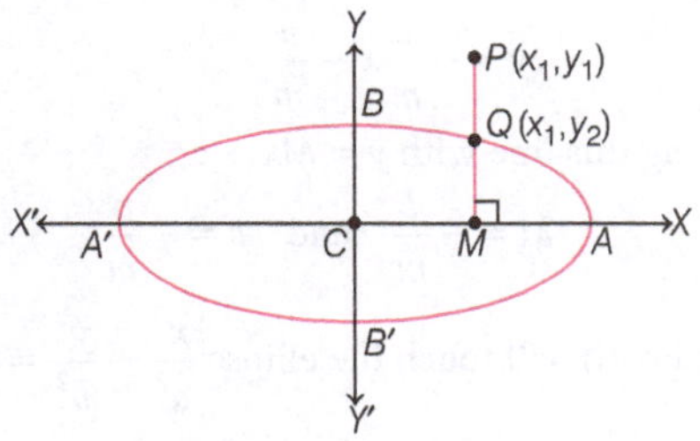

Since, $Q(x_1, y_2)$ lies on the ellipse

$$\frac{x^2}{a^2}+\frac{y^2}{b^2}=1$$

Then, $$\frac{x_1^2}{a^2}+\frac{y_2^2}{b^2}=1$$

$$\Rightarrow \quad \frac{y_2^2}{b^2}=1-\frac{x_1^2}{a^2} \quad \text{...(i)}$$

Now, point P lies outside, on or inside the ellipse according as

$$PM >, =\text{or}, < QM$$

$$\Rightarrow \quad y_1 >, =\text{or}, < y_2$$

$$\Rightarrow \quad \frac{y_1^2}{b^2} >, =\text{or}, < \frac{y_2^2}{b^2}$$

$$\Rightarrow \quad \frac{y_1^2}{b^2} >, =\text{or}, < 1-\frac{x_1^2}{a^2} \quad \text{[from Eq. (i)]}$$

$$\Rightarrow \quad \frac{x_1^2}{a^2}+\frac{y_1^2}{b^2} >, =\text{or}, < 1,$$

or $$\frac{x_1^2}{a^2}+\frac{y_1^2}{b^2}-1 >, =\text{or}, < 0$$

Hence, the point $P(x_1, y_1)$ lies outside, on or inside the ellipse $\frac{x^2}{a^2}+\frac{y^2}{b^2}=1$ according as

$$\frac{x_1^2}{a^2}+\frac{y_1^2}{b^2}-1 > 0, =\text{or}, < 0$$

JEE SPIKE

Let $S=\frac{x^2}{a^2}+\frac{y^2}{b^2}-1$, then $S_1=\frac{x_1^2}{a^2}+\frac{y_1^2}{b^2}-1$

The point (x_1, y_1) lies outside, on or inside the ellipse $S=0$ according as $S_1 >, =$ or < 0.

Example 17. Find the position of the point $(4, -3)$ relative to the ellipse $5x^2+7y^2=140$.

Sol. The given ellipse can be written as $\frac{x^2}{28}+\frac{y^2}{20}-1=0$

Let $$S=\frac{x^2}{28}+\frac{y^2}{20}-1$$

$$\therefore \quad S_1=\frac{(4)^2}{28}+\frac{(-3)^2}{20}-1=\frac{3}{140}>0$$

So, the point $(4, -3)$ lies outside the ellipse $5x^2+7y^2=140$.

Example 18. Find the integral value of α for which the point $\left(7-\frac{5\alpha}{4}, -\alpha\right)$ lies inside the ellipse $\frac{x^2}{25}+\frac{y^2}{16}=1$.

Sol. Since, the point $\left(7-\frac{5\alpha}{4}, -\alpha\right)$ lies inside the ellipse $\frac{x^2}{25}+\frac{y^2}{16}=1$, then

$$\frac{1}{25}\left(7-\frac{5\alpha}{4}\right)^2+\frac{1}{16}(-\alpha)^2-1<0$$

$$\Rightarrow \quad (28-5\alpha)^2+25\alpha^2-400<0$$

$$\Rightarrow \quad 50\alpha^2 - 280\alpha + 384 < 0$$
$$\Rightarrow \quad 25\alpha^2 - 140\alpha + 192 < 0$$
$$\Rightarrow \quad (5\alpha - 12)(5\alpha - 16) < 0$$
$$\therefore \quad \frac{12}{5} < \alpha < \frac{16}{5}$$

Hence, integral value of α is 3.

6.7 Intersection of a Line and an Ellipse

Let the ellipse be $\left(\frac{x^2}{a^2} + \frac{y^2}{b^2}\right) = 1$ ...(i)

and the given line be $y = mx + c$ ...(ii)

Eliminating y from Eqs. (i) and (ii), then

$$\frac{x^2}{a^2} + \frac{(mx+c)^2}{b^2} = 1$$

$$\Rightarrow (a^2m^2 + b^2)x^2 + 2mca^2x + c^2a^2 - a^2b^2 = 0 \quad \text{...(iii)}$$

Above equation being a quadratic in x gives two values of x. Shows that every straight line will cut the ellipse in two points may be real, coincident or imaginary according as

Discriminant of Eq. (iii) $>, =, < 0$

i.e. $4m^2c^2a^4 - 4(a^2m^2 + b^2)(c^2a^2 - a^2b^2) >, =, < 0$

or $\quad -a^2b^2c^2 + a^4b^2m^2 + a^2b^4 >, =, < 0$

or $\quad a^2m^2 + b^2 >, =, < c^2$ ...(iv)

Condition of Tangency If the line Eq. (ii) touches the ellipse Eq. (i), then Eq. (iii) has equal roots.

$\therefore$ Discriminant of Eq. (iii) $= 0$

$$\Rightarrow \quad c^2 = a^2m^2 + b^2$$

or $\quad c = \pm\sqrt{(a^2m^2 + b^2)}$ ...(v)

So, the line $y = mx + c$ touches the ellipse

$$\frac{x^2}{a^2} + \frac{y^2}{b^2} = 1 \quad \text{if} \quad c^2 = a^2m^2 + b^2$$

[which is condition of tangency]

Substituting the value of c from Eq. (v) in Eq. (ii), then

$$y = mx \pm \sqrt{(a^2m^2 + b^2)}$$

Hence, the lines $y = mx \pm \sqrt{(a^2m^2 + b^2)}$ will always tangents to the ellipse.

Point of contact Substituting $c = \pm\sqrt{(a^2m^2 + b^2)}$ in Eq. (iii), then $(a^2m^2 + b^2)x^2 \pm 2ma^2x$

$$\sqrt{(a^2m^2 + b^2)} + (a^2m^2 + b^2)a^2 - a^2b^2 = 0$$

or $\quad (a^2m^2 + b^2)x^2 \pm 2ma^2x\sqrt{(a^2m^2 + b^2)} + a^4m^2 = 0$

or $\quad (x\sqrt{(a^2m^2 + b^2)} \pm a^2m)^2 = 0$

$$\therefore \quad x = \pm\frac{a^2m}{\sqrt{(a^2m^2 + b^2)}} = \pm\frac{a^2m}{c}$$

From Eq. (i), $\frac{a^4m^2}{c^2} \cdot \frac{1}{a^2} + \frac{y^2}{b^2} = 1$

$$\Rightarrow \quad \frac{y^2}{b^2} = 1 - \frac{a^2m^2}{c^2} = \frac{c^2 - a^2m^2}{c^2} = \frac{b^2}{c^2}$$

$$y = \pm\frac{b^2}{c}$$

Hence, the point of contact is $\left(\pm\frac{a^2m}{c}, \pm\frac{b^2}{c}\right)$ known as m-point on the ellipse.

Example 19. Prove that the straight line $lx + my + n = 0$ touches the ellipse $\frac{x^2}{a^2} + \frac{y^2}{b^2} = 1$ if $a^2l^2 + b^2m^2 = n^2$.

Sol. The given line is

$$lx + my + n = 0$$

or $\quad y = -\frac{l}{m}x - \frac{n}{m}$ ...(i)

Comparing this line with $y = Mx + c$

$$\therefore \quad M = -\frac{l}{m} \quad \text{and} \quad c = -\frac{n}{m}$$

The line Eq. (i) will touch the ellipse $\frac{x^2}{a^2} + \frac{y^2}{b^2} = 1$, if

$$c^2 = a^2M^2 + b^2$$

$$\Rightarrow \quad \frac{n^2}{m^2} = \frac{a^2l^2}{m^2} + b^2$$

$$\Rightarrow \quad a^2l^2 + b^2m^2 = n^2$$

Example 20. Show that the line $x\cos\alpha + y\sin\alpha = p$ touches the ellipse $\frac{x^2}{a^2} + \frac{y^2}{b^2} = 1$ if $a^2\cos^2\alpha + b^2\sin^2\alpha = p^2$ and that point of contact is $\left(\frac{a^2\cos\alpha}{p}, \frac{b^2\sin\alpha}{p}\right)$.

Sol. The given line is $x\cos\alpha + y\sin\alpha = p$

$$y = -x\cot\alpha + p\operatorname{cosec}\alpha$$

Comparing this line with $y = mx + c$, we get

$$\therefore \quad m = -\cot\alpha$$

and $\quad c = p\operatorname{cosec}\alpha$

Hence, the given line touches the ellipse, then

$$c^2 = a^2m^2 + b^2$$

$\Rightarrow \quad p^2 \operatorname{cosec}^2\alpha = a^2 \cot^2 \alpha + b^2$

$\Rightarrow \quad p^2 = a^2 \cos^2 \alpha + b^2 \sin^2 \alpha$

and point of contact is $\left(-\dfrac{a^2 m}{c}, \dfrac{b^2}{c}\right)$

i.e. $\left(-\dfrac{a^2(-\cot\alpha)}{p \operatorname{cosec}\alpha}, \dfrac{b^2}{p \operatorname{cosec}\alpha}\right)$

i.e. $\left(\dfrac{a^2 \cos\alpha}{p}, \dfrac{b^2 \sin\alpha}{p}\right)$

Example 21. For what value of λ does the line $y = x + \lambda$ touches the ellipse $9x^2 + 16y^2 = 144$.

Sol. $\because$ Equation of ellipse is

$$9x^2 + 16y^2 = 144 \quad \text{or} \quad \frac{x^2}{16} + \frac{y^2}{9} = 1$$

On comparing this with $\dfrac{x^2}{a^2} + \dfrac{y^2}{b^2} = 1$, we get

$a^2 = 16$ and $b^2 = 9$

and comparing the line $y = x + \lambda$ with $y = mx + c$, we get

$$m = 1 \quad \text{and} \quad c = \lambda$$

If the line $y = x + \lambda$ touches the ellipse $9x^2 + 16y^2 = 144$,

then $\quad c^2 = a^2 m^2 + b^2$

$\Rightarrow \quad \lambda^2 = 16 \times 1^2 + 9$

$\Rightarrow \quad \lambda^2 = 25$

$\therefore \quad \lambda = \pm 5$

6.8 Equation of Tangent in Different Forms

1. Point Form

Theorem The equation of tangent to the ellipse $\dfrac{x^2}{a^2} + \dfrac{y^2}{b^2} = 1$ at the point (x_1, y_1) is $\dfrac{xx_1}{a^2} + \dfrac{yy_1}{b^2} = 1$

Proof (By first Principal Method)

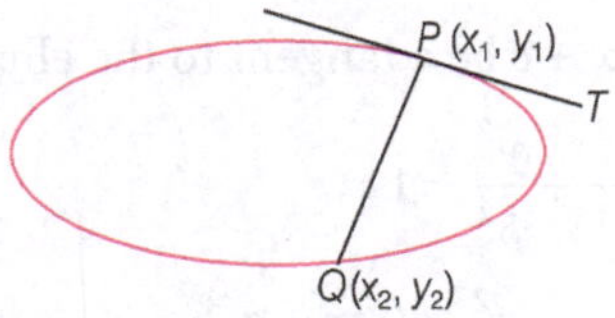

$\because$ Equation of ellipse is $\dfrac{x^2}{a^2} + \dfrac{y^2}{b^2} = 1 \quad$ ...(i)

Let $P \equiv (x_1, y_1)$ and $Q \equiv (x_2, y_2)$ be any two point on Eq. (i), then

$$\frac{x_1^2}{a^2} + \frac{y_1^2}{b^2} = 1 \quad \text{...(ii)}$$

and $$\frac{x_2^2}{a^2} + \frac{y_2^2}{b^2} = 1 \quad \text{...(iii)}$$

On subtracting Eq. (ii) from Eq. (iii), then

$$\frac{1}{a^2}(x_2^2 - x_1^2) + \frac{1}{b^2}(y_2^2 - y_1^2) = 0$$

$$\Rightarrow \frac{(x_2 + x_1)(x_2 - x_1)}{a^2} + \frac{(y_2 + y_1)(y_2 - y_1)}{b^2} = 0$$

$$\Rightarrow \frac{y_2 - y_1}{x_2 - x_1} = -\frac{b^2(x_1 + x_2)}{a^2(y_1 + y_2)} \quad \text{...(iv)}$$

Equation of PQ is

$$y - y_1 = \frac{y_2 - y_1}{x_2 - x_1}(x - x_1) \quad \text{...(v)}$$

From Eqs. (iv) and (v), then

$$y - y_1 = -\frac{b^2(x_1 + x_2)}{a^2(y_1 + y_2)}(x - x_1) \quad \text{...(vi)}$$

Now, for tangent at P, $Q \to P$ i.e. $x_2 \to x_1$ and $y_2 \to y_1$, then Eq. (vi) becomes

$$y - y_1 = -\frac{b^2(2x_1)}{a^2(2y_1)}(x - x_1)$$

or $$\frac{yy_1 - y_1^2}{b^2} = -\left(\frac{xx_1 - x_1^2}{a^2}\right)$$

or $$\frac{xx_1}{a^2} + \frac{yy_1}{b^2} = \frac{x_1^2}{a^2} + \frac{y_1^2}{b^2} \text{ or } \frac{xx_1}{a^2} + \frac{yy_1}{b^2} = 1 \quad \text{[from (ii)]}$$

which is required equation of tangent at (x_1, y_1).

JEE SPIKE

The equation of tangent at (x_1, y_1) can be obtained by replacing x^2 by xx_1, y^2 by yy_1, x by $\dfrac{x + x_1}{2}$, y by $\dfrac{y + y_1}{2}$ and xy by $\dfrac{xy_1 + x_1 y}{2}$.

This method is applicable only when the equation of ellipse is a polynomial of second degree in x and y.

JEE SCANNER

Example Similar to PYQ Asked in JEE Main 2021

On the ellipse $\frac{x^2}{12}+\frac{y^2}{16}=1$, let P be a point in the third quadrant such that the tangent at P to the ellipse is perpendicular to the line $x-2y=0$. Let S and S′ be the foci of the ellipse and e be its eccentricity. If A is the area of the $\Delta SPS'$, then the value of $2A(1-e^2)$, is equal to ......

Sol. (9) Given, equation of ellipse $\frac{x^2}{12}+\frac{y^2}{16}=1$

Then, equation of tangent at (x_1, y_1) will be

$$\frac{xx_1}{12}+\frac{yy_1}{16}=1.$$

Since, tangent is perpendicular to the $x-2y=0$, then

$$\left(\frac{-4x_1}{3y_1}\right)\times\left(\frac{1}{2}\right)=-1 \Rightarrow x_1=\frac{3y_1}{2}$$

Also, $\frac{x_1^2}{12}+\frac{y_1^2}{16}=1 \Rightarrow \frac{9y_1^2}{48}+\frac{y_1^2}{16}=1 \Rightarrow \frac{9y_1^2+3y_1^2}{48}=1$

$\Rightarrow \frac{12y_1^2}{48}=1 \Rightarrow y_1=\pm 2 \Rightarrow y_1=-2$

and $x_1=-3$ [P lies in IIIrd quadrant]

$\therefore P(-3,-2)$

Again, $b^2-a^2=b^2e^2 \Rightarrow 16-12=16e^2 \Rightarrow e=\frac{1}{2}$

$\therefore$ $S=(0, be)$ and $S'=(0,-be) \Rightarrow S=(0,2)$ and $S'=(0,-2)$

$\therefore$ Area of $\Delta SPS'=\frac{1}{2}\times 4\times 3=6$ sq units

[$\because$ base = 4, height = 3]

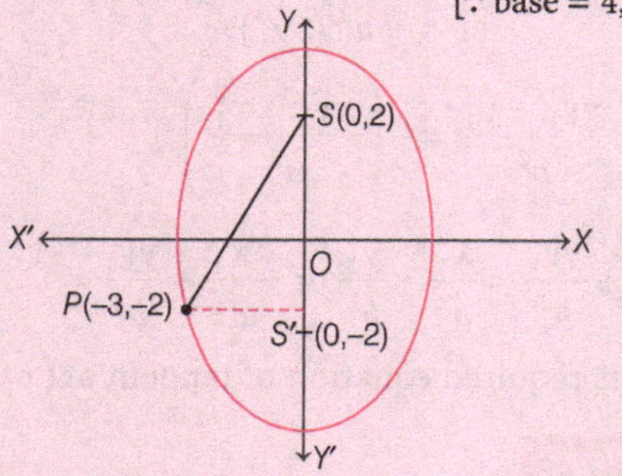

$\therefore$ $2A(1-e^2)=2\times 6\times\left(1-\frac{1}{4}\right)=2\times 6\times\frac{3}{4}=2\times\frac{9}{2}=9$

Skill Builder

For Sol.

On the ellipse $\frac{x^2}{16}+\frac{y^2}{25}=1$, let P be a point in the first quadrant such that the tangent at P to the ellipse is perpendicular to the line $4x-5y=0$. Let S and S′ be the foci of the ellipse and e be its eccentricity. If A is the area of the $\Delta SPS'$, then the value of $\frac{25\sqrt{2}}{96}(A(1-e^2))$ is equal to......

■ **For more practice** See Q.9 of Milestone Practice 6.2.

2. Parametric form

Theorem The equation of tangent to the ellipse $\frac{x^2}{a^2}+\frac{y^2}{b^2}=1$ at the point $(a\cos\phi, b\sin\phi)$ is

$$\frac{x}{a}\cos\phi+\frac{y}{b}\sin\phi=1$$

Proof The equation of tangent to the ellipse $\frac{x^2}{a^2}+\frac{y^2}{b^2}=1$ at the point (x_1, y_1) is $\frac{xx_1}{a^2}+\frac{yy_1}{b^2}=1$ [by point form]

Replacing x_1 by $a\cos\phi$ and y_1 by $b\sin\phi$, then we get

$$\frac{x}{a}\cos\phi+\frac{y}{b}\sin\phi=1$$

Remembering method $\because$ Equation of chord joining $(a\cos\theta, b\sin\theta)$ and $(a\cos\phi, b\sin\phi)$ is

$$\frac{x}{a}\cos\left(\frac{\theta+\phi}{2}\right)+\frac{y}{b}\sin\left(\frac{\theta+\phi}{2}\right)=\cos\left(\frac{\theta-\phi}{2}\right)$$

$$\Rightarrow \frac{x}{a}\left\{\frac{\cos\left(\frac{\theta+\phi}{2}\right)}{\cos\left(\frac{\theta-\phi}{2}\right)}\right\}+\frac{y}{b}\left\{\frac{\sin\left(\frac{\theta+\phi}{2}\right)}{\cos\left(\frac{\theta-\phi}{2}\right)}\right\}=1$$

or $$\frac{x}{a^2}\left\{\frac{a\cos\left(\frac{\theta+\phi}{2}\right)}{\cos\left(\frac{\theta-\phi}{2}\right)}\right\}+\frac{y}{b^2}\left\{\frac{b\sin\left(\frac{\theta+\phi}{2}\right)}{\cos\left(\frac{\theta-\phi}{2}\right)}\right\}=1$$

3. Slope form

Theorem The equations of tangents of slope m to ellipse $\frac{x^2}{a^2}+\frac{y^2}{b^2}=1$ are $y=mx\pm\sqrt{(a^2m^2+b^2)}$ and the coordinates of the points of contact are

$$\left(\mp\frac{a^2m}{\sqrt{(a^2m^2+b^2)}}, \pm\frac{b^2}{\sqrt{(a^2m^2+b^2)}}\right)$$

Proof Let $y=mx+c$ be a tangent to the ellipse

$$\frac{x^2}{a^2}+\frac{y^2}{b^2}=1.$$

Then, the equation $\frac{x^2}{a^2}+\frac{(mx+c)^2}{b^2}=1$

$$\Rightarrow x^2(a^2m^2+b^2)+2a^2mcx+a^2(c^2-b^2)=0 \quad \text{...(i)}$$

must have equal roots

$$4a^4m^2c^2-4(a^2m^2+b^2)a^2(c^2-b^2)=0$$

[$\because B^2-4AC=0$]

$$\Rightarrow \quad a^2m^2c^2 - (a^2m^2 + b^2)(c^2 - b^2) = 0$$

$$\Rightarrow \quad a^2m^2c^2 - a^2m^2c^2 + a^2b^2m^2 - b^2c^2 + b^4 = 0$$

$$\Rightarrow \quad a^2b^2m^2 - b^2c^2 + b^4 = 0$$

$$\Rightarrow \quad c^2 = a^2m^2 + b^2$$

$$\therefore \quad c = \pm\sqrt{(a^2m^2 + b^2)}$$

Substituting this value of c in $y = mx + c$, we get

$$y = mx \pm \sqrt{(a^2\,m^2 + b^2)}$$

As the required equations of tangent of ellipse in terms of slope, putting $c = \pm\sqrt{(a^2m^2 + b^2)}$ in (i), we get

$$x^2\,(a^2m^2 + b^2) \pm 2a^2m\sqrt{(a^2m^2 + b^2)}\;x + a^4m^2 = 0$$

$$\Rightarrow \quad (\sqrt{(a^2m^2 + b^2)}\;x \pm a^2m)^2 = 0 \Rightarrow x = \mp\frac{a^2m}{\sqrt{(a^2m^2 + b^2)}}$$

Substituting this value of x in $y = mx \pm \sqrt{a^2m^2 + b^2}$

we obtained $y = \pm\dfrac{b^2}{\sqrt{(a^2m^2 + b^2)}}$

Thus, the coordinates of the points of contact are

$$\left(\mp\frac{a^2m}{\sqrt{(a^2m^2 + b^2)}}, \pm\frac{b^2}{\sqrt{(a^2m^2 + b^2)}}\right)$$

JEE SPIKE

Point of intersection of tangent at θ and φ on the ellipse $\dfrac{x^2}{a^2} + \dfrac{y^2}{b^2} = 1$

is $\left(\dfrac{a\cos\left(\dfrac{\theta+\phi}{2}\right)}{\cos\left(\dfrac{\theta-\phi}{2}\right)}, \dfrac{b\sin\left(\dfrac{\theta+\phi}{2}\right)}{\cos\left(\dfrac{\theta-\phi}{2}\right)}\right)$.

Example 22. If the line $3x + 4y = \sqrt{7}$ touches the ellipse $3x^2 + 4y^2 = 1$, then find the point of contact.

Sol. Let the given line touches the ellipse at point $P(x_1, y_1)$.

The equation of tangent at P is

$$3xx_1 + 4yy_1 = 1 \qquad \text{...(i)}$$

On comparing Eq. (i) with the given equation of line $3x + 4y = \sqrt{7}$, we get

$$\frac{3x_1}{3} = \frac{4y_1}{4} = \frac{1}{\sqrt{7}}$$

$$\therefore \quad x_1 = y_1 = \frac{1}{\sqrt{7}}$$

Hence, point of contact (x_1, y_1) is $\left(\dfrac{1}{\sqrt{7}}, \dfrac{1}{\sqrt{7}}\right)$.

Example 23. Find the equation of the tangents to the ellipse $3x^2 + 4y^2 = 12$ which are perpendicular to the line $y + 2x = 4$.

Sol. Let m be the slope of the tangent. Since, the tangent is perpendicular to the line $y + 2x = 4$.

$$\therefore \quad m \times -2 = -1 \Rightarrow m = \frac{1}{2}$$

Since, $\quad 3x^2 + 4y^2 = 12$ or $\dfrac{x^2}{4} + \dfrac{y^2}{3} = 1$

On comparing this with $\dfrac{x^2}{a^2} + \dfrac{y^2}{b^2} = 1$

$$\therefore \quad a^2 = 4 \text{ and } b^2 = 3$$

So, the equations of the tangents are, we get

$$y = \frac{1}{2}x \pm \sqrt{4 \times \frac{1}{4} + 3}$$

$$\Rightarrow \quad y = \frac{1}{2}x \pm 2$$

or $\quad x - 2y \pm 4 = 0$

Example 24. Find the locus of the foot of the perpendicular drawn from centre upon any tangent to the ellipse $\dfrac{x^2}{a^2} + \dfrac{y^2}{b^2} = 1$.

Sol. Any tangent of $\dfrac{x^2}{a^2} + \dfrac{y^2}{b^2} = 1$ is

$$y = mx \pm \sqrt{(a^2m^2 + b^2)} \qquad \text{...(i)}$$

Equation of the line perpendicular to Eq. (i) and passing through (0, 0) is

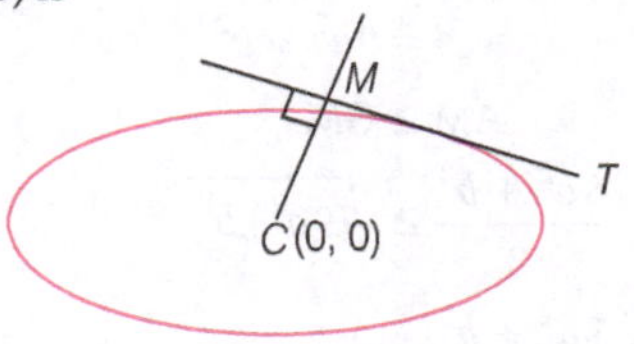

$$y = -\frac{1}{m}x \text{ or } m = -\frac{x}{y} \qquad \text{...(ii)}$$

Substituting the value of m from Eq. (ii) in Eq. (i), then

$$y = -\frac{x^2}{y} \pm \sqrt{\left(a^2\frac{x^2}{y^2} + b^2\right)}$$

$$\Rightarrow \quad (x^2 + y^2)^2 = a^2x^2 + b^2y^2$$

or changing to polars by putting $x = r\cos\theta$, $y = r\sin\theta$, it becomes

$$r^2 = a^2\cos^2\theta + b^2\sin^2\theta$$

Example 25. Find the point on the ellipse $16x^2 + 11y^2 = 256$, where the common tangent to it and the circle $x^2 + y^2 - 2x = 15$ touch.

Sol. The given ellipse is $\dfrac{x^2}{16}+\dfrac{y^2}{(256/11)}=1$

Equation of tangent to it at point $\left(4\cos\theta, \dfrac{16}{\sqrt{11}}\sin\theta\right)$ is

$$\frac{x}{4}\cos\theta + y\frac{\sqrt{11}}{16}\sin\theta = 1$$

It also touch the circle $(x-1)^2+(y-0)^2=4^2$.

Therefore, $$\frac{\left|\frac{1}{4}\cos\theta - 1\right|}{\sqrt{\left(\frac{\cos^2\theta}{16}+\frac{11}{256}\sin^2\theta\right)}} = 4$$

$\Rightarrow$ $$|\cos\theta - 4| = \sqrt{(16\cos^2\theta + 11\sin^2\theta)}$$

or $$4\cos^2\theta + 8\cos\theta - 5 = 0$$

or $$(2\cos\theta - 1)(2\cos\theta + 5) = 0$$

or $$\cos\theta = \frac{1}{2} \qquad \left[\because \cos\theta \neq -\frac{5}{2}\right]$$

$\therefore$ $$\theta = \frac{\pi}{3}, \frac{5\pi}{3}$$

Therefore, points are $\left(2, \pm\dfrac{8\sqrt{3}}{\sqrt{11}}\right)$.

Example 26. Find the maximum area of the ellipse $\dfrac{x^2}{a^2}+\dfrac{y^2}{b^2}=1$ which touches the line $y=3x+2$.

Sol. $\because$ Line $y=3x+2$ touches ellipse $\dfrac{x^2}{a^2}+\dfrac{y^2}{b^2}=1$

Here, $m=3$ and $c=2$

Substituting in $c^2=a^2m^2+b^2$, we get

$$4 = 9a^2 + b^2 \qquad \text{...(i)}$$

Now, AM $\geq$ GM

$\Rightarrow$ $$\frac{9a^2+b^2}{2} \geq \sqrt{(9a^2)b^2}$$

$\Rightarrow$ $$\frac{9a^2+b^2}{2} \geq 3ab \Rightarrow 2 \geq 3ab \qquad \text{[from Eq. (i)]}$$

or $$\frac{2\pi}{3} \geq \pi ab \text{ or } \frac{2\pi}{3} \geq \text{Area of ellipse}$$

Therefore, the maximum area of the ellipse is $\dfrac{2\pi}{3}$.

Example 27. A circle of radius r is concentric with the ellipse $\dfrac{x^2}{a^2}+\dfrac{y^2}{b^2}=1$. Prove that the common tangent is inclined to the major axis at an angle $\tan^{-1}\sqrt{\left(\dfrac{r^2-b^2}{a^2-r^2}\right)}$.

Sol. Equation of the circle of radius r and concentric with ellipse $\dfrac{x^2}{a^2}+\dfrac{y^2}{b^2}=1$ is

$$x^2+y^2=r^2 \qquad \text{...(i)}$$

Any tangent to ellipse $\dfrac{x^2}{a^2}+\dfrac{y^2}{b^2}=1$ is

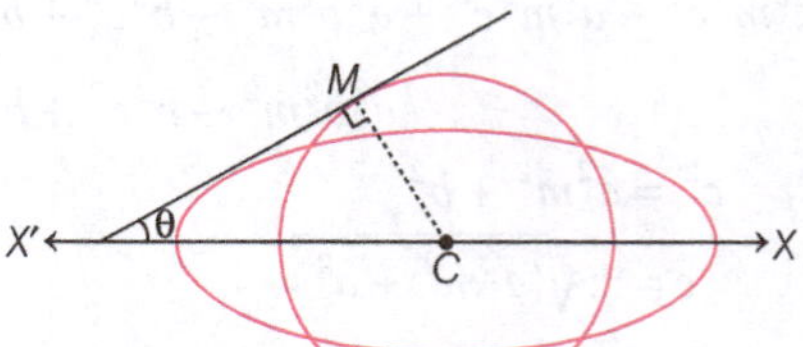

$$y = mx \pm \sqrt{(a^2m^2+b^2)} \qquad \text{[where, } m=\tan\theta]$$

If it is a tangent to circle, then perpendicular from (0, 0) is equal to radius r, then

$$\frac{\sqrt{(a^2m^2+b^2)}}{\sqrt{(m^2+1)}} = |r| \text{ or } a^2m^2+b^2 = m^2r^2+r^2$$

$$(a^2-r^2)m^2 = r^2-b^2$$

$\therefore$ $$m = \sqrt{\left(\frac{r^2-b^2}{a^2-r^2}\right)} \Rightarrow \tan\theta = \sqrt{\left(\frac{r^2-b^2}{a^2-r^2}\right)}$$

or $$\theta = \tan^{-1}\sqrt{\left(\frac{r^2-b^2}{a^2-r^2}\right)}$$

Example 28. Show that the product of the perpendiculars from the foci of any tangent to an ellipse is equal to the square of the semi-minor axis, and the feet of these perpendiculars lie on the auxiliary circle.

Sol. Let equation of ellipse be

$$\frac{x^2}{a^2}+\frac{y^2}{b^2}=1 \qquad \text{... (i)}$$

Equation of any tangent in term of slope (m) of Eq. (i) is

$$y = mx \pm \sqrt{(a^2m^2+b^2)}$$

or $$y - mx = \pm\sqrt{a^2m^2+b^2} \qquad \text{...(ii)}$$

Equation of a line perpendicular to Eq. (ii) and passing through $S(ae, 0)$ is

$$y - 0 = -\frac{1}{m}(x-ae)$$

or $$x + my = ae \qquad \text{...(iii)}$$

The lines Eqs. (ii) and (iii) will meet at the foot of perpendicular whose locus is obtained by eliminating the variable m between Eqs. (ii) and (iii), then squaring and adding Eqs. (ii) and (iii), we get

$$(y-mx)^2+(x+my)^2 = a^2m^2+b^2+a^2e^2$$

$\Rightarrow$ $$(1+m^2)(x^2+y^2) = a^2m^2+b^2+a^2-b^2$$

$\Rightarrow$ $$(1+m^2)(x^2+y^2) = a^2(1+m^2)$$

or $$x^2+y^2=a^2$$

which is auxiliary circle of ellipse. Similarly, we can show that the other foot drawn from second focus also lies on $x^2+y^2=a^2$.

Again, if p_1 and p_2 be perpendiculars from foci $S(ae, 0)$ and $S'(-ae, 0)$ on Eq. (ii), then

$$p_1 = \frac{|\sqrt{(a^2m^2 + b^2)} + mae|}{\sqrt{(1+m^2)}} \text{ and } p_2 = \frac{|\sqrt{(a^2m^2 + b^2)} - mae|}{\sqrt{(1+m^2)}}$$

$$\therefore \quad p_1p_2 = \frac{|a^2m^2 + b^2 - a^2e^2m^2|}{(1+m^2)}$$

$$= \frac{|a^2m^2 + b^2 - (a^2 - b^2)m^2|}{(1+m^2)}$$

$$= \frac{b^2(1+m^2)}{(1+m^2)} = b^2 = (\text{semi-minor axis})^2$$

JEE SCANNER

Example Similar to PYQ Asked in JEE Main 2022

If m is the slope of a common tangent to the curves $\frac{x^2}{9} + \frac{y^2}{16} = 1$, $x^2 + y^2 = 12$, then the value of m^2 is equal to

(a) 1/3 (b) 4/3 (c) 1 (d) 3/2

Sol. (b) Let the slope of common tangent be m. Then, equation of tangent to $x^2 + y^2 = 12$ is $y = mx \pm \sqrt{12 + 12m^2}$

Equation of tangent to ellipse $\frac{x^2}{9} + \frac{y^2}{16} = 1$ is

$$y = mx \pm \sqrt{9m^2 + 16}$$

Since, both equations are identical, then

$$mx \pm \sqrt{12 + 12m^2} = mx \pm \sqrt{9m^2 + 16}$$

$$\Rightarrow \quad 12 + 12m^2 = 9m^2 + 16 \Rightarrow 3m^2 = 4 \Rightarrow m^2 = \frac{4}{3}$$

Skill Builder

If m is the slope of a common tangent to the curves $\frac{x^2}{19} + \frac{y^2}{15} = 1$, $x^2 + y^2 = 16$, then the value of $3m^2$ is equal to

(a) 1 (b) 2

(c) 4 (d) 9

For Sol.

■ **For more practice** See Q.10 of Milestone Practice 6.2.

Example 29. Prove that the locus of mid-points of the portion of the tangents to the ellipse $\frac{x^2}{a^2} + \frac{y^2}{b^2} = 1$ intercepted between the axes is $a^2y^2 + b^2x^2 = 4x^2y^2$.

Sol. Let $P(x_1, y_1)$ be any point on the ellipse

$$\frac{x^2}{a^2} + \frac{y^2}{b^2} = 1 \qquad \text{...(i)}$$

$\therefore$ Equation of tangent at (x_1, y_1) to (i) is $\frac{xx_1}{a^2} + \frac{yy_1}{b^2} = 1$

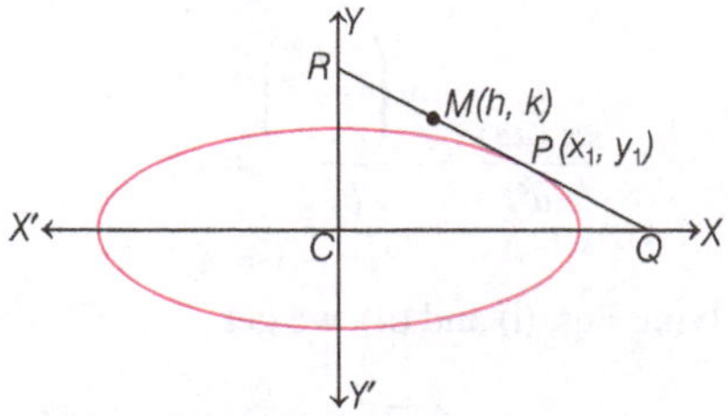

This meet the coordinate axes at

$$Q\left(\frac{a^2}{x_1}, 0\right) \text{ and } R\left(0, \frac{b^2}{y_1}\right)$$

Let $M(h, k)$ be the mid-point of QR, then

$$h = \frac{\frac{a^2}{x_1} + 0}{2} \text{ and } k = \frac{0 + \frac{b^2}{y_1}}{2}$$

$$\Rightarrow \quad x_1 = \frac{a^2}{2h} \text{ and } y_1 = \frac{b^2}{2k}$$

Since, (x_1, y_1) lies on Eq. (i)

$$\therefore \quad \frac{\left(\frac{a^2}{2h}\right)^2}{a^2} + \frac{\left(\frac{b^2}{2k}\right)^2}{b^2} = 1$$

$$\Rightarrow \quad \frac{a^2}{4h^2} + \frac{b^2}{4k^2} = 1$$

$$\Rightarrow \quad a^2k^2 + b^2h^2 = 4h^2k^2$$

Hence, the locus of $M(h, k)$ is $a^2y^2 + b^2x^2 = 4x^2y^2$

Example 30. Prove that the tangents at the extremities of latusrectum of an ellipse intersect on the corresponding directrix.

Sol. Let LSL' be a latusrectum of the ellipse $\frac{x^2}{a^2} + \frac{y^2}{b^2} = 1$.

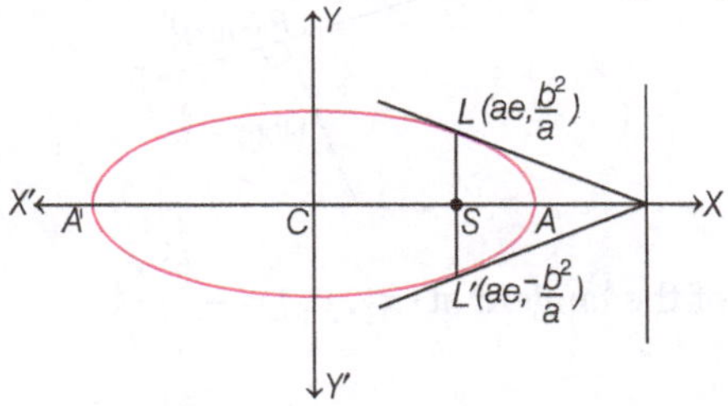

$\therefore$ The coordinates of L and L' are

$$\left(ae, \frac{b^2}{a}\right) \text{ and } \left(ae, -\frac{b^2}{a}\right) \text{ respectively.}$$

$\therefore$ Equation of tangent at $L\left(ae, \frac{b^2}{a}\right)$ is

$$\frac{x(ae)}{a^2} + \frac{y\left(\frac{b^2}{a}\right)}{b^2} = 1 \Rightarrow xe + y = a \qquad \text{...(i)}$$

The equation of the tangent at $L'\left(ae, -\dfrac{b^2}{a}\right)$ is

$$\frac{x(ae)}{a^2} + \frac{y\left(-\dfrac{b^2}{a}\right)}{b^2} = 1$$

$$\Rightarrow \qquad ex - y = a \qquad \text{...(ii)}$$

On solving Eqs. (i) and (ii), we get

$$x = \frac{a}{e}$$

and $$y = 0$$

Thus, the tangents at L and L' intersect at $(a/e, 0)$ which is a point lying on the corresponding directrix i.e. $x = \dfrac{a}{e}$.

6.9 Equations of Normals in Different Forms

1. Point form

Theorem The equation of normal at (x_1, y_1) to the ellipse $\dfrac{x^2}{a^2} + \dfrac{y^2}{b^2} = 1$ is

$$\frac{a^2x}{x_1} - \frac{b^2y}{y_1} = a^2 - b^2$$

Proof Since the equation of tangent to the ellipse $\dfrac{x^2}{a^2} + \dfrac{y^2}{b^2} = 1$ at (x_1, y_1) is

$$\frac{xx_1}{a^2} + \frac{yy_1}{b^2} = 1$$

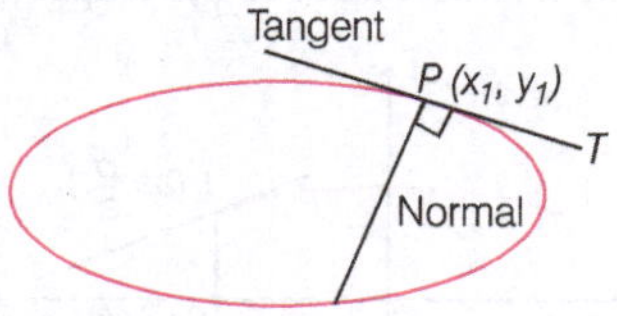

The slope of the tangent at $(x_1, y_1) = -\dfrac{b^2x_1}{a^2y_1}$

$\therefore$ Slope of normals at $(x_1, y_1) = \dfrac{a^2y_1}{b^2x_1}$

Hence, the equation of normal at (x_1, y_1) is

$$y - y_1 = \frac{a^2y_1}{b^2x_1}(x - x_1)$$

or $$\frac{a^2x}{x_1} - \frac{b^2y}{y_1} = a^2 - b^2$$

2. Parametric form

Theorem The equation of normal to the ellipse $\dfrac{x^2}{a^2} + \dfrac{y^2}{b^2} = 1$ at $(a\cos\phi, b\sin\phi)$ is

$$ax\sec\phi - by\operatorname{cosec}\phi = a^2 - b^2$$

Proof Since, the equation of normal of the ellipse $\dfrac{x^2}{a^2} + \dfrac{y^2}{b^2} = 1$ at (x_1, y_1) is

$$\frac{a^2x}{x_1} - \frac{b^2y}{y_1} = a^2 - b^2 \qquad \text{...(i)}$$

Replacing x_1 by $a\cos\phi$ and y_1 by $b\sin\phi$, then Eq.(i) becomes

$$\frac{a^2x}{a\cos\phi} - \frac{b^2y}{b\sin\phi} = a^2 - b^2$$

$$ax\sec\phi - by\operatorname{cosec}\phi = a^2 - b^2$$

is the equation of normal at $(a\cos\phi, b\sin\phi)$.

3. Slope form

Theorem The equation of the normals of slope m to the ellipse $\dfrac{x^2}{a^2} + \dfrac{y^2}{b^2} = 1$ are given by

$$y = mx \mp \frac{m(a^2 - b^2)}{\sqrt{(a^2 + b^2m^2)}}$$

at the points $\left(\pm\dfrac{a^2}{\sqrt{(a^2 + b^2m^2)}}, \pm\dfrac{mb^2}{\sqrt{(a^2 + b^2m^2)}}\right)$.

Proof The equation of normal to the ellipse $\dfrac{x^2}{a^2} + \dfrac{y^2}{b^2} = 1$ at (x_1, y_1) is

$$\frac{a^2x}{x_1} - \frac{b^2y}{y_1} = a^2 - b^2 \qquad \text{...(i)}$$

Since, m is the slope of the normal, then

$$m = \frac{a^2y_1}{b^2x_1}$$

$$y_1 = \frac{b^2x_1m}{a^2} \qquad \text{...(ii)}$$

Since, (x_1, y_1) lies on $\dfrac{x^2}{a^2} + \dfrac{y^2}{b^2} = 1$

$$\therefore \qquad \frac{x_1^2}{a^2} + \frac{y_1^2}{b^2} = 1$$

or $$\frac{x_1^2}{a^2} + \frac{b^4x_1^2m^2}{a^4b^2} = 1 \text{ or } \frac{x_1^2}{a^2} + \frac{b^2x_1^2m^2}{a^4} = 1$$

or $$x_1^2 = \frac{a^4}{(a^2 + b^2m^2)}$$

$$\therefore \quad x_1 = \pm \frac{a^2}{\sqrt{a^2 + b^2m^2}}$$

From Eq. (ii), $$y_1 = \pm \frac{mb^2}{\sqrt{(a^2 + b^2m^2)}}$$

$\therefore$ Equation of normal in terms of slope is

$$y - \left(\pm \frac{mb^2}{\sqrt{a^2 + b^2m^2}}\right) = m\left(x - \left(\pm \frac{a^2}{\sqrt{a^2 + b^2m^2}}\right)\right)$$

$$\Rightarrow \quad y = mx \mp \frac{m(a^2 - b^2)}{\sqrt{(a^2 + b^2m^2)}} \quad \text{...(iii)}$$

Thus, $y = mx \mp \frac{m(a^2 - b^2)}{\sqrt{(a^2 + b^2m^2)}}$ is a normal to the ellipse $\frac{x^2}{a^2} + \frac{y^2}{b^2} = 1$, where m is the slope of the normal.

The coordinates of the point of contact are

$$\left(\pm \frac{a^2}{\sqrt{a^2 + b^2m^2}}, \pm \frac{mb^2}{\sqrt{a^2 + b^2m^2}}\right)$$

Comparing Eq. (iii) with $y = mx + c$

$$\therefore \quad c = \mp \frac{m(a^2 - b^2)}{\sqrt{(a^2 + b^2m^2)}} \text{ or } c^2 = \frac{m^2(a^2 - b^2)^2}{(a^2 + b^2m^2)}$$

which is condition of normality, when $y = mx + c$ is the normal of $\frac{x^2}{a^2} + \frac{y^2}{b^2} = 1$.

JEE SPIKE

Point of intersection of normals at θ and ϕ on the ellipse $\frac{x^2}{a^2} + \frac{y^2}{b^2} = 1$ is

$$\left(\frac{a^2 - b^2}{a}\cos\theta\cos\phi\frac{\cos\left(\frac{\theta+\phi}{2}\right)}{\cos\left(\frac{\theta-\phi}{2}\right)}, -\frac{(a^2 - b^2)}{b}\sin\theta\sin\phi\frac{\sin\left(\frac{\theta+\phi}{2}\right)}{\cos\left(\frac{\theta-\phi}{2}\right)}\right).$$

Example 31. If the normal at an end of a latusrectum of an ellipse $\frac{x^2}{a^2} + \frac{y^2}{b^2} = 1$ passes through one extremity of the minor axis, show that the eccentricity of the ellipse is given by $e^4 + e^2 - 1 = 0$ or $e^2 = \frac{\sqrt{5} - 1}{2}$.

Sol. The coordinates of an end of the latusrectum are $(ae, b^2/a)$.

The equation of normal at $P(ae, b^2/a)$ is

$$\frac{a^2x}{ae} - \frac{b^2(y)}{b^2/a} = a^2 - b^2 \text{ or } \frac{ax}{e} - ay = a^2 - b^2$$

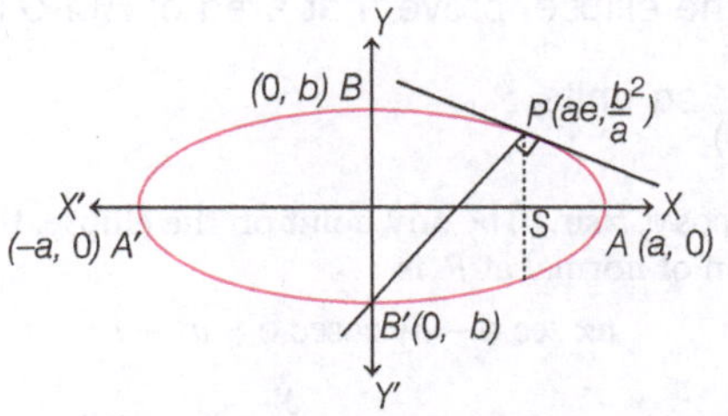

It passes through one extremity of the minor axis whose coordinates are $(0, -b)$

$$\therefore \quad 0 + ab = a^2 - b^2$$

or $$(a^2b^2) = (a^2 - b^2)^2$$

or $$a^2a^2(1 - e^2) = (a^2e^2)^2 \text{ or } 1 - e^2 = e^4$$

or $$e^4 + e^2 - 1 = 0$$

or $$(e^2)^2 + e^2 - 1 = 0$$

$$\therefore \quad e^2 = \frac{-1 \pm \sqrt{1+4}}{2} \Rightarrow e^2 = \frac{\sqrt{5} - 1}{2} \quad \text{[taking +ve sign]}$$

Example 32. Prove that the straight line $lx + my + n = 0$ is a normal to the ellipse $\frac{x^2}{a^2} + \frac{y^2}{b^2} = 1$ if $\frac{a^2}{l^2} + \frac{b^2}{m^2} = \frac{(a^2 - b^2)^2}{n^2}$.

Sol. The equation of any normal to $\frac{x^2}{a^2} + \frac{y^2}{b^2} = 1$ is

$$ax\sec\phi - by\operatorname{cosec}\phi = a^2 - b^2 \quad \text{... (i)}$$

The straight line $lx + my + n = 0$ will be a normal to the ellipse $\frac{x^2}{a^2} + \frac{y^2}{b^2} = 1$

Therefore, Eq. (i) and $lx + my + n = 0$ represent the same line

$$\frac{a\sec\phi}{l} = \frac{-b\operatorname{cosec}\phi}{m} = \frac{a^2 - b^2}{-n}$$

$$\Rightarrow \quad \cos\phi = \frac{-na}{l(a^2 - b^2)}$$

and $$\sin\phi = \frac{nb}{m(a^2 - b^2)}$$

$$\because \quad \sin^2\phi + \cos^2\phi = 1$$

$$\therefore \quad \frac{n^2b^2}{m^2(a^2 - b^2)^2} + \frac{n^2a^2}{l^2(a^2 - b^2)^2} = 1$$

$$\Rightarrow \quad \frac{a^2}{l^2} + \frac{b^2}{m^2} = \frac{(a^2 - b^2)^2}{n^2}$$

Example 33. A normal inclined at an angle of 45° to X-axis of the ellipse $\frac{x^2}{a^2}+\frac{y^2}{b^2}=1$ is drawn. It meets the major and minor axes in P and Q respectively. If C is the centre of the ellipse, prove that area of ΔCPQ is $\frac{(a^2-b^2)^2}{2(a^2+b^2)}$ sq units.

Sol. Let $R(a\cos\phi, b\sin\phi)$ be any point on the ellipse, then equation of normal at R is

$$ax\sec\phi - by\,\text{cosec}\,\phi = a^2-b^2$$

or $$\frac{x}{\frac{\cos\phi\,(a^2-b^2)}{a}}+\frac{y}{\frac{-\sin\phi\,(a^2-b^2)}{b}}=1$$

It meets the major and minor axes at $P\left(\left(\frac{(a^2-b^2)}{a}\right)\cos\phi, 0\right)$ and $Q\left(0, -\frac{(a^2-b^2)}{b}\sin\phi\right)$ respectively.

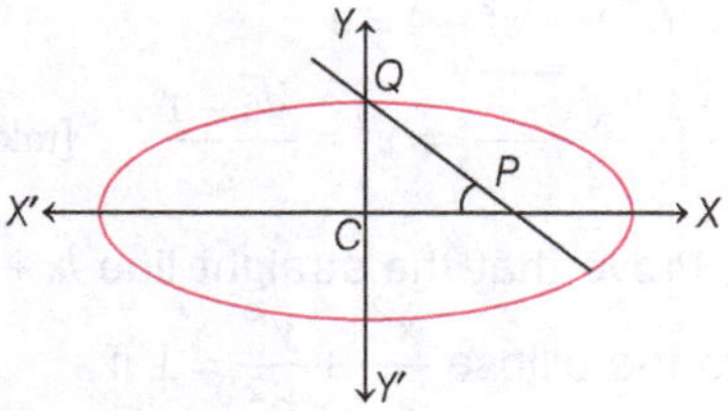

$\therefore\quad CP=\left(\frac{a^2-b^2}{a}\right)|\cos\phi|$ and $CQ=\left(\frac{a^2-b^2}{b}\right)|\sin\phi|$

$\therefore\quad$ Area of $\Delta CPQ=\frac{1}{2}\times CP\times CQ$

$$=\frac{(a^2-b^2)^2\,|\sin\phi\cos\phi|}{2ab}\qquad ...(i)$$

But slope of normal $=\frac{a}{b}\tan\phi=\tan 45°$ [given]

$\Rightarrow\quad \frac{a}{b}\tan\phi=1$

$\Rightarrow\quad \tan\phi=\frac{b}{a}$

$\therefore\quad \sin 2\phi=\frac{2\tan\phi}{1+\tan^2\phi}=\frac{2ab}{a^2+b^2}$

$\therefore$ From Eq. (i), area of $\Delta CPQ=\frac{(a^2-b^2)^2\left|\frac{\sin 2\phi}{2}\right|}{2ab}$

$$=\frac{(a^2-b^2)^2\,\frac{ab}{(a^2+b^2)}}{2ab}$$

$$=\frac{(a^2-b^2)^2}{2(a^2+b^2)}\text{ sq units}$$

JEE SCANNER

Example Similar to PYQ Asked in JEE Main 2023

Let C be the largest circle centered at $(6,0)$ and inscribed in the ellipse $\frac{x^2}{100}+\frac{y^2}{25}=1$. If $(7,\alpha)$ lies on C, then α^2 is equal to ....

Sol. (12) Equation of normal to ellipse $\frac{x^2}{100}+\frac{y^2}{25}=1$ at any point $P(10\cos\theta, 5\sin\theta)$ is $10\sec\theta x-5\,\text{cosec}\theta y=75$

This normal is also the normal of the circle passing through the point $(6,0)$.

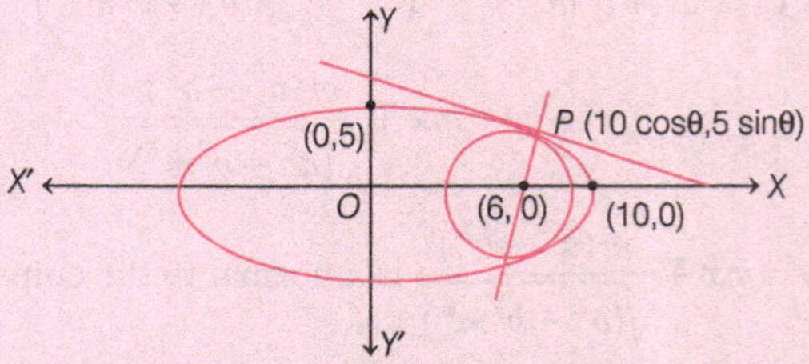

So, $60\sec\theta=75$ or $\sin\theta=0$ (not possible)

$$\cos\theta=\frac{4}{5}\text{ and }\sin\theta=\frac{3}{5}$$

$\therefore$ Point $P\equiv\left(\frac{40}{5},\frac{15}{5}\right)\equiv(8,3)$

The largest radius of circle

$$r=\sqrt{(8-6)^2+(3-0)^2}=\sqrt{4+9}=\sqrt{13}$$

So, the equation of circle is $(x-6)^2+y^2=13$ passing it through $(7,\alpha)$, then $1+\alpha^2=13$

Hence, $\alpha^2=12$

Skill Builder

Let C be the largest circle centered at $\left(\frac{9}{2},0\right)$ and inscribed in the ellipse $\frac{x^2}{100}+\frac{y^2}{25}=1$. If $(6,\alpha)$ lies on C, then $2\alpha^2$ is equal to ....

For Sol.

- **For more practice** See Q.13 of milestone practice 6.2.

Example 34. Any ordinate MP of an ellipse meets the auxiliary circle in Q. Prove that the locus of the point of intersection of the normals at P and Q is the circle $x^2+y^2=(a+b)^2$.

Sol. Let equation of ellipse be $\frac{x^2}{a^2}+\frac{y^2}{b^2}=1$ and its auxiliary circle be $x^2+y^2=a^2$.

Coordinates of P and Q are $(a\cos\phi, b\sin\phi)$ and $(a\cos\phi, a\sin\phi)$ respectively.

Equation of normal at P to the ellipse $\dfrac{x^2}{a^2}+\dfrac{y^2}{b^2}=1$ is

$$ax\sec\phi - by\,\text{cosec}\,\phi = a^2 - b^2 \quad \text{...(i)}$$

and equation of normal at Q to the circle $x^2+y^2=a^2$ is

$$y = x\tan\phi \quad \text{...(ii)}$$

From Eq. (ii), $\tan\phi = \dfrac{y}{x}$

$$\therefore \quad \sin\phi = \frac{y}{\sqrt{(x^2+y^2)}} \quad \text{and} \quad \cos\phi = \frac{x}{\sqrt{(x^2+y^2)}}$$

$$\text{or} \quad \text{cosec}\,\phi = \frac{\sqrt{(x^2+y^2)}}{y} \quad \text{and} \quad \sec\phi = \frac{\sqrt{(x^2+y^2)}}{x} \quad \text{...(iii)}$$

Substituting the values of $\sec\phi$ and $\text{cosec}\,\phi$ from Eq. (iii) in Eq. (i), we get

$$ax \times \frac{\sqrt{(x^2+y^2)}}{x} - by \times \frac{\sqrt{(x^2+y^2)}}{y} = a^2 - b^2$$

$$\text{or} \quad (a-b)\sqrt{(x^2+y^2)} = (a+b)(a-b)$$

$$\text{or} \quad \sqrt{x^2+y^2} = a+b$$

$$\therefore \quad x^2+y^2 = (a+b)^2$$

which is required locus.

6.10 Co-normal Points Lie on a Fixed Curve

Let $P(x_1, y_1)$, $Q(x_2, y_2)$, $R(x_3, y_3)$ and $S(x_4, y_4)$ be conormal points so that normal drawn from them meet in $T(h, k)$. Then, equation of normal at $P(x_1, y_1)$ is

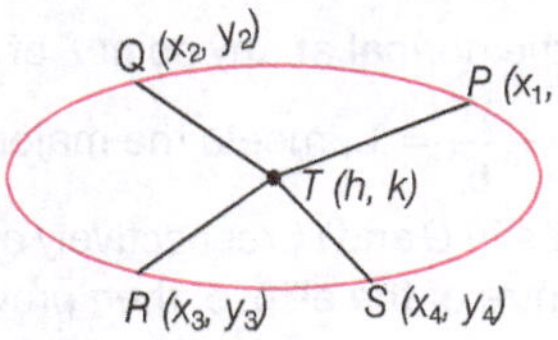

$$\frac{a^2x}{x_1} - \frac{b^2y}{y_1} = a^2 - b^2$$

$$\text{or} \quad (a^2-b^2)x_1y_1 + b^2yx_1 - a^2xy_1 = 0$$

but the point $T(h, k)$ lies on it

$$\therefore \quad (a^2-b^2)x_1y_1 + b^2kx_1 - a^2hy_1 = 0$$

Similarly, for points Q, R and S are

$$(a^2-b^2)x_2y_2 + b^2kx_2 - a^2hy_2 = 0$$

$$(a^2-b^2)x_3y_3 + b^2kx_3 - a^2hy_3 = 0$$

$$\text{and} \quad (a^2-b^2)x_4y_4 + b^2kx_4 - a^2hy_4 = 0$$

Hence, P, Q, R, S all lie on the curve

$$(a^2-b^2)xy + b^2kx - a^2hy = 0$$

This curve is called **Apollonian rectangular hyperbola.**

JEE Focus Points

- The feet of the normals from any fixed point to the ellipse lie at the intersections of the Apollonian rectangular hyperbola with the ellipse.
- Four normals can be drawn to an ellipse from any point and if $\alpha, \beta, \gamma, \delta$ are the eccentric angles of these four co-normal points, then $\alpha+\beta+\gamma+\delta$ is an odd multiple of π.
- If α, β, γ are the eccentric angles of three points on the ellipse $\dfrac{x^2}{a^2}+\dfrac{y^2}{b^2}=1$, the normals at which are concurrent, then $\sin(\alpha+\beta)+\sin(\beta+\gamma)+\sin(\gamma+\alpha)=0$

Concept Inside Video

Example 35. If the normals at $P(x_1, y_1)$, $Q(x_2, y_2)$ and $R(x_3, y_3)$ on the ellipse $\dfrac{x^2}{a^2}+\dfrac{y^2}{b^2}=1$ are concurrent, then show that $\begin{vmatrix} x_1 & y_1 & x_1y_1 \\ x_2 & y_2 & x_2y_2 \\ x_3 & y_3 & x_3y_3 \end{vmatrix}=0$ and if point $P(\alpha)$, $Q(\beta)$ and $R(\gamma)$, prove that $\begin{vmatrix} \sec\alpha & \text{cosec}\,\alpha & 1 \\ \sec\beta & \text{cosec}\,\beta & 1 \\ \sec\gamma & \text{cosec}\,\gamma & 1 \end{vmatrix}=0$

Sol. The equation of the normal to the ellipse $\dfrac{x^2}{a^2}+\dfrac{y^2}{b^2}=1$ at $P(x_1, y_1)$, $Q(x_2, y_2)$ and $R(x_3, y_3)$ are

$$\frac{a^2x}{x_1} - \frac{b^2y}{y_1} = a^2 - b^2 \quad \text{...(i)}$$

$$\frac{a^2x}{x_2} - \frac{b^2y}{y_2} = a^2 - b^2 \quad \text{...(ii)}$$

$$\text{and} \quad \frac{a^2x}{x_3} - \frac{b^2y}{y_3} = a^2 - b^2 \quad \text{...(iii)}$$

Eliminating x and y from Eqs. (i), (ii) and (iii), we get

$$\begin{vmatrix} \dfrac{a^2}{x_1} & \dfrac{-b^2}{y_1} & (a^2-b^2) \\ \dfrac{a^2}{x_2} & \dfrac{-b^2}{y_2} & (a^2-b^2) \\ \dfrac{a^2}{x_3} & \dfrac{-b^2}{y_3} & (a^2-b^2) \end{vmatrix} = 0$$

$$\Rightarrow \begin{vmatrix} \dfrac{1}{x_1} & \dfrac{1}{y_1} & 1 \\ \dfrac{1}{x_2} & \dfrac{1}{y_2} & 1 \\ \dfrac{1}{x_3} & \dfrac{1}{y_3} & 1 \end{vmatrix} = 0 \Rightarrow \begin{vmatrix} x_1 & y_1 & x_1y_1 \\ x_2 & y_2 & x_2y_2 \\ x_3 & y_3 & x_3y_3 \end{vmatrix} = 0$$

$$\text{Also,} \quad \begin{vmatrix} a\cos\alpha & b\sin\alpha & ab\cos\alpha\sin\alpha \\ a\cos\beta & b\sin\beta & ab\cos\beta\sin\beta \\ a\cos\gamma & b\sin\gamma & ab\cos\gamma\sin\gamma \end{vmatrix} = 0$$

$$\Rightarrow \begin{vmatrix} \text{cosec}\,\alpha & \sec\alpha & 1 \\ \text{cosec}\,\beta & \sec\beta & 1 \\ \text{cosec}\,\gamma & \sec\gamma & 1 \end{vmatrix} = 0 \Rightarrow \begin{vmatrix} \sec\alpha & \text{cosec}\,\alpha & 1 \\ \sec\beta & \text{cosec}\,\beta & 1 \\ \sec\gamma & \text{cosec}\,\gamma & 1 \end{vmatrix} = 0$$

Hence proved.

Milestone Practice 6.2

1. The number of values of c such that the straight line $y = 4x + c$ touches the curve $\frac{x^2}{4} + y^2 = 1$, is
   (a) 0 (b) 1 (c) 2 (d) infinite

2. If any tangent to the ellipse $\frac{x^2}{a^2} + \frac{y^2}{b^2} = 1$ cuts off intercepts of length h and k on the axes, then $\frac{a^2}{h^2} + \frac{b^2}{k^2}$ is equal to
   (a) -1 (b) 0 (c) 1 (d) None of these

3. The equations of the tangents to the ellipse $3x^2 + y^2 = 3$ making equal intercepts on the axes are
   (a) $x + y = \pm 2$ (b) $x + y = \pm 4$
   (c) $y = \pm x \pm \sqrt{30}$ (d) $y = \pm x \pm \sqrt{35}$

4. If $\frac{x}{a} + \frac{y}{b} = \sqrt{2}$ touches the ellipse $\frac{x^2}{a^2} + \frac{y^2}{b^2} = 1$, then its eccentric angle θ is equal to
   (a) 0 (b) 45° (c) 60° (d) 90°

5. The number of values of $\theta \in [0, 2\pi]$ for which the line $2x\cos\theta + 3y\sin\theta = 6$ touches the ellipse $4x^2 + 9y^2 = 36$ is
   (a) 1 (b) 2 (c) 4 (d) infinite

6. The common tangent of $x^2 + y^2 = 4$ and $2x^2 + y^2 = 2$ is
   (a) $x + y + 4 = 0$ (b) $x - y + 7 = 0$
   (c) $2x + 3y + 8 = 0$ (d) None of these

7. If the normal at any point P on the ellipse $\frac{x^2}{a^2} + \frac{y^2}{b^2} = 1$ meets the axes at G and g respectively, then $PG : Pg$ is equal to
   (a) $a : b$ (b) $a^2 : b^2$ (c) $b : a$ (d) $b^2 : a^2$

8. Number of distinct normal lines that can be drawn to the ellipse $\frac{x^2}{169} + \frac{y^2}{25} = 1$, from the point $(0, 6)$ is
   (a) one (b) two (c) three (d) four

9. On the ellipse $\frac{x^2}{16} + \frac{y^2}{12} = 1$. Let P be a point in the second quadrant such that the tangent at P to the ellipse is parallel to the line $4x - 5y + 15 = 0$. Let S and S' be the foci of the ellipse with eccentricity e. If A is area of $\Delta SPS'$, find $A(1 + e^2)$.

10. Let m be the slope of common tangent to the curves $4x^2 + 9y^2 = 36$ and $(2x)^2 + (2y)^2 = 31$, then find m^2.

11. An ellipse passes through the point $(4, -1)$ and touches the line $x + 4y - 10 = 0$. Find its equation if its axes coincide with coordinate axes.

12. If a tangent of slope 2 of the ellipse $\frac{x^2}{a^2} + \frac{y^2}{b^2} = 1$, is normal to the circle $x^2 + y^2 + 4x + 1 = 0$, then find the maximum value of ab.

13. Let C be the largest circle centred at $\left(\frac{8}{3}, 0\right)$ and inscribed in the ellipse $\frac{x^2}{36} + \frac{y^2}{16} = 1$. If $(3, \alpha)$ lies on C, then find the value of $45\alpha^2$.

14. The line $5x - 3y = 8\sqrt{2}$ is a normal to the ellipse $\frac{x^2}{25} + \frac{y^2}{9} = 1$. If θ be eccentric angle of the foot of this normal, then find the value of θ.

15. If the tangent drawn at point $(\lambda^2, 2\lambda)$ on the parabola $y^2 = 4x$ is same as the normal drawn at a point $(\sqrt{5}\cos\theta, 2\sin\theta)$ on the ellipse $4x^2 + 5y^2 = 20$. Find the values of λ and θ.

16. If the normal at any point P of the ellipse $\frac{x^2}{a^2} + \frac{y^2}{b^2} = 1$, meets the major and minor axes in G and H, respectively and C in the centre of the ellipse, then prove that
$$a^2(CG)^2 + b^2(CH)^2 = (a^2 - b^2)^2$$

17. The tangent and normal at any point P of an ellipse $\frac{x^2}{a^2} + \frac{y^2}{b^2} = 1$ cut its major axis in points Q and R respectively. If $QR = a$, prove that the eccentric angle of the point P is given by $e^2\cos^2\phi + \cos\phi - 1 = 0$.

Answer Key

1. (c)	2. (c)	3. (a)	4. (b)	5. (d)	6. (d)
7. (d)	8. (c)	9. $\frac{75}{\sqrt{139}}$	10. (3)	11. $\frac{x^2}{20} + \frac{y^2}{5} = 1$	
12. 4	13. 459	14. $\frac{\pi}{4}$	15. $\theta = \cos^{-1}\left(-\frac{1}{\sqrt{5}}\right)$ and $\lambda = \pm\frac{1}{\sqrt{5}}$		

For Detailed Solution

Milestone 3 Pair of Tangents

• Combined Equation of Pair of Tangents • Chord of Contact • Diameter • Conjugate Diameters
• Director Circle • Concyclic Points • Reflection Property of an Ellipse

6.11 Combined Equation of pair of Tangents

Theorem The combined equation of the pair of tangents drawn from a point (x_1, y_1) to the ellipse $\frac{x^2}{a^2}+\frac{y^2}{b^2}=1$ is

$$\left(\frac{x^2}{a^2}+\frac{y^2}{b^2}-1\right)\left(\frac{x_1^2}{a^2}+\frac{y_1^2}{b^2}-1\right)=\left(\frac{xx_1}{a^2}+\frac{yy_1}{b^2}-1\right)^2$$

or $$SS_1 = T^2$$

where $$S=\frac{x^2}{a^2}+\frac{y^2}{b^2}-1;$$

$$S_1=\frac{x_1^2}{a^2}+\frac{y_1^2}{b^2}-1$$

and $$T=\frac{xx_1}{a^2}+\frac{yy_1}{b^2}-1$$

Proof Let $T(h, k)$ be any point on the pair of tangents PQ or PR drawn from any external point $P(x_1, y_1)$ to the ellipse $\frac{x^2}{a^2}+\frac{y^2}{b^2}=1$

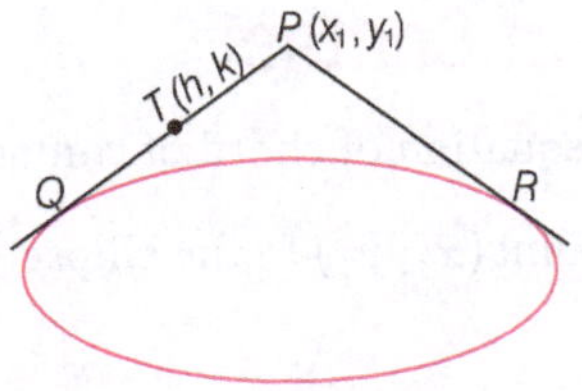

∴ Equation of PT is

$$y-y_1=\frac{k-y_1}{h-x_1}(x-x_1)$$

or $$y=\left(\frac{k-y_1}{h-x_1}\right)x+\left(\frac{hy_1-kx_1}{h-x_1}\right)$$

which is the tangent to the ellipse

$$\frac{x^2}{a^2}+\frac{y^2}{b^2}=1$$

$$\therefore \quad c^2=a^2m^2+b^2$$

or $$\left(\frac{hy_1-kx_1}{h-x_1}\right)^2=a^2\left(\frac{k-y_1}{h-x_1}\right)^2+b^2$$

$$\Rightarrow \quad (hy_1-kx_1)^2=a^2(k-y_1)^2+b^2(h-x_1)^2$$

Hence, locus of (h, k) is

$$(xy_1-x_1y)^2=a^2(y-y_1)^2+b^2(x-x_1)^2$$

or $$(xy_1-x_1y)^2=(b^2x^2+a^2y^2)+(b^2x_1^2+a^2y_1^2)-2(b^2xx_1+a^2yy_1)$$

or $$\left(\frac{xy_1-x_1y}{ab}\right)^2=\left(\frac{x^2}{a^2}+\frac{y^2}{b^2}\right)+\left(\frac{x_1^2}{a^2}+\frac{y_1^2}{b^2}\right)-2\left(\frac{xx_1}{a^2}+\frac{yy_1}{b^2}\right)$$

or $$\left(\frac{xy_1-x_1y}{ab}\right)^2-\left(\frac{x^2}{a^2}+\frac{y^2}{b^2}\right)-\left(\frac{x_1^2}{a^2}+\frac{y_1^2}{b^2}\right)+\left(\frac{xx_1}{a^2}+\frac{yy_1}{b^2}\right)^2+1$$

$$=\left(\frac{xx_1}{a^2}+\frac{yy_1}{b^2}\right)^2+1-2\left(\frac{xx_1}{a^2}+\frac{yy_1}{b^2}\right)$$

or $$\left(\frac{x^2}{a^2}+\frac{y^2}{b^2}-1\right)\left(\frac{x_1^2}{a^2}+\frac{y_1^2}{b^2}-1\right)=\left(\frac{xx_1}{a^2}+\frac{yy_1}{b^2}-1\right)^2$$

or $$SS_1=T^2$$

Alternate proof Let the ellipse be

$$\frac{x^2}{a^2}+\frac{y^2}{b^2}=1 \quad \text{...(i)}$$

Let $P(x_1, y_1)$ be any point outside the ellipse, let a chord of the ellipse through the point $P(x_1, y_1)$ cut the ellipse at Q and let $R(h, k)$ be any arbitrary point on the line PQ (R inside or outside). Let Q divides PR in the ratio $\lambda : 1$ then coordinates of Q is

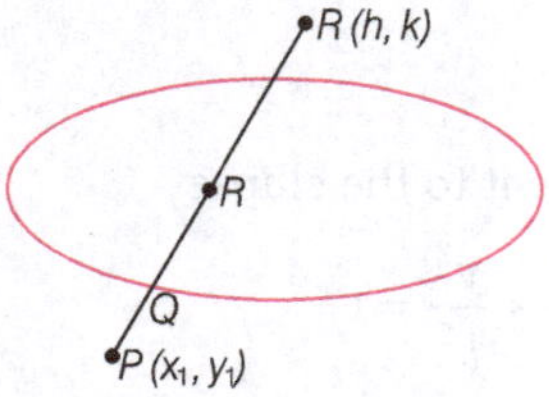

$$\left(\frac{\lambda h+x_1}{\lambda+1}, \frac{\lambda k+y_1}{\lambda+1}\right) \quad [\because PQ : QR = \lambda : 1]$$

Since, Q lies on ellipse Eq. (i), then

$$\frac{1}{a^2}\left(\frac{\lambda h+x_1}{\lambda+1}\right)^2+\frac{1}{b^2}\left(\frac{\lambda k+y_1}{\lambda+1}\right)^2=1$$

$$\Rightarrow \quad b^2(\lambda h+x_1)^2+a^2(\lambda k+y_1)^2=a^2b^2(\lambda+1)^2$$

$$\Rightarrow \quad (a^2k^2+b^2h^2-a^2b^2)\lambda^2+2(hx_1b^2+ky_1a^2-a^2b^2)\lambda+(b^2x_1^2+a^2y_1^2-a^2b^2)=0 \quad \text{...(ii)}$$

Line PR will become tangent to ellipse Eq. (i), then roots of Eq. (ii) are equal

$$\therefore \quad 4(hx_1b^2+ky_1a^2-a^2b^2)^2-4(a^2k^2+b^2h^2-a^2b^2)(b^2x_1^2+a^2y_1^2-a^2b^2)=0$$

Dividing by $4a^4b^4$, we get

$$\therefore \quad \left(\frac{hx_1}{a^2}+\frac{ky_1}{b^2}-1\right)^2=\left(\frac{k^2}{b^2}+\frac{h^2}{a^2}-1\right)\left(\frac{x_1^2}{a^2}+\frac{y_1^2}{b^2}-1\right)$$

Hence, locus of $R(h, k)$ i.e. equation of pair of tangents from $P(x_1, y_1)$ is

$$\left(\frac{xx_1}{a^2}+\frac{yy_1}{b^2}-1\right)^2=\left(\frac{x^2}{a^2}+\frac{y^2}{b^2}-1\right)\left(\frac{x_1^2}{a^2}+\frac{y_1^2}{b^2}-1\right)$$

i.e. $\quad T^2 = SS_1$

or $\quad SS_1 = T^2$

JEE SCANNER

Example Similar to PYQ Asked in JEE Main 2023

The angle between the pair of tangents drawn from the point (1, 2) to the ellipse $3x^2+2y^2=5$ is

(a) $\tan^{-1}\left(\frac{\sqrt{5}}{12}\right)$ (b) $\tan^{-1}\left(\frac{6}{\sqrt{5}}\right)$

(c) $\tan^{-1}\left(\frac{12}{\sqrt{5}}\right)$ (d) $\tan^{-1}\left(\frac{\sqrt{5}}{6}\right)$

Sol. (c) The combined equation of the pair of tangents drawn from (1, 2) to the ellipse $3x^2+2y^2=5$ is

$$(3x^2+2y^2-5)(3+8-5)=(3x+4y-5)^2 \quad [\because SS_1=T^2]$$

$$\Rightarrow \quad 9x^2-24xy-4y^2+30x+40y-55=0$$

If the angle between these lines is θ, then

$$\tan\theta=\frac{2\sqrt{h^2-ab}}{a+b}$$

$$=\frac{2\sqrt{(-12)^2-(9)(-4)}}{9+(-4)}=\frac{2}{5}\sqrt{144+36}$$

$$=\frac{2}{5}\sqrt{180}=\frac{2}{5}\times 6\sqrt{5}=\frac{12}{\sqrt{5}}$$

$$\therefore \quad \theta=\tan^{-1}\left(\frac{12}{\sqrt{5}}\right)$$

Skill Builder

The angle between the pair of tangents drawn from the point (3, 4) to the ellipse $4x^2+9y^2=36$ is

(a) $\tan^{-1}\left(\frac{1}{2}\right)$ (b) $\tan^{-1}(1)$

(c) $\tan^{-1}(0)$ (d) $\tan^{-1}(2)$

For Sol.

■ **For more practice** See Q.1 of Milestone Practice 6.3.

6.12 Chord of Contact

Theorem The equation of chord of contact of tangents drawn from a point (x_1, y_1) to the ellipse $\frac{x^2}{a^2}+\frac{y^2}{b^2}=1$ is

$$\frac{xx_1}{a^2}+\frac{yy_1}{b^2}=1$$

Proof Let PQ and PR be the tangents drawn from a point $P(x_1, y_1)$ to the ellipse $\frac{x^2}{a^2}+\frac{y^2}{b^2}=1$ such that

$$Q \equiv (x', y') \text{ and } R \equiv (x'', y'')$$

are the points of contacts of these tangents the chord QR is called chord of contact of the ellipse

$$\frac{x^2}{a^2}+\frac{y^2}{b^2}=1$$

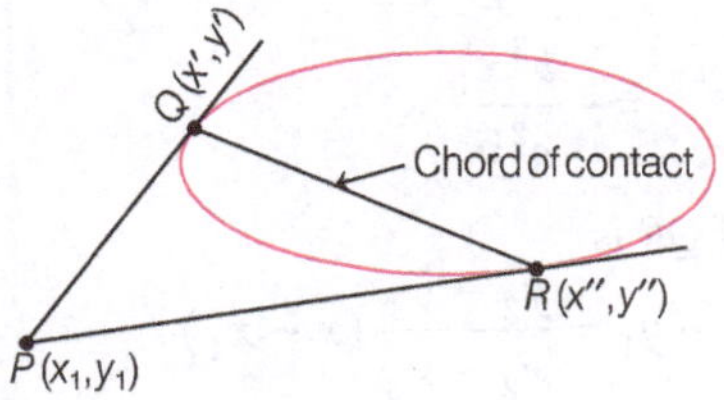

Equations of tangents at $Q(x',y')$ and $R(x'',y'')$ are

$$\frac{xx'}{a^2}+\frac{yy'}{b^2}=1 \text{ and } \frac{xx''}{a^2}+\frac{yy''}{b^2}=1, \text{ respectively.}$$

These tangents pass through $P(x_1,y_1)$, therefore

$$\frac{x'x_1}{a^2}+\frac{y'y_1}{b^2}=1 \quad \text{and} \quad \frac{x''x_1}{a^2}+\frac{y''y_1}{b^2}=1$$

$\Rightarrow$ (x',y') and (x'',y'') lie on $\frac{xx_1}{a^2}+\frac{yy_1}{b^2}=1$

Hence, the equation of QR is $\frac{xx_1}{a^2}+\frac{yy_1}{b^2}=1$

which is same as the equation of tangent but position of point differ.

Example 36. Find the locus of the points of the intersection of tangents to ellipse $\frac{x^2}{a^2}+\frac{y^2}{b^2}=1$ which make an angle θ.

Sol. Given ellipse is $\frac{x^2}{a^2}+\frac{y^2}{b^2}=1$ ...(i)

Equation of any tangent to ellipse Eq. (i) in terms of slope (m) is $y=mx\pm\sqrt{(a^2m^2+b^2)}$

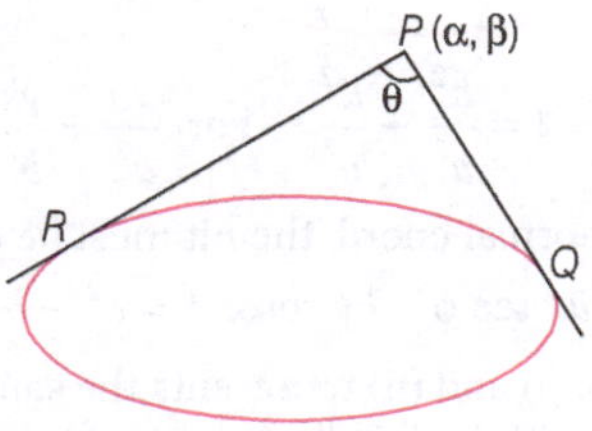

Since, its passes through $P(\alpha,\beta)$, then

$$\beta=m\alpha\pm\sqrt{(a^2m^2+b^2)}$$

$\Rightarrow$ $(\beta-m\alpha)=\pm\sqrt{(a^2m^2+b^2)}$

$\Rightarrow$ $(\beta-m\alpha)^2=a^2m^2+b^2$

$\Rightarrow$ $m^2(a^2-\alpha^2)+2\alpha\beta m+(b^2-\beta^2)=0$ ...(ii)

Eq. (ii) being a quadratic equation in m.

Let roots of Eq. (ii) be m_1 and m_2, then

$\therefore$ $m_1+m_2=-\frac{2\alpha\beta}{(a^2-\alpha^2)},\ m_1m_2=\frac{b^2-\beta^2}{a^2-\alpha^2}$

$\therefore$ $(m_1-m_2)=\sqrt{(m_1+m_2)^2-4m_1m_2}$

$$=\sqrt{\frac{4\alpha^2\beta^2}{(a^2-\alpha^2)^2}-\frac{4(b^2-\beta^2)}{(a^2-\alpha^2)}}$$

$$=\sqrt{\frac{4\alpha^2\beta^2-4(b^2-\beta^2)(a^2-\alpha^2)}{(a^2-\alpha^2)^2}}$$

$$=\sqrt{\frac{4\{\alpha^2\beta^2-a^2b^2+b^2\alpha^2+a^2\beta^2-\alpha^2\beta^2\}}{(a^2-\alpha^2)^2}}$$

$$=\frac{2}{|(a^2-\alpha^2)|}\sqrt{(a^2\beta^2+b^2\alpha^2-a^2b^2)}$$

Let θ be the angle between these two tangents, then

$$\tan\theta=\left|\frac{m_1-m_2}{1+m_1m_2}\right|=\left|\frac{\frac{2}{(a^2-\alpha^2)}\sqrt{(a^2\beta^2+b^2\alpha^2-a^2b^2)}}{\left(1+\frac{b^2-\beta^2}{a^2-\alpha^2}\right)}\right|$$

$$\tan\theta=\left|\frac{2\sqrt{(a^2\beta^2+b^2\alpha^2-a^2b^2)}}{a^2+b^2-\alpha^2-\beta^2}\right|$$

or $(a^2+b^2-\alpha^2-\beta^2)^2\tan^2\theta=4(a^2\beta^2+b^2\alpha^2-a^2b^2)$

$\Rightarrow$ $(\alpha^2+\beta^2-a^2-b^2)^2\tan^2\theta=4(b^2\alpha^2+a^2\beta^2-a^2b^2)$

$\therefore$ Locus of $P(\alpha,\beta)$ is

$$(x^2+y^2-a^2-b^2)^2\tan^2\theta=4\quad(b^2x^2+a^2y^2-a^2b^2)$$

Example 37. Prove that the chord of contact of tangents drawn from the point (h,k) to the ellipse $\frac{x^2}{a^2}+\frac{y^2}{b^2}=1$ will subtend a right angle at the centre, if $\frac{h^2}{a^4}+\frac{k^2}{b^4}=\frac{1}{a^2}+\frac{1}{b^2}$. Also, find the locus of (h,k).

Decoding the Question

If the lines are perpendicular, then coefficient of x^2 + coefficient of $y^2=0$

Sol. The equation of chord of contact of tangents drawn from $P(h,k)$ to the ellipse $\frac{x^2}{a^2}+\frac{y^2}{b^2}=1$ is $\frac{hx}{a^2}+\frac{ky}{b^2}=1$ ...(i)

The equation of the straight lines CA and CB is obtained by making homogeneous ellipse $\frac{x^2}{a^2}+\frac{y^2}{b^2}=1$ with the help of Eq. (i).

$\therefore$ $\frac{x^2}{a^2}+\frac{y^2}{b^2}=\left(\frac{hx}{a^2}+\frac{ky}{b^2}\right)^2$

$\Rightarrow$ $\left(\frac{h^2}{a^4}-\frac{1}{a^2}\right)x^2+\left(\frac{k^2}{b^4}-\frac{1}{b^2}\right)y^2+\frac{2hk}{a^2b^2}xy=0$ ...(ii)

But given $\angle ACB = 90°$

$\therefore$ Coefficient of x^2 + Coefficient of $y^2 = 0$

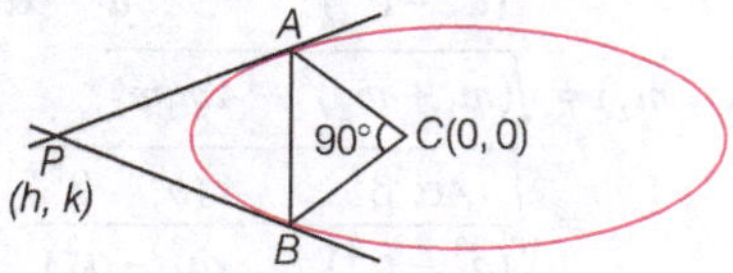

$$\Rightarrow \quad \frac{h^2}{a^4} - \frac{1}{a^2} + \frac{k^2}{b^4} - \frac{1}{b^2} = 0$$

$$\Rightarrow \quad \frac{h^2}{a^4} + \frac{k^2}{b^4} = \frac{1}{a^2} + \frac{1}{b^2}$$

Hence, locus of (h, k) is

$$\frac{x^2}{a^4} + \frac{y^2}{b^4} = \frac{1}{a^2} + \frac{1}{b^2}$$

Chord Bisected at a Given Point

Theorem The equation of a chord of the ellipse

$$\frac{x^2}{a^2} + \frac{y^2}{b^2} = 1$$

bisected at the point (x_1, y_1) is given by

$$\frac{xx_1}{a^2} + \frac{yy_1}{b^2} - 1 = \frac{x_1^2}{a^2} + \frac{y_1^2}{b^2} - 1$$

or $\qquad T = S_1$

Proof Let $Q \equiv (x_2, y_2)$ and $R \equiv (x_3, y_3)$ be the end points of a chord QR of the ellipse $\frac{x^2}{a^2} + \frac{y^2}{b^2} = 1$ and let $P \equiv (x_1, y_1)$ be its mid-point.

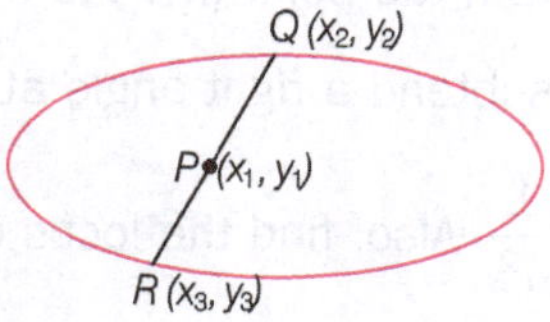

Now, $Q \equiv (x_2, y_2)$ and $R \equiv (x_3, y_3)$ lie on $\frac{x^2}{a^2} + \frac{y^2}{b^2} = 1$, then

$$\frac{x_2^2}{a^2} + \frac{y_2^2}{b^2} = 1 \qquad \text{...(i)}$$

and

$$\frac{x_3^2}{a^2} + \frac{y_3^2}{b^2} = 1 \qquad \text{...(ii)}$$

Subtracting Eq. (ii) from Eq. (i), we get

$$\therefore \quad \frac{1}{a^2}(x_2^2 - x_3^2) + \frac{1}{b^2}(y_2^2 - y_3^2) = 0$$

$$\Rightarrow \frac{(x_2 + x_3)(x_2 - x_3)}{a^2} + \frac{(y_2 + y_3)(y_2 - y_3)}{b^2} = 0$$

$$\Rightarrow \quad \frac{y_2 - y_3}{x_2 - x_3} = -\frac{b^2(x_2 + x_3)}{a^2(y_2 + y_3)} = -\frac{b^2}{a^2} \cdot \frac{2x_1}{2y_1}$$

$$\left[\because x_1 = \frac{x_2 + x_3}{2} \text{ and } y_1 = \frac{y_2 + y_3}{2}\right]$$

$$= -\frac{b^2 x_1}{a^2 y_1} \qquad \text{...(iii)}$$

$\therefore$ Equation of QR is

$$y - y_1 = \frac{y_2 - y_3}{x_2 - x_3}(x - x_1)$$

$$\Rightarrow \quad y - y_1 = -\frac{b^2 x_1}{a^2 y_1}(x - x_1) \qquad \text{[from Eq. (iii)]}$$

$$\Rightarrow \quad \frac{yy_1}{b^2} - \frac{y_1^2}{b^2} = -\frac{xx_1}{a^2} + \frac{x_1^2}{a^2}$$

$$\Rightarrow \quad \frac{xx_1}{a^2} + \frac{yy_1}{b^2} - 1 = \frac{x_1^2}{a^2} + \frac{y_1^2}{b^2} - 1 \text{ or } T = S_1$$

where, $\qquad T = \frac{xx_1}{a^2} + \frac{yy_1}{b^2} - 1$

and $\qquad S_1 = \frac{x_1^2}{a^2} + \frac{y_1^2}{b^2} - 1$

Example 38. Prove that the locus of the middle points of normal chords of the ellipse $\frac{x^2}{a^2} + \frac{y^2}{b^2} = 1$ is the curve $\left(\frac{x^2}{a^2} + \frac{y^2}{b^2}\right)^2 \left(\frac{a^6}{x^2} + \frac{b^6}{y^2}\right) = (a^2 - b^2)^2$.

Sol. Let (h, k) be the middle point of any chord of an ellipse, then its equation is $T = S_1$

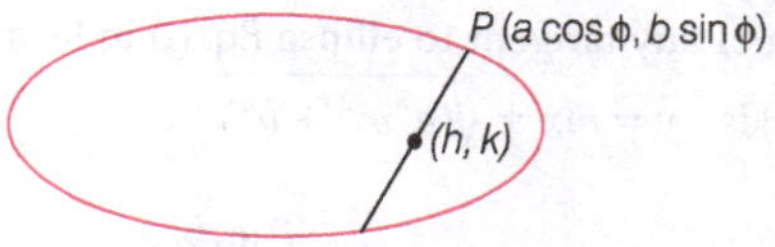

or $\frac{xh}{a^2} + \frac{yk}{b^2} - 1 = \frac{h^2}{a^2} + \frac{k^2}{b^2} - 1$ or $\frac{xh}{a^2} + \frac{yk}{b^2} = \frac{h^2}{a^2} + \frac{k^2}{b^2}$ ...(i)

If Eq. (i) is a normal chord, then it must be of the form

$$ax \sec \phi - by \operatorname{cosec} \phi = a^2 - b^2 \qquad \text{...(ii)}$$

Thus, the Eqs. (i) and (ii) represents the same normal chord of the ellipse with its middle point (h, k).

Hence, they are identical and comparing their coefficients,

we get $\qquad \frac{h/a^2}{a \sec \phi} = \frac{k/b^2}{-b \operatorname{cosec} \phi} = \frac{\frac{h^2}{a^2} + \frac{k^2}{b^2}}{(a^2 - b^2)}$

$$\Rightarrow \quad \cos\phi = \frac{a^3}{h}\frac{\left(\frac{h^2}{a^2}+\frac{k^2}{b^2}\right)}{(a^2-b^2)} \quad \text{...(iii)}$$

and $$\sin\phi = -\frac{b^3}{k}\frac{\left(\frac{h^2}{a^2}+\frac{k^2}{b^2}\right)}{(a^2-b^2)} \quad \text{...(iv)}$$

On squaring and adding Eqs. (iii) and (iv), we get

$$\cos^2\phi+\sin^2\phi = \frac{\left(\frac{a^6}{h^2}+\frac{b^6}{k^2}\right)\left(\frac{h^2}{a^2}+\frac{k^2}{b^2}\right)^2}{(a^2-b^2)^2}$$

$$\Rightarrow \quad 1 = \frac{\left(\frac{a^6}{h^2}+\frac{b^6}{k^2}\right)\left(\frac{h^2}{a^2}+\frac{k^2}{b^2}\right)^2}{(a^2-b^2)^2}$$

$$\Rightarrow \quad \left(\frac{h^2}{a^2}+\frac{k^2}{b^2}\right)^2\left(\frac{a^6}{h^2}+\frac{b^6}{k^2}\right) = (a^2-b^2)^2$$

Hence, locus of (h, k) is $\left(\frac{x^2}{a^2}+\frac{y^2}{b^2}\right)^2\left(\frac{a^6}{x^2}+\frac{b^6}{y^2}\right) = (a^2-b^2)^2$

Example 39. Show that the locus of the middle points of chords of an ellipse which pass through a fixed point, is another ellipse.

Sol. Let $P(x_1, y_1)$ be the middle point of any chord AB of the ellipse $\frac{x^2}{a^2}+\frac{y^2}{b^2}=1$, then equation of chord AB is

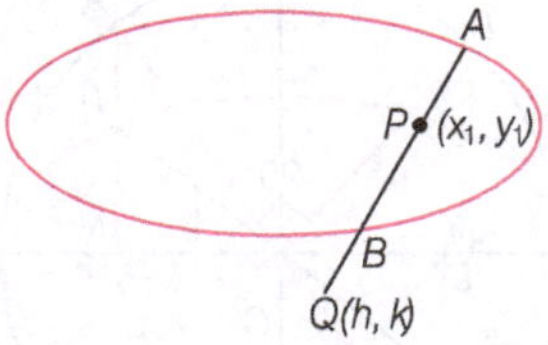

$$\Rightarrow \quad \frac{xx_1}{a^2}+\frac{yy_1}{b^2}-1 = \frac{x_1^2}{a^2}+\frac{y_1^2}{b^2}-1$$

$$\Rightarrow \quad \frac{xx_1}{a^2}+\frac{yy_1}{b^2} = \frac{x_1^2}{a^2}+\frac{y_1^2}{b^2} \quad \text{... (i)}$$

But it passes through a fixed point $Q(h, k)$, its coordinates must satisfy Eq. (i),

$$\therefore \quad \frac{hx_1}{a^2}+\frac{ky_1}{b^2} = \frac{x_1^2}{a^2}+\frac{y_1^2}{b^2}$$

This can be re-written as

$$\frac{\left(x_1-\frac{h}{2}\right)^2}{a^2}+\frac{\left(y_1-\frac{k}{2}\right)^2}{b^2} = \frac{1}{4}\left(\frac{h^2}{a^2}+\frac{k^2}{b^2}\right)$$

Hence, locus of $P(x_1, y_1)$ is

$$\frac{\left(x-\frac{h}{2}\right)^2}{a^2}+\frac{\left(y-\frac{k}{2}\right)^2}{b^2} = \frac{1}{4}\left(\frac{h^2}{a^2}+\frac{k^2}{b^2}\right)$$

Its obviously an ellipse with centre at $\left(\frac{h}{2}, \frac{k}{2}\right)$ and axes parallel to coordinates axes.

JEE SCANNER

Example Similar to PYQ Asked in JEE Main 2023

If $\left(\frac{1}{2}, \frac{2}{5}\right)$ be the mid-point of the chord of the ellipse $\frac{x^2}{25}+\frac{y^2}{16}=1$, then the length of the chord is

(a) $\frac{7\sqrt{41}}{5}$ (b) $\frac{7\sqrt{41}}{10}$ (c) $\frac{5\sqrt{41}}{7}$ (d) $\frac{10\sqrt{41}}{7}$

Sol. (a) Given ellipse is $\frac{x^2}{25}+\frac{y^2}{16}=1$ ...(i)

The equation of the chord bisects at (h, k), is

$$T = S_1$$

$$\Rightarrow \quad \frac{hx}{5^2}+\frac{ky}{4^2} = \frac{h^2}{5^2}+\frac{k^2}{4^2} \Rightarrow \frac{hx}{25}+\frac{ky}{16} = \frac{h^2}{25}+\frac{k^2}{16}$$

$$\Rightarrow \quad \frac{\left(\frac{1}{2}\right)x}{25}+\frac{\left(\frac{2}{5}\right)y}{16} = \frac{\left(\frac{1}{2}\right)^2}{25}+\frac{\left(\frac{2}{5}\right)^2}{16}$$

On solving, we get

$$4x+5y = 4 \quad \text{...(ii)}$$

Solving Eqs. (i) and (ii), we get

$$x = 4, -3 \text{ and } y = \frac{-12}{5}, \frac{16}{5}$$

Let the chord be AB where

$$A = \left(4, \frac{-12}{5}\right) \text{ and } B = \left(-3, \frac{16}{5}\right)$$

Hence, the length of the AB, is

$$\sqrt{(7)^2+\left(\frac{28}{5}\right)^2} = 7\sqrt{1+\frac{16}{25}} = \frac{7\sqrt{41}}{5}$$

Skill Builder

If $(0, 3)$ be the mid-point of the chord of the ellipse $\frac{x^2}{16}+\frac{y^2}{25}=1$, then the length of the chord is

(a) $\frac{16}{5}$ (b) $\frac{32}{5}$

(c) $\frac{19}{5}$ (d) $\frac{22}{5}$

For Sol.

■ **For more practice** See Q.11 of Milestone Practice 6.3.

6.13 Diameter

The locus of the middle points of a system of parallel chords of an ellipse is called a diameter and the point where the diameter intersects the ellipse is called the vertex of the diameter.

Let $y = mx + c$ be system of parallel chords to $\frac{x^2}{a^2} + \frac{y^2}{b^2} = 1$ for different chords c varies, m remains constant.

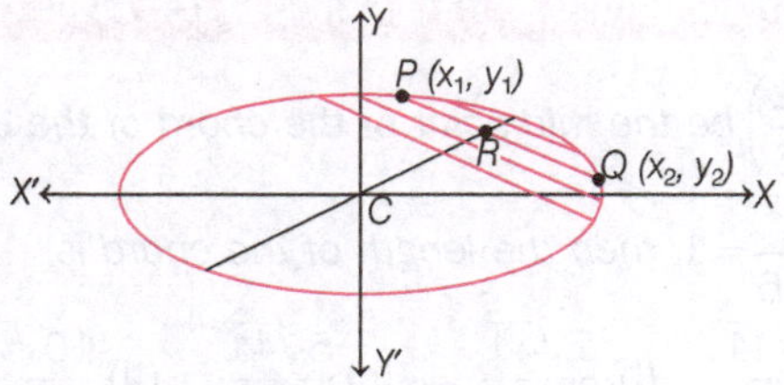

Let the extremities of any chord PQ of the set be $P(x_1, y_1)$ and $Q(x_2, y_2)$ and let its middle point be $R(h, k)$, then solving equations.

$$\frac{x^2}{a^2} + \frac{y^2}{b^2} = 1 \text{ and } y = mx + c$$

$$\therefore \quad \frac{x^2}{a^2} + \frac{(mx+c)^2}{b^2} = 1$$

$$\Rightarrow (a^2m^2 + b^2)x^2 + 2mca^2x + a^2(c^2 - b^2) = 0$$

Since, x_1 and x_2 be the roots of this equation, then

$$x_1 + x_2 = -\frac{2mca^2}{a^2m^2 + b^2} \quad \text{...(i)}$$

Since, (h, k) be the middle point of QR, then

$$h = \frac{x_1 + x_2}{2}$$

From Eq. (i),

$$2h = -\frac{2mca^2}{a^2m^2 + b^2}$$

$$\Rightarrow \quad h = -\frac{mca^2}{a^2m^2 + b^2} \quad \text{...(ii)}$$

Point (h, k) lies on $y = mx + c$

$$\therefore \quad k = mh + c, \; c = k - mh \quad \text{...(iii)}$$

From Eqs. (ii) and (iii), we get,

$$h = -\frac{ma^2(k - mh)}{a^2m^2 + b^2}$$

$$\Rightarrow \quad a^2m^2h + b^2h = -mka^2 + m^2a^2h$$

$$\Rightarrow \quad b^2h = -mka^2 \text{ or } k = -\frac{b^2h}{a^2m}$$

Hence, locus of $R(h, k)$ is $y = -\frac{b^2x}{a^2m}$

which is diameter of the ellipse passing through $(0, 0)$.

Alternate method

Let (h, k) be the middle point of the chord $y = mx + c$ of the ellipse $\frac{x^2}{a^2} + \frac{y^2}{b^2} = 1$, then

$$T = S_1 \Rightarrow \frac{xh}{a^2} + \frac{ky}{b^2} = \frac{h^2}{a^2} + \frac{k^2}{b^2}$$

$$\therefore \quad \text{Slope} = -\frac{b^2h}{a^2k} = m \Rightarrow k = -\frac{b^2h}{a^2m}$$

Hence, locus of the mid-point is $y = -\frac{b^2x}{a^2m}$

6.14 Conjugate Diameters

Two diameters are said to be conjugate when each bisects all chords parallel to the other. If $y = mx$ and $y = m_1x$ be two conjugate diameters of an ellipse, then $mm_1 = -\frac{b^2}{a^2}$.

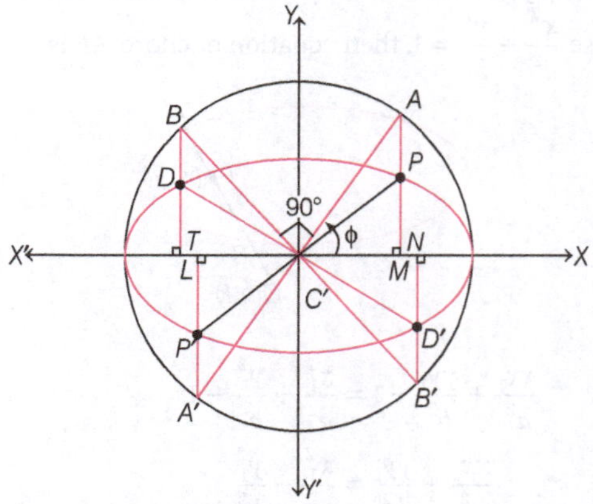

Conjugate diameters of circle i.e. AA' and BB' are perpendicular to each other. Hence, conjugate diameters of ellipse are PP' and DD'.

Hence, angle between conjugate diameters of ellipse $\neq 90°$.

Now, the co-ordinates of the four extremities of two conjugate diameters are

$$P(a\cos\phi, b\sin\phi), \; P'(-a\cos\phi, -b\sin\phi),$$

$$D(-a\sin\phi, b\cos\phi), \; D'(a\sin\phi, -b\cos\phi)$$

Properties of Conjugate Diameters

PROPERTY 1 The eccentric angles of the ends of a pair of conjugate diameters of an ellipse differ by a right angle.

Let PCP' and DCD' be two conjugate diameters of the ellipse $\frac{x^2}{a^2}+\frac{y^2}{b^2}=1$ and let the eccentric angles of the

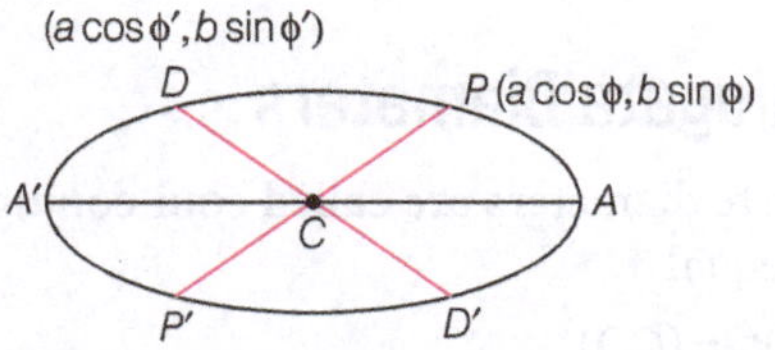

extremities P and D be ϕ and ϕ' respectively. Then, the coordinates of P and D are $(a\cos\phi, b\sin\phi)$ and $(a\cos\phi', b\sin\phi')$ respectively.

Now, m_1 = slope of $CP=\frac{b}{a}\tan\phi$

and m_2 = slope of $CD=\frac{b}{a}\tan\phi'$

Since, the diameters PCP' and DCD' are conjugate diameters.

$$\therefore \quad m_1 m_2 = -\frac{b^2}{a^2}$$

$$\Rightarrow \quad \frac{b^2}{a^2}\tan\phi\tan\phi' = -\frac{b^2}{a^2}$$

$$\Rightarrow \quad \tan\phi\tan\phi' = -1$$

$$\Rightarrow \quad \tan\phi = -\cot\phi' = \tan\left(\frac{\pi}{2}+\phi'\right)$$

$$\Rightarrow \quad \phi = \frac{\pi}{2}+\phi' \Rightarrow \phi-\phi' = \frac{\pi}{2}$$

PROPERTY 2 The sum of the squares of any two conjugate semi- diameters of an ellipse is constant and equal to the sum of the squares of the semi-axes of the ellipse i.e.

$$CP^2+CD^2=a^2+b^2$$

Let CP and CD be two conjugate semi-diameters of an ellipse $\frac{x^2}{a^2}+\frac{y^2}{b^2}=1$ and let eccentric angle of P is ϕ. The eccentric angle of D is $\frac{\pi}{2}+\phi$. So, the coordinates of P and D are $(a\cos\phi, b\sin\phi)$ and $\left(a\cos\left(\frac{\pi}{2}+\phi\right), b\sin\left(\frac{\pi}{2}+\phi\right)\right)$

i.e. $(-a\sin\phi, b\cos\phi)$, respectively.

$$\therefore \quad CP^2+CD^2=(a^2\cos^2\phi+b^2\sin^2\phi)+(a^2\sin^2\phi+b^2\cos^2\phi)=a^2+b^2$$

PROPERTY 3 The product of the focal distances of a point on an ellipse is equal to the square of the semi diameter which is conjugate to the diameter through the point.

Let PCP' and DCD' be the conjugate diameters of an ellipse and let the eccentric angle of P is ϕ, then coordinates of P is $(a\cos\phi, b\sin\phi)$

$\therefore$ Coordinates of D is $(-a\sin\phi, b\cos\phi)$

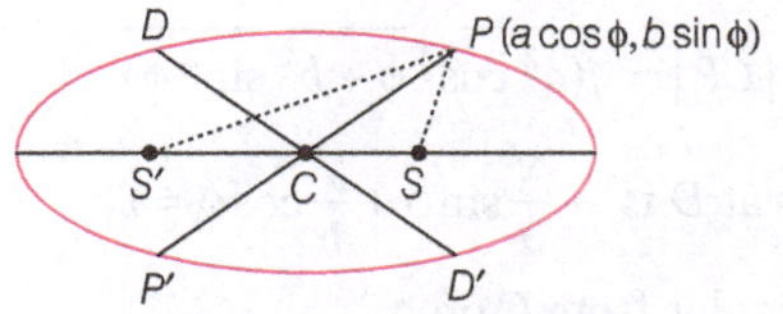

Let S and S' be two foci of the ellipse. Then,

$$SP\cdot S'P=(a-ae\cos\phi)\cdot(a+ae\cos\phi)$$
$$=a^2-a^2e^2\cos^2\phi$$
$$=a^2-(a^2-b^2)\cos^2\phi \qquad [\because b^2=a^2(1-e^2)]$$
$$=a^2\sin^2\phi+b^2\cos^2\phi=CD^2$$

PROPERTY 4 The tangents at the extremities of a pair of conjugate diameters form a parallelogram whose area is constant and equal to product of the axes.

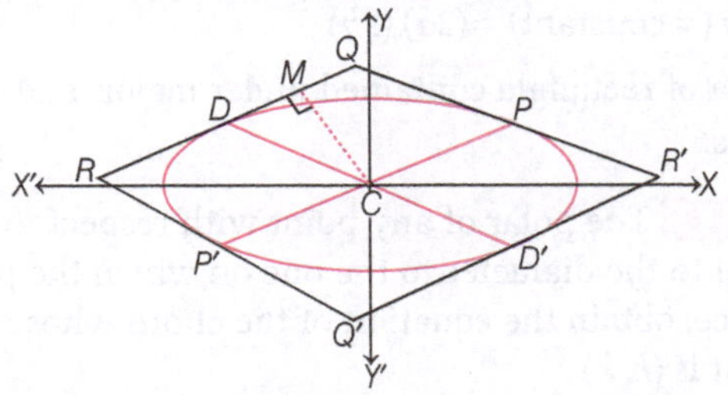

Let PCP' and DCD' be a pair of conjugate diameters of the ellipse $\frac{x^2}{a^2}+\frac{y^2}{b^2}=1$. Let the eccentric angle of P be ϕ. Then, the eccentric angle of D is $\left(\frac{\pi}{2}+\phi\right)$, so the coordinates of P and D are

$$(a\cos\phi, b\sin\phi) \text{ and } \left(a\cos\left(\frac{\pi}{2}+\phi\right), b\sin\left(\frac{\pi}{2}+\phi\right)\right)$$

i.e. $(-a\sin\phi, b\cos\phi)$, respectively.

Similarly, the coordinates of P' and D' are $(-a\cos\phi, -b\sin\phi)$ and $(a\sin\phi, -b\cos\phi)$, respectively.

Equation of tangents at P, D, P' and D' are respectively.

$$\frac{x}{a}\cos\phi+\frac{y}{b}\sin\phi=1, -\frac{x}{a}\sin\phi+\frac{y}{b}\cos\phi=1,$$
$$-\frac{x}{a}\cos\phi-\frac{y}{b}\sin\phi=1$$
$$\text{and} \quad \frac{x}{a}\sin\phi-\frac{y}{b}\cos\phi=1$$

Clearly, the tangents at P and P' are parallel. Also, the tangents at D and D' are parallel. Hence, the tangents at P, D, P', D' form a parallelogram.

Area of parallelogram $QRQ'R' = 4$ (the area of parallelogram $QDCP$)

$= 4 \cdot |QD| \cdot$ (perpendicular from C on QD)

$= 4 \cdot |CP| \cdot$ (perpendicular from C on QD) ...(i)

Now, $|CP| = \sqrt{(a^2 \cos^2 \phi + b^2 \sin^2 \phi)}$

$\because$ Tangent at D is $-\frac{x}{a}\sin\phi + \frac{y}{b}\cos\phi = 1$

$\therefore$ Perpendicular from C on

$$QD = \frac{1}{\sqrt{\frac{\sin^2\phi}{a^2} + \frac{\cos^2\phi}{b^2}}} = \frac{ab}{\sqrt{a^2\cos^2\phi + b^2\sin^2\phi}}$$

Now, from Eq. (i),

Area of parallelogram $QRQ'R'$

$= 4 \times \sqrt{(a^2\cos^2\phi + b^2\sin^2\phi)} \times \frac{ab}{\sqrt{a^2\cos^2\phi + b^2\sin^2\phi)}}$

$= 4ab$ (= constant) $= (2a)(2b)$

= Area of rectangle contained under major and minor axes.

PROPERTY 5 The polar of any point with respect to ellipse is parallel to the diameter to the one on which the point lies. Hence, obtain the equation of the chord whose mid-point is (h, k).

Let (h, k) be the point on the diameter $y = m_1 x$

$\therefore \quad m_1 = k/h$

any diameter conjugate to it is $y = m_2 x$

but $\quad m_1 m_2 = -\frac{b^2}{a^2} \Rightarrow \frac{k}{h} m_2 = -\frac{b^2}{a^2}$

$\therefore \quad m_2 = -\frac{b^2 h}{a^2 k}$

Polar of (h, k) is $\frac{hx}{a^2} + \frac{ky}{b^2} = 1$ ...(i)

Its slope is $-\frac{b^2 h}{a^2 k} = m_2$ and hence parallel.

Now, equation of chord parallel to the Eq. (i) is

$$\frac{hx}{a^2} + \frac{ky}{b^2} = \lambda \quad \text{...(ii)}$$

It is passes through points (h, k).

$$\therefore \quad \lambda = \frac{h^2}{a^2} + \frac{k^2}{b^2} \quad \text{... (iii)}$$

From Eqs. (ii) and (iii), $\frac{hx}{a^2} + \frac{ky}{b^2} = \frac{h^2}{a^2} + \frac{k^2}{b^2}$

i.e. $\quad T = S_1$

which is the equation of chord of the ellipse, if mid-points are (h, k).

Equi-Conjugate Diameters

Two conjugate diameters are called equi-conjugate if their lengths are equal.

i.e. $\quad (CP)^2 = (CD)^2$

$\therefore \quad a^2\cos^2\phi + b^2\sin^2\phi = a^2\sin^2\phi + b^2\cos^2\phi$

$\Rightarrow \quad a^2(\cos^2\phi - \sin^2\phi) - b^2(\cos^2\phi - \sin^2\phi) = 0$

$\Rightarrow \quad (a^2 - b^2)\cos 2\phi = 0$

$\because \quad (a^2 - b^2) \neq 0$

$\therefore \quad \cos 2\phi = 0$

$\therefore \quad \phi = \frac{\pi}{4}$ or $\frac{3\pi}{4}$

$\therefore \quad CP = CD = \sqrt{\frac{(a^2 + b^2)}{2}}$

JEE Focus Points

- Two points are conjugate points, if each point lies on the polar of the other.
- Two lines are conjugate, if each line passes through the pole of the polar.

Example 40. The eccentricity of an ellipse whose pair of conjugate diameters are $y = 3x$ and $7y = -2x$ is

(a) $\frac{3}{\sqrt{7}}$ (b) $\frac{4}{\sqrt{7}}$ (c) $\frac{1}{\sqrt{7}}$ (d) $\frac{9}{\sqrt{7}}$

Sol. (c) Let the ellipse be $\frac{x^2}{a^2} + \frac{y^2}{b^2} = 1$

$\because y = 3x$ and $7y = -2x$ is a pair of conjugate diameters, therefore

$$m_1 m_2 = \frac{-b^2}{a^2}$$

$\because \quad m_1 = 3$ and $m_2 = -\frac{2}{7}$

$\therefore \quad 3 \times -\frac{2}{7} = \frac{-b^2}{a^2} \Rightarrow \frac{b^2}{a^2} = \frac{6}{7}$

$\because$ Eccentricity of the ellipse lies between (0, 1).

$\therefore \quad e = \sqrt{1 - \frac{b^2}{a^2}} = \sqrt{1 - \frac{6}{7}} = \sqrt{\frac{1}{7}} = \frac{1}{\sqrt{7}}$

Example 41. For the ellipse $3x^2+4y^2=12$, then the conjugate diameter of line joining (6, 5) to origin is

(a) $10y+5x=0$ (b) $11y+9x=0$

(c) $10y-9x=0$ (d) $10y+9x=0$

Sol. (d) Ellipse : $3x^2+4y^2=12$

or $\frac{x^2}{4}+\frac{y^2}{3}=1$

Here, $a^2=4$ and $b^2=3$

Now, the line $y=\frac{5}{6}x$

$\therefore \quad m_1=\frac{5}{6}$

Let $y=m_2x$ be the conjugate diameter.

Now, we know that

$$m_1m_2=\frac{-b^2}{a^2} \Rightarrow \frac{5}{6}\times m_2=\frac{-3}{4}$$

$$\Rightarrow \quad m_2=\frac{-3\times 6}{4\times 5}=\frac{-18}{20}=\frac{-9}{10}$$

$\therefore$ Equation of conjugate diameter is

$$y=\frac{-9}{10}x \Rightarrow 10y+9x=0$$

Example 42. Show that the tangents at the ends of conjugate diameters of the ellipse $x^2/a^2+y^2/b^2=1$ intersect on the ellipse $x^2/a^2+y^2/b^2=2$.

Or

Prove that the locus of the poles of the line joining the extremities of two conjugate diameters is the ellipse $x^2/a^2+y^2/b^2=2$.

Sol. Let CP and CD be two semi-conjugate diameters, so that if eccentric angle of P is ϕ then eccentric angle of D is $\frac{\pi}{2}+\phi$

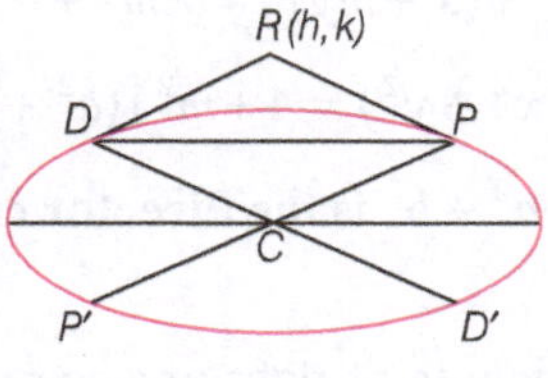

$\therefore$ Coordinates of P and D are

$(a\cos\phi, b\sin\phi)$ and $\left(a\cos\left(\frac{\pi}{2}+\phi\right), b\sin\left(\frac{\pi}{2}+\phi\right)\right)$

respectively.

$\therefore$ Equation of PD is

$$\frac{x}{a}\cos\left(\frac{\phi+\frac{\pi}{2}+\phi}{2}\right)+\frac{y}{b}\sin\left(\frac{\phi+\frac{\pi}{2}+\phi}{2}\right)=\cos\left(\frac{\frac{\pi}{2}+\phi-\phi}{2}\right)$$

$$\Rightarrow \quad \frac{x}{a}\cos\left(\frac{\pi}{4}+\phi\right)+\frac{y}{b}\sin\left(\frac{\pi}{4}+\phi\right)=\frac{1}{\sqrt{2}} \quad \text{...(i)}$$

If its pole or point of intersection of tangents at its extremities be (h, k), then its equation is the same as that of the polar or the chord of contact of (h, k).

i.e. $$\frac{hx}{a^2}+\frac{ky}{b^2}=1 \quad \text{...(ii)}$$

Since, Eqs. (i) and (ii) are identical.

$$\therefore \quad \frac{h}{a\cos\left(\frac{\pi}{4}+\phi\right)}=\frac{k}{b\sin\left(\frac{\pi}{4}+\phi\right)}=\sqrt{2}$$

$$\Rightarrow \quad \sqrt{2}\cos\left(\frac{\pi}{4}+\phi\right)=\frac{h}{a} \quad \text{...(iii)}$$

and $$\sqrt{2}\sin\left(\frac{\pi}{4}+\phi\right)=\frac{k}{b} \quad \text{...(iv)}$$

Squaring and adding Eqs. (iii) and (iv), we get

$$\frac{h^2}{a^2}+\frac{k^2}{b^2}=2\left(\cos^2\left(\frac{\pi}{4}+\phi\right)+\sin^2\left(\frac{\pi}{4}+\phi\right)\right)$$

$$\therefore \quad \frac{h^2}{a^2}+\frac{k^2}{b^2}=2$$

Hence, locus of (h, k) is $\frac{x^2}{a^2}+\frac{y^2}{b^2}=2$

Time Saving Technique

Equation of tangents at P and D are

$$\frac{x}{a}\cos\phi+\frac{y}{b}\sin\phi=1 \quad \text{... (i)}$$

and $$\frac{x}{a}\cos\left(\frac{\pi}{2}+\phi\right)+\frac{y}{b}\sin\left(\frac{\pi}{2}+\phi\right)=1$$

i.e. $$-\frac{x}{a}\sin\phi+\frac{y}{b}\cos\phi=1 \quad \text{...(ii)}$$

Squaring and adding Eqs. (i) and (ii), we get

$$\frac{x^2}{a^2}+\frac{y^2}{b^2}=2$$

which is required locus.

Example 43. If $x\cos\alpha+y\sin\alpha=p$ is a chord joining the ends P and D of conjugate semi-diameters, of the ellipse then prove that $a^2\cos^2\alpha+b^2\sin^2 a=2p^2$ and hence or otherwise deduce that the line PD always touches a similar ellipse.

Sol. Let equation of ellipse be $\frac{x^2}{a^2}+\frac{y^2}{b^2}=1$, eccentric angle of P is ϕ, then eccentric angle of D is $\frac{\pi}{2}+\phi$.

$\therefore$ Coordinates of P and D are

$(a\cos\phi, b\sin\phi)$ and $\left(a\cos\left(\frac{\pi}{2}+\phi\right), b\sin\left(\frac{\pi}{2}+\phi\right)\right)$

$\therefore$ Equation of PD is

$$\frac{x}{a}\cos\left(\frac{\phi+\frac{\pi}{2}+\phi}{2}\right)+\frac{y}{b}\sin\left(\frac{\phi+\frac{\pi}{2}+\phi}{2}\right)=\cos\left(\frac{\frac{\pi}{2}+\phi-\phi}{2}\right)$$

$$\Rightarrow \quad \frac{x}{a}\cos\left(\frac{\pi}{4}+\phi\right)+\frac{y}{b}\sin\left(\frac{\pi}{4}+\phi\right)=\frac{1}{\sqrt{2}} \quad \text{...(i)}$$

If it is same as $x\cos\alpha + y\sin\alpha = p$, ...(ii)

then on comparing, we get

$$\frac{\cos\left(\frac{\pi}{4}+\phi\right)}{a\cos\alpha}=\frac{\sin\left(\frac{\pi}{4}+\phi\right)}{b\sin\alpha}=\frac{1}{p\sqrt{2}}$$

or $$a\cos\alpha = p\sqrt{2}\cos\left(\frac{\pi}{4}+\phi\right) \quad \text{...(iii)}$$

and $$b\sin\alpha = p\sqrt{2}\sin\left(\frac{\pi}{4}+\phi\right) \quad \text{...(iv)}$$

On squaring and adding Eqs. (iii) and (iv), we get

$$a^2\cos^2\alpha + b^2\sin^2\alpha = (p\sqrt{2})^2$$

$$\left\{\cos^2\left(\frac{\pi}{4}+\phi\right)+\sin^2\left(\frac{\pi}{4}+\phi\right)\right\}$$

$$\Rightarrow \quad a^2\cos^2\alpha + b^2\sin^2\alpha = 2p^2$$

Again, line (i) can be written as

$$\frac{x}{a/\sqrt{2}}\cos\theta + \frac{y}{b/\sqrt{2}}\sin\theta = 1,$$

where $$\theta = \frac{\pi}{4}+\phi$$

which is clearly a tangent to the ellipse

$$\frac{x^2}{(a/\sqrt{2})^2}+\frac{y^2}{(b/\sqrt{2})^2}=1 \text{ or } \frac{x^2}{a^2}+\frac{y^2}{b^2}=\frac{1}{2} \quad \text{...(v)}$$

If e' be its eccentricity, then

$$(b/\sqrt{2})^2 = (a/\sqrt{2})^2(1-e'^2)$$

$$\Rightarrow \quad b^2 = a^2(1-e'^2)$$

but $$b^2 = a^2(1-e^2)$$

$$\therefore \quad e = e'$$

Hence, the line *PD* always touches the similar ellipse.

6.15 Director Circle

The locus of the point of intersection of the tangents to an ellipse $\frac{x^2}{a^2}+\frac{y^2}{b^2}=1$ which are perpendicular to each other is called director circle.

Let any tangent in terms of slope of ellipse $\frac{x^2}{a^2}+\frac{y^2}{b^2}=1$ is

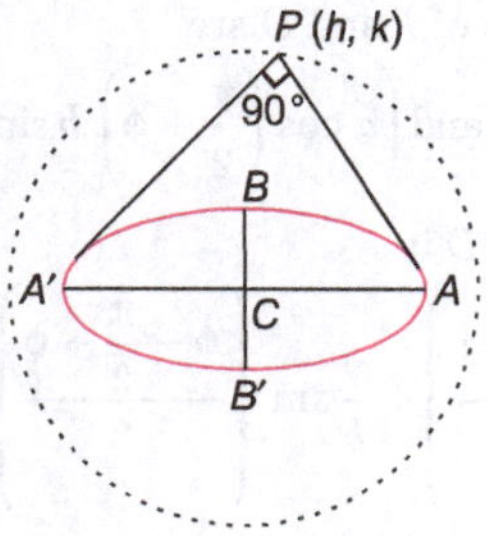

$$y = mx \pm \sqrt{(a^2m^2+b^2)}$$

It is passes through (h, k)

$$\therefore \quad k = mh \pm \sqrt{(a^2m^2+b^2)}$$

or $$(k-mh)^2 = a^2m^2+b^2$$

$$\Rightarrow \quad k^2+m^2h^2-2mhk = a^2m^2+b^2$$

$$\Rightarrow \quad m^2(h^2-a^2)-2hkm+k^2-b^2=0$$

It is quadratic equation in m, let slope of two tangents are m_1 and m_2,

$$\therefore \quad m_1m_2 = \frac{k^2-b^2}{h^2-a^2}$$

$$-1 = \frac{k^2-b^2}{h^2-a^2} \quad [\because \text{ tangents are perpendicular}]$$

$$\Rightarrow \quad -h^2+a^2 = k^2-b^2 \text{ or } h^2+k^2 = a^2+b^2$$

Hence, locus of $P(h, k)$ is

$$\mathbf{x^2+y^2=a^2+b^2}$$

Alternate Method

If any tangent $y = mx \pm \sqrt{(a^2m^2+b^2)}$ ...(i)

and $$y = -\frac{x}{m} \pm \sqrt{\left\{a^2\left(-\frac{1}{m}\right)^2+b^2\right\}} \quad \text{...(ii)}$$

touch the ellipse and intersect at right angles.

From Eq. (i), $y - mx = \pm\sqrt{(a^2m^2+b^2)}$ ...(iii)

Eq. (ii) can be re-written as

$$x + my = \pm\sqrt{(a^2+b^2m^2)} \quad \text{...(iv)}$$

On squaring and adding Eqs. (iii) and (iv), then

$$(y-mx)^2+(x+my)^2 = a^2m^2+b^2+a^2+b^2m^2$$

$$\Rightarrow \quad (1+m^2)(x^2+y^2) = (1+m^2)(a^2+b^2)$$

Hence, $x^2+y^2=a^2+b^2$ is the **director circle** of the ellipse.

Example 44. Tangents at right angles are drawn to the ellipse $\frac{x^2}{a^2}+\frac{y^2}{b^2}=1$. Show that the locus of the middle points of the chord of contact is the curve $\left(\frac{x^2}{a^2}+\frac{y^2}{b^2}\right)^2 = \frac{x^2+y^2}{a^2+b^2}$.

Decoding the Question

If equation of an ellipse is $\frac{x^2}{a^2}+\frac{y^2}{b^2}=1$, then equation of director circle is $x^2+y^2=a^2+b^2$.

Sol. Let $Q(h, k)$ be the middle point of the chord of contact

$\therefore$ Equation of chord AB whose mid point $Q(h, k)$ is

$$T = S_1$$

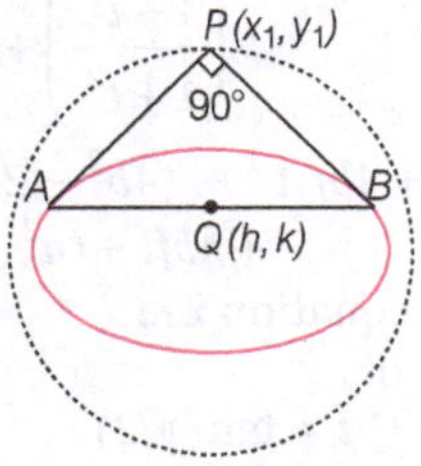

$$\frac{hx}{a^2} + \frac{ky}{b^2} = \frac{h^2}{a^2} + \frac{k^2}{b^2} \quad \text{...(i)}$$

and equation of chord of contact AB with respect to $P(x_1, y_1)$ is

$$\frac{xx_1}{a^2} + \frac{yy_1}{b^2} = 1 \quad \text{...(ii)}$$

Eqs. (i) and (ii) are identical, hence comparing their coefficient, we get

$$\frac{x_1}{h} = \frac{y_1}{k} = \frac{1}{\left(\frac{h^2}{a^2} + \frac{k^2}{b^2}\right)}$$

$$\therefore \quad x_1 = \frac{h}{\left(\frac{h^2}{a^2} + \frac{k^2}{b^2}\right)} \quad \text{...(iii)}$$

and $$y_1 = \frac{k}{\left(\frac{h^2}{a^2} + \frac{k^2}{b^2}\right)} \quad \text{...(iv)}$$

Since, tangents are at right angles, then the point (x_1, y_1) must lie on the director circle $x^2 + y^2 = a^2 + b^2$ of the ellipse.

$$\therefore \quad x_1^2 + y_1^2 = a^2 + b^2$$

$$\Rightarrow \frac{h^2}{\left(\frac{h^2}{a^2} + \frac{k^2}{b^2}\right)^2} + \frac{k^2}{\left(\frac{h^2}{a^2} + \frac{k^2}{b^2}\right)^2} = a^2 + b^2$$

[from Eqs. (iii) and (iv)]

$$\therefore \quad \left(\frac{h^2}{a^2} + \frac{k^2}{b^2}\right)^2 = \frac{h^2 + k^2}{a^2 + b^2}$$

Hence, locus of mid-point $Q(h, k)$ is $\left(\frac{x^2}{a^2} + \frac{y^2}{b^2}\right)^2 = \frac{x^2 + y^2}{a^2 + b^2}$

Sub-Tangent and Sub-Normal

Let the tangent and normal at $P(x_1, y_1)$ meet the axes at T and G respectively.

Equation of tangent at $P(x_1, y_1)$ to the ellipse $\frac{x^2}{a^2} + \frac{y^2}{b^2} = 1$ is

$$\frac{xx_1}{a^2} + \frac{yy_1}{b^2} = 1 \quad \text{...(i)}$$

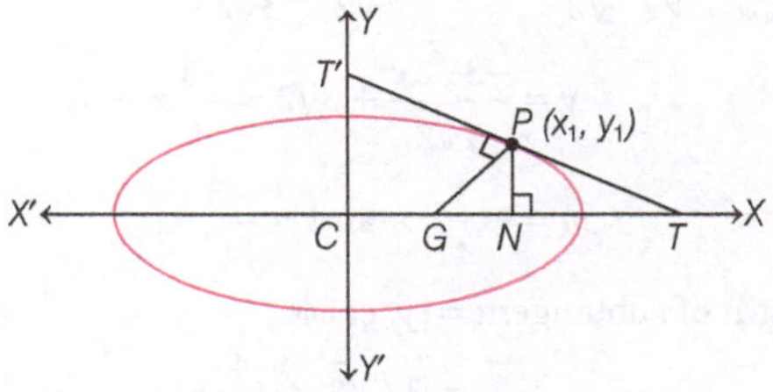

$\because$ T lies on X-axis.

Put $y = 0$ in Eq. (i), we get $x = CT$

$$\therefore \quad CT = \frac{a^2}{x_1} \text{ and } CN = x_1$$

and **length of sub-tangent** $NT = CT - CN = \frac{a^2}{x_1} - x_1$

Equation of normal at $P(x_1, y_1)$ to the ellipse $\frac{x^2}{a^2} + \frac{y^2}{b^2} = 1$ is

$$\frac{x - x_1}{x_1 / a^2} = \frac{y - y_1}{y_1 / b^2} \quad \text{...(ii)}$$

$\because$ G lies on X-axis. Put $y = 0$ in Eq. (ii)

$$x = CG \;\therefore\; CG = x_1 - \frac{b^2}{a^2} x_1$$

$\therefore$ **Length of sub-normal**

$$GN = CN - CG = x_1 - \left(x_1 - \frac{b^2}{a^2} x_1\right) = \frac{b^2}{a^2} x_1 = (1 - e^2)\, x_1$$

JEE Focus Points

- Length of subtangent $= \left|\frac{y}{m}\right|$
- Length of subnormal $= |ym|$, where $m = \tan\theta$

Example 45. The relation between the length of subtangent and subnormal of the ellipse $\frac{x^2}{16} + \frac{y^2}{9} = 1$ at $P(\pi / 4)$ is

(a) $\frac{\text{length of subtangent}}{\text{length of subnormal}} = \frac{16}{9}$

(b) length of subtangent $= 36$

(c) length of subnormal $= \frac{9}{4}$

(d) All of these

Sol. (a) Given, ellipse is $\frac{x^2}{16} + \frac{y^2}{9} = 1$

Now, point $P(\pi / 4) = (a \cos \pi / 4, b \sin \pi / 4)$ is

$$= \left(4 \times \frac{1}{\sqrt{2}}, 3 \times \frac{1}{\sqrt{2}}\right) = \left(\frac{4}{\sqrt{2}}, \frac{3}{\sqrt{2}}\right)$$

Now, equation of tangent at $P(\pi/4)$ is

$$\frac{x}{16}\times\frac{4}{\sqrt{2}}+\frac{y}{9}\times\frac{3}{\sqrt{2}}=1 \Rightarrow \frac{x}{4\sqrt{2}}+\frac{y}{3\sqrt{2}}=1$$

$$\Rightarrow \quad y=\frac{-3\sqrt{2}x}{4\sqrt{2}}+3\sqrt{2}=\frac{-3}{4}x+3\sqrt{2}$$

$$\therefore \quad m=-\frac{3}{4}\Rightarrow \tan\phi=\frac{-3}{4}$$

$\therefore$ Length of subtangent $= |y.\cot\phi|$

$$=|3/\sqrt{2}\times\frac{-4}{3}|=\frac{4}{\sqrt{2}}$$

$\therefore$ Length of subnormal $= |y.\tan\phi|$

$$=|3/\sqrt{2}\times\frac{-3}{4}|=\frac{9}{4\sqrt{2}}$$

Now, $\dfrac{\text{length of subtangent}}{\text{length of subnormal}}=\dfrac{4}{9/4}=\dfrac{16}{9}$

6.16 Concyclic Points

Any circle intersects an ellipse in two or four real points. They are called concyclic points and the sum of their eccentric angles is an even multiple of π.

Theorem If $\alpha,\beta,\gamma,\delta$ be the eccentric angles of the four concyclic points on an ellipse, then prove that $\alpha+\beta+\gamma+\delta=2n\pi$, where n is any integer.

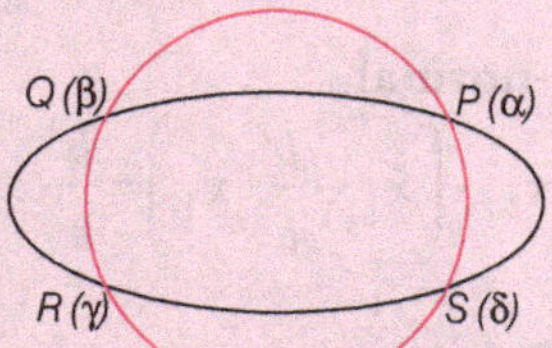

Proof Let the given circle be

$$x^2+y^2+2gx+2fy+c=0 \quad \text{...(i)}$$

and the given ellipse be

$$\frac{x^2}{a^2}+\frac{y^2}{b^2}=1 \quad \text{...(ii)}$$

Let $(a\cos\phi, b\sin\phi)$ be a point of intersection of Eqs. (i) and (ii).

As it lies on the circle Eq. (i).

$$\therefore \quad a^2\cos^2\phi+b^2\sin^2\phi+2ga\cos\phi+2fb\sin\phi+c=0 \quad \text{...(iii)}$$

or
$$a^2\left(\frac{1-\tan^2(\phi/2)}{1+\tan^2(\phi/2)}\right)^2+b^2\left(\frac{2\tan(\phi/2)}{1+\tan^2(\phi/2)}\right)^2+2ga\left(\frac{1-\tan^2(\phi/2)}{1+\tan^2(\phi/2)}\right)+2fb\left(\frac{2\tan(\phi/2)}{1+\tan^2(\phi/2)}\right)+c=0 \quad \text{...(iv)}$$

Put $\tan(\phi/2)=t$

$\therefore$ Eq. (iv) reduces to

$$a^2\left(\frac{1-t^2}{1+t^2}\right)^2+b^2\left(\frac{2t}{1+t^2}\right)^2+2ga\left(\frac{1-t^2}{1+t^2}\right)+2fb\left(\frac{2t}{1+t^2}\right)+c=0$$

or $(a^2-2ga+c)t^4+4bf\,t^3+(4b^2-2a^2+2c)t^2+4bft+(a^2+2ga+c)=0$ ...(v)

which is biquadratic equation in t

i.e. it has four values of t.

$$t=\tan(\phi/2)$$

Since, four values of eccentric angles are $\alpha,\beta,\gamma,\delta$

$$\therefore \quad \tan\left(\frac{\alpha}{2}+\frac{\beta}{2}+\frac{\gamma}{2}+\frac{\delta}{2}\right)=\frac{S_1-S_3}{1-S_2+S_4}=\frac{\Sigma t_1-\Sigma t_1t_2t_3}{1-\Sigma t_1t_2+\Sigma t_1t_2t_3t_4}=0$$

$$\Rightarrow \frac{1}{2}(\alpha+\beta+\gamma+\delta)=n\pi$$

$\therefore \quad \alpha+\beta+\gamma+\delta=2n\pi$, where n is any integer.

Alternate Method Let P, Q, R, S be four concyclic points on an ellipse, whose eccentric angles $\alpha,\beta,\gamma,\delta$ respectively. Then equation of the chords PQ and RS are (Take any two chords)

$$\frac{x}{a}\cos\left(\frac{\alpha+\beta}{2}\right)+\frac{y}{b}\sin\left(\frac{\alpha+\beta}{2}\right)-\cos\left(\frac{\alpha-\beta}{2}\right)=0$$

and
$$\frac{x}{a}\cos\left(\frac{\gamma+\delta}{2}\right)+\frac{y}{b}\sin\left(\frac{\gamma+\delta}{2}\right)-\cos\left(\frac{\gamma-\delta}{2}\right)=0$$

Now, the equation of any curve passing through P, Q, R and S is given by

$$\left(\frac{x^2}{a^2}+\frac{y^2}{b^2}-1\right)+\lambda\left(\frac{x}{a}\cos\left(\frac{\alpha+\beta}{2}\right)+\frac{y}{b}\sin\left(\frac{\alpha+\beta}{2}\right)-\cos\left(\frac{\alpha-\beta}{2}\right)\right)\times\left(\frac{x}{a}\cos\left(\frac{\gamma+\delta}{2}\right)+\frac{y}{b}\sin\left(\frac{\gamma+\delta}{2}\right)-\cos\left(\frac{\gamma-\delta}{2}\right)\right)=0$$

But the given points are concyclic. Hence, this equation will represent a circle, if coefficient of x^2 = coefficient y^2. and coefficient of $xy=0$

Now, equation of the coefficient of $xy=0$

$$\cos\left(\frac{\alpha+\beta}{2}\right)\sin\left(\frac{\gamma+\delta}{2}\right)+\sin\left(\frac{\alpha+\beta}{2}\right)\cos\left(\frac{\gamma+\delta}{2}\right)=0$$

or $\quad \sin\left(\dfrac{\alpha+\beta+\gamma+\delta}{2}\right)=0=\sin n\pi$

$$\therefore \quad \frac{1}{2}(\alpha+\beta+\gamma+\delta)=n\pi \quad \text{or} \quad \alpha+\beta+\gamma+\delta=2n\pi$$

where, n is any integer.

Hence, the sum of eccentric angles of four concylic points on an ellipse is always an even multiple of π.

COROLLARY 1 Prove that the common chords of a circle and an ellipse are equally inclined to the axes of the ellipse. If the point of intersection of chords PQ and RS is T, then equation of chord PQ is

$$\frac{x}{a}\cos\left(\frac{\alpha+\beta}{2}\right)+\frac{y}{b}\sin\left(\frac{\alpha+\beta}{2}\right)=\cos\left(\frac{\alpha-\beta}{2}\right)$$

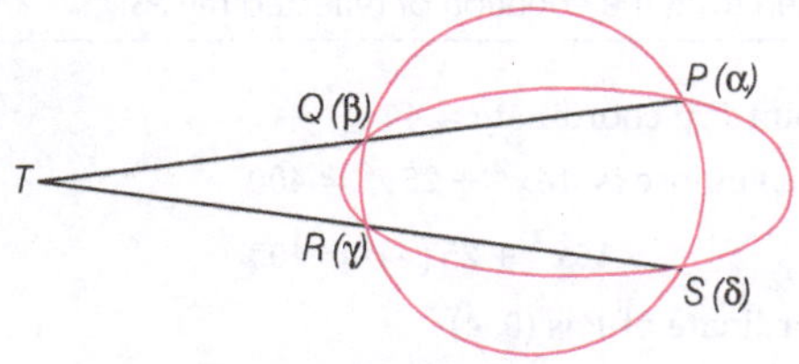

$\therefore$ Slope of $PQ = -\frac{b}{a}\cot\left(\frac{\alpha+\beta}{2}\right)$

$$= -\frac{b}{a}\cot\left(n\pi-\frac{\gamma+\delta}{2}\right) \quad [\because \alpha+\beta+\gamma+\delta=2n\pi]$$

$$= \frac{b}{a}\cot\left(\frac{\gamma+\delta}{2}\right) = -(\text{slope of } RS)$$

Hence, PQ and RS are equally inclined to the axis of x.

COROLLARY 2 Find the centre of the circle passing through the three points on an ellipse whose eccentric angles are α, β, γ.

Let the point of intersection of ellipse

$$\frac{x^2}{a^2}+\frac{y^2}{b^2}=1 \quad \text{...(i)}$$

and circle $\quad x^2+y^2+2gx+2fy+c=0 \quad$ ...(ii)

be $\alpha, \beta, \gamma, \delta$.

$\therefore \quad \alpha+\beta+\gamma+\delta=2n\pi \quad$ [where n is an integer]

Let ϕ be any point on Eq. (i)

$\therefore \quad x=a\cos\phi, y=b\sin\phi$

This point also lie on Eq. (ii)

$\therefore \quad a^2\cos^2\phi+b^2\sin^2\phi+2ga\cos\phi+2fb\sin\phi+c=0$ ...(iii)

$\Rightarrow \{(a^2-b^2)\cos^2\phi+2ga\cos\phi+(b^2+c)\}^2=4f^2b^2(1-\cos^2\phi)$

$\Rightarrow (a^2-b^2)^2\cos^4\phi+4ga(a^2-b^2)\cos^3\phi + \{2(a^2-b^2)(b^2+c)+4g^2a^2+4f^2b^2\}\cos^2\phi + 4ga(b^2+c)\cos\phi+\{b^2+c^2-4f^2b^2\}=0$

This is a fourth degree equation in $\cos\phi$.

It has four roots (i.e. $\cos\alpha, \cos\beta, \cos\gamma, \cos\delta$)

$$\therefore \quad \cos\alpha+\cos\beta+\cos\gamma+\cos\delta=-\frac{4ga}{(a^2-b^2)} \quad \text{...(iv)}$$

Similarly, changing Eq. (iii) in $\sin\phi$, we get

$$\sin\alpha+\sin\beta+\sin\gamma+\sin\delta=-\frac{4fb}{b^2-a^2} \quad \text{...(v)}$$

$\because \quad \alpha+\beta+\gamma+\delta=2n\pi$

$\therefore \quad \delta=2n\pi-(\alpha+\beta+\gamma)$

$\therefore \quad \sin\delta=-\{\sin(\alpha+\beta+\gamma)\}$ and $\cos\delta=\cos(\alpha+\beta+\gamma)$

Then, from Eqs. (iv) and (v), we get

$$-g=\left(\frac{a^2-b^2}{4a}\right)\{\cos\alpha+\cos\beta+\cos\gamma+\cos(\alpha+\beta+\gamma)\}$$

and $$-f=\left(\frac{b^2-a^2}{4b}\right)\{\sin\alpha+\sin\beta+\sin\gamma-\sin(\alpha+\beta+\gamma)\}$$

which give coordinate of centre of circle through α, β and γ.

COROLLARY 3 $P'CP$ and $D'CD$ are conjugate diameters of an ellipse and α is the eccentric angle of P. Prove that the eccentric angle of the point where the circle through P, P', D again cuts the ellipse is $\frac{\pi}{2}-3\alpha$.

The eccentric angles of P, P' and D are $\alpha, \pi+\alpha, \frac{\pi}{2}+\alpha$ respectively. Let β be the eccentric angle of the fourth point. As above

$$\alpha+(\pi+\alpha)+\left(\frac{\pi}{2}+\alpha\right)+\beta=2n\pi$$

$$\therefore \quad \beta=2n\pi-\left(\frac{3\pi}{2}+3\alpha\right)=\frac{\pi}{2}-3\alpha \quad [\text{for } n=1]$$

Some Standard Properties of the Ellipse

(i) If S be the focus and G be the point where the normal at P meets the axis of an ellipse, then $SG=e\cdot SP$ and the tangent and normal at P bisects the external and internal angles between the focal distances of P.

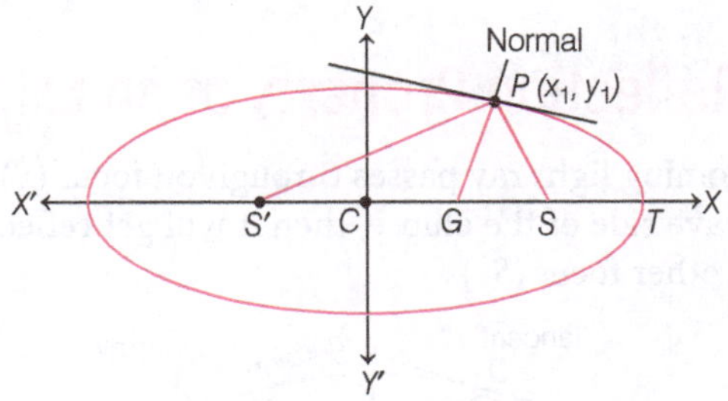

Let P be any point on the ellipse $\frac{x^2}{a^2}+\frac{y^2}{b^2}=1$

$\therefore$ Equation of normals PG is

$$(x-x_1)\frac{a^2}{x_1}=(y-y_1)\frac{b^2}{y_1}$$

On putting $y=0$, for the point G, we have

$$(x-x_1)\frac{a^2}{x_1}=-b^2$$

$$\therefore \quad x = CG = \left(\frac{a^2 - b^2}{a^2}\right) x_1 = \frac{a^2 e^2}{a^2} x_1 = e^2 x_1$$

$$\therefore \quad SG = CS - CG = ae - e^2 x_1 = e(a - ex_1) = eSP$$

Similarly, $S'G = eS'P$

$$\therefore \quad \frac{SG}{S'G} = \frac{eSP}{eS'P} = \frac{SP}{S'P}$$

$\therefore$ The normal PG bisects the internal $\angle SPS'$ between the focal distances but tangent and normal are at right angles, the tangent PT bisects the external angle SPL between them.

(ii) The locus of the feet of the perpendiculars from the foci on any tangent to an ellipse is the auxiliary circle. The equation of any tangent in terms slope (m) of the ellipse $\frac{x^2}{a^2} + \frac{y^2}{b^2} = 1$ is

$$y = mx \pm \sqrt{(a^2 m^2 + b^2)}$$

or $$y - mx = \pm \sqrt{(a^2 m^2 + b^2)} \quad \text{...(i)}$$

Equation of perpendicular line of Eq. (i) and passes through $(\pm ae, 0)$ is

$$my + x = \pm ae \quad \text{...(ii)}$$

The locus of the point of intersection of the line given by Eqs. (i) and (ii) can be obtained by eliminating m between them, on squaring and adding Eqs. (i) and (ii), we get

$$y^2(1 + m^2) + x^2(1 + m^2) = a^2 m^2 + b^2 + a^2 e^2$$

$$\Rightarrow \quad (1 + m^2)(x^2 + y^2) = a^2 m^2 + a^2 = a^2(1 + m^2)$$

or $$x^2 + y^2 = a^2$$

which is the equation of the auxiliary circle of the ellipse $\frac{x^2}{a^2} + \frac{y^2}{b^2} = 1$.

6.17 Reflection Property of an Ellipse

If an incoming light ray passes through on focus (S) strike the concave side of the ellipse, then it will get reflected towards other focus (S').

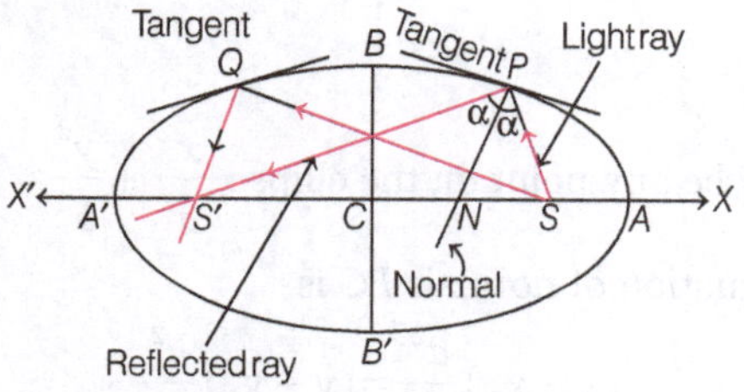

and $\quad \angle SPS' = \angle SQS'$

Example 46. A ray emanating from the point $(-3, 0)$ is incident on the ellipse $16x^2 + 25y^2 = 400$ at the point P with ordinate 4. Find the equation of the reflected ray after first reflection.

Decoding the Question

Firstly, find the coordinates of point P and the coordinates of foci, then from the equation of reflected ray PS.

Sol. For point P, y-coordinate = 4

$\because$ Given ellipse is $16x^2 + 25y^2 = 400$

$$16x^2 + 25(4)^2 = 400$$

$\therefore$ Coordinate of P is (0, 4)

and $$e^2 = 1 - \frac{16}{25} = \frac{9}{25}$$

$$\Rightarrow \quad e = \frac{3}{5}$$

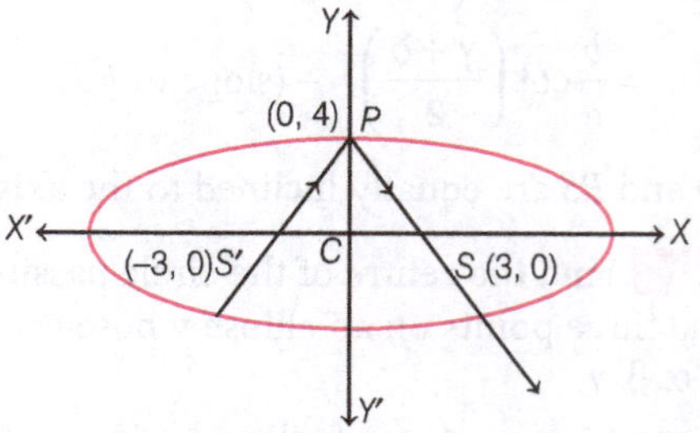

Foci $(\pm ae, 0)$ i.e. $(\pm 3, 0)$

Equation of reflected ray (i.e. PS) is

$$\frac{x}{3} + \frac{y}{4} = 1 \text{ or } 4x + 3y = 12.$$

Equation of an Ellipse Referred to Two Perpendicular Lines

Let $P(x, y)$ be any point on the ellipse $\frac{x^2}{a^2} + \frac{y^2}{b^2} = 1$,

then $$y = PM \text{ and } x = PN$$

$$\therefore \quad \frac{(PN)^2}{a^2} + \frac{(PM)^2}{b^2} = 1$$

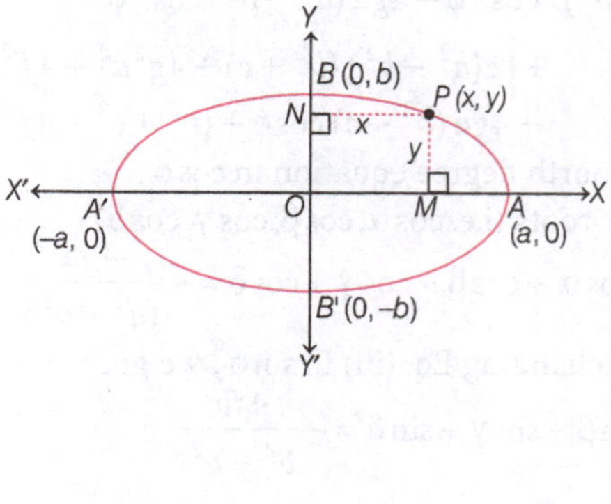

Suppose if axes along the lines

$$a_1x+b_1y+c_1=0 \quad \text{and} \quad b_1x-a_1y+c_2=0$$

then $PN=\dfrac{|a_1x+b_1y+c_1|}{\sqrt{(a_1^2+b_1^2)}}$, $PM=\dfrac{|b_1x-a_1y+c_2|}{\sqrt{(b_1^2+a_1^2)}}$

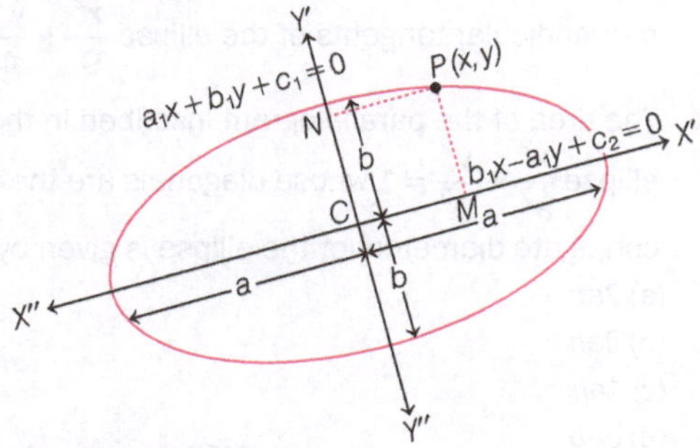

Then, equation of ellipse is

$$\frac{\left\{\dfrac{a_1x+b_1y+c_1}{\sqrt{(a_1^2+b_1^2)}}\right\}^2}{a^2}+\frac{\left\{\dfrac{b_1x-a_1y+c_2}{\sqrt{(b_1^2+a_1^2)}}\right\}^2}{b^2}=1$$

Concept Inside Video

JEE Focus Points

- **Centre** is the point of intersection of $a_1x+b_1y+c_1=0$ and $b_1x-a_1y+c_2=0$
- **Equations of Major and Minor Axes**
  (i) If $a>b$, then major axis lies along $b_1x-a_1y+c_2=0$ and minor axis lies along $a_1x+b_1y+c_1=0$.
  (ii) If $a<b$, then major axis lies along $a_1x+b_1y+c_1=0$ and minor axis lies along $b_1x-a_1y+c_2=0$.
- **Eccentricity**
  (i) If $a>b$, $b^2=a^2(1-e^2)$ (ii) If $a<b$, $a^2=b^2(1-e^2)$
- **Foci**
  (i) If $a>b$, $\dfrac{a_1x+b_1y+c_1}{\sqrt{(a_1^2+b_1^2)}}=\pm ae$, $\dfrac{b_1x-a_1y+c_2}{\sqrt{(b_1^2+a_1^2)}}=0$
  we get after solving (x, y)
  (ii) If $a<b$, $\dfrac{a_1x+b_1y+c_1}{\sqrt{a_1^2+b_1^2}}=0$, $\dfrac{b_1x-a_1y+c_2}{\sqrt{b_1^2+a_1^2}}=\pm be$
  we get after solving (x, y)
- **Directrices**
  (i) If $a>b$, $\dfrac{a_1x+b_1y+c_1}{\sqrt{(a_1^2+b_1^2)}}=\pm\dfrac{a}{e}$
  (ii) If $a<b$, $\dfrac{b_1x-a_1y+c_2}{\sqrt{(a_1^2+b_1^2)}}=\pm\dfrac{b}{e}$

Example 47. Determine the equations of major and minor axes of the ellipse

$$4(x-2y+1)^2+9(2x+y+2)^2=25$$

Also, find its centre, length of the latusrectum and eccentricity.

Sol. The equation of the ellipse can be written as

$$4\times5\left(\frac{x-2y+1}{\sqrt5}\right)^2+9\times5\left(\frac{2x+y+2}{\sqrt5}\right)^2=25$$

or $$\frac{\left(\dfrac{x-2y+1}{\sqrt5}\right)^2}{(5/4)}+\frac{\left(\dfrac{2x+y+2}{\sqrt5}\right)^2}{(5/9)}=1$$

or $$\frac{X^2}{a^2}+\frac{Y^2}{b^2}=1$$

Here $a>b$

$\therefore$ **Equation of major axis is** $Y=0$

i.e. $2x+y+2=0$

and **Equation of minor axis is** $X=0$

i.e. $x-2y+1=0$

Centre $X=0$ and $Y=0$

$\Rightarrow$ $x-2y+1=0$,

$2x+y+2=0$

On solving, we get

$$x=-1, y=0$$

$\therefore$ Centre is $(-1, 0)$

Length of latusrectum $=\dfrac{2b^2}{a}$

$$=\frac{2\times5/9}{\sqrt5/2}$$

$$=\frac{4\sqrt5}{9}$$

Eccentricity $b^2=a^2(1-e^2)$

$\Rightarrow$ $\dfrac{5}{9}=\dfrac{5}{4}(1-e^2)$

$\Rightarrow$ $\dfrac{4}{9}=1-e^2$

$\Rightarrow$ $e^2=\dfrac{5}{9}$

$\therefore$ $e=\dfrac{\sqrt5}{3}$

Milestone Practice 6.3

1. The angle between the pair of tangents drawn from the point (2, 1) to the ellipse $2x^2 + 3y^2 = 5$ is
   (a) $\tan^{-1}\left(\frac{12}{5}\right)$ (b) $\tan^{-1}\left(\frac{6}{\sqrt{5}}\right)$
   (c) $\tan^{-1}\left(\frac{2\sqrt{138}}{5}\right)$ (d) $\tan^{-1}(12\sqrt{5})$

2. If chords of contact of tangents from two points (x_1, y_1) and (x_2, y_2) to the ellipse $\frac{x^2}{a^2} + \frac{y^2}{b^2} = 1$ are at right angles, then $\frac{x_1 x_2}{y_1 y_2}$ is equal to
   (a) $\frac{a^2}{b^2}$ (b) $-\frac{b^2}{a^2}$ (c) $-\frac{a^4}{b^4}$ (d) $-\frac{b^4}{a^4}$

3. From the point $(\lambda, 3)$ tangents are drawn to $\frac{x^2}{9} + \frac{y^2}{4} = 1$ and are perpendicular to each other then λ is
   (a) ± 1 (b) ± 2 (c) ± 3 (d) ± 4

4. The eccentric angle of one end of a diameter of $x^2 + 3y^2 = 3$ is $\pi / 6$, then the eccentric angle of the other end will be
   (a) $\frac{5\pi}{6}$ (b) $-\frac{5\pi}{6}$ (c) $-\frac{2\pi}{3}$ (d) $\frac{2\pi}{3}$

5. The locus of the mid-points of a focal chord of the ellipse $\frac{x^2}{a^2} + \frac{y^2}{b^2} = 1$ is
   (a) $\frac{x^2}{a^2} + \frac{y^2}{b^2} = \frac{ex}{a}$ (b) $\frac{x^2}{a^2} - \frac{y^2}{b^2} = \frac{ex}{a}$
   (c) $x^2 + y^2 = a^2 + b^2$ (d) $x^2 - y^2 = a^2 + b^2$

6. The centre of the ellipse $\frac{(x + y - 2)^2}{9} + \frac{(x - y)^2}{16} = 1$ is
   (a) (0, 0) (b) (1, 0)
   (c) (0, 1) (d) (1, 1)

7. Find the locus of the point of intersection of two perpendicular tangents of the ellipse $\frac{x^2}{9} + \frac{y^2}{4} = 1$.

8. The area of the parallelogram inscribed in the ellipse $\frac{x^2}{a^2} + \frac{y^2}{b^2} = 1$ whose diagonals are the conjugate diameters of the ellipse is given by
   (a) $2ab$
   (b) $3ab$
   (c) $4ab$
   (d) $5ab$

9. Find the locus of the vertices of equilateral triangle circumscribing the ellipse $\frac{x^2}{a^2} + \frac{y^2}{b^2} = 1$.

10. A tangent to the ellipse $x^2 + 4y^2 = 4$ meets the ellipse $x^2 + 2y^2 = 6$ at P and Q. Prove that the tangents at P and Q of the ellipse $x^2 + 2y^2 = 6$ are at right angles.

11. Find the locus of the mid-point of chords of the ellipse $\frac{x^2}{a^2} + \frac{y^2}{b^2} = 1$ $(a > b)$ passing through the point $(2a, 0)$.

12. Find the locus of the point the chord of contact of tangents from which to the ellipse $\frac{x^2}{a^2} + \frac{y^2}{b^2} = 1$, touches the circle $x^2 + y^2 = c^2$.

13. Find the centre and eccentricity of the ellipse
   $4(x - 2y + 1)^2 + 9(2x + y + 2)^2 = 5.$

14. A ray emanating from the point $(0, -\sqrt{5})$ is incident on the ellipse $9x^2 + 4y^2 = 36$ at the point P with abscissa 2. Find the equation of the reflected ray after first reflection.

Answer Key

1. (c) 2. (c) 3. (b) 4. (b) 5. (a) 6. (d)
7. $x^2 + y^2 = 13$ 8. (a) 9. $\frac{(a^2 + 3b^2)^2}{a^2} x^2 + \frac{(3a^2 + b^2)}{b^2} y^2 = (a^2 - b^2)^2$ 11. $\frac{(x - a)^2}{a^2} + \frac{y^2}{b^2} = 1$
12. $\frac{x^2}{a^2} + \frac{y^2}{b^2} = \frac{1}{e^2}$ 13. $(-1, 0)$ and $\frac{\sqrt{5}}{3}$ 14. $\sqrt{5}x + 2y - 2\sqrt{5} = 0$

For Detailed Solution

JEE Pattern EXAMPLES

Single Option Correct Type Questions

Example 1 *The eccentricity of an ellipse* $\frac{x^2}{a^2}+\frac{y^2}{b^2}=1$ *whose latusrectum is half of its minor axis, is*

(a) $\frac{1}{2}$ (b) $\frac{1}{\sqrt{2}}$

(c) $\frac{\sqrt{3}}{2}$ (d) $\frac{1}{\sqrt{3}}$

Sol. (c) Let $a > b$. Then, we have

Length of latusrectum = Half of its minor axis

$$\Rightarrow \quad \frac{2b^2}{a}=\frac{1}{2}\times 2b \quad \Rightarrow \quad \frac{b}{a}=\frac{1}{2}$$

Now, eccentricity, $e=\sqrt{1-\frac{b^2}{a^2}}=\sqrt{1-\frac{1}{4}}=\frac{\sqrt{3}}{2}$

Example 2 *An arc of a bridge is semi-elliptical with the major axis horizontal. If the length of the base is 9 m and the heighest part of the bridge is 3m from the horizontal, then the height of the arc, 2m from the centre of the base is*

(a) $\frac{\sqrt{65}}{4}$ (b) $\frac{\sqrt{65}}{3}$

(c) $\frac{\sqrt{65}}{2}$ (d) $\sqrt{65}$

Sol. (b) Let the equation of the semi-ellipse arc be $\frac{x^2}{a^2}+\frac{y^2}{b^2}=1, (a > b)$.

Length of the major axis, $2a=9 \Rightarrow a=\frac{9}{2}$

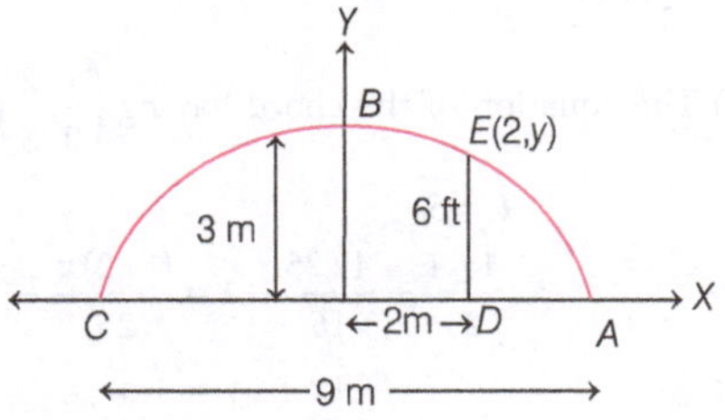

Length of the semi-minor axis, $b=3$

So, equation of the arc becomes

$$\frac{4x^2}{81}+\frac{y^2}{9}=1$$

Now, if $x=2$, then

$$\frac{16}{81}+\frac{y^2}{9}=1$$

$$\Rightarrow \quad \frac{y^2}{9}=\frac{65}{81}$$

$$\Rightarrow \quad y^2=\frac{65}{9} \Rightarrow y=\frac{\sqrt{65}}{3}$$

So, required height is $\frac{\sqrt{65}}{3}$ m.

Example 3 *The eccentricity of the ellipse* $\frac{(3x-4y+2)^2}{16}+\frac{(4x+3y-5)^2}{9}=1$*, is*

(a) $\frac{\sqrt{7}}{4}$ (b) $\frac{\sqrt{7}}{5}$

(c) $\frac{\sqrt{7}}{6}$ (d) $\frac{1}{\sqrt{7}}$

Sol.

> **Decoding the Question**
>
> If equation of ellipse is of the form $\frac{(mx-ny+p)^2}{a^2}+\frac{(nx+my+p)^2}{b^2}$, then divide numerator and denominator of each term by m^2+n^2

(a) The given equation is

$$\frac{(3x-4y+2)^2}{16}+\frac{(4x+3y-5)^2}{9}=1$$

$$\frac{((3x-4y+2)/5)^2}{16/25}+\frac{((4x+3y-5)/5)^2}{9/25}=1$$

$$\therefore \quad a^2=\frac{16}{25}, b^2=\frac{9}{25}$$

Now, eccentricity, $e=\sqrt{1-\frac{b^2}{a^2}}$

$$=\sqrt{1-\frac{9}{16}}=\frac{\sqrt{7}}{4}$$

Example 4 *The maximum area of the ellipse* $\dfrac{x^2}{a^2}+\dfrac{y^2}{b^2}=1$, *which touches the line* $y=3x+2$, *is*

(a) $\dfrac{\pi}{3}$ (b) $\dfrac{2\pi}{3}$

(c) 2π (d) 6π

Sol. (b) Line $y=3x+2$ touches ellipse $\dfrac{x^2}{a^2}+\dfrac{y^2}{b^2}=1$

Here, $m=3$ and $c=2$

Now, $c^2=a^2m^2+b^2$

$\Rightarrow \quad 4=9a^2+b^2$

Now, we know that AM ≥ GM

$\Rightarrow \quad \dfrac{9a^2+b^2}{2}\ge\sqrt{9a^2\times b^2}$

$\Rightarrow \quad 2\ge 3ab \Rightarrow \dfrac{2\pi}{3}\ge\pi ab \quad [\because \text{area of an ellipse}=\pi ab]$

$\therefore$ Maximum area of the ellipse is $\dfrac{2\pi}{3}$.

JEE SCANNER

Example 5 Similar to PYQ Asked in JEE Main 2024

Let P be a point on the ellipse $\dfrac{x^2}{16}+\dfrac{y^2}{9}=1$. *Let the line passing through P and parallel to Y-axis meet the circle* $x^2+y^2=16$ *at point Q such that P and Q are on the same side of the X-axis. Then, the eccentricity of the locus of the point R on PQ such that* $PR:RQ=2:3$ *as P moves on the ellipse is*

(a) $\dfrac{11}{19}$ (b) $\dfrac{13}{21}$

(c) $\dfrac{\sqrt{139}}{23}$ (d) $\dfrac{\sqrt{111}}{20}$

Sol. (d) We have,

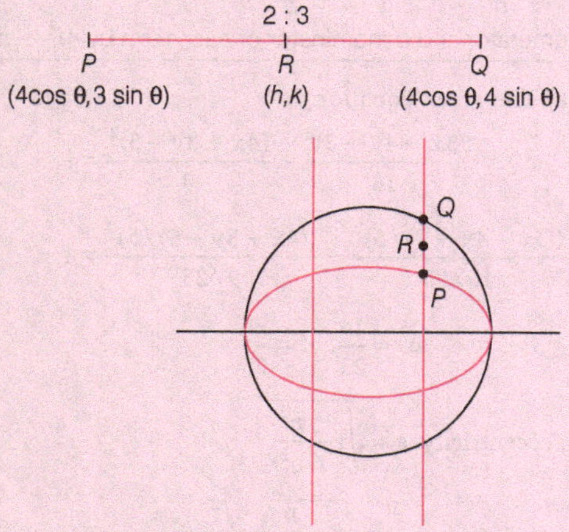

$\therefore \quad h=\dfrac{8\cos\theta+12\cos\theta}{5}=4\cos\theta$

and $k=\dfrac{8\sin\theta+9\sin\theta}{5}=\dfrac{17}{5}\sin\theta$

Hence, locus of the point R on PQ is

$$\frac{x^2}{4^2}+\frac{y^2}{\left(\frac{17}{5}\right)^2}=1$$

Here, $\quad a^2=4^2$ and $b^2=\left(\dfrac{17}{5}\right)^2$

Now, eccentricity, $e=\sqrt{1-\dfrac{b^2}{a^2}}=\sqrt{1-\dfrac{\left(\frac{17}{5}\right)^2}{4^2}}$

$$=\sqrt{1-\frac{289}{400}}=\sqrt{\frac{111}{400}}$$

So, $\quad c=\dfrac{\sqrt{111}}{20}$

Skill Builder

Let P be a point on the ellipse $\dfrac{x^2}{25}+\dfrac{y^2}{16}=1$. Let the line passing through P and parallel to Y-axis meet the circle $x^2+y^2=25$ at point Q such that P and Q are on the same side of the X-axis, Then, the eccentricity of the locus of the point R on PQ such that $PR:RQ=3:2$ as P moves on the ellipse is

(a) $\dfrac{11}{19}$ (b) $\dfrac{13}{16}$

(c) $\dfrac{4\sqrt{6}}{25}$ (d) $\dfrac{\sqrt{111}}{20}$

For Sol.

Example 6 *The length of the chord of the ellipse* $\dfrac{x^2}{25}+\dfrac{y^2}{16}=1$, *whose middle point is* $\left(\dfrac{1}{2},\dfrac{2}{5}\right)$ *is*

(a) $\dfrac{7}{4}\sqrt{41}$

(b) $\dfrac{4}{7}\sqrt{41}$

(c) $\dfrac{7}{5}\sqrt{41}$

(d) $\dfrac{5}{7}\sqrt{41}$

Sol. (c) The equation of the chord having $\left(\dfrac{1}{2},\dfrac{2}{5}\right)$ as mid-point is

$$T=S_1$$

$\Rightarrow \quad \dfrac{1/4}{25}+\dfrac{4/25}{16}-1=\dfrac{(1/2)x}{25}+\dfrac{(2/5)y}{16}-1$

$\Rightarrow \quad 4x+5y=4$

$\Rightarrow \quad 5y=4(1-x)$

On solving with ellipse, we get

$$16x^2 + 16(1 - x)^2 = 400$$

$$\Rightarrow \quad x^2 - x - 12 = 0$$

$$\Rightarrow \quad x = 4, -3$$

For $\quad x - 4, y = -\frac{12}{5}$

and for $\quad x = -3, y = \frac{16}{5}$

$$\therefore \quad \text{Length of the chord} = \sqrt{(4+3)^2 + \left(\frac{-12}{5} - \frac{16}{5}\right)^2}$$

$$= \sqrt{49 + \frac{784}{25}}$$

$$= \frac{\sqrt{2009}}{5} = \frac{7}{5}\sqrt{41}$$

Example 7 ■ *A point O is the centre of the ellipse with major axis AB and minor axis CD. Point F is one focus of the ellipse. If $OF = 6$ and the diameter of the inscribed circle of ΔOCF is 2, then the product $(AB)(CD)$ is equal to*

(a) 52 (b) 56

(c) 78 (d) None of these

Sol. (b) $\because$ Diameter of the inscribed circle of ΔOCF is 2.

$\therefore$ Radius = 1

Centre of the circle is (1, 1) and equation of CF is $\frac{x}{6} + \frac{y}{b} = 1$

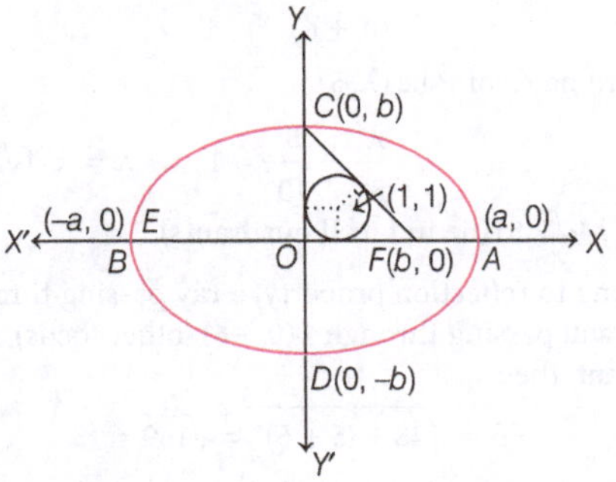

Now, length of perpendicular from (1, 1) on $CF = 1$ (radius)

$$\Rightarrow \quad \frac{\left|\frac{1}{6} + \frac{1}{b} - 1\right|}{\sqrt{\left(\frac{1}{36} + \frac{1}{b^2}\right)}} = 1$$

or $\quad -\left(\frac{1}{b} - \frac{5}{6}\right) = \sqrt{\left(\frac{1}{36} + \frac{1}{b^2}\right)}$

$$\Rightarrow \quad \left(\frac{5}{6} - \frac{1}{b}\right) = \sqrt{\left(\frac{1}{36} + \frac{1}{b^2}\right)}$$

On squaring both sides, then $\left(\frac{5}{6} - \frac{1}{b}\right)^2 = \frac{1}{36} + \frac{1}{b^2}$

$$\Rightarrow \quad \frac{25}{36} + \frac{1}{b^2} - \frac{5}{3b} = \frac{1}{36} + \frac{1}{b^2}$$

$$\Rightarrow \quad \frac{5}{3b} = \frac{24}{36} = \frac{2}{3}$$

$$\therefore \quad b = \frac{5}{2}$$

Also, $\quad b^2 = a^2(1 - e^2)$

$$b^2 = a^2 - (ae)^2$$

$$\Rightarrow \quad a^2 = b^2 + (ae)^2 = \frac{25}{4} + 36 \qquad [\because ae = 6]$$

$$\Rightarrow \quad a = \frac{13}{2}$$

Hence, $(AB)(CD) = (2a)(2b)$

$= 13 \times 5 = 65$

Example 8 ■ *The normal at a variable point P on an ellipse $\frac{x^2}{a^2} + \frac{y^2}{b^2} = 1$ of eccentricity e meets the axes of the ellipse in Q and R, then the locus of the mid-point of QR is a conic with eccentricity e′ such that*

(a) e' is independent of e (b) $e' = 1$

(c) $e' = e$ (d) $e' = \frac{1}{e}$

Sol. (c) Normal at $P(a\cos\theta, b\sin\theta)$ is

$$ax\sec\theta - by\,\text{cosec}\,\theta = a^2 - b^2 \qquad (\text{let } a > b)$$

It meets the axes at

$$Q\left(\frac{(a^2 - b^2)}{a}\cos\theta,\ 0\right) \text{ and } R\left(0, -\frac{(a^2 - b^2)}{b}\sin\theta\right)$$

Let mid-point of QR be $T(x, y)$, then

$$2x = \frac{(a^2 - b^2)}{a}\cos\theta$$

or $\quad 2ax = (a^2 - b^2)\cos\theta \qquad \ldots(\text{i})$

and $\quad 2y = -\frac{(a^2 - b^2)}{b}\sin\theta$

or $\quad 2by = -(a^2 - b^2)\sin\theta \qquad \ldots(\text{ii})$

On squaring and adding Eq. (i) and Eq.(ii), we get

$$4a^2x^2 + 4b^2y^2 = (a^2 - b^2)^2$$

$$\Rightarrow \quad \frac{x^2}{\left(\frac{a^2 - b^2}{2a}\right)^2} + \frac{y^2}{\left(\frac{a^2 - b^2}{2b}\right)^2} = 1$$

which is an ellipse, having eccentricity e', then

Let $\quad A = \frac{a^2 - b^2}{2a}, B = \frac{a^2 - b^2}{2b}$

$$A^2 = B^2(1 - e'^2) \qquad [\because B > A]$$

$$\Rightarrow \quad e'^2 = 1 - \frac{A^2}{B^2} = 1 - \frac{b^2}{a^2} = e^2$$

$$\therefore \quad e' = e$$

JEE SCANNER

Example 9 Similar to PYQ Asked in JEE Main 2024

Let the line $3x+5y-k=0, k>0$, intersect the X-axis and Y-axis at the points A and B respectively. If the equation of the circle having the line segment AB as a diameter is $x^2+y^2-5x-3y=0$ and the length of the latusrectum of the ellipse $x^2+25y^2=k^2$ is $\frac{m}{n}$, where m and n are coprime, then $2m+n$ is equal to

(a) 17 (b) 30 (c) 27 (d) 32

Sol. (a) Given equation of line $3x+5y-k=0$ which intersects the X-axis and Y-axis at the points A and B.

When $y=0$, then coordinate of A is $\left(\frac{k}{3}, 0\right)$

When $x=0$, when coordinate of B is $\left(0, \frac{k}{5}\right)$

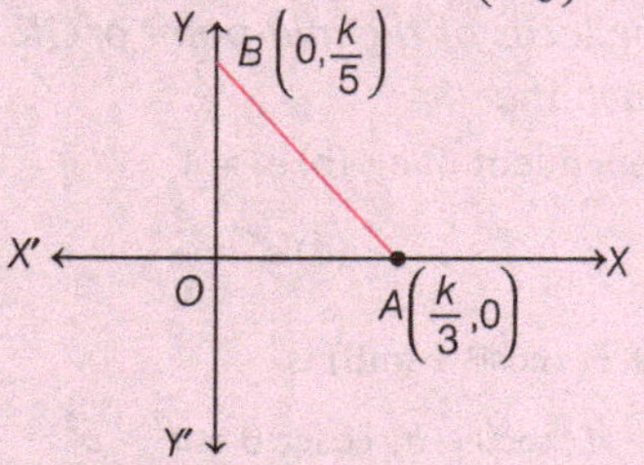

Equation of circle with diameter AB is

$$(x-0)\left(x-\frac{k}{3}\right)+\left(y-\frac{k}{5}\right)(y-0)=0$$

$$\Rightarrow \quad x^2+y^2-\frac{kx}{3}-\frac{ky}{5}=0$$

On comparing with $x^2+y^2-5x-3y=0$, we get

$$\frac{k}{3}=5 \Rightarrow k=15$$

Now, equation of ellipse is

$$x^2+25y^2=225 \Rightarrow \frac{x^2}{225}+\frac{y^2}{9}=1$$

$$\text{Latusrectum}=\frac{2b^2}{a}=\frac{2\times 9}{15}=\frac{6}{5} \Rightarrow m=6 \text{ and } n=5$$

$$\therefore \quad 2m+n=12+5=17$$

Skill Builder

Let the line $x+2y-k=0, k>0$, intersect the X-axis and Y-axis at the points A and B respectively. If the equation of the circle having the line segment AB as a diameter is $x^2+y^2-2x-y=0$ and the length of the latusrectum of the ellipse $x^2+16y^2=k^2$ is $\frac{m}{n}$, where m and n are coprime, then $2m+n$ is equal to

For Sol.

(a) 2 (b) 6
(c) 12 (d) 32

Example 10 *A ray emanating from the point (0, 6) is incident on the ellipse $25x^2+16y^2=1600$ at the point P with ordinate 5 After reflection, ray cuts the Y-axis at B. The length of PB is*

(a) 5 (b) 7
(c) 12 (d) 13

Sol. (d) $\because$ Ellipse is $25x^2+16y^2=1600$

or $$\frac{x^2}{8^2}+\frac{y^2}{10^2}=1$$

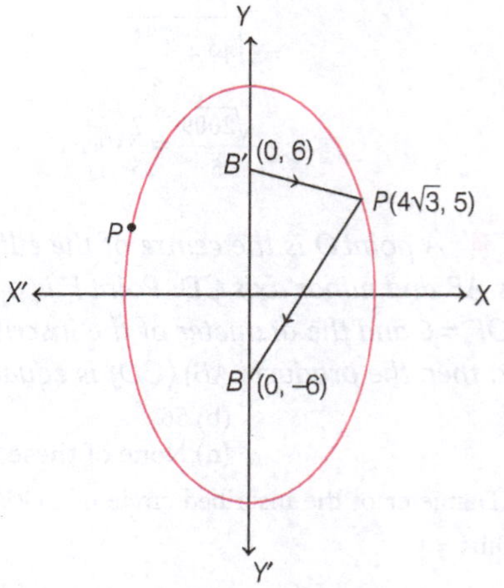

Coordinating foci are $(0, \pm\sqrt{(10^2-8^2)})$

i.e. $(0, \pm 6)$

Let coordinates of P be $(\lambda, 5)$.

$$\therefore \quad \frac{\lambda^2}{8^2}+\frac{5^2}{10^2}=1 \Rightarrow \lambda=\pm 4\sqrt{3}$$

$\therefore$ $P \equiv (\pm 4\sqrt{3}, 5)$ (lie in I or II quadrants)

According to reflection property, a ray passing through focus $B'(0, 6)$ will passing through $B(0, -6)$ (other focus). If P lies in I quadrant, then

$$PB=\sqrt{48+(5+6)^2}=\sqrt{169}=13$$

Example 11 *Coordinates of the vertices B and C of a ΔABC are (2, 0) and (8, 0) respectively. The vertex A is varying in such a way that $4\tan\left(\frac{B}{2}\right)\cdot\tan\left(\frac{C}{2}\right)=1$. Then, the locus of A is*

(a) $\frac{(x-5)^2}{25}+\frac{y^2}{16}=1$

(b) $\frac{(x-5)^2}{16}+\frac{y^2}{9}=1$

(c) $\frac{(x-5)^2}{25}+\frac{y^2}{9}=1$

(d) $\frac{(x-5)^2}{16}+\frac{y^2}{25}=1$

Sol. (a) $\because\ 4\tan\left(\frac{B}{2}\right)\cdot\tan\left(\frac{C}{2}\right)=1$

$$\Rightarrow\quad 4\times\sqrt{\frac{(s-c)(s-a)}{s(s-b)}}\times\sqrt{\frac{(s-a)(s-b)}{s(s-c)}}=1$$

$$\Rightarrow\quad \frac{s-a}{s}=\frac{1}{4}$$

$$\Rightarrow\quad 3s=4a$$

$$\Rightarrow\quad 3\left(\frac{a+b+c}{2}\right)=4a$$

or $\quad b+c=\frac{5a}{3}=10=2a \quad [\because a=BC=6]$

Since, the sum of distances of A from two given fixed points B and C is always 10.

Here, B and C are foci.

$\therefore$ Centre (5, 0) and distance between foci = 6

$$\Rightarrow\quad 2a_1 e=6$$

$$\Rightarrow\quad e=\frac{6}{10}=\frac{3}{5} \quad [\because a_1=5]$$

and $\quad b^2=a_1^2(1-e^2)=25\left(1-\frac{9}{25}\right)=16$

or $\quad b=4$

$\because$ A lies on the ellipse.

$\therefore$ Locus of A is

$$\frac{(x-5)^2}{(5)^2}+\frac{(y-0)^2}{(4)^2}=1$$

or $\quad \frac{(x-5)^2}{25}+\frac{y^2}{16}=1$

Example 12 *If a tangent of slope 2 of the ellipse $\frac{x^2}{a^2}+\frac{y^2}{b^2}=1$ is normal to the circle $x^2+y^2+4x+1=0$, then the maximum value of ab is*

(a) 1 (b) 2
(c) 4 (d) 8

Sol. (c) Equation of tangent is $y=2x+\sqrt{(4a^2+b^2)}$

This is normal to the circle

$x^2+y^2+4x+1=0$

This tangent passes through $(-2, 0)$, then

$$0=-4+\sqrt{(4a^2+b^2)}$$

$$\Rightarrow\quad 4a^2+b^2=16$$

$\because\quad$ AM $\geq$ GM

$$\therefore\quad \frac{4a^2+b^2}{2}\sqrt{(4a^2)(b^2)}$$

$$\Rightarrow\quad \frac{16}{2}\geq 2ab$$

or $\quad ab\leq 4$

Hence, the maximum value of ab is 4.

More than One Correct Option Type Questions

Example 13 *If the equation $(5x-1)^2+(5y-2)^2=(\lambda^2-2\lambda+1)(3x+4y-1)^2$ represents an ellipse, then the value of λ is/are*

(a) 0.2 (b) 1.1
(c) 0.78 (d) 1.91

Sol. (a, b, c, d) We have,

$$(5x-1)^2+(5y-2)^2=(\lambda^2-2\lambda+1)(3x+4y-1)^2$$

$$\Rightarrow\quad \left(x-\frac{1}{5}\right)^2+\left(y-\frac{2}{5}\right)^2=(\lambda-1)^2\left|\frac{3x+4y-1}{\sqrt{3^2+4^2}}\right|^2$$

$$\Rightarrow\quad \sqrt{\left(x-\frac{1}{5}\right)^2+\left(y-\frac{2}{5}\right)^2}=|\lambda-1|\left|\frac{3x+4y-1}{\sqrt{3^2+4^2}}\right|$$

For ellipse, $SP=ePM$, $0<e<1$

$$\Rightarrow\quad 0<|\lambda-1|<1$$

$$\Rightarrow\quad \lambda\in(0,2)-\{1\}$$

Example 14 *The value of eccentric angle of a point on the ellipse $\frac{x^2}{6}+\frac{y^2}{2}=1$, whose distance from the centre of the ellipse is $\sqrt{5}$, is/are*

(a) $\frac{\pi}{6}$ (b) $\frac{5\pi}{6}$ (c) $\frac{4\pi}{3}$ (d) $\frac{11\pi}{6}$

Sol. (a, b, d)

Any point on the ellipse is $P(\sqrt{6}\cos\theta, \sqrt{2}\sin\theta)$

Now, $\quad CP=\sqrt{6\cos^2\theta+2\sin^2\theta}=\sqrt{5}$

$$\Rightarrow\quad 6(1-\sin^2\theta)+2\sin^2\theta=5$$

$$\Rightarrow\quad 4\sin^2\theta=1$$

$$\Rightarrow\quad \sin\theta=\pm\frac{1}{2}$$

$$\Rightarrow\quad \theta=\frac{\pi}{6},\frac{5\pi}{6},\frac{7\pi}{6},\frac{11\pi}{6}$$

Example 15 *For the ellipse $3x^2+2y^2+6x-8y+5=0$ which of the following is/are true ?*

(a) $e=\frac{1}{\sqrt{3}}$ (b) Centre is $(-1, 2)$
(c) Foci are $(-1, 1)(-1, 3)$ (d) Directrices are $y=2\pm\sqrt{3}$

Sol. (a, b, c) We have,

$$3x^2+2y^2+6x-8y+5=0$$

$$\Rightarrow\quad 3(x^2+2)+2(y^2-4y)+5=0$$

$$\Rightarrow\quad 3(x+1)^2-3+2(y-2)^2-8+5=0$$

$$\Rightarrow\quad 3(x+1)^2+2(y-2)^2=6$$

$$\Rightarrow\quad \frac{(x+1)^2}{2}+\frac{(y-2)^2}{3}=1$$

$\therefore$ Center is $(-1, 2)$.

Now, $a^2 = 2$ and $b^2 = 3$

$\Rightarrow$ $a = \sqrt{2}$ and $b = \sqrt{3}$ and $b > a$.

Now, $e = \sqrt{1 - \frac{a^2}{b^2}} = \sqrt{1 - \frac{2}{3}} = \frac{1}{\sqrt{3}}$

Foci $= (-1, 2 \pm be) = (-1, 2 \pm 1)$ i.e. $(-1, 1)$ and $(-1, 3)$

Directrices are $y = 2 \pm \frac{b}{e} \Rightarrow y = 2 \pm 3 \Rightarrow y = 5$ or $y = -1$

Example 16 *Extremities of the latusrectum of the ellipse $\frac{x^2}{a^2} + \frac{y^2}{b^2} = 1 (a > b)$ having a given major axis $2a$ lies on*

(a) $x^2 = a(a - y)$ (b) $x^2 = a(a + y)$
(c) $y^2 = a(a + x)$ (d) $y^2 = a(a - x)$

Sol. (a, b) $\because$ Extremities of the latusrectum are $\left(ae, \pm \frac{b^2}{a}\right)$.

Let $x = \pm ae$ and $y = \pm \frac{b^2}{a}$

or $x^2 = a^2e^2$ and $b^2 = \pm ay$

or $x^2 = a^2 - b^2$ and $b^2 = \pm ay$

$\therefore$ $x^2 = a^2 \pm ay$ or $x^2 = a(a \pm y)$

Example 17 *The locus of the image of the focus of the ellipse $\frac{x^2}{25} + \frac{y^2}{9} = 1$, with respect to any of the tangent to the ellipse is*

(a) $(x + 4)^2 + y^2 = 100$ (b) $(x + 2)^2 + y^2 = 50$
(c) $(x - 4)^2 + y^2 = 100$ (d) $(x - 2)^2 + y^2 = 50$

Sol. (a, c) Let $M(h, k)$ be the image SM cuts a tangent at a point which lies on the auxiliary circle of the ellipse, therefore

$\left(\frac{h \pm 4}{2}\right)^2 + \frac{k^2}{4} = (5)^2$ [$\because$ foci of the given ellipse are $(\pm 4, 0)$]

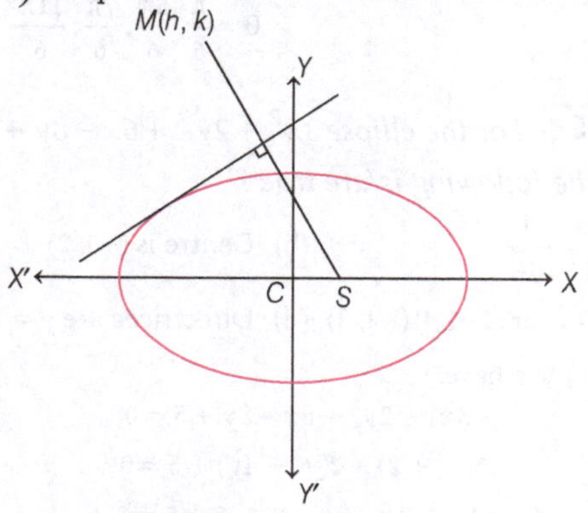

or $(h \pm 4)^2 + k^2 = 100$

Hence, the locus is $(x \pm 4)^2 + y^2 = 100$

Example 18 *A tangent to the ellipse $4x^2 + 9y^2 = 36$ is cut by the tangent at the extremities of the major axis at T and T′. The circle TT′ as diameter passes through the point*

(a) $(-\sqrt{5}, 0)$ (b) $(\sqrt{5}, 0)$
(c) $(\sqrt{3}, 0)$ (d) $(-\sqrt{3}, 0)$

Sol. (a, b) Given equation of the ellipse is $4x^2 + 9y^2 = 36$

i.e. $\frac{x^2}{9} + \frac{y^2}{4} = 1$ ...(i)

The equation of tangent at $(3\cos\theta, 2\sin\theta)$ is

$$\frac{x}{3}\cos\theta + \frac{y}{2}\sin\theta = 1$$

which meets the tangent at $x = 3$ and $x = -3$ at the extremities of major axis

$$T \equiv \left(3, \frac{2(1 - \cos\theta)}{\sin\theta}\right)$$

and $T' \equiv \left(-3, \frac{2(1 + \cos\theta)}{\sin\theta}\right)$

$\therefore$ Equation of circle on TT' as diameter is

$$(x - 3)(x + 3) + \left(y - \frac{2(1 - \cos\theta)}{\sin\theta}\right)\left(y - \frac{2(1 + \cos\theta)}{\sin\theta}\right) = 0$$

$\Rightarrow$ $x^2 + y^2 - \frac{4}{\sin\theta} \cdot y - 5 = 0$

or $(x^2 + y^2 - 5) - \frac{4}{\sin\theta} y = 0$ ...(ii)

Clearly, Eq. (ii), passes through point of intersection of

$x^2 + y^2 - 5 = 0$

and $y = 0$ i.e. $(\pm\sqrt{5}, 0)$

Example 19 *Consider the ellipse $\frac{x^2}{\tan^2 \alpha} + \frac{y^2}{\sec^2 \alpha} = 1$, where $\alpha \in (0, \pi / 2)$. Which of the following quantities would vary as α varies?*

(a) degree of flatness
(b) ordinate of the vertex
(c) coordinate of the foci
(d) length of latusrectum

Sol. (a, b, d) If $\alpha \in (0, \pi/2)$ $\sec^2\alpha > \tan^2\alpha$

$\therefore$ Coordinates of foci $(0, \pm \sqrt{(\sec^2\alpha + \tan^2\alpha)})$ i.e. $(0, \pm 1)$ which is independent of α. Vertices are $(0, \pm \sec\alpha)$ and latusrectum $= \frac{2a^2}{b} = \frac{2\tan^2\alpha}{\sec\alpha}$

$\because$ $\alpha \in (0, \pi / 2)$

$\Rightarrow$ $\tan\alpha \in (0, \infty)$

and $\sec\alpha \in (1, \infty)$

Hence, $\alpha \propto$ degree of flatness.

Example 20 *Let $A(\theta)$ and $B(\phi)$ be the extremities of a chord of an ellipse. If the slope of AB is equal to the slope of the tangent at a point $C(\alpha)$ on the ellipse, then the value of α is*

(a) $\frac{\theta+\phi}{2}$ (b) $\frac{\theta-\phi}{2}$

(c) $\frac{\theta+\phi}{2}+\pi$ (d) $\frac{\theta+\phi}{2}-\pi$

Sol. (a. c) $\because$ Slope of AB = Slope of tangent at C

$$\Rightarrow \left(\frac{b\sin\phi - b\sin\theta}{a\cos\phi - a\cos\theta}\right) = -\frac{b}{a}\frac{\cos\alpha}{\sin\alpha}$$

$$\Rightarrow \frac{b.2\cos\left(\frac{\theta+\phi}{2}\right).\sin\left(\frac{\phi-\theta}{2}\right)}{-a.2\sin\left(\frac{\theta+\phi}{2}\right).\sin\left(\frac{\phi-\theta}{2}\right)} = -\frac{b}{a}\cot\alpha$$

$$\therefore \tan\alpha = \tan\left(\frac{\theta+\phi}{2}\right)$$

$$\Rightarrow \alpha = n\pi + \left(\frac{\theta+\phi}{2}\right), n \in I$$

Passage Based Questions

Passage I

(Ex. Nos. 21 and 22)

A sequence of ellipses $E_1, E_2, E_3, \ldots, E_n$ is constructed as follows : Ellipse E_n is drawn so as to touch ellipse E_{n-1} as the extremities of the major axis of E_{n-1} and to have its foci at the extremities of the mirror axis of E_{n-1}.

Example 21 *If E_n is independent of n, then the eccentricity of ellipse E_{n-2} is*

(a) $\left(\frac{3-\sqrt{5}}{2}\right)$ (b) $\left(\frac{\sqrt{5}-1}{2}\right)$

(c) $\left(\frac{2-\sqrt{3}}{2}\right)$ (d) $\left(\frac{\sqrt{3}-1}{2}\right)$

Example 22 *If eccentricity of ellipse E_n is e_n, then the locus of (e_n^2, e_{n-1}^2) is*

(a) a parabola

(b) an ellipse

(c) a hyperbola

(d) a rectangular hyperbola

21. (b) If $E_n : \frac{x^2}{a_n^2} + \frac{y^2}{b_n^2} = 1$ and eccentricity of E_n is e_n

If $a_n > b_n$

Then, $b_n^2 = a_n^2(1 - e_n^2)$ ...(i)

According to the question, $b_n = b_{n-1}$ ...(ii)

and $a_{n-1} = a_n e_n$ ...(iii)

For ellipse, E_{n-1}, $a^2_{n-1} = b^2_{n-1}(1 - e^2_{n-1})$ ...(iv)

From Eqs. (i) and (ii), we get

$b_{n-1}^2 = a_n^2(1 - e_n^2)$ ...(v)

On substituting the values of a_{n-1} and b_{n-1}^2 from Eqs. (iii) and (v) in Eq. (iv), then

$$a_n^2 e_n^2 = a_n^2(1 - e_n^2)(1 - e_{n-1}^2)$$

$$\Rightarrow e_n^2 = (1 - e_n^2)(1 - e_{n-1}^2) \quad \text{...(vi)}$$

$\because$ E_n is independent of n.

$\therefore$ $e_n = e_{n-1} = e$ [say]

From Eq. (vi), we get

$$e^2 = (1 - e^2)^2$$

$$\Rightarrow e^4 - 3e^2 + 1 = 0$$

$$\therefore e^2 = \frac{3 \pm \sqrt{5}}{2} = \frac{6 \pm 2\sqrt{5}}{4} = \left(\frac{\sqrt{5} \pm 1}{2}\right)^2$$

$$\therefore e = \frac{\sqrt{5}-1}{2} \quad [\because 0 < e < 1]$$

22. (d) From Eq. (vi), $e_n^2 = (1 - e_n^2)(1 - e_{n-1}^2)$

Locus of (e_n^2, e_{n-1}^2) is

$$x = (1 - x)(1 - y)$$

$$\Rightarrow xy - 2x - y + 1 = 0$$

Here, $a = 0, b = 0$ and $c = 1$,

$f = -\frac{1}{2}, g = -1$ and $h = \frac{1}{2}$

$$\therefore \Delta = 0 + 2 \times -\frac{1}{2} \times -1 \times \frac{1}{2} - 0 - 0 - 1 \times \frac{1}{4} = \frac{1}{4} \neq 0$$

and $h^2 > ab, a + b = 0$

$\Rightarrow$ Rectangular hyperbola.

Passage II

(Ex. Nos. 23 and 24)

Consider an ellipse $E : \frac{x^2}{a^2} + \frac{y^2}{b^2} = 1$, centred at point O and having AB and CD as its major and minor axes respectively if S_1 be one of the focus of the ellipse, radius of incircle of ΔOCS_1 be 1 unit and $OS_1 = 6$ units.

Example 23 *If area of ellipse (E) is Δ sq unit, then the value of 4Δ is*

(a) 63π (b) 64π

(c) 65π (d) 66π

Example 24 *The equation of the director circle of (E) is*

(a) $x^2 + y^2 = 48.5$ (b) $x^2 + y^2 = 97$

(c) $x^2 + y^2 = \sqrt{48.5}$ (d) $x^2 + y^2 = \sqrt{97}$

Sol. $\because$ $OS_1 = ae = 6, OC = b$

$$\therefore CS_1 = \sqrt{(OS_1)^2 + (OC)^2} = \sqrt{(a^2e^2 + b^2)} = a$$

Area of $\Delta OCS_1 = \frac{1}{2} \times (OS_1) \times (OC) = \frac{1}{2} \times 6 \times b = 3b$

and semi-perimeter of $\Delta OCS_1 = \frac{1}{2}(OS_1 + OC + CS_1)$

$$= \frac{1}{2}(6 + a + b)$$

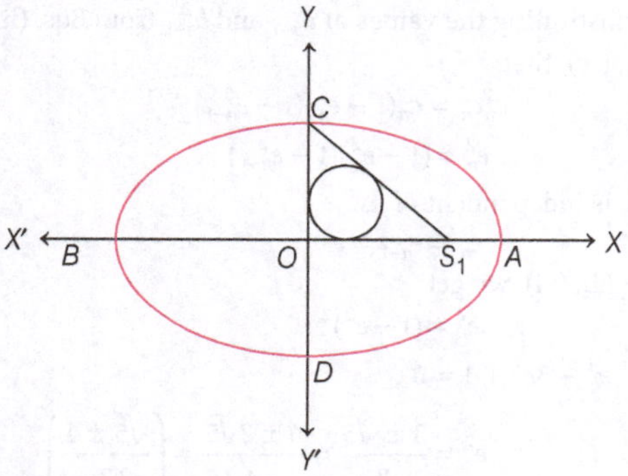

$\because$ In radius of $\Delta OCS_1 = 1$

$$\therefore \quad \frac{3b}{\frac{1}{2}(6 + a + b)} = 1$$

$$\Rightarrow \quad b = \frac{1}{5}(6 + a) \quad \text{...(i)}$$

Also, $$b^2 = a^2(1 - e^2) = a^2 - 36 \quad \text{...(ii)}$$

From Eqs. (i) and (ii), we get

$$\frac{1}{25}(6 + a)^2 = a^2 - 36$$

$$\Rightarrow \quad 2a^2 - a - 78 = 0$$

or $$a = \frac{13}{2}, -6$$

23. (c) $\therefore \; a = \frac{13}{2}$ and $b = \frac{5}{2}$ [from Eq. (i)]

$$\because \quad \Delta = \pi ab = \pi \times \frac{13}{2} \times \frac{5}{2}$$

$$\therefore \quad 4\Delta = 65\pi$$

24. (a) Equation of director circle of E is $x^2 + y^2 = a^2 + b^2$

$$= \frac{169 + 25}{4} = 48.5$$

Stem Based Questions

Stem I

(Ex. Nos. 25 and 26)

A curve is represented by C

$21x^2 - 6xy + 29y^2 + 6x - 58y - 151 = 0$

Example 25 *The eccentricity of the given cure is ....*

Example 26 *The length of major axis is ....*

Sol. Given, $21x^2 - 6xy + 29y^2 + 6x - 58y - 151 = 0$

$$\Rightarrow \quad 3(x - 3y + 3)^2 + 2(3x + y - 1)^2 = 29 + 151$$

$$\Rightarrow \quad \frac{(x - 3y + 3)^2}{60} + \frac{(3x + y - 1)^2}{90} = 1$$

$$\Rightarrow \quad \frac{\left(\frac{x - 3y + 3}{\sqrt{10}}\right)^2}{\frac{6}{\sqrt{10}}} + \frac{\left(\frac{3x + y - 1}{\sqrt{10}}\right)^2}{\frac{9}{\sqrt{10}}} = 1$$

Here, $$a^2 = \frac{9}{\sqrt{10}} \text{ and } b^2 = \frac{6}{\sqrt{10}}$$

25. Now, $b^2 = a^2(1 - e^2)$

$$\Rightarrow \quad \frac{6}{\sqrt{10}} = \frac{9}{\sqrt{10}}(1 - e^2)$$

$$\Rightarrow \quad \frac{2}{3} = 1 - e^2$$

$$\Rightarrow \quad e^2 = 1 - \frac{2}{3} = \frac{1}{3}$$

$$\Rightarrow \quad e = \frac{1}{\sqrt{3}}$$

26. Length of major axis = 6

Stem II

(Ex. Nos. 27 and 28)

Let $C : x^2 + y^2 = r^2$ and $E : \frac{x^2}{16} + \frac{y^2}{9} = 1$ intersect at four distinct points A, B, C, D. Their common tangents form a parallelogram $EFGH$.

Example 27 *If $ABCD$ is a square and $r = \frac{k\sqrt{2}}{5}$, then k is*

Example 28 *If $EFGH$ is a square, then r is*

27. (12) $C : x^2 + y^2 = r^2$

$$E : \frac{x^2}{16} + \frac{y^2}{9} = 1$$

$$\Rightarrow \quad \frac{r^2 - y^2}{16} + \frac{y^2}{9} = 1$$

$$\Rightarrow \quad y^2 = \frac{144 - 9r^2}{7}$$

$$x^2 = \frac{16r^2 - 144}{7}$$

If $ABCD$ is a square, then

$x^2 = y^2$

$$\Rightarrow \quad \frac{144 - 9r^2}{7} = \frac{16r^2 - 144}{7}$$

$$\Rightarrow \quad 25r^2 = 288$$

$$\Rightarrow \quad r = \frac{12\sqrt{2}}{5}$$

$$\Rightarrow \quad k = 12$$

28. Tangent of slope m to the circle

$$y = mx + \sqrt{r^2m^2 + r^2}$$

Tangent of slope m to the ellipse

$$y = mx + \sqrt{16m^2 + 9}$$

For common tangent,

$$r^2m^2 + r^2 = 16m^2 + 9$$

If $EFGH$ is a square, then $m^2 = 1$

$$\therefore \quad 2r^2 = 25$$

$$\Rightarrow \quad r^2 = \frac{25}{2}$$

$$\Rightarrow \quad r = \frac{5}{\sqrt{2}}$$

Single Integer Answer Type Questions

Example 29 *If F_1 and F_2 are the feet of the perpendiculars from the foci S_1 and S_2 of the ellipse $\frac{x^2}{25} + \frac{y^2}{16} = 1$ on the tangent at any point P on the ellipse, then the minimum value of $S_1F_1 + S_2F_2$ is ....*

Sol. (8) We know that the product of perpendiculars from two foci of an ellipse upon any tangent is equal to the square of the semi-minor axis.

$$\therefore \quad S_1F_1 \times S_2F_2 = 16$$

Now, $\quad$ AM $\geq$ GM

$$\Rightarrow \quad \frac{S_1F_1 + S_2F_2}{2} \geq \sqrt{S_1F_1 \times S_2F_2}$$

$$\Rightarrow \quad S_1F_1 + S_2F_2 \geq 2\sqrt{16}$$

$$\Rightarrow \quad S_1F_1 + S_2F_2 \geq 8$$

Example 30 *Let P be a variable point on the ellipse $\frac{x^2}{2} + \frac{y^2}{1} = 1$ with foci F_1 and F_2. If A be the area of the ΔPF_1F_2, then the maximum value of A is ....*

Sol. (1) Here, $\frac{x^2}{2} + \frac{y^2}{1} = 1$

$$\Rightarrow \quad a^2 = 2, \; b^2 = 1$$

$$e^2 = 1 - \frac{b^2}{a^2} = 1 - \frac{1}{2} = \frac{1}{2}$$

$$\Rightarrow \quad e = \frac{1}{\sqrt{2}}$$

$\therefore \quad F_1(1, 0)$ and $F_2(-1, 0)$.

Now, $A = \text{ar}(\Delta PF_1F_2)$

$$= \frac{1}{2}\begin{vmatrix} \sqrt{2}\cos\theta & \sin\theta & 1 \\ 1 & 0 & 1 \\ -1 & 0 & 1 \end{vmatrix} = \frac{1}{2}(2\sin\theta) = \sin\theta$$

Hence, the maximum value of A is 1 sq. unit.

JEE SCANNER

Example 31 Similar to PYQ Asked in JEE Main 2023

Let an ellipse with centre (2, 0) and latusrectum of length $\frac{1}{2}$ have its major axis along X-axis. If its minor axis subtends an angle 60° at the foci, then the square of the sum of the lengths of its minor and major axes is equal to ....

Sol. (5) $LR = \frac{1}{2} \Rightarrow \frac{2b^2}{a} = \frac{1}{2} \Rightarrow b^2 = \frac{a}{4} \Rightarrow b = \frac{\sqrt{a}}{2}$

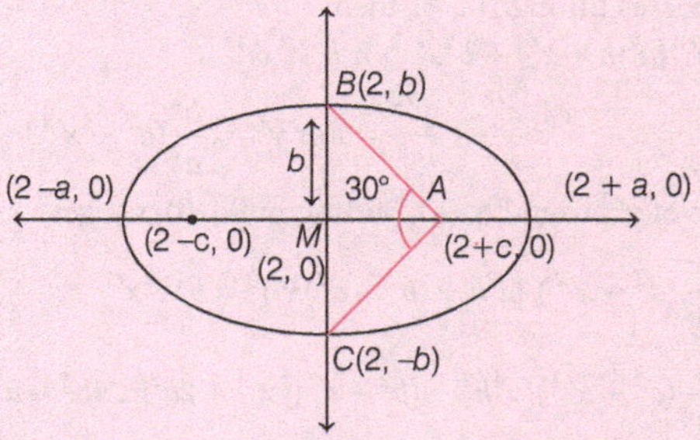

In ΔAMB, $\tan 30° = \frac{b}{MA}$

$$\Rightarrow \quad \frac{1}{\sqrt{3}} = \frac{\sqrt{a}}{2 \times OA} \Rightarrow MA = \frac{\sqrt{3a}}{2}$$

$$A(2 + MA, 0) \equiv A(2 + c, 0)$$

$$\Rightarrow \quad MA = c$$

$$\Rightarrow \quad MA^2 = c^2$$

$$\Rightarrow \quad a^2 - b^2 = c^2$$

$$\Rightarrow \quad a^2 - b^2 = \frac{3a}{4}$$

$$\Rightarrow \quad a^2 - \frac{a}{4} = \frac{3a}{4}$$

$$\Rightarrow \quad 4a^2 - a = 3a$$

$$\Rightarrow \quad 4a^2 - 4a = 0 \Rightarrow 4a(a-1) = 0$$

$$\Rightarrow \quad a = 1, a = 0$$

$$\Rightarrow \quad a = 1 \text{ and } b = \frac{\sqrt{a}}{2} = \frac{1}{2}$$

$\therefore$ Sum of square of minor and major axis is

$$(2a)^2 + (2b)^2 = (2 \times 1)^2 + \left(2 \times \frac{1}{2}\right)^2 = 4 + 1 = 5$$

Skill Builder

Let an ellipse with centre (3, 0) and latusrectum of length $\frac{1}{2}$ have its major axis along X-axis. If its minor axis subtends an angle 60° at the foci, then the square of the sum of the lengths of its minor and major axes is equal to ......

For Sol.

Example 32 *If the normals at the four points* (x_1, y_1), (x_2, y_2), (x_3, y_3) *and* (x_4, y_4) *on the ellipse* $\frac{x^2}{a^2}+\frac{y^2}{b^2}=1$ *are concurrent, then the value of* $\left(\sum_{i=1}^{4} x_i\right)\left(\sum_{i=1}^{4}\frac{1}{x_i}\right)$ *is ....*

Sol. (4) Let point of concurrent be (h, k).

Equation of normal at (x', y') is

$$\frac{x-x'}{x'a^2}=\frac{y-y'}{y'b^2}$$

It is passes through (h, k), then

$$y'^2\{a^2(h-x')+b^2x'\}^2=b^4k^2x'^2 \quad \text{...(i)}$$

But $$\frac{x'^2}{a^2}+\frac{y'^2}{b^2}=1 \text{ or } y'^2=\frac{b^2}{a^2}(a^2-x'^2) \quad \text{...(ii)}$$

Value of y'^2 from Eq. (ii), putting in Eq. (i), we get

$$\frac{b^2}{a^2}(a^2-x'^2)\{a^2h+(b^2-a^2)x'\}^2=b^4k^2x'^2$$

$$\Rightarrow \frac{b^2}{a^2}(a^2-x'^2)\{a^4h^2+(b^2-a^2)^2x'^2+2a^2hx'(b^2-a^2)\}$$
$$=b^4k^2x'^2$$

Arranging above as a fourth degree equation in x', we get

$$\Rightarrow -(a^2-b^2)^2x'^4+2ha^2(a^2-b^2)x'^3+x'^2(\dots)$$
$$-2a^4h(a^2-b^2)x'+a^6h^2=0$$

above equation being of fourth degree in x', therefore roots of the above equation are x_1, x_2, x_3, x_4, then

$$(x_1+x_2+x_3+x_4)=-\frac{2ha^2(a^2-b^2)}{-(a^2-b^2)^2}=\frac{2ha^2}{(a^2-b^2)} \quad \text{...(iii)}$$

$$\left(\frac{1}{x_1}+\frac{1}{x_2}+\frac{1}{x_3}+\frac{1}{x_4}\right)=\frac{\Sigma x_1x_2x_3}{x_1\cdot x_2\cdot x_3\cdot x_4}$$
$$=\frac{\dfrac{2a^4h(a^2-b^2)}{-(a^2-b^2)^2}}{\dfrac{a^6h^2}{-(a^2-b^2)^2}}=\frac{2(a^2-b^2)}{a^2h} \quad \text{...(iv)}$$

On multiplying Eqs. (iii) and (iv), we get

$$(x_1+x_2+x_3+x_4)\left(\frac{1}{x_1}+\frac{1}{x_2}+\frac{1}{x_3}+\frac{1}{x_4}\right)=4$$

or $$\left(\sum_{i=1}^{4}x_i\right)\left(\sum_{i=1}^{4}\frac{1}{x_i}\right)=4$$

Example 33 *If* $x, y \in R$, *satisfies the equation* $\frac{(x-4)^2}{4}+\frac{y^2}{9}=1$, *then the difference between the largest and the smallest value of the expression* $\frac{x^2}{4}+\frac{y^2}{9}$ *is ....*

Sol. (8) Parametric coordinates on $\frac{(x-4)^2}{4}+\frac{y^2}{9}=1$ are $(4+2\cos\theta, 3\sin\theta)$.

Now, let $$E=\frac{x^2}{4}+\frac{y^2}{9}=\frac{(4+2\cos\theta)^2}{4}+\frac{(3\sin\theta)^2}{9}$$
$$=(2+\cos\theta)^2+\sin^2\theta$$
$$=4+4\cos\theta+\cos^2\theta+\sin^2\theta=5+4\cos\theta$$

$\therefore$ $$E_{max}=5+4(1)=9 \quad [\because -1\le\cos\theta\le1]$$

and $$E_{min}=5+4(-1)=1$$

Hence, $E_{max}-E_{min}=9-1=8$

Example 34 *If the tangent at* $\left(4\cos\phi, \frac{16}{\sqrt{11}}\sin\phi\right)$ *to the ellipse* $16x^2+11y^2=256$ *is also a tangent to the circle* $x^2+y^2-2x-15=0$, *then the number of values of* ϕ *is ......*

Sol. (2) Given ellipse is $16x^2+11y^2=256$

$$\frac{x^2}{16}+\frac{y^2}{\left(\frac{16}{\sqrt{11}}\right)^2}=1$$

The equation of the tangent to the given ellipse at $\left(4\cos\phi, \frac{16}{\sqrt{11}}\sin\phi\right)$ is

$$\frac{x\cos\phi}{4}+\frac{y\sin\phi}{\left(\frac{16}{\sqrt{11}}\right)}=1 \quad \text{...(i)}$$

which is also a tangent to the circle

$$x^2+y^2-2x-15=0$$
$$\Rightarrow (x-1)^2+y^2=16$$

So, the length of the perpendicular from the centre to the circle is equal to the radius of a circle.

$$\left|\frac{\left(\frac{\cos\phi}{4}\right)-1}{\sqrt{\frac{\cos^2\phi}{16}+\frac{\sin^2\phi}{\frac{256}{11}}}}\right|=4$$

$$\Rightarrow \left(\left(\frac{\cos\phi}{4}\right)-1\right)^2=16\left(\frac{\cos^2\phi}{16}+\frac{\sin^2\phi}{256/11}\right)$$

$$\Rightarrow \left(\frac{\cos^2\phi}{16}-2\frac{\cos\phi}{4}+1\right)=\cos^2\phi+\frac{11}{16}\sin^2\phi$$

$$\Rightarrow 4\cos^2\phi+8\cos\phi-5=0$$

$$\Rightarrow (2\cos\phi-1)(2\cos\phi+5)=0$$

$$\Rightarrow (2\cos\phi-1)=0$$

$$\Rightarrow \cos\phi=\frac{1}{2}$$

$$\Rightarrow \phi=\frac{\pi}{6}, \frac{5\pi}{6}$$

Hence, the number of values of ϕ is 2.

Numerical Value Type Questions

Example 35 *The minimum area of the triangle formed by the tangent to the ellipse $\frac{x^2}{16}+\frac{y^2}{9}=1$ is ....*

Decoding the Question

We know that $\sin\theta \in [-1, 1]$. So, maximum value of $\sin\theta$ will be 1.

Sol. (12) The equation of the tangent to the ellipse is

$$\frac{x}{4\sec\theta}+\frac{y}{3\operatorname{cosec}\theta}=1$$

Now, $\Delta = \text{ar}\,\Delta OAB = \frac{1}{2}\times 4\sec\theta \times 3\operatorname{cosec}\theta = \frac{12}{\sin 2\theta}$

$\therefore$ Minimum area of the triangle = 12 sq. units.

Example 36 *If $\left(\frac{1}{5}, \frac{2}{5}\right)$ be the mid-point of the chord of the ellipse $\frac{x^2}{25}+\frac{y^2}{16}=1$, then its length is $\frac{a\sqrt{b}}{5}$. Then, the value of $a+b$ is ....*

Sol. (48) Given ellipse $\frac{x^2}{25}+\frac{y^2}{16}=1$ ...(i)

The equation of the chord bisected as (h, k) is

$$T = S_1$$

$$\Rightarrow \frac{hx}{a^2}+\frac{kv}{b^2}=\frac{h^2}{a^2}+\frac{k^2}{h^2} \Rightarrow \frac{hx}{25}+\frac{ky}{16}=\frac{h^2}{25}+\frac{k^2}{16}$$

$$\Rightarrow \frac{(1/5)^x}{25}+\frac{(2/5)x}{16}=\frac{(1/5)x}{25}+\frac{(2/5)^2}{16}$$

On solving, we get

$$4x+5y=4$$

On solving Eqs. (i) and (ii), we get

$$x = 4, -3 \text{ and } y - \frac{12}{5}, \frac{16}{5}$$

Let the chord be AB where

$$A=\left(4, \frac{12}{5}\right) \text{ and } B = 0-3, \frac{16}{5}$$

Hence, the length of AB is

$$=\sqrt{(7)^2+\left(\frac{28}{5}\right)^2}=7\sqrt{1+\frac{16}{25}}=\frac{7\sqrt{41}}{5}$$

$\therefore$ $a=7, b=41$

Hence, $a+b=48$

Example 37 *The area of the quadrilateral formed by the tangents at the end-points of latus rectum to the ellipse $\frac{x^2}{9}+\frac{y^2}{5}=1$ is*

Sol. (27) Given, ellipse is $\frac{x^2}{9}+\frac{y^2}{5}=1$

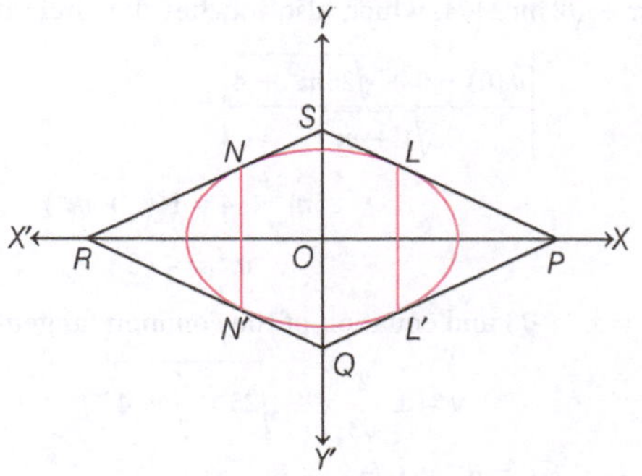

Now, $e=\sqrt{1-\frac{b^2}{a^2}}=\sqrt{1-\frac{5}{9}}=\frac{2}{3}$

$$L=\left(ae, \frac{b^2}{a}\right)=\left(2, -\frac{5}{3}\right)$$

$$L'=\left(ae, -\frac{b^2}{a}\right)=\left(2, -\frac{5}{3}\right)$$

$$N=\left(-ae, \frac{b^2}{a}\right)=\left(-2, \frac{5}{3}\right)$$

and $N=\left(-ae, -\frac{b^2}{a}\right)=\left(-2, -\frac{5}{3}\right)$

Now, the tangent at L is

$$\frac{xx_1}{9}+\frac{yy_1}{5}=1$$

$$\Rightarrow \frac{2x}{9}+\frac{\frac{5}{3}y}{5}=1$$

$$\Rightarrow \frac{x}{9/2}+\frac{y}{3}=1$$

Thus, $P=\left(\frac{9}{2}, 0\right)$ and $S=(0, 3)$

Therefore, ar(quad $PQRS$) = $4\times$ ar(ΔOPS)

$$=4\times\frac{1}{2}\times\frac{9}{2}\times 3$$

$$= 27 \text{ sq. units}$$

Example 38 *If l is the length of the intercept made by a common tangent to the circle $x^2+y^2=16$ and the ellipse $\frac{x^2}{25}+\frac{y^2}{4}=1$, on the coordinates axes, then $3l^2$ is equal to.*

Sol. (196) Equation of any tangent to the ellipse is $y = mx + \sqrt{25m^2+4}$, which also touches the circle if

$$\left|\frac{m(0)-0+\sqrt{25m^2+4}}{\sqrt{1+m^2}}\right| = 4$$

$$\Rightarrow \quad 25m^2+4 = 16(1+m^2)$$

$$\Rightarrow \quad m^2 = 4/3$$

$\Rightarrow$ $m = \pm 2/\sqrt{3}$ and equation of the common tangent is

$$y = \pm\frac{2}{\sqrt{3}}x + \sqrt{25\times\frac{4}{3}+4}$$

$$\Rightarrow \quad \sqrt{3}y \mp 2x = 4\sqrt{7}$$

$$\Rightarrow \quad l^2 = \left(\frac{4\sqrt{7}}{2}\right)^2 + \left(\frac{4\sqrt{7}}{\sqrt{3}}\right)^2$$

$$\therefore \quad 3l^2 = 196$$

Example 39 *Suppose that the foci of the ellipse $\frac{x^2}{9}+\frac{y^2}{5}=1$ are $(f_1, 0)$ and $(f_2, 0)$ where $f_1>0$ and $f_2<0$. Let P_1 and P_2 be two parabolas with a common vertex at $(0, 0)$ and with foci at $(f_1, 0)$ and $(2f_2, 0)$, respectively. Let T_1 be a tangent to P_1 which passes through $(2f_2, 0)$ and T_2 be a tangent to P_2 which passes through $(f_2, 0)$. m_1 is the slope of T_1 and m_2 is the slope of T_2, then the value of $\left(\frac{8}{m_1^2}+2m_2^2\right)$ is.*

Sol. (20) We have, $a^2=9, b^2=5$

$$\therefore \quad e^2 = 1-\frac{b^2}{a^2} = 1-\frac{5}{9} = \frac{4}{9}$$

$$\Rightarrow \quad e = \frac{2}{3}$$

Thus, $f_1 = ae = 2$ and $f_2 = -2$

An equation of P_1 is $y^2 = f_1x = 8x$

and an equation of P_2 is

$$y^2 = -16x$$

Let equation of T_1 be

$$y = m_1x + \frac{2}{m_1}$$

As T_1 passes through $(2f_2, 0) = (-4, 0)$

$$0 = -4m_1 + \frac{2}{m_1} \Rightarrow m_1^2 = \frac{1}{2}$$

An equation of T_2 is

$$y = m_2x - \frac{4}{m_2}$$

As it passes through $(f_1, 0) = (2, 0)$

$$0 = 2m_2 - \frac{4}{m_2}$$

$$\Rightarrow \quad m_2^2 = 2$$

Thus, $\frac{8}{m_1^2} + 2m_2^2 = 16+4 = 20$

Matching Type Questions

Example 40 *Match the following*

Column I	Column II
A. Let $f(x) = \begin{cases} a^x, & x<2 \\ 8, & x=2 \\ \frac{b(x^2-b^2)}{(x-2)}, & x>2 \end{cases}$ If f is continuous at $x=2$, then the locus of the pair of perpendicular tangents to the ellipse $\frac{x^2}{a^2}+\frac{y^2}{b^2}=1$ is $x^2+y^2=r^2$, then r^2 is divisible by	(p) 3
B. If the ellipse $\frac{(x-h)^2}{M}+\frac{(y-k)^2}{N}=1$ has major axis on the line $y=2$, minor-axis on the line $x=-1$, major axis has length 10 and minor axis has length 4. Then, $h+k+M+N$ is divisible by	(q) 4
C. If PQ is a focal chord of ellipse $\frac{x^2}{25}+\frac{y^2}{16}=1$, which passes through $S(3, 0)$ and $PS=2$, then length of PQ is divisible by	(r) 5
D. A tangent to the ellipse $\frac{x^2}{27}+\frac{y^2}{48}=1$ having slope $\left(-\frac{4}{3}\right)$ cuts the x and y-axis at the points A and B respectively. If O is the origin, then area of ΔOAB is divisible by	(s) 6

Sol. (A)→ (p, q, s); (B)→ (p, r, s); (C)→ (r); (D)→ (p, q, s)

(A) $\underset{x\to 2^-}{Lt} f(x) = \underset{x\to 2^+}{Lt} f(x) = f(2)$

$$\Rightarrow \quad \underset{h\to 0}{Lt}\, a^{2-h} = \underset{h\to 0}{Lt}\frac{b((2+h)^2-b^2)}{2+h-2} = 8$$

$$\Rightarrow \quad a^2 = b \lim_{h\to 0} \frac{(2+h)^2 - b^2}{h} = 8$$

At $h \to 0$, $(2+h)^2 - b^2 \to 0$

$\therefore \quad b^2 = 4$ and $a^2 = 8$

$\therefore$ Locus of the pair of perpendicular tangents to the ellipse

$$\frac{x^2}{a^2} + \frac{y^2}{b^2} = 1$$

$\therefore$ Required locus is

$$x^2 + y^2 = a^2 + b^2 = 8 + 4 = 12$$

$$\Rightarrow \quad r^2 = 12$$

(B) $\because$ Major axis on the line $y = 2$

and minor axis on the line $x = -1$

$\therefore$ Centre of ellipse is $(-1, 2)$.

$\Rightarrow \quad h = -1, k = 2$

Also, $\quad 2a = 10$ and $2b = 4$

$\therefore \quad M = a^2 = 25$

and $\quad N = b^2 = 4$

Now, $\quad h + k + M + N = -1 + 2 + 25 + 4 = 30$

(C) Here, $a = 5, b = 4$

$\because \quad b^2 = a^2(1 - e^2)$

$\Rightarrow \quad 16 = 25(1 - e^2)$

$\therefore \quad e = \frac{3}{5}$

Foci $(\pm 3, 0)$

Here, $SA = 2$ [A and A' are vertices]

Also, gives $PS = 2$

$\therefore$ P coincides with A and Q coincides with A'

$\therefore$ $PQ = 2a = 10$

(D) Let $(\sqrt{27}\cos\theta, \sqrt{48}\sin\theta)$ be a point on the ellipse

$$\frac{x^2}{27} + \frac{y^2}{48} = 1$$

$\therefore$ Equation of tangent at $(\sqrt{27}\cos\theta, \sqrt{48}\sin\theta)$ is

$$\frac{x\cos\theta}{\sqrt{27}} + \frac{y\sin\theta}{\sqrt{48}} = 1$$

$$\therefore \quad \text{Slope} = -\frac{\sqrt{48}}{\sqrt{27}} \cdot \frac{\cos\theta}{\sin\theta} = -\frac{4}{3} \quad \text{[given]}$$

$$\therefore \quad \tan\theta = 1 \quad \Rightarrow \theta = \frac{\pi}{4}$$

$\therefore$ Equation of tangent is $\frac{x}{\sqrt{54}} + \frac{y}{\sqrt{96}} = 1$

$\therefore$ Area of triangle $= \frac{1}{2} \times 3\sqrt{6} \times 4\sqrt{6} = 36$

Example 41 *Suppose the tangent at point $P(a\cos\theta, b\sin\theta)$ $\left(0 < \theta < \frac{\pi}{2}\right)$ to the ellipse $E : \frac{x^2}{a^2} + \frac{x}{b^2} = 1$ meets the X-axis at T and Y-axis at T_1, and normal at point P to the ellipse E meets the X-axis at N and Y-axis N_1. Match the expressions in column I with appropriate expressions in column II.*

Column I		Column II	
(A)	$\frac{a^2}{OT^2} + \frac{b^2}{OT_1^2}$	(p)	$2ab$
(B)	$\min\limits_{0 \le \theta \le \frac{\pi}{2}} (OT)(OT_1)$	(q)	ab
(C)	$\max\limits_{0 \le \theta \le \frac{\pi}{2}} (ON)(ON_1)$	(r)	1
(D)	$\min\limits_{0 \le \theta \le \frac{\pi}{2}}$ (Area of ΔOTT_1)	(s)	$\frac{(a^2 - b^2)^2}{2ab}$

Sol. A $\to$ (r); B $\to$ (p); C $\to$ (s); D $\to$ (q)

Equation of tangent at P to E is

$$\frac{x}{a}\cos\theta + \frac{y}{b}\sin\theta = 1 \quad \text{...(i)}$$

and equation of normal at P to E is

$$ax\sec\theta - by\,\text{cosec}\theta = a^2 - b^2 \quad \text{...(ii)}$$

Eq. (i) meets the X-axis at $T(a\sec\theta, 0)$ and Y-axis $T_1(0, b\,\text{cosec}\theta)$

We have $\frac{a^2}{OT^2} + \frac{b^2}{OT_1^2} = \cos^2\theta + \sin^2\theta = 1$

$$(OT)(OT_1) = \frac{2ab}{\sin(2\theta)} \Rightarrow \min_{0 \le \theta \le \frac{\pi}{2}} (OT)(OT_1) = 2ab$$

Eq. (ii) meets the X-axis at $N\left(\frac{a^2 - b^2}{a}\cos\theta, 0\right)$ and Y-axis at $N_1\left(0, \frac{a^2 - b^2}{b}\sin\theta\right)$.

Now, $\quad (ON)(ON_1) = \frac{(a^2 - b^2)^2}{2ab}\sin 2\theta$

$$\max_{0 \le \theta \le \frac{\pi}{2}} (ON)(ON_1) = \frac{(a^2 - b^2)^2}{2ab}$$

$$\text{Area of } \Delta OTT_1 = \frac{1}{2}(OT)(OT_1) = \frac{ab}{\sin(2\theta)}$$

$$\min_{0 \le \theta \le \frac{\pi}{2}} (\text{Area of } \Delta OTT_1) = ab$$

EXERCISE 1

JEE Main Pattern

Single Option Correct Type Questions

1. If $\frac{x^2}{f(4a)}+\frac{y^2}{f(a^2-5)}$ represents an ellipse with major axis as Y-axis and f is a decreasing fucntion, then

(a) $a \in (-\infty, 1)$ (b) $a \in (5, \infty)$
(c) $a \in (1, 4)$ (d) $a \in (-1, 5)$

2. The curve represented by the equation

$$\frac{x^2}{\sin\sqrt{2}-\cos\sqrt{3}}+\frac{y^2}{\sin\sqrt{3}-\cos\sqrt{2}}=1 \text{ is}$$

(a) an ellipse with foci on X -axis
(b) an ellipse with foci on Y-axis
(c) a hyperbola with foci on X-axis
(d) a hyperbola with foci on Y-axis

3. The minimum distance of the centre of the ellipse $\frac{x^2}{16}+\frac{y^2}{9}=1$ from the chord of contact of mutually perpendicular tangents of the ellipse is

(a) $\frac{144}{5}$ (b) $\frac{16}{5}$
(c) $\frac{9}{5}$ (d) None of these

4. A circle of radius $\frac{5}{\sqrt{2}}$ is concentric with the ellipse $\frac{x^2}{16}+\frac{y^2}{9}=1$, then the acute angle made by the common tangent with the line $\sqrt{3}x-y+6=0$ is

(a) $\frac{\pi}{3}$ (b) $\frac{\pi}{4}$
(c) $\frac{\pi}{6}$ (d) $\frac{\pi}{12}$

5. C is the centre of the ellipse $\frac{x^2}{16}+\frac{y^2}{9}=1$ and A and B are two points on the ellipse such that $\angle ACB = 90°$, then $\frac{1}{(CA)^2}+\frac{1}{(CB)^2}=$

(a) $\frac{7}{12}$ (b) $\frac{12}{7}$
(c) $\frac{25}{144}$ (d) $\frac{144}{25}$

6. If $a=[t^2-3t+4]$ and $b=[3+5t]$, where $[\cdot]$ denotes the greatest integer function, then the latusrectum of the ellipse $\frac{x^2}{a^2}+\frac{y^2}{b^2}=1$ at $t=\frac{3}{2}$ is

(a) 20 (b) 10 (c) $\frac{1}{5}$ (d) $\frac{1}{10}$

7. If the line $x+2y+4=0$ cutting the ellipse $\frac{x^2}{a^2}+\frac{y^2}{b^2}=1$ at points whose eccentric angles are 30° and 60° subtends a right angle at the origin, then its equation is

(a) $\frac{x^2}{8}+\frac{y^2}{4}=1$ (b) $\frac{x^2}{16}+\frac{y^2}{4}=1$
(c) $\frac{x^2}{4}+\frac{y^2}{16}=1$ (d) None of these

8. An arc of a bridge is semi-elliptical with major axis horizontal. If the length of the base is 9 m and the highest part of the bridge is 3 m from the horizontal, the best approximation of the height of the arc 2 m from the centre of the base is

(a) $\frac{11}{4}$m (b) $\frac{8}{3}$m
(c) $\frac{7}{2}$m (d) 2m

9. A tangent to the ellipse $\frac{x^2}{25}+\frac{y^2}{16}=1$ at any point P meet the line $x=0$ at a point Q. Let R be the image of Q in the line $y=x$, then circle whose extremities of a diameter are Q and R passes through a fixed point. The fixed point is

(a) (3, 0) (b) (4, 0)
(c) (5, 0) (d) (0, 0)

10. If tangents PQ and PR are drawn from a point on the circle $x^2+y^2=25$ to the ellipse $\frac{x^2}{16}+\frac{y^2}{b^2}=1$, $(b<4)$, so that the fourth vertex S of parallelogram $PQSR$ lies on the circumcircle of triangle PQR, then the eccentricity of the ellipse is

(a) $\frac{\sqrt{5}}{4}$ (b) $\frac{\sqrt{5}}{3}$
(c) $\frac{\sqrt{7}}{4}$ (d) $\frac{\sqrt{7}}{3}$

11. $x-2y+4=0$ is a common tangent to $y^2=4x$ and $\frac{x^2}{4}+\frac{y^2}{b^2}=1$. Then, the value of b and the other common tangent are given by
(a) $b=\sqrt{3}$; $x+2y+4=0$
(b) $b=3$; $x+2y+4=0$
(c) $b=\sqrt{3}$; $x+2y-4=0$
(d) $b=\sqrt{3}$, $x-2y-4=0$

12. The point at shortest distance from the line $x+y=7$ and lying on an ellipse $x^2+2y^2=6$, has coordinates
(a) $(\sqrt{2}, \sqrt{2})$ (b) $(0, \sqrt{3})$
(c) $(2, 1)$ (d) $\left(\sqrt{5}, \frac{1}{\sqrt{2}}\right)$

13. From a point on the axis of x common tangents are drawn to the parabola $y^2=4x$ and the ellipse $\frac{x^2}{a^2}+\frac{y^2}{b^2}=1\,(a>b>0)$. If these tangents form an equilateral triangle with their chord of contact w.r.t parabola, then set of exhaustive values of a is
(a) $(0, 3)$ (b) $\left(0, \frac{3}{2}\right)$
(c) $\left(\frac{3}{2}, 3\right)$ (d) $\left(1, \frac{3}{2}\right)$

14. If circumcentre of an equilateral triangle inscribed in $\frac{x^2}{a^2}+\frac{y^2}{b^2}=1$, with vertices having eccentric angle α, β, γ respectively is (h, k), then $\Sigma \cos(\alpha-\beta)=$
(a) $\frac{9h^2}{a^2}+\frac{9k^2}{b^2}+\frac{3}{2}$ (b) $9h^2-9k^2+a^2b^2$
(c) $\frac{9h^2}{a^2}+\frac{9k^2}{b^2}+3$ (d) $\frac{9h^2}{2a^2}+\frac{9k^2}{2b^2}-\frac{3}{2}$

15. A parabola is drawn with focus at one of the foci of the ellipse $\frac{x^2}{a^2}+\frac{y^2}{b^2}=1$, where $a>b$ and directrix passing through the other focus and perpendicular to the major axis of the ellipse. If the latusrectum of the ellipse and that of the parabola are same, then the eccentricity of the ellipse is
(a) $\sqrt{2}-1$ (b) $\sqrt{3}-1$
(c) $2\sqrt{2}-2$ (d) $3\sqrt{3}-5$

16. If the maximum distance of any point on the ellipse $x^2+2y^2+2xy=1$ from its center is r, then r is equal to
(a) $\frac{\sqrt{6}+1}{2}$ (b) $\frac{\sqrt{5}+1}{2}$
(c) $\frac{\sqrt{3}+1}{2}$ (d) $\frac{\sqrt{2}+2}{2}$

17. The length of the common chord of the ellipse $\frac{(x-1)^2}{9}+\frac{(y-2)^2}{4}=1$ and the circle $(x-1)^2+(y-2)^2=1$ is
(a) zero (b) one
(c) three (d) eight

18. A ray eminating from the point $(-4, 0)$ is incident on the ellipse $9x^2+25y^2=225$ at the point P with ordinate 3. The equation of the reflected ray after first reflection is
(a) $4x+3y=12$ (b) $3x+4y=10$
(c) $3x+4y=5$ (d) $3x+4y=12$

19. The area of the rectangle formed by the perpendiculars from the centre of ellipse $\frac{x^2}{16}+\frac{y^2}{9}=1$ to the tangent and normal at the point, whose eccentric angle is $\frac{\pi}{4}$, is
(a) $\frac{84}{25}$ sq units (b) $\frac{32}{25}$ sq units
(c) $\frac{9}{25}$ sq unit (d) $\frac{73}{25}$ sq units

20. The locus of the middle point of the intercept of the tangents drawn from an external point to the ellipse $x^2+3y^2=3$ between the coordinate axes is
(a) $\frac{1}{x^2}+\frac{1}{3y^2}=1$ (b) $\frac{1}{3x^2}+\frac{1}{y^2}=1$
(c) $\frac{3}{4x^2}+\frac{1}{4y^2}=1$ (d) $\frac{1}{4x^2}+\frac{1}{3y^2}=1$

21. If $\sqrt{3}bx+ay=2ab$ touches the ellipse $\frac{x^2}{a^2}+\frac{y^2}{b^2}=1$ and the eccentric angle of the point of contact is θ, then $\tan\theta$ is equal to
(a) $\sqrt{3}$ (b) 1 (c) $\frac{1}{\sqrt{3}}$ (d) 0

22. If circle be described on two semi-conjugate diameter of the ellipse as diameters, then the locus of their second points of intersection is
(a) $2(x^2+y^2)=(b^2x^2+a^2y^2)$
(b) $2(ax^2+y^2)=(x^2+b^2y^2)^2$
(c) $2(x^2+y^2)=(a^2x^2+b^2y^2)^2$
(d) $2(x^2+y^2)^2=(a^2x^2+b^2y^2)$

23. The line passing through the extremity A of the major axis and extremity B of the minor axis of the ellipse $x^2+9y^2=9$ meets its auxiliary circle at the point M. Then, the area (in sq units) of the triangle with vertices at A, M and the origin O is
(a) $\frac{31}{10}$ (b) $\frac{29}{10}$ (c) $\frac{21}{10}$ (d) $\frac{27}{10}$

24. The ellipse $E_1 : \frac{x^2}{9} + \frac{y^2}{4} = 1$ is inscribed in a rectangle R whose sides are parallel to the coordinate axes. Another ellipse E_2 passing through the point (0, 4) and (3, 2) circumscribes the rectangle R. The eccentricity of the ellipse E_2 is

(a) $\sqrt{2}/2$ (b) $\sqrt{3}/2$
(c) 1/2 (d) 3/4

25. The normal at a point P on the ellipse $x^2 + 4y^2 = 16$ meets the X-axis at Q. If M is the mid-point of the line segment PQ, then the locus of M intersects the latusrectum of the given ellipse at the points

(a) $\left(\pm\frac{3\sqrt{5}}{2}, \pm\frac{2}{7}\right)$ (b) $\left(\pm\frac{3\sqrt{5}}{2}, \pm\frac{\sqrt{19}}{4}\right)$
(c) $\left(\pm 2\sqrt{3}, \pm\frac{1}{7}\right)$ (d) $\left(\pm 2\sqrt{3}, \pm\frac{4\sqrt{3}}{7}\right)$

Numerical Type Questions

26. The length of sides of square which can be made by four perpendicular tangents to the ellipse $\frac{x^2}{7} + \frac{2y^2}{11} = 1$ is ......

27. The length of the focal chord of the ellipse $\frac{x^2}{a^2} + \frac{y^2}{b^2} = 1$ which makes an angle θ with the major axis is $\frac{\lambda ab^2}{a^2 \sin^2\theta + b^2 \cos^2\theta}$, then the value of λ is......

28. Number of distinct normal lines that can be drawn to ellipse $\frac{x^2}{169} + \frac{y^2}{25} = 1$ from the point $P(0, 6)$ is n, then the value of 2^n is ......

29. If p is the length of the perpendicular from a focus upon the tangent at any point P of the ellipse $\frac{x^2}{a^2} + \frac{y^2}{b^2} = 1$ and r is the distance of P from the focus, then the value of $\frac{2a}{r} - \frac{b^2}{p^2}$ is......

30. An ellipse passing through the origin has its foci (3, 4) and (6, 8). The length of its semi-minor axis is b, then the value of $b/\sqrt{2}$ is......

31. The maximum value of 5λ for which four normals can be drawn to ellipse $\frac{x^2}{25} + \frac{y^2}{16} = 1$ through a point $(\lambda, 0)$ is......

32. An ellipse with major and minor axes $6\sqrt{3}$ and 6 respectively, slides along the coordinate axes and always remains confined in the first quadrant. If the length of arc described by centre of ellipse is $\frac{\pi\lambda}{6}$, then the value of λ is ......

33. If the tangent at $\left(4\cos\phi, \frac{16}{\sqrt{11}}\sin\phi\right)$ to the ellipse $16x^2 + 11y^2 = 256$ is also a tangent to the circle $x^2 + y^2 - 2x - 15 = 0$, then the number of values of ϕ is ......

34. A normal is drawn to ellipse $\frac{x^2}{(a^2 + 5a + 3)^2} + \frac{y^2}{(a^2 + 3)^2} = 1$ whose centre is at O. If maximum radius of circle centered at origin and touching the normal is 10, then the positive value of a is......

35. If the tangent drawn from the point $P(2, 3)$ to the circle $x^2 + y^2 - 8x + 6y + 1 = 0$ touch the circle at the points M and N. The circumcircle of ΔPMN cuts the director circle of ellipse $\frac{(x+5)^2}{9} + \frac{(y-3)^2}{b^2} = 1$ orthogonally, then the value of $\frac{b^2}{9}$ is ...

36. If the angle subtended by the common tangent of the two ellipse $\frac{(x-4)^2}{25} + \frac{y^2}{4} = 1$ and $\frac{(x+1)^2}{1} + \frac{y^2}{4} = 1$ at the origin is $\frac{\pi}{k}$, then $2k$ is equal to ......

Previous years Questions

37. If the length of the minor axis of an ellipse is equal to half of the distance between the foci, then the eccentricity of the ellipse is **[Single Correct Type, 2024 Main]**

(a) $\frac{\sqrt{3}}{2}$ (b) $\frac{2}{\sqrt{5}}$ (c) $\frac{1}{\sqrt{3}}$ (d) $\frac{\sqrt{5}}{3}$

38. Let P be a point on the ellipse $\frac{x^2}{9} + \frac{y^2}{4} = 1$. Let the line passing through P and parallel to Y-axis meet the circle $x^2 + y^2 = 9$ at point Q such that P and Q are on the same side of the X-axis. Then, the eccentricity of the locus of the point R on PQ such that $PR : RQ = 4 : 3$ as P moves on the ellipse is **[Single Correct Type, 2024 Main]**

(a) $\frac{11}{19}$ (b) $\frac{13}{21}$ (c) $\frac{\sqrt{139}}{23}$ (d) $\frac{\sqrt{13}}{7}$

39. Let the line $2x+3y-k=0, k>0$, intersect the X-axis and Y-axis at the points A and B, respectively. If the equation of the circle having the line segment AB as a diameter is $x^2+y^2-3x-2y=0$ and the length of the latusrectum of the ellipse $x^2+9y^2=k^2$ is $\frac{m}{n}$, where m and n are coprime, then $2m+n$ is equal to **[Single Correct Type, 2024 Main]**

(a) 13 (b) 12
(c) 11 (d) 10

40. If the radius of the largest circle with centre (2, 0) inscribed in the ellipse $x^2+4y^2=36$ is r, then $12r^2$ is equal to **[Single Correct Type, 2023 Main]**

(a) 69 (b) 72
(c) 115 (d) 92

41. Consider ellipses $E_k : kx^2+k^2y^2=1, k=1,2,\ldots 20$. Let C_k be the circle which touches the four chords joining the end points (one minor axis and another on major axis) of the ellipse E_k. If r_k is the radius of the circle C_k, then the value of $\sum_{k=1}^{20}\frac{1}{r_k^2}$ is **[Single Correct Type, 2023 Main]**

(a) 3320 (b) 2870
(c) 3080 (d) 3210

42. Let a circle of radius 4 be concentric to the ellipse $15x^2+19y^2=285$. Then, the common tangents are inclined to the minor axis of the ellipse at the angle **[Single Correct Type, 2023 Main]**

(a) $\frac{\pi}{4}$ (b) $\frac{\pi}{3}$ (c) $\frac{\pi}{12}$ (d) $\frac{\pi}{16}$

43. If the maximum distance of normal to the ellipse $\frac{x^2}{4}+\frac{y^2}{b^2}=1, b<2$, from the origin is 1, then the eccentricity of the ellipse is **[Single Correct Type, 2023 Main]**

(a) $\frac{1}{\sqrt{2}}$ (b) $\frac{1}{2}$ (c) $\frac{\sqrt{3}}{4}$ (d) $\frac{\sqrt{3}}{2}$

44. Let the tangent and normal at the point $(3\sqrt{3}, 1)$ on the ellipse $\frac{x^2}{36}+\frac{y^2}{4}=1$ meet the Y-axis at the points A and B, respectively. Let the circle C be drawn taking AB as a diameter and the line $x=2\sqrt{5}$ intersect C at the points P and Q. If the tangents at the points P and Q on the circle intersect at the point (α, β), then $\alpha^2-\beta^2$ is equal to **[Single Correct Type, 2023 Main]**

(a) 60 (b) $\frac{314}{5}$ (c) 61 (d) $\frac{304}{5}$

45. Let $P\left(\frac{2\sqrt{3}}{\sqrt{7}}, \frac{6}{\sqrt{7}}\right)$, Q, R and S be four points on the ellipse $9x^2+4y^2=36$. Let PQ and RS be mutually perpendicular and pass through the origin. If $\frac{1}{(PQ)^2}+\frac{1}{(RS)^2}=\frac{p}{q}$, where p and q are coprime, then $p+q$ is equal to **[Single Correct Type, 2023 Main]**

(a) 137 (b) 157
(c) 147 (d) 143

46. Let A be a point on the X-axis. Common tangents are drawn from A to the curves $x^2+y^2=8$ and $y^2=16x$. If one of these tangents touches the two curves at Q and R, then $(QR)^2$ is equal to **[Single Correct Type, 2023 Main]**

(a) 76 (b) 72
(c) 64 (d) 81

47. Let an ellipse with centre (1, 0) and latusrectum of length 1/2 have its major axis along X-axis. If its minor axis subtends an angle 60° at the foci, then the square of the sum of the lengths of its minor and major axes is equal to ......5...... . **[Numerical Value Type, 2023 Main]**

48. Let $H_n : \frac{x^2}{1+x}-\frac{y^2}{3+x}=1, n\in N$. Let k be the smallest even value of n such that the eccentricity of H_k is a rational number. If l is the length of the latusrectum of H_k, then $21l$ is equal to .... **[Numerical Value Type, 2023 Main]**

49. Let the eccentricity of an ellipse $\frac{x^2}{a^2}+\frac{y^2}{b^2}=1$ is reciprocal to that of the hyperbola $2x^2-2y^2=1$. If the ellipse intersects the hyperbola at right angles, then square of length of the latusrectum of the ellipse is .... **[Numerical Value Type, 2023 Main]**

50. The line $x=8$ is the directrix of the ellipse $E:\frac{x^2}{a^2}+\frac{y^2}{b^2}=1$ with the corresponding focus (2, 0). If the tangent to E at the point P in the first quadrant passes through the point $(0, 4\sqrt{3})$ and intersects the X-axis at Q, then $(3PQ)^2$ is equal to .... **[Numerical Value Type, 2023 Main]**

51. Let C be the largest circle centred at (2, 0) and inscribed in the ellipse $\frac{x^2}{36}+\frac{y^2}{16}=1$. If $(1, \alpha)$ lies on C, then $10\alpha^2$ is equal to .... **[Numerical Value Type, 2023 Main]**

52. Let a tangent to the curve $9x^2 + 16y^2 = 144$ intersect the coordinate axes at the points A and B. Then, the minimum length of the line segment AB is ....
[Numerical Value Type, 2023 Main]

53. If m is the slope of a common tangent to the curves $\frac{x^2}{16} + \frac{y^2}{9} = 1$ and $x^2 + y^2 = 12$, then $12m^2$ is equal to
[Single Correct Type, 2022 Main]

(a) 6 (b) 9
(c) 10 (d) 12

54. Let a line L passes through the point of intersection of the lines $bx + 10y - 8 = 0$ and $2x - 3y = 0$, $b \in R - \left\{\frac{4}{3}\right\}$. If the line L also passes through the point (1, 1) and touches the circle $17(x^2 + y^2) = 16$, then the eccentricity of the ellipse $\frac{x^2}{5} + \frac{y^2}{b^2} = 1$ is
[Single Correct Type, 2022 Main]

(a) $\frac{2}{\sqrt{5}}$ (b) $\sqrt{\frac{3}{5}}$
(c) $\frac{1}{\sqrt{5}}$ (d) $\sqrt{\frac{2}{5}}$

55. Let the eccentricity of an ellipse $\frac{x^2}{a^2} + \frac{y^2}{b^2} = 1$, $a > b$, be 1/4. If this ellipse passes through the point $\left(-4\sqrt{\frac{2}{5}}, 3\right)$, then $a^2 + b^2$ is equal to
[Single Correct Type, 2022 Main]

(a) 29 (b) 31
(c) 32 (d) 34

56. The locus of the mid-point of the line segment joining the point (4, 3) and the points on the ellipse $x^2 + 2y^2 = 4$ is an ellipse with eccentricity
[Single Correct Type, 2022 Main]

(a) $\frac{\sqrt{3}}{2}$ (b) $\frac{1}{2\sqrt{2}}$
(c) $\frac{1}{\sqrt{2}}$ (d) $\frac{1}{2}$

57. The acute angle between the pair of tangents drawn to the ellipse $2x^2 + 3y^2 = 5$ from the point (1, 3) is
[Single Correct Type, 2022 Main]

(a) $\tan^{-1}\left(\frac{16}{7\sqrt{5}}\right)$ (b) $\tan^{-1}\left(\frac{24}{7\sqrt{5}}\right)$
(c) $\tan^{-1}\left(\frac{32}{7\sqrt{5}}\right)$ (d) $\tan^{-1}\left(\frac{3+8\sqrt{5}}{35}\right)$

58. Let PQ be a focal chord of the parabola $y^2 = 4x$ such that it subtends an angle of $\frac{\pi}{2}$ at the point (3, 0). Let the line segment PQ be also a focal chord of the ellipse $E: \frac{x^2}{a^2} + \frac{y^2}{b^2} = 1$, $a^2 > b^2$. If e is the eccentricity of the ellipse E, then the value of $\frac{1}{e^2}$ is equal to
[Single Correct Type, 2022 Main]

(a) $1 + \sqrt{2}$ (b) $3 + 2\sqrt{2}$
(c) $1 + 2\sqrt{3}$ (d) $4 + 5\sqrt{3}$

59. Let the maximum area of the triangle that can be inscribed in the ellipse $\frac{x^2}{a^2} + \frac{y^2}{4} = 1$, $a > 2$, having one of its vertices at one end of the major axis of the ellipse and one of its sides parallel to the Y-axis be $6\sqrt{3}$. Then, the eccentricity of the ellipse is
[Single Correct Type, 2022 Main]

(a) $\frac{\sqrt{3}}{2}$ (b) $\frac{1}{2}$
(c) $\frac{1}{\sqrt{2}}$ (d) $\frac{\sqrt{3}}{4}$

60. Let the tangents at the points P and Q on the ellipse $x^2/2 + y^2/4 = 1$ meet at the point $R(\sqrt{2}, 2\sqrt{2} - 2)$. If S is the focus of the ellipse on its negative major axis, then $SP^2 + SQ^2$ is equal to ....
[Numerical Value Type, 2022 Main]

61. If the length of the latus rectum of the ellipse $x^2 + 4y^2 + 2x + 8y - \lambda = 0$ is 4 and l is the length of its major axis, then $\lambda + l$ is equal to ....
[Numerical Value Type, 2022 Main]

62. Let the common tangents to the curves $4(x^2 + y^2) = 9$ and $y^2 = 4x$ intersect at the point Q. Let an ellipse, centered at the origin O, has lengths of semi-minor and semi-major axes equal to OQ and 6, respectively. If e and l respectively denote the eccentricity and the length of the latusrectum of this ellipse, then l/e^2 is equal to...... .
[Numerical Value Type, 2022 Main]

63. If two tangents drawn from a point (α, β) lying on the ellipse $25x^2 + 4y^2 = 1$ to the parabola $y^2 = 4x$ are such that the slope of one tangent is four times the other, then the value of $(10\alpha + 5)^2 + (16\beta^2 + 50)^2$ equals ....
[Numerical Value Type, 2022 Main]

64. Let θ be the acute angle between the tangents to the ellipse $\frac{x^2}{9}+\frac{y^2}{1}=1$ and the circle $x^2+y^2=3$ at their point of intersection in the first quadrant. Then, $\tan\theta$ is equal to **[Single Correct Type, 2021 Main]**

(a) $\frac{5}{2\sqrt{3}}$ (b) $\frac{2}{\sqrt{3}}$

(c) $\frac{4}{\sqrt{3}}$ (d) 2

65. The line $12x\cos\theta+5y\sin\theta=60$ is tangent to which of the following curves? **[Single Correct Type, 2021 Main]**

(a) $x^2+y^2=169$ (b) $144x^2+25y^2=3600$

(c) $25x^2+12y^2=3600$ (d) $x^2+y^2=60$

66. Let $E_1:\frac{x^2}{a^2}+\frac{y^2}{b^2}=1, a>b$. Let E_2 be another ellipse such that it touches the end points of major axis of E_1 and the foci of E_2 are the end points of minor axis of E_1. If E_1 and E_2 have same eccentricities, then its value is **[Single Correct Type, 2021 Main]**

(a) $\frac{-1+\sqrt{5}}{2}$ (b) $\frac{-1+\sqrt{8}}{2}$

(c) $\frac{-1+\sqrt{3}}{2}$ (d) $\frac{-1+\sqrt{6}}{2}$

67. The locus of mid-points of the line segments joining $(-3,-5)$ and the points on the ellipse $\frac{x^2}{4}+\frac{y^2}{9}=1$ is **[Single Correct Type, 2021 Main]**

(a) $9x^2+4y^2+18x+8y+145=0$

(b) $36x^2+16y^2+90x+56y+145=0$

(c) $36x^2+16y^2+108x+80y+145=0$

(d) $36x^2+16y^2+72x+32y+145=0$

68. If $x^2+9y^2-4x+3=0$, $x, y\in R$, then x and y respectively lie in the intervals **[Single Correct Type, 2021 Main]**

(a) $\left[-\frac{1}{3},\frac{1}{3}\right]$ and $\left[-\frac{1}{3},\frac{1}{3}\right]$

(b) $\left[-\frac{1}{3},\frac{1}{3}\right]$ and $[1, 3]$

(c) $[1, 3]$ and $[1, 3]$

(d) $[1, 3]$ and $\left[-\frac{1}{3},\frac{1}{3}\right]$

69. If a tangent to the ellipse $x^2+4y^2=4$ meets the tangents at the extremities of its major axis at B and C, then the circle with BC as diameter passes through the point **[Single Correct Type, 2021 Main]**

(a) $(\sqrt{3}, 0)$ (b) $(\sqrt{2}, 0)$

(c) $(1, 1)$ (d) $(-1, 1)$

70. Let an ellipse $E\Rightarrow\frac{x^2}{a^2}+\frac{y^2}{b^2}=1, a^2>b^2$, passes through $\left(\sqrt{\frac{3}{2}},1\right)$ and has eccentricity $1/\sqrt{3}$. If a circle, centered at focus $F(\alpha,0)$, $\alpha>0$, of E and radius $2/\sqrt{3}$, intersects E at two points P and Q, then PQ^2 is equal to **[Single Correct Type, 2021 Main]**

(a) 8/3 (b) 4/3

(c) 16/3 (d) 3

71. Let a tangent be drawn to the ellipse $\frac{x^2}{27}+y^2=1$ at $(3\sqrt{3}\cos\theta, \sin\theta)$, where $\theta\in\left(0,\frac{\pi}{2}\right)$. Then, the value of θ such that the sum of intercepts on axes made by this tangent is minimum is equal to **[Single Correct Type, 2021 Main]**

(a) $\frac{\pi}{8}$ (b) $\frac{\pi}{4}$ (c) $\frac{\pi}{6}$ (d) $\frac{\pi}{3}$

72. Let L be a tangent line to the parabola $y^2=4x-20$ at $(6, 2)$. If L is also a tangent to the ellipse $\frac{x^2}{2}+\frac{y}{b}=1$, then the value of b is equal to **[Single Correct Type, 2021 Main]**

(a) 11 (b) 14

(c) 16 (d) 20

73. If the point of intersections of the ellipse $\frac{x^2}{16}+\frac{y^2}{b^2}=1$ and the circle $x^2+y^2=4b$, $b>4$, lie on the curve $y^2=3x^2$, then b is equal to **[Single Correct Type, 2021 Main]**

(a) 12 (b) 5 (c) 6 (d) 10

74. On the ellipse $\frac{x^2}{8}+\frac{y^2}{4}=1$. Let P be a point in the second quadrant such that the tangent at P to the ellipse is perpendicular to the line $x+2y=0$. Let S and S' be the foci of the ellipse and e be its eccentricity. If A is the area of the ΔSPS, then the value of $(5-e^2)\cdot A$ is **[Single Correct Type, 2021 Main]**

(a) 6 (b) 12 (c) 14 (d) 24

75. A ray of light through $(2, 1)$ is reflected at a point P on the Y-axis and then passes through the point $(5, 3)$. If this reflected ray is the directrix of an ellipse with eccentricity $1/3$ and the distance of the nearer focus from this directrix is $8/\sqrt{53}$, then the equation of the other directrix can be **[Single Correct Type, 2021 Main]**

(a) $11x+7y+8=0$ or $11x+7y-15=0$

(b) $11x-7y-8=0$ or $11x+7y+15=0$

(c) $2x-7y+29=0$ or $2x-7y-7=0$

(d) $2x-7y-39=0$ or $2x-7y-7=0$

76. If the minimum area of the triangle formed by a tangent to the ellipse $\frac{x^2}{b^2}+\frac{y^2}{4a^2}=1$ and the coordinate axis is kab, then k is equal to

[Numerical Value Type, 2021 Main]

77. Let E be an ellipse whose axes are parallel to the coordinates axes, having its center at $(3,-4)$, one focus at $(4,-4)$ and one vertex at $(5,-4)$. If $mx-y=4$, $m>0$ is a tangent to the ellipse E, then the value of $5m^2$ is equal to ....

[Numerical Value Type, 2021 Main]

78. Let L be a common tangent line to the curves $4x^2+9y^2=36$ and $(2x)^2+(2y)^2=31$. Then, the square of the slope of the line L is ....

[Numerical Value Type, 2021 Main]

79. Which of the following points lies on the locus of the foot of perpendicular drawn upon any tangent to the ellipse, $\frac{x^2}{4}+\frac{y^2}{2}=1$ from any of its foci?

[Single Correct Type, 2020 Main]

(a) $(-2,\sqrt{3})$ (b) $(-1,\sqrt{2})$
(c) $(-1,\sqrt{3})$ (d) $(1,2)$

80. If the point P on the curve, $4x^2+5y^2=20$ is farthest from the point $Q(0,-4)$, then PQ^2 is equal to

[Single Correct Type, 2020 Main]

(a) 29 (b) 21 (c) 48 (d) 36

81. If the co-ordinates of two points A and B are $(\sqrt{7},0)$ and $(-\sqrt{7},0)$ respectively and P is any point on the conic, $9x^2+16y^2=144$, then $PA+PB$ is equal to

[Single Correct Type, 2020 Main]

(a) 16 (b) 8
(c) 6 (d) 9

82. The length of the minor axis (along Y - axis) of an ellipse in the standard form is $\frac{4}{\sqrt{3}}$. If this ellipse touches the line, $x+6y=8$; then its eccentricity is

[Single Correct Type, 2020 Main]

(a) $\sqrt{\frac{5}{6}}$ (b) $\frac{1}{2}\sqrt{\frac{11}{3}}$
(c) $\frac{1}{3}\sqrt{\frac{11}{3}}$ (d) $\frac{1}{2}\sqrt{\frac{5}{3}}$

83. Let the line $y=mx$ and the ellipse $2x^2+y^2=1$ intersect at a point P in the first quadrant. If the normal to this ellipse at P meets the coordinate axes at $\left(-\frac{1}{3\sqrt{2}},0\right)$ and $(0,\beta)$, then β is equal to

[Single Correct Type, 2020 Main]

(a) $\frac{2\sqrt{2}}{3}$ (b) $\frac{\sqrt{2}}{3}$
(c) $\frac{2}{\sqrt{3}}$ (d) $\frac{2}{3}$

EXERCISE 2

JEE Advanced Pattern

Single Option Correct Type Questions

1. The eccentricity of the ellipse $ax^2 + by^2 + 2fx + 2gy + c = 0$ if axis of ellipse parallel to X-axis, is

(a) $\sqrt{\left(\frac{b-a}{b}\right)}$ (b) $\sqrt{\left(\frac{a+b}{b}\right)}$

(c) $\sqrt{\left(\frac{a+b}{a}\right)}$ (d) None of these

2. A circle has the same center as an ellipse and passes through the foci F_1 and F_2 of the ellipse such that two curves intersect at four points. Let P be any one of their point of intersection. If the major axis of the ellipse is 17 and the area of triangle PF_1F_2 is 30, then the distance between the foci is

(a) 13 (b) 11
(c) 9 (d) 7

3. The area of the rectangle formed by the perpendicular from the centre of the standard ellipse to the tangent and normal at its point whose eccentric angle is $\frac{\pi}{4}$, is

(a) $\frac{(a^2-b^2)\,ab}{a^2+b^2}$ (b) $\frac{(a^2-b^2)}{(a^2+b^2)\,ab}$

(c) $\frac{(a^2+b^2)\,ab}{(a^2-b^2)}$ (d) $\frac{(a^2+b^2)}{(a^2-b^2)\,ab}$

4. An ellipse is inscribed in a circle and a point within the circle is chosen at random. If the probability that this point lies outside the ellipse is 2/3, then the eccentricity of the ellipse is

(a) $\frac{2\sqrt{2}}{3}$ (b) $\frac{\sqrt{5}}{3}$

(c) $\frac{8}{9}$ (d) $\frac{2}{3}$

5. An ellipse slides between two perpendicular straight lines. Then, the locus of its centre is a/an

(a) parabola
(b) ellipse
(c) hyperbola
(d) circle

6. The length of the chord of the ellipse $\frac{x^2}{25} + \frac{y^2}{16} = 1$, where mid-point is $\left(\frac{1}{2}, \frac{2}{3}\right)$ is

(a) $\frac{1}{10}$ (b) $\frac{\sqrt{8161}}{10}$

(c) $\frac{\sqrt{8061}}{10}$ (d) None of these

7. The equation of the locus of the middle point of the portion of the tangent to the ellipse $\frac{x^2}{16} + \frac{y^2}{9} = 1$ include between the coordinate axes is the curve

(a) $9x^2 + 16y^2 = 4x^2y^2$ (b) $16x^2 + 9y^2 = 4x^2y^2$
(c) $3x^2 + 4y^2 = 4x^2y^2$ (d) $9x^2 + 16y^2 = x^2y^2$

8. The tangent at the point $(a\cos\alpha, b\sin\alpha)$ on the ellipse $\frac{x^2}{a^2} + \frac{y^2}{b^2} = 1$ meets the auxilliary circle in two points which subtends a right angle at the centre, then the eccentricity e of the ellipse is given by the equation

(a) $e^2(1+\cos^2\alpha) = 1$ (b) $e^2(\operatorname{cosec}^2\alpha + 1) = 1$
(c) $e^2(1+\sin^2\alpha) = 1$ (d) $e^2(1+\tan^2\alpha) = 1$

9. The area of quadrilateral formed by the tangent at the end points of latusrectum to the ellipse $\frac{x^2}{9} + \frac{y^2}{5} = 1$ is

(a) $\frac{27}{4}$ sq. units (b) $\frac{27}{2}$ sq. units

(c) $\frac{27}{5}$ sq. units (d) 27 sq. units

10. If the tangent is drawn at ellipse $\frac{x^2}{27} + y^2 = 1$ at $(3\sqrt{3}\cos\theta, \sin\theta)$, where $\theta \in \left(0, \frac{\pi}{2}\right)$ such that the sum of intercepts on axes made by this tangent is minimum, then the value of θ is

(a) $\frac{\pi}{3}$ (b) $\frac{\pi}{4}$

(c) $\frac{\pi}{6}$ (d) $\frac{\pi}{2}$

11. If common tangents are drawn to the parabola $y^2 = 4x$ and the ellipse $3x^2 + 8y^2 = 48$ touching the parabola at A and B and the ellipse at C and D. Then, area of quadrilateral $ABCD$ is equal to

(a) $55\sqrt{5}$ sq. units (b) $53\sqrt{2}$ sq. units
(c) $55\sqrt{2}$ sq. units (d) $53\sqrt{5}$ sq. units

12. Let P_i and P_i' be the feet of perpendiculars drawn from foci S and S' on a tangent T_i to an ellipse whose length of semi-major axis is 30 units. If $\sum_{i=1}^{10} (SP_i)(S'P_i') = 1440$, then the value of eccentricity of ellipse is

(a) $\frac{\sqrt{31}}{5}$ (b) $\frac{\sqrt{21}}{5}$
(c) $\frac{2\sqrt{21}}{5}$ (d) $\frac{\sqrt{14}}{5}$

13. A series of ellipse $E_1, E_2, \ldots, E_n$ are drawn such that E_n touches E_{n-1} at the extremities of the major axis of E_{n-1} and foci of E_n coincide with the extremities of minor axis of E_{n-1}. If eccentricity of the ellipse is independent of n, then the value of eccentricity is

(a) $\frac{\sqrt{5}-1}{2}$ (b) $\frac{\sqrt{5}+1}{4}$
(c) $\frac{\sqrt{5}-3}{2}$ (d) $\frac{\sqrt{5}+3}{4}$

14. The ellipse $x^2 + 4y^2 = 4$ is inscribed in a rectangle aligned with the coordinate axes, which in turn is inscribed in another ellipse that passes through the point $(4, 0)$. Then, the equation of the ellipse is

(a) $x^2 + 12y^2 = 16$ (b) $4x^2 + 48y^2 = 48$
(c) $4x^2 + 64y^2 = 48$ (d) $x^2 + 16y^2 = 16$

15. In a triangle ABC with fixed based BC, the vertex A moves such that $\cos B + \cos C = 4\sin^2 \frac{A}{2}$

If a, b and c denote the lengths of the sides of the triangle opposite to the angles A, B and C, respectively, then

(a) $b + c = 4a$
(b) $b + c = 3a$
(c) locus of point A is an ellipse
(d) locus of point A is a pair of straight lines

More than One Correct Type Questions

16. The distance of a point on the ellipse $\frac{x^2}{6} + \frac{y^2}{2} = 1$ from the centre is 2, then the eccentric angles are

(a) $\frac{\pi}{4}$ (b) $\frac{3\pi}{4}$
(c) $\frac{5\pi}{4}$ (d) $\frac{7\pi}{4}$

17. If the equation of family of ellipse is $x^2 \sec^2\theta + y^2 \operatorname{cosec}^2\theta = 1$, where $\frac{\pi}{4} < \theta < \frac{\pi}{2}$, then the locus of extremities of the latusrectum is

(a) $2y^2(1 + x^2) = (1 - x^2)^2$
(b) $2x^2(1 + y^2) = (1 - y^2)^2$
(c) $2y(1 - x^2) = 1 + x^2$
(d) $2y^2(1 + x^2) = 1 + y^4 - 2x^2$

18. Let F_1 and F_2 be two foci of the ellipse and PT and PN be the tangent and the normal respectively to the ellipse at point P. Then,

(a) PN bisects $\angle F_1PF_2$
(b) PT bisects $\angle F_1PF_2$
(c) PT bisects angle $(180° - \angle F_1PF_2)$
(d) None of the above

19. $\frac{x^2}{(a^2 - a - 6)} + \frac{y^2}{(a^2 - 6a + 5)} = 1$ will represent an ellipse if a lies in the interval

(a) $(-\infty, -2)$ (b) $(1, \infty)$
(c) $(3, \infty)$ (d) $(5, \infty)$

20. If the axes of an ellipse coincide with the coordinate axes and the ellipse passes through the point $(4, -1)$ and touches the line $x + 4y - 10 = 0$, then its equation is

(a) $x^2 + 64y^2 = 80$
(b) $x^2 + 4y^2 = 20$
(c) $x^2 + 20y^2 = 100$
(d) $x^2 + 8y^2 = 40$

21. If P is a point on the ellipse $\frac{x^2}{a^2} + \frac{y^2}{b^2} = 1$, whose foci are S and S'. Let $\angle PSS' = \theta$ and $\angle PS'S = \phi$, then

(a) $SP + S'P = 2a$, if $a > b$
(b) $SP + S'P = 2b$, if $b > a$
(c) $\tan\left(\frac{\theta}{2}\right)\tan\left(\frac{\phi}{2}\right) = \frac{1-e}{1+e}$
(d) $\tan\left(\frac{\theta}{2}\right)\tan\left(\frac{\phi}{2}\right) = \frac{e-1}{e+1}$

22. If a pair of variable straight lines $x^2 + 4y^2 + axy = 0$ (where a is a real parameter) cuts the ellipse $x^2 + 4y^2 = 4$ at two points A and B, then the locus of the point of intersection of tangents at A and B is

(a) $x - 2y = 0$ (b) $2x - y = 0$
(c) $x + 2y = 0$ (d) $2x + y = 0$

23. In the ellipse $25x^2 + 9y^2 - 150x - 90y + 225 = 0$

(a) foci are at $(3, 1)$, $(3, 9)$ (b) $e = \frac{4}{5}$
(c) centre is $(5, 3)$ (d) major axis is 6

24. The parametric angle α, where $-\pi < \alpha \le \pi$ of the point on the ellipse $\frac{x^2}{a^2}+\frac{y^2}{b^2}=1$ at which the tangent drawn cuts the intercept of minimum length on the coordinate axes, is/are

(a) $\tan^{-1}\sqrt{\left(\frac{b}{a}\right)}$ (b) $-\tan^{-1}\sqrt{\left(\frac{b}{a}\right)}$

(c) $\pi-\tan^{-1}\sqrt{\left(\frac{b}{a}\right)}$ (d) $\pi+\tan^{-1}\sqrt{\left(\frac{b}{a}\right)}$

25. Let E_1 and E_2 be two ellipses whose centers are at the origin. The major axes of E_1 and E_2 lie along the X-axis and the Y-axis, respectively. Let S be the circle $x^2+(y-1)^2=2$. The straight line $x+y=3$ touches the curves, S, E_1 and E_2 at P, Q and R respectively. Suppose that $PQ=PR=\frac{2\sqrt{2}}{3}$. If e_1 and e_2 are the eccentricities of E_1 and E_2 respectively, then the correct expression(s) is (are)

(a) $e_1^2+e_2^2=\frac{43}{40}$ (b) $e_1e_2=\frac{\sqrt{7}}{2\sqrt{10}}$

(c) $|e_1^2-e_2^2|=\frac{5}{8}$ (d) $e_1e_2=\frac{\sqrt{3}}{4}$

Passage Based Questions

Passage I

(Q. Nos. 26 and 27)

- The line $2px+y\sqrt{(1-p^2)}=1$ $(|p|<1)$ for different values of p, touches a fixed ellipse whose axes are the coordinate axes.

26. The eccentricity of the ellipse is

(a) $\frac{1}{\sqrt{5}}$ (b) $\frac{1}{\sqrt{3}}$ (c) $\frac{\sqrt{3}}{2}$ (d) $\frac{2}{\sqrt{5}}$

27. The foci of the ellipse are

(a) $\left(\pm\frac{\sqrt{3}}{2},0\right)$ (b) $\left(0,\pm\frac{\sqrt{3}}{2}\right)$

(c) $(\pm\sqrt{3},0)$ (d) $(0,\pm\sqrt{3})$

Passage II

(Q. Nos. 28 and 29)

- An ellipse whose distance between foci S and S' is 4 *units is inscribed in the* ΔABC *touching the sides* AB, AC *and* BC *at* P, Q *and* R, *respectively. If centre of ellipse is at origin and major axis along* X-*axis*, $SP+S'P=6$.

28. Equation of the ellipse is

(a) $9x^2+5y^2=45$ (b) $4x^2+9y^2=36$

(c) $5x^2+9y^2=45$ (c) $9x^2+4y^2=36$

29. If $AB=BC$ and $\angle B=\pi/2$, then locus of A is

(a) $(x^2+y^2-14)^2=4(5x^2+9y^2-45)$

(b) $(x^2+y^2-14)^2=4(5x^2+9y^2-54)$

(c) $(x^2+y^2-14)^2=4(9x^2+5y^2-45)$

(d) $(x^2+y^2-14)^2=4(9x^2+5y^2-54)$

Passage III

(Q. Nos. 30 and 31)

- An ellipse E has its centre $C(3,1)$, focus at $(3,6)$ and passing through the point $P(7,4)$

30. The product of the lengths of the perpendicular segments from the foci on tangent at point P is

(a) 20 (b) 45 (c) 40 (d) 90

31. If F and F' are the feet of perpendiculars from foci S and S' on tangent at point P, then point of intersection of lines SF' and $S'F$ is

(a) $\left(5,\frac{5}{3}\right)$ (b) $\left(3,\frac{4}{3}\right)$

(c) $\left(5,\frac{10}{3}\right)$ (d) $\left(3,\frac{8}{3}\right)$

Stem Based Questions

Stem I

(Q. Nos. 32 and 33)

- Curves $C_1: x^2+y^2=r^2$ and $C_2: \frac{x^2}{16}+\frac{y^2}{9}=1$ intersect at four distinct points A, B, C and D. Their common tangents form a parallelogram $PQRS$.

32. If $PQRS$ is a square, then the value of $2r^2$ is ......

33. If $PQRS$ is a square, then the ratio of the area of curve C_1 to the area of circumcircle of ΔPQR is $\frac{\lambda_1}{\lambda_2}$, then $\lambda_1+\lambda_2$ is ......

Stem II

(Q. Nos. 34 and 35)

- Let $F_1(x_1,0)$ and $F_2(x_2,0)$ be the foci of the ellipse $\frac{x^2}{9}+\frac{y^2}{8}=1$, where $x_1<0$ and $x_2>0$. Suppose a parabola having vertex at the origin and focus at F_2 intersects the ellipse at point A in the first quadrant and at point B in the fourth quadrant.

34. If the orthocentre of the ΔF_1AB is (a,b), then $2(b-a)$ is equal to ....

35. If the tangents to the ellipse at A and B meet at C and the normal to the parabola at A meets the X-axis at D and the ratio of area of the ΔADC to the area of quadrilateral AF_1BF_2 is $\lambda_1:\lambda_2$, then $(\lambda_2-\lambda_1)$ is ......

Stem III

(Q. Nos. 36 and 37)

- Let an ellipse having major axis and minor axis parallel to X-axis and Y-axis, respectively. Its two foci S and S' are $(3, 1)$ and $(9, 1)$ and a line $x + y = 12$ is a tangent to this at point P.

36. If eccentricity of the ellipse is $\frac{\lambda}{\sqrt{\mu}}$, then $(\lambda + \mu)$ is ......

37. If length of major axis is $m\sqrt{17}$, then m is equal to ......

Single Integer Type Questions

38. Two concentric ellipse be such that the foci of one be on the other and if 3/5 and 4/5 be their eccentricities. If θ is the angle between their axes, then the value of $2(1 + \sin^2\theta + \sin^4\theta)$ must be.........

39. Rectangle $ABCD$ has area 200 unit^2. An ellipse with area 200π unit^2, passes through A and C and has foci at B and D. If the perimeter of the rectangle is P, then the value of $\sqrt{(P+1)}$ is ......

40. A vertical line passing through the point $(h, 0)$ intersects the ellipse $\frac{x^2}{4} + \frac{y^2}{9} = 1$ at the points P and Q. Let the tangents to the ellipse at P and Q meet at the point R. If $\Delta(h)$ = area of the triangle $PQR, \Delta_1 = \frac{1}{2} \le h \le \max \Delta(h)$ and $\Delta_2 = \frac{1}{2} \le h \le \min \Delta(h)$, then $\frac{8}{\sqrt{5}}\Delta_1 - 8\Delta_2$ is ......

41. Suppose that the foci of the ellipse $\frac{x^2}{9} + \frac{y^2}{5} = 1$ are $(f_1, 0)$ and $(f_2, 0)$, where $f_1 > 0$ and $f_2 < 0$. Let P_1 and P_2 be two parabolas with a common vertex at $(0, 0)$ and with foci at $(f_1, 0)$ and $(2f_2, 0)$, respectively. Let T_1 be a tangent to P_1 which passes through $(2f_2, 0)$ and T_2 be a tangent to P_2 which passes through $(f_1, 0)$. If m_1 is the slope of T_1 and m_2 is the slope of T_2, then the value of $\left(\frac{1}{m_1^2} + m_2^2\right)$ is ......

42. Variable pairs of chord at right angles and drawn through any point P (with eccentric angle $\frac{\pi}{4}$) on the ellipse $\frac{x^2}{4} + y^2 = 1$, to meet the ellipse at two points A and B. If the line joining A and B passes through a fixed point $Q(a, b)$ such that $a^2 + b^2$ is equal to $\frac{m}{n}$, where m and n are relatively prime, then the value of $\left[\frac{m+n}{3}\right]$ is ......

(where $[\cdot]$ denotes greatest integer function).

44. Consider the ellipse $E: \frac{x^2}{a^2} + \frac{y^2}{b^2} = 1$, centered at point O having AB and CD as its major and minor axes, respectively. If S_1 is one of the foci of the ellipse, radius of incircle of ΔOCS is 1 unit and $OS_1 = 6$ units, then the value of $(a - b)$ is ......

Numerical Value Type Questions

44. Two tangents to an ellipse $\frac{x^2}{a^2} + \frac{y^2}{b^2} = 1$ are drawn which intersect at right angles. Let l_1 and l_2 be the intercepts on these tangents made by the auxiliarly circle $x^2 + y^2 = a^2$. If $l_1^m + l_2^n = (SS')^p$, then $m^2 + n^2 + p^2$ is ...

45. A line passing through the extremity A of the major axis and extremity B of the minor axis of the ellipse $x^2 + 9y^2 = 9$ meets the auxiliary circle at point M, then the area of triangle with vertices at A, M and the origin O, is ......

46. If the quadratic equation, whose one root is positive abscissa of focus and other root is $\frac{25}{41}$ times the square of the length of chord of ellipse $\frac{x^2}{25} + \frac{y^2}{16} = 1$, middle point is $\left(\frac{1}{2}, \frac{2}{5}\right)$ is $x^2 - \alpha x + \beta = 0$, then $\beta - \alpha$ is ......

47. If the normals at (x_r, y_r), where $r = 1, 2, 3, 4$ to the ellipse $\frac{x^2}{a^2} + \frac{y^2}{b^2} = 1$ are concurrent, then value of λ is ......, if $(x_1 + x_2 + x_3 + x_4)\left(\frac{1}{x_1} + \frac{1}{x_2} + \frac{1}{x_3} + \frac{1}{x_4}\right) = \frac{100}{\lambda}$.

48. An archway is in the shape of a semi-ellipse, the road level being the major axis. If breadth of the archway is 30 ft. and a man 6 ft. tall touches the top when 2 ft from the side, the greatest height of the arch is $\frac{\lambda}{\sqrt{14}}$ ft., then λ is equal to ......

Matching Type Questions

49. Match the following

Column I	Column II
(A) For the ellipse $\frac{x^2}{9}+\frac{y^2}{4}=1$ with vertices A and A', tangents drawn at the point P in the first quadrant meets the Y-axis at Q and the chord $A'P$ meets the Y-axis at M. If O is the origin, then $OQ^2 - MQ^2$ is	(p) 7
(B) If $y = x$ and $3y+2x=0$ are the equations of a pair of conjugate diameters of the ellipse $\frac{x^2}{a^2}+\frac{y^2}{b^2}=1$ and e be the eccentricity, then $4(1+e^2+e^4+\ldots+\infty)$ is	(q) 2
(C) If the variable line $y = kx+2h$ is tangent to an ellipse $2x^2+3y^2=6$, then the locus of $P(h,k)$ is a conic C whose eccentricity is e, then $3e^2$ is	(r) 4
(D) If extremities of the latusrectum of the ellipse $\frac{x^2}{a^2}+\frac{y^2}{b^2}=1$, $(a>1)$ having positive ordinates lie on the parabola $x^2=-2(y-2)$, then a is	(s) 6

50. Match the following

Column I	Column II
(A) An ellipse is sliding along the cordinate axes. If the foci of the ellipse are (1,1) and (3,3) and if area of the director circle of the ellipse (in square units) is $\pi\lambda$, then λ is divisible by	(p) 3
(B) If from a point $P(0,\lambda)$, two normals other than axes are drawn to the ellipse $\frac{x^2}{25}+\frac{y^2}{16}=1$ such that $\lvert\lambda\rvert<p$, then $4p$ is divisible by	(q) 4
(C) The orbit of the earth is an ellipse with eccentricity $\frac{1}{60}$ with the sun at one focus the major axis being approximately 186×10^6 miles in length. If the shortest and longest distances of the earth from the sun are $\lambda\times10^5$ miles and $\mu\times10^5$ miles respectively then $\mu-(\lambda+1)$ is divisible by	(r) 5
(D) If the mid-point of a chord of the ellipse $\frac{x^2}{16}+\frac{y^2}{25}=1$ is (0,3) and length of the chord is $\frac{4\lambda}{5}$, then λ is divisible by	(s) 6

51. Match the following

Column I	Column II
(A) The minimum and maximum distances of a point (2,6) from the ellipse $9x^2+8y^2-36x-16y-28=0$ are L and G, then	(p) $L+G=10$
(B) The minimum and maximum distances of a point (1,2) from the ellipse $4x^2+9y^2+8x-36y+4=0$ are L and G, then	(q) $L+G=6$
(C) The minimum and maximum distances of a point $\left(\frac{9}{5},\frac{12}{5}\right)$ from the ellipse $4(3x+4y)^2+9(4x-3y)^2=900$ are L and G, then	(r) $G-L=8$
(D) The minimum and maximum distances of a point (0,4) from the ellipse $25x^2+9y^2=225$ are L and G, then	(s) $G-L=6$

Previous Year Questions

52. Consider the ellipse $\frac{x^2}{9}+\frac{y^2}{4}=1$. Let $S(p,q)$ be a point in the first quadrant such that $\frac{p^2}{9}+\frac{q^2}{4}>1$. Two tangents are drawn from S to the ellipse, of which one meets the ellipse at one end point of the minor axis and the other meets the ellipse at a point T in the fourth quadrant. Let R be the vertex of the ellipse with positive x coordinate and O be the center of the ellipse. If the area of the ΔORT is 3/2, then which of the following options is correct? **[Single Correct Type, 2024 Adv.]**

(a) $q=2,\ p=3\sqrt{3}$
(b) $q=2,\ p=4\sqrt{3}$
(c) $q=1,\ p=5\sqrt{3}$
(d) $q=1,\ p=6\sqrt{3}$

53. Let T_1 and T_2 be two distinct common tangents to the ellipse $E:\frac{x^2}{6}+\frac{y^2}{3}=1$ and the parabola $P: y^2=12x$. Suppose that the tangent T_1 touches P and E at the points A_1 and A_2, respectively and the tangent T_2 touches P and E at the points A_4 and A_3 respectively. Then, which of the following statement(s) is (are) true? **[More than One Correct Type, 2023 Adv.]**

(a) The area of the quadrilateral $A_1A_2A_3A_4$ is 35 sq units
(b) The area of the quadrilateral $A_1A_2A_3A_4$ is 36 sq units
(c) The tangents T_1 and T_2 meet the X-axis at the point $(-3, 0)$
(d) The tangents T_1 and T_2 meet the X-axis at the point $(-6, 0)$

54. Consider the ellipse $\frac{x^2}{4}+\frac{y^2}{3}=1$.

Let $H(\alpha, 0)$, $0<\alpha<2$ be a point. A straight line drawn through H parallel to the Y-axis crosses the ellipse and its auxiliary circle at points E and F respectively, in the first quadrant. The tangent to the ellipse at the point E intersects the positive X-axis at a point G. Suppose the straight line joining F and the origin makes an angle ϕ with the positive X-axis.

[Single Correct Type, 2022 Adv.]

	List-I		List-II
I.	If $\phi=\pi/4$, then the area of the $\Delta\, FGH$ is	P.	$\frac{(\sqrt{3}-1)^4}{8}$
II.	If $\phi=\pi/3$, then the area of the ΔFGH is	Q.	1
III.	If $\phi=\pi/6$, then the area of the $\Delta\, FGH$ is	R.	3/4
IV.	If $\phi=\pi/12$, then the area of the $\Delta\, FGH$ is	S.	$1/2\sqrt{3}$
		T.	$3\sqrt{3}/2$

The correct option is

(a) (I) → (R); (II) → (S); (III) → (Q); (IV) → (P)

(b) (I) → (R); (II) → (T); (III) → (S); (IV) → (P)

(c) (I) → (Q); (II) → (T); (III) → (S); (IV) → (P)

(d) (I) → (Q); (II) → (S); (III) → (Q); (IV) → (P)

55. Let E be the ellipse $\frac{x^2}{16}+\frac{y^2}{9}=1$. For any three distinct points P, Q and Q' on E, let $M_1(P, Q)$ be the mid-point of the line segment joining P and Q and $M_2(P, Q')$ be the mid-point of the line segment joining P and Q'. Then, the maximum possible value of the distance between $M_1(P, Q)$ and $M_2(P, Q')$ as P, Q and Q' vary on E, is ____ .

[Numerical Value Type, 2021 Adv.]

56. Let a, b and λ be positive real numbers. Suppose P is an end point of the latusrectum of the parabola $y^2=4\lambda x$ and suppose the ellipse $\frac{x^2}{a^2}+\frac{y^2}{b^2}=1$ passes through the point P. If the tangents to the parabola and the ellipse at the point P are perpendicular to each other, then the eccentricity of the ellipse is

[Single Correct Type, 2020 Adv.]

(a) $1/\sqrt{2}$ (b) 1/2 (c) 1/3 (d) 2/5

EXERCISE 3

Challenging Problems

1. Find the locus of the centroid of an equilateral triangle inscribed in the ellipse $\frac{x^2}{a^2}+\frac{y^2}{b^2}=1$.

2. If the normals to $\frac{x^2}{a^2}+\frac{y^2}{b^2}=1$ at the ends of the chords $lx+my=1$ and $l'x+m'y=1$ be concurrent then show that $a^2ll'=b^2mm'=-1$.

3. An ellipse slides between two straight lines at right angles to each other. Show that the locus of its centre is a circle.

4. Triangles are formed by pairs of tangents drawn from any point on the ellipse $a^2x^2+b^2y^2=(a^2+b^2)^2$ to the ellipse $\frac{x^2}{a^2}+\frac{y^2}{b^2}=1$ and the chord of contact. Show that the orthocentre of each such triangles lies on the ellipse.

5. Show that the tangents drawn at those points of the ellipse $\frac{x^2}{a}+\frac{y^2}{b}=(a+b)$, where it is cut by any tangent to $\frac{x^2}{a^2}+\frac{y^2}{b^2}=1$, intersect at right angles.

6. From any point on the conic $\frac{x^2}{a^2}+\frac{y^2}{b^2}=4$, tangents are drawn to the conic $\frac{x^2}{a^2}+\frac{y^2}{b^2}=1$. Prove that the normals at the points of contact meet on the conic $a^2x^2+b^2y^2=\frac{1}{4}(a^2-b^2)^2$.

7. A variable point P on an ellipse of eccentricity e, is joined to its foci S and S', prove that the locus of the incentre of the triangle PSS' is an ellipse whose eccentricity is $\sqrt{\left(\frac{2e}{1+e}\right)}$.

8. Prove that the eccentricity of the ellipse $\frac{x^2}{a^2}+\frac{y^2}{b^2}=1$ is given by $2\cot\omega=\frac{e^2\sin 2\theta}{\sqrt{(1-e^2)}}$, where ω is one of the angles between the normals at the points whose eccentric angles are θ and $\frac{\pi}{2}+\theta$.

9. Show that the area of the triangle inscribed in an ellipse is $\left[2ab\sin\left(\frac{\beta-\gamma}{2}\right)\sin\left(\frac{\gamma-\alpha}{2}\right)\sin\left(\frac{\alpha-\beta}{2}\right)\right]$, where α, β and γ are the eccentric angles of the vertices and hence find the condition that the area of a triangle inscribed in an ellipse may be maximum.

10. Let ABC be an equilateral triangle inscribed in the circle $x^2+y^2=a^2$. Suppose perpendiculars form A, B and C to the major axis of the ellipse $\frac{x^2}{a^2}+\frac{y^2}{b^2}=1$ $(a>b)$ meet the ellipse respectively at P, Q and R so that P, Q and R lie on the same side of the major axis as A, B and C, respectively. Prove that the normal to the ellipse drawn at the points P, Q and R are concurrent.

11. If two concentric ellipses be such that the foci of one be on the other and if e and e' are their eccentricities. Prove that the angle between their axes is $\cos^{-1}\left\{\frac{\sqrt{(e^2+e'^2-1)}}{ee'}\right\}$

12. If the normals at the four points $(x_1, y_1), (x_2, y_2), (x_3, y_3)$ and (x_4, y_4) on the ellipse $\frac{x^2}{a^2}+\frac{y^2}{b^2}=1$ are concurrent. Prove that

$$(x_1+x_2+x_3+x_4)\left(\frac{1}{x_1}+\frac{1}{x_2}+\frac{1}{x_3}+\frac{1}{x_4}\right)=4$$

or $(\Sigma\cos\alpha)(\Sigma\sec\alpha)=4$

where α, β, γ and δ are the eccentric angles of the points.

13. If S and S' are the foci of an ellipse and P any point on the curve, then show that

$$\tan\left(\frac{PSS'}{2}\right)\tan\left(\frac{PS'S}{2}\right)=\frac{1-e}{1+e}$$

Hence, or otherwise show that the locus of the centre of the circle inscribed in the triangle PSS' is another ellipse.

14. If the normal at any point P of the ellipse $\frac{x^2}{a^2}+\frac{y^2}{b^2}=1$ meets the major and minor axes in G and g respectively, and if CF is the perpendicular upon this normal from the centre C of the ellipse. Show that $PF\cdot PG=b^2$ and $PF\cdot Pg=a^2$.

15. Prove that the normals at the four points, where the lines $\frac{lx}{a}+\frac{my}{b}=1$ and $\frac{x}{la}+\frac{y}{mb}=-1$ cut the ellipse $\frac{x^2}{a^2}+\frac{y^2}{b^2}=1$ are concurrent.

16. The eccentric angle of any point P measured from the semi-major axis CA is ϕ. If S is the focus nearest to A, and $\angle ASP=\theta$, then prove that

$$\tan\left(\frac{\theta}{2}\right)=\sqrt{\left(\frac{1+e}{1-e}\right)}\tan\left(\frac{\phi}{2}\right)$$

17. If PSQ and PHR are focal chords of the ellipse $\frac{x^2}{a^2}+\frac{y^2}{b^2}=1$, where S and H are the foci. The tangents at Q and R meet at T. Show that the locus of T as P moves round the ellipse is

$$(1+e^2)^2\frac{x^2}{a^2}+(1-e^2)^2\frac{y^2}{b^2}=(1+e^2)^2,$$

where e is the eccentricity of the ellipse.

Answer Key

Exercise 1

1. (d)	2. (a)	3. (b)	4. (d)	5. (c)	6. (c)	7. (b)	8. (b)	9. (d)	10. (c)
11. (a)	12. (c)	13. (c)	14. (d)	15. (a)	16. (b)	17. (a)	18. (d)	19. (a)	20. (c)
21. (c)	22. (d)	23. (d)	24. (c)	25. (c)	26. (5)	27. (2)	28. (8)	29. (1)	30. (5)
31. (9)	32. (6)	33. (2)	34. (2)	35. (6)	36. (4)	37. (b)	38. (d)	39. (c)	40. (d)
41. (c)	42. (b)	43. (d)	44. (d)	45. (b)	46. (b)	47. (5)	48. (306)	49. (2)	50. (39)
51. (118)	52. (7)	53. (b)	54. (b)	55. (b)	56. (c)	57. (b)	58. (b)	59. (a)	60. (13)
61. (75)	62. (4)	63. (2929)	64. (b)	65. (b)	66. (a)	67. (c)	68. (d)	69. (a)	70. (c)
71. (c)	72. (b)	73. (a)	74. (a)	75. (c)	76. (2)	77. (3)	78. (3)	79. (c)	80. (d)
81. (b)	82. (b)	83. (b)							

Exercise 2

1. (a)	2. (a)	3. (a)	4. (a)	5. (d)	6. (d)	7. (a)	8. (c)	9. (d)	10. (c)
11. (c)	12. (b)	13. (a)	14. (a)	15. (c)	16. (a,b,c,d)	17. (b,d)	18. (a,c)	19. (a,d)	20. (a,b)
21. (a,b,c)	22. (a,c)	23. (a,b)	24. (a,b,c)	25. (a,b)	26. (c)	27. (b)	28. (c)	29. (a)	30. (a)
31. (c)	32. (25)	33. (3)	34. (1.8)	35. (3)	36. (20)	37. (2)	38. (6)	39. (9)	40. (9)
41. (4)	42. (6)	43. (4)	44. (12)	45. (2.7)	46. (95)	47. (25)	48. (45)		

49. $A\to r, B\to s, C\to p, D\to q$

50. $A\to q, B\to p, C\to p, r, s, D\to q$

51. $A\to p, s, B\to q, C\to q, s; D\to p, r$

52. (a)

53. (a,c) 54. (c) 55. (4) 56. (a)

Solutions

Exercise 1 - JEE Main Pattern

1. $\because$ Major axis on Y-axis.

$\therefore \quad f(a^2-5) > f(4a)$

$\Rightarrow \quad a^2 - 5 < 4a \quad [\because f \text{ is decreasing}]$

$\Rightarrow \quad a^2 - 4a - 5 < 0$

or $\quad (a-5)(a+1) < 0$ or $-1 < a < 5$

$\therefore \quad a \in (-1, 5)$

2. Let $a^2 = \sin\sqrt{2} - \cos\sqrt{3} = \sin\sqrt{2} - \sin\left(\frac{\pi}{2} - \sqrt{3}\right)$

$= \sin\sqrt{2} + \sin\left(\sqrt{3} - \frac{\pi}{2}\right)$

$= \sin(1.41) + \sin(1.73 - 1.57)$

$= \sin(1.41) + \sin(0.16) > 0$

and $b^2 = \sin\sqrt{3} - \cos\sqrt{2}$

$= \sin\sqrt{3} - \sin\left(\frac{\pi}{2} - \sqrt{2}\right)$

$= \sin(1.73) - \sin(1.57 - 1.41) = \sin(1.73) - \sin(0.36) > 0$

Also, $a^2 > b^2$

Hence, curve represents an ellipse with foci on X-axis.

3. Mutually perpendicular tangents have been drawn by taking any point on the director circle of given ellipse. Any point on the director circle can be taken as $(5\cos\theta, 5\sin\theta)$. Equation of corresponding chord of contact is

$$\frac{5x}{16}\cos\theta + \frac{5y}{9}\sin\theta - 1 = 0$$

Its distance from the origin is equal to

$$\left|\frac{-1}{\sqrt{\left(\frac{25\cos^2\theta}{256} + \frac{25\sin^2\theta}{81}\right)}}\right|$$

$$= \frac{5}{16.9}\frac{1}{\sqrt{(256 - 175\cos^2\theta)}} \geq \frac{144}{5.9} \geq \frac{16}{5}$$

4. Any tangent to $\frac{x^2}{16} + \frac{y^2}{9} = 1$, is $y = mx + \sqrt{(16m^2+9)}$

It is also tangent to the circle $x^2 + y^2 = \left(\frac{5}{\sqrt{2}}\right)^2$, then perpendicular distance from $(0, 0)$ is equal to $\frac{5}{\sqrt{2}}$

$$\therefore \quad \frac{\sqrt{(16m^2+9)}}{\sqrt{(m^2+1)}} = \frac{5}{\sqrt{2}}$$

$\Rightarrow \quad 32m^2 + 18 = 25m^2 + 25$

or $\quad 7m^2 = 7 \Rightarrow m = \pm 1$

For acute, $m = 1$.

Now, let θ be the angle between common tangent and the line $\sqrt{3}x - y + 6 = 0$, then

$$\tan\theta = \left|\frac{\sqrt{3}-1}{1+\sqrt{3}}\right| = \frac{\sqrt{3}-1}{\sqrt{3}+1} = \tan\left(\frac{\pi}{12}\right)$$

$\therefore \quad \theta = \frac{\pi}{12}$

5. Let $A \equiv (4\cos\theta, 3\sin\theta)$, then

$B \equiv (-4\sin\theta, 3\cos\theta)$

$\therefore \quad (CA)^2 = 16\cos^2\theta + 9\sin^2\theta$

and $(CB)^2 = 16\sin^2\theta + 9\cos^2\theta$

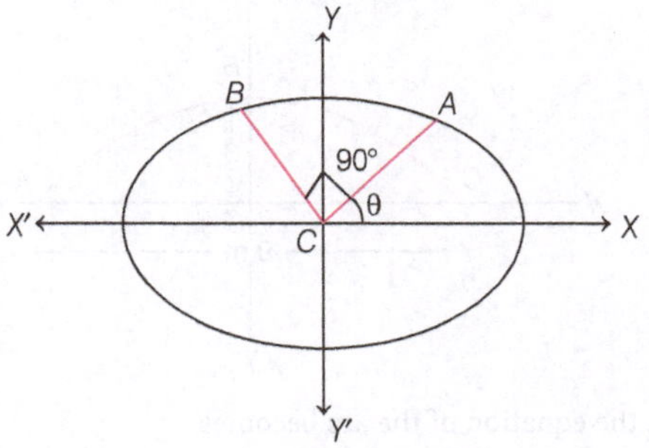

$$\therefore \frac{1}{(CA)^2} + \frac{1}{(CB)^2} = \frac{1}{16\cos^2\theta + 9\sin^2\theta} + \frac{1}{16\sin^2\theta + 9\cos^2\theta}$$

$$= \frac{25}{144(\sin^4\theta + \cos^4\theta) + 337\sin^2\theta\cos^2\theta}$$

$$= \frac{25}{144(1 - 2\sin^2\theta\cos^2\theta) + 337\sin^2\theta\cos^2\theta}$$

$$= \frac{25}{144 + 49\sin^2\theta\cos^2\theta} = \frac{25}{144} \quad [\text{for } \theta = 0]$$

6. At $t = \frac{3}{2}$, $b > a$

$$\therefore \text{Length of latusrectum} = \frac{2a^2}{b} = \frac{2[t^2 - 3t + 4]^2}{[3 + 5t]}$$

$$= \frac{2\left[\frac{9}{4} - \frac{9}{2} + 4\right]^2}{\left[3 + \frac{15}{2}\right]} \quad \left[\text{at } t = \frac{3}{2}\right]$$

$$= \frac{2[1.75]^2}{[10.5]} = \frac{2(1)^2}{10} = \frac{1}{5}$$

7. Slope of line $= \frac{b}{a}\left(\frac{\sin 60° - \sin 30°}{\cos 60° - \cos 30°}\right) = -\frac{b}{a} = -\frac{1}{2}$ or $a = 2b$

Homogenising the ellipse with $x + 2y + 4 = 0$, then

$$\frac{x^2}{4b^2} + \frac{y^2}{b^2} = \left(\frac{x+2y}{-4}\right)^2$$

or $\quad x^2\left(\frac{1}{4b^2} - \frac{1}{16}\right) + y^2\left(\frac{1}{b^2} - \frac{1}{4}\right) - \frac{xy}{4} = 0$

Now, coefficient of x^2 + coefficient of $y^2 = 0$

$\Rightarrow \quad \frac{1}{4b^2} - \frac{1}{16} + \frac{1}{b^2} - \frac{1}{4} = 0$ or $\frac{5}{4b^2} = \frac{5}{16}$

or $\quad b^2 = 4$ and $a^2 = 16$

$\therefore$ Ellipse is $\frac{x^2}{16} + \frac{y^2}{4} = 1$

8. Let the equation of the semi elliptical arc be

$$\frac{x^2}{a^2} + \frac{y^2}{b^2} = 1 \qquad [y > 0]$$

Length of the major axis $= 2a = 9$

$\Rightarrow \quad a = \frac{9}{2}$

Length of the semi minor axis $= b = 3$

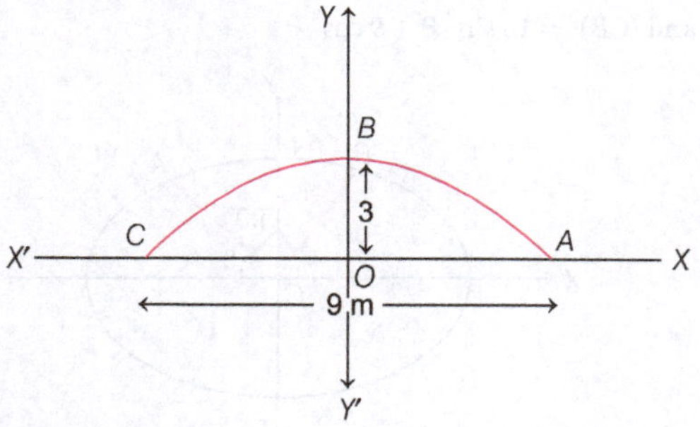

So, the equation of the arc becomes

$$\frac{4x^2}{81} + \frac{y^2}{9} = 1$$

If $x = 2$, then $\quad y^2 = \frac{65}{9}$

$\therefore \quad y = \frac{\sqrt{65}}{3} = \frac{8}{3}$ [approximately]

9. Equation of tangent of the ellipse at $P(5\cos\theta, 4\sin\theta)$ is

$$\frac{x}{5}\cos\theta + \frac{y}{4}\sin\theta = 1$$

It meets the line $x = 0$ at $Q(0, 4 \operatorname{cosec}\theta)$ and image of Q in the line $y = x$ is $R(4 \operatorname{cosec}\theta, 0)$.

$\therefore$Equation of the circle is

$$(x - 0)(x - 4\operatorname{cosec}\theta) + (y - 4\operatorname{cosec}\theta)(y - 0) = 0$$

i.e. $\quad x^2 + y^2 - 4(x + y)\operatorname{cosec}\theta = 0$

$\therefore$Each member of the family passes through the intersection of

$$x^2 + y^2 = 0 \text{ and } x + y = 0$$

i.e. the point $(0, 0)$.

10. A cyclic parallelogram will be a rectangle or square.

So, $\quad \angle QPR = 90°$

Therefore, P lies on the director circle of the ellipse

$$\frac{x^2}{16} + \frac{y^2}{b^2} = 1$$

Hence, $x^2 + y^2 = 25$ is the director circle of $\frac{x^2}{16} + \frac{y^2}{b^2} = 1$,

then $\quad 16 + b^2 = 25$ or $b^2 = 9$

$\Rightarrow \quad a^2(1 - e^2) = 9$

$\Rightarrow \quad 16(1 - e^2) = 9 \qquad [\because a^2 = 16]$

$\Rightarrow \quad e^2 = 1 - \frac{9}{16} = \frac{7}{16}$

$\therefore \quad e = \frac{\sqrt{7}}{4}$

11. Given, $x - 2y + 4 = 0$ or $y = \frac{x}{2} + 2$

Condition of tangency is $c^2 = a^2m^2 + b^2$

$\Rightarrow \quad 4 = 4 \times \frac{1}{4} + b^2$

$\therefore \quad b = \sqrt{3}$

Now, common tangent meet on X-axis at a point $(-4, 0)$.

According to symmetry, other common tangent meet Y-axis at $(0, -2)$.

$\therefore$Equation of other common tangent is

$$\frac{x}{-4} + \frac{y}{-2} = 1 \text{ or } x + 2y + 4 = 0$$

12. The tangent at the point of shortest distance from the line $x + y = 7$ is parallel to the given line.

Any point on the given ellipse is $(\sqrt{6}\cos\theta, \sqrt{3}\sin\theta)$.

Equation of the tangent is $\frac{x\cos\theta}{\sqrt{6}} + \frac{y\sin\theta}{\sqrt{3}} = 1$.

It is parallel to $x + y = 7$

So, $\quad \frac{\cos\theta}{\sqrt{6}} = \frac{\sin\theta}{\sqrt{3}}$

$\Rightarrow \quad \frac{\cos\theta}{\sqrt{2}} = \frac{\sin\theta}{1}$

$\therefore$ The required point is $(2, 1)$.

13. Let $y = mx + \frac{1}{m}$ be a tangent to the parabola, then for the required equilateral triangle, $m = \pm\frac{1}{\sqrt{3}}$

and it is tangent to ellipse also, if

$$\left(\frac{1}{m}\right)^2 = a^2m^2 + b^2$$

$\Rightarrow \quad 3 = \frac{a^2}{3} + b^2$

$\Rightarrow \quad 3 = \frac{a^2}{3} + a^2 - a^2e^2$

$\Rightarrow \quad a^2e^2 = \frac{4a^2}{3} - 3$

or $e^2 = \frac{4}{3} - \frac{3}{a^2}$

Now, $0 < e^2 < 1$

$\Rightarrow$ $0 < \frac{4}{3} - \frac{3}{a^2} < 1$

$\therefore$ $\frac{3}{2} < a < 3$ or $a \in \left(\frac{3}{2}, 3\right)$

14. For equilateral triangle, Circumcentre = Centroid

$\therefore$ $h = \frac{a\cos\alpha + a\cos\beta + a\cos\gamma}{3}$

or $\frac{3h}{a} = \Sigma\cos\alpha$

or $\left(\frac{3h}{a}\right)^2 = (\Sigma\cos\alpha)^2 = \Sigma\cos^2\alpha + 2\,\Sigma\cos\alpha\cos\beta$ ...(i)

and $k = \frac{b\sin\alpha + b\sin\beta + b\sin\gamma}{3}$

or $\frac{3k}{b} = \Sigma\sin\alpha$

or $\left(\frac{3k}{b}\right)^2 = (\Sigma\sin\alpha)^2 = \Sigma\sin^2\alpha + 2\,\Sigma\sin\alpha\sin\beta$ ...(ii)

On adding Eqs. (i) and (ii), we get

$$\frac{9h^2}{a^2} + \frac{9k^2}{b^2} = 3 + 2\,\Sigma\cos(\alpha - \beta)$$

or $\Sigma\cos(\alpha - \beta) = \frac{9h^2}{2a^2} + \frac{9k^2}{2b^2} - \frac{3}{2}$

15. $\because$ Latusrectum of parabola = $4(ae)$ ...(i)

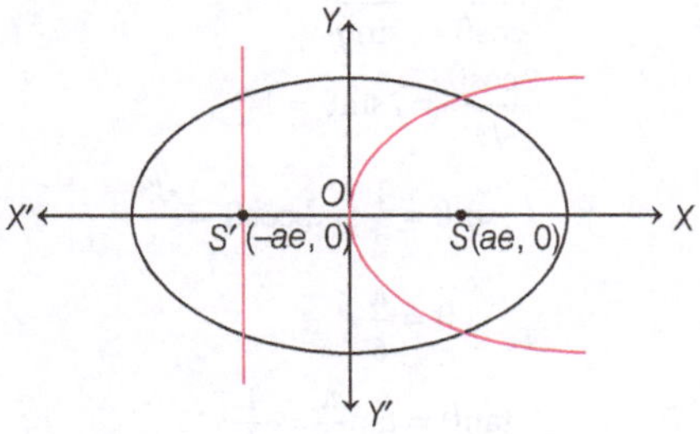

and latusrectum of ellipse $= \frac{2b^2}{a}$ ...(ii)

$\because$ Latusrectum of parabola and ellipse are equal

$\therefore$ $\frac{2b^2}{a} = 4ae$ [from Eqs. (i) and (ii)]

$\Rightarrow$ $2b^2 = 4a^2 e$

or $2a^2(1 - e^2) = 4a^2 e$

or $e^2 + 2e - 1 = 0$

Therefore, $e = \frac{-2 \pm \sqrt{(4+4)}}{2} = -1 \pm \sqrt{2}$

Hence, $e = \sqrt{2} - 1$

16. Here, the center of the ellipse is (0, 0).

Let $P(r\cos\theta, r\sin\theta)$ be any point on the given ellipse, then

$r^2\cos^2\theta + 2r^2\sin^2\theta + 2r^2\sin\theta\cos\theta = 1$

or $r^2 = \frac{1}{1 + \sin^2\theta + \sin 2\theta}$

$= \frac{2}{2 + (1 - \cos 2\theta) + 2\sin 2\theta} = \frac{2}{2\sin 2\theta - \cos 2\theta + 3}$

$\because$ $3 - \sqrt{5} \le 2\sin 2\theta - \cos 2\theta + 3 \le 3 + \sqrt{5}$

For r_{max}, $2\sin 2\theta - \cos 2\theta + 3 = 3 - \sqrt{5}$

$\therefore$ $r_{max}^2 = \frac{2}{3 - \sqrt{5}} = \frac{2(3 + \sqrt{5})}{4} = \frac{6 + 2\sqrt{5}}{4} = \left(\frac{\sqrt{5} + 1}{2}\right)^2$

Hence, $r_{max} = \frac{\sqrt{5} + 1}{2}$

17. Centre of the ellipse is (1, 2) and length of major axis and minor axis are 6 and 4 respectively and centre and radius of the circle are (1, 2) and 1 respectively.

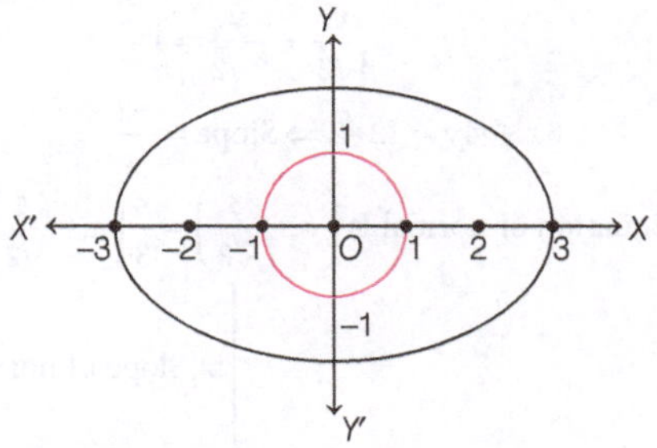

Hence, ellipse and circle do not touch or cut.

$\therefore$ Common chord impossible.

Hence, length of common chord = 0

18. Given, y coordinate is 3 for point P and ellipse is $9x^2 + 25y^2 = 225$

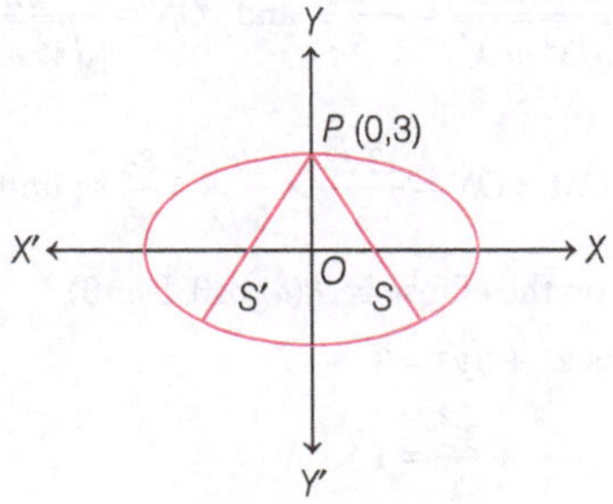

$\Rightarrow$ $\frac{9x^2}{225} + \frac{25y^2}{225} = 1$

$\Rightarrow$ $\frac{x^2}{25} + \frac{y^2}{9} = 1$ ...(i)

$\Rightarrow$ $a^2 = 25$ and $b^2 = 9$

$\therefore$ $e = \sqrt{1 - \frac{b^2}{a^2}} = \sqrt{1 - \frac{9}{25}} = \frac{4}{5}$

Put $y = 3$ in Eq. (i), we get coordinate of P

$$\frac{x^2}{25} + \frac{9}{9} = 1$$

$\Rightarrow$ $x^2 = 0 \Rightarrow x = 0$

$\Rightarrow$ $P = (0, 3)$

Now, foci $(\pm ae, 0) \equiv (\pm 4, 0)$

$\therefore$ Reflected ray PS = Line joining $P(0, 3)$ and $S(4, 0)$

$$\Rightarrow \quad y - 0 = \frac{3-0}{0-4}(x-4)$$

$$\Rightarrow \quad -4y = 3x - 12 \Rightarrow 3x + 4y = 12$$

$\therefore$ Equation of reflected ray is $3x + 4y = 12$.

19. Given equation of ellipse is $\frac{x^2}{16} + \frac{y^2}{9} = 1$

$$\Rightarrow \quad a^2 = 16 \text{ and } b^2 = 9 \Rightarrow a = 4 \text{ and } b = 3$$

Let $P(a\cos\theta, b\sin\theta) = (4\cos\theta, 3\sin\theta)$ be any point on ellipse.

$\therefore$ Equation of tangent at $P\left(4\cos\frac{\pi}{4}, 3\sin\frac{\pi}{4}\right) = P\left(\frac{4}{\sqrt{2}}, \frac{3}{\sqrt{2}}\right)$ is

$$\frac{x}{16}\left(\frac{4}{\sqrt{2}}\right) + \frac{y}{9}\left(\frac{3}{\sqrt{2}}\right) = 1 \qquad \left[\because \theta = \frac{\pi}{4} \text{ (given)}\right]$$

$$\Rightarrow \quad \frac{x}{4\sqrt{2}} + \frac{y}{3\sqrt{2}} = 1$$

$$\Rightarrow \quad 3x + 4y = 12\sqrt{2} \Rightarrow \text{Slope} = \frac{-3}{4}$$

$\therefore$ Equation of normal is $\left(y - \frac{3}{\sqrt{2}}\right) = \frac{4}{3}\left(x - \frac{4}{\sqrt{2}}\right)$

$$\left[\because \text{Slope of normal} = \frac{-1}{\frac{-3}{4}} = \frac{4}{3}\right]$$

$$\Rightarrow \quad 4\sqrt{2}x - 3\sqrt{2}y = 7 \Rightarrow 4x - 3y = \frac{7}{\sqrt{2}}$$

$\because$ Perpendicular from centre to tangent and normals are OM and ON

$$\therefore \quad OM = \left|\frac{12\sqrt{2}}{\sqrt{3^2+4^2}}\right| = \frac{12\sqrt{2}}{5} \text{ and } ON = \left|\frac{\frac{7}{\sqrt{2}}}{\sqrt{4^2+3^2}}\right| = \frac{7}{5\sqrt{2}}$$

$$\therefore \quad OM \times ON = \frac{12\sqrt{2}}{5} \times \frac{7}{5\sqrt{2}} = \frac{84}{25} \text{ sq units}$$

20. Let point R on the ellipse be $R(a\cos\theta, b\sin\theta)$.

$\because$ Ellipse is $x^2 + 3y^2 = 3$

$$\frac{x^2}{3} + \frac{y^2}{1} = 1$$

$$\Rightarrow \quad a^2 = 3 \text{ and } b^2 = 1 \Rightarrow a = \sqrt{3} \text{ and } b = 1$$

$$\therefore \quad R(\sqrt{3}\cos\theta, \sin\theta)$$

$\Rightarrow$ Equation of tangent at R is $\frac{x(\sqrt{3}\cos\theta)}{3} + y\sin\theta = 1$

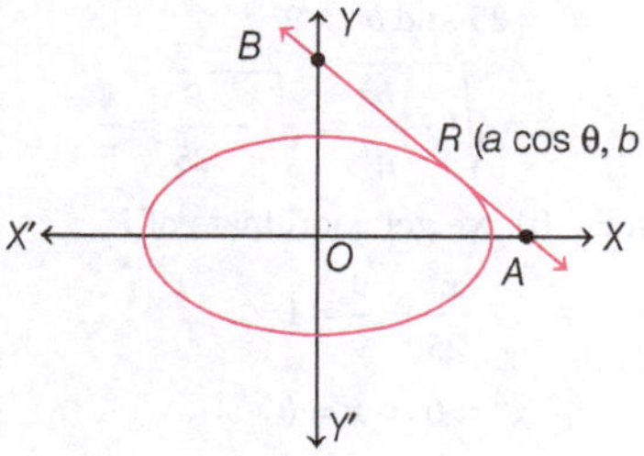

For A, put $y = 0 \Rightarrow x = \frac{\sqrt{3}}{\cos\theta} \Rightarrow A \equiv (\sqrt{3}\sec\theta, 0)$

For B, put $x = 0 \Rightarrow y = \frac{1}{\sin\theta} \Rightarrow B \equiv (0, \operatorname{cosec}\theta)$

Let $Q(h, k)$ be the middle point of AB, then

$$\therefore \quad h = \frac{\sqrt{3}\sec\theta + 0}{2} \text{ and } k = \frac{\operatorname{cosec}\theta}{2}$$

$$\Rightarrow \quad \sin\theta = \frac{1}{2k} \text{ and } \cos\theta = \frac{\sqrt{3}}{2h}$$

$$\because \quad \frac{1}{4k^2} + \frac{3}{4h^2} = 1 \qquad [\because \sin^2\theta + \cos^2\theta = 1]$$

$$\therefore \quad \text{Locus is } \frac{3}{4x^2} + \frac{1}{4y^2} = 1$$

21. Given, ellipse $\frac{x^2}{a^2} + \frac{y^2}{b^2} = 1$ and tangent $\sqrt{3}bx + ay = 2ab$

$$\Rightarrow \quad \frac{\sqrt{3}bx}{2ab} + \frac{ay}{2ab} = 1$$

$$\Rightarrow \quad \frac{x}{\left(\frac{2}{\sqrt{3}}\right)a} + \frac{y}{2b} = 1 \qquad \text{...(i)}$$

Let $P(\theta)$ be the point of contact and whose eccentric angle is θ.

$\Rightarrow P \equiv (a\cos\theta, b\sin\theta)$

Equation of tangent at P is $\frac{x}{a}\cos\theta + \frac{y}{b}\sin\theta = 1$ ...(ii)

From Eq. (i) and (ii) we get

$$\frac{\frac{\frac{2}{\sqrt{3}}a}{a}}{\cos\theta} = \frac{\frac{2b}{b}}{\sin\theta} = 1$$

$$\Rightarrow \quad \frac{2\cos\theta}{\sqrt{3}} = 2\sin\theta = 1$$

$$\Rightarrow \quad \sin\theta = \frac{1}{2} \text{ and } \cos\theta = \frac{\sqrt{3}}{2}$$

$$\Rightarrow \quad \theta = \frac{\pi}{6}$$

$$\therefore \quad \tan\theta = \tan\frac{\pi}{6} = \frac{1}{\sqrt{3}}$$

22. If CP and CQ be the two conjugate diameters of the ellipse $\frac{x^2}{a^2} + \frac{y^2}{b^2} = 1$ having centre $C(0, 0)$.

Let $P \equiv a(\cos\phi, b\sin\phi)$, then $Q \equiv (-a\sin\phi, b\cos\phi)$

Equation of circle drawn CP and CQ as diameters

$$(x-0)(x - a\cos\phi) + (y-0)(y - b\sin\phi) = 0$$

$$\Rightarrow \quad x^2 + y^2 - ax\cos\phi - by\sin\phi = 0 \qquad \text{...(i)}$$

$$\text{and} \quad (x-0)(x + a\sin\phi) + (y-0)(y - b\cos\phi) = 0$$

$$\Rightarrow \quad x^2 + y^2 + ax\sin\phi - by\cos\phi = 0 \qquad \text{...(ii)}$$

From Eqs. (i) and (ii), we get

$$(ax + by)\sin\phi = (by - ax)\cos\phi$$

$$\Rightarrow \quad \frac{\sin\phi}{by-ax} = \frac{\cos\phi}{ax+by} = \frac{1}{\sqrt{(by-ax)^2+(by+ax)^2}}$$

$$= \frac{1}{\sqrt{2(b^2y^2+a^2x^2)}}$$

$$\Rightarrow \quad \sin\phi = \frac{by-ax}{\sqrt{2(b^2y^2+a^2x^2)}}$$

and $$\cos\phi = \frac{ax+by}{\sqrt{2(b^2y^2+a^2x^2)}}$$

From Eq. (i), we get

$$x^2+y^2 = \frac{ax(by+ax)}{\sqrt{2(b^2y^2+a^2x^2)}} + \frac{by(by-ax)}{\sqrt{2(b^2y^2+a^2x^2)}}$$

$$= \frac{a^2x^2+b^2y^2}{\sqrt{2}(\sqrt{a^2x^2+b^2y^2})}$$

$$\Rightarrow \quad x^2+y^2 = \sqrt{\frac{a^2x^2+b^2y^2}{2}}$$

On squaring both sides, we get

$$(x^2+y^2)^2 = \frac{a^2x^2+b^2y^2}{2}$$

$$\therefore \quad 2(x^2+y^2)^2 = a^2x^2+b^2y^2$$

23. The given ellipse is $x^2+9y^2=9$.

or $$\frac{x^2}{3^2}+\frac{y^2}{1^2}=1$$

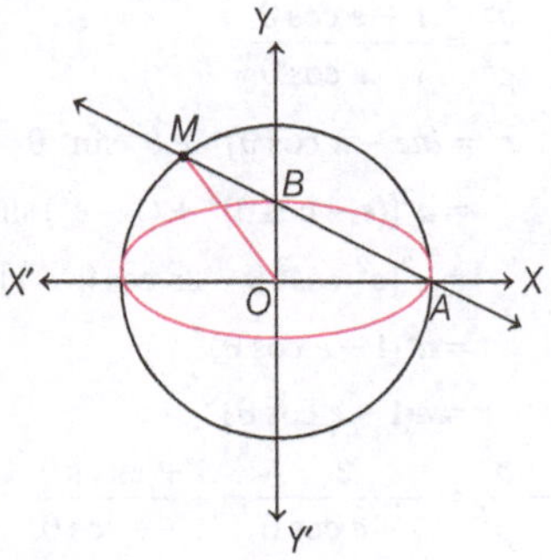

So, $A(3, 0)$ and $B(0, 1)$

$\therefore$ Equation of AB is $\frac{x}{3}+\frac{y}{1}=1$ or $x+3y-3=0$ ...(i)

Also, auxiliary circle of given ellipse is

$$x^2+y^2=9 \quad ...(ii)$$

On solving Eq. (i) and (ii), we get the point M where line AB meets the auxiliary circle.

Put $x=3-3y$ from Eq. (i) in Eq. (ii), we get

$$(3-3y)^2+y^2=9$$

$$\Rightarrow \quad 9-18y+9y^2+y^2=9$$

$$\Rightarrow \quad 10y^2-18y=0$$

$$\Rightarrow \quad y=0, \frac{9}{5}$$

$$\Rightarrow \quad x=3, \frac{-12}{5}$$

Clearly, $M\left(\frac{-12}{5}, \frac{9}{5}\right)$

$$\therefore \text{ Area of } \Delta OAM = \frac{1}{2}\times \left|\begin{vmatrix} 0 & 0 & 1 \\ 3 & 0 & 1 \\ \frac{-12}{5} & \frac{9}{5} & 1 \end{vmatrix}\right| = \frac{27}{10} \text{ sq units}$$

24. As rectangle $ABCD$ circumscribed the ellipse

$$\frac{x^2}{9}+\frac{y^2}{4}=1$$

$$\therefore \quad A \equiv (3, 2)$$

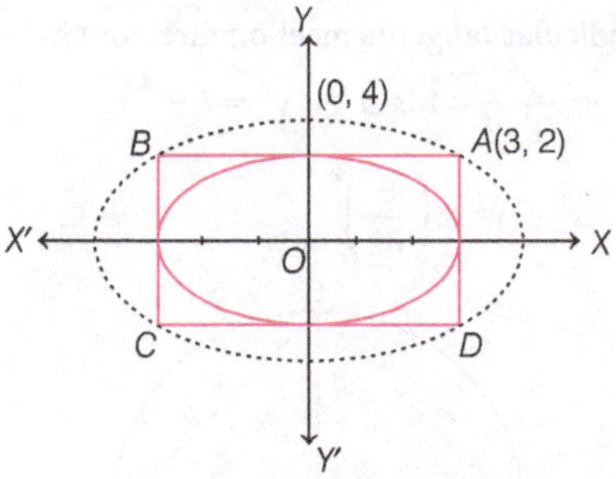

Let the ellipse circumscribing the rectangle $ABCD$ is

$$\frac{x^2}{a^2}+\frac{y^2}{b^2}=1$$

Given that it passes through (0, 4), then

$$b^2=16$$

Also, it passes through $A(3, 2)$, then

$$\frac{9}{a^2}+\frac{4}{16}=1 \Rightarrow a^2=12$$

$$\therefore \quad e=\sqrt{1-\frac{12}{16}}=\sqrt{\frac{1}{4}}=\frac{1}{2}$$

25. The given ellipse is $\frac{x^2}{4^2}+\frac{y^2}{2^2}=1$ such that $a^2=16$ and $b^2=4$

$$\therefore \quad e^2=1-\frac{4}{16}=\frac{3}{4}$$

$$\Rightarrow \quad e=\frac{\sqrt{3}}{2}$$

Let $P\equiv(4\cos\theta, 2\sin\theta)$ be any point on the ellipse, then equation of normal at P is

$$4x\sin\theta-2y\cos\theta=12\sin\theta\cos\theta$$

$$\Rightarrow \quad \frac{x}{3\cos\theta}-\frac{y}{6\sin\theta}=1$$

$\therefore$ Q, the point where normal at P meets X-axis, has coordinates $(3\cos\theta, 0)$.

$\therefore$ Mid-point of PQ is $M\left(\frac{7\cos\theta}{2}, \sin\theta\right)$

For locus of point M, we consider

$$x=\frac{7\cos\theta}{2} \text{ and } y=\sin\theta$$

$$\Rightarrow \cos\theta=\frac{2x}{7} \text{ and } \sin\theta=y \Rightarrow \frac{4x^2}{49}+y^2=1 \quad ...(i)$$

Also, the latusrectum of given ellipse is

$$x = \pm ae = \pm 4 \times \frac{\sqrt{3}}{2} = \pm 2\sqrt{3}$$

or $\quad x = \pm 2\sqrt{3} \quad$ ...(ii)

On solving Eqs. (i) and (ii), we get

$$\frac{4 \times 12}{49} + y^2 = 1$$

$\Rightarrow \quad y^2 = \frac{1}{49}$ or $y = \pm \frac{1}{7}$

$\therefore$ The required points are $\left(\pm 2\sqrt{3}, \pm \frac{1}{7}\right)$.

26. $\because$ Perpendicular tangents meet on director circle of ellipse $\frac{x^2}{7} + \frac{y^2}{11/2} = 1$ is $x^2 + y^2 = 7 + \frac{11}{2}$

i.e. $\quad x^2 + y^2 = \left(\frac{5}{\sqrt{2}}\right)^2$

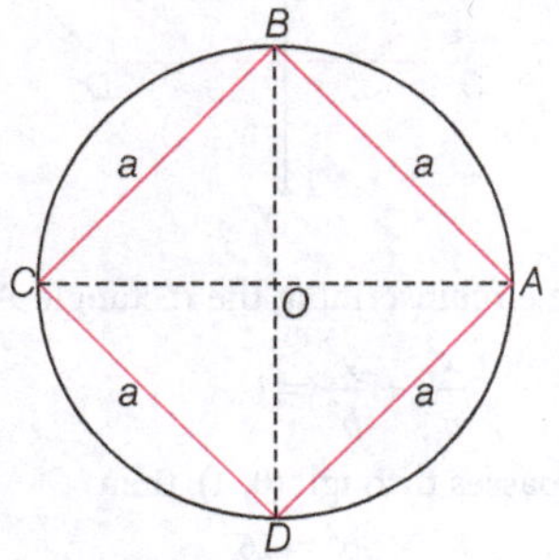

Let length of sides $= a$

$\therefore \quad OA = OB = OC = OD = \frac{a}{\sqrt{2}}$

Given, $\quad \frac{a}{\sqrt{2}} = \frac{5}{\sqrt{2}}$

$\therefore \quad a = 5$

27. We know that for $\theta = \frac{\pi}{2}$ the focal chord will be latusrectum with length $\frac{2b^2}{a}$.

$$\Rightarrow \quad \frac{\lambda ab^2}{a^2 \sin^2\left(\frac{\pi}{2}\right) + b^2 \cos^2\left(\frac{\pi}{2}\right)} = \frac{2b^2}{a}$$

$$\Rightarrow \quad \frac{\lambda ab^2}{a^2 + 0} = \frac{2b^2}{a}$$

$\therefore \quad \lambda = 2$

28. Equation of normal at the point $(13 \cos \theta, 5 \sin \theta)$ is

$$y - 5 \sin \theta = \frac{13}{5} \frac{\sin \theta}{\cos \theta}(x - 13 \cos \theta)$$

or $\quad 5y \cos \theta - 25 \sin \theta \cos \theta = 13x \sin \theta - 169 \sin \theta \cos \theta$

It passes through $(0, 6)$, then

$$30 \cos \theta - 25 \sin \theta \cos \theta = 0 - 169 \sin \theta \cos \theta$$

$\Rightarrow \quad 30 \cos \theta + 144 \sin \theta \cos \theta = 0$

or $\quad 6 \cos \theta (5 + 24 \sin \theta) = 0$

or $\quad \cos \theta = 0$ and $\sin \theta = -\frac{5}{24}$

$\therefore \quad \theta = \frac{\pi}{2}, \ \theta = \pi + \sin^{-1}\left(\frac{5}{24}\right)$ and

$$\theta = 2\pi - \sin^{-1}\left(\frac{5}{24}\right)$$

Hence, three normals can be drawn.

i.e. $\quad n = 3$

$\therefore \quad 2^n = 2^3 = 8$

29. The equation of the tangent at $P(a \cos \theta, b \sin \theta)$ on the given ellipse $\frac{x^2}{a^2} + \frac{y^2}{b^2} = 1$ is $\frac{x}{a} \cos \theta + \frac{y}{b} \sin \theta = 1$

Length of the perpendicular from the focus $(ae, 0)$ on the ellipse is

$$p = \frac{|e \cos \theta - 1|}{\sqrt{\left(\frac{\cos^2 \theta}{a^2} + \frac{\sin^2 \theta}{b^2}\right)}}$$

$$= \frac{|ab(e \cos \theta - 1)|}{\sqrt{(b^2 \cos^2 \theta + a^2(1 - \cos^2 \theta))}}$$

$$= \frac{ab(1 - e \cos \theta)}{\sqrt{a^2 - a^2 e^2 \cos^2 \theta}}$$

$$= b\sqrt{\left(\frac{1 - e \cos \theta}{1 + e \cos \theta}\right)}$$

$$\Rightarrow \quad \frac{b^2}{p^2} = \frac{1 + e \cos \theta}{1 - e \cos \theta}$$

Now, $\quad r^2 = (ae - a \cos \theta)^2 + b^2 \sin^2 \theta$

$$= a^2[(e - \cos \theta)^2 + (1 - e^2) \sin^2 \theta]$$

$$= a^2[e^2 \cos^2 \theta - 2e \cos \theta + 1]$$

$$= a^2(1 - e \cos \theta)^2$$

$\Rightarrow \quad r = a(1 - e \cos \theta)$

Now, $\quad \frac{2a}{r} - \frac{b^2}{p^2} = \frac{2}{1 - e \cos \theta} - \frac{1 + e \cos \theta}{1 - e \cos \theta} = 1$

30. The points are $A(3, 4)$, $B(6, 8)$ and $O(0, 0)$.

$\because \quad OA + OB = 2a \quad$ (where, a is semi major axis)

$\Rightarrow \quad 5 + 10 = 2a$

$\therefore \quad a = \frac{15}{2}$

Now, $\quad AB = 2ae$

$\Rightarrow \quad \sqrt{(6 - 3)^2 + (8 - 4)^2} = 2 \times \frac{15}{2} \times e$

or $\quad 5 = 15e$

$\therefore \quad e = \frac{1}{3}$

$\therefore \quad b^2 = a^2(1 - e^2) = \frac{225}{4}\left(1 - \frac{1}{9}\right) = 50$

Hence, $\quad \left(\frac{b}{\sqrt{2}}\right) = 5$

31. For the ellipse $\frac{x^2}{25}+\frac{y^2}{16}=1$, a normal at $P(5\cos\theta, 4\sin\theta)$ is

$$5x\sin\theta-4y\cos\theta=9\sin\theta\cos\theta$$

Since, the normal passes through $(\lambda, 0)$, then

$$5\lambda\sin\theta-0=9\sin\theta\cos\theta$$

For, $\sin\theta\neq 0$ (i.e. $\theta\neq 0, \pi$), we get

$$5\lambda=9\cos\theta<9 \qquad [\because \cos\theta<1]$$

$$\therefore \quad 5\lambda<9$$

Hence, maximum value of 5λ is 9.

32. Here, $a=3\sqrt{3}$ and $b=3$

Since, axes are at 90° to each other.

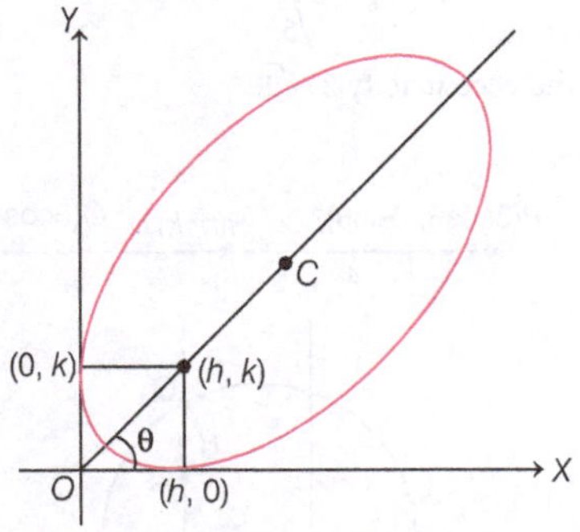

$\therefore$ $O(0, 0)$ being the centre of arc and radius of arc is OC

$\Rightarrow OC=\sqrt{(27+9)}=6$ units

The two extreme positions are horizontal and vertical orientation.

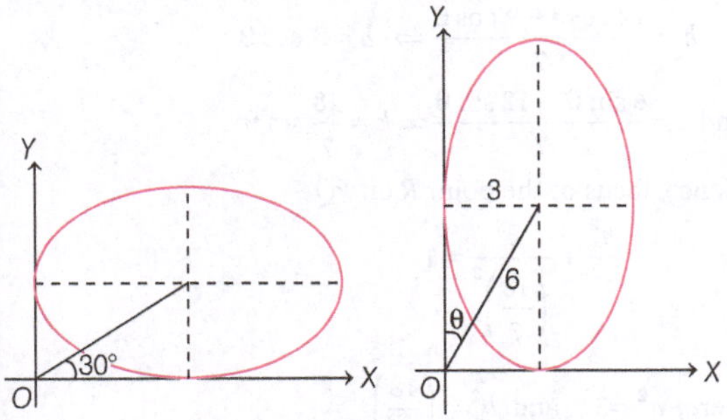

Hence, rotation 30° takes place in totality

$\Rightarrow$ Length of arc $=\frac{2\pi r}{12}=\frac{2\pi}{12}\times 6=\pi=\frac{\pi\lambda}{6}$ [given]

$$\therefore \quad \lambda=6$$

33. Given equation of ellipse is $16x^2+11y^2=256$

$$\Rightarrow \quad \frac{x^2}{16}+\frac{y^2}{(16/\sqrt{11})^2}=1$$

$\therefore$ The equation of the tangent to the given ellipse at

$$\left(4\cos\phi, \frac{16}{\sqrt{11}}\sin\phi\right) \text{ is } \frac{x}{4}\cos\phi+\frac{y\sin\phi}{(16/\sqrt{11})}=1 \qquad \text{...(i)}$$

Which is also a tangent to circle $x^2+y^2-2x-15=0$

$$\Rightarrow \quad (x-1)^2+y^2=16$$

So, length of perpendicular from centre to circle is equal to radius of circle

$$\Rightarrow \quad \left|\frac{\frac{\cos\phi}{4}-1}{\sqrt{\frac{\cos^2\phi}{16}+\frac{\sin^2\phi}{256/11}}}\right|=4$$

$$\Rightarrow \quad \left(\frac{\cos\phi}{4}-1\right)^2=16\left(\frac{\cos^2\phi}{16}+\frac{\sin^2\phi}{256/11}\right)$$

$$\Rightarrow \quad 4\cos^2\phi+8\cos\phi-5=0$$

$$\Rightarrow \quad (2\cos\phi-1)(2\cos\phi+5)=0$$

$$\Rightarrow \quad 2\cos\phi-1=0 \text{ and } 2\cos\phi+5=0 \text{ (not possible)}$$

$$\Rightarrow \quad 2\cos\phi=1$$

$$\Rightarrow \quad \cos\phi=\frac{1}{2}$$

$$\Rightarrow \quad \phi=\frac{\pi}{6}, \frac{5\pi}{6}$$

Hence, the number of values of ϕ is 2.

34. Given, equation of ellipse is

$$\frac{x^2}{(a^2+5a+3)^2}+\frac{y^2}{(a^2+3)^2}=1$$

$$\because \quad \frac{x^2}{A^2}+\frac{y^2}{B^2}=1$$

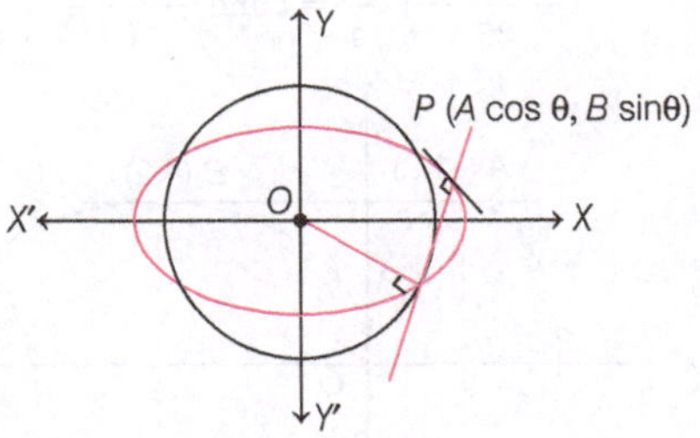

Equation of normal at point P is

$$Ax\sec\theta-By\,\text{cosec}\,\theta=A^2-B^2$$

$\because$ Radius of circle = Perpendicular distance from centre to normal at P

$$=\left|\frac{A^2-B^2}{\sqrt{A^2\sec^2\theta+B^2\text{cosec}^2\theta}}\right|$$

$$=\left|\frac{A^2-B^2}{\sqrt{A^2+B^2+A^2\tan^2\theta+B^2\cot^2\theta}}\right|$$

$$\leq\frac{|A^2-B^2|}{\sqrt{A^2+B^2+2AB}}$$

$$=|A-B|$$

$$\therefore \quad r_{\max}=|A-B|=a^2+5a+3-(a^2+3)$$

$$10=5a \Rightarrow a=2.$$

35. Given, circle $x^2+y^2-8x+6y+1=0$

Centre at $O\equiv(4, -3)$

The circumcircle of ΔPMN will circumscribed the quadrilateral $PMON$.

$\therefore$ Here, diameter is OP.

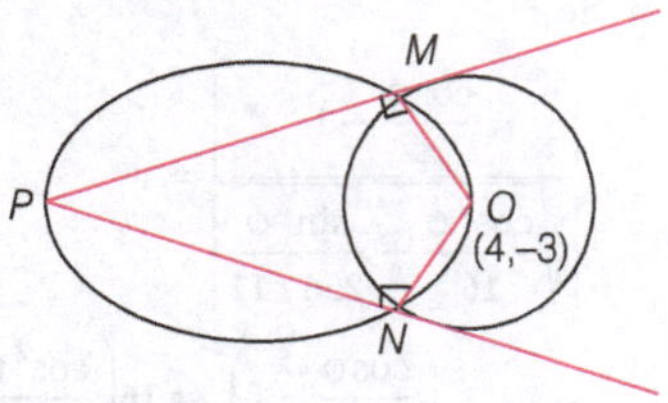

Equation of circumcircle of ΔPMN is

$$(x-2)(x-4)+(y-3)(y+3)=0$$

$$\Rightarrow \quad x^2+y^2-6x-1=0 \qquad \text{...(i)}$$

and director circle is $\quad (x+5)^2+(y-3)^2=9+b^2$

$$\Rightarrow \quad x^2+y^2+10x-6y+25-b^2=0 \qquad \text{...(ii)}$$

On applying condition of orthogonality, we get

$2(g_1g_2+f_1f_2)=c_1+c_2$

$$\Rightarrow \quad 2[-3(5)+0(-3)]=-1+25-b^2$$

$$\Rightarrow \quad -30=24-b^2$$

$$\Rightarrow \quad b^2=54$$

$$\therefore \quad \frac{b^2}{9}=\frac{54}{9}=6.$$

36. Given ellipse are

$$\frac{(x-4)^2}{25}+\frac{y^2}{4}=1 \text{ and } \frac{(x+1)^2}{1}+\frac{y^2}{4}=1$$

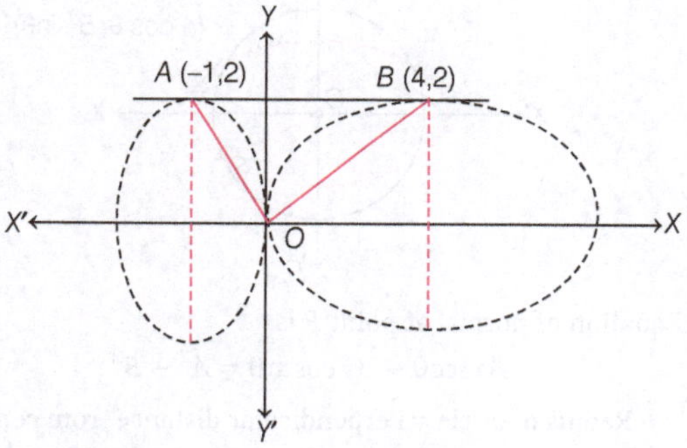

Here, $B(4, 2)$ is one end of the minor axis of the ellipse $\frac{(x-4)^2}{25}+\frac{y^2}{4}=1$ and $A(-1, 2)$ is one end of the major axis of the ellipse $\frac{(x+1)^2}{1}+\frac{y^2}{4}=1$

$$\therefore \quad AB=5, OB=\sqrt{20} \text{ and } OA=\sqrt{5}$$

$$\because \quad OA^2+OB^2=(\sqrt{20})^2+(\sqrt{5})^2=25=AB^2$$

$\therefore$ OAB is right angled triangle.

$\therefore$ Angle subtended by tangent is $\angle AOB=\frac{\pi}{2}$

$$\because \quad \frac{\pi}{k}=\frac{\pi}{2} \qquad \text{[given]}$$

$$\Rightarrow \quad k=2$$

$$\therefore \quad 2k=2(2)=4$$

37. If the minor axis is a and e is eccentricity.

According to the question,

$$ae=2b$$

$$\Rightarrow \quad \frac{4b^2}{a^2}=e^2$$

$$\Rightarrow \quad 4(1-e^2)=e^2 \qquad \left[\because e=\sqrt{1-\frac{b^2}{a^2}}\right]$$

$$\Rightarrow \quad 4=5e^2$$

$$\Rightarrow \quad e^2=\frac{4}{5}$$

$$\Rightarrow \quad e=\frac{2}{\sqrt{5}}$$

Hence, the eccentricity $2/\sqrt{5}$.

38. We have,

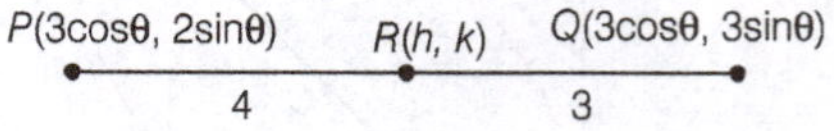

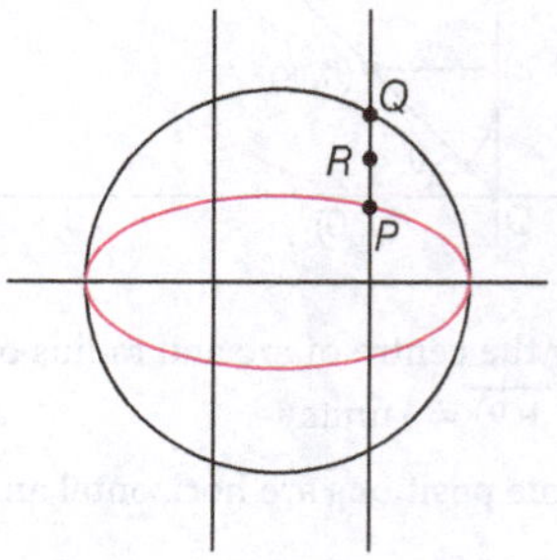

$$\therefore \quad h=\frac{12\cos\theta+9\cos\theta}{7} \Rightarrow h=3\cos\theta$$

$$\text{and } k=\frac{6\sin\theta+12\sin\theta}{7} \Rightarrow k=\frac{18}{7}\sin\theta$$

Hence, locus of the point R on PQ.

$$\frac{h^2}{3^2}+\frac{k^2}{\left(\frac{18}{7}\right)^2}=1$$

Here, $a^2=3^2$ and $b^2=\left(\frac{18}{7}\right)^2$

Now, eccentricity, $e^2=\sqrt{1-\frac{b^2}{a^2}}$

$$=\sqrt{1-\frac{\left(\frac{18}{7}\right)^2}{3^2}}=\sqrt{1-\frac{36}{49}}=\sqrt{\frac{13}{49}}$$

Hence, $e=\frac{\sqrt{13}}{7}$

39. Given equation of line $2x+3y-k=0$ which intersect the X-axis and Y-axis at the points A and B.

When $y=0$, then coordinate of A is $\left(\frac{k}{2}, 0\right)$ and when $x=0$, then coordinate of B is $\left(0, \frac{k}{3}\right)$.

Equation of circle with diameter AB is

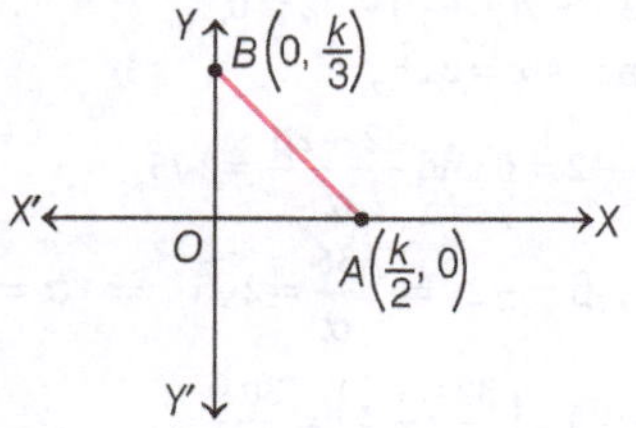

$$(x-0)\left(x-\frac{k}{2}\right)+\left(y-\frac{k}{3}\right)(y-0)=0$$

$$\Rightarrow \quad x^2+y^2-\frac{kx}{2}-\frac{ky}{3}=0$$

On comparing with $x^2+y^2-3x-2y=0$, we get

$$\frac{k}{2}=3 \Rightarrow k=6$$

Now, equation of ellipse,

$$x^2+9y^2=k^2 \Rightarrow \frac{x^2}{36}+\frac{y^2}{4}=1$$

$$\text{Latusrectum}=\frac{2b^2}{a}=\frac{2\times 4}{6}=\frac{4}{3}$$

$$\Rightarrow \quad m=4 \text{ and } n=3$$

$$\therefore \quad 2m+n=8+3=11$$

40. Given, equation of ellipse is $\frac{x^2}{6^2}+\frac{y^2}{3^2}=1$

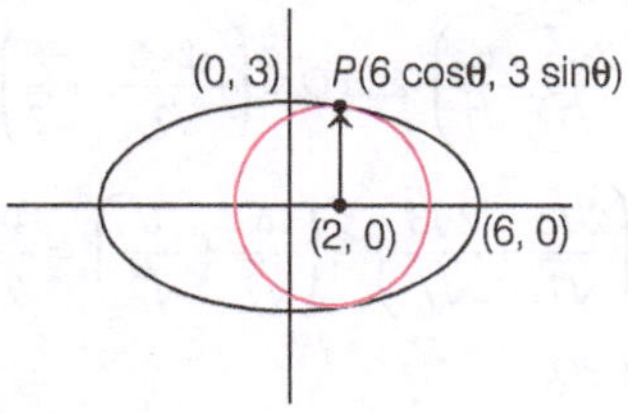

Let P be a point on ellipse.

Then, $P\equiv(6\cos\theta, 3\sin\theta)$

$\therefore$ Equation of circle : $(x-2)^2+y^2=r^2$

For circle of maximum radius to be inscribed in an ellipse, then P should also lie on circle.

$$\Rightarrow \quad (6\cos\theta-2)^2+(3\sin\theta)^2=r^2$$

$$\Rightarrow \quad 36\cos^2\theta+4-24\cos\theta+9\sin^2\theta=r^2$$

$$\Rightarrow \quad 13+27\cos^2\theta-24\cos\theta=r^2$$

$$\Rightarrow \quad 3(9\cos^2\theta-8\cos\theta)+13=r^2$$

$$\Rightarrow \quad 3\left[\left(3\cos\theta-\frac{4}{3}\right)^2-\frac{16}{9}\right]+13=r^2$$

For, r to be minimum

$$\Rightarrow \quad \left(3\cos\theta-\frac{4}{3}\right)^2=0$$

Then, $\quad r^2=13-\frac{16}{3}=\frac{23}{3}$

$$\therefore \quad 12r^2=23\times 4=92$$

41. We have, $E_k: kx^2+k^2y^2=1, k=1,2,\ldots,20$

$$\Rightarrow \quad \frac{x^2}{\frac{1}{k}}+\frac{y^2}{\frac{1}{k^2}}=1$$

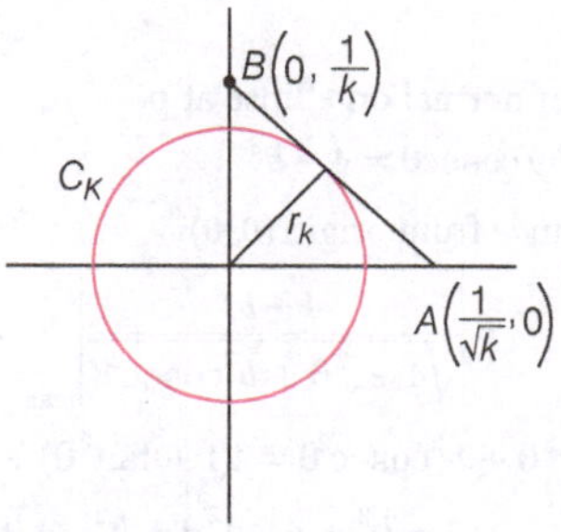

Equation of AB is $\frac{x}{\frac{1}{\sqrt{k}}}+\frac{y}{\frac{1}{k}}=1$

or $\quad \sqrt{k}x+ky=1$

r_k is the radius of circle C_k.

So, $r_k=$ Perpendicular distance from (0, 0) to AB

$$r_k=\frac{|0+0-1|}{\sqrt{(\sqrt{k})^2+k^2}}=\frac{1}{\sqrt{k+k^2}}$$

$$\frac{1}{r_k^2}=k+k^2$$

$$\therefore \quad \sum_{k=1}^{20}\frac{1}{r_k^2}=\sum_{k=1}^{20}k+\sum_{k=1}^{20}k^2$$

$$=\frac{20\times 21}{2}+\frac{20\times 21\times 41}{6}$$

$$=210+2870=3080$$

42. We have, equation of ellipse $15x^2+19y^2=285$

or $\quad \frac{x^2}{19}+\frac{y^2}{15}=1$

Let the coordinate of center of circle be (0, 0).

Equation of circle is $x^2+y^2=16$

Equation of tangent of ellipse is $y=mx\pm\sqrt{19m^2+15}$

or $\quad mx-y\pm\sqrt{19m^2+15}=0$

It is also tangent to the circle $x^2+y^2=16$

Perpendicular distance from center of circle to tangent = 4

$$\frac{\left|0-0\pm\sqrt{19m^2+15}\right|}{\sqrt{m^2+1}}=4$$

On squaring both side, we get

$$19m^2+15=16m^2+16$$

$$3m^2=1 \Rightarrow m^2=\frac{1}{3} \Rightarrow m=\pm\frac{1}{\sqrt{3}}$$

$$\tan\theta=\frac{1}{\sqrt{3}} \Rightarrow \theta=\frac{\pi}{6} \text{ with } X\text{-axis or } \frac{\pi}{3} \text{ with } Y\text{-axis}$$

Hence, the common tangents are inclined to the minor axis of the ellipse at an angle of $\pi/3$.

43. We have, equation of ellipse is $\frac{x^2}{4}+\frac{y^2}{b^2}=1, b<2$

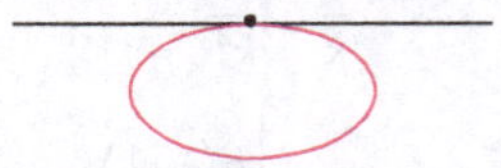

Equation of normal on ellipse at p

$2x\sec\theta - by\,\text{cosec}\,\theta = 4-b^2$

Now, distance from origin $(0, 0)$

$$=\left|\frac{4-b^2}{\sqrt{4\sec^2\theta+b^2\text{cosec}^2\theta}}\right|_{\max}=1$$

Now, $4\sec^2\theta + b^2\text{cosec}^2\theta = 4(1+\tan^2\theta)+b^2(1+\cot^2\theta)$

$$=4+b^2+4\tan^2\theta+b^2\cot^2\theta \ge 4+b^2+4b$$

$$[\because 4\tan^2\theta + b^2\cot^2\theta \ge 4b]$$

$$\ge (2+b)^2$$

$\therefore \quad \left|\frac{4-b^2}{2+b}\right|=1 \Rightarrow |2-b|=1$

$\Rightarrow \quad 2-b=\pm 1 \Rightarrow b=3, 1$

$\Rightarrow \quad b=1 \qquad [\because b<2]$

Now, eccentricity of ellipse $=\sqrt{1-\frac{b^2}{a^2}}=\sqrt{1-\frac{1}{4}}=\frac{\sqrt{3}}{2}$

44. Given, equation on ellipse $\frac{x^2}{36}+\frac{y^2}{4}=1$

Tangent equation is $\frac{x\cdot(3\sqrt{3})}{36}+\frac{y\cdot 1}{4}=1$

$\Rightarrow \quad \frac{x\sqrt{3}}{12}+\frac{y}{4}=1$

$\Rightarrow \quad x\sqrt{3}+3y=12 \qquad \text{...(i)}$

Since, Eq. (i) meet Y-axis at $A\equiv(0, 4)$.

Now, normal equation is

$$\frac{x\cdot 36}{3\sqrt{3}}-\frac{y\cdot 4}{1}=36-4=32$$

$\Rightarrow \quad \frac{12x}{\sqrt{3}}-4y=32 \qquad \text{...(ii)}$

Since, Eq. (ii) meet Y-axis at B,

$\therefore \quad B=(0,-8)$

Now, equation of circle AB is

$$(x-0)(x-0)+(y-4)(y+8)=0$$

$\Rightarrow \quad x^2+y^2+4y-32=0$

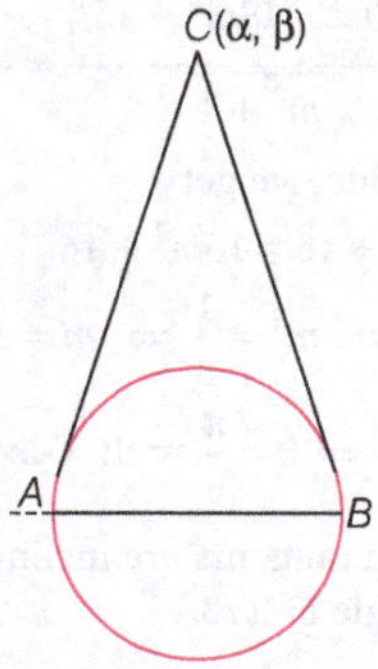

Now, equation of chord of contact from (α, β) with respect to circle $\alpha x+\beta y+2(y+\beta)-32=0$,

which is same as $x=2\sqrt{5}$

Thus, $\quad \beta+2=0$ and $\frac{32-2\beta}{\alpha}=2\sqrt{5}$

$\therefore \quad \beta=-2 \Rightarrow \frac{36}{\alpha}=2\sqrt{5} \Rightarrow \alpha=\frac{18}{\sqrt{5}}$

Thus, $(\alpha^2-\beta^2)=\left(\frac{324}{5}-4\right)=\frac{304}{5}$

45. Given, Ellipse : $9x^2+4y^2=36$,

$$P\equiv\left[\frac{2\sqrt{3}}{\sqrt{7}}, \frac{6}{\sqrt{7}}\right]$$

Since, PQ passes through origin, then

slope of $\quad PQ=\dfrac{\frac{6}{\sqrt{7}}-0}{\frac{2\sqrt{3}}{\sqrt{7}}-0}=\sqrt{3}$

$\therefore$ Equation of PQ is $y=\sqrt{3}x$

On solving with ellipse, $9x^2+4(\sqrt{3}x)^2=36$

$\Rightarrow \quad 21x^2=36$

$\Rightarrow \quad x=\frac{\pm 2\sqrt{3}}{\sqrt{7}}$

$\Rightarrow \quad y=\frac{\pm 6}{\sqrt{7}}$

$\therefore \quad P\equiv\left(\frac{2\sqrt{3}}{\sqrt{7}}, \frac{6}{\sqrt{7}}\right)$ and $Q\equiv\left(\frac{-2\sqrt{3}}{\sqrt{7}}, \frac{-6}{\sqrt{7}}\right)$

$\Rightarrow (PQ)^2=\left(\frac{2\sqrt{3}}{\sqrt{7}}+\frac{2\sqrt{3}}{\sqrt{7}}\right)^2+\left(\frac{6}{\sqrt{7}}+\frac{6}{\sqrt{7}}\right)^2=\frac{48}{7}+\frac{144}{7}=\frac{192}{7}$

Since, $\quad RS\perp PQ$,

$\therefore$Slope of $RS=\frac{-1}{\sqrt{3}}$

So, equation of RS is $y=\frac{-x}{\sqrt{3}}$

On solving with ellipse, $9x^2+4\left(\frac{-x}{\sqrt{3}}\right)^2=36$

we get $\quad R\left(\frac{6\sqrt{3}}{\sqrt{31}}, \frac{-6}{\sqrt{31}}\right)$ and $S\equiv\left(\frac{-6\sqrt{3}}{\sqrt{31}}, \frac{6}{\sqrt{31}}\right)$ (say)

$\Rightarrow \quad (RS)^2=\left(\frac{6\sqrt{3}}{\sqrt{31}}+\frac{6\sqrt{3}}{\sqrt{31}}\right)^2+\left(\frac{-6}{\sqrt{31}}-\frac{6}{\sqrt{31}}\right)^2=\frac{576}{31}$

$\therefore \quad \frac{1}{(PQ)^2}+\frac{1}{(RS)^2}=\frac{13}{144}=\frac{p}{q}$, p and q are coprime.

$\therefore \quad p+q=13+144=157$

46. We know that tangent at parabola $y^2=4ax$ is given by

$$y=mx+\frac{a}{m} \qquad [m=\text{slope}]$$

and tangent at ellipse, $x^2+y^2=a^2$ is given by

$$y=mx\pm\sqrt{a^2m^2+b^2}$$

So, in this case

Tangent at parabola $y^2 = 16x$

$$y = mx + \frac{4}{m}$$

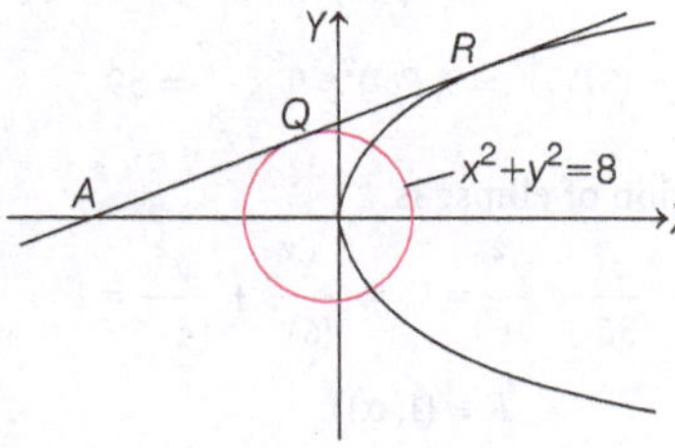

and tangents at curve $x^2 + y^2 = 8$

$$y = mx \pm \sqrt{8m^2 + 8}$$

Both tangents are same, so

$$\frac{4}{m} = \pm \sqrt{8m^2 + 8}$$

$$\Rightarrow \quad \frac{16}{m^2} = 8m^2 + 8 \Rightarrow \frac{2}{m^2} = m^2 + 1$$

$$\Rightarrow \quad (m^2 + 2)(m^2 - 1) = 0$$

On taking, $m = \pm 1$

So, common tangent is

$$y = x + 4$$

$$\Rightarrow \quad x - y + 4 = 0 \quad \text{...(i)}$$

Now, tangent to $x^2 + y^2 = 8$ is

$$xx_1 + yy_1 - 8 = 0 \quad \text{...(ii)}$$

From Eqs. (i) and (ii), we get

$$\frac{x_1}{1} = \frac{y_1}{-1} = \frac{-8}{4} \Rightarrow x_1 = -2 \text{ and } y_1 = 2$$

Tangent at point $Q(-2, 2)$, on $y^2 = 16x$ is

$$\Rightarrow \quad yy_1 = 16\left(\frac{x + x_1}{2}\right)$$

$$yy_1 = 8x + 8x_1$$

$$8x - yy_1 + 8x_1 = 0 \quad \text{...(iii)}$$

From Eqs. (i) and (iii), we get

$$\frac{8}{1} = \frac{-y_1}{-1} = \frac{8x_1}{4} \Rightarrow y_1 = 8 \text{ and } x_1 = 4$$

So, $R(4, 8)$

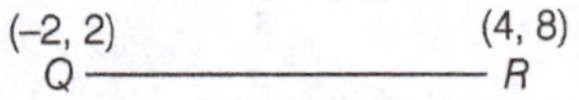

Now, $\quad (QR)^2 = (-2-4)^2 + (2-8)^2 = 36 + 36 = 72$

47.

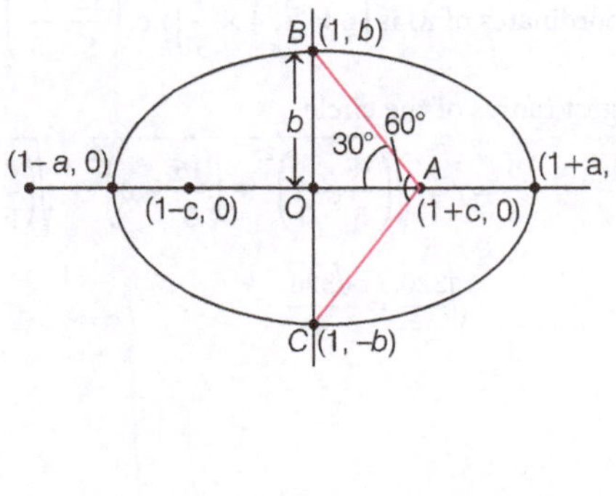

$$LR = \frac{1}{2} \Rightarrow \frac{2b^2}{a} = \frac{1}{2} \Rightarrow b^2 = \frac{a}{4}$$

$$\Rightarrow \quad b = \frac{\sqrt{a}}{2}$$

In ΔAOB, $\tan 30° = \dfrac{b}{OA}$

$$\Rightarrow \quad \frac{1}{\sqrt{3}} = \frac{\sqrt{a}}{2 \times OA} \Rightarrow OA = \frac{\sqrt{3a}}{2}$$

$$A(1 + OA, 0) \equiv A(1 + c, 0)$$

$$1 + OA = 1 + c \quad \Rightarrow OA = c$$

$$c = OA \Rightarrow c^2 = OA^2 \Rightarrow a^2 - b^2 = \frac{3a}{4}$$

$$a^2 - \frac{a}{4} = \frac{3a}{4} \Rightarrow 4a^2 - a = 3a$$

$$4a^2 - 4a = 0 \Rightarrow 4a(a-1) = 0$$

$$a = 1, a = 0 \Rightarrow a = 1$$

$$\Rightarrow \quad b = \frac{\sqrt{a}}{2} = \frac{1}{2}$$

Sum of square of minor axis and major axis is

$$(2a)^2 + (2b)^2 = (2 \times 1)^2 + \left(2 \times \frac{1}{2}\right)^2$$

$$= 4 + 1 = 5$$

48. We have,

$$H_n : \frac{x^2}{1+x} - \frac{y^2}{3+x} = 1, n \in N$$

Here, $a^2 = 1 + x$ and $b^2 = 3 + x$

Eccentiricity $(e) = \sqrt{1 + \dfrac{b^2}{a^2}}$

$$= \sqrt{1 + \left(\frac{3+x}{1+x}\right)} = \sqrt{\frac{2x+4}{x+1}} = \sqrt{\frac{2(x+2)}{x+1}}$$

The smallest even value for which $c \in \theta$ is 48.

$\therefore \quad K = 48$

$$e = \sqrt{\frac{2(48+2)}{48+1}} = \frac{10}{7}$$

$$\Rightarrow \quad a^2 = n + 1 = 49, b^2 = n + 3 = 51$$

$$\therefore \quad 21l = 21 \times \left(\frac{2b^2}{a}\right) = 21 \times 2 \times \frac{51}{7} = 306$$

49. Equation of hyperbola is $2x^2 - 2y^2 = 1$

$$\Rightarrow \quad \frac{x^2}{1/2} - \frac{y^2}{1/2} = 1$$

Here, $\quad a = b$

$\therefore$ Eccentricity of rectangular hyperbola is $\sqrt{2}$.

$\therefore$ Eccentricity of ellipse is $1/\sqrt{2}$.

Since, ellipse intersects the hyperbola at right angles.

$\therefore$ Ellipse and the hyperbola are co-focal

$\therefore$ Foci of hyperbola $\equiv (1, 0)$

$\Rightarrow$ Foci of ellipse, $ae = 1$

$$\Rightarrow \quad a\left(\frac{1}{\sqrt{2}}\right) = 1 \Rightarrow a = \sqrt{2}$$

$\Rightarrow \qquad e^2 = 1 - \dfrac{b^2}{a^2} \Rightarrow \dfrac{1}{2} = 1 - \dfrac{b^2}{2}$

$\Rightarrow \qquad \dfrac{b^2}{2} = \dfrac{1}{2}$

$\Rightarrow \qquad b^2 = 1$

$\therefore$ Length of the latusrectum $= \dfrac{2b^2}{a}$

$= \dfrac{2}{\sqrt{2}} = \sqrt{2}$

$\therefore$ Square of length of the latusrectum is 2.

50. Given, ellipse $E : \dfrac{x^2}{a^2} + \dfrac{y^2}{b^2} = 1$

Since, focus of ellipse is (2, 0) and directrix is $x = 8$, then

$ae = 2$ and $\dfrac{a}{e} = 8$

$\therefore \qquad (ae)\left(\dfrac{a}{e}\right) = 2 \times 8$

$\Rightarrow \qquad a^2 = 16 \Rightarrow a = 4$

$\therefore \qquad e = \dfrac{2}{a} = \dfrac{2}{4} = \dfrac{1}{2}$

Again, $\qquad e = \sqrt{1 - \dfrac{b^2}{a^2}}$

$\Rightarrow \qquad \dfrac{1}{2} = \sqrt{1 - \dfrac{b^2}{16}} \qquad \left[\because e = \dfrac{1}{2} \text{ (given)}\right]$

$\Rightarrow \qquad \dfrac{1}{4} = \dfrac{16 - b^2}{16}$

$\Rightarrow \qquad b^2 = 12$

$\therefore$ Equation of ellipse is $\dfrac{x^2}{16} + \dfrac{y^2}{12} = 1$

Let $P \equiv (4\cos\theta, 2\sqrt{3}\sin\theta)$. So, equation of tangent at P is

$$\frac{4\cos\theta\, x}{16} + \frac{2\sqrt{3}\sin\theta\, y}{12} = 1$$

or $\qquad \dfrac{x\cos\theta}{4} + \dfrac{y\sin\theta}{2\sqrt{3}} = 1 \qquad \text{...(i)}$

Since, tangent passes through $(0, 4\sqrt{3})$, then

$$0 + \frac{4\sqrt{3}\sin\theta}{2\sqrt{3}} = 1$$

$\Rightarrow \qquad \sin\theta = \dfrac{1}{2} \Rightarrow \theta = 30°$

$\therefore$ Equation of tangent is $\dfrac{x}{4} \times \dfrac{\sqrt{3}}{2} + \dfrac{y}{2\sqrt{3}} \times \dfrac{1}{2} = 1$

$\Rightarrow \qquad \dfrac{\sqrt{3}x}{8} + \dfrac{y}{4\sqrt{3}} = 1$

Again, point P is

$(4\cos 30°, 2\sqrt{3}\sin 30°)$ i.e. $(2\sqrt{3}, \sqrt{3})$

Also, tangent intersects X-axis at $\left(\dfrac{8}{\sqrt{3}}, 0\right)$.

So, Q is $\left(\dfrac{8}{\sqrt{3}}, 0\right)$.

$\therefore \qquad (PQ)^2 = \left(\dfrac{8}{\sqrt{3}} - 2\sqrt{3}\right)^2 + (0 - \sqrt{3})^2$

$= \left(\dfrac{8-6}{\sqrt{3}}\right)^2 + 3 = \dfrac{4}{3} + 3 = \dfrac{13}{3}$

$\therefore \qquad (3PQ)^2 = 9(PQ)^2 = 9 \times \dfrac{13}{3} = 39$

51. Given equation of ellipse is

$$\frac{x^2}{36} + \frac{y^2}{16} = 1 \Rightarrow \frac{x^2}{(6)^2} + \frac{y^2}{(4)^2} = 1$$

Let $\qquad R \equiv (1, \alpha)$

$P \equiv (2, 0)$

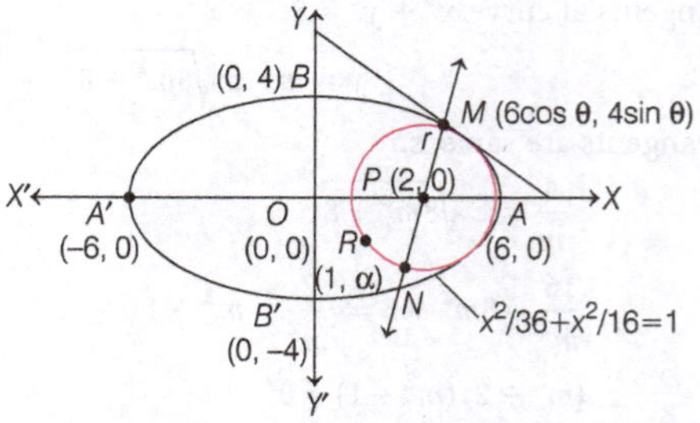

Also, given C is the largest circle having centre (2, 0) inscribed in the given ellipse.

Now, coordinates of any point M taken on the ellipse is $(6\cos\theta, 4\sin\theta)$.

So, equation of normal MN to the ellipse at $M(6\cos\theta, 4\sin\theta)$ is given by

$$\frac{36x}{6\cos\theta} - \frac{16y}{4\sin\theta} = 36 - 16$$

$\Rightarrow \qquad \dfrac{6x}{\cos\theta} - \dfrac{4y}{\sin\theta} = 20$

$\Rightarrow \qquad \dfrac{3x}{\cos\theta} - \dfrac{2y}{\sin\theta} = 10 \qquad \text{...(i)}$

Since, Eq. (i) is also normal to the given circle C and passing through the point $P(2, 0)$.

So, $\qquad \dfrac{3 \times 2}{\cos\theta} - \dfrac{2 \times 0}{\sin\theta} = 10$

$\Rightarrow \qquad 6 = 10\cos\theta$

$\Rightarrow \qquad \cos\theta = \dfrac{3}{5}$

$\therefore \qquad \sin\theta = \dfrac{4}{5}$

[using $\sin^2\theta = 1 - \cos^2\theta$]

So, coordinates of M is $\left(6 \times \dfrac{3}{5}, 4 \times \dfrac{4}{5}\right)$ i.e. $\left(\dfrac{18}{5}, \dfrac{16}{5}\right)$.

$\therefore$ Largest radius of the circle

$$= r = \sqrt{\left(\frac{18}{5} - 2\right)^2 + \left(\frac{16}{5} - 0\right)^2} = \sqrt{\left(\frac{8}{5}\right)^2 + \left(\frac{16}{5}\right)^2}$$

$\Rightarrow \qquad r = \sqrt{\dfrac{320}{25}} = \dfrac{\sqrt{320}}{5}$

Hence, equation of the required circle having centre at $P(2, 0)$ and radius r is

$$(x-2)^2 + (y-0)^2 = \left(\frac{\sqrt{320}}{5}\right)^2$$

$$\Rightarrow \quad (x-2)^2 + y^2 = \frac{320}{25} = \frac{64}{5} \quad \text{...(ii)}$$

Since, Eq. (ii) passes through $R(1, \alpha)$ as question said.

So, $$(1-2)^2 + \alpha^2 = \frac{64}{5}$$

$$\Rightarrow \quad \alpha^2 = \frac{64}{5} - 1 = \frac{64-5}{5} = \frac{59}{5}$$

$$\therefore \quad 10\alpha^2 = 10 \times \frac{59}{5} = 2 \times 59 = 118$$

52. Given, equation of curve is $9x^2 + 16y^2 = 144$.

$\Rightarrow \frac{x^2}{16} + \frac{y^2}{9} = 1$, which is equation of an ellipse.

Now, any point taken on this ellipse is of the form $(4\cos\theta, 3\sin\theta)$.

So, equation of tangent at this point is given by

$$\frac{x(4\cos\theta)}{16} + \frac{y(3\sin\theta)}{9} = 1$$

$$\Rightarrow \quad \frac{x\cos\theta}{4} + \frac{y\sin\theta}{3} = 1 \quad \text{...(i)}$$

According to the question, Eq. (i) intersect the coordinate axes at A and B.

So, $A \equiv (4\sec\theta, 0)$

and $B \equiv (0, 3\,\text{cosec}\,\theta)$

Now, length of line segment

$$AB = \sqrt{(4\sec\theta - 0)^2 + (0 - 3\,\text{cosec}\,\theta)^2}$$

$$\Rightarrow \quad AB = \sqrt{16\sec^2\theta + 9\,\text{cosec}^2\theta}$$

$$= \sqrt{16(1+\tan^2\theta) + 9(1+\cot^2\theta)}$$

$$\Rightarrow \quad AB = \sqrt{25 + 16\tan^2\theta + 9\cot^2\theta}$$

Now, $16\tan^2\theta$ and $9\cot^2\theta$ are two positive real numbers using AM $\geq$ GM, then

$$\Rightarrow \quad \frac{16\tan^2\theta + 9\cot^2\theta}{2} \geq \sqrt{16\tan^2\theta \times 9\cot^2\theta}$$

$$\Rightarrow \quad 16\tan^2\theta + 9\cot^2\theta \geq 2\sqrt{16\tan^2\theta \times 9 \times \frac{1}{\tan^2\theta}}$$

$$\Rightarrow \quad 16\tan^2\theta + 9\cot^2\theta \geq 24$$

$$\Rightarrow \quad 25 + 16\tan^2\theta + 9\cot^2\theta \geq 24 + 25$$

$$\Rightarrow \quad 25 + 16\tan^2\theta + 9\cot^2\theta \geq 49$$

$$\Rightarrow \quad \sqrt{25 + 16\tan^2\theta + 9\cot^2\theta} \geq \sqrt{49}$$

$$\Rightarrow \quad AB \geq 7$$

$\therefore$ Minimum length of line segment AB is 7.

53. Curves : $\frac{x^2}{16} + \frac{y^2}{9} = 1$ and $x^2 + y^2 = 12$

Let the slope of common tangent be m.

Equation of tangent to $x^2 + y^2 = 12$

$$y = mx \pm \sqrt{12 + 12m^2}$$

Equation of tangent to ellipse $\frac{x^2}{16} + \frac{y^2}{9} = 1$

$$y = mx \pm \sqrt{16m^2 + 9}$$

Both equations are identical, then

$$mx \pm \sqrt{12 + 12m^2} = mx \pm \sqrt{16m^2 + 9}$$

$$\Rightarrow \quad 12 + 12m^2 = 16m^2 + 9$$

$$3 = 4m^2 \Rightarrow m^2 = \frac{3}{4}$$

$$\therefore \quad 12m^2 = 12 \times \frac{3}{4} = 9$$

54. L is line passing through the intersection of the lines $bx + 10y - 8 = 0$ and $2x - 3y = 0$.

$$L: (bx + 10y - 8) + \lambda(2x - 3y) = 0$$

also passes through (1, 1), then

$$(b + 10 - 8) + \lambda(2 - 3) = 0 \Rightarrow \lambda = b + 2$$

So, equation of line $L: (bx + 10y - 8) + (b+2)(2x - 3y) = 0$

$$L: (3b + 4)x - (3b - 4)y - 8 = 0$$

This line L is tangent to circle $x^2 + y^2 = \frac{16}{17}$

So, distance from centre to tangent = Radius

$$\left|\frac{-8}{\sqrt{(3b+4)^2 + (3b-4)^2}}\right| = \frac{4}{\sqrt{17}}$$

$$\Rightarrow \quad 9b^2 + 16 + 24b + 9b^2 + 16 - 24b = 68$$

$$\Rightarrow \quad 18b^2 = 36 \Rightarrow b^2 = 2$$

Equation of ellipse, $\frac{x^2}{5} + \frac{y^2}{2} = 1$

$$\therefore \quad e = \sqrt{1 - \frac{b^2}{a^2}} = \sqrt{1 - \frac{2}{5}} = \sqrt{\frac{3}{5}}$$

55. $\frac{x^2}{a^2} + \frac{y^2}{b^2} = 1$ $[a > b]$

$$e^2 = 1 - \frac{b^2}{a^2} \Rightarrow \frac{b^2}{a^2} = 1 - \frac{1}{16} = \frac{15}{16}$$

$$\Rightarrow \quad b^2 = \frac{15}{16}a^2$$

$\frac{x^2}{a^2} + \frac{y^2}{b^2} = 1$ is passing through $\left(-4\sqrt{\frac{2}{5}}, 3\right)$, then

$$\frac{16 \times \frac{2}{5}}{a^2} + \frac{9}{b^2} = 1$$

$$\Rightarrow \quad \frac{32}{5a^2} + \frac{9}{b^2} = 1 \Rightarrow \frac{32}{5a^2} + \frac{9}{\frac{15}{16}a^2} = 1$$

$$\Rightarrow \quad \frac{80}{5a^2} = 1$$

$$\Rightarrow \quad a^2 = 16 \text{ and } b^2 = 15$$

$$\therefore \quad a^2 + b^2 = 16 + 15 = 31$$

56.

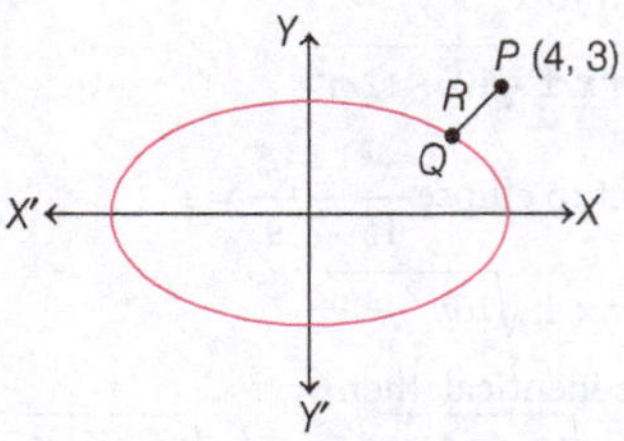

Equation of ellipse is $x^2 + 2y^2 = 4$.

$\Rightarrow \quad \frac{x^2}{4} + \frac{y^2}{2} = 1$

Let the point be $Q \equiv (2\cos\theta, \sqrt{2}\sin\theta)$.

Let the mid-point of PQ be $R \equiv (h, k)$.

$\Rightarrow 2h = 4 + 2\cos\theta$ and $2k = 3 + \sqrt{2}\sin\theta$

$\Rightarrow \quad (h-2)^2 + \left(\frac{2k-3}{\sqrt{2}}\right)^2 = 1$

$\Rightarrow \quad \frac{(x-2)^2}{1} + \frac{4\left(y-\frac{3}{2}\right)^2}{2} = 1$

$\therefore$ Locus is $\frac{(x-2)^2}{1} + \frac{\left(y-\frac{3}{2}\right)^2}{\frac{1}{2}} = 1$

$\Rightarrow \quad e^2 = 1 - \frac{1}{2} = \frac{1}{2} \Rightarrow e = \frac{1}{\sqrt{2}}$

57. Given, equation of ellipse is $2x^2 + 3y^2 = 5$

$\Rightarrow \quad \frac{x^2}{5/2} + \frac{y^2}{5/3} = 1$

Equation of tangent to the ellipse is

$$y = mx \pm \sqrt{a^2m^2 + b^2}$$

Here, $\quad a^2 = \frac{5}{2}$ and $b^2 = \frac{5}{3}$

$$y = mx \pm \sqrt{\frac{5}{2}m^2 + \frac{5}{3}}$$

The ellipse passes through (1, 3), so

$$3 = m \pm \sqrt{\frac{5}{2}m^2 + \frac{5}{3}}$$

$\Rightarrow \quad 3 - m = \pm\sqrt{\frac{5}{2}m^2 + \frac{5}{3}}$

On squaring both sides, we get

$$9 + m^2 - 6m = \frac{5}{2}m^2 + \frac{5}{3}$$

$\Rightarrow \quad 54 + 6m^2 - 36m = 15m^2 + 10$

$\Rightarrow \quad 9m^2 + 36m - 44 = 0$

Let the pair of lines be $y = m_1x + c_1$

and $\quad y = m_2x + c_2$

Here, $\quad m_1 + m_2 = -\frac{36}{9} = -4$ and $m_1m_2 = -\frac{44}{9}$

$$|m_1 - m_2| = \sqrt{(m_1 + m_2)^2 - 4m_1m_2}$$

$$= \sqrt{16 - 4 \times \left(-\frac{44}{9}\right)} = \sqrt{\frac{144 + 176}{9}} = \sqrt{\frac{320}{9}} = \frac{8\sqrt{5}}{3}$$

$\because \tan\theta = \left|\frac{m_1 - m_2}{1 + m_1m_2}\right|$,

where θ is the angle between the tangents

$$= \left|\frac{\frac{8\sqrt{5}}{3}}{1 + \left(-\frac{44}{9}\right)}\right| = \left|\frac{8\sqrt{5} \times 3}{-35}\right| = \frac{24}{7\sqrt{5}}$$

$\therefore \quad \theta = \tan^{-1}\left(\frac{24}{7\sqrt{5}}\right)$

58. Given that PQ is a focal chord of the parabola $y^2 = 4x$ which subtends an angle of $\pi/2$ at the point (3, 0).

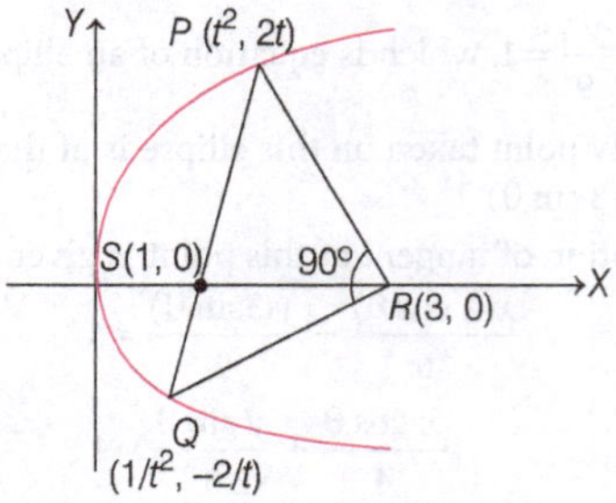

$$m_{PR} \cdot m_{RQ} = -1$$

$\Rightarrow \quad \frac{(0-2t)}{(3-t^2)} \times \frac{\left(0 - \left(-\frac{2}{t}\right)\right)}{\left(3 - \frac{1}{t^2}\right)} = -1$

$\Rightarrow \quad \frac{4t^2}{9t^2 - 3 - 3t^4 + t^2} = 1$

$\Rightarrow \quad 4t^2 = 10t^2 - 3 - 3t^4$

$\Rightarrow \quad 3t^4 - 6t^2 + 3 = 0$

$\Rightarrow \quad (t^2)^2 - 2(t)^2(1) + (1)^2 = 0$

$\Rightarrow \quad (t^2 - 1)^2 = 0 \Rightarrow t = 1$

$\Rightarrow P$ and Q must be end points of latusrectum.

$P(1, 2)$ and $Q(1, -2)$

$\therefore \quad \frac{2b^2}{a} = 4$ and $ae = 1$

$\because \quad b^2 = a^2(1 - e^2) \Rightarrow 2a = a^2 - 1$

$\Rightarrow \quad a^2 - 2a - 1 = 0 \Rightarrow a = 1 + \sqrt{2}$

Now, $\quad e^2 = 1 - \frac{b^2}{a^2}$

$\Rightarrow \quad e^2 = 1 - \frac{2a}{a^2} = 1 - \frac{2}{a} = \frac{a-2}{a} = \frac{\sqrt{2}-1}{\sqrt{2}+1}$

$\Rightarrow \quad \frac{1}{e^2} = \frac{\sqrt{2}+1}{\sqrt{2}-1} \times \frac{\sqrt{2}+1}{\sqrt{2}+1} = 3 + 2\sqrt{2}$

$\Rightarrow \quad \frac{1}{e^2} = 3 + 2\sqrt{2}$

59. Given, equation of ellipse $\frac{x^2}{a^2}+\frac{y^2}{4}=1$

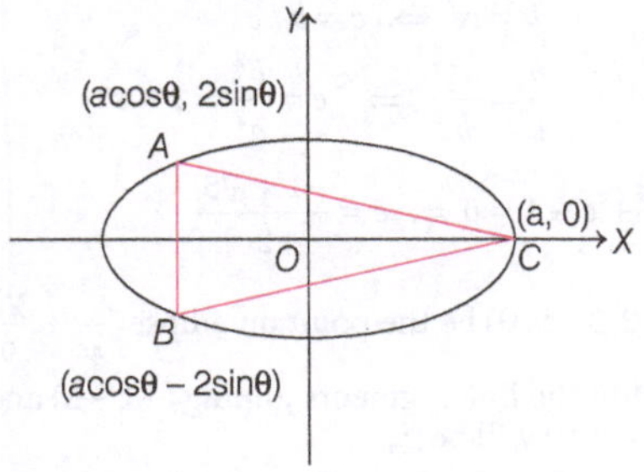

Let Δ be the area of ΔABC.

Then, $\Delta=\frac{1}{2}(4\sin\theta)(a-a\cos\theta)$

$\Rightarrow \Delta=2a(\sin\theta-\sin\theta\cos\theta)$

$\Rightarrow \Delta=a(2\sin\theta-2\sin\theta\cos\theta)$

$\Rightarrow \Delta=a(2\sin\theta-\sin2\theta)$

Now, on differentiating w.r.t. θ, we get

$$\Delta'=a(2\cos\theta-2\cos2\theta)$$

For maximum value of Δ, we get $\Delta'=0$

$\Rightarrow a(2\cos\theta-2\cos2\theta)=0$ $[\because a\neq0]$

$\Rightarrow \cos2\theta-\cos\theta=0$

$\Rightarrow 2\cos^2\theta-\cos\theta-1=0$

$\Rightarrow (2\cos\theta+1)(\cos\theta-1)=0$

$\therefore \cos\theta=-\frac{1}{2}$ and $\cos\theta=1$

$$\theta=\frac{2\pi}{3} \text{ and } \theta=0^\circ$$

$$\Delta''=a(-2\sin\theta+4\sin2\theta)<0, \text{ at } \theta=\frac{2\pi}{3}.$$

Then, Δ has maximum value occur at $\theta=\frac{2\pi}{3}$

Hence, $\Delta_{max}=\frac{a}{2}\left(4\cdot\frac{\sqrt{3}}{2}\right)\left(1+\frac{1}{2}\right)=\frac{3\sqrt{3}a}{2}$

According to question, $6\sqrt{3}=\frac{3\sqrt{3}a}{2} \Rightarrow a=4$

Now, $e=\sqrt{1-\frac{4}{16}}=\frac{\sqrt{3}}{2}$ $\left[\because e=\sqrt{1-\frac{b^2}{a^2}}\right]$

60. Given, equation of ellipse $\frac{x^2}{2}+\frac{y^2}{4}=1$

Here, $a^2=2$ and $b^2=4$

$$e=\sqrt{1-\frac{a^2}{b^2}}=\sqrt{1-\frac{1}{2}}=\sqrt{\frac{1}{2}}=\frac{1}{\sqrt{2}}$$

$\therefore$ Coordinates of S are $(0,-\sqrt{2})$.

Equation of chord of contact from the point $(\sqrt{2}, 2\sqrt{2}-2)$ is

$$\frac{x\sqrt{2}}{2}+\frac{y(2\sqrt{2}-2)}{4}=1$$

$\Rightarrow \frac{x}{\sqrt{2}}=1-\frac{y(\sqrt{2}-1)}{2}$

$\Rightarrow x=\frac{2-y(\sqrt{2}-1)}{\sqrt{2}}$

On substituting value of x in equation of ellipse, we get

$$\frac{\left(\frac{2-y(\sqrt{2}-1)}{\sqrt{2}}\right)^2}{2}+\frac{y^2}{4}=1$$

$\Rightarrow 4+y^2(\sqrt{2}-1)^2-4y(\sqrt{2}-1)+y^2=4$

$\Rightarrow y^2[2+1-2\sqrt{2}+1]-4y(\sqrt{2}-1)=0$

$\Rightarrow y^2(4-2\sqrt{2})-4y(\sqrt{2}-1)=0$

$\Rightarrow 2\sqrt{2}y^2(\sqrt{2}-1)-4y(\sqrt{2}-1)=0$

$\Rightarrow y=0, \sqrt{2}$

If $y=0$, then $x=\sqrt{2}$

If $y=\sqrt{2}$, then $x=\frac{2-\sqrt{2}(\sqrt{2}-1)}{\sqrt{2}}=1$

Let P be $(\sqrt{2}, 0)$ and Q be $(1, \sqrt{2})$.

$\therefore (SP)^2+(SQ)^2$

$=(\sqrt{2}-0)^2+(0+\sqrt{2})^2+(1-0)^2+(\sqrt{2}+\sqrt{2})^2$

$=2+2+1+8=13$

61. Ellipse is $(x+1)^2+4(y+1)^2=\lambda+5$

$\Rightarrow \frac{(x+1)^2}{\lambda+5}+\frac{(y+1)^2}{\left(\frac{\lambda+5}{4}\right)}=1$

$\therefore$ Now, length of latusrectum,

$$4=\frac{\frac{2(\lambda+5)}{4}}{\sqrt{\lambda+5}}$$

$\Rightarrow 8=\sqrt{\lambda+5} \Rightarrow \lambda=59$

$\therefore$ Length of major axis, $l=2\sqrt{\lambda+5}=2\times8=16$

$\therefore \lambda+l=59+16=75$

62. Let $y=mx+c$ be the common tangent.

So, $c=\frac{1}{m}=\pm\frac{3}{2}\sqrt{1+m^2}$

$\Rightarrow m^2=\frac{1}{3} \Rightarrow m=\pm\frac{1}{\sqrt{3}}$

So, equation of common tangents will be

$y=\pm\frac{1}{\sqrt{3}}x\pm\sqrt{3}$, which intersect at $Q(-3, 0)$.

Here, for ellipse, $a=3$, $b=6$

Then, $e=\sqrt{1-\frac{a^2}{b^2}}=\sqrt{1-\frac{9}{36}}$

$$e=\frac{\sqrt{3}}{2}$$

$\therefore l=\frac{2a^2}{b}=\frac{2\times9}{6}=3$

Hence,, $\frac{l}{e^2}=\frac{3}{3}\times4=4$

63. The given ellipse is $25x^2 + 4y^2 = 1$.

Since, (α, β) lies on the given ellipse.

$$\therefore \quad 25\alpha^2 + 4\beta^2 = 1 \quad \text{... (i)}$$

Tangent to the parabola $y^2 = 4x$ is $y = mx + \frac{1}{m}$ passing through (α, β).

So, $\alpha m^2 - \beta m + 1 = 0$ has roots m_1 and $4m_1$.

$$\therefore \quad m_1 + 4m_1 = \frac{\beta}{\alpha} \text{ and } m_1 \cdot 4m_1 = \frac{1}{\alpha}$$

$$\Rightarrow \quad 4\beta^2 = 25\alpha \quad \text{... (ii)}$$

From Eqs. (i) and (ii), we get

$$25(\alpha^2 + \alpha) = 1 \quad \text{... (iii)}$$

Now, $(10\alpha + 5)^2 + (16\beta^2 + 50)^2$

$$= 25(2\alpha + 1)^2 + 2500(2\alpha + 1)^2$$

$$= 2525(4\alpha^2 + 4\alpha + 1)$$

$$= 2525\left(\frac{4}{25} + 1\right) \quad \left[\because \alpha^2 + \alpha = \frac{1}{25}\right]$$

$$= 101(29) = 2929$$

64. Given ellipse $\frac{x^2}{9} + \frac{y^2}{1} = 1$ ...(i)

and circle $x^2 + y^2 = 3$ ... (iii)

The point of intersection by solving Eqs. (i) and (ii) in first quadrant is $(3/2, \sqrt{3}/2)$.

On differentiating Eqs. (i) and (ii) w.r.t. x, we get

Let $m_1 = \frac{dy}{dx} = \frac{-x}{9y}$ and $m_2 = \frac{dy}{dx} = \frac{-x}{y}$

At $\left(\frac{3}{2}, \frac{\sqrt{3}}{2}\right)$, $m_1 = -\frac{1}{3\sqrt{3}}$, $m_2 = -\sqrt{3}$

If angle between both curves is θ, then

$$\tan\theta = \left|\frac{m_1 - m_2}{1 + m_1 m_2}\right|$$

$$= \left|\frac{\frac{-1}{3\sqrt{3}} + \sqrt{3}}{1 + \left(\frac{-1}{3\sqrt{3}}\right)(-\sqrt{3})}\right| = \frac{2}{\sqrt{3}}$$

65. $12x\cos\theta + 5y\sin\theta = 60$

$$\Rightarrow \quad \frac{x\cos\theta}{5} + \frac{y\sin\theta}{12} = 1$$

The given equation is the equation of the tangent which passes through $(5\cos\theta, 12\sin\theta)$.

Hence, the given equation is tangent to $\frac{x^2}{25} + \frac{y^2}{144} = 1$ at $(5\cos\theta, 12\sin\theta)$.

66. $e^2 = 1 - \frac{b^2}{a^2}$ and $e'^2 = 1 - \frac{a^2}{c^2}$

$$e' = e \quad \text{[given]}$$

$$\Rightarrow \quad \frac{b^2}{a^2} = \frac{a^2}{c^2} \Rightarrow c = \frac{a^2}{b}$$

Also, $b = ce \Rightarrow c = b/e$

$$\Rightarrow \quad \frac{b}{e} = \frac{a^2}{b} \Rightarrow e = \frac{b^2}{a^2} = 1 - e^2$$

$$\Rightarrow \quad e^2 + e - 1 = 0 \Rightarrow e = \frac{-1 + \sqrt{5}}{2}$$

67. Let $(2\sin\theta, 3\cos\theta)$ be the point on ellipse $\frac{x^2}{4} + \frac{y^2}{9} = 1$ and let mid-point of the line segments joining $(-3, -5)$ and $(2\sin\theta, 3\cos\theta)$ will be (h, k).

Then, $\frac{2\sin\theta - 3}{2} = h, \frac{3\cos\theta - 5}{2} = k$

$$\Rightarrow \quad \sin\theta = \frac{2h + 3}{2}, \cos\theta = \frac{2k + 5}{3}$$

$$\because \quad \sin^2\theta + \cos^2\theta = 1$$

$$\therefore \quad \left(\frac{2h + 3}{2}\right)^2 + \left(\frac{2k + 5}{3}\right)^2 = 1$$

$$\Rightarrow \quad \frac{(4h^2 + 9 + 12h)}{4} + \frac{(4k^2 + 25 + 20k)}{9} = 1$$

$$\Rightarrow \quad 36h^2 + 16k^2 + 108h + 80k + 145 = 0$$

Locus of (h, k) is $36x^2 + 16y^2 + 108x + 80y + 145 = 0$

68. $x^2 + 9y^2 - 4x + 3 = 0$

$$\Rightarrow \quad x^2 - 4x + 2^2 + 9y^2 = 1 \Rightarrow (x - 2)^2 + 9y^2 = 1$$

$$\Rightarrow \quad \frac{(x - 2)^2}{1^2} + \frac{y^2}{\left(\frac{1}{3}\right)^2} = 1$$

This represents an ellipse.

$$-1 \le x - 2 \le 1 \text{ and } -\frac{1}{3} \le y \le \frac{1}{3}$$

$$\Rightarrow \quad 1 \le x \le 3 \text{ and } -\frac{1}{3} \le y \le \frac{1}{3}$$

$$\Rightarrow \quad x \in [1, 3] \text{ and } y \in \left[-\frac{1}{3}, \frac{1}{3}\right]$$

69. Equation of ellipse, $x^2 + 4y^2 = 4$

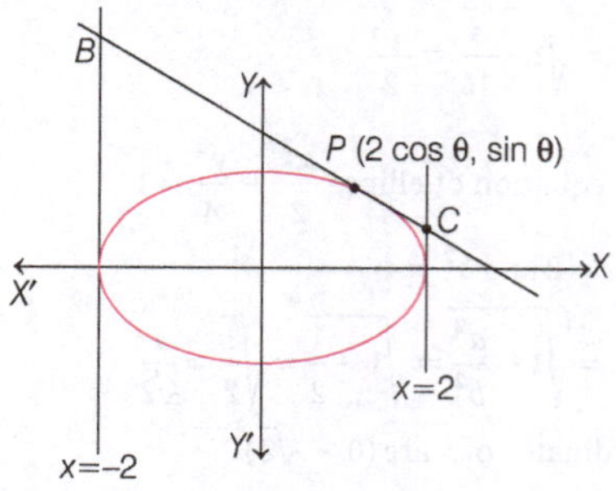

$$\Rightarrow \quad \frac{x^2}{4} + \frac{y^2}{1} = 1$$

Extremities end of major axis $= (\pm 2, 0)$

Let $P(2\cos\theta, \sin\theta)$ be any point of ellipse.

Equation of tangent to the ellipse at the point P is

$$\frac{2\cos\theta x}{4}+\frac{y\sin\theta}{1}=1$$

Coordinates of B are $\left(-2, \cot\frac{\theta}{2}\right)$ and C are $\left(2, \tan\frac{\theta}{2}\right)$.

Equation of circle whose end points of diameter are B and C is

$$(x-2)(x+2)+\left(y-\cot\frac{\theta}{2}\right)\left(y-\tan\frac{\theta}{2}\right)=0$$

$$x^2+y^2-\left(\tan\frac{\theta}{2}+\cot\frac{\theta}{2}\right)y-3=0$$

At $\quad y=0, x=\pm\sqrt{3}$

Hence, circle is passing through the points $(\pm\sqrt{3}, 0)$.

70. $E:\frac{x^2}{a^2}+\frac{y^2}{b^2}=1$ passes through $\left(\sqrt{\frac{3}{2}}, 1\right)$.

$$\therefore \quad \frac{3}{2a^2}+\frac{1}{b^2}=1 \quad \text{...(i)}$$

$$a^2-b^2=a^2e^2$$

$$\Rightarrow \quad a^2-b^2=\frac{a^2}{3}$$

$$\Rightarrow \quad 2a^2=3b^2$$

On putting $2a^2=3b^2$ in Eq. (i), we get

$$\frac{3}{3b^2}+\frac{1}{b^2}=1$$

$$\Rightarrow \quad 2=b^2 \Rightarrow a^2=3$$

Focus $\left(\sqrt{3}\cdot\frac{1}{\sqrt{3}}, 0\right) \Rightarrow$ Focus $=(1, 0)$

Centre $=(1, 0)$, Radius $=\frac{2}{\sqrt{3}}$

$$(x-1)^2+(y-0)^2=\left(\frac{2}{\sqrt{3}}\right)^2 \quad \text{...(ii)}$$

$$E:\frac{x^2}{3}+\frac{y^2}{2}=1 \quad \text{...(iii)}$$

From Eqs. (ii) and (iii), we get

$$x=1, y=\pm\frac{2}{\sqrt{3}}$$

$$\therefore \quad PQ=\frac{4}{\sqrt{3}} \Rightarrow PQ^2=\frac{16}{3}$$

71. Given, equation of ellipse is $\frac{x^2}{27}+y^2=1$

Now, equation of tangent to the ellipse at $P(3\sqrt{3}\cos\theta, \sin\theta)$ is given by

$$\frac{3\sqrt{3}\cos\theta\cdot x}{27}+\sin\theta\cdot y=1$$

$$\Rightarrow \quad \frac{x\cos\theta}{3\sqrt{3}}+y\sin\theta=1 \quad \text{... (i)}$$

x-intercept of Eq. (i) is $x=3\sqrt{3}\sec\theta=OA$ (say)

y-intercept of Eq. (i) is $y=\operatorname{cosec}\theta=OB$ (say)

$\therefore$ Sum of intercepts $=3\sqrt{3}\sec\theta+\operatorname{cosec}\theta=f(\theta)$ (say)

$$\Rightarrow \quad f'(\theta)=3\sqrt{3}\sec\theta\tan\theta-\operatorname{cosec}\theta\cdot\cot\theta$$

Put $f'(\theta)=0$

$$\Rightarrow \quad \frac{3\sqrt{3}\sin\theta}{\cos^2\theta}=\frac{\cos\theta}{\sin^2\theta}$$

$$\Rightarrow \quad \tan^3\theta=\frac{1}{3\sqrt{3}} \Rightarrow \theta=\pi/6$$

$-\infty \leftarrow$ − | + $\rightarrow +\infty$ (at $\theta=\pi/6$)

$\because$ $f'(\theta)$ changes sign from negative to positive when moving from left to right.

$\therefore$ $f(\theta)$ will attain minima at $\theta=\pi/6$.

72. **Decoding the Question**

(i) First find the slope of line L of (6, 2), then write the equation of tangent.

(ii) Then, use the condition of tangency to the ellipse as $c^2=a^2m^2+b^2$ if $E:\frac{x^2}{a^2}+\frac{y^2}{b^2}=1$ $L: y=mx+c$

Given, equation of parabola is

$$y^2=4x-20 \quad \text{... (i)}$$

On differentiating Eq. (i) w.r.t. x, we get

$$2y\frac{dy}{dx}=4 \Rightarrow \frac{dy}{dx}=\frac{2}{y}$$

$$\therefore \quad \left(\frac{dy}{dx}\right)_{(6,2)}=\text{Slope of tangent at } (6, 2)=\frac{2}{2}=1$$

$\therefore$ Equation of tangent is $y-2=1(x-6)$

$$\Rightarrow \quad x-y-4=0 \quad \text{... (ii)}$$

As we know the condition of tangency to the ellipse, a straight line $y=mx+c$ will be tangent to the ellipse $x^2/a^2+y^2/b^2=1$.

$$c^2=a^2m^2+b^2$$

$$\therefore \quad 16=2(1)^2+b \quad [\text{here } c=-4, m=1, b=\sqrt{b}]$$

$$\Rightarrow \quad b=14$$

73. Given equation of ellipse

$$\frac{x^2}{16}+\frac{y^2}{b^2}=1 \quad \text{... (i)}$$

and equation of circle

$$x^2+y^2=4b \quad \text{... (ii)}$$

From Eqs. (i) and (ii), we get

$$\frac{4b-y^2}{16}+\frac{y^2}{b^2}=1$$

$$\Rightarrow \quad 4b^3-y^2b^2+16y^2=16b^2 \Rightarrow y^2=\frac{16b^2-4b^3}{16-b^2}$$

As (x, y) lies on $y^2=3x^2$.

So, $\quad y^2=3(4b-y^2)$ [from Eq. (ii)]

$$\Rightarrow \quad 4y^2=12b \Rightarrow y^2=3b$$

Now, $\quad \frac{16b^2-4b^3}{16-b^2}=3b$

$$\Rightarrow \quad 16b^2-4b^3=48b-3b^3$$

$\Rightarrow \quad b^3 - 16b^2 + 48b = 0$

$\Rightarrow \quad b(b^2 - 16b + 48) = 0$

$\Rightarrow \quad b(b-4)(b-12) = 0$

As $\quad b > 4$

So, $\quad b = 12$

74. Given equation of ellipse is $\frac{x^2}{8} + \frac{y^2}{4} = 1.$

Then, equation of tangent at (x_1, y_1) will be $\frac{xx_1}{8} + \frac{yy_1}{4} = 1.$

Since, tangent is perpendicular to the line $x + 2y = 0$, then

$$\left(\frac{-x_1}{2y_1}\right)\left(\frac{-1}{2}\right) = -1$$

$\Rightarrow \quad x_1 = -4y_1$

Also, $\quad \frac{x_1^2}{8} + \frac{y_1^2}{4} = 1$

$\Rightarrow \quad \frac{16y_1^2}{8} + \frac{y_1^2}{4} = 1 \quad [\because x_1 = -4y_1]$

$\Rightarrow \quad y_1^2 = \frac{4}{9}$

$\Rightarrow \quad y_1 = \pm\frac{2}{3} \Rightarrow y_1 = \frac{2}{3}$

$[\because (x_1, y_1)$ lies in II quadrant$]$

and $\quad x_1 = -4y_1 = -4 \times \frac{2}{3} = \frac{-8}{3}$

$\therefore \quad P\left(\frac{-8}{3}, \frac{2}{3}\right)$

Again, $\quad a^2 - b^2 = a^2e^2$

$8 - 4 = 8e^2 \Rightarrow e = 1/\sqrt{2}$

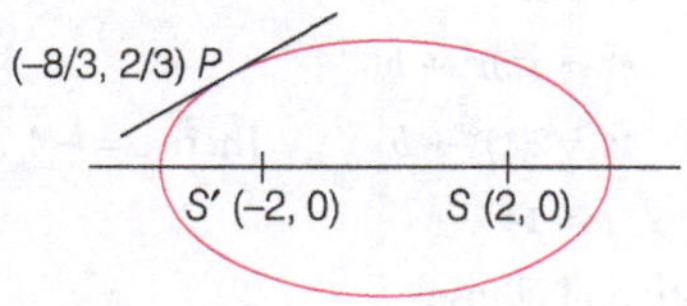

Now, S and S' are the foci of the ellipse.

So, $\quad S:(ae, 0) = \left(2\sqrt{2}\cdot\frac{1}{\sqrt{2}}, 0\right) = (2, 0)$

and $S':(-ae, 0) = \left(-2\sqrt{2}.\frac{1}{\sqrt{2}}, 0\right) = (-2, 0)$

Area of $\quad \Delta SPS' = \frac{1}{2} \times 4 \times \frac{2}{3} = \frac{4}{3} \quad \left[\because \text{base} = 4, \text{height} = \frac{2}{3}\right]$

So, $\quad (5 - e^2)A = \left(5 - \frac{1}{2}\right)\frac{4}{3} = \frac{9}{2}\cdot\frac{4}{3} = 6$

75. Equation of the reflected ray will be $L: \frac{y-3}{x-5} = m$

Now, the image of (2, 1) w.r.t. line $x = 0$ should lie on the reflected line.

Image of $(2,1) = (-2, 1)$

So, $\quad \frac{1-3}{-2-5} = m \Rightarrow m = \frac{2}{7}$

So, equation of reflected ray

$\Rightarrow \quad \frac{y-3}{x-5} = \frac{2}{7}$

$7y - 21 = 2x - 10$

$\Rightarrow \quad 2x - 7y + 11 = 0 \quad$ [equation of directrix]

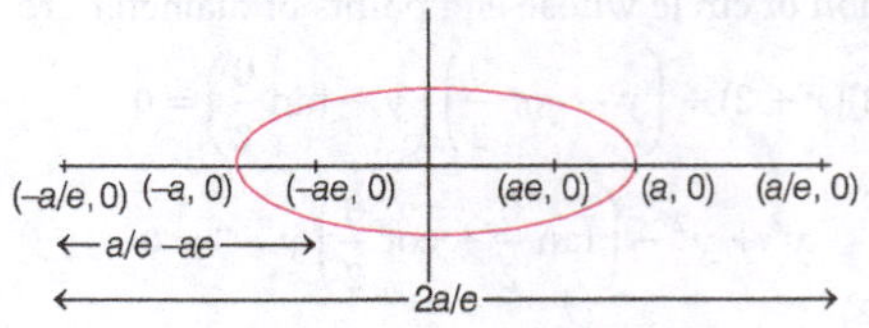

Now, $\quad e = \frac{1}{3} \quad$ [given]

So, $\quad \frac{a}{e} - ae = \frac{a}{1/3} - \frac{1}{3}a = \frac{8a}{3}$

$\Rightarrow \quad \frac{8a}{3} = \frac{8}{\sqrt{53}} \quad$ [given]

So, $\quad a = \frac{3}{\sqrt{53}}$

and $\quad \frac{2a}{e} = \left(2\cdot\frac{3}{\sqrt{53}}\right) \times \left(\frac{3}{1}\right) = \frac{18}{\sqrt{53}}$

Now, another directrix will be parallel to the first directrix and lie at a distance of $\frac{18}{\sqrt{53}}$ units.

So, let the equation of another directrix be $2x - 7y + \lambda = 0$

Accordingly, $\frac{|\lambda - 11|}{\sqrt{2^2 + 7^2}} = \frac{18}{\sqrt{53}}$

$|\lambda - 11| = 18 \Rightarrow \lambda = 11 \pm 18 \Rightarrow \lambda = 29$ or -7

Hence, equation of another directrix will be $2x - 7y + 29 = 0$ or $2x - 7y - 7 = 0$

76. Equation of an ellipse : $\frac{x^2}{b^2} + \frac{y^2}{4a^2} = 1$

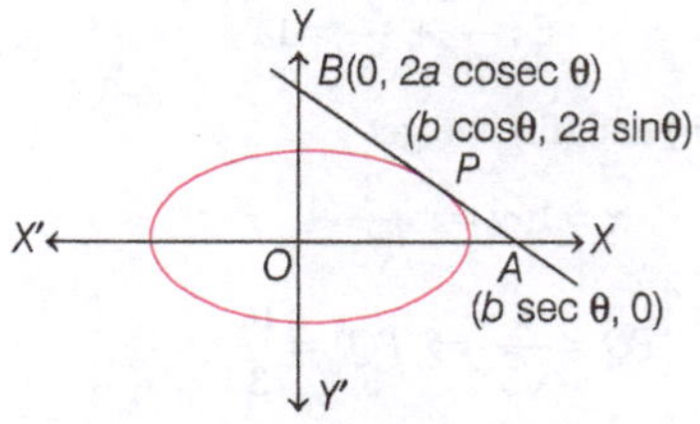

Equation of tangent at $P \equiv (b\cos\theta, 2a\sin\theta)$ is

$$\frac{x\cos\theta}{b} + \frac{y\sin\theta}{2a} = 1$$

Point of intersection of tangent and coordinate axes are $A(b\sec\theta, 0)$ and $B(0, 2a\operatorname{cosec}\theta)$.

Area of $\Delta OAB = \frac{1}{2}(b\sec\theta)(2a\operatorname{cosec}\theta)$

$$= \frac{ab}{\sin\theta\cos\theta} = \frac{2ab}{\sin 2\theta}$$

$\text{Area}_{\min} = 2ab$, when $\sin 2\theta = 1$

$\therefore \quad k = 2$

77. Let E be an ellipse whose centre is $C \equiv (3, -4)$, focus is $F \equiv (4, -4)$ and one vertex is $A \equiv (5, -4)$.

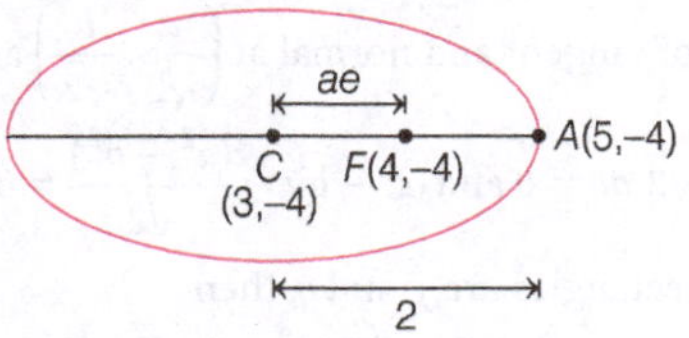

Hence, $a = 2$ and $ae = 1 \Rightarrow e = 1/2$

Now, $b^2 = a^2 - (ae)^2 = 4 - 1 \Rightarrow b^2 = 3$

So, equation of ellipse $E : \dfrac{(x-3)^2}{4} + \dfrac{(y+4)^2}{3} = 1$

intersecting with given tangent $mx - y = 4$

$$\Rightarrow \quad y + 4 = mx$$

$$\frac{x^2 - 6x + 9}{4} + \frac{m^2x^2}{3} = 1$$

$$\Rightarrow \quad (3 + 4m^2)x^2 - 18x + 15 = 0$$

Now, $D = 0$

$$\Rightarrow \quad 324 - 4(3 + 4m^2)(15) = 0$$

$$\Rightarrow \quad 144 - 240m^2 = 0$$

$$\therefore \quad 5m^2 = 3$$

78. Given curves are $A : 4x^2 + 9y^2 = 36$

and $\qquad B : (2x)^2 + (2y)^2 = 31$

L is common tangent line to curve A and B.

Let slope of L be m.

Given, curve A is equation of ellipse.

$$\frac{x^2}{9} + \frac{y^2}{4} = 1$$

Then, equation of tangent to ellipse will be

$$y = mx \pm \sqrt{9m^2 + 4} \qquad \text{...(i)}$$

Curve B is circle i.e $x^2 + y^2 = \dfrac{31}{4}$

Then, equation of tangent to circle will be

$$y = mx \pm \sqrt{\left(\frac{31}{4}\right)m^2 + \left(\frac{31}{4}\right)} \qquad \text{...(ii)}$$

On comparing Eqs. (i) and (ii), we get

$$9m^2 + 4 = \left(\frac{31}{4}\right)m^2 + \left(\frac{31}{4}\right)$$

$$\Rightarrow \quad 36m^2 + 16 = 31m^2 + 31$$

$$\Rightarrow \quad 5m^2 = 15 \quad \Rightarrow \quad m^2 = 3$$

$\therefore$ Square of slope of line L is 3.

79. As, we know that locus of the foot of perpendicular drawn upon any tangent to the ellipse $\dfrac{x^2}{4} + \dfrac{y^2}{2} = 1$ from any of its foci is the auxiliary circle and its equation is

$$x^2 + y^2 = 4 \qquad \text{...(i)}$$

So, from the option the auxiliary circle (i) passes through the point $(-1, \sqrt{3})$.

80. Equation of given curve is $4x^2 + 5y^2 = 20$.

$$\Rightarrow \quad \frac{x^2}{5} + \frac{y^2}{4} = 1 \qquad \text{...(i)}$$

Let a point be $P \equiv (\sqrt{5}\cos\theta, 2\sin\theta)$ on the curve (i).

$$(PQ)^2 = (\sqrt{5}\cos\theta - 0)^2 + (2\sin\theta + 4)^2 \qquad [\because Q = (0, -4)]$$

$$\therefore \quad (PQ)^2 = 5\cos^2\theta + 16 + 4\sin^2\theta + 16\sin\theta$$

$$= 21 - \sin^2\theta + 16\sin\theta$$

$$= 21 - (8 - \sin\theta)^2 + 64 = 85 - (8 - \sin\theta)^2$$

As, the point P is farthest from the point Q,

so $\qquad \sin\theta = 1$

And so $\qquad (PQ)^2 = 85 - 49 = 36$

81. Equation of given conic is $9x^2 + 16y^2 = 144$.

$\Rightarrow \dfrac{x^2}{16} + \dfrac{y^2}{9} = 1$ is an ellipse, so its eccentricity,

$$e = \sqrt{1 - \frac{9}{16}} = \pm\frac{\sqrt{7}}{4}$$

$\therefore$ Coordinates of foci $(\pm ae, 0)$ are $F_1 \equiv (\sqrt{7}, 0)$ is A and $F_2 \equiv (-\sqrt{7}, 0)$ is B.

$$\Rightarrow \quad a = 4$$

As, point P lies on the ellipse itself.

So, $PA + PB = 2a = 2 \times 4 = 8$ according to definition of ellipse.

82. According to given information, let the equation of ellipse be

$$\frac{x^2}{a^2} + \frac{3y^2}{4} = 1 \qquad \text{...(i)}$$

$\because$ Ellipse (i) touches the line $x + 6y = 8$, then

$$\left(\frac{8}{6}\right)^2 = a^2\left(\frac{1}{6}\right)^2 + \frac{4}{3}$$

$$\Rightarrow \quad \frac{16}{9} = \frac{a^2}{36} + \frac{4}{3}$$

$$\Rightarrow \quad \frac{a^2}{36} = \frac{4}{9} \Rightarrow a^2 = 16$$

Now, eccentricity $e = \sqrt{1 - \dfrac{b^2}{a^2}} = \sqrt{1 - \dfrac{4}{3 \times 16}} = \dfrac{1}{2}\sqrt{\dfrac{11}{3}}$

83. Since, equation of normal to the ellipse at P meets the coordinate axes at $\left(-\dfrac{1}{3\sqrt{2}}, 0\right)$ and $(0, \beta)$ is

$$\frac{x}{-\frac{1}{3\sqrt{2}}} + \frac{y}{\beta} = 1 \qquad \text{...(i)}$$

Now, let point $P(x_1, y_1)$, so equation of normal to ellipse $\dfrac{x^2}{1/2} + \dfrac{y^2}{1} = 1$ at point P is

$$\Rightarrow \quad \frac{x}{2x_1} - \frac{y}{y_1} = \frac{1}{2} - 1$$

$$\Rightarrow \quad -\frac{x}{2x_1} + \frac{y}{y_1} = \frac{1}{2} \qquad \text{...(ii)}$$

$\because$ Eqs. (i) and (ii) represents same line.

$$\therefore \quad \frac{2x_1}{-\frac{1}{3\sqrt{2}}} = \frac{y_1}{\beta} = \frac{2}{1}$$

$$\Rightarrow \quad x_1 = \frac{1}{3\sqrt{2}} \text{ and } y_1 = 2\beta$$

$\because$ Point $P(x_1, y_1)$ lies on ellipse, so

$$2\left(\frac{1}{9 \times 2}\right) + 4\beta^2 = 1$$

$$\Rightarrow \quad \beta^2 = \frac{2}{9}$$

$$\Rightarrow \quad \beta = \pm\frac{\sqrt{2}}{3}$$

$\because$ Point $P(x_1, y_1)$ is in first quadrant, so $y_1 = 2\beta > 0$

$$\therefore \quad \beta = \frac{\sqrt{2}}{3}$$

Exercise 2 - JEE Advanced Pattern

1. $ax^2 + by^2 + 2fx + 2gy + c = 0$

$$a\left\{x^2 + \frac{2fx}{a}\right\} + b\left\{y^2 + \frac{2gy}{b}\right\} + c = 0$$

$$\Rightarrow \quad a\left(x + \frac{f}{a}\right)^2 + b\left(y + \frac{g}{b}\right)^2 = \left(\frac{f^2}{a} + \frac{g^2}{b} - c\right)$$

$$\Rightarrow \quad \frac{(x + f/a)^2}{\left(\frac{f^2}{a} + \frac{g^2}{b} - c\right)/a} + \frac{(y + g/b)^2}{\left(\frac{f^2}{a} + \frac{g^2}{b} - c\right)/b} = 1$$

If e is eccentricity, then

$$\frac{\left(\frac{f^2}{a} + \frac{g^2}{b} - c\right)}{b} = \frac{\left(\frac{f^2}{a} + \frac{g^2}{b} - c\right)}{a}(1 - e^2)$$

$$\Rightarrow \quad 1 - e^2 = \frac{a}{b}$$

$$\Rightarrow \quad e^2 = \frac{b - a}{b}$$

$$\therefore \quad e = \sqrt{\left(\frac{b - a}{b}\right)}$$

2. Let ellipse be $\frac{x^2}{a^2} + \frac{y^2}{b^2} = 1$ and the circle be $x^2 + y^2 = a^2e^2$, point of intersection of the circle and the ellipse is $P\left(\frac{a}{e}\sqrt{(2e^2 - 1)}, \frac{a}{e}(1 - e^2)\right)$.

Now, area of $\Delta PF_1F_2 = \left|\frac{1}{2} \times 2ae \times \frac{a}{e}(1 - e^2)\right|$

$$= a^2(1 - e^2) = 30 \quad \text{[given]}$$

$$\text{or} \quad a^2e^2 = a^2 - 30 = \left(\frac{17}{2}\right)^2 - 30 = \frac{169}{4} \quad [\because 2a = 17]$$

$$\therefore \quad ae = \frac{13}{2} \text{ or } 2ae = 13$$

3. Let standard ellipse be $\frac{x^2}{a^2} + \frac{y^2}{b^2} = 1$ $(a > b)$

Equations of tangent and normal at $\left(\frac{a}{\sqrt{2}}, \frac{b}{\sqrt{2}}\right)$ are

$$bx + ay - \sqrt{2}\,ab = 0 \text{ and } ax - by - \frac{(a^2 - b^2)}{\sqrt{2}} = 0.$$

If sides of rectangles are p and q, then

$$p = \frac{|0 + 0 - \sqrt{2}\,ab|}{\sqrt{(a^2 + b^2)}} = \frac{\sqrt{2}\,ab}{\sqrt{(a^2 + b^2)}}$$

and
$$q = \left|\frac{0 - 0 - \frac{(a^2 - b^2)}{\sqrt{2}}}{\sqrt{(a^2 + b^2)}}\right| = \frac{(a^2 - b^2)}{\sqrt{2}\sqrt{(a^2 + b^2)}}$$

$$\therefore \quad \text{Area of rectangle} = pq = \frac{(a^2 - b^2)\,ab}{(a^2 + b^2)}$$

4. Let equation of ellipse be $\frac{x^2}{a^2} + \frac{y^2}{b^2} = 1$

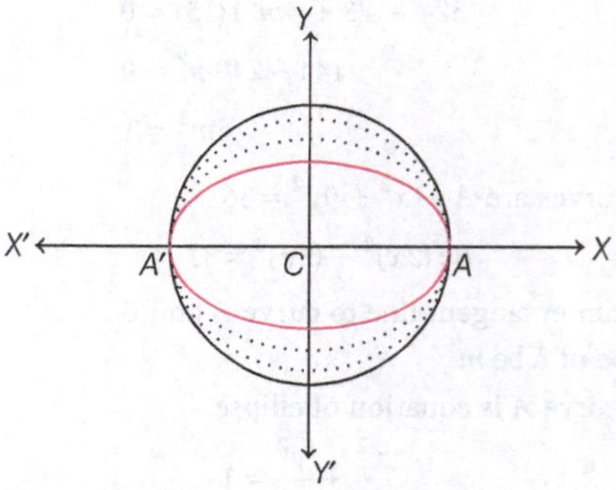

and equation of circle be $x^2 + y^2 = a^2$

$\therefore$ Area of ellipse $= \pi ab$ and area of circle $= \pi a^2$

$$\therefore \quad \text{Probability} = \frac{\pi a^2 - \pi ab}{\pi a^2} = \frac{a - b}{a} = \frac{2}{3} \quad \text{[given]}$$

$$\Rightarrow \quad 3a - 3b = 2a \text{ or } a = 3b$$

$$\text{or} \quad a^2 = 9b^2 = 9a^2(1 - e^2) \Rightarrow 9e^2 = 8$$

$$\therefore \quad e = \frac{2\sqrt{2}}{3}$$

5. Let $S \equiv (x_1, y_1)$ and $S' \equiv (x_2, y_2)$

Let $C \equiv (h, k)$

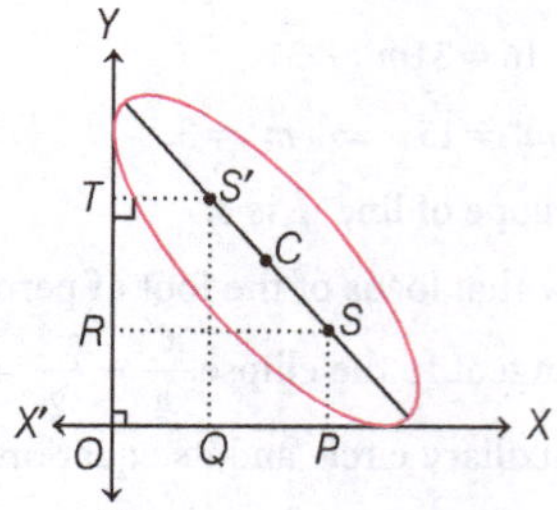

$$\therefore \quad \frac{x_1 + x_2}{2} = h$$

$$\Rightarrow \quad x_1 + x_2 = 2h \text{ and } y_1 + y_2 = 2k$$

$\because \quad SP\,S'Q = b^2$

$\Rightarrow \quad y_1 y_2 = b^2$ and $SR \cdot S'T = b^2$

$\Rightarrow \quad x_1 x_2 = b^2$

Distance between foci $SS' = 2ae$

$\Rightarrow \quad \sqrt{(x_1 - x_2)^2 + (y_1 - y_2)^2} = (2ae)$

$\Rightarrow \quad (x_1 - x_2)^2 + (y_1 - y_2)^2 = 4a^2e^2$

$\Rightarrow \quad (x_1 + x_2)^2 - 4x_1x_2 + (y_1 + y_2)^2 - 4\,y_1y_2 = 4a^2e^2$

$\Rightarrow \quad 4h^2 - 4b^2 + 4k^2 - 4b^2 = 4(a^2 - b^2)$

$\Rightarrow \quad h^2 + k^2 - 2b^2 = a^2 - b^2$

$\therefore \quad h^2 + k^2 = a^2 + b^2$

Locus of centre is $x^2 + y^2 = a^2 + b^2$, which is a circle.

6. **Decoding the Question**

Equation of chord of ellipse $\dfrac{x^2}{a^2} + \dfrac{y^2}{b^2} = 1$ whose mid-point (x_1, y_1) is $\dfrac{xx_1}{a^2} + \dfrac{yy_1}{b^2} = \dfrac{x_1^2}{a^2} + \dfrac{y_1^2}{b^2}$

$$\therefore \quad \frac{x}{50} + \frac{y}{24} = \frac{1}{100} + \frac{1}{36} \quad \text{...(i)}$$

Let $A \equiv (x_1, y_1)$ and $B \equiv (x_2, y_2)$

$$\therefore \quad \frac{x_1}{50} + \frac{y_1}{24} = \frac{1}{100} + \frac{1}{36} \quad \text{...(ii)}$$

$$\text{and} \quad \frac{x_2}{50} + \frac{y_2}{24} = \frac{1}{100} + \frac{1}{36} \quad \text{...(iii)}$$

$$\therefore \quad \frac{(x_2 - x_1)}{50} + \frac{(y_2 - y_1)}{24} = 0$$

$$\therefore \quad AB = \sqrt{(x_2 - x_1)^2 + (y_2 - y_1)^2}$$

$$= \sqrt{(x_2 - x_1)^2 + \left(\frac{24}{50}\right)^2 (x_2 - x_1)^2} = \frac{|x_2 - x_1|}{25}\sqrt{769}$$

Now, on solving $\dfrac{x}{50} + \dfrac{y}{24} = \dfrac{1}{100} + \dfrac{1}{36}$ and $\dfrac{x^2}{25} + \dfrac{y^2}{16} = 1$,

then $\quad x^2 - x - \dfrac{5336}{9} = 0$

$$\therefore \quad |x_2 - x_1| = \frac{\sqrt{D}}{a} = \frac{\sqrt{21353}}{3}$$

$$\therefore \quad AB = \frac{\sqrt{21353}}{3 \times 25} \times \sqrt{769}$$

7. Equation of tangent at the point $P(4\cos\theta, 3\sin\theta)$ is

$$\frac{x}{4}\cos\theta + \frac{y}{3}\sin\theta = 1 \text{ or } \frac{x}{4\sec\theta} + \frac{y}{3\,\text{cosec}\,\theta} = 1$$

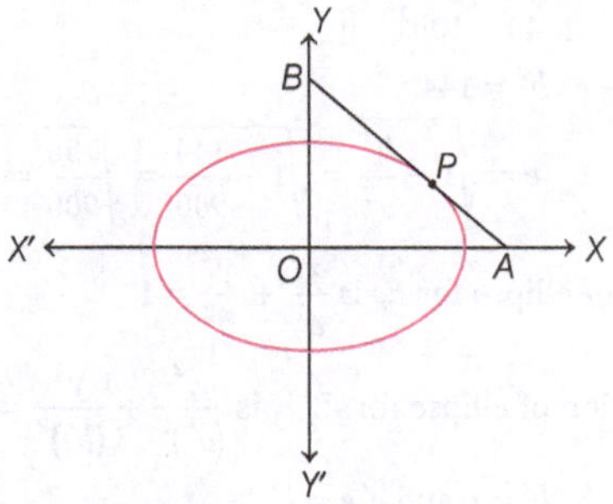

Coordinates of A and B are

$$A \equiv (4\sec\theta, 0) \text{ and } B \equiv (0, 3\text{cosec}\,\theta)$$

Let middle point (h, k).

$$\therefore \quad h = 2\sec\theta \text{ and } k = \frac{3}{2}\text{cosec}\,\theta$$

$$\Rightarrow \quad \left(\frac{2}{h}\right)^2 + \left(\frac{3}{2k}\right)^2 = 1$$

$\therefore \quad$ Locus is $9x^2 + 16y^2 = 4x^2y^2$

8. Equation of tangent at $(a\cos\alpha, b\sin\alpha)$ is

$$\frac{x}{a}\cos\alpha + \frac{y}{b}\sin\alpha = 1 \quad \text{...(i)}$$

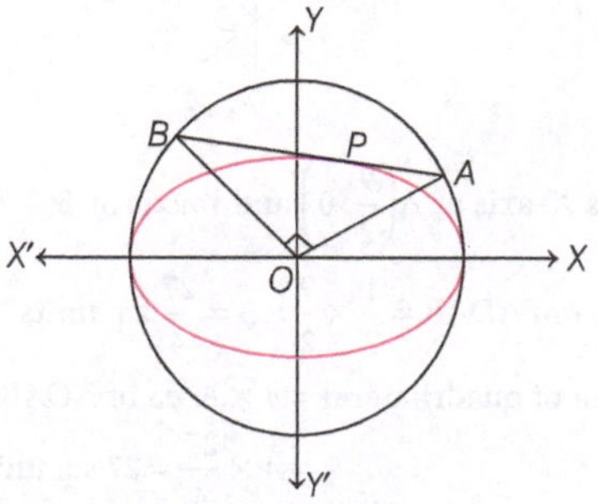

Equation of auxiliary circle is

$$x^2 + y^2 = a^2 \quad \text{...(ii)}$$

For combined equation of OA and OB, making homogeneous Eq. (ii) with the help of Eq. (i), then

$$x^2 + y^2 = a^2\left(\frac{x}{a}\cos\alpha + \frac{y}{b}\sin\alpha\right)^2$$

$$\Rightarrow \quad x^2\sin^2\alpha + y^2\left(1 - \frac{a^2}{b^2}\sin^2\alpha\right) - \frac{2axy}{b}\sin\alpha\cos\alpha = 0$$

$\because \quad \angle AOB = 90°$

$\therefore$ Coefficient of x^2 + Coefficient of $y^2 = 0$

$$\Rightarrow \quad \sin^2\alpha + 1 - \frac{a^2}{b^2}\sin^2\alpha = 0$$

$$\Rightarrow \quad 1 + \sin^2\alpha - \frac{a^2}{a^2(1 - e^2)}\sin^2\alpha = 0$$

$$\Rightarrow \quad (1 - e^2)(1 + \sin^2\alpha) - \sin^2\alpha = 0$$

$$\Rightarrow \quad 1 - e^2(1 + \sin^2\alpha) = 0$$

$$\text{or} \quad e^2(1 + \sin^2\alpha) = 1$$

9. The end point of latus rectum of ellipse $\dfrac{x^2}{a^2} + \dfrac{y^2}{b^2} = 1$ in I quadrant is $\left(ae, \dfrac{b^2}{2}\right)$ and tangent at this point intersects X-axis at $\left(\dfrac{a}{e}, 0\right)$ and Y-axis at $(0, a)$

$\because \quad$ Given ellipse is $\dfrac{x^2}{9} + \dfrac{y^2}{5} = 1$

$$\Rightarrow \quad a^2 = 9 \text{ and } b^2 = 5$$

$$\Rightarrow \quad e = \sqrt{1 - \frac{5}{9}} = \frac{2}{3}$$

$\therefore$ End point of latusrectum in I quadrant is $\left(2, \frac{5}{3}\right)$.

$\therefore$ Equation of tangent at L is $\frac{2x}{9} + \frac{y}{3} = 1$

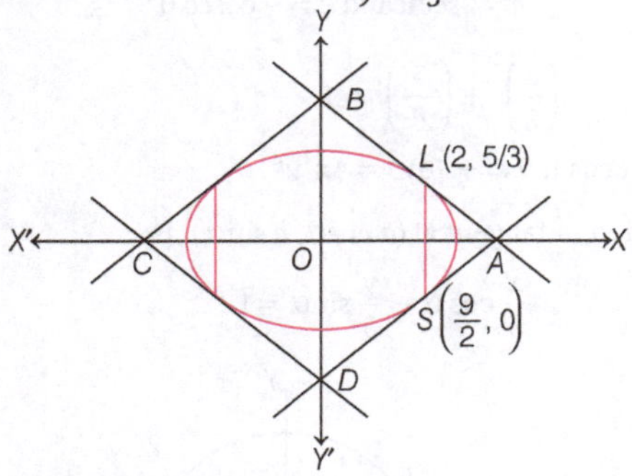

It meets X-axis at $A\left(\frac{9}{2}, 0\right)$ and Y-axis at $B(0, 3)$

$\therefore$ Area of $\Delta DAB = \frac{1}{2} \times \frac{9}{2} \times 3 = \frac{27}{4}$ sq. units

$\therefore$ Area of quadrilateral $= 4 \times$ Area of ΔOAB

$= 4 \times \frac{27}{4} = 27$ sq. units.

10. Given point is $(3\sqrt{3}\cos\theta, \sin\theta)$ and ellipse is $\frac{x^2}{27} + y^2 = 1$

$\therefore$ Equation of tangent is $\frac{x}{3\sqrt{3}}\cos\theta + y\sin\theta = 1$

$\Rightarrow$ Intercepts are $\left(0, \frac{1}{\sin\theta}\right)$ and $\left(\frac{3\sqrt{3}}{\cos\theta}, 0\right)$

Sum of intercepts, $S = \frac{3\sqrt{3}}{\cos\theta} + \frac{1}{\sin\theta} = 3\sqrt{3}\sec\theta + \operatorname{cosec}\theta$

For minimum of S, put $\frac{dS}{d\theta} = 0$

$\Rightarrow$ $3\sqrt{3}\sec\theta\tan\theta - \operatorname{cosec}\theta\cot\theta = 0$

$\Rightarrow$ $\tan^3\theta = \frac{1}{3\sqrt{3}} \Rightarrow \tan\theta = \frac{1}{\sqrt{3}} \Rightarrow \theta = \frac{\pi}{6}$

$\because$ At $\theta = \frac{\pi}{6}, \frac{d^2s}{d\theta^2} > 0$

$\Rightarrow$ S will be minimum at $\theta = \frac{\pi}{6}$.

11. **Decoding the Question**

Equation of tangent of ellipse $\frac{x^2}{a^2} + \frac{y^2}{b^2} = 1$ is $y = mx \pm \sqrt{a^2m^2 + b^2}$ and equation of tangent of parabola $y^2 = 4ax$ is $y = mx + \frac{a}{m}$.

Let $y = mx + \frac{1}{m}$ be a tangent to the parabola $y^2 = 4x$ which touch the ellipse $\frac{x^2}{4^2} + \frac{y^2}{(\sqrt{6})^2} = 1$

$\Rightarrow$ $\frac{1}{m^2} = 16m^2 + 6$ $\quad [\because c^2 = a^2m^2 + b^2]$

$\therefore$ $16m^4 + 6m^2 - 1 = 0$

$\Rightarrow$ $m = \pm\frac{1}{\sqrt{8}}$

The coordinates of the point of contact of common tangent of slopes $m = \pm\frac{1}{2\sqrt{2}}$ to $y^2 = 4x$ are $A(8, 4\sqrt{2}), B(8, -4\sqrt{2})$, $C\left(-2, \frac{3}{\sqrt{2}}\right)$ and $D\left(-2, \frac{-3}{\sqrt{2}}\right)$.

From the points A, B, C and D, we get $AB \parallel CD$

$\Rightarrow$ $ABCD$ is a trapezium.

Now, $AB = 8\sqrt{2}$ and $CD = 3\sqrt{2}$

and distance between AB and CD is $(8 + 2) = 10$ units.

$\therefore$ Area of $ABCD = \frac{1}{2}(AB + CD) \times$ distance between AB and CD

$= \frac{1}{2} \times 11\sqrt{2} \times 10 = 55\sqrt{2}$ sq. units

12. Given, length of semi-major axis $= 30 = a$

$\Rightarrow$ $2a = 60$

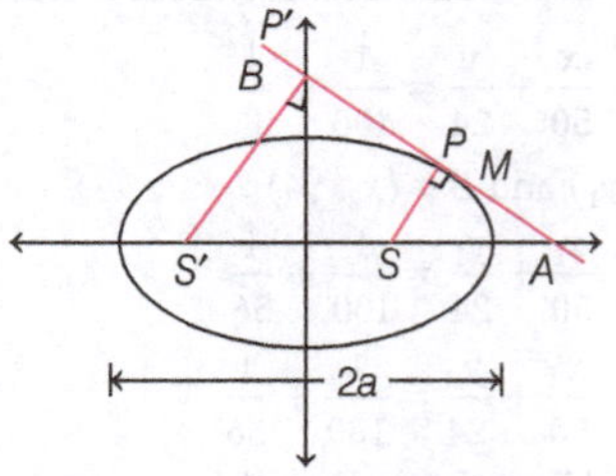

Equation of tangent is $y = mx \pm \sqrt{a^2m^2 + b^2}$.

$SP \perp AB, S'P' \perp AB$ and M is a point of contact.

$\because$ We know, $SP \cdot S'P' = \left|\frac{mae \pm \sqrt{a^2m^2 + b^2}}{\sqrt{1 + m^2}}\right| \left|\frac{-mae \pm \sqrt{a^2m^2 + b^2}}{\sqrt{1 + m^2}}\right|$

$= \frac{a^2m^2 + b^2 - m^2a^2e^2}{1 + m^2}$

$= \frac{a^2m^2 + b^2 - m^2(a^2 - b^2)}{1 + m^2} = b^2$ $\quad \left[\because e^2 = 1 - \frac{b^2}{a^2}, a^2e^2 = a^2 - b^2\right]$

$\therefore \sum_{i=1}^{10}(SP_i)(S'P'_i) = b^2 + b^2 + \ldots\ldots + 10$ times

$1440 = 10b^2$

$\Rightarrow$ $b^2 = 144$

$\therefore$ $e = \sqrt{1 - \frac{b^2}{a^2}} = \sqrt{1 - \frac{144}{900}} = \sqrt{\frac{756}{900}} = \frac{6\sqrt{21}}{30} = \frac{\sqrt{21}}{5}$.

13. Equation of ellipse for E_n is $\frac{x^2}{a^2} + \frac{y^2}{b^2} = 1$

and equation of ellipse for E_{n-1} is $\frac{x^2}{(a')^2} + \frac{y^2}{(b')^2} = 1$

$b' = a$ and $a'e = b$ $\quad$ ...(i)

$\Rightarrow \quad (b')^2 = (a')^2 - (a')^2 e^2$

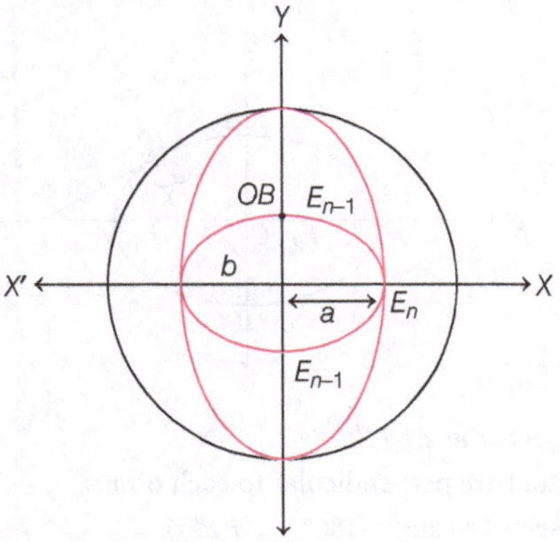

From Eq. (i),

$$a^2 = \frac{b^2}{e^2} - b^2 \qquad \left[\because e^2 = 1 - \frac{b^2}{a^2}\right]$$

$$\Rightarrow \quad e^2 = \frac{b^2}{a^2} - \frac{b^2 e^2}{a^2} = \frac{b^2}{a^2}(1 - e^2)$$

$$\Rightarrow \quad e^2 = (1 - e^2)^2 \Rightarrow e = \pm(1 - e^2)$$

$$\Rightarrow \quad e^2 + e - 1 = 0 \text{ and } e^2 - e - 1 = 0$$

$$\Rightarrow \quad e = \frac{-1 \pm \sqrt{1+4}}{2}, e = \frac{1 \pm \sqrt{1+4}}{2}$$

$$\Rightarrow \quad e = \frac{-1 \pm \sqrt{5}}{2}, \frac{1 \pm \sqrt{5}}{2}$$

$$\therefore \quad e = \frac{\sqrt{5} - 1}{2} \qquad [\because 0 < e < 1]$$

14. The given ellipse is $\frac{x^2}{4} + \frac{y^2}{1} = 1$

So, $A = (2, 0)$ and $B = (0, 1)$

If $PQRS$ is the rectangle in which it is inscribed, then $P = (2, 1)$.

Let $\frac{x^2}{a^2} + \frac{y^2}{b^2} = 1$ be the ellipse circumscribing the rectangle $PQRS$. Then, it passes through $P(2, 1)$.

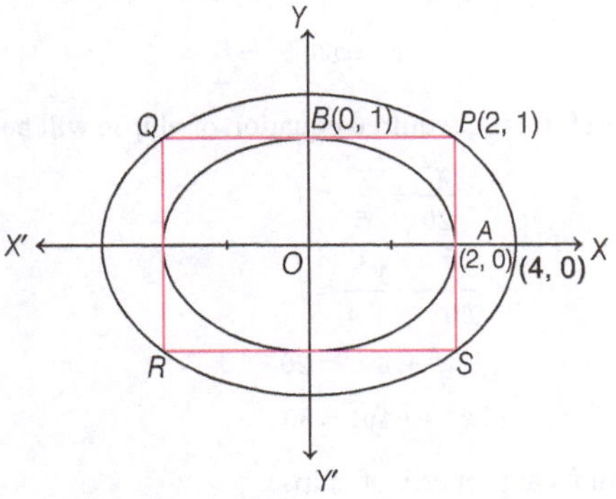

$$\therefore \quad \frac{4}{a^2} + \frac{1}{b^2} = 1 \qquad \text{...(i)}$$

Also, given that it passes through (4, 0).

$$\therefore \quad \frac{16}{a^2} + 0 = 1$$

$$\Rightarrow \quad a^2 = 16$$

$$\Rightarrow \quad b^2 = 4/3 \qquad [\because \text{substituting } a^2 = 16 \text{ in Eq. (i)}]$$

$\therefore$ The required ellipse is $\frac{x^2}{16} + \frac{y^2}{4/3} = 1$

or $\quad x^2 + 12y^2 = 16$

15. In ΔABC, given that $\cos B + \cos C = 4\sin^2 \frac{A}{2}$

$$\Rightarrow \quad 2\cos\frac{B+C}{2}\cos\frac{B-C}{2} - 4\sin^2\frac{A}{2} = 0$$

$$\Rightarrow \quad 2\sin\frac{A}{2}\left[\cos\frac{B-C}{2} - 2\sin\frac{A}{2}\right] = 0$$

$$\Rightarrow \quad \sin\frac{A}{2} = 0 \text{ or } \left(\cos\frac{B-C}{2} - 2\cos\frac{B+C}{2}\right) = 0$$

$$\left[\because \frac{A}{2} = 90^\circ - \left(\frac{B+C}{2}\right)\right]$$

But in a triangle, $\sin\frac{A}{2} \neq 0$

$$\cos\frac{B-C}{2} - 2\cos\frac{B+C}{2} = 0$$

$$\Rightarrow \quad \frac{\cos\left(\frac{B+C}{2}\right)}{\cos\left(\frac{B-C}{2}\right)} = \frac{1}{2}$$

Applying componendo and dividendo, we get

$$\frac{\cos\left(\frac{B+C}{2}\right) + \cos\left(\frac{B-C}{2}\right)}{\cos\left(\frac{B+C}{2}\right) - \cos\left(\frac{B-C}{2}\right)} = \frac{1+2}{1-2} = -3$$

$$\Rightarrow \quad -\frac{2\cos\frac{B}{2}\cos\frac{C}{2}}{2\sin\frac{B}{2}\sin\frac{C}{2}} = -3$$

$$\Rightarrow \quad \tan\frac{B}{2}\tan\frac{C}{2} = \frac{1}{3}$$

$$\Rightarrow \quad \sqrt{\frac{(s-a)(s-c)}{s(s-b)}}\sqrt{\frac{(s-a)(s-b)}{s(s-c)}} = \frac{1}{3}$$

$$\Rightarrow \quad \frac{s-a}{s} = \frac{1}{3}$$

or $\quad 2s = 3a$

$\Rightarrow \quad a + b + c = 3a$

or $\quad b + c = 2a$

i.e. $\quad AC + AB = \text{constant}$

$[\because$ base $BC = a$ is given to be constant$]$

$\Rightarrow A$ moves on an ellipse.

16. Let $P \equiv (\sqrt{6}\cos\theta, \sqrt{2}\sin\theta)$ be any point on the ellipse.

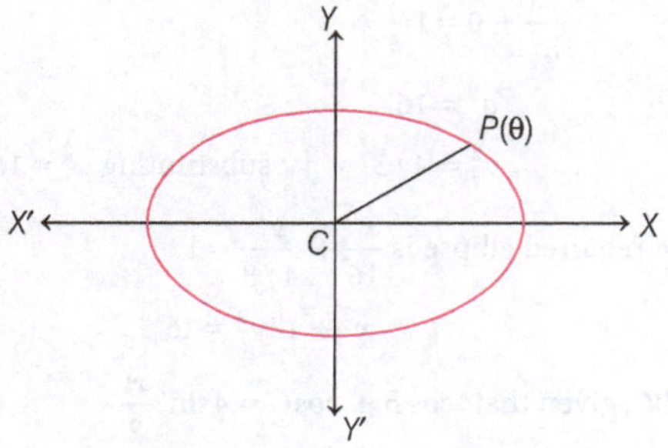

$$\frac{x^2}{6} + \frac{y^2}{2} = 1$$

Given, $\quad CP = 2 \Rightarrow (CP)^2 = 4$

$\Rightarrow \quad 6\cos^2\theta + 2\sin^2\theta = 4$

$\Rightarrow \quad 6\cos^2\theta + 2(1 - \cos^2\theta) = 4$

or $\quad \cos^2\theta = \frac{1}{2} = \left(\frac{1}{\sqrt{2}}\right)^2 = \left(\cos\frac{\pi}{4}\right)^2$

$\therefore \quad \theta = n\pi \pm \frac{\pi}{4}, n \in I$

$\therefore \quad \theta = \frac{\pi}{4}, \frac{3\pi}{4}, \frac{5\pi}{4}$ and $\frac{7\pi}{4}$

17. Here, $a = \cos\theta$ and $b = \sin\theta$

$\therefore \quad \frac{\pi}{4} < \theta < \frac{\pi}{2}$

$\therefore \quad a < b$

Then, $\quad a^2 = b^2(1 - e^2)$

$\Rightarrow \quad \cos^2\theta = \sin^2\theta(1 - e^2)$

$\therefore \quad e^2 = 1 - \cot^2\theta$

or $\quad e = \sqrt{(1 - \cot^2\theta)} \quad \left[\because \frac{\pi}{4} < \theta < \frac{\pi}{2}\right]$

$\because$ Extremities of latusrectum are $\left(\pm\frac{a^2}{b}, \pm be\right)$

$\Rightarrow \quad x = \pm\frac{a^2}{b}, y = \pm be$

or $\quad b^2x^2 = a^4$

and $\quad y^2 = b^2e^2 = \sin^2\theta - \cos^2\theta$

or $\quad \sin^2\theta x^2 = \cos^4\theta$

and $\quad y^2 = 1 - 2\cos^2\theta$

or $\quad (1 - \cos^2\theta)x^2 = \cos^4\theta$

and $\quad \cos^2\theta = \frac{1 - y^2}{2}$

$\therefore \quad \left(1 - \frac{1 - y^2}{2}\right)x^2 = \left(\frac{1 - y^2}{2}\right)^2$

or $\quad 2x^2(1 + y^2) = (1 - y^2)^2$

or $\quad 2y^2(x^2 + 1) = 1 + y^4 - 2x^2$

18. $\because \quad \frac{PF_1}{PF_2} = \frac{NF_1}{NF_2}$

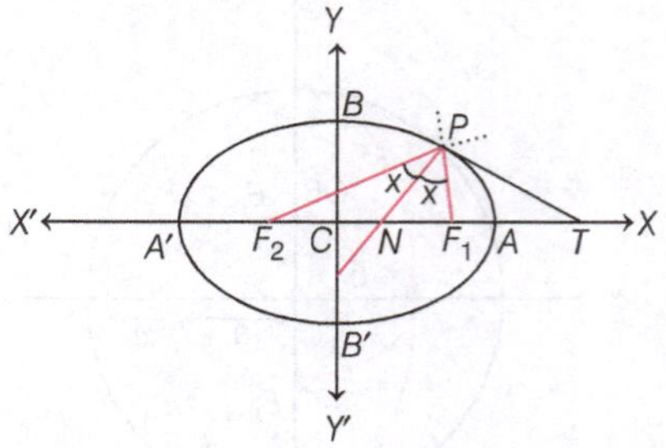

$\therefore$ PN bisects the $\angle F_1PF_2$.

$\because$ Bisectors are perpendicular to each other.

$\therefore$ PT bisects the angle $(180° - \angle F_1PF_2)$.

19. Since, $a^2 - a - 6 > 0 \Rightarrow (a - 3)(a + 2) > 0$

$\therefore \quad a < -2$ or $a > 3 \quad$ ...(i)

and $\quad a^2 - 6a + 5 > 0 \Rightarrow (a - 1)(a - 5) > 0$

$\therefore \quad a < 1$ or $a > 5 \quad$ ...(ii)

Also, $\quad a^2 - a - 6 \neq a^2 - 6a + 5$

or $\quad a \neq \frac{11}{5} \quad$ ...(iii)

From Eqs. (i), (ii) and (iii) we get

$$a \in (-\infty, -2) \cup (5, \infty)$$

20. Let the required equation be

$$\frac{x^2}{a^2} + \frac{y^2}{b^2} = 1 \quad \text{...(i)}$$

Since, Eq. (i) passes through $(4, -1)$, then

$$\frac{16}{a^2} + \frac{1}{b^2} = 1 \quad \text{...(ii)}$$

The equation of given line is $y = -\frac{x}{4} + \frac{10}{4}$

which touches the ellipse (i),

$$\left(\frac{10}{4}\right)^2 = a^2\left(-\frac{1}{4}\right)^2 + b^2$$

$\Rightarrow \quad \frac{a^2}{16} + b^2 = \frac{25}{4} \quad$ ...(iii)

On solving, Eqs. (ii) and (iii), we get $a^2 = 20, b^2 = 5$

or $\quad a^2 = 80, b^2 = \frac{5}{4}$

Therefore, the required equation of ellipse will be

$$\frac{x^2}{20} + \frac{y^2}{5} = 1$$

or $\quad \frac{x^2}{80} + \frac{y^2}{5/4} = 1$

i.e. $\quad x^2 + 4y^2 = 20$

or $\quad x^2 + 64y^2 = 80$

21. From focal property of ellipse,

$SP + S'P = 2a$, if $a > b$

and $\quad SP + S'P = 2b$, if $b > a$

Also, $PS\cos\theta + PS'\cos\phi = 2ae$ ...(i)

and $PS\sin\theta - PS'\sin\phi = 0$ ...(ii)

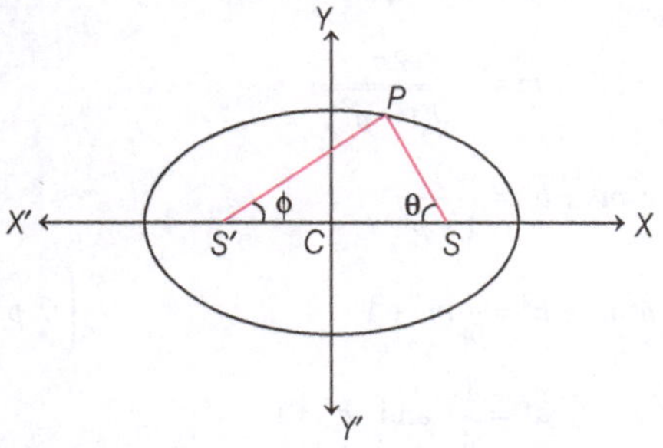

From Eqs. (i) and (ii), we get

$$PS = \frac{2ae\sin\phi}{\sin(\theta+\phi)},\ PS' = \frac{2ae\sin\theta}{\sin(\theta+\phi)}$$

$\because$ $SP + S'P = 2a$

$\therefore$ $e(\sin\theta + \sin\phi) = \sin(\theta+\phi)$

$\Rightarrow$ $e\cdot 2\sin\left(\frac{\theta+\phi}{2}\right)\cos\left(\frac{\theta-\phi}{2}\right) = 2\sin\left(\frac{\theta+\phi}{2}\right)\cos\left(\frac{\theta+\phi}{2}\right)$

or $$\frac{\cos\left(\frac{\theta-\phi}{2}\right)}{\cos\left(\frac{\theta+\phi}{2}\right)} = \frac{1}{e}$$

or $$\frac{\cos\left(\frac{\theta-\phi}{2}\right) - \cos\left(\frac{\theta+\phi}{2}\right)}{\cos\left(\frac{\theta-\phi}{2}\right) + \cos\left(\frac{\theta+\phi}{2}\right)} = \frac{1-e}{1+e}$$

or $$\tan\left(\frac{\theta}{2}\right)\tan\left(\frac{\phi}{2}\right) = \frac{1-e}{1+e}$$

22. Let the point of intersection of tangents at A and B be $P(x_1, y_1)$. Then, equation of AB is $xx_1 + 4yy_1 = 4$

or $$\frac{xx_1}{4} + yy_1 = 1 \quad \text{...(i)}$$

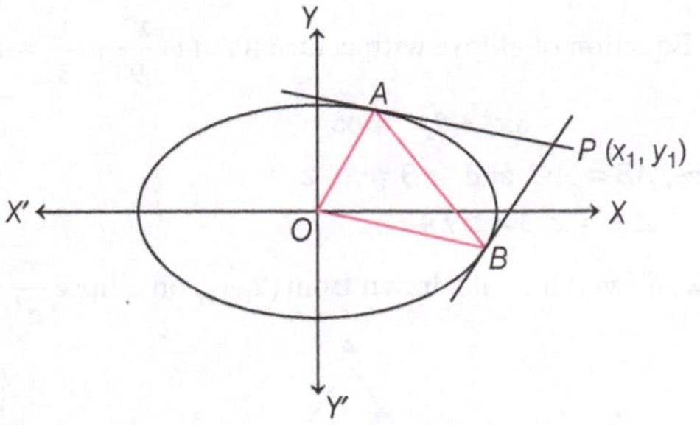

For point of OA and OB, homogenising the equation of ellipse with the help of Eq. (i), then

$$x^2 + 4y^2 = 4\left(\frac{xx_1}{4} + yy_1\right)^2$$

or $$x^2\left(\frac{x_1^2}{4} - 1\right) + y^2(4y_1^2 - 4) + 2xyx_1y_1 = 0 \quad \text{...(ii)}$$

But given equation of OA and OB is

$$x^2 + 4y^2 + axy = 0 \quad \text{...(iii)}$$

Since, Eqs. (ii) and (iii) are identical, then

$$\frac{\frac{x_1^2}{4} - 1}{1} = \frac{4y_1^2 - 4}{4} = \frac{2x_1y_1}{a}$$

or $x_1^2 - 4 = 4(y_1^2 - 1)$

or $x_1^2 - 4y_1^2 = 0$

Therefore, the locus is $x^2 - 4y^2 = 0$

or $(x + 2y)(x - 2y) = 0$

or $x + 2y = 0$ and $x - 2y = 0$

23. Given equation, $25x^2 + 9y^2 - 150x - 90y + 225 = 0$

$\Rightarrow$ $25(x^2 - 6x) + 9(y^2 - 10y) + 225 = 0$

$\Rightarrow$ $25\{(x-3)^2 - 9\} + 9\{(y-5)^2 - 25\} + 225 = 0$

$\Rightarrow$ $25(x-3)^2 + 9(y-5)^2 = 225$

$\Rightarrow$ $$\frac{(x-3)^2}{3^2} + \frac{(y-5)^2}{5^2} = 1 \quad \text{...(i)}$$

Let $x - 3 = X,\ y - 5 = Y$

Then, Eq. (i) becomes

$$\frac{X^2}{3^2} + \frac{Y^2}{5^2} = 1 \quad \text{...(ii)}$$

Now, on comparing Eq. (ii) with $\frac{X^2}{a^2} + \frac{Y^2}{b^2} = 1$

$\therefore$ $a = 3, b = 5$

$\Rightarrow$ $a^2 = b^2(1 - e^2)$

$\Rightarrow$ $9 = 25(1 - e^2)$

$\Rightarrow$ $e = \frac{4}{5}$

Centre $X = 0,\ Y = 0$

$x - 3 = 0,\ y - 5 = 0$

$\therefore$ Centre $\equiv (3, 5)$

Foci $X = 0, Y = \pm be$

$\Rightarrow$ $x - 3 = 0, y - 5 = \pm 4$

$\Rightarrow$ $y = 5 \pm 4$

$\therefore$ Foci are (3, 1) and (3, 9)

Major axis $2b = 10$

24. Equation of tangent at α is

$$\frac{x}{a}\cos\alpha + \frac{y}{b}\sin\alpha = 1$$

$\Rightarrow$ $$\frac{x}{a\sec\alpha} + \frac{y}{b\operatorname{cosec}\alpha} = 1$$

Now, length of intercept,

$$z = \sqrt{(a^2\sec^2\alpha + b^2\operatorname{cosec}^2\alpha)}$$

or $z^2 = a^2\sec^2\alpha + b^2\operatorname{cosec}^2\alpha$

$$\therefore \quad \frac{d(z^2)}{d\alpha} = 2\left(\frac{a^2 \sin\alpha}{\cos^3\alpha} - \frac{b^2\cos\alpha}{\sin^3\alpha}\right)$$

and $\quad \dfrac{d^2(z^2)}{d\alpha^2} > 0$

For minimum of z, $\dfrac{d(z^2)}{d\alpha} = 0$

$$\therefore \quad \tan^4\alpha = \frac{b^2}{a^2}$$

or $\quad \tan\alpha = \pm\sqrt{\left(\dfrac{b}{a}\right)}$

$$\Rightarrow \quad \alpha = \tan^{-1}\sqrt{\left(\frac{b}{a}\right)}, \ \pi - \tan^{-1}\sqrt{\left(\frac{b}{a}\right)}$$

$$-\pi + \tan^{-1}\sqrt{\left(\frac{b}{a}\right)} \text{ and } -\tan^{-1}\sqrt{\left(\frac{b}{a}\right)}$$

25. Let $E_1 : \dfrac{x^2}{a^2} + \dfrac{y^2}{b^2} = 1$, where $a > b$

and $E_2 : \dfrac{x^2}{c^2} + \dfrac{y^2}{d^2} = 1$, where $c < d$

Also, $S : x^2 + (y-1)^2 = 2$

Tangent at $P(x_1, y_1)$ to S is $x + y = 3$

To find point of contact, put $x = 3 - y$ in S, we get $P(1, 2)$ writing equation of tangent in parametric form

$$\frac{x-1}{\frac{-1}{\sqrt{2}}} = \frac{y-2}{\frac{1}{\sqrt{2}}} = \pm\frac{2\sqrt{2}}{3}$$

$$x = \frac{-2}{3} + 1 \text{ or } \frac{2}{3} + 1 \text{ and } y = \frac{2}{3} + 2 \text{ or } \frac{-2}{3} + 2$$

$$\Rightarrow \quad x = \frac{1}{3} \text{ or } \frac{5}{3} \text{ and } y = \frac{8}{3} \text{ or } \frac{4}{3}$$

$$\therefore \quad Q\left(\frac{5}{3}, \frac{4}{3}\right) \text{ and } R\left(\frac{1}{3}, \frac{8}{3}\right)$$

Equation of tangent to E_1 at Q is $\dfrac{5x}{3a^2} + \dfrac{4y}{3b^2} = 1$, which is identical to $\dfrac{x}{3} + \dfrac{y}{3} = 1$

$$\Rightarrow \quad a^2 = 5 \text{ and } b^2 = 4 \Rightarrow e_1^2 = 1 - \frac{4}{5} = \frac{1}{5}$$

Equation of tangent to E_2 at R is $\dfrac{x}{3c^2} + \dfrac{8y}{3d^2} = 1$ identical to $\dfrac{x}{3} + \dfrac{y}{3} = 1$

$$\Rightarrow \quad c^2 = 1, d^2 = 8 \Rightarrow e_2^2 = 1 - \frac{1}{8} = \frac{7}{8}$$

$$\therefore \quad e_1^2 + e_2^2 = \frac{43}{40}, e_1e_2 = \frac{\sqrt{7}}{2\sqrt{10}}, |e_1^2 - e_2^2| = \frac{27}{40}$$

Sol. (Q. Nos. 26 to 27)

Given line is $2px + y\sqrt{(1-p^2)} = 1$

$$\Rightarrow \quad y = -\frac{2p}{\sqrt{(1-p^2)}}x + \frac{1}{\sqrt{(1-p^2)}}$$

$\because$ Equation of tangent in terms of slope (m) of ellipse $\dfrac{x^2}{a^2} + \dfrac{y^2}{b^2} = 1$ is $y = mx + \sqrt{(a^2m^2 + b^2)}$

$$\therefore \quad m = -\frac{2p}{\sqrt{(1-p^2)}}$$

and $\quad a^2m^2 + b^2 = \dfrac{1}{1-p^2}$

or $\quad a^2m^2 + b^2 = \dfrac{1}{4}m^2 + 1 \qquad \left(\because p^2 = \dfrac{m^2}{m^2+4}\right)$

$$\therefore \quad a^2 = \frac{1}{4} \text{ and } b^2 = 1$$

$\therefore$ Equation of ellipse is $\dfrac{x^2}{1/4} + \dfrac{y^2}{1} = 1$

26. Here, $a^2 = \dfrac{1}{4}$ and $b^2 = 1$

$$\because \quad b > a$$

$$\therefore \quad a^2 = b^2(1-e^2) \Rightarrow \frac{1}{4} = 1 - e^2 \Rightarrow e^2 = \frac{3}{4}$$

$$\therefore \quad e = \frac{\sqrt{3}}{2}$$

27. Foci of ellipse are $(0, \pm\sqrt{(b^2 - a^2)})$

i.e. $\quad \left(0, \pm\dfrac{\sqrt{3}}{2}\right)$

Sol. (Q. Nos. 28 to 29)

28. Given, distance between foci S and S' is 4 units.

$$\therefore \quad SS' = 4 \Rightarrow 2ae = 4$$

$$\therefore \quad ae = 2 \qquad \ldots \text{(i)}$$

and given $SP + S'P = 6$

$$\Rightarrow \quad 2a = 6$$

$$\because \quad a = 3 \qquad \ldots \text{(ii)}$$

From Eqs. (i) and (ii), we get

$$e = \frac{2}{3}$$

and $\quad b^2 = a^2(1-e^2) = a^2 - (ae)^2 = 9 - 4 = 5$

$\therefore$ Equation of ellipse with centre (0, 0) is $\dfrac{x^2}{9} + \dfrac{y^2}{5} = 1$

$$\Rightarrow \quad 5x^2 + 9y^2 = 45$$

29. Since, $AB = AC$ and $\angle B = \pi/2$

$$\because \quad \angle A = \angle C = \pi/4$$

Now, if two tangents drawn from (x_1, y_1) on ellipse $\dfrac{x^2}{a^2} + \dfrac{y^2}{b^2} = 1$

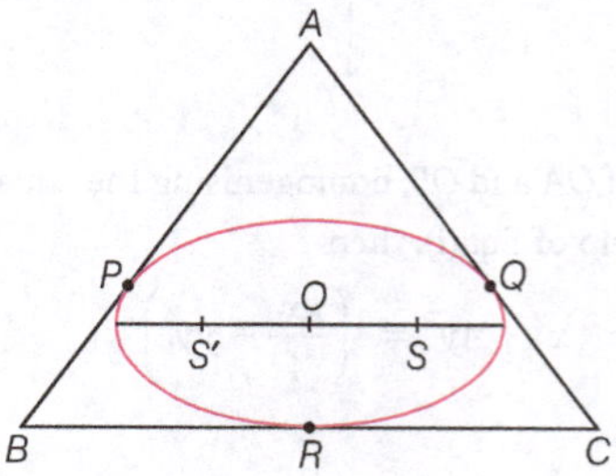

and angle between tangents is α, then

$$\tan\alpha = \frac{2ab\sqrt{\left(\frac{x_1^2}{a^2}+\frac{y_1^2}{b^2}-1\right)}}{|x_1^2+y_1^2-a^2-b^2|}$$

Let $A \equiv (x_1, y_1)$

Here, $\alpha = \frac{\pi}{4}$ and $a = 3, b = \sqrt{5}$

Then, $$1 = \frac{6\sqrt{5}\sqrt{\left(\frac{x_1^2}{9}+\frac{y_1^2}{5}-1\right)}}{(x_1^2+y_1^2-9-5)}$$

or $$(x_1^2+y_1^2-14)^2 = 180\left(\frac{x_1^2}{9}+\frac{y_1^2}{5}-1\right)$$

$\therefore$ Required locus is $(x^2+y^2-14)^2 = 4(5x^2+9y^2-45)$

Sol. (Q. Nos. 30 to 31)

Here, $b > a$

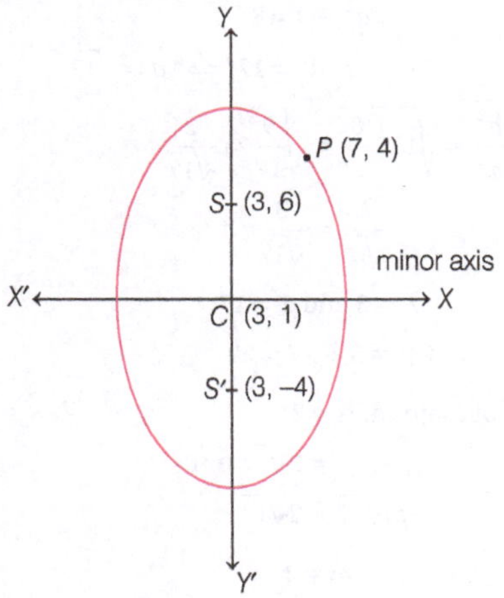

and $CS = 5 = be$ ...(i)

Equation of ellipse is

$$\frac{(x-3)^2}{a^2}+\frac{(y-1)^2}{b^2} = 1 \quad \text{...(ii)}$$

which passes through $P(7, 4)$, then

$$\frac{16}{a^2}+\frac{9}{b^2} = 1$$

$\Rightarrow$ $$\frac{16}{b^2-25}+\frac{9}{b^2} = 1 \quad [\because a^2 = b^2(1-e^2) = b^2-25]$$

$\Rightarrow$ $$b^4-50b^2+225 = 0$$

or $$(b^2-45)(b^2-5) = 0$$

$\therefore$ $$b = 3\sqrt{5} \quad (b \neq \sqrt{5})$$

From Eq. (i), $e = \frac{\sqrt{5}}{3}$ and $a^2 = 45-25 = 20$

From Eq. (ii), ellipse (E) is $\frac{(x-3)^2}{20}+\frac{(y-1)^2}{45} = 1$

30. Product of the lengths of the perpendicular segments from the foci on tangent at $P(7, 4)$ is equal to a^2 i.e. 20 $[\because b > a]$

31. Since, lines SF' and $S'F$ meet the normal PG and bisect it.

$\therefore$ Required point is mid-point of PG.

$\because$ Equation of ellipse E is $\frac{(x-3)^2}{20}+\frac{(y-1)^2}{45} = 1$

$\Rightarrow$ $$\frac{2(x-3)}{20}+\frac{2(y-1)}{45}\frac{dy}{dx} = 0$$

$\therefore$ $$\left.\frac{dy}{dx}\right|_{(7,4)} = -3$$

$\therefore$ Slope of normal $= \frac{1}{3}$

Equation of normal at $P(7, 4)$ is $y-4 = \frac{1}{3}(x-7)$

$\Rightarrow$ $$x-3y+5 = 0$$

which meets the major axis in $G\left(3, \frac{8}{3}\right)$.

$\therefore$ Required point is mid-point of PG i.e. $\left(5, \frac{10}{3}\right)$.

Sol. (Q. Nos. 32 to 33)

32. Tangents of slope m to the circle and ellipse are respectively

$$y = mx \pm r\sqrt{(m^2+1)} \text{ and } y = mx \pm \sqrt{(16m^2+9)}$$

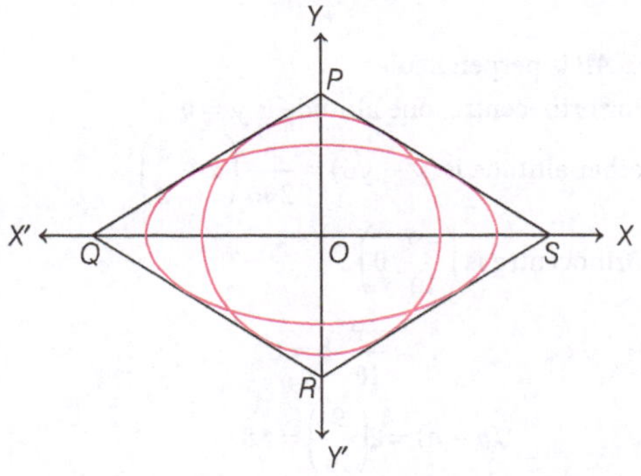

For common tangent, $r^2(m^2+1) = 16m^2+9$

$\Rightarrow$ $$r = \sqrt{\left(\frac{16m^2+9}{m^2+1}\right)}$$

If $PQRS$ is a square,

then $m = \pm 1$

or $r\sqrt{2} = \sqrt{25}$ or $2r^2 = 25$

33. Since, $PQRS$ is a square, then $\angle PQR = 90°$

$\therefore$ PR is diameter of circle through P, Q and R

$\therefore$ Area of circumcircle of

$$\Delta PQR = \pi (OP)^2 = \pi(r\sqrt{2})^2 = 2\pi r^2$$

and area of circle C_1 is πr^2.

$\therefore$ The required ratio is $\dfrac{1}{2} = \dfrac{\lambda_1}{\lambda_2}$

$\Rightarrow \qquad \lambda_1 = 1$

and $\qquad \lambda_2 = 2$

Hence, $\qquad \lambda_1 + \lambda_2 = 3$

Sol. (Q. Nos. 34 to 35)

Given, ellipse is $\dfrac{x^2}{9} + \dfrac{y^2}{8} = 1$

Here, $\qquad e = \sqrt{1 - \dfrac{8}{9}} = \dfrac{1}{3}$

$\Rightarrow$ Foci are $(\pm 1, 0)$

$\Rightarrow \qquad F_1(-1, 0)$ and $F_2(1, 0)$

The given parabola is $y^2 = 4x$.

Thus, $A = \left(\dfrac{3}{2}, \sqrt{6}\right)$ and $B = \left(\dfrac{3}{2}, -\sqrt{6}\right)$

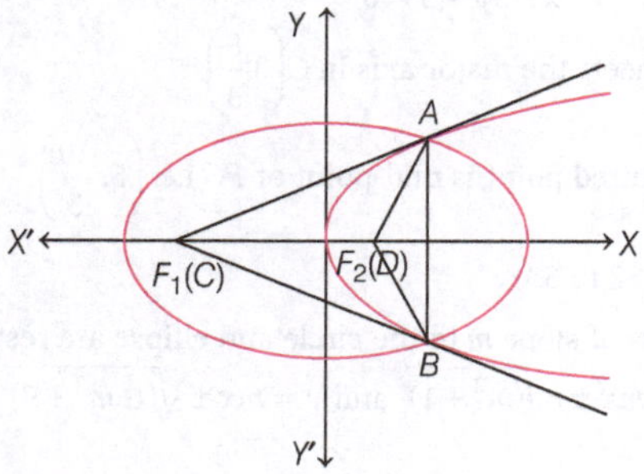

34. Since, AB is perpendicular.

$\therefore$ For orthocentre, one altitude is $y = 0$

and other altitude is $(y - \sqrt{6}) = \dfrac{5}{2\sqrt{6}}\left(x - \dfrac{3}{2}\right)$

$\Rightarrow$ Orthocentre is $\left(\dfrac{-9}{10}, 0\right)$

$\Rightarrow \qquad a = \dfrac{-9}{10}, b = 0$

$\therefore \qquad 2(b - a) = 2\left(\dfrac{9}{10}\right) = 1.8$

35. Equation of tangent at A and B is $\dfrac{x}{6} + \dfrac{y\sqrt{6}}{8} = 1$

$\therefore$ C is $(6, 0)$.

Equation of normal at A is $(y - \sqrt{6}) = \dfrac{-\sqrt{6}}{2}\left(x - \dfrac{3}{2}\right)$

$\therefore$ D is $\left(\dfrac{7}{2}, 0\right)$.

$\therefore$ Area of $\Delta ADC = \dfrac{1}{2} \times \sqrt{6} \times \dfrac{5}{2} = \dfrac{5\sqrt{6}}{4}$

Area of $AF_1BF_2 = \dfrac{\sqrt{6}}{2} + \dfrac{3\sqrt{6}}{2} = \dfrac{4\sqrt{6}}{2}$

$\therefore$ Required ratio $\dfrac{5\sqrt{6}}{4} : \dfrac{4\sqrt{6}}{2} = 5 : 8 = \lambda_1 : \lambda_2$ [given]

$\therefore \qquad \lambda_2 - \lambda_1 = 8 - 5 = 3$

Sol. (Q. Nos. 36 to 37)

We know that distance between two focus $= 2ae$.

$\therefore \qquad 2ae = 6 \Rightarrow ae = 3$ and $P_1P_2 = b^2$

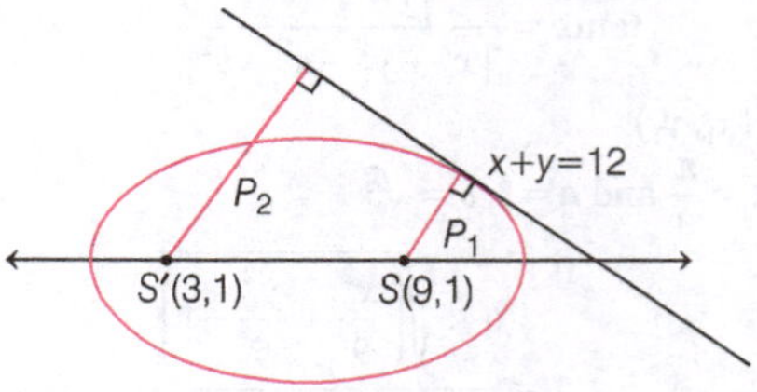

$\Rightarrow \qquad \left|\dfrac{9 + 1 - 12}{\sqrt{2}}\right|\left|\dfrac{3 + 1 - 12}{\sqrt{2}}\right| = b^2 \qquad [\because P_1P_2 = b^2]$

$\Rightarrow \qquad \dfrac{2}{\sqrt{2}} \times \dfrac{8}{\sqrt{2}} = b^2$

$\Rightarrow \qquad b^2 = 8$

$\Rightarrow \qquad a^2 - a^2e^2 = 8$

$\Rightarrow \qquad a^2 - 9 = 8 \qquad [\because ae = 3]$

$\Rightarrow \qquad a^2 = 17 \Rightarrow a = \sqrt{17}$

36. $e = \sqrt{1 - \dfrac{b^2}{a^2}} = \sqrt{1 - \dfrac{8}{17}} = \sqrt{\dfrac{9}{17}} = \dfrac{3}{\sqrt{17}}$

$\because \qquad \dfrac{\lambda}{\sqrt{\mu}} = \dfrac{3}{\sqrt{17}}$

$\Rightarrow \qquad \lambda = 3$ and $\mu = 17$

$\therefore \qquad \lambda + \mu = 3 + 17 = 20$

37. $\because$ Length of major axis $= 2a$

$= 2\sqrt{17}$ units

$m\sqrt{17} = 2\sqrt{17}$ [given]

$\therefore \qquad m = 2$

38. Let S and S' be the foci of one ellipse and H and H' be the foci of other, C being their common centre. Then, $SHS'H'$ is a parallelogram and since

$$SH + S'H = HS' + H'S' = 2a$$

Since, the sum of the focal distances of any point on an ellipse is equal to its major axis which is $2a$.

Then, $\qquad CS = ae,\ CH = ae'$

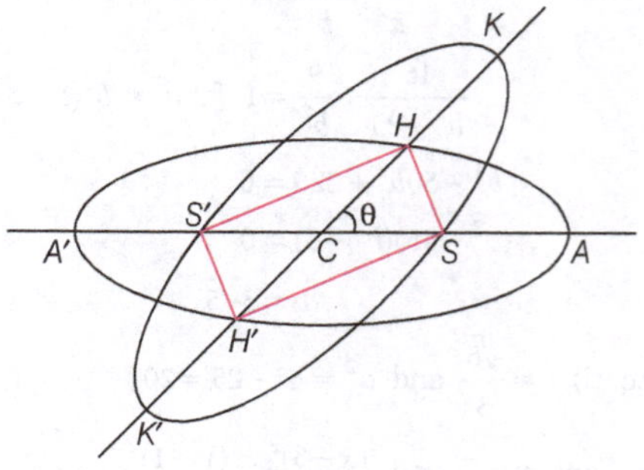

Let θ be the angle between their axes.

Then, $$SH^2 = a^2e^2 + a^2e'^2 - 2a^2ee' \cos\theta$$
$$HS^2 = a^2e^2 + a^2e'^2 + 2a^2ee' \cos\theta$$

Now, $$2a = SH + S'H$$

On squaring both sides, then

$$4a^2 = (SH)^2 + (S'H)^2 + 2(SH)\cdot(S'H)$$

$$\Rightarrow 4a^2 = 2a^2(e^2 + e'^2) + 2\sqrt{(a^2e^2 + a^2e'^2)^2 - 4a^4e^2e'^2 \cos^2\theta}$$

$$\Rightarrow (2 - e^2 - e'^2)^2 = (e^2 + e'^2)^2 - 4e^2e'^2 \cos^2\theta$$

$$\Rightarrow 4 + (e^2 + e'^2)^2 - 4(e^2 + e'^2) = (e^2 + e'^2)^2 - 4e^2e'^2 \cos^2\theta$$

$$\Rightarrow 1 - e^2 - e'^2 = -e^2e'^2 \cos^2\theta$$

$$\therefore \cos\theta = \frac{\sqrt{e^2 + e'^2 - 1}}{ee'} = \frac{\sqrt{\left(\frac{9}{25} + \frac{16}{25} - 1\right)}}{12/25} = 0$$

$$\therefore \theta = \frac{\pi}{2}$$

$$\sin\theta = 1$$

$$\therefore 2(1 + \sin^2\theta + \sin^4\theta) = 2(1 + 1 + 1) = 6$$

39. Let the sides of the rectangle be p and q.

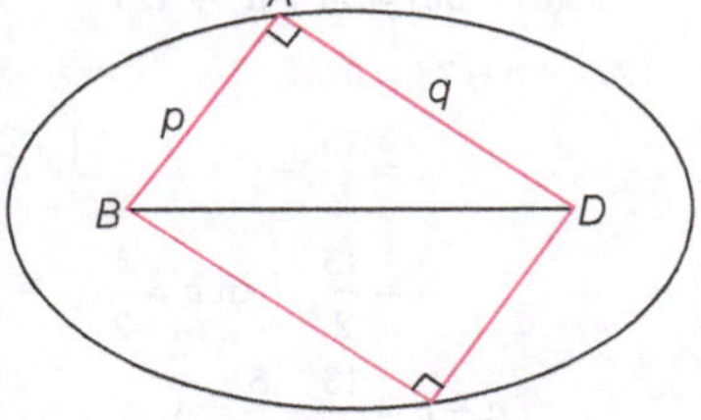

$\therefore$ Area of rectangle $= pq = 200$ ...(i)

and area of ellipse $= \pi ab = 200\pi$

$\therefore$ $ab = 200$ ...(ii)

Perimeter of rectangle $= 2(p + q)$ ...(iii)

In ΔABD,

Distance $BD = \sqrt{(p^2 + q^2)}$ = Distance between foci $= 2ae$

or $p^2 + q^2 = 4a^2e^2 = 4(a^2 - b^2)$ ...(iv)

Also, $BA + DA = 2a$ $[\because SP + S'P = 2a]$

$\Rightarrow$ $p + q = 2a$ ...(v)

From Eq. (iv),

$$(p + q)^2 - 2pq = 4(a^2 - b^2)$$

$\Rightarrow$ $(2a)^2 - 2 \times 200 = 4(a^2 - b^2)$ [from Eqs. (i) and (v)]

or $b^2 = 100$ or $b = 10$

From Eq. (ii), $a = 20$

From Eq. (iii),

$$P = 2(p + q) = 2(2a) = 4a = 80$$

$$\therefore P + 1 = 81$$

Hence, $\sqrt{(P + 1)} = 9$

40. Vertical line $x = h$, meets the ellipse $\frac{x^2}{4} + \frac{y^2}{3} = 1$ at

$$P\left(h, \frac{\sqrt{3}}{2}\sqrt{(4 - h^2)}\right) \text{ and } Q\left(h, \frac{-\sqrt{3}}{2}\sqrt{(4 - h^2)}\right)$$

By symmetry, tangents at P and Q will meet each other at X-axis.

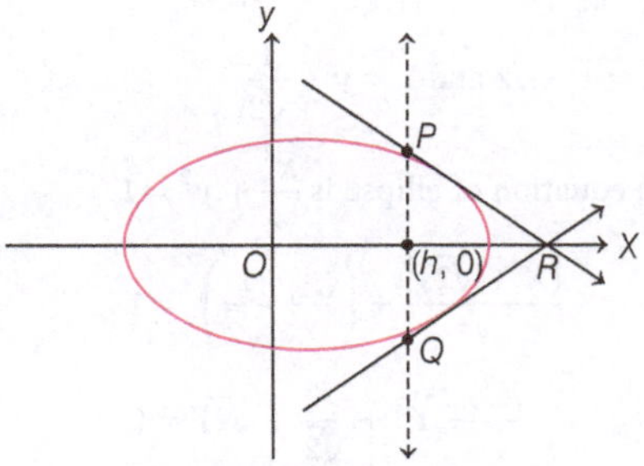

Tangent at P is $\frac{xh}{4} + \frac{y\sqrt{3}}{6}\sqrt{(4 - h^2)} = 1$

which meets X-axis at $R\left(\frac{4}{h}, 0\right)$.

Area of $\Delta PQR = \frac{1}{2} \times \sqrt{3}\sqrt{(4 - h^2)} \times \left(\frac{4}{h} - h\right)$

i.e. $$\Delta(h) = \frac{\sqrt{3}}{2}\frac{(4 - h^2)^{3/2}}{h}$$

$$\frac{d\Delta}{dh} = -\sqrt{3}\left[\frac{\sqrt{(4 - h^2)}(h^2 + 2)}{h^2}\right] < 0$$

$\therefore \Delta(h)$ is a decreasing function.

$$\therefore \frac{1}{2} \le h \le 1$$

$$\Rightarrow \Delta_{max} = \Delta\left(\frac{1}{2}\right) \text{ and } \Delta_{max} = \Delta(1)$$

$$\therefore \Delta_1 = \frac{\sqrt{3}}{2}\left(\frac{\left(4 - \frac{1}{4}\right)^{3/2}}{\frac{1}{2}}\right) = \frac{45}{8}\sqrt{5}$$

$$\Delta_2 = \frac{\sqrt{3}}{2} \cdot \frac{3\sqrt{3}}{1} = \frac{9}{2}$$

$$\therefore \frac{8}{\sqrt{5}}\Delta_1 - 8\Delta_2 = 45 - 36 = 9$$

41. Ellipse : $\frac{x^2}{9} + \frac{y^2}{5} = 1 \Rightarrow a = 3, b = \sqrt{5}$ and $e = \frac{2}{3}$

$$\therefore f_1 = 2 \text{ and } f_2 = -2$$

$$P_1 : y^2 = 8x \text{ and } P_2 : y^2 = -16x$$

$$T_1 : y = m_1x + \frac{2}{m_1}$$

It passes through $(-4, 0)$.

$$\therefore 0 = -4m_1 + \frac{2}{m_1} \Rightarrow m_1^2 = \frac{1}{2}$$

$$T_2 : y = m_2 x - \frac{4}{m_2}$$

It passes through (2, 0).

$\therefore \quad 0 = 2m_2 - \frac{4}{m_2} \Rightarrow m_2^2 = 2$

Hence, $\frac{1}{m_1^2} + m_2^2 = 4$

42. Let $X = x - \sqrt{2}$ and $Y = y - \frac{1}{\sqrt{2}}$

Given equation of ellipse is $\frac{x^2}{4} + y^2 = 1$

$\Rightarrow \quad \frac{(X+\sqrt{2})^2}{4} + \left(Y + \frac{1}{\sqrt{2}}\right)^2 = 1$

$\Rightarrow \quad \frac{X^2}{4} + Y^2 + \frac{X}{\sqrt{2}} + \sqrt{2}Y = 0$

Let equation of AB be $aX + bY = 1$

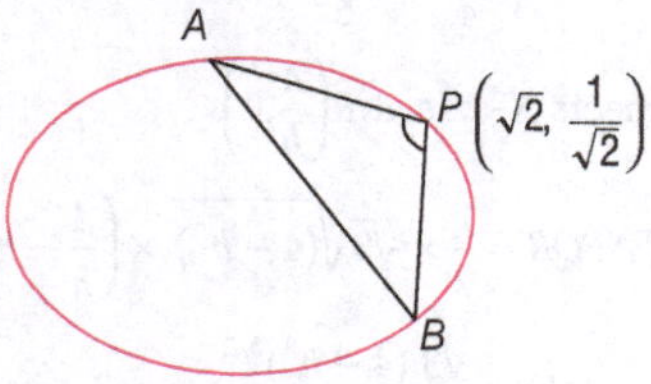

$\therefore$ By homogenisation, we get

$$\frac{X^2}{4} + Y^2 + \left(\frac{X}{\sqrt{2}} + \sqrt{2}Y\right)(aX + bY) = 0$$

$\because \quad AP \perp AB$, coefficient of X^2 + coefficient of $Y^2 = 0$

$\Rightarrow \quad \frac{a}{\sqrt{2}} + \sqrt{2}b + \frac{5}{4} = 0$

$\Rightarrow \quad \frac{-4a}{5\sqrt{2}} - \frac{4\sqrt{2}b}{5} = 1$

$\Rightarrow$ AB passes through fix point

$$\left(\frac{-4}{5\sqrt{2}}, \frac{-4\sqrt{2}}{5}\right) = \left(\frac{-4}{5\sqrt{2}} + \sqrt{2}, \frac{-4\sqrt{2}}{5} + \frac{1}{\sqrt{2}}\right)$$

$$= \left(\frac{6}{5\sqrt{2}}, \frac{-3}{5\sqrt{2}}\right)$$

$\Rightarrow \quad a = \frac{6}{5\sqrt{2}}$ and $b = \frac{-3}{5\sqrt{2}}$

$\Rightarrow \quad a^2 + b^2 = \frac{36+9}{50} = \frac{9}{10} = \frac{m}{n}$

Hence, $\left[\frac{m+n}{3}\right] = \left[\frac{19}{3}\right] = 6$

43. (4) Let $OC = b$ and $OS_1 = a$

Given, $OS_1 = ae = 6$

$\therefore$ Area of $\Delta OCS_1 = \frac{1}{2} \times OS_1 \times OC = 3b$

and semi-perimeter of

$$\Delta OCS_1 = \frac{1}{2}(OS_1 + OC + CS_1)$$

$$= \frac{1}{2}(6 + a + b) \quad \text{...(i)}$$

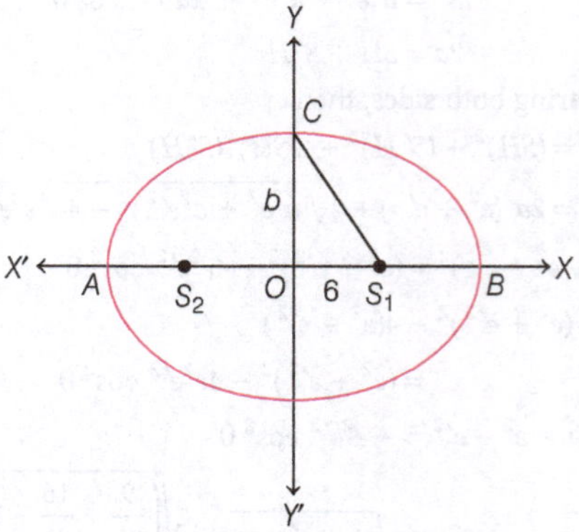

Radius of incircle of $\Delta OCS_1 = 1$ [given]

$\Rightarrow \quad \frac{3b}{\frac{1}{2}(6+a+b)} = 1$

$\Rightarrow \quad 5b = 6 + a$ ...(ii)

On squaring with sides, we get

$25b^2 = 36 + 12a + a^2$ $[\because b^2 = a^2 - a^2e^2 = a^2 - 36]$

$\Rightarrow \quad 25(a^2 - 36) = 36 + a^2 + 12a$

$\Rightarrow \quad 2a^2 - a - 78 = 0$

$\Rightarrow \quad a = \frac{13}{2}, -6$

When $\quad a = \frac{13}{2}$, then $b = \frac{5}{2}$

$\therefore \quad a - b = \frac{13}{2} - \frac{5}{2} = 4$

44. Equation of tangent to the ellipse $\frac{x^2}{a^2} + \frac{y^2}{b^2} = 1$ having slope m is

$$y = mx + \sqrt{a^2m^2 + b^2} \quad \text{...(i)}$$

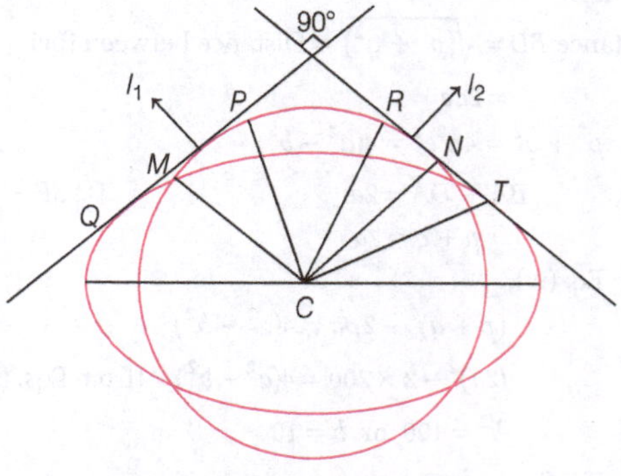

$\because$ Tangents are perpendicular to each other.

$\therefore \quad y = \frac{-x}{m} + \sqrt{\frac{a^2}{m^2} + b^2}$

$\Rightarrow \quad x + my = \sqrt{a^2 + b^2m^2}$ ...(ii)

From Eqs. (i) and (ii), intercept on auxiliary circle be $l_1 = PQ$ and $l_2 = RT$

Let CM and CN be perpendiculars to PQ and RT, respectively, where C is (0, 0).

$$(CM)^2 = \frac{a^2m^2 + b^2}{1 + m^2} \text{ and } (CN)^2 = \frac{a^2 + b^2m^2}{1 + m^2}$$

$\therefore \quad l_1 = PQ = 2PM$

$$\Rightarrow \quad l_1^2 = 4(PM)^2 = 4(CP^2 - CM^2)$$

$$= 4\left(a^2 - \frac{a^2m^2 + b^2}{1 + m^2}\right)$$

$$= \frac{4}{1 + m^2}(a^2 - b^2) \quad \text{...(iii)}$$

Also, $$l_2^2 = 4\left[a^2 - \frac{a^2 + b^2m^2}{1 + m^2}\right]$$

$$= \frac{4m^2(a^2 - b^2)}{1 + m^2}$$

Now, $$l_1^2 + l_2^2 = 4(a^2 - b^2)\left(\frac{1}{1 + m^2} + \frac{m^2}{1 + m^2}\right)$$

$$= 4(a^2 - b^2) = 4a^2e^2$$

$$= (2ae)^2 = (SS')^2$$

$$\therefore \quad l_1^2 + l_2^2 = (SS')^2$$

$$\Rightarrow \quad l_1^m + l_2^n = (SS')^p$$

$$\therefore \quad m = n = p = 2$$

$$\therefore \quad m^2 + n^2 + p^2 = 2^2 + 2^2 + 2^2 = 4 + 4 + 4 = 12$$

45. Given ellipse is $x^2 + 9y^2 = 9$

$$\Rightarrow \quad \frac{x^2}{9} + \frac{y^2}{1} = 1$$

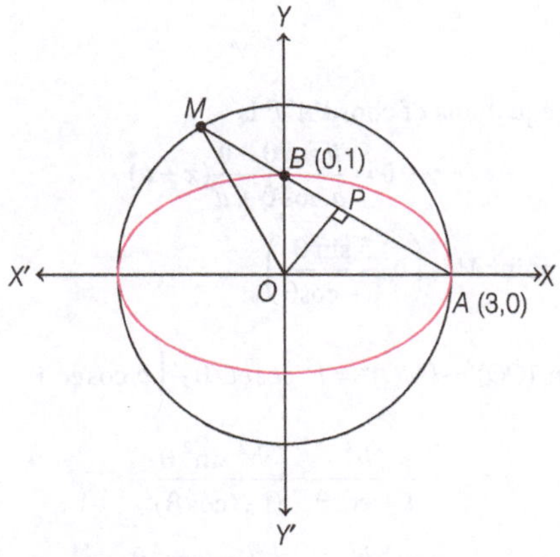

Now, equation of line AM is $y - 0 = \frac{1 - 0}{0 - 3}(x - 3)$

$$\Rightarrow \quad x + 3y - 3 = 0 \quad \text{...(i)}$$

and perpendicular distance from O is

$$OP = \left|\frac{-3}{\sqrt{1^2 + 3^2}}\right| = \frac{3}{\sqrt{10}} \text{ units}$$

Equation of auxiliary circle at M is $x^2 + y^2 = a^2$

$$\Rightarrow \quad x^2 + y^2 = 9 \quad \text{...(ii)}$$

$$\Rightarrow \quad 9(1 - y)^2 + y^2 = 9 \quad \text{[from Eq. (i)]}$$

$$\Rightarrow \quad 9 + 9y^2 - 18y + y^2 = 9$$

$$\Rightarrow \quad y = \frac{9}{5} \text{ and } x = \frac{-12}{5}$$

$$\Rightarrow \quad M = \left(\frac{-12}{5}, \frac{9}{5}\right) \text{ and } A(3, 0)$$

$$\therefore \quad AM = \sqrt{\left(\frac{27}{5}\right)^2 + \left(\frac{9}{5}\right)^2} = \frac{9\sqrt{10}}{5}$$

$\therefore$ Area of triangle $= \frac{1}{2} \times AM \times OP$

$$= \frac{1}{2} \times \frac{9\sqrt{10}}{5} \times \frac{3}{\sqrt{10}}$$

$$= \frac{27}{10} \text{ sq. units} = 2.7 \text{ sq. units}$$

46. Given ellipse is $\frac{x^2}{25} + \frac{y^2}{16} = 1$ ...(i)

$$\because \quad a = 5 \text{ and } b = 4$$

$$\therefore \quad e = \sqrt{1 - \frac{16}{25}} = \frac{3}{5}$$

$$\therefore \quad \text{Focus} = (\pm\, ae, 0) = (\pm\, 3, 0) \Rightarrow m = 3$$

Equation of chord whose middle point is $\left(\frac{1}{2}, \frac{2}{5}\right)$.

$$\Rightarrow \quad \frac{x}{25}\left(\frac{1}{2}\right) + \frac{y}{16}\left(\frac{2}{5}\right) = \frac{\left(\frac{1}{2}\right)^2}{25} + \frac{\left(\frac{2}{5}\right)^2}{16}$$

$$\Rightarrow \quad \frac{x}{50} + \frac{y}{40} = \frac{1}{50} \Rightarrow y = \frac{-4}{5}(x - 1)$$

From Eq. (i),

$$\frac{x^2}{25} + \frac{\left(\frac{-4}{5}\right)^2(x - 1)^2}{16} = 1$$

$$\Rightarrow \quad x^2 - x - 12 = 0$$

$$\Rightarrow \quad x_1 = 4, x_2 = -3$$

$\therefore$ Length of chord $= \sqrt{(x_1 - x_2)^2 + (y_1 - y_2)^2}$

$$= |(x_1 - x_2)\sqrt{1 + m^2}|$$

$$\Rightarrow \quad l^2 = (7)^2\left(1 + \frac{16}{25}\right) = \frac{49}{25} \times 41$$

$$\Rightarrow \quad \frac{25l^2}{41} = 49$$

$\therefore$ Roots of quadratic equation be 3 and 49.

$\therefore$ Required equation is $x^2 - 52x + 147 = 0$

$\Rightarrow \alpha = 52, \beta = 147$

Hence, $\beta - \alpha = 147 - 52 = 95$

47. $\because$ Normal at $P(\alpha, \beta)$ to the ellipse $\frac{x^2}{a^2} + \frac{y^2}{b^2} = 1$

$$\frac{a^2(x - \alpha)}{\alpha} = \frac{b^2(y - \beta)}{\beta} \quad \text{...(i)}$$

This passes through (h, k)

$\Rightarrow \quad \dfrac{a^2(h-\alpha)}{\alpha} = \dfrac{b^2(k-\beta)}{\beta}$

$\Rightarrow \quad a^2\beta(h-\alpha) = b^2\alpha(k-\beta)$

$\Rightarrow \quad [(h-\alpha)^2 + b^2\alpha]\beta = b^2k\alpha$

$\Rightarrow \quad [a^2h - (a^2-b^2)\alpha]^2\beta^2 = b^4k^2\alpha^2 \qquad \text{...(ii)}$

Also, (α, β) lies on the ellipse, which means

$$\frac{\alpha^2}{a^2} + \frac{\beta^2}{b^2} = 1 \qquad \text{...(iii)}$$

Eliminating β from Eqs. (ii) and (iii), we get

$\Rightarrow \quad (a^4h^2 + \alpha^2(a^2-\beta^2)^2 - 2a^2h\alpha(a^2-b^2)$

$$\left(\frac{a^2-\alpha^2}{a^2}\right)b^2 = b^4k^2\alpha^2$$

$\Rightarrow \quad a^4\dfrac{(a^2-b^2)^2a^2}{a^2} - 2\alpha^3h(a^2-b^2)b^2$

$$+\alpha^2(a^2b^2h^2 + b^4k^2 - b^2(a^2-b^2)$$

$$+\alpha(2a^2b^2h(a^2-b^2)) - a^4b^2h^2 = 0.$$

This being 4th degree equation in α, we get 4 values of α say, x_1, x_2, x_3, x_4.

$\therefore \quad x_1 + x_2 + x_3 + x_4 = \dfrac{2b^2h(a^2-b^2)a^2}{b^2(a^2-b^2)^2} = \dfrac{2a^2h}{a^2-b^2}$

$$\frac{1}{x_1} + \frac{1}{x_2} + \frac{1}{x_3} + \frac{1}{x_4} = \frac{2a^2b^2h(a^2-b^2)}{a^4b^2h^2} = \frac{2(a^2-b^2)}{a^2h}$$

$\therefore \quad (x_1 + x_2 + x_3 + x_4)\left(\dfrac{1}{x_1} + \dfrac{1}{x_2} + \dfrac{1}{x_3} + \dfrac{1}{x_4}\right)$

$$= \left(\frac{2a^2h}{a^2-b^2}\right)\left(\frac{2(a^2-b^2)}{a^2h}\right) = 4$$

$$= \frac{100}{\lambda}$$

$\therefore \quad \dfrac{100}{\lambda} = 4$

$\lambda = 25 \Rightarrow \lambda = 25$

48. Let ABA' be the semi-ellipse archway such that $AA' = 30\,ft$ and $OB = b$ (let)

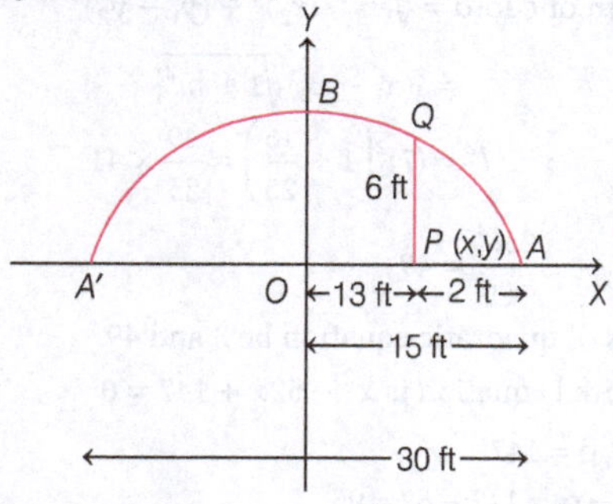

Let the equation of ellipse be

$$\frac{x^2}{a^2} + \frac{y^2}{b^2} = 1 \qquad \text{...(i)}$$

Let $P(x, y)$ be a point at a distance $2\,ft$ from point A and man stands at P touches the ellipse at Q.

$\therefore \quad PQ = 6, AA' = 30$

$\Rightarrow \quad 2a = 30$

$\Rightarrow \quad a = 15$

$\therefore \quad OP = 15 - 2 = 13$

Here, the point $Q(13, 6)$ lies on ellipse (i).

$\therefore \quad \dfrac{(13)^2}{(15)^2} + \dfrac{6^2}{b^2} = 1$

$\Rightarrow \quad \dfrac{36}{b^2} = 1 - \dfrac{169}{225}$

$\Rightarrow \quad b^2 = \dfrac{225 \times 9}{14}$

$\Rightarrow \quad b = \dfrac{45}{\sqrt{14}}$

$\therefore$ The greatest height of the arch is $\dfrac{45}{\sqrt{14}}\,ft$

$\therefore \quad \lambda = 45$

49. (A) Let point P be $(a\cos\theta, b\sin\theta)$. The equation of tangent at point P is $\dfrac{x}{a}\cos\theta + \dfrac{y}{b}\sin\theta = 1$

The point Q is $(0, b\operatorname{cosec}\theta)$.

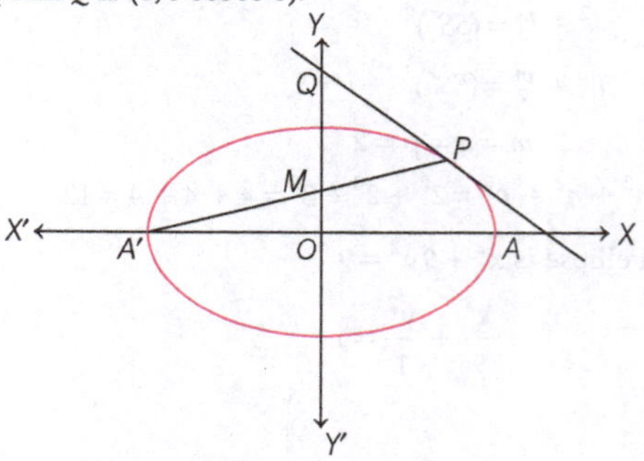

The equations of chord $A'P$ is

$$y - 0 = \frac{b\sin\theta - 0}{a\cos\theta + a}(x + a)$$

The point M is $\left(0, \dfrac{b\sin\theta}{1+\cos\theta}\right)$

Then, $(OQ)^2 - (MQ)^2 = b^2\operatorname{cosec}^2\theta - \left(b\operatorname{cosec}\theta - \dfrac{b\sin\theta}{1+\cos\theta}\right)^2$

$$= \frac{2b^2}{1+\cos\theta} - \frac{b^2\sin^2\theta}{(1+\cos\theta)^2}$$

$$= \frac{2b^2}{1+\cos\theta} - \frac{b^2(1-\cos^2\theta)}{(1+\cos\theta)^2}$$

$$= \frac{2b^2}{(1+\cos\theta)} - \frac{b^2(1-\cos\theta)}{(1+\cos\theta)}$$

$$= b^2 = 4$$

(B) We know that two diameters $y = m_1x$, $y = m_2x$ are conjugate diameters of $\frac{x^2}{a^2}+\frac{y^2}{b^2}=1$ if $m_1m_2 = -\frac{b^2}{a^2}$

$$\Rightarrow \quad 1\times -\frac{2}{3} = \frac{-b^2}{a^2} \quad \text{or} \quad b^2 = \frac{2}{3}a^2$$

$$\text{or} \quad a^2(1-e^2) = \frac{2}{3}a^2 \quad \text{or} \quad 1-e^2 = \frac{2}{3} \quad \text{or} \quad e^2 = \frac{1}{3}$$

$$\text{Hence, } 4\left(1+\frac{1}{3}+\frac{1}{9}+\ldots\infty\right) = 4\left(\frac{1}{1-\frac{1}{3}}\right) = 6$$

(C) Since, $2x^2+3y^2 = 6 \Rightarrow \frac{x^2}{3}+\frac{y^2}{2} = 1$

By condition of tangency, $(2h)^2 = 3\times(k)^2+2$

Therefore, the locus of $P(h,k)$ is

$$4x^2-3y^2 = 2 \quad \text{(which is hyperbola)}$$

$$\text{or} \quad \frac{x^2}{1/2}-\frac{y^2}{2/3} = 1$$

$$\text{Hence,} \quad \frac{2}{3} = \frac{1}{2}(e^2-1)$$

$$\Rightarrow \quad e^2 = 1+\frac{4}{3} \quad \text{or} \quad 3e^2 = 7$$

(D) $\left(\pm ae, \frac{b^2}{a}\right)$ are extremities of the latusrectum having positive ordinates, then

$$a^2e^2 = -2\left(\frac{b^2}{a}-2\right) \quad \ldots\text{(i)}$$

$$\text{But} \quad b^2 = a^2(1-e^2) \quad \ldots\text{(ii)}$$

From Eqs. (i) and (ii), we get

$$1a^2e^2 = -2(a(1-e^2)-2)$$

$$\Rightarrow \quad a^2e^2-2ae^2+2a-4 = 0$$

$$\Rightarrow \quad ae^2(a-2)+2(a-2) = 0$$

$$\therefore \quad (ae^2+2)(a-2) = 0$$

$$\text{Hence,} \quad a = 2$$

50. (A) Since, (0, 0) lies on the director circle and mid-point of foci (2, 2) is the center of the circle.

Hence, radius of director circle $= OC$

$$r = \sqrt{(4+4)} = 2\sqrt{2}$$

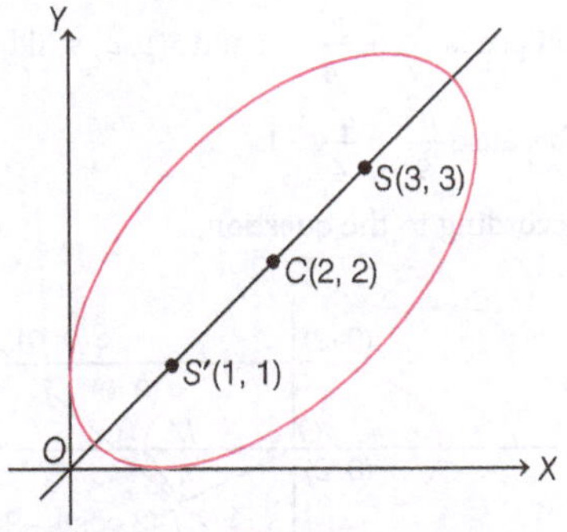

Therefore, the area is πr^2 i.e. $8\pi = \pi\lambda$ [given]

$$\therefore \quad \lambda = 8$$

(B) Equation of normal at $(5\cos\theta,\ 4\sin\theta)$ is $5x\sec\theta - 4y\,\text{cosec}\,\theta = 9$ and it passes through $P(0,\lambda)$.

Then, $0-4\lambda\ \text{cosec}\,\theta = 9$

$$\text{or} \quad \lambda = -\frac{9}{4}\sin\theta$$

$$\text{or} \quad |\lambda| = \frac{9}{4}|\sin\theta| < \frac{9}{4}$$

$$\therefore \quad p = \frac{9}{4} \Rightarrow 4p = 9$$

(C) Let the orbit of the earth be the ellipse

$$\frac{x^2}{a^2}+\frac{y^2}{b^2} = 1 \quad \ldots\text{(i)}$$

Its major axis $= 2a = 186\times10^6$ miles [given]

i.e. $a = 93\times10^6$ miles and $e = 1/60$ [given]

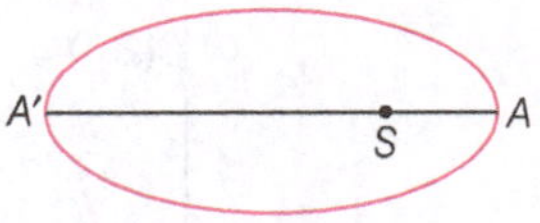

Let the Sun be at the focus $S(ae,0)$. Then, the Earth will be at shortest and longest distance from the Sun when the Earth is at the extremities of the major axis which are respectively nearest and farthest from this focus S.

$\therefore$ Shortest distance of the Earth from the Sun

$= SA$, where S is $(ae, 0)$ and A is $(a,0)$

$= a-ae = a(1-e)$

$= (93\times10^6)(1+(1/60))$

$= 91450000$ miles

$= 914.5\times10^5$ miles and longest distance of Earth from the Sun

$= SA'$, where S is $(ae,0)$ and A' is $(-a,0)$

$= a+ae$

$= a(1+e)$

$= (93\times10^6)(1+(1/60))$

$= 94550000$ miles $= 945.5\times10^5$ miles

$$\therefore \quad \mu-(\lambda+1) = 945.5-914.5-1 = 30$$

(D) Equation of chord whose mid-point (0,3) is $T = S_1$

$$\Rightarrow \quad 0+\frac{3\cdot y}{25}-1 = 0+\frac{9}{25}-1$$

$$\Rightarrow \quad y = 3$$

It intersects the ellipse $\frac{x^2}{16}+\frac{y^2}{25} = 1$

$$\text{At } y = 3, \quad \frac{x^2}{16} = 1-\frac{3^2}{25} = \frac{16}{25} \quad \text{or} \quad x = \pm\frac{16}{5}$$

$\therefore$ Length of chord $= \frac{32}{5} = \frac{4\lambda}{5}$ [given]

$$\therefore \quad \lambda = 8$$

51. (A) Let $S = 9x^2+8y^2-36x-16y-28$

$\therefore$ Value of S at (2,6)

$$S_1 = 9(2)^2+8(6)^2-36(2)-16(6)-28$$

$$= 36+288-72-96-28 = 128 > 0$$

$\therefore$ Point (2,6) lies outside the ellipse.

The equation of the given ellipse be rewritten as

$$9(x-2)^2+8(y-1)^2=72$$

$$\Rightarrow \quad \frac{(x-2)^2}{8}+\frac{(y-1)^2}{9}=1$$

Centre of ellipse is (2,1) and axis parallel to Y-axis.

$\therefore$ Vertices are $x-2=0$ and $y-1=\pm 3$

or (2,–2) and (2,4)

$\therefore$ Minimum distance, $L = PA = 2$

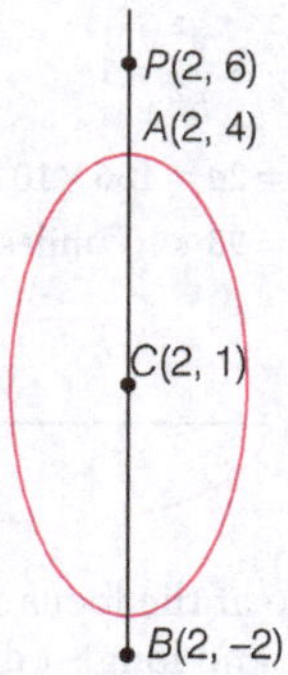

and maximum distance, $G = PB = 8$

Then, $L+G=10$ and $G-L=6$

(B) Let $S=4x^2+9y^2+8x-36y+4$

$\therefore$ Value of S at (1,2) is

$$S_1=4(1)^2+9(2)^2+8(1)-36(2)+4$$
$$=4+36+8-72+4$$
$$=-20<0$$

$\therefore$ Point (1,2) lies inside the ellipse.

The equation of the given ellipse be rewritten as

$$4(x+1)^2+9(y-2)^2=36$$

or $$\frac{(x+1)^2}{9}+\frac{(y-2)^2}{4}=1$$

$\therefore$ Centre of ellipse is $(-1, 2)$ and axis parallel to X-axis.

$\therefore$ Vertices are $x+1=\pm 3$ and $y-2=0$

or (-4,2) and (2,2)

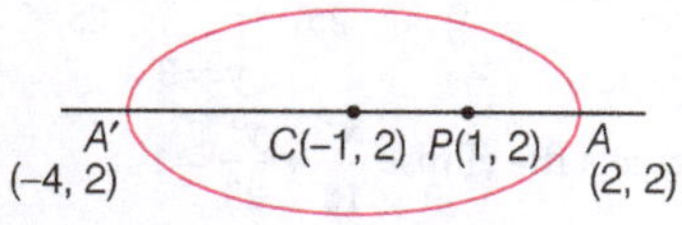

$\therefore$ Minimum distance, $L = PA = 1$

and Maximum distance

$$G = PA' = AA' - PA = 6-1=5$$

$\therefore$ $$L+G=6 \text{ and } G-L=4.$$

(C) Here, $3x+4y=0$ and $4x-3y=0$ are mutually perpendicular lines, then substituting

$$\frac{3x+4y}{\sqrt{(3^2+4^2)}}=X \text{ and } \frac{4x-3y}{\sqrt{((4)^2+(-3)^2)}}=Y$$

Then, the given equation can be written as

$$4X^2+9Y^2=36 \Rightarrow \frac{X^2}{9}+\frac{Y^2}{4}=1$$

$\therefore$ Vertices, $X=\pm 3$ and $Y=0$

or $$\frac{3x+4y}{5}=\pm 3, \frac{4x-3y}{5}=0$$

or $$3x+4y=\pm 15, y=\frac{4x}{3}$$

Vertices are $\left(\frac{9}{5},\frac{12}{5}\right)$ and $\left(-\frac{9}{5},\frac{-12}{5}\right)$

$\because$ Given point is a vertex.

$\therefore$ Minimum distance $L=0$

and maximum distance G = Length of major axis $=2\times 3=6$

Then, $L+G=6$ and $G-L=6$

(D) Given ellipse is $25x^2+9y^2=225$

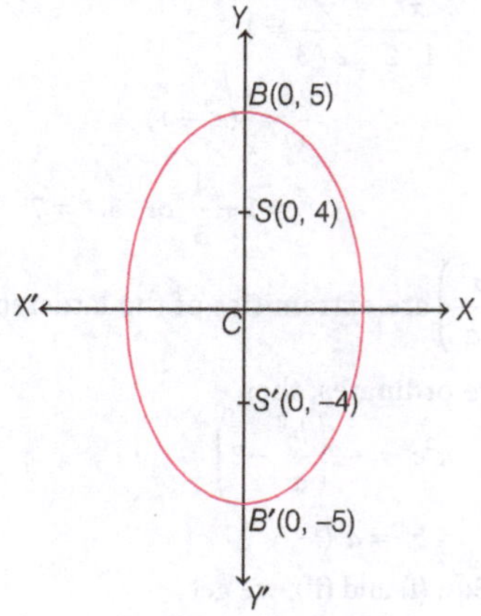

or $$\frac{x^2}{9}+\frac{y^2}{25}=1$$

$\therefore$ Foci are $(0, \pm\sqrt{(25-9)})$ or $(0, \pm 4)$

and vertices are B (0, 5) and B' (0, –5)

$\therefore$ Minimum distance $L = SB = 1$

and maximum distance $G = SB' = 4+5=9$

Then, $L+G=10$ and $G-L=8$

52. Given ellipse is $\frac{x^2}{9}+\frac{y^2}{4}=1$ and $S(p, q)$ will be outside of ellipse because $\frac{p^2}{9}+\frac{q^2}{4}>1$.

Now, according to the question,

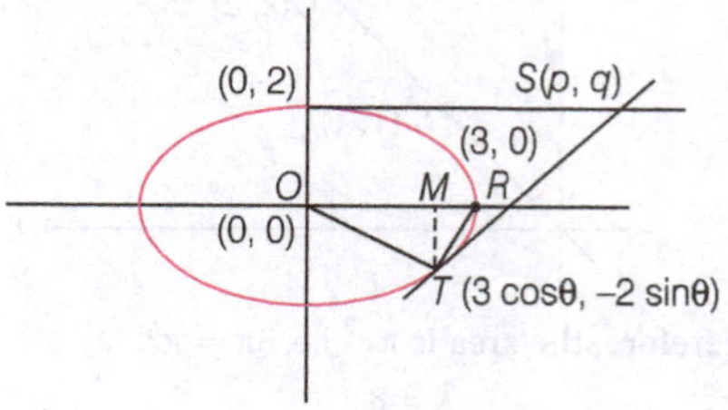

Here, $TM = 2\sin\theta$

$$\text{ar}(\Delta ORT) = \frac{3}{2} \qquad \text{[given]}$$

$$\Rightarrow \quad \left|\frac{1}{2}\times 3\times 2\sin\theta\right| = \frac{3}{2}$$

$$\Rightarrow \quad |\sin\theta| = \frac{1}{2}$$

$$\Rightarrow \quad \theta = -\frac{\pi}{6} \text{ or } \frac{11\pi}{6}$$

$$\Rightarrow \quad T \equiv \left(\frac{3\sqrt{3}}{2}, -1\right)$$

Now, tangent at (2, 0)

$$\Rightarrow \quad T = 0$$

$$\Rightarrow \quad \frac{x(0)}{9} + \frac{y(2)}{4} = 1$$

$$\Rightarrow \quad y = 2 \qquad \text{...(i)}$$

and tangent at $\left(\frac{3\sqrt{3}}{2}, -1\right)$

$$\Rightarrow \quad \frac{x\left(\frac{3\sqrt{3}}{2}\right)}{9} + \frac{y(-1)}{4} = 1 \qquad \text{...(ii)}$$

By solving Eqs. (i) and (ii), we get

$$p = 3\sqrt{3}, q = 2$$

53.

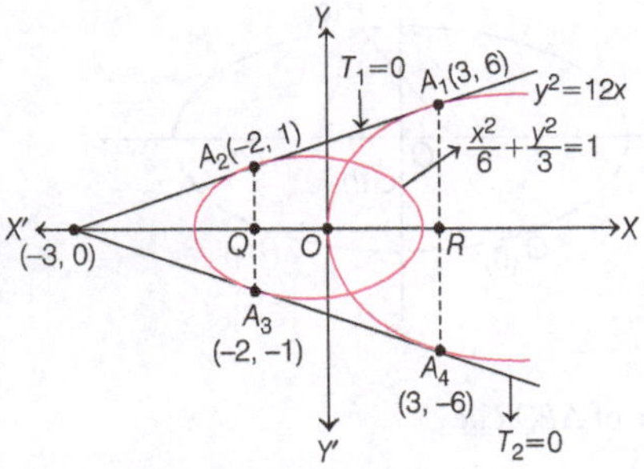

Given equation of ellipse

$$E: \frac{x^2}{6} + \frac{y^2}{3} = 1 \qquad \text{...(i)}$$

and equation of parabola

$$P: y^2 = 12x \qquad \text{...(ii)}$$

Now, equation of tangent on Eq. (i) is given by

$$y = mx \pm \sqrt{6m^2 + 3} \qquad \text{...(iii)}$$

and also equation of tangent on Eq. (ii) is given by

$$y = mx + \frac{3}{m} \qquad \text{...(iv)}$$

On comparing Eqs. (iii) and (iv), we get

$$\frac{3}{m} = \pm\sqrt{6m^2+3} \Rightarrow \frac{9}{m^2} = 6m^2 + 3$$

$$\Rightarrow \quad 9 = 6m^4 + 3m^2$$

$$\Rightarrow \quad 2m^4 + m^2 - 3 = 0$$

$$\Rightarrow \quad 2m^4 + 3m^2 - 2m^2 - 3 = 0$$

$$\Rightarrow \quad m^2(2m^2+3) - 1(2m^2+3) = 0$$

$$\Rightarrow \quad (2m^2+3)(m^2-1) = 0$$

$$\because \quad 2m^2 + 3 > 0, \forall m$$

$$\therefore \quad m^2 - 1 = 0 \Rightarrow m = \pm 1$$

$\therefore$ Equations of common tangents are $y = x + 3$ and $y = -x - 3$ (putting $m = \pm 1$)

and hence point of contact for parabola is $\left(\frac{a}{m^2}, \frac{2a}{m}\right)$

i.e. $\quad A_1 \equiv (3, 6)$, $8A_4 \equiv (3, -6)$

Now, let $A_2 \equiv (x_1, y_1)$.

So, equation of tangent is $T = 0$

$$\Rightarrow \quad \frac{xx_1}{6} + \frac{yy_1}{3} = 1$$

On comparing it with $y = x + 3$,

i.e. $\quad x - y = -3$

$$\frac{x}{-3} + \frac{y}{3} = 1, \text{ we get}$$

$$\frac{x_1}{6} = -\frac{1}{3} \Rightarrow x_1 = -2$$

and $\quad \frac{y_1}{3} = \frac{1}{3} \Rightarrow y_1 = 1$

Hence, $\quad A_2 \equiv (-2, 1)$

Since, A_3 is mirror image of A_2 in X-axis.

So, by symmetry, $A_3 \equiv (-2, -1)$.

Now, point of intersection of $T_1 = 0$ and $T_2 = 0$ is $(-3, 0)$.

(by putting $y = 0$ in $y = x + 3$, we get $x = -3$)

and also Area of quadrilateral $A_1A_2A_3A_4$

$$= \frac{1}{2} \times (\text{Sum of parallel sides}) \times (\text{Distance between parallel sides})$$

$$= \frac{1}{2} \times (12 + 2) \times 5 = \frac{1}{2} \times 14 \times 5$$

$= 35$ sq units

54. (c) Given equation of the ellipse is $\frac{x^2}{4} + \frac{y^2}{3} = 1$ and $H(\alpha, 0)$, $0 < \alpha < 2$ be a point.

Clearly, $\alpha = 2\cos\phi$

Now, tangent $E(2\cos\phi, \sqrt{3}\sin\phi)$ to ellipse $\frac{x^2}{4} + \frac{y^2}{3} = 1$

i.e. $\frac{x\cos\phi}{2} + \frac{y\sin\phi}{\sqrt{3}} = 1$ intersects X-axis at $G(2\sec\phi, 0)$.

Thus, area of $\Delta FGH = \frac{1}{2}(2\sec\phi - 2\cos\phi)\cdot 2\sin\phi$

$$= 2\sin^2\phi \cdot \tan\phi$$

$$\Delta = (1 - \cos 2\phi)\cdot\tan\phi$$

For condition (I)

If $\phi = \frac{\pi}{4}$, then $\Delta = \left(1 - \cos\frac{\pi}{2}\right)\cdot\tan\frac{\pi}{4} = 1$

$\therefore \quad$ (I) $\rightarrow$ (Q)

For condition (II)

If $\phi = \frac{\pi}{3}$, then $\Delta = 2 \cdot \left(\frac{\sqrt{3}}{2}\right)^2 \cdot \sqrt{3} = \frac{3\sqrt{3}}{2}$

$\therefore$ (II) $\rightarrow$ (T)

For condition (III)

If $\phi = \frac{\pi}{6}$, then $\Delta = 2 \cdot \left(\frac{1}{2}\right)^2 \frac{1}{\sqrt{3}} = \frac{1}{2\sqrt{3}}$

$\therefore$ (III) $\rightarrow$ (S)

For condition (IV)

If $\phi = \frac{\pi}{12}$, then $\Delta = \left(1 - \frac{\sqrt{3}}{2}\right) \cdot (2 - \sqrt{3})$

$$= \frac{(2-\sqrt{3})^2}{2} = \frac{(\sqrt{3}-1)^4}{8}$$

$\therefore$ (IV) $\rightarrow$ (P)

55. As we know that in a triangle, sides joining the mid-points of two sides is half and parallel to the third side.

$\therefore$ $$M_1M_2 = \frac{1}{2} QQ'$$

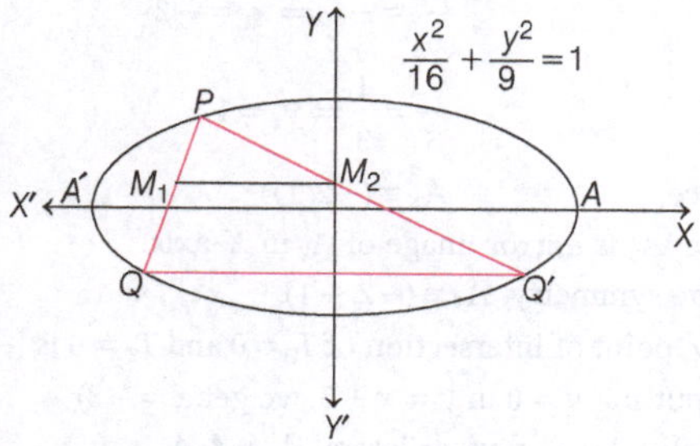

Maximum value of QQ' is AA'.

Hence, maximum value of $M_1M_2 = \frac{1}{2} AA' = 4$

56. Equation of given parabola is

$$y^2 = 4\lambda x \quad \text{... (i)}$$

So, the end point of the latusrectum of the parabola (i) is $P(\lambda, 2\lambda)$ and the given ellipse $\frac{x^2}{a^2} + \frac{y^2}{b^2} = 1$, passes through point $P(\lambda, 2\lambda)$.

On differentiating the equation of parabola, w.r.t. x, we get

$$\frac{dy}{dx} = \frac{2\lambda}{y}$$

$\therefore$ Slope of tangent to the parabola at point P is $m_1 = 1$

Similarly, on differentiating the equation of given ellipse, $\frac{x^2}{a^2} + \frac{y^2}{b^2} = 1$, w.r.t x, we get

$$\frac{2x}{a^2} + \frac{2y}{b^2}\frac{dy}{dx} = 0 \Rightarrow \frac{dy}{dx} = -\frac{b^2x}{a^2y}$$

$\therefore$ Slope of tangent to the ellipse at point P is $m_2 = -\frac{b^2}{2a^2}$

$\because$ It is given that the tangents are perpendiculars to each other. So,

$$m_1m_2 = -1 \Rightarrow (1)\left(-\frac{b^2}{2a^2}\right) = -1$$

$$\Rightarrow \quad \frac{b^2}{a^2} = 2 \Rightarrow b = \sqrt{2}a$$

$\therefore$ Eccentricity of ellipse $\frac{x^2}{a^2} + \frac{y^2}{b^2} = 1$ will be

$$e = \sqrt{1 - \frac{a^2}{b^2}} = \sqrt{1 - \frac{1}{2}} = \frac{1}{\sqrt{2}} \quad [\because b > a]$$

Exercise 3 - Challenging Problems

1. Let the vertices of the equilateral triangle P, Q and R and whose eccentric angles be α, β and γ.

Let the centroid of ΔPQR be (h, k).

Then,

$$h = \frac{a}{3}(\cos\alpha + \cos\beta + \cos\gamma) \quad \text{...(i)}$$

and $$k = \frac{b}{3}(\sin\alpha + \sin\beta + \sin\gamma) \quad \text{...(ii)}$$

$\because$ ΔPQR is equilateral.

$\therefore$ Centroid of the ΔPQR is same as the circumcentre.

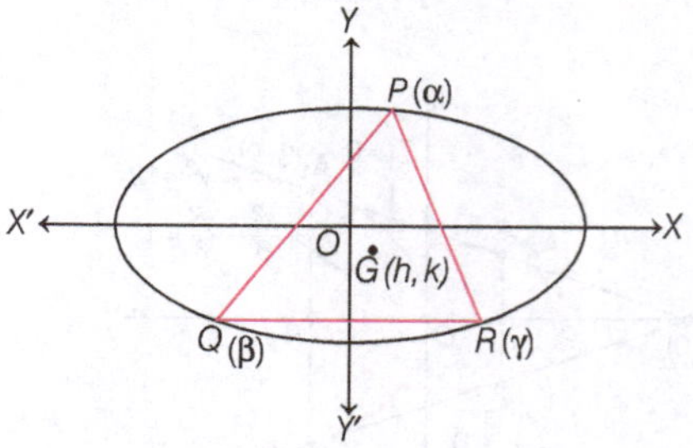

$\because$ Circumcentre of ΔPQR be

$$h = \frac{(a^2 - b^2)}{4a}\{\cos\alpha + \cos\beta + \cos\gamma + \cos(\alpha + \beta + \gamma)\}$$

$$k = \frac{(b^2 - a^2)}{4b}\{\sin\alpha + \sin\beta + \sin\gamma - \sin(\alpha + \beta + \gamma)\}$$

Using Eqs. (i) and (ii), then

$$\cos(\alpha + \beta + \gamma) = h\left(\frac{4a}{a^2 - b^2} - \frac{3}{a}\right) = \frac{h(a^2 + 3b^2)}{a(a^2 - b^2)} \quad \text{...(iii)}$$

and $$\sin(\alpha + \beta + \gamma) = \frac{(3a^2 + b^2)k}{b(a^2 - b^2)} \quad \text{...(iv)}$$

On squaring and adding Eqs. (iii) and (iv), we get

$\therefore$ $$I = \frac{(a^2 + 3b^2)^2}{a^2(a^2 - b^2)^2}h^2 + \frac{(3a^2 + b^2)^2}{b^2(a^2 - b^2)^2}k^2$$

Hence, locus of (h, k) is

$$\frac{(a^2 + 3b^2)^2}{a^2}x^2 + \frac{(3a^2 + b^2)^2}{b^2}y^2 = (a^2 - b^2)^2.$$

2. Let these normals meet in (h, k), then their feet lie on the curve

$$b^2x(k-y) + a^2y(x-h) = 0$$

$$\Rightarrow \quad (a^2-b^2)xy + b^2kx - a^2hy = 0$$

$\therefore$ The locus passes through the points where the lines $lx + my - 1 = 0$ and $l'x + m'y - 1 = 0$ meet the given ellipse,

$$\left(\frac{x^2}{a^2}+\frac{y^2}{b^2}-1\right) - \lambda(lx+my-1)(l'x+m'y-1)$$

$$\equiv (a^2-b^2)xy + b^2kx - a^2hy$$

On comparing the coefficients of x^2, y^2 and constant terms, we get

$$\frac{1}{a^2} - \lambda ll' = 0, \frac{1}{b^2} - \lambda mm' = 0, -1-\lambda = 0$$

$$\therefore \quad \frac{1}{a^2} + ll' = 0 \text{ and } \frac{1}{b^2} + mm' = 0 \quad [\because \lambda = -1]$$

$$\therefore \quad a^2ll' = b^2mm' = -1$$

3. Let the length of major and minor axes of an ellipse be $2a$ and $2b$ and if the centre of the ellipse be $C(h, k)$

If $S(x_1, y_1)$ and $S'(x_2, y_2)$ are two foci of the ellipse, then

$$SS' = 2ae$$

$$\Rightarrow \quad (x_1-x_2)^2 + (y_1-y_2)^2 = 4a^2e^2$$

$$\Rightarrow \quad (x_1+x_2)^2 - 4x_1x_2 + (y_1+y_2)^2 - 4y_1y_2 = 4(a^2-b^2)$$

$$\Rightarrow \quad (2h)^2 + (2k)^2 - 4(x_1x_2+y_1y_2) = 4(a^2-b^2) \quad \text{...(i)}$$

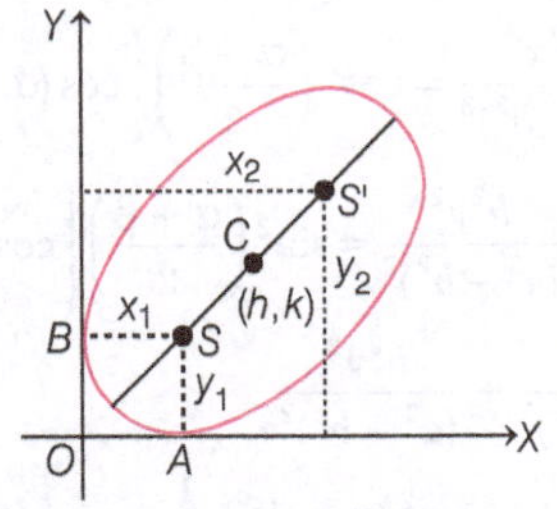

Since, the ellipse always slides between the two fixed lines OX and OY, they are always tangents to it. Therefore, y_1, y_2 and x_1, x_2 are perpendicular distances of the foci from their tangents whose product are always b^2.

Hence, $\quad x_1x_2 = y_1y_2 = 6^2$

$\Rightarrow$ Eq. (i) becomes $4h^2 + 4k^2 - 8b^2 = 4(a^2-b^2)$

$$\Rightarrow \quad h^2 + k^2 = a^2 + b^2$$

$\therefore$ Locus of the centre (h, k) is the circle

$$x^2 + y^2 = a^2 + b^2$$

4. Let the coordinates of P and Q on the ellipse $\frac{x^2}{a^2}+\frac{y^2}{b^2}=1$ be

$$P \equiv (a\cos\alpha, b\sin\alpha) \text{ and } Q = (a\cos\beta, b\sin\beta)$$

Equation of tangents at P and Q are

$$\frac{x}{a}\cos\alpha + \frac{y}{b}\sin\alpha = 1 \quad \text{...(i)}$$

and $$\frac{x}{a}\cos\beta + \frac{y}{b}\sin\beta = 1 \quad \text{...(ii)}$$

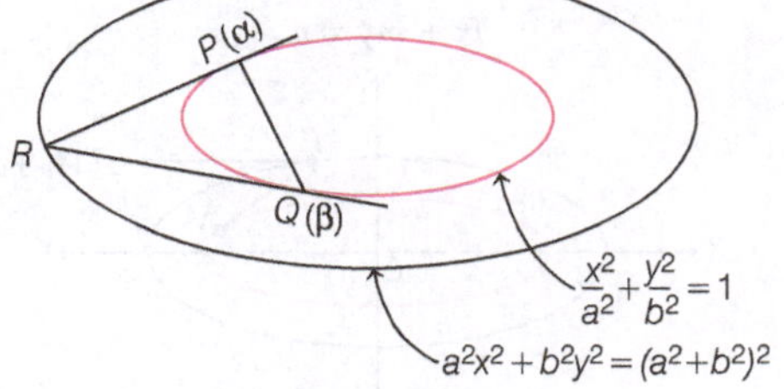

Point of intersection of Eqs. (i) and (ii) are

$$R\left\{a\frac{\cos\left(\frac{\alpha+\beta}{2}\right)}{\cos\left(\frac{\alpha-\beta}{2}\right)}, b\frac{\sin\left(\frac{\alpha+\beta}{2}\right)}{\cos\left(\frac{\alpha-\beta}{2}\right)}\right\}$$

This point R lies on the ellipse $a^2x^2 + b^2y^2 = (a^2+b^2)^2$

$$\Rightarrow a^4\cos^2\left(\frac{\alpha+\beta}{2}\right) + b^4\sin^2\left(\frac{\alpha+\beta}{2}\right)$$

$$= (a^2+b^2)^2\cos^2\left(\frac{\alpha-\beta}{2}\right) \quad \text{...(iii)}$$

The equation of the line of perpendicular from Q on the tangent at P is

$$a\sin\alpha(x - a\cos\beta) - b\cos\alpha(y - b\sin\beta) = 0 \quad \text{...(iv)}$$

Similarly, the equation to other perpendicular will be

$$a\sin\beta(x - a\cos\beta) - b\cos\beta(y - b\sin\alpha) = 0 \quad \text{...(v)}$$

On solving Eqs. (iv) and (v), we get

$$x = \frac{a^3}{a^2+b^2}\cdot\frac{\cos\left(\frac{\alpha+\beta}{2}\right)}{\cos\left(\frac{\alpha-\beta}{2}\right)}$$

and $$y = \frac{b^3}{a^2+b^2}\cdot\frac{\sin\left(\frac{\alpha+\beta}{2}\right)}{\cos\left(\frac{\alpha-\beta}{2}\right)}$$

Since, this orthocentre lies on ellipse $\frac{x^2}{a^2}+\frac{y^2}{b^2}=1$

Then, $$a^4\cos^2\left(\frac{\alpha+\beta}{2}\right) + b^4\sin^2\left(\frac{\alpha+\beta}{2}\right)$$

$$= (a^2+b^2)^2\cos^2\left(\frac{\alpha-\beta}{2}\right) \quad \text{...(vi)}$$

which is true by Eq. (iii).

Hence, the orthocentre of the triangle lies on the ellipse.

5. The given ellipses, are

$$\frac{x^2}{a^2}+\frac{y^2}{b^2}=1 \quad \text{...(i)}$$

$$\frac{x^2}{a(a+b)} + \frac{y^2}{b(a+b)} = 1 \quad \text{...(ii)}$$

Chord of contact of (x_1, y_1) w.r.t. ellipse (ii) is

$$\frac{xx_1}{a(a+b)} + \frac{yy_1}{b(a+b)} = 1 \quad \text{...(iii)}$$

or $$lx + my = n \quad \text{(say)}$$

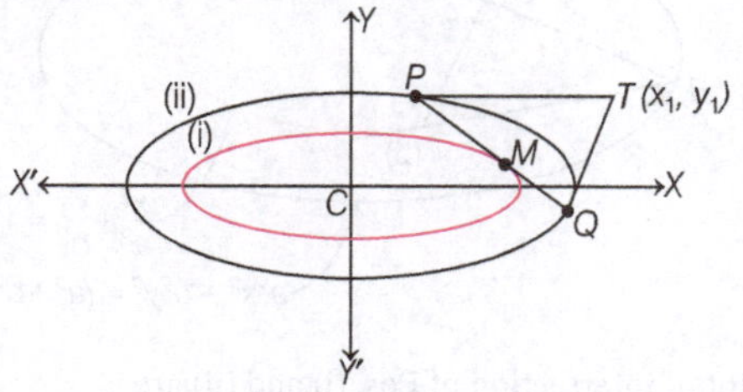

If it touches $\frac{x^2}{a^2} + \frac{y^2}{b^2} = 1,$

then $$a^2l^2 + b^2m^2 = n^2 \quad \text{[from corollary]}$$

$$\Rightarrow \frac{a^2x_1^2}{a^2(a+b)^2} + \frac{b^2y_1^2}{b^2(a+b)^2} = 1$$

$$\Rightarrow x_1^2 + y_1^2 = (a+b)^2$$

Locus of $T(x_1, y_1)$ is $x^2 + y^2 = (a+b)^2$

$$= a(a+b) + b(a+b),$$

which is the director circle of Eq. (ii).

Hence, PT and TQ are intersect at right angle.

6. Equations of concentric ellipses are

$$\frac{x^2}{a^2} + \frac{y^2}{b^2} = 4 \quad \text{...(i)}$$

and $$\frac{x^2}{a^2} + \frac{y^2}{b^2} = 1 \quad \text{...(ii)}$$

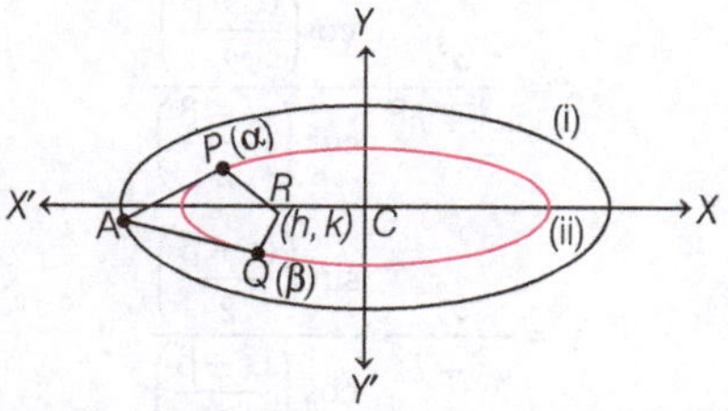

Let points $P(a\cos\alpha, b\sin\alpha)$ and $Q(a\cos\beta, b\sin\beta)$ be on the ellipse (ii). Equation of tangents at P and Q are

$$\frac{x}{a}\cos\alpha + \frac{y}{b}\sin\alpha = 1 \quad \text{...(iii)}$$

and $$\frac{x}{a}\cos\beta + \frac{y}{b}\sin\beta = 1 \quad \text{...(iv)}$$

Point of intersection of Eqs. (iii) and (iv) is

$$A\left\{\frac{a\cos\left(\frac{\alpha+\beta}{2}\right)}{\cos\left(\frac{\alpha-\beta}{2}\right)}, \frac{b\sin\left(\frac{\alpha+\beta}{2}\right)}{\cos\left(\frac{\alpha-\beta}{2}\right)}\right\}$$

This point A satisfy Eq.(i).

$$\therefore \frac{\cos^2\left(\frac{\alpha+\beta}{2}\right)}{\cos^2\left(\frac{\alpha-\beta}{2}\right)} + \frac{\sin^2\left(\frac{\alpha+\beta}{2}\right)}{\cos^2\left(\frac{\alpha-\beta}{2}\right)} = 4$$

$$\Rightarrow 1 = 4\cos^2\left(\frac{\alpha-\beta}{2}\right), \frac{1}{2} = 1 + \cos(\alpha-\beta)$$

$$\therefore \cos(\alpha-\beta) = -\frac{1}{2} \quad \text{...(v)}$$

Equations of normals PR and QR are

$$ax\sec\alpha - by\operatorname{cosec}\alpha = a^2 - b^2$$

and $$ax\sec\beta - by\operatorname{cosec}\beta = (a^2 - b^2)$$

or $$ax\sin\alpha - by\cos\alpha = (a^2 - b^2)\sin\alpha\cos\alpha \quad \text{...(vi)}$$

$$ax\sin\beta - by\cos\beta = (a^2 - b^2)\sin\beta\cos\beta \quad \text{...(vii)}$$

On multiplying Eq. (vi) by $\cos\beta$ and Eq. (vii) by $\cos\alpha$ and subtracting, we get

$$ax\sin(\alpha-\beta) = (a^2 - b^2)\cos\alpha\cos\beta(\sin\alpha - \sin\beta)$$

$$\frac{ax}{a^2-b^2} = \frac{\cos\alpha\cos\beta \cdot 2\cos\left(\frac{\alpha+\beta}{2}\right)\sin\left(\frac{\alpha-\beta}{2}\right)}{2\sin\left(\frac{\alpha-\beta}{2}\right)\cos\left(\frac{\alpha-\beta}{2}\right)}$$

$$= \frac{\cos\alpha\cos\beta\cos\left(\frac{\alpha+\beta}{2}\right)}{\cos\left(\frac{\alpha-\beta}{2}\right)}$$

$$= \pm 2\cos\alpha\cos\beta\cos\left(\frac{\alpha+\beta}{2}\right) \quad \text{[from Eq. (v)]}$$

$$= \pm\cos\left(\frac{\alpha+\beta}{2}\right)[\cos(\alpha+\beta) + \cos(\alpha-\beta)]$$

$$\frac{ax}{a^2-b^2} = \pm\cos\left(\frac{\alpha+\beta}{2}\right)\left\{\cos(\alpha+\beta) - \frac{1}{2}\right\} \quad \text{[Using (v)]}$$

$$\Rightarrow \frac{a^2x^2}{(a^2-b^2)^2} = \cos^2\left(\frac{\alpha+\beta}{2}\right)\left[\cos(\alpha+\beta) - \frac{1}{2}\right]^2$$

Similarly, $$\frac{b^2y^2}{(a^2-b^2)^2} = \sin^2\left(\frac{\alpha+\beta}{2}\right)\left[\cos(\alpha+\beta) + \frac{1}{2}\right]^2$$

$$\therefore \frac{a^2x^2}{(a^2-b^2)^2} + \frac{b^2y^2}{(a^2-b^2)^2}$$

$$= \cos^2(\alpha+\beta) + \frac{1}{4} - \cos^2(\alpha+\beta)$$

Hence, required locus is $a^2x^2 + b^2y^2 = \frac{1}{4}(a^2 - b^2)^2$

7. Let the given ellipse be $\frac{x^2}{a^2} + \frac{y^2}{b^2} = 1$

Let the coordinates of P be $(a\cos\phi, b\sin\phi)$

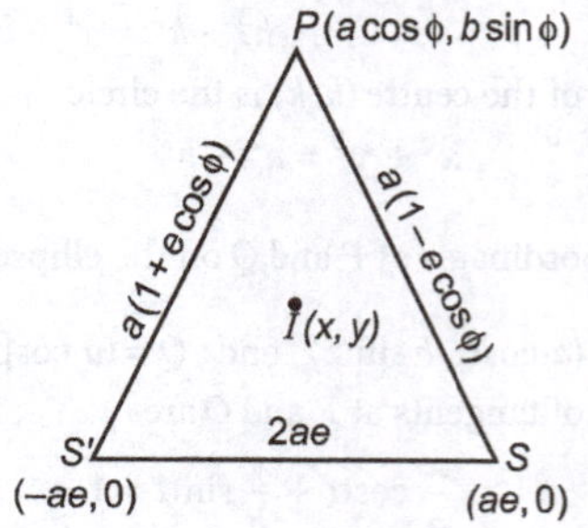

By hypothesis,

$b^2 = a^2(1 - e^2)$ and $S(ae, 0)$, $S'(-ae, 0)$

$\therefore$ SP = focal distance of the point P

$= a - ae\cos\phi$ and $S'P = a + ae\cos\phi$

Also, $SS' = 2ae$

If (x, y) be the incentre of the $\Delta PSS'$, then

$$\therefore \quad x = \frac{(2ae)\, a\cos\phi + a(1 - e\cos\phi)(-ae) + 1(1 + e\cos\phi)\, ae}{2ae + a(1 - e\cos\phi) + a(1 + e\cos\phi)}$$

$$x = ae\cos\phi \qquad \text{...(i)}$$

$$\text{and} \quad y = \frac{2ae(b\sin\phi) + a(1 + e\cos\phi)\cdot 0 + a(1 - e\cos\phi)\cdot 0}{2ae + a(1 - e\cos\phi) + a(1 + e\cos\phi)},$$

$$\Rightarrow \quad y = \frac{eb\sin\phi}{(e+1)} \qquad \text{...(ii)}$$

On eliminating ϕ from Eqs. (i) and (ii), we get

$$\frac{x^2}{a^2e^2} + \frac{y^2}{\left[\frac{be}{e+1}\right]^2} = 1,$$

which represents an ellipse. Let e_1 be its eccentricity.

$$\therefore \quad \frac{b^2e^2}{(e+1)^2} = a^2e^2(1 - e_1^2) \Rightarrow e_1^2 = 1 - \frac{b^2}{a^2(e+1)^2}$$

$$= 1 - \frac{1 - e^2}{(e+1)^2} = 1 - \frac{1-e}{1+e} = \frac{2e}{1+e}$$

$$\Rightarrow \quad e_1 = \sqrt{\left(\frac{2e}{1+e}\right)}$$

8. The equation of the normals at two given points θ and $\frac{\pi}{2} + \theta$ are

$$ax\sec\theta - by\,\mathrm{cosec}\,\theta = a^2 - b^2 \qquad \text{...(i)}$$

$$\text{and} \quad ax\sec\left(\frac{\pi}{2} + \theta\right) - by\,\mathrm{cosec}\left(\frac{\pi}{2} + \theta\right) = a^2 - b^2 \qquad \text{...(ii)}$$

Their slopes are $\quad m_1 = \frac{a}{b}\tan\theta \quad$ and $\quad m_2 = -\frac{a}{b}\cot\theta$

$$\therefore \quad \tan\omega = \frac{m_2 - m_1}{1 + m_2m_1} = \frac{-\frac{a}{b}(\cot\theta + \tan\theta)}{\left(1 - \frac{a^2}{b^2}\right)} = \frac{2ab}{(a^2 - b^2)\sin 2\theta}$$

$$\Rightarrow \quad 2\cot\omega = \frac{(a^2 - b^2)\sin 2\theta}{ab} = \frac{a^2e^2}{a\cdot a\sqrt{1 - e^2}}\sin 2\theta$$

$$\therefore \quad \frac{2\cot\omega}{\sin 2\theta} = \frac{e^2}{\sqrt{(1 - e^2)}}$$

9. The vertices of the triangle PQR are

$P \equiv (a\cos\alpha, b\sin\alpha)$, $Q \equiv (a\cos\beta, b\sin\beta)$

and $R \equiv (a\cos\gamma, b\sin\gamma)$

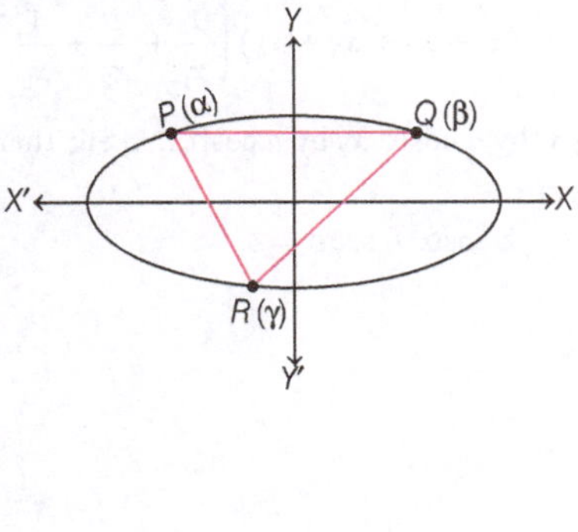

$$\therefore \text{ Area of } \Delta PQR = \frac{1}{2}\begin{vmatrix} a\cos\alpha & b\sin\alpha & 1 \\ a\cos\beta & b\sin\beta & 1 \\ a\cos\gamma & b\sin\gamma & 1 \end{vmatrix} = \frac{ab}{2}\begin{vmatrix} \cos\alpha & \sin\alpha & 1 \\ \cos\beta & \sin\beta & 1 \\ \cos\gamma & \sin\gamma & 1 \end{vmatrix}$$

$$= \frac{ab}{2}[\sin(\gamma - \beta) + \sin(\alpha - \gamma) + \sin(\beta - \alpha)]$$

$$= \frac{ab}{2}\left\{2\sin\left(\frac{\alpha - \beta}{2}\right)\cos\left(\frac{2\gamma - \alpha - \beta}{2}\right) - 2\sin\left(\frac{\alpha - \beta}{2}\right)\cos\left(\frac{\alpha - \beta}{2}\right)\right\}$$

$$= ab\sin\left(\frac{\alpha - \beta}{2}\right)\left[\cos\left(\frac{2\gamma - \alpha - \beta}{2}\right) - \cos\left(\frac{\alpha - \beta}{2}\right)\right]$$

$$= 2ab\sin\left(\frac{\alpha - \beta}{2}\right)\sin\left(\frac{\gamma - \beta}{2}\right)\sin\left(\frac{\alpha - \gamma}{2}\right)$$

$$\therefore \text{ Area of } \Delta PQR = 2ab\sin\left(\frac{\alpha - \beta}{2}\right)\sin\left(\frac{\beta - \gamma}{2}\right)\sin\left(\frac{\gamma - \alpha}{2}\right) \qquad \text{...(i)}$$

If P_1, Q_1 and R_1 be the points upon the auxiliary circle corresponding to points P, Q and R, then

$$\text{Area of } \Delta P_1Q_1R_1 = 2a^2\sin\left(\frac{\alpha - \beta}{2}\right)\sin\left(\frac{\beta - \gamma}{2}\right)\sin\left(\frac{\gamma - \alpha}{2}\right)$$

{taking $b = a$ in Eq. (i)}

$$\therefore \quad \frac{\text{Area of } \Delta PQR}{\text{Area of } \Delta P_1Q_1R_1} = \frac{b}{a}$$

$$\therefore \quad (\text{Area of } \Delta PQR) = \left(\frac{b}{a}\right)\text{Area of } (\Delta P_1Q_1R_1)$$

$\therefore$ Area of ΔPQR is the greatest when area of $\Delta P_1Q_1R_1$ be the greatest and hence $\Delta P_1Q_1R_1$ must be equilateral.

$$\therefore \quad \alpha - \beta = \beta - \gamma = \gamma - \alpha = \frac{2\pi}{3}$$

$\therefore$ The eccentric angles of P, Q, R will be

$$\alpha, \alpha + \frac{2\pi}{3}, \alpha + \frac{4\pi}{3}$$

10. Equation of normal at $P(a\cos\theta, b\sin\theta)$ is

$$ax\sec\theta - by\,\mathrm{cosec}\,\theta = (a^2 - b^2)$$

$$\text{or} \quad ax\sin\theta - by\cos\theta = \frac{1}{2}(a^2 - b^2)\sin 2\theta \qquad \text{...(i)}$$

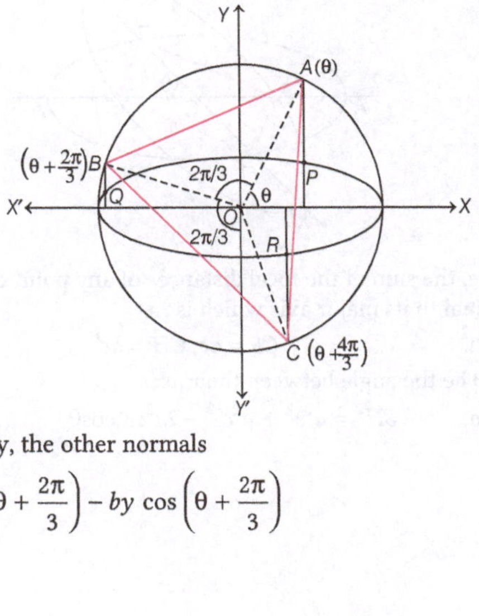

Similarly, the other normals

$$ax\sin\left(\theta + \frac{2\pi}{3}\right) - by\cos\left(\theta + \frac{2\pi}{3}\right)$$

$$= \frac{1}{2}(a^2 - b^2)\sin\left(2\theta + \frac{4\pi}{3}\right) \quad \text{...(ii)}$$

and $ax \sin\left(\theta + \frac{4\pi}{3}\right) - by \cos\left(\theta + \frac{4\pi}{3}\right)$

$$= \frac{1}{2}(a^2 - b^2)\sin\left(2\theta + \frac{8\pi}{3}\right) \quad \text{...(iii)}$$

$\because \quad \sin\left(\theta + \frac{4\pi}{3}\right) = \sin\left(\theta - \frac{2\pi}{3}\right), \cos\left(\theta + \frac{4\pi}{3}\right)$

$$= \cos\left(\theta - \frac{2\pi}{3}\right)$$

and $\quad \sin\left(2\theta + \frac{8\pi}{3}\right) = \sin\left(2\theta - \frac{4\pi}{3}\right)$

Further, the three normals are concurrent, then

$$\begin{vmatrix} \sin\theta & \cos\theta & \sin 2\theta \\ \sin\left(\theta + \frac{2\pi}{3}\right) & \cos\left(\theta + \frac{2\pi}{3}\right) & \sin\left(2\theta + \frac{4\pi}{3}\right) \\ \sin\left(\theta - \frac{2\pi}{3}\right) & \cos\left(\theta - \frac{2\pi}{3}\right) & \sin\left(2\theta + \frac{8\pi}{3}\right) \end{vmatrix} = 0$$

Applying $R_2 \to R_2 + R_3$, then

$$\text{LHS} = \begin{vmatrix} \sin\theta & \cos\theta & \sin 2\theta \\ 2\sin\theta\cos\frac{2\pi}{3} & 2\cos\theta\cos\frac{2\pi}{3} & 2\sin(2\theta + 2\pi)\cos\frac{2\pi}{3} \\ \sin\left(\theta - \frac{2\pi}{3}\right) & \cos\left(\theta - \frac{2\pi}{3}\right) & \sin\left(2\theta + \frac{8\pi}{3}\right) \end{vmatrix}$$

$$= -\begin{vmatrix} \sin\theta & \cos\theta & \sin 2\theta \\ \sin\theta & \cos\theta & \sin 2\theta \\ \sin\left(\theta - \frac{2\pi}{3}\right) & \cos\left(\theta - \frac{2\pi}{3}\right) & \sin\left(2\theta + \frac{8\pi}{3}\right) \end{vmatrix} = 0$$

$[\because R_1 = R_2]$

11. Let S and S' be the foci of one ellipse and H and H' be the other, C being their common centre. Then, $SHS'H'$ is a parallelogram and since $SH + S'H = HS' + H'S' = 2a$

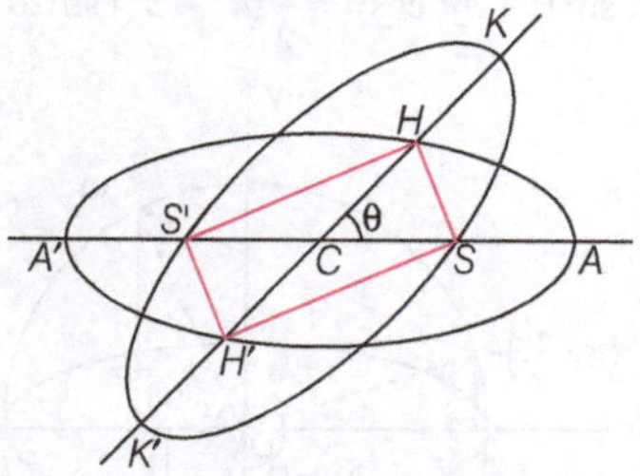

Since, the sum of the focal distances of any point on an ellipse is equal to its major axis which is $2a$.

Then, $\quad CS = ae, CH = ae'$

Let θ be the angle between their axes.

Then, $\quad SH^2 = a^2e^2 + a^2e'^2 - 2a^2ee'\cos\theta$

$$HS'^2 = a^2e^2 + a^2e'^2 + 2a^2ee'\cos\theta$$

Now, $\quad 2a = SH + S'H$

On squaring both sides, then

$$4a^2 = (SH)^2 + (S'H)^2 + 2(SH)\cdot(S'H)$$

$$\Rightarrow 4a^2 = 2a^2(e^2 + e'^2) + 2\sqrt{(a^2e^2 + a^2e'^2)^2 - 4a^4e^2e'^2\cos^2\theta}$$

$$\Rightarrow (2 - e^2 - e'^2)^2 = (e^2 + e'^2)^2 - 4e^2e'^2\cos^2\theta$$

$$\Rightarrow 4 + (e^2 + e'^2)^2 - 4(e^2 + e'^2) = (e^2 + e'^2)^2 - 4e^2e'^2\cos^2\theta$$

$$\Rightarrow 1 - e^2 - e'^2 = -e^2e'^2\cos^2\theta$$

$$\therefore \quad \cos\theta = \frac{\sqrt{e^2 + e'^2 - 1}}{ee'}$$

$$\therefore \quad \theta = \cos^{-1}\left(\frac{\sqrt{(e^2 + e'^2 - 1}}{ee'}\right)$$

12. Let point of concurrent be (h, k).

Equation of normal at (x', y') is $\dfrac{x - x'}{x'/a^2} = \dfrac{y_1 - y'}{y'/b^2}$

It passes through (h, k) then

$$y'^2\{a^2(h - x') + b^2x'\}^2 = b^4k^2x'^2 \quad \text{...(i)}$$

But $\quad \dfrac{x'^2}{a^2} + \dfrac{y'^2}{b^2} = 1$ or $y'^2 = \dfrac{b^2}{a^2}(a^2 - x'^2) \quad$ ...(ii)

Value of y'^2 from Eq. (ii), putting in Eq. (i), we get

$$\frac{b^2}{a^2}(a^2 - x'^2)\{a^2h + (b^2 - a^2)x'\}^2 = b^4k^2x'^2$$

$$\Rightarrow \frac{b^2}{a^2}(a^2 - x'^2)\{a^4h^2 + (b^2 - a^2)^2x'^2 + 2a^2hx'(b^2 - a^2)\}$$

$$= b^4k^2x'^2$$

Arranging above as a fourth degree equation in x', we get

$$\Rightarrow -(a^2 - b^2)^2x'^4 + 2ha^2(a^2 - b^2)x'^3 + x'^2(\ldots)$$

$$-2a^4h(a^2 - b^2)x' + a^6h^2 = 0$$

Above equation being of fourth degree in x', therefore roots of the above equation are x_1, x_2, x_3 and x_4 then

$$(x_1 + x_2 + x_3 + x_4) = -\frac{2ha^2(a^2 - b^2)}{-(a^2 - b^2)^2} = \frac{2ha^2}{(a^2 - b^2)} \quad \text{...(iii)}$$

$$\left(\frac{1}{x_1} + \frac{1}{x_2} + \frac{1}{x_3} + \frac{1}{x_4}\right) = \frac{\Sigma x_1x_2x_3}{x_1 \cdot x_2 \cdot x_3 \cdot x_4}$$

$$= \frac{\dfrac{2a^4h(a^2 - b^2)}{-(a^2 - b^2)^2}}{\dfrac{a^6h^2}{-(a^2 - b^2)^2}} = \frac{2(a^2 - b^2)}{a^2h} \quad \text{...(iv)}$$

Multiplying Eqs. (iii) and (iv), we get

$$(x_1 + x_2 + x_3 + x_4)\left(\frac{1}{x_1} + \frac{1}{x_2} + \frac{1}{x_3} + \frac{1}{x_4}\right) = 4$$

Replacing x_1 by $a\cos\alpha$, x_2 by $a\cos\beta$, ... etc, then, we get the second form

i.e. $\quad \Sigma\cos\alpha\ \Sigma\sec\alpha = 4.$

13. Let $\angle PSS' = \alpha$ and $\angle PS'S = \beta$

$\therefore \quad SS' = 2ae$

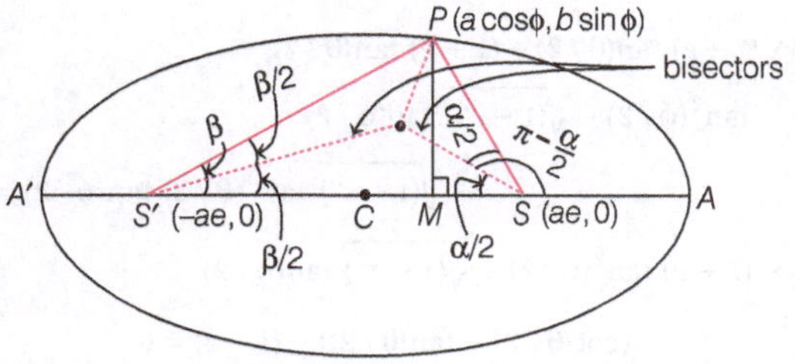

By sine rule in $\Delta PSS'$, then

$$\frac{SP}{\sin\beta} = \frac{S'P}{\sin\alpha} = \frac{SS'}{\sin\{\pi - (\alpha+\beta)\}}$$

$$\Rightarrow \quad \frac{SP}{\sin\beta} = \frac{S'P}{\sin\alpha} = \frac{SS'}{\sin(\alpha+\beta)}$$

or $$\frac{SP + S'P}{\sin\beta + \sin\alpha} = \frac{SS'}{(\sin\alpha+\beta)}$$

or $$\frac{2a}{\sin\beta + \sin\alpha} = \frac{2ae}{\sin(\alpha+\beta)} \qquad [\because SP + S'P = 2a]$$

or $$\frac{2a}{2ae} = \frac{\sin\beta + \sin\alpha}{\sin(\alpha+\beta)}$$

$$\Rightarrow \quad \frac{1}{e} = \frac{2\sin\left(\frac{\alpha+\beta}{2}\right)\cos\left(\frac{\alpha-\beta}{2}\right)}{2\sin\left(\frac{\alpha+\beta}{2}\right)\cos\left(\frac{\alpha+\beta}{2}\right)}$$

$$\Rightarrow \quad \frac{1}{e} = \frac{\cos\left(\frac{\alpha-\beta}{2}\right)}{\cos\left(\frac{\alpha+\beta}{2}\right)}$$

$$\frac{1-e}{1+e} = \frac{\cos\left(\frac{\alpha-\beta}{2}\right) - \cos\left(\frac{\alpha+\beta}{2}\right)}{\cos\left(\frac{\alpha-\beta}{2}\right) + \cos\left(\frac{\alpha+\beta}{2}\right)}$$

{by componendo and dividendo rule}

$$\Rightarrow \quad \frac{1-e}{1+e} = \tan(\alpha/2)\tan(\beta/2) \qquad \text{...(i)}$$

or $$\tan\left(\frac{PSS'}{2}\right)\tan\left(\frac{PS'S}{2}\right) = \frac{1-e}{1+e}$$

The centre of the circle inscribed in $\Delta\, PSS'$ will lie on the bisectors of angles α and β whose equations are

$$y = \tan\left(\frac{\beta}{2}\right)(x + ae) \qquad \text{...(i)}$$

and $y = \tan\left(\pi - \frac{\alpha}{2}\right)(x - ae)$ or $y = -\tan\left(\frac{\alpha}{2}\right)(x - ae)$ ...(ii)

On multiplying Eqs. (i) and (ii), we get

$$y^2 = -\tan\left(\frac{\alpha}{2}\right)\tan\left(\frac{\beta}{2}\right)(x^2 - a^2e^2)$$

$$y^2 = -\left(\frac{1-e}{1+e}\right)(x^2 - a^2e^2) \qquad \text{[from Eq. (i)]}$$

or $$y^2 + x^2\left(\frac{1-e}{1+e}\right) = a^2e^2\left(\frac{1-e}{1+e}\right)$$

or $$\frac{x^2}{a^2e^2} + \frac{y^2}{a^2e^2\left(\frac{1-e}{1+e}\right)} = 1, \text{ which is an ellipse.}$$

14. Let P be $(a\cos\phi, b\sin\phi)$.

$\therefore$ Equation of tangent at P is

$$\frac{x}{a}\cos\phi + \frac{y}{b}\sin\phi = 1 \qquad \text{...(i)}$$

and equation of normal at P is

$$ax\sec\phi - by\,\text{cosec}\,\phi = a^2 - b^2 \qquad \text{...(ii)}$$

It is clear from the figure $CFPQ$ is rectangle

$\therefore \quad PF = CQ$

{i.e. the perpendicular from $C(0, 0)$ on Eq. (i)}

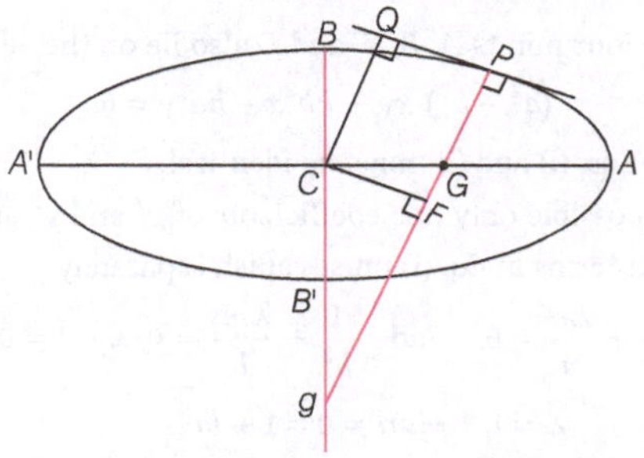

$$= \frac{1}{\sqrt{\left(\frac{\cos^2\phi}{a^2} + \frac{\sin^2\phi}{b^2}\right)}} = \frac{ab}{\sqrt{(a^2\sin^2\phi + b^2\cos^2\phi)}} \qquad \text{...(iii)}$$

On putting $y = 0$ in Eq. (ii), the point G is $\left(\frac{a^2 - b^2}{a}\cos\phi, 0\right)$

and on putting $x = 0$ in Eq. (ii), the point g is

$$\left(0, -\frac{(a^2-b^2)}{b}\sin\phi\right)$$

$$\therefore \quad (PG)^2 = \left(a\cos\phi - \left(\frac{a^2-b^2}{2}\right)\cos\phi\right)^2 + (b\sin\phi - 0)^2$$

$$= \frac{b^4}{a^2}\cos^2\phi + b^2\sin^2\phi = \frac{b^2}{a^2}(b^2\cos^2\phi + a^2\sin^2\phi)$$

$$\therefore \quad PG = \frac{b}{a}\sqrt{(a^2\sin^2\phi + b^2\cos^2\phi)} \qquad \text{...(iv)}$$

and $$(Pg)^2 = (a\cos\phi - 0)^2 + \left(b\sin\phi + \frac{(a^2-b^2)}{b}\sin\phi\right)^2$$

$$= a^2\cos^2\phi + \frac{a^4}{b^2}\sin^2\phi$$

$$= \frac{a^2}{b^2}(a^2\sin^2\phi + b^2\cos^2\phi)$$

$$\therefore \quad Pg = \frac{a}{b}\sqrt{(a^2\sin^2\phi + b^2\cos^2\phi)} \qquad \text{...(v)}$$

From Eqs. (iii) and (iv), $PF \cdot PG = b^2$

and from Eqs. (iii) and (v), $PF \cdot Pg = a^2$.

15. Let the normals at the points when the line, $\frac{lx}{a}+\frac{my}{b}=1$ meet at $P(h, k)$.

Let the line joining the feet of the other two normals from (h, k) have for its equation, $rx + sy = 1$

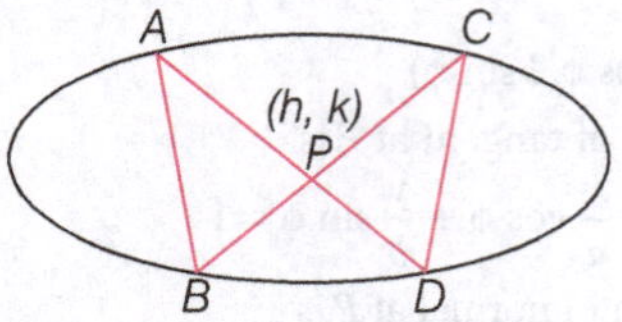

Then, the general equation of a curve through the intersection of the ellipse and the two lines is

$$\left(\frac{x^2}{a^2}+\frac{y^2}{b^2}-1\right)+\lambda\left(\frac{lx}{a}+\frac{my}{b}-1\right)\times(rx+sy-1)=0 \quad \text{...(i)}$$

But the four points A, B, C and D also lie on the ellipse

$$(a^2-b^2)\,xy+kb^2x-ha^2y=0 \quad \text{...(ii)}$$

Curves Eqs. (i) and (ii) must be identical.

This is possible only one coefficients of x^2 and y^2 and the constant terms in Eq. (i) must vanish separately.

$$\frac{1}{a^2}+\frac{\lambda rl}{a}=0, \quad \text{and} \quad \frac{1}{b^2}+\frac{\lambda ms}{b}=0,\ \lambda-1=0$$

$\therefore$ $\lambda = 1,\ 1 + arl = 0 = 1 + bms$

$\therefore$ $r=\frac{-1}{al}$ and $s=\frac{-1}{mb}$

Therefore, the line $rx + sy = 1$ becomes

$$-\frac{x}{al}-\frac{y}{mb}=1 \text{ or } \frac{x}{al}+\frac{y}{mb}=-1$$

16. $\therefore$ $\tan\theta=\frac{b\sin\phi}{(a\cos\phi-ae)}=\frac{\left(\frac{b}{a}\right)\sin\phi}{(\cos\phi-e)}$

$\because$ $b^2=a^2(1-e^2)$

$\therefore$ $\frac{b}{a}=\sqrt{(1-e^2)}$

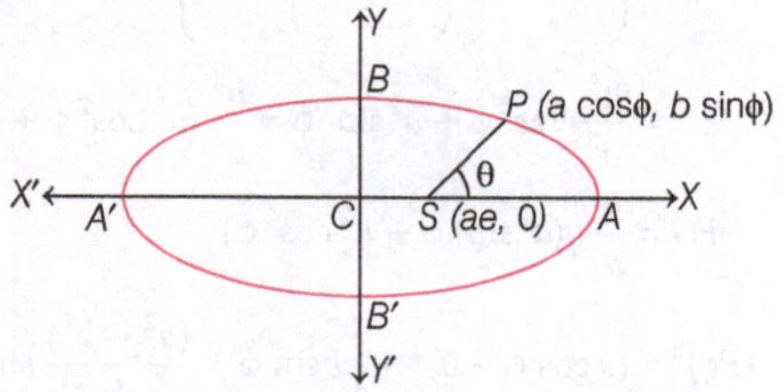

$$\Rightarrow \quad \tan\theta=\frac{\sqrt{(1-e^2)}\sin\phi}{(\cos\phi-e)}$$

$$\Rightarrow \sin\theta\cos\phi-e\sin\theta=\sqrt{(1-e^2)}\sin\phi\cos\theta$$

$$\Rightarrow \frac{2\tan(\theta/2)}{1+\tan^2(\theta/2)}\cdot\frac{1-\tan^2(\phi/2)}{1+\tan^2(\phi/2)}-\frac{e\,(2\tan(\theta/2))}{(1+\tan^2(\theta/2))}$$

$$=\sqrt{(1-e^2)}\cdot\frac{2\tan(\phi/2)}{1+\tan^2(\phi/2)}\cdot\frac{1-\tan^2(\theta/2)}{1+\tan^2(\theta/2)}$$

$$\Rightarrow 2\tan(\theta/2)\,(1-\tan^2(\phi/2))-2e\tan(\theta/2)\,(1+\tan^2(\phi/2))$$

$$=2\sqrt{(1-e^2)}\cdot\tan(\phi/2)\,(1-\tan^2(\theta/2))$$

$$\Rightarrow (1-e)\tan(\theta/2)-(1+e)\tan(\theta/2)$$

$$\tan^2(\phi/2)-\sqrt{(1-e^2)}\tan(\phi/2)$$

$$+\sqrt{(1-e^2)}\tan^2(\theta/2)\tan(\phi/2)=0$$

$$\Rightarrow (1+e)\tan^2(\phi/2)+\sqrt{(1-e^2)}\tan(\phi/2)$$

$$(\cot(\theta/2)-\tan(\theta/2))-(1-e)=0$$

$$\Rightarrow \sqrt{(1+e)}\tan(\phi/2)\{\sqrt{(1+e)}\tan(\phi/2)-\sqrt{(1-e)}\tan(\theta/2)\}$$

$$+\sqrt{(1-e)}\cot(\theta/2)\{\sqrt{(1+e)}\tan(\phi/2)-\sqrt{(1-e)}\tan(\theta/2)\}=0$$

$$\Rightarrow (\sqrt{(1+e)}\tan(\phi/2)+\sqrt{(1-e)}\cot(\theta/2))$$

$$(\sqrt{(1+e)}\tan(\phi/2)-\sqrt{(1-e)}\tan(\theta/2))=0$$

But ϕ and θ lies between 0 and π.

Then, $\tan(\phi/2)>0$ and $\tan(\theta/2)>0$

$$\Rightarrow \sqrt{(1+e)}\tan(\phi/2)+\sqrt{(1-e)}\cot(\theta/2)\neq 0$$

$$\therefore \sqrt{(1+e)}\tan(\phi/2)-\sqrt{(1-e)}\tan(\theta/2)=0$$

$$\tan(\theta/2)=\sqrt{\left(\frac{1+e}{1-e}\right)}\tan(\phi/2)$$

17. Let coordinates of T be (x_1, y_1). Let eccentric angles of P, Q, R be ϕ, ϕ_1, ϕ_2

Thus equation of chords PSQ and PHR are

$$\frac{x}{a}\cos\left(\frac{\phi+\phi_1}{2}\right)+\frac{y}{b}\sin\left(\frac{\phi+\phi_1}{2}\right)=\cos\left(\frac{\phi-\phi_1}{2}\right) \quad \text{...(i)}$$

and $$\frac{x}{a}\cos\left(\frac{\phi+\phi_2}{2}\right)+\frac{y}{b}\sin\left(\frac{\phi+\phi_2}{2}\right)=\cos\left(\frac{\phi-\phi_2}{2}\right) \quad \text{...(ii)}$$

$\because$ Eqs. (i) and (ii) passes through $(ae, 0)$ and $(-ae, 0)$ then Eqs.(i) and (ii) becomes

$$e\cos\left(\frac{\phi+\phi_1}{2}\right)=\cos\left(\frac{\phi-\phi_1}{2}\right) \quad \text{...(iii)}$$

and $$-e\cos\left(\frac{\phi+\phi_2}{2}\right)=\cos\left(\frac{\phi-\phi_2}{2}\right) \quad \text{...(iv)}$$

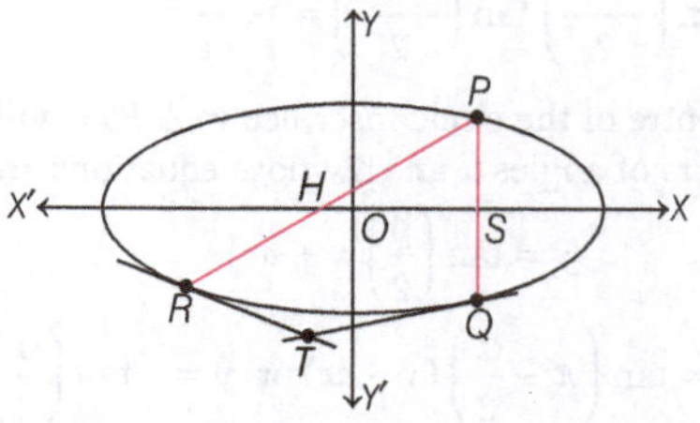

By componendo and dividendo

$$\frac{1-e}{1+e}=-\frac{2\cos(\phi/2)\cos(\phi_2/2)}{2\sin(\phi/2)\sin(\phi_2/2)}$$

or $$\frac{1-e}{1+e}=-\cot(\phi/2)\cot(\phi_2/2)$$

or $\tan(\phi_2/2) = -\frac{(1+e)}{(1-e)}\cot(\phi/2)$

Similarly, $\tan(\phi_1/2) = -\frac{(1-e)}{(1+e)}\cot(\phi/2)$

the equation of QR is

$$\frac{x}{a}\cos\left(\frac{\phi_1+\phi_2}{2}\right)+\frac{y}{b}\sin\left(\frac{\phi_1+\phi_2}{2}\right)=\cos\left(\frac{\phi_1-\phi_2}{2}\right)$$

Dividing both sides by $\cos(\phi_1/2)\cos(\phi_2/2)$, we get

$$\Rightarrow \frac{x}{a}(1-\tan(\phi_1/2)\tan(\phi_2/2))+\frac{y}{b}(\tan(\phi_1/2)+\tan(\phi_2/2))$$

$$=1+\tan(\phi_1/2)\tan(\phi_2/2) \quad \text{or} \quad \frac{x}{a}(1-\cot^2(\phi/2))+\frac{y}{b}$$

$$\left\{-2\left(\frac{1+e^2}{1-e^2}\right)\cot(\phi/2)\right\}=1+\cot^2(\phi/2)$$

or $\frac{x}{a}\frac{(1-\cot^2(\phi/2))}{(1+\cot^2(\phi/2))}-\frac{1+e^2}{1-e^2}\frac{2\cot\phi/2}{1+\cot^2\phi/2}\cdot\frac{y}{b}=1$

or $-\frac{x}{a}\cos\phi-\left(\frac{1+e^2}{1-e^2}\right)\sin\phi\cdot\frac{y}{b}=1$

or $\frac{x}{a}(1-e^2)\cos\phi+\frac{y}{b}(1+e^2)\sin\phi=-(1-e^2)$ ...(v)

But QR is also chord of contact.

Thus equation of QR is

$$\frac{xx_1}{a^2}+\frac{yy_1}{b^2}=1 \quad \text{...(vi)}$$

Comparing the coefficients of Eqs. (v) and (vi), we get

$$\frac{(1-e^2)\cos\phi}{x_1/a}=\frac{(1+e^2)\sin\phi}{y_1/b}=-(1-e^2)$$

$$\Rightarrow \cos^2\phi=\frac{x_1^2}{a^2} \text{ and } \sin^2\phi=\frac{y_1^2}{b^2}\frac{(1-e^2)^2}{(1+e^2)^2}$$

$$\because \cos^2\phi+\sin^2\phi=1$$

$$\therefore \frac{x_1^2}{a^2}+\frac{y_1^2}{b^2}\cdot\frac{(1-e^2)^2}{(1+e^2)^2}=1$$

Locus of (x_1, y_1) is $\frac{x^2}{a^2}(1+e^2)^2+(1-e^2)^2\frac{y^2}{b^2}=(1+e^2)^2$.

7

> Maths is fun. It teaches you life and death information like when you are cold, you should go to a corner since it's 90° degree there.
>
> **–Steven Wright**

Hyperbola

Learning Milestones

Milestone 1 Hyperbola

- Definition 1
- Definition 2
- Tracing of the Hyperbola
- Focal Distances of a point
- Conjugate Hyperbola

Milestone 2 Line and Hyperbola

- Position of Point with respect to Hyperbola
- Intersection of a Line and a Hyperbola
- Equation of Tangents in Different Forms
- Equation of Normals is Different Forms
- Pair of Tangents
- Chord of Contact
- Equation of the Chord Bisected at a Given Point

Milestone 3 Rectangular Hyperbola

- Diameter of Hyperbola
- Conjugate Diameter
- Director Circle
- Asymptotes
- Rectangular Hyperbola
- Reflection Property of a Hyperbola
- Equation of Hyperbola Referred to two Perpendicular Lines

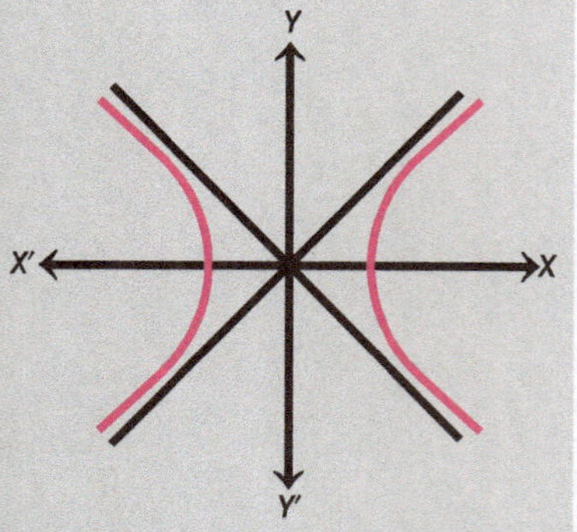

Practice Milestones

Practice Milestone 1- JEE Main Pattern

Practice Milestone 2 - JEE Advanced Pattern

Practice Milestone 3 - Challenging Problems

Milestone 1 Hyperbola

• Definition 1 • Definition 2 • Tracing of the Hyperbola • Focal Distance of a Point • Conjugate Hyperbola

7.1 Definition 1

The locus of a point which moves in a plane such that its distance from a fixed point (i.e. focus) is e times its distance from a fixed line (i.e. directrix) is known as hyperbola. For hyperbola $e > 1$.

Standard Equation of Hyperbola

Let S be the focus and ZM be the directrix of the hyperbola. Draw $SZ \perp ZM$. Divide SZ internally and externally in the ratio $e:1 (e > 1)$ and let A and A' be their internal and external points of division.

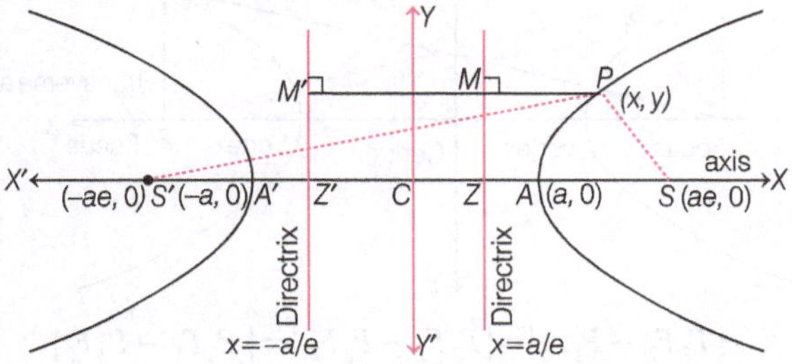

Then, $$SA = e\,AZ \quad \text{...(i)}$$

and $$SA' = e\,A'Z \quad \text{...(ii)}$$

Clearly, A and A' will lie on the hyperbola.

Let $AA' = 2a$ and take C the mid-point of AA' as origin

$\therefore \quad CA = CA' = a$

Let $P(x, y)$ be any point on the hyperbola and CA as X-axis, the line through C perpendicular to CA as Y-axis.

Then, on adding Eqs. (i) and (ii),

$\therefore \quad SA + SA' = e(AZ + A'Z)$

$\Rightarrow \quad CS - CA + CS + CA' = e(AA')$

$\Rightarrow \quad 2CS = e(2a) \quad [\because CA = CA']$

$\therefore \quad CS = ae$

$\therefore$ The focus S is $(CS, 0)$ i.e. $(ae, 0)$ and subtracting Eq. (i) from Eq. (ii), then

$$SA' - SA = e(A'Z - AZ)$$

$$AA' = e[(CA' + CZ) - (CA - CZ)]$$

$\Rightarrow \quad AA' = e(2CZ) \quad [\because CA = CA']$

$\Rightarrow \quad 2a = e(2CZ)$

$\therefore \quad CZ = a/e$

$\therefore$ The directrix MZ is $x = CZ = a/e$

or $\quad x - a/e = 0 \quad \left[\because e > 1, \therefore \frac{1}{e} < 1\right]$

Now, draw $PM \perp MZ$,

$\therefore \quad \frac{SP}{PM} = e$ or $(SP)^2 = e^2 (PM)^2$

or $\quad (x - ae)^2 + (y - 0)^2 = e^2\left(x - \frac{a}{e}\right)^2$

or $\quad (x - ae)^2 + y^2 = (ex - a)^2$

$\Rightarrow \quad x^2 + a^2e^2 - 2aex + y^2 = e^2x^2 - 2aex + a^2$

$\Rightarrow \quad x^2(e^2 - 1) - y^2 = a^2(e^2 - 1)$

$\Rightarrow \quad \frac{x^2}{a^2} - \frac{y^2}{a^2(e^2 - 1)} = 1$

or $\quad \frac{x^2}{a^2} - \frac{y^2}{b^2} = 1,$

where $b^2 = a^2(e^2 - 1)$

This is the standard equation of the hyperbola.

The equation being the same as that of hyperbola when $S'(-ae, 0)$ is focus and $M'Z'$ i.e. $x = -\frac{a}{e}$ is directrix.

Generally The equation of the hyperbola whose focus is the point (h, k) and directrix is $lx + my + n = 0$ and whose eccentricity is e, is

$$(x - h)^2 + (y - k)^2 = e^2 \frac{(lx + my + n)^2}{(l^2 + m^2)}$$

JEE Focus Points

- Distance between foci $SS' = 2ae$ and distance between directrices $ZZ' = 2a/e$
- Two hyperbolas are said to be similar if they have the same value of eccentricity.

Concept Inside Video

Since, $\frac{x^2}{a^2} - \frac{y^2}{b^2} = 1$

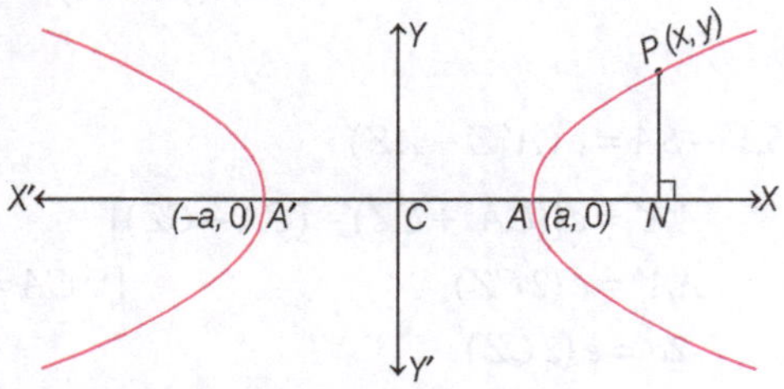

$\Rightarrow \quad \frac{y^2}{b^2} = \frac{x^2}{a^2} - 1$

$\frac{y^2}{b^2} = \frac{(x-a)(x+a)}{a^2}$ ...(i)

$\because \quad AN = CN - CA = (x - a)$

and $\quad A'N = CN + CA' = (x + a)$

and $\quad PN = y$

$\therefore$ From Eq. (i), $\frac{(PN)^2}{AN \cdot A'N} = \frac{b^2}{a^2}$

Example 1. Find the equation of the hyperbola whose directrix is $2x + y = 1$, focus $(1, 2)$ and eccentricity $\sqrt{3}$.

Sol. Let $P(x, y)$ be any point on the hyperbola. Draw PM perpendicular from P on the directrix.

Then, by definition $SP = e\ PM$

$\Rightarrow \quad (SP)^2 = e^2 (PM)^2$

Equation of hyperbola whose focus (1, 2), eccentricity is $\sqrt{3}$ and equation of directrix is $2x + y = 1$.

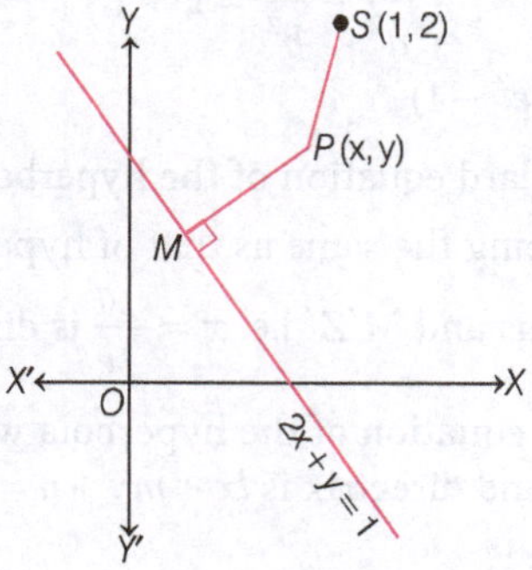

$$(x-1)^2 + (y-2)^2 = (\sqrt{3})^2 \left(\frac{2x + y - 1}{\sqrt{4+1}}\right)^2$$

$$\Rightarrow \quad (x-1)^2 + (y-2)^2 = \frac{3}{5}(2x + y - 1)^2$$

$$\Rightarrow \quad 5(x^2 - 2x + 1 + y^2 - 4y + 4) = 3(4x^2 + y^2 + 1 + 4xy - 4x - 2y)$$

$$\Rightarrow \quad 5x^2 - 10x + 5 + 5y^2 - 20y + 20 = 12x^2 + 3y^2 + 3 + 12xy - 12x - 6y$$

$$\Rightarrow \quad 7x^2 - 2y^2 + 12xy - 2x + 14y - 22 = 0$$

7.2 Definition 2

A hyperbola is the set of all points in a plane, the difference of whose distance from two fixed points in the plane is a constant. The two fixed points are called the foci of the hyperbola. The mid-point of the line segment joining the foci is called the center of the hyperbola. The line through the foci is called the transverse axis and the line through the center and perpendicular to the transverse axis is called the conjugate axis.

The points at which the hyperbola intersects the transverse axis are called the vertices of the hyperbola.

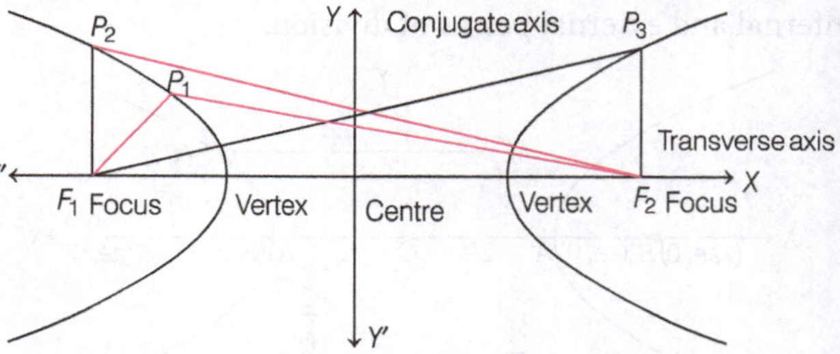

$$|P_1F_2 - P_1F_1| = |P_2F_1 - P_2F_2| = |P_3F_1 - P_3F_2|$$

Standard Equation of Hyperbola

Let the distance between the two foci be $2c$, the distance between the two vertices is $2a$ and $b = \sqrt{c^2 - a^2}$.

If the foci be $(\pm c, 0)$, then center will be $(0, 0)$.

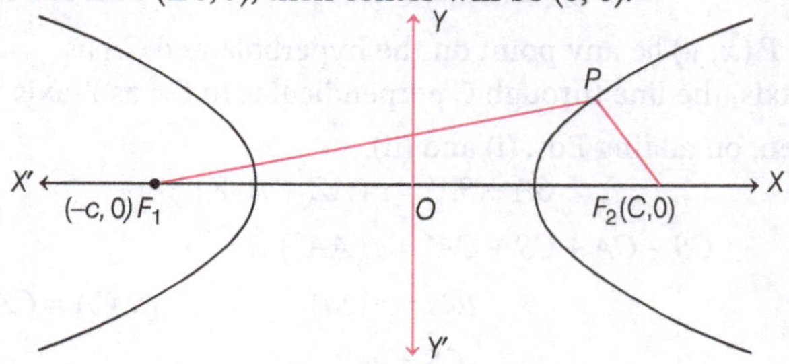

According to the definition of hyperbola,

$$PF_1 - PF_2 = 2a \ (2a < 2c \Rightarrow c > a)$$

$$\Rightarrow \quad \sqrt{(x+c)^2+y^2}-\sqrt{(x-c)^2+y^2}=2a$$

$$\Rightarrow \quad \sqrt{(x+c)^2+y^2}=2a+\sqrt{(x-c)^2+y^2}$$

$$\Rightarrow (x+c)^2+y^2=4a^2+4a\sqrt{(x-c)^2+y^2}+(x-c)^2+y^2$$

$$\Rightarrow x^2+c^2+2cx+y^2-x^2-c^2+2cx-y^2$$

$$=4a^2+4a\sqrt{(x-c)^2+y^2}$$

$$\Rightarrow \quad 4(cx-a^2)=4a\sqrt{(x-c)^2+y^2}$$

$$\Rightarrow \quad \frac{cx}{a}-a=\sqrt{(x-c)^2+y^2}$$

$$\Rightarrow \quad \frac{c^2x^2}{a^2}-2cx+a^2=x^2+c^2-2cx+y^2$$

$$\Rightarrow \quad \left(\frac{c^2-a^2}{a^2}\right)x^2-y^2=c^2-a^2$$

$$\Rightarrow \quad \frac{x^2}{a^2}-\frac{y^2}{c^2-a^2}=1$$

$$\Rightarrow \quad \frac{x^2}{a^2}-\frac{y^2}{b^2}=1 \qquad [\because b=\sqrt{c^2-a^2}\,]$$

7.3 Tracing of the Hyperbola

Equation of the hyperbola is

$$\frac{x^2}{a^2}-\frac{y^2}{b^2}=1 \qquad \text{...(i)}$$

I. Since, only even powers of x and y occur in this equation, so it (hyperbola) is symmetrical about the both axes.

II. The hyperbola (i) does not cut Y-axis at real points where as it cuts X-axis at $(a, 0)$ and $(-a, 0)$.

III. Eq. (i) may be written as

$$y=\pm\frac{b}{a}\sqrt{(x^2-a^2)}$$

It follows that $x^2-a^2\ge 0$

$$\therefore \quad x^2\ge a^2$$

$$\Rightarrow \quad x\le -a \text{ or } x\ge a$$

Hence, $x\notin(-a, a)$

The curve does not exist in the region

$$x=-a \text{ to } x=a.$$

IV. As x increases, y also increases i.e. the curve extends to infinity.

Some Terms Related to Hyperbola

Let the equation of hyperbola is $\dfrac{x^2}{a^2}-\dfrac{y^2}{b^2}=1$

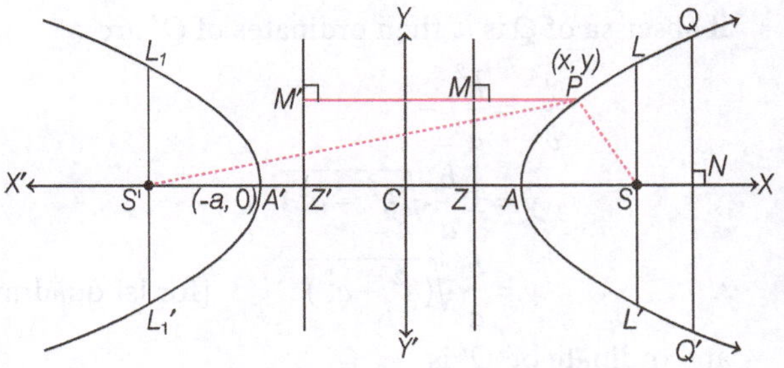

(i) **Centre** All chords passing through C and bisected at C.
Here, $C\equiv(0, 0)$

(ii) **Eccentricity** For the hyperbola $\dfrac{x^2}{a^2}-\dfrac{y^2}{b^2}=1$, we have

$$b^2=a^2(e^2-1)$$

$$\Rightarrow \quad e^2=\frac{a^2+b^2}{a^2}$$

$$\Rightarrow \quad e=\sqrt{1+\left(\frac{b^2}{a^2}\right)}$$

$$\Rightarrow \quad e=\sqrt{\left\{1+\frac{(2b)^2}{(2a)^2}\right\}}$$

$$\Rightarrow \quad e=\sqrt{\left\{1+\frac{(\text{conjugate axis})^2}{(\text{transverse axis})^2}\right\}}$$

(iii) **Foci and directrices** S and S' are the foci of the hyperbola and their coordinates are $(ae, 0)$ and $(-ae, 0)$ respectively and ZM and $Z'M'$ are two directrices of the hyperbola and their equations are $x=\dfrac{a}{e}$ and $x=-\dfrac{a}{e}$ respectively.

(iv) **Axes** The points $A(a, 0)$ and $A'(-a, 0)$ are called the vertices of the hyperbola and line AA' is called transverse axis and the line perpendicular to it through the centre $(0, 0)$ of the hyperbola is called conjugate axis. The length of transverse and conjugate axes are taken as $2a$ and $2b$, respectively.

(v) **Double ordinates** If Q be a point on the hyperbola, draw QN perpendicular to the axis of the hyperbola and produced to meet the curve again at Q'.
Then, QQ' is called a double ordinate of Q.
If abscissa of Q is h, then ordinates of Q' are

$$\frac{y^2}{b^2} = \frac{h^2}{a^2} - 1$$

$$\therefore \quad y = \pm \frac{b}{a}\sqrt{(h^2 - a^2)}$$

$$\therefore \quad y = \frac{b}{a}\sqrt{(h^2 - a^2)} \quad \text{[for Ist quadrant]}$$

and ordinate of Q' is

$$y = -\frac{b}{a}\sqrt{(h^2 - a^2)} \quad \text{[for IVth quadrant]}$$

Hence, coordinates of Q and Q' are

$$\left(h, \frac{b}{a}\sqrt{(h^2 - a^2)}\right) \text{ and } \left(h, -\frac{b}{a}\sqrt{(h^2 - a^2)}\right)$$

respectively.

(vi) **Latusrectum** The double ordinates LL' and L_1L_1' are the latusrectums of the hyperbola. These lines are perpendicular to transverse axis AA' and through the foci S and S', respectively.

Length of latusrectum

Now, let $LL' = 2k$, then $LS = L'S = k$

Coordinates of L and L' are (ae, k) and $(ae, -k)$

lie on the hyperbola $\frac{x^2}{a^2} - \frac{y^2}{b^2} = 1$

$$\therefore \quad \frac{a^2e^2}{a^2} - \frac{k^2}{b^2} = 1$$

or $$k^2 = b^2(e^2 - 1)$$

$$= b^2\left(\frac{b^2}{a^2}\right) \quad [\because b^2 = a^2(e^2 - 1)]$$

$$\therefore \quad k = \frac{b^2}{a} \quad [\because k > 0]$$

$$\therefore \quad 2k = \frac{2b^2}{a} = LL'$$

$\therefore$ Length of latusrectum $LL' = L_1L'_1 = \frac{2b^2}{a}$

and end points of latusrectums are

$$L \equiv \left(ae, \frac{b^2}{a}\right), L' \equiv \left(ae, -\frac{b^2}{a}\right),$$

$$L_1 \equiv \left(-ae, \frac{b^2}{a}\right) \text{ and } L_1' \equiv \left(-ae, -\frac{b^2}{a}\right),$$

respectively.

(vii) **Focal chord** A chord of hyperbola passing through its focus is called a focal chord.

(viii) **Parametric equations of the hyperbola** Let $\frac{x^2}{a^2} - \frac{y^2}{b^2} = 1$ be the hyperbola with centre C and transverse axis $A'A$.

Therefore, circle drawn with centre C and segment $A'A$ as a diameter is called auxiliary circle of the hyperbola $\frac{x^2}{a^2} - \frac{y^2}{b^2} = 1$.

$\therefore$ Equation of the auxiliary circle is $x^2 + y^2 = a^2$

Let $P(x, y)$ be any point on the hyperbola $\frac{x^2}{a^2} - \frac{y^2}{b^2} = 1$. Draw PN perpendicular to X-axis.

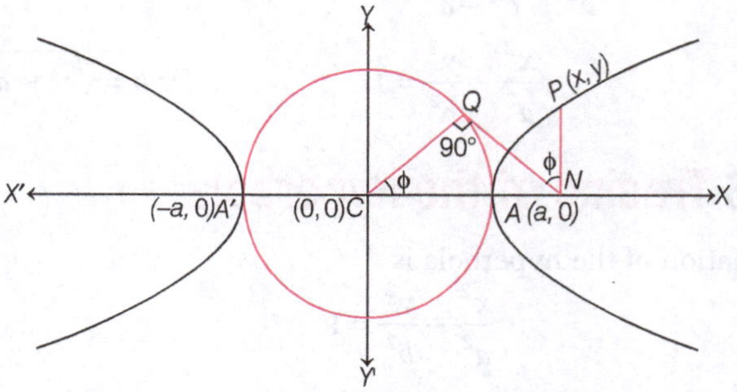

Let NQ be a tangent to the auxiliary circle $x^2 + y^2 = a^2$. Join CQ.

Let $\angle QCN = \phi$

Here, P and Q are the **corresponding points** of the hyperbola and the auxiliary circle. ϕ is the eccentric angle of $P \cdot (0 \le \phi < 2\pi)$

Since, $$Q \equiv (a\cos\phi, a\sin\phi)$$

Now, $$x = CN = \frac{CN}{CQ} \cdot CQ = \sec\phi \cdot a$$

$$\because \quad x = CN = a\sec\phi$$

$$\therefore \quad P(x, y) \equiv (a\sec\phi, y)$$

$\because$ P lies on $\frac{x^2}{a^2} - \frac{y^2}{b^2} = 1$

$$\therefore \quad \frac{a^2\sec^2\phi}{a^2} - \frac{y^2}{b^2} = 1$$

or $\frac{y^2}{b^2} = \sec^2\phi - 1 = \tan^2\phi$

$\therefore \quad y = \pm b \tan\phi$

$\therefore \quad y = b\tan\phi \quad$ [P lies in Ist quadrant]

The equations of $x = a\sec\phi$ and $y = b\tan\phi$ are known as the parametric equations of the hyperbola

$$\frac{x^2}{a^2} - \frac{y^2}{b^2} = 1.$$

Position of points Q describes an auxiliary circle and the corresponding point P which describes the hyperbola and $0 \le \phi < 2\pi$.

ϕ varies from	$Q\ (a\cos\phi, a\sin\phi)$	$P\ (a\sec\phi, b\tan\phi)$
0 to $\frac{\pi}{2}$	I	I
$\frac{\pi}{2}$ to π	II	III
π to $\frac{3\pi}{2}$	III	II
$\frac{3\pi}{2}$ to 2π	IV	IV

7.4 Focal Distances of a Point

The difference of the focal distances of any point on the hyperbola is constant and equal to length of the transverse axis of the hyperbola.

The hyperbola is $\frac{x^2}{a^2} - \frac{y^2}{b^2} = 1 \quad$ ...(i)

The foci S and S' are $(ae, 0)$ and $(-ae, 0)$.

The equation of its directrices MZ and $M'Z'$ are

$$x = \frac{a}{e} \text{ and } x = -\frac{a}{e}, \text{ respectively.}$$

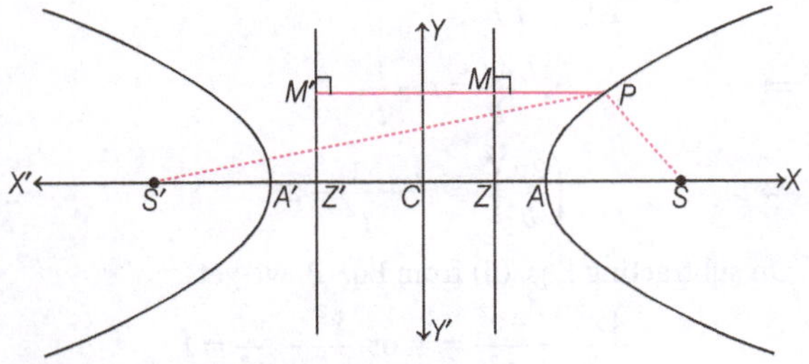

Let $P(x_1, y_1)$ be any point on Eq. (i).

Now, $\quad SP = ePM = e\left(x_1 - \frac{a}{e}\right) = ex_1 - a$

and $\quad S'P' = ePM' = e\left(x_1 + \frac{a}{e}\right) = ex_1 + a$

$\therefore \quad S'P - SP = (ex_1 + a) - (ex_1 - a)$

$= 2a = AA' =$ Transverse axis

Example 2. Find the vertices, foci, eccentricity, the length of transverse, conjugate axes and latusrectum and the equations of the directrices of the hyperbola $9x^2 - 4y^2 = 36$.

Sol. Given, $\quad 9x^2 - 4y^2 = 36$

$\Rightarrow \quad \frac{9x^2}{36} - \frac{4y^2}{36} = 1 \quad$ ...(i)

$\Rightarrow \quad \frac{x^2}{4} - \frac{y^2}{9} = 1$

On comparing Eq. (i) with $\frac{x^2}{a^2} - \frac{y^2}{b^2} = 1$, we get

$a^2 = 4$ and $b^2 = 9$

$\Rightarrow \quad a = 2$ and $b = 3$

Using $\quad b^2 = a^2(e^2 - 1)$

$\Rightarrow \quad 9 = 4(e^2 - 1)$

$\Rightarrow \quad \frac{9}{4} = (e^2 - 1)$

$\Rightarrow \quad e^2 = 9/4 + 1$

$\Rightarrow \quad e = \frac{\sqrt{13}}{2}$

Coordinate of vertices $= (\pm a, 0) = (\pm 2, 0)$

Coordinate of foci $= (\pm ae, 0) = \left(\pm 2 \times \frac{\sqrt{13}}{2}, 0\right)$

$= (\pm\sqrt{13}, 0)$

Length of transverse axis $= 2a = 2 \times 2 = 4$

Length of conjugate axis $= 2b = 2 \times 3 = 6$

Length of latusrectum $= \frac{2b^2}{a} = \frac{2 \times 9}{2} = 9$

Equation of directrices, $x = \pm a/e$

$= \pm\frac{2}{\frac{\sqrt{13}}{2}} = \pm\frac{4}{\sqrt{13}} = \pm\frac{4\sqrt{13}}{13}$

Example 3. Find the lengths of transverse axis and conjugate axis, eccentricity, the coordinates of foci, vertices, lengths of the latusrectum and equations of the directrices of the following hyperbolas

(i) $9x^2 - y^2 = 1 \qquad$ (ii) $16x^2 - 9y^2 = -144$

Sol. (i) The equation $9x^2 - y^2 = 1$ can be written as

$$\frac{x^2}{(1/9)} - \frac{y^2}{1} = 1.$$

This is of the form $\frac{x^2}{a^2} - \frac{y^2}{b^2} = 1$

On comparing, we get

$\therefore \quad a^2 = \frac{1}{9}$ and $b^2 = 1$

$\Rightarrow \quad a = \frac{1}{3}$ and $b = 1$

Length of transverse axis The length of transverse axis $= 2a = \frac{2}{3}$

Length of conjugate axis The length of conjugate axis $= 2b = 2$

Eccentricity, $e = \sqrt{\left(1 + \frac{b^2}{a^2}\right)} = \sqrt{1 + \frac{1}{(1/9)}} = \sqrt{10}$

Foci The coordinates of the foci are $(\pm ae, 0)$ i.e. $\left(\pm \frac{\sqrt{10}}{3}, 0\right)$.

Vertices The coordinates of the vertices are $(\pm a, 0)$ i.e. $\left(\pm \frac{1}{3}, 0\right)$.

Length of latusrectum The length of latusrectum

$$= \frac{2b^2}{a} = \frac{2(1)^2}{1/3} = 6$$

Equation of the directrices The equations of the directrices are

$$x = \pm \frac{a}{e}$$

i.e. $\quad x = \pm \frac{1/3}{\sqrt{10}}$

or $\quad x = \pm \frac{1}{3\sqrt{10}}$

(ii) The equation $16x^2 - 9y^2 = -144$ can be written as

$$\frac{x^2}{9} - \frac{y^2}{16} = -1$$

This is of the form $\frac{x^2}{a^2} - \frac{y^2}{b^2} = -1$

On comparing we get

$\therefore \quad a^2 = 9$ and $b^2 = 16$

$\Rightarrow \quad a = 3$ and $b = 4$

Length of transverse axis The length of transverse axis $= 2b = 8$.

Length of conjugate axis The length of conjugate axis $= 2a = 6$.

Eccentricity : $\quad e = \sqrt{\left(1 + \frac{a^2}{b^2}\right)} = \sqrt{\left(1 + \frac{9}{16}\right)} = \frac{5}{4}$

Foci The coordinates of the foci are $(0, \pm be)$ i.e. $(0, \pm 5)$

Vertices The coordinates of the vertices are $(0, \pm b)$ i.e. $(0, \pm 4)$.

Length of latusrectum The length of latusrectum $= \frac{2a^2}{b}$

$$= \frac{2(3)^2}{4} = \frac{9}{2}$$

Equation of directrices The equation of directrices are

$$y = \pm \frac{b}{e}$$

$$y = \pm \frac{4}{(5/4)} \Rightarrow y = \pm \frac{16}{5}$$

Example 4. Find the eccentricity of the hyperbola whose length of latusrectum is half of its transverse axis.

Sol. Let the equation of hyperbola be $\frac{x^2}{a^2} - \frac{y^2}{b^2} = 1$.

Then, transverse axis $= 2a$ and latusrectum $= \frac{2b^2}{a}$

According to the question, $\frac{2b^2}{a} = \frac{1}{2}(2a)$

$\Rightarrow \quad 2b^2 = a^2$

$\Rightarrow \quad 2a^2(e^2 - 1) = a^2 \quad [\because b^2 = a^2(e^2 - 1)]$

$\Rightarrow \quad 2e^2 - 2 = 1 \Rightarrow e^2 = \frac{3}{2}$

$\therefore \quad e = \sqrt{\frac{3}{2}}$

Hence, the required eccentricity is $\sqrt{\frac{3}{2}}$.

Example 5. Prove that the point $\left\{\frac{a}{2}\left(t + \frac{1}{t}\right), \frac{b}{2}\left(t - \frac{1}{t}\right)\right\}$ lies on the hyperbola for all values of $t \; (t \neq 0)$.

Sol. Let $x = \frac{a}{2}\left(t + \frac{1}{t}\right)$

$\Rightarrow \quad \frac{2x}{a} = t + \frac{1}{t}$

$\Rightarrow \quad \left(\frac{2x}{a}\right)^2 = t^2 + \frac{1}{t^2} + 2 \quad \text{...(i)}$

and let $y = \frac{b}{2}\left(t - \frac{1}{t}\right)$

$\Rightarrow \quad \frac{2y}{b} = t - \frac{1}{t}$

$\Rightarrow \quad \left(\frac{2y}{b}\right)^2 = t^2 + \frac{1}{t^2} - 2 \quad \text{...(ii)}$

On subtracting Eqs. (ii) from Eq. (i), we get

$$\frac{4x^2}{a^2} - \frac{4y^2}{b^2} = 4 \text{ or } \frac{x^2}{a^2} - \frac{y^2}{b^2} = 1$$

which is hyperbola.

Example 6. Find the equation of the hyperbola whose foci are (6, 4) and (–4, 4) and eccentricity is 2.

Sol. The centre of the hyperbola is the mid-point of the line joining the two foci. So, the coordinates of the centre are $\left(\frac{6-4}{2}, \frac{4+4}{2}\right)$ i.e. (1, 4)

Let $2a$ and $2b$ be the lengths of transverse and conjugate axes and let e be the eccentricity. Then, equation of hyperbola is

$$\frac{(x-1)^2}{a^2} - \frac{(y-4)^2}{b^2} = 1$$

$\because$ Distance between the foci $= 2ae$

$$\sqrt{(6+4)^2 + (4-4)^2} = 2a \times 2$$

$\Rightarrow$ $10 = 4a$

$\therefore$ $a = 5/2$

$\therefore$ $b^2 = a^2(e^2 - 1) = \frac{25}{4}(4-1) = \frac{75}{4}$

Thus, the equation of the hyperbola is

$$\frac{(x-1)^2}{\left(\frac{25}{4}\right)} - \frac{(y-4)^2}{\left(\frac{75}{4}\right)} = 1$$

$\Rightarrow$ $12(x-1)^2 - 4(y-4)^2 = 75$

$\Rightarrow$ $12(x^2 - 2x + 1) - 4(y^2 - 8y + 16) = 75$

$\Rightarrow$ $12x^2 - 4y^2 - 24x + 32y - 127 = 0$

Example 7. Obtain the equation of a hyperbola with coordinate axes as principal axes, given that the distances of one of its vertices from the foci are 9 and 1 units.

Sol. Let equation of hyperbola is

$$\frac{x^2}{a^2} - \frac{y^2}{b^2} = 1 \quad \text{...(i)}$$

If vertices are $A(a, 0)$ and $A'(-a, 0)$ and foci are $S(ae, 0)$ and $S'(-ae, 0)$.

Given, $l(S'A) = 9$ and $l(SA) = 1$

$\Rightarrow$ $a + ae = 9$ and $ae - a = 1$

$\Rightarrow$ $a(1+e) = 9$ and $a(e-1) = 1$

$\therefore$ $\frac{a(1+e)}{a(e-1)} = \frac{9}{1}$

$\Rightarrow$ $1 + e = 9e - 9 \Rightarrow e = \frac{5}{4}$

$\because$ $a(1+e) = 9$

$\therefore$ $a\left(1 + \frac{5}{4}\right) = 9 \Rightarrow a = 4$

$\Rightarrow$ $b^2 = a^2(e^2 - 1) = 16\left(\frac{25}{16} - 1\right)$

$\therefore$ $b^2 = 9$

From Eq. (i). equation of hyperbola is $\frac{x^2}{16} - \frac{y^2}{9} = 1$.

Example 8. For the hyperbola $\frac{x^2}{100} - \frac{y^2}{25} = 1$, find the value of $F_1A \cdot F_2A$, where F_1 and F_2 are foci and A is vertex of the hyperbola.

Sol. We have, $\frac{x^2}{100} - \frac{y^2}{25} = 1$

$\therefore$ $a^2 = 100, b^2 = 25$

$\therefore$ $e = \sqrt{1 + \frac{b^2}{a^2}} = \sqrt{1 + \frac{25}{100}} = \frac{\sqrt{5}}{2}$

Now, foci $= (\pm ae, 0) = \left(\pm 10 \times \frac{\sqrt{5}}{2}, 0\right)$

$= (\pm 5\sqrt{5}, 0)$

$\therefore$ $F_1 = (5\sqrt{5}, 0)$ and $F_2 = (-5\sqrt{5}, 0)$

Again, vertices $= (\pm a, 0) = (\pm 10, 0)$

$\therefore$ $A = (10, 0)$

Now, $F_1A = \sqrt{(10 - 5\sqrt{5})^2} = 10 - 5\sqrt{5}$

and $F_2A = \sqrt{(10 + 5\sqrt{5})^2 + 0^2} = 10 + 5\sqrt{5}$

$\therefore$ $F_1A \cdot F_2A = (10 - 5\sqrt{5})(10 + 5\sqrt{5})$

$= 100 - 75 = 25$

Example 9. Show that equation of one of the latusrectum of the hyperbola $(10x-5)^2 - (10y-2)^2 = 9(3x+4y-7)^2$ is $30x + 40y - 23 = 0$.

Sol. We have, $(10x-5)^2 - (10y-2)^2 = 9(3x+4y-7)^2$

$\Rightarrow$ $\left(x - \frac{1}{2}\right)^2 - \left(y - \frac{1}{5}\right)^2 = \frac{9}{4}\left(\frac{3x+4y-7}{5}\right)^2$

$\therefore$ Focus is $\left(\frac{1}{2}, \frac{1}{5}\right)$, $e = \frac{3}{2}$ and directrix is $3x + 4y - 7 = 0$.

Since, latusrectum is line parallel to directrix passing through focus.

Thus, equation of corresponding latusrectum will be $3x + 4y + \lambda = 0$ and it passes through $\left(\frac{1}{2}, \frac{1}{5}\right)$.

$\therefore$ $\frac{3}{2} + \frac{4}{5} + \lambda = 0$

$\Rightarrow$ $\lambda = \frac{-23}{10}$

So, equation of latusrectum is

$$3x + 4y - \frac{23}{10} = 0$$

$\therefore$ $30x + 40y - 23 = 0$

Example 10. If a latusrectum LL' of a hyperbola forms an equilateral triangle with third vertex at the other focus, then find the eccentricity.

Sol. Given, $\Delta S'LL'$ is an equilateral triangle.

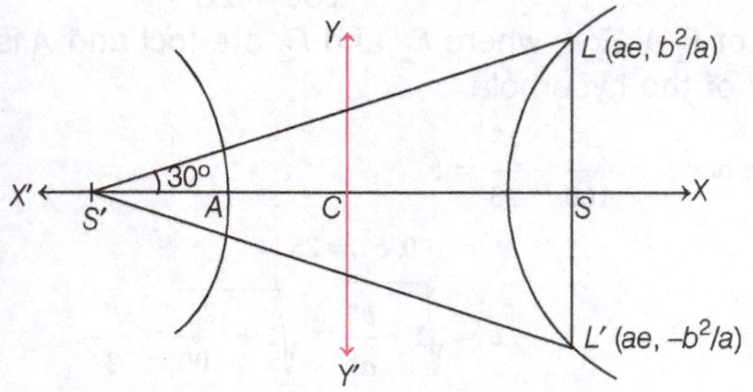

$\therefore \quad \angle LS'S = 30°$

$\Rightarrow \quad \tan 30° = \dfrac{b^2/a}{2ae}$

$\Rightarrow \quad \dfrac{1}{\sqrt{3}} = \dfrac{b^2}{2a^2e}$

$\Rightarrow \quad \dfrac{1}{\sqrt{3}} = \dfrac{1}{2}\left(\dfrac{e^2-1}{e}\right)$

$\Rightarrow \quad 2e = \sqrt{3}e^2 - \sqrt{3}$

$\Rightarrow \quad \sqrt{3}e^2 - 2e - \sqrt{3} = 0$

$\therefore \quad e = \sqrt{3}$

Example 11. If foci of a hyperbola are foci of the ellipse $\dfrac{x^2}{25} + \dfrac{y^2}{9} = 1$ and if the eccentricity of the hyperbola is 2, then find its equation.

Sol. Given, equation of ellipse is

$$\frac{x^2}{25} + \frac{y^2}{9} = 1$$

$\therefore \quad a^2 = 25, b^2 = 9$

So, $\quad e = \sqrt{1 - \dfrac{b^2}{a^2}} = \sqrt{1 - \dfrac{9}{25}} = \dfrac{4}{5}$

Now, foci of ellipse $= (\pm ae, 0) = (\pm 4, 0)$

Now, according to the question,

Foci of hyperbola is also $(\pm 4,0)$.

Let the equation of hyperbola be $\dfrac{x^2}{A^2} - \dfrac{y^2}{B^2} = 1$

$\therefore \quad (\pm Ae, 0) = (\pm 4, 0)$ and $e = 2$ [given]

$\Rightarrow \quad Ae = 4$

$\Rightarrow \quad 2A = 4$

$\Rightarrow \quad A = 2$

Again, $\quad B^2 = A^2(e^2 - 1)$

$\Rightarrow \quad B^2 = 4(4-1) = 12$

So, the equation of hyperbola is $\dfrac{x^2}{4} - \dfrac{y^2}{12} = 1$.

JEE SCANNER

Example Similar to PYQ Asked in JEE Main 2023

Let H be the hyperbola, whose foci are $(1 \pm \sqrt{5}, 0)$ and eccentricity is $\sqrt{5}$, then the length of its latusrectum is equal to ....

Sol. (8) We have, foci $= (1 \pm \sqrt{5}, 0)$

$\therefore \quad S_1 = (1+\sqrt{5}, 0)$ and $S_2 = (1-\sqrt{5}, 0)$

Now, $\quad S_1S_2 = 2ae$

$\Rightarrow \quad 2\sqrt{5} = 2a \times \sqrt{5} \Rightarrow a = 1$

Again, $\quad e = \sqrt{1 + \dfrac{b^2}{a^2}}$

$\Rightarrow \quad 5 = 1 + b^2 \quad [\because e = \sqrt{5}, a = 1]$

$\Rightarrow \quad b^2 = 4$

Now, length of $LR = \dfrac{2b^2}{a} = \dfrac{2 \times 4}{1} = 8$

Skill Builder

Let H be the hyperbola, whose foci are $(\pm 4, 0)$ and eccentricity is $\sqrt{2}$, so the length of its latusrectum is $a\sqrt{b}$, then $a+b$ is equal to ....

For Sol.

■ **For more practice** See Q.17 of Milestone Practice 7.1.

7.5 Conjugate Hyperbola

The hyperbola whose transverse and conjugate axes are respectively the conjugate and transverse axes of a given hyperbola is called the conjugate hyperbola of the given hyperbola. The conjugate hyperbola of the hyperbola

$$\frac{x^2}{a^2} - \frac{y^2}{b^2} = 1 \text{ is } -\frac{x^2}{a^2} + \frac{y^2}{b^2} = 1$$

its shape is shown below.

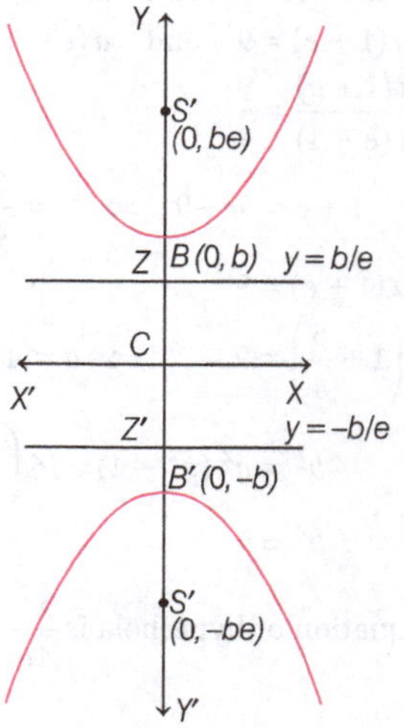

Various results related to hyperbola $\frac{x^2}{a^2}-\frac{y^2}{b^2}=1$ and its conjugate hyperbola

$$-\frac{x^2}{a^2}+\frac{y^2}{b^2}=1$$

or $$\frac{x^2}{a^2}-\frac{y^2}{b^2}=-1$$

are given in the following table

Hyperbola Basic Fundamentals	$\frac{x^2}{a^2}-\frac{y^2}{b^2}=1$	$-\frac{x^2}{a^2}+\frac{y^2}{b^2}=1$ or $\frac{x^2}{a^2}-\frac{y^2}{b^2}=-1$
Centre	$(0,0)$	$(0,0)$
Length of transverse axis	$2a$	$2b$
Length of conjugate axis	$2b$	$2a$
Foci	$(\pm ae, 0)$	$(0, \pm be)$
Equation of directrices	$x=\pm a/e$	$y=\pm b/e$
Eccentricity	$e=\sqrt{\left(\frac{a^2+b^2}{a^2}\right)}$	$e=\sqrt{\left(\frac{a^2+b^2}{b^2}\right)}$
Length of latusrectum	$\frac{2b^2}{a}$	$\frac{2a^2}{b}$
Parametric coordinates	$(a\sec\phi, b\tan\phi)$, $0\le\phi<2\pi$	$(a\tan\phi, b\sec\phi)$, $0\le\phi<2\pi$
Focal radii	$SP=ex_1-a$ and $S'P=ex_1+a$	$SP=ey_1-b$ and $S'P=ey_1+b$
Difference of focal radii $(S'P-SP)$	$2a$	$2b$
Tangents at the vertices	$x=-a, x=a$	$y=-b, y=b$
Equation of the transverse axis	$y=0$	$x=0$
Equation of the conjugate axis	$x=0$	$y=0$

JEE Focus Points

- If the centre of hyperbola is (h,k) and axes are parallel to the coordinates axes, then its equation is

$$\frac{(x-h)^2}{a^2}-\frac{(y-k)^2}{b^2}=1.$$

By shifting the origin at (h, k) without rotating the coordinate axes, the above equation reduces to

$$\frac{X^2}{a^2}-\frac{Y^2}{b^2}=1, \quad \text{where } X=X+h, y=Y+k$$

- If e_1 and e_2 are the eccentricities of a hyperbola and its conjugate, respectively, then $e_1^{-2}+e_2^{-2}=1$.

Proof For hyperbola $b^2=a^2(e_1^2-1)$

or $$e_1^2=1+\frac{b^2}{a^2}=\frac{a^2+b^2}{a^2} \quad \text{... (i)}$$

and for conjugate hyperbola $a^2=b^2(e_2^2-1)$

or $$e_2^2=1+\frac{a^2}{b^2}=\frac{a^2+b^2}{b^2} \quad \text{... (ii)}$$

From Eqs. (i) and (ii), we get

$$\frac{1}{e_1^2}+\frac{1}{e_2^2}=1 \text{ or } e_1^{-2}+e_2^{-2}=1$$

- The foci of a hyperbola and its conjugate are concyclic and form the vertices of a square.
- A simple method to find the coordinates of the centre of the hyperbola expressed as a general equation of degree two should be remembered as :

Let $\phi(x, y)=0$ represents a hyperbola.

Find $\frac{\partial\phi}{\partial x}$ (differentiate w.r.t x keeping y as constant) and $\frac{\partial\phi}{\partial y}$ (differentiate w.r.t. y keeping x as constant).

Then, the point of intersection of $\frac{\partial\phi}{\partial x}=0$ and $\frac{\partial\phi}{\partial y}=0$ gives the centre of the hyperbola.

Example 12. The eccentricity of the conjugate hyperbola of the hyperbola $x^2-3y^2=1$ is

(a) 2

(b) $2/\sqrt{3}$

(c) 4

(d) 4/3

Sol. Given, hyperbola is $x^2-3y^2=1$

$$\Rightarrow \quad \frac{x^2}{1}-\frac{y^2}{1/3}=1$$

$$\because \quad a^2=1 \text{ and } b^2=1/3$$

Let e' be the eccentricity of conjugate hyperbola, then

$$1=\frac{1}{3}(e'^2-1)$$

$$\Rightarrow \quad 3=e'^2-1$$

$$\Rightarrow \quad e'^2=4$$

Hence, $$e'=2$$

Example 13. Show that the equation $7y^2 - 9x^2 + 54x - 28y - 116 = 0$ represent a hyperbola. Find the coordinates of the centre, lengths of transverse and conjugate axes, eccentricity, latusrectum, coordinates of foci, vertices and equations of the directrices of the hyperbola.

Sol. We have, $7y^2 - 9x^2 + 54x - 28y - 116 = 0$

$\Rightarrow \quad 7(y^2 - 4y) - 9(x^2 - 6x) - 116 = 0$

$\Rightarrow \quad 7(y^2 - 4y + 4) - 9(x^2 - 6x + 9) = 116 + 28 - 81$

$\Rightarrow \quad 7(y-2)^2 - 9(x-3)^2 = 63$

$$\Rightarrow \quad \frac{(y-2)^2}{9} - \frac{(x-3)^2}{7} = 1$$

$$\Rightarrow \quad \frac{Y^2}{9} - \frac{X^2}{7} = 1$$

where, $X = x - 3$ and $Y = y - 2$

This equation represents conjugate hyperbola.

Comparing it with $\frac{Y^2}{b^2} - \frac{X^2}{a^2} = 1$, we get

$b^2 = 9$ and $a^2 = 7$

$\therefore \quad b = 3$ and $a = \sqrt{7}$

$\because \quad X = 0, Y = 0$

i.e. $\quad x - 3 = 0, y - 2 = 0$

$\therefore$ Centre is (3, 2).

Length of transverse axis Length of transverse axis $= 2b = 6$

Length of conjugate axis Length of conjugate axis $= 2a = 2\sqrt{7}$

Eccentricity The eccentricity e is given by

$$e = \sqrt{1 + \frac{a^2}{b^2}} = \sqrt{1 + \frac{7}{9}} = \frac{4}{3}$$

Length of latusrectum The length of latusrectum

$$= \frac{2a^2}{b} = \frac{2(7)}{3} = \frac{14}{3}$$

Foci The coordinates of foci are $(0, \pm be)$

$\therefore \quad X = 0, Y = \pm be$

$\Rightarrow \quad x - 3 = 0, y - 2 = \pm 3 \times \frac{4}{3}$ or $(3, 2 \pm 4)$

i.e. $(3, -2)$ and $(3, 6)$

Vertices The coordinates of vertices are $(0, \pm b)$

or $\quad X = 0, Y = \pm b$

or $\quad x - 3 = 0, y - 2 = \pm 3$ or $(3, 2 \pm 3)$

or vertices are $(3, -1)$ and $(3, 5)$.

Equation of directrices The equation of directrices are

$$Y = \pm \frac{b}{e}$$

$$\Rightarrow \quad y - 2 = \pm \frac{3}{4/3} \Rightarrow y = \left(2 \pm \frac{9}{4}\right)$$

i.e. $\quad y = \frac{17}{4}$ and $y = -\frac{1}{4}$

JEE SCANNER

Example Similar to PYQ Asked in JEE Main 2023

Let $a > 0$, $b > 0$. Let e and l respectively be the eccentricity and length of the latusrectum of the hyperbola $\frac{x^2}{a^2} - \frac{y^2}{b^2} = 1$. Let e' and l' respectively be the eccentricity and length of the latusrectum of its conjugate hyperbola. If $e^2 = \frac{13}{18} l$ and $(e')^2 = \frac{13}{10} l'$, then the value of $117a + 65b$ is equal to ....

Sol. (1170) Given, hyperbola is $\frac{x^2}{a^2} - \frac{y^2}{b^2} = 1$.

Then, $\quad l = \frac{2b^2}{a}, l' = \frac{2a^2}{b}$

Now, $\quad e^2 = \frac{13}{18} l$

$$\Rightarrow \quad \frac{a^2 + b^2}{a^2} = \frac{13}{18} \times \frac{2b^2}{a}$$

$$\Rightarrow \quad a^2 + b^2 = \frac{13}{9} ab^2 \qquad ...(i)$$

and $\quad (e')^2 = \frac{13}{10} l'$

$$\Rightarrow \quad \frac{b^2 + a^2}{b^2} = \frac{13}{10} \times \frac{2a^2}{b}$$

$$\Rightarrow \quad a^2 + b^2 = \frac{13}{5} a^2 b \qquad ...(ii)$$

From Eqs. (i) and (ii), we get

$$9a = 5b$$

Now, from Eqs. (i), we get

$$a^2 + \frac{81}{25} a^2 = \frac{13}{9} a \times \frac{81}{25} a^2$$

$$\Rightarrow \quad \frac{106}{25} a^2 = \frac{117 a^3}{25}$$

$$\Rightarrow \quad 106 = 117a$$

and $\quad b = \frac{9a}{5} = \frac{9}{5} \times \frac{106}{117} = \frac{106}{65}$

$$\Rightarrow \quad 65b = 106$$

Hence, $\quad 117a + 65b = 212$

Skill Builder

Let $a, b > 0$. Let e and l respectively be the eccentricity and length of LR of the hyperbola $\frac{x^2}{a^2} - \frac{y^2}{b^2} = 1$. Let e' and l' respectively be the eccentricity and length of LR of its conjugate hyperbola. If $e^2 = \frac{17}{20} l$ and $(e')^2 = \frac{17}{14} l'$, then the value of $170a + 119b$ is equal to ....

For Sol.

■ **For more Practice** See Q. 18 of Milestone Practice 7.1.

Milestone Practice 7.1

1. Find the equation of hyperbola whose focus is $(-1, 2)$, eccentricity is 3 and directrix is $x + y - 7 = 0$.

2. If e_1 and e_2 are the eccentricities of the conic sections $16x^2 + 9y^2 = 144$ and $9x^2 - 16y^2 = 144$, then
   (a) $e_1^2 - e_2^2 = 1$ (b) $e_1^2 + e_2^2 < 3$
   (c) $e_1^2 + e_2^2 = 3$ (d) $e_1^2 + e_2^2 > 3$

3. The transverse axis of a hyperbola is of length $2a$ and a vertex divides the segment of the axis between the centre and the corresponding focus in the ratio 2 : 1, then the equation of the hyperbola is
   (a) $4x^2 - 5y^2 = 4a^2$ (b) $4x^2 - 5y^2 = 5a^2$
   (c) $5x^2 - 4y^2 = 4a^2$ (d) $5x^2 - 4y^2 = 5a^2$

4. The eccentricity of the hyperbola whose latusrectum is 8 and conjugate axis is equal to half of the distance between the foci, is
   (a) $\frac{2}{\sqrt{3}}$ (b) $\frac{3}{\sqrt{3}}$ (c) $\frac{4}{\sqrt{3}}$ (d) $\frac{5}{\sqrt{3}}$

5. If e and e′ are the eccentricities of the hyperbola $\frac{x^2}{a^2} - \frac{y^2}{b^2} = 1$ and $\frac{x^2}{b^2} - \frac{y^2}{a^2} = 1$, then the point $\left(\frac{1}{e}, \frac{1}{e'}\right)$ lies on the circle
   (a) $x^2 + y^2 = 1$ (b) $x^2 + y^2 = 2$
   (c) $x^2 + y^2 = 3$ (d) $x^2 + y^2 = 4$

6. If e and e′ are the eccentricities of the ellipse $5x^2 + 9y^2 = 45$ and the hyperbola $5x^2 - 4y^2 = 45$ respectively, then ee' is equal to
   (a) -1 (b) 1 (c) -4 (d) 9

7. The equation $\frac{x^2}{10 - \lambda} + \frac{y^2}{6 - \lambda} = 1$ represents
   (a) a hyperbola if $\lambda < 6$ (b) an ellipse if $\lambda > 6$
   (c) a hyperbola if $6 < \lambda < 10$ (d) an ellipse if $0 < \lambda < 6$

8. The eccentricity of the hyperbola conjugate to $x^2 - 3y^2 = 2x + 8$ is
   (a) $\frac{2}{\sqrt{3}}$ (b) $\sqrt{3}$ (c) 2 (d) $\sqrt{2}$

9. For hyperbola $\frac{x^2}{\cos^2\alpha} - \frac{y^2}{\sin^2\alpha} = 1$ which of the following remains constant with change in α
   (a) Abscissae of vertices (b) Abscissae of foci
   (c) Eccentricity (d) Directrix

10. If the foci of the ellipse $\frac{x^2}{16} + \frac{y^2}{b^2} = 1$ and the hyperbola $\frac{x^2}{144} - \frac{y^2}{81} = \frac{1}{25}$ coincide, then the value of b^2 is
    (a) 1 (b) 5 (c) 7 (d) 9

11. Find the equation of the hyperbola whose foci are $(0, \pm\sqrt{10})$ and which passes through the point $(2, 3)$.

12. Find the equation of the hyperbola whose foci are $(10, 5)$ and $(-2, 5)$ and eccentricity 3.

13. Prove that the straight lines $\frac{x}{a} - \frac{y}{b} = m$ and $\frac{x}{a} + \frac{y}{b} = \frac{1}{m}$ always meet on a hyperbola.

14. Find the centre, eccentricity and length of axes of the hyperbola $3x^2 - 5y^2 - 6x + 20y - 32 = 0$.

15. Find the eccentricity of the hyperbola conjugate to the hyperbola $x^2 - 3y^2 = 1$.

16. A hyperbola passes through the foci of the ellipse $\frac{x^2}{25} + \frac{y^2}{16} = 1$ and its transverse and conjugate axes coincide with major and minor axis of the ellipse. If the product of their eccentricities is one, then find the equation of the hyperbola.

17. Let H be the hyperbola, whose foci are $(\pm 5, 0)$ and eccentricity is 2, then find the length of its latusrectum.

18. Let $a, b > 0$. Let e and l respectively be the eccentricity and length of latusrectum of the hyperbola $\frac{x^2}{a^2} - \frac{y^2}{b^2} = 1$. Let e′ and l' respectively eccentricity and length of latusrectum of its conjugate hyperbola. If $e^2 = \frac{9}{10}l$ and $(e')^2 = \frac{9}{8}l'$, then find the value of $a + b$.

Answer Key

1. $7x^2 + 7y^2 + 18xy - 130x - 118y + 431 = 0$ 2. (b) 3. (d) 4. (a) 5. (a) 6. (b)
7. (c, d) 8. (c) 9. (b) 10. (c) 11. $y^2 - x^2 = 5$ 12. $\frac{(x-4)^2}{4} - \frac{(y-5)^2}{32} = 1$
14. Centre = (1, 2), eccentricity = $2\sqrt{\frac{2}{5}}$, Length of conjugate axis = $2\sqrt{3}$, Length of transversal axis = $2\sqrt{5}$
15. 2 16. $\frac{x^2}{9} - \frac{y^2}{16} = 1$ 17. 15 18. 2 (approx)

For Detailed Solution

Milestone 2 Line and Hyperbola

- Position of Point with respect to Hyerpbola • Intersection of a Line and a Hyperbola
- Equations of Tangents in Different Forms • Equation of Normals in Different Forms • Pair of Tangents
- Chord of Contact • Equation of the Chord Bisected at a Given Point

7.6 Position of Point with respect to Hyperbola

Theorem The point (x_1, y_1) lies outside, on or inside the hyperbola $\frac{x^2}{a^2} - \frac{y^2}{b^2} = 1$ according as $\frac{x_1^2}{a^2} - \frac{y_1^2}{b^2} - 1 <, = \text{ or } > 0$

Proof Let $P \equiv (x_1, y_1)$ then $Q \equiv (x_1, y_2)$

Draw PL perpendicular to X-axis

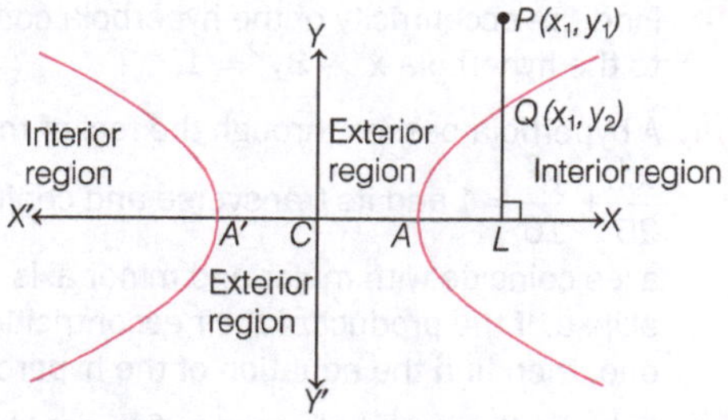

Clearly, $PL > QL$

$$\Rightarrow \quad y_1 > y_2$$

$$\Rightarrow \quad \frac{y_1^2}{b^2} > \frac{y_2^2}{b^2} \Rightarrow -\frac{y_1^2}{b^2} < -\frac{y_2^2}{b^2}$$

$$\Rightarrow \quad \frac{x_1^2}{a^2} - \frac{y_1^2}{b^2} < \frac{x_1^2}{a^2} - \frac{y_2^2}{b^2}$$

$$\Rightarrow \quad \frac{x_1^2}{a^2} - \frac{y_1^2}{b^2} < 1 \left[\because Q(x_1, y_2) \text{ lies on } \frac{x^2}{a^2} - \frac{y^2}{b^2} = 1\right]$$

$$\Rightarrow \quad \frac{x_1^2}{a^2} - \frac{y_1^2}{b^2} - 1 < 0$$

Thus, the point $P(x_1, y_1)$ lies outside the hyperbola. Hence, the point (x_1, y_1) lies outside, on or inside the hyperbola

$$\frac{x^2}{a^2} - \frac{y^2}{b^2} = 1$$

according as $\frac{x_1^2}{a^2} - \frac{y_1^2}{b^2} - 1 <, = \text{or } > 0.$

Example 14. Find the position of the point $(5, -4)$ relative to the hyperbola $9x^2 - y^2 = 1$.

Sol. Since, $9(5)^2 - (-4)^2 - 1 = 225 - 16 - 1 = 208 > 0$

So, the point $(5, -4)$ lies inside the hyperbola $9x^2 - y^2 = 1$.

7.7 Intersection of a Line and a Hyperbola

Let the hyperbola be $\frac{x^2}{a^2} - \frac{y^2}{b^2} = 1$ ...(i)

and the given line be $y = mx + c$. ...(ii)

On eliminating y from Eqs. (i) and (ii), then

$$\frac{x^2}{a^2} - \frac{(mx+c)^2}{b^2} = 1$$

$$\Rightarrow \quad b^2x^2 - a^2(mx+c)^2 = a^2b^2$$

$$\Rightarrow \quad (a^2m^2 - b^2)x^2 + 2mca^2x + a^2(b^2 + c^2) = 0 \quad \text{...(iii)}$$

Above equation being a quadratic in x gives two values of x. It shows that every straight line will cut the hyperbola in two points, may be real, coincident or imaginary, according as discriminant of Eq. (iii) $>, =, < 0$

i.e. $4m^2c^2a^4 - 4(a^2m^2 - b^2)a^2(b^2 + c^2) >, =, < 0$

or $\quad -a^2m^2 + b^2 + c^2 >, =, < 0$

or $\quad c^2 >, =, < a^2m^2 - b^2$ ...(iv)

Condition of Tangency If the line (ii) touches the hyperbola (i), then Eq. (iii) has equal roots.

$\therefore$ Discriminant of Eq. (iii) $= 0$

$$\Rightarrow \quad c^2 = a^2m^2 - b^2$$

or $\quad c = \pm\sqrt{(a^2m^2 - b^2)}$ ...(v)

So, the line $y = mx + c$ touches the hyperbola

$$\frac{x^2}{a^2} - \frac{y^2}{b^2} = 1 \quad \text{if} \quad c^2 = a^2m^2 - b^2$$

[which is condition of tangency]

On substituting the value of c from Eq. (v) in Eq. (ii)

$$y = mx \pm \sqrt{(a^2m^2 - b^2)}$$

Hence, the line $y = mx \pm \sqrt{(a^2m^2 - b^2)}$ will always be tangent to the hyperbola.

Point of contact On substituting $c = \pm\sqrt{(a^2m^2 - b^2)}$ in Eq. (iii)

$$(a^2m^2 - b^2)\,x^2 \pm 2ma^2\sqrt{(a^2m^2 - b^2)}\;x + a^4m^2 = 0$$

or $(x\sqrt{(a^2m^2 - b^2)} \pm a^2m)^2 = 0$

$$\therefore \quad x = \pm\frac{a^2m}{\sqrt{(a^2m^2 - b^2)}} = \pm\frac{a^2m}{c}$$

From Eq. (i), $\dfrac{a^4m^2}{c^2}\cdot\dfrac{1}{a^2} - \dfrac{y^2}{b^2} = 1$

$$\Rightarrow \quad \frac{y^2}{b^2} = \frac{a^2m^2}{c^2} - 1 = -\frac{(c^2 - a^2m^2)}{c^2} = \frac{b^2}{c^2}$$

$$\therefore \quad y = \pm\frac{b^2}{c}$$

Hence, the point of contact is $\left(\pm\dfrac{a^2m}{c}, \pm\dfrac{b^2}{c}\right)$.

This is known as ***m*-point** on the hyperbola.

JEE SPIKE

If $m = 0$, then Eq. (iii) gives

$$-b^2x^2 + a^2(b^2 + c^2) = 0$$

$$x^2 = \frac{a^2(b^2 + c^2)}{b^2}$$

$$\therefore \quad x = \pm\frac{a}{b}\sqrt{(b^2 + c^2)}$$

which gives two values of x.

Concept Inside Video

Example 15. Prove that the straight line $lx + my + n = 0$ touches the hyperbola $\dfrac{x^2}{a^2} - \dfrac{y^2}{b^2} = 1$ if $a^2l^2 - b^2m^2 = n^2$.

Sol. The given line is $lx + my + n = 0$ or $y = -\dfrac{l}{m}x - \dfrac{n}{m}$

On comparing this line with $y = Mx + c$ ...(i)

$$\therefore \quad M = -\frac{l}{m} \text{ and } c = -\frac{n}{m}$$

This line (i) will touch the hyperbola

$$\frac{x^2}{a^2} - \frac{y^2}{b^2} = 1 \text{ if } c^2 = a^2M^2 - b^2$$

$$\Rightarrow \quad \frac{n^2}{m^2} = \frac{a^2l^2}{m^2} - b^2 \text{ or } a^2l^2 - b^2m^2 = n^2$$

Example 16. Show that the line $x\cos\alpha + y\sin\alpha = p$ touches the hyperbola $\dfrac{x^2}{a^2} - \dfrac{y^2}{b^2} = 1$ if $a^2\cos^2\alpha - b^2\sin^2\alpha = p^2$.

Sol. The given line is $x\cos\alpha + y\sin\alpha = p$

$$\Rightarrow \quad y\sin\alpha = -x\cos\alpha + p$$

$$\Rightarrow \quad y = -x\cot\alpha + p\,\text{cosec}\,\alpha$$

On comparing this line with $y = mx + c$, then

$$\Rightarrow \quad m = -\cot\alpha,\ c = p\,\text{cosec}\,\alpha$$

Since, the given line touches the hyperbola $\dfrac{x^2}{a^2} - \dfrac{y^2}{b^2} = 1$.

Then, $c^2 = a^2m^2 - b^2$

$$\Rightarrow \quad p^2\text{cosec}^2\alpha = a^2\cot^2\alpha - b^2$$

or $p^2 = a^2\cos^2\alpha - b^2\sin^2\alpha$

Example 17. For what value of λ does the line $y = 2x + \lambda$ touches the hyperbola $16x^2 - 9y^2 = 144$?

Sol. Equation of hyperbola is

$$16x^2 - 9y^2 = 144$$

or $\dfrac{x^2}{9} - \dfrac{y^2}{16} = 1$

On comparing with $\dfrac{x^2}{a^2} - \dfrac{y^2}{b^2} = 1$, we get $a^2 = 9, b^2 = 16$

and comparing this line $y = 2x + \lambda$ with $y = mx + c$

$$\therefore \quad m = 2 \text{ and } c = \lambda$$

If the line $y = 2x + \lambda$ touches the hyperbola $16x^2 - 9y^2 = 144$.

Then, $c^2 = a^2m^2 - b^2$

$$\Rightarrow \quad \lambda^2 = 9(2)^2 - 16$$

$$= 36 - 16 = 20$$

$$\therefore \quad \lambda = \pm 2\sqrt{5}$$

Example 18. If it is possible to draw a tangent to the hyperbola $\dfrac{x^2}{a^2} - \dfrac{y^2}{b^2} = 1$ having slope 2, then find its range of eccentricity.

Sol. Tangent having slope m is $y = mx \pm \sqrt{(a^2m^2 - b^2)}$

The tangent having slope 2 is $y = 2x \pm \sqrt{(4a^2 - b^2)}$, which is real if

$$4a^2 - b^2 \geq 0$$

or $\dfrac{b^2}{a^2} \leq 4$

or $e^2 - 1 \leq 4$

or $e^2 \leq 5$

or $1 < e \leq \sqrt{5}$ [for hyperbola $e > 1$]

JEE SCANNER

Example Similar to PYQ Asked in JEE Main 2022

Let the eccentricity of the hyperbola $H: \frac{x^2}{a^2} - \frac{y^2}{b^2} = 1$ be $\frac{5}{3}$ and length of its latusrectum be $\frac{32}{3}$. If $y = 2x + c$ is a tangent to the hyperbola H, then the value of c^2 is ......

Sol. (20) Given, $e = \frac{5}{3}$

$$\Rightarrow \quad 1 + \frac{b^2}{a^2} = \frac{25}{9}$$

$$\Rightarrow \quad \frac{b^2}{a^2} = \frac{16}{9} \quad \text{...(i)}$$

and $$\frac{2b^2}{a} = \frac{32}{3} \quad \text{[given]}$$

$$\Rightarrow \quad b^2 = \frac{16}{3}a \quad \text{...(ii)}$$

From Eqs. (i) and (ii),

$$\therefore \quad \frac{16a^2}{9} = \frac{16}{3}a \Rightarrow a = 3$$

$$\therefore \quad b^2 = 16$$

Hence, $$c^2 = a^2m^2 - b^2 = 9 \times 4 - 16 = 20$$

Skill Builder

Let the eccentricity of the hyperbola $H: \frac{x^2}{a^2} - \frac{y^2}{b^2} = 1$ be $\frac{\sqrt{5}}{2}$ and length of its latusrectum be 3. If $y = x + c$ is a tangent to the hyperbola H, then the value of c^2 is ......

For Sol.

- **For more practice** See Q.13 of Milestone Practice 7.2.

7.8 Equations of Tangents in Different Forms

1. Point form (first principal method)

Theorem The equation of the tangent to the hyperbola $\frac{x^2}{a^2} - \frac{y^2}{b^2} = 1$ at (x_1, y_1) is $\frac{xx_1}{a^2} - \frac{yy_1}{b^2} = 1$.

Proof Equation of hyperbola is

$$\frac{x^2}{a^2} - \frac{y^2}{b^2} = 1 \quad \text{...(i)}$$

Let $P \equiv (x_1, y_1)$ and $Q \equiv (x_2, y_2)$ be any two points put in Eq. (i).

Then, $$\frac{x_1^2}{a^2} - \frac{y_1^2}{b^2} = 1 \quad \text{...(ii)}$$

and $$\frac{x_2^2}{a^2} - \frac{y_2^2}{b^2} = 1 \quad \text{...(iii)}$$

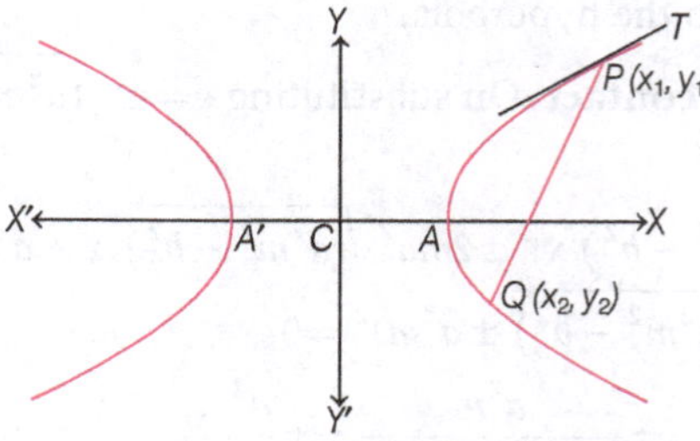

On subtracting Eq. (ii) from Eq. (iii), then

$$\frac{1}{a^2}(x_2^2 - x_1^2) - \frac{1}{b^2}(y_2^2 - y_1^2) = 0$$

$$\Rightarrow \quad \frac{(x_2 - x_1)(x_2 + x_1)}{a^2} - \frac{(y_2 - y_1)(y_2 + y_1)}{b^2} = 0$$

$$\Rightarrow \quad \frac{y_2 - y_1}{x_2 - x_1} = \frac{b^2}{a^2}\frac{(x_1 + x_2)}{(y_1 + y_2)} \quad \text{...(iv)}$$

Equation of PQ is

$$y - y_1 = \frac{y_2 - y_1}{x_2 - x_1}(x - x_1) \quad \text{...(v)}$$

From Eqs. (iv) and (v), we get

$$y - y_1 = \frac{b^2}{a^2} \cdot \frac{(x_1 + x_2)}{(y_1 + y_2)}(x - x_1) \quad \text{...(vi)}$$

Now, tangent at $P, Q \to P$

i.e. $x_2 \to x_1$ and $y_2 \to y_1$, then Eq. (vi) becomes

$$y - y_1 = \frac{b^2}{a^2} \cdot \frac{(2x_1)}{(2y_1)}(x - x_1)$$

or $$\frac{yy_1 - y_1^2}{b^2} = \frac{xx_1 - x_1^2}{a^2}$$

or $$\frac{xx_1}{a^2} - \frac{yy_1}{b^2} = \frac{x_1^2}{a^2} - \frac{y_1^2}{b^2}$$

or $$\frac{xx_1}{a^2} - \frac{yy_1}{b^2} = 1 \quad \text{[from Eq. (ii)]}$$

which is the required equation of tangent at (x_1, y_1).

2. Parametric form

Theorem The equation of tangent to the hyperbola $\frac{x^2}{a^2} - \frac{y^2}{b^2} = 1$ at $(a \sec \phi, b \tan \phi)$ is

$$\frac{x}{a}\sec\phi - \frac{y}{b}\tan\phi = 1$$

Proof Since, equation of tangent at (x_1, y_1) is

$$\frac{xx_1}{a^2} - \frac{yy_1}{b^2} = 1$$

Now, replacing x_1 by $a \sec\phi$ and y_1 by $b \tan\phi$, we get

$$\frac{x}{a}\sec\phi - \frac{y}{b}\tan\phi = 1$$

JEE SPIKE

The point of intersection of tangents at θ and ϕ on the hyperbola $\frac{x^2}{a^2} - \frac{y^2}{b^2} = 1$ is

$$\left(\frac{a\cos\left(\frac{\theta-\phi}{2}\right)}{\cos\left(\frac{\theta+\phi}{2}\right)}, \frac{b\sin\left(\frac{\theta+\phi}{2}\right)}{\cos\left(\frac{\theta+\phi}{2}\right)}\right)$$

Concept Inside Video

Remembering method

$\because$ Equations of chord joining θ and ϕ is

$$\frac{x}{a}\cos\left(\frac{\theta-\phi}{2}\right) - \frac{y}{b}\sin\left(\frac{\theta+\phi}{2}\right) = \cos\left(\frac{\theta+\phi}{2}\right)$$

or
$$\frac{x}{a}\left\{\frac{\cos\left(\frac{\theta-\phi}{2}\right)}{\cos\left(\frac{\theta+\phi}{2}\right)}\right\} - \frac{y}{b}\left\{\frac{\sin\left(\frac{\theta+\phi}{2}\right)}{\cos\left(\frac{\theta+\phi}{2}\right)}\right\} = 1$$

or
$$\frac{x}{a^2}\left\{\frac{a\cos\left(\frac{\theta-\phi}{2}\right)}{\cos\left(\frac{\theta+\phi}{2}\right)}\right\} - \frac{y}{b^2}\left\{\frac{b\sin\left(\frac{\theta+\phi}{2}\right)}{\cos\left(\frac{\theta+\phi}{2}\right)}\right\} = 1$$

i.e.
$$\left\{\frac{a\cos\left(\frac{\theta-\phi}{2}\right)}{\cos\left(\frac{\theta+\phi}{2}\right)}, \frac{b\sin\left(\frac{\theta+\phi}{2}\right)}{\cos\left(\frac{\theta+\phi}{2}\right)}\right\}$$

3. Slope form

Theorem The equations of tangents of slope m to the hyperbola $\frac{x^2}{a^2} - \frac{y^2}{b^2} = 1$ is given by

$$y = mx \pm \sqrt{(a^2m^2 - b^2)}$$

The coordinates of the points of contact are

$$\left(\pm\frac{a^2m}{\sqrt{(a^2m^2 - b^2}}, \pm\frac{b^2}{\sqrt{(a^2m^2 - b^2)}}\right)$$

Proof Let $y = mx + c$ be a tangent to the hyperbola

$$\frac{x^2}{a^2} - \frac{y^2}{b^2} = 1 \qquad \text{...(i)}$$

On substituting the value of $y = mx + c$ in Eq. (i), then

$$\frac{x^2}{a^2} - \frac{(mx+c)^2}{b^2} = 1$$

or $(a^2m^2 - b^2)x^2 + 2mca^2x + a^2(c^2 + b^2) = 0$

must have equal roots

$$\therefore \quad 4a^4m^2c^2 - 4(a^2m^2 - b^2)a^2(c^2 + b^2) = 0$$

$$[\because B^2 - 4AC = 0]$$

$$\Rightarrow \quad a^2m^2c^2 - (a^2m^2 - b^2)(b^2 + c^2) = 0$$

$$\Rightarrow \quad a^2m^2c^2 - a^2b^2m^2 - a^2m^2c^2 + b^4 + b^2c^2 = 0$$

$$\Rightarrow \quad -a^2b^2m^2 + b^4 + b^2c^2 = 0 \Rightarrow c^2 = a^2m^2 - b^2$$

$$\therefore \quad c = \pm\sqrt{(a^2m^2 - b^2)}$$

On substituting this value of c in $y = mx + c$, we get

$$y = mx \pm \sqrt{(a^2m^2 - b^2)} \qquad \text{...(ii)}$$

as the required equation of tangents of hyperbola in terms of slope.

$\because$ Tangent at (x_1, y_1) to the hyperbola $\frac{x^2}{a^2} - \frac{y^2}{b^2} = 1$ is

$$\frac{xx_1}{a^2} - \frac{yy_1}{b^2} = 1 \qquad \text{...(iii)}$$

On comparing Eqs. (ii) and (iii), we get

$$\frac{x_1/a^2}{m} = \frac{y_1/b^2}{1} = \pm\frac{1}{\sqrt{a^2m^2 - b^2}}$$

Thus, the coordinates of the points of contact are

$$\left(\frac{\pm a^2m}{\sqrt{(a^2m - b^2)}}, \pm\frac{b^2}{\sqrt{(a^2m - b^2)}}\right)$$

Example 19. Find the equation of the tangent to the hyperbola $x^2 - 4y^2 = 36$ which is perpendicular to the line $x - y + 4 = 0$.

Sol. Let m be the slope of the tangent. Since, the tangent is perpendicular to the line $x - y + 4 = 0$

$$\therefore \quad m \times 1 = -1 \quad \Rightarrow \quad m = -1$$

Since, $\quad x^2 - 4y^2 = 36$ or $\frac{x^2}{36} - \frac{y^2}{9} = 1$

On comparing this with $\frac{x^2}{a^2} - \frac{y^2}{b^2} = 1$, we get

$$a^2 = 36 \text{ and } b^2 = 9$$

So, the equation of tangents are

$$y=(-1)\,x \pm \sqrt{36\times(-1)^2-9}$$

$\Rightarrow$ $$y=-x\pm\sqrt{27}$$

or $$x+y\pm 3\sqrt{3}=0$$

Example 20. Find the equation and the length of the common tangents to hyperbola

$$\frac{x^2}{a^2}-\frac{y^2}{b^2}=1 \text{ and } \frac{y^2}{a^2}-\frac{x^2}{b^2}=1.$$

Sol. Tangent at $(a\sec\phi, b\tan\phi)$ on the 1st hyperbola is

$$\frac{x}{a}\sec\phi-\frac{y}{b}\tan\phi=1 \quad \text{...(i)}$$

Similarly, tangent at any point $(b\tan\theta, a\sec\theta)$ on 2nd hyperbola is

$$\frac{y}{a}\sec\theta-\frac{x}{b}\tan\theta=1 \quad \text{...(ii)}$$

If Eqs. (i) and (ii) are common tangents, then they should be identical. On comparing the coefficients of x and y, we get

$\Rightarrow$ $$\frac{\sec\theta}{a}=-\frac{\tan\phi}{b}$$

or $$\sec\theta=-\frac{a}{b}\tan\phi \quad \text{...(iii)}$$

and $$-\frac{\tan\theta}{b}=\frac{\sec\phi}{a}$$

or $$\tan\theta=-\frac{b}{a}\sec\phi \quad \text{...(iv)}$$

$\because$ $$\sec^2\theta-\tan^2\theta=1$$

$\Rightarrow$ $$\frac{a^2}{b^2}\tan^2\phi-\frac{b^2}{a^2}\sec^2\phi=1 \quad \text{[from Eqs. (iii) and (iv)]}$$

or $$\frac{a^2}{b^2}\tan^2\phi-\frac{b^2}{a^2}(1+\tan^2\phi)=1$$

or $$\left(\frac{a^2}{b^2}-\frac{b^2}{a^2}\right)\tan^2\phi=1+\frac{b^2}{a^2}$$

$\therefore$ $$\tan^2\phi=\frac{b^2}{a^2-b^2}$$

and $$\sec^2\phi=1+\tan^2\phi=\frac{a^2}{a^2-b^2}$$

Hence, the points of contact are

$$\left\{\pm\frac{a^2}{\sqrt{(a^2-b^2)}},\pm\frac{b^2}{\sqrt{(a^2-b^2)}}\right\}$$

and $$\left\{\mp\frac{b^2}{\sqrt{(a^2-b^2)}},\mp\frac{a^2}{\sqrt{(a^2-b^2)}}\right\} \quad \text{[from Eqs. (iii) and (iv)]}$$

Length of common tangent i.e. the distance between the above points is $\sqrt{2}\dfrac{(a^2+b^2)}{\sqrt{(a^2-b^2)}}$ and equation of common tangent on putting the values of $\sec\phi$ and $\tan\phi$ in Eq. (i) is

$$\pm\frac{x}{\sqrt{(a^2-b^2)}}\mp\frac{y}{\sqrt{(a^2-b^2)}}=1 \text{ or } x\mp y=\pm\sqrt{(a^2-b^2)}$$

Alternate Solution

The given two hyperbolas are $\dfrac{x^2}{a^2}-\dfrac{y^2}{b^2}=1$ ...(i)

and $\dfrac{x^2}{(-b^2)}-\dfrac{y^2}{(-a^2)}=1$ ...(ii)

We know that

$$y=mx\pm\sqrt{(a^2m^2-b^2)} \quad \text{...(iii)}$$

is tangent to Eq. (i) for all m.

Similarly, $$y=m_1x\pm\sqrt{(-b^2)\,m_1^2-(-a^2)}$$
$$y=m_1x\pm\sqrt{(a^2-b^2m_1^2)} \quad \text{...(iv)}$$

will be tangent to Eq. (ii).

For common tangents to Eqs. (i) and (ii), the lines (iii) and (iv) must be identical

i.e. $m=m_1$ and $a^2m^2-b^2=a^2-b^2m_1^2$

i.e. $(a^2+b^2)(m^2-1)=0$

$\Rightarrow$ $m^2=1$

$\Rightarrow$ $m=\pm 1$

$\therefore$ The equation of common tangent lines are

$$y=\pm x\pm\sqrt{(a^2-b^2)} \quad \text{[from Eq. (iii)]}$$

or $$y\mp x=\pm\sqrt{(a^2-b^2)} \quad \text{...(v)}$$

Equation of tangent to Eq. (i) at (x_1, y_1) is

$$\frac{xx_1}{a^2}-\frac{yy_1}{b^2}=1 \quad \text{...(vi)}$$

On comparing Eqs.(v) and (vi), then

$$\frac{x_1/a^2}{\mp 1}=\frac{-y_1/b^2}{1}=\frac{1}{\pm\sqrt{(a^2-b^2)}}$$

i.e. $$\left(\mp\frac{a^2}{\sqrt{(a^2-b^2)}},\mp\frac{b^2}{\sqrt{(a^2-b^2)}}\right)$$

and equation of tangent to Eq. (ii) at (x_2, y_2) is

$$\frac{xx_2}{(-b^2)}-\frac{yy_2}{(-a^2)}=1 \quad \text{...(vii)}$$

On comparing Eqs. (v) and (vii), then

$$\frac{x_2/(-b^2)}{\mp 1}=\frac{y_2}{1}=\frac{1}{\pm\sqrt{(a^2-b^2)}}$$

i.e. $$\left(\pm\frac{b^2}{\sqrt{(a^2-b^2)}},\pm\frac{a^2}{\sqrt{(a^2-b^2)}}\right)$$

The points of contact are $\left(\pm\dfrac{a^2}{\sqrt{(a^2-b^2)}},\pm\dfrac{b^2}{\sqrt{(a^2-b^2)}}\right)$

and $\left(\mp\dfrac{b^2}{\sqrt{(a^2-b^2)}},\mp\dfrac{a^2}{\sqrt{(a^2-b^2)}}\right)$

Hence, the length of common tangent is $\sqrt{2}\cdot\dfrac{(a^2+b^2)}{\sqrt{(a^2-b^2)}}$.

Example 21. *PQ* is the chord joining the points ϕ_1 and ϕ_2 on the hyperbola $\dfrac{x^2}{a^2}-\dfrac{y^2}{b^2}=1$. If $\phi_1-\phi_2=2\alpha$, where α is constant, prove that *PQ* touches the hyperbola $\dfrac{x^2}{a^2}\cos^2\alpha-\dfrac{y^2}{b^2}=1$.

Sol. Given hyperbola is $\dfrac{x^2}{a^2}-\dfrac{y^2}{b^2}=1$ ...(i)

Equation of the chord PQ to the hyperbola (i) is

$$\frac{x}{a}\cos\left(\frac{\phi_1-\phi_2}{2}\right)-\frac{y}{b}\sin\left(\frac{\phi_1+\phi_2}{2}\right)=\cos\left(\frac{\phi_1+\phi_2}{2}\right)$$

$$\Rightarrow \quad \frac{x}{a}\cos\alpha-\frac{y}{b}\sin\left(\frac{\phi_1+\phi_2}{2}\right)=\cos\left(\frac{\phi_1+\phi_2}{2}\right)$$

[given $\phi_1-\phi_2=2\alpha$]

i.e. $$y=\frac{b}{a}\frac{\cos\alpha}{\sin\left(\frac{\phi_1+\phi_2}{2}\right)}x+\frac{b\cos\left(\frac{\phi_1+\phi_2}{2}\right)}{\sin\left(\frac{\phi_1+\phi_2}{2}\right)} \quad \text{...(ii)}$$

On comparing this line with $y=mx+c$, then

$$m=\frac{b}{a}\cdot\frac{\cos\alpha}{\sin\left(\frac{\phi_1+\phi_2}{2}\right)}$$

and $$c=\frac{b\cos\left(\frac{\phi_1+\phi_2}{2}\right)}{\sin\left(\frac{\phi_1+\phi_2}{2}\right)}$$

For line $y=mx+c$ to be a tangent on $\dfrac{x^2}{a^2}\cos^2\alpha-\dfrac{y^2}{b^2}=1$,

we have, $c^2=\dfrac{a^2}{\cos^2\alpha}m^2-b^2$

$$\therefore \quad \text{LHS}=c^2=\frac{b^2\cos^2\left(\frac{\phi_1+\phi_2}{2}\right)}{\sin^2\left(\frac{\phi_1+\phi_2}{2}\right)}$$

and $$\text{RHS}=\frac{a^2}{\cos^2\alpha}m^2-b^2$$

$$=\frac{a^2}{\cos^2\alpha}\times\frac{b^2\cos^2\alpha}{a^2\sin^2\left(\frac{\phi_1+\phi_2}{2}\right)}-b^2$$

$$=\frac{b^2}{\sin^2\left(\frac{\phi_1+\phi_2}{2}\right)}-b^2$$

$$=\frac{b^2\cos^2\left(\frac{\phi_1+\phi_2}{2}\right)}{\sin\left(\frac{\phi_1+\phi_2}{2}\right)}$$

Hence proved.

Example 22. If the line $y=mx+\sqrt{(a^2m^2-b^2)}$ touches the hyperbola $\dfrac{x^2}{a^2}-\dfrac{y^2}{b^2}=1$ at the point $(a\sec\theta, b\tan\theta)$, then show that $\theta=\sin^{-1}\left(\dfrac{b}{am}\right)$.

Sol. Given, $(a\sec\theta, b\tan\theta)$ lies on $y=mx+\sqrt{(a^2m^2-b^2)}$

$$\therefore \quad b\tan\theta=am\sec\theta+\sqrt{(a^2m^2-b^2)}$$

$$\Rightarrow \quad (b\tan\theta-am\sec\theta)^2=a^2m^2-b^2$$

$$\Rightarrow \quad b^2\tan^2\theta+a^2m^2\sec^2\theta-2abm\tan\theta\sec\theta=a^2m^2-b^2$$

$$\Rightarrow \quad a^2m^2\tan^2\theta-2abm\tan\theta\sec\theta+b^2\sec^2\theta=0$$

or $$a^2m^2\sin^2\theta-2abm\sin\theta+b^2=0 \quad [\because \cos\theta\neq 0]$$

$$\therefore \quad \sin\theta=\frac{2abm\pm\sqrt{4a^2b^2m^2-4a^2b^2m^2}}{2a^2m^2}=\left(\frac{b}{am}\right)$$

$$\therefore \quad \theta=\sin^{-1}\left(\frac{b}{am}\right)$$

Example 23. If SY and $S'Y'$ be drawn perpendiculars from foci to any tangent to a hyperbola. Prove that Y and Y' lie on the auxiliary circle and that product of these perpendiculars is constant.

Sol. Let hyperbola be $\dfrac{x^2}{a^2}-\dfrac{y^2}{b^2}=1$ ...(i)

Tangent at $P(a\sec\phi, b\tan\phi)$ on Eq. (i) is

$$\frac{x}{a}\sec\phi-\frac{y}{b}\tan\phi=1 \quad \text{...(ii)}$$

Its slope is $\dfrac{(b\sec\phi)}{(a\tan\phi)}$.

Equation of SY which is perpendicular to Eq. (i) and passes through focus S i.e. $(ae, 0)$ is

$$y-0=-\frac{a\tan\phi}{b\sec\phi}(x-ae)$$

or $$\frac{x}{b}\tan\phi+\frac{y}{a}\sec\phi=\frac{ae}{b}\tan\phi \quad \text{...(iii)}$$

$\because$ Lines (ii) and (iii) intersect at Y and in order to find its locus, we have to eliminate ϕ between Eqs. (ii) and (iii), for which squaring and adding Eqs. (ii) and (iii) then, we get

$$(x^2+y^2)\left(\frac{\sec^2\phi}{a^2}+\frac{\tan^2\phi}{b^2}\right)=1+\frac{a^2e^2}{b^2}\tan^2\phi$$

$$=1+\frac{a^2+b^2}{b^2}\tan^2\phi=(1+\tan^2\phi)+\frac{a^2}{b^2}\tan^2\phi$$

$$=\left(\sec^2\phi+\frac{a^2}{b^2}\tan^2\phi\right)=a^2\left(\frac{\sec^2\phi}{a^2}+\frac{\tan^2\phi}{b^2}\right)$$

$\therefore$ $x^2+y^2=a^2$ is the required locus.

Similarly, the point Y' also lies on it. Again, if p_1 and p_2 be the length of perpendiculars from $S(ae, 0)$ and $S'(-ae, 0)$ on the tangent (ii), then

$$p_1p_2=\frac{(e\sec\phi-1)\cdot(e\sec\phi+1)}{\sqrt{\left(\frac{\sec^2\phi}{a^2}+\frac{\tan^2\phi}{b^2}\right)}\sqrt{\left(\frac{\sec^2\phi}{a^2}+\frac{\tan^2\phi}{b^2}\right)}}$$

$$=\frac{a^2b^2(e^2\sec^2\phi-1)}{b^2\sec^2\phi+a^2\tan^2\phi}=\frac{a^2b^2(e^2\sec^2\phi-1)}{a^2(e^2-1)\sec^2\phi+a^2\tan^2\phi}$$

$$=\frac{b^2(e^2\sec^2\phi-1)}{(e^2\sec^2\phi-1)}=b^2 \quad [\because b^2=a^2(e^2-1)]$$

7.9 Equations of Normals in Different Forms

1. Point form

Theorem The equation of the normal to the hyperbola $\frac{x^2}{a^2}-\frac{y^2}{b^2}=1$ at (x_1, y_1) is $\frac{a^2x}{x_1}+\frac{b^2y}{y_1}=a^2+b^2$

Proof Since, the equation of tangent to the hyperbola $\frac{x^2}{a^2}-\frac{y^2}{b^2}=1$ at (x_1, y_1) is $\frac{xx_1}{a^2}-\frac{yy_1}{b^2}=1$

The slope of tangent at $(x_1, y_1)=\frac{b^2x_1}{a^2y_1}$

$\therefore$ Slope of normal at $(x_1, y_1)=-\frac{a^2y_1}{b^2x_1}$

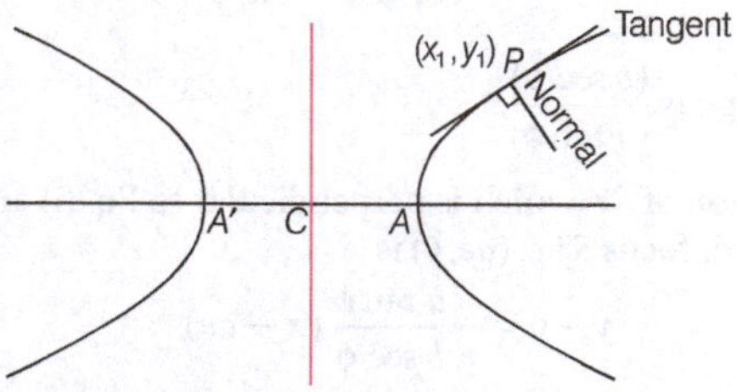

Hence, the equation of normal at (x_1, y_1)

$$y-y_1=-\frac{a^2y_1}{b^2x_1}(x-x_1)$$

or $$\frac{a^2x}{x_1}+\frac{b^2y}{y_1}=a^2+b^2$$

Alternate proof

The equation of normal at (x_1, y_1) can also be obtained by this method

$$\frac{x-x_1}{a'x_1+hy_1+g}=\frac{y-y_1}{hx_1+b'y_1+f} \quad \text{...(i)}$$

a', b', g, f, h are obtained by comparing the given hyperbola with

$$a'x^2+2hxy+b'y^2+2gx+2fy+c=0 \quad \text{...(ii)}$$

The denominator of Eq. (i) can easily be remembered by the first two rows of this determinant

i.e. $$\begin{vmatrix} a' & h & g \\ h & b' & f \\ g & f & c \end{vmatrix}$$

Since, first row is $a'(x_1)+h(y_1)+g(1)$

and second row is $h(x_1)+b'(y_1)+f(1)$

Here, hyperbola $\frac{x^2}{a^2}-\frac{y^2}{b^2}=1$

or $$\frac{x^2}{a^2}-\frac{y^2}{b^2}-1=0 \quad \text{...(iii)}$$

On comparing Eqs. (ii) and (iii), we get

$$a'=\frac{1}{a^2}, b'=-\frac{1}{b^2}, g=0, f=0, h=0$$

From Eq. (i), equation of normal of Eq. (iii) at (x_1, y_1) is

$$\frac{x-x_1}{\frac{1}{a^2}x_1+0+0}=\frac{y-y_1}{0-\frac{y_1}{b^2}+0}$$

or $$\frac{a^2x}{x_1}-a^2=-\frac{b^2y}{y_1}+b^2$$

or $$\frac{a^2x}{x_1}+\frac{b^2y}{y_1}=a^2+b^2$$

2. Parametric form

Theorem The equation of normal at $(a\sec\phi, b\tan\phi)$ to the hyperbola $\frac{x^2}{a^2}-\frac{y^2}{b^2}=1$ is $ax\cos\phi+by\cot\phi=a^2+b^2$

Proof Since, the equation of normals of the hyperbola $\frac{x^2}{a^2}-\frac{y^2}{b^2}=1$ at (x_1, y_1) is

$$\frac{a^2x}{x_1}+\frac{b^2y}{y_1}=a^2+b^2 \quad \text{...(i)}$$

Replacing x_1 by $a\sec\phi$ and y_1 by $b\tan\phi$, then Eq. (i) becomes

$$\frac{a^2x}{a\sec\phi}+\frac{b^2y}{b\tan\phi}=a^2+b^2$$

or $$ax\cos\phi+by\cot\phi=a^2+b^2$$

is equation of normal at $(a\sec\phi, b\tan\phi)$.

3. Slope form

Theorem The equations of normals of slope m to the hyperbola $\frac{x^2}{a^2}-\frac{y^2}{b^2}=1$ are given by

$$y=mx\mp\frac{m(a^2+b^2)}{\sqrt{(a^2-m^2b^2)}}$$

at the points $$\left(\pm\frac{a^2}{\sqrt{(a^2-m^2b^2)}}, \mp\frac{mb^2}{\sqrt{(a^2-m^2b^2)}}\right)$$

Proof The equation of normal to the hyperbola $\frac{x^2}{a^2} - \frac{y^2}{b^2} = 1$ at (x_1, y_1) is

$$\frac{a^2 x}{x_1} + \frac{b^2 y}{y_1} = a^2 + b^2 \quad \text{...(i)}$$

Since, m is the slope of the normal, then

$$m = -\frac{a^2 y_1}{b^2 x_1}$$

$$y_1 = -\frac{b^2 x_1 m}{a^2} \quad \text{...(ii)}$$

Since, (x_1, y_1) lies on $\frac{x^2}{a^2} - \frac{y^2}{b^2} = 1$

$$\therefore \quad \frac{x_1^2}{a^2} - \frac{y_1^2}{b^2} = 1 \text{ or } \frac{x_1^2}{a^2} - \frac{b^4 x_1^2 m^2}{a^4 b^2} = 1$$

or $$x_1^2 = \frac{a^4}{a^2 - b^2 m^2}$$

$$\therefore \quad x_1 = \pm \frac{a^2}{\sqrt{(a^2 - b^2 m^2)}}$$

From Eq. (ii), $$y_1 = \mp \frac{mb^2}{\sqrt{(a^2 - b^2 m^2)}}$$

$\therefore$ Equation of normal in terms of slope is

$$y - \left(\mp \frac{mb^2}{\sqrt{(a^2 - m^2 b^2)}}\right) = m\left(x - \left(\pm \frac{a^2}{\sqrt{(a^2 - m^2 b^2)}}\right)\right)$$

$$\Rightarrow \quad y = mx \mp \frac{m(a^2 + b^2)}{\sqrt{(a^2 - m^2 b^2)}} \quad \text{...(iii)}$$

Thus, Eq. (iii) is a normal to the hyperbola

$$\frac{x^2}{a^2} - \frac{y^2}{b^2} = 1$$

where m is the slope of the normal.
The coordinates of the point of contact are

$$\left(\pm \frac{a^2}{\sqrt{(a^2 - b^2 m^2)}}, \mp \frac{mb^2}{\sqrt{(a^2 - b^2 m^2)}}\right)$$

On comparing Eq. (iii) with $y = mx + c$, then

$$\therefore \quad c = \mp \frac{m(a^2 + b^2)}{\sqrt{(a^2 - m^2 b^2)}}$$

or $$c^2 = \frac{m^2(a^2 + b^2)^2}{(a^2 - m^2 b^2)}$$

which is condition of normality, where $y = mx + c$ is the normal of

$$\frac{x^2}{a^2} - \frac{y^2}{b^2} = 1$$

JEE SPIKE

Normal other than transverse axis, never passes through the focus.

Example 24. A normal to the hyperbola $\frac{x^2}{a^2} - \frac{y^2}{b^2} = 1$ meets the axes in M and N and lines MP and NP are drawn perpendiculars to the axes meeting at P. Prove that the locus of P is the hyperbola $a^2x^2 - b^2y^2 = (a^2 + b^2)^2$.

Sol. The equation of normal at the point $(a \sec \phi, b \tan \phi)$ to the hyperbola $\frac{x^2}{a^2} - \frac{y^2}{b^2} = 1$ is

$$ax \cos \phi + by \cot \phi = a^2 + b^2 \quad \text{...(i)}$$

The normal (i) meets the X-axis in $M\left(\frac{a^2 + b^2}{a} \sec \phi, 0\right)$ and Y-axis in $N\left(0, \frac{a^2 + b^2}{b} \tan \phi\right)$

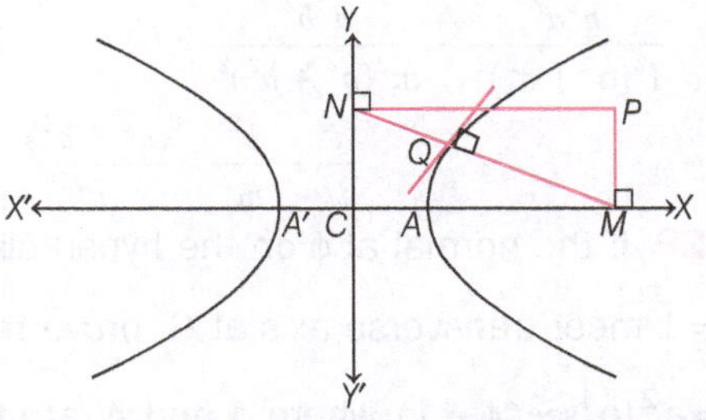

$\therefore$ Equation of MP, the line through M and perpendicular to X-axis, is

$$x = \left(\frac{a^2 + b^2}{a}\right) \sec \phi$$

or $$\sec \phi = \frac{ax}{(a^2 + b^2)} \quad \text{...(ii)}$$

and the equation of NP, the line through N and perpendicular to the Y-axis, is

$$y = \left(\frac{a^2 + b^2}{b}\right) \tan \phi$$

or $$\tan \phi = \frac{by}{(a^2 + b^2)} \quad \text{...(iii)}$$

The locus of the point of intersection of MP and NP will be obtained by eliminating ϕ from Eqs. (ii) and (iii), we have

$$\sec^2\phi - \tan^2\phi = 1$$

$$\Rightarrow \quad \frac{a^2x^2}{(a^2+b^2)^2} - \frac{b^2y^2}{(a^2+b^2)^2} = 1$$

or $$a^2x^2 - b^2y^2 = (a^2+b^2)^2$$

is the required locus of P.

Example 25. Prove that the line $lx + my - n = 0$ will be a normal to the hyperbola $\frac{x^2}{a^2} - \frac{y^2}{b^2} = 1$ if $\frac{a^2}{l^2} - \frac{b^2}{m^2} = \frac{(a^2+b^2)^2}{n^2}$.

Sol. The equation of any normal to $\frac{x^2}{a^2} - \frac{y^2}{b^2} = 1$ is

$$ax\cos\phi + by\cot\phi = a^2 + b^2$$

or $$ax\cos\phi + by\cot\phi - (a^2+b^2) = 0 \quad \text{...(i)}$$

The straight line $lx + my - n = 0$ will be a normal to the hyperbola $\frac{x^2}{a^2} - \frac{y^2}{b^2} = 1$, then Eq. (i) and $lx + my - n = 0$ represent the same line

$$\frac{a\cos\phi}{l} = \frac{b\cot\phi}{m} = \frac{(a^2+b^2)}{n}$$

or $$\sec\phi = \frac{na}{l(a^2+b^2)} \text{ and } \tan\phi = \frac{nb}{m(a^2+b^2)}$$

$\because \quad \sec^2\phi - \tan^2\phi = 1$

$$\therefore \quad \frac{n^2a^2}{l^2(a^2+b^2)^2} - \frac{n^2b^2}{m^2(a^2+b^2)^2} = 1$$

$$\Rightarrow \quad \frac{a^2}{l^2} - \frac{b^2}{m^2} = \frac{(a^2+b^2)^2}{n^2}$$

Example 26. If the normal at ϕ on the hyperbola $\frac{x^2}{a^2} - \frac{y^2}{b^2} = 1$ meet transverse axis at G, prove that $AG \cdot A'G = a^2(e^4\sec^2\phi - 1)$, where A and A' are the vertices of the hyperbola.

Sol. The equation of normal at $(a\sec\phi, b\tan\phi)$ to the given hyperbola is $ax\cos\phi + by\cot\phi = (a^2+b^2)$.

This meets the transverse axis i.e. X-axis at G. So, the coordinates of G are $\left(\left(\frac{a^2+b^2}{a}\right)\sec\phi, 0\right)$ and the coordinates of the vertices A and A' are $A(a, 0)$ and $A'(-a, 0)$ respectively.

$$\therefore AG \cdot A'G = \left(-a + \left(\frac{a^2+b^2}{a}\right)\sec\phi\right)\left(a + \left(\frac{a^2+b^2}{a}\right)\sec\phi\right)$$

$$= \left(\frac{a^2+b^2}{a}\right)^2 \sec^2\phi - a^2$$

$$= (ae^2)^2\sec^2\phi - a^2 = a^2(e^4\sec^2\phi - 1)$$

Example 27. Find the locus of the foot of perpendicular from the centre upon any normal to the hyperbola $\frac{x^2}{a^2} - \frac{y^2}{b^2} = 1$.

Sol. Normal at $P(a\sec\phi, b\tan\phi)$ is

$$ax\cos\phi + by\cot\phi = a^2 + b^2 \quad \text{...(i)}$$

and equation of line perpendicular to Eq. (i) and passing through origin is

$$bx - ay\sin\phi = 0 \quad \text{...(ii)}$$

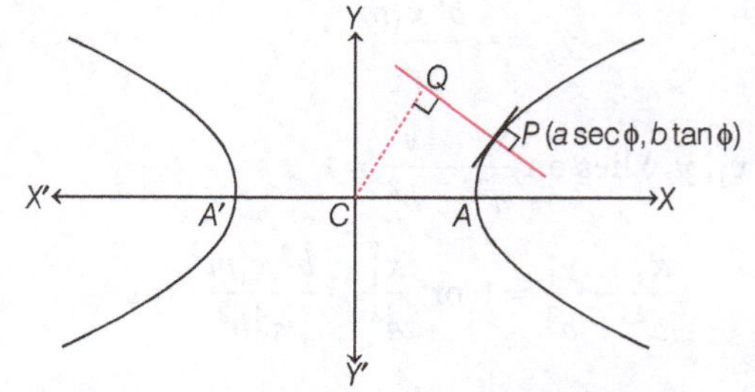

On eliminating ϕ from Eqs. (i) and (ii), we will get the equation of locus of Q, as from Eq. (ii),

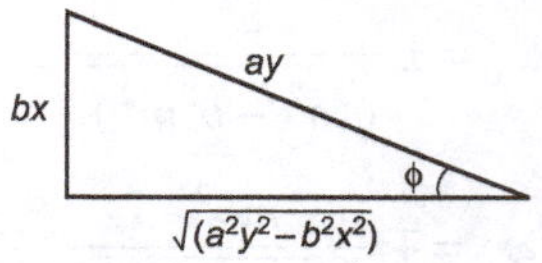

$$\sin\phi = \frac{bx}{ay}$$

$$\therefore \quad \cos\phi = \frac{\sqrt{(a^2y^2 - b^2x^2)}}{ay}$$

and $$\cot\phi = \frac{\sqrt{(a^2y^2 - b^2x^2)}}{bx}$$

From Eq. (i),

$$ax \times \frac{\sqrt{a^2y^2 - b^2x^2}}{ay} + by \times \frac{\sqrt{(a^2y^2 - b^2x^2)}}{bx} = a^2 + b^2$$

$$\Rightarrow \quad (x^2+y^2)\sqrt{(a^2y^2 - b^2x^2)} = (a^2+b^2)xy$$

or $$(x^2+y^2)^2(a^2y^2 - b^2x^2) = (a^2+b^2)^2x^2y^2$$

which is required locus.

7.10 Pair of Tangents

Theorem The combined equation of the pair of tangents drawn from a point $P(x_1, y_1)$, lying outside the hyperbola $\frac{x^2}{a^2} - \frac{y^2}{b^2} = 1$ to the hyperbola $\frac{x^2}{a^2} - \frac{y^2}{b^2} = 1$ is

$$\left(\frac{x^2}{a^2} - \frac{y^2}{b^2} - 1\right)\left(\frac{x_1^2}{a^2} - \frac{y_1^2}{b^2} - 1\right) = \left(\frac{xx_1}{a^2} - \frac{yy_1}{b^2} - 1\right)^2$$

or $SS_1 = T^2$

where $S = \frac{x^2}{a^2} - \frac{y^2}{b^2} - 1;$

$S_1 = \frac{x_1^2}{a^2} - \frac{y_1^2}{b^2} - 1$ and $T = \frac{xx_1}{a^2} - \frac{yy_1}{b^2} - 1$

Proof Let $T(h, k)$ be any point on the pair of tangents PQ or PR drawn from any external point $P(x_1, y_1)$ to the hyperbola

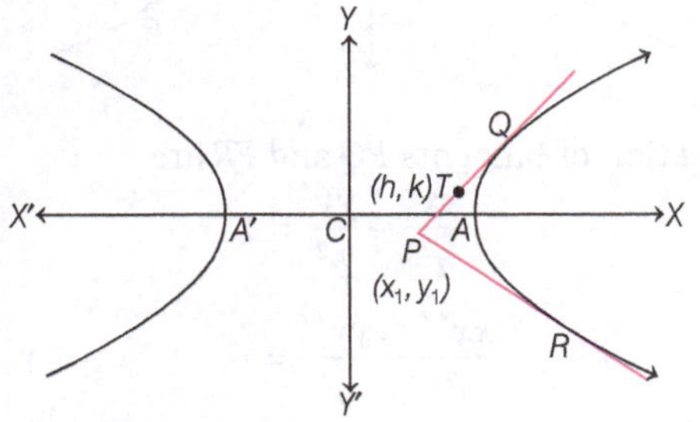

$$\frac{x^2}{a^2} - \frac{y^2}{b^2} = 1$$

$\therefore$ Equation of PT is $y - y_1 = \frac{k - y_1}{h - x_1}(x - x_1)$

or $$y = \left(\frac{k - y_1}{h - x_1}\right)x + \left(\frac{hy_1 - kx_1}{h - x_1}\right)$$

which is the tangent to the hyperbola

$$\frac{x^2}{a^2} - \frac{y^2}{b^2} = 1$$

$\therefore$ $$c^2 = a^2m^2 - b^2$$

or $$\left(\frac{hy_1 - kx_1}{h - x_1}\right)^2 = a^2\left(\frac{k - y_1}{h - x_1}\right)^2 - b^2$$

$\Rightarrow$ $$(hy_1 - kx_1)^2 = a^2(k - y_1)^2 - b^2(h - x_1)^2$$

Hence, locus of (h, k) is

$$(xy_1 - x_1y)^2 = a^2(y - y_1)^2 - b^2(x - x_1)^2$$

or $$(xy_1 - x_1y)^2 = -(b^2x^2 - a^2y^2) - (b^2x_1^2 - a^2y_1^2) - 2(a^2yy_1 - b^2xx_1)$$

or $$\left(\frac{xy_1 - x_1y}{ab}\right)^2 = -\left(\frac{x^2}{a^2} - \frac{y^2}{b^2}\right) - \left(\frac{x_1^2}{a^2} - \frac{y_1^2}{b^2}\right) + 2\left(\frac{xx_1}{a^2} - \frac{yy_1}{b^2}\right)$$

or $$-\left(\frac{xy_1 - x_1y}{ab}\right)^2 - \left(\frac{x^2}{a^2} - \frac{y^2}{b^2}\right) - \left(\frac{x_1^2}{a^2} - \frac{y_1^2}{b^2}\right) + 1 + \left(\frac{xx_1}{a^2} - \frac{yy_1}{b^2}\right)^2$$

$$= \left(\frac{xx_1}{a^2} - \frac{yy_1}{b^2}\right)^2 - 2\left(\frac{xx_1}{a^2} - \frac{yy_1}{b^2}\right) + 1$$

or $$\left(\frac{x^2}{a^2} - \frac{y^2}{b^2} - 1\right)\left(\frac{x_1^2}{a^2} - \frac{y_1^2}{b^2} - 1\right) = \left(\frac{xx_1}{a^2} - \frac{yy_1}{b^2} - 1\right)^2$$

or $$SS_1 = T^2$$

ALTERNATE PROOF

Let the hyperbola be $$\frac{x^2}{a^2} - \frac{y^2}{b^2} = 1 \quad \text{...(i)}$$

Let $P(x_1, y_1)$ be any point outside the hyperbola.

Let a chord of the hyperbola through the point $P(x_1, y_1)$ cut the hyperbola at Q and R. Let $R(h, k)$ be any arbitrary point on the line PQ (R inside or outside).

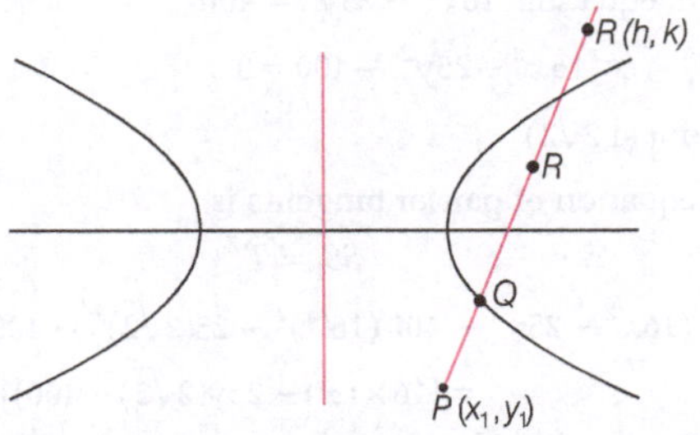

Let Q divides PR in the ratio $\lambda : 1$, then coordinates of Q are

$$\left(\frac{\lambda h + x_1}{\lambda + 1}, \frac{\lambda k + y_1}{\lambda + 1}\right) \quad [\because PQ : QR = \lambda : 1]$$

Since, Q lies on hyperbola (i), then

$$\frac{1}{a^2}\left(\frac{\lambda h + x_1}{\lambda + 1}\right)^2 - \frac{1}{b^2}\left(\frac{\lambda k + y_1}{\lambda + 1}\right)^2 = 1$$

$\Rightarrow$ $$b^2(\lambda h + x_1)^2 - a^2(\lambda k + y_1)^2 = a^2b^2(\lambda + 1)^2$$

$\Rightarrow$ $$(b^2h^2 - a^2k^2 - a^2b^2)\lambda^2 + 2(b^2hx_1 - a^2ky_1 - a^2b^2)\lambda + (b^2x_1^2 - a^2y_1^2 - a^2b^2) = 0 \quad \text{...(ii)}$$

Let PR will become tangent to the hyperbola (i), then roots of Eq. (ii) are equal

$$4(b^2hx_1 - a^2ky_1 - a^2b^2)^2 - 4(b^2h^2 - a^2k^2 - a^2b^2) \times (b^2x_1^2 - a^2y_1^2 - a^2b^2) = 0$$

On dividing by $4a^4b^4$, then

$\therefore$ $$\left(\frac{hx_1}{a^2} - \frac{ky_1}{b^2} - 1\right)^2 = \left(\frac{h^2}{a^2} - \frac{k^2}{b^2} - 1\right)\left(\frac{x_1^2}{a^2} - \frac{y_1^2}{b^2} - 1\right)$$

Hence, locus of $R(h, k)$ i.e. equation of pair of tangents from $P(x_1, y_1)$ is

$$\left(\frac{xx_1}{a^2} - \frac{yy_1}{b^2} - 1\right)^2 = \left(\frac{x^2}{a^2} - \frac{y^2}{b^2} - 1\right)\left(\frac{x_1^2}{a^2} - \frac{y^2}{b^2} - 1\right)$$

i.e. $$T^2 = SS_1 \quad \text{or} \quad SS_1 = T^2$$

JEE SPIKE

$S=0$ is the equation of the curve, S_1 is obtained from S by replacing x by x_1 and y by y_1 and $T=0$ is the equation of the tangent at (x_1, y_1) to $S=0$.

Example 28. The tangents from $(1, 2\sqrt{2})$ to the hyperbola $16x^2-25y^2=400$ include an angle between them which is equal to

(a) $\pi/6$ (b) $\pi/3$
(c) $\pi/2$ (d) $\pi/4$

Sol. (c) Given, equation $16x^2-25y^2=400$

$$\Rightarrow \quad 16x^2-25y^2-400=0$$

and point $(1, 2\sqrt{2})$ [given]

$\because$ The equation of pair of tangents is

$$SS_1=T^2$$

$$\Rightarrow \quad (16x^2-25y^2-400)(16(1)^2-25(2\sqrt{2})^2-400) = [16\times(x)-25y(2\sqrt{2})-400)]^2$$

$$\Rightarrow \quad (16x^2-25y^2-400)(16-200-400) = (16x-50\sqrt{2}y-400)^2$$

$$\Rightarrow \quad -584(16x^2-25y^2-400) = (16x-50\sqrt{2}y-400)^2$$

$$\Rightarrow \quad (16x-50\sqrt{2}y-400)^2+584(16x^2-25y^2-400)=0$$

Let m_1 and m_2 are roots, then

$$m_1m_2=a/b=\frac{\text{Coefficient of } x^2}{\text{Coefficient of } y^2}$$

$$=\frac{(16)^2+(584)(16)}{(50\sqrt{2})^2-(584)(25)}=\frac{9600}{-9600}$$

$$\therefore \quad m_1m_2=-1$$

Hence, angle between pair of tangents is $\pi/2$.

7.11 Chord of Contact

Theorem If the tangents from a point $P(x_1, y_1)$ to the hyperbola $\frac{x^2}{a^2}-\frac{y^2}{b^2}=1$ touch the hyperbola at Q and R, then the equation of the chord of contact QR is

$$\frac{xx_1}{a^2}-\frac{yy_1}{b^2}=1$$

Proof Let $Q\equiv(x', y')$ and $R\equiv(x'', y'')$

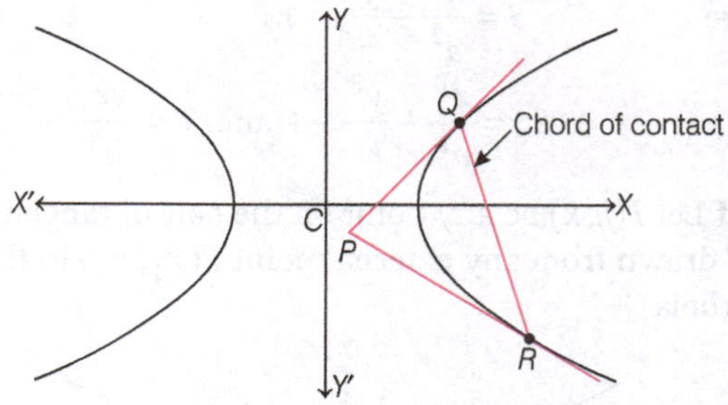

Now, equation of tangents PQ and PR are

$$\frac{xx'}{a^2}-\frac{yy'}{b^2}=1 \quad \text{...(i)}$$

and

$$\frac{xx''}{a^2}-\frac{yy''}{b^2}=1 \quad \text{...(ii)}$$

Since, Eqs. (i) and (ii) pass through $P(x_1, y_1)$, then

$$\frac{x'x_1}{a^2}-\frac{y'y_1}{b^2}=1 \quad \text{...(iii)}$$

and

$$\frac{x''x_1}{a^2}-\frac{y''y_1}{b^2}=1 \quad \text{...(iv)}$$

Hence, it is clear that $Q(x', y')$ and $R(x'', y'')$ lie on

$$\frac{xx_1}{a^2}-\frac{yy_1}{b^2}=1$$

or $\quad T=0$

which is **chord of contact** QR.

7.12 Equation of the Chord Bisected at a Given Point

Theorem The equation of the chord of the hyperbola

$$\frac{x^2}{a^2}-\frac{y^2}{b^2}=1,$$

bisected at the point (x_1, y_1) is

$$\frac{xx_1}{a^2}-\frac{yy_1}{b^2}-1=\frac{x_1^2}{a^2}-\frac{y_1^2}{b^2}-1$$

or $\quad T=S_1$, where $T=\frac{xx_1}{a^2}-\frac{yy_1}{b^2}-1$

and $\quad S_1=\frac{x_1^2}{a^2}-\frac{y_1^2}{b^2}-1.$

Proof Since, equation of the hyperbola is

$$\frac{x^2}{a^2}-\frac{y^2}{b^2}=1 \quad \text{...(i)}$$

Let QR be the chord of the hyperbola whose mid-point is $P(x_1, y_1)$. Since, Q and R lie on the hyperbola (i).

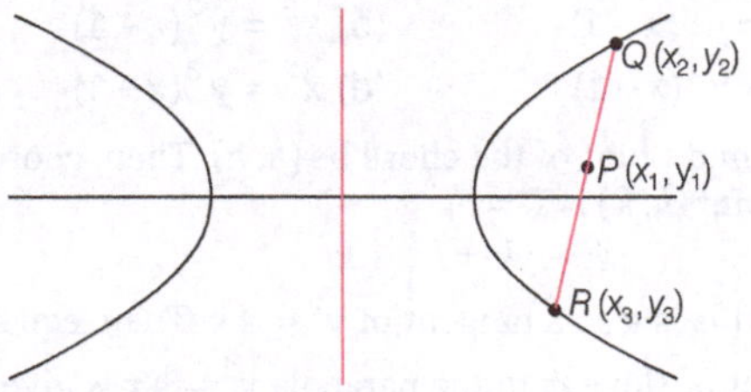

$$\therefore \quad \frac{x_2^2}{a^2}-\frac{y_2^2}{b^2}=1 \quad \text{...(ii)}$$

and $$\frac{x_3^2}{a^2}-\frac{y_3^2}{b^2}=1 \quad \text{...(iii)}$$

On subtracting Eq. (iii) from Eq. (ii), we get

$$\frac{1}{a^2}(x_2^2-x_3^2)-\frac{1}{b^2}(y_2^2-y_3^2)=0$$

$$\Rightarrow \quad \frac{(x_2+x_3)(x_2-x_3)}{a^2}-\frac{(y_2+y_3)(y_2-y_3)}{b^2}=0$$

$$\Rightarrow \quad \frac{y_2-y_3}{x_2-x_3}=\frac{b^2(x_2+x_3)}{a^2(y_2+y_3)}$$

$$=\frac{b^2\,(2x_1)}{a^2\,(2y_1)} \quad [P \text{ is the mid-point of } QR]$$

$$=\frac{b^2x_1}{a^2y_1} \quad \text{...(iv)}$$

$\therefore$ Equation of QR is

$$y-y_1=\frac{y_2-y_3}{x_2-x_3}(x-x_1)$$

$$\Rightarrow \quad y-y_1=\frac{b^2x_1}{a^2y_1}(x-x_1) \text{ [from Eq. (iv)]}$$

$$\Rightarrow \quad \frac{yy_1}{b^2}-\frac{y_1^2}{b^2}=\frac{xx_1}{a^2}-\frac{x_1^2}{a^2}$$

$$\Rightarrow \quad \frac{xx_1}{a^2}-\frac{yy_1}{b^2}=\frac{x_1^2}{a^2}-\frac{y_1^2}{b^2}$$

$$\Rightarrow \quad \frac{xx_1}{a^2}-\frac{yy_1}{b^2}-1=\frac{x_1^2}{a^2}-\frac{y_1^2}{b^2}-1$$

$$\Rightarrow \quad T=S_1$$

Example 29. Find the locus of the mid-points of the chords of the hyperbola $\frac{x^2}{a^2}-\frac{y^2}{b^2}=1$ which subtend a right angle at the origin.

Sol. Let (h, k) be the mid-point of the chord of the hyperbola. Then, its equation is

$$\frac{hx}{a^2}-\frac{ky}{b^2}-1=\frac{h^2}{a^2}-\frac{k^2}{b^2}-1$$

or $$\frac{hx}{a^2}-\frac{ky}{b^2}=\frac{h^2}{a^2}-\frac{k^2}{b^2} \quad \text{...(i)}$$

The equation of the lines joining the origin to the points of intersection of the hyperbola and the chord (i) is obtained by making homogeneous hyperbola with the help of Eq. (i)

$$\therefore \quad \frac{x^2}{a^2}-\frac{y^2}{b^2}=\frac{\left(\frac{hx}{a^2}-\frac{ky}{b^2}\right)^2}{\left(\frac{h^2}{a^2}-\frac{k^2}{b^2}\right)^2}$$

$$\Rightarrow \quad \frac{1}{a^2}\left(\frac{h^2}{a^2}-\frac{k^2}{b^2}\right)^2x^2-\frac{1}{b^2}\left(\frac{h^2}{a^2}-\frac{k^2}{b^2}\right)^2y^2$$

$$=\frac{h^2}{a^4}x^2+\frac{k^2}{b^4}y^2-\frac{2hk}{a^2b^2}xy \quad \text{...(ii)}$$

The lines represented by Eq. (ii) will be at right angle if Coefficient of x^2 + Coefficient of $y^2=0$

$$\Rightarrow \frac{1}{a^2}\left(\frac{h^2}{a^2}-\frac{k^2}{b^2}\right)^2-\frac{h^2}{a^4}-\frac{1}{b^2}\left(\frac{h^2}{a^2}-\frac{k^2}{b^2}\right)^2-\frac{k^2}{b^4}=0$$

$$\Rightarrow \quad \left(\frac{h^2}{a^2}-\frac{k^2}{b^2}\right)^2\left(\frac{1}{a^2}-\frac{1}{b^2}\right)=\frac{h^2}{a^4}+\frac{k^2}{b^4}$$

Hence, the locus of (h, k) is

$$\left(\frac{x^2}{a^2}-\frac{y^2}{b^2}\right)^2\left(\frac{1}{a^2}-\frac{1}{b^2}\right)=\frac{x^2}{a^4}+\frac{y^2}{b^4}$$

Example 30. From the points on the circle $x^2+y^2=a^2$, tangents are drawn to the hyperbola $x^2-y^2=a^2$, then prove that the locus of the middle-points of the chords of contact is the curve $(x^2-y^2)^2=a^2(x^2+y^2)$.

Sol. Since, any point on the circle $x^2+y^2=a^2$ is $(a\cos\theta, a\sin\theta)$, chord of contact of this point w.r.t. hyperbola $x^2-y^2=a^2$ is

$$x\,(a\cos\theta)-y\,(a\sin\theta)=a^2$$

or $$x\cos\theta-y\sin\theta=a \quad \text{...(i)}$$

Let its mid-point be (h, k), then it is same as

$$T=S_1$$

i.e. $$hx-ky-a^2=h^2-k^2-a^2$$

or $$hx-ky=h^2-k^2 \quad \text{...(ii)}$$

On comparing Eqs. (i) and (ii), we get

$$\frac{\cos\theta}{h} = \frac{\sin\theta}{k} = \frac{a}{(h^2 - k^2)}$$

or $\quad (h^2 - k^2)\cos\theta = ah \quad$ ...(iii)

and $\quad (h^2 - k^2)\sin\theta = ak \quad$ ...(iv)

On squaring and adding Eqs. (iii) and (iv), we get

$$(h^2 - k^2)^2 = a^2h^2 + a^2k^2$$

$$\Rightarrow \quad (h^2 - k^2)^2 = a^2(h^2 + k^2)$$

Hence, the required locus is

$$(x^2 - y^2)^2 = a^2(x^2 + y^2).$$

Example 31. Prove that the locus of the mid-points of the chords of the hyperbola $\frac{x^2}{a^2} - \frac{y^2}{b^2} = 1$ which passes through a fixed point (α, β) is a hyperbola whose centre is $\left(\frac{\alpha}{2}, \frac{\beta}{2}\right)$.

Sol. Let the mid-point of the chord be (h, k). Then, the equation of the chord whose mid-point is (h, k), is

$$\frac{hx}{a^2} - \frac{ky}{b^2} - 1 = \frac{h^2}{a^2} - \frac{k^2}{b^2} - 1$$

or $$\frac{hx}{a^2} - \frac{ky}{b^2} = \frac{h^2}{a^2} - \frac{k^2}{b^2}$$

It passes through (α, β), then

$$\frac{\alpha h}{a^2} - \frac{\beta k}{b^2} = \frac{h^2}{a^2} - \frac{k^2}{b^2}$$

$\therefore$ Locus of (h, k) is $$\frac{x\alpha}{a^2} - \frac{y\beta}{b^2} = \frac{x^2}{a^2} - \frac{y^2}{b^2}$$

$$\Rightarrow \quad \frac{1}{a^2}(x^2 - \alpha x) - \frac{1}{b^2}(y^2 - \beta y) = 0$$

$$\Rightarrow \quad \frac{1}{a^2}\left\{\left(x - \frac{\alpha}{2}\right)^2 - \frac{\alpha^2}{4}\right\} - \frac{1}{b^2}\left\{\left(y - \frac{\beta}{2}\right)^2 - \frac{\beta^2}{4}\right\} = 0$$

or $$\frac{\left(x - \frac{\alpha}{2}\right)^2}{a^2} - \frac{\left(y - \frac{\beta}{2}\right)^2}{b^2} = \frac{1}{4}\left\{\frac{\alpha^2}{a^2} - \frac{\beta^2}{b^2}\right\} = \lambda \quad \text{(say)}$$

$$\therefore \quad \frac{\left(x - \frac{\alpha}{2}\right)^2}{a^2\lambda} - \frac{\left(y - \frac{\beta}{2}\right)^2}{b^2\lambda} = 1$$

The centre of this hyperbola is $\left(\frac{\alpha}{2}, \frac{\beta}{2}\right)$.

JEE SCANNER

Example Similar to PYQ Asked in JEE Main 2021

The locus of the mid-points of the chords of the hyperbola $x^2 - y^2 = 9$, which touches the parabola $y^2 = 4x$, is

(a) $x^3 = y^3(x-1)$ (b) $x^2 = y^2(x-1)$

(c) $x^3 = y^2(x-1)$ (d) $x^2 = y^3(x-1)$

Sol. Let the mid-point of the chord be (h, k). Then, chord through mid-point (h, k) is $T = S_1$

$$xh - yk = h^2 - k^2 \quad \text{... (i)}$$

Now, this is also a tangent of $y^2 = 4x$. Then, equation of the tangent of slope m to the parabola $y^2 = 4x$ is given by

Tangent $y = mx + \frac{1}{m} \Rightarrow mx^2 - ym = -1 \quad$ ...(ii)

Eqs. (i) and (ii) coincide, then

$$\therefore \quad \frac{h}{m^2} = \frac{k}{m} = \frac{h^2 - k^2}{-1}$$

$$\Rightarrow \quad h = mk \Rightarrow m = h/k$$

and $$\frac{k^2}{h} = \frac{h^2 - k^2}{-1}$$

$$\Rightarrow \quad -k^2 = h^3 - k^2h \Rightarrow h^3 = k^2(h-1)$$

Therefore, locus of mid-point of the chord is $x^3 = y^2(x-1)$.

Skill Builder

The locus of the mid-points of the chords of the hyperbola $x^2 - y^2 = 16$, which touches the parabola $y^2 = 6x$, is

(a) $y^2 = x^3(x-3)$

(b) $x^3 = y^2(x-3)$

(c) $y^3 = x^2(x-3)$

(d) $x^2 = y^3(x-3)$

For Sol.

■ **For more practice** See Q.16 of Milestone Practice 7.2.

Example 32. Find the equation of common tangents to the curves $y^2 = 8x$ and $\frac{x^2}{9} - \frac{y^2}{5} = 1$.

Sol. The equation of any tangent to the parabola $y^2 = 8x$ is

$$y = mx + \frac{2}{m} \quad \text{...(i)}$$

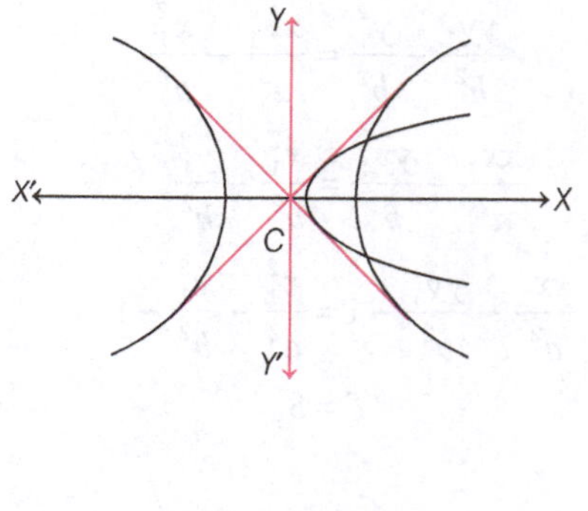

Since, the tangent to the parabola is also a tangent to the hyperbola $\frac{x^2}{9}-\frac{y^2}{5}=1$.

$\therefore \quad 5x^2-9\left(mx+\frac{2}{m}\right)^2=45$

$\Rightarrow \quad 5x^2-9(m^2x^2+4/m^2+4x)=45$

$\Rightarrow \quad (5-9m^2)x^2-36x-9(4/m^2+5)=0$

Now, for $D=0$

$\Rightarrow \quad (36)^2+36(5-9m^2)(4/m^2+5)=0$

$\Rightarrow \quad 36+\frac{20}{m^2}+25-36-45m^2=0$

$\Rightarrow \quad 4/m^2+5-9m^2=0$

$\Rightarrow \quad 9m^4-5m^2-4=0$

$\Rightarrow \quad (m^2-1)(9m^2+4)=0$

$\Rightarrow \quad (m^2-1)=0$

$\therefore \quad m=\pm 1$

Hence, the equations of the common tangents are $y=\pm x\pm 2$.

Milestone Practice 7.2

1. If $4x^2+\lambda y^2=45$ and $x^2-4y^2=5$ cut orthogonally, then the value of λ is

(a) $\frac{1}{9}$ (b) $\frac{1}{3}$

(c) 9 (d) 18

2. If the tangent at the point $(2\sec\phi, 3\tan\phi)$ of the hyperbola $\frac{x^2}{4}-\frac{y^2}{9}=1$ is parallel to $3x-y+4=0$, then the value of ϕ is

(a) $\frac{\pi}{6}$ (b) $\frac{\pi}{4}$

(c) $\frac{\pi}{3}$ (d) $\frac{5\pi}{12}$

3. If the line $2x+\sqrt{6}y=2$ touches the hyperbola $x^2-2y^2=4$, then the point of contact is

(a) $(-2,\sqrt{6})$ (b) $(-5,2\sqrt{6})$

(c) $\left(\frac{1}{2},\frac{1}{\sqrt{6}}\right)$ (d) $(4,-\sqrt{6})$

4. The equation of the chord of hyperbola $25x^2-16y^2=400$, whose mid-point is (5, 3), is

(a) $115x-47y=434$ (b) $125x-48y=481$

(c) $127x-49y=488$ (d) $155x-67y=574$

5. The value of m for which $y=mx+6$ is a tangent to the hyperbola $\frac{x^2}{100}-\frac{y^2}{49}=1$ is

(a) $\sqrt{\left(\frac{17}{20}\right)}$ (b) $-\sqrt{\left(\frac{17}{21}\right)}$

(c) $\sqrt{\left(\frac{20}{17}\right)}$ (d) $-\sqrt{\left(\frac{21}{17}\right)}$

6. P is a point on the hyperbola $\frac{x^2}{a^2}-\frac{y^2}{b^2}=1$ and N is the foot of the perpendicular from P on the transverse axis. The tangent to the hyperbola at P meets the transverse axis at T. If O is the centre of the hyperbola, then $OT\cdot ON$ is equal to

(a) a^2 (b) b^2

(c) e^2 (d) b^2/a

7. If $x=9$ is the chord of contact of the hyperbola $x^2-y^2=9$, then the equation of the corresponding pair of tangents, is

(a) $9x^2-8y^2+18x-9=0$

(b) $9x^2-8y^2-18x+9=0$

(c) $9x^2-8y^2-18x-9=0$

(d) $9x^2-8y^2+18x+9=0$

8. Let $P(a\sec\theta, b\tan\theta)$ and $Q(a\sec\phi, b\tan\phi)$, when $\theta+\phi=\frac{\pi}{2}$, be two points on the hyperbola $\frac{x^2}{a^2}-\frac{y^2}{b^2}=1$. If (h,k) is the point of intersection of the normals at P and Q, then k is equal to

(a) $\left(\frac{a^2+b^2}{a}\right)$

(b) $-\left(\frac{a^2+b^2}{a}\right)$

(c) $\left(\frac{a^2+b^2}{b}\right)$

(d) $-\left(\frac{a^2+b^2}{b}\right)$

9. The tangent at a point P on the hyperbola $\frac{x^2}{a^2}-\frac{y^2}{b^2}=1$ passes through the point $(0, -b)$ and the normal at P passes through $(2a\sqrt{2}, 0)$, then eccentricity of the hyperbola is
(a) $5/4$
(b) $3/2$
(c) $\sqrt{2}$
(d) $2\sqrt{2}$

10. A tangent to the hyperbola $\frac{x^2}{a^2}-\frac{y^2}{b^2}=1$ cuts the ellipse $\frac{x^2}{a^2}+\frac{y^2}{b^2}=1$ in points P and Q. Find the locus of the mid-point of PQ.

11. A line through the origin meets the circle $x^2+y^2=a^2$ at P and the hyperbola $x^2-y^2=a^2$ at Q. Prove that the locus of the point of intersection of tangent at P to the circle with the tangent at Q to the hyperbola is the curve $(a^4+4y^4)x^2=a^6$.

12. Normals are drawn to the hyperbola $\frac{x^2}{a^2}-\frac{y^2}{b^2}=1$ at the points $P(a\sec\theta_1, b\tan\theta_1)$ and $Q(a\sec\theta_2, b\tan\theta_2)$ meeting the conjugate axis at G_1 and G_2 respectively. If $\theta_1+\theta_2=\frac{\pi}{2}$, then prove that $CG_1\cdot CG_2=\frac{a^2e^4}{(e^2-1)}$, where C is the centre of the hyperbola and e is its eccentricity.

13. Let the eccentricity of the hyperbola, $H: \frac{x^2}{a^2}-\frac{y^2}{b^2}=1$ be $\frac{\sqrt{15}}{3}$ and length of its latus rectum be 6. If $y=x+c$ is a tangent to the hyperbola H, then find the value of c^2.

14. Find the value of λ, for which $y=3x+\lambda$ touches the hyperbola $9x^2-5y^2=45$.

15. Find the equation of the tangent to the hyperbola $4x^2-9y^2=1$, which is parallel to the line $4y=5x+7$. Also, find the point of contact.

16. Chords of the hyperbola $x^2-y^2=a^2$ touch the parabola $y^2=4ax$. Prove that the locus of their middle points is the curve $y^2(x-a)=x^3$.

Answer Key

1. (c)	2. (a)	3. (d)	4. (b)	5. (a)	6. (a)
7. (b)	8. (d)	9. (c)	10. $\frac{x^2}{a^2}-\frac{y^2}{b^2}=\left(\frac{x^2}{a^2}+\frac{y^2}{b^2}\right)^2$		
13. $\frac{27}{4}$	14. ± 6	15. $24y=30x\pm\sqrt{161}, \left(\pm\frac{15}{2\sqrt{161}}, \frac{\pm 8}{3\sqrt{161}}\right)$			

For Detailed Solution

Milestone 3 Rectangular Hyperbola

• Diameter of Hyperbola • Conjugate Diameter • Director Circle • Asymptotes • Rectangular Hyperbola • Reflection Property of a Hyperbola • Equation of a Hyperbola Referred to Two Perpendicular Lines

7.13 Diameter of Hyperbola

The locus of the middle points of a system of parallel chords of a hyperbola is called a diameter and the point where the diameter intersects the hyperbola is called the vertex of the diameter.

Theorem The equation of a diameter bisecting a system of parallel chords of slope m of the hyperbola $\frac{x^2}{a^2}-\frac{y^2}{b^2}=1$ is

$$y=\frac{b^2}{a^2m}x$$

Proof Let $y=mx+c$ be a system of a parallel chords to $\frac{x^2}{a^2}-\frac{y^2}{b^2}=1$ for different chords. As c varies, m remains constant.

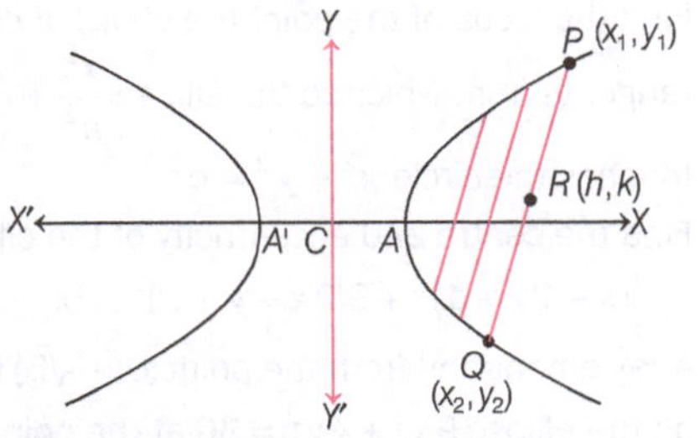

Let the extremities of any chord PQ of the set be $P(x_1, y_1)$ and $Q(x_2, y_2)$ and let its middle point be $R(h, k)$.

Then, solving equations $\frac{x^2}{a^2}-\frac{y^2}{b^2}=1$ and $y=mx+c$,

we get
$$\frac{x^2}{a^2}-\frac{(mx+c)^2}{b^2}=1$$

$$\Rightarrow (a^2m^2-b^2)x^2+2mca^2x+a^2(c^2+b^2)=0$$

Since, x_1 and x_2 are the roots of this equation, then

$$x_1+x_2=\frac{-2mca^2}{a^2m^2-b^2} \quad \text{...(i)}$$

Since, (h, k) is the middle point of QR.

$$\therefore \quad h=\frac{x_1+x_2}{2}$$

Then, from Eq. (i), $h=-\frac{mca^2}{a^2m^2-b^2}$

but (h, k) lies on $y=mx+c$.

$$\therefore \quad k=mh+c$$

or
$$c=k-mh \quad \text{...(ii)}$$

From Eqs. (i) and (ii),

$$h=\frac{ma^2(k-mh)}{a^2m^2-b^2}$$

$$\Rightarrow a^2m^2h-b^2h=-ma^2k+m^2a^2h$$

$$\Rightarrow -b^2h=-ma^2k \text{ or } k=\frac{b^2h}{a^2m}$$

Hence, locus of $R(h, k)$ is $y=\frac{b^2x}{a^2m}$

which is the diameter of the hyperbola passing through (0, 0).

Alternate Proof

Let (h, k) be the middle-point of the chord $y=mx+c$ of the hyperbola $\frac{x^2}{a^2}-\frac{y^2}{b^2}=1$

Then, $T=S_1$

$$\Rightarrow \frac{xh}{a^2}-\frac{yk}{b^2}=\frac{h^2}{a^2}-\frac{k^2}{b^2}$$

$$\therefore \quad \text{Slope}=\frac{hb^2}{a^2k}=m$$

$$\Rightarrow \quad k=\frac{b^2h}{a^2m}$$

Hence, the locus of mid-point is $y=\frac{b^2x}{a^2m}$.

Milestone Practice 6.3

1. The angle between the pair of tangents drawn from the point (2, 1) to the ellipse $2x^2 + 3y^2 = 5$ is
   (a) $\tan^{-1}\left(\frac{12}{5}\right)$ (b) $\tan^{-1}\left(\frac{6}{\sqrt{5}}\right)$
   (c) $\tan^{-1}\left(\frac{2\sqrt{138}}{5}\right)$ (d) $\tan^{-1}(12\sqrt{5})$

2. If chords of contact of tangents from two points (x_1, y_1) and (x_2, y_2) to the ellipse $\frac{x^2}{a^2} + \frac{y^2}{b^2} = 1$ are at right angles, then $\frac{x_1 x_2}{y_1 y_2}$ is equal to
   (a) $\frac{a^2}{b^2}$ (b) $-\frac{b^2}{a^2}$ (c) $-\frac{a^4}{b^4}$ (d) $-\frac{b^4}{a^4}$

3. From the point $(\lambda, 3)$ tangents are drawn to $\frac{x^2}{9} + \frac{y^2}{4} = 1$ and are perpendicular to each other then λ is
   (a) ± 1 (b) ± 2 (c) ± 3 (d) ± 4

4. The eccentric angle of one end of a diameter of $x^2 + 3y^2 = 3$ is $\pi/6$, then the eccentric angle of the other end will be
   (a) $\frac{5\pi}{6}$ (b) $-\frac{5\pi}{6}$ (c) $-\frac{2\pi}{3}$ (d) $\frac{2\pi}{3}$

5. The locus of the mid-points of a focal chord of the ellipse $\frac{x^2}{a^2} + \frac{y^2}{b^2} = 1$ is
   (a) $\frac{x^2}{a^2} + \frac{y^2}{b^2} = \frac{ex}{a}$ (b) $\frac{x^2}{a^2} - \frac{y^2}{b^2} = \frac{ex}{a}$
   (c) $x^2 + y^2 = a^2 + b^2$ (d) $x^2 - y^2 = a^2 + b^2$

6. The centre of the ellipse $\frac{(x + y - 2)^2}{9} + \frac{(x - y)^2}{16} = 1$ is
   (a) (0, 0) (b) (1, 0)
   (c) (0, 1) (d) (1, 1)

7. Find the locus of the point of intersection of two perpendicular tangents of the ellipse $\frac{x^2}{9} + \frac{y^2}{4} = 1$.

8. The area of the parallelogram inscribed in the ellipse $\frac{x^2}{a^2} + \frac{y^2}{b^2} = 1$ whose diagonals are the conjugate diameters of the ellipse is given by
   (a) $2ab$
   (b) $3ab$
   (c) $4ab$
   (d) $5ab$

9. Find the locus of the vertices of equilateral triangle circumscribing the ellipse $\frac{x^2}{a^2} + \frac{y^2}{b^2} = 1$.

10. A tangent to the ellipse $x^2 + 4y^2 = 4$ meets the ellipse $x^2 + 2y^2 = 6$ at P and Q. Prove that the tangents at P and Q of the ellipse $x^2 + 2y^2 = 6$ are at right angles.

11. Find the locus of the mid-point of chords of the ellipse $\frac{x^2}{a^2} + \frac{y^2}{b^2} = 1 \ (a > b)$ passing through the point $(2a, 0)$.

12. Find the locus of the point the chord of contact of tangents from which to the ellipse $\frac{x^2}{a^2} + \frac{y^2}{b^2} = 1$, touches the circle $x^2 + y^2 = c^2$.

13. Find the centre and eccentricity of the ellipse $4(x - 2y + 1)^2 + 9(2x + y + 2)^2 = 5$.

14. A ray emanating from the point $(0, -\sqrt{5})$ is incident on the ellipse $9x^2 + 4y^2 = 36$ at the point P with abscissa 2. Find the equation of the reflected ray after first reflection.

Answer Key

1. (c) 2. (c) 3. (b) 4. (b) 5. (a) 6. (d)
7. $x^2 + y^2 = 13$ 8. (a) 9. $\frac{(a^2 + 3b^2)^2}{a^2} x^2 + \frac{(3a^2 + b^2)}{b^2} y^2 = (a^2 - b^2)^2$ 11. $\frac{(x - a)^2}{a^2} + \frac{y^2}{b^2} = 1$
12. $\frac{x^2}{a^2} + \frac{y^2}{b^2} = \frac{1}{e^2}$ 13. $(-1, 0)$ and $\frac{\sqrt{5}}{3}$ 14. $\sqrt{5}x + 2y - 2\sqrt{5} = 0$

For Detailed Solution

Now, the lines (i) and (ii) are parallel and so are Eqs. (iii) and (iv).

Hence, these tangents form a parallelogram.

On solving Eqs. (i) and (iii), we get the coordinates of Q as $[a(\sec\phi+\tan\phi), b(\sec\phi+\tan\phi)]$, which clearly lies on the asymptote $y=\frac{b}{a}x$, similarly the other points of intersection lies on the asymptotes.

The equations of PCP' and DCD' are

$$y=\frac{b\tan\phi}{a\sec\phi}x \text{ or } bx\tan\phi-ay\sec\phi=0 \quad \text{...(v)}$$

and $$y=\frac{b\sec\phi}{a\tan\phi}x \text{ or } bx\sec\phi-ay\tan\phi=0 \quad \text{...(vi)}$$

Hence, by symmetry,

Area of parallelogram $QRQ'R'$

$$= 4\,(\text{Area of parallelogram } QDCP)$$
$$= 4\cdot CP\times(\text{Perpendicular length from } C \text{ on } QD)$$
$$= 4\cdot\sqrt{(a^2\sec^2\phi+b^2\tan^2\phi)}\times\frac{1}{\sqrt{\frac{\tan^2\phi}{a^2}+\frac{\sec^2\phi}{b^2}}}$$
$$= 4ab = \text{ constant}$$

PROPERTY 3 *If the normal at P meets the transverse axis in G, then $SG=e\cdot SP$. Prove also that the tangent and normal bisect the angle between the focal distances of P.*

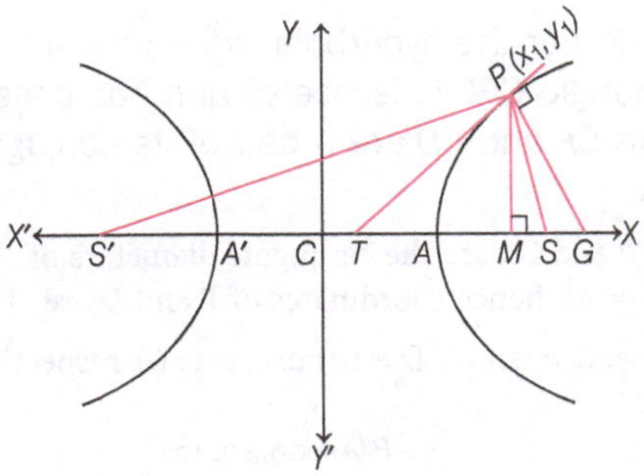

Let the coordinates of P be (x_1, y_1). The equation of normal at P on the hyperbola $\frac{x^2}{a^2}-\frac{y^2}{b^2}=1$ is

$$\frac{a^2x}{x_1}+\frac{b^2y}{y_1}=a^2+b^2 \quad \text{... (i)}$$

The normal (i) meets the X-axis i.e. $y=0$ in Eq. (i), then coordinates of G are $\left(\frac{(a^2+b^2)}{a^2}x_1, 0\right)$ or $(e^2x_1, 0)$

$\therefore \quad CG=e^2x_1$

Now, $\quad SG=CG-CS$

$$=e^2x_1-ae=e(ex_1-a)=e\cdot SP$$

Similarly, $\quad S'G=e\cdot S'P$

$\therefore \quad \frac{SG}{S'G}=\frac{SP}{S'P}$

This relation shows that the normal PG is the external bisector of the angle SPS'. The tangent PT being perpendicular to PG, therefore the internal bisector of the angle SPS' is PT.

PROPERTY 4 *If a pair of conjugate diameters meet the hyperbola in P, P′ and its conjugate in D, D′, then the asymptotes bisect PD, PD′, P′D and P′D′.*

The coordinates of four points P, D, P' and D' are $(a\sec\phi, b\tan\phi)$, $(a\tan\phi, b\sec\phi)$, $(-a\sec\phi, -b\tan\phi)$ and $(-a\tan\phi, -b\sec\phi)$, respectively.

If (h, k) is the middle point of PD, then

$$h=\frac{a}{2}(\sec\phi+\tan\phi) \text{ and } k=\frac{b}{2}(\tan\phi+\sec\phi)$$

$\therefore \quad \frac{h}{k}=\frac{a}{b}$

$\therefore$ Locus of mid-point (h, k) is $y=\frac{b}{a}x$, which is equation of asymptote of hyperbola $\frac{x^2}{a^2}-\frac{y^2}{b^2}=1$.

Similarly, other mid-points lie on the other asymptotes.

Example 34. If the line $lx+my+n=0$ passes through the extremities of a pair of conjugate diameters of the hyperbola $\frac{x^2}{a^2}-\frac{y^2}{b^2}=1$, then

(a) $a^2l^2-b^2m^2=1$ (b) $a^2l^2-b^2m^2=0$
(c) $a^2l^2+b^2m^2=1$ (d) None of these

Sol. (b) The extremities of a pair of conjugate diameter of $\frac{x^2}{a^2}-\frac{y^2}{b^2}=1$ are $(a\sec\phi, b\tan\phi)$ and $(a\tan\phi, b\sec\phi)$, respectively.

According to the question, since extremities of a pair of conjugate diameters lie on $lx + my + n = 0$

$\therefore \quad l(a\sec\phi) + m(b\tan\phi) + n = 0 \quad$ ...(i)

and $\quad l(a\tan\phi) + m(b\sec\phi) + n = 0 \quad$ ...(ii)

Then, from Eq. (i), we get

$$al\sec\phi + bm\tan\phi = -n$$

$$\Rightarrow a^2l^2\sec^2\phi + b^2m^2\tan^2\phi + 2ablm\sec\phi\tan\phi = n^2 \quad \text{...(iii)}$$

Now, from Eqs. (ii), $al\tan\phi + bm\sec\phi = -n$

$$\Rightarrow a^2l^2\tan^2\phi + b^2m^2\sec^2\phi + 2ablm\sec\phi\tan\phi = n^2 \quad \text{...(iv)}$$

On substracting Eq. (iv) from Eq. (iii), we get

$$a^2l^2(\sec^2\phi - \tan^2\phi) + b^2m^2(\tan^2\phi - \sec^2\phi) = 0$$

or $\quad a^2l^2 - b^2m^2 = 0$

Intersection of Conjugate Diameters and Hyperbola

To prove that of a pair of conjugate diameters of a hyperbola, only one meets the curve in real points.

Let $\quad y = mx \quad$ ...(i)

and $\quad y = m_1x \quad$ ...(ii)

be a pair of conjugate diameters of the hyperbola

$$\frac{x^2}{a^2} - \frac{y^2}{b^2} = 1, \text{ then } mm_1 = \frac{b^2}{a^2} \quad \text{...(iii)}$$

On solving Eq. (i) and the equation of hyperbola

$\frac{x^2}{a^2} - \frac{y^2}{b^2} = 1$, we get

$$\frac{x^2}{a^2} - \frac{m^2x^2}{b^2} = 1 \quad \text{or} \quad x^2 = \frac{a^2b^2}{b^2 - a^2m^2} \quad \text{...(iv)}$$

Similarly, Eq. (ii) meets the hyperbola at points whose abscissa are given by

$$x^2 = \frac{a^2b^2}{b^2 - a^2m_1^2} \quad \text{...(v)}$$

The two values of x given by Eq. (iv) will be real if

$b^2 - a^2m^2 > 0$ i.e. $m < \left(\frac{b}{a}\right)$

i.e. $\quad \frac{b^2}{a^2m_1} < \left(\frac{b}{a}\right) \quad \left[\because mm_1 = \frac{b^2}{a^2}\right]$

$\Rightarrow \quad \frac{b}{a} < m_1$ i.e. if $b^2 < a^2m_1^2$

If $\quad b^2 - a^2m_1^2 < 0,$

then from Eq. (v) the values of x are imaginary.

Hence, if Eq. (i) meets the hyperbola in real points, then Eq. (ii) meets it in imaginary points and *vice-versa*.

JEE SPIKE

If CD is the conjugate diameter of a diameter CP of the hyperbola $\frac{x^2}{a^2} - \frac{y^2}{b^2} = 1$, where P is $(a\sec\phi, b\tan\phi)$, then equation of CP, where C is $(0, 0)$ is $y - 0 = \frac{b\tan\phi - 0}{a\sec\phi - 0}(x - 0) \Rightarrow y = \frac{b}{a}\sin\phi \cdot x$

On comparing this with $y = mx$. $m = \frac{b}{a}\sin\phi$

$\therefore \quad mm' = \frac{b^2}{a^2} \Rightarrow \frac{b}{a}\sin\phi \times m' = \frac{b^2}{a^2}$

$\therefore \quad m' = \left(\frac{b}{a}\right)\operatorname{cosec}\phi$

Concept Inside Video

$\therefore$ Equation of conjugate diameter is $y = m'x = (b/a)\operatorname{cosec}\phi \cdot x$.

On solving, we get

$$y = (b/a)\operatorname{cosec}\phi \cdot x \quad \text{and} \quad -\frac{x^2}{a^2} + \frac{y^2}{b^2} = 1.$$

Then, we get coordinates of D

i.e. $\quad D \equiv (a\tan\phi, b\sec\phi)$

Example 35. If a pair of conjugate diameters meets the hyperbola and its conjugate in P and D respectively, then prove that $CP^2 - CD^2 = a^2 - b^2$.

Sol. Since, coordinates of P and D are $(a\sec\phi, b\tan\phi)$ and $(a\tan\phi, b\sec\phi)$ respectively.

$$\text{Then, } (CP)^2 - (CD)^2 = a^2\sec^2\phi + b^2\tan^2\phi - a^2\tan^2\phi - b^2\sec^2\phi$$

$$= a^2(\sec^2\phi - \tan^2\phi) - b^2(\sec^2\phi - \tan^2\phi)$$

$$= a^2(1) - b^2(1) = a^2 - b^2$$

Example 36. For the hyperbola $x^2 - y^2 = a^2$, prove that the triangle CPD is isosceles and has constant area, where CP and CD are a pair of its conjugate diameters.

Sol. Since, CP and CD are the conjugate diameters of $x^2 - y^2 = a^2$, hence coordinates of P and D are

$P \equiv (a\sec\phi, a\tan\phi)$, $D \equiv (a\tan\phi, a\sec\phi)$, respectively.

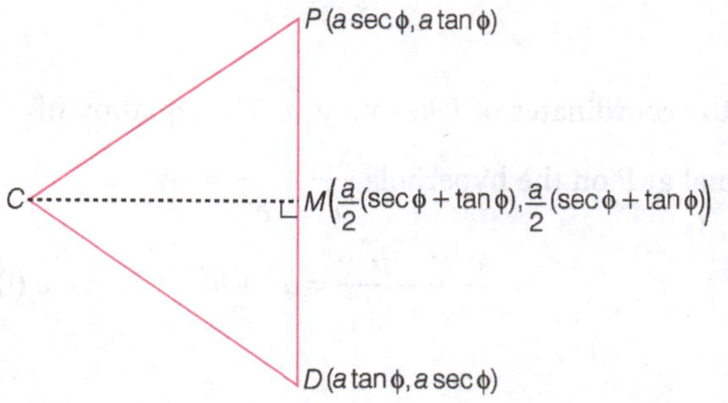

$$\therefore \quad CP = \sqrt{a^2(\sec^2\phi + \tan^2\phi)} = CD \quad [\because C = O(0, 0)]$$

Hence, ΔCPD is an isosceles triangle.
Draw perpendicular from C on PD, where M is the mid-point of PD

$$\therefore \quad M \equiv \left(\frac{a}{2}(\sec\phi + \tan\phi), \frac{a}{2}(\sec\phi + \tan\phi)\right)$$

$$\therefore \quad CM = \frac{|(\sec\phi + \tan\phi)|}{2}\sqrt{(a^2 + a^2)}$$

and $\quad PD = \sqrt{[a(\sec\phi - \tan\phi)]^2 + [a(\sec\phi - \tan\phi)]^2}$

$$= |\sec\phi - \tan\phi|\sqrt{(a^2 + a^2)}$$

$$\therefore \quad \text{Area of } \Delta PCD = \frac{1}{2}\cdot PD\cdot CM$$

$$= \frac{1}{4}(a^2 + a^2) = \frac{a^2}{2} = \text{constant}$$

Example 37. Find the condition for the lines $Ax^2 + 2Hxy + By^2 = 0$ to be conjugate diameters of $\frac{x^2}{a^2} - \frac{y^2}{b^2} = 1$.

Sol. Let the lines represented by $Ax^2 + 2Hxy + By^2 = 0$

are $\quad y = mx$ and $y = m_1x$

$$\therefore \quad mm_1 = \frac{A}{B} \qquad \text{...(i)}$$

But $y = mx$ and $y = m_1x$ are the conjugate diameters of

$$\frac{x^2}{a^2} - \frac{y^2}{b^2} = 1$$

Then, $$mm_1 = \frac{b^2}{a^2} \qquad \text{...(ii)}$$

$\therefore$ From Eqs. (i) and (ii), $\frac{A}{B} = \frac{b^2}{a^2}$

or $\quad a^2A = b^2B$

which is the required condition.

7.15 Director Circle

The locus of the point of intersection of the tangents to the hyperbola $\frac{x^2}{a^2} - \frac{y^2}{b^2} = 1$, which are perpendicular to each other is called director circle.

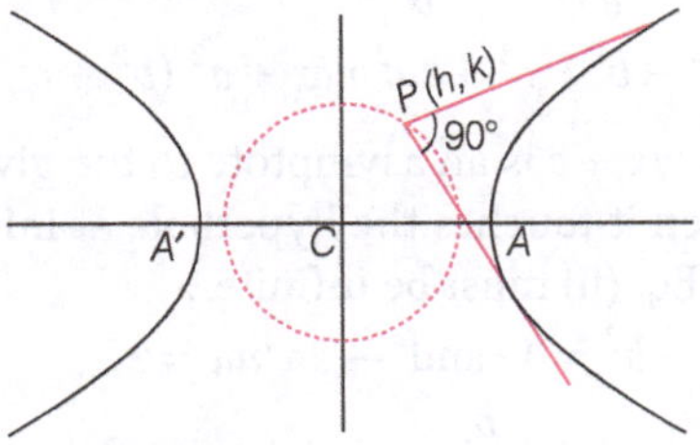

Let any tangent in terms of slope of hyperbola $\frac{x^2}{a^2} - \frac{y^2}{b^2} = 1$ be

$$y = mx + \sqrt{(a^2m^2 - b^2)}$$

It passes through (h, k).

$$\therefore \quad k = mh + \sqrt{(a^2m^2 - b^2)}$$

or $\quad (k - mh)^2 = a^2m^2 - b^2$

$$\Rightarrow \quad k^2 + m^2h^2 - 2mhk = a^2m^2 - b^2$$

$$\Rightarrow \quad m^2(h^2 - a^2) - 2hkm + k^2 + b^2 = 0$$

It is quadratic equation in m. Let slopes of two tangents be m_1 and m_2.

$$\therefore \quad m_1m_2 = \frac{k^2 + b^2}{h^2 - a^2}$$

$$-1 = \frac{k^2 + b^2}{h^2 - a^2} \quad [\because \text{tangents are perpendicular}]$$

$$\Rightarrow \quad -h^2 + a^2 = k^2 + b^2$$

or $\quad h^2 + k^2 = a^2 - b^2$

Hence, locus of $P(h, k)$ is $x^2 + y^2 = a^2 - b^2, (a > b)$.

Alternate Method

If tangents $y = mx + \sqrt{(a^2m^2 - b^2)}$ ...(i)

and $$y = -\frac{x}{m} + \sqrt{\left\{a^2\left(-\frac{1}{m}\right)^2 - b^2\right\}} \qquad \text{...(ii)}$$

touch the hyperbola and intersect at right angles.

From Eq. (i), we get

$$y - mx = \sqrt{(a^2m^2 - b^2)} \qquad \text{...(iii)}$$

Eq. (ii) can be rewritten as.

$$x + my = \sqrt{(a^2 - b^2m^2)} \qquad \text{...(iv)}$$

On squaring and adding Eqs. (iii) and (iv), we get

$$(y - mx)^2 + (x + my)^2 = a^2m^2 - b^2 + a^2 - b^2m^2$$

$$(1 + m^2)(x^2 + y^2) = (1 + m^2)(a^2 - b^2)$$

Hence, $x^2 + y^2 = a^2 - b^2$ is the **director circle** of the hyperbola.

Concept Inside Video

JEE Focus Points

- For director circle of $\frac{x^2}{a^2} - \frac{y^2}{b^2} = 1$, a must be greater than b. If $a < b$, then director circle $x^2 + y^2 = a^2 - b^2$ does not exist.
- The equation of director circle of $-\frac{x^2}{a^2} + \frac{y^2}{b^2} = 1$ is $x^2 + y^2 = b^2 - a^2$ $(b > a)$. If $b < a$, then director circle does not exist.

Example 38. Let the major axis of a standard ellipse equal to the transverse axis of a standard hyperbola and their director circles have radii equal to $2R$ and R, respectively. If e_1 and e_2 are the eccentricities of the ellipse and hyperbola, then the correct relation is

(a) $4e_1^2 - e_2^2 = 6$ (b) $e_1^2 - 4e_2^2 = 2$
(c) $4e_2^2 - e_1^2 = 6$ (c) $e_2^2 - 4e_1^2 = 2$

Sol. (c) Let equation of ellipse be

$$\frac{x^2}{a^2} + \frac{y^2}{b^2} = 1 \, (a > b)$$

$\therefore$ Director circle is $x^2 + y^2 = a^2 + b^2$

and $b^2 = a^2(1 - e_1^2)$

Given, $a^2 + b^2 = (2R)^2$

$\Rightarrow$ $a^2 + a^2(1 - e_1^2) = (2R)^2$

$$\Rightarrow \quad 2 - e_1^2 = \frac{4R^2}{a^2} \quad \text{...(i)}$$

and equation of hyperbola is $\dfrac{x^2}{a^2} - \dfrac{y^2}{b_1^2} = 1$

and $b_1^2 = a^2(e_2^2 - 1)$

Given, $a^2 - b_1^2 = R^2$

$\Rightarrow$ $a^2 - a^2(e_2^2 - 1) = R^2$

$$\Rightarrow \quad 2 - e_2^2 = \frac{R^2}{a^2} \quad \text{...(ii)}$$

On dividing Eq. (i) by Eq. (ii), we get

$$\frac{2 - e_1^2}{2 - e_2^2} = 4 \Rightarrow 4e_2^2 - e_1^2 = 6$$

Example 39. If any tangent to the hyperbola $\dfrac{x^2}{a^2} - \dfrac{y^2}{b^2} = 1$ with centre C, meets its director circle in P and Q, show that CP and CQ are conjugate semi-diameters of the hyperbola.

Sol. Since, equation of hyperbola is

$$\frac{x^2}{a^2} - \frac{y^2}{b^2} = 1 \quad \text{...(i)}$$

Equation of tangent at $(a \sec \phi, b \tan \phi)$ on Eq. (i) is

$$\frac{x}{a} \sec \phi - \frac{y}{b} \tan \phi = 1 \quad \text{...(ii)}$$

Equation of director circle of Eq. (i) is

$$x^2 + y^2 = a^2 - b^2 \quad \text{...(iii)}$$

Equation of lines joining the point of intersection of Eqs. (i) and (ii) to the origin is obtained by making Eq. (iii) homogeneous with the help of Eq. (ii).

$$\therefore \quad x^2 + y^2 = (a^2 - b^2)\left(\frac{x}{a} \sec \phi - \frac{y}{b} \tan \phi\right)^2$$

$$\text{or} \quad x^2\left(1 - \frac{(a^2 - b^2)\sec^2 \phi}{a^2}\right) + y^2\left(1 - \frac{(a^2 - b^2)\tan^2 \phi}{b^2}\right) + \frac{2(a^2 - b^2)\sec \phi \tan \phi}{ab} xy = 0 \quad \text{...(iv)}$$

Let m and m' represent the slopes of the lines given by Eq. (iv).

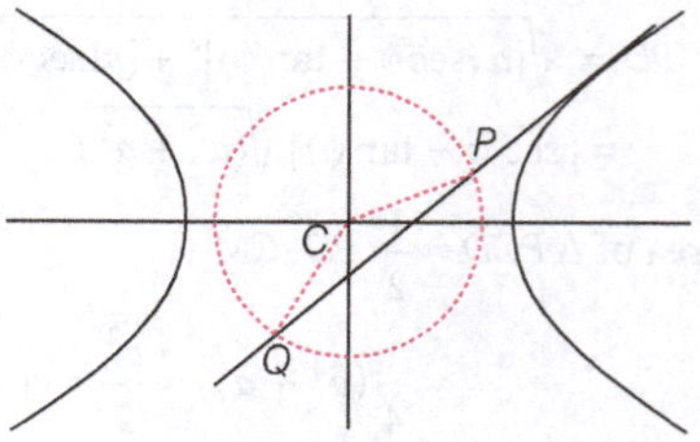

$$\text{Then, } mm' = \frac{1 - \dfrac{(a^2 - b^2)\sec^2 \phi}{a^2}}{1 - \dfrac{(a^2 - b^2)\tan^2 \phi}{b^2}} = \frac{b^2}{a^2} \cdot \frac{a^2 - (a^2 - b^2)\sec^2 \phi}{b^2 - (a^2 - b^2)\tan^2 \phi}$$

$$= \frac{b^2}{a^2} \cdot \frac{b^2 \sec^2 \phi - a^2 \tan^2 \phi}{b^2 \sec^2 \phi - a^2 \tan^2 \phi} = \frac{b^2}{a^2}$$

Hence, the lines CP and CQ are conjugate semi-diameters of the hyperbola.

7.16 Asymptotes

An asymptotes of any hyperbola or a curve is a straight line which touches in it two points at infinity.

Asymptotes of Hyperbola The equations of two asymptotes of the hyperbola

$$\frac{x^2}{a^2} - \frac{y^2}{b^2} = 1 \text{ are } y = \pm \frac{b}{a} x \text{ or } \frac{x}{a} \pm \frac{y}{b} = 0.$$

Proof Let $y = mx + c$ be an asymptote of the hyperbola

$$\frac{x^2}{a^2} - \frac{y^2}{b^2} = 1 \quad \text{...(i)}$$

On substituting the value of y in Eq. (i),

$$\frac{x^2}{a^2} - \frac{(mx + c)^2}{b^2} = 1$$

$$\text{or} \quad (a^2m^2 - b^2)\, x^2 + 2a^2mcx + a^2\,(b^2 + c^2) = 0 \quad \text{...(ii)}$$

If the line $y = mx + c$ is an asymptote to the given hyperbola, then it touches the hyperbola at infinity. So, both roots of Eq. (ii) must be infinite.

$\therefore$ $a^2m^2 - b^2 = 0$ and $-2a^2mc = 0$

Then, $m = \pm \dfrac{b}{a}$ and $c = 0$

On substituting the value of m and c in $y = mx + c$, we get

$$y = \pm \frac{b}{a} x \Rightarrow \frac{x}{a} \pm \frac{y}{b} = 0$$

Alternate Proof

The difference between the second degree curve and pair of asymptotes is constant.

$\because$ Given hyperbola is $\dfrac{x^2}{a^2}-\dfrac{y^2}{b^2}=1$

$\therefore$ Pair of asymptotes is $\dfrac{x^2}{a^2}-\dfrac{y^2}{b^2}+\lambda=0$ ...(i)

Eq. (i) represents a pair of lines, then $\Delta=0$

$$\therefore \quad \frac{1}{a^2}\cdot\left(-\frac{1}{b^2}\right)\cdot\lambda+0-0-0-\lambda\cdot 0=0$$

$$\therefore \quad \lambda=0$$

From Eq. (i), pair of asymptotes is $\dfrac{x^2}{a^2}-\dfrac{y^2}{b^2}=0$

or $\quad y=\pm\dfrac{b}{a}x$ or $\dfrac{x}{a}\pm\dfrac{y}{b}=0$

JEE Focus Points

- If $b=a$, then $\dfrac{x^2}{a^2}-\dfrac{y^2}{b^2}=1$ reduces to $x^2-y^2=a^2$. The asymptotes of rectangular hyperbola $x^2-y^2=a^2$ are $y=\pm x$ which are at right angles.
- A hyperbola and its conjugate hyperbola have the same asymptotes.
- The angle between the asymptotes of $\dfrac{x^2}{a^2}-\dfrac{y^2}{b^2}=1$ is $2\tan^{-1}\left(\dfrac{b}{a}\right)$

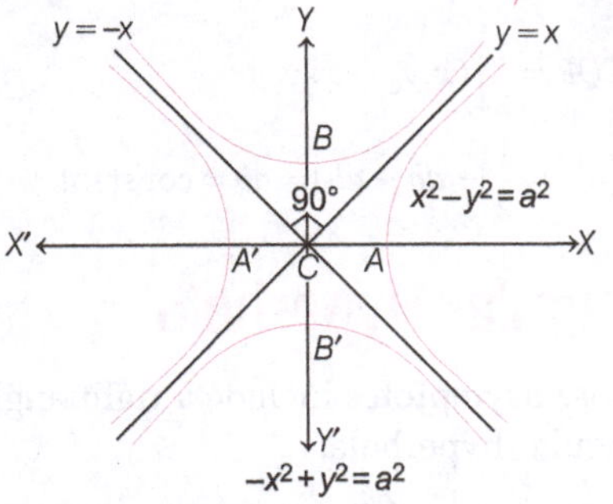

Concept Inside Video

- If the angle between the asymptotes of a hyperbola $\dfrac{x^2}{a^2}-\dfrac{y^2}{b^2}=1$ is 2θ, then $e=\sec\theta$.
- The asymptotes pass through the centre of the hyperbola.
- The bisectors of the angles between the asymptotes are the coordinate axes.
- Let $H\equiv\dfrac{x^2}{a^2}-\dfrac{y^2}{b^2}-1=0$, $A\equiv\dfrac{x^2}{a^2}-\dfrac{y^2}{b^2}=0$ and $C\equiv\dfrac{x^2}{a^2}-\dfrac{y^2}{b^2}+1=0$ be the equation of the hyperbola, asymptotes and the conjugate hyperbola respectively, then clearly $C+H=2A$.

Example 40. Find the asymptotes of the hyperbola $xy-3y-2x=0$.

Sol. Since, equation of a hyperbola and its asymptotes differ in constant terms only.

$\therefore$ Pair of asymptotes is given by

$$xy-3y-2x+\lambda=0, \quad \text{...(i)}$$

where λ is any constant such that it represents two straight lines.

$$\therefore \quad abc+2fgh-af^2-bg^2-ch^2=0$$

$$\Rightarrow \quad 0+2\times-\frac{3}{2}\times-1\times\frac{1}{2}-0-0-\lambda\left(\frac{1}{2}\right)^2=0$$

$$\therefore \quad \lambda=6$$

From Eq. (i), the asymptotes of given hyperbola are given by $xy-3y-2x+6=0$

or $\quad (y-2)(x-3)=0.$

$\therefore$ Asymptotes are $x-3=0$ and $y-2=0$.

Example 41. From a point $P(1,2)$ two tangents are drawn to a hyperbola H in which one tangent is drawn to each arm of hyperbola. If the equations of asymptotes of hyperbola H are $\sqrt{3}x-y+5=0$ and $\sqrt{3}x+y-1=0$, then eccentricity of H is

(a) 2 (b) $\dfrac{2}{\sqrt{3}}$ (c) 2 (d) $\sqrt{3}$

Sol. Equation of asymptotes are

$$\sqrt{3}x-y+5=0 \text{ and } \sqrt{3}x+y-1=0$$

$$a_1=\sqrt{3}, b_1=-1, c_1=5 \text{ and } a_2=\sqrt{3}, b_2=1, c_2=-1$$

$$\because \quad c_1c_2(a_1a_2+b_1b_2)=5(-1)[\sqrt{3}(\sqrt{3})+(1)(-1)]$$

$$=-5(3-1)=-10<0$$

Therefore, origin lies in acute angle, $P(1,2)$ lies in obtuse angle.

Acute angle between asymptotes,

$$\tan\theta=\left|\frac{m_1+m_2}{1-m_1m_2}\right|$$

$$=\left|\frac{\sqrt{3}+\sqrt{3}}{1-3}\right|=|\sqrt{3}|$$

$$\Rightarrow \quad \theta=\pi/3$$

$$\therefore \quad e=\sec\theta/2=\sec\pi/6=\frac{2}{\sqrt{3}}$$

Example 42. The asymptotes of a hyperbola having centre at the point $(1,2)$ are parallel to the lines $2x+3y=0$ and $3x+2y=0$. If the hyperbola passes through the point $(5,3)$, then show that its equation is $(2x+3y-8)(3x+2y+7)=154$.

Sol. Let the asymptotes be $2x+3y+\lambda=0$ and $3x+2y+\mu=0$.

Since, asymptotes passes through $(1,2)$, then

$$\lambda=-8 \text{ and } \mu=-7$$

Thus, the equation of asymptotes are

$$2x + 3y - 8 = 0 \quad \text{and} \quad 3x + 2y - 7 = 0$$

Let the equation of hyperbola be

$$(2x + 3y - 8)(3x + 2y - 7) + \gamma = 0 \quad \text{... (i)}$$

It passes through (5,3), then

$$(10 + 9 - 8)(15 + 6 - 7) + \gamma = 0$$

$$\Rightarrow \quad 11 \times 14 + \gamma = 0$$

$$\therefore \quad \gamma = -154$$

On putting the value of γ in Eq. (i), we obtain

$$(2x + 3y - 8)(3x + 2y - 7) - 154 = 0$$

which is the equation of required hyperbola.

Example 43. If the angle between asymptotes of hyperbola $\frac{x^2}{a^2} - \frac{y^2}{b^2} = 1$ is 120° and product of perpendicular drawn from foci upon its any tangent is 9, then locus of point of intersection of perpendicular tangents of the hyperbola can be

(a) $x^2 + y^2 = 3$ (b) $x^2 + y^2 = 16$

(c) $x^2 + y^2 = 9$ (d) $x^2 + y^2 = 18$

Sol. (d) Angle between asymptotes $= 2\tan^{-1}(b/a) = 120°$

$$\tan^{-1}(b/a) = 60°$$

$$\Rightarrow \quad \frac{b}{a} = \sqrt{3} \Rightarrow b = a\sqrt{3} \Rightarrow b^2 = 3a^2$$

$$\because \quad b^2 = 9$$

$$\therefore \quad a^2 = 9/3 = 3$$

Required locus is director circle of the hyperbola and which is $x^2 + y^2 = a^2 - b^2 = 3 - 9 = -6$

which is not possible.

Now, angle between asymptotes,

$$2\tan^{-1}(b/a) = 60°$$

$$\Rightarrow \quad \tan^{-1}(b/a) = 30°$$

$$\Rightarrow \quad \frac{b}{a} = 1/\sqrt{3} \Rightarrow a^2 = 3b^2$$

$$\because \quad b^2 = 9$$

$$\therefore \quad a^2 = 27$$

Required locus is $x^2 + y^2 = a^2 - b^2$

$$\Rightarrow \quad x^2 + y^2 = 27 - 9$$

Hence, $x^2 + y^2 = 18$

Example 44. Show that the tangent at any point of a hyperbola cuts off a triangle of constant area from the asymptotes and that the portion of it intercepted between the asymptotes is bisected at the point of contact.

Sol. Let $P(a\sec\phi, b\tan\phi)$ be any point on the hyperbola

$$\frac{x^2}{a^2} - \frac{y^2}{b^2} = 1 \quad \text{... (i)}$$

Asymptotes of Eq. (i) are

$$y = \pm\frac{b}{a}x$$

Equation of tangent of Eq. (i) at $P(a\sec\phi, b\tan\phi)$ is

$$\frac{x}{a}\sec\phi - \frac{y}{b}\tan\phi = 1 \quad \text{...(ii)}$$

On solving Eq. (ii) and $y = \frac{b}{a}x$, we get

$$\frac{x}{a}(\sec\phi - \tan\phi) = (\sec^2\phi - \tan^2\phi)$$

$$\therefore \quad x = a(\sec\phi + \tan\phi)$$

$$\text{and} \quad y = b(\sec\phi + \tan\phi)$$

Let $Q \equiv [a(\sec\phi + \tan\phi), b(\sec\phi + \tan\phi)]$

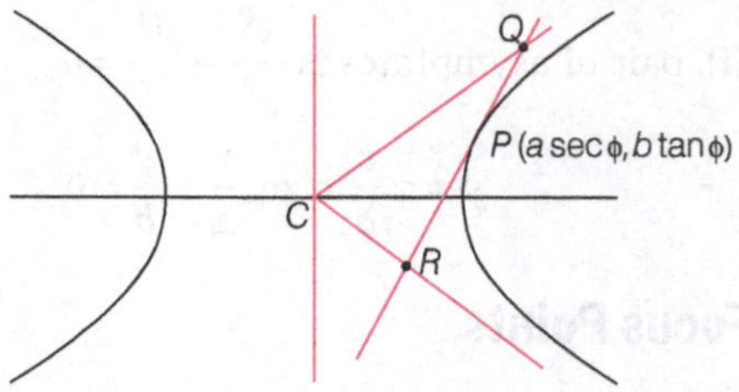

Now, solving Eq. (ii) and $y = -\frac{b}{a}x$, we get,

$$\frac{x}{a}(\sec\phi + \tan\phi) = (\sec^2\phi - \tan^2\phi)$$

$$\text{or} \quad x = a(\sec\phi - \tan\phi)$$

$$\text{and} \quad y = -b(\sec\phi - \tan\phi)$$

Let $R \equiv [a(\sec\phi - \tan\phi), -b(\sec\phi - \tan\phi)]$

Mid-point of QR is $(a\sec\phi, b\tan\phi)$ which is coordinates of P.

$$\therefore \text{Area of } \Delta CQR = \frac{1}{2}|(x_1y_2 - x_2y_1)|$$

$$= \frac{1}{2}|-ab - ab| = ab = \text{constant.}$$

7.17 Rectangular Hyperbola

A hyperbola whose asymptotes include a right angle is said to be rectangular hyperbola.

Or

If the lengths of transverse and conjugate axes of any hyperbola be equal, it is called **rectangular or equilateral hyperbola.**

According to the first definition,

$$2\tan^{-1}\left(\frac{b}{a}\right) = \frac{\pi}{2}$$

$$\Rightarrow \quad \tan^{-1}\left(\frac{b}{a}\right) = \frac{\pi}{4} \Rightarrow \frac{b}{a} = 1$$

$$a = b$$

Then, $\frac{x^2}{a^2}-\frac{y^2}{b^2}=1$ becomes $x^2-y^2=a^2$

According to the second definition,

When $a=b$, $\frac{x^2}{a^2}-\frac{y^2}{b^2}=1$ becomes $x^2-y^2=a^2$

$$\text{Eccentricity, } e=\sqrt{\left(1+\frac{b^2}{a^2}\right)}=\sqrt{2}$$

Hence, $x^2-y^2=a^2$ is the general form of the equation of the rectangular hyperbola.

JEE SPIKE

All the results of $\frac{x^2}{a^2}-\frac{y^2}{b^2}=1$ are applicable to the hyperbola $x^2-y^2=a^2$ after changing b by a.

The Rectangular Hyperbola $xy=c^2$

When the centre of any rectangular hyperbola be at the origin and its asymptotes coincide with the coordinate axes its, equation is $xy=c^2$.

Since, asymptotes coincides the coordinate axes.

Hence, asymptotes are $y=0$ and $x=0$.

$\therefore$ Combined equation of asymptotes is $xy=0$.

Now, equation of any hyperbola and its asymptotes differ in respect of constant terms only.

$\therefore$ Equation of rectangular hyperbola is $xy=c^2$, where c is any constant.

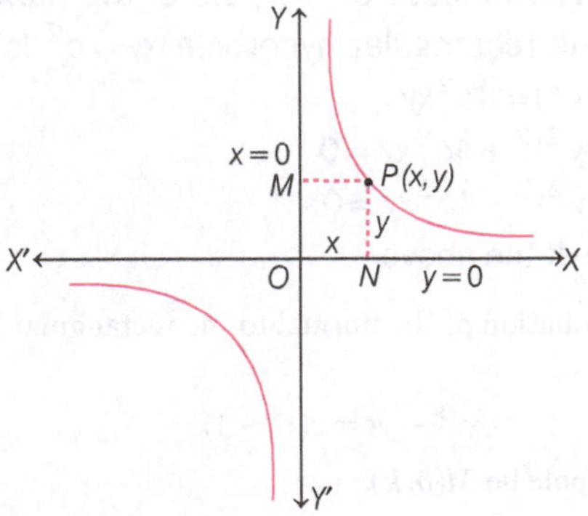

By rotation of axes

The equation of rectangular hyperbola is $x^2-y^2=a^2$ and its asymptotes are $x-y=0$ and $x+y=0$. Since, asymptotes are inclined at 45° and 135° to the X-axis respectively.

If we rotate the axes through $\theta=-45°$ without changing the origin.

Thus, when we replace (x,y) by

$$[x\cos(-45°)-y\sin(-45°),\ x\sin(-45)°+y\cos(-45°)]$$

i.e. $\left(\frac{x+y}{\sqrt{2}},\frac{-x+y}{\sqrt{2}}\right)$

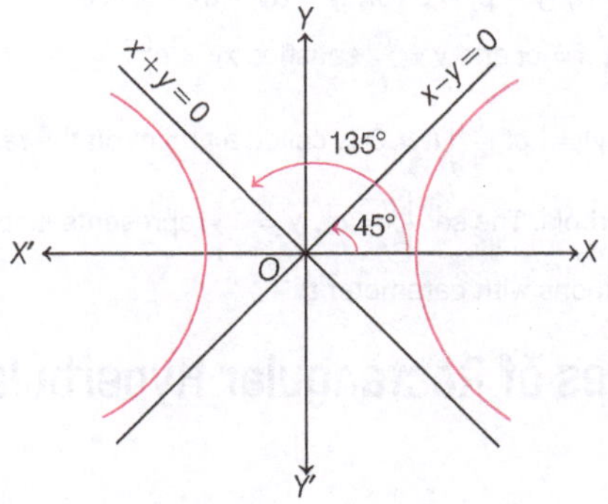

Then, equation $x^2-y^2=a^2$ reduces to

$$\left(\frac{x+y}{\sqrt{2}}\right)^2-\left(\frac{-x+y}{\sqrt{2}}\right)^2=a^2$$

or $\frac{1}{2}\{(x+y)^2-(-x+y)^2\}=a^2$

$\Rightarrow$ $\frac{1}{2}(2y)(2x)=a^2$

or $xy=\frac{a^2}{2}=\left(\frac{a}{\sqrt{2}}\right)^2=c^2$ (say)

or $xy=c^2$

Study of Hyperbola $xy=c^2$

(i) **Vertices** $A(c,c)$ and $A'(-c,-c)$.

(ii) **Transverse axis** $y=x$.

(iii) **Conjugate axis** $y=-x$.

(iv) **Foci** $S(c\sqrt{2},c\sqrt{2})$ and $S'(-c\sqrt{2},-c\sqrt{2})$.

(v) **Length of latusrectum** Length of $AA'=2\sqrt{2}\,c$.

(vi) **Equation of auxiliary circle** $x^2+y^2=2c^2$.

(vii) **Equation of director circle** $x^2+y^2=0$.

(viii) **Asymptotes** $x=0, y=0$.

JEE Focus Points

- The equations of the asymptotes and the conjugate hyperbola of the rectangular hyperbola $xy = c^2$, where the axes are the asymptotes, are $xy = 0$ and $xy = -c^2$, respectively.
- The equation of a rectangular hyperbola having coordinate axes as its asymptotes is $xy = c^2$. If the asymptotes of a rectangular hyperbola are $x = \alpha$ and $y = \beta$, then its equation is $(x - \alpha)(y - \beta) = c^2$ or $xy - \alpha y - \beta x + \lambda = 0$
- Since, $x = ct$ and $y = \frac{c}{t}$ satisfies $xy = c^2$

  $\therefore (x, y) = \left(ct, \frac{c}{t}\right)$ $(t \neq 0)$ is called a t point on the rectangular hyperbola. The set $\left\{x = ct,\ y = \frac{c}{t}\right\}$ represents its parametric equations with parameter t.

Concept Inside Video

Properties of Rectangular Hyperbola $xy = c^2$

(i) Equation of the chord joining t_1 and t_2 is $x + yt_1t_2 - c(t_1 + t_2) = 0$.

(ii) Equation of tangent at (x_1, y_1) is $xy_1 + x_1y = 2c^2$.

(iii) Equation of tangent at t is $\frac{x}{t} + yt = 2c$.

(iv) Point of intersection of tangents at t_1 and t_2 is $\left(\frac{2ct_1t_2}{t_1 + t_2}, \frac{2c}{t_1 + t_2}\right)$.

(v) Equation of normal at (x_1, y_1) is $xx_1 - yy_1 = x_1^2 - y_1^2$.

(vi) Equation of normal at t is $xt^3 - yt - ct^4 + c = 0$.

(vii) Point of intersection of normals at t_1 and t_2 is.

$$\left(\frac{c\{t_1t_2(t_1^2 + t_1t_2 + t_2^2) - 1\}}{t_1t_2(t_1 + t_2)}, \frac{c\{t_1^3t_2^3 + (t_1^2 + t_1t_2 + t_2^2)\}}{t_1t_2(t_1 + t_2)}\right).$$

Example 45. Area of triangle formed by tangent to the hyperbola $xy = 16$ at $(16, 1)$ and coordinate axes, is equal to

(a) 8 (b) 16
(c) 32 (d) 64

Sol. (c) Tangent to hyperbola $xy = c^2$ is

$$\frac{x}{x_1} + \frac{y}{y_1} = 2$$

$\because$ Point is $(16, 1)$ [given]

$\therefore$ $x_1 = 16$ and $y_1 = 1$

Equation is $x/16 + y/1 = 2$

$\Rightarrow$ $x + 16y = 32$

$\therefore$ $A \equiv (32, 0)$ and $B(0, 2)$

$\therefore$ Area of $\Delta OAB = 1/2 \times 32 \times 2 = 32$ sq units

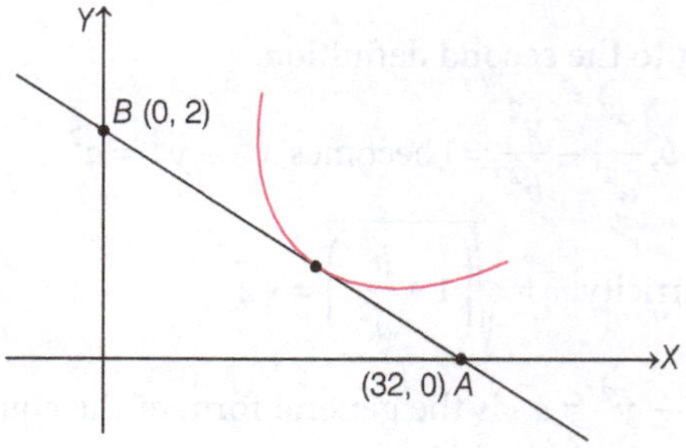

Example 46. If the normal at the point t_1 to the rectangular hyperbola $xy = c^2$ meets it again at the point t_2, then prove that $t_1^3 t_2 = -1$.

Sol. Since, the equation of normal at $\left(ct_1, \frac{c}{t_1}\right)$ to the hyperbola $xy = c^2$ is $xt_1^3 - yt_1 - ct_1^4 + c = 0$

but this passes through $\left(ct_2, \frac{c}{t_2}\right)$,

then, $ct_2t_1^3 - \frac{c}{t_2}t_1 - ct_1^4 + c = 0$

$\Rightarrow$ $t_2^2t_1^3 - t_1 - t_1^4t_2 + t_2 = 0$

$\Rightarrow$ $t_2t_1^3(t_2 - t_1) + (t_2 - t_1) = 0$

$\Rightarrow$ $(t_1^3t_2 + 1)(t_2 - t_1) = 0$

$\Rightarrow$ $t_1^3t_2 + 1 = 0$ $[\because t_2 \neq t_1]$

$\therefore$ $t_1^3t_2 = -1$

Example 47. The locus of the pole of the normal chords of the rectangular hyperbola $xy = c^2$ is

(a) $(x^2 - y^2) = 4c^2xy$
(b) $(x^2 - y^2)^2 + 4c^2xy = 0$
(c) $(x^2 - y^2)^2 - 4c^2xy = 0$
(d) None of the above

Sol. (b) The equation of the normal to the rectangular hyperbola is

$$xt^3 - yt = c(t^4 - 1) \quad \text{...(i)}$$

Let the pole be $M(h, k)$.

Then, equation of pole at M is

$$xk + yh = 2c^2 \quad \text{...(ii)}$$

$\because$ The lines (i) and (ii) are same line.

So, $\frac{t^3}{k} = -\frac{t}{h} = \frac{c(t^4 - 1)}{2c^2}$

$\Rightarrow$ $\frac{t^3}{k} = -\frac{t}{h} = \frac{t^4 - 1}{2c}$

On solving, we get

$$\frac{-k}{h^3} = \frac{(t^4 - 1)^2}{4c^2}$$

$$\Rightarrow \quad \frac{-k}{h^3} = \frac{\left(\frac{k^2}{h^2} - 1\right)^2}{4c^2}$$

$$\Rightarrow \quad -4c^2kh = (k^2 - h^2)^2$$

$$\Rightarrow \quad (h^2 - k^2)^2 + 4c^2kh = 0$$

$\therefore$ Locus is $(x^2 - y^2)^2 + 4c^2xy = 0$

Example 48. A triangle has its vertices on a rectangular hyperbola. Prove that the orthocentre of the triangle also lies on the same hyperbola.

Sol. Let t_1, t_2 and t_3 be the vertices of the ΔABC, described on the rectangular hyperbola $xy = c^2$.

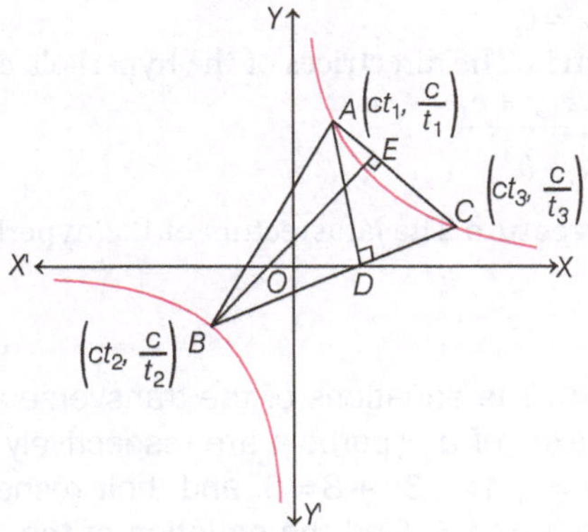

$\therefore$ Coordinates of A, B and C are $\left(ct_1, \frac{c}{t_1}\right)$, $\left(ct_2, \frac{c}{t_2}\right)$ and $\left(ct_3, \frac{c}{t_3}\right)$, respectively.

Now, slope of BC is $\dfrac{\frac{c}{t_3} - \frac{c}{t_2}}{ct_3 - ct_2} = -\dfrac{1}{t_2t_3}$

$\because$ Slope of AD is t_2t_3.

$\therefore$ Equation of altitude AD is

$$y - \frac{c}{t_1} = t_2t_3(x - ct_1)$$

or $\quad t_1y - c = x\, t_1t_2t_3 - ct_1^2t_2t_3 \quad$ ...(i)

Similarly, equation of altitude BE is

$$t_2y - c = x\, t_1t_2t_3 - c\, t_1t_2^2t_3 \quad \text{...(ii)}$$

On solving Eqs. (i) and (ii), we get the orthocentre $\left(-\frac{c}{t_1t_2t_3}, -c\, t_1t_2t_3\right)$, which lies on $xy = c^2$.

7.18 Reflection Property of a Hyperbola

If an incoming light ray passing through one focus S strike convex side of the hyperbola, then it will get reflected towards other focus S'.

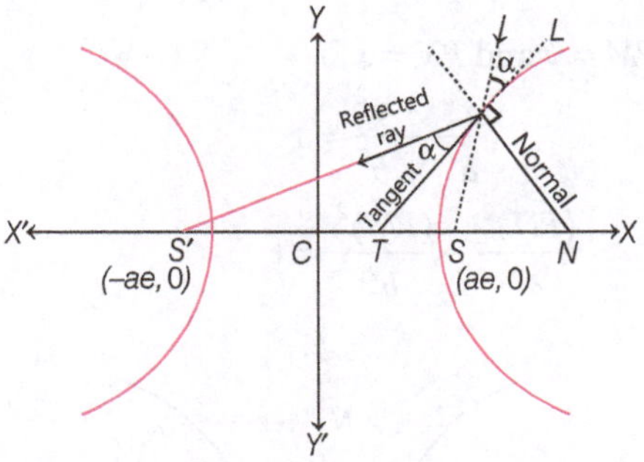

Example 49 A ray emanating from the point $(5, 0)$ is incident on the hyperbola $9x^2 - 16y^2 = 144$ at the point P with abscissa 8. Find the equation of the reflected ray after first reflection and point P lies in first quadrant.

Sol. Given hyperbola is $9x^2 - 16y^2 = 144$.

This equation can be rewritten as

$$\frac{x^2}{16} - \frac{y^2}{9} = 1 \quad \text{...(i)}$$

Coordinates of foci are $(0, \pm\sqrt{16 + 9})$ i.e. $(0, \pm 5)$

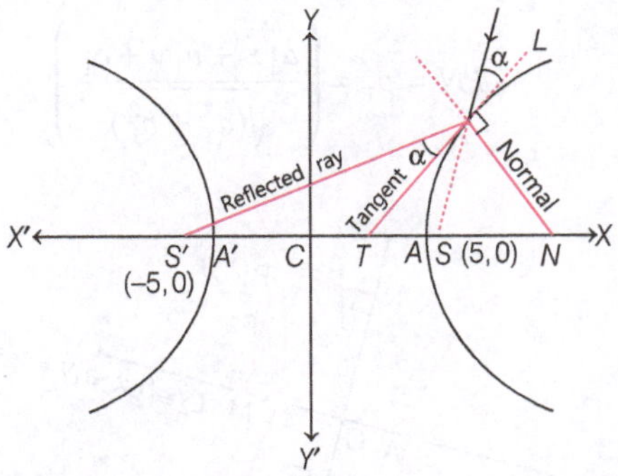

Since, x-coordinate of P is 8. Let y-coordinate of P be α.

$\because$ $(8, \alpha)$ lies on Eq. (i).

$$\therefore \quad \frac{64}{16} - \frac{\alpha^2}{9} = 1 \Rightarrow \alpha^2 = 27$$

$$\Rightarrow \quad \alpha = 3\sqrt{3} \quad [\because P \text{ lies in Ist quadrant}]$$

Hence, the coordinates of point P are $(8, 3\sqrt{3})$.

$\therefore$ Equation of reflected ray passing through $P(8, 3\sqrt{3})$ and $S'(-5, 0)$ is

$$y - 3\sqrt{3} = \frac{0 - 3\sqrt{3}}{-5 - 8}(x - 8)$$

or $\quad 13y - 39\sqrt{3} = 3\sqrt{3}x - 24\sqrt{3}$

or $3\sqrt{3}x - 13y + 15\sqrt{3} = 0$

7.19 Equation of a Hyperbola Referred to Two Perpendicular Lines

Let $P(x, y)$ be any point on the hyperbola $\frac{x^2}{a^2} - \frac{y^2}{b^2} = 1$.

Then, $PM = y$ and $PN = x$

$$\therefore \quad \frac{x^2}{a^2} - \frac{y^2}{b^2} = 1$$

$$\Rightarrow \quad \frac{(PN)^2}{a^2} - \frac{(PM)^2}{b^2} = 1$$

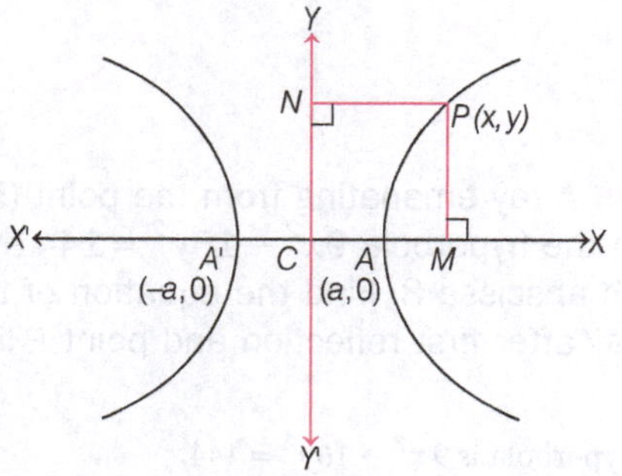

If perpendicular lines represented by

$$L_1 \equiv a_1 x + b_1 y + c_1 = 0$$

and

$$L_2 \equiv b_1 x - a_1 y + c_2 = 0$$

Then,

$$PN = p_1 = \left(\frac{a_1 x + b_1 y + c_1}{\sqrt{(a_1^2 + b_1^2)}} \right)$$

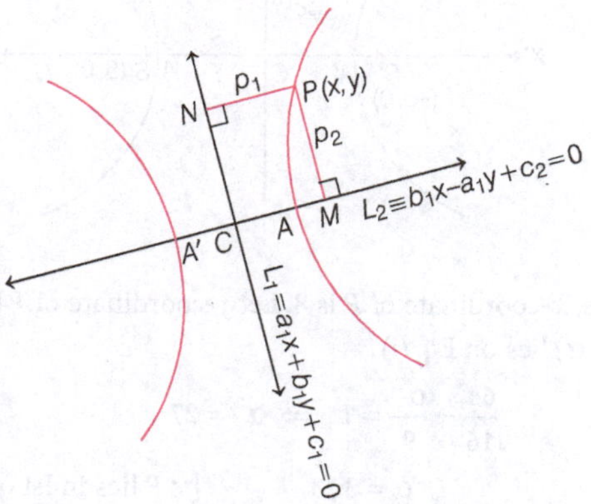

and

$$PM = p_2 = \left(\frac{b_1 x - a_1 y + c_2}{\sqrt{(b_1^2 + a_1^2)}} \right)$$

Now, equation of hyperbola becomes

$$\frac{\left(\dfrac{a_1 x + b_1 y + c_1}{\sqrt{(a_1^2 + b_1^2)}} \right)^2}{a^2} - \frac{\left(\dfrac{b_1 x - a_1 y + c_2}{\sqrt{(b_1^2 + a_1^2)}} \right)^2}{b^2} = 1$$

Then, the point P describes a hyperbola in the plane of the given lines such that :

(i) **Centre** The centre of the hyperbola is the point of intersection of the lines $L_1 = 0$ and $L_2 = 0$.

(ii) **Transverse axis** The transverse axis lies along $L_2 = 0$.
Conjugate axis The conjugate axis lies along $L_1 = 0$.

(iii) **Length of transverse and conjugate axes** The length of transverse and conjugate axes are $2a$ and $2b$ respectively.

(iv) **Foci** The foci of the hyperbola is the point of intersection of the lines $\frac{a_1 x + b_1 y + c_1}{\sqrt{(a_1^2 + b_1^2)}} = \pm ae$ and $L_2 = 0$.

(v) **Directrix** The directrices of the hyperbola are $\frac{a_1 x + b_1 y + c_1}{\sqrt{(a_1^2 + b_1^2)}} = \pm \frac{a}{e}$

(vi) **Latusrectum** The latusrectum of the hyperbola is $\frac{2b^2}{a}$.

Example 50. The equations of the transverse and conjugate axes of a hyperbola are respectively $3x + 4y - 7 = 0$, $4x - 3y + 8 = 0$ and their respective lengths are 4 and 6. Find the equation of the hyperbola.

Sol. The equation of the required hyperbola is

$$\frac{\left(\dfrac{3x + 4y - 7}{\sqrt{(3^2 + 4^2)}} \right)^2}{\left(\dfrac{4}{2} \right)^2} - \frac{\left(\dfrac{4x - 3y + 8}{\sqrt{4^2 + (-3)^2}} \right)^2}{\left(\dfrac{6}{2} \right)^2} = 1$$

$$\Rightarrow \quad \frac{1}{100}(3x + 4y - 7)^2 - \frac{1}{225}(4x - 3y + 8)^2 = 1$$

$$\Rightarrow \quad 9(3x + 4y - 7)^2 - 4(4x - 3y + 8)^2 = 900$$

$$\Rightarrow \quad 9(9x^2 + 16y^2 + 49 + 24xy - 42x - 56y)$$
$$- 4(16x^2 + 9y^2 + 64 - 24xy + 64x - 48y) = 900$$

$$\Rightarrow \quad 17x^2 + 312xy + 108y^2 - 634x - 312y - 715 = 0.$$

Milestone Practice 7.3

1. The diameter of $16x^2 - 9y^2 = 144$ which is conjugate to $x = 2y$ is

(a) $y = \frac{16}{9}x$ (b) $y = \frac{32}{9}x$

(c) $x = \frac{16}{9}y$ (d) $x = \frac{32}{9}y$

2. Tangents drawn from a point on the circle $x^2 + y^2 = 9$ to the hyperbola $\frac{x^2}{25} - \frac{y^2}{16} = 1$, then tangents are at angle

(a) $\frac{\pi}{6}$ (b) $\frac{\pi}{4}$

(c) $\frac{\pi}{3}$ (d) $\frac{\pi}{2}$

3. If $H \equiv \frac{x^2}{a^2} - \frac{y^2}{b^2} - 1 = 0$, $C \equiv \frac{x^2}{a^2} - \frac{y^2}{b^2} + 1 = 0$ and $A \equiv \frac{x^2}{a^2} - \frac{y^2}{b^2} = 0$, then H, A and C are in

(a) AP (b) GP

(c) HP (d) AGP

4. The angle between the asymptotes of $\frac{x^2}{4} - \frac{y^2}{9} = 1$ is equal to

(a) $\tan^{-1}\left(\frac{2}{3}\right)$ (b) $\tan^{-1}\left(\frac{3}{2}\right)$

(c) $2\tan^{-1}\left(\frac{2}{3}\right)$ (d) $2\tan^{-1}\left(\frac{3}{2}\right)$

5. If e and e_1 are the eccentricities of the hyperbolas $xy = c^2$ and $x^2 - y^2 = a^2$, then $(e + e_1)^2$ is equal to

(a) 2 (b) 4

(c) 6 (d) 8

6. The product of the lengths of perpendiculars drawn from any point on the hyperbola $\frac{x^2}{2} - y^2 = 1$ to its asymptotes is

(a) $\frac{1}{2}$ (b) 2 (c) $\frac{2}{3}$ (d) $\frac{3}{2}$

7. The number of points on hyperbola $\frac{x^2}{a^2} - \frac{y^2}{b^2} = 3$ from which mutually perpendicular tangents can be drawn to the circle $x^2 + y^2 = a^2$ is/are

(a) 0 (b) 2

(c) 3 (d) 4

8. If the sum of the slopes of the normal from a point P to the hyperbola $xy = c^2$ is equal to $t_1^2 + t_2^2 + t_3^2 + t_4^2 = \lambda\,(\lambda \in R^+)$, then the locus of point P is

(a) $x^2 = \lambda c^2$ (b) $y^2 = \lambda c^2$

(c) $xy = \lambda c^2$ (d) None of these

9. If $S \equiv x^2 + 4xy + 3y^2 - 4x + 2y + 1 = 0$, then the value of λ for which $S + \lambda = 0$ represents its asymptotes is

(a) 20

(b) 18

(c) -16

(d) -22

10. A ray emanating from the point $(-\sqrt{41}, 0)$ is incident on the hyperbola $16x^2 - 25y^2 = 400$ at the point P with abscissa 10. Then, the equation of the reflected ray after first reflection and point P lies in second quadrant is

(a) $4\sqrt{3}x - (10 - \sqrt{41})\,y + 4\sqrt{123} = 0$

(b) $4\sqrt{3}x + (10 - \sqrt{41})\,y - 4\sqrt{123} = 0$

(c) $4\sqrt{3}x + (10 - \sqrt{41})\,y + 4\sqrt{123} = 0$

(d) $4\sqrt{3}x - (10 - \sqrt{41})\,y - 4\sqrt{123} = 0$

11. A ray of light incident along the line $3x + (5 - 4\sqrt{2})y = 15$ gets reflected from the hyperbola $\frac{x^2}{16} - \frac{y^2}{9} = 1$, then its reflected ray goes along the line

(a) $x\sqrt{2} - y + 5 = 0$

(b) $y\sqrt{2} - x + 5 = 0$

(c) $y\sqrt{2} - x - 5 = 0$

(d) None of the above

12. The equations of the transverse and conjugate axes of a hyperbola are $x + 2y - 3 = 0$ and $2x - y + 4 = 0$ respectively and their respective lengths are $\sqrt{2}$ and $\frac{2}{\sqrt{3}}$. The equation of the hyperbola is

(a) $2(x + 2y - 3)^2 - 3(2x - y + 4)^2 = 5$

(b) $2(2x - y + 4)^2 - 3(x + 2y - 3)^2 = 5$

(c) $2(x + 2y - 3)^2 - 3(2x - y + 4)^2 = 1$

(d) $2(2x - y + 4)^2 - 3(x + 2y - 3)^2 = 1$

13. Find the equation of that diameter which bisects the chord $7x + y - 2 = 0$ of the hyperbola $\frac{x^2}{3} - \frac{y^2}{7} = 1$.

14. Find the equation of the hyperbola which has $3x - 4y + 7 = 0$ and $4x + 3y + 1 = 0$ for its asymptotes and which passes through the origin.

15. The asymptotes of a hyperbola are parallel to lines $2x + 3y = 0$ and $3x + 2y = 0$. The hyperbola has its centre at $(1, 2)$ and it passes through $(5, 3)$, find its equation.

16. If the pair of straight lines $Ax^2 + 2Hxy + By^2 = 0$ be conjugate diameters of the hyperbola $\frac{x^2}{a^2} - \frac{y^2}{b^2} = 1$, then prove that $Aa^2 = Bb^2$.

17. A circle cuts the rectangular hyperbola $xy = 1$ in points (x_r, y_r), $r = 1, 2, 3, 4$ then prove that $x_1 x_2 x_3 x_4 = y_1 y_2 y_3 y_4 = 1$.

Answer Key

1. (b) 2. (d) 3. (a) 4. (d) 5. (d)
6. (c) 7. (a) 8. (a) 9. (d) 10. (b)
11. (d) 12. (b) 13. $x + 3y = 0$
14. $12x^2 - 7xy - 12y^2 + 31x + 17y = 0$
15. $6x^2 + 13xy + 6y^2 - 38x - 37y - 98 = 0$

For Detailed Solution

JEE Pattern EXAMPLES

Single Option Correct Type Questions

Example 1 *If the eccentricity of the hyperbola $x^2 - y^2 \sec^2 \alpha = 5$ is $\sqrt{3}$ times the eccentricity of the ellipse $x^2 \sec^2 \alpha + y^2 = 25$, then the value of α is*

(a) $\frac{\pi}{6}$ (b) $\frac{\pi}{4}$ (c) $\frac{\pi}{3}$ (d) $\frac{\pi}{2}$

Sol. (b) For the hyperbola $\frac{x^2}{5} - \frac{y^2}{5\cos^2\alpha} = 1$, we have

$$e_1^2 = 1 + \frac{5\cos^2\alpha}{5} = 1 + \cos^2\alpha \quad \ldots \text{(i)}$$

For the ellipse $\frac{x^2}{25\cos^2\alpha} + \frac{y^2}{25} = 1$, we have

$$e_2^2 = 1 - \frac{25\cos^2\alpha}{25} = 1 - \cos^2\alpha = \sin^2\alpha \quad \ldots \text{(ii)}$$

Given that $e_1 = \sqrt{3}\, e_2$ or $e_1^2 = 3e_2^2$

$\Rightarrow \quad 1 + \cos^2\alpha = 3\sin^2\alpha$ [from Eqs. (i) and (ii)]

$\Rightarrow \quad 2 = 4\sin^2\alpha$

or $\quad \sin\alpha = \frac{1}{\sqrt{2}} \Rightarrow \alpha = \frac{\pi}{4}$

Example 2 *PQ is a double ordinate of the hyperbola $\frac{x^2}{a^2} - \frac{y^2}{b^2} = 1$ such that OPQ is an equilateral triangle, point O being the centre of the hyperbola, then the eccentricity of the hyperbola satisfies*

(a) $1 < e < \frac{2}{\sqrt{3}}$ (b) $e = \frac{2}{\sqrt{3}}$

(c) $e = \frac{\sqrt{3}}{2}$ (d) $e > \frac{2}{\sqrt{3}}$

Sol. (d) Let the length of each side of the equilateral ΔOPQ be l units ($l > a$). Then, the coordinates of P are $\left(\frac{\sqrt{3}}{2}l, \frac{1}{2}l\right)$. Point P lies on the hyperbola $\frac{x^2}{a^2} - \frac{y^2}{b^2} = 1$.

$\therefore \quad \frac{3l^2}{4a^2} - \frac{l^2}{4b^2} = 1 \Rightarrow (3b^2 - a^2)l^2 = 4a^2b^2$

$\Rightarrow \quad (3e^2 - 4)l^2 = 4a^2(e^2 - 1) \Rightarrow l = 2a\sqrt{\frac{e^2 - 1}{3e^2 - 4}}$

$\therefore$ l is real and $e > 1$.

$\Rightarrow \quad e^2 > \frac{4}{3} \Rightarrow e > \frac{2}{\sqrt{3}}$

JEE SCANNER

Example 3 Similar to PYQ Asked in JEE Main 2023

Let the foci of hyperbola H coincide with the foci of the ellipse $E: \frac{(x-2)^2}{64} + \frac{(y-2)^2}{48} = 1$ and the eccentricity of the hyperbola H be the reciprocal of the eccentricity of the ellipse E. If the length of the transverse axis of H is α and the length of its conjugate axis is β, then $\alpha^2 + \beta^2$ is equal to

(a) 64 (b) 36 (c) 68 (d) 72

Sol. (a) $E: \frac{(x-2)^2}{64} + \frac{(y-2)^2}{48} = 1$

$$e_1 = \sqrt{1 - \frac{48}{64}} = \frac{1}{2} \Rightarrow e_2 = 2$$

$\therefore$ Both the foci of hyperbola (H) are $F_1(6, 2)$ and $F_2(-2, 2)$

$2ae_2 = 8 \Rightarrow 4a = 8 \Rightarrow a = 2$

$\therefore \quad \alpha = 4$

Now, $\quad e_2^2 = 1 + \frac{b^2}{a^2} \Rightarrow b^2 = 3a^2 \Rightarrow b = 2\sqrt{3}$

$\therefore \quad \beta = 4\sqrt{3}$

$\therefore \alpha^2 + \beta^2 = 16 + 48 = 64$

Skill Builder

For Sol.

Let the foci of hyperbola H coincide with the foci of the ellipse $E: \frac{(x-3)^2}{81} + \frac{(y-3)^2}{72} = 1$ and the eccentricity of the hyperbola H be the reciprocal of the eccentricity of the ellipse E. If the length of the transverse axis of H is α and the length of its conjugate axis is β, then $\alpha^2 + \beta^2$ is equal to

(a) 64 (b) 36 (c) 68 (d) 72

Example 4 *A hyperbola, having the transverse axis of length $2\sin\theta$, is confocal with the ellipse $3x^2 + 4y^2 = 12$. Then, its equation is*

(a) $x^2\operatorname{cosec}^2\theta - y^2\sec^2\theta = 1$

(b) $x^2\sec^2\theta - y^2\operatorname{cosec}^2\theta = 1$

(c) $x^2\sin^2\theta - y^2\cos^2\theta = 1$

(d) $x^2\cos^2\theta - y^2\sin^2\theta = 1$

Sol. (a) Equation of ellipse is $3x^2 + 4y^2 = 12$

$$\Rightarrow \quad \frac{x^2}{4} + \frac{y^2}{3} = 1$$

$$\therefore \quad a^2 = 4, b^2 = 3$$

Now, for hyperbola $A^2e_1^2 = A^2 + B^2$

$$\Rightarrow \quad (1)^2 = \sin^2\theta + B^2 \qquad [\because Ae_1 = ae]$$

$$\Rightarrow \quad B^2 = \cos^2\theta$$

So, equation of hyperbola is $\dfrac{x^2}{A^2} - \dfrac{y^2}{B^2} = 1$

$$\Rightarrow \quad \frac{x^2}{\sin^2\theta} - \frac{y^2}{\cos^2\theta} = 1$$

$$\Rightarrow \quad x^2\operatorname{cosec}^2\theta - y^2\sec^2\theta = 1$$

Example 5 *Area of quadrilateral formed with the foci of the hyperbola $\dfrac{x^2}{a^2} - \dfrac{y^2}{b^2} = 1$ and $\dfrac{x^2}{a^2} - \dfrac{y^2}{b^2} = -1$ is*

(a) $4(a^2 + b^2)$ (b) $2(a^2 + b^2)$

(c) $(a^2 + b^2)$ (d) $\dfrac{1}{2}(a^2 + b^2)$

Sol. (b)

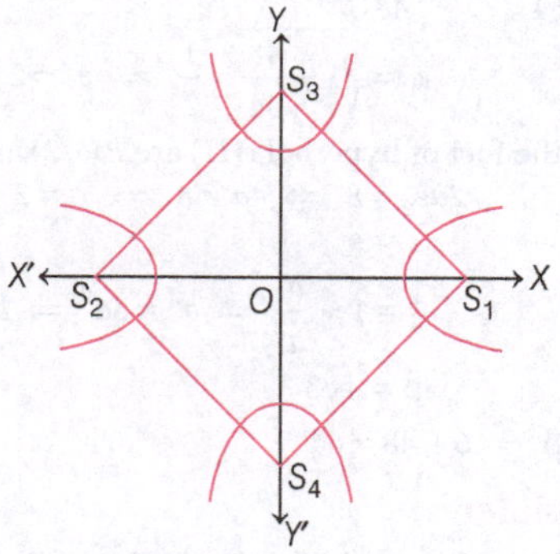

Required area $= 4 \times$ Area of ΔS_1OS_3

$$= 4 \times \frac{1}{2} ae \times be_1 = (2ab)(ee_1) \qquad \text{...(i)}$$

$$\because \quad b^2 = a^2(e^2 - 1)$$

$$\therefore \quad e = \frac{\sqrt{(a^2 + b^2)}}{a} \qquad \text{...(ii)}$$

and $\quad a^2 = b^2(e_1^2 - 1)$

$$\therefore \quad e_1 = \frac{\sqrt{(a^2 + b^2)}}{b} \qquad \text{...(iii)}$$

On substituting the values of e and e_1 from Eqs. (ii) and (iii) in Eq. (i), then

$$\text{Required area} = 2ab \times \frac{\sqrt{(a^2 + b^2)}}{a} \times \frac{\sqrt{(a^2 + b^2)}}{b} = 2(a^2 + b^2)$$

Example 6 *Let $P(a\sec\theta, b\tan\theta)$ and $Q(a\sec\phi, b\tan\phi)$, where $\theta + \phi = \dfrac{\pi}{2}$, be two points on the hyperbola $\dfrac{x^2}{a^2} - \dfrac{y^2}{b^2} = 1$. If (h, k) is the point of intersection of normals at P and Q, then k is equal to*

(a) $\left(\dfrac{a^2 + b^2}{a}\right)$ (b) $-\left(\dfrac{a^2 + b^2}{a}\right)$

(c) $\left(\dfrac{a^2 + b^2}{b}\right)$ (d) $-\left(\dfrac{a^2 + b^2}{b}\right)$

Sol. (d) Equations of the normals at $P(\theta)$ and $Q(\phi)$ are

$$ax\cos\theta + by\cot\theta = a^2 + b^2 \qquad \text{... (i)}$$

and $$ax\cos\phi + by\cot\phi = a^2 + b^2 \qquad \text{... (ii)}$$

Now, on dividing by $\cos\theta$ and $\cos\phi$ in Eqs. (i) and (ii) respectively, we get

$$ax + by\operatorname{cosec}\theta = (a^2 + b^2)\sec\theta \qquad \text{... (iii)}$$

and $$ax + by\operatorname{cosec}\phi = (a^2 + b^2)\sec\phi \qquad \text{... (iv)}$$

On subtracting Eq. (iv) from Eq. (iii), we get

$$y = \left(\frac{a^2 + b^2}{b}\right) \cdot \left(\frac{\sec\theta - \sec\phi}{\operatorname{cosec}\theta - \operatorname{cosec}\phi}\right)$$

$$\therefore \quad k = y$$

$$= \left(\frac{a^2 + b^2}{b}\right) \cdot \left(\frac{\sec\theta - \sec\left(\frac{\pi}{2} - \theta\right)}{\operatorname{cosec}\theta - \operatorname{cosec}\left(\frac{\pi}{2} - \theta\right)}\right) \qquad \left(\because \theta + \phi = \frac{\pi}{2}\right)$$

$$= \left(\frac{a^2 + b^2}{b}\right) \left(\frac{\sec\theta - \operatorname{cosec}\theta}{\operatorname{cosec}\theta - \sec\theta}\right) = -\left(\frac{a^2 + b^2}{b}\right)$$

Example 7 *Let the major axis of a standard ellipse equals the transverse axis of a standard hyperbola and their director circles have radius equal to $2R$ and R, respectively. If e_1 and e_2 are the eccentricities of the ellipse and hyperbola, then the correct relation is*

(a) $4e_1^2 - e_2^2 = 6$ (b) $e_1^2 - 4e_2^2 = 2$

(c) $4e_2^2 - e_1^2 = 6$ (d) $e_2^2 - 4e_1^2 = 2$

Sol. (c) Let equation of ellipse be $\dfrac{x^2}{a^2} + \dfrac{y^2}{b^2} = 1 \ (a > b)$

$\therefore$ Director circle is $x^2 + y^2 = a^2 + b^2$

and $\quad b^2 = a^2(1 - e_1^2)$

Given, $\quad a^2 + b^2 = (2R)^2$

$\Rightarrow \quad a^2 + a^2(1 - e_1^2) = 4R^2$

$\Rightarrow \quad 2 - e_1^2 = \dfrac{4R^2}{a^2} \quad \text{... (i)}$

and equation of hyperbola is $\dfrac{x^2}{a^2} - \dfrac{y^2}{b_1^2} = 1$

$\therefore$ Director circle is $x^2 + y^2 = a^2 - b_1^2$

and $\quad b_1^2 = a^2(e_2^2 - 1)$

Given $\quad a^2 - b_1^2 = R^2$

$\Rightarrow \quad a^2 - a^2(e_2^2 - 1) = R^2$

$\Rightarrow \quad 2 - e_2^2 = \dfrac{R^2}{a^2} \quad \text{... (ii)}$

On dividing Eq. (i) by Eq. (ii), then

$$\frac{2 - e_1^2}{2 - e_2^2} = 4$$

$\Rightarrow \quad 4e_2^2 - e_1^2 = 6$

Example 8 *The coordinates of a point on the hyperbola* $\dfrac{x^2}{24} - \dfrac{y^2}{18} = 1$*, which is nearest to the line* $3x + 2y + 1 = 0$ *are*

(a) (6, 3) (b) (−6, −3)
(c) (6, −3) (d) (−6, 3)

Sol. (d)

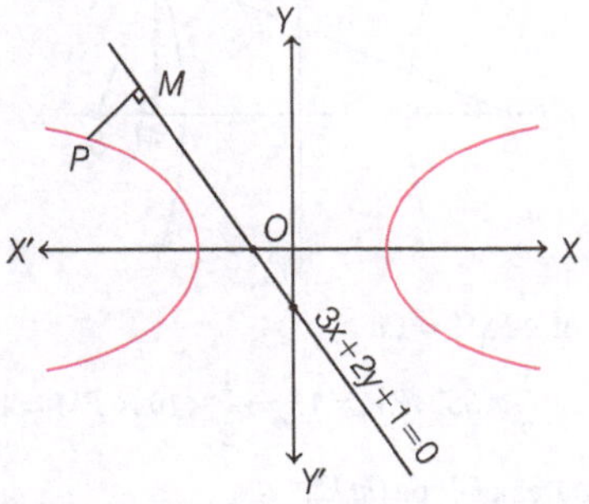

Point P is nearest to the given line, if the tangent at P is parallel to the given line.

Now, equation of tangent at $P(x_1, y_1)$ is $\dfrac{xx_1}{24} - \dfrac{yy_1}{18} = 1$

$\therefore$ Slope of tangent at $P(x_1, y_1)$ is $\dfrac{3}{4}\dfrac{x_1}{y_1}$,

which must be equal to $-\dfrac{3}{2}$

Therefore, $\dfrac{3}{4} \cdot \dfrac{x_1}{y_1} = -\dfrac{3}{2}$ or $x_1 = -2y_1 \quad \text{...(i)}$

Also, $P(x_1, y_1)$ lies on the curve

Hence, $\quad \dfrac{x_1^2}{24} - \dfrac{y_1^2}{18} = 1 \quad \text{...(ii)}$

On solving Eqs. (i) and (ii), we get two points (6, −3) and (−6, 3) of which (− 6, 3) is the nearest.

Alternate Solution

The equation of normal at $P(2\sqrt{6}\sec\theta, 3\sqrt{2}\tan\theta)$ is

$$(2\sqrt{6}\cos\theta)x + (3\sqrt{2}\cot\theta)y = 42$$

Now, this line will be perpendicular to $3x + 2y + 1 = 0$

Then, $\quad (2\sqrt{6}\cos\theta) \times 3 + (3\sqrt{2}\cot\theta) \times 2 = 0$

or $\quad \sin\theta = -\dfrac{1}{\sqrt{3}}$

$\therefore \quad \tan\theta = \dfrac{1}{\sqrt{2}}$ and $\sec\theta = -\dfrac{\sqrt{3}}{\sqrt{2}}$

Hence, $\quad P \equiv (-6, 3)$

Example 9 *Let any double ordinate PNP′ of the hyperbola* $\dfrac{x^2}{25} - \dfrac{y^2}{16} = 1$ *be produced both sides to meet the asymptotes at Q and Q′, then (PQ) (P′Q) is equal to*

(a) 9 (b) 16 (c) 25 (d) 41

Sol. (b) Let $Q \equiv (x_1, y_1)$

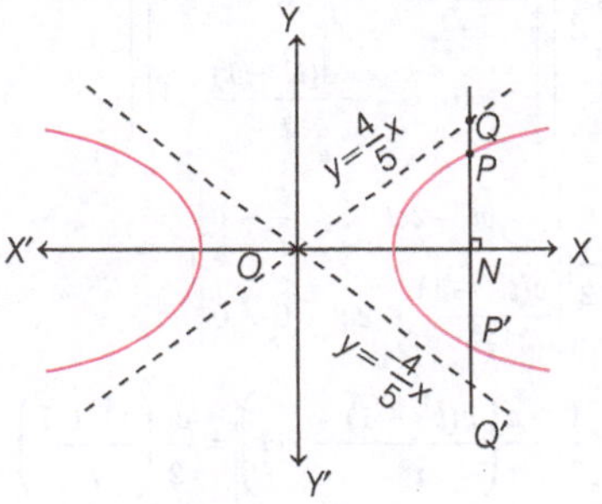

We have, $\quad NP = \dfrac{4}{5}\sqrt{(x_1^2 - 25)}$

and Q is on $\quad y = \dfrac{4}{5}x$

$\therefore \quad NQ = \dfrac{4}{5}x_1$

Now, $\quad PQ = NQ - NP$

$$= \frac{4}{5}(x_1 - \sqrt{(x_1^2 - 25)})$$

and $\quad P'Q = NP' + NQ = NP + NQ \quad [\because NP' = NP]$

$$= \frac{4}{5}(x_1 + \sqrt{(x_1^2 - 25)})$$

$\therefore \quad (PQ)(P'Q) = \dfrac{16}{25}(x_1^2 - (x_1^2 - 25)) = \dfrac{16}{25} \times 25 = 16$

Example 10 *The tangent to the hyperbola* $xy = c^2$ *at point P(t) intersects the X-axis at T and the Y-axis at T′. The normal to the hyperbola at P(t) intersects the X-axis at N and the Y-axis at N′. The areas of the triangles PNT and PN′T′ are* Δ *and* Δ' *respectively, then* $\dfrac{1}{\Delta} + \dfrac{1}{\Delta'}$ *is*

(a) equal to 1 (b) depend on t
(c) depend on c (d) equal to 2

Sol. (c) Equation of tangent at $P\left(ct, \frac{c}{t}\right)$ is $\frac{x}{t} + ty = 2c$

or
$$\frac{x}{2ct} + \frac{y}{(2c/t)} = 1$$

$\therefore$
$$T \equiv (2ct, 0) \text{ and } T' \equiv \left(0, \frac{2c}{t}\right)$$

and equation of normal at $P\left(ct, \frac{c}{t}\right)$ is
$$xt^3 - yt - ct^4 + c = 0$$

or
$$\frac{x}{\left(\frac{c(t^4-1)}{t^3}\right)} + \frac{y}{\left(\frac{c(t^4-1)}{-t}\right)} = 1$$

$\therefore$
$$N \equiv \left(\frac{c(t^4-1)}{t^3}, 0\right) \text{ and } N' \equiv \left(0, -\frac{c(t^4-1)}{t}\right)$$

$\because$ Area of triangle, $PNT = \Delta$

$$\therefore \quad \Delta = \frac{1}{2}\left\|\begin{matrix} ct & \frac{c}{t} & 1 \\ \frac{c(t^4-1)}{t} & 0 & 1 \\ 0 & \frac{-c(t^4-1)}{t} & 1 \end{matrix}\right\|$$

$$\Rightarrow \Delta = \frac{1}{2}\left|\begin{matrix} ct - 2ct & \frac{c}{t} - 0 \\ \frac{c(t^4-1)}{t^3} - 2ct & 0 - 0 \end{matrix}\right|$$

$$= \frac{1}{2}\left|-\frac{c}{t}\left(\frac{c(t^4-1)}{t^3} - 2ct\right)\right| = \frac{c^2}{2}\left(\frac{t^4+1}{t^4}\right)$$

and area of $\Delta PN'T' = \Delta'$

$$\therefore \quad \Delta' = \frac{1}{2}\left|\begin{matrix} ct - 0 & \frac{c}{t} - \frac{2c}{t} \\ 0 - 0 & -\frac{c(t^4-1)}{t} - \frac{2c}{t} \end{matrix}\right| = \frac{1}{2}\left|ct\left(-\frac{c(t^4-1)}{t} - \frac{2c}{t}\right)\right|$$

$$= \frac{c^2}{2}(t^4+1)$$

$$\therefore \quad \frac{1}{\Delta} + \frac{1}{\Delta'} = \frac{2t^4}{c^2(t^4+1)} + \frac{2}{c^2(t^4+1)} = \frac{2}{c^2}$$

Example 11 *For each positive integer n, consider the point P with abscissa n on the curve $y^2 - x^2 = 1$. If d_n represents the shortest distance from the point P to the line $y = x$, then $\lim_{n \to \infty} (n \cdot d_n)$ has the value equal to*

(a) $\frac{1}{2\sqrt{2}}$ (b) $\frac{1}{2}$ (c) $\frac{1}{\sqrt{2}}$ (d) 0

Sol. (a) Let $P \equiv (n, \sqrt{(n^2+1)})$

$$\therefore \quad d_n = \left(\frac{\sqrt{(n^2+1)} - n}{\sqrt{2}}\right) \text{ or } n \cdot d_n = \frac{n}{\sqrt{2}}(\sqrt{(n^2+1)} - n)$$

or
$$\lim_{n \to \infty} (n \cdot d_n) = \frac{1}{\sqrt{2}} \lim_{n \to \infty} n(\sqrt{(n^2+1)} - n)$$

$$= \frac{1}{\sqrt{2}} \lim_{n \to \infty} \frac{n(\sqrt{(n^2+1)} - n)(\sqrt{(n^2+1)} + n)}{(\sqrt{(n^2+1)} + n)}$$

$$= \frac{1}{\sqrt{2}} \lim_{n \to \infty} \frac{n(1)}{n\left(\sqrt{\left(1 + \frac{1}{n^2}\right)} + 1\right)}$$

$$= \frac{1}{\sqrt{2}} \lim_{n \to \infty} \left(\frac{1}{\sqrt{\left(1 + \frac{1}{n^2}\right)} + 1}\right) = \frac{1}{\sqrt{2}} \cdot \left(\frac{1}{1+1}\right) = \frac{1}{2\sqrt{2}}$$

JEE SCANNER

Example 12 Similar to PYQ Asked in JEE Main 2023

Let P be a point on the hyperbola $H: \frac{x^2}{16} - \frac{y^2}{9} = 1$ in the first quadrant such that the area of triangle formed by P and two foci of H is 15. Then, the square of the distance of P from the origin is

(a) 40 (b) 46 (c) 41 (d) 28

Sol. (c) $H: \frac{x^2}{16} - \frac{y^2}{9} = 1$

Here, $a^2 = 16, b^2 = 9 \quad \therefore \quad a = 4, b = 3$

Let S and S' be foci of hyperbola.

$$\therefore \quad e = \sqrt{1 + \frac{b^2}{a^2}} = \sqrt{1 + \frac{9}{16}} = \frac{5}{4}$$

$\because$ $S(ae, 0)$ and $S'(-ae, 0)$

$S(5, 0)$ and $S'(-5, 0)$

$\therefore$ $SS' = 10$

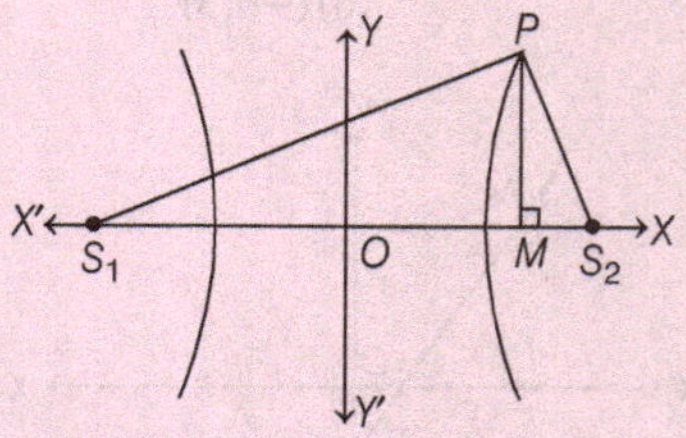

Now, area of $\Delta PSS' = 15$

$$\Rightarrow \quad \frac{1}{2} \times SS' \times PM = 15 \Rightarrow \frac{1}{2} \times 10 \times PM = 15 \Rightarrow PM = 3$$

Let coordinates of P be (h, k).

$\therefore$ $k = 3$ $[\because PM = 3]$

P satisfies the equation of hyperbola.

$$\therefore \quad \frac{h^2}{16} - \frac{(3)^2}{9} = 1 \Rightarrow h^2 = 32$$

$\therefore$ Square of distance of p from the origin $= h^2 + k^2 = 32 + 9 = 41$

Skill Builder

Let P be a point on the hyperbola $H: \frac{x^2}{25} - \frac{y^2}{16} = 1$ in the first quadrant such that the area of triangle formed by P and two foci of H is $4\sqrt{41}$. Then, the square of the distance of P from the origin is

(a) 60 (b) 66

(c) 61 (d) 72

For Sol.

More than One Option Correct Type Questions

Example 13 *If two tangents can be drawn to the different branches of hyperbola $\frac{x^2}{1} - \frac{y^2}{4} = 1$ from the point (α, α^2), then*

(a) $\alpha \in (-\infty, -2)$ (b) $\alpha \in (-2, 0)$

(c) $\alpha \in (0, 2)$ (d) $\alpha \in (2, \infty)$

Sol. (a, d) Since, (α, α^2) lies on the parabola $y = x^2$.

$\therefore (\alpha, \alpha^2)$ must lie between the asymptotes of hyperbola

$$\frac{x^2}{1} - \frac{y^2}{4} = 1 \text{ in I and II quadrants.}$$

$\because$ Asymptotes of $\frac{x^2}{1} - \frac{y^2}{4} = 1$ are $y = \pm 2x$

$$\therefore \quad 2\alpha < \alpha^2 \quad \text{and} \quad -2\alpha < \alpha^2$$

$$\Rightarrow \quad \alpha(\alpha - 2) > 0 \quad \text{and} \quad \alpha(\alpha + 2) > 0$$

$$\therefore \quad \alpha < 0 \text{ or } \alpha > 2 \quad \text{and} \quad \alpha < -2 \text{ or } \alpha > 0$$

$$\therefore \quad \alpha \in (-\infty, -2) \cup (2, \infty)$$

Example 14 *If the ellipse $x^2 + \lambda^2 y^2 = \lambda^2 a^2$; $\lambda^2 > 1$ is confocal with the hyperbola $x^2 - y^2 = a^2$, then*

(a) ratio of eccentricities of ellipse and hyperbola is $1 : \sqrt{3}$.

(b) ratio of major axis of ellipse and transverse axis of hyperbola is $\sqrt{3} : 1$.

(c) the ellipse and hyperbola cuts each other orthogonally.

(d) ratio of length of latusrectum of ellipse and hyperbola is 1 : 3.

Sol. (a, b, c) Given ellipse is $\frac{x^2}{\lambda^2 a^2} + \frac{y^2}{a^2} = 1$, $\lambda^2 a^2 > a^2$ and

let e_1 and e_2 be the eccentricities of ellipse and hyperbola, then

$$a^2 = \lambda^2 a^2 (1 - e_1^2)$$

or $$e_1 = \sqrt{\left(1 - \frac{1}{\lambda^2}\right)} \text{ and } e_2 = \sqrt{2}$$

Now, $$\lambda a e_1 = a e_2$$

$$\Rightarrow \quad \lambda \sqrt{\left(1 - \frac{1}{\lambda^2}\right)} = \sqrt{2}$$

$$\Rightarrow \quad \lambda^2 - 1 = 2 \text{ or } \lambda = \pm\sqrt{3}$$

$$\therefore \quad \lambda = \sqrt{3} \qquad (\because \lambda > 0)$$

From option (a) $\frac{e_1}{e_2} = \frac{1}{\lambda} = \frac{1}{\sqrt{3}}$

From option (b) $= \frac{\text{Major axis of ellipse}}{\text{Transverse axis of hyperbola}}$

$$= \frac{2\lambda a}{2a} = \lambda = \sqrt{3}$$

From option (c) Equations of tangents of ellipse and hyperbola at (x_1, y_1) are $\frac{xx_1}{\lambda^2 a^2} + \frac{yy_1}{a^2} = 1$

and $\quad xx_1 - yy_1 = a^2$

i.e. slopes are $= -\frac{x_1}{\lambda^2 y_1}$ and $\frac{x_1}{y_1}$ [say m_1 and m_2]

According to alternate, $m_1 m_2 = -\frac{x_1}{\lambda^2 y_1} \times \frac{x_1}{y_1}$

$$= -\frac{x_1^2}{\lambda^2 y_1^2}$$

$$= -\frac{\frac{2a^2}{\lambda^2 + 1}}{\frac{a^2(\lambda^2 - 1)}{(\lambda^2 + 1)}} = -\frac{2}{\lambda^2 - 1} \qquad \left[\because \begin{array}{l} x_1^2 = \frac{2a^2\lambda^2}{\lambda^2 + 1} \\ \text{and } y_1^2 = \frac{a^2(\lambda^2 - 1)}{(\lambda^2 + 1)} \end{array}\right]$$

$$= -\frac{2}{3 - 1} = -1 \qquad [\because \lambda = \sqrt{3}]$$

From option (d) $= \frac{\text{Latusrectum of ellipse}}{\text{Latusrectum of hyperbola}}$

$$= \frac{\frac{2a^2}{\lambda a}}{\frac{2a^2}{a}} = \frac{1}{\lambda} = \frac{1}{\sqrt{3}}$$

Example 15 *If the circle $x^2 + y^2 = a^2$ intersects the hyperbola $xy = c^2$ at four points $P(x_1, y_1)$, $Q(x_2, y_2)$, $R(x_3, y_3)$ and $S(x_4, y_4)$, then*

(a) $\Sigma x_1 = 0$ (b) $\Sigma y_1 = 0$

(c) $\Pi x_1 = c^4$ (d) $\Pi y_1 = c^4$

Sol. (a, b, c, d) On solving $x^2 + y^2 = a^2$ and $xy = c^2$, we get

$$x^2 + \frac{c^4}{x^2} = a^2$$

or $$x^4 - a^2x^2 + c^4 = 0$$

or $$\Sigma x_1 = 0 \text{ and } \Pi x_1 = c^4$$

Similarly, if we eliminate x,

then $$y^4 - a^2y^2 + c^4 = 0$$

or $$\Sigma y_1 = 0 \text{ and } \Pi y_1 = c^4$$

Example 16 *A straight line touches the rectangular hyperbola $9x^2 - 9y^2 = 8$ and the parabola $y^2 = 32x$. The equation of the line is*

(a) $9x + 3y - 8 = \infty$ (b) $9x - 3y + 8 = 0$

(c) $9x + 3y + 8 = 0$ (d) $9x - 3y - 8 = 0$

Sol. (b, c) Equation of tangent to the parabola $y^2 = 32x$ is

$$y = mx + \frac{8}{m} \qquad \text{... (i)}$$

which is also touches the hyperbola $9x^2 - 9y^2 = 8$

i.e. $$x^2 - y^2 = \frac{8}{9}$$

So that $$\left(\frac{8}{m}\right)^2 = \frac{8}{9} \times m^2 - \frac{8}{9}$$

$$\Rightarrow \quad \frac{8}{m^2} = \frac{m^2}{9} - \frac{1}{9}$$

$$\Rightarrow \quad m^4 - m^2 - 72 = 0$$

$$\Rightarrow \quad (m^2 - 9)(m^2 + 8) = 0$$

$$\therefore \quad m^2 - 9 = 0$$

but $$m^2 + 8 \neq 0$$

$$\therefore \quad m = \pm 3$$

Hence, from Eq. (i), the equation of tangents are

$$y = 3x + \frac{8}{3}$$

and $$y = -3x - \frac{8}{3}$$

or $$9x - 3y + 8 = 0$$

and $$9x + 3y + 8 = 0$$

Example 17 *For the hyperbola*

$$9x^2 - 16y^2 - 18x + 32y - 151 = 0$$

(a) one of the directrix is $x = 21/5$
(b) the length of latus rectum is $9/2$
(c) foci are $(6, 1)$ and $(-4, 1)$
(d) the eccentricity is $5/4$

Sol. (a, b, c, d) The given hyperbola can be written as

$$\frac{(x-1)^2}{16} - \frac{(y-1)^2}{9} = 1$$

or $$\frac{X^2}{16} - \frac{Y^2}{9} = 1 \text{ [where } X = x - 1 \text{ and } Y = y - 1]$$

$$e = \sqrt{1 + \frac{b^2}{a^2}}$$

$$= \sqrt{1 + \frac{9}{16}} = \frac{5}{4}$$

Directrices are $X = \pm a/e$.

Therefore, $x - 1 = \pm \frac{16}{5}$

or $x = \frac{21}{5}$ and $x = -\frac{11}{5}$

Length of latus rectum $= \frac{2b^2}{a} = \frac{9}{2}$

The foci are given by $X = \pm ae, Y = 0$

or $(6, 1), (-4, 1)$.

Example 18 *If P is a point on a hyperbola, then*

(a) the locus of the excentre of the circle described opposite to $\angle P$ for $\Delta PSS'$ (S and S' are foci) is tangent at vertex.
(b) the locus of the excentre of the circle described opposite to $\angle S'$ is a hyperbola.
(c) the locus of the excentre of the circle described opposite of $\angle P$ for $\Delta PSS'$ (S and S' are foci) is a hyperbola.
(d) None of the above

Sol. (a, b) Let (h, k) be the excentre. Then,

$$h = \frac{a(ae\sec\theta + a) - ae(ae\sec\theta - a) - 2ae(a\sec\theta)}{2ae(\sec\theta - 1)} = -a$$

$$= -a \text{ (for } a\sec\theta > 0)$$

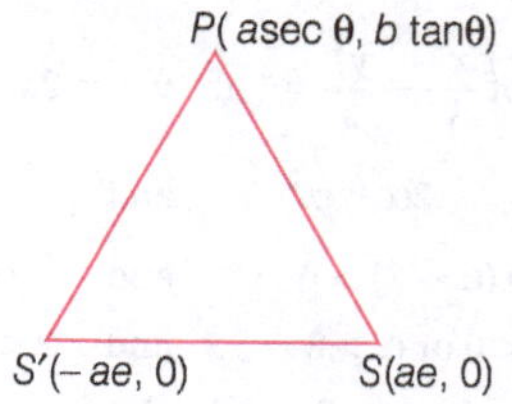

Similarly, $x = a$, for $a\sec\theta < 0$.

Therefore, the locus is $x^2 = a^2$.

Again, let (h, k) be the excentre opposite $\angle S'$. Then,

$$h = \frac{2a^2e\sec\theta + a^2e^2\sec\theta + a^2e + a^2e^2\sec\theta - a^2e}{2a + 2ae} = ae\sec\theta$$

$$k = \frac{2aeb\tan\theta}{2a + 2ae}$$

Therefore, the locus is a hyperbola.

Example 19 *If the normal at P to the rectangular hyperbola $x^2 - y^2 = 4$ meets the axes at G and g and C is the centre of the hyperbola, then*

(a) $PG = PC$ (b) $Pg = PC$
(c) $PG = Pg$ (d) $Gg = 2PC$

Sol. (a, b, c, d) Normal at point $P(2\sec\theta, 2\tan\theta)$ is $\frac{2x}{\sec\theta} + \frac{2y}{\tan\theta} = 8$

It meets the axes at point $G(4\sec\theta, 0)$ and $g(0, 4\tan\theta)$.

Then, $$PG = \sqrt{4\sec^2\theta + 4\tan^2\theta}$$

$$Pg = \sqrt{4\sec^2\theta + 4\tan^2\theta}$$

$$PC = \sqrt{4\sec^2\theta + 4\tan^2\theta}$$

$$Gg = \sqrt{16\sec^2\theta + 16\tan^2\theta}$$

$$= 2\sqrt{4\sec^2\theta + 4\tan^2\theta} = 2PC$$

Passage Based Questions

Passage I

(Ex. Nos. 20 and 21)

If p is a variable point and F_1 and F_2 are two fixed points such that $|PF_1 - PF_2| = 2a$. Then, the locus of the point P is a hyperbola with points F_1 and F_2 as the two focii ($F_1F_2 > 2a$). If $\frac{x^2}{a^2} - \frac{y^2}{b^2} = 1$ is a hyperbola, then its conjugate hyperbola is $\frac{x^2}{a^2} - \frac{y^2}{b^2} = -1$. Let $P(x, y)$ be a variable point such that $|\sqrt{(x-1)^2 + (y-2)^2} - \sqrt{(x-5)^2 + (y-5)^2}| = 3$.

Example 20 *If the locus of the point P represents a hyperbola of eccentricity e, then the eccentricity e′ of the corresponding conjugate hyperbola is*

(a) $\frac{5}{3}$ (b) $\frac{4}{3}$ (c) $\frac{5}{4}$ (d) $\frac{3}{\sqrt{7}}$

Example 21 *Locus of intersection of two perpendicular tangents to the given hyperbola is*

(a) $(x-3)^2 + \left(y - \frac{7}{2}\right)^2 = \frac{55}{4}$

(b) $(x-3)^2 + \left(y - \frac{7}{2}\right)^2 = \frac{25}{4}$

(c) $(x-3)^2 + \left(y - \frac{7}{2}\right)^2 = \frac{7}{4}$

(d) None of the above

Sol. 20. (c) $2a = 3$

Distance between the focii (1, 2) and (5, 5) is 5.

$$2ae = 5$$

$$\therefore \quad e = \frac{5}{3}$$

$$\frac{1}{e^2} + \frac{1}{e'^2} = 1 \Rightarrow e' = \frac{5}{4}$$

21. (d) Director circle $(x-h)^2 + (y-k)^2 = a^2 - b^2$, where (h, k) is centre is $\left(\frac{1+5}{2}, \frac{2+5}{2}\right) = \left(3, \frac{7}{2}\right)$

$$b^2 = a^2(e^2 - 1) = \left(\frac{3}{2}\right)^2\left(\left(\frac{5}{3}\right)^2 - 1\right) = 4$$

Director circle $(x-3)^2 + \left(y - \frac{7}{2}\right)^2 = \frac{9}{4} - 4$

$$(x-3)^2 + \left(y - \frac{7}{2}\right)^2 = -\frac{7}{4}$$

This does not represent any real point.

Passage II

(Q. Nos. 22 and 23)

For the hyperbola $\frac{x^2}{a^2} - \frac{y^2}{b^2} = 1$, the normal at point P meets the transverse axis AA' in G and the conjugate axis BB' in g and CF be perpendicular to the normal from the centre.

Example 22 *The value of* $\frac{PF \cdot PG}{(CB)^2}$ *is equal to*

(a) 4 (b) 3 (c) 2 (d) 1

Example 23 *The value of* $PF \cdot Pg$ *is equal to*

(a) $(CA)^2$ (b) $(CF)^2$

(c) $(CB)^2$ (d) $CA \cdot CB$

Sol. $C \equiv (0,0)$ $AA' = 2a$, $BB' = 2b$

$\therefore$ $CA = CA' = a$ and $CB = CB' = b$

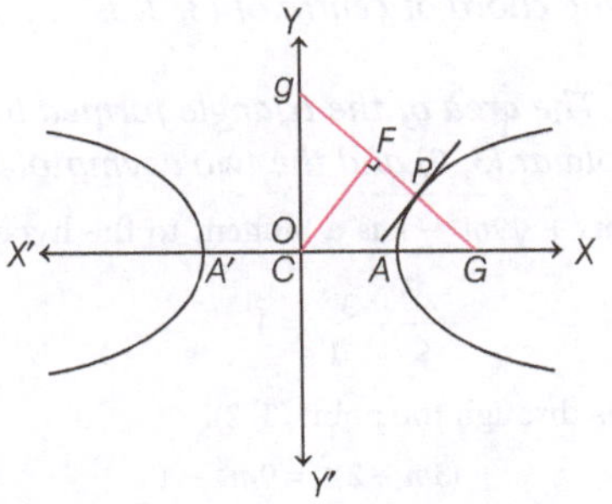

Let $P \equiv (a\sec\theta, b\tan\theta)$

Equation of normal at P is

$$ax\cos\theta + by\cot\theta = a^2 + b^2 \quad \text{... (i)}$$

$$\therefore \quad G \equiv \left(\frac{(a^2+b^2)}{a}\sec\theta, 0\right) \text{ and } g \equiv \left(0, \frac{(a^2+b^2)}{b}\tan\theta\right)$$

Equation of CF which is perpendicular to Eq. (i) and through origin is $bx\cot\theta - ay\cos\theta = 0$

$$\therefore \quad PF = \frac{ab}{\sqrt{(b^2\sec^2\theta + a^2\tan^2\theta)}}$$

$$\text{and } PG = \sqrt{\left(a\sec\theta - \frac{a^2+b^2}{a}\sec\theta\right)^2 + (b\tan\theta - 0)^2}$$

$$= \frac{b}{a}\sqrt{(b^2\sec^2\theta + a^2\tan^2\theta)}$$

22. (d) Since,

$$PF \cdot PG = \frac{ab}{\sqrt{(b^2\sec^2\theta + a^2\tan^2\theta)}} \cdot \frac{b}{a}\sqrt{(b^2\sec^2\theta + a^2\tan^2\theta)}$$

$$= b^2 = (CB)^2$$

$$\therefore \quad \frac{PF \cdot PG}{(CB)^2} = 1$$

23. (a) $\because$ $Pg = \sqrt{(a\sec\theta - 0)^2 + \left(b\tan\theta - \frac{(a^2+b^2)}{b}\tan\theta\right)^2}$

$$= \sqrt{\left(a^2\sec^2\theta + \frac{a^4}{b^2}\tan^2\theta\right)} = \frac{a}{b}\sqrt{(b^2\sec^2\theta + a^2\tan^2\theta)}$$

$$\therefore PF \cdot Pg = \frac{ab}{\sqrt{(b^2\sec^2\theta + a^2\tan^2\theta)}} \times \frac{a}{b}\sqrt{(b^2\sec^2\theta + a^2\tan^2\theta)}$$

$$= a^2 = (CA)^2$$

Stem Based Questions

Stem I

(Ex. Nos. 24 and 25)

Tangents are drawn to the hyperbola $x^2 - 9y^2 = 9$ from (3, 2). Answer the following questions.

Example 24 *The area of the triangle formed by the tangents and the chord of centre of (3, 2) is ....*

Example 25 *The area of the triangle formed by the tangent to the hyperbola at (3, 0) and the two asymptotes is ....*

Sol. 24. (8) $y = mx + \sqrt{9m^2 - 1}$ is a tangent to the hyperbola

$$\frac{x^2}{9} - \frac{y^2}{1} = 1$$

This passes through the point (3, 2).

$$\therefore \quad (3m-2)^2 = 9m^2 - 1$$

$$\Rightarrow \quad 4 - 12m = -1$$

$$\Rightarrow \quad -12m = -5$$

$$\Rightarrow \quad m = \frac{5}{12}$$

$\therefore$ One tangent is $5x - 12y + 9$. Also, the tangent at the vertex (3, 0) passes through (3, 2).

Hence, the other tangent through (3, 2) is $x = 3$. The chord of contact is $\frac{3x}{9} - \frac{2y}{1} = 1$

$$\Rightarrow \quad x - 6y = 3$$

Therefore, the sides of the triangle are $5x - 12y + 9 = 0$

$$x = 3 \text{ and } x - 6y = 3$$

On solving these equations, the vertices of the triangle are (3, 2), (3, 0) and $(-5, -4/3)$. Hence, the area of the triangle is

$$= \frac{1}{2}\begin{vmatrix} 3 & 2 & 1 \\ 3 & 0 & 1 \\ -5 & \frac{-4}{3} & 1 \end{vmatrix}$$

$$= \frac{1}{2}\left|3\left(0 + \frac{4}{3}\right) - 2(3+5) + 1(-4-0)\right|$$

$$= \frac{1}{2}|4 - 16 - 4| = 8$$

25. (3) The area of the triangle formed by two asymptotes and a tangent to the hyperbola $\frac{x^2}{a^2} - \frac{y^2}{b^2} = 1$

is always constant, which is equal to ab.

$\therefore$ Area of triangle $= 3 \times 1 = 3$

Stem II

(Ex. Nos. 26 and 27)

The locus of the foot of the perpendicular drawn from a focus and a tangent to the hyperbola is the auxiliary circle. Consider the hyperbola whose foci are (7, 8) and $(-5, -4)$. The foot of the perpendicular from be focus upon a tangent is the point (4, 7). Answer the following questions.

Example 26 *Length of the conjugate axis of the hyperbola is ....*

Example 27 *Length of the latusrectum of the hyperbola is ....*

25. (12.328) The centre of the hyperbola is

$$\left(\frac{-5+7}{2}, \frac{8-4}{2}\right) = (1, 2)$$

Since, (4, 7) lies on the auxiliary circle. Therefore, its radius is

$$a = \sqrt{(1-4)^2 + (2-7)^2} = \sqrt{9+25} = \sqrt{34}$$

The distance between the foci is $2ae$.

From the coordinates of the foci, the distance between them is

$$\sqrt{(7+5)^2 + (8+4)^2} = \sqrt{12^2 + 12^2} = 12\sqrt{2}$$

Now, $2 \times \sqrt{34}\, e = 12\sqrt{2}$

$$\Rightarrow \quad e = \frac{6}{\sqrt{17}}$$

We have, $b^2 = a^2(e^2 - 1) = 34\left(\frac{36}{17} - 1\right) = 34 \times \frac{19}{17} = 38$

$$\Rightarrow \quad 2b = 2\sqrt{38} = 12.328$$

26. (5.830) The length of the latusrectum is

$$\frac{2b^2}{a} = \frac{2 \times 38}{\sqrt{34}} = \frac{76}{\sqrt{34}} = 5.830$$

Single Integer Type Questions

Example 28 *The equation of transverse axis of hyperbola (passing through origin) having asymptotes $3x - 4y - 1 = 0$ and $4x - 3y - 6 = 0$ is $ax + by - c = 0$, $a, b, c \in N$ and gcd (greatest commondivisor) $(a, b, c) = 1$, then the value of $a + b + c$ is*

Sol. (7) Since, the equation of asymptotes are

$$3x - 4y - 1 = 0 \text{ and } 4x - 3y - 6 = 0$$

$\therefore$ Equation of transverse axis is given by

$$\frac{|(3x - 4y - 1)|}{\sqrt{(3)^2 + (-4)^2}} = \frac{|4x - 3y - 6|}{\sqrt{(4)^2 + (-3)^2}}$$

or $|3x-4y-1| = |4x-3y-6|$

or $(3x-4y-1) = \pm(4x-3y-6)$

$\Rightarrow \quad x+y-5=0$

and $\quad x-y-7=0$

$\therefore$ Transverse axis is given by $ax+by-c=0$; $a, b, c \in N$

$\Rightarrow \quad ax+by-c \equiv x+y-5=0$

$\Rightarrow \quad a=1, b=1, c=5$

Hence, $\quad a+b+c=1+1+5=7$

Example 29 *If a variable line has its intercepts on the coordinate axes are e and e′, where $\frac{e}{2}$ and $\frac{e'}{2}$ are the eccentricities of a hyperbola and its conjugate hyperbola, then the line always touches the circle $x^2+y^2=r^2$, where r is*

Sol. (2) Since $\frac{e}{2}$ and $\frac{e'}{2}$ are the eccentricities of a hyperbola and its conjugate, we have

$$\left(\frac{e}{2}\right)^{-2}+\left(\frac{e'}{2}\right)^{-2}=1 \text{ or } \frac{4}{e^2}+\frac{4}{(e')^2}=1$$

or $$4=\frac{e^2e'^2}{e^2+e'^2} \quad \text{... (i)}$$

Equations of variable line is $\frac{x}{e}+\frac{y}{e'}=1$

i.e. $\quad xe'+ye-ee'=0.$

It is tangent to the circle $x^2+y^2=r^2$

$$\therefore \quad \frac{|0-ee'|}{\sqrt{e^2+e'^2}}=r$$

$$\therefore \quad r=\frac{ee'}{\sqrt{(e^2+e'^2)}}=2 \quad \text{[from Eq. (i)]}$$

Example 30 *If the radii of director circles of $\frac{x^2}{a^2}+\frac{y^2}{b^2}=1$ and $\frac{x^2}{a^2}-\frac{y^2}{b^2}=1$ are 2r and r respectively and e_e and e_h be the eccentricities of ellipse and hyperbola respectively, then the value of $4e_h^2-e_e^2$ is ....*

Sol. (6) The equations of the director circles of ellipse and hyperbola are $x^2+y^2=a^2+b^2$ and $x^2+y^2=a^2-b^2$ respectively.

$\therefore \quad 2r=\sqrt{a^2+b^2}$ and $r=\sqrt{a^2-b^2}$

$\Rightarrow \quad 2\sqrt{a^2-b^2}=\sqrt{a^2+b^2}$

$\Rightarrow \quad 4(a^2-b^2)=a^2+b^2$

$\Rightarrow \quad 4\left(1+\frac{b^2}{a^2}\right)=1+\frac{b^2}{a^2}$

$\Rightarrow \quad 4[(1-(e_h^2-1)]=1+1-e_e^2$

$\Rightarrow \quad 8-4e_h^2=2-e_e^2$

$\Rightarrow \quad 4e_h^2-e_e^2=6$

Example 31 *If abscissa of orthocentre of a triangle inscribed in a rectangular hyperbola xy = 4 is $\frac{1}{2}$, then the value of ordinate of orthocentre is ....*

Sol. (8) Let $P(t_1)$, $Q(t_2)$ and $R(t_2)$ be the three points on the hyperbola $xy=c^2$.

We know that the slope of chord with end points $P(t_1)$ and $Q(t_2)$ will be $m_{PQ}=\frac{-1}{t_1t_2}$

$\therefore$ Slope of perpendicular to PQ will be $m_1=t_1t_2$

Hence, equation of altitude through $R(t_3)$ will be

$$\left(y-\frac{c}{t_3}\right)=t_1t_2(x-ct_3)$$

i.e. $$t_1t_2t_3x-t_3y-ct_1t_2t_3(t_3-1)=0 \quad \text{...(i)}$$

Similarly, altitude through $P(t_1)$ will be

$$y-\frac{c}{t_1}=t_2t_3(x-ct_1)$$

$$\Rightarrow \quad t_1t_2t_3x-t_1y-ct_1t_2t_3(t_1-1)=0 \quad \text{...(ii)}$$

From Eqs. (i) and (ii), we have

$$y(t_3-t_1)=ct_1t_2t_3(t_1-t_3)$$

$\Rightarrow \quad y=-ct_1t_2t_3$

and $\quad x=\frac{-c}{t_1t_2t_3} \quad [xy=c^2]$

Hence, orthocentre will lie on the hyperbola itself.

Now, for given hyperbola $xy=4 \Rightarrow x=\frac{1}{2}$

$\therefore \quad y=8$

Example 32 *PP′ is a diameter of the rectangular hyperbola $xy=c^2$. If the intersection of the tangent of P with the straight line through P′ parallel to either asymptote is the locus $xy+\lambda c^2=0$. Then, the value of λ is ......*

Sol. (3) The given rectangular hyperbola is

$$xy=c^2 \quad \text{...(i)}$$

Given that PP′ is a diameter of Eq. (i). Therefore, if P is the point $(ct, c/t)$, then P′ is $(-ct, -c/t)$. Equation of tangent at P is

$$x+yt^2=2ct \quad \text{...(ii)}$$

Asymptotes of Eq. (i) are $x=0$ and $y=0$.

$\therefore$ The equation of the line through P′ and parallel to the asymptote $y=0$ is

$$y=-c/t \quad \text{...(iii)}$$

On putting the value of t from Eq. (iii) in Eq. (ii), then

$$x+y\times\frac{c^2}{y^2}=2c\times\left(-\frac{c}{y}\right)$$

or $$xy+c^2=-2c^2 \text{ or } xy+3c^2=0$$

which is the required locus of the point of intersection of Eqs. (ii) and (iii).

Again, the equation of the line through P' and parallel to the asymptote $x = 0$ is

$$x = -ct \quad \text{...(iv)}$$

On putting the value of t from Eq. (iv) in Eq. (ii), we get

$$x + y\left(\frac{x^2}{c^2}\right) = 2c \times -\frac{x}{c}$$

or $$xy + 3c^2 = 0$$

which is the required locus of the point of intersection of Eqs. (ii) and (iv).

Numerical Value Type Questions

Example 33 *The equation of the hyperbola whose asymptotes are $x + 2y + 3 = 0$ and $3x + 4y + 5 = 0$ and which passes through the point $(1, -1)$ is $ax^2 + 2hxy + by^2 + 2gx + 2fy + c = 0$. Then, value of $a + b + c$ is*

Sol. (18) Combined equation of asymptotes is

$$(x + 2y + 3)(3x + 4y + 5) = 0$$

or $$3x^2 + 10xy + 8y^2 + 14x + 22y + 15 = 0 \quad \text{...(i)}$$

Also, we know that the equation of the hyperbola differs from that of asymptotes by a constant.

Let the equation of the hyperbola be

$$3x^2 + 10xy + 8y^2 + 14x + 22y + \lambda = 0 \quad \text{...(ii)}$$

Since, it passes through $(1, -1)$, then

$$3(1)^2 + 10(1)(-1) + 8(-1)^2 + 14(1) + 22(-1) + \lambda = 0$$

$$\Rightarrow \quad 3 - 10 + 8 + 14 - 22 + \lambda = 0$$

$$\therefore \quad \lambda = 7$$

From Eq. (ii), equation of hyperbola is

$$3x^2 + 10xy + 8y^2 + 14x + 22y + 7 = 0$$

Here, $a = 3$, $b = 8$ and $c = 7$

$\therefore \; a + b + c = 3 + 8 + 7 = 18$

Example 34 *Area of the triangle formed by a tangent to the hyperbola $xy = 90$ and its asymptotes is*

Sol. (180) Equation of the tangent at $\left(\sqrt{90}t, \frac{\sqrt{90}}{t}\right)$ to the hyperbola is $x^2 + t^2y^2 = 2\sqrt{90}t$

Which meets the asymptote $x = 0$ and $y = 0$ at

$$A(2\sqrt{90}t, 0) \text{ and } B\left(0, \frac{2\sqrt{90}}{t}\right)$$

Area of the triangle $OAB = \frac{1}{2} \times OA \times OB$

$$= \frac{1}{2} \times 2\sqrt{90}t \times \frac{2\sqrt{90}}{t}$$

$$= 2 \times 90$$

$$= 180 \text{ sq. units.}$$

JEE SCANNER

Example 35 Similar to PYQ Asked in JEE Main 2023

Let S be the focus of the hyperbola $\frac{x^2}{2} - \frac{y^2}{3} = 1$, on the positive X-axis. Let C be the circle with its centre at $(2, \sqrt{3})$ and passing through the point S. If O is the origin and SAB is a diameter of C, then the square of the area of the ΔOSB is equal to ....

Sol. (15) Given, $\frac{x^2}{2} - \frac{y^2}{3} = 1$

Focus of hyperbola $= (ae, 0)$

Here, $\quad a^2 = 2$ and $b^2 = 3$

Now, $\quad b^2 = a^2(e^2 - 1) \Rightarrow 3 = 2(e^2 - 1)$

$$\Rightarrow \quad e^2 - 1 = \frac{3}{2} \Rightarrow e^2 = \frac{3}{2} + 1 = \frac{5}{2} \Rightarrow e = \sqrt{\frac{5}{2}}$$

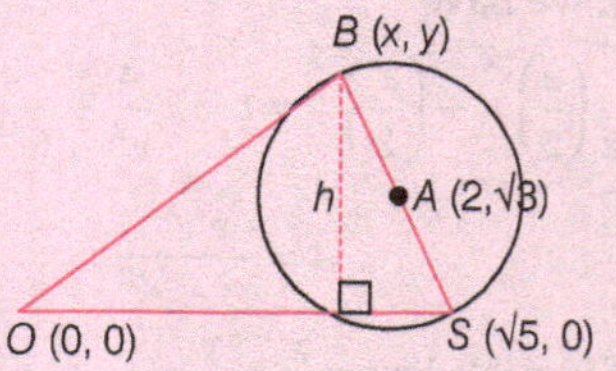

So, $\quad (ae, 0) = (\sqrt{5}, 0) = S$

Now, $\quad \frac{x + \sqrt{5}}{2} = 2 \Rightarrow x = 4 - \sqrt{5}$

and $\quad \frac{y + 0}{2} = \sqrt{3} \Rightarrow y = 2\sqrt{3}$

$$B(x, y) = (4 - \sqrt{5}, 2\sqrt{3})$$

$$h = 2\sqrt{3} \text{ and } OS = \sqrt{5}$$

$\therefore$ Area of $\Delta OSB = \frac{1}{2} \times OS \times h = \frac{1}{2} \times \sqrt{5} \times 3\sqrt{3} = \sqrt{15}$

Hence, the square of area of ΔOSB is 15 sq. units.

Skill Builder

Let S be the focus of the hyperbola $\frac{x^2}{5} - \frac{y^2}{7} = 1$, on the positive X-axis. Let C be the circle with its centre at $(\sqrt{10}, \sqrt{7})$ and passing through the point S. If O is the origin and SAB is a diameter of C, then the square of the area of the ΔOSB is equal to ......

For Sol.

Example 36 *The graph $xy = 1$ is reflected in $y = 2x$ to given the graph $12x^2 + rxy + sy^2 + t = 0$, then the value of rs is ...*

Sol. (84) Let $P(h, k)$ lie on the hyperbola.

Reflection of a general point (h, k) in $y = 2x$ gives $R(x_1, y_1)$.

$$\therefore \quad \frac{h - x_1}{2} = \frac{k - y_1}{(-1)} = \frac{2(2h - k)}{5}$$

$$\Rightarrow \quad x_1 = \frac{4k - 3h}{5} \text{ and } y_1 = \frac{3k + 4h}{5}$$

$\therefore \quad h = \dfrac{4y_1 - 3x_1}{5}$ and $k = \dfrac{3y_1 + 4x_1}{5}$

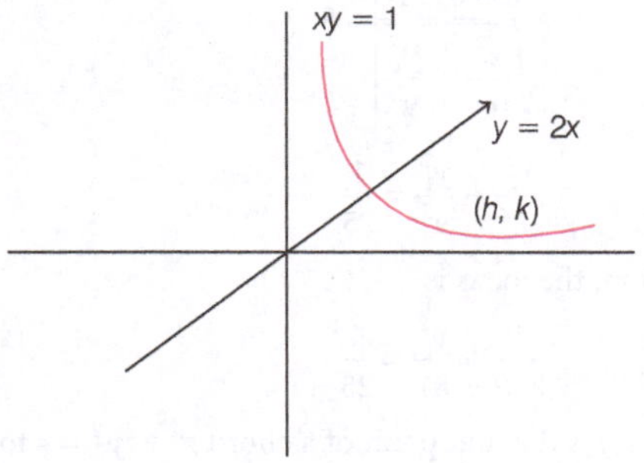

$\therefore \quad hk = 1$

$\Rightarrow \quad \dfrac{4y_1 - 3x_1}{5} \times \dfrac{3y_1 + 4x_1}{5} = 1$

$\Rightarrow \quad 12x_1^2 - 7x_1y_1 - 12y_1^2 + 25 = 0$

$\therefore \quad r = -7, s = -12$ and $t = 25$

So, $\quad rs = (-7)(-12) = 84$

Matching Type Questions

Example 37 *Match the following.*

	Column I		Column II
(A)	The locus of the point of intersection of the lines $\sqrt{3}x - y - 4\sqrt{3}t = 0$ and $\sqrt{3}\,tx + ty - 4\sqrt{3} = 0$ (where t is a parameter) is a hyperbola whose eccentricity is	(p)	a natural number
(B)	If the product of the perpendicular distances from any point on the hyperbola $\dfrac{x^2}{a^2} - \dfrac{y^2}{b^2} = 1$ of eccentricity $e = \sqrt{3}$ from its asymptotes is equal to 6, then the length of the transverse axis of the hyperbola is	(q)	a prime number
(C)	The area of the triangle that a tangent at a point of the hyperbola $\dfrac{x^2}{16} - \dfrac{y^2}{a} = 1$ makes with its asymptotes is	(r)	a composite number
(D)	For the hyperbola $xy = 8$ any tangent of it at P meets coordinates axes at Q and R, then area of ΔCQR when c is centre of the hyperbola is	(s)	a perfect number

Sol. (A) $\rightarrow$ (p, q); (B) $\rightarrow$ (p, r); (C) $\rightarrow$ (p, r); (D) $\rightarrow$ (p, r, s)

(A) The given lines are

$$\sqrt{3}\,x - y - 4\sqrt{3}\,t = 0 \quad \text{... (i)}$$

and

$$\sqrt{3}\,tx + ty - 4\sqrt{3} = 0 \quad \text{... (ii)}$$

eliminate t from Eqs. (i) and (ii), then

$$\frac{\sqrt{3}x - y}{4\sqrt{3}} = \frac{4\sqrt{3}}{\sqrt{3}x + y}$$

$\Rightarrow \quad 3x^2 - y^2 = 48$

or $\quad \dfrac{x^2}{16} - \dfrac{y^2}{48} = 1$

or $\quad 48 = 16(e^2 - 1) \Rightarrow e^2 = 4$

$\therefore \quad e = 2$

(B) Here, $\quad e = \sqrt{3}$

$\therefore \quad b^2 = a^2(3 - 1) = 2a^2 \quad \text{... (i)}$

Now, hyperbola convert in the form

$$\frac{x^2}{a^2} - \frac{y^2}{2a^2} = 1$$

Let $P(a\sec\theta, a\sqrt{2}\tan\theta)$ be any point on the hyperbola.

$\because$ Asymptotes of hyperbola are

$$\frac{x^2}{a^2} - \frac{y^2}{2a^2} = 0$$

or $\quad 2x^2 - y^2 = 0$

or $\quad x\sqrt{2} + y = 0$ and $x\sqrt{2} - y = 0$

$\because$ Product of the perpendiculars from P on asymptotes $= 6$

$\therefore \quad \dfrac{|a\sqrt{2}\sec\theta + a\sqrt{2}\tan\theta|}{\sqrt{(2+1)}} \dfrac{|a\sqrt{2}\sec\theta - a\sqrt{2}\tan\theta|}{\sqrt{2+1}} = 6$

or $\quad \dfrac{2a^2}{3} = 6$

$\therefore \quad a = 3$

Hence, length of transverse axis $= 2a = 6$

(C) Equation of tangent at $(a, 0)$ is $x = a$

Equation of asymptotes are $y = \pm \dfrac{b}{a}x$

$\therefore \quad P \equiv (a, b)$ and $Q \equiv (a, -b)$

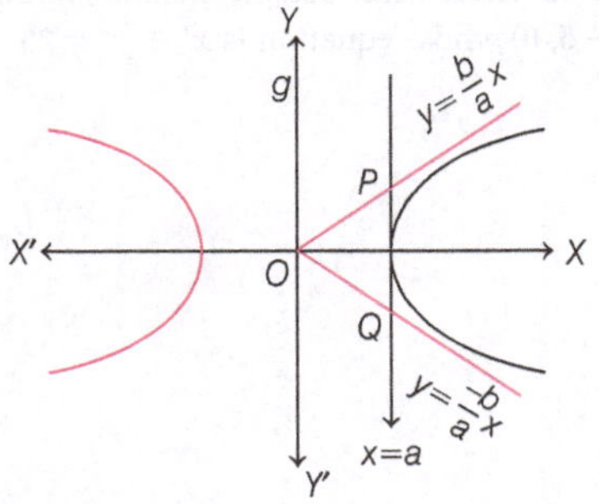

$\therefore$ Required area $= \dfrac{1}{2} \times a \times 2b = ab$

$= (4)(3) = 12 \quad$ [here, $a = 4, b = 3$]

(D) Any point of $xy = 8$ is $P\left(\sqrt{8}t, \dfrac{\sqrt{8}}{t}\right)$

$\therefore$ Equation of the tangent at P is $\dfrac{x}{\frac{16t}{\sqrt{8}}} + \dfrac{y}{\frac{16t}{\sqrt{8t}}} = 1$

$\therefore$ Area of the triangle $= \dfrac{1}{2}, \dfrac{16t}{\sqrt{8}}, \dfrac{16}{\sqrt{8t}} = 6$

Example 38 *Match the Items of Column I with those of Column II.*

Column I	Column II
(A) The locus of the point whose chord of contact with respect to the hyperbola $\frac{x^2}{16}-\frac{y^2}{9}=1$ touches the circle described on the line joining the foci is	(p) $(x^2+y^2)=4x^2-3y^2$
(B) The chords of the circle $x^2+y^2=4$ touch the hyperbola $\frac{x^2}{4}-\frac{y^3}{3}=1$. Then, the locus of the mid-points of these chords is	(q) $x^2+y^2=9$
(C) The director circle of the hyperbola $\frac{x^2}{25}-\frac{y^2}{16}=1$ is	(r) $x^2-y^2=32$
(D) The distance between the foci of a hyperbola is 16 and its eccentricity is $\sqrt{2}$. Then, the equation of the hyperbola is	(s) $\frac{x^2}{256}+\frac{y^2}{81}=\frac{1}{25}$

Sol. (A) → (s); (B) → (p); (C) → (q); D → (r)

(A) $P(x_1, y_1)$ be a point on the locus.

That is $\frac{xx_1}{16}-\frac{yy_1}{9}=1$

touches the circle described on the line joining the foci $S(5, 0)$ and $S'(-5, 0)$ whose equation is $x^2+y^2=25$.

$$\Rightarrow \left|\frac{0-0-1}{\sqrt{\frac{x_1^2}{16^2}+\frac{y_1^2}{9^2}}}\right|=5$$

$$\Rightarrow \frac{x_1^2}{16^2}+\frac{y_1^2}{9^2}=\frac{1}{25}$$

Therefore, the locus is

$$\frac{x^2}{256}+\frac{y^2}{81}=\frac{1}{25}$$

(B) (x_1, y_1) is the mid-point of a chord $x^2+y^2=4$ touching the hyperbola $\frac{x^2}{4}-\frac{y^2}{3}=1$

That is the line $xx_1+yy_1=x_1^2+y_1^2$, touches the hyperbola. This means

$$\left(\frac{x_1^2+y_1^2}{y_1^2}\right)^2=4\left(\frac{-x_1}{y_1}\right)^2-3$$

$$\Rightarrow (x_1^2+y_1^2)^2=4x_1^2-3y_1^2$$

Therefore, the locus is $(x^2+y^2)^2=4x^2-3y^2$.

(C) Director circle of $\frac{x^2}{a^2}-\frac{y^2}{b^2}=1$ is $x^2+y^2=a^2-b^2$.

So, $a^2=25$ and $b^2=16$.

Hence, the director circle is $x^2+y^2=9$

(D) Since, $\sqrt{2}$ is the eccentricity of the hyperbola, it must be a rectangular hyperbola. So, it is of the form $x^2-y^2=a^2$. By hypothesis

$$2ae=16$$

$$\Rightarrow 2a(\sqrt{2})=16 \Rightarrow a=4\sqrt{2}$$

Hence, the hyperbola is $x^2-y^2=32$.

EXERCISE 1

JEE Main Pattern

Single Option Correct Type Questions

1. P is any point on the hyperbola $x^2 - y^2 = a^2$. If F_1 and F_2 are the foci of the hyperbola and $PF_1 \cdot PF_2 = \lambda(OP)^2$, where O is the origin, then λ is equal to

(a) 1 (b) $\sqrt{2}$ (c) 2 (d) 3

2. If the sum of the slopes of the normals from a point P to the hyperbola $xy = c^2$ is equal to λ $(\lambda \in R^+)$, then locus of point P is

(a) $x^2 - y^2 = \lambda c^2$ (b) $y^2 = \lambda c^2$
(c) $xy = \lambda c^2$ (d) $x^2 = \lambda c^2$

3. If there are two points A and B on rectangular hyperbola $xy = c^2$ such that abscissa of A = ordinate of B, then the locus of point of intersection of tangents at A and B is

(a) $y^2 = x^2 + 2c^2$ (b) $y^2 = x^2 + \frac{c^2}{2}$
(c) $y = x$ (d) $y = 3x$

4. A series of hyperbola is drawn having a common transverse axis of length $2a$. Then, the locus of a point P on each hyperbola such that its distance from the transverse axis is equal to its distance from an asymptote, is

(a) $(x^2 - y^2)^2 = 4x^2(x^2 - a^2)$
(b) $(x^2 - y^2)^2 = x^2(x^2 - a^2)$
(c) $(x^2 - y^2)^2 = 4y^2(x^2 - a^2)$
(d) $(x^2 - y^2)^2 = y^2(x^2 - a^2)$

5. If a rectangular hyperbola $(x - 1)(y - 2) = 4$ cuts a circle $x^2 + y^2 + 2gx + 2fy + c = 0$ at points (3, 4) (5, 3), (2, 6) and $(-1, 0)$, then the value of $(g + f)$ is equal to

(a) -8 (b) -9 (c) 8 (d) 9

6. If $f(x) = ax^3 + bx^2 + cx + d$, ($a, b, c, d$ are rational numbers) and roots of $f(x) = 0$ are eccentricities of a parabola and a rectangular hyperbola, then $a + b + c + d$ equals

(a) -1
(b) 0
(c) 1
(d) data inadequate

7. From a point on the line $y = x + c$, where c is a parameter tangents are drawn to the hyperbola $\frac{x^2}{2} - \frac{y^2}{1} = 1$ such that chords of contact pass through a fixed point (x_1, y_1). Then, $\frac{x_1}{y_1}$ is equal to

(a) 2 (b) 3
(c) 4 (d) None of these

8. Two conics $\frac{x^2}{a^2} - \frac{y^2}{b^2} = 1$ and $x^2 = -\frac{a}{b}y$ intersect, if

(a) $0 < b \le \frac{1}{2}$ (b) $0 < a < \frac{1}{2}$
(c) $a^2 < b^2$ (d) $a^2 > b^2$

9. Let $A \equiv (-3, 4)$ and $B \equiv (2, -1)$ be two fixed points. A point C moves such that

$\tan\left(\frac{1}{2}\angle ABC\right) : \tan\left(\frac{1}{2}\angle BAC\right) = 3:1$. Thus, locus of C is a hyperbola, distance between whose foci is

(a) 5 (b) $5\sqrt{2}$
(c) $\frac{5}{2}$ (d) $\frac{5}{\sqrt{2}}$

10. A point P is taken on the right half of the hyperbola $\frac{x^2}{a^2} - \frac{y^2}{b^2} = 1$ having its foci as S_1 and S_2. If the internal angle bisector of the angle $\angle S_1PS_2$ cuts the X-axis at point $Q(\alpha, 0)$, then range of α is

(a) $[-a, a]$ (b) $[0, a]$
(c) $(0, a]$ (d) $[-a, 0)$

11. If angle between asymptotes of hyperbola $\frac{x^2}{a^2} - \frac{y^2}{b^2} = 1$ is 120° and product of perpendiculars drawn from foci upon its any tangent is 9, then locus of point of intersection of perpendicular tangents of the hyperbola can be

(a) $x^2 + y^2 = 3$
(b) $x^2 + y^2 = 6$
(c) $x^2 + y^2 = 9$
(d) $x^2 + y^2 = 18$

12. If $\alpha+\beta=3\pi$, then the chord joining the points α and β for the hyperbola $\frac{x^2}{a^2}-\frac{y^2}{b^2}=1$ passes through

(a) focus
(b) centre
(c) one of the end point of the transverse axis
(d) one of the end points of the conjugate axis

13. If the curves $\frac{x^2}{a^2}+\frac{y^2}{b^2}=1\,(a>b)$ and $x^2-y^2=c^2$ cut at right angles, then

(a) $a^2+b^2=2c^2$ (b) $b^2-a^2=2c^2$
(c) $a^2-b^2=2c^2$ (d) $a^2b^2=2c^2$

14. If chords of the hyperbola $x^2-y^2=a^2$ touch the parabola $y^2=4ax$, then the locus of the middle points of these chords is the curve

(a) $y^2(x+a)=x^3$ (b) $y^2(x-a)=x^3$
(c) $y^2(x+2a)=3x^3$ (d) $y^2(x-2a)=2x^3$

15. An ellipse has eccentricity 1/2 and one focus at the point $P(1/2, 1)$. Its one directrix is the common tangent nearer to the point P, to the circle $x^2+y^2=1$ and the hyperbola $x^2-y^2=1$. The equation of the ellipse in standard form is

(a) $9x^2+12y^2=108$
(b) $9(x-1/3)^2+12(y-1)^2=1$
(c) $9(x-1/3)^2+4(y-1)^2=36$
(d) None of the above

16. The eccentricity of the hyperbola whose length of the latusrectum is equal to 8 and the length of its conjugate axis is equal to half of the distance between its foci, is

(a) $\frac{2}{\sqrt{3}}$ (b) $\sqrt{3}$ (c) $\frac{4}{3}$ (d) $\frac{4}{\sqrt{3}}$

17. A hyperbola passes through the point $P(\sqrt{2},\sqrt{3})$ and has foci at $(\pm 2, 0)$. Then, the tangent to this hyperbola at P also passes through the point

(a) $(-\sqrt{2},-\sqrt{3})$ (b) $(3\sqrt{2}, 2\sqrt{3})$
(c) $(2\sqrt{2}, 3\sqrt{3})$ (d) $(\sqrt{3}, \sqrt{2})$

18. Consider a branch of the hyperbola $x^2-2y^2-2\sqrt{2}x-4\sqrt{2}y-6=0$ with vertex at the point A. Let B be one of the end points of its latusrectum. If C is the focus of the hyperbola nearest to the point A, then the area of the triangle ABC is

(a) $1-\sqrt{\frac{2}{3}}$ (b) $\sqrt{\frac{3}{2}}-1$
(c) $1+\sqrt{\frac{2}{3}}$ (d) $\sqrt{\frac{3}{2}}+1$

19. An ellipse intersects the hyperbola $2x^2-2y^2=1$ orthogonally. The eccentricity of the ellipse is reciprocal of that of the hyperbola. If the axes of the ellipse are along the coordinate axes, then

(a) equation of ellipse is $x^2+2y^2=3$
(b) the foci of ellipse are $(\pm 1, 0)$
(c) equation of ellipse is $x^2+2y^2=4$
(d) the foci of ellipse are $(\pm\sqrt{2}, 0)$

20. Let $P(6,3)$ be a point on the hyperbola $\frac{x^2}{a^2}-\frac{y^2}{b^2}=1$. If the normal at the point P intersects the X-axis at $(9, 0)$, then the eccentricity of the hyperbola is

(a) $\sqrt{\frac{5}{2}}$ (b) $\sqrt{\frac{3}{2}}$
(c) $\sqrt{2}$ (d) $\sqrt{3}$

21. The equation of the line passing through the centre of a rectangular hyperbola is $x-y-1=0$. If one of its asymptote is $3x-4y-6=0$, then the equation of the other asymptote is

(a) $4x-3y+8=0$ (b) $4x+3y+17=0$
(c) $3x-2y+15=0$ (d) None of these

22. The condition that a straight line with slope m will be normal to parabola $y^2=4ax$ as well as a tangent to rectangular hyperbola $x^2-y^2=a^2$ is

(a) $m^6-4m^2+2m-1=0$
(b) $m^4+3m^3+2m+1=0$
(c) $m^6-2m=0$
(d) $m^6+4m^4+3m^2+1=0$

23. The locus of the middle points of chords of hyperbola $3x^2-2y^2+4x-6y=0$ parallel to $y=2x$ is

(a) $3x-4y=4$
(b) $3y-4x+4=0$
(c) $4x-4y=3$
(d) $3x-4y=2$

24. The coordinates of the centre of the hyperbola $x^2+3xy+2y^2+2x+3y+2=0$ is

(a) $(-1,0)$ (b) $(1, 0)$
(c) $(-1,1)$ (d) $(1,-1)$

Numerical Value Type Questions

25. The ellipse $\frac{x^2}{a^2}+\frac{y^2}{b^2}=1$ and the hyperbola $\frac{x^2}{A^2}-\frac{y^2}{B^2}=1$ are given to be confocal and length of minor axis of the ellipse is same as the conjugate axis of the hyperbola. If e_1 and e_2 represent the eccentricities of ellipse and hyperbola respectively, then the value of $e_1^{-2}+e_2^{-2}$ is......

26. If abscissa of orthocentre of a triangle inscribed in a rectangular hyperbola $xy = 4$ is $\frac{1}{2}$, then the ordinate of orthocentre of triangle is ......

27. Normal drawn to the hyperbola $xy = 2$ at the point $P(t_1)$ meets the hyperbola again at $Q(t_2)$, then minimum distance between the points P and Q is ......

28. The normal at P to a hyperbola of eccentricity $\frac{3}{2\sqrt{2}}$ intersects the transverse and conjugate axes at M and N, respectively. The locus of mid-point of MN is a hyperbola, then its eccentricity is ......

29. If radii of director circle of the ellipse $\frac{x^2}{a^2} + \frac{y^2}{b^2} = 1$ and hyperbola $\frac{x^2}{a^2} - \frac{y^2}{b_1^2} = 1$ are in the ratio 1 : 3 and $9e_1^2 - e_2^2 = \lambda$, where e_1 and e_2 are the eccentricities of ellipse and hyperbola respectively, then the value of λ is ......

30. The shortest distance between the curves $\frac{x^2}{a^2} - \frac{y^2}{b^2} = 1$ and $4x^2 + 4y^2 = a^2\ (b > a)$ is $f(a, b)$, then the value of $f(4, 6) + f(2, 3)$ is ....

31. Chords of the circle $x^2 + y^2 = 4$, touch the hyperbola $\frac{x^2}{4} - \frac{y^2}{16} = 1$. The locus of their middle points is the curve $(x^2 + y^2)^2 = \lambda x^2 - 16y^2$, then the value of λ is ......

32. Tangents are drawn from the point (α, β) to the hyperbola $3x^2 - 2y^2 = 6$ and are inclined at angles θ and ϕ to the X-axis. If $\tan\theta \cdot \tan\phi = 2$, then the value of $2\alpha^2 - \beta^2$ is ......

33. The line $2x + y = 1$ is tangent to the hyperbola $\frac{x^2}{a^2} - \frac{y^2}{b^2} = 1$. If this line passes through the point of intersection of the nearest directrix and the X-axis, then the eccentricity of the hyperbola is ......

34. A normal to the hyperbola $\frac{x^2}{4} - \frac{y^2}{1} = 1$ has equal intercepts on positive X and Y axis. If this normal touches the ellipse $\frac{x^2}{a^2} + \frac{y^2}{b^2} = 1$, then $\frac{18}{25}(a^2 + b^2)$ is equal to ......

Previous Years Questions

35. Let P be a point on the hyperbola $H : \frac{x^2}{9} - \frac{y^2}{4} = 1$ in the first quadrant such that the area of triangle formed by P and the two foci of H is $2\sqrt{13}$. Then, the square of the distance of P from the origin is
[Single Correct Type, 2024 Main]

(a) 20 (b) 26 (c) 22 (d) 18

36. Let the foci of a hyperbola H coincide with the foci of the ellipse $E : \frac{(x-1)^2}{100} + \frac{(y-1)^2}{75} = 1$ and the eccentricity of the hyperbola H be the reciprocal of the eccentricity of the ellipse E. If the length of the transverse axis of H is α and the length of its conjugate axis is β, then $3\alpha^2 + 2\beta^2$ is equal to **[Single Correct Type, 2024 Main]**

(a) 242 (b) 205 (c) 237 (d) 225

37. Let $H : \frac{-x^2}{a^2} + \frac{y^2}{b^2} = 1$ be the hyperbola, whose eccentricity is $\sqrt{3}$ and the length of the latus rectum is $4\sqrt{3}$. Suppose the point $(\alpha, 6)$, $\alpha > 0$ lies on H. If β is the product of the focal distances of the point $(\alpha, 6)$, then $\alpha^2 + \beta$ is equal to **[Single Correct Type, 2024 Main]**

(a) 172 (b) 169 (c) 171 (d) 170

38. For $0 < \theta < \frac{\pi}{2}$, if the eccentricity of the hyperbola $x^2 - y^2 \operatorname{cosec}^2\theta = 5$ is $\sqrt{7}$ times eccentricity of the ellipse $x^2 \operatorname{cosec}^2\theta + y^2 = 5$, then the value of θ is
[Single Correct Type, 2024 Main]

(a) $\pi/6$ (b) $\pi/3$ (c) $\pi/4$ (d) $5\pi/12$

39. Let e_1 be the eccentricity of the hyperbola $\frac{x^2}{16} - \frac{y^2}{9} = 1$ and e_2 be the eccentricity of the ellipse $\frac{x^2}{a^2} + \frac{y^2}{b^2} = 1$, $a > b$, which passes through the foci of the hyperbola. If $e_1 e_2 = 1$, then the length of the chord of the ellipse parallel to the X-axis and passing through $(0, 5)$ is
[Single Correct Type, 2024 Main]

(a) $8\sqrt{5}/3$ (b) $4\sqrt{5}$ (c) $3\sqrt{5}$ (d) $10\sqrt{5}/3$

40. Consider a hyperbola H having centre at the origin and foci on the X-axis. Let C_1 be the circle touching the hyperbola H and having the centre at the origin. Let C_2 be the circle touching the hyperbola H at its vertex and having the centre at one of its foci. If areas (in sq units) of C_1 and C_2 are 36π and 4π, respectively, then the length (in units) of latus rectum of H is
[Single Correct Type, 2024 Main]

(a) 14/3 (b) 28/3 (c) 11/3 (d) 10/3

41. If the foci of a hyperbola are same as that of the ellipse $\frac{x^2}{9}+\frac{y^2}{25}=1$ and the eccentricity of the hyperbola is $\frac{15}{8}$ times the eccentricity of the ellipse, then the smaller focal distance of the point $\left(\sqrt{2}, \frac{14}{3}\sqrt{\frac{2}{5}}\right)$ on the hyperbola, is equal to **[Single Correct Type, 2024 Main]**

(a) $7\sqrt{\frac{2}{5}}-\frac{8}{3}$ (b) $14\sqrt{\frac{2}{5}}-\frac{4}{3}$

(c) $14\sqrt{\frac{2}{5}}-\frac{16}{3}$ (d) $7\sqrt{\frac{2}{5}}+\frac{8}{3}$

42. Let S be the focus of the hyperbola $\frac{x^2}{3}-\frac{y^2}{5}=1$, on the positive X-axis. Let C be the circle with its centre at $A(\sqrt{6}, \sqrt{5})$ and passing through the point S. If O is the origin and SAB is a diameter of C, then the square of the area of the ΔOSB is equal to .... **[Numerical Value Type, 2024 Main]**

43. The length of the latus rectum and directrices of a hyperbola with eccentricity e are 9 and $x=\pm\frac{4}{\sqrt{3}}$, respectively. Let the line $y-\sqrt{3}x+\sqrt{3}=0$ touch this hyperbola at (x_0, y_0). If m is the product of the focal distances of the point (x_0, y_0), then $4e^2+m$ is equal to ... **[Numerical Value Type, 2024 Main]**

44. Let the foci and length of the latus rectum of an ellipse $\frac{x^2}{a^2}+\frac{y^2}{b^2}=1$, $a>b$ be $(\pm 5, 0)$ and $\sqrt{50}$, respectively. Then, the square of the eccentricity of the hyperbola $\frac{x^2}{b^2}-\frac{y^2}{a^2b^2}=1$ equals .... **[Numerical Value Type, 2024 Main]**

45. Let the latus rectum of the hyperbola $\frac{x^2}{9}-\frac{y^2}{b^2}=1$ subtend an angle of $\frac{\pi}{3}$ at the centre of the hyperbola. If b^2 is equal to $\frac{l}{m}(1+\sqrt{n})$, where l and m are coprime numbers, then $l^2+m^2+n^2$ is equal to .... **[Numerical Value Type, 2024 Main]**

46. Let H be the hyperbola, whose foci are $(1\pm\sqrt{2}, 0)$ and eccentricity is $\sqrt{2}$. Then, the length of its latus rectum is **[Single Correct Type, 2023 Main]**

(a) 3 (b) 2

(c) 5/2 (d) 3/2

47. In a group of 100 persons, 75 speak English and 40 speak Hindi. Each person speaks at least one of the two languages. If the number of persons, who speak only English is α and the number of persons who speak only Hindi is β, then the eccentricity of the ellipse $25(\beta^2x^2+\alpha^2y^2)=\alpha^2\beta^2$ is **[Single Correct Type, 2023 Main]**

(a) $\frac{3\sqrt{15}}{12}$ (b) $\frac{\sqrt{129}}{12}$ (c) $\frac{\sqrt{117}}{12}$ (d) $\frac{\sqrt{119}}{12}$

48. Let $P(x_0, y_0)$ be the point on the hyperbola $3x^2-4y^2=36$, which is nearest to the line $3x+2y=1$. Then, $\sqrt{2}(y_0-x_0)$ is equal to **[Single Correct Type, 2023 Main]**

(a) 9 (b) -9 (c) -3 (d) 3

49. The foci of a hyperbola are $(\pm 2, 0)$ and its eccentricity is $\frac{3}{2}$. A tangent, perpendicular to the line $2x+3y=6$, is drawn at a point in the first quadrant on the hyperbola. If the intercepts made by the tangent on the X and Y-axes are a and b respectively, then $|6a|+|5b|$ is equal to .... **[Numerical Value Type, 2023 Main]**

50. Let m_1 and m_2 be the slopes of the tangents drawn from the point $P(4, 1)$ to the hyperbola $H=\frac{y^2}{25}-\frac{x^2}{16}=1$. If Q is the point from which the tangents drawn to H have slopes $|m_1|$ and $|m_2|$ and they make positive intercepts α and β on the X-axis, then $\frac{(PQ)^2}{\alpha\beta}$ is equal to .... **[Numerical Value Type, 2023 Main]**

51. The vertices of a hyperbola H are $(\pm 6, 0)$ and its eccentricity is $\frac{\sqrt{5}}{2}$. Let N be the normal to H at a point in the first quadrant and parallel to the line $\sqrt{2}x+y=2\sqrt{2}$. If d is the length of the line segment of N between H and the Y-axis, then d^2 equal to .... **[Numerical Value Type, 2023 Main]**

52. Let $a>0$, $b>0$. Let e and l respectively be the eccentricity and length of the latus rectum of the hyperbola $\frac{x^2}{a^2}-\frac{y^2}{b^2}=1$. Let e' and l' respectively be the eccentricity and length of the latus rectum of its conjugate hyperbola. If $e^2=\frac{11}{14}l$ and $(e')^2=\frac{11}{8}l'$, then the value of $77a+44b$ is equal to **[Single Correct Type, 2022 Main]**

(a) 100 (b) 110 (c) 120 (d) 130

53. Let the eccentricity of the hyperbola $H: \frac{x^2}{a^2} - \frac{y^2}{b^2} = 1$ be $\sqrt{5/2}$ and length of its latus rectum be $6\sqrt{2}$. If $y = 2x + c$ is a tangent to the hyperbola H, then the value of c^2 is equal to **[Single Correct Type, 2022 Main]**

(a) 18 (b) 20 (c) 24 (d) 32

54. The normal to the hyperbola $\frac{x^2}{a^2} - \frac{y^2}{9} = 1$ at the point $(8, 3\sqrt{3})$ on it passes through the point **[Single Correct Type, 2022 Main]**

(a) $(15, -2\sqrt{3})$ (b) $(9, 2\sqrt{3})$
(c) $(-1, 9\sqrt{3})$ (d) $(-1, 6\sqrt{3})$

55. If the line $x - 1 = 10$ is directrix of the hyperbola $kx^2 - y^2 = 6$, then the hyperbola passes through the point **[Single Correct Type, 2022 Main]**

(a) $(-2\sqrt{5}, 6)$ (b) $(-\sqrt{5}, 3)$
(c) $(\sqrt{5}, -2)$ (d) $(2\sqrt{5}, 3\sqrt{6})$

56. Let $\lambda x - 2y = \mu$ be a tangent to the hyperbola $a^2x^2 - y^2 = b^2$. Then, $\left(\frac{\lambda}{a}\right)^2 - \left(\frac{\mu}{b}\right)^2$ is equal to **[Single Correct Type, 2022 Main]**

(a) -2 (b) -4 (c) 2 (d) 4

57. Let the focal chord of the parabola $P: y^2 = 4x$ along the line $L: y = mx + c, m > 0$ meet the parabola at the points M and N. Let the line L be a tangent to the hyperbola $H: x^2 - y^2 = 4$. If O is the vertex of P and F is the focus of H on the positive X-axis, then the area of the quadrilateral $OMFN$ is **[Single Correct Type, 2022 Main]**

(a) $2\sqrt{6}$ (b) $2\sqrt{14}$ (c) $4\sqrt{6}$ (d) $4\sqrt{14}$

58. Let the hyperbola $H: \frac{x^2}{a^2} - \frac{y^2}{b^2} = 1$ passes through the point $(2\sqrt{2}, -2\sqrt{2})$. A parabola is drawn whose focus is same as the focus of H with positive abscissa and the directrix of the parabola passes through the other focus of H. If the length of the latusrectum of the parabola is e times the length of the latusrectum of H, where e is the eccentricity of H, then which of the following points lies on the parabola? **[Single Correct Type, 2022 Main]**

(a) $(2\sqrt{3}, 3\sqrt{2})$ (b) $(3\sqrt{3}, -6\sqrt{2})$
(c) $(\sqrt{3}, -\sqrt{6})$ (d) $(3\sqrt{6}, 6\sqrt{2})$

59. Let the foci of the ellipse $\frac{x^2}{16} + \frac{y^2}{7} = 1$ and the hyperbola $\frac{x^2}{144} - \frac{y^2}{\alpha} = \frac{1}{25}$ coincide. Then, the length of the latus rectum of the hyperbola is

[Single Correct Type, 2022 Main]

(a) $\frac{32}{9}$ (b) $\frac{18}{5}$ (c) $\frac{27}{4}$ (d) $\frac{27}{10}$

60. A common tangent T to the curves $C_1: \frac{x^2}{4} + \frac{y^2}{9} = 1$ and $C_2: \frac{x^2}{42} - \frac{y^2}{143} = 1$ does not pass through the fourth quadrant. If T touches C_1 at (x_1, y_1) and C_2 at (x_2, y_2), then $|2x_1 + x_2|$ is equal to ....

[Numerical Value Type, 2022 Main]

61. Let $H: \frac{x^2}{a^2} - \frac{y^2}{b^2} = 1, a > 0, b > 0$, be a hyperbola such that the sum of lengths of the transverse and the conjugate axes is $4(2\sqrt{2} + \sqrt{14})$. If the eccentricity H is $\frac{\sqrt{11}}{2}$, then value of $a^2 + b^2$ is equal to ....

[Numerical Value Type, 2022 Main]

62. Let a line L_1 be tangent to the hyperbola $\frac{x^2}{16} - \frac{y^2}{4} = 1$ and let L_2 be the line passing through the origin and perpendicular to L_1. If the locus of the point of intersection of L_1 and L_2 is $(x^2 + y^2)^2 = \alpha x^2 + \beta y^2$, then $\alpha + \beta$ is equal to ....

[Numerical Value Type, 2022 Main]

63. Let the eccentricity of the hyperbola $\frac{x^2}{a^2} - \frac{y^2}{b^2} = 1$ be $\frac{5}{4}$. If the equation of the normal at the point $\left(\frac{8}{\sqrt{5}}, \frac{12}{5}\right)$ on the hyperbola is $8\sqrt{5}x + \beta y = \lambda$, then $\lambda - \beta$ is equal to ....

[Numerical Value Type, 2022 Main]

64. Let the hyperbola $H: \frac{x^2}{a^2} - y^2 = 1$ and the ellipse $E: 3x^2 + 4y^2 = 12$ be such that the length of latusrectum of H is equal to the length of latusrectum of E. If e_H and e_E are the eccentricities of H and E respectively, then the value of $12(e_H^2 + e_E^2)$ is equal to ....

[Numerical Value Type, 2022 Main]

65. The locus of the mid-points of the chords of the hyperbola $x^2 - y^2 = 4$, which touch the parabola $y^2 = 8x$, is **[Single Correct Type, 2021 Main]**

(a) $y^3(x-2) = x^2$ (b) $x^3(x-2) = y^3$
(c) $y^2(x-2) = x^3$ (d) $x^2(x-2) = y^3$

66. Let a line $L: 2x + y = k, k > 0$ be a tangent to the hyperbola $x^2 - y^2 = 3$. If L is also a tangent to the parabola $y^2 = \alpha x$, then α is equal to

[Single Correct Type, 2021 Main]

(a) 12 (b) -12
(c) 24 (d) -24

67. The point $P(-2\sqrt{6}, \sqrt{3})$ lies on the hyperbola $\frac{x^2}{a^2} - \frac{y^2}{b^2} = 1$ having eccentricity $\sqrt{5}/2$. If the tangent and normal at P to the hyperbola intersect its conjugate axis at the point Q and R respectively, then QR is equal to **[Single Correct Type, 2021 Main]**

(a) $4\sqrt{3}$ (b) 6 (c) $6\sqrt{3}$ (d) $3\sqrt{6}$

68. The locus of the centroid of the triangle formed by any point P on the hyperbola $16x^2 - 9y^2 + 32x + 36y - 164 = 0$ and its foci is **[Single Correct Type, 2021 Main]**

(a) $16x^2 - 9y^2 + 32x + 36y - 36 = 0$
(b) $9x^2 - 16y^2 + 36x - 32y - 144 = 0$
(c) $16x^2 - 9y^2 + 32x - 36y - 144 = 0$
(d) $9x^2 - 16y^2 + 36x - 32y - 36 = 0$

69. A hyperbola passes through the foci of the ellipse $\frac{x^2}{25} + \frac{y^2}{16} = 1$ and its transverse and conjugate axes coincide with major and minor axes of the ellipse, respectively. If the product of their eccentricities is one, then the equation of the hyperbola is **[Single Correct Type, 2021 Main]**

(a) $\frac{x^2}{9} - \frac{y^2}{16} = 1$ (b) $\frac{x^2}{9} - \frac{y^2}{4} = 1$
(c) $\frac{x^2}{9} - \frac{y^2}{25} = 1$ (d) $x^2 - y^2 = 9$

70. The locus of the mid-points of the chord of the circle, $x^2 + y^2 = 25$ which is tangent to the hyperbola, $\frac{x^2}{9} - \frac{y^2}{16} = 1$ is **[Single Correct Type, 2021 Main]**

(a) $(x^2 + y^2)^2 - 16x^2 + 9y^2 = 0$
(b) $(x^2 + y^2)^2 - 9x^2 + 144y^2 = 0$
(c) $(x^2 + y^2)^2 - 9x^2 - 16y^2 = 0$
(d) $(x^2 + y^2)^2 - 9x^2 + 16y^2 = 0$

71. Let $A(\sec\theta, 2\tan\theta)$ and $B(\sec\phi, 2\tan\phi)$, where $\theta + \phi = \pi/2$, be two points on the hyperbola $2x^2 - y^2 = 2$. If (α, β) is the point of the intersection of the normals to the hyperbola at A and B, then $(2\beta)^2$ is equal to .... **[Numerical Value Type, 2021 Main]**

72. The locus of the point of intersection of the lines $(\sqrt{3})kx + ky - 4\sqrt{3} = 0$ and $\sqrt{3}x - y - 4(\sqrt{3})k = 0$ is a conic, whose eccentricity is .... **[Numerical Value Type, 2021 Main]**

73. If a hyperbola passes through the point P910, 16) and it has vertices at $(\pm 6, 0)$, then the equationof the normal to it at P is **[Single Correct Type, 2020 Main]**

(a) $3x + 4y = 94$
(b) $x + 2y = 42$
(c) $2x + 5y = 100$
(d) $x = 3y = 58$

EXERCISE 2

JEE Advanced Pattern

Single Option Correct Type Questions

1. Let F_1, F_2 be foci of the hyperbola $\frac{x^2}{16} - \frac{y^2}{9} = 1$ and F_3, F_4 be the foci of its conjugate hyperbola. If e_H and e_C are their eccentricities respectively, then the statement which holds true is
(a) their equations of their asymptotes are different
(b) $e_H > e_C$
(c) area of the quadrilateral formed by their foci is 50 sq units
(d) their auxiliary circles will have the same equation

2. Locus of the point of intersection of the tangents at the points with eccentric angles ϕ and $\frac{\pi}{2} - \phi$ on the hyperbola $\frac{x^2}{a^2} - \frac{y^2}{b^2} = 1$ is
(a) $x = a$ (b) $y = b$
(c) $x = ab$ (d) $y = ab$

3. If the tangent and normal to a rectangular hyperbola cut off intercepts x_1 and x_2 on one axis and y_1 and y_2 on the other axis, then
(a) $x_1y_1 + x_2y_2 = 0$ (b) $x_1y_2 + x_2y_1 = 0$
(c) $x_1x_2 + y_1y_2 = 0$ (d) None of these

4. The equation of a hyperbola, conjugate to the hyperbola $x^2 + 3xy + 2y^2 + 2x + 3y = 0$ is
(a) $x^2 + 3xy + 2y^2 + 2x + 3y + 1 = 0$
(b) $x^2 + 3xy + 2y^2 + 2x + 3y + 2 = 0$
(c) $x^2 + 3xy + 2y^2 + 2x + 3y + 3 = 0$
(d) $x^2 + 3xy + 2y^2 + 2x + 3y + 4 = 0$

5. Let C be a curve which is the locus of the point of intersection of lines $x = 2 + m$ and $my = 4 - m$. A circle $S_1 = (x-2)^2 + (y+1)^2 = 25$ intersects the curve C at four points P, Q, R and S. If O is the centre of the curve C, then $(OP)^2 + (OQ)^2 + (OR)^2 + (OS)^2$ is
(a) 25 (b) 50
(c) 100 (d) 200

6. A hyperbola, having the transverse axis of length $2\sin\theta$, is confocal with the ellipse $3x^2 + 4y^2 = 12$. Then, its equation is
(a) $x^2\operatorname{cosec}^2\theta - y^2\sec^2\theta = 1$
(b) $x^2\sec^2\theta - y^2\operatorname{cosec}^2\theta = 1$
(c) $x^2\sin^2\theta - y^2\cos^2\theta = 1$
(d) $x^2\cos^2\theta - y^2\sin^2\theta = 1$

7. If the foci of the ellipse $\frac{x^2}{k^2a^2} + \frac{y^2}{a^2} = 1$ and the hyperbola $\frac{x^2}{a^2} - \frac{y^2}{b^2} = 1$ coincide $k > \sqrt{\lambda}$, then λ is equal to
(a) 3 (b) 2
(c) 4 (d) 5

8. If $y = mx + c$ is a tangent to hyperbola $\frac{x^2}{\lambda^2} - \frac{y^2}{(\lambda^3 + \lambda^2 + \lambda)^2} = 1$, then least value of $16\,m^2$ is equal to
(a) 0 (b) 1
(c) 4 (d) 9

9. Let $PQ: 2x + y + 6 = 0$ be a chord of the curve $x^2 - 4y^2 = 4$, coordinates of the point $R(\alpha, \beta)$ that satisfy $\alpha^2 + \beta^2 - 1 \le 0$, such that area of ΔPQR is minimum, are given by
(a) $\left(\frac{-2}{\sqrt{5}}, \frac{1}{\sqrt{5}}\right)$ (b) $\left(\frac{-2}{\sqrt{5}}, \frac{-1}{\sqrt{5}}\right)$
(c) $\left(\frac{2}{\sqrt{5}}, \frac{1}{\sqrt{5}}\right)$ (d) $\left(\frac{2}{\sqrt{5}}, \frac{-1}{\sqrt{5}}\right)$

10. Let the chord be $x\cos\alpha + y\sin\alpha = p$ of the hyperbola $\frac{x^2}{16} - \frac{y^2}{18} = 1$ subtends a right angle at the centre, let diameter of the circle, concentric with the hyperbola, to which the given chord is a tangent is d, then $\frac{d}{4}$ is equal to
(a) 4 (b) 5
(c) 6 (d) 7

11. How many number of triangles can be inscribed in the rectangular hyperbola $xy = c^2$, whose sides all touch the parabola $y^2 = 4ax$?

(a) 4 (b) 3
(c) 2 (d) infinite

12. A series of hyperbola is drawn having a common transverse axis of length $2a$, then the locus of a point p on each hyperbola. Such that its distance from the transverse axis is equal to its distance from an asymptote, is

(a) $(x^2 - y^2)^2 = 4x^2(x^2 - a^2)$
(b) $(x^2 - y^2)^2 = x^2(x^2 - a^2)$
(c) $(x^2 - y^2) = 4y^2(x^2 - a^2)$
(d) $(x^2 - y^2)^2 = y^2(x^2 - a^2)$

13. The point $P(-2\sqrt{6}, \sqrt{3})$ lies on the hyperbola $\frac{x^2}{a^2} - \frac{y^2}{b^2} = 1$ having eccentricity $\frac{\sqrt{5}}{2}$. If the tangent and normal at p to the hyperbola intersect its conjugate axis at the point Q and R respectively, then OR is equal to

(a) $4\sqrt{3}$ (b) $6\sqrt{3}$ (c) $5\sqrt{3}$ (d) $2\sqrt{3}$

14. If AB is a double ordinates of the hyperbola $\frac{x^2}{a^2} - \frac{y^2}{b^2} = 1$ such that OAB is an equilateral triangle, where O being the centre of the hyperbola, then the eccentricity e of the hyperbola satisfies

(a) $e > \frac{\sqrt{3}}{2}$ (b) $e > \frac{2}{\sqrt{3}}$
(c) $e < \frac{1}{\sqrt{3}}$ (d) $e < \frac{2}{\sqrt{3}}$

15. From any point on the hyperbola $h_1 : \frac{x^2}{a^2} - \frac{y^2}{b^2} = 1$ and tangents are drawn to the hyperbola $h_2 : \frac{x^2}{a^2} - \frac{y^2}{b^2} = 2$, the area cut off by the chord of contact on the asymptotes of h_2 is equal to

(a) $\frac{4b^2}{\sqrt{e^2 - 1}}$ (b) $\frac{4a^2}{\sqrt{e^2 - 1}}$
(c) $4a$ (d) $\frac{4b}{\sqrt{e^2 - 1}}$

More than One Correct Type Questions

16. The equation $16x^2 - 3y^2 - 32x - 12y - 44 = 0$ represents a hyperbola with

(a) length of the transverse axis $= 2\sqrt{3}$
(b) length of the conjugate axis $= 8$
(c) centre at $(1, -2)$
(d) eccentricity $= \sqrt{19}$

17. If $P(x_1, y_1)$, $Q(x_2, y_2)$, $R(x_3, y_3)$ and $S(x_4, y_4)$ are 4 concyclic points on the rectangular hyperbola $xy = c^2$, the coordinates of the orthocentre of the ΔPQR are

(a) $(x_4, -y_4)$
(b) (x_4, y_4)
(c) $(-x_4, -y_4)$
(d) $(-x_4, y_4)$

18. The line $y = x + 5$ touches

(a) the parabola $y^2 = 20x$ (b) the ellipse $9x^2 + 16y^2 = 144$
(c) the hyperbola $\frac{x^2}{29} - \frac{y^2}{4} = 1$ (d) the circle $x^2 + y^2 = 25$

19. Which of the following equations in parametric form can represent a hyperbola, where t is a parameter?

(a) $x = \frac{a}{2}\left(t + \frac{1}{t}\right)$ and $y = \frac{b}{2}\left(t - \frac{1}{t}\right)$
(b) $\frac{tx}{a} - \frac{y}{b} + t = 0$ and $\frac{x}{a} + \frac{ty}{b} - 1 = 0$
(c) $x = e^t + e^{-t}$ and $y = e^t - e^{-t}$
(d) $x^2 - 6 = 2\cos t$ and $y^2 + 2 = 4\cos^2\left(\frac{t}{2}\right)$

20. Given ellipse $\frac{x^2}{16} + \frac{y^2}{7} = 1$ and the hyperbola $\frac{x^2}{144} - \frac{y^2}{81} = \frac{1}{25}$, if the ordinate of one of the points of intersection is produced to cut an asymptote at P, then which of the following is true?

(a) They have the same foci.
(b) Square of the ordinate of point of intersection is $\frac{63}{25}$.
(c) Sum of the squares of coordinate of P is 16.
(d) P lies on the auxiliary circle formed by ellipse.

21. Let the eccentricity of the hyperbola $\frac{x^2}{a^2} - \frac{y^2}{b^2} = 1$ be reciprocal to that of the ellipse $x^2 + 4y^2 = 4$. If the hyperbola passes through a focus of the ellipse, then

(a) the equation of the hyperbola is $\frac{x^2}{3} - \frac{y^2}{2} = 1$.
(b) a focus of the hyperbola is $(2, 0)$.
(c) the eccentricity of the hyperbola is $\sqrt{\frac{5}{3}}$.
(d) the equation of the hyperbola is $x^2 - 3y^2 = 3$.

22. Tangents are drawn to the hyperbola $\frac{x^2}{9} - \frac{y^2}{4} = 1$, parallel to the straight line $2x - y = 1$. The points of contact of the tangents on the hyperbola are

(a) $\left(\frac{9}{2\sqrt{2}}, \frac{1}{\sqrt{2}}\right)$ (b) $\left(-\frac{9}{2\sqrt{2}}, -\frac{1}{\sqrt{2}}\right)$
(c) $(3\sqrt{3}, -2\sqrt{2})$ (d) $(-3\sqrt{3}, 2\sqrt{2})$

23. Consider the hyperbola $H: x^2 - y^2 = 1$ and a circle S with centre $N(x_2, 0)$. Suppose that H and S touch each other at a point $P(x_1, y_1)$ with $x_1 > 1$ and $y_1 > 0$. The common tangent to H and S at P intersects the X-axis at point M. If (l, m) is the centroid of the triangle PMN, then the correct expression(s) is(are)

(a) $\frac{dl}{dx_1} = 1 - \frac{1}{3x_1^2}$ for $x_1 > 1$ (b) $\frac{dm}{dx_1} = \frac{x_1}{3(\sqrt{(x_1^2 - 1)})}$ for $x_1 > 1$

(c) $\frac{dl}{dx_1} = 1 + \frac{1}{3x_1^2}$ for $x_1 > 1$ (d) $\frac{dm}{dy_1} = \frac{1}{3}$ for $y_1 > 0$

Passage Based Questions

Passage I

(Q. Nos. 24 to 25)

- Let $P(\theta_1)$ and $Q(\theta_2)$ are the extremities of any focal chord of the hyperbola $\frac{x^2}{a^2} - \frac{y^2}{b^2} = 1$ whose eccentricity is e. Let θ be the angle between its asymptotes. Tangents are drawn to the hyperbola at some arbitrary point R. These tangent meet the coordinate axes at the points A and B respectively. The rectangle $OACB$ (O being the origin) is completed, then

24. Locus of point C is

(a) $\frac{b^2}{x^2} - \frac{a^2}{y^2} = 1$ (b) $\frac{b^2}{x^2} + \frac{a^2}{y^2} = 1$

(c) $\frac{a^2}{x^2} + \frac{b^2}{y^2} = 1$ (d) $\frac{a^2}{x^2} - \frac{b^2}{y^2} = 1$

25. If $\cos^2\left(\frac{\theta_1 + \theta_2}{2}\right) = \lambda \cos^2\left(\frac{\theta_1 - \theta_2}{2}\right)$, then λ is equal to

(a) $\left(\frac{a^2 + b^2}{a^2}\right)$ (b) $\left(\frac{a^2 + b^2}{b^2}\right)$

(c) $\left(\frac{a^2 + b^2}{ab}\right)$ (d) $\left(\frac{a^2 + b^2}{2ab}\right)$

Passage II

(Q. Nos. 26 to 27)

- Let $P(x, y)$ be a variable point such that $|\sqrt{(x-1)^2 + (y-2)^2} - \sqrt{(x-5)^2 + (y-5)^2}| = 4$ which represents a hyperbola.

26. The eccentricity of the corresponding conjugate hyperbola is

(a) $\frac{5}{4}$ (b) $\frac{4}{3}$

(c) $\frac{5}{3}$ (d) $\frac{3}{2}$

27. Locus of point of intersection of two perpendicular tangents to the hyperbola is

(a) $(x-3)^2 + (y - 7/2)^2 = \frac{1}{4}$ (b) $(x-3)^2 + (y - 7/2)^2 = \frac{3}{4}$

(c) $(x-3)^2 + (y - 7/2)^2 = \frac{5}{4}$ (d) $(x-3)^2 + (y - 7/2)^2 = \frac{7}{4}$

Passage III

(Q. Nos. 28 to 29)

- The graph of the conic $x^2 - (y-1)^2 = 1$ has one tangent line with positive slope that passes through the origin. The point of tangency being (a, b).

28. The value of $\sin^{-1}\left(\frac{a}{b}\right)$ is

(a) $\frac{5\pi}{12}$ (b) $\frac{\pi}{6}$

(c) $\frac{\pi}{4}$ (d) $\frac{\pi}{3}$

29. Length of the latusrectum of the conic is

(a) 1 (b) $\sqrt{2}$

(c) 2 (d) 4

Passage IV

(Q. Nos. 30 to 31)

- A point P moves such that the sum of the slopes of the normals drawn from it to the hyperbola $xy = 4$ is equal to the sum of the ordinates of feet of normals. The locus of P is a curve C.

30. The equation of the curve C is

(a) $x^2 = 2y$ (b) $x^2 = 4y$

(c) $x^2 = 6y$ (d) $x^2 = 8y$

31. The area of the equilateral triangle inscribed in the curve C having one vertex as the vertex of curve C is

(a) $8\sqrt{3}$ sq units (b) $12\sqrt{3}$ sq units

(c) $27\sqrt{3}$ sq units (d) $48\sqrt{3}$ sq units

Stem Based Questions

Stem I

(Q. Nos. 32 and 33)

- Tangents are drawn to the hyperbola $x^2 - 9y^2 = 9$ from (3, 2). Answer the following questions.

32. The area of the triangle formed by the tangents and chord contact of (3, 2) is ....

33. If the mid-point of the intercept of the tangent at (3, 0) between the asymptotes is (α, β), then value of $|\alpha + \beta|$ is ....

Stem II

(Q. Nos. 34 and 35)

- The locus of the foot of the perpendicular drawn from a focus onto a tangent to the hyperbola is the auxiliary circle. Consider the hyperbola whose foci are $(5,6)$ and $(-3,-2)$. The foot of the perpendicular from the focus upon a tangent is the point $(2,5)$. Answer the following questions.

34. Square of length of the conjugate axis of the hyperbola is ....

35. If the directrix of the hyperbola corresponding to focus $(5, 6)$ is $ax + by + c = 0$, then the value of $|a+b+c|$ is ....

Stem III

(Q. Nos. 36 and 37)

- Let $H: \frac{x^2}{a^2} - \frac{y^2}{b^2} = 1$, where $a > b$, be a hyperbola in the XY-plane whose conjugate axis LM subtends an angle of at one 60° of its vertices N. The area of the ΔLMN be $4\sqrt{3}$.

36. The length of conjugate axis of H is ......

37. The distance between the foci of H is ......

Single Integer Type Questions

38. ABC is a triangle such that $\angle ABC = 2\angle BAC$. If AB is fixed and locus of C is a hyperbola, then the eccentricity of the hyperbola is ....

39. Point P lie on $2xy = 1$. A triangle is constructed by P, S and S' (where S and S' are foci). The locus of ex-centre opposite S (S and P lie in first quadrant) is $(x + py)^2 = (\sqrt{2} - 1)^2 (x - y)^2 + q$, then the value of $p + q$ is ....

40. A transversal cut the same branch of a hyperbola $\frac{x^2}{a^2} - \frac{y^2}{b^2} = 1$ in P, P' and the asymptotes in Q, Q'; then $(PQ + PQ') - (P'Q' + P'Q)$ is equal to ....

41. The equation of transverse axis is hyperbola passing through origin having asymptotes $3x - 4y - 1 = 0$ and $4x - 3y - 6 = 0$ is $ax + by - c = 0$, $a, b, c \in N$ and $gcd(a, b, c,) = 1$, then the value of $a + b + c$ is ......

42. If a rectangular hyperbola with centre C is cut by a circle of radius r at four points P_1, P_2, P_3 and P_4, and $CP_1^2 + CP_2^2 + CP_3^2 + CP_4^2$ is λr^2, then λ is equal to......

Numerical Value Type Questions

43. A variable straight line of slope 4 intersects the hyperbola $xy = 1$ at two points. If the locus of the point which divides the line segment between these two points in the ratio $1:2$ is $ax^2 + by^2 + cxy + d = 0$, then $\frac{a+b+c+d}{1000}$ is equal to ......

44. The graphs of $x^2 + 4y^2 + 6x - 24y + 72 = 0$ and $x^2 - y^2 + 6x + 16y - 46 = 0$ intersect at four points. The sum of distance of the four points from point $(-3, 2)$ is ......

45. Let the double ordinate PP' of the hyperbola $\frac{x^2}{4} - \frac{y^2}{3} = 1$ is produced both sides to meet asymptotes of hyperbola in Q and Q' and the product $(PQ)(PQ')$ is equal to λ, then λ^3 is equal to ....

46. A straight line is drawn parallel to the conjugate axis of a hyperbola to meet it and the conjugate hyperbola in the points P and Q. If the tangents at P and Q meet the curve $\frac{y^4}{b^4}\left(\frac{y^2}{b^2} + \frac{x^2}{a^2}\right) = \frac{\lambda x^2}{a^2}$, then the value of $\frac{\lambda}{10}$ is ....

47. A variable straight line of slope 4 intersects the hyperbola $xy = 1$ at two points. If the locus of the point which divides the line segment between these two points in the ratio $1:2$ is $\alpha x^2 + y^2 + \beta xy = 2$, then $\alpha \cdot \beta$ is equal to ....

Matching Type Questions

48. Match the following.

Column I		Column II	
(A) If λ be the length of the latusrectum of the hyperbola $16x^2 - 9y^2 + 32x + 36y - 164 = 0$, then 3λ is divisible by		(p)	4
(B) If the chord $x\cos\alpha + y\sin\alpha = p$ of the hyperbola $\frac{x^2}{16} - \frac{y^2}{18} = 1$ subtends a right angle at the centre, a circle touches the given chord and concentric with hyperbola, then the diameter of circle is divisible by		(q)	6
(C) For the hyperbola $xy = 8$ any tangent of it at P meets coordinate axes at Q and R, then the area of triangle CQR is divisible by (where C is centre of the hyperbola)		(r)	8
(D) For the hyperbola $x^2 - 3y^2 = 9$, acute angle between its asymptotes is $\frac{\pi\lambda}{24}$, then λ is divisible by		(s)	16

49. Match the following.

Column I	Column II
(A) If the vertex of a hyperbola bisects the distance between its centre and the corresponding focus, then the ratio of the square of its conjugate axis to the square of its transverse axis is	(p) 6
(b) With one focus of the hyperbola $\frac{x^2}{9} - \frac{y^2}{16} = 1$ as the centre, a circle is drawn which is tangent to the hyperbola with no part of the circle being outside the hyperbola. The radius of the circle is	(q) 3
(C) If S_1 and S_2 are the foci of the hyperbola whose length of the transverse axis is 4 and that of the conjugate axis is 6, and S_3 and S_4 are the foci of the conjugate hyperbola, then the area of quadrilateral $S_1S_2S_3S_4$ is	(r) 2
(D) If equation of hyperbola whose conjugate axis is 5 and distance between its foci is 13, is $ax^2 - by^2 = c$, where a and b are co-prime, then $\frac{3ab}{2c}$ is	(s) 26

50. If e_1 and e_2 are the roots of the equation $x^2 - \lambda x + 2 = 0$

Column I	Column II
(A) If e_1 and e_2 are the eccentricities of ellipse and hyperbola respectively, then the values of λ are	(p) $2\sqrt{2}$
(B) If both e_1 and e_2 are the eccentricities of the hyperbolas, then the values of λ are	(q) $2\sqrt{3}$
(C) If e_1 and e_2 are the eccentricities of the hyperbola and conjugate hyperbola, then the values of λ are	(r) $2\sqrt{5}$
(D) If e_1 is the eccentricity of the hyperbola for which there exist infinite points from which perpendicular tangents can be drawn and e_2 is the eccentricity of the hyperbola in which no such points exist, then the values of λ are	(s) $2\sqrt{6}$

Previous Years Questions

51. Consider the hyperbola $\frac{x^2}{100} - \frac{y^2}{64} = 1$ with foci at S and S_1 where S lies on the positive X-axis. Let P be a point on the hyperbola, in the first quadrant. Let $\angle SPS_1 = \alpha$ with $\alpha < \frac{\pi}{2}$. The straight line passing through the point S and having the same slope as that of the tangent at P to the hyperbola, intersects the straight line S_1P at p_1. Let δ be the distance of P from the straight line Sp_1 and $\beta = S_1P$. Then, the greatest integer less than or equal to $\frac{\beta\delta}{9} \sin \frac{\alpha}{2}$ is ......

[Numerical Value Type, 2022 Adv.]

52. Let a and b be positive real numbers such that $a > 1$ and $b < a$. Let P be a point in the first quadrant that lies on the hyperbola $\frac{x^2}{a^2} - \frac{y^2}{b^2} = 1$. Suppose the tangent to the hyperbola at P passes through the point (1, 0) and suppose the normal to the hyperbola at P cuts off equal intercepts on the coordinate axes. Let Δ denote the area of the triangle formed by the tangent at P, the normal at P and the X-axis. If e denotes the eccentricity of the hyperbola, then which of the following statements is/are TRUE ?

[Single Correct Type, 2020 Adv.]

(a) $1 < e < \sqrt{2}$

(b) $\sqrt{2} < e < 2$

(c) $\Delta = a^4$

(d) $\Delta = b^4$

EXERCISE 3

Challenging Problems

1. PP' is a diameter of the rectangular hyperbola $xy = c^2$. Show that the intersection of the tangent of P with the straight line through P' parallel to either asymptote is the locus $xy + 3c^2 = 0$.

2. The tangent at a point P of a rectangular hyperbola meets the asymptotes at L and M and C is the centre of the hyperbola. Prove that
$PL = PM = CP$.

3. Prove that the perpendicular focal chords of a rectangular hyperbola are equal.

4. The normals at three points P, Q and R on a rectangular hyperbola intersect at a point T on the curve. Prove that the centre of the hyperbola is the centroid of the triangle PQR.

5. Find the equation of the hyperbola whose asymptotes are $x + 2y + 3 = 0$ and $3x + 4y + 5 = 0$ and which passes through the point $(1, -1)$. Find also the equation of the conjugate hyperbola.

6. A triangle is inscribed in $xy = c^2$ and two of its sides are parallel to $y = m_1 x$ and $y = m_2 x$ prove that the third side envelopes the hyperbola $4m_1 m_2 xy = c^2 (m_1 + m_2)^2$.

7. In both an ellipse and a hyperbola, prove that the focal distance of any point and the perpendicular from the centre upon the tangent at it meet on a circle whose centre is the focus and whose radius is the semi-transverse axis.

8. Show that an infinite number of triangles can be inscribed in the rectangular hyperbola $xy = c^2$, whose sides all touch the parabola $y^2 = 4ax$.

9. A circle with centre $(3\alpha, 3\beta)$ and of variable radius cuts the rectangular hyperbola $x^2 - y^2 = 9a^2$ at the points P, Q, R and S. Prove that the locus of the centroid of the triangle PQR is $(x - 2\alpha)^2 - (y - 2\beta)^2 = a^2$.

10. If the normals at (x_i, y_i), $i = 1, 2, 3, 4$ on the rectangular hyperbola, $xy = c^2$, meet at the point (α, β) show that
(i) $\Sigma x_i = \alpha$ (ii) $\Sigma y_i = \beta$
(iii) $\Pi x_i = \Pi y_i = -c^4$ (iv) $\Sigma x_i^2 = \alpha^2$
(v) $\Sigma y_i^2 = \beta^2$

11. If a circle cuts a rectangular hyperbola $xy = c^2$ in A, B, C and D and the parameters of these four points be t_1, t_2, t_3 and t_4 respectively prove the following :
(i) $t_1 t_2 t_3 t_4 = 1$, find the value of $\Sigma \frac{1}{t_1}$.
(ii) If H be the orthocentre of the triangle ABC, then H and D are extremities of a diameter of the rectangular hyperbola.
(iii) The centre of mean position of the four points bisects the distance between the centres of the two curves.
(iv) The centre of the circle through A, B and C is
$$\left[\frac{c}{2}\left(t_1 + t_2 + t_3 + \frac{1}{t_1 t_2 t_3}\right), \frac{c}{2}\left(\frac{1}{t_1} + \frac{1}{t_2} + \frac{1}{t_3} + t_1 t_2 t_3\right)\right].$$

12. If a hyperbola be rectangular and its equation be $xy = c^2$, prove that the locus of the middle points of chords of constant length $2d$ is $(x^2 + y^2)(xy - c^2) = d^2 xy$.

13. If four points be taken on a rectangular hyperbola such that the chord joining any two is perpendicular to the chord joining the other two, and if α, β, γ and δ be the inclinations to either asymptote of the straight line joining these points to the centre, prove that $\tan \alpha \tan \beta \tan \gamma \tan \delta = 1$.

14. A rectangular hyperbola passes through two fixed points and its asymptotes are in given directions. Prove that its vertices lie on an ellipse and hyperbola which intersect orthogonally.

15. Let normals are drawn from (α, β) to the hyperbola $xy = 1$, and (x_i, y_i), $i = 1, 2, 3, 4$ be the feet of the co-normal points. If the algebraic sum of the perpendicular distances drawn from (x_i, y_i), $i = 1, 2, 3, 4$ onto a variable line vanishes, show that the variable line passes through the point $(\alpha/4, \beta/4)$.

Answer Key

Exercise 1

1. (a)	2. (d)	3. (c)	4. (a)	5. (a)	6. (b)	7. (a)	8. (b)	9. (b)	10. (c)
11. (d)	12. (b)	13. (c)	14. (b)	15. (b)	16. (a)	17. (c)	18. (b)	19. (b)	20. (b)
21. (b)	22. (d)	23. (a)	24. (a)	25. (2)	26. (8)	27. (4)	28. (3)	29. (16)	30. (3)
31. (4)	32. (7)	33. (2)	34. (6)	35. (c)	36. (d)	37. (c)	38. (b)	39. (d)	40. (b)
41. (a)	42. (4)	43. (61)	44. (51)	45. (182)	46. (b)	47. (d)	48. (b)	49. (12)	50. (8)
51. (216)	52. (d)	53. (b)	54. (c)	55. (c)	56. (d)	57. (b)	58. (b)	59. (d)	60. (20)
61. (88)	62. (12)	63. (85)	64. (42)	65. (c)	66. (d)	67. (c)	68. (a)	69. (a)	70. (d)
71. (9)	72. (2)	73. (c)							

Exercise 2

1. (c)	2. (b)	3. (c)	4. (b)	5. (c)	6. (a)	7. (b)	8. (d)	9. (b)	10. (c)
11. (d)	12. (a)	13. (b)	14. (b)	15. (a)	16. (a,b,c)	17. (b,c)	18. (a,b,c)	19. (a,c,d)	20. (c,d)
21. (b,d)	22. (a,b)	23. (a,b,d)	24. (d)	25. (a)	26. (c)	27. (d)	28. (c)	29. (c)	30. (b)
31. (d)	32. (8)	33. (3)	34. (88)	35. (7)	36. (4)	37. (8)	38. (2)	39. (5)	40. (0)
41. (7)	42. (4)	43. (0.025)	44. (40)	45. (18)	46. (04)	47. (160)			

48. (A) → (p,r,s), (B) → (p,q,r), (C) → (p,r,s), (D) → (p,r)

49. (A) → (q), (B) → (r), (C) → (s), (D) → (p)

50. (A) → (q,r,s), (B) → (p), (C) → (p), (D) → (q,r,s,)

51. (7)

52. (a,d)

Solutions

Exercise 1 - JEE Main Pattern

1. Since, $PF_1 \cdot PF_2 = e\left(x_1 - \frac{a}{e}\right) \cdot e\left(x_1 + \frac{a}{e}\right)$

$$= e^2x_1^2 - a^2$$

$$= 2x_1^2 - a^2 \quad [\text{for rectangular hyperbola, } e = \sqrt{2}]$$

$$= x_1^2 + x_1^2 - a^2$$

If $P(x_1, y_1)$, then given hyperbola become $x_1^2 - y_1^2 = a^2$

$\therefore \quad PF_1 \cdot PF_2 = x_1^2 + y_1^2 = (OP)^2$

$\Rightarrow \quad \lambda = 1$

2. Let the point of contact of normal from point $P(h, k)$ be $R(t)$ for the hyperbola $xy = c^2$

Then, the equation of normal is $ct^4 - xt^3 + yt - c = 0$

$\Rightarrow ct^4 - ht^3 + kt - c = 0 \qquad [\because \text{ it passes through } (h,k)]$...(i)

$\Rightarrow t_1^2 + t_2^2 + t_3^2 + t_4^2 = \lambda \qquad$ [given] ... (ii)

From Eq. (i),

$$\Sigma t_i = \frac{h}{c}, \Sigma t_i t_j = 0$$

$\therefore \quad (\Sigma t_i)^2 - 2\Sigma t_i t_j = t_1^2 + t_2^2 + t_3^2 + t_4^2$

$\Rightarrow \quad \left(\frac{h}{c}\right)^2 - 0 = \lambda$

or $\quad h^2 = \lambda c^2$

$\therefore$ Locus of P is $x^2 = \lambda c^2$

3. Let A and B be (α, β) and (β, α), respectively.

$\because$ A and B are symmetrical about the line $y = x$.

So, tangents at A and B will be mirror images of each other about $y = x$.

Thus, point of intersection will lie on $y = x$.

4. Let $P(h,k)$ be any point on any one member of hyperbola family, having equation $\frac{x^2}{a^2} - \frac{y^2}{b^2} = 1$; b is any arbitrary constant, then its asymptotes are given by $y = \pm \frac{b}{a}x$, then according to question,

$$|k| = \frac{\left|\pm \frac{b}{a}h - k\right|}{\sqrt{\left(\frac{b^2}{a^2} + 1\right)}}$$

$\Rightarrow \quad k^2 = \left(\pm \frac{b}{a}h - k\right)^2 \left(\frac{a^2}{a^2 + b^2}\right)$

or $\quad k^2 = \frac{(\pm bh - ak)^2}{(a^2 + b^2)} \qquad$ ...(i)

Further, (h,k) lies on hyperbola.

$\therefore \quad \frac{h^2}{a^2} - \frac{k^2}{b^2} = 1 \Rightarrow b = \sqrt{\left(\frac{a^2k^2}{h^2 - a^2}\right)} \qquad$ ...(ii)

From Eqs. (i) and (ii), we get

$$(k^2 - h^2) = \pm 2h\sqrt{(h^2 - a^2)}$$

$\Rightarrow \quad (k^2 - h^2)^2 = 4h^2(h^2 - a^2)$

$\therefore$ Required locus is $(x^2 - y^2)^2 = 4x^2(x^2 - a^2)$

5. We know that if a circle cuts a rectangular hyperbola, then arithmetic mean of points of intersections is the mid-point of centre of hyperbola and circle.

So, $\quad \frac{3 + 5 + 2 + (-1)}{4} = \frac{-g + 1}{2}$

and $\quad \frac{4 + 3 + 6 + 0}{4} = \frac{-f + 2}{2}$

$\therefore \quad g + f = -8$

6. We know that eccentricities of a parabola and rectangular hyperbola are 1 and $\sqrt{2}$, respectively. Also, irrational roots occur in conjugate pair, thus roots of $f(x) = 0$ are 1, $\sqrt{2}$ and $-\sqrt{2}$.

$\therefore \quad f(x) = (x - 1)(x - \sqrt{2})(x + \sqrt{2})$

$$= x^3 - x^2 - 2x + 2$$

$\therefore \quad a + b + c + d = 1 - 1 - 2 + 2 = 0$

7. Let the point be (α, β).

Then, $\beta = \alpha + c$

Chord of contact of hyperbola, $T = 0$.

$\therefore \quad \frac{x\alpha}{2} - \frac{y\beta}{1} = 1$

$\Rightarrow \quad \frac{x\alpha}{2} - y(\alpha + c) = 1$

$\Rightarrow \quad \left(\frac{x}{2} - y\right)\alpha - (yc + 1) = 0$

Since, this passes through point (x_1, y_1).

$\therefore \quad x_1 = 2y_1$ and $y_1c + 1 = 0$

$\therefore \quad y_1 = \frac{x_1}{2}$

Hence, $\quad \frac{x_1}{y_1} = 2$

8. Eliminating x, we get

$$\frac{y^2}{b^2} + \frac{y}{ab} + 1 = 0$$

This equation has real and distinct roots.

$\therefore \quad \dfrac{1}{a^2b^2} - \dfrac{4}{b^2} > 0$

i.e. $\quad \dfrac{1}{a^2} > 4$ or $a^2 < \dfrac{1}{4}$

$\Rightarrow \; a < \dfrac{1}{2}$ and hence the conics intersect if $0 < a < \dfrac{1}{2}$.

9. Since, $\dfrac{\tan\left(\frac{1}{2}\angle ABC\right)}{\tan\left(\frac{1}{2}\angle BAC\right)} = \dfrac{3}{1}$

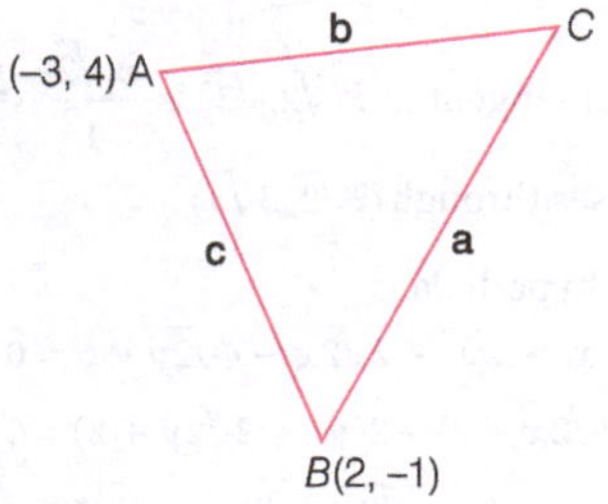

or $\quad \dfrac{\tan\left(\frac{B}{2}\right)}{\tan\left(\frac{A}{2}\right)} = 3$ or $\dfrac{\frac{\Delta}{s(s-b)}}{\frac{\Delta}{s(s-a)}} = 3$

or $\quad \dfrac{s-a}{s-b} = 3$

$\Rightarrow \quad s - a = 3s - 3b$

or $\quad 2s = 3b - a$

or $\quad a + b + c = 3b - a$

or $\quad b - a = \dfrac{c}{2}$

or $\quad AC - BC = \text{constant}$

$\therefore$ Locus of C is a hyperbola, whose foci are A and B.

$\therefore$ Distance between foci $= |AB| = 5\sqrt{2}$.

10.

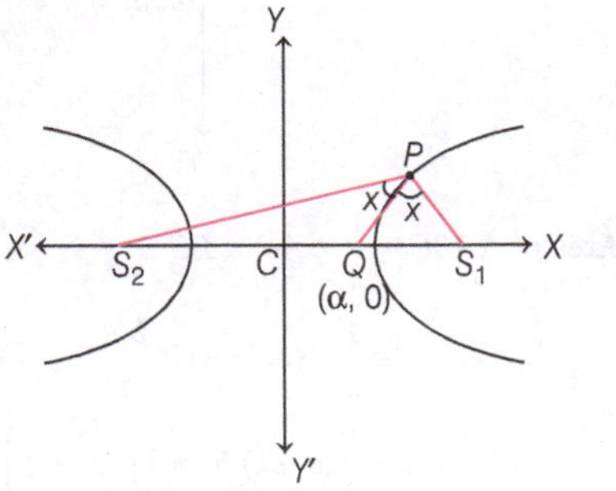

Let $\quad P \equiv (x_1, y_1)$

It is clear from figure,

$$\alpha > 0 \quad \text{... (i)}$$

and $Q(\alpha, 0)$ lies outside of the hyperbola, then

$$\frac{x^2}{a^2} - \frac{y^2}{b^2} - 1 \le 0$$

$\Rightarrow \quad \dfrac{\alpha^2}{a^2} - 1 \le 0$

or $\quad \alpha^2 \le a^2$

$\therefore \quad -a \le \alpha \le a \quad \text{... (ii)}$

From Eqs. (i) and (ii), we get

$$0 < \alpha \le a$$

$$\alpha \in (0, a]$$

11. Since, angle between asymptotes $= 2\tan^{-1}\left(\dfrac{b}{a}\right) = 120°$

or $\quad \tan^{-1}\left(\dfrac{b}{a}\right) = 60°$ or $\dfrac{b}{a} = \sqrt{3}$

$\therefore \quad b = a\sqrt{3}$ or $b^2 = 3a^2$

$\Rightarrow \quad a^2 = 3 \quad [\because b^2 = 9]$

Required locus is director circle of the hyperbola and which is $x^2 + y^2 = a^2 - b^2 = 3 - 9 = -6$, which is not possible.

Now, angle between asymptotes $= 2\tan^{-1}\left(\dfrac{b}{a}\right) = 60°$.

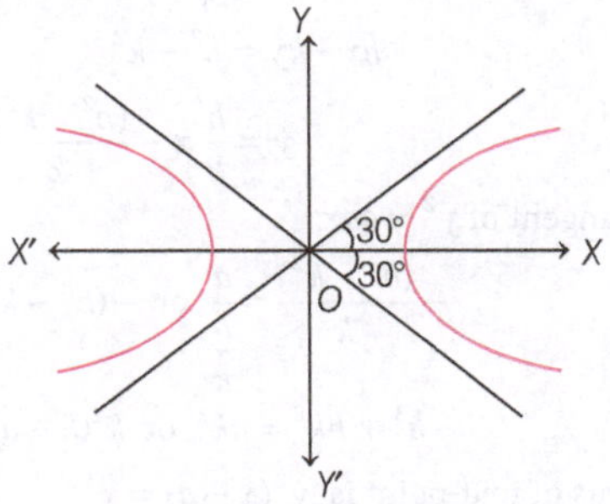

or $\quad \tan^{-1}\left(\dfrac{b}{a}\right) = 30°$

or $\quad \dfrac{b}{a} = \dfrac{1}{\sqrt{3}}$

or $\quad a^2 = 3b^2 = 27 \quad [\because b^2 = 9]$

$\therefore$ Required locus is $x^2 + y^2 = a^2 - b^2 = 27 - 9 = 18$

12. Equation of chord joining α and β is

$$\frac{x}{a}\cos\left(\frac{\alpha-\beta}{2}\right) - \frac{y}{b}\sin\left(\frac{\alpha+\beta}{2}\right) = \cos\left(\frac{\alpha+\beta}{2}\right)$$

Put $\alpha + \beta = 3\pi$, then $\dfrac{x}{a}\cos\left(\dfrac{\alpha-\beta}{2}\right) + \dfrac{y}{b} = 0$

It passes through the centre (0, 0).

13. Let $P(a\cos\theta, b\sin\theta)$ be on the ellipse.

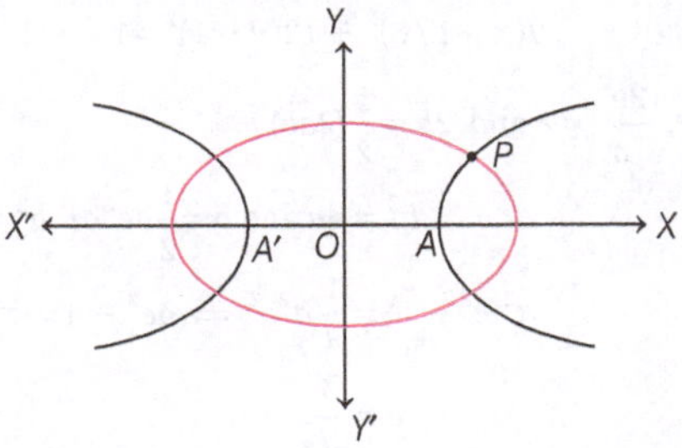

$\therefore$ Equation of tangent at P on ellipse is

$$\frac{x}{a}\cos\theta + \frac{y}{b}\sin\theta = 1 \quad \text{... (i)}$$

and equation of tangent at P on $x^2 - y^2 = c^2$ is

$$x(a\cos\theta) - y(b\sin\theta) = c^2 \quad \text{...(ii)}$$

Since, curves intersect at right angle, then

$$-\frac{b}{a}\cot\theta \times \frac{a}{b}\cot\theta = -1$$

$$\therefore \quad \tan^2\theta = 1 \quad \text{... (iii)}$$

Since, $P(a\cos\theta, b\sin\theta)$ also lies on hyperbola.

$$\therefore \quad (a\cos\theta)^2 - (b\sin\theta)^2 = c^2$$

On dividing both sides by $\cos^2\theta$, then

$$a^2 - b^2\tan^2\theta = c^2(1 + \tan^2\theta)$$

or $$a^2 - b^2 = 2c^2 \quad \text{[from Eq. (iii)]}$$

14. Let mid-point of the chord be (h, k).

$\therefore$ Equation of chord of $x^2 - y^2 = a^2$ is

$$T = S_1$$

$$hx - ky = h^2 - k^2$$

or $$y = \frac{h}{k}x - \frac{(h^2 - k^2)}{k},$$

which is tangent of $y^2 = 4ax$.

$$\therefore \quad -\frac{(h^2 - k^2)}{k} = \frac{a}{\frac{h}{k}} \text{ or } -(h^2 - k^2) = \frac{ak^2}{h}$$

or $$-h^3 + hk^2 = ak^2 \text{ or } k^2(h - a) = h^3$$

Hence, locus of mid-point is $y^2(x - a) = x^3$.

15. It is clear from the figure, the common tangent to the circle $x^2 + y^2 = 1$ and hyperbola $x^2 - y^2 = 1$, is $x = 1$, which is nearer to P (1/2, 1) and given one focus at P (1/2, 1), so the equation of the directrix is $x = 1$. Hence, the equation of the ellipse is

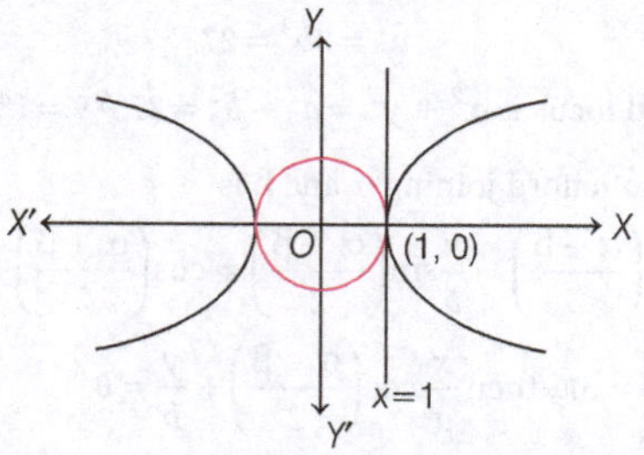

$$\sqrt{(x - 1/2)^2 + (y - 1)^2} = \frac{1}{2}|x - 1|$$

$$\Rightarrow \quad 9(x - 1/3)^2 + 12(y - 1)^2 = 1$$

16. Since, $\frac{2b^2}{a} = 8$ and $2b = \frac{1}{2}(2ae)$

$$\Rightarrow \quad b^2 = 4a \text{ and } b = \frac{1}{2}ae \text{ or } b^2 = \frac{1}{4}a^2e^2$$

$$\Rightarrow \quad a^2(e^2 - 1) = \frac{1}{4}a^2e^2 \Rightarrow 4e^2 - 4 = e^2 \text{ or } e^2 = \frac{4}{3}$$

$$\therefore \quad e = \frac{2}{\sqrt{3}}$$

17. Let equation of hyperbola be $\frac{x^2}{a^2} - \frac{y^2}{b^2} = 1$

Since, it passes through $P(\sqrt{2}, \sqrt{3})$, then $\frac{2}{a^2} - \frac{3}{b^2} = 1$

$$\Rightarrow \quad 2b^2 - 3a^2 = a^2b^2 \quad \text{...(i)}$$

and $ae = 2 \Rightarrow a^2 + b^2 = 4$ ...(ii)

From Eqs. (i) and (ii), we get $2(4 - a^2) - 3a^2 = a^2(4 - a^2)$

$$\Rightarrow a^4 - 9a^2 + 8 = 0 \Rightarrow (a^2 - 1)(a^2 - 8) = 0$$

$$\therefore \quad a^2 = 1 \quad [\because a^2 \neq 8]$$

From Eq. (ii), $b^2 = 3$

$\therefore$ Equation of hyperbola is $\frac{x^2}{1} - \frac{y^2}{3} = 1$

Equation of tangent at $P(\sqrt{2}, \sqrt{3})$ is $\frac{x\sqrt{2}}{1} - \frac{y\sqrt{3}}{3} = 1$

which passes through $(2\sqrt{2}, 3\sqrt{3})$.

18. The given hyperbola is

$$x^2 - 2y^2 - 2\sqrt{2}x - 4\sqrt{2}y - 6 = 0$$

$$\Rightarrow (x^2 - 2\sqrt{2}x + 2) - 2(y^2 + 2\sqrt{2}y + 2) = 6 + 2 - 4$$

$$\Rightarrow \quad (x - \sqrt{2})^2 - 2(y + \sqrt{2})^2 = 4$$

$$\Rightarrow \quad \frac{(x - \sqrt{2})^2}{2^2} - \frac{(y + \sqrt{2})^2}{(\sqrt{2})^2} = 1$$

$$\therefore \quad a = 2, b = \sqrt{2}$$

$$\Rightarrow \quad e = \sqrt{\left(1 + \frac{2}{4}\right)} = \sqrt{\frac{3}{2}}$$

Clearly, ΔABC is a right triangle.

$$B \equiv \left(ae, \frac{b^2}{a}\right)$$

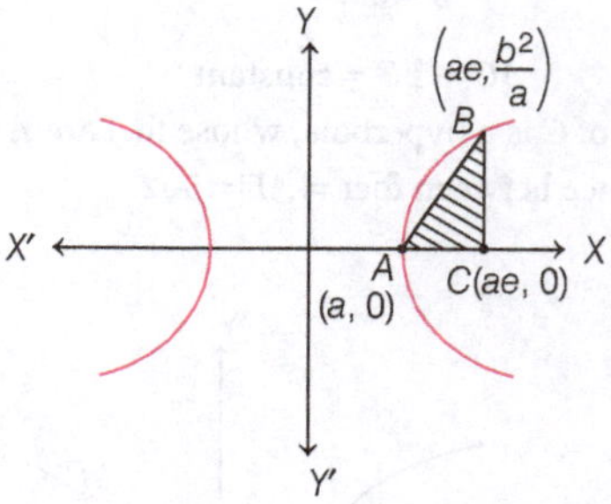

$$\therefore \quad \text{Area of } \Delta ABC = \frac{1}{2} \times AC \times BC$$

$$= \frac{1}{2} \times (ae - a) \times \frac{b^2}{a}$$

$$= \frac{1}{2}(e - 1)b^2 = \frac{1}{2}\left(\sqrt{\frac{3}{2}} - 1\right) \cdot 2 = \left(\sqrt{\frac{3}{2}} - 1\right)$$

19. The given hyperbola is

$$x^2 - y^2 = \frac{1}{2}, \quad \text{... (i)}$$

which is rectangular hyperbola

$$\therefore \quad e = \sqrt{2}$$

Let the ellipse be $\frac{x^2}{a^2} + \frac{y^2}{b^2} = 1$.

Its eccentricity $= \frac{1}{\sqrt{2}}$

$\therefore \quad b^2 = a^2(1 - e^2) = a^2\left(1 - \frac{1}{2}\right) = \frac{a^2}{2}$

So, the equation of ellipse becomes

$$x^2 + 2y^2 = a^2 \quad \text{... (ii)}$$

Let the hyperbola (i) and ellipse (ii) intersect each other at $P(x_1, y_1)$.

$\therefore$ (Slope of hyperbola (i) at (x_1, y_1)) $\times$ (Slope of ellipse (ii) at (x_1, y_1)) $= -1$

$\Rightarrow \quad \frac{x_1}{y_1} \times \frac{-x_1}{2y_1} = -1$

or $\quad x_1^2 = 2y_1^2 \quad$ ... (iii)

Also, (x_1, y_1) lies on $x^2 - y^2 = \frac{1}{2}$

$\therefore \quad x_1^2 - y_1^2 = \frac{1}{2} \quad$ ... (iv)

From Eqs. (iii) and (iv), we get $y_1^2 = \frac{1}{2}$ and $x_1^2 = 1$

and (x_1, y_1) lies on ellipse $x^2 + 2y^2 = a^2$

$\therefore \quad x_1^2 + 2y_1^2 = a^2$

$\Rightarrow \quad 1 + 1 = a^2$ or $a^2 = 2$

$\therefore$ Equation of ellipse is $x^2 + 2y^2 = 2$

whose foci are $(\pm 1, 0)$.

20. Equation of normal at P (6, 3) is $\frac{a^2x}{6} + \frac{b^2y}{3} = a^2 + b^2$

$\because$ Normal intersects the X-axis at (9, 0), then

$$\frac{9a^2}{6} + 0 = a^2 + b^2$$

$\Rightarrow \quad 3a^2 = 2a^2 + 2b^2$

or $\quad a^2 = 2b^2$ or $a^2 = 2a^2(e^2 - 1)$

$\therefore \quad e^2 = \frac{3}{2}$

Hence, $\quad e = \sqrt{\frac{3}{2}}$

21. Since, asymptotes of rectangular hyperbola are perpendicular to each other.

$\because$ Given asymptote is $3x - 4y - 6 = 0$

$\therefore$ Other asymptote is $4x + 3y + \lambda = 0 \quad$ ... (i)

Given, centre of hyperbola lies on $x - y - 1 = 0$.

Since, asymptotes pass through the centre of hyperbola.

$\therefore$ Centre is the point of intersection of $x - y - 1 = 0$ and $3x - 4y - 6 = 0$.

$\therefore$ Centre is $(-2, -3)$, also $(-2, -3)$ lies on Eq. (i).

Then, $\quad -8 - 9 + \lambda = 0$

$\therefore \quad \lambda = 17$

Hence, other asymptote is $4x + 3y + 17 = 0 \quad$ [from Eq. (i)]

22. Equation of normal of $y^2 = 4ax$ is

$$y = mx - 2am - am^3,$$

which is tangent of $x^2 - y^2 = a^2$

$\therefore \quad (-2am - am^3)^2 = a^2m^2 - a^2$

or $\quad 4m^2 + m^6 + 4m^4 = m^2 - 1$

or $\quad m^6 + 4m^4 + 3m^2 + 1 = 0$

23. Let the middle point of the chord be (h, k).

$\therefore \quad T = S_1$

$$3xh - 2yk + 2(x + h) - 3(y + k) = 3h^2 - 2k^2 + 4h - 6k$$

Slope of this chord $= \frac{3h + 2}{2k + 3} = 2 \quad$ [given]

or $\quad 3h + 2 = 4k + 6$

$\Rightarrow \quad 3h - 4k = 4$

Hence, locus of middle point is $3x - 4y = 4$

24. Let $f(x, y) \equiv x^2 + 3xy + 2y^2 + 2x + 3y + 2 = 0$

$\therefore \frac{\partial f}{\partial x} = 2x + 3y + 2$ and $\frac{\partial f}{\partial y} = 3x + 4y + 3$

For centre, $\frac{\partial f}{\partial x} = 0$ and $\frac{\partial f}{\partial y} = 0$

$\therefore \quad 2x + 3y + 2 = 0$

and $\quad 3x + 4y + 3 = 0$

After solving, we get

$$x = -1 \text{ and } y = 0$$

$\therefore$ Coordinates of centre are $(-1, 0)$.

25. For ellipse (if $a > b$),

$$ae_1 = \sqrt{(a^2 - b^2)}$$

or $\quad a^2e_1^2 = a^2 - b^2$

and for hyperbola,

$$Ae_2 = \sqrt{(A^2 + B^2)}$$

$\Rightarrow \quad = \sqrt{(A^2 + b^2)} \quad$ [$\because$ 2b = 2B (given)]

or $\quad A^2e_2^2 = A^2 + b^2$

$\Rightarrow \quad \frac{1}{e_1^2} + \frac{1}{e_2^2} = \frac{a^2}{(a^2 - b^2)} + \frac{A^2}{(A^2 + b^2)} \quad$ ... (i)

Since, both the curves are confocal.

$\therefore ae_1 = Ae_2$

or $\quad a^2e_1^2 = A^2e_2^2$

$\Rightarrow \quad a^2 - b^2 = A^2 + b^2$

or $\quad A^2 = a^2 - 2b^2 \quad$ ... (ii)

From Eqs. (i) and (ii), we get

$$\frac{1}{e_1^2} + \frac{1}{e_2^2} = \frac{a^2}{a^2 - b^2} + \frac{a^2 - 2b^2}{a^2 - b^2}$$

$$= \frac{2(a^2 - b^2)}{(a^2 - b^2)} = 2$$

26. Orthocentre of triangle formed by the points $\left(ct_1, \frac{c}{t_1}\right), \left(ct_2, \frac{c}{t_2}\right)$ and $\left(ct_3, \frac{c}{t_3}\right)$ on the rectangular hyperbola $xy = c^2$ is $\left(-\frac{c}{t_1t_2t_3}, -c\, t_1t_2t_3\right)$.

Here, $c = 2$ and $\frac{-c}{t_1t_2t_3} = \frac{1}{2}$ or $t_1t_2t_3 = -2c$

$\therefore$ Ordinate of orthocentre $= -c\, t_1t_2t_3$

$$= -c \times -2c = 2c^2 = 2(2)^2 = 8$$

27. Since, the normal drawn at $P(t_1)$ meets the hyperbola $xy = 2$ again at $Q(t_2)$, then $t_1^3 t_2 = -1$ ... (i)

$\because$ $P \equiv \left(\sqrt{2}\, t_1, \frac{\sqrt{2}}{t_1}\right)$ and $Q \equiv \left(\sqrt{2}\, t_2, \frac{\sqrt{2}}{t_2}\right)$

$\therefore$ Distance $PQ = \sqrt{(\sqrt{2}t_1 - \sqrt{2}t_2)^2 + \left(\frac{\sqrt{2}}{t_1} - \frac{\sqrt{2}}{t_2}\right)^2}$

$$= \sqrt{2}\, |t_1 - t_2| \sqrt{\left(1 + \frac{1}{t_1^2 t_2^2}\right)}$$

$$= \sqrt{2}\, \frac{(t_1^4 + 1)^{3/2}}{|t_1^3|} \quad \text{[from Eq. (i)]}$$

$$= \sqrt{2}\left(t_1^2 + \frac{1}{t_1^2}\right)^{3/2} \geq \sqrt{2}\, (2)^{3/2} = 4 \quad (\because \text{AM} \geq \text{GM})$$

$\therefore$ Distance $PQ \geq 4$

Hence, minimum distance between the points P and Q is 4.

28. Let $P(a\sec\theta, b\tan\theta)$ be a point on the hyperbola $\frac{x^2}{a^2} - \frac{y^2}{b^2} = 1$ with eccentricity $e = \frac{3}{2\sqrt{2}}$.

$\therefore$ $a^2 = 8b^2$ $\quad [\because b^2 = a^2(e^2 - 1)]$ ...(i)

$\because$ Equation of normal at P is $ax\cos\theta + by\cot\theta = a^2 + b^2$

$\therefore$ $M \equiv \left(\left(\frac{a^2 + b^2}{a}\right)\sec\theta, 0\right)$

and $N \equiv \left(0, \left(\frac{a^2 + b^2}{b}\right)\tan\theta\right)$

Let mid-point of MN be $R(h,k)$.

$\therefore$ $2h = \left(\frac{a^2+b^2}{a}\right)\sec\theta$ ... (ii)

and $2k = \left(\frac{a^2+b^2}{b}\right)\tan\theta$ ... (iii)

From Eqs. (ii) and (iii), we get

$$4a^2h^2 - 4b^2k^2 = (a^2 + b^2)^2$$

$\therefore$ Locus of R is $\frac{x^2}{\left(\frac{a^2 + b^2}{2a}\right)^2} - \frac{y^2}{\left(\frac{a^2 + b^2}{2b}\right)^2} = 1$

which has eccentricity

$$e_1 = \sqrt{\left(1 + \frac{a^2}{b^2}\right)} = \sqrt{(1 + 8)} = 3 \quad \text{[from Eq. (i)]}$$

29. Equations of director circle of ellipse

$$\frac{x^2}{a^2} + \frac{y^2}{b^2} = 1 \text{ is } x^2 + y^2 = a^2 + b^2$$

$\therefore$ Radius, $r_1 = \sqrt{(a^2 + b^2)} = \sqrt{a^2 + a^2(1 - e_1^2)}$

$$= a\sqrt{(2 - e_1^2)} \quad \text{... (i)}$$

and director circle of hyperbola $\frac{x^2}{a^2} - \frac{y^2}{b^2} = 1$ is

$$x^2 + y^2 = a^2 - b^2$$

$\therefore$ Radius. $r_2 = \sqrt{(a^2 - b_1^2)}$

$$= \sqrt{a^2 - a^2(e_2^2 - 1)}$$

$$= a\sqrt{(2 - e_2^2)} \quad \text{... (ii)}$$

Given, $\frac{r_1}{r_2} = \frac{1}{3}$

$\Rightarrow$ $18 - 9e_1^2 = 2 - e_2^2$

$$16 = 9e_1^2 - e_2^2$$

$\therefore$ $\lambda = 16$

30. Since, $\frac{x^2}{a^2} - \frac{y^2}{b^2} = 1$ and $x^2 + y^2 = \frac{a^2}{4}$ having origin as their common centre.

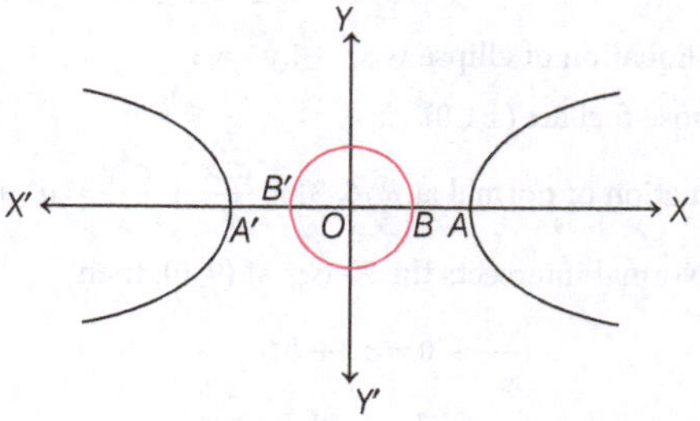

So, vertex is the nearest point.

Hence, shortest distance = BA

$$= a - \frac{a}{2} = \frac{a}{2}$$

$\therefore$ $f(a, b) = \frac{a}{2}$

Hence, $f(4,6) + f(2,3) = \frac{4}{2} + \frac{2}{2} = 3$

31. Let $P(h,k)$ be the middle point, then equation of chord whose mid-point is $P(h,k)$ is $T = S_1$. Then,

$\Rightarrow$ $hx + ky - 4 = h^2 + k^2 - 4$

or $y = -\frac{h}{k}x + \frac{(h^2 + k^2)}{k}$

It will touch the hyperbola $\frac{x^2}{4} - \frac{y^2}{16} = 1$, then

$$\left(\frac{h^2 + k^2}{k}\right)^2 = 4 \times \frac{h^2}{k^2} - 16$$

$\Rightarrow \quad (h^2 + k^2)^2 = 4h^2 - 16k^2$

$\therefore$ Locus of $P(h,k)$ is $(x^2 + y^2)^2 = 4x^2 - 16y^2$

$\therefore \quad \lambda = 4$

32. The given hyperbola is $\frac{x^2}{2} - \frac{y^2}{3} = 1$

Equation of tangents are $y = mx \pm \sqrt{(2m^2 - 3)}$

$\because$ Tangents from the point (α, β) will be

$$(\beta - m\alpha)^2 = 2m^2 - 3$$

or $\quad m^2(\alpha^2 - 2) - 2m\alpha\beta + \beta^2 + 3 = 0$

$\because \quad m_1 m_2 = \frac{\beta^2 + 3}{\alpha^2 - 2}$

$\Rightarrow \quad \tan\theta \tan\phi = \frac{\beta^2 + 3}{\alpha^2 - 2}$

$\Rightarrow \quad 2 = \frac{\beta^2 + 3}{\alpha^2 - 2}$

or $\quad 2\alpha^2 - \beta^2 = 7$

33. Since, line $2x + y = 1$ is tangent to the hyperbola $\frac{x^2}{a^2} - \frac{y^2}{b^2} = 1$

$\therefore \quad (1)^2 = a^2(-2)^2 - b^2$

$\Rightarrow \quad 4a^2 - b^2 = 1 \quad \ldots \text{(i)}$

Intersection point of nearest directrix $x = \frac{a}{e}$ and X-axis is $\left(\frac{a}{e}, 0\right)$

As $2x + y = 1$ passes through $\left(\frac{a}{e}, 0\right)$.

$\therefore \quad \frac{2a}{e} + 0 = 1 \Rightarrow a = \frac{e}{2} \quad \ldots \text{(ii)}$

and $\quad b^2 = a^2(e^2 - 1) = \frac{e^2}{4}(e^2 - 1) \quad \ldots \text{(iii)}$

On substituting the values of a and b from Eqs. (ii) and (iii) in Eq. (i), then $\quad e^2 - \frac{e^2}{4}(e^2 - 1) = 1$

$\Rightarrow \quad (e^2 - 4)(e^2 - 1) = 0$

$\therefore \quad e^2 = 4, e^2 \neq 1 \quad [\because e > 1]$

Hence, $\quad e = 2$

34. The equation of the normal to the hyperbola $\frac{x^2}{4} - \frac{y^2}{1} = 1$ at $(2\sec\theta, \tan\theta)$ is $2x\cos\theta + y\cot\theta = 5$

The slope of the normal is $-2\sin\theta = -1$

$\Rightarrow \quad \sin\theta = \frac{1}{2}$ or $\theta = \frac{\pi}{6}$

y-intercept of the normal $= \frac{5}{\cot\theta} = \frac{5}{\sqrt{3}}$,

As, it touches the ellipse $\frac{x^2}{a^2} + \frac{y^2}{b^2} = 1$.

$\therefore \quad a^2 + b^2 = \frac{25}{3}$

Hence, $\frac{18}{25}(a^2 + b^2) = \frac{18}{25} \times \frac{25}{3} = 6$

35. $H: \frac{x^2}{9} - \frac{y^2}{4} = 1$

Here, $\quad a^2 = 9, b^2 = 4$

$\therefore \quad a = 3, b = 2$

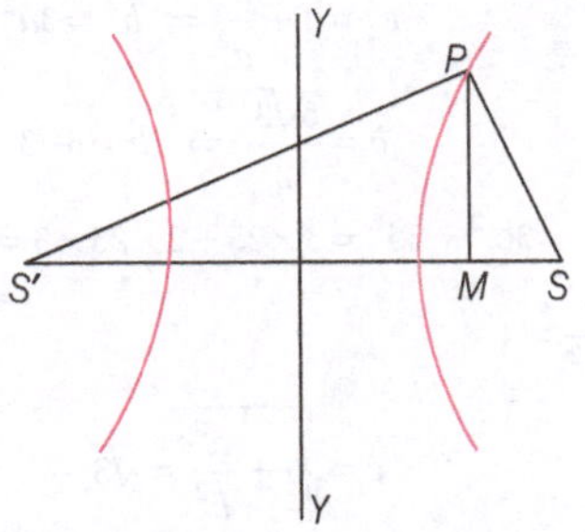

Let S and S' be foci of hyperbola.

$\therefore \quad e = \sqrt{1 + \frac{b^2}{a^2}} = \sqrt{1 + \frac{4}{9}} = \frac{\sqrt{13}}{3}$

$\because \quad S = (ae, 0)$ and $S'(-ae, 0)$

$= (\sqrt{13}, 0)$ and $(-\sqrt{13}, 0)$

$\therefore \quad SS' = 2\sqrt{13}$

$\therefore$ Area of $\Delta PSS' = 2\sqrt{13}$

$\Rightarrow \quad \frac{1}{2} \times SS' \times PM = 2\sqrt{13}$

$\Rightarrow \quad \frac{1}{2} \times 2\sqrt{13} \times PM = 2\sqrt{13} \Rightarrow PM = 2$

Let coordinates of P be (h, k).

$\therefore \quad k = 2 \quad [\because PM = 2]$

P satisfies the equation of hyperbola.

$\therefore \quad \frac{h^2}{9} - \frac{(2)^2}{4} = 1 \Rightarrow h^2 = 18$

$\therefore$ Square of distance of P from the origin

$= h^2 + k^2 = 18 + 4 = 22$

36. **Decoding the Question**

> For ellipse, use eccentricity, $e = \sqrt{1 - \frac{b^2}{a^2}}$ and for hyperbola, use eccentricity, $e = \sqrt{1 + \frac{b^2}{a^2}}$

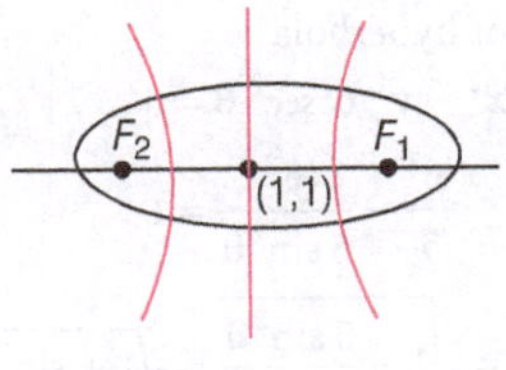

$E: \frac{(x-1)^2}{100} + \frac{(y-1)^2}{75} = 1$

$e_1 = \sqrt{1 - \frac{75}{100}} = \frac{1}{2}$

$e_2 = 2$

$F_1 \equiv (6,1)$ and $F_2 \equiv (-4,1)$

$$2ae_2 = 10 \Rightarrow a = \frac{5}{2} \Rightarrow 2a = 5$$

$\therefore \quad \alpha = 5$

Now, $\quad e_2^2 = 1 + \frac{b^2}{a^2} \Rightarrow b^2 = 3a^2$

$\Rightarrow \quad b = \frac{5\sqrt{3}}{2} \Rightarrow 2b = 5\sqrt{3} = \beta$

$\therefore \quad 3\alpha^2 + 2\beta^2 = 3 \times 25 + 2 \times 25 \times 3 = 225$

37. $\frac{-x^2}{a^2} + \frac{y^2}{b^2} = 1$

$$e = \sqrt{1 + \frac{a^2}{b^2}} = \sqrt{3}$$

$\Rightarrow \quad 1 + \frac{a^2}{b^2} = 3 \Rightarrow \frac{a^2}{b^2} = 2 \quad$ ...(i)

and latusrectum $= \frac{2a^2}{b} = 4\sqrt{3}$

By Eq. (i), $\frac{4b^2}{b} = 4\sqrt{3} \Rightarrow b = \sqrt{3}$

$\Rightarrow \quad b^2 = 3$ and $a^2 = 2 \times 3 = 6$

Now, $\quad \frac{-x^2}{6} + \frac{y^2}{3} = 1$

Put $(\alpha, 6)$ in it, $\quad \frac{-\alpha^2}{6} + \frac{36}{3} = 1$

$\Rightarrow \quad -\alpha^2 = -66 \Rightarrow \alpha^2 = 66$

For the given equation,

focal distances $= |ey_1 - b|, |ey_1 + b|$

So, $\quad \beta = (ey_1 + b)(ey_1 - b) = e^2y_1^2 - b^2$

$= 3 \times 6^2 - 3 = 105$

So, $\quad \alpha^2 + \beta = 66 + 105 = 171$

38. **Decoding the Question**

Use following step wise approach.

Step 1 Apply formula, $e_{\text{Hyperbola}} = \sqrt{1 + \frac{b^2}{a^2}}$ to get eccentricity of hyperbola. Then, apply $e_{\text{Ellipse}} = \sqrt{1 - \frac{b^2}{a^2}}$

Given equation of hyperbola

$$x^2 - y^2 \operatorname{cosec}^2 \theta = 5$$

$\Rightarrow \quad \frac{x^2}{5} - \frac{y^2}{5\sin^2\theta} = 1$

$$e_1 = \sqrt{1 + \frac{5\sin^2\theta}{5}} = \sqrt{1 + \sin^2\theta}$$

Equation of ellipse $x^2 \operatorname{cosec}^2\theta + y^2 = 5$

$\Rightarrow \quad \frac{x^2}{5\sin^2\theta} + \frac{y^2}{5} = 1$

$\Rightarrow \quad e_2 = \sqrt{1 - \frac{5\sin^2\theta}{5}} \Rightarrow e_2 = \sqrt{1 - \sin^2\theta}$

Given, $\quad e_1 = \sqrt{7}e_2$

$\Rightarrow \quad 1 + \sin^2\theta = 7(1 - \sin^2\theta)$

$\Rightarrow \quad 1 + \sin^2\theta = 7 - 7\sin^2\theta$

$\Rightarrow \quad 8\sin^2\theta = 6 \Rightarrow \sin^2\theta = \frac{3}{4}$

$\Rightarrow \quad \sin\theta = \sqrt{3}/2 \Rightarrow \theta = \pi/3$

39. Given, e_1 = eccentricity of the hyperbola $\frac{x^2}{16} - \frac{y^2}{9} = 1$

and e_2 = eccentricity of the ellipse $\frac{x^2}{a^2} + \frac{y^2}{b^2} = 1, a > b$.

Also, $\quad e_1e_2 = 1 \quad$ [given]

Now, $\quad e_1 = \frac{5}{4}$

$\therefore \quad e_2 = \frac{4}{5} \quad \left[\because e_1 = \sqrt{1 + \frac{b^2}{a^2}}\right]$

Also, given ellipse is passing through $(\pm 5, 0)$, which is foci of the hyperbola $(\pm ae, 0)$.

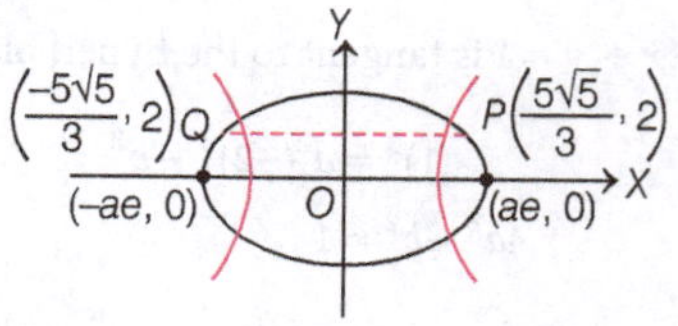

Also, $\quad 1 - \frac{b^2}{a^2} = \frac{16}{25} \Rightarrow b = 3$

So, equation of ellipse $\frac{x^2}{25} + \frac{y^2}{9} = 1$

Hence, coordinates of points of chords are $\left(\pm \frac{5\sqrt{5}}{3}, 2\right)$.

Thus, length of chord $(L_{PQ}) = \frac{10\sqrt{5}}{3}$

40. Let $H: \frac{x^2}{a^2} - \frac{y^2}{b^2} = 1$

$$b^2 = a^2(e^2 - 1)$$

$\therefore$ Equation of circle, $x^2 + y^2 = a^2$

Area $= 36\pi$

$\Rightarrow \quad \pi a^2 = 36\pi \Rightarrow a = 6$

Now, radius of C_2 can be $a(e-1)$ or $a(e+1)$.

For $r = a(e-1)$,

Area $= 4\pi$

$$\pi a^2(e-1)^2 = 4\pi$$

$\Rightarrow \quad (e-1)^2 = \frac{4}{36} = \frac{1}{9}$

$\Rightarrow \quad e - 1 = \frac{1}{3} \Rightarrow e = \frac{4}{3}$

For $r = a(e+1)$,

Area $= 4\pi$

$\Rightarrow \quad \pi r^2 = 4\pi$

$\Rightarrow \quad a^2(e+1)^2 = 4$

$\Rightarrow \quad (e+1)^2 = \dfrac{1}{9}$

$\Rightarrow \quad e + 1 = \dfrac{1}{3}$

$\Rightarrow \quad e = -\dfrac{2}{3}$ [rejected]

$\therefore \quad b^2 = a^2(e^2 - 1) = 36\left(\dfrac{16}{9} - 1\right)$

$= 4 \times 7 = 28$

$\therefore$ Length of latusrectum $= \dfrac{2b^2}{a} = \dfrac{2 \times 28}{6} = \dfrac{28}{3}$

Alternate Solution

Area of $C_1 = \pi a^2 = 36\pi \Rightarrow a^2 = 36$

Area of $C_2 = \pi(c-a)^2 = 4\pi$

$(c-6)^2 = 4 \Rightarrow c = 8$

$\therefore \quad b^2 = c^2 - a^2 = 64 - 36 = 28$

Length of latusrectum $= \dfrac{2b^2}{a} = \dfrac{2 \times 28}{6} = \dfrac{28}{3}$

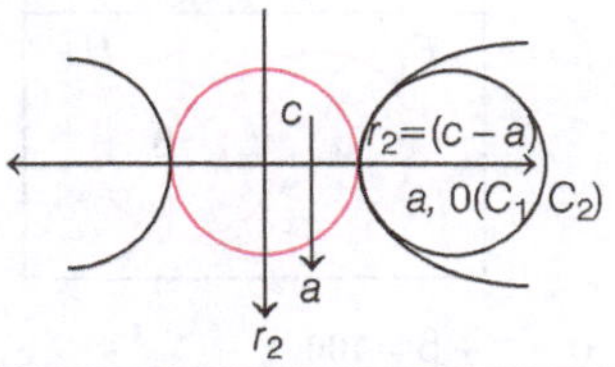

41. Ellipse : $\dfrac{x^2}{9} + \dfrac{y^2}{25} = 1$ ...(i)

$a = 3,\ b = 5$

Eccentricity, $e = \sqrt{1 - \dfrac{a^2}{b^2}} = \sqrt{1 - \dfrac{9}{25}} = \dfrac{4}{5}$ ...(ii)

For Eq. (ii), $(0, \pm be) = (0, \pm 4)$

$\therefore \quad e_H = \dfrac{15}{8} \times e_{\text{Ellipse}} = \dfrac{15}{8} \times \dfrac{4}{5} = \dfrac{3}{2}$

Let equation of hyperbola be $\dfrac{x^2}{a^2} - \dfrac{y^2}{b^2} = -1$

Foci $(0, \pm 4)$, $be_H = 4$

$b \times \dfrac{3}{2} = 4 \Rightarrow b = \dfrac{8}{3}$

$\Rightarrow \quad a^2 = b^2(e_H^2 - 1) = \dfrac{64}{9}\left(\dfrac{9}{4} - 1\right)$

$\Rightarrow \quad a^2 = \dfrac{80}{9}$

$\therefore \quad \dfrac{x^2}{\frac{80}{9}} - \dfrac{y^2}{\frac{64}{9}} = -1$

Directrix, $y = \pm \dfrac{b}{e} = \pm \dfrac{16}{9}$

$PS = ePM$

M = distance between $P\left(\sqrt{2}, \dfrac{14}{3}\sqrt{\dfrac{2}{5}}\right)$

and directrix $= 7\sqrt{\dfrac{2}{5}} - \dfrac{8}{3}$

42. $\dfrac{x^2}{3} - \dfrac{y^2}{5} = 1$

Focus of hyperbola $= (ae, 0)$

Here, $a = \sqrt{3}$ and $b^2 = a^2(e^2 - 1)$

$\Rightarrow \quad 5 = 3(e^2 - 1)$

$\Rightarrow \quad e^2 = \dfrac{5}{3} + 1 = \dfrac{8}{3} \Rightarrow e = \sqrt{8/3}$

So, $(ae, 0) = (\sqrt{8}, 0) = S$

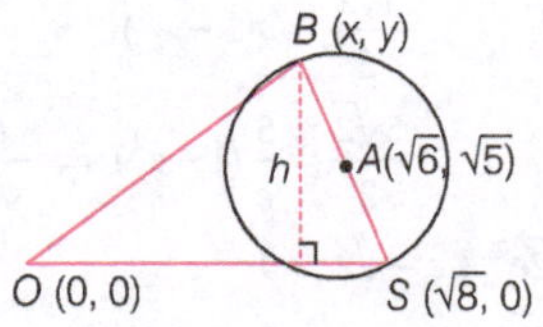

$\dfrac{x + \sqrt{8}}{2} = \sqrt{6}$

$\Rightarrow \quad x = 2\sqrt{6} - \sqrt{8}$

and $\quad \dfrac{y}{2} = \sqrt{5}$

$\Rightarrow \quad y = 2\sqrt{5}$

$B(x, y) = (2\sqrt{6} - \sqrt{8}, 2\sqrt{5})$

$h = 2\sqrt{5}$ and $OS = \sqrt{8}$

Therefore, $\text{ar}(\Delta OSB) = \dfrac{1}{2}(OS) \times h$

$= \dfrac{1}{2} \times \sqrt{8} \times 2\sqrt{5} = \sqrt{40}$

$A^2 = 40$

43. Given, $\dfrac{2b^2}{a} = 9$ and $\dfrac{a}{e} = \pm\dfrac{4}{\sqrt{3}}$

Equation of tangent, $y - \sqrt{3}x + \sqrt{3} = 0$

By equation of tangent,

Slope, $S = \sqrt{3}$ [say]

Constant $= -\sqrt{3}$

By condition of tangency,

$6 = 6a^2 - 9a \Rightarrow a = 2, b^2 = 9$

Equation of hyperbola is $\dfrac{x^2}{4} - \dfrac{y^2}{9} = 1$ and for tangent,

point of contact is $(4, 3\sqrt{3}) = (x_0, y_0)$.

Now, $\quad e = \sqrt{1 + \dfrac{9}{4}} = \dfrac{\sqrt{13}}{2}$

Again, product of focal distances

$m = (x_0 e + a)(x_0 e - a)$

$m + 4e^2 = 20e^2 - a^2$

$= 20 \times \dfrac{13}{4} - 4 = 61$

44. $\frac{x^2}{a^2} + \frac{y^2}{b^2} = 1$

Foci $= (\pm 5, 0) = (\pm ae, 0)$

Length of latusrectum $= \sqrt{50} = \frac{2b^2}{a}$

$\Rightarrow \quad ae = 5, \frac{2b^2}{a} = 5\sqrt{2}$

$\Rightarrow \quad a = \frac{5}{e}, \; b^2 = \frac{5\sqrt{2}a}{2}$

$\Rightarrow \quad b^2 = a^2(1 - e^2)$

$\Rightarrow \quad \frac{5\sqrt{2}a}{2} = a^2(1 - e^2)$

$\Rightarrow \quad \frac{5\sqrt{2}}{2} = a(1 - e^2)$

$\Rightarrow \quad \frac{5\sqrt{2}}{2} = \frac{5}{e}(1 - e^2) \Rightarrow \frac{e}{\sqrt{2}} = 1 - e^2$

$\Rightarrow \quad \sqrt{2}e^2 + e - \sqrt{2} = 0$

$\Rightarrow \quad (e + \sqrt{2})(\sqrt{2}e - 1) = 0$

$\Rightarrow \quad e = \frac{1}{\sqrt{2}}$

$\Rightarrow \quad a = 5\sqrt{2}$

and $\quad b = 5$

Now, hyperbola, $\frac{x^2}{b^2} - \frac{y^2}{a^2b^2} = 1$

$\Rightarrow \quad a^2b^2 = b^2(e^2 - 1)$

$\Rightarrow \quad a^2 = e^2 - 1$

$\Rightarrow \quad e^2 = 1 + a^2 = 1 + 50 \Rightarrow e^2 = 51$

45. We have, $\frac{x^2}{9} - \frac{y^2}{b^2} = 1$

From figure in ΔAOB,

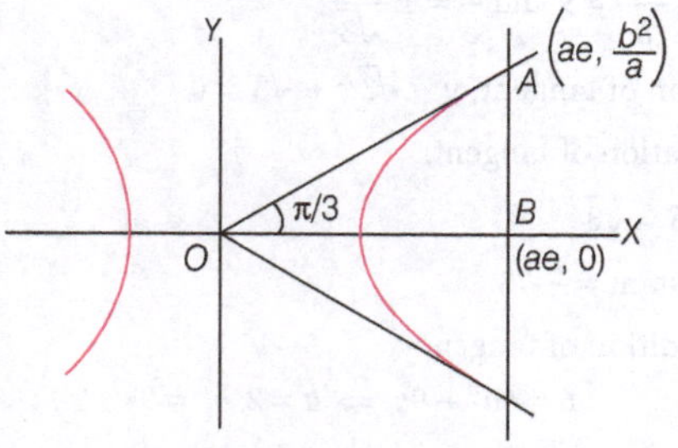

$\tan\frac{\pi}{6} = \frac{b^2/a}{ae} \Rightarrow \frac{1}{\sqrt{3}} = \frac{b^2}{a^2e}$

$\Rightarrow \quad e = \frac{\sqrt{3}b^2}{a^2}$ or $e^2 = 1 + \frac{b^2}{a}$

$\Rightarrow \quad 1 + \frac{b^2}{9} = \frac{3b^4}{81} \Rightarrow b^4 = 3b^2 + 27$

$b^4 - 3b^2 - 27 \Rightarrow b^2 = \frac{2}{3}(1 + \sqrt{13})$

$\therefore \quad l = 3, m = 2$ and $n = 13$

$\therefore \quad l^2 + m^2 + n^2 = 182$

46. **Decoding the Question**

(i) Distance between foci of hyperbola is $2ae$.

(ii) And $a^2e^2 = b^2 + a^2$, where e = eccentricity of hyperbola.

We have, foci of hyperbola are $S(1 + \sqrt{2}, 0)$ and $S'(1 - \sqrt{2}, 0)$.

Now, we know that $SS' = 2ae \Rightarrow 2\sqrt{2} = 2ae$

$\Rightarrow \quad a = 1 \qquad [\because e = \sqrt{2}]$

Again, $\quad e = \sqrt{1 + \frac{b^2}{a^2}}$

$\Rightarrow \quad \sqrt{2} = \sqrt{1 + \frac{b^2}{(1)^2}} \Rightarrow b^2 = 1$

Now, length of latusrectum $= \frac{2b^2}{a} = \frac{2 \times 1}{1} = 2$

47. Let E be the person speak English

$\therefore n(E) = 75$

and H be the person speak Hindi

$\therefore n(H) = 40$

Let number of persons who speak both English and Hindi are t.

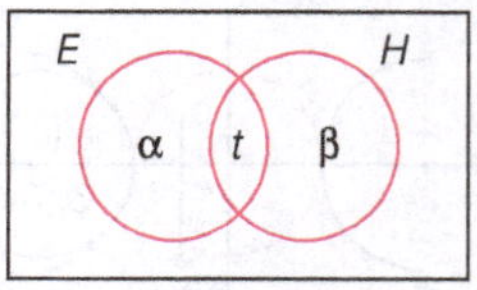

$\therefore \quad \alpha + t + \beta = 100 \qquad$ ...(i)

$\alpha + t = 75 \qquad$ ...(ii)

and $\quad \beta + t = 40 \qquad$ ...(iii)

From Eqs. (i) and (ii), $\beta = 25$

From Eqs. (i) and (iii), $\alpha = 60$

and from Eq. (i), $\quad t = 15$

We have, equation of ellipse $25(\beta^2x^2 + \alpha^2y^2) = \alpha^2\beta^2$

$\Rightarrow \quad 25\left(\frac{x^2}{\alpha^2} + \frac{y^2}{\beta^2}\right) = 1$

$\Rightarrow \quad 25\left(\frac{x^2}{3600} + \frac{y^2}{625}\right) = 1$

$\Rightarrow \quad \frac{x^2}{144} + \frac{y^2}{25} = 1$

$\therefore$ Eccentricity, $e = \sqrt{1 - \frac{b^2}{a^2}}$

$= \sqrt{1 - \frac{25}{144}} = \frac{\sqrt{119}}{12}$

48. We have, equation of the hyperbola is $3x^2 - 4y^2 = 36$

$T: 3x_0x - 4y_0y = 36$

For (x_0, y_0) to be nearest to line $3x + 2y = 1$, tangent T must be parallel to $3x + 2y = 1$.

$\therefore$ Slope of T = Slope of line $3x + 2y = 1$

$\Rightarrow \quad \frac{-3x_0}{-4y_0} = -\frac{3}{2} \Rightarrow x_0 = -2y_0$

Now, (x_0, y_0) lies on hyperbola.

$\therefore \quad 3x_0^2 - 4y_0^2 = 36$

$\Rightarrow \quad 12y_0^2 - 4y_0^2 = 36 \quad [\because x_0 = -2y_0]$

$\Rightarrow \quad y_0 = \pm \frac{3}{\sqrt{2}}$

$\therefore \quad x_0 = -2y_0 = \mp 3\sqrt{2}$

So, points are $\left(3\sqrt{2}, -\frac{3}{\sqrt{2}}\right)$ and $\left(-3\sqrt{2}, \frac{3}{\sqrt{2}}\right)$

But $\left(3\sqrt{2}, -\frac{3}{\sqrt{2}}\right)$ is nearest to the line $3x + 2y = 1$

$\therefore \quad P(x_0, y_0) = \left(3\sqrt{2}, \frac{-3}{\sqrt{2}}\right)$

So, $\quad \sqrt{2}(y_0 - x_0) = \sqrt{2}\left(\frac{-3}{\sqrt{2}} - 3\sqrt{2}\right)$

$= -3 - 6 = -9$

49. Let the equation of hyperbola $\frac{x^2}{a^2} - \frac{y^2}{b^2} = 1$, where $ae = 2$ and $e = \frac{3}{2}$ [given]

$\Rightarrow \quad a = \frac{4}{3}$

Also, $\quad b^2 = a^2e^2 - a^2$

$\Rightarrow \quad b^2 = \frac{16}{9} \times \frac{9}{4} - \frac{16}{9}$

$\Rightarrow \quad b^2 = 4 - \frac{16}{9}$

$\Rightarrow \quad b^2 = \frac{20}{9}$

Given, tangent perpendicular to the line $2x + 3y = 6$.

So, slope of tangent $= 3/2$

The equation of tangent of hyperbola is $y = mx \pm \sqrt{a^2m^2 - b^2}$

$= \frac{3x}{2} \pm \sqrt{\frac{16}{9} \times \frac{9}{4} - \frac{20}{9}}$

$= \frac{3x}{2} \pm \sqrt{4 - \frac{20}{9}} = \frac{3x}{2} \pm \frac{4}{3}$

$\Rightarrow \quad y = \frac{3x}{2} \pm \frac{4}{3}$

Intercept on X-axis $(y = 0)$

$\Rightarrow \quad a = \frac{8}{9}$

Intercept on Y-axis $(x = 0)$

$\therefore \quad b = \frac{4}{3}$

So, $|6a| + |5b| = \left|6 \times \frac{8}{9}\right| + \left|5 \times \frac{4}{3}\right|$

$= \frac{16}{3} + \frac{20}{3} = \frac{36}{3} = 12$

50. Equation of tangent to the hyperbola, $\frac{y^2}{a^2} - \frac{x^2}{b^2} = 1$ is

$y = mx \pm \sqrt{a^2 - b^2m^2}$ passing through $(4, 1)$.

$\therefore \quad 1 = 4m \pm \sqrt{a^2 - b^2m^2}$

$\Rightarrow \quad (1 - 4m) = \pm \sqrt{25 - 16m^2}$

$\Rightarrow \quad 1 - 8m + 16m^2 = 25 - 16m^2$

$\Rightarrow \quad 32m^2 - 8m - 24 = 0$

$\Rightarrow \quad 4m^2 - m - 3 = 0 \Rightarrow m = 1, \frac{-3}{4}$

Given that tangent drawn to given hyperbola to have positive slopes.

So, equation of tangent with positive slopes 1 and 3/4 are

$(y - 1) = 1 \cdot (x - 4) \Rightarrow y = x - 3 \quad \text{...(i)}$

and $\quad (y + 1) = \frac{3}{4}(x - 4) = 4y = 3x - 16 \quad \text{...(ii)}$

with intercept on X-axis.

Thus, $\quad \alpha = \frac{16}{3}$ and $\beta = 3$

On solving Eqs. (i) and (ii), we get $x = -4, y = -7$

Thus, $\quad p = (4, 1)$ and $Q = (-4, -7)$

$\therefore \quad PQ = \sqrt{(4 + 4)^2 + (1 + 7)^2} = \sqrt{64 + 64} = \sqrt{128}$

$(PQ)^2 = 128$

$\Rightarrow \quad \frac{PQ^2}{\alpha\beta} = \frac{128}{16} = 8$

51. Vertices of hyperbola H are $(\pm 6, 0) \equiv (\pm a, 0)$

So, $\quad a = 6$

Eccentricity, $e = \frac{\sqrt{5}}{2}$

$\sqrt{1 + \frac{b^2}{a^2}} = \frac{\sqrt{5}}{2}$

$\Rightarrow \quad b^2 = 9, b = 3$

So, equation of hyperbola, $H : \frac{x^2}{36} - \frac{y^2}{9} = 1$

Now, equation of normal for hyperbola H is

$\frac{ax}{\sec\theta} + \frac{by}{\tan\theta} = a^2 + b^2$

$6\cos\theta\, x + 3\cot\theta\, y = 45$

This normal is parallel to $\sqrt{2}x + y = 2\sqrt{2}$.

$\therefore \quad \frac{-\sqrt{2}}{1} = \frac{-6\cos\theta}{3\cot\theta}$

$\Rightarrow \quad \sin\theta = \frac{1}{\sqrt{2}}$

$\Rightarrow \quad \theta = \frac{\pi}{4}$

So, equation of normal is

$6\cos\frac{\pi}{4}x + 3\cot\frac{\pi}{4}y = 45$

$6 \cdot \frac{x}{\sqrt{2}} + 3 \cdot 1 \cdot y = 45$

$\Rightarrow \quad \sqrt{2}x + y = 15$

Let $P = (a\sec\theta, b\tan\theta)$

$$\equiv \left(6\sec\frac{\pi}{4}, 3\tan\frac{\pi}{4}\right), P\ (6\sqrt{2}, 3)$$

Q lies on Y-axis, put $x = 0$ in equation of normal

$$0 + y = 15 \Rightarrow y = 15$$

$\therefore$ $Q(0, 15)$

$\Rightarrow$ $d^2 = (6\sqrt{2} - 0)^2 + (3 - 15)^2$

$$= 72 + 144 = 216$$

52. Given, $H: \dfrac{x^2}{a^2} - \dfrac{y^2}{b^2} = 1,$

then $e = \dfrac{2b^2}{a}$

$$e^2 = \frac{11}{14}l$$

$\Rightarrow$ $a^2 + b^2 = \dfrac{11}{7}b^2 a$ ... (i)

and $e'^2 = \dfrac{11}{8}l'$

$\Rightarrow$ $a^2 + b^2 = \dfrac{11}{4}a^2 b$ ... (ii)

From Eqs. (i) and (ii), $7a = 4b$

Then, from Eq. (i), we get

$$\frac{16}{49}b^2 + b^2 = \frac{11}{7}b^2 . \frac{4b}{7}$$

$\Rightarrow$ $44b = 65$ and $77a = 65$

$\therefore$ $77a + 44b = 130$

53. Given, $e = \sqrt{5/2}$

$\Rightarrow$ $1 + \dfrac{b^2}{a^2} = \dfrac{5}{2} \Rightarrow \dfrac{b^2}{a^2} = \dfrac{3}{2}$

and $\dfrac{2b^2}{a} = 6\sqrt{2} \Rightarrow 2 \cdot \dfrac{3}{2} \cdot a = 6\sqrt{2}$

$$a = 2\sqrt{2}, b^2 = 12$$

Now, $c^2 = a^2m^2 - b^2 = 8 \cdot 4 - 12 = 20$

54. Given, $\dfrac{x^2}{a^2} - \dfrac{y^2}{9} = 1$; point $(8, 3\sqrt{3})$

$$\frac{64}{a^2} - \frac{9 \times 3}{9} = 1 \Rightarrow a^2 = 16$$

$\therefore$ Equation of normal at point $(8, 3\sqrt{3})$,

$$(y - y_1) = \frac{-y_1 a^2}{x_1 b^2}(x - x_1)$$

$\Rightarrow$ $(y - 3\sqrt{3}) = \dfrac{-3\sqrt{3}}{8} \times \dfrac{16}{9}(x - 8)$

$$y - 3\sqrt{3} = \frac{-2}{\sqrt{3}}(x - 8)$$

Verify $(-1, 9\sqrt{3})$ in the equation of normal,

$$y - 3\sqrt{3} = -\frac{2}{\sqrt{3}}(-1 - 8) \Rightarrow y = 9\sqrt{3}$$

Thus, $(-1, 9\sqrt{3})$ is the required point.

55. Given, equation of hyperbola is $kx^2 - y^2 = 6$

$\Rightarrow$ $\dfrac{x^2}{\frac{6}{k}} - \dfrac{y^2}{6} = 1$

$\Rightarrow$ $e = \sqrt{1 + \dfrac{b^2}{a^2}} = \sqrt{1 + k}$

Equation of directrix, $x = \pm\dfrac{a}{e}$

$\Rightarrow$ $x = \pm\sqrt{\dfrac{6}{k}} \times \dfrac{1}{\sqrt{1 + k}}$

$\Rightarrow$ $\dfrac{\sqrt{6}}{\sqrt{k}\sqrt{1 + k}} = 1$

$\Rightarrow$ $6 = k^2 + k$

$\Rightarrow$ $k(k + 3) - 2(k + 3) = 0$

$\Rightarrow$ $k = 2$ $[\because k \neq -3]$

$\therefore$ The equation of hyperbola is $\dfrac{x^2}{3} - \dfrac{y^2}{6} = 1$

From the options,

(a) $(-2\sqrt{5}, 6)$; $\dfrac{20}{3} - \dfrac{36}{6} \neq 1$ (b) $(-\sqrt{5}, 3)$; $\dfrac{5}{3} - \dfrac{9}{6} \neq 1$

(c) $(\sqrt{5}, -2)$; $\dfrac{5}{3} - \dfrac{4}{6} = 1$ (d) $(2\sqrt{5}, 3\sqrt{6})$; $\dfrac{20}{3} - 9 \neq 1$

$\therefore$ The hyperbola passes through the point $(\sqrt{5}, -2)$.

56. The given equation of hyperbola, $a^2x^2 - y^2 = b^2$

i.e. $\dfrac{x^2}{\left(\dfrac{b^2}{a^2}\right)} - \dfrac{y^2}{b^2} = 1$ ... (i)

Tangent of Eq. (i) is

$$y = mx \pm \sqrt{\frac{b^2m^2}{a^2} - b^2} \quad \text{... (ii)}$$

Given that $\lambda x - 2y = \mu$ be a tangent to the hyperbola.

So, $y = \dfrac{\lambda x}{2} - \dfrac{\mu}{2}$ ... (iii)

Now, On comparing Eqs. (ii) and (iii), we get

$$m = \frac{\lambda}{2}, \frac{b^2m^2}{a^2} - b^2 = \frac{\mu^2}{4}$$

On substituting $m = \dfrac{\lambda}{2}$ in $\dfrac{b^2m^2}{a^2} - b^2 = \dfrac{\mu^2}{4}$, we get

$$\frac{b^2}{a^2} \times \frac{\lambda^2}{4} - b^2 = \frac{\mu^2}{4}$$

$\Rightarrow$ $\dfrac{\lambda^2}{a^2} - \dfrac{\mu^2}{b^2} = 4$

$\Rightarrow$ $\left(\dfrac{\lambda}{a}\right)^2 - \left(\dfrac{\mu}{b}\right)^2 = 4$

57.

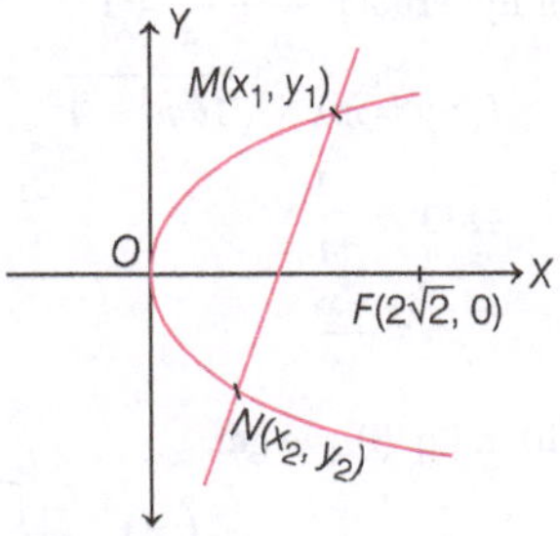

$$H : x^2 - y^2 = 4$$

$$\Rightarrow \quad \frac{x^2}{4} - \frac{y^2}{4} = 1$$

Focus $(ae, 0) = F(2\sqrt{2}, 0)$

$$y^2 = 4x, a = 1, \text{focus } (a, 0) = (1, 0)$$

Focal chord line $L : y = mx + c \,;\, m > 0$

Line L passes through $(1, 0)$

$$0 = m + c \qquad \text{...(i)}$$

$$\Rightarrow \quad m = -c$$

Also, line L is tangent to hyperbola $\frac{x^2}{4} - \frac{y^2}{4} = 1.$

$$\therefore \quad c = \pm\sqrt{a^2m^2 - b^2} = \pm\sqrt{4m^2 - 4}$$

$$\Rightarrow \quad 4m^2 - 4 = m^2 \qquad [\because m = -c]$$

$$\Rightarrow \quad m = 2/\sqrt{3} (m > 0)$$

Equation of line $L : y = \frac{2}{\sqrt{3}}x - \frac{2}{\sqrt{3}}$

Now, this line L cuts the parabola $y^2 = 4x$ at two points M and N.

$$\therefore \quad \left(\frac{2x-2}{\sqrt{3}}\right)^2 = 4x$$

$$\Rightarrow \quad (x-1)^2 = 3x$$

$$\Rightarrow \quad x^2 - 5x + 1 = 0$$

Now, $$y^2 = \frac{4(\sqrt{3}y + 2)}{2}$$

$$\Rightarrow \quad y^2 - 2\sqrt{3}y - 4 = 0$$

$\therefore$ Area of quadrilateral $OMFN = \left|\frac{1}{2}\begin{vmatrix} 0 & x_1 & 2\sqrt{2} & x_2 & 0 \\ 0 & y_1 & 0 & y_2 & 0 \end{vmatrix}\right|$

$$= \frac{1}{2}|0 - 2\sqrt{2}y_1 + 2\sqrt{2}y_2 - 0 + 0|$$

$$= \frac{2\sqrt{2}}{2}|y_2 - y_1|$$

$$= \sqrt{2}\sqrt{(y_1 + y_2)^2 - 4y_1y_2}$$

$$= \sqrt{2}\sqrt{12 + 16} = 2\sqrt{14}$$

58. Given, equation of hyperbola, $\frac{x^2}{a^2} - \frac{y^2}{b^2} = 1$

Hyperbola passes through $(2\sqrt{2}, -2\sqrt{2})$

$$\therefore \quad \frac{8}{a^2} - \frac{8}{b^2} = 1$$

$$8b^2 - 8a^2 = a^2b^2 \qquad \text{...(i)}$$

Focus of parabola = Focus of hyperbola with positive abscissa

$$A = ae. \qquad \text{...(ii)}$$

Equation of directrix of parabola is $x = -ae$

Length of latusrectum of hyperbola is e times the length of latusrectum of hyperbola.

$$4A = \frac{2b^2}{a} \times e \Rightarrow 4a = \frac{2b^2}{a} \qquad [\because \text{from Eq. (ii)}]$$

$$\Rightarrow \quad 2a^2 = b^2$$

On substituting it in Eq. (i), we get

$$8(2a^2) - 8a^2 = a^2(2a^2)$$

$$\Rightarrow \quad a^2 = 4 \Rightarrow a = 2 \qquad [\because a \neq 0]$$

$$b^2 = 2a^2 = 8$$

$$\therefore \quad e = \sqrt{1 + \frac{8}{4}} = \sqrt{3}$$

$$\Rightarrow \quad A = ae = 2\sqrt{3}$$

Equation of parabola is $y^2 = 4Ax = 4 \times 2\sqrt{3}x = 8\sqrt{3}x$

From options, $8\sqrt{3} \times 3\sqrt{3}$

$$\Rightarrow \quad 72 = 72$$

Hence, $(3\sqrt{3}, -6\sqrt{2})$ lies on the parabola.

59. The given equation of ellipse is $\frac{x^2}{16} + \frac{y^2}{7} = 1.$

Thus, eccentricity is $\sqrt{1 - \frac{7}{16}} = \frac{3}{4}$

So, foci are $(\pm\, ae, 0) = (\pm\, 3, 0)$

Now, equation of hyperbola is $\frac{x^2}{\left(\frac{144}{25}\right)} - \frac{y^2}{\left(\frac{\alpha}{25}\right)} = 1$

Now, eccentricity, $e = \sqrt{1 + \frac{\left(\frac{\alpha}{25}\right)}{\left(\frac{144}{25}\right)}} = \frac{\sqrt{\alpha + 144}}{12}$

Then, foci are $(\pm\, ae, 0) = \left(\pm\frac{12}{5} \cdot \frac{1}{12}\sqrt{144 + \alpha}, 0\right)$

$$= \left(\pm\frac{1}{5}\sqrt{144 + \alpha}, 0\right)$$

Given that the foci of the ellipse and hyperbola are coincide, then

$$3 = \frac{1}{5}\sqrt{144 + \alpha} \quad \Rightarrow \quad \alpha = 81$$

Thus, the hyperbola is $\frac{x^2}{\left(\frac{12}{5}\right)^2} - \frac{y^2}{\left(\frac{9}{5}\right)^2} = 1$

Hence, the length of latusrectum

$$= 2\left(\frac{81/25}{12/5}\right) = 2 \times \frac{81}{25} \times \frac{5}{12} = \frac{27}{10}$$

60. Given, $C_1 : \frac{x^2}{4} + \frac{y^2}{9} = 1$

and $C_2 : \frac{x^2}{42} - \frac{y^2}{143} = 1$

Tangent to C_1 is $y = mx \pm \sqrt{4m^2 + 9}$

Tangent to C_2 is $y = mx \pm \sqrt{42m^2 - 143}$

For common tangent, $4m^2 + 9 = 42m^2 - 143 \Rightarrow m = \pm 2$

If tangent does not pass through IV quadrant, then $m > 0$ and y-intercept is positive.

$\therefore$ Tangent is $y = 2x + 5$

This tangent touches C_1 at $(x_1\ y_1)$.

$\therefore$ Tangent is $\frac{x_1 x}{4} + \frac{y y_1}{9} = 1$

On comparing, we get $\frac{x_1 / 4}{2} = \frac{1}{-5}$

$$\Rightarrow \quad x_1 = -8/5$$

Also, point of contact with C_2 is (x_2, y_2).

$\therefore$ Tangent is $\frac{xx_2}{42} - \frac{yy_2}{143} = 1$

$$\therefore \quad \frac{x_2 / 42}{2} = \frac{1}{-5}$$

$$\Rightarrow \quad x_2 = \frac{-84}{5}$$

$$\therefore \quad |2x_1 + x_2| = \frac{100}{5} = 20$$

61. **Decoding the Question**

Sum of length of transverse axis and conjugate axis of hyperbola = $2a + 2b$.

$$H : \frac{x^2}{a^2} - \frac{y^2}{b^2} = 1$$

$$e = \frac{\sqrt{11}}{2} \Rightarrow e^2 = \frac{11}{4} \Rightarrow 1 + \frac{b^2}{a^2} = \frac{11}{4}$$

$$\Rightarrow \quad b^2 = \frac{7}{4}a^2 \Rightarrow b^2 = \left(\frac{\sqrt{7}}{2}a\right)^2$$

$$\therefore \quad \frac{x^2}{a^2} - \frac{y^2}{\left(\frac{\sqrt{7}}{2}a\right)^2} = 1$$

Length of transverse axis = $2a$

Length of conjugate axis = $2b = 2\left(\frac{\sqrt{7}}{2}a\right) = \sqrt{7}a$

Sum of length of transverse axis and conjugate axis.

$$2a + \sqrt{7}a = 4(2\sqrt{2} + \sqrt{14})$$

$$\Rightarrow \quad a(2 + \sqrt{7}) = 4\sqrt{2}(2 + \sqrt{7})$$

$$\Rightarrow \quad a = 4\sqrt{2}$$

$$\Rightarrow \quad b^2 = \left(\frac{\sqrt{7}}{2} \times 4\sqrt{2}\right)^2 = 4 \times 14 = 56$$

$$\therefore \quad a^2 + b^2 = 32 + 56 = 88$$

62. Equation of hyperbola, $\frac{x^2}{16} - \frac{y^2}{4} = 1$

$$L_1 : y = mx \pm \sqrt{16m^2 - 4} \quad \text{...(i)}$$

$$L_2 : y = \frac{-1}{m}x$$

$$\Rightarrow \quad m = \frac{-x}{y} \quad \text{...(ii)}$$

Using Eq. (ii) in Eq. (i), we get

$$y = -\left(\frac{x}{y}\right)x \pm \sqrt{16\left(\frac{-x}{y}\right)^2 - 4}$$

$$\Rightarrow \quad y = \frac{-x^2}{y} \pm \frac{\sqrt{16x^2 - 4y^2}}{y}$$

$$\Rightarrow \quad (y^2 + x^2)^2 = 16x^2 - 4y^2 \quad \text{...(iii)}$$

Given equation $(x^2 + y^2)^2 = \alpha x^2 + \beta y^2$ ...(iv)

On comparing Eqs. (iii) and (iv), we get

$$\alpha = 16 \text{ and } \beta = -4$$

$$\therefore \quad \alpha + \beta = 16 - 4 = 12$$

63. Since, $e = 5/4$

$$\Rightarrow \quad 1 + \frac{b^2}{a^2} = \left(\frac{5}{4}\right)^2 \Rightarrow 9a^2 = 16b^2$$

The point $\left(\frac{8}{\sqrt{5}}, \frac{12}{5}\right)$ satisfies the hyperbola.

$$\therefore \quad \frac{64}{5a^2} - \frac{144}{25b^2} = 1$$

$$\Rightarrow \quad \frac{64 \times 9}{5 \times 16b^2} - \frac{144}{25b^2} = 1$$

$$\Rightarrow \quad b = \frac{6}{5} \text{ and } a = \frac{8}{5}$$

Equation of normal at the point $\left(\frac{8}{\sqrt{5}}, \frac{12}{5}\right)$

$$= \frac{\sqrt{5}a^2 x}{8} + \frac{5b^2 y}{12} = a^2 + b^2$$

$$\Rightarrow \quad \sqrt{5} \times \frac{64}{25 \times 8}x + \frac{5}{12} \times \frac{36}{25}y = 4$$

$$\Rightarrow \quad 8\sqrt{5}x + 15y = 100$$

Compare it with given equation $8\sqrt{5}x + \beta y = \lambda$, $\beta = 15$ and $\lambda = 100$

Hence, $\lambda - \beta = 100 - 15 = 85$

64. The given equation of hyperbola $H : \frac{x^2}{a^2} - y^2 = 1$

and ellipse $E : 3x^2 + 4y^2 = 12$

$$\Rightarrow \quad \frac{x^2}{4} + \frac{y^2}{3} = 1$$

Latusrectum of hyperbola, $(l) = \frac{2 \times (1)^2}{a} = \frac{2}{a}$

and latusrectum of ellipse, $(l) = \frac{2 \times \sqrt{(3)^2}}{2} = \frac{2 \times 3}{2} = 3$

Since, given that length of latusrectum of hyperbola = length of latusrectum of parabola.

$\therefore \quad \frac{2}{a} = 3 \Rightarrow a = \frac{2}{3}$

e_H is eccentricity of $H = \sqrt{1 + \frac{b^2}{a^2}} = \sqrt{1 + \frac{9}{4}} = \sqrt{\frac{13}{4}}$

and e_E is eccentricity of

$$E = \sqrt{1 - \frac{b^2}{a^2}} = \sqrt{1 - \frac{3}{4}} = \sqrt{\frac{1}{4}}$$

Thus, $12(e_E^2 + e_H^2) = 12\left(\frac{1}{4} + \frac{13}{4}\right)$

$$= 12\left(\frac{14}{4}\right)$$

$$= \frac{168}{4} = 42$$

65. Let the locus of the mid-point of the chord be (h, k).

Then, chord through mid-point (h, k) is $T = S_1$

$\Rightarrow \quad xh - yk = h^2 - k^2 \quad$ ...(i)

Now, this is also a tangent of $y^2 = 8x$

The equation of the tangent of slope m to the parabola $y^2 = 8x$ is given by

Tangent : $\quad y = mx + \frac{2}{m}$

$\Rightarrow \quad m^2x - my = -2 \quad$ ...(ii)

Eqs. (i) and (ii) are coincide.

$\therefore \quad \frac{h}{m^2} = \frac{-k}{-m} = \frac{h^2 - k^2}{-2}$

$\Rightarrow \quad h = km$

$\Rightarrow \quad m = \frac{h}{k}$

$\therefore \quad \frac{k^2}{h} = \frac{h^2 - k^2}{-2}$

$\Rightarrow \quad -2k^2 = h^3 - hk^2$

$\Rightarrow \quad h^3 = k^2(h - 2)$

Therefore, locus of mid-point of the chords is $x^3 = y^2(x - 2)$.

66. $T : 2x + y = k$

$$H : x^2 - y^2 = 3$$

$$P : y^2 = \alpha x$$

If T is tangent, then $y = mx \pm \sqrt{a^2m^2 - b^2}$

$\Rightarrow \quad y = -2x - k$

On comparing both sides, we get

$$m = -2 \text{ and } k = 3$$

If $2x + y = 3$ is also tangent to $y^2 = \alpha x$, then, $y = mx + \frac{\alpha}{4m}$

$\because \quad m = -2$

$\therefore \quad \frac{\alpha}{-8} = 3$

$\Rightarrow \quad \alpha = -24$

67. $a^2 + b^2 = a^2e^2$

$$a^2 + b^2 = a^2\left(\frac{5}{4}\right)$$

$\Rightarrow \quad 4b^2 = a^2$

$$\frac{x^2}{a^2} - \frac{y^2}{b^2} = 1$$

$\because$ Point $P(-2\sqrt{6}, \sqrt{3})$ lies on given ellipse.

$\therefore \quad \frac{24}{4b^2} - \frac{3}{b^2} = 1 \Rightarrow b^2 = 3 \Rightarrow a^2 = 12$

Equation of tangent at P, $\frac{x(-2\sqrt{6})}{12} - \frac{y(\sqrt{3})}{3} = 1$

For conjugate axis, put $x = 0$

$\therefore \quad Q(0, -\sqrt{3})$

Equation of normal at P, $\frac{y - \sqrt{3}}{x + 2\sqrt{6}} = \left(\frac{-1}{\sqrt{3}}\right) \times \left(\frac{12}{-2\sqrt{6}}\right)$

$\Rightarrow \quad y - \sqrt{3} = 2\sqrt{12} = 4\sqrt{3}$

$\Rightarrow \quad y = 5\sqrt{3}$

$\therefore \quad R(0, 5\sqrt{3}) \Rightarrow QR = 6\sqrt{3}$

68. Given, hyperbola is $16x^2 - 9y^2 + 32x + 36y - 164 = 0$

$\Rightarrow \quad 16(x + 1)^2 - 9(y - 2)^2 = 164 + 16 - 36 = 144$

$\Rightarrow \quad \frac{(x + 1)^2}{9} - \frac{(y - 2)^2}{16} = 1$

Eccentricity, $e = \sqrt{1 + \frac{16}{9}} = \frac{5}{3}$

$\Rightarrow$ Foci are (4, 2) and (−6, 2).

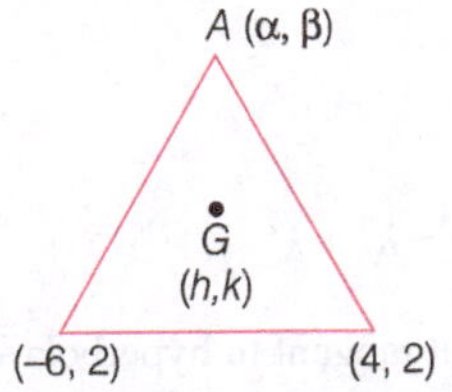

Let the centroid be (h, k) and $A(\alpha, \beta)$ be point on hyperbol(a).

So, $\quad h = \frac{\alpha - 6 + 4}{3}$ and $k = \frac{\beta + 2 + 2}{3}$

$\Rightarrow \quad \alpha = 3h + 2$ and $\beta = 3k - 4$

(α, β) lies on hyperbola, so $16(3h + 2 + 1)^2 - 9(3k - 4 - 2)^2 = 144$

$\Rightarrow \quad 16(h^2 + 2h + 1) - 9(k^2 - 4k + 4) = 16$

$\Rightarrow \quad 16x^2 - 9y^2 + 32x + 36y - 36 = 0$

69. Given, ellipse is $\frac{x^2}{25} + \frac{y^2}{16} = 1$

or $\quad \frac{x^2}{(5)^2} + \frac{y^2}{(4)^2} = 1, \; a = 5$ and $b = 4$

Now, foci of ellipse $= (\pm e, 0)$, where $e = \sqrt{a^2 - b^2}$

Put the values of a and b, we get

$$e = \sqrt{5^2 - 4^2} = \sqrt{25 - 16} = \sqrt{9}$$

$\therefore$ Foci $= (\pm 3, 0)$

According to question, hyperbola passes through the focus of ellipse.

Let equation of hyperbola be $\frac{x^2}{a^2} - \frac{y^2}{b^2} = 1.$

Since, it passes through $(\pm 3, 0)$, we get

$$\frac{(\pm 3)^2}{a^2} - \frac{0}{b^2} = 1 \Rightarrow a^2 = 9$$

Also, given that product of eccentricities is 1.

$$\Rightarrow \quad \left(\sqrt{1 - \frac{16}{25}}\right)\left(\sqrt{1 + \frac{b^2}{9}}\right) = 1$$

(using formula of eccentricity of ellipse and hyperbola)

On squaring both sides, we get

$$1 + \frac{b^2}{9} = \frac{25}{9} \quad \Rightarrow \quad b^2 = 16$$

Thus, equation of hyperbola is $\frac{x^2}{9} - \frac{y^2}{16} = 1.$

70. **Decoding the Question**

Equation of tangent having slope m to hyperbola $\frac{x^2}{a^2} - \frac{y^2}{b^2} = 1$ is $y = mx \pm \sqrt{a^2 m - b^2}$.

Let the mid-point of the chord of the circle be (h, k).

The equation of a chord through its mid-point is simply $T = S_1$.

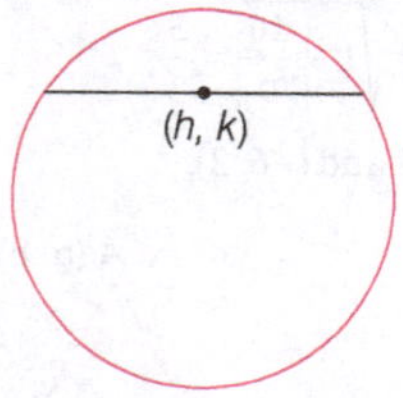

Here, $hx + ky = h^2 + k^2$

The equation of tangent to hyperbola $\frac{x^2}{a^2} - \frac{y^2}{b^2} = 1$ is

$$y = mx \pm \sqrt{a^2 m - b^2}$$

Here, $\quad y = mx \pm \sqrt{9m^2 - 16}$

So, $$y = \frac{-hx}{k} + \frac{h^2 + k^2}{k} \quad \text{... (i)}$$

and $$y = mx \pm \sqrt{9\,m^2 - 16} \quad \text{... (ii)}$$

Eqs. (i) and (ii) are identical, so

$$\frac{1}{1} = \frac{-h/k}{m} = \frac{h^2 + k^2}{k\sqrt{9m^2 - 16}} \Rightarrow m = \frac{-h}{k}$$

$$\Rightarrow \quad 9m^2 - 16 = \frac{(h^2 + k^2)^2}{k^2}$$

$$\Rightarrow \quad 9\left(\frac{h^2}{k^2}\right) - 16 = \frac{(h^2 + k^2)^2}{k^2}$$

$$\Rightarrow \quad 9h^2 - 16k^2 = (h^2 + k^2)^2$$

So, $\quad (x^2 + y^2)^2 - 9x^2 + 16y^2 = 0$

71. Let $A(\sec\theta, 2\tan\theta)$ and $B(\sec\phi, 2\tan\phi)$

Equation of normal of $\sec\theta, 2\tan\theta$ of hyperbola $\frac{x^2}{1} - \frac{y^2}{2} = 1$ is

$$x\cos\theta + 2y\cot\theta = 3 \quad \text{...(i)}$$

and $(\sec\phi, 2\tan\phi)$ is

$$x\cos\phi + 2y\cot\phi = 3 \quad \text{...(ii)}$$

On solving Eqs. (i) and (ii), and multiply $\cos\phi$ by Eq. (i) and $\cos\theta$ by Eq. (ii) and subtracting, we get

$$2y(\cot\theta\cos\phi - \cot\phi\cos\theta) = 3(\cos\phi - \cos\theta)$$

$$\Rightarrow \quad 2y\left(\frac{\cos\phi\cos\theta}{\sin\theta} - \frac{\cos\phi\cos\theta}{\sin\phi}\right) = 3(\cos\phi - \cos\theta)$$

$$\Rightarrow \quad 2y\cos\phi\cos\theta\left(\frac{\sin\phi - \sin\theta}{\sin\theta\sin\phi}\right) = 3(\cos\phi - \cos\theta)$$

$$= \frac{3(\cos\phi - \cos\theta)\tan\theta\tan\phi}{\sin\phi - \sin\theta}$$

$$= \frac{3\left(2\sin\frac{\phi + \theta}{2}\sin\frac{\theta - \phi}{2}\right)\tan\theta\tan\phi}{2\sin\left(\frac{\phi - \theta}{2}\right)\cos\left(\frac{\theta + \phi}{2}\right)}$$

$$= -3\tan\left(\frac{\theta + \phi}{2}\right)\tan\theta\tan\phi$$

$$= -3\tan\frac{\pi}{4}\tan\theta\tan\left(\frac{\pi}{2} - \theta\right) \quad [\because \phi + \theta = 2]$$

$$\Rightarrow \quad 2y = -3\tan\theta\cot\theta = -3$$

$$\therefore \quad (2y)^2 = 9 \quad \Rightarrow \quad (2\beta)^2 = 9$$

72. Given lines are

$$\sqrt{3}kx + ky - 4\sqrt{3} = 0 \quad \text{... (i)}$$

$$\sqrt{3}x - y - 4\sqrt{3}\,k = 0 \quad \text{... (ii)}$$

On multiplying Eq. (ii) by k and then adding Eqs. (i) and (ii),

$$(2\sqrt{3}x)k = 4\sqrt{3} + 4\sqrt{3}k^2$$

$$\therefore \quad x = \frac{4\sqrt{3}(1 + k^2)}{2\sqrt{3}k} = 2\left(k + \frac{1}{k}\right)$$

On subtracting Eq. (i) from Eq. (ii) $\times\, k$,

$$2ky = 4\sqrt{3} - 4\sqrt{3}k^2\; y = \frac{4\sqrt{3}(1 - k^2)}{2k} = 2\sqrt{3}\left(\frac{1}{k} - k\right)$$

$$\Rightarrow \quad \frac{x}{2} = \left(k + \frac{1}{k}\right) \quad \text{... (iii)}$$

and $$\frac{y}{2\sqrt{3}} = \left(\frac{1}{k} - k\right) \quad \text{... (iv)}$$

On squaring and subtracting Eq. (iii) from Eq. (iv),

$$\frac{x^2}{4} - \frac{y^2}{12} = \left(k^2 + \frac{1}{k^2} + 2\right) - \left(\frac{1}{k^2} + k^2 - 2\right)$$

$$\frac{x^2}{16} - \frac{y^2}{48} = 1$$

Clearly, this is a hyperbola.

$$\therefore \quad e^2 = 1 + \frac{b^2}{a^2} = 1 + \frac{48}{16} = 1 + 3$$

$$e^2 = 4$$

$$\therefore \quad e = \sqrt{4} = 2 \quad [\because e \text{ is positive}]$$

73. Since, the vertices of hyperbola on X-axis at $(\pm 6, 0)$, so equation of hyperbola we can assume as

$$\frac{x^2}{a^2} - \frac{y^2}{b^2} = 1 \text{ and } |a| = 6$$

and hyperbola passes through point $P(10, 16)$ so

$$\frac{(10)^2}{6^2} - \frac{(16)^2}{b^2} = 1$$

$$\Rightarrow \quad b^2 = \frac{36 \times 256}{256} = 144$$

So, equation of hyperbola is $\frac{x^2}{36} - \frac{y^2}{144} = 0$, and the equation of normal to hyperbola at point P is

$$\frac{36x}{10} + \frac{144y}{16} = 36 + 144$$

$$\Rightarrow \quad 2x + 5y = 100$$

Exercise 2 - JEE Advanced Pattern

1. Given, hyperbola is $\frac{x^2}{16} - \frac{y^2}{9} = 1$ ... (i)

Foci are $(\pm 5, 0)$.

$$F_1 \equiv (5, 0), F_2 \equiv (-5, 0)$$

Also, $\quad 4e_H = 5$

$$\therefore \quad e_H = \frac{5}{4}$$

Conjugate hyperbola of Eq. (i) is

$$-\frac{x^2}{16} + \frac{y^2}{9} = 1 \quad \text{... (ii)}$$

Foci are $(0, \pm 5)$.

$$F_3 \equiv (0, 5), F_4 \equiv (0, -5)$$

Also, $\quad 3e_c = 5$

$$\therefore \quad e_c = \frac{5}{3}$$

Equation of asymptotes of Eqs. (i) and (ii) are same

$$y = \pm \frac{3}{4}x \text{ and } e_H < e_c$$

Auxiliary circle of Eq. (i) is $x^2 + y^2 = 16$

and Eq. (ii) is $x^2 + y^2 = -9$

and area of quadrilateral formed by their foci $= 4 \times \frac{1}{2} \times 5 \times 5$

$= 50$ sq units

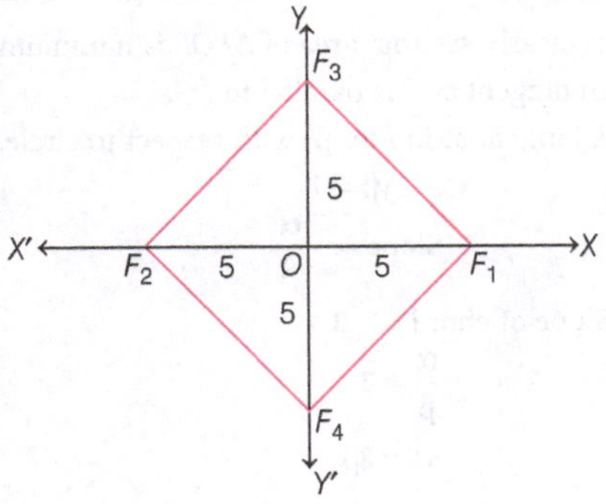

2. Point of intersection of tangents at $(a\sec\alpha, b\tan\alpha)$ and $(a\sec\beta, b\tan\beta)$ is

$$\left(\frac{a\cos\left(\frac{\alpha - \beta}{2}\right)}{\cos\left(\frac{\alpha + \beta}{2}\right)}, \frac{b\sin\left(\frac{\alpha + \beta}{2}\right)}{\cos\left(\frac{\alpha + \beta}{2}\right)} \right)$$

Here, $\quad \alpha = \phi, \beta = \frac{\pi}{2} - \phi$

Then, point of intersection is $\left(\frac{a\cos\left(\frac{\pi}{4} - \phi\right)}{\frac{1}{\sqrt{2}}}, b \right)$.

So, $x = a\sqrt{2}\cos\left(\frac{\pi}{4} - \phi\right)$ and $y = b$

$\therefore$ Required locus is $y = b$.

3. Let rectangular hyperbola be $xy = c^2$.

Equation of tangent at t is

$$\frac{x}{t} + yt = 2c$$

$$\Rightarrow \quad \frac{x}{2ct} + \frac{y}{\left(\frac{2c}{t}\right)} = 1 \quad \text{... (i)}$$

and equation of normal at t is

$$xt^3 - yt - ct^4 + c = 0$$

$$\Rightarrow \quad xt^3 - ty = ct^4 - c$$

$$\Rightarrow \quad \frac{x}{\left(\frac{ct^4 - c}{t^3}\right)} + \frac{x}{\left(\frac{-ct^4 + c}{t}\right)} = 1 \quad \text{... (ii)}$$

From Eqs. (i) and (ii) it is clear that

$$x_1 = 2ct, x_2 = \left(\frac{ct^4 - c}{t^3}\right)$$

and $\quad y_1 = \frac{2c}{t}, y_2 = \left(\frac{-ct^4 + c}{t}\right)$

$$\therefore \quad x_1x_2 + y_1y_2 = \frac{2ct(ct^4 - c)}{t^3} + \frac{2c}{t} \cdot \frac{(-ct^4 + c)}{t}$$

$$= \frac{2c^2(t^4 - 1)}{t^2} + \frac{2c^2(t^4 - 1)}{t^2} = 0$$

4. Let $H : x^2 + 3xy + 2y^2 + 2x + 3y = 0$

Let pair of asymptotes be

$$x^2 + 3xy + 2y^2 + 2x + 3y + \lambda = 0$$

$$\therefore \quad \Delta = 0$$

$$1 \times 2 \times \lambda + 2 \times \frac{3}{2} \times 1 \times \frac{3}{2} - 1 \times \frac{9}{4} - 2 \times 1 - \lambda \times \frac{9}{4} = 0$$

$$\Rightarrow \quad -\frac{\lambda}{4} + \frac{9}{2} - \frac{9}{4} - 2 = 0$$

$$\Rightarrow \quad \frac{\lambda}{4} = \frac{9}{4} - 2 = \frac{1}{4}$$

$$\therefore \quad \lambda = 1$$

$A : x^2 + 3xy + 2y^2 + 2x + 3y + 1 = 0$

$\because \quad H + C = 2A$

$\therefore \quad C = 2A - H$

$= x^2 + 3xy + 2y^2 + 2x + 3y + 2$

Hence, conjugate hyperbola is
$x^2 + 3xy + 2y^2 + 2x + 3y + 2 = 0.$

5. Given, $x - 2 = m$ and $y + 1 = \dfrac{4}{m}$

$\therefore \quad (x-2)(y+1) = 4$

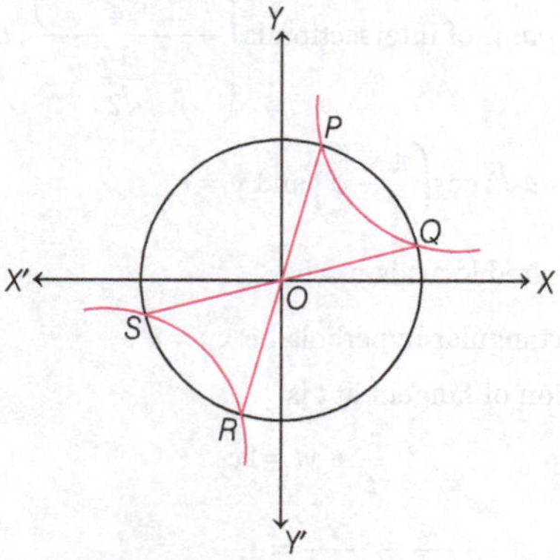

Let $\quad x - 2 = X, y + 1 = Y$

$\therefore \quad XY = 4$

and $\quad S_1 = (x-2)^2 + (y+1)^2 = 25$

or $\quad X^2 + Y^2 = 25$

Curve C and circle are concentric, therefore

$(OP)^2 + (OQ)^2 + (OR)^2 + (OS)^2 = 4r^2$

$= 4(5)^2 = 100$

6. The length of transverse axis $= 2\sin\theta = 2a$

$\Rightarrow \quad a = \sin\theta$

Also, for ellipse $3x^2 + 4y^2 = 12$

or $\quad \dfrac{x^2}{4} + \dfrac{y^2}{3} = 1, a^2 = 4, b^2 = 3$

$e = \sqrt{1 - \dfrac{b^2}{a^2}} = \sqrt{1 - \dfrac{3}{4}} = \dfrac{1}{2}$

$\therefore$ Focus of ellipse $= \left(2 \times \dfrac{1}{2}, 0\right) \Rightarrow (1, 0)$

As hyperbola is confocal with ellipse, focus of hyperbola $= (1, 0)$

$\Rightarrow \quad ae = 1 \Rightarrow \sin\theta \times e = 1$

$\Rightarrow \quad e = \operatorname{cosec}\theta$

$\therefore \quad b^2 = a^2(e^2 - 1) = \sin^2\theta(\operatorname{cosec}^2\theta - 1) = \cos^2\theta$

$\therefore$ Equation of hyperbola is $\dfrac{x^2}{\sin^2\theta} - \dfrac{y^2}{\cos^2\theta} = 1$

or $\quad x^2\operatorname{cosec}^2\theta - y^2\sec^2\theta = 1$

7. Foci of the ellipse $\dfrac{x^2}{k^2a^2} + \dfrac{y^2}{a^2} = 1$ are

$(\pm a\sqrt{(k^2 - 1)}, 0)$ and foci of the hyperbola

$\dfrac{x^2}{a^2} - \dfrac{y^2}{b^2} = 1$ are $(\pm ae, 0), e > 1$

$\therefore$ Foci are coincide, then

$a\sqrt{(k^2 - 1)} = ae$ or $\sqrt{(k^2 - 1)} > 1$

or $\quad k^2 - 1 > 1$ or $k^2 > 2$

$\because \quad k > \sqrt{2} = \sqrt{\lambda}$

$\therefore \quad \lambda = 2$

8. Given, $y = mx + c$ is tangent to hyperbola

$\dfrac{x^2}{\lambda^2} - \dfrac{y^2}{(\lambda^3 + \lambda^2 + \lambda)^2} = 1$

$\therefore$ As per condition of tangency

$c^2 = a^2m^2 - b^2$

$c^2 = \lambda^2m^2 - (\lambda^3 + \lambda^2 + \lambda)^2$

$c^2 \geq 0$

$\Rightarrow \quad \lambda^2m^2 - \lambda^2(\lambda^2 + \lambda + 1)^2 \geq 0$

$\Rightarrow \quad m^2 \geq (\lambda^2 + \lambda + 1)^2$

$\because \quad \lambda^2 + \lambda + 1 = (\lambda + 1/2)^2 + \dfrac{3}{4}$

$\therefore$ Minimum value of $\lambda^2 + \lambda + 1 = \dfrac{3}{4}$

$\therefore$ Minimum value of $m^2 = (\lambda^2 + \lambda + 1)^2_{\min} = \dfrac{9}{16}$

$\therefore \quad (16m^2)_{\min} = 9$

9. Curve $x^2 - 4y^2 = 4$ [given]... (i)

Chord of contact $2x + y + 6 = 0 \Rightarrow y = -6 - 2x$ ... (ii)

Slope of chord $= -2$

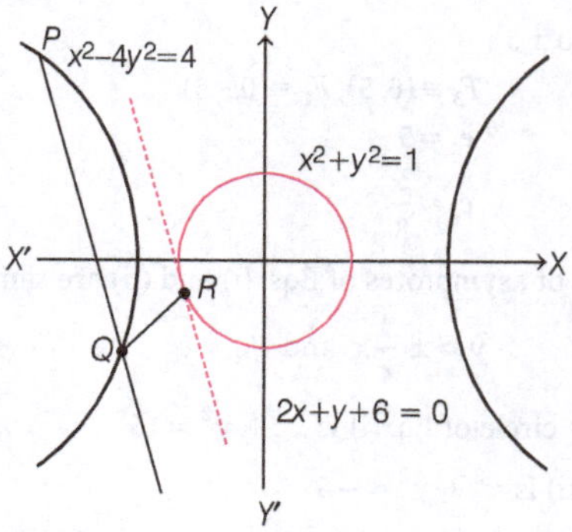

$\because R(\alpha, \beta)$ is the point satisfy $\alpha^2 + \beta^2 - 1 \leq 0$

[i.e. interior region of circle $x^2 + y^2 = 1$]

$\because$ It is clearly see that area of ΔPQR is minimum.
When tangent at R is parallel to PQ.
Now, tangent at in $R(\alpha, \beta)$ with respect to circle is

$x\alpha + y\beta = 1$

Slope $= -\dfrac{\alpha}{\beta}$

Slope of chord $= -2$

$\because \quad \dfrac{\alpha}{\beta} = 2$

$\Rightarrow \quad \alpha = 2\beta$

$\therefore$ (α, β) lies in circle $x^2 + y^2 = 1$

$$\alpha^2 + \beta^2 = 1$$

$$4\beta^2 + \beta^2 = 1,\ 5\beta^2 = 1$$

$$\beta = \pm \frac{1}{\sqrt{5}} \Rightarrow \alpha = \pm 2/\sqrt{5}$$

$\because$ (α, β) lies on III quadrant.

$$\therefore \quad (\alpha, \beta) = \left(\frac{-2}{\sqrt{5}}, \frac{-1}{\sqrt{5}}\right)$$

10. Given chord is $x\cos\alpha + y\sin\alpha = p$ of the hyperbola

$$\frac{x^2}{16} - \frac{y^2}{18} = 1 \quad \text{... (i)}$$

subtends a right angle at the centre p.

$$\because \quad \frac{x\cos\alpha + y\sin\alpha}{p} = 1 \quad \text{... (ii)}$$

Homogenising Eq. (i) with help of Eq. (ii) then

$$\frac{x^2}{16} - \frac{y^2}{18} = \left(\frac{x\cos\alpha + y\sin\alpha}{p}\right)^2 \quad \text{...(iii)}$$

$\because$ Eq. (iii) represents a pair of lines which are perpendicular.

$\therefore$ coefficient of x^2 + coefficient of $y^2 = 0$

$$\left(\frac{1}{16} - \frac{\cos^2\alpha}{p^2}\right) + \left(\frac{-1}{18} - \frac{\sin^2\alpha}{p^2}\right) = 0$$

$$\Rightarrow \quad \frac{1}{16} - \frac{1}{18} - \frac{1}{p^2}(\cos^2\alpha + \sin^2\alpha) = 0$$

$$\Rightarrow \quad \frac{1}{p^2} = \frac{18 - 16}{18 \times 16}$$

$$\Rightarrow \quad \frac{1}{p^2} = \frac{1}{9 \times 16}$$

$$\Rightarrow \quad p = 3 \times 4 = 12$$

$\therefore x\cos\alpha + y\sin\alpha = \pm 12$ is tangent to circle

$$x^2 + y^2 = r^2 = \left(\frac{d}{2}\right)^2$$

$$\therefore \quad d = 24 \Rightarrow \frac{d}{4} = 6$$

11. From any point $A\left(ct_1, \frac{c}{t_1}\right)$ on the rectangular hyperbola.

$$xy = c^2 \quad \text{... (i)}$$

Tangent AB and AC are drawn to the parabola $y^2 = 4ax$.

Then, $\quad B = \left(ct_2, \frac{c}{t_2}\right)$ and $c = \left(ct_3, \frac{c}{t_3}\right)$

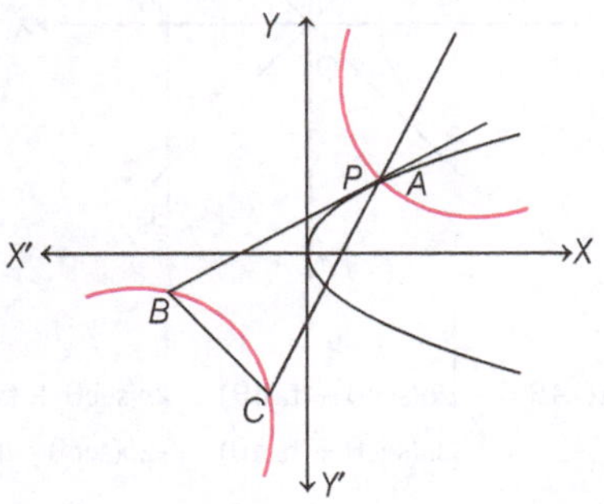

Then, ΔABC is inscribed in the rectangular hyperbola and its sides AB and AC touch the parabola.

$\because$ BC is also a tangent to it.

$\therefore$ Equations of chord AB, BC and CA are

$$AB = x + yt_1t_2 = c(t_1 + t_2)$$

$$BC = x + yt_2t_3 = c(t_2 + t_3)$$

$$CA = x + yt_3t_1 = c(t_3 + t_1)$$

$\because$ AB is tangent to a parabola $y^2 = 4ax$, its equation is

$$y = \frac{-1}{t_1t_2} + \frac{c(t_1 + t_2)}{t_1t_2}$$

Touching condition $c = \frac{a}{m}$ or $cm = a$

$$\frac{c(t_1 + t_2)}{t_1\, t_2}\left(\frac{-1}{t_1t_2}\right) = a$$

$$\Rightarrow \quad -at_1^2t_2^2 = c(t_1 + t_2)$$

$$\Rightarrow \quad at_1^2t_2^2 + ct_2 + ct_1 = 0$$

Similarly, $\quad (at_2^2)\, t_3^2 + ct_3 + ct_1 = 0$

$$\therefore \quad (at_1^2)t^2 + ct + ct_1 = 0 \quad \text{... (ii)}$$

and t_2 and t_3 are the roots of Eq. (ii).

$$\therefore \quad t_2 + t_3 = \frac{-c}{at_1^2} \text{ and } t_2t_3 = \frac{c}{at_1}$$

$$\Rightarrow \quad c = at_1t_2t_3$$

$$\therefore \quad c(t_2 + t_3) = \frac{-c^2}{at_1^2} = \frac{-a^2t_1^2t_2^2t_3^2}{at_1^2}$$

$$= -at_2^2\, t_3^2$$

$$\Rightarrow \quad -at_2t_3 = \frac{c(t_2 + t_3)}{t_2t_3} \text{ is the condition.}$$

This proves BC to be also a tangent to the parabola. But any point A can be taken in infinite ways anywhere on the curve representing the rectangular hyperbola.

Hence, such triangles exist in infinite number.

12. Let $P(h, k)$ be any point on any one member of hyperbola family having equation $\frac{x^2}{a^2} - \frac{y^2}{b^2} = 1$, b is any arbitrary constant, then its asymptotes are given by $y = \pm \frac{b}{a}x$, then according to the question,

$$|k| = \frac{\left|\pm \frac{bh}{a} - k\right|}{\sqrt{\frac{b^2}{a^2} + 1}}$$

$$\Rightarrow \quad k^2 = \left(\pm \frac{b}{a}h - k\right)^2 \left(\frac{a^2}{a^2 + b^2}\right)$$

$$\text{or} \quad k^2 = \frac{(\pm bh - ak)^2}{a^2 + b^2} \quad \text{... (i)}$$

Further, (h, k) lies on hyperbola, then

$$\frac{h^2}{a^2} - \frac{k^2}{b^2} = 1$$

$$\Rightarrow \quad b = \sqrt{\frac{a^2k^2}{h^2 - a^2}} \quad \text{... (ii)}$$

From Eqs. (i) and (ii), we get

$$(k^2 - h^2) = \pm 2h\sqrt{h^2 - a^2}$$

On squaring both sides, we get

$$(k^2 - h^2)^2 = 4h^2(h^2 - a^2)$$

$\because$ Locus is $(x^2 - y^2)^2 = 4x^2(x^2 - a^2)$

13. Given, point $P(-2\sqrt{6}, \sqrt{3})$ lies on hyperbola $\frac{x^2}{a^2} - \frac{y^2}{b^2} = 1$

$$\Rightarrow \quad \frac{24}{a^2} - \frac{3}{b^2} = 1 \qquad \text{...(i)}$$

Given, $e = \frac{\sqrt{5}}{2}$

$\because$ $b^2 = a^2(e^2 - 1)$

$\Rightarrow$ $b^2 = a^2\left(\frac{5}{4} - 1\right) \Rightarrow 4b^2 = a^2$

Put $4b^2 = a^2$ in Eq. (i), we get $\frac{6}{b^2} - \frac{3}{b^2} = 1$

$\Rightarrow$ $b^2 = 3$ and $a^2 = 12$

$\therefore$ Equation of hyperbola is $\frac{x^2}{12} - \frac{y^2}{3} = 1$

$\because$ Tangent at P is $\frac{x}{12}(-2\sqrt{6}) - \frac{y}{3}(\sqrt{3}) = 1 \Rightarrow \frac{x}{\sqrt{6}} - \frac{y}{\sqrt{3}} = 1$

For Q, put $x = 0$, we get $y = -\sqrt{3}$

$\therefore$ $Q(0, -\sqrt{3})$

Normal at $P, (y - \sqrt{3}) = \sqrt{2}(x + 2\sqrt{6})$

For R, put $x = 0$, we get $y = \sqrt{3} + 4\sqrt{3} = 5\sqrt{3}$

$\therefore$ $R(0, 5\sqrt{3})$

$\therefore$ $QR = 6\sqrt{3}$,

14. Let double ordinate be $2l$.

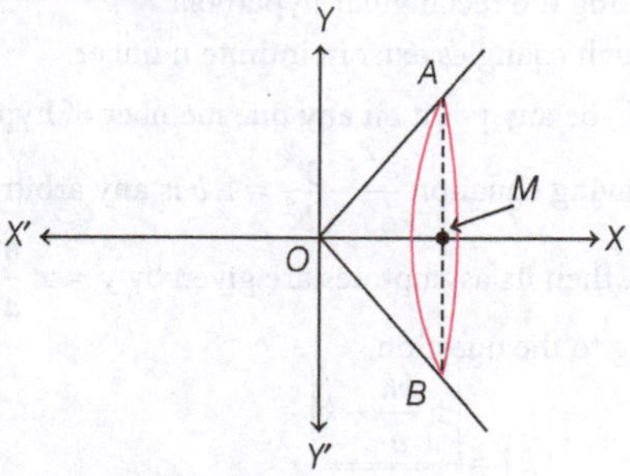

$\therefore AB = 2l$ and $AM = BM = l$

$\therefore$ Ordinate of A is l.

The abscissa of point A is given by

$$\frac{x^2}{a^2} - \frac{l^2}{b^2} = 1$$

$$\Rightarrow \quad x^2 = \frac{a^2(l^2 + b^2)}{b^2} \Rightarrow x = \frac{a\sqrt{l^2 + b^2}}{b}$$

$\therefore$ A is $\left(\frac{a\sqrt{l^2 + b^2}}{b}, l\right)$

$\because \Delta AOB$ is equilateral triangle.

$\therefore$ $OA = AB = OB = 2l$

also $OM^2 + AM^2 = OA^2$

$\therefore$ $\frac{a^2(l^2 + b^2)}{b^2} + l^2 = 4l^2$

$\Rightarrow$ $\frac{a^2(l^2 + b^2)}{b^2} = 3l^2$

$\Rightarrow$ $a^2b^2 + a^2l^2 = 3l^2b^2$

$\Rightarrow$ $a^2b^2 = 3l^2b^2 - a^2l^2$

$\Rightarrow$ $\frac{a^2b^2}{(3b^2 - a^2)} = l^2$

$\because$ $l^2 > 0$

$\therefore$ $\frac{a^2b^2}{(3b^2 - a^2)} > 0$

$\Rightarrow$ $3b^2 - a^2 > 0$

$\Rightarrow$ $3a^2(e^2 - 1) - a^2 > 0$

$\Rightarrow$ $3a^2e^2 - a^2 - 3a^2 > 0$

$\Rightarrow$ $3a^2e^2 > 4a^2$

$\Rightarrow$ $e^2 > \frac{4}{3} \Rightarrow e > \frac{2}{\sqrt{3}}$

15. Given, $h_1 : \frac{x^2}{a^2} - \frac{y^2}{b^2} = 1$

and $h_2 : \frac{x^2}{a^2} - \frac{y^2}{b^2} = 2 \Rightarrow \frac{x^2}{2a^2} - \frac{y^2}{2b^2} = 1$

Let any point on hyperbola h_1 be $P(a\sec\theta, b\tan\theta)$.

Then, chord of contact for h_2 with respect to P is given by

$$T = 0$$

$$\frac{x}{a}\sec\theta - \frac{y}{b}\tan\theta = 2 \qquad \text{...(i)}$$

Equation of asymptotes for h_2

$$y = \pm\frac{b}{a}x \Rightarrow y = \frac{b}{a}x$$

Point of asymptotes and Eq. (i) is

$A = [2a(\sec\theta + \tan\theta), 2b(\sec\theta + \tan\theta)]$

and $B = [2a(\sec\theta - \tan\theta), -2b(\sec\theta - \tan\theta)]$

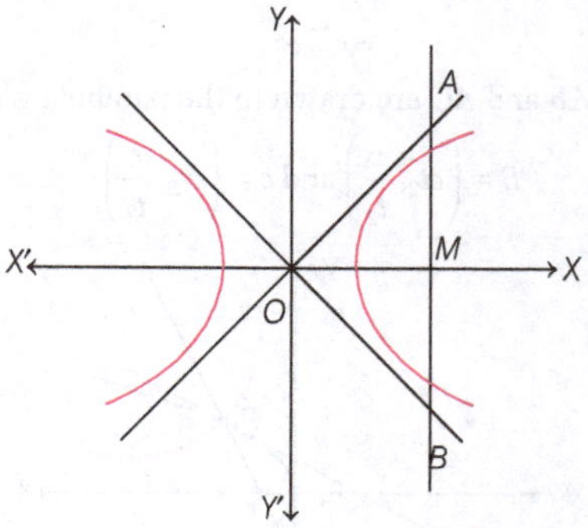

$$\text{Area of } \Delta OAB = \frac{1}{2}\begin{vmatrix} 0 & 0 & 1 \\ 2a(\sec\theta + \tan\theta) & 2b(\sec\theta + \tan\theta) & 1 \\ 2a(\sec\theta + \tan\theta) & -2b(\sec\theta - \tan\theta) & 1 \end{vmatrix}$$

$\Rightarrow \frac{1}{2}|[-4ab(\sec^2\theta - \tan^2\theta) - 4ab(\sec^2\theta - \tan^2\theta)]|$

$$= \frac{1}{2} \times 8ab = 4ab$$

$\because \quad e^2 = 1 + \frac{b^2}{a^2} = a^2e^2 = a^2 + b^2$

$\Rightarrow \quad b = \sqrt{a^2e^2 - a^2} = a\sqrt{e^2 - 1}$

$$a = \frac{b}{\sqrt{e^2 - 1}}$$

and $\quad 4ab = 4a^2\sqrt{e^2 - 1} = \frac{4b^2}{\sqrt{e^2 - 1}}$

16. Given, $\quad 16x^2 - 3y^2 - 32x - 12y - 44 = 0$

$\Rightarrow \quad 16(x^2 - 2x) - 3(y^2 + 4y) - 44 = 0$

$\Rightarrow 16\{(x-1)^2 - 1\} - 3\{(y+2)^2 - 4\} - 44 = 0$

$\Rightarrow \quad 16(x-1)^2 - 3(y+2)^2 = 48$

$$\frac{(x-1)^2}{(\sqrt{3})^2} - \frac{(y+2)^2}{4^2} = 1$$

Option (a) Length of transverse axis $= 2 \times \sqrt{3} = 2\sqrt{3}$

Option (b) Length of conjugate axis $= 2 \times 4 = 8$

Option (c) Centre $x - 1 = 0$ and $y + 2 = 0$, i.e. $(1, -2)$

Option (d) $\quad 4^2 = (\sqrt{3})^2(e^2 - 1)$

or $\quad e^2 - 1 = \frac{16}{3}$

$\Rightarrow \quad e^2 = \frac{19}{3}$

$\therefore \quad e = \sqrt{\frac{19}{3}}$

17. P, Q, R and S lie on the circle

$$x^2 + y^2 + 2gx + 2fy + c = 0 \quad \text{... (i)}$$

and also lies on $\quad xy = c^2 \quad$ ... (ii)

On solving Eqs. (i) and (ii), then

$$x^2 + \left(\frac{c^2}{x}\right)^2 + 2gx + \frac{2fc^2}{x} + c = 0$$

$\Rightarrow \quad x^4 + 2gx^3 + cx^2 + 2fc^2x + c^4 = 0$

$\therefore \quad x_1x_2x_3x_4 = c^4 \quad$ ... (iii)

and $\quad P \equiv (x_1, y_1) \equiv \left(x_1, \frac{c^2}{x_1}\right)$

$$Q \equiv \left(x_2, \frac{c^2}{x_2}\right)$$

and $\quad R \equiv \left(x_3, \frac{c^2}{x_3}\right)$

Let orthocentre be $O \equiv (h, k)$.

Then, slope of $QR \times$ slope of $OP = -1$

$$\left(\frac{\frac{c^2}{x_3} - \frac{c^2}{x_2}}{x_3 - x_2}\right) \times \left(\frac{k - \frac{c^2}{x_1}}{h - x_1}\right) = -1$$

$\Rightarrow \quad -\frac{c^2}{x_2x_3} \times \left(\frac{k - \frac{c^2}{x_1}}{h - x_1}\right) = -1$

$\Rightarrow \quad k - \frac{c^2}{x_1} = \frac{hx_2x_3}{c^2} - \frac{x_1x_2x_3}{c^2} \quad$ ... (iv)

Also, slope of $PQ \times$ slope of $OR = -1$

$$k - \frac{c^2}{x_3} = \frac{h\,x_1x_2}{c^2} - \frac{x_1x_2x_3}{c^2} \quad \text{...(v)}$$

From Eqs. (iii) and (iv), then

$\therefore \quad h = -\frac{c^4}{x_1x_2x_3}$ and $k = -\frac{x_1x_2x_3}{c^2}$

From Eq. (iii),

$$h = -x_4 \text{ and } k = -\frac{c^2}{x_4}$$

$\therefore$ Orthocentre lies on $xy = c^2$

i.e. $\quad (x_4, y_4)$ and $(-x_4, -y_4)$

18. Given, $y = x + 5$

On comparing with $y = mx + c$ we get

$\therefore \quad m = 1, c = 5$

Option (a) Condition of tangency

$$c = \frac{a}{m} \Rightarrow 5 = \frac{5}{1}$$

which is true.

Option (b)

$$9x^2 + 16y^2 = 144$$

$\Rightarrow \quad \frac{x^2}{16} + \frac{y^2}{9} = 1$

$\because$ Condition of tangency

$$c^2 = a^2m^2 + b^2$$

$\Rightarrow \quad 25 = 16 \times 1 + 9 = 25$

which is true.

Option (c)

$$\frac{x^2}{29} - \frac{y^2}{4} = 1$$

$\because$ Condition of tangency

$$c^2 = a^2m^2 - b^2$$

$$25 = 29 \times 1 - 4 = 25$$

which is true.

Option (d) Now, length of perpendicular from centre (0, 0) to the line $y = x + 5$ is $\frac{|5|}{\sqrt{2}}$ i.e. $\frac{5}{\sqrt{2}} \neq$ radius (5).

19. **Option (a)**

$$\left(\frac{2x}{a}\right)^2-\left(\frac{2y}{b}\right)^2=\left(t+\frac{1}{t}\right)^2-\left(t-\frac{1}{t}\right)^2=4$$

$$\Rightarrow \qquad \frac{x^2}{a^2}-\frac{y^2}{b^2}=1$$

Option (b)

$$\because \quad \frac{tx}{a}-\frac{y}{b}+t=0 \Rightarrow t=\frac{ay}{b(x+a)} \qquad \text{... (i)}$$

and $$\frac{x}{a}+\frac{ty}{b}-1=0 \Rightarrow t=\frac{(a-x)\,b}{ay} \qquad \text{... (ii)}$$

From Eqs. (i) and (ii), we get

$$\frac{ay}{b\,(x+a)}=\frac{(a-x)b}{ay}$$

$$\Rightarrow \qquad a^2y^2=b^2(a^2-x^2)$$

$$\Rightarrow \qquad b^2x^2+a^2y^2=a^2b^2$$

or $$\frac{x^2}{a^2}+\frac{y^2}{b^2}=1$$

Option (c) $x^2-y^2=(e^t+e^{-t})^2-(e^t-e^{-t})^2=4$

Option (d) $\because x^2-6=2\cos t$

$$\Rightarrow \quad x^2-4=2(1+\cos t)=4\cos^2\left(\frac{t}{2}\right) \qquad \text{... (i)}$$

and $$y^2+2=4\cos^2\left(\frac{t}{2}\right) \qquad \text{... (ii)}$$

From Eqs. (i) and (ii), then

$$x^2-4=y^2+2$$

or $$x^2-y^2=6$$

20. Vertices and foci of ellipse $\frac{x^2}{16}+\frac{y^2}{7}=1$ are $(\pm 4, 0)$ and $(\pm 3, 0)$, respectively.

Vertices and foci of the hyperbola $\frac{x^2}{\left(\frac{144}{25}\right)}-\frac{y^1}{\left(\frac{81}{25}\right)}=1$ are $\left(\pm\frac{12}{5}, 0\right)$ and $(\pm 3, 0)$, respectively.

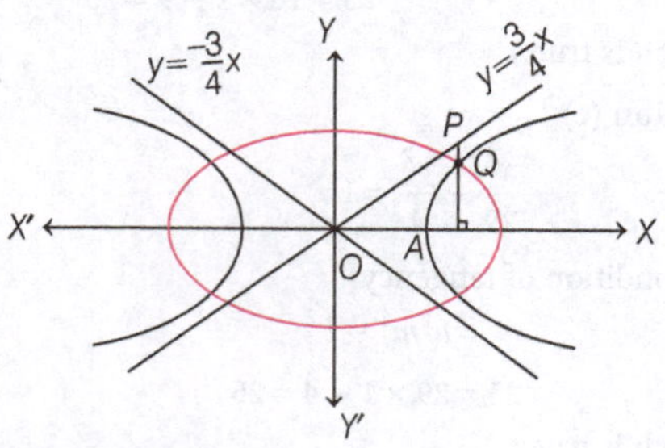

For point of intersection

$$7\left(1-\frac{x^2}{16}\right)=81\left(\frac{x^2}{144}-\frac{1}{25}\right)$$

$$\Rightarrow \qquad x^2=\frac{256}{25}$$

and $$y^2=7\left(1-\frac{16}{25}\right)=\frac{63}{25}$$

= square of the ordinate of point of intersection

$$y^2 \text{ for } P=\frac{9}{16}x^2=\frac{9}{16}\times\frac{256}{25}=\frac{144}{25}$$

$\therefore$ Sum of the squares of coordinates of P is $x^2+y^2=16$ which is auxiliary circle formed by ellipse.

21. Given, ellipse is $x^2+4y^2=4$

or $$\frac{x^2}{4}+\frac{y^2}{1}=1$$

$$\therefore \qquad e=\sqrt{\left(1-\frac{1}{4}\right)}=\frac{\sqrt{3}}{2}$$

and foci are $(\pm\sqrt{3}, 0)$.

$\therefore$ Eccentricity of hyperbola $=\frac{2}{\sqrt{3}}=e_1$

and $b^2=a^2(e_1^2-1)=a^2\left(\frac{4}{3}-1\right)=\frac{a^2}{3}$,

then equation of hyperbola becomes

$$x^2-3y^2=a^2$$

which passes through $(\pm\sqrt{3}, 0)$

$$3-0=a^2 \Rightarrow a^2=3$$

$\therefore$ Equation of hyperbola is

$$x^2-3y^2=3$$

and foci of hyperbola are $\left(\pm\sqrt{3}\times\frac{2}{\sqrt{3}}, 0\right)$ i.e. $(\pm 2, 0)$

22. Equation of tangent at (x_1, y_1) is

$$\frac{xx_1}{9}-\frac{yy_1}{4}=1 \qquad \text{... (i)}$$

Equation of line parallel to

$$2x-y=\lambda \qquad \text{... (ii)}$$

$\because$ Line (ii) is tangent of $\frac{x^2}{9}-\frac{y^2}{4}=1$, then

$$\lambda^2=9\times 2^2-4$$

$$\therefore \qquad \lambda=\pm 4\sqrt{2}$$

From Eq. (ii), Equation of tangent is

$$2x-y=\pm 4\sqrt{2} \qquad \text{... (iii)}$$

On comparing Eqs. (i) and (iii), we get $\frac{x_1}{18}=\frac{y_1}{4}=\pm\frac{1}{4\sqrt{2}}$

or $$x_1=\pm\frac{9}{2\sqrt{2}} \text{ and } y_1=\pm\frac{1}{\sqrt{2}}$$

Hence, points of contact of the tangents on the hyperbola are $\left(\frac{9}{2\sqrt{2}}, \frac{1}{\sqrt{2}}\right)$ and $\left(-\frac{9}{2\sqrt{2}}, -\frac{1}{\sqrt{2}}\right)$

23. Given, $H: x^2-y^2=1$

S : Circle with centre $N(x_2, 0)$

Common tangent to H and S at $P(x_1, y_1)$ is

$$xx_1-yy_1=1$$

$$\Rightarrow \qquad m_1=\frac{x_1}{y_1}$$

Also, radius of circle S with centre $N(x_2, 0)$ through point of contact (x_1, y_1) is perpendicular to tangent.

$$\therefore \quad m_1 m_2 = -1 \Rightarrow \frac{x_1}{y_1} \times \frac{0 - y_1}{x_2 - x_1} = -1$$

$$\Rightarrow \quad x_1 = x_2 - x_1 \text{ or } x_2 = 2x_1$$

M is the point of intersection of tangent at P and X-axis

$$\therefore \quad M\left(\frac{1}{x_1}, 0\right)$$

$\because$ Centroid of ΔPMN is (l, m)

$$\therefore \quad x_1 + \frac{1}{x_1} + x_2 = 3l \text{ and } y_1 = 3m$$

Using $x_2 = 2x_1$,

$$\Rightarrow \quad \frac{1}{3}\left(3x_1 + \frac{1}{x_1}\right) = l \text{ and } \frac{y_1}{3} = m$$

$$\therefore \quad \frac{dl}{dx_1} = 1 - \frac{1}{3x_1^2}, \frac{dm}{dy_1} = \frac{1}{3}$$

Also, (x_1, y_1) lies on H,

$$\Rightarrow \quad x_1^2 - y_1^2 = 1 \text{ or } y_1 = \sqrt{(x_1^2 - 1)}$$

$$\therefore \quad m = \frac{1}{3}\sqrt{(x_1^2 - 1)}$$

$$\therefore \quad \frac{dm}{dx_1} = \frac{x_1}{3\sqrt{(x_1^2 - 1)}}$$

Sol. (Q. Nos. 24 to 25)

$\because P(a\sec\theta_1, b\tan\theta_1)$ and $Q(a\sec\theta_2, b\tan\theta_2)$ are the extremities of focal chord, then

$$\tan\left(\frac{\theta_1}{2}\right)\tan\left(\frac{\theta_2}{2}\right) = \frac{1-e}{1+e} \text{ for focus } S(ae, 0) \quad \text{...(i)}$$

and $$\theta = 2\tan^{-1}\left(\frac{b}{a}\right) \quad \text{... (ii)}$$

Let $$R \equiv (a\sec\phi, b\tan\phi)$$

$\therefore$ Equation of tangent at R is

$$\frac{x}{a}\sec\phi - \frac{y}{b}\tan\phi = 1$$

$$\therefore \quad A \equiv (a\cos\phi, 0)$$

and $$B \equiv (0, -b\cot\phi)$$

24. Let $C = (h, k)$

$\because OACB$ is rectangle.

$\therefore$ Mid-point of OC = mid-point of AB

$$\Rightarrow \quad \left(\frac{h}{2}, \frac{k}{2}\right) \equiv \left(\frac{a\cos\phi}{2}, \frac{-b\cot\phi}{2}\right)$$

or $$h = a\cos\phi \quad \Rightarrow \sec\phi = \frac{a}{h} \quad \text{... (iii)}$$

and $$k = -b\cot\phi \quad \Rightarrow \tan\phi = -\frac{b}{k} \quad \text{... (iv)}$$

From Eqs. (iii) and (iv), we get

$$\frac{a^2}{h^2} - \frac{b^2}{k^2} = 1$$

Hence, required locus is $\frac{a^2}{x^2} - \frac{b^2}{y^2} = 1$

25. From Eq. (i) $1 + \tan\left(\frac{\theta_1}{2}\right)\tan\left(\frac{\theta_2}{2}\right) = \frac{2}{1+e}$

$$\Rightarrow \quad \frac{\cos\left(\frac{\theta_1 - \theta_2}{2}\right)}{\cos\left(\frac{\theta_1}{2}\right)\cos\left(\frac{\theta_2}{2}\right)} = \frac{2}{1+e} \quad \text{... (v)}$$

and $$1 - \tan\left(\frac{\theta_1}{2}\right)\tan\left(\frac{\theta_2}{2}\right) = \frac{2e}{1+e}$$

$$\Rightarrow \quad \frac{\cos\left(\frac{\theta_1 + \theta_2}{2}\right)}{\cos\left(\frac{\theta_1}{2}\right)\cos\left(\frac{\theta_2}{2}\right)} = \frac{2e}{1+e} \quad \text{... (vi)}$$

From Eqs. (v) and (vi), we get

$$\frac{\cos\left(\frac{\theta_1 + \theta_2}{2}\right)}{\cos\left(\frac{\theta_1 - \theta_2}{2}\right)} = e \text{ or } \frac{\cos^2\left(\frac{\theta_1 + \theta_2}{2}\right)}{\cos^2\left(\frac{\theta_1 - \theta_2}{2}\right)} = e^2$$

or $$\lambda = e^2 \quad \text{[given]}$$

$$= \frac{a^2 + b^2}{a^2}$$

Sol. (Q. Nos. 26 to 27)

$\because S_1(1,2)$ and $S_2(5, 5)$ are the foci,

then $$S_1S_2 = 5 = 2ae \quad \text{... (i)}$$

and $$|S'P - SP| = 2a$$

Here, $$2a = 4 \quad \text{... (ii)}$$

From Eqs. (i) and (ii), we get

$$e = \frac{5}{4}$$

26. Let e' be the eccentricity of conjugate hyperbola.

$$\therefore \quad \frac{1}{e^2} + \frac{1}{e'^2} = 1 \Rightarrow \frac{16}{25} + \frac{1}{e'^2} = 1$$

$$\Rightarrow \quad \frac{1}{e'^2} = \frac{9}{25}$$

$$\therefore \quad e' = \frac{5}{3}$$

27. Locus of point of intersection of two mutually perpendicular tangents is the director circle given by

$$(x - h)^2 + (y - k)^2 = (a^2 - b^2)$$

where (h, k) is the centre of hyperbola given by

$$(h, k) = \left(\frac{1+5}{2}, \frac{2+5}{2}\right) \equiv \left(3, \frac{7}{2}\right)$$

$$\therefore \quad a^2 = 4, b^2 = a^2(e^2 - 1) = 4\left(\frac{25}{16} - 1\right) = \frac{9}{4}$$

$\therefore$ Required locus (director circle) is

$$(x - 3)^2 + \left(y - \frac{7}{2}\right)^2 = 4 - \frac{9}{4} = \frac{7}{4}$$

Sol. (Q. Nos. 28 to 29)

Given conic is $x^2 - y^2 + 2y - 2 = 0$. ... (i)

Equation of tangent at (a, b) is

$$ax - by + (y + b) - 2 = 0$$

$\because$ Tangent line pass through $(0, 0)$, then $b = 2$

Also, (a, b) lies on Eq. (i), then $a^2 - b^2 + 2b - 2 = 0$

or $a^2 - 4 + 4 - 2 = 0$

$\Rightarrow$ $a^2 = 2$

$\therefore$ $a = \pm\sqrt{2}$

28. $\because$ Slope of tangent $= \dfrac{a}{b}$

$$= \frac{\sqrt{2}}{2} \quad \text{[for positive slope]}$$

$$= \frac{1}{\sqrt{2}}$$

$\therefore$ $\sin^{-1}\left(\dfrac{a}{b}\right) = \sin^{-1}\left(\dfrac{1}{\sqrt{2}}\right) = \dfrac{\pi}{4}$

29. $\because$ Conic is $x^2 - (y-1)^2 = 1$

$\therefore$ Length of latusrectum $= \dfrac{2(1)^2}{1} = 2$

Sol. (Q. Nos. 30 to 31)

Any point on the hyperbola is $(2t, 2/t)$ normal at this point is

$$xt^3 - yt - 2t^4 + 2 = 0$$

If the normal passes through $P(h, k)$, then

$$2t^4 - ht^3 + kt - 2 = 0$$

The equation has roots t_1, t_2, t_3 and t_4 then

$$\Sigma t_1 = \frac{h}{2}, \Sigma t_1t_2 = 0,$$

$$\Sigma t_1t_2t_3 = -\frac{k}{2}, t_1t_2t_3t_4 = -1$$

$\because$ Feet of normals are $\left(2t_1, \dfrac{2}{t_1}\right)$ and $\left(2t_2, \dfrac{2}{t_2}\right)$,

$\left(2t_3, \dfrac{2}{t_3}\right)$ and $\left(2t_4, \dfrac{2}{t_4}\right)$

$\because$ Sum of slopes of normals = Sum of ordinates of feet of normals

$\therefore$ $t_1^2 + t_2^2 + t_3^2 + t_4^2 = \dfrac{2}{t_1} + \dfrac{2}{t_2} + \dfrac{2}{t_3} + \dfrac{2}{t_4} \Rightarrow \Sigma t_1^2 = 2\Sigma\left(\dfrac{1}{t_1}\right)$

30. $(\Sigma t_1)^2 - 2\Sigma t_1t_2 = 2\left(\dfrac{\Sigma t_1t_2t_3}{t_1t_2t_3t_4}\right)$

$\Rightarrow$ $\left(\dfrac{h}{2}\right)^2 - 0 = 2\left(\dfrac{-k/2}{-1}\right)$ or $h^2 = 4k$

Hence, the locus of (h, k) is $x^2 = 4y$.

31.

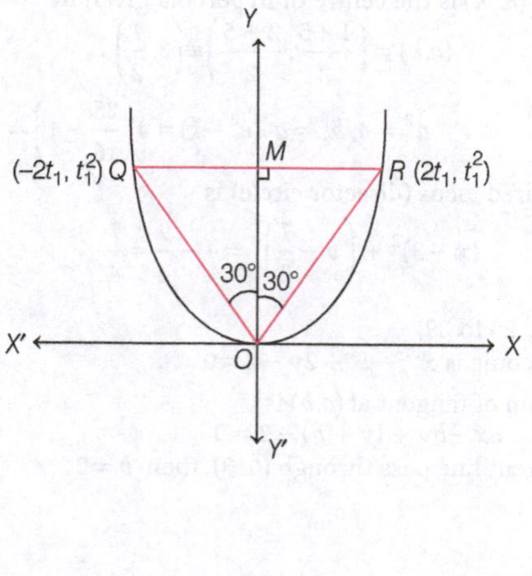

$\because$ $\tan 30° = \dfrac{2t_1}{t_1^2}$ or $\dfrac{1}{\sqrt{3}} = \dfrac{2}{t_1}$

$\therefore$ $t_1 = 2\sqrt{3}$

$\Rightarrow$ $QR = 4t_1 = 8\sqrt{3}$

Area of equilateral ΔOQR

$$= \frac{\sqrt{3}}{4}(8\sqrt{3})^2 = 48\sqrt{3} \text{ sq units}$$

Sol. (Q. Nos. 32 to 33)

32. $y = mx + \sqrt{9m^2 - 1}$ is a tangent to the hyperbola

$$\frac{x^2}{9} - \frac{y^2}{1} = 1$$

This passes through the point (3, 2) this implies

$$(3m - 2)^2 = 9m^2 - 1$$

$\Rightarrow$ $12m = 5$

$\Rightarrow$ $m = \dfrac{5}{12}$

Therefore, one tangent is $5x - 12y + 9 = 0$. Also the tangent at the vertex (3, 0) passes through (3, 2).

Hence, the other tangent through (3, 2) is $x = 3$, the chord of contact is

$$\frac{3x}{9} - \frac{2y}{1} = 1$$

$\Rightarrow$ $x - 6y = 3$

Therefore, the sides of the triangle are

$$5x - 12y + 9 = 0$$
$$x = 3$$

and $x - 6y = 3$

On solving these question, the vertices of the triangle are (3, 2), (3, 0) and $(-5, -4/3)$.

Hence, the area of the $\Delta = \dfrac{1}{2}\begin{vmatrix} 3 & 2 & 1 \\ 3 & 0 & 1 \\ -5 & \dfrac{-4}{3} & 1 \end{vmatrix}$

$$\Delta = \frac{1}{2}\left|3\left(0 + \frac{4}{3}\right) - 2(3 + 5) + 1(-4 - 0)\right|$$

$$= \frac{1}{2}|4 - 16 - 4| = 8 \text{ sq units}$$

33. We know that the portion of the tangent is intercepted between the asymptote is bisected at the point of contact infact the asymptotes are $x = \pm 3y$ and the tangent at (3, 0) is $x = 3$.

Hence, the tangent at (3, 0) intersects the asymptotes at points (3, 1) and (3, − 1) so that the mid-point of the segment is (3, 0).

$\therefore$ $\alpha + \beta = 3$

Sol. (Q. Nos. 34 to 35)

34. The centre of the hyperbola is

$$\left(\frac{-3+5}{2}, \frac{6-2}{2}\right) = (1, 2)$$

Since, (2, 5) lies on the auxiliary circle, its radius is

$$a = \sqrt{(1-2)^2 + (2-5)^2} = \sqrt{10}$$

The distance between the foci is $2ae$ from the coordinates of the foci, the distance between them is

$$\sqrt{(5+3)^2+(6+2)^2}=\sqrt{128}=8\sqrt{2}$$

Now, $\quad 2\sqrt{10}e=8\sqrt{2} \Rightarrow e=\frac{4}{\sqrt{5}}$

We have, $\quad b^2=a^2(e^2-1)=10\left(\frac{16}{5}-1\right)$

$\therefore \quad 2b=2\sqrt{22}=9.38$

$\Rightarrow \quad (2b)^2=4\times 22=88$

35. Let the corresponding directrix be $x+y=\lambda$ (because the directrix is perpendicular to transverse axis), the distance of this from the centre is a/e.

$$\left|\frac{1+2-\lambda}{\sqrt{2}}\right|=\sqrt{10}\times\frac{\sqrt{5}}{4}=\frac{5}{2\sqrt{2}}$$

$\Rightarrow \quad \lambda=3+\frac{5}{2}=\frac{11}{2}$

Therefore, the directrix equation is $2x+2y-11=0$

$\therefore \quad |a+b+c|=|2+2-11|=7$

Sol. (Q. Nos. 36 to 37)

36. Given, Area of $\Delta LMN=4\sqrt{3}$

$\Rightarrow \quad \frac{1}{2}\times LM\times ON=4\sqrt{3} \Rightarrow \frac{1}{2}\times 2b\times\sqrt{3}b=4\sqrt{3}$

$\Rightarrow \quad b^2=4 \Rightarrow b=2$

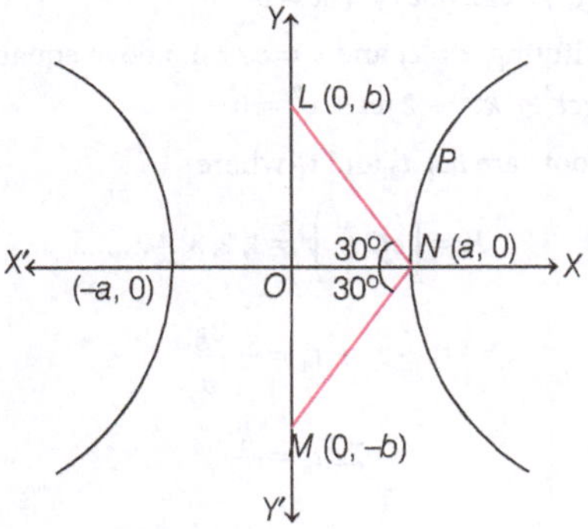

So, length of conjugate axis of hyperbola $=2b=4$

37. In ΔOLN, $\tan 30^\circ=\frac{OL}{ON}=\frac{b}{a}$

$\Rightarrow \quad a=\sqrt{3}b \Rightarrow a=2\sqrt{3} \quad [\because b=2]$

$\therefore \quad b^2=a^2(e^2-1) \Rightarrow 4=12(e^2-1)$

$\Rightarrow \quad e^2=\frac{4}{3} \Rightarrow e=\frac{2}{\sqrt{3}}$

$\therefore$ The distance between the foci of hyperbola $=2ae$

$$=2\times 2\sqrt{3}\times\frac{2}{\sqrt{3}}=8$$

38. Let $A\equiv(a,0)$ and $B\equiv(-a,0)$

If $\quad C\equiv(x,y)$

$\therefore \quad \tan\theta=\frac{y}{a+x} \quad \text{... (i)}$

and $\quad \tan 2\theta=\frac{y}{a-x} \quad \text{... (ii)}$

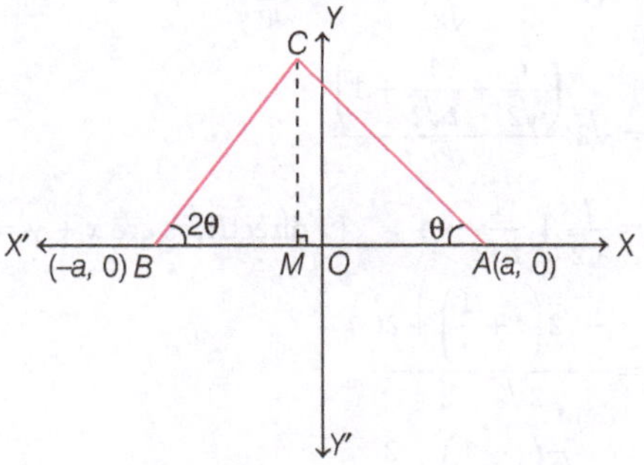

From Eq. (ii),

$$\frac{2\tan\theta}{1-\tan^2\theta}=\frac{y}{a-x}$$

$\Rightarrow \quad \dfrac{\frac{2y}{a+x}}{1-\left(\frac{y}{a+x}\right)^2}=\dfrac{y}{a-x}$ [from Eq. (i)]

or $\quad \frac{2y(a+x)}{a^2+x^2+2ax-y^2}=\frac{y}{a-x}$

$\Rightarrow \quad 2(a^2-x^2)=a^2+x^2+2ax-y^2$

or $\quad 3x^2+2ax-y^2-a^2=0$

or $\quad 3\left(x+\frac{a}{3}\right)^2-y^2=\frac{2a^2}{3}$

or $\quad \dfrac{\left(x+\frac{a}{3}\right)^2}{\left(\frac{2a^2}{9}\right)}-\dfrac{y^2}{\left(\frac{2a^2}{3}\right)}=1$

$\therefore$ Eccentricity $(e)=\sqrt{\left(\dfrac{\frac{2a^2}{9}+\frac{2a^2}{3}}{\frac{2a^2}{9}}\right)}=2$

39. Let $P\left(\frac{t}{\sqrt{2}},\frac{1}{t\sqrt{2}}\right)$ be any point on $2xy=1$ and $S\equiv(1,1)$

and $\quad S'\equiv(-1,-1)$

Here, $\quad t>0$

Let $R(h,k)$ be the ex-centre of $\Delta PSS'$ opposite to vertex S.

$\Rightarrow \quad h=\dfrac{-a-c+\frac{tb}{\sqrt{2}}}{a+b-c}$ and $k=\dfrac{-a-c+\frac{b}{t\sqrt{2}}}{a+b-c}$

Here, $\quad b=2\sqrt{2}, a=ePM$

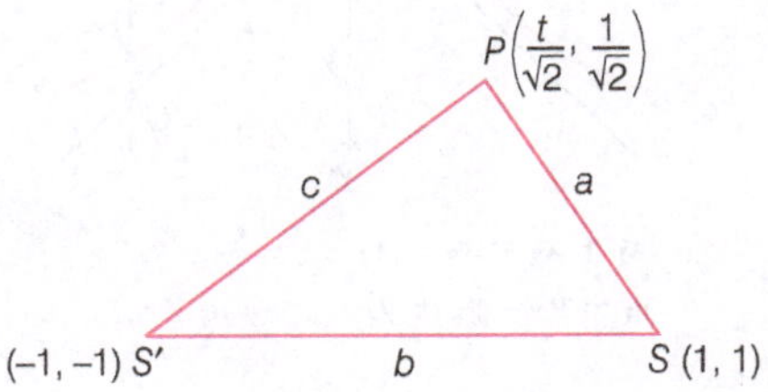

$$= \sqrt{2}\,\frac{\left(\frac{t}{\sqrt{2}} + \frac{1}{t\sqrt{2}} - 1\right)}{\sqrt{2}} = \frac{t}{\sqrt{2}} + \frac{1}{t\sqrt{2}} - 1$$

and $$c = \sqrt{2}\,\frac{\left(\frac{t}{\sqrt{2}} + \frac{1}{t\sqrt{2}} + 1\right)}{\sqrt{2}}$$

$$= \frac{t}{\sqrt{2}} + \frac{1}{t\sqrt{2}} + 1 \qquad [\because \text{directrices are } x + y = \pm 1]$$

$\therefore$ $$h = \frac{-\sqrt{2}\left(t + \frac{1}{t}\right) + 2t}{2\sqrt{2} - 2}$$

and $$k = \frac{-\sqrt{2}\left(t + \frac{1}{t}\right) + \frac{2}{t}}{2\sqrt{2} - 2}$$

$\therefore$ $$h + k = -\left(t + \frac{1}{t}\right) \qquad \text{... (i)}$$

and $$h - k = \frac{t - \frac{1}{t}}{\sqrt{2} - 1} \qquad \text{... (ii)}$$

$\because$ $$\left(t + \frac{1}{t}\right)^2 = \left(t - \frac{1}{t}\right)^2 + 4$$

$\Rightarrow$ $$(h + k)^2 = (\sqrt{2} - 1)^2 (h - k)^2 + 4$$

$\therefore$ Locus of R is $(x + y)^2 = (\sqrt{2} - 1)^2 (x - y)^2 + 4$

On comparing, we get $p = 1$ and $q = 4$

$\therefore$ $$p + q = 5$$

40. Equation of pair of asymptotes is

$$\frac{x^2}{a^2} - \frac{y^2}{b^2} = 0$$

For intersection points of transversal and pair of asymptotes

$$\frac{x^2}{a^2} - \frac{(mx + c)^2}{b^2} = 0 \begin{matrix} x_1 \\ x_2 \end{matrix} \qquad \text{...(i)}$$

$$\frac{x^2}{a^2} - \frac{(mx + c)^2}{b^2} = 1 \begin{matrix} x_3 \\ x_4 \end{matrix}$$

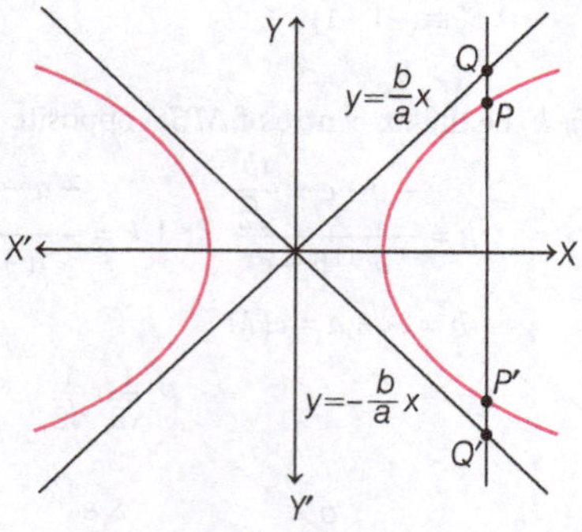

$\Rightarrow$ $$x_1 + x_2 = x_3 + x_4$$
$$y_1 + y_2 = y_3 + y_4$$

$\therefore$ Mid-points of PP' and QQ' are same (say R)

$\therefore$ $$RQ = RQ' \qquad \text{... (i)}$$
$$RP = RP' \qquad \text{... (ii)}$$

On subtracting Eq. (i) from Eq. (ii), we get

$$PQ = P'Q'$$

$\Rightarrow$ $$PQ + PP' = P'Q' + PP'$$

$\Rightarrow$ $$P'Q = PQ'$$

$$(PQ - P'Q') + (PQ' - P'Q) = 0$$

41. Given, the equation of asymptotes are

$$3x - 4y - 1 = 0$$

and $$4x - 3y - 6 = 0$$

Equation of transverse axis is given by

$$\frac{|3x - 4y - 1|}{\sqrt{3^2 + (-4)^2}} = \frac{|4x - 3y - 6|}{\sqrt{4^2 + (-3)^2}}$$

or $$3x - 4y - 1 = \pm (4x - 3y - 6)$$

$\Rightarrow$ $$x + y - 5 = 0$$

and $$x - y - 1 = 0$$

$\therefore$ Transverse axis is given

i.e. $ax + by - c = 0;\ a, b, c \in N$

$\Rightarrow$ $$ax + by - c = x + y - 5 = 0$$

$\Rightarrow$ $$a = 1, b = 1, c = 5$$

$\therefore$ $$a + b + c = 1 + 1 + 5 = 7$$

42. Let the hyperbola be $xy = c^2$ and the circle be $S : x^2 + y^2 + 2gx + 2fy + k = 0$

On substituting $x = ct$ and $y = c/t$ in above equation, we get

$$c^2t^4 + 2gct^3 + kt^2 + 2fct + c^2 = 0$$

Whose roots are t_1t_2, t_3 and t_4 where

$$P_r = \left(ct_r, \frac{c}{t_r}\right) r = 1, 2, 3, 4 \ldots\ldots\ldots$$

$\therefore$ $$t_1 + t_2 + t_3 + t_4 = -\frac{2g}{c}$$

$\therefore$ $$\Sigma t_1t_2 = \frac{k}{c^2}$$

$\therefore$ $$\Sigma t_1t_2t_3 = \frac{-2f}{c}$$

and $t_1t_2t_3 = 1$

Now, $$\sum_{i=1}^{4} CP_i^2 = C^2\left[t_1^2 + t_2^2 + t_3^2 + \frac{1}{t_1^2} + \frac{1}{t_2^2} + \frac{1}{t_3^2} + \frac{1}{t_4^2}\right]$$

$$= C^2\left[(\Sigma t_1)^2 - 2\Sigma t_1t_2 + \left(\Sigma\frac{1}{t_1}\right)^2 - 2\Sigma\frac{1}{t_1t_2}\right]$$

$$= C^2\left[\frac{4g^2}{C^2} - \frac{2k}{C^2} + \frac{4f^2}{C^2} - \frac{2k}{C^2}\right] \qquad [\because t_1t_2t_3t_3 = 1]$$

$$= 4(g^2 + f^2 - k) = 4r^2$$

$\therefore$ $$\lambda r^2 = 4r^2$$

$\Rightarrow$ $$\lambda = 4$$

43. Let $M(h, k)$ be the point.

The equation of any line through $M(h, k)$ having slope 4 is $y - k = 4(x - h)$.

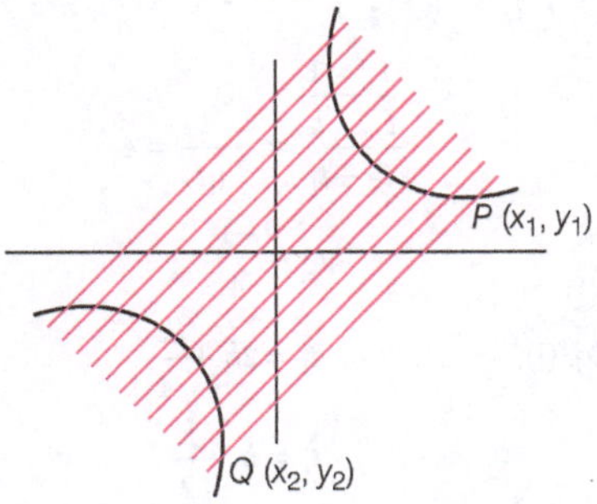

Suppose, the line meets the curve $xy = 1$ at $P(x_1, y_1)$ and $Q(x_2, y_2)$.

Now, $\quad y - k = (x - h) \Rightarrow \dfrac{1}{x} - k = 4(x - h)$

$\Rightarrow \quad 4x^2 - (4h - k)x - 1 = 0$

Let its roots be x_1 and x_2.

$\therefore \quad x_1 + x_2 = \dfrac{4h - k}{4}$ ... (i)

$x_1 x_2 = -\dfrac{1}{4}$ ... (ii)

Also $\quad h = \dfrac{2x_1 + x_2}{3}$

$\Rightarrow \quad 2x_1 + x_2 = 3h$ ... (iii)

From Eqs. (i) and (iii), we get

$$x_1 = 3h - \frac{4h - k}{4} = \frac{8h + k}{4}$$

$$x_2 = 3h - 2\left(\frac{8h + k}{4}\right) = -\left(\frac{2h + k}{2}\right)$$

On putting the values of x_1 and x_2 in Eq. (ii), we get

$$-\left(\frac{8h + k}{4}\right)\frac{(2h + k)}{2} = -\frac{1}{4}$$

$\Rightarrow \quad 16h^2 + 10hk + k^2 - 2 = 0$

Locus is $\quad 16x^2 + 10xy + y^2 - 2 = 0$

$a = 16, b = 1, c = 10$ and $d = -2$

$\Rightarrow \quad \dfrac{a + b + c + d}{1000} = \dfrac{25}{1000} = 0.025$

44. $\quad (x + 3)^2 + (y - 12)^2 = 81$

$(x + 3)^2 - (y - 8)^2 = -9$

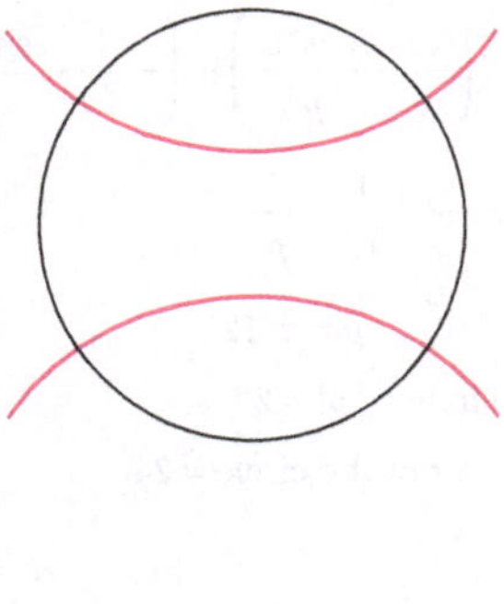

Let (h, k) be intersection point.

Then, $\quad (h + 3)^2 + (k - 12)^2 = 81$ ... (i)

$(h + 3)^2 - (k - 8)^2 = -9$ ... (ii)

On adding Eqs. (i) and (ii), we get

$2h^2 + 12h - 8k + 26 = 0$

$h^2 + 6x - 4k + 13 = 0$ ... (iii)

On subtracting Eq. (i) from Eq. (ii), we get

$2k^2 - 40k + 118 = 0$

$k^2 - 20k + 59 = 0 \begin{cases} k_1 \\ k_2 \end{cases}$ ...(iv)

$\therefore \quad k_1 + k_2 = 20$ and $k_1 k_2 = 59$

Distance of (h, k) from $(-3, 2)$.

$$d = \sqrt{(h + 3)^2 + (k - 2)^2} = k$$

$\therefore$ Sum of distance of all intersection points

$$2(k_1 + k_2) = 2(20) = 40$$

45. Given, hyperbola $\dfrac{x^2}{4} - \dfrac{y^2}{3} = 1$

$\Rightarrow \quad y = \dfrac{\sqrt{3}}{2}(\sqrt{x^2 - 4}) \Rightarrow a = 2$ and $b = \sqrt{3}$

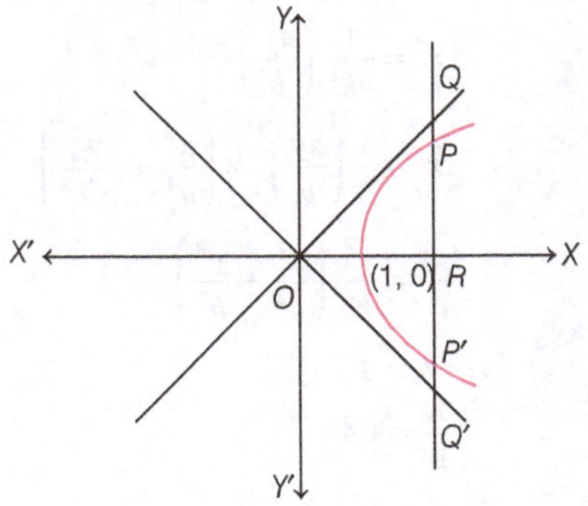

$\because \quad y = \pm\dfrac{b}{a}x \Rightarrow y = \pm\dfrac{\sqrt{3}}{2}x$

The ends of the double ordinate be $P\left(h, \dfrac{\sqrt{3}}{2}\sqrt{h^2 - 4}\right)$

and $P'\left(h_1, \dfrac{-\sqrt{3}}{2}\sqrt{h^2 - 4}\right)$

Since, mid-point of PP' and QQ' is R.

$\because \quad Q = \left(h_1, \dfrac{\sqrt{3}}{2}h\right)$ and $Q'\left(h, \dfrac{-\sqrt{3}}{2}h\right)$

$\Rightarrow \quad (PQ)\cdot(PQ') = \left(\dfrac{\sqrt{3}}{2}\right)^2 [h^2 - (h^2 - 4)]$

$= \dfrac{3}{4} \times 4 = 3 = \lambda$

$\therefore \quad \lambda = 3$

Then, $\quad \lambda^3 = 3^3 = 27$

46. Let the equation of the hyperbola be

$$\frac{x^2}{a^2}-\frac{y^2}{b^2}=1$$

and its conjugate is $\frac{x^2}{a^2}-\frac{y^2}{b^2}=-1$

The equation of any line parallel to conjugate axis is $x=k$.

Let P be $\left(k, \frac{b}{a}\sqrt{k^2-a^2}\right)$ and Q be $\left(k, \frac{b}{a}\sqrt{k^2+a^2}\right)$.

The equation of the tangent at P to the hyperbola is

$$\frac{xk}{a^2}-\frac{y}{ab}\sqrt{k^2-a^2}=1 \quad \text{...(i)}$$

and the equation of the tangent at Q to the conjugate hyperbola is

$$\frac{xk}{a^2}-\frac{y}{ab}\sqrt{k^2-a^2}=-1 \quad \text{... (ii)}$$

On squaring and adding Eqs. (i) and (ii), we get

$$k^2=\frac{1}{\frac{x^2}{a^4}+\frac{y^2}{a^2b^2}}$$

On solving, we get $x=\frac{1}{2k}\left(\frac{ay}{b}\right)^2$

$$x^2=\frac{1}{4k^2}\left(\frac{ay}{b}\right)^2$$

$$\Rightarrow \quad x^2=\frac{1}{4}\left(\frac{ay}{b}\right)^4\times\left(\frac{x^2}{a^4}+\frac{y^2}{a^2b^2}\right)$$

$$\Rightarrow \quad \frac{4x^2}{a^2}=\frac{y^4}{b^4}\left(\frac{x^2}{a^2}+\frac{y^2}{b^2}\right)$$

$$\therefore \quad \lambda=4$$

$$\therefore \quad \frac{\lambda}{10}=0.4$$

47. Let $y=4x+c$ meets $xy=1$ at two points A and B.

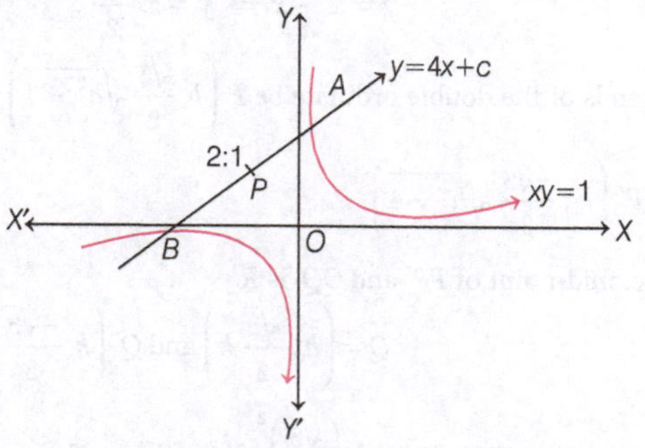

Here, $A\left(t_1, \frac{1}{t_1}\right)$ and $B\left(t_2, \frac{1}{t_2}\right)$

$\therefore$ Coordinates of P are $\left(\frac{2t_1+t_2}{2+1}, \frac{2\cdot\frac{1}{t_1}+1\cdot\frac{1}{t_2}}{2+1}\right)=(h,k)$ (let)

$$\therefore \quad h=\frac{2t_1+t_2}{3} \text{ and } k=\frac{2t_2+t_1}{3t_1\,t_2} \quad \text{...(i)}$$

Also, $\left(t_1, \frac{1}{t_1}\right)$ and $\left(t_2, \frac{1}{t_2}\right)$ lie on $y=4x+c$.

$$\frac{\frac{1}{t_2}-\frac{1}{t_1}}{t_2-t_1}=-\frac{1}{t_1t_2}=4$$

$$\text{or} \quad t_1t_2=\frac{-1}{4} \quad \text{...(ii)}$$

From Eq. (i), $\quad t_1=2h+\frac{k}{4}$

and $\quad t_1=h-\frac{k}{2} \quad$ ...(iii)

From Eqs. (ii) and (iii), we get

$$\left(-h-\frac{k}{2}\right)\left(2h+\frac{k}{4}\right)=\frac{-1}{4}$$

$$\Rightarrow \quad -\left(\frac{2h+k}{2}\right)\left(\frac{8h+k}{4}\right)=-\frac{1}{4}$$

$$\Rightarrow \quad (2h+k)(8h+k)=2$$

$$\Rightarrow \quad 16h^2+k^2+10hk=2$$

$\Rightarrow$ The required locus is $16x^2+y^2+10xy=2$

which is equal to $\alpha x^2+y^2+\beta xy=2$

$$\therefore \quad \alpha=16 \text{ and } \beta=10$$

Hence, $\quad \alpha\cdot\beta=16\times10=160$

48. **(A)** $16x^2-9y^2+32x+36y-164=0$

$\Rightarrow 16(x^2+2x+1)-9(y^2-4y+4)-144=0$

$$\text{or} \quad 16(x+1)^2-9(y-2)^2=144$$

$$\text{or} \quad \frac{(x+1)^2}{9}-\frac{(y-2)^2}{16}=1$$

$$\therefore \quad \lambda=\text{length of latusrectum}=\frac{2\times16}{3}=\frac{32}{3}$$

or $3\lambda=32$

(B) Making $\frac{x^2}{16}-\frac{y^2}{18}=1$ homogeneous with the help of $x\cos\alpha+y\sin\alpha=p$, then

$$\frac{x^2}{16}-\frac{y^2}{18}=\left(\frac{x\cos\alpha+y\sin\alpha}{p}\right)^2$$

Since, these lines are perpendicular to each other, then

$$\left(\frac{1}{16}-\frac{\cos^2\alpha}{p^2}\right)+\left(-\frac{1}{18}-\frac{\sin^2\alpha}{p^2}\right)=0$$

$$\text{or} \quad \frac{1}{16}-\frac{1}{18}=\frac{1}{p^2}$$

$$\text{or} \quad p=\pm12$$

$\therefore$ Radius of circle $=|p|=2$

Hence, diameter of the circle $=24$

(C) Any point on $xy = 8$ is $P\left(\sqrt{8}\, t, \frac{\sqrt{8}}{t}\right)$

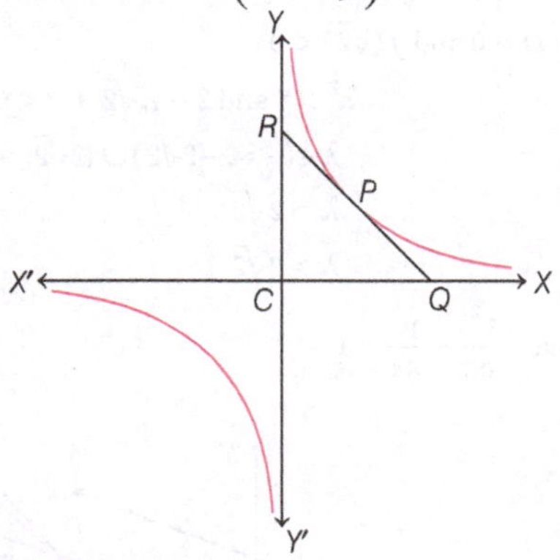

Equation of tangent at P

$$x \times \frac{\sqrt{8}}{t} + y \times \sqrt{8}\, t = 16 \text{ or } \frac{x}{\left(\frac{16t}{\sqrt{8}}\right)} + \frac{x}{\left(\frac{16}{\sqrt{8}\,t}\right)} = 1$$

$$\therefore \quad CQ = \frac{16t}{\sqrt{8}} \text{ and } CR = \frac{16}{\sqrt{8}t}$$

Hence, area of $\Delta CQR = \frac{1}{2} \times CQ \times CR$

$$= \frac{1}{2} \times \frac{16t}{\sqrt{8}} \times \frac{16}{\sqrt{8}t} = 16$$

(D) Hyperbola is $x^2 - 3y^2 = 9$

or $$\frac{x^2}{9} - \frac{y^2}{3} = 1$$

$\because$ Angle between asymptotes

$$= 2\tan^{-1}\left(\frac{\sqrt{3}}{3}\right) = 2\tan^{-1}\left(\frac{1}{\sqrt{3}}\right)$$

$$= 2 \times \frac{\pi}{6} = \frac{\pi\lambda}{24} \qquad \text{[given]}$$

$$\therefore \quad \lambda = 8$$

49. **(A)** Let the hyperbola be $\frac{x^2}{a^2} - \frac{y^2}{b^2} = 1$

then $$2a = ae$$

$\Rightarrow$ $$e = 2$$

$\therefore$ $$\frac{(2b)^2}{(2a)^2} = \frac{b^2}{a^2} = e^2 - 1$$

$$= (2)^2 - 1 = 3$$

(B) Given hyperbola is $\frac{x^2}{9} - \frac{y^2}{16} = 1$ ...(i)

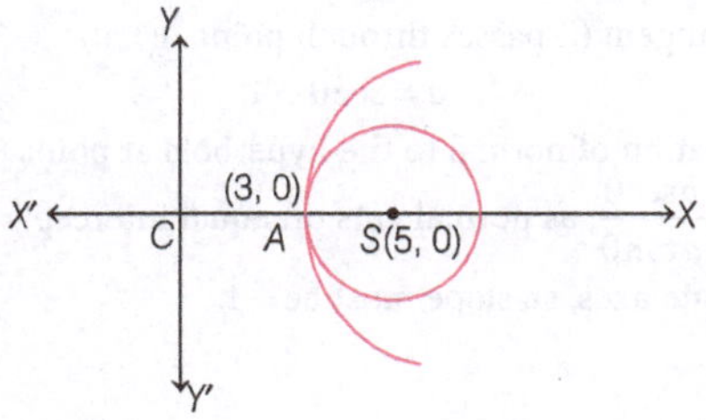

or $$e^2 = 1 + \frac{16}{9} = \frac{25}{9}$$

or $$e = \frac{5}{3}$$

Hence, its foci are $(\pm 5, 0)$.

The equation of the circle with (5, 0) as centre is

$$(x-5)^2 + (y-0)^2 = r^2 \qquad \text{... (ii)}$$

On solving Eqs. (i) and (ii), we get

$$16x^2 - 9(r^2 - (x-5)^2) = 144$$

or $$25x^2 - 90x - 9r^2 + 81 = 0$$

Since, the circle touches the hyperbola, the above equation must have equal roots.

Hence, $$(90)^2 - 4(25)(81 - 9r^2) = 0$$

or $$r = 0$$

which is not possible.

Hence, the circle can not touch at two points. It can only be tangent at the vertex.

Hence, $$r = 5 - 3 = 2$$

(C) Equation of hyperbola is $\frac{x^2}{2^2} - \frac{y^2}{3^2} = 1$

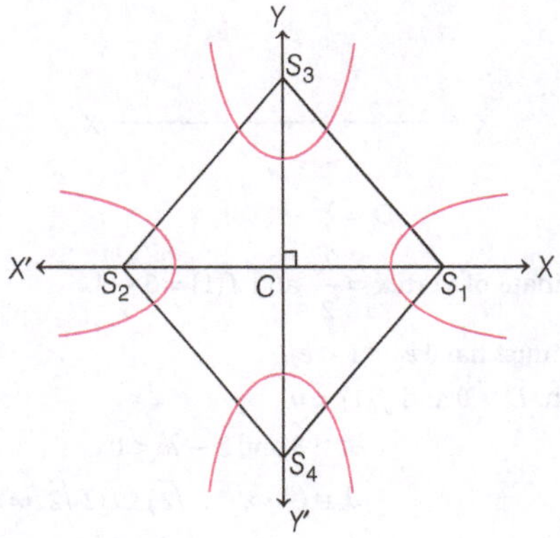

Its foci are $(\pm\sqrt{(2^2 + 3^2)}, 0)$.

or $$S_1 \equiv (\sqrt{13}, 0) \text{ and } S_2 \equiv (-\sqrt{13}, 0)$$

and equation of conjugate hyperbola is $-\frac{x^2}{2^2} + \frac{y^2}{3^2} = 1$.

Its foci are $(0, \pm\sqrt{(3^2 + 2^2)})$.

or $$S_3 \equiv (0, \sqrt{13}) \text{ and } S_4 \equiv (0, -\sqrt{13})$$

Hence, area of quadrilateral $S_1S_2S_3S_4$

$$= 4 \times \text{Area of } \Delta S_1CS_3$$

$$= 4 \times \frac{1}{2} \times CS_1 \times CS_3$$

$$= 2 \times \sqrt{13} \times \sqrt{13} = 26$$

(D) Given hyperbola is $ax^2 - by^2 = c$.

or $$\frac{x^2}{(c/a)} - \frac{y^2}{(c/b)} = 1$$

$\because$ $$\sqrt{\frac{c}{b}} = \frac{5}{2} \qquad \text{...(i)}$$

and $$2\sqrt{\left(\frac{c}{a}+\frac{c}{b}\right)}=13 \quad \text{...(ii)}$$

From Eqs. (i) and (ii) we get

$$2\sqrt{\left(\frac{c}{a}+\frac{25}{4}\right)}=13$$

or $$\frac{c}{a}=\frac{169}{4}-\frac{25}{4}=36 \quad \text{... (iii)}$$

and $$\frac{c}{b}=\frac{25}{4} \quad \text{... (iv)}$$

$$\therefore \quad \frac{a}{b}=\frac{\frac{c}{b}}{\frac{c}{a}}=\frac{25}{144}$$

$\because$ a and b are coprime.

$\therefore$ $a=25,\ b=144$

and from Eq. (iii), $c=900$

Hence, $$\frac{3ab}{2c}=\frac{3\times25\times144}{2\times900}=6$$

50. Let $f(x)=x^2-\lambda x+2$

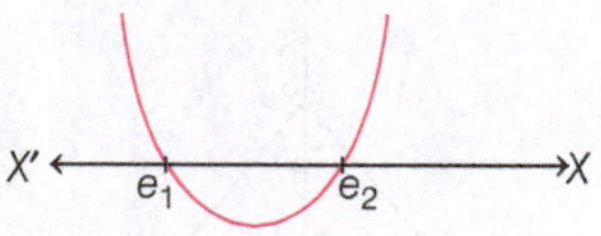

$\therefore$ $D=\lambda^2-8$

x-coordinate of vertex $=\frac{\lambda}{2}$ and $f(1)=3-\lambda$

(A) We must have $e_1<1<e_2$.

Then, $D>0$ and $f(1)<0$

$\Rightarrow$ $\lambda^2>8$ and $3-\lambda<0$

$\Rightarrow$ $\lambda\in(-\infty,-2\sqrt{2})\cup(2\sqrt{2},\infty)$ and $\lambda>3$

$\therefore$ $\lambda>3$

(B) $\because$ $e_1>1,\ e_2>1$

Then, $D\ge0$ and $f(1)>0$ and $\frac{\lambda}{2}>1$

$\Rightarrow$ $\lambda\in(-\infty,-2\sqrt{2})]\cup[2\sqrt{2},\infty)$

and $\lambda<3$ and $\lambda>2$

$\therefore$ $\lambda\in[2\sqrt{2},3)$

(C) We must have $\frac{1}{e_1^2}+\frac{1}{e_2^2}=1.$

or $e_1^2+e_2^2=(e_1e_2)^2$

$\Rightarrow$ $(e_1+e_2)^2-2e_1e_2=(e_1e_2)^2$

$\Rightarrow$ $\lambda^2-4=(2)^2$ or $\lambda^2=8$

$\therefore$ $\lambda=\pm2\sqrt{2}$

(D) We must have $e_1<\sqrt{2}<e_2$.

Then $D>0$ and $f(\sqrt{2})<0$

$\Rightarrow$ $\lambda^2>8$ and $2-\lambda\sqrt{2}+2<0$

or $\lambda\in(-\infty,-2\sqrt{2})\cup(2\sqrt{2},\infty)$

and $\lambda>2\sqrt{2}$

$\therefore$ $\lambda>2\sqrt{2}$

51. Hyperbola : $\frac{x^2}{100}-\frac{y^2}{64}=1$

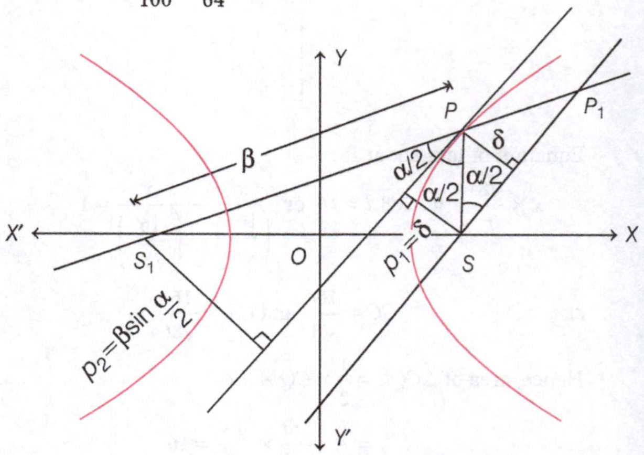

$$a=10,\ b=8,\ e=\sqrt{1+\frac{64}{100}}=\frac{\sqrt{41}}{5}$$

Product of perpendiculars on any tangent from foci S and S_1 = (semi-minor axis)^2

$$p_1\cdot p_2=b^2$$

$$\delta\times\beta\sin\frac{\alpha}{2}=64$$

$$\frac{\beta\delta\sin\frac{\alpha}{2}}{9}=\frac{64}{9}\Rightarrow\left[\frac{\beta\delta}{9}\sin\frac{\alpha}{2}\right]=\left[\frac{64}{9}\right]=7$$

52. Equation of given hyperbola is

$$\frac{x^2}{a^2}-\frac{y^2}{b^2}=1,\ a>b \text{ and } a>1$$

Let point $P(a\sec\theta, b\tan\theta)$ on the hyperbola in first quadrant i.e.

$$Q\in\left(0,\frac{\pi}{2}\right).$$

Now, equation of tangent to the hyperbola at point P is

$$\frac{x\sec\theta}{a}-\frac{y\tan\theta}{b}=1 \quad \text{...(i)}$$

$\because$ The tangent (i) passes through point $A(1, 0)$

So, $a=\sec\theta>1.$ ... (ii)

and equation of normal to the hyperbola at point P having slope is $\frac{b\sec\theta}{a\tan\theta}$, as normal cuts off equal intercepts on the coordinate axes, so slope must be -1.

Therefore, $\dfrac{b\sec\theta}{a\tan\theta} = -1$

$\Rightarrow \qquad b = -\tan\theta \qquad$ [from Eq. (ii)]

$\because$ The eccentricity of hyperbola

$$e = \sqrt{1 + \frac{b^2}{a^2}} = \sqrt{1 + \sin^2\theta}$$

$\therefore \qquad 1 < e < \sqrt{2}$ as $\theta \in \left(0, \dfrac{\pi}{2}\right)$

And the area of required triangle is, which is isosceles is

$$\Delta = \frac{1}{2}(AP)^2$$

$$= \frac{1}{2}[(1 - \sec^2\theta)^2 + \tan^4\theta]$$

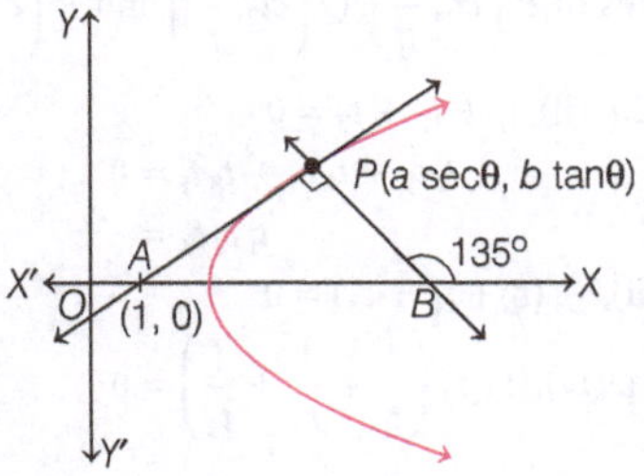

$$= \frac{1}{2}(2\tan^4\theta) = \tan^4\theta = b^4$$

Exercise 3 - Challenging Problems

1. The given rectangular hyperbola is

$$xy = c^2 \qquad \text{...(i)}$$

Given that PP' is a diameter of Eq. (i). Therefore, if P is the point $(ct, c/t)$, then P' is $(-ct, -c/t)$. Equation of tangent at P is

$$x + yt^2 = 2ct \qquad \text{...(ii)}$$

Asymptotes of Eq. (i) are $x = 0$ and $y = 0$.

$\therefore$ The equation of the line through P' and parallel to the asymptote $y = 0$ is

$$y = -c/t \qquad \text{...(iii)}$$

On putting the value of t from Eq. (iii) in Eq. (ii), then

$$x + y \times \frac{c^2}{y^2} = 2c \times -\frac{c}{y}$$

or $\qquad xy + c^2 = -2c^2$

or $\qquad xy + 3c^2 = 0$

which is the required locus of the point of intersection of Eqs. (ii) and (iii).

Again, the equation of the line through P' and parallel to the asymptote $x = 0$ is $x = -ct$ ...(iv)

On putting the value of t from Eq. (iv) in Eq. (ii), we get

$$x + y\left(\frac{x^2}{c^2}\right) = 2c \times -\frac{x}{c} \quad \text{or} \quad xy + 3c^2 = 0$$

which is the required locus of the point of intersection of Eqs. (ii) and (iv).

2. Since, hyperbola is $xy = c^2$ ...(i)

Let $P\left(ct, \dfrac{c}{t}\right)$ be any point on Eq. (i), then equation of tangent at P on Eq. (i) is

$$x + t^2y = 2ct \qquad \text{...(ii)}$$

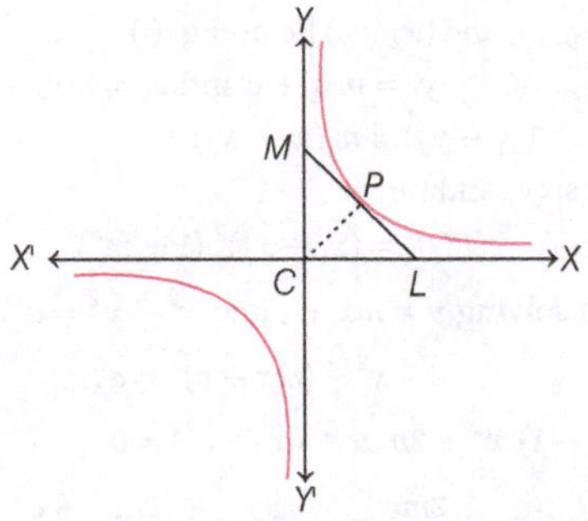

Since, asymptotes of $xy = c^2$ are $x = 0$ and $y = 0$

i.e. Y-axis and X-axis.

$\because$ Tangents meet X-axis at L and Y-axis at M.

$\therefore$ Coordinates of L and M are $(2ct, 0)$ and $\left(0, \dfrac{2c}{t}\right)$ respectively. The mid-point of LM is $\left(\dfrac{2ct + 0}{2}, \dfrac{0 + \frac{2c}{t}}{2}\right)$

i.e. $\left(ct, \dfrac{c}{t}\right)$. i.e. the point of P.

$\therefore \qquad PL = PM$

Also, $CP = \sqrt{\left(c^2t^2 + \dfrac{c^2}{t^2}\right)}$ and $ML = \sqrt{\left(4c^2t^2 + \dfrac{4c^2}{t^2}\right)} = 2CP$

$\therefore \qquad CP = \dfrac{1}{2}ML = PL = PM$

Hence, $\quad PL = PM = CP$.

3. Let rectangular hyperbola is $x^2 - y^2 = a^2$.

Let equations of PQ and DE be

$$y = mx + c \qquad \text{...(i)}$$

and $\qquad y = m_1x + c_1 \qquad$ ...(ii)

respectively.

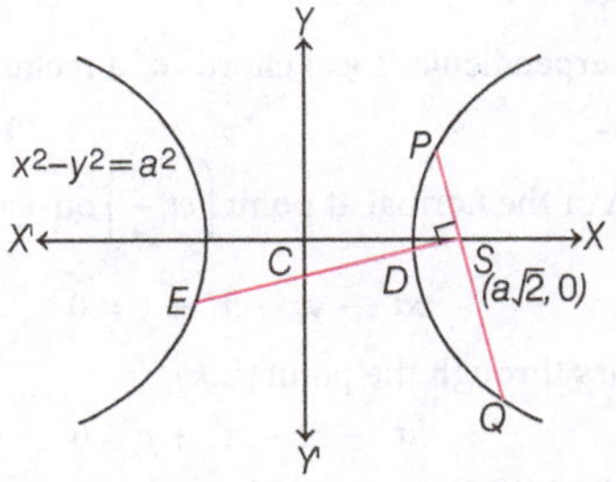

Be any two focal chords of any rectangular hyperbola $x^2 - y^2 = a^2$ through its focus. We have to prove $PQ = DE$.

Since, $PQ \perp DE$.

$\therefore \qquad mm_1 = -1 \qquad$ ...(iii)

Also, PQ passes through $S\,(a\sqrt{2}, 0)$, then from Eq. (i),

$$0 = ma\sqrt{2} + c$$

or $$c^2 = 2a^2m^2 \quad \text{...(iv)}$$

Let (x_1, y_1) and (x_2, y_2) be the coordinates of P and Q, then

$$(PQ)^2 = (x_1 - x_2)^2 + (y_1 - y_2)^2 \quad \text{...(v)}$$

Since, (x_1, y_1) and (x_2, y_2) lie on Eq. (i)

$\therefore$ $$y_1 = mx_1 + c \text{ and } y_2 = mx_2 + c$$

$\therefore$ $$(y_1 - y_2) = m(x_1 - x_2) \quad \text{...(vi)}$$

From Eqs. (v) and (vi),

$$(PQ)^2 = (x_1 - x_2)^2 (1 + m^2) \quad \text{...(vii)}$$

Now, on solving $y = mx + c$ and $x^2 - y^2 = a^2$, then

$$x^2 - (mx + c)^2 = a^2$$

or $$(m^2 - 1)x^2 + 2mcx + (a^2 + c^2) = 0$$

$\therefore$ $$x_1 + x_2 = \frac{2mc}{m^2 - 1} \quad \text{and} \quad x_1x_2 = \frac{a^2 + c^2}{m^2 - 1}$$

$\Rightarrow$ $$(x_1 - x_2)^2 = (x_1 + x_2)^2 - 4x_1x_2$$

$$= \frac{4m^2c^2}{(m^2 - 1)^2} - \frac{4(a^2 + c^2)}{(m^2 - 1)}$$

$$= \frac{4\{a^2 + c^2 - a^2m^2\}}{(m^2 - 1)^2}$$

$$= \frac{4a^2(m^2 + 1)}{(m^2 - 1)^2} \quad [\because c^2 = 2a^2m^2]$$

From Eq. (vii), $$(PQ)^2 = 4a^2\left(\frac{m^2 + 1}{m^2 - 1}\right)^2$$

Similarly, $$(DE)^2 = 4a^2\left(\frac{m_1^2 + 1}{m_1^2 - 1}\right)^2$$

$$= 4a^2\left(\frac{\left(-\frac{1}{m}\right)^2 + 1}{\left(-\frac{1}{m}\right)^2 - 1}\right)^2 \quad [\because mm_1 = -1]$$

$$= 4a^2\left(\frac{m^2 + 1}{m^2 - 1}\right)^2 = (PQ)^2$$

Thus, $(PQ)^2 = (DE)^2 \Rightarrow PQ = DE$.

Hence, perpendicular focal chords of a rectangular hyperbola are equal.

4. Equation of the normal at point $\left(ct, \frac{c}{t}\right)$ on $xy = c^2$ is

$$xt^3 - yt - ct^4 + c = 0$$

It will pass through the point (h, k)

$\therefore$ $$ht^3 - kt - ct^4 + c = 0 \quad \text{...(i)}$$

Also, $T\,(h, k)$ lies on $xy = c^2$, then

$\therefore$ $$hk = c^2$$

Therefore, $$h = cq \quad \text{and} \quad k = \frac{c}{q}$$

$$cqt^3 - \frac{c}{q}t - ct^4 + c = 0$$

or $$qt^3 - \frac{t}{q} - t^4 + 1 = 0$$

or $$q^2t^3 - t - qt^4 + q = 0$$

or $$q(qt^3 + 1) - t(qt^3 + 1) = 0$$

or $$(q - t)(qt^3 + 1) = 0$$

$$q \neq t$$

$\therefore$ $$qt^3 + 1 = 0$$

The three points other than T are given by

$$qt^3 + 1 = 0 \quad \text{...(ii)}$$

If coordinates of $P\left(ct_1, \frac{c}{t_1}\right)$, $Q\left(ct_2, \frac{c}{t_2}\right)$ and $R\left(ct_3, \frac{c}{t_3}\right)$,

then from Eq. (ii), $t_1 + t_2 + t_3 = 0$ ...(iii)

$$t_1t_2 + t_2t_3 + t_3t_1 = 0 \quad \text{...(iv)}$$

and $$t_1t_2t_3 = -1 \quad \text{...(v)}$$

From Eq. (iii), $c(t_1 + t_2 + t_3) = 0$

and from Eq. (iv), $t_1t_2t_3\left(\frac{1}{t_1} + \frac{1}{t_2} + \frac{1}{t_3}\right) = 0$

or $$(-1)\left(\frac{1}{t_1} + \frac{1}{t_2} + \frac{1}{t_3}\right) = 0 \quad \text{[from Eq. (v)]}$$

$\therefore$ $$\frac{1}{t_1} + \frac{1}{t_2} + \frac{1}{t_3} = 0$$

or $$c\left(\frac{1}{t_1} + \frac{1}{t_2} + \frac{1}{t_3}\right) = 0$$

$\therefore c(t_1 + t_2 + t_3) = 0$ and $c\left(\frac{1}{t_1} + \frac{1}{t_2} + \frac{1}{t_3}\right) = 0$

Hence, centroid of ΔPQR is the origin. **Hence proved.**

5. Combined equation of asymptotes is

$$(x + 2y + 3)(3x + 4y + 5) = 0$$

or $$3x^2 + 10xy + 8y^2 + 14x + 22y + 15 = 0 \quad \text{...(i)}$$

Also, we know that the equation of the hyperbola differs from that of asymptotes by a constant.

Let the equation of the hyperbola be

$$3x^2 + 10xy + 8y^2 + 14x + 22y + \lambda = 0 \quad \text{...(ii)}$$

Since, it passes through $(1, -1)$, then

$$3(1)^2 + 10(1)(-1) + 8(-1)^2 + 14(1) + 22(-1) + \lambda = 0$$

$\Rightarrow$ $$3 - 10 + 8 + 14 - 22 + \lambda = 0$$

$\therefore$ $$\lambda = 7$$

From Eq. (ii), equation of hyperbola is

$$3x^2 + 10xy + 8y^2 + 14x + 22y + 7 = 0 \quad \text{...(iii)}$$

But we know that equation of conjugate hyperbola = 2 (Combined equation of asymptotes) − (Equation of hyperbola)

$\Rightarrow 6x^2 + 20xy + 16y^2 + 28x + 44y + 30$

$$- 3x^2 - 10xy - 8y^2 - 14x - 22y - 7 = 0$$

or $3x^2 + 10xy + 8y^2 + 14x + 22y + 23 = 0.$

6. Let a triangle PQR be inscribed in $xy = c^2$.

Let the coordinates of the vertices of the triangle be

$$P\left(ct_1, \frac{c}{t_1}\right), Q\left(ct_2, \frac{c}{t_2}\right) \text{ and } R\left(ct_3, \frac{c}{t_3}\right)$$

Now, the equation of chord joining P and Q is

$$x + yt_1t_2 = c(t_1 + t_2) \quad \text{...(i)}$$

and the equation of chord joining Q and R is

$$x + yt_2t_3 = c(t_2 + t_3) \quad \text{...(ii)}$$

Let Eq. (i) be parallel to $y = m_1x$ and Eq. (ii) be parallel to $y = m_2x$.

$$\therefore \quad m_1 = -\frac{1}{t_1t_2} \text{ and } m_2 = -\frac{1}{t_2t_3}$$

$$\therefore \quad \frac{m_1}{m_2} = \frac{t_3}{t_1} \text{ i.e. } t_3 = \left(\frac{m_1}{m_2}\right)t_1 \quad \text{...(iii)}$$

Again, the equation to the third side RP is

$$x + yt_3t_1 = c(t_3 + t_1)$$

$$x + y\left(\frac{m_1}{m_2}\right)t_1^2 = c\left(\frac{m_1}{m_2}t_1 + t_1\right)$$

or $$ym_1t_1^2 - ct_1(m_1 + m_2) + xm_2 = 0 \quad \text{...(iv)}$$

t_1 being a parameter. Since, t_1 is real the envelope of Eq. (iv) is given by the discriminant of Eq. (iv) = 0

i.e. $c^2(m_1 + m_2)^2 - 4ym_1 \cdot xm_2 = 0$

or $$4m_1m_2xy = c^2(m_1 + m_2)^2.$$ **Hence proved.**

7. Let the hyperbola be $\frac{x^2}{a^2} - \frac{y^2}{b^2} = 1$ ...(i)

Let there be any point $P(a\sec\phi, b\tan\phi)$ on the hyperbola Eq. (i).

$\therefore$ Equation of tangent at P is

$$\frac{x}{a}\sec\phi - \frac{y}{b}\tan\phi = 1 \quad \text{...(ii)}$$

Equation of focal chord SP is [if $S \equiv (-ae, 0)$]

$$y - 0 = \frac{b\tan\phi - 0}{a\sec\phi + ae}(x + ae)$$

$$\Rightarrow \quad y = \frac{b\sin\phi(x + ae)}{(a + ae\cos\phi)} \quad \text{...(iii)}$$

Equation of line passing through (0, 0) and perpendicular to Eq. (ii) is

$$y = -\frac{a}{b}\sin\phi \cdot x \quad \text{...(iv)}$$

Let Eqs. (iii) and (iv) are passing through (h, k), then

$$k = \frac{b(h + ae)\sin\phi}{(a + ae\cos\phi)} \quad \text{...(v)}$$

$$k = -\frac{a}{b}\sin\phi \cdot h \quad \text{...(vi)}$$

From Eq. (iv), $\sin\phi = -\frac{bk}{ah}$

and from Eq. (v), $\cos\phi = -\left\{\frac{a^2h + (h + ae)b^2}{a^2eh}\right\}$

$$= -\left\{\frac{(a^2 + b^2)h + aeb^2}{a^2eh}\right\}$$

$$= -\left\{\frac{a^2e^2h + aeb^2}{a^2eh}\right\} = -\left\{\frac{aeh + b^2}{ah}\right\}$$

$$\therefore \quad \sin^2\phi + \cos^2\phi = 1$$

$$\Rightarrow \quad \frac{b^2k^2}{a^2h^2} + \frac{(aeh + b^2)^2}{a^2h^2} = 1$$

$\therefore$ Locus of (h, k) is $\quad b^2y^2 + (aex + b^2)^2 = a^2x^2$

$$\Rightarrow \quad b^2y^2 + a^2e^2x^2 + b^4 + 2aeb^2x = a^2x^2$$

$$\Rightarrow \quad b^2y^2 + (a^2 + b^2)x^2 + b^4 + 2aeb^2x = a^2x^2$$

$$\Rightarrow \quad y^2b^2 + b^2(x^2 + 2aex) + b^4 = 0$$

$$\Rightarrow \quad b^2y^2 + b^2\{(x + ae)^2 - a^2e^2\} + b^4 = 0$$

$$\Rightarrow \quad b^2y^2 + b^2(x + ae)^2 - b^2(a^2 + b^2) + b^4 = 0$$

$$\Rightarrow \quad b^2y^2 + b^2(x + ae)^2 - a^2b^2 = 0$$

$$\Rightarrow \quad (x + ae)^2 + y^2 = a^2$$

8. From any point $A\left(ct_1, \frac{c}{t_1}\right)$ on the rectangular hyperbola

$$xy = c^2. \quad \text{...(i)}$$

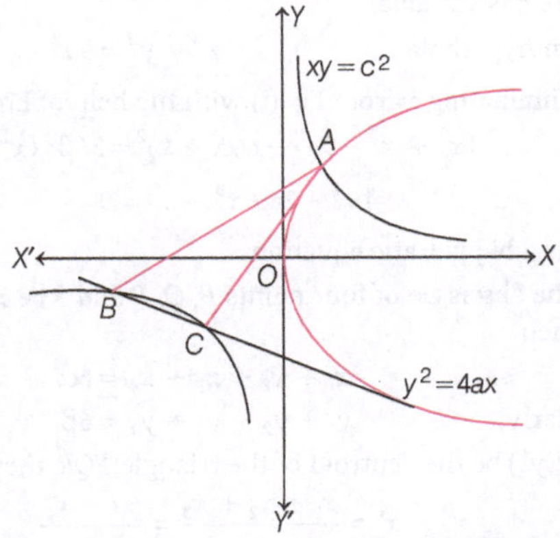

Tangent AB and AC are drawn to the parabola $y^2 = 4ax$,

then $$B \equiv \left(ct_2, \frac{c}{t_2}\right) \text{ and } C \equiv \left(ct_3, \frac{c}{t_3}\right).$$

Then, ΔABC is inscribed in the rectangular hyperbola and its sides AB and AC touch the parabola.

$\because$ BC is also a tangent to it

Equations of chords AB, BC and CA are

$$AB \equiv x + yt_1t_2 = c(t_1 + t_2)$$

$$BC \equiv x + yt_2t_3 = c(t_2 + t_3)$$

$$CA \equiv x + yt_3t_1 = c(t_3 + t_1)$$

$\because$ AB is tangent to parabola $y^2 = 4ax$, its equation

$$y = -\frac{1}{t_1t_2}x + \frac{c(t_1 + t_2)}{t_1t_2}$$

Touching condition $c = \frac{a}{m}$ or $cm = a$

$$\frac{c(t_1+t_2)}{t_1t_2}\cdot\left(\frac{-1}{t_1t_2}\right) = a$$

$$\Rightarrow \quad -at_1^2t_2^2 = c(t_1+t_2)$$

$$(at_1^2)\, t_2^2 + ct_2 + ct_1 = 0$$

Similarly, $\quad (at_1^2)\, t_3^2 + ct_3 + ct_1 = 0$

Hence, $\quad (at_1^2)\, t^2 + ct + ct_1 = 0 \quad$ ...(ii)

and t_2 and t_3 are the roots of Eq. (ii),

$$\therefore \quad t_2 + t_3 = -\frac{c}{at_1^2} \text{ and } t_2t_3 = \frac{c}{at_1} \Rightarrow c = at_1t_2t_3$$

$$\therefore \quad c(t_2+t_3) = -\frac{c^2}{at_1^2} = -\frac{(at_1t_2t_3)^2}{at_1^2} = -at_2^2t_3^2$$

$$\Rightarrow \quad -at_2t_3 = \frac{c(t_2+t_3)}{t_2t_3} \text{ is the condition.}$$

This proves BC to be also a tangent to the parabola. But any point A can be taken in infinite ways anywhere on the curve representing the rectangular hyperbola. Hence, such triangles exist in infinite number.

9. The equation of the circle with centre $(3\alpha, 3\beta)$ is

$$x^2 + y^2 - 6\alpha x - 6\beta y + k = 0 \quad \text{...(i)}$$

where k is variable.

Given hyperbola is $\quad x^2 - y^2 = 9a^2 \quad$ ...(ii)

On eliminating y from Eq. (i) with the help of Eq. (ii), we get

$$(x^2 + x^2 - 9a^2 - 6\alpha x + k)^2 = 36\beta^2(x^2 - 9a^2)$$

$$\Rightarrow \quad 4x^4 - 24\alpha x^3 + \dots = 0$$

this is a biquadratic equation.

Let the abscissae of four points P, Q, R and S be x_1, x_2, x_3 and x_4, then

$$x_1 + x_2 + x_3 + x_4 = 6\alpha \quad \text{...(iii)}$$

Similarly, $\quad y_1 + y_2 + y_3 + y_4 = 6\beta \quad$ ...(iv)

If (x', y') be the centroid of the triangle PQR, then

$$x' = \frac{x_1 + x_2 + x_3}{3} = \frac{6\alpha - x_4}{3}$$

$$\therefore \quad -3(x' - 2\alpha) = x_4$$

and $\quad y' = \dfrac{y_1 + y_2 + y_3}{3} = \dfrac{6\beta - y_4}{3}$

$$\therefore \quad -3(y' - 2\beta) = y_4$$

But $\quad x_4^2 - y_4^2 = 9a^2$

$$\Rightarrow \quad 9(x' - 2\alpha)^2 - 9(y' - 2\beta)^2 = 9a^2$$

$$\Rightarrow \quad (x' - 2\alpha)^2 - (y' - 2\beta)^2 = a^2$$

Hence, locus of centroid (x', y') is $(x - 2\alpha)^2 - (y - 2\beta)^2 = a^2$.

10. Let $(x_i, y_i) = \left(ct_i, \frac{c}{t_i}\right)$, $i = 1, 2, 3, 4$ be the points on the rectangular hyperbola $xy = c^2$.

Equation of normal to the hyperbola $xy = c^2$ at $\left(ct, \frac{c}{t}\right)$ is

$$ct^4 - t^3x + ty - c = 0$$

It passes through (α, β), then

$$ct^4 - t^3\alpha + t\beta - c = 0$$

its biquadratic equation in t. Let the roots of this equation are t_1, t_2, t_3 and t_4, then

$$\Sigma t_1 = \frac{\alpha}{c},$$

$$\Sigma t_1t_2 = 0,\ \Sigma t_1t_2t_3 = -\beta/c,\ t_1t_2t_3t_4 = -1$$

Now, (i) $\quad \Sigma x_i = c\,\Sigma t_1 = \alpha$

(ii) $\quad \Sigma y_i = c\left(\Sigma \frac{1}{t_1}\right) = c\left(\frac{\Sigma t_1t_2t_3}{t_1t_2t_3t_4}\right) = \beta$

(iii) $\quad \Pi\, x_i = c^4 \Pi\, t_i = -c^4$

and $\quad \Pi\, y_i = c^4\left(\frac{1}{\Pi t_i}\right) = -c^4$

(iv) $\quad \Sigma x_i^2 = c^2(\Sigma t_1^2) = c^2\{(\Sigma t_1)^2 - 2\Sigma t_1t_2\}$

$$= \alpha^2$$

(v) $\quad \Sigma y_i^2 = (\Sigma y_1)^2 - 2\Sigma y_1y_2$

$$= \beta^2 - 2c^2\Sigma\left(\frac{1}{t_1t_2}\right)$$

$$= \beta^2 - 2c^2\cdot\frac{\Sigma t_1t_2}{t_1t_2t_3t_4} = \beta^2$$

11. (i) Let the equation of the circle be

$$x^2 + y^2 + 2gx + 2fy + k = 0 \quad \text{...(i)}$$

and the equation of the rectangular hyperbola be

$$xy = c^2 \quad \text{...(ii)}$$

Put $x = ct$ and $y = \frac{c}{t}$ in Eq. (i)

Then, $\quad c^2t^2 + \dfrac{c^2}{t^2} + 2gct + \dfrac{2fc}{t} + k = 0$

$$\Rightarrow \quad c^2t^4 + 2gct^3 + kt^2 + 2fct + c^2 = 0$$

This equation being fourth degree in t. Let roots be t_1, t_2, t_3 and t_4, then

$$\Sigma t_1 = -\frac{2g}{c},\ \Sigma t_1t_2 = \frac{k}{c^2},$$

$$\Sigma t_1t_2t_3 = -\frac{2f}{c} \text{ and } t_1t_2t_3t_4 = 1$$

$$\therefore \quad \Sigma\frac{1}{t_1} = \frac{\Sigma t_1t_2t_3}{t_1t_2t_3t_4} = \frac{\frac{-2f}{c}}{1} = \frac{-2f}{c}$$

(ii) Orthocentre of the ΔABC is $\left(\dfrac{-c}{t_1t_2t_3}, -ct_1t_2t_3\right)$

Hence, orthocentre is $\left(\dfrac{-ct_4}{t_1t_2t_3t_4}, \dfrac{-ct_1t_2t_3t_4}{t_4}\right)$

i.e. $\quad \left(-ct_4, \dfrac{-c}{t_4}\right)$

But D is $\quad \left(ct_4, \dfrac{c}{t_4}\right)$

Hence, H and D are the extremities of a diagonal of rectangular hyperbola.

(iii) The centre of the mean position of the four points is

$$\left(\frac{c}{4}(t_1+t_2+t_3+t_4), \frac{c}{4}\left(\frac{1}{t_1}+\frac{1}{t_2}+\frac{1}{t_3}+\frac{1}{t_4}\right)\right)$$

i.e. $$\left(\frac{c}{4}\Sigma t_1, \frac{c}{4}\Sigma\left(\frac{1}{t_1}\right)\right)$$

i.e. $$\left(-\frac{g}{2}, -\frac{f}{2}\right)$$

[from relation Eq. (i)]

$\because$ Centres of the circle and rectangular hyperbola are $(-g, -f)$ and $(0, 0)$; mid point of centres of circle and rectangular hyperbola is $\left(\frac{-g}{2}, \frac{-f}{2}\right)$.

Hence, the centre of the mean position of the four points bisects the distance between the centres of the two curves (circle and rectangular hyperbola).

(iv) Let the circle passing through ABC meet the hyperbola in fourth point D; then centre of circle is

$$(-g, -f), (-g, -f)$$

$$\Rightarrow \quad \left(\frac{c}{2}\left(\frac{-2g}{c}\right), \frac{c}{2}\left(\frac{-2f}{2}\right)\right)$$

[from Eq. (i) relation]

$$\Rightarrow \quad \left(\frac{c}{2}(t_1+t_2+t_3+t_4), \frac{c}{2}\left(\frac{1}{t_1}+\frac{1}{t_2}+\frac{1}{t_3}+\frac{1}{t_4}\right)\right)$$

But $$t_1t_2t_3t_4 = 1$$

$\therefore$ $$t_4 = \frac{1}{t_1t_2t_3}$$

Hence, centre of circle is

$$\left(\frac{c}{2}\left(t_1+t_2+t_3+\frac{1}{t_1t_2t_3}\right), \frac{c}{2}\left(\frac{1}{t_1}+\frac{1}{t_2}+\frac{1}{t_3}+t_1t_2t_3\right)\right)$$

12. Let chord be PQ and coordinates of P and Q are $\left(ct_1, \frac{c}{t_1}\right)$ and $\left(ct_2, \frac{c}{t_2}\right)$ respectively.

Now, let mid-point of PQ is $M(h, k)$

$\therefore$ $$h = \frac{1}{2}(ct_1 + ct_2)$$

$\therefore$ $$t_1 + t_2 = \frac{2h}{c} \quad \text{and} \quad k = \frac{1}{2}\left\{\frac{c}{t_1}+\frac{c}{t_2}\right\}$$

or $$\frac{2k}{c} = \frac{t_1+t_2}{t_1t_2}$$

or $$\frac{2k}{c} = \frac{\frac{2h}{c}}{t_1t_2} \quad \left[\because t_1 + t_2 = \frac{2h}{c}\right]$$

or $$t_1t_2 = \frac{h}{k}$$

$\therefore$ $$(t_1-t_2)^2 = (t_1+t_2)^2 - 4t_1t_2 = \frac{4h^2}{c^2} - \frac{4h}{k}$$

$$= \frac{4h}{c^2k}(hk - c^2) \quad \text{...(i)}$$

Since, $$|PQ| = 2d$$

$\therefore$ $$\sqrt{(ct_1-ct_2)^2 + \left(\frac{c}{t_1}-\frac{c}{t_2}\right)^2} = 2d$$

or $$c^2(t_1-t_2)^2\left\{1+\frac{1}{t_1^2t_2^2}\right\} = (2d)^2$$

or $$c^2 \times \frac{4h}{c^2k}(hk-c^2)\left\{1+\frac{k^2}{h^2}\right\} = 4d^2 \quad \text{[from Eq. (i)]}$$

or $$(h^2+k^2)(hk-c^2) = d^2hk$$

Hence, locus of the mid-point of PQ is

$$(x^2+y^2)(xy-c^2) = d^2xy.$$

13. Let the rectangular hyperbola is $xy = c^2$ ...(i)

Since, the centre of hyperbola (i) is origin $(0, 0)$ and equation of asymptotes are $x = 0$ and $y = 0$.

The equation of a line through $(0, 0)$ and makes an angle θ with asymptote (X-axis) is $y = x\tan\theta$.

It will meet the hyperbola, where $x(x\tan\theta) = c^2$

i.e. $$x = c\sqrt{\cot\theta}$$

On putting $x = c\sqrt{\cot\theta}$ in eq. (i),

then $$y = c\sqrt{(\tan\theta)}$$

$\therefore$ The four points are $(c\sqrt{\cot\theta}, c\sqrt{\tan\theta})$ where

$$Q = \alpha, \beta, \gamma, \delta.$$

The line joining the points α and β is perpendicular to the line joining the points γ and δ.

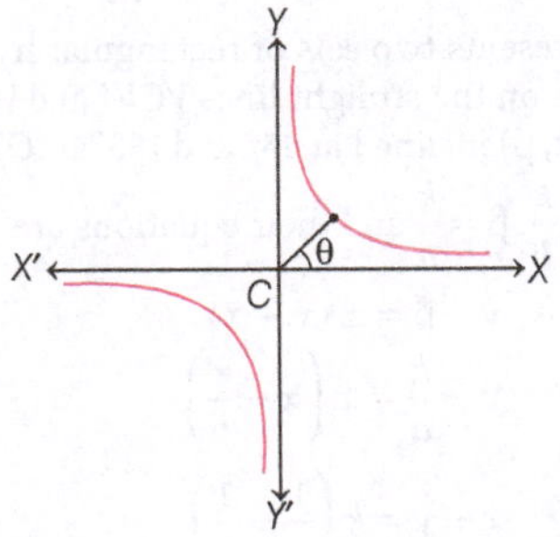

Therefore, the product of their slopes $= -1$

i.e. $$\frac{c\sqrt{\tan\beta} - c\sqrt{\tan\alpha}}{c\sqrt{\cot\beta} - c\sqrt{\cot\alpha}} \times \frac{c\sqrt{\tan\delta} - c\sqrt{\tan\gamma}}{c\sqrt{\cot\delta} - c\sqrt{\cot\gamma}} = -1$$

$$\Rightarrow \quad (-\sqrt{\tan\alpha}\sqrt{\tan\beta}) \times (-\sqrt{\tan\gamma}\sqrt{\tan\delta}) = -1$$

or $$\tan\alpha\tan\beta\tan\gamma\tan\delta = 1$$

14. Let two perpendicular asymptotes of a rectangular hyperbola are CD and CE.

Let the coordinates of A, B and C are $(a, 0)$, $(0, b)$, (α, β). OX and OY are parallel to CD and CE.

Then, equations of CD and CE are

$$y - \beta = 0 \quad \text{and} \quad x - \alpha = 0$$

Thus, combined equation of CD and CE is

$$(x-\alpha)(y-\beta) = 0$$

or $$xy - \alpha y - \beta x + \alpha\beta = 0$$

is the equation of asymptotes of rectangular hyperbola.

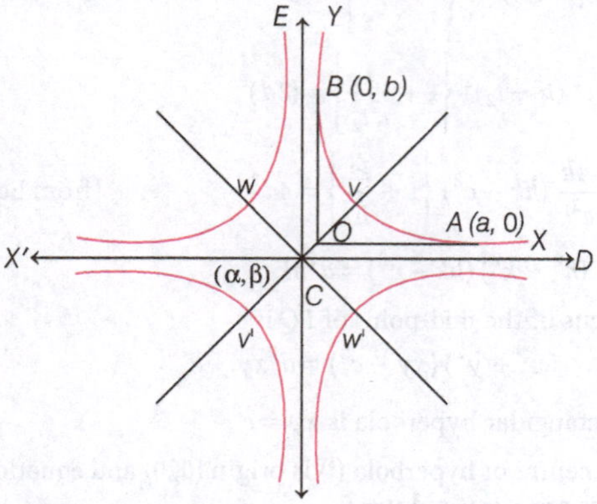

Hence, equation of rectangular hyperbola is

$$xy - \alpha y - \beta x + k = 0,$$

where k is any constant.

It passes through $A(a, 0)$ and $B(0, b)$

$\therefore \quad 0 - 0 - \beta a + k = 0$

and $\quad 0 - \alpha b - 0 + k = 0$

$\therefore \quad \beta = \dfrac{k}{a}$ and $\alpha = \dfrac{k}{b}$

Hence, equation of rectangular hyperbola becomes

$$xy - k\left(\frac{x}{a} + \frac{y}{b} - 1\right) = 0 \qquad \text{...(i)}$$

Eq. (i) represents two sets of rectangular hyperbolas whose vertices lie on the straight lines VCV' and WCW' both passing through (α, β) inclined at 45° and 135° to OX.

Then, $\alpha = \dfrac{k}{b}, \beta = \dfrac{k}{a}$ and their equations are

$$y - \beta = \pm (x - \alpha)$$

$\Rightarrow \quad y - \dfrac{k}{a} = \pm \left(x - \dfrac{k}{b}\right)$

or $\quad x + y = k\left(\dfrac{1}{a} + \dfrac{1}{b}\right)$

and $\quad x - y = k\left(\dfrac{1}{b} - \dfrac{1}{a}\right) \qquad \text{...(ii)}$

or $\quad k = \dfrac{ab(x + y)}{(a + b)}$

and $\quad k = \dfrac{ab(x - y)}{(a - b)}$

On putting in Eq. (i), then

$$\frac{x^2}{a} + \frac{y^2}{b} - x - y = 0$$

and $\quad \dfrac{x^2}{b} - \dfrac{y^2}{a} - x + y = 0$

On differentiating these equations, we get

$$\frac{2x}{a} + \frac{2y}{b}\frac{dy}{dx} - 1 - \frac{dy}{dx} = 0$$

and $\quad \dfrac{2x}{b} - \dfrac{2y}{a}\dfrac{dy}{dx} - 1 + \dfrac{dy}{dx} = 0$

$\therefore$ Slopes of lines are

$$m_1 = \frac{dy}{dx} = \frac{b(a - 2x)}{a(2y - b)}$$

and $\quad m_2 = \dfrac{dy}{dx} = \dfrac{a(2x - b)}{b(2y - a)}$

At $(0, 0)$ $\quad m_1 = -1$ and $m_2 = 1$

$\therefore \quad m_1 m_2 = -1$

which shows that curves intersect orthogonally.

15. Equation of the normal to the hyperbola $xy = 1$ at t is

$$xt^3 - yt - t^4 + 1 = 0 \qquad \text{...(i)}$$

$\because$ It passes through (α, β).

$\therefore \quad t^4 - \alpha t^3 + \beta t - 1 = 0$

If foot of the co-normal points are

$$\left(t_1, \frac{1}{t_1}\right), \left(t_2, \frac{1}{t_2}\right), \left(t_3, \frac{1}{t_3}\right) \text{ and } \left(t_4, \frac{1}{t_4}\right)$$

$\therefore \quad t_1 + t_2 + t_3 + t_4 = \alpha$

$\Rightarrow \quad x_1 + x_2 + x_3 + x_4 = \alpha$

and $\quad \dfrac{1}{t_1} + \dfrac{1}{t_2} + \dfrac{1}{t_3} + \dfrac{1}{t_4} = \beta$

$\Rightarrow \quad y_1 + y_2 + y_3 + y_4 = \beta$

Let the variable line be

$$px + qy + r = 0 \qquad \text{...(ii)}$$

Since, algebraic sum of perpendicular distances from $(x_1, y_1), (x_2, y_2), (x_3, y_3)$ and (x_4, y_4) to Eq. (ii) is zero.

$$\left(\frac{px_1 + qy_1 + r}{\sqrt{(p^2 + q^2)}}\right) + \left(\frac{px_2 + qy_2 + r}{\sqrt{p^2 + q^2}}\right) + \left(\frac{px_3 + qy_3 + r}{\sqrt{(p^2 + q^2)}}\right) + \left(\frac{px_4 + qy_4 + r}{\sqrt{(p^2 + q^2)}}\right) = 0$$

$\Rightarrow \quad p(x_1 + x_2 + x_3 + x_4) + q(y_1 + y_2 + y_3 + y_4) + 4r = 0$

$\Rightarrow \quad p\left(\dfrac{x_1 + x_2 + x_3 + x_4}{4}\right) + q\left(\dfrac{y_1 + y_2 + y_3 + y_4}{4}\right) + r = 0$

$\Rightarrow \quad p \cdot \dfrac{\alpha}{4} + q \cdot \dfrac{\beta}{4} + r = 0$

$\therefore$ Eq. (ii) passes through $\left(\dfrac{\alpha}{4}, \dfrac{\beta}{4}\right)$.